KU-339-568

List of Contributors

Members of 11 King's Bench Walk Chambers

Sean Aughey MA (Cantab), LLM (Cantab), barrister - Foreign Employees (26)

Joseph Barrett, LLB, LLM (Harvard), barrister - Contract of Employment (8), Employee, Self-Employed or Worker? (15), References (40)

Andrew Blake BA, LLM, barrister - Holidays (29)

Charles Bourne QC, barrister - Discrimination and Equal Opportunities III (13)

Edward Capewell, MA, MPhil, barrister - Unfair Dismissal I, III (53), (55)

Akhlaq Choudhury QC, BSc, LLB (London), barrister - Children and Young Persons (4), Education and Training (14), Restraint of Trade (41), Service Lettings (43),

Leo Davidson, barrister - Financial Regulation in the UK (25)

Simon Forshaw, barrister - Restraint of Trade (41)

Paul Greatorex, barrister - Probationary Employees (36), Time Off Work (49)

Patrick Halliday MA (Cantab), barrister - European Union Law (23)

Harini Iyengar MA (Oxon), BCL (Oxon), barrister - ACAS early conciliation (3), Insolvency (31)

Seán Jones QC, BA, BCL (Oxon), barrister - Discrimination and Equal Opportunities I (11), Employee Participation (16), Part-Time Workers (33)

Christopher Knight MA (Cantab), BCL (Oxon) barrister - Engagement of Employees (21)

Michael Lee MA (Cantab), barrister - Unfair Dismissal II (54)

Richard Leiper QC, LLB, MJuris, barrister - Financial penalties on employers (24), Transfer of Undertakings (52)

Julian Milford MA, barrister - Continuous Employment (7), Redundancy I and II (38, 39)

Thomas Ogg BA (Oxon), MSc (Oxon), barrister - Maternity and Parental Rights (32)

Marcus Pilgerstorfer, barrister - Employment Tribunals I, II (18, 19)

Nigel Porter MA (Cantab), LLM (Cantab), barrister - Introduction (1), Introduction to the Advisory, Conciliation and Arbitration Service (ACAS) (2), Codes of Practice (5), Disclosure of Information (10), Employees' Past Criminal Convictions (17), Human Rights (30), Pay I and II (34, 35), Temporary and Seasonal Employees (47)

Anya Proops QC, MA (Cantab), PhD, barrister - Vicarious Liability (56)

List of Contributors

Clive Sheldon QC, BA (Cantab), LLM, barrister - Sickness and Sick Pay (44), Termination of Employment (48), Wrongful Dismissal (58)

Hannah Slarks, barrister - Public Sector Employees (37)

Daniel Stilitz QC, BA, MA, barrister - Strikes and Industrial Action (45), Trade Unions I and II (50, 51)

Judy Stone BA (Hons) Oxon, barrister - Directors (9), Retirement (42)

Holly Stout MA (Cantab), DipLaw, barrister - Discrimination and Equal Opportunities II (12), Discrimination and Equal Opportunities III (13), Equal Pay (22)

Peter Wallington QC, MA, LLM, barrister - Collective Agreements (6), Employment Tribunals III (20), Working Time (57)

Other Contributors

Sarah Bradford BA (Hons), ACA, CTA (Fellow), Director of Writetax Ltd - Taxation (46)

Prof Dominic Regan, City Law School London, Solicitor - Health and Safety at Work I and II (27, 28)

Contents

Contents

Tolley's Employment Handbook

by

Mrs Justice Slade DBE

High Court Judge,
A Recorder of the Crown Court,
A Master of the Bench of the Inner Temple,
Honorary Vice-President of the
Employment Law Bar Association

Thirty first Edition
by
members of
11 KBW Chambers
and

Sarah Bradford

Director of Writetax Ltd

Prof Dominic Regan

City Law School London, Solicitor

 LexisNexis®

Members of the LexisNexis Group worldwide

United Kingdom	RELX (UK) Limited trading as LexisNexis, 1-3 Strand, London WC2N 5JR
Australia	LexisNexis, Chatswood, New South Wales
Austria	LexisNexis Verlag ARD Orac GmbH & Co KG, Vienna
Benelux	LexisNexis Benelux, Amsterdam
Canada	LexisNexis Canada, Markham, Ontario
China	LexisNexis China, Beijing and Shanghai
France	LexisNexis SA, Paris
Germany	LexisNexis GmbH, Dusseldorf
Hong Kong	LexisNexis Hong Kong, Hong Kong
India	LexisNexis India, New Delhi
Italy	GiuffrèEditore, Milan
Japan	LexisNexis Japan, Tokyo
Malaysia	Malayan Law Journal Sdn Bhd, Kuala Lumpur
New Zealand	LexisNexis NZ Ltd, Wellington
Singapore	LexisNexis Singapore, Singapore
South Africa	LexisNexis, Durban
USA	LexisNexis, Dayton, Ohio

© RELX (UK) Ltd 2017

Published by LexisNexis
This is a Tolley title

ISBN for this volume: 9780754553724

Visit LexisNexis at www.lexisnexis.co.uk

Preface

Welcome to the 2017 edition of the Handbook. The new year has brought some changes to the editorial team. We have said goodbye to Amy Rogers whose astonishing acuity of thought and (alas almost unique) respect for deadlines will be sorely missed. Joining the team is Leo Davidson who arrives with a bang and a new chapter: FINANCIAL REGULATION IN THE UK (25) which deals with the rapidly developing area of employment in financially-regulated businesses. This is the first of a number of new chapters that we have planned to introduce over coming editions.

This year we have lost to retirement two judges who have each had a profound effect on the present shape of Employment Law. First was HHJ Peter Clark who has retired after a Boycott-like innings in the EAT. Never afraid to disagree with a recent decision of a President, he would quietly tug the law back towards orthodoxy when necessary. He was a judge whose heart and head invariably pointed in the same direction: towards justice. The second to retire was Lord Justice Elias. There cannot be many who have thought as long, carefully and deeply about Employment Law as Patrick Elias. His most remarkable characteristic was that however much he knew about an area and however inexperienced the advocate before him, he would always take care to look for the very best way in which the advocate's argument might be put. Every contention got a close look and a fair consideration. For all the ruthlessness with which a bad point might ultimately be despatched, he was always a patient and considerate judge. It is amazing and disappointing in equal measure that he never took the place in the Supreme Court to which his talents befitted him.

Since the last edition, the most significant development has undoubtedly been the decision of the UK to leave the European Union. The effects of Brexit remain, at this point, to be determined. We will, of course, track those effects across future editions. This preface is written a week or two before a general election. All parties presently maintain that employment rights will be unaffected. But even if there is no immediate change, for many key rights the enforceable minima set by European Legislation will soon vanish. At the moment, for instance, it would not be open to the Government to reduce the statutory right to paid holidays to less than four weeks. That would be to fail properly to implement the *Working Time Directive*. If, as the present Government hopes, we will leave unbound by the *aquis communautaire* and beyond the reach of the European Court of Justice, the floor will vanish. Holiday pay has been an area in which European Law has loomed large and has continued to do so this year. Those developments include the decision of the Court of Appeal in *Lock v British Gas* (the *Working Time Regulations 1998* can be read so as to comply with the requirement imposed by the Directive that commissions should be taken into account when calculating holiday pay); the Northern Ireland Court of Appeal in *Patterson v Castlereagh Borough Council* [2015] IRLR 721 (in which it was assumed on a concession that pay for voluntary overtime might have to be reflected in holiday pay) and the ECJ in *Maschek v Magistratsdirektion der Stadt Wien* [2016] IRLR 801 (on whether an employee is entitled to payment in lieu of holiday that he could have taken during a period of garden leave). These have all been analysed by Andrew Blake in his updated HOLIDAYS (29) chapter.

It has been, as ever, a bumper year for developments in the law of discrimination. Perhaps the most significant of those developments were the consolidated cases of *Essop and Naeem* [2017] UKSC 2 in which the Supreme Court took the opportunity greatly to simplify the law of indirect discrimination concluding that it was not necessary for a complainant to show precisely why a PCP produced a particular disadvantage for those who have a particular protected characteristic as long as it was clear that it did. Nor was it necessary for the "context factor" which provides the necessary link between the effect of the PCP and the protected characteristic to be independently discriminatory. It was with considerable gratitude to Lady Hale for the clarity and simplicity of her judgment that I was able to select a decent chunk of the relevant part of

Preface

Discrimination and Equal Opportunities I (11) and press delete. It was a therapeutic moment. Amongst the other significant developments are two ECJ cases on religious discrimination and, more specifically, on employer religious neutrality policies: *Achbita v G4S Secure Solutions NV* Case C-157/15; [2017] IRLR 466 and *Bougnaoui v Micropole SA* Case C-188/15; [2017] IRLR 447.

In an extensively revised EDUCATION AND TRAINING (14), Akhlaq Choudury QC traces through the changes introduced to apprenticeships by the *Enterprise Act 2016*.

The vexed and significant question of the application of the national minimum wage regime to sleep-in shifts in care homes was considered by the EAT in *Royal Mencap Society v Tomlinson Blake (and other appeals)* UKEAT/0290/16/DM. The case is on its way to the Court of Appeal, but the EAT has given useful guidance on the issue which is summarised by Nigel Porter at PAY – I: PAYMENTS, PAY STATEMENTS AND MISCELLANEOUS STATUTORY PAY RIGHTS (34). Nigel is also responsible for DISCLOSURE OF INFORMATION (10) which contains an excellent summary of the new rules on Gender pay Gap Reporting, a subject also addressed in detail by Holly Stout in EQUAL PAY (22).

Another area that never sleeps is Taxation and at CHAPTER 46 Sarah Bradford deals with a slew of new developments including the prospective changes to the rules relating to the taxation of PILONs.

Michael Lee and Ed Capewell have updated the chapters Unfair Dismissal chapters to reflect a number of significant decisions including *O'Brien v Bolton St Catherine's Academy* [2017] EWCA Civ 145 which considers the relationship between the range of reasonable responses test and the Public Law notion of "Wednesbury unreasonabless" and the Supreme Court's decision in *McBride v Scottish Police Authority* [2016] ICR 788 on the scope and nature of reinstatement as a remedy (see UNFAIR DISMISSAL I – III (53) to (55)).

In past years I have observed that the apparent determination of the present Conservative government to repeal the *Human Rights Act* has been long on rhetoric and short on action. That trend continues. As we go to press the Supreme Court has heard argument but is yet to deliver judgment on the question of the lawfulness of the present regime of Employment Tribunal fees.

The law is stated at 1 April 2017 with later developments included wherever possible. Feedback is extremely welcome. There is a bounty for error-spotting. I can be contacted at sean.jones@11kbw.com or via twitter on @seanjones11kbw.

Seán Jones QC

Abbreviations and References

Abbreviations – General

ACAS	=	Advisory, Conciliation and Arbitration Service
ERRB	=	Enterprise and Regulatory Reform Bill
CA	=	Court of Appeal
CAC	=	Central Arbitration Committee
COET	=	Central Office of the Employment Tribunals
CRE	=	Commission for Racial Equality
DfEE	=	Department for Education and Employment
DRC	=	Disability Rights Commission
DSS	=	Department of Social Security
DTI	=	Department of Trade and Industry
EAT	=	Employment Appeal Tribunal
EEC	=	European Economic Community
EC	=	European Community
ECJ	=	European Court of Justice
EOC	=	Equal Opportunities Commission
HL	=	House of Lords
Pt	=	Part
Sch	=	Schedule
SI	=	Statutory Instrument
SR & O	=	Statutory Rules and Orders

Abbreviations – Statutes

DDA	=	Disability Discrimination Act 1995
DRCA	=	Disability Rights Commission Act 1999
EA	=	Employment Act (with date)
EPA	=	Employment Protection Act 1975
EPCA	=	Employment Protection (Consolidation) Act 1978
ETA	=	Employment Tribunals Act 1996
EqA	=	Equality Act 2010
EqPA	=	Equal Pay Act 1970
ERA 1996	=	Employment Rights Act 1996
ERA 1999	=	Employment Relations Act 1999
FA	=	Finance Act (with date)
HSWA	=	Health and Safety at Work etc. Act 1974
HRA	=	Human Rights Act 1998
ICTA	=	Income and Corporation Taxes Act 1988
OLA	=	Occupiers' Liability Act 1957
OSRPA	=	Offices, Shops and Railway Premises Act 1963
PIDA	=	Public Interest Disclosure Act 1998
RRA	=	Race Relations Act 1976
SBA	=	Supplementary Benefits Act 1976
SDA	=	Sex Discrimination Act 1975
SDA 1986	=	Sex Discrimination Act 1996
SSA	=	Social Security Act 1975
SSA 1986	=	Social Security Act 1986
SSAA	=	Social Security Administration Act 1992

Abbreviations and References

SSCBA	=	Social Security Contributions and Benefits Act 1992
SSHBA	=	Social Security and Housing Benefits Act 1982
SSPA	=	Social Security Pensions Act 1975
TUA	=	Trade Union Act 1984
TULRA	=	Trade Union and Labour Relations Act 1974
TULR(A)A	=	Trade Union and Labour Relations (Amendment) Act 1976
TULRCA	=	Trade Union and Labour Relations (Consolidation) Act 1992
TURERA	=	Trade Union Reform and Employment Rights Act 1993
UCTA	=	Unfair Contract Terms Act 1977
WA	=	Wages Act 1986

Law reports – Series referred to

AC	=	Law Reports, Appeal Cases
All ER	=	All England Law Reports
ATC	=	Annotated Tax Cases
BCLC	=	Butterworths Company Law Cases
Ch	=	Law Reports, Chancery Division
CMLR	=	Common Market Law Reports
Cr App Rep	=	Criminal Appeal Reports
FSR	=	Fleet Street Reports
ICR	=	Law Reports, Industrial Cases Reports
IDS	=	Incomes Data Services
IRLB	=	Industrial Relations Law Bulletin
IRLR	=	Industrial Relations Law Reports
ITR	=	Industrial Tribunal Reports
LJKB	=	Law Journal Reports, New Series, King's Bench (ended 1949)
Lloyd's Rep	=	Lloyd's List Law Reports
LS Gaz	=	Law Society's Gazette
PCC	=	Palmer's Company Cases
QB/KB	=	Law Reports, Queen's (King's) Bench Division
TLR	=	Times Law Reports (last year of publication 1952)
WLR	=	Weekly Law Reports

Table of Statutes

Table of Statutes

Table of Statutes

Table of Statutes

Table of Statutes

Table of Statutes

Table of Statutes

Table of Statutes

Table of Statutes

Table of EU Legislation

Table of EU Legislation

Secondary Legislation

Directives

Table of EU Legislation

Table of Statutory Instruments

Table of Statutory Instruments

Table of Statutory Instruments

Table of Statutory Instruments

Table of Statutory Instruments

Table of Statutory Instruments

Table of Statutory Instruments

Table of Statutory Instruments

Table of Cases

Table of Cases

Table of Cases

Table of Cases

Table of Cases

Table of Cases

D

Table of Cases

xci

Table of Cases

Table of Cases

Table of Cases

Table of Cases

c

Table of Cases

Table of Cases

Table of Cases

H

Table of Cases

Table of Cases

Table of Cases

Table of Cases

Table of Cases

Table of Cases

K

Table of Cases

Table of Cases

Table of Cases

Table of Cases

Table of Cases

Table of Cases

Table of Cases

Table of Cases

Table of Cases

Table of Cases

O

Table of Cases

Table of Cases

Table of Cases

Table of Cases

Table of Cases

Table of Cases

Table of Cases

Table of Cases

Table of Cases

Table of Cases

Table of Cases

Table of Cases

Table of Cases

Table of Cases

Table of Cases

Table of Cases

W

Table of Cases

Table of Cases

Table of Cases

Table of Cases

Table of Cases

X

Y

Z

Table of Cases

1 Introduction

1.1 SCOPE AND AIMS OF THIS BOOK

Employment law is fully recognised today as a subject of the greatest importance. Legislation passed in recent years has transformed the law and created important new statutory rights and obligations. Employment law continues to develop at a rapid pace, with new domestic legislation creating or modifying statutory rights being enacted each year. Further, EC legislation and decisions of the European Court have had, and will continue to have, an important impact on certain areas of domestic employment law. Inevitably, a wealth of reported tribunal and court decisions on the meaning and effect of these new provisions has also built up.

This handbook seeks to explain the legislation in its context, along with the common law and the EC law on employment matters. It is intended as a reference guide for the employer, company secretary, manager or personnel officer involved daily in decisions concerning the rights of employees. It is also intended to serve as a comprehensive handbook on employment law for solicitors, employees, trade union officials, and all kinds of advisers and professional people.

The remainder of this chapter serves as an introduction to the subject by examining a number of fundamental aspects of current employment law. It concludes with a checklist of the areas of law relevant to the various stages of employment and a brief explanation of the standard scale of maximum fines which may be imposed upon conviction of an adult of a summary offence.

Employment law and trade union law. The main emphasis of this book is on the law affecting the individual employment relationship, ie directly applying to employers and their employees. It therefore provides detailed coverage of the law governing the contract of employment, termination of employment, redundancy, unfair dismissal, equal pay, the various forms of unlawful discrimination relevant to employment and numerous other individual employment rights. The importance of trade unions is nonetheless fully recognised, and the status, functions and liabilities of trade unions and the law relating to trade union membership are considered in appropriate chapters.

1.2 WHAT CONSTITUTES EMPLOYMENT?

One of the most fundamental questions asked is whether a particular worker is an employee or not. An employee is a person who agrees to work for another person pursuant to a *contract of employment* (or 'contract of service' to use the more traditional term). It is important to be able to distinguish a contract of employment from other types of agreement under which services are rendered. There are a number of characteristics which enable a contract of employment to be identified. One problem which can often arise is deciding whether a particular person doing work for another is working as an employee, ie under a contract of employment, or as an independent contractor (or 'self-employed' person) under a *contract for services*. These matters are discussed further in EMPLOYEE, SELF-EMPLOYED OR WORKER? (15).

1.3 The contract of employment

The most important matters to be borne in mind are the following.

(a)   In general, the parties are free to agree whatever contractual terms they wish – this means, among other things, that they may agree that work is to be done either by an employee or by an independent contractor.

Introduction

(b)   However, *all the terms* of the contract, and the way in which it is performed, will be looked at in deciding whether it is in substance a contract of employment or not, so it will not be sufficient merely to state that the contract is a contract for services and not a contract of employment.

(c)   Whether or not the contract is a contract of employment, certain further terms may be implied, if not expressly agreed.

(d)   If the contract *is* a contract of employment, all the statutory employment rights are capable of applying, if the relevant pre-conditions are satisfied, and (subject to limited exceptions) any term of the contract excluding these rights is usually *ineffective*.

(e)   If the contract *is not* a contract of employment, the main statutory employment rights cannot apply, because they apply only for the benefit of people working under a contract of employment. However, there are some important statutory provisions which also apply to self-employed persons and/or 'workers' as defined in the relevant legislation.

For further details, see CONTRACT OF EMPLOYMENT (8) and EMPLOYEE, SELF-EMPLOYED OR WORKER? (15).

1.4   SOURCES OF EMPLOYMENT LAW

The legal rules governing employment law are derived from three principal sources:

(a)   the common law, including the law of contract pursuant to which the contract of employment is enforced, and the law of torts (wrongful acts which cause damage or loss) which governs (for example) an employer's liability for acts of his employees, civil liability for industrial accidents and for strikes and other forms of industrial action;

(b)   statute law, ie Acts of Parliament and Regulations, which operate outside the contract (eg the law on unfair dismissal); and

(c)   European legislation and judgments of the European Court of Justice ('ECJ').

Some elements of these three sources are considered briefly below.

1.5   Terms of the contract of employment

Generally, the employer and employee are free to agree whatever terms they wish. Therefore, the most basic legal rules governing the employment relationship are those agreed by the parties themselves, for example, the type of work to be done, place of work, rate of pay, etc. In practice, the more detailed terms and conditions of the contract are often not discussed and agreed individually with each employee. Many employers have written standard terms and conditions of employment for all employees, sometimes drawn up and agreed in consultation with officials of recognised trade unions.

In cases where a disagreement arises, the main problem is often evidential. If an employer does not provide written particulars of the terms and conditions of employment, or if a particular matter was agreed orally but never put in writing, years later memories will have faded and there may be no reliable evidence of precisely what was agreed. This is one reason why employers are under a statutory obligation to provide a written summary of the main contractual terms to each employee within a short time after he begins his job. They must notify changes in the same way. (See 8.7 CONTRACT OF EMPLOYMENT.)

2

1.10 STANDARD SCALE OF FINES

At various points in the book, reference is made to the standard scale of maximum fines which may be imposed upon conviction of an adult of a summary offence (that is, one which ~alls to be tried by magistrates rather than by the Crown Court).

~dard scale of maximum fines is as follows.

Amount of maximum fine (£)
200
500
1,000
2,500
Unlimited

offences committed after 12 March 2013 by ~~~~ of *Offenders Act 2012* which came into force on the same date. ~~Justice Act 1991, s 17.~~ The *Punishment of Offenders Act 2012 ss 86–87*, empowers the Secretary of State to increase the levels 1–4 of the standard scale fines to such sums considered appropriate. These provisions are, however, not yet in force.

It should be noted that the *Legal Aid, Sentencing and Punishment of Offenders Act 2012* makes provision in *s 85* for the removal of the £5000 maximum on the standard scale of fines and, by *ss 86–87*, empowers the Secretary of State to increase the levels 1–4 of the standard scale fines to such sums considered appropriate. These provisions are, however, not yet in force.

Where the Crown Court tries an offence and imposes a fine following a conviction there is no maximum amount in the absence of some specific provision to the contrary (*Powers of Criminal Courts Act 1973, s 30; Criminal Law Act 1977, s 32(1)*).

Before a court (magistrates' court or Crown Court) fixes the amount of any fine, it must inquire into the financial circumstances of the offender. The amount must reflect the court's opinion of the seriousness of the offence, and the court must also take account of the circumstances of the case, including the financial circumstances of the offender. (*Criminal Justice Act 1991, s 18*, as substituted by *Criminal Justice Act 1993, s 65*.)

The period for early conciliation is one calendar month from receipt of the form under *Rule 2* or the telephone call under *Rule 3* (*Rule 6(1)*) during which period the conciliation officer must "endeavour to promote a settlement". The early conciliation period may be extended by the conciliation officer if the prospective claimant and prospective respondent consent and if the conciliation officer considers that there is a reasonable prospect of a settlement being achieved before the expiry of the extended period (*Rule 6(2)*). The extended period is a maximum of 14 days and no further extension is permitted (*Rule 6(3)*).

If during the conciliation period (or the extended period) the conciliation officer concludes that a settlement of all or part of a dispute is not possible ACAS must issue and an "early conciliation certificate" (*Rule 7(1)*). Similarly if the conciliation period (or the extended period if applicable) expires without settlement then the early conciliation certificate must be issued (*Rule 7(2)*). The early conciliation certificate must include the information listed in *Rule 8*, being the names and addresses of the prospective claimant and respondent, the date of receipt of the form under *Rule 2* or the telephone call under *Rule 3*, the date of issue of the certificate and the unique reference number (the "early conciliation number") given by ACAS to the early conciliation certificate. A copy of the early conciliation certificate must be provided by ACAS to the prospective claimant and, if ACAS has had contact with the prospective respondent during the conciliation period, to that party also (*Rule 9*).

The *Employment Tribunals (Constitution and Rules of Procedure) (Amendment) Regulations 2014 (SI 2014/271)* amends *Schedule 1* to the *Employment Tribunals (Constitution and Rules of Procedure) Regulations 2013* so as to require claimants either to provide to the employment tribunal as part of the claim the early conciliation number or to confirm that the claim does not involve "relevant proceedings" or to confirm that one of the exemptions from the early conciliation scheme applies (*Rule 10(1)(c)* as amended). Failure to comply with this obligation will mean the claim form is rejected (*Rule 10(2)* and *Rule 12* of *Sch 1* to the *2013 Regulations* as amended).

The scheme applies to all "relevant proceedings" where ACAS is under a duty to promote a settlement. See *s 18* of the *Employment Tribunals Act 1996* ("*ETA*"). The *Employment Tribunals Act 1996 (Application of Conciliation Provisions) Order 2014 (SI 2014/431)* substitutes a new list of jurisdictions in *s 18* of the *ETA*. See *ETA, s 18(a)–(z2)* (as amended). Subject to limited exceptions all claims which may be advanced by an individual claimant fall with the scope of mandatory early conciliation.

The exemptions from early conciliation are set out in *Reg 3* of the *Regulations*. There are five exemptions but the two most relevant are likely to be applications for interim relief and multiple claims where another claimant has already made contact with ACAS. The exemptions are as follows:

(a)   another person ("B") has complied with that requirement in relation to the same dispute and A wishes to institute proceedings on the same claim form as B;

(b)   A institutes those relevant proceedings on the same claim form as proceedings which are not relevant proceedings;

(c)   A is able to show that the respondent has contacted ACAS in relation to a dispute, ACAS has not received information from A under s *18A(1)* of the *Employment Tribunals Act* in relation to that dispute, and the proceedings on the claim form relate to that dispute;

(d)   the proceedings are proceedings under *Part X* of the *Employment Rights Act 1996* (unfair dismissal) and the application to institute those proceedings is accompanied by an application under *s 128* of the *ERA* or *s 161* of the *Trade Union and Labour Relations (Consolidation) Act 1992* (interim relief cases);

(e)   A is instituting proceedings against the Security Service, the Secret Intelligence Service or the Government Communications Headquarters.

2.6 Advisory, Conciliation and Arbitration Service (ACAS)

2.6 CONSEQUENTIAL AMENDMENTS TO TIME LIMITS FOR PRESENTATION OF CLAIMS

The tribunal time limits are extended to allow time for early conciliation. The time limit provisions in primary legislation have been amended by *Sch 2* to the *Enterprise and Regulatory Reform Act 2013*. The time limits in the various statutory instruments are amended by the *Enterprise and Regulatory Reform Act 2013 (Consequential Amendments) (Employment) Order 2014 (SI 2014/386)* and the *Employment Tribunals Act 1996 (Application of Conciliation Provisions) Order 2014 (SI 2014/431)* and, in the case of *TUPE*, the *Enterprise and Regulatory Reform Act 2013 (Consequential Amendments) (Employment) (No. 2) Order 2014 (SI 2014/853)*.

The statutory formula for the amendment of time limits is common to all the amending legislation and provides (using the example of the amendment to the time limits in the *ERA 1996* (see the new *s 207B*):

> "207B Extension of time limits to facilitate conciliation before institution of proceedings
>
> (1) This section applies where this Act provides for it to apply for the purposes of a provision of this Act (a "relevant provision").
>
> But it does not apply to a dispute that is (or so much of a dispute as is) a relevant dispute for the purposes of section 207A.
>
> (2) In this section—
>
> (a) Day A is the day on which the complainant or applicant concerned complies with the requirement in subsection (1) of section 18A of the Employment Tribunals Act 1996 (requirement to contact ACAS before instituting proceedings) in relation to the matter in respect of which the proceedings are brought, and
>
> (b) Day B is the day on which the complainant or applicant concerned receives or, if earlier, is treated as receiving (by virtue of regulations made under subsection (11) of that section) the certificate issued under subsection (4) of that section.
>
> (3) In working out when a time limit set by a relevant provision expires the period beginning with the day after Day A and ending with Day B is not to be counted.
>
> (4) If a time limit set by a relevant provision would (if not extended by this subsection) expire during the period beginning with Day A and ending one month after Day B, the time limit expires instead at the end of that period.
>
> (5) Where an employment tribunal has power under this Act to extend a time limit set by a relevant provision, the power is exercisable in relation to the time limit as extended by this section."

Thus the period between initiation of contact with ACAS (Day A) and receipt (or deemed receipt) of the early conciliation certificate (Day B) does not count for limitation purposes (See, e.g., *ERA, s 207B(3)* above). If the certificate is sent by email, the day of receipt will be the same as the date of issue (*Rule 9(3)*). If posted, it will be the day it would have been delivered in the ordinary course of the post (*Rule 9(3)*). The certificate will state the date of issue and the method by which it is being sent (*Rule 8(e)*).

In addition there is a further extension if the relevant time limit would, if not extended by the relevant provision, expire "during the period beginning with Day A and ending one month after Day B". If so the relevant time limit expires at the end of that period. (See, e.g., *ERA, s 207B(4)* above).

The tribunal retains the familiar powers to extend time and those powers are "exercisable in relation to the time limit as extended by this section". Accordingly, a claim submitted after the extended limitation period may still be heard if it is just and equitable to do so (where that is the applicable statutory test) or if it was not reasonably practicable to present the claim in time (where that test applies).

2.7   CONCILIATION AFTER PRESENTATION OF A COMPLAINT TO THE EMPLOYMENT TRIBUNAL

Once a complaint has been presented to an employment tribunal, a conciliation officer must conciliate whether or not he is requested to do so if he considers that he could conciliate with a reasonable prospect of success or when he is requested to do so by both parties (*ETA 1996, s 18(1), (2)*).

Where the complaint is one of unfair dismissal, and the complainant has ceased to be employed by the employer against whom the complaint is made, the conciliation officer is required to seek the complainant's reinstatement or re-engagement. Where the complainant does not wish for either of these remedies, or where reinstatement or re-engagement is not practicable, the conciliation officer will attempt to obtain for him a sum by way of compensation (*ETA 1996, s 18(4)*). The same principles apply in relation to a potential complaint of unfair dismissal which has not been lodged in the employment tribunal at the time of conciliation (*ETA 1996, s 18(5)*). As a result of amendments made by the *Employment Act 2008* and the removal of the fixed periods for conciliation there is no limit upon the period during which a conciliation officer may seek to promote settlement by way of conciliation and this conciliation may in appropriate cases continue up to the point of an award of remedy by an employment tribunal.

Thus, if a complaint is presented to an employment tribunal, the respondent employer will often be contacted by a conciliation officer. The conciliation officer will usually outline the complainant's grievance and may convey the respondent's comments back to the complainant. If the respondent does not want his comments conveyed to the complainant he should make this clear to the conciliation officer. Nothing communicated to a conciliation officer in connection with the performance of his functions is admissible in evidence in any proceedings before an employment tribunal, except with the consent of the person who communicated it to the officer (*ETA 1996, s 18(7)*). It may also be of some comfort to those involved in the settlement of claims through ACAS to know that such communications attract absolute privilege for the purposes of any defamation proceedings as held in *Freer v Glover* [2005] EWHC 3341 (QB), [2006] IRLR 521 in which a solicitor acting for the employer involved in negotiations through ACAS was sued in defamation by the employee. Incidental publication of the alleged defamatory statement to ACAS staff was also protected by the privilege (*Lincoln v Daniels* [1962] 1 QB 237, [1961] 3 All ER 740, CA applied).

The important role of conciliation officers is emphasised by the fact that, subject to one important exception, an agreement to settle an employment tribunal complaint will only normally be binding on the parties if the agreement relates to a complaint or potential complaint where a conciliation officer has taken action in accordance with his statutory powers. The important exception concerns settlements reached after the employee has received advice from a relevant independent adviser (see EMPLOYMENT TRIBUNALS – I (18)). In other cases, an agreement to settle a claim or a potential claim is unenforceable, leaving the complainant free to pursue his claim before an employment tribunal (*ERA 1996, s 203(1), (2); SDA 1975, s 77(4)(a); RRA 1976, s 72(4)(a)*). In *Moore v Duport Furniture Products Ltd* [1982] ICR 84, [1982] IRLR 31, HL, a conciliation officer was considered to have taken such action in circumstances where the parties had already reached a settlement. In that case, the officer ascertained that they had truly reached agreement, which he then recorded in writing on a form designed for the purpose (Form COT 3). Where a conciliation officer assisted the parties in reaching an oral agreement, that agreement was held to be binding, notwithstanding that it had not been recorded in writing (*Gilbert v Kembridge Fibres Ltd* [1984] ICR 188, [1984] IRLR 52, EAT; see also *Hennessy v Craigmyle & Co Ltd* [1986] ICR 461, [1986] IRLR 300, CA). A conciliation officer is not under a duty to advise an employee on the relevant legislation, but an agreement reached with his assistance may be set aside if he acts partially or adopts unfair methods (*Slack v Greenham (Plant Hire) Ltd* [1983] ICR 617, [1983] IRLR 271, EAT). Nor will a tribunal be bound by a sham COT 3 designed to mislead a government department (*Trafford Carpets Ltd v Barker* IDS 440, p 16).

An attack upon the binding nature of a COT3 agreement on the basis that the conciliation officer had not advised the employees properly as to their rights was rejected by the EAT in *Clark v Redcar and Cleveland Borough Council* [2006] ICR 897, [2006] IRLR 324, EAT. As part of an overall settlement negotiated in equal pay claims the employees signed COT3 agreements limiting the amount of back pay to be paid. Subsequently they sought to set them aside on the basis of ACAS failing to provide advice that they could achieve considerably more in compensation by proceeding with the claims. The EAT reaffirmed that the function of ACAS was to promote settlement and not to advise upon the merits of a party's case and to do so might compromise the role of the conciliation officer. While best practice might sometimes suggest that the conciliation officer should caution the employee to take further advice, failure to do so would not provide grounds to set aside the COT3 which would only be set aside in cases of bad faith or impropriety by the conciliation officer.

In order to ensure that an agreement to settle a complaint or potential complaint is enforceable, parties should normally seek the assistance of a conciliation officer to promote a settlement and have him record the agreement on the appropriate form (COT3). This is not however mandatory for a settlement to be effective. The extent to which the conciliation officer must "take action" for the purposes of ousting the jurisdiction of the employment tribunal under *s 203* of the *ERA 1996* has been recently considered by the EAT in *Alma Construction Ltd v Bonner* [2011] IRLR 204. The EAT held that the threshold for taking action was very low. The ACAS officer is not required to broker the settlement nor to record it, whether in a COT3 or otherwise. The duty is only to endeavour to promote settlement. So long as this has been done, the ACAS officer has taken action and, if a settlement was reached, it will be binding for the purposes of *ERA 1996, s 203* and the employment tribunal will have no jurisdiction subsequently to hear the claim. In that case the communication to the employer via the ACAS officer of the claimant's willingness to accept an offer of settlement was sufficient for the purposes of *ERA 1996, s 203*.

In *Livingstone v Hepworth Refractories Ltd* [1992] 3 CMLR 601, [1992] ICR 287, EAT, it was held that a COT 3 made where the conciliation officer was acting under the *Employment Protection Consolidation Act 1978* (now *ERA 1996*) was only effective to settle discrimination or equal pay claims if it was expressly stated to include such claims, whether brought under domestic or European law.

2.8   Conciliation in complaints to Central Arbitration Committee

ACAS will seek to promote a settlement of complaints by recognised trade unions of failure to disclose information (*TULRCA 1992, s 183(2)*; see TRADE UNIONS – I (50)).

2.9   ARBITRATION

Where a trade dispute exists or is apprehended, ACAS may, with the consent of all parties to the dispute, refer the matters in dispute for the arbitration of:

(a)   an independent arbitrator or arbitrators, not being an employee of ACAS; or

(b)   the Central Arbitration Committee.

(TULRCA 1992, s 212(1).)

However, ACAS will first consider the likelihood of the dispute being settled by conciliation and, in the absence of special reasons, a matter will not be referred to arbitration until any agreed disputes procedure has been exhausted *(TULRCA 1992, s 212(2), (3))*.

An award by an arbitrator may be published if ACAS so decides and all the parties concerned consent *(TULRCA 1992, s 212(4)(b))*.

The *Arbitration Act 1950, Part I* does not apply to such an arbitration *(TULRCA 1992, s 212(5))*.

2.10   THE EMPLOYMENT RIGHTS (DISPUTE RESOLUTION) ACT 1998

By *s 212A* of *TULRCA 1992* (introduced by *s 7* of the *Employment Rights (Dispute Resolution) Act 1998*, which came into force on 1 August 1998), ACAS was given the power to draw up a scheme for the voluntary (but binding) arbitration of unfair dismissal disputes subject to the approval of the Secretary of State. Following ACAS consultation on the scheme, which was expressed to be intended to be 'voluntary, speedy, informal, confidential and free from legal argument', the arbitration scheme came into effect in England and Wales on 21 May 2001. Guidance on the operation of the scheme is available on the ACAS website (www.acas.org.uk). The application of the scheme was, from 6 April 2004, extended to Scotland by the *ACAS Arbitration Scheme (Great Britain) Order 2004 (SI 2004/753)*. The scheme may be summarised (in brief outline) as follows (for further detail see EMPLOYMENT TRIBUNALS – I (18)).

First, it is important to note that the scheme is voluntary and is limited to unfair dismissal claims. If a claim for unfair dismissal is to be determined under the scheme, then any other claim (even if raised at the same time or on related facts) must go to the employment tribunal or be settled. If other related claims are to be heard in the employment tribunal, then the arbitration proceedings may be postponed pending the tribunal's determination. On submission of a claim to arbitration, both parties must waive in writing the right they would otherwise have in relation to an unfair dismissal claim. This includes waiver of the right to raise jurisdictional issues such as time limits, continuity of service and whether, in fact, the employee was dismissed.

The scheme provides for hearings to take place in private (unlike the normal tribunal procedure) and is intended to be speedy, non-legalistic and cost effective. The scheme is not intended for claims involving legal complexity or EC law; such claims, according to the Schedule, should remain the province of the employment tribunal. The arbitrators will be appointed by ACAS from the ACAS arbitration panel. In contrast to tribunal proceedings, the arbitration may take place anywhere, including the employee's place of work. There is no mechanism for compulsory attendance of witnesses or production of documents (although failure to produce/attend may be taken into account by the arbitrator in reaching his decision). Evidence will not be subject to the formality of tribunal procedure and will be given unsworn and without cross-examination. The arbitrator will, however, have the power to question witnesses or parties to determine the facts.

2.10   Advisory, Conciliation and Arbitration Service (ACAS)

The arbitrator's decision will not take the form of detailed reasons. The arbitrator must, in reaching his decision, apply the recognised principles of fairness in the employment context (including ACAS Codes of Practice) and, additionally, must apply the *Human Rights Act 1998* and relevant EC law. The remedies available to a successful employee are the same as in the employment tribunal (reinstatement, re-engagement and compensation). The arbitrator's decision is final; there is no mechanism for appeal from the decision. The parties remain free to settle the matter at any time during the arbitration, however. To date the scheme has not proved to be very popular: the *ACAS Annual Report* 2006/07 revealed that in that year only three unfair dismissal cases were the subject of arbitration (down from 6 in 2005/06, 4 in 2004/05, 7 in 2003/04 and 23 in 2002/03). Data for subsequent years is not included in the relevant ACAS Reports.

The power of ACAS to arbitrate also extends to flexible working requests. See, on flexible working, *ERA 1996, ss 80F–80I* (as inserted by the *Employment Act 2002*). The ACAS flexible working arbitration scheme, introduced pursuant to *s 212A* of *TULRCA* (see the *ACAS (Flexible Working) Arbitration Scheme (England and Wales) Order 2003 (SI 2003/694)*) is similar in form and operation to the scheme relating to unfair dismissal. An arbitrator hears the claim and gives a final decision with limited rights of appeal or challenge available to the parties. If the parties have elected to go to arbitration, there is no right to go to the employment tribunal. The remedies and compensation which may be awarded by the arbitrator mirror those in the employment tribunal. As in the case of unfair dismissal arbitration, there is detailed guidance on the arbitration of flexible working disputes available on the ACAS website. Utilisation of this service is, however, infrequent. The *ACAS Annual Report* 2006–07 revealed that in that year no flexible working claims went to arbitration (the same as 2005/06; in 2004/05 one such claim went to arbitration). Data for subsequent years is not included in the relevant ACAS Reports.

2.11   ADVICE

ACAS is empowered, on request or on its own initiative, to give such advice as it thinks appropriate to employers, workers and their organisations on matters concerned with or affecting or likely to affect industrial relations. It may also publish general advice on matters connected with or affecting or likely to affect industrial relations (*TULRCA 1992, s 213* as substituted by *TURERA 1993, s 43(2)*). ACAS's helpline is extremely popular, with close to one million calls answered per year. The ACAS helpline telephone number is 08457 47 47 47.

ACAS publishes a number of guides in relation to various employment law issues with a series of advisory booklets, leaflets and handbooks, the latter directed particularly to small firms. In addition, ACAS has a series of e-learning packages available on its website together with an online helpline. These publications are available from ACAS Public Enquiry Points and also from the ACAS website (www.acas.org.uk).

The ACAS telephone Helpline for all employment related questions is 0300 123 1100.

2.12   INQUIRY

ACAS may, if it thinks fit, inquire into any question relating to industrial relations generally or to industrial relations in any particular industry or in any particular undertaking or part of any undertaking (*TULRCA 1992, s 214(1)*).

The findings of such an inquiry, together with any advice given in connection with those findings, may be published by ACAS if it appears to it that publication is desirable for the improvement of industrial relations. Before deciding whether to publish, ACAS must send a draft of the findings to all the parties appearing to ACAS to be concerned, and take account of their views (*TULRCA 1992, s 214(2)*).

2.13   CODES OF PRACTICE

ACAS has a general power to issue new or revised Codes of Practice to give practical guidance for promoting the improvement of industrial relations (*TULRCA 1992, s 199*). It has issued five Codes of Practice so far:

No 1: Disciplinary and Grievance Procedures

No 2: Disclosure of Information

No 3: Time Off for Trade Union Duties

No.4: Code of Practice on Settlement Agreements (2013)

No 5: Handling in a Reasonable Manner Requests to Work Flexibly (2014)

The Codes have not remained static since their first issue in 1985 and have been the subject of a number of revisions.

A wholly new Code of Practice No 1 was issued with effect from 6 April 2009 to reflect the repeal by the *Employment Act 2008* of the statutory dispute resolution procedures in relation to matters of discipline and grievance (which had been introduced by *Part 3* of the *Employment Act 2002* (with effect from 1 October 2004) and the *Employment Act 2002 (Dispute Resolution) Regulations 2004 (SI 2004/752)*. Code of Practice No 1 was revised in minor respects in relation to accompaniment at disciplinary or grievance hearings and reissued on 11 March 2015. The relevant statutory instrument setting out the revised Code of Practice No 1 is (*SI 2015/649*).

The Code of Practice No 2 on Disclosure of Information (third revision 2003) deals with disclosure of information to trade unions for the purposes of collective bargaining pursuant to the obligations contained in *ss 181* and *182* of *TULRCA 1992*.

The Code of Practice No 3 on Time Off for Trade Union Duties was revised with effect from 1 January 2010 by order of the Secretary of State (*Employment Protection Code of Practice (Time Off for Trade Union Duties and Activities) Order 2009 (SI 2009/3223)*).

The fourth of the ACAS codes on Settlement Agreements was introduced as a consequence of *s 14* of the *Enterprise and Regulatory Reform Act 2013* and the introduction of protected conversations between employers and employees about terms of settlement for the termination of employment (see *s 111A* of the *ERA 1996*).

As in the case of the other Codes, it was made pursuant to *s 199* of *TULR(C)A 1992*, and was brought into force on 29 July 2013 by the *Employment Code of Practice (Settlements) Order 2013 (SI 2013/1665)*.

The fifth of the ACAS Codes on flexible work requests was introduced with effect from 30 June 2014 following implementation of the changes made by the *Children and Families Act 2014* in relation to such requests. Again, it was made pursuant to *s 199* of *TULR(C)A 1992*, and was brought into force by the *Code of Practice (Handling in a Reasonable Manner Requests to Work Flexibly) Order 2014 (SI 2014/1665)*.

For the legal effect of these Codes of Practice and the procedure to be followed in issuing them, see **5.3 CODES OF PRACTICE**.

2.14 Advisory, Conciliation and Arbitration Service (ACAS)

2.14 CONTACTING ACAS

ACAS headquarters are at Euston Tower, 286 Euston Road, London NW1 3JJ. Tel: 0207 396 0022. For information in relation to employment issues the ACAS Helpline (0300 123 1100) should be used. The majority of ACAS publications and guides may be downloaded from its website (www.acas.org.uk).

ACAS regional offices

Acas East Midlands

Apex Court,
City Link,
Nottingham, NG2 4LA.

Acas East of England

Forest Heath District Council Offices,
College Heath Road,
Mildenhall,
Suffolk, IP28 7EY.

Acas London

Euston Tower,
286 Euston Road,
London, NW1 3JJ.

Acas North East

Newcastle Civic Centre,
Barras Bridge,
Newcastle upon Tyne, NE1 8QH.

Acas North West

3rd Floor,
Piccadilly Gate,
Store Street,
Manchester, M1 2WD

Acas North West

Redgrave Court,
Merton Road, Bootle,
Merseyside,
Liverpool, L20 7HS.

Acas South East

Civic Offices,
1st Floor,
Harlington Way,
Fleet,
Hampshire,   GU51 4AE.

Acas South West

Temple Quay House,
2 The Square,
Bristol, BS1 6DG.

Acas West Midlands

Victoria Square House,
Victoria Square,
Birmingham, B2 4AJ.

Acas Yorkshire and Humber

The Cube,
123 Albion Street,
Leeds, LS2 8ER.

Acas Scotland

151 West George Street,
Glasgow, G2 2JJ.

Acas Wales

Companies House,
Crown Way,
Cardiff, CF14 3U0.

3   ACAS Conciliation

3.1   INTRODUCTION OF COMPULSORY EARLY CONCILIATION

Following amendments which originated in the *Enterprise and Regulatory Reform Act 2013*, a new conciliation scheme run by the Advisory Conciliation and Arbitration Service (ACAS) came into operation on 6 April 2014 (*Enterprise and Regulatory Reform Act 2013 (Commencement No 5, Transitional Provisions and Savings) Order 2014, art 3 (SI 2014/253)*).

Where a claimant had referred a dispute to ACAS between 6 April 2014 and 5 May 2014, and presented the claim form before 5 May 2014, the claim was treated as subject to a requirement of early conciliation, which was met on day on which he or she referred the dispute to ACAS (*SI 2014/253, art 4*).

From 6 May 2014 (*SI 2014/253, art 4*), a claimant will generally be required to prove that the dispute has been referred to ACAS for early conciliation before presenting a claim to the Employment Tribunal, by producing the early conciliation certificate, failing which the Employment Tribunal will not have jurisdiction over the claim (*Employment Tribunal Rules of Procedure, r 12*).

Most employment tribunal proceedings are relevant proceedings for the purposes of early conciliation (*Employment Tribunals Act 1996, s 18(1)* as amended by the *ETA 1996 (Application of Conciliation Provisions) Order 2014 (SI 2014/431)*). Early conciliation is the process which applies to matters which could be the subject of relevant proceedings, *ie* to a potential claim, and conciliation is the process which applies to relevant proceedings themselves, *ie* to a claim which has been presented (*ETA 1996, s 18(1A)*). When proceeding under the provisions on early conciliation, the conciliation officer is, where appropriate, under a duty to have regard to the desirability of encouraging the use of other procedures available for the settlement of grievances (*ETA 1996, s 18(6)*). Anything communicated to a conciliation officer in connection with the performance of his conciliation functions will not be admissible in evidence in Employment Tribunal proceedings without the consent of the person who made the communication (*ETA 1996, s 18(7)*). Therefore, an employer has no right to know or rely on the content of the discussions which occurred between the employee and ACAS.

Before presenting an Employment Tribunal claim, the claimant must provide prescribed information to ACAS in the prescribed manner, about the matter (*ETA 1996, s 18A(1)*).

On receiving the prescribed information in the prescribed manner, ACAS must send a copy of it to a conciliation officer (*ETA 1996, s 18A(2)*), who will be under a duty during the early conciliation period to endeavour to promote a settlement between the would-be parties (*ETA 1996, s 18A(3)*).

If the conciliation officer concludes that a settlement is not possible or the early conciliation period expires without a settlement having been reached, then the conciliation officer will issue an early conciliation certificate to the employee (*ETA 1996, s 18A(4)*). Nevertheless, the conciliation officer may continue to endeavour to promote a settlement even after the early conciliation period has ended (*ETA 1996, s 18A(5)*).

3.2   EXEMPTIONS FROM EARLY CONCILIATION

Relevant proceedings may be commenced without the requirement for early conciliation in prescribed circumstances (*ETA 1996, s 18A(7)*). At present, exemptions from early conciliation exist in five cases: first, where the claimant institutes relevant proceedings to which the requirement for early conciliation would apply, however, another person has complied with the requirement for early conciliation in relation to the same dispute and the claimant wishes to institute proceedings on the same claim form; second, where the claimant institutes relevant proceedings on the same claim form as proceedings which are not relevant proceedings; third, where the claimant can prove that the respondent notified ACAS about a dispute, ACAS has not received information from the claimant under *ETA 1996, s 18A(1)* in relation to that dispute, and the proceedings on the claim form relate to that dispute; fourth, where the claim is for unfair dismissal and is accompanied by an application for interim relief under *ERA 1996, s 128* or *TULRCA 1992, s 161*; or, fifth, where the claimant is instituting proceedings against the Security Service, the Secret Intelligence Service or the Government Communications Headquarters (*Employment Tribunals (Early Conciliation: Exemptions and Rules of Procedure) Regulations 2014, art 3 (SI 2014/254)*).

3.3   THE EFFECTS OF THE REQUIREMENT FOR EARLY CONCILIATION

Where a claimant is subject to the requirement to contact ACAS before instituting Employment Tribunal proceedings, he or she may not present a claim without an early conciliation certificate (*ETA 1996, s 18A(8)*).

Where the proposed claim is of unfair dismissal, the conciliation officer is empowered to seek to promote the employee's reinstatement or re-engagement by the employer or its successor or an associated employer on terms which appear equitable to the conciliation officer, as an alternative to promoting agreement as to compensation (*ETA 1996, s 18A(9)*).

An employer may refer a workplace dispute to ACAS if he or she considers that it is likely to escalate into employment tribunal proceedings, where the employee has not already notified ACAS (*ETA 1996, s 18B(1)*), and an employee may refer a dispute to ACAS even though the case involves an exception to the requirement for early conciliation (*ETA 1996, s 18B(2)*). In both situations, the conciliation officer will still be under a duty to promote a settlement, however, the duration of that duty is open-ended, rather for the duration of the prescribed period (*ETA 1996, s 18B(3)* cf *ETA 1996, s 18A(3)*). Nevertheless, where the dispute is referred by the employer or by an employee whose potential claim is subject to an exception from the requirement for early conciliation, then the conciliation officer's duty to promote settlement comes to an end when either the conciliation officer concludes that a settlement is not possible, or the conciliation officer comes under a duty to promote settlement during the prescribed period under *section 18A(3)* of the *ETA 1996*, ie when the dispute is referred to ACAS by a prospective claimant in relevant proceedings. For disputes referred by the employer, or where there is an exception to the requirement for early conciliation, the conciliation officer is empowered in unfair dismissal cases to promote reinstatement, re-engagement, or agreed compensation (*ETA 1996, s 18B(6)*). It should be noted that where an employer refers the dispute to ACAS it will have no effect upon the limitation period, because the conciliation officer's duty is not linked to the prescribed period for early conciliation, nor to any obligation to issue a certificate of early conciliation. ACAS advises employers to telephone them if they would like to start early conciliation.

Where early conciliation fails and a claim is presented and a copy sent to ACAS, the existing system will continue, under which the conciliation officer will be under a duty to promote settlement where requested by both parties or where the officer considers that there would be a reasonable prospect of promoting a settlement (ETA 1996, s 18C(1)). The powers of the conciliation officer include promoting reinstatement, re-engagement and an agreed sum of compensation, where the claim is for unfair dismissal (*ETA 1996, s 18C(2)*).

3.4 THE EARLY CONCILIATION RULES OF PROCEDURE

The Early Conciliation Rules of Procedure (*Employment Tribunals (Early Conciliation: Exemption and Rules of Procedure) Regulations 2014, reg 5, Schedule*) prescribe the content of early conciliation.

Guidance is available at www.acas.org.uk/earlyconciliation, where the early conciliation notification form can also be found.

The form may be returned online or by post (*Early Conciliation Rules of Procedure, r 2(a)*).

Parties without internet access may telephone ACAS on 0300 123 11 22 (*Early Conciliation Rules of Procedure, r 1*). ACAS will then insert the prospective claimant's name and address and the prospective respondent's name and address to the early conciliation form (*Early Conciliation Rules of Procedure, r 3*).

On the notification form the employee is required to state his or her name and contact details and the employer's name and contact details (*Early Conciliation Rules of Procedure, r 2(2)*). The current ACAS form also requests the date on which employment started, the date on which employment ended if applicable, the job which the employee did, and the date on which the event about which the employee intends to complain took place.

If there is more than one respondent, the employee must present a separate early conciliation form for each respondent, or name each respondent by telephone (*Early Conciliation Rules of Procedure, r 4*). The correct name must be used for the respondent, otherwise the conciliation certificate will not match with the claim form and the employment tribunal will lack jurisdiction. The employee is not required to give any other details of the complaint in the notification form.

ACAS is required to make reasonable attempts to contact the prospective claimant and if he or she consents must make reasonable attempts to contact the prospective respondent (*Early Conciliation Rules of Procedure, r 5*).

3.5   Early conciliation through ACAS is voluntary for both the employer and the employee, although an employee who does not wish to use early conciliation will after 6 May 2014 still be required to obtain a conciliation certificate before presenting an employment tribunal claim. No charge is made to either party to conciliation. Where ACAS is unable to make contact with either prospective party, then it must conclude that a settlement is not possible (*Early Conciliation Rules of Procedure, r 5*).

Given first that ACAS early conciliation is voluntary for claimants and second that discussions between employees and ACAS are confidential, it does not seem fruitful for an employer to try to raise complaints or jurisdictional arguments based on inconsistency between issues discussed at the early conciliation stage and the content of the claim form. Despite the existence of the early conciliation regime, employers may still be taken unawares by particular claims or allegations in the claim form, or by applications to amend claims.

In *Science Warehouse Limited v Mills* (2015) UKEAT/0224/15, [2016] IRLR 96 the Employment Appeal Tribunal ("the EAT") held that *s 18A* of the *ETA 1996* did not require that the early conciliation process was undertaken in respect of each claim, but used the broader terminology of "matter", and also envisaged that the requirement to notify ACAS was one that fell on a prospective rather than on an existing claimant. Therefore, the EAT considered that where the claimant had previously lodged a valid employment tribunal claim, including her early conciliation reference, and was applying to amend to add a new but related claim, that was a matter for the employment tribunal's general case management powers and not subject to jurisdictional restrictions imposed by the early conciliation rules. Following the same principles, in *Mist v Derby Community Health Services NHS Trust* (2016) UKEAT/0170/15, [2016] All ER (D) 252 (Jan) the EAT held that an application to join a transferee in a transfer of undertakings claim as a second respondent fell to be considered as a possible amendment to an existing claim and did not require a further early conciliation certificate. Likewise, in *Compass Group UK & Ireland Ltd v Morgan* [2016] IRLR 924, the EAT held that an early conciliation certificate obtained by a prospective claimant could cover future events.

ACAS is requesting that potential claimants should notify ACAS themselves of their intention to claim, and that claimants' representatives should not do so. The guidance states, however, that once ACAS has checked the details and nature of the claim with the claimant, and a conciliator has made contact with the claimant and confirmed that the representative has been appointed, then ACAS will deal with the representative. Representatives of groups of claimants are requested to call ACAS to discuss how group conciliation works and the involvement of a specialist collective conciliator.

According to its guidance, when ACAS first receives an early conciliation request, an acknowledgment will be sent online, by email or by post, depending upon the method of notification used by the party. ACAS has stated in its guidance that it aims to telephone the notifier by the end of the following working day to check the information provided, find out what the claim is about and explain early conciliation. No time indicator is given for the next stage, which is for the ACAS conciliator to call the claimant. Nevertheless, once the conciliator has made contact with the claimant and the claimant has agreed to proceed with early conciliation, the conciliator will aim to make contact with both parties by the end of the following working day.

If the conciliator cannot contact the claimant over a reasonable period of time or the claimant indicates that he or she does not want to use early conciliation, then ACAS will close the case and issue an early conciliation certificate by email or post.

The guidance from ACAS says that most conciliation discussions will be by telephone but sometimes the conciliator will chair a meeting between the parties where it is considered helpful.

Any settlements which ACAS facilitates will be made on the COT3 form.

3.6 THE EFFECT ON THE LIMITATION PERIOD

The claimant must make a request for early conciliation during the limitation period. Once the request is made, time for presenting the claim stops running from the day after the employee refers the dispute to ACAS until the day after he or she receives the early conciliation certificate (see *art 2* of the *Employment and Regulatory Reform Act 2013 (Consequential Amendments) Order 2014 (SI 2014/386)*).

The conciliation officer will endeavour to promote a settlement for up to one month from receipt of the early notification form or the telephone call from the prospective claimant (*Early Conciliation Rules of Procedure, r 6(1)*).

If both parties agree that more time is needed for conciliation, the cessation can be extended only once for 14 days (*Early Conciliation Rules of Procedure, r 6(2)* and *(3)*).

After a maximum cessation of one month plus 14 days, if the matter is not resolved, the conciliator will end early conciliation and issue a conciliation certificate, as the conciliator will do if he or she concludes earlier that settlement is not possible (*Early Conciliation Rules of Procedure, r 7*).

The formal early conciliation certificate must contain the prospective claimant's name and address, the prospective respondent's name and address, the date of receipt by ACAS of the early conciliation form presented in accordance with Early Conciliation Rules, a unique reference number which the employee must provide when submitting his or her claim form to the employment tribunal, the date of issue of the certificate and the mode of transmission of the certificate (*Early Conciliation Rules of Procedure, r 8*). The conciliation certificate must be sent to the prospective claimant but will be copied to the employer only if the employer had been contacted by ACAS (*Early Conciliation Rules of Procedure, r 9(1)*). If ACAS has an email address for the recipient, the early conciliation certificate must be sent by email, otherwise it will be sent by post (*Early Conciliation Rules of Procedure, r 9(2)*). It will be deemed received the same day if emailed and received in the ordinary course of the post if posted *Early Conciliation Rules of Procedure, r 9*).

3.7 The limitation period will recommence after the early conciliation certificate has been received by the employee. The employee will have at least one month following receipt of the conciliation certificate in which to present his or her claim (*SI 2014/386*).

Thus, it can be seen that in most cases, involving a three-month limitation period, the maximum limitation period will now, in strict theory, be one day short of five months and fourteen days, calculated as follows. If the employee contacts ACAS on the last day of the limitation period (which would be a risky strategy to adopt) then one day short of three months would have passed at the commencement of the early conciliation period. Time would then cease to run for a maximum of one month plus 14 days. Following the issue of the conciliation certificate, the employee would have a further month in which to present the claim.

On the other hand, where the employer refers the dispute to ACAS, the employee is not under a requirement to notify ACAS about the dispute before presenting his or her claim (*ETA 1996, ss 18A(7), 18B)*). In other words, one way in which an employer could try to encourage a claimant to present a claim within the normal limitation period would be notify ACAS about the dispute early during the limitation period, draw that fact to the employee's attention and point out that he or she was not required to contact ACAS. Nevertheless, it seems that it remains open to a prospective claimant to contact ACAS even where the employer has already done so (*ETA 1996, ss 18A(7) and 18B(1)(b)*).

The question whether a claim was presented in time or not will still be a matter for the Employment Tribunal and the ACAS conciliator will not be able to decide or advise on that issue, ACAS states. It appears that a claimant who is out of time is still required to contact ACAS to obtain an early conciliation certificate (*ETA 1996, s 18A*). The prospective claimant and prospective respondent in such a situation would need to consider carefully the tactical advantages and disadvantages of engaging in a settlement discussion at that time, and of refusing to participate so that the certificate was issued straight away, since the involvement of ACAS after expiry of the limitation period would have appear to have no effect upon the limitation period.

In addition, every employer must ensure that young persons employed by him are protected at work from any risks to their health or safety which are a consequence of the factors referred to in (a) above (*reg 19(1)*). Furthermore, the employment of young persons is prohibited for work:

(i)   which is beyond their physical or psychological capacity;

(ii) involving harmful exposure to agents which are toxic or carcinogenic, cause heritable genetic damage or harm to the unborn child, or which in any other way chronically affect human health;

(iii) involving harmful exposure to radiation;

(iv) involving the risk of accidents which it may reasonably be assumed cannot be recognised or avoided by young persons owing to their insufficient attention to safety or lack of experience or training; or

(v)   in which there is a risk to health from extreme cold or heat, noise or vibration.

In determining whether work will involve harm or risk for these purposes, the employer must have regard to the results of the assessment referred to above (*reg 19(2)*).

However, the prohibition in *reg 19(2)* does not apply in relation to young persons over school-leaving age where (1) the work is necessary for their training, (2) the young person will be supervised by a competent person, and (3) the risks are reduced to their lowest practicable level (*reg 19(3)*).

4.6   Rest periods, breaks and night work

Following the publication in February 1997 by the DTI of a consultation document to implement the provisions of *Directive 94/33* (see above) which cover night work, and entitlement to rest periods, for young persons, the DTI subsequently announced that it intended to implement those provisions by including them in the regulations for implementing the *EC Working Time Directive (93/104)*.

Both Directives were implemented by the *Working Time Regulations 1998 (SI 1998/1833)*, which came into force on 1 October 1998. With regard to young persons (referred to in those *Regulations* as 'young workers'), *Directive 94/33* sets a limit on working time of eight hours per day and 40 hours per week, and prohibits night work altogether. However, in the draft *Regulations* which were originally issued for consultation, the Government stated that it proposed to take advantage of the opt-outs available in the *Directive* which disapplied those limits, as it believed 'that the working time limits set out in the Working Time Directive provide sufficient protection for all workers'. Thus, the original wording of the *Working Time Regulations 1998* did not provide for separate limits on working time for young workers, and the adult limits were applicable to them. (For a summary of the adult limits, see **28.15** Health and Safety at Work – II.)

The opt-outs referred to above ceased to be available on 22 June 2000, and the Government issued a consultation document in December 2000 seeking views on how the remaining provisions of the *Directive* should be implemented. In June 2002, the Government issued a further consultation document (see webarchive.nationalarchives.gov.uk) to which draft amending *Regulations* were annexed. These amending *Regulations* were subsequently issued as the *Working Time (Amendment) Regulations 2002 (SI 2002/3128)* and came into force on 6 April 2003. From that date the *1998 Regulations* were amended so as to:

(a)   limit the working hours of young workers to no more than 40 hours per week, or eight hours in any one day – an employer must take all reasonable steps, in keeping with the need to protect the health and safety of workers, to ensure that these limits are complied with in respect of each young worker employed by him (*reg 5A*); and

(b)   prohibit night working by young workers between 10pm to 6am (or 11pm to 7am) (*regs 2, 6A*).

These provisions protecting young workers were added to the existing special entitlements in the *1998 Regulations* which apply to young workers, which are set out below:

(c)   a health and capacities assessment before being required to perform night work, and periodically thereafter (*reg 7(2)*);

(d)   a minimum daily continuous rest period of 12 hours (*reg 10(2)*);

(e)   two days off per week (*reg 11(3)*); and

(f)   a minimum 30-minute rest break where daily working time exceeds 4.5 hours (*reg 12(4)*).

Note that the protections and entitlements set out in (a) to (f) above are subject to the following exceptions.

Domestic servants. Regulations *5A, 6A*, and *7(2)* do not apply in relation to a young worker employed as a domestic servant in a private household (*reg 19*, as amended).

Armed forces. Regulations *5A, 6A, 10(2)* and *11(3)* do not apply in relation to a young worker serving as a member of the armed forces, although where such a young worker is accordingly required to work during the restricted period, or is not permitted the minimum rest period provided for in *reg 10(2)* or *11(3)*, he must be allowed an appropriate period of compensatory rest (*reg 25(2), (3)*, as amended).

Force majeure. Regulations *5A, 6A, 10(2)* and *12(4)* do not apply in relation to a young worker where his employer requires him to undertake work which no adult worker is available to perform and which:

(i)   is occasioned by either an occurrence due to unusual and unforeseeable circumstances, beyond the employer's control, or exceptional events, the consequences of which could not have been avoided despite the exercise of all due care by the employer;

(ii)   is of a temporary nature; and

(iii)   must be performed immediately.

Where the application of *regs 5A, 6A, 10(2)* or *12(4)* is excluded by virtue of (i) to (iii) above, and a young worker is accordingly required to work during a period which would otherwise be a rest period or rest break, his employer must allow him to take an equivalent period of compensatory rest within the following three weeks (*reg 27*, as amended).

Other restrictions applicable to young workers. Regulation *5A* does not apply in relation to a young worker:

(1)   where the young worker's employer requires him to undertake work which is necessary either to maintain continuity of service or production or to respond to a surge in demand for a service or product;

(2)   where no adult worker is available to perform the work; and

(3)   where performing the work would not adversely affect the young worker's education or training.

(*Regulation 27A(1)*, inserted by *SI 2002/3128*).

In addition, in the circumstances referred to in (1) to (3) above:

(a)   *reg 6A* does not apply in relation to a young worker employed—

   (i)   in a hospital or similar establishment; or

   (ii)   in connection with cultural, artistic, sporting or advertising activities; and

(b)   *reg 6A* does not apply, except in so far as it prohibits work between midnight and 4am, in relation to a young worker employed in—

   (i)   agriculture;

   (ii)   retail trading;

   (iii) postal or newspaper deliveries;

   (iv)   a catering business;

   (v)   a hotel, public house, restaurant, bar or similar establishment; or

   (vi)   a bakery.

(Regulation 27A(2), (3), inserted by SI 2002/3128.)

Where the application of *reg 6A* is excluded by para (*a*) or (*b*) above, and a young worker is accordingly required to work during a period which would otherwise be a rest period or rest break:

(i)   he must be supervised by an adult worker where such supervision is necessary for the young worker's protection; and

(ii)   he must be allowed an equivalent period of compensatory rest.

(Regulation 27A(4), inserted by SI 2002/3128.)

Remedies. Regulation 30 (as amended) provides that a young worker may complain to an employment tribunal where his employer has refused to permit him to exercise any right he has:

(1)   under *reg 10(2), 11(3)*, or *12(4)*; or

(2)   to compensatory rest under *reg 25(3), 27A(4)(b)* or *27(2)*.

The time limit for the presentation of such a complaint is three months beginning with the day on which it is alleged that the exercise of the right should have been permitted (or in the case of a rest period or leave extending over more than one day, the date on which it should have been permitted to begin). If the tribunal is satisfied that it was not reasonably practicable for the complaint to be presented within the period of three months (see **18.7** EMPLOYMENT TRIBUNALS – I), then this time may be extended.

Where the tribunal finds the complaint well-founded, it must make a declaration to that effect, and may make an award of compensation to be paid by the employer to the worker. The amount of the compensation will be such as the tribunal considers just and equitable in all the circumstances having regard to:

(a)   the employer's default in refusing to permit the worker to exercise his right; and

(b)   any loss sustained by the worker which is attributable to the matters complained of.

(For separate provisions governing rest periods for young persons engaged as workers on United Kingdom ships, see the *Merchant Shipping and Fishing Vessels (Health and Safety at Work) (Employment of Young Persons) Regulations 1998 (SI 1998/2411), reg 6.*)

4.7 Children and Young Persons

4.7 WORK EXPERIENCE FOR YOUNG PERSONS AND OTHERS

The *Education Act 1996, s 560A* (as amended by the *Children and Families Act 2014*, with effect from 1 September 2014) provides that a local authority in England may secure the provision of work experience for persons in their area (a) who are over compulsory school age but under 19, or (b) who are aged 19 or over and for whom an Education and Health Care plan is maintained. A local authority in England must (i) encourage participation in work experience by persons in their area who are within (a) or (b) above and (ii) encourage employers to participate in the provision of work experience for such persons (*Education Act 1996, s 560A(2)*).

4.8 TIME OFF FOR YOUNG PERSONS FOR STUDY OR TRAINING

England

As of 28 June 2013, young persons (i.e. 16 and 17 years olds) in England have a duty to participate in education or training until the age of 18 (see *Education and Skills Act 2008, Part 1*, brought into force by the *Education and Skills Act 2008 (Commencement No.9 and Transitory Provision) Order 2013 (SI 2013/1204)*). This duty to participate in education or training applies to any person who is resident in England and who:

(a)   has ceased to be of compulsory school age;

(b)   is still within a year of ceasing to be of compulsory school age (although with effect from 20 June 2015 this provision will apply to all those aged under 18 (*SI 2013/1204, Art 2(a), 3*)); and

(c)   has not attained a level 3 qualification.

Those in full-time occupation must participate in 'sufficient' relevant training or education. (*ESA 2008, s 2(1)*). A person is in full-time occupation if he works for at least 20 hours per week: (a) under a contract of employment; or (b) in any other way prescribed (see *Duty to Participate in Education or Training (Alternative Ways of Working) Regulations 2013 (SI 2013/1243)*), otherwise than under a short-term contract or arrangement. (*ESA 2008, s 5(1)*). The *Duty to Participate in Education or Training (Miscellaneous Provisions) Regulations 2013 (SI 2013/1205)* set out the definition of 'normal weekly working hours' and what is also to be treated as working for at least 20 hours. In addition, these regulations set out what constitutes: (i) a level 3 qualification, (ii) full time education (otherwise than at school) or training, (iii) the relevant period during which the duty applies, and (iv) further ways to calculate the requirement for 'sufficient' relevant training or education.

ESA 2008 also imposes corresponding duties on local education authorities (with effect from 28 June 2013) and employers (from a date to be appointed) to enable and support participation in education and training. Enforcement provisions protecting employees from detriment or unfair dismissal for exercising (or proposing to exercise) a right to participate in education and training under *ESA 2008* are also yet to be appointed.

Scotland and Wales

The right for young persons in employment to take time off from work for study and training, by virtue of *ERA 1996, ss 63A–63C* (inserted by the *Teaching and Higher Education Act 1998, s 32*), which previously applied across Great Britain, now applies only to young persons in Scotland and Wales.

An employee in Scotland or Wales who:

(a)   is aged 16 or 17,

(b)   is not receiving full-time secondary or further education, and

(c)   has not attained the prescribed standard of achievement,

is entitled to be permitted by his employer to take time off during the employee's working hours in order to undertake study or training leading to a relevant qualification (*ERA 1996, s 63A(1)*). The study or training may be either on the premises of the employer (or principal – see below) or elsewhere (*ERA 1996, s 63A(7)*). For the 'prescribed standard of achievement', see the *Right to Time Off for Study or Training Regulations 2001 (SI 2001/2801)*, which revoked and replaced the *1999 Regulations (SI 1999/986)* with effect from 1 September 2001.

A 'relevant qualification' means an external qualification the attainment of which (i) would contribute to the attainment of the prescribed standard referred to in (c) above, or (ii) would be likely to enhance the employee's employment prospects, whether with his employer or otherwise (*ERA 1996, s 63A(2)(c)*). An 'external qualification' means an academic or vocational qualification awarded or authenticated by such person or body as may be specified in *Regulations* (as to which, see the *Schedule* to *SI 2001/2801* referred to above).

An employee who satisfies the requirements in (a) to (c) above, and is sub-contracted by his employer to another person ('the principal'), is entitled to be permitted by the principal to take time off for the purposes specified in *ERA 1996, s 63A(1 (ERA 1996, s 63A(3)*). An 18-year-old employee who is undertaking study or training leading to a relevant qualification which he began before attaining that age has a similar right to time off (*ERA 1996, s 63A(4)*).

The amount of time off that an employee is to be permitted to take, and the occasions on which and the conditions under which time off is to be taken, are those that are reasonable in the circumstances having regard, in particular, to (a) the requirements of the employee's study or training, and (b) the circumstances of the business of the employer (or the principal) and the effect of the employee's time off on the running of that business (*ERA 1996, s 63A(5)*).

An employee who is allowed time off is entitled to be paid for the time taken off at the 'appropriate hourly rate', ie one week's pay divided by the number of normal working hours in a week for that employee when employed under the contract of employment in force on the day when the time off is taken (*ERA 1996, s 63B(1), (2)*). (For the calculation of the normal hourly rate where the number of normal working hours differs from week to week or over a longer period, see *ERA 1996, s 63B(3), (4)*.)

4.9   Remedy for refusal of, or remuneration for, time off

If the employer (or principal) has unreasonably refused the employee time off or has refused to pay him, the employee may present a complaint to an employment tribunal (*ERA 1996, s 63C(1)*). The time limit for the presentation of such a complaint is three months beginning with the day on which it is alleged the time off should have been allowed (or, as the case may be, on which the time off was taken). If the tribunal is satisfied that it was not reasonably practicable for the complaint to be presented within the period of three months (see **18.7 EMPLOYMENT TRIBUNALS – I**), then this time may be extended (*ERA 1996, s 63C(2)*).

If the employment tribunal finds the complaint well-founded, it will make a declaration to that effect (*ERA 1996, s 63C(3)*). If the complaint is of an unreasonable refusal to permit the employee to take time off, the tribunal will also order the employer or principal to pay the employee remuneration for the period during which the time off should have been allowed (*ERA 1996, s 63C(4)*). If the complaint is of a refusal to pay the employee for the time off, the tribunal will also order the employer or principal to pay the employee the amount due to him (*ERA 1996, s 63C(5)*).

4.10   Children and Young Persons

4.10   Right not to suffer detriment

By virtue of *ERA 1996, s 47A* (inserted by the *Teaching and Higher Education Act 1998, s 44*), an employee who is entitled to (i) time off under *ERA 1996, s 63A(1)* or *63A(3)*, and (ii) remuneration under *ERA 1996, s 63B(1)* for that time off (see **4.8** above), has the right not to be subjected to a detriment (ie an action short of dismissal) by his employer or principal on the ground that the employee exercised (or proposed to exercise) that right or received (or sought to receive) such remuneration.

If the employee suffers such a detriment, the remedy is to complain to an employment tribunal pursuant to *ERA 1996, s 48*. (For details, see **28.10** HEALTH AND SAFETY AT WORK – II.)

4.11   CONTRACTS OF EMPLOYMENT, AND MINORS

Contracts of employment form an important exception to the general principle that any contract made by a minor is unenforceable against him during his minority.

A contract of service or apprenticeship which enables a minor to earn a living is likely to be upheld as being for his benefit (*Doyle v White City Stadium Ltd* [1935] 1 KB 110, 104 LJKB 140, CA); this principle was followed by analogy in *Chaplin v Leslie Frewin (Publishers) Ltd* [1966] Ch 71, [1965] 3 All ER 764, CA, which concerned a contract for the publication of a book; see also *Mills v Inland Revenue Commissioners* [1972] 3 All ER 977. (*Doyle* and *Chaplin* were distinguished in *Proform Sports Management Ltd v Proactive Sports Management Ltd* [2006] EWHC 2812 (Ch), [2007] 1 All ER 542, which concerned a representation agreement with a professional footballer that had been entered into during his minority. Reference was also made to *Doyle* and *Chaplin* (albeit obiter) by Lady Hale in *Fisher v Brooker* [2009] UKHL 41, [2009] 4 All ER 789, in considering whether a minor can validly assign copyright by contract.) The effect of the entire contract must be considered; the contract will be upheld if on the whole it is for the minor's benefit (*Clements v London and North Western Rly Co* [1894] 2 QB 482, CA), but it will not be binding on the minor if it is not in his interests, or is clearly unreasonable or oppressive (*De Francesco v Barnum* (1890) 45 Ch D 430). Where a contract is, on the whole, for the minor's benefit, but it contains invalid covenants which are severable, such covenants may be struck out and the remainder of the contract upheld (see *Bromley v Smith* [1909] 2 KB 235, 78 LJKB 745).

The *Minors' Contracts Act 1987* made some limited amendments to the law relating to minors' contracts generally. In particular, it repealed the *Infants Relief Act 1874*, thereby enabling a minor, on or after reaching the age of majority, to ratify an otherwise unenforceable contract which he had entered into as a minor (*MCA 1987, s 1*).

5   Codes of Practice

Cross-references. See **10.4** DISCLOSURE OF INFORMATION for details of ACAS Code No 2 and **10.14** DISCLOSURE OF INFORMATION for the Codes of Practice in relation to Data Protection issued by the information Commissioner; **28.21** HEALTH AND SAFETY AT WORK – II for the HSC Code on Safety Representatives and Safety Committees; **49.2**, **49.3** and **49.9** TIME OFF WORK for ACAS Code No 3 and the HSC Code on Time Off for Training of Safety Representatives.

5.1   The first Code of Practice (now revoked) was introduced under powers conferred by the *Industrial Relations Act 1971*. Since then a number of other Codes have been issued. Codes of Practice are written in clear terms for the layman in order to give practical guidance. Employers are advised to read the existing and any new Codes of Practice issued and to follow their provisions whenever applicable. Although following a Code of Practice does not guarantee success in any potential claim in an employment tribunal, the employer who can show that he has followed its provisions will be on firm ground.

In broad terms, these Codes of Practice cannot be enforced by law. Nor does breach of a Code *of itself* give rise to any liability. However, Codes may be taken into account in legal proceedings. This chapter considers the powers which exist enabling specified bodies or people to issue Codes and the particular legal effect of the different Codes.

5.2   **THE CODES OF PRACTICE ISSUED BY ACAS**

Power to issue the Codes

ACAS is given statutory power to issue Codes of Practice, subject to approval by both Houses of Parliament. That power is now contained in the *Trade Union and Labour Relations (Consolidation) Act 1992* ('*TULRCA*'), *s 199*. Five such Codes (as amended) have been issued.

ACAS Code of Practice No 1 on Discipline and Grievance Procedures. The newest version of this Code was issued on 11 March 2015 by the *Code of Practice (Disciplinary and Grievance Procedures) Order 2015 (SI 2015/649)*. The revisions made to the previous version (which version came into force on 6 April 2009, replacing the previous 2004 revision of Code No 1) are, however, very limited and address only the EAT's decision in *Toal v GB Oils* [2013] IRLR 696 which had cast doubt on the previous version of the Code on the issue of whether an employer could reasonably object to the choice of a person to accompany an employee to a disciplinary or grievance hearing. The newest version of the Code continues to reflect the repeal of the statutory dispute resolution procedures by the *Employment Act 2008*. The Code, which comprises some 45 paragraphs, sets out practical guidance to employers, employees and representatives and lays down principles for the handling of disciplinary and grievance issues in the workplace. It should be noted that the Code does not apply to dismissals on grounds of redundancy. The excessive formalism of the statutory dispute resolution procedures is removed. A failure to follow the Code does not, of itself, give rise to automatic liability in any proceedings nor does it remove jurisdiction to hear the complaint from the employment tribunals. The employment tribunals are, however, obliged to take the Code into account and are empowered to adjust any award by up to 25% for an unreasonable failure to comply with any provision of the Code (see further **5.3** below).

In addition to the Code of Practice, ACAS has also published guidance dealing with disciplinary and grievance situations titled 'Discipline and Grievances at Work: The ACAS Guide'. Unlike the Code, employment tribunals are not expressly required to have regard to the ACAS guidance in reaching their decisions. In *McMillan v Airedale NHS Foundation*

5.2   Codes of Practice

Trust [2014] EWCA Civ 1031 the Court of Appeal observed, however, that whilst the guidance did not have the formal status of a code of practice, the guidance was "referred to in, and fills in the gaps in, the ACAS code of practice" and could in that case form part of the factual matrix for construing the relevant contractual disciplinary procedures.

ACAS Code of Practice No 2 on Disclosure of Information to Trade Unions for Collective Bargaining Purposes. This Code of Practice is in its third revision (2003) and sets out relatively short guidance in relation to the obligations to disclose information to trade unions for collective bargaining purposes pursuant to the provisions of *ss 181* and *182* of *TULRCA*. Under *TULRCA* information must be disclosed in accordance with good industrial relations practice and, in considering what is good industrial relations practice, regard is to be had to any relevant provisions of the Code. The provisions of the code are to be taken into account in any proceedings before the Central Arbitration Committee (*TULRCA s 181(2)(b)*, *181(4)* and *207(1)* and *(2)*). Paragraphs 4–12 of the Code provide guidance on the types of information to be disclosed and non exhaustive examples of categories of information are set out in paragraph 11. Guidance on restrictions on the duty to disclose are provided in paragraphs 13–15 of the Code and the responsibilities of trade unions and employers are considered in paragraphs 16–21. Guidance on joint arrangements for disclosure of information are set out in paragraphs 22–23 of the Code.

ACAS Code of Practice No 3 on Time Off for Trade Union Duties and Activities. This Code of Practice has been revised with effect from 1 January 2010 by order of the Secretary of State (*Employment Protection Code of Practice (Time Off for Trade Union Duties and Activities) Order 2009 (SI 2009/3223)*). (See further TIME-OFF WORK (49)).

ACAS Code of Practice on Settlement Agreements (2013). This, the fourth of the ACAS Codes, was introduced as a consequence of s 14 of the Enterprise and Regulatory Reform Act 2013 and the introduction of protected conversations between employers and employees about terms of settlement for the termination of employment (see *s 111A* of the *ERA 1996*). As in the case of the other Codes, it was made pursuant to *s 199* of *TULR(C)A 1992*, and was brought into force on 29 July 2013 by the *Employment Code of Practice (Settlements) Order 2013 (SI 2013/1665)*.

Acas Code of Practice on Handling in a Reasonable Manner Requests to Work Flexibly (2014). This, the fifth and newest of the ACAS Codes was introduced with effect from 30 June 2014 following implementation of the changes made by the *Children and Families Act 2014* in relation to such requests. Again, it was made pursuant to *s 199* of *TULR(C)A 1992*, and was brought into force by the *Code of Practice (Handling in a Reasonable Manner Requests to Work Flexibly) Order 2014 (SI 2014/1665)*.

As each of the first three Codes has during their history been the subject of substantial revision, in all cases the most up-to-date versions of the Codes should always be consulted. Each of the ACAS Codes is available for download from the ACAS website (www.acas.org.uk).

Where ACAS proposes to issue a Code, or a revised Code, it must first publish a draft and consider any representations made to it. If ACAS decides to proceed, the draft (modified if need be) is transmitted to the Secretary of State, who may either approve it or publish his reasons for withholding approval. If the Secretary of State approves the draft, it is laid before Parliament (*TULRCA 1992, ss 200, 201*).

5.3   Legal effect

TULRCA 1992, s 207(1), *(2)* states that breach of the ACAS Codes does not render a person liable to proceedings. However, in any proceedings before an employment tribunal or the Central Arbitration Committee ('CAC'), any Code of Practice issued by ACAS is admissible in evidence and any provision of the Code which appears to the employment tribunal or the CAC to be relevant to any question arising in the proceedings must be taken into account in determining that question. It had long been established that non-compliance with a Code would not necessarily render a dismissal unfair, but 'a failure to follow a procedure prescribed in the Code may lead to the conclusion that a dismissal was unfair, which, if that procedure had been followed, would have been held to have been fair' (*W Devis & Sons Ltd v Atkins* [1977] AC 931 at 955). As a consequence of the amendments made by the *Employment Act 2008* (*s 3(1), (2)*) and the repeal of the statutory dispute resolution procedures, *s 207A* was added to TULRCA 1992 with effect from 6 April 2009 whereby an employment tribunal is empowered, in cases where it is satisfied that there was unreasonable failure to comply with the requirements of a relevant Code of Practice (that is to say Code of Practice No 1 as promulgated after 6 April 2009 and as revised from 11 March 2015), to reduce or increase the award by up to 25% (*TULRCA 1992, s 207A(2), (3)* and *(4)*). For s 207A to have application in a grievance procedures case the relevant grievance must be raised in writing (*Cadogan Hotel Partners v Ozog* (UKEAT/0001/14)).

5.4 CODES ISSUED BY THE SECRETARY OF STATE RELATING TO INDUSTRIAL ACTION

Power to issue the Codes

TULRCA 1992, ss 203 and *204* empower the Secretary of State to issue Codes of Practice, after consultation with ACAS, to be approved by both Houses of Parliament. Such Codes are to contain practical guidance for the purposes of promoting the improvement of industrial relations or promoting desirable practices in relation to the conduct by trade unions of ballots and elections. The Codes currently applicable are The Code on Picketing (2017 reissue), the Code of Practice on Industrial Action Ballots and Notice to Employers (2017 reissue) and the Code of Practice on Access and Unfair Practices During Recognition and Derecognition Ballots (2005). The Code on Picketing is a reissued and revised version of the previous Code (see *Employment Code of Practice (Picketing) Order 1992 (SI 1992/476)*). It came into force on 1 March 2017 and takes into account the amendments to relevant statutory provisions made by the Trade Union Act 2016. The revised Code was brought into effect by *The Code of Practice Picketing Order 2017 (SI 2017/237)*. The Code of Practice on Industrial Action Ballots and Notice to Employers also came into force on 1 March 2017 and similarly incorporates the relevant amendments made by the *Trade Union Act 2016*. That Code was brought into effect by *The Code of Practice (Industrial Action Ballots and Notice to Employers) Order 2017 (SI 2017/233)*. The other Code of Practice on Access and Unfair Practices During Recognition and Derecognition Ballots (2005) was laid before Parliament on 18 July 2005 and came into force on 1 October 2005. The 2005 Code incorporate changes made by the *Employment Relations Act 2004* (see TRADE UNIONS – I, II (50, 51)) as well as updating and revising the earlier Codes but, to date, has not been revised in 2017.

The Department of Trade and Industry Codes may supersede any part of or all of a Code issued by ACAS or a previous DTI or Department of Employment Code (*TULRCA 1992, s 208(2)*) (see above).

5.5 Legal effect

Although a failure to comply with the Codes issued by the Secretary of State does not itself render a person liable to proceedings, the Codes are stated to be admissible in evidence and to be taken into account, if relevant, in any proceedings not only before an employment tribunal or the CAC but also, in the case of a DTI or Department for Education and Employment Code, in any court (*TULRCA 1992, s 207(1), (3)*). Thus, in *Thomas v National Union of Mineworkers (South Wales Area)* [1986] Ch 20, [1985] ICR 886 at 920–921 Scott J granted an injunction, following violent picketing, to restrain the union from organising pickets in greater numbers than were suggested by the relevant Code.

5.6   Codes of Practice

5.6   CODES ISSUED BY THE BORDER AND IMMIGRATION AGENCY

The Border and Immigration Agency has issued two relevant Codes of Practice: the Border & Immigration Agency Code of Practice: Civil Penalties for Employers (2008) and the Border & Immigration Agency Code of Practice: Guidance for Employers for the Avoidance of Unlawful Discrimination in Employment Practice while Seeking to Prevent Illegal Working (2008). The Codes are made under the authority of *s 19* and *s 23* of the *Immigration, Asylum and Nationality Act 2006* and came into force on 29 February 2008.

The Civil Penalties Code gives guidance on the assessment of penalties in the event of employing illegal migrant workers and the factors taken into account in that assessment. The Code must be taken into account by the courts and may be used in legal proceedings.

The Guidance for Employers for the Avoidance of Unlawful Discrimination in Employment Practice while Seeking to Prevent Illegal Working Code provides guidance to employers on how to avoid a civil penalty for employing an illegal migrant worker in a way which does not result in unlawful race discrimination (paragraph 1). As a statutory code its provisions are admissible in evidence and must be taken into account in any relevant proceedings in the courts and in the employment tribunal. The Code seeks to summarise the relevant provisions prohibiting race discrimination and the responsibilities of an employer under *ss 15* and *21* of the *Immigration, Asylum and Nationality Act 2006* ("the *Act*") and provides short guidance in paragraphs 8.1–8.8 on avoiding race discrimination whilst complying with the responsibilities imposed by the Act.

5.7   THE POSITION PRIOR TO THE EQUALITY ACT 2010: (1) CODES RELATING TO RACIAL EQUALITY

History of the Codes

The *Race Relations Act 1976, s 47* empowered the Commission for Racial Equality to issue Codes of Practice containing practical guidance for either or both of the following purposes:

(a)   the elimination of discrimination in the field of employment; and

(b)   the promotion of equality of opportunity in that field between persons of different racial groups.

The first Code of Practice was issued in April 1984 by the Commission for Racial Equality ('CRE') and new Code of Practice on Racial Equality in Employment (2005) was issued in April 2006. This Code of Practice continues to apply to matters occurring before the coming into force of the relevant provisions of the *Equality Act 2010* on 1 October 2010.

The CRE had also published a Code of Practice on the Duty to Promote Racial Equality (in force from May 2002) as a consequence of the duty imposed by the *Race Relations (Amendment) Act 2000* on public bodies to promote racial equality (see DISCRIMINATION AND EQUAL OPPORTUNITIES – I (11), II(12), III (13)). This Code of Practice continues to apply to matters occurring before the coming into force of the relevant provisions of the *Equality Act 2010* on 1 October 2010.

5.8   Legal effect

The *Race Relations Act 1976, s 47(10)* (now repealed) provided that a failure to observe any provision in a Code of Practice shall not of itself render a person liable to proceedings. However, such Codes were admissible in evidence and, where relevant, were to be taken into account in any proceedings before an employment tribunal. See now, for matters occurring before 1 October 2010, *section 15(4)(b)* of the *Equality Act 2006* which maintains the admissibility of such Codes in evidence and provides that, where relevant, they be taken into account in determining any question arising in any such proceedings.

5.9   THE POSITION PRIOR TO THE EQUALITY ACT 2010: (2) CODES ISSUED BY THE EQUAL OPPORTUNITIES COMMISSION

History of the Codes relating to sex discrimination and equal pay

The *Sex Discrimination Act 1975, s 56A* empowered the Equal Opportunities Commission to issue Codes of Practice containing practical guidance for either or both of the following purposes:

(a)   the elimination of discrimination in the field of employment; and

(b)   the promotion of equality of opportunity in that field between men and women.

The Equal Opportunities Commission issued a Code of Practice which came into force on 30 April 1985. (See Discrimination and Equal Opportunities – I **(11)**, II **(12)**, III **(13)**.)

A new Code of Practice on Equal Pay was introduced on 1 December 2003 by the *Code of Practice on Equal Pay Order 2003 (SI 2003/2865)*. This Code was admissible in evidence in any proceedings under the *SDA 1975* or the *Equal Pay Act 1970* (see **5.10** below) and included information on equal pay for pregnant women and those on maternity leave, the Equal Pay Questionnaire procedure and equal pay reviews and grievance procedures (see Equal Pay **(22)**). The Equal Opportunities Commission also issued the Gender Equality Duty Code of Practice (2007) in force from 6 April 2007 pursuant to *s 76E(1)* of the *SDA 1975*.

The Equal Opportunities Commission (along with the CRE and the Disability Rights Commission) was replaced with effect from 1 October 2007 by the Equality and Human Rights Commission established under the *Equality Act 2006*. The Codes of Practice relating to sex discrimination and equal pay continue to apply to matters occurring before the coming into force of the relevant provisions of the *Equality Act 2010* on 1 October 2010.

5.10   Legal effect

The *Sex Discrimination Act 1975, s 56A* (as amended by *TURERA 1993, Sch 7 para 15* and as modified by *SDA 1975, s 76E(3)*) provided that a failure to observe any provision in a Code of Practice shall not of itself render a person liable to proceedings. However, such Codes were admissible in evidence and, where relevant, were to be taken into account in any proceedings before an employment tribunal under that *Act* or the *Equal Pay Act 1970*. See now, for matters occurring before 1 October 2010, *section 15(4)(b)* of the *Equality Act 2006* which maintains the admissibility of such Codes in evidence and provides that, where relevant, they be taken into account in determining any question arising in any such proceedings.

THE POSITION PRIOR TO THE EQUALITY ACT 2010: CODES RELATING TO DISABILITY

5.11   History of the Disability Codes

The *Disability Discrimination Act 1995, s 53* empowered the Secretary of State to issue Codes of Practice containing such practical guidance as he considers appropriate with a view to:

5.11 Codes of Practice

(a)   eliminating discrimination in the field of employment against disabled persons and persons who have had a disability; and

(b)   encouraging good practice in relation to the employment of disabled persons and persons who have had a disability.

The Disability Rights Commission Code of Practice on Employment and Occupation was promulgated under powers conferred by *s 53A* of the *Disability Discrimination Act 1995*.

The Disability Rights Commission (along with the CRE and the Equal Opportunities Commission) was replaced with effect from 1 October 2007 by the Equality and Human Rights Commission established under the *Equality Act 2006*. The Codes of Practice relating to disability continue to apply to matters occurring before the coming into force of the relevant provisions of the *Equality Act 2010* on 1 October 2010.

5.12 Legal effect

A failure on the part of any person to observe any provision of a Code of Practice did not of itself make that person liable to any proceedings. However, such a Code was admissible in evidence in any proceedings under the *DDA 1995* before an employment tribunal, a county court or a sheriff court and, where relevant, was to be taken into account in determining any question arising in any such proceedings (*DDA 1995, s 53A(8)* and *(8A)* (now repealed). For matters occurring before 1 October 2010, *s 15(4)(b)* of the *Equality Act 2006* applies, maintaining the admissibility of such Codes in evidence and provides that, where relevant, they be taken into account in determining any question arising in any such proceedings under the *DDA*.

5.13 GUIDANCE ON DISABILITY

In relation to the definition of disability, the Secretary of State, pursuant to *s 6(5)* of the *Equality Act 2010* and the *Equality Act 2010 (Guidance on the Definition of Disability) Appointed Day Order 2011 (SI 2011/1159)*, has produced "Guidance On Matters to be Taken Into Account In Determining Questions Relating to the Definition of Disability (2011)" which came into force on 1 May 2011. The guidance does not impose legal obligations in itself but by *Schedule 1, Paragraph 12* to the *Equality Act 2010* the guidance must be taken into account by an adjudicating body on the issue whether a person is disabled.

5.14 THE EQUALITY ACT 2010: NEW CODES OF PRACTICE ON EMPLOYMENT AND EQUAL PAY

The *Equality Act 2010* received the Royal Assent (on 8 April 2010) and the major provisions relating to employment law have been brought into force with effect from 1 October 2010. The Equality and Human Rights Commission consulted during 2010 on draft Codes of Practice, the purpose of which are to offer statutory guidance on the *Equality Act's* employment and equal pay implications.

With effect from 6 April 2011 the Codes of Practice under the previous legislation, considered in outline above, have been revoked by *The Former Equality Commissions' Codes of Practice (Employment, Equal Pay, and Rights of Access for Disabled Persons) (Revocation) Order 2011 (SI 2011/776)* ("the *Revocation Order*"). By the *Revocation Order* each of the following Codes or Practice are revoked: the Code of Practice for the elimination of discrimination on the grounds of sex and marriage and the promotion of equality of opportunity in employment, issued by the former Equal Opportunities Commission under *section 56A* of the *Sex Discrimination Act 1975*, which came into effect on 30 April 1985 (*SI 1985/387*); the Code of Practice on Equal Pay, also issued by the former Equal Opportunities Commission under *section 56A* of the *Sex Discrimination Act 1975*, which came into effect on 1 December 2003 (*SI 2003/2865*); the Disability Discrimination Act 1995 Code of Practice on Employment and Occupation, issued by the former Disability Rights Commission under *section 53A* of the *Disability Discrimination Act 1995*, which came into effect on 1 October 2004 (*SI 2004/2302*); the revised Code of Practice on Racial Equality in Employment, issued by the former Commission for Racial Equality under *section 47* of the *Race Relations Act 1976*, which came into effect on 6 April 2006 (*SI 2006/630*); and the Disability Discrimination Act 1995 Code of Practice on Rights of Access: services to the public, public authority functions, private clubs and premises, issued by the former Disability Rights Commission under *section 53A* of the *Disability Discrimination Act 1995*, which came into effect on 4 December 2006 (*SI 2006/1967*).

The *Revocation Order* contains, in *art 3*, transitional provisions in relation to matters occurring, inter alia, prior to 1 October 2010. In any cases progressing through the employment tribunals relating to matters occurring prior to that date the previous various Codes of Practice considered above will remain relevant and applicable. In transitional cases the former Codes are to continue to have effect in relation to such proceedings for the purposes of *section 15(4)(b)* of the *Equality Act 2006*, which requires a court or tribunal to take a code into account in any case in which it appears to the court or tribunal to be relevant.

For matters occurring on or after 1 October 2010 the relevant Codes of Practice in the employment field will be the Equality Act 2010 Code of Practice on Employment and the Equality Act 2010 Code of Practice on Equal Pay. An additional new Code of Practice, the Equality Act 2010 Code of Practice on Services, Public Functions and Associations is outside the scope of this work. Each of the new codes are issued under *section 14(1)* of the *Equality Act 2006* (as amended by the *Equality Act 2010*) and are brought into force by the *Equality Act 2010 Codes of Practice (Services, Public Functions and Associations, Employment and Equal Pay) Order 2011 (SI 2011/857)*.

The Equality Act 2010 Code of Practice on Employment

The Code on Employment deals with all equalities issues in employment other than Equal Pay (see below). The Code is substantial, totalling 308 pages. As previously, by *section 15(4)(b)* of the *Equality Act 2006*, the courts and employment tribunals are obliged to take the new Code into account in any relevant case.

The Code is divided into two parts. The scheme of Part One of the Code, which is divided into Chapters 2–15, is to summarise the law relating to the various protected characteristics (Chapter 2), and then direct and indirect discrimination (Chapters 3 and 4). Disability discrimination has two separate chapters (Chapters 5 and 6) and harassment, pregnancy and victimisation are also considered separately (Chapters 7, 8 and 9 respectively). The summary of the obligations under the Act is set out in Chapter 10 and work relationships other than employment are considered in Chapter 11. Positive action is addressed in Chapter 12. Thereafter occupational requirements (Chapter 13), pay and benefits (Chapter 14) and enforcement (Chapter 15) are summarised.

Part Two of the Code (beginning at page 221) provides guidance on avoiding discrimination in recruitment (Chapter 16) and in employment (Chapter 17). Guidance on the content of equalities policies is found in Chapter 18 and Chapter 19 deals with guidance on termination of employment. The Code concludes (beginning at page 294) with three appendices on the Meaning of Disability (Appendix 1), Monitoring (Appendix 2) and Making Reasonable Adjustments to Work Premises – Legal Considerations (Appendix 3). The Code may be found at https://www.equalityhumanrights.com/en/advice-and-guidance/equality-act-codes-practice.

5.14   Codes of Practice

The Equality Act 2010 Code of Practice on Equal Pay

The Code of Practice on Equal Pay totals 62 pages. As previously the courts and employment tribunals are obliged to take the Code into account to the extent relevant in any equal pay case. (See paragraph 116 of the Code and *section 15(4)(b)* of the *Equality Act 2006*). The order of the Code is to, first, summarise the existing law relating to equal pay (paragraphs 22–91 of the Code). The provisions in relation to pregnancy, maternity and equal pay are summarised at paragraphs 92–101 with various examples. The new pay transparency provisions prohibiting secrecy are summarised at paragraphs 102–110. Thereafter the questionnaire procedure, burden of proof, employment tribunal procedure and awards are summarised (see paragraphs 111–157 of the Code). The second part of the Code (beginning at page 49) is a good practice guide headed "Good Equal Pay Practice" (see paragraphs 158–185 of the Code). The Code may be found at https ://www.equalityhumanrights.com/en/advice-and-guidance/equality-act-codes-practice.

5.15   CODES ISSUED BY THE HEALTH AND SAFETY EXECUTIVE

Power to issue the Codes

Regulations made under the *Health and Safety at Work, etc Act 1974 ('HSWA 1974')* are sometimes supplemented by Codes of Practice approved and/or issued by the Health and Safety Commission (for details of which see **27.28 HEALTH AND SAFETY AT WORK – I**) (*HSWA 1974, s 16*). A full consideration of these codes is beyond the scope of this book. Two such codes are directly relevant to employment law: the HSE Code of Practice on Safety Representatives and Safety Committees and the HSE Code of Practice on Time Off for Training Safety Representatives. They both supplement the *Safety Representatives and Safety Committees Regulations 1977 (SI 1977/500)* as amended by *SI 1992/2051*, made under *HSWA 1974*.

5.16   Legal effect

Non-compliance with a relevant HSE Code does not of itself render a person liable to any civil or criminal proceedings. However, where in any criminal proceedings a person is alleged to have committed an offence by contravening a provision for which a code of practice was in force, if breach of the Code is established, the offence is proved unless the court is satisfied that the requirement or prohibition was complied with otherwise than by observance of the Code (*HSWA 1974, s 17*).

5.17   CODES ISSUED BY THE INFORMATION COMMISSIONER

The Information Commissioner issued the Employment Practices Data Protection Code in four parts. Part 1: Recruitment and Selection: March 2002. Part 2: Employment Records: August 2002. Part 3: Monitoring at Work: June 2003. Part 4: Information about Workers Health: December 2005. The Code in consolidated form (November 2011) may be obtained from   https://ico.org.uk/media/for-organisations/documents/1064/the_employment _practices_code.pdf. The Code is issued pursuant to statutory authority conferred on the Information Commissioner by *s 51(3)(b)* of the *Data Protection Act 1998*. The Codes promulgated by the Information Commissioner do not have formal legal status or effect unlike the other codes of practice considered above. The Information Commissioner is, however, the enforcing authority for the purposes of the *Data Protection Act 1998* and the Code may reasonably be assumed to represents the views of the Information Commissioner in relation to the standards of practice to be expected of employers in relation to the subject matters covered by the Code. In addition to the Code the Information Commissioner has also published guidance in relation to the Code: 'Employment Practices Code: Supplementary Guidance'. This too may be downloaded from the Information Commissioner's website.

The Information Commissioner has been seeking consultation responses on a new Code of Practice concerning the right of individuals to make a subject access request under *s 7* of the *Data Protection Act 1998*. This is likely to be significant to employers who are frequently faced with subject access requests prior to or contemporaneous with the commencement of litigation by employees. In summary the draft Code provide some practical guidance including best practice recommendations on staff training, having a subject access request policy and responding to subject access requests on a centralised basis. It is noteworthy that the code does not require data controllers to suspend routine data destruction policies (even after a subject access request is made) and recognises that staff may legitimately hold personal data on personal devices or email accounts and staff are not required under the code to search such data sources unless there is good reason to believe relevant personal data is held. If archived sources are known to differ from current sources of data then they should be searched but there is no obligation to search archives if there is evidence that the material is the same. Furthermore, data controllers are not to be required to use complicated methods of recovering deleted data if the data has been deleted in accordance with normal data retention and deletion policies.

5.18 REVISION AND REVOCATION OF CODES

Provision has been made for the revision by the appropriate authority of those codes which are issued under *TULRCA 1992, s 203* (ie the Secretary of State and BIS for the DTI Codes; see **5.4** above) or which are issued under *TULRCA 1992, s 199* (ie the ACAS Codes; see **5.2** above). ACAS may revise its codes under *TULRCA 1992, s 201* and the Secretary of State may revise the DTI (now BIS) codes under *TULRCA 1992, s 205*. Similar procedural provisions apply as in the case of making new codes. The Secretary of State may, with Parliamentary approval, revoke either an ACAS or a DTI/BIS Employment Code (*TULRCA 1992, ss 202, 206*). In the case of an ACAS Code, he may do so only at the request of ACAS.

6   Collective Agreements

6.1   INTRODUCTION

The practice of collective bargaining, by which wage rates and terms and conditions of employment of workers are determined by negotiations between employers and trade unions, leading to collective agreements, is still relatively common in traditional heavy industries and most of the public sector, although its importance in the economy as a whole has declined as the incidence of union recognition has fallen over the last 30 years. National bargaining between trade unions and employer representatives is the norm in the public sector, although there has for some years been considerable pressure from central Government to move to separate bargaining at regional level or for separate business units of large public sector employers. In some industries in the private sector also, negotiations between representatives of associations of employers and the recognised trade unions at national level lead to collective agreements which in practice set norms for the industry or sector concerned, although since the 1980s there has not been any statutory mechanism enabling workers within the sector to enforce the terms agreed collectively against a particular employer. This is in contrast to the practice which prevails widely in some other member states of the EU, and which is reflected in the provisions found in EU Directives permitting the domestic implementation of obligations introduced by the Directive by way of collective agreement as an alternative to legislation.

Under the British system, collective agreements are generally not legally enforceable between the collective parties (employers and unions); however they may form the basis for the individual worker's contract of employment if it is agreed between the collective parties that they should do so. Whether a collective agreement, or a particular provision of the agreement, is in fact incorporated into the contract of a particular worker, however, is a matter of the construction and application of the express or implied terms of the contract between the worker and his or her employer, and not an automatic consequence of the stated intentions of the collective parties: see further **6.7** below.

6.2   DEFINITION

For the purposes of the *Trade Union and Labour Relations (Consolidation) Act 1992* ('*TULRCA 1992*'), a collective agreement is defined in *s 178* as 'any arrangement or agreement made by or on behalf of one or more trade unions and one or more employers or employers' associations' which relates to one or more of the following matters:

(*a*)   terms and conditions of employment, or the physical conditions in which any workers are required to work;

(*b*)   engagement or non-engagement, or termination or suspension of employment or the duties of employment, of one or more workers;

(*c*)   allocation of work or the duties of employment between workers or groups of workers;

(*d*)   matters of discipline;

(*e*)   a worker's membership or non-membership of a trade union;

(*f*)   facilities for officials of trade unions; and

(*g*)   facilities for negotiation or consultation, and other procedures, relating to any of the above matters, including the recognition by employers or employers' associations of the right of a trade union to represent workers in such negotiation or consultation or in the carrying out of such procedures.

This list of the possible subject matter for collective agreements does not mean that agreements must necessarily cover all of the listed areas. Employers are free (subject to the statutory procedure in *TULRCA 1992, Sch A1* for trade unions to obtain recognition) to agree to confer negotiating rights on a trade union to whatever more limited extent they may wish, as well as to define the categories of employees for whom the union is to be recognised, and similarly to make agreements covering only limited and specific aspects of the matters potentially within the scope of a collective agreement. This is a central feature of the voluntarist approach to the role of trade unions which has characterised British employment law for most of the post-war era. However an employer may also seek to make a collective agreement covering a very limited range of issues with a union that is not independent of employer influence, in order to block an attempt by an independent union to obtain recognition; for the potential consequences of such a situation see *R (Boots Management Services Ltd) v Central Arbitration Committee* [2014] IRLR 887, EAT.

6.3   LEGAL STATUS

It was established in the landmark case of *Ford Motor Co v AUEW* [1969] 2 QB 303 that collective agreements are not, at common law, generally legally enforceable between the parties to them. The basis for this conclusion was that it was not the intention of the parties to create legal relations, a necessary ingredient of any contractually binding agreement. This has remained the position since, save for the period during which the *Industrial Relations Act 1971* was in force; this reversed the presumption established in the *Ford* case, replacing it with a presumption that any collective agreement was intended by the parties thereto to be legally enforceable, unless the contrary was stated. During the period the *Act* was in force (1 December 1971 to 16 September 1974) the practice of collective parties in the vast majority of cases was to insert a clause in any agreement stating 'this is not a legally enforceable agreement' (known as a 'TINALEA' clause).

6.4   Following the repeal of the *Industrial Relations Act 1971*, the position at common law was restored by statute (the *Trade Union and Labour Relations Act 1974, s 18*, now consolidated in *TULRCA 1992, s 179(3)*). By virtue of *s 179(3)*, any collective agreement made before 1 December 1971, or after 16 September 1974, will be conclusively presumed not to have been intended by the parties to the agreement to be a legally enforceable contract unless the agreement:

(a)   is in writing, and

(b)   contains a provision which (however expressed) states that the parties intend that the agreement shall be a legally enforceable contract,

in which event it is conclusively presumed to be intended to be legally enforceable. Despite including the phrase "however expressed", condition (*b*) may not be satisfied by a mere statement in the agreement that the parties are to be bound by it (*National Coal Board v National Union of Mineworkers* [1986] ICR 736, [1986] IRLR 439). It is possible for an agreement to state that the parties intend a particular part of it to be legally enforceable, in which case the presumption against enforceability would apply to the rest. The position for any agreement made during the currency of the *1971 Act* remains that there is a presumption that the parties intended the agreement to be legally enforceable, unless (as is usually the case for such agreements made during that period as remain in force) the contrary is stated within the agreement. It should be noted that the fact that the parties intend (or are presumed to intend) their agreement to be legally enforceable does not automatically mean that everything in it is enforceable; particular terms of an agreement may still not be enforceable, for instance for reasons of public policy, or because the language used is not sufficiently clear to be given effect.

Where an employer is required to recognise a trade union in accordance with the provisions of *TULRCA 1992, Sch A1* (see Trade Unions – I (50)), and the method of collective bargaining is specified by the Central Arbitration Committee under *paras 30* and *31* of *Sch A1*, any agreement reached through collective bargaining will have effect as a legally enforceable contract made between the parties; this will also be the case if the parties agree an alternative procedure for collective bargaining to that specified by the CAC. However, the only remedy for breach of any such agreement is an order for specific performance (*TULRCA 1992, Sch A1, para 31(6)*). It should be noted that the specified method that may be imposed under TULRCA Sch A1 covers only collective bargaining about pay, hours and holidays, not the wider range of issues within *s 178*: see *British Airline Pilots Association v Jet2.com Ltd* [2015] EWHC 1110 (QB), [2015] IRLR 543. However the Court of Appeal, in an appeal by the union in that case, held that this was not limited to negotiations about proposals which if adopted would become part of the employees' contracts; it was sufficient that the proposals related to matters of pay, hours or holidays. Accordingly the union, representing airline pilots, was entitled to negotiate on issues of rostering and crewing arrangements for the employer's flight crew: *British Airline Pilots Association v Jet2.com Ltd* [2017] EWCA Civ 20, [2017] IRLR 233.

6.5   INCORPORATION INTO INDIVIDUAL CONTRACTS OF EMPLOYMENT

Although the great majority of collective agreements are not legally enforceable by the union against the employer or vice versa, they may, and in most cases in practice do, have legally binding consequences as between the employer and the individual employee. Their terms may be incorporated into individual contracts of employment either because the contract expressly provides for such incorporation, or because incorporation is an implied term of the contract deriving from custom and practice in the industry. In either case, the collective agreement will be incorporated, notwithstanding that the particular employee may not approve of what the union has negotiated, or may even have ceased to belong to the relevant union (see, eg *Tocher v General Motors Scotland Ltd* [1981] IRLR 55, EAT). On the other hand a collective agreement will not be incorporated into individual contracts of employment merely because the employer belongs to the association which negotiated that agreement (*Hamilton v Futura Floors Ltd* [1990] IRLR 478, Ct of Sess, OH).

It does not matter that the agreement is as between the parties to it not legally enforceable, since it is the terms as incorporated into the individual employee's contract that fall to be enforced, and the contract of employment will very rarely not be legally enforceable. Thus, for example, in *Marley v Forward Trust Group Ltd* [1986] ICR 891, [1986] IRLR 369, the Court of Appeal held that an employee could enforce the terms of a collective agreement on redundancy which was incorporated into his contract, even though the agreement itself was expressed to be 'binding in honour only'.

It may even be possible for the union concerned to rely on the Contracts (Rights of Third Parties) Act 1999 to enforce the terms of a collective agreement not directly enforceable between it and the employer, but which has been incorporated into the individual contracts of the employees it represents. This was the case in *Cavanagh v Secretary of State for Work and Pensions* [2016] EWHC 1136 (QB), [2016] IRLR 591, [2016] ICR 826, where the issue was the check off (the deduction by the employer from employees' pay of trade union subscriptions, which are then paid over to the union). In this case the union was a third party to the individual contracts of employment into which (as the court held) the check off had been incorporated, but the term was clearly intended to benefit the union by ensuring the regular receipt of subscriptions.

6.6   The basis for the incorporation of terms of a collective agreement into an individual contract of employment is usually that the contract of employment expressly states that this is to be the case, often in terms covering not only agreements current at the time of the making of the contract, but also future agreements. Incorporation by implication as a matter of custom and practice is most likely to be established by evidence in those industries and sectors of the economy where traditions of collective bargaining are most strongly established and there is a long practice of the benefits of collective agreements being observed by the employer; it is a matter of evidence in each case whether the practice of applying collectively agreed terms is sufficiently 'reasonable, certain and notorious' to be regarded as custom and practice, or whether the term relied on has been sufficiently consistently applied by the employer to be incorporated by implication. See further as to the application of custom and practice as a source of terms of the contract of employment [6.11] below.

A further, but in practice less common, way for collectively negotiated terms to be contractually enforceable by individual employees is where the union acts as agent for the employees in negotiating the terms, typically for a specific group of employees who have engaged the union to negotiate on their behalf. An example of this process is *Edwards v Skyways Ltd* [1964] 1 WLR 349.

6.7   Even where there is an express incorporation of collective agreements into individual contracts of employment, it does not follow that all provisions of the agreements between the employer and the relevant union or unions will be incorporated. Whether a particular provision will be held by the courts to be incorporated depends on whether it is considered 'apt' for incorporation. Terms specifying rates of pay, hours of work or entitlements to benefits will readily be held to be apt for incorporation, but at the other end of the scale terms setting out a procedure for the resolution of disputes between the union and the employer will equally readily be treated as not apt for incorporation as contractual terms enforceable by an individual employee.

The leading case on the correct approach to what is apt for incorporation is *Alexander v Standard Telephones and Cables plc* [1991] IRLR 286. Hobhouse J summarised the position, in terms which have since been regularly cited as authoritative, thus:

> 'The principles to be applied can therefore be summarised. The relevant contract is that between the individual employee and his employer; it is the contractual intention of those two parties which must be ascertained. In so far as that intention is to be found in a written document, that document must be construed on ordinary contractual principles. Insofar as there is no such document or that document is not complete or conclusive, their contractual intention has to be ascertained by inference from the other available material including collective agreements. The fact that another document is not itself contractual does not prevent it from being incorporated into the contract if that intention is shown as between the employer and the individual employee. Where a document is expressly incorporated by general words it is still be necessary to consider, in conjunction with the words of incorporation, whether any particular part of that document is apt to be a term of the contract; if it is inapt, the correct construction of the contract may be that it is not incorporated. Where it is not a case of express incorporation, but a matter of inferring the contractual intent, the character of the document and the relevant part of it, and whether it is apt to form part of the individual contract is central to the decision whether or not the inference should be drawn.' (para 31)

Provisions dealing with, for example, relations between an employer and a union operate at a collective level and are inappropriate for incorporation as terms of individual contracts. A number of cases illustrate the kind of provision which has been held not to be apt for incorporation into individual contracts. In *National Coal Board v National Union of Mineworkers* [1986] ICR 736, [1986] IRLR 439, the agreement set out the details of a conciliation scheme for the settlement of disputes. In the *Alexander* case itself, terms of a collective agreement specifying the procedure to be applied in a redundancy situation, and the criteria to be used for selection for redundancy, were held not to be apt for incorporation into the individual employees' contracts. Similarly in *Kaur v MG Rover Group Ltd* [2004] EWCA Civ 1507, [2005] IRLR 40 the Court of Appeal held that a provision in a collective agreement which stated that 'there will be no compulsory redundancy' did not have effect as a term of the individual contracts of employment between the employer and each employee.

In *Malone v British Airways plc* [2010] EWCA Civ 1225, [2011] IRLR 32, the Court of Appeal found that provisions of a collective agreement between the unions and the airline regarding minimum cabin crew complements for flights had not been incorporated into the contracts of employment. There was insufficient evidence of mutual intention to give the terms of the agreement enforceability by individual cabin crew members and the particular provisions were not apt for incorporation. The Court of Appeal focused in particular on what it saw as the disastrous consequences for the business if the provision were to be individually enforceable, such as flights having to be cancelled if not enough cabin crew members to fulfil the minimum manning levels were available, a consequence it concluded could not have been intended. See also *British Airline Pilots Association v Jet2.com Ltd* [2015] EWHC 1110 (QB), [2015] IRLR 543 (terms as to rostering arrangements for airline pilots not apt for incorporation, a point not in dispute in the subsequent successful appeal in this case: see [6.4] above).

A further example of a finding that a term was not appropriate for incorporation is the Court of Appeal's decision in *George v Ministry of Justice* [2013] EWCA Civ 324 (16 April 2013, unreported), a case relating to an agreement for time off in lieu for prison officers who had worked more than 39 hours in a week.

6.8   The kinds of terms most likely to be found to be apt for incorporation are those conferring specific benefits or imposing specific obligations on employees, such as rates of pay, provisions for specific future pay increases, changes in working hours, or conditions to be observed for the taking of leave; a good example of the incorporation of an agreement for future pay rises is *Cabinet Office v Beavan* [2014] IRLR 434. What is apt may also be affected by the history of how agreements between the collective parties have been incorporated into employees' contracts. In *Henry v London General Transport Services Ltd* [2002] EWCA Civ 488, [2002] IRLR 472, the employers entered into negotiations with a union, the TGWU, in preparation for a management buy-out. There had been a history of negotiations with the TGWU but there was no express incorporation of terms collectively agreed. The TGWU and the employers agreed a framework agreement which contained new and less advantageous terms and conditions, including reduced pay. The tribunal held that the terms of the framework agreement were so fundamental that the past practice of negotiations leading to the incorporation of terms collectively agreed was not such as to enable these changes to be incorporated into individual contracts. The Court of Appeal disagreed. The matters which were the subject of the framework agreement were apt for incorporation into individual contracts. Further, if the appropriate custom and practice was established, it could be expected to cover all contractual terms. The tribunal had been wrong to draw a distinction between fundamental and other terms without identifying a basis for that distinction.

Guidance has been given by the High Court as to when a collectively agreed disciplinary procedure will be regarded as incorporated into individual contracts: see *Hussain v Surrey and Sussex Healthcare NHS Trust* [2011] EWHC 1670 (QB), para 168. Relevant factors include the importance of the procedure, the level of detail prescribed, the certainty of the terms of the procedure, whether the terms would if contractual be workable and whether the provisions appear in the context of other provisions having contractual effect. See also *Cavanagh v Secretary of State for Work and Pensions*, discussed at [6.5] above.

In order for a term in a collective agreement to be incorporated into a contract of employment it may be necessary for an employee to have his attention drawn specifically to it. In *Worrall v Wilmott Dixon Partnerships Ltd* (UKEAT/0521/09) [2010] All ER (D) 107 (Jul), EAT, a council and its trade unions entered into a collective agreement regarding pay and redundancy and the terms were then inserted into a staff handbook. The handbook was generally available but not given to each employee. The EAT held that the term was not contractual as it had not been brought to the employee's attention and he could not therefore be said to have accepted the term. However this analysis is open to question, since it was the employee who sought to rely on the agreement, as it conferred a substantial benefit on him in connection with his redundancy. Further an express general incorporation of collective agreements into an individual's contract need not require that the individual has knowledge of each agreement; whether the incorporating provision does so require is a question of construction of the particular terms.

6.9   The principles applicable to the construction of collective agreements are the same as those which apply to other contracts: *Adams v British Airways plc* [1996] IRLR 574, CA. In particular, the Court of Appeal has confirmed that the principles for the construction of contracts set out by Lord Hoffmann in *Investors Compensation Scheme v West Bromwich Building Society* [1998] WLR 896 apply: see *Bull v Nottinghamshire and City of Nottingham Fire Authority* [2007] EWCA Civ 240, [2007] ICR 1631. Where the terms of a collective agreement are truly ambiguous, it is permissible to look at a clearly established practice, which continues both before and after an agreement is made, as evidence of what the parties meant by the agreement (*Dunlop Tyres Ltd v Blows* [2001] EWCA Civ 1032, [2001] IRLR 629; see also CONTRACT OF EMPLOYMENT (8)). In both the *Bull* case and in *Briggs v Nottingham University Hospitals NHS Trust* [2010] EWCA Civ 264, [2010] IRLR 504, the Court of Appeal looked at the context of the agreement and whether the surrounding circumstances, purpose of the agreement and background to the negotiations lent support to a particular construction.

The construction of a collective agreement for a three year pay deal was considered by the Court of Appeal in *Anderson v London Fire and Emergency Planning Authority* [2013] EWCA Civ 321, [2013] IRLR 459. Reversing the EAT, the Court held that an agreement providing for two formulae for the third year's pay increase should be interpreted as requiring whichever formula produced the greater increase, since that gave effect to industrial common sense in the circumstances of the agreement. The court rejected the EAT's view (see [2012] IRLR 888) that the fact of two alternatives being stated gave the employer the right to choose which to implement as making no sense in the context of a negotiated pay agreement.

6.10   Like any contract, a collective agreement may have implied, as well as express, terms. The approach of the courts to whether a particular term should be implied into a collective agreement depends on the context as well as the term sought to be implied. In the case of *Ali v Christian Salvesen Food Services Ltd* [1997] 1 All ER 721, [1997] ICR 25, the Court of Appeal took a restrictive approach, acknowledging that such agreements are reached between the two sides of the industry and will inevitably involve compromises between their interests. The case concerned an 'annualised hours' contract, under which the employees were employed to work a notional 40-hour week but in fact were expected to work far more flexible hours based on an annual rota. There was no entitlement to overtime pay until the number of hours worked during a particular year exceeded a specified figure. The individual workers in the case had worked for more than 40 hours per week, but their contracts had been terminated before the number of hours worked in the year exceeded the specified figure. The question was whether they could claim overtime in respect of the number of hours which they had worked in excess of 40 per week. There was no express term which governed what should happen in this situation. The employees therefore based their case on an implied term. The Court of Appeal rejected the implication of a term to cover this situation. Waite LJ pointed out that this was one of several situations for which the collective agreement had not made provision. He refused to imply a term, stating that when a matter had not been covered in a collective agreement, the natural inference was that it had been intentionally omitted because it was either too controversial or too complicated to justify inclusion.

An example of a case where a term was held by the Court of Appeal to be implied into a collective agreement which was silent on the point is *Garratt v Mirror Group Newspapers Ltd* [2011] EWCA Civ 425, [2011] ICR 880. The case concerned a collective agreement between the employer and a newly recognised trade union for enhanced redundancy terms. The employer had in practice for many years made enhanced payments but had always required employees to enter into compromise agreements as a condition of payment. This was (as the Court found) very well known, and had never been disputed. The agreement itself, which had been expressly incorporated into Mr Garratt's contract, was silent on the point of compromise agreements, but the Court readily upheld a finding in the County Court that the requirement for a compromise agreement was to be implied on the basis of the mutual understanding of the parties.

6.11   A related issue, which has arisen in a number of recent cases, usually in the context of claims for enhanced redundancy payments, is whether a policy or practice of the employer, such as making enhanced redundancy payments, has become a contractual entitlement by satisfying the requirements of a custom or practice. A custom or practice must be 'reasonable, certain and notorious', and its establishment in this type of context is likely to require evidence not just of a practice of payment over a period of time, but also that the payments were made in a manner indicative of a contractual entitlement of the affected employees to receive them. A full survey of recent cases on this point can be found in the judgment of Underhill LJ in *Park Cakes Ltd v Shumba* [2013] EWCA Civ 974, [2013] IRLR 800, where the Court also restates the principles applicable. The factors most likely to be relevant are listed at para 36 of Underhill LJ's judgment as the following:

–   On how many occasions and over how long a period the benefit in issue has been paid.

–   Whether the benefits have always been the same.

–   The extent to which the enhanced benefits in issue have been publicised, and in what terms.

–   How the terms concerned have been described by the employer (such as whether they have been labelled '*ex gratia*').

–   What (if anything) is said in the written contracts of the employees concerned.

–   Whether the employer's practice has been, viewed objectively, equivocal.

The Court also stressed that the burden of proof of a custom and practice is on the employees. Subsequent decisions applying, and illustrating the operation of, these principles are *CSC Computer Sciences Ltd v McAlinden* [2013] EWCA Civ 1435, *Peacock Stores v Peregrine* (UKEAT/0315/13) and *Migliacco v Samuel Smith (Southern) Ltd* (UKEAT/0267/14).

6.12   CHANGES TO COLLECTIVE AGREEMENTS

Once the terms of a collective agreement are incorporated into individual contracts, the relevant contractual terms are, as a matter of general principle, unaffected by the termination of the collective agreement (*Robertson v British Gas Corpn* [1983] ICR 351, [1983] IRLR 302, CA; *Gibbons v Associated British Ports* [1985] IRLR 376; *Lee v GEC Plessey Telecommunications* [1993] IRLR 383). The question in each case is what the contract of employment provides, and the termination of a collective agreement is not determinative of that issue any more than its lack of legally binding status.

6.13   A related issue is the continuing effect of collective agreements following the transfer of employees under the *Transfer of Undertakings (Protection of Employment) Regulations 2006 (SI 2006/246) ('TUPE')* (see TRANSFER OF UNDERTAKINGS (52)). In *Whent v T Cartledge Ltd* [1997] IRLR 153, the employees had been employed by a local authority under contracts expressly incorporating collective agreements setting the rates of pay for local authority workers. They had transferred under *TUPE* to the respondent, which withdrew recognition from the trade union and pulled out of the collective agreement. The EAT nonetheless held that individuals retained the right under their individual contracts of employment to the benefits provided for by the collective agreement, including subsequent improvement in pay rates negotiated by the collective parties after the claimants' employment had transferred.

However, the Court of Appeal in *Alemo-Herron v Parkwood Leisure Ltd* [2010] EWCA Civ 24, [2010] IRLR 298 held, overruling *Whent*, that whilst the effect of *TUPE* was to preserve employees' contractual rights to the benefit of both current (at the time of the transfer) and later collective agreements and make them enforceable against the transferee, the judgment of the ECJ in *Werhof v Freeway Traffic Systems GmbH & Co KG*: C-499/04, [2005] ECR I-2397, [2006] IRLR 400 made clear that a static rather than dynamic interpretation of *Directive 2001/23/EC*, the parent Directive of *TUPE*, was required: the *Directive* did not require a transferee to be bound by a collective agreement other than the one in force at the time of the transfer. As *reg 4* of *TUPE* implemented *art 3(1)* of the *Directive*, a contractual term giving employees the right to pay increases negotiated from time to time by collective agreement was not protected on a transfer. The employees were not entitled to pay increases negotiated between the trade unions and local government employers after their transfer to a private sector employer.

Following a further appeal in *Alemo-Herron*, the Supreme Court held that the effect of *Werhof*, and in particular whether it required domestic legislation to go no further than the static approach adopted by the ECJ in *Werhof* itself, was unclear, and referred the case to the Court for clarification of this. The judgment of the Court (*Parkwood Leisure Ltd v Alemo-Herron*: C-4326/11, [2013] IRLR 744) essentially confirms the approach of the Court of Appeal. The Court ruled that the Directive precludes national legislation which imposes on an employer to whom employees have transferred as part of a relevant transfer the terms of a subsequent collective agreement, if the transferee employer has not had the possibility of participating in the negotiating process leading to the adoption of the agreement. The principal reason given by the Court for this conclusion is that a 'dynamic' interpretation would undermine the right of transferee employers to conduct their business, a right safeguarded by the EU Charter of Fundamental Rights. The case was referred back to the Supreme Court for further consideration of the ECJ's judgment, but was settled before a further hearing could take place. It is to be expected that in any future proceedings a British court will interpret *TUPE* consistently with the ECJ's ruling.

As a separate point, the effect of subsequent statutory changes on collective agreements which have transferred under *TUPE* cannot be ignored. Thus in *Worrall v Wilmott Dixon Partnerships Ltd* (UKEAT/0521/09/DM), [2010] All ER (D) 107 (Jul), an agreement to confer additional pensionable service on employees taking voluntary redundancy was held no longer to be effective following a change in legislation making it unlawful to confer this category of benefit on employees.

6.14 CHANGING TERMS WITHOUT A COLLECTIVE AGREEMENT

Employers may wish to change the terms of employment of their employees which have been derived from a collective agreement, typically because of a wish to reduce costs. If in these circumstances no agreement can be reached with the relevant trade union, the employer may seek to impose the changes unilaterally. Such cases are likely to raise the question whether there is a provision in the individuals' contracts of employment permitting the degree of unilateral variation of terms proposed. If not, and unless individual employees agree to a variation of contract, the employer cannot impose the new terms without taking the relatively drastic step of dismissing the employees and offering re-employment on the new terms. The question whether individual contracts contain provisions sufficiently wide to permit unilateral variation at the instance of the employer may therefore be of considerable importance.

6.15   The answer to this question will depend on the precise wording of the contract, as well as the particular changes proposed. The general approach of the courts to this question can be seen in two recent decisions, each rejecting the employer's attempt to apply a unilateral change following a failure of negotiations on the proposed change. In *Norman v National Audit Office* [2015] IRLR 634, EAT, the employees' standard contractual terms included a statement that conditions of service were 'subject to amendment', and that any changes would be notified to staff, either in general circulars for changes applying generally, or individually for changes directly affecting individuals. The employer sought to rely on this to validate reductions in the number of annual 'privilege day' holidays and the period for which sick pay would be paid. The EAT rejected this claim. The clause in issue went no further than to set out the mechanism by which amendments were to be notified: it did not clearly or unambiguously reserve the right of the employer to amend terms unilaterally without the employees' consent.

In *Sparks v Department for Transport* [2016] EWCA Civ 360, [2016] IRLR 519, [2016] ICR 695 the employees' contracts contained a statement that 'Your contract of employment cannot be changed detrimentally without your agreement. Consequently the Department will not change your terms and conditions of contract without your consent or that of a recognised trade union.' The Department wished to introduce a new absence management policy under which the number of days' absence before the 'trigger points' for disciplinary action were to be applied was to be reduced. The policy had previously been agreed with the relevant trade unions, but the change was not acceptable to the unions. The Department therefore proceeded to make the change unilaterally. The High Court, and on appeal the Court of Appeal, held that the original collectively agreed policy was apt for incorporation into individual contracts, and was therefore part of the employees' contracts, with the result that a detrimental change, such as that proposed, could not be made without a further collective agreement (which would be incorporated into individual contracts) or individual consent.

An example of a decision that an employer could make unilateral changes in the terms of its employees' contracts by relying on an express variation clause in the contract is *Bateman v Asda Stores Ltd* [2010] IRLR 370, [2010] All ER (D) 277 (Feb), EAT. In that case the employer's Colleague Handbook, which was incorporated into individual contracts, contained the statement that 'the Company reserves the right to review, revise, amend or replace the content of this handbook and introduce new policies from time to time'. This was held to be sufficient to permit the employer to impose changes in its pay structure, albeit with no individual employees suffering reductions in pay.

6.16   'NO STRIKE' CLAUSES

There are specific provisions restricting the incorporation into individual contracts of collective agreements which would restrict the right to take part in industrial action. Any provision of a collective agreement which prohibits or restricts the right of workers to engage in a strike or other industrial action, or has the effect of prohibiting or restricting that right, cannot be incorporated into the contract of employment of an individual worker unless the collective agreement:

(a)   is in writing; and

(b)   contains a provision stating that those terms shall or may be incorporated in such a contract; and

(c)   is reasonably accessible at his place of work to the worker to whom it applies and is available for him to consult during working hours; and

(d)   is one where each trade union which is a party to the agreement is an independent trade union (see **50.22** TRADE UNIONS – I); and

(e)   the individual contract with the worker expressly or impliedly incorporates those terms of the collective agreement relating to strikes.

(*TULRCA 1992, s 180.*)

Despite the fact that a collective agreement and an individual's contract of employment may comply with all the requirements of *s 180*, a court cannot order specific performance of a contract of employment or grant an injunction restraining a breach, or threatened breach, of such a contract which would have the effect of compelling the employee to do any work or attend at any place for the doing of any work (*TULRCA 1992, s 236*).

6.17   WORKFORCE AGREEMENTS

In a number of situations, statutory provisions giving effect in domestic law to EU Directives may be modified in their application by collective agreements. Examples are provisions in the *Working Time Regulations 1998* permitting the modification of some of the substantive rules in the *Regulations*, and the *Maternity and Parental Leave etc Regulations 1999* (allowing for the disapplication of the default rules for the taking of parental leave). Collective agreements may only be made where there is a recognised trade union with which the employer may negotiate. The disadvantages to employers and employees of the absence of any alternative facility for the modification of EU-derived statutory rights are met by provision in these *Regulations* for 'workforce agreements' negotiated between employers and elected representatives of the workforce. For details of the procedural requirements for a workforce agreement under the *Working Time Regulations 1998* (other provisions for workforce agreements are in essentially identical terms) see 57.4 WORKING TIME. Employee representatives elected to negotiate workforce agreements are afforded similar protection from retaliatory action to that afforded to trade union representatives.

6.18   DISCRIMINATORY AGREEMENTS

Under *section 145* of the *Equality Act 2010* terms in collective agreement, which discriminate against employees because of any protected characteristic are void. A qualifying person may apply to the Employment Tribunal for a declaration that the term is void (see *section 146*). A person qualifies under *section 146* if, but only if, he or she is, or seeks to be, an employee of the employer (or an employer) party to the collective agreement, and either is or may in the future be affected by the disputed term, or (if the term provides for particular treatment of individuals) may be subject in future to the treatment objected to. The remedy for a successful complainant is a declaration that the term is void.

Claims under *section 145* (as under the equivalent provisions in the various Acts and regulations replaced by the *Equality Act 2010*) are rare. An example of the use of the procedure (in an earlier formulation) is *Meade-Hill and National Union of Civil and Public Servants v British Council* [1996] 1 All ER 79, [1995] IRLR 478, CA, where a mobility clause was successfully challenged as indirectly discriminatory against female employees.

7   Continuous Employment

7.1   Many of the statutory employment protection rights such as the right to claim a redundancy payment and compensation for unfair dismissal are conferred only on those employees who have accrued sufficient continuous employment. Further, the calculation of a redundancy payment and of the basic award in unfair dismissal proceedings is based on the employee's length of continuous service. The length of an employee's period of continuous employment is calculated with a few exceptions according to provisions in *ERA 1996, ss 210–219*. The rules relating to continuity apply to employees, irrespective whether they work full-time or part-time, and if part-time, irrespective of the number of hours worked per week.

The more important provisions relating to continuity of employment are set out in this chapter.

7.2   COMPUTATION OF PERIODS OF EMPLOYMENT

Questions arising as to whether an employee's employment is of a kind which counts towards a period of continuous employment, or whether periods are to be treated as forming a single period of continuous employment, are to be determined week by week, but the length of an employee's period of employment is to be computed in *calendar months* and *years of twelve months* (*ERA 1996, s 210(1), (2), (3)*).

7.3   Beginning and end of a period of continuous employment

Subject to the provisions of *ERA 1996, s 211(2), (3)* an employee's period of continuous employment for the purpose of calculating his entitlement to any right under *ERA 1996* begins with the day on which he actually starts work and ends with the day by reference to which the length of his period of continuous employment falls to be ascertained for the purposes of the employment right in question (*ERA 1996, s 211(1)*). It is important to note that the day on which an employee actually started work must be included in the reckoning under *ERA 1996, s 211*, so that if, for example, an employee starts work on 2 April, and is dismissed on 1 April the following year, he will have one year's continuous employment (see *Pacitti Jones v O'Brien* [2005] IRLR 888). In *General of the Salvation Army v Dewsbury* [1984] ICR 498, the EAT held that 'starts work' in *EPCA 1978, s 151(3)* (the predecessor to *ERA 1996, s 211(1)*) was not intended to refer to the undertaking of the full-time duties of employment but was intended to refer to the beginning of the employee's employment under her contract of employment, which in that case was earlier than the former date.

7.4   EVENTS AFFECTING A PERIOD OF EMPLOYMENT

The rest of this chapter sets out the events which may affect the period of employment. The following matters are considered:

—   weeks which count (see **7.6** below);

—   change of employer (see **7.9** below);

—   weeks, or part weeks, which do not count but which do not break continuity (see **7.10** below);

—   events which break continuity (see **7.12** below).

7.5 Continuous Employment

7.5 PRELIMINARY POINTS

Presumption of continuity. A person's employment (by a particular employer) is presumed to have been continuous unless the contrary is shown (*ERA 1996, s 210(5)*). That presumption does not apply where the person's employer has changed: see *Jones v Schwarzenbach* (2015) UKEAT/0100/15, [2015] All ER (D) 145 (Sep). Except as provided in *ERA 1996, ss 215–217*, any week which does not count in computing a period of employment breaks the continuity of the period of employment (*ERA 1996, s 210(4)*).

Meaning of 'week'. For these purposes, a week runs from Sunday to Saturday (*ERA 1996, s 235*). So long as the employee is employed by the employer in two successive weeks, it does not matter that one job may have ended and another begun, nor how the first job ended (*Tipper v Roofdec Ltd* [1989] IRLR 419).

Statutory concept. The concept of continuity of employment is a statutory concept (see *Secretary of State for Employment v Globe Elastic Thread Co Ltd* [1979] ICR 706). This means that parties cannot destroy it by means of a contractual agreement (see *Collison v BBC* [1998] IRLR 238). (See **7.7** below.)

7.6 WEEKS WHICH COUNT

The following weeks count towards a period of continuous employment.

(a) Any week during the whole or part of which the employee's relations with his employer are governed by a contract of employment (*ERA 1996, s 212(1)*).

In *Roach v CSB (Moulds) Ltd* [1991] ICR 349, the EAT held that continuity had been broken where in two successive weeks the applicant had been employed first by the respondent, then by a third party, then by the respondent again in a different job. However, the EAT in Scotland held in *Sweeney v J & S Henderson (Concessions) Ltd* [1999] IRLR 306 that the long-criticised *Roach* decision was wrongly decided and that, so long as during the relevant weeks there is at least one day governed by a contract of employment with the relevant employer, it does not matter how the gap was created nor what the employee did during its currency (see also *Carrington v Harwich Dock Co Ltd* [1998] IRLR 567).

(b) Periods in which there is no contract of employment may count as periods of employment in certain circumstances. If in any week the employee is, for the whole or part of the week:

(i) incapable of work in consequence of illness or injury; or

(ii) absent from work on account of a temporary cessation of work; or

(iii) absent from work in circumstances such that, by arrangement or custom, he is regarded as continuing in the employment of his employer for all or any purposes,

that week will count as a period of employment (*ERA 1996, s 212(3)*).

Not more than 26 weeks count under (b)(i) above between any periods of employment which themselves count for continuity purposes (*ERA 1996, s 212(4)*). The problems arising from these provisions are considered in more detail in **7.7** below.

(c) An employee's contract of employment is deemed to continue during maternity leave with appropriate amendments so that there is no need for special provisions preserving continuity during the maternity period (*ss 71 and 73, ERA 1996* and *reg 9* of the *Maternity and Parental Leave Regulations 1999*). The same position applies in respect of continuity during any statutory adoption leave period (*ss 75A-B, ERA 1996* and *regs 19* and *21* of the *Paternity and Adoption Leave Regulations 2002 (SI 2002/2788)*); during parental leave (*ERA 1996 ss 76* and *77* and *reg 17* of the *Maternity and Parental Leave Regulations*); during paternity leave (*s 80C(1), ERA 1996* and *reg 12* of the *Paternity and Adoption Leave Regulations*); and during shared parental leave (*s 75I, ERA 1996* and *reg 38* of the *Shared Parental Leave Regulations 2014 (SI 2014/3050)*.

(d)   Intervals in employment where employment is deemed to continue by virtue of the provisions of *ERA 1996, ss 92(7), 97(2), 138(1)* and *145(5)* respectively also count. *ERA 1996, ss 92(7), 97(2)* and *145(5)* operate to treat an employee's employment as continuing until the expiry of the statutory minimum period of notice in circumstances where notice should have been given but was not, and the employee was thereby deprived of the minimum qualifying period of employment for claims for a written statement of reasons for dismissal, unfair dismissal and redundancy payments respectively. *Section 138(1), ERA 1996* operates to preserve continuity where an employee dismissed for redundancy has his contract renewed or is re-engaged after an interval of not more than four weeks. If a dismissed employee is reinstated or re-engaged in consequence of the presentation of a "relevant complaint of dismissal", or as a result of action taken by a conciliation officer under the *Employment Tribunals Act 1996, s 18*, or as a result of a relevant compromise contract (see CHAPTER 3: ACAS CONCILIATION), the employee's continuity of employment is preserved and the weeks in any intervening period count. Further, if the employee has been paid a redundancy payment and it is a term of his reinstatement or re-engagement that he repay that sum, the continuity of his employment for redundancy payments purposes is not broken (*Employment Protection (Continuity of Employment) Regulations 1996 (SI 1996/3147)*; *ERA 1996, s 219*). The phrase "relevant complaint of dismissal" in *reg 2* of *SI 1996/3147* is not defined, but it would certainly include a complaint of unfair dismissal, and arguably, other complaints (such as discrimination) in relation to dismissal: see *Lipinski v Ebbsfleet Autospray Centre Ltd* (UKEAT/0288/12), 6 June 2013.

7.7 Periods of 'no employment'

The true meaning of *ERA 1996, s 212(3)* (see **7.6**(b) above) has given rise to various difficulties of interpretation.

Generally. *Section 212(3)* applies only where there is no contract of employment in existence and not where there is a contract of employment in existence, but the employee is not required to perform any work under that contract (*Ford v Warwickshire County Council* [1983] ICR 273; *Pearson v Kent County Council* [1993] IRLR 165). In *Pearson*, the Court of Appeal held that the critical question is why there is no contract during the week in question, and not why the previous contract of employment came to an end.

Illness and injury (s 212(3)(a)). This provision can apply so long as the employee is unfit for the work for which he was previously employed. Thus, continuity may be preserved even where the employee takes a temporary job with another employer until he is capable of returning to his former work (*Donnelly v Kelvin International Services* [1992] IRLR 496; see also *Pearson*, above).

Temporary cessation of work (s 212(3)(b)). In *Ford* the House of Lords held that the continuity of employment of a teacher whose contract came to an end at the end of every summer term but who was re-engaged in the autumn term was preserved during the summer vacation by *EPCA 1978, Sch 13 para 9(1)(b)*, now *ERA 1996, s 212(3)(b)*. Lord Diplock at 285 said that 'temporary' meant lasting only for a relatively short time, and that it was necessary to ask whether the interval between the two contracts was short in relation to their combined duration. This has become known as the 'mathematical' approach.

7.7 Continuous Employment

The test for "temporary cessation of work" under *s 212(3)(b)* does not require an examination of the expectation of parties of further work. What is required is to find the reason for the termination of the first contract of employment. If it has ended because of a temporary cessation of work, and the claimant is employed again, the case falls within *s 212(3)(b): Hussain v Acorn Independent College* [2011] IRLR 463. So, in *Hussain*, a teacher who was employed as temporary cover in the summer term, and who was then employed permanently in the next college year when the teacher he was covering unexpectedly decided not to return to work, could aggregate both his temporary cover contract and his permanent contract for continuity purposes. It did not matter that he had no expectation of further work when his temporary cover contract expired.

In *Flack v Kodak Ltd* [1986] ICR 775 the Court of Appeal had to consider whether six workers in the photo-finishing department of Kodak Ltd had sufficient continuous employment to pursue their employment protection rights. They had been employed intermittently over a number of years. Their period of employment depended on the extent of the department's work. The court decided that the correct approach in deciding whether a gap in an employee's employment, during which he is absent from work on account of a cessation of work, is a temporary cessation for the purposes of *EPCA 1978, Sch 13 para 9(1)(b)*, now *ERA 1996, s 212(3)(b)*, is to take into account all the relevant circumstances and in particular to consider the length of the period of absence in the context of the period of employment as a whole. Thus, the court did not apply a strictly 'mathematical' approach and held that the periods of absence did not break the continuity of employment (see also *Berwick Salmon Fisheries Co Ltd v Rutherford* [1991] IRLR 203).

However, in *Sillars v Charringtons Fuels Ltd* [1989] ICR 475 the Court of Appeal held that it was still open to an employment tribunal, after considering the matter in the round, to conclude that the 'mathematical' approach should be applied in an appropriate case (for example, where there was a systematic pattern of events). That there was an intention to re-employ the applicant later did not necessarily mean that the cessation of work was temporary in the sense of being for a relatively short time.

The 'cessation of work' must involve a reduction in the employer's overall quantum of work, and not merely a decision to allocate work to some other employee (*Byrne v Birmingham City District Council* [1987] ICR 519). *Byrne* was followed in *Letheby & Christopher Ltd v Bond* [1988] ICR 480.

Regarded as continuing in employment (s 212(3)(c)). This provision might apply to, for example, a period of unpaid leave. However, it was held in *Letheby* (see above) that an employee employed under single separate contracts, who went on holiday at a time convenient to her employers, was not absent from work in circumstances such that by arrangement or custom she was regarded as continuing in employment, where there was no prior agreement between the parties that after each holiday period there was to be some continuation of her employment.

The Court of Appeal in *Curr v Marks & Spencer plc* [2002] EWCA Civ 1852, [2003] IRLR 74 stressed that *s 212(3)(c)* requires a mutual arrangement between employer and employee, and a 'meeting of minds' by the arrangement that both parties regard the ex-employee as continuing in employment for some purpose. The Court did not regard it as helpful to refer to the test of *s 212(3)(c)* as involving consideration of whether an employment relationship continues (regarded as the 'key question' by the EAT in *Letheby* and *Booth v United States of America* [1999] IRLR 16): this was not the statutory test. In *Curr*, an employee absent on a four-year maternity break scheme did not fall within *s 212(3)(c)*, although she was required to work for at least two weeks in each year of the break; was prohibited from accepting other paid employment without consulting her manager; and was in regular contact with the employer. This was because the other terms on which she took her maternity break clearly showed that employment was not regarded as continuing. On commencement of her break, she was required to resign, and was given her P45. At the end of the break, she had an option to be re-employed by the employer, but the scheme's emphasis on 're-employment' in fact showed that she was not regarded as continuing in employment during the break.

The EAT has reached conflicting decisions on whether an "arrangement" under *s 212(3)(c)* can be made retrospectively. In *Murphy v A Birrell & Sons* [1978] IRLR 458 and *Morris v Walsh Western UK Ltd* [1997] IRLR 562, it held that a retrospective agreement to treat the period of an employee's absence as continuous was insufficient to preserve continuity of employment under *s 212(3)(c)* (because continuity of employment is a statutory concept – see *Secretary of State for Employment v Globe Elastic Thread Co Ltd* [1979] ICR 706). On the other hand, in *Ingram v Foxon* [1984] ICR 685 and *London Probation Board v Kirkpatrick* [2005] IRLR 443, the EAT held that there is no temporal qualification to the term "arrangement" in *s 212(3)(c)*, and that arrangements can be made retrospectively. The conflict in the authorities has been resolved by the EAT's latest decision in *Welton v Deluxe Retail Ltd* [2013] ICR 428. Langstaff P stated that an "arrangement" within *s 212(3)(c)* was not able to bridge a gap in continuity of employment unless it was in existence before, or arose contemporaneously with, the relevant weeks of absence from work during which there was no contract. He reviewed the authorities in detail, and stated that *Kirkpatrick* should no longer be followed.

7.8   Part-timers

As mentioned in **7.1** above, there is no difference in the provisions for calculating periods of continuous employment, in relation to their application to part-time employees as against full-time employees.

7.9   CHANGE OF EMPLOYER

Normally, to be continuous, employment must be with one employer. Separate companies must normally be treated as quite distinct entities. The 'corporate veil' may only be pierced if it is a mere facade concealing the true facts (*National Dock Labour Board v Pinn & Wheeler Ltd* [1989] BCLC 647). However, note the following points.

(a)   *Associated employers.* If an employee of an employer is taken into the employment of another employer who, at the time when the employee enters his employment is an 'associated' employer of the former employer, that change will not break the continuity of the employee's employment (*ERA 1996, s 218(6)*).

For the purposes of *ERA 1996*, any two employers are to be treated as associated if one is a company of which the other (directly or indirectly) has control, or if both are companies of which a third person (directly or indirectly) has control (*ERA 1996, s 231*). The definition of 'control' in *s 231* has been problematic over the years. The EAT held in *Hair Colour Consultants Ltd v Mena* [1984] ICR 671 that 'control' means voting control by a majority of shares, rather than de facto control (see also *South West Launderettes Ltd v Laidler* [1986] ICR 455, *Secretary of State for Employment v Newbold* [1981] IRLR 305, *Umar v Pliastar Ltd* [1981] ICR 727 and *Washington Arts Association Ltd v Forster* [1983] ICR 346). However, the Court of Appeal in *Secretary of State for Employment v Chapman* [1989] ICR 771 held that whilst voting control is the usual and normal test for determining whether two employers are associated, that test is not conclusive. Further, the EAT held in *Tice v Cartwright* [1999] ICR 769 that the word 'control' in *s 231* dealt with practical rather than theoretical control so that two brothers in partnership controlled the company in which they each had a 50% shareholding. (*Tice v Cartwright* has been applied by the EAT in *Da Silva Junior v Composite Mouldings & Design Ltd* [2009]

7.9 Continuous Employment

ICR 417. See also, *Hartford v Swiftrim Ltd* [1987] ICR 439; and *Zarb v British Brazilian Produce Co (Sales) Ltd* [1978] IRLR 78 cf *Strudick v IBL* [1988] ICR 796; and *Russell v Elmdon Freight Terminal Ltd* [1989] ICR 629.)

The EAT has been willing to treat the term 'company' as including both a partnership of companies (*Pinkney v Sandpiper Drilling Ltd* [1989] IRLR 425) and a foreign entity equivalent to an English company (*Hancill v Marcon Engineering Ltd* [1990] ICR 103). However, not all bodies corporate (such as local authorities) are 'companies' within *ERA 1996, s 231* (*Gardiner v London Borough of Merton* [1980] IRLR 472). In *Hasley v Fair Employment Agency* [1989] IRLR 106, the Northern Ireland Court of Appeal pointed out that the section only requires the employer which is *controlled* to be a company; the *controlling* employer may be some other type of legal person.

(b)   *Transfers of a business.* If a trade or business or an undertaking is transferred from one person to another, the period of employment of an employee in the trade or business or undertaking at the time of the transfer counts as a period of employment with the transferee and is regarded as unbroken (*ERA 1996, s 218(2)*).

ERA 1996, s 218(2) will generally apply in cases where there has been a transfer of an undertaking for the purposes of the *Transfer of Undertakings (Protection of Employment) Regulations 2006* ("*TUPE*"), in which case continuity of employment is in any event preserved under *TUPE* (see *TUPE, reg 4(1)*). However, the operation of *ERA 1996, s 218(2)* is not restricted to cases in which there has been a transfer under *TUPE*, and if for one reason or another *TUPE* does not apply, continuity of employment may nevertheless be preserved under the statute. See for example *Oakland v Wellswood (Yorkshire) Ltd* [2010] ICR 902. In *Oakland*, the tribunal and EAT held that there had been no *TUPE* transfer, because the transferor was the subject of bankruptcy proceedings for the purposes of *reg 8(7)* of *TUPE*. Notwithstanding that, the Court of Appeal found that the employee's continuity of employment had been preserved by virtue of *ERA 1996, s 218(2)* (without needing to decide whether the tribunal's and EAT's conclusions on *reg 8(7)* of *TUPE* were correct). See further TRANSFER OF UNDERTAKINGS (52).

Case law on *ERA 1996, s 218(2)* has warned against artificial attempts to break continuity. In *Macer v Abafast Ltd* [1990] ICR 234 and *Gibson v Motortune Ltd* [1990] ICR 740, the EAT stated that the machinery of *EPCA, Sch 13 para 17(2)*, the predecessor to *ERA 1996, s 218(2)*, could operate even where the machinery of transfer led to a gap of more than one week between periods of employment. This approach was adopted by the Court of Appeal in *Clark & Tokeley Ltd v Oakes* [1998] IRLR 577, on the basis that there will often not be a precise time of transfer, which can take place over an extended period; and that what had to be examined when considering whether an employee was employed "at the time of transfer" was not the point when the legal formalities of transfer were completed, but the actual state of affairs as a matter of fact, which could cover a period of days or even weeks.

A similar result which preserves continuity may be obtained under *TUPE, reg 4(1)*, but on a different conceptual basis. Under *TUPE*, contrary to the position under *ERA 1996, s 218(2)*, a transfer takes place at a particular moment in time: see *Celtec Ltd v Astley* [2006] ICR 993, HL. However, *TUPE* operates so as to preserve the continuity of employment of employees automatically unfairly dismissed prior to the transfer for reasons related to the transfer: see *TUPE, reg 4(3)* and *reg 7(1)* and *Litster v Forth Dry Dock and Engineering Co Ltd* [1990] 1 AC 546; and see further TRANSFER OF UNDERTAKINGS (52).

(c)   *Substitution of employer by statute.* If by or under an Act of Parliament, whether public or local, a contract of employment between any body corporate and an employee is modified and some other body corporate is substituted as the employer, the period of employment of the employee at the time when the modification takes effect counts as a period of employment with the second body corporate and is regarded as unbroken (*ERA 1996, s 218(3)*). For a case where, on the facts, the predecessor provision to *s 218(3)* was held not to apply, see *Gale v Northern General Hospital NHS Trust* [1994] IRLR 292.

(d)   *Employment in schools/the National Health Service.* If an employee of the governing body of a maintained school is taken into the employment of the local authority responsible for the school, or vice versa, continuity of employment is preserved (*ERA 1996, s 218(7)*). Similarly, in certain circumstances, continuity of employment is preserved when an employee's employment switches from one health service employer to another, if he is undergoing professional training which involves successive employment by a number of different health service employers (*ERA 1996, ss 218(8)–218(10)* and *Employment Protection (National Health Service) Order 1996 (SI 1996/638)*).

(e)   *Death of employer, partnerships, etc.* If, on the death of the employer, the employee passes into the employment of the personal representatives or trustees of the deceased, continuity is not broken. A change in partners, personal representatives or trustees does not break the continuity of an employee's employment (*ERA 1996, s 218(4), (5)*). The provision in *ERA 1996, s 218(5)* for preservation of continuity on a change in partners covers the situation where, after the change, there are no partners, but only a sole proprietor: see *Bower v Stevens* [2004] ICR 1582 and *Jeetle v Elster* [1985] ICR 389.

7.10   WEEKS WHICH DO NOT BREAK CONTINUITY

The following weeks do not count in the computation but do not break continuity. (This applies also where the events occur in only part of the week.)

(a)   Any week during which the employee takes part in a strike (*ERA 1996, s 216(1), (2)*).

(b)   Any week during which the employee is absent from work because of a lock-out (*ERA 1996, s 216(3)*).

(c)   For the purpose of calculating the qualifying period for pursuing a claim to a redundancy payment and for the purpose of calculating the amount of the payment, any week during which the employee (i) was employed outside Great Britain (*ERA 1996, s 215(2)(a)*), and (ii) was not an employed earner for the purposes of the *Social Security Contributions and Benefits Act 1992* in respect of whom a secondary Class 1 contribution was payable under that Act (whether or not the contribution was in fact paid) (*ERA 1996, s 215(2)(b)*). For all other purposes, continuity continues during periods in which the employee is engaged in work wholly or mainly outside Great Britain (*ERA 1996, s 215(1)(a)*).

(d)   Where a person left employment because he was called into permanent service in the reserve or auxiliary armed forces, but has subsequently been re-employed by his former employer, his period of permanent service in the armed forces does not break continuity, provided that no more than 6 months have elapsed since the end of that permanent service: *ERA 1996, s 217* and the *Reserve Forces (Safeguard of Employment) Act 1985*.

7.11 Continuous Employment

7.11 'Postponement' of start of employment

If an employee's period of continuous employment includes one or more periods which do not count in computing the length of the period but do not break continuity, the beginning of the period is treated as *postponed* by the number of days falling within that intervening period, or, as the case may be, by the aggregate number of days falling within those periods (*ERA 1996, s 211(3)*).

7.12 EVENTS WHICH BREAK CONTINUITY

Except as is otherwise specifically provided in *ERA 1996, ss 215–217*, any week which does not count in the computation breaks the continuity of a period of employment (*ERA 1996, s 210(4)*).

The receipt of a redundancy payment breaks continuity for redundancy qualification and payment purposes (*ERA 1996, s 214*). However, *s 214* does not apply where an employee, having received a redundancy payment (or equivalent payment), is reinstated or re-engaged by his employer on terms which include a requirement to repay the amount of that payment, and that requirement is complied with (*Employment Protection (Continuity of Employment) Regulations 1996 (SI 1996/3147)* – see also **7.6(d)** above). *Section 214* also does not apply where a 'redundancy payment' paid by the employer is not a payment which he is statutorily obliged to make (*Rowan v Machinery Installations (South Wales) Ltd* [1981] ICR 386; *Ross v Delrosa Caterers Ltd* [1981] ICR 393). Further, given that a 'redundancy payment' in this context means a statutory redundancy payment, and a right to such a payment depends on there having been a dismissal, it follows that where an employee's employment is transferred pursuant to *TUPE 1981*, there is no dismissal and therefore any payment received by the employee is not a statutory redundancy payment and will not break continuity under *s 214* (*Senior Heat Treatment v Bell* [1997] IRLR 614). However, this will not be the case where the Secretary of State has paid the equivalent of a statutory redundancy payment to an employee of an insolvent employer under *ERA 1996, s 167* (*Secretary of State for Trade and Industry v Lassman* [2000] IRLR 411).

7.13 TABLE OF QUALIFYING PERIODS FOR STATUTORY EMPLOYMENT PROTECTION RIGHTS

Employment right	Qualifying period
	NB Not all statutory employment protection rights require a qualifying period of continuous employment. For example, the general right to maternity leave does not depend upon 'continuous' employment as defined by *ERA 1996*.
Written statement of employment particulars	One month (see *ERA 1996, s 198*).
Guarantee payments/Payments during medical suspension	One month ending with the day before the period for which guarantee payment, etc is claimed (*ERA 1996, s 29(1)* and *s 65(1)*).
Minimum period of notice	One month (*ERA 1996, ss 86(1), 87(1)*).
	Any contract of a person who has been employed for three months which is a contract for a fixed term of one month or less is deemed for the purposes of *s 86* to have effect as if it were for an indefinite period and thus subject to the notice provisions (*ERA 1996, s 86(4)*).

Employment right	Qualifying period
Unfair dismissal Written reasons for dismissal	Two years (one year for employees whose continuous employment commenced before 6 April 2012). (*ERA 1996, s 108(1)* and *92(3)*).
	If an employee is dismissed by reason of a medical suspension requirement or recommendation under an enactment or a Code of Practice providing for health and safety at work, the qualifying period is one month (*ERA 1996, s 108(2)*).
	In certain other cases of unfair dismissal, no qualifying period is necessary. These are where the reason or principal reason for the dismissal:
	(*a*) was a union-related reason (*TULRCA 1992, s 154*; and see **54.**3(a) UNFAIR DISMISSAL – **II**);
	(*b*) was the assertion of a statutory right (*ERA 1996, s 108(3)(g)*; and see **54.**3(c) UNFAIR DISMISSAL – **II**);
	(*c*) was a health and safety-related reason (*ERA 1996, s 108(3)(c)*; and see **54.**3(b) UNFAIR DISMISSAL – **II**);
	(*d*) was a reason related to pregnancy, childbirth or maternity; maternity leave; adoption leave; parental leave; paternity leave; shared parental leave; or time off for dependants under *ERA 1996, s 57* (*ERA 1996, s 108(3)(b)*; and see **32.9** MATERNITY AND PARENTAL RIGHTS);
	(*e*) was a reason connected with the performance by an employee who is a pension scheme trustee of his functions as such a trustee (*ERA 1996, s 108(3)(e)*; see **54.**3(e) UNFAIR DISMISSAL – **II**);
	(*f*) was a reason connected with the performance by an employee representative (see **39.4** REDUNDANCY – **II** and **52.18** TRANSFER OF UNDERTAKINGS), or a candidate in an election for such an employee representative, of his functions as such an employee representative or candidate (*ERA 1996, s 108(3)(f)*; see **54.**3(f) UNFAIR DISMISSAL – **II**);
	(*g*) was a reason connected with the refusal of Sunday work by a shop worker or betting worker (*ERA 1996, s 108(3)(d)*; see **54.**3(g) UNFAIR DISMISSAL – **II**);
	(*h*) was a reason related to working time (*ERA 1996, s 108(3)(dd)*; and see **54.**3(h) UNFAIR DISMISSAL – **II**);
	(*I*) was a reason connected with the assertion of rights under the *National Minimum Wage Act 1998* (*ERA 1996, s 108(3)(gg)*; see **54.**3(m) UNFAIR DISMISSAL – **II**);
	(*j*) was a reason connected with the making of a protected disclosure under *ERA 1996, ss 43A–43L* (*ERA 1996, s 108(3)(ff)* and *s 103A*; see **54.**3(n) UNFAIR DISMISSAL – **II**);

7.13   Continuous Employment

Employment right	Qualifying period	
	(k)	was a reason connected with the assertion of rights under the *Tax Credits Act 1999* (*ERA 1996, s 108(3)(gh)*; see **54.**3(t) UNFAIR DISMISSAL – II);
	(l)	was a reason connected with the assertion of rights under the *Transnational Information and Consultation of Employees Regulations 1999* (*ERA 1996, s 108(3)(hh)*; see **54.**3(u) UNFAIR DISMISSAL – II);
	(m)	was a reason connected with the assertion of rights under the *Part-time Workers (Prevention of Less Favourable Treatment) Regulations 2000 (SI 2000/1551)* (*ERA 1996, s 108(3)(i)*; see **54.**3(s) UNFAIR DISMISSAL – II);
	(n)	was a reason connected with the assertion of rights under the *Fixed-term Employees (Prevention of Less Favourable Treatment) Regulations 2002 (SI 2002/2034)* (*ERA 1996, s 108(3)(j)*; see **54.**3(v) UNFAIR DISMISSAL – II);
	(o)	was a reason connected with the assertion of flexible working rights under *ERA 1996, ss 80F–80G* (*ERA 1996, s 108(3)(gi)*; see **54.**3 UNFAIR DISMISSAL – II);
	(p)	was a reason connected with trade union recognition or bargaining arrangements (*TULRCA 1992, Sch A1, paras 161–162* (see **54.**3(o) UNFAIR DISMISSAL – II);
	(q)	was that the employee exercised or sought to exercise the right, pursuant to *Employment Relations Act 1999, s 10*, to be accompanied to a disciplinary or grievance hearing or that the employee accompanied or sought to accompany another worker to such a hearing (*Employment Relations Act 1999, s 12(4)*. See **54.**3(p) UNFAIR DISMISSAL – II);
	(r)	was that the employee was dismissed for taking part in protected industrial action in the circumstances set out in *TULRCA 1992, s 238A*, introduced by the *Employment Relations Act 1999, s 16* and *Sch 5*. (See **54.**3(q) UNFAIR DISMISSAL – II; or
	(s)	was a reason connected with the exercise of various negotiation or consultation rights within a "European Company" as defined in the *European Public Limited-Liability Company Regulations 2004 (SI 2004/2326)*. (*ERA 1996, s 108(3)(k)*: see **54.**3 UNFAIR DISMISSAL – II);
	(t)	was a reason connected with the exercise of various negotiation or consultation rights under the *Information and Consultation of Employees Regulations 2004 (SI 2004/3426)*. *ERA 1996, s 108(3)(l)*: see **54.**3 UNFAIR DISMISSAL – II);

Employment right	Qualifying period	
	(u)	was the fact that the employee has been summoned for jury service, or has been absent on jury service in the circumstances set out in *ERA 1996, s 98B*. (*ERA 1996, s 108(3)(aa)*: see **54.3 Unfair Dismissal – II**);
	(v)	was a selection for redundancy for a reason which would have been automatically unfair if it had been the reason for dismissal (*ERA 1996, s 108(3)(h), s 105*);
	(w)	was a reason connected with an employee's performance of various functions or exercise of various entitlements under the *European Cooperative Society (Involvement of Employees) Regulations 2006 (SI 2006/2059)*: see *reg 31 of SI 2006/2059 and ERA 1996, s 108(3)(o)*. The *2006 Regulations* relate to the formation of, and employees' participation in, European Cooperative Societies;
	(x)	was a reason connected with an employee's performance of various functions or exercise of various entitlements in respect of participation in a cross-border merger: see the *Companies (Cross-Border Mergers) Regulations 2007, regs 46–47* and *ERA 1996, s 108(3)(p)*;
	(y)	was for a reason relating to a "prohibited list" within *reg 3* of the *Employment Relations Act 1999 (Blacklists) Regulations 2010*. This applies essentially when an employee has been dismissed because his name has been included on a "blacklist" made or obtained by the employer, containing details of trade union membership or activities. See *ERA s 104F* and *s 108(3)(gl)*;
	(z)	was that the employee made or proposed to make an application falling with *ERA 1996, s 63D* (statutory right to make request in relation to study or training); or exercised or sought to exercise various rights under the *Employee Study and Training (Procedural Requirements) Regulations 2010, SI 2010/155*; or exercised or proposed to exercise a right conferred on the employee under *ERA 1996, s 63F* (setting out the employer's duties in relation to an application under *ERA 1996, s 63D*); or brought proceedings against the employer under *ERA 1996, s 63I* (complaints to employment tribunals related to applications under *ERA 1996, s 63D*); or alleged the existence of any circumstance which would constitute a ground for bringing such proceedings. See *ERA 1996, s 104E* and *s 108(3)(gk)*, and the *Employee Study and Training (Procedural Requirements) Regulations 2010, SI 2010/155, reg 18*;

Employment right	Qualifying period
	(za) was a reason connected with an employee's performance or proposed performance of various functions or entitlements connected with negotiating rights in a European Public Limited-Liability Company. See *ERA 1996, s 108(3)(q)* and *reg 29(1)* of the *European Public Limited-Liability Company (Employee Involvement)(Great Britain) Regulations 2009 (SI 2009/2401)*;
	(zb) was a reason specified in *reg 17(3)* of the *Agency Workers Regulations 2010 (SI 2010/93)*, where the employee is an agency worker. See *ERA 1996, s 108(3)(r)* and *reg 17(1)* of the *Agency Workers Regulations 2010*.
	(zc) was a reason connected with the assertion of certain rights under the *Occupational and Personal Pension Schemes (Consultation by Employers and Miscellaneous Amendment) Regulations 2006, SI 2006/349* (see *ERA 1996, s 108(3)(m)*);
	(zd) was a reason specified in *ERA 1996, s 104D* (certain matters connected with the enrolment of employees in a pension scheme): see *ERA 1996, s 108(3)(gj)*;
	(ze) was that the employee refused to accept an offer by the employer for the employee to become an employee shareholder within the meaning of *ERA 1996, s 205A*. See *ERA 1996, s 104G* and *108(3)(gm)*.
	(zf) was a reason related to the employee's political opinions or affiliation. See *ERA 1996, s 108(4)*.
	(zg) was a reason connected to the employee's membership of a reserve force (as defined in *Armed Forces Act 2006, s 374*). See *ERA 1996, s 108(5)* (applying to dismissals from 1 October 2014).
	If the reason or principal reason for dismissal is the transfer of an undertaking, so that dismissal is automatically unfair by operation of reg *7(1)* of the *Transfer of Undertakings (Protection of Employment) Regulations 2006 ("TUPE")*, the normal qualifying period applies (see *reg 7(6) TUPE*).
Redundancy payment	Two years (*ERA 1996, s 155*).
Consultation of appropriate representatives and notification of Secretary of State on redundancy	Three months, but only where the employment is under a fixed-term contract of three months or less or one made in contemplation of a specific task not expected to last for more than three months (*TULRCA 1992, s 282*).

8   Contract of Employment

Cross-references. See CHILDREN AND YOUNG PERSONS (4) for statutory restrictions on their employment; RESTRAINT OF TRADE, CONFIDENTIALITY AND EMPLOYEE INTERVENTIONS (41); and COLLECTIVE AGREEMENTS (6) for their respective effects on individual contracts; 22.5 EQUAL PAY for the statutory equality clause; 34.6 PAY – I for illegal deductions from wages; 45.16 STRIKES AND INDUSTRIAL ACTION for the effect of industrial action on contracts; and 55.2–55.5 UNFAIR DISMISSAL – III for reinstatement and re-engagement orders. See TERMINATION OF EMPLOYMENT (48) and WRONGFUL DISMISSAL (58) for termination of contract rules. For restrictions on contracting out of statutory provisions, see 22.14 EQUAL PAY, 38.14 REDUNDANCY – I and 53.19 UNFAIR DISMISSAL – I.

8.1   The contract of employment is dealt with in this chapter under the following heads:

(a)   Formation of the contract;

(b)   The statutory requirement for written particulars of contract;

(c)   Terms of the contract, including implied terms and unenforceable terms;

(d)   Changes to contractual terms; and

(e)   Remedies for breach of the employment contract.

This chapter does not deal with the question of whether a particular agreement under which a person works is a 'contract of *employment*' for the purposes of *ERA 1996 s 230(1)*. That question is considered in EMPLOYEE, SELF-EMPLOYED OR WORKER? (15).

8.2   FORMATION

Requirements

The usual requirements of contract law apply: offer, acceptance, consideration, intention to create legal relations and certainty. For examples of the application of these principles, see: *Moore v President of the Methodist Conference* [2011] EWCA Civ 1581, [2012] ICR 432, [2012] IRLR 229 and *Anar v Dresdner Kleinwort Ltd* [2011] EWCA Civ 229, [2011] All ER (D) 88 (Mar). The parties' agreement is to be construed objectively in the factual context prevailing at the time of the agreement. On the importance of certainty, see *Judge v Crown Leisure Ltd* [2005] EWCA Civ 571, [2005] IRLR 823, where it was held that statements made at a Christmas party and in vague terms (such as "in due course" and "eventually") did not amount to a contractually binding agreement to increase the employee's pay. Contrast this with *Anar*, where neither the informal nature of the employer's assurances nor the imprecise scope of those assurances automatically precluded their enforceability.

A contract of employment may also be implied from the parties' conduct: *Franks v Reuters Ltd* [2003] EWCA Civ 417, [2003] IRLR 423; *Dacas v Brook Street Bureau (UK) Ltd* [2004] EWCA Civ 217, [2004] ICR 1437, [2004] IRLR 358 and *Cable & Wireless plc v Muscat* [2006] EWCA Civ 220, [2006] ICR 975, [2006] IRLR 354. The existence of a "factual substratum" suggestive of a contract of employment will not suffice to establish an implied contract (*Beattie v Leicester City Council* (UKEAT0386/09/SM) (20 January 2010, unreported)). Questions as to implied contracts of employment frequently arise in connection 'tripartite' relationships involving agency workers (see EMPLOYEE, SELF-EMPLOYED OR WORKER? (15)).

The fact that a contract of employment is void does not automatically mean that no "employment relationship" exists. For example, where a public authority's employment of an individual was *ultra vires*, there may nonetheless be a *de facto* employment relationship

8.2 Contract of Employment

on the basis of which the individual may be treated as an employee for the purposes of *ERA s. 230(1)* (*Eastbourne Borough Council v Foster* [2001] EWCA Civ 1091, [2001] LGR 529, [2002] ICR 234; *Lairikyengbam v Shrewsbury and Telford Hospital NHS Trust* [2010] ICR 66, [2009] All ER (D) 271 (Oct), EAT).

8.3 Form of the contract

A contract of employment may be either written or oral, or a mixture of the two. This means that – subject to the contractual principles summarised above – its form may range from a document drawn up by solicitors and signed by both parties, to a chat over a cup of tea in the canteen. One of the issues in *Cheltenham Borough Council v Laird* [2009] EWHC 1253 (QB), [2009] IRLR 621 (upheld on appeal: [2010] EWCA Civ 847) was whether the employment contract had been concluded by an oral agreement which predated the employee's completion of a medical questionnaire or by the consequent letter of appointment which postdated that questionnaire. The court found the latter to be the case, observing that it would be reasonably expected practice for appointments at this senior managerial level to be concluded in writing.

As the court in *Laird* suggested, senior executives will usually be employed pursuant to written agreements drafted by solicitors. These agreements are often for a fixed term. A director's contract of employment whose guaranteed term is longer than two years must be approved by a resolution of the members of the company. A guaranteed period is the period for which the director's employment may continue other than at the instance of the company and within which the company may not terminate the employment (see **9.3** DIRECTORS and *Companies Act 2006, s 188*). In the event that the contract is not approved by the members, its provisions as to duration are void and there is instead substituted a term that the employment is terminable on reasonable notice (*s 189*). Such agreements frequently contain provisions dealing with the tenure by the employee of a directorship of the employing company. They may also contain restrictive covenants (see RESTRAINT OF TRADE, CONFIDENTIALITY AND EMPLOYEE INTERVENTIONS (**41**)).

Less senior employees may be asked to sign a standard form contract of employment. Alternatively, the contract may be contained in an exchange of letters, or terms may be agreed orally at an interview. Provided that the parties are in agreement over the essential terms of the contract, such as hours and wages, there will be a valid contract of employment enforceable by either party. However, an employer is under a duty to give his employees particulars in writing of certain important terms of their contracts (see **8.6** below).

8.4 Parties to the contract

Despite the rule that unincorporated associations can neither sue nor be sued in their own name, an employee can bring employment tribunal proceedings against the management committee of an unincorporated association: *Asim v Nazir* [2010] ICR 1225.

Occasionally, a question arises as to the identity of the employer where it is unclear which of a number of companies or other legal persons is the employer under the contract. In such cases, the employer is likely to be the person who has power to control the employee's activities (see *Clifford v Union of Democratic Mineworkers* [1991] IRLR 518; *Andrews v King (Inspector of Taxes)* [1991] STC 481, [1991] ICR 846). The question is resolved by considering all the circumstances (and documents) of the case (see for example the unreported Scottish case of *McVeigh v Livingstone* (UKEATS/0027/08/BI) (16 June 2009, unreported), where the tribunal scrutinised the claimant's wage slips, P60s and written particulars in resolving the question of whether the employer was the company or the individuals in control of that company).

See **26.8** FOREIGN EMPLOYEES for the rules as to which country's system of law governs the contract of employment.

8.5   An employer may engage or refuse to engage any person who has legal capacity, subject only to the statutory provisions relating to CHILDREN AND YOUNG PERSONS (4), discrimination on grounds of race or sex or disability or age or religion or belief or sexual orientation or trade union membership or non-membership (see DISCRIMINATION AND EQUAL OPPORTUNITIES – I (11), II (12), and III (13), 50.2 TRADE UNIONS – I) and the provisions relating to the employment of foreign nationals (see FOREIGN EMPLOYEES (26)).

8.6   WRITTEN PARTICULARS OF CONTRACT

Although the law does not require the contract itself to be in writing, employers are required to give each employee a written statement of particulars of certain important terms of the contract (see *ERA 1996, s 1* and CONTINUOUS EMPLOYMENT (7)). This statement is not itself the contract of employment, but it offers (strong) persuasive (though not conclusive) evidence of the terms of the contract (*Robertson v British Gas Corpn* [1983] ICR 351, [1983] IRLR 302, CA; *System Floors (UK) Ltd v Daniel* [1982] ICR 54, [1981] IRLR 475).

This written statement of particulars must be given to the employee not later than two months after the beginning of the employment. If, during that period, the employee is to begin work outside the UK for more than a month, the statement must be given to him not later than the time he leaves the UK to begin work (*ERA 1996, s 2(5)*).

The statement may be given in instalments during the two-month period (*ERA 1996, s 1(1)*). However, certain of the particulars must be included in a single document. These are the names of the parties, the dates when employment and continuous employment began, the particulars of remuneration, hours and holidays, the job title or description, and the place of work (*ERA 1996, s 2(4)*).

If employment ends within the two-month period, a statement must still be given (*ERA 1996, s 2(6)*), unless the employment continued for less than one month (*ERA 1996, s 198*).

Amendments to the *ERA 1996* introduced by the *Employment Act 2002* permit the use of documents as an alternative to a statement of particulars. If the employer gives the employee a contract of employment or an engagement letter which contains the information required by *ERA 1996, s 1* at the time when employment commences (*ERA 1996, s 7B*) or afterwards (*ERA 1996, s 7A(1)(c)*) that is sufficient to meet the obligations under *s 1*. If the document contains the material required by *s 3* (disciplinary procedure, etc) that is sufficient to comply with that section.

8.7   Particulars which must be given

The written statement must:

(a)   name the employer and the employee;

(b)   specify the date when the employment began; and

(c)   specify the date on which the employee's period of *continuous* employment began (taking into account any employment with a previous employer which counts towards that period).

(*ERA 1996, s 1(3)*.)

(For the day on which employment 'begins', see **7.3** CONTINUOUS EMPLOYMENT.)

It must also give the following particulars of terms of employment which are applicable as at a specified date not more than seven days before the date on which the statement is given:

(d)   the scale or rate of remuneration, or the method of calculating remuneration;

(e)   the intervals at which remuneration is paid (that is whether weekly, or monthly or at other specified intervals);

(f)   any terms and conditions relating to hours of work (including any terms and conditions relating to normal working hours);

(g)   any terms and conditions relating to:

    (i)   entitlement to holidays, including public holidays and holiday pay (the particulars being sufficient to enable the employee's entitlement, including any entitlement to accrued holiday pay on the termination of employment, to be precisely calculated);

    (ii)   incapacity for work due to sickness or injury, including any provisions for sick pay; and

    (iii)   pensions and pension schemes (unless the employee's pension rights depend on the terms of a pension scheme established under statute, and he is employed by a body or authority required under statute to give information concerning pension rights to new employees);

(h)   the length of notice which the employee is obliged to give and entitled to receive to terminate his contract of employment;

(i)   the title of the job which the employee is employed to do or a brief description of the work for which the employee is employed;

(j)   where the employment is not intended to be permanent, the period for which it is expected to continue or, if it is for a fixed term, the date when it is to end;

(k)   either the place of work or, where the employee is required or permitted to work at various places, an indication of that and of the employer's address;

(l)   any collective agreements which directly affect the terms and conditions of the employment, including the persons by whom they were made where the employer is not a party; and

(m)   where the employee is required to work outside the UK for more than a month, certain further particulars concerning that period, the currency of remuneration, any additional remuneration and benefits, and any terms and conditions relating to return.

(ERA 1996, s 1(4), (5).)

The Secretary of State may add to the list of particulars to be given (*ERA 1996, s 7*).

Disciplinary and complaints procedures. The *ERA 1996* (as amended by *s 35, Employment Act 2002*) further requires that every statement given to an employee shall contain a note:

(A)   specifying any disciplinary rules applicable to the employee or referring to a document which is reasonably accessible to the employee and which specifies such rules. The employer must also specify any procedure applicable to the taking of disciplinary actions relating to the employee, or to a decision to dismiss the employee, or refer the employee to the provisions of another document which specifies such a procedure; and

(B)   specifying, by description or otherwise:

    (i)   a person to whom the employee can apply if he is dissatisfied with any disciplinary decision relating to him or any decision to dismiss him; and

(ii)   a person to whom the employee can apply for the purpose of seeking redress of any grievance relating to his employment and the manner in which any such application should be made,

and where there are further steps to be taken in any such application, explaining those steps or referring to a document which is reasonably accessible to the employee and which explains them (*ERA 1996, s 3(1)*).

The requirement to give a note of disciplinary and complaints procedures does not apply to rules, disciplinary decisions, decisions to dismiss, grievances or procedures relating to HEALTH AND SAFETY AT WORK – **II (28)** (*ERA 1996, s 3(2)*).

Contracting-out certificate. The written particulars must include a note stating whether a contracting-out certificate is in force for the particular employment concerned (*ERA 1996, s 3(5)*). Such a certificate is issued where there is in place an occupational pension scheme which satisfies certain conditions.

Previously, employers who (together with any associated employer) employed less than 20 persons were exempted from the obligations in respect of informing employees of disciplinary procedures. That exemption is abolished by *s 36, Employment Act 2002*.

ERA 1996 does not require there to be provisions in the contract on all these matters (see *Morley v Heritage plc* [1993] IRLR 400). It simply requires notice of such provisions that do exist to be given to the employee. Where there are no provisions relating to any of the matters listed above, that fact must be stated, eg where no contractual sick pay is provided (*ERA 1996, s 2(1)*).

Certain classes of employee are also entitled to a statement setting out their right to refuse to work on Sundays under the provisions formerly in the *Sunday Trading Act 1994* and the *Betting, Gaming and Lotteries Act 1963* which have now been consolidated in the *ERA 1996*.

8.8   Alternatives to inclusion of particulars in written statement

ERA 1996, s 2(2), (3) provides that the written statement of particulars:

(a)   may refer the employee to the provisions of some other document which he has reasonable opportunities of reading in the course of his employment, or which is made reasonably accessible to him in some other way, for particulars of any of the matters specified in *ERA 1996, s 1(4)(d)(ii)* and *(iii)* (sickness, sick pay and pensions); and

(b)   may refer the employee to the law or to a collective agreement which directly affects his terms and conditions for particulars of the matters specified in *s 1(4)(e), ERA 1996* (length of notice), provided that any such collective agreement is one which he has reasonable opportunities of reading in the course of his employment or which is made reasonably accessible to him in some other way.

8.9   Written particulars and changes in contract terms

Any changes in the contractual terms or in other matters of which written particulars must be given must be the subject of a written statement given to the employee at the earliest opportunity and in any event not later than one month after the change (or the time of leaving the UK to work for more than one month, if that is the cause of the change) (*ERA 1996, s 4(1), (3)*). Similar provisions concerning the documents in which particulars may be set out again apply.

A mere change of the employer's name, or a mere change in employer which does not break CONTINUOUS EMPLOYMENT (7), does not require a complete new statement under *ERA 1996, s 1*, but does require a statement of change under *s 4* (*ERA 1996, s 4(6), (8)*).

8.10   Exceptions

The requirement to give written particulars applies to all employees except:

(a)   seamen of various kinds (*ERA 1996, s 199, s 5(1)*); and

(b)   a person whose employment continues for less than one month (*ERA 1996, s 198*).

8.11   Employees' remedies for failure to give particulars

An employee who has not been provided with the necessary particulars may make a complaint relating to the failure to an employment tribunal (*ERA 1996, s 11(1)*). Claims under *s 11* are a relatively speedy way of having contractual employment rights determined.

An application may be made by either the employer or the employee if a statement of particulars has purportedly been given, but a question arises as to the particulars which ought to have been included or referred to in it (*ERA 1996, s 11(2)*). Where no *express* term has been agreed, it may be that the tribunal is able to *imply* a term after considering all the facts and circumstances of the relationship between the employer and the employee concerned (*Mears v Safecar Security Ltd* [1982] ICR 626). However, if there has been no express or implied agreement upon a particular term, the tribunal has no power to invent a term for the parties (*Eagland v British Telecommunications plc* [1993] ICR 644; and see **8.14** below). Nor is *s 11* to be used as a means of clarifying or interpreting an ambiguous term (*Construction Industry Training Board v Leighton* [1978] IRLR 60). This was confirmed by the Court of Appeal in *Southern Cross Healthcare Co Ltd v Perkins* [2010] EWCA Civ 1442, [2011] ICR 285, [2011] IRLR 247, where Maurice Kay LJ held at para 29 that "the reference in *section 11(1)* of the *1996 Act* to a determination of 'what particulars ought to have been included', is not an invitation to judicial creativity, even under the rubric of "construction"".

An employer's failure to include a term in the statement of particulars does not mean that the employer is unable to enforce that term: *Lange v Georg Schüneman GmbH* [2001] IRLR 244, ECJ.

The tribunal will, if it finds such a complaint under *s 11* well-founded, state the particulars which should have been given and the employer will be deemed to have given a statement including those particulars (*ERA 1996, s 12(1), (2)*). If the employer has been in breach of any of those terms, the employee may bring an action against him in the county court or the High Court or, if the breach involves a deduction from pay, in the tribunal under *ERA 1996, ss 13–27* (the former *Wages Act 1986* provisions) (see **34.6 Pay – I**). The right to present a complaint for failure to provide written particulars may be exercised by an employee who has been employed for more than two months. If the employment has ceased, the application to the tribunal must be made before the end of the period of three months beginning with the date on which the employment ceased or within such further period as the tribunal considers reasonable where it was not reasonably practicable for the application to be made within three months (*ERA 1996, s 11(4)*). (See **19.91 Employment Tribunals**.)

There is no right to claim damages for a breach of the statutory duty to give written particulars, although in certain special circumstances an employer may be under a contractual duty to take reasonable steps to publicise a term (*Scally v Southern Health and Social Services Board* [1991] ICR 771, HL).

In the event that an employee brings a claim of a type specified in *Sch 5* to the *Employment Act 2002* (a wide range of claims including, but not limited to, unfair dismissal, discrimination and breach of contract cases) against an employer which is resolved in favour of the employee and, at the time when the proceedings were commenced, the employer was in breach either of his duty to provide a statement of particulars under *ERA 1996, s 1* or to a statement of changes under *ERA 1996, s 4*, then the tribunal must award the employee two weeks' pay (and may award four weeks' pay) even if it makes no other award (*EmA 2002, s 38*). If the claim is unsuccessful or withdrawn, no award can be made: *Advanced Collection Limited v Gultekin* (UKEAT 10377114, 6 February 2015) If the tribunal does make an award in favour of the employee, it must increase that award by two weeks' pay (and may increase it by four weeks' pay). However, if there are exceptional circumstances that would make the award or the increase to the award unjust or inequitable, then the tribunal does not have to order the additional award.

8.12   TERMS OF THE CONTRACT

Freedom to agree

Agreement remains the pivotal issue in construing employment contracts. As the Supreme Court has confirmed in *Autoclenz Ltd v Belcher* [2011] UKSC 41, [2011] 4 All ER 745 (in the context of whether or not individuals were 'workers'), the fundamental question is "what was the agreement between the parties?" If the evidence showed that the written contractual terms did not reflect the parties' true agreement, then it can to that extent be disregarded.

The parties are free to agree any terms they wish, subject to certain limitations set out below. In determining the terms of a contract, a tribunal will have to consider the provisions of a written contract (if any). However, even in the case where there is a written contract, it will not be correct to consider only its terms unless it is established that the parties intended that the document should contain all the terms of the contract. It is open to the parties to agree some terms in writing and others orally (see the discussion in *Carmichael v National Power plc* [1999] 4 All ER 897, [1999] 1 WLR 2042, para 19). If an employment tribunal is called upon to interpret the terms of a contract, it must apply the same principles as an ordinary court. This means, for example, the words used must be interpreted in the context which existed and was known to both parties at the time when the contract was made (*Investors Compensation Scheme Ltd v West Bromwich Building Society* [1998] 1 All ER 98, HL) but that the parties' subsequent conduct is not admissible in construing their original written agreement (*Hooper v British Railways Board* [1988] IRLR 517). Where the terms of a written contract are truly ambiguous, it may be permissible to construe what the parties meant by using evidence of a clearly established practice, which continued both before and after the contract was made (*Dunlop Tyres Ltd v Blows* [2001] IRLR 629, CA; see also Collective Agreements (6)). This latter principle should, however, be approached with caution: courts and tribunals will be reluctant to draw inferences from later conduct (*Choudhry v Triesman* [2003] EWHC 1203 (Ch)). The Tribunal may also consider whether a purported provision of a contract (or, indeed, the very basis of hiring an 'employee') is a 'sham' where neither party intended to create the legal rights and obligations which they set out (*Redrow Homes (Yorkshire) Ltd v Buckborough & Sewell* [2009] IRLR 34, EAT; *Protectacoat Firthglow Ltd v Szilagyi* [2009] EWCA Civ 98, [2009] ICR 835, [2009] IRLR 365; *Autoclenz*; see also Employee, Self-Employed or Worker? (15)).

8.13   Employer handbooks and policies

Employees will often be provided with a substantial volume of documentation on starting work. These documents may be presented under a variety of titles, such as employer policies and company handbooks. In practice, they are often more voluminous than the statement of written particulars or any document which is according to its own terms a contractual document. In many cases, it may be a matter of considerable practical importance to know whether or not these documents have contractual effect. This question may arise, for example, when the employer seeks to vary the provisions of a policy or of the company handbook. If the policy or handbook is contractual, it may not be unilaterally varied. The question may also arise when an employer is seeking to dismiss an employee. Where the handbook provides, for example, for a particular disciplinary procedure, and the employer proposes to dismiss in breach of that procedure, the employee may seek an injunction to restrain dismissal (see **8.42** below). Such an injunction can only be granted where the procedure relied upon has contractual effect. If the procedure does not have contractual force, there is no legal foundation for such an injunction.

There is no single test for determining whether documents such as disciplinary procedures have contractual effect: factors to consider include the certainty, level of detail and workability of the relevant provision, its importance to the working relationship and its context (*Hussain v Surrey and Sussex Healthcare NHS Trust* [2011] EWHC 1670 (QB)).

A code or policy is only to be regarded as having contractual effect when it may be regarded as conferring rights on employees. If it only lays down standards of good practice which an employer would be expected to follow, it does not have contractual effect (*Wandsworth London Borough Council v D'Silva* [1998] IRLR 193, CA). In *D'Silva* the employer sought unilaterally to alter the terms of a sickness policy. The employee alleged that this would be in breach of contract. The Court of Appeal held that since the policy was not intended to confer rights but was only a statement of good practice, the employer could alter the terms without securing the agreement of the employees.

In contrast, in *Attrill & Other v Dresdner Kleinwort Limited & Anor* [2013] EWCA Civ 394, [2013] 3 All ER 607, the Court of Appeal held that the employer's announcement of a bonus pool (specifically aimed at retaining employees) during a 'Town Hall' meeting broadcast online was an offer capable of acceptance and of incorporation into the employees' contracts.

In *Keeley v Fosroc International Ltd* [2006] EWCA Civ 1277, [2006] IRLR 961, the Court of Appeal held that even where a handbook was expressly incorporated, that did not mean that the entire content of the handbook had contractual effect. It was particularly relevant to consider the importance of the provision for the employee. If it was clearly worded as conferring an entitlement on the employee, it was likely to have contractual effect. It was not determinative that the passage in the handbook was described as a policy.

Even where the policy is contractual, its effect will depend on the construction of the contract as a whole. Thus, the House of Lords held in *Taylor v Secretary of State for Scotland* [2000] IRLR 502 that the inclusion in the contract of an equal opportunities policy which undertook that there should be no discrimination on the grounds of age did not prevent the employer from dismissing an employee on the grounds that he had reached the minimum retirement age (see RETIREMENT (42)). See also *Bateman v Asda Stores Ltd* [2010] IRLR 370, [2010] All ER (D) 277 (Feb) where the handbook empowered the employer 'to review, revise, amend or replace' the contents of the handbook, including contractual matters such as pay. See also the *Attrill* case (above).

8.14   Express or implied terms

The terms of the contract may be express or implied or incorporated.

Express terms are those that the parties specifically by reference agree upon. The express terms of the contract may be found in a document described as the contract of employment or in an offer letter or in oral exchanges between the parties or in other documents. The provisions set out in a statement of written particulars will be evidence of the express terms, albeit that the statement of written particulars is not the contract itself. The parties may agree upon certain points by reference to a document such as a collective agreement which thereby becomes incorporated into the agreement between the parties (see **6.2** COLLECTIVE AGREEMENTS). See however, *Malone v British Airways* [2010] EWCA Civ 1225, [2011] ICR 125, [2011] IRLR 32, where the Court of Appeal upheld findings that provisions concerning staffing levels, set out in staff agreements and manuals, were not apt to be enforced by individual employees.

The core of a contract of employment is a contract whereby an employee agrees to work for an employer in return for pay. In the event that a contract of employment exists, this is the irreducible minimum. However, as set out below there are many other aspects to a contract of employment.

In *R v Hull University Visitor, ex p Page* [1992] ICR 67 at 80D–80F, Staughton LJ was of the view that a job advertisement should be read together with a letter of appointment (the case later went to the House of Lords: [1993] ICR 114). Implied and incorporated terms are dealt with below.

8.15   Common implied terms

Frequently, many terms of the contract will not be specifically set out or stated. There may be many rights and obligations on either side which are left unexpressed and unspecified. The general rule is that a term will be implied into a contract if it is so obvious that both parties would have regarded it as a term even though they had not expressly stated it as a term or if it is *necessary* to imply the term in order to give the contract business efficacy (*Liverpool City Council v Irwin* [1977] AC 239; *Scally v Southern Health and Social Services Board* [1991] ICR 771 at 781). Terms also may be implied if they are customary in the particular trade or calling, or form the usual practice of the particular employer, if it is sufficiently well known. Such a custom or practice must be 'reasonable, certain and notorious' (*Bond v CAV Ltd* [1983] IRLR 360; *Henry v London General Transport Services Ltd* [2002] ICR 910, [2002] IRLR 472). In order to become an implied term, a custom must be followed with regularity such that it becomes legitimate to infer that the parties follow the practice because they regard it as a legal obligation rather than that the practice is followed as a matter of policy: *Solectron Scotland Ltd v Roper* [2004] IRLR 4. In *Garratt v Mirror Group Newspapers Ltd* [2011] EWCA Civ 425, the Court of Appeal upheld an implied term that enhanced redundancy payments were available only to employees who signed compromise agreements. The Court of Appeal has recently affirmed, and in some respects updated, these principles in *Park Cakes Ltd v Shuba* [2013] IRLR 800 and *CSC Computer Services Ltd v McAlinden* [2013] EWCA Civ 1435.

Terms commonly implied are the *employee's* duties of:

(a)   fidelity;

(b)   obedience;

(c)   working with due diligence and care;

(d)   not using or disclosing the employer's trade secrets or confidential information;

and the *employer's* duties:

(e)   to take care for the employee's health and safety;

(f)   to provide redress for grievances;

(g)   (in some cases) not merely to pay but to provide work;

and the duties of *both parties:*

(h)   not to destroy the relationship of trust and confidence (see below for more detail);

(i)   to give a reasonable period of notice of termination, when no specific notice period has been agreed.

The above list is not exhaustive: other duties can arise in various circumstances. Some of them are dealt with below.

8.15   Contract of Employment

Employee's duties

8.16   *Duty of fidelity—*

An employee has a duty to serve his employer faithfully and not to act against the interests of the employer's business. In general, unless the employee is subject to some form of fiduciary duty, this does not impose an obligation to inform the employer of the employee's past misconduct: *Basildon Academies v Amadi* UKEAT 0343/14.

It would be in breach of an implied term of the contract of employment for the employee to set up a rival business to that of his employer during the period of his employment, unless he had been expressly permitted to do so, or to take more than preparatory steps towards doing so: *Balston Ltd v Headline Filters Ltd* [1990] FSR 385. However, mere preparations to set up a competing business after the termination of the employment are not necessarily a breach of contract (*Ixora Trading Inc v Jones* [1990] FSR 251).

The line between legitimate and illegitimate steps towards competing is difficult to draw. It has been held that it is not decisive to consider whether the employee's acts are described as preparatory: *Helmet Integrated Systems Ltd v Tunnard* [2006] EWCA Civ 1735, [2007] IRLR 126. It is a question for decision in each case whether the employee's conduct in seeking to set up a new business is legitimate or illegitimate. In the *Tunnard* case it was held that an employee did not act in breach of contract when he designed a product intended to compete with his employer's. The court reached this view partly on the basis that the contract of employment did not sufficiently restrict his ability to prepare for future competition. That analysis does not sit happily with the existence of the implied duty of fidelity. The court also noted that he was a salesman and not a technical designer. In principle, an employee crosses the line and acts unlawfully when his acts are inconsistent with his duty of fidelity (see *Shepherds Investments Ltd v Walters* [2006] EWHC 836 (Ch), [2007] IRLR 110, a case concerned primarily with directors; see also *Cobbetts LLP v Hodge* [2009] EWHC 786 (Ch), a case concerned with a solicitor negotiating for himself an equity share in a client company without obtaining the informed consent of his employer) and *Samsung Semiconductor Europe Ltd v Docherty* [2011] CSOH 32 (where the Court of Session stated that an employee's liability did not depend on his consciously assuming fiduciary duties). Another example (albeit that this was a case about a director's fiduciary duty) is *Foster Bryant Surveying Ltd v Bryant* [2007] EWCA Civ 200, [2007] IRLR 425. It is also a breach of contract for an employee to tender for future business from a customer of the employer in competition with the employer (*Adamson v B & L Cleaning Services Ltd* [1995] IRLR 193). For the implied obligation not to use or disclose the employer's trade secrets or confidential information, see **41.13 RESTRAINT OF TRADE, CONFIDENTIALITY AND EMPLOYEE INTERVENTIONS**.

8.17   *Duty to Obey Reasonable Employer Instructions—*

The employee is also obliged by the implied terms of his contract of employment to obey the reasonable instructions of his employer and to carry out his work conscientiously and honestly. In *Sybron Corpn v Rochem Ltd* [1984] Ch 112, it was held that the terms and nature of a particular employment might be such that there was a contractual duty to disclose the misconduct of other employees (see also *Item Software (UK) Ltd v Fassihi* [2004] EWCA Civ 1244, [2005] ICR 450).

A work to rule or withdrawal of goodwill may amount to a breach of the implied obligation to serve the employer faithfully (*Secretary of State for Employment v Associated Society of Locomotive Engineers and Firemen (No 2)* [1972] 2 QB 455, [1972] ICR 19, CA; *British Telecommunications plc v Ticehurst* [1992] ICR 383).

The duties of obedience and fidelity are also owed to an employer to whom the employee is seconded (*Macmillan Inc v Bishopsgate Investment Trust plc* [1993] IRLR 393).

A distinction must be drawn between the duty to serve the employer in good faith, which is owed by all employees, and fiduciary duties, which are not an incident of every employment relationship. When a person is a fiduciary (such as a trustee or a company director), he is obliged to pursue another's interests at the expense of his own. In the case of an employee, his obligation is to comply with the express and implied terms of his contract (for a discussion of the distinction, see *Nottingham University v Fishel* [2000] IRLR 471). By way of further example of the difference, an employee is not under an implied obligation to reveal his own misconduct, but a fiduciary is under such an obligation (*Tesco Stores Ltd v Pook* [2004] IRLR 618); *Item Software (UK) Ltd v Fassihi* [2004] EWCA Civ 1244, [2005] ICR 450, *GHLM Trading Ltd v Maroo* [2012] EWHC 61 (Ch)). Senior employees may owe fiduciary obligations by reason of their seniority even if they are not directors: *Shepherds Investments Ltd v Walters* [2006] EWHC 836 (Ch), [2007] IRLR 110.

In *Cresswell v Inland Revenue Board* [1984] 2 All ER 713, [1984] ICR 508, it was held that an employee was expected to adapt to new methods and techniques in performing his duties, provided the employer arranged for him to receive the necessary training in the new skills and the nature of the work did not alter so radically that it was outside the contractual duties of the employee. If the employer has an express power to transfer the employee to other duties, he is not subject to an implied requirement to exercise that power reasonably, provided that he has some proper grounds for the exercise of the express power and he does not exercise it in such a way as to destroy trust and confidence between himself and the employee (*White v Reflecting Roadstuds Ltd* [1991] ICR 733). Similarly, an express right in the employer to require a particular number of hours per week to be worked must be construed as being subject to the employer's duty to safeguard the employee's health and safety (*Johnstone v Bloomsbury Health Authority* [1991] ICR 269).

8.18 *Duty to take due care in performance of duties—*

An employee owes a contractual duty of care to his employer, breach of which can support a claim for damages (*Janata Bank v Ahmed* [1981] ICR 791, [1981] IRLR 457 applying *Lister v Romford Ice and Cold Storage Co Ltd* [1957] AC 555).

Employer's duties

8.19 *Health and safety—*

It is an implied term of the contract of employment that the employer will take reasonable steps to ensure the employee's safety (see comments in *Dutton & Clark Ltd v Daly* [1985] IRLR 363, *Johnstone v Bloomsbury Health Authority* [1991] ICR 269 and HEALTH AND SAFETY AT WORK – I (27)). This includes providing a safe system of work. The duty to provide a safe system of work should not be limited to preventing physical injury. Employers also owe a duty to take reasonable care not to cause psychiatric harm to an employee by reason of the volume or character of work imposed on the employee. The standard of care depends on what is reasonable conduct for a person in the employer's position. What is reasonable depends on the nature of the relationship, the magnitude of the risk of injury that was reasonably foreseeable, the seriousness of the consequences for the employee if that injury should occur, and the cost and practicability of preventing the risk (*Walker v Northumberland County Council* [1995] IRLR 35).

In *Waltons & Morse v Dorrington* [1997] IRLR 488, it was held that a term was to be implied into every contract of employment that 'the employer will provide and monitor for employees, so far as is reasonably practicable, a working environment which is reasonably suitable for the performance by them of their contractual duties'. In that case, the employer acted in breach of the term by requiring a non-smoking secretary to work in a smoke-filled environment.

8.20   Contract of Employment

8.20   *Redress for grievances—*

In *W A Goold (Pearmak) Ltd v McConnell* [1995] IRLR 516, the EAT held that it was an implied term that the employer would 'reasonably and promptly afford a reasonable opportunity to their employees to obtain redress of any grievance they may have' (see also *Ministry of Defence v Guellard* [2009] All ER (D) 50 (Dec)). The basis for the implication of this term was the statutory obligation to include in the written statement of terms, a note specifying to whom and in what manner an employee might apply for the purpose of seeking redress of any grievance relating to employment (see **8.7** above).

8.21   *Duty to provide work—*

In some cases, it may be argued that the employer's only obligation is to pay and that there is no duty upon an employer to provide work. In other words, so long as the employee is fully remunerated, the employer can ask him to stay at home without being in breach of contract. A contract of employment may, however, be subject to an implied obligation to provide work where earnings vary according to the work done, where an individual such as an actor is dependent upon publicity, or where the employee has skills that may atrophy through lack of use: *Langston v Amalgamated Union of Engineering Workers* [1974] 1 All ER 980, [1974] ICR 180 and 510, CA; *Breach v Epsylon Industries Ltd* [1976] ICR 316; *Spencer v Marchington* [1988] IRLR 392; and cf *Warren v Mendy* [1989] ICR 525. See also *Christie v Carmichael* [2010] IRLR 1016, where the Scottish EAT found that the employer was entitled to place an employee on garden leave, notwithstanding the lack of an express contractual provision to that effect, partly on the basis that the employee's skills would not atrophy. The range of cases in which the court will imply an obligation to provide work has widened following the decision of the Court of Appeal in *William Hill Organisation Ltd v Tucker* [1999] ICR 291, [1998] IRLR 313. There it was held that the question of whether there was an obligation to provide work depended on the facts of each case. The question was whether the consideration moving from the employer extended to an obligation to permit the employee to do the work or whether it was confined to a duty to pay the agreed remuneration. See also *SG&R Valuation Service Co LLC v Boudrais* [2008] EWHC 1340 (QB), [2008] IRLR 770, where it was held that even where the employee's contract does confer on him a right to work, that right would be foregone if the employee demonstrated in a serious way that he was not ready or willing to work. This was approved in *Standard Life Health Care Ltd v Gorman* [2009] EWCA Civ 1292, [2010] IRLR 233.

8.22   *Suspension only on reasonable grounds—*

In *McClory v Post Office* [1992] ICR 758, the court was prepared to imply a term that the employer's express right to suspend the employee must only be exercised on reasonable grounds, although not to imply any term that the employer should when exercising that power observe the principles of natural justice. The case also contains a useful discussion of the circumstances in which an employee may have a contractual right to work overtime.

McClory was approved in *Watson v Durham University* [2008] EWCA Civ 1266, in the context of the employer making weak allegations of racism and then seeking to suspend the employee on that basis much later.

In *Marshall (Cambridge) Ltd v Hamblin* [1994] IRLR 260, the EAT held that an employee who has resigned has no right to work out his notice period (in the absence, of course, of any express term or custom and practice to the contrary). The employee's only right was to pay in lieu of notice, even though the majority of the employee's income was based on commission.

8.22a   *Employee's economic well-being—*

In *Scally v Southern Health and Social Services Board* [1991] ICR 771, the House of Lords held that the employer was under an implied duty to take reasonable steps to bring to the employee's attention a right which he had (in that case, to purchase extra years' service for superannuation purposes) that would be lost unless he took certain action, given that the employee could not reasonably have been expected to be aware of the relevant contractual term without it being drawn to his attention.

However, there is no implied term that the employer will take reasonable care of his employees' economic well-being: *Crossley v Faithful & Gould Holdings* [2004] EWCA Civ 293, [2004] IRLR 377.

8.22b *Continuation of employment and ill health payments—*

Where a contract of employment contains terms entitling the employee to benefits during a period of ill health and the continued receipt of such benefits is dependent on the individual remaining in the employer's employment, a term will be implied that the employer will not dismiss the employee while he remains incapacitated so as to deprive him of the continued receipt of those benefits (*Aspden v Webbs Poultry & Meat Group (Holdings) Ltd* [1996] IRLR 521). A similar approach was taken in Scotland in *Adin v Sedco Forex International Resources Ltd* [1997] IRLR 280 (and see *Brompton v AOC International Ltd* [1997] IRLR 639, para 38, CA).

The extent to which an employer may dismiss an employee who is in receipt of sick pay and/or who anticipates that, if his contract of employment continues in force, he will in due course be entitled to early retirement or to some other benefit was the issue in the Court of Session case of *Hill v General Accident Fire and Life Assurance Corpn plc* [1998] IRLR 641. The employee in that case was in receipt of sick pay. If he had remained employed and in receipt of sick pay for a further four months, he would have been entitled to an ill-health retirement pension or to sickness and accident benefit. The employer terminated his contract by reason of redundancy. Mr Hill sued alleging that the termination of his employment was in breach of the implied duty of trust and confidence and that, whilst he was absent sick and in receipt of sick pay or with an anticipation of early retirement or other benefits, his employment could be terminated only by reason of his own repudiatory breach of contract. The court held that a person in Mr Hill's position could not be dismissed by reason of his absence, or for a specious reason, or for no reason at all. The power to dismiss included, but was not limited to, the case where the employee acted in repudiatory breach of contract. Accordingly, a dismissal by reason of redundancy was not in breach of the implied term of trust and confidence. In *Villella v MFI Furniture Centres Ltd* [1999] IRLR 468, a case concerning Permanent Health Insurance, the High Court formulated an implied term that the employer would not terminate the contract of employment, save for cause other than ill health, in circumstances which would deprive the employee of his continuing entitlement to benefit.

It has also been held that where an employer provides a benefit such as PHI and the insurer fails to pay, there is an implied obligation on the employer to pursue the insurer for payment, including, if need be, by litigation: *Marlow v East Thames Housing Group Ltd* [2002] IRLR 798. The extent of the obligation would of course depend on the merits of the employee's argument.

The *Aspden* line of cases has been applied by analogy to the case where an employer proposes to dismiss for redundancy and employees have the benefit of a contractual redundancy package. In *Jenvey v Australian Broadcasting Corpn* [2002] EWHC 927 (QB), [2003] ICR 79 it was held that where the employer had proposed to dismiss for redundancy with the consequence that the employee would enjoy a contractual payment, it was an implied term that the employer would not then dismiss for any other reason (apart from cause) if to do so would defeat those contractual rights.

8.22c *Discretionary payments and benefits—*

Contracts of employment often contain provision for benefits that are dependent upon the exercise of discretion by the employer. By way of example, contracts providing an entitlement to bonus often confer a discretion on the employer in relation to the amount of the bonus. It is an implied term that such a discretion will be exercised in good faith, for a proper purpose and rationally: *Horkulak v Cantor Fitzgerald International* [2004] IRLR 942 (approving *Clark v Nomura International Plc* [2000] IRLR 766) and *Brogden Bank plc v Investec Bank plc* [2014] IRLR 924. In *Horkulak*, damages for breach of contract by not making a bonus payment were assessed on the basis of what the employer would have paid had it exercised the discretion genuinely and rationally. The court stood in the shoes of the employer and decided what sums would have been awarded once it was established that the sum awarded by the employer was in breach of contract. See also *Small v Boots Co Plc* [2009] IRLR 328.

However, the Court of Appeal has subsequently stressed the limited role of the Court in such claims. It is no part of the Court's function to decide what bonus should have been awarded. The Court is concerned only to ensure that the employer complies with its legal obligation to exercise its discretion in good faith and rationally: see *Humphreys v Norilsk Nickel International (UK) Ltd* [2010] IRLR 976. The employer has a wide discretion and the burden of establishing that a bonus paid was irrational is 'a very high one': *Keen v Commerzbank AG* [2007] ICR 623, sub nom *Commerzbank AG v Keen* [2007] IRLR 132. However, the Court of Appeal has also held that once an employee makes out grounds that a decision is irrational the burden shifts to the employer to demonstrate that it has reached a reasonable decision, this may require evidence from the actual decision-maker: *Hills v Niksun Inc* [2016] EWCA Civ 115.

In the recent case of *Braganza v BP Shipping Ltd and Ors* [2015] ICR 449, the Supreme Court held (by a 3:2 majority) that an employer's decision regarding eligibility for contractual death benefits was subject to review on public law *Wednesbury* principles, and that the employer's decision was unlawful for failing to take relevant matters into account. How widely, or narrowly, this novel, expansive approach will be applied in other cases regarding contractual payments and benefits will need to be worked out by the Courts.

8.22d *Trust and confidence—*

It is now well established that employment contracts contain an implied of mutual trust and confidence. This term is framed as follows: the parties to the contract will not, without reasonable and proper cause, conduct themselves in a manner calculated or likely to destroy or seriously damage the relationship of confidence and trust which should exist between employer and employee. This is a mutual duty, albeit that the overwhelming majority of the cases deal with breach of the term by the employer. This implied term has been approved by the House of Lords in the landmark decision of *Malik v BCCI SA (in liq)* [1998] AC 20, [1997] ICR 606. Although in *Malik* Lord Steyn said the term applied to conduct calculated **and** likely to have the requisite effects, the EAT has since confirmed that it is 'calculated **or** likely': *Baldwin v Brighton and Hove City Council* [2007] ICR 680, [2007] IRLR 232.

It has also been held that the test for determining whether the employer has acted in breach of this term is a severe one: the conduct of the employer must be such as to destroy or seriously damage the relationship (*Claridge v Daler Rowney Ltd* [2008] ICR 1267), and there must have been no reasonable and proper cause for the conduct (*Gogay v Hertfordshire County Council* [2000] IRLR 703, CA, paras 53–55; *Devon and Somerset Fire and Rescue Service v Tilke* (UKEAT/0303/09/RN) (25 January 2010, unreported)). This term is fundamental to the employment relationship and any breach of it is likely to be repudiatory: *Morrow v Safeway Stores plc* [2002] IRLR 9, EAT. However, it is important to bear in mind that both limbs of the term are important: conduct which destroys trust and confidence is not in breach of contract if there is a reasonable cause (*Hilton v Shiner Ltd Builders Merchants* [2001] IRLR 727*)*. The Court of Appeal has deprecated the use of loose language in some cases which may appear to extend the scope of the implied term (into, for example, an obligation of 'fair dealing'). The proper approach is to apply the language of the House of Lords in *Malik*: see *O'Brien v Transco plc (formerly BG plc)* [2002] EWCA Civ 379,

[2002] ICR 721. Recent guidance comes from *Tullett Prebon Plc v BGC Brokers LP* [2011] IRLR 420: the question is whether, looking at all the circumstances objectively, the party's intention was to refuse performance of the contract.

The implied term that the employer will not act in a manner calculated or likely to destroy or seriously to damage the relationship of trust and confidence is capable of being relevant in a very wide range of circumstances. Breaches of this implied term are often cited in constructive dismissal cases and a number of examples are given in that context (see **53.7 UNFAIR DISMISSAL – I**).

It has been held that an employer's failure to adhere to statutory obligations may give rise to a breach of the implied term. Thus in *Nottinghamshire County Council v Meikle* [2004] IRLR 703 it was held that an employer's continuing failure to make the reasonable adjustments which were required to be made in order to accommodate the employee's disability was a breach of contract. (See also *Greenhof v Barnsley Metropolitan Borough Council* [2006] IRLR 98.) This reasoning should not be pushed too far. It is wrong to suggest that every breach by an employer of his statutory obligations involves a breach of contract: *Doherty v British Midland Airways Ltd* [2006] IRLR 90.

In *Hill v General Accident Fire and Life Assurance Corpn plc* [1998] IRLR 641, 1999 SLT 1157, the Court of Session specifically rejected a submission that, as a result of *Malik*, a new approach had to be taken to the interpretation of contracts of employment and that they had to be construed in a way which furthered mutual trust. The English courts have shown similar restraint. In *University of Nottingham v Eyett* [1999] IRLR 87, it was held that there had been no breach of the implied term by an employer who failed to advise the employee that if he delayed his retirement by a short time, he would be paid a higher pension than that which he actually received.

In considering the scope of the implied term of trust and confidence, it is important to bear in mind that the obligation in question relates to the maintenance of the trust and confidence which should exist in an employment relationship. There is no implied obligation on the employer to act reasonably: see *Post Office v Roberts* [1980] IRLR 347. The Privy Council placed an important limit on the scope of the implied term. Where there is an untrammelled express power in a contract (for example, to dismiss without cause or to require an employee to move location) the implied term cannot operate to limit the scope of that power: *Reda v Flag Ltd* [2002] IRLR 747. Implied terms in contracts must give way to and may not contradict express terms.

There is a further important limitation on the efficacy of the implied term of trust and confidence. It is inoperative in connection with decisions to terminate employment: *Johnson v Unisys Ltd* [2001] ICR 480. This reasoning is informed by policy considerations. Since Parliament has enacted the right not to be unfairly dismissed, it would be an abuse of the judicial function to develop or apply an implied contractual term that in effect displaced, or usurped, the statutory provisions in regulating the manner of dismissal. It would be wrong, for example, for the common law to develop a right which overlapped with the right not to be unfairly dismissed but which was not subject to the same limitations, in respect of, for example, continuity of employment and time limits for the presentation of claims, which Parliament has decided should apply to unfair dismissal claims.

Thus, an employee cannot complain that his dismissal was in breach of the implied term of trust and confidence. It is, however, possible to formulate a claim for breach of the implied term of trust and confidence in respect of things done by the employer to the employee before dismissal. A line is drawn between unfairness in respect of the dismissal itself, which can only be the subject of a statutory claim of unfair dismissal and unfairness before the dismissal which gives rise to a separate cause of action in contract. Usually, it is the employer's decision to dismiss, rather than any earlier act, which gives rise to loss. However, there may be exceptional cases where this is not so. Examples might include cases of unjustified suspension (as in *Gogay v Hertfordshire County Council* [2000] IRLR 703) or cases where an employee suffers psychiatric illness as a result of pre-dismissal unfairness. Examples of the latter are *Eastwood v Magnox Electric plc* and [2004] IRLR 733. In both cases employees alleged that they had suffered psychiatric illness as a result of the ways in which the employers had conducted investigations and disciplinary proceedings. The claims were originally struck out as having no basis in law in the light of *Johnson* but the House of Lords held that the claims, being based on allegations about pre-dismissal conduct, did disclose a cause of action and could proceed to trial.

In some cases, where a breach of the duty is alleged the question may arise whether the employer is liable for the act said to constitute the breach. Thus, in *Moores v Bude Stratton Town Council* [2001] ICR 271, [2000] IRLR 676 an individual councillor verbally abused an employee. When the employee resigned and claimed constructive dismissal, the issue arose whether the council was liable for the acts of the individual back-bench councillor. A majority of the EAT (Lindsay J dissenting) held that the council was liable. For the parameters of an employer's liability, see Vicarious Liability (56). Even if the employer is not vicariously liable for the acts complained of, he may be directly liable for failing to supervise or prevent those acts: see *Waters v Metropolitan Police Comr* [2000] IRLR 720. In *Waters*, the House of Lords held that an employer might be liable to his employee in negligence if he knew of or foresaw acts being done by other employees which might cause physical or mental harm to the employee but did nothing to prevent or supervise such acts when it was in his power to do so. The argument in *Waters* was concerned with the tort of negligence. However, in that case there was no contract between the police officer and the commissioner. One can see how, in a case where there was a contract of employment, the implied term of trust and confidence would impose a similar duty in contract on the employer.

8.22e *Place of work—*

There must be a contractual term, express or implied, dealing with the place where the employee may be required to work. If there is no express term, that term will be implied which the parties would have agreed if they had directed their minds to the problem. All the circumstances of the case will be considered, including the nature of the business, the nature of the employee's duties and his status, what the employee was told when engaged and whether he has in fact been moved from time to time, and whether there is any provision for the payment of expenses for working away from home. The term implied may be that the employee can be required to work anywhere within reasonable daily travelling distance of his home (*O'Brien v Associated Fire Alarms Ltd* [1969] 1 All ER 93; *Jones v Associated Tunnelling Co Ltd* [1981] IRLR 477; *Courtaulds Northern Spinning Ltd v Sibson* [1988] ICR 451). See also *Little v Charterhouse Magna Assurance Co Ltd* [1980] IRLR 19 and *Rank Xerox Ltd v Churchill* [1988] IRLR 280. However, such a 'mobility clause' (whether express or implied) may be coupled with implied obligations to give reasonable notice of any move (see *United Bank Ltd v Akhtar* [1989] IRLR 507; *Prestwick Circuits Ltd v McAndrew* [1990] IRLR 191; and cf *White*, above). Although there must be a term which identifies where the employee is to work, it is not necessary in every case to imply a mobility clause. Whether or not it is necessary to imply such a clause will depend on the nature of the work and the other facts of the case (*Aparau v Iceland Frozen Foods plc* [1996] IRLR 119). It appears that an employer may only effectively rely upon a mobility clause if he makes it clear that he is doing so (*Curling v Securicor Ltd* [1992] IRLR 549).

In *Bass Leisure Ltd v Thomas* [1994] IRLR 104, the EAT held that the place where an employee works is a question of fact to be determined by considering where the employee in fact works rather than where she can be required to work (see **38.7** Redundancy – I). This approach was approved by the Court of Appeal in *High Tables Ltd v Horst* [1997] IRLR 513. (Compare *Gale v Northern General Hospital NHS Trust* [1994] IRLR 292, which was concerned specifically with the construction of the *National Health Service and Community Care Act 1990, s 6(1)*.)

8.22f *Termination of the contract—*

In the absence of any express term governing the notice required to be given to terminate the contract, it is an implied term that reasonable notice of termination will be given. Reasonable notice will not be implied if to do so would contradict an express term, eg a term giving a party the right to terminate at any time without cause. The implication of the term is necessary in order to provide a means by which a contract of otherwise indefinite duration may be terminated. If the express terms make provision, there is no need to imply a term: *Reda v Flag Ltd* [2002] UKPC 38, [2002] IRLR 747. What is reasonable will depend on all the facts of the case (see **48.6 TERMINATION OF EMPLOYMENT**). Where there is no contractual provision governing when a notice of termination served by an employer takes effect, the notice only takes effect when the employee has personally taken delivery of the letter containing the notice (*Newcastle upon Tyne NHS Foundation Trust v Haywood* [2017] EWCA Civ 153).

8.22g Incorporated terms

These are terms which are incorporated into the contract rather than being agreed individually between the parties. The principal source of incorporated terms is collective agreements (see COLLECTIVE AGREEMENTS (6)). The *Equality Act 2010* incorporates into every contract of employment an 'equality clause'.

8.23 Unenforceable terms

Certain terms, while not being unlawful in the sense of rendering an employer liable to criminal prosecution or a civil action, may be unenforceable, as set out in **8.24–8.30** below.

8.24 *Terms which are unlawful or contrary to public policy*

A contract the terms of which are unlawful (eg to do an unlawful act) or which are contrary to public policy (eg a contract for an immoral purpose) is unenforceable. The same may be true where the contract, although capable of being performed lawfully, has in fact been performed illegally. Further, relief will not be granted to a party if to do so would 'affront the public conscience'. The general law as to illegality was summarised by the Court of Appeal in *Euro-Diam Ltd v Bathurst* [1990] 1 QB 1, [1988] 2 All ER 23. In *Colen v Cebrian (UK) Ltd* [2003] EWCA Civ 1676, [2004] ICR 568, the Court of Appeal gave the following guidance. In order for a contract to become unenforceable by reason of illegality, it must be shown either that the contract was entered into with the object of committing an illegal act or that it was performed with that objective. If the contract was lawful when entered into and was intended to be performed lawfully, an illegal act in the course of performance does not in every case make the entire contract unenforceable. It is necessary to consider the intentions of the parties to the contract. The court will not assist a party who has to rely on his own illegal act for the purposes of his claim. If he does not have to pray in aid the unlawful act, it is a question of fact in each case whether the method of performance of the contract or the degree of participation in the illegal act means that the contact is unenforceable by reason of illegality. The burden of establishing that the contract is illegal rests on the person making that allegation.

In *Payne v Enfield Technical Services Ltd* [2008] EWCA Civ 393, [2008] ICR 1423 and at [2008] IRLR 500, the Court of Appeal upheld the EAT's ruling that to defeat an unfair dismissal claim on the grounds that a contract of employment is illegal and unenforceable 'there must be some form of misrepresentation, some attempt to conceal the true facts of the relationship, before the contract is rendered illegal for the purposes of a doctrine rooted in public policy'.

In the employment context, illegality may arise in the context of defrauding the revenue. In that context (although the observation is of general application), the Court of Appeal has held that a party will only be prevented from relying on a contract by reason of illegality where the parties have knowingly entered arrangements which have to their knowledge represented the facts of the employment relationship as other than that they really were (cf *Enfield Technical Services* above, para 25). Thus, for example, it is not sufficient to prevent a person relying on a contract of employment that he has previously indicated to the Revenue that he was self-employed unless there was also some attempt to conceal the true facts – ie to claim to be self-employed when the parties know that the person is an employee. On similar facts, see also *Connolly v Whitestone Solicitors* (UKEAT/0445/10/ZT) (24 June 2011, unreported).

In another context, a foreign employee knowingly working illegally without a work permit will not be able to complain of unfair dismissal (*Sharma v Hindu Temple*, IDS Brief 464, p 5; for work permits, see **26.4, FOREIGN EMPLOYEES**). Similarly, the contract of employment of an employee taking employment in breach of the terms on which he has been permitted entry to the UK is likely to be unlawful (*Vakante v Governing Body of Addey and Stanhope School* [2005] ICR 231, CA and *Zarkasi v Anindita* (UKEAT/0400/11/JOJ) (18 January 2012, unreported)), but working for less money than is stated on the employee's work permit application is not necessarily unlawful (*San Ling Chinese Medicine Centre v Lian Wei Ji* (UKEAT/0370/09) (25 January 2010, unreported).

If the unlawful element of the contract can be severed, a court may in certain circumstances allow the employee to pursue a claim based on the lawful elements of the contract (*Blue Chip Trading Ltd v Helbawi* [2009] IRLR 128). Further, if the employee was not aware of the fact that the contract was being performed unlawfully by the employer (by, for example, not deducting tax from remuneration) the employee may rely on the contract for the purposes of claiming employment protection rights (*Newland v Simons and Willer (Hairdressers) Ltd* [1981] ICR 521). However, ignorance of the law as opposed to the facts is no excuse (*Miller v Karlinski* (1945) 62 TLR 85). Nor is the fact that the parties did not intend to break the law relevant (*Salvesen v Simon* [1994] ICR 409). The mere fact that in the course of performing an otherwise lawful contract, the employee has committed an unlawful or immoral act does not bar him from bringing a claim for unfair dismissal (*Coral Leisure Group Ltd v Barnett* [1981] ICR 503; *Hewcastle Catering Ltd v Ahmed and Elkamah* [1992] ICR 626, [1991] IRLR 473, CA). Thus, the fact that an employee did not pay tax on occasional payments received outside his contract of employment did not have the effect of rendering the contract of employment illegal in *Annandale Engineering v Samson* [1994] IRLR 59. Further, the claim may be brought if the employer's conduct in participating in an illegal contract is so reprehensible in comparison with that of the employee that it would be wrong to allow the employer to rely on the illegality (cf *Euro-Diam*, above).

The distinction between unlawful tax evasion and lawful tax avoidance must be borne in mind. The fact that an employee lawfully arranges matters so as to minimise liability to tax does not render the contract of employment illegal (*Lightfoot v D & J Sporting Ltd* [1996] IRLR 64).

The fact that a contract is unenforceable by reason of illegality does not preclude a person employed under such a contract from bringing claims of sex or race (or presumably disability or religion or age or belief or sexual orientation) discrimination. The reason for this is that such actions do not seek to enforce the unenforceable contract (*Leighton v (1) Michael and (2) Charalambous* [1996] IRLR 67) unless the claim arises out of or is inextricably bound up with the conduct which causes the contract to be illegal (see *Hougna v Allen* [2014] UKSC 47).

8.25 *Terms automatically varied by statute*

Terms which, although they are agreed between the parties, are in breach of certain statutory provisions take effect as if varied to comply with those provisions. For example:

(a)   terms which are less advantageous than those which apply to a member of the opposite sex doing the same or like work, or work of equal value (see **22.8 EQUAL PAY**), or which infringe the law on sex discrimination; or

(b)   terms providing for the employment of directors for a guaranteed period of more than two years (see **9.3 DIRECTORS**).

8.26 *Restrictions upon contracting out of certain statutory provisions*

With some exceptions, for instance where a conciliation officer (see **2.3 ADVISORY, CONCILIATION AND ARBITRATION SERVICE**) has exercised his statutory powers in the settlement of certain claims or where there has been a valid compromise agreement (see **18.27 EMPLOYMENT TRIBUNALS**), an employer or employee may not contract out of the following Acts. Any attempt to do so will be ineffective.

Equality Act 2010 (see *s 144*)

Equal Pay Act 1970

ERA 1996, Part II (see *s 203(1), (2)*)

Trade Union and Labour Relations (Consolidation) Act 1992 (see *s 288*)

Working Time Regulations 1998 (save insofar as the *Regulations* permit the parties to agree that the operation of the *Regulations* is to be excluded or limited)

8.27 *Discriminatory terms*

Terms in contracts which are contrary to the provisions of the discrimination legislation are void and unenforceable against the person discriminated against: see *Equality Act 2010, s 143*. Similarly, any term in a collective agreement which discriminates on grounds of sex, sexual orientation or religion or belief is void and unenforceable against the party discriminated against: see *Equality Act 2010, s 145*.

8.28 *Terms in restraint of trade*

Sometimes, a contract will contain a term restricting the employee's freedom to work after he leaves his employment. Such terms will be regarded as 'in restraint of trade' and therefore unenforceable if their main purpose is simply to restrain competition. However, if the main purpose is to protect something in which the employer has a legitimate interest, such as trade secrets or confidential information, or to protect the employer's goodwill or '*customer connection*' (as it is called in this context), then such a term may be enforceable. These questions are discussed in more detail in **RESTRAINT OF TRADE, CONFIDENTIALITY AND EMPLOYEE INTERVENTIONS (41)**.

8.29 *Restrictions on industrial action*

Provisions in collective agreements which purport to restrict the right to take industrial action cannot form part of the individual contract of employment unless certain conditions are satisfied (see **6.5 COLLECTIVE AGREEMENTS**).

8.30 *Unfair Contract Terms Act 1977*

The effect of the *Unfair Contract Terms Act 1977* ('*UCTA 1977*') is to render certain types of contractual term unenforceable, and others unenforceable unless they satisfy a test of reasonableness laid down in *UCTA 1977, s 11* (namely, that the term was a fair and reasonable one to be included having regard to the circumstances which were, or ought reasonably to have been, known to or in the contemplation of the parties when the contract was made; in applying this test the court is directed to have regard to certain specific considerations).

Despite earlier indications to the contrary, it has now been held that *UCTA* does not apply to contracts of employment. The reason for this is that *UCTA* applies only to those who either 'deal as a consumer' or deal 'on the other [party's] written standard terms of business'. In *Keen v Commerzbank AG* [2006] EWCA Civ 1536, [2007] ICR 623, *sub nom Commerzbank AG v Keen* [2007] IRLR 132, the Court of Appeal held that an employee neither dealt as a consumer nor on his employer's standard terms of business. Employers do not deal with their employees as consumers; the business of an employer is not employing its staff.

In the light of this judgment, no further consideration is given to *UCTA* in this work.

8.31   CHANGES TO CONTRACTUAL TERMS

The general principle is that no change in the terms of an employee's contract may be made without his consent. Consent can come either from an employee's (express or implied) agreement to the proposed change, or from a pre-existing contractual provision allowing the employer unilaterally to effect variations. Where neither of these forms of consent is in place, a change in terms is likely to amount to a breach of contract.

If the proposed change is of great importance to the employer, the only course of action open to him in circumstances in which the employee does not consent, is to give notice to terminate the original contract and offer new terms. Great care must be taken to adhere to a fair procedure when doing this so as to avoid a successful claim for unfair dismissal (see Unfair Dismissal – II **(54)**).

A particular question which has caused difficulty is whether a change in terms and conditions mutually agreed between the parties can be enforced in the context of the transfer of an undertaking under the *Transfer of Undertakings (Protection of Employment) Regulations 1981 (SI 1981/1794)* ('*TUPE 1981*'), which have now been replaced by the *Transfer of Undertakings (Protection of Employment) Regulations 2006 (SI 2006/246)* ('*TUPE 2006*'). This subject is considered fully in Transfer of Undertakings **(52)**.

8.32   Agreement

Consent may be express, by the employee agreeing to the change orally or, preferably, in writing (see *Judge v Crown Leisure Ltd* [2005] EWCA Civ 571, [2005] IRLR 823 on the importance, in discussions about contractual variation, of an intention to create legal relations). On the question of consideration for agreed variations, see *Lee v GEC Plessey Telecommunications* [1993] IRLR 383, where the High Court held that there was good consideration for any pay rise which followed pay negotiations, so that the employer was legally bound by the increased rate of pay; but cf. *Reuse Collections Ltd v Sendall* [2015] IRLR 226 where the Court held that a 'general' pay rise did not provide consideration for insertion of a restraint of trade provision on the ground that there was an insufficient link between both matters.

Alternatively, consent may be *implied*, by the employee continuing to work for the employer without protest for a significant period of time whilst being aware of a change imposed by his employer. Where a change is imposed by the employer and the employee continues to work without objection, it may be that the employee will be held impliedly to have consented to the change. Where the change is one which has an immediate effect on the employee, continuing to work without protest may very well indicate consent. However, where the change is one which does not have an immediate practical effect, the court should exercise caution before inferring consent (*Jones v Associated Tunnelling Co Ltd* [1981] IRLR 477, *Aparau v Iceland Frozen Foods plc* [1996] IRLR 119, *Solectron Scotland Ltd v Roper* [2004] IRLR 4, *Cumbria County Council v Dow (No 2)* [2008] IRLR 109, EAT). In addition, the actual change in the employee's working conditions must be more than "trivial" under those changed conditions is to be regarded as implied consent: see the Court of Appeal decision in *Khatri v Co-operative Centrale Raiffeisen-Boerenleenbank BA* [2010] IRLR 715 applying *Solectron Scotland* (above).

A further example of a variation is *Attrill & Other v Dresdner Kleinwort Limited & Anor* [2012] EWCA Civ 394, where the variation was effected by the employees' implicit acceptance of an offer (concerning the bonus pool to be made available to employees) made during a 'Town Hall' meeting broadcast over the internet. This was an offer to vary the terms of the employees' contract and, in the circumstances, the employer had waived any requirement for the employees to communicate acceptance (although, if this requirement had not been waived, such communication of acceptance could not be inferred from the employees' remaining in employment). There was consideration for this variation. *Attrill* should also be noted for its discussion of implied acceptance of variations.

Where an employee protests but then continues to work for a considerable time, he may bear an evidential burden of showing that he did not impliedly agree to the new term (see *Henry v London General Transport Services Ltd* [2002] ICR 910, [2002] IRLR 472, where the employee continued to work for two years).

8.33   Variation clauses

In some contracts, the employer will expressly reserve a power to vary the terms. Such variation clauses are sometimes drafted in wide terms, purporting for example to allow the employer to make such changes as it sees fit from time to time. The answer to the question of whether or not such clauses are effective is a "qualified yes" (*Malone v British Airways* [2010] EWCA Civ 1225, [2011] ICR 125, [2011] IRLR 32; *Wandsworth London Borough Council v D'Silva* [1998] IRLR 193). These qualifications include the following. Courts take a strict approach to the interpretation of such clauses, and will construe them *contra proferentem*. Clear words are required to create a power unilaterally to alter the terms of the contract: *Norman and anor v National Audit Office* [2015] IRLR 634. Variation clauses specifying the terms that the employer is empowered to vary (as opposed to arrogating a general power to vary any term) are more likely to find favour with courts, although even more focussed variation provisions may be struck down: see *Hart v St Mary's School (Colchester) Ltd* UKEAT 0305/14 (where the Court held that a clause permitting variations to a teacher's working hours based on the requirements of the school timetable should not be accepted). The court is unlikely to favour an interpretation that does more than vary the contractual provisions with which the employer is required to comply. A court is unlikely to allow an interpretation which goes further and which may affect the rights of the employee under the contract: see, e.g. *Sparks v Department for Transport* [2016] ICR 695. Thus, the extent to which an employer will be permitted to rely on an express provision entitling him to vary the terms of a contract, and so to evade the general rule that changes to contracts must be mutually agreed, is likely to be limited.

8.34   Variation, breach and termination

Any change in terms to which the employee does not consent is *prima facie* a breach of contract. If the change is a significant one, the employee may be entitled to resign and allege that he has been constructively dismissed (see **48.19 TERMINATION OF EMPLOYMENT**). However, where an employer unilaterally imposes radically different terms of employment, it may be that the correct interpretation is that the employer has terminated the original contract and replaced it with another. Accordingly, there would be a dismissal by the employer (and immediate re-employment) which entitled the employee to bring unfair dismissal proceedings (*Hogg v Dover College* [1990] ICR 39; *Alcan Extrusions v Yates* [1996] IRLR 327; and see UNFAIR DISMISSAL– I (53)). For guidance on the question of whether the situation is one of dismissal and reengagement or mere variation of terms, see *Cumbria County Council v Dow (No 2)* [2008] IRLR 109, EAT and *Potter v North Cumbria Acute Hospitals NHS Trust* [2009] IRLR 900: where the parties have not (expressly or impliedly) agreed to terminate the old contract, their intention is to be ascertained from all the circumstances, including the "elasticity" of the original contract and the cumulative effect of any minor variations.

8.35   EMPLOYEE'S REMEDIES FOR BREACH OF CONTRACT OF EMPLOYMENT

If an employer is in breach of contract, his employee may bring proceedings in the High Court or the county court for sums due under the contract and for damages. The employee can bring such an action while remaining in employment. However, if the employer's breach of contract is sufficiently serious, the employee may treat himself as dismissed, leave, and bring proceedings for his prospective loss (see WRONGFUL DISMISSAL (58)) as well as for any sums outstanding at the date of dismissal; though note that at common law an employee cannot accept a repudiation by resigning with notice: *Reuse Collections Limited v Sendall* [2015] IRLR 226. The courts are also able to grant declaratory relief. If the breach of contract involves a deduction from pay, the employee may present a complaint to the employment tribunal under *Part II* of the *ERA 1996* (which contains provisions formerly found in the *Wages Act 1986*) (see 34.6 PAY – I). Employment tribunals now also have jurisdiction in relation to certain claims for contractual damages arising on the termination of an employee's employment (see below).

8.36   Damages

Extent of damages which can be claimed

Where an employee is dismissed summarily in breach of contract, the *prima facie* measure of damages is the sum which the employer would have had to pay in order to bring the contract to an end lawfully – that is to say, the sum payable in respect of the notice period. However, it will often be a term of the contract that the employer must follow a prescribed disciplinary or other procedure prior to dismissal. In such cases, if the employee can show that the conduct of the disciplinary procedure would take time and, therefore, extend the period of employment, he may be able to claim as damages lost wages for the time which the disciplinary or other procedure would have taken, in addition to pay for the notice period (see *Boyo v Lambeth London Borough Council* [1994] ICR 727, [1995] IRLR 50, CA and *Focsa Services (UK) Ltd v Birkett* [1996] IRLR 325). However, in assessing compensation, the tribunal must work on the basis that the outcome of the pursuit of the disciplinary or other procedure would have been the same (*Janciuk v Winerite* [1998] IRLR 63). This means that an employee cannot be compensated in a breach of contract claim on the basis that, had a contractual disciplinary procedure been pursued, he would not have been dismissed. The limit of compensation is the time which would have been taken to complete the procedure.

Damages payable will include damages for loss of pension rights that would have accrued had the employee not been dismissed summarily in breach of contract: *Silvey v Pendragon plc* [2001] IRLR 685.

On the question of whether payment in lieu of notice should include bonus payments, see *Locke v Candy and Candy Ltd* [2010] EWCA Civ 1350, where the Court of Appeal held by a majority (based on the particular contractual terms in issue) that an employee who was summarily dismissed shortly before the payment date of a discretionary bonus was not entitled to the bonus as part of his payment in lieu of notice, because the bonus clause stated that employees had to be employed in order to receive the bonus. However, where there is no express term making the payment of a bonus conditional upon being employed at that time, one cannot simply be implied: *Rutherford v Seymour Pierce Ltd* [2010] EWHC 375 (QB), [2010] IRLR 606. The court found that such a term was not necessary for the contract to operate satisfactorily, was manifestly unreasonable, and was not customary in that area of business.

Of course, an employee need not actually have commenced duties in order to be able to bring a claim. So, for example, where an offer of employment is made and accepted, there is a valid contract of employment even if the start date is postponed. If the contract is terminated before the actual start date, the employee will have a claim for wrongful dismissal. He may also have other claims such as discrimination (see *Sarker v South Tees Acute Hospitals NHS Trust* [1997] IRLR 328 and **21.5** ENGAGEMENT OF EMPLOYEES).

8.37 *No damages for loss of the chance to claim unfair dismissal*

Sometimes, employers dismiss employees summarily in order to prevent the employee from accruing a sufficient period of qualifying employment to bring a claim for unfair dismissal. Thus, for example, a person with a month's notice period might be summarily dismissed two weeks before accruing one year's continuous employment. However, it has been held that a claim for damages for breach of contract cannot include damages for the loss of a chance to bring an unfair dismissal claim: *Harper v Virgin Net Ltd* [2004] EWCA Civ 271, [2004] IRLR 390, CA.

8.38 *Damages for loss of reputation*

In *Malik v BCCI SA* [1997] IRLR 462, the House of Lords accepted that it might be possible to recover damages for loss of reputation caused by a breach of contract, provided that a relevant breach of contract could be established and that requirements of causation, remoteness and mitigation are satisfied. It was not necessary that the conduct relied upon be directed at the employees. In that case, the individual employees alleged that their employer had run a corrupt and dishonest business and that, as a result, the employees were tainted by their involvement with their former employer and were at a disadvantage in the job market. These facts were assumed to be true for the purposes of the argument, although no findings were made in respect of them. The House of Lords held that it would be a breach of the implied term of trust and confidence to operate a dishonest business and that the employees were entitled to argue that they could recover damages for any consequent loss as a result of damage inflicted on their employment prospects. The correct measure of damages where the breach affects employment prospects is to ask: but for the breach by the employer, what would prospective employers considering the claimant's application have done and what would have been the outcome for the employee? (*BCCI SA v Ali (No 3)* [2002] EWCA Civ 82, [2002] IRLR 460).

8.39 *Pecuniary loss only*

The *Malik* case does not alter the principle that damages are not recoverable for the manner of a dismissal, according to the House of Lords in *Johnson v Unisys Ltd* [2003] 1 AC 518. By a majority of four to one, their Lordships held that there was no right at common law to recover damages for injury to feeling (even in the case where that injury manifested itself as a psychological injury) caused by dismissal. Their Lordships held that it would be wrong to develop by judicial invention a right to compensation in circumstances where Parliament had already intervened by creating the right not to be unfairly dismissed. The courts therefore ought not to allow persons to side-step the limits on that right which Parliament had put in place by the creation of an inconsistent common law right. Lord Hoffmann expressed the view (obiter) that damages for unfair dismissal should extend beyond pecuniary loss to include 'in an appropriate case . . . compensation for distress, humiliation, damage to reputation in the community or to family life'. However, the House of Lords subsequently declined to follow Lord Hoffmann's *obiter* comment and has re-affirmed that damages for unfair dismissal are limited to financial losses: *Dunnachie v Kingston upon Hull City Council* [2004] UKHL 36, [2004] IRLR 727.

A number of cases in which employees alleged that they had suffered psychiatric injury as a consequence of the investigative or disciplinary process followed by their employer, rather than their dismissal, were struck out at first instance on the ground that they were barred by *Johnson*. However, the House of Lords subsequently held that the effect of *Johnson* is only to preclude common law claims where the employee seeks to recover damages consequent on dismissal: *Eastwood v Magnox Electric plc* and *McCabe v Cornwall County Council* [2004] IRLR 733. Where it is possible to claim that loss or injury has flowed not from dismissal but from pre-dismissal steps (such as suspension or the anterior conduct of disciplinary procedures), then *Johnson* does not prevent claims being brought: see for example *Gogay v Hertfordshire County Council* [2000] IRLR 703, CA (compensation awarded for psychological injury as a consequence of the manner in which an allegation of misconduct was investigated). The Supreme Court has confirmed the position: in the conjoined appeals of *Edwards v Chesterfield Royal Hospital NHS Foundation Trust* and *Botham v Ministry of Defence* [2011] UKSC 58, [2012] 2 WLR 55, [2012] 2 All ER 278, [2012] ICR 201, [2012] IRLR 129, it was held (by a majority of 5-2) that the effect of *Johnson* was to preclude damages for loss attributable to the unfair manner of a dismissal in breach of the terms of the employment contract. Where provisions of the employer's disciplinary code are incorporated into the contract, they are nonetheless not ordinary contractual terms, with breaches falling to be dealt with under the *ERA 1996* rather than as free-standing claims for breach of contract.

8.40   *'Stigma' damages*

The employee is under a duty to mitigate his pecuniary loss, for example (where he has been dismissed) by seeking alternative employment. In *Chagger v Abbey National plc* [2010] ICR 397, [2010] IRLR 47, the claimant (who had been employed as a risk analyst) contended that he had been stigmatised by prospective employers, who were unwilling to employ him because he had brought successful claims against his former employer for unfair dismissal, discrimination and breach of contract. He therefore retrained to work as a teacher on a substantially lower salary. His former employer argued that the claimant's damages should not include the ongoing financial consequences of stigmatisation by third parties, since that was too remote from the former employer's unlawful act. The Court of Appeal found for the claimant on this point: an employee has to be compensated for the full loss flowing from the unlawful act of his former employer, and the involvement of third party prospective employers did not sever the causal chain. Damages may now therefore in principle extend to such 'stigma' effects. To date however, there are no reported cases of stigma damages being awarded: even in *Chagger* (upon remission to the Tribunal following the Court of Appeal decision referred to above) no such award was made.

8.41   *Express terms regarding damages*

In some contracts, most usually those of senior executives, there is a term which provides for prescribed sums to be payable by the employer on breach. A question may arise whether such terms are liquidated damages clauses, which are valid; or penalties, which are unenforceable. A clause is a liquidated damages clause where it represents a genuine pre-estimate of a party's loss in the event of breach. Where the amount to be paid appears designed to deter or punish the wrong-doer rather than to compensate the innocent party, the clause is a penalty. In *Murray v Leisureplay plc* [2005] IRLR 946 a clause entitling an executive to three years' pay on termination without the obligation to mitigate was held not to be a penalty. The Court held that a useful test was whether the sum to be paid was extravagant and unconscionable. See also *Tullett Prebon Group Ltd v El-Hajjali* [2008] IRLR 760 for an example of a liquidated damages clause, and *CMC Group Plc v Zhang* [2006] EWCA Civ 408 for an example of a penalty clause. In *Imam-Sadeque v Bluebay Asset Management* [2013] IRLR 344, the High Court held that a condition in a compromise agreement making entitlement to a significant (£1.7m) benefit conditional on compliance with a non-solicitation obligation was not a penalty.

8.42   Injunctions

Circumstances in which injunctions may be granted

In certain circumstances, the courts will grant an employee an injunction to restrain the employer from taking action in breach of contract. This may be done to restrain the implementation of a dismissal where a contractual disciplinary or disputes procedure has not been exhausted (see, eg, *Irani v Southampton and South-West Hampshire Health Authority* [1985] ICR 590 and observations in *R v BBC, ex p Lavelle* [1983] ICR 99). In

Barros D'Sa v University Hospital and Warwickshire NHS Trust [2001] IRLR 691, there was a two-stage disciplinary procedure. The first stage involved an investigation by an inquiry panel. The second stage involved a disciplinary hearing at which decisions would be taken as to the appropriate course of action depending upon the circumstances and the inquiry panel's recommendations. At the second stage, the employer sought to introduce new material and new allegations against the employee which had not been considered at the inquiry panel stage. The Court of Appeal granted an injunction to prevent the new material and allegation being considered. An employer was not entitled to depart from a contractual disciplinary procedure on the ground that he considered that the relationship of trust and confidence had broken down.

In *Mezey v South West London and St George's Mental Health NHS Trust* [2007] IRLR 237, 244, the Court of Appeal upheld the grant of an injunction to restrain a suspension on full pay on the basis that the decision to suspend, even if permitted by the express terms of the contract, could involve a breach of the implied term of trust and confidence. A further development in that case saw the Court of Appeal uphold the grant of a further injunction against the employer taking capability proceedings against an employee who had already been cleared by an investigatory panel ([2010] EWCA Civ 293).

An injunction has also been granted to restrain the enforcement of an instruction the employer was not contractually entitled to give (see *Hughes v Southwark London Borough Council* [1988] IRLR 55) and to prevent a dismissal which would be in breach of a contractual redundancy selection procedure (*Anderson v Pringle of Scotland Ltd* [1998] IRLR 64, 1998 SLT 754, OH). However, an injunction will only be granted in the exceptional case where the employer still has full confidence in the employee's continuing ability and other necessary attributes (*Powell v Brent London Borough Council* [1988] ICR 176; *Alexander v Standard Telephones & Cables plc* [1990] ICR 291). In *Robb v Hammersmith and Fulham London Borough Council* [1991] ICR 514, it was suggested that this might not be necessary where the employee will merely be remaining at home under suspension pending a disciplinary hearing. The better view is that no injunction should be granted unless trust and confidence remain between the employer and the employee. To grant an injunction in circumstances where trust and confidence did not remain would be inconsistent with the general rule that there cannot be specific performance of a contract of service. However, within modern contracts of employment, there are often a number of provisions which may be enforced by an injunction without compelling the parties to a contract of employment to perform their obligations to employ and/or to work. Where the parties are in agreement that the contract of employment subsists, albeit in a qualified form (such as where the employee is suspended), then the court may enforce by order parts of the contract which do not compel the parties to co-operate any more than they would be prepared to do in any event. Thus if, for example, the parties agree that the contract subsists albeit that the employee is suspended, then the court may enforce contractual provisions relating to, for example, discipline. Enforcement of such provisions in those circumstances does not require a reluctant employer to employ or a reluctant employee to work (see *Peace v City of Edinburgh Council* [1999] IRLR 417).

The injunction may, if necessary, be made conditional upon the employee undertaking to work in accordance with instructions (*Wadcock v London Borough of Brent* [1990] IRLR 223). Similarly, if new working practices are introduced in breach of contract, an injunction will not be granted where, for practical purposes, the old system cannot be restored (*MacPherson v Lambeth London Borough Council* [1988] IRLR 470). See also *Dietman v Brent London Borough Council* [1988] ICR 842, *Ali v Southwark London Borough Council* [1988] ICR 567, [1988] IRLR 100 and *Wishart v National Association of Citizens Advice Bureaux Ltd* [1990] ICR 794.

8.43 *Interlocutory injunctions*

The court will usually first be asked to grant an *interlocutory* injunction, ie one which seeks to restrain the alleged breach of contract pending trial (which may not happen for several months or even longer). At the interlocutory stage, the judge does not hear oral evidence and will not have time to determine complex questions that may arise. The correct approach is therefore to decide, first, whether there is a serious question to be tried and, second, whether any injustice caused by granting or refusing to grant the injunction could be properly compensated by an award of damages later. A 'serious question to be tried' means that there is an arguable case that the claimant is entitled to the relief sought. There must be evidence which supports each of the constituent parts of the claimant's claim. The judge will not determine whether the claimant's evidence is true. He will, however, have to see that there is at that stage a sufficient basis in fact and law to mean that the claim has some merit. If there is a serious question and damages would not be an adequate remedy, the court may grant an injunction, and the decision whether to do so will depend upon the 'balance of convenience'. This will often lead it to preserve the *status quo* (see *American Cyanamid Co v Ethicon Ltd* [1975] AC 396). For an example of an interlocutory injunction against dismissal, see *Lauffer v Barking, Havering and Redbridge University Hospitals NHS Trust* [2009] EWHC 2360 (QB), [2010] Med LR 68, where the employer's failure to apply its disciplinary procedure deprived the employee of the opportunity to clear his name and avoid dismissal. See also *Mezey v South West London and St George's Mental Health NHS Trust* [2010] IRLR 512, where the Court of Appeal upheld the granting of an injunction to restrain an NHS Trust from taking capability proceedings in breach of its disciplinary procedures. The approach to be adopted to applications of this sort was considered by the Supreme Court in *West London Mental Health NHS Trust v Chhabra* [2013] UKSC 80, [2014] 1 All ER 943. While emphasising that the Courts should generally be cautious in intervening in on-going disciplinary proceedings, the Supreme Court overturned the Court of Appeal and granted an injunction preventing the Trust proceeding with the relevant disciplinary proceedings. The Court held that the irregularities in the case were serious and noted the limited nature of the damages to which the claimant would be entitled if an injunction was not granted. However, in the recent case of *Hendy v Ministry of Justice* [2014] IRLR 856 the Court has re-emphasised that it will only intervene if any breach is sufficiently serious that it cannot be remedied within the disciplinary procedure and that it is not the Court's function to micro-manage a disciplinary procedure.

Somewhat different considerations may apply where the decision at the interlocutory stage will effectively determine the dispute in favour of one party or the other. In those circumstances, the court will do its best to form a view as to which party has the stronger case (see *Lansing Linde Ltd v Kerr* [1991] ICR 428). Also, where the dispute turns upon a question of law or the construction of a document, the court has power to make a final determination of that question at an interlocutory stage (*Civil Procedure Rules, part 24*). For an example of this course being taken in an employment dispute, see *Jones v Gwent County Council* [1992] IRLR 521.

The courts will not generally make mandatory interlocutory orders for the continued payment of wages where these are sought as an indirect means of obtaining an injunction (see *Alexander*, above; *Jakeman v South West Thames Regional Health Authority and London Ambulance Service* [1990] IRLR 62).

8.44   Jurisdiction

Employment tribunals have jurisdiction to hear claims for breach of contracts of employment or contracts 'connected with employment' other than personal injury claims (*Employment Tribunals Extension of Jurisdiction (England and Wales) Order 1994 (SI 1994/1623)*).

The claim must be one which 'arises or is outstanding on the termination of the employee's employment' (*art 3(c)*). This means that the employee must have an enforceable but unsatisfied claim at the date of termination. The formulation does not enable tribunals to determine claims which, at the termination of employment, are contingent: *Peninsula Business Services Ltd v Sweeney* [2004] IRLR 49, EAT. *Article 5* specifically excludes a claim relating to:

(a)   a term requiring the employer to provide living accommodation for the employee;

(b)   a term imposing an obligation on the employer or the employee in connection with living accommodation;

(c)   a term relating to intellectual property;

(d)   a term imposing an obligation of confidence; and

(e)   a term which is in restraint of trade.

Article 7 provides that an employee must present a contract claim:

(i)   within three months of the effective date of termination of the contract giving rise to the claim (see **53.13** UNFAIR DISMISSAL – I);

(ii)   where there is no effective date of termination, within three months of the date when the employee last worked in the employment which has been terminated; or

(iii)   within such further period as the tribunal considers reasonable, where it was not reasonably practicable for the employee to present a claim in time (see **18.20** EMPLOYMENT TRIBUNALS – I).

The tribunal has jurisdiction only in respect of contracts of employment or those connected with employment (*ERA 1996, s 3(2)*). Thus, an agreement compromising a wrongful dismissal claim effected during employment falls within the tribunal's jurisdiction: *Rock-it Cargo Ltd v Green* [1997] IRLR 581.

The provisions as to the time when a claim must be made mean that the employment tribunal does not have jurisdiction to consider a claim made during the currency of employment. Its jurisdiction is limited to claims submitted after the termination of the employment: see *Capek v Lincolnshire County Council* [2000] ICR 878, CA. Further, the claim must arise or be outstanding on the termination of employment. This means that the tribunal does not have jurisdiction to entertain claims that only arise for the first time after the employment has terminated, eg a settlement of a dismissal claim made after the employment has ended: *Miller Bros and F P Butler v Johnston* [2002] IRLR 386. There are conflicting tribunal decisions on the question of whether the six year limitation period under *section 5* of the *Limitation Act 1980* for breach of contract claims in the civil courts also applies to claims in the tribunal.

Employers are entitled to counterclaim (*arts 4, 8*). Counterclaims must be made at a time when a contract claim by an employee is already before the tribunal and has not been settled or withdrawn. The counterclaim must arise out of a contract with the employee who has made the contract claim. In *Ridge v HM Land Registry* UKEAT 0485/12, the EAT held that the defence of set-off is also available to an employer in the tribunal. The tribunal was therefore entitled to reduce the damages due to an employee in a claim for unpaid pension contributions by setting off the amount claimed by the employer for overpayment of wages, even though the tribunal had rejected the employer's contract claim as out of time.

The time limit for presenting counterclaims is six weeks from the date when the employer (or other respondent to the employee's contract claim) received a copy of the originating application in respect of that employee's contract claim. This period is subject to extension where it was not reasonably practicable for the employer's counterclaim to be presented in time (see **18.20** EMPLOYMENT TRIBUNALS – I).

8.44   Contract of Employment

The Order contains specific provisions relating to death and bankruptcy.

8.45   The maximum award which a tribunal may make in respect of a contract claim, or a number of contract claims relating to the same contract, is £25,000 *(art 10)*. In many cases, the potential value of a contractual claim may exceed £25,000. The question may arise whether a successful employee in the tribunal who recovers the maximum award may then bring fresh proceedings in the High Court for the remainder of the value of the contractual claim. In *Fraser v HLMAD Ltd* [2006] IRLR 687, [2006] ICR 1395, the Court of Appeal held that no further claim may be brought in the civil courts once a tribunal has ruled on a wrongful dismissal claim. The key point is that, once the court has decided a matter, a claimant may not ask another court to deal with that same matter again. The reason for this is that the employee no longer has a cause of action which he is able to litigate. The cause of action – breach of contract – has been replaced by, or 'merged in' the judgment of the tribunal. The concept of a cause of action merging in a judgment, so precluding a further action being brought in respect of the same cause of action, is well established in law (see *Halsbury's Laws*, Vol 26, paras 550–551). Further, there are several cases in which a party who has succeeded in one forum which has a limited power to award damages has been precluded from seeking to institute fresh proceedings in respect of the same matter in another forum in order to recover the shortfall. In *Hills v Co-operative Wholesale Society Ltd* [1940] 2 KB 435, an employee brought an action in the High Court and in the county court against his employer in respect of the same complaint. A defence of common employment was available to the employer in the High Court but not in the county court. The employer paid into the county court the maximum sum which the employee could recover in that forum and the employee accepted that sum. The Court of Appeal held that the employee could not continue with the High Court proceedings. His cause of action had been completely satisfied when he accepted the payment made in respect of the county court proceedings, notwithstanding that there was a limit on the sum that the county court could award. See also *Wright v London General Omnibus Co* (1877) 2 QBD 271; *Clarke v Yorke* (1882) 52 LJ Ch 32.

It is suggested that a person should not be entitled to bring the same cause of action simultaneously in the tribunal and in the county court or the High Court. Rather, he should be put to his election. An analogy is to be found in *Australian Commercial Research and Development Ltd v ANZ McCaughan Merchant Bank Ltd* [1989] 3 All ER 65 where a claimant who had commenced proceedings based on the same cause of action in both England and Queensland was put to his election. It is important that a person chooses carefully in which forum to begin, since cause of action estoppel may be created where an application to the tribunal is dismissed upon withdrawal by the applicant (*Barber v Staffordshire County Council* [1996] ICR 379, followed in *Osborne v Valve (Engineering) Services Ltd* (24 November 2000, unreported), EAT). In *Osborne* the court held that: (1) the principles of *res judicata* bar an employee from bringing High Court wrongful dismissal proceedings after the same cause of action has been determined by the tribunal; and (2) a 'determination' by the tribunal includes a dismissal by the tribunal following withdrawal of the claim. Therefore, the safest course to adopt in a case where an applicant wishes to pursue High Court wrongful dismissal proceedings after having already commenced tribunal proceedings is to invite the tribunal to stay the case before it. A stay does not determine the proceedings. It simply prevents further steps being taken until the stay is lifted.

However, a number of cases have suggested a more flexible approach to those who commence proceedings in the tribunal and withdraw in order to sue in the civil courts; the cases are not wholly easy to reconcile. In *Sajid v Sussex Muslim Society* [2002] IRLR 113, an applicant presented a breach of contract claim to a tribunal and later withdrew it. His express reason for withdrawing was in order to present the claim in a court whose jurisdiction to award damages was not limited to £25,000. The Court of Appeal held that his claim was entitled to proceed. The second proceedings did not offend the principle of *res judicata*, which was finality in litigation. Since it was clear that the purpose of withdrawal of the tribunal claim was so as to bring county court proceedings, the principle behind *res judicata* was not engaged. Unlike the applicant in *Barber*, Mr Sajid had not intended by withdrawing his claim to abandon his cause of action.

A different analysis prevailed in *Lennon v Birmingham City Council* [2001] EWCA Civ 435, [2001] IRLR 826, decided by the Court of Appeal before *Sajid* but not referred to in the latter case. In *Lennon*, the applicant brought and subsequently withdrew a complaint in which she alleged that she had been harassed and bullied by her employer. This was regarded by the employer as a complaint of sex discrimination. A tribunal dismissed the claim on withdrawal. Later she brought a claim in the county court in which she relied on the same allegations which had provided the foundation for her tribunal claim. The Court of Appeal held that the claim was rightly struck out under the doctrine of issue estoppel. The court expressly rejected the argument that the reason for the withdrawal of the complaint could be relevant: all that mattered was the simple fact of the dismissal of the claim by the tribunal on withdrawal.

The Court of Appeal has sought to reconcile the apparent tension between *Sajid* and *Lennon* in *Ako v Rothschild Asset Management Ltd* [2002] EWCA Civ 236, [2002] ICR 899 (applied in *Khan v Heywood and Middleton Primary Care Trust* [2007] ICR 24, *[2006] IRLR 793*). In *Ako*, the applicant lodged a complaint of discrimination, which was subsequently dismissed on withdrawal. A week after the dismissal of the first complaint, she lodged a second complaint containing the same allegations against the same respondent but also added a new respondent. It was found that her intention had not been to cease the litigation against Rothschild, but only to add in the additional respondent. The Court of Appeal held that, as a matter of general legal principle, a court could review the matrix of fact surrounding a legal act in order to understand its effect. Therefore, there could be cases where the circumstances surrounding the withdrawal of a claim meant that the cause of action was not exhausted. The court drew attention to procedural rules in the common law courts, which enabled proceedings that had been discontinued to be revived with permission. There was no such rule in the tribunal. Its omission meant that the strict application of the rules of estoppel could work an injustice.

However, the findings of an employment tribunal can create an issue estoppel in subsequent proceedings in the High Court, even where the issues were presented differently or supported by fresh arguments: *Green v Hampshire County Council* [1979] ICR 861; *Smith v Chelsea Football Club plc* [2010] EWHC 1168 (QB).

On the other hand, there will be no abuse of process where the issues being litigated in one forum (for example, a breach of contract claim in the High Court) were fundamentally different from those already being litigated in the other (for example, an unfair dismissal or victimisation claim in the Tribunal): *University of London v Tariquez-Zaman* [2010] EWHC 908 (QB).

8.46   Disclosure

This section is principally concerned with the remedies of the employee against the employer when the latter has acted in breach of contract. However, the situation may also arise when the employer has become mixed up in alleged wrongdoing by third parties. In *A v Company B Ltd* [1997] IRLR 405, an employee was dismissed by his employer after allegations of gross misconduct had been made to the employer by a third party. The employer did not identify the complainant or specify the nature of the complaints that had been made. The employee took the view that false allegations had been made about him and wished to institute an action against the third party alleging defamation. In order that the employee could prosecute that action, the High Court ordered that the employer disclose details of the allegations which had been made about him by the third party, following the principles laid down in *Norwich Pharmacal Co v Customs and Excise Comrs* [1974] AC 133.

8.47   EMPLOYER'S REMEDIES FOR BREACH OF CONTRACT OF EMPLOYMENT

Withholding or deduction of wages

If an employee does not perform any of his contractual duties, he is not entitled to his contractual wage. Thus, an employee is not entitled to be paid for days when he is on strike.

If the employee refuses to perform the full range of his contractual duties, particularly if this refusal is in pursuance of industrial action, the purpose of which is to disrupt the employer's business, the employee will not be entitled to his full contractual wage (see *Miles v Wakefield Metropolitan District Council* [1987] ICR 368). In *Wiluszynski v Tower Hamlets London Borough Council* [1989] IRLR 259, the Court of Appeal held that the Council was entitled to withhold the whole of the employee's wages when the employee refused to perform a substantial part of his duties and it was clear that the employer was not accepting the work which was performed as substantial performance of the contract. In *British Telecommunications plc v Ticehurst* [1992] ICR 383, it was held that a manager who intended to continue participating in a withdrawal of goodwill could be sent home without pay.

Alternatively, the employer may be able to deduct from the employee's wages a sum representing the financial loss suffered by him as a result of the employee's breach of contract (see *Sim v Rotherham Metropolitan Borough Council* [1986] ICR 897).

In *Cooper v Isle of Wight College* [2007] EWHC 2831 (QB), [2008] IRLR 124, it was held that the appropriate sum which an employer was entitled to deduct in respect of a one day strike was $1/260^{th}$ of a year's pay on the basis that there are 260 working days in the year.

In the case where the employee engages in action short of a strike, it is open to the employer to decline to make any payment on the basis that he is only prepared to accept full performance of the employee's obligations (*Miles* above). An employee who carries out only part of his duties does so at risk. There is no right to claim a quantum meruit. In *Spackman v London Metropolitan University* [2007] IRLR 744, the employee refused to perform some tasks and the employer deducted 30% of the employee's pay. Having held that the employer could lawfully have paid nothing, the court held that there was no breach of contract by deducting 30% of the employee's pay.

The employer's right to withhold pay may arise in many situations where the employee refuses to work. In *Luke v Stoke-on-Trent Council* [2007] EWCA Civ 761, [2007] ICR 1678, [2007] IRLR 777, the Court of Appeal held that an employer was entitled not to pay an employee who felt unable to attend her place of work after a breakdown in her relationship with her employer. The employer had reasonably required her to return to work. Since she had failed to do so, there was no entitlement to pay: see also *Sunrise Brokers LLP v Rodgers* [2014] EWCA Civ 1373.

(See also **34.14 PAY – I.**)

8.47a   Acceptance of fundamental breach

If the employee is in fundamental breach of his contractual obligations, the employer can accept the breach and bring the contract to an end. Such a fundamental breach will generally consist of gross misconduct, extreme incompetence, or a major failure to carry out the work required of the employee. To go on strike will generally amount to a fundamental breach of contract. See also **45.2 STRIKES AND INDUSTRIAL ACTION** and **58.6, 58.7 WRONGFUL DISMISSAL**.

8.47b   Damages

An employer may bring proceedings against an employee for damages for breach of contract (see, eg, *Janata Bank v Ahmed* [1981] ICR 791). Situations which may give rise to such proceedings are a breach of the employee's duty of fidelity, breach of his duty of care and failure to give the notice of termination he is contractually obliged to give. In practice, such claims are rare (but see *Cheltenham Borough Council v Laird* [2009] EWHC 1253 (QB), [2009] IRLR 621, an unsuccessful claim by a local authority against a former employee for the costs it would not have incurred if it had employed someone else). What is more common is an application for an injunction to restrain disclosure of confidential information or to enforce a restrictive covenant (see RESTRAINT OF TRADE, CONFIDENTIALITY AND EMPLOYEE INTERVENTIONS (41)).

Parties to contracts are entitled to make their own provision for compensation in the event of breach by one party. The law distinguishes between liquidated damages clauses (those containing genuine pre-estimates of loss and designed to compensate the innocent party) and penalty clauses (those designed to deter or punish a wrongdoer) – the former are enforceable, the latter are not. A payment to an employee on dismissal is likely to be regarded as a penalty if it is extravagant and unconscionable: *Murray v Leisureplay plc* [2005] EWCA Civ 963, [2005] IRLR 946. These clauses are relatively uncommon in employment contracts. In *Giraud UK Ltd v Smith* [2000] IRLR 763, however, the contract provided that in the event that the employee failed to give and work the notice period stipulated by the contract, there would be a deduction from his final payment 'equivalent to the number of days short'. The employee left without notice. The employer refused to make any final payment to the employee. The employer argued that it was entitled to a payment from the employee of four weeks' pay. The EAT confirmed that employment contracts may contain liquidated damages clauses, but found that in this case the clause was a penalty because there was no limit of liability to the employer's actual loss. See also *Tullett Prebon Group Ltd v El-Hajjali* [2008] EWHC 1924 (QB), [2008] IRLR 760 for an example of a liquidated damages clause successfully relied upon by an employer.

In *Gamatronic (UK) Ltd v Hamilton* [2016] EWHC 2225 (QB) (QBD), two directors were found to be in breach of fiduciary duty in taking steps to compete prior to joining a competitors business. However, the claimant was not entitled to any remedy in respect of the breaches as the directors had continued to perform their duties diligently; nor would compensation be awarded in respect of their salaries paid by the competitor as there was no reasonable relationship between those salaries and their breach of fiduciary duty.

8.47c   Injunction or specific performance

In no circumstances may the employee be compelled to work by injunction or by an order of specific performance. That was the common law and the principle is enacted in *TULRCA 1992, s 236*. That applies also if such compulsion will be the practical result of granting an injunction against a third party, eg the only alternative employer (*Warren v Mendy* [1989] ICR 525); the court will not make an order which would prevent the employee from earning his living. However, the Court of Appeal held in *Evening Standard Co Ltd v Henderson* [1987] ICR 588 that it may be possible to restrain an employee who does not give proper notice (see **48.17** TERMINATION OF EMPLOYMENT) from working elsewhere during his notice period so long as the employer will provide him with all his contractual benefits without actually requiring him to work. The *Henderson* principle was approved in *Provident Financial Group plc and Whitegates Estate Agency Ltd v Hayward* [1989] ICR 160, where an express contractual prohibition was relied upon. However, the Court of Appeal indicated that no injunction would be granted if the plaintiff's business had nothing to do with that of the new employer. It also recognised that an employee might need to work and exercise his skills (the employer in *Hayward* had put the employee on 'garden leave' during his notice period, whereas in *Henderson* work was available if the employee wanted it), and refused to grant an injunction after considering the non-competitive nature of the job the employee wished to take up, and the length of the unexpired notice period (see also *Warren*).

In *William Hill Organisation Ltd v Tucker* [1998] IRLR 313, the Court of Appeal appeared to impose further limitations on the availability of the 'garden leave injunction' remedy. The court held that it was necessary to consider in each case whether the consideration moving from the employer obliged the employer to permit the employee to do work, or whether the full extent of the obligation is to pay the employee. If the employer was obliged to permit the employee to carry out work, then the court would be unlikely to grant a garden leave injunction in the absence of an express provision which entitled the employer not to provide work and/or required the employee to agree not to attend work during the notice period. It was unlikely that such a provision would be implied. However, even where an express term was present, the court would not grant relief to any greater extent than would be granted in respect of a justifiable covenant in restraint of trade (see **41.6 RESTRAINT OF TRADE, CONFIDENTIALITY AND EMPLOYEE INTERVENTIONS**).

A garden leave injunction was granted in *SG&R Valuation Service Co LLC v Boudrais* [2008] IRLR 770 notwithstanding the absence of any express provision for garden leave in the employees' contracts. Although the employees had a right to work during their notice periods, this right was vitiated because the employees had, during their notice periods, committed wrongdoing by which they would or might profit. By those breaches of their contracts, they had "demonstrated in a serious way that they were not ready or willing to work, or that they had not rendered it impossible or reasonably impracticable for the employer to provide work". This principle – expressly described as a qualification to the right to work rather than an implied term of the employees' contracts – was approved by the Court of Appeal in *Standard Life Health Care Ltd v Gorman* [2009] EWCA Civ 1292, [2010] IRLR 233.

In *Sunrise Brokers LLP v Rodgers* [2015] ICR 272, however, the Court of Appeal held that there is no rule of law requiring an employer to pay an employee if it seeks an injunction preventing him from resigning in breach of contract. The question is whether the injunction would compel the employee to return to work for the employer. The court therefore held that an injunction restraining a broker, who had purported to resign without giving the required contractual notice, from joining a competitor or contacting clients during his notice period and a period thereafter covered by post-termination restrictive covenants, was properly granted. The reason the broker would be unpaid during this period was that he had refused to return to work.

The same general principles relating to the grant of interlocutory injunctions apply as are discussed under 'Employee's remedies', above (see also **RESTRAINT OF TRADE, CONFIDENTIALITY AND EMPLOYEE INTERVENTIONS (41)**).

In *Associated Foreign Exchange Ltd v International Foreign Exchange (UK) Ltd* [2010] EWHC 1178 (Ch), [2010] IRLR 964, the court refused to grant an interlocutory injunction to restrain a former employee from breaching a 12-month non-solicitation covenant, because the market changed at such a pace that such protection was unnecessary and because this covenant was unlikely to be enforceable.

8.47d Account of profits

In some cases, the appropriate remedy for a breach of contract may be the restitutionary remedy of an account of profits. An account was ordered by the House of Lords in *A-G v Blake* [2001] IRLR 36. Such a remedy will only be available in exceptional circumstances where the normal remedies of damages, specific performance and injunction do not provide an adequate remedy. The case of *Blake*, a spy who had published a book in breach of his contractual duties to the Crown, was such an exceptional case.

9   Directors

9.1   INTRODUCTION

Directors of companies are office-holders. They are not necessarily employees. However, directors often enter into service agreements, thereby becoming employees in addition to holding office. The appointment of a director is nevertheless independent of any contract of employment between a director and a company, although the contract of employment may contain provisions which have application to the office.

The provisions regulating the appointment to, and removal from, the office of a director are set out in the *Companies Act 2006* ('*CA 2006*'). The *Companies (Model Articles) Regulations 2008 (SI 2008/3229)*, as amended, ('*MA Regulations*') set out 'default' articles of association for different kinds of companies. The *MA Regulations* apply to all companies incorporated under *CA 2006* on or after 1 October 2009. A company may adopt for its articles the whole or any part of those default articles. Accordingly, it is necessary to look at the precise terms of the articles of a company in order to determine the position in any particular case.

The old 'default' articles in *Table A* of the *Companies (Tables A to F) Regulations 1985 (SI 1985/805)* remain valid for any company incorporated under the Companies Act 1985 in the form they existed at the time of that company's incorporation.

CA 2006 also codified the rules governing the duties directors owe to their companies.

This chapter concerns the position of directors as employees. It does not set out the numerous responsibilities of directors under company law, nor address the power of the courts to control delinquent directors.

9.2   APPOINTMENT

A director may be employed by the other directors of a company under the authority of one of the articles of association. Such a director is often referred to as an executive director. The relevant provisions of the model articles provide that:

(1)   Directors may undertake any services for the company that the directors decide;

(2)   Directors are entitled to such remuneration as the directors determine:

    (a)   for their services to the company as directors, and

    (b)   for any other service which they undertake for the company.

(For private companies limited by shares: *para 19* of *Sch 1* to the *MA Regulations*; for private companies limited by guarantee: *para 19, Sch 2, MA Regulations*; for public companies, it is *para 23* of *Sch 3*.)

The relevant provision in *Table A* was *art 84*. As explained above, *Table A* remains valid for companies incorporated prior to 1 October 2009. It provides:

'Subject to the provisions of the Act, the directors may appoint one or more of their number to the office of managing director or to any other executive office under the company and may enter into an agreement or arrangement with any director for his employment by the company or for provision by him of any services outside the scope of the ordinary duties of a director. Any such appointment, agreement or arrangement may be made upon such terms as the directors determine and they may remunerate any such director for his services as they think fit. Any appointment of a director to an executive office shall terminate if he ceases to be a director but without prejudice to any claim to damages for breach of the contract of service between the director and the company. A managing director and a director holding any executive office shall not be subject to retirement by rotation.'

As explained above, the model articles of association may or may not be incorporated into the articles of a particular company. Even where they are not incorporated into the articles, executive directors are not usually subject to retirement by rotation. However, where a company is listed, the Governance Code (see **9.15** below) recommends that all directors should be submitted for re-election at regular intervals, at the first annual general meeting after their appointment, and at least every three years thereafter (B.7.1). Directors of FTSE 350 companies are subject to annual election.

Usually, the terms of the director's appointment will be recorded in a letter written under the authority of the board of directors, or in a service agreement which the board has approved. Where a board resolution contains the terms of the appointment, this may be sufficient evidence of the terms of the contract between the director and the company.

9.3   **Relationship between articles and contracts of employment**

Where the articles do not confer the directors with a power to employ one of their number, or if that power is not properly exercised, the employment contract between the employed director and the company will be void for want of authority. An example of this situation is *Guinness plc v Saunders* [1990] 2 AC 663. In *Guinness v Saunders*, a committee of the board purported to grant a director special remuneration pursuant to an alleged oral contract. The House of Lords held that this alleged contract was void. This was because the board had no power under the articles to delegate this power to the committee. Since there was no binding contract, their Lordships refused to permit the director to claim payment for actual services which he had performed (on a *quantum meruit* basis). He also could not claim an equitable allowance because it would be inequitable to permit the director to take advantage of his directorship in order to claim remuneration in such circumstances. This was in accordance with the general equitable principle that a director may not profit from the holding of his office. (This principle is often modified by the articles of association.)

The articles and board resolutions are deemed to be known by each director. Accordingly, a director cannot rely on ostensible authority, implied authority or assume that another director, the committee or the board have powers which they do not have: *Guinness v Saunders*, above, at 658, per Lord Templeman. When considering the position of an employed director, it is necessary to examine carefully the relationship between the articles and terms of any service agreement. In order to avoid any doubt, service agreements should expressly provide for the circumstances in which they can be terminated. They must be drafted having regard to the articles which are then in force. (It should also be noted that the employers of directors are obliged to provide a written statement of the particulars of employment, see further below at **9.6**.)

In *Read v Astoria Garage (Streatham) Ltd* [1952] Ch 637, a managing director was appointed by a board resolution. This resolution contained no terms as to how the post might be terminated. A resolution of the board, later approved by the company in general meeting, removed the managing director from post. The relevant article provided that the appointment:

'shall be subject to determination *ipso facto* if he ceases for any cause to be a director or if the Company in general meeting resolves that the tenure of office as managing director . . . be determined.'

In the absence of an express term in the original resolution, the director was taken to have contracted on the terms of the articles. He therefore had no claim for wrongful dismissal since the employment had been terminated in accordance with the articles. By contrast, the director in *Nelson v James Nelson & Sons Ltd* [1914] 2 KB 770, CA was appointed in accordance with an article which enabled the board to make an appointment 'for such period as they think fit, and may revoke such appointment'. The duration of the agreement by which the director was appointed was for an indefinite period. It was held that the board had an unfettered power to appoint for such period as it deemed fit. However, the right to revoke only existed if the contract so provided. Since the contract did not contain a power to revoke, the director was entitled to damages for wrongful dismissal when his appointment was terminated.

The position must be judged by considering the articles as they are at the date of entering into the contract of service with the director. In *Southern Foundries (1926) Ltd v Shirlaw* [1940] AC 701, the company, subsequent to the appointment of a director, had adopted new articles which were less favourable to an employed director. It was held that the adoption of these new articles could not worsen the contractual position of an employed director. Accordingly, a dismissal taking place under the new articles was wrongful.

Service agreements may also contain implied terms. For example, in *Shindler v Northern Raincoat Co Ltd* [1960] 1 WLR 1038, a director sold his shares in the company to a different company under a contract of sale which provided that he would be appointed managing director for a period of ten years. This second company was subsequently resold to a third company. The third company did not wish to retain the director's services. In the director's successful claim for wrongful dismissal, it was held that it had become an implied term of his contract of service that the company would not do anything of its own motion to cause him to be removed as managing director in breach of the contract of sale. Diplock J distinguished *Read v Astoria Garage* (above) on the basis that, in *Shindler* and unlike in *Read*, there was evidence of a contract between the company and the director which was inconsistent with the articles. On the basis of the reasoning in *Southern Foundries v Shirlaw*, the director had been wrongfully dismissed in breach of that contract.

9.4   Employed or not?

Articles, such as the model articles, usually give the directors a very broad discretion as to the terms of appointment of one of their number. In particular, articles often provide a power to employ a director pursuant to a contract of employment or, instead, to enter into an agreement for the provision of services. A director may, in respect of additional services, be engaged as either an employee or as an independent contractor. The question of whether the director is an employee or an independent contractor may be of great importance. Many statutory employment rights, such as the right to claim unfair dismissal, are only conferred on employees.

It should also be noted that whether or not an individual is 'employed' may depend on the context in which the question is asked. This is because the definition of an 'employee' varies.

This matter is addressed in detail in Employee, Self-Employed or Worker? (15)). However, the questions pertaining to directors are to some degree distinct and merit separate attention.

Where there is no formal agreement, evidence as to the employment status of a director may be gleaned from board resolutions or minutes, correspondence between the parties and the manner in which the individual is paid and taxed. The courts have tended to consider directors who work full-time for a company and are paid a salary to be employees: *Trussed Steel Concrete Co Ltd v Green* [1946] Ch 115. An example is *Folami v Nigerline (UK) Ltd* [1978] ICR 277, where an accountant from a holding company was appointed managing director of the company's subsidiary and it was held that, having been paid by the subsidiary, the managing director was an employee for the purposes of statutory employment rights. A director who was remunerated by way of director's fees and had not been treated as an employee for the purposes of national insurance was held not to be an employee for the purpose of exercising statutory employment rights in *Parsons v Albert J Parsons & Sons Ltd* [1979] IRLR 117.

A person who is a controlling shareholder can also be an employee of that company. In *Secretary of State for Business, Enterprise and Regulatory Reform v Neufeld (Richard)* [2009] EWCA Civ 280, [2009] ICR 1183, the Court of Appeal considered the relevant authorities and confirmed that it is a question of fact whether or not such a shareholder/director is an employee. An employee's shareholding and/or degree of control of the company is not ordinarily relevant to the inquiry of whether a contract is one of employment, unless it gives rise to questions of whether the contract was genuine. For applications of *Neufeld*, see *Ashby v Monterry Designs Ltd* (UKEAT/0226/08/CEA) (18 December 2009, unreported), *Secretary of State for Business, Innovation and Skills v Knight* [2014] IRLR 605, and, in the Northern Irish Court of Appeal in *Department of Employment & Learning v Morgan* [2016] IRLR 350.

With regard to directors, the 'control test' is not particularly appropriate for determining whether a director is employed. This is because a director may be largely in control of the day-to-day running of the company or part of it (albeit that the 'control' in such a case is exercisable theoretically by the company: see *Secretary of State for Business, Enterprise and Regulatory Reform v Neufeld*, above). Indeed, a controlling share-holder, such as in *Neufeld*, can even ultimately decide whether or not he is dismissed. The 'organisation test', also known as the 'integration test' may be more appropriate. This test was set out by Denning LJ in *Stevenson (or Stephenson) Jordan and Harrison Ltd v MacDonald and Evans* (1952) 69 RPC 10, [1952] 1 TLR 101, CA as follows:

> 'Under a contract of service, a man is employed as part of the business and his work is done as an integral part of the business; whereas, under a contract for services, his work, although done for the business, is not integrated into it but is an accessory to it'.

Accordingly, a director who provides consultancy or advisory services to the company is likely to be an independent contractor, whereas an executive director who is engaged for the purposes of managing the business (or a part of it), and whose work forms an integral part of the business is likely to be an employee.

In *Crawford v Department for Employment and Learning* [2014] NICA 26, the Northern Ireland Court of Appeal emphasised the importance of careful analysis of the contractual position. Clear written agreements may assist in clarifying the issues, however, courts are likely to look to the substance of the agreement rather than simply its form. In *Clark v Clark Construction Initiatives* [2008] ICR 635, [2008] IRLR 364, Elias J set out three circumstances in which a court would not give effect to a purported contract of employment: sham, ulterior purpose and where the parties do not conduct themselves in accordance with the contract. See also *Secretary of State for Business, Enterprise and Regulatory Reform v Neufeld*, above.

In *Secretary of State for Business, Innovation & Skills v Knight* [2014] IRLR 605, it was held that the fact that a managing director had decided not to require her salary to be paid did not necessarily mean that she was not an employee. See also *Stack v Ajar-Tec Ltd* [2015] IRLR 474, where the Court of Appeal overturned a finding that there was no employment contract despite the fact that a director had never been paid.

In *Holterman Ferho Exploitatie BV v Spies van Bullenheim* C-47/14 [2016] ICR 90, the CJEU considered this question in relation to the definition of an employee under European law. It was held that the answer would depend on whether there was the necessary relationship of "subordination".

9.5   Scope of employment

The scope of a director's employment will be determined by the terms of any service agreement, and any board resolutions which are in force from time to time which grant him or her authority. The powers and duties of a director may be subject to variation by the board. Directors may be appointed to an executive function such as finance director of the company or group. Subject to the terms of the service agreement, the scope of the employment is capable of being completely changed, expanded or narrowed. Even the executive function may be subject to change in some circumstances.

In *Harold Holdsworth & Co (Wakefield) Ltd v Caddies* [1955] 1 WLR 352, it was held that the board could confine the responsibilities of a managing director to the affairs of a subsidiary where the contract provided that he was:

> 'appointed a managing director of the Company and as such managing director he shall perform the duties and exercise the powers in relation to the business of the company and the business.. of its existing subsidiary company . . . .which may from time to time be assigned to or vested in him by the board of directors.'

(The court noted that Mr Caddies had been appointed 'a' rather than 'the' managing director.)

9.6   Written particulars

The employer of a director, like that of other employees, is obliged to provide a written statement of the particulars of the employment. The provisions of *ss 1 to 6* of the *Employment Rights Act 1996* apply (see CONTRACT OF EMPLOYMENT (8)).

9.7   DIRECTORS' SERVICE CONTRACTS

A director's 'service contract' is defined, for the purposes of the relevant parts of *CA 2006*, in *s 227* as a contract under which:

(a)   a director of the company undertakes personally to perform services (as director or otherwise) for the company, or for a subsidiary; or

(b)   services (as director or otherwise) that a director of the company undertakes personally to perform are made available by a third party to the company, or to a subsidiary.

The definition is expressly stated not to be restricted to contracts for the performance of services outside the scope of the ordinary duties of a director.

9.8   Inspection

Under s *228* of *CA 2006*, a company must keep available for inspection a copy of every director's service contract with the company (or a subsidiary), or, if this is not in writing, a written memorandum setting out the terms of the contract. These documents must be kept available for inspection at the company's registered office or at a place specified by regulations. If they are kept at a place other than the registered office, the company must give notice to the registrar of where they are kept: *s 228(4)*. The documents must be retained and kept available for at least one year from the date of termination or expiry of the contract: *s 228(3)*.

The provisions apply to a variation in a director's service contract as well as to the original contract.

9.8 Directors

Section 228 does not specify the terms which are to be included in any memorandum setting out the terms of a service agreement where this is not in writing. Nevertheless, a memorandum should specify the main terms of the employment pertaining to salary, benefits and duration. It could also contain all the written particulars required by *s 1* of the *Employment Rights Act 1996*.

There is no longer any exception for service contracts with a short expiry date or for those who work wholly or mainly outside the United Kingdom.

All copies and memoranda which are required to be kept must be open to inspection to any member of the company without charge (*CA 2006, s 229(1)*).

If a company fails to comply with any of the above provisions, the company and every officer who is in default is liable to a fine and, for continued contravention to a daily default fine (*CA 2006, s 228(5), (6)*). If inspection of a copy or memorandum is refused, the court may order an immediate inspection or direct that a copy be sent to the person requiring it (*CA 2006, s 229(5)*).

9.9 Contracts with sole members who are also directors

Where, outside the ordinary course of the company's business, a limited company with only one member enters into a contract with that sole member who is a director, then, unless the contract is in writing, the terms must be set out in a written memorandum or recorded in the minutes of the first meeting of the directors following the making of the contract. A failure to comply is an offence punishable by a fine not exceeding level 5 on the standard scale: see *s 231* of *CA 2006*.

9.10 Listing Rule requirements

The Financial Conduct Authority ('FCA') is the United Kingdom's Listing Authority. (Prior to April 2013, the FCA was known as the Financial Services Authority or FSA). The FCA makes rules governing the admission and continuing obligations of listed companies. These are known as the *Listing Rules*. They can be found on the FCA's website at www.fca.org.uk. These generally include provisions as to directors' service contracts. Companies should check the up-to-date provisions as they change from time to time.

In particular, according to the current version of the rules, a listed company must notify a Regulatory Information Service (RIS) of any change including:

(a)   the appointment of a new director stating the appointee's name and whether the position is executive, non-executive or chairman and the nature of any specific function or responsibility of the position;

(b)   the resignation, removal or retirement of a director (unless the director retires by rotation and is re-appointed at a general meeting of the shareholders);

(c)   important changes to the role, functions or responsibilities of a director; and

(d)   the effective date of the change if it is not with immediate effect (LR 9.6.11).

This notification must take place as soon as possible and in any event by the end of the business day following the decision or receipt of notice about the change by the company.

If the effective date of the change is not known, the notification should state this fact and the company should notify a RIS as soon as the date has been decided. (LR 9.6.12)

A listed company must also notify a RIS of the following information in respect of any new director appointed to the board:

(a)   details of all directorships held by the director in any other publicly quoted company at any time in the previous five years, indicating whether or not he is still a director;

(b)   any unspent convictions in relation to indictable offences;

(c)   details of any receiverships, compulsory liquidations, creditors voluntary liquidations, administrations, company voluntary arrangements or any composition or arrangement with its creditors generally or any class of its creditors of any company where the director was an executive director at the time of, or within the 12 months preceding, such events;

(d)   details of any compulsory liquidations, administrations or partnership voluntary arrangements of any partnerships where the director was a partner at the time of, or within the 12 months preceding, such events;

(e)   details of receiverships of any asset of such person or of a partnership of which the director was a partner at the time of, or within the 12 months preceding, such event; and

(f)   details of any public criticisms of the director by statutory or regulatory authorities (including designated professional bodies) and whether the director has ever been disqualified by a court from acting as a director of a company or from acting in the management or conduct of the affairs of any company (LR 9.6.13).

This notification must be given as soon as possible following the decision to appoint the director and in any event within five business days of the decision.

If there is no such information that is required to be disclosed about a director, then this should be notified to the RIS (LR 9.6.15).

Any changes in such information with respect to a current director should also be disclosed as well as any new directorships held by the director in any other publicly quoted company (LR 9.6.14).

9.11   Take-over Code

During the course of an offer, or even before the date of the offer if the board of an offeree company has reason to believe that a *bona fide* offer might be made imminently, *rule 21* of the *City Code on Takeovers and Mergers* issued and administered by the Panel on Takeovers and Mergers ("Panel") will apply. According to the 12th edition, published on 12 September 2016, where *rule 21* applies, the board must not enter into contracts other than in the ordinary course of business without the approval of the shareholders of the company in general meeting (or with the consent of the Panel following consultation where the proposed action is in pursuance of a contract entered into earlier or another pre-existing obligation or an earlier decision).

Note 5 of the notes to *Rule 21* indicates that the Panel will regard amending or entering into a service contract with, or creating or varying the terms of employment of, a director as entering into a contract 'otherwise than in the ordinary course of business' for the purpose of *Rule 21* if the new or amended contract or terms constitute an abnormal increase in the director's emoluments or a significant improvement in the terms of service. Accordingly, during an offer period, extending the duration of a service agreement or increasing a director's salary should not be effected without the prior agreement of the Panel.

The notes go on to state that this will not prevent any such increase or improvement which results from a genuine promotion or new appointment. However, the Panel must be consulted in advance in such cases.

9.12 Directors

9.12 Disclosure

Directors have obligations to disclose their interests in some circumstances. *Section 177(1)* of *CA 2006* provides that 'if a director of a company is in any way, directly or indirectly, interested in a proposed transaction or arrangement with the company, he must declare the nature and extent of that interest to the other directors'. Such a declaration may (but need not be) made at a meeting of directors or by notice in accordance with specified procedures (see *ss 184* and *185* of *CA 2006*). Any declaration must be made before the company enters into the relevant transaction or arrangement: *CA 2006, s 177(4)*. Furthermore, where a director has an interest in an existing transaction or arrangement entered into by the company and has not declared the interest under *s 177*, he must do so (*CA 2006, s 182*). A failure to do so is an offence (*CA 2006, s 183*). The rules as to the nature of the declaration are the same as in *s 177*.

A director need not declare an interest if, or to the extent that, the other directors are already aware of it or ought reasonably to be aware of it (*CA 2006, s 177(6)*). The failure of a director to declare his interest renders a contract voidable at the instance of the company: see *Hely-Hutchinson v Brayhead Ltd* [1968] 1 QB 549, CA at 589-90, 594. By contrast, where a director has complied with the duty to disclose an interest, the transaction or arrangement is not liable to be set aside by virtue of any common law rule or equitable principle requiring members' approval (*CA 2006, s 180*).

9.13 Duration of director's service agreement

The duration of a service agreement will largely be a matter of contract between the company and the director concerned. This may be subject, however, to any restrictions in the articles of association as well as to *s 188* of *CA 2006*, discussed further below.

9.14 *Section 188*

Pursuant to *s 188* of *CA 2006*, shareholder approval is required for any provision under which the guaranteed term of a director's employment with the company of which he is a director or, where he is the director of a holding company, within that group is, or may be, more than two years. (The previous provisions, contained in *s 319* of *CA 1985* only applied where the agreement could last for more than five years.)

The provision applies wherever the employment is to continue, or may be continued, otherwise than at the instance of the company, for a period of more than two years during which the employment cannot be terminated by the company by notice, or can be terminated but only in specified circumstances (*CA 2006, s 188(3)*). The section therefore applies to contracts terminable by notice, and to contracts with a minimum duration but which are intended to continue thereafter upon notice, as well as to fixed-term contracts. Specified circumstances would include, for example, the right to terminate for gross misconduct or incapacity. Therefore, any right to terminate on these grounds would not avoid the need for shareholder approval of the term of the contract.

Section 188(3) sets out a situation in which serial contracts are, to some degree, aggregated in determining the duration of the agreement. Where, more than six months before the end of the guaranteed term of a director's employment, the company enters into a further service contract, then *s 188* applies as if the unexpired period of the guaranteed term of the original contract were added to the guaranteed term of the new contract. The aim of this provision appears to be to catch the situation whereby a company attempts to circumvent *s 188* by employing a director on a series of short term contracts.

Where *s 188* requires a term to be approved, it must be approved by a resolution of the members of the company (or, where the director is or is to be employed by the holding company, by a resolution of the holding company) (*CA 2006, s 188(2)*). Before a resolution is passed, a written memorandum setting out the proposed agreement incorporating the term must be made available to members. In the case of a written resolution, this is done by sending or submitting the provision to every eligible member at or before the time at which the proposed resolution is sent or submitted. In the case of a resolution at a meeting, this is done by making the provision available for inspection both at the company's registered office for not less than 15 days ending with the date of the meeting, and at the meeting itself (*CA 2006, s 188(5)*).

If a term is incorporated into an agreement in contravention of *s 188*, it is void, and is, in certain circumstances, replaced by a term entitling the company to terminate the employment at any time by giving reasonable notice (*CA 2006, s 189*). This provision incorporates the common law concept of reasonable notice which is discussed in WRONGFUL DISMISSAL (58).

9.15   *Recommendations*

Currently, there are no other statutory restrictions on the duration of a director's service agreement.

However, the UK Corporate Governance Code ("Governance Code", formerly the "Combined Code on Corporate Governance") recommends that companies should set notice periods at one year or less.

The Governance Code sets out standards of good practice in relation to companies as well as more specific provisions. It is updated at regular intervals. The current edition of the Code was published in April 2016 and applies to financial years beginning on or after 17 June 2016. Listed companies must, in order to comply with the *Listing Rules*, report on how they have applied the Main Principles of the Governance Code, in a manner that would enable shareholders to evaluate how the principles have been applied. They must also either confirm that they have complied with all the provisions of the Governance Code, or, alternatively, state that they have not, setting out which provisions they have has not complied with, the periods within which they did not comply and the reasons for non-compliance (*LR 9.8.6(5)* and *(6)* of the *Listing Rules*). This is often described as 'comply or explain'.

Paragraph D.1.5 of the Governance Code recommends that notice or contract periods should be set at one year or less. If it is necessary to offer longer notice or contract periods to new directors recruited from outside a company, such period should reduce to one year or less after the initial period.

Since a company is only required to 'comply or explain', departures may be made from these provisions in certain circumstances. A departure from the provisions may be justified, for example, where a new recruit is only prepared to contract with the company on terms other than those recommended. If a company decides to set a longer notice or contract period than the recommendation, an explanation for this must be given in the company's disclosure statement.

9.16   DIRECTORS' DUTIES

Whether or not a director is employed by the company, he or she owes it duties. The nature and extent of the duties will depend on the circumstances of an individual case. He or she will owe the general duties owed by all directors to their companies as well as any additional or specific duties imposed by reason of the articles of association or any relevant board resolution. There will also be relevant express and implied duties under the contract of employment or other service agreement.

CA 2006 codified the existing law in this area with effect from October 2008.

9.17 Directors

9.17 The Companies Act 2006

The background to *CA 2006* was a number of major reports which indicated the need for a statutory codification of directors' duties. This is the first time that the duties owed by directors to their company have been set out in statute. The hope was apparently to make the rules clearer and more accessible.

Sections 170 to *177* of *CA 2006* set out the general duties that are owed by a director to the company. It is expressly stated that these duties are based on certain common law rules and equitable principles and have effect in place of those rules and principles (*CA 2006, s 170(3)*).

There has been some discussion in the case law about whether the codification changed the scope or content of the common law and equitable duties upon which the statutory duties were based. In *Towers v Premier Waste* [2011] EWCA Civ 923, Mummery LJ stated of the statutory rules that they "extract and express the essence of the rules and principles which they have replaced". See also *Eastford Ltd v Thomas Graham Gillespie* [2011] CSOH 12 in the Inner House of the Scottish Court of Session.

These general duties are to be interpreted and applied in the same way as common law rules or equitable principles and the courts will have regard to the corresponding rules and principles when interpreting and applying the general duties (*CA 2006, s 170(4)*). Where the duties have not been reformulated, the case law will assist in determining how these duties should be applied in individual cases. However, if there is any conflict, the new statutory provisions will clearly take precedence.

The consequences of a breach or threatened breach of *ss 170* to *177* are the same as would apply if the corresponding common law rule or equitable principle applied. They are enforceable in the same way as any other fiduciary duty owed to a company (*CA 2006, s 178*).

The precise duties owed by an employed director will depend on the articles of association, memorandum, and relevant board minutes as well as the express and implied terms of the service agreement as well as *CA 2006*.

9.18 Duty to act within powers

A director of a company must act in accordance with the company's constitution, and only exercise powers for the purposes for which they are conferred (*CA 2006, s 171*). This duty replaces similar pre-existing duties.

In *Extrasure Travel Insurances Ltd v Scattergood* [2003] 1 BCLC 598 (applied in *Re HLC Environmental Projects Ltd (in liquidation)* [2013] EWHC 2876 (Ch)), it was held (at [92]) that the court must apply a four stage test:

First, identify the power whose exercise is in question;

Second, identify the proper purpose for which the power was delegated to the directors;

Third, identify the substantial purpose for which the power was in fact exercised; and

Finally, decide whether that purpose was proper.

See also *Madoff Securities International Ltd (in liquidation) v Raven* [2013] EWHC 3147 (Comm); [2014] Lloyd's Rep FC 95 at [196].

The Outer House of the Scottish Court of Session held in *Eastford Ltd v Thomas Graham Gillespie* [2009] CSOH 119 that this provision did not prevent the subsequent ratification of an act performed by a director.

9.19   **Duty to promote the success of the company**

A director of a company is required to act in the way he considers, in good faith, would be most likely to promote the success of the company for the benefit of its members as a whole. In doing this, he must have regard to:

(a)   the likely consequences of any decision in the long term,

(b)   the interests of the company's employees,

(c)   the need to foster the company's business relationships with suppliers, customers and others,

(d)   the impact of the company's operations on the community and the environment,

(e)   the desirability of the company maintaining a reputation for high standards of business conduct, and

(f)   the need to act fairly as between members of the company.

(CA 2006, s 172(1)).

This duty replaces the common law duty to act in good faith in the company's interests. The duty also overlaps with the duty to avoid conflicts of interest, see below at **9.22**.

'Success' is not defined in *CA 2006*. The DTI guidance notes suggest that it should be taken to mean 'long-term increases in value'.

The duty is subjective in the sense that directors must act in a way which they reasonably believe is likely to promote success: see *Regentcrest plc (in liquidation) v Cohen* [2001] 2 BCLC 80 at [120] – but see the qualifications set out in *Re Cosy Seal Insulation Ltd (In Administration)* [2016] EWJC 1255 (Ch); [2016] 2 BCLC 319.

Section 172 raises but does not answer a number of questions. It is not clear whether the company maintains its own interests separate from the interests of its current members at any time. This may be relevant, for example, to the question of whether a director can recommend the lower of two competing bids if it is considered that this is in the long term interests of the company albeit not in the interests of its existing members.

Another issue may arise if the factors to which the directors must have regard conflict. However, all that is required is that a director 'have regard to' the factors set out in *s 172*. Accordingly, so long as the factors are considered, it will not matter if some of the considerations point in different directions. It would be good practice for board minutes to refer to the factors in *s 172* when documenting the decision making process.

While the interests of a company are normally identified with those of its members, the interests of creditors as a class may be relevant if the company is in financial difficulties· *GHLM Trading Ltd v Maroo* [2012] EWHC 61 (Ch) at [164]. A useful summary of the law can be found in *Re HLC Environmental Projects Ltd (in liquidation)* [2013] EWHC 2876 (Ch) at [88], where it was held that the underlying principle is that directors are not free to take action which puts at real (as opposed to remote) risk the creditors' prospects of being paid. However, in *BTI v Sequana* [2016] EWHC 1686 (Ch); [2017] Bus LR 82, it was held that the duty to consider creditors' interests did not extend for the whole of the period in which there was a risk of insufficient assets.

The duty is "subjective" in the sense that the question is whether the director honestly believed that his act or omission was in the interests of the company: see *Madoff Securities International Ltd (in liquidation) v Raven* [2013] EWHC 3147 (Comm); [2014] Lloyd's Rep FC 95. However, this may be subject to exceptions: see the HLC case at [91]-[92].

9.19   Directors

For an employed director, the duty of good faith arises both in his or her capacity as an employee, and as a director by which he or she owes various fiduciary duties to the company. There is a distinction between a director's fiduciary duties and an employee's obligation of fidelity.

9.20   Duty to exercise independent judgment

A company director is required to exercise 'independent judgment'. However, this duty is not infringed by acting in accordance with agreements entered into by the company or as authorised by the company's constitution (*CA 2006, s 173*).

This was some extent a new duty and there is no exactly equivalent duty at common law (but see *Lonrho Ltd v Shell Petroleum* [1980] 1 WLR 627 at 634F).

The government stated in debate that this duty will not prevent directors from relying on the judgment of others in areas in which they are not expert and/or to delegate matters to committees. The duty is likely, however, to require individual directors to exercise independent judgment in deciding whether or not to accept advice or judgment from others even in such circumstances.

See *CF Booth Ltd, Re* [2017] EWHC 457 (Ch) for an example of a case of breach of this duty where directors had paid themselves excessive remuneration while following a policy of no dividends.

9.21   Duty to exercise reasonable care, skill and diligence

A director of a company must exercise 'reasonable care, skill and diligence' (*CA 2006, s 174(1)*). This is defined to mean the care, skill and diligence that would be exercised by a reasonably diligent person with the general knowledge, skill and experience that may reasonably be expected of a person carrying out the functions carried out by the director in relation to the company, and the general knowledge, skill and experience that the individual director has (*CA 2006, s 174(2)*). These provisions mean that the standard of care and skill required of a director will not be the same for all directors. It will depend not only on the nature of the company but also on the individual circumstances of the director in question (as well as on general, objective criteria: see [207] of *Madoff Securities International Ltd (in liquidation) v Raven* [2013] EWHC 3147 (Comm); [2014] Lloyd's Rep FC 95).

Prior to the coming into force of *CA 2006*, the classic exposition of the general (implied) duties of a director was stated by Romer J in *Re City Equitable Fire Insurance Co Ltd* [1925] Ch 407:

> 'In order therefore to ascertain the duties that a person appointed to the board of an established company undertakes to perform, it is necessary to consider not only the nature of the company's business but also the manner in which the work of the company is in fact distributed between the directors and other officials of the company, provided also that this distribution is a reasonable one in the circumstances and not inconsistent with any express provisions in the articles of association. In discharging the duties of his position thus ascertained, a director must, of course, act honestly; he must also exercise some degree of both skill and diligence. To the question of what is the particular degree of skill and diligence required of him, the authorities do not I think give any clear answers. It has been laid down that so long as a director acts honestly he cannot be made responsible in damages unless guilty of gross or culpable negligence in a business sense'.

Romer J went on to set out the following specific principles:

> '(1)   A director need not exhibit in the performance of his duties a greater degree of skill than may reasonably be expected from a person of his

knowledge and experience. A director of a life insurance company, for instance, does not guarantee that he has the skill of an actuary or physician . . .

(2)   A director is not bound to give continuous attention to the affairs of his company. His duties are of an intermittent nature to be performed at periodical board meetings, and at meetings of any committee of the board upon which he happens to be placed . . .

(3)   In respect of all duties that, having regard to the exigencies of the business, and the articles of association, may properly be left to some other official, a director is, in the absence of grounds for suspicion, justified in trusting that official to perform such duties honestly.'

These principles were applied in *Northampton Regional Livestock Centre Co Ltd v Cowling* [2014] EWHC 30 (QB) (a point not considered in the appeal).

In *Madoff Securities International Ltd (in liquidation) v Raven* [2013] EWHC 3147 (Comm), it was held that directors' failure to apply their minds to whether a proposed act was in the interests of the company was a dereliction of the duty (see [265]).

Where a director is also an employee, the legal position is different. This is because an employee impliedly undertakes that he possesses, and will exercise, reasonable skill and competence in the work which he undertakes (*Harmer v Cornelius* (1858) 5 CBNS 236 and *Lister v Romford Ice and Cold Storage Co Ltd* [1957] AC 555). He owes an implied duty to his employer to take such reasonable care and skill in his work. (For other implied duties of employees see CONTRACT OF EMPLOYMENT (8)). These duties go beyond those set out in *Re City Equitable* and in CA 2006. These higher duties would apply to a director who is also an employee. Any breach of these implied duties may constitute a repudiatory breach of the contract, and therefore justify a company in terminating the employment contract without notice. If the contract is terminated, the director will usually be under a contractual obligation to resign his office with the company.

9.22 Duty to avoid conflicts of interest

Section 175 of *CA 2006* imposes a duty on directors to avoid conflicts of interest. These are situations in which the director has or could have a direct or indirect interest that conflicts, or possibly may conflict with, the interests of the company. The duty is expressed to apply particularly to the exploitation of any property, information or opportunity. It is immaterial whether the company could itself take advantage of any of these (*CA 2006, s 175(2)*). The duty does not apply to a conflict arising in relation to a transaction or arrangement with the company.

There are two exceptions to the duty. First, it is not infringed if the situation cannot reasonably be regarded as likely to give rise to a conflict of interest. Secondly, there is no breach where the matter has been authorised (*s 175(4)* and see *Bristol and West Building Society v Mothew* [1998] Ch 1 at 18 for the pre-existing law). For a private company, authorisation may be given by the matter being proposed to and authorised by the directors (unless this is invalidated by something in the company's constitution) (*s 175(5)(a)*). For a public company, where the constitution enables directors to authorise the matter, authorisation may be given by the matter being proposed and authorised in accordance with the constitution (*s 175(5)(b)*). (Public companies may wish to ensure that their articles of association allow for this.) Authorisation is only effective if any quorum requirement is met without including the potentially interested director and the matter was agreed without (or not counting) the vote of the interested director (*s 175(6)*). For a case where it was held that there was no liability as the shareholders acquiesced in what would otherwise have constituted a breach, see *Sharma v Sharma* [2013] EWCA Civ 1287, [2014] BCC 73.

A number of authorities have emphasised the strict application of the rules. For example, the case of *Towers v Premier Waste Management* [2011] EWCA Civ 923, [2012] IRLR 73, above, did not engage the new statutory duties. However, Mummery LJ emphasised the strictness of the no-conflict duty in that it does not depend on proof of fault on behalf of the director or of loss on behalf of the company. A director is in breach regardless of whether he acted in good faith or whether the company could not itself have exploited the opportunity. See also the recent case of *Invideous v Thorogood* [2013] EWHC 3015 (Ch).

The duties of an executive director may be more extensive than the parallel duty of a director who is not employed. For example, in the very old case *London and Mashonaland Exploration Co Ltd v New Mashonaland Exploration Co Ltd* [1891] WN 165, it was held that a director (albeit a dummy director who did not attend board meetings) did not commit any breach of duty by being appointed a director of a competing company. By contrast, if a full time employee works for a competing company part-time without the consent of his full-time employer, this has been held to amount to a serious breach of his contract: see *Hivac Ltd v Park Royal Scientific Instruments Ltd* [1946] Ch 169. This principle also applies to employed directors. For example, in *Thomas Marshall (Exports) Ltd v Guinle* [1979] Ch 227, [1978] ICR 905, a managing director traded on his own account on behalf of two other companies which he had set up in competition with the company. His service agreement had expressly provided that, while employed as a managing director, he would not engage in any other business without the company's consent. He was held to be in breach of his obligation of fidelity and good faith as an employee and in breach of his fiduciary duty as a director.

There is no free-standing duty requiring an employed director to disclose his own wrongdoing (albeit that there is a duty to disclose their own interests in some circumstances, see **9.12**, above). However, the fundamental common law duty to act in good faith in the interests of the company may require an employed director to disclose his own wrongdoing in certain circumstances, particularly where the wrongdoing constitutes a breach of fiduciary duties. For example, in *Item Software (UK) Ltd v Fassihi* [2004] EWCA Civ 1244, [2005] ICR 450, [2004] IRLR 928, the Court of Appeal held that an employed director was under a duty to disclose his own misconduct in seeking to divert a contract from the company to another company which he himself owned. In these circumstances, the company could recover damages for loss caused by the breach of duty. (Such a duty may also apply to senior employees, see *Tesco Stores Ltd v Pook* [2003] EWHC 823 (Ch), [2004] IRLR 618 and *Helmet Integrated Systems Ltd v Tunnard* [2006] EWCA Civ 1735, [2007] IRLR 126.) Although *Fassihi* was described as a "controversial" decision in *Brandeaux Advisers (UK) Ltd v Chadwick* [2010] EWHC 3241 (QB) at [47], it has been followed, see, for example he Court of Appeal in *Customer Systems plc v Ranson* [2012] EWCA Civ 841, [2012] IRLR 769. See also *GHLM Trading Ltd v Maroo* [2012] EWHC 61 (Ch) for a case in which the claimants failed to establish breach. In *Odyssey Entertainment Limited (in liquidation) v Kamp* [2012] EWHC 2316 (Ch), it was held that where a director is seriously considering carrying on a similar business to that of the company, and is recommending closing the business, those intentions must be disclosed.

Directors (and senior employees) may be under a duty not to prepare to compete with their existing employers and, if they do so, to disclose their wrongdoing to their employer. Whether or not such a duty exists and whether or not a director will be found to be in breach of the duty depends very much upon the circumstances of an individual case. For contrasting examples, see *Tunnard* (where the employee was not in breach), *Shepherds Investments Ltd v Walters* [2006] EWHC 836 (Ch), [2007] IRLR 110 (where the director was in breach) and *Crowson Fabrics Ltd v Rider* [2007] EWHC 2942 (Ch), [2008] IRLR 288. In *Attwood Holdings Ltd v Woodward* [2009] EWHC 1083 (Ch), an employed director was held to be in breach of duty by failing to alert a company to an impending threat of competition from him and a colleague, by taking preparatory steps including approaches to customers and by retaining confidential information. At first instance, in *Customer Systems plc v Ranson* [2011] EWHC 3304 (QB), Sir Raymond Jack held that an employee had owed fiduciary duties but had been entitled to discuss plans for his future with third parties, to set up a potential contracting company without advising the company but not to obtain contracting work or transfer his business contacts from his company mobile phone for his own purposes. However, the Court of Appeal ([2012] EWCA Civ 841, [2012] IRLR 769) overturned that decision, on the basis that the employee was not a fiduciary at all.

Directors are likely to be under a duty to disclose the wrongdoing of their colleagues, whether subordinate or superior (for an example, see *Walters*, above). This duty applies regardless of whether this would inevitably involve the disclosure of the director's own misconduct (*Sybron Corpn v Rochem Ltd* [1984] Ch 112, [1983] 2 All ER 707).

In *QBE Management Services (UK) Ltd v Dymoke* [2012] EWHC 80 (QB), [2012] IRLR 458, Haddon-Cave J held that directors were under a positive duty to inform the company in a timely manner of any activity, actual or threatened, which might damage the company's interest.

A breach of any duty to disclose may lead to a subsequent agreement for payment to a director being avoided on grounds of mistake. This could include, for example, a termination payment. The Court of Appeal accepted in *Horcal Ltd v Gatland* [1984] IRLR 288 that a director was not under a duty to disclose his own intended wrongdoing. Accordingly, the company was not entitled to recover a termination payment in a situation where the director had not committed any wrongful act at the date of the termination agreement. A company may even be liable to the director for any unpaid salary earned by the director from the time of a breach of duty until termination, even where the breach could have justified summary dismissal had the company been aware of it (*Healey v Francaise Rubastic SA* [1917] 1 KB 946).

In *Re Allied Business and Financial Consultants Ltd: O'Donnell v Shanahan* [2009] EWCA Civ 75, [2009] BCC 822, a case concerning facts prior to the coming into force of the statutory duties, the Court of Appeal held that a director who takes personal advantage of information or an opportunity which comes to him in his capacity as a director will be liable even if the information or opportunity regards a matter outside the scope of the company's business.

In *Foster Bryant Surveying Ltd v Bryant* [2007] EWCA Civ 200, [2007] IRLR 425, the Court of Appeal reviewed the law relating to a director's fiduciary duties during a period of notice after he had resigned but before he had left office. In general terms, the director must act towards his company with honesty, good faith and loyalty, and must avoid any conflict of interest. On the facts of Bryant, a director who had resigned in innocent circumstances was not in breach of fiduciary duty when he agreed to be retained by a company's main client after his resignation became effective.

9.23 Duty not to accept benefits from third parties

A company director must not accept a benefit from a third party which is conferred by reason of his being a director or his doing (or refraining from doing) anything as director (*CA 2006, s 176*). A third party is any person other than the company, an associated body corporate or a person acting on one of their behalves. Benefits received by a director from a person by whom his services are provided to the company are not regarded as conferred by a third party (*s 176(3)*). The duty is not infringed if the acceptance of the benefit cannot reasonably be regarded as likely to give rise to a conflict of interest (*s 176(4)*). Such

9.24 Continuing obligations

A person who ceases to be a director continues to be subject to the duty to avoid conflicts of interest (set out in *s 175*) as regards the exploitation of any property, information or opportunity of which he became aware at a time when he was a director (*s 170(2)(a)*). Such a person will also continue to be subject to the duty not to accept benefits from third parties (set out in *s 176*) as regards things done or not done by him before he ceased to be a director (*s 170(2)(b)*).

In *Thermasacan v Norman* [2009] EWHC 3694 (Ch), [2011] BCC 535, the Court of Appeal held that *ss 170* and *175* could not be relied upon to extend the pre-existing law so as to support a blanket prohibition on canvassing or soliciting the business of any client of the company. The Court of Appeal analysed previous authority (*CMS Dolphin Ltd v Simonet* [2002] BCC 600, *Hunter Kane Ltd v Watkins* [2003] EWHC 186 (Ch) and *Foster Bryant Surveying Ltd v Bryant* [2007] EWCA Civ 200) and summarised its effects as follows:

(a)   A director is precluded from taking any property or business advantage, especially where he was a participant in the negotiations, even after his resignation, if the resignation was prompted or influenced by a desire to acquire for himself any maturing business opportunity.

(b)   However, a director is entitled to resign and is then entitled to use his general fund of skill and knowledge acquired while a director. This may even include business contacts and personal connections.

9.25   Indemnity

An employee is entitled to be indemnified by his employer in respect of expenses, costs and claims incurred by him on behalf of his employer during the proper performance of his duties as an employee. An employed director is similarly entitled to such an indemnity. This entitlement may be expressly set out under the articles. For example, under the Model Articles for Private Companies Limited by Shares (*para 20 of Sch 1* to the *MA Regulations*), the company may pay any reasonable expenses which the directors properly incur in connection with their attendance at meetings of directors or committees of directors, general meetings, or separate meetings of the holders of any class of shares or of debentures of the company, or otherwise in connection with the exercise of their powers and the discharge of their responsibilities in relation to the company. (For private companies limited by shares, see *para 20 of Sch 2* and for public companies, see *para 24 of Sch 3*.) In respect of companies incorporated before 1 October 2009, see *art 83 of Table A*.

However, there is a statutory limit on the scope of indemnities that may be afforded to a director (whether or not he is employed). Any provision that purports to exempt a director from any liability in connection with any negligence, default, breach of duty or breach of trust in relation to the company is void unless at least one of the following three exceptions applies. The first exception is that a company may purchase and maintain insurance (*CA 2006, s 232 (2)(a)*, *s 233*). The second exception is a 'qualifying third party indemnity provision'. A 'qualifying third party indemnity provision' is provision for indemnity against liability incurred by the director to a person other than the company (or an associated company) where the following two conditions are satisfied.

(1)   The indemnity is not against any liability to pay a fine imposed in criminal proceedings or a sum payable to a regulatory body by way of penalty in respect of non-compliance with any requirement of a regulatory nature.

(2)   The indemnity is not against any liability incurred by the director in defending any criminal proceedings in which he is convicted (and the conviction has become final) or in defending any civil proceedings brought by the company or an associated company in which judgment is given against him, or in connection with any application under any specified provisions in which the court refuses to grant him relief. These provisions are *s 661(3)* or *(4)* (acquisition of shares by innocent nominee) or *s 1157* of *CA 2006* (general power to grant relief in case of honest and reasonable conduct). (With regard to *s 1157* see further **9.26** below.)

(*CA 2006, s 234.*)

The third exception is a 'qualifying pension scheme indemnity provision'. A 'qualifying pension scheme indemnity' is a provision indemnifying a director who is a trustee of an occupational pension scheme against liability incurred in connection with the company's activities as trustee of the scheme which meets the following conditions.

(1)   The indemnity is not against any liability of the director to pay a fine imposed in criminal proceedings or a sum payable to a regulatory body by way of penalty in respect of non-compliance with any requirement of a regulatory nature.

(2)   The provision does not provide any indemnity against any liability incurred by the director in defending criminal proceedings in which he is convicted (and the conviction has become final).

(*CA 2006, s 235.*)

Qualifying third party indemnity provision and qualifying pension scheme indemnity provision must be disclosed in the directors' report. The rules governing this disclosure are set out at *s 236* of *CA 2006*. Copies of any qualifying indemnity provision must be kept available for inspection (*CA 2006, s 237*) and must be open to inspection by any member of the company without charge (*CA 2006, s 238*).

9.26   Relief from liability

Section 1157 of *CA 2006* applies where a director is facing proceedings for negligence, default, breach of duty or breach of trust. In such circumstances, if it appears to the court hearing the case that the director has acted honestly and reasonably and, in all the circumstances (including those connected with his appointment) he ought fairly to be excused, that court may relieve him either wholly or partly from his liability on such terms as it thinks fit. Where such a director is tried by a judge with a jury, the judge may withdraw the case in whole or in part from the jury if satisfied that relief should be granted, and direct that judgment be entered for the defendant on such terms as are considered appropriate (*CA 2006, s 1157(3)*).

If a director has reason to believe that any such proceedings will or might be brought against him, he may apply to the court for relief and the court has the same power of relief as set out above (*CA 2006, s 1157(2)*).

See *Towers v Premier Waste* [2011] EWCA Civ 923 for a case where the court refused to relieve a director from liability pursuant to *section 1157* and *Northampton Regional Livestock Centre Co Ltd* [2014] EWHC 30 (QB) where a court would have been prepared to grant such relief. The relief may be available even where a director has failed to exercise reasonable care at common law: *Re D'Jan of London* [1993] BCC 646 per Hoffman LJ at 649. In *McGivney Construction Ltd v Kaminski* [2015] CSOH 107, the Outer House of the Scottish Court of Session held that a director would require a strong case for relief where he or she had obtained a material personal benefit.

9.27   REMUNERATION

There is nothing in *CA 2006* to restrict or determine the amount of remuneration which may be paid to a director. The model articles set out in the *Schedules* to the *MA Regulations* provide that directors are entitled to such remunerations as the directors determine (a) for their services to the company as directors, and (b) for any other service which they undertake for the company. Subject to the articles, a director's remuneration may take any form and include arrangements in connection with the payment of a pension, allowance or gratuity or any death, sickness or disability benefits. Unless the directors decide otherwise, the remuneration accrues from day to day (see *para 19 of Sch 1, para 19 of Sch 2* and *para 23 of Sch 3*, as appropriate).

9.27   Directors

Article 82 of *Table A*, for companies incorporated before 1 October 2009, provides in relation to non-executive directors that:

> 'The director shall be entitled to such remuneration as the company may by ordinary resolution determine and, unless the resolution provides otherwise, the remuneration shall be deemed to accrue from day to day.'

With regard to executive directors appointed in accordance with the model articles (see **9.2** above), the amount of remuneration is a matter for the board. So long as the board exercises its power in good faith in accordance with the relevant provisions of the model code (or *art 84*, as appropriate), the company will be unable to avoid the terms agreed for remuneration. However, if remuneration is set at an excessive level, this might provide evidence of a failure to exercise the power in good faith.

However, amendments made to *CA 2006* which have been in force since 1 October 2013 mean that a quoted company may not make a remuneration payment to a present, past or future director unless that payment is consistent with the approved directors' remuneration policy or is approved by resolution of the members of the company (*CA 2006, s 226B*). The "approved directors' remuneration policy" is the most recent remuneration policy to have been approved by a resolution passed by the members of the company in general meeting (*CA 2006, s 226B*). The same is true of payments for loss of office (*CA 2006, s 226C*).

A resolution approving such remuneration or payment for loss of office must not be passed unless a memorandum setting out particulars of the proposed payment including its amount is made available for inspection by the company's members at the registered office for not less than 15 days and at the relevant meeting itself (*CA 2006, s 226D*). It must be made available on the company's website (*CA 2006, s 226D(3)*). The memorandum must explain the ways in which the payment is inconsistent with the approved directors' remuneration policy (*CA 2006, s 226D(2)*).

An obligation to make a payment which would be in contravention of these rules has no effect (*CA 2006, s 226E(1)*). Any payment made in contravention of these rules is held by the recipient on trust for whoever is making the payment and, in the case of a company, any director who authorised the payment is jointly and severally liable to indemnify the company that made the payment for any lsos resulting from it (*CA 2006, s 226E(2)*). However, a director may be relieved wholly or partly from liability if the director shows that he or she has acted honestly and reasonably and the court considers that, having regard to all the circumstances of the case, the director ought to be relieved of liability (*CA 2006, s 226E(5)*).

There are further detailed provisions in *s 226E* for payments made for loss of office in connection with transfers of undertaking, property or shares.

It is also noted that the excessive payment of remuneration to directors may be in breach of the directors' other duties pursuant to *ss 170* to *176* of the *Companies Act 2006*. See, for example, *CF Booth Ltd* [2017] EWHC 457 (Ch).

9.28   Guidance: the Governance Code

A brief explanation of the operation of the Governance Code is set out at para **9.15** above. With regard to directors' remuneration, the Governance Code recommends that the board of directors establish a remuneration committee with delegated responsibility for setting remuneration levels for all executive directors and the chairman. Section D of the Governance Code contains the relevant recommendations.

Level of remuneration

In relation to the level of remuneration, the Governance Code sets out the following "Main Principle":

"Executive directors' remuneration should be designed to promote the long-term success of the company. Performance related elements should be transparent, stretching and rigorously applied.""

There are two "Supporting Principles" that relate to executive directors' pay:

(a)   The remuneration committee should judge where to position their company relative to other companies. But they should use such comparisons with caution, in view of the risk of an upward ratchet of remuneration levels with no corresponding improvement in corporate and individual performance, and should avoid paying more than is necessary.

(b)   They should also be sensitive to pay and employment conditions elsewhere in the group, especially when determining annual salary increases.

Schedule A to the Governance Code then sets out the provisions which remuneration committees should follow in designing schemes of performance-related remuneration for executive directors. For example:

(a)   The remuneration committee should determine an appropriate balance between fixed and performance-related, immediate and deferred remuneration.

(b)   Performance conditions, including non-financial metrics where appropriate, should be relevant, stretching and designed to promote the long-term success of the company.

(c)   Remuneration incentives should be compatible with risk policies and systems. Upper limits should be set and disclosed.

(d)   The remuneration committee should consider whether the directors should be eligible for annual bonuses and/or benefits under long-term incentive structures.

(e)   Share options should be weighed against other kinds of long-term investment. Executive share options should not be offered at a discount save as permitted by the Listing Rules.

(f)   Any new long-term incentive schemes which are proposed should be approved by shareholders and should preferably replace existing schemes or at least form part of an overall plan.

(g)   For share-based remuneration, the remuneration committee should consider requiring directors to hold a minimum number of shares and to hold shares for a further period after vesting or exercise, including for a period after leaving the company, subject to certain needs. In normal circumstances, shares granted or other forms of deferred remuneration should not vest or be paid, and options should not be exercisable, in less than three years. Longer periods may be appropriate.

(h)   Only basic pay should be pensionable. The remuneration committee should consider the pension consequences to the company of changes to pensionable remuneration, especially for directors close to retirement.

In addition, the Governance Code provides that:

(a)   Remuneration schemes should include provisions that would enable the company to recover sums paid or withhold the payment of any sum, and specify the circumstances in which it would be appropriate to do so (D.1.1).

(b)   Where a company releases an executive director to serve as a non-executive director elsewhere, the remuneration report (see below at [9.31]–[9.32] should include a statement as to whether or not the director will retain such earnings and if so, what the remuneration is (D.1.2).

(c)   The remuneration committee should carefully consider what compensation commitments (including pension contributions) their directors' terms of appointment would entail in the event of early termination. The aim should be to avoid rewarding poor performance. They should take a robust line on reducing compensation to reflect departing directors' obligations to mitigate loss (D.1.4).

Procedure

In relation to the procedure to be adopted in determining remuneration, the "Main Principle" is that:

"There should be a formal and transparent procedure for developing policy on executive remuneration and for fixing the remuneration packages of individual directors (Main Principles, Section D). No director should be involved in deciding his or her own remuneration."

There are two "Supporting Principles":

(a)   The remuneration committee should take care to recognise and manage conflicts of interest when receiving views from executive directors or senior management, or consulting the chief executive about its proposals. The remuneration committee should also be responsible for appointing any consultants in respect of executive director remuneration.

(b)   The chairman of the board should ensure that the committee chairman maintains contact as required with its principal shareholders about remuneration.

The detailed relevant provisions include:

(a)   The board should establish a remuneration committee of at least three, or in the case of smaller companies (ie outside the FTSE 350) two, independent non-executive directors. In addition the company chairman may also be a member of, but not chair, the committee if he or she was considered independent on appointment as chairman. The remuneration committee should make available its terms of reference, explaining its role and the authority delegated to it by the board. Where remuneration consultants are appointed, they should be identified in the annual report and a statement should be made available of whether they have any other connection with the company (D.2.1).

(b)   The remuneration committee should have delegated responsibility for setting remuneration for all executive directors and the chairman, including pension rights and any compensation payments. The committee should also recommend and monitor the level and structure of remuneration for senior management. The definition of 'senior management' for this purpose should be determined by the board but should normally include the first layer of management below board level (D.2.2).

(c)   Shareholders should be invited specifically to approve all new long-term incentive schemes and significant changes to existing schemes, save in permitted circumstances (D.2.4).

9.29   Guidance: the Stewardship Code

The UK Stewardship Code, published in September 2012 sets out the Financial Reporting Council's ("FRC") principles of effective stewardship by investors. The Stewardship Code is directed to institutional investors, ie asset owners and asset managers with equity holdings in UK listed companies. It states that the FRC expects signatories of the Code to publish on their website or in another accessible form a statement that describes how the signatory has applied each of the seven principles of the Code or explains why an element of the Code has not been complied with. This is the same "comply or explain" basis as that which applies in relation to the Governance Code.

The third principle is that institutional investors should monitor their investee companies. This includes seeking to satisfy themselves that the company's board and committees adhere to the spirit of the UK Corporate Governance Code. This will include satisfying themselves that the company has complied with the provisions described in paragraph **[9.28]** above in relation to directors' remuneration.

The fourth principle is that institutional investors should establish clear guidelines on when and how they will escalate their stewardship activities. The Code advises that instances when institutional investors may want to intervene include when they have concerns about the company's remuneration.

9.30   The Remuneration Codes

It should also be noted that an executive director of any organisation which is authorised by the Financial Conduct Authority ("FCA") and/or the Prudential Regulatory Authority ("PRA") may be subject to the FCA's Remuneration Codes or the remuneration part of the PRA Handbook. As such, provisions of those codes will apply to the assessment, method and timing of payment of that director's variable remuneration.

The details of these are outside the scope of this work.

9.31   Disclosure of directors' remuneration

The law on the disclosure of directors' remuneration changed with effect from 1 October 2013 for quoted companies with the introduction of a requirement to produce a new style remuneration report. (Quoted companies are defined as those registered in the UK with equity listed on the main market. AIM listed companies are not included). The relevant provisions are explained at **[9.32]** below. Even before that time, there were a number of requirements as to disclosure which apply to all companies and which continue to apply.

Section 412 of *CA 2006* empowered the Secretary of State to make regulations requiring certain information to be given in notes to a company's annual accounts about directors' remuneration.

The relevant regulations are the *Large and Medium-sized Companies and Groups (Accounts and Reports) Regulations 2008 (SI 2008/410)* ('*2008 Regulations*'). They apply to all companies other than those subject to the small companies regime: see below at **[9.33]**.

Companies are required to provide information about directors' remuneration in notes to the company's accounts (*reg 8* and *Sch 5, 2008 Regulations*). Some of the provisions apply to both quoted and unquoted companies. Quoted companies are exempted from some of these provisions but are instead subject to the regime described at **[9.32]** below.

Both quoted and unquoted companies must provide information as to:

(a)   the aggregate amount of remuneration paid to or receivable by directors;

(b)   the aggregate of the amount of gains made by directors on the exercise of share options;

(c)   the aggregate of the amount of money paid to or receivable by directors, and the net value of assets (other than money and share options) received or receivable by directors under long term incentive schemes; and

(d)   the aggregate value of any company contributions paid (or treated as paid) to a pension scheme in respect of directors and by reference to which the rate or amount of any money purchase benefits that may become payable will be calculated.

(*Sch 5, para 1(1)*.)

They must also provide information as to the number of directors (if any) to whom retirement benefits are accruing under money purchase schemes and under defined benefit schemes.

(*Sch 5, para 1(2)*.)

(The rules are slightly different for companies which are unquoted and whose equity share capital is not listed on AIM: see *para 1(3)*.)

Unquoted (but not quoted) companies must provide additional information in notes to the accounts as to details of the highest paid directors' emoluments (where the aggregates in (a), (b) and (c) above total £200,000 or more) (*para 2*). They are also required to provide information as to retirement benefits (*para 3*), compensation for loss of office (*para 4*), and sums paid to third parties in respect of directors' services (*para 5*).

A director, or anyone who has been a director in the last five years, is obliged to give notice to the company of those matters relating to himself that may be necessary for these purposes (*CA 2006, s 412(5)*). Any default is an offence which is punishable by a fine not exceeding level 3 on the standard scale (*CA 2006, s 412(6)*).

(For the application of *s 412*, with modifications, to unregistered companies, see the *Unregistered Companies Regulations 2009, SI 2009/2436*.)

9.32   *Quoted companies*

Quoted companies are required to prepare a directors' remuneration report (see *s 420* of *CA 2006*). *Schedule 8* to the *2008 Regulations* sets out the information that must be contained in the report and requirements as to how it should be set out.

A new style of directors' remuneration report has been required for quoted companies since 1 October 2013. This report must now contain the information specified in *Parts 2, 3,* and *4* of *Schedule 8* to the *2008 Regulations* as amended by the *Large and Medium-sized Companies and Groups (Accounts and Reports)(Amendment) Regulations 2013 (SI 2013/1981)*. In particular, it must contain:

(a)   a statement by the director who fulfils the role of chair of the remuneration committee (or, if there is no chair, by a director nominated by the directors to make the statement) summarising for the relevant financial year the major decisions on directors' remuneration; any substantial changes relating to directors' remuneration and the context in which those changes occurred and decisions have been taken (Part 2);

(b)   specified information in a table in the form set out in Part 3 setting out, for each director, the total amount of salary and fees, all taxable benefits, money or other assets received as a result of performance measures and targets, all pension related benefits and any other items in the nature of remuneration together with a total figure as well as a comparison with the previous year. (there are precise and detailed provisions setting out the meaning of each of these terms and what must be set out, to which the reader is referred);

(c)   specified information about pensions for those directors who have a prospective entitlement setting out the details of those rights, a description of any additional early retirement benefits and separate details relating to each type of pension benefit (para 13 of Part 3);

(d)   specified details of any scheme interest awarded to each director (para 14);

(e)   specified details of any payments of money or other assets to past directors (para 15);

(f)   specified details of any payments to directors for loss of office (para 16);

(g)   a statement of any requirements or guidelines for each director to own shares and whether these have been met and a table setting out the number of interests in shares of the director and any connected person (para 17);

(h)   a line graph showing shareholder returns on holdings (para 18(1);

(i)   for the director undertaking the role of chief executive officer, a table setting out total remuneration, and other information as set out in para 18(2);

(j)   percentage changes from previous years (para 19);

(k)   a graph or table showing the expenditure of the company and difference in spend on employee remuneration, shareholder distribution and any other significant distributions deemed to assist in understanding the relative importance of spending on pay in respect of the relevant financial year and the previous financial year (para 20);

(l)   a statement describing how the company intends to implement the approved directors' remuneration policy in the next financial year including, where applicable, performance measures and their relative weightings, performance targets and how awards will be calculated (para 21);

(m)   details of any committee which has considered matters relating to directors' remuneration (para 22);

(n)   a statement setting out specified information about voting in respect of the directors' remuneration report and policy (para 23);

The report must also include a separate section setting out the directors' remuneration policy ("Remuneration Policy") as required by *Part 4* of *Schedule 8*. The Remuneration Policy sets out how the company proposes to pay directors, including all forms of remuneration, and explains how that proposal supports the company's long-term strategy and performance. The remuneration policy also includes details of the company's proposed approach to payments relating to recruitment and loss of office. There are specific and detailed provisions as to the precise requirements in *Part 4*. Companies must take care to follow those precise requirements which are not set out in full here.

Shareholders have a binding vote on a resolution to approve the remuneration policy. Companies are required to put their remuneration policy to a shareholder resolution at the first AGM and thereafter at least every three years. If a company wishes to make changes to the remuneration policy, it has to put a new policy to shareholders for approval at a general meeting.

Once a remuneration policy has been approved, a company is only able to make remuneration and loss of office payments which are permitted within the limits of the policy, unless separately approved by shareholder resolution (see above at [9.27]).

Shareholders have an annual advisory vote on a resolution to approve the implementation report. If a company fails to pass this resolution in a year in which the remuneration policy was not put to a shareholder resolution, this will trigger a requirement to put the remuneration policy to shareholders the following year.

9.33   *Special provisions for small companies*

These requirements do not apply for companies which fall under the 'small companies regime' for financial years which commenced after 1 January 2016 (or after 1 January 2015, with the directors' agreement). A small company is a company in respect of which the following conditions are satisfied:

(a)   The turnover is not more than £10.2 million;

(b)   The balance sheet total is not more than £5.1 million;

(c)   The company has not more than 50 employees.

(*CA 2006, s 382*, as amended.)

Detailed rules as to how these are calculated are found in *s 382* of *CA 2006*.

A parent company only qualifies as small if the group headed by it qualifies as a small group (*s 383(1)*). A group only qualifies as small if the following conditions are satisfied:

(a)   The aggregate turnover is not more than £10.2 million net (or £12.2 million gross);

(b)   The balance sheet total is not more than £5.1 million net (or £6.1 million gross);

(c)   The group has not more than 50 employees.

Again, there are detailed rules about how these should be calculated. They are found in *s 383* of *CA 2006*.

Some companies are ineligible to be small companies. These are any company that was at any time within the relevant financial year:

(a)   a traded company;

(b)   a company which is an authorised insurance company, a banking company, an e-money issuer, a MiFID investment firm or a UCITS management company;

(c)   a company that carries on insurance market activity; or

(d)   a member of an ineligible group.

(*CA 2006, s 384(1)*, as amended.)

A group is ineligible if any of its members is:

(a) a public company;

(b) a body corporate (other than a company) whose shares are admitted to trading on a regulated market in an EEA State;

(c) a person (other than a small company) who has permission under *Part 4A* of the *Financial Services and Markets Act 2000* to carry on a regulated activity;

(ca) an e-money issuer;

(d) a small company which is an authorised insurance company, a banking company, a MiFID investment firm or a UCITS management company; or

(e) a person who carries out insurance market activity.

9.34 *Listing Rules requirements*

Listed companies must make a disclosure statement stating whether they have complied with the Governance Code and, if not, set out those provisions with which they have not complied, the period of non-compliance and the reasons for it (see further above at **9.15**).

Rule 9.8.6 of the *Listing Rules* requires a company to include with its annual reports and accounts a report to the shareholders of the board containing a statement setting out all the interests of each director of the listed company (including the interests of all "connected persons", as defined), including all changes in interests that have occurred between the end of the period under review and one month prior to the date of the notice of the annual general meeting; or a statement that there have been no such changes.

There were further requirements concerning a report to shareholders in relation to directors' remuneration for periods ending before 30 September 2013. However, these requirements have been entirely withdrawn. In effect, they have been replaced by the new requirements for a directors' remuneration report.

9.35   Pensions

Usually, the making of pension arrangements will be regulated by the company's articles of association. The model articles for companies incorporated on or after 1 October 2009 provide that a director's remuneration may take any form and include "any arrangements in connection with the payment of a pension, allowance or gratuity, or any death, sickness or disability benefits, to or in respect of that director" (*para 19, Sch 1, MA Regulations, para 19 of Sch 2, MA Regulations* or, *para 23, Sch 3, MA Regulations*, depending on the type of company).

The making of pension arrangements for directors was expressly authorised by *Article 87* of *Table A. Article 87* of *Table A*, which applies to companies incorporated before 1 October 2009, provides:

> 'The directors may provide benefits, whether by the payment of gratuities or pensions or by insurance or otherwise, for any director who has held but no longer holds any executive office or employment with the company or with any body corporate which is or has been a subsidiary of the company or a predecessor in business of the company or of any such subsidiary, and for any member of his family (including a spouse and a former spouse) or any person who is or was dependent on him, and may (as well before as after he ceases to hold such office or employment) contribute to any fund and pay premiums for the purchase or provision of any such benefit'.

For unquoted companies, the notes of accounts must show the excess retirement benefits paid to or receivable by directors or past directors (*para 3 of Sch 5* to the *Large and Medium-sized Companies and Groups (Accounts and Reports) Regulations 2008 (SI 2008/410)* ('*2008 Regulations*')). The notes must disclose the aggregate of:

(a)   the amount of retirement benefits paid to or receivable by directors under pension schemes; and

(b)   the amount of retirement benefits paid to or receivable by past directors under such schemes,

as, in each case, is in excess of the retirement benefits to which they were each entitled on the date the benefits first became payable or 31 March 1997, whichever is the later.

The aggregate need not include excess amounts if:

(i)   the funding of the scheme was such that the amounts were or could have been paid without recourse to additional contributions; and

(ii)   the amounts were paid to or receivable by all pensioner members of the scheme on the same basis.

Companies which are subject to the 'small companies regime' (see **9.32** above) are not obliged to disclose this information.

For quoted companies, detailed provisions as to the disclosure of retirement benefits in respect of the directors' remuneration report are contained in *para 13 of Sch 8* to the *2008 Regulations*.

9.36 TERMINATION OF DIRECTORS' OFFICE

A company may, by ordinary resolution at a meeting, remove a director from office under *section 168* of *CA 2006*. This power applies regardless of any contrary provisions in the articles of association or in any service agreement. However, the section does not deprive a person removed under it of compensation or damages payable to him in respect of the termination of his appointment, or as circumscribing from any other power to remove a director (*CA 2006, s 168(5)*. Such a power may, for example, derive its authority under the articles.

The ordinary resolution may only be proposed if special notice has been given (pursuant to *CA 2006, s 168(2)*). A director has specified rights to protest against a proposal to remove him from office (see *CA 2006, s 169*).

Any service agreement will usually be terminated by the removal of a director from office. However, this is not invariably so. The outcome will depend on the terms of the service agreement. A person cannot, for example, continue as managing director if he or she is not a director. By contrast, there may be situations in which the office of director is wholly separate from the employment relationship. This might be the case where a manager has no right under the employment contract to be appointed or remain as a director. Such a person may continue in employment as a manager despite the termination of the directorship. If the companies intend that the employment should end if the employee ceases to be a director, the service agreement should include a clause stating this. The converse position may also occur where the employment of an executive director may terminate whilst he or she remains in office. Usually, the board is responsible for terminating the executive appointment of a director, by a majority. Again, if it is intended that the executive appointment should be co-terminous with the appointment as a director, the service agreement should so provide. Service agreements often provide that the executive is required to resign from office as a director (and all other offices held by him in the company) in the event that the employment terminates. Service agreements may also contain power of attorney clauses to effect a resignation if a director fails to resign when he is obliged to do so.

In *Richards v I P Solutions Group* [2017] IRLR 133, the EAT held that where, pursuant to a company's articles of association, a director could be dismissed for a "material breach of a material statutory obligation", this meant a significant breach and not any breach of the duties set out in *CA 2006*.

9.37 Termination payments

It is not lawful for a company to make to a director any payment by way of compensation for loss of office, or as consideration for or in connection with his retirement from office, without particulars of the proposed payment (including the amount) being disclosed to members of the company and the proposal being approved by the company. This restriction is by virtue of s *217* of CA 2006. It does not, however, prevent any payment made in good faith in discharge of an existing legal obligation, by way of damages for breach of an obligation, by way of settlement or compromise of any claim arising in connection with the termination or by way of pension in respect of past services (*CA 2006, s 220(1)*). Approval is not required where the amount concerned does not exceed £200 (*s 221*).

In *Taupo Totara Timber Co Ltd v Rowe* [1978] AC 537, a director was given the right, under the terms of his service agreement, to resign his office following a takeover. Further, he would then be entitled to a payment equivalent to five times his annual salary to be paid tax free. Following a takeover, the director sought to enforce this provision by giving notice. The Privy Council held that the payment did not require shareholder approval since it had been contractually agreed by the company. In that case, there was no suggestion that this was a liquidated damages clause which might amount to an unenforceable penalty clause.

The Privy Council approved the decision in *Taupo Totara Timber Co Ltd v Rowe* in the Australian case of *Lincoln Mills (Australia) Ltd v Gough* [1964] VR 193 in which it was held that the similar (but non-identical) provision in Victorian companies legislation applied only to payment to a director for loss of office and not in respect of loss of the employment (and see also *Lander v Premier Pict Petroleum Ltd* 1997 SLT 1361 in the Court of Session (Outer House).

In *Murray v Leisureplay plc* [2005] EWCA Civ 963, [2005] IRLR 946, the Court of Appeal considered an argument that a clause in a chief executive director's contract providing for the payment of one year's gross salary in the event of termination was unenforceable as a penalty. The Court of Appeal held that a clause will only be held to be a penalty if the party seeking to avoid it can demonstrate that the sum payable on breach is extravagant or unconscionable.

In respect of unquoted companies, details of compensation paid to directors for loss of office must be shown in notes to the accounts (under *Sch 5* to the *2008 Regulations*). There must be shown the aggregate amount of any compensation to director or past directors including compensation receivable for:

(a) loss of office as a director of the company; or

(b) loss, while a director of the company or on or in connection with his ceasing to be a director of it, of any other office in connection with the management of the company's affairs, or any office as director or otherwise in connection with the management of the affairs of any subsidiary undertaking of the company.

References to compensation include benefits otherwise than in cash and in relation to such compensation, references to its amount are to the estimated money value of the benefit. The nature of any such compensation must be disclosed. References to compensation for loss of office include:

(i) compensation in consideration for, or in connection with, a person's retirement from office;

(ii) where that retirement is as a result of a breach of the person's contract with the company or with a subsidiary undertaking, payments by way of damages or settlement in respect of the breach.

With regard to quoted companies, the directors' remuneration report must contain details of any 'significant award' made to any person who was not a director at the time but had previously been a director including compensation in respect of loss of office: *paras 15* and *16* of *Sch 8* to the *2008 Regulations*.

If a payment is made in contravention of *s 217*, it is held by the recipient on trust for the company making the payment and any director who authorised the payment is jointly and severally liable to indemnify the company that made the payment for any loss resulting from it.

Any payments made to directors for loss of office will need to be consistent with the approved remuneration policy or separately approved by a shareholder resolution (see above at **[9.33]**). Furthermore, such payments will need to be disclosed in the remuneration report as set out above.

9.38 *Recommendations*

Paragraph D.1.4 of the Governance Code recommends that remuneration committees consider what compensation commitments, including pension contributions and all other elements, their directors' terms of appointment would entail in the event of early termination. The aim should be to avoid rewarding poor performance. It is recommended that committees take a robust line on reducing compensation to reflect the departing directors' obligations to mitigate loss.

9.39 Directors

9.39 Company approval for property transfer

Payments to a director by way of compensation for loss of office, or as consideration for or in connection with retirement from office, where made in connection with the transfer of the whole or any part of the undertaking or property of a company, must have shareholder approval (*CA 2006, s 218*). Shareholder approval is not required, however, where payment is made of *bona fide* damages for breach of contract or by way of pension for past services (*s 220*). If approval is required but not obtained, the amount received is deemed to be held by the director in trust for the company (*s 222(2)*). Approval is not required where the amount concerned does not exceed £200 (*s 221*).

9.40 Payments on takeover

Payments to a director by way of compensation for loss of office, or as consideration for or in connection with a transfer of shares in the company resulting from a takeover bid, must also have the approval of the relevant shareholders (*CA 2006, s 219*). Again, there is an exception for *bona fide* damages for breach of contract or by way of pension for past services (*s 220*). If approval is required but not obtained, the amount received is deemed to be held by the director in trust for persons who have sold their shares as a result of the offer made. The director is also required to bear the expenses incurred in distributing that sum (*s 222(3)*).

9.41 TRANSFER OF UNDERTAKING

If an undertaking is sold or otherwise transferred or if there is a "service provision change" (see Transfer of Undertaking), the employment of all those employed in the undertaking automatically transfers from the transferor company to the transferee under the *Transfer of Undertakings (Protection of Employment) Regulations 2006 (SI 2006/246) ('TUPE')*. For the purposes of *TUPE*, a contract of employment is defined as any agreement between an employee and his or her employer which determines the conditions of employment. An 'employee' is any individual who works for another person whether under a contract of service or apprenticeship or otherwise but does not include anyone who provides services under a contract for services. Accordingly, an employed director will be an employee for the purposes of *TUPE*. Therefore, if the undertaking or part of undertaking in which the director is employed is transferred, the directors' employment contract will transfer to the transferee.

If the director is entitled under the contract of employment to be appointed director of the company which employs him or her, then failure to appoint him as a director of the transferee will amount to a repudiatory breach of contract, entitling the director to resign and claim constructive dismissal. The director will also be required to resign as a director of the transferor company or otherwise be removed from office.

Service agreements often contain provisions dealing with reconstructions. A typical agreement will exclude any claim brought by a director if he or she is offered employment with the successor company on no less favourable terms and conditions. In any event, *TUPE* would be likely to apply in these circumstances to the same effect.

(*TUPE* is addressed in detail in TRANSFER OF UNDERTAKINGS (52).)

10   Disclosure of Information

10.1   An employer is under a duty to disclose certain information to his employees and their representatives, by virtue of the *Trade Union and Labour Relations (Consolidation) Act 1992* ('*TULRCA 1992*') (see **10.2–10.5** below), the *Transfer of Undertakings (Protection of Employment) Regulations 2006 (SI 2006/246)* replacing the previous *1981 Regulations (SI 1981/1794)* (see **10.6** below) and the *Health and Safety at Work, etc Act 1974* (see **10.7–10.8** below). Information may also have to be disclosed for the purposes of consultation about forthcoming redundancies (see **39.2** Redundancy – II). The trustees of occupational pension schemes are put under certain duties of disclosure by virtue of the *Occupational Pension Schemes (Disclosure of Information) Regulations 1996 (SI 1996/1655)* (see **10.9** below). Duties to afford access to certain records (as well as other obligations) arise from the *Data Protection Act 1988* (see **10.12** below), and the *Access to Medical Reports Act 1988* and *Access to Health Records Act 1990* (see **10.14** below).

Further, the employer is under a duty *not* to disclose certain types of information about his employees to third parties (see **10.17** below).

For the obligations of applicants to disclose information on matters of nationality and the like, see the *Asylum and Immigration Act 1996* and the *Immigration, Asylum and Nationality Act 2006* and see Foreign Employees **(26)**.

For the obligation to disclose information in relation to criminal convictions see Employee's Past Criminal Convictions **(17)**.

As to disclosures of information made by employees concerning their employer or its business, the law of breach of confidence is relevant. (See Restraint of Trade, Confidentiality and Employee Interventions **(41)**.) Specific protection is also afforded in certain circumstances to employees who disclose information to third parties relating to wrongdoing by the *Public Interest Disclosure Act 1998*. This Act is considered in outline at the end of this chapter (see **10.17** below).

10.2   INFORMATION FOR COLLECTIVE BARGAINING

TULRCA 1992, Part IV Chapter I imposes an obligation on an employer to disclose information necessary for collective bargaining. He can no longer be in the advantageous position of withholding information about such matters as profits and wages when negotiating. The right to enforce such an obligation is given to trade unions recognised for the particular group of employees in whose interests the information is sought (for recognition, see **50.11** Trade Unions – I). The sanctions for non-disclosure are wide: if the information required for negotiation is not disclosed, the Central Arbitration Committee ('CAC') may order that the terms and conditions under negotiation become part of the individual employee's contract of employment. The CAC may order these terms to take effect as claimed or in a modified form. If the employer refuses to implement these terms the employees affected may bring an action for breach of contract in the county court or High Court.

10.3   Duty to disclose

If, at any stage of collective bargaining, a representative of a trade union which is recognised by the employer requests, either orally or, if required by the employer, in writing, information which is both:

(a)   information without which the trade union representative would be, to a material extent, impeded in carrying on with the employer such collective bargaining; and

10.3 Disclosure of Information

(b) information which it would be in accordance with good industrial relations practice that the employer should disclose for the purposes of collective bargaining,

the employer must (in writing, if requested by the representative) disclose such information, unless it falls within one of the exceptions below (*TULRCA 1992, s 181*).

Exceptions. The employer need not disclose the information where:

(i) it would be against the interests of national security;

(ii) it is information which he could not disclose without contravening a prohibition imposed by or under an enactment;

(iii) it is information which has been communicated to the employer in confidence or which the employer has otherwise obtained in consequence of the confidence reposed in him by another person;

(iv) it is information relating specifically to an individual and he has not consented to its being disclosed;

(v) it is information the disclosure of which would cause substantial injury to the employer's undertaking for reasons other than its effect on collective bargaining; or

(vi) it is information obtained by the employer for the purpose of bringing, prosecuting or defending any legal proceedings.

(*TULRCA 1992, s 182(1)*.)

In the performance of his duty under *TULRCA 1992, s 181*, an employer will not be required:

(A) to produce, or allow inspection of, any document (other than a document prepared for the purpose of conveying or confirming the information) or to make a copy of, or extracts from, any document; or

(B) to compile or assemble any information where the compilation or assembly would involve an amount of work or expenditure out of reasonable proportion to the value of the information in the conduct of collective bargaining.

(*TULRCA 1992, s 182(2)*.)

A union only has the right to information concerning matters which are relevant to collective bargaining for which it is recognised. Thus, although a union may have the right to represent a certain class of employee, unless it has a right to represent them *for the purpose of collective bargaining* it does not enjoy the statutory right to information (*R v Central Arbitration Committee, ex p BTP Tioxide Ltd* [1981] ICR 843).

Furthermore, information which would not assist collective bargaining need not be disclosed. Thus, the High Court refused to order the disclosure of figures obtained by the Ministry of Defence showing detailed tenders submitted by contract labour cleaners (*Civil Service Union v Central Arbitration Committee* [1980] IRLR 274).

10.4 Code of Practice

ACAS issued its Code of Practice No 2, on 'Disclosure of Information to Trade Unions for Collective Bargaining Purposes' in 1977 (as subsequently revised in 1998 and 2003). The Code does not provide a complete list of items which should be disclosed, as these will vary according to the circumstances, but merely provides some examples of information which should be considered for disclosure (see also CODES OF PRACTICE (5)). Some of the categories of negotiations for which information may have to be disclosed are set out below.

(a)   Negotiations over pay and benefits.

(b)   Negotiations on conditions of service.

(c)   Negotiations over manpower.

(d)   Negotiations over performance.

(e)   Financial negotiations.

The extent of the duty, and the exceptions, will be matters for interpretation in individual cases. A common sense view of what information is necessary in all the circumstances will be taken.

10.5   Consequences of failure to comply with a request for information

Initial failure to give information. If an employer fails to comply with a request for information from an independent trade union, the union may present a complaint to the CAC. If conciliation seems a possibility, the CAC will refer the matter to ACAS. If ACAS fails in its attempt at conciliation, or if the complaint is not considered initially suitable for conciliation, the CAC will proceed to hear and determine the complaint. The trade union and employer concerned are entitled to be heard, as is any person whom the CAC considers to have a proper interest in the complaint (*TULRCA 1992, s 183(1)–(4)*).

If the CAC finds the complaint wholly or partly well-founded, it will make a declaration specifying the following:

(a)   the nature of the information which it considers should originally have been provided;

(b)   the date (or, if more than one, the earliest date) on which the employer refused or failed to disclose that information or to confirm it in writing; and

(c)   a period (not being less than one week from the date of the declaration) within which the employer must disclose the information or confirm it in writing.

(*TULRCA 1992, s 183(5)*.)

Continued failure to give information. If the employer persists in failing to disclose the information specified in the CAC's declaration within the specified time limit, the trade union may present a further complaint to the CAC who will hear and determine the further complaint. The trade union and employer concerned are again entitled to be heard, as is any person whom the CAC considers has a proper interest in the complaint. If it finds the complaint well-founded, the CAC will issue a declaration specifying the information in respect of which it so finds (*TULRCA 1992, s 184*).

On or after presenting such a further complaint, the trade union may also present a claim relating to the terms and conditions of employment of employees of a description specified in the original claim for information (*TULRCA 1992, s 185(1)*). If the CAC finds or has found the further complaint well-founded, it may make an award that there be incorporated into those employees' contracts of employment:

(i)   the terms and conditions specified in the claim; or

(ii)   other terms and conditions which it considers appropriate.

The award may be back-dated to the date on which the CAC declared that the employer refused or failed to disclose (or confirm in writing) the information (see (b) above) (*TULRCA 1992, s 185(3)*). It may only be made in respect of a description of employees and shall comprise only terms and conditions relating to matters in respect of which the trade union making the claim is recognised by the employer (*TULRCA 1992, s 185(4)*).

10.5 Disclosure of Information

However, if at any time after a trade union has presented a claim under *TULRCA 1992, s 185(1)* to the CAC, and before the CAC has made its award, the employer gives the union the required information, the claim is treated as withdrawn (*TULRCA 1992, s 185(2)*).

Terms incorporated by an award remain in force until they are superseded or varied:

(a)   by a subsequent award under this procedure;

(b)   by a collective agreement between the employer and the union; or

(c)   by express or implied agreement between the employees and the employer as far as it improves any terms and conditions awarded under this procedure.

(*TULRCA 1992, s 185(5)*.)

10.6   TRANSFER OF UNDERTAKINGS REGULATIONS

The *Transfer of Undertakings (Protection of Employment) Regulations 2006 (SI 2006/246)* (which apply to relevant transfers of an undertaking or a service provision change taking place after 6 April 2006) impose obligations upon transferors to disclose to transferees 'employee liability information' (*reg 11*). Failure to make such disclosure is actionable in the employment tribunal by the transferee (*reg 12*). Transferor and transferee employers must also consult in relation to employees affected by a relevant transfer and disclose information to recognised trade unions or elected representatives when there is a transfer to which the *Regulations* apply. Both the transferor and transferee vendor must inform representatives of recognised trade unions, or elected representatives, of certain specified matters which arise on the transfer (*regs 13–16*). A failure to do so is actionable in the Employment Tribunal. See *Royal Mail Group Ltd v Communication Workers Union* [2009] IRLR 1046. (See further, TRANSFER OF UNDERTAKINGS (52)).

It should be noted that the recent government consultation on Proposed Changes to the Regulations has, in addition to the proposal to abolish completely the concept of "service provision change", proposed repealing the specific requirements regarding the notification of Employee Liability Information, but making it clear that the transferor should disclose information to the transferee where it is necessary for the transferee and transferor to perform their duties regarding information and consultation.

10.7   INFORMATION NECESSARY FOR HEALTH AND SAFETY PURPOSES

Employers are obliged by the *Health and Safety at Work, etc Act 1974 ('HSWA 1974')* to provide their employees with information necessary to ensure, so far as is possible, their health and safety at work (*HSWA 1974, s 2(2)(c)*). An employer must prepare and, when appropriate, revise a written statement of his general policy with respect to the health and safety at work of his employees and the organisation and arrangements for the time being in force for carrying out that policy, and bring the statement and any revision of it to the notice of all his employees (*HSWA 1974, s 2(3)*; see also **27.18** HEALTH AND SAFETY AT WORK – I). Failure to provide such written information is an offence which carries a maximum fine of £20,000 on conviction in a magistrates' court, and an unlimited fine on conviction in the Crown Court (*HSWA 1974, s 33(1), (1A), (3)*; *Magistrates' Courts Act 1980, s 32(2)*; and see **1.10** INTRODUCTION).

10.8   Safety representatives, and representatives of employee safety

Under *s 2(6)* of the *HSWA 1974* employers are required to consult with safety representatives from the workforce on health and safety matters. Safety representatives, appointed by a recognised trade union (see also **28.21** HEALTH AND SAFETY AT WORK – II), were given statutory powers to obtain certain information by the *Safety Representatives and Safety Committees Regulations 1977 (SI 1977/500), reg 7*. They are entitled, after giving the employer reasonable notice, to inspect and take copies of any document which the employer is legally obliged to keep, except a document consisting of or relating to any health record of an identifiable individual (*reg 7(1)*). In addition, an employer is obliged to make available to safety representatives any information within his knowledge relating to health, safety or welfare, which is necessary to enable them to fulfil their functions, *except*:

(a)   any information the disclosure of which would be against the interests of national security;

(b)   any information which he could not disclose without contravening a prohibition imposed by or under an enactment;

(c)   any information relating specifically to an individual, unless he has consented to its being disclosed;

(d)   any information the disclosure of which would, for reasons other than its effect on health, safety or welfare at work, cause substantial injury to the employer's undertaking or, where the information was supplied to him by some other person, to the undertaking of that other person; or

(e)   any information obtained by the employer for the purpose of bringing, prosecuting or defending any legal proceedings.

(*Regulation 7(2), (3)*.)

Employees who are not covered by trade union-appointed safety representatives are entitled to be consulted by their employer on health and safety matters, by virtue of the *Health and Safety (Consultation with Employees) Regulations 1996 (SI 1996/1513)*. The consultation may be either with the employees directly or with representatives elected by the relevant employees (referred to in the *Regulations* as 'representatives of employee safety'). The employer must provide the necessary information to enable the employees or representatives to participate fully and effectively in the consultation. In the case of representatives, the information must also be sufficient to enable them to carry out their functions under the *Regulations*. Information within the categories (a) to (e) above need not be provided. (See also **28.22** HEALTH AND SAFETY AT WORK – II.)

10.9   OCCUPATIONAL PENSION SCHEMES

Under the *Occupational Pension Schemes (Disclosure of Information) Regulations 1996 (SI 1996/1655)* the trustees of such schemes must make available to members and prospective members and (in most instances) to their spouses and to beneficiaries and independent recognised trade unions, various categories of information. These include the constitution of the scheme (*reg 3*), basic information about the scheme (*reg 4* and *Sch 1*), information about entitlements (*reg 5* and *Sch 2*) and audited accounts and annual reports (*reg 6* and *Sch 3*). Each of these regulations details the categories of persons and (where applicable) trade unions to whom the information is to be furnished.

10.10   GENDER PAY GAP INFORMATION

Section 78 of the *EqA 2010* provides for regulations to be made requiring employers employing 250 or more employees to publish gender pay gap information. *Section 78* of the *EqA 2010* was brought into force by the *Equality Act 2010 (Commencement No 11) Order 2016 (SI 2016/839)* on 22 August 2016. The relevant regulations requiring the publication of gender pay gap information are the *Equality Act 2010 (Gender Pay Gap Information)*

10.10 Disclosure of Information

Regulations 2017 (SI 2017/172) which came into force on 6 April 2017 and apply to all employers with more than 250 employees. The extended definition of "employee" under the *EqA 2010* applies in assessing whether the 250 employee threshold is crossed. Employers will have up to 12 months to publish the gender pay gaps relating to their organisation. There are six calculations which must be carried out and the results must be published on the employer's website and also on a government website within 12 months from commencement. Employers have the option to provide a narrative account with their calculations. This narrative, if utilised, should, it is intended, explain the reasons for the results and give details about any action being taken to reduce or remove the relevant gender pay gap.

10.11 THE INFORMATION AND CONSULTATION OF EMPLOYEES REGULATIONS 2004 (SI 2004/3426)

On 11 June 2001, the EU Social Policy Council agreed a draft Directive on informing and consulting employees. In March 2002 *Directive 2002/14/EC* ('the *Information and Consultation Directive*') was adopted by the member states. The *Directive* gives employees a right to be informed about the undertaking's economic situation and employment prospects, and be informed and consulted with a view to reaching agreement about decisions likely to lead to substantial changes in work organisation or contractual relations. The *Directive* was implemented in the UK by the *Information and Consultation of Employees Regulations 2004, SI 2004/3426* ('the *Regulations*').

The *Regulations* came into force on 6 April 2005 in relation to undertakings with 150 or more employees and 6 April 2007 for undertakings with 100 or more employees. In the case of undertakings with 50 or more employees, the commencement date was 6 April 2008. The *Regulations* do not apply to undertakings employing fewer than 50 employees. It is particularly important to identify whether there is an undertaking employing the requisite number of employees for the provisions of the *Regulations* to apply. The definition of undertaking in the *Regulations* (taken from the *Directive*) is 'a public or private undertaking carrying out an economic activity whether or not operating for gain'. As to calculating the number of employees engaged in the undertaking, this is averaged over a 12 month period. Further, only 'employees' are to be counted and accordingly subcontractors and temporary workers may be excluded from the calculation insofar as they are not 'employees'. The *Regulations* provide two ways in which information and consultation procedures may be established: first, by employee request and second, by the employer deciding to commence negotiations. If there is no existing mechanism for information and consultation in the undertaking then, for an employees' request to initiate the procedure, there must be a written request to the employer (or to the Central Arbitration Committee (CAC)) by not less than 10% of the employees employed in the undertaking. The undertaking is the whole business of the employer and is not to be equated with the body of workers working at a particular establishment or workplace. Accordingly, the 10% threshold properly understood applies to 10% of all of the employer's employees (*Moyer-Lee v Cofely Workplace Ltd* (2015) UKEAT/0058/15, [2015] IRLR 879). In cases where there is a pre-existing agreement, if a 10% request is made the employer must either enter into negotiations or ballot the employees on the issue of the continuance of the existing agreement. If 40% of the workforce (or a majority of those voting in the ballot) vote in favour of the request then the employer must enter into negotiations for a new agreement. Also, in the case of pre-existing agreements relating to information and consultation, it must in any event be determined if that agreement satisfies the requirements of the *Regulations* (*reg 8(1)*). To be valid the agreement must be in writing, cover all the employees in the undertaking, have been approved by the employees and set out how the employer is to give information to the employees or their representatives and how their views will be sought on the information provided. The EAT in *Stewart (J) v Moray Council* [2006] ICR 1253, [2006] IRLR 592 for the first time considered the *Regulations* in determining whether pre-existing agreements which had been negotiated with trade unions satisfied the requirements of the *Regulations*. On the facts the trade union representatives had agreed and approved the agreements but the agreements had not been specifically put to non-union employees for approval. The CAC rejected an argument that in these circumstances employee approval had not been obtained. It was held that the approval of the representatives was sufficient to satisfy the requirements of the *Regulations*. On the facts, however, one of the agreements failed the statutory requirement of setting out adequately how the employer would give information to the employees and consult with them. The CAC's decision was upheld by the EAT which went on to give guidance on the issue of union involvement and the issue of coverage under *reg 8(1)(b)*. The EAT also found that the requirement of approval by the employees (*reg 8(1)(c)*) could be met by collective approval by trade unions so long as the *majority* of employees were union members. See also *University of London v Morrissey* [2016] IRLR 487 (UKEAT/0285/15) in which the EAT stressed that, notwithstanding the wide discretion afforded by the *Regulations*, the system chosen must ultimately give fair representation to all of the affected employees and, if it does not, it is open to challenge. In *Amicus v Macmillan Publishers Ltd* [2007] IRLR 378 the CAC upheld a complaint that the employer was in breach of the *Regulations* by failing to hold a ballot rejecting the employer's arguments that it was entitled to rely on pre-existing information and consultation agreements or that there was a negotiated agreement in place. The decision of the CAC entitled the union to apply for a penalty notice.

If there is no valid pre-existing agreement or no agreement at all and there has been an appropriate request and ballot, then the employer must enter into negotiations for an agreement with employees' representatives. Negotiations may last for up to six months (extendable by agreement).

For a negotiated agreement to be valid it must cover all the employees in the undertaking, be in writing and dated and signed by the employer, set out the circumstances in which the employer will inform and consult the employees and provide for the appointment or election of information and consultation representatives or for information and consultation directly with the employees (*reg 16(1)*). To be valid a negotiated agreement must also be approved by the employees by being signed by all or a majority of the negotiating representatives *and* by at least 50% of the employees in the undertaking *or* approved by 50% of the employees who vote in a ballot (*reg 16(2)*).

If the employer and representatives fail to reach a negotiated agreement (or if the employer fails to enter into negotiations following a 10% request) then the *Regulations* impose standard information and consultation procedures by default. In cases of a negotiated agreement, or where the standard procedures are imposed, the *Regulations* provide specific provisions in order to protect confidential information. By *reg 25* it will be a breach of statutory duty for an individual to disclose confidential information subject to a right of challenge to the confidentiality in issue which will be heard by the CAC. In certain cases where the effect of disclosure would be potentially seriously prejudicial to the undertaking, the employer may be justified in withholding the information from employee representatives (*reg 26*). As to individual rights, the *Regulations* extend the standard rights to time off and protection against dismissal or detriment on the grounds of taking part in the activities of an information and consultation representative to the employees' representatives. The right to time off, however, does not apply to representatives who are exercising their functions pursuant to a pre-existing agreement. The enforcement of the *Regulations* on a collective level rests with the CAC which will be empowered to adjudicate on the issue of what is an 'undertaking', the number of employees employed in an undertaking, the employer's provision of data, validity of balloting and appointment or election of representatives and whether an employer has complied with obligations under a negotiated agreement or standard arrangement (as the case may be). The *Regulations* provide for substantial penalties for employers who default on their obligations: in cases of complaint of failure to comply with the terms of an agreement (which has been upheld by the CAC), there will be a right for employee representatives to apply to the Employment Appeal Tribunal for a penalty notice (of up to £75,000) to be issued against the employer. The time limit for such an application is three months from the date of the CAC's determination.

The consequences of failure to comply with the *Regulations* are likely to be substantial. In *Amicus v Macmillan Publishers Ltd* [2007] IRLR 378 the CAC upheld a complaint that the employer was in breach of the *Regulations* by failing to hold a ballot rejecting the employer's arguments that it was entitled to rely on pre-existing information and consultation agreements or that there was a negotiated agreement in place. The decision of the CAC entitled the union to apply to the EAT for a penalty notice and the EAT, issuing its first penalty notice in *Amicus v Macmillan Publishers Ltd* [2007] IRLR 885 fined the employer £55,000 commenting (Elias P.) that such a sum should 'deter others from adopting [a] . . . cavalier attitude to the obligations' imposed by the *Regulations*. See also *Darnton v Bournemouth University* [2010] ICR 524, [2010] IRLR 294 in which the EAT observed that previous cases on penalty would be likely to be of little assistance on the fixing of a penalty in another case. Following *Darnton*, some guidance on the approach to fixing a penalty in failure to ballot cases (see *regs 7* and *18*) was provided by *Brown v G4 Security (Cheltenham)* (UKEAT/0526/09/RN) [2010] All ER (D) 84 (Aug). When determining the penalty for a failure to ballot for employee representatives, as well as the non-exhaustive factors relevant to penalty set out in *reg 23(3)* (which comprise gravity of failure, period of time over which failure occurs, reasons for failure, number of employees affected and total number of employees employed) it is appropriate to take into account all additional relevant factors which should be weighted depending on the facts of the case. The proportion of employees affected is relevant as is the extent of any corrective measures taken by the employer following the CAC's determination of breach.

Guidance on the operation of the *Regulations* is available from: https ://www.gov.uk/government/publications/information-and-consultation-regulations-2004 (see, further, on the provisions of the *Directive* and *Regulations*: **16.2 EMPLOYEE PARTICIPATION**). It should be borne in mind that the guidance is merely an interpretation of the law and not definitive. See *Darnton v Bournemouth University* [2009] IRLR 4 (CAC) in which the CAC concluded that the government guidance on the operation of *reg 14* of the *Regulations* was incorrect. The Employment Appeal Tribunal agreed with the CAC's interpretation, explaining that the guidance "has no special status" and that, in relation to *reg 14*, the guidance was wrong. See *Darnton v Bournemouth University* [2010] ICR 524, [2010] IRLR 294, EAT. Specifically, in relation to disclosure of information, the Guidance at paragraphs 53–55 provides guidance on the information required to be provided under the *Regulations*. One matter which will often be of substantial concern to employers is disclosure of information which is also considered to be commercially confidential; whether the *Regulations* require the disclosure of such information and, if so, what protections are available to the employer to maintain confidence in the information. The Guidance explains (paragraph 76) that employers may: (1) restrict any information or document they provide to I&C representatives or others, so that it may not be passed on to anyone else (see *regulation 25*). The employer may do this where it is in the legitimate interest of the undertaking. This will include information that is share price sensitive; (2) withhold information or documents altogether that they would otherwise be required to give I&C representatives (see *regulation 26*). They may do this where disclosing it to them would seriously harm the functioning of the undertaking, or be prejudicial to it. In the event of a dispute in relation to confidential information the matter is to be resolved by the CAC. The guidance at paragraph 77 provides further information in relation to confidential information and the imposition of requirements of confidentiality upon the recipients.

10.12 DATA PROTECTION: THE BACKGROUND

The obligations in relation to the storage of personal data on a computer were originally governed by the *Data Protection Act 1984*, passed in response to the Council of Europe's Convention for the Protection of Individuals with regard to Automatic Processing of Personal Data. The *1984 Act* required those processing personal data to register with the Data Protection Registrar (*DPA 1984, s 5(1)*) and restrictions were imposed upon the use or disclosure of data (*DPA 1984, s 5(2)*). Those processing data in relation to employees were obliged to adhere to the 'data protection principles', which provided that the employee should be informed that he is the subject of personal data and be allowed access to such data, and that the data should be corrected or erased where appropriate (*DPA 1984, Sch 1 Part I, para 7*). In addition there were obligations to inform employees whether personal data was kept on them, and to supply a copy of the relevant information (*DPA 1984, s 21*). Finally, an employer could be required to pay compensation where damage was caused by reason of the inaccuracy, loss or unauthorised disclosure of data (*DPA 1984, ss 22, 23*). The current, and considerably more extensive and onerous, data protection obligations required by the *EU Data Protection Directive (95/46)* are now contained in the *Data Protection Act 1998*.

10.13 DATA PROTECTION ACT 1998

On 15 January 1998, the Government published a Data Protection Bill which was designed to implement the *EU Data Protection Directive (95/46)*. On 16 July 1998, the *Data Protection Act 1998* received Royal Assent. The *Data Protection Act 1998* repealed and replaced the *Data Protection Act 1984*. The *Directive* was required to be implemented by 24 October 1998 and, accordingly, it was expected that the *Act* would come into force by this date. However, it actually came into force on 1 March 2000 subject to extensive transitional provisions in relation to paper-based records (see *DPA 1998, Sch 8*). The final provisions of the *Data Protection Act* came into force on 24 October 2007. A full consideration of the law of data protection is beyond the scope of this work. There follows a short summary of the key features of the *Data Protection Act 1998*.

10.14 Data Protection Act 1998: an overview

Most significantly, the law of data protection is extended to cover paper files as well as information stored on computer (*DPA 1998, s 1(1)*). Information contained in a 'relevant filing system' is brought within the compass of the *Act*'s protection. A relevant filing system is defined as non-automated information relating to individuals which is 'structured either by reference to individuals or by reference to criteria relating to individuals, in such a way that specific information relating to a particular individual is readily accessible'. Personal data includes any expression of opinion about a person and indications of intention by the employer or any other person in relation to that individual (*DPA 1998, s 1(1)*). It follows that paper-based personnel records will clearly come within the data protection regime.

Schedule 1 to the *DPA 1998* sets out eight principles relating to the *processing* of personal data. 'Processing' includes collection, storage, organisation, retrieval, alternation, disclosure or destruction of data. The principles may be summarised as follows:

(a)   personal data shall be processed fairly and lawfully;

(b)   personal data shall be obtained only for specified and lawful purposes and shall not be processed in any manner incompatible with those purposes;

(c)   personal data shall be adequate, relevant and not excessive in relation to the purposes for which it is processed;

(d)   personal data shall be accurate and, where necessary, kept up to date;

(e)   personal data shall be kept for no longer than is necessary for the purposes for which it is processed;

(f)   personal data shall be processed in accordance with the rights of data subjects under the *Act*;

(g)   personal data shall be subject to appropriate technical and organisational measures to protect against unauthorised or unlawful processing and accidental loss, destruction or damage; and

(h)   personal data shall not be transferred to a country or territory outside the European Economic Area unless that country or territory ensures an adequate level of data protection.

In *Durant v Financial Services Authority* [2003] EWCA Civ 1746, [2004] FSR 573 the Court of Appeal gave guidance on the meaning of 'personal data' and on a 'relevant filing system'. The Court of Appeal concluded that 'personal data' did not include every piece of information relating to an individual but must have a 'continuum of relevance or proximity to the data subject'. The issue of whether the information was biographical and focused on the individual would assist in identifying personal data. As to 'relevant filing system', the Court of Appeal held that, in relation to manual records, the definition would only apply if the system was of sufficient sophistication to provide similar accessibly to that afforded by a computer system, but would exclude material only accessible by a manual search of files. Under *Part II* of the *Act* employees (as 'data subjects') have the right (by written request and upon payment of a fee) to be told by the employer whether personal data about them is being processed, to be given descriptions of the data and its recipients and to have the data supplied in an intelligible form (*DPA 1998, s 7*). The employer must comply with the request within 40 days. Put simply, employees are entitled in relation to paper records to receive a copy of their personnel file. Confidential references, however, given by the employer for the purposes of education, training or employment are excluded from the right under *s 7*. References given by third parties and held in a file by the current employer are not so excluded.

An employee is given a right under *s 14* of the *DPA 1998* to apply to the High Court or the county court on the ground that personal data relating to him is inaccurate. The court may order the employer to rectify, destroy or erase, as the case may be, data containing expressions of opinion based on inaccurate information. Where the inaccurate data is disclosed to third parties, the court may order the employer to notify those persons that the inaccurate data has been corrected. By *DPA 1998, s 10*, an employee may issue written notice requiring an employer not to process personal data where it is likely to cause substantial and unwarranted damage and distress. By *DPA 1998, s 13*, data subjects may recover compensation not only for loss and damage as a result of inaccurate data processing or unauthorised disclosure but also, in certain cases, for distress caused thereby. *DPA 1998, s 12* limits the use of computers exclusively in certain forms of decision-making and employees may issue notices requiring that employers do not take a decision that significantly affects the employee *solely* on the automatic processing of personal data. The Information Commissioner has extensive powers of enforcement in relation to the *Act*.

Finally, it is significant to note that new restrictions are introduced in relation to the processing of 'sensitive personal data'. Such data is broadly defined as including ethnic or racial origins, political opinions, religious beliefs or other beliefs of a similar nature, trade union membership, physical or mental health and data relating to the commission or alleged commission of any offence or the sentence in relation to any such offence. The House of Lords has given guidance on the meaning of personal and sensitive data in *Common Services Agency v Scottish Information Comr* [2008] UKHL 47, [2008] 4 All ER 851, [2008] 1 WLR 1550. Information which has been manipulated to conceal the identity of living individuals will still be personal data where the individuals can be identified by the data controller.

Their Lordships held that 'sensitive data' is a subset of 'personal data' and, as the information related to issues of health (the incidence of childhood leukaemia), it followed that, if the information was personal data, it would also be sensitive personal data. In relation to sensitive personal data, in addition to the *Sch 1* data protection principles, at least one of the conditions found in *Sch 3* to the *DPA 1998* must be satisfied. These conditions include the express consent of the employee for the following:

(i)   that the processing is necessary for performing or exercising a right or obligation imposed by or in connection with employment;

(ii)   that the processing is necessary in connection with legal proceedings or for the purposes of obtaining legal advice;

(iii)   that the processing is necessary for the administration of justice or statutory duty; or

(iv)   the processing of racial or ethnic origin information is necessary for the purposes of monitoring equality of opportunity or treatment.

Following recent changes to the sanctions applicable to breach of data protection obligations substantial financial penalties may be imposed. Under *sections 55A* and *55B* of the *Data Protection Act 1998*, introduced by the *Criminal Justice and Immigration Act 2008*, the Information Commissioner may, in certain circumstances, serve a monetary penalty notice on a data controller. The amount of the monetary penalty is determined by the Information Commissioner up to a maximum of £500,000. The Commissioner may impose a monetary penalty notice if a data controller has seriously contravened the data protection principles and the contravention was of a kind likely to cause substantial damage or substantial distress. In addition the contravention must either have been deliberate or the data controller must have known or ought to have known that there was a risk that a contravention would occur and failed to take reasonable steps to prevent it.

The Information Commissioner has published the Employment Practices Data Protection Code. The purpose of this Code is to ensure that, in relation to data obtained by employers on their employees, the storage and use of that data complies with the obligations imposed by the *Data Protection Act 1998* and also the *Human Rights Act 1998* (see HUMAN RIGHTS (30)). The Code is in four parts, all of which have now been published by the Information Commissioner. The first part deals with the recruitment and selection of employees and the second part concerns records management. The third part deals with monitoring at work and covers issues such as recording workers' activities by CCTV cameras, automated checking software and recording of workers' telephone calls. The final part of the Code relates to medical information and is titled 'Information about workers' health'. Much of this part of the Code deals with processing of sensitive personal data and covers the following areas: general considerations, occupational health schemes, medical examination and testing, drug and alcohol testing and genetic testing. The text of the Code, together with supplementary guidance, can be found on the Information Commissioner's website at ico.org.uk. See also the ICO's "Data Protection Good Practice Note Subject Access and Employment References" which clarifies how the *Data Protection Act 1998* applies to employment references. The recommendations also apply to other types of reference, such as those provided for educational purposes.

10.15 ACCESS TO MEDICAL REPORTS

Medical reports obtained by an employer should obviously not be disclosed to third parties without the employee's consent.

The *Access to Medical Reports Act 1988* ('*AMRA 1988*') gives individuals a right of access to medical reports relating to them which are supplied by medical practitioners for employment purposes (*AMRA 1998, s 1*). An employer may not apply to a medical

10.15   Disclosure of Information

practitioner for such a report without the employee's consent (*AMRA 1998, s 3(1)*). The ACAS handbook 'Discipline at Work' includes a model letter of enquiry to an employee's doctor. The employee is entitled to see the report *before* it is supplied (*AMRA 1998, s 4*) and to withhold consent to the report being supplied (*AMRA 1998, s 5(1)*). There is also provision for the correction of errors (*AMRA 1998, s 5(2)*). If there is a failure to comply with the *Act*, an application may be made to the court (*AMRA 1998, s 8*).

The statutory definition of 'medical report' refers to a medical practitioner who is or has been responsible for the clinical care of the individual. Therefore, a report obtained from a company doctor after an examination carried out for a particular purpose is unlikely to be subject to the *Act*. Nor does an employer request a medical report within the meaning of the *Act* where he merely seeks confirmation of information already received (*McIntosh v John Brown Engineering Ltd*, IDS Brief No 441, p 3).

The *Access to Health Records Act 1990* came into force on 1 November 1991 and, in general, applies only to information recorded after that date. It applies to health records, other than those falling within the scope of the *Data Protection Act 1984* (see **10.13** above). Individuals have a right to apply for access to records relating to them to the health professional who holds those records (*AHRA 1990, s 3*). There is also a right to apply for inaccurate records to be corrected (*AHRA 1990, s 6*). The right of access is subject to certain exclusions (*AHRA 1990, ss 4, 5*). A 'health professional' as defined by *AHRA 1990, s 2* includes any registered medical practitioner, so that the *Act* may be expected to apply to company doctors. An application may be made to the court if the holder of a health record fails to comply with the *Act* (*AHRA 1990, s 8*).

10.16   CONFIDENTIAL INFORMATION RELATING TO EMPLOYEES

Apart from the specific statutory obligations referred to above, the employer will normally be under a common law duty not to disclose to third parties confidential information which he holds concerning his employees. In *Dalgleish v Lothian and Borders Police Board* [1991] IRLR 422, there was held to be a *prima facie* case that employees' names and addresses were confidential.

However, it may well be that in a competitive tendering situation in which it is expected that there will be a transfer of an undertaking to the successful contractor (see further on this issue TRANSFER OF UNDERTAKINGS (52)), there is little option but to disclose details of the workforce to potential tenderers. In such a case, it will be preferable to disclose the information, so far as possible, in such a way as not to identify individual employees.

10.17   DISCLOSURE OF INFORMATION BY EMPLOYEES: THE PUBLIC INTEREST DISCLOSURE ACT 1998 AND PART IVA OF THE EMPLOYMENT RIGHTS ACT 1996

The *Public Interest Disclosure Act 1998 ('PIDA 1998')* received the Royal Assent on 2 July 1998 and came into force on 2 July 1999. This somewhat complicated piece of legislation introduces specific rights into the *ERA 1996* for those who disclose information about alleged wrongdoings, including the right not to suffer detriment in employment (*PIDA 1998, s 2*, inserting *ERA 1996, s 47B*) and the right not to be unfairly dismissed for making such disclosures (*PIDA 1998, ss 5, 7*). Such a dismissal will be automatically unfair and there is no qualifying period of employment, nor upper age limit. (See UNFAIR DISMISSAL – I (53).) The provisions of *PIDA 1998* do not apply to employment in the Security Service, the Secret Intelligence Service or the Government Communications Headquarters (*PIDA 1998, s 11*) nor to police officers or persons employed under a contract of employment in the police service (*PIDA 1998, s 13*). Significant amendments to the provisions of *Part IVA* of the *ERA 1996* have been introduced with effect from 25 June 2013 by amendments introduced by the *Enterprise and Regulatory Reform Act 2013 ("ERRA 2013")* and are considered below.

10.18   Protected disclosures by workers

In order for the protection afforded by the Act to apply, the disclosure must be made by 'a worker'. Worker is defined generally in *ERA 1996, s 230(3)* and, for the purposes of the protection against detriment for making protected disclosures, the definition of worker is further extended by *ERA 1996, s 43K* (as inserted by *PIDA 1998, s 1* and as variously amended) and includes contractors acting under the control of the employer, persons on training courses and doctors, dentists, opticians and pharmacists providing services under statutory schemes. Provision is also made for Regulations to be made protecting applicants for employment in the health service from suffering detriment by reason of having made protected disclosures (*ERA 1996, s 49B* added by the *Small Business, Enterprise and Employment Act 2015, s 149*, as from 26 May 2015). In *Clyde & Co LLP and another v Bates van Winkelhof* [2014] UKSC 32 the Supreme Court has held that a member of a Limited Liability Partnership ("LLP") is also a "worker" for the purposes of *s 230(3)* of the *ERA* and, accordingly, could bring claims relating to protected disclosures in the employment tribunal. Giving the leading Judgment Lady Hale observed "That conclusion is to my mind entirely consistent with the underlying policy of those provisions, which some might think is particularly applicable to businesses and professions operating within the tightly regulated fields of financial and legal services." The "direction of travel" in the case law seems to favour extending protection against detriment and that protection will not be lost by a restrictive interpretation of "worker" when that protection is consistent with the underlying policy of the legislation. This is further illustrated by *Keppel Seghers UK Ltd v Hinds* [2014] IRLR 754, a decision relating to *s 43K* (namely a worker who is "introduced or supplied to do that work by a third person") in which the EAT emphasised that it was appropriate to adopt a purposive construction to provide protection rather than deny it where this was possible. Moreover, in *Roberts v Wilsons Solicitors LLP* [2016] IRLR 586 it was held that a member of an LLP could bring a claim for detriment under ERA s 47B where the loss in issue was post-termination financial loss. The protection is not without limits however. In *Day v Lewisham & Greenwich NHS Trust* (2016) UKEAT/0250/15/RN a doctor in training alleged detriment against the hospital in which he trained and also Health Education England which had arranged the training. The latter claim was struck out as he was not a worker for the purposes of *ERA 1996, s 230* and did not come within the extended definition in *ERA 1996, s 43K*. In *Sharpe v The Bishop of Worcester* [2015] IRLR 663 the Court of Appeal held that there must be a contract in existence for *ERA 1996, s 43(1)(a)* to apply and in Gilham v Ministry of Justice (UKEAT/0087/16) the EAT held that a district judge was an officeholder but did not have a contract and accordingly was not a worker for the purposes of *ERA 1996, s 230(3)* . In *McTigue v University Hospital NHS Foundation Trust* [2016] IRLR 742 the EAT held that an agency worker could bring a claim against an end user client under the extended definition in *s 43K(1)* even though the agency worker was also an employee or worker of the relevant agency. The case provides helpful guidance on the operation of *s 43K*. The same conclusion was recently upheld, applying *McTigue*, by the Court of Appeal in *Day v Health Education England (Respondent) & (1) Public Concern At Work (Interveners) (2) Lewisham And Greenwich NHS Trust (Interested Party)* [2017] EWCA Civ 329 permitting a junior doctor to bring, in principle, a complaint of detriment against a body with whom he had a training contract but who was not his employer. The matter was remitted to the employment tribunal to determine if the body with whom the doctor had the training contract "substantially determined" the terms of the engagement for the purposes of *ERA s 43K*.

Second, the disclosure must be a 'qualifying disclosure' as defined in *ERA 1996, s 43B* (*PIDA 1998, s 1*). A qualifying disclosure is a disclosure of information which, in the reasonable belief of the disclosing worker, is made in the public interest and tends to shows one or more of the following six categories of wrongdoing:

(a)   that a criminal offence has been committed, is being committed or is likely to be committed;

10.18 Disclosure of Information

(b)   that a person has failed, is failing or is likely to fail to comply with any legal obligation to which he is subject;

(c)   that a miscarriage of justice has occurred, is occurring or is likely to occur;

(d)   that the health or safety of any individual has been, is being or is likely to be endangered;

(e)   that the environment has been, is being or is likely to be damaged; or

(f)   that information tending to show any matter falling within any one of the preceding paragraphs has been, is being or is likely to be deliberately concealed.

The requirement that the disclosure is, in the reasonable belief of the worker, in the public interest was added with effect from 25 June 2013 by *s 17* of the *ERRA 2013*. This is a significant amendment which may narrow to some extent the scope of disclosures which qualify for protection.

In *Geduld v Cavendish Munro Professional Risks Management Ltd* [2010] ICR 325, [2010] IRLR 38 the EAT considered what was required for a disclosure of "information". At issue was whether the contents of a solicitors' letter was a qualifying disclosure. The EAT held that there was a distinction between communicating "information" (which is protected) and making an "allegation" which does not convey facts (and which is not protected). The distinction is well illustrated by an example given in Mrs Justice Slade's judgment in relation to the state of a hospital. To say "health and safety requirements are not being complied with" is an unprotected allegation. To say "the wards of the hospital have not been cleaned for two weeks and sharps were left lying around" is conveying "information" and is protected. On the facts the solicitor's letter contained only an allegation and was not a protected disclosure. See also *Goode v Marks & Spencer plc* (UKEAT/0442/09/DM) [2010] All ER (D) 63 (Sep) and *Smith v London Metropolitan University* [2011] IRLR 884, EAT in which *Cavendish Munro Professional Risks Management Ltd v Geduld* was applied on the "information" point. In *Goode* the EAT observed that the principle was applicable to circumstances where an employee expressed an adverse opinion of what the employer was doing or proposed to do (in that case a redundancy exercise). In *Millbank Financial Services Ltd v Crawford* [2014] IRLR 18 the principles outlined in *Geduld* were further considered in the factual context of complaints alleging omissions to act. The EAT held that the disclosure in question was a qualifying one and that conveying facts for the purposes of the whistleblowing provisions plainly included conveying facts about what had not been done as well as about what had been done. See also *Norbrook Laboratories (GB) Ltd v Shaw* (UKEAT/0150/13) which considered the effect of taking a series of complaints together in the analysis of whether a qualifying disclosure had been made out in the sense understood in *Geduld*. Wholly separate communications cannot, however, be aggregated to make out a protected disclosure (*Barton v Royal Borough of Greenwich* (2015) UKEAT/0041/14, [2015] All ER (D) 161 (May). In *Kilraine v London Borough of Wandsworth* (2015) UKEAT/0260/15/JOJ the President of the EAT appeared to depart from the trend to apply strictly the distinction between "information" and "allegation" derived from *Geduld*, observing that the tribunals should be careful in applying the principle as the statute does not draw a distinction between information and allegation and the two concepts are often tied together. Generalised allegations of inappropriate behaviour haves been held to fall short of a disclosure of information (*Kilraine v London Borough of Wandsworth* [2016] IRLR 422).

Helpful and detailed guidance on the approach to be taken by a tribunal in determining whether protected disclosures had been made is provided by *Blackbay Ventures Ltd v Gahir* [2014] IRLR 416. The tribunal should (i) separately identify each alleged disclosure by reference to date and content, (ii) identify each alleged failure to comply with a legal obligation or health and safety matter (as the case may be), (iii) identify the basis on which it is alleged each disclosure is qualifying and protected and (iv) identify the source of the legal obligation relied upon by reference to statute or regulations (save in obvious cases). Absent this exercise the tribunal will not know the particular disclosure said to have resulted in a particular detriment nor the relevant date of the alleged detriment. The tribunal should then go on to consider whether the claimant had the reasonable belief required under *ERA, s 43B(1)*. The enquiry should then move to whether the disclosure was made in the public interest (for post 25 June 2013 disclosures) or whether made in good faith (for pre 25 June 2013 actions). The tribunal must identify the alleged detriment and the date thereof as part of its findings. A failure by an Employment Tribunal to identify a legal obligation by reference to its source (by referring, for example, to statute or regulations) when it is alleged that a protected disclosure has been made on this ground is an error of law (*Eiger Securities LLP v Korshunova* [2017] IRLR 115).

In *Chesterton Global Ltd v Numohamed* [2015] IRLR 614 (EAT) the EAT considered the public interest requirement for the first time. It was made clear that the disclosure need not be in the public interest per se – rather the question was whether the disclosing employee had a reasonable belief the disclosure was in the public interest. The EAT observed that the statutory objective of the addition of the public interest requirement was to reverse the decision in *Perkins v Sodexho* [2002] IRLR 109 and thus to prevent a worker from relying upon a complaint of a breach of his own contract of employment as a protected disclosure where that breach involves no wider public interest implications and held the disclosure in the instant case, which related to profit manipulation by the employer, passed the public interest test even though the motivation for raising the issue was the effect that manipulation had on the disclosing employee's (and some 100 other employees') rates of commission payment. In *Underwood v Wincanton* (2015) UKEAT/0163/15, [2015] All ER (D) 129 (Aug) an alleged disclosure by four employees about unfair allocation of overtime, which had been struck out, was remitted by the EAT for reconsideration to determine if it was capable of passing the hurdle of the public interest, which suggests the possibility that the test could be satisfied when even a small number of employees have a common complaint. See also *Morgan v Royal Mencap Society* [2016] IRLR 428 further illustrating the broad and generous approach to the issue of when the public interest is engaged.

The geographical location of the wrongdoing (ie whether inside or outside the United Kingdom) is irrelevant (*ERA 1996, s 43B(2)* inserted by *PIDA 1998, s 1*). A disclosure is not a qualifying disclosure, however, if a person making the disclosure commits a criminal offence in so doing, or if the disclosure is made in breach of legal professional privilege (*ERA 1996, s 43B(3), (4)* inserted by *PIDA 1998, s 1*). The Court of Appeal has held that the requirements under *s 43B* are (i) that the employee believes that the information disclosed meets the requirements of the section (ii) that the employee's belief is objectively reasonable and (iii) that the disclosure is made in good faith (*Babula v Waltham Forest College* [2007] EWCA Civ 174, [2007] IRLR 346). It is important to note, however, that the "good faith" requirement in relation to any category of protected disclosure has been removed with effect from 25 June 2013 by the provisions of *s 18* of the *ERRA 2013*.

There is no absolute requirement that the legal obligation *in fact* exists, the objective reasonableness of the employee's belief is what is in issue (*Kraus v Penna plc* [2004] IRLR 260 disapproved). In *Korashi v Abertawe Bro Morgannwg University Local Health Board* [2012] IRLR 4, the EAT has given guidance on "reasonable belief". Although the test is objective this has to be considered taking into account the personal circumstances of the discloser. The question is whether it was reasonable for him to believe. Further, where an employee relies upon multiple alleged protected disclosures (as is very common), reasonable belief must be made out in relation to each of the disclosures and a general belief in the broad gist of the content of the disclosures is not enough.

Third, in order to be a 'protected disclosure', a qualifying disclosure must be made only to the category of persons contemplated in the *Act* and not to other persons (*ERA 1996, ss 43C–43H* inserted by *PIDA 1998, s 1*). There are six ways contemplated in which a worker may make a 'protected disclosure', the first four of which are as follows:

(i)   to the worker's employer or (in cases where the information relates to the conduct of another person or to matters for which a person other than the employer has legal responsibility) that other person (*ERA 1996, s 43C*);

(ii)   to a legal adviser in the course of obtaining legal advice (*ERA 1996, s 43D*);

(iii) to a Minister of the Crown where the worker's employer is (a) an individual appointed under any enactment by a Minister of the Crown or (b) a body whose members are appointed by a Minister of the Crown (*ERA 1996, s 43E*);

(iv)   to a person prescribed by order made by the Secretary of State for the purposes of receiving qualifying disclosure information of relevant categories (*ERA 1996, s 43F*). The details of those persons and the relevant matters in respect of which they are prescribed are set out at length in the *Public Interest Disclosure (Prescribed Persons) Order 1999 (SI 1999/1549)* (as amended). Further, from 6 April 2010 the Employment Tribunal Service was empowered by the *Employment Tribunals (Constitution and Rules of Procedure) (Amendment) Regulations 2010 (SI 2010/131)* to provide a copy of the whole or part of any ET1 in which it is alleged a protected disclosure has been made to the relevant regulator. The consent of the claimant is required and the online form ET1 has been amended to provide for the claimant to indicate consent to disclosure.

The fifth category of protected disclosure will permit disclosures to be made to persons other than those contemplated in categories (i) to (iv) above but only if the worker reasonably believes the information to be substantially true, does not make the disclosure for the purposes of personal gain, one of a number of stringent conditions is satisfied, and in all the circumstances it is reasonable to make the disclosure (*ERA 1996, s 43G*). It had previously been held that a disclosure is not made in good faith if an ulterior motive is the predominant purpose for making the disclosure even if the worker making the disclosure reasonably believed it was true (*Street v Derbyshire Unemployed Workers' Centre* [2004] EWCA Civ 964, [2004] 4 All ER 839). The burden of proving bad faith in relation to an employee's disclosure rests on the employer (*Bachnak v Emerging Markets Partnership (Europe) Ltd* (0288/05) (2006) 150 Sol Jo LB 435, EAT. The fact that a protected disclosure is made during the course of disciplinary proceedings does not of itself indicate ulterior motive and absence of good faith (*Soh v Imperial College of Science Technology and Medicine* (2015) UKEAT/0350/14, [2015] All ER (D) 202 (Dec)).

As set out above, the absence of good faith does not prevent a qualifying disclosure being a protected disclosure. The issue of whether the protected disclosure was made in good faith remains relevant, however, at the stage of remedy. In assessing compensation for detriment the tribunal may reduce any award by up to 25% if it was not made in good faith and the tribunal considers it just and equitable to do so (*ERA 1996, s 49(6A)* as added by the *ERRA 2013, s 18(4)* from 25 June 2013). Thus the issue of good faith and the decided cases in relation to the concept will remain relevant in such cases where absence of good faith is in issue.

The conditions contemplated by this section are:

(A)   that the worker reasonably believes, at the time of making the disclosure, that he will be subjected to a detriment by the employer if the disclosure is made to the employer or a prescribed person (*ERA 1996, s 43G(2)(a)*); or

(B)   that, in cases where there is no prescribed person in relation to the relevant qualifying disclosure, the worker reasonably believes that evidence relating to the wrongdoing will be concealed or destroyed if a disclosure is made to the employer (*ERA 1996, s 43G(2)(b)*); or

(C)   that the worker has previously made a disclosure of substantially the same information to the employer or to a prescribed person (*ERA 1996, s 43G(2)(c)*).

Finally, in determining whether it was reasonable for the worker to make the disclosure under *ERA 1996, s 43G*, regard must be had to the identity of the person to whom the disclosure is made, the seriousness of the relevant failure, whether the relevant failure is continuing or likely to occur in the future, whether the disclosure is made in breach of a duty of confidence owed by the employer to another person, the action which the employer or person to whom a previous disclosure was made might reasonably have been expected to take as a result of the previous disclosure, and whether the worker complied with any procedure whose use by him was authorised by the employer (*ERA 1996, s 43G(3)–(4)*).

The final category of protected disclosure relates to disclosure of 'exceptionally serious failures' (*ERA 1996, s 43H*). In this situation the worker must make the disclosure, believing the information to be substantially true, not for personal gain in circumstances when the relevant failure is of an exceptionally serious nature and where in all the circumstances it was reasonable to make the disclosure. For an example of a disclosure to the local press being a protected disclosure see *Collins v National Trust* (2507255/05) (17 January 2006, unreported), EAT.

In determining reasonableness of the disclosure, particular regard shall be had to the identity of the person to whom the disclosure is made.

By *ERA 1996, s 43J* (inserted by *PIDA 1998, s 1*) a provision in an agreement (including a contract of employment) which purports to preclude a worker from making protected disclosures is rendered void.

In cases where an employee/worker has made a protected disclosure as defined in the *Act* and is subjected to a detriment or dismissal as a result by the employer, the remedy will be by way of complaint to an employment tribunal (*ERA 1996, ss 47B, 103A* inserted by *PIDA 1998, ss 2, 5*). It has been held by the EAT that an employee/worker could pursue a detriment claim under *s 47B* against his employer where the protected disclosure relied upon was made whilst employed by a previous employer (*BP Plc v Elstone and Petrotechnics Ltd* [2010] IRLR 558, EAT).

Consideration of the meaning of subjection to a detriment has been given by the EAT in *Abertawe Bro Mogannwg University Health Board v Ferguson* [2014] IRLR 14. In that case the EAT held that the employer does not have to be able to control the circumstances giving rise to the detriment and guidance was given on the concept of a deliberate failure to act by the employer. It should be noted that this case involved, in part, the issue of conduct of other workers. Claims in relation to subjection to a detriment by reason of making a protected disclosure will be simplified by the reforms enacted in the *ERRA 2013* which provides, for claims arising after 25 June 2013, for vicarious liability in the employer for acts of detriment done by its workers or agents (see further below).

Protected disclosures made in bad faith are now subject to the potential reduction in compensation by up to 25% (*ERA 1996, s 49(6A)* as added by the *ERRA 2013, s 18(4)* from 25 June 2013).

Under *ERA 1996, s 48(2)* it is "for the employer to show the ground on which any act, or deliberate failure to act, was done". In *NHS Manchester v Fecitt* [2012] IRLR 64, reversing the EAT, the Court of Appeal has held that the test in discrimination law of "in no sense whatsoever" derived from *Wong v Igen Ltd* [2005] 3 All ER 812 was not to be imported into the statutory test for whistleblowing. The correct test is whether 'the protected disclosure materially influences (in the sense of being more than a trivial influence) the employer's treatment of the whistleblower'. In some cases it will be necessary to carefully analyse whether the detriment in issue is due to having made protected disclosures or whether the detriment is because of the way in which the employee makes the disclosure (e.g. in an unreasonable offensive or abusive way). If the latter is in fact the reason for the detriment then it will not be by reason of having made a protected disclosure (*Panayiotou v Kernaghan* [2014] IRLR 500).

Dismissal on grounds of having made a protected disclosure is automatically unfair and there is no qualifying period of employment or upper age limit. The protected disclosure must be the reason or principal reason for the dismissal – it is not sufficient that the disclosure was a material influence (as that test only applies to detriment cases and not dismissal) (*ERA, s 103A* as explained in *Eiger Securities LLP v Korshunova* [2017] IRLR 115). If a dismissing officer was unaware of the protected disclosures relied upon (even though others in the organisation were aware) then the dismissal cannot be by reason of the protected disclosures (*Royal Mail Group Ltd v Jhuti* [2016] IRLR 854, EAT). For the application of the burden of proof in such cases see *Kuzel v Roche Products Ltd* [2008] EWCA Civ 380, [2008] IRLR 530. As enacted, *PIDA 1998* contemplated that the compensation for unfair dismissal by reason of making a protected disclosure would be on the same basis as that applying to other categories of unfair dismissal. *PIDA 1998, s 8* kept open the possibility of introducing a different basis for assessment of compensation by way of regulations to be introduced by the Secretary of State prescribing the manner of calculation of compensation in such cases (see *ERA 1996, s 127B*, inserted by *PIDA 1998, s 8(4)*). The relevant *Regulations (Public Interest Disclosure (Compensation) Regulations 1999 (SI 1999/1548))* remove the limit on an unfair dismissal compensatory award in relation to this category of dismissal (see *ERA 1996, s 124(1A)* and *s 103A*). By *ERA 1996, s 123(6A)*, in the event of an unfair dismissal where the reason or principal reason for the dismissal was a protected disclosure but one that was not made in good faith, then the compensatory award may be reduced by up to 25% if the tribunal considers it just and equitable to do so (as added by *s 18(5)* of the *ERRA 2013* from 25 June 2013). There is no similar provision applying to a basic award for unfair dismissal.

Awards for injury to feelings as a result of subjection to a detriment (but not dismissal) will be calculated on the same basis as in discrimination cases (ie applying the guidance in *Vento v Chief Constable of West Yorkshire Police (No 2)* [2002] EWCA Civ 1871, [2003] IRLR 102). See *Virgo Fidelis Senior School v Boyle* [2004] IRLR 268, EAT. Following a detailed review of the authorities, the EAT in *Commissioner of Police for the Metropolis v Shaw* [2012] IRLR 291 has held that, when making an award of aggravated damages in a whistleblowing claim, such damages are an aspect of injury to feelings as they refer to increasing the injury to feelings by some act in addition to the wrong itself. Tribunals are advised to express the award by identifying the ordinary injury to feelings element and the aggravated element as subheadings of the overall injury to feelings award. In the case of a dismissal which is automatically unfair by reason of making a protected disclosure, as in other areas of unfair dismissal, no award can be made for injury to feelings (cf *Dunnachie v Kingston upon Hull City Council* [2004] IRLR 727, HL).

Interim relief is available in appropriate protected disclosure cases where the claimant is "likely" to succeed in the claim. See the *Employment Rights Act 1996, ss 128* and *129*. In *Dandpat v University of Bath* (UKEAT/408/09) (10 November 2009, unreported) and *Raja v Secretary of State for Justice* (UKEAT/0364/09/CEA) [2010] All ER (D) 134 (Mar) the EAT held that a claimant must show "a pretty good chance of success" (*Taplin v C Shippam Ltd* [1978] IRLR 450 (EAT) – a case under *TULR(C)A, s 163* – applied). More recently in *Ministry of Justice v Sarfraz* [2011] EAT 562, the EAT clarified that, in making an order for interim relief under *ss 128* and *129* of the *1996 Act*, the employment judge in a whistleblowing case must find that it was "likely" that the employment tribunal at the final hearing would find five things: (i) that the claimant had made a disclosure to his employer; (ii) that he believed that that disclosure tended to show one or more of the things itemised at (a)–(f) under *s 43B(1)* of the *1996 Act*; (iii) that that belief was reasonable; (iv) that the disclosure was made in good faith; and (v) that the disclosure was the principal reason for his dismissal. In that regard, the word "likely" does not mean "more likely than not" (that is at least 51% probability) but connotes a significantly higher degree of likelihood.

In a careful and detailed judgment the Court of Appeal decided that the principles outlined in *Relaxion Group plc v Rhys-Harper* [2003] UKHL 33, [2003] 4 All ER 1113 in relation to acts of victimisation occurring after the termination of the employment contract do apply to detriments suffered after the termination of the employment relationship, for example an unfavourable reference provided by reason of having made a protected disclosure (see *Woodward v Abbey National plc* [2006] EWCA Civ 822, [2006] 4 All ER 1209, [2006] ICR 1436). *Fadipe v Reed Nursing Personnel* [2001] EWCA Civ 1885, [2005] ICR 1760 (Note) which had held that post-employment victimisation under *s 44* of the *ERA* (health and safety cases) was not protected should not now be followed after *Woodward*. In *Onyango v Adrian Berkeley t/a Berkeley Solicitors* [2013] IRLR 338, the issue was whether the protection against detriment could apply to the situation where the protected disclosure relied upon for the purposes of *s 43B, ERA* occurred after the termination of the employment. The EAT, applying *Woodwood*, concluded that, as a post termination detriment was actionable, there was no reason to exclude the situation where the protected disclosure relied upon also occurred post termination.

The breadth of application of the protection afforded by the concept of a protected disclosure is further illustrated by two cases involving dismissal occurring *after PIDA 1998* came into force but in relation to disclosures of information made *before PIDA 1998* came into force. In circumstances where the dismissal or other detriment imposed by the employer by reason of the disclosure occurred after 2 July 1999 an Employment Tribunal had jurisdiction to hear a complaint (see *Stolt Offshore Ltd v Miklaszewicz* [2002] IRLR 344 and *Meteorological Office v Edgar* [2002] ICR 149). In *Pinnington v City and Council of Swansea* [2005] EWCA Civ 135, [2005] ICR 685, however, the Court of Appeal held that a suspension from work which had commenced prior to the coming into force of *PIDA 1998* but which continued for two days during which the *Act* was in force did not amount to a detriment under *ERA, s 47B* in relation to the final two days as there was no distinct act or omission by the employer on those two days on the grounds of the employee having made a protected disclosure.

The wide ambit of a 'qualifying disclosure' prior to the amendments introduced by the *ERRA 2013* was vividly illustrated by *Parkins v Sodexho Ltd* [2002] IRLR 109 in which case the EAT held that a complaint by an employee to his employer of a breach of his own contract of employment could be a qualifying (and protected) disclosure in relation to 'any legal obligation'. It followed that a dismissal by reason of making the complaint could be automatically unfair under the provisions of the *PIDA 1998* as contained in *ERA 1996*. The effect of the requirement that the employee reasonably believes that the disclosure is in the public interest is intended to reverse the effect of this decision. Whilst this will be an important area to be further clarified in the courts it is clear that the intention of the amendment is to remove matters of essentially private dispute between employer and employee from the scope of whistleblowing protection. (See *Chesterton Global Ltd v Numohamed* [2015] IRLR 614 above).

In *Hibbins v Hesters Way Neighbourhood Project* [2009] ICR 319, [2009] IRLR 198 the EAT held that the protection afforded to whistleblowers is not limited to cases where the wrongdoing relates to wrongdoing or failure by the employer but extends to a disclosure relating to the default of any legal person. Subject to the requirement that the disclosure is in the public interest this principle would appear to remain good law following the amendments introduced by the *ERRA 2013*.

10.18 Disclosure of Information

The protection against detriment is, similarly, not without limits and does not extend to employees deciding to conduct an 'investigation' into possible misconduct by the employer by hacking into the employer's computer system or searching files for 'evidence'. Such activity does not amount to a 'disclosure'. See *Evans v Bolton School* [2006] EWCA Civ 1653, [2007] ICR 641, sub nom *Bolton School v Evans* [2007] IRLR 140 in which a disciplinary warning given to a teacher for hacking into a computer was held to be legitimate and not a detriment imposed by reason of a protected disclosure. *Bolton School* was applied in *Panayiotou v Kernaghan* [2014] IRLR 500 (above) drawing the important distinction between a detriment imposed by reason of a protected disclosure and one imposed by reason of the unreasonable way in which the employee makes the disclosure. It was held in *Waite v South East Coast Ambulance Service NHS Trust* [2009] All ER (D) 43 (Jan) that before a claimant may lodge a whistleblowing detriment claim under *s 48* of the *ERA* a written grievance must be submitted pursuant to the statutory grievance procedures. This no longer applies after 6 April 2009 with the repeal of the statutory grievance procedure provisions of the *Employment Act 2002* by the *Employment Act 2008 (Commencement No 1, Transitional and Savings) Order 2008 (SI 2008/3232)*.

In *NHS Manchester v Fecitt* [2012] IRLR 64 (above) the Court of Appeal had held, applying *Majrowski v Guy's and St Thomas' NHS Trust* [2007] 1 AC 224, that the employer cannot be vicariously liable for the acts of employees which are not themselves unlawful. Thus acts of victimisation on grounds of having made a protected disclosure were not in themselves unlawful and there was, accordingly, no basis for vicarious liability. The decision of the EAT in *Carlisle-Morgan v Cumbria County Council* [2007] IRLR 314, [2007] All ER (D) 248 (Jan) (EAT) to the contrary was considered to be wrongly decided. This lacuna in the statutory protection against detriment has been addressed by amendments introduced by the *ERRA 2013* with effect from 25 June 2013. *Section 47B of the ERA 1996*, which provides the protection against detriment on grounds of having made a protected disclosure, has new subsections *(1A)–(1E)* added by *s 19(1)* of the ERRA 2013. These subsections extend protection against detriment by reason of having made a protected disclosure to detriments imposed by other workers in the course of that worker's employment or by agents of the employer acting with the employer's authority *(ERA, s 47B(1A))*. The provisions are similar to those found in relation to liability of employees and agents in the *Equality Act 2010 ("EQA 2010")* and provide for a statutory defence for the employer to show that the employer took all reasonable steps to prevent the detriment *(ERA, s 47B(1D))*. By *ERA s 47B(1E)* a worker or agent is not liable for doing something which subjects the disclosing worker to a detriment if the worker or agent does that thing in reliance on a statement by the employer that doing that thing does not contravene the *Act* and it is reasonable for the worker or agent to rely on that statement. If that defence is made out it does not prevent liability of the employer arising under *ERA s 47B(1B)* *(ERA s 47B(1E))*.

11   Discrimination and Equal Opportunities – I

11.1   THE SCOPE AND APPROACH OF THIS CHAPTER

Scope

Over the course of the last half-century, UK employment law has seen the ongoing and often vigorous development of a body of equal opportunities law. The underlying concept is a straightforward one: people should not be subject to disadvantage in the job market or in the workplace for reasons that have nothing to do with the skills they have to offer or their performance of their duties. There has been a steady incrementing of characteristics of the employee upon which it is no longer accepted that an employer may base employment-related decisions. As the law stands they are: sex; marital or civil partnership status; race; disability; gender reassignment; religion or belief; sexual orientation; pregnancy or maternity leave; and age. These grounds are referred to below as the 'protected characteristics'.

On 8 April 2010, the *Equality Act 2010* ("*EA 2010*") received Royal Assent. Many of its most important provisions came into force on 1 October 2010. The principal purpose of the Act was to consolidate the numerous individual pieces of legislation that had previously made up the patchwork of the earlier law. This edition of the Handbook does not set out the old law. It does, however, refer to caselaw decided under the former regime where it remains relevant to the interpretation of *EA 2010*.

Discrimination on grounds of sex in respect of contractual terms and conditions, which is known more familiarly as "Equal Pay" or, to use the language of the *EA 2010*, "Equality of Terms", is treated separately (see EQUAL PAY (22)).

Approach

The approach taken below is first to explain the relevant general principle and immediately thereafter to indicate where particular issues arise in the context of its application to one or more of the protected characteristics.

11.2   LEGAL SOURCES AND GUIDANCE MATERIAL

Each protection against discrimination has been introduced by a legislative instrument. Sometimes the Domestic law implements an obligation originally to be found in a European legislative measure. However, even those measures, such as protection against discrimination on grounds of sex or race, which have domestic origins have since been shaped by European Law.

On 6 April 2011, the Employment and Human Rights Commission issued a Code of Practice on Employment (the "*EHRC* Code") which can be downloaded from the EHRC's website at the following address: www.equalityhumanrights.com/publication/employment-statutory-code-practice.
Tribunals and courts must take into account any part of the Code that appears to them relevant to any questions arising in proceedings.

The Government produced a series of guides providing short, clear explanations of the impact of *EA 2010* on different sectors. They may be found online at: https ://www.gov.uk/government/publications/equality-act-guidance.

11.2 Discrimination and Equal Opportunities – I

BASIC DISCRIMINATION CONCEPTS

Set out immediately below is a summary of the legislative framework applicable to each of the protected characteristics:

11.3 Sex

Sex discrimination in employment is prohibited by the *EA 2010*. Sex is identified as a protected characteristic at *EA 2010, s 4*. Both men and women are protected (*EA 2010, s 11*).

Men cannot complain of sex discrimination where a woman has received "special treatment . . . in connection with pregnancy or childbirth" (*EA 2010, s 3(6)(b)*). However, in *Eversheds Legal Services Ltd v De Belin* [2011] IRLR 448, [2011] ICR 1137, EAT (a case brought under the *Sex Discrimination Act 1975* ("*SDA 1975*")), it was held that where the "special treatment" was disproportionate, in the sense of being more favourable treatment than was reasonably necessary to compensate the woman for the disadvantages occasioned by her pregnancy, a claim could be brought by a man using the woman as a comparator.

Equal treatment between the sexes in employment is within the scope of competence of the European Union. The *Equal Treatment Directive (2006/54/EC)* ('*ETD 2006/54/EC*') is vertically directly effective which means that public sector workers are able to rely directly on its provisions. *EA 2010* is interpreted, so far as possible, so as to be consistent with the requirements of the *Directive*.

On 1 May 1999, the *Amsterdam Treaty* came into force. It amended *art 119* of the *Treaty of Rome* (now *art 157* of the *Treaty on the Functioning of the European Union*) incorporating a principle of equal treatment into the *Treaty* itself. This, in turn, has opened up the possibility of a horizontally directly effective right to equal treatment conferred on both public and private sector employees.

11.4 Marital or civil partnership status

"Marriage and civil partnership status" is identified as a protected characteristic at *EA 2010, s 4*. Marriage is to be interpreted as including the marriage of a same sex couple (*Marriage (Same Sex Couples) Act 2013, Sch 3, Pt 1, Para 1(1)(a)*). Only those who are married or who have a civil partner are protected (*EA 2010, s 8(2)*). The *Act* does not protect those who are discriminated against on grounds of being single. Discrimination against unmarried partners was found to be precluded by Art 14, para 1 of the *European Convention on Human Rights* when read with Article 1 of the Protocol (i.e. the right to peaceful enjoyment of possessions) in a case concerning a survivor's pension (*Re Brewster's application for judicial review* [2017] UKSC 8, [2017] IRLR 366, [2017] ICR 434).

A protection against discrimination on grounds of marital or family status was included in *ETD 76/207/EEC* but is absent from the *ETD 2006/54/EC* which superseded it. It is unclear whether or not the intention was to push marital status outside the range of protected characteristics for the purposes of European Law (see *Dunn v Institute of Cemetery and Crematorium Management* [2012] All ER (D) 173 (Feb)).

11.5 Race

Race is identified as a protected characteristic by *EA 2010, s 4*. For the definition of "race" see **11.20** below.

Article 18 of the *Treaty on the Functioning of The European Union* prohibits discrimination on grounds of nationality "within the scope of application of the Treaties". *Article 19* (formerly *art 13* of the *Treaty of Rome*) confers a power on the European Union to legislate to combat discrimination on a variety of grounds including 'racial or ethnic origin'. On

29 June 2000, the European Council issued the *Race Discrimination Framework Directive (Council Directive 2000/43/EC)*. The scope of the *Directive* is not identical to that of *EA 2010*. For instance, *EA 2010* treats nationality as a form of discrimination because of race. In contrast the *Directive* does not apply to discrimination on grounds of nationality (*art 3, para 2*).

11.6   Gender reassignment

Gender reassignment is identified as a protected characteristic at *EA 2010, s 4*. For the definition of "gender reassignment" see **11.21** below.

11.7   Religion or belief

Adherence to a particular religion or holding a particular religious or philosophical belief is identified as a protected characteristic at *EA 2010, s 4*. For the definition of "religion", "religious belief" and "philosophical belief" see **11.22** below. Lacking a particular religion or religious or philosophical belief is also a protected characteristic (*EA 2010, s 10*).

The protection has its origins in *art 19(1)* of the *Treaty on the Functioning of the European Union* which provides that 'the Council . . . may take appropriate action to combat discrimination based on . . . religion or belief . . . '. On 27 November 2000, the Council issued *Directive 2000/78/EC* establishing a general framework for equal treatment in employment and occupation ('the *Framework Directive 2000/78/EC*'). The directive included a prohibition of religious discrimination.

11.8   Sexual orientation

Sexual orientation is identified as a protected characteristic at *EA 2010, s 4*. For the definition of "sexual orientation" see **11.23** below.

The origin of the protection is, once again, *art 19* of the *Treaty on the Functioning of the European Union* and the *Framework Directive 2000/78/EC*.

11.9   Pregnancy or maternity leave

Pregnancy and Maternity are identified as protected characteristics at *EA 2010, s 4*. For the definitions of "pregnancy" and "maternity" see **11.24** below.

11.10   Age

Age is identified as a protected characteristic at *EA 2010, s 4*. For the definitions of "age" and "age group" see **11.25** below.

The *Act* is the present implementation of the age-related provisions of the *Framework Directive 2000/78/EC* which required member states to enact legislation prohibiting age discrimination in employment.

Following the case of *Mangold v Helm* [2006] IRLR 143 in the European Court of Justice, there is some question as to whether the *Directive* made it unlawful to discriminate on the grounds of age even prior to 1 October 2006 (that being the date on which the *Employment Equality (Age) Regulations 2006* (*SI 2006/1031*) first implemented the *Directive*). This is a matter of some controversy and is not addressed in detail here. For a discussion by the Advocate General of the European Court of Justice which is somewhat critical of the judgment in *Mangold*, see *Félix Palacios* at paras 79 to 100. In *Bartsch v Bosch und Siemens Hausgeräte (BSH) Altersfürsorge GmbH*: C-427/06 [2009] All ER (EC) 113, [2009] 1 CMLR 163, the ECJ held that the prohibition on age discrimination was not mandatory in a case where the allegedly discriminatory measure was not intended to implement the *Directive* at a time before the time limit for transposing the *Directive* had expired. However, in the case of *Seda Kucukdeveci v Swedex GmbH & Co KG*: C-555/07 [2010] IRLR 346, the ECJ reiterated that the principle of non-discrimination on the ground of age should be regarded as a general principle of European Law and held that the European provisions may be relied upon to challenge legislation which was enacted prior to the coming into force of the directive.

11.11 Disability

Disability is identified as a protected characteristic at *EA 2010, s 4*. For the definition of "disability" see **11.26** below.

The *Act* is the present implementation in UK law of the prohibition against discrimination on grounds of disability to be found in the *Framework Directive 2000/78/EC*. In *HK Danmark*, acting on behalf of *Ring v Dansk Almennyttigt Boligselskab*: C-335/11 [2013] IRLR 571, the CJEU held that the *Framework Directive* had to be read, so far as possible, so as to be compatible with the *United Nations Convention on the Rights of Persons with Disabilities*.

11.12 MEANING OF DISCRIMINATION

There are four principal ways in which a person may discriminate against another:

(i)   by *directly* discriminating against them (**11.13** below);

(ii)   by *indirectly* discriminating against them (**11.34** below);

(iii)   by *victimising* them (**11.38** below); or

(iv)   by *harassing* them (**11.39** below).

In addition there are two forms of discrimination which are specific to disability discrimination:

(v)   failure to make reasonable adjustments (a close cousin of indirect discrimination) (**11.37** below); and

(vi)   discrimination arising from disability (**11.33** below).

There is also a discrete form of direct discrimination which prohibits unfavourable treatment of because of pregnancy or maternity leave (see **11.30** ff below).

11.13 DIRECT DISCRIMINATION

Direct discrimination is defined at *EA 2010, s 13(1)*:

> "A person (A) discriminates against another (B) if, because of a protected characteristic, A treats B less favourably than A treats or would treat others."

Persons A and B may be any legal person, including a company (*EAD Solicitors v Abrams* [2016] ICR 380, [2015] IRLR 978).

The basic definition is modified insofar as it relates to age discrimination. If the protected characteristic is age, A does not discriminate against B if A can show A's treatment of B to be a "proportionate means of achieving a legitimate aim" (see further below at **11.34**).

The definition differs from that which applied under the pre-existing law in that rather than the less favourable treatment having to be "on grounds of" the relevant protected characteristic, the treatment has to be "because of it". The explanatory notes accompanying the Act suggest that the change in language is intended to make the legislation easier to understand but not to bring about any material change in the law (*EA 2010, EN Para 61*).

The account set out immediately below breaks the legislative tests into two elements: less favourable treatment and the reason for that treatment. Whilst that division reflects the manner in which a tribunal will usually approach the issue, in *Shamoon v Chief Constable of the Royal Ulster Constabulary* [2003] UKHL 11, [2003] 2 All ER 26, [2003] ICR 337 a number of their Lordships took the view that it may sometimes be appropriate to ask the latter question first. For an account of when it will be appropriate to do so, see **11.15** below.

Less favourable treatment

11.14 *Unfavourable and less favourable treatment distinguished*

Most people asked to summarise the overall aim of anti-discrimination legislation would likely begin by suggesting that people should not be treated badly because of their protected characteristic. However, the test for direct discrimination is not whether a person treats another "unfavourably". Instead, *EA 2010, s 13* requires a complainant to show that they have been treated "less favourably" than another. The reason why the legislation takes this approach is that rather than trying to ensure that people are treated well, it is aimed at ensuring that people are treated equally. So, for instance, few would argue against the proposition that a pay rise is a good thing. However, if an employer gives his ethnic minority employees smaller pay rises than he gives white employees because of their race he commits an act of unlawful discrimination. The ethnic minority employees have been favourably treated (their pay has increased) but they have been less favourably treated. The flipside is that an employer who treats all of his employees equally badly will not normally be found to have discriminated. It is the equality rather than the quality of the treatment that matters. For that reason, the House of Lords has suggested that the conduct of a hypothetical reasonable employer is irrelevant to the question whether he has unlawfully discriminated:

> 'The fact that, for the purposes of the law of unfair dismissal, an employer has acted unreasonably casts no light whatsoever on the question whether he has treated an employee less favourably for the purposes of the [*EA 2010*]'.

(*Glasgow City Council v Zafar* [1998] 2 All ER 953, [1997] 1 WLR 1659, [1998] ICR 120. See also *Martins v Marks & Spencer plc* [1998] IRLR 326.) Despite the House of Lords' robust rejection of the suggestion that showing that an employer's conduct was unreasonable makes it more likely that they have treated an affected employee less favourably, other authorities have been prepared to give the unreasonableness of the employer's conduct a limited and indirect relevance. Thus in *Law Society v Bahl* [2003] IRLR 640, EAT, the Employment Appeal Tribunal took the view that the more unreasonable the treatment the more the credibility of any non-discriminatory explanation proffered may be called into question. The question was considered more closely by the Court of Appeal (*Bahl v Law Society* [2004] EWCA 1070; [2004] IRLR 799). The Court of Appeal reiterated that unreasonable behaviour cannot found an inference of discrimination. An employer is not obliged, therefore, to lead evidence that others have been treated equally unreasonably. However, if there is no explanation for the unreasonable treatment the absence of an explanation (as opposed to the unreasonableness of the treatment) might found an inference. The Court of Appeal returned to the issue in a later case in which no explanation was provided and held that whilst a tribunal should not be 'too ready' to infer unlawful discrimination from unreasonable conduct in the absence of evidence of other discriminatory behaviour, it was 'not wrong in law' to do so (*Wong v Igen Ltd* [2005] EWCA Civ 142, [2005] 3 All ER 812, [2005] ICR 931). *Nelson v Newry and Mourne District Council* [2009] IRLR 548 approached the question from the opposite direction, appearing to suggest that the reasonableness of the employer's position pointed away from a conclusion of discrimination. In *Eagle Place Services Ltd v Rudd* [2010] IRLR 486, the EAT took yet another approach to the question of the relevance of the reasonableness of the employer's behaviour. The employer dismissed a disabled employee unreasonably. The employer said that the appropriate comparator would be someone towards whom they would have behaved equally unreasonably but who was not disabled. The EAT disagreed with the employer's analysis, holding that it was not open to the employer to say that they would have behaved unreasonably towards the comparator.

Even in cases where employees have plainly been treated differently, it may still be difficult immediately to determine whether there has been less favourable treatment. Thus, where male and female employees are subject to different but comparably restrictive dress requirements there is no less favourable treatment on grounds of sex (*Schmidt v Austicks Bookshops Ltd* [1977] IRLR 360, EAT; and see *Smith v Safeway plc* [1996] ICR 868, CA and *Department for Work and Pensions v Thompson* [2004] IRLR 348, EAT).

The test of what amounts to less favourable treatment is an objective one (*Burrett v West Birmingham Health Authority* [1994] IRLR 7, EAT). However, there may be a limited role for the subjective preferences of the complainant. Thus, where a local education authority provided more places for boys than for girls in selective schools, the House of Lords held that it was not necessary for the complainant to demonstrate that selective education was, objectively, 'better' than non-selective education. It was enough that, by denying the girls the same opportunity as the boys, the council was depriving them of a choice which was valued by them (or at least by their parents) and which was a choice obviously valued, on reasonable grounds, by many others (*Birmingham City Council v Equal Opportunities Commission* [1989] AC 1155, [1989] 2 WLR 520, HL).

It is the treatment itself rather than its consequences which must be different and less favourable (*Balgobin v Tower Hamlets London Borough Council* [1987] ICR 829, EAT).

Segregating a person from others on racial grounds is deemed to be less favourable treatment (*EA 2010, s 13(5)*). Thus, it is not open to an employer to argue that the provision of segregated facilities for his black employees is not discriminatory even though the facilities provided for black workers are equal to, if not better than, those provided for his white employees. No similar provision is made in respect of the other protected characteristics (see, in relation to sex: *Interim Executive Board of C School v Her Majesty's Chief Inspector of Education, Children's Services and Skills* [2016] EWHC 2813 (Admin), [2017] IRLR 30.

In the case of a pre-operative transsexual, avoiding less favourable treatment does not necessarily require that the complainant be treated as if their gender had already been changed. What is required in any case will depend on the particular circumstances (*Croft v Royal Mail Group plc* [2003] EWCA Civ 1045, [2003] IRLR 592: pre-operative male to female transsexual not treated less favourably when not allowed to use female toilets).

11.15   *Comparators*

Identifying direct discrimination involves the making of a comparison. It is open to an employee either to demonstrate that another specific individual employee has been more favourably treated (in which case that other employee is known as the 'comparator') or to establish that, absent any concrete examples, the tribunal may nevertheless still be sure that the employer would have treated another employee more favourably. In the latter case, the Tribunal considers what is known as a 'hypothetical comparator'.

Identifying a suitable comparator

(a) General Requirement that there should be no material difference between the complainant and the comparator

The *EA 2010* requires that the circumstances of the comparator should not be materially different:

"On a comparison of cases for the purposes of section 13 [direct discrimination] . . . there must be no material difference between the circumstances relating to each case." (*EA 2010, s 23(1)*)

The question whether a comparator is appropriate is one of "fact and degree" – the circumstances of the complainant and the comparator need not be identical (*Hewage v Grampian Health Board* [2012] UKSC 37, [2012] ICR 1054). Although picking the wrong comparator will be an error of law (*Naeem v Secretary of State for Justice* UKEAT/215/13; [2014] ICR 472).

For guidance on the question of when circumstances will be materially different see *Dhatt v McDonalds Hamburgers Ltd* [1991] 3 All ER 692, [1991] 1 WLR 527, [1991] ICR 238: it was not discriminatory to treat potential employees differently according to whether they were or were not free to work in the United Kingdom without permission and, hence, it was legitimate to require evidence of such permission only from those who were not British or EU citizens. (See also *Wakeman v Quick Corpn* [1999] IRLR 424, CA: UK employees of a Japanese company could not complain about higher rates of pay enjoyed by colleagues seconded from Japan. The fact that they were secondees meant that their circumstances were materially different to those of the UK employees; but see *Spicer v Government of Spain* [2004] EWCA Civ 1046, [2005] ICR 213; *Bullock v Alice Ottley School* [1993] ICR 138: The comparator selected in a sex discrimination case concerned with a disparity in retirement ages was inappropriate because he performed a different job to that performed by the complainant; *Shomer v B & R Residential Lettings Ltd* [1992] IRLR 317, *Leeds Private Hospital Ltd v Parkin* [1992] ICR 571 and *Brook v Haringey London Borough Council* [1992] IRLR 478.) Where a female prison officer complained about being made to search male prisoners the appropriate comparator was a man required to search female prisoners and not a man required to search men (*Saunders v Home Office* [2006] ICR 318, EAT). In a case where a Muslim school support worker was suspended for refusing to remove her veil when interacting with pupils the appropriate comparator was a woman who was not a Muslim who also covered her face: *Azmi v Kirklees MBC* [2007] ICR 1154. In *Kelly v Covance Laboratories Ltd* UKEAT/0186/15 [2016] IRLR 338, where an animal testing laboratory was worried about infiltration by animal rights activists, an instruction to a Russian national to speak English called for a comparator who also spoke a language other than English at the workplace.

Identifying an appropriate comparator has proven difficult in cases where employers have distinguished between different age groups when deciding what termination payments to make. *Lockwood v DWP* [2013] EWCA Civ 1195, [2013] IRLR 941, a younger employee complained that those older than 35 had voluntary redundancy payments calculated on a more generous basis. The EAT decided that those under 35 could not validly compare themselves with their older colleagues. Statistics suggested that older employees found it harder to get another job which made their circumstances materially different. The Court of Appeal overturned the EAT's decision. Since the reason that older employees found getting a new job harder was, the statistics suggested, their age, the supposed material distinction was, in truth, the protected characteristic itself. Applying *Lockwood*, the EAT in *Donkor v Royal Bank of Scotland* UKEAT/0162/15, [2016] IRLR 268 determined that where an employee was denied voluntary redundancy because he was old enough to qualify for early retirement he could be validly compared to a younger colleague who was not entitled to retire and whose voluntary redundancy package was consequently much cheaper. "But for" the claimant's age, the difference in entitlement would not have existed. Therefore, the cost was itself an age -related factor and not a material difference. The thrust of the Domestic authorities is to treat age-related job market factors as being irrelevant to the question of the appropriate comparison but relevant to the question of justification. However, a somewhat different approach was taken by the ECJ in *O v Bio Philippe Auguste*

Sarl C-432/14 [2015] IRLR 1017. The ECJ concluded that students doing vacation work could be excluded from an entitlement to receive a payment at the end of a fixed term period of employment. The students were not comparable to ordinary fixed-term workers. Vacation work was "temporary" and "ancillary" and students did not suffer from the same "job insecurity" as their older colleagues.

When dealing with hypothetical comparators it might be possible to construe the legislation so as to require the tribunal to construct a comparator who is 'in effect, a clone of the applicant in every respect (including personality and personal characteristics)' save that they are, for instance, of a different race. However, that approach was rejected in *Madden v Preferred Technical Group CHA Ltd* [2004] EWCA Civ 1178, [2005] IRLR 46 (per Wall LJ at paragraph 87). The effect of such an approach would be to run together the two relevant questions, namely whether the complainant was less favourably treated and whether they were less favourably treated on the prohibited ground. The reasoning would be that if the complainant and comparator are identical in all respects save, for instance, for their race any less favourable treatment must, logically, be on racial grounds. In practice, it can be very difficult to keep the two issues distinct. There are signs that this difficulty is being embraced by the appeal courts. In *Stockton on Tees Borough Council v Aylott* [2010] EWCA Civ 910, [2011] ICR 1279, the Court of Appeal invokes the decision of the House of Lords in *Shamoon v Chief Constable of the Royal Ulster Constabulary* [2003] UKHL 11, [2003] 2 All ER 26, [2003] ICR 337 and suggests that it will often be appropriate to start by identifying the reason for the treatment the employee complains of. If the answer is that the reason is a protected characteristic, the finding of less favourable treatment will likely follow as a matter of inevitability. Since the hypothetical comparator is designed to allow a tribunal to decide whether there has been less favourable treatment and that finding is, in turn, intended to be a signpost pointing to a prohibited and discriminatory reason for the employer's actions, the *Shamoon* approach effectively starts the journey at the point which had originally been identified as the destination. Adopting that approach will often make it unnecessary to identify a hypothetical comparator at all, as Mummery LJ made clear in *Stockton* (see also *JP Morgan Europe Ltd v Chweidan* [2011] EWCA Civ 648, [2012] ICR 268). Where a tribunal determines, nevertheless, to identify one it should determine which circumstances are relevant by reasoning backwards from the reason for the treatment accorded to the complainant. As Mummery LJ puts it in *Stockton*:

> 'The relevant circumstances and attributes of an appropriate comparator should reflect the circumstances and attributes relevant to the reason for the action or decision which is complained of.'

The selection of the comparator is the responsibility of the complainant. However, in some circumstances, a tribunal that determines that the complainant's chosen comparator is inappropriate may be required to go on to make the comparison with a hypothetical comparator (see *Balamoody v UK Central Council for Nursing, Midwifery and Health Visiting* [2001] EWCA Civ 2097, [2002] IRLR 288: the complainant was unrepresented. The Court of Appeal appears to have felt that the tribunal had a rather better grasp of the nature of the complainant's case than he did himself).

(b) Comparators in cases of direct disability discrimination

Where the protected characteristic is disability, *EA 2010, s 23(2)* requires that the "circumstances" that must not materially differ between complainant and comparator specifically include a person's abilities. In other words, the complainant and comparator must have the same abilities. This may mean that the appropriate comparator is also a disabled person. At first glance this might appear illogical. However, the rationale is that direct disability discrimination is not intended to protect against less favourable treatment received because the employee lacks certain abilities but rather against less favourable treatment because they have a "particular disability". An example would be an employee who is dismissed because they are HIV+. Their abilities may be indistinguishable from those of any other employee but the employer is not prepared to employ people with that particular disability. Discrimination on the grounds that an employee lacks a particular ability is the subject of a separate protection dealt with at **11.39** below. It is known as "discrimination arising from disability" and differs to direct discrimination in that it is engaged where the employee is treated unfavourably (rather than *less* favourably) and a defence of justification is potentially available.

Watts v High Quality Lifestyles Ltd [2006] IRLR 850, [2006] All ER (D) 216 (Apr), EAT was the first appellate decision to consider direct disability discrimination. The claimant was a support worker who had suffered a number of injuries including cuts and bites in the course of his work with persons with learning difficulties. Upon revealing to management that he was HIV+, he was suspended and later dismissed on the grounds that his position was untenable after a risk assessment concluded that injuries involving broken skin were commonplace. The employment tribunal found that such treatment was on the grounds of disability and upheld his claim. However, the EAT found that the employment tribunal had failed to consider whether he had in fact been less favourably treated than a hypothetical comparator would have been. The EAT also found that in identifying the appropriate comparator, the Employment Tribunal should have found that the comparator had 'some attribute, whether caused by medical condition or otherwise, which is not HIV+ . . . [which] must carry the same risk of causing to others illness or injury of the same gravity, here serious and possibly fatal'. It is thought that this approach to identifying comparators might be to construe 'relevant circumstances' too narrowly. A comparator with an attribute carrying precisely the same risk of causing illness or injury to others would almost always be likely to be treated in the same way as the claimant, in which case the claim of direct discrimination would fail. The EAT's approach to comparator in this case, which requires that the comparator is effectively someone who is HIV+ by another name, could also let discrimination based on the stigma of being HIV+ slip through the net. In *Aylott v Stockton-on-Tees Borough Council* [2010] EWCA Civ 910, [2011] ICR 1278, the Court of Appeal considered that an employment tribunal had been entitled to exclude from the characteristics of its hypothetical comparator certain unsatisfactory aspects of the complainant's behaviour and performance on the basis that they stemmed from his particular disability. The tribunal had been entitled to exclude the particular disability itself from the comparison, but it seemed they could also exclude certain effects of the disability. The *Stockton* approach would appear, therefore, to take a more employee-friendly approach than *Watts*, though the latter authority has since been cited by the Court of Appeal with approval (see *Aitken v Commissioner of Police of the Metropolis* [2011] EWCA Civ 582, [2012] ICR 78 where *Aylott* was distinguished on its facts. The ET in *Aitken* considered threatening behaviour should be part of the circumstances applicable to a hypothetical comparator and the complainant did not suggest at that stage that the behaviour arose from his disability).

Whether and, if so, how the costs of supporting someone with a disability should be factored into the necessary comparison for direct discrimination purposes was at issue in *Cordell v Foreign and Commonwealth Office* [2012] ICR 280, EAT. The complainant was profoundly deaf. She was not appointed to a diplomatic post in Kazakhstan because of the cost and difficulty maintaining continuity of the services of a lip-speaker. Her case was the cost should be compared to cost of paying for diplomats posted overseas having their children educated in boarding school. The circumstances of those with children needing education was said to be materially different. A comparison that allowed the complainant to be compared with parents was too general to be useful. The EAT preferred to take the *Shamoon* approach (see **11.15** (a) above) and to ask the reason why the complainant was not appointed. The answer was not her disability but the costs of dealing with it, which meant that any less favourable treatment was not because of her disability and the claim for direct discrimination failed.

(c) Comparators in sexual orientation cases

Specific provision is made in relation to sexual orientation at *EA 2010, s 23*:

> (3) If the protected characteristic is sexual orientation, the fact that one person (whether or not the person referred to as B) is a civil partner while another is married to a person of the opposite sex is not a material difference between the circumstances relating to each case.

> (4) If the protected characteristic is sexual orientation, the fact that one person (whether or not the person referred to as B) is married to a person of the same sex while another is married to a person of the opposite sex is not a material difference between the circumstances relating to each case.

> (EA 2010, s 23 as amended with effect from 13 March 2014 by the Marriage (Same Sex Couples) Act 2013, Sch 7 and SI 2014/93).

(d) Comparators in Gender reassignment cases: absence due to undergoing a gender reassignment

EA 2010, s 16 makes specific provision protecting transsexuals who are absent from work because of a gender reassignment. A person's absence is treated as being because of gender reassignment "if it is because the person is proposing to undergo, is undergoing or has undergone [a] process (or part of [a] process)" for the purpose of reassigning the person's sex by changing physiological or other attributes of sex (*EA 2010, ss 7(1)* and *16(3)*). For the purposes of determining whether or not the employee has been treated less favourably because of their protected characteristic, *EA 2010, s 16* provides that the employee should be their own comparator. The Tribunal asks whether they would have been treated more favourably if they had been absent because of sickness or injury (*EA 2010, s 16(2)(a)*) or absent for some other reason where the Tribunal is satisfied that "it is not reasonable for [the employee] to be treated less favourably" (*EA 2010, s 16(2)(b)*).

(e) Comparators in pregnancy and maternity leave cases

There is a specific prohibition on treating a person unfavourably (as opposed to less favourably) because of pregnancy or maternity leave (*EA 2010, s 18*). Because what is prohibited is unfavourable treatment there is no need for a comparator. This reflects long-standing European authority to the effect that because only women may fall pregnant there is no appropriate male comparator. There is, in other words, no equivalent man whose circumstances could be said not to be materially different (see *Dekker v Stichting Vormingscentrum voor Jong Volwassenen (VJV - Centrum) Plus*: C-177/88 [1990] ECR I-3941, [1992] ICR 325 and *Webb v EMO Air Cargo (UK) Ltd* [1994] ICR 770, ECJ. For UK authority confirming the absence of a need for a comparator in pregnancy discrimination cases see *McGuigan v TG Boynes & Sons* [1999] 633 IDS Brief 6, EAT; *Smith v Gardner Merchant Ltd* [1998] IRLR 510 per Ward LJ obiter and *Fletcher v NHS Pensions Agency* [2005] ICR 1458, EAT). The *s 18* protection against unfavourable treatment on grounds of pregnancy is dealt with at **11.30** below.

However, *EA 2010, ss 4* and *13* appear to have the effect that pregnancy and maternity are also amongst the protected characteristics which are prohibited from being the reason for less favourable treatment. Perhaps surprisingly, it seems to be open to an employee who can make out a claim under *EA 2010, s 18* also to bring a claim under *s 13*. *EA 2010, s 18(7)* expressly precludes an employee bringing both a *s 18* pregnancy claim and a *s 13* sex discrimination claim. However, it does not preclude a *s 13* pregnancy discrimination claim. Why would a complainant ever want to bring a *s 13* pregnancy discrimination claim given the express protection conferred by *s 18*? The answer may be that there are cases of pregnancy discrimination that would not fall within *s 18*. The *s 18* protection is only available to a complainant during the so-called "protected period" (broadly from conception to the end of maternity leave – see *EA 2010, s 18(6)*). Thus, an employee who is discriminated against because she announces that she intends to become pregnant; because her employer discovers that she has miscarried; or because her employer mistakenly believes that she is pregnant cannot bring a *s 18* claim and will have to rely on *s 13*.

The uncertainty that remains is whether a complainant bring a *s 13* pregnancy discrimination claim has to identify a comparator. The need to establish less favourable treatment suggests that she does but since only women can announce an intention to get pregnant, miscarry or be mistakenly assumed to be pregnant, how can the apparent requirement for a comparator be reconciled with the European authorities referred to above? The legislation provides no answer and the matter awaits appellate consideration.

(f) Comparators in sex discrimination cases: is a comparison necessary where the conduct complained of is 'gender-specific'?

The short answer is 'yes'. At one point the courts and tribunals had come to accept that a comparative approach might not always be possible or appropriate in sex discrimination cases. As explained above, it has long since been accepted that a woman treated unfavourably on grounds of pregnancy has no valid male comparator. Attempts have been made to extend the principle to other instances of so-called "gender-specific" treatment, typically in cases of harassment where the female victim of harassment was treated in a way that a male victim would not have been.

The House of Lords in *Macdonald v Advocate General for Scotland* [2003] UKHL 34, [2004] 1 All ER 339, [2003] ICR 937 (see also *Smith v Gardner Merchant Ltd* [1998] 3 All ER 852, [1998] IRLR 510) specifically reaffirmed the need for a comparator even where the alleged discriminatory behaviour could be said to be gender-specific.

(g) Irrelevance of whether the alleged discriminator shares the protected characteristic with the complainant.

EA 2010, s 24(1) makes it clear that it is irrelevant whether the alleged discriminator (referred to as "A") shares the relevant protected characteristic with the complainant:

> "For the purpose of establishing a contravention of this Act by virtue of Section 13(1), it does not matter whether A has the protected characteristic".

Thus, a woman may discriminate against another woman on grounds of sex, etc.

Performing the comparison

The burden of establishing that they have been less favourably treated falls upon the complainant.

In most cases involving an actual comparator the comparison will be relatively straightforward. For instance, a complainant who has not been appointed to a particular post may seek to compare themselves to the person who was. Evidence will then centre on the selection process. Similarly, an employee who is made redundant may seek to compare themselves to someone who was retained in employment.

Matters are more complex when dealing with hypothetical comparators because the Tribunal will be asked to infer that the necessary less favourable treatment. By definition one is dealing with a situation where there may be little direct evidence. In *Chief Constable of West Yorkshire v Vento* [2001] IRLR 124, the EAT suggested that a tribunal might look to see how 'unidentical but not wholly dissimilar cases' had been dealt with. Thus, someone whose circumstances differ sufficiently from those of the complainant to make them an inappropriate comparator may nevertheless have relevance in the context of the consideration of how a hypothetical comparator would have been treated.

11.15   Discrimination and Equal Opportunities – I

In other cases a complainant may wish to lead evidence of, for instance, sexist comments made by the respondent on the basis that they tend to suggest a discriminatory attitude and thus that a male employee would have been treated more favourably. In such a case evidence principally relevant to the question whether less favourable treatment was on a prohibited ground may assist in establishing that the complainant would have been less favourably treated. Support for this approach may be found in *Shamoon v Chief Constable of the Royal Ulster Constabulary* [2003] UKHL 11, [2003] 2 All ER 26, [2003] ICR 337, in which a number of members of the House of Lords suggested that rather than identify the less favourable treatment and only then ask whether the reason for the treatment was the protected characteristic, a tribunal could first ask whether the characteristic was the reason why the complainant was treated in the manner complained about. If the tribunal decides that the characteristic was part of the reason for the treatment it can then be inferred that someone without the characteristic would have been treated more favourably. The decision in *Shamoon* was concerned with the law as it was before the enactment of *SDA 1975, s 63A*. That section formally reversed the burden of proof in sex discrimination cases. The reverse burden of proof, which now applies to all of the protected characteristics (see **11.3**) is to be found at *EA 2010, s 136*. As the burden only shifts where a prima facie case of discrimination has been established an exploration of the employer's reasons for actions as a first step would seem to jump the gun. However, the EAT has stressed the particular suitability of the *Shamoon* guidance when dealing with cases involving hypothetical comparators (see *Laing v Manchester City Council* [2006] ICR 1519, EAT). The Court of Appeal has sought to allow tribunals the greatest flexibility, holding both that whilst it is generally good practice to follow the two stage test, there is no necessary error of law if a tribunal does not do so (*Brown v Croydon London Borough Council* [2007] EWCA Civ 32, [2007] IRLR 259) and that it cannot be said to be an error of law in cases involving hypothetical comparators to deal first with the question of less favourable treatment (see *Madarassy v Nomura International plc* [2007] EWCA Civ 33, [2007] ICR 867 and *JP Morgan Europe Ltd v Chweidan* [2011] EWCA Civ 648, [2012] ICR 268).

11.16 *Positive discrimination*

"Positive discrimination" involves favouring those with a particular protected characteristic for well-intentioned reasons. As explained below (see **11.17**), UK law largely disregards such intentions and motives. Well-intentioned discrimination is still unlawful. However, the law does allow a limited scope for positive discrimination. The essence of exception is that, in certain defined circumstances, positive discrimination may be lawful where the purpose is to redress the effect of pre-existing discriminatory disadvantage. A full consideration of positive discrimination may be found at **12.10** DISCRIMINATION AND EQUAL OPPORTUNITIES – II.

'Because of' the protected characteristic

11.17 *General principles*

EA 2010, s 13 prohibits less favourable treatment "because of a protected characteristic". The use of the formula "because of" in preference to that used in the earlier legislation, (ie "on grounds of") was not intended materially to alter the law. The explanatory notes accompanying the Act suggest that the intention was simply to make the meaning of the legislation more readily accessible (*EA 2010, EN, Para 61*). In *Onu v Akwiwu* [2014] EWCA Civ 279, [2014] ICR 571, [2014] IRLR 448, the Court of Appeal expressly accepted that the two formulations have the same meaning (Affirmed [2016] UKSC 31, [2016] IRLR 719, [2016] ICR 756).

Cases of direct discrimination may be usefully divided into two categories. In the first category the treatment in issue is discriminatory on its face. In the second category, the treatment with which the court is concerned is not objectively discriminatory – one has to know something about the respondent's reasons for their actions in order to know whether the less favourable treatment could be said to be "because" of the protected characteristic. (For an example of the court applying this categorization see *Khan v Royal Mail Group* [2014] EWCA Civ 1082. See also *Amnesty International v Ahmed* [2009] ICR 1450 and *Interserve FM Limited v Tuleikyte* UKEAT/0267/16 where the two categories were referred to as "criterion" and "reason why" cases respectively and *Commissioner of Police of the Metropolis v Keohane* UKEAT/463/12 [2014] ICR 1073 where the EAT warns against the risk of letting such labels distract from the express statutory test).

A good example of the first type of case would be where an employer had an express policy of not appointing women to certain roles. Where the less favourable treatment is objectively discriminatory, the law does not require any investigation of the subjective motives of the discriminator. As the Court of Appeal put it in *Khan v Royal Mail Group*:

> "It does not matter why he discriminated on the ground of sex; if in fact he did."

Thus unintentional direct discrimination is unlawful as are acts of direct discrimination performed for entirely non-discriminatory motives (see *R (on the application of E) v Governing Body of JFS (Secretary of State for Children, School and Families, interested parties) (United Synagogue intervening)* [2009] UKSC 15, [2010] IRLR 136 and *Ahmed v Amnesty International* [2009] ICR 1450, [2009] NLJR 1400, EAT). See also *Martin v Devonshires Solicitors* UKEAT/86/10 [2011] ICR 352 which considers both *JFS* and *Ahmed* and proposes a distinction between "motive" which is irrelevant, and "motivation" which is not.

On the other hand, the presence of a discriminatory motive or intention will plainly be compelling evidence pointing to a finding of unlawful discrimination *Nagarajan v London Regional Transport* [2000] 1 AC 501 at 519). The tribunal must bear in mind that a discriminatory motive may be sub- or unconscious (*Geller v Yeshurun Hebrew Congregation* UKEAT/190/15, [2016] ICR 1028).

In some cases falling into the first category, less favourable treatment may be because of a characteristic which, while not itself a protected characteristic, is very closely related to one. In *James v Eastleigh Borough Council* [1990] 2 AC 751, [1990] 2 All ER 607, the claimant, a man, was charged to use a swimming pool whereas a woman of the same age would not have been. The difference in treatment arose from the fact that the local authority's policy was to allow pensioners to swim without charge and women had a lower State retirement age than men. Since retirement age depended directly upon gender, there was an exact correspondence between the characteristic relied upon by the claimant and the protected characteristic of sex. Similarly, in *Donkor v Royal Bank of Scotland* UKEAT/0162/15 [2016] IRLR 268, where voluntary redundancy was not offered to an older employee because he would have been entitled to take early retirement which would have been very costly, he was treated less favourably because of his age. The entitlement to retire and the associated cost arose from his age. In *Onu* (above), by contrast, the reason for less favourable treatment was the claimant's immigration status. The Supreme Court was not satisfied that that characteristic could be said exactly to correspond to the protected characteristic of nationality. Although all migrant domestic workers are non-British not all non-British people are migrant domestic workers.

An example of the second type of case is one where an ethnic minority employee is not promoted. It would not be sufficient for a tribunal to be satisfied that the employee has been less favourably treated than their chosen actual or hypothetical comparator. The tribunal will also want to consider *why* the complainant was not promoted. It is only if the protected characteristic is a substantive or operational reason for the less favourable treatment that liability will be established.

It might be said that in both categories the tribunal is still asking a causal question – what caused the less favourable treatment? Lawyers traditionally approach questions of causation by applying a "but for" analysis. They ask whether "but for" the protected characteristic the less favourable treatment would have occurred. The analysis works relatively straightforwardly with cases falling into the first category, like *James*. However, in *Onu* (above) the Court of Appeal suggested that in the second category of case it was better to avoid talk of causation altogether. A similar position was adopted by the House of Lords in *Chief Constable of West Yorkshire Police v Khan* [2001] UKHL 48, [2001] 1 WLR 1947, [2001] ICR 1065, HL(E), where it was said that the real question was "what, consciously or unconsciously, was the [alleged discriminator's] reason". Unlike causation, the Court considered, that question required a subjective test. Causation is a legal question whereas a respondent's reasons for action are a question of fact.

In some cases, the tribunal has been criticized for using the but for test. One example is *Martin v Lancehawk Ltd (trading as European Telecom Solutions)* [2004] All ER (D) 400 (Mar) EAT: an employer dismissed a female employee when their affair concluded. It was argued that as the employer would not have slept with a man, it could be said that 'but for' the complainant's sex she would not have been dismissed. The EAT found that there had been no discrimination. They felt that the 'reason why' the complainant was dismissed was the end of the affair and not her sex. Her sex was causally relevant but not causally determinative. The Appeal Tribunal also considered that the appropriate comparator was a homosexual lover and that such a lover would have been treated no differently. On that analysis the 'but for' test would not have been made out. However, the Appeal Tribunal went on, in any event, to reject the 'but for' test formulating instead a test based on 'the reason why' the employer has acted as he had, relying on dicta in *Chief Constable of West Yorkshire Police v Khan* (above) and *Shamoon* (above). In *B v A* [2007] IRLR 576, EAT, the tribunal was said to have erred by applying the 'but for' test when, had they asked whether the claimant had been dismissed 'by reason' of her sex, they would have concluded that she had not been – rather she had been dismissed because her employer, who was also her lover, had been motivated by sexual jealousy on seeing her in the company of another man.

If a decision maker's reason for treating an employee less favourably is not directly influenced by a protected characteristic but, in reaching the decision, she relies upon views expressed by a colleague which are themselves tainted by discrimination the decision-maker does not treat the complainant less favourably because of their protected characteristic (*CLFIS (UK) Ltd v Reynolds* [2015] EWCA Civ 439, [2015] ICR 1010, [2015] IRLR 562. See also *Gallop v Newport City Council (No. 2)* UKEAT/0118/15, [2016] IRLR 395). Note, however, that the colleague upon whose views the decision-maker relied may themselves have acted unlawfully.

Discrimination will be treated as being because of the protected characteristic if the substantial or effective, although not necessarily the sole or intended, reason for the discriminatory treatment was the characteristic (see *R v Commission for Racial Equality, ex p Westminster City Council* [1984] ICR 770; affd in part [1985] ICR 827 – a race case). In *Barton v Investec Henderson Crosthwaite Securities Ltd* [2003] ICR 1205, EAT, the Employment Appeal Tribunal went further in the context of sex discrimination holding that sex should not be 'any part of the reasons for the treatment in question' (approved by the Court of Appeal in *Igen v Wong* (above)). Even so, it must be a significant factor in the sense of being more than trivial. (See also *Villalba v Merrill Lynch & Co Inc* [2007] ICR 469, EAT).

11.18 *Meaning of 'because of sex'*

EA 2010, s 11 provides:

"In relation to the protected characteristic of sex –

(a)   a reference to a person who has a particular protected characteristic is a reference to a man or to a woman; and

(b)   a reference to persons who share a protected characteristic is a reference to persons of the same sex."

'Sex' is not defined in *EA 2010*. 'Woman' and 'man' are defined as being a female and male respectively of any age (*EA 2010, s 212*).

Before the UK enacted specific protection for transsexuals, the European Court of Justice decided that discrimination against transsexuals was a form of sex discrimination. In *P v S*: C-13/94 [1996] All ER (EC) 397, [1996] ECR I-2143, the European Court adopted a broad test which rendered unlawful any discrimination based 'essentially if not exclusively on the sex of the person concerned'.

At one point pregnancy discrimination was treated as falling within the scope of sex discrimination as only women may fall pregnant. It now has a discrete protection – for which see **11.24** below. Treating an employee less favourably because she is the commissioning mother in a surrogacy arrangement is neither discrimination because of pregnancy (because she has not herself been pregnant) nor discrimination because of sex (*CD v ST* C-167/12 [2014] IRLR 551). To succeed in a sex discrimination claim the mother would have to show that a commissioning father would have been treated differently.

11.19 *Meaning of 'because of marital or civil partnership status'*

EA 2010, s 8 provides:

"(1) A person has the protected characteristic of marriage and civil partnership if the person is married or a civil partner;

(2) In relation to the protected characteristic of marriage and civil partnership –

(a) a reference to a person who has a particular protected characteristic is a reference to a person who is married or a civil partner;

(b) a reference to persons who share a protected characteristic is a reference to persons who are married or are civil partners."

"Marriage" is not defined in the Act. The *EHRC Code* does provide some further guidance, however. It says of "marriage" that it will cover any formal union of a man and woman which is legally recognised in the UK as a marriage. As a result of the *Marriage (Same Sex Couples) Act 2013, Sch 3, Pt 1, Para 1* it includes marriages between same sex couples. In *Bick v Royal West of England Residential School for the Deaf* [1976] IRLR 326, a tribunal decided (with very considerable reluctance) that the predecessor provisions in the *SDA 1975* did not protect employees who were merely engaged. That decision was not followed in *Turner v Turner* (ET/2401702/04) which concluded that the right to marry enshrined in *Art 12* of the *European Convention on Human Rights*, meant that the provision had to be interpreted so as to protect those dismissed because they are planning to marry.

Equally, civil partnership is not defined in *EA 2010*, however a civil partner is someone who has been registered as the civil partner of a person of the same sex (see *Civil Partnership Act 2004, s 1*). The *EHRC Code* makes it clear that it also encompasses those whose civil partnerships have been registered abroad (Para 2.33).

For an example of direct discrimination on grounds of marital status see *Chief Constable of the Bedfordshire Constabulary v Graham* [2002] IRLR 239, EAT. In *Hawkins v Atex Group Ltd and Others* [2012] All ER (D) 71 (Apr), [2012] ICR 1315, the EAT indicated that the appropriate comparator will usually be somebody who is in a relationship akin to (but falling short of) marriage. That comparator ensures that the focus is on the significance of the married status itself and not, for instance, on the question of which particular individual the employee is married to.

11.20 *Meaning of 'because of race'*

"Race" is defined by *EA 2010, s 9(1)* to include: "colour", "nationality" and "ethnic or national origins". A "racial group" is "a group of persons defined by reference to race" (*EA 2010, s 9(3)*).

In relation to the protected characteristic of race:

> "a reference to a person who has a particular protected characteristic is a reference to a person of a particular racial group" (*EA 2010, s 9(2)(a)*)

A racial group can comprise two or more distinct racial groups (*EA 2010, s 9(4)*). Thus, a French national will be a member of the racial group consisting of French people and of a racial group consisting of all foreign nationals.

EA 2010, s 9(5) conferred a power on a Minister of the Crown to amend *s 9* by order to provide for caste to be an aspect of race. *Section 65* of the *Employment Rights and Regulatory Reform Act 2013* ("*ERRRA 2013*") amends *EA 2010, s 9* by adding caste to the definition of race. The amendment is to take effect at a date that had not yet been appointed at the date of going to press (but see *Tirkey v Chandok* below). On 28 March 2017 the Government opened a consultation on cast discrimination.

A distinction is drawn between racial origin and citizenship: *Ealing London Borough Council v Race Relations Board* [1972] AC 342; *Tejani v Superintendent Registrar for the District of Peterborough* [1986] IRLR 502.

The House of Lords in *Mandla v Dowell Lee* [1983] 2 AC 548, [1983] 1 All ER 1062 held that 'ethnic . . . origins' in the definition of 'racial group' meant a group which was a segment of the population distinguished from others by a sufficient combination of shared customs, beliefs, traditions and characteristics derived from a common or presumed common past, even if not drawn from what in biological terms was a common racial stock (see also *Para 2.39* of the *EHRC Code*). On that basis, it held that Sikhs were a racial group entitled to the protection of the *RRA 1976*. In *R (on the application of E) v Governing Body of JFS (Secretary of State for Children, School and Families, interested parties) (United Synagogue intervening)* [2009] UKSC 15, [2010] IRLR 136, SC, the Supreme Court, by a majority, determined that there was a discrete and "narrower sense" of discrimination on grounds of ethnic origin which applied to less favourable treatment on the ground of "lineage" or "descent". In the particular case a Jewish faith school applied an admission criterion that required that each pupil's mother should either be Jewish by birth or else have converted to Judaism under the auspices of an Orthodox synagogue. The application of the criterion was held to be an act of direct discrimination on grounds of ethnic origin.

In *Tirkey v Chandok* [2015] ICR 527, [2015] IRLR 195 EAT, the EAT upheld the refusal of an employment tribunal to strike out an argument that caste discrimination fell within the scope of race discrimination. Although not all caste discrimination would fall within the definition of race, the EAT considered (relying upon JFS above) that in some cases the link between descent and caste would be close enough to allow an argument that an act of discrimination was because of "ethnic or national origins".

Where 'racial group', is defined by 'colour' the group may comprise people of more than one ethnic origin (*Lambeth London Borough Council v Commission for Racial Equality* [1990] ICR 768).

'National origins' means more than the legal nationality acquired at birth (*BBC Scotland v Souster* above). One may 'acquire' national origins by adherence. Whilst nationality is a protected characteristic, discrimination because of migrant domestic worker status is not discrimination because of nationality (*Onu v Akwiwu* [2016] UKSC 31, [2016] IRLR 719).

Jews are members of a racial group (see, for example, *Seide v Gillette Industries* [1980] IRLR 427). So are gypsies in the sense of those who belong to the Romany race, although mere habitual wanderers are not (*Commission for Racial Equality v Dutton* [1989] QB 783, [1989] 1 All ER 306). Rastafarians are not an ethnic group (*Crown Suppliers (Property Services Agency) v Dawkins* [1993] ICR 517, CA). The Scots and the English are separate racial groups (*Northern Joint Police Board v Power* [1997] IRLR 610, EAT and *BBC Scotland v Souster* [2001] IRLR 150, Ct Sess).

In *Bradford Hospitals NHS Trust v Al-Shabib* [2003] IRLR 4, EAT, the tribunal decided that a grievance panel had treated the complainant less favourably on racial grounds when they formed an adverse impression of him as a result of his being 'difficult to control' and 'emotive'. The tribunal found that the respondent had erred by failing to take into account that, as an Iraqi, the complainant could not be expected to behave in a 'conventional Anglo-Saxon way'. However, the EAT found that it was not open to the tribunal to assume, in the absence of evidence, that there was a material difference in the manner in which 'Anglo-Saxons' and Iraqis might behave.

In *Simon v Brimham Associates* [1987] ICR 596, the Court of Appeal reached the somewhat surprising conclusion that an employment tribunal was entitled to find that a Jew who had withdrawn a job application when he learned that to be Jewish might preclude his selection was not discriminated against in circumstances in which the interviewer had merely asked him the same question about his religion as he would have asked any candidate, not knowing whether or not he was Jewish.

Where an employee was dismissed for fighting, he was not dismissed on racial grounds merely because his employer applied a policy of not taking into account acts of provocation and thus ignored the fact that he had been provoked by acts of racial abuse and violence. The policy was applied consistently to employees of all races: *Sidhu v Aerospace Composite Technology Ltd* [2001] ICR 167, CA.

The relevant race need not be the race of the employee that is the victim of the discrimination. For instance, in *Showboat Entertainment Centre v Owens* [1984] 1 All ER 836, [1984] 1 WLR 384, EAT a white employee was dismissed for refusing to carry out a discriminatory instruction. See the account of Associative Discrimination below at **11.27**.

In *Redfearn v Serco Ltd* [2006] EWCA Civ 659, [2006] ICR 1367, the Court of Appeal refused to extend the approach taken in *Showboat* to a case in which a white bus driver whose passengers and colleagues were mainly Asian was dismissed, in essence, for being a member of the British National Party. It was a condition of membership of that party that one should be white. The employee contended that the race of his passengers and colleagues had substantially contributed to the decision to dismiss him. The Court of Appeal distinguished *Showboat* on the basis that whilst it was within the policy of *RRA 1976* that those affected by an employer's racist policies should be protected, it did not follow that racists should be protected from the anti-discriminatory policies of their employers. The Court of Appeal in *English v Thomas Sanderson Blinds Ltd* [2008] EWCA Civ 1421; [2009] ICR 543, [2009] IRLR 206 expressed doubts about whether *Redfearn* had been correctly decided but accepted that they were bound by it. Mr Redfearn subsequently brought proceedings in the European Court of Human Rights ([2013] IRLR 51). The Court did not focus on the question whether the dismissal had constituted an act of race discrimination. Instead it found that there had been a breach of his *Art 11* right to Freedom of Association. The Court considered that he should have had access to an unfair dismissal remedy without the need to serve a period of qualifying employment. The Government dealt with the ECtHR decision by amending *ERA 1996, s 108* to provide that a claim for unfair dismissal may be brought without the need for a qualifying period of service where the reason for dismissal "is or relates to the employee's political opinions or affiliation" (w.e.f. 25 June 2013, *ERRA 2013, s 13*).

11.21 *Meaning of 'because of gender reassignment'*

A transsexual person is defined by *EA 2010, s 7(2)* to mean "a person who has the protected characteristic of gender reassignment". A person has the protected characteristic of gender reassignment if:

> "the person is proposing to undergo, is undergoing or has undergone a process (or part of a process) for the purpose of reassigning the person's sex by changing physiological or other attributes of sex" (*EA 2010, s 7(1)*)

The *EHRC Code* emphasises that it is not necessary for an employee to have undergone any medical treatment before the protection is attracted (*Para 2.24*) – a proposal is sufficient. That is so, suggests the Code, even if the proposal is revoked (*Para 2.25*). Cross-dressing is covered only where "as part of the process of reassigning their sex, someone is driven by their gender identity to cross-dress" (*Para 2.26*).

In *Ashton v Chief Constable of West Mercia Constabulary* [2001] ICR 67, EAT considered a case concerning a transsexual undergoing a gender reassignment. As part of her treatment she received medication, which caused her to be depressed. Her depression affected her ability to work and she was dismissed on grounds of incapability. The EAT upheld the tribunal's finding that the fact that the incapability was a result of the side-effects of her medication did not establish a *causal* link between the dismissal and her sex and thus that she had not been unlawfully discriminated against.

In *A v Chief Constable of the West Yorkshire Police* [2002] EWCA Civ 1584, [2003] ICR 161, the Court of Appeal considered that, for the purposes of employment law, post-operative transsexuals fall to be treated for all purposes as having their re-assigned sex. Thus, a post-operative male to female transsexual is to be treated as a woman rather than as a transsexual. The Court's reasoning was as follows: Post-operative male to female transsexuals are to be treated as women for the purposes of the European Convention on Human Rights (see *Goodwin v United Kingdom* (2002) 35 EHRR 447). The *ETD 76/207/EEC* (since repealed and replaced by the *ETD 2006/54/EC*) had to be interpreted, so far as possible, as being compatible with the *ECHR*. *SDA 1975* (the predecessor of the *EA 2010*), in turn, had to be interpreted, where possible, as being consistent with the *ETD 76/207/EEC*. However, the *Goodwin* case recognised that a departure from the normal rule may be required where 'significant factors of public interest . . . weigh against the interests of the individual applicant in obtaining legal recognition of her gender reassignment'. The decision was affirmed by the House of Lords ([2004] UKHL 21, [2004] ICR 806). The *Gender Recognition Act 2004* created a system of "gender recognition certificates". Anyone who holds a certificate must be treated according to their acquired gender.

The *EHRC Code* suggests that where a person has been diagnosed as having "Gender Dysphoria" or "Gender Identity Disorder" that may be an impairment within the meaning of the disability discrimination provisions of the *EA 2010* (*Para 2.28*).

11.22 *Meaning of because of religion or belief*

Meaning of 'belief'

"Belief" means any religious or philosophical belief and a reference to a belief includes a reference to a lack of belief (*EA 2010, s 10(2)*).

A reference to a person who has a particular characteristic is a reference to a person of a particular religion or belief and a reference to persons who share a protected characteristic is a reference to persons who are of the same religion or belief (*EA 2010, s 10(3)*).

Meaning of 'religion'

EA 2010, s 10(1) defines "religion", with some circularity, to mean "any religion". It also provides that any reference to religion includes a reference to a lack of religion with the effect that an employer is no more free to discriminate against atheists than he is against Christians. No more detailed definition is given. This represents, it would appear, a deliberate decision on the part of the Government taken when the protection was first introduced by the *Employment Equality (Religion or Belief) Regulations 2003, SI 2003/1660* ("*RBR 2003*"). The Government assumed that controversy about the scope of the definition will be rare and that in controversial cases it is best left to the courts and the tribunals to resolve the matter without further guidance.

It is tempting to suppose that it is the difficulty of defining 'religion' rather than the ease of doing so which has led the Government to avoid offering a more specific definition. The *EHRC Code* does not take matters very much further. It emphasises that a religion need not be "mainstream or well known". It does, however, have to have "a clear structure and belief system". Denominations or sects may be considered religions in their own right for the purposes of the *Act* (*EHRC Code, Para 2.54*)

Although not a matter which the *EHRC Code* touches upon, it is suggested that a religion will be concerned with the supernatural and, in particular, is likely to be theistic, ie it will be a belief about a god or gods.

The present context is not the only one in which this difficult definitional question has been faced and some assistance can be gained from consideration of those other contexts.

One context in which the issue has arisen is the law pertaining to charities. The advancement of religion is recognised as a charitable purpose (see *Income Tax Special Purposes Comr v Pemsel* [1891] AC 531). In their decision of 17 November 1999 in relation to an application for charitable status made by the Church of Scientology, the Charity Commissioners reviewed the existing case law on the definition of religion and derived the following characteristics:

(i)   a belief in a god, deity or supreme being (*R v Registrar General, ex p Sergedal* [1970] 2 QB 697 – though Buddhism qualified as a religion despite there being some doubt as to whether it required a belief in a supreme being);

(ii)   reverence and recognition of the dominant power and control of any entity or being outside their own body and life (*Sergedal* above); and

(iii)   faith and worship: faith in a god and worship of that god (*South Place Ethical Society* [1980] 1 WLR 1565).

The Commissioners identified a further significant factor, absent from the express words of the *EA 2010*; whilst the court will not consider the truth of the tenets of the relevant religion it will not treat as a religion everything which calls itself a religion. In practice the tribunal has adopted a similar approach. Because Charity Law is concerned with the 'advancement of religion', if the court is satisfied that the tenets of a particular sect 'inculcate doctrines adverse to very foundations of all religion and/or subversive of all morality' it will not be treated as 'advancing religion'. On its face the *EA 2010* covers all religions whether or not they espouse morally repellent precepts. This is likely to lead to problems in which religious precepts conflict with the interests of other protected groups. As we shall see below, the tribunals have adapted Human Rights law to create a requirement that the belief at issue be "worthy of respect in a democratic society".

The *Sergedal* case upon which the Charity Commissioners placed reliance was given much less weight in *R (on the application of Hodkin) v Registrar of Births, Deaths and Marriages* [2013] UKSC 77. The particular context of the decision was the proper interpretation of the Places of Worship Registration Act 1855. The issue was whether a chapel belonging to the Church of Scientology was a "place of worship". If it was then weddings could be performed there. The issue in turn prompted consideration of what was and was not a religion. Some guidance is given by Lord Toulson who seems to have felt that Lord Denning's approach in *Sergdal* was too narrowly theistic. Lord Toulson is careful to make clear that he is dealing with the particular legislation in issue and that he is not formulating a test, but his observations remain a helpful indication of the Supreme Court's likely approach to the definitional issue:

> "I would describe religion in summary as a spiritual or nonsecular belief system, held by a group of adherents, which claims to explain mankind's place in the universe and relationship with the infinite, and to teach its adherents how they are to live their lives in conformity with the spiritual understanding associated with the belief system. By spiritual or nonsecular I mean a belief system which goes beyond that which can be perceived by the senses or ascertained by the application of science. I prefer not to

use the word "supernatural" to express this element, because it is a loaded word which can carry a variety of connotations. Such a belief system may or may not involve belief in a supreme being, but it does involve a belief that there is more to be understood about mankind's nature and relationship to the universe and can be gained from the senses or from science. I emphasise that this is intended to be description and not a definitive formula."

Another context in which the definition of religion arises as an issue is the *European Convention on Human Rights*. This second context has a more direct relevance because the *EA 2010* implements a European Directive and European legislation has to be interpreted, wherever possible, so as to be compatible with the *European Convention on Human Rights*. *ECHR, art 9(1)* provides that 'everyone has the right to freedom of thought, conscience and religion'. The right also includes 'freedom to change . . . religion or belief . . . and freedom, either alone or in community with others and in public or in private, to manifest [one's] religion or belief, in worship, teaching, practice and observance'. However, whilst it might be hoped that a developed body of authority of the European Court of Justice would be available to assist in interpreting the scope of the words 'religion or belief', in fact there is remarkably little helpful case law. The Commission has assumed that Scientology is a religion (*X and Church of Scientology v Sweden* (1979) 16 DR 68). The court decided that 'Wicca' was not a religion on the ground that it had no clear structure or belief systems (*X v United Kingdom* (1977) 11 DR 55) (but note Wicca appeared as an example of a religion in the *ACAS Code* issued to assist with the interpretation of the *RBR 2003*).

The *EHRC Code* lists (at *Para 2.53*) a number of what it describes as "commonly recognised religions": the Baha'i faith, Buddhism, Christianity, Hinduism, Islam, Jainism, Judaism, Rastafarianism, Sikhism and Zoroastrianism. However, the *EHRC Code* also stresses that a religion does not have to be "mainstream" or "well-known" and that "sects" and "denominations" may also be affected (*Para 2.54*).

Meaning of 'religious belief'

Religious belief is defined as follows:

> 'any religious   . . .   belief and a reference to belief includes a reference to a lack of belief

(EA 2010, s 10(2))

The Act distinguishes, therefore, between religion and religious belief. The distinction arises from the fact that religious beliefs are not exclusively about a god or gods. Most religions profoundly affect what might be described as one's 'world view'. In other words, religious adherence affects what one believes about the world as well as what one believes about the supernatural (but see *R (on the application of Williamson) v Secretary of State for Education and Employment* [2001] EWHC 860 (Admin), [2002] 1 FLR 493 where Elias J opined that a religious belief, for the purposes of the *ECHR* was not simply a belief which is 'in accordance with the religious faith' but which 'embod(ied) or define(d)' the belief or conviction itself). When *Williamson* came before the House of Lords, their Lordships felt it unnecessary to explore the definitional question as the *ECHR*, like *EA 2010*, protects both religious and non-religious beliefs: [2005] 2 AC 246).

In *Eweida v British Airways* [2009] ICR 303, [2009] IRLR 78 (affd without considering this issue in [2010] EWCA Civ 80, [2010] ICR 890), the EAT decided that a belief could qualify as a religious belief even if it was unique to the employee (i.e no-one else shared the same belief) and without it being a mandatory requirement of an established religion.

In *Eweida*, the belief at issue was the visible wearing of a crucifix. In *Azmi v Kirklees MBC* [2007] ICR 1154, the belief was that of certain Muslims that Muslim women should only be in the presence of unrelated males when they are veiled. These are both examples of religious beliefs that deal not with whether there is a deity but how an adherent is expected to behave. A difficult question can arise as to whether the conduct that the employer is seeking to prevent should be treated as a religious belief or a "manifestation" of that belief. The latter concept is to be found in the *European Convention on Human Rights* (at *Art 9(2)*) and is dealt with separately below.

In refusing permission to appeal in the case of *Macfarlane v Relate Avon*, Lord Justice Laws touched upon a further distinction. The law, he said, protects "the right to hold and express a belief" but does not protect "that belief's substance" ([2010] EWCA Civ B1, [2010] IRLR 872). A similar position was adopted by the EAT in *Eweida* (above).

A belief in the sacrosanctity of Christian marriage was held to be a religious belief in *Pendleton v Derbyshire County Council* UKEAT/0238/15, [2016] IRLR 580.

Meaning of 'philosophical belief'

Philosophical belief is defined as follows:

> 'any . . . philosophical belief and a reference to belief includes a reference to a lack of belief'

(EA 2010, s 10(2))

As originally enacted *RBR 2003* protected those who held philosophical beliefs which could be said to be 'similar' to religious beliefs. The question how one identified a 'philosophical belief' which was sufficiently 'similar' to a religious belief as to fall within the scope of the legislation was harder to answer the more closely it was considered. Perhaps the defining characteristic of a religious belief is its theistic nature; it is a belief in a god or gods. If the belief is theistic it is a religious belief. If it is not, it is difficult to see how it could be said to be in any way 'similar' because the defining characteristic is absent.

An alternative approach was to assume that the similarity with which the legislation was concerned arose not from the essence of the belief but rather its ancillary characteristics. This would seem to be the approach adopted in the *ACAS Code* which stressed the likely importance of there being a 'clear belief system' and the belief being one which is 'profound' and which affects the adherent's 'way of life or view of the world'. The *ACAS Code* offered Humanism as an example of the sort of belief that might qualify. Other examples would include Confucianism and some commentators have even suggested that Vegetarianism might qualify.

With effect from 30 April 2007, *RBR 2003, reg 2(1)* was amended. The requirement that the philosophical belief be 'similar' to a religious belief was removed. Under *EA 2010* simply holding a particular philosophical belief (or equally, not holding it) will suffice. The logical consequence of the present formulation must be that holding a belief that is philosophical but not similar to a religious belief will qualify for protection.

In *McClintock v Department of Constitutional Affairs* [2008] IRLR 29, the EAT gave the following guidance:

> 'The test for determining whether views can properly be considered to fall into the category of a philosophical belief is whether they have sufficient cogency, seriousness, cohesion and importance and are worthy of respect in a democratic society: see *Campbell & Cosans v United Kingdom* [1982] 4 EHRR 293.'

McClintock was applied by the Employment Appeal Tribunal in *Nicholson v Grainger plc* [2010] ICR 360, EAT, which upheld a finding by the Employment Tribunal that a belief in man-made climate change was capable of amounting to a philosophical belief for the purposes of the regulations. In addition to the matters specifically identified as relevant in the quotation from *McClintock* above, the Appeal Tribunal emphasised that the belief must be genuinely held and that it must not (as was the case in *McClintock*) be merely an opinion or viewpoint based on the present state of information available. It had also to be a belief as to a weighty and substantial aspect of human life and behaviour. The Appeal Tribunal rejected 4 proposed limitations on the types of beliefs that would qualify for protection, finding: (1) The belief does not need to be shared by anyone else; (2) It need not form part of a "fully-fledged system of thought"; (3) It may be a political belief so long as it otherwise qualifies and (4) A philosophical belief based upon science may qualify. Some refinements of the factors identified in Nicholson were suggested in *Harron v Chief Constable of Dorset Police* UKEAT/0234/15, [2016] IRLR 481: the reference to the need for a belief to be about a "substantial aspect of human life" is intended to exclude only beliefs about trivial aspects; and the requirement for the belief to be "coherent" requires only that it should be intelligible and capable of being understood.

In *Hashman v Orchard Park Garden Centre* [2011] EqLR 426 the Tribunal concluded that a belief in the sanctity of life and, more specifically, beliefs that fox-hunting and hare-coursing were incompatible with the sanctity of life were each beliefs qualifying for protection. The EAT dismissed an appeal on the basis that it had no reasonable prospect of success. In *Henderson v GMB* [2016] EWCA Civ 1049, [2017] IRLR 340, a tribunal had accepted that "left wing democratic socialism" was a qualifying belief. That finding went unchallenged before the EAT and subsequently the Court of Appeal, where the complainant lost on other grounds.

As an example of a belief that would not qualify the *EHRC Code* suggests a belief in a philosophy of racial superiority for a particular racial group. Such a belief would, it is suggested, be incompatible with human dignity and conflicts with the fundamental rights of others.

Philosophical beliefs are no less stringently protected than religious beliefs (*Henderson v GMB* above).

Manifesting a Religious Belief

The European Convention on Human Rights protects the manifestation of one's religion or beliefs at *Art 9(2)*:

> "Freedom to manifest one's religion or beliefs shall be subject only to such limitations as are prescribed by law and are necessary in a democratic society in the interests of public safety, for the protection of public order, health or morals, or for the protection of the rights and freedoms of others."

The Charter of Fundamental Rights of the European Union also protects manifestation of religion (at *Art 10(1)*). The ECJ has held that the since the *Framework Directive 2000/78* makes reference to the ECHR in its recitals and should be interpreted so as to be consistent with the Convention and the Charter, the Directive should also be taken to prohibit discrimination because of manifestation of religion (*Achbita v G4S Secure Solutions NV* Case C-157/15), [2017] IRLR 466).

The *EA 2010* does not provide express protection for manifestation, although it must, of course, be interpreted so as to be consistent with the *Framework Directive* and therefore undoubtedly does. Before *Achbita*, the distinction between holding a belief and manifesting it had, however, arisen in the Domestic Law. It is a distinction which is expressly spelt out in the EHRC Code (at Paras 2.60 and 2.61). In *McConkey v Simon Community Northern Ireland* [2009] UKHL 24, [2009] ICR 787, Lord Simon said in relation to the *Fair Employment and Treatment (Northern Ireland) Order 1998, (SI 1998/3162)*:

> ' . . . [T]he Order is concerned with discrimination against someone on the basis of the religious belief or political opinion that he holds. It is not concerned with discrimination on the ground of actions that the person may take in support of that religious belief or political opinion'

Discrimination and Equal Opportunities – I   11.22

Insofar as *McConkey* might be thought to mean that manifestation of belief falls outside the scope of *EA 2010*, that cannot be right in the light of the ECHR's decision in four joined cases: *Eweida and others v United Kingdom* 48420/10, 59842/10, 51671/10 and 36516/10 and *Achbita*, above. In two of the cases (*Eweida* and *Chaplin*), the complainants were challenging policies that precluded them from wearing crucifixes over their work clothes. In Eweida the reason for the policy (which was later abolished) was the employer's corporate image. The European Court of Human Rights concluded that wearing a religious symbol was a manifestation of religious belief. Departing from the trend of earlier authority, the Court decided that the freedom was not protected merely by the fact that the complainant could obtain work with another employer with a less restrictive policy (though that was a factor that could be taken into account in determining whether the restriction to which she objected was a proportionate interference with her right). The Court took the view that concern about corporate image was an inadequate basis for restricting Ms Eweida's rights and found that the UK had failed to provide proper protection for them. This led to inaccurate press comment to the effect that there was now a "right" to wear a cross to work. In *Chaplin* however, the complainant's case was rejected. Her employer forbade the wearing of a cross on a necklace because it created health and safety concerns. The Court felt that that provided a defensible basis for restricting her right. The other two cases concerned employees whose religious beliefs meant that they did not wish to provide services to same sex couples. In Ladele a registrar of births, deaths and marriages did not wish to perform civil partnership ceremonies. In *Macfarlane* a Relate counsellor's employer concluded that he was not genuinely prepared to provide psychosexual counselling to same sex couples. In each case colleagues objected to the complainant's apparent unwillingness to comply with the employer's equality policies. Both complainants were unsuccessful in the Domestic courts. The European Court of Human Rights recognised that the situation gave rise to a necessary balancing of interests and concluded that the United Kingdom had been within the margin of appreciation available to it in fixing the balance in the manner in which it had.

Achbita was concerned with an employer's policy that forbade the wearing of any signs of political, philosophical or religious beliefs by any customer-facing staff. Ms Achbita wanted to wear an Islamic headscarf whilst working on reception. She was dismissed. Since the policy was applied to all employees whatever their belief (or lack of belief), the ECJ determined that there was no direct discrimination. That suggests that a specific policy of forbidding, say, the niqab, might be taken to amount to direct discrimination and call the decision in *Azmi*, above, into question. The ECJ also considered indirect discrimination arguments and decided that wanting to project neutrality in matters of belief to clients was a legitimate aim and, provided the policy was applied consistently and limited to customer-facing staff, it was likely justified.

As the express words of *Art 9(2)* make clear and the result in the *Chaplin* case demonstrates, the right to manifest one's religion is not limitless. That raises a difficult question: if an employee complains that they have been treated less favourably because they have manifested their religion, how is *Art 9(2)* to be reconciled with the fact that direct discrimination cannot be justified? *Wasteney East London NHS Foundation Trust* UKEAT/0157/15, *[2016] IRLR 388, [2016] ICR 643* suggests that the answer is, in practice, likely to be by narrowly defining what the reason for the less favourable treatment is. In *Wasteney* itself, the complainant was alleged to have been trying to convert a junior Muslim colleague to Christianity. Proselytisation is a manifestation of religion. However, the Appeal Tribunal decided that because the complainant's behaviour had been unwelcome and she had been senior to the colleague she had been trying to convert, the manner of the manifestation was inappropriate and it was that inappropriateness that had been the real reason for the complainant's being disciplined.

In *Bougnaoui v Micropole SA* Case C-188/15; [2017] IRLR 447, an employee was dismissed when a client asked that she should not wear an Islamic headscarf when working at their premises and, when pressed by her employer, she refused to agree not to wear one. The ECJ assumed for the purposes of argument that it might be shown that she was being treated less favourably because she was manifesting her religion. They considered whether, in the circumstances, it might be said that there was a "genuine and determining occupational requirement" within *2000/78, Art 4(1)* and decided that there was nothing about the job itself which objectively required her not to wear the headscarf. A subjective desire on the employer's part to comply with the wishes of the client would not establish the defence.

11.23   *Meaning of 'because of sexual orientation'*

EA 2010, s 12(1) provides that sexual orientation means a person's sexual orientation towards:

(a)   "persons of the same sex" (ie gay men or lesbians);

(b)   "persons of the opposite sex" (ie heterosexuals); or

(c)   "persons of either sex" (ie bisexual persons).

No definition is given of 'sexual orientation' *per se*. The *Oxford English Dictionary* defines 'orientation' as 'the state of being oriented', 'a person's attitude or adjustment in relation to circumstances'. It follows that there is no requirement that a person be sexually active in order to be regarded as being of a particular sexual orientation. The *EHRC Code* says that "sexual orientation relates to how people feel as well as their actions". (*Para 2.65*).

The *EA 2010* does not cover asexuals or sexual orientation towards anything other than persons (eg bestiality), nor do they cover (regardless of orientation) sexual conduct or particular sexual preferences (eg sadomasochism, paedophilia, etc) or the absence of such conduct (eg celibacy).

Before the enactment of a specific protection, there were a number of attempts made to establish that sexual orientation discrimination was a species of sex discrimination. However, the House of Lords ultimately determined that it is not an act of sex discrimination to treat an employee less favourably on grounds of their sexual orientation (*MacDonald v Advocate General for Scotland* [2003] UKHL 34, [2004] 1 All ER 339, [2003] ICR 937).

However, if an employer were to treat gay men less favourably than lesbian women (or vice versa), that would constitute sex discrimination on ordinary principles.

A reference to a person who has a particular protected characteristic is a reference to a person who is of a particular sexual orientation and a reference to persons who share a protected characteristic is a reference to persons who are of the same sexual orientation (*EA 2010, s 12(2)*). Nevertheless, where an employee who was known to be heterosexual was subjected to innuendo that he was gay, he was harassed 'on the grounds of sexual orientation' (see *English v Thomas Sanderson Blinds Ltd* [2008] EWCA Civ 1421; [2009] ICR 543, [2009] IRLR 206).

11.24   *Meaning of 'because of pregnancy or maternity leave'*

For the purposes of *EA 2010*, the protected characteristics are "pregnancy" and "maternity". Curiously, the Act omits to include a more detailed definition of the protected characteristic even though it has done so in respect of each of the others. In *Sahota v Home Office and another* [2010] ICR 772, the EAT opined that IVF treatment should be treated as equivalent to pregnancy only between the points in time at which follicular puncture and transfer of the embryo occurred. Commissioning a surrogate to have a child does not give an entitlement to maternity leave or fall within the scope of the protections against pregnancy or sex discrimination (*CD v ST* C-167/12 CJEU; [2014] 3 CMLR 272; [2014] IRLR 551; [2014] ICR D26)

EA 2010, s 18(2)(b) ensures that a woman is protected against unfavourable treatment because of a pregnancy-related illness. It is unclear whether less favourable treatment because of a pregnancy-related illness would fall within *EA 2010, s 13* as well and thus provide the basis for an allegation of direct discrimination. In the absence of clarification, the safest course would be to assume that it does.

The absence of more detailed definition of "maternity" is troubling as, on its face, "maternity" discrimination might be thought to have a broader scope than "maternity leave" discrimination (which is what was prohibited under the predecessor provisions in the *SDA 1975*). However, *EA 2010, s 18*, though headed "Pregnancy and Maternity Discrimination: Work Cases", only prohibits discrimination because of compulsory maternity leave or because the employee exercises, has exercised or seeks to exercise her right to take ordinary or additional maternity leave. Whilst this may indicate that the protection against direct discrimination on grounds of maternity conferred by *EA 2010, s 13* is intended to have a similarly limited scope, the question remains an open one until it has been considered by the courts.

11.25 *Meaning of 'because of age'*

For the purposes of *EA 2010*, the protected characteristic is "age", a reference to a person having a particular protected characteristic is a reference to a person of a particular "age group" and an "age group" is defined as a "group of persons defined by reference to age, whether by reference to a particular age or to a range of ages" (*EA 2010, s 5*).

In *Wooster v Mayor and Burgesses of the London Borough of Tower Hamlets* [2009] IRLR 980, the EAT upheld a tribunal finding that a local authority treated a 48-year-old employee less favourably on the grounds of his age by refusing to redeploy him where the consequence of doing so would have been to avoid having to pay him an early retirement pension to which he would become entitled once he reached the age of 50. (Such treatment may be justified in certain circumstances: see *Woodcock v Cumbria Primary Care Trust* [2012] EWCA Civ 330 and Discrimination and Equal Opportunities – II (12).)

11.26 *Meaning of 'because of disability'*

EA 2010 s 6(1) provides:

"A person (P) has a disability if–

(a)   P has a physical or mental impairment, and

(b)   the impairment has a substantial and long-term adverse effect on P's ability to carry out normal day-to-day-activities,"

The elements of the test are then further defined by *EA 2010, Sch 1 Part 1*. That schedule substantially reproduces the former *DDA 1995, Sch 1* save that the former *paragraph 4(1)* is not reproduced so that the complainant does not have to show that one of the attributes formerly listed in that paragraph (i.e. mobility, manual dexterity, physical co-ordination, continence, the ability to lift, carry or otherwise move everyday objects; speech hearing or eyesight; memory or ability to concentrate, learn or understand; or perception of the risk of physical danger) is adversely affected. The exclusion of *paragraph 4(1)* makes the test a little less complicated to apply and arguably effects a modest broadening of its scope.

Guidance has been issued by the Secretary of State which applies to any case based upon a discriminatory act occurring (or, in the case of a continuing act, commencing) on or after 1 May 2011 (*Equality Act (Guidance on the Definition of Disability) Appointed Day Order 2011 SI 2011/1159*). The tribunal must take the guidance into account (*EA 2010, Sch 1, Part 1, Para 12*). Advice as to how to take the guidance into account was given by the EAT in *Ladbrokes Betting and Gaming Ltd* UKEAT/0353/15, [2017] IRLR 312:

"Tribunals should start with the statutory language, consider the guidance and decide, having looked at both, what the statute means, concentrating primarily on the language of the statutory provision itself."

The EAT in *Goodwin v Patent Office* [1999] IRLR 4 laid down detailed guidance as to the approach to be taken by employment tribunals in determining whether or not a claimant is disabled. Readers should refer to this case for the full details of the EAT's guidance. In summary, the EAT held that in determining whether or not a claimant is disabled, the tribunal should look carefully at what the parties have said in the pleadings and clarify the issues, in most cases after standard directions to this effect or at a directions hearing; they should take a purposive approach to the construction of the legislative protections; they should refer expressly to any relevant provisions of the Guidance which have been taken into account (see below); in determining whether or not an impairment has an adverse effect on a person's ability to carry out activities, they should bear in mind that the fact that a person can, with difficulty or great effort, carry out these activities does not mean that his ability to carry them out has not been impaired; they should bear in mind that disabled persons are likely to play down the effect that a disability has on their activities; in determining what is a day-to-day activity, the tribunal's inquiry should not focus only on a particular or a special set of circumstances such as activities carried on in the home; in determining whether an adverse effect is substantial the tribunal may, where the claimant still claims to be suffering from the same degree of impairment as at the time of the events complained of, take into account how the claimant appears to the tribunal to 'manage' his condition; where a claimant is or had been on medication, the tribunal should, in determining whether there is an adverse effect, examine how the claimant's abilities were affected whilst on medication and how those activities would have been affected without the medication; and when addressing each of the conditions under *EA 2010, s 6(1)*, namely the 'impairment' condition, the 'adverse effect' condition, the 'substantial' condition and the 'long-term' condition, the tribunal should be careful not to lose sight of the overall picture.

The definition of disability used in *EA 2010* must, of course, be read, so far as possible, as to be compatible with the *Framework Directive 2000/78/EC*. The Directive does not specifically define "disability". However, in *HK Danmark*, acting on behalf of *Ring v Dansk Almennyttigt Boligselskab* C-335/11: [2013] IRLR 571; [2014] ICR 851, the CJEU held that the *Framework Directive* had to be read, so far as possible, as to be compatible with the *United Nations Convention on the Rights of Persons with Disabilities*. The *Convention* contains the following definition at *Art 1*:

> "Persons with disabilities include those who have long-term physical, mental, intellectual or sensory impairments which in interaction with various barriers may hinder their full and effective participation in society on an equal basis with others".

The net effect is that the domestic provisions have to be read in the light of the Convention definition (confirmed in *Banaszczyk v Booker Ltd* UK/EAT/0132/15 [2016] IRLR 273).

In *Fag og Arbejde, acting on behalf of Kaltoft v Kommunernes Landsforening, acting on behalf of the Municipality of Bullund* C-354/13: [2015] IRLR 146, [2015] ICR 322, ECJ, the European Court of Justice determined, invoking the *Convention* test, that obesity may constitute a disability where it "hindered [a worker's] full and effective participation in professional life on an equal basis with other workers on account of reduced mobility or the onset, in that person, of medical conditions preventing him from carrying out his work or causing discomfort when carrying out his professional activity." Infertility does not, in contrast, meet the *Convention* test. In *Z v A Government Department* C-363/12: [2014] IRLR 563, the ECJ decided that a failure to grant maternity leave to the commissioning mother in a surrogacy arrangement did not amount to disability discrimination as "the inability to have a child by conventional means does not in itself, in principle, prevent the commissioning mother from having access to, participating in or advancing in employment".

Impairments

The *Guidance* deals with the definition of impairment at *Paras A3–A8*. It suggests that the terms should be given their "ordinary meanings". An impairment does not have to be the result of an illness, nor does the cause of an impairment have to be established, provided the tribunal is satisfied that it exists. According to the guidance (at *Para A7*), there is no need to consider the cause even if the likely cause is a condition which is excluded from the protective scope of the *Act*. So, for example, addiction to alcohol is deemed not to be an impairment (see below) but illnesses caused by alcohol addiction may cause other impairments which do fall within the scope of the protected characteristic. The Guidance provides that rather than focussing on the cause of the impairment, the focus should instead be on the effects of impairment on the person's ability to carry out normal day to day activities (*Para A4*).

In *College of Ripon and York St John v Hobbs* [2002] IRLR 185, the EAT held that the task of ascertaining whether there is a physical impairment did not involve drawing any rigid distinctions between an underlying fault or defect in the body on the one hand, and evidence of the manifestations or effects of that fault or defect on the other. Thus, an impairment can be something that consists simply of the effects of an illness as opposed to the illness itself. In that case, there was clear evidence that there was something physically wrong with the claimant's body. However, there was no conclusive medical evidence as to the precise cause. Notwithstanding this lacuna in the evidence, the EAT held that it was open to the tribunal to find that there was a physical impairment simply on the basis of the evidence that there was something wrong with the claimant physically (see also *Rugamer v Sony Music Entertainment UK Ltd* [2002] ICR 381, [2001] IRLR 644 and *Ministry of Defence v Hay* [2008] ICR 1247). This rather relaxed approach to ascertaining a physical impairment is to be contrasted with the more rigid approach recommended in cases of mental impairment. In *Morgan v Staffordshire University* [2002] IRLR 190, the EAT held (no doubt to the relief of employers faced with a barrage of medical certificates merely citing 'stress' or 'anxiety' as the reason for absence) that the occasional use of terms such as 'anxiety', 'stress' or 'depression' even by GPs will not amount to proof of a mental impairment (See also *J v DLA Piper UK LLP* [2010] IRLR 936, EAT). In particular, it was held that the occasional mention in medical notes of or reference in the World Health Organisation's International Classification of Diseases to such terms would not be sufficient in the absence of informed medical evidence that said more. The EAT in that case also provided some detailed guidance for those seeking to establish a mental impairment. Readers are referred to the report of the *Morgan* case for the full details. In essence, however, the guidance reiterates the importance of expert medical evidence in this area. Both the *College of Ripon* and *Morgan* cases were noted with approval by the Court of Appeal in *McNicol* (see above). (See also *De Keyser Ltd v Wilson* [2001] IRLR 324.) However, readers should also refer to the decision of *Dunham v Ashford Windows* [2005] ICR 1584, [2005] IRLR 608, in which the EAT held that a person might have a mental impairment (such as learning difficulties) which did not amount to a mental illness. The Guidance supports this distinction between a mental impairment and mental illness (*Para A5*). Where there is dispute between the parties as to whether or not the employee has an impairment, or as to the nature of that impairment, the employer is entitled to adduce expert evidence to disprove the existence of such an impairment: *Hospice of St Mary of Furness v Howard* [2007] IRLR 944.

It may not always be possible, nor is it necessary, to categorise a condition as either a physical or mental impairment (*Guidance Para A6*). It is sufficient that an impairment can be established.

There was formerly a requirement that a mental illness had to be a "clinically well-recognised illness" before it could be a mental impairment but that requirement was repealed as from 5 December 2005 (*DDA 2005, s 18(2)*).

Certain things are deemed by the *Equality Act 2010 (Disability) Regulations 2010 (SI 2010/2128)* not to amount to impairments:

(a)   Addiction to alcohol, nicotine or any other substance (*Reg 3(1)*) unless the addiction was originally the result of administration of medically prescribed drugs or other medical treatment (*Reg 3(2)*);

(b)   A tendency to: set fires; steal; physical or sexual abuse of other persons; exhibitionism; and voyeurism (*Reg 4(1)*);

(c)   Seasonal allergic rhinitis (or "hayfever") unless it aggravates the effect of any other condition (*Reg 4(2)* and *(3)*).

An employee may have a condition (eg a depressive illness) that does amount to a disability in its own right but which was caused by an excluded condition, (eg addiction to alcohol). The EAT has confirmed that an employee in these circumstances would be disabled notwithstanding the link with the excluded condition because it is not relevant to consider the cause of a particular disability (*Power v Panasonic (UK) Ltd* [2003] IRLR 151). Conversely, a person might have an excluded condition that is caused by or is a manifestation of an impairment that falls within the scope of *EA 2010* (See *Edmund Nuttall Ltd v Butterfield* [2005] IRLR 751, where the excluded condition – in that case, exhibitionism – was caused by depression).

Adverse effect

Under the old law, an impairment was *only* to be taken to affect the ability to carry out normal day-to-day activities if it affected one of the following:

(a)   mobility;

(b)   manual dexterity;

(c)   physical co-ordination;

(d)   continence;

(e)   the ability to lift, carry or otherwise move everyday objects;

(f)   speech, hearing or eyesight;

(g)   memory or ability to concentrate, learn or understand; or

(h)   perception of the risk of physical danger.

(*DDA 1995, Sch 1 para 4(1)*.)

The list set out above was not reproduced in the *EA 2010*. The nearest one comes to such a list is to be found in the *Appendix* to the *Guidance*. There one finds two lists. The first is entitled "An illustrative and non-exhaustive list of factors which, if they are experienced by a person, it would be reasonable to regard as having a substantial adverse effect on normal day to day activities". There is a second list, equally extravagantly entitled, which focuses on factors that it would not be reasonable to regard as having the necessary substantial adverse effect. The examples are too numerous to list here. The first example included in the first list is "difficulty in getting dressed, for example, because of physical restrictions, a lack of understanding of the concept, or low motivation". The first example included in the second list is "inability to move heavy objects without assistance or mechanical aid, such as moving a large suitcase or heavy piece of furniture without a trolley". The *Guidance* stresses that the examples are indicators and not tests.

Substantial Adverse effects

An effect is substantial if it is more than minor or trivial (*EA 2010, s 212(1)* and *Guidance, Para B1*). Unless a matter can be classified as falling within the heading "trivial" or "insubstantial", it must be treated as substantial (*Aderemi v London and South Eastern Railway Ltd* [2013] ICR 591, EAT).

In assessing the effect, the Guidance suggests that the following should be looked at: the time taken to carry out an activity, the way it is carried out; and the cumulative effects of the impairment (*Guidance, Paras B2–B5*). The tribunal should also consider the extent to which a person could reasonably be expected to modify his or her behaviour by, for example, use of a coping or avoidance strategy (*Guidance, Para B7*).

Para B11 of the *Guidance* stresses the importance of keeping in mind the fact that environmental conditions may exacerbate or lessen the effect of an impairment.

The EAT in the case of *Leonard v Southern Derbyshire Chamber of Commerce* [2001] IRLR 19 emphasised that when considering whether an impairment had a substantial adverse effect on the ability to carry out normal day-to-day activities, the tribunal must concentrate on what the claimant cannot do or can only do with difficulty. An approach that looks mainly to what the applicant can do may lead to the erroneous conclusion that because the claimant can still do many things, the adverse effect cannot be substantial. This approach was supported by the EAT in *Paterson v Metropolitan Police Comr* [2007] ICR 1522 where it held that, when assessing whether the effect of an impairment is 'substantial', the comparison to be made is between the way in which the individual in fact carried out the activity in question and the way he would have carried it out if not impaired. The mere fact that an employee can perform the duties of his job does not necessarily mean that he is not disabled. (See *Law Hospital NHS Trust v Rush* [2001] IRLR 611 and *Ekpe v Metropolitan Police Comr* [2001] IRLR 605.) In *Cruickshank v VAW Motorcast Ltd* [2002] IRLR 24, the EAT considered the position of an employee whose impairment (an asthmatic complaint) was such that he only appeared to suffer substantial adverse effects whilst present at the workplace. The employment tribunal had held that the employee was not a disabled person because it could not be said that there was an adverse effect on his normal day-to-day activities. The EAT disagreed and held that the tribunal had been wrong to confine its analysis to the claimant's activities outside of the work environment. (See *Chief Constable of Dumfries & Galloway Constabulary v Adams* [2009] ICR 1034, [2009] IRLR 612, where the EAT confirmed that an activity undertaken in the course of employment would be a normal day-to-day activity if it was common to different types of employment.) In general terms, the principle that normal day-to-day activities are not to be determined only on the basis of a particular environment must be correct. However, where there is evidence that an employee only suffers substantial adverse effects when in a particular work environment (in the form, say, of a severe allergic reaction to the carpets in a particular office) and nowhere else, it might still be possible to argue that there was no substantial adverse effect on normal day-to-day activities or that the effects were not long term. The better approach in these circumstances (as suggested by the EAT in *Cruickshank*) would be to consider whether any reasonable adjustments could be made rather than attempting to argue that there is no disability.

Where two impairments are relied upon, neither of which on its own would satisfy the substantial adverse effect requirement under *DDA*, account should be taken of whether the impairments together have a substantial overall effect on the person's ability to carry out normal day-to-day activities. (See *Ginn v Tesco Stores Ltd* [2005] All ER (D) 259 (Oct), applied in *Patel v Oldham Metropolitan Borough Council* [2010] IRLR 280, which addressed the question whether an impairment that had developed from an initial impairment could be aggregated with the original to determine whether the longevity requirement was satisfied).

Long-term effects

By EA 2010, Sch 1, para 2:

"(1) The effect of an impairment is long-term if –

(a)   it has lasted for at least 12 months,

(b)   it is likely to last for at least 12 months, or

(c)   it is likely to last for the rest of the life of the person affected."

Even if an impairment ceases to have substantial adverse effect on the employee's ability to carry out normal day-to-day activities, it is treated as continuing to have that effect if it is likely to recur (*EA 2010, Sch 1, para 2(2)*). The cumulative effect of related impairments should be taken into account (*Guidance, Para C2*). In assessing whether an effect is "likely" to last for the periods identified in *EA 2010, Sch 1, para 2(1)(b)* and *(c)* above the tribunal should ask whether it "could well happen" (see *Guidance, Para C3* and *Boyle v SCA Packaging Ltd* [2009] UKHL 37; [2009] ICR 1056; [2009] IRLR 746).

European Law looks to the UN Convention on the Rights of Persons with Disabilities when interpreting the *Framework Directive 2000/78* (see *HK Danmark* (above)). The Convention definition of disability refers to "long-term physical, mental, intellectual or sensory impairments". Two points of note arise: first, the UN definition differs from the *EA 2010* definition in that the adjective "long-term" qualifies the impairment and not its effects. Second, there is no further more precise definition of what is meant by "long-term". These differences open the possibility of an argument that domestic law is not compatible with EU Law. The ECJ has looked at the UN definition in *Daouidi v Bootes Plus SL and others* C-395/15, [2017] IRLR 151. The court decided that the mere fact that a period of absence from work caused by injury was indeterminate did not mean it was "long-term". That was a question of fact to be judged on all of the evidence. There can be little doubt that the domestic courts and tribunals would take the same approach on that question of principle. *Daouidi* does not, therefore, create any specific concern that domestic law is incompatible with EU Law.

Normal day-to-day activities

The *Guidance* addresses "normal day-to day activities" in *section D*. General guidance is given at *Para D3*:

> "In general, day-to-day activities are things people do on a regular or daily basis, and examples include shopping, reading and writing, having a conversation or using the telephone, watching television, getting washed and dressed, preparing and eating food, carrying out and taking part in social activities. Normal day-to-day activities can include general work-related activities, and study and education-related activities, such as interacting with colleagues, following instructions, using a computer, driving, carrying out interviews, preparing written documents, and keeping to a timetable or a shift pattern."

The term is not intended to include activities which are normal only for a particular person or a small group of people (*Para D4*). However, a normal day-to-day activity does not have to be something that the majority of people do (*Para D5*). Specialised activities such as watch-making or playing an instrument to a high standard are not included (*Paras D8 and D9*).

Normal day to day activities can include activities engaged in at work (see *Chacón Navas v Eurest Coletivades* [2006] C-13/05 CJEU; [2007] ICR 1; [2006] IRLR 706; *Dumfries & Galloway Constabulary v Adams* [2009] ICR 1034; [2009] IRLR 612 and *Banaszczyk v Booker Ltd* UK/EAT/0132/15: [2016] IRLR 273).

In *Ekpe v Metropolitan Police Comr* [2001] IRLR 605, the EAT held that it was an error of law to conclude that an activity only done by women was not a normal day-to-day activity. However, a refusal to allow a person to progress in her professional life is not an adverse effect on normal day-to-day activities (see *Chief Constable of Lothian and Borders Police v Cumming* [2010] IRLR 109).

In *Leonard v Southern Derbyshire Chamber of Commerce* [2000] All ER (D) 1327, the employment tribunal had considered the examples given in earlier guidance in determining whether or not the applicant's condition had a substantial adverse effect on her day-to-day activities. In deciding that the applicant was not disabled, the employment tribunal had balanced those examples in the Guidance that the claimant could do (such as being able to eat and drink) against those which the claimant could not do (such as negotiate pavement edges properly). The EAT held that this balancing exercise was inappropriate, 'since her ability to catch a ball did not diminish her inability to negotiate pavement edges safely'. As stated above, the correct approach involves considering all matters, but paying particular attention to those activities that the applicant cannot do.

Severe Disfigurement

Severe disfigurement is deemed to have the necessary substantial adverse effect (*EA 2010, Sch, para 3*). The Guidance gives the following examples of what might qualify to be protected under this provision: "scars, birthmarks, limb or postural deformation or diseases of the skin" (*Para B25*).

Tattoos and piercings are addressed at *Reg 5* of the *Equality Act 2010 (Disability) Regulations 2010, SI 2010/2128*. It is provided that they should not count as disfigurements having a substantial adverse effect on the ability of a person to carry out normal day-to-day activities.

Effect of medical treatment

The substantial adverse effects of an impairment may sometimes be avoided by medical treatment or other "measures". That does not have the effect, however, of removing the employee from the protective scope of the Act. *EA 2010, Sch 1, para 5* provides:

"(1) An impairment is to be treated as having a substantial adverse effect on the ability of the person concerned to carry out normal day-to-day activities if:

(a)   measures are being taken to treat or correct it, and

(b)   but for that, it would be likely to have that effect.

(2) "Measures" includes, in particular, medical treatment and the use of a prosthesis or other aid

(3) Sub-paragraph (1) does not apply –

(a)   in relation to the impairment of a person's sight, to the extent that the impairment is, in the person's case, correctable by spectacle or contact lenses or in such other ways as may be prescribed
         ..."

The measures taken may, broadly, have one of three types of effect. First, it may temporarily alleviate the adverse effect. That is the set of circumstances with which the provision set out above is intended to deal. So, for instance, an asthmatic employee would probably be regarded as disabled within the meaning of the *Act* if his condition was such that if it were not controlled through the use of inhalers and medication, it would have a substantial adverse effect on his normal day-to-day activities. Similarly, an employee with a disabling depression still has a disability even if the effects of the depression are controlled with anti-depressants. Since the medical treatment means the adverse effect is prevented, the tribunal has to deduce what would happen if the medical treatment ceased. Where a deduced effect is alleged, the employee is required to prove the disability with some particularity and clear medical evidence will usually be necessary. A mere assertion by the employee as to what would happen if the treatment ceased will probably not be sufficient (*Woodrup v Southwark London Borough Council* [2003] IRLR 111, CA). When assessing what would happen if treatment or a corrective measure ceased to be taken, the tribunal must ask itself whether it is "likely" that the substantial adverse effect would resume. That outcome is sufficiently likely if the tribunal is able to say that it "could well happen" (*SCA Packaging Ltd v Boyle* [2009] UKHL 37, [2009] NI 317, [2009] IRLR 746).

The second type of effect that the measures might have is producing a permanent improvement such that it is unlikely that the substantial adverse effect will recur. In *Abadeh v British Telecommunications plc* [2001] ICR 156, the EAT decided that where continuing treatment has produced a permanent improvement, that improvement must be taken into account. Put another way, the tribunal should ask would happen if treatment stopped now and not what would have happened if the claimant had never received treatment. The EAT further clarified that a "deduced effect" argument was only available at all if the medical treatment was continuing. *EA 2010, Sch 1, para 5* does not apply where the treatment has ceased (see also *Carden v Pickerings Europe Ltd* [2005] IRLR 720).

The third type of effect that measures might have is curing the underlying impairment itself. Again, the claimant cannot argue that they are a disabled person on the basis that they would have been had they not been cured.

However, where a measure brings about a permanent improvement or a cure such that a claimant cannot argue they are still disabled that does not mean that the employee will not have the protected characteristic of disability, that is because less favourable treatment of those who disabilities in the past is also prohibited (see below and *Guidance, Para 17*).

The EAT in *Kapadia v Lambeth London Borough Council* [2000] IRLR 14 found that counselling sessions conducted by a consultant psychologist amounted to 'medical treatment', notwithstanding the fact that the counselling only comprised 'talking' to the claimant and the fact that no drugs were administered.

The EAT in *Vicary v British Telecommunications plc* [1999] IRLR 680, commented (*obiter*) that the words 'or other aid' (*EA 2010, Sch 1, para 5(2)*) are probably intended to refer to aids such as Zimmer frames or sticks or wheelchairs and not to labour-saving household devices such as electric can-openers. An 'aid' in this context can also include surgically inserted plates and pins. (*Carden v Pickerings Europe Ltd* [2005] IRLR 720).

Deemed Disabilities

EA 2010, Sch 1, para 6 deems Cancer, HIV infection and multiple sclerosis to be disabilities.

Para 7 confers a power to prescribe that other conditions should also be deemed to be disabilities. On 1 October 2010 the *Equality Act 2010 (Disability) Regulations 2010, SI 2010/2128* came into force. *Reg 3* deems that addiction to alcohol, nicotine or any other substance is to be treated as not amounting to an impairment unless the addiction is the result of the administration of medically prescribed drugs or other medical treatment. *Reg 4* deems certain other conditions not to amount to impairments: a tendency to set fires, to steal or to physical or sexual abuse of other persons; exhibitionism or voyeurism.

Seasonal allergic rhinitis ("hay fever") cannot amount to an impairment in its own right but can be taken into account if it aggravates another condition.

Reg 6 deals with babies and young children. Although, of course, neither are likely to be employees, whether or not a child is disabled may affect whether an associative discrimination claim will succeed. Where a child under 6 has an impairment which does not have a substantial long term adverse effect on the ability of the child to carry out normal day to day activities, the impairment is deemed have that effect if it would have it on a child who was older than 6.

Reg 7 deems to be disabled any person certified by a consultant ophthalmologist to be blind, severely sight impaired or partially-sighted.

For matters which are deemed by the Regulations not to amount to impairments, see the section on impairments above.

Progressive conditions

EA 2010, Sch 1, para 8 deals with progressive conditions. The effect of the provision is that even if the employee's condition creates an impairment which has an adverse effect which is not yet sufficiently "substantial" to qualify as a disability, it is treated as doing so if "the condition is likely to result in [them] suffering such an impairment".

Mere diagnosis of a progressive condition (other than one of the conditions giving rise to a deemed disability) would not be sufficient in itself. In *Mowat-Brown v University of Surrey* [2002] IRLR 235, the EAT held that it is not even enough simply for an applicant to establish that he has a progressive condition and that it has or has had an effect on his ability to carry out normal day-to-day activities. A claimant with a progressive condition must go on to show that it is likely that at some stage in the future there will be a substantial adverse effect on his ability to carry out normal day-to-day activities. The *Guidance* (at *Para B19*) provides that in such cases, medical prognosis of the likely impact of the condition will be the normal route to establishing protection under the progressive conditions provisions. A person may be taken as having a disability even where the substantial adverse effect is as a result of the treatment for a progressive condition (eg an operation for prostate cancer that results in urinary incontinence) rather than the progressive condition itself (see *Kirton v Tetrosyl Ltd* [2003] EWCA Civ 619, [2003] ICR 1237, [2003] IRLR 353). Note that the decision in *Mowat-Brown* predates that in *SCA Packaging* (above). It interpreted "likely" to mean more likely than not. The EAT confirmed in *Taylor v Ladbrokes Betting and Gaming Ltd* UKEAT/0353/15, [2017] IRLR 312 that, in the light of *SCA Packaging*, it was sufficient if there was a "small possibility of deterioration in a population [affected by the relevant condition]".

Para B32 of the *Guidance* suggests the protection will not apply where the progressive condition is successfully treated so as to remove any adverse effect. More difficult is the question of the applicability of *Paragraph B7* (which is summarised in the section of this paragraph headed "Substantial Adverse effects" above). It suggests that when considering whether an effect is substantial one may take into account what might reasonably be expected of the claimant in terms of the modification of their own behaviour so as to avoid the effect. In *Taylor*, above, the EAT was urged to decide that the guidance should be taken into account when determining whether or not a deterioration is "likely". The EAT refused to decide the point.

Past Disabilities

EA 2010, s 6(4) provides that reference (however expressed) to a person who has a disability includes reference to a person who has had the disability. The *Guidance, Para B17* states that if medical treatment cures a condition, the employee may still be protected on the basis that they have had a disability in the past.

Disability "at the relevant time"

The EAT in *Cruickshank v VAW Motorcast Ltd* [2002] IRLR 24 confirmed that in determining whether a person is disabled, the court should apply the appropriate test to the claimant's condition at the date of the alleged discriminatory act and not at the date of the hearing. This approach could present difficulties particularly where the effects of a particular condition tend to fluctuate or last for uncertain periods. The fact that by the date of the hearing, an adverse effect had in fact lasted for 12 months is not necessarily conclusive of it having been likely to have lasted that long at the date of the discriminatory act. However, now that it has been confirmed that 'likely' in this context means 'could well happen', such difficulties will probably arise only rarely (see *SCA Packaging Ltd v Boyle* [2009] UKHL 37, [2009] NI 317, overruling *Latchman v Reed Business Information Ltd* [2002] ICR 1453). In *Swift v Chief Constable of Wiltshire Constabulary* [2004] IRLR 540, the EAT had held that in determining whether at a particular point in time a substantial adverse effect was likely to recur, the Tribunal was entitled to take account of evidence of what had happened since that time. However, the effect of *Swift* was doubted by the Court of Appeal in *McDougall v Richmond Adult Community College* [2008] EWCA Civ 4, [2008] ICR 431 (at paragraph 17). Rather, in *McDougall*, Pill LJ emphasised that a prediction as to the likelihood of recurrence must be made on the basis of the evidence available at the time of the act complained of. The central purpose of the legislation is to prevent discriminatory decisions and to provide sanctions if such decisions are made. Whether an employer has committed such a wrong is to be judged, therefore, on the basis of the evidence available at the time of the decision complained of. (See *Ministry of Defence v Hay* [2008] ICR 1247, where *McDougall* was distinguished on the basis that it did not apply where the decision as to whether someone was disabled did not turn upon any predictive element to be established on the facts known at the time of the alleged act of discrimination. In *Hay*, the question was not one of recurrence of a condition but of whether the claimant was suffering from an impairment or impairments which had a substantial adverse effect upon his normal day-to-day activities.)

There is special provision made in relation to cases of past disability at *EA 2010, Sch1, para 9* provides:

> "(1) A question as to whether a person has a disability at a particular time ("the relevant time") is to be determined, for the purposes of section 6, as if the provisions of, or made under, this Act were in force when the act complained of was done had been in force at the relevant time.
>
> (2) The relevant time may be a time before the coming into force of the provisions of this Act to which the question relates."

The *Guidance* provides that the protection would cover those who continue to experience debilitating effects as a result of treatment for a past disability (*Para A16*). Note that the wording of sub-paragraph 9(1) does not make sense on its face, The word "were" in the second line appears to have been inserted when the legislation was in draft form but without any obvious purpose and with the effect of obscuring the meaning of the provision. The purpose of the provision becomes clear if one ignores the "were".

11.27 Associative Discrimination – Cases where the member of the protected category is a third party

In most cases, a person who alleges that they have been discriminated against will be complaining that the have been treated less favourably because of their protected characteristic (i.e. because of their race, sex, sexual orientation, etc). However, where, for instance, a white employee is dismissed for refusing to comply with an instruction not to deal with black customers, it is the customers' protected characteristic that is in issue rather than that of the employee. Discrimination which is based upon a third person's protected characteristic is known as "associative discrimination". The label "associative" is not itself found in the legislation (either European or Domestic) and no particular relationship is required between the complainant and the person with the protected characteristic. The question is simply a causal one – was the complainant treated less favourably because of the other person's protected characteristic? (see *Thompson v London Central Bus Company Ltd* (2015) UKEAT/0108/15, [2016] IRLR 9).

The coming into force of the *EA 2010* represented a substantial expansion of the scope of associative discrimination. Whereas under the pre-existing law, associative discrimination claims could only be brought in respect of certain protected characteristics, *EA 2010, s 13* extends the scope of protection to all of the protected characteristics save one. The exception is "marriage and civil partnership". A claim may only be brought where it is the person less favourably treated that is married or a civil partner (*EA 2010, s 13(4)*).

In addition to associative direct discrimination, associative indirect discrimination and, it appears, associative victimisation are also prohibited (see **[11.34]** and **[11.38]** below).

A company could complain of associative discrimination where it was treated less favourably because of protected characteristic of the person whose services it supplied (*EAD Solicitors v Abrams* UKEAT/0054/15: [2015] IRLR 978). There was associative direct discrimination because of sexual orientation when a bakery refused to supply a customer with a cake bearing the message "support gay marriage". The customer was treated less favourably because the message "benefited" gay people *Lee v McArthur* [2016] NICA 39, [2017] IRLR 69.

11.28 Perceived Discrimination – Cases where the complainant is assumed, incorrectly, to have the protected characteristic

The Government believes that the formulation of direct discrimination adopted in *EA 2010, s 13* has the effect that perceived discrimination is prohibited in relation to each of the protected characteristics. It remains to be seen how, in relation to perceived disability discrimination, the difficulties identified by the EAT in the *J v DLA Piper UK LLP* case ([2010] IRLR 936) will be overcome. The EAT found that *DDA 1995* (the predecessor legislation) did not protect an employee against dismissal because he was perceived to be disabled. The rationale was that the definition of a protected disability is so specific and requires so many factors to be considered that it will be, in practice, extremely difficult to determine whether the employer believed the employee was disabled as opposed, for instance, to merely ill. In other words, protection against perceived disability discrimination was unworkable in practice. It is to be assumed that, however unworkable, it is a protection *EA 2010* was intended to introduce.

11.29 Combined Discrimination

Combined discrimination was a new form of discrimination that was to be introduced by *EA 2010*. It would have occurred where an employee was treated less favourably because of two protected characteristics. For instance, if a driving school were to decide that the job of driving instructor was not a suitable one for an older woman and refused to appoint a woman in her sixties to a position, their reason would not be the candidate's sex or her age but the combination of her sex and age. On 23 March 2011, the Government Equalities Unit announced that it no longer intended to proceed with its proposals to bring *EA 2010, s 14* into force. It is that provision which would otherwise have prohibited such discrimination.

11.30 Discrimination on the ground of pregnancy

EA 2010 provides two discrete protections for women who are discriminated against because of their pregnancy. First, pregnancy is identified as a "protected characteristic" at *EA 2010, s 4*. As a result, it would seem that it is possible for a woman to complain of direct discrimination where she is treated "less favourably" because of her pregnancy, relying on *EA 2010, s 13(1)*. This is dealt with at **11.24** above.

The second protection provides is an express prohibition on employers treating employees unfavourably (as opposed to less favourably) because of their pregnancy (*EA 2010, s 18(2)(a)*):

> 'A person (A) discriminates against a woman if, in the protected period in relation to a pregnancy of hers, A treats her unfavourably –
>
> (a) because of the pregnancy; . . . '

This formulation differs from that found in the earlier law in that, although it was clear that a pregnant employee was not required to identify a comparator, she was still required to show that she had been "less favourably treated" which unhelpfully implied a residual need for comparison. Now the *Act* simply prohibits "unfavourable" treatment. Otherwise, the provisions are materially the same. In *Madarassy v Nomura International Plc* [2007] EWCA Civ 33, [2007] ICR 867, (a case decided under the old law but after the requirement for a comparator had been abolished) the Court of Appeal indicated that even in pregnancy cases a comparator might still be of use. The Court had in mind a case where there is real doubt as to whether pregnancy was the reason for the treatment. Thus, where a pregnant employee is dismissed for dishonesty and claims that the employer only took the step of dismissing her (rather than disciplining her) because she was pregnant, it might be relevant to ask what had happened to male employees who had behaved in the same way. Where, however, the reason is a matter directly connected with the pregnancy (such as absence) it will not be appropriate to ask how a man with a similar absence record would have been treated.

The protection is specifically restricted to a "protected period" which begins when the woman conceives and ends, in cases where she is entitled to ordinary and additional maternity leave ("OML" and "AML"), either at the end of the additional maternity leave period or when she returns to work (if that is earlier) and in any other case at the end of the period of 2 weeks beginning with the end of pregnancy (*EA 2010, s 18(6)*). Thus an employer who dismisses an employee who informs him that she intends to try for a child does not act in breach of *s 18* as the protected period has not begun. In such a case the complainant would have two options: (1) bringing a *s 13* pregnancy discrimination case; or (2) bringing a *s 13* sex discrimination case. The approach of treating pregnancy-related discrimination falling outside the period as sex discrimination was taken by the ECJ in *Mayr v Backerei und Konditorei Gerhard Flockner OHG* C-506/06: [2008] IRLR 387. A woman undergoing IVF treatment was dismissed between the removal of ova from her follicles and the replacement of a fertilised ovum in her uterus. The ECJ determined that she was not a pregnant worker for the purposes of *PWD 92/85* but could rely, instead on *ETD 76/207/EEC* (now the *ETD 2006/54/EC*).

On the other hand, once a protected period has begun *EA 2010, s 18(7)* specifically requires that any pregnancy discrimination claim be brought under *s 18* rather than as a sex discrimination claim under *s 13*. If, during the protected period, the employee is treated less favourably because of her sex but not because of her pregnancy a claim under *EA 2010, s 13* would of course still be available.

An employee may complain about the implementation of a decision taken during the protected period even if the implementation itself does not occur until after the period has come to an end (*EA 2010, s 18(5)*). This, again, reflects the ECJ's approach: In *Paquay v Societe d'architectes Hoet + Minne SPRL*: C-460/06 [2008] ICR 420, ECJ, the protection against dismissal afforded during the 'protected period' provided for by *PWD 92/85* was held to apply where an employer advertised the employee's job during the protected period but gave notice only once the protected period had finished. The *PWD* was interpreted as requiring that steps preparatory to a decision to dismiss should also be unlawful.

As it is a form of direct discrimination, pregnancy discrimination cannot be justified, The strictness of the principle is well illustrated by the case of *Mahlburg v Land Mecklenburg-Vorpommern*: C-207/98 [2000] ECR I-549, [2001] 3 CMLR 887. The ECJ considered the case of a pregnant woman who applied for and was refused a job intended to last for an indefinite period on the basis that, at the time at which she would otherwise have started the job, domestic law precluded her from working. Did the fact that the *ETD 76/207/EEC* (since repealed and replaced by *ETD 2006/54/EC*) was expressed to be without prejudice to such protective legislation mean that a refusal to appoint the claimant had not been discriminatory? The court decided that there had been an act of direct discrimination. The result pursued by the *ETD 76/207/EEC* was 'substantive, not formal, equality'. As a result, 'the application of provisions concerning the protection of pregnant women cannot result in unfavourable treatment regarding their access to employment'.

Cases in which the reason for the employee being unfavourably treated is the pregnancy per se will be rare. More commonly, the employer points to a reason connected with the pregnancy. In *Dekker v Stichting Vormingscentrum voor Jong Volwassenen (VJV - Centrum) Plus*: C-177/88 [1990] ECR I-3941, [1992] ICR 325, the complainant applied for a job as a teacher. Although suitable she was not appointed because the respondent would have had to pay her a maternity allowance, which, because she would have been pregnant when appointed, the respondent would have been unable to recover under their insurance policy. The reason for the refusal to appoint was thus not the pregnancy per se but the substantial irrecoverable costs of the appointment. However, the ECJ approached the case on the basis that the refusal to appoint was on ground of pregnancy. The domestic courts have adopted a similar approach. In *O'Neill v Governors of St Thomas More RCVA Upper School* [1997] ICR 33, EAT, the Employment Appeal Tribunal considered a case where a Roman Catholic school dismissed a religious education teacher who was pregnant by a priest. The school argued that it was not the pregnancy itself but the circumstances of the pregnancy that provided the dominant motive for the decision to dismiss. The EAT held that the dismissal had been discriminatory and rejected the concept of dismissal for "pregnancy per se" as misleading. Instead the tribunal should simply ask itself whether, on an objective basis, the dismissal was on the ground of pregnancy. Pregnancy did not need, in the EAT's opinion, to be the sole or even the main ground for the decision to dismiss.

A common complaint made by employers is that an employee has 'deceived' them by not declaring that they are pregnant at a point at which an important decision is made. For example, in *Busch v Klinikum Neustadt GmbH & Co Betriebs-KG*: C-320/01 [2003] IRLR 625, ECJ, an employee absent on parental leave applied to return early. Having been allowed to do so, she declared she was pregnant and sought to take maternity leave which would have been unavailable to her during a period of parental leave. The employers tried to rescind their consent to her return from parental leave. The Court decided that the employee was not obliged to declare her pregnancy and, in any event, the employer would not have been entitled to take her pregnancy into account even if she had told them about it. That being so, they had discriminated against her.

In *Ministry of Defence v Pope* [1997] ICR 296, EAT, the Employment Appeal Tribunal held that where an employee terminated her pregnancy in order to avoid being dismissed for pregnancy, she could bring a claim against her employer for damages for injury to feelings. In its decision in *Webb v EMO Air Cargo (UK) Ltd* C-32/93: [1994] QB 718; [1994] ECR I-3567; [1994] ICR 770; [1994] IRLR 482 the ECJ had expressly referred to the need to prevent women feeling pressured into terminations as one of the policies underlying the maternity leave period.

In *New Southern Railways Ltd v Quinn* [2006] IRLR 266, EAT, an employer was found to have discriminated where it removed a pregnant employee from a trial position and returned her to her less senior and lower-paid position. The Tribunal was not prepared to treat the case as one of medical suspension.

A failure to comply with the obligation imposed by the *Management of Health and Safety Regulations 1999 (SI 1999/3242)* to carry out a risk assessment in respect of a pregnant employee may amount to an act of unlawful sex discrimination (see *Hardman v Mealon (t/a Orchard Lodge Nursing Home)* [2002] IRLR 516). However, there is no general obligation to carry out a risk assessment and there is only an obligation to do so where: (1) the employee notifies her employer in writing that she is pregnant; (2) the work is of a kind which could involve a risk of harm or danger to the health and safety of a new expectant mother or to the health and safety of her baby; and (3) the risk arises from either processes or working conditions or physical, biological or chemical agents in the workplace at the time specified in the non-exhaustive list at *Annexes I* and *II* of *Directive 92/85/EEC (O'Neill v Buckinghamshire County Council* [2010] IRLR 384, EAT).

Where an employee is prevented, by reason of her pregnancy, from performing her usual job tasks, a failure to consider alternative employment may be discriminatory on the basis that the employer has treated the employee less favourably in relation to access to opportunities for transfer within *EA 2010, s 39(2)(b) (Iske v P&O European Ferries (Dover) Ltd* [1997] IRLR 401, EAT).

There is a limit to how remote the reason can be from the pregnancy. Thus, in *Walter v Secretary of State for Social Security* [2001] EWCA Civ 1913, [2002] ICR 540, the *Jobseeker's Allowance Regulations 1996 (SI 1996/207)* did not offend against the *Social Security Directive 79/7/EEC* (which prohibited sex discrimination in access to social security entitlements; see **23.5 EUROPEAN UNION LAW**) where a student breaking her studies to have a child was precluded from claiming the allowance. Those taking breaks from studies are treated under the Regulations as retaining their status as a student, a status which disqualifies them from making a claim. The Court of Appeal decided that the complainant's ineligibility to claim derived from her student status and not from her pregnancy.

11.31 Discrimination on ground of maternity leave

EA 2010, s 4 identifies "maternity" as a protected characteristic. *Part 2, Chapter 1* of the *Act* does not define what is meant by "maternity". The explanatory notes, equally, do not provide a definition. The significance of the lack of a definition is that "maternity" is a broader term than "maternity leave" and the earlier law only prohibited discrimination on the latter, narrower, ground. However, it is probable that *EA 2010* intends to do no more than reproduce the existing maternity leave-related protection. That view is reinforced by *EA 2010, s 18* which is headed "Pregnancy and maternity discrimination: work cases". Section18 deals only with pregnancy discrimination (*EA 2010, s 18(2)*) and maternity leave discrimination (*EA 2010, ss 18(3) and (4)*). Despite the heading, there is no protection of maternity more generally.

EA 2010, s 18(3) prohibits a person from discriminating against a woman by treating her unfavourably because she is on compulsory maternity leave. Compulsory maternity leave is the two week period provided for by *ERA 1996, s 72(1)* (*EA 2010, s 213(3)*) (see MATERNITY AND PARENTAL RIGHTS **32.27**).

Unfavourable treatment because an employee "is exercising or seeking to exercise, or has exercised or sought to exercise [her] right to ordinary or additional maternity leave" is prohibited by *EA 2010, s 18(4)*. Ordinary maternity leave ("OML") is the right conferred by *ERA 1996, s 71(1)* (*EA 2010, s 213(4)* see MATERNITY AND PARENTAL RIGHTS **32.21**). Additional maternity leave ("AML") is the right conferred by *ERA 1996, s 73(1)* (*EA 2010, s 313(7)* see MATERNITY AND PARENTAL RIGHTS **32.28**).

Discrimination for a maternity-related reason was, prior to October 2005, treated as a form of sex discrimination. In order to preclude overlapping claims *EA 2010, s 18(7)(b)* disapplies *EA 2010, s 13* (the prohibition on direct sex discrimination) where the unfavourable treatment is for a reason falling within *EA 2010, s 18(3) or (4)*. However, since maternity is a protected characteristic in its own right (*EA 2010, s 4*), it would seem that a *s 13* action would potentially still be available on that discrete basis. *Section 13* requires, however, that there should be "less favourable treatment" which would seem, on its face, to require a comparator to be identified which means that in most cases occurring during the protected period, there would be little point bringing a *s 13* claim rather than a *s 18* claim.

The scope of the protection is broad and the courts and tribunals have interpreted the provision purposively. For instance, early cases concerning maternity leave considered attempts by employers to narrow the protective scope of the provision by drawing a distinction between the taking of the leave and the consequences for the employer's business of the employee's absence. The ECJ rejected the distinction in *Dekker* (above) where an employer argued, unsuccessfully, that it did not discriminate against a pregnant applicant for employment by refusing to employ her since the real reason for not employing her was the adverse economic consequence of its inability to insure itself to recover the cost of the payments it would have to make to her during her maternity leave. Domestic authorities have taken the same line and establish, in general terms, that an employer may not use a maternity leave-related absence as either a reason for or (it would appear from the *Rees* and *Lewis Woolf* cases below) the occasion of treating a pregnant employee unfavourably.

However broad an interpretative approach is taken of the European and domestic provisions, there will still be some cases where *EA 2010, s 18* is not engaged and a claimant will have to rely upon the sex discrimination provisions. An example might be where an employer discriminates against an employee because he believes that she wishes to start a family and the respondent used an alleged failure by the complainant properly to exercise her right to return following maternity leave as a 'pretext' for the termination of her contract of employment. As this pretext was only available where the employee was a woman, the EAT reasoned, the dismissal was discriminatory.

11.32 Unfavourable treatment for reasons relating to a maternity-related illness

Under the earlier law, unfavourable treatment on grounds of a pregnancy-related illness was deemed to be discrimination on grounds of pregnancy (*SDA 1975, s 3A(3)(b)*). *EA 2010, s 18(2)* adopts a slightly different approach making unfavourable treatment on grounds of a pregnancy-related illness a specifically prohibited form of discrimination:

> "A person (A) discriminates against a woman if, in the protected period in relation to a pregnancy of hers, A treats her unfavourably–
>
> . . .
>
> (b) because of illness suffered by her as a result of it."

In order to prevent overlapping heads of claim, *EA 2010, s. 18(7)(a)* disapplies the protection against direct sex discrimination where the unfavourable treatment complained falls within *EA 2010, s 18(2)(b)*.

For an explanation of the "protected period" see **11.30** above.

European case law provides helpful interpretative guidance: in *Brown v Rentokil Ltd*: C-394/96 [1998] All ER (EC) 791, [1998] ECR I-4185, the following principles were established.

(a)   An employee may not be dismissed by reason of absence arising from a maternity-related illness at any point between conception and the end of her maternity leave period ('the protected period').

(b)   Where the maternity-related illness occurs after the end of the protected period, a dismissal will not be discriminatory if a man would have been dismissed had he been absent, because of illness, for a comparable period.

(c)   Where the illness arises during the protected period but persists thereafter, only days of absence which occur after the end of the protected period may be relied upon by an employer in deciding to dismiss (*William B Morrison & Son Ltd* (1999) 648 IDS Brief, EAT).

In a case decided before the ECJ's decision in *Brown* (and, thus, against the context of the former domestic protective regime), the EAT went further still and held that a dismissal effected after the end of the protected period was contrary to *SDA 1975* if it was for a maternity-related illness that arose during the employee's period of maternity leave (*Caledonia Bureau Investment and Property v Caffrey* [1998] ICR 603). However *Caledonia* was disapproved by the English EAT in *Lyons v DWP Jobcentre Plus* (UKEAT/348/13) [2014] ICR 668 which held that an employer dismissing an employee for sickness absence did not discriminate (either on grounds of sex or pregnancy) when it took into account periods of absence occurring outside the protected period that resulted from a pregnancy-related illness.

11.33 Discrimination Arising from Disability

EA 2010 introduced a new form of discrimination: "Discrimination arising from disability". The explicit aim of the provision was to reverse the principal effect of the decision of the House of Lords in *London Borough of Lewisham v Malcolm* [2008] UKHL 43; [2008] 1 AC

1399; [2008] IRLR 700. That decision had concerned a predecessor tort defined in the *Disability Discrimination Act 1995*: "disability-related discrimination". Under the old law an employee had to establish that they had been treated less favourably for a reason relating to their disability. The requirement to demonstrate "less favourable treatment" meant that a comparator had to be identified. In *Clark v Novacold* [1999] ICR 951, (a case decided on the old law) the Court of Appeal considered a case in which an employee was dismissed for sickness absence. The absence stemmed from his disability. Since the absence related to the disability, the Court decided that the reason for dismissal was disability-related. The appropriate comparator was someone in respect of whom that reason was not available. This meant essentially asking whether the employer would have dismissed for absence someone who had not been absent. The apparent absurdity of the test was mitigated by the fact that disability-related discrimination was capable of being justified. In *Malcolm* the House of Lords concluded that liability should be made out only when a tribunal could be satisfied that the disability itself was part of the reason for termination. The appropriate comparator was someone who had been absent but not for a reason relating to their disability. This was widely considered to have neutered the protection and the new tort was intended, in effect, to reinstate *Clark v Novacold*.

EA 2010, s 15 provides:

> "(1) A person (A) discriminates against a disabled person (B) if –
>
> (a) A treats B unfavourably because of something arising in consequence of B's disability, and
>
> (b) A cannot show that the treatment is a proportionate means of achieving a legitimate aim.
>
> (2) Subsection (1) does not apply if A shows that A did not know, and could not reasonably have been expected to know, that B had the disability."

The claimant need only establish that they have been unfavourably treated. The test is not "less favourable treatment". No comparator is required. A claimant cannot complain where they have been favourably treated but feel they should have been treated more favourably still. Therefore, where a claimant's working week was reduced to take account of her disability and her subsequent ill-health retirement pension was calculated by reference to her earnings whilst on reduced hours there was no breach of *section 15*. Ill health retirement was available only to those with a disability and was a benefit. The claimant could not complain that the benefit should have been calculated on a more generous basis (*Trustees of Swansea University Pension Scheme v Williams* UKEAT/0415/14: [2015] ICR 1197; [2015] IRLR 885, EAT).

Section 15(1)(a) contains a double causation test: the unfavourable treatment must be "because of" the relevant "something" and that "something" must itself "arise in consequence" of the disability. The Tribunal must be careful not to elide the distinction between the two limbs of the test – it is not a question of whether the complainant was treated less favourably because of their disability (*Basildon and Thurrock NHS Foundation Trust v Weerasinghe* UKEAT/397/14 [2016] ICR 305). In respect of the first element of causation (the "because" issue) the test is the same of that in respect of direct discrimination and focuses on the alleged discriminator's reasons for action. The "something" must more than trivially influence the treatment but it need not be the sole or principal cause (see *Hall v Chief Constable of West Yorkshire Police* UKEAT/0057/15 [2015] IRLR 893 and *Pnasier v NHS England and another* UKEAT/0137/15 [2016] IRLR 170). In respect of the second element (the "in consequence" issue) there is no need to look at what was in the mind of the alleged discriminator (see *Pnasier*).

Where the question of knowledge is in issue, the claimant must establish that the individual that took the decision being challenged either knew or ought to have known of the claimant's disability (*IPC Media Ltd v Millar* [2013] IRLR 707, EAT).

The EAT has provided guidance on the correct approach to *s 15* cases in *Pnasier* above:

"(a) A tribunal must first identify whether there was unfavourable treatment and by whom: in other words, it must ask whether A treated B unfavourably in the respects relied on by B. No question of comparison arises.

(b) The tribunal must determine what caused the impugned treatment, or what was the reason for it. The focus at this stage is on the reason in the mind of A. An examination of the conscious or unconscious thought processes of A is likely to be required, just as it is in a direct discrimination case. Again, just as there may be more than one reason or cause for impugned treatment in a direct discrimination context, so too, there may be more than one reason in a s.15 case. The 'something' that causes the unfavourable treatment need not be the main or sole reason, but must have at least a significant (or more than trivial) influence on the unfavourable treatment, and so amount to an effective reason for or cause of it.

(c) Motives are irrelevant. The focus of this part of the enquiry is on the reason or cause of the impugned treatment and A's motive in acting as he or she did is simply irrelevant ....

(d) The tribunal must determine whether the reason/cause (or, if more than one), a reason or cause, is 'something arising in consequence of B's disability'. That expression 'arising in consequence of' could describe a range of causal links. Having regard to the legislative history of s.15 of the Act . . . , the statutory purpose which appears from the wording of s.15, namely to provide protection in cases where the consequence or effects of a disability lead to unfavourable treatment, and the availability of a justification defence, the causal link between the something that causes unfavourable treatment and the disability may include more than one link. In other words, more than one relevant consequence of the disability may require consideration, and it will be a question of fact assessed robustly in each case whether something can properly be said to arise in consequence of disability.

(e) . . . However, the more links in the chain there are between the disability and the reason for the impugned treatment, the harder it is likely to be to establish the requisite connection as a matter of fact.

(f) This stage of the causation test involves an objective question and does not depend on the thought processes of the alleged discriminator.

. . .

(i) . . . it does not matter precisely in which order these questions are addressed. Depending on the facts, a tribunal might ask why A treated the claimant in the unfavourable way alleged in order to answer the question whether it was because of 'something arising in consequence of the claimant's disability'. Alternatively, it might ask whether the disability has a particular consequence for a claimant that leads to 'something' that caused the unfavourable treatment."

If an employee has a disability that causes him to be frequently absent from work, dismissing him for that absence record will amount to a breach of *s 15(1)* unless it can be justified. That is the same outcome that applying the former provisions of the *DDA 1995* would have produced had *Malcolm* (above) not overturned *Clark* (above). The EAT has suggested that where an employee wishes to complain that they have been dismissed for a disability-related absence, they should bring a claim under *s 15* rather than as a claim that the employer has failed to make a reasonable adjustment under *s 20* (for which see **11.37** below) (*General Dynamics Information Technology Ltd v Carranza* UK/EAT/107/14 [2015] ICR 169, [2015] IRLR 43, [2015] ICR 169 EAT). In cases where a dismissal arises from the application of a sickness absence policy, there is commonly argument about what needs to be justified by the employer. There are two possible views. The first view is that one has to justify the policy or procedure itself and that, so long as the policy is justified, its application in individual cases will be too. Lady Hale said in *Seldon v Clarkson Wright and Jakes* ([2012] IRLR 590 UKSC) "I would accept that where it is justified to have a general rule, then the existence of that rule will usually justify the treatment which results from it ...". However, the EAT has suggested that this general principle does not apply in cases concerned with sickness absence procedures that (as is typical) have a number of steps that are taken before an employee can be dismissed. In such cases the Appeal Tribunal held, it was the application of the policy at each individual stage that required justification – *Buchanan v Commissioner of Police of the Metropolis* UKEAT/0112/16, [2016] IRLR 918, [2017] ICR 184.

For a detailed treatment of the justification defence see **12.9**.

11.34 Indirect discrimination

The concept of indirect discrimination has always been easier to define than to apply in practice. It is often easiest to think first about direct discrimination and then consider how and why indirect discrimination differs. If an employer has a policy of never employing women, a female applicant who falls foul of that policy is the victim of an act of direct discrimination. There is a direct link between the application of the policy; the less favourable treatment that the woman receives and her protected characteristic. You do not need to know anything additional about the context in order to see the discriminatory impact. What if the employer instead insisted that all applicants should have post-graduate degrees? To use the language of *EA 2010* (explained in greater detail below) that would be to apply a "provision, criterion or practice" that was on its face non-discriminatory. It is impossible to tell whether such a "PCP" would tend to disadvantage women without knowing more about the context – specifically about comparative rates of completion of higher degrees. If it turns out that far fewer women obtain post-graduate degrees, the apparently neutral PCP will in practice favour men. It is the combination of the PCP with what we will call below the "context factor", that explains the disparity. As Lady Hale observed in *Essop v Home Office and Naeem v Secretary of State for Justice* [2017] UKSC 27, the context factors may take a number of different forms. They may be genetic (minimum height requirements indirectly discriminate because women are on average shorter than men); or social (length of service provisions will tend indirectly to discriminate because women are expected to be the ones to interrupt their careers to take care of children); they may even be another PCP (so in *Chief Constable of West Yorkshire Police v Homer* [2012] ICR 704 a requirement for a degree and a compulsory retirement age combined to produce an indirectly discriminatory effect).

Another way of understanding the difference between direct and indirect discrimination would be to look at what the different types of discrimination protection aim to achieve. This too was summarised eloquently by Lady Hale in *Essop*:

"the prohibition of direct discrimination aims to achieve equality of treatment. Indirect discrimination assumes equality of treatment—the PCP is applied indiscriminately to all—but aims to achieve a level playing field, where people sharing a particular protected characteristic are not subjected to requirements which many of them cannot meet but which cannot be shown to be justified. The prohibition of indirect discrimination thus aims to achieve equality of results in the absence of such justification. It is dealing with hidden barriers which are not easy to anticipate or to spot."

The dividing line between direct and indirect discrimination is not always an easy one to draw but the two forms of discrimination are distinct statutory torts and the distinction makes a material difference, particularly because a defence of justification is available in cases of indirect but not all cases of direct discrimination (*R v Secretary of State for Defence* [2006] EWCA Civ 1293, [2006] 1 WLR 3213, [2006] IRLR 934; For an account of the justification defence see **12.9** DISCRIMINATION AND EQUAL OPPORTUNITIES – II). It may be that the same broad set of facts may give rise both to a claim for direct and indirect discrimination. Thus, if a set of job requirements is indirectly discriminatory and, in addition, the interviewer favours members of one race over another, both claims may lie. However, in such a case the complainant will rely on different facts to make out each claim. A particular set of facts should normally (although not invariably) found one or other, but not both, sorts of claim (see *Jaffrey v Department of Environment Transport and the Regions* [2002] IRLR 688, EAT). In *Chief Constable of West Midlands Police v Harrod* (2015) UKEAT/0189/14, [2015] ICR 1311, [2015] IRLR 790, early retirement was only permitted to those whose length of service was long enough to have earned them an entitlement to a pension worth two thirds of average pensionable pay. That meant, in practice, one had to be at least 48 to qualify. The EAT considered, *obiter*, that a criterion that inevitably discriminated on grounds of age (even if it did not take that explicit form) should be treated as direct discrimination. The Court of Appeal specifically declined to consider the point ([2017] EWCA Civ 191).

Before 2010, there were a number of subtly different statutory formulations of the test for indirect discrimination in operation. Since the coming into force of the *EA 2010* there is a single, unified test. *EA 2010, s 19(1)*, provides:

"A person (A) discriminates against another (B) if A applies to B a provision, criterion or practice which is discriminatory in relation to a relevant protected characteristic of B's".

The relevant protected characteristics are all of those listed in *EA 2010, s 4* with the single exception of "pregnancy and maternity" (*EA 2010, s 19(3)*). This represents an extension of the protection afforded to those whose relevant characteristic is disability or gender re-assignment as neither were protected against indirect discrimination under the previous regime.

A provision, criterion or practice is discriminatory in relation to a relevant protected characteristic of B's if:

"(a) A applies, or would apply, it to persons with whom B does not share the characteristic,

(b) it puts, or would put, persons with whom B shares the characteristic at a particular disadvantage when compared with persons with whom B does not share it,

(c) it puts, or would put, B at that disadvantage, and

(d) A cannot show it to be a proportionate means of achieving a legitimate aim."

There is no definition of "provision", "criterion" or "practice" in the Act itself. The *EHRC Code* states:

"[the terms] should be construed widely so as to include, for example, any formal or informal policies, rules practices, arrangements, criteria, conditions, prerequisites, qualifications or provisions. A provision, criterion or practice may also include decisions to do something in the future – such as a policy or criterion that has not yet been applied – as well as a 'one-off' or discretionary scheme." (Para 4.5)

The term 'provision' would be apt to include both contractual provisions and the provisions of non-contractual policies. It should be borne in mind that in cases of sex discrimination, unlawful discrimination in relation to contractual terms is combated by means of a separate legislative regime known, misleadingly, as 'Equal Pay' (see EQUAL PAY (**22**)). The term 'equal pay' is misleading because all discriminatory differences in contractual terms fall within the scope of that protective regime whether or not they are, strictly speaking, to do with pay. A provision may consist of a 'one-off decision' (*Starmer v British Airways plc* [2005] IRLR 862, EAT: decision not to allow an employee to reduce her work to 50% of normal hours constituted the application of a 'provision').

'Criterion' is self-explanatory and significant as many cases involving discrimination will be concerned with selection decisions whether for appointment, promotion or dismissal. There is no requirement (as there had been under the old sex and racial discrimination tests) for the discriminatory criterion to be an absolute bar to the member of the protected class. Thus a criterion that an applicant for a post should have English as a first language will be struck down if it disadvantages an employee of a particular race even if it appears on a list of desirable rather than required characteristics.

'Practice' naturally bears the widest of meanings. It enables the Tribunal to look past an employer's Human Resources policies and to look at the day to day experience of the employees.

It is not necessary to decide whether a particular measure is specifically a provision, criterion or practice, as long as the apparent discrimination results from something that might properly be described by one or all of those labels (see Per Langstaff J in *Chief Constable of the West Midlands Police v Harrod* (2015) UKEAT/0189/14, [2015] ICR 1311, [2015] IRLR 790, approved by the Court of Appeal [2017] EWCA Civ 191).

A PCP is applied where employees are required to enter into new terms and conditions if they are to avoid dismissal (*Edie v HCL Insurance BPO Services Ltd* UKEAT/0152/14; [2015] ICR 713).

A claim may be based on more than one provision, criterion or practice (or "PCP") and relate to the impact the combined PCPs have on more than one protected characteristic. Thus, in *Ministry of Defence v DeBique* [2010] IRLR 471, EAT, a soldier who was unable to obtain the necessary visa to allow her sister to move from St Vincent to assist her with childcare was adversely affected by a PCP that required her to be available for duty twenty four hours a day and seven days a week (which indirectly discriminated against women as they are more likely to have childcare responsibilities) and a PCP which precluded members of family living overseas from coming to the UK so as to assist with childcare (which indirectly discriminated against foreign nationals).

In some cases, the relevant PCP may be expressly defined by the employer. In other cases, the tribunal may need to formulate a PCP by analysing the employer's practice or behaviour. There may be a number of different formulations which are consistent with the underlying circumstances of the case. If a complainant can 'realistically identify a [PCP] capable of supporting [their] case . . . it is nothing to the point that [their] employer can with equal cogency derive from the facts a different and unobjectionable requirement or condition' (*Allonby v Accrington and Rossendale College* [2001] EWCA Civ 529, [2001] IRLR 364, CA).

When is the PCP applied?

In *Little v Richmond Pharmacology Limited* UK/EAT/490/12 [2014] ICR 85 an employee's request to work flexibly, rather than full time, was initially refused but then granted (to the extent of a trial period) on appeal. The EAT determined that the original decision had been contingent on an appeal and, in the light of the employee's success at that stage, the requirement to work full time was not applied.

Disparity of effect - Group Disadvantage

At the heart of indirect discrimination is the notion that a single measure taken by an employer may affect different groups of employees very differently. In *Eweida v British Airways Plc* [2010] EWCA Civ 80, [2010] ICR 890, [2010] IRLR 322, [2010] 09 LS Gaz R 19 Lord Justice Sedley defined the purpose of indirect discrimination protection as not to "deal with the problem of group discrimination" but rather to "deal with the discriminatory impact of facially neutral requirements". That task is approached by asking whether "an identifiable group is adversely affected, whether actually or potentially, by some ostensibly neutral requirement". The practical consequence is that a complainant has to show more than just that they have been disadvantaged by the relevant requirement. They have to show that others who share their protected characteristic would also be adversely affected. In *Eweida* itself, the complainant's indirect discrimination claim failed because she was unable to show that any other employee shared her religious belief that she should wear a crucifix visibly. Issues of justification never arose, because Ms Eweida could not establish she had been indirectly discriminated against. Ms Eweida took her case to Strasbourg. The European Court of Human Rights upheld her claim that the UK had failed to take adequate steps to protect her right to manifest her religion. The Court's analysis focused entirely on justification arguments which means that the Court must be taken to have believed that the Claimant should have been able to establish that she had been indirectly discriminated against. One possible reading of the ECtHR's decision, therefore, is that the requirement to show that the PCP particularly disadvantages others with whom you share your belief is incompatible with the convention right. In *Mba v Mayor and Burgesses of Merton LBC* [2013] EWCA Civ 1562; [2014] IRLR 145, [2014] ICR 357 Lord Justice Elias confirmed that: "The protection of freedom of religion conferred by . . . Article [9] does not require a claimant to establish any group disadvantage; the question is whether the interference of that individual right by the employer is proportionate given the legitimate aims of the employer". He goes on to say, however, that Article 9 rights cannot be directly enforced in the Tribunal and expresses his belief that it was "not possible to read down the concept of indirect discrimination to ignore the need to establish group disadvantage" so as to ensure compatibility with the Convention. Tribunals should assume, therefore, that group disadvantage is still required in religion and belief cases until Parliament deals with the incompatibility. Permission to appeal to the Supreme Court was subsequently denied ([2014] ICR 947).

Causation

We suggested above that one way of understanding indirect discrimination was to think of it as discrimination which arises from the combination of a neutral PCP with a context factor. It is the context factor that provides the link to the protected characteristic. Both are "causes" of the disadvantage. To take the simple example of a height restriction: if the employer abandoned the minimum height requirement, there would be no disadvantage. Similarly, if the women and men were the same height on average (so that the context factor no longer existed), there would be no disadvantage. For the purposes of the *EA 2010*, the legally relevant causal relationship is between the PCP and the particular disadvantage (see *Essop* (above) at paragraph 25 of the judgment). Another way of putting the same point is to say that the law is focused on whether the PCP is a cause of the disadvantage and not why it is. This point is dramatically illustrated by *Essop* itself. The Civil Service required those seeking promotion to sit a test. BAME civil servants tended to do less well on average. Similarly, older employees tended to do less well. Statistical analysis suggested that in each case the chances of the apparent connection between the protected characteristic and the lower average success rate being a matter of mere coincidence was 0.1%. There were plainly context factors related to protected characteristics in play. The difficulty was no-one could say what they were. The Supreme Court decided that that did not matter; the claimants did not have to establish why the PCP particularly disadvantaged those with the relevant protected characteristics, they just had to establish that the PCP was having that effect.

Meaning of "particular disadvantage"

In cases of indirect discrimination the complainant must show that the PCP, puts persons who share the same protected characteristic as the complainant at a 'particular disadvantage'. This term is not defined. It was unclear whether the use of the word 'particular' was intended to convey something more than mere disadvantage. The same language is used in the *Race Discrimination Directive 2000/43*. In *Chez Razpredelenie Bulgaria AD v Komisia za Zashtita ot Diskriminatsia* C-83/14, [2015] IRLR 746, the ECJ rejected a contention that the use of the word "particular" connotes a "a serious, obvious and particularly significant case". The requirement for a "particular disadvantage" must be understood as meaning that "it is particularly persons [with the relevant protected characteristic] who are at a disadvantage because of the measure at issue". In other words, it is not a question of how grave a disadvantage might be but who suffers it.

Assessing disadvantage

Assessing disparity of effect is a comparative process. Whereas, in a case of direct discrimination, one compares the treatment received by an individual with that received or which would have been received by another, indirect discrimination cases require comparisons between groups of employees. Taking, by way of example, a case of indirect sex discrimination, the Tribunal looks at the impact of the relevant PCP on the men and women affected by it. The first task of the Tribunal is to determine which group or groups of employees it is going to look at in order to perform the comparison. This is known as selecting the 'pool' for comparison. The task of identifying the relevant pool can be difficult and is often, in practice, determinative of the case (See, for example, *Chaudhury v British Medical Association* [2007] EWCA Civ 788, [2007] IRLR 800: In a case under the old test, the claimant complained that the BMA operated a policy (amounting to a requirement or condition) of refusing to support members in race discrimination claims against regulatory authorities. The Court of Appeal determined that had such a requirement or condition been applied the appropriate pool for assessing the disparity of its effect was not BMA members generally but those members who wished to bring such claims. Since all such members were equally disadvantaged, regardless of their race, no disparity of effect could be established).

EA 2010, s 23(2) requires that on a comparison of cases for the purposes of *s 19* "there must be no material difference between the circumstances relating to each case". The EAT concluded in *Naeem v Secretary of State for Justice* UKEAT/215/13; [2014] ICR 472 that the consequence of *s 23* is that the identity of the appropriate comparator group is a question of law (neither the Court of Appeal, nor the Supreme Court subsequently suggested otherwise, albeit that the EAT decision on pool was ultimately overturned).

The best starting point for determining the composition of the pool is the advice given in the Statutory Code of Practice (2011) issued by the EHRC. At paragraph 4.18 it says:

> "In general, the pool should consist of the group which the provision, criterion or practice affects (or would affect) either positively or negatively, while excluding workers who are not affected by it, either positively or negatively."

One should also bear in mind, however, what the purpose of the selecting the pool is. One should focus on the specific allegation that is being made. The pool should "realistically and effectively test the particular allegation" (*Ministry of Defence v DeBique* [2010] IRLR 471, EAT).

Because it may be possible in a particular case, to identify more than one potentially appropriate pool, the selection of the pool is, in the first instance, a matter for the claimant. However, the tribunal is not necessarily bound to adopt the pool suggested by the claimant and it may reject the claimant's pool where it considers that it is an artificial or arbitrary one (*Abbott v Cheshire and Wirral Partnership NHS Trust* [2006] EWCA Civ 523, [2006] ICR 1267). If the Tribunal decides to reject the claimant's proposed pool, it should explain its reasons for doing so in its decision (*Secretary of State for Trade and Industry v Rutherford (No 2)* at the EAT, reported at [2005] ICR 119 at 160). Once the Tribunal has resolved to determine the pool for itself, it does not have a broad discretion as to how the pool is identified. In most cases, the Court of Appeal suggested in *Allonby* ([2001] IRLR 364, CA, it should be a matter of logical deduction from the measure. Consistently with the EHRC guidance set out above, the starting point should be the whole of the group to which the provision, criterion or practice is applied, and the tribunal will be wary of any further sub-division (cf *London Underground Ltd v Edwards* [1995] IRLR 355, *Jones v University of*

Manchester [1993] ICR 474, CA and *Rutherford v Secretary of State for Trade and Industry* [2006] UKHL 19, [2006] ICR 785 – provisions precluding claims for redundancy payments and unfair dismissal by those over 65 applied to the whole working population and not just those older employees for whom the 'retirement had some meaning'). *Rutherford* was not authority, the Court of Appeal concluded in *Grundy v BA* [2008] IRLR 74, for the 'routine selection of the widest pool'. Sedley LJ instead preferred to allow the tribunal a discretion as to the pool considered:

> 'In discrimination claims the key determinant . . . is the issue which the claimant has elected to pose and which the tribunal is therefore required to evaluate by finding a pool in which the specificity of the allegation can be realistically tested. Provided it tests the allegation in a suitable pool, the tribunal cannot be said to have erred in law even if a different pool, with a different outcome, could equally legitimately have been chosen.'

Equally, an expansion of the pool to include those who were not even potentially subject to the provision, criterion or practice, would be inappropriate (cf *Briggs v North Eastern Education and Library Board* [1990] IRLR 181). However, where the provision, criterion or practice relates to recruitment criteria the relevant pool might be very large and in *Greater Manchester Police Authority v Lea* [1990] IRLR 372, the EAT held that the employment tribunal had not erred in accepting that the economically active population was an appropriate pool for the purpose of determining the proportion of men and women who could comply with a condition of not being in receipt of an occupational pension. In *Lord Chancellor v Coker* [2001] IRLR 116, the EAT considered a case where the Lord Chancellor had decided to appoint a particular individual to be his special adviser. The appointment was challenged by two complainants who alleged that the failure publicly to advertise the position had resulted in their having been the subjects of acts of indirect sex and race discrimination, respectively. As the criterion was, in effect, that the candidate should be the relevant specific individual, the EAT concluded that no pool could sensibly be identified. The EAT's decision was upheld by the Court of Appeal ([2001] EWCA Civ 1756, [2002] ICR 321). The relevant criterion was identified before their Lordships as being a friend of the Lord Chancellor. The Court of Appeal concluded that the necessary disparity of impact could not be established. Looking at the pool of those qualified to perform the role, the criterion excluded almost the entirety of its members. The criterion could only be said to have a disproportionate effect where a significant proportion of the pool were able to satisfy it. That was not the case on the facts. Lord Phillips went on to opine that:

> 'Making an appointment from within a circle of family, friends and personal acquaintances is seldom likely to constitute indirect discrimination.'

Under the old law, the Claimant had to establish that a "considerably smaller proportion" of those who shared their protected characteristic could comply with the PCP. *EA 2010* requires, instead, that the claimant establish that those in the pool who share the claimant's protected characteristic should be at a "particular disadvantage". The old test was explicitly concerned with numbers and the case law set out below, decided under the old provisions, understandably focus on figures. The new test is not expressly concerned with numbers but it seems from the EHRC Code that statistics will still be important. In defining "disadvantage", *EHRC Code, Para 4.12* says:

> 'Statistics can provide an insight into the link between the provision, criterion or practice and the disadvantage that it causes."

However, the *EHRC Code* recognises that the numbers of people involved may be too small or the evidence available too unreliable to allow for a statistical analysis. In such circumstances, the *EHRC Code* suggests (at *Para 4.13*), it would be neither practicable nor appropriate for a statistical approach to be taken and the tribunal may wish, instead, to rely upon expert evidence. Experts may also be appropriate where the tribunal requires some assistance in properly understanding the impact of a PCP on those with a particular protected characteristic (see *Para 4.14* which gives as an example expert evidence about the principles of a particular religious belief). It seems that even expert evidence may be unnecessary. In *Games v University of Kent* [2015] IRLR 202, EAT, the tribunal was unpersuaded by statistics relied upon by a claimant who alleged that a requirement for lecturers to have a PhD was indirectly age discriminatory. The EAT considered that evidence of the experience of the claimant or of other members of the affected group might provide "compelling evidence of disadvantage even if there are no statistics at all".

When the *EHRC Code* turns to providing guidance on carrying out the comparative exercise it turns again to numbers. The tribunal should ask (says *Para 4.21*) how many workers in the pool are (or would be) disadvantaged by the PCP despite not sharing the protected characteristic with the claimant. That number should be expressed as a proportion, which the guidance labels as "x". The same exercise is then repeated in relation to pool members who do share the protected characteristic. That proportion is labelled "y". The tribunal then compares "x" with "y" in order to determine whether the necessary particular disadvantage exists. *Para 4.22* advises:

> 'Whether a difference is significant will depend on the context, such as the size of the pool and the numbers behind the proportions. It is not necessary to show that the majority of those within the pool who share the protected characteristic are placed at a disadvantage.'

Turning to the case law on the old formulation, there was little guidance on how one determines whether a particular disparate impact is sufficient. The issue was referred to the European Court of Justice in *R v Secretary of State for Employment, ex p Seymour-Smith* [1999] ICR 447. The guidance provided by the ECJ was disappointingly vague. The ECJ decision echoed the language of the *SDA 1975* as it was prior to 1 October 2005 in requiring that a 'considerably smaller percentage' of women than men were able to satisfy the relevant condition. A mere statistically significant disparity was insufficient. However, the ECJ went on to hold that a 'lesser but persistent and relatively constant disparity over a long period' might suffice. It was hoped that the House of Lords might feel able to put a little meat on these bones when the matter came back for their further consideration in the light of the reference ([2000] ICR 244). The issue in *Seymour-Smith* was whether the requirement, introduced in 1985, that employees should have two years' continuous service before qualifying for protection against unfair dismissal indirectly discriminated against women. In 1985, 77.4% of men could comply with that requirement whereas only 68.9% of women could do so. In 1991, the year which their Lordships identified as being the critical one for the purposes of the particular case, the relevant percentages were 74.5% and 67.4%. None of their Lordships thought that those figures, on their own, suggested that a 'considerably smaller percentage' of women could comply. However, the majority felt that the disparity (which narrowed slowly to about 4.3% by 1993) fell into the category of the sort of 'persistent and relatively consistent' disparity that the ECJ had indicated might suffice. They determined, therefore, that the requirement was indirectly discriminatory although they went on to find that it was justified.

In practice, the tribunals are given a considerable margin of discretion in deciding when the percentages should be taken to indicate a sufficiently significant disparity. The courts had consistently rejected the adoption of a rule of thumb (see *McCausland v Dungannon District Council* [1993] IRLR 583 which was concerned with the construction of the *Fair Employment (Northern Ireland) Act 1976* which applied the same test of disparate impact to religious discrimination). In *Harvest Town Circle Ltd v Rutherford* [2002] ICR 123, EAT, the EAT expressed the pious (if rather faint) hope that 'as more cases of indirect discrimination are heard a more soundly based assessment of what is or is not properly regarded as a considerable or substantial disparity will develop'. In *London Underground Ltd v Edwards (No 2)* [1999] ICR 494, there was only one person in the pool of comparison who could not comply with the relevant requirement. 100% of the 2,023 men to whom the provision applied could comply. Of the 21 women affected, only the complainant could not comply. This meant that the proportion of women that could comply was 95.2%. Nevertheless, the Court of Appeal upheld the tribunal's decision that the proportion of women that could comply was considerably smaller.

The approach adopted in *Edwards* illustrates another general principle applicable to the assessment of disparate impact; one should not focus on the absolute numbers underlying the relevant proportions but on the percentages themselves. The principle was specifically endorsed by the ECJ in *Seymour-Smith* (but see *Harvest Town Circle Ltd* above, in which the EAT interpret *Seymour-Smith* as allowing a domestic court to look at either absolute numbers or relative proportions of those who could comply).

In many cases, the tribunal will look at the relevant proportions and simply subtract one from the other. In the *Edwards* case, for instance, one might say that 4.8% more men can comply than women. *McCausland* suggests taking a further mathematical step. Rather than subtracting the smaller percentage from the larger, one should calculate a ratio. In the *McCausland* case itself, 2.9% of Protestants could comply with the relevant requirement as compared with only 1.5% of Catholics. Simply subtracting one percentage from the other produces an unimpressive difference of only 1.4%. However, when one looks at the ratio of the two percentages one finds that the group of Catholics that could comply was only 71% of the size of the group of Protestants that could do so. A further variation was suggested by Lord Nicholls in *Barry v Midland Bank plc* [1999] ICR 859 at page 869. He suggested that having calculated what proportion of men and women fell within the advantaged and disadvantaged groups respectively one should then calculate a ratio of the proportions of those falling within the disadvantaged group. His approach is thus akin to the *McCausland* approach save that it focuses on those who cannot comply rather than those who can. However, in *Secretary of State for Trade and Industry v Rutherford* above, the Court of Appeal indicated that it would be wrong to focus only on the disadvantaged group. When *Rutherford* came before the House of Lords, Lord Walker of Gestingthorpe took the view that, save where special circumstances justify it, attention should be focused on the 'advantaged' group (*Rutherford v Secretary of State for Trade and Industry* [2006] UKHL 19, [2006] ICR 785). However, in *Grundy v British Airways plc* [2007] EWCA Civ 1020, [2008] IRLR 74, an equal pay case, the Court of Appeal held that an employment tribunal had been entitled to focus on the disadvantaged group. the position remains, therefore, somewhat unclear.

The EAT has sought to rely on *Seymour-Smith* as a basis for taking a much less mechanistic approach to the assessment of the sufficiency of disparity. In *Chief Constable of Avon and Somerset Constabulary v Chew* [2001] All ER (D) 101 (Sep), EAT, the EAT indicated that a 'flexible approach' could be adopted to assessing the sufficiency of any disparity. It was not always necessary to rely on statistics. Further, the tribunal was entitled to consider whether the objectionable provision was inherently more likely to produce a detrimental effect, which disparately affected a particular sex. Thus in *Chew*, a shift rota would likely be harder for those with childcare responsibilities to comply with, and women are more likely to have childcare responsibilities.

PCPs that distinguish between employees on the basis of length of service are often considered to adversely affect younger employees. However, not all such provisions will have the necessary disparity of effect, one example is *Tyrolean Airways Tiroler Luftfahrt Gesellschaft mbH v Betriebsrat Bord der Tyrolean Airways Tiroler Luftfahrt Gesellschaft mbH*: C-132/11 [2012] IRLR 781: A provision in a collective agreement which required flight and cabin crew to have three years' employment with the airline before achieving a particular grade was not sufficiently linked (either directly or indirectly) to age for it to be discriminatory. The rule excluded experience gained with other airlines it was not an age-related provision.

Disparity of Effect - Personal disadvantage

The third element of the test is personal disadvantage. It does not matter if, for instance, persons of a particular religion or sex are disproportionately disadvantaged by a provision, criterion or practice, if the complainant is not. Thus a female employee cannot complain that she has been indirectly discriminated against as a result of an employer imposing a minimum height requirement if she is taller than the minimum requirement. Under the old test, inability to comply with the requirement or condition was not its own detriment (*Lord Chancellor v Coker* [2001] IRLR 116, EAT). It is thought that a similar principle applies under the new test. The disadvantage must be the consequence of the application of the provision, criterion or practice and not the imposition of the measure itself.

In addition to being able to demonstrate that they are personally disadvantaged, the Act appears to require that the claimant demonstrate that they are subject to the same disadvantage as the group (hence the reference at *s 19(1)(c)* to "that disadvantage" rather than to "a disadvantage"). Usually, that will be obvious. However, there can be difficult cases. One is *Essop* (above). It was understood, in *Essop* that BAME candidates were more likely to fail the test. It was not understood why. It was argued on behalf of the Home Office that a black candidate who failed should have to show that the reason why they failed was the same reason that fewer black candidates on average succeeded. Unless the claimant could do that, it was argued, the tribunal could not know whether the claimant and the group were suffering from the same disadvantage. Otherwise, there was a danger of "coat-tailing". A candidate who failed because they were late to the exam could just say that they had suffered the same particular disadvantage (i.e. "failing") as the group. The Supreme Court rejected that approach. If it could be shown that the failure arose from lateness, it was not the PCP that was disadvantaging the candidate – the necessary causation was lacking. Another way of looking at it would be that their lateness amounted to a "material difference between the circumstances" of the candidate and the others in the pool for the purposes of *s 23*. A third suggestion made by Lady Hale was that the issue could be wrapped up in the consideration of justification.

If a causal connection must be established between the personal disadvantage and the protected characteristic, it seems that it does not have to be a characteristic of the complainant as it is possible to bring an associative indirect discrimination complaint. That was the view of the ECJ in *Chez Razpredelenie Bulgaria AD v Komisia za Zashtita ot Diskriminatsia* C-83/14, [2015] IRLR 746: An electricity company placed meters out of reach in predominantly Roma areas. This was to the complainant's detriment even though she was not herself of Roma origin. She lived in a Roma area and was not provided with a meter she could easily check. The ECJ considered that both associative direct and indirect discrimination claims were open to her.

Indirect discrimination: particular cases

11.35 *Sex discrimination and full-time work*

Provisions, criteria or practices which result in the less favourable treatment of part-time employees are frequently found indirectly to discriminate against women (cf *Bilka-Kaufhaus GmbH v Weber von Hartz*: 170/84 [1986] ECR 1607, [1986] 2 CMLR 701; *Clarke v Eley (IMI) Kynoch Ltd* [1983] ICR 165, EAT; *R v Secretary of State for Employment, ex p Equal Opportunities Commission* [1994] ICR 317), although it cannot be assumed that such a condition would have a discriminatory effect (see, for example, *Sinclair, Roche & Temperley v Heard* [2004] IRLR 763, EAT). Each case turns on its own facts and claimants have to be prepared to lead evidence which establishes a disparate impact (*Kidd v DRG (UK) Ltd* [1985] ICR 405).

Because the effects of a requirement to work full time are often complex, it is by no means always immediately obvious that the complainant had been less favourably treated. See, for instance, *Kachelmann v Bankhaus Hermann Lampe KG*: C-322/98 [2000] ECR I-7505,

[2002] 1 CMLR 155, ECJ, in which the ECJ wrestled with the question of whether a bank's decision, following the deletion of a part-time post, to limit the selection pool for redundancy to part-time workers amounted to less favourable treatment or (as it ultimately decided) that to have included full-timers would be to have conferred an advantage on part-timers by effectively entitling them to be offered a full-time post if a full-timer were selected for redundancy.

Historically, the predominance of women in the part-time sector has been assumed to be related to the fact that they have traditionally been expected to be the providers of homecare to young children. This assumption underpins the reasoning of the EAT in the case of *Price v Civil Service Commission (No 2)* [1978] IRLR 3 which held that imposing a maximum age limit of 28 for appointment as an Executive Officer in the Civil Service was, in practice, to the disadvantage of women as they were more likely to have had career breaks in order to start a family. Similarly, in *Meade-Hill and National Union of Civil and Public Servants v British Council* [1996] 1 All ER 79, [1995] ICR 847, [1995] IRLR 478, the Court of Appeal was persuaded that the exercise of a contractual mobility clause might be discriminatory as women were more likely than their partners to be the 'second earner' and thus less able to re-locate. Whilst it appears that the tribunals and courts are frequently comfortable making such assumptions, in practice it is dangerous for an employer to do so. In *Skyrail Oceanic Ltd v Coleman* [1981] ICR 864, it was held that selection of a woman for redundancy on the assumption that men are more likely than women to be the primary supporters of their spouses and children could itself amount to unlawful discrimination.

The same issue arises in circumstances where a woman wishes to make changes to her work patterns following the birth of her child. In *Clymo v Wandsworth London Borough Council* [1989] ICR 250, an employer declined to allow an employee to change to a job-sharing (ie part-time) arrangement. The EAT held that the employer, having merely declined to provide an advantage not proffered to any employees in that grade, had not 'subjected' the employee to anything, and that there was no detriment. By contrast, in *Robinson v Oddbins Ltd* [1996] 27 DCLD 1 an employment tribunal held that the employee's request to job-share had not been properly considered and the company's reliance on a contractual clause requiring employees, when asked, to work hours over and above the standard working week had indirectly discriminated against women who were more likely to have childcare responsibilities (cf also *Puttick v Eastbourne Borough Council* (unreported, 1995, COIT 3106/2)). In another case, the EAT held that a refusal to allow a woman to job-share was not directly discriminatory in the absence of evidence that a man making a similar request would have had it granted; however, it did not consider the issue of indirect discrimination (*British Telecommunications plc v Roberts* [1996] IRLR 601). In practice, employers will need to be able to establish that there is a sensible justification for requiring that employees work full-time if they are to be safe from claims. In *Lockwood v Crawley Warren Group Ltd* [2001] 680 IDS Brief 9, EAT, this approach was extended still further. A female employee encountered difficulties with her childcare arrangements. She offered to work full-time from home or else to take up to six months' unpaid leave with a view to resolving the difficulties. She was offered two weeks of leave instead and resigned. The EAT decided that the refusal to allow her either to work from home or to take the leave she had asked for, amounted to the application of a condition or requirement. For an example of the circumstances in which a refusal to allow an employee to work flexibly was justified, see *Georgiou v Colman Coyle* [2002] 705 IDS Brief 12, EAT: the office was small; there was a need for two full-time solicitors; commercial clients expected a prompt and efficient service; the need to consult files and to be supervised meant that the complainant had to attend the respondent's premises; and reduced fee income would adversely affect the respondent's profitability.

11.35a   Discrimination and Equal Opportunities – I

11.35a *Sex Discrimination and absence on Maternity or Parental Leave*

An employee who is absent on maternity or parental leave is unable to perform their work duties. That inability may have consequences where access to benefits or continued employment may depend on an assessment of work performed, targets achieved or income generated. There is, of course, a specific protection available where an employer treats an employee unfavourably because of maternity leave (see **[11.31]** above and **32.24 MATERNITY AND PARENTAL RIGHTS** below) or parental leave. However, indirect sex discrimination may have a role to play too. In *Riezniece v Zemkopibas ministrija and another* C-7/12; [2013] IRLR 828; [2014] ICR 1096, the CJEU determined that a method of selecting employees for transfer or dismissal amounted to indirect sex discrimination. The employee was absent on parental leave when a post was abolished. An assessment was performed. Some of the criteria matched those used in annual appraisals but some did not. As the employee was on leave she was assessed on the basis of her last annual appraisal. This approach was thought to disadvantage her and she scored lowest in the assessment. A much higher number of women took parental leave than did men.

11.36 *Sexual orientation*

It is lawful to offer access to benefits, facilities or services to married persons and civil partners to the exclusion of all other persons. *EA 2010, Sch 9, Part 3, Para 18(2)* specifically provides that that does not amount to an act of sexual orientation discrimination (but see *Maruko v Versorgungsanstalt der Deutschen Buhnen*: C-267/06 [2008] IRLR 450).

Many employers offered access to benefits, facilities or services exclusively to married persons which had the effect of excluding homosexual employees. *EA 2010, Sch 9, Part 3, Para 18(1)* provides that no claim for sexual orientation discrimination lies in relation to any such practice in so far as the relevant right had accrued before 5 December 2005 (on which date civil partnerships came into being) or is a right to a benefit which is payable in respect of periods of service before that date. For cases which suggest that such a cut-off date is compatible with EU Law see *Walker v Innospec* [2015] EWCA Civ 1000, [2015] IRLR 1005 and *Parris v Trinity College Dublin* C-443/15, [2017] IRLR 173, [2017] ICR 313.

To bring a claim of indirect discrimination, it will be necessary for a complainant to identify himself as being of a particular sexual orientation, something that is not necessary for a complaint of direct discrimination, victimisation or harassment.

11.37 Disability: Duty to Make Reasonable Adjustments

Under the *DDA 1995*, there was no prohibition of indirect disability discrimination, instead there was a new creature: a duty to make reasonable adjustments where a disabled employee is placed a "substantial disadvantage" as the result of a provision, criterion or practice, physical feature of the employer's premises or the absence of an auxiliary aid. The principal difference between the ordinary duty not indirectly to discriminate and the duty to make reasonable adjustments is that the former is simply a path to compensation whereas the latter imposes a positive duty upon an employer to remove barriers to the effective participation in its workforce of those with disabilities.

When does the duty arise?

The duty is set out at *EA 2010, s 20* and is supplemented by a detailed schedule: *EA 2010, Sch 8*.

EA 2010, s 20 imposes a "requirement" on an employer:

(1)   whose provisions, criteria or practices puts a disabled person at a "substantial disadvantage" in relation to a relevant matter in comparison with persons who are not disabled (*s 20(3)*);

(2)   whose premises have a physical feature which puts a disabled person at a substantial disadvantage (*s 20(4)*); or

(3)   whose disabled employee will be put at a substantial disadvantage if they are not provided with an auxiliary aid (*s 20(5)*);

to "take such steps as it is reasonable to have to take to avoid the disadvantage" or to provide the auxiliary aid (as appropriate). A failure to comply with any of the requirements spelt out above is treated as a failure to comply with a duty to make reasonable adjustments (*EA 2010, s 21(1)*) which, in turn, amounts to an act of discrimination (*EA 2010, s 21(2)*). A tribunal considering whether or not the duty has been complied with should make explicit findings identifying: the relevant provision, criterion or practice; the persons who are not disabled with whom comparison is made; the nature and the extent of any substantial disadvantage suffered by the employee; and any step or steps it would have been reasonable for the employer to take (see *Secretary of State for Work and Pensions (Job Centre Plus) v Higgins* [UKEAT/579/12, [2014] ICR 341).

The Act does not further define the phrase "provisions, criteria or practices". *EHRC Code* suggests that the terms should be construed widely and would include: "any formal or informal policies, rules, practices, arrangements or qualifications including one-off decision and actions" (*Para 6.10*). "Physical feature" is defined at *s 20(10)* to include "a feature arising from the design or construction of a building; a feature of an approach to, exit from or access to a building; a fixture or fitting, or furniture, furnishings, materials, equipment or other chattels, in or on the premises; or any other physical element or quality". References to auxiliary aids include references to auxiliary services (*s 20(11)*). It would appear that a 'provision, criterion or practice' could include an implied condition that a person is fit for the job they are employed to do. If it transpires that a person through disability can no longer fulfil that condition (i.e. the person is no longer capable of doing the job for which they were employed) then there may be a duty to consider any adjustments that could be made to remove the disadvantage caused by that implied condition (see *Archibald v Fife Council* [2004] UKHL 32, [2004] ICR 954, HL).

In *Nottingham City Transport Limited v Harvey* [2013] EqLR 4, EAT, the Appeal Tribunal found that a procedurally-flawed disciplinary investigation which disadvantaged a disabled employee was not a "practice" as there was no evidence that investigations conducted by the respondent were generally inadequate. Similarly, in *Carphone Warehouse Limited v Martin* [2013] EqLR 481, EAT, the Appeal Tribunal decided that "incompetence or a woeful lack of application or a failure to stick to your own time limits [could not] . . . be properly characterised as a [PCP]". In *Griffiths v Secretary of State for Work and Pensions* [2015] EWCA Civ 1265, [2016] IRLR 216, [2017] ICR 160, the Court of Appeal considered the vexed and common question of adjustments to absence policies. The Court recommended care as to how the PCP is framed. The PCP in *Griffiths* itself was not the particular absence policy itself but rather the underlying requirement (reflected in the policy) to "maintain a certain level of attendance at work so as to avoid disciplinary sanctions".

The Act further defines what may be expected by way of adjustments:

(1)   Where the relevant provision, criterion or practice or auxiliary aid relates to the provision of information the steps that it is reasonable for an employer to take include steps for ensuring that the information is provided in accessible format (*s 20(6)*); and

(2)   Where the disadvantage arises from a physical feature, avoiding the disadvantage may include: "removing the physical feature in question; altering it; or providing a reasonable means of avoiding it" (*s 20(9)*).

EA 2010, Sch 8 fleshes out the *s 20* test. In relation to employers two things are identified as "relevant matters": Deciding to whom to offer employment and employment itself (*EA 2010, Sch 8, Part 2, para (1)*). In *General Dynamics Information Technology Ltd v Carranza* UKEAT/0107/14 [2015] ICR 169, [2015] IRLR 43, EAT suggested that adjustments should be understood as "practical actions which are taken to avoid the disadvantage". The EAT contrasted such actions with adjustments to "mere mental processes" which they felt the Act did not require. Specifically, they rejected an argument that it would have been a reasonable adjustment to disregard an earlier warning for absence when considering whether to dismiss. The EAT further suggested that where the essence of the complaint is someone has been dismissed for disability-related absence in accordance with an employer's absence management policy, the better course is to bring a claim under *s 15* (for which see **11.33** above) rather than suggesting that the policy should have been adjusted.

In order for the duty to arise the employee must be subjected to a "substantial" disadvantage in comparison with persons who are not disabled. "Substantial" is defined at *EA 2010, s 212(1)* to mean "more than minor or trivial". The threshold is set deliberately low. The *EHRC Code* emphasises that the purpose of the comparison is to determine whether the disadvantage arises because of the disability and that, in contrast to the position with cases of direct and indirect discrimination, there is "no requirement to identify a comparator or comparator group whose circumstances are the same or nearly the same as the disabled person's" (*Para 6.16*). The disabled person affected must be the claimant. It is not possible to bring an "associative" reasonable adjustments claim. So in *Hainsworth v Ministry of Defence* [2014] EWCA Civ 763, [2014] IRLR 728 an employer did not have to transfer an employee back to the UK so as to ensure that her disabled son had access to education designed to meet his special needs.

No duty where Employer lacks knowledge of disability or disadvantage

Limitations on the duty are set out *EA 2010, Sch 8, Part 3*. An employer is not subject to a duty to make reasonable adjustments if he does not know and could not reasonably be expected to know:

(1) In the case of an applicant or potential applicant for employment that the disabled person may be an applicant for the work in question;

(2) In any other case, that an interested disabled person has a disability and is likely to be placed at the relevant substantial disadvantage.

In *Wilcox v Birmingham CAB Services Ltd* [2011] EqLR 810, the EAT departed from earlier authority (*Eastern and Coastal Kent PCT v Grey* [2009] IRLR 429) which had suggested that an employer could only rely on the exception if he could show that he lacked the actual or constructive knowledge referred to in both limbs of (2) above. That interpretation seemed to mean that an employer might be subject to the duty even where he was unaware (and could not reasonably have been expected to be aware) of the disability provided he could foresee that the employee might be subject to a disadvantage. In *Wilcox* the EAT took the view that unless the employer had actual or constructive knowledge of the disability, the question of substantial disadvantage did not arise. An employer will be taken to have the requisite knowledge provided they are aware of the impairment and its consequences. There is no need for them to be aware of the specific diagnosis of the condition that creates the impairment (*Jennings v Barts and the London NHS Trust* [2013] EqLR 326, EAT).

Where a question as to whether an employee is a disabled person arises, an employer will often look to an occupational health practitioner for a view. However, an employer cannot simply "rubber stamp" an occupational health practitioner's opinion that an employee is not a disabled person. In *Gallop v Newport City Council* [2013] EWCA Civ 1583; [2014] IRLR 211 the fact that the employer had obtained a bare, unreasoned assertion by an occupational health doctor that an employee was not disabled did not mean that they did not have constructive knowledge of the claimant's disability.

Where an employer had no actual knowledge of a disability the Tribunal must go on specifically to consider the question of constructive knowledge (*McCubbin v Perth and Kinross Council* UKEATS/0025/13).

Where an employer is fixed with constructive knowledge (on the basis that he ought to have known) it is open to him to argue that he has nevertheless complied with the duty on the basis either that no reasonable adjustments were possible or else that he had in fact taken steps that resulted in him unwittingly discharging the duty (see *British Gas Services Ltd v McCaull* [2001] IRLR 60). The test is an objective one. It is the steps taken or not taken that are to be tested and not the employer's state of mind in taking or not taking such steps.

The Content of the Duty

The employer must take such steps as it is reasonable to have to take either to avoid the disadvantage or, in auxiliary aid cases, to provide the aid (*EA 2010, s 20(3) to (5)*). The employer cannot require the employee to pay its costs of complying with the duty (*EA 2010, s 20(7)*).

EA 2010, s 22 allows for regulations to further define the duty including defining what would and would not be reasonable in particular circumstances. No regulations have yet been issued that apply in employment cases.

The *DDA 1995* had, at *s 18B*, guidance as to what sorts of measures might be required and what factors might be taken into account in determining reasonableness. The factors that were identified included:

(1)   the extent to which taking the step would prevent the effect in relation to which the duty is imposed;

(2)   the extent to which it is practicable for [the employer] to take the step;

(3)   the financial and other costs which would be incurred by [the employer] in taking the step and the extent to which it would disrupt any of his activities;

(4)   the extent of [the employer's] financial and other resources;

(5)   the availability to [the employer] of financial or other assistance with respect to taking the step; and

(6)   the nature of [the employer's] activities and the size of his undertaking.

The steps that might be taken included making adjustments to premises; allocating some of the disabled person's duties to another person; transferring him to an existing vacancy and altering his hours of work and training. The reasonableness factors and example adjustments do not appear to have been carried across to the *EA 2010*. However, there is no doubt that they remain relevant and they have been substantially reproduced at Chapter 6 of the *EHRC Code*. Guidance is set out at *Para 6.23* ff of the *EHRC Code*. The EAT has suggested that tribunals would be wise to consider the factors identified in the Code whilst acknowledging that they are under no duty to address every factor contained in it (*Secretary of State for Work and Pensions (Job Centre Plus) v Higgins* above).

The first guidance factor – the extent to which the step would prevent the effect in relation to which the duty is imposed – has been the subject of some consideration in appeal cases. In *First Group plc v Paulley* [2017] UKSC 4, [2017] IRLR 258 Lord Neuberger held there has to be a "real prospect" that the step "would have made a difference" (see also *Lancaster v TBWA Manchester* UKEAT/0460/10 and *Foster v Leeds Teaching Hospital NHS Trust* [2011] EqLR 1075). One has to be careful, however, precisely to identify the disadvantage in issue. In *Noor v Foreign and Commonwealth Office* [2010] UK/EAT/470/10, [2011] ICR 695, the EAT overturned a tribunal decision to the effect that since any proposed adjustment to an interviewing process would still not have resulted in the complainant having been appointed, there was no breach of the duty. The complainant had been at a disadvantage in the interview and there were steps that the respondent might have taken which would have reduced that specific disadvantage even if no step would have landed the applicant the job itself.

Employers should also be careful to identify what arrangement or what provision, criterion or practice is actually placing the disabled employee at a disadvantage in order that the appropriate adjustments can be considered. In *Paul v National Probation Service* [2004] IRLR 190, a tribunal rejected the claim of a claimant who had been refused a job after failing an occupational health assessment. The tribunal concluded that the claimant had not been placed at a disadvantage compared to others since all job applicants had to undergo an assessment. The EAT held that the tribunal had wrongly regarded the relevant arrangement as being the requirement to undergo an assessment. It was not the fact of the assessment that had placed the claimant at a disadvantage but the health adviser's assessment that the claimant's depressive illness rendered him unsuitable for the job. By focusing on the wrong 'arrangement' the tribunal omitted to consider whether there were any reasonable adjustments that the employer could have made (eg by obtaining specialist advice from the claimant's consultant on his fitness for the job). (See also *Smith v Churchills Stairlifts plc* [2005] EWCA Civ 1220, [2006] IRLR 41, where the Court of Appeal confirmed that the comparator for these purposes is readily identified by reference to the disadvantage caused by the relevant arrangements.)

The EAT has held that whether or not any adjustments were reasonable in the circumstances will be determined by the employment tribunal objectively (see *Morse v Wiltshire County Council* [1998] IRLR 352 and *HM Land Registry v Wakefield* [2009] All ER (D) 205 (Feb), EAT). Thus, it may not be sufficient for an employer simply to assert that adjustments were considered and thought to be unreasonable if the tribunal finds that there were other reasonable adjustments which could have been made by the employer (see also *Ridout v TC Group* [1998] IRLR 628). The employment tribunal will not be entitled, however, to rely upon a failure to make a reasonable adjustment where the particular adjustment in question was not raised as an issue and the parties have not had an opportunity to make submissions in relation to that adjustment (*Tarbuck v Sainsbury's Supermarkets Ltd* [2006] IRLR 664). Recognising that tribunals often fall into error when they fail to identify and address each of the separate elements of the 'failure to make reasonable adjustments' cause of action, the EAT has laid down useful guidance on the step-by-step process to be followed in such cases: *Environment Agency v Rowan* [2008] IRLR 20.

Clark v Novacold [1999] IRLR 318, EWCA was authority for the proposition that the duty to make reasonable adjustments did not apply to a dismissal. Following *Aylott v Stockton on Tees BC* [2010] EWCA Civ 910, that would seem no longer to be the case. In an admittedly obiter consideration of the issue, Mummery LJ was inclined to accept that the effect of *Framework Directive 2000/78/EC, Art 3(1)(c)* was to require dismissals to fall within the scope of the duty. There would appear to be no duty to offer part-time employment as an alternative to dismissal in circumstances where the claimant had not asked to work part-time and where he was not fit for any form of work at the relevant time (*Callagan v Glasgow City Council* [2001] IRLR 724). Avoiding dismissal may involve offering the employee an alternative job at a higher grade which she is capable of doing without requiring her to undergo a competitive interview cf *Archibald v Fife Council* [2004] UKHL 32, [2004] ICR 954 and in certain circumstances (eg where there is an on-going reorganisation) it could even involve the creation of an entirely new job (*Southampton City College v Randall* [2006] IRLR 18). However, there is no obligation on an employer to create a post specifically, which is not otherwise necessary, merely to create a job for a disabled person (*Tarbuck v Sainsbury's Supermarkets Ltd* [2006] IRLR 664 but see *Chief Constable of South Yorkshire Police v Jelic* [2010] IRLR 744 where in the context of a "disciplined service" the EAT held that employer should have considered a job swap, ie creating a vacancy by forcing the incumbent to transfer to another role). Nor is there an obligation to avoid dismissal by placing a disabled person into a role that the employer does not believe that they can perform (*Wade v Sheffield Hallam University* UKEAT/0194/12: [2013] EqLR 951, EAT. Employers intending to adjust an employee's role should bear in mind that where an employee is moved to a role that would ordinarily be less well-remunerated, they may have at least to consider continuing to pay the employee at their former higher rate – see *G4S Cash Solutions (UK) Ltd v Powell* UKEAT/0243/15, [2016] IRLR 820. *G4S* also reminds employers that the duty to make reasonable adjustments is not a licence unilaterally to vary the employee's contract. If you want make a change that would ordinarily require the employee's consent, that consent is still required.

In *Gomez v Glaxosmithkline Services Unlimited* [2011] EqLR 804, the EAT considered the case of a claimant who suffered from severe depression and panic attacks. The claimant was found to have been leaving the site at which he worked without authorisation and using a colleague's security pass. He was dismissed for gross misconduct. He argued that the penalty should have been "adjusted" and that he should have been given a warning instead. The EAT concluded that the employer could not be reasonably required to take such a step as it risked the employer appearing to condone the practice. *Burke v College of Law and another* [2011] EqLR 454, EAT is a further example of an employer determining that a proposed adjustment would not have been reasonable. It is a case concerning a "qualification body" – one of the categories of non-employers covered by the Act. The claimant, who had MS, was re-sitting LPC exams. A series of adjustments were made including allowing them more time. However, the claimant had asked for still further time and the opportunity to take the exams at home. Those adjustments were declined. The EAT concluded that the examination's purpose was to "assess the ability of the candidate to demonstrate their competence and capability in the subject matter under time pressure." The time restriction was, therefore, a competence standard. See also: *Lowe v Cabinet Office* [2011] EqLR 803: The claimant had Asperger's Syndrome. She applied for admission to the Civil Service Fast Stream. The selection exercise involved application of a criterion that required a high standard of communication skills and assessment by group exercise. The tribunal accepted that no adjustment was reasonably required. The exercise was to find high quality applicants and the proposed adjustments would have destroyed the essence of the exercise).

In *Clark v Newsquest Media* [2011] EqLR 932 an employer required a diabetic employee to test her blood and inject herself in private. The tribunal concluded that employer was acting in breach of the duty.

The following have been held by employment tribunals to be reasonable adjustments:

(i)   provision of subtitled training videos for Channel 5 Television re-tuners (*Williams v Channel 5 Engineering Services Ltd*, IDS Brief 609, p 13); and

(ii)   provision of a special 'Grahl' chair costing £1,000 for an employee with a club foot (*Tarling v Wisdom Toothbrushes Ltd*, 24 June 1997, COIT 1500148/97).

The employer's duty to make reasonable adjustments is confined to those which are 'job related' (see *Kenny v Hampshire Constabulary* [1999] IRLR 76). A disabled person may be in a position to obtain employment if he was provided with transport to get to the place of employment. However, the employer's duty in relation to that person, whilst extending to the making of adjustments to enable access to the employer's premises, would not extend to the provision of transport to get there from home. In *Kenny*, the job applicant had cerebral palsy and required assistance in carrying out his toilet functions. The EAT held that whilst there may be a duty to consider physical adjustments to enable access to the toilets, the employer was not under a duty to provide a personal carer to assist the claimant with his toilet needs. Such provision would address the claimant's personal needs but would not be job-related.

The extent to which tribunals should take into account the actual or assumed knowledge of an employer in the context of the duty to make reasonable adjustments has been considered by the EAT in *Ridout v TC Group* [1998] IRLR 628. In that case, a job applicant had disclosed in her application that she was disabled and had photosensitive epilepsy controlled by a daily dose of Epilim. She was shortlisted for an interview. Upon entering the room in which the interview was to be held, the claimant, who was wearing sunglasses around her neck, commented that she might be disadvantaged by the fluorescent lighting in the room. However, the claimant did not use the sunglasses during her interview nor did she say that she felt in any way disadvantaged. The claimant complained to the tribunal that the employer had failed in its duty to make reasonable adjustments in respect of the physical arrangements for the interview. The tribunal dismissed the complaint. The EAT held that the tribunal was correct to find that the employer was not in breach of its duty to make reasonable adjustments notwithstanding that it knew of the claimant's condition. The EAT added that the provisions of *DDA 1995, s 6* (the predecessor provisions) required the tribunal to measure the extent of the duty, if any, against the actual or assumed knowledge of the employer both as to the disability and its likelihood of causing the individual a substantial disadvantage in comparison with persons who are not disabled. In this case, no reasonable employer could be expected to know, without being told in terms by the claimant, that the arrangements which were made for her interview might disadvantage her. Thus, it would appear that the extent of the duty to make reasonable adjustments will depend partly on the amount of information volunteered by the disabled person as to any disadvantages being suffered. However, this does not mean that the employer can simply wait to be told of such disadvantages before a duty will arise. On the facts in *Ridout*, it may have been reasonable for the employer itself not to make further inquiries as to any disadvantage. Whether or not this will be so in other cases will be a question of fact for the tribunal. In *Mid-Staffordshire General Hospitals NHS Trust v Cambridge* [2003] IRLR 566, the EAT went so far as to hold that 'A proper assessment of what is required to eliminate the disabled person's disadvantage is . . . a necessary part of the duty imposed by *s 6(1)* since that duty cannot be complied with unless the employer makes a proper assessment of what needs to be done.' However, this decision (which was followed by the EAT in *Southampton City College v Randall* [2006] IRLR 18) was held by the EAT in *Tarbuck v Sainsbury's Supermarkets Ltd* [2006] IRLR 664 to have been incorrectly decided. Elias J concluded in Tarbuck that ' . . . there is no separate and distinct duty' to consult employees and that the single question under section 3A(1) was whether the employer had complied with his obligations there set out (see *Hay v Surrey County Council* [2007] EWCA Civ 93, [2007] All ER (D) 199 (Feb) in which the EAT's reasoning in *Tarbuck* was approved and it was held that there is, similarly, no separate duty to undertake a risk assessment, although an employer who had failed to conduct such an assessment could not use ignorance by reason of that failure to excuse non-compliance). The effect of these decisions is that consultation and/or risk assessments clearly remain prudent practice in any case where an employer is made aware of a disability, although the failure to take such steps would not of itself amount to a breach of the duty (see *Code of Practice, paras 5.12* and *7.29*). Indeed, the Court of Appeal has stated that a failure to conduct adequate investigations or assessments into the adjustments that can be made can amount to unjustified treatment of an employee. (See *Williams v J Walter Thompson Group Ltd* [2005] EWCA Civ 133, [2005] IRLR 376, which was not referred to in *Hay v Surrey County Council*).

An employer may breach the duty to make reasonable adjustments by failing to take steps that the employee has never in fact asked should be taken (*Project Management Institute v Latif* [2007] IRLR 579 EAT and *Home Office (UK Visas and Immigration) v Kuranchie* UKEAT/0202/16). The duty is to make reasonable adjustments and not simply respond to reasonable requests.

The EAT has stated that there was almost bound to be a breach of the implied term of trust and confidence where the employer had over a period of time seriously breached its obligation to make reasonable adjustments (*Greenhof v Barnsley Metropolitan Borough Council* [2006] IRLR 98).

In *Griffiths v Secretary of State for Work and Pensions* [2015] EWCA Civ 1265, [2016] IRLR 216, Lord Justice Elias rejected a suggestion that an adjustment would only constitute a "step" for the purposes of S. 20 if it promoted "access to and progress in employment". It was contended that modifying an absence management procedure so as to discount periods of disability-related absence would not promote those goals. On the contrary, it would facilitate absence. Rejecting that contention, his Lordship warned against artificial narrowing of what would constitute a step and expressed the view that "any modification of, or qualification to, the PCP in question which would or might remove the substantial disadvantage caused by the PCP is in principle capable of amounting to a relevant step". His Lordship did suggest, however, that it may not be reasonable to expect an employer to take steps where the disadvantage was one which was "not directly related to the ability to integrate [the disabled person] into employment". He gave as an example of that latter sort of case *O'Hanlon v Revenue and Customs Comrs* [2007] EWCA Civ 283, [2007] ICR 1359, in which the Court of Appeal determined that an employer had not failed to make a reasonable adjustment where it declined to modify a sick pay policy to provide for a longer period of absence on full pay for an employee whose absence was disability-related. The Court worried that avoiding financial hardship and stress might risk disincentivising return rather than enabling the employee to "play a full part in the world of work".

On the facts of *Griffiths* the particular adjustments sought were not thought to be reasonable. In *Jennings v Barts* (above) the EAT decided that he employer had not been obliged to produce a bespoke modification of its absence management procedures so as to discount from consideration disability-related absences. It accepted arguments that a modification would have been costly, disruptive and divisive (i.e. that would have caused resentment amongst colleagues). Discounting of disability-related absences in assessing absence record was, however, found to be reasonable in *Cox v Post Office*, IDS Brief 609.

When a complaint comes to the Tribunal and the complainant has alleged that certain adjustments should have been made, is it open to them to run an alternative case that other lesser, but unpleaded, adjustments would have been appropriate? In her partial dissent in *First Group v Paulley* (above) Lady Hale suggested that is open to a complainant to make that case.

11.38   Victimisation

In the United States, this form of discrimination is sometimes known as 'retaliation', a word which perhaps more accurately captures its essence than our own term 'victimisation'. There is little point conferring equal opportunity rights upon employees if their employers are free to punish them whenever they assert those rights. Thus the *EA 2010* protects those who rely on its provisions from being subjected to a detriment.

The coming into force of *EA 2010* marked a significant change to the law of victimisation. Under the previous law victimisation was treated as a form of discrimination, that is to say a claimant needed to establish that there had been "less favourable treatment" on a prohibited ground. However, rather than the prohibited ground being a protected characteristic, the previous law focused instead on the complainant having performed a so-called "protected act". *EA 2010, s 27* adopts a different model – that of subjection to a detriment. As a result a complainant now needs only to show that he has been treated badly, not that others have been treated better. Furthermore, it may not be necessary for it to have been the complainant who has performed the protected act. If an employer subjects the complainant to a detriment because of a protected act performed by a colleague, that would suffice (*Thompson v London Central Bus Company Ltd* (2015) UKEAT/0108/15, [2016] IRLR 9 – although that is difficult to reconcile with the express words of the section itself (see immediately below) which requires the person subjected to the detriment to be the person who performed the protected act).

EA 2010, s 27(1) provides:

"A person (A) victimises another person (B) if A subjects B to a detriment because –

(a)   B does a protected act, or

(b)   A believes that B has done, or may do, a protected act."

"Protected act" is defined at *EA 2010, s 27(2)*:

"Each of the following is a protected act –

(a)   bringing proceedings under this Act;

(b)   giving evidence or information in connection with proceedings under this Act;

(c)   doing any other thing for the purposes of or in connection with this Act;

(d)   making an allegation (whether or not express) that A or another person has contravened this Act".

The reference in (d) above to contravening the Act includes committing a breach of an equality clause or rule (*EA 2010, s 27(5)*).

If what is alleged would not be unlawful under the relevant legislation there is no protected act. For example, in *Waters v Metropolitan Police Comr* [1997] IRLR 589 (a case on the old law) a police officer, who was harassed by a colleague whilst both were off-duty, complained. She was later less favourably treated by her employer and alleged victimisation. As her harasser had been off duty, the employer was not vicariously liable for his actions. For that reason, the harassment was not unlawful. In those circumstances, the later act of less favourable treatment could not amount to victimisation.

Bringing an internal complaint does not constitute bringing proceedings (*British Telecommunications plc v Grant* (1994) 518 IDS Brief, EAT) although it may, nevertheless, involve alleging a breach of the Act on the part of the employer and qualify for protection on that basis instead.

An employee performs a 'protected act' by giving evidence even where the evidence given is not in support of the complaint (*Kirby v National Probation Service for England and Wales (Cumbria Area)* [2006] IRLR 508, [2006] All ER (D) 111 (Mar), EAT obiter). Nor need the evidence be given orally; providing a witness statement would be sufficient (*National Probation Service* above, again obiter).

Participating in an investigation into allegations of discrimination made by a third party would qualify as having done something by reference to the relevant anti-discrimination legislation (see *National Probation Service* above).

Giving false evidence or information, or making a false allegation, is not a protected act if the evidence or information is given, or the allegation is made, in bad faith (*EA 2010, s 27(3)*). In *HM Prison Service v Ibimidun* [2008] IRLR 940, the EAT considered a case where an employee had brought a series of discrimination claims, some of which were upheld, others dismissed. One claim, the tribunal found, had been brought for the purpose of harassing the employer. The employer dismissed the employee for bringing that claim. The EAT accepted that, properly analysed, the reason for the employee's dismissal was the harassment that resulted from the bringing of the claim. It would have been open to the EAT to conclude that the claim was both false and brought in bad faith. The EAT considered whether the claim was false, asking itself whether it could be said to be 'not in accordance with the truth or facts'. However, that consideration was *obiter* as the EAT decided that the claim should fail, instead, for want of causation: the reason for the dismissal was not the claim but the fact that it had been brought to harass the employer. This approach appears to sidestep the requirements of *s 27(3)*; it means that claims not brought in good faith (but which may not be false) fail on causation grounds. In *Martin v Devonshires Solicitors* [2011] ICR 352, the EAT expressed the opinion that where an employee raises groundless complaints as result of a mental illness, the case would not fall within the bad faith exception. However, where the employee was dismissed for, amongst other factors, her inability to accept that her claims were groundless the dismissal would not be on grounds of her having performed protected act. In *Woodhouse v North West Homes Leeds Ltd* [2013] IRLR 773 the EAT stressed that Martin was an exceptional case and that the concept of victimisation might be "neutered" if the "irrationality and multiplicity of grievances" were to lead "as a matter of routine" to the case being treated as falling outside the scope of victimisation.

Only individuals are entitled to be protected against detriment (*EA 2010, s 27(4)*).

It is important to note that the person doing the victimising need not be the person who was the subject of the original complaint of discrimination. Thus if a prospective employer decides not to appoint a candidate because he had brought or given evidence in proceedings against his former employer, that will amount to an act of victimisation.

The employer must subject the employee to a detriment "because" the latter has performed a protected act. The language used in *EA 2010, s 27* matches that in the definition of direct discrimination at *s 13*. It would seem to follow, therefore, that, the protected act has to be an effective and substantial cause of employer's detrimental actions but does not have to be the principal cause. Predecessor provisions required that the complainant should have been treated less favourably "by reason that" they had performed a protected act. Those words were closely analysed in *Chief Constable of West Yorkshire Police v Khan* [2001] IRLR 830, HL. It was decided that the provision did not "raise a question of causation as that expression is usually understood". One had to look at subjectively what was in the alleged discriminator's mind. Lord Scott observed that the words "by reason that" suggested that one was looking for "the real reason, the core reason . . . " Some caution needs to be exercised in relying on older authorities, therefore, since Lord Scott's comments would be difficult to reconcile with the proper approach to the test in direct discrimination cases and that is the approach which is now used in victimisation cases.

The sort of case in which the question of precisely why an employer subjected an employee to a detriment is likely to be most important is where there has been a protected act but the employer is contending that another related, but discrete, reason is their real reason for action. In *Aziz v Trinity Street Taxis Ltd* [1989] QB 463, [1988] 2 All ER 860, the Court of Appeal dealt with a number of points arising out of the construction of a predecessor provision in the *RRA 1976: s 2(1)*, and held in particular that it was necessary for a complainant to show that it was the very fact that his act had been done under, or by reference to, the race relations legislation that had influenced the unfavourable treatment. On the facts, the respondent association would have expelled any member who covertly recorded conversations, irrespective of whether that was done to support an allegation of racial discrimination and, therefore, the complaint of victimisation failed. It remains to be seen whether the courts will take a similarly narrow view of the new test.

There is no victimisation where the reason for the unfavourable treatment is the disruptive way in which complaints are made rather than the complaints as such (*Re York Truck Equipment Ltd*, IDS Brief 439, p 10). See also, *Martin v Devonshire Solicitors* [2011] ICR 352: An employee suffering from a mental illness repeatedly raised groundless complaints and was unable to accept that they were not well-founded. The employee was dismissed. The EAT upheld a finding that the reason for her dismissal was not the protected acts but a combination of "genuinely separable" factors including the risk to future management caused by her mental illness and her inability to accept that her complaints were groundless (but see *Woodhouse v North West Homes Leeds Ltd* above).

In *Woods v Pasab Ltd* [2012] EWCA Civ 1578, [2013] IRLR 305 an employee alleged that the pharmacy in which she worked was "a little Sikh Club" and was dismissed. The tribunal concluded that the comment amounted to a protected act but the Court of Appeal determined that the reason for the dismissal was her employer's belief that the comment was itself racist.

A line of authority on the old law addressed the question of whether respondents could be liable for steps taken in the context of defending legal proceedings. In *Khan* above, the House of Lords held that it was open to an employer faced with discrimination proceedings (and thus a protected act) to take honest and reasonable steps to protect its position in the relevant litigation even if that led to less favourable treatment. Thus, in *Khan* itself an employer could decline to issue a reference until the outcome of proceedings were known where the reference might otherwise have had to deal with matters that were in dispute. There are, however, limits. In *Derbyshire v St Helens Metropolitan Borough Council* [2007] UKHL 16, [2007] 3 All ER 81, it was stressed that the question whether the employer has acted in an honest and reasonable manner must be assessed from the perspective of the employee. On the facts, it was not open to an employer to write to claimants who had brought equal pay claims and to seek to persuade them to settle their claim by pointing out the possible negative consequences that the success of their claim might have for colleagues. In *South London & Maudsley NHS Trust v Dathi* [2008] IRLR 350, the EAT distinguished both *Khan* and *St Helens* and applied the principle of 'absolute immunity' to two letters written by representatives during the course of litigation. In one letter the representative refused certain disclosure, in the other the representative set out the grounds upon which it intended to resist a costs application. It was alleged that both letters amounted to acts of discrimination and/or victimisation. *Khan* was distinguished on the basis that the reference had been sent against the background of proceedings but could not be said to have 'come into existence for the purposes of the proceedings' themselves. *St Helens* was distinguished on the basis that the letter sent in that case had 'gone too far' and amounted to an exercise in intimidation rather than an appropriate step in litigation.

11.39 Harassment

Harassment Relating to a Relevant Protected Characteristic

EA 2010, s 26(1) provides that:

"A person (A) harasses another (B) if –

(a)   A engages in unwanted conduct related to a relevant protected characteristic, and

(b)   the conduct has the purpose or effect of –
    (i)   violating B's dignity, or
    (ii)   creating an intimidating, hostile, degrading, humiliating or offensive environment for B."

The definition of harassment has a wide scope in that it covers harassment which "relates" to the relevant protected ground and not merely harassment which is "because of" the characteristic. In *GMB v Henderson* [2016] EWCA Civ 1049; [2017] IRLR 340, the Court of appeal suggested that deciding whether the unwanted conduct "relates to" the protected characteristic will require a "consideration of the mental processes of the putative harasser", though it is unclear from the decision whether the observation was intended to be limited to cases where the violation of dignity and/or the creation of the harassing environment is the alleged harasser's purpose rather than where it is merely the effect of the conduct in issue.

Although harassing conduct may cause an employee to resign and that resignation may amount to a constructive dismissal, the resignation cannot itself amount to "unwanted conduct" (*Timothy James Consulting Ltd v Wilton* (2015) UKEAT/0082/14, [2015] ICR 765, [2015] IRLR 368). On the other hand, where an employer expressly dismisses an employee, that act of dismissal can constitute unwanted conduct of the kind contemplated by *s 26(1)* (*Urso v Department for Work and Pensions* UKEAT/00045/16, [2017] IRLR 304).

In determining whether conduct has the effect of violating B's dignity or creating the relevant environment for the purposes of *EA 2010, s 26(1)(b)* the Tribunal must take into account: B's perception; the other circumstances of the case; and whether it is reasonable for the conduct to have that effect (*EA 2010, s 26(4)*). In *Land Registry v Grant* [2011] EWCA Civ 769, [2011] ICR 1390, Elias LJ focussed on the words "intimidating, hostile, degrading, humiliating or offensive" and observed that:

'Tribunals must not cheapen the significance of these words. They are an important control to prevent trivial acts causing minor upsets being caught by the concept of harassment.'

The scope of the protection is limited in that not all of the protected characteristics defined at *EA 2010, s 4* are included. Specifically, harassment relating to "marriage and civil partnership" and "pregnancy and maternity" are not covered. Does that mean that it is lawful to harass someone on those grounds? The answer is probably not. Before there was any specific protection against harassment in the *SDA 1975* and the *RRA 1976* an employee wishing to complain that they had been harassed was obliged to take an indirect route. If they could show that they had been harassed "on grounds of" their race or sex they would bring a claim for direct discrimination. Harassing someone was treated as subjecting them to a detriment which was, in turn, a form of less favourable treatment. *EA 2010, s 212(1)* defines "detriment" so as specifically to exclude "conduct which amounts to harassment". The purpose is to ensure that someone who has been harassed is obliged to bring a *s 26* harassment claim rather than a *s 13* direct discrimination claim. However, the definition of "detriment" is said to be subject to *s 212(5)* which provides:

"Where this Act disapplies a prohibition on harassment in relation to a specified protected characteristic, the disapplication does not prevent conduct relating to that characteristic from amounting to a detriment for the purposes of discrimination within section 13 because of that characteristic".

The effect of these rather roundabout provisions is that a complainant who has been harassed on grounds of marriage, civil partnership, pregnancy or maternity may be able to bring a direct discrimination claim under *EA 2010, s 13* but only if they can show that the harassment was "because of" the relevant protected characteristic and, further, that they were less favourably treated than a comparator. These additional requirements are unnecessary where a claim is based directly upon *s 26*.

The test as to whether conduct has the relevant effect is not subjective. Conduct is not to be treated, for instance, as violating a complainant's dignity merely because he thinks it does. It must be conduct which could reasonably be considered as having that effect. However, the tribunal is obliged to take the complainant's perception into account in making that assessment. The intention of the alleged harasser may be relevant to determining whether the conduct could reasonably be considered to violate a complainant's dignity (*Richmond Pharmacology Ltd v Dhaliwal* [2009] IRLR 336, EAT). However, it is not necessary that the alleged harasser should have known that his behaviour would be unwanted (*Reed and Bull Information Systems Limited v Stedman* [1999] IRLR 299, EAT). Where the language of the alleged harasser is relied upon it will be important to assess the words used in the context in which the use occurred. In *Lindsay v London School of Economics* [2013] EWCA Civ 1650; [2014] IRLR 218, one employee used the word "gollywog" in conversation with a black colleague. The claimant argued that the term was inherently discriminatory and inevitably amounted to harassment. However, her colleague had not been describing the claimant as a gollywog. Instead she had been describing a jam manufacturer's former use of the doll in its branding. The particular context established that there was no harassment.

"Outing" a lesbian or gay employee may itself amount to harassment: *HM Land Registry v Grant* (above).

Where an employer's action or inaction results in an intimidating, hostile, degrading or offensive environment becoming worse he may be said to have in part "created" the resulting environment: *Conteh* above.

A number of cases have considered variations of a situation where the victim of the harassment does not themselves have the relevant protected characteristic. In the first type of case the unwanted conduct relates to the protected characteristic of a third party, e.g. an employee who is harassed because of the religion of a colleague (where, for instance, he refuses to assist his employer in justifying the colleague's discriminatory dismissal) is himself unlawfully harassed (*Saini v All Saints Haque Centre* [2009] IRLR 74, EAT). In the second type of case, the harasser treats the employee as if they have the protected characteristic knowing that they do not actually have it. An employee was harassed on grounds of sexual orientation when he was subjected to homophobic abuse by colleagues who knew that he was not a homosexual *English v Thomas Sanderson Blinds Ltd* [2008] EWCA Civ 1421, [2009] ICR 543. A third type of case is one concerned specifically with those who claim to have the protected characteristic of disability. The EAT was persuaded that this represents a special category of case (relying on *J v DLA Piper* (above) – where the EAT rejected the possibility of a perceived disability discrimination claim). Thus, a person who claims, but has not established, that they are a disabled person cannot claim that the unwanted conduct "related to" the protected characteristic of disability- *Peninsula Business Service Ltd v Baker* UKEAT/0241/16, [2017] IRLR 39.

An employer will be liable for acts of harassment committed by its employees against other employees (see below). A complainant will sometimes wish to take a further step and allege that there should be a discrete liability for the employer's failure to protect the employee from the harassment they suffered or properly to investigate the matter once it was raised with them. If the reason for the employer's failure to take steps to protect the employee was the employee's protected characteristic, the employer would be liable for an act of direct discrimination on ordinary principles. Thus, if employers allows both male and female employees to be subject to harassment by colleagues (or indeed by third parties), they do not discriminate. However, if they take steps to protect men but not women a liability will arise.

A mere failure to investigate a complaint of harassment will not in and of itself involve any unlawful action on the part of an employer. Again, the question is whether the reason for the employer's inaction was a protected characteristic (*Home Office v Coyne* [2000] ICR 1443, EWCA). Where a manager failed to take action following a complaint of racial abuse his inaction was capable of amounting to "unwanted conduct" but, on the facts, his decision not to investigate was not taken on the grounds of race and, for that reason, did not amount to harassment: *Conteh v Parking Partners Ltd* v Parking Partners Ltd UKEAT/288/10: [2011] ICR 341 (see also *Unite the Union v Nailard* UKEAT/0300/15, [2016] IRLR 906, [2017] ICR 121).

Harassment of a Sexual Nature

EA 2010, s 26(2) provides that A harasses B if A engages in unwanted conduct of a sexual nature which has the effect of violating B's dignity or creating an intimidating, hostile, degrading, humiliating or offensive environment for B. The Act does not define what is meant by conduct being "of a sexual nature".

As with the general form of harassment, the Tribunal must take into account B's perception, the other circumstances of the case and whether it is reasonable for conduct to have the alleged effect when assessing whether the conduct complained of had the effect of violating B's dignity or creating the relevant hostile atmosphere (*EA 2010, s 26(4)*).

Less favourable treatment of those who reject or submit to harassment

EA 2010, s 26(3) defines a third form of protection. It deals with an employee's reaction to certain forms of harassment and how, in turn, the employer treats the employee. Where an employee is subjected either to harassment of a sexual nature or harassment relating to gender reassignment or sex and either rejects or submits to that conduct any less favourable treatment that results because of that rejection or submission is unlawful.

The fact that the protection is against "less favourable treatment" makes it a form of discrimination although the essence of the problem being dealt with seems more closely related to victimisation and might, therefore, have been expected to follow the "subjection to a detriment" model.

Employer's liability for harassment by third parties

EA 2010, s 40(2) formerly made employers potentially liable for harassment by third parties. *Section 66* of the *Enterprise and Regulatory Reform Act 2013* ("*ERRA 2013*") repealed *EA 2010, s 40(2)* to *(4)* inclusive from 1 October 2013.

Harassment that is not specifically related to a Protected Characteristic

The *Criminal Justice and Public Order Act 1994* created an offence of 'intentional harassment'. It is committed where a person 'with intent to cause a person harassment, alarm or distress' uses threatening, abusive or insulting language or behaviour, or disorderly behaviour, or displays any writing, sign or other visible representation which is threatening, abusive or insulting, so that another person feels harassment, alarm or distress. The maximum penalties for the offence are six months in prison or a fine of £5,000. A further offence was created by the *Protection from Harassment Act 1997* (which came into force on 16 June 1997 (*SI 1997/1418*)). In addition to providing for harassers to be subject potentially to a fine or up to six months in prison, the Act creates a number of civil remedies, including damages and restraining orders backed by powers of arrest. In *Vaughan v London Borough of Lewisham* [2013] EWHC 795 (QB); [2013] IRLR 720 the High Court refused to injunct witnesses in a Tribunal claim from giving evidence. The claimant had alleged their evidence would be untrue and would amount to continuation of the harassment that she alleged she had suffered at work.

11.40   DISCRIMINATION IN EMPLOYMENT

Discrimination alone will not found liability. It is only certain forms of discrimination which are unlawful; principally discrimination in employment.

Discrimination and harassment is prohibited at every stage of employment: advertising vacancies; engagement of employees; promotion and other opportunities; and dismissal. For discrimination against non-employees, such as contract workers, office holders, etc, see **12.24 ff DISCRIMINATION AND EQUAL OPPORTUNITIES – II**.

11.41   The meaning of 'employment'

EA 2010 protects "employees" but defines "employment" broadly so as to include not just those employed under a contract of employment or apprenticeship but also those engaged pursuant to contracts "personally to do work" (*EA 2010, s 83(2)*).

In *Mirror Group Newspapers Ltd v Gunning* [1986] ICR 145, a case about the predecessor provision in the *SDA 1975*, the Court of Appeal held that the provision referred to a contract, the dominant purpose of which was the execution of personal work or services. *EA 2010, s 83* would fall to be interpreted in the same way.

A sub-postmaster who was responsible for seeing that the work of the Post Office was carried out but was not obliged to carry out the work himself was also held not to be an employee even within the extended meaning of the *Act* (*Tanna v Post Office* [1981] ICR 374). A taxi driver was not employed under 'a contract personally to execute any work or labour' where there was no mutual obligation between himself and the cab firm to offer or to accept any work (*Mingeley v Pennock & Ivory* [2004] EWCA Civ 328, [2004] ICR 727 – but see *Windle v Secretary of State for Justice* UK/EAT/339/13: [2015] ICR 156 where the EAT took the view that mutuality was only relevant to cases concerned with employees and not where the issue was whether the claimant was engaged under a contract personally to provide services). Similarly, where the contract pursuant to which the claimant was engaged contained a right to send a substitute to perform work, they were not an employee *Halawi v WDFG UK Ltd* [2014] EWCA Civ 1387, [2015] IRLR 50.

An unpaid volunteer working at a Citizens' Advice Bureau was not an employee (*X v Citizens Advice Bureau (Equality and Human Rights Commission intervening)* ([2013] IRLR 146, [2013] ICR 249). Nor was the complainant a "worker" or someone pursuing an "occupation" for the purposes of the *Framework Directive 2007/78/EC*. Similarly, a locally elected trade union official is not an employee. They undertook responsibilities voluntarily. They did not agree to perform any particular amount of work and they had no right to remuneration: *Unite the Union v Nailard* UKEAT/0300/15, [2016] IRLR 906, [2017] ICR 121.

A person working under the Youth Opportunities Programme was also held not to be employed within the meaning of *RRA 1976, s 78* (another predecessor provision. See *Daley v Allied Suppliers Ltd* [1983] ICR 90).

Wippel v Peek and Cloppenburg GmbH & Co KG: C-313/02 [2005] ICR 1604, ECJ – the *ETD 76/207/EEC* protects workers who are engaged on an 'on demand' basis and who are not obliged to take on work offered. *EA 2010* must, of course, be interpreted, wherever possible, to be consistent with the directive.)

An associate minister in the Church of Scotland was employed under 'a contract personally to execute . . . work' despite being an office holder. The House of Lords concluded that she was both an office holder and an employee (*Percy v Board of National Mission of the Church of Scotland* [2005] UKHL 73, [2006] ICR 134, HL(S)). The question (arising in a different context) as to whether part-time judges are workers has been determined by the CJEU: *O'Brien v Ministry of Justice* [2012] ICR 955 – they are.

The definition of employment is broad enough to cover the personal provision of services by a professional and even the retention of a firm of solicitors, instructions to a firm being, in reality, a contract entered into with each partner (*Loughran and Kelly v Northern Ireland Housing Executive* [1999] 1 AC 428, [1998] 3 WLR 735, [1998] ICR 828, HL(NI), distinguished in *Patterson v Legal Services Commission* [2003] EWCA Civ 1558, [2004] ICR 312 where there was no obligation on the complainant to carry out the work personally). Discrimination in appointing an arbitrator falls outside the scope of *RBR 2003* (and thus the *EA 2010*) – the arbitrator is engaged pursuant to a contract personally to provide services but is not subject to the necessary "control" of the parties to the arbitration (*Hashwani v Jivraj* [2011] UKSC 40, [2011] ICR 1004). A beauty consultant whose services were provided to a respondent management company through a company she had herself set up was not, on the facts, subject to the control of the respondent (*Halawi* above). Professional interpreters who worked on an assignment by assignment basis for Her Majesty's Court and Tribunals Service in a relationship which involved no mutuality of obligation were not "employees" (*Windle and another v Secretary of State for Justice* [2016] EWCA Civ 459, [2016] IRLR 628). The Court of Appeal emphasised the need to consider all relevant factors and appeared to row back somewhat from any suggestion in *Jivraj* that the extent to which someone is acting "under direction" or is in a "subordinate position" is potentially decisive.

A person discriminated against by being dismissed does not have to have been employed for a qualifying period before being entitled to bring a claim.

The Act applies to members of the armed forces "as it applies to employment by a private person" (*EA 2010, s 83(3)*) save that references in the legislation to "associated employers" are "to be ignored". Also included within the scope of "employment" as defined are those in Crown employment (*EA 2010, s 83(2)(b)*), certain members of the House of Commons and House of Lords staff (*EA 2010, s 83(2)(c)* and *(d)* and police officers and cadets (*EA 2010, s 42*)).

A person without employees can still be an employer provided they are "seeking to employ one or more persons" (*EA 2010, s 83(4)*).

11.42 Territorial Jurisdiction

Whereas the previous law contained an express territorial restriction (for which see above), the *EA 2010* does not. *EA 2010, EN Para 15* states:

> "As far as territorial application is concerned, in relation to Part 5 (work) and following the precedent of the Employment Rights Act 1996, the Act leaves it to tribunals to determine whether the law applies, depending for example on the connection between the employment relationship and Great Britain."

It seems, therefore, that the tribunals are intended to have regard to the guidance given by the House of Lords in *Lawson v Serco* [2006] IRLR 289, HL (see UNFAIR DISMISSAL I, para 53.15). In *Bates Van Winkelhof v Clyde & Co LLP* [2012] EWCA Civ 1207, [2012] IRLR 992, [2013] ICR 883 the Court of Appeal suggested that expatriate employees may not need to meet the requirement identified in *Lawson* that the claim should have connections with Great Britain and with British Employment Law that were as strong as those with the country in which they worked if they could show that they lived and/or worked part of the time in Great Britain. All that is needed in such a case are connections to Great Britain that are sufficiently strong to enable it to be thought that Parliament would have regarded it as appropriate for the tribunal to deal with the claim. However, in *R (on the application of Hottak and another) v Secretary of State for Foreign and Commonwealth Affairs* [2016] EWCA Civ 938, [2016] IRLR 534, [2016] ICR 975, it was confirmed that there is a single test covering both unfair dismissal and discrimination cases.

Even where an employee works entirely outside Great Britain, they may still be able to bring a claim in the tribunal where their employment falls within certain European rules on jurisdiction and judgment. These were considered in the context of discrimination cases by the EAT in *Simpson v Intralinks* [2012] ICR 1343. The complainant lived and worked in Germany for a company registered in the UK. Her contract provided for German Law to be applicable and for disputes to be resolved in Germany. Nevertheless, the EAT concluded that the tribunal had jurisdiction to hear claims of sex discrimination and equal pay. The analysis was as follows: *EC Council Regulation 44/2001* ("the *Brussels Regulation*") makes provision for jurisdiction in civil matters including employment disputes. *Art 19* permits an employer to be sued either in the state in which they are domiciled (in this case, in the UK) or in the state where the employee "habitually carries out [their] work" (in this case, Germany). The choice is the employee's and not that of the court. The choice of forum clause did not preclude UK proceedings because *Art 21* only allows departure from jurisdiction by agreement where the agreement was entered into after the dispute has arisen (which was not the case here). The EAT then turned to the question of the applicable law. That was to be determined by reference to the *Rome Convention* (since superseded by *Rome II*). *Art 3* of the *Rome Convention* provides that a contract should be governed by the law chosen by the parties (i.e. in this case German Law). However, there is provision for certain mandatory employment protection provisions to be given effect. *Art 7(1)* provides:

> "When applying under this Convention the law of a country, effect may be given to mandatory rules of the law of another country with which the situation has a close connection, if and insofar as, under the law of the other country, those rules must be applied whatever the law of applicable to the contract . . . ."

The EAT was satisfied that the statutory provisions dealing with sex discrimination and equal pay were "mandatory provisions" as the underlying legislation provides that they may not be derogated from by agreement. If the *Brussels* rules pointed to Great Britain as having jurisdiction but the *Rome* rules point to foreign law being the applicable law, the EAT was prepared to countenance the tribunal having jurisdiction and applying foreign law save to the extent that mandatory provisions of domestic law took precedence.

EA 2010, s 81 provides that the protections to be found in *Part 5* of the Act only apply to work on ships or hovercraft and to seafarers in "such circumstances as are prescribed". No circumstances have yet been prescribed. *Section 82* allows for "specified provisions" of *Part 5* to be applied to "offshore work". "Offshore work" is defined to mean:

"work for the purposes of:

(a)   activities in the territorial sea adjacent to the United Kingdom,

(b)   activities such as are mentioned in subsection (2) of section 11 of the Petroleum Act 1998 in waters within which subsection 8(b) or (c) of that section, or

(c)   activities mentioned in paragraphs (a) and (b) of section 87(1) of the Energy Act 2004 in waters to which that section applies.

The *Equality Act 2010 (Offshore Work) Order 2010, SI 2010/1835* provides that *Part 5* of *EA 2010* applies to offshore work as if it were taking place in Great Britain unless it takes place in the Northern Irish Area (as defined by the *Civil Jurisdiction (Offshore Activities) Order 1987*) or is in connection with a ship which is in the course of navigation or a ship which is engaged in dredging or fishing (*Reg 2(1)*). Dredging is defined so as not to include excavation of the sea-bed or its subsoil in the course of pipe laying (*Reg 2(2)*). Jurisdiction is conferred on the English and Welsh Tribunals where the offshore work is being done in the "English Area" as defined in the *Civil Jurisdiction (Offshore Activities) Order 1987* and the offshore work consists of work falling within sub-paragraphs (a) or (b) of the definition set out above above. If the work falls within sub-paragraph (c) the jurisdiction is conferred on the High Court.

11.43   Advertisements

There is no specific prohibition on discriminatory advertising in *EA 2010*. However, the explanatory notes suggest that this is because the issue is dealt with elsewhere in the Act without, unhelpfully, identifying where else it is supposedly dealt with (*EA 2010*, EN Para 1024). It is likely that discriminatory advertisements will be actionable by individuals as a form of direct discrimination contrary to *EA 2010, s 13* consistent with the analysis of the ECJ in *Centruum voor Gelijkheid van kansen en voor racismebestrijding v Firma Feryn NV*: C-54/07, [2008] ICR 1390.

11.44   Engagement

EA 2010, s 39 provides that:

"An employer (A) must not discriminate against a person (B) –

(a)   in the arrangements A makes for deciding to whom to offer employment,

(b)   as to the terms on which A offers B employment,

(c)   by not offering B employment."

Refusing to employ someone because they have a protected characteristic is perhaps the most obvious example of employment-related discrimination. The equivalent protection in the *Framework Directive (2000/78/EU, Art 3(1))* and the *Equal Treatment Directive (2006/54/EU, Art 1)* requires equal treatment in respect of "access to employment". In *Kratzer v R+V Allegemeins Vershicherung AG* C-423/15, [2016] IRLR 888, [2016] ICR 967, there was found to be no breach of either directive where an applicant had applied not in order to get appointed but in order to try to bring discrimination proceedings. The ECJ considered that since he was not truly seeking employment, his case fell outside the scope of the directives. There is little doubt the UK courts would reach the same outcome although it would not necessarily be by saying that *s 39* was not engaged. It might instead be seen as an abuse of process.

Thus, if an employer offers a woman three weeks' holiday, whereas a man doing the same job is entitled to five weeks, he is guilty of discrimination. Also, the woman's contract will be modified by the equality of terms provisions of the Act to give her the same holiday entitlement as that of the man (see EQUAL PAY (22)).

Where a complainant's employment transfers by operation of the *Transfer of Undertakings (Protection of Employment) Regulations 2006, SI 2006/246*, there is no "offer" made by the new employer (*NHS Direct NHS Trust v Gunn* [2015] IRLR 799, which also suggested that an offer of "suitable alternative employment" where an employee is redundant will constitute such an offer).

In *Saunders v Richmond-upon-Thames London Borough Council* [1978] ICR 75, it was assumed that questions asked at an interview constituted 'arrangements' within the meaning of (1) above. Whether or not the questions were unlawful was held to be a question of fact to be determined in each case. In *Brennan v JH Dewhurst Ltd* [1984] ICR 52, the arrangements made for interviewing applicants were operated so as to discriminate against women, and were therefore unlawful.

A refusal to re-instate a former employee following a dismissal does not constitute 'refusing to offer employment' (*Post Office v Adekeye* [1997] ICR 110, CA).

EA 2010, s 60(1) prohibits employers from asking about the health of an applicant for employment before offering them work (either conditionally or unconditionally – see *EA 2010, s 60(10)*) or, if the relevant person acting on behalf of the employer is shortlisting applicants, before including the applicant in the pool from which the employer intends to select the appointee. Breach can only be challenged by the EHRC (*EA 2010, s 60(2)*). Offering work includes making a conditional offer (*EA 2010, s 10*).

Merely asking the prohibited question does not in and of itself involve any disability discrimination, but it may be used as evidence to establish such discrimination (*EA 2010, s 60(3)*).

EA 2010, s. 60(6) disapplies the prohibition in a surprisingly broad range of circumstances. In each case asking the question must be necessary for the specified purpose. Those purposes are:

(1)   Establishing whether the applicant will be able to comply with a requirement to undergo an assessment or establishing whether a duty to make reasonable adjustments is or will be imposed on the employer in relation to the applicant in connection with the requirement to undergo assessment. For this purpose, an assessment is an "interview or other process designed to give an indication of a person's suitability for the work concerned" (*EA 2010, s 60(12)*);

(2)   Establishing whether the applicant will be able to carry out a function that is intrinsic to the work concerned. The exception is only available if the employer is satisfied that the function would still be intrinsic if the job were adjusted in accordance with the duty to make reasonable adjustments (*EA 2010, s 60(7)*);

(3)   Monitoring diversity in the range of people applying to the Employer for work;

(4)   Taking action to which *section 158* (ie the Positive Action provisions) would apply if references to persons who share (or do not share) a protected characteristic were references to disabled persons (or persons who are not disabled) and the reference to the characteristic were a reference to disability; or

(5)   If the Employer applies in relation to the work a requirement to have a particular disability, establishing that the applicant has that disability. The requirement has to be an occupational requirement and its application has to be a proportionate means of achieving a legitimate aim (*EA 2010, s 60(8)*).

The provision does not affect anything done for the purposes of national security vetting (*EA 2010, s 60(14)*).

Is an unsuccessful candidate who meets the criteria for selection entitled to information from the employer about whether someone has been appointed and, if so, on what criteria? UK Law had, until recently, a questionnaire procedure (for which see below). In *Meister v Speech Design Carrier Systems*: C-415/60 [2012] ICR 1066, the CJEU decided that as a matter of European Law, a candidate was not entitled to such information but a refusal to provide it might be something that could be taken into account in deciding whether or not the complainant had been the victim of discrimination.

11.45   *Racial discrimination: engagement and asylum and immigration*

The *Immigration, Asylum and Nationality Act 2006, s 15* makes it an offence for an employer to employ those whose immigration status precludes them from working in the UK. The *schedule* to the *Immigration (Restrictions on Employment) Order 2007 (SI 2007/3290)* specifies a number of documents ('statutory documents') which, if produced prior to engagement, the employer may rely upon as establishing that the job applicant is entitled to work in the UK. Provided the employer has complied with the requirements of *reg 6* which included taking all reasonable steps to check the validity of the document, it has a defence to any prosecution under the *Act*. There is a danger that in seeking to avoid liability under the *Act*, employers may treat job applicants from ethnic minorities differently. This in turn creates the risk of discrimination claims. The Home Office has produced a code of practice which   includes   guidance   on   avoiding   discrimination (www.gov.uk/government/publications/right-to-work-checks-code-of-practice-on -avoiding-discrimination).

A failure to comply with the provisions of the code may be taken into account by an employment tribunal considering a claim of race discrimination.

The EAT has suggested that a foreign national complaining of discriminatory treatment may only be able to compare herself with other foreign nationals rather than with British citizens (*Sheiky v Argos Distributions Ltd* (1997) 597 IDS Brief 16).

An employer that declined to consider applicants from outside the EEA on grounds that they would be unlikely to be able to obtain work permits committed an act of indirect discrimination (*Osborne Clarke Services v Purohit* [2009] IRLR 341, EAT).

11.46   *Sex discrimination: terms offered – special provisions for those on maternity leave*

EA 2010, Sch 9, Part 3, Para 17 substantially reproduces the pre-existing law. *Para 17(1)* provides that a person does not contravene *EA 2010, ss 39(1)(b)* (discrimination as to the terms on which employment is offered) or *(2)* (discrimination as to the terms of employment, access to opportunities for promotion transfer or training or receiving any other benefit, facility or service, discriminatory dismissal or subjection to any detriment) by depriving a woman who is on maternity leave of any benefit from the terms of her employment relating to pay. However, "terms of employment" does not mean "contract of employment", *EA 2010. Sch 9, Part 3, Para 17(4)* provides:

> "A reference to terms of her employment is a reference to terms of her employment that are not in her contract of employment, her contract of apprenticeship or her contract to do work personally".

The Act then creates an exception to the exception by providing that the reference to "benefit" from the terms of the woman's employment does not include a reference to –

(a)   maternity-related pay (including maternity-related pay that is increase-related),

(b)   pay (including increase-related pay) in respect of times when she is not on maternity leave, or

(c)   pay by way of bonus in respect of times when she is on compulsory maternity leave.

(*EA 2010, Sch 9, Part 3, Para 17(2)*) with the effect that that there may be breaches of *EA 2010, s 39(1)(b)* and *(2)* in relation to those matters.

Pay means benefits: (a) that consist of the payment of money to an employee by way of wages or salary; and (b) that are not benefits whose provision is regulated by the employee's contract of employment or apprenticeship or her contract personally to do work.

"Maternity-related pay" is pay to which the employee is entitled: (a) as a result of being pregnant; or (b) in respect of times when she is on maternity leave (*EA 2010, Sch 9, Part 3, Para 17(6)*).

Pay is "increase-related" in so far as it is "to be calculated by reference to increases in pay that the woman would have received had she not been on maternity leave" (*EA 2010, Sch 9, Part 3, Para 17(3)*).

11.47 Opportunities in employment

There is an express prohibition on discrimination "in the way A affords B access to opportunities for promotion, transfer or training or for receiving any other benefit, facility or service (*EA 2010, s 39(2)(b)*).

In the case of receipt of a benefit, facility or service there is an exception to liability in the case of services which the employer offers to the public. The essence of the idea is that someone, for instance, who works for an airline, cannot bring a claim as an employee if she is treated less favourably when flying as a passenger on one of her employer's aircraft. She would be left to whatever remedies members the public would have, *EA 2010, Sch 9, Part 3, Para 19(1)* provides that:

"A person does not contravene [*EA 2010, s 39(2)(b)*] in relation to the provision of a benefit, facility or service to B if A is concerned with the provision (for payment or not) of a benefit, facility or service of the same description to the public".

A reference to the public includes a section of the public which includes B (*EA 2010, Sch 9, Part 3, Para 19(6)*).

There are exceptions to the general exclusion of liability in respect of benefits, facilities or services provided to the public. They, broadly, cover circumstances in which the fact that the complainant is an employee means that they are not sensibly to be treated as if they were simply another member of the public. The exceptions are set out at *EA 2010, Sch 9, Part 3, Para 19(3)*:

"Sub-paragraph (1) does not apply if –
(a)   the provision by A to the public differs in a material respect from the provision by A to [other employees],
(b)   the provision to B is regulated by B's terms, or
(c)   the benefit, facility or service relates to training."

The reference in (c) to "B's terms" means "the terms of B's employment" (*EA 2010, Sch 9, Part 3, Para 19(5)*. Similar provision is made in relation to contract workers, partners and office holders).

11.48 *Sex discrimination: opportunities afforded – special provisions for those on maternity leave*

There is a specific exception to liability under *EA 2010, s 39(2)* in respect of the terms of employment of women on maternity which relate to pay (*EA 2010, Sch 9, Part 3, Para 17(1)*). For a more detailed account of the exception see "Sex discrimination: terms offered – special provisions for those on maternity leave" above.

11.49 Dismissal

An express prohibition on discriminatory dismissal is to be found at *EA 2010, s 39(2)(c)*. Dismissal is defined by *EA 2010, s 39(7)* so as to include the termination of employment: (a) by the expiry of a period (including a period expiring by reference to an event or circumstance); and (b) by an act of B's (including giving notice) in circumstances such that B is entitled, because of A's conduct, to terminate the employment without notice. Termination by expiry of a period will not constitute dismissal if, immediately after the termination, the employment is renewed on the same terms (*EA 2010, s 39(8)*).

Where an employee is prevented from performing their job by reason of a disability, the doctrine of frustration may apply so as to terminate their contract. However, the tribunal should first consider whether or not the employer has complied with any duty *Equality Act 2010, s 20* to make reasonable adjustments (*Warner v Armfield Retail & Leisure Ltd* UKEAT/376/12, [2014] ICR 239).

An employer's breach of its duties under the anti-discrimination legislation may amount to a breach of the implied duty of trust and confidence so as to repudiate the contract of employment and entitle the victim to treat themselves as having been constructively dismissed (*Shaw v CCL Ltd* [2008] IRLR 284, EAT).

If an employee is dismissed for a combination of lawful and unlawfully discriminatory reasons, they are entitled to compensation, limited to injury to feelings, even where dismissal would have occurred even if there had been no discrimination (*GMBU v Henderson* [2015] IRLR 451, EAT, the dictum was not contradicted when the case was considered by the Court of Appeal ([2016] EWCA Civ 1049)).

11.50 Subjection to other detriment

EA 2010, s 39(2)(d) contains a "catch all" obligation not to subject employees to a detriment. This reproduces the pre-existing law.

A complainant seeking to establish that he has been subjected to a 'detriment' need not demonstrate that he has suffered a physical or economic consequence. It is sufficient to show that a reasonable employee would or might take the view that they had been disadvantaged in the circumstances in which they had to work (*Shamoon v Chief Constable of the Royal Ulster Constabulary (Northern Ireland)* [2003] UKHL 11, [2003] 2 All ER 26, [2003] ICR 337 and see *Ministry of Defence v Jeremiah* [1980] QB 87, [1979] 3 All ER 83 in which it was held that requiring only male supervisors to carry out dirty work was an unlawful detriment; see also *BL Cars Ltd v Brown* [1983] ICR 143; *Jiad v Byford* [2003] EWCA Civ 135, [2003] IRLR 232).

In *De Souza v Automobile Association* [1986] ICR 514, the Court of Appeal held that the Employment Appeal Tribunal had correctly concluded that Mrs De Souza had not been subjected to a 'detriment' as a result of overhearing a manager say to another manager, about her, to get his typing done by 'the wog'. The EAT in *Barclays Bank plc v Kapur* [1989] ICR 142 (appeal allowed, [1989] ICR 753) suggested, in a passage which was not a necessary part of its decision, that the words 'any other detriment' related to acts in connection with dismissal or disciplinary proceedings and were not wholly general in their scope. The correctness of this construction is, with respect, doubted. It is also open to argument whether *De Souza* was correctly decided, bearing in mind more recent cases dealing with harassment.

An employee was not subjected to a detriment where the employer failed, because of his race, to investigate complaints that he had fabricated against a colleague (*Cordant Security Ltd v Singh* UKEAT/0144/15 [2016] IRLR 4). However, there could be detriment where an employee's grievances were not properly investigated even though they would not have been upheld (*Deer v University of Oxford* [2015] EWCA Civ 52, [2015] ICR 1213, [2015] IRLR 481 – a victimisation case). There may, therefore, be a distinction to be drawn between fabricated and ill-founded complaints.

Failure, after the termination of the employment contract, to confer a non-contractual benefit on a former employee will only exceptionally constitute a 'detriment' (*Relaxion Group plc v Rhys-Harper* [2003] UKHL 33, [2003] 4 All ER 1113).

11.51 *Harassment on grounds of marriage, civil partnership, pregnancy or maternity as a detriment*

EA 2010 provides (somewhat obliquely) that harassing an employee on grounds of marriage, civil partnership, pregnancy or maternity is deemed to be direct discrimination. The method by which this result is achieved is not straightforward and is explained immediately below.

Before there was a specific prohibition of harassment, victims would bring claims instead for direct discrimination. To be harassed was to be subjected to a detriment (see *Porcelli v Strathclyde Regional Council* [1986] ICR 564). That indirect protection was abandoned in favour of introducing a direct protection against harassment which is described at **11.39** above. However, the *EA 2010*, specifically excludes two protected characteristics from the scope of its express prohibition of harassment: marriage and civil partnership and pregnancy and maternity (see *EA 2010, s 26(5)*). It seems, however, that the intention is not to allow employees to be harassed on those grounds. The definition of "detriment" at *EA 2010, s 212* excludes harassment save that there is provision made at *s 212(5)* in the following terms:

> "Where this Act disapplies a prohibition on harassment in relation to a specified protected characteristic, the disapplication does not prevent conduct relating to that characteristic from amounting to a detriment for the purposes of discrimination within section 13 because of that characteristic."

Therefore, harassing a woman because she is pregnant would amount to direct discrimination within *s 13*. The same would be true in the case of harassment because of marriage, civil partnership or maternity.

It should be noted that this indirect route does not entirely replicate the protection provided by the express prohibition on harassment. In particular, the employee will have to show that they have been "less favourably treated". This allows the employer to continue to run what has become known as the "bastard defence", ie because he is equally unpleasant to all employees an employee, though harassed, cannot establish that they have been less favourably treated.

Authorities which predate the introduction of the specific prohibition on harassment will be relevant to claims brought as direct discrimination claims. In *Reed and Bull Information Systems Ltd v Stedman* [1999] IRLR 299, the EAT gave guidance to tribunals dealing with three troublesome questions which commonly arise in harassment cases. The particular case was concerned was sexual harassment and the principles have been adapted below and expressed as matters of general principle:

(a)   *If an employee regards as harassment words or conduct to which many would not take exception or regard as harassment, has their claim been made out?*

The question is whether the behaviour has to be objectively offensive or whether it is sufficient that it should be offensive in the subjective opinion of the employee. The EAT steered a middle course. The fact that, objectively, the behaviour is not offensive does not dispose of the issue. If a particularly sensitive employee has made it clear that the conduct is unwelcome, any repetition may amount to harassment. Other forms of conduct are objectively hostile or offensive, and these do not require the employee to indicate that they are unwelcome before they may constitute harassment. This approach is consistent with that taken by *EA 2010, s 26* in relation to the specific prohibition of harassment.

(b)   *If the alleged harasser does not appreciate that their words or conduct are unwelcome, has the claim been proved?*

The EAT restated the general principle that, as with all cases of direct discrimination, the fact that the alleged discriminator lacks a discriminatory motive or intention will not prevent a finding of direct discrimination. If the alleged harasser should have known that conduct is unwelcome either because that risk was obvious or else because the victim has made it clear to him, he will be liable even if he did not intend to harass.

(c)   *Is a 'one-off act' sufficient to constitute harassment?*

A one-off act may be sufficient. The clearer it is that objectively the conduct was hostile or offensive, the more likely it is that a one-off act will suffice to establish harassment (see also *Insitu Cleaning Co Ltd v Heads* [1995] IRLR 4).

Further guidance was given in *Driskel v Peninsula Business Services Ltd* [2000] IRLR 151, EAT. First, where there are a number of alleged incidents, the tribunal should be careful to focus on their cumulative effect rather than concentrating upon whether individual incidents are trivial in nature. Second, simply because a male superior engages in vulgar behaviour with male colleagues does not mean that a woman is not treated less favourably when she is subjected to such behaviour. Behaviour of that kind directed at a woman is more likely to be intimidatory and to undermine her dignity than similar behaviour directed at a male colleague. (On the question of the objective nature of the test, the Administrative Court expressed a preference for the guidance given in *Driskel* over that given in *Reed*; *EOC v Secretary of State for Trade and Industry* [2007] EWHC 483 (Admin), [2007] ICR 1234 at para 33).

11.52 Post-employment discrimination

EA 2010 reproduces the pre-existing application of post-termination protections against discrimination.

EA 2010, s 108(1) provides: provides:

"A person (A) must not discriminate against another (B) if –

(a)   the discrimination arises out of and is closely connected to a relationship which used to exist between them,

(b)   conduct of a description constituting the discrimination would, if it occurred during the relationship, contravene the Act."

A similar provision is made in relation to harassment at *EA 2010, s 108(2)*:

"A person (A) must not harass another (B) if –

(a)   the harassment arises out of and is closely connected to a relationship which used to exist between them, and

(b)   conduct of a description constituting the harassment would, if it occurred during the relationship, contravene the Act."

Since the Act is intended to be a consolidating measure, it does not matter whether the relationship ends before or after the commencement of *s 108* (*EA 2010, s 108(3)*).

The requirement that the discrimination should arise out of and be closely connected with a "relationship that used to exist between [A and B]" means that where a former employee of a police authority was subjected to a detriment by a successor body by which she had never been employed, *s 108* did not apply (see *Butterworth v Police and Crime Commissioner's Office for Greater Manchester and another* UKEAT/0222/15: [2016] IRLR 280, EAT).

Conduct is not treated as breaching *s 108* "in so far as it also amounts to victimisation" (*EA 2010, s 108(7)*). The statutory language appears on its face to suggest that post-employment victimisation is not actionable. However, the Court of Appeal has confirmed that proceedings can be brought (*Rowstock Ltd v Jessemey* [2014] EWCA Civ 185, [2014] ICR 550, [2014] IRLR 368).

Where a tribunal makes a reinstatement order as a remedy for unfair dismissal, a discriminatory failure to comply with the order was not 'discrimination in employment' for the purposes of the predecessor provision in *RRA 1976* (*D'Souza v Lambeth London Borough Council* [2003] UKHL 33, [2003] 4 All ER 1113).

Other unlawful acts

11.53 *Instructions or pressure to commit unlawful acts*

EA 2010, s 111 prohibits employers from instructing, causing or inducing (whether directly or indirectly) an employee to commit an unlawful act of discrimination (or from attempting to do so).

EA 2010, s 111(1) creates a concept known as a "basic contravention" which involves the employee contravening any of the following in relation to a third party:

(a)   Part 3 of the Act (Services and Public Functions);

(b)   Part 4 of the Act (Premises);

(c)   Part 5 of the Act (Work);

(d)   Part 6 of the Act (Education);

(e)   Part 7 of the Act (Associations);

(f)   Section 108(1) (Post-employment discrimination);

(g)   Section 108(2) (Post-employment harassment); or

(h)   Section 112(1) (Knowingly helping another to commit a basic contravention).

EA 2010, s 111(1) prohibits an employer from instructing an employee to commit a basic contravention. *EA 2010, ss 111(2)* and *(3)* do the same thing in relation to causing or inducing a contravention respectively. Inducement may be either direct or indirect (*EA 2010, s 111(4)*).

Proceedings can be brought by the employee if they are subjected to detriment by their employer's conduct or by the third party that was the target of the employer's conduct. Proceedings may also be brought by the Commission (*EA 2010, s 111(5)*). A claim may be pursued even if the basic contravention never occurs and whether or not other proceedings have been (or could be) brought in relation to the employer's conduct (*EA 2010, s 111(6)*).

In *Weathersfield Ltd v Sargent (t/a Van and Truck Rentals) v Sargent* [1999] ICR 425, CA, the receptionist at a truck rental company was instructed to tell black or Asian enquirers that no vehicles were available. As a result, she found her position intolerable and resigned. The respondent argued that as any employee would have been given the same instruction, the complainant could not establish that she had been less favourably treated. The EAT concluded that the instruction affected employees 'differentially' in that some, but not all, would regard themselves as 'victims of mistreatment'. The appropriate comparator, therefore, was somebody who was prepared to go along with the employer's unlawful instruction. The EAT's decision was affirmed by the Court of Appeal.

An attempt to instruct, cause or induce an employee to commit a basic contravention is also actionable (*EA 2010, s 111(8)*).

In *Commission for Racial Equality v Imperial Society of Teachers of Dancing* [1983] ICR 473, the Employment Appeal Tribunal held that a prospective employer acted unlawfully by telling the head of careers at a school that he would prefer that the school did not put forward any coloured applicants.

11.54 *Liability for unlawful act of employee*

EA 2010, s 109 substantially reproduces the former regime of vicarious liability. *EA 2010, s 109(1)* provides:

"Anything done by a person (A) in the course of A's employment must be treated as also done by the employer".

A broad interpretation is given to the concept of "in the course of . . . employment" (*Jones v Tower Boot Co Ltd* [1997] ICR 254, CA). In effect, it is open to a tribunal to find that an employer is liable for acts of discrimination where they are committed 'at work' instead of merely where they are committed 'as work'. The common law test has now 'caught up' (see *Lister v Helsey Hall Ltd* [2001] UKHL 22, [2002] 1 AC 215, HL at 46.7). Acts committed by colleagues away from the workplace are less likely to fall within the scope of the discrimination legislation (eg cf *Waters v Metropolitan Police Comr* [1997] IRLR 589, CA: sexual assault by one off-duty police officer on another in a police section house. Cf also *Sidhu v Aerospace Composite Technology Ltd* [2000] IRLR 602, CA: acts committed during the course of a 'family day' organised by an employer and held at an amusement park were not in the course of employment; and *HM Prison Service v Davis* (2000) 666 IDS Brief 14, EAT: harassment not in course of employment where employee visited colleague at her home, even though employer had power to discipline employees for misconduct committed away from the workplace) although that will not always be so. In *Chief Constable of Lincolnshire Police v Stubbs* [1999] ICR 547, EAT, the EAT upheld a finding that drinks after work and an organised leaving party were sufficiently work-related to be treated as 'extensions of work'.

A police officer will not, for most purposes, be treated as an employee. However police officers and police cadets are deemed, for the purposes of *Part 5* of the *Equality Act 2010*, to be employed by their chief officer (*s 42(1)*).

It does not matter whether the thing is done with the employer's knowledge or approval (*EA 2010 s 109(3)*). Vicarious liability does not extend to cover the offences created under *EA 2010* (with the exception offences under *Part 12* (disabled persons: transport)) (*EA 2010, s 109(5)*).

The employee who commits the discriminatory act is fixed with liability by *EA 2010, s 110(1)*:

"A person (A) contravenes this section if –

(a)   A is an employee . . .
(b)   A does something which by virtue of section 109(1) . . . , is treated as having been done by A's employer . . . , and
(c)   the doing of that thing by A amounts to a contravention of this Act by the employer . . . "

If the employer manages to establish the reasonable steps defence (for which see below), the employee may still be liable (*EA 2010, s 110(2)*). Even under the former regime, it was possible to bring a claim of victimisation against an individual employee even where the employer was not sued (*Barlow v Stone* [2012] IRLR 898).

The employee has a defence where he reasonably relies on a statement by the employer that the doing the act in question would not involve a contravention of the Act (*EA 2010, s 110(3)*). If the employer makes such a statement which is false or misleading in a material respect and does so knowingly or recklessly, he commits an offence liable to a fine not exceeding level 5 on the standard scale (*EA 2010, s 110(5)*).

11.55 *Defence to vicarious liability*

EA 2010, s 109(4) provides:

> "In proceedings against A's employer (B) in respect of anything alleged to have been done by A in the course of his employment it is a defence for B to show that B took all reasonable steps to prevent A –
> (a)   from doing that thing, or
> (b)   from doing anything of that description."

See *Balgobin v Tower Hamlets London Borough Council* [1987] ICR 829). In determining whether the defence is made out, the tribunal should focus on what the employer has done prior to the occurrence of the act and not how he reacts once it has occurred (*Haringey London Borough Council (Haringey Design Partnership Directorate of Technical and Environmental Services) v Al-Azzawi* (2002) 703 IDS Brief 7, EAT). An employment tribunal may have regard to such matters as whether the employer has issued a written policy to employees on equal opportunities, whether it has given its managers training in such matters and whether it has taken steps to discipline employees if they have been guilty of unlawful discrimination. Where there were steps which it would have been reasonably practicable to take, it seems that the respondent must take them if he is to escape liability even if it cannot be shown that those steps would have prevented the discriminatory acts from occurring (*Canniffe v East Riding of Yorkshire Council* [2000] IRLR 555, EAT).

Where an employee's discriminatory behaviour occurs outside the course of his employment, an employer may have a primary, as opposed to a vicarious, liability if he has a sufficient control over the circumstances in which the behaviour occurred to have prevented it from happening and the reason for not exercising that control is a prohibited ground.

11.56 *Liability for unlawful act of agent*

EA 2010, s 109(3) treats the principal as having done anything that an agent has done with the principal's authority (*EA 2010, s 109(2)*). That does not mean that the act must have been done with the principal's knowledge or approval (*EA 2010, s 109(3)*).

The concept of agency used by the *Act* is the same as the common law concept (*Kemeh v Ministry of Defence* [2014] EWCA Civ 91, [2014] IRLR 377). In *Kemch*, a cook employed by a third party contractor but working in an MoD kitchen was not the MoD's agent. Locally elected trade union officials were found to be agents by the Appeal Tribunal in *Unite the Union v Nailard* UKEAT/0300/15, [2016] IRLR 906, [2017] ICR 121.

In contrast to the position with employers there is no "reasonable steps" defence available to a principal.

EA 2010, s 110(1) fixes the agent with liability where:

> "A person (A) contravenes this section if –
> (a)   A is an . . . agent
> (b)   A does something which by virtue of section 109(2) . . . , is treated as having been done by A's . . . , principal . . . and

(c)   the doing of that thing by A amounts to a contravention of this Act by the
. . . principal"

It is no answer for the principal to say that it did not give the agent authority to discriminate.
It will be enough if the agent has authority to do an act which may be carried out in a lawful
or a discriminatory manner (*Lana v Positive Action Training in Housing (London) Ltd* [2001]
IRLR 501, EAT and *Kemeh v Ministry of Defence* [2014] EWCA Civ 91, [2014] IRLR 377).

The principal will only be liable where the agent's actions are a breach of the Act. If, for
instance, an agent is unaware that a complainant has performed protected acts, the agent
cannot victimise them and the principal will have no liability whatever they themselves knew
– *Peninsula Business Service Ltd v Baker* UKEAT/0241/16, *[2017] IRLR 394).*

The agent has a defence where he reasonably relies on a statement by the principal that the
doing the act in question would not involve a contravention of the Act (*EA 2010, s 110(3)).*
If the principal makes such a statement which is false or misleading in a material respect and
does so knowingly or recklessly, he commits an offence liable to a fine not exceeding level
5 on the standard scale (*EA 2010, s 110(5)).*

11.57 *Liability for act of other third party*

The *EA 2010* formerly created a broad liability for failure to protect employees from
harassment by third parties. However, this liability was abolished with effect from 1 October
2013; see Para **11.39** above.

The actions of a third party purporting to exert influence over an employer may be treated
as evidence of discrimination on the employer's part if they do not take steps to distance
themselves from the behaviour (see *Asociatia ACCEPT v Combaterea Discriminarii* C-81/12;
[2013] IRLR 660; [2013] ICR 938, CJEU – burden of proof reversed by evidence of a
leading shareholder saying in a media interview that a football club would not recruit gay
players).

11.58 *Aiding unlawful acts*

EA 2010, s 112 makes it unlawful for a person knowingly to help another to commit what
it calls a "basic contravention". A basic contravention is a breach of *Parts 3 to 7* of the *Act*
inclusive (*Part 5* is the part that deals with work), *ss 108(1)* or *(2)* (post-termination
discrimination and harassment) or *s 111* (instructing, causing or inducing contraventions).

The act must be unlawful in the sense that it must be possible to sue the person who
committed the *Act*. In *May & Baker Ltd (t/a Sanofi-Aventis Pharma) v Okerago* [2010]
IRLR 394, EAT an employee was harassed by an agency worker that her employer had
hired. The agency worker's act was not capable of founding liability since she did not
employ the complainant. That being so, there was no unlawful act for the employer to aid.

Although the new language talks of "helping" rather than "aiding" an unlawful act, there
is no reason to believe that the change in language is intended to bring about a different
result. The guidance given by case law on the predecessor provisions is likely to remain
authoritative.

Guidance on the circumstances in which a person might be said to 'aiding' a discriminator
was given by the House of Lords in *Anyanwu v South Bank Student's Union* [2001] UKHL
14, [2001] 2 All ER 353, HL. Two paid student executives of a student union were dismissed
by the union after an investigation into their activities had resulted in the University
expelling them. The complainants alleged that their dismissals had been discriminatory and
that, as their expulsion had meant that dismissal was inevitable, the University should be
treated as having aided the discriminatory dismissals. The House of Lords upheld the claim
and offered, in the course of Lord Bingham's judgment, the following guidance: First, the
word 'aids' in the statutory provision should be given its ordinary meaning. Second, a

person may knowingly aid another to do an unlawful act without inducing the wrongdoer to act unlawfully or procuring the act of discrimination. Third, provided that the assistance given is not so insignificant as to be negligible, it does not matter whether the help is substantive or productive.

The case of *Hallam v Avery* [2001] UKHL 15, [2001] 1 WLR 655, HL, draws an important distinction that limits the circumstances in which a person may be said to have aided another to discriminate. On the particular facts, a local authority had agreed to hire out rooms to a gypsy couple for their wedding reception. The police warned the local authority that they had experienced problems with gypsy weddings in the past. The local authority sought to impose further conditions on the hiring of the room, which, it was found, amounted to an act of discrimination. The House of Lords considered that the judge at first instance had been entitled to find that the police had not aided the local authority in its act of discrimination. Since it was the Police's warning that seemed to have prompted the discriminatory act one might, at first glance, conclude that the warning and the discrimination were sufficiently entangled to allow a finding that the Police had knowingly aided the local authority to discriminate. It was important, however, in the view of Lord Millet, to focus on what the discriminatory act actually was. In this case it was deciding to impose conditions. The Council had made the decision on its own and had neither 'needed or obtained the aid of the police' in doing so. Aiding someone to commit a discriminatory act required 'a much closer involvement in the actual act of the principal than . . . encouraging or inducing on the one hand or causing or procuring on the other'. What was required was actual participation in the decision-making. It would seem from later cases (see immediately below) that even advising the local authority to impose conditions might not have been sufficient. The question whether a solicitor might be said to be aiding an act of discrimination in giving advice or in acting on instructions was considered in *Bird v Sylvester* [2007] EWCA Civ 1052, [2008] ICR 208. An employee unsuccessfully sued her employer for race discrimination. The employer's solicitor advised his client to take disciplinary proceedings against the employee in part because of the claim. On instruction, the solicitor wrote to the employee informing her that disciplinary action would be taken against her. The employee claimed that she had been unlawfully victimised and that the solicitor had knowingly aided the employer to discriminate. The Court of Appeal decided that the solicitor was not liable. The decision to discipline the employee had been the employer's alone. The solicitor had advised the employer to perform the discriminatory act, but that was insufficient. Turning to the letter sent to the employee in which the threat of disciplinary action was made, the Court of Appeal considered that it was 'very difficult to see how a solicitor who confines himself to giving objective legal advice in good faith as to the proper protection of his client's interests, and acts strictly upon his client's instructions, could be at risk of an adverse finding'. Their Lordships were not prepared to go so far as to hold that a solicitor might never be liable. Liability might arise where 'the solicitor himself actively promotes, perhaps for a malign motive, oppressive actions, and actively carries them along'.

A person does not 'aid' discrimination merely by creating an environment in which discrimination could occur. Fostering and encouraging a discriminatory culture may, however, suffice (*Gilbank v Miles* [2006] EWCA Civ 543, [2006] ICR 1297).

A person cannot "aid" another to commit an act which the latter had already committed at the point at which the employer first becomes involved. Thus, a failure to investigate an allegation of harassment does not mean that the employer should be taken to have aided the harasser (*May & Baker Ltd v Okerago* [2010] IRLR 394, EAT).

When might someone be said to be knowingly aiding a discriminator?

Hallam (above) had been decided on a different basis by the Court of Appeal ([2000] ICR 583, CA). Whilst the imposition of further conditions was an act of discrimination, it was decided that there was insufficient evidence that the police had been aware that, as a result of their advice, the local authority would treat the couple less favourably on grounds of their race. That being so, they could not be said knowingly to have aided an act of discrimination. Recklessness was insufficient; the police had to know that they were aiding a discriminator. See also *Sinclair, Roche & Temperley v Heard* [2004] IRLR 763, EAT.

In *Shepherd v North Yorkshire County Council* [2006] IRLR 190, EAT a council was accused of knowingly aiding a trade union to delay the implementation of a collective agreement. The agreement had the effect of prolonging a disparity in pay between male and female employees. The EAT decided that even if the Council had been aware that the union was discriminating, they could not be said to have knowingly aided the discrimination. There was a material difference between taking advantage of a failure by another and aiding that party to discrimination. The Council had had its own interests to protect in any collective negotiation. Further, the union had not needed the employer's assistance to discriminate. Where, during the course of his employment, an employee commits an act of discrimination, his employer may be liable for it (see above). The employee may also be liable in a personal capacity.

Guidance on when the employee may be said to have knowingly aided his employer is given in *Allaway v Reilly* [2007] IRLR 864:

'If a fellow employee does an act in the course of employment which has the effect of discriminating against the claimant employee on grounds of sex and that is a result which can be concluded to have been within his knowledge at the time he carried out the act in question, the requirements of the subsection are met. Discrimination does not have to be what he intended nor does it have to have been his motive. It is enough that, on the evidence, the conclusion can be drawn that discrimination as the probable outcome was within the scope of his knowledge at the time. It would not need to be in the forefront of his mind nor would he need to have specifically addressed his mind to it. It must be enough if, in all the circumstances, it can properly be concluded that it was within the knowledge that was possessed by the alleged discriminator.'

The employee may be liable on this basis even in circumstances where the employer has succeeded in establishing the employer's defence (*Crofton v Yeboah* [2002] EWCA Civ 794, [2002] IRLR 634).

If a person found liable under the provision is an individual acting in the course of his employment, it may be proper for any award of compensation to be made only against the employer, who will generally be liable on the principles set out above (*Deane v Ealing London Borough Council* [1993] ICR 329).

There is a defence to liability where A reasonably relies upon a statement by B that the act for which help is given does not contravene the Act (*EA 2010, s 112(2)*). If B makes such a statement, it is false or misleading in a material respect and B either knew or was reckless as to its falsity, B commits an offence punishable to a fine of up to level 5 on the standard scale (*EA 2010, s 112(3)* and *(4)*).

12   Discrimination and Equal Opportunities – II: Exceptions, Defences and Non-Employers covered by the Employment Rules

12.1   The *Equality Act 2010* (*'EA 2010'*) came into force, for the most part, on 1 October 2010. It applies to all acts of discrimination occurring after 1 October 2010 or, in the case of 'acts extending over a period' (see **13.6** DISCRIMINATION AND EQUAL OPPORTUNITIES – III), to all acts that continue after 1 October 2010 even if they began before: see *art 7* of the *Equality Act 2010 (Commencement No 4, Savings, Consequential, Transitional, Transitory and Incidental Provisions and Revocation) Order 2010 (SI 2010/2317)*. The scope and application of the *EA 2010* and the predecessor legislation, the *Sex Discrimination Act 1975* (*'SDA 1975'*), the *Race Relations Act 1976* (*'RRA 1976'*), *Employment Equality (Religion or Belief) Regulations 2003* (*'RBR 2003'*), the *Employment Equality (Sexual Orientation) Regulations 2003* (*'SOR 2003'*), the *Disability Discrimination Act 1995* (*'DDA 1995'*) and the *Employment Equality (Age) Regulations 2006* (*'AR 2006'*) is described in DISCRIMINATION AND EQUAL OPPORTUNITIES – I (11).

This chapter deals with the exceptions to the scope, and defences to the application of, that legislation ('the equality legislation'). In summary, an employer (or non-employer covered by the rules) may have a defence to claims of both direct and indirect discrimination where he can show that being of a particular race, religion or belief, sex or sexual orientation is a genuine requirement or qualification for a particular job (see below **12.2** ff). A defence of justification is also available to certain forms of discrimination (see below **12.9**) and a defence of lack of knowledge of disability to certain forms of disability discrimination (see below **12.9A**). This chapter also covers the application of the equality legislation to non-employers covered by the employment rules, such as trade organisations, vocational training providers, partnerships, barristers, police officers, the Crown etc. (see below **12.24** ff). Finally, the chapter deals briefly with the equality duties imposed on public authorities by the *EA 2010* and the predecessor legislation (below **12.37**).

There are also a number of general exceptions (or limits) to the scope of the equality legislation. Broadly speaking, the legislation does not prohibit discrimination where the employee is employed outside Great Britain (below **12.18**), or works under an illegal contract (below **12.19**), or where the discrimination relates to benefits that the employer also provides to the public (below **12.20**), is authorised by another enactment (below **12.21**), is necessary for the purposes of national security (below **12.22**) or where the employer qualifies for immunity under the *State Immunity Act 1978* (below **12.23**). In addition, there are a number of exceptions that are specific to each of the different grounds of discrimination, such as where communal accommodation is provided, or where the employment is for the purposes of an organised religion, or where a particular benefit is dependent on the employee having marital or civil partnership status (see below **12.11–12.16**).

There are also circumstances in which a respondent is permitted to discriminate positively in favour of persons of a particular race, sex, etc (see below **12.10** ff) and certain exemptions that apply only to charities, which in some instances permit positive discrimination in relation to certain groups or (at least) enable charities to continue to pursue their charitable objectives without incurring liability for discrimination (**12.10A**).

For the so-called 'reasonable steps' defence, which enables employers to avoid vicarious liability where they are able to show that they took all reasonable steps to prevent an employee from committing a particular act of discrimination see **11.54**, DISCRIMINATION AND EQUAL OPPORTUNITIES – I.

For enforcement of the equality legislation and remedies, see DISCRIMINATION AND EQUAL OPPORTUNITIES – III (13).

12.1 Discrimination and Equal Opportunities – II

Note that because of its distinct legislative regime, discrimination on grounds of sex in respect of contractual terms and conditions is dealt with in a separate chapter (see EQUAL PAY (22)).

The equality legislation implements in domestic law a number of European Directives, specifically the *Equal Treatment Directive (2006/54/EC)* ("ETD 2006") (on sex discrimination), the *Race Discrimination Framework Directive (2000/43/EC)* ("the Race Directive") and the *Framework Directive (2000/78/EC)* (which covers discrimination on grounds of religion or belief, disability, sexual orientation and age) ("the Framework Directive"). In accordance with usual principles of EU law, the relevant provisions of the domestic equality legislation are to be interpreted in conformity with the governing European Directives. Where there are irreconcilable differences between the domestic legislation and the European Directives, public sector workers will be able to rely on the Directives themselves under the principle of direct effect. In certain circumstances, EU law may require national courts to disapply provisions of national law even in the context of proceedings between private parties. See generally EUROPEAN UNION LAW (23).

12.2 GENUINE OCCUPATIONAL REQUIREMENT OR QUALIFICATION

Broadly speaking, where being of a particular race, religion or belief, sex, sexual orientation, age or disability can be shown to be a genuine requirement or qualification for a particular job, a respondent may have a defence to certain forms of both direct and indirect discrimination. The defence is not, however, a licence to discriminate. Thus, in general, and except where otherwise indicated below, the existence of a genuine occupational requirement or qualification is *not* a defence to a claim of discrimination in the terms of employment offered or afforded to the complainant, or discrimination taking the form of subjecting a complainant to a detriment other than dismissal, or to a claim of harassment.

Under the predecessor legislation to the *EA 2010*, there were (save in relation to disability) a large number of specific genuine occupational requirement exceptions. These are detailed below. However, most of those are not available under the *EA 2010*. Instead, the *EA 2010* contains a general exception for occupational requirement in *paragraph 1* of *Schedule 9*. It applies only to discrimination taking the particular forms set out in *paragraph 1(2)*, ie discrimination in determining how and to whom to offer employment, in the way that persons are afforded access to opportunities for promotion, transfer or training or for receiving any other benefit, facility or service and to discrimination in relation to dismissal. It does not apply to discrimination in the terms of someone's employment (or offer of employment), or to discrimination in the form of subjecting someone to a detriment other than dismissal, or to a claim of harassment. Under *paragraph 1* of *Schedule 9* a person will not contravene the *Act* by discriminating in one of the aforementioned ways if he applies in relation to work a requirement to have a particular protected characteristic and if he shows that, having regard to the nature or context of the work, it is: (a) an occupational requirement; (b) the application of the requirement is a proportionate means of achieving a legitimate aim; and, (c) the person to whom the requirement is applied does not meet it (or, for all protected characteristics except sex, the employer has reasonable grounds for not being satisfied that the person meets it).

In addition to this general exception, a handful of specific genuine occupational requirements or qualifications remain under the *EA 2010*. These are set out at the appropriate points below.

It is likely that the various specific exceptions that were available under the predecessor legislation but are not available under the *EA 2010* should now be regarded as examples of the sort of situation in which the new general genuine occupational requirement exception in the *EA 2010* is likely to apply.

Note that the *DDA 1995* contained no genuine occupational requirement/qualification exceptions. This exception is available for disability discrimination for the first time under the *EA 2010*.

12.3   Sex: genuine occupational qualification

In addition to the general exception set out above at **12.2**, the following genuine occupational requirement exceptions relating to sex are available under the *EA 2010*:

(a)   An exception for employment for the purposes of an organised religion where the application of the requirement engages 'the compliance or non-conflict principle' and the person to whom the requirement applies does not meet it (*para 2(1)* of *Sch 9*). The 'compliance principle' is engaged if the requirement is applied so as to comply with the doctrines of the religion (*para 2(5)*). The 'non-conflict principle' is engaged if, because of the nature or context of the employment, the requirement is applied so as to avoid conflicting with the strongly held religious convictions of a significant number of the religion's followers (*para 2(6)*).

(b)   An exception for service in the armed forces if it can be shown that a requirement for someone to be a man is a proportionate means of ensuring the combat effectiveness of the armed forces (*para 4, Sch 9*).

(c)   An exception for sporting events, specifically for acts done in relation to the participation of people as competitors in a 'gender-affected activity' (*s 195(1)*). A 'gender-affected activity' is a sport, game or other activity of a competitive nature where the physical strength, stamina or physique of average persons of one sex would put them at a disadvantage compared to average persons of the other sex as competitors in events involving the activity (*s 195(3)*).

Note also that the exception set out at (a) immediately above also applies to requirements that a person not be married or a civil partner, that they not be married to, or the civil partner of, a person who has a living former spouse or civil partner, or to requirements relating to circumstances in which a marriage or civil partnership came to an end (*para 2(4)(c)–(e)*).

These exceptions reflect some of those that were available under the *SDA 1975*, although there were a much wider range of specific genuine occupational requirement exceptions relating to sex available under the *SDA 1975*.

The *SDA 1975* provided that where being a man (or, as appropriate, being a woman) is a genuine occupational qualification ('a GOQ') for a job, a respondent may have a defence to a complaint of discrimination in relation to determining who to offer employment, in refusing employment or in access to opportunities for promotion, transfer or training. The defence was not available where the complainant's complaint was that he had been dismissed or subjected to any other detriment.

Being a man was only capable of being a GOQ under the *SDA 1975* for a job in certain defined circumstances, namely:

(a)   Where the essential nature of the job calls for a man for reasons of physiology (excluding physical strength or stamina) or, in dramatic performances or other entertainment, for reasons of authenticity, such that the essential nature of the job would be materially different if carried out by a woman.

Thus a woman may not be discriminated against simply because a job is perceived to require the physical strength and stamina of a man, provided that she is actually capable of performing the duties (ie provided the essential nature of the job would not be materially different if carried out by her). However, employers may discriminate for other physiological reasons, in particular where seeking male models or actors.

(b)   Where the job needs to be held by a man to preserve decency or privacy because:

   (i)   it is likely to involve physical contact with men in circumstances where they might reasonably object to its being carried out by a woman; or

   (ii)   the holder of the job is likely to do his work in circumstances where men might reasonably object to the presence of a woman because they are in a state of undress or are using sanitary facilities.

If an employer required his employees to work stripped to the waist, then in order to establish that he was justified in refusing to offer employment to women, a court hearing a complaint against him would, it is thought, decide whether that requirement was necessary for the performance of the task, or a mere whim on the part of the employer.

(c)   Where the job is likely to involve the holder of the job doing his work, or living, in a private home and needs to be held by a man because objection might reasonably be taken to allowing a woman:

   (i)   the degree of physical or social contact with a person living in the home; or

   (ii)   the knowledge of intimate details of such a person's life which is likely, because of the nature or circumstances of the job or of the home, to be allowed to, or available to, the holder of the job.

(d)   Where the nature or location of the establishment makes it impracticable for the holder of the job to live elsewhere than in premises provided by the respondent and:

   (i)   the only such premises which are available for persons holding that kind of job are lived in, or normally lived in, by men and are not equipped with separate sleeping accommodation for women and sanitary facilities which could be used by women in privacy from men; and

   (ii)   it is not reasonable to expect the respondent either to equip these premises with such accommodation and facilities, or to provide other premises for women.

(See, eg, *Sisley v Britannia Security Systems Ltd* [1983] ICR 628.)

(e)   Where the nature of the establishment, or the part of it within which the work is done, requires the job to be held by a man because:

   (i)   it is, or is part of, a hospital, prison or other establishment for persons requiring special care, supervision or attention; and

   (ii)   those persons are all men (disregarding any woman whose presence is exceptional); and

   (iii) it is reasonable, having regard to the essential character of the establishment or that part, that the job should not be held by a woman.

(f)   Where the holder of the job provides individuals with personal services promoting their welfare or education or similar personal services, and those services can most effectively be provided by a man.

(g)   Where the job needs to be held by a man because it is likely to involve the performance of duties outside the United Kingdom in a country whose laws or customs are such that the duties could not, or could not effectively, be performed by a woman.

(h)   Where the job is one of two to be held by a married couple or (with effect from 5 December 2005) civil partners: see *s 7, SDA 1975*, as amended by *s 251* of the *Civil Partnership Act 2004*. (See also below **12.14** for further discussion of civil partnership and same sex marriage.)

(*SDA 1975, s 7(2)*, as amended by the *Sex Discrimination Act 1986, s 1(2)* and the *Employment Act 1989, s 3(2)*.)

These exceptions applied even where only some of the duties of the job fall within the above provisions, as well as where all of them do (*SDA 1975, s 7(3)*). However, where an employer already had female employees who were capable of carrying out the duties of a vacant post, and whom it would be reasonable to employ on those duties and whose numbers were sufficient to meet his likely requirements in respect of those duties without undue inconvenience, then he could not discriminate by filling the vacancy with another man, even if the vacancy fell within (*a*) to (*g*) above (*SDA 1975, s 7(4)*). (See, eg, *Etam plc v Rowan* [1989] IRLR 150 and also *Lasertop Ltd v Webster* [1997] IRLR 498, EAT.) It is existing employees that count. It was not open to a tribunal to find that the defence was defeated on the basis that it was open to the respondent to appoint new female employees capable of performing the relevant duties.

For the exception under the *SDA 1975* for ministers of religion see below **12.11(g)**.

12.4   Race: genuine occupational requirement or qualification

There are no specific exceptions for race discrimination in the employment sphere under the *EA 2010*. Only the general genuine occupational requirement exception set out at **12.2** above is available.

The *RRA 1976*, as amended by the *Race Relations Act (Amendment) Regulations 2003 (SI 2003/1626)* ('*Race Relations Amendment Regulations*'), however, provided for two different genuine occupational exceptions. The first, the exception for genuine occupational requirement (*RRA 1976, s 4A*: 'the GOR exception'), applied with effect from 19 July 2003 in relation to discrimination on grounds of race or ethnic or national origins. Note that these grounds are a subset of the definition of 'racial grounds' used in the *Act* (see **11.20** Discrimination and Equal Opportunities – I). The second, the exception for genuine occupational qualification (*RRA 1976, s 5*: 'the GOQ exception'), applied where the first did not, ie in relation to discrimination on grounds of colour or nationality and to all racial discrimination occurring before 19 July 2003.

The GOR exception was available only where the discrimination related to a determination as to who to offer employment, a refusal to offer employment or dismissal. The exception was not available for discrimination in the way in which the complainant was afforded access to opportunities for promotion, transfer or training. Unlike the exception under the *SDA 1975*, however, it was available as a defence to a dismissal complaint.

The first exception (the GOR exception) applied where it was shown that:

'having regard to the nature of the employment or the context in which it is carried out:

(a)   being of a particular race or of particular ethnic or national origins is a genuine and determining occupational requirement;

(b)   it is proportionate to apply that requirement in the particular case; and

(c)   either –
   (i)   the person to whom that requirement is applied does not meet it; or
   (ii) the respondent is satisfied, and in all the circumstances it is reasonable for him not to be satisfied, that the person meets it.'
   (*RRA 1976, s 4A(2)*).

235

12.4 Discrimination and Equal Opportunities – II

It was suggested by the Department of Trade and Industry at the time of the introduction of the *SOR 2003* and *RBR 2003* that, in relation to the equivalent provision in those regulations (as to which see below **12.7** and **12.**6) that, in order to ensure compatibility with the governing European Directive (*Directive 2000/78/EC*), the word 'genuine' in *s 4A(2)(a)* should be interpreted in its primary sense of 'actual, true', rather than its secondary sense of 'honestly held belief'.

The second exception (the GOQ exception) was only available where the discrimination took the forms of discrimination in the arrangements made for the purpose of determining who should be offered employment; refusal or deliberate omission to offer employment; and discrimination in the way in which the complainant is afforded access to opportunities for promotion transfer or training. It was not available where the complainant's complaint was that he had been dismissed. In contrast to the general 'nature and context' principle that formed the basis of the GOR exception, the GOQ exception applied only in certain defined circumstances, namely where:

(a)   the job involves participation in a dramatic performance or other entertainment in a capacity for which a person of that racial group is required for reasons of authenticity; or

(b)   the job involves participation as an artist's or photographic model in the production of a work of art, visual image or sequence of visual images for which a person of that racial group is required for reason of authenticity; or

(c)   the job involves working in a place where food or drink is (for payment or not) provided to, and consumed by, members of the public or a section of the public in a particular setting for which, in that job, a person of that racial group is required for reasons of authenticity (thus, a respondent may lawfully discriminate in selecting waiters for an Indian or Chinese restaurant); or

(d)   the holder of the job provides persons of that racial group with personal services promoting their welfare, and those services can most effectively be provided by a person of that racial group (*RRA 1976, s 5(2)*).

The scope of the GOQ exception was discussed in *Tottenham Green Under-Fives' Centre v Marshall* [1989] ICR 214 and in *Lambeth London Borough Council v Commission for Racial Equality* [1990] ICR 768. In *Lambeth*, the Court of Appeal held that the use of the word 'personal' in *s 5(2)(d)* indicated that the identity of the giver and the recipient of the services is important. The Court of Appeal agreed with the Employment Appeal Tribunal that the *RRA 1976* appeared to contemplate direct contact between the giver and the recipient – mainly face-to-face or where there would be susceptibility to personal, physical contact.

The GOQ exception applied where some of the duties fell within (a) to (d) above as well as where all of them did (*RRA 1976, s 5(3)*), and also where those duties were merely ones which it was desirable that the post-holder should carry out and were not fundamental to the post. However, it did not apply where the duties were too trivial to be taken into account or where they had been deliberately put into the job description as a sham or smokescreen (*Tottenham Green Under Fives' Centre v Marshall (No 2)* [1991] ICR 320).

It also did not apply where a respondent already had employees of a particular racial group who were capable of carrying out the duties of a vacant post and whom it would be reasonable to employ on those duties and whose numbers were sufficient to meet his likely requirements in respect of those duties without undue inconvenience, regardless of whether the vacancy fell within *s 5(2)* (*RRA 1976, s 5(4)*). As with cases of sex discrimination (see above **12.3**), it was existing employees who counted.

236

12.5   Gender reassignment: genuine occupational qualification

In addition to the general exception set out at **12.2** above, the *EA 2010* includes the following two specific exceptions for requirements that a person not be a transsexual person:

(a)   An exception for employment for the purposes of an organised religion where the application of the requirement engages 'the compliance or non-conflict principle' and the person to whom the requirement applies does not meet it (*para 2(1)* of *Sch 9*). The 'compliance principle' is engaged if the requirement is applied so as to comply with the doctrines of the religion (*para 2(5)*). The 'non-conflict principle' is engaged if, because of the nature or context of the employment, the requirement is applied so as to avoid conflicting with the strongly held religious convictions of a significant number of the religion's followers (*para 2(6)*).

(b)   An exception for service in the armed forces if it can be shown that a requirement is a proportionate means of ensuring the combat effectiveness of the armed forces (*para 4, Sch 9*).

These exceptions reflect some of the specific exceptions that were available under the predecessor legislation to the *EA 2010*. Those exceptions were as follows.

Following the insertion of *ss 7A* and *7B* into the *SDA 1975* by the *Sex Discrimination (Gender Reassignment) Regulations 1999 (SI 1999/1102)* ('*Gender Reassignment Regulations*') with effect from 1 May 1999 a genuine occupational qualification ('GOQ') defence was available in appropriate circumstances to allegations of sex discrimination brought by persons intending to undergo, undergoing or who have undergone gender reassignment ('transsexuals'). (See generally **11.21** Discrimination and Equal Opportunities – I.)

Broadly speaking, there were two circumstances where the GOQ defence might arise in relation to complaints by transsexuals. First, a gender reassignment might mean that the employee fell foul of a GOQ that the complainant be a man or, as appropriate, a woman. Second, there might be circumstances where the requirement was, in effect, not that the complainant should be a particular sex but that they should not be a transsexual.

(1)   *Where the requirement was that a complainant be a man or a woman*

Turning first to consider cases where the requirement was for a complainant of a specific sex, for the most part, *SDA 1975, s 7A* simply extended the GOQ exception for sex discrimination (see above **12.3**) to cases involving transsexuals. However, there were three differences between the scope of the defence in cases involving transsexuals and its scope in other cases of sex discrimination. First, there was a defence available to a respondent even in cases where a respondent discriminates:

(a)   in the terms in which he offers employment; or

(b)   by dismissing the complainant, or by subjecting him to any other detriment (*SDA 1975, s 7A(1)*).

Second, the defence was subject to an overarching requirement that treatment meted out to the complainant was reasonable in view of the circumstances giving rise to the GOQ (*SDA 1975, s 7A(1)(b)*).

Third, the limitation on the GOQ defence to a claim of sex discrimination imposed by *s 7(4)* (ie that a GOQ defence could not be used where a respondent already had female employees who were capable of carrying out the duties of a vacant post whom it would be reasonable to employ on those duties) applied to the dismissal of transsexuals as it did to the filling of vacant posts (*SDA 1975, s 7A(3)*).

Note, however, that the defence was not available where the complainant's sex had become the acquired gender under the *Gender Recognition Act 2004* ('*GRA 2004*'): *SDA 1975, s 7A(4)*, as inserted by *GRA 2004, s 14* with effect from 4 April 2005. The *GRA 2004* provides for the application by transsexuals for "gender recognition certificates". Where a gender recognition certificate had been issued to a person, this particular GOQ exception did not apply at all since the person becomes 'for all purposes' the acquired gender (*GRA 2004, s 9*).

(2)   *Where the requirement was that the complainant not be a transsexual*

SDA 1975, s 7B set out the variation of the defence which dealt with circumstances where it was thought that not being a transsexual was a GOQ. Those circumstances were in addition to those described above in relation to sex discrimination and were referred to as 'supplementary general occupational qualifications' ('supplementary GOQs'). The supplementary GOQs were as follows:

(a)   the job involves the holder of the job being liable to be called upon to perform intimate physical searches pursuant to statutory powers;

(b)   the job is likely to involve the holder of the job doing his work, or living, in a private home and needs to be held otherwise than by a person who is undergoing or has undergone gender reassignment, because objection might reasonably be taken to allowing such a person:

   (i)   the degree of physical or social contact with a person living in the home; or

   (ii)   the knowledge of intimate details of such person's life, which is likely, because of the nature or circumstances of the job or of the home, to be allowed to, or available to, the holder of the job;

(c)   the nature or location of the establishment makes it impracticable for the holder of the job to live elsewhere than in premises provided by the respondent, and:

   (i)   the only such premises which are available for persons holding that kind of job are such that reasonable objection could be taken, for the purpose of preserving decency and privacy, to the holder of the job sharing accommodation and facilities with either sex whilst undergoing gender reassignment; and

   (ii)   it is not reasonable to expect the respondent either to equip those premises with suitable accommodation or to make alternative arrangements; or

(d)   the holder of the job provides vulnerable individuals with personal services promoting their welfare, or similar personal services, and in the reasonable view of the respondent those services cannot be effectively provided by a person undergoing gender reassignment.

The supplementary GOQs set out in paras (c) and (d) above only applied where an employee intended to undergo or was undergoing a gender reassignment. They were not available where the employee had already undergone the reassignment (*SDA 1975, s 7B(3)*). Further, the supplementary GOQs could not be relied upon as a defence to discriminating against the employee:

(i)   in the terms on which they are offered employment (*SDA 1975, s 7B(1)(a)*);

(ii)   in the way in which the employee is afforded access to opportunities for promotion, transfer or training, other than where there is a deliberate refusal or a deliberate omission to afford such access to a job; or

(iii)   by subjecting him to any other detriment.

The case of *A v Chief Constable of West Yorkshire Police (No 2)* [2004] UKHL 21, [2004] ICR 806, HL was a case that concerned, in effect, a requirement that a police officer not be a transsexual. It was decided on the basis of the *SDA 1975* as it stood prior to the coming into force of the *Gender Reassignment Regulations* on 1 May 1999. However, the decision is relevant to the GOQ defence under the *SDA 1975* and under the *EA 2010*. *A* was a male-to-female transsexual who applied for a position as a police constable. Her birth certificate recorded her sex as 'male', but she had undergone gender reassignment surgery and was also in outward appearance female. The Chief Constable refused her application because he considered that in order to be a police officer it was necessary to be either a man or a woman, both in appearance and by birth. The Chief Constable relied for the genuineness of that requirement on *s 54(9)* of the *Police and Criminal Evidence Act 1984* ('*PACE*'), which stipulates that intimate searches must be carried out by a police officer of the same sex as the person searched. The House of Lords held that the jurisprudence of the European Court of Human Rights and the Court of Justice of the European Union required transsexuals to be recognised in their reassigned gender. Accordingly, *s 54(9)* had to be interpreted as applying to a transsexual's reassigned gender, thereby depriving the Chief Constable of his GOQ defence.

Note, however, that since the coming into force of the *GRA 2004* on 1 July 2004, transsexuals may apply for a gender recognition certificate. Where a gender recognition certificate has been issued to a person, that person becomes 'for all purposes' the acquired gender (*GRA 2004, s 9*). Where a person has not applied for a gender recognition certificate, it will be a matter for argument as to whether the reasoning of the House of Lords in *A* should apply to any provisions similar to *PACE 1984, s 54(9)*. On the one hand, if the decision in *A* is viewed as being driven by the CJEU's interpretation of the *Equal Treatment Directive*, it should make no difference where Parliament has chosen to draw the line on recognition, since EU law is supreme. On the other hand, if the decision in *A* is viewed as being driven by the jurisprudence of the European Court of Human Rights, it could be argued that, Parliament having now enacted the *GRA 2004* and determined the precise circumstances in which gender recognition should be accorded to transsexuals, that determination is to be respected as a matter that falls within the 'margin of appreciation' accorded to sovereign states.

Finally, it should be noted that, with effect from 1 October 2005, a further *caveat* to the supplementary GOQs was inserted into *SDA 1975, s 7B* by the *Employment Equality (Sex Discrimination) Regulations 2005 (SI 2005/2467)* ("the *2005 Sex Discrimination Regulations*"). That *caveat* was similar to provisions applying in respect of race (see above **12.4**) and sex (see above **12.3**): the supplementary GOQs did not apply where the employer:

(i)   already had transsexual employees who either had not undergone gender reassignment (and were not undergoing or intending to undergo gender reassignment) or (having already undergone reassignment) had become the acquired gender under *GRA 2004*; and,

(ii)   those employees were capable of carrying out the duties in question, were sufficient in number to meet the employer's likely requirements in respect of those duties without undue inconvenience and whom it would be reasonable to employ on those duties.

See also **12.6** below for the exception for requirements imposed in respect of employment by an organised religion that a person not be a transsexual.

12.6   Religion or belief: genuine occupational requirement

In addition to the general exception set out at **12.2** above, under the *EA 2010* the exception available under the predecessor legislation (see below) for organisations with an ethos based on religion or belief is preserved in *paragraph 3* of *Schedule 9* to the Act. It applies where, having regard to the nature or context of the work, it is shown that a requirement to be of a particular religion or belief is: (a) an occupational requirement; (b) the application of the requirement is a proportionate means of achieving a legitimate aim; and, (c) the person to whom the requirement is applied does not meet (or the employer has reasonable grounds for not being satisfied that the person meets the requirement).

In addition, there is an exception under *paragraph 2* of *Schedule 9* to the *Act* for employment for the purposes of an organised religion. It applies to the application of the following requirements: (a) to be of a particular sex, (b) not to be a transsexual, (c) not to be married or a civil partner, (d) not to be married to a person of the same sex, (e) not to be married to, or the civil partner of, a person who has a living former spouse or civil partner, (f) relating to circumstances in which a marriage or civil partnership came to an end or (f) a requirement related to sexual orientation. The exception applies where the application of any such requirement engages 'the compliance or non-conflict principle' and the person to whom the requirement applies does not meet it (*para 2(1)* of *Sch 9*). The 'compliance principle' is engaged if the requirement is applied so as to comply with the doctrines of the religion (*para 2(5)*). The 'non-conflict principle' is engaged if, because of the nature or context of the employment, the requirement is applied so as to avoid conflicting with the strongly held religious convictions of a significant number of the religion's followers (*para 2(6)*). The exception also covers qualifications for employments covered by the exception: *para 2(3)*. This exception reflects specific exceptions available under the predecessor legislation. However, it is controversial because it does not include any proportionality requirement and is therefore arguably not compliant with the terms of the governing European Directive (*Directive 2000/78/EC*). This argument was run, unsuccessfully, in *R (Amicus-MSF) v Secretary of State for Trade and Industry* [2004] EWHC 860 (Admin), [2004] IRLR 430 in relation to the equivalent provisions in the predecessor legislation. A European Commission Reasoned Opinion (RO 2006/2450) subsequently concluded that the absence of a proportionality requirement from the UK legislation meant that this provision did not comply with the *Directive*. At the time the Commission anticipated that this would be corrected in the *Equality Act 2010*, but it was not. This issue was not considered in *Pemberton v Inwood* [2017] IRLR 211.

In *Pemberton v Inwood*, the EAT upheld the ET's decision that a refusal by the Bishop of Southwell and Nottingham to grant the licence necessary to allow the claimant to take up a post as an NHS chaplain fell within the scope of para 2(3) as the employment was 'for the purposes of an organised religion' even though the employer was the NHS: it sufficed if one of the purposes of the employment was for an organised religion even if there were other purposes to the employment. Further, since the reason for the refusal to grant the licence was because the claimant had entered into a same-sex marriage, which was against the teachings of the Church, a requirement related to sexual orientation had been applied (since the claimant would not have entered a same-sex marriage were he not gay) and had been applied in order to comply with 'the doctrines of the Church' within the meaning of that term in para 2(3). 'Doctrines' in para 2(3) was to be interpreted objectively, rather than being restricted to what would actually be called "doctrine" by the Church or to issues on which all members of the Church agreed. That case also highlighted the important point that the exception is not available for claims of harassment. The EAT indicated that had there been any harassing conduct beyond merely making and communicating the decision that fell within the para 2(3) exception, a claim for harassment could have succeeded. On the facts, however, the tribunal had been entitled to conclude that there was no such conduct.

Under the predecessor legislation, the *RBR 2003*, a genuine occupational requirement ('GOR') was available in two sorts of cases. The exception only applied where the discrimination related to the arrangements for determining who to offer employment, a refusal of employment, access to opportunities for promotion, transfer or training and dismissal.

The first type of case was like the GOR exception under the *RRA 1976* (see above **12.4**). In the first type of case the exception applied where, having regard to the nature of the employment or the context in which it was carried out, being of a particular religion or belief was 'a genuine and determining occupational requirement' (*reg 7(2)*).

The second type of case was where the respondent had an ethos based on a religion or belief and, having regard to that ethos as well as to the nature of the employment, or the context in which it was carried out, being of a particular religion or belief was a GOR (*reg 7(3)*).

In both types of case, the mere existence of a GOR did not take the complainant outside the protective scope of the *Regulations*. First, it had also to be shown that the complainant did not meet the requirement. Where it was not immediately clear whether the complainant met the requirement, it was sufficient that the respondent was not satisfied, on reasonable grounds, that the complainant met the requirement (*reg 7(2)(c)* and *(3)(c)*). Second, it had to be proportionate to apply the requirement in the particular case (*reg 7(2)(b)* and *(3)(b)*).

Note that in *Glasgow City Council v McNab* [2007] IRLR 476 it was held that a local education authority ('LEA') could not defend a discrimination claim in relation to a Catholic School for which it was responsible on the basis that it was an organisation with an ethos based on a religion or belief. Although the School had such an ethos, the employer and respondent to the claim was the LEA and it could not have a specific religious ethos.

See also **12.21** below for further specific provisions exempting from the *EA 2010* acts of discrimination done pursuant to legislative provisions authorising discrimination on grounds of religious belief in relation to various appointments to educational establishments.

See also **12.11(G)** below for Ministers of Religion.

12.7 Sexual orientation: genuine occupational requirement

In addition to the general exception set out at **12.2** the *EA 2010* contains an exception for employment for the purposes of an organised religion where the application of a requirement related to sexual orientation engages 'the compliance or non-conflict principle' and the person to whom the requirement applies does not meet it (*para 2(1)* of *Sch 9*). The 'compliance principle' is engaged if the requirement is applied so as to comply with the doctrines of the religion (*para 2(5)*). The 'non-conflict principle' is engaged if, because of the nature or context of the employment, the requirement is applied so as to avoid conflicting with the strongly held religious convictions of a significant number of the religion's followers (*para 2(6)*). The exception also covers qualifications for employments covered by the exception: *para 2(3)*. This exception reflects specific exceptions available under the predecessor legislation.

The *SOR 2003* provided for two types of cases in which a respondent might rely on the genuine occupational requirement ('GOR') exception in defence to a claim of discrimination on grounds of sexual orientation. In both types of case the defence was only available where the discrimination related to the arrangements for determining who to offer employment, a refusal of employment, access to opportunities for promotion, transfer or training and dismissal.

The first type of case was like the first type of case under the *RBR 2003* (see above **12.6**), ie the exception applied where, having regard to the nature of the employment or the context in which it was carried out, being of a particular sexual orientation was a 'genuine and determining occupational requirement'. The respondent had to show that it was proportionate to apply the requirement in that particular case and that either the complainant did not meet the requirement as to sexual orientation or that it was reasonable, in all the circumstances, for the respondent to be satisfied that the complainant did not (*reg 7(2)*). In the absence of an express admission by the complainant, this involved the tribunal determining whether the respondent's conclusion or assumption about the complainant's sexual orientation was a reasonable one.

The second type of case was where the employment was for the purposes of an organised religion and the respondent applied 'a requirement related to sexual orientation' in order:

(a)   to comply with the doctrines of that religion, or

(b)   owing to the nature or context of that employment, to avoid conflicting with the strongly held religious convictions of a significant number of the religion's followers (*reg 7(3)(a)* and *(b)*).

As with the first type of case, the respondent had also to show that either the person to whom the requirement was applied did not meet that requirement or that it was reasonable for the respondent to have been satisfied that he did not (*reg 7(3)(c)*).

It was argued in *R (Amicus-MSF) v Secretary of State for Trade and Industry* [2004] EWHC 860 (Admin), [2004] IRLR 430 that *regs 7(2)* and *(3)* were incompatible with the governing European Directive (*Directive 2000/78/EC*) among other reasons because they contain no proportionality requirement. However, the High Court held that the *Regulations* were compatible. With regard to *reg 7(2)* (the first type of case), Richards J noted that, although the exception applied not only where the complainant did not in fact meet the requirement as to sexual orientation, but also where it was 'reasonable' for the respondent 'not to be satisfied' that the complainant met that requirement, the need for the respondent's decision to be 'reasonable' ensured that the decision could not be based on mere assumptions or social stereotyping. With regard to *reg 7(3)* (the second type of case), Richards J noted that the exception, as a derogation from the principle of equal treatment, had to be construed strictly. He noted that 'for the purposes of an organised religion' was a narrower expression than 'for the purposes of a religious organisation' or 'an ethos based on religion or belief', as used in the *RBR 2003*. Thus, employment as a teacher in a faith school was, he considered, likely to fall outside the exception as being 'for the purposes of a religious organisation' rather than 'for the purposes of an organised religion'. Further, he observed that the condition that the employer apply the requirement 'so as to comply with the doctrines of the religion' was an objective test and very narrow in scope. Similarly, the alternative condition that the exception be applied where required 'to avoid conflicting with the strongly held religious convictions of a significant number of the religion's followers' was also an objective test that would be difficult to satisfy in practice. He also noted that, although the phrase used in *reg 7(3)* 'a requirement related to sexual orientation' was linguistically wider in scope than the phrase 'being of a particular sexual orientation' used in *reg 7(2)*, it was difficult to see a practical difference between the two since 'being of a particular sexual orientation' necessarily encompassed matters relating to sexual behaviour, etc. A European Commission Reasoned Opinion (RO 2006/2450) subsequently concluded that the absence of a proportionality requirement from the UK legislation meant that this provision did not comply with the *Directive*. At the time the Commission anticipated that this would be corrected in the *Equality Act 2010*, but it was not.

Compare the exception for employment for purposes of an organised religion with the exception for ministers of religion in the *SDA 1975*: see below **12.11(g)**.

12.8   Age: genuine occupational requirement

There are no specific exceptions for age under the *EA 2010*. Only the general genuine occupational requirement exception set out at **12.2** above is available.

AR 2006 recognised that there might be circumstances in which being of a particular age group was a genuine requirement of the job. However, the existence of a genuine occupational requirement was no defence to discrimination taking one of the following forms under *AR 2006*:

(a)   discrimination in the terms on which employment was offered;

(b)   discrimination in the terms of employment afforded to an employee;

(c)   subjecting the employee to a detriment other than dismissal; and

(d)   harassing the employee.

The defence was *potentially* available where the discrimination took one or more of the following forms:

(a)   discrimination in the arrangements made for determining to whom employment should be offered;

(b)   discrimination by refusing to offer, or deliberately not offering, employment;

(c)   discrimination in the opportunities offered an employee for promotion, transfer, or training;

(d)   discrimination by refusing to afford, or deliberately not offering, an opportunity; and

(e)   discrimination by dismissal.

AR 2006 did not list the circumstances in which such a defence might apply. Instead, they set out a general defence where, having regard to the nature of the employment, or the context in which the employment is carried out, possessing a characteristic related to age was a genuine and determining occupational requirement, and it was proportionate to apply that requirement in the particular case (*reg 8(2)*).

In *Wolf v Stadt Frankfurt Am Main* [2010] IRLR 244, the CJEU found that legislation imposing an upper age limit of 30 for recruitment for frontline fire-fighting duties was justified as a genuine occupational requirement in accordance with the equivalent provision of the *Directive, Article 4(1)*. The genuine occupational requirement was physical fitness. The legislation was justified by the aim of preserving the operational capacity of the fire service and did not go beyond what was necessary to achieve that objective having regard to the number of years remaining following training during which officers could carry out physically demanding tasks.

12.8A Marriage and civil partnership: genuine occupational requirement

In addition to the general exception set out at **12.2** above, there is an exception under *paragraph 2* of *Schedule 9* to the *Act* for employment for the purposes of an organised religion. It applies to the application of requirements: (i) not to be married or a civil partner, (ii) not to be married to a person of the same sex, (iii) not to be married to, or the civil partner of, a person who has a living former spouse or civil partner, or (iv) to requirements relating to circumstances in which a marriage or civil partnership came to an end. The exception applies where the application of any such requirement engages 'the compliance or non-conflict principle' and the person to whom the requirement applies does not meet it (*para 2(1)* of *Sch 9*). The 'compliance principle' is engaged if the requirement is applied so as to comply with the doctrines of the religion (*para 2(5)*). The 'non-conflict principle' is engaged if, because of the nature or context of the employment, the requirement is applied so as to avoid conflicting with the strongly held religious convictions of a significant number of the religion's followers (*para 2(6)*). This exception reflects specific exceptions available under the predecessor legislation. However, it is controversial because it does not include any proportionality requirement and is therefore arguably not compliant with the terms of the governing European Directive (*Directive 2000/78/EC*). This argument was run, unsuccessfully, in *R (Amicus-MSF) v Secretary of State for Trade and Industry* [2004] EWHC

860 (Admin), [2004] IRLR 430 in relation to the equivalent provisions in the predecessor legislation. A European Commission Reasoned Opinion (RO 2006/2450) subsequently concluded that the absence of a proportionality requirement from the UK legislation meant that this provision did not comply with the *Directive*. At the time the Commission anticipated that this would be corrected in the *Equality Act 2010*, but it was not.

12.9   JUSTIFICATION

A defence of justification is (and has always) been available to the following forms of discrimination:

- *Indirect discrimination* in respect of all the protected characteristics;

- *Discrimination arising from disability* under the *s 15* of the *EA 2010*;

- *Direct discrimination* on grounds of age only.

Under the *EA 2010* a single formula applies for indirect discrimination in relation to all the protected characteristics. A provision, criterion or practice ("PCP") that is applied to all, but which puts (or would put) persons of a particular protected characteristic at a particular disadvantage when compared with others (and which puts the complainant at that disadvantage) will nonetheless be justified if the employer can show it 'to be a proportionate means of achieving a legitimate aim' (*s 19(2)*). The same test applies on the face of the legislation for direct age discrimination (*s 13(2)*) and discrimination arising from a disability (*s 15(1)(b)*). However, so far as direct age discrimination is concerned, a slightly different test applies in *Directive 2000/78/EC* and *s 13(2)* of the *EA 2010* must be 'read down' accordingly. Whereas there is no limitation on the aims that may be regarded as legitimate for the purposes of justifying indirect discrimination, direct age discrimination can only be justified if the aim of the measure in question relates to "employment policy, the labour market or vocational training" and not "purely individual reasons particular to the employer's situation, such as cost reduction or improving competitiveness": see *art 6(1)* of *Directive 2000/78/EC* and *Seldon v Clarkson, Wright & Jakes* [2012] UKSC 16, [2012] ICR 716 (see further below).

An issue that has arisen in the cases is whether it is necessary for the employer 'merely' to justify the PCP itself or whether it is also necessary to justify the application of the PCP to the claimant. The SC in *Seldon* accepted that it will normally suffice if the employer succeeds in showing that the PCP was a proportionate means of achieving a legitimate aim in general, although did not rule out that it might be necessary in certain cases for the employer to demonstrate that the application of the provision, criterion or practice to the particular employee was justified in that particular case. In *Homer v Chief Constable of West Yorkshire Police* [2012] UKSC 15, [2012] ICR 704, however, the SC held that what needed to be justified was the rule itself. See also *Rajaratnam v Care UK Clinical Services Ltd* (7 October 2015), UKEAT/0435/14/DA, UKEAT/0076/15/DA in which the EAT held that a requirement for GPs to work night-shifts was justified by the need to provide healthcare services 24 hours per day. The employer did not need also to justify the application of the rule to the claimant. Further support for this approach is to be found in *Chief Constable of West Midlands Police v Harrod and ors* where the EAT ([2015] ICR 1311) and CA ([2017] EWCA Civ 191) both took the view, in slightly differing terms, that provided the rule was justified (in that case a provision of the Police Pensions Regulations 1987 that permitted compulsory retirement only of those who had become entitled to a pension), there was no need to justify the exercise of the discretion to apply the rule in any particular case. However, the EAT in *Buchanan v Commissioner of Police of the Metropolis* [2017] ICR 184 considered that the aforementioned cases were not authority for the proposition that this was the approach to be taken in all cases. In particular, Judge Richardson considered that in claims of disability discrimination in relation to absence procedures, the issue will generally be whether the application of the procedure in the particular circumstances of the claimant's case was justified; asking whether it is justifiable for an employer to have sickness absence procedures at all simply does not address the discrimination claim at all.

Under the predecessor legislation, the test for whether a provision, criterion or practice, was justified differed until recently depending on whether the complaint fell under the *SDA 1975*, related to discrimination on grounds of race or ethnic or national origins under the *RRA 1976*, or discrimination on grounds of colour or nationality under that *Act*, or fell under the *RBR 2003* or the *SOR 2003*, or the *DDA 1995*.

With the exception of discrimination on grounds of colour and nationality under the *RRA 1976*, the test had become the same in each of the Acts and Regulations as it is under the *EA 2010*, ie a 'proportionate means of achieving a legitimate aim' (*SDA 1975, s 1(2)*, as amended by the *Sex Discrimination Regulations 2005, reg 3*; *RRA 1976, s 1(1A)(c)*, as inserted by the *Race Relations Amendment Regulations* with effect from 19 July 2003; *RBR 2003, reg 3(1)(b)(iii); SOR 2003, reg 3(1)(b)(iii)*).

This contrasts with the 'old' test, which required respondents only to show that the application of the relevant provision, criterion or practice was 'justifiable irrespective' of the sex/race etc. of the person to whom it was applied. The 'old' test still applies to indirect race discrimination on grounds of colour and nationality under the *RRA 1976* (*RRA 1976, s 1(1)(b)(ii)*), indirect race discrimination on any ground occurring prior to 19 July 2003 (*RRA 1976, s 1(1)(b)(ii)*) and indirect sex discrimination occurring prior to 1 October 2005 (*SDA 1975, s 1(2)(b)(ii)*).

The reason for the change in the test was so that the domestic legislation conformed with the governing European Directives (*Directive 76/207/EEC, art 2, para 2*, as amended by *Directive 2002/73*; *Directive 2000/43/EC, art 2, para 2(b)* and *Directive 2000/78/EC, art 2, para 2(b)*). It will be noted that the governing European Directives each provide that a respondent must demonstrate that the relevant provision, criterion or practice is 'objectively justified by a legitimate aim *and* the means of achieving that aim are appropriate and necessary'. Although the domestic legislation makes no mention of the requirements that the measure be 'appropriate and necessary', in line with the general principles for the application and interpretation of EC law (see **23.2 EUROPEAN UNION LAW**) tribunals no longer accept that a measure is proportionate unless a respondent has shown that it is both appropriate and necessary.

Although the test for justification has changed, the case law on the 'old' test has continued to be regarded as relevant by tribunals. Care should be taken, however, to ensure that the specific requirements of the 'new' test are always met.

A defence of justification was also available in principle to claims of disability-related discrimination under the *DDA 1995* (see **DISCRIMINATION AND EQUAL OPPORTUNITIES – I (11)**). However, the position following *Lewisham London Borough Council v Malcolm* [2008] UKHL 43, [2008] 1 AC 1399, was that most such claims would in fact be complaints of direct discrimination. As such, the circumstances in which a justification defence to disability-related discrimination was available to employers became very limited indeed. Where the justification of disability-related discrimination was in issue, different considerations applied to those that are generally applicable to the defence of justification available to the types of discrimination set out in the bullet points above. In particular, first, the test for justification was whether the reason for the difference in treatment was both 'material to the circumstances of the particular case and substantial' (*DDA 1995, s 3A(5)*). In *Jones v Post Office* [2001] EWCA Civ 558, [2001] ICR 805 Arden LJ explained that for a reason to be 'material', there must be a 'reasonably strong connection between that reason and the circumstances of the individual case', and for it to be 'substantial', it 'must carry real weight and thus be of substance' although it need not necessarily be the best possible conclusion that could be reached in the light of all known medical science. Unlike for other justification defences (see below), the 'range of reasonable responses' test (familiar to those dealing with unfair dismissals) applied to the question of justification in disability-related discrimination. The second main difference was that in the case of an employer who had not complied with his duty to make adjustments (see DISCRIMINATION AND EQUAL OPPORTUNITIES – I (11)), the defence of justification was only available if the treatment in question would have been justified even if the duty had been complied with (*DDA 1995, s 3A(6)*). Thus, where an employee using a wheelchair was not promoted solely because the workstation for the more senior post is inaccessible to wheelchairs, the refusal to promote would not be justified if the furniture could be rearranged to make the workstation accessible. For cases on justification of disability-related discrimination see *Jones v Post Office* [2001] EWCA Civ 558, [2001] ICR 805; *Williams v J Walter Thompson Group Ltd* [2005] EWCA Civ 133, [2005] IRLR 376 and *O'Hanlon v Revenue and Customs Comrs* [2007] EWCA Civ 283, [2007] IRLR 404).

The general test for justification

The classic test for establishing whether or not discrimination may be justified is found in *Bilka-Kaufhaus GmbH v Weber Von Hartz (Case 170/84)* [1986] IRLR 317. There the Court of Justice of the European Union said that the national court (or tribunal) must be satisfied that the measures having a disparate impact 'correspond to a real need . . . are appropriate with a view to achieving the objectives pursued and are necessary to that end' (para 36). In subsequent cases (see especially *R v Secretary of State for Employment, ex p Seymour-Smith and Perez* [1999] IRLR 253 and also *Kutz-Bauer v Freie und Hansestadt Hamburg*: C-187/00 [2003] IRLR 368) the CJEU expanded on this, ruling that is for the national court (or tribunal) to ascertain:

(1)   whether the measure in question has a legitimate aim, unrelated to any discrimination based on any prohibited ground;

(2)   whether the measure is capable of achieving that aim; and

(3)   whether in the light of all the relevant factors, and taking into account the possibility of achieving by other means the aims pursued by the provisions in question, the measure is proportionate.

It is important for Tribunals to be clear about the three elements of the test. "Appropriate", "necessary" and "proportionate" are not interchangeable: see *Homer v Chief Constable of West Yorkshire* [2012] UKSC 15, [2012] ICR 704. To be proportionate, a measure has to be both an appropriate means of achieving the legitimate aim and a (reasonably) necessary means of doing so.

(1) Legitimate aim

To be legitimate, an aim must correspond to a "real need" on the part of the employer's business: *Bilka-Kaufhaus* (ibid), *R (Elias) v Secretary of State for Defence* [2006] 1 WLR 3213. This is not to be confused with a test of necessity: see *HM Land Registry v Benson* [2012] ICR 627 at paragraph 37. Whatever the aim, it is important that the tribunal make clear findings as to the employer's aim and why it is legitimate: *Cockram v Air Products Plc* (24 November 2015), UKEAT/0122/15/LA.

Direct age discrimination

In relation to direct age discrimination only there is a limitation on the aims that may be regarded as legitimate. Direct age discrimination can only be justified if the aim of the measure in question relates to "employment policy, the labour market or vocational training" and not "purely individual reasons particular to the employer's situation, such as cost reduction or improving competitiveness": see *art 6(1)* of *Directive 2000/78/EC* and *Seldon v Clarkson, Wright & Jakes* [2012] UKSC 16, [2012] ICR 716. So far as direct age discrimination is concerned, therefore, *s 13(2)* of the *EA 2010* must be 'read down' accordingly.

The *Directive* gives examples of the sort of age discriminatory measures that might be permitted in pursuit of such aims, including (a) the setting of special conditions on access to employment and vocational training, employment and occupation, dismissal and remuneration conditions, for young people, older workers and persons with caring responsibilities in order to promote their vocational integration or ensure their protection; (b) the fixing of minimum conditions of age, professional experience or seniority in service for access to employment or to certain advantages linked to employment; (c) the fixing of a maximum age for recruitment which is based on the training requirements of the post in question or the need for a reasonable period of employment before retirement. These examples are not to be regarded as exhaustive: *Rosenbladt (Gisela) v Oellerking Gebaudereinigungsges mbH*: C-45/09 [2011] 1 CMLR 1011, [2011] IRLR 51.

Aims that have been accepted as legitimate for the purposes of direct age discrimination include:

- encouraging better access to employment and better distribution of work between the generations (*Félix Palacios de la Villa v Cortefiel Servicios SA*: C-411/05 [2008] All ER (EC) 249, [2007] IRLR 989, *Petersen v Berufungsausschuss für Zahnärzte für den Bezirk Westfalen-Lippe* [2010] IRLR 254 and *Hörnfeldt v Posten Meddelande AB*: C-141/11 [2012] IRLR 785), including encouraging the reasonable flow of new applicants for judicial posts (*Hampton v Lord Chancellor* [2008] IRLR 258, ET) and ensuring promotion opportunities for associate solicitors (*Seldon* ibid);

- the efficient planning of the departure and recruitment of staff (*Fuchs and another v Land Hessen*, Joined Cases C-159/10 and C-160/10: [2011] IRLR 1043; *Seldon* and *Hörnfeldt*);

- protecting acquired rights and legitimate expectations with regard to remuneration (*Specht v Land Berlin* (Joined Cases C-501, 506, 540 and 541/12), [2014] ICR 966 and *Schmitzer v Bundesministerin für Inneres* (Case C-530/13) [2015] IRLR 331; see further below and also **22.12** EQUAL PAY for justification of pay protection arrangements generally);

- encouraging the recruitment of older persons (*Mangold v Helm* [2006] IRLR 143);

- improving access to vocational training for young people (*de Lange v Staatssecretaris van Financien* (C-548/15); and

- running an organisation in a collegiate way and avoiding the indignity of disciplining staff for underperformance (*Rosenbladt*, *Seldon* and *Hörnfeldt*) or the possibility of disputes about an employee's fitness for work after a certain age (*Fuchs*).

In the light of the SC's decision in *Seldon* some earlier decisions may fall to be re-evaluated. Thus in *MacCulloch v Imperial Chemical Industries plc* [2008] ICR 1334 the CA accepted that 'rewarding loyalty' and 'encouraging turnover' could be legitimate aims of measures that were directly discriminatory on grounds of age. It is difficult to see how aims thus expressed could be legitimate post *Seldon* for direct age discrimination.

For other cases on the justification of direct age discrimination see: *Lockwood v Department of Work and Pensions* [2013] EWCA Civ 1195, [2013] IRLR 941 (redundancy payments varying based on age were justified), *Ingeniorforeningen i Danmark, acting on behalf of Ole Andersen v Region Syddanmark*: C-499/08 [2011] 1 CMLR 1140 and *Dansk Jurist- Og Okonomforbund, acting on behalf of Toftgaard v Indenrigs- Og Sundhedsministeriet*: Case C-546/11 [2014] IRLR 37 (withholding termination payments from over 65s on grounds that they were eligible for a pension was not justified because the same aim could have been met by the lesser measure of withholding the payment only if the individual had actually decided to draw their pension); see also **12.15**(d) below.

Indirect discrimination

So far as indirect discrimination of all forms is concerned, there is no restriction on the possible motivations that can in principle constitute legitimate aims. What constitutes a legitimate aim is a question of fact for the tribunal: see *Ladele v Islington London Borough Council* [2009] EWCA Civ 1357, [2010] ICR 532 at [45]. It will therefore be open to employers to demonstrate that any aim they seek to pursue is legitimate. This is consistent with the fact that justification must be applied on a case-by-case basis and that it is very difficult to anticipate all possible justifications.

In addition to the aims identified above as legitimate for the purposes of direct age discrimination claims, examples of aims that have been accepted as legitimate aims for the purposes of justifying indirect discrimination include:

- facilitating the recruitment and retention of staff of appropriate calibre (*Homer v Chief Constable of West Yorkshire* [2012] UKSC 15, [2012] ICR 704);

- recognising the legitimate expectations of employees who were already in receipt of a benefit or had otherwise acquired rights deserving of protection (*Pulham v Barking and Dagenham London Borough Council* [2010] ICR 333, EAT, *Specht v Land Berlin* (ibid) and *Schmitzer v Bundesministerin für Inneres* (ibid));

- preventing a windfall or receipt of excessive compensation (*Loxley v BAE Systems Land Systems (Munitions & Ordnance) Ltd* [2008] ICR 1348, [2008] IRLR 853, EAT and *Kraft Foods Ltd v Hastie* (UKEAT/0024/10/ZT) [2010] ICR 1355);

- achieving a stable workforce in the context of a fair process of redundancy selection (*Rolls Royce Plc v Unite the Union* [2010] ICR 1, CA);

- avoiding the risk to the public of employing persons in the police force who have a criminal conviction (*RMC v Chief Constable of Hampshire* (UKEAT/0184/16/LA, 8 November 2016): the policy indirectly discriminated against men who are more likely to have criminal convictions, but the EAT upheld the ET's decision that it was justified);

- securing efficiencies (such as reducing the backlog of oral Parole Board hearings (*Greenland v Secretary of State for Justice* UKEAT/0232/14/DA, 20 March 2015) or other desirable management aims, such as achieving a coherent pay structure, avoiding privatisations, job losses, cuts in hours, and employees receiving lower pay (*Allen v GMB* [2008] IRLR 690) or securing the provision of a 24-hour health service (*Rajaratnan v Care UK Clinical Services Ltd* (7 October 2015, UKEAT/0435/14/DA, UKEAT/0076/15/DA));

- making the maximum possible number of redundancies: *Harrod and ors v Chief Constable of West Midlands Police* [2017] EWCA Civ 191 (although see commentary below on the lawfulness of using cost as a justification for discrimination);

- seeking to break even year-on-year: *Braithwaite v HCL Insurance BPO Services Ltd* (UKEAT/0152-3/14/DM, 5 February 2015);

- rewarding employees for specific work performed, e.g. night work (*Blackburn v Chief Constable of West Midlands Police* [2008] EWCA Civ 1208, [2009] IRLR 135);

- ensuring a teacher is able to communicate effectively with her pupils (a requirement not to wear a veil while teaching: *Azmi v Kirklees Metropolitan Borough Council* [2007] IRLR 484); and,

- ensuring the employer is able to fulfil its contractual requirements to a third party (eg by requiring a security guard to work on a Friday lunchtime and not attend Muslim prayers: *Cherfi v G4S Security Services Ltd* [2011] EqLR 825).

In addition, the legitimate aims accepted in *MacCulloch* (above) of 'rewarding loyalty' and 'encouraging turnover' are plainly capable of constituting legitimate aims for the purposes of indirect discrimination even if there is now some doubt about their legitimacy in the context of direct age discrimination. Beware, however, of vague or aspirational 'legitimate aims' such as 'intergenerational fairness': while securing 'intergenerational fairness' could be a legitimate aim, it must be possible to articulate precisely what that means in the context of the particular case: *Cockram v Air Products Plc*)24 November 2015, UKEAT/0122/15/LA).

Cost-related aims

One type of legitimate aim has proved particularly controversial – cost-related aims. Given the limitation on legitimate aims for the purposes of justifying direct age discrimination, cost reduction will plainly not be a legitimate aim in the context of direct age discrimination: see *Seldon* and *Schmitzer v Bundesministerin für Inneres* (Case C-530/13) [2015] IRLR 331. There is nothing express in the governing European legislation, or the domestic legislation, that imposes any such limitation on reliance on cost reduction as a legitimate aim when justifying indirect discrimination. Nonetheless, there is a line of cases in which it has been held that cost may only be relied on as justification if it is combined with other factors: *Cross v British Airways plc* [2005] IRLR 423, EAT; *R (Elias) v Secretary of State for Defence* [2006] EWCA Civ 1293, [2006] IRLR 934. In *Woodcock v Cumbria Primary Care Trust* [2011] IRLR 119 the EAT expressed the view (*obiter*) that, as a matter of principle and of common sense, there should be no rule that considerations of cost could never be sufficient on their own to justify indirect discrimination. On appeal, however, the Court of Appeal ([2012] EWCA Civ 330, [2012] ICR 1126) confirmed what was then generally understood to be the orthodox position that justification by reference to costs alone was impermissible, although it could be taken into account with other factors – the 'costs plus' approach. The CA referred to the line of cases establishing this principle, including *Schönheit v Stadt Frankfurt*: C-4/02 and C-5/02 [2004] IRLR 983, CJEU and *Kutz-Bauer v Freie und Hansestadt Hamburg*: C-187/00 [2003] IRLR 368, CJEU, *British Airways plc v Grundy*, *Cross v British Airways Plc* [2005] IRLR 423 and *Redcar and Cleveland BC v Bainbridge* [2008] ICR 249. See also *Osborne Clarke Services v Purohit* [2009] IRLR 341. However, in *Ministry of Justice v O'Brien* [2013] UKSC 6, [2013] 1 WLR 522 the Supreme Court reviewed the relevant authorities in the context of a claim under the *Part-time Workers (Prevention of Less Favourable Treatment) Regulations 2000* and reached the conclusion (at paragraph 69) that cost could not be relied on in order to justify discrimination (i.e. apparently even in combination with other factors). That said, the Court did not consider it needed to decide whether *Woodcock v Cumbria Primary Care Trust* had been wrongly decided. It also appeared to accept in principle that 'sound management of public finances' could be a legitimate aim. It thus remained to be seen whether the *O'Brien* decision would be regarded as outlawing altogether cost considerations. In *R (Unison) v Lord Chancellor (No. 2)* [2015] ICR 390, the Divisional Court indicated that it regarded the law to be as stated in *Woodcock*, i.e. the 'costs plus' approach. The decision of the CJEU in *Schmitzer v Bundesministerin für Inneres* (Case C-530/13) suggests that the 'costs plus' approach is correct, although that case was a direct age discrimination case and thus a case in which cost saving could never be a legitimate aim, even if it can support the proportionality of a measure (see above). In *Schmitzer*, the CJEU made clear that budgetary considerations could be relied upon by way of justification, provided that they were relied on in conjunction with 'political, social or demographic considerations'. See also the discussion of this line of case law in *R(Unison) v Lord Chancellor (No. 3)* [2015] EWCA Civ 935, [2016] ICR 1.

Notwithstanding the statements of principle in the case law, it should be noted that there are in fact a number of cases where the Tribunals and Courts have reached conclusions that could be characterized as being findings that costs alone can justify discrimination and which may continue to be followed despite the Supreme Court's ruling. Thus the courts appear to have had little difficulty with the notion that measures intended to avoid a 'windfall' or 'excessive compensation' to the employee – measures which the employer will inevitably have introduced to save itself money – have been held to be justified: *Loxley v BAE Systems (Munitions & Ordnance) Ltd* [2008] ICR 1348, [2008] IRLR 853 and *Kraft Foods UK Ltd v Hastie* [2010] ICR 1355. It should be noted that in those cases, the payments in question were held to serve some other legitimate purpose and so the courts were able to regard the quantum of the payment as being an aspect of the proportionality of the means of meeting the legitimate aim of (for eg in the case of severance pay) paying a reasonable sum of money on termination of employment to allow the employees time to find a new job. *HM Land Registry v S M Benson and ors* [2012] ICR 627 is another apparently anomalous case. Here, the EAT found that the Tribunal had wrongly found an employer's use of a 'cheapness criterion' in a redundancy situation to be unjustified indirect age discrimination. The EAT held that the 'cheapness criterion' fulfilled a legitimate aim of saving the employer money, and that it was justified because there was no practicable alternative means of achieving the same aim and the measure was not disproportionate. It is notable, however, that the case seems to have been decided by the EAT without reference to the authorities for the general principle that costs alone cannot justify discrimination. See also *Braithwaite v HCL Insurance BPO Services Ltd* [2015] ICR 713 in which the EAT held, applying *Land Registry v Benson* that seeking 'to break even year-on-year' was a legitimate aim and that cost-saving changes to terms and conditions of employment (which employees had to accept or resign their employments) were justified. Similarly, in *Harrod and ors v Chief Constable of West Midlands Police* [2017] EWCA Civ 191, the CA (without referring to the 'costs alone' case law) accepted as legitimate the aim of making the maximum possible number of redundancies, which was in substance adopting an aim of saving as much money as possible.

Given these anomalous cases, and given that so far as disability discrimination is concerned cost can effectively justify indirect discrimination because it can be a reason why it is not reasonable to make an adjustment for a disabled person (see eg *Cordell v Foreign & Commonwealth Office* [2012] ICR 280 and 11.43 DISCRIMINATION AND EQUAL OPPORTUNITIES – I), prior to *O'Brien* (ibid) the time appeared to be ripe for the CJEU to consider again whether or not costs alone can be relied on as justifying indirect discrimination. However, following *O'Brien* there is little prospect of any reference on that point being made from the UK in the near future.

In past cases where cost was relied on as a justification, it was not necessary precisely to quantify the costs, it was usually sufficient for there to be evidence as to the 'broad scale' of costs: see *Pulham and ors v London Borough of Barking & Dagenham* [2010] ICR 333. In that case the EAT also observed that, although it is open to an employer to rely on the fact that the particular budget to which the cost in question has been allocated is exhausted, this should never be regarded as a determinative factor since the allocation of cost centres to particular budgets is a matter that it is within the employer's power to vary if necessary.

Discriminatory aims

An aim that is itself discriminatory, or is 'inextricably linked to' the forbidden ground of discrimination, will not be legitimate and it will not be possible for justification to be established: see *Orphanos v Queen Mary College* [1985] IRLR 349, HL, applied in *R (Elias) v Secretary of State for Defence and Commission for Racial Equality* [2006] EWCA Civ 1293, [2006] IRLR 934, save in the context of age discrimination where direct discrimination can be justified: see *obiter* comments in *Chief Constable of West Midlands Police and ors v Harrod and ors* [2017] EWCA Civ 145. *Elias* concerned the requirement in a non-statutory compensation scheme for persons interned by the Japanese during the Second World War that, in order to qualify for compensation, internees had to have been born in the UK or have a parent or grandparent born in the UK. The Court of Appeal held that although the Government's desire to limit the scheme to those with a close connection with Britain was a legitimate aim, and cost factors could potentially justify such a limitation, the actual criteria imposed by the Government were so closely connected with the unlawful ground of discrimination (national origins) that their use could not be justified. See also *Ministry of Justice v O'Brien* [2013] UKSC 6, [2013] 1 WLR 522 (aims intended to reward the greater contribution of full-time judges and encourage better candidates to apply for full-time judicial appointment were held not to justify discrimination against part-timers in relation to pensions because, in effect, the aims were themselves discriminatory). See also *Lockwood v Department of Work and Pensions* [2013] EWCA Civ 1195, [2013] IRLR 941, applied in *Smith and Budgen v Ministry of Justice* (13 February 2014, UKEAT/0308/12/RN, UKEAT/0309/12/RN) (where the EAT held that it had been impermissible for the Tribunal to find that the provisions were justified solely by reference to the difference in ages of the employees and remitted the matter to the Tribunal for further consideration).

For similar reasons, if an employer has recognised that a particular practice or policy may be discriminatory, the EAT has held that it will not be possible for the employer to justify continuing that practice or policy even on a transitional or phasing-out basis: see *Pulham and ors v London Borough of Barking & Dagenham* [2010] ICR 333. However, in other cases the courts have accepted that transitional pay protection arrangements may be justified (even where past discrimination has been expressly recognised by the employer). Indeed, in *Specht v Land Berlin* (Joined Cases C-501, 506, 540 and 541/12), [2014] ICR 966, the CJEU found such arrangements to be justified even where they would perpetuate previous discrimination indefinitely. See further below *Other specific cases* and **22.12** Equal Pay.

Other examples of cases where the aim has been found to be itself discriminatory and therefore illegitimate include *Allonby v Accrington and Rossendale College* [2001] EWCA Civ 529, [2001] IRLR 364 (purpose of imposing the condition was to enable the employer to avoid a statutory protection against discrimination). Compare in this context *Osborne Clarke Services v Purohit* [2009] IRLR 341. That case concerned a firm of solicitors' practice of not offering training contracts to persons who required work permits. They sought to justify this indirect nationality discrimination on the grounds that: (i) they did not feel they could legitimately sign the work permit application form because that required the employer to certify that it was unable to fill the post with a national worker and in fact they were significantly over-subscribed with applicants for training contracts; and (ii) applications for work permits would increase the cost of the process of appointing trainees. The tribunal rejected the cost argument as being an 'unattractive way of justifying indirect discrimination'. As to the argument about the work permit criteria, the EAT ruled that in order to avoid unlawful discrimination, issues of requirement for work permits should only be considered once it had been decided on merit who should be awarded a training contract. Application should then be made to the British Immigration Authority ('BIA') and employers should leave it to the BIA to determine whether the work permit criteria were satisfied.

(2) Whether the measure is capable of achieving the aim

It is not sufficient for an employer to convince a tribunal that the treatment (in the case of age) or PCP (in indirect discrimination) had a legitimate aim. He also needs to show that it was appropriate and reasonably necessary in order to achieve that aim. As noted above, the requirement that the treatment or measure be appropriate means that it must actually contribute to the pursuit of the legitimate aim. There must not be a mismatch between the aim and the means. There are few examples of cases where it has been held that the means employed are not at least capable of achieving the aim in question. However, one example which could be viewed as such is *Petersen v Berufungsausschuss für Zahnärzte für den Bezirk Westfalen-Lippe* [2010] IRLR 254, where the CJEU held that a maximum age limit of 68 for panel dentists was not justified as being necessary for the protection of health where there was an exception for those practising outside the panel system. This was because it could not be regarded as essential for the protection of health in the light of the broad exception. (In this respect, *Petersen* concerned an exemption in *Article 2(5)* of the *Framework Directive* for measures which are necessary for the protection of health rather than justification under

Article 6. It therefore did not address the question of whether it was permissible to assume based only on "general experience" that the performance of dentists declined after a certain age.) A better example is *Homer v Chief Constable of West Yorkshire* [2012] UKSC 15, [2012] ICR 704 in which the SC accepted that a requirement to have a law degree in order to enter a higher pay band may facilitate the recruitment and retention of staff of appropriate calibre. However, the SC considered that where the member of staff in question had been recruited much earlier and under a different system where a law degree was not required, the requirement to have one before being allowed to cross a pay threshold was unlikely to fulfil the aim of retaining valued staff. Indeed, in this author's view, the position is likely to be quite the contrary. Cf the similar case of *Games v University of Kent* [2015] IRLR 202 (concerning a requirement for university lecturers to hold a PhD) and also *Hennigs v Eisenbahn-Bundesamt; Land Berlin v Mai*, joined Cases C-297/10 and C-298/10: [2012] IRLR 83, CJEU (the aim of rewarding experience is not achieved by age-related pay scales which apply irrespective of experience) and *Kücükdeveci v Swedex GmbH & Co KG*: C-555/07 [2011] 2 CMLR 703 (the aim of making it easier to recruit young people is not achieved by a measure which applies long after the employees have ceased to be young). *Cockram v Air Products Plc* (24 November 2015, UKEAT/0122/15/LA) is another good example: in that case an employer's stock option scheme permitted employees to keep unvested stock options if they retired on or after 'customary retirement age'. Under the company's old pension scheme (which applied to the claimant), retirement age was 50, but under the company's new scheme retirement age was 55. The employer claimed that 'customary retirement age' for the purposes of the stock option scheme was therefore 55 and argued that this was justified by the legitimate aims of intergenerational fairness, rewarding experience and loyalty, and ensuring a mix of generations amongst its staff. These aims were accepted by the tribunal, but the decision was overturned by the EAT on appeal which found that on the facts the tribunal could not have concluded that the aim was anything other than 'merely' achieving consistency between schemes. In particular, the tribunal had not given sufficient reasons for what intergenerational fairness consisted of, and it could not conclude that the rule served the legitimate aim of rewarding experience and loyalty in circumstances where employees had not been told that 55 was the relevant age.

(3) Proportionality

The requirement that a measure be proportionate means that tribunals must seek to balance the discriminatory effect of the requirement or condition against the legitimate aim in question (see *Ojutiku v Manpower Services Commission* [1982] ICR 661; *Hampson v Department of Education and Science* [1989] ICR 179, overturned by the House of Lords ([1990] ICR 511) on grounds other than justification, which was not argued before their Lordships). The tribunal must consider both the quantitative and the qualitative effects of the discrimination, ie how many women or people of a particular racial group will suffer in consequence of it, and how seriously they will suffer (cf *Jones v University of Manchester* [1993] ICR 474 and also *EC Commission v Belgium* [1991] IRLR 393). Where the discriminatory effect is particularly acute, the measure is more likely to be disproportionate. Thus in *Seda Kucukdeveci v Swedex GmbH & Co KG*: C-555/07 [2010] IRLR 346, the CJEU ruled that a German law was unlawful which provided that periods of employment completed by an employee before reaching the age of 25 were not taken into account in calculating the notice period for dismissal. The discrimination was significant and the link to the legitimate aim tenuous. In *Mba v Mayor and Burgesses of the London Borough of Merton* [2014] ICR 357 (which concerned a requirement for a care assistant at a children's home to work on Sundays which put her at a disadvantage because she was a practising Christian who believed she should not work on Sundays) the Court of Appeal noted that the fact that only one or a minority of employees in the particular workplace would be affected by a requirement would not necessarily mean that it was easier for the employer to justify the discriminatory effect, since if only a few employees were affected it would in many cases be easier for the employer to accommodate their religious beliefs.

Measures that apply to all without taking sufficient account of the different circumstances of particular groups will generally be disproportionate. Thus in *Ingeniørforeningen i Danmark, acting on behalf of Ole Andersen v Region Syddanmark*: C-499/08 [2011] 1 CMLR 1140 the CJEU considered a measure providing severance payments for all long-serving employees but not those over 65 was disproportionate because it applied to all employees over 65 regardless of whether they were actually drawing a pension. See, to similar effect, *Dansk Jurist-Og Økonomforbund, acting on behalf of Toftgaard v Indenrigs- Og Sundhedsmin-isteriet*: Case C-546/11 [2014] IRLR 37. In *Mangold*, a measure aimed to encourage the recruitment of older persons was held to be disproportionate as it applied to all old people, regardless of whether they had been out of employment. The CJEU took a more lenient approach in the case of *Félix Palacios*. It held that the enforcement of a compulsory retirement age under a collective agreement was justified as being proportionate. The CJEU noted that the national authorities had a broad discretion in social and employment matters and it was for them to strike the appropriate balance. In *R (Unison) v First Secretary of State* [2006] EWHC 2373 (Admin), [2006] IRLR 926, the Secretary of State had changed the Local Government Pension Scheme, considering this to be necessary in order to comply with the *Directive* and the *Regulations*. The Secretary of State considered that the scheme would not be justified by the aim of rewarding loyalty as it treated those who remained in service in the same way as those who had left. The Court held that this position was not irrational.

When determining whether or not a measure is proportionate, it will be relevant to consider whether or not any lesser form of the measure would nevertheless serve the employer's legitimate aim. It will normally be for the parties to identify possible alternatives, although in *Naeem v Secretary of State for Justice* [2014] IRLR 520 EAT suggested, *obiter*, that a tribunal might be expected of its own motion to consider 'manifest' alternatives. The suggestion was not considered on appeal in that case ([2015] EWCA Civ 1264, [2016] ICR 289 and [2017] UKSC 27; [2017] 1 WLR 1343) and in *Magoulas v Queen Mary University of London* (29 January 2016), UKEAT/0244/15/RN, the EAT declined to follow this suggestion. In *Azmi v Kirklees Metropolitan Borough Council* [2007] IRLR 484 (in which the Muslim claimant complained that she had been unlawfully discriminated against on grounds of her religious belief because she was not allowed to wear the veil while teaching at a primary school), the EAT held that the tribunal was right to have taken into account, in finding the requirement imposed by the school to be proportionate, the facts that (i) the respondent school had, before insisting on the claimant not wearing a veil, observed her teaching both with and without the veil and taken the view that she was much more effective without the veil, and (ii) the school had permitted her to wear the veil when moving around the school premises and had only required her not to wear the veil while teaching. Contrast, in the education field, *R (on the application of Watkins-Singh) v Governing Body of Aberdare Girls' High School* [2008] EWHC 1865 (Admin), [2008] ELR 561 where the High Court found that a school's policy forbidding jewellery was not justified because it prevented Sikhs from wearing Kara bangles which were of great importance to them and yet so small and unostentatious that the discriminatory effect of the policy was disproportionate and *G v St Gregory's Catholic Science College Governors* [2011] EWHC 1452 (Admin), [2011] EqLR 859 where the High Court found that a prohibition on pupils wearing hair in corn-rows was indirectly discriminatory on racial grounds and not justified as it was disproportionate. See also *Cherfi v G4S Security Services Ltd* [2011] EqLR 825 in which the EAT upheld a Tribunal's decision that a requirement for a security guard to work Friday lunchtimes was proportionate even though it prevented him (as a Muslim) from attending Friday prayers. The EAT held that the Tribunal had properly considered both the effect on the employee and the effect on the employer's business and had lawfully concluded that the requirement was a proportionate means of achieving the legitimate aim of meeting the employer's business need (which involved fulfilling contractual obligations to a third party). See further, to similar effect, *Mba v Merton LBC* [2014] ICR 357 (requirement to work on Sundays justified indirect discrimination against Christian employee).

Justification where the aim is to protect fundamental rights

There is one possible exception to the requirement to consider the proportionality of a particular aim. This is where the aim is itself the protection of fundamental rights. The argument made in the cases in which this has been suggested appears to be that the aim is sufficiently legitimate to justify the use of any means to achieve it. See in this regard *Islington London Borough Council v Ladele* [2010] IRLR 211. That case concerned the Council's requirement that its services be provided on a non-discriminatory basis. It had accordingly disciplined a registrar who, owing to her religious beliefs, refused to carry out civil partnership ceremonies. The Tribunal found that the Council's aim of providing non-discriminatory services was legitimate but considered that the use of disciplinary measures to achieve this aim was disproportionate. The EAT (whose decision was approved by the CA) overturned this decision, holding that since the Council's aim was legitimate and could not be achieved other than by imposing disciplinary sanctions on employees who sought to pick and choose the duties that they would perform, the Council's actions had not been unlawful. The CA confirmed that in those circumstances it was not necessary to go on to consider the proportionality of the means: since the legitimate aim was itself the protection of fundamental rights, to ask whether a particular means to achieving that aim was disproportionate "might well be characterised as invoking the tail to wag the dog" (Lord Neuberger, [51]): see also *McFarlane v Relate Avon Ltd* [2010] EWCA Civ 880, [2010] IRLR 872. It should further be noted that the EAT in *Ladele* considered that, if the Council had wished to accommodate the claimant's religious beliefs, it would have been lawful for it to do so, but the fact that this could have been done did not mean that the policy the Council had in fact adopted was unlawful. However, the CA held (*obiter*) that where a registrar had been designated as a civil partnership registrar it would be unlawful under the *Equality Act (Sexual Orientation) Regulations 2007* for her to refuse to provide registration services to homosexual couples (for which unlawful act the Council would be liable).

Mrs Ladele, Mr McFarlane and two other claimants, Ms Eweida (whose complaint was that British Airways had refused to allow her to wear a cross at work, cf *Eweida v British Airways Plc* [2010] EWCA Civ 80, [2010] ICR 890) and Ms Chaplin (a nurse who was refused permission to wear a necklace with a cross on it at work) took their cases to the ECrtHR, complaining that the UK had unlawfully interfered with their rights under *Art 9* of the *ECHR* to manifest their religious belief and/or had unlawfully discriminated against them contrary to *Art 14* of the *ECHR*. In conjoined proceedings (*Eweida and ors v United Kingdom*, App nos 48420/10, 59842/10, 51671/10 and 36516/10, [2013] IRLR 231) the ECrtHR upheld Ms Eweida's complaint, but rejected the others. In each case the ECrtHR considered that the applicant had established an interference with their rights under *Art 9* and/or *Art 14* and went on to consider whether that interference was justified. The test applied by the ECrtHR when considering justification is indistinguishable from that which applies in domestic law under the *EA 2010*. In each case the ECrtHR sought to balance the importance to the applicant of the right to manifest his or her religious belief against the business need / aim of the applicant's employer. The ECrtHR did not take the view that just because an employer's aim was the protection of fundamental rights, there was no need to consider proportionality. Rather, in both the *Ladele* and *McFarlane* cases the fact that this was the employer's aim was merely treated as a factor that weighed heavily in the balance in favour of the interference being justified. The ECrtHR also held that although it is relevant to the assessment of justification in the employment context that an employee can avoid the interference by resigning his or her job, this fact on its own could never justify discrimination or interference with an employee's fundamental rights. In *Ladele*, *McFarlane* and *Chaplin* the ECrtHR considered that the UK had struck the right balance in holding the employer's action to be lawful. In *Eweida*, however, the ECrtHR considered that although the employer's aim of projecting a uniform corporate image was a legitimate one, it was not weighty one (and not as weighty as the health and safety reasons for not allowing

Ms Chaplin to wear a cross, for example) and the fact that the employer had subsequently amended the policy made clear that it had not been vital to have the policy in the first place. The interference with Ms Eweida's rights had therefore been disproportionate.

Another recent case to consider the impact of *Article 9* of the *ECHR* on domestic indirect discrimination law is *Mba v Mayor and Burgesses of the London Borough of Merton* [2014] ICR 357. That case concerned a requirement for a care assistant to work on Sundays which conflicted with her Christian belief that she should not work on the Sabbath. In that case the Court of Appeal held that the tribunal had erred in taking into account, in the employer's favour, the fact that the belief that one should not work on a Sunday is not a 'core component' of Christian belief, since it is a belief shared only by some, not all, Christians. The Court of Appeal held that this did not mean that any less respect was to be accorded to the Claimant's belief (which was accepted to be genuine) in the context of *Article 9* and thus the fact that the belief was not a 'core component' of Christianity was to be regarded as largely irrelevant to the question of justification for the purposes of domestic law. In the context of a domestic law indirect discrimination claim, the only relevance of a claimant's belief not being a 'core component' of a particular religion was that it would be likely to mean that an employer would only encounter a few employees who may need to have that belief accommodated. In many cases this would make it harder for the employer to justify not accommodating the employee's belief.

General principles

The question of whether discrimination is justified is one of fact for the employment tribunal (*Singh v British Rail Engineering* [1986] ICR 22).

The burden of proof is on the respondent to satisfy the tribunal that the measure applied is objectively justified (*Rainey v Greater Glasgow Health Board* [1987] ICR 129, an equal pay case in which the House of Lords held that the same principles are applicable to the *SDA 1975* as to the *Equal Pay Act 1970*; see **22.12 Equal Pay**). (See Discrimination and Equal Opportunities – **III (13)** for general discussion of the burden of proof.)

The test to be applied by the tribunal is an objective one: while the tribunal should take into account the reasonable needs of the respondent's business, the tribunal has to make its own judgment as to whether the provision, criterion or practice applied by the respondent is reasonably necessary: there is no scope for 'margin of discretion' or 'range of reasonable responses' approach when considering whether an indirectly discriminatory provision, criterion or practice is justified: *Hardys & Hansons plc v Lax* [2005] EWCA Civ 846, [2005] IRLR 726.

The tribunal must demonstrate that it has critically evaluated any defence of justification: its reasons for finding that a measure is a 'proportionate means of achieving a legitimate aim' must be apparent from the decision: *Redfearn v Serco Ltd*, above. In that case, the EAT held that the tribunal had not given sufficient reasons for finding that a requirement that no employee be a member of the British National Party was justified as a proportionate means of achieving the legitimate aim of protecting the health and safety of Asian passengers using the Respondent's services. See also *MacCulloch v Imperial Chemical Industries plc* [2008] ICR 1334.

Although it has occasionally been suggested that some forms of indirect discrimination (most notably age discrimination) require a lesser degree of justification than others, the Court of Appeal has confirmed that such suggestions have no juridical basis and the same degree of justification is required for all grounds of discrimination: *R (on the application of the British Gurkha Welfare Society) v Ministry of Defence* [2010] EWCA Civ 1098, [2010] 1 WLR 1067. Nonetheless, there is at least one category of case in which it is established that a slightly different approach should be taken, and that is in cases concerning measures based on length of service. These are dealt with at the end of this section.

What is clear is that the overall discriminatory effect of the measure will necessarily be greater in cases of direct discrimination and this will be a material factor when applying the proportionality test: see *MacCulloch v Imperial Chemical Industries plc* [2008] ICR 1334 and *Incorporated Trustees of the National Council on Ageing (Age Concern England) v Secretary of State for Business, Enterprise and Regulatory Reform*: C-388/07 [2009] ICR 1080, CJEU. See also further above under 'proportionality'. The case law on justification of retirement and related measures is dealt with in a separate section below and in **(42)** Retirement.

The time at which justification needs to be established is when the measure is applied, not when it was adopted (unless, of course, the challenge is to the adoption of the policy): *Trustees of Swansea University Pension & Assurance Scheme v Williams* [2015] ICR 1197. Further, it is not necessary as a matter of law for the alleged discriminator to have analysed the proportionality question at the time of adopting or applying a rule or policy: see *Ministry of Justice v O'Brien* [2013] UKSC 6, [2013] 1 WLR 522, *Cadman v Health and Safety Executive* [2004] EWCA Civ 1317, [2004] IRLR 97 and the *Trustees of Swansea University* and *Elias* cases (above). Flaws in the employer's decision-making processes are irrelevant, what matters is the outcome, not how the decision was made: *Chief Constable of West Midlands Police v Harrod* [2015] IRLR 790 (upheld on appeal on slightly different grounds: [2017] EWCA Civ 191). It is always open to the alleged discriminator to justify the rule or policy by factors not expressly taken into account at the time of adopting the rule or policy: see *Schönheit v Stadt Frankfurt* conjoined cases C-4/02 and C-5/02 [2004] IRLR 983 and *Seldon v Clarkson Wright & Jakes* [2010] EWCA Civ 899, [2011] ICR 60 (affd on this point [2012] UKSC 16, [2012] ICR 716). However, where the alleged discriminator has not even considered questions of proportionality at the time of adopting a rule or policy, it may be more difficult for him to establish justification (cf *Ministry of Justice v O'Brien* ibid, *Hockenjos v Secretary of State for Social Security* [2004] EWCA Civ 1749, [2005] IRLR 471 and the *Elias* and *Seldon* cases, above).

Under the 'old' test, it was held that a measure may be justified even though the respondent has not produced detailed evidence to show that there was no other way of achieving his or her object (cf *Cobb* above). Under the 'new' test, it is much more likely that a failure to adduce cogent evidence of justification will result in a finding that justification is not made out: see *Starmer v British Airways plc* [2005] IRLR 862, EAT and also the Court of Appeal's decision in *Hockenjos v Secretary of State for Social Security* [2004] EWCA Civ 1749, [2005] IRLR 471 (below). In *Hampton v Lord Chancellor* [2008] IRLR 258, the employment tribunal held that the government's decision to set the retirement age for part-time recorders at 65 was not proportionate as it considered that the government's evidence was insufficiently conclusive. However, see *Pulham and ors v London Borough of Barking & Dagenham* [2010] ICR 333, in which the EAT held that an employer was not precluded from advancing a defence of justification in respect of pay protection arrangements merely because the arrangements had not been "carefully costed and crafted" at the time of implementation.

Nonetheless, in every case respondents need to take care to ensure that evidence adduced is aimed at the right issue. In *Whiffen v Milham Ford Girls' School* [2001] EWCA Civ 385, [2001] IRLR 468, the respondent attempted to justify a policy of responding to a redundancy situation by first allowing the contracts of temporary staff to lapse without renewal. The respondent argued that it needed to make redundancies and that the policy was gender-neutral. The Court of Appeal pointed out that all indirect discrimination cases concerned provisions which were gender-neutral on their face and that, where it had been found that an apparently gender-neutral provision had a disparate effect on a particular group (here, women), it was no justification that the policy might have operated non-discriminatorily in another situation. What required justification was that redundancies were first visited on temporary employees. See also *Garcia-Bello v Aviance UK Ltd* [2007] All ER (D) 318 (Dec): where there was no clear evidence that flexible shift patterns could not have been introduced, there was no justification for the disparate impact of the new shift patterns on those with childcare responsibilities (who were all female). Compare also *Mba v Mayor and Burgesses of the London Borough of Merton* [2014] ICR 357 in which the Court of Appeal held that in considering whether a requirement for a care assistant to work on Sundays was justified when that put her at a disadvantage because of her Christian beliefs, the employment tribunal should not have taken into account (in the employer's favour) that the employer had previously tried to accommodate her wishes for two years, or that the employer had arranged her shifts so that she could attend Church on Sunday. Such general evidence of 'good will' on the part of the employer was not relevant to determining whether a present requirement for her to work on Sundays was justified (although, presumably, the tribunal could legitimately have taken into account the employer's evidence of the difficulty of accommodating the claimant's wishes over the previous two years as evidence of justification).

In particular, care must be taken in properly identifying and distinguishing the aim of the measure from the means used to achieve it. The fact that different measures with different aims could be introduced by an employer is not relevant in determining whether a particular measure with a legitimate aim is justified, what matters is whether there are more proportionate ways of achieving the aim of the measure in question: see *Blackburn and anor v Chief Constable of West Midlands Police* [2008] EWCA Civ 1208, [2009] IRLR 135 (aim of rewarding those who did night work was legitimate and therefore it was proportionate to pay those persons more – it did not matter that other police forces had decided not to reward night workers). Likewise, what the tribunal must evaluate is the employer's legitimate aim, not some other aim that it considers would have been preferable: thus in *XC Trains Ltd v D* [2016] IRLR 748 the EAT held that the ET had erred in law in concluding that the train company's shift system unjustifiably disadvantaged women where it had concentrated on an aim of its own, namely achieving a more gender-balanced workforce, rather than addressing the employer's legitimate aims of needing to run an efficient train service and minimise the anti-social hours worked by all drivers. Where there is no other way of achieving the identified aim, the means will inevitably be proportionate: *Harrod and ors v Chief Constable of West Midlands Police* [2017] EWCA Civ 191 (a case that illustrates the importance of a well-crafted legitimate aim: once it was accepted that the legitimate aim was making as many officers redundant as possible, and there being only one way to make police officers redundant, it followed that all the redundancies were lawful. Had the legitimate aim been the less ambitious one of 'saving money' that would have opened up scope for argument as to the proportionality of the numbers of redundancies chosen). See also *Allen v GMB* [2008] IRLR 690. In that case the CA considered the situation of a union which had decided, in negotiating with an employer in relation to various pay issues, to adopt a policy whereby employees' interests in relation to future pay deals were prioritised over claims to back pay under the *Equal Pay Act 1970*. The result was that those employees who had equal pay claims (a predominantly female group) received less by way of settlement than they might otherwise have done. The Tribunal held that the union's objective (which it identified as being to achieve single status, avoiding privatisations, job losses, cuts in hours, and members receiving lower pay under the new system) was legitimate, but that the means used to achieve that aim amounted to 'manipulation' and were unjustified. One factor in the Tribunal's conclusion was that it was considered that the amount accepted by the Union in settlement of the equal pay claims was bordering on negligent. The EAT found that the Tribunal had taken the wrong approach to the question of objective justification. The EAT considered that, once it had been accepted that an aim was legitimate then if the means adopted to achieve that aim were the only means available then the policy would be justified. The CA disagreed and upheld the Tribunal's decision. The CA considered that the EAT had taken too narrow an approach to the concept of 'means'. The 'means' was not the balance struck by the union in the deal with the Council, but the methods used to persuade members to accept that deal. The Tribunal had been entitled to find that those methods had been manipulative and disproportionate to the legitimate aims pursued.

The fact that a discriminatory measure has been negotiated with the trade union or other workforce representatives will usually be a relevant factor in assessing whether or not the measure is justified. (This is consistent with the fact that achieving a stable workforce may be a legitimate aim, see *Rolls Royce Plc v Unite the Union* [2010] ICR 1, CA.) The fact that a rule has been agreed in the process of collective bargaining will not render an otherwise unlawful scheme lawful, but nonetheless weight will be given to the fact that the parties have agreed to a scheme that they (presumably) consider to be fair: *Loxley v BAE Land Systems* [2008] IRLR 853. See also *Rosenbladt v Oellerking Gebaudereinigungsgesellschaft mbH*: C-45/09 [2011] 1 CMLR 32, [2011] IRLR 51. Similarly, the fact that the terms in question have been agreed by the members of a partnership will be a relevant factor (*Seldon v Clarkson Wright & Jakes (No. 2)* [2014] ICR 1275. However, employers and tribunals cannot through negotiation and agreement with workforce representatives abdicate their responsibility to assess for themselves whether a measure is proportionate: see *Pulham and ors v London Borough of Barking & Dagenham* [2010] ICR 333. Further, it has been held that where the discriminatory measure is included in legislation, leaving the individual employer with a discretion whether or not to adopt it, courts and tribunals should apply a lower standard of scrutiny to reliance on the measure by the individual employer since the fact that the measure has been approved by Parliament is an important justifying factor: see *Chief Constable of West Midlands Police v Harrod* [2015] IRLR 790 (concerning the compulsory retirement of police officers using a discretionary provision in the *Police Pensions Regulations 1987*: upheld on appeal on slightly different grounds: [2017] EWCA Civ 191).

Treatment, provisions, criteria or practices based on length of service

Although generally speaking the same principles apply when considering justification of prima facie discriminatory measures regardless of the ground of discrimination relied on, it appears from the case law on equal pay that a slightly different approach is to be taken to cases involving disproportionate impact arising from the use of the criterion of length of service. There seems to be no reason why the same principles should not apply to indirect discrimination in relation to matters other than pay arising from the use of a length of service criterion. It will sometimes be the case that use of the criterion of length of service will have a disproportionate impact on women because women tend to have more career breaks or shorter working lives than men. (It is also likely to be indirectly discriminatory on the grounds of age.) However, the CJEU in *Danfoss* [1989] IRLR 532 held that, although the use of the criterion of length of service may involve some discrimination against women, the employer did not have to provide 'special justification' for that because, in essence, it could be assumed that length of service brings with it greater experience and improved job performance. In *Cadman v Health and Safety Executive*: C-17/05 [2006] ICR 1623 the CJEU retreated slightly from this, saying 'where recourse to the criterion of length of service . . . leads to disparities . . . between the men and women to be included in the comparison, (i) since, as a general rule, recourse to the criterion of length of service is appropriate to attain the legitimate objective of rewarding experience acquired which enables the worker to perform his duties better, the employer does not have to establish specifically that recourse to that criterion is appropriate to attain that objective as regards a particular job, unless the worker provides evidence capable of raising serious doubts in that regard; (ii) where a job classification system based on an evaluation of the work to be carried out is used in determining pay, there is no need to show that an individual worker has acquired experience during the relevant period which has enabled him to perform his duties better'.

The CA in *Wilson v Health and Safety Executive* [2009] EWCA Civ 1074, [2010] ICR 302 then clarified the approach that should be taken to domestic cases involving a length of service criterion in the light of the CJEU decision in *Cadman*. The CA ruled that, so far as domestic law is concerned, the "serious doubts" test put forward by the CJEU in *Cadman* is only of relevance before trial (presumably as a ground for 'strike out'). The CA said that what a claimant needs to show, pre-trial, is that there is evidence from which, if established at trial, it can properly be found that the general rule in *Danfoss* and *Cadman* (that seniority and length of service are generally material differences other than sex) does not apply. The CA confirmed, however, that a claim involving a length of service criterion is to be approached in essentially the same way as any other claim involving indirect discrimination. The burden is on the claimant to show disparate impact and, if that is established, the burden shifts to the employer to justify the difference as necessary. The CA noted (at [52]) that the Tribunal had allowed the employer a 'margin of appreciation' in relation to objective justification in this case. The CA indicated that there was no error of law in that approach.

Retirement and related provisions

Until 6 April 2011 there was a specific exception in *reg 30* of the *AR 2006* (preserved by the *EA 2010*) for retirement (see below **12.15** and also generally RETIREMENT **(42)**). Since 6 April 2011 the *Employment Equality (Repeal of Retirement Age Provisions) Regulations 2011 (SI 2011/1069)* have phased out the designated retirement age in reg 30 of the AR 2006 so that (at the latest from October 2012) there is no longer any automatically justified retirement age for employees and whether retirements and related provisions are justified falls to be considered in accordance with the standard principles for justifying indirect discrimination in relation to other protected characteristics (see above). There are, however, two important differences between the justification test as it applies to direct age discrimination and that which applies in relation to indirect discrimination. First, as set out above, direct age discrimination can only be justified if the aim of the measure in question relates to "employment policy, the labour market or vocational training" and not "purely individual reasons particular to the employer's situation, such as cost reduction or improving competitiveness": see *art 6(1)* of Directive 2000/78/EC and *Seldon v Clarkson, Wright & Jakes* [2012] UKSC 16, [2012] ICR 716. (In *Seldon* the Tribunal had not appreciated this distinction between direct age discrimination and indirect discrimination. Accordingly, the matter was remitted for the Tribunal to consider whether a compulsory retirement age of 65 for solicitors in a partnership was justified or not. On remission, the Tribunal concluded that 65 was justified as a retirement age and the EAT upheld that decision: [2014] ICR 1275.) Secondly, although normally it will suffice if the employer succeeds in showing that the provision, criterion or practice was a proportionate means of achieving a legitimate aim in general, it might be necessary in certain cases for the employer to demonstrate that the application of the provision, criterion or practice to the particular employee was justified in that particular case: see *Seldon*, ibid.

For further discussion of the case law on the justifications for retirements and related provisions see RETIREMENT **(42)**.

Other specific cases

For cases concerning justification of pay protection arrangements (i.e. arrangements made by an employer to protect employee's existing pay when introducing a new pay scheme, usually in response to a recognition that the previous pay scheme was, or might have been, discriminatory on grounds of age), see: *Specht v Land Berlin* (Joined Cases C-501, 506, 540 and 541/12), [2014] ICR 966 and *Schmitzer v Bundesministerin für Inneres* (Case C-530/13) [2015] IRLR 331. *Schmitzer* concerned the pay scheme for Austrian civil servants. Previously, the scheme had included an element whereby service prior to the age of 18 was disregarded, thus directly discriminating on grounds of age. A new system was introduced which allowed the full experience of workers, regardless of age, to be taken into account. However, those disadvantaged under the previous system continued to be disadvantaged under the new system. The CJEU accepted that on changing pay systems, pay protection arrangements intended to protect the rights of those acquired under the previous system pursued a legitimate aim. However, the CJEU emphasised that such arrangements would only be justified for a transitional period and that accordingly the Austrian arrangements (which perpetuated the previous discrimination indefinitely) were unlawful. In contrast, in

Specht, the CJEU accepted that a new pay scheme was justified even though it perpetuated indefinitely the effects of discrimination under the previous scheme. Specht concerned the pay scheme for German civil servants. Pay had previously been determined by reference to a scale that depended on the employee's age at the date of appointment and was thus directly discriminatory on grounds of age. A new system was introduced so that pay was determined by reference to experience. The German civil service considered that it was not practical retrospectively to assess where all existing civil servants ought to sit on the new payscale, so existing civil servants were simply moved to the point on the new payscale that corresponded to their existing salary, thus perpetuating the directly discriminatory pay arrangements. The CJEU held that this was justified, essentially because it accepted that it was genuinely not practical to do anything else given the nature of the assessment of experience required under the new system and the numbers of civil servants. See also *Naeem v Secretary of State for Justice* [2017] UKSC 27, [2017] 1 WLR 1343 in which the Supreme Court, while declining to interfere with the Employment Tribunal's decision that the particular transitional pay protection arrangements for prison service chaplains were justified, nonetheless observed (at paragraph 47) that where a case concerned the lawfulness of a transitional scheme, "the question was not whether the original pay scheme could be justified but whether the steps being taken to move towards the new system were proportionate. Where part of the aim is to move towards a system which will reduce or even eliminate the disadvantage suffered by a group sharing a protected characteristic, it is necessary to consider whether there were other ways of proceeding which would eliminate or reduce the disadvantage more quickly. Otherwise it cannot be said that the means used are "no more than necessary" to meet the employer's need for an orderly transition. . . . The burden of proof is on the respondent, although it is clearly incumbent upon the claimant to challenge the assertion that there was nothing else the employer could do. Where alternative means are suggested or are obvious, it is incumbent upon the tribunal to consider them." See further **22.12** Equal Pay for the case law on sex discrimination in similar circumstances.

For justification of differential treatment creating more favourable access to employment opportunities for UK students/employees than non-UK students/employees, see: *Daler-Rowney Ltd v Revenue and Customs Commissioners* [2015] ICR 632, concerning national minimum wage legislation.

For cases concerning justification of indirectly discriminatory requirements in relation to working practices in the armed forces, see *Macmillan v Ministry of Defence* (200322 May 2006, EATS/0003/04), EAT and *Boote v Ministry of Defence* (22 April 2004, unreported), IT(NI).

For justification of requirements or conditions that Sikhs who wear turbans should wear safety helmets on construction sites (a *prima facie* indirectly discriminatory provision) see below **12.12**.

For a consideration of the justification for a requirement to work on Sundays (which was indirectly discriminatory under the *RBR 2003*), cf *Williams-Drabble v Pathway Care Solutions Ltd* (ET, 10 January 2005, IDS Brief 776, p 8 and *Mba v Merton LBC* [2014] ICR 357). See, in like vein, *Cherfi v G4S Security Services Ltd* [2011] EqLR 825) (requirement to work on Friday lunchtimes justified despite disadvantage to Muslims wishing to attend Friday prayers).

12.9A LACK OF KNOWLEDGE OF DISABILITY

A special defence is available to claims of discrimination arising from a disability under *s 15* of the *EA 2010* and to claims of failure to comply with the duty to make reasonable adjustments under *s 20* of the *EA 2010* (see generally DISCRIMINATION AND EQUAL OPPORTUNITIES – I (11)). Although not explicit in the statute it appears that knowledge of disability is also a requisite element of a direct disability discrimination claim: see *Lewisham Borough Council v Malcolm* [2008] 1 AC 1399 and *Morgan v Armadillo Managed Services Ltd* (2014) UKEAT/0567/12, [2014] All ER (D) 113 (Aug), EAT. However since this is as a result of a necessary element of liability being the requirement for a causal relationship between the treatment and the employee's disability, rather than by way of a defence or exception, this is not dealt with further in this chapter, but only in Discrimination And Equal Opportunities – I (11).

Under the *EA 2010* there will be no unlawful discrimination arising from a disability if the employer shows that he did not know, and could not reasonably have been expected to know, that the employee had the disability (*s 15(2)*). There will be no duty to make reasonable adjustments if the employer: (a) did not know, and could not reasonably have been expected to know, that the employee had the disability; and (b) was likely to be placed at a disadvantage by the arrangements in question (*Sch 8, para 20(1)(b)*). In relation to claims made by applicants for employment (or partnership, or candidates for a contract position, etc), the defence also applies where the employer did not know and could not reasonably have been expected to know that an interested disabled person is or may be an applicant for the work in question.

A similar defence was available to a claim of a failure to make reasonable adjustments under the *DDA 1995, s 4A(3)* and it is likely that courts and tribunals will take the same approach to the defences available under the *EA 2010*. In *Eastern and Coastal Kent Primary Care Trust v Grey* [2009] IRLR 429, the EAT held that the defence under the *DDA 1995, s 4A(3)* applies where the employer:

(i)   does not know that the disabled person has a disability;

(ii)   does not know that the disabled person is likely to be at a substantial disadvantage compared with persons who are not disabled;

(iii)   could not reasonably be expected to know that the disabled person had a disability; and

(iv)   could not reasonably be expected to know that the disabled person is likely to be placed at a substantial disadvantage in comparison with persons who are not disabled.

In *Secretary of State for Work and Pensions v Alam* [2010] ICR 665 and *Wilcox v Birmingham Cab Services Ltd* [2011] EqLR 810 the EAT emphasised again that it is necessary (for the purposes of the defence to a claim of failure to make reasonable adjustments) for the employer to show both that it did not know (actually or constructively) that the employee was disabled and that it did not know (actually or constructively) that the employee was placed at the relevant disadvantage by the disability. The EAT in *Wilcox* further confirmed that there was no conflict in this respect between *Grey* and *Alam* as some commentators appeared to have thought.

It is important to remember, though, that the same is not true of the defence to a claim of discrimination arising from disability under *s 15(2)*. To succeed on that defence it is only necessary to show that the employer did not know (actually or constructively) that the employee was disabled. If the employer does have actual or constructive knowledge of the disability then it does not matter whether or not the employer is aware that its reason for treating the employee as it does is something that arises in consequence of the disability or not.

In considering whether an employer has the requisite knowledge of disability, the same principles should apply as to determining whether an employee is disabled, see **11.26** Discrimination and Equal Opportunities – I. Thus, for example, where there is an issue as to whether an employee's condition was likely at a particular juncture to last for more than

12 months, or likely to recur, that will be an issue to be judged by what was known to the employer at the time and not by reference to hindsight: see *McDougall v Richmond Adult Community College* [2008] EWCA Civ 4, [2008] ICR 431. Indeed, generally, it will be an error of law for a Tribunal to take into account when determining whether an employer had the requisite knowledge matters that the employer could not have known at the time: *Northumberland Tyne and Wear NHS Foundation Trust v Geoghegan* (14 December 2014, UKEAT/0048/13/BA).

It should be noted that employers are responsible for making their own judgment as to whether an employee is disabled or not and cannot necessarily rely on the opinion of a medical practitioner or the lack of formal confirmation by an employee. Where an employer has obtained advice from occupational health or a medical practitioner to the effect that an employee is not disabled, the Tribunal will need to consider whether it was reasonable for the employer to have relied on that advice or whether the Tribunal ought reasonably to have known that the employee was disabled, despite the advice to the contrary. *Gallop v Newport City Council* [2013] EWCA Civ 1583, [2014] IRLR 211 was a case in which the CA held that it was an error of law for the Tribunal to have held that an employer did not have the requisite knowledge of disability because it had relied on the unreasoned opinion of an occupational health adviser. The CA remitted the case to the Tribunal to consider again whether the employer had acted reasonably in relying on that advice. That is not to say, however, that an employer will not be able to rely on the opinion of a medical practitioner in order to make out a defence of lack of knowledge: indeed, the *Wilcox* case was one in which the EAT held that the Tribunal had been entitled to find that it was inappropriate to impute constructive knowledge to the employer prior to receipt of a formal medical report. In that case the employee suffered from an unusual mental impairment and the EAT held that it had been open to the Tribunal to conclude that the employer could not reasonably have known both of that impairment and that its effects would be substantial and long term (so as to bring it within the definition of disability in *s* 6 of the *EA 2010*) prior to receipt of medical evidence to that effect. See also *Peregrine (deceased) v Amazon.co.uk Ltd* (UKEAT/0075/13/SM) for a case in which medical professionals had not at the time appreciated that an employee's back pain was connected to his known disability (cancer) and the Tribunal found (and the EAT upheld) that in those circumstances the employer could not reasonably have known of the connection either.

Generally speaking, however, employers must be aware of the potential discriminatory impact of their decisions whenever less favourable treatment is meted out. As suggested by the EAT in *H J Heinz Co Ltd v Kenrick* [2000] IRLR 144 (in a passage cited with apparent approval by Baroness Hale in the non-dissenting part of her opinion in *Lewisham London Borough Council v Malcolm* [2008] UKHL 43, [2008] 1 AC 1399), an employer is required to pause before dismissing an employee or treating an employee in a less favourable way in order to consider whether the reason for the dismissal or treatment might relate to disability and, if it might, to reflect on the discrimination legislation and the EHRC *Code of Practice* before dismissing or treating the employee in that way.

12.10 POSITIVE DISCRIMINATION

Domestic law

Broadly speaking, positive discrimination was not permitted under the predecessor domestic equality legislation because discriminating in favour of one group of people generally involves unlawful discrimination against another group who are treated less favourably in comparison (*Lambeth London Borough Council v Commission for Racial Equality* [1990] ICR 768; though compare *Arnold v Barnfield College* [2004] All ER (D) 63 (Jul), EAT: mere existence of a policy of attracting more ethnic minority candidates not sufficient to indicate that there had been unlawful discrimination). Disability discrimination has always been an exception to this, discrimination against non-disabled persons, on grounds of disability, not being in and of itself unlawful. The *EA 2010* expressly provides that it is not an instance of unlawful discrimination for a disabled person to be treated more favourably than a non-disabled person is or would be treated: *EA 2010, s 13(3)*. Moreover, the duty to make reasonable adjustments (see DISCRIMINATION AND EQUAL OPPORTUNITIES – I (11)) can also be regarded as a form of positive discrimination.

Under the *EA 2010* there is now a generally applicable exception under *s 158* for 'positive action' and a specific exception under *s 159* for 'positive action' in relation to recruitment and promotion. The two exceptions are mutually exclusive (*s 158(4)(a)*), but they apply to any act done by anyone (ie by an employer or a trade union or an agency) that would otherwise be unlawful under the Act. The exception under *s 158* came into force on 1 October 2010 at the same time as the major part of the Act. The exception under *s 159* came into force on 6 April 2011 (*SI 2011/96, art 3*).

The general exception under *s 158* applies where a person reasonably thinks that: (a) persons who share a protected characteristic suffer a disadvantage connected to the characteristic; or (b) persons who share a protected characteristic have needs that are different from the needs of persons who do not share it; or (c) participation in an activity by persons who share a protected characteristic is disproportionately low (*s 158(1)*). In such circumstances the *EA 2010* does not prohibit a person from taking any action which is a proportionate means of achieving the aim of: (a) enabling or encouraging persons who share the protected characteristic to overcome or minimise that disadvantage; or (b) meeting those needs; or (c) enabling or encouraging persons who share the protected characteristic to participate in that activity (*s 158(2)*).

The specific exception for recruitment and promotion under *s 159* applies where a person reasonably thinks that: (a) persons who share a protected characteristic suffer a disadvantage connected to the characteristic; or (b) participation in an activity by persons who share a protected characteristic is disproportionately low (*s 159(1)*). In such circumstances the *EA 2010* will not prohibit a person from treating a particular candidate more favourably in connection with recruitment or promotion because they have a particular protected characteristic where that treatment is done with the aim of enabling or encouraging persons who share the protected characteristic to: (a) overcome or minimise that disadvantage; or (b) to participate in that activity (*s 159(2)*). However, the section only applies if 'all else is equal' (specifically if those who are being considered for recruitment or promotion are as qualified as each other) and if the employer does not have a general policy of preferring candidates of a particular protected characteristic for recruitment or promotion (*s 159(4)(a), (b)*). Further, in all cases the positive discrimination must be a proportionate means of achieving the statutory aims set out above (*s 159(4)(c)*).

In addition, there are exceptions under the *EA 2010* for those providing supported employment for the disabled (*s 133(3)*) and for those providing training to non-EEA nationals who will not remain in the UK on completion of training (*para 4, Sch 23*).

See also **12.37** below for discussion of the equality duties imposed on all public authorities which, while not specifically authorising positive discrimination, do authorise and oblige public authorities to take positive action to eliminate unlawful discrimination.

Under the predecessor legislation there were a number of more specific exceptions for positive discrimination as follows, only some of which have been retained in the *EA 2010*.

(a)   *Access to training*

There is no specific exception for access to training under the *EA 2010*.

Under the predecessor legislation employers could discriminate positively in favour of a particular racial group or in favour of female or male employees in order to afford that group access to training and to encourage the members of that group to take advantage of opportunities for doing particular work, provided that, at any time within the 12 months immediately preceding the positive discrimination:

(i)   there were no persons of that group among those doing that work at that establishment; or

(ii)   the proportion of persons of that group among those doing that work at that establishment is comparatively small (*RRA 1976, s 38(1), (2)*; *SDA 1975, s 48(1), (2)*).

The *RRA 1976* specifies that the proportion of persons of that group must be 'small in comparison to':

(i)   all those employed by the respondent at that establishment; or

(ii)   the population of the area from which that respondent normally recruits persons for work in his employment at that establishment.

Other persons concerned with the provision of vocational training could also discriminate in favour of racial groups, men or women (as appropriate) where it reasonably appeared to that person that there were no, or a comparatively small number, of members of that particular race, sex, etc doing that work in Great Britain (*RRA 1976, s 37; SDA 1975, s 47*). This particular exception specifically did not apply to discrimination by employers (*RRA 1976, s 37(3)* and *SDA 1975, s 47(4)*).

Similar provision was also made for positive discrimination in favour of persons of a particular religion or belief or sexual orientation where it reasonably appears to the person discriminating that it will prevent or compensate for disadvantages, linked to religion, belief, sexual orientation or age (or age group), respectively, suffered by persons of that religion or belief or sexual orientation or age (or age group) (as appropriate) (*RBR 2003, reg 25(1); SOR 2003, reg 26(1); AR 2006, reg 29(1)*). The ACAS Guidance on the *SOR 2003* and *RBR 2003* suggested that the exception would allow advertisements encouraging applications from people of a particular sexual orientation, religion or belief, provided it was made clear that selection would be on merit without reference to sexual orientation, religion or belief. The *Regulations* did not permit quota systems.

(b)   *Membership, etc of trade organisations*

There is no specific exception for membership, etc of trade organisations under the *EA 2010*.

Positive discrimination was permitted under the *SDA 1975* and the *RRA 1976* to encourage both membership of and post-holding in trade organisations (including discrimination in affording access to training for holding such posts) where, at any time during the previous 12 months, there were no or proportionally few postholders or members of the relevant racial group or sex in that organisation (*RRA 1976, s 38(3), (4), (5); SDA 1975, s 48(2), (3)*).

Similar provision was made by the *RBR 2003* and the *SOR 2003* to allow positive discrimination by trade organisations where it reasonably appeared to the organisation that the act prevents or compensates for disadvantages linked to religion, belief, sexual orientation or age suffered by those of that religion, belief, sexual orientation or age (or age group) who are members of the organisation, or are eligible to become members, or hold, or are likely to hold, posts within that organisation (*RBR 2003, reg 25(2); SOR 2003, reg 26(2); AR 2006, reg 29(2)*). The exception extended to "encouraging" only people of a particular sexual orientation, religion or belief to become members of the organisation where it reasonably appeared to the organisation that doing so would prevent or compensate for disadvantages suffered by people of that sexual orientation, religion or belief (*RBR 2003, reg 25(3); SOR 2003, reg 26(3); AR 2006, reg 29(3)*).

Under the *SDA 1975* (but not under the *RRA 1976, SOR 2003, RBR 2003* or *AR 2006*), trade organisations were also permitted to discriminate positively by setting quotas reserving a certain number of elected seats to men only or women only where in the opinion of the organisation the quotas were in the circumstances needed to secure a reasonable lower limit to the number of members of that sex serving on the body (*SDA 1975, s 49(1)*). However, discrimination in the arrangements for determining who is entitled to vote in an election of members of the body or in any arrangements concerning membership of the union or organisation itself is *not* permitted: *SDA 1975, s 49(2)*.

Note that although a set of barristers chambers was a 'trade organisation' within the meaning of the equivalent provisions of the *DDA 1995*, a pupil is not a 'member' of that organisation (*Higham v Meurig Lestyn Horton* [2004] EWCA Civ 941, [2005] ICR 292). (However, see **12.27** below for the general provisions relating to barristers.)

(c)   *Special treatment in connection with pregnancy or childbirth*

Special treatment afforded to women in connection with pregnancy or childbirth has always been permitted, and may not be taken account of when considering a claim of sex discrimination brought by a man: *SDA 1975, s 2(2)*. This rule is preserved under the *EA 2010* by *s 13(6)(b)* in relation to direct sex discrimination and by para 2 of Part 1 of Sch 7 insofar as the sex equality clause is concerned. However, in *Eversheds Legal Services Ltd v De Belin* [2011] IRLR 448, the EAT made clear that the exception is limited to such treatment as is necessary as a proportionate means of achieving the legitimate aim of compensating women for the disadvantages occasioned by their pregnancy or maternity leave. Thus, Eversheds had unlawfully discriminated against Mr De Belin when, in operating a redundancy selection procedure, they awarded his female colleague absent on maternity leave full marks for performance on the ground that she was not present at work to be assessed. The EAT held that Eversheds could have compensated the female colleague for the disadvantage she was under as a result of her maternity leave by assessing her performance during the period she was last at work. Since this would have been a fairer way of achieving the same aim, it followed that Eversheds had acted disproportionately and therefore unlawfully.

(d)   *Special treatment of Sikhs in relation to the wearing of helmets on construction sites*

See below **12.13**.

(e)   *Acts done to meet education, training or welfare needs of particular racial groups*

There is no specific exception in the *EA 2010* for such acts. However, the *RRA 1976* contained a further general exception for acts done for the purposes of protecting a particular racial group or groups. *Section 35* of the *RRA 1976* provided that nothing done by any body would be unlawful if it was done in order to afford persons of a particular racial group ('the protected group') access to facilities or services to meet the special needs of persons of that group in regard to their education, training or welfare, or any ancillary benefits. While this may appear to have been a broad provision permitting positive discrimination, it is unlikely that *s 35* would have rendered lawful an act of (negative) discrimination against a particular person or racial group unless that act was specifically done in order to provide services for the protected group. For example, it is unlikely that a trade organisation could have relied on this provision in order to justify having a membership consisting of only one racial group (or excluding a particular racial group) since a refusal of membership would not be directly related to the provision of services to the protected persons (though, where funds were limited, it ought to justify a refusal to provide legal services to members of the organisation if that was a 'special need' of the protected persons). This is particularly so given the specific express (and limited) provision as to positive discrimination by trade organisations (see above).

Positive action under EC law

Broadly speaking, the position in relation to positive action under EC law is, as one would expect, parallel to that under domestic law. However, the CJEU has held that *art 2(4)* of the version of *Council Directive 76/207/EEC* that was in force until 5 October 2005 (ie before the amendments made by *Council Directive 2002/73/EC*) permitted certain positively discriminatory measures. Measures permitted are those to the effect that where 'all else is equal' a female should be preferred for an appointment or promotion, provided that the measure is qualified by a requirement that consideration is given to the individual circumstances of each applicant: *Marschall v Land Nordrhein-Westfalen*: C-409/95 [2001] ICR 45, CJEU. However, where a national measure is not so qualified (*Kalanke v Freie Hansestadt Bremen*:C-450/93 [1996] ICR 314, CJEU), or that qualification is too vague to prevent appointments being made on the basis of sex alone (*Abrahamsson v Fogelqvist*:C-407/98 [2002] ICR 932, CJEU), the CJEU has held it to be incompatible with the *Directive* (cf also *EFTA Surveillance Authority v Norway*: E-1/02 [2003] IRLR 318, CJEU).

The wording of the old *art 2(4)* is wider than that of *art 2(8)*, which replaced it as from 5 October 2005 (compare 'measures to promote equal opportunity for men and women, in particular by removing existing inequalities' with the new version to be found in *art 2(8)* and *art 157(4)* of the Treaty: 'the principle of equal treatment shall not prevent any Member State from maintaining or adopting measures providing for specific advantages in order to make it easier for the under-represented sex to pursue a vocational activity or to prevent or compensate for disadvantages in professional careers'). However, it is likely that the type of positive discrimination permitted by *art 2(4)* will continue to be held by the CJEU to be permissible under the new wording of the *Treaty* and the *Directive*. Similarly, it is likely to be acceptable in relation to the other grounds of discrimination, as to which EC legislation currently provides that 'the principle of equal treatment shall not prevent any Member State from maintaining or adopting specific measures to prevent or compensate for disadvantages linked to' race, sexual orientation, etc (*Council Directive 2000/43/EC, art 5*; *Council Directive 2000/78/EC, art 7*). Further, with positive action now enshrined in *art 157(4)* of the *Treaty*, it is likely to be permissible for both private and public sector organisations positively to discriminate in this manner. Indeed, Parliament has assumed this to be the case by enacting *ss 158* and *159* of the *EA 2010*.

CHARITIES

12.10a *Section 193* of the *EA 2010* sets out a number of exceptions to the Act for charities. By *s 193(1)* and *(2)*, a person is deemed not to contravene the *Act* if he restricts the provision of benefits to persons who share a protected characteristic if he does so pursuant to a charitable instrument and the provision of the benefits is (a) a proportionate means of achieving a legitimate aim or (b) for the purpose of preventing or compensating for a disadvantage linked to the protected characteristic. However, save for the protected characteristic of disability, this exception does not apply where the benefit in question is vocational training: *s 193(9)* and *(10)*.

Further, there are special rules about charitable instruments that refer to the provision of benefits by reference to 'colour'. By *s 193(4)* if a charitable instrument enables the provision of benefits to persons of a class defined solely by reference to colour, then henceforth the instrument has effect as if that reference were deleted and the instrument applied to persons generally. Where a charitable instrument refers to characteristics other than colour, it has effect as if the reference to colour were ignored. Further, the Charities Commission (or other charity regulator) does not contravene the *Act* only by exercising a function in relation to a charity in a manner which the regulator thinks is expedient in the interests of the charity, having regard to the charitable instrument.

By *s 193(3)* it is not a contravention of the *EA 2010* for a person who provides supported employment to treat persons who have the same disability (or a disability of a prescribed description) more favourably than those who do not have that disability (or a disability of such a description).

By *s 193(5)* it is not a contravention of the *EA 2010* for a charity that as of 18 May 2005 required members, or persons wishing to become members, to make a statement which asserts or implies membership or acceptance of a religion or belief to continue to do so. For this purpose, restricting the access by members to a benefit, facility or service to those who make such a statement is to be treated as imposing such a requirement. No new charity can impose such a requirement, however. Nor can a charity that formerly had such a requirement, but ceased to impose it for any period.

By *s 193(7)* it is not a contravention of the *Act* for a service provider, in relation to an activity which is carried on for the purpose of promoting or supporting a charity, to restrict participation in the activity to persons of one sex.

12.11 EXCEPTIONS SPECIFIC TO THE DIFFERENT GROUNDS OF DISCRIMINATION

Exceptions for sex discrimination

(a) *Where communal accommodation is provided*

The *EA 2010* provides an exception for any act of sex discrimination or gender reassignment discrimination done in relation to the admission of persons to communal accommodation, or the provision of a benefit, facility or service linked to the accommodation (*para 3(1)* of *Sch 23*). 'Communal accommodation' is defined as 'residential accommodation which includes dormitories or other shared sleeping accommodation which for reasons of privacy should be used only by persons of the same sex (*para 3(5)*). It can also include residential accommodation all or part of which should be used only by persons of the same sex because of the nature of the sanitary facilities serving the accommodation (*para 3(6)(c)*). A benefit, facility or service is linked to communal accommodation if it cannot properly and effectively be provided except for those using the accommodation (*para 3(7)(a)*).

For the exception to apply, the accommodation must be managed in a way which is as fair as possible to both men and women (*para 3(2)* and *3(7)(b)*). In determining whether the exception applies, account must be taken of whether and how far it is reasonable to expect that the accommodation should be altered or extended or that further accommodation should be provided, and of the frequency of the demand or need for use of the accommodation by persons of one sex as compared with those of the other (*para 3(3)*). Where the discrimination is on grounds of gender reassignment, account must also be taken of whether and how far the conduct in question is a proportionate means of achieving a legitimate aim (*para 3(4)*).

The provision in the *EA 2010* is substantially the same as that which applied under *ss 46(3)–(5)* of the *SDA 1975*.

The exception means that if, for example, a company provided a holiday home for its employees but the sleeping arrangements were only suitable for men, then provided that it was only used occasionally and it was impractical to modify it for the use of the women or to build additional accommodation for them, such discrimination may be lawful.

Similarly, if a firm ran a residential training course in northern Scotland and accommodation could only be provided for men and it was fair so to do, failure to make the course available to women would not be unlawful discrimination because the benefit (the residential training course) is linked to the communal accommodation and cannot be properly and effectively provided without it.

Arrangements to compensate for detriment

It should be noted that sex discrimination is only permitted in the above circumstances where such arrangements as are reasonably practicable have been made to compensate for any detriment caused by the discrimination (*EA 2010*, *para 3(8)* of *Sch 23*; *SDA 1975*, *s 46(6))*. For example, training courses run by the ABC Company for a few days in the north of Scotland are not available to women employees because of the unsuitability of the accommodation: the company will *not* have a defence against a claim alleging discrimination unless it can show either that an alternative course had been provided or that, having been considered carefully, it was thought with good reason not to be practicable to provide it.

(b) *Pay and other contractual terms*

For all grounds of discrimination other than sex and maternity and pregnancy, differences in pay and other contractual terms fall to be considered under the general provisions on discrimination. Under the *SDA 1975, s 6(5)* and *(6)*, however, offering or paying a woman less remuneration than a man was not an act of unlawful discrimination. Instead, it was, if certain conditions were satisfied, unlawful under the *Equal Pay Act 1970* ('*EqPA 1970*'). Thus, if a woman was engaged on like work or on work rated as equivalent to that of a man or on work of equal value to that of a man, a woman's contract was modified by the *EqPA 1970* (through the mechanism of a statutory implied equality clause) so that she could claim pay and other benefits equal to that which the man received (see EQUAL PAY (22)). Less favourable treatment in relation to contractual terms was still an act of unlawful discrimination under the *SDA 1975* if the victim was a transsexual (*SDA 1975, s 6(8)*).

The same exclusionary rule applies under the *EA 2010* with one significant amendment. Differences in the contractual terms of men and women are covered by *ss 64–69* of the *EA 2010* (which effectively re-enact the provisions of the *EqPA 1970* by providing for a statutory implied sex equality clause in all contracts). Then, by virtue of *s 70* the 'ordinary' sex discrimination provisions are disapplied in circumstances where the claim relates to a term of the woman's contract that falls to be modified or included by virtue of the statutory sex equality clause, or would fall to be modified or excluded were it not for the fact that the employer is able to establish a defence of genuine material factor (see **22.10** EQUAL PAY), or because one of the various statutory exceptions in *Part 2* of *Sch 7* applies. They are also disapplied where the claim relates to contractual pay, but the statutory equality clause has no effect, unless – and this is the significant amendment on the position under the previous legislation - the difference in pay constitutes direct discrimination under *ss 13* or *14* of the *Act* (*s 71*). Complaints of direct discrimination in relation to contractual pay where there is no actual comparator and a hypothetical comparator only is relied on are thus dealt with under the 'ordinary' provision in relation to sex discrimination in *s 13* of the *Act*. All other complaints of sex discrimination in relation to contractual terms must be brought by reference to the sex equality clause in accordance with *ss 64–69* of the *Act*.

A similar exclusionary rule operates in respect of the new maternity equality clause created by the *EA 2010*: see *ss 72–76* of the *Act* and below **12.11A**.

(c) *Retirement, death and related benefits*

Sex discrimination in relation to death and retirement benefits was partially excluded from the scope of the *SDA 1975* by *s 6(4)*. Instead, such discrimination was dealt with primarily by the *Pensions Act 1995*. *Sections 62* and *64* of the *Pensions Act 1995* implied into the rules of every occupational pension scheme an 'equal treatment rule' which operated in the same way as the more familiar 'equality clause' in the *Equal Pay Act 1970* (cf **12.35** below **22.5** EQUAL PAY). The partial exclusion under *SDA 1975, s 6(4)* applied to discrimination taking the following forms:

(i)   Discrimination in the terms on which the woman is offered employment;

(ii)   Discrimination in the way the woman is afforded access to benefits etc.;

(iii) Discriminatory dismissals; and

(iv)   Discriminatory subjection to any other detriment.

Where a person discriminated against a woman in one of those respects in relation to her membership of, or rights under, an occupational pension scheme, that discrimination would not be unlawful where, if provision had been made for that discrimination in the terms of the scheme, that term would have been compliant with the equal treatment rule in the *Pensions Act 1995*.

Although the provisions of the *Pensions Act 1995* and the *SDA 1975* have been brought together in the *EA 2010*, there is still a similar division made between the general provisions prohibiting discrimination in relation to pensions and those prohibiting sex and maternity discrimination in relation to pensions. *Sections 61(1)* and *(3)* of the EA 2010 provide that 'an occupational pension scheme must be taken to include a non-discrimination rule' and that the scheme will take effect 'subject to' that rule (see generally **12.35** below). However, where the equality rules apply (or would apply but for the exceptions in *Part 2* of *Sch 7*), the non-discrimination rule does not: *s 61(10)*. Thus the general non-discrimination rule only applies to occupational pension schemes where the sex equality rule under *s 67* or the maternity equality rule under *s 75* does not.

By virtue of *para 5* of *Part 2* of *Sch 7* to the *EA 2010*, a difference between men and women in relation to the calculation of employer's pension contributions or determination of benefits payable under the scheme is permitted if the difference results from the application of actuarial factors which differ for men and women (for example because of different life expectancies for men and women).

There are further specific temporal exclusions from the scope of the sex equality rule as it applies to pensions. By *s 67(9)*, the sex equality rule, so far as relating to the terms on which persons become members of an occupational pension scheme, does not have effect in relation to pensionable service before 8 April 1976 and by *s 67(10)* the sex equality rule, so far as relating to the terms on which members of an occupational pension scheme are treated, does not have effect in relation to pensionable service before 17 May 1990. This reflects the decisions in *Barber v Guardian Royal Exchange Assurance Group*: C-262/88 [1990] ICR 616 and *Defrenne v Sabena*: C-43/75 [1976] ICR 547. A similar temporal limitation also applies to claims based on the *Part-time Workers Regulations* and governing Directive 98/23, which only enable equivalence to be claimed in respect of periods of service after those *Regulations* came into force on 7 April 2000: *Ministry of Justice v O'Brien* [2015] EWCA Civ 1000, [2016] ICR 182. See further **22.16** EQUAL PAY.

By *s 69(4)* it is a defence to a claim that an occupational pension scheme breaches a sex equality rule for the trustees or managers to show that the difference between the treatment of men and women under the scheme is because of a material factor that is not the difference of sex. This is the same as the defence that is available to equal pay claims generally and is dealt with in **22.11–22.12** EQUAL PAY.

Note that it is unlawful to apply different compulsory retirement ages to men and women.

A fuller account of the equal opportunities issues relating to death or retirement benefits is set out in **22.15** EQUAL PAY and see also RETIREMENT (**42**). See also further below **12.35**.

(d) *Members of the armed forces*

Broadly speaking, since 1 October 1997, the equality legislation has applied to service in the armed forces as it does to other employment: cf the *Sex Discrimination (Complaints to Employment Tribunals) (Armed Forces) Regulations 1997 (SI 1997/2163)*, the *Race Relations (Complaints to Employment Tribunals) (Armed Forces) Regulations 1997 (SI 1997/2161)*; *RBR 2003, reg 36*; *SOR 2003, reg 36*; and see below **12.36**.

Under the *EA 2010* there is a single exception for discrimination against women and transsexuals for service in the armed forces. The exception applies if it can be shown that the discrimination is a proportionate means of ensuring the combat effectiveness of the armed forces (*para 4, Sch 9*).

A similar exception for any act done 'for the purpose of ensuring the combat effectiveness of the armed forces' applied under the *SDA 1975, s 85(4)*. This was inserted into the *SDA 1975* by the *Sex Discrimination Act 1975 (Application to Armed Forces, etc) Regulations 1994 (SI 1994/3276)*. Its introduction raised a question as to whether the provisions of the *SDA 1975* complied with the *Equal Treatment Directive (Directive 76/207/EEC)*. The exemption was relied upon by the Army Board in *Sirdar v Army Board*: C-273/97 [2000] ICR 130. A woman who had applied to work as a chef in the Royal Marines was refused a transfer on the grounds that chefs were expected, where necessary, to be capable of fighting as a member of a commando unit. The complainant argued that *SDA 1975, s 85(4)* was contrary to the *Directive 76/207/EEC*. The matter was referred to the European court, which decided that whilst it was true that there was no Treaty right to derogate from equality legislation on grounds of national security, *art 2(2)* of the *ETD* nevertheless allowed the Army Board to refuse the complainant her transfer. *Article 2(2)* provides that *Directive 76/207/EEC* is 'without prejudice to the right of Member States to exclude from [the Directive's] field of application those occupational activities and, where appropriate, the training leading thereto, for which, by reason of their nature or the context in which they are carried out, the sex of the worker constitutes a determining factor'. In effect, the CJEU seems to have decided that being male is a genuine occupational requirement for a Royal Marine.

Prior to 1 October 2005, there was another exception available under the *SDA 1975* for sex discrimination in admission to the Army Cadet Force, Air Training Corps, Sea Cadet Corps, Combined Cadet Force, or any other cadet training corps for the time being administered by the Ministry of Defence was not unlawful (*SDA 1975, s 85(5)*). However, this was deleted by *reg 34* of the *Sex Discrimination Regulations 2005*.

(e) *Police officers*

Discrimination in height requirements and uniform or uniform allowances, which would otherwise constitute sex discrimination, was specifically provided to be lawful in the employment of police constables under the *SDA 1975, s 17(2), (3)*.

This exception is not included in the *EA 2010*. Such discrimination will only be lawful if it falls within the general exception for occupational requirements: see above **12.2**

See also **13.2** Discrimination and Equal Opportunities **III** for the exclusion from the jurisdiction of employment tribunals of claims against police disciplinary panels.

(f) *Prison officers*

Under the *SDA 1975* discrimination was lawful between male and female prison officers as to requirements relating to height (*SDA 1975, s 18(1)*). Men could be governors of women's prisons (*SDA 1975, s 18(2)*).

These exceptions are not included in the *EA 2010*. Such discrimination will only be lawful if it falls within the general exception for occupational requirements: see above **12.2**.

(g) *Ministers of religion*

Generally speaking, ministers of religion will be regarded as employees under employment legislation: see *Percy v Board of National Mission of the Church of Scotland* [2005] UKHL 73, [2006] ICR 134, although cf *New Testament Church of God v Stewart* [2007] EWCA Civ 1004, [2008] ICR 282 and *Moore v President of the Methodist Conference* [2013] UKSC 29, [2013] 2 WLR 1350. However, prior to 1 October 2005, there was an exception under the *SDA 1975* for employment for the purposes of an organised religion where a particular post-holder was required to be either male or female (or required not to be a transsexual) in order to comply with the doctrines of the religion or to avoid offending the religious susceptibilities of a significant number of its followers (*SDA 1975, s 19(1), (3), (4)*). That exemption was preserved, but with some changes, by *reg 20* of the *Sex Discrimination*

Regulations 2005 (which amended *SDA 1975, s 19* with effect from 1 October 2005). The amended version of *s 19* provided an exemption for employment for purposes of an organised religion where a requirement was applied that:

(a)   the employee be of a particular sex;

(b)   the employee not be undergoing or have undergone gender reassignment;

(c)   the employee not be married, or not be a civil partner;

(d)   the employee not have a living former spouse or civil partner (or that the employee's spouse or civil partner not have a living former spouse or civil partner); or

(e)   as to how the person, or the person's spouse or civil partner has at any time ceased to be married or ceased to be a civil partner.

The exemption only applied if the requirement in question was applied either so as to comply with the doctrines of the religion or because of the nature of the employment and context in which it is carried out, so as to avoid conflicting with the strongly-held religious convictions of a significant number of the religion's followers.

This exception is not included in the *EA 2010*. Such discrimination is only lawful if it falls within the general exception for occupational requirements: see above **12.2**, **12.3** and **12.7**.

(h) *Sports and competitions*

Section 44 excluded from the scope of the *SDA 1975* any act that related to participation as a competitor in a sport, game or other competitive activity, provided that the activity had been confined to competitors of one sex because the physical strength, stamina or physique of the average woman puts her at a disadvantage to the average man in carrying out that activity.

A similar exception applies under *s 195* of the *EA 2010*: see above **12.3**.

(i) *Pregnancy and maternity discrimination*

Discrimination against women for pregnancy or maternity-related reasons was for some time dealt with as a type of sex discrimination. Specific provisions dealing with maternity and pregnancy discrimination were then introduced from 1 October 2005 and this separate provision is continued in the *EA 2010* (see generally **11.30–11.32** Discrimination and Equal Opportunities - I). However, a formal separation of the two is achieved by *s 18(7)* which provides (in short) that where treatment would constitute pregnancy or maternity discrimination as defined in that section, then it cannot constitute direct sex discrimination under *s 13* of the *EA 2010*. Where pregnancy-related unfavourable treatment does not fall within pregnancy or maternity discrimination as defined in *s 18* however (eg because the treatment occurs outside what the *Act* terms the 'protected period' of ordinary or additional maternity leave) a claim may still be dealt with as a claim of sex discrimination: see eg *Mayr v Backerei und Konditorei Gerhard Flockner OHG*: C-506/06 [2008] IRLR 387.

(j) *Special treatment in connection with pregnancy or child birth*

Section 13(6)(b) of the *EA 2010* and *para 2* of *Part 1* of *Schedule 7* to the *EA 2010* exclude from the provisions prohibiting (respectively) direct sex discrimination and unequal pay for men and women special treatment afforded to women in connection with pregnancy or child birth. In other words, although such treatment could constitute direct discrimination against men, no complaint may be brought about it under the *Act*. See further above **12.10**(c).

12.11 Discrimination and Equal Opportunities – II

Exceptions for race discrimination

12.11a (a) *Pay*

Discrimination against women for pregnancy or maternity-related reasons was for some time dealt with as a type of sex discrimination. Specific provisions dealing with maternity and pregnancy discrimination were then introduced from 1 October 2005 and this separate provision is continued in the *EA 2010* (see generally **11.30–11.32 DISCRIMINATION AND EQUAL OPPORTUNITIES - I**). However, under the predecessor legislation discrimination in relation to pay on grounds of maternity or pregnancy was, as with sex discrimination in relation to all contractual terms, dealt with under the *EqPA 1970* by way of a statutory equality clause rather than under the *SDA 1975* (see generally **22.13 EQUAL PAY**). The same division is maintained in the *EA 2010*.

Whilst an employee is absent from work on maternity leave, an employer may lawfully cease paying her anything other than pay to which she is entitled by statute or contract as a result of being pregnant or on maternity leave: *EA 2010, Sch 9, Part 3, para 17*. However, a woman remains entitled to any bonus in respect of a period when she is on compulsory maternity leave *(para 17(2)(c))*. She also remains entitled to be paid in accordance with the statutory maternity equality clause in *ss 73* and *74* of the *EA 2010* and to be treated for the purposes of any occupational pension scheme in accordance with the statutory maternity equality rule in *s 75* of the *EA 2010* (see further below (b)).

The statutory maternity equality clause (broadly speaking) requires a woman who is paid during maternity leave by reference to her normal salary to receive any salary increases (proportionately adjusted) as she would have received if she were working, and likewise to be paid any bonus (proportionately adjusted where appropriate) (see **22.13 EQUAL PAY** for details of the effect of the maternity equality clause). By *s 76* it is then provided that where a term of a woman's employment relates to pay, no complaint of sex or pregnancy or maternity discrimination can be made in relation to it. Rather, the claim must be brought as an 'equal pay' claim based on the maternity equality clause under *ss 73* and *74*.

(b) *Occupational pensions*

As with terms of a woman's employment related to pay, the right to equal treatment in respect of occupational pension schemes was 'carved out' of the *SDA 1975* and dealt with separately under the *Pensions Act 1995* (see generally **22.18 EQUAL PAY** and **12.35** below). The same division is maintained in the *EA 2010*. Thus *EA 2010, s 75* creates a maternity equality rule that applies to all occupational pension schemes requiring them to treat time on maternity leave in the same way as time at work (save that any contributions may be reduced proportionate to any reduction in the pay that the woman receives during maternity leave). By *s 76* where a complaint concerns a matter that is covered by the maternity equality rule, no complaint of sex or pregnancy or maternity discrimination can be made in relation to it. Rather, the claim must be brought as an 'equal pay' claim based on the maternity equality rule under *s 75*.

12.12 Exceptions for race discrimination

(a) *Skills to be exercised outside Great Britain*

The predecessor legislation applied to training a person in skills intended to be exercised wholly outside Great Britain as it did to training for skills to be exercised in Great Britain, with one exception: discrimination on grounds of colour and nationality in the provision of such training fell outside the scope of the legislation: *RRA 1976, s 6*, as amended by the *Race Relations Act 1976 (Amendment) Regulations 2003 (SI 2003/1626))*.

This exception does not apply under the *EA 2010*. There is, however, an exception (in *para 4* of *Sch 23* to the *EA 2010*) for nationality discrimination in the provision of training to non-EEA residents where the trainer thinks that the non-resident does not intend to exercise in Great Britain skills obtained as a result.

(b) *Private household*

The predecessor legislation applied to employment for the purposes of a private household as it did to businesses, with one exception: discrimination on grounds of colour and nationality in relation to employment for the purposes of a private household was excluded from the scope of the *RRA 1976* by *s 4(3)*. The question was whether the employment is for the purposes of a private household 'to a substantial degree'. Thus, an applicant for a job as a chauffeur whose primary task was to drive a car for a company chairman could bring a complaint of racial discrimination (*Heron Corpn Ltd v Commis* [1980] ICR 713).

This exception is not available under the *EA 2010*.

(c) *Seamen recruited abroad*

Under the predecessor legislation, seamen (whether employees or contract workers) recruited abroad to work on any ship could lawfully be discriminated against on grounds of their nationality unless their work concerned exploration of the sea bed or subsoil (or the exploitation of their natural resources) on the continental shelf, save for those parts of the continental shelf to which the law of Northern Ireland applied (*RRA 1976, s 9(1), (3)*). If the ground for the discrimination is any of the other 'racial grounds' (for which see **11.20** DISCRIMINATION AND EQUAL OPPORTUNITIES – I) they could lawfully be discriminated against in relation to their pay but not otherwise. 'Pay' included retirement or death benefits (*RRA 1976, s 9(5)*, as amended by the *Race Relations Act 1976 (Amendment) Regulations 2003 (SI 2003/1626)*).

This exception is not available under the *EA 2010*.

(d) *Sports and competitions*

Discrimination on the basis of a person's nationality, place of birth, or length of time for which he had been resident in a particular area or place is not unlawful if it is done in selecting one or more persons to represent a country, place or area or related association, in a sport or game or other activity of a competitive nature, or if it consists of doing anything in pursuance of the rules of a competition so far as relating to eligibility to compete in a sport or game or other such activity: *EA 2010, s 195(5)* and *(6)*. A similar exception applied under the predecessor legislation: *RRA 1976, s 39*.

12.13 **Exception for protection of Sikhs from discrimination in connection with requirements as to wearing of safety helmets**

Properly speaking, this is not an exception, but a limitation on the availability of the defence of justification. Thus, where:

(a) any person applies to a Sikh any provision, criterion or practice relating to the wearing by him of a safety helmet while he is on a construction site; and

(b) at the time when he so applies the provision, criterion or practice that person has no reasonable grounds for believing that the Sikh would not wear a turban at all times when on such a site,

the provision, criterion or practice is taken to be one which cannot be shown to be a proportionate means of achieving a legitimate aim. It follows that the act of indirect discrimination will not be justified (see **12.9** above) (*reg 26(1)*).

Any special treatment afforded to a Sikh in consequence of *s 11(1)* or *11(2)* of the *Employment Act 1989* (exemption of Sikhs from requirements as to wearing of safety helmets on construction sites) is not to be regarded as giving rise, in relation to any other person, to any direct or indirect discrimination (*reg 26(2)*).

12.13 Discrimination and Equal Opportunities – II

For the purposes of *reg 26* 'construction site' means any place in Great Britain where any building operations or works of engineering construction are being undertaken, but does not include any site within the territorial sea adjacent to Great Britain unless there are being undertaken on that site such operations or works as are activities falling within *art 8(1)(a)* of the *Health and Safety at Work etc Act 1974 (Application outside Great Britain) Order 2001*. 'Safety helmet' means 'any form of protective headgear'. 'Sikh' means 'a follower of the Sikh religion' and any reference to a Sikh being on a construction site is a reference 'to his being there whether while at work or otherwise' (*reg 26(3)* and *(4)*).

Since the coming into force of the *EA 2010*, this exception is preserved by dint of amendments to *s 12* of the *Employment Act 1989* by virtue of which discrimination in relation to the wearing of safety helmets by Sikhs is deemed to be lawful for the purposes of the *EA 2010*: see *para 5* of *Sch 27* to the *EA 2010*.

12.14 Exception for sexual orientation discrimination: benefits dependent on marital or civil partnership status

Any benefit to which access is dependent on marital status was, prior to the coming into force of the *Marriage (Same-Sex Couples) Act 2013* on 13 March 2014, likely to be indirectly discriminatory against homosexuals as homosexuals were not permitted to marry under national law, but only to become civil partners under the *Civil Partnership Act 2004* (the *CPA 2004*). It was also likely to be direct discrimination: see *Hall v Bull* [2013] UKSC 73, [2013] 1 WLR 3741. Prior to 5 December 2005, however, *reg 25* of the *SOR 2003* provided expressly that nothing in the *SOR 2003* should make it unlawful for an employer to prevent or restrict access to a benefit by reference to marital status. It was argued in *R (Amicus-MSF) v Secretary of State for Trade and Industry* [2004] EWHC 860 (Admin), [2004] IRLR 430 that *reg 25* was incompatible with the governing European *Directive 2000/78/EC*). Richards J held that *reg 25* was compatible because it reflected the limitation in *Recital 2* of the *Directive* which says that 'this *Directive* is without prejudice to national laws on marital status and the benefits dependent thereon'.

The provision was then amended with effect from 5 December 2005 to reflect the coming into force of the *CPA 2004*. It provided for a complete exclusion from the SOR 2003 'for anything which prevents or restricts access to a benefit by reference to marital status where the right to the benefit accrued or the benefit is payable in respect of periods of service prior to the coming into force of the *Civil Partnership Act 2004*' (ie prior to 5 December 2005). Under the *EA 2010* the exception in *reg 25* of the *SOR 2003* (as amended) was preserved by *para 18* of *Sch 9* to the *EA 2010*. It was amended again by the *Marriage (Same-Sex Couples) Act 2013* so as to preserve the status quo regarding benefits notwithstanding the newly increased scope of marriage. Where the right to the benefit accrues, or the benefit is payable, after 5 December 2005, however, an employer is not permitted to make any distinction between married persons and civil partners, or between male-female married persons and same-sex married persons. *Section 23(3)* of the *EA 2010* further makes explicit that for the purposes of identifying a comparator under the Act there is to be taken to be no material difference between marriage and civil partnership. An employer may still, however, make a particular benefit available to, say, married persons and civil partners, but withhold the benefit from other employees, including those in long-term heterosexual or homosexual relationships: see *para 18(2)* of *Sch 9* to the *EA 2010*.

The decision of the CJEU in *Maruko v Versorgungsanstalt der deutschen Bühnen*: C-267/06 [2008] IRLR 450 the CJEU showed that the amendment to the *SOR 2003* effected on 5 December 2005 was in fact required under EC law in any event. (In *Maruko* the CJEU held that it was unlawful for Germany to withhold a widower's pension from the widower of a civil partner, where it would have been payable to a married partner.) The *Maruko* judgment, and the subsequent judgment in *Jurgen Röomer v Freie und Hansestadt Hamburg*: C-147/08 [2013] 2 CMLR 11, provided an indication, however, that under EU law it may not be permissible for UK legislation to limit the retrospective effect of the amendment made on 5 December 2005. In *Walker v Innospec Ltd* [2013] Pens LR 21 a Manchester Employment Tribunal determined that a provision of a pension scheme that prevented the civil partner of a member from being entitled to the same benefit as the married partner of a member on the member's death breached the non-discrimination rule, even though the benefit had accrued as a result of a period of pensionable service that was wholly prior both to the coming into force of the *CPA 2004* on 5 December 2005 and the coming into force of the *SOR 2003* in December 2003. On appeal, however, [2014] IRLR 334, the EAT reversed the Tribunal's decision on the basis that it had misunderstood the *Maruko* and *Römer* judgments, which the EAT held were not inconsistent with a long line of both domestic and European authorities that have held pension benefits to be deferred pay. Further, the EAT noted that it was a fundamental principle of domestic and European law that legislation should not have retrospective effect. Accordingly, *para 18* of *Sch 9* to the *EA 2010* was compatible with EU law and the employer had acted lawfully in refusing to treat the civil partner of a pension scheme member equally with a married partner in respect of a benefit that had accrued during a period of service prior to 5 December 2005, even though the benefit would only have been payable after that date. The EAT's decision was upheld by the CA: [2015] EWCA Civ 1000, [2016] ICR 182.

Employers should note that 'civil partnership' is defined in detail in the *CPA 2004*. It includes not only those couples who have registered their partnership in the UK since the coming into force of that *Act*, but also those couples who have registered their partnership overseas whether before or after the coming into force of the *CPA 2004*. A large number of partnerships registered overseas are automatically to be recognised as 'civil partnerships' under the *CPA 2004*. These are listed in Sch 20 to the Act. Other partnerships may be recognised if the conditions in *ss 212 to 218* of the *CPA 2004* (readers are referred to the text of the *Act*). Where a 'civil partnership' is recognised under the *CPA 2004*, it must also be recognised by employers for the purposes of *reg 25* of the *SOR 2003* and *para 18* of *Sch 9* to the *EA 2010*.

12.15 Exceptions for age discrimination

(a) Retirement

Prior to 6 April 2011 there was an exception for retirement in the *AR 2006* as set out below. Under the *EA 2010*, the exception for retirement dismissals was preserved until 6 April 2011 so that at or over the age of 65 if retirement was the reason for the dismissal the dismissal was not unlawful by virtue of *Part 10* of the *Employment Rights Act 1996* (*para 8, Part 2, Sch 9*). Further, it was not unlawful for an employer to discriminate against employees who were close to retirement in certain respects. In particular, under *para 9* of *Part 2* of *Sch 9* to *EA 2010*, it was not unlawful for an employer to refuse to offer employment to an employee who was, or would be before the end of six months beginning with the date on which the application for employment had to be made, aged over 65, or, where this is higher, the normal retirement age for the employment concerned. These exceptions no longer apply. Since 6 April 2011 the *Employment Equality (Repeal of Retirement Age Provisions) Regulations 2011 (SI 2011/1069)* have phased out the designated retirement age in *reg 30* of the *AR 2006* so that (at the latest from October 2012) these exceptions are no longer available and whether or not retirements and related provisions are justified falls to be considered in accordance with the standard principles for justifying direct age discrimination. See **12.9** above for discussion of justification of retirement and related provisions under the general discrimination principles. See **42.3** RETIREMENT for the current law on retirement.

Prior to 6 April 2011, *reg 30(2)* of *AR 2006* provided that nothing in *Parts 2* or *3* of *AR 2006* 'shall render unlawful the dismissal of a person to whom this regulation applies at or over the age of 65 where the reason for the dismissal is retirement'. This exception, often dubbed the 'National Default Retirement Age' or 'NDRA', only applied to the dismissal of employees in the narrower sense of those employed on a contract of employment. There was no maximum age exemption for enforced retirement in other cases. An important example is that of partners, office holders and workers who are not employees. In such cases, any enforced retirement is unlawful unless the action can be justified. This can be illustrated by two recent decisions. In *Seldon v Clarkson Wright & Jakes* [2012] UKSC 16, [2012] ICR 716, the claimant was an equity partner in a solicitors' firm. As he was not an employee, the respondent's only defence to a compulsory retirement age of 65 was objective justification. This defence succeeded before the Tribunal, but the EAT held that retirement at 65 was not justified by the assumption that performance would decline around that age – an older age could have been chosen. The CA upheld the EAT's decision, but observed that once it was accepted (as it was) that retirement had a legitimate aim, it was difficult to see how selection of the age of 65 was not justified, particularly as that was still at that stage the national default retirement age for employees. The SC, however, held that the Tribunal had taken the wrong approach to considering whether or not a retirement age of 65 was justified and accordingly remitted the matter. On remission, the Tribunal concluded that 65 was justified as a retirement age and the EAT upheld that decision: [2014] ICR 1275. See further above **11.9** for the approach to be taken to considering whether or not direct age discrimination (including the application of retirement ages) is justified. For further examples of when retirement ages may or may not be justified see **12.9** above.

Whether or not the reason for dismissal was retirement depended on the application of specific criteria set out in detailed provisions of *AR 2006*. See **42.3** Retirement.

'Heyday', part of Age Concern, brought judicial review proceedings challenging the legality of *AR 2006* on the ground that the blanket exception for retirement over 65 did not properly transpose the *Equality Directive*. The Administrative Court referred the matter to the CJEU for a preliminary ruling. The CJEU held that *reg 30* was not necessarily unlawful but that it would be for the national court to determine whether the blanket exception for those dismissed at or over the age of 65 was justified. On its return to the Administrative Court (*R (on the application of Age UK) v Secretary of State for Business, Innovation & Skills* [2010] ICR 260), Blake J held that the NDRA was based upon a social policy aim of certainty, clarity and maintaining confidence in the labour market and that it was proportionate for there to be such a blanket exception. The judge further held that the choice of age of 65 was within the margin of appreciation when it was adopted in 2006 but that the conclusion might have been different had there been no suggestion of an upcoming government review. Blake J also indicated that he did not presently see how 65 could remain as the appropriate age after that review.

See **42.3** Retirement for the current law on retirement.

(b) National minimum wage

The National Minimum Wage ('NMW') legislation allows for lower sums to be paid to younger workers. *Para 11* of *Part 2* of *Schedule 9* to the *EA 2010* (formerly *reg 31* of *AR 2006*) allows employers to retain different pay between the bands but only if the younger workers are being paid less than the adult NMW. Surprisingly, if the employer pays the younger workers more than the adult NMW, but less than older employees, this will require objective justification.

See also *para 12* of *Part 2* in relation to apprentices.

(c) Certain benefits based on length of service

Para 10 of *Part 2* of *Schedule 9* to the *EA 2010* provides an exception for benefits, facilities or services based on length of service. The exception applies where a person ('A'), in relation to the provision of a benefit, facility or service, puts a worker ('B') at a disadvantage when compared to another worker ('C') if and so far as the disadvantage is because B has a shorter period of service than C (*para 10(1)*). A similar exception applied under the predecessor legislation: see *reg 32* of the *AR 2006*.

Discrimination and Equal Opportunities – II   12.15

The exception is absolute where B's length of service does not exceed five years. Where B's length of service is longer than five years, it must reasonably appear to A that the way in which the criterion of length of service is used fulfils a business need. In the predecessor legislation examples of the types of business need that might be relied upon were given as encouraging loyalty or motivation, or rewarding experience (*reg 32(2), AR 2006*). No examples are given in the *EA 2010* but such business needs will continue to be acceptable in principle.

For the purposes of this exception, the period of service may be counted from the start of B's employment with A, or from his employment above a particular level (the level being assessed by reference to the demands made on B and set at that which A reasonably regards as appropriate for the purposes of this exception): *para 10(3)*. The period of employment in question is the person's period of continuous employment as deemed by *s 218* of the *ERA 1996* or any other enactment (*para 10(6)* and see CONTINUOUS EMPLOYMENT (7))

The period of service must be based on the number of weeks during the whole or part of which B has worked for A (*para 10(4)*), but for that purpose A may, so far as reasonable, discount periods of absence and 'periods that A reasonably regards as related to periods of absence' (*para 10(5)*). Note that in the predecessor legislation specific reference was made in connection with treatment of periods of absence to a requirement that, in deciding whether it is reasonable for an employer to treat a period of absence in a particular way, regard must be had to the way in which other workers' similar absences have been treated (*reg 32(4)(b), AR 2006*). Further, the reference to 'periods that A reasonably regards as related to periods of absence' was not included in the *AR 2006*, which instead included the more specific reference to 'any period during which the worker was present at work where that preceded a period of absence and, in all the circumstances including the length of the absence, the reason for the absence, its effect on the worker's ability to discharge his duties, and the way in which other workers are treated, it is reasonable for the period to be discounted' (*AR 2006, reg 32(4)(c)*). The provision in the *EA 2010* is evidently somewhat broader, not being limited to periods that precede periods of absence, but it is difficult to envisage the circumstances in which resort may be had to this part of the exception.

Note that the exception does not apply to benefits, facilities or services that are provided only as a result of a person ceasing to work, whether through ill health, redundancy, retirement or other termination: *para 10(7)*.

In *Rolls Royce Plc v Unite the Union* [2009] EWCA Civ 387, [2010] 1 WLR 318, the Court of Appeal held that use of a length of service criterion in assessing employees for redundancy was capable of constituting 'the award of any benefit' within the meaning of *reg 32(1)* of the *AR 2006*. A majority further held that whether or not the employer had reasonably concluded at the time that the use of the length of service criterion fulfilled a business need of its undertaking for the purposes of *reg 32(2)* was to be assessed objectively and it did not matter that the employer had subsequently decided that the use of the length of service criterion did not fulfil a business need of its undertaking.

(d) Enhanced redundancy benefits

Para 13 of *Part 2* of *Schedule 9* to *EA 2010* makes provision for employers to provide 'qualifying employees' with enhanced redundancy payments. Similar provision was made previously by *reg 33* of *AR 2006*

The exception allows employers to give enhanced redundancy payments only to those 'qualifying employees' who are entitled to a redundancy payment by virtue of *ERA 1996, s 135*, or who would be so entitled but does not have the two year qualifying period, or to an employee who agrees to the termination of his employment in circumstances where, had he been dismissed, he would have fallen into one of the former two categories (*para 13(3)*).

There are rules as to how the amounts must be calculated. The amount must be calculated as in the relevant provisions of the *ERA 1996* (*ss 162(1)–(3)*). However, in making the calculation, the employer may treat a week's pay as not being subject to a maximum amount, and/or multiply the appropriate amount allowed for each year of employment by a figure of more than one (*para 13(5)*). Having made the calculation, the employer may also increase the amount calculated by multiplying it by a figure of more than one (*para 13(6)*).

Where an enhanced redundancy scheme does not fall within this exception, it is potentially discriminatory and will fall to be justified in the usual way. For examples of this, see *MacCulloch* and *Loxley* above. See also *Lockwood v Department of Work and Pensions* [2013] EWCA Civ 1195, [2014] ICR 1257 in which redundancy payments under the Civil Service Compensation Scheme varying based on age depending on whether the individual was under or over the age of 35 were held to be justified in the light of statistical evidence produced by the employer as to the speed with which differing age groups could find alternative employment. Compare, however, *Heron v Sefton Metropolitan Borough Council* [2014] Eq LR 130 where the application by the local authority of the provisions of the Civil Service Compensation Scheme which provide for enhanced redundancy payments made to employees over normal pension age to be subject to a cap not applied to employees below normal pension age was held to be unjustified direct age discrimination and compare *Smith v Ministry of Justice* (UKEAT/0308/12/RN, UKEAT/0309/12/RN) (where the EAT held that it had been impermissible for the Tribunal to find that the provisions were justified solely by reference to the difference in ages of the employees and remitted that matter to the Tribunal for further consideration).

(e) Provision of life assurance cover to retired workers

Regulation 34 of *AR 2006* provided an exception for the provision of life assurance to retired workers. Where an employer arranged for workers to be provided with life assurance after their early retirement on grounds of ill health, it was not unlawful to arrange for such cover to cease when the workers reached a normal retirement age, if one existed, or age 65, where there was no retirement age (*reg 34(1)*).

'Normal retirement age' meant the age at which workers in the undertaking who held the same kind of position as the worker held at the time of his retirement were normally required to retire (*reg 34(2)*).

Similar provision was made in *para 14* of *Part 2* of *Schedule 9* of *EA 2010*. However, this was repealed by the *Employment Equality (Repeal of Retirement Age Provisions) Regulations 2011 (SI 2011/1069), reg 2(3)* with effect from 6 April 2011.

(f) Child care

Paragraph 15 of *Part 2* of *Schedule 9* to *EA 2010* provides that it is not unlawful age discrimination in a number of respects for a person to make arrangements for or to facilitate the provision of care for children of a particular age group. (Otherwise, this might give rise to a claim for "associative discrimination", ie where a person is discriminated against because of someone else's age: see DISCRIMINATION AND EQUAL OPPORTUNITIES – I at **11.25**.) Facilitating the provision of care for a child includes paying for some or all of the cost of the provision, helping a parent to find a suitable person to provide care for the child, and enabling a parent to spend more time providing care or otherwise assisting the parent with respect to the care that they provide (*para 15(3)*). A 'child' is defined to be a person who has not attained the age of 17 (*para 15(3)*) and care includes supervision (*para 15(4)*).

There was no similar provision in *AR 2006*.

(g) Occupational pension schemes

The *AR 2006* provided a number of exceptions for age discrimination in relation to occupational pension schemes (in *Sch 2*). The *EA 2010* does not itself contain any exceptions, but provides for exceptions to be set out in subordinate legislation. A Minister of the Crown may by order (following consultation) provide that it is not an age contravention for an employer or for the trustees and managers of an occupational pension scheme to use certain specified practices in relation to contributions to personal pension schemes (*para 16* of *Part 2* of *Schedule 9* to *EA 2010* and *s 61(8)*).

The *Equality Act (Age Exceptions for Pension Schemes) 2010 Order (SI 2010/2133)* (as amended) made under that enabling power makes extensive and detailed provision for exceptions from the *EA 2010* for certain practices in relation to pension schemes. See below **12.35**.

(h) Sport and other competitive activities

Section 195(7) of the *EA 2010* provides an exception from the age discrimination provisions for participation in a competitive 'age-banded activity'. An 'age-banded activity' is a 'sport, game or other activity of a competitive nature in circumstances in which the physical or mental strength, agility, stamina, physique, mobility, maturity or manual dexterity of average persons of a particular age group would put them at a disadvantage compared to average persons of another age group as competitors in events involving the activity' (*s 195(8)*). Discrimination in relation to such activities is permitted where it is 'necessary to secure in relation to the activity fair competition or the safety of competitors', or 'to comply with the rules of a national or international competition' or 'to increase participation in that activity' (*s 195(7)*).

(i) Armed forces

Like the *AR 2006*, the *EA 2010* does not apply to service in the armed forces: *para 4* of *Part 1* of *Sch 9*. In *Child Soldiers International v Secretary of State for Defence* [2015] EWHC 2183 (Admin), [2016] 1 CMLR 20, the High Court determined that this exception was lawful and compatible with the governing Directive 2000/78. The context was a judicial review concerning the army's practice of requiring those recruited on their 16th birthday to serve six years before transfer to the reserves, while those recruited at 18 need only serve four years.

12.16   Exceptions for disability discrimination

(a) Armed forces

Paragraph 4(3) of *Schedule 9* to *EA 2010* provides an exemption from the prohibition on disability discrimination in respect of "service in the armed forces". The similar exemption for age discrimination in the armed forces was held by the High *Child Soldiers International v Secretary of State for Defence* [2015] EWHC 2183 (Admin), [2016] 1 CMLR 20 to be lawful and compatible with the governing *Directive 2000/78*. It is likely that the same result would be reached if the disability discrimination exemption were to be considered.

A similar exemption applied under the predecessor legislation for those serving in the naval, military or air forces of the Crown (*DDA 1995 s 64(7)*).

(b) Exemption for small businesses

At one time small businesses were exempt from the *DDA 1995*. That exemption was repealed with effect from 1 October 2004 by *reg 6* of the *DDA 1995 (Amendment Regulations) 2004*.

(c) Charities

Any act done by a charity pursuant to any charitable purpose connected with categories of persons determined by reference to any physical or mental capacity was not unlawful under the employment provisions of the *DDA 1995* (*DDA 1995, s 18C*). This exception is not re-enacted in the *EA 2010*. See **12.10**A above for the provisions on charities in the *EA 2010*.

(d) Statutory office holders, police and prison officers, members of fire brigades

Whereas these and other categories of worker were excluded from the employment provisions of the *DDA 1995* prior to 1 October 2004, since that date there has been no such exception, save in relation to the armed forces (see above). See also now **12.25** below for office holders generally and **12.26** below for police officers.

12.17 GENERAL EXCEPTIONS TO THE EQUALITY LEGISLATION

A number of other exceptions or defences are available to claims of both direct and indirect discrimination. As a matter of principle, these exceptions ought to be narrowly or strictly construed: *Lambeth London Borough Council v Commission for Racial Equality* [1989] IRLR 379; upheld on appeal ([1990] ICR 768) (although the principle of construction was not referred to in the judgments of the Court of Appeal).

12.18 Employment out of the territorial jurisdiction

In the *EA 2010* there are specific provisions applying the *Act* to employment on ships, hovercraft and other offshore work: see *ss 81–83*, the *Equality Act 2010 (Work on Ships and Hovercraft) Regulations 2011 (SI 2011/1771)* and *Hasan v Shell International Shipping Services (PTE) Ltd* (14 January 2014, UKEAT/0242/13/SM). However, otherwise the *EA 2010* does not include any specific provisions as to its territorial extent. It follows that whether or not a particular employment or act of discrimination falls under the jurisdiction of the *EA 2010* has to be determined according to generally applicable principles on the conflict of laws: see generally Foreign Employees, **26.9**. The Court of Appeal accepted in *R (Hottak and anor) v Secretary of State for Foreign and Commonwealth Affairs and anor* [2016] EWCA Civ 438, [2016] 1 WLR 3791 that courts and tribunals should apply the principles that have been developed in relation to claims of unfair dismissal brought under the *Employment Rights Act 1996* ('*ERA 1996*') as that statute too contains no specific provision about territorial extent. The CA rejected the employee's argument that the *EA 2010* should be given a wider territorial scope than the *ERA 1996* (thus disapproving the suggestion of the Div Crt in that case ([2015] EWHC 1953, [2015] IRLR 827 and the EAT in *Olsen v Gearbulk Services Ltd* [2015] IRLR 818). In *Hottak* the CA concluded that local interpreters employed by British Forces in Afghanistan did not have a sufficient connection with the UK to bring their discrimination claims under the EA 2010. See also *Smania v Standard Chartered Bank* [2015] IRLR 271 for a case in which the EAT considered, but rejected, an argument that the territorial extent of the public interest disclosure provisions of the *ERA 1996* should be given a wider scope than that of the unfair dismissal provisions.

The case law as it has developed in relation to claims under the *ERA 1996*, and now also the *EA 2010*, may be summarised as follows. The House of Lords in *Lawson v Serco Ltd* [2006] IRLR 289 held that an employment tribunal would have jurisdiction to consider a claim of unfair dismissal by an employee if he was 'employed in Great Britain'. Lord Hoffmann identified three potential categories of employee who would be regarded as 'employed in Great Britain' (ibid at paras 25-40):

The 'standard' case: an employee 'working in Great Britain' at the time of his dismissal (otherwise than on a casual visit);

The 'peripatetic' employee (such as an airline pilot): an employee based in Great Britain at the time of his dismissal;

The 'expatriate' case (ie an employee living, working and based abroad): normally such employment would be outside the territorial jurisdiction of the UK, unless the employee had 'strong connections' with Great Britain and British employment law.

Lord Hoffmann gave two examples of expatriate employees who would fall within the territorial jurisdiction of the *ERA 1996*: those posted abroad by a British employer for the purposes of a business carried on in Great Britain (such as a foreign correspondent on the staff of a British newspaper) and those expatriate employees of a British employer operating within what is in practice a British enclave in a foreign country (such as a British military base).

In *Ravat v Halliburton Manufacturing & Services Ltd* [2012] ICR 389, the Supreme Court emphasised that Lord Hoffmann's three categories are merely examples of the application of the general principle that, in order for the Tribunal to have jurisdiction, the employee's employment must have much stronger connections with both Great Britain and with British employment law than with any other system of law. Their Lordships held that although the three categories were helpful, it was important to remember that there was no requirement of 'exceptionality' for expatriate employees. If they had strong connections with Great Britain and British employment law, then the Tribunal would have jurisdiction. Moreover, the EAT has now confirmed that whether or not there is a sufficiently close connection is a question of fact for the Tribunal, susceptible to review on appeal only if the Tribunal has erred in law: *Olsen v Gearbulk Services Ltd* [2015] IRLR 818.

Ravat concerned an employee who lived in Preston, Lancashire, but who was employed by a British subsidiary of an American multinational corporation to provide services to that corporation's German company and as a result spent half his time living and working in Libya and half of it living and working in the UK. The employment tribunal held that the claimant had a sufficiently strong connection with the UK to fall within the jurisdiction of the *ERA 1996*. The Scottish EAT reversed that decision, but the Court of Session restored the decision of the Tribunal and the Supreme Court upheld the Court of Session's decision. Their Lordships considered it to be important that the employer's business was in truth based in Great Britain, and that the employee had been treated as a 'commuter', being given assurances that his posting to Libya would not affect the benefits to which he would have been entitled as a UK-based employee and that the law of his contract would remain that of Britain. In practice his employment had continued to be managed from the employer's human resources department in Aberdeen, and the employee had maintained his home in Great Britain. See also *Ministry of Defence v Wallis* [2010] IRLR 1035 and *Powell v OMV Exploration & Production Ltd* [2014] IRLR 80.

In *Bates van Winkelhof v Clyde & Co LLP* [2012] EWCA Civ 1207, [2013] ICR 183 (reversed on other grounds: [2014] UKSC 32, [2014] 1 WLR 2047) the Court of Appeal had to consider whether or not UK employment tribunals had jurisdiction over discrimination claims brought by a solicitor who was a member of a UK LLP, but seconded to, and employed under, a contract with, a Tanzanian law firm. The employer argued that the Supreme Court in *Ravat* had held that in such cases it was necessary for a comparative exercise to be carried out by the Tribunal in order to ascertain whether the employee's connections with Great Britain were stronger than those with the territory in which he or she works. The Court of Appeal in *Bates*, however, clarified that such a comparative exercise is not required unless the employee is employed wholly abroad. In this case, where the claimant worked for at least part of her time in Great Britain, the only question was whether the connection with Great Britain was (to use Lord Hope's words in *Ravat*) "sufficiently strong to enable it to be said that Parliament would have regarded it as appropriate for the tribunal to deal with the claim".

In *R (Hottak and anor) v Secretary of State for Foreign and Commonwealth Affairs and anor* [2015] EWHC 1953 (Admin) the Divisional Court held that Afghan interpreters employed by HM Government in the service of the armed forces in Afghanistan but on contracts subject to local law and local terms and conditions did not have a sufficient connection with the UK to enable them to bring claims under the *EA 2010*. They had no physical contact or connection with the UK but were local staff, locally engaged. Their only connection with the UK was the identity of their employer. They had a much stronger connection with Afghanistan.

The approach to be applied where the employee is not working at the date of dismissal was considered in *YKK Europe Ltd v Heneghan* [2010] ICR 611. The EAT held that in these cases a broader factual inquiry will be required. The Tribunal will need to consider (among other things):— why the employee was absent from work, the length of his absence before dismissal, where he was working or based (and for how long) before his absence from work began, where the employee would have been working at the time of dismissal if he had not been absent from work, whether there was an active employment relationship between the date of his absence from work and the date of dismissal, from where the contract was being operated at dismissal, and whether the tribunal would have had territorial jurisdiction as at the date on which the claimant became absent from work. No factor is determinative and the weight to be given to the factors is for the tribunal. The EAT remitted the matter to the Tribunal to determine the question of jurisdiction.

The EAT in *Pervez v Macquarie Bank Ltd* [2011] ICR 266 has confirmed that the principles discussed above are not 'cut down' in any way by *reg 19(1)* of the *Employment Tribunals (Constitution and Rules of Procedure) Regulations 2004* ("*the 2004 Regulations*"), which provides that an employment tribunal in England or Wales 'shall only have jurisdiction to deal with proceedings . . . where . . . one of the respondents resides or carries on business in England and Wales'. The EAT held that a respondent should be regarded as carrying on a business in England or Wales if it has (for eg) a peripatetic employee who is based here.

The above contrasts with the situation under the predecessor legislation, where specific provision was made as to the territorial extent of the Acts and Regulations. Broadly speaking, the predecessor equality legislation applied where a complainant did his work wholly or partly in Great Britain and did not apply where the complainant worked wholly outside Great Britain (*RRA 1976, ss 4, 8(1), (1A); SDA 1975, ss 6(1), 10(1)*, both as amended; *RBR 2003, reg 9(1); SOR 2003, reg 9(1); AR 2006, reg 10(10)*. The question was whether, viewing the complainant's employment as a whole, he did his work wholly outside Great Britain (*Saggar v Ministry of Defence* [2005] EWCA Civ 413, [2005] ICR 1073). See also *Tradition Securities and Futures SA v X and Y* [2009] ICR 88, *Deria v General Council of British Shipping* [1986] ICR 172, *British Airways plc v Mak* [2011] EWCA Civ 184, [2011] All ER (D) 256 (Feb) for cases on the old provisions.

There are also specific provisions relating to employment on ships and hovercraft and to employment concerned with exploration or exploitation of the sea bed or subsoil, employment on the Frigg gas field and other parts of the Continental Shelf: see the *Equality Act 2010 (Work on Ships and Hovercraft) Regulations 2011 (SI 2011/1771)* and the *Equality Act 2010 (Offshore Work) Order 2010 (SI 2010/1835)* made under, respectively, *ss 81* and *82* of the *EA 2010*.

See also **11.42** Discrimination and Equal Opportunities – I.

12.19 Employment under an illegal contract

The test for excluding a tribunal's jurisdiction on grounds of illegality in relation to discrimination claims is not as strict as that used in cases of breach of contract. In breach of contract cases, a court or tribunal will not enforce a claim where the employment is pursuant to an illegal contract, or if there was an intention at the time of the formation of the contract to perform it illegally, or if the complainant has to rely on his or her illegal conduct in order to found his claim (*Colen v Cebrian (UK) Ltd* [2003] EWCA Civ 1676, [2004] ICR 568; though note that the court may in certain circumstances be prepared to 'sever' the legal and illegal parts of a contract: *Blue Chip Trading Ltd v Helbawi* [2009] IRLR 128 and see generally **8.24** CONTRACT OF EMPLOYMENT). By contrast, in discrimination cases, the fact that a contract is illegal or tainted by illegality will not exclude the tribunal's jurisdiction, unless the complainant's claim is so closely connected or inextricably bound up or linked with the complainant's illegal conduct that to allow the complainant to recover compensation would be to appear to condone that conduct (*Hall v Woolston Hall Leisure Ltd* [2001] ICR 99, CA, approving *Leighton v Michael* [1995] ICR 1091, EAT). In *Hall v Woolston Hall Leisure*, the CA held that where the complaint is concerned with a dismissal only, the fact of dismissal may not be sufficiently closely connected with the illegality as to preclude a claim. However, a claim in respect of discrimination relating to access to opportunities for promotion, transfer or training or any other benefits, facilities or services may be precluded: see *Governing Body of Addey and Stanhope School v Vakante* [2003] ICR 290, EAT, Further, the tribunal at the remitted hearing in that case decided that the dismissal as well as the manner in which the employer gave the employee access to training and other benefits were so inextricably linked with the employee's illegal conduct – obtaining employment in breach of immigration rules – that both claims were precluded. This decision was upheld on appeal: see [2004] EWCA Civ 1065, [2005] ICR 231. *Hounga v Allen and anor (Anti-Slavery International intervening)* [2014] UKSC 47, [2014] 1 WLR 2889 was a case that concerned Ms Houng, a 14-year-old from Nigeria, who the Allen family had offered to employ as a home help in return for schooling and £50 per month. They helped her obtain false identity documents with which she entered the UK and secured a six-month visitors' visa. Ms Hounga was then kept in the Allen's house, required to do the housework and look after the children, not paid, not enrolled in school and threatened with imprisonment should she try to leave. After 18 months, she had displeased Mrs Allen, who threw her out on the street. She brought a claim that her dismissal was discriminatory. The Tribunal upheld her complaint, and so did the EAT, but a unanimous CA ([2012] EWCA Civ 609) held that the illegality of her conduct in working illegally was inextricably linked with her claim such that her claim was precluded as a matter of public policy. The SC reversed that decision, holding that Ms Hounga's illegal conduct merely provided the context for the claim and was not so inextricably linked with it as to bar the claim on public policy grounds. A majority (Lord Wilson JSC, Baroness Hale DPSC and Lord Kerr JSC) went further and held that, in the alternative, the 'inextricable link' test was not applicable because the public policy reasons for barring claims where the court might otherwise appear to be condoning illegality was trumped by the more significant public policy concern to stop human trafficking.

The burden of proof is on the party alleging illegality (*Colen v Cebrian (UK) Ltd*, above).

The Court of Appeal in *Woolston Hall Leisure* left undecided a question whether the limited grounds for derogation from the right not to suffer less favourable treatment conferred by *Directive 76/207/EEC* meant that illegality could not be used as a ground for refusing an employee a remedy. The point was also raised in *Vakante v Governing Body of Addey and Stanhope School (No 2)* [2004] ICR 279, EAT (in relation to the equivalent provision of the *Race Directive 2000/43/EC*). However, the Court of Appeal held that, since *Directive 2000/43* only came into force after the claimant's cause of action arose and, since it was clearly not intended to have retrospective effect, it could not assist the claimant ([2004] EWCA Civ 1065, [2005] ICR 231). This point was not revisited in *Allen v Hounga* (ibid).

12.20 Benefits provided to the public

The provisions relating to discrimination with regard to access to benefits of any description (including facilities and services) do not apply if the respondent is concerned with the provision (for payment or not) of benefits of that description to the public, or to a section of the public comprising the complainant in question, unless:

(i)   that provision differs in a material respect from the provision of the benefits to his employees (or non-employees covered by the employment rules: see below **12.24** ff); or

(ii)   the provision of the benefits to the complainant in question is regulated by his contract of employment (or equivalent for non-employees covered by the employment rules); or

(iii) the benefits relate to training.

Para 19 of *Sch 9* to the *EA 2010.*

The same exception applied under the predecessor legislation: see *RRA 1976, s 4(2)(b)* and *4(4); SDA 1975, s 6(2)(a)* and *6(7); RBR 2003, reg 6(2)(b)* and *6(4); SOR 2003, reg 6(2)(b)* and *6(4); AR 2006 7(6); DDA 1995, s 4(4).*

Thus, for example, a bank which provides loans to members of the public and to most employees on the same terms may not be taken to an employment tribunal by an employee who is denied a loan on grounds of race, sex, religion or belief, gender reassignment, disability, age or sexual orientation if the employee is not entitled to the loan under his contract of employment. However, it will be liable to an action by that employee in the county court under the provisions relating to discrimination in the provision of goods, facilities or services: *Part 3* of the *EA 2010.*

12.21 Discrimination in compliance with the law

Under *Sch 22, para 1* to the *EA 2010* it is a defence to a claim of discrimination on grounds of age, disability, religion or belief that the act complained of was carried out in order to comply with a statutory requirement or (in the case of disability, religion or belief) in order to comply with a requirement or condition imposed by virtue of an enactment. A statutory requirement includes a reference to a Measure of the General Synod of the Church of England as well as an enactment passed or made on or after the date on which *EA 2010* was passed: *Sch 22, para 1(3).* Note that the defence will only succeed where the enactment actually requires the discrimination. The application by an employer of discriminatory provisions of an enactment (such as the provisions of the Civil Service Pension Scheme) will not be lawful if in fact the employer had the power or discretion not to apply the provisions in question: see *Heron v Sefton Metropolitan Borough Council* [2014] Eq LR 130 and the decision of the ET concerning judicial pensions in *McCloud and ors v The Lord Chancellor and ors* (5 April 2016, Case No. 2201483/2015). For this reason the *obiter* suggestion in *Harrod and ors v Chief Constable of West Midlands Police and ors* [2017] EWCA Civ 191 that the exception in *Sch 22, para 1* could have been relied upon by the Chief Constable in that case in relation to the decision to use *reg A19* of the *Police Pensions Regulations 1987* to retire all officers with over 30 years' service is probably incorrect: certainly it could not have been relied on to legitimise the decision to retire all such officers, even if it might have provided a partial defence since under the Police Pensions Regulations it is not possible to retire officers unless they have completed 30 years' service.

The defence is only available to claims of age, disability and religion or belief discrimination. Similar provision was made in respect of age and disability (but not religion or belief discrimination) under the predecessor legislation: *AR 2006, reg 27; DDA 1995, s 59.* No such defence is available in *EA 2010* to claims of discrimination on grounds of race, sex or sexual orientation in the employment sphere, although this was not the case under the predecessor legislation (see below).

There is, however, a general exception in the *EA 2010* for discrimination on grounds of nationality and/or indirect discrimination on the basis of a person's place of ordinary residence or the length of time a person has been present or resident in the UK or an area within it that is authorised by another enactment or statutory instrument: see *para 1* of *Sch 23* to the *EA 2010.*

Racial discrimination

Prior to the amendments introduced with effect from 19 July 2003 by the *Race Relations Amendment Regulations*, there was a general defence available where the relevant act of discrimination was carried out pursuant to any enactment, Order in Council or statutory instrument, or in order to comply with a ministerial condition or requirement imposed pursuant to statute (*RRA 1976, s 41(1)*).

The scope of that provision was considered by the House of Lords in *Hampson v Department of Education and Science* [1990] ICR 511. Their Lordships held that the application of the defence was restricted to acts done in the necessary performance of an express obligation contained in an instrument, and did not extend to discretionary acts carried out by the Secretary of State, even in circumstances where he had a positive public duty to exercise his discretion. (See also *Dhatt v McDonalds Hamburgers Ltd* [1991] ICR 238.)

From 19 July 2003, the position was as follows (EA 2010, para 1, Sch 23; formerly RRA 1976, s 41):

(a)   Where discrimination was on grounds of race, ethnic or national origins, no defence is available;

(b)   Otherwise, discriminatory acts were not unlawful if performed:

    (i)   in pursuance of any enactment or Order in Council;

    (ii)   in pursuance of any instrument made under any enactment by a Minister of the Crown; or

    (iii)   in order to comply with any condition or requirement imposed by a Minister of the Crown by virtue of any enactment;

(c)   Where discrimination was on grounds of the complainant's nationality, place of ordinary residence or the length of time for which he has been present or resident in or outside the UK, the defence was available in the three circumstances set out in (b) immediately above but also:

    (i)   in pursuance of any arrangements made by or with the approval of, or for the time being approved by, a Minister of the Crown; or

    (ii)   in order to comply with any condition imposed by a Minister of the Crown;

For the application of the exemption for acts done pursuant to arrangements made by or with the approval of a Minister of the Crown, see *R (on the application of Mohammed) v Secretary of State for Defence* [2007] EWCA Civ 1023, [2007] All ER (D) 09 (May).

Sex discrimination

Save in certain respects intended to preserve the position as it was under previous enactments, or in order to ensure the health and safety of women, no defence is available under the *EA 2010* for sex discrimination carried out in order to comply with a legal requirement. The exceptions on the grounds of statutory authority which relate to the protected characteristic of sex (*EA 2010, Sch 22, para 1*) relate only to services and education.

However, it remains the case that a respondent is not guilty of an unlawful act if he discriminates in order to comply with a statute passed before the *SDA 1975*, or a statutory instrument made or approved (whether before or after the passing of the *SDA*) by or under an act passed before the *SDA*, or by a provision specified in Sch 1 to the EA 1989, in each case if such provision is one concerning the protection of women (*SDA 1975, s 51*, as substituted by *EA 1989, s 3(3)*, now contained in *Sch 22, para 2* of the *EA 2010*). Thus, discrimination in order to comply with college statutes enacted under a statute prior to *SDA 1975* was considered lawful in *Hugh-Jones v St John's College, Cambridge* [1979] ICR 848. Many such statutory requirements were removed as a result of *EA 1989*.

Discriminatory action taken by an employer to ensure the health and safety of his employees will not be considered unlawful if it is taken in compliance with his statutory obligations and in order to protect the complainant (or class of women to which the complainant belongs): *SDA 1975, s 51(1)(c)(ii)* and now *Sch 22, para 2* of the *EA 2010* and see *Page v Freight Hire (Tank Haulage) Ltd* [1981] ICR 299.

Pregnancy and maternity

Para 2 of *Sch 22* to the *EA 2010* further provides an exception from the maternity and pregnancy discrimination provisions for acts done in order to comply with a statute passed before *SDA 1975*, or by a provision specified in *Sch 1* to the *EA 1989*, in each case if such provision is one concerning the protection of women, or in order to comply with other statutory obligations and in order to protect the complainant or class of women to which the complainant belongs.

Religion or belief

In addition to the general exception under para 1 (above), *paras 3* and *4* of *Sch 22* to the *EA 2010* provide various exceptions for acts of religious discrimination in relation to appointments to positions in educational establishments, where that discrimination is authorised or required either by the constitution of the educational establishment or by statute.

The exceptions under *para 3* apply in relation to the appointment of (a) the head teacher or principal of an educational establishment (as defined in *sub-para (6)*), (b) the head, a fellow or other member of the academic staff of a college, or institution in the nature of a college, in a university; or (c) a professorship of a university which is a canon professorship or one to which a canonry is annexed. Discrimination on grounds of religion or belief is permitted in relation to such appointments where this is necessary to comply with a requirement of any instrument relating to the establishment that the head teacher or principle must be a member of a particular religious order, or that the holder of the position must be a woman (if the instrument was made before 16 January 1990) or an Act or instrument in accordance with which the professorship is a canon professorship or to which a canonry is annexed.

The exceptions under para 4 allow any discrimination that is permitted for the purposes of (a) *section 58(6)* or *(7)* of the *School Standards and Framework Act 1998* (dismissal of teachers because of failure to give religious education efficiently); (b) *section 60(4)* and *(5)* of that *Act* (religious considerations relating to certain appointments); (c) *section 124A* of that *Act* (preference for certain teachers at independent schools of a religious character); or (d) *section 124AA(5)* to *(7)* of that *Act* (religious considerations relating to certain teachers at Academies with religious character).

By a decision of 20 October 2014 (Ref. Ares(2014)3466266) the European Commission dismissed a complaint about the width of the exceptions allowed for faith schools in UK law. However, on 20 February 2015, it was reported in the *Times Educational Supplement* that the European Commission had decided to re-open its investigation.

12.22 National security

Under the *EA 2010* there is a single general exception to the *Act* for anything done for the purpose of safeguarding national security, provided it is proportionate to that purpose: *s 192*. National security may also justify an exception to the rules on making enquiries about health and disability when vetting for employment: see *s 60(14)* of the *EA 2010*.

A similar exception applied under the predecessor legislation. Discrimination on grounds of sexual orientation, religion or belief, disability or age was not unlawful if it is done for the purpose of safeguarding national security, and the discriminatory act is justified by that purpose (*RBR 2003, reg 24*; *SOR 2003, reg 24*; *DDA 1995, s 59(2A)*; *EA 2006, reg 27*). An act of sex discrimination done for the purpose of safeguarding national security was also permitted by the *SDA 1975, s 52(1)*. However, it should be noted that no such derogation was available for sex discrimination in Community law, though cf *Sirdar v Army Board*: C-273/97 [2000] ICR 130, CJEU and above **12.11**(d). The *RRA 1976* permitted race discrimination where the act in question was done for the purpose of safeguarding national security and was justified by that purpose: *RRA 1976, s 42*.

See also **12.11**(d) and **12.16**(a) above for the exceptions relating to sex and disability discrimination in the armed forces.

12.23 Employees working for those with state or diplomatic immunity

A number of provisions in principle confer state or diplomatic immunity in relation to employment discrimination claims, in particular the *State Immunity Act 1978* ("*SIA 1978*") and the *Diplomatic Privileges Act 1964* ("the *DPA 1964*"), which incorporated the Vienna Convention on Diplomatic Relations 1961. It was at one time accepted that the provisions of the *SIA 1978* did not infringe *art 6(1)* of the *European Convention on Human Rights*: see *Holland v Lampen-Wolfe* [2000] 1 WLR 1573, ECrtHR and *Fogarty v United Kingdom* [2002] IRLR 148, ECtHR. However, more recent cases of the ECrtHR (eg *Al-Adsani v UK* (2002) 34 EHRR 11) have held that *art 6(1)* is engaged in such cases and will be infringed if the immunity is not justified by the need to comply with international law. On that basis, the Court of Appeal in *Benkharbouche v Embassy of Sudan* [2015] EWCA Civ 33, [2016] QB 347 declared that, in preventing employment claims being brought against embassies when that was not required by international law, the *SIA 1978* infringed *article 6* of the *ECHR*. In contrast, in *Al-Malki v Reyes* [2015] EWCA Civ 32; [2016] 1 WLR 1785, decided on the same day, the Court of Appeal held that the diplomatic immunity conferred by the *DPA 1964* did not breach *articles 4* or *6* of the *ECHR* in relation to trafficking claims brought by persons employed in the service of Saudi Arabian diplomats. Both cases have been appealed to the Supreme Court and the outcome of those appeals is awaited. In the meantime, in *Warner v B&M Europe Ltd* (UKEAT/0081/15/RN, UKEAT/0139/16/RN, 13 July 2016), the EAT held that the grant of immunity to the European Patent Office under the *European Patent Organisation (Immunities and Privileges) Order 1978* was compatible with *art 6 ECHR*. In the light of the Court of Appeal's decision in *Benkharbouche*, earlier cases should be approached with care, but general principles had been established that a restrictive approach should be taken to claims to state immunity and the first question will be whether the employment is part of the function of the diplomat in his mission. In *Abusabib v Taddese* [2013] ICR 603 the EAT held that a domestic servant employed solely in the diplomat's home was not part of the function of the mission and therefore he could not hide behind state immunity to avoid a discrimination claim. See also *Wokuri v Kassam* [2012] EWHC 105 (Ch), [2013] Ch 80.

12.24 NON-EMPLOYEES AND NON-EMPLOYERS COVERED BY THE EMPLOYMENT RULES

Contract workers

In recent times there has been a marked trend towards the use of contract workers. Contract workers are parties to a tri-partite arrangement. The first party is the person who has work which needs doing. He is known as the 'principal'. The principal enters into a contract with a second party who is obliged to supply employees to perform the work. The employees are known as 'contract workers' in relation to the principal.

Under the *EA 2010*, contract workers are covered by *s 41*. *Sections 41(1)* and *(3)* prohibit discrimination and victimisation of contract workers by 'principals':

(i)   as to the terms on which the principal allows the worker to do the work;

(ii)   by not allowing him to do it or continue to do it;

(iii)   in the way he affords him access to any benefits or by refusing or deliberately not affording him access to them; or

(iv)   by subjecting him to any other detriment.

There is also a specific prohibition on harassment of contract workers by 'principals' (*s 41(2)*). A 'principal' is defined as 'a person who makes work available for an individual who is (a) employed by another person and (b) supplied by that other person in furtherance of a contract to which the principal is a party (whether or not that other person is a party to it) (*s 41(5)*). A 'contract worker' is an individual supplied to a principal in furtherance of such a contract.

Contract workers and reasonable adjustments. The duty to make reasonable adjustments applies to the hirer of contract labour as it does to an employer. However, it might not be reasonable for a hirer of contract labour to make certain adjustments if the period for which the contract worker works for the hirer of contract labour is short (*Code of Practice, para 9.8*). The provider of contract labour may also have a duty to make a reasonable adjustment where a similar substantial disadvantage is likely to affect a contract worker as a result of the arrangements or premises of all or most of the hirers of contract labour to whom he might be supplied In such circumstances, the provider of contract labour would have to make any reasonable adjustment within his power which would overcome the disadvantage wherever it might arise. Thus, in a case of a blind word-processor operator working for an employment agency, it would be reasonable for the agency to provide her with a specially adapted computer to take with her to any temporary engagement to which she is sent because otherwise she would be suffering the same substantial disadvantage at all or most such engagements (*Code of Practice, para 9.10*).

In *Abbey Life Assurance Co Ltd v Tansell* [2000] IRLR 387, the applicant had set up his own company and was employed by it. That company supplied the applicant's services as a computer consultant to third parties under a contract with an employment agency, MHC. Abbey Life had an agreement with MHC to supply computer personnel. Abbey Life rejected the applicant's services and a complaint of disability discrimination was made to an employment tribunal. The tribunal held that the applicant was a contract worker for MHC and not Abbey Life. MHC appealed successfully to the EAT (see *MHC Consulting Services Ltd v Tansell* [1999] IRLR 677). The Court of Appeal dismissed Abbey Life's appeal against that decision, holding that Abbey Life was the 'principal' or the hirer of contract labour for the purposes of *DDA 1995*. The fact that Abbey Life's contract was with MHC and not the applicant's employer did not preclude the application of *s 4B, DDA 1995* as there was a chain of unbroken contracts between the applicant and the 'end user', namely, Abbey Life.

The genuine occupational requirement exception (above para **12.2**) applies to contract workers in relation to not allowing them to do, or to continue doing, particular work: see *para 1(2)(b)* of *Sch 9* to the *EA 2010*.

Similar provision was made in the predecessor legislation: see *SDA 1975, s 9(2), (2A)*, as amended; *RRA 1976, s 7(1), (3A)*, as amended; *RBR 2003, reg 8(1), (2); SOR 2003, reg 8(1), (2)*; and *EA 2006, reg 9(1), (2)*.

The provisions relating to the meaning of 'at an establishment in Great Britain' (above **12.18**) applied to principals as they did to employers under the predecessor legislation. So, too, did the genuine occupational requirement exceptions (*SDA 1975, s 9(3), (3A) and (3B); RRA*

1976, s 7(3); RBR 2003, reg 8(3); SOR 2003, reg 8(3); AR 2006, reg 9(3); see above **12.2** ff) and the exceptions for benefits provided to the public (*SDA 1975, s 9(4); RRA 1976, s 7(5); RBR 2003, reg 8(4); SOR 2003, reg 8(4); AR 2006, reg 9(4);* see above **12.2**).

The provisions relating to contract workers are designed to prevent an employer from escaping its responsibilities under the equality legislation by bringing in workers on sub-contract and should therefore be given a broad construction so as to provide statutory protection to a wide range of workers (*Jones v Friends Provident Life Office* [2004] IRLR 783, NICA). In that case, Carswell LCJ held (para 17) that, in order to fall within the relevant provisions, it is necessary to show that: (i) the contract between the employer and the principal is one under which it is contemplated that employees will be supplied by the former to the latter; and, (ii) the principal is in a position to influence or control the conditions under which the employee worked. However, in *Leeds City Council v Woodhouse* [2010] EWCA Civ 410, [2010] IRLR 625 the Court of Appeal ruled that the second of those conditions was not necessary. What matters is that the worker works 'for' the principal. Influence and control does not have to be shown in all cases.

The notion of a 'contract worker' extends to cover a case where the complainant works for a company operating a 'concession' within a department store. Thus, where a department store withdrew, on racial grounds, the necessary permission for the complainant to work in the store, the latter was entitled to bring proceedings against the former under *RRA 1976, s 7* (*Harrods Ltd v Remick* [1998] ICR 156, CA). However, it should be noted that the Northern Ireland Court of Appeal in *Jones v Friends Provident* considered that *Harrods Ltd v Remick* represented, possibly, too wide an interpretation of the relevant provisions. In particular, the Court in *Jones v Friends Provident* considered that it is unlikely to be sufficient for a complainant to establish merely that the principal benefited from the work done by them in order to bring that principal within the scope of the relevant provisions. Nevertheless, more complex contractual arrangements are probably covered by the provisions: see *MHC Consulting Services Ltd v Tansell* [2000] ICR 789, CA, a case under the *DDA 1995*. In that case the complainant contracted with a company that he had set up which company then contracted with a service provider, which in turn contracted with the ultimate beneficiary of the services. The beneficiary was a principal for the purposes of the *DDA 1995* notwithstanding the inclusion of an additional link in the contractual chain. In all cases, however, there must in fact be a *contractual* relationship: where arrangements take effect under statute (as, for example, the obligations placed on general practitioners and local health authorities under the *National Health Service (General Medical Services) Regulations 1992*) there may be no contractual relationship at all: *David-John v North Essex Health Authority* [2004] ICR 112, EAT. See also *Vidal-Hall v Hawley* (21 February 2008, UKEAT/0462/07/DA) where the claim failed for lack of a contract between principal and the supplier of the worker.

A contract worker is not limited to comparing the treatment he has received with the manner in which the principal treats contract workers of different sexual orientation, racial group etc; he may also compare himself to employees of the principal (*Allonby v Accrington and Rossendale College* [2001] EWCA Civ 529, [2001] IRLR 364). Thus, a company which refused to allow an agency worker to return to work for it after she had been on maternity leave discriminated against her on the grounds of her sex, contrary to *SDA 1975, s 9* (*BP Chemicals Ltd v Gillick* [1995] IRLR 128, EAT). Similarly, where a local authority appointed a permanent worker in place of a contract worker who had left to take maternity leave, it was argued on behalf of the principal that the contract worker could not rely upon the provisions of the equivalent Northern Irish legislation. The principal had not refused to allow her to continue to do the work (she had merely left to start maternity leave) and by the time that she wanted to return there was no work for a contract worker to do, a permanent worker having been appointed. Nevertheless, the NICA held that the principal was liable to the contract worker who had been subjected to 'other detriment' (*Patefield v Belfast City Council* [2000] IRLR 664, NICA).

12.25 Office holders

In addition to the general provisions applying the equality legislation to the Crown, etc (see below **12.36**), specific provision is also made in relation to discrimination against office holders. Overwhelmingly, office holders are public sector appointees, often those with specific statutory powers or responsibilities. They have historically been considered not to be employed in a post but, rather, as holding an office which exists independently of the terms of their appointment. An example would be Registrars of Births, Deaths and Marriages. Following the decisions of the CJEU and Supreme Court in *O'Brien v Ministry of Justice* (respectively, C-393/10, [2012] ICR 955 and [2013] UKSC 6, [2013] 1 WLR 522) establishing that judges are 'workers' under European law, it is likely that many office holders will now also fall within the definition of 'employee' in *s 83* of the *EA 2010* and thus be covered by the standard rules on employees. However, the provisions in relation to office holders are likely still to remain relevant to such people, and also to those who are genuinely office holders and not employees or workers in European law.

Under the *EA 2010* office holders are covered by *ss 49–51*. *Section 49* makes provision in respect of appointments to personal offices (ie what are referred to below as 'general office holders'). *Section 50* makes provision in respect of 'public offices', prohibiting discrimination, victimisation and harassment in relation to appointments and dismissals. *Section 51* makes provision prohibiting discrimination, victimisation and harassment in relation to recommendations for appointment to public offices. An office or post which is both a personal office and public office is to be treated for the purposes of the *EA 2010* as being a public office only (*s 52(4)*). Posts to which persons are elected rather than appointed are not covered (*s 52(5)*). There are also further excluded offices listed in *Schedule 6*. These include any office that would be covered by any of the other employment provisions (eg contract work, partnerships, etc) (see *para 1* of *Sch 6*), political offices (*para 2*) and honourable offices (eg life peerages or other dignities) (para 3). The genuine occupational requirement exception applies to office holders in the same way as to employees: see *para 1(2)(e)–(g)* of *Sch 9* to the *EA 2010* and generally **12.2** above.

The predecessor legislation also applied to office holders: see *RRA 1976, s 76* and *76ZA*, or *SDA 1975, ss 10A* and *10B*; *RBR 2003, reg 10*; *SOR 2003, reg 10*; *AR 2006, reg 12*; *DDA 1995, s 4C–4F*.

12.26 Police

Police officers are office holders and not employees. However, *s 42(1)* of the *EA 2010* deems holding the office of constable to be treated as employment by the chief officer (in respect of any act done by the chief officer in relation to a constable or appointment to the office of constable) and by the responsible authority (in respect of any act done by the authority in relation to a constable or appointment to the office of constable). The 'chief officer' is:

(a)   in relation to an appointment under a relevant Act, the chief officer of police for the police force to which the appointment relates;

(b)   in relation to any other appointment, the person under whose direction and control the body of constables or other persons to which the appointment relates is;

(c)   in relation to a constable or other person under the direction and control of a chief officer of police, that chief officer of police;

(d)   in relation to any other constable or any other person, the person under whose direction and control the constable or other person is.

The 'responsible authority' is:

(a)   in relation to an appointment under a relevant Act (ie the *Metropolitan Police Act 1829*, the *City of London Police Act 1839*, the *Police (Scotland) Act 1967*, the *Police Act 1996*), the police authority that maintains the police force to which the appointment relates;

(b)   in relation to any other appointment, the person by whom a person would (if appointed) be paid;

(c)   in relation to a constable or other person under the direction and control of a chief officer of police, the police authority that maintains the police force for which that chief officer is the chief officer of police;

(d)   in relation to any other constable or any other person, the person by whom the constable or other person is paid.

The predecessor equality legislation made similar provision: *SDA 1975, s 17; RRA 1976, s 76A; RBR 2003, reg 11; SOR 2003, reg 11; AR 2006, reg 13; DDA 1995, s 64A.*

The requirement that the act should be done by the chief officer (or, similarly, by the police authority) is not to be interpreted literally and will include acts performed by those to whom the chief officer has delegated authority (see *Chief Constable of Cumbria v McGlennon* [2002] ICR 1156, EAT).

Further detailed provisions apply the legislation to cadets, employees and office holders of the Serious Organised Crime Agency and other police bodies (*EA 2010, ss 42(2)–(6)* and *43(4)–(7)*; see formerly *SDA 1975, s 17(6), (7), (9); RRA 1976, s 76B; RBR 2003, reg 11(6), (7), 11A; SOR 2003, reg 11(6), (7), 11A; AR 2006, regs 13(6), (7), (14); DDA 1995, s 64A(6), (7)* and *s 56* of the *Serious Organised Crime and Police Act 2005*).

For circumstances in which police constables may lawfully be discriminated against see above **12.11**(e).

See also **13.2** Discrimination and Equal Opportunities **III** for the exclusion from the jurisdiction of employment tribunals of claims against police disciplinary panels.

12.27 Barristers and advocates

Unlawful discrimination against applicants for pupillage or tenancy

It is unlawful for a barrister or barrister's clerk, in relation to any offer of a pupillage or tenancy, to discriminate against a person on any of the unlawful grounds:

(a)   in the arrangements which are made for the purpose of determining to whom the pupillage or tenancy should be offered;

(b)   in respect of any terms on which it is offered; or

(c)   by refusing, or deliberately not offering, it to him (*EA 2010, s 47(1)*; see previously: *SDA 1975, s 35A(1); RRA 1976, s 26A(1); RBR 2003, reg 12(1); SOR 2003, reg 12(1); AR 2006, reg 15(1); DDA 1995, s 7A(1)*).

Unlawful discrimination against pupils or tenants

It is unlawful for a barrister or barrister's clerk, in relation to a pupil or tenant in the set of chambers in question, to discriminate against him:

(a)   in respect of any terms applicable to him as a pupil or tenant;

(b)   in the opportunities for training or gaining experience, which are afforded or denied to him;

(c)   in the benefits which are afforded or denied to him; or

(d)   by terminating his pupillage, or by subjecting him to any pressure to leave the chambers or other detriment (*EA 2010, s 47(2)*; see previously: *SDA 1975, s 35A(2); RRA 1976, s 26A(2); RBR 2003, reg 12(2); SOR 2003, reg 12(2); AR, reg 15(2); DDA 1995, s 7A(2)*).

Unlawful harassment of pupils, tenants or applicants for pupillage or tenancy

It is unlawful for a barrister or barrister's clerk, in relation to a pupillage or tenancy in the set of chambers in question, to subject to harassment a person who is, or has applied to be, a pupil or tenant (*EA 2010, s 47(3)*; see previously: *SDA 1975, s 35A(2A)*, as amended with effect from 1 October 2005; *RRA 1976, s 26A(3A); RBR 2003, reg 12(3); SOR 2003, reg 12(3); DDA 1995, s 7A(3)*).

Unlawful victimisation of pupils, tenants or applicants for pupillage or tenancy

It is unlawful for a barrister or barrister's clerk, in relation to a pupillage or tenancy in the set of chambers in question, to victimise a person who is, or has applied to be, a pupil or tenant (*EA 2010, s 47(4) and (5)*).

Unlawful discrimination by those instructing barristers

It is unlawful for any person, in relation to the giving, withholding or acceptance of instructions to a barrister, to discriminate against any person by subjecting him to a detriment, or to subject him to harassment (*EA 2010, s 47(6)*; see previously: *SDA 1975, s 35A(3); RRA 1976, s 26A(3); RBR 2003, reg 12(4); SOR 2003, reg 12(4); AR 2006, reg 15(4); DDA 1995, s 7A(4)*).

'Barrister's clerk' includes any person carrying out any of the functions of a barrister's clerk. 'Pupil', 'pupillage', 'set of chambers', 'tenancy' and 'tenant' have the meanings commonly associated with their use in the context of barristers practising in independent practice, but 'tenancy' and 'tenant' also include reference to any barrister permitted to work in a set of chambers who is not a tenant (ie a 'squatter') (*EA 2010, ss 47(8) and (9)*; see previously: *SDA 1975, s 35A(4); RRA 1976, s 26A(4); RBR 2003, reg 12(5); SOR 2003, reg 12(5); AR 2006, reg 15(5); DDA 1995, s 7A(5)*).

The exceptions for genuine occupational requirements (above **12.2** ff) and benefits provided to the public (above **12.20**) do not apply to barristers.

The provisions in respect of barristers extend to England and Wales only. Similar provision is made for advocates and their pupils in Scotland (*EA 2010, s 48*; see previously: *SDA 1975, s 35B; RRA 1976, s 26B; RBR 2003, reg 13; SOR 2003, reg 13; AR 2006, reg 16; DDA 1995, s 7C*).

12.28 Partnerships

Unlawful discrimination against partners and candidates for partnership

Prior to the decision of the Supreme Court in *Bates van Winkelhof v Clyde & Co LLP* [2014] UKSC 32, [2014] 1 WLR 2047 it was thought that partners in firms were not only not 'employees', but that they could also not be 'workers' under EU or domestic law. In *Bates* the SC concluded that an equity partner in a limited liability partnership (LLP) could be a 'worker' for the purposes of a whistle-blowing claim under the *ERA 1996*. In principle, it would appear that such partners could therefore also be 'workers' for the purposes of the *EA 2010*. However, whether they are or not, specific provision is made in the *EA 2010* expressly prohibiting discrimination against partners and candidates for partnership. The legislation applies to limited partnerships and limited liability partnerships as it does to partnerships (with appropriate amendments of terminology) (*EA 2010, s 44(8), s 45 and 46*; see previously: *SDA 1975, s 11(5), (6); RRA 1976, s 10(4), (5); RBR 2003, reg 14(5), (6); SOR 2003, reg 14(5), (6); AR 2006, reg 17(6); DDA 1995, s 6C(2)*). Note, however, that for discrimination on grounds of colour or nationality, the *RRA 1976* only applied to firms with six or more partners: *RRA 1976, s 10(1A)*.

(a)   in the arrangements they make for the purpose of determining to whom they should offer that position;

(b)   in the terms on which they offer him that position;

(c)   by refusing to offer, or deliberately not offering, him that position; or

(d)   in a case where the person already holds that position:

  (i)   in the way they afford him access to any benefits or by refusing to afford, or deliberately not affording, him access to them, or

  (ii)   by expelling him from that position, or

  (iii)   subjecting him to any other detriment (*EA 2010, s 44(1)* and *(2)*; see previously *SDA 1975, s 11(1), (2); RRA 1976, s 10(1), (2); RBR 2003, reg 14(1), (3); SOR 2003, reg 14(1), (3); AR 2006, reg 17(1); DDA 1995, s 6A(1)*).

Under *EA 2010*, it is also unlawful to discriminate against a person who is already a partner as to the terms on which the person is a partner: *s 44(2)(a)*.

'Expulsion' of a person from a position as partner is defined additionally to refer to the termination of that person's position as partner by:

(a)   the expiration of any period (including a period expiring by reference to an event or circumstance), not being a termination immediately after which the partnership is renewed on the same terms; and

(b)   any act of his (including the giving of notice) in circumstances such that he is entitled to terminate it without notice by reason of the conduct of the other partners (*EA 2010, s 1(6)*; see previously: *RRA 1976, s 10(6); DDA 1995, s 6A(4); RBR 2003, reg 14(8); SOR 2003, reg 14(8); AR 2006, reg 17(8)*).

Note that where one partner dissolves a two-person partnership the other partner is 'expelled' for the purposes of the provisions on partnerships and may sue the remaining partner (*Dave v Robinska* [2003] ICR 1248).

It is also unlawful for a firm, in relation to a position as partner in the firm, to subject to harassment a person who holds or has applied for that position (*EA 2010, s 44(3), (4)*; see previously *SDA 1975, 11(2A)*, as inserted with effect from 1 October 2005 by the *Sex Discrimination Regulations 2005; RRA 1976, s 10(1B); RBR 2003, reg 14(2); SOR 2003, reg 14(2); AR 2006, reg 17(2); DDA 1995, s 6A(2)*).

It is also unlawful for a firm, in relation to a position as partner in the firm, to victimise a person who holds or has applied for that position (*EA 2010, s 44(5)* and *(6)*). Under the predecessor legislation victimisation was merely a form of discrimination and no separate provision was made for it.

Genuine occupational requirement defences (see above **12.2** ff) are available to partnerships under the *EA 2010*: see *para 1(2)(c)* and *(d)* of *Sch 9*. For the position under the predecessor legislation see: *RBR 2003, reg 14(4); SOR 2003, reg 14(4); AR 2006, reg 17(4); SDA 1975, s 11(3), (3A), (3B); RRA 1976, s 10(3)*.

12.29 Trade organisations

A 'trade organisation' is defined in the discrimination legislation as:

(i)   an organisation of workers,

(ii)   an organisation of employers, or

(iii)   any other organisation whose members carry on a particular profession or trade for the purposes of which the organisation exists.

(EA 2010, s 57(7); see previously : *SDA 1975, 12(1); RRA 1976, s 11(1); RBR 2003, reg 15(4); SOR 2003, reg 15(4); AR 2006, reg 18(4); DDA 1995, s 13(4))*.

'Profession' is defined so as to include 'any vocation or occupation', and 'trade' to include 'any business': *EA 2010, s 212(1)*; see previously *SDA 1975, s 82(1); RRA 1976, s 78(1); RBR 2003, reg 15(4); SOR 2003, reg 15(4); AR 2006, reg 18(4)*.

The EAT has held that the National Federation of Self-Employed and Small Businesses Ltd is an 'employers' organisation': *National Federation of Self-Employed and Small Businesses Ltd v Philpott* [1997] IRLR 340. In *Medical Protection Society v Sadek* [2004] EWCA Civ 865, [2004] ICR 1263, the Court of Appeal considered the status of the Medical Protection Society, a membership organisation which had provided the claimant with advice and representation in relation to a claim he had brought against his employer, an NHS Trust. The Court held that the Society was 'an organisation of workers' within the first category of the definition of 'trade organisation' in *s 11(1)* of the *RRA 1976*, because medical and dental practitioners were properly classified as 'workers' even though they were 'members [of] a profession' within the third category of the definition of 'trade organisation' and even though some of them may be employees and others independent contractors. The Court considered that the EAT had been wrong to conclude that the Society fell within *both* the first and third categories of the definition: the third category was only a residual one.

It is unlawful for a trade organisation to discriminate against a person:

(a)   in the terms on which it is prepared to admit him to membership of the organisation; or

(b)   by refusing to accept, or deliberately not accepting, his application for membership; *(EA 2010, s 57(1)*; see previously *SDA 1975, s 12(2); RRA 1976, s 11(2); RBR 2003, reg 15(1); SOR 2003, reg 15(1); AR 2006, reg 18(1); DDA 1995, s 13(1))*.

Pursuant to *s 57(1)* of *EA 2010*, it is additionally unlawful for a trade organisation to discriminate in the arrangements made for deciding to whom to offer membership of the organisation.

It is also unlawful for a trade organisation, in relation to a member of the organisation, to discriminate against him:

(a)   in the way it affords him access to any benefits or by refusing or deliberately omitting to afford him access to them;

(b)   by depriving him of membership, or varying the terms on which he is a member; or

(c)   by subjecting him to any other detriment *(EA 2010, s 57(2)*; see previously: *SDA 1975, s 12(3); RRA 1976, s 11(3); RBR 2003, reg 15(2); SOR 2003, reg 15(2); AR 2006, reg 18(2); DDA 1995, s 13(2))*.

It is unlawful for a trade organisation, in relation to a person's membership or application for membership of that organisation, to subject that person to harassment *(EA 2010, s 57(3)*; see previously: *SDA 1975, s 12(3A)*, as inserted with effect from 1 October 2005 by the *Sex Discrimination Regulations 2005; RRA 1976, s 11(4); RBR 2003, reg 15(3); SOR 2003, reg 15(3); AR 2006, reg 18(3); DDA 1995, s 13(3))*.

In *Fire Brigades Union v Fraser* [1998] IRLR 697 (Court of Session, Inner House), the union provided support and assistance for the alleged victim of the harassment, but refused to provide assistance to the alleged harasser. The Court of Session overturned a decision of the employment tribunal that the alleged harasser had been the victim of an act of discrimination on the part of the union. Whilst it was true that the union treated the alleged victims of harassment more favourably, the tribunal was making the wrong comparison in comparing harasser and harassee. The proper question was whether a female alleged harasser would have been treated differently.

The genuine occupational requirement exception (above para **12.2**) does not apply to trade organisations.

Note that there is no express provision rendering the union liable for the discriminatory acts of its members. Where a union official is employed by the union, the union will be vicariously liable for the acts of that official under *EA 2010, s 109*: see **11.54** DISCRIMINATION AND EQUAL OPPORTUNITIES – I. However, elected union officials who undertake union duties during paid time off work from their 'normal' employer will (even if they do this on a full-time basis) not be employees of the union since they are not paid by the union. Rather, they will be agents of the union and thus the union will be vicariously liable for their actions on that basis: see *Unite the Union v Nailard* [2017] ICR 121 and **11.56** DISCRIMINATION AND EQUAL OPPORTUNITIES – I.

12.30 Qualifications bodies

A qualifications body is an authority or body which can confer professional or trade qualifications: *EA 2010, s 54(2)*. A 'professional or trade qualification' is an authorisation, recognition, enrolment, approval or certification, which is needed for, or facilitates, engagement in a particular profession or trade. 'Confer' is defined to include the renewal or extension of a qualification (see *EA 2010, s 54(3)*; see previously *SDA 1975, s 13(1), (3)*; *RRA 1976, s 12(1), (2)*; *RBR 2003, reg 16(3)*; *SOR 2003, reg 16(4)*; *AR 2006, reg 19(3)*; *DDA 1995, s 14A(5)*). Establishments of further and higher education and schools are excluded from the definition: *EA 2010, 54(4)*. (Separate provision in relation to discrimination in education is made by both the *EA 2010* and the predecessor legislation. Consideration of this is, however, outside the scope of this book.)

It is unlawful for a qualifications body to discriminate against a person:

(a)   in the terms on which it is prepared to confer a professional or trade qualification on him;

(b)   by refusing or deliberately not granting any application by him for such a qualification; or

(c)   by withdrawing such a qualification from him or varying the terms on which he holds it

(*EA 2010, s 53(1)* and *(2)*; see previously *SDA 1975, s 13(1)*; *RRA 1976, s 12(1)*; *RBR 2003, reg 16(1)*; *SOR 2003, reg 16(1)*; *AR 2006, reg 19(1)*; *DDA 1995, s 14A(1)*)

Under *EA 2010*, it is additionally unlawful for a qualifications body to discriminate against a person:

(a)   in the arrangements made for deciding upon whom to confer a relevant qualification; and

(b)   by subjecting him to any other detriment

(*EA 2010, s 53(1), (2)*)

It is unlawful for a qualifications body, in relation to a professional or trade qualification conferred by it, to subject to harassment a person who holds or applies for such a qualification (*EA 2010, s 53(3)*; see previously: *SDA 1975, s 13(1A)*, as inserted with effect from 1 October 2005 by the *Sex Discrimination Regulations 2005*; *RRA 1976, s 12(1A)*; *RBR 2003, reg 16(2)*; *SOR 2003, reg 16(2)*; *EA 2006, reg 19(2)*).

The *EA 2010* also specifically prohibits victimisation by qualifications bodies: *s 53(4)* and *(5)* of *EA 2010*.

A number of cases have considered the definition of 'qualifications body' for the purpose of these provisions. In *British Judo Association v Petty* [1981] ICR 660, it was held that a qualification would only fall within the predecessor provision in *SDA 1975, s 13* if it facilitated employment, i.e. remunerated work, not voluntary activity; on the facts, that requirement was satisfied in relation to a judo referee's certificate so that the discriminatory restriction it contained was unlawful. In *Pemberton v Inwood* [2017] IRLR 211 the EAT observed that whether or not something is a 'relevant qualification' is not to be determined by reference to the intention of the awarding body, but whether, as a matter of fact, the something may be properly characterised as a 'qualification' and is needed for, or facilitates engagement in, a particular trade or profession. The question of fact is one for the tribunal and the EAT will not normally interfere. In that case, which concerned the grant of licences by the Bishop of Southwold and Nottingham, the EAT upheld the Tribunal's determination (applying *British Judo Association*) that the grant of a "Permission to Officiate" was not the grant of qualification because it only qualified the priest for voluntary duties. However, the grant of an "Extra parochial ministry licence" was necessary for the paid employment in the NHS sought by the claimant. Further, the grant of the licence was not a decision taken 'on a whim': it depended on the individual being "of good standing": that was capable of objective assessment and could therefore properly be regarded as a 'qualification'. In refusing to grant the licence, the Bishop was therefore acting as a qualifications body.

The provisions relating to qualifications bodies are not to be so widely construed as to extend to the mere awarding of a contract, even by a body or authority which has a *de facto* monopoly in the particular trade (*Malik v Post Office Counters Ltd* [1993] ICR 93). The provisions are aimed at discrimination by professional bodies and not individual businesses. Thus, where a private medical health insurer would only make payments in respect of treatment given by practitioners holding certain recognised qualifications, a plastic surgeon could not bring a claim where the insurer refused to recognise her Greek medical qualifications (*Tattari v Private Patients Plan Ltd* [1997] IRLR 586, CA; see also *Loughran and anr v Northern Ireland Housing Executive* [1998] IRLR 593). However, in *Patterson v Legal Services Commission* [2003] EWCA Civ 1558, [2004] ICR 312 the Court of Appeal held that the conferral of a franchise by the Legal Services Commission enabling the applicant's firm to receive public funds for the provisions of services in certain categories of legal work was an 'authorisation' that 'facilitates engagement in' the profession of solicitor for the purposes of *RRA 1976, s 12*. The authorisation was conferred on both the applicant's firm and the applicant personally.

Being a Justice of the Peace is not 'engagement in a particular profession' (*Arthur v A-G* [1999] ICR 631). However, appointment as a Justice of the Peace would now be covered by the provisions relating to office holders (see above **12.25**).

A number of cases have considered the position of political parties. In *McDonagh and Triesman v Ali* [2002] EWCA Civ 93, [2002] ICR 1026 the CA held (disapproving the EAT's decision in *Sawyer v Ahsan* [1999] IRLR 609) that the Labour Party is not a 'qualifications body' within the definition, at least in relation to the selection or nomination of candidates for elections. Although being an MP is a 'profession', the selection or nomination of candidates is not an 'authorisation' or 'qualification' for that profession. *Triesman* has now been approved by the House of Lords in *Watt (formerly Carter) v Ahsan* [2007] UKHL 51, [2008] 2 WLR 17. In that case, however, the House of Lords did confirm that although not a 'qualifications body', the Labour Party was an 'association' within the meaning of *s 25* of the *RRA 1976* (which applied to any association of persons of 25 or more members, regulated by a constitution, that did not fall within *s 11* of the *RRA 1976*. *Section 25* fell within *Part III* of the *RRA 1976*, is outside the jurisdiction of the employment tribunal and the scope of this work).

In *Kulkarni v NHS Education Scotland* [2013] Eq LR 34 the EAT (Scotland) held that NHS Education Scotland was not a 'qualifications body' or, at least, was not covered by *s 53* of the *EA 2010* in respect of its function of allocating trainees. Although having a trainee would facilitate a consultant surgeon's engagement in his profession, the EAT(S) was satisfied that the allocation of a trainee was not the conferral of 'an authorisation, qualification, recognition, registration, enrolment, approval or certification'.

Note that it is not possible to complain to an employment tribunal under this provision if the act complained of is one in respect of which an appeal, or proceedings in the nature of an appeal, may be brought under any enactment. In the predecessor legislation this exception was to be found in *SDA 1975, s 63(2); RRA 1976, s 54(2); RBR 2003, reg 28(2); SOR 2003, reg 28(2); AR 2006, reg 36(2); DDA 1995, s 17A(1A)*. The exception is now in *s 120(7)* of the *EA 2010*. The scope and effect of this provision were considered in *R v Department of Health, ex p Gandhi* [1991] ICR 805, *Khan v General Medical Council* [1996] ICR 1032, CA, *Tariquez-Zaman v GMC* (UKEAT/0292/06), *Chaudhary v Specialist Training Authority Appeal Panel and ors* [2005] ICR 1086 and *Depner v GMC* (UKEAT/0457/11/KN). In *Jooste v General Medical Council* [2012] Eq LR 1049, EAT (4 July 2012) and *General Medical Council v Michalak* [2015] ICR 502, the EAT held that the exception applies where a person may bring a claim for judicial review of the decision of the qualifications body under *s 31* of the *Senior Courts Act 1981* as well as where a person has a statutory right of appeal to a specialist tribunal. However, the Court of Appeal in *Michalak* ([2016] EWCA Civ 172, [2016] ICR 628) allowed the claimant's appeal and held, overruling *Jooste* that *s 120(7)* of the *EA 2010* does not operate so as to oust the jurisdiction of the employment tribunal in respect of complaints about qualifications bodies.

The genuine occupational requirement exception (above para **12.2**) does not apply to qualifications bodies.

12.30a *Sex discrimination*

Uniquely, the *SDA 1975* provided that, if the qualifications body had to consider an applicant's character, if there was evidence to show that an applicant has practised unlawful discrimination in connection with the carrying on of any profession or trade, that must be taken into account by the body (*SDA 1975, s 13(2)*). No such provision appears in the *EA 2010*.

12.30b *Disability discrimination*

Qualifications bodies benefit from an exception from the *EA 2010* for disability discrimination in relation to the application of 'competence standards'. The application of a 'competence standard' is not unlawful unless it constitutes unlawful indirect discrimination under *s 19* (*s 53(7)*). A 'competence standard' is an academic, medical or other standard applied for the purpose of determining whether or not a person has a particular level of competence or ability (*s 54(6)*). By *para 15(2)* of *Part 2* of *Sch 8* to the *EA 2010* the application of a competence standard by a qualifications body is not the application of a 'provision, criterion or practice' for the purpose of the duty to make reasonable adjustments.

A similar exception applied under the *DDA 1995*. Under the *DDA 1995* qualifications bodies benefitted from an exception to the duty to make reasonable adjustments for disabled people. If the provision, criterion or practice in question was a 'competence standard' then the duty to make reasonable adjustments did not arise: *DDA 1995, s 14B(1)*. A 'competence standard' was "An academic, medical or other standard applied by or on behalf of a qualifications body for the purpose of determining whether or not a person has a particular level of competence or ability" (*DDA 1995, s 14A(5)*). Further, insofar as a qualifying body applied a competence standard to those seeking qualification and sought to justify any disability-related discrimination against a disabled person, the application of the competence standard was only justified if the same standard was applied to persons that did not have the particular disability and its application was a proportionate means of achieving a legitimate aim (*DDA 1995, s 14A(3)*).

In *Burke v The College of Law* UKEAT/0301/10/SM, the EAT considered the College of Law's requirement that Legal Practice Course exams be completed under timed conditions in an examination hall. The College of Law had already granted Mr Burke, who suffered from multiple sclerosis, 60% additional time. However, he contended that a reasonable adjustment would be that he be able to complete the exams over a number of days at home. The Tribunal (and the EAT) held that the requirement that the exam be completed under timed conditions was a competence standard. While the EAT recognised that there was a distinction to be made between an academic standard and the process by which it was assessed, and that in many cases the latter would be subject to the duty to make reasonable adjustments, the EAT accepted that, in the context of a professional examination which seeks to mimic (to some extent) conditions of practice, the time requirement was a competence standard. This was so even though the College of Law had already voluntarily made 'reasonable adjustments' to the time requirement: the fact that they had made the adjustment voluntarily did not mean they had been under a duty to so. Moreover, there was a qualitative difference between an extension of timed exam conditions and the home examination conditions proposed by the claimant. On appeal, the CA ([2012] EWCA Civ 37, [2012] EqLR 279) held that it was not necessary to decide whether or not the time requirement was a competence standard, the fact was that the Tribunal had looked at all the adjustments made by the College and had rightly concluded that reasonable adjustments had been made (including to the time requirement).

In addition to the competence standard exception, provision is made in *s 96(7)–(9)* of the *EA 2010* for the relevant regulators of qualifications bodies to specify certain provisions, criteria or practices in relation to which qualifications bodies are not to be subject to the duty to make reasonable adjustments in relation to specified qualifications. The identity of the relevant regulators, the specified qualifications and the means by which the regulators must publish their specified provisions, criteria or practices (principally on their websites) are prescribed for by regulations for England (*SI 2010/2245*), Scotland (*SI 2010/315*) and Wales (*SI 2010/2217*).

Sexual orientation discrimination

12.30c There is an exception equivalent to the genuine occupational requirement exception for discrimination in employment (see above **12.7**). Para *2(3)* of *Part 1* of *Sch 9* to the *EA 2010* provides that the provisions relating to discrimination by qualifications bodies do not apply to 'professional or trade qualifications conferred for the purposes of an organised religion where a requirement related to sexual orientation is applied to the qualification so as to comply with the doctrines of the religion or to avoid conflicting with the strongly held religious convictions of a significant number of the religion's followers'. See *SOR 2003, reg 16(3)* for the exception under the predecessor legislation.

12.31 Providers of vocational training

The predecessor legislation contains specific provisions relating to providers of vocational training. The *EA 2010* covers such persons by way of the provisions for employment service-providers (see below **12.34**).

Under the predecessor legislation, a 'training provider' was any person who provides, or makes arrangements for the provision of, training or facilities for training which would help fit another person for any employment: *SDA 1975, s 14(1); RRA 1976, s 13(1); RBR 2003, reg 17(4); SOR 2003, reg 17(4); AR 2006, reg 20(4)*. DDA 1995 prohibited discrimination in the provision of "work placements" (*s 14C*) and "employment services" (*s 21A*, read with *ss 19* and *20*). "Vocational training" and "vocational guidance" were included within the scope of "employment services" (*DDA 1995, s 21A(1)(a), (b)*).

The *RBR 2003, SOR 2003* and *AR 2006* made clear that 'training' includes practical work experience provided by an employer to a person whom he does not employ; this is undoubtedly also within the meaning of 'training' in the *SDA 1975* (see especially *s 14(1B)*) and *RRA 1976* (training being defined under *s 78* of the *RRA 1976* as including '*any form of education or instruction*'). This point was confirmed by the EAT in *Chenge v Treasury Solicitor's Department* [2007] IRLR 386, in which the Department had sought to argue that the Government Legal Service vacation placement scheme (where successful applicants gain work experience placements for which they are paid only expenses) was not 'training' within the meaning of *RRA 1976, s 13(1)*. The EAT held that the phrase '*any form of education*' could include education by watching as well as education by doing and that was no need to analyse in detail the syllabus of a scheme in order to decide whether it was a training scheme or a work placement scheme. There was no principled reason why *RRA 1976* should not apply to work experience or work placement. Nor did it matter how long a course took, though the EAT did note that if it was '*merely an educational visit*' that might fall in a different category. Previously, the EAT held in *Fletcher v NHS Pensions Agency* [2005] ICR 1458, that the NHS Pensions Agency, which provides bursaries to trainee midwives combining academic study at universities with practical training through clinical placements in the community and hospitals, is a 'training provider' within the meaning of *SDA 1975, s 14(1)* since the bursaries are a 'facility' for training.

However, where someone is appointed purely as a volunteer (even if they hope through that appointment to secure paid employment with the organisation), that is not 'vocational training'. Voluntary employment is outside the scope of the discrimination legislation: *X v Mid Sussex Citizens Advice Bureau* [2012] UKSC 59, [2013] ICR 249.

The definition of 'training provider' excluded employers in relation to training for their own employees and also education establishments: *SDA 1975, s 14(2); RRA 1976, s 13(2); RBR 2003, reg 17(4); SOR 2003, reg 17(4); AR 2006, reg 20(4)*. This is because separate provision in relation to discrimination in education was made by both the Acts and the Regulations. Claims in relation to discrimination in education are excluded from the jurisdiction of the employment tribunals and are therefore outside the scope of this book. Note, however, that the mere fact that a provider of vocational training was acting as agent of an educational establishment did not mean that a claim against that provider was excluded from the jurisdiction of the employment tribunals, provided of course that the respondent otherwise fell within the definition of 'training provider' in the legislation: *Moyhing v Homerton University Hospitals NHS Trust* (3 May 2005, UKEAT/0851/04/MAA).

It was unlawful, in relation to a person seeking or undergoing training which would help fit him for any employment for any training provider to discriminate against him:

(a) in the terms on which the training provider affords him access to any training (or any facilities concerned with such training);

(b) by refusing or deliberately not affording him such access;

(c) by terminating his training; or

(d) by subjecting him to any other detriment during his training (*SDA 1975, s 14(1); RRA 1976, s 13(1); RBR 2003, reg 17(1); SOR 2003, reg 17(1); AR 2006, reg 20(1)*; see also *DDA 1995, ss 19(1)* and *21A*).

RBR 2003, SOR 2003, AR 2006 and, with effect from 1 October 2005, the *SDA 1975* also applies expressly to 'arrangements' made 'for the purpose of selecting people to receive vocational training' (*SDA 1975, s 14(1)(a)*, as amended by the *Sex Discrimination Regulations 2005*; *RBR 2003, reg 17(1)(aa); SOR 2003, reg 17(1)(aa); AR 2006, reg 20(1)(a)*).

In *Fletcher* the bursaries were stopped during the trainees' maternity leave: since the bursaries were 'facilities concerned with training', which were stopped because the claimants were pregnant, this was unlawful sex discrimination. The EAT ruled that the tribunal had been wrong to conclude that there was no unlawful discrimination because employees absent for other reasons were treated the same way.

All the exceptions that applied to discrimination by employers applied in relation to discrimination by providers of vocational training. The *RBR 2003, SOR 2003* and *AR 2006* provided that the training provider would have a defence where the alleged discrimination only concerned training for employment which, by virtue of the fact that the exception for genuine occupational requirement applied, the respondent could lawfully refuse to offer the person seeking training (*RBR 2003, reg 17(3); SOR 2003, reg 17(3); AR 2006, reg 20(3)*). The exceptions in the *RBR 2003, SOR 2003* and *AR 2006* for national security, positive action and the protection of Sikhs from discrimination in relation to the wearing of safety helmets applied generally to Parts II and III of both sets of *Regulations* and therefore applied to training providers as they did to employers. The *SDA 1975* and *RRA 1976* provided, simply, that all the exceptions that applied in relation to discrimination by employers applied also to training providers (*SDA 1975, s 14(2); RRA 1976, s 13(2)*). (For exceptions see above **12.3, 12.10, 12.11, 12.12** and **12.17** ff.)

It was also unlawful for a training provider, in relation to a person seeking or undergoing training which would help fit him for any employment, to subject him to harassment (*SDA 1975, s 14(1A)*, as inserted with effect from 1 October 2005 by the *Sex Discrimination Regulations 2005*; *RRA 1976, s 13(3)*; *RBR 2003, reg 17(2)*; *SOR 2003, reg 17(2)*; *AR 2006, reg 20(2); DDA 1995, s 21A(2)*).

12.32 Employment agencies, careers guidance, etc

The provisions relating to employment agencies applied in the predecessor legislation. The *EA 2010* covers such person by way of the provisions for employment service-providers (see below **12.34**).

The *RBR 2003, SOR 2003* and *AR 2006* defined an employment agency as 'a person who, for profit or not, provides services for the purpose of finding employment for workers or supplying respondents with workers'.

Under *DDA 1995*, employment agencies were covered as providers of "employment services", defined to include "services to assist a person to obtain or retain employment, or to establish himself as self-employed" (*s 21A(1)(c)*).

No definition was given in the *SDA 1975* or the *RRA 1976*, though both those *Acts*, like the *RBR 2003* and *SOR 2003*, state that references to the services of an employment agency include 'guidance on careers and any other services related to employment' (*SDA 1975, s 15(3); RRA 1976, s 14(3); RBR 2003, reg 18(6); SOR 2003, reg 18(6); AR 2006, reg 21(6)*). Education establishments were excluded from the definition of employment agencies (impliedly in the *SDA 1975* and the *RRA 1976*, expressly in the *RBR 2003* and *SOR 2003: reg 18(6)* and in *AR 2006, reg 21(6)*). (Separate provision in relation to discrimination in education was made by both the Acts and the Regulations. Consideration of this is, however, outside the scope of this book.)

Note that users of employment agencies could also bring claims against the employer to whom they are supplied, either under the provisions relating to contract workers (see above **12.24**) or, in certain circumstances, as employees (see generally EMPLOYEE, SELF-EMPLOYED OR WORKER? **(15)**).

It was unlawful for an employment agency to discriminate against a person:

(a)   in the terms on which the agency offered to provide any of its services;

(b)   by refusing or deliberately not providing any of its services; or

(c)   in the way it provided any of its services (*SDA 1975, s 15(1); RRA 1976, s 14(1); RBR 2003, reg 18(1); SOR 2003, reg 18(1); AR 2006, reg 21(1)*).

All the exceptions that applied to discrimination by employers applied in relation to discrimination by employment agencies. The *RBR 2003, SOR 2003* and *AR 2006* provided that the agency would have a defence where the alleged discrimination 'only concerns employment which, by virtue of . . . (the) exception for genuine occupational requirement . . . the employer could lawfully refuse to offer the person in question' (*RBR 2003, reg 18(3); SOR 2003, reg 18(3); AR 2006, reg 20(3)*). The exceptions in the *RBR 2003, SOR 2003* and *AR 2006* for national security, positive action and the protection of Sikhs from discrimination in relation to the wearing of safety helmets applied generally to *Parts II* and *III* of both sets of *Regulations* and therefore applied to employment agencies as to employers. The *SDA 1975* and *RRA 1976* provided, simply, that the agency would have a defence where the alleged discrimination 'only concerns employment which an employer could lawfully refuse to offer the' person concerned (*SDA 1975, s 15(4); RRA 1976, s 14(4)*). (For circumstances in which an employer could lawfully refuse to offer employment see above **12.3, 12.10, 12.11, 12.12** and **12.17 ff.**)

A further defence was available that is peculiar to employment agencies. An employment agency would not be liable for unlawful discrimination where it proves that 'it acted in reliance on a statement made to it by the employer to the effect that, by reason of (the existence of a genuine occupational requirement) its action would not be unlawful', provided that it also proves that it was reasonable for it to rely on the statement (*SDA 1975, s 15(5); RRA 1976, s 14(5); RBR 2003, reg 18(4); SOR 2003, reg 18(4); AR 2006, reg 21(4)*). Thus, if, for example, an employment agency relied on the statement of an employer who had been guilty of discrimination in the past, to the knowledge of the employment agency, it may be difficult for that agency to establish that it had acted reasonably in relying upon that statement.

If an employer knowingly or recklessly made a statement to that effect which 'in a material respect is false or misleading', they thereby committed an offence punishable by a fine not exceeding level 5 on the standard scale (*SDA 1975, s 15(6); RRA 1976, s 14(6); RBR 2003, reg 18(5); SOR 2003, reg 18(5); AR 2006, reg 21(5)* see also **1.10 INTRODUCTION**).

It was also unlawful for an employment agency, in relation to the provision of its services, to subject to harassment a person to whom it provided such services, or who had requested the provision of such services: *SDA 1975, s 15(1A)*, as inserted with effect from 1 October 2005 by the *Sex Discrimination Regulations 2005, reg 18; RRA 1976, s 14(1A); RBR 2003, reg 18(2); SOR 2003, reg 18(2); AR 2006, reg 21(2); DDA 1995, s 21A(2)*.

12.33 State provision of employment-related services

The provisions relating to state provision of employment-related services applied in the predecessor legislation. The *EA 2010* covers such person by way of the provisions for employment service-providers (see below **12.34**).

Under the predecessor legislation, the prohibitions on discrimination and harassment also applied to the provision of facilities or services by the Secretary of State under the *Employment and Training Act 1973, s 2* (arrangements for assisting persons to obtain employment) and by the Scottish Enterprise or Highlands and Islands Enterprise under the *Enterprise and New Towns (Scotland) Act 1990, s 2(3)* (the equivalent provision for Scotland) (*SDA 1975, s 16(1), (1A); RRA 1976, s 15(1), (1A); RBR 2003, reg 19(1), (2); SOR 2003, reg 19(1), (2); AR 2006, reg 22(1), (2)*).

Similarly, the prohibitions on racial and sex discrimination and harassment applied where a local authority provided services under the *Employment and Training Act 1973, s 10* (*SDA 1975, s 15(2); RRA 1976, s 14(2)*).

The provisions relating to the provision of facilities or services under the *Employment and Training Act 1973, s 2* were default provisions, applying only where the Secretary of State would not be covered by the provisions relating to employment agencies (see above **12.32**) or providers of vocational training generally (see above **12.31**): *SDA 1975, 16(2); RRA 1976, s 15(2); RBR 2003, reg 19(3); SOR 2003, reg 19(3); AR 2006, reg 20(3)*).

12.34 Employment service-providers

The *EA 2010* contains specific provision in relation to employment service-providers. This replaces the provision in the predecessor legislation on providers of vocational training, employment agencies and state provision of employment-related services, although case law on those types of provider (see above) will in the main continue to be relevant when construing the provision in the *EA 2010* in respect of employment service-providers.

A non-exhaustive definition of employment service provision is given at *s 56(2)*. It includes the provision of vocational training, the provision of vocational guidance, the provision of a service for finding employment for persons, the supply of persons for work to employers, careers services and various other statutory services.

'Vocational training' is defined for the purposes of the section as 'training for employment' or 'work experience (including work experience the duration of which is not agreed until after it begins') (*s 56(6)*) and 'training' includes facilities for training (*s 56(8)*).

Section 55 makes it unlawful for any 'employment service-provider' to discriminate against, or victimise, persons:

(a)   in the arrangements they make for selecting persons to whom to provide, or to whom they offer to provide, their services;

(b)   as to the terms on which the service is provided;

(c)   by not providing, or not offering to provide, the service;

(d)   by terminating the provision of the service; or

(e)   by subjecting the individual to any other detriment (*EA 2010, s 55(1). (2), (4), (5)*).

There is also a specific prohibition on harassment by the employment service-providers: *EA 2010, s 55(3)*.

The employment services provision is a residual one that applies only where the other provisions relating to employment do not apply (*s 56(3)*). Training that is covered by the parts of the *Act* relating to schools and higher education is also excluded: *s 56(4)* and *(5)*. *Section 56(5)* provides that the employment services provision does not apply 'in relation to training or guidance for students of an institution to which section 91 (further and higher education) applies in so far as it is training or guidance to which the governing body of the institution has power to afford access'. In *Blackwood v Birmingham and Solihull Mental Health NHS Foundation Trust* [2016] ICR 903 the CA considered the meaning of 'power to afford access' in *s 56(5)* and concluded that 'power' means 'the ability to do something' (even if that something requires third party co-operation and consent) and that 'afford access' means 'afford entry to a placement'. Thus, a student mental health nurse placed with the respondent Trust by her university was engaged in vocational training to which the university had 'power to afford access' even though the placement could only be arranged by the university with the consent of the Trust and even though the Trust had a unilateral power to terminate the placement (i.e. even though the university had no power to compel the Trust to continue to afford the claimant access to the placement). This meant that *s 56(5)* applied and accordingly *s 55* was disapplied. This in principle left the claimant only with a potential claim under the higher education provisions of the *Act* (*s 91*) against the University. This in effect left the claimant without a remedy since the only claim that could be made against the University under *s 91* was a claim in relation to "access" to vocational training. The University could not under that provision be held responsible for the actions of the Trust in providing the vocational training. If the Trust had been the claimant's employer, a claim could have been brought straightforwardly under the employment provisions, but that was not the situation and in this case the *EA 2010* on its face left the claimant without a remedy. The CA considered that this situation was incompatible with the requirements of EU Law (specifically *art 14(1)* of *Directive 2006/54*) and accordingly ruled that s 56(5) must be construed as reading "This section does not apply to discrimination in relation to training or guidance for students of an institution to which section 91 applies to the extent that the student is entitled under that section to make a claim as regards that discrimination". So read, *s 56(5)* did not prevent the tribunal from hearing the claimant's claim against the Trust under *s 55* as a vocational training provider. The Court of Appeal in Blackwood also gave guidance as to the circumstances in which the agency provisions in *ss 109* and *110* of the *EA 2010* might be relevant in such claims. See **11.56** Discrimination and Equal Opportunities – I. For a case in which it was determined that the university was not 'affording access' to vocational medical training for the purposes of *s 56(5)*, see *Garrard v University of London* [2013] EqLR 746.

The genuine occupational requirement exceptions (above para **12.2** ff) are applied indirectly to employment service-providers. They may refuse to provide employment services to persons where the services relate to employment of a type the offer of which could lawfully be refused to that person by virtue of a genuine occupational requirement: see *para 5* of *Sch 9* to the *EA 2010*. An employment services provider will have a defence to any claim if he relies reasonably on a statement made by the person with the power to offer the work that a genuine occupational requirement would apply: *para 5(3)*. It is an offence for a person with the power to offer such work to knowingly or recklessly make a statement about a genuine occupational requirement that is false or misleading: *para 5(4)*. A person guilty of that offence is liable on summary conviction to a fine not exceeding level 5 on the standard scale: *para 5(5)*.

12.35   Trustees and managers of occupational pension schemes

The *EA 2010* makes specific provision in relation to occupational pension schemes. *Section 61(1)* provides that an occupational pension scheme must be taken to include a non-discrimination rule. A non-discrimination rule is a provision by which a 'responsible person' (A):

(a)   must not discriminate against another person (B) in carrying out any of his functions in relation to the scheme;

(b)   must not, in relation to the scheme, harass B;

(c)   must not, in relation to the scheme, victimise B (*s 61(2)*).

'Responsible persons' are the trustees or managers of the scheme, employers whose employees are (or may be) members of the scheme and persons exercising an 'appointing function' in relation to an office the holder of which is, or may be, a member of the scheme (*s 61(4)*). An 'appointing function' includes the functions of appointing a person, terminating a person's appointment, recommending a person for appointment and approving an appointment (*s 61(6)*).

The non-discrimination rule does not operate in relation to a person who is a pension credit member of the scheme, ie the spouse or civil partner of a member of the scheme who has received a pension credit from the scheme on the death of the pensioner member: *s 61(5)*.

Section 62 makes specific provision to enable trustees and managers to make alterations to the scheme by resolution to conform with the non-discrimination rule, even if they do not have the power under the scheme to do so, or if the procedure for doing so would be liable to be unduly complex or protracted or involves obtaining consents which cannot be obtained or which can be obtained only with undue delay or difficulty.

The provisions in relation to occupational pension schemes in the predecessor legislation were similar: see the *RBR 2003* and *SOR 2003* (as amended with effect from 2 December 2003 by the *Employment Equality (Religion or Belief) (Amendment) Regulations 2003 (SI*

2003/2828) and The *Employment Equality (Sexual Orientation) (Amendment) Regulations 2003 (SI 2003/2827)* respectively) applied to trustees and managers of occupational pension schemes, as did the *DDA 1995* (as amended). *AR 2006* also applied to trustees and managers of pension schemes. However, there were detailed exceptions in relation to age set out in *Schedule 2* to *AR 2006*.

'Occupational pension scheme' has the same meaning as in the *Pensions Schemes Act 1993 (EA 2010, s 212,* see previously *RBR 2003, Sch 1A, para 1; SOR 2003, Sch 1A, para 1; AR 2006, Sch 2, para 1*).

Certain further provision is made in relation to occupational pension schemes so far as the protected characteristics of sex, pregnancy and maternity, sexual orientation, age and disability are concerned as follows.

12.35a Sex discrimination

In the predecessor legislation sex discrimination in relation to pensions was dealt with in the *Pensions Act 1995* and not in the *SDA 1975.* Although the provisions of the *Pension Act 1995* and the *SDA 1975* have been brought together in the *EA 2010,* there is still a similar division made between the general provisions prohibiting discrimination in relation to pensions and those prohibiting sex and maternity discrimination in relation to pensions. As set out above, *Sections 61(1)* and *(3)* of the *EA 2010* provide that 'an occupational pension scheme must be taken to include a non-discrimination rule' and that the scheme will take effect 'subject to' that rule. However, the 'non-discrimination rule' only applies where an 'equality rule' does not have effect (or would have had effect but for the exceptions in *Part 2* of *Sch 7*): see *EA 2010, s 61(10).* Thus the general 'non-discrimination rule' only applies to occupational pension schemes where the sex equality rule under *s 67* or the maternity equality rule under *s 75* (see below) does not.

See **22.14** ff E QUAL P AY for details of the sex equality rule in relation to occupational pension schemes and see also R ETIREMENT **(42)**.

12.35b Pregnancy and maternity discrimination

In the predecessor legislation sex discrimination in relation to pensions was dealt with in the *Pensions Act 1995* and not in the *SDA 1975.* Although the provisions of the *Pensions Act 1995* and the *SDA 1975* have been brought together in the *EA 2010,* there is still a similar division made between the general provisions prohibiting discrimination in relation to pensions and those prohibiting sex and maternity discrimination in relation to pensions. As set out above, *Sections 61(1)* and *(3)* of the *EA 2010* provide that 'an occupational pension scheme must be taken to include a non-discrimination rule' and that the scheme will take effect 'subject to' that rule. However, the 'non-discrimination rule' only applies where an 'equality rule' does not have effect (or would have had effect but for the exceptions in *Part 2* of *Sch 7*): see *EA 2010, s 61(10).* Thus the general 'non-discrimination rule' only applies to occupational pension schemes where the sex equality rule under *s 67* (see above) or the maternity equality rule under *s 75* does not.

See **22.17** E QUAL P AY for details of the maternity equality rule.

12.35c Sexual orientation

It should first be noted that so far as the general non-discrimination rule applicable to occupational pension schemes is concerned, *section 67(7)* expressly provides that if the effect of a 'relevant matter' (i.e. a relevant term or the exercise of a relevant discretion permitted under the scheme: *s 67(8)*) differs according to a person's family, marital or civil partnership status, a comparison for the purposes of determining whether the trustees or managers have discriminated on grounds of sex contrary to *s 67* must be with persons of the opposite sex who have the same status, i.e. between male civil partners and female civil partners, not between male civil partners and female spouses, for example. It is to be noted, however, that in the light of the decision of the *Supreme Court in Hall v Bull* [2013] UKSC 73, [2013] 1 WLR 3741 (see above **12.14**) such discrimination will generally constitute direct discrimination on grounds of sexual orientation.

There is, however, a further specific exception in *para 18* of *Part 3* of *Sch 9* to the *EA 2010* for benefits dependent on marital status. This applies to pensions as to other benefits and is discussed in detail above at **12.14**. In short, it provides that a person does not contravene the Act, so far as relating to sexual orientation, by doing anything which prevents or restricts a person who is not married from having access to a benefit, facility or service (a) the right to which accrued before 5 December 2005 (the day on which *section 1* of the *Civil Partnership Act 2004* came into force), or (b) which is payable in respect of periods of service before that date. A challenge to the lawfulness of this temporal limitation under EU law was rejected by the CA in *Innospec Ltd v Walker* [2015] EWCA Civ 1000, [2016] ICR 182 (a case that concerned the entitlement of a same-sex civil partner (now spouse) to a survivor's pension on the same basis of an opposite-sex spouse); the outcome of an appeal to the Supreme Court is awaited. See also *Parris v Trinity College Dublin* (C-443/15) [2017] ICR 313. That case concerned an occupational pension scheme with a rule to the effect that a survivor's pension would only be payable if the marriage (whether same-sex or opposite-sex) had taken place before the individual reached the age of 60. The claimant complained that this was indirectly discriminatory against homosexuals who under Irish law were not permitted to marry prior to 2011, by which time the claimant was already 60. Disagreeing with the Advocate General in that case, the CJEU rejected the claim, essentially on the basis that under EU law it is a matter for Member States if and when to provide legal recognition to same-sex partnerships and EU law does not require such legal recognition to be given retroactive effect.

12.35d Age discrimination

The *AR 2006* provided a number of exceptions for age discrimination in relation to occupational pension schemes (in *Sch 2*). The *EA 2010* does not itself contain any exceptions, but provides for exceptions to be set out in subordinate legislation. A Minister of the Crown may by order (following consultation) provide that it is not an age contravention for an employer or for the trustees and managers of an occupational pension scheme to use certain specified practices in relation to contributions to personal pension schemes (*para 16* of *Part 2* of *Schedule 9* to *EA 2010* and *s 61(8)*).

The *Equality Act (Age Exceptions for Pension Schemes) 2010 Order (SI 2010/2133)* (as amended) made under that enabling power makes extensive and detailed provision for exceptions from the *EA 2010* for certain practices in relation to pension schemes.

It is to be noted that the *2010 Order* states that the inclusion of a practice in the list of exceptions provided for in that *Order* does not mean that it would otherwise be unlawful: *art 5*.

It should also be noted that most of these exceptions go beyond the exceptions for age discrimination that are specifically referred to in the *Framework Directive* and would therefore need to be justified (in the event of a challenge) as being a proportionate means of achieving a legitimate aim. *Article 6(2)* of the *Framework Directive* does however specifically permit Member States to 'provide that the fixing for occupational social security schemes of ages for admission or entitlement to retirement or invalidity benefits, including the fixing under those schemes of different ages for employees or groups or categories of employees, and the use, in the context of such schemes, of age criteria in actuarial calculations, does not constitute discrimination on the grounds of age, provided this does not result in discrimination on the grounds of sex'. The scope of this exception was considered by the CJEU in *Dansk Jurist- Og Okonomforbund, acting on behalf of Toftgaard v Indenrigs- Og Sundhedsministeriet* Case C-546/11 [2014] ICR 1. In that case the CJEU held that 'availability pay' paid to Danish civil servants when made redundant (up to three years further salary provided they remained available for assignment to another post during that period) did not constitute a form of occupational social security scheme. Exclusion of over 65s from receipt of availability pay because they were eligible for a state pension was therefore direct discrimination, and not justified.

Readers are referred to the text of the *2010 Order* for the detail of the provisions. In summary, however, the exceptions cover the following:

(a) any rights accrued or benefits payable in respect of periods of pensionable service prior to 1 December 2006 (*art 3(b)*);

(b) provisions which treat members or potential members of a scheme differently on the grounds of their length of service with an employer so long as that length of service is less than five years (and length of service may refer to length of service at or above a particular level, assessed by reference to the demands made on the member or worker, for eg, in terms of effort, skills and decision-making) (*art 6(2)*);

(c) length of service criteria of greater than five years, if it reasonably appears to the employer that this meets a business need (for eg by encouraging the loyalty or motivation or rewarding the experience of some or all of its workers) (with regard to action by trustees or managers, they may rely on a confirmation by the employer) (*art 6(3)*);

(d) setting minimum or maximum ages for admission to the scheme (*Sch 1, para 1(a)*), or for the commencement of payment of employer contributions (*Sch 2, paras 4* and *5*), including different ages for different groups or categories of worker;

(e) setting a minimum level of pensionable pay for admission (provided this is not above one and a half times the lower earnings limit in s 5(1) of the Social Security Contributions and Benefits Act 1992, does not exceed an amount calculated by reference to the lower earnings limit where the aim is more or less to reflect the amount of the basic state retirement pension; or an amount calculated more or less to reflect the amount of the basic state retirement pension plus the additional state retirement pension) (*Sch 1, para 1(b)*);

(f) the use of age criteria in actuarial calculations (*Sch 1, para 2*) (for a case in which this exemption was held to apply so as to preclude the claim see *Hadfield v Health & Safety Executive* UKEATS/0013/10/BI);

(g) differences in employer or member contributions attributable to differences in pensionable pay (*Sch 2, para 2* and *Sch 1, paras 3, 18* and *21(3)*);

(h) differences in the amount of any age related benefit or death benefit attributable to differences over time in the pensionable pay of those members (*Sch 1, para 20*) or the setting of a maximum amount of benefit by reference to a fraction, proportion or multiple of a member's pensionable pay (*Sch 1, para 21(3)*);

(i) differences in employer or member contributions attributable to differences in age, but only in limited circumstances (broadly speaking where the aim of the payment of differential rates is to equalise the amount of benefits that persons of different ages whose circumstances are otherwise comparable will receive) (*Sch 1, paras 4, 5* and *6*);

(Note that, once an employee has passed the minimum age for admission to a scheme, there is no exception that enables an employer simply to pay different levels of contribution to employees based on their ages. Such arrangements would constitute prima facie age discrimination and would have to be justified by reference to a legitimate aim in the normal way: see *Handels- og Kontorfunktionaerernes Forbund Danmark v Experian A/S* Case C-476/11 [2014] ICR 27. In that case, the CJEU accepted that legitimate aims for paying different amounts of employer contribution by reference to the ages of workers could include enabling older workers entering late to build up a reasonable pension over a short period, or including younger workers in the scheme at an early stage while making it possible for them to have a larger proportion of their income at their disposal, or the need to cover risks the cost of which increased with age unless that is justified. The CJEU held that it was for the national court to determine whether the particular arrangements in question were justified by reference to those aims.)

(j)   setting of early or late retirement ages including different ages for different groups or categories of member (including different ages for deferred and active members) (*Sch 1, para 11*);

(k)   a minimum age for entitlement to or payment of any age-related benefit to a member, provided that this benefit is subject to actuarial reduction for early receipt, and the member is not credited with additional periods of pensionable service (except where certain other exemptions for minimum ages for entitlement apply) (*Sch 1, paras 7, 8, 9* and *12*);

(l)   a minimum age for payment or entitlement to a particular age-related benefit on grounds of redundancy where it is enhanced in a specified manner (*Sch 1, para 10*);

(m)   a minimum age for entitlement to age-related benefits on grounds of ill health, where the benefit is enhanced in a specified manner (*Sch 1, para 12*) and for the discontinuation of any life assurance cover for such members when they reach retirement age (*Sch 1, para 16*);

(n)   for the purpose of equalising the amount of age-related benefit employees of different ages whose situations are otherwise comparable will receive as a result of historical arrangements, an employer may pay different rates of contribution according to the age of workers (*Sch 2, para 1*);

(o)   an employer may always make equal rates of contribution irrespective of the age of the workers in respect of whom contributions are made (*Sch 2, para 6*);

(p)   age-related benefits or death benefits may be calculated by reference to length of pensionable service, so long as members in a comparable situation are entitled to accrue rights based upon the same fraction of pensionable pay (*Sch 1, para 17*) and benefits may be limited by a maximum number of years of pensionable service (*Sch 1, para 21(2)*);

(q)   pensions in payment may be increased for members over 55 (*Sch 1, para 28*), and may be increased for other members by reference to their ages (or the length of time the pension has been in payment) to the extent that the aim in setting the different rates is to maintain the relative value of members' pensions (*Sch 1, paras 29* and *30*);

(r)   death benefit by reference to the number of years pensionable service that a member would have completed had they remained in employment to normal pension age (*Sch 1, para 13*), and any pension payable where the dependent is more than a specified number of years younger than the member may be actuarially reduced (*Sch 1, para 15*);

(s)   benefits payable to members aged between age 60 and 65 may in certain circumstances be reduced by reference to the state retirement pension rate (*Sch 1, para 14*);

(t)   certain differences in the fraction of pensionable pay at which any age-related benefit accrues, or the amount of death benefit, or age-related benefits, or setting a maximum amount of age-related benefits or death benefit equal to a fraction, proportion or multiple of the member's pensionable pay, or a minimum period of pensionable service, in each case where the aim is to give members in a comparable situation the right to the same fraction proportion or multiple of pensionable pay without regard to pensionable service (*Sch 1, para 18*);

(u)   where (t) applies, setting different rates of member or employer contributions is also permitted (*Sch 1, para 19*);

(v)   limiting age related benefits or death benefits to members entitled to short service benefit under s 71 of the Pension Schemes Act 1993 (*Sch 1, para 22*);

(w)   excluding from a calculation of pensionable pay an amount which does not exceed one and a half times the lower earning limit, aimed to reflect the basic state retirement pension, or calculated to reflect the basic state retirement pension plus the additional state retirement pension (*Sch 1, para 23*);

(x)   differences in age-related or death benefits attributable to accrual of age-related benefit at a higher fraction for pensionable pay over the upper limit to reflect the additional state retirement pension (*Sch 1, para 24*);

(y)   limiting the amount of a benefit (or employer contributions: *Sch 2, para 3*) where this relates to all members joining or eligible to join on, after or before a particular date and which results from imposing a maximum level of pensionable pay by reference to which such benefit is calculated (*Sch 1, para 25*);

(z)   closure of schemes, or parts of schemes, from certain dates (*Sch 1, paras 26* and *27*);

(aa) an age limit for the transfer of the value of a member's accrued rights into or out of a scheme may be set provided that it is not more than one year before the member's normal pension age (*Sch 1, para 31*);

(ab) anything necessary to secure any tax relief or exemption or to prevent any charge to tax arising under Part 4 of the Finance Act 2004 (*Sch 1, para 32*).

12.35e

Disability discrimination

In addition to the general non-discrimination rule applicable to occupational schemes (see above) 'responsible persons' are also under a duty to make reasonable adjustments for persons with disabilities: *EA 2010, s 61(11)*. *Section 63* further provides so far as communications are concerned (i.e. the provision of information and the operation of a dispute resolution procedure) the prohibition on disability discrimination applies to a disabled pension credit member as it does to someone who is a deferred member or pensioner member of the scheme.

Local authority members

Section 58 of the *EA 2010* contains specific provision prohibiting local authorities from discriminating against a member of the authority in relation to the member's carrying out of 'official business' by not affording him access to training or other facilities or subjecting him to a detriment. By *s 59(4)*, 'official business' is anything the member does as a member of the authority, as a member of a body to which the member is appointed by the authority, or as a member of any other public body. A local authority must also not harass the member (*s 58(2)*) or victimise him (*s 58(3)*). However, *s 58(4)* provides that a member will not be subjected to a 'detriment' for these purposes only because the member is (a) not appointed or elected to an office of the authority, (b) not appointed or elected to, or to an office of, a committee or sub-committee of the authority, or (c) not appointed or nominated in exercise of an appointment power of the authority. By *s 58(6)* a duty to make reasonable adjustments also applies to a local authority (see also *paragraph 18* of *Schedule 8*). The genuine occupational requirement exception (above **12.2**) does not apply to qualifications bodies.

12.36 The Crown

As with the predecessor legislation, *EA 2010* applies to employment by the Crown, House of Commons staff and House of Lords staff as it does to other employments: see *s 82(2)*. See *SDA 1975, s 85–85B; RRA 1976, s 75–75B; RBR 2003, reg 36–38; SOR 2003, reg 36–38; AR 2006, reg 44–46; DDA 1995, s 64–65* for the relevant provisions of the predecessor legislation.

Save as set out above at **12.3, 12.5, 12.11**(d), **12.5**(i) and **12.16**(d), it also applies to service in the armed forces: see *s 82(3)*. As under the predecessor legislation, separate provision is made for enforcement of claims by members of the armed forces: see **13.2** DISCRIMINATION AND EQUAL OPPORTUNITIES – III.

12.37 GENERAL EQUALITY DUTIES ON PUBLIC AUTHORITIES

Sections 149–157 of the *EA 2010*, which came fully into force on 6 April 2011, impose general equality duties on public authorities. Similar provision was to be found in the predecessor legislation at *RRA 1976, s 71, SDA 1975, s 76A* and *DDA 1995, s 49A*. Full discussion of these provisions is outside the scope of this work. However, in summary, section 149(1) creates a new, truly general public sector equality duty ("PSED") (in the sense that it applies to all protected characteristics apart from marital/civil partnership status: see *s 159(7)*), which requires public authorities and others exercising public functions (*s 149(2)*), in the exercise of their functions, to have 'due regard to the need to':

(a)   eliminate discrimination, harassment, victimisation and any other conduct that is prohibited by or under the *EA 2010*;

(b)   advance equality of opportunity between persons who share a relevant protected characteristic and persons who do not share it;

(c)   foster good relations between persons who share a relevant protected characteristic and persons who do not share it.

Section 149(3) makes clear that the 'due regard' duty includes in particular a duty to have due regard to the need to remove or minimise disadvantages suffered by persons who share a relevant protected characteristic that are connected to that characteristic, to take steps to meet the needs of persons who share a relevant protected characteristic that are different from the needs of persons who do not share it, and to encourage persons who share a relevant protected characteristic to participate in public life or in any other activity in which participation by such persons is disproportionately low. *Section 149(5)* further stipulates that having due regard to the need to foster good relations between persons includes having due regard to the need to tackle prejudice and promote understanding. The section recognises that compliance with the PSED may involve treating some persons more favourably than others, but makes clear that this is not to be taken as permitting conduct that would otherwise be prohibited under the Act (*s 149(6)* and see **12.10** above for the exceptions for positive discrimination).

Note that the duty does not sanction treating some people more favourably than others where this would be conduct otherwise prohibited under the *EA 2010* (see *s 149(6)*).

In addition to the PSED, the *EA 2010* also imposes certain specific duties on public authorities for the purpose of enabling the better performance by the authority of its PSED: see *s 153*. Those specific duties are set out in the *Equality Act 2010 (Specific Duties) Regulations 2011*. They require public authorities to publish information to demonstrate their compliance with the PSED and to set (and publish) specific equality objectives.

An appraisal of the case law on the PSED is beyond the scope of this book.

12.38 Enforcement

Enforcement of the general duties is the responsibility of the Equality and Human Rights Commission (*ss 31* and *32* of the *Equality Act 2006*). *Section 156* of the *EA 2010* further makes it clear that there is no 'cause of action at private law' in relation to an alleged breach of the GEDs or PSED. This leaves open the possibility of a judicial review claim by a private individual in relation to alleged breaches of these general duties, and many such claims have been brought (see **12.37** above). Permission to apply for judicial review may, however, be refused in such cases if the court considers that the option of complaint to the EHRC constitutes an adequate alternative remedy for the individual.

13   Discrimination and Equal Opportunities – III: Enforcement

13.1   The *Equality Act 2010* ('*EA 2010*') makes provision in relation to nine 'protected characteristics' defined in *s 4*, namely: age, disability, gender reassignment, marriage and civil partnership, pregnancy and maternity, race, religion or belief, sex, and sexual orientation (see further DISCRIMINATION AND EQUAL OPPORTUNITIES – I (11) above). The vast majority of the provisions of the *EA 2010* in relation to employment and all those relevant to this chapter came into force on 1 October 2010. The *EA 2010* therefore now provides a unified code covering all anti-discrimination law. Insofar as the contents of this chapter are concerned, the *EA 2010* very largely replicates (and consolidates and simplifies) the provisions of the previous Acts and Regulations, namely the *Sex Discrimination Act 1975* ('*SDA 1975*'), the *Race Relations Act 1976* ('*RRA 1976*'), the *Employment Equality (Sexual Orientation) Regulations 2003 (SI 2003/1661)* ('*SOR 2003*'), the *Employment Equality (Religion or Belief) Regulations 2003 (SI 2003/1660)* ('*RBR 2003*'), the *Disability Discrimination Act 1995* ('*DDA 1995*') and the *Employment Equality (Age) Regulations 2006 (SI 2006/1031)* ('*AR 2006*'). With effect from 1 October 2010 the *EA 2010* repealed (so far as is relevant for this chapter) those Acts and Regulations. However this chapter continues to refer to those Acts and Regulations for two reasons. First, there may yet remain cases working their way through the tribunal system under the old legislation. Secondly, as the *EA 2010* largely replicates the old legislation the vast majority of cases under the old legislation remain relevant to the interpretation of the equivalent provisions of the *EA 2010* and the understanding of those cases is assisted by citation of the old legislation.

No civil or criminal proceedings may be taken against any person for a breach of any provision of the *EA 2010* (and previously the *SDA 1975, RRA 1976, SOR 2003, RBR 2003, DDA 1995* or *AR 2006*), except where such an action is expressly provided for by the *EA 2010* (and previously by those Acts or Regulations) (*EA 2010, s 113(1)*; and previously *SDA 1975, s 62(1); RRA 1976, s 53(1); SOR 2003, reg 27(1); RBR 2003, reg 27(1); DDA 1995, Sch 3, para 2(1)*; and *AR 2006, reg 35(1)*). This does not restrict the making of quashing, mandatory or prohibiting orders (which are remedies obtained against public bodies upon an application for judicial review) or a complaint to the Pensions Ombudsman (*EA 2010, s 113(3)*; and previously the *SDA 1975, s 62(2); RRA 1976, s 53(2); SOR 2003, reg 27(2); RBR 2003, reg 27(2); DDA 1995, Sch 3, para 2(2)*; and *AR 2006, reg 35(2)*). One difference is that employment tribunals now have jurisdiction in relation to certain complaints relating to occupational pension schemes under the *EA 2010, s 120(2)–(5)*. The only means of direct enforcement open to an individual for discrimination, in relation to employment, is generally by application to an employment tribunal (see **13.2** below).

Since 1 October 2007 the Equality and Human Rights Commission ('EHRC'), established under the *Equality Act 2006 ('EA 2006')* (see **13.23 – 13.24** below) has had additional powers to hold investigations (see **13.25 – 13.27** below), issue unlawful act notices (see **13.28** below) and may apply for an injunction in certain cases (see **13.29 – 13.30** below) Previously, in the case of sex, race and disability discrimination only, the Equal Opportunities Commission ('EOC'), the Commission for Racial Equality ('CRE') and Disability Rights Commission ('DRC') respectively exercised similar powers.

Where the *EA 2010* (or previously the *SDA 1975, RRA 1976, SOR 2003, RBR 2003, DDA 1995* or *AR 2006*) does not confer the rights granted by EU directives, such as the *EEC Directive 76/207* ('the *Equal Treatment Directive*') or the *Framework Directive 2000/78/EC*, individuals may rely upon these Directives in claims against state authorities (see further **37.8** PUBLIC SECTOR EMPLOYEES and **11.2** DISCRIMINATION AND EQUAL OPPORTUNITIES – I).

The provisions under the *SDA 1975, RRA 1976, SOR 2003, RBR 2003, DDA 1995* and *AR 2006* were very similar and when referring to the previous legislation this chapter addresses the issue of enforcement in these six areas together, highlighting any relevant differences. The *EA 2010* (principally *Pts 9* and *10*) largely replicates those provisions.

Reference can also be made to *Harvey on Industrial Relations and Employment Law* (HARVEYS – L (EQUAL OPPORTUNITIES) and PI (PRACTICE AND PROCEDURE)).

13.2 APPLICATIONS TO AN EMPLOYMENT TRIBUNAL

Under the *EA 2010, s 120* an employment tribunal has jurisdiction to determine a complaint relating to (a) a contravention of *Pt 5* (work) and (b) a contravention of *ss 108* (relationship that has come to an end), *111* (instructing, causing and inducing contraventions) or *112* (aiding contraventions) that relates to *Pt 5*. An employment tribunal also has jurisdiction to determine various applications and questions in relation to occupational pension schemes which are outside the scope of this chapter (*EA 2010, ss 120(2)–(5)*).

The Court of Appeal has now made clear that a claim can be brought for victimisation (as opposed to discrimination or harassment) occurring after the employment relationship has ended: *Jessemey v Rowstock Ltd* [2014] EWCA Civ 185, [2014] 3 All ER 409, [2014] ICR 550, [2014] IRLR 368.

No claim can be brought by a person who is a volunteer rather than an employee or other "worker" (*X v Mid-Sussex CAB and another* [2012] UKSC 59, [2013] ICR 249).

Previously a person ('the complainant') could present a complaint to an employment tribunal that another person had committed an act of discrimination or harassment against them which was unlawful by virtue of any of the provisions relating to employment (*SDA 1975, s 63(1); RRA 1976, s 54(1); SOR 2003, reg 28(1); RBR 2003, reg 28(1); DDA 1995, s 17A*; and *AR 2006, reg 36(1)*).

The employer of a discriminator is also liable for the discrimination under the *EA 2010, s 109* (previously *SDA 1975, ss 41, 42; RRA 1976, ss 32, 33; SOR 2003, reg 22, 23; RBR 2003, reg 22, 23; DDA 1995, ss 57, 58*; and *AR 2006, reg 25, 26*).

A complainant is entitled to include an individual respondent (eg a fellow employee) in his claim to see that that person is called to account as it is not correct to say that the primary liability for discrimination rests with the employer (see *Barlow v Stone* [2012] IRLR 898), but the complainant will need to plead a case that could prove that the individual respondent satisfies the requirements for liability under these provisions (see *Allaway v Reilly* [2007] IRLR 864, EAT). A tribunal was therefore wrong to rule that it could not hear a claimant's sexual harassment claim against a fellow employee unless the employer was also a respondent (see *Hurst v Kelly* [2013] ICR 1225, EAT). Where a claimant brings a claim against an unincorporated association it is permissible to do so either in the name of the association or in the name of a representative respondent, provided that the members of the board or management committee are actually aware of the proceedings and that where allegations are made against specific members those are joined as respondents (see *Nazir v Asim* [2010] ICR 1225, EAT).

In *Beresford v Sovereign House Estates* [2012] ICR D9 the EAT held that a tribunal could not exercise the power of joinder under *rule 10(2)(k)* or *rule 10(2)(r)* of the *Employment Tribunals (Constitution and rules of procedure) Regulations 2004 (SI 2004/1861)*, Sch 1, to join a fellow employee as respondent at the request of the respondent employer where the claimant had disavowed any intention to pursue a claim against the fellow employee. The power in question was a power to join any person whom the tribunal considered might be liable for the claim or who had an interest in the outcome of the claim. Under the new rules contained in *Schedule 1* to the *Employment Tribunals (Constitution and Rules of Procedure) Regulations 2013 (SI 2013/1237)*, *rule 34* now empowers the tribunal to add any person as a party if it appears that there are issues between that person and any of the existing parties falling within the jurisdiction of the Tribunal which it is in the interests of justice to have determined in the proceedings. It remains to be seen whether this somewhat wider power will lead to a departure from the *Beresford* approach.

In the case of sex and race discrimination members of the armed forces have also been able to bring claims in the employment tribunal since 1 October 1997. Previously, pursuant to the (now repealed) *Sex Discrimination (Complaints to Employment Tribunals) (Armed Forces) Regulations 1997 (SI 1997/2163)* (as amended by the *Armed Forces Act 2006 (Consequential Amendments) Order 2009 (SI 2009/2054), art 2* and *Sch 1*) and the (now repealed) *Race Relations (Complaints to Employment Tribunals)(Armed Forces) Regulations 1997 (SI 1997/2161)* (as amended by the *Armed Forces Act 2006 (Consequential Amendments) Order 2009 (SI 2009/2054), art 2* and *Sch 1*)) members of the armed forces had been subject to a separate statutory regime. Similar provisions were also contained in *SOR 2003, reg 36* and *RBR 2003, reg 36*, but not in *DDA 1995* and *AR 2006*, both of which expressly provided that they did not apply to service in any of the naval, military or air forces (*DDA 1995, s 64(7)*; *AR 2006, reg 44(4)*).

The *EA 2010, s 121* makes similar provision to those previously made in relation to race, sex, sexual orientation and religion or belief in relation to complaints by members of the armed forces and does now include complaints of age discrimination. Where a member of the armed forces has the right to bring a claim, he may only present a complaint to the employment tribunal if he has made a complaint in respect of the same matter to an officer under the service complaints procedures prescribed by regulations made under the *Armed Forces Act 2006, s 334*, and that complaint has not been withdrawn. A complaint will be treated as having been withdrawn if, having made the complaint to an officer neither that officer nor a superior officer has decided to refer the complaint to the Defence Council, and the complainant fails to apply for such a reference to be made. Presenting a complaint to the employment tribunal does not prevent the continuation of the service redress procedures. An employment tribunal will not have jurisdiction to hear a claim from a member of the armed forces if a 'service complaint' has not been accepted as valid by the prescribed officer under the services complaints procedure (eg because it was made out of time) and this requirement does not breach EU law (see *Molaudi v Ministry of Defence* [2011] ICR D19, (2011) 939 IDS Brief 21, EAT). Similarly there can be no claim if a complainant fails to appeal within time against the rejection of a service complaint (*Williams v Ministry of Defence* [2013] Eq LR 27, EAT).

An exception to the jurisdiction of the employment tribunals for employment-related claims exists for acts committed (or treated as committed) by qualifications bodies. It is not possible to complain to the employment tribunal if the act complained of is one in respect of which an appeal, or proceedings in the nature of an appeal, may be brought under any enactment (the *EA 2010, s 120(7)*; and previously *SDA 1975, s 63(2); RRA 1976, s 54(2); SOR 2003, reg 28(2)(a); RBR 2003, reg 28(2)(a); DDA 1995, s 17A(1A)*; and *AR 2006, reg 36(2)(a)*). The scope and effect of these provisions under the *RRA 1976* were considered in *R v Department of Health, ex p Gandhi* [1991] ICR 805; *Khan v General Medical Council* [1994] IRLR 646, CA; and *Chaudhary v Specialist Training Authority Appeal Panel (No 2)* [2005] EWCA Civ 282, [2005] ICR 1086). The availability of judicial review of a decision of a qualifications body does not oust the tribunal's jurisdiction (although judicial review is controlled by *section 31* of the *Senior Courts Act 1981*): *Michalak v General Medical Council* [2016] EWCA Civ 172, [2016] ICR 628, the purpose of *section 120(7)* being to ensure that the most appropriate specialist body hears a complaint. In the case of a discrimination claim the employment tribunal is better equipped than the Administrative Court.

In *Watt (formerly Carter) v Ahsan* [2007] UKHL 51, [2008] 1 AC 696, [2008] ICR 82, the House of Lords held that an employment tribunal had been a court of competent jurisdiction to decide that the Labour Party was a body conferring a qualification or authorisation needed for engagement in a profession or trade for the purposes of the *RRA 1976, s 12*, notwithstanding that a subsequent decision of the Court of Appeal had shown that decision to be wrong (and hence the claim should have been brought in the county court).

Tribunals also lack jurisdiction to hear complaints about discriminatory conduct in the course of judicial or quasi-judicial proceedings, and a police disciplinary board has been held to be a judicial body (*Heath v Metropolitan Police Comr* [2004] EWCA Civ 943, [2005] ICR 329). That immunity from suit does not extend to the decision to commence disciplinary proceedings nor to a chief constable's decision to dismiss (*Lake v British Transport Police* [2007] ICR 47, EAT). Moreover, a police disciplinary board's immunity from suit is not impeached so as to oust the employment tribunal's jurisdiction where the claimant merely seeks to advance before the employment tribunal a case that had been rejected by the board (*Lake v British Transport Police* [2007] EWCA Civ 424, [2007] ICR 1293, reversing the EAT's decision on this issue). In *P v Commissioner of Police for the Metropolis* [2016] EWCA Civ 2, [2016] IRLR 301 it was decided that there is no inconsistency between *Heath* and *Lake* and that the employment tribunal has no jurisdiction to hear a claim of a discriminatory dismissal where a disciplinary panel is the effective dismissing agent.

In *South London & Maudsley NHS Trust v Dathi* [2008] IRLR 350, EAT, a claim for victimisation based on the respondent's letters in response to a costs application and an application for disclosure in the course of previous discrimination proceedings should have been struck out by the tribunal as the letters attracted absolute immunity as they had come into existence for the purpose of those proceedings. In *Parmar v East Leicester Medical Practice* [2011] IRLR 641, EAT, Underhill P confirmed that the absolute privilege identified in *Heath* applies also to a witness who prepares a witness statement, even if a trial never takes place, and applies also to claims of alleged victimisation as well as other forms of discrimination.

Discrimination claims do not lapse on the death of the complainant. The deceased's estate may commence or continue proceedings (*Lewisham and Guys Mental Health NHS Trust v Andrews* [2000] ICR 707, CA). A discrimination claim is a 'hybrid' claim and a bankrupt has standing to bring such a claim provided that he limits the remedy sought to a declaration or compensation for injury to feelings (*Khan v Trident Safeguards Ltd* [2004] EWCA Civ 624, [2004] IRLR 961). Where a claimant employed as a member of a diplomatic mission by a foreign state claims for personal injury in a discrimination claim the employment tribunal does have jurisdiction to hear such a claim as it falls within the exception from state immunity for claims in respect of personal injury under the *State Immunity Act 1978, s 5* (see *Federal Republic of Nigeria v Ogbonna* [2012] 1 WLR 139, [2012] ICR 32, EAT).

Where, following the transfer of business under the *Transfer of Undertakings (Protection of Employment) Regulations 1981 (SI 1981/1794)* (now the *Transfer of Undertakings (Protection of Employment) Regulations 2006 (SI 2006/2405)*), a complainant complained that the refusal of a reference by the transferor after the TUPE transfer was victimisation under the *RRA 1976, s 2*, any liability was that of the transferor and did not pass to the transferee (*Coutinho v Vision Information Services Ltd* (2008) 849 IDS Brief 12, EAT). In proceedings related to the latter case the Court of Appeal has held that an employment tribunal was wrong to strike out for want of jurisdiction a claim brought by the claimant in which he argued that the failure by the TUPE transferee to honour an award of compensation was itself victimisation for the purposes of the *RRA 1976, s 2* (see *Rank Nemo (DMS) Ltd v Coutinho* [2009] EWCA Civ 454, [2009] ICR 1296, [2009] IRLR 672).

The *EA 2010, s 140* gives courts and employment tribunals the power to transfer cases between each other in certain circumstances. Where conduct has given rise to two or more separate proceedings under the *Act*, with at least one being for a contravention of *s 111* (instructing, causing or inducing contraventions), a court may transfer proceedings to an employment tribunal or an employment tribunal may transfer proceedings to a court (*EA 2010, s 140(1), (2), (3)*). A court or employment tribunal is to be taken for the purposes of *Pt 9* of the *EA 2010* to have jurisdiction to determine a claim or complaint transferred to it under the section (*EA 2010, s 140(4)*). A court or employment tribunal may not make a decision that is inconsistent with an earlier decision in proceedings arising out of the conduct (*EA 2010, s 140(5)*).

Final findings in previous relevant proceedings are treated as conclusive in proceedings under the *EA 2010* (*EA 2010, s 137(1)*). The 'relevant proceedings' are those under the *Race Relations Act 1968, ss 19* or *20*, the *EqPA 1970*, the *SDA 1975*, the *RRA 1976*, the *Sex Discrimination Act 1986, s 6(4A)*, the *DDA 1995*, *Pt 2* of the *EA 2006*, the *SOR 2003*, the *RBR 2003, AR 2006*, and the *Equality Act (Sexual Orientation) Regulations 2007 (SI 2007/1263)* (*EA 2010, s 137(2)*).

Note that guidance has been given by the Court of Appeal on case management of cases brought by disabled persons who have difficulty attending hearings: see *Royds LLP v Pine* [2012] EWCA Civ 1734, [2013] 1 WLR 717 and *Pine v Cineven Ltd* [2016] EWCA Civ 1047.

13.3   Burden of proof

The burden of proof has been an area that has generated much case law over previous years, particularly following the introduction of a 'reverse' burden of proof. The *EA 2010, s 136(2), (3)* provides for a 'reverse' burden of proof but in slightly different (and simpler) terms than under the previous *Acts* and *Regulations*:

(a)   If there are facts from which the court could decide, in the absence of any other explanation, that a person (A) contravened the provision concerned, the court must hold that the contravention occurred (*s 136(2)*).

(b)   This does not apply if A shows that A did not contravene the provision (*s 136(3)*).

This burden of proof applies to all the protected characteristics and proceedings for any type of contravention of the *Act* (*s 136(1)*). So the complications in relation to the potentially different treatment of race victimisation and colour and nationality claims discussed below is removed.

It is however important to understand the development of the burden of proof because much of the recent case law on burden of proof will remain relevant and because of the historic legacy of existing cases decided under the previous legislation.

But it is also important not to exaggerate the significance of the reverse burden of proof. Where the tribunal is in a position to make clear findings of fact in relation to allegedly discriminatory conduct, the reverse burden of proof has no effect, and the discussion below should be read with this fact in mind. See *Hewage v Grampian Health Board* [2012] UKSC 37, [2012] ICR 1054 per Lord Hope, paragraph 32.

SDA 1975 and *RRA 1976* originally gave the complainant the burden of showing both that they had been less favourably treated and that the less favourable treatment had been on grounds of sex or race. In practice, the burden proved difficult to discharge. Discrimination was very rarely overtly sexist or racist and the complainant had instead to persuade the tribunal to draw an inference. Complainants were assisted by case law (most famously *King v Great Britain-China Centre* [1992] ICR 516, CA) in which the following approach was advocated. First, the complainant had to establish a difference in sex or race and that they had been less favourably treated. Once this prima facie case had been established the tribunal was entitled to turn to the employer and seek an explanation for this disparity in treatment. If the employer's explanation was unsatisfactory the tribunal was entitled but not obliged (see *Glasgow City Council v Zafar* [1998] ICR 120, HL) to draw an inference that the less favourable treatment was on the relevant prohibited ground. The advantage of the guidance allowing rather than compelling the drawing of an inference is that it made allowance for the fact that humans are capable of acting inconsistently and unreasonably and yet not discriminatorily.

Eventually by way of a series of amendments to the Acts and in the new *SOR 2003, RBR 2003* and *AR 2006* a new split burden of proof was introduced in discrimination cases. Except for race victimisation claims and possibly race discrimination claims on grounds of colour or nationality, the new burden of proof was applicable to all other discrimination and harassment claims under the *SDA 1975, RRA 1976, SOR 2003, RBR 2003, DDA 1995* and *AR 2006*, including claims where the respondent was vicariously liable or knowingly aided a prohibited act. The relevant provisions were:

Sex	*SDA 1975, s 63A*
Marital status	*SDA 1975, s 63A*
Pregnancy or maternity leave	*SDA 1975, s 63A*
Gender reassignment	*SDA 1975, s 63A*
Race	*RRA 1976, s 54A*
Sexual orientation	*SOR 2003, reg 29*
Religion or belief	*RBR 2003, reg 29*
Age	*AR 2006, reg 37(2)*
Disability	*DDA 1995, s 17A(1C)*

Where, on the hearing of the complaint, the complainant proved facts from which the tribunal could conclude in the absence of an adequate explanation that the respondent:

(a)   had committed an unlawful act against the complainant falling within the jurisdiction of the employment tribunal; or

(b)   was either vicariously liable for such an act or had knowingly aided the commission of such an act;

the tribunal had to uphold the complaint unless the respondent proved that he did not commit, or as the case may be, was not to be treated as having committed, the act.

There were conflicting decisions on whether the old test continued to apply in cases of discrimination on grounds of colour or nationality, and on whether the new reverse burden of proof applied to victimisation claims. These complexities should no longer be significant, thanks to the *EA 2010*.

Seminal general guidance on the application of the reverse burden of proof test was provided by the EAT in *Barton v Investec Henderson Crosthwaite Securities Ltd* [2003] ICR 1205, EAT at 1218F and by the Court of Appeal in *Wong v Igen Ltd* [2005] EWCA Civ 142, [2005] ICR 931. The guidance is set out below in full under the heading 'the revised *Barton* Guidance'. Although couched by reference to the *SDA 1975, s 63A*, it applied equally to the *RRA 1976, SOR 2003, RBR 2003, DDA 1995* and *AR 2006*, and is likely to be highly relevant to the approach to be adopted under the *EA 2010, s 136*. The Supreme Court in *Hewage v Grampian Health Board* [2012] UKSC 37, [2012] ICR 1054 stated that this guidance had been very clearly expressed and no further guidance from the Supreme Court was needed.

The revised test is similar to the approach adopted in *King* in that the burden is initially on the complainant to make out what might be described as the '*prima facie case*'. The respondent then has to give an explanation. However, the revised test is stricter because once a *prima facie* case is established the respondent then has the burden of proving that he did not act unlawfully. If he fails to discharge the burden, the tribunal has to find in favour of the complainant.

As indicated above, under the old test the tribunal would decide, once a *prima facie* case had been made out, whether the case was in truth one of discrimination on a prohibited ground or whether it was perhaps unreasonable or inconsistent but nevertheless non-discriminatory treatment. Because discretion is replaced with compulsion, it becomes particularly important to determine when the *prima facie* case has been made out. Case law indicates that it is now harder for the complainant to make out a *prima facie* case than it was under the old *King* test.

In order to establish a *prima facie* case at stage one there must be something that raises a suggestion that a prohibited factor may have been at work. In *Igen v Wong* above, their Lordships addressed the issue in the context of the analysis of the *RRA 1976*:

'The relevant act is, in a race discrimination case . . . that (a) in circumstances relevant for the purposes of any provision of the 1976 Act (for example in relation to employment in the circumstances specified in section 4 of the Act), (b) the alleged discriminator treats another person less favourably and (c) does so on racial grounds. All those facts are facts which the complainant, in our judgment, needs to prove on the balance of probabilities.'

The Court of Appeal confirmed in *Madarassy v Nomura International plc* [2007] EWCA Civ 33, [2007] ICR 867, [2007] IRLR 246, that a claimant must establish more than a difference in status (eg. sex) and a difference in treatment before a tribunal will be in a position where it 'could conclude' that an act of discrimination had been committed. See also *Adebayo v Dresdner Kleinwort Wasserstein Ltd* [2005] IRLR 514, [2005] All ER (D) 371 (Mar), EAT; *University of Huddersfield v Wolff* [2004] IRLR 534, EAT; *Fernandez v Office of the Parliamentary Commissioner* [2006] All ER (D) 460 (Jul), EAT; *Griffiths-Henry v Network Rail Infrastructure Ltd* [2006] IRLR 865, [2006] All ER (D) 15 (Jul), EAT; *Fox v Rangecroft* [2006] EWCA Civ 1112; and *Islington London Borough Council v Ladele* [2009] ICR 387, [2009] IRLR 154, EAT (affd [2009] EWCA Civ 1357, [2010] IRLR 211, CA). There does not have to be positive evidence that any difference in treatment was on a prohibited ground in order to establish a *prima facie* case (*Network Rail Infrastructure Ltd* above), but even if the tribunal believes that the respondent's conduct requires explanation, before the burden can shift there must be something to suggest that the treatment was due to the claimant's possessing a protected characteristic (see *B and C v A* [2010] IRLR 400, EAT). It is not sufficient to shift the burden of proof that the conduct is simply unfair or unreasonable if it is unconnected to a protected characteristic (see *Comr of Police of the Metropolis v Osinaike* (2010) 907 IDS Brief 15, EAT; *St Christopher's Fellowship v Walters-Ennis* [2010] EWCA Civ 921, [2010] EqLR 82). However, a tribunal will be setting an impermissibly high hurdle if it asks whether discrimination is the only inference which could be drawn from the facts: *Pnaiser v NHS England and Coventry City Council* [2016] IRLR 170, EAT.

Whilst tribunals must be alert to the existence of, for example, racial or sexual stereotypes, the burden will only shift if there is sufficient reason to believe that the respondent could have been motivated by such a stereotype (see *B and C*, above). In *Canadian Imperial Bank of Commerce v Beck* (2010) 912 IDS Brief 10, EAT, an employment tribunal was held to have been entitled to regard the use of the word "younger" in a job specification as, in the circumstances, sufficient to shift the burden of proof onto the respondent in an age discrimination case relating to redundancy selection. Similarly, an employment tribunal had erred by not concluding that a manager's asking whether the claimant's age might be a reason why he could not work to the respondent's expectations had caused the burden of proof to shift (see *James v Gina Shoes Ltd* [2012] EqLR 314, EAT). However, inferences about subconscious motivation of alleged discriminators can only be based on solid evidence. In *South Wales Police Authority v Johnson* [2014] EWCA Civ 73 a remark by an individual about her experiences in relationships with black men was insufficient basis for inferring that her treatment of a black employee was motivated by racial prejudice.

In a case of alleged indirect discrimination, it is necessary for a claimant to establish the existence of the relevant "provision, criterion or practice" before the burden can shift in relation to discriminatory impact (*Dippenaar v Bethnal Green and Shoreditch Education Trust* (2015) UKEAT/0064/15, [2016] ELR 173, EAT). It is not, however, necessary for a claimant to show that the reason why the PCP has disadvantaged the group is related to the protected characteristic, or that this is the reason why the individual claimant has suffered a disadvantage: all that is required is that there be a causal connection between the PCP and the disadvantage: *Essop and ors v Home Office* [2017] UKSC 27, [2017] 1 WLR 1343. Thus in that case it was not necessary for the claimants to prove that the reason why more black and minority ethnic ("BME") civil servants fail the core skills test for promotion is related to their race or ethnicity: it was sufficient that a greater proportion of BME claimants failed and that there was a causal link between the test (the PCP) and the failure or likelihood of failure (the disadvantage). At that point, the burden shifts to the respondent to justify the PCP.

In deciding whether or not a *prima facie* case has been made out, the tribunal should ignore the substance of any explanation proffered by the employer for the treatment, turning to it only once the burden has shifted (*Igen* above). However, in *Veolia Environmental Services UK v Gumbs* [2014] EqLR 364, the EAT held that when considering whether the burden has shifted, the tribunal is entitled to take into account the fact of an employer giving inconsistent reasons for its conduct. Moreover, this does not mean that at the first stage the tribunal should consider only evidence adduced by the claimant and ignore the respondent's evidence. The tribunal should have regard to all the facts at the first stage to determine what inferences can properly be drawn (*Laing v Manchester City Council* [2006] ICR 1519, [2006] IRLR 748, EAT; approved by the Court of Appeal in *Madarassy* and *Appiah v Bishop Douglass Roman Catholic High School* [2007] EWCA Civ 10, [2007] ICR 897, [2007] IRLR 264; see also *Nelson v Newry and Mourne District Council* [2009] NICA 24, [2009] IRLR 548; *Asim v Nazir* [2010] ICR 1225, EAT; and *Mohmed v West Coast Trains Ltd* (2006) 814 IDS Brief 7, EAT). At this stage the tribunal will need to look at evidence that the act complained of occurred at all, evidence as to the actual comparator relied upon by the claimant, evidence as to whether the comparisons being made by the claimant were like with like, and available evidence as to the reasons for the differential treatment (*Madarassy* above). In *Madarassy* the Court of Appeal held that at the first stage the respondent may adduce evidence which: showed that the alleged acts did not occur; that, if they did occur, there was not less favourable treatment of the claimant; that the comparators chosen by the claimant or the situations chosen by the claimant were not like the claimant or the situations with which comparison was sought to be made; and that even if there was less favourable treatment it was not on prohibited grounds. So, in *Osoba v Chief Constable of Hertfordshire* [2013] Eq LR 1072 the EAT held that where at the first stage the tribunal accepted that the employer had acted honestly, it would be wrong to require it to provide a further explanation. It is submitted that there may be some difficulty for tribunals in distinguishing this last category of evidence which the Court of Appeal has held that they are entitled to consider and accept at the first stage and any putative explanation from the respondent that would be considered at the second stage.

The complainant must establish on the balance of probabilities that the employer has committed the potentially discriminatory act. It would not be appropriate to require an explanation from the employer for something that the employer *may* have done. Thus where an act merely may have been committed by the employer or by a third party a *prima facie* case will not have been established (*Igen* above).

Logically the employer may offer one of a number of sorts of explanations at the second stage, if he offers one at all; those that confirm discrimination, those that explain the disparity in a manner which makes it clear that there was no unlawful discrimination but which, to use the words of the EAT in *Sinclair, Roche & Temperley v Heard* [2004] IRLR 763, EAT 'redound to the employer's discredit', and those which explain away discrimination and are themselves worthy reasons. It is not sufficient to establish discrimination that the tribunal considers that the explanation given is not one that is objectively justified or reasonable as unfairness is not sufficient to establish discrimination (see *Network Rail Infrastructure Ltd* above).

The explanation cannot simply be asserted but must be proved. As the facts supporting the explanation will be in the respondent's knowledge cogent evidence is expected in support of any explanation proffered (see *Barton* above). The Court of Appeal has emphasised in *EB v BA* [2006] EWCA Civ 132, [2006] IRLR 471 that where the burden of proof has shifted the respondent must be required to adduce the evidence necessary to discharge that burden, otherwise the protection afforded to a claimant by (in that case) the *SDA 1975, s 63A* is negated. The weight of the burden imposed on the respondent at the second stage will depend on the strength of the *prima facie* case established by the claimant at the first stage (see *Network Rail Infrastructure Ltd* and *Ladele* above; *Khan & King v The Home Office* [2008] EWCA Civ 578, (2008) 858 IDS Brief 16, CA; *Virdi v Metropolitan Police Comr* [2009] EWCA Civ 477, [2009] All ER (D) 62 (Jun)). Once the burden of proof has shifted the tribunal is not required expressly to reject the respondent's explanation in order to make a finding of discrimination; it can merely not accept the explanation, though it is preferable if it does make positive findings one way or the other (see *Pothecary Witham Weld*, and *Beck*, above).

In 'reasonable adjustments' cases under the *DDA 1995*, Elias J has suggested (see *Project Management Institute v Latif* [2007] IRLR 579, EAT) that the claimant is required, at the first stage: (a) to establish the provision, criterion or practice relied upon; and (b) to demonstrate substantial disadvantage. The burden then shifts to the respondent to show that no adjustment or further adjustment should be made.

Before the new test many authorities emphasised the importance of making clear findings of fact and explaining why inferences were (or were not) being drawn (see *Anya v University of Oxford* [2001] ICR 847, CA). The later authorities make the same point. There must be clear findings of fact in relation to less favourable treatment; a clear finding as to whether the burden has reversed (see *Wolff* above); clear findings of fact in relation to the explanation; and a clear finding as to whether the explanation offered has discharged the burden and, if not, why not (see *Sinclair, Roche & Temperley* above; *Bahl* below; and *Chatwal v Wandsworth Borough Council* [2011] EqLR 942, EAT).

Where an employer advances an obviously non-discriminatory explanation, the tribunal's decision should show that it has recognised that an explanation has been provided and, if it still wishes to conclude that the act was unlawfully discriminatory, explain expressly why it is rejecting the explanation (*Bahl v Law Society* [2003] IRLR 640, EAT).

In a case where it is alleged that an act was on grounds of sex and/or on racial grounds and the evidence does not satisfy the tribunal that either ground, considered independently, is made out, it is not open to the tribunal to decide that 'taken together' the treatment was unlawful on both grounds (*Bahl* above) (and the same would hold true for any other attempt to combine other prohibited grounds). However in *Ministry of Defence v DeBique* [2010] IRLR 471, EAT, it was held that an employment tribunal had been entitled, in a case of alleged indirect race and sex discrimination, to consider the combined effect of two PCPs (provision, criterion or practice). In that case a female single parent soldier from St Vincent and the Grenadines complained of indirect sex discrimination in relation to a requirement that she be available for duty 24 hours a day seven days a week, which the tribunal considered placed female soldiers at a particular disadvantage, and the effect of the immigration rules which meant that, unlike a UK soldier, she could not have a relative with her to assist with childcare.

EA 2010, s 14 was to introduce the concept of combined discrimination where a claimant suffered less favourable treatment because of the combination of two (and only two) relevant protected characteristics (but not marriage and civil partnership or pregnancy and maternity). This was only to be available in relation to direct discrimination (not, as in *DeBique*, indirect discrimination). However, the Government has decided not to bring *s 14* into force and combined discrimination is not a concept recognised in EU law either: *Parris v Trinity College Dublin* C-443/15, [2017] ICR 313.

The Court of Appeal has confirmed that it is not always necessary for a tribunal expressly to go through the two-stage test in sequence and it can instead focus on the respondent's reasons for the treatment, for example where the comparator is hypothetical and the facts are not fundamentally in dispute (*Brown v Croydon London Borough Council* [2007] EWCA Civ 32, [2007] ICR 909, [2007] IRLR 259; *Secretary of State for Work and Pensions v McCarthy* (2010) 908 IDS Brief 11, EAT; see also *Laing, Khan and Ladele* above). Although it is generally good practice to go through the two-stage test there are cases where the claimant is not prejudiced by the tribunal omitting the first stage and going straight to the second stage and concluding that the respondent has discharged the burden of proving that the treatment was not on a prohibited ground. However, in such cases the tribunal must take care to apply *s 136* correctly and consider whether the burden of proof had shifted to the respondent: *Country Style Foods Ltd v Bouzir* [2011] EWCA Civ 1519, [2012] EqLR 163 and *Fennell v Foot Anstey LLP* (UKEAT/0290/15/DM, 28 July 2016).

The revised Barton Guidance

(1)   Pursuant to *SDA 1975, s 63A*, it is for the claimant who complains of sex discrimination to prove on the balance of probabilities facts from which the tribunal could conclude, in the absence of an adequate explanation, that the employer has committed an act of discrimination against the claimant which is unlawful by virtue of *Part 2* or which, by virtue of *s 41* or *s 42* of *SDA 1975*, is to be treated as having been committed against the claimant. These are referred to below as 'such facts'.

(2)   If the claimant does not prove such facts he or she will fail.

(3)   It is important to bear in mind in deciding whether the claimant has proved such facts that it is unusual to find direct evidence of sex discrimination. Few employers would be prepared to admit such discrimination, even to themselves. In some cases the discrimination will not be an intention but merely based on the assumption that 'he or she would not have fitted in'.

(4)   In deciding whether the claimant has proved such facts, it is important to remember that the outcome at this stage of the analysis by the tribunal will therefore usually depend on what inferences it is proper to draw from the primary facts found by the tribunal.

(5)   It is important to note the word 'could' in the *SDA 1975*, s 63A(2). At this stage the tribunal does not have to reach a definitive determination that such facts would lead it to the conclusion that there was an act of unlawful discrimination. At this stage a tribunal is looking at the primary facts before it to see what inferences of secondary fact could be drawn from them.

(6)   In considering what inferences or conclusions can be drawn from the primary facts, the tribunal must assume that there is no adequate explanation for those facts.

(7)   These inferences can include, in appropriate cases, any inferences that it is just and equitable to draw in accordance with *SDA 1975, s 74(2)(b)* from an evasive or equivocal reply to a questionnaire or any other questions that fall within *SDA 1975, s 74(2)* (see *Dattani v Chief Constable of West Mercia Police* [2005] IRLR 327, EAT – *RRA 1976, s 65* (the equivalent provision to *SDA 1975, s 74(2)*) also covers evasive or equivocal pleading in a response to a claim).

(8)   Likewise, the tribunal must decide whether any provision of any relevant code of practice is relevant and, if so, take it into account in determining such facts pursuant to *SDA 1975, s 56A(10)* (now the *EA 2006, s 15(4)*). This means that inferences may also be drawn from any failure to comply with any relevant code of practice.

(9)   Where the claimant has proved facts from which conclusions could be drawn that the employer has treated the claimant less favourably on the ground of sex, then the burden of proof moves to the employer.

(10)   It is then for the employer to prove that he did not commit, or as the case may be, is not to be treated as having committed, that act.

(11)   To discharge that burden it is necessary for the employer to prove, on the balance of probabilities, that the treatment was in no sense whatsoever on the grounds of sex, since 'no discrimination whatsoever' is compatible with the Burden of Proof Directive.

(12)   That requires a tribunal to assess not merely whether the employer has proved an explanation for the facts from which such inferences can be drawn, but further that it is adequate to discharge the burden of proof on the balance of probabilities that sex was not a ground for the treatment in question.

(13)   Since the facts necessary to prove an explanation would normally be in the possession of the respondent, a tribunal would normally expect cogent evidence to discharge that burden of proof. In particular, the tribunal will need to examine carefully explanations for failure to deal with the questionnaire procedure and/or a code of practice.

See also HARVEYS – Division L.5.D.

13.4   Time limit

A complaint must be presented to a tribunal before the end of the period of three months beginning when the act complained of was done (*EA 2010, s 123(1)(a)*; and previously *SDA 1975, s 76(1); RRA 1976, s 68(1); SOR 2003, reg 34(1), (1A); RBR 2003, reg 34(1), (1A); DDA 1995, Sch 3, para 3(1)*; and *AR 2006, reg 42(1)*, or such other period as the employment tribunal thinks just and equitable (*EA 2010 s 123(1)(b)*).

Where the claim concerns, in whole or in part, a cross-border dispute to which *art 8(1)* of *Directive 2008/52/EC* ("the *Mediation Directive*") applies and a mediation (within the meaning of *art 3(a)* of the *Mediation Directive*) has started before the time limit expires but the time limit will expire before the mediation ends or less than four weeks after the mediation ends, the time limit under the *EA 2010, s 123(1)(a)* is extended until four weeks after the mediation ends (*EA 2010, s 140A(1), (5), (6)*). Where a tribunal has power to extend a time limit under the *EA 2010, s 123(1)(b)* that power is exercisable in relation to the limitation period as extended by *s 140A* (*EA 2010, s 140A(13)*). Insofar as it is still in force pursuant to transitional and saving provisions, the time limit under the *SDA 1976, s 76(1)* is now subject to similar extension provisions in relation to disputes to which *art 8(1)* of the *Mediation Directive* applies. Those provisions are contained in the *SDA 1976, s 76ZA*.

A six month time limit applies to complaints by members of the armed forces: *EA 2010, s 123(2)*.

From 1 October 2004 the three month time limit could be extended by the 'extended period' under the *Employment Act 2002 (Dispute Resolution) Regulations 2004 (SI 2004/752)*, reg 15. However, following the repeal of the *EmA 2002, ss 29 to 33* and *Schedules 2 to 4* by the *Employment Act 2008, ss 1 and 20*, and subject to the transitional provisions under the *Employment Act 2008 (Commencement No 1, Transitional Provisions and Savings) Order 2008 (SI 2008/3232), art 3* and *Schedule*, such an extension ceased to be available after 6 April 2009.

13.4 Discrimination and Equal Opportunities – III: Enforcement

In computing the time limit, the clock is stopped during the period from the day after the claimant complies with the requirement to contact ACAS for early conciliation ("day A") until the day on which the claimant receives or is treated as receiving an early conciliation certificate ("day B"). If the time limit would otherwise expire between day A and one month after day B, it will instead expire at the end of that period. "One month" means on the "corresponding date" so where day B is 30 June, the time limit will expire on 30 July (*Tanveer v East London Bus & Coach Co Ltd* [2016] ICR D11. Only one conciliation certificate can be, or needs to be, issued for each "matter". This means that a conciliation certificate issued in response to issues raised in the run-up to dismissal or resignation will also cover the subsequent dismissal or resignation: *Compass Group UK and Ireland Ltd v Morgan* [2017] ICR 73. However, beware the mistaken issue of a second conciliation certificate in these circumstances: that will be invalid and will not give rise to any further extension of time: *HMRC v Garau* UKEAT/0348/16/LA. There is no need to seek a further conciliation certificate where amendments are made to a claim, even where the amendment is adding a different respondent provided the amended claim concerns the same "matter": *Drake International Systems Ltd and ors v Blue Arrow Ltd* [2016] ICR 445. See further **13.10**.

Whether a claim in relation to benefits is properly characterised as concerning equal pay or sex discrimination will have significant consequences for the applicable time limit (see, for example, *Hosso v European Credit Management Ltd* [2011] EWCA Civ 1589, [2012] ICR 547, [2012] IRLR 235). See also HARVEYS – Divisions **L.5.E, PI.1.E**.

For the purposes of deciding when an act was done, in calculating the time limit:

(a)   where the inclusion of any term in any contract renders the making of the contract an unlawful act, that act shall be treated as extending throughout the duration of the contract;

(b)   any act extending over a period shall be treated as done at the end of that period: *EA 2010 s 123(3)* (for an example, see *Calder v James Finlay Corpn Ltd* [1989] ICR 157);

(c)   a deliberate omission shall be treated as done when the person in question decided upon it: *EA 2010 s 123(3)*; and

(d)   in the absence of evidence establishing the contrary, a person is to be taken as having decided upon failure to do something when he does something inconsistent with the omitted act or when the period within which he would reasonably be expected to have done the act has expired: *EA 2010 s 123(4)*.

(See previously *SDA 1975, s 76(6); RRA 1976, s 68(7); SOR 2003, reg 34(4); RBR 2003, reg 34(4); AR 2006, reg 42(4)*; and *DDA 1995, Sch 3, para 3(3),(4)*.)

Whether a claim form contains a complaint of a particular act (which may affect the time limit by being the last in a series of connected acts) is a question of construction of the document, and therefore an error by the tribunal in this regard can found an appeal to the EAT (*Gregory Charles v Tesco Stores Ltd* [2013] Eq LR 260, CA).

Where a claim had been struck out because it was brought outside the time limit, a second claim alleging that the claimant was the victim of an ongoing course of conduct was an abuse of process because it was in reality just an attempt to resurrect the first claim (*Agbenowossi-Koffi v Donvand Ltd t/a Gulliver's Travel Associates* [2014] EWCA Civ 855).

13.5 Omissions

A difficulty of interpretation arose in cases where there was a delay between the point at which the discriminator decided upon a deliberate omission and the point at which he omitted to act. In *Swithland Motors plc v Clarke* [1994] ICR 231, EAT, the appellant decided, whilst negotiating the purchase of a car sales business from receivers, that in the event that its bid was successful it would follow its usual practice of employing only female sales staff. It would omit, therefore, to offer the existing male staff the opportunity to continue in employment. The purchase was completed more than three months after the decision to apply the policy had been taken. On its face *SDA 1975, s 76(6)(c)* appeared to suggest that the male employees were out of time to complain before they even knew that there was something to complain about. The EAT decided that the section had to be read as meaning 'decides at a time and in circumstances when he is in a position to implement that decision'. Time ran, therefore, from the date on which the business was purchased.

13.6 *Acts extending over a period*

Applications in discrimination cases will often make reference to a number of alleged instances of discrimination stretching back over a period, only part of which is within three months of the date of submission of the claim. The tribunal must then assess whether the individual allegations together constitute an 'act extending over a period' or else are to be treated as a series of discrete events.

In *Barclays Bank plc v Kapur* [1991] ICR 208, the House of Lords held that the bank's stipulation that service in Africa would not count for pension purposes, although originally made years before the complaints were brought, subjected the applicant employees to a continuing disadvantage which by virtue of *RRA 1976, s 68(7)(b)* was to be treated as an act done when the employees retired. It was necessary to distinguish a continuing rule such as this from an act which merely had continuing consequences. In *Sougrin v Haringey Health Authority* [1992] ICR 650, a pay re-grading was held to fall into the latter category, but in *Littlewoods Organisation plc v Traynor* [1993] IRLR 154 the failure to take the remedial measures promised after an earlier act of discrimination was held to be a continuing act (see also *Matuszowicz v Kingston-Upon-Hull City Council* [2009] EWCA Civ 22, [2009] ICR 1170, [2009] IRLR 28, CA and *Fairlead Maritime Ltd v Parsoya* (UKEAT/0275/15/DA, 30 August 2016)). However, in *Okoro v Taylor Wood Construction Ltd* [2013] ICR 580, CA, a construction company's decision to ban some contract workers from one of its sites was held to be a one-off act. In *Smith v Carillion and Secretary of State for Business, Innovation & Skills* [2015] EWCA Civ 209, [2015] IRLR 467, the Court of Appeal also applied *Okoro* holding that there could not be any more expansive interpretation by reference to the *Human Rights Act 1998* where the last incident complained of took place before the *Act* came into force.

A number of apparently discrete acts may provide evidence of a policy, rule or practice. The existence of such a policy or practice may itself constitute a 'continuing act' (*Owusu v London Fire and Civil Defence Authority* [1995] IRLR 574). In *Cast v Croydon College* [1998] ICR 500, CA, an employee who was about to commence maternity leave asked to be allowed to return on a part-time basis. Her request was refused. She took her maternity leave, returned to work and repeated her request. When it was again refused she resigned, alleging that she was unable to comply with the requirement that she work full-time. She commenced proceedings in the tribunal. Only the second refusal was 'in time'. It was held that each refusal constituted a separate act of discrimination, because on each occasion the employer considered the matter afresh. Had it merely restated its earlier decision, the position might have been different. Further, the tribunal decided that the second refusal was merely a confirmation of the first and that the claim was out of time. However, the Court of Appeal determined, first, that the two refusals were discrete decisions and that the claim in relation to the second refusal was within time and, further, that the two refusals should have been treated as evidence of the existence of a 'policy' on the employer's part, the fact that the same decision was reached on each occasion was evidence of the existence of a discriminatory policy. The operation of such a discriminatory policy constituted an act 'extending over a period' within the meaning of *SDA 1975, s 76*. Similarly, where an employer fails to make a reasonable adjustment for a disabled employee and then keeps the refusal under review, there is a continuing act or omission and time does not run (*Jobcentre Plus v Jamil and others*, EAT (26 November 2013, unreported). In contrast, in another case, the Court of Appeal has held that the time limit begins to run again on each occasion on which the policy is applied. Thus, where a complainant was refused the same request on a number of occasions, each refusal caused the three-month time limit to start afresh (*Rovenska v General Medical Council* [1998] ICR 85, CA). The EAT has held that an employment tribunal was entitled to conclude that a refusal by an employer to revoke a dismissal was entirely separate from the dismissal itself and not part of a continuing act (*Baynton v South West Trains Ltd* [2005] ICR 1730).

The EAT has said, *obiter*, that complaints of different types of discrimination can in principle be taken together as constituting conduct extending over a period, giving the example of complaints of direct discrimination by giving a Claimant undesirable shifts and a failure to make reasonable adjustments by giving the Claimant different shifts (*Robinson v Royal Surrey County Hospital NHS Foundation Trust* (30 July 2015, EAT unreported)).

Other authorities have used terms such as 'rule', 'scheme', 'regime' or 'practice' as well as 'policy'. However, the Court of Appeal has stressed that such terms are merely examples of acts which may extend over a period. Their Lordships have adopted a broader description of what the tribunal should look for: an 'ongoing situation' or a 'continuing state of affairs' which may be contrasted with 'a succession of unconnected or isolated specific acts' (*Hendricks v Metropolitan Police Comr* [2002] EWCA Civ 1686, [2003] ICR 530, CA). It will be a relevant, but not conclusive, factor whether the same or different individuals were involved in the alleged incidents of discrimination over the period and where there is a break in contact of several months a tribunal may be entitled to conclude that continuity is not preserved (see *Aziz v FDA* [2010] EWCA Civ 304). The Court of Appeal confirmed the *Hendricks* approach in *Lyfar v Brighton and Sussex University Hospitals Trust* [2006] EWCA Civ 1548, [2006] All ER (D) 182 (Nov), emphasising the need to focus on the substance of the complaints when assessing whether they form a continuous act. However, in order to establish the existence of a policy or practice, the complainant must establish some degree of 'co-ordination' (*Metropolitan Police Comr v Hendricks* (2002) 707 IDS Brief 8, EAT). In *Moxam v Visible Changes Ltd* [2012] Eq LR 202, EAT, the employment tribunal had erred by not applying a broad approach to 'racial grounds' to recognise that earlier instances of the use of racist language revealed that a manager had the same mindset as he had in relation to later, in-time incidents and therefore time should have been extended to include the earlier incidents. Following the House of Lords' decision in *Relaxion Group plc v Rhys-Harper* [2003] UKHL 33, [2003] ICR 867, the EAT has held that a serious of acts constituting an act extending over time can include an act taking place after the complainant has ceased to be an employee of the respondent (*BHS Ltd v Walker* (2005) 787 IDS Brief 11).

It will generally be an error of law for a tribunal to seek to determine whether there is an act extending over a period on the basis of legal argument alone without hearing any evidence and making findings of fact (see *City of Edinburgh Council v Kaur* [2013] Eq LR 632, and the 'public interest disclosure' case of *Arthur v London Eastern Rly Ltd (t/a One Stansted Express)* [2006] EWCA Civ 1358, [2007] IRLR 58). However, it is not enough for a claimant simply to assert that there is a continuing act or that there is an ongoing state of affairs, rather he or she must have an arguable basis for the contention that the complaints are so linked as to be a continuing act or an ongoing state of affairs (*Ma v Merck Sharp & Dohme Ltd* [2008] EWCA Civ 1426, [2008] All ER (D) 158 (Dec)). Conversely, a claimant is not required expressly to state in his claim form that there is a 'continuing act' if it is sufficiently clear to the respondent that such an argument would be raised in response to a limitation defence (see *Khetab v AGA Medical Ltd* (2011) 922 IDS Brief 9, EAT). In *Kerr v Ernst & Young Services Ltd* [2011] ICR D13, EAT, an employment judge was held to have erred in giving directions at a case management discussion that precluded a claimant from relying on complaints of discrimination against three individuals (on the grounds inter alia that too much time had elapsed) as she had no power at a case management discussion effectively to strike out parts of his claim. Further, even if she had had the power to do so, she had erred in not giving the opportunity for representations before making such an order.

In *Tyagi v BBC World Service* [2001] EWCA Civ 549, [2001] IRLR 465, the complainant sought to allege that he had been discriminated against in relation to an application for promotion. His claim was lodged 15 months after he had failed to obtain the promotion and a year after he had ceased to be employed by the respondent. He contended that the respondent operated a discriminatory recruitment policy which was still in place at the date of his application. That being so, he argued, his application was not out of time. The Court of Appeal found against him drawing a distinction between those who remained in employment at the time of complaint and those who did not. The former group was entitled to complain about discriminatory policies which affected the way in which their employer afforded them 'access to opportunities for promotion'. They could, therefore, complain about the existence of the policy itself. The latter were only able to complain about the arrangements made for the purpose of determining who should be offered a particular job and, thus, could not complain about the policy. See also *Ruhaza v Alexander Hancock Recruitment Ltd* [2012] EqLR 9, EAT.

In the case of a single act, time starts to run when the course of action is complete, that is when a complaint to a tribunal could first be made (*Clarke v Hampshire Electro-Plating Co Ltd* [1992] ICR 312; see also *Adekeye v Post Office* [1993] ICR 464). Where the alleged act of discrimination was the dismissal of an internal appeal relating to an unsuccessful promotion application time ran from the date of that decision, not the date that the claimant was notified of the decision (*Virdi v Metropolitan Police Comr* [2007] IRLR 24, EAT). In the case of a constructive dismissal which is alleged to be discriminatory, time runs from the complainant's resignation, not from the employer's repudiatory breach (*Meikle v Nottinghamshire County Council* [2004] EWCA Civ 859, [2005] ICR 1).

See also *Dimtsu v Westminster City Council* [1991] IRLR 450.

13.7 *Extension of time*

A tribunal may nevertheless consider a complaint or application which is out of time if, in all the circumstances of the case, it considers that it is just and equitable to do so (*EA 2010, s 123(1)(b)*; and previously *SDA 1975, s 76(5); RRA 1976, s 68(6); SOR 2003, reg 34(3); RBR 2003, reg 34(3); DDA 1995, Sch 3, para 3(2)*; and *AR 2006, reg 42(3)*). In considering applications for extension, the correct approach for the tribunal to take is to bear in mind that employment tribunal time limits are generally enforced strictly and to ask whether a sufficient case has been made out to exercise its discretion in favour of extension. It is not a question of extending time unless a good reason can be shown for not doing so (*Robertson v Bexley Community Centre (t/a Leisure Link)* [2003] EWCA Civ 576, [2003] IRLR 434). The discretion to extend time is not at large and the time limit will operate to exclude otherwise valid claims unless the claimant can displace it, although this does not mean that the discretion has to be used sparingly (see *Chief Constable of Lincolnshire Police v Caston* [2009] EWCA Civ 1298, [2010] IRLR 327). In deciding whether or not it is just and equitable to grant an extension of time, the tribunal must take care first to consider the reasons why the claim was brought out of time and then the reasons why the claim was not presented sooner than it was: *Abertawe Bro Morgannwg University Local Health Board v Morgan* (UKEAT/0305/13/LA, 18 February 2014). However, the failure to put forward a good reason for not having submitted the claim in time (or sooner) does not necessarily mean time should not be extended: all relevant factors including the balance of prejudice and the merits of the claim must be considered: *Rathakrishnan v Pizza Express (Restaurants) Ltd* [2016] IRLR 278, doubting *Habinteg Housing Association Ltdv Holleran* (2015) UKEAT/0274/14, [2015] All ER (D) 353 (Feb), EAT.

One possible ground for extending time is that the complainant was unaware of his or her rights, another that she has received incorrect advice from her lawyer (*Hawkins v Ball and Barclays Bank plc* [1996] IRLR 258; *Chohan v Derby Law Centre* [2004] IRLR 685, EAT; *Virdi v Metropolitan Police Comr*, above; cf also *British Coal Corpn v Keeble* [1997] IRLR 336; *Bahous*, below, or where a complainant has delayed because she was awaiting the outcome of an internal appeal or grievance procedure (*Aniagwu v Hackney London Borough Council* [1999] IRLR 303, EAT). The undesirability of bringing a claim while still employed is a factor that a tribunal may legitimately take into account when determining whether it is just and equitable to extend time: *Fairlead Maritime Ltd v Parsoya* (UKEAT/0275/15/DA, 30 August 2016). However exhausting internal procedures will not always justify a delay (*Robinson v Post Office* [2000] IRLR 804), and the Court of Appeal has since decided that *Aniagwu* is limited to its own facts (*Apelogun-Gabriels v Lambeth London Borough Council* [2001] EWCA Civ 1853, [2002] ICR 713). A tribunal is not required to accept a doctor's evidence that a claimant was unable due to psychiatric illness to present his claim in time where there was evidence that he had been fit enough to seek legal advice and had written coherent letters on unrelated matters within the limitation period (see *Chouafi v London United Busways Ltd* [2006] EWCA Civ 689, [2006] All ER (D) 33 (May)). In *Department of Constitutional Affairs v Jones* [2007] EWCA Civ 894, [2008] IRLR 128 (a case under the *DDA 1995*), the Court of Appeal held that a tribunal had been entitled to consider that the claimant's own inability to admit to himself that he was mentally ill and a disabled person for the purposes of the *DDA 1995* was a factor justifying delay in presenting a claim.

The tribunal may be assisted by considering the factors that the court is obliged to consider when extending time in personal injury cases (for which see the *Limitation Act 1980, s 33(3)* or *CPR rule 3.9(1)*). However it is not obliged to do so. Its obligation is simply to ensure that no significant circumstance is left out of account (*Afolabi v Southwark London Borough Council* [2003] EWCA Civ 15, [2003] ICR 800). One of the most significant factors which the tribunal should consider is whether a fair trial of the issue is still possible (*DPP v Marshall* [1998] ICR 518). Whilst the fact that a fair trial is impossible will most likely preclude extension of time, it does not follow that merely because a fair trial is still possible time should be extended (*Simms v Transco plc* [2001] All ER (D) 245 (Jan), EAT). If a respondent wishes to establish that a fair trial is no longer possible, he should consider leading evidence to establish the point (*Southwark London Borough Council*, above). An employment tribunal will err if it fails to take account of the prejudice to the employer of allowing a claim out of time (*Abegaze v South East Essex College* [2006] ICR 468, EAT).Conversely, an employment tribunal will err if it fails to recognise the absence of any real prejudice to an employer when refusing to exercise its discretion to extend time (*Baynton v South West Trains Ltd* [2005] ICR 1730, EAT). The merits of a case are an important factor and it will be an error of law for a tribunal not to take account of the merits of the case when considering the balance of prejudice (*Bahous v Pizza Express Restaurant Ltd* (2012) 945 IDS Brief 17, [2012] EqLR 4, EAT and *Donald v AVC Media Enterprises Ltd* UKEATS/0016/14/JW, 9 November 2016). The Inner House of the Court of Session held in *Malcolm v Dundee City Council* [2012] CSIH 13, [2012] EqLR 363 that an employment tribunal had taken an overly strict approach in refusing to extend time *after* it had held a 21 day hearing and concluded that allegations of harassment were well-founded on their merits. Where time is extended an employee cannot rely on legislation that was not in force at the time of the act complained of if the act would not have been unlawful at the time that it was committed (see *Abegaze*, above).

Where there is more than one respondent, the employment tribunal should consider the position of each respondent separately when deciding whether it is just and equitable to extend time (*Harden v Wootlif and Smart Diner Group Ltd* (UKEAT/0448/14/DA, 15 April 2015)). Different claims brought within the same proceedings may also require separate consideration: *Abertawe Bro Morgannwg University Local Health Board v Morgan* (UKEAT/0305/13/LA, 18 February 2014).

In *Stevens v Bexley Health Authority* [1989] ICR 224, the EAT appeared to consider that the statutory time limits were not applicable to claims brought directly under European law, but more recent decisions have shown that view to be incorrect (see **22.20–22.21 EQUAL PAY**, and **23.2 EUROPEAN UNION LAW**).

See also HARVEYS – Divisions L.5.E(4), (5), PI.1.F(1), (3).

13.8   Formulating the complaint

Care must be taken in drafting the complaint. In *Chapman v Simon* [1994] IRLR 124, the Court of Appeal held that an employment tribunal is limited to considering those matters complained of in the originating application (see also, *Akinmolasire v Camden and Islington Mental Health & Social Care Trust* [2004] EWCA Civ 1351, [2004] All ER (D) 59 (Oct)). However where general accusations of sex discrimination were made in relation to a redundancy dismissal, an employee was entitled to receive from the tribunal a finding on whether or not a failure to offer alternative employment was discriminatory even though she had not specifically relied on the point (*Prowse-Piper v Anglian Windows Ltd* [2010] EWCA Civ 428 (12 March 2010, unreported, CA)). In the light of the Court of Appeal's decision in *Chapman* it is also advisable, when specifying the detriments to which it is alleged that the complainant was subjected, specifically to recite that employees who do not share the complainant's protected characteristic have not or would not be subjected to such detriments. In relation to racial discrimination, the EAT has held that the employment tribunal either at or before the substantive hearing needs to identity which categories of racial discrimination (ie colour, race, nationality or ethnic or national origin) are relied upon so that the correct comparator can be identified, although a claimant who is not sure may plead all or most of them (see *Okonu*, above; and also *Chagger*, above). The EAT held in *Baker v Metropolitan Police Comr* (2010) 899 IDS Brief 9, EAT, that it is not sufficient merely to tick the box on the ET1 form for the particular type of discrimination complained of (in that case disability) without pleading any details (although the EAT also held that the tribunal erred in not considering the claimant's application to amend the claim). An employment tribunal had been entitled to refuse to allow an amendment to a claim to plead associative disability discrimination where the tribunal had already made findings of fact which meant that the amended claim could not have succeeded (see *Brill v Interactive Business Communications Ltd* [2010] EWCA Civ 1604). Where default judgment has been entered against a respondent for failure to file a response in time, in assessing compensation at a remedies hearing a tribunal may not make findings inconsistent with the case on liability pleaded in the claim form (see *Eaton v Spencer* [2012] ICR D7, EAT). In that situation, where alternative bases of liability are pleaded it is for the tribunal at a remedies hearing to decide which is appropriate (*Thomas and others v Taylors of St James Ltd* (UKEAT/0117/13/KN, 2 July 2013).

The Court of Appeal has determined that direct and indirect discrimination are separate claims which must be separately identified in a claim form (*Ali v Office of National Statistics* [2004] EWCA Civ 1363, [2005] IRLR 201). It is therefore essential fully to plead the facts on which different types of allegation of discrimination are based. Where a complainant believes that his dismissal was both discriminatory and unfair, it is essential that both are pleaded. If he first pursues a claim for unfair dismissal, he will not be entitled later to bring a fresh discrimination claim (*Divine-Bortey v Brent London Borough Council* [1998] IRLR 525, CA, applying *Henderson v Henderson* (1843) 3 Hare 100).

Where a complainant relies on more than one alleged act of discrimination, it is up to the complainant to ensure that each of them is pursued at the hearing itself. The tribunal is not obliged to make a finding in relation to everything raised in pleadings, only in relation to those matters which the complainant pursues at the hearing (*Mensah v East Hertfordshire NHS Trust* [1998] IRLR 531, CA). Where more than one incident is complained about, it is important for a tribunal to be clear which complaints are relied upon as distinct justiciable causes of action (and if necessary consider whether time should be extended in relation to those matters) and those complaints that are merely relied on as evidence (see *Aylott v Stockton-on-Tees Borough Council* [2009] IRLR 533, EAT).

A claim cannot be amended to include a complaint in relation to an act or omission that would not have been unlawful at the time that it took place (see *Standard Life Bank Ltd v Wilson* (2008) 851 IDS Brief 5, EAT – a decision concerning age discrimination).

Where a claimant relies on an actual comparator in addition to a hypothetical comparator, this is an important detail of the claim and it should be set out in the claim form (if necessary by amendment) (see *Woodward v Santander UK plc* [2010] IRLR 834, EAT).

In general, discrimination cases should not be struck out at a preliminary stage on grounds that they stand no reasonable prospect of success. Normally, a full examination of the facts will be required. However, a strike out may be appropriate in cases where, taking the claimant's case at its highest, it is nonetheless conclusively disproved by, or is totally and inexplicably inconsistent with, undisputed contemporaneous documents: *Mechkarov v Citibank NA* [2016] ICR 1121. In that case, the EAT (Mitting J) further observed that if core issues of fact turned to any extent on oral evidence, there needed to be a full hearing and it was not appropriate for an employment judge to conduct a 'mini trial' on those issues at a preliminary hearing without consideration of relevant documents. Where all material facts are clear and there is unlikely to be further relevant evidence available at a full hearing, a strike out may be appropriate: see *RMC v Chief Constable of Hampshire* (UKEAT/0184/16/LA, 8 November 2016) (where it was agreed the facts were not in dispute and oral evidence was not required and *Shestak v Royal College of Nursing* (2008) 152 Sol Jo (no 37) 30, [2008] All ER (D) 193 (Oct), (2009) 873 IDS Brief 12, EAT (where the strike-out was based on undisputed documents and a failure to articulate an arguable basis for the claims); although see, in contrast, *A v B* [2010] EWCA Civ 1378, [2011] ICR D9, in which the Court of Appeal held that the EAT had correctly overturned a decision to strike out a sex discrimination victimisation claim where there was a more than fanciful prospect that the respondent would fail to discharge the reverse burden of proof; see also *Community Law Clinic Solicitors v Methuen* [2012] EWCA Civ 571, [2012] EqLR 880, *Millbank Financial Services Ltd v Crawford* [2014] IRLR 18 and *Chandok v Tirkey* [2015] ICR 527 (emphasising that strike-out will not be appropriate where there is further potentially material evidence to come).

Discrimination claims often create problems for case management because, as noted above, a claimant seeks to rely on a series of alleged incidents of discrimination, even if only as background material from which inferences can be drawn. Whilst the basic rule is that evidence is admissible if it is relevant and inadmissible if it is irrelevant, evidence may be logically or theoretically relevant but too marginal and unlikely to assist the tribunal to justify its admission (see *HSBC Asia Holdings BV v Gillespie* [2011] IRLR 209, [2011] ICR 192, EAT). In *Gillespie* the EAT held that an employment judge had erred in not excluding evidence which allegedly went to the background of discriminatory acts where the evidence was not sufficiently relevant to justify the burden that would be placed on the respondent in addressing it. Underhill P held that, while in many cases, the best approach is to address the question of admissibility during the course of the substantive hearing, in some cases, particularly discrimination cases, this may not be practicable or fair and it may be appropriate to decide questions of admissibility in advance of the hearing, for example when the issue affects the hearing length, disclosure or the need for witness orders. Underhill P also suggested (obiter) that where a claimant raises complaints in relation to a large number of incidents of alleged discrimination, and it cannot be agreed that the claimant proceed with a sample only of his allegations, it may be possible instead to deal with his allegations in tranches rather than at a single hearing. However, whilst an employment judge may direct a claimant to set out clearly in a schedule the acts and omissions he or she complains of, there is no power to require a claimant to 'self select' which complaints he or she will pursue at the final hearing (see *McKinson v Hackney Community College* (2012) 942 IDS Brief 16, [2011] EqLR 1114, EAT).

13.9   Questionnaire and disclosure

An important difficulty encountered by complainants has been obtaining the information necessary to assess the strength of their case and to conduct it successfully once they are satisfied of its merits. To assist a person who considers that they may have been unlawfully discriminated against or subjected to harassment to decide whether to institute proceedings and, if they do so, to formulate and present the case in the most effective manner, there was until recently a procedure whereby such a person (whether an applicant or potential applicant) could serve, on the person against whom he or she has a complaint, a questionnaire in the form prescribed (*EA 2010, s 138*; and previously under respectively, *SDA 1975, s 74; RRA 1976, s 65; SOR 2003, reg 33; RBR 2003, reg 33; DDA 1995, s 56*; and *AR 2006, reg 41*) to gather information about their complaint. The questions and answers were admissible (subject to compliance with time limits) in tribunal proceedings and tribunals could draw inferences from a failure by the employer to answer the questions.

However, *EA 2010, s 138* was repealed with effect from 6 April 2014.

As a result of this repeal, claimants may now need to commence proceedings in order to obtain information which is not provided voluntarily. In pursuing a claim before an employment tribunal, a claimant may ask for the disclosure of documents by his employer or prospective employer. For the power of an employment tribunal to order the disclosure of documents which are relevant to the proceedings, see **19.60–19.62** EMPLOYMENT TRIBUNALS – II. However, in *Science Research Council v Nassé* [1979] ICR 921, the House of Lords held that tribunals should not order the disclosure of reports or references given and received in confidence, except when it is necessary for disposing fairly of the proceeding that the confidence should be overridden. In *Canadian Imperial Bank of Commerce v B* [2009] EWCA Civ 619, [2010] IRLR 740 the Court of Appeal summarised the position as ing that an order for disclosure should be made if it was "necessary for fairly disposi of the proceedings" and that while relevance was a factor it was not sufficient on its own arrant the granting of an order and conversely confidentiality does not, of itself, warrant usal of an order.

In *West Midlands Passenger Transport Executive v Singh* [1988] ICR 614, the Court ppeal upheld an employment tribunal's order for discovery of a schedule of statistics sh the ethnic origins of candidates for promotion and those actually promoted during eriod preceding the alleged discrimination. The decision also gives guidance as to wh osure should be refused because, although relevant, it would be oppressive. T ppeal further held that it might be possible, first, to infer from stati licant been discrimination against members of a racial group in gen as ember absence of a satisfactory explanation in the particular duced where the does not of that group had been the victim of discrimin Lighting Ltd [1990] ICR 125, continues to be the case under the

Under previously applicable tribunal r dent claimed to be prohibited by law have the power to require a sc led a security vetting, or indeed from information is not already imant a tribunal erred in law by ordering the [1990] IRLR 6, EAT) al 60, [2006] IRLR 73). was not appointed to a post (*Barracks* present rules. 016] 2 WLR 778, in *Kiani v Secretary* to a claim based on EU rike an appropriate [2015] ICR 1179 of State for the Home The C invoked as a ground for withholding held that where fr balance between information from respond the requirements

329

flowing from state security and the requirements of the right to effective judicial protection whilst limiting any interference with the exercise of that right to that which [was] strictly necessary'. The same approach was required by article 6 of the Human Rights Convention (see *Tariq v Home Office* [2011] UKSC 35, [2012] 1 AC 452). The balancing of those competing interests had to take account of all the material facts of the particular case. The tribunal in *Kiani* did not err in refusing further disclosure where it had taken sufficient account of material seen at a closed hearing in which the claimant could not participate but was assisted by a special advocate, and had conducted a balancing exercise knowing that the material contained 'the very essence of the case'.

The EAT has held that evidence about a 'without prejudice' discussion with a complainant about bringing her employment to an end could be adduced as there was no dispute at the time attracting privilege and, in any event, the public interest in having discrimination allegations properly determined meant that it would be an abuse to apply the 'without prejudice' rule in that case (*BNP Paribas v Mezzotero* [2004] IRLR 508). However in *Woodward v Santander UK plc* [2010] IRLR 834, the EAT sought to emphasise that *Mezzotero* did not create a new exception to the without prejudice rule and that the policy reasons behind the rule that parties be able to negotiate freely applied with particular force where parties were seeking to settle discrimination claims. The EAT held that the exception to the without prejudice rule for unambiguous impropriety applied only in the clearest cases, and was not engaged in the present case.

In *Vaseghi v Brunel University* (2006) 818 IDS Brief 10, EAT, the EAT held that discussions with two employees about settlement of their discrimination claims took place in circumstances where the without prejudice privilege was waived and that the importance of establishing the truth in discrimination cases may tip the scales of justice against maintaining the privilege where the claimants' case would be severely prejudiced by not being able to refer to the discussions. The Court of Appeal affirmed the EAT's judgment holding that in the particular and unusual circumstances of the case where the grievance procedure had in effect been a trial of the victimisation issue before an independent panel at which both parties gave evidence of the previous negotiations there was a waiver (*Brunel University v Vaseghi* [2007] EWCA Civ 482, [2007] IRLR 592). The Court of Appeal also held that by pleading its response in the way it did and attaching a copy of the grievance report the university had confirmed its intention to waive privilege and it was too late to amend the response to withdraw that waiver.

In many discrimination cases there will often be a need for the claimant to be examined by a frequently instructed medical expert to assist the employment tribunal to determine and cooperate whether the claimant is disabled. Persistent failure by a claimant to *Cumbers–* attend medical expert may justify the striking out of the claim (see See also *Hart Bakers* [2011] EWCA Civ 277).

13.10   Conciliation   L.5.C, PI.1.N.

For tribunal claims applies (e.g. for cer Early Conciliation not

Previously, when a comp officer was required to en 2014, it is compulsory, unless an exemption he was requested to claims), for a claimant to have made an

(a)   in the absence of requ ment tribunal, the conciliation that he could act with a the complaint if:

respondent; or

nt, he considered

(*Employment Tribunals Act 1996* ('*ETA 1996*'), *s 18(1)*, *(2)*). His services could also be sought by a prospective party before the presentation of a complaint (*ETA 1996, s 18(3)*).

From 6 April 2014, all such conciliation requests are treated as requests for Early Conciliation. From 6 May 2014, tribunal claims will not be accepted unless the complaint has been referred to ACAS and a conciliation certificate issued. This certificate confirms that the Early Conciliation requirements have been met (*Employment Tribunals Act 1996* ('*ETA 1996*'), *s 18A*).

Conciliation can also be requested by a person who anticipates having proceedings issued against them (ibid *s 18B*) or after the issue of proceedings (*s 18C*).

Information given to the conciliation officer in the performance of his duties is not admissible in evidence before the tribunal except with the consent of the giver of the information (*ETA 1996, s 18(7)*). Thus, frequently a conciliation officer will contact the employer to investigate the possibility of the removal of the cause of complaint. An employer is not obliged to give the conciliation officer information.

An ACAS conciliation officer has no responsibility to see that the terms of a settlement are fair to the employee and, indeed, a conciliation officer should not advise the parties on the merits of the case (see *Clarke v Redcar & Cleveland Borough Council* [2006] ICR 897, [2006] IRLR 324, EAT, for guidance on the role of a conciliation officer). The ACAS conciliation officer does not have to broker a settlement or record it in order for an agreement reached effectively to oust the employment tribunal's jurisdiction pursuant to the *ETA, s 18(2)*, he merely needs to endeavour to promote settlement (*Allma Construction Ltd v Bonner* [2011] IRLR 204, EAT). Where one party makes an offer to another that is sufficiently definite to indicate an intention to be bound, covering the essentials of the contract in question, and it is accepted, then a contract is concluded which, if an ACAS conciliation officer has been involved, will be sufficient to oust the employment tribunal's jurisdiction. It does not matter if there are additional matters that could have been included in the agreement and what are the "essentials" of the agreement will vary from case to case (see *Bonner* above).

See also **2.4** Advisory, Conciliation and Arbitration Service **(ACAS)**. For the validity of settlements, see **13.33** below. For the effect of Early Conciliation on time limits, see **13.4** above.

See also Harveys – Divisions **PI.3, PI.1.T**.

13.11 Restriction of publicity

The *ETA 1996, s 11* empowered the Secretary of State to make regulations allowing for the restriction of publicity in cases where the commission of a sexual offence, or sexual misconduct, is alleged. Regulations were subsequently made which give powers to restrict publicity to both the employment tribunals and the Employment Appeal Tribunal. There are, broadly, two powers. The first is a power to ensure that the tribunal's own documents do not identify the parties concerned. The second power enables the tribunal to restrict others from reporting the identity of the parties or matters which might lead to them being identified. These powers are likely to be most relevant in some cases of sex discrimination, and now sexual orientation discrimination. Similar powers to make restricted reporting orders exist in relation to proceedings under the *DDA 1995*, or now under the *EA 2010, s 120* where the complaint relates to disability, on the application of the complainant or of its own motion where evidence of a personal nature is likely to be heard by the employment tribunal hearing the complaint (*ETA 1996, s 12(1)*, *(2)*). Evidence of a personal nature would be evidence of a medical, or other intimate nature, which might reasonably be assumed to be likely to cause significant embarrassment to the complainant if reported (*ETA 1996, s 12(7)*).

Where a case appears to involve allegations of the commission of a sexual offence, the tribunal is required to omit or delete from the register, and any judgment, document or record of proceedings which will otherwise be available to the public, any 'identifying matter which is likely to lead members of the public to identify any person affected by or making such an allegation' (*Employment Tribunals (Constitution and Rules of Procedure) Regulations 2004 (SI 2004/1861), Sch 1, rule 49*). The EAT is similarly required by the *Employment Appeal Tribunal Rules 1993 (SI 1993/2854), rule 23(2)*. A sexual offence means an offence of rape and related offences, and certain other offences including indecent assault, under-age intercourse and incest (*ETA 1996, s 11(6)*). A case will 'involve' such allegations even if they are not the basis of the claim or central to the decision-making; it is enough that they will fall to be considered (*X v Metropolitan Police Comr* [2003] ICR 1031, EAT). The employment tribunal and EAT has the power to order that their judgments be anonymised in the case of an alleged sexual offence as the *ECHR Article 8* right to privacy of the victim of such an offence is 'well-recognised' (see *B and C v A* [2010] IRLR 400, EAT). The EAT has held that (in the absence of an express power to do so) it has a duty to protect a party's rights under the *ECHR Article 8* by interpreting its powers under the *ETA 1996, s 30(3)* to regulate its own procedure so as to anonymise its judgment and delete from its public records any matter likely to lead to the identification of a party (*A v B* [2010] IRLR 844, [2010] ICR 849, EAT). In that case the claimant brought unfair dismissal proceedings following his dismissal stemming from unproven allegations of child sex abuse. The EAT held that his right to reputation under *ECHR Article 8* had to be weighed against the protection of freedom of expression under *ECHR Article 10* and that the balance, in the circumstances of the case, clearly favoured maintaining the claimant's anonymity.

Where a case appears to involve allegations of sexual misconduct the employment judge may make a temporary restricted reporting order on application by one of the parties or of the tribunal's own motion (*SI 2004/1861, Sch 1, rule 50(1), (2), (3)*). The parties may apply to have the temporary restricted reporting order revoked or converted into a full restricted reporting order within 14 days of the temporary order being made, otherwise the order lapses after 14 days (*rule 50(4), (5)*). A full restricted reporting order can only be made if the parties are given the opportunity to advance oral argument at a pre-hearing review or a hearing as to whether the order should be made (*rule 50(6)*). A full restricted reporting order remains in force until the tribunal's judgment on liability and remedy is sent to the parties, unless revoked earlier (*rule 50(9), (11)*). If the claim is withdrawn before judgment is issued (pursuant to rule 25(3)) with the order still in place, then the tribunal has no jurisdiction to consider the revocation of the order after the withdrawal with the effect that it continues in perpetuity (*Davidson v Dallas McMillan* [2009] CSIH 70, [2010] IRLR 439, Ct of Session). Meanwhile the power to restrict reporting extends beyond the period expressed in the legislation by virtue of *ECHR, article 8*: see *F v G* and *EF and NP v AB, CD, JK, QR and Associated Newspapers Ltd* (below).

The tribunal has a discretion to allow non-parties (such as journalists) to make submissions as to the revocation or variation of a restricted reporting order (see *Davidson*, above). Sexual misconduct is defined in *ETA 1996, s 11(6)* to mean the commission of a sexual offence, sexual harassment, or other adverse conduct related to sex (whether in its character or in its having reference to the sex or sexual orientation of the person at whom it is directed).

A restricted reporting order is one prohibiting the publication in Great Britain, in a written publication available to the public, of matter likely to lead members of the public to identify a person as one who is affected by or is the person making the allegation, or the inclusion of such matter in programs for reception in Great Britain. A corporate body is not a person for these purposes (*Leicester University v A* [1999] ICR 701). Contravention of a restricted reporting order is a criminal offence carrying a fine not exceeding level 5 on the standard scale (see **1.10** Introduction). The EAT has decided that the European Union law requirement that domestic procedural rules should not make enforcement of, *inter alia*, the directly effective right to equal treatment conferred on public sector workers by the *Equal Treatment Directive*, 'virtually impossible' or 'excessively difficult' (see **23.2** European Union Law) allows tribunals to make restricted reporting orders in cases other than where sexual misconduct is alleged. In that particular case, the EAT was satisfied that, without a restricted reporting order, the particular complainant would have been deterred from bringing her claim of discrimination on grounds of her transsexuality (*Chief Constable of the West Yorkshire Police v A* [2001] ICR 128, EAT).

The order should be no broader than is necessary to achieve the purpose of the legislation, which is to protect the identity of the alleged victim and perpetrator, and of any witness whose anonymity is essential to the proper conduct of the litigation. A restricted reporting order should not, therefore, conceal the identity of the complainant in circumstances where she does not wish to be anonymous (*R v London (North) Industrial Tribunal, ex p Associated Newspapers Ltd* [1998] IRLR 569; see also *X v Metropolitan Police Comr*, above, for application of the same reasoning in the case of a claim brought by a transsexual). An employment tribunal had been entitled to consider that a change of mind by two claimants whose identity was previously covered by an order and the addition of six new media organisations seeking to revoke or vary the order was sufficient grounds to justify reconsidering the order (*Tradition Securities and Futures SA v Times Newspapers Ltd* [2009] IRLR 354, EAT). In that case the EAT also held that there was much to be said for orders being as specific as possible, although in that case it was not useful to specify what kind of material was or was not likely to lead to the named individual alleged perpetrators being identified.

In *F v G* [2012] ICR 246, EAT, Underhill P held that an employment tribunal has wide powers unconstrained by the particular wording of *rules 49* or *50* to make anonymity orders or restricted reporting orders to the extent necessary to protect the *ECHR, article 8* rights of third parties (in that case of disabled students at the college where the claimant had worked) even where there was no allegation of a sexual offence or sexual misconduct. The President also observed that there was no reason why a decision on anonymity had to be made once and for all at the start of proceedings but instead a tribunal could make an interim decision on anonymity and then a final decision when judgment was delivered, at which time the tribunal would be best placed to assess all the relevant factors.

Applying *F v G* (above), the EAT in *EF and NP v AB, CD, JK, QR and Associated Newspapers Ltd* [2015] IRLR 619 held that in relation to allegations of sexual activities involving a husband and wife and the managing director of the company where the husband worked, consideration of the *article 8* rights of the wife and of her child necessitated a permanent extended restricted reporting order preventing identification of all three individuals.

The EAT is similarly empowered to make restricted reporting orders by *SI 1993/2854, rule 23(3), (5), (5A)* (as amended by the *Employment Appeal Tribunal (Amendment) Rules 2004 (SI 2004/2526), rule 15*).

For a more detailed consideration of restricted reporting orders, see **19.91–19.92** EMPLOYMENT TRIBUNALS – **II**, and also HARVEYS – DIVISIONS **PI.1.W**(5), (6), **PI.2.H**(1), (2).

13.12   Remedies

Where an employment tribunal finds that a complaint presented to it is well-founded, it must make such of the following orders as it considers just and equitable:

(a)   An order declaring the rights of the complainant and the respondent in relation to the act to which the complaint relates (*EA 2010, s 124(1)(a)*; and previously *SDA 1975, s 65(1)(a); RRA 1976, s 56(1)(a); SOR 2003, reg 30(1)(a); RBR 2003, reg 30(1)(a); DDA 1995, 17A(2)(a)*; and *AR 2006, reg 38(1)(a)*). Such a declaration may state, for example, that the complainant is entitled to certain training facilities or should be considered for a certain position.

(b)   An order requiring the respondent to pay to the complainant compensation of an amount corresponding to any damages he could have been ordered by a county court to pay to the complainant if the complaint had fallen to be dealt with under the jurisdiction of the county court (*EA 2010, s 124(1)(b)*; and previously *SDA 1975, s 65(1)(b); RRA 1976, s 56(1)(b); SOR 2003, reg 30(1)(b); RBR 2003, reg 30(1)(b); DDA 1995, s 17A(2)(b)*; and *AR 2006, reg 38(1)(b)*. Once a tribunal has decided to award compensation the amount must be computed on the basis of what damages would be recoverable in a county court, and not on the basis of what the tribunal thinks is just and equitable (the *EA 2010, s 124(6)*; *Hurley v Mustoe (No 2)* [1983] ICR 422). If the complainant was barred from applying for a particular benefit, the tribunal must, in assessing compensation, consider the percentage chance that the application would have succeeded (*Calder v James Finlay Corpn Ltd* [1989] ICR 157).

(c)   An "appropriate recommendation" pursuant to *EA 2010, s 124(1)(c)*, namely a recommendation that within a specified period the respondent takes specified steps for the purpose of obviating or reducing the adverse effect of any matter to which the proceedings relate (a) on the claimant or (b) on any other person (*EA 2010, s 124(3)*). Previously a tribunal could make a recommendation that the respondent take, within a specified period, action appearing to the tribunal to be practicable for the purpose of obviating or reducing the adverse effect on the complainant only of any act of discrimination to which the complaint relates (*SDA 1975, s 65(1)(c); RRA 1976, s 56(1)(c); SOR 2003, reg 30(1)(c); RBR 2003, reg 30(1)(c); DDA 1995, s 17A(2)(c)*; and *AR 2006, reg 38(1)(c)*).

See also HARVEYS – Divisions L.6, L.7.

13.13 Compensation: general principles

Until the mid-1990s, awards of compensation in cases of sex or race discrimination were subject to a statutory maximum like compensatory awards for unfair dismissals. However, following the decision of the ECJ in *Marshall v Southampton and South West Hampshire Regional Health Authority (No 2)* [1993] IRLR 445, that capping compensation meant victims of discrimination did not have an 'effective remedy', the upper ceiling on the size of awards was removed by the *Sex Discrimination and Equal Pay (Remedies) Regulations 1993 (SI 1993/2798)* (subsequently the *Employment Tribunals (Interest on Awards in Discrimination Cases) Regulations 1996 (SI 1996/2803)* – see below). Prior to 3 July 1994, compensation for employment-related acts of race discrimination was also subject to the same statutory maximum (by the former *RRA 1976, s 56(2)*). The *Race Relations (Remedies) Act 1994*, removed the limit.

Where an employer is found to be vicariously liable for its employees' discriminatory acts, it will normally be required to make a payment in compensation. However, it does not follow that the individual discriminators should escape the consequences of liability. Where they have been named as individual respondents, it is open to the tribunal to make an order that they, too, should make a payment in compensation (see *Gbaja-Biamila v DHL International (UK) Ltd* [2000] ICR 730, EAT). Tribunals are entitled to order that liability be on a joint and several basis. However, in *London Borough of Hackney v Sivanandan* [2013] IRLR 408, [2013] ICR 672 the Court of Appeal held that where the same, "indivisible", damage is done to a claimant by concurrent tortfeasors – ie either tortfeasors who are liable for the same act (joint tortfeasors) or tortfeasors who separately contribute to the same damage – each is liable for the whole of that damage. As between any particular tortfeasor and the claimant no question of apportionment arises. As between joint tortfeasors the position is determined under the *Civil Liability (Contribution) Act 1978* but this has no impact on the liability of any of them to the claimant. As the Court said in *Sivanandan* it is not clear whether the ET has jurisdiction to decide the position as between joint tortfeasors or whether this requires separate proceedings in the County Court.

Exemplary damages became available in discrimination cases as a result of the decision of the House of Lords in *Kuddus v Chief Constable of Leicestershire Constabulary* [2001] UKHL 29, [2002] 2 AC 122. For an example, see *MOD v Fletcher* [2010] IRLR 25, EAT.

The Court of Appeal overturned an employment tribunal's decision to strike out a successful claimant's claim as to remedy on the grounds that there had been a failure actively to pursue the claim and a fair hearing was no longer possible after a number of years had passed following the liability decision (see *Abegaze*, CA above).

For decisions relating to the assessment of compensation see *Alexander v Home Office* [1988] ICR 685, *North West Thames Regional Health Authority v Noone* [1988] ICR 813, *Sharifi v Strathclyde Regional Council* [1992] IRLR 259, and the cases summarised below. See also HARVEYS – Divisions L.6.C, L.7.

Care should be taken to ensure that the effect of tax on the award is taken into account. Compensation for pecuniary loss should be calculated in the first instance on the basis of net rather than gross loss of earnings (*Visa International Service Association v Paul* [2004] IRLR 42, EAT). However, compensation for loss consequent on the termination of employment will then be taxable since by virtue of *sections 401* and *403* of the *Income Tax (Earnings and Pensions) Act 2003*, a sum received in connection with the termination of a person's employment is tax-free up to £30,000 but is subject to income tax to the extent that it exceeds that sum. Contrary to the previous view of tribunals, this is not limited to compensation for financial loss, and compensation is taxable even where it is compensation for infringement of the right not to suffer discrimination. That was the decision of the Upper Tribunal (Tax) chaired by Rose J in *Moorthy v Revenue and Customs Commissioners* [2016] IRLR 258, overruling *Oti-Obihara v Revenue and Customs Comrs* [2010] UKFTT 568 (TC), [2011] IRLR 386. The Upper Tribunal in the same case also held that tax liability on such an award extends to compensation for injury to feelings, and that the contrary rulings of Singh J in *Timothy James Consulting Ltd v Wilton* [2015] IRC 765, EAT and of Judge McMullen QC in *Orthet Ltd v Vince-Cain* [2005] ICR 374, EAT were incorrect. Pension loss is also taxable on the same basis: Chief Constable of Northumbria v Erichsen (UKEAT/0027/15/BA). The same tax rules apply to compensation, or sums paid under a compromise agreement, for a discriminatory dismissal. In accordance with the principles in *British Transport Commission v Gourley* [1956] AC 185, it is therefore necessary, once the amount of the award has been calculated (using net figures for earnings and pension loss) to 'gross up' the award so as to ensure that the claimant is not left out of pocket once the tax on the award has been paid.

Compensation for discrimination during employment is however not taxable save to the extent that it is connected with remuneration so as to make it an "emolument of the employment" (*Income Tax (Earnings and Pensions) Act 2003, s 62*). For a case where on the facts the First-tier Tribunal found a settlement payment to be referable to the discrimination claim and not to the employment, see *A v HM Revenue & Customs* [2015] UKFTT 189 (TC), [2015] IRLR 962.

13.14   Compensation: Indirect discrimination

In cases of intentional indirect discrimination a tribunal's power to award compensation is the same as for direct discrimination: *EA 2010, s 124(2)(b)*. However, where the indirect discrimination is unintentional, the tribunal is required, before awarding compensation, first to consider whether to make a declaration and/or recommendation (*EA 2010, s 124(4), (5)*). Provided it considers those remedies first, the tribunal has complete discretion as to whether it orders compensation in cases of unintentional indirect discrimination and may award compensation whether or not it also makes a declaration or recommendation. Previously there was no power to award compensation for unintentional indirect discrimination until the *Sex Discrimination and Equal Pay (Miscellaneous Amendments) Regulations 1996 (SI 1996/438)*, which inserted a new *s 65(1B)* into the *SDA 1975*, gave tribunals, for the first time, a power to make awards of compensation in cases of unintentional indirect sex discrimination on a similar basis to that which now exists under the *EA 2010*. The *SOR 2003, reg 30, RBR 2003, reg 30, DDA 1995, s 17A* and *AR 2006, reg 38* contained similar provisions. In the case of race discrimination there was no such mechanism for awarding compensation for unintentional indirect discrimination (*RRA 1976, s 57(3)*). In a case decided under the old rules, *JH Walker Ltd v Hussain* [1996] ICR 291, it was held that intention may be inferred where it is established that the employer was aware that discriminatory consequences would flow from its actions. See also *London Underground Ltd v Edwards* [1995] ICR 574 for the circumstances in which indirect discrimination may be said to have been intentional

13.15 Compensation: pecuniary loss

The measure of loss is tortious. In other words, a complainant must be put, so far as possible, into the position that he would have been in had the act of discrimination not occurred (*Ministry of Defence v Cannock* [1994] ICR 918, EAT). Thus, the tribunal must ask itself, 'If there had been no unlawful discrimination, what would have happened?'.

Where the act complained of is a discriminatory dismissal, the tribunal will have to decide whether the complainant would have been dismissed in any event if there had been no discrimination (see *O'Donoghue v Redcar and Cleveland Borough Council* [2001] EWCA Civ 701, [2001] IRLR 615, CA; *Abbey National plc v Chagger* [2009] ICR 624, [2009] IRLR 86, EAT; affd *sub nom Chagger v Abbey National plc* [2009] EWCA Civ 1202, [2010] ICR 397, [2010] IRLR 47). The tribunal often carries out a similar exercise when calculating compensation for unfair dismissal. However, in the context of discrimination proceedings, there is a significant difference of approach. In unfair dismissal cases, one asks whether a reasonable employer would have dismissed in any event. In discrimination cases, however, one asks whether the actual respondent would have dismissed (*Abbey National plc v Formoso* [1999] IRLR 222). As the unlawful act is the discrimination, not the dismissal itself, the question is whether (and when) the dismissal would have occurred on non-discriminatory grounds (or whether and when the employee would have left the respondent's employment of his own choice) (*Chagger*, above, and *Wardle*, below). In cases where the complainant alleges that her dismissal was both unfair and discriminatory, this difference may significantly complicate the process of calculation. However, a reduction of compensation to reflect the chance that the employee might have left under a compromise agreement, based on evidence of pre-hearing negotiations but without any evidence of waiver of privilege, is unfair (see *Gallop v Newport City Council* [2013] IRLR 23, a case in which an appeal was subsequently allowed on a different issue: [2014] Eq LR 141). In *Chagger*, above, the EAT stated that although there were conceptual differences between discriminatory and unfair dismissals it would be unsatisfactory if a radically different approach from the approach in *Polkey v A E Dayton Services Ltd* [1988] AC 344, [1988] ICR 142, [1987] IRLR 503, HL, were to be adopted in discrimination cases. While the starting point in analysing future loss may be the period during which the claimant would have remained employed with the respondent had there been no dismissal, a tribunal has to recognise that a discriminatory dismissal means that the dismissed employee enters the labour market not at a time or in circumstances of his or her choosing, thereby potentially altering the claimant's career path. The proper assessment of loss is determined by asking when the claimant might be expected to obtain another job with equivalent salary (*Chagger v Abbey National plc* [2009] EWCA Civ 1202, [2010] ICR 397, [2010] IRLR 47, reversing the EAT on this point).

The mere fact that there is an element of speculation involved in assessing whether a claimant would have been dismissed anyway is not a reason for an employment tribunal to refuse to engage with the assessment exercise if evidence is advanced by the employer that he might have been dismissed (see *Eversheds Legal Services Ltd v De Belin* [2011] ICR 1137, [2011] IRLR 448, EAT). Determining what would have happened in the absence of discrimination may involve the tribunal in assessing percentage chances. For instance, in cases of pregnancy dismissal, the tribunal will usually have to assess the chance that the complainant would, but for the dismissal, have returned to work. It is not necessarily perverse for the tribunal to conclude that there is a 100% chance that the relevant event would have occurred (*Ministry of Defence v Hunt* [1996] ICR 544, EAT). A tribunal is not required to take account of contingencies that it regards as too remote or which are unlikely to arise during the period for which it considers that the claimant should be compensated (see *Wooster v Mayor and Burgesses of the London Borough of Tower Hamlets* [2009] IRLR 980, EAT and *Chief Constable of Northumbria v Erichsen* (UKEAT/0027/15/BA). Where there are a number of contingent possibilities, the proper approach is to cumulate the percentages (eg where there is a 75% chance that a woman would have returned to work following the birth of her child had she not been dismissed and a 50% chance of her having received a pay rise thereafter, her loss should be assessed on the basis of the chance of her having earned at the higher rate, that is 50% × 75% – see *Hunt* above). In *Wardle v Credit Agricole Corporate and Investment Bank* [2011] EWCA Civ 545, [2011] ICR 1290, [2011] IRLR 604 the Court of Appeal held that it is wrong for a tribunal to approach compensation for career loss by awarding damages until the point where it can be sure that the claimant will find an equivalent job, rather, in the normal case, if a tribunal assesses that a claimant is likely (ie it is more probable than not) to get an equivalent job by a specific date that is the date up to which loss is fairly to be assessed. Exceptionally a tribunal may be entitled to conclude on the evidence before it that there is no real prospect of the claimant ever securing an equivalent job, in which the tribunal has to assess loss as continuing for the rest of the claimant's working life. (The Court of Appeal also delivered a supplemental decision in this case on the effect of an adjustment in the overall level of compensation awarded consequent upon an appeal on the level of statutory uplift under the *EmA 2002, s 31(3)* – [2011] EWCA Civ 770, [2011] IRLR 819).

In *GM Packaging (UK) Ltd v Ottey* (UKEAT/0045/14/LA) it was held that a tribunal should have reviewed its remedy decision where an EAT ruling that another employee had been fairly dismissed in respect of the same incident could have supported a *Polkey* argument.

Where an employer has made an *ex gratia* payment on dismissal or any other payment which falls to be deducted from the award, the proper approach is to make the deduction before applying the percentage chance (*Hunt* above; *Ministry of Defence v Wheeler* [1998] ICR 242; cf *Digital Equipment Co Ltd v Clements (No 2)* [1998] IRLR 134, CA).

In assessing percentage prospects of particular events occurring, the tribunal is encouraged to rely upon statistical evidence. However, such evidence is simply one factor to take into account. Thus in *Vento v Chief Constable of West Yorkshire Police (No 2)* [2002] EWCA Civ 1871, [2003] ICR 318, the tribunal had been entitled to conclude that there was a 75% chance that the complainant would have remained in the police force until retirement (a period of 21 years of service) despite statistics suggesting that only 9% of female officers leaving the respondent's service had served for longer than 18 years. The fact that a claimant is in receipt of incapacity benefit does not, in itself, mean that he or she is incapable of working during the same period and therefore not eligible for compensation for loss of earnings during that period, rather an employment tribunal needs to consider all the evidence as to whether the claimant can work (*Sheffield Forgemasters International Ltd v Fox* [2009] ICR 333, [2009] IRLR 192, EAT). In *Brash-Hall v Getty Images Ltd* [2006] EWCA Civ 531, (2006) 811 IDS Brief 5, the Court of Appeal held that, where an employee had been dismissed constructively and in a discriminatory manner and the tribunal had decided that she would have been made redundant anyway, her compensation could only include the amount she would have received in contractual severance payment if she proved that she would have signed a severance agreement.

Percentage chances may also affect awards for injury to feelings: see *Das v Ayrshire and Arran Health Board* (below).

There will be cases where the evidence does not enable the calculation of loss to descend to the precise addition or subtraction of numerical values and a broad-brush assessment is necessary. The EAT will not interfere unless the resulting figure is manifestly excessive or manifestly too low on the evidence (*MoJ v Burton and Engel* [2016] IRLR 100, EAT).

In *Bullimore v Pothecary Witham Weld (No 2)* [2011] IRLR 18, EAT, Underhill P emphasised that questions of causation and remoteness are addressed according to different principles. Causation is a factual issue of whether the damage would have occurred 'but for' the wrongful act, whereas questions of remoteness involve a value judgment as to what was 'direct' or 'natural' or 'foreseeable' as a consequence. Where an employer for an illegitimate reason (in that case to victimise the claimant) gave an adverse reference leading to a prospective employer not offering a job or withdrawing an offer it was hard to see why that was too remote to attract compensation. The EAT held that there was no rule that a subsequent tortious act (eg the prospective employer itself unlawfully victimising the claimant) breaks the 'chain of causation'. In that case the employment tribunal had erred in not awarding compensation for loss of earnings stemming from victimisation by way of a damaging reference.

It is well established that a discriminator's motives are not relevant when it comes to deciding whether or not an act is discriminatory. However, a majority of the EAT (consisting of the two lay members) has decided that motives may be relevant when it comes to assessing compensation (*Chief Constable of Greater Manchester Police v Hope* [1999] ICR 338). Upholding the tribunal's decision that the complainant had been the victim of an act of direct race and sex discrimination, it nevertheless went on to decide that, in the absence of discriminatory intent, the tribunal should have made a nil award of compensation.

In *GM Packaging (UK) Ltd v Ottey* (UKEAT/0045/14/LA) it was held that a tribunal should have reviewed its remedy decision where an EAT ruling that another employee had been fairly dismissed in respect of the same incident could have supported a *Polkey* argument.

Where an employer has made an *ex gratia* payment on dismissal or any other payment which falls to be deducted from the award, the proper approach is to make the deduction before applying the percentage chance (*Hunt* above; *Ministry of Defence v Wheeler* [1998] ICR 242; cf *Digital Equipment Co Ltd v Clements (No 2)* [1998] IRLR 134, CA).

In *Chagger*, above, the EAT held that the risk that future potential employers might decline to employ the claimant because of his discrimination claim (so-called 'stigma loss') was too remote to be reflected in compensation payable by the respondent former employer. However the Court of Appeal reversed the EAT on this point holding that there was no reason why a respondent should not be liable for so-called stigma losses resulting from the refusal of third party potential employers to employ the claimant, even if those refusals are unlawful. The Court held that a tribunal should take a sensible and robust approach and not simply rely on the assertion of stigma or speculation, but where there was very extensive evidence of attempted mitigation failing to result in a job the tribunal would be entitled to conclude that the claimant was unlikely to obtain future employment in the industry. The Court also considered that there could be exceptional cases where stigma loss was the only head of damage, for example where the respondent would have dismissed even had there been no discrimination, however the onus would be on the claimant to prove such loss.

For guidance on avoiding double recovery in cases where complainants suffer both injury to feelings and a psychiatric injury, see 'Compensation: personal injury' immediately below. In *Voith Turbo Ltd v Stowe* [2005] IRLR 228, EAT, the EAT observed, *obiter*, that a dismissal on grounds of race discrimination was always very serious and could not be regarded as one-off and suitable for a lower band award. In *Miles v Gilbank* [2006] ICR 12, the EAT upheld an award of £25,000 for injury to feelings resulting from the bullying and harassment of a pregnant employee repeatedly and consciously inflicted with total disregard for the welfare of the employee or her unborn child. This was affirmed by the Court of Appeal ([2006] EWCA Civ 543, [2006] ICR 1297, [2006] IRLR 538), which held that if the discrimination involved the well-being of the claimant's unborn child, this increased the seriousness.

For guidance on the circumstances in which the appeal tribunal will be prepared to interfere with the amount of an award under this heading, see *ICTS (UK) Ltd v Tchoula* [2000] IRLR 643, EAT. An appellate court will only interfere if the award is so much out of line that it amounts to an error of law through a misdirection in principle or is for some other reason, such as an erroneous evaluation of the facts, plainly wrong (*R (Elias) v Secretary of State for Defence* [2006] EWCA Civ 1293, [2006] IRLR 934) or if the tribunal does not give adequate reasons for the size of the award (*NSL Ltd and another v Miller* UKEAT/0012/14/MC). Otherwise the EAT will not interfere, because such awards are "not susceptible to close calculation" (*HM Land Registry v McGlue* [2013] Eq LR 701). The EAT has demonstrated that it will overturn awards even if 'correctly categorised' so that its powers are not limited to correcting mis-categorisations (see *Doshoki v Draeger Ltd* [2002] IRLR 340, EAT). An example of this is *Massey v UNIFI* [2007] EWCA Civ 800, [2008] ICR 62, [2007] IRLR 902, a case of unjustified union discipline where the Court of Appeal raised the award for injury to feelings to £12,500 where it considered that an award of £7,500 was too far down the middle *Vento* category as the injury to feelings was intense and prolonged.

See also HARVEYS – Division L.7.B.

13.17 Compensation: personal injury

Where the injury to feelings is such that it results in the onset of psychiatric illness, the complainant may recover compensation for personal injury in the tribunal (*Sheriff v Klyne Tugs (Lowestoft) Ltd* [1999] ICR 1170). It is thought that the same principle would apply where an employee is physically injured in the course of harassment. An award for personal injury may be made in addition to an award for injury to feelings (*Hampshire CC v Wyatt* (UKEAT/0013/16/DA, 13 October 2016)), although it may not always be easy to distinguish where injury to feelings stops and injury to mental health begins and there is consequently a danger of double recovery of which the tribunal must be aware and seek to avoid. In *HM Prison Service v Salmon* [2001] IRLR 425, the EAT suggested that in such cases it was open to a tribunal to make a single award for injury to feelings and to include an element for psychiatric harm. Tribunals may therefore make two awards or a combined award and, in either case, should make it clear what they are doing.

Damages for personal injury are recoverable for any harm caused by the discriminatory act and not simply harm which was reasonably foreseeable (*Essa v Laing Ltd* [2003] ICR 1110, EAT). Although this decision was upheld on appeal by a majority of the Court of Appeal, there was some suggestion that the simple causation test may only apply to cases of racial abuse and not discrimination more widely ([2004] EWCA Civ 02, [2004] ICR 746), although that suggestion has not gained wider acceptance. It will not avail a discriminator that the harm was related to a pre-existing condition if the unlawful act caused the harm, although where there is evidence that the harm was likely to have occurred at some point in the future a discount for acceleration will be necessary (see *Massey v UNIFI*, above). However when more than one event contributes to the harm suffered by a claimant the extent of the respondent's liability is limited to the contribution to the harm made by its discriminatory conduct (see *Thaine v London School of Economics* [2010] ICR 1422, EAT – in that case only 40%; see also *Olayemi v Athena Medical Centre* [2016] ICR 1074). The Court of Appeal remitted a case for rehearing when new evidence was obtained which might have materially affected the employment tribunal's assessment of the extent of the depressive illness that the tribunal had found had been exacerbated by the respondent's discriminatory conduct (see *Blundell v Governing Body of St Andrew's Catholic Primary School* [2011] EWCA Civ 427, [2012] ICR 295). Although in most cases it will be necessary to have expert medical evidence to prove the nature and extent of a personal injury, its likely cause(s) and prognosis, it is not a prerequisite to making an award and in an appropriate case a tribunal can make an award for personal injury without expert medical evidence directed to the point: *Hampshire CC v Wyatt*, ibid.

There are conflicting decisions of the EAT on whether the general uplift of 10% on general damages in civil proceedings declared by the Court of Appeal in *Simmons v Castle* [2013] 1 All ER 334, [2013] 1 WLR 1239 applies to personal injury awards made by the tribunal. In *Pereira De Souza v Vinci Construction Ltd* [2015] ICR 1034, Judge Serota QC decided that it does not, but his decision was doubted by Langstaff P in *Beckford v Southwark LBC* [2016] IRLR 178, holding that the uplift does apply; see also *Shannon v Rampersad (t/a Clifton House Residential Home)* [2015] IRLR 982 and *Olayemi v Athena Medical Centre and anor* [2016] ICR 1074. It is to be hoped that an answer to this issue will be provided in the decision of the Court of Appeal in the appeal against the EAT's decision in *King v Sash Window Workshop Ltd* [2015] IRLR 348 although that case concerns only an injury to feelings award and not a personal injury award.

See also Harveys – Division **L.7.C.**

13.18 Compensation: aggravated and exemplary damages

Aggravated damages may be awarded in discrimination cases where the complainant is able to establish a causal link between 'exceptional or contumelious conduct or motive' on the employer's part and her injury to feelings. Such damages may be appropriate, for instance, where an employer has failed properly to investigate the applicant's complaint of discrimination (*Johnson* above). The promotion of the alleged discriminator while he was still subject to disciplinary proceedings for his alleged discrimination was a matter a tribunal could take into account in awarding aggravated damages (see *British Telecommunications*, above). There has been some uncertainty over whether any sum awarded under this head should be incorporated into the award for injury to feelings. This approach was approved, *obiter*, by the EAT in *Gbaja-Biamila v DHL International (UK) Ltd* [2000] ICR 730, EAT (adopting the approach of the Northern Ireland Court of Appeal in *McConnell v Police Authority for Northern Ireland* [1997] IRLR 625, NICA). However, in *ICTS (UK) Ltd v Tchoula* [2000] IRLR 643, EAT, the EAT declined to find that the tribunal had erred by making a separate award of aggravated damages. The Court of Appeal subsequently confirmed the approach in *ICTS* and overruled *McConnell* by holding that aggravated damages should not be aggregated with damages for injury to feelings (*Scott v IRC* [2004] EWCA Civ 400, [2004] IRLR 713). In *Commissioner of Police for the Metropolis v Shaw* [2012] ICR 464, [2012] IRLR 291, EAT, Underhill P stated that aggravated damages are an aspect of injury to feelings reflecting the making more serious of the injury to feelings by some additional element which would fall into one of three categories: (a) the manner in which the wrong was committed, (b) motive (but only if the claimant was aware of the motive), or (c) subsequent conduct (eg by the employer not taking the complaint seriously, failure to apologise or conduct at trial). The ultimate question would always be what additional distress was caused to a particular claimant in the particular circumstances of the case and tribunals should be cautious about focusing on the respondent's conduct. However, a tribunal should ask itself whether the conduct, objectively viewed, was capable of having that aggravating effect, and should be cautious to avoid awarding aggravated damages and

(b)   encourage good practice in relation to equality and diversity;

(c)   promote equality of opportunity;

(d)   promote awareness and understanding of rights under the *EA 2010* (previously the equality enactments);

(e)   enforce the *EA 2010* (previously the equality enactments));

(f)   work towards the elimination of unlawful discrimination; and

(g)   work towards the elimination of unlawful harassment.

(*EA 2006, s 8(1)*).

'Unlawful' is defined as contrary to the *EA 2010* (previously the equality enactments) (*EA 2006, s 34* as amended). The equality enactments were (until they were repealed and replaced by the *EqA 2010*) the *EPA 1970*, the *SDA 1975*, the *RRA 1976*, the *DDA 1995*, Part 2 of the *EA 2006*, regulations made under *Part 3* of the *EA 2006*, the *SOR 2003*, the *RBR 2003* and the *AR 2006* (*EA 2006, s 33(1)*, which was repealed when the *EA 2010* came into force). In fulfilling its duties under *s 8* the EHRC must take account of any relevant human rights (*EA 2006, s 9(4)*). The EHRC is required to monitor the effectiveness of the equality and human rights enactments and give advice and make recommendations to central government on changes to the law (*EA 2006, s 11*). The equality and human rights enactments are the *Human Rights Act 1998*, the *EA 2006* and the *EA 2010* (*EA 2006, s 11(3)(c)* as amended). The EHRC is required to monitor progress in performing its functions under the *EA 2006, s 8* and 9, and issue a report on this progress every three years (*EA 2006, s 12*). The EHRC is also required to issue an annual report on its performance (*EA 2006, Sch 1, para 32*).

The EHRC may issue a code of practice in connection with a matter addressed by the *EA 2010* (and previously the *EqPA 1970, SDA 1975*, Pts 2–4, *s 76A* and orders under *ss 76B, 76C*, the *RRA 1976*, Pts 2–4 and *s 71, DDA 1995*, Pts 2–4 and *5A, EqA 2006, Pt 2* and regulations made under *Pt 3, SOR 2003*, Pts 2, 3, *RBR 2003*, Pts 2, 3, and *AR 2006*, arts 2, 3 (*EA 2006, s 14(1)* as amended). Before issuing a code the EHRC must publish its proposals, consult such persons as it thinks appropriate and submit a draft to the Secretary of State for approval (*EA 2006, ss 14(6), (7)*). A failure to comply with a code of practice does not make a person liable to criminal or civil proceedings but a code is admissible in evidence in such proceedings and shall be taken into account by a court or tribunal if it appears relevant (*EA 2006, s 15(4)*). The EHRC has published a Code of Practice on Employment, which is available on the EHRC website, and which reflects the new anti-discrimination law set out in the *EA 2010*.

The EHRC has the power to institute or intervene in legal proceedings (including judicial review) if it appears to the Commission that the proceedings relate to a matter in connection with which it has a function (*EA 2006, s 30*). This makes explicit on the face of the statute a power that the EOC, CRE and DRC were held to have. In *R v Secretary of State for Employment, ex p Equal Opportunities Commission* [1994] 1 All ER 910, [1994] ICR 317, the House of Lords considered that the EOC had *locus standi* to challenge by judicial review proceedings a refusal by the Secretary of State to accept that English law was sexually discriminatory in certain respects, and their Lordships also held (by a majority) that the Divisional Court was a proper forum for the challenge in question. The EHRC has already exercised this power to intervene in an number of discrimination cases in the employment field (see, for example, *Oyarce v Cheshire County Council* [2008] EWCA Civ 434, [2008] ICR 1179, [2008] IRLR 653; *Slack v Cumbria County Council* [2009] EWCA Civ 293, [2009] IRLR 463; *Bainbridge v Redcar and Cleveland Borough Council* [2008] EWCA Civ 885, [2009] ICR 133, [2008] IRLR 776; and *Seldon v Clarkson Wright & Jakes* [2012] UKSC 16, [2012] ICR 716) and *Jessemey v Rowstock Ltd* [2014] EWCA Civ 185, [2014] 3 All ER 409,

[2014] IRLR 368 (see **13.2** above). In *R (on the application of McCarthy) v Basildon District Council* [2008] EWHC 987 (Admin), [2008] All ER (D) 118 (May) (a planning case) the Court of Appeal rejected an application by the local authority to prevent the EHRC intervening by way of written submissions because its intervention would be profitable as it could give guidance to the Court.

The EHRC has a website, www.equalityhumanrights.com. Its offices are at: Arndale House, The Arndale Centre, Manchester, M4 3AQ (telephone 0161 829 8100, fax 0161 829 8110, and email info@equalityhumanrights.com; 3 More London, Riverside Tooley Street, London, SE1 2RG (telephone 020 3117 0235, fax 0203 117 0237, and email info @equalityhumanrights.com); 3rd floor, 3 Callaghan Square, Cardiff, CF10 5BT (telephone 02920 447710, fax 02920 447713, and email wales@equalityhumanrights.com); and The Optima Building, 58 Robertson Street, Glasgow, G2 8DU (telephone 0141 228 5910, fax 0141 228 5912, and email scotland@equalityhumanrights.com).

13.25 Formal inquiries and investigations

The EHRC has an express power to conduct inquiries into any matter relating to its duties under the *EA 2006, ss 8* and *9 (EA 2006, s 16(1))*. If, during an inquiry the EHRC begins to suspect that a person has committed an unlawful act it must: (a) in continuing the inquiry, so far as possible, avoid further consideration of whether the person has committed an unlawful act, (b) commence an investigation, (c) may use information acquired during the inquiry in the investigation, and (d) ensure that any aspect of the inquiry which concerns the person investigated is not pursued while the investigation is in progress (*EA 2006, s 16(2)*).

The EHRC has the power to investigate whether a person has committed an unlawful act or has not complied with an unlawful act notice issued under *s 21* or an undertaking made in an agreement made under *s 23*, but may only investigate whether a person has committed an unlawful act if it suspects the person to have done so (such suspicion may, but need not, arise as a result of an inquiry under *s 16*) (*EA 2006, ss 20(1), (2), (3)*). In relation to the EOC, CRE and DRC it had been held that if they did not have a suspicion that the subject of an investigation had committed an unlawful act of discrimination, the investigation and any non-discrimination notice based upon it might be challenged (*Prestige Group plc, Re, Commission for Racial Equality v Prestige Group plc* [1984] 1 WLR 335, [1984] ICR 473, HL; *Hillingdon London Borough Council v Commission for Racial Equality* [1982] AC 779).

Before settling the report of an investigation recording a finding that a person has committed an unlawful act or has failed to comply with an unlawful act notice or an undertaking, the EHRC is required to send a draft to the person and specify a period of at least 28 days in which the person may make written representations, which the EHRC must consider (*EA 2006, s 20(4)*). *Schedule 2* to the *EA 2006* sets out supplemental provisions concerning investigations (*EA 2006, s 20(5)*).

Where the EHRC conducts an inquiry it is required to publish the terms of reference in a manner that it considers likely to bring the inquiry to the attention of persons whom it concerns or who might be interested in it, and in particular to the attention of any person specified in the terms of reference (*EA 2006, Sch 2, para 2*). Before holding an investigation the EHRC is required to prepare terms of reference specifying the person to be investigated and the nature of the alleged unlawful act, give the person the notice, give that person the opportunity to make representations about the terms of reference, and having considered such representations publish the terms of reference once settled (*EA 2006, Sch 2, para 3*). The EHRC is required to make arrangements for persons to make representations (which may, but need not, include oral representations) in relation to inquiries, investigations and assessments and must give any person specified in the terms of reference the opportunity to make representations (*EA 2006, Sch 2, paras 6, 7*). The EHRC must consider any representations made but need not do so, if it considers it appropriate, where the representations are not made by a person specified in the terms of reference or by a 'relevant lawyer' (i.e. either (a) an advocate or solicitor in Scotland, or (b) a person who, for the purposes of the *Legal Services Act 2007*, is an authorised person in relation to an activity which constitutes the exercise of a right of audience or the conduct of litigation (within the meaning of that *Act*)) (*EA 2006, Sch 2, para 8*, as amended). In relation to formal investigations by the EOC, CRE or DRC it has been held that the persons concerned were not entitled to cross-examine witnesses (*R v Commission for Racial Equality, ex p Cottrell and Rothon* [1980] 1 WLR 1580).

13.26 *Information.* The EHRC has powers to require persons to provide information by issuing a notice in the course of an inquiry, investigation or assessment (*EA 2006, Sch 2, para 9*). Such a notice may require a person to provide information in his possession, produce documents in his possession, or give oral evidence, and may specify the form of information, documents or evidence and the timing, but a notice may not require a person to provide information that he is prohibited from disclosing by an enactment, do anything that he could not be compelled to do in proceedings in the High Court or Court of Session, or require a person to attend at a place unless the EHRC undertakes to pay the expenses of his journey (*EA 2006, Sch 2, para 10*). A recipient of a notice may apply to a county court (in England and Wales) or a sheriff (in Scotland) to have the notice cancelled on the grounds that the requirement imposed by it is unnecessary having regard to the purpose of the inquiry, investigation or assessment, or is unreasonable (*EA 2006, Sch 2, para 11*). Where the EHRC believes that a person has failed, or is likely to fail, without reasonable excuse to comply with a notice it may apply to a county court (in England and Wales) or a sheriff (in Scotland) for an order requiring the person to take such steps as are specified in the order (*EA 2006, Sch 2, para 12*). A person commits an offence if he fails to comply with a notice under *para 9* or an order under *para 12(2)*, falsifies any document provided in accordance with such a notice or order, or makes a false statement in giving oral evidence in accordance with a notice under *para 9*, and such an offence is punishable on summary conviction by a fine not exceeding level 5 on the standard scale (*EA 2006, Sch 2, para 13*, and see **1.10** INTRODUCTION).

13.27 *The Commission's report.* The EHRC is required to publish a report of its findings following an inquiry, investigation or assessment and may make recommendations as part of the report or in respect of a matter arising in the course of the inquiry, investigation or assessment, which may be addressed to any class of persons (*EA 2006, Sch 2, paras 15, 16*). A tribunal or court may have regard to the findings of a report but shall not treat it as conclusive, and a person to whom a recommendation is addressed shall have regard to it (*EA 2006, Sch 2, paras 18, 19*).

It is an offence for a Commissioner, Investigating Commissioner or employee of the EHRC to disclose any information acquired by the EHRC by way of representations made in relation to, or in the course of, an inquiry under the *EA 2006, s 16*, an investigation under *s 20*, an assessment under *s 31* or a notice under *s 32*, or from a person with whom the EHRC enters into, or considers entering into, an agreement under *s 23* (*EA 2006, ss 6(1), (2)*). Disclosure of such information is permitted only if the disclosure is:

(a)   for the purposes of a function of the EHRC under the *EA 2006, ss 16, 20, 21, 24, 25, 31, or 32*;

(b)   in a report of an inquiry, investigation or assessment published by the EHRC;

(c)   in pursuance of an order of a court or tribunal;

(d)   with the consent of the person to whom the disclosed information relates;

(e)   in a manner that ensures that no person to whom the disclosed information relates can be identified;

(f)   for the purposes of civil or criminal proceedings to which the EHRC is a party; or

(g)   if the information was acquired by the EHRC more than 70 years before the date of the disclosure.

(EA 2006, s 6(3)).

Contravention of these rules is made an offence punishable on summary conviction with a fine not exceeding level 5 on the standard scale *(EA 2006, s 6(6)*; and see **1.10** INTRODUCTION).

13.28 Unlawful act notices and other remedies

Remedies available to the EHRC. The EHRC has a wider range of remedies available to it than the EOC, CRE and DRC. Where, following investigation, the EHRC is satisfied that a person has committed an unlawful act it has the power to issue a notice specifying the unlawful act and the provision of the *EA 2010* (or previously the equality enactments) that has been infringed – an 'unlawful act notice' – and the notice may require the person to prepare an action plan to avoid repetition or continuation of the unlawful act or recommend action to be taken for that purpose *(EA 2006, s 21(1), (2)* (as amended), *(4))*. A person in receipt of a notice may within six weeks beginning with the date on which the notice was given appeal to an employment tribunal or county court (depending on which of these would have jurisdiction to consider a claim in respect of the alleged unlawful act) on the grounds that either (a) the person did not commit the unlawful act specified in the notice or (b) the requirement to prepare an action plan was unreasonable *(EA 2006, ss 21 (5), (7))*. On such an appeal the court or tribunal may affirm, annul or vary the notice, affirm, annul or vary the requirement, or make an order for costs or expenses *(EA 2006, s 21(6))*. The *Employment Tribunals (Constitution and Rules of Procedure) Regulations 2013 (SI 2013/1237), Sch 1* now regulates the procedure to be adopted upon the hearing of appeals against unlawful act notices.

Where the EHRC issues a notice under *s 21* requiring a person to prepare an action plan the notice must specify the time within which the person must give the EHRC a first draft plan *(EA 2006, s 22(2))*. On the receipt of the first draft plan the EHRC may approve it or give the person notice that it is inadequate and require the person to submit a revised draft by a specified time, possibly with recommendations as to the content of the revised draft *(EA 2006, s 22 (3), (4))*. The EHRC is empowered to apply to a county court (in England and Wales) or (in Scotland) a sheriff for an order requiring a person to produce a first draft plan by a specified time, or a revised draft plan by a specified time and in accordance with any directions as to its contents *(EA 2006, s 22(6))*. Where, within six weeks of the person giving the draft plan to the EHRC, it has not issued a notice that the draft plan is inadequate or applied for an order under *s 22(6)(b)*, or where such an order is refused, the action plan will come into effect *(EA 2006, s 22(5))*. The EHRC may agree with the person who prepared it to vary an action plan *(EA 2006, s 22(7))*.

The EHRC is empowered to seek an order from the county court or sheriff within five years of an action plan coming into force requiring a person to act in accordance with the plan or to take specified action for a similar purpose *(EA 2006, s 22(6)(c))*. It is a criminal offence punishable on summary conviction by a fine not exceeding level 5 on the standard scale to fail to comply with an order under *s 22(6)* without reasonable excuse *(EA 2006, s 22(9); and see **1.10** INTRODUCTION).

The EHRC has another remedy for potential unlawful acts contrary to the *EA 2010* (or previously the equality enactments). Under the *EA 2006, s 23*, the EHRC may enter into an agreement with a person under which the person undertakes not to commit an unlawful act of a specified kind or to take, or refrain from taking, other specified action, and the EHRC agrees not to proceed against the person under *ss 20* or *21* in respect of any act of that specified kind *(EA 2006, s 23(1))*. The EHRC will only be able to enter into an agreement if it believes that the person has committed an unlawful act but a person will not be taken to have admitted to the commission of an unlawful act only by virtue of entering into an agreement *(EA 2006, ss 22(2), (3))*.

INJUNCTIONS

13.29 Persistent discrimination

The EHRC is empowered, where it thinks that a person is likely to continue to commit an unlawful act, to apply (in England and Wales) to a county court for an injunction or (in Scotland) to the sheriff for an interdict to prevent the person from committing the act (*EA 2006, s 24(1)*). The EHRC is also able, if a person subject to an agreement under the *EA 2006, s 23* has failed, or is likely to fail, to comply with an undertaking, to apply to a county court or sheriff for an order requiring the person to comply with the undertaking or such other order as the court or sheriff may specify (*EA 2006, s 24(2), (3)*).

13.30 Advertisements and instructions or pressure to discriminate

Prior to the *EA 2010* coming into force on 1 October 2010 only the EHRC had power to bring proceedings in relation to discriminatory advertising or instructions or pressure to discriminate contrary to the *SDA 1975, ss 38–40, the RRA 1976, ss 29–31*, the *DDA 1995, ss 16B* and *16C*, and the *EA 2006, ss 54, 55* (religious discrimination: advertising and instructions or pressure to discriminate) (*EA 2006, s 25(1), (2)*; and see *Ruhaza v Alexander Hancock Recruitment Ltd* [2012] EqLR 9, EAT). Where the EHRC believed that a person had committed an act to which *s 25* applied it could present a complaint to an employment tribunal where the alleged act was unlawful by reference to the *SDA 1975, Pt 2*, the *RRA 1976, Pt 2*, the *DDA 1995, Pt 3*, or the *EA 2006, Pts 2*, and *3* (in so far as it related to employment services), or otherwise in the county court (in England and Wales) or to a sheriff (in Scotland) (*EA 2006, s 25(3)*). Such a complaint or application was to be made within the six month period beginning with the date (or last date) on which the alleged unlawful act occurred, or with the permission of the tribunal, court or sheriff (*EA 2006, s 26(1)*). On an application under *s 25(3)* the court, sheriff or tribunal could determine whether the allegation was correct (*EA 2006, s 25(4)*).

The EHRC was also empowered to apply to a county court (in England and Wales) for an injunction or to a sheriff (in Scotland) for an interdict where a tribunal, court or sheriff had determined under *s 25(4)* that a person has done an act to which the section applied or the EHRC considered that a person has done such an act, and the EHRC believed that if unrestrained the person was likely to do another such act (*EA 2006, s 25(5), (6)*). A court or sheriff could not rely upon a determination under *s 25(4)* while an appeal against that determination was pending or might be brought (disregarding the possibility of an appeal out of time with permission) (*EA 2006, s 26(2)*). Any application under the *EA 2006, s 25(5), (6)* had to be brought within five years of the unlawful act occurring or with the permission of the court or sheriff (*EA 2006, s 26(3)*).

The *EA 2010* repealed *EA 2006, ss 25* and *26* (*EA 2010, s 211, Sch 26, paras 6, 14* and *15, Sch 27, Pt 1*).

From 1 October 2010 *EA 2006, s 24A* made provision in relation to:

(a)   an act which is unlawful because, by virtue of any of *EA 2010, ss 13* to *18*, it amounts to a contravention of any of *Pts 3, 4, 5, 6* or *7* of that *Act*,

(b)   an act which is unlawful because it amounts to a contravention of the *EA 2010, s 60(1)* (or to a contravention of *ss 111* or *112* of that *Act* that relates to a contravention of *s 60(1)* of that *Act*) (enquiries about disability and health),

(c)   an act which is unlawful because it amounts to a contravention of the *EA 2010, s 106* (information about diversity in range of election candidates etc),

(d)   an act which is unlawful because, by virtue of the *EA 2010, s 108(1)*, it amounts to a contravention of any of *Pts 3, 4, 5, 6* or *7* of that *Act*, or

(e)   the application of a provision, criterion or practice which, by virtue of the *EA 2010*, *s 19*, amounts to a contravention of that *Act*.

For the purposes of the *EA 2006*, *ss 20* to *24*, it is immaterial whether the EHRC knows or suspects that a person has been or may be affected by the unlawful act or application (*EA 2006*, *s 24A(2)*). An unlawful act includes making arrangements to act in a particular way which would, if applied to an individual, amount to a contravention mentioned in the *EA 2006*, *s 24A(1)(a)* (*EA 2006*, *s 24A(3)*). Nothing in the *EA 2006* affects the entitlement of a person to bring proceedings under the *EA 2010* in respect of a contravention mentioned in the *EA 2006*, *s 24A(1)* (*EA 2006*, *s 24A(4)*).

13.31   ASSISTANCE FOR PERSONS DISCRIMINATED AGAINST

The EHRC is able to make grants to another person in pursuance of its duties under the *EA 2006*, *ss 8* and *9*, which may be subject to conditions (*EA 2006*, *s 17*). The EHRC may assist an individual who is, or may become, a party to legal proceedings where the proceedings relate to the *EA 2010* (and previously the equality enactments) and the individual alleges that he has been the victim of behaviour contrary to that Act (or those enactments)) (*EA 2006*, *s 28(1)*, as amended). This assistance may take the form of legal advice, legal representation, facilities for settlement of a dispute, or any other form of assistance (*EA 2006*, *s 28(4)*). Where the proceedings partly relate to matters other than the *EA 2010* (or previously the equality enactments) the assistance may be given in relation to any aspect of the proceedings but must cease if the proceedings cease to relate to the *EA 2010* (or previously the equality enactments) (*EA 2006*, *s 28(6)*). The Lord Chancellor may by order disapply this restriction in specified kinds of cases (*EA 2006*, *s 28(7)*). For these purposes the section is taken to apply to any provisions of EU law that confer rights on individuals and relate to discrimination on the grounds of sex (including gender reassignment), racial origin, ethnic origin, religion, belief, disability, age or sexual orientation (*EA 2006*, *s 28(12)*, *(13)*). Where an individual receives assistance from the EHRC under *s 28* and the individual becomes entitled to costs either as a result of settlement or an award by the court or tribunal the EHRC's expenses in providing assistance will be charged on any sum paid to the individual by way of costs (*EA 2006*, *s 29*).

13.32   EFFECT ON CONTRACTS

A term of a contract is unenforceable against a person in so far as it constitutes, promotes or provides for treatment of that or another person that is of a description prohibited by the *EA 2010* (*EA 2010*, *s 142(1)*). A relevant non-contractual term is unenforceable against a person in so far as it constitutes, promotes or provides for treatment of that or another person that is of a description prohibited by the Act, in so far as the Act relates to disability (*EA 2010*, *s 142(2)*). A relevant non-contractual term is defined as a term which (a) is a term of an agreement that is not a contract, and (b) relates to the provision of an employment service within *ss 56(2)(a)* to *(e)* or to the provision under a group insurance arrangement of facilities by way of insurance (*EA 2010*, *s 142(3)*).

Previously a term of a contract was void where:

(a)   its inclusion rendered the making of the contract unlawful by virtue of the *Acts* or *Regulations*;

(b)   it was included in furtherance of an act rendered unlawful by the *Acts* or *Regulations*; or

(c)   it provided for the doing of an act which would be rendered unlawful by the *Acts* or *Regulations*.

(*SDA 1975, s 77(1); RRA 1976, s 72(1); SOR 2003, reg 35 and Sch 4, part 1, para 1(1); RBR 2003, reg 35 and Sch 4, part 1, para 1(1); DDA 1995, s 17C and Sch 3A, part 1, para 1(1); and AR 2006, reg 43 and Sch 5, part 1, para 1(1).*)

Thus, a term in a contract for the provision of a discriminatory training programme would be rendered void by those provisions. A term in a contract for an advertisement which provided for the inclusion of a discriminatory expression would similarly be void. In *Jivraj v Hashwani* [2010] EWCA Civ 712, [2010] IRLR 797, [2010] ICR 1435, the Court of Appeal held that a provision in an arbitration clause that the appointed arbitrator had to be a member of the Ismaili community was void as it involved discrimination on the grounds of religion or belief contrary to the *RBR 2003, regs* 2 and 6, and as a result the whole arbitration clause was void because removal of the offending provision rendered the agreement substantially different from that originally intended (this decision was reversed by the Supreme Court on the basis that an arbitrator was not employed under a contract personally to do work such as to fall within the *RBR 2003* and, in any event, the requirement in question was a genuine occupational requirement – [2011] UKSC 40, [2011] ICR 1004, [2012] IRLR 827).

Also previously a term which constituted (or was in furtherance of or provided for) unlawful discrimination against a party to a contract was not made void, but was unenforceable against that party (*SDA 1975, s 77(3); RRA 1976, s 72(3); SOR 2003, reg 35 and Sch 4, part 1, para 1(2); RBR 2003, reg 35 and Sch 4, part 1, para 1(2); DDA 1995, s 17C and Sch 3A, part 1, para 1(2); and AR 2006, reg 43 and Sch 5, part 1, para 1(2)*). For example, a term in a contract with a woman which states that she cannot use a smoking room normally reserved for men was not enforceable in a court of law.

A party to the contract may apply to a county court in England and Wales or a sheriff court in Scotland which may remove or modify the discriminatory term, provided that all persons affected have been notified of the application (*EA 2010, s 143(1), (2)*; and previously *SDA 1975, s 77(5); RRA 1976, s 72(5); SOR 2003, reg 35 and Sch 4, part 1, para 3(1); RBR 2003, reg 35 and Sch 4, part 1, para 3(1); DDA 1995, s 17C and Sch 3A, part 1, para 3(1); and AR 2006, reg 43 and Sch 5, part 1, para 3(1)*).

The *EA 2010, s 145* provides that a term of a collective agreement is void in so far as it constitutes, promotes or provides for treatment of a description prohibited by the *Act*, and a rule of an undertaking is unenforceable against a person in so far as it constitutes, promotes or provides for treatment of the person that is of a description prohibited by the *Act*. A qualifying person (as defined by the *EA 2010, s 146(5), (6)*) may make a complaint to an employment tribunal that a term is void, or that a rule is unenforceable, as a result of *s 145 (s 146(1)*). A person will only be able to make such an application if either the term or rule may in the future have effect in relation to him, and where the complaint alleges that the term or rule provides for treatment of a description prohibited by the *Act*, he may in the future be subjected to treatment that would (if he were subjected to it in present circumstances) be of that description (*EA 2010, s 146(2)*). If the tribunal finds that the complaint is well-founded, it must make an order declaring that the term is void or the rule is unenforceable (*EA 2010, s 146(3)*).

This is similar to the position that obtained previously. By the *Sex Discrimination Act 1986*, s 6 (as amended), *SDA 1975, s 77* was made to apply to any term of a collective agreement (see COLLECTIVE AGREEMENTS (6)) (even if not intended to be legally enforceable) or to any rule made by an employer for application to his employees or to applicants for employment. Similar provisions were contained in *RRA 1976, s 72A, SOR 2003, reg 35 and Sch 4, part 2, RBR 2003, reg 35 and Sch 4, part 2, DDA 1995, s 17C and Sch 3A, part 2, and AR 2006, reg 43 and Sch 5, part 2*. These provisions also applied to any rule made by an organisation of workers, an organisation of employers, or an organisation whose members carry on a particular profession or trade for whose purposes it exists, for application to its members and prospective members. They also applied to any rule made by an authority or body which can confer an authorisation or qualification needed for, or facilitating, engagement in a particular profession or trade, for application to those who have received or seek to receive such authorisation or qualification. Persons who are (as the case may be) employees, members or the recipients of authorisations or qualifications, or who are genuinely and actively seeking to become such, and who have reason to believe that the offending term or rule may at some future time have effect in relation to them could complain to an employment tribunal. If the tribunal found the complaint well-founded, it would declare the term or rule void. In the context of multiple equal pay claims, the EAT has held that there was no alternative, consistent with the EU law obligation to provide an effective remedy, to the employment tribunal considering granting declarations under *SDA 1975, s 77* that a collective agreement was contrary to the principles of equal pay at the same time as considering the equal pay claims themselves, notwithstanding that the claimants could test the disputed terms in the context of the equal pay claims (*UNISON v Brennan* [2008] ICR 955, [2008] IRLR 492, EAT).

See also EQUAL PAY (**22**).

Local authorities used to be prohibited from inserting clauses into their contracts obliging the other party to comply with the discrimination legislation, because these are 'non-commercial matters' (*Local Government Act 1988, s 17*; and see *R v Islington London Borough Council, ex p Building Employers Confederation* [1989] IRLR 382). However the *EA 2010* amends the *Local Government Act 1988, s 17* so that the section does not prevent a public authority to which it applies from exercising any function regulated by the section with reference to a non-commercial matter to the extent that the authority considers it necessary or expedient to do so to enable or facilitate compliance with (a) the duty imposed on it by the *EA 2010, s 149* (public sector equality duty), or (b) any duty imposed on it by regulations under the *EA 2010, ss 153* or *154* (powers to impose specific duties) (the *Local Government Act 1988, s 17(10)*, inserted by the *EA 2010, s 211(1), Sch 26, paras 1, 2(b)*).

See also HARVEYS – Division L.5.B.

13.33   SETTLEMENT OF A CLAIM

A term of a contract is unenforceable by a person in whose favour it would operate in so far as it purports to exclude or limit a provision of or made under the *EA 2010* (*EA 2010, s 144(1)*). A clause in a members' agreement in a firm of solicitors which purported to require any disputes between members to be referred for alternative dispute resolution and thence for final resolution through arbitration was held to be unenforceable by virtue of the *EA 2010, s 144* in *Clyde & Co LLP v Bates van Winkelhof* [2011] EWHC 668 (QB), [2011] IRLR 467. Slade J held that the *EA 2010, s 144(1)* was not just concerned with agreements to exclude the right not to be discriminated against but also agreements to exclude the enforcement of those rights in proceedings. The effect of the clause in the agreement was to preclude the continuation of sex discrimination proceedings in the employment tribunal and was therefore void and unenforceable.

There is one exception to the rule against contracting out of the anti-discrimination legislation. Contracts or agreements settling or compromising a complaint relating to discrimination in employment (and previously complaints relating to the *Equal Pay Act 1970, s 2* (see **22.29** EQUAL PAY)) are enforceable against the complainant only where the contract is made with the assistance of a conciliation officer (see **2.4** ADVISORY, CONCILIATION AND ARBITRATION SERVICE (ACAS)), or where the contract is a compromise contract (now "settlement agreement") meeting certain statutory conditions (see CHAPTER 3: ACAS CONCILIATION) (*EA 2010, s 144(4)*; and previously *SDA 1975, s 77(4)(aa)* as inserted by *TURERA 1993, Sch 6, para 1*, and *Employment Rights (Dispute Resolution) Act 1998, s 9*; *RRA 1976, s 72(4)* as amended by *TURERA 1993, Sch 6, para 2(4A)* and *Employment Rights (Dispute Resolution) Act 1998, s 9; SOR 2003, reg 35* and *Sch 4, part 1, para 2*; *RBR 2003, reg 35* and *Sch 4, part 1, para 2*; *DDA 1995, s 17C* and *Sch 3A, Part 1, para 2*; and *AR 2006, reg 43* and *Sch 5, Part 1, para 2*;).

2004/2515); for the purposes of the *SOR 2003,* the *Employment Equality (Sexual Orientation) Regulations 2003 (Amendment) Regulations 2004 (SI 2004/2519));* for the purposes of the *DDA 1995,* the *Compromise Agreements (Description of Person) Order 2005 (SI 2005/2364);* and, for the purposes of the *RBR 2003,* the *Employment Equality (Religion or Belief) Regulations 2003 (Amendment) (No 2) Regulations 2004 (SI 2004/2520);* all of which had been amended by the *Legal Services Act 2007 (Consequential Amendments) Order 2009 (SI 2009/3348), art 2).*

'Independent trade union' has the same meaning as in the *Trade Union and Labour Relations (Consolidation) Act 1992* (see **50.22** TRADE UNIONS – **I**).

See also HARVEYS – Division **PI.1.U**.

14   Education and Training

14.1   An employer has no obligation at common law to provide facilities for the education and training of his employees unless they are engaged under a contract of apprenticeship or their contract of employment provides otherwise. Similarly he does not have to allow employees time off for day-release or sandwich courses. However, with effect from 28 June 2013, young persons (i.e. 16 and 17 years olds) in England have a duty to participate in education or training until the age of 18 with corresponding duties on local education authorities (with effect from 28 June 2013) and employers (from a date to be appointed) to enable and support participation in education and training (see *Education and Skills Act 2008*). Young persons in full-time occupation must participate in 'sufficient' relevant training or education. (*ESA 2008, s 2(1)*). In Scotland and Wales, young persons in employment have the right to take time off from work in order to undertake study or training leading to a 'relevant qualification' (see **4.8 CHILDREN AND YOUNG PERSONS**).

In addition, an employer should not ask his employee to carry out a task requiring a special skill unless he has ensured that the employee possesses those skills or unless the employer has undertaken to train the employee. (If he does so and an accident occurs he may be liable, see **27.5–27.7 HEALTH AND SAFETY AT WORK – I.**) For the income tax treatment of training costs, see the *Income Tax (Earnings and Pensions) Act 2003, s 311*.

Various bodies and schemes have been created by the Government to encourage the education and training of employees and those seeking employment. At governmental level, the responsibility for higher and further education, apprenticeships, and skills is currently vested in the Department for Education.

The body responsible for funding the delivery of training and apprenticeships in England is the Education and Skills Funding Agency, from April 2017. There are different arrangements in Wales and Scotland (see **14.8** below).

As mentioned above, the *Apprenticeships, Skills, Children and Learning Act 2009* has made important changes in relation to the delivery of training in England. Amongst other matters, the Act has also made provision about apprenticeships in England and Wales, and has introduced a right for a 'qualifying employee' to apply to his or her employer to undertake study and/or training. Some of these changes took effect in April 2010, certain other changes took effect in 2011, and others are not yet in force; these provisions are dealt with in **14.9** onwards below.

14.2   APPRENTICESHIPS

Apprenticeships offer what must be the oldest form of training in skilled trades for young people.

The apprenticeship is normally for a fixed term of years or until a set qualification is achieved, the apprentice, his parent or guardian (if he is a minor), and the employer entering into a written agreement. The agreement will usually be in a form common to all apprenticeships for the trade concerned. In general the apprentice will have time off to attend college and take examinations.

A contract for apprenticeship may not be terminable for misconduct in the same way as an ordinary contract of employment; and in the event of wrongful termination, different principles apply to the assessment of damages (*Dunk v George Waller & Son Ltd* [1970] 2 QB 163. See also *Revenue and Customs Commissioners v Jones* [2014] ICR D43, in which the distinction between contracts of apprenticeship and contracts of employment was restated by the EAT).

14.2   Education and Training

In *Wallace v C A Roofing Services Ltd* [1996] IRLR 435, Sedley J in the High Court held that a contract of apprenticeship (unlike a contract of employment or training contract) cannot be terminated on the grounds of redundancy, falling short of closure or a fundamental change in the character of the employers' enterprise. He stated that a contract of apprenticeship remains a distinct entity at common law; its first purpose is training, and the execution of work for the employer is secondary. Thus, the ordinary law as to dismissal does not apply. The contract is for a fixed term and is not terminable at will, unlike a contract of employment at common law.

Wallace was applied in *Whitely v Marton Electrical Ltd* [2003] IRLR 197, in which the EAT held that a 'modern apprenticeship agreement', under which an employer agrees to employ an apprentice 'for the duration of the training plan', is different from an ordinary contract of employment and is not terminable on notice. The provision in the agreement requiring the apprentice to comply with the employer's terms and conditions of employment did not mean that the employer's terms as to notice of termination applied to the apprentice. Where any provision of the employer's terms and conditions were inconsistent with those of the agreement, the agreement must prevail because it was plainly the agreement which the parties intended should govern their relationship. However, in *Thorpe v Dul* [2003] ICR 1556, the EAT remitted the case for the employment tribunal to decide, as a question of fact, the legal status of the modern apprenticeship agreement in that case. See also *Revenue and Customs Commissioners v Jones* [2014] ICR D43, where the EAT held that livery stable workers who trained for formal British Horse Society examinations were not engaged under a contract of apprenticeship because the training aspect was incidental and subsidiary to the contract. Moreover, there was an express power under the contract to dismiss for gross misconduct without notice which was inconsistent with a contract of apprenticeship.

In *Flett v Matheson* [2006] EWCA Civ 53, [2006] IRLR 277, some eight months after commencing employment at the age of 16, the employee entered into a tripartite individual learning plan (ILP) with the employer and a training provider, which was stated to be carried out under advanced modern apprenticeship arrangements (see also **14.9** below). The employee was subsequently dismissed without notice, and claimed unfair dismissal and/or breach of contract of employment. The EAT held that the employee was employed under a contract of employment but not under a contract of apprenticeship; the employee appealed against the latter finding.

Allowing the appeal, the Court of Appeal held that a modern tripartite apprenticeship arrangement can constitute a common law contract of apprenticeship. In its view, the important issue is the nature and duration of the employer's obligations under the agreement. The fact that part of the training is provided by a third party is not crucial to the analysis of those obligations. In the present case, the ILP had the essential features of an apprenticeship. The contract of employment was varied or overlaid by the ILP, and that variation gave rise to additional obligations on the employer. The individual learning plan was called an 'apprenticeship' and provided for a combination of off and on the job training for a lengthy period. What occurred at the workplace was part of the training. While the employer did not provide the more academic part of the training, he was required to give the apprentice time off to obtain it and to fund the cost of attendance at classes. It was not open to the employer to dismiss on reasonable notice, subject to making reasonable efforts to find another employer willing and able to continue the training. If attempts to find another employer failed, the obligations on the employer remained and, save in certain specified circumstances, the apprentice could not be dismissed within the period of training. *Flett* was considered by the EAT in *Revenue and Customs Commissioners v Jones* [2014] ICR D43, where livery stable workers receiving training were held not to be engaged under a contract of apprenticeship.

If they satisfy the necessary qualifying conditions, apprentices enjoy the statutory employment protection rights (*Employment Rights Act 1996, s 230(2); Equality Act 2010, s 83(2)*). Note that to the extent that it would otherwise be treated as being a contract of service, an 'approved English apprenticeship agreement' is to be treated as being a contract of service (*Apprenticeships, Skills, Children and Learning Act 2009, s A5*).

The Employment Appeal Tribunal, on the basis of the evidence before it that the Law Society recommended the operation of a dual system whereby a clerk was articled to an individual partner in a firm of solicitors under a deed of articles but was employed by the firm under a contract of employment, held that an articled clerk was engaged under such a system (*Oliver v J P Malnick & Co* [1983] 3 All ER 795, [1983] ICR 708).

In *Edmonds v Lawson* [2000] QB 501, [2000] 2 WLR 1091, [2000] ICR 567, the Court of Appeal (allowing an appeal from Sullivan J: [2000] IRLR 18) held that, although a pupil barrister was employed under a contract by the set of barristers' chambers where she was taken on as a pupil, the contract was not a contract of apprenticeship or an equivalent contract. The pupil was, therefore, not a 'worker' for the purposes of the *National Minimum Wage Act 1998*, and was not entitled to be paid the national minimum wage ('NMW'). (For the NMW for apprentices, see **14.7** below; and see generally **34.9 Pay – I.**)

Flett v Matheson was followed (and *Edmonds v Lawson* was considered) in *Lee v Chassis & Cab Specialists Ltd* (UKEAT/0268/10/JOJ) [2011] All ER (D) 178 (Feb), (Transcript) where the EAT, in allowing an appeal from the employment tribunal, held that on the evidence the claimant in that case was an apprentice and not an employee. He was therefore excluded from the NMW by virtue of *SI 1999/584, reg 12(2)* (now revoked). See also *Revenue and Customs Commissioners v Jones* [2014] ICR D43, where livery stable workers were held not to be engaged under a contract of apprenticeship in a complaint by the Revenue for failure to pay NMW. Since amendments to the legislation in 2014 and included in the consolidating National Minimum Wage Regulations 2015, participation in a traineeship (a short-term government-funded work experience placement for those aged between 16 and 25) in England does not qualify a worker for the NMW (*SI 2015/621, reg 54*)

Apprenticeship Levy

In 2015, the Government announced an apprenticeship levy which is to come into effect in April 2017. This will be a levy on UK employers to fund up to an additional 3 million apprenticeship starts by 2020. The relevant provisions are contained in the *Finance Act 2016* and came into force from 15 September 2016. They provide for a levy to be charged on employers' pay bills at a rate of 0.5% for those employers having annual pay bills of more than £3 million. It is expected that the levy would be paid by less than 2% of UK employers. (See *Part 6 of the Finance Act 2016*). See https ://www.gov.uk/government/uploads/system/uploads/attachment_data/file/ 562401/Apprenticeship_funding_from_May_2017.pdf for information as to how the levy will work.

(See also **14.9** to **14.11** below.)

14.3   RECOVERY OF TRAINING COSTS

Problems are sometimes encountered in practice where an employer expends significant sums of money on training an employee, for example, by sending him on outside courses, and the employee then leaves his job shortly afterwards, in some instances without giving proper notice.

The wasted training costs will not usually be recoverable in the absence of an express agreement to that effect. That is so even if the employee leaves without giving proper notice, because the costs would have been incurred whether or not that breach of contract had occurred.

14.3 Education and Training

An agreement for the repayment of training costs in the event of an early departure will have to be very carefully drafted in order to be enforceable. If it applies where there is a breach of contract by the employee, it may be struck down as a 'penalty clause' unless it can be said to represent a genuine pre-estimate of loss suffered by the employer (*Giraud UK Ltd v Smith* [2000] IRLR 763; *Sands-Ellison v One Call Insurance* [2003] All ER (D) 389 (Mar); *Tullett Prebon Group Ltd v El-Hajjali* [2008] IRLR 760; *Imam-Sadeque v Bluebay Asset Management (Services) Ltd* [2013] IRLR 344; *Cavendish Square Holding BV v Talal El Makdessi* [2015] UKSC 67, [2015] 3 WLR 1373). This will usually mean, for example, that the proportion of the costs to be repaid must depend upon how long the employee remains after being trained (a clause meeting that requirement was upheld in *Neil v Strathclyde Regional Council* [1984] IRLR 14). Another possible argument against an agreement to repay training costs is that it is in restraint of trade, although the contention in *Neil* that the clause in that case was also illegal and unenforceable as an unlawful restrictive covenant or, alternatively, as being contrary to public policy because it was an undue restraint on the employee's liberty, was rejected at first instance (*Strathclyde Regional Council v Neil* [1984] IRLR 11; the point was not pursued on appeal). The reasoning in *Neil* was upheld in *Transocean Maritime Agencies SA Monegasque v Pettit* 1997 SCLR 534.

14.4 INDUSTRIAL TRAINING BOARDS

Industrial Training Boards were established by the Secretary of State for Employment under the *Industrial Training Act 1982* ('*ITA 1982*'), as amended (most recently by *EA 1989*), which repealed and replaced the *Industrial Training Act 1964*, as amended. The Boards' role is to ensure that the quantity and quality of training are adequate to meet the needs of the industries for which they are established, and they may:

(a) provide or secure the provision of such courses and other facilities (which may include residential accommodation) for the training of those persons as the Board considers adequate, having regard to any alternative courses or facilities available;

(b) approve alternative courses and facilities;

(c) publish recommendations regarding the length and nature of courses and standards to be attained in training;

(d) make tests for ascertaining the standards recommended and award certificates of the attainment of those standards;

(e) assist persons in finding facilities for being trained for employment in the industry;

(f) carry out, or assist others to carry out, research into any matter relating to training for employment in the industry; and

(g) provide advice about training connected with the industry.

(*ITA 1982, s 5(1)*.)

An Industrial Training Board may enter into contracts of service or apprenticeship with persons who intend to be employed in the industry and to attend courses or avail themselves of other facilities provided or approved by the Board (*ITA 1982, s 5(2)*).

Industrial Training Boards may provide advice on training. They may also:

(i) pay maintenance and travelling allowances to persons attending courses provided or approved by the Board;

(ii) make grants or loans to persons providing courses or other facilities approved by the Board, to persons who make studies for the purpose of providing such courses or facilities, and to persons who maintain arrangements to provide such courses or facilities which are not for the time being in use;

(iii)   pay fees to persons providing post-school education in respect of persons who receive it in association with their training in courses provided or approved by the Board; and

(iv)   make payments to persons in connection with arrangements under which they or employees of theirs make use of courses or other facilities provided or approved by the Board.

(ITA 1982, s 5(4).)

Forms are available from the relevant Industrial Training Board for the employer to provide the information enabling him to claim such a payment as is mentioned under (iv) above.

An Industrial Training Board, with the approval of the Secretary of State, may require employers in the industry to furnish returns and other information, to keep certain records and to produce them for examination by the Board *(ITA 1982, s 6(1))*. Penalties may be imposed for the infringement of any of these provisions. Penalties also exist for knowingly or recklessly furnishing false records or information.

Two statutory Boards remain: the Construction Industry Training Board ('CITB') and the Engineering Construction Industry Training Board ('ECITB').

Provision is made for the imposition of a levy from time to time on employers in the industry, for the purpose of raising money towards meeting the expenses of each Board *(ITA 1982, s 11)*. A levy is imposed by means of a 'levy order' made by the Secretary of State. The most recent levy orders include the *Industrial Training Levy (Construction Industry Training Board) Order 2015 (SI 2015/701)* (which took effect on 12 March 2015) and *Industrial Training Levy (Engineering Construction Industry Training Board) Order 2015 (SI 2015/677)* (which took effect on 12 March 2015). A claim that the CITB levy was ultra vires and operated unfairly towards the employer was dismissed by Kerr J in *R (Hudson Contract Services Ltd) v Secretary of State for Business Innovation and Skills* [2016] EWHC 844 (Admin). The Court held that the statutory purpose of the scheme was to fund the CITB's expenses, not just to fund courses, and the CITB incurred expenses in broader industry provision which could be recouped. Furthermore, as the statutory scheme did not prescribe any particular method of raising the levy or restrict how it could be raised, the CITB was entitled to raise the levy for payments other than just those made directly for labour.

The CITB and the ECITB (as well as the non-statutory Film industry training board) were subject to a Government review from 2013 and the final report was published in December 2015. Some changes to the ITBs were recommended but it was stated that final recommendations as to the future of the CITB and ECITB would be made once the future apprenticeship levy arrangements in respect of post-16 apprenticeships were clear. In October 2016, the Minister for Apprenticeships and Skills announced a review of ITBs to determine "whether market failures in construction still require a separate levy and grant system and if so, how this can operate alongside the apprenticeship levy" (https ://www.gov.uk/government/news/paul-morrell-to-advise-major-review-of-industrial -training-boards).

14.5   SERVICES FOR SCHOOL-LEAVERS

The *Trade Union Reform and Employment Rights Act 1993* substituted new *ss 8–10A* in the *Employment and Training Act 1973* so as to place a duty on the Secretary of State to secure the provision of careers guidance and placing services ('relevant services') for people attending schools and colleges. The Secretary of State is also given power to arrange for the provision of relevant services for other people, and may direct local authorities to provide

14.5 Education and Training

(or arrange for the provision of) relevant services. The *1973 Act* requires the providers of relevant services to provide them in accordance with the directions given by the Secretary of State. The Chief Inspector of Education, Children's Services and Skills in England must inspect and report on the provision of services in England in pursuance of *s 8* or *s 9* by any person or institution, when requested to do so by the Secretary of State; he may also undertake other inspections of the provision of those services as he thinks fit. However, any such inspection may not relate to services provided for persons who are over 20 years old. (*ETA 1973, s 10B*, inserted by the *Learning and Skills Act 2000* and amended by the *Education Act 2005* and the *Education and Inspections Act 2006*).

14.6 WORK PROGRAMME

The Work Programme was designed to help people prepare for, find and stay in employment. It was delivered for Jobcentre Plus by specialist organisations, called 'providers'. The Work Programme stopped taking new participants on 1 April 2017.

Further details are available at https://www.gov.uk/moving-from-benefits-to-work/job-search-programmes.

14.7 WORK-BASED TRAINING

Work-based training opportunities are currently provided through various types of apprenticeships (currently known as Intermediate Level Apprenticeships, Advanced Level Apprenticeships and Higher Apprenticeships), and other training initiatives, all of which involve working and training with an employer, and studying for other qualifications (usually with a training provider). In the past, apprenticeships were aimed primarily at people aged between 16 and 24, but apprenticeship opportunities for people aged 25 or over were introduced in August 2007.

There is a national minimum wage (NMW) for apprentices. (*National Minimum Wage Regulations 2015 (SI 2015/621), reg 4A*)The wage applies to all apprentices aged under 19 (including those working under an 'approved English apprenticeship agreement' within the meaning of *section A5* of the *Apprenticeships, Skills, Children and Learning Act 2009* (see **14.11** below)), and apprentices aged 19 or over in the first year of their apprenticeship. (Apprentices aged 19 or over who have already spent a year on their apprenticeship must be paid at least the full NMW rate appropriate to their age.) As at 1 April 2017, the apprentice minimum wage is £3.50 per hour and applies to time working, plus time spent training that is part of the apprenticeship. If an apprentice is on a higher wage, the employer must continue to pay that amount for the remainder of the training or until the apprentice becomes eligible for the full NMW. (See **33.9 PAY – I.**)

For further information regarding apprenticeships, see https://www.gov.uk/apprenticeships-guide.

For the purposes of health and safety legislation, trainees are treated as the employees of the person whose undertaking is providing training (*Health and Safety (Training for Employment) Regulations 1990 (SI 1990/1380)*). For the application of discrimination laws see Discrimination and Equal Opportunities – **I, II, III (11, 12, 13)**; an 'Equal Opportunities Toolkit' has also been produced for use in conjunction with training for young people.

14.8 SKILLS TRAINING

As from April 2017, the Education and Skills Funding Agency is responsible for funding and regulating adult skills training in England; for further information, see https://www.gov.uk/government/organisations/education-and-skills-funding-agency. As from

3 April 2017, the Institute for Apprenticeships was launched (although at the time of writing this launch seems to have preceded the coming into force of the relevant statutory provisions: *Apprenticeships, Skills, Children and Learning Act 2009, s ZA1*). Its aims include ensuring high -quality apprenticeship standards and advising government on funding for each standard. The Institute of Apprenticeships is an executive non-departmental public body sponsored by the Department for Education. In Wales, the regulation and funding of adult skills training is the responsibility of the Welsh Assembly Government; for further information, see gov.wales/topics/educationandskills/?lang=en. In Scotland, since 2008 these functions are the responsibility of Skills Development Scotland; for further details, see www.skillsdevelopmentscotland.co.uk/our-services/services-for-individuals.aspx.

Another relevant service is *learndirect*, which provides courses (mainly on-line) and information through its network of learning centres; for further information, see www.learndirect.com. See also the Government website, which provides information and advice to adults who wish to earn new skills, gain new qualifications, or retrain; further information can be found on www.gov.uk/browse/working/finding-job.

14.9   APPRENTICESHIPS, SKILLS, CHILDREN AND LEARNING ACT 2009

The *Apprenticeships, Skills, Children and Learning Act 2009* (referred to below as 'the *Act*') has been substantially revised with *Part 1* now containing provision (yet to be come into force) for a new Institute for Apprenticeships and as from 26 March 2015 provisions dealing with Apprenticeships in England.

The provisions of the *Act* that are of relevance to this chapter are the changes to the structure for funding education and training (dealt with briefly in **14.10** below), and also the provisions set out in *Part 1* of the *Act*, which is headed 'Apprenticeships, Study and Training'. *Part 1* is in turn divided into four chapters: a new *chapter ZA1* (inserted by the *Enterprise Act 2016* from a date to be appointed), *chapter A1* ('Apprenticeships: England', *ss A1* to *A11*); *chapter 1* ('Apprenticeships: Wales', *sections 1* to *39*, which now apply only to Wales); and *chapter 2* ('Study and Training', *section 40*). *Chapters A1* and *1* are dealt with briefly in **14.11** below, and *chapter 2* (which sets out a new statutory right for an employee to request his employer to allow him to undertake study or training) is dealt with in greater detail in **14.12** onwards below.

14.10   Structural changes

The *Act* dissolved the Learning and Skills Council (LSC). The LSC's responsibility for funding education and training for young people in England over compulsory school age but under 19 was transferred to local education authorities (initially supported by a new Young People's Learning Agency, although this was abolished by the *Education Act 2011* with effect from 1 April 2012; see *SI 2012/924*). In addition, the *Act* creates the office of Chief Executive of Skills Funding. The Chief Executive, with his staff, constitutes the Skills Funding Agency and has taken on the LSC's responsibility for funding post-19 education and training in England. These provisions (in *Part 4* of the *Act*) came into force on 1 April 2010 (see the *Apprenticeships, Skills, Children and Learning Act 2009 (Commencement No 2 and Transitional and Saving Provisions) Order 2010 (SI 2010/303)*). *Part 4* of the *Act* was subsequently amended by the *Education Act 2011* so as to impose a duty on the Chief Executive to fund apprenticeship training, by securing the provision of proper facilities for every young person in certain specified groups who has secured an apprenticeship opportunity. The effect of this section is to give higher funding priority for apprenticeship training for these young persons. This duty is known as 'the apprenticeship offer'. (*Apprenticeships, Skills, Children and Learning Act 2009, ss 83A, 83B*, in force 1 September 2012 (see *SI 2012/1087*)); *Apprenticeships (the Apprenticeship Offer) (Prescribed Persons) Regulations 2013 (SI 2013/560)*, in force 6 April 2013).

14.10 Education and Training

The *Deregulation Act 2015* introduced substantial changes to the *Act*. With effect from 26 May 2015, the office of the Chief Executive of Skills Funding was abolished along with his apprenticeship functions. (*Deregulation Act 2015, Sch 14*). There is also (as from 26 March 2015) a new *chapter A1* in the *Act* making provision for approved English apprenticeships. (*Deregulation Act 2015, Sch 1*)

The *Enterprise Act 2016* introduced further changes although many of these are yet to take effect. A new *Chapter ZA1* establishes a new 'Institute of Apprenticeships' whose functions including providing the Secretary of State with advice and assistance in connection with her functions relating to apprenticeships in England.

14.11 Apprenticeships

Sections ZA1 to ZA11 of the *Act* make provision for the establishment of the Institute of Apprenticeships whose functions will include advising the Secretary of State in relation to apprenticeships in England and setting standards in respect of apprenticeships. *Sections 1 to 39* of the *Act* make provision about apprenticeships in Wales, including provisions about the issuing of 'apprenticeship certificates'. Normally, to receive such a certificate, an applicant will need to have been a party to an 'apprenticeship agreement' which, at the date on which it was entered into, related to a recognised 'apprenticeship framework'. The conditions will also require the applicant, while working under the agreement, to have completed a course of training for the principal qualification identified by the framework in question, and to have met all the other requirements specified for the award of a certificate. (These are known as the 'standard completion conditions', although there are 'alternative completion conditions' that apply in prescribed circumstances: see further **14.7** above.) For England, there is new provision for "approved English apprenticeships" under *chapter A1* of *Part 1* of the *Act*.

Approved English Apprenticeships

An approved English apprenticeship is an arrangement which takes place under an approved English apprenticeship agreement, such agreement being one which provides for the apprentice to work for another person for reward in a sector for which the Secretary of State has published an approved apprenticeship standard, provides for the apprentice to receive training to assist the apprentice to achieve the approved apprenticeship standard and satisfies any prescribed conditions. (*s A1(1)* to *(3)*, the *Act*). An approved English apprenticeship can also be an arrangement which is an alternative English apprenticeship of a kind described in regulations. Such an arrangement can involve a person working otherwise than for reward. (*s A1(1)* to *(3)*, the *Act*). Upon completion of an approved English apprenticeship, the Secretary of State may issue a certificate. An approved English apprenticeship agreement is to be treated as not being a contract of apprenticeship if it would otherwise be so treated. (*ss A3, A5*, the *Act*).

The Government has committed to an additional 3 million apprenticeship starts by 2020 to be funded by a levy on employers with pay bills of more than £3 million. See **14.2** above and the *Apprenticeship Levy*.

14.12 Study and training

Section 40 of the *Act* inserted new *sections 63D* to *63K* (*Part VIA*) into the *ERA 1996*. These provisions came into force on 6 April 2010 (except in relation to small employers and their employees). (See *SI 2010/303, Sch 3*.) A 'small employer' means an employer who employs fewer than 250 employees (for the detailed definition, see *SI 2010/303, Sch 3, col 2*). Originally, *SI 2010/303* stated that these provisions would come into force on 6 April 2011 in relation to small employers and their employees, but this was revoked by the *Apprenticeships, Skills, Children and Learning Act 2009 (Commencement No 2 and Transitional and Saving Provisions) Order 2010 (Amendment) Order 2011 (SI 2011/882)*.

14.13 *Statutory right to make request in relation to study or training*

A 'qualifying employee' (ie an employee who is not excluded by *section 63D(7)* (see below), and who has been continuously employed for a period of not less than 26 weeks: *Employee Study and Training (Qualifying Period of Employment) Regulations 2010 (SI 2010/800)*) may make an application under *section 63D* to his or her employer (*ERA 1996, s 63D(1)*). The application must state that it is an application under *section 63D* (*ERA 1996, s 63D(5)*), and must be made for the purpose of enabling the employee to undertake study or training (or both) within *section 63D(4)*, ie where its purpose is to improve:

(a)   the employee's effectiveness in the employer's business; and

(b)   the performance of the employer's business.

The following persons are excluded by *section 63D(7)*:

(i)   a person of compulsory school age (or, in Scotland, school age);

(ii)   a person to whom *Part 1* of the *Education and Skills Act 2008* (duty to participate in education or training for 16 and 17 year olds) applies;

(iii)   a person who, by virtue of *section 29* of that *Act*, is treated as a person to whom that *Part* applies for the purposes specified in that section (extension for person reaching 18);

(iv)   a person to whom *section 63A* of the *ERA 1996* (right to time off for young person for study or training — see **4.7** CHILDREN AND YOUNG PERSONS) applies;

(v)   an agency worker; or

(vi)   a person of a description specified by the Secretary of State in regulations.

Nothing in *ERA 1996, Part VIA* prevents an employee and an employer from making any other arrangements in relation to study or training (*ERA 1996, s 63D(8)*).

14.14 *Section 63D application: supplementary provisions*

A *section 63D* application may (a) be made in relation to study or training of any description (subject to what is stated below); (b) relate to more than one description of study or training (*ERA 1996, s 63E(1)*).

In particular, the study or training need not be intended to lead to the award of a qualification to the employee (*ERA 1996, s 63E(3)*), and may be such that it would:

(i)   be undertaken on the employer's premises or elsewhere (including at the employee's home);

(ii)   be undertaken by the employee while performing the duties of the employee's employment or separately;

(iii)   be provided or supervised by the employer or by someone else;

(iv)   be undertaken without supervision;

(v)   be undertaken within or outside the United Kingdom.

(*ERA 1996, s 63E(2)*).

A *section 63D* application must give the following details of the proposed study or training (*ERA 1996, s 63E(4)(a)*):

(A)   its subject matter;

(B)   where and when it would take place;

(C)   who would provide or supervise it;

(D)   what qualification (if any) it would lead to.

The application must also explain how the employee thinks the proposed study or training would improve (i) the employee's effectiveness in the employer's business, and (ii) the performance of the employer's business (*ERA 1996, s 63E(4)(b)*).

For detailed requirements as to the form of the application, and the information it must contain, see the *Employee Study and Training (Eligibility, Complaints and Remedies) Regulations 2010 (SI 2010/156)*.

14.15 *Employer's duties in relation to section 63D application*

Where an employer receives a *section 63D* application from an employee, and the employer has not received such an application from the employee within the previous 12 months, he must deal with the application in accordance with regulations made by the Secretary of State (*ERA 1996, s 63F(4)*). The employer may refuse the application (or, as the case may be, part of the application) only if he thinks that one or more of the permissible grounds for refusal applies in relation to the application (or, as the case may be, that part) (*ERA 1996, s 63F(1), (5), (6)*). The permissible grounds for refusal are:

(a)   that the proposed study or training to which the application, or the part in question, relates would not improve (i) the employee's effectiveness in the employer's business, or (ii) the performance of the employer's business;

(b)   the burden of additional costs;

(c)   detrimental effect on ability to meet customer demand;

(d)   inability to re-organise work among existing staff;

(e)   inability to recruit additional staff;

(f)   detrimental impact on quality;

(g)   detrimental impact on performance;

(h)   insufficiency of work during the periods the employee proposes to work;

(i)   planned structural changes;

(j)   any other grounds specified by the Secretary of State in regulations.

(*ERA 1996, s 63F(7)*).

For the detailed requirements imposed on the employer on receiving a *section 63D* application (including a requirement to hold a meeting with the employee within 28 days of receiving the application), see the *Employee Study and Training (Procedural Requirements) Regulations 2010 (SI 2010/155)*.

14.16 *Employee's duties in relation to agreed study or training*

Where an employer has agreed to a *section 63D* application (or part of one) made by an employee in relation to particular study or training, the employee must inform the employer if he (a) fails to start or complete the agreed study or training, or (b) undertakes, or proposes to undertake, study or training that differs from the agreed study or training in any respect (including those specified in *section 63E(4)(a)* — see **14.14** above) (*ERA 1996, s 63H*). For the requirements as to the way in which the employee is to comply with this duty, see the *Employee Study and Training (Procedural Requirements) Regulations 2010 (SI 2010/155), reg 20*.

14.17 *Complaint to employment tribunal*

An employee who makes a *section 63D* application may present a complaint to an employment tribunal that:

(a)   the employer has failed to comply with *section 63F(4)*, *(5)* or *(6)* (see **14.15** above), or

(b)   the employer's decision to refuse the application, or part of it, is based on incorrect facts.

(ERA 1996, s 63I(1)).

No such complaint may be made in respect of an application which has been disposed of by agreement or withdrawn *(ERA 1996, s 63I(2))*. Where an application that has not been disposed of by agreement or withdrawn, a complaint under *section 63I* may only be made if the employer:

(i)   notifies the employee of a decision to refuse the application (or part of it) on appeal; or

(ii)   commits a breach of certain requirements set out in *SI 2010/155*, namely the failure to hold a meeting or a failure to notify a decision *(ERA 1996, s 63I(3)*; *Employee Study and Training (Eligibility, Complaints and Remedies) Regulations 2010 (SI 2010/156), reg 5)*.

An employee also has a right to complain to an employment tribunal that the employer has failed, or threatened to fail, to comply with *reg 16(2)*, *(3)*, or *(5)* of *SI 2010/155* (right of employee to be accompanied by companion at meeting to consider *s 63D* application; right of companion to address meeting or confer with employee; right of employee to have meeting postponed if companion unavailable) *(Employee Study and Training (Procedural Requirements) Regulations 2010 (SI 2010/155), reg 17)*.

An employment tribunal may not consider a complaint under *s 63I* unless the complaint is presented:

(A)   before the end of the period of three months beginning with the relevant date; or

(B)   within any further period that the tribunal considers reasonable, if the tribunal is satisfied that it was not reasonably practicable for the complaint to be presented before the end of that period of three months.

(ERA 1996, s 63I(5)). The new extension of time limits to facilitate conciliation before presenting a complaint apply to *ERA 1996, s 63I(5)* as of 6 April 2014. *(ERA 1996, s 63I(7))*.

The relevant date is the date on which the employee is notified of the decision on the appeal or (as the case may be) the date on which the breach was committed *(ERA 1996, s 63I(6))*.

14.18 *Remedies*

If an employment tribunal finds a complaint under *s 63I* well-founded it must make a declaration to that effect and may (a) make an order for reconsideration of the *s 63D* application; (b) make an award of compensation to be paid by the employer to the employee *(ERA 1996, s 63J(1))*.

The amount of any compensation must be the amount the tribunal considers just and equitable in all the circumstances, but must not exceed the permitted maximum of 8 weeks' pay *(ERA 1996, s 63J(2), (3)*; *Employee Study and Training (Eligibility, Complaints and Remedies) Regulations 2010 (SI 2010/156), reg 6)*.

If an employment tribunal makes an order for reconsideration of the *s 63D* application, *s 63F* (see **14.15** above) and regulations under that section (ie. *SI 2010/155*) apply as if the application had been received on the date of the order (instead of on the date it was actually received) (*ERA 1996, s 63J(4)*).

14.19 *Right not to suffer detriment, and right not to be unfairly dismissed*

Detriment. An employee has the right not to be subjected to any detriment (ie an action short of dismissal) by any act, or any deliberate failure to act, by the employee's employer done on the ground that the employee:

(a)   made (or proposed to make) a *s 63D* application;

(b)   exercised (or proposed to exercise) a right conferred on the employee under *section 63F*;

(c)   brought proceedings against the employer under *s 63I*; or

(d)   alleged the existence of any circumstance which would constitute a ground for bringing such proceedings.

(*ERA 1996, s 47F(1)*, inserted by the *Apprenticeships, Skills, Children and Learning Act 2009, s 40(1), (3)*).

Unfair dismissal. An employee who is dismissed is to be regarded for the purposes of *Part X* of the *ERA 1996* as unfairly dismissed if the reason (or, if more than one, the principal reason) for the dismissal is that the employee took (or proposed to take) any of the actions specified in (a) to (d) under *Detriment* above.

(*ERA 1996, s 104E*, inserted by the *Apprenticeships, Skills, Children and Learning Act 2009, s 40(1), (4)*).

each of which recorded that there was no obligation to offer or accept any further contract. In those circumstances, it was impermissible to imply an over-arching or umbrella contract of employment pursuant to which each individual contract was issued.

The third element – that the employer must have a sufficient degree of control over the employee – does not mean that work must necessarily be carried out under the employer's actual supervision or control. In a more general sense, it requires that ultimate authority over the employee in the performance of his work resides in the employer, so that the employee is subject to the latter's orders and directions.

The necessity of control derives from the judgment of McKenna J in *Ready Mixed Concrete (South East) Ltd v Minister of Pensions and National Insurance* [1968] 2 QB 497 at 514. McKenna J's remarks on control have been cited with approval in the majority of subsequent important cases dealing with the essential ingredients of an employment contract. The Court of Appeal has re-affirmed that in the absence of sufficient control, there cannot be a contract of employment. What constitutes sufficient control – and whether that means the imposition of a framework within which a person works or direct supervision of the performance of a person's functions – will vary from case to case. But control is a necessary condition of a contract of employment: *Johnson Underwood Ltd v Montgomery* [2001] EWCA Civ 318, [2001] IRLR 269. Once there is mutuality of obligation such that there is a contract, control is relevant for deciding whether the contract is a contract of employment: *Stephenson v Delphi Systems Ltd* [2003] ICR 471. The Court of Appeal has emphasised that what is required is the 'ultimate' ability of the employer to control the manner in which work is carried out; it is not necessary that the employee is subject to detailed factual control on a day-to-day basis: *Troutbeck SA v White* [2013] EWCA Civ 1171, [2013] IRLR 949 (and see also *Catholic Child Welfare Society and Ors v Various Claimants* [2013] IRLR 219).

If the contract does not impose an obligation to provide services personally or if there is no mutuality of obligation throughout the period under consideration, or if there is no control present, then the contract in question cannot be a contract of employment. If all these elements are present, the contract *may* be one of employment. It will then be necessary to consider the surrounding circumstances to determine the nature of the relationship.

In order to determine, once the irreducible minimum requirements are present, whether the contract is a contract of employment, it is necessary to paint a picture from the accumulation of relevant details. This means not only looking at specific matters, but also standing back and considering the overall picture. This approach derives from *Hall (Inspector of Taxes) v Lorimer* [1994] 1 All ER 250, [1994] 1 WLR 209, [1994] STC 23, 66 TC 349, [1994] ICR 218. The matters that are capable of being relevant are too numerous to list in full. However, they might include payment by wages or salary; whether the worker provides his own equipment; whether he is subject to the employer's disciplinary and grievance procedures; receipt of sick pay or contractual holiday pay; provision of benefits traditionally associated with employment such as a pension scheme, health care or other benefits; whether the worker is a part of the employer's business; whether there are restrictions on working for others.

Some cases have focused on factors that distinguish an employee from a person in business on his own account. The sorts of details that may be relevant include whether (or how far) he:

(a)   is employed as part of the business of the employer and his work is done as an integral part of that business;

(b)   provides his own equipment;

(c)   hires his own helpers;

(d)   takes a degree of financial risk;

(e)   has responsibility for investment and management; and

(f)   has the opportunity of profiting from sound management in performing his task.

This list is derived from *Market Investigations Ltd v Minister of Social Security* [1969] 2 QB 173, *per* Cooke J at 185. In *Lee Ting Sang v Chung Chi-Keung* [1990] 2 AC 374, [1990] ICR 409, the Privy Council said that the best expression of the test was that stated in the *Market Investigations* case: is the person concerned in business on his own account? This test was again applied in *Andrews v King (Inspector of Taxes)* [1991] STC 481, [1991] ICR 846, where the Vice-Chancellor went on to say that the essence of business was that it was carried on with a view to profit (whereas it was not open to the employee there to make an increased profit from the way in which he carried out his tasks). The importance of this criterion has recently been emphasised by the Court of Appeal in *Stringefellow Restaurants Limited*. However, it is not a matter of running through these indicia as if they were an all-purpose checklist. Part of the function of painting the picture is to determine what are the significant details in the instant case and to look at the whole arrangement. Thus, in *Hall v Lorimer*, a vision mixer who supplied no tools, equipment or money to his business and did not hire staff was still self-employed. The key factor was that he was a professional person who worked for a variety of people for short periods and was not dependent on any one paymaster (see also *Suhail v Barking Havering and Redbridge NHS Trust* UKEAT 0536/13, where a similar analysis was applied to a locum working in the NHS). In *Pimlico Plumbers Ltd v Smith* UKEAT 0495/12 the EAT held that a plumber was not an employee, a key point being that he assumed the financial risk of non-payment by customers.

It has been observed that one cannot safely rely on a simple dichotomy between the employed and those on business on their own account. There are categories of person who are not in business on their own account but who are not, for that reason alone, necessarily to be regarded as employees. In particular, many statutory provisions either contain a wider definition of employee than that which is used in the common law (for example, the discrimination legislation) or extend protection to a category of persons called 'workers' who are not employed but are not in business on their own account either: see *James v Redcats (Brands) Ltd* [2007] IRLR 296.

As a general rule, the greater the degree of personal responsibility an individual undertakes in any of the matters set out above, the more likely he is to be considered an independent contractor rather than an employee.

The way in which a person is treated for tax may be relevant but is not decisive. The tax and employment regimes are separate and do not necessarily have to give the same answer as to a person's status.

In assessing all of these factors, it is legitimate in a case where the contract is said to be based partly on oral exchanges and on conduct to consider evidence of the way in which the parties understood their relationship and the way in which they conducted themselves in practice (see *Carmichael v National Power plc* and also now *Autoclenz*). However, the conduct of the parties cannot be relied upon for the purpose of implying a term that flatly contradicts an express term: *Stevedoring and Haulage Services Ltd*. In *Stevedoring and Haulage Services*, workers were engaged on terms that specifically negated mutuality of obligation in that they made it clear that there was no obligation to offer or accept employment beyond the individual engagement that was the subject of the contract. The conduct of the parties (which remained the same throughout several renewals of the contract) could not override those express written terms by creating mutual obligations to offer and to accept work outside the individual engagement.

Where the nature of the relationship between the parties is in doubt or is ambiguous, it is open to the parties, by agreement, to stipulate what the legal situation between them is to be (*Massey v Crown Life Insurance Co Ltd* [1978] 2 All ER 576, [1978] 1 WLR 676, [1978]

ICR 590). However, all the circumstances of the relationship must be considered, and the courts will look behind the parties' intentions, and labels, to ascertain the true nature of the agreement (*Young & Woods Ltd v West* [1980] IRLR 201). Where a person worked for an employment agency and the tribunal found that there were mutual obligations and considerable control, it was incorrect to decide that there was no contract of employment on the basis that this is what the parties had originally intended. The label applied by the parties would only be decisive where all the other factors were evenly balanced: *Dacas v Brook Street Bureau (UK) Ltd* [2004] IRLR 358.

It is wrong to say that a person is an employee simply because he is not self-employed. There may also be intermediate categories of worker (*Dacas v Brook Street*). But to enjoy the statutory rights that apply only to employees (e.g. to claim unfair dismissal), the person must be an employee.

Note also that a full-time working director of his family firm (who drew fees rather than being paid a salary) was held to be self-employed (*Parsons v Albert J Parsons & Sons Ltd* [1979] ICR 271), as were musicians with a London orchestra (*Winfield v London Philharmonic Orchestra Ltd* [1979] ICR 726) and a sub-postmaster (*Hitchcock v Post Office* [1980] ICR 100, *Wolstenholme v Post Office Ltd* [2003] ICR 546). A police cadet was held not to be an employee or an apprentice (*Wiltshire Police Authority v Wynn* [1981] QB 95, [1980] 3 WLR 445, 79 LGR 591, [1980] ICR 649). A Presbyterian minister was held not to be an employee, as was a Sikh priest (*Davies v Presbyterian Church of Wales* [1986] 1 All ER 705, [1986] 1 WLR 323, [1986] ICR 280; *Singh v Guru Nanak Gurdwara* [1990] ICR 309, CA). But in *Percy v Board of National Mission of the Church of Scotland* [2005] UKHL 73, [2006] 2 WLR 353, [2006] ICR 134 a minister of the Church of Scotland was held to be employed within the wider definition of that term in the *Sex Discrimination Act* (see also *New Testament Church of God v Stewart* [2008] IRLR 134). There is no rule of law that a person who provides services via a company cannot be an employee (*Catamaran Cruisers Ltd v Williams* [1994] IRLR 386). It has been held that a volunteer is not an employee because of the absence of consideration moving from the recipient of the volunteer's services. There is no obligation on that party to make payment and, in the absence of payment, there is no consideration and no contract: *Melhuish v Redbridge Citizens' Advice Bureau* [2005] IRLR 419, EAT. It is necessary to consider the purpose of a contract in order to decide whether it is a contract of employment. Thus an arrangement by which a prisoner undertook work as part of his rehabilitation was not a contract of employment because that was not its purpose: *M&P Steelcraft Ltd v Ellis* [2008] ICR 578.

The Court of Appeal considered the status of a modern apprenticeship agreement between a trainee, an employer and a Training and Enterprise Council or some other educational establishment in *Flett v Matheson* [2006] EWCA Civ 53, [2006] ICR 673. The Court of Appeal overturned the EAT's decision that such an arrangement created a contract of employment between the individual and the employer. The Court held that the purpose of the arrangement was to provide practical aspects of training. The apprentice was to be released from work to attend academic training. The Court approved the distinction which had been drawn between an employment contract and a contract for apprenticeship in *Whitely v Marton Electrical Ltd* [2003] ICR 495. In the event, the Court in *Flett* remitted the matter for the Tribunal to make further findings of fact.

A general practitioner is not employed by a health authority. GPs are under obligations in relation to the nature of the work they undertake. But since these obligations are imposed by statutory instrument and not by contract, those obligations do not make the GP an employee of the health authority: *David-John v North Essex Health Authority* [2004] ICR 112, EAT.

Equity partners are generally not employees. However, there are many different forms of partnership arrangements where individuals are not traditional equity partners. The *Partnership Act 1890, section 2(3)* provides that receiving a share of the profits is prima facie

15.3   Employee, Self-Employed or Worker?

evidence of a partnership. But, there is old authority that suggests where an individual receives a salary as well as a share in the profits, there is strong evidence that he is an employee, not a partner (*Ross v Parkyns* (1875) LR 20 Eq 331). It is necessary to consider all the circumstances to determine whether or not an individual is an employee. In *Stekel v Ellice* [1973] 1 WLR 191 Megarry J considered that under a partnership agreement a salaried partner on a fixed salary, not dependent on profits, could still be a true partner at least if he was entitled to a share in the profits on a winding-up. There is no requirement for an individual to have a minimum share of profits or involvement in management decisions before they can be regarded as a partner. The fact that an individual has the rights and duties of a partner and an entitlement to a residue of the firm if wound up can be sufficient (see *Tiffin v Lester Aldridge LLP* [2011] IRLR 105). In *Kovats v TFO Management LLP* [2009] ICR 1140 the EAT examined *section 4(4)* of the *Limited Liability Partnerships Act 2000* which provides that a member of a limited liability partnership shall not be regarded for any purpose as employed by the limited liability partnership unless, if he and the other members were partners in a partnership, he would be regarded for that purpose as employed by the partnership. Judge Birtles held that "any purpose" includes *section 230* of *ERA* and therefore the same test applied for partners in an LLP as in the case of traditional partnerships. In *Clyde & Co LLP v Bates Van Winklehof* [2014] UKSC 32, [2014] ICR 730 the Supreme Court held that an 'equity' member of a limited liability partnership could be a worker and therefore entitled to pursue a claim in respect of an alleged protected disclosure. Notably, the Court suggested that a relationship of subordination was not required in order to establish worker status. The Court left open the question of whether a partner in an ordinary partnership can be a worker.

There may be contracts that are neither contracts of employment nor contracts for services but which fall into an intermediate category (*Construction Industry Training Board v Labour Force Ltd* [1970] 3 All ER 220; *Ironmonger v Movefield Ltd (t/a Deering Appointments)* [1988] IRLR 461, EAT). It is thought that a person who works under such a contract will, for most purposes, be in the same position as one who is self-employed. However, such persons may also be regarded as 'workers' for other statutory purposes such as the *Working Time Regulations* and the provisions in relation to unlawful deductions of wages.

In *O'Kelly v Trusthouse Forte plc* [1984] QB 90, [1983] 3 All ER 456, [1983] 3 WLR 605, [1983] ICR 728, the majority of the Court of Appeal held that an appellate court could only interfere with a decision of an employment tribunal on the question of whether an individual was an employee if it could be shown that the employment tribunal had erred in law or reached a perverse conclusion. See also *Lee Ting Sang v Chung Chi-Keung* [1990] 2 AC 374, [1990] 2 WLR 1173, [1990] ICR 409, [1990] IRLR 236; *Hall v Lorimer* [1994] ICR 218. However, when the issue whether a person is an employee or self-employed depends on the construction of a written document, this will involve questions of law (*Davies v Presbyterian Church of Wales*) but only to the extent that it appears that the parties intended all the express terms of their contract to be contained in the document (*Ministry of Defence HQ Defence Dental Service v Kettle* (UKEAT/0308/06/LA) [2007] All ER (D) 301 (Jan)). Whether or not that was their intention is a question of fact (*Carmichael v National Power plc*).

Can a controlling shareholder be an employee? A question sometimes arises as to whether a person who controls the shareholding in the employing enterprise can also be employed by that enterprise. This arises often in cases where a company has become insolvent and a majority shareholder or director claims to be an employee and therefore entitled to payments from the Secretary of State under *section 182* of *ERA*. The most recent guidelines on the issue were given in *Secretary of State for Business, Enterprise and Regulatory Reform v Neufeld (Richard) (2) Howe (Keith)* [2009] EWCA Civ 280, [2009] IRLR 475. There is no reason in principle why a controlling shareholder should not be an employee. The mere fact that a person is a shareholder or profits from the success of a business does not mean that he cannot be an employee. It is no answer to argue that the extent of the individual's control of the company meant that the control condition of a contract of employment could not be satisfied. There are three cases in which it would be legitimate not to give effect to a contract of employment between a controlling shareholder and his company. First where the contract is itself a sham. Second where the contract was entered into for an ulterior purpose (such as to obtain payment from the Secretary of State upon the company's insolvency). Third where the parties do not conduct themselves in accordance with the contract – either because they never intended to or because the relationship ceases to reflect the terms of the contract. Where a contract is in place, the onus is on the party seeking to deny it to show that it is not what it appears to be. If the parties conduct themselves in accordance with the terms of the contract, that is a strong indicator of a contract of employment. By contrast if their conduct is inconsistent, it may be held that there is no such contract.

Specific engagements. When one asks whether a person was employed or self-employed, the question usually concerns the general relationship between the parties to the contract. The question – although rarely framed in these terms – is whether the 'general engagement' between the parties was a contract of employment or a contract for services. Often it will be necessary to consider whether, over a period, a person was an employee. This will be the case, for example, when one is concerned to determine whether a person has sufficient continuity of service to bring an unfair dismissal claim. However, in some cases it may be relevant to enquire whether a particular or specific engagement was a contract of employment or a contract for services. Thus, for example, in the case of a regular casual worker who is paid only when work is available but who is not paid in times when there is no work, it may be that the general engagement is not a contract of employment because of a lack of mutual obligations. However, it may be that, when the worker does actually work, the relationship is one of employment. Thus, it would be said that the worker was employed for each 'specific engagement' (for an example where the distinction was drawn, see *Clark v Oxfordshire Health Authority* [1998] IRLR 125). The process for analysing whether a specific engagement is a contract of employment is the same as that set out above. However, the focus is on each particular assignment when the worker does actually work and not on the general relationship.

There may be several reasons why it is necessary to determine whether there was a contract of employment for each specific engagement. For example, the regular casual worker may wish to claim unfair dismissal. Because there is no mutuality of obligations, he cannot establish sufficient continuity of employment by relying on the general relationship. However, if each specific engagement was a contract of employment then it may be that he could establish sufficient continuity by relying on the statutory provisions that allow for gaps in employment to be bridged (see CONTINUOUS EMPLOYMENT (7)). This was the case in *Prater v Cornwall County Council* [2006] EWCA Civ 102, [2006] 2 All ER 1013, [2006] ICR 731 where a teacher was employed on a number of assignments. There was no overarching contract of employment because there were no mutual obligations between assignments. But the Court of Appeal held that this was irrelevant to determining the person's status when she was performing an assignment. If the conditions of employment were satisfied for each assignment, then the worker was an employee whilst undertaking them. The question then was whether gaps when there was no contract could be bridged. *James v Redcats (Brands) Ltd* [2007] IRLR 296 also supports the point that a person's status between engagements is irrelevant to that person's status when an assignment is being performed.

An example in the case law where the court focused on the specific engagement is *McMeechan v Secretary of State for Employment* [1997] IRLR 353. The case concerned a person who worked via an employment agency for a number of different companies. The last company for which he worked went into insolvent liquidation without having paid him for his assignment. He made a claim against the Secretary of State in respect of those payments under *ERA 1996, section 182 et seq.* The question before the Court of Appeal was whether the worker could be regarded as an employee of the agency for the purposes of the *specific* engagement in respect of which he was not paid regardless of his status for the purpose of his *general* engagement by the agency. The Court of Appeal held that a person may be an employee for the purposes of specific engagements even though the general relationship between the parties is not one of employer and employee. It is then a question of assessing the person's status when he does in fact turn up for work regardless of the fact that there may be no general obligation on him to do so.

Employment agencies. Where a person is found work by an employment agency, there will be a contract between the worker and the agency (which may or may not be a contract of employment) and a separate contract between the agency and the person to whom the services are provided. But absent a further contract between the worker and the recipient of the services, the worker will not be an employee of that person (see *Costain Building and Civil Engineering Ltd v Smith* [2000] ICR 215, EAT). However, it may be possible to infer a contract between the worker and the recipient of services from the conduct of both those parties: *James v London Borough of Greenwich* [2008] IRLR 302; *Cable & Wireless plc v Muscat* [2006] IRLR 354. It is also possible that the contract with the agency may in truth be a contract of employment. In *Royal National Lifeboat Institution v Bushaway* [2005] IRLR 674, the EAT held that a tribunal had been entitled to ignore an entire agreement clause in finding that a person was employed by the client of an agency. (See also **47.2 TEMPORARY AND SEASONAL EMPLOYEES**).

The complexity of this area of the law is demonstrated by *Evans v Parasol Ltd* (UKEAT/0536/08/RN upheld by the Court of Appeal [2010] EWCA Civ 866, [2011] ICR 37) in which the EAT noted it would be a bold employment judge who was willing to strike out a claim by an agency worker against a possible employer when an individual worked under agency type arrangements.

In *Motorola Ltd v (1) Davidson and (2) Melville Craig* [2001] IRLR 4, the EAT was concerned to consider whether a person taken on by a recruitment agency, Melville Craig, to work for Motorola, was to be regarded as employed by Motorola for the purposes of a complaint of unfair dismissal. The EAT upheld the decision of the tribunal that there was sufficient control by Motorola over Mr Davidson in fact to mean that the relationship was one of employer-employee even though Motorola had no direct legal control over Mr Davidson. It was sufficient that Motorola had indirect control over Mr Davidson in that it could give directions to Melville Craig, including a direction no longer to send Mr Davidson to work for Motorola. Further, at the site, there was a sufficient degree of control in fact. The appeal was unusual in that the only issue argued was that of control. Hence, the case does not lay down any wider propositions about persons engaged by employment agencies becoming employees of the agency's clients. The importance of the case is in the stress which it lays on 'practical aspects of control that fall short of direct legal rights' and the recognition that an employment relationship may be created by a combination of practical control and indirect legal control.

The Court of Appeal has reiterated in *Johnson Underwood Ltd v Montgomery* [2001] EWCA Civ 318, [2001] ICR 819, [2001] IRLR 269 that the essential test to apply in judging whether a person is employed by a recruitment agency (or, indeed, by a hirer) is the existence of irreducible minima of mutual obligation and control. To the extent that Waite LJ in *McMeechan* appeared to reduce mutual obligation and control to mere factors to be taken into account, the absence of which would not necessarily be decisive, Buckley J indicated that he was wrong to do so.

In *Montgomery*, the courts below had already determined that the applicant was not an employee of the hirer (a finding which the applicant did not challenge). The result of the Court of Appeal's finding was that the applicant was held not to be an employee of the respondent agency either, since the agency had little or no control over her. The court indicated its unhappiness with this state of affairs, which left the applicant without a remedy and in a state of legal limbo. However, it stated that the solution to her dilemma lay with Parliament. The government issued regulations governing the relationships between recruitment bureaux, work-seekers and hirers, *The Conduct of Employment Agencies and Employment Businesses Regulations 2003 (SI 2003/3319)*. The regulations require that recruitment businesses should be required to clarify whether their relation to work-seekers is one of an employment business or an agency (*reg 14*). (The distinction between agencies and employment businesses in the *Regulations* is derived from the *Employment Agencies Act 1973*. Under *section 13* of the *Act*, agencies find workers employment with employers; employment businesses supply persons to act for, or under the control of, other persons.) The Regulations also require that employment businesses must state in any agreement with work-seekers whether the work-seeker is engaged by them under a contract of service or contract for services (*reg 15*).

In *Bunce v Postworth Ltd (t/a Skyblue)* [2005] EWCA Civ 490, [2005] IRLR 557, the Court of Appeal held that an agency worker was not an employee of the agency either because of the general relationship between the parties or when the worker was engaged on a specific assignment. There were no mutual obligations as between agency and worker for the purposes of individual assignments nor was there sufficient control

In *Dacas v Brook Street Bureau* [[2004] EWCA Civ 217, [2004] IRLR 358, the Court of Appeal analysed the circumstances in which a person provided to another by an agency could be employed by the end user. The analysis was approved in *Cable & Wireless v Muscat* [2006] IRLR 354, [2006] ICR 975. However, the Court of Appeal added the important qualification that a contract could only be implied between the worker and the end user when it was 'necessary' to do so in order to give the relationship business reality. The question of necessity was considered in *Beck v Camden London Borough Council* (UKEAT/0121/08/ZT) [2008] All ER (D) 09 (Sep) and in *Sridhar v East Living Ltd* (UKEAT/0476/07/RN) [2008] All ER (D) 290 (Nov). It is only where express contractual arrangements do not adequately explain the legal relationship between the parties that the question of whether there is an implied contract between an agency worker and an end user might arise. The tribunal must specifically consider whether it is necessary to imply a contract rather than looking solely at whether the conduct of the parties was consistent with an employment relationship.

Later cases have indicated that it will be difficult to show that it is necessary to imply such a contract. In *James v Greenwich London Borough Council* [2008] IRLR 302, the Court of Appeal repeated the necessity test. The Court also approved observations in the EAT that in the usual agency relationship there were no mutual obligations between the worker and the end user: the end user was not obliged to pay the worker. The end user was also not able to insist on a particular worker being provided. It was the agency which was obliged to pay, but it did not control the worker. It would only be in exceptional circumstances that it was necessary to imply a contract. The express terms of the contract described the relationship and it would not be necessary to imply a contract. It might be possible to infer a contract from the parties' conduct if that departed from the express terms of the contracts. But the mere fact that an agency worker worked for an end user for a long time could not justify the implication of a contract. The judgment of the Supreme Court in *Autoclenz* does not refer to 'necessity' as a separate test to be applied when analysing the nature of the contractual relationship between the parties, and it may suggest that this requirement has been over-stated in *James* and other cases.

In *Cairns v Visteon UK Ltd* [2007] IRLR 175, [2007] ICR 616, the EAT toyed with the idea that there could be two contracts of employment – one with the agency and one with the end user. However, this could not resolve the problem that it would only be possible to imply a contract where it was necessary to do so. Also, there would be enormous practical problems – would both employers have to follow the dismissal procedures in the event of a dismissal?

The present state of the law is thus that it will only be in exceptional circumstances that an agency worker will be held to have a contract of employment with the end user.

15.3 Employee, Self-Employed or Worker?

The problems faced by agency workers have to some extent been ameliorated by the *Agency Workers Regulations 2010*. Workers supplied by a temporary work agency to work "temporarily for and under the supervision and direction of a hirer" are covered by the *Regulations*. The definitions exclude the genuinely self-employed, those working through their own limited liability company (provided they are genuinely self employed) and those working on "managed service contracts". Upon completion of a 12-week qualifying period, an agency worker is entitled to the same pay, holidays and other basic conditions as if he or she had been recruited directly by the hirer on day one of the assignment, whether as an employee or a worker. In identifying the "same basic working and employment conditions terms", agency workers may compare their terms with direct recruits of the hirer working in "the same" or "broadly similar" role, not necessarily in the same office or establishment. The *Regulations* reduce the need to infer a contract of employment between the worker and the recipient of services. Although in order to qualify for certain employment protection rights such as the right not to be unfairly dismissed agency workers will still need to demonstrate they are employees.

15.4 SOME LEGAL CONSEQUENCES OF THE DISTINCTION

(The lists set out below are not exhaustive.)

For the employee

Rights

An employee enjoys (subject to satisfaction of the qualifying conditions) the following rights:

(1)   Unfair dismissal protection

(2)   Redundancy payment entitlement

(3)   Written particulars of terms of employment

(4)   Statutory minimum period of notice

(5)   Guarantee payment

(6)   Medical suspension payment

(7)   Protection from discrimination on grounds of race, sex, marital status, disability, gender reassignment, religion or belief or sexual orientation.

(8)   Equal pay

(9)   Maternity rights

(10) Time off for trade union activities, duties, etc

(11) Not to be refused employment because of membership or non-membership of a trade union

(12) To be employed for the agreed period or be given the agreed length of notice

(13) To be provided with a safe place of work and to have reasonable care taken of his safety

(14) To be paid statutory sick pay

(15) To be paid his wages free of any deductions not properly authorised

(16) In the case of those employed as shop workers or betting workers, the right to object to working on Sundays

(17) To limits on working time and the right to paid holidays under the *Working Time Regulations 1998*

Obligations

(1) To obey the employer's lawful orders

(2) To work faithfully and with due diligence

(3) To give the contractually agreed or statutory minimum period of notice to terminate the employment

(4) To pay income tax by way of deductions under the PAYE scheme

(5) To pay employee's National Insurance contributions

15.5 For the employer

Rights

These are:

(1) To benefit from the employee's obligations set out above

Obligations

(1) To observe the employee's rights set out above

(2) To deduct tax under the PAYE scheme

(3) To keep the necessary statutory sick pay records

(4) To make the appropriate National Insurance contributions

15.6 Self-employed – the self-employed person

Rights

These are:

(1) To benefit from all his contractual entitlements

(2) Not to be discriminated against on grounds of race, sex, marital status, disability, gender reassignment, religion or belief or sexual orientation and to the right to claim equal pay with a comparator of the opposite sex

(3) Where applicable, to be provided with a safe place and safe system of work

(4) To be paid his wages free of any deductions not properly authorised

(5) To limits on working time and to the benefit of annual leave in accordance with the *Working Time Regulations 1998*

Obligations

(1) To fulfil his contractual obligations

(2) To work with due skill and diligence

(3) To pay income tax under *Schedule D*

(4) To pay self-employed person's National Insurance contributions

15.7 Employee, Self-Employed or Worker?

15.7 Self-employed – the person who engages a self-employed person

Rights

These are:

(1)   To benefit from the self-employed person's contractual obligations

Obligations

(1)   To observe the self-employed person's rights set out above

15.8 Employees and office-holders

Another distinction may be identified between employees who are employed under a contract of employment and 'office-holders' who may not be employees or have the rights of employees (such as the right to complain of unfair dismissal). In *Johnson v Ryan* [2000] ICR 236, the worker was a local authority rent officer appointed pursuant to the *Rent Act 1977*. It was argued that, as an office-holder, the worker was not entitled to present a claim of unfair dismissal. The EAT identified three categories of 'office-holder'. First, those whose rights and duties are defined by the office they hold and not by any contract. An example is police officers. Second, persons who are called office-holders but who in reality are employed under contracts of service. Third, those who are both employees and office-holders. An example is company directors. In determining whether a worker who is described as an office-holder is an employee, the factual situation must be considered. Relevant matters include whether the worker receives a salary, whether the salary was fixed and whether the worker's duties were subject to close control by the employer or whether the worker worked independently. The EAT held that a rent officer was an employee. In doing so, it noted that the recent approach of the appellate courts had been to take an inclusive approach to employee protection (see generally PUBLIC SECTOR EMPLOYEES (37)).

In *Percy v Board of National Mission of the Church of Scotland* [2005] UKHL 73, [2006] 2 WLR 353, [2006] ICR 134, the House of Lords held that a minister of the Church of Scotland was employed within the broader meaning of that term in the Sex Discrimination Act. Holding an office and being an employee were not mutually exclusive. The legal question is whether there was an intention to create legal relations. The Court of Appeal adopted the same approach in *New Testament Church of God v Stewart* [2008] IRLR 134, but added that in deciding whether there was the necessary intention, one had to have regard to the religious principles of the church in question. If those principles precluded a legally binding relationship between the church and the minister, it could mean that no contract of employment would be found. This analysis has recently been affirmed by the Supreme Court in President of the *Methodist Conference v Preston* [2013] UKSC 29, [2013] ICR 833 which emphasises the need to carefully analyse the specific rules and practices of the relevant church and the nature of the particular arrangements with the specific minister. On the facts, no contract of employment was established.

O'Brien v Ministry of Justice [2013] UKSC 6, [2013] ICR 499, [2013] IRLR 315 considers the position of part-time fee paid recorders. The Supreme Court has confirmed that although part-time fee paid recorders are not subject to any superior authority in the manner in which they perform their judicial functions, they are engaged in an employment relationship by the Ministry of Justice and are 'workers'. The court also held that there was no objective justification for not providing part-time fee paid record with *pro rata temporis* pension rights. The result in *O'Brien* contrasts with the decision in *Gilham v Ministry of Justice* [2017] IRLR 23 that a district judge was an office holder and did not also work under a contract for services or a contract of employment, and so was not a worker under *ERA, s 230(3)*. The fact that the claims in *O'Brien* were based on EU law made all the difference for this purpose.

15.9   Workers

It has already been indicated that many of the provisions of employment legislation providing protection to individuals are not confined to those who are to be regarded in law as employees. Much protection is accorded to those who satisfy the definition of 'worker'.

That definition (found, for example, in *section 230* of *ERA* and in similar form in the *Working Time Regulations* and elsewhere) is wider than the definition of employee because it includes those who undertake to 'do or perform personally any work or services for another party to the contracts whose status is not by virtue of the contract that of a client or customer of any profession or business undertaking carried on by the individual'. The scope of this definition is currently highly topical because of the emergence of the so called 'gig economy', whereby businesses structure their arrangements in ways which prevent those who work from them acquiring employment rights.

This wider definition applies to a number of employment rights that are referred to in the start of this chapter. Reference should be made to each individual chapter for an explanation of the classes of person who benefit from the right. However, because there are now so many provisions that protect 'workers', this chapter seeks to provide an introduction to that concept.

The definition can be seen as comprising two elements. First the individual must be under an obligation personally to do work. Second, the person for whom the work is done must not be a client or customer of a business being run by the individual. The second limb is obviously necessary because otherwise the truly self-employed would be caught by a definition which required only that the person do work personally.

Several cases have considered what is meant by the definition of worker. The cases are decided under different provisions, but because the definition is the same, no distinction needs to be drawn based on the legal context of the decision. It is legitimate to consider decisions under the discrimination legislation and under other provisions which use the term worker, such as the *National Minimum Wage Act* and the *Working Time Regulations.*

In *James v Redcats (Brands) Ltd* [2007] IRLR 296, the EAT held that one had to draw a careful distinction between employees, workers and those engaged in their own business. When a right extended to workers, it was only the last category that was excluded. The EAT referred to cases such as *Lee v Chung* (cited above) and said that the dichotomy suggested in those cases between employees and the self-employed could be too simple. It was necessary also to draw a further distinction between those in business on their own account and workers. The EAT suggested that it was useful to consider a 'dominant purpose' test, derived from discrimination cases. If the dominant feature of the arrangement was that the person was to provide personal service then, even if the prerequisites of employment were missing, the person was likely to be a worker. Where a genuine right to substitution exists there is no personal service and there cannot be worker status. It is not sufficient that the individual might be obliged to personally find a substitute if unable to work (see *Community Dental Centres Ltd v Sultan-Darmon* [2010] IRLR 1024).

The leading case is now *Jivraj v Haswani* [2011] UKSC 40, [2011] ICR 1004, [2011] IRLR 827, in which the Supreme Court held that the correct test is whether the contract provides for services to be rendered by an independent contractor or whether the service provider consents to work under the control of another, and is therefore a worker. The Court concluded that an arbitrator was outside this definition, notwithstanding that he provided personal services and received fees, due to a lack of control or subordination. In *Halawi v WDFG UK Ltd t/a World Duty Free* [2015] IRLR 50, the Court of Appeal held that a beauty consultant who provided her services to a cosmetics company via a limited company and employment agency, and who had exercised her right to substitute performance, was not a worker and so was unable to bring a claim for discrimination. The Court emphasised the requirements of personal service and subordination.

15.9 Employee, Self-Employed or Worker?

Byrne Bros (Formworks) Ltd v Baird [2002] IRLR 96 was a case under the *Working Time Regulations*. The EAT concluded that labour-only sub-contractors had been correctly identified as workers notwithstanding that they had a limited power to send a substitute, the individuals were still under a personal obligation. Referring to the second part of the definition, the EAT said that the aim was to extend protection to an intermediate class of person between employees and those who are carrying on business on their own account. Such people, although not employees, are subordinate to the person for whom they work and hence in need of protection. The EAT said that a consideration of who was a worker would involve the same sorts of factors as are considered in deciding who is an employee 'but with the boundary pushed further in the putative worker's favour'. In *Wright v Redrow Homes (Yorkshire) Ltd* [2004] EWCA Civ 469, [2004] 3 All ER 98, [2004] ICR 1126, [2004] IRLR 720 the Court of Appeal held that the question whether there was an obligation to undertake work personally depended on the terms of the contract and not what happened in practice. Pill LJ cautioned against relying too heavily on policy reasons when deciding who was a worker. The Court of Appeal has provided important guidance on the application of the test identified above in *Pimlico Plumbers Ltd v Smith* [2017] IRLR 323. The Court upheld the Tribunal's finding that a plumber who was self-employed for tax purposes, and whose written contract expressly provided that he was an independent contractor, was nevertheless a worker. While the conclusion was fact sensitive, the Court gave detailed guidance on the relevance of the obligation to provide personal services, emphasising that *limited* rights of substitution would not necessarily preclude the conclusion that a person is a worker.

In *Windle v Secretary of State for Justice* [2016] ICR 721; [2016] IRLR 628, the Court of Appeal restored a Tribunal's decision that two court interpreters who performed services for HM Courts and Tribunals Service on a case-by-case basis were not workers. The ultimate question is the nature of the relationship during the period when the work was being done. However, as a matter of common sense, and common experience, the fact that a person supplying services is only doing so on an assignment-by-assignment basis may tend to suggest a degree of independence, or lack of subordination, in the relationship while at work which indicates that the person is not a worker. The absence of a contract governing the periods between cases supported the conclusion that the interpreters acted as independent contractors.

In *Aslam & Ors v Uber BV & Ors* [2017] IRLR 4 a Tribunal found that Uber 'taxi' drivers are workers. The Tribunal rejected Uber's case that the drivers were self-employed, and that it merely provided a 'technology platform' that allowed drivers to find and agree work with individual passengers. Uber has appealed to the EAT.

In dealing with the second part of the definition (that the person for whom the work is done is not a client or customer of a business undertaken by an individual), the EAT in *Cotswold Developments Construction Ltd v Williams* [2006] IRLR 181 suggested that the paradigm case of a person who did work for clients was a professional such as a solicitor or barrister. The paradigm case of a person who did work for customers was the owner of a shop or a tradesman such as a domestic plumber. The EAT suggested that a helpful test would be to consider whether the individual marketed his services to the public generally (in which case he would not be a worker) or whether he was integrated into the business of his principal (in which case he would be a worker).

The cases thus distinguish between those who are running their own business and those who, although not employed, are providing services as a part of another's business. In *Bacica v Muir* [2006] IRLR 35, the EAT suggested that factors such as working on the basis of a CIS certificate (in the construction industry), having accounts prepared for submission to the Inland Revenue, being free to work for others and in fact doing so, being paid a rate which included an overhead allowance and not being paid when not working were all factors indicating that a person was undertaking his own business.

In *Day v Lewisham and Greenwich NHS Trust* [2017] EWCA Civ 329, the Court of Appeal held that a 'worker' relationship was established simultaneously between junior doctors and both: (a) their employing NHS trust, and (b) Health Education England, for the purpose of *section 43K (1)(a)(ii)* of *ERA*.

The Supreme Court has confirmed that unpaid volunteers are not workers: *X v Mid Sussex Citizens Advice Bureau* [2013] 1 All ER 1038.

16   Employee Participation

16.1   OVERVIEW

There was, until fairly recently, little statutory provision in the UK for employees to participate or become involved in the affairs of the organisations in which they work. Some legislation in the 1970s (the *Health and Safety at Work Act 1974* and the *Employment Protection Act 1975*) compelled employers with recognised trade unions to consult with their employees on such matters as health and safety, disclosure of information and on redundancies. European Community obligations led to further legislation, widening consultation requirements in the case of redundancies, transfers of undertakings, and health and safety. Further legislation was introduced by the Labour Government. For example, the *ERA 1999* requires employers to recognise trade unions where this is desired by a majority of the relevant workforce (see Trade Unions – I (50)). Separately, workforce consultation was incorporated into the bidding process of the Private Finance Initiative.

The statutory landscape has now changed dramatically, however, as a result of legislation originating at EU level. The *Social Protocol* to the *Maastricht Treaty on European Union* gave the EU the power, *inter alia*, to adopt directives concerning the information and consultation of workers. The *Treaty* came into force on 1 November 1993. At the time, the United Kingdom 'opted out' of the *Social Protocol*. However, the Labour Government which came to power in 1997 ended the opt-out. On 1 May 1999 the Treaty of Amsterdam came into effect, incorporating the *Social Protocol* into the *EC Treaty* (see further European Union Law (23)). One effect of this has been to give increased emphasis to securing framework agreements on social legislation through negotiation between European-level trade union and employer bodies (the 'social partners'). One such agreement resulted in the *Directive on Parental Leave (96/34)* (see generally Maternity and Parental Rights (33)).

There are now five separate EU measures relating to informing and consulting employees and employee participation:

(1)   The *European Works Council Directive (94/45)*, adopted in September 1994, was the first employment measure adopted under the *Social Protocol*. This places obligations on companies with more than 1,000 employees, including at least 150 employees in a second European member state, and was implemented in national legislation by the *Transnational Information and Consultation of Employees Regulations 1999 (SI 1999/3323)*. A recast *European Works Council Directive* was agreed in May 2009 and came into force, in the main, in June 2011. The *1999 Regulations* were amended with effect, in the main, from 5 June 2011 to reflect this (see below **16.20**).

(2)   The original *European Works Council Directive* was followed by *Directive 2002/14/EC* 'establishing a general framework for informing and consulting employees in the European Community'. This places obligations on smaller, national companies and was implemented into domestic law by the *Information and Consultation of Employees Regulations 2004 (SI 2004/3426)*, as amended by *SI 2006/514* (see below **16.2**).

(3)   The *European Company Statute* (consisting of *EU Council Regulation 2157/2001* and *Directive 2001/86/EC*) enables companies operating in more than one member state to be established as a single company under EC law. This was originally implemented domestically by the *European Public Limited-Liability Company Regulations 2004 (SI 2004/2326)* and is now implemented, in Great Britain, by the *European Public Limited-Liability Company (Employee Involvement) (Great Britain) Regulations 2009 (SI 2009/2401)* (see below **16.28**).

16.1 Employee Participation

(4) Similar provisions apply to European Cooperative Societies under *Regulation 1435/03* and *Directive 2003/72/EC*, implemented domestically by the *European Cooperative Society Regulations 2006 (SI 2006/2059)*.

(5) Finally, EC rules in relation to employee participation following cross-border mergers between companies, contained in *Directive 2005/56/EC*, have been implemented domestically by the *Companies (Cross-Border Mergers) Regulations 2007 (SI 2007/2974)*.

Amendments have been made to the various sets of regulations to give effect to the *Agency Workers Regulations 2010 (SI 2010/93)*.

In April 2015, the European Commission began a consultation on the possible consolidation of a number of these directives, following a 'fitness check' published in 2013. Practitioners should expect further developments in this area.

These various sets of regulations are detailed and complex, running cumulatively to many hundreds of pages. This chapter provides an overview of the main provisions. However, regard should be had to the regulations in their entirety. Practitioners advising on issues under any of the regulations will also, of course, be well advised to consider authorities decided under each set of regulations in relation to the comparable provisions of the other EU and domestic measures.

Decisions of the Central Arbitration Committee ('CAC') (and other information and consultation legislation) are available at: www.cac.gov.uk/index.aspx?articleid=2389.

16.2 THE INFORMATION AND CONSULTATION OF EMPLOYEES REGULATIONS 2004

In February 2002, EC member states adopted *Directive 2002/14/EC* 'establishing a general framework for informing and consulting employees in the European Community'. The *Directive* provides for undertakings with at least 50 employees in any one member state to provide their employees with information and to consult with them over a wide range of issues concerning the operation of the organisation. As the ECJ noted in *Holst v Dansk Arbejdsgiverforening*: C-405/08 [2010] 2 CMLR 49, the *Directive* envisages that Member States may allow management and the workforce to play a leading role in its implementation, although it remains the responsibility of Member States to ensure that all workers are afforded the full protection for which the *Directive* provides.

The *Directive* has been implemented into domestic law by the *Information and Consultation of Employees Regulations 2004 (SI 2004/3426)*, as amended (the '*ICE Regulations*').

• The *ICE Regulations* were made under s 42 of the *Employment Relations Act 2004*. Their purpose, as explained by the EAT in *Darnton v Bournemouth University* [2010] ICR 524 at [2], is "*to provide for the establishment of arrangements under which employees can be informed and consulted by their employers about matters of mutual concern*". Or as the EAT put it in *University of London v Morrissey* (UKEAT/0285/15/RN, 15 January 2016): "*to engage the workforce as a whole, to involve them all in the (often sensitive) process of obtaining information and engaging in consultation t a greater extent than had been the case prior to the 2002 Directive*", and "*to facilitate the engagement of employees – that is, all employees in the workforce – in general terms in that process*".

• Guidance on the *ICE Regulations* is available on www.gov.uk/informing-consulting -employees-law. This includes the detailed guidance issued by the DTI (as was) in January 2006: webarchive.nationalarchives.gov.uk/20121212135622/http

://www.bis.gov.uk/files/file25934.pdf. However, this guidance "has no special status ": see the EAT in *Darnton v Bournemouth University* [2010] ICR 524 at [18] and the CAC in *Coombs & Holder v GE Aviation Systems Ltd* IC/43/(2012) at §55.

16.3

Employees in undertakings with 50 or more employees in the United Kingdom have a right to be informed and consulted on a regular basis about issues in the organisation for which they work: see *reg 3* and *sch 1* to the *ICE Regulations*. (The *ICE Regulations* applied originally only to undertakings with 150 or more employees, but this threshold has gradually been reduced.)

The number of employees in an undertaking is calculated by taking the average number of employees employed by the employer over the preceding 12-month period (*reg 4(1), (2)*). Employees who work for less than 75 hours in each month may count as 'half' an employee for this purpose (*reg 4(3)*).

From 1 October 2011, by virtue of the *Agency Workers Regulations 2011 (SI 2010/93)*, an agency worker who has a contract with a temporary work agency shall be treated as an employee of that agency for these purposes for the duration of his or her assignment (*reg 3A*).

Note that issues have arisen in other Member States as to the meaning of an "employee" within *article 3(2)* of the *Directive*. In *Association de Médiation Sociale v Union Locale des Syndicats CGT*: C-176/12 [2014] IRLR 310 that workers engaged under particular atypical 'assisted contracts' (such as apprentices, or employees with professional training contracts) were required to be taken into account when calculating staff numbers in an undertaking. The Court held, further, that *Article 3(1)* of the *Directive* had direct effect. However, it could not be relied upon in a dispute between individuals, unlike eg. that in issue in *Kücükdeveci v Swedex GmbH & Co KG*: C-555/07 [2010] IRLR 346. The employees were left to claim *Francovich* damages from the French state (*Francovich v Italy*: C-6/90 [1992] IRLR 84).

16.4 Undertakings

The *ICE Regulations* apply to 'undertakings' whose registered office, head office or principal place of business is situated in Great Britain (*reg 3*). Where the registered office is in Great Britain, and the head office or principal place of business is in Northern Ireland, or vice versa, the *ICE Regulations* only apply where the majority of employees are employed to work in Great Britain.

An undertaking is defined as a 'public or private undertaking carrying out an economic activity, whether or not operating for gain' (*reg 2*). This will cover almost all employers. However, there is uncertainty about whether particular parts of the public sector are carrying out economic activities: see eg *Henke v Gemeinde Schierke and Verwaltungsgemein-schaft Brocken*: C-298/94 [1996] ECR I-4989, [1997] ICR 746, ECJ, *Mayeur v Association Promotion de l'Information Messine (APIM)*: C-175/99 [2002] ICR 1316, ECJ and *Collino v Telecom Italia SpA*: C-343/98 [2000] ECR I-6659, [2002] ICR 38, ECJ; cf. the definition of 'undertaking' in the *Transfer of Undertakings (Protection of Employment Regulations 1981 (SI 1981/1794)* and the *Transfer of Undertakings (Protection of Employment Regulations 2006 (SI 2006/246)* and the authorities in relation thereto and cf. also the approach of the Court of Justice in the *USA v Nolan* litigation in relation to information and collective redundancies (52.3 TRANSFER OF UNDERTAKINGS).

The DTI Guidance suggests (in paragraph 5) that, in the case of a company, the definition of an undertaking in the *ICE Regulations* covers separately incorporated legal entities, rather than organisational entities such as an establishment, division or business unit. The CAC

16.4   Employee Participation

reached the same conclusion in *Coombs & Holder v GE Aviation Systems Ltd* IC/43/(2012) by reference to the language of the *ICE Regulations*, holding – without any enthusiasm – that an undertaking meant a single legal entity capable of being an employer, and that a group of legal entities was not itself an undertaking.

The CAC and then the EAT have considered the Guidance recently in *Cofeley Workplace Limited v Moyer-Lee* (CAC - IC/47(2014), 31 July 2014; EAT – [2015] IRLR 879), determining that the relevant employee request did not satisfy the threshold in *reg 7(1)* of the *ICE Regulations*. The CAC held, *inter alia*, on the facts, that a particular contract (ie. essentially, a particular site or subdivision of the business) was not a relevant "undertaking". Taking into account the terms of the DTI Guidance, it considered that the terms "undertaking" and "establishment" are mutually exclusive, that an undertaking means more than simply a unit of business and, so far as the *ICE Regulations* are concerned, that a public or private undertaking is not an "establishment". The EAT upheld that approach, noting in so doing that the Guidance is of persuasive weight. Langstaff J considered that an "undertaking", in this context, cannot mean any grouping smaller than that which is the legal employer of the employees concerned.

16.5   Employee requests for data

Employees or their representatives have the right to make a written request for their employer to supply them with data for the purpose of ascertaining the number of people employed by the employer in the UK (and therefore whether or not the *ICE Regulations* apply) (*reg 5*).

A complaint that an employer has failed to provide the data, referred to in *reg 5(3)*, or that the data is false or incomplete in a material particular, may be presented to the CAC up to one month after the date of the request (*reg 6*). Where the CAC finds the complaint to be well-founded, it will order the employer to disclose the data to the complainant (*reg 6(2)*).

16.6   Initiation of obligations under the ICE Regulations

The obligations under the *ICE Regulations* to inform and consult do not apply automatically, even where the employer has sufficient employees for the *ICE Regulations* to apply in principle. Instead, the obligations must be initiated by either the employer or the employees.

16.7   *Initiation by the Employer*

Employers may initiate negotiations under the *ICE Regulations* by giving notice in writing in accordance with *reg 11(1)*. Notice must be published in such a manner as to bring it to the attention of all the employees of the undertaking, so far as is reasonably practicable (*reg 11(2)*).

16.8   *Employee Requests*

In addition, an employer must generally initiate negotiations for an agreement in respect of information and consultation where it receives a valid employee request (*reg 7(1)*). To be valid, an employee request must be made by at least 10% of the employees in the undertaking (subject to a minimum of 15 and a maximum of 2,500 employees), either as a single request or a number of separate requests over a six-month period (*reg 7(1)–(3)*). Requests must be in writing and sent to the registered office, head office or principal place of business of the employer, or to the CAC (*reg 7(4)*). A request must specify the names of the employee(s) making it and the date on which it is sent (*reg 7(4)*). Where the request is sent to the CAC, the CAC is then required to notify the employer of the request, request from the employer such information as it needs to verify the number and names of the employees who have made the request, and inform the employer and the employees who have made the request how many employees have made the request (*reg 7(5)–(6)*).

16.9   *General Considerations*

As a general rule, no employee may request negotiation (or renegotiation) of any agreement, and no employer may give notice of an intention to negotiate (or renegotiate) any agreement within three years of:

(a)   the date of the conclusion of any negotiated agreement under the *ICE Regulations* (see below **16.12**); or

(b)   the date when the standard information and consultation provisions began to apply (see below **16.13**, but note the provision in *reg 18(2)* for the renegotiation of the standard provisions 'at any time'); or

(c)   the date of the employee request, where the employer has held a ballot following an employee request which has resulted in endorsement of a pre-existing agreement (see below **16.15** (*reg 12(1)*)).

There is an exception to the general rule where there are material changes in the undertaking during the three-year period having the result that an agreement in force no longer covers all the employees of the undertaking, or, if it is a pre-existing agreement (as to which see below **16.15**) can no longer be said to have been approved by all the employees of the undertaking (*reg 12(2)*).

If the employer considers that there was no valid employee request, or an employee (or employee's representative) considers that an employer notification was not valid, a complaint may be presented to the CAC (*reg 13(1), (2)*). Complaints must be presented to the CAC within one month of the date of the employee request or the date of the employer notification (*reg 13(3)*). If the CAC finds the complaint made out, it may make a declaration to that effect (*reg 13(1)–(2)*).

Note that in order to initiate negotiations for an agreement in relation to employees in more than one undertaking, it is necessary for there to be a valid employee request or employer notification in relation to each undertaking (*reg 14(6)*).

16.10 **Negotiated agreements**

Where a valid employee request has been made or employer notice has been given (see above **16.6–16.9**), the employer is obliged to initiate negotiations by taking the steps set out in *reg 14*. The employer must, as soon as reasonably practicable:

(a)   make arrangements satisfying the requirements of *reg 14(2)* for the employees of the undertaking to elect or appoint negotiating representatives;

(b)   inform the employees in writing of the identity of the negotiating representatives; and

(c)   invite the negotiating representatives to enter into negotiations to reach a negotiated agreement (*reg 14(1), (2)*).

Reg 14(1) requires an employer to take these steps as soon as reasonably practicable. In *Darnton v Bournemouth University* [2010] ICR 524, the EAT rejected an argument that there is any implied requirement in *reg 14* for an employer to do so in any event within three months of the employee request. Whilst this appears to be what the DTI Guidance issued in 2006 envisaged, and whilst the EAT recognised that it would be unusual for it not to be reasonably practicable to complete these steps within three months of the employee request, the statutory requirement is simply as stated in *reg 14(1)*: "as soon as reasonably practicable".

As to the election or appointment of negotiating representatives, there are only two express requirements in *reg 14(2)*: (i) the election or appointment must be arranged in such a way that all employees of the undertaking are represented by one or more representatives; and

16.10   Employee Participation

(ii) all employees of the undertaking must be entitled to take part in the election or appointment of the representatives and, if there is a ballot, all employees must be entitled to vote in the ballot. In *University of London v Morrissey* UKEAT/0285/15, [2016] IRLR 487, however, the EAT held that "the arrangements put in place should be with a view for the effective representation of *all* employees, and we would emphasis all employees rather than a section of employees." Moreover: *"Although the word "effective" does not appear in the Regulations . . . if [the CAC] concluded that effectiveness was absent, this would indicate that the Regulations had not been faithfully applied".* There may be cases in which it is appropriate for an employer to enter discussions with recognised unions and evolve a process that satisfies *reg 14*. In other cases, that would not lead to effective representation; all will depend upon the particular facts. On the facts in *Morrissey*, the CAC had been entitled to hold that the process put in place by the employer – by inviting those unions which it recognised for the purposes of collective bargaining to nominate candidates – was not sufficient and did not comply with *reg 14*.

16.11   Complaints about the election or appointment of negotiating representatives

Complaints about the election or appointment of negotiating representatives may be made to the CAC within 21 days of the election or appointment (*reg 15(1)*). If the CAC finds the complaint well-founded it must make an order requiring the employer to arrange for the process of election or appointment to take place again (*reg 15(2)*).

16.12   Negotiated agreements

Once negotiating representatives have been appointed, the *ICE Regulations* are designed to encourage employers, employees and their representatives to agree information and consultation arrangements which suit their particular circumstances. Thus, the *ICE Regulations* specifically require employer and employee representatives to work in a spirit of co-operation (*reg 21*).

The *ICE Regulations* are notably non-prescriptive with respect to the substance of the arrangements for information and consultation, for example as to the subjects, method, timing or frequency of any information provision or consultation. Guidance as to the possible content of an agreement may be gained from the standard information and consultation provisions, which will apply in default if the parties fail to reach a negotiated agreement (see below **16.13**).

There are, however, some express requirements with which any negotiated agreement must comply (*reg 16(1)*). Any agreement must:

(a)   Cover all employees of the undertaking (either in a single agreement or in different parts);

(b)   Set out the circumstances in which the employer must inform and consult the employees to which it relates;

(c)   Be in writing;

(d)   Be dated;

(e)   Be approved by the employees in accordance with the *ICE Regulations* (see below);

(f)   Be signed by or on behalf of the employer;

(g)   Either:

    (i)   provide for the appointment or election of information and consultation representatives to whom the employer must provide the information and whom the employer must consult; or

(ii) provide that the employer must provide information directly to the employees to which it relates and consult those employees directly; and

(h) Provide that where an employer is to provide information about the employment situation under any part of that agreement, that information shall include suitable information relating to the use of agency workers in that undertaking.

In addition, to be valid, a negotiated agreement must have been signed by all the negotiating representatives, or, if it is only signed by a majority of the negotiating representatives, it must have been approved by at least 50% of the employees in the undertaking either: (i) in writing, or (ii) in a ballot (*reg 16(3), (4)*).

If a ballot is held:

(a) The employer must make such arrangements as are reasonably practicable to ensure that the ballot is fair, all employees must be entitled to vote, and the ballot must be conducted so as to secure that those voting do so in secret (again so far as is reasonably practicable) and the votes given in the ballot are accurately counted (*reg 16(5)*).

(b) The employer must inform all employees entitled to vote of the result of the ballot as soon as is reasonably practicable (*reg 16(6)*).

(c) A complaint may be presented to the CAC in circumstances where an employee representative considers that the ballot for approval of a negotiated agreement has not complied with the *ICE Regulations* (*reg 17(1)*). Complaints may only be made by a negotiating representative (and not by an employee). They must be made within 21 days of the date of the ballot. If the CAC finds the complaint well-founded it must order the employer to re-run the ballot (*reg 17(2)*).

A time limit is set on negotiations: they may last (in the first instance) for no more than six months commencing at the end of the period of three months beginning with the date on which the valid employee request was made or the valid employer notification was issued (*reg 14(3)*). However, time spent holding a ballot to determine whether or not to use a pre-existing agreement rather than negotiate a new one (see below **16.15**) or on making an application to the CAC is ignored when calculating the six-month negotiating period (see *reg 14(3), (4)* for the detailed provisions on the calculation of time). If the employer and a majority of the negotiating representatives agree, before the end of the six-month period to extend the period for negotiation, it may be extended by such further period(s) as the parties agree (*reg 14(5)*). In its decision in *Darnton v Bournemouth University* (IC/22/2009) (20 May 2009, unreported) the CAC held in paragraph 62 that it was crucial, to satisfy the requirements of the *ICE Regulations* that any agreement to extend the negotiation period was reached prior to the expiry of the time-limit, that the agreement to extend was itself explicit and that the period covered by the extension was made clear.

Whether or not particular policies fall within the scope of any negotiated agreement (or, by analogy) the standard provisions (see **16.13** below) will depend on the particular provisions of the agreement and the policy in question. In *Wright v Rolls Royce* IC/46/(2013), 24 January 2014, a travel policy was held not to be within the scope of 'contractual relations arrangements' under a negotiated agreement.

16.13 Standard information and consultation provisions

Where no arrangements are agreed, standard provisions on information and consultation will apply automatically from six months after the date on which negotiations should have started (if they did not start) or on which the negotiating period ended (if agreement was not reached): *reg 18(1)*. The standard provisions are set out in *reg 20*. In summary, they require the employer:

16.13 Employee Participation

(a) to provide information and consultation representatives (as to the election and appointment of which, see below) with information on:

(i) the recent and probable development of the undertaking's activities and economic situation;

(ii) the situation, structure and probable development of employment within the undertaking and on any anticipatory measures envisaged, in particular, where there is a threat to employment within the undertaking (and from 1 October 2011 such information must include suitable information relating to the use of agency workers (if any) in that undertaking); and

(iii) decisions likely to lead to substantial changes in work organisation or in contractual relations, including those referred to in *ss 188–192* of the *Trade Union and Labour Relations (Consolidation) Act 1992* (see generally REDUNDANCY – II: PRACTICE AND PROCEDURE **(39)**) and *regs 13–16* of the *Transfer of Undertakings (Protection of Employment) Regulations 2006* (see **52.18** TRANSFER OF UNDERTAKINGS) *(reg 20(1))*;

(b) to consult the information and consultation representatives as to developments, threats and changes to employment within the undertaking *(reg 20(3))*; and

(c) to ensure that the timing, method and content of the consultation are appropriate, that it takes place with the appropriate level of management and that a reasoned response is given by the employer to any opinion expressed by the representatives *(reg 20(4))*.

The information in *(a)* above must be given at a time, in a fashion and with such content as are appropriate to enable the information and consultation representatives to conduct an adequate study and, where necessary, to prepare for consultation *(reg 20(2))*.

Note that although there is an obligation to inform and consult on developments, threats and changes to employment within the undertaking, the obligation under the *ICE Regulations* ceases once the duties in *s 188* of *TULR(C)A 1992* or *reg 13* of *TUPE* or *regs 11–13* of the *Pension Scheme Regulations* apply, provided that the employer gives notification in accordance with *reg 20(5)*.

16.14 Whenever the standard provisions are going to apply, there is an obligation on the employer to arrange for the holding of a ballot of its employees to elect information and consultation representatives *(reg 19(1))*. There must be one representative for every 50 employees (or part thereof), provided that there are always at least two and not more than 25 representatives *(reg 19(3))*. The requirements for the holding of ballots under *reg 19* are set out in *Sch 2*.

Complaints in relation to the conduct of a ballot for the election of information and consultation representatives may be made to the CAC by any employee or employees' representative *(reg 19(4))*. Where the CAC finds the complaint well-founded, it must order the employer to arrange, or re-arrange and hold the ballot *(reg 19(5))*. If such an order is made, the complainant employee or employee's representative may also make an application to the Employment Appeal Tribunal, within three months of the CAC's decision, for a penalty notice to be issued against the employer *(reg 19(6))*. See **16.18** below for the issue of penalties.

16.15 Pre-existing agreements

If a valid employee request to negotiate an agreement under the *ICE Regulations* is made by fewer than 40% of employees employed in the undertaking (see above **16.7**), but there is a pre-existing agreement which:

(a)   is in writing;

(b)   sets out how the employer is to give information to the employees or their representatives and seek their views on such information;

(c)   covers all the employees of the undertaking; and

(d)   has been approved by the employees,

the employer may, instead of initiating negotiations (see above **16.10**), hold a ballot to seek the endorsement of the employees for the employee request (*reg 8(1), (2)*). However, the option is only open to the employer where the employee request has been made by fewer than 40% of the employees employed in the undertaking (*reg 8(1)*).

Where the pre-existing agreement covers more than one undertaking, the employer may hold a combined ballot for all the undertakings so covered if the employee request either alone or aggregated with any requests made by employees in the other undertakings is made by fewer than 40% of the employees in all the undertakings (*reg 9(1), (2)*). However, even if the pre-existing agreement covers more than one undertaking, it is still open to the original undertaking to ballot only its own employees (*reg 9(3)*).

If the employer wishes to hold a ballot, he must inform the employees in writing within one month of the date of the employee request and arrange for the ballot to be held as soon as reasonably practicable thereafter (but no fewer than 21 days after the employer has informed the employees of its intention to hold a ballot): *reg 8(3)*. The requirements for the ballot are the same as for the ballot for employee approval of a negotiated agreement where only a majority of the negotiating representatives have signed the agreement (see above **16.12**), save that the employees are only to be regarded as having endorsed the employee request if at least 40% of the employees employed in the undertaking and the majority of the employees who vote in the ballot have voted in favour of endorsing the request (*reg 8(4), (6)*).

If the employees endorse the employee request, the employer is under a duty to initiate negotiations as described in **16.10** above (*reg 8(5)(b)*). If the employees do not endorse the employee request, the employer is not under such an obligation (*reg 8(5)(c)*) and the pre-existing agreement will continue to govern information and consultation within the undertaking.

An employee or employees' representative who believes that the employer has not complied with the requirements of the *ICE Regulations* in relation to the holding of a ballot to endorse an employee request may complain to the CAC (*regs 8(7)–(8)* and *10*). There is a time limit of 21 days for the bringing of complaints, which runs from the date the employer informed the employees of its intention to hold a ballot (if it is the employer's entitlement to hold a ballot that is disputed) or from the date of the ballot (if it is alleged that the employer has failed to comply with a ballot requirement): *reg 10(1), (2)*. There is no time limit for complaints that an employer has failed to inform employees that it intends to hold a ballot, or (having announced that it intends to hold a ballot) fails to hold it within the requisite time period (*reg 8(7), (8)*). Where the CAC finds the complaint well-founded, it shall or may (as appropriate) order the employer to hold the ballot (*regs 8(9)* and *10(3)(c)*) or commence negotiations in accordance with the procedure described at **16.10** above: *reg 10(3)(a), (b)* and *(c)(i)*.

From 1 October 2011, where information about the employment situation is to be provided by an employer under a pre-existing agreement, such information must include suitable information relating to the use of agency workers (if any) in that undertaking (*reg 8A*).

16.16 In *Stewart (J) v Moray Council* [2006] ICR 1253, [2006] IRLR 592 the EAT concluded that, where an undertaking had in place multiple agreements relating to the provision of information to its employees, the requirement under *reg 8(1)(b)* of the *ICE Regulations* that a pre-existing agreement should cover all the employees of that undertaking was met by all the agreements read together. However, each of the other requirements under *reg 8(1)* had to be met by each individual agreement so that the provisions relating to the holding of a ballot could apply. The EAT also held that employees are covered by the terms of a collective agreement within the meaning of *reg 8(1)(b)* if that agreement is intended to regulate their terms and conditions (whether or not they are union members) or if they fall within a category of employees intended to be regulated by that agreement. Further, *reg 8(1)(c)* does not prescribe any particular way in which employee approval needs to be demonstrated (eg by ballot or by written support): this is a matter of fact for the CAC. The EAT considered that it would usually (but not always) be legitimate to infer approval if, at the time the agreement was made, the majority of the employees covered by the agreement were members of the union or unions which are parties to that agreement.

16.17 Confidential information

An employer is not required to disclose any information or document for the purposes of the *ICE Regulations* where the nature of the information or document is such that, according to objective criteria, its disclosure would seriously harm the functioning of, or would be prejudicial to, the undertaking *(reg 26(1))*. Any dispute between an employer and information and consultation or employee representatives in relation to the nature of information or a document that an employer has refused to disclose may be referred to the CAC *(reg 26(2))*. The CAC has power to order the disclosure of the information or document where it considers that disclosure would not be seriously harmful or prejudicial, and has power to prescribe the terms on which it should be disclosed *(reg 26(3), (4))*.

If an employer discloses any information or document, pursuant to its obligations under the *ICE Regulations*, and requires that information or document to be held in confidence and not to be disclosed to others except, where terms permit him to do so, in accordance with those terms, then any disclosure by the recipient in breach of those terms will be actionable by the employer as a breach of statutory duty *(reg 25(1)–(3))*. This is in addition to any right which any person might have in relation to that disclosure otherwise than under the *ICE Regulations (reg 25(4))*. The employer will not, however, have any right of action for breach of statutory duty under the *ICE Regulations* if the recipient reasonably believed the disclosure to be a 'protected disclosure' within the meaning of *s 43A* of the *Employment Rights Act 1996 (reg 25(5))* and see **10.17 DISCLOSURE OF INFORMATION.**

There is a right for a recipient to apply to the CAC for a declaration that it was unreasonable for the employer to require him to hold the information or document in confidence *(reg 25(6))*. If the CAC considers that disclosure of the information or document by the recipient would not, or would not be likely to, harm the legitimate interests of the undertaking, it must make a declaration to that effect *(reg 25(7))*. Where it does so, the information or document shall not be regarded as having been entrusted to any recipient on terms requiring it to be held in confidence *(reg 25(8))*.

16.18 Complaints

In addition to the various rights to bring complaints to the CAC mentioned above, a complaint may be presented to the CAC where an employee representative considers that an employer is not acting in accordance with an agreement negotiated under the *ICE Regulations* or with the standard arrangements. The time limit for presenting complaints is three months from the date of the alleged failure. If the complaint is upheld, the CAC may make a declaration and order the employer to take such steps as are reasonable for it to take in order to comply with the terms of the negotiated agreement or the standard arrangements (see *reg 22(1)–(5))*.

If the CAC makes such a declaration (whether with or without such an order) an application may be made to the Employment Appeal Tribunal for a penalty notice to be issued, under which the employer may be required to pay up to £75,000 (*regs 22(6), (7)* and *23*). The time limit for such applications is three months from the date of the CAC's declaration (*reg 22(6)*).

In *Darnton v Bournemouth University (No 2)* (UKEAT/0391/09/RN) (4 March 2010, unreported) the EAT rejected an argument that the University had reasonable excuse for its failure to comply with the *ICE Regulations* within the meaning of *reg 22(7)*, such that no penalty notice should be issued. It held that simply taking a wrong view about a material matter was not, without more, sufficient to constitute a reasonable excuse (paragraph 9). It was not necessary for the EAT to determine whether reliance on mistake expert advice would constitute reasonable excuse as there was no sufficient evidence before it that the University had in fact relied on such advice.

Matters to be taken into account by the EAT when setting the amount of the penalty include: the gravity of the failure; the period of time over which the failure occurred; the reason for the failure; the number of employees affected by the failure; and the number of employees employed by the undertaking or, where a negotiated agreement covers employees in more than one undertaking, the number of employees employed by both or all of the undertakings (*reg 23(3)*). In *Darnton (No 2)*, paragraph 12, the EAT indicated that *"the assessment of the right level of penalty is in the nature of a broad evaluation, and a nice analysis of the weight to be given to individual components is unrealistic".* It considered that it should have regard to all relevant considerations, which may cover a wide range and are not necessarily limited to those specific in *reg 23*. Moreover, assistance from other decided cases was not likely to be useful, including cases under the other jurisdictions. Similarly, in *Brown v G4 Security (Cheltenham)*, (UKEAT/0526/09/RN) [2010] All ER (D) 84 (Aug) the EAT reiterated that each case is fact-specific, that there is a need to take into account the matters listed in *reg 23* but that *reg 23* is not an exhaustive list: "Depending on the circumstances of the particular case additional factors may be taken into account and the weight of each of them will depend on the facts of the case under consideration." The EAT added, in *G4 Security*, that in its view, the number of employees in the undertaking was not particularly relevant in determining the gravity of the breach, as breach of obligations under the *ICE Regulations* affecting all employees in a small workforce may be almost as significant as a breach affecting a small proportion of a much larger workforce.

In *Amicus v Macmillan Publishers Ltd* [2007] IRLR 885, the EAT issued a penalty notice against Macmillan requiring it to pay £55,000. The penalty notice was issued in circumstances where the EAT found that Macmillan had adopted a 'wholly cavalier attitude' to its obligations under the *ICE Regulations* (see also the CAC decision reported at [2007] IRLR 378). In contrast, in *Darnton (No 2)*, the EAT imposed a penalty of £10,000. It held that the fact that the breach complained of was not deliberate and did not result from any deliberate disregard of the University's obligations under the *ICE Regulations* or even an attitude of carelessness or insouciance towards those obligations, was an important mitigating factor, In addition, on the facts, 'shadow' information and consultation procedures had been in place for a considerable period. Nevertheless, the EAT was concerned to ensure that any penalty was more than negligible. It held that the scheme of the *ICE Regulations* required unexcused errors by the University to be marked by a real penalty. In *Brown v G4 Security (Cheltenham)*, UKEAT/0526/09/RN (27 April 2010), a penalty of £20,000 was imposed.

16.19   Employment protection

Employee representatives have the right to reasonable paid time off during working hours for the purpose of performing their functions as representatives (*regs 27, 28*). A complaint that an employer has unreasonably refused to permit the employee representative a reasonable amount of paid time off, or has failed to pay the whole or part of any amount to which the employee is entitled, may be presented to an employment tribunal (*reg 29(1)*). The time limit for bringing a complaint is 'three months beginning with the day on which the time off was taken or on which it is alleged the time off should have been permitted', with specific provision to facilitate early conciliation (*reg 29(1)(2)(a)* and *reg 29A* in relation to early conciliation and see **2.5 EARLY CONCILIATION**). If the tribunal is satisfied that it was not reasonably practicable for the complaint to be presented before the end of the initial time limit, then it may extend time for such further period as it considers reasonable (*reg 29(2)*). Where a tribunal finds a complaint well-founded, it must make a declaration and order the employer to pay the employee an amount equivalent to the amount of time off it should have allowed the employee, or the amount it should have paid the employee (as appropriate): *reg 29(3)–(5)*.

In relation to the right to time off work, see generally TIME OFF WORK **(49)**.

An employee who is an employees' representative, negotiating representative, information and consultation representative or a candidate in an election to be any such representative, and who is dismissed is to be regarded as unfairly dismissed if the reason or (if more than one) the principal reason for dismissal is that the employee:

(a)   performed or proposed to perform any functions or activities as such a representative or candidate;

(b)   exercised or proposed to exercise an entitlement under *regs 27* or *28* to reasonable paid time off for performing any of those functions;

(c)   made or proposed to make a request to exercise such an entitlement (or did so through a person acting on his behalf).

   (Reg 30.)

Such an employee is also protected from detriment on these grounds (*reg 32*).

In addition, an employee who is dismissed is to be regarded as unfairly dismissed if the reason or (if more than one) the principal reason for dismissal is that the employee:

(d)   exercised, or proposed to exercise, (in good faith) any entitlement to complain (or appeal) to an employment tribunal, the CAC or the EAT in connection with any rights conferred by the *ICE Regulations*;

(e)   requested, or proposed to request data in accordance with *reg 5* (above **16.5**);

(f)   acted with a view to securing that an agreement was or was not negotiated or that the standard information and consultation provisions did or did not become applicable;

(g)   indicated that he supported or did not support the coming into existence of a negotiated agreement or the application of the standard information and consultation provisions;

(h)   stood as a candidate in an election in which any person elected would, on being elected, be a negotiating representative or an information and consultation representative;

(i)   influenced or sought to influence by lawful means the way in which votes were to be cast by other employees in a ballot arranged under the *ICE Regulations*;

(j)   voted in such a ballot;

(k)   expressed doubts as to whether such a ballot had been properly conducted; or

(l)   proposed to do, failed to do, or proposed to decline to do, any of the things mentioned in sub-paragraphs (f) to (j) above.

(*Reg 30* and *ss 105(7H)* and *108(3), ERA 1996.*)

Such an employee is also protected from detriment on these grounds (*reg 32*).

There is an exception where an employee has, in the performance of any of his functions or activities as a representative or candidate disclosed any confidential information in breach of the provisions of the *ICE Regulations* (*reg 30(4)* and see **16.17**). Such dismissals will be potentially fair, unless they also fall foul of the 'protected disclosure' provisions of the *Employment Rights Act 1996* (see **10.17–10.18** DISCLOSURE OF INFORMATION). See also generally **54.3** UNFAIR DISMISSAL- II: THE FAIRNESS OF THE DISMISSAL.

An employee also has the right not to be subjected to a detriment for any of the above actions (or inactions): *reg 32*. This is subject to an identical exception for protected disclosures (*reg 32(4)*). A complaint that an employee has been subjected to a detriment in contravention of *reg 32* may be presented to an employment tribunal in the same manner as complaints under the *Employment Rights Act 1996* for subjection to a detriment on other grounds (*reg 33*). Compare **50.37** TRADE UNIONS – I: NATURE AND LIABILITIES.

These requirements reflect *art 7* of the *Directive*, by which Member States are required to ensure that employees' representatives, when carrying out their functions, enjoy adequate protection and guarantees to enable them to perform properly the duties which have been assigned to them. In *Holst v Dansk Arbejdsgiverforening*: C-405/08 [2010] 2 CMLR 49 the ECJ indicated that the *Directive* does not require that any more extensive protection against dismissal be granted to employees' representatives. However, any measure adopted to transpose the *Directive*, whether provided for by legislation or by collective agreement, must comply with the minimum protection threshold laid down in *art 7*.

16.20 EUROPEAN WORKS COUNCILS

The original *European Works Council (EWC) Directive (94/45)* applied in EEA states except the UK from 22 September 1996, and was subsequently extended to the UK by *Directive 97/74*. A recast *EWC Directive 2009/38/EC* (the '*New Works Council Directive*'), which was agreed on 6 May 2009 and came into force, in the main, on 6 June 2011, has made a number of substantive changes to the original.

The purpose of the *Directives* is to improve the right to information and to consultation of employees in Community-scale undertakings and Community-scale groups of undertakings.

They require the establishment of an European-level information and consultation procedure or a European Works Council ('EWC') in all undertakings (or groups of undertakings) employing:

(a)   at least 1,000 workers in the EEA, with

(b)   at least 150 workers in each of at least two member states.

(The EEA comprises the EU member states, Norway, Iceland and Liechtenstein.)

16.21 The *Directives* have been implemented in national legislation by the *Transnational Information and Consultation of Employees Regulations 1999 (SI 1999/3323)* (as amended) (the '*TICE Regulations*').

The original *TICE Regulations*, as previously amended, were further amended to give effect to the *New Works Council Directive* by the *Transnational Information and Consultation of Employees (Amendment) Regulations 2010 (SI 2010/1088)*, made under *s 2(2)* of the *European Communities Act 1972*. These amendments came into force, in the main, on 5 June 2011. This chapter refers to the amended form of the *TICE Regulations*, save where otherwise stated.

Employee Participation

BIS issued detailed guidance on the Amendment Regulations in April 2010, which is available online: webarchive.nationalarchives.gov.uk/20090609003228/http ://www.berr.gov.uk/assets/biscore/employment-matters/docs/10-888-transnational -information-consultation-regulations-2010-guidance.pdf.

There are significant differences between the *TICE Regulations* as they stand now and as they stood before 5 June 2011. Practitioners need to consider carefully whether the issue before them falls under the *TICE Regulations* in their pre-amendment or amended form. In outline terms, the amended *TICE Regulations* will apply to all EWCs save to the extent specified in *Part IX* and especially amended *regs 44–45A* (which exempt from most of the new provisions agreements establishing an EWC or information and consultation procedure which were signed between 5 June 2009 and 4 June 2011 or signed between 15 December 1999 and 4 June 2009 and then revised between 5 June 2009 and 4 June 2011, and certain forms of agreement in force prior to specified dates in the 1990s).

Note that the *TICE Regulations* do not apply to Community-scale undertakings which had pre-existing voluntary agreements in force before 23 September 1996 under the original *Directive* which cover the entire workforce, or to voluntary agreements made prior to 16 December 1999 by undertakings which are subject to the 15 January 2000 implementation date (*regs 44, 45*).

16.22 Number of employees

In order to determine whether an undertaking (or group of undertakings) has the necessary number of employees to qualify as a Community-scale undertaking (or group of undertakings) for the purposes of the *Directive* and *TICE Regulations*, an average is taken of the two years preceding the relevant date (*reg 6*). For UK employees this means adding together the number of UK employees in each month in the two year period preceding the relevant date (as defined in *reg 6(4)*) and dividing the total by 24 (see *reg 6(2)–(3)*). For this purpose, employees who are contracted to work 75 hours or less in a normal month without overtime may be counted as half an employee for that month if the UK management so decides (*reg 6(3)*). For employees elsewhere, calculations are to be made according to the law and practice of the member state concerned (*reg 6(1)(b)*).

When an employee or employees' representative seeks information to establish whether the organisation is part of a Community-scale undertaking (or group of undertakings), management must provide details of the average numbers of employees employed in the UK and in each of the other member states in the past two years (*reg 7*). As amended, *reg 7* also now requires management to obtain and provide information relating to the structure of the undertaking (or group of undertakings) and its workforce in the UK and in each of the other member states in the past two years, and to provide suitable information relating to the use of agency workers.

The CAC may order disclosure where the employer has failed to comply (*reg 8*).

In *Betriebsrat der Bofrost Josef H Boquoi Deutschland West GmbH & Co KG v Bofrost Josef H Boquoi Deutschland West GmbH & Co KG*: C-62/99 [2001] ECR I-2579, [2004] 2 CMLR 53, [2001] IRLR 403, the ECJ stated, in relation to *Directive 97/74*, that an undertaking which is part of a group is required to supply information on number of employees, etc to workers' representatives, even where it has not yet been established that the management to which the request for information is addressed is the management of a controlling undertaking within the group (see also *Betriebsrat der Firma ADS Anker GmbH v ADS Anker GmbH*: C-349/01 [2004] ECR I-6803, [2004] 3 CMLR 14, (2004) 763 IDS Brief 11 ('*ADS Anker*')). Workers are entitled to have access to information enabling them to ascertain whether they have the right to request that negotiations on an EWC be opened with central management. The sorts of information that the group may be obliged to supply includes information on the average total number of employees, their distribution across the member states, the establishments of the undertaking and the group undertakings, and on the structure of the undertaking and of the undertakings in the group, as well as the names and addresses of the employee representatives which might participate in the setting-up of an EWC (*Gesamtbetriebsrat der Kühne & Nagel AG & CoKG v Kühne & Nagel AG & Co KG*: C-440/00 [2004] ECR I-787, [2004] 2 CMLR 54, [2004] IRLR 332). The group's obligation to supply information extends only to such information as is 'essential' (*Kühne & Nagel*, paragraphs 64 and 69) to the opening of negotiations for establishing an EWC. In *ADS Anker* (above), the ECJ ruled that it was for the national court to determine what information was 'essential'.

Where the central management of a Community-scale undertaking or group of undertakings is not located in an EU member state, then the management ('the deemed management') required to provide information to employees and employees' representatives is the management of the undertaking employing the greatest number of employees in any member state: *art 4(2)* of the *New Works Council Directive* and see *Kühne & Nagel*. In order to fulfil its obligations under the *New Works Council Directive*, the deemed management must request the information from other undertakings in the group and the other undertakings must supply that information to the deemed management.

Note that only certain of the *TICE regulations* apply in relation to a Community-scale undertaking or group of undertakings whose central management is not situated in the UK: *reg 4* and for a recent example in practice see *Morgan & King v SAFRAN Group* EWC/8/2013, 26 July 2013.

16.23 Requests for an EWC

Central management situated in the UK is required to initiate negotiations for the establishment of a European Works Council ('an EWC') or an information and consultation procedure if it receives either:

(a)   a valid request from 100 employees or from employees' representatives who represent at least that number in at least two undertakings or establishments in at least two different member states; or

(b)   separate requests by employees or employees' representatives which, taken together, mean that 100 employees or employees' representatives representing that number have made requests in at least two undertakings or establishments in at least two different member states.

(*Regulation 9(1), (2)*.)

All such requests must be in writing, dated (with the date of sending) and sent to central or local management (*reg 9(3)*). Alternatively, central management may initiate negotiations on its own initiative (*reg 9(5)*).

Such requests must be in writing, dated and sent to central or local management (*reg 9(3)*). Central management may initiate negotiations on its own initiative (*reg 9(5)*). Disputes over the validity of requests to set up an EWC are to be referred to the CAC within three months, and undertakings which consider that they have a valid voluntary agreement but which receive a request to establish an EWC may also apply to the CAC to decide the point (*reg 10*).

These requirements also apply where the central management is not situated in a member state and the representative agent of central management is located in the UK and, in other cases, where a UK-based establishment or group has more employees than other establishments or groups in member states (*reg 5(1)*).

16.24 Employee Participation

16.24 Special negotiating body

A 'special negotiating body' ('SNB') is to be established to represent employees in their negotiations with management on the setting up of an EWC or arrangements for implementing an information and consultation procedure (*reg 11*). It consists of representatives of employees from all Member States in which employees are employed to work (*reg 12*). For SNBs constituted on or after 5 June 2011, employees in each Member State shall elect or appoint one SNB member for each 10% (or fraction of 10%) of the total number of employees in all Member States which those employees represent (*reg 12(2)*). (Under the old *TICE Regulations*, the number of representatives for each member state had been decided by a formula set by the state in which the central management (or representative agent if the central management is outside the EEA) was located.) The SNB is then required to inform central management and local managements and the European social partner organisations of its composition and of the date on which it proposes to start negotiations: *Regulation 12(4)*.

UK members of the SNB are to be elected by a ballot of UK employees. Requirements for the ballot are set out in *regs 13* and *14*. There is no need for a ballot where there already exists a consultative committee carrying out an information and consultation function whose members were elected by a ballot of UK employees (*reg 15*). In these circumstances the committee may nominate from its number UK representatives for the SNB as set out in *reg 15*.

Central management and the SNB must negotiate in a spirit of cooperation, with a view to reaching written agreement on the detailed arrangements for informing and consulting employees (*reg 17(1)*).

In order to reach an EWC agreement, central management must convene a meeting with the SNB, informing local managements accordingly. SNBs are to take decisions by majority vote except that two-thirds of the votes are needed on a decision not to open, or to terminate, negotiations. The SNB may be assisted in these negotiations by experts, including representatives of European trade organisations (*reg 16(2)–(3)*). Any expert appointed by the SNB may, at the SNB's request, attend any meeting with central management under *reg 16(1)* in an advisory capacity.

SNB members are entitled to meet within a reasonable time both before and after any meeting with central management, without the central management or its representatives being present, using any means necessary for communication at those meetings (*reg 16(1A)*). Reasonable expenses relating to the negotiations necessary to enable the SNB to carry out its functions in an appropriate manner are to be borne by central management, including the expenses of one expert where applicable (*reg 16*).

16.25 Setting up an EWC

Where the SNB and central management agree to establish an EWC, the agreement must specify:

(a) the undertakings or establishments covered;

(b) the composition of the EWC, number of members, allocation of seats (taking into account, so far as reasonably practicable, the need for balanced representation of employees by role, gender and sector) and term of office of the members;

(c) the functions and procedure for information and consultation of the EWC and arrangements to link this with information and consultation of national employee representation bodies;

(d) the venue, frequency and duration of meetings;

(e)   where the parties decide that it is necessary to establish a select committee, the composition of the select committee, the procedure for appointing its members, the functions and the procedural rules;

(f)   the financial and material resources allocated to the EWC;

(g)   the date of entry into force of the agreement and its duration, the arrangements for amending or terminating the agreement, the circumstances in which the agreement is to be renegotiated including where the structure of the Community-scale undertaking or Community-scale group of undertakings changes and the procedure for renegotiation of the agreement.

(Regulation 17(4).)

Central management and the SNB may decide in writing to establish an information and consultation procedure instead of an EWC *(reg 17(3))*. However, such agreement must specify a method by which the representatives can meet to discuss the information conveyed to them *(reg 17(5))*.

In addition, where information disclosed under an EWC agreement or an information and consultation procedure includes information as to the employment situation in the Community-scale undertaking or, as the case may be, the Community-scale group of undertakings, this must include suitable information relating to the use of agency workers *(reg 17(9))*.

A statutory EWC, governed by the *Schedule* to the *TICE Regulations* (as opposed to an EWC as described in *reg 17(4)* and *(6)*), is to be set up if:

(a)   the parties agree;

(b)   central management refuses to start negotiations within six months of the date on which a valid request was made; or

(c)   no agreement has been concluded within three years of the request being made, provided the SNB has not taken a decision to terminate (or not to start) negotiations.

(Regulation 18.)

The *Schedule* contains a 'statutory model' comprising a standard set of rules for the constitution of a statutory EWC governing its competence, composition, meetings and procedures. In particular, it lists topics about which the EWC is to be informed and consulted (see the *Schedule* at *para 7(3)–(4)*).

Central management and the EWC or information/consultation representatives are under a duty to work in a spirit of co-operation with due regard to their reciprocal rights and obligations *(reg 19)*.

The amended *TICE Regulations* contain more detailed requirements as to the information to be provided by management to EWC members or to information and consultation representatives and as to consultation with such members or representatives than previously: see eg. the new *reg 18A*. From 1 October 2011, however, they limit information and consultation to transnational matters: *reg 18A*. They also introduce requirements to link information and consultation of EWCs with information and consultation of national employee representation bodies: see *reg 19E*. At the same time, the amended *TICE Regulations* require EWCs to inform employees' representatives or, if there are no such representatives, employees themselves, of the content and outcome of the information and consultation procedure (with a right of complaint to the CAC if they fail to do so): see *regs 19C–19D*.

16.25 Employee Participation

The amended *Regulations* also contain a new focus on the 'means' required by an EWC. Thus they require central management to provide EWC members with the means to fulfil their duty to represent collectively the interests of the employees of the undertaking or group of undertakings concerned: see *reg 19A*. They also require central management to provide EWC members and SNB members with the means required to undertake any necessary training: see *regs 19B* and *25*.

Finally, the amended *Regulations* contain provision on 'adaptation' where there are significant changes in the structure of the Community-scale undertaking or group of undertakings: *reg 19F*.

The CAC will rule on disputes about the operation of an EWC or the failure to establish an EWC. If a complaint is well-founded, the CAC must make a decision to that effect and may make an order requiring central management to take appropriate steps by a specified date. In addition, on an application by a relevant applicant within three months of a CAC decision, the EAT will issue a penalty notice requiring central management to pay an amount to the Secretary of State (*regs 20, 21, 21A*). The maximum penalty to be imposed is £100,000 (*reg 22(2)*). The EAT also hears appeals on points of law from the CAC (*reg 38(8)*). Both the EAT and CAC may refer cases to ACAS if they believe that a dispute is reasonably likely to be settled by conciliation (*reg 39(1)*).

16.26 Confidential information

Present and former members of SNBs, EWCs, information/consultation representatives and relevant experts assisting them must not disclose information which central management requires to be kept confidential (*reg 23(1)*). Civil action may be taken by management for breach of this statutory duty of confidence except where the individual reasonably believed disclosure to be a protected disclosure within the meaning of *s 43A* of the *Employment Rights Act 1996*, as inserted by the *Public Interest Disclosure Act 1998* (*reg 23(1)–(5)*). Members or representatives can appeal to the CAC for a declaration if they believe UK central management is imposing confidentiality requirements unreasonably. A declaration will be made if the CAC considers that disclosure would not, or would not be likely to, 'prejudice or cause serious harm to the undertaking' (*reg 23(6)–(7)*).

Management may withhold any information which, according to objective criteria, would seriously harm the functioning of, or be prejudicial to, the undertaking. The CAC will rule on disputes over whether a document or information should be disclosed and will order disclosure where it considers, on objective criteria, that no serious harm or prejudice would result (*reg 24*).

16.27 Employment protection

Members of SNBs, EWCs, information/consultation representatives and candidates for election as such members are entitled to take reasonable time off work, with pay, to carry out their functions (*regs 25–27A*). See TIME OFF WORK (49).

Such employees also have the right not to be subjected to a detriment by the employer on the ground that they performed their functions or activities or made a request for statutory time off or payment for time off or proposed to do so (*reg 31*). Additional rights not to be victimised apply to any employee whether or not he or she falls within the above categories. It is unlawful (by *reg 31(5), (6)*) to subject an employee to a detriment on the grounds that the employee:

(a)   took proceedings in tribunal to enforce a right or entitlement under the *TICE Regulations* (provided any claim is made in good faith);

(b)   exercised any entitlement to apply or complain to the EAT or CAC;

(c)   requested information under *reg 7*;

(d)   acted with a view to securing (or not securing) the setting up of an SNB, an EWC or information/consultation procedure;

(e)   indicated that he supported (or did not support) the setting up of an SNB, an EWC or information/consultation procedure;

(f)   stood as a candidate for election to be an SNB or EWC member or information/consultation representative, influenced or sought to influence how votes are cast in a ballot under the *TICE Regulations*, voted in such a ballot or questioned the conduct of the ballot; or

(g)   proposed to do any of the above, or failed to do or proposed to decline to do, any of (d) to (f) above.

It is also automatically unfair under *reg 28* to dismiss an employee for such a reason (or for such a principal reason, where there is more than one reason) (see UNFAIR DISMISSAL – II (54)).

Complaints of detrimental treatment may be made to an employment tribunal within three months of the act or failure to act or, if that is not reasonably practicable, within such further period as the tribunal considers reasonable (*reg 32*). Compensation may be awarded if the complaint is well-founded, see *ERA 1996, s 49*. Complaints may be settled by ACAS conciliation or by valid settlement agreements (*reg 41*).

16.28 EUROPEAN COMPANIES (SES)

Longstanding proposals for a European Company Statute ('ECS'), which would allow European Companies or 'Societas Europaea' ('SEs') to be formed under European law, came to fruition on 8 October 2001 with the adoption by the EU Council of Ministers of *Regulation 2157/2001*.

The ECS gives companies operating in more than one member state, with a share capital of more than 120,000 Euro, the option of being established as a single company under EU law, able to operate throughout the EU with one set of rules and a unified reporting system. The *Regulation* is accompanied by a *Directive* on worker involvement (*Directive 2001/86/EC*).

16.29   The *Directive* and *Regulation* were originally implemented domestically by the *European Public Limited-Liability Company Regulations 2004 (SI 2004/2326)* (the '*EPLC Regulations*'). Under the *EPLC Regulations*, before an SE can be registered, the various companies or establishments involved in its creation must have complied with the requirements of *Regulation 2157/2001* in relation to the information, consultation and participation of employees (*reg 12*).

However, the *EPLC Regulations* were amended by *SI 2008/948* and, much more extensively, by *SI 2009/2400*, subject to transitional provisions in *SI 2009/2400 reg 2* and *Sch 2*. In particular, *SI 2009/2400* extended the reach of the *EPLC Regulations* to the entirety of the UK, and not just Great Britain. Most significantly for present purposes, *SI 2009/2400* revoked *Part 3* of the *EPLC Regulations* dealing with employee involvement.

Part 3 of the *EPLC Regulations* has been replaced since 1 October 2009 by the combination of:

(a)   The *European Public Limited-Liability Company (Employee Involvement) (Great Britain) Regulations 2009 (SI 2009/2401)*, applicable to SEs with a registered office in Great Britain (the 'GB Regulations'); and

Employee Participation

(b) The *European Public Limited-Liability Company (Employee Involvement) (Northern Ireland) Regulations (SI 2009/2402)*, applicable to SEs with a registered office in Northern Ireland.

This chapter addresses the *GB Regulations* only.

The Explanatory Memorandum states that there are no substantive differences between the *GB Regulations* and the prior provisions of *Part 3* of the *EPLC Regulations*.

The requirements of the *GB Regulations* apply whenever a company intends to establish an SE whose registered office is to be in Great Britain, or an SE has its registered office in Great Britain (*reg 4(1)*). In relation to the election or appointment of members of the 'special negotiating body' (below **16.31**) or employee representatives, the requirements apply whenever there are employees of the relevant company in Great Britain (*reg 4(2)*). In relation to matters of enforcement and employee protection, the GB Regulations also apply where any subsidiary or establishment of a relevant company or SE, or an employee or employees' representative, is registered or situated in Great Britain (*reg 4(3)*).

16.30 Employer's duty to provide information

Regulation 5 places a duty on the participating company (or companies) to provide information to employee representatives (or, if there are no such representatives, the employees themselves) whenever they decide to form an SE. The company must, as soon as possible after publishing the terms of any draft merger, or creating a holding company, or agreeing a plan to form a subsidiary or to transform into an SE, provide information to employees which, at least (by *reg 5(1), (2)*):

(a) identifies the participating companies, concerned subsidiaries and establishments;

(b) gives the number of employees employed by each participating company and concerned subsidiary and at each concerned establishment; and

(c) gives the number of employees employed to work in each EEA State; and

(d) provides specified information in relation to agency workers (from 1 October 2011).

Complaints that a company has failed to provide information, or has provided information that is false or incomplete in a material particular may be presented to the CAC by an employee's representative or (if there is no such representative) an employee (*reg 6(1)*). If the CAC finds the complaint well-founded, it must order the disclosure of the information in question (*reg 6(2)*).

There is a continuing obligation on the company to provide information as to progress in establishing an SE (*reg 5(3)*). The obligation is to provide that information to the 'special negotiating body' (see below **16.31**).

16.31 The special negotiating body

The company or companies proposing to form an SE are obliged to set up a 'special negotiating body' ('SNB') (*reg 8(1)*). The function of the SNB is to reach an 'employee involvement agreement' with the participating companies (see below **16.32**). The SNB consists of employee representatives elected from the employees in each member state. The employees from each member state have the right to elect one representative for each 10% or fraction of 10% which those employees represent (and so on, *reg 8(2)*). Where more than one company is involved there must be at least one representative from each company (*reg 8(3)*). Employees must be informed of the identity of the members of the SNB as soon as practicable and in any event within one month of the election (*reg 8(5)*). There is provision for appointing additional members and for changing members in certain circumstances (*reg 8(4), (6)*).

Complaints in relation to the establishment of (or failure to establish) an SNB may be presented to the CAC by a person elected or appointed to the SNB, an employees' representative (or, if there is no such representative, the employee) or a participating company or concerned subsidiary (*reg 9(1)–(2)*). Complaints must be made within one month of the last date on which the participating companies complied or should have complied with the obligation to inform employees of the identity of members of the SNB (*reg 9(3)*). Where the CAC finds an application well-founded it must make a declaration to that effect and the participating companies will continue to be under an obligation to comply with their duties under the *GB Regulations* (*reg 9(4)*).

The requirements of the ballot for the election of representatives are set out in *regs 10* and *11*. Any UK employee or UK employees' representative who believes that the arrangements for the ballot of the UK employees do not comply with the requirements of the *GB Regulations* may present a complaint to the CAC (*reg 10(4)*). Complaints must be presented within a period of 21 days beginning on the date on which the management published the final arrangements for the ballot (*reg 10(4)*). Where the CAC finds the complaint well-founded it must make a declaration to that effect and may make an order requiring the management to modify the arrangements it has made for the ballot of UK employees so as to comply with the requirements of the *GB Regulations* (*reg 10(5)*).

Where there is already a 'consultative committee' within the organisation concerned, the company is relieved of the obligation to arrange a ballot and instead the 'consultative committee' is permitted to appoint one or more of its own members to the SNB (*regs 12(1)* and *(3)*). A 'consultative committee' is defined as a body of persons which represents all the employees of the participating company, consists wholly of persons who are employees of the participating company or its concerned subsidiaries, whose normal functions include carrying out 'an information and consultation function', and which is able to carry out its functions without interference from the management of the participating company (*reg 12(4)*). 'Information and consultation function' is defined in *reg 12(5)* as 'receiving, on behalf of all the employees of the participating company, information which may significantly affect the interests of the employees of that company, but excluding information which is relevant only to a specific aspect of the interests of the employees, such as health and safety or collective redundancies; and being consulted by the management of the participating company on that information'. Most trade unions will be 'consultative committees' within the *GB Regulations.*

Where such a consultative committee exists, it is entitled to appoint so many of its number (or, with the permission of the management of the participating company, a trade union representative who is not an employee of the company) to the SNB as that company would be entitled to elect under a ballot (*reg 12(2)*). The consultative committee must then publish the names of those it has appointed to the SNB in such a manner as to bring them to the attention of the management of the participating company and, so far as reasonably practicable, the employees and employees' representatives (and those of its concerned subsidiaries) (*reg 12(5)–(6)*).

Where the management of a participating company, an employee or an employee's representative believes that a 'consultative committee' does not fulfil the requirements of *reg 12*, or that the representative appointed by that committee is not entitled to be appointed, they may complain to the CAC (provided they do so within 21 days of the publication of the names of the representatives purportedly appointed by the consultative committee) (*reg 12(7)–(9)*). If the CAC finds the complaint well-founded, it must make a declaration (*reg 12(8)*). Any appointment made by the consultative committee will then be of no effect and appointment of representatives must thereafter be by ballot (*reg 12(9)*).

16.32 Negotiated employee involvement agreement

The task of the SNB is to reach an employee involvement agreement with the (proposed) SE (*reg 7*).

16.32 Employee Participation

The parties are under a duty to negotiate in a spirit of co-operation (*reg 14(2)*). An initial six-month time limit is set within which to reach agreement, but with provision for extension for up to 12 months from the date the original time-limit began running by agreement between the parties (*reg 14(3)*).

There are no specific requirements as to the substance of the agreement to be reached on employee involvement, save that the elements of employee involvement at all levels must be at least as favourable as those which exist in the company to be transformed into an SE (*reg 15(4)*).

However, to be valid, the agreement must be in writing and must specify the agreement reached on certain key points (*by reg 15*):

(a)   the scope of the agreement;

(b)   the composition, number of members and allocation of seats on the representative body;

(c)   the functions and the procedure for the information and consultation of the representative body;

(d)   the frequency of meetings of the representative body;

(e)   the financial and material resources to be allocated to the representative body;

(f)   if, during negotiations, the parties have decided to establish one or more information and consultation procedures instead of a representative body, the agreement must specify the arrangements for implementing those procedures;

(g)   if, during negotiations, the parties have decided to establish arrangements for participation, the agreement must record the substance of those arrangements including (if applicable) the number of members in the SE's administrative or supervisory body which the employees will be entitled to elect, appoint, recommend or oppose, the procedures as to how these members may be elected, appointed, recommended or opposed by the employees, and their rights; and

(h)   in all cases, the date of entry into force of the agreement and its duration, the circumstances, if any, in which the agreement is required to be re-negotiated and the procedure for its re-negotiation.

In addition, from 1 October 2011, where under the employee involvement agreement the SE's competent organ is to provide information on the employment situation in that company, such information must include suitable information relating to the use of agency workers (*reg 15(3A)*).

There are specific rules as to how decisions must be taken by the SNB, and what level of majority is required for each sort of decision (an absolute majority generally, but two thirds where a decision would result in a reduction of participation rights) (*reg 16(1)–(3)*).

For the purpose of negotiations, the SNB may be assisted by experts of its choice (*reg 16(5)*). The participating company or companies must pay for any reasonable expenses of the SNB, though the company is not required to pay for the expenses of more than one expert (*reg 16(6)*).

The details of any decision taken by the SNB must be published to the employees represented on the body as soon as reasonably practicable and, in any event no later than 14 days after the decision has been taken (*reg 16(4)*).

Complaints in relation to decisions of the SNB may be presented to the CAC by a member of the SNB, an employees' representative, or where there is no such representative in respect of an employee, that employee (*reg 18(1)*). Complaints may only be presented on the grounds that (a) the decision was not taken by the requisite majority, or (b) that the SNB failed to publish a decision as required by the *GB Regulations*. The time limit for presentation of complaints is 21 days from the date the SNB did or should have published their decision. Where the CAC finds the complaint well-founded it must make a declaration that the decision was not taken properly and that it is to have no effect (*reg 18(2)*).

16.33 Standard rules on employee involvement

Where no employee involvement agreement has been reached within the six-month (or twelve-month extended) time limit in reg *14(3)*, or the parties have so agreed, the 'standard rules on employee involvement' will apply (*reg 19*). These are detailed and complex and are set out in the *Schedule* to the *GB Regulations*. In summary, however, the standard rules provide as follows:

(a)   The management of the SE must arrange for the establishment of a 'representative body';

(b)   The representative body must be composed of employees of the SE and its subsidiaries and establishments (one member for each 10% or fraction thereof of employees of the SE, its subsidiaries and establishments employed for the time being in each member state). Its members must be elected or appointed by the EEA of the SNB, by whatever method the SNB decides;

(c)   Once the representative body has been established for four years, it must decide whether to open negotiations with the management of the SE to reach an employee involvement agreement or whether the standard rules should continue to apply. If a decision is taken to open negotiations the procedure described at **16.32** above will apply, save that references to the SNB should be read as being references to the representative body;

(d)   For the purpose of informing and consulting on questions which concern the SE and any of its subsidiaries or establishments in another EEA state and questions which exceed the powers of the decision-making organ in a single EEA state, the management is obliged to:

  (i)   prepare and provide to the representative body regular reports on the progress of the business of the SE and the SE's prospects;

  (ii)   provide the representative body with the agenda for meetings of its administrative, management or supervisory committees and copies of all documents submitted to any general meeting of the SE's shareholders.

  (iii)   Inform the representative body when there are exceptional circumstances affecting the employees' interests to a considerable extent, particularly in the event of relocations, transfers, the closure of establishments or undertakings or collective redundancies;

(e)   If the representative body so desires, the management must meet with it at least once a year to discuss the reports on the progress of the business. Such meetings should relate, in particular, to the structure, economic and financial situation, the probable development of business and of production and sales, the situation and probable trend of employment, investments and substantial changes concerning organisation, introduction of new working methods or production processes, transfers of production, mergers, cut-backs or closures of undertakings, establishments or important parts thereof and collective redundancies;

(f)   Where there are exceptional circumstances affecting the employees' interests, the representative body (or, if it so decides, a select committee constituted in accordance with *paragraph 2* of the *Schedule* to the *GB Regulations*) must be permitted to meet with the most appropriate level of management and, if the SE does not act in accordance with the representative body's opinion as to what should be done in the circumstances, the representative body may request a further meeting to seek agreement;

(g)   The members of the representative body must inform the employees' representatives or, if no such representatives exist, the employees of the SE and its subsidiaries and establishments, of the content and outcome of the information and consultation procedures;

(h)   The representative body and the select committee of the representative body may be assisted by experts of its choice;

(i)   The costs of the representative body must be borne by the SE, which must also provide the members of that body with financial and material resources needed to enable them to perform their duties in an appropriate manner, including (unless agreed otherwise) the cost of organising meetings, providing interpretation facilities and accommodation and travelling expenses. However, again, where the representative body or the select committee is assisted by more than one expert the SE is not required to pay the expenses of more than one of them.

Again, since 1 October 2011, where under the standard employee involvement agreement the SE's competent organ is to provide information on the employment situation in that company, such information must include suitable information relating to the use of agency workers (*Schedule, para 8A*).

16.34 Alternative arrangements

The members of the SNB may 'opt out' of any sort of employee involvement, in which case the usual national rules on employee involvement will apply, and the obligations to agree employee involvement procedures under the *GB Regulations* will fall away (*reg 17(3)*). The 'opt out' may be exercised by the SNB deciding, by a two thirds majority vote, not to open negotiations for an employee involvement agreement or to terminate any such negotiations (*reg 17(1)*). The SNB cannot, however, 'opt out' if the SE is to be formed by way of transformation of an existing company, and the existing company is one in which any of the employees have the right to participate in the board of that company (*reg 17(2)*). Procedures for agreeing employee involvement under the *GB Regulations* may, provided at least two years have passed since the decision to 'opt out' be 'reactivated' by an employee request that is:

(a)   in writing; and

(b)   made by at least 10% of the employees of, or by employees' representatives representing at least 10% of the total number of employees employed by the participating companies and its concerned subsidiaries, or (where the SE has been registered) the SE and its subsidiaries (*reg 17(4)*).

Where the SE has been registered, the SE may agree to the SNB being reconvened earlier than the specified two years.

16.35 Disputes and complaints

Disputes about the operation of an employee involvement agreement or the standard rules on employee involvement may be referred to the CAC by a member of the representative body or (where no representative body has been elected or appointed) an information and consultation representative or employee of the SE (*reg 20(1)*). There is a three-month time limit, running from the date on which the defaulting party allegedly failed to comply with the agreed procedure (*reg 20(2)*). If the CAC finds a complaint well-founded it may make a declaration and an order requiring the defaulting party to take requisite steps to remedy the default (*reg 20(4)–(5)*).

In the event of the CAC making such a declaration, the aggrieved party has three months in which to apply to the Employment Appeal Tribunal for a penalty notice to be awarded against the defaulting party (*reg 20(6)*). Matters to be taken into account by the EAT when setting the amount of the penalty include: the gravity of the failure; the period of time over which the failure occurred; the reason for the failure; the number of employees affected; and the number of employees employed by the undertaking (*reg 21(3)*).

16.36 Employment protection

Similar provisions apply in relation to rights to reasonable paid time off (*regs 26–28*), protection from dismissal (*regs 29–30*) and protection from other detriment (*regs 31–32*) as apply under the *ICE Regulations* (see above **16.19**).

16.37 EUROPEAN CO-OPERATIVE SOCIETIES (SCES)

Directive 2003/72/EC, accompanying *Regulation 1435/03* on the establishment of European Co-operative Societies (or 'Societas Cooperativa Europaea') (SCEs), prescribed requirements as to employee involvement in SCEs, with effect from 18 August 2006. Together, these measures are known as the *Statute for a European Cooperative Society*.

In *Validity of Regulation 1435/2003, Re: European Parliament v EU Council*: C-436/03 [2006] ECR I-3733, [2006] 3 CMLR 3, the ECJ held that the *Regulation* was correctly adopted under *art 308 EC*, as it has as its purpose the creation of a new form of co-operative society in addition to national forms, and leaves unchanged the different national laws already in existence (see [44]-[46]).

16.38 The *Directive* has been implemented domestically by the *European Cooperative Society (Involvement of Employees) Regulations 2006 (SI 2006/2059)* (the '*SCE Regulations*'), with effect from 18 August 2006. The *SCE Regulations* were implemented under *s 2(2)* of the *European Communities Act 1972* (unlike the *ICE Regulations*, which were made under *s 42* of the *Employment Relations Act 2004*).

An SCE is an organisation which has as its principal object the satisfaction of its members' needs and/or the development of their economic and social activities, in particular through the conclusion of agreements with them to supply goods or services or to execute particular work or commissions: *reg 3* read with *EC Regulation 1435/03, art 1(3)*.

The *SCE Regulations* apply to an actual or proposed SCE which will have its registered office in the UK, except where, at the relevant time:

(a)   the total workforce is less than 50;

(b)   the total workforce comprises employees employed to work in only one EEA state; and either—

(c)   if a participating individual (a natural person directly participating in the establishing of an SCE: *reg 3*) intends to form an SCE, all or all but one of the other parties to its formation are participating individuals, or

(d)   if a participating legal entity (as defined in *art 2* of the *Directive*) intends to form an SCE, all of the other parties to its formation are participating individuals.

(*Regs 4(2)* and *5(1)–(2)*.)

Employee Participation

The *SCE Regulations* do not apply where an SCE has been registered and, at the relevant time, paragraphs (*a*) to (*c*) above applied: *reg 5(3)*. However, the *SCE Regulations* will apply in modified form if a formerly exempt SCE sees its total workforce increase to 50 or more employees, including employees employed to work in at least two different EEA states (even if that does not continue to be so), or if a valid employee request is made to that effect (*reg 6*). Regard should be had to the detailed provisions as to exemption in *regs 5* and *6*.

Note that particular provisions of the *SCE Regulations* apply to SCEs which have UK employees or other connections to the UK, but which do not fall within *reg 4(2)*, see *regs 4(3)–(4)*. Where the registered office of an SCE governed by participation transfers to the UK from another EEA state, at least the same level of employee participation rights must continue post-transfer (*reg 5(4)*).

Nothing in the *SCE Regulations* shall prejudice the rights of employees of an SCE, its subsidiaries or establishments to involvement (cf participation) as provided for by law or practice in the EEA state in which they were employed immediately prior to the SCE's registration (*reg 43*).

16.39 Duty to provide information

Reg 7 places a duty on the participating individual or the competent organ of a participating legal entity to provide information to employee representatives (or, if there are no such representatives, the employees themselves) as soon as possible after publishing draft terms of merger or conversion or agreeing a plan to form an SCE. The relevant employee representatives and employees are those of the participating individual or legal entity, any concerned subsidiaries and concerned establishments (*reg 7(1)*). The information must, as a minimum (*reg 7(2)*):

(a)   identify the participating individuals, legal entities, subsidiaries and establishments, and any concerned subsidiaries or establishments;

(b)   give the number of employees employed by each participating individual, legal entity, subsidiary and at each establishment (and, from 1 October 2011, provide specified information in relation to agency workers); and

(c)   give the number of employees employed to work in each EEA State.

Where there is a 'special negotiating body' (see below **16.40**), there is a continuing obligation on each participating individual and the competent organs of each participating legal entity to provide information to as to progress in establishing the SCE (*reg 7(3)*).

Complaints as to a failure to provide information, or provision of information that is false or incomplete in a material particular may be presented to the CAC by an employee's representative or (if there is no such representative) an employee (*reg 8(1)*). If the CAC finds the complaint well-founded, it must order the disclosure of the information in question (*reg 8(2)*).

16.40 The special negotiating body

The individuals or legal entities proposing to form an SCE are obliged to set up a 'special negotiating body' ('SNB') (*reg 10(1)*). The function of the SNB is to reach an 'employee involvement agreement' with the participating individuals and entities (*reg 9*).

The constitution of the SNB is complex, and is governed by *reg 10*. Employees must be informed of the identity of the members of the SNB as soon as reasonably practicable and in any event within one month of the election (*reg 10(5)*). The method used to elect or appoint representatives should seek to promote gender balance (*reg 10(1)*).

Complaints in relation to the establishment of (or failure to establish) an SNB may be presented to the CAC by a person elected or appointed to the SNB, an employees' representative (or, if there is no such representative, the employee) or a participating individual, legal entity or concerned subsidiary (*reg 11(1)–(2)*). Complaints must be made within one month of the last date on which the participating individuals and participating legal entities complied or should have complied with the obligation to inform employees of the identity of members of the SNB (*reg 11(3)*). Where the CAC finds an application well-founded it must make a declaration to that effect and the participating individuals and legal entities will continue to be under an obligation to comply with their duty under *reg 10(1)* to set up an SNB (*reg 11(4)*).

The requirements for ballots of UK employees to elect the UK members of the SNB are set out in *regs 12* and *13*. Any UK employee or UK employees' representative who believes that the arrangements for the ballot of the UK employees do not comply with the requirements of the *SCE Regulations* may present a complaint to the CAC (*reg 12(4)*). Complaints must be presented within 21 days from the date on which the relevant employers published the final arrangements for the ballot. Where the CAC finds the complaint well-founded it must make a declaration to that effect and may make an order requiring the relevant employers to modify their arrangements for the ballot of UK employees so as to comply with the requirements of the *SCE Regulations* (*reg 23(5)*).

However, the participating individual or participating legal entity is not obliged to arrange a ballot where it already has a relevant consultative committee (*regs 14(1)–(2)*). Instead, the committee is entitled to appoint the UK member or members of the SNB who would otherwise have been elected, having regard to the fact that the method used should seek to promote gender balance (*reg 14(2)(a)*). The committee can appoint either one of its number or, with the permission of the relevant participating individual or participating legal entity, a trade union representative who is not an employee of that individual or entity (*reg 14(2)(b)*). The consultative committee must then publish the names of those it has appointed to the SNB in such a manner as to bring them to the attention of the participating individual or legal entity and, so far as reasonably practicable, employees and employees' representatives (and those of concerned subsidiaries) (*reg 14(5)*).

Where the participating individual or legal entity, or an employee or an employee's representative believes that a consultative committee does not fulfil the requirements of *reg 14(3)*, or that the representative appointed is not entitled to be appointed, they may complain to the CAC within 21 days of the publication of the names of the purported representatives (*reg 14(6)*). If the CAC finds the complaint well-founded, it must make a declaration to that effect (*reg 14(7)*). Any appointment made by the consultative committee will then be of no effect and a ballot is required (*reg 14(8)*).

16.41   Negotiated employee involvement agreement

The task of the SNB is to reach an employee involvement agreement with the participating individuals and competent organs of the participating legal entities (*reg 16*). The parties must negotiate in a spirit of co-operation (*reg 16(2)*). There is an initial six-month time limit for agreement, but this can be extended for up to 12 months from the day on which the original time limit began running by agreement between the parties (*reg 16(3)*).

There are few specific requirements as to the substance of the agreement to be reached on employee involvement. To be valid, the agreement must be in writing and must specify the agreement reached on certain key points. These are broadly the same as those which apply in relation to SEs (see above, **16.32**) with, in addition, specification of the substance of any agreed arrangements for employees or their representatives to participate in and vote in the general meeting or any section or sectorial meetings of the SCE (*reg 17*). The standard rules on employee involvement (see below, **16.42**) will only apply if there is express provision to that effect (*reg 17(3)*). Note also that in relation to an SCE to be formed by conversion, the employee involvement agreement must preserve elements of employee involvement which are at least as favourable as those which exist in the cooperative to be converted into an SCE (*reg 17(4)*). From 1 October 2011, where under the employee involvement agreement information is to be provided on the employment situation in the SCE, such information must include suitable information relating to the use of agency workers (*reg 17(6)*).

There are specific rules as to how decisions must be taken by the SNB, what level of majority is required for each sort of decision, and the assistance of experts (*regs 18–19*). These are broadly similar to those which apply to SNBs established in relation to SEs (see above, **16.32**).

Members of the SNB, employees' representatives (or where there is no such relevant representative, employees) may complain to the CAC that an SNB decision was not taken by the requisite majority, or that the SNB failed to publish a decision as required by the *SCE Regulations*. The time limit for presentation of complaints is 21 days from the date the SNB did or should have published their decision (*reg 20(1)*). Where the CAC finds the complaint well-founded it must make a declaration that the decision was not taken properly and that it is to have no effect (*reg 20(2)*).

16.42   Standard rules on employee involvement

Detailed and complex 'standard rules on employee involvement' are set out in *reg 21* and *Sch 2* to the *SCE Regulations*. In general, these will apply where (*reg 21*):

(a)   the parties so agree; or

(b)   no employee involvement agreement has been reached within the six-month (or twelve-month extended) time limit in *reg 16(3)* and where: (i) the participating individual and legal entities agree that they should apply, and so continue with the registration of the SCE, and (ii) the SNB has not taken any decision under *reg 19(1)* to 'opt out' of negotiations.

Note that there are further detailed provisions in *reg 21(3)* and *(5)* as to when the standard rules on participation in *Pt 3* of *Sch 2* will apply. Where the standard rules on participation apply and more than one form of employee participation exists in the participating legal entities, the SNB shall decide which of the existing forms of participation are to exist in the SCE (*reg 21(4)*).

16.43   Alternative arrangements

The members of the SNB may 'opt out' of any sort of employee involvement, in which case the usual national rules on employee involvement will apply, and the obligations to agree employee involvement procedures under the *SCE Regulations* will fall away (*reg 19(3)*). The 'opt out' may be exercised by the SNB deciding, by a two thirds majority vote, not to open negotiations for an employee involvement agreement or to terminate any such negotiations (*reg 19(1)*). The SNB cannot, however, 'opt out' if the SCE is to be formed by way of conversion if any employees of the cooperative to be converted have participation (*reg 19(2)*). Procedures for agreeing employee involvement under the *SCE Regulations* may be 'reactivated' by an employee request in similar circumstances as applied in relation to SEs (*reg 19(4)* and see above, **16.34**).

16.44   Disputes and complaints

Complaints that a participating individual or the competent organ of a participating legal entity or of the SCE has failed to comply with the employee involvement agreement or the standard rules on employee involvement may be referred to the CAC by a member of a representative body, or (in the absence of such a body) an information and consultation representative or an employee (*reg 22(1)*). There is a three-month time limit, running from the date of the alleged failure (*reg 22(2)*). If the CAC finds a complaint well-founded it must make a declaration and may make an order requiring the defaulting party to take requisite steps to remedy the default (*reg 22(4)–(5)*).

In addition, if an employees' representative (or, in the absence of such representative, the employees) believes that a participating individual, legal entity or SCE is misusing or intending to misuse the SCE or powers in the *SCE Regulations* for the purposes of depriving employees of their right to employee involvement, or withholding rights to employee involvement, he may present a complaint to the CAC (*reg 24(1)–(2)*). Where such a complaint is made either prior to registration or within a period of 12 months of the registration of the SCE, the CAC must uphold the complaint unless the respondent proves that it did not misuse or intend to misuse the SCE or the powers in the *SCE Regulations* (*reg 24(2)*). If the CAC finds the complaint to be well-founded, it shall make a declaration to that effect and may make an order requiring the participating individual, legal entity or SCE to take remedial action (*reg 24(3)*).

In the event of the CAC making either such declaration, the applicant has three months in which to apply to the Employment Appeal Tribunal for a penalty notice against the defaulting party (*reg 22(6)* and *reg 24(3)(b)*). Broadly similar provisions govern such applications as in relation to SEs: see *regs 22(6)–(9)*, *23* and *24(3)(b)* and above, **16.35**.

16.45 Confidential information

Similar provisions apply in relation to confidential information (*reg 26*), and the withholding of information or documents which would seriously harm the functioning of or be prejudicial to the SCE or the participating legal entity or individual, or any subsidiary or establishment thereof (*reg 27*) as apply under the *ICE Regulations* (see above **16.17**).

16.46 Employment protection

Broadly similar provisions apply in relation to rights to reasonable paid time off (*regs 28* to *30*), protection from dismissal (*regs 31* and *32*) and protection from other detriment (*regs 33* and *34*) as apply under the *ICE Regulations* (see above, **16.19**).

16.47 CROSS-BORDER MERGERS

The *Companies (Cross-Border Mergers) Regulations 2007 SI 2007/2974* (the '*Merger Regulations*') came into force on 15 December 2007. They implement *Directive 2005/56/EC* on cross-border mergers between limited liability companies.

The *Merger Regulations* (as amended) contain detailed requirements applicable to cross-border mergers involving at least one company formed and registered in the UK and at least one company formed and registered in another EEA state or involving the formation of a new company which is to be a UK company (*regs 2, 3*). They apply to unregistered companies, as well as registered companies (*reg 5*).

Importantly, for present purposes, they prescribe minimum requirements as to the information to be provided to employees and their representatives prior to any merger, and as to employee participation following such a merger.

The requirements of the *Merger Regulations*, and in particular the provisions under which the UK courts may order meetings of members or creditors, have now been considered by the Courts in a number of cases. Those cases cast little light on employee information and participation requirements and an exhaustive review is thus beyond the scope of this chapter but see, *inter alia*, *Re Oceanrose Investments Ltd* [2008] EWHC 3475 (Ch), [2009] Bus LR 947, *Re Wood DIY Ltd* [2011] EWHC 3089 (Ch), [2012] BCC 67, [2012] BCC 67, *Diamond Resorts (Europe) Ltd, Re* [2012] EWHC 3576 (Ch), [2013] BCC 275, *In the Matter of Itau BBA International Limited* [2012] EWHC 1783 (Ch), [2013] Bus LR 490, *Re House-Clean Ltd* [2013] EWHC 2337 (Ch), [2013] BCC 611, *Re Nomura International plc* [2013] EWHC 2789 (Ch), *Re Sigma Tau Pharmaceutical Limited* [2013] EWHC 3279 (Ch), [2014] BCC 70, *Re Olympus* [2014] EWHC 1350 (Ch), [2014] 2 BCLC 402 and recently eg. Birss J in *In the matter of International Game Technology Plc* [2015] EWHC 717 (Ch), [2015] BCC 866, Morgan J in *Re Livanova Plc* [2015] EWHC 2865 (Ch), and *Re Easynet Global Services Ltd* [2016] EWHC 2681 (Ch).

16.48 A 'cross-border merger' means:

(a)   a merger by absorption, as defined in *reg 2(2)*;

(b)   a merger by absorption of a wholly-owned subsidiary, as defined in *reg 2(3)*; or

(c)   a merger by formation of a new company, as defined in *reg 2(4)*.

16.49

In the most part, the employee participation requirements contained in the *Merger Regulations* apply only when the *transferee company* is a UK company (as defined in *reg 3*). The entirety of *Part 4* ('employee participation') applies where the transferee company is a UK company and where:

(a)   in the six months before the publication of draft terms of merger, a merging company has over 500 employees on average, and has a system of employee participation (specific provision is made in *reg 22(1A)* as to the treatment of agency workers); or

(b)   a UK merging company has a proportion of employee representatives amongst its directors; or

(c)   a merging company has employee representatives amongst members of the administrative or supervisory organ or their committees or of the management group which covers the profit units of the company: *reg 22(1)*.

However, chapter 4 (election of UK members of the special negotiating board) and chapters 6–9 (confidential information, employee protection, complaints and enforcement) of *Part 4* of the *Merger Regulations* apply to a UK merging company, its employees or their representatives, regardless of whether the transferee company is a UK company (*reg 22(2)*).

The *Merger Regulations* apply in Northern Ireland in modified form (*reg 22(3)*).

16.50 Employee participation is defined for the purposes of the *Merger Regulations* as the influence of the employees and/or employee representatives in the transferee company or a merging company by way of a right to elect or appoint some of the members of the company's supervisory or administrative organ (or recommend or oppose the appointment of some or all such members) (*reg 3(1)*).

An employee, for these purposes, is someone who has entered into or works under a contract of employment and includes, where the employment has ceased, an individual who worked under a contract of employment (*reg 3(1)*). Employee representatives are trade union representatives (if the employer recognises an independent trade union is recognised by their employer for the purpose of collective bargaining in respect of the relevant employees), or other employees who have been elected or appointed to positions in which they are expected to receive particular types of information (*reg 3(1)*). See further the definitions in *reg 3*.

16.51 The pre-merger process

Parts 2 and *3* of the *Merger Regulations* set out requirements in relation to the pre-merger process. In short, the *Merger Regulations* require certain information to be provided to employee representatives or employees of UK merging companies as part of the pre-merger process in cross-border mergers, and require the merging companies to consider any report by employee representatives: see, in particular, *regs 8* and *10*. In addition, the draft terms of merger (which must be certified by a court) must contain information on the procedures by which any employee participation rights are to be determined in accordance with *Part 4* of the *Merger Regulations* (see above **16.49**) (*reg 7(2)(j)*). Each UK company involved in a cross-border merger can apply for a court order certifying that the pre-merger requirements in *regs 7–10* and *12–15* have been complied with (*reg 6* and note also the amended *reg 16*).

16.52 Duty on merging company to provide information

As soon as possible after adopting draft terms of merger under *reg 7*, each merging company must provide certain minimum information to its employee representatives (or, if no such representatives exist, the employees themselves) (*reg 23(1)*). That information must as a minimum, by *reg 23(2)*:

(a)   identify the merging companies;

(b)   notify any decision taken by the merging companies pursuant to *reg 36* (ie a decision to apply statutory standard rules of employee participation); and

(c)   give the number of employees employed by each merging company.

From 1 October 2011 such information must include suitable information in relation to the use of agency workers (*reg 23(3)*).

Each merging company is also subject to a continuing obligation to provide information such as is necessary to keep the 'special negotiating body' (see below **16.53**) informed of the plan and progress of establishing the UK transferee company, up until the date upon which the consequences of the cross-border merger take effect (on which see *reg 17*) (*reg 23(3)*).

An employee representative (or, where no such representative exists, an employee) may complain to the CAC that a merging company has failed to provide information as required by *reg 23*, or that the information is false or incomplete in a material particular (*reg 24(1)*). If the CAC finds the complaint well-founded it must order the company to disclose information (*reg 24(2)*).

16.53 The special negotiating body

Unless the merging companies decide, pursuant to *reg 36*, that the statutory standard rules of employee participation applicable in cross-border mergers set out in *reg 38* are to apply to a UK transferee company, each merging company must make arrangements to establish a 'special negotiating body' ('SNB') (*reg 25(1)*). The task of the SNB will then be to reach an 'employee participation agreement' with the merging companies: *reg 25(2)* and see below **16.54**.

The composition (and election) of an SNB is prescribed by *reg 26*, the requirements in relation to a ballot to elect the UK members of an SNB are set out in *regs 33* and *34* and the representative role of each SNB member is defined by *reg 35*. Employees must be informed of the identity of the members of the SNB as soon as reasonably practicable and in any event within one month of the election (*reg 26(4)*). There is provision for appointing additional members and for changing members in certain circumstances (*reg 26(5)*).

16.53 Employee Participation

Complaints in relation to the establishment of (or failure to establish) an SNB may be presented to the CAC (*reg 27(1)*). Where it is alleged that the failure is attributable to the conduct of the merging company, an application may be presented by a person elected to the SNB or by an employee representative (or, if there is no such representative, an employee) (*reg 27(2)*). Where it is alleged that the failure is attributable to the conduct of the employees or the employee representatives, an application may be presented by the merging company (*reg 27(3)*).

Complaints must be made within one month of the last date on which the merging companies complied or should have complied with the obligation to inform employees of the outcome of elections for membership of the SNB (*reg 27(4)*). Where the CAC finds an application under *reg 27(2)* well-founded it must make a declaration to that effect. If the complaint was made by an SNB representative, employee representative or employee, the merging companies will continue to be under an obligation to comply with their duty under *reg 25* (*reg 27(5)*). If it was made by a merging company, the companies no longer continue to be under that obligation (*reg 27(6)*).

16.54 Negotiated employee participation agreement

The merging companies and the SNB are to negotiate in a spirit of cooperation with a view to reaching an employee participation agreement (*reg 28(2)*).

There are no specific requirements as to the substance of the agreement to be reached. However, to be valid, the employee participation agreement must be in writing and must specify the agreement reached on certain key points:

(a)   the scope of the agreement;

(b)   the substance of any arrangements for employee participation (if, during negotiations, the parties decide to establish such arrangements), including (if applicable) the number of directors of the UK transferee company which the employees will be entitled to elect, appoint, recommend or oppose, the procedures as to how these directors may be elected, appointed, recommended or opposed by the employees, and their rights; and

(c)   the date on which the agreement enters into force, its duration and the circumstances of (and procedure for) any re-negotiation.

(*Reg 29(1)–(2)*.)

From 1 October 2011, where under the employee participation agreement the transferee company is to provide information on the employment situation in that company, such information must include suitable information relating to the use of agency workers (if any) in that company (*reg 29(2A)*).

The employee participation agreement will only be subject to the statutory standard rules of employee participation set out in *reg 38* if it contains a provision to that effect (*reg 29(3)*).

There is an initial six-month time limit within which they are to reach agreement (beginning one month after the last date on which SNB members were elected or appointed), but with provision for extension for up to 12 months from the date from which the original six-month time limit ran by agreement between the parties (*reg 28(3)*).

There are specific rules as to how decisions must be taken by the SNB, and what level of majority is required for each sort of decision (an absolute majority generally, but two thirds in certain circumstances where a decision would result in a reduction of participation rights) (*reg 30(1)–(4)*). The SNB may decide not to open negotiations to reach an employee participation agreement or to terminate negotiations already opened (in which case the duty of the parties to negotiate will cease) (*reg 31*). Such a decision must be taken by a 'particular prescribed' form of two thirds majority (*reg 31(1)*).

The details of any decision taken by the SNB must be published in such a manner as to bring the decision, so far as reasonably practicable, to the attention of the represented employees, as soon as reasonably practicable and within 14 days after the decision has been taken (*reg 30(5)*).

For the purpose of negotiations, the SNB may be assisted by experts of its choice (*reg 30(6)*). The merging companies must pay for any reasonable expenses of the SNB, though the company is not required to pay for the expenses of more than one expert (*reg 30(7)*).

Complaints in relation to decisions of the SNB may be presented to the CAC by a member of the SNB, an employee representative, or where there is no such representative in respect of an employee, that employee (*reg 32(1)*). Complaints may only be presented on the grounds that: (*a*) the decision was not taken by the requisite majority, or (*b*) that the SNB failed to publish a decision as required by the *Merger Regulations* (*reg 32(1)*). The time limit for presentation of complaints is 21 days from the date the SNB did or should have published their decision (*reg 32(2)*). Where the CAC finds the complaint well-founded it must make a declaration that the decision was not taken properly and that it is to have no effect (*reg 32(3)*).

16.55 Standard rules of employee participation in a UK transferee company

The *Merger Regulations* contain 'standard rules' on employee participation, in *reg 38*.

The merging companies may opt for these rules to apply to a UK transferee company from the date upon which the consequences of the cross-border merger take effect (on which see *reg 17*), without negotiating with the SNB, the employee representatives or the employees (*reg 36*).

In addition, these 'standard rules' apply to a UK transferee company where:

(a)   the parties agree that they should; or

(b)   the period specified in *reg 28(3)* has expired without the parties reaching an employee participation agreement and:

    (i)   the merging companies agree that they should; and

    (ii)   the SNB has not taken any decision either not to open or to terminate the negotiations under *reg 31* (*reg 37(1)*);

and provided that:

(c)   before registration of the UK transferee company, one or more forms of employee participation existed in at least one of the merging companies and either:

    (i)   that participation applied to at least one third of the total number of employees of the merging companies, or

    (ii)   that participation applied to less than one third of the total number of employees of the merging companies but the SNB has decided that the standard rules of employee participation should apply (*reg 37(2)*).

(*Reg 37*).

16.55 Employee Participation

From 1 October 2011, for these purposes, agency workers whose contract within *reg 3(1)(b)* of the *Agency Workers Regulations 2010* was not a contract of employment with one or more temporary work agencies that were merging companies at the relevant time, are to be treated as having been employed by such an agency or agencies for the duration of their assignment with a hirer (*reg 37(2A)*).

Where the standard rules of employee participation apply and more than one form of employee participation existed in the merging companies, ordinarily the SNB shall decide (and inform the merging companies) which of those forms shall apply in the UK transferee company (*reg 37(3)*). However, if the SNB fails to make such a decision, the merging companies become responsible for determining the form of employee participation in the UK transferee company (*reg 37(4)*). In addition, the merging companies will also be so responsible where one or more forms of employee participation existed within them but they chose, without any prior negotiation, to be directly subject to the standard rules (*reg 37(4)*).

The standard rules of employee participation are set out in *reg 38*. They include that:

(a)   the employee representatives of the UK transferee company (or if there are no such representatives, the employees) have the right to elect, appoint, recommend or oppose the appointment of a number of directors of the transferee company, such number to be equal to the number in the merging company which had the highest proportion of directors (or their EEA equivalent) so elected or appointed (subject to *reg 39*, see below);

(b)   subject to (*c*) below, the employee representatives (or if there are no such representatives, the employees) shall decide, taking into account the proportion of employees of the transferee company formerly employed in each merging company, on the allocation of directorships, or on the means by which the transferee's employees may recommend or oppose the appointment of directors;

(c)   in making the decision in (*b*) above, if the employees of one or more merging companies are not covered by the proportional criterion set out in (*b*), the employee representatives (or if there are no such representatives, the employees) shall appoint a member from one of those merging companies including one from the UK, if appropriate; and

(d)   every director of the transferee company who was elected, appointed or recommended by the employee representatives or employees is a full director with the same rights and obligations (including the right to vote) as the directors representing shareholders.

From 1 October 2011, where under the standard rules of employee participation the transferee company is to provide information on the employment situation in that company, it must include suitable information relating to the use of agency workers (if any) in that company (*reg 38(5)*).

Note that where the 'standard rules' apply following prior negotiation, the UK transferee company may choose to limit the proportion of directors elected, appointed, recommended or opposed through employee participation to a level which is the lesser of the highest proportion in force in the merging companies prior to registration, or one third of the directors (*reg 39*).

Specific protective provision is made in relation to subsequent domestic mergers (*reg 40*).

16.56 Disputes and complaints

Disputes about whether the transferee company has failed to comply with the terms of an employee participation agreement or the standard rules on employee participation may be referred to the CAC by an SNB, or (where no SNB has been elected or appointed, or an

SNB has been dissolved) an employee representative or employee (*reg 53(1)–(3)*). There is a three-month time limit, running from the date of the alleged failure to comply with the agreed procedure (*reg 53(2)*). If the CAC finds a complaint well-founded it must make a declaration to that effect and may make an order requiring the transferee company to remedy the default (*reg 53(4)–(5)*).

In addition, if an employee representative (or where there is no such representative in relation to an employee, an employee) believes that a transferee or merging company is misusing or intending to misuse the transferee company or the powers in the *Merger Regulations* for the purpose of depriving the employees of that merging or transferee company of their rights to employee participation or withholding such rights, he may complain to the CAC (*reg 54(1)*). Such complaint must be made within 12 months from the date upon which the consequences of the merger take effect (on which, see *reg 17*) (*reg 54(2)*). The CAC must uphold the complaint unless the respondent proves that it did not misuse or intend to so misuse the transferee company or the powers in the *Merger Regulations* (*reg 54(3)*). If the CAC finds the complaint to be well-founded it must make a declaration to that effect and may make an order requiring the transferee company or merging company to take specified remedial action (*reg 54(4)*).

In the event of the CAC making either such declaration, the applicant has three months in which to apply to the Employment Appeal Tribunal for a penalty notice against the relevant company (*regs 53(6) and 54(5)*). The EAT must issue a penalty notice unless satisfied that the failure resulted from a reason beyond the relevant company's control or that it has some other reasonable excuse for its failure (*regs 53(7) and 54(6)*). When setting the amount of the penalty, up to a maximum of £75,000, the EAT must take into account: the gravity of the failure; the period of time over which it occurred; the reason for the failure; the number of employees affected by the failure; and the number of employees employed by the undertaking (*reg 55*).

Note that no order of the CAC under *regs 53* or *54* can suspend or alter the effect of any act done or of any agreement made by the transferee company or merging company (*regs 53(9) and 54(7)*).

16.57 Confidential information

Similar provisions apply in relation to confidential information (*reg 41*), and the withholding of information or documents which would seriously harm the functioning of or be prejudicial to a transferring or merging entity (*reg 42*) as apply under the *TICE Regulations* (see above **16.26**).

16.58 Employment protection

The *Merger Regulations* also contain rights to reasonable paid time off for SNB members, directors of transferee companies or candidates as such (*regs 43 to 45*), protection from dismissal (*regs 46 and 47*) and protection from other detriment (*regs 49 to 51*).

16.59 OTHER NOTABLE CONSULTATION RIGHTS

Whilst the focus of this chapter is the specific legislative regimes described above, advisers will note that these are not the only provisions requiring particular information to be provided to employees or requiring consultation on particular issues, as a result both of domestic legislation and developments in EU law.

16.59 Employee Participation

For example:

(a)   Employers must consult with trade union representatives in certain cases where a large number of redundancies are planned (see eg. *section 188* of the *TULR(C)A* and REDUNDANCY – **II (39)**) and in relation to transfers of businesses (see eg the *Transfer of Undertakings (Protection of Employment) Regulations 2006 (SI 2006/246)*, *reg 13* and **52.18** TRANSFER OF UNDERTAKINGS).

(b)   Employers must consult over certain health and safety issues (see eg the *Safety Representatives and Safety Committees Regulations 1977 (SI 1977/500)*, the *Health and Safety (Consultation with Employees) Regulations 1996 (SI 1996/1513)* and see HEALTH AND SAFETY AT WORK – **II (28)**).

(c)   Where a trade union is statutorily recognised for collective bargaining purposes (see TRADE UNIONS – **I (50)**) an employer must consult the union regularly in relation to employee training, and to provide certain information to the union for such purposes (*TULR(C)A 1992, s 70B*).

(d)   Employers must disclose certain information to employees and their representatives in relation to collective bargaining and occupational pension schemes: see DISCLOSURE OF INFORMATION **(10)**.

(e)   By the *Large and Medium-sized Companies and Groups (Accounts and Reports) Regulations 2008 (SI 2008/410)* ('the *Reports Regulations*'), *reg 10* and *Sch 7, para 11* (together with the *CA 2006, ss 415* and *416*), the annual directors' report for medium and large-sized companies must contain a statement describing the action that has been taken by the company during that financial year to introduce, maintain or develop arrangements aimed at:

(i)   providing employees systematically with information on matters of concern to them as employees;

(ii)   regular consultation with employees or their representatives so that employee views can be taken into account in making decisions which are likely to affect their interests;

(iii)   encouraging the involvement of employees in the company's performance through an employees' share scheme or by some other means; and

(iv)   achieving a common awareness on the part of all employees of the financial and economic factors affecting the performance of the company.

17   Employee's Past Criminal Convictions

17.1   SPENT CONVICTIONS

The *Rehabilitation of Offenders Act 1974* ('*ROA 1974*') provides that, after a period of time, people who have been convicted of criminal offences and who have served their sentences are, with some exceptions (see **17.4** below), not obliged to disclose those convictions. The length of time which must elapse before a person's conviction becomes 'spent' in this way depends upon the nature of the sentence imposed and runs from the date of sentence. Certain sentences, such as imprisonment or custody for life, sentences of imprisonment, youth custody or detention in a young offender institution, or corrective training for a term exceeding 30 months, and detention during Her Majesty's pleasure, can never become spent (*ROA 1974, s 5(1)*; as amended by *Criminal Justice Act 1982, ss 77, 78, Sch 14 para 36, Sch 16*). An offender whose conviction has become spent is known as a 'rehabilitated person' (*ROA 1974, s 1(1)*).

17.2   Non-disclosure of spent convictions

Subject to certain exceptions, a rehabilitated person is to be treated for all purposes in law as a person who has not committed or been charged with or convicted of the offence in question.

Evidence of such matters may not be adduced in judicial proceedings and questions should not be asked in such proceedings which cannot be answered without revealing such matters; if asked, they need not be answered (*ROA 1974, s 4(1)*). This also applies to employment tribunal proceedings (*ROA 1974, s 4(6)*).

This all appears clear, however *A v B* (UKEAT/0025/13) reveals a possible further exception to this principle, namely a general exception contained in *s 7(3)* of the *ROA 1974* which appears to have been applied for the first time in the employment context in *A v B*. *Section 7(3)* provides that a judicial authority may admit or require evidence as to a person's spent convictions or circumstances ancillary thereto notwithstanding the provision of *s 4(1)* and may disregard those provisions if it is satisfied that "in the light of considerations which appear to it to be relevant ... that justice cannot be done in the case except by admitting or requiring evidence" on the spent convictions. *A v B* was a race discrimination case in which the employer had dismissed the employee. The employer contended the reason for dismissal was inappropriate comments to female members of staff and denied race discrimination. The employer wished to rely upon spent convictions of the claimant for kerb-crawling in defence of the claim. The tribunal held that the conviction was admissible by reason of the general exception in *ROA 1974, s 7(3)*. The tribunal's decision was upheld by the EAT. The EAT held that the first question is one of relevance of the conviction to the proceedings in question. Further the admission of the spent conviction must be the only way of doing justice. The tribunal must consider unfair prejudice to the convicted person but *s 7(3)* does not confer a discretion on the court. If justice can only be done by admitting the spent conviction then it must be admitted. *Art 8 of the ECHR* (right to privacy) did not add anything to the exercise. In the circumstances the tribunal's decision to admit the conviction was upheld. It remains to be seen if this becomes a significant or frequently used exception to the general prohibition contained in *ROA 1974, s 4(1)* in employment claims.

Further, outside of the particular case of judicial proceedings, if questions about past convictions and related matters are put in other circumstances (such as at a job interview or on an application form), they may be answered on the basis that they do not refer to spent convictions, and the person questioned shall not be subjected to any liability or otherwise prejudiced in law by failing to acknowledge or disclose his spent convictions (*ROA 1974, s 4(2)*). Any obligation imposed on a person, by a rule of law or an agreement or arrangement (which would include a contract of employment), to disclose any matters does not require the disclosure of spent convictions or ancillary matters (*ROA 1974, s 4(3)(a)*).

A person who reveals another's spent criminal convictions may raise the defence of justification (ie truth) in any subsequent action for libel or slander, provided that the revelation was not made with malice (*ROA 1974, s 8(3), (5)*).

17.3 Spent convictions and dismissal

A spent conviction or a failure to disclose such a conviction are not proper grounds for dismissing or excluding a person from any office, profession, occupation or employment or for prejudicing him in any way in any occupation or employment (*ROA 1974, s 4(3)(b)*). Thus, an employer may not dismiss an employee merely because he discovers that the employee has a conviction which has become spent. In *Hendry v Scottish Liberal Club* [1977] IRLR 5, a Scottish employment tribunal held that a spent conviction for possession of cannabis had to some extent influenced the club's decision to dismiss the employee. Therefore, the reason for the dismissal could not fall within the range of permitted reasons and the dismissal was unfair (see **54.2 UNFAIR DISMISSAL – II**). A security officer is not an occupation excluded from the benefit of the *ROA 1974* (see **17.4** below) and, consequently, an employer who dismissed two security officers for failing to disclose a spent conviction was held to have dismissed them unfairly (*Property Guards Ltd v Taylor and Kershaw* [1982] IRLR 175).

Furthermore, the fact that a person has a spent conviction is not a proper ground for an employer to refuse to engage that person, unless the person falls within a category to which the *Exceptions Order* applies (see below) (*ROA 1974, s 4(3)(b)*). However, it is not clear what remedy there would be for such a refusal: possibly it would be an action for breach of statutory duty.

17.4 EXCEPTIONS

The *Rehabilitation of Offenders Act 1974 (Exceptions) Order 1975 (SI 1975/1023)* (as variously amended) provides that people following certain occupations and professions are obliged (despite the provisions of *ROA 1974, s 4(2)*) to disclose any spent convictions and may be dismissed or excluded from employment because of such a conviction (despite the provisions of *ROA 1974, s 4(3)*). Those professions and occupations include: doctors, nurses, midwives, dentists, barristers, solicitors, accountants, teachers, police officers and (by virtue of *SI 1986/2268*, which amends the *(Exceptions) Order 1975*) directors or other officers of building societies. The *Rehabilitation of Offenders Act 1974 (Exceptions) (Amendment) Order 1986 (SI 1986/1249)* also amends the *(Exceptions) Order 1975* by substituting, for a number of specific excepted occupational groups, a general exception covering any office or employment which is concerned with the provision of accommodation, care, leisure and recreational facilities, schooling, social services, supervision or training to persons under 18 years, where the holder of the office or employment would have access to such minors in the normal course of his duties or if the duties are carried out wholly or partly on the premises where such provision takes place. Further amendments to the *(Exceptions) Order 1975* are made by the *Osteopaths Act 1993, s 39(2), (4)*, by the *Chiropractors Act 1994, s 40(2), (4)*, and by the *Insurance Companies (Third Insurance Directives) Regulations 1994 (SI 1994/1696)*. The application of the *(Exceptions) Order 1975* to work 'in connection with the provision of social services' was considered by the EAT in *Wood v Coverage Care Ltd* [1996] IRLR 264.

By virtue of the *1975 Order*, as amended, an applicant for, or candidate for admission to, any profession or occupation specified in the *Order*, or which falls within the general exception referred to above, is not statutorily excused from the obligation to disclose spent convictions where a question is asked in order to assess his suitability for any profession, occupation, office or employment in the circumstances described, if the question relates to the applicant for such a post or (where applicable) if it relates to a person who lives in the same household as the applicant, and the provision of the services mentioned would normally take place in that household.

The *Rehabilitation of Offenders Act 1974 (Exceptions) Order 1975* was further amended by the *Rehabilitation of Offenders Act 1974 (Exceptions) (Amendment) Order 2002 (SI 2002/441)*, which came into force on 29 February 2002. The professions to which the rehabilitative provisions of the *ROA 1974* do not apply are extended to include chartered psychologists, actuaries, registered foreign lawyers, legal executives and receivers appointed by the Court of Protection. Further employments subject to exemption from some of the provisions of the *ROA 1974* will now include the Crown Prosecution Service, Customs and Excise, the National Crime Squad, the National Criminal Intelligence Service, those working with vulnerable adults and certain employments in the RSPCA. Further exceptions relate to National Lottery Commission personnel, air traffic workers, and to the licensing of taxi drivers and National Lottery licences. Most recently, by the *Rehabilitation of Offenders Act 1974 (Exceptions) (Amendment) (England and Wales) Order 2008 (SI 2008/3259)*, which came into force on 18 December 2008, the *Exceptions Order* extends the definition of a conviction to include a caution and makes further extensions and modifications to the category of persons to whom the exemption provisions apply. Thus in relation to the broad categories of persons to whom the exceptions to the Act apply, cautions as well as convictions will not become spent and will always be disclosable.

A further exception to the *Act* is set out in the *Financial Services Act 1986, s 189*, which provides that convictions for offences involving fraud or dishonesty, or for offences under legislation relating to companies (including insider dealing), various financial institutions, insolvency, consumer credit and consumer protection, shall not be regarded as spent for the purposes of certain proceedings, questions and actions specified in *FSA 1986, Sch 14*.

With the introduction of major provisions of the *Safeguarding of Vulnerable Groups Act 2006* (see further **17.8** below) the *Rehabilitation of Offenders Act 1974 (Exceptions) Order* has been further amended to confer the right to ask questions regarding spent convictions and spent cautions where a person seeks to work in controlled activity with children or vulnerable adults within the meaning of the *Safeguarding of Vulnerable Groups Act 2006*. The right is, however, limited to circumstances where the person seeking such work is barred from regulated activity relating to children or vulnerable adults. See the *Rehabilitation of Offenders Act 1974 (Exceptions) (Amendment) (England and Wales) Order 2008 (SI 2010/1153)* which came into force on 31 March 2010.

17.5   EFFECT OF PROVISIONS FOR REHABILITATION

If, for example, at an interview, an applicant is asked whether he has any criminal convictions, a negative answer may mean:

(i)   that he has no previous convictions;

(ii)   that he has convictions but they are spent; or

(iii)   that he has convictions which are not spent and he is not telling the truth.

If the employer subsequently discovers, after engaging the applicant, that he has previous convictions:

(a)   if these are not spent, he may consider the applicant for dismissal if such a dismissal would be fair in all the circumstances (see **54.4** UNFAIR DISMISSAL – **II**); or

17.5 Employee's Past Criminal Convictions

(b)   if these are spent, he may not take any action, unless there are other reasons which justify him in doing so.

If the applicant reveals at an interview that he has previous convictions:

(A)   if the convictions are spent, they do not form a good reason for refusing the applicant the job; or

(B)   if they are not spent, they may form good grounds for refusing the applicant the job (and there will be no legal redress if the applicant is refused the job on such grounds).

Any agreement or arrangement that an applicant must reveal past convictions is ineffective so far as spent convictions are concerned (see **17.2** above).

Applicants for any position in a profession or occupation excluded from the protection of the *Act* (see **17.4** above) must answer questions relating to previous convictions and may be refused or dismissed from such employment for a conviction or for failing to disclose such a conviction.

17.6 REHABILITATION PERIODS

The period of rehabilitation is related to the length of the sentence which was passed on the offender. The main rehabilitation periods presently applicable are set out below. These periods have been the subject of recent amendment by *s 139* of the *Legal Aid, Sentencing and Punishment of Offenders Act 2012* and came into force on 10 March 2014. The provisions of *s 5(2)* to *5(11)* of the *ROA 1974* have been replaced with new subsections *(2)* to *(8)*. By *ROA 1974, s 5(1)* certain sentences are excluded from rehabilitation under the *ROA 1974*. These are:

(a)   a sentence of imprisonment for life;

(b)   a sentence of imprisonment, youth custody detention in a young offender institution or corrective training for a term exceeding forty eight months;

(c)   a sentence of preventive detention;

(d)   a sentence of detention during Her Majesty's pleasure or for life under *section 90* or *91* of the *Powers of Criminal Courts (Sentencing) Act 2000* or under *section 209* or *218* of the *Armed Forces Act 2006* or under *section 205(2)* or *(3)* of the *Criminal Procedure (Scotland) Act 1975*, or a sentence of detention for a term exceeding forty eight months passed under *section 91* of the said *Act* of *2000* or *section 209* of the said *Act* of *2006* (young offenders convicted of grave crimes) or under *section 206* of the said *Act* of *1975* (detention of children convicted on indictment);

(e)   a sentence of custody for life;

(f)   a sentence of imprisonment for public protection under *section 225* of the *Criminal Justice Act 2003*, a sentence of detention for public protection under *section 226* of that *Act* or an extended sentence under *section 226A, 226B, 227* or *228* of that *Act* (including any sentence within this paragraph passed as a result of any of *sections 219* to *222* of the *Armed Forces Act 2006*) (*ROA 1974, s 5(1)*).

The rehabilitation periods for non excluded sentences are set out in the table below (see further *ROA 1974, s 5(2)*). It is to be observed that very different rehabilitation periods apply depending upon whether the convicted person was over or under the age of 18 at the date of the relevant conviction:

Sentence	End of rehabilitation period for adult offenders	End of rehabilitation period for offenders under 18 at date of conviction
A custodial sentence of more than 30 months and up to, or consisting of, 48 months	The end of the period of 7 years beginning with the day on which the sentence (including any licence period) is completed	The end of the period of 42 months beginning with the day on which the sentence (including any licence period) is completed
A custodial sentence of more than 6 months and up to, or consisting of, 30 months	The end of the period of 48 months beginning with the day on which the sentence (including any licence period) is completed	The end of the period of 24 months beginning with the day on which the sentence (including any licence period) is completed
A custodial sentence of 6 months or less	The end of the period of 24 months beginning with the day on which the sentence (including any licence period) is completed	The end of the period of 18 months beginning with the day on which the sentence (including any licence period) is completed
Removal from Her Majesty's service	The end of the period of 12 months beginning with the date of the conviction in respect of which the sentence is imposed	The end of the period of 6 months beginning with the date of the conviction in respect of which the sentence is imposed
A sentence of service detention	The end of the period of 12 months beginning with the day on which the sentence is completed	The end of the period of 6 months beginning with the day on which the sentence is completed
A fine	The end of the period of 12 months beginning with the date of the conviction in respect of which the sentence is imposed	The end of the period of 6 months beginning with the date of the conviction in respect of which the sentence is imposed
A compensation order	The date on which the payment is made in full	The date on which the payment is made in full
A community or youth rehabilitation order	The end of the period of 12 months beginning with the day provided for by or under the order as the last day on which the order is to have effect	The end of the period of 6 months beginning with the day provided for by or under the order as the last day on which the order is to have effect
A relevant order	The day provided for by or under the order as the last day on which the order is to have effect	The day provided for by or under the order as the last day on which the order is to have effect

(*ROA 1974, s 5* as amended by, in particular, the *Legal Aid, Sentencing and Punishment of Offenders Act 2012, s 139* with effect from 10 March 2014).

See also on disclosure of old convictions and compatibility with *art 8* of the *ECHR T (and others) v Chief Constable of Greater Manchester and others* [2013] EWCA Civ 25, considered at the end of **17.7** below.

17.7 REFORM OF ACCESS TO PAST CRIMINAL CONVICTIONS: PART V OF THE POLICE ACT 1997

Part V of the *Police Act 1997* (*'PA 1997'*), which received Royal Assent on 27 March 1997, contains a number of provisions for access to the records of employees' past convictions. The *Act* provides for the issue of a number of certificates which may be sought by the employee or provided to an employer in order to satisfy a prospective employer of the accuracy of the employee's disclosure of criminal convictions (*PA 1997, ss 112–127*). See also the *Police Act 1997 (Criminal Records) Regulations 2002 (SI 2002/233)*.

An applicant may apply, upon payment of a fee, for a 'criminal conviction certificate' ('CCC') which records all convictions of the applicant (as defined in the *Rehabilitation of Offenders Act 1974* but excluding spent convictions) or states that there are no such convictions, as the case may be (*PA 1997, s 112*).

An application may be made for a 'criminal record certificate' ('CRC') in cases where *s 4(2)(a)* or *(b)* of the *Rehabilitation of Offenders Act 1974* have been excluded by order of the Secretary of State. The application must be countersigned by a 'registered person' within the meaning of the *Act* (*PA 1997, s 120*) who confirms that the information is sought in relation to a matter which is exempt from the provisions of the *Rehabilitation of Offenders Act 1974* (*PA 1997, s 113(2)*). The CRC is broader than the CCC in that it includes details of *all* convictions (including spent convictions) and also details of all cautions administered, or confirms the absence of any convictions or cautions, as the case may be (*PA 1997, s 113A*). Similarly, in the case of application for Crown employment, a CRC may be issued in cases of exempted questions concerning an applicant's suitability for Crown appointment (*PA 1997, s 114*).

An 'enhanced criminal record certificate' ('ECRC') may be obtained in relation to applications for certain sensitive employments (*PA 1997, s 115*). The application must be countersigned by a registered person who confirms that the certificate is sought in relation to considering the applicant's suitability for employment in a number of positions such as working with children or vulnerable adults (*PA 1997, s 113B*).

The ECRC (as in the case of the CRC) gives details of all convictions and cautions (or their absence) but, in addition, the Secretary of State will request the Chief Officer of every relevant police force to provide any information which the Chief Officer considers relevant to the issue of the applicant's suitability for such a position; this information will be included in the certificate (*PA 1997, s 113B(4)*). The application, meaning and effect of *s 115(7)* (the predecessor provision relating to relevant information prior to the enactment in materially identical terms of *s 113B(4)*) has been considered authoritatively in *R (X) v Chief Constable of the West Midlands Police* [2004] EWCA Civ 1068, [2005] 1 All ER 610, [2005] 1 WLR 65. It was held that the Chief Constable was under a duty to disclose if the information might be relevant, unless there was some good reason for not making such a disclosure, and that he was not required to afford the subject of the information a right to make representations. Further *s 115* (now *s 113(B)(4)*) has been held to engage *Art 8* of the *European Convention for the Protection of Human Rights and Fundamental Freedoms* but has been held to be compliant with that *Article* (see *R(X) v Chief Constable of the West Midlands Police* (above). See also *R (L) v Metropolitan Police Comr* [2006] EWHC 482 (Admin), [2006] All ER (D) 262 (Mar), *R v Local Authority and Police Authority in the Midlands, ex p LM* [2000] 1 FLR 612), *R (on the application of Pinnington) v Chief Constable of Thames Valley Police* [2008] EWHC 1870 (Admin), [2008] All ER (D) 405 (Jul).

The discretion afforded by *s 113B* is broad and extends to any information which may, in the opinion of the Chief Officer, be relevant. It has been explained judicially that 'any' means just what it says and is not limited in its scope to information relating to criminal conduct: see *R (L) v Metropolitan Police Comr* [2006] EWHC 482 (Admin) [2006] All ER (D) 262 (Mar). By *s 116*, the issuing of ECRCs are extended to Crown employment.

In *Desmond v Chief Constable of Nottinghamshire Police* [2011] EWCA Civ 3 the Court of Appeal held that the police are not obliged in tort to take reasonable care when providing information under the *PA 1997* about a job applicant for the purposes of the ERRC certificate. The Court of Appeal held that statute does not confer a common law cause of action for breach of statutory duty in the information provided by the police or by refraining from providing information. The Court observed that the procedure's purpose of protecting vulnerable young people would be jeopardised if the police owed a tortious duty of care towards the person the subject of the check. The Court further observed that an aggrieved individual was not without alternative avenues of redress including the statutory remedy of correcting an inaccurate certificate contained in *s 117* of the *PA 1997*, a judicial review application and/or a claim under the *Human Rights Act 1998* for breach of *art 8*, breach of the *Data Protection Act 1998* or claims for misfeasance in public office and/or maladministration. The *Protection of Freedoms Act 2012* introduced a new *s 117A* to the *PA 1997* which provides for an independent monitor to whom application may be made to determine if information is not relevant or ought not to be included in a certificate.

In the case of each certificate outlined above, the Secretary of State may refuse to issue a certificate unless satisfied of the applicant's identity, which may involve the provision of fingerprints to confirm identity (*PA 1997, s 118*). If the applicant believes that any of the information contained in any certificate is inaccurate, he may apply in writing to the Secretary of State for a new certificate (*PA 1997, s 117*). On the utilisation of *s 117* see *R(B) v Secretary of State for Home Department and Metropolitan Police Comr* [2006] EWHC 579 (Admin), [2006] All ER (D) 370 (Mar). It is an offence to falsify or alter certificates or use certificates belonging to another (*PA 1997, s 123*). It is also an offence for employees of registered bodies or recipients of CRC or ECRC information to disclose the information contained in the certificates otherwise than in the course of their duties (*PA 1997, s 124* and see *s 124A* in relation to offences relating to delegated functions). There is a recently revised code of practice addressing relevant matters titled 'Revised Code of Practice for Disclosure and Barring Service Registered Persons November 2015 issued by the Secretary of State under the Act (*PA 1997, s 122(2)*). The Code is available from https ://www.gov.uk/government/publications/dbs-code-of-practice.

The *Protection of Freedoms Act 2012* made certain minor amendments to the provisions of *Part V* of the *PA 1997* and criminal record certificates are now obtained from the newly created Disclosure and Barring Service ("DBS").

The government announced in March 2013 that new legislation was to be enacted to filter out certain convictions from disclosure on a criminal record certificate. On 29 May 2013, by the *Rehabilitation of Offenders Act 1974 (Exceptions) Order 1975 (Amendment) (England and Wales) Order 2013 (SI 2013/1198)* and *Police Act 1997 (Criminal Record Certificates: Relevant Matters) (Amendment) (England and Wales) Order 2013 (SI 2013/2000)*, filtering rules were introduced to exclude certain convictions from disclosure on a criminal record certificate.

By the *Rehabilitation of Offenders Act 1974 (Exceptions) Order 1975 (Amendment) (England and Wales) Order 2013 (SI 2013/1198)* certain criminal matters are identified as either "protected convictions" or "protected cautions".

A conviction is a "protected conviction" if:

(i)   it does not relate to a 'listed offence', such as violent and sexual offences; and

(ii)   no custodial sentence was imposed; and

(iii)   the individual has no other convictions (where the individual has more than one conviction, all convictions will be included on the certificate); and

(iv)   it was received by a person aged under 18 at the time of the conviction and five and a half years or more have elapsed; or

(v)   it was received by a person aged 18 or over at the time of the conviction and 11 years or more have elapsed.

A caution is a "protected caution" if:

(i)   it does not relate to a listed offence; and

(ii)   it was given to a person aged under 18 at the time of the caution and two years or more have elapsed; or

(iii)   it was given to a person aged 18 or over at the time of the caution and six years or more have elapsed.

These "protected" categories are not to be disclosed on a DBS certificate. It should be noted that certain convictions will always be disclosed ("listed offences"). Further it is only if it is the individual's only conviction or caution (as the case maybe) that will attract the protection of being "protected" and accordingly omitted from the DBS record. There are also certain excepted employments from the regime (eg employment which engages national security) where even protected convictions or cautions will be disclosed.

If a conviction or caution is "protected" then, as well as being excluded from the DBS certificate, employers will not be legally entitled to ask questions about such convictions or cautions or rely on them to refuse employment or as grounds for dismissal as to do so would be unlawful under the *ROA 1974*.

These changes were made in response to the Court of Appeal's decision in *R (T and others) v Chief Constable of Greater Manchester and others* [2013] EWCA Civ 25, in which the Court of Appeal held that the disclosure of all cautions and convictions, however old or minor, on a DBS Certificate was incompatible with Article 8 of the Convention for Human Rights. In that case the claimants contended that, in certain respects, the provisions of the *Police Act 1997*, the *Rehabilitation of Offenders Act 1974* and the *Rehabilitation of Offenders Act 1974 (Exceptions) Order* were incompatible with article 8 of the European Convention on Human Rights. The Court of Appeal held that the provisions of the *PA 1997*, requiring disclosure of all convictions, were incompatible with art 8 rights as the disclosure of all convictions and cautions relating to recordable offences was disproportionate to the legitimate aim of protection of the public.

17.8   THE SAFEGUARDING OF VULNERABLE GROUPS ACT 2006

The *Safeguarding Vulnerable Groups Act 2006* ("the *Act*") received Royal Assent on 8 November 2006 and significant provisions came into force on 12 October 2009. The Act provides that it is an offence to employ a person to work with children or vulnerable adults unless they were registered with the then Independent Safeguarding Authority ("ISA"). A main function of the ISA was the maintaining of two lists of persons barred from carrying out regulated activity in relation to children and, separately, vulnerable adults. From 12 October 2009 it was an offence for a barred individual to seek or undertake regulated activity with children and vulnerable adults and it was an offence for a Regulated Activity Provider (as defined in the *Act*) to knowingly employ a barred person in relation to regulated activity (*Safeguarding Vulnerable Groups Act 2006 (Commencement No 6, Transitional Provisions and Savings) Order 2009 (SI 2009/2611)*). A "Regulated Activity" was any activity which involves contact with children or vulnerable adults, eg fostering and childcare, specified activities involving contact with children or vulnerable adults in specified places or at specified times or overnight and activities involving workers in defined positions of responsibility. A "Controlled Activity" included support work in the health or further education field, support work in adult social care and work for specified organisations which would involve frequent access to sensitive records relating to children and/or vulnerable adults. Other provisions relating to registration under a vetting barring scheme, which were due to commence in July 2010, were not brought into force new legislation in the *Protection of Freedoms Act 2012* creates a new scheme considered outline below.

In *R (Royal College of Nursing) v Secretary of State for the Home Department* [2010] EWH 2761 (Admin), [2011] Fam Law 231, provisions of the *Act* providing for a person to be automatically placed on a barred list in the event of a caution or conviction were held to breach *art 6* of the *ECHR* and were incompatible with the *Human Rights Act* because the provisions did not permit representations to be made prior to being placed on the list. In other respects, in relation to appeal and minimum barring period, the Act was however found to be compliant with the *ECHR* and *HRA*.

17.9 THE PROTECTION OF FREEDOMS ACT 2012

The *Protection of Freedoms Act 2012* ("the *Act*") amends the *Safeguarding Vulnerable Groups Act 2006* and created a new corporate body, the Disclosure and Barring Service ("DBS"). The relevant amending provisions are found in *Part V* of the *Act*.

Sections 64–76 of the *Act* make amendments to the definition of regulated activity and the definition of vulnerable adults under the *Safeguarding Vulnerable Groups Act 2006* (see *ss 64–66*) and abolish the concept of controlled activity and monitoring (*ss 68–69*). Changes are made to the test for barring decisions (*s 67*) and the information required in order to make a barring decision is addressed in s 70. A power of review of barring decisions by the DBS of its own motion is provided for in *s 71* of the *Act*. By *s 72* an affected person may apply for information relating to a barring decision.

Section 73 of the *Act* introduces a new *s 34ZA* into the *Safeguarding Vulnerable Groups Act 2006* which requires a regulated activity provider to check that any relevant person is not barred prior to engaging that person. The duty also extends to suppliers of personnel.

Section 87 of the *Act* creates the DBS and by *s 87* the ISA is dissolved and its functions transferred to the DBS. *Schedule 8* of the *Act* provides further detail in relation to the constitution and operation of the DBS. Information in relation to the DBS may be obtained from its website www.gov.uk/government/organisations/disclosure-and-barring-service.

17.10 RECORDING EMPLOYEES' CRIMINAL CONVICTIONS

The *Data Protection Act 1998* limits the right of an employer to process data on employees' criminal convictions without the express consent of the employee, save for limited purposes specified in the *Act* (*DPA 1998, Sch 3*). (See further **10.12 DISCLOSURE OF INFORMATION**.)

18 Employment Tribunals – I

18.1 HISTORY

Employment tribunals (known until 1998 as 'industrial tribunals') are the principal forum for adjudicating disputes between employees (and prospective or former employees, and in some cases other workers) and employers. The tribunals, which were originally created in 1964 to decide disputes about liability to pay Industrial Training Levy, have over the years been given significant additional jurisdiction, increasingly so in recent years. Their future is now subject to the review carried out by Lord Justice Briggs into the structure of the Civil Courts, discussed further at 18.3 below.

The workload of the employment tribunals has, unsurprisingly, fluctuated over the 50 years of their operation. In more recent years the number of cases rose from a low of 29,304 applications registered in 1988–89, to a high of 236,100 in 2009–10. The figures were affected in particular by significant numbers of multiple claims, mostly for equal pay, which have led to considerable variations in the total number of claims from year to year, and by large numbers of claims for holiday pay by air crew, reissued every three months. The underlying trend in single claims was for a gradual rise in the period prior to 2013, reaching a high point of over 70,000 such claims in 2009–10, but both the total number of claims (218,100) and the number of individuals bringing separate claims fell back in 2010–11 and again in 2011–12 (186,300). There was a slight rise in 2012–13 (191,541).

On 29 July 2013, however, the Government introduced a requirement for claimants to pay an issue fee when presenting their claim to the Employment Tribunal, accompanied by other fees including a claimant's hearing fee. There has been much discussion on the effect this measure on the numbers of claims presented. The reconciled quarterly statistics produced by the Government showed that there were receipts of single claims of 4,969 and multiple claims 5,873 in the period September – December 2013 (amounting to 76% reduction on the same period the year before for all claims combined). For the period January – March 2014, there were 5,619 single claims and 5,348 multiples (amounting to an 81% reduction on the same period in 2013 for all claims combined. For the total period April 2013 - March 2014, circa 105,800 claims were received and approx 61,300 claims were received over the period April 2014 - March 2015. In the period April 2015 – March 2016, however, 83,031 claims were received. Although this is plainly an increase on the previous year, it is still well under the number accepted in 2012/13 (see above).

Statistics of numbers of cases do not give the full picture of the volume and complexity of the tribunals' case load in recent years. The number of individual claims under separate jurisdictions raised in each case has been steadily rising over the years; it now stands at an average of approx. 2.1 per case. The trend to more complex cases and lengthier hearings was reinforced by the extension of the tribunals' jurisdiction to cover discrimination on grounds of religion or belief, sexual orientation and age and claims by agency workers as well as the dramatic increase in the numbers of multiple equal pay claims.

The increase in workload since the 1990s, which was not matched by increases in resources, put a considerable strain on the tribunal system. This led to a number of measures intended to improve efficiency and effectiveness. Various changes to procedures were made by the *Trade Union Reform and Employment Rights Act 1993 ('TURERA 1993')* and new rules of procedure were made the same year; further reforms were enacted by the *Employment Rights (Dispute Resolution) Act 1998 ('ERDRA 1998')*. Since 2000, several further initiatives have been taken.

(a) New Rules of Procedure were introduced as from July 2001 (the *Employment Tribunals (Constitution and Rules of Procedure) Regulations 2001 (SI 2001/1171)* and their Scottish counterpart *(SI 2001/1170)*). Those new rules embodied a number of changes, of which the most significant were:

    (i) The introduction of an Overriding Objective for tribunals, which must be taken into account in interpreting the rules of procedure and in deciding issues affecting the conduct of the proceedings. The Overriding Objective is 'to deal with cases justly', which includes so far as practicable ensuring that the parties are on an equal footing, saving expense, dealing with cases in ways proportionate to their complexity, and ensuring that they are dealt with expeditiously and fairly. The parties are required to assist in the achievement of this objective. The parties are required to assist in the achievement of this objective. See further **19.1** et sec.

    (ii) Tribunals were given powers to order a claim (or defence) to be struck out on the ground that it was 'misconceived', a term defined as including having 'no reasonable prospects of success'.

    (iii) The power to award costs was extended to cases where the bringing or conducting of proceedings was 'misconceived' (defined as above), and the amount that could be awarded on a summary assessment by the tribunal was raised from £500 to £10,000. In addition the deposit that could be ordered at a pre-hearing review was increased to a maximum of £500; previously it had been £150.

These changes were retained and built on in further reforms of the rules in 2004, 2009, 2012 and 2013 (see below). During 2012, a comprehensive review of the rules was undertaken under the chairmanship of Underhill J (as he then was) and new rules contained in the *Employment Tribunals (Constitution and Rules of Procedure) Regulations 2013, SI 2013/1237* ('the *2013 Regulations*' and 'the *2013 Rules*') came into force on 29 July 2013.

(b) Following the recommendations of a Government Task Force which had been appointed to reassess the workings of the employment tribunal system as a whole, which recommended a greater emphasis on the early resolution of disputes, major changes in the procedure for making claims to employment tribunals were introduced by the *Employment Act 2002* and accompanying *Dispute Resolution Regulations*. The details of these procedures, which are now largely of historical interest following the repeal of the relevant provisions of the *2002 Act* by the *Employment Act 2008*, are briefly noted at **18.2** below. At the same time, various changes in tribunal procedure were made by Rules of Procedure which came into force on 1 October 2004 (the *Employment Tribunals (Constitution and Rules of Procedure) Regulations 2004, SI 2004/1861* ('the *2004 Regulations*'; the *Rules* themselves were in *Schedule 1* to the *2004 Regulations* ('the *2004 Rules*')). These rules were replaced on 29 July 2013 by the rules of procedure set out in the *2013 Regulations*.

(c) A major review of the tribunal system generally, under Sir Andrew Leggatt, a former Lord Justice of Appeal (*Tribunals for Users*, TSO August 2000) led to the creation by the *Tribunals, Courts and Enforcement Act 2007*, of a unified tribunal system, with a transfer of responsibility for employment tribunals from the DTI to the Ministry of Justice, but with the employment tribunals retaining their separate identity, and the existing tripartite structure of membership.

The *2007 Act* expressly preserves the separate identity of employment tribunals and the EAT, but not their administrative independence from the rest of the new tribunal system. The Tribunals Service was given the responsibility for the administration of employment tribunals and the Employment Appeal Tribunal, with BIS (as successor to the DTI) retaining responsibility for the Rules of Procedure. Subsequently the Tribunals Service has been merged with HM Courts Service to form HM Courts and Tribunals Service, which came into being on 1 April 2011. In Scotland, a Scottish Tribunals Service does not presently have responsibility for employment tribunals. A consultation in 2012 considered whether the employment tribunals and EAT in Scotland should transfer to that service; ultimately, however, no such proposals were contained in the *Tribunals (Scotland) Bill*, part of the Programme for Government 2012–13. However, more recently, a further consultation has completed and is being considered concerning a draft Order in Council that would make provision to transfer specified functions of the Employment Tribunal to the First-tier Tribunal for Scotland pursuant to the *Scotland Act 2016*: see **18.6** below.

One change of detail made by the *2007 Act* (*Sch 8 para 36*, inserting a new *s 3A* into the *ETA 1996*) was the re-naming of employment tribunal chairmen (as they had been designated since 1964) as Employment Judges; Regional Chairmen became Regional Employment Judges. The change took effect on 1 November 2007.

(d)   There have been a number of other developments aimed at promoting the early resolution of employment disputes. A scheme for voluntary arbitration through ACAS in unfair dismissal cases, foreshadowed by *ERDRA 1998*, came into operation in 2001 for England and Wales and early 2004 in Scotland. It has subsequently been extended to cover disputes about the right to request flexible working arrangements. However, the scheme has had a very limited impact, with fewer than 100 cases referred to it since its inception. See further **19.25** below. Despite the limited impact of the voluntary arbitration service, there has been increasing interest in alternative dispute resolution schemes for employment disputes, and initiatives in this area include the development of mediation services by ACAS (the number of new cases has in general been on the rise, but the numbers are still relatively small; ACAS advertise a success rate of about 80%) and in January 2009 the introduction of a facility for judicial mediation within the employment tribunals themselves. Since 2016, judicial assessment has also been offered by the employment tribunal (see **19.24** below for details of judicial mediation and assessment).

A further initiative introduced by ACAS in 2009, with significant initial success, was a facility for Pre-claim Conciliation, before a claim is presented to an employment tribunal. Nearly 10,000 cases were referred to this scheme in its first year, over 17,000 in the second year, 2010–11, some 23,700 in 2011/2012, reducing slightly to 22,630 in 2012/13 and 21,762 in 2013/14. Of these the number of cases recorded as successfully resolved has revolved around the 50% mark, more precisely 51.9% for 2012/13 and 57.1% for 2013/14. 77% (in 2012) and 82.6% (in 2013) were not followed by tribunal claims (a more generous measure of success). This scheme was discontinued in April 2014 with the introduction of Early Conciliation.

By *section 7* of the *Enterprise and Regulatory Reform Act 2013*, a new requirement for Early Conciliation was introduced in 2014 requiring prospective claimants under certain jurisdictions of the tribunal to provide information to ACAS prior to presenting their claim to the tribunal. This requirement was to remedy the fact that only around one fifth of claimants contacted ACAS for advice before submitting their claims. Provision is made for a certificate of compliance to be issued by an ACAS conciliation officer, and for consequential adjustments to the time limits for presenting the claims (see **19.8** et sec below for details).

18.2 Employment Tribunals – I

18.2 The 2002 Act and its Repeal

The changes affecting the powers and procedure of employment tribunals introduced via the *Employment Act 2002* and the *Employment Act 2002 (Dispute Resolution) Regulations 2004*, with effect from 1 October 2004, were largely reversed by the repeal of the relevant parts of that *Act* by the *Employment Act 2008*, with effect from 6 April 2009 and the consequential lapse of the *Regulations*. Consequently, only a brief summary of the features of the legislation is given below.

(a)   A requirement for claimants to go through workplace grievance procedures where relevant, before a claim can be made to a tribunal, with power to reduce compensation if the claimant does not do so (and increase it if the employer does not provide a procedure, or dismisses or takes disciplinary action without following the applicable statutory procedure) (*2002 Act, s 31*);

(b)   Changes in the time limits for commencing tribunal claims to allow time for internal procedures to be concluded without the necessity to present a claim to preserve the employee's rights; the employee is not permitted to present his or her claim to the tribunal in certain cases until after the employer has been given the opportunity to resolve it under the grievance procedure, and in certain circumstances the time limit for claiming is automatically extended by three months (*ss 32, 33*);

(c)   Provision for a limited conciliation period for ACAS to attempt to secure a settlement; if the case was not settled within that period (or any extension of it), ACAS ceased to be under a duty to offer its assistance in any further attempts at settlement (*s 24*: this provision was repealed, and the implementing provisions in the *ET Rules* were revoked, with immediate effect both for new cases and those already before the tribunals, on 6 April 2009).

The changes introduced by the *2002 Act* proved to be widely disliked, and the approach of the courts to their interpretation has generally been based in the importance of preserving rights of access to justice rather than literal application of the legislation. In March 2007 the DTI instituted a consultation exercise on whether the procedures introduced by the *2002 Act* should be scrapped, as recommended by a Review commissioned by the Department. The consultation exercise confirmed the Government in its view that the procedures should be repealed, and the legislation to repeal the statutory dispute resolution procedures and associated procedural requirements, received the Royal Assent as the *Employment Act 2008* in November 2008.

The relevant provisions of the *2008 Act* were brought into force on 6 April 2009, but subject to significant exceptions, contained in the *Employment Act 2008 (Commencement No 1, Transitional Provisions and Savings) Order 2008, SI 2008/3232*. This *Order* preserves the old law in cases where either of the statutory dismissal and disciplinary procedures applied, if the employer dismissed the employee, or initiated the statutory procedure, on or before 5 April 2009. The old law also applies in cases where either of the statutory grievance procedures applied, if the matter the subject of the claim occurred on or before 5 April 2009, or, if it extended over a period spanning that date, if the employee either presented a claim or submitted a written grievance before 5 July 2009 (or in certain cases 5 October 2009). For those cases where the old law applies, not only was the acceptance of a claim still subject to the preconditions in *s 32* of the *Employment Act 2002* (where applicable) but also the provisions of *s 31* giving tribunals powers to increase or decrease compensation by up to 50% where there has been a failure to comply with the applicable statutory procedure, continue to apply.

Other changes introduced at the same time as the repeal of the *2002 Act* included simplified tribunal claim and response forms. However the procedure for screening claims prior to acceptance for compliance with procedural requirements such as using the prescribed claim form and providing the mandatory information on it, has also been retained, albeit the requirements of the new claim form are less prescriptive. New forms and new procedures for screening claims upon presentation are introduced by the Rules within the *2013 Regulations*.

One feature of the 2002 reforms that has been retained in modified form is the power given to tribunals to increase or decrease compensation in certain circumstances; the tribunal may increase or decrease the sum awarded by up to 25% if satisfied that the employer or employee, as the case may be, has unreasonably failed to comply with a provision of a relevant ACAS Code of Practice (*Trade Union and Labour Relations (Consolidation) Act 1992, s 207A*, inserted by the *Employment Act 2008, s 2*). The relevant ACAS Code is that on disciplinary and grievance procedures, which was reissued in a simplified and shortened form to accompany the legislative changes. One consequence of these provisions is that cases on uplifts to compensation under *s 31* of the *Employment Act 2002* may be relevant to the equivalent provisions introduced by the *2008 Act*. Two such cases are *Wardle v Credit Agricole Corporate and Investment Bank* [2011] IRLR 604 and *Abbey National v Chagger* [2010] ICR 397. The Court of Appeal held that it was incumbent when setting the percentage increase or decrease to have regard to the size of the award; it also considered that the maximum uplift should be reserved for the most exceptional and serious cases; there must be proportionality. Whilst the spirit of the ACAS Code of Practice should be followed even if the case is not strictly one of misconduct (see *Lund v St Edmunds School, Canterbury* (UKEAT/0514/12) – a 'some other substantial reason' dismissal), the EAT has now confirmed that the code itself does not apply (and therefore uplifts are not available) in cases of ill health dismissals (see *Holmes v QinetiQ Ltd* [2016] ICR 1016) or 'some other substantial reason' dismissals (see *Phoenix House Ltd v Stockman* [2017] ICR 84, disagreeing with provisional observations to the contrary in *Hussain v Jurys Inn Group Ltd* [2016] UKEAT/0283/15). Uplifts cannot be made in favour of workers as opposed to employees: see *Local Government Yorkshire and Humber v Shah* (UKEAT/0587/11).

18.3   Developments since 2008

There have been a number of further developments affecting the operation and procedure of employment tribunals since the repeal of the *2002 Act* in 2008.

(a)   In January 2011, the Department for Business, Innovation and Skills (BIS, the successor to the DTI) launched a further round of consultation on proposals to reform the employment tribunal system to remove what the consultation document stated were regarded as unjustifiable burdens the working of the existing system places on business (*Resolving Workplace Disputes*). In addition to a change in substantive employment rights (the extension of the qualifying period of service for unfair dismissal claims to two years, since implemented for employees whose employment commences on or after 6 April 2012) the consultation paper proposed a requirement to submit all claims initially to ACAS, to then be presented to the tribunal only if not successfully conciliated; greater powers for tribunals to dispose of weak claims by striking out, including powers to do so on paper without a hearing; an increase in the maximum deposit that can be required (to £1,000) and the limit on costs orders (to £20,000); abolishing payments of expenses to witnesses; delegating to Legal Officers some of the interlocutory work now undertaken by employment judges; taking written witness statements as read at hearings; extending the provision for cases to be heard by a judge sitting alone to cover unfair dismissal; introducing penalties for employers found liable by a tribunal; and reducing the use of lay members in the EAT.

The outcome of this consultation was announced in November 2011; broadly, this was the Government's intention to proceed with all of the proposals summarised, and some, which can be implemented by secondary legislation, were brought into effect on 6 April 2012 by the *Employment Tribunals (Constitution and Rules of Procedure) (Amendment) Regulations 2012, SI 2012/468*. These changes are the addition of unfair dismissal claims to the categories of cases where an employment judge can sit alone (with a discretion to order a full panel under the *Employment Tribunals Act 1996, s 4(5)*: see the *Employment Tribunals Act 1996 (Tribunal Composition) Order 2012, SI 2012/988*); an increase in the maximum sum that can be ordered as a deposit to £1,000 and the maximum sum that can be awarded for costs to £20,000; ending the payment of travel expenses for witnesses, with a new power for the tribunal to order a party to pay these expenses; and a new rule providing that witness statements, where used, are to be taken as read unless the tribunal directs otherwise (this does not affect the position in Scotland that witness statements are generally not used). Although all these changes came into effect on 6 April 2012, all but the first only apply to cases presented on or after that date (see *Reg 3* of the *2012 Regulations*). These changes have been retained within the *2013 Regulations* and *2013 Rules*.

Most of the other changes required legislation. The *Enterprise and Regulatory Reform Act 2013, Part 2* was enacted on 25 April 2013. The *Act* made provision for conciliation through ACAS prior to instituting proceedings (*s 7, s 8, s 9*); the prohibition on disclosure of information held by ACAS (*s 10*); the extension of decision making to legal officers (*s 11*); changes to the composition of the Employment Appeal Tribunal so that, by default, appeals are heard by a judge sitting alone but with power to direct that lay members sit on the case (*s 12*); no qualifying period of employment for dismissals for political opinions (*s 13*); confidentiality of negotiations before termination of employment (*s 14*); the Secretary of State to have power to order the increase or decrease in the limit of the compensatory award in unfair dismissal cases(*s 15*); the power of the Tribunal to award financial penalties payable to the Secretary of State of between £100 and £5,000 where the Tribunal concludes the employer has breached any of the worker's rights to which the claim relates and there are one or more aggravating features (*s 16*); various changes to the law on protected disclosures (*s 17–21*); and renaming compromise agreements (*s 23*).

(b)   In a separate but parallel development, in December 2011 the Ministry of Justice published consultation proposals for the introduction of fees for employment tribunal claims. Proposals were then based on a Government decision, announced in October 2012, that fees would be introduced, the consultation being limited to the levels of fees, when and how they would be payable, remission for those of limited means, and other issues arising. The Government aimed to save £10 million a year from the cost of the employment tribunals (just over £80 million in 2010–11) by levying fees, but questions were raised by those consulted about whether the level of exemptions and administrative cost of determining disputes about fees will affect this figure.

The consultation on fees closed in March 2012. There was a generally hostile response from professional bodies representing employment practitioners.

On 29 July 2013, the *Employment Tribunals and the Employment Appeal Tribunal Fees Order 2013* came into force. That order provides for the payment of fees for (i) issuing a claim, (ii) the listing of a final hearing (iii) the making of certain specified applications (the applications being: reconsidering a default judgment, reconsidering a judgment after a final hearing, dismissing a claim upon withdrawal, bringing an employer's contract claim), or (iv) by a Respondent upon a listing for judicial mediation.

The level of fees is specified in the order. Issue fees for single claims of either £160 or £250 and hearing fees for single claims of either £230 or £950, in each case dependant on whether the claim is of Type A or B respectively. The lower level of fee will apply to straightforward claims (Type A) such as unauthorised deductions and claims for statutory redundancy payments. Type A claims are listed in Table 2 of *Schedule 2* of the *Order*. The higher level will apply to other claims (called Type B claims). This includes most claims e.g. for unfair dismissal, discrimination, whistleblowing etc. Different level of fee apply for grouped claims (but will not exceed the sum that would have been due had the claims been presented individually). Fees for the specified applications vary from £60 to £350 depending on the application and type of claim. The fee for judicial mediation is set at £600. *Schedule 3* of the *Order* sets out the scheme for granting full and part remission in respect of the fees that would otherwise be payable. See further regarding Fees and Remissions at **19.36** et sec below.

In early 2017, the Government published its review into the introduction of fees in the Employment Tribunal noting that the scheme has "broadly met its objectives". This review recognises that there has been a significant fall in the number of claims made ("significantly greater [fall in claims] than was estimated when fees were first introduced") and that claimants have been discouraged from bringing claims. However, the review states that there is no conclusive evidence that claimants have been *prevented* from commencing claims. A proposal was included in the review for expanding the fee remission scheme by lifting the income threshold and by removing the requirement to pay fees in certain types of cases where the employer is insolvent. A challenge to the fees regime is pending before the Supreme Court.

(c)   An additional announcement made by BIS on the occasion of the publication of the Government's response to the January 2011 consultation was the creation of a small group, chaired by Underhill J (as he then was), the immediate past President of the EAT, to conduct a 'root and branch' review of the *ET Rules*, with a view to the simplification both of the *Rules* and their operation. The group reported in July 2012. A further consultation on those proposed rules was launched in September 2012 and the Government's response to that exercise published in March 2013. As a result of the review, on 28 May 2013, the *Employment Tribunals (Constitution and Rules of Procedure) Regulations 2013, SI 2013 No 1237* ('the *2013 Regulations*') were made. The *2013 Regulations* contain the Rules in *Schedule 1*. The new rules came into force on 29 July 2013 and are covered comprehensively in the next chapter: see CHAPTER 19.

(d)   In July 2016, Lord Justice Briggs published his review into the Civil Courts Structure. The terms of reference for that review included a request to review the boundaries between the Civil Courts and the Tribunals Service. An interim report published in January 2016 specifically highlighted is the question of whether the Employment Tribunal and Employment Appeal Tribunal should be integrated into the structure of the civil courts. Three options were identified: "(a) To leave the ET (and the EAT) where they are, uncomfortably stranded between the civil courts and the main Tribunal Structure. (b) To bring both tribunals broadly under the wing of the structure of the civil courts. (c) To make both tribunals part of the Tribunal Structure, as First Tier and Upper Tribunals respectively." The interim report set out reasons why option (b) appeared to be the most attractive, albeit that this did not mean necessarily that the *Civil Procedure Rules 1998* would apply to employment disputes in place of specific rules, perhaps based on the *2013 Rules*. The final report declined to offer a firm recommendation, and notably there was no recommendation that a new Employment and Equalities Court should be created. Briggs LJ did offer some observations on how the jurisdiction of such a court might be set. He further expressed the view that whilst he was of the view that there was room for a body – such as the EAT – having a first instance jurisdiction in more complex cases (with a route of appeal direct to the Court of Appeal), he again declined to make specific recommendations.

18.3 Employment Tribunals – I

A further potentially significant feature of Lord Justice Briggs' final report was the recommendation for the introduction of an on-line court (separate from the County Court) for the resolution of modest money claims (starting at £10,000 with the aim of lifting the threshold to £25,000) via a different online claims resolution process. The aim is to create a more investigative process, led by IT, which will critically be cheaper and therefore more accessible to ordinary people of more limited means. Costs recovery will be limited and fixed and modelled on the small claims track.

(e)   In September 2016, a joint statement prepared by the Lord Chancellor, Lord Chief Justice and Senior President of Tribunals set out an intention for digitising the entire claims process and delegating routine tasks from judges to case workers. Such changes would – for ETs – require amendments to primary legislation and a consultation was launched in December 2016. The Government's response was published in February 2017 and the intention is to bring forward measures as soon as Parliamentary time allows.

18.4   The 2013 Rules of Procedure

The *2013 Regulations* contain provisions providing for the continued establishment of employment tribunals (*Reg 3*). They go on to provide for the appointment and tenure of office of the Presidents of the Tribunals (one for England and Wales and one for Scotland), the Vice-President (for Scotland only), Regional Employment Judges (in England and Wales only) and Employment Judges and members (see *Regs 5* and *6*. These office holders are required to use the resources available to secure, so far as practicable, the speedy and efficient disposal of proceedings, determine the allocation of proceedings between Tribunals, and to determine when and where Tribunals shall sit. The President is able to make directions to Regional Employment Judges and the Vice President in Scotland (see *Reg 7*).

The *2013 Regulations* also cover the composition of tribunals for particular cases, special rules for cases involving issues of national security, and a number of ancillary provisions which are referred to at relevant points in the text below. *Schedule 1* contains the rules of procedure applicable to most claims, and is referred to as the *Employment Tribunals Rules of Procedure 2013* ('the *2013 Rules*'). The other Schedules now cover the following:

(a)   *Schedule 2:*   Rules for National Security cases;

(b)   *Schedule 3:*   Rules for Equal Value cases;

Although the *2004 Regulations* and *2004 Rules* had made considerable changes in the substance of the procedure to be applied by tribunals, and had been intended to be drafted in simpler language more readily understandable by litigants without legal training, there had nonetheless been judicial criticisms of the quality of drafting. This was a central driver behind the development of the new *2013 Rules* contained within the *2013 Regulations*. The key terminology used by the *2013 Regulations* includes the following:

(i)   Those applying to a tribunal are referred to as 'claimants' (rather than 'applicants' as had been the case prior to 2004); those responding to claims are 'respondents'.

(ii)   The document by which an application is made to the tribunal is called a 'Claim Form' (instead of an 'originating application' which was the term used prior to 2004).

(iii)   The response by a respondent is called a 'Response Form' (rather than the old term, 'notice of appearance').

(iv)   Hearings are either final hearings or preliminary hearings (previous terminology including, directions hearings, interlocutory hearings, Case Management Discussions ('CMDs'), and Pre-hearing Reviews ('PHRs') have been discarded).

18.5

Alongside the changes of terminology are changes of substance. Below is a brief summary of the principal changes of substance effected by the *2013 ET Rules* and related provisions:

(a)   There is a requirement for Early Conciliation via ACAS of certain claims prior to them being presented to an employment tribunal.

(b)   Differently designed Claim Forms (known as Form ET1) and Response Forms (Form ET3) were introduced to accompany the *2013 Rules* (there is a link to these forms at https://www.gov.uk/courts-tribunals/employment-tribunal). Use of the paper or electronic version of the prescribed forms is mandatory when presenting claims. Certain mandatory information is required to be given on the Claim Form. When presenting, a claimant must do so using one of the prescribed methods: online, in person or by post (fax is no longer available). The payment of an issue fee or application for a fee remission is required.

(c)   An initial administrative screening process will apply by which the tribunal secretariat will weed out and reject claims not containing the required minimum information, not enclosing a fee or remission application, or otherwise appearing to be outside the tribunal's jurisdiction. Where substantive defects are detected, the case is referred to a Judge for decision whether to refuse to accept and register the claim. Rejection decisions can be reconsidered by the claimant making an application for reconsideration.

(d)   Response Forms must be received by the tribunal within 28 days following the date that the Claim Form was sent to the respondent. Minimum information must be provided, otherwise the Tribunal can reject the response. A response will also be rejected if it is received late unless an application for an extension has been made or the response is accompanied by such an application. If the employer wishes to bring an employer's contact claim, this must be included within the response and a fee must be paid. If no response is received within the time, a Judge will issue a judgment covering the whole of the claim (if possible) or which part of the claim a judgment can properly cover, and then set a hearing before a judge alone to determine the rest. The respondent remains entitled to notice of hearings but (unless an extension of time for presenting a response is granted) is only entitled to participate in any hearing to the extent permitted by a judge.

(e)   In every case, once the pleadings have closed, an employment judge will consider all the documents held by the Tribunal in order to determine whether the claims and defences are arguable and within the jurisdiction of the Tribunal. If so, case management orders will be made. If not (viz that a claim or defence, or part thereof, does not have reasonable prospects of success), a notice of dismissal will be issued by the Judge, requiring the relevant party to make written representations as to why the claim or defence, or part thereof, should not be dismissed. If no written representations are received by the date specified, the claim or defence or part thereof will stand dismissed. If the written representations do not satisfy the judge, then a hearing will be held to decide whether the claim or defence or part thereof should be allowed to continue. The other party may but need not participate in the hearing.

(f)   Judges are required to consider facilitating ADR throughout the process of a claim.

(g)   There are generally two types of hearing: preliminary hearings and final hearings. Preliminary hearings can be for case management only, or decide substantive points, called "preliminary issues". A preliminary issue is held in private unless a preliminary issue is to be decided, when that part of the hearing must be held in public. Final hearings are held in public. The Tribunal has powers to restrict the public disclosure of any aspects of the proceedings so far as it considers necessary in the interests of justice to protect convention rights, and in other circumstances.

(h)   Decisions of tribunals can be in the form of orders and judgments. A written record of all decisions must be provided to the parties. Reasons must be given for any decision on any disputed issue, whether substantive of procedural, but must be proportionate to the significance of the issue and may be very short (particularly if the decision is other than a judgment). Where a decision is given in writing, the reasons must also be in writing. If reasons are given orally, a request for written reasons must be presented within 14 days of the sending of the written record of the decision.

(i)   The Tribunal has powers to award costs, preparation time orders, and wasted costs. The Scottish term for costs is 'expenses'. The availability of preparation time orders enable a tribunal to make an award in favour of a party who is not legally represented, to cover the costs of his or her time in preparing for the hearing, covering such hours as the tribunal assesses as reasonable at a fixed hourly rate. This was set, initially, at £33 an hour, but with an automatic increase of £1 an hour each year from 6 April 2014, so that the current rate is £37 an hour. Preparation time orders cannot be made if a costs order is also made (or vice versa) and can only be made under the same conditions as a costs order. A wasted costs order, can be made against a representative, provided the representative is acting for profit, and is either an order to pay costs to the other party, or an order disallowing the representative's charges to his or her client in whole or in part. Tribunals may have regard to the means of the paying party in deciding whether, and if so how much, to award by way of costs. The Tribunal can summarily assess costs/preparation time up to £20,000, but can award more than this either by agreement of the parties, or by conducting a detailed assessment of costs, or by referring the case to the County Court for it to undertake a detailed assessment. The Tribunal also has a discretion 'at large' to order the reimbursement of a fee where the party who paid that fee has been wholly or partly successful. Such a reimbursement is a "costs order" and is subject to the other general rules on costs.

(j)   A number of other changes of detail were made, including widening the circumstances in which the Tribunal can make orders to restrict the disclosure to the public of any part of proceedings (including but not limited to restricted reporting orders), and wider powers to conduct hearings by telephone or video link. Changes were made to reconsideration of certain types of orders to remove some of the technical traps that existed in the *2004 Rules*. Further, a generalised power to make a case management order has been introduced, which covers many of the orders which were previously specified in terms in the *2004 Rules*. The generalised nature of the Case Management Powers are supplemented by Presidential Guidance which a Tribunal considering a matter is bound to consider, although is not bound to follow.

(k)   The public register of applications was closed on 1 October 2004. The register of decisions (now a register of judgments) has been retained (*Reg 14*), and judgments and written reasons remain available for public inspection. Since 2016, new judgments and reasons have been made available for inspection on-line at https ://www.gov.uk/employment-tribunal-decisions. It remains to be decided whether older decisions will be made available on-line. Following a ruling by the Information Commissioner under the *Freedom of Information Act 2000* (Case FS

50080369, 2 October 2008; the decision can be accessed at ico.org.uk) information about the identity of respondents to proceedings must now be disclosed to interested parties.

Reg 11 of the *2013 Regulations* confers power on the Presidents to issue Practice Directions regulating the procedure of tribunals and the manner of exercise of the powers conferred on tribunals and Employment Judges by the *2013 Regulations* and *Rules*. The first Practice Directions issued under the forerunner of this provision under the *2004 Regulations*, which apply in Scotland only, were issued in December 2006; they cover lists of documents, sists (the Scots Law term for stays) for mediation and the procedure for counterclaims in contract cases. Other Practice Directions are issued from time to time by both Presidents to give directions for particular categories of cases, such as staying (sisting in Scotland) claims affected by a pending reference to the Court of Justice of the European Union (CJEU), or transferring all cases against a particular respondent to the same tribunal office. More recently, Practice Directions have been issued both in England and Wales to cover the presentation of claims generally.

A facet of procedure, introduced for claims presented on or after 6 April 2010 where a claim has been made under the provisions of the *ERA 1996* introduced by the *Public Interest Disclosure Act 1998*, allows for the claimant's underlying 'whistleblowing' disclosure to be forwarded by the tribunal secretariat to the relevant Regulator for investigation, if the claimant has signified a wish for this to be done. This does not affect the procedure for hearing the claim itself. It now finds expression in Rule *14* of the *2013 Rules*. By *s 148* of the *Small Business, Enterprise and Employment Act 2015*, regulators are to be legally obliged to produce annual reports (and reports to Parliament) detailing the whistleblowing reports they receive.

18.6   ADMINISTRATION

The employment tribunals are constituted under the *Employment Tribunals Act 1996 ('ETA 1996')* (a consolidating Act replacing equivalent earlier legislation) and the *Regulations* and *Rules of Procedure* made under the powers conferred by the *ETA 1996*. The overall responsibility for the running of the employment tribunals in England and Wales is vested in the President of the Employment Tribunals, a judicial officer appointed by the Lord Chancellor (*2013 Regulations, reg 5*). The tribunal system is divided into 12 regions, each with a Regional Employment Judge appointed by the Lord Chancellor (*2013 Regulations, reg 6*). There is a separate President of the Employment Tribunals for Scotland, and a Vice-President, both appointed by the Lord President of the Court of Session (*2013 Regulations, regs 5, 6*). Tribunals sit at all the regional centres and at various other permanent centres and an increasing number of *ad hoc* centres.

The administration of tribunals (and of the EAT) is now the responsibility of HM Courts and Tribunals Service ('HMCTS'), which came into existence on 1 April 2011, merging the former Tribunals Service with HM Courts Service. The Tribunals Service itself came into existence in 2006 as an executive agency of the then Department for Constitutional Affairs, now the Ministry of Justice, and was given a statutory basis by the *Tribunals, Courts and Enforcement Act 2007*. The merger of the two services does not affect the office of Senior President of Tribunals created by the *2007 Act*. The Senior President (currently Lord Justice Ryder) has overall responsibility for all tribunals. HMCTS is responsible for the administration of some twenty separate statutory tribunals, including the provision of premises, staff and facilities such as computing.

The various tribunals within the remit of the Tribunals Service (and now HMCTS) have been brought together into a unified structure, with an Upper Tribunal replacing the various appellate tribunals and most of the first instance tribunals grouped into a number of

18.6   Employment Tribunals – I

Chambers reflecting their areas of jurisdiction. Employment tribunals and the Employment Appeal Tribunal have however retained their separate status, identity, judiciary and rules of procedure, although increasingly not their separate premises.

At present HMCTS is responsible for tribunals in Scotland as well as England and Wales. Section 39 Scotland Act 2016 allows for the transfer of competence over the functions of employment tribunals dealing with Scottish Cases. Functions can be transferred to a Scottish Tribunal named in an Order in Council. A draft Order in Council has been promulgated and consulted upon which would enable the First-tier Tribunal to hear Scottish employment cases as defined under the order, along with certain specified other cases.

The proposed transfer of functions would allow the First-tier tribunal to hear Scottish employment cases (as defined in the draft Order), along with a number of cases that do not fit within that category but which have a sufficient link to Scotland and should therefore be heard in a Scottish tribunal. The challenges this proposal is likely to pose are discussed by the President of Employment Tribunals (Scotland), Judge Shona Simon, in the Senior President of Tribunal's Annual Report 2015 (see pp 80–82); and for 2016 (see pp 103-107). As at August 2016, the Scottish Government was considering the consultation responses.

The Bury St Edmunds Office maintains the public Register of Judgments and applications for copies of judgments should be made to that office, enclosing the relevant fee (currently £10 per judgment plus £5 for each additional judgment). Judgments older than 6 years have been retained but are unavailable pending a decision as to the future administration of this archive. As noted above, since 2016, judgments and reasons have been available on-line.

There is a Central Office of Employment Tribunals for England and Wales and for Scotland. Claims presented by post must be sent to the address set out in the Presidential Practice Direction. Online claims are also directed to that office automatically. Alternatively, presentation in person can be to a local office at the addresses (and within the times) set out in the Presidential Practice Direction. The relevant office which will determine the claim is determined by the postcode of the claimant's place of work or former place of work. The Central Office will automatically send the claim to be handled by the appropriate office.

18.7   COMPOSITION

Tribunals are drawn from three panels (*2013 Regulations, reg 8*):

(a)   Employment Judges, who are appointed by the Lord Chancellor on the recommendation of the Judicial Appointments Commission (a body established by the *Constitutional Reform Act 2005*), or in Scotland by the Lord President of the Court of Session (there is a Scottish Judicial Appointments Board, but its responsibilities do not extend to recommending appointments to the employment tribunals judiciary), and must have a five-year legal qualification (this was reduced from seven years in 2008). Appointments are both full-time and part-time.

(b)   Persons appointed by the Lord Chancellor after consulting organisations representative of employees.

(c)   Persons so appointed after consultation with organisations representative of employers.

The members drawn from panels (*b*) and (*c*) (variously referred to as 'lay members', 'wing members' and 'the industrial jury') all serve part-time. The Presidents are required to maintain separate panels of Judges, and of each of the two categories of lay members, who are considered suitable to hear cases involving issues of national security, and the tribunal assigned to such a case will be composed of a member of each special panel (*2013*

Regulations, reg 10). There is also a power to establish panels of Judges and members with specialist knowledge to hear particular categories of proceedings for which such knowledge would be beneficial (*reg 8(4)*). This power has been used to create specialist panels to hear equal pay cases, but there are no plans at present for other specialist panels.

The composition, and methods of appointment and reappointment to membership, of the employment tribunals have in the past given rise to a potential difficulty under the *Human Rights Act 1998 ('HRA 1998')*. *Article 6* of the *European Convention on Human Rights*, which the *HRA 1998* incorporates into UK law, confers the right to a determination of issues relating to civil rights (which includes most if not all issues brought before employment tribunals) at a fair and public hearing before an independent and impartial tribunal. The issue was raised whether employment tribunals could satisfy this requirement in cases where the Secretary of State for Trade and Industry was a party to the proceedings, as where claims were made against the Secretary of State because the employer was insolvent. Changes in the method of appointment of Judges and lay members in 2000 largely removed the potential conflicts of interest, and the creation of the Tribunals Service, together with the transfer of responsibility for recommending the appointment of Judges to the Judicial Appointments Commission (and appointments in Scotland being made by the Lord President), is thought to have resolved the problem, but this must remain open to possible judicial determination.

18.8   A full tribunal consists of one member from each panel (*2013 Regulations, reg 9(3)*). Decisions may be by majority, but if the Tribunal is composed of two persons (which by *ETA 1996, s 4(1)(b)* can occur where the parties consent), the Judge has a second or casting vote (*2013 Rules, Rule 49*). If agreement is sought to the tribunal sitting with only one lay member, the parties must be informed as to whether the lay member is from the employers' or employees' panel: *Rabahallah v British Telecommunications plc* [2005] ICR 440 (following *De Haney v Brent Mind* [2003] EWCA Civ 1637, [2004] IRLR 348, a case about the equivalent situation in the EAT). In *Rabahallah*, the EAT recommended that the parties be asked to sign a standard form to confirm that informed consent has been given to the tribunal sitting or continuing with only one lay member. A tribunal with two lay members drawn from the same panel is not a properly constituted tribunal and any decision by such a panel would be a nullity.

Tribunals normally sit in public; the circumstances in which they may sit in private or reporting of proceedings may be restricted are explained below (see **19.91–19.93**). The importance of a public hearing was reiterated in *Storer v British Gas plc* [2000] 2 All ER 440, [2000] 1 WLR 1237, [2000] ICR 603, [2000] IRLR 495, where the Court of Appeal set aside a decision on a preliminary issue reached at a hearing held in the private office of the Regional Employment Judge because no tribunal room was available. The court dismissed as irrelevant the argument that no members of the public had been prevented from attending the hearing.

18.9   Judges sitting alone

A full tribunal is required for the hearing of most claims: however, certain categories of proceedings must be heard by a tribunal consisting of a Judge sitting alone, unless a Judge (not necessarily the same person who hears the case) directs to the contrary considering factors such as the likelihood of a dispute on the facts, the likelihood of disputes of law, the views of the parties, and whether there are other proceedings which might be heard concurrently (*ETA 1996, s 4(2), (3)* and *(5)*). Where a case involves a number of claims, some which can be heard by a judge alone, and others which require a full tribunal, there is a duty on the Tribunal (in respect of the claims which can be heard by judge alone) to consider whether they should be heard together before a full tribunal: *Birring v Rogers and Moore t/a Charity Link* [2015] UKEAT/0388/14 (see below). An important change to the categories of cases which can be heard by a judge sitting alone was made by the *Employment*

18.9 Employment Tribunals – I

Tribunals Act 1996 (Tribunal Composition) Order 2012, SI 2012/988, adding unfair dismissal claims to the list with effect from 6 April 2012. (Since then, the EAT has felt the need to emphasise that the substantive law has not changed: see *Mitchell v St Joseph's School* (UKEAT/0506/12).)

The principal categories of case covered by these provisions are now as follows (see *ETA 1996, s 4(3)* for a complete list):

(a) applications for interim relief in relation to dismissal in health and safety and public interest disclosure cases (*ERA 1996, ss 128–132*) or for trade union reasons (*TULRCA 1992, ss 161, 165* and *166*);

(b) applications against the Secretary of State under *ERA 1996, ss 170* and *188* or *Pension Schemes Act 1993, s 126* (where the former employer is insolvent);

(c) applications under the *ERA 1996, s 23* or *TULRCA 1992, s 68A* (unlawful deductions from wages, etc);

(d) applications under the following provisions of *ERA 1996*: *s 11* (particulars of employment terms and itemised pay statements), *s 34* (guarantee payments), *s 70* (remuneration during suspension on medical grounds), *s 111* (unfair dismissal), *s 163* (redundancy payments), and *s 206(4)* (appointment of 'appropriate person' in proceedings, following the death of an employee);

(e) applications under *TULRCA 1992, s 192* or *reg 15(10)* of the *Transfer of Undertakings (Protection of Employment) Regulations 2006 (SI 2006/246)* (failure to pay a protective award);

(f) claims for breach of contract under the *Employment Tribunals Extension of Juris-diction (England and Wales) Order 1994 (SI 1994/1623)* or the equivalent Scottish order;

(g) Claims under the *Working Time Regulations 1998, reg 30* (and equivalent provisions applying to certain categories of worker not covered by the *1998 Regulations*) for holiday pay or pay in lieu of holiday not taken prior to the termination of employment, but not other claims under the *1998 Regulations*;

(h) proceedings where both or all parties have given their written consent to a hearing before a Judge alone (whether or not consent has been subsequently withdrawn); and

(i) proceedings where the respondent (or all respondents if more than one) does not contest the claim, or no longer does so.

(*ETA 1996, s 4(3)*.)

For claims in categories not listed above, there is no power for a judge sitting alone to determine the case and any decision made following such a final hearing would be a nullity: *Nascimento v British Bakeries Ltd* [2005] All ER (D) 20 (Sep), EAT; *Insaidoo v Metropolitan Resources North West Ltd* [2011] All ER (D) 04 (May); *Birring* (above). This is to be contrasted with the ability of a judge sitting alone to conduct a preliminary hearing (whether for case management or to determine preliminary issues, subject to *2013 Rules, Rule 55*). In this connection it may be noted that whilst claims under *TULRCA 1992, s 192* for payment of a protective award already made under *s 189* can be heard by a judge sitting alone (as stated in (e) above), claims for a protective award to be made under *s 189* require a full panel, so a judgment upholding or refusing such a claim by a judge sitting alone is a nullity: *Weedon v Pinnacle Entertainment Ltd* (UKEAT/0217/11). It should be stressed that if any of the claims in a case where more than one claim has been made fall outside the list above, the case must be heard by a full panel (unless the claim requiring a full panel has been withdrawn or struck out before the hearing). As an example in claims for unfair dismissal and for failure to provide written reasons for dismissal, the latter claim must be heard by a full tribunal, and the addition of such a claim will normally necessitate that the unfair dismissal claim is also heard by a full panel.

The provision at (i) above was given greater significance by the decision of the EAT in *Parfett v John Lamb Partnership Ltd* (UKEAT/0111/08) [2008] All ER (D) 22 (Jul), holding that it covers cases where the Respondent either has not submitted a response or has not had the response accepted. In such cases a Judge may issue a judgement on such parts of the claim s/he can determine. If that does not cover the full scope of the claim (and frequently remedy will remain), the Judge will proceed to fix a hearing before a Judge alone: see *Rule 21(2)* of the *2013 Rules*.

In addition, preliminary hearings must be heard by a Judge sitting alone, regardless of the type or complexity of the claim (*Rule 55*) except where a notice has been given that preliminary issues are to be, or may be, decided at the hearing, and a party has requested in writing that the hearing be conducted by a full tribunal. In such cases an Employment Judge will make a decision whether this would be desirable (*Rule 55*). See the EAT's comments in *Sutcliffe v Big C's Marine Ltd* [1998] ICR 913.

Until 2009, an important omission from the list of claims which could be heard by a Judge sitting alone was claims for holiday pay under the *Working Time Regulations 1998 ('WTR'), reg 30*. Following the ruling of the Court of Appeal in *IRC v Ainsworth* [2005] EWCA Civ 441, [2005] IRLR 465 that claims for unpaid holiday pay under the *WTR* could only be brought under *reg 30*, and not as a complaint of unlawful deductions under *Part II* of the *ERA 1996*, it became necessary for any claim for arrears of pay which included a statutory holiday pay claim to be heard by a full tribunal. As a result, the *ETA 1996, s 4(3)* was amended with effect from 6 April 2009 by the *Employment Tribunals Act 1996 (Tribunal Composition) Order 2009, SI 2009/789*, by adding holiday pay claims under the *WTR* to the list of categories of claim which may be heard by a judge sitting alone. However the amendment does not extend to other claims under the *WTR*; claims in relation to rest breaks, rest periods and compensatory rest remain subject to the general requirement that a Hearing must be before a full tribunal. The *2009 Order* also made equivalent amendments to the regulations conferring rights to paid holiday for sea fishermen, aircrew in civil aviation, and workers on inland waterways. However, the addition of claims for holiday pay under the *WTR 1998* has since largely lost its importance, following the decision of the House of Lords (under the name of *Revenue and Customs Comrs v Stringer* [2009] UKHL 31, [2009] ICR 985, [2009] IRLR 677), overruling the Court of Appeal's decision in *IRC v Ainsworth* and holding that such claims may be brought under *Part II* of the *ERA 1996*. This may afford advantages in terms of time limits, and claims under *Part II* may also be heard by a judge sitting alone (see paragraph (c) above).

An order can be made, in any case falling within *ETA 1996, s 4(3)*, for the hearing to be before a full panel. The power to make such orders has become much more significant with the addition of unfair dismissal to the categories of cases which can be heard by a judge sitting alone, a controversial change opposed by the majority of consultees in the consultation which preceded it. In an unfair dismissal case in which the members outvoted the judge, *McCafferty v Royal Mail Group Plc* (UKEATS/0002/12), Lady Smith stated that tribunals should give "careful consideration" to the parties' canvassed views.

Factors which must be considered in deciding whether to direct a full panel include whether there is a likelihood of a dispute of fact making this desirable (a point likely to be raised very commonly for unfair dismissal cases); whether there is a likelihood of a point of law arising making a hearing before a Judge alone desirable; the views of the parties; and the existence of any concurrent proceedings which have to be heard by a full tribunal (*ETA 1996, s 4(5)*).

There have been conflicting authorities in the past on the extent of the obligation to consider ordering a hearing before a full panel in cases within *s 4(3)*. The EAT has revisited its previous decisions, and the position, based on *Gladwell v Secretary of State for Trade and Industry* [2007] ICR 264, [2006] All ER (D) 154 (Nov) and *Sterling Developments (London) Ltd v Pagano* [2007] IRLR 471, [2007] All ER (D) 01 (May), is currently as follows:

(a)   Listing, including a decision whether to list a case before a Judge sitting alone or a full tribunal, is a judicial function, but it is permissible for a Regional Employment Judge to lay down a general policy on listing, subject to the consideration of individual cases.

(b)   There is a discretion to refer a case that may be heard by a Judge alone to a full panel, and the exercise or non-exercise of this discretion is open to challenge by an appeal. In the event of an appeal, if the Judge has not given reasons for the way the discretion was exercised, the EAT may ask for reasons. The implication of this is that the point must be considered, and a decision made, for each case.

(c)   The parties should be told of their right to request a full panel, either at a preliminary hearing for case management, if one is held, or in the notice of hearing; any request for a full panel should be judicially considered.

(d)   The Employment Judge responsible for the hearing should consider whether a full panel is needed, having regard to any developments in the case (such as that it has become clear that there are significant disputes of fact), but also having regard to the desirability of not creating delay or expense.

(e)   It may be necessary to canvass the views of the parties on whether the hearing should go ahead before the Judge alone, but it is not an error of law to fail to do so or to fail to give reasons for declining to order a full tribunal, and the Judge is not bound to accede to the wishes of the parties.

(f)   It may be necessary to at least consider ordering a full panel even if neither party asks for one, since unrepresented litigants may not appreciate the possibility of a full panel or why that would be desirable in the particular case.

The EAT in *Gladwell* declined to decide whether (as had been held in the earlier case of *Sogbetun v Hackney London Borough Council* [1998] ICR 1264, [1998] IRLR 676), a failure to exercise the discretion given by *s 4(5)* made the subsequent proceedings a nullity. It is this point in particular on which earlier cases differ, but in the light of the more recent guidelines the question has become largely academic, as a failure to follow the points indicated is likely to provide the basis for a successful appeal by the aggrieved party.

In *Birring v Rogers and Moore t/a Charity Link* [2015] UKEAT/0388/14, the EAT considered an appeal from the decision of a judge alone in a claim of both unfair dismissal and a trade union detriment. The unfair dismissal claim could be heard by a judge alone, whereas this was not the case in respect of the trade union detriment claim. The decision of a single judge was therefore a nullity in respect of the trade union detriment claim and the appeal allowed in that respect. However, Langstaff P went on to disturb the decision on the unfair dismissal complaint also. The judge below had failed to consider *s 4(5)* and decide whether the unfair dismissal complaint should be heard together with the trade union detriment claim. The EAT held he should have done, and there was a duty to do so, in cases involving a mixture of judge-alone and full tribunal jurisdictions (see para 18). The EAT also observed that it was a pity in the Notices of Hearing did not draw attention to the fact submissions might be made as to the composition of the Tribunal (para 20).

18.10 There is provision in the *ETA 1996, ss 4(6A)* and *7(3A)* (added respectively by the *ERDRA 1998, s 2* and the *Employment Act 2002, s 26*) for certain proceedings to be disposed of by an Employment Judge without a hearing. These powers have been implemented by the *2013 Rules*, which permit a Judge to issue a default judgment in favour of a claimant, either on liability only or including awarding the remedy claimed, if the respondent has failed to submit a Response Form within the time limit and to the extent this is possible (*2013 Rules, rule 21(2)*).

A Judgment can also be issued without a hearing if all parties have agreed in writing as to its terms (*Rule 64*), and a Judgment dismissing the claim will be issued without the need for a hearing if it has been withdrawn by the claimant (*rule 52*) unless the exceptions in that rule apply.

In certain circumstances also, a claim may be struck out for non-compliance by the claimant with an order of the tribunal without the right to a further hearing: see, under the old rules, *Sodexho Ltd v Gibbons* [2005] ICR 1647, [2005] IRLR 836, EAT (striking out for non-payment of a deposit ordered at a PHR), but such a step is a judicial act and therefore a judgment and therefore open to reconsideration: see now *Rule 70*.

In addition, there is provision for a case to be heard in the absence of a party who fails to attend (and is not represented) at the Hearing (*2013 Rules, rule 47*) or in the absence of a respondent who has been excluded from participating in the proceedings by virtue of *rule 21(3)* for failure to submit a valid Response Form in time.

18.11 JURISDICTION

It is important to appreciate at the outset that employment tribunals are creatures of statute, and therefore have only such powers and jurisdiction as have been conferred on them by statutory provision. Jurisdiction cannot be conferred, or enlarged, by agreement between the parties to a case, or by the acquiescence or silence of a party. This does not mean that the tribunal cannot resolve a dispute about whether it has jurisdiction. Such disputes arise relatively frequently, and must be determined when they do arise; but if the tribunal erroneously holds that it has jurisdiction and proceeds to exercise it, the assertion of jurisdiction is open to challenge on appeal. Similarly, jurisdiction cannot be conferred simply by agreement, or a concession by one party which the party subsequently withdraws before there is a binding determination of the case: *Radakovits v Abbey National plc* [2009] EWCA Civ 1346, [2009] IRLR 307 (employer initially conceding claim in time, but later withdrawing concession; tribunal held bound to determine whether it had jurisdiction once the point was in dispute). (But, as was noted by Sedley LJ in *Clark v Clark Construction Initiatives Ltd* [2008] EWCA Civ 1466, [2009] ICR 718, at para 14, if the question determining jurisdiction is one of fact, there may be no practical grounds for appealing against an erroneous determination of the facts necessary to confer jurisdiction; and see *Kudjodji v Lidl Ltd* (UKEAT/0054/11): once tribunal has decided it has jurisdiction, and subject to any appeal, a different tribunal hearing the case at a later stage cannot reopen that decision.)

Tribunals have jurisdiction both under English and Scots law, and under EU law. The jurisdiction under English and Scots law is entirely statutory; jurisdiction under EU law derives from principles of EU law itself. The total number of separate jurisdictions is now in excess of 70, albeit many of these arise extremely infrequently in practice. The principal statutory provisions, which all apply equally to Scotland, are:

(a) *Employment Rights Act 1996 ('ERA 1996')*, as amended (unfair dismissal, redundancy payments, disputes over written particulars of employment and itemised pay statements, unlawful deductions from wages or requirements to make payments to employers (formerly under the *Wages Act 1986*), breaches of the *National Minimum Wage Act 1998*, guarantee payments, rights to time off for public duties, protection from detriment in certain health and safety (and other) cases and as a result of a protected disclosure under the *Public Interest Disclosure Act 1998*, time off for family emergencies, maternity, paternity, adoption and parental leave issues, failure to pay during medical suspension, issues over requests for flexible working arrangements, written reasons for dismissal, claims (other than pension claims) against the Secretary of State in insolvency cases, interim relief in certain unfair dismissal cases and a number of minor and ancillary matters);

(b)   *TULRCA 1992* (unfair dismissal or action short of dismissal for trade union reasons or for participation in industrial action; offering inducements not to join a union or to opt out of collective agreements; blacklisting complaints; time off for union and other duties; failure to consult recognised unions or employee representatives over proposed redundancies; claims for payment of protective awards made for such failures to consult; failure to consult recognised unions over training; and disputes over union membership, disciplinary action against members and expulsions);

(c)   *Equality Act 2010, ss 120* (claims under *Part 5* of the *Act* (work)) and *127* (claims of breach of an equality clause or rule under the equality of terms provisions of the *Act*) and *ss 122* and *128* (cases referred to the tribunal by a court);

(d)   *Employment Tribunals Extension of Jurisdiction (England and Wales) Order 1994* and the equivalent Scottish Order (claims in contract and employers' counterclaims, subject to a maximum jurisdiction of £25,000);

(e)   *Working Time Regulations 1998 (SI 1998/1833), regs 30–32* (complaints of dismissal or subjection to detriment for insisting on entitlements to breaks or rest periods, or refusing to agree to work hours in excess of the maximum, and of refusal to permit the exercise of rights to annual leave, rest breaks or rest periods conferred on workers by the *Regulations* or to provide compensatory rest, or to pay for annual leave or in lieu of accrued leave rights on termination of employment; also complaints of detrimental treatment or dismissal of those elected as representatives to negotiate workforce agreements, or standing as candidates for election);

(f)   *National Minimum Wage Act 1998, ss 22, 24* (appeals against penalty notices issued by compliance officers, and complaints of detriment by workers; complaints of underpayment are made under the *ERA 1996, Part II*);

(g)   *Employment Relations Act 1999 ('ERA 1999'), s 11* (failure to permit workers to be accompanied at grievance or disciplinary hearing or to postpone hearing for that purpose);

(h)   *Part-time Workers (Prevention of Less Favourable Treatment) Regulations 2000 (SI 2000/ 1551), reg 8* (infringement of right not to be less favourably treated; subjection to detriment for assertion of rights);

(i)   *Fixed-term Employees (Prevention of Less Favourable Treatment) Regulations 2002 (SI 2002/2034), reg 7* (infringement of right not to be less favourably treated; subjection to detriment for assertion of rights) and *reg 9(5)* (application for declaration of status as permanent employee);

(j)   *Transfer of Undertakings (Protection of Employment) Regulations 2006 (SI 2006/246), regs 12* (failure to notify employee liability information to transferee) and *15* (failure to inform or consult with trade unions or employee representatives, and associated claims for non-payment of protective awards);

(k)   *Equality Act 2006, ss 21, 25* (appeals against unlawful act notices issued by the Commission for Equality and Human Rights, and applications by the Commission to restrain certain unlawful acts under the discrimination legislation);

(l)   *Agency Workers Regulations 2010 (SI 2010/93), reg 18* (with effect from 1 October 2011, complaints of infringements of the rights conferred by the *Regulations*, including equality of treatment with directly employed staff);

(m)   *Employment Relations Act 1999 (Blacklists) Regulations 2010 (SI 2010/493), regs 5, 6, 9* (refusal to employ or provide agency services to, or subjecting to detriment, workers, by reference to blacklists);

(n)   miscellaneous legislation (including claims arising from failure to consult recognised union over application to contract out of occupational pension scheme and certain other claims under the *Pension Schemes Act 1993*; appeals against industrial training levies; appeals against improvement and prohibition notices; disputes over time off for safety representatives and union learning representatives and other employee representatives given statutory rights to paid or unpaid time off; proceedings against employment agencies under the *Deregulation and Contracting Out Act 1994*).

The jurisdictions under the *Equality Act 2010* replace several heads of jurisdiction under the various statutes and regulations it replaces, principally the *Equal Pay Act 1970, Sex Discrimination Act 1975, Race Relations Act 1976* and *Disability Discrimination Act 1995*, and the regulations on discrimination on grounds of sexual orientation, religion or belief and age. Part of the latter, the *Employment Equality (Age) Regulations 2006, SI 2006/1031*, providing for the procedure for requests to remain in employment after a notice to retire was issued remained in force after the revocation of the main regulations, but was revoked as from 6 April 2011 (see the *Employment Equality (Repeal of Retirement Age Provisions) Regulations 2011, SI 2011/1069*) but subject to transitional provisions which may result in claims arising after that date.

The EAT has held in relation to complaints of unlawful deduction from wages under *ERA 1996, Part II* that tribunals have no jurisdiction to hear complaints of non-payment or under-payment of Statutory Sick Pay, where the employer disputes liability to pay, as such disputes are reserved to the Inland Revenue (now HM Revenue and Customs): *Taylor Gordon & Co Ltd (t/a Plan Personnel) v Timmons* [2004] IRLR 180. The reasoning applies equally to disputes about entitlement to Statutory Maternity Pay, Statutory Paternity Pay and Statutory Adoption Pay. The tribunal also has no jurisdiction to determine the amount of an unquantified bonus claimed to be due in order to determine whether a failure to pay the bonus was an unlawful deduction from wages, since only a claim for non-payment of a specific sum said to be owed to the claimant can be made under *Part II: Coors Brewers Ltd v Adcock* [2007] EWCA Civ 19, [2007] IRLR 440; see also *Kingston upon Hull City Council v Schofield & Others* [2012] UKEAT 0616/11. The definition of 'wages' in the *ERA 1996* provides further parameters to the Tribunal's jurisdiction to determine claims of this type. Notable exceptions from the definition are payments in respect of expenses: see *London Borough of Southwark v O'Brien* [1996] IRLR 420 and *Qantas Cabin Crew (UK) Ltd v Lopez and Hooper* [2013] IRLR 4.

A further limitation on the jurisdiction of tribunals is that they cannot interpret the contractual terms of employees in proceedings for a determination of whether a statement of the particulars of terms of employment given to the claimant were correct: *Southern Cross Healthcare Co Ltd v Perkins* [2010] EWCA Civ 1442, [2011] IRLR 247 (a case concerning a dispute over the amount of holiday entitlement the claimants' contracts conferred). There is a dispute within the EAT's case law as to whether this applies so as to prohibit the Tribunal interpreting contractual terms for the purposes of adjudicating upon an unauthorised deductions from wages claim. In *Agarwal v Cardiff University & Another* [2017] UKEAT/0210/16, Slade J held there was no jurisdiction to construe the contract for the purposes of a wages claim, applying Southern Cross with the consequence that a claim concerning whether the contract contained implied terms relevant to the wages payable would have to be determined in the civil courts. By contrast, in *Weatherilt v Cathay Pacific*

Airways Ltd [2017] UKEAT/0333/16 HHJ Richardson disagreed and considered that *Agarwal* should not be followed because the EAT in that case had not been referred to relevant Court of Appeal authority in *Delaney v Staples* [1991] ICR 331 and *Camden Primary Care Trust v Atchoe* [2007] EWCA Civ 714. The EAT held in *Weatherilt* that it would be surprising if the tribunal could not construe a provision of the contract to see whether it authorised a deduction when that question might be central to the issue in an unauthorised deduction claim.

It should be noted that tribunals in England and Wales, and in Scotland respectively, only have jurisdiction over cases with the required territorial connection with the respective part of Great Britain. If a claim over which only the tribunals in Scotland have jurisdiction is presented in England or Wales, or vice versa, the claim is ineffective and the receiving tribunal has no jurisdiction to deal with it (or even to transfer the papers to the correct country): *McFadyen v PB Recovery Ltd* (UKEATS/0072/08) (31 July 2009, unreported).

The *2013 Rules* specify where a claim should be presented as between England and Wales and Scotland in *Rule 8(2)* and *(3)*. These provisions may allow for a claim to be brought in either jurisdiction. The test for Tribunals to apply gives a number of routes to jurisdiction (here set out by reference to England and Wales, but see *Rule 8(3)* for Scotland): where the respondent, or one of them, resides or carries on business in England and Wales, if one or more of the acts or omissions complained of took place in England and Wales, if the claim relates to a contract under which the work is or has been performed partly in England and Wales or where jurisdiction derives from a connection with Great Britain and the connection in question is at least partly a connection with England and Wales. A broad approach to the question whether the respondent carries on business within the jurisdiction was adopted in *Pervez v Macquarie Bank Ltd (London Branch)* [2011] ICR 266, [2011] IRLR 284, EAT, where it was held that the respondent (an Australian company) carried on business in England through the presence of the claimant who was working on secondment in London (having been based in Hong Kong), although the respondent had no other presence in the jurisdiction. *Rule 99* permits the Tribunal to transfer proceedings between England and Wales and Scotland provided that the tribunal receiving the claim would have had jurisdiction to receive the originally presented claim and the claim would be more conveniently determined there.

It should be noted that all of these points are separate from the jurisdictional issues which arise in relation to whether legislation conferring a substantive employment right applies to the particular circumstances of employment with an extra-territorial element; these issues are discussed elsewhere in this book in the context of the particular rights concerned.

18.12 Jurisdiction over EU law

Tribunals' jurisdiction is statutory, but there is no statutory provision giving the tribunal power to determine claims under EU law. The basis for tribunals hearing such claims has therefore been a source of legal difficulty.

There is clear authority recognising tribunals' jurisdiction where a claimant relies on *art 157* of the *Treaty on the functioning of the EU* (formerly *art 141* of the *Treaty of Rome* (equal pay claims)): *Pickstone v Freemans plc* [1989] AC 66, [1987] 3 All ER 756, [1987] 3 WLR 811, [1987] 2 CMLR 572, [1987] ICR 867. Claims relying on the *Equal Treatment Directive 76/207* (now replaced by the consolidating *Directive 2006/54*) against state authorities have been acknowledged to be within the jurisdiction of tribunals since the principle of direct effect was established by the European Court of Justice in *Marshall v Southampton and South West Hampshire Area Health Authority (Teaching)*: C-152/84 [1986] QB 401, [1986] ICR 335 and are now relatively common. The position in relation to other *Directives* depends on whether the particular provision concerned is sufficiently 'clear, precise and unconditional' to have direct effect, a question of EU law and thus ultimately for the CJEU.

Rulings of the Court of Appeal to the effect that tribunals have no jurisdiction to hear 'freestanding' claims under EU law, and that any such claims must be made under the relevant statute with the offending provision disapplied (*Biggs v Somerset County Council* [1996] 2 All ER 734, [1996] 2 CMLR 292, [1996] ICR 364; *Staffordshire County Council v Barber* [1996] ICR 379) have since been overtaken by developments in the case law of the CJEU, in particular *Mangold v Helm*: C-144/04 [2006] IRLR 143, *Impact v Minister for Agriculture and Food*: C-268/06 [2008] IRLR 552, *Kücükdeveci v Swedex GmbH*: C-555/07 [2010] IRLR 346, and *Dominguez v Centre Informatique du Centre Ouest Atlantique*: C-282/10 [2012] IRLR 321. The effect of these and other decisions is that a claim may be made in a domestic forum to give effect to a right conferred by EU law, whether or not fully and correctly transposed into domestic law by the member state, once the date for transposition has passed; such enforcement may in some circumstances be against private sector respondents as well as public bodies. The basis for the employment tribunal being an appropriate forum for such claims can be derived from the *Impact* case, where the CJEU ruled that a specialist tribunal with power to determine claims under national legislation implementing a *Directive* must also have power to decide claims made directly under the *Directive*, if alternative means of pursuing the claim would involve sufficiently serious procedural disadvantages.

In addition, whether or not it is possible to maintain a claim in an employment tribunal directly under EU law, the EAT has held that the tribunal has power, even in proceedings against a non-state entity, to disapply, or read words into, a statutory provision, if this is necessary to give effect to a right conferred by EU law, and the rewriting of the statutory provision 'goes with the grain' of the domestic legislation: *Coleman v EBR Attridge Law LLP* [2010] 1 CMLR 846, [2010] ICR 242; contrast the more restrictive approach (*obiter*) in *Hainsworth v Ministry of Defence* [2014] EWCA Civ 763.

The Court of Appeal's decisions referred to above have two main effects (neither of which would appear to be affected by the *Impact* decision):

(a)   Procedural provisions, particularly those relating to time limits for making claims, contained in the relevant national legislation apply equally where that legislation is used as a basis for a claim relying on EU law. (The same principle applies to other procedural rules; for an example, see *Livingstone v Hepworth Refractories Ltd* [1992] ICR 287.)

(b)   Claims against the Government for damages for failure to implement EU Directives cannot be brought in the tribunal; the claim must be made in the High Court against the Attorney-General, or in Scotland the Lord Advocate (*Secretary of State for Employment v Mann* [1997] ICR 209, CA; for an example of such a claim, see *R v A-G for Northern Ireland, ex p Burns* [1999] IRLR 315).

However, there are still considerations of EU law which may affect how any discretion under the national legislation has to be exercised (eg to extend time), whether time limits run against the claimant and whether restrictions on remedies available under the national statute are compatible with EU law (*Marshall v Southampton and South West Hampshire Area Health Authority (No 2)*: C-271/91 [1994] QB 126, [1993] ICR 893 and *Levez v T H Jennings (Harlow Pools) Ltd*: C-326/96 [1999] IRLR 36, [1999] ICR 521 (both decisions of the CJEU)). For an interesting example see *Chief Constable of West Yorkshire Police v A* [2000] IRLR 465 (tribunal has power under EU law to make restricted reporting order protecting identity of transsexual claimant; see further **18.18** below and now *Rule 50* of the *2013 Rules*).

The CJEU has endorsed the principle of the application of national time limits to cases reliant on EU law, provided that the time limits are no less favourable than for those for similar claims in domestic law and do not render the exercise of rights under EU law impossible in practice: *Fisscher v Voorhuis Hengelo BV*: C-128/93 [1994] IRLR 662, [1995] ICR 635. For a case where a limit was held to infringe this principle, see *Magorrian v Eastern Health and Social Services Board*: C-246/96 [1998] ICR 979, [1998] IRLR 86.

Separately from the European Convention of Human Rights (on which see below), the European Union's Charter of Fundamental Rights of the European Union, agreed in 2000 in Nice (OJ C 364, 18.12.2000, p1-22), is becoming a source of EU relied upon before national courts and tribunals. By Art 6(1) of the Treaty on European Union, it has the same legal value as a treaty. According to the CJEU, where it is necessary to interpret a provision of secondary Community law, preference should as far as possible be given to the interpretation which renders the provision consistent with the EC Treaty and the general principles of Community law: see e.g. *Schutzverband der Spirituosen-Industrie v Diageo Deutschland GmbH* (Case C-457/05) [2007] ECR I-08075. Further, domestic law must, as mentioned above, be interpreted as far as possible, in a manner to give effect to EU law, where necessary disapplying offending provisions of national law. In *R (NS) v Secretary of State for the Home Department* [2010] EWCA Civ 990, the UK Government accepted that in principle the rights set out in the Charter can be relied on as against the UK. See also the judgment of Mostyn J in *R (AB) v Secretary of State for the Home Department* [2013] EWHC 3453 at paras 13-14. A recent example of the Charter's effect can be seen in *Benkharbouche v Embassy of the Republic of Sudan* [2015] IRLR 301. There, the Court of Appeal recognised the direct effect of the Charter rights even in cases between private individuals (i.e. horizontally). Accordingly, the Court felt able to disapply sections of the *State Immunity Act 1978* as being contrary to art 47 of the EU Charter (guaranteeing an effective remedy, in that case with the same content as Art 6 ECHR). *Benkharbouche* is, at the time of writing, on appeal in the Supreme Court.

18.13 Human Rights Act 1998

Proceedings under the *HRA 1998*, *s 7* can only be brought in those courts or tribunals designated as 'appropriate'. As no designation has been made for employment tribunals, it follows that no 'freestanding' claims can be brought in the tribunal under that *Act*. (See on this *Whittaker v Watson (P & D) (t/a P & M Watson Haulage)* [2002] ICR 1244, confirming that the EAT is in the same position, and cannot therefore issue a declaration that a statutory provision is incompatible with the *HRA 1998*.) However, tribunals are 'public authorities' within *s 6* of the *Act*, and thus are required not to act in a way which is incompatible with rights secured by the *European Convention on Human Rights* unless compelled to do so by legislation. This means that issues of alleged infringement of a party's human rights may be raised in the course of tribunal proceedings, and the tribunal may find it necessary to take the *Convention* into account in the course of deciding substantive or procedural issues in the case. To that extent the position is similar to that under EU law, but the power to overrule primary legislation incompatible with a directly applicable EU obligation does not have a direct parallel. For guidance on how the *Convention* affects the application of the general law of unfair dismissal see *X v Y* [2004] EWCA Civ 662, [2004] IRLR 625, CA and *Turner v East Midlands Trains Ltd* [2013] ICR 525.

As a separate point, the right under *art 6* of the *Convention* to a fair trial in the determination of one's civil rights imposes obligations on tribunals as the forum in which that right is afforded in most employment cases. In addition to the obligations of independence and impartiality, discussed at **18.7** above, tribunals are required to afford a determination 'within a reasonable time' in order to satisfy *art 6*. Even the relatively generous timescale applied by the European Court of Human Rights in its jurisprudence under *art 6* was held to have been exceeded in *Somjee v United Kingdom* [2002] IRLR 886, where a series of applications to the tribunal and appeals to the EAT, with lengthy delays at a number of stages, had led to a nine year delay between the initial application and its final determination. However delay is not in itself a ground of appeal: rather the question in any appeal where there has been serious delay, whether in issuing the tribunal's judgment or more generally, is whether there is a real risk that the party appealing has in substance been deprived of the right to a fair trial in accordance with *Art 6: Bangs v Connex South Eastern Ltd* [2005] EWCA Civ 14, [2005] 2 All ER 316, [2005] IRLR 389, where the Court of Appeal laid down guidance on the correct approach to such appeals. The earlier decision of the EAT in *Kwamin v Abbey National plc* [2004] ICR 841, in which a broader approach was taken, was disapproved by the Court. In more mundane situations, compliance with the timeliness requirement of *Art 6* is a relevant factor for a tribunal in deciding whether to grant an adjournment, if the effect of doing so would be to create any significant delay or further delay in the proceedings.

Issues in relation to *Art 6* are frequently raised in employment tribunals (particularly by litigants in person) but in practice rarely add to the general principles of fairness embodied in the Overriding Objective (see **18.14** below for this), and given effect in more detail by the *ET Rules*. Two examples may be given. The Supreme Court held, in *Home Office v Tariq* [2011] UKSC 35, [2011] IRLR 843, that the special procedure for National Security cases laid down by *Sch 2* to the *2004 Regulations* (see now *Sch 2* to the *2013 Regulations*), under which a Special Advocate is appointed to advance the claimant's case and the claimant is denied access to sensitive evidence heard in private, does not breach the requirements of *Art 6*. In *Power v Greater Manchester Police Authority* (UKEAT/0087/10), the EAT held that there was no incompatibility with *Art 6* in a case where the claimant was denied the opportunity of cross-examining the person alleged to have discriminated against him (because the employer chose not to call her as a witness); the right under *Art 6* to cross-examine witnesses applies to criminal, not civil, proceedings. It is also worth noting the approach taken to *Art 6* in internal proceedings before the employer, clarified by the Supreme Court in *R (G) v Governors of X School* [2012] 1 AC 167 and the Court of Appeal in *Mattu v University Hospitals Coventry and Warwickshire NHS Trust* [2013] ICR 270.

In addition, *Art 6* is often cited in appeals based on the inadequacy of an employment tribunal's reasons; but in practice the higher courts' interpretation and application of the obligation to give reasons under *2013 Rules, rule 62(1)* and general principles of common law fully meets the requirements derived from *Art 6*. See further **19.117–19.118**.

Issues of the right to privacy under *Art 8* of the *Convention* may arise in the context of what evidence a tribunal should admit, where it is asserted that the obtaining or use of the evidence involved or would involve an impermissible interference with that right. An example of this argument being deployed (albeit unsuccessfully on the facts) is *Chairman and Governors of Amwell View School v Dogherty* [2007] IRLR 198 (admissibility of covert tape recording of Governors' private deliberations following disciplinary hearing). On the same topic, see *Vaughan v Lewisham Borough Council* [2013] All ER (D) 80.

In *Woodrup v Southwark London Borough Council* [2002] EWCA Civ 1716, [2003] IRLR 111, the Court of Appeal considered an argument that employment tribunals are engaged in the provision of services to the public within *Part III* of the *Disability Discrimination Act 1995*, which would entail a duty to make reasonable adjustments in favour of disabled parties in the conduct of the proceedings. Without formally ruling on the point, both members of the Court (Simon Brown and Clarke LJJ) expressed strong doubts as to the suggestion that there is such a legal duty on tribunals. There is also an express exclusion of judicial acts, including things done on the instructions a person exercising judicial authority, from the general duty of public bodies not to discriminate against disabled persons in the exercise of any of their functions: *Equality Act 2010, Sch 3, para 3*, replacing equivalent provisions in the *Disability Discrimination Act 1995, ss 21B(1), 21C(1)*. Such acts may well attract judicial immunity from any claim that might be brought: see e.g. *Engel v PATROL* (UKEAT/520/12). That said, in *Rackham v NHS Professionals Ltd* [2015] UKEAT/0110/15, the EAT gave guidance on the Tribunal's obligation "as an organ of the state" to make adjustments to accommodate disabled claimants. Specific reference was made to guidance in the Equal Treatment Bench Book. This has been amplified by the Northern

Ireland Court of Appeal in *Galo v Bombardier Aerospace UK* [2016] NICA 25; [2016] IRLR 703, which gave detailed guidance at para 53 of the judgment. In practice tribunals do their best to accommodate to the needs of disabled litigants, provided the tribunal staff are made aware of the particular disability.

The Tribunal now has express ability in *Rule 50* to make an order preventing or restricting public disclosure of any aspects of proceedings so far as it considers necessary in the interest of justice or in order to protect Convention rights of any person.

TIME LIMITS FOR CLAIMS

18.14 General

All applications to employment tribunals must be presented within a certain time limit, which varies according to the particular statutory provision relied on. The statutory provisions as to time limits are relatively complex, as they differ according to the particular statutory provisions relied on. It is important to appreciate a number of basic points about time limits.

(a)   Time limits go to the jurisdiction of the tribunal. A claim presented after the time limit has expired cannot be considered at all on its merits, however strong these may be, unless the tribunal can be persuaded to extend time under the limited discretionary powers to do so conferred by the relevant statute. There is power to extend time in relation to almost all the statutory jurisdictions of the tribunals, but the criteria vary according to the particular type of claim; full details are given in **18.25–18.28** below.

(b)   Time limits do not only lay down the latest date for bringing a claim. In relation to some (though not all) jurisdictions, the tribunal is precluded from hearing a claim because it was brought prematurely, *before* the relevant time period began to run. In addition, under the *Employment Act 2002*, some claims could not be presented until 28 days had elapsed after a written grievance had been submitted to the employer; as this is now mostly of historical interest, for details please see the 23rd edition of this *Handbook*. See now the requirement to have engaged in early conciliation prior to commencing proceedings discussed at **19.8 ff** below.

(c)   Time limits apply to the *presentation* of a claim, that is, its delivery (physically or electronically) to the relevant office of the tribunal (see (*e*) below for further details on how the date of presentation is calculated in marginal situations).

(d)   Time runs from a particular event, the nature of which varies depending on the particular jurisdiction. It may be both important and difficult to determine what is the relevant date in a particular case – notoriously so where it is the 'effective date of termination' that is in issue, as in an unfair dismissal claim. Normally it is the date of the event which starts the clock running, not the date (if later) on which the individual becomes aware of the event (eg an unlawful deduction from wages which the employee does not spot on first receiving the relevant payslip; or the learning of an employer taking detrimental action because of whistleblowing: see *McKinney v London Borough of Newham* [2014] UKEAT/0501/13 in which the EAT held it was the date of the decision which started time running). However some events, such as termination of employment, may require communication to the employee to be effective (cf *Gisda Cyf v Barratt* [2010] UKSC 41, [2010] IRLR 1073]). See further **18.22** below. (This point may be important not just in determining when time starts to run for presenting a claim, but also whether there is a claim at all, as where legislation comes into force after the first point in time at which the right to complain arises: see for a good example *Coutts & Co plc v Cure* [2005] ICR 1098.)

(e)   The usual formulation of the time limit in employment legislation is that the complaint must be presented within a period (usually of three months) beginning with the date of the relevant event, such as the dismissal. This means that that date is the first day of the three-month period, which therefore ends one day earlier in the third following month. The correct way of calculating the three-month period is to take the day of the month of the day immediately prior to the date (eg of dismissal) and go forward three months. Thus if the employee is dismissed on 1 June, the last date for presentation is 31 August, but if the date of dismissal was 30 April, the correct last date is 29 July; some anomalies may arise from months of different lengths. See further *Pruden v Cunard Ellerman Lines Ltd* [1993] IRLR 317 and *University of Cambridge v Murray* [1993] ICR 460.

(f)   The principal exceptions to the three-month time limit are claims for a statutory redundancy payment (six months from the 'relevant date', usually the date of dismissal) and equal pay (during, or within six months following the termination of, the relevant employment). One category of claims, for interim relief in certain categories of unfair dismissal claim (see *ERA, ss 128–132; TULRCA 1992, ss 161–163*), has a time limit of only seven days from the effective date of termination.

(g)   It is not necessarily possible to circumvent time limits for a particular claim by presenting an application under one jurisdiction and then applying to add further claims. The rules on amendment of claims (see **19.72** below) require tribunals balance the prejudice or hardship that would be suffered by each party if the amendment is, or is not, allowed, taking into account, if it be the case, that the new claim has been raised for the first time after the time limit has expired. This may result in the application to amend being refused, particularly if made at the last minute before the Hearing (see further on amendments generally **19.72**). However, provided the proper test is applied, being out of time does not automatically mean that permission to amend should be refused: *Mist v Derby Community Health Services NHS Trust* [2016] ICR 543. The Tribunal cannot, however, allow an amendment whilst parking the question of whether the new claims are time-barred: the issue of time is integral to the assessment as to whether or not to allow the amendment: *Amey Services Ltd v Aldridge* [2016] UKEATS/0007.

(h)   Since time points are a matter going to the jurisdiction of the tribunal, they may be raised at any time in the proceedings. The point may be (and quite frequently in practice is) raised by the tribunal itself, and in such cases it must be considered and decided on although the respondent is content to have the matter adjudicated on its merits. It is even possible (as an exception to the normal practice) for the issue of time to be raised for the first time in the course of an appeal: for an example see *Landon v Lill* (EAT/1486/00) (9 October 2002, unreported).

(i)   The time point is often considered as a preliminary issue separately from the substantive hearing; as it may raise questions of fact, evidence can be called by either or both parties. Under the *2013 Rules*, the time point (a "preliminary issue") can be dealt with at a preliminary hearing (*Rule 53*). Sometimes it is inappropriate to determine the issue of jurisdiction separately, for example where it involves the same factual issues as have to be determined on the merits of the case: see *Ironsides Ray & Vials v Lindsay* [1994] ICR 384, [1994] IRLR 318. The general approach of the EAT before the introduction of the *2013* and indeed the *2004 Rules* was to discourage the separation of preliminary points unless they were clearly distinct from other issues arising in the case: see eg *Wellcome Foundation v Darby* [1996] IRLR 538 and *Sutcliffe v Big C's Marine Ltd* [1998] ICR 913. The *2004 Rules* gave more weight to the pre-hearing review procedure, and the practice of ordering PHRs to determine time issues became more common, at least in unfair dismissal cases; however in discrimination cases, where evidence of alleged discrimination over a relatively extended period may be admissible even if the claims founded on that evidence are held to be out of time, and where arguments about whether acts continue over a period are frequent, tribunals were markedly more reluctant to deal separately with time points (see the Court of Appeal's judgment in *Hendricks v Commissioner of Police for the Metropolis* [2003] IRLR 96). This remains the position under the *2013 Rules*.

(j)   Special provisions apply to the presentation of claims by members or former members of the armed forces; see **30.4** for details.

(k)   Bringing a claim out of time does not mean necessarily that the claim is an abuse of process. Thus in *Higgins v Home Office* [2015] ICR D19, the ET had erred in rejecting a claim 6 years out of time as an abuse of process under Rule 12(1)(b). The Judge ought to have had regard to the claimant's mental health issues which may have had a bearing on the late presentation.

18.15 Automatic Extensions of the Time Limit

Subject to some complex transitional provisions, which in almost all cases do not apply to claims presented after 5 October 2009, the provisions of the *Employment Act 2002* and the *Dispute Resolution Regulations* which served to extend time automatically no longer apply following the repeal of *ss 29–33* of the *Employment Act 2002* and the associated Schedules with effect from 6 April 2009. For that reason the reader is referred to previous editions of this Handbook.

18.16 For jurisdictions in which there is an obligation to undergo Early Conciliation, there is an effect on the statutory time limits where a claimant, who is still within time, contacts ACAS to commence Early Conciliation. The provisions are discussed in the next chapter: see **19.14**.

18.17 COMPUTING AND EXTENDING TIME IN DIFFERENT JURISDICTIONS

Different statutes have provided different criteria for the extension of time. It is important to appreciate that the tribunal cannot extend time unless the relevant condition is satisfied; in addition, in relation to the first category of criteria noted below, even if it is satisfied, the tribunal must decide the further question whether the length of extension sought to validate the claim is reasonable. The principal categories of criteria, and the jurisdictions to which each applies, are as follows:

(i)   that it was not reasonably practicable to present the Claim Form within time: unfair dismissal; unlawful deduction from wages; subjection to a detriment for a reason within *ERA 1996* and *TULRCA 1992*; most other claims within *ERA 1996* and *TULRCA 1992*; claims under the *Working Time Regulations 1998*; claims for breach of contract;

(ii)   that it would be just and equitable to extend time: unlawful discrimination under the *Equality Act 2010, s 120*; less favourable treatment or subjection to detriment under the *Part-time Workers (Prevention of Less Favourable Treatment) Regulations 2000, reg 8* or the *Fixed-term Workers (Prevention of Less Favourable Treatment) Regulations 2002, reg 7*; redundancy payments (subject to a maximum extension of six months: *ERA 1996, s 164*); claims under the *Agency Workers Regulations 2010, reg 17*;

(iii)   no provision for extension (except in cases of concealment of the information on which the claim is based): equal pay claims (see the *Equality Act 2010, s 127*). See further **18.27** below.

The tests to be applied by the tribunals in relation to each of the first two criteria are considered below, at **18.25–18.26** and **18.29–18.30** respectively.

It should be noted that if there is a disputed issue as to whether a claim was presented in time, and/or whether, if not, time should be extended, it will be necessary, where the relevant facts are in dispute, that evidence is adduced at the hearing, whether this is the final hearing or a preliminary hearing: cf *Sodexo Health Care Services Ltd v Harmer* (UKEATS/0079/08).

18.18   Establishing when time starts to run in dismissal cases: the 'effective date of termination'

In claims alleging unfair dismissal, time starts to run from and including the 'effective date of termination' ('EDT': see *ERA 1996, s 97*). The EDT has been described judicially as a 'statutory construct' and normal contractual principles do not necessarily determine when the EDT falls. The (now relatively extensive) case law has established the following points.

(a)   If an employee is summarily dismissed, either orally or by notice in writing given to him or her at the time of dismissal, and whether or not the employer also makes a payment in lieu of the notice not given, the EDT is the date on which he or she is dismissed or ceases to work (*ERA 1996, s 97(1)*; *Dedman v British Building and Engineering Appliances Ltd* [1974] 1 All ER 520, [1974] 1 WLR 171, [1974] ICR 53).

(b)   However, if the employer gives notice to terminate a contract of employment and either requires or does not require the employee to work during the notice period, the EDT is not the date on which the employee ceases work but the date on which the notice expires. This situation is to be contrasted with where the employer dismisses and exercises a payment in lieu of notice clause so as to bring the contract to an end either immediately or on short notice accompanied by a payment instead of giving full notice. There, as described in (a) above, the EDT will be when the contract actually comes to an end. In *Societe Generale, London Branch v Geys* [2012] UKSC 63, [2013] IRLR 122, the Supreme Court held that to exercise the PILON clause in question it was not sufficient for the employee to receive their payment in lieu, but that they also receive notification from the employer in clear and unambiguous terms, that such a payment has been made and was made in the exercise of the contractual right to terminate the employment with immediate effect. If some notice of termination is given, and the parties subsequently agree to bring forward the date of termination (as may happen if the employee has another job to go to), the earlier date will be the EDT: an example in the redundancy context is *Palfrey v Transco Plc* [2004] IRLR 916.

(c)   If the employer dismisses summarily but communicates the decision by letter, the EDT is the date on which the employee receives and reads the letter, not the date on which the employer takes the decision to dismiss, or the date on which the letter is sent, or even received (if, for instance, the employee is away from home and does not see the letter until a few days later: *McMaster v Manchester Airport plc* [1998] IRLR 112). This conclusion was applied by the Supreme Court in a case with similar facts, *Gisda Cyf v Barratt* [2010] UKSC 41, [2010] IRLR 1073, with the caution that a claimant could not postpone the EDT by deliberately avoiding opening or reading a letter of dismissal. See further the discussion in *Newcastle Upon Tyne NHS Foundation Trust v Haywood* [2017] EWCA Civ 153 in which the Court held that contractual notice was given on actual receipt rather than on delivery or the deemed date of receipt (although the reasoning of the different members of the court varied). Where an employment agency employed an employee, and the employee's assignment ended, the burden was on the claimant to prove she had been dismissed. Dismissal did not fall to be implied even though the agency failed to take any steps to find other work and made assumptions about the employee's interest in further agency work: *Sandle v Adecco UK Ltd* [2016] IRLR 941.

(d)   If the employee resigns without notice (as in a constructive dismissal case), or by giving notice, and does so directly to the employer, the EDT will be the date on which the resignation without notice is communicated, or alternatively on the expiry of the period of notice given.

(e)   If the employee resigns without notice and communicates his or her resignation by letter to the employer, the EDT is the date on which the letter is received by the employer, and (probably) seen and read at least by someone in the employer's organisation, not necessarily the actual addressee: *Horwood v Lincolnshire County Council*, (UKEAT/0462/11), following a decision to the same effect in *Potter v R J Temple (in Liquidation)* (UKEAT/0478,03), where the employee had resigned by fax, and *George v Luton Borough Council* (UKEAT/0311/03). If the employee gives, say, a week's notice, the week will run from the date of receipt of the notice, not (if later) the date on which the notice was seen and read by the relevant manager. (See further **18.24** below as to how the period of notice is calculated.)

(f)   If the employee is dismissed (or resigns) on notice, and during the currency of the notice the employer summarily dismisses the employee, the (earlier) date on which the summary dismissal occurs becomes the EDT in substitution for the (later) date on which the original notice would have expired: *Parker Rhodes Hickmott Solicitors v Harvey* (UKEAT/0455/11); if the result of the second dismissal is that the employee has less than the minimum period of service required to make a claim of unfair dismissal, that is the effect of the second dismissal and the employee cannot claim unfair dismissal (unless for a reason to which the qualifying service requirement does not apply): *M-Choice Ltd v Aalders* (UKEAT/0227/11), applying *Patel v Nagesan* [1995] IRLR 370.

The determination of the EDT is a question of fact which should be decided in a practical and common sense manner having regard to what the parties understood at the time: *Newman v Polytechnic of Wales Students Union* [1995] IRLR 72. However, the applicable date is a matter of law, and a date other than that derived from a correct application of legal principles to the facts cannot simply be agreed by the parties: *Fitzgerald v University of Kent at Canterbury* [2004] EWCA Civ 143, [2004] IRLR 300. Similarly the EDT cannot be changed by the unilateral action of the employer in treating the date of the employee's resignation as later than it in fact was and paying her accordingly: *Horwood v Lincolnshire County Council* (above). Whilst the parties cannot themselves, unilaterally or by agreement, change what in fact is the EDT, they can of course set the EDT at a particular date by their actions, as where the parties agree to bring forward the date of termination so that the employee can leave to get another job, or the employee resigns without notice during the currency of notice of dismissal by the employer.

If the employee invokes an internal appeal procedure to appeal against his dismissal, time normally starts to run from the date of the original dismissal, *not* the date of the dismissal of the appeal, unless the contract provides for the employment to continue until the appeal is determined (*J Sainsbury Ltd v Savage* [1981] ICR 1); for an example of a situation where the EDT was held to be the date of dismissal of the appeal, see *Drage v Governors of Greenford High School* [2000] IRLR 314, CA. This was also found to be the case in *Hawes & Curtis Ltd v Arfan, Mirza* (UKEAT/0229/12), where the EAT found that the parties had agreed after the employees appealed that their contracts would be kept open and in existence until the appeal hearing. For a case where the EDT was held to be affected by a decision to reinstate the employee following an appeal, which in turn was overruled by more senior management, see *London Probation Board v Kirkpatrick* [2005] IRLR 443; see also UNFAIR DISMISSAL – I (53). See also as to the potential complexities of identifying the EDT where the employer removes the employee from the payroll *Kirklees Metropolitan Borough Council v Radecki* [2009] EWCA Civ 298, [2009] ICR 1244 and compare *Societe Generale, London Branch v Geys*, above.

is not, the sender can argue that it was thereby not reasonably practicable to present the claim in time. (It would still be necessary in such a case to show that he or she had acted promptly in following up the matter when no acknowledgement was received, and had resubmitted the claim expeditiously.) *Rule 90(b)* of the *2013 Rules* now provides that there is a presumption that documents sent by means of electronic communication were delivered, unless the contrary is proved, on the day of transmission.

(vii)   Where the employee is prevented by serious illness from claiming in time, it will normally be held not to have been reasonably practicable to present the claim in time. In *Schultz v Esso Petroleum Ltd* [1999] 3 All ER 338, [1999] ICR 1202, [1999] IRLR 488, the employee became ill some six weeks before the time limit expired and was unable to instruct solicitors. The Court of Appeal rejected an argument that an extension of time should be refused since he could have claimed before he fell ill: the Court held that although the whole period of three months is relevant, it is necessary to focus particularly on the latter part of the period of three months. This decision was applied by the EAT in *Agrico UK Ltd v Ireland* (EATS/0042/05), in support of a finding that it had been perverse of a tribunal to hold that it had not been reasonably practicable to present the claim in time where the Claim Form had been left by the claimant's solicitor for his secretary to complete and send in on the last day for presentation, but she fell ill and was absent that day, and the matter was not attended to until she returned to work the following day. The tribunal's error was to focus exclusively on the end of the three months, and not consider the practicability of the claim having been presented earlier. It is difficult to reconcile this approach and that in the *Avdic* case, above, and it would be helpful to have further clarification from the Court of Appeal of the position where an intention to submit at the last moment goes wrong for unforeseen reasons.

(viii) If the claimant instructs solicitors or advisers to act on his or her behalf and through their default the Claim Form is not presented in time, the tribunal will consider that it was reasonably practicable for the claim to be presented in time, and will not entertain the claim. As Lord Denning MR said in *Dedman v British Building and Engineering Appliances Ltd* [1974] 1 All ER 520, [1974] 1 WLR 171, [1974] ICR 53:

> 'I would suggest that in every case the tribunal should inquire into the circumstances and ask themselves whether the man or his advisers were at fault in allowing [the time limit] to pass by without presenting the complaint. If he was not at fault, nor his advisers – so that he had just cause or excuse for not presenting his complaint within [the time limit] – then it was "not practicable" for him to present it within that time.'

See also *Walls Meat Co Ltd v Khan* [1979] ICR 52, [1978] IRLR 499, CA, *Riley v Tesco Stores Ltd* [1980] ICR 323, *Croydon Health Authority v Jaufurally* [1986] ICR 4, and *El-Kholy v Rentokil Initial Facilities Services (UK) Ltd* (UKEAT/0472/12). The point is not limited to lawyers; if the claimant has placed his case in the hands of his trade union, he may be fixed with the consequences of delay on the union's part, as in *Cullinane v Balfour Beatty Engineering Services Ltd* (UKEAT/0537/10). However, in *Harvey's Household Linens Ltd v Benson* [1974] ICR 306 it was held that Department of Employment officials were not 'advisers' for this purpose, so their error ought not to be attributed to a claimant who followed their advice; this was followed in *Dixon Stores Group v Arnold* (EAT/772/93). The same applies to advice given by tribunal employees (*Rybak v Jean Sorelle Ltd* [1991] ICR 127; and see *London International College v Sen* [1993] IRLR 333). In *Alexanders Holdings Ltd v Methven* (EAT/782/93), the EAT upheld a finding in the case of a claimant who believed, as a result of ambiguous advice from the

Department of Social Security, that he was not permitted to present his claim for three months following dismissal, that it was not reasonably practicable for him to do so in time.

The question whether a claimant is fixed by the error of his or her adviser is sometimes said to turn on whether the adviser concerned was a 'skilled adviser'. That is a question of fact, depending on the particular circumstances of the case: *Theobald v Royal Bank of Scotland plc* [2007] All ER (D) 04 (Jan). The EAT in this case also makes the distinction between instructing an adviser to act on the employee's behalf, in which case it will usually be held to have been reasonably practicable to present the claim in time, and taking advice from an adviser but retaining control over the submission of the claim, where the fault of the adviser in giving erroneous advice will not count against the claimant; however this distinction was rejected by the EAT in the subsequent case of *T Mobile (UK) Ltd v Singleton* [2011] All ER (D) 12 (May), where it was held that the mere taking of advice from a solicitor was sufficient to fix the claimant with the solicitor's negligence in failing to alert him to the correct time limit. In the same case it was held that the employer is under no duty to take active steps to correct a misunderstanding by the employee of the correct time limit.

In *Marks & Spencer plc v Williams-Ryan* [2005] EWCA Civ 470, [2005] IRLR 562, however, the Court of Appeal upheld a finding that it was not reasonably practicable for the claimant to claim in time where she had been led by misleading information provided by the employer to understand that she could not present a tribunal claim until her internal appeal against dismissal had been concluded (and that process was in turn delayed beyond the three month limit). The important distinction here is between inaction and actively (or unintentionally) misleading. See also *Aryeetey v Tuntum Housing Association*, [2007] All ER (D) 174 (Oct) (not reasonably practicable to present claim when claimant advised by Employment Judge during related proceedings that a further claim was not necessary).

(ix)   A rather stricter view of ignorance of rights may be taken where the rights are based on principles of European law overriding restrictions in domestic law. Thus, in *Biggs v Somerset County Council* [1996] 2 All ER 734, [1996] 2 CMLR 292 [1996] ICR 364, the Court of Appeal held as a matter of law that it was reasonably practicable for Ms Biggs to present a claim for unfair dismissal at a time when (as a part-time employee) she was expressly debarred by statute from the right to complain and the statute was only held to infringe EU law many years later.

18.21

If it is not reasonably practicable to present a claim in time, the tribunal may allow an extension of time of such further period as it considers reasonable. There is no fixed limit, and each case must be considered on its facts in the light of the employee's explanation for the delay: *Marley (UK) Ltd v Anderson* [1996] ICR 728, CA. The EAT has commented that the tribunal has an unfettered discretion as to how long an extension of time to allow in the light of all the circumstances, albeit the discretion must be exercised judicially: *Howlett Marine Services Ltd v Bowlam* [2001] IRLR 201. In practice, however the starting point is that there is an obligation on claimants to act expeditiously in asserting their rights in the tribunal, so that even a relatively short delay beyond the point when it became reasonably practicable to present the claim may be more than is reasonable in the absence of an explanation for the further delay; in *Theobald v The Royal Bank of Scotland plc* (EAT/0444/06) [2007] All ER (D) 04 (Jan), a delay of 13 days was held on the facts to be too long, and in *Nolan v Balfour Beatty Engineering Services Ltd* (UKEAT/0109/11) a decision allowing an extension of 11 weeks from when the claimant became aware of the facts entitling him to claim was held to be perverse.

For the practical application of the process of assessing a reasonable time, see *James W Cook & Co (Wivenhoe) Ltd (in liq) v Tipper* [1990] ICR 716, at 724–725, CA, as explained in *Marley (UK) Ltd v Anderson* (above). It has been suggested that the tribunal should consider the same questions as in applying the 'reasonable practicability' test, particularly as regards the claimant's state of mind and state of knowledge, but focusing on what was reasonable rather than what was practicable: *Thompson v Northumberland County Council*, [2007] All ER (D) 95 (Sep). More recently, the EAT has twice held that the same approach should be used as to whether the extension sought is reasonable as to whether it was not reasonably practicable to present the claim in time: *Nolan*, above, and *Cullinane v Balfour Beatty Engineering Services Ltd* (UKEAT/0537/10), both claims under the trade union blacklisting legislation.

A claimant who loses the opportunity to have his or her case heard by the tribunal because of the negligence of professional advisers is able to sue them in the ordinary courts. The claim is for the loss of a chance of making a successful claim, so that an assessment of the prospects of success in the tribunal would have to be made when calculating damages.

If a claimant wishes to pursue his or her claim in another forum (eg in proceedings for wrongful dismissal (see WRONGFUL DISMISSAL (58)) but also wishes to preserve the right to proceed in the tribunal, he or she should submit a Claim Form, using the 'Further Information' section to explain the position, and seek to have the tribunal proceedings stayed (*Warnock v Scarborough Football Club* [1989] ICR 489; and see **19.83** below).

18.22 Redundancy payments

A time limit of six months applies. This period runs from the 'relevant date', which is defined in *ERA 1996, s 145* and is in most cases (where there has not been a trial period in alternative employment) the same as the EDT (see for details of this **18.18** and **18.19** above). The EAT in *Watts v Rubery Owen Conveyancer Ltd* [1977] 2 All ER 1 held that a claim for a redundancy payment may not be presented until the dismissal has taken effect (unless the claim is based on the special procedure for claim in redundancy payments where the employee has been laid off or placed on short time working). However the Court of Appeal in *Bon Groundwork Ltd v Foster* [2012] EWCA Civ 252, [2012] IRLR 517 acknowledged that the decision in *Watt* has since been heavily criticised, and declined to rule on whether it is still good law. In order to preserve the right to institute tribunal proceedings, it is sufficient that within the six-month period following the 'relevant date' the employee has made a claim by notice in writing to the employer; or referred the claim to a tribunal; or presented a claim of unfair dismissal to the tribunal; or that a payment (not necessarily the full entitlement) has been agreed and paid. The effect of any of these actions is to preserve the right to claim indefinitely (*ERA 1996, s 164(1)*). The six-month time limit may be extended by up to a further six months if the tribunal is persuaded that it is just and equitable to do so (*ERA 1996, s 164(2), (3)*). See **18.30** below for the principles applicable to a 'just and equitable' extension of time. There is no jurisdiction to extend time beyond the further period of six months: *Crawford v Secretary of State for Employment* [1995] IRLR 523.

18.23 Equal pay

The standard time limit laid down by *s 129* of the *Equality Act 2010* is six months from the date the employee ceased to be employed by the respondent employer (*ss 129(3), 130*). A claim may, of course, be made whilst the applicant is still employed. The time limit provisions are modified in cases about pension rights. All of these points applied equally to claims under the predecessor legislation, the *Equal Pay Act 1970*. The validity of the six-month time limit was challenged as contrary to EU law in *Preston v Wolverhampton Healthcare NHS Trust* [2001] UKHL 5, [2001] ICR 217, but was upheld, subject to qualifications (see below) by the House of Lords.

Following amendments made by the *Equal Pay Act 1970 (Amendment) Regulations 2003 (SI 2003/1656)*, retained in the *Equality Act 2010*, there are three categories of case in which the time limit may be extended. First, whilst normally the limit applies to each contract where an employee is employed under a number of contracts, even if the contracts are immediately consecutive, where there is a succession of contracts at regular intervals forming part of a stable employment relationship (a 'stable employment case'), time only runs from the end of the last such contract (*Equality Act 2010, ss 129(3), 130(3)*). Second, where the employer deliberately concealed from the claimant a fact relevant to his or her claim and without knowledge of which he or she could not reasonably have been expected to institute the proceedings, and the claimant did not discover and could not with reasonable diligence have discovered the fact until after the end of the period of employment (a 'concealment case') time is extended to six months from the day on which the claimant discovered, or could with reasonable diligence have discovered, the fact (*ss 129(3), 130(4)*). Third, if at the date of the ending of his or her employment (or any later date from which time would otherwise run by virtue of either of the other exceptions) the claimant is under a disability, ie is a minor (or under 16 in Scotland) or is of unsound mind (a 'disability case'), time runs from the date that he or she ceases to be under such a disability (*ss 129(3), 130(7)*).

Subject to these exceptions, the tribunal has no jurisdiction to extend time. However, provided that a claim is presented in time, ie (usually) within six months following the termination of the employment, an equal pay claim relating to a job in which the employee had ceased to be employed some time previously may be pursued: *Young v National Power plc* [2001] 2 All ER 339, [2001] ICR 328, CA: see further on this *Allan v Newcastle-upon-Tyne City Council* [2005] ICR 1170, [2005] IRLR 504, EAT.

The Court of Appeal has given guidance in *Slack v Cumbria County Council (Equality and Human Rights Commission intervening)* [2009] EWCA Civ 293, [2009] ICR 1217 on the position where a claimant was employed for a continuous period by the same employer but, because of changes in such matters as hours of work, new contracts were issued during that period. The Court's conclusion was that time would not start to run against the employee in relation to the prior period of employment simply because she signed a new contract, since the situation would normally fall within the scope of the 'stable employment relationship' exception in what is now *Equality Act 2010 ss 129(3), 130(3)*. In the light of that conclusion, the Court went on to hold that the time limits (then laid down by the *Equal Pay Act 1970*) were compatible with the requirements of European law.

The House of Lords has ruled that where an employee's employment has been transferred under the *Transfer of Undertakings (Protection of Employment) Regulations 1981*, time for making a claim in respect of employment with the previous employer runs from the date of the transfer, not the eventual end of the employment with the transferee employer: *Powerhouse Retail Ltd v Burroughs* [2006] UKHL 13, [2006] IRLR 381. The same principle would apply to a transfer under the replacement *2006 Regulations*. This limitation does not however apply where the claim is against the current employer, based on a term derived from the application of an equality clause during the previous employment but which then transferred with the claimant under the Regulations to her new employer: *Gutridge v Sodexo Ltd* [2009] EWCA Civ 729, [2009] ICR 1486.

It should be noted that claims for equal pay under the *Equality Act 2010* can also be brought in the High Court or County Court, based on the contractual equality clause implied into all employment contracts by the equality of terms provisions of the *2010 Act*. Like any contractual claim in the ordinary courts, such claims may be brought at any time within six years of the breach (the time limit in Scotland is five years). The Court has power to strike a claim out if it could 'more conveniently' be brought in the employment tribunal. In *Abdulla v Birmingham City Council* [2012] ICR 1419, the Supreme Court confirmed this position. The Court indicated that prior to the expiry of time to bring a claim in the tribunal, in most cases it would be more convenient to dispose of the case in the Tribunal. However, after that time period has expired, and the claim is time-barred in the tribunal, a Court could not conclude the claim would more conveniently be disposed of in the tribunal. Parliament had allowed the claims to be brought in the civil courts as well as in the tribunal. In *Asda Stores Ltd v Brierley* [2016] ICR 945, the Court of Appeal considered whether an ET could impose a stay on its proceedings so as in effect to compel claimants to pursue High Court proceedings. Elias LJ held that whilst Rule 29 did confer a power to stay proceedings (including indefinitely), the ET could not use that power to relinquish jurisdiction to the High Court merely because it considered that court to be a more appropriate forum. Unlawful

18.24 Unlawful discrimination

A claim must be presented to the tribunal 'not after the end' of the period of three months 'beginning when the act complained of was done': *Equality Act 2010, s 123(1)*. There are specific provisions to deal with discrimination by omission, which is to be treated as occurring when the person in question decided upon it; and an act extending over a period is to be treated as done at the end of that period: see *s 123(3)*. The latter provision covers the maintenance of a continuing policy or state of affairs, as well as a continuing course of discriminatory conduct such as harassment: see *Barclays Bank plc v Kapur* [1991] 2 AC 355, [1991] 1 All ER 646, [1991] ICR 208, [1991] IRLR 136; and *Okoro v Taylor Woodrow Construction Ltd* [2013] ICR 580. The same provisions as to time limits and extensions of time apply to each of the *Part-time Workers (Prevention of Less Favourable Treatment) Regulations 2000*, the *Fixed-term Employees (Prevention of Less Favourable Treatment) Regulations 2002* and the *Agency Workers Regulations 2010*. See further **18.28** below.

The line between a continuing policy or course of conduct and a single act with continuing consequences is illustrated by cases on each side of the line in *Owusu v London Fire and Civil Defence Authority* [1995] IRLR 574. The leading case on what it is necessary to show to establish an act continuing over a period is now *Hendricks v Metropolitan Police Comr* [2002] EWCA Civ 1686, [2003] 1 All ER 654, [2003] ICR 530. In this case the Court of Appeal emphasised that whilst a policy or practice of discrimination will normally provide a basis for a claim that there was a discriminatory act continuing over a period, it is not a necessary precondition, as earlier cases had appeared to indicate. The correct test is whether the acts complained of are linked, and are evidence of a continuing discriminatory state of affairs. In *Lyfar v Brighton and Sussex University Hospitals Trust* [2006] EWCA Civ 1548, [2006] All ER (D) 182 (Nov), the Court of Appeal confirmed that its decision in *Hendricks* was to be followed, in preference to *Robertson v Bexley Community Centre* [2003] EWCA Civ 576, [2003] IRLR 434, a case decided after *Hendricks* but which does not refer to it, and applies the requirement of a policy or practice. A relevant factor in whether or not a series of acts is to be regarded as an act continuing over a period is whether the same person or persons is or are responsible for each of the acts: *Aziz v FDA* [2010] EWCA Civ 304, 154 Sol Jo (no 14) 29. As to the relevance of such matters as evidence that later events were acts of discrimination, see *HSBC Asia Holdings BV v Gillespie* [2011] ICR 192. If the issue whether a number of incidents amounted to an act continuing over a period is being considered as a preliminary issue at a preliminary hearing (as may be the case when some but not all or the incidents would be out of time if treated separately) the test is whether the claimant has made out a prima facie case for the incidents being treated collectively as an act continuing over a period: *Lyfar v Brighton and Sussex University Hospitals NHS Trust* [2006] EWCA Civ 1548, *Aziz v First Division Association* [2010] EWCA Civ 304.

The fact that it has not been specifically pleaded in the claim that the various acts of alleged discrimination alleged form part of an act continuing over a period does not preclude the tribunal from treating them as such for the purpose of the running of time, at least if the respondent had been sufficiently alerted to the point: *Khetab v Aga Medical Ltd* (UKEAT/0313/10).

Where a discriminatory policy is operated by a respondent, time begins to run afresh each time the policy is operated to the detriment of the claimant: *Rovenska v General Medical Council* [1998] ICR 85. If the complainant is an employee, the continued existence of the policy or practice, or state of affairs evidenced by the specific acts, postpones the running of time until the policy is discontinued or rescinded or (if earlier) the employment ends: *Cast v Croydon College* [1998] ICR 500. This is not necessarily the case, however, where a claimant complains of repeated rejections of job applications: cf *Tyagi v BBC World Service* [2001] EWCA Civ 549, [2001] IRLR 465; each rejection is likely to be treated as a separate cause of action, with time running accordingly. Time does not start to run in respect of an act of discrimination until the discriminator is in a position to put into effect his or her discriminatory intention: *Swithland Motors plc v Clarke* [1994] IRLR 275 (as to the position in dismissal cases, see below).

The *Equality Act 2010* and the *Part-time Workers, Fixed-term Employees Regulations* and *Agency Workers Regulations* also make specific provision for when time runs where what is complained of is a deliberate omission (such as a refusal to make adjustments to the working arrangements for a disabled employee). In such cases the principle is that time runs from the date on which the employer decided not to act, rather than from the date of the employee becoming aware of this fact. As there will often be no direct evidence of the relevant date, there are further provisions treating the employer as having decided not to act when he does an act inconsistent with doing the act omitted, or at the end of a reasonable period within which he could be expected to have acted. These provisions were considered by the Court of Appeal in *Matuszowicz v Kingston-Upon-Hull City Council* [2009] EWCA Civ 22, [2009] 3 All ER 685, [2009] IRLR 288. The Court held that the statutory provisions must be taken to apply equally to a non-deliberate omission – as where the employer simply failed to make the required adjustment in a disability case (as this case was). Recognising the difficulty that employees may have in appreciating when time starts to run in these circumstances, the Court urged tribunals to allow some latitude to employees to take account of their difficulty in judging when a reasonable time had passed for the employer to act.

Another difficult issue in relation to when time starts to run is where the complaint is of discrimination by way of, or leading to, dismissal. It is now clearly established (after earlier conflicting case law) that time runs from the date of the dismissal (rather than (if earlier) the date on which notice was given): see the cases cited in *British Gas Services Ltd v McCaull* [2001] IRLR 60 at para 25. In *Derby Specialist Fabrication Ltd v Burton* [2001] 2 All ER 840, [2001] ICR 833 this principle was followed in a race discrimination case where the claim was for constructive dismissal. The EAT held that this constituted a 'dismissal' within *s 4(2)* of the *RRA 1976* and it was not therefore necessary to rely on the discriminatory acts which had led to the employee's resignation as 'detriments' (in which case the claim would have been out of time). The same conclusion has now also been reached by the Court of Appeal in relation to the *DDA 1995*: *Meikle v Nottinghamshire County Council* [2004] EWCA Civ 859, [2004] 4 All ER 97, [2005] ICR 1, [2004] IRLR 703, following *Catherall v Michelin Tyres plc* [2003] ICR 28, EAT, and disapproving the earlier contrary view expressed by a different division of the EAT in *Metropolitan Police Comr v Harley* [2001] ICR 927.

A point not directly arising in these cases, and on which there is no direct authority, is whether a claim alleging discrimination by way of dismissal may be presented before the claimant has been dismissed, in the sense applied in the cases cited above. There is nothing obvious in the wording of the statutory provisions on time limits to prevent this, as a claim is merely required not to be presented after the end of the period specified. Under the legislation on discrimination prior to the *Equality Act 2010*, the complaint to be presented was that the respondent 'has committed' an act of unlawful discrimination (see eg the *Sex Discrimination Act 1975, s 63(1)* wording which did preclude a complaint of dismissal being presented before the dismissal took effect, and there was (and is) no equivalent in the discrimination legislation of *ERA 1996 s 111(3)*, which specifically allows the presentation of a complaint of unfair dismissal during the notice period: see **18.19** above. However the position is less clearly expressed in the *Equality Act 2010, ss 120(1)* and *123(1)*; the former provision refers to complaints 'relating to' a contravention of relevant parts of the *Act*, and 'not after the end' of a period does not necessarily mean also 'not before the beginning'. The prudent course, in the circumstances, is not to present a claim before the dismissal has taken effect.

18.25 'Just and equitable' extension of time

A tribunal has discretion to extend time where it would be 'just and equitable' to do so: *Equality Act 2010, s 123(3)*; *Part-time Workers (Prevention of Less Favourable Treatment) Regulations 2000, reg 8, Fixed-term Employees (Prevention of Less Favourable Treatment) Regulations 2002, reg 8*; *Agency Workers Regulations 2010, reg 18*. This is a broader discretion than the 'not reasonably practicable' test and the EAT has (albeit with limited success) discouraged the development of authorities on the application of the test: see *Hutchinson v Westward Television Ltd* [1977] ICR 279, [1977] IRLR 69. Where there is more than one Respondent, the Tribunal must consider the question of an extension of time for each one separately: *Harden v Wootlif & another* UKEAT/0448/14.

The Court of Appeal has emphasised that there is no presumption in favour of the extension of time. The onus is on the claimant to convince the tribunal that it is just and equitable to extend time, in the context that time limits in employment cases are intended to apply strictly: *Robertson v Bexley Community Centre* [2003] EWCA Civ 576, [2003] IRLR 434. However, in *Chief Constable of Lincolnshire Police v Caston* [2009] EWCA Civ 1298, [2010] IRLR 327, the Court of Appeal emphasised that the comments in *Robertson* merely indicated that there was a broad discretion, the question being one of fact and judgment rather than policy; 'there is no principle of law which indicates how generously or sparingly the power to enlarge time is to be exercised' (per Sedley LJ). Because of the breadth of the discretion, the appellate courts are reluctant to interfere with the exercise of the discretion if the issue is appealed.

The fact that the onus is on the claimant to make out a case for an extension of time means that it is often necessary, or at least helpful, for the claimant to give evidence in support of the claim for an extension. However, the EAT has confirmed that evidence from the claimant is not a precondition for an extension; other material before the tribunal, such as documents, may be sufficient to establish the balance in favour of the claimant: *Accurist Watches Ltd v Wadher* [2009] All ER (D) 189 (Apr). See by analogy the approach of the EAT, requiring specific medical evidence relevant to the individual's condition, in order to justify an extension of time for appealing in *J v K* [2017] UKEATPA/0661/16.

If there are circumstances which otherwise render it just and equitable to extend time, the length of the extension required is not of itself a limiting factor, unless the delay would prejudice the possibility of a fair trial: *Afolabi v Southwark London Borough Council* [2003] EWCA Civ 15, [2003] ICR 800, where the Court of Appeal upheld an extension of time of nearly nine years where the claimant had without fault on his part been unaware of the facts relied on to support his claim, and had acted reasonably promptly when those facts came to his knowledge. However it will be exceptional that a delay of or approaching that order would not render a fair trial impossible, especially where facts are disputed and there is no clear contemporaneous documentation.

Other factors which a tribunal should take into account in the exercise of its discretion will depend on the facts of each case, and cannot be exhaustively listed. They will however include the reason for the delay, whether the claimant was aware of his or her rights to claim, and/or of the time limit, the conduct of the employer, the length of the extension sought, and the prejudice that would be suffered by the employer if the claim were permitted to proceed (necessarily balanced against the prejudice to the claimant if he or she is refused an extension of time). Tribunals are encouraged to consider by analogy the checklist of factors listed in the *Limitation Act 1980, s 33* (which confers discretion to extend time for personal injury claims in the courts) – see *British Coal Corporation v Keeble* [1997] IRLR 336 –, but the EAT has stated that this process is not mandatory (*Chohan v Derby Law Centre* [2004] IRLR 685). Tribunals do not need to follow a formulaic approach and set out a checklist of factors that may be relevant, in particular where no reliance is placed on them: *Hall v ADP Dealer Services Ltd* (UKEAT/00390/13). A failure to provide a good excuse for the delay in bringing a relevant claim will not inevitably result in an extension being refused: *Rathakrishnan v Pizza Express (Restaurants) Ltd* [2016] ICR 283. There is authority for the proposition that the most important factor in whether to extend time is whether the delay has affected the ability of the tribunal to conduct a fair trial of the issues: *DPP v Marshall* [1998] ICR 518. However it is suggested that this should not be relied on as a reason not to attach weight to other factors such as serious and avoidable delay by the claimant in claiming, or in obtaining advice about a possible claim.

An example of a specific factor being taken into account in favour of a claimant is *Department of Constitutional Affairs v Jones* [2007] EWCA Civ 894, [2008] IRLR 128, where the Court of Appeal accepted as a valid reason for extending time the claimant's inability or unwillingness to admit to himself or others that he was disabled (by clinical depression).

The EAT has held that where delay in presenting a claim is attributable to incorrect legal advice from the claimant's solicitor, this should not be visited on the claimant by refusing an extension of time, notwithstanding that the claimant may have a valid claim in negligence against the solicitor, since this would confer a windfall on the respondent: *Chohan v Derby Law Centre*, above. This does not mean that time *should* be extended in all such cases, but that all other factors must also be considered. See also *Hawkins v Ball* [1996] IRLR 258 for a more cautious approach to this point, and *Wright v Wolverhampton City Council* (UKEAT/0117/08) [2009] All ER (D) 179 (Feb), applying the principles to poor advice given by a trade union representative. By contrast, where the delay in presentation is down entirely to the claimant, a tribunal is more likely to refuse an application for a just and equitable extension of time: see *De Souza v Manpower UK Ltd* [2013] All ER (D) 199 (Feb), where the application was one day out of time.

Case law prior to the implementation of the *Dispute Resolution Regulations* had established that a decision by the employee to delay presenting a claim whilst an internal grievance procedure or appeal was being pursued would not necessarily be a sufficient reason to extend time under the 'just and equitable' principle, even if the delay had not prejudiced the employer. It was only one of the relevant factors to be taken into account, and the weight to be attached to it was a matter for the tribunal in the light of the facts of each case: *Apelogun-Gabriels v Lambeth London Borough Council* [2001] EWCA Civ 1853, [2002] ICR 713, [2002] IRLR 116 overruling *Aniagwu v Hackney London Borough Council* [1999] IRLR 303 and affirming *Robinson v Post Office* [2000] IRLR 804. It is probable that following the repeal of the dispute resolution legislation, the position as stated in *Apelogun-Gabriels* again applies.

The principle established in relation to unfair dismissal claims by the Court of Appeal in *Biggs v Somerset County Council* [1996] ICR 364, that a failure to appreciate that European law confers a right to claim apparently excluded by the UK statute does not make it 'not reasonably practicable' to claim in time, does not apply to discrimination claims. The 'just and equitable' test is wider, and an understandable misapprehension as to the state of the law is a relevant factor in deciding whether to extend time: *British Coal Corpn v Keeble* [1997] IRLR 336. Not all misunderstandings of the law will be accepted as excuses however; see *University of Westminster v Bailey* [2009] All ER (D) 47 (Nov), where the EAT held that it was not an acceptable reason for a 19 month delay that the claimant, a senior lecturer in HR, did not realise that the *Sex Discrimination Act 1975* applied equally to men. It has been suggested that a change in the law could render it just and equitable to extend time to allow a claim which could not have been brought as the law had previously been understood to be: *Foster v South Glamorgan Health Authority* [1988] ICR 526.

notice period (*ERA 1996, s 111(3)*), and a breach of contract claim presented before the EDT is premature, with the result that the tribunal has no jurisdiction to determine it (*Capek v Lincolnshire County Council* [2000] IRLR 590, CA). The EAT has held (in *Miller Bros and F P Butler Ltd v Johnston* [2002] ICR 744) that the tribunal has no jurisdiction to consider a claim for breach of contract where the contract was only concluded after the employment had terminated (in that case a compromise agreement which the employer had failed to implement).

Contract claims are the only class of claim in respect of which an employer may counterclaim. In the *2013 Rules* such a claim is called an "Employer's Contract Claim". An employer's contract claim may only be brought if presented at a time when the employee's claim is before the tribunal (ie it has been presented and not withdrawn) and is subject to a time limit of six weeks beginning with the day the employer received from the tribunal a copy of the employee's Claim Form (*Employment Tribunals Extension of Jurisdiction (England and Wales) Order 1994, art 8*). The same 'not reasonably practicable' test applies to any application for an extension of time. The validity of the employer's contract claim is not, however, affected by whether the claim itself was brought in time: all that is relevant is that a claim has been brought and a counterclaim is presented within the time limit running from the date of presentation of the claim (*Patel v RCMS Ltd* [1999] IRLR 161).

The *2013 Rules* specify that any employer's contract claim must be made as part of the response, presented in accordance with *Rule 16*: see *Rule 23*. Such a response is ordinarily due within 28 days of the date the copy of the claim form was sent by the Tribunal to the respondent: *Rule 16(1)*. Care must therefore be taken when seeking any extension of the 28 day period in order not to run into difficulties with the statutory limitation date for an employer's contract claim as set out in *Art 8* of the *1994 Order*. Having time extended for a response does not automatically grant an extension of the statutory time limit for bringing an employer's contract claim. The statutory time limit can only be extended on the 'not reasonably practicable' basis whereas there is a general discretion to extend the time for presenting a response.

The employer's contract claim can be rejected in the same way as a claimant's claim may be rejected under *Rule 12* of the *2013 Rules* – see *Rule 23*. The other procedural requirements for an employer's contract claim are covered in **19.52**. A Practice Direction issued by the President of the employment tribunals in Scotland (No 3 of December 2006) was revoked in February 2014 as a result of the new rules.

18.28   Other claims

For details of time limits for other classes of claim, and provisions as to extension of time, the relevant statutory provisions should be consulted. Three points of importance merit mention here:

(a)   Claims under the *Part-time Workers (Prevention of Less Favourable Treatment) Regulations 2000*, the *Fixed-term Employees (Prevention of Less Favourable Treatment) Regulations 2002*, and the *Agency Workers Regulations 2010*, alleging either less favourable treatment or subjection to a detriment by way of victimisation, are subject to provisions as to the applicable time limit, when time runs and extensions of time which are substantially the same as those in the anti-discrimination statutes: see **18.24** and **18.25** above. This contrasts with claims of subjection to detriment under *Part IVA* of the *ERA 1996*, where the 'not reasonably practicable' test applies: *ERA 1996, s 48(3)(b)*. An application under *reg 9* of the *Fixed-term Employees (Prevention of Less Favourable Treatment) Regulations 2002* for a declaration that the employee is a permanent employee may be made at any time provided that the employee has requested a statement to that effect from the employer, and that he or she is still employed by the employer when the tribunal application is made: *reg 9(6)*.

(b)   Complaints by trade unions or employee representatives, or in certain circumstances individual employees, under the *Transfer of Undertakings (Protection of Employment) Regulations 2006 ('TUPE'), reg 15*, of a failure to inform or consult over a relevant transfer, are subject to a three-month time limit, time running from the date of the transfer, and any extension is subject to the 'not reasonably practicable' criteria. However the EAT has held that a complaint may also be presented before the transfer has occurred, where it is alleged that there has been a material breach of the duty to inform or to consult: *South Durham Health Authority v UNISON* [1995] ICR 495. A similar position arises in relation to complaints of failure to consult recognised trade unions or employee representatives about proposed redundancies (*TULRCA, s 188*): a complaint must be presented either before the last of the dismissals the subject of the complaint takes effect or within the period of three months beginning with that date (*s 189(5)*) but there is no restriction on earlier presentation, provided that the employer is subject to an obligation to consult (ie the employer proposes redundancies) and it is alleged that there has been a breach of the obligation.

(c)   Complaints of failure to pay sums due under a protective award made under either of the two above provisions are subject to separate time limits. In a case under *TUPE*, the time limit is three months beginning with the date of the order for a protective award (with the possibility of an extension if presentation in time was not reasonably practicable: *reg 15(12)*). If the award is made, or varied, by the EAT following an appeal, the time for claiming runs from the date of the EAT's order: *Dillon v Todd* (UKEATS/0010/11). In redundancy cases, the period of three months runs from the last day in respect of which the protective award was made, again with the possibility of extension. However, it is possible that the protective award is not made (or confirmed on appeal) until after the time limit has expired. In such a case the claimant must rely on the 'not reasonably practicable' extension, and should therefore not delay in presenting his or her claim: *Howlett Marine Services Ltd v Bowlam* [2001] IRLR 201.

19   Employment Tribunals – II

19.1   THE OVERRIDING OBJECTIVE

The traditional approach to litigation in Britain was for the parties to prepare and present their respective cases with relatively little management of the proceedings by the court. That approach, which was to a considerable extent followed in the early years of the operation of employment tribunals, was superseded in the civil courts in England and Wales by the requirements of the *Civil Procedure Rules 1998* for the active management of cases to ensure that the principles embodied in the Overriding Objective are achieved in practice. The move towards much more active management of cases was followed in employment tribunals, both in England and Wales and Scotland, with the introduction of a similar Overriding Objective of dealing with cases justly. The Overriding Objective was first introduced in *reg 10* of the *2001 Regulations* and was said by *reg 10(1)* to be "to enable tribunals to deal with cases justly". The components of that objective were broken down in reg 10(2) to include, so far as practicable, (a) ensuring that the parties are on an equal footing; (b) saving expense; (c) dealing with the case in ways which are proportionate to the complexity of the issues; and (d) ensuring that the case is dealt with expeditiously and fairly. By *reg 10(3)* a tribunal was obliged to seek to give effect to the overriding objective when exercising powers under the rules and when interpreting the rules. There was further an obligation on the parties to assist the tribunal achieving the overriding objective. The objective thus framed followed, broadly, *Part 1* of the *Civil Procedure Rules 1998*, albeit without including specific reference to proportionality in terms of the amount of money involved in a case, the importance of the case or the financial position of each party; and further without reference to the need to allot to each case an appropriate share of the Court's resources, while taking into account the need to allot resources to other cases. By the time of the *2004 Regulations*, the Overriding Objective appeared as *reg 3*. Its content remained static, save for two minor adjustments: (i) including reference to dealing with cases in ways which are proportionate to the importance of the issues, as well as their complexity; and (ii) re-ordering the components of the objective so that saving expense was moved down the list to the last position.

19.2   The *2013 Regulations* and *2013 Rules* differ from their predecessors in that the Overriding Objective has been moved from its previous positioning as part of the *Regulations* to its new place as *Rule 2*. It provides as follows:

> The overriding objective to these Rules is to enable Employment Tribunals to deal with cases fairly and justly. Dealing with a case fairly and justly includes, so far as practicable –
>
> (a)   ensuring that the parties are on an equal footing;
>
> (b)   dealing with cases in ways which are proportionate to the complexity and importance of the issues;
>
> (c)   avoiding unnecessary formality and seeking flexibility in the proceedings;
>
> (d)   avoiding delay so far as compatible with proper consideration of the issues; and
>
> (e)   saving expense.
>
> A Tribunal shall seek to give effect to the overriding objective in interpreting, or exercising any power given to it by, these Rules. The parties and their representatives shall assist the Tribunal to further the overriding objective and in particular shall co-operate generally with each other and with the Tribunal.

19.3   The Overriding Objective in the *2013 Rules* therefore differs in a number of respects from the previous formulations:

(i)   the requirement of dealing with cases "fairly" has been elevated from being a defined component part of the objective, to form a part of the expression of the objective itself. It is difficult to see that this change (and departure from the formulation in the *Civil Procedure Rules 1998*) is anything more than form over substance; no practical effect is likely given that it has always been a requirement to ensure that cases were dealt with fairly.

(ii)   *Rule 2* introduces for the first time a requirement to avoid unnecessary formality and to seek flexibility in the proceedings. This was not a feature of the objective as framed in the legacy Regulations, and nor is it to be found in the *Civil Procedure Rules 1998* (as amended). This may well give effect to a substantive change to the practice of Employment Tribunals.

(iii)   Rather than seeking expedition, *Rule 2* sets out to avoid delay, so far as that is compatible with proper consideration of the issues. Like point (i) above, this is likely to be a mere formal change.

(iv)   *Rule 2* extends the obligation to assist the Tribunal in furthering the overriding objective beyond the parties to representatives, and further requires the parties and representatives to co-operate generally with each other and the Tribunal. This change makes express that which was previously implicitly required by the objective.

19.4

Rule 2 also differs from the Overriding Objective as contained in the amended *Civil Procedure Rules 1998* (see the amendments in the *Civil Procedure (Amendment) Rules 2013*). The latter includes within the concept of dealing with a case justly specific reference to allotting an appropriate share of the Court's resources to a case, enforcing compliance with rules, practice directions and orders, and to dealing with cases in a way proportionate to the amount of money involved and the financial position of each party. The Overriding Objective in the *Civil Procedure Rules 1998* also refers to dealing with the case proportionately to the importance of the "case" rather than *Rule 2*'s reference to the importance of the "issues", although it may be difficult in practical terms to distinguish these concepts.

It is of particular note is the fact that the need for compliance with rules, practice directions and orders has intensified in the Civil Courts since the change in the rules in April 2013: see e.g. *Mitchell v News Group Newspapers Ltd* [2014] 1 WLR 795, *Fred Perry (Holdings) Ltd v Brands Plaza Trading* [2012] EWCA Civ 224, *M A Lloyd & Sons v PPC International Ltd* [2014] EWHC 41 (QB), *Holloway v Transform Medical Group (CS) Limited* [2014] EWHC 1641, *Hallam Estates Ltd v Baker* [2014] EWCA Civ 661 and Lord Dyson MR's Lecture to the Implementation Programme (22 March 2013, at para 27). Since then, however, the Court of Appeal has signalled a softening of that approach, explaining that Mitchell had been "misunderstood" and "misapplied" leading to "manifestly unjust and disproportionate" decisions: *Denton v TH White Ltd* [2014] 1 WLR 3926. Nonetheless the Court continued to emphasise the new "culture of compliance" that had come into being.

The EAT considered these developments in *Harris v Academies Enterprise Trust* [2015] IRLR 208. Langstaff P noted the difference in the terms of the overriding objective under the CPR and *Rule 2* (para 32-33) but considered that decisions in the Tribunal could accommodate wider considerations because the tribunal has to deal with a case fairly and justly. "Justice is a wide concept" which can include justice viewed from the perspective of the system of which the tribunals are part in ensuring that indulgence given to one party does not deprive another party of that justice to which they also are entitled (para 34). That said, whereas (a) the need for litigation to be conducted efficiently and at proportionate cost; and (b) the enforcement of compliance with rules, practice directions and orders, had been given "top seats at the table" in the civil courts, they were not singled out even as particular factors within *Rule 2*. *Rule 2* was drafted in full knowledge of the approach that the CPR were taking and therefore it was wrong to say that the Tribunal rules had "lagged behind, being overtaken by history". There was a conscious decision by Parliament to adopt a different regime in the Tribunal (see para 38). Nonetheless, the EAT underlined that "Rules are there to be observed, orders are there to be observed, and breaches are not mere trivial matters . . . Tribunal judges are entitled to take a stricter line than they may have taken previously, but it remains a matter to be assessed from within the existing rules and the principles in existing cases" (para 40).

This sentiment dovetails with the Presidential Guidance for General Case Management, which emphasises (at para 19) that Orders are important and that non-compliance may lead to sanctions. The Guidance encourages parties having difficulty in complying to discuss it with the other parties and then apply to the Tribunal to vary the Order. See further the discussion of *Rule 6* below.

19.5 It is important to appreciate that, by *Rule 2*, the various powers of case management given to the tribunal, as described below, are required to be interpreted and exercised so as to give effect to the Overriding Objective. The extent to which the conduct of tribunal proceedings will be influenced by these overarching provisions will vary according to the circumstances, but it can generally be said that it would not be consistent with the Overriding Objective, or the duty of co-operation, for a party to seek to exploit technical or procedural points, or to drive up costs by excessive applications, for example, for additional disclosure or information. This is now underlined by the inclusion within the objective of the need to avoid unnecessary formality and to seek flexibility within proceedings. Deliberate delaying tactics, the concealment until the last minute of relevant evidence, or attempting to overload the tribunal with excessive and marginally relevant documentation are examples of behaviour that would be judged unreasonable by reference to the Objective, and which could result in an award of costs against the offending party. The "universal guiding principles" identified by Walker J in *Zazakhstan Kagazy Plc v Baglan Zhunus* [2015] EWHC 996 (Comm) are in principle equally applicable to litigation in the employment tribunal (para 3):

"(1) The court expects solicitors and counsel to take appropriate steps to conduct the debate, whether in advocacy or in correspondence, in a way which will lower the temperature rather than raise it.

(2) This remains the case even where – indeed particularly where – any concession is perceived as anathema by one or other or both sides. It is perfectly possible to be vigorous without being insulting.

(3) Imputations on others, whoever they may be, should only be made if they are both necessary and justified. If they are not strictly necessary, or they are not objectively justified, they should be rigorously excluded. Sometimes they are necessary, for example when . . . an allegation of bad faith is necessary. They must be confined to what is necessary. As to what is objectively justifiable, regard should be had to the degree of proof that is needed. . . .

(4) Rather than focus on criticisms of the other side, the focus should be on working out a timetable which will enable opposing parties to consider what facts and issues can be agreed, and what information and revised estimates for reading and hearing time can be given to the court prior to the hearing so as to ensure that the court's time is used efficiently and productively.

(5) If it is likely that a point which might be taken by a party, or it becomes likely that a point previously taken by a party, will not significantly advance that party's case, or will require a disproportionate amount of time or resources if it

is to be resolved, then notification should be given that the point will not be relied upon for present purposes. The notification can be accompanied by an appropriate reservation as to the position in future."

19.6

The case law on the provisions of pre-*2001 Rules*, where equivalent to the *2013 Rules*, should now be read subject to the effect of the Overriding Objective. An example of the impact of the Objective on previous interpretations of comparable provisions in previous versions of the *ET Rules* is *Williams v Ferrosan Ltd* [2004] IRLR 607, where the EAT held that the power of a tribunal to review its decisions 'in the interests of justice' (then contained in *rule 34(3)* of the *2004 Rules*) should not be restricted to cases where new facts had arisen subsequently or there had been a procedural mishap, but should be applied more widely to give effect to the Objective, effectively overruling the earlier and narrower approach taken by the EAT in *Trimble v Supertravel Ltd* [1982] ICR 440. This approach has been strongly endorsed in a case under the *2004 Rules*: *Sodexho Ltd v Gibbons* [2005] ICR 1647, [2005] IRLR 836, EAT. The overriding objective continues to have a role in shaping and updating procedural decisions taken by the EAT and the Courts. For a recent example see *Burrell v Micheldever Tyre Services Ltd* [2014] EWCA Civ 716, [2014] ICR 935 in which, but for contrary authority, the Court would have modified the traditional approach to remitting a case to the Tribunal following a successful appeal given the introduction of the overriding objective.

19.7 ALTERNATIVE DISPUTE RESOLUTION

The importance now attached to alternative dispute resolution ("ADR") is reflected in the fact that *Rule 3* of the *2013 Rules* mandates that the Tribunal "shall wherever practicable and appropriate encourage the use by the parties of the services of ACAS, judicial or other mediation, or other means of resolving their disputes by agreement". This is underlined by other references in the *Rules*: upon the initial consideration of claims and defences for arguability, the Judge is empowered (as well as making case management orders) to propose judicial mediation or other forms of dispute resolution: *Rule 26(1)*.

Whilst there is now increased emphasis on assisting the parties reach agreement through ADR, it has for some time been the case that the majority of tribunal claims are either withdrawn after a private settlement between the parties or following a mediation or conciliation through an ACAS conciliation officer.

ACAS Early Conciliation

19.8 *Introduction*

Following a consultation in January 2013, the ACAS Early Conciliation scheme was introduced by the *Enterprise and Regulatory Reform Act 2013, section 7*. The background concern (see para 58 of the Enterprise and Regulatory Reform Act 2013's Explanatory Notes) was that less than one fifth of claimants contacted ACAS for advice before submitting their claims. The new scheme has predictably had the effect of substantially increasing those numbers. EC Notifications during the period 6 April 2014 to 31 March 2015 were 80,734 from employees, and 2,689 from employers (it should be noted that for the first month of those figures, the scheme was voluntary). Between 1 April 2015 and 31 March 2016 the numbers were 87,892 and 4,280 respectively. These numbers represent an approx. 4 fold increase on the pre-claim conciliation scheme that ACAS operated from 2009 until the introduction of Early Conciliation. At the time of writing, statistics for the current year show that notifications have remained broadly consistent: from 1 April 2016 to 31 December 2016 there were 65,798 employee notifications and 3,615 from employers.

Further details of the scheme in practice can be found in the ACAS annual report and research papers *Evaluation of ACAS Early Conciliation 2015 (Ref 04/15)* and more recently, extending beyond the *EC experience, Evaluation of ACAS conciliation in Employment Tribunal Applications 2016 (Ref 04/16)*.

The relevant statutory provisions of the Early Conciliation scheme are to be found in *ETA 1996, sections 18, 18A, 18B, 18C.* The procedure for early conciliation is contained within the *Schedule* to the *Employment Tribunals (Early Conciliation: Exemptions and Rules of Procedure) Regulations 2014.* They are referred to below as the *EC Rules*.

For claims lodged on or after 6 May 2014, unless an exemption applies, there is a requirement that before a prospective claimant presents an application to a tribunal to institute "relevant proceedings", that prospective claimant must comply with the requirement for early conciliation: see *ETA 1996, section 18A(1)* and *Reg 4(1)* of the *Enterprise and Regulatory Reform Act 2013 (Commencement No 5, Transitional Provisions and Savings) Order 2014.* Such a prospective claimant will need an early conciliation certificate in order to institute those relevant proceedings: see *ETA 1996, section 18A(4).* In *Cranwell v Cullen* [2015] UKEATPAS/0046/14, the EAT held the Early Conciliation scheme was mandatory and where the statutory exemption did not apply, there was no discretion on the Tribunal, whether applying Rule 6 or otherwise, to waive the requirements. This was so even in a case where the very thought of conciliation would be problematic (that was a case in which the claimant alleged "appallingly" bad treatment described as "demeaning, derogatory and discriminatory, culminating in a physical assault"). Similarly, in the first instance decision of *Thomas v Nationwide Building Society* (2014) Case No 1601342/2014, the initial rejection of the claim for failing to follow EC was upheld. There, the judge allowed a reconsideration of that rejection where the claimant had belatedly embarked on the procedure and rectified the defect (although there was then an effect on the presentation date – see **19.41** below). However, the EAT has been keen that the requirements of the EC scheme do not become a web of technical requirements and to avoid the "real risk that satellite litigation in respect of the provisions of early conciliation might proliferate, with the same stultifying effect that litigation under the *Employment Act 2002* had in respect of the provisions of the dispute resolution procedures for which it provided" (per Langstaff J in *Drake International Systems Ltd v Blue Arrow Ltd* [2016] ICR 445 (para 35); see also See HHJ Eady QC's comments in *Science Warehouse v Mills* [2016] ICR 252 at para 26). The EAT has therefore emphasised in both of those cases that the *section 18A(1)* requirement on a prospective Claimant is to provide information to ACAS before s/he "presents an application to institute relevant proceedings relating to any matter". A "matter" was not the same as a "claim" or "cause of action". As Langstaff J held in *Drake International*, a "matter" might involve an event or events, different times and dates, and different people. Similarly, in *Compass Group v Morgan* [2017] ICR 73, Simler P emphasised the deliberate use of broad terminology: it was a matter of fact and degree as to whether the proceedings instituted related to "any matter" in respect of which the claimant had provided the requisite information to ACAS. The judge also observed that there was no indication of any temporal or other limitation on the validity of an EC Certificate. Thus in *Science Warehouse v Mills*, it was held that the Tribunal has a power to allow an amendment as a matter of judicial discretion to include a new cause of action in the ET1 as presented even if there had not been notification in respect of that new cause of action. Similarly in *Drake International Systems Ltd v Blue Arrow Ltd*, a TUPE case, new respondents could be substituted for the original respondent without there needing to be a further reference to ACAS under the EC procedures. Two other observations by Langstaff J in *Drake International* are of note. At para 26, he held that that once proceedings were on foot, it made no sense to talk of a "prospective" claimant in relation to the "matter". Further, and of more general application, at para 27, he remarked that what has been billed as the "obligation to engage in early conciliation" is overstated: "there is no such obligation but merely the need to obtain formal recognition that early conciliation has been considered by the claimant". As well as Compass Group, the approach in Science Warehouse and Mills was followed in *Mist v Derby Community Health Services NHS Trust* [2016] ICR 543.

Relevant proceedings for these purposes are defined by *ETA 1996, section 18*. That section contains a list of jurisdictions to which the early conciliation procedures apply. Almost all employment disputes within the jurisdiction of the tribunal are within the scope of ACAS conciliation, including breach of contract claims and claims for statutory redundancy payments (*ETA 1996, s 18(1)*).

19.9   *Notification*

By *Rule 1* of the *EC Rules*, a claimant satisfies the requirement for early conciliation if they either (i) present a completed early conciliation form to ACAS in accordance with *Rule 2* or (ii) telephone ACAS in accordance with *Rule 3*.

Rule 2 provides that an early conciliation form can be completed either on the ACAS website, https://ec.acas.org.uk/, or in hard-copy, which should then be posted to ACAS on the address shown on the early conciliation form (at the time of writing this is EC Notification, ACAS (Phoenix), PO Box 10279, Nottingham, NG2 9PE). The form must contain basic contact information for the claimant and employer (names and addresses) (*Rule 2(2)*), and ACAS may reject a form that does not contain the required information (*Rule 2(3)*) by returning it to the prospective claimant. In *Mist v Derby Community NHS Trust* [2016] ICR 543, the EAT held that the requirement to give the prospective Respondent's name and address was not a requirement for the precise or full legal title and (by way of example) a trading name would be sufficient. There, the name given to ACAS had been "Royal Derby Hospital" yet in the subsequent ET1 form, the Respondent was named as "Derby Hospitals NHS Foundation Trust". The EAT held the Tribunal had been right not to reject the ET1 form (or alternatively to have treated it as a minor error under *Rule 12(2A)*). HHJ Eady QC held (para 54) that "[t]he requirement is designed to ensure ACAS is provided with sufficient information to be able to make contact with the prospective Respondent if the Claimant agrees such an attempt to conciliate should be made . . . I do not read it as setting any higher bar." In addition to the mandatory information required by *Rule 2(2)*, the current early conciliation notification form asks for details of the claimant's employment (job title, dates of employment, date of incident about which complaint is made).

Rule 3 enables a prospective claimant to contact ACAS by telephone on the number set out on the early conciliation form (currently 0300 123 1122). The same mandatory basic information must be told to ACAS during the call (*Rule 3(1)*), and it is then down to ACAS to insert the information onto an early conciliation form (*Rule 3(2)*).

Separate notification forms under *Rule 2* (or oral notifications by telephone under *Rule 3*) are required for each prospective respondent: see *Rule 4*. This was a requirement introduced by amendment: The *Employment Tribunals (Early Conciliation: Exemptions and Rules of Procedure) (Amendment) Regulations 2014*.

19.10   *The Early Conciliation Process*

After ACAS has been notified, it is under a duty by *Rule 5(1)* of the *EC Rules* to make reasonable attempts to contact the prospective claimant. This will result in a conciliator speaking to the prospective claimant to find out what the claim is about, explain next steps and then ask whether they wish to proceed with conciliation.

If the prospective claimant consents, ACAS must then make reasonable attempts to contact the prospective respondent (*Rule 5(2)*). This is in order to hold a similar conversation with the respondent.

If ACAS is unable to make contact with either the prospective claimant, or the prospective respondent, then it is required to conclude that settlement is not possible (*Rule 5(3)*). This triggers the duty to issue an early conciliation certificate (see *Rule 7(1)* and below).

Assuming contact can be made with both parties, *Rule 6(1)* provides that for up to one calendar month, starting with either receipt by ACAS of the early conciliation form presented under *Rule 2*, or of the telephone call in accordance with *Rule 3*, ACAS is under a duty to "endeavour to promote a settlement" between the parties (see also *ETA 1996, section 18A(3)*). This period can be extended by the conciliation officer under *Rule 6(2)* provided the parties consent to the extension, and the conciliation officer "considers that there is a reasonable prospect of achieving a settlement before the expiry of the extended period". Such an extension can only occur once, and only be for up to a maximum of 14 days (*Rule 6(3)*).

The duty to promote settlement is not limited to financial remedies. Where the proposed proceedings are for unfair dismissal, and where the claimant has ceased to be employed, the conciliation officer may seek to promote reinstatement or reengagement as well as compensation (*ETA 1996, section 18A(9)*).

19.11 *Early Conciliation Certificate*

By *Rule 7(1)* and *ETA 1996, section 18A(4)*, if at any point during the period for early conciliation under *Rule 6(1)*, or any extension of that period under *Rules 6(2)* and *(3)*, the conciliation officer concludes that a settlement of a dispute (or part of a dispute) is not possible, ACAS is obliged ("must") issue an early conciliation certificate.

In addition, by *Rule 7(2)* and *ETA 1996, section 18A(4)*, if the period for early conciliation under *Rule 6(1)*, or any extension of that period under *Rules 6(2)* and *(3)*, expires without settlement having been achieved, ACAS is again obliged to issue an early conciliation certificate.

The contents of the early conciliation certificate are mandated by *Rule 8*. It must contain:

(a)   the name and address of the prospective claimant;

(b)   the name and address of the prospective respondent;

(c)   the date of receipt by ACAS of the early conciliation form presented in accordance with *Rule 2* or the date that the prospective claimant telephoned ACAS in accordance with *Rule 3*;

(d)   the unique reference number given by ACAS to the early conciliation certificate; and

(e)   the date of issue of the certificate, which will be the date that the certificate is sent by ACAS, and a statement indicating the method by which the certificate is to be sent.

A copy of the certificate must be sent to the prospective claimant and, if contact has been had with the prospective respondent, that respondent (Rule 9(1)). Where an email address has been provided by the claimant and/or respondent, that must be used, failing which ACAS will send the certificate by post: see *Rule 9(2)*. The certificate is deemed to be received on the day it is sent (if sent by email), and on the day it would be delivered in the ordinary course of the post (if sent by post): see *Rule 9(3)*.

Even though the period of early conciliation might have passed without settlement, and that ACAS has issued an early conciliation certificate in accordance with the provisions set out above, nonetheless, it is still open to a conciliator to endeavour to promote a settlement after the expiry of the prescribed period: see *ETA 1996, section 18A(5)*.

19.12 *Settlement*

If the matter can be successfully resolved by settlement, the conciliator will record the agreement in the form of a COT3 form (an ACAS settlement document). A COT3 is a legally binding contract; it will usually be part of that agreement that the Claimant cannot pursue a Tribunal claim about the matter agree (see further below at **19.18**).

19.13 *Exemptions*

There are a number of exemptions to the requirement to comply with early conciliation. By *ETA 1996, section 18A(7)* a person may institute relevant proceedings without complying with *ETA 1996, section 18A(1)* in those circumstances. The prescribed circumstances are set out in *Reg 3* of the *Early Conciliation Regulations 2014*. Relevant proceedings can be started by a person (referred to as A within *Reg 3*) without complying with the requirement for early conciliation where:

(a)   someone else (referred to as B within *Reg 3*) has complied with the requirement "in relation to the same dispute" and A wishes to institute proceedings on the same claim form as B (in this case, by *Reg 3(2)*, A benefits from any extension in time which B has achieved by complying with the requirement);

(b)   the relevant proceedings are instituted by A on the same claim form as proceedings which are not relevant proceedings;

(c)   A can show that the respondent has contacted ACAS in relation to a dispute, A has not provided early conciliation information to ACAS about that dispute, and the proceedings on the claim form relate to that dispute;

(d)   the proceedings are for unfair dismissal and are accompanied by an application for interim relief under *ERA 1996, section 128* or *TULRECA, section 161*;

(e)   A is instituting proceedings against the Security Service, the Secret Intelligence Service or the Government Communications Headquarters.

19.14 *Effect on Time Limits*

Time limits for presenting a claim are affected by the Early Conciliation process. By way of general overview, when a claimant who is still within time contacts ACAS, the time limit for presenting their claim is "paused". The time limit then starts to run again when the Early Conciliation certificate is produced. Once Early Conciliation has ended, the claimant has at least one calendar month in which to present the claim.

The detailed legislative changes to time limits were made by *section 8* of the *2013 Act* and *Schedule 2* to that *Act*. They are now to be found in the amended *ERA 1996*, at *section 207B*. In general the following rules apply:

(i)   the time period beginning with the day after the day on which the prospective claimant complies with the requirement to provide information to ACAS ("Day A") and ending with the day on which the complainant receives or is treated as having received the conciliation officer's certificate ("Day B") is not to be counted when working out time limits. As has been seen above, the early conciliation period could be as long as one calendar month plus 14 days from the day on which ACAS is contacted.

(ii)   if a time limit would otherwise have expired during the period beginning with Day A and ending one month after Day B, the time limit expires instead one month after Day B. For example if dismissal occurred on 31 May, the original time limit would expire on 30 August. If conciliation is entered into on 15 August (day A), but this fails on 5 September (day B) then as the original time limit falls between days A and B, time is extended to one month after day B, i.e. 5 October;

(iii)   if the time limit falls more than one month after day B, then time will be extended by a period equivalent to the early conciliation period. Thus for example, if dismissal occurred on 31 May and conciliation is entered into on 15 June (day A) but this fails on 5 July (day B), the original time limit (30 August) does not fall within these days. The early conciliation period took 20 days – the period between day A and B and therefore 20 days is added to the original time limit of 30 August so the date for presentation is extended to 19 September;

(iv)   if a time limit has already expired by the time of entering early conciliation, no extension will be available;

(v)   any power to extend time is exercisable in relation to a time limit as extended by these rules.

Tanveer v East London Bus and Coach Company Ltd UKEAT/0022/16 provides a useful example of these provisions in practice and assists with the interpretation of the one month extension referred to above. The dates were these: a claimant was dismissed on 20 March 2015 (thus the time limit but for the provisions of *ERA 1996, s 207B* created a last day for presentation on 19 June 2015). The claimant made his notification to ACAS (i.e. Day A) on 18 June 2015 and the EC Certificate was received (Day B) on 30 June 2015. The ET1 was presented on 31 July 2015. By *ERA 1996, s 207B(3)*, the period beginning with the day after Day A and ending with Day B (19 June 2015 – 30 June 2015 inclusive – 12 days) is not to be counted. However, adding that period onto the date on which limitation would have applied (19 June 2015) did not render the claim in time. However, *ERA 1996, s 207B(4)* provides that where a time limit would (if not extended by that subsection) expire during a period beginning with Day A (18 June 2015) and ending one month after Day B (20 June 2015), then the time limit expires instead at the end of that period. But how does one calculate "one month after Day B"? In *Tanveer*, HHJ Eady QC held that the answer was that provided by the House of Lords in *Dodds v Walker* [1981] 1 WLR 1027, applying the corresponding month date principle. In other words, "month" meant "calendar month" and the relevant time period ends upon the corresponding date in the appropriate subsequent month, i.e. the day of that month that bears the same number as the day of the earlier month on which the notice was given or the specified event occurred. Thus the period in *Tanveer* ended one month after 30 June 2015. This was 30 July 2015 so that the claim was out of time, having been presented the next day. One month after Day B did not mean (in this case) one month from 1 July 2015.

A number of ET decisions have considered whether time spent in early conciliation before the EDT should be added to the time limit. In *Fergusson v Combat Stress* (4105592/16), EJ Walker sitting in Scotland held that no account should be taken of the time after notification to Acas but before the EDT when calculating the time limit for bringing a claim. There ACAS received the EC form (day A) on 14 July 2016, the EDT was 11 August 2016, the EC Certificate was received (day B) on 14 August 2016 and the ET1 was presented on 18 November 2016. The Judge held that *s 207B* was a "stop the clock provision" and that a clock cannot be stopped until it has started. Thus, it was only the days between the EDT and day B that fell not to be counted, rather than the entire period between day A and day B that fell to be 'added' to the primary time limit. The claim was therefore out of time. This approach differed from two English decisions in *Chandler v Thanet District Council* (2301782/14) and *Myers v Nottingham County Council* (2601136/15). Since all of those cases, in *Ullah v Hounslow LBC* (2302599/2015) EJ Baron sitting in England thought that the draftsman had probably not considered this type of case and without considering the previous cases, reached a result consistent with *Fergusson*.

The *Fergusson* and *Ullah* approach is supported by the reasoning of the EAT in *Revenue and Customs Commissioners v Garau* [2017] UKEAT/0348/16. Kerr J held that the EC provisions only allow for the provision of one EC certificate per matter to be issued. Issuing a second EC certificate has no impact on the limitation period as it does not trigger the modified limitation regime. There, the employee was told of the impending termination of his employment and contacted ACAS. An EC certificate was issued on 4 November 2015. The employment then ended on 30 December 2015. Ordinarily, the primary time limit would have ended on 29 March 2016. The employee had, however, contacted ACAS for a second time shortly before this and a second EC certificate was issued on 25 April 2016. The claimant presented his claims on 25 May 2016. Kerr J held that the second certificate was unnecessary and not a "certificate" within the meaning of *s 18A(4)*. Kerr J also reasoned that it was wrong to say that the time spent on EC would not count in calculating the date of expiry of the time limit (as the EJ had done). He observed that in *Tanveer*, limitation had already started to run when the claimant had contacted ACAS. In *Garau* the position was different: the limitation clock could not stop under the first certificate because it had never started. This reasoning is supportive of *Fergusson* and *Ullah*.

19.15 *Beyond Early Conciliation: Other ACAS Duties*

ACAS also has a duty to endeavour to promote settlement where the prescribed information under the early conciliation procedure has not been received from the prospective claimant, and in circumstances where an exemption from the requirement to undertake early conciliation applies: see *ETA 1996, section 18B*. The duty under *section 18B* lasts until the conciliation officer concludes that a settlement is not possible, or until the early conciliation procedure is triggered so that the duty under *section 18A* applies.

A further duty on ACAS to endeavour to promote settlement is imposed by *ETA 1996, section 18C*: post-claim conciliation. This duty applies where, after the institution of relevant proceedings, ACAS is requested to endeavour to promote settlement by both parties to proceedings or the conciliation officer considers that s/he could act under that section with a reasonable prospect of success.

In order to assist with the discharge of the latter duty, *Rule 93* of the *2013 Rules* provides that where proceedings concern an enactment which provides for conciliation (i.e. those falling within the scope of *ETA 1996, section 18*), the Tribunal "shall" send a copy of the claim form and the response to an ACAS conciliation officer, as well as informing the parties of the services of an ACAS conciliation officer being available to them. Further, *Rule 93(2)* provides that a representative of ACAS may attend any preliminary hearing (subject to *Rules 50* and *94* – cases involving privacy and national security restrictions, see below).

19.16 *ACAS Conciliation in General*

The functions of conciliation officers are discussed in some detail in *Clarke v Redcar & Cleveland Borough Council* [2006] IRLR 324. It is not the conciliation officer's responsibility to ensure that the terms of any settlement are fair to the employee (or employer), and the conciliation officer should never advise a party as to the merits of the case, or advise the employee whether he or she could expect to get more compensation from the tribunal. The primary function is to promote a settlement by whatever legitimate means the officer thinks appropriate in the circumstances. These limitations are considered important to protect the impartiality of the conciliation service. In practice, some conciliation officers are more ready to express views on the value of claims or draw claimants' attention to typical levels of awards or the maximum that can be awarded for the claims being raised. Anything said to a conciliation officer is confidential and cannot, by statute, be disclosed to the tribunal without the consent of the communicator (*ETA 1996, s 18(7)*). If a settlement is reached with the aid of the conciliation officer it is recorded on a Form COT3. It is the policy of ACAS not to be involved in settlements where it has had no conciliation role whatsoever, ie the conciliation officer is merely asked to record a settlement reached privately.

Settlement Generally

19.17 *Prohibition on Contracting Out*

By *ERA 1996, s 203(1)* and *Equality Act 2010, s 144(1)* (and equivalent provisions in other statutes) any provision in an agreement is void insofar as it purports to (a) exclude or limit the operation of a provision in the relevant act, or (b) preclude a person from bringing any proceedings under the act before an employment tribunal. The High Court has confirmed that the words "bringing any proceedings" in subsection (b) includes "continuing any proceedings": see *Clyde & Co LLP v Bates van Winkelhof* [2011] IRLR 467 at para 16. The

Bates van Winkelhof case illustrated the breadth of the section: there, a provision in a partnership agreement in a firm of solicitors which provided for binding arbitration of disputes between partners was held ineffective to prevent an equity partner from bringing whistleblowing and sex discrimination claims.

The legislative policy behind these measures was explained by Mummery LJ in *Hinton v University of East London* [2005] IRLR 552 (para 17): "to protect employees from signing away the right to bring employment tribunal proceedings . . . except in cases where a number of closely defined conditions are satisfied. The most obvious target of the section is the blanket or sweep-up form of general waiver or release covering all future claims and inserted in a contract of employment issued to an employee on his engagement. The elaborate code of employment protection in the *1996 Act* would be worthless, if, at the stroke of a pen, it could be removed by a general waiver or release of rights." Similarly, Smith LJ explained that the purpose was "to protect claimants from the danger of signing away their rights without a proper understanding of what they are doing".

The effect was examined by the EAT in *Sutherland v Network Appliance Ltd* [2001] IRLR 12. First, it was confirmed that a common law claim (such as a breach of contract claim) can be compromised by an agreement that does not comply with the statutory provisions. Secondly, the EAT explained that a non-compliant agreement is not totally void: at most it is only the provision within the agreement which purports to exclude/limit the operation of the relevant act or which precludes a person from bringing proceedings before an employment tribunal. Thus the EAT held that agreements were intended to be capable of surviving in part even if they had been struck out in part.

It is not the role of the Employment Tribunal to ensure that upon a compromise having been reached by the parties at the door of the Tribunal, a valid settlement agreement or other binding agreement has been reached by the parties. Thus no error of law is committed by a tribunal which dismisses a case when told that the dispute has been settled, even if the agreement is not compliant with the statutory provisions: see *Mayo-Deman v University of Greenwich* [2005] IRLR 845; see also *Times Newspapers Ltd v Fitt* [1981] ICR 637 and *Carter v Reiner Moritz Associates Ltd* [1997] ICR 881 (in which final orders were made by the Tribunal by consent). However, if, after terms of settlement are agreed, the Tribunal makes an order staying proceedings for a period to allow the terms of settlement to be put into effect, with liberty to apply to restore the proceedings, upon such an application to restore, a Tribunal should consider whether the agreement is a valid compromise of statutory rights, and is not entitled to dismiss the proceedings on the basis that the terms of a non-compliant settlement agreement have been complied with by one or more of the parties: see *Osaghae v United Lincolnshire Hospitals NHS Trust* [2013] UKEAT 0575/12; see also *Horizon Recruitment Ltd v Vincent* [2010] ICR 491 discussed below.

19.18 *Compromise through ACAS Conciliation*

An agreement reached where a conciliation officer has taken action under one of the relevant statutes is a statutory exception to *s 203(1)*: the agreement will, subject to its terms, be binding on the parties. Endorsing an agreement on a Form COT3 is sufficient 'action': *Moore v Duport Furniture Products Ltd* [1982] ICR 84. Provided that a conciliation officer has taken action there is no more formality required for a binding agreement that for any other contract; thus settlement can be reached orally (see *Duru v Granada Retail Catering Ltd* [2001] All ER (D) 97 (Jul) and *Allma Construction Ltd v Bonner* [2011] IRLR 204) but it is strongly advisable to reduce the terms of the agreement to writing as soon as possible, to avoid later disputes about the terms of the agreement (as occurred in *Duru*) or even whether an agreement was reached at all (as was in dispute in the *Allma* case). It is also important that any written record of the agreement made is properly worded to compromise all claims intended to be covered by it. Issues may also arise subsequently as to the meaning, scope or application of a COT3 agreement. The ordinary principles of law for the interpretation of contracts apply to such agreements. Unlike settlement agreements (see below) a settlement reached through ACAS conciliation may in principle cover any disputes between the parties, including disputes that have not arisen at the time of the settlement. However, as a matter of construction, a court or tribunal will expect very clear words to convey the parties' intention to compromise future disputes: *Royal National Orthopaedic Hospital Trust v Howard* [2002] IRLR 849; *McLean v TLC Marketing* (UKEAT/0429/08); see also by way of example *Department for Work and Pensions v Brindley* [2016] UKEAT/0123/16 (interpreting a COT3 which settled claims "arising from the facts of the Proceedings"). In an extreme case a conciliated settlement agreement may be set aside, eg if the conciliation officer acted in bad faith or adopted unfair methods to procure a settlement, but it would not be enough to justify setting aside the agreement that the conciliation officer had not adopted best practice, provided that he or she had acted in good faith: *Clarke v Redcar & Cleveland Borough Council* [2006] IRLR 324 (an unsuccessful attempt to set aside agreements to settle a large number of equal pay claims).

A party will normally be bound by a settlement signed by his or her authorised representative, even if not a lawyer: *Freeman v Sovereign Chicken Ltd* [1991] ICR 853. However this is only so if the party has held out the representative as being his or her representative (as by including details of the representative on the Claim Form or Response Form). If a representative merely holds him or herself out as having the requisite authority, an agreement reached by the opposing party with the representative will not bind the 'client': *Gloystarne & Co Ltd v Martin* [2001] IRLR 15.

19.19 *Settlement agreements*

In the absence of ACAS conciliation, before 1993 the only option to secure an effective compromise of a tribunal claim, in practice, was to include a term in the agreement that the claimant would apply to the tribunal to have his or her claim dismissed on withdrawal; or if the parties were at the tribunal when a settlement was reached, an application could be made to the tribunal for an appropriate order. The former procedure has the disadvantage that the claimant can change his or her mind before making the application; the practice therefore is to make any payment conditional on the application to withdraw being made. (It is important that the respondent also applies to have the claim dismissed, not merely withdrawn or stayed, since in the latter case – in the absence of a binding agreement to the contrary – the case can subsequently be reopened: for an example see *Osaghae v United Lincolnshire Hospitals NHS Trust* [2013] UKEAT 0576/12.)

Both of the procedures referred to above are still available, but TURERA 1993 added a further and potentially more effective avenue of binding settlement, namely, a "compromise agreement". The scope for compromise agreements was extended by ERDRA 1998. With effect from 29 July 2013, "compromise agreements" have become known as "settlement agreements": see SI 2013/1648, Art 2(c). The principal relevant statutory provisions are now in *ERA 1996, s 203, Equality Act 2010, s 147, TULRCA 1992, s 288, Working Time Regulations 1998, reg 35,* and *National Minimum Wage Act 1998, s 49.* The *Part-time Workers (Prevention of Less Favourable Treatment) Regulations 2000, reg 9* provides that *ERA 1996, s 203* applies as if the *Regulations* were contained in that *Act,* and there are similar provisions in the *Fixed-term Employees (Prevention of Less Favourable Treatment) Regulations 2002, reg 8* and in the *Transfer of Undertakings (Protection of Employment) Regulations 2006, reg 18* (rectifying the anomaly that there was no equivalent provision in the predecessor *1981 Regulations*). The *Equality Act 2010, s 147* used to refer to "compromise contracts" rather than "compromise agreements", however *SI 2013/1648, Art 2(c)* amended the language to "settlement agreements" in line with the other statutory provisions.

It is to be noted that some common claims cannot be settled by a settlement agreement, for example claims for the failure to inform and consult under *TUPE 2006,* claims for failure to consult in collective redundancy cases under *TULCRA 1992, s 188* and claims for the right to statutory maternity, paternity and adoption pay. A COT3 can be used to settle such claims.

19.20

A settlement agreement is an agreement to refrain from issuing or continuing proceedings under one of the statutes or regulations listed in the preceding paragraph. In order for a settlement agreement to be binding, the following conditions must now be satisfied:

(a)   The agreement must be in writing;

(b)   It must relate to the particular complaint or proceedings (see further below);

(c)   The claimant must have received advice from a relevant independent adviser as to the terms and effect of the proposed agreement and in particular its effect on his or her ability to pursue his or her rights before an employment tribunal;

(d)   There must be in force, when the adviser gives the advice, a contract of insurance, or an indemnity provided for members of a profession or professional body, covering the risk of a claim by the claimant in respect of loss arising in consequence of the advice;

(e)   The agreement must identify the adviser; and

(f)   The agreement must state that the conditions regulating settlement agreements under the relevant Act or Regulations are satisfied.

A provision in the Bill which became the *Employment Act 2002* removing the requirement at (b) above was withdrawn during the Bill's passage through Parliament because of fears that it could facilitate the misuse of the settlement agreement procedure by requiring prospective employees to sign such agreements as a condition of being offered employment. As a consequence it is not possible to compromise all and any potential future disputes or claims under this procedure. The requirements at (e) and (f) are applied strictly. It is not sufficient that there is an independent adviser and that the statutory requirements have been satisfied; it is essential that this be stated. In *Lunt v Merseyside TEC Ltd* [1999] ICR 17, the EAT upheld a decision that a (then) compromise agreement which did not contain the statement required at (f) above was therefore void; this must apply equally to (e). In *Palihakkara v British Telecommunications plc* [2007] All ER (D) 131 (Jan), EAT, the EAT went further and held that a statement that the conditions under *ERA 1996, s 203* were satisfied was not effective to validate the agreement so far as it related to complaints of sex and race discrimination, although the requirements for such complaints were the same as those set out in *s 203* for complaints under *ERA 1996*. It is therefore necessary to state that the requirements for settlement agreements under the particular statute or statutes applicable for each claim intended to be compromised are satisfied; it is not completely clear following this decision whether it would be enough to say that the conditions under *s 203* 'and all similar statutory provisions' are satisfied, although it would be very surprising if this were not so. Advisors should also note the change in terminology from 'compromise agreements' to 'settlement agreements' when completing the statement required at (f).

The following are the categories of 'relevant independent advisers' who may act in settlement agreements:

(i)   Qualified lawyers;

(ii)   Fellows of the Institute of Legal Executives;

(iii)   Officers, officials, employees or members of an independent trade union; or

(iv)   Employees or volunteer workers at advice centres.

In each of the last two categories the individual must be certified in writing by the union or advice centre as competent and authorised to give advice. A 'qualified lawyer', means a barrister or advocate in practice as such or employed to give legal advice, or a solicitor holding a practising certificate.

In addition:

(A) The adviser must not be, or be employed by, or be acting in the matter for, the employer or an associated employer;

(B) In the case of a trade union or advice centre, that organisation must not be the employer or an associated employer; and

(C) Advice from an advice centre worker must be free (but a union may apparently charge for its services).

There was initially widespread concern that there might be a drafting error in the former provisions of the *Equality Act 2010*, replacing the equivalents in the former discrimination statutes. The concern was that a lawyer who had acted for or advised a party during a dispute could not then act as the independent adviser required as a condition of the validity of a compromise contract under *s 147*. Conflicting advice was obtained from Leading Counsel by the Law Society, with the result that the Government, whilst maintaining that the section was fully effective, made an amendment to *s 147* to remove the perceived doubts, with effect from 6 April 2012 (see the *Equality Act 2010 (Amendment) Order 2012, SI 2012/334*). It is now clear that a lawyer who has advised the employee can act as the independent adviser for the purposes of a settlement agreement settling claims under the *2010 Act*.

A settlement agreement may be used to compromise more than one complaint, provided it clearly identifies each of the complaints being compromised and the relevant statutory provisions: *Lunt v Merseyside TEC Ltd* [1999] ICR 17. This case also confirms that claims can be validly compromised without the need to commence tribunal proceedings; but there must be an actual complaint: as noted above, a settlement agreement cannot settle potential disputes which have not yet arisen. This last point is a significant restriction on the utility of settlement agreements where the parties wish to ensure a 'clean break'. Moreover, settlement agreements are likely to be strictly construed, and any ambiguity resolved against the employer, as in *Palihakkara v British Telecommunications plc*, above, where an agreement to compromise all claims arising out of the termination of the employment was held not to cover claims of discrimination against the claimant whilst she had been employed. The effective scope of settlement agreements was clarified and restricted by the Court of Appeal in *Hinton v University of East London* [2005] EWCA Civ 532, [2005] IRLR 552, and advice on the framing of agreements was also offered. The agreement must specifically identify the 'particular proceedings' (or the complaints which could lead to proceedings) being compromised. This entails for tribunal proceedings that the actual case be identified, and the agreement should identify complaints by a brief description of the complaint and a reference to the statutory provision under which the claim is asserted. A bare reference to the relevant statute is unlikely to be sufficient, especially if the statute is the *ERA 1996* or the *Equality Act 2010*, since these each cover a wide range of separate types of complaint. Mummery LJ added the advice that it is good practice to include a summary of the factual and legal basis of the complaint or proceedings to identify the subject matter of the compromise more clearly. It is also generally unwise to rely on standard form settlement agreements or simply include a list of all the statutory provisions in relation to which settlement agreements may be required under the statute. The policy underpinning these points is that settlement agreements are a device to protect employees when agreeing to relinquish their statutory rights, and the statutory provisions should be construed to give effect to that policy. The role of the independent adviser in the settlement of large multiple claims was considered by the EAT in *McWilliam v Glasgow City Council* [2011] IRLR 568.

may make it impracticable, in claims for modest compensation, or where the employee is not in a position to meet his or her share of the mediation cost and the employer is not willing to meet the whole cost. One way of meeting this problem is to make use of one of the free mediation services now offered in employment cases.

ACAS offers free mediation where the matter at issue is about employment rights that could go to an employment tribunal. If the dispute is not about a statutory employment right, a charge is made for the mediation. This service, although relatively little known, has become well established with the number of cases rising. Some two thirds of cases referred for ACAS mediation are either settled or partially settled in the course of mediation, and in a total of over 90%, ACAS considers that some progress towards settlement is made.

19.24 A more recent innovation is the introduction of a facility for judicial mediation within the employment tribunals. A pilot scheme offering the (then free) services of an Employment Judge to mediate between the parties if they so wish was run in 2006–07, which was assessed as successful (but it should be noted that when the results of a research project based on the pilot scheme were finally published by the Ministry of Justice in March 2010, the report (Urwin et al, Evaluating the use of judicial mediation in Employment Tribunals) indicated that the success rate for mediations was no higher than the settlement rate for cases not referred to mediation, raising doubts about the cost effectiveness at least of the pilot). The Ministry of Justice Guidance Note indicates that over 65% of cases subject to judicial mediation reach a successful settlement on the day of mediation. Provision was made, by an amendment to the *ETA 1996* by the *Tribunals, Courts and Enforcement Act 2007*, for judicial mediation to be given more formal status, and a national scheme was introduced in January 2009. This facility is now provided subject to the payment of a fee. By *Art 4(3)* of the *Employment Tribunals and Employment Appeals Tribunal Fees Order 2013*, a fee of £600 is payable by the respondent on a date specified in a notice accompanying a notification of listing for judicial mediation. The scheme uses Employment Judges trained in mediation skills; the Judge is then excluded from any future involvement in the proceedings should the mediation not be successful. The parties must bear any costs incurred in preparing for the mediation, attendance of representatives etc, but subject to the point that reimbursement of such costs by the other party may form part of the terms of settlement. Because of resource considerations, mediation is only offered in a limited range of cases, generally those discrimination claims which are considered likely to involve a hearing of at least three days, and with priority given to cases where the claimant is still employed (although the practice in each region can vary). Both parties must agree to a reference to mediation. There is no guarantee that mediation will be offered even if the parties' views are canvassed (this is usually done at a Preliminary Hearing for Case Management) and both agree, because of the limited numbers of Judges who have been trained to undertake mediations. Any indication by a judge at a Preliminary Hearing is usually subject to the approval of the Regional Employment Judge. If it is agreed that there will be a mediation, it will normally be scheduled for a full day, at the tribunal offices, and appropriate directions given to the parties about any documents etc. An order for the preparation and exchange of mediation position statements is becoming increasingly common. One point which is emphasised in the information given to parties invited to consider mediation is that it is essential that a person with the authority to agree terms of settlement is available to attend the mediation.

A further important point is that the proceedings are in private, and anything said in the course of the mediation is strictly confidential and will not be admissible in any tribunal proceedings that may follow in the event that the mediation does not achieve a settlement. If the mediation is successful, the agreed terms will be incorporated into a formal order of the tribunal.

The practice is that judicial mediators adopt a purely facilitative approach, and do not offer opinions on the merits of claims or what might be appropriate terms for settlement. This has led to criticism from some users of the scheme, but there is also concern that too interventionist an approach might be felt by some parties as undue pressure to settle on terms with which they are unhappy. Judicial mediation can in this way be contrasted with Judicial Assessment discussed in the following paragraph. The usual procedure is for the judicial mediation to be held at a tribunal office, for the parties to have separate rooms and for the mediator to liaise between them. Often joint sessions are held in a tribunal room at the start of the day and, if the mediation is successful, at the end. No statistics have been published for the numbers and outcomes of judicial mediations, but anecdotal evidence indicates that there is a relatively high success rate, and that demand for mediations fully meets, if not exceeds, the availability of appropriately trained employment judges. However the future of the facility will be subject to the willingness of respondents to invest the £600 fee for the facility, a matter which was one of the more strongly criticised aspects of the fees proposals prior to their introduction.

Further guidance on judicial mediation can be seen from the Presidential Guidance on General Case Management. There is a section dedicated to judicial medication at the end of that Guidance. The guidance indicates that equal pay claims will generally be unsuitable for judicial mediation and that an important factor in determining suitability is if there is an ongoing employment relationship.

19.24A With effect from 3 October 2016, Presidential Guidance was issued setting out a Protocol containing a formal framework for the Judicial Assessment of employment tribunal claims. The aim is to conduct with the parties a preliminary consideration of the claim and response at an early stage (viz at that stage when a case management preliminary hearing is conducted) so as to encourage the parties to resolve the dispute by agreement. The Guidance states that it will be particularly helpful (but not exclusively so) where a party is not professionally represented. The Protocol emphasises the impartial and confidential nature of the assessment which will cover the strengths, weaknesses and risks of the claims, allegations and contentions made by the parties. Judicial Assessment is generally offered at the first case management hearing, and at the stage after the issues have been clarified and the formal orders made. It is not expected to take place later in proceedings. Whilst an assessment can take place on the telephone, it will normally take place in person and at a hearing that has been listed for up to 2 hours. Judicial Assessment is aimed at most cases of any complexity, but a number of (non-exhaustive) factors are identified as making a case unsuitable:

(i)   the presence of multiple claimants, not all of whom request judicial assessment;

(ii)   presence of an insolvent party; and

(iii)   intimated High Court or other proceedings.

The parties must freely consent to Judicial Assessment and the Protocol is clear (para 14) that "no pressure should ever be placed on any party to agree to it". Where Judicial Assessment does take place, anything said by the parties or the Judge are non-attributable and must be kept strictly confidential. No reference may be made to things said in subsequent proceedings including the final hearing. Reference can be made in without prejudice correspondence or in a judicial mediation. The assessment will consist of the Judge giving provisional, guarded, indications on the state of the allegations (without evaluating the evidence) as to the strength of the parties' cases, including the potential outcome. The Judge who conducts the assessment will then normally not be involved in any subsequent part of the proceedings (save for day-to-day case management). Whilst settlement might be reached immediately after the assessment, more usually the parties will wish to consider their positions and then enter into settlement discussions through Acas, direct negotiation or judicial mediation.

19.25 ACAS arbitration schemes

Section 7 of the *ERDRA 1998* provides for the making of a scheme by ACAS, subject to the approval of the Secretary of State, for the determination of unfair dismissal claims by private arbitration. The process of establishing a scheme proved unexpectedly protracted, but it was finally brought into effect, for England and Wales only, in May 2001. It was extended to Scotland in 2004. The ACAS Annual Reports have consistently recorded a disappointingly small take-up of the scheme, with only 61 cases registered in the six years to 31 March 2009, of which only four were registered in the years 2007–8 and 2008–9 together (ACAS Annual Reports, 2007–8 and 2008–9). Figures for the period from April 2009 have not been published by ACAS. The Scheme is now contained in a *Schedule* to the *ACAS Arbitration Scheme (Great Britain) Order 2004 (SI 2004/753)*, and is given effect by *TULRCA 1992, s 212A*, as inserted by *ERDRA 1998, s 7*. The Scheme is lengthy (running to 227 paragraphs, including some containing separate provisions for England and Wales and for Scotland) and is supported by a separate Guide published by ACAS, which should be consulted by any party considering the submission of a dispute to arbitration under the Scheme. The Arbitration Scheme is entirely voluntary, in the sense that it requires the agreement of both parties, and it is available only for unfair dismissal claims. The *Employment Act 2002* amended *s 212A* to provide for a similar arbitration scheme in relation to disputes over requests for flexible working arrangements raised under the provisions of the ERA 1996 (as added by the 2002 Act) conferring the right to make such requests. A Scheme (for England and Wales only) was made by the *ACAS (Flexible Working) Arbitration Scheme (England and Wales) Order 2003 (SI 2003/694)*. This was extended to Scotland by the *ACAS (Flexible Working) Arbitration Scheme (Great Britain) Order 2004, SI 2004/2333*.

The *Apprenticeships, Skills, Children and Learning Act 2009* amended *s 212A* to provide for an arbitration scheme in relation to disputes over requests for time off work in relation to study and training (see *ERA 1996, Part VIA, s 63D* ff). No such scheme has yet been enacted.

19.26 GENERAL PROVISIONS OF THE RULES

The *2013 Rules* contain a number of general provisions which provide for when compliance with orders and other rules must be achieved.

19.27 Computing time

The time for compliance with the provisions of the Rules, practice directions and orders is governed by *Rule 4* of the *2013 Rules*.

Rule 4(1) provides that, unless otherwise specified by the Tribunal, an act required by the *Rules*, a practice direction or an order of the Tribunal to be done on a particular day, may be done at any time before midnight on that day. Where there is an issue as to whether the act has been done by that time, the party claiming to have done it shall prove compliance.

By *Rule 4(2)*, where the time for doing any act ends on a day other than a working day, the act is done in time if it is done on the next working day. A "working day" means any day except a Saturday, Sunday, Christmas Day, Good Friday or a bank holiday under *s 1* of the *Banking and Financial Dealings Act 1971*.

Where an act is required to be, or may be, done within a certain number of days of or from an event, by *Rule 4(3)*, the date of that event is not counted within the calculation. The example given in that sub-rule is of a Response which must be presented within 28 days of the date on which the respondent was sent a copy of the claim: if the claim was sent on 1 October, the last day for presentation of the response is 29 October. Similarly, where the formulation of the requirement is for an act to be done not less than a certain number of days before or after an event, by *Rule 4(4)* provides that the date of that event is also not included in the calculation. The example in the rules is of a party wishing to present representations in writing for consideration by a Tribunal at a hearing. The requirement is for these to be presented not less than 7 days before the hearing. If the hearing is fixed for 8 October, the representations must be presented no later than 1 October.

By *Rule 4(5)*, Tribunals are required "wherever practicable" to express the last date for compliance with an imposed time limit as a calendar date.

Time limits that run from the date when a document is sent to a person by the Tribunal are dealt with specifically by *Rule 4(6)*. In such cases, unless the contrary is proved, the date when the document is sent is to be regarded as the date endorsed on the document as the date of sending, or in the absence of such an endorsement, the date shown on the letter accompanying the document.

By *Rule 5*, the Tribunal may of its own initiative, or upon application by a party, extend or shorten any time limit specified in the Rules or in any decision, whether or not (in the case of an extension) it has expired.

19.28 Irregularities and Non-Compliance

Rule 6 caters for instances of irregularities and non-compliance with requirements of the *Rules* and orders of the Tribunal. It provides that, with exceptions, a failure to comply with any provision of the Rules or of an order of the Tribunal does not of itself render void the proceedings or any step taken in proceedings. Rather, in the case of such non-compliance, the Tribunal is given a discretion to take such action as it considers just. A non-exhaustive list of "such action" which the Tribunal "may take" is set out in the rule. It includes "all or any of" the following: (a) waiving or varying the requirement; (b) striking out the claim or the response, in whole or in part, in accordance with *Rule 37* (on which, see below); (c) barring or restricting a party's participation in the proceedings; and (d) awarding costs in accordance with *Rule 74* to *84* (on which, see below).

This rule therefore gives the Tribunal considerable latitude to take action which it considers appropriate to the act of non-compliance concerned. In cases of proposed action which would limit a party's access to the Tribunal, or affect the ability of the party to have a fair hearing of its case, the discretion afforded by this Rule will need to be exercised in a manner which is proportionate so as to ensure compliance with *Art 6* of the *ECHR*.

Rule 6 does not apply in cases of failures to comply with:

(a)   *Rule 8(1)* – requirement to present a claim form using the prescribed form;

(b)   *Rule 16(1)* – requirement to present a response using the prescribed form and within 28 days of the day the copy of the claim form was sent by the Tribunal;

(c)   *Rule 23* – requirement for an employer's contract claim to be made as part of the response, presented in accordance with Rule 16;

(d)   *Rule 25* – requirement for a claimant to respond to an employer's contract claim within 28 days of the date the response was sent to the claimant.

Nor does *Rule 6* apply where there has been a failure to comply with an unless order made under *Rule 38* or a deposit order made under *Rule 39*.

Specific reference to *Rule 6* is given in *Rule 9* which provides that where two or more claimants wrongly include claims on the same claim form, this is to be treated as an irregularity within the terms of *Rule 6*.

The scope of *Rule 6* was considered by the EAT in *Cranwell v Cullen* [2015] UKEATPAS/0046. The EAT held that it offered no assistance to a claimant who had not complied with the requirements of the Early Conciliation scheme. *Rule 6* could not modify these requirements which were laid down in statute in the ETA. *Rule 6* was further "plainly designed to allow a Tribunal to relieve litigants of the consequences of their failure to comply" and made no sense to construe it as entitling the Tribunal to avoid having to satisfy an obligation placed upon it. Finally, there had to be non-compliance before *Rule 6* could apply and there had been no non-compliance with the Rules because the Tribunal had complied with its obligation. The non-compliance of the claimant with the statutory requirements were not enough.

19.29 Delivery of Documents

The *2013 Rules* make specific provision for the delivery of documents both to the Tribunal and to the parties. The *Rules* further prescribe how the parties should communicate with the Tribunal and themselves.

Communication with the Tribunal

Rule 85 sets out how documents may be delivered to the Tribunal. Save for the delivery of a claim form, documents may be delivered to the Tribunal (a) by post; (b) by direct delivery to the appropriate tribunal office (including delivery by courier or messenger service); or (c) by electronic communication.

Specific treatment is given to a claim form, which must be delivered in accordance with the practice direction made under *Regulation 11*, which supplements *Rule 8*. The requirements are considered separately below.

In order to facilitate these requirements, *Rule 85(3)* requires the Tribunal to notify the parties after the presentation of a claim of the address of the Tribunal office dealing with the case, including by giving fax numbers and email. Thereafter, by that sub-rule, the parties must use the contact details so notified. The Tribunal may from time to time notify the parties of a change in contact details, after which the new details must be used.

When communicating with the Tribunal, parties should note the contents of *Rule 92*: where a party sends a communication to the Tribunal (except an application for a person to attend to give evidence, produce documents or produce information under *Rule 32*), it must send a copy to all other parties, and state that it has done so either by using "cc" or otherwise. The Tribunal may order a departure from *Rule 92* where it considers it is in the interests of justice to do so.

Relevant to electronic delivery of documents to the Tribunal is the EAT's decision in the (different) context of lodging a notice of appeal with the EAT. In *Mejekodunmi v City Facilities Management* [2016] ICR D5 it was held that a notice of appeal was not lodged by sending a link to a dropbox document.

Communication with Parties

By *Rule 86*, the Tribunal and the other parties are permitted to deliver documents to a party (a) by post; (b) by direct delivery to that party's address (including delivery by a courier or messenger service); (c) by electronic communication; or (d) by being handed personally to that party (if not represented), or to any individual representative named in the claim form or response, or, on the occasion of a hearing, to any person identified by the party as representing that party at that hearing. Where the methods listed at (a) to (c) above are used, the document in question shall be delivered to the address given in the claim form (if a representative is named in the claim form, their address shall be used) or to a different address as notified in writing by the party in question.

Where a party gives both a postal address and one or more electronic addresses, any of these may be used unless the party has indicated in writing that a particular address should or should not be used.

Communication with Non-Parties

Save in the special cases referred to below, by *Rule 87*, documents shall be sent to non-parties at any address for service which they may have notified and otherwise at any known address or place of business in the United Kingdom, or if the party is a corporate body, at its registered or principal office in the United Kingdom, or if permitted by the President, at an address outside the United Kingdom.

Special cases are governed by *Rule 88*. This provides that addresses for serving the Secretary of State, the Law Officers, and the Counsel General to the Welsh Assembly Government, in cases where they are not parties, are to be issued by practice direction. The Presidential Practice Direction – Addresses for Serving Documents in Special Cases (England and Wales) was issued under *Regulation 11* on 18 December 2013. It provides a schedule of addresses for the Redundancy Payments Service (UK), the Secretary of State (BIS), the Attorney General's Office (England), the Counsel General for Wales, the Advocate General for Scotland and the Lord Advocate (Scotland). A similar practice direction covers Scottish cases.

Substituted and Irregular Service

By *Rule 89*, where no address for service in accordance with *Rule 85–88* is known, or it appears that service at any such address is unlikely to come to the attention of the addressee, the President, Vice President or a Regional Employment Judge may order that there shall be substituted service in such manner as appears appropriate.

Even where there has been non-compliance with *Rule 86–88*, a Tribunal may nonetheless treat any document as delivered to a person, if it is satisfied that the document in question (or its substance) has in fact come to the attention of that person: see Rule 91.

Date of Delivery

Rule 90 provides for deemed dates of delivery of documents delivered in accordance with the provisions of *Rules 85* and *86* (communications with the Tribunal and with parties). The rule requires the Tribunal ("shall") to treat the following deemed dates as the date of delivery, "unless the contrary is proved":

(a)   Document sent by post: on the day it would be delivered in the ordinary course of post.

(b)   Document sent by electronic communication: on the day of transmission.

(c)   Document delivered directly or personally: on the day of delivery.

It should be noted that on its face, *Rule 90* does not apply to communications with non-parties (under *Rule 87*).

19.30 Presidential Guidance

Pursuant to *Rule 7* of the *2013 Rules*, the Presidents of Employment Tribunals for England and Wales, and Scotland, may publish guidance as to how the powers conferred by the Rules may be exercised. *Rule 7* specifies, however, that Tribunals "must have regard to any such guidance, but they shall not be bound by it". The *Rule* requires the guidance to be published in an appropriate manner to bring it to the attention of claimants, respondents and their advisors.

The current practice is for Presidential Guidance to be published on the Judiciary website: www.judiciary.gov.uk/publications/employment-rules-and-legislation-practice-directions/. The guidance for England and Wales now covers (i) issuing judgments under *Rule 21* (judgments issued in default of a response) – issued 4 December 2013; (ii) seeking a postponement of a hearing – issued 4 December 2013; (iii) general case management – issued 13 March 2014; (iv) making a statutory appeal falling within the jurisdiction of the Employment Tribunal – issued 16 June 2014; and (v) judicial assessment – issued 3 October 2016. The General Case Management guidance covers topics including: disclosure of documents and preparing bundles, witness statements, amendments to the claim and response (including adding and removing parties), disability, remedy, costs, timetabling, concluding cases without a hearing, and judicial mediation.

The President has also issued Practice Directions covering (i) address for service in various special cases – issued 18 December 2013 and (ii) the presentation of claims – issued 14 December 2016 (replacing one dated 10 March 2016 which in turn replaced one dated 29 July 2013).

The relevant parts of the Presidential Guidance is set out in the appropriate sections below.

STARTING A CLAIM

Presentation of a Claim Form

19.31 *Methods of Presentation*

Rule 8(1) mandates that a claim be started by presenting a completed claim form (using a prescribed form) in accordance with any practice direction made under *Reg 11* which supplements that rule. Presentation of a claim form is defined by *Rule 1(1)* as delivering to a Tribunal office by any means permitted by *Rule 85* (but see below concerning *Rule 85(2)*).

Rule 8(2) and *8(3)* govern where, as between the jurisdictions, claims may be presented. *Rule 8(2)* provides that a claim may be presented in England and Wales if:

(a)   the respondent, or one of the respondents, resides or carries on business in England and Wales;

(b)   one or more of the acts or omissions complained of took place in England and Wales;

(c)   the claim relates to a contract under which the work is or has been performed partly in England or Wales; or

(d)   the Tribunal has jurisdiction to determine the claim by virtue of a connection with Great Britain and the connection in question is at least partly a connection with England and Wales.

Rule 8(3) contains corresponding provisions permitting claims to be presented in Scotland.

Two practice directions have been made – one covering the presentation of claims in England and Wales, and the other presentation of claims in Scotland – to specify the permitted methods of presentation. The Presidential Practice Direction on the Presentation of Claims (England and Wales) dated 14 December 2016 sets out three ways in which a completed claim form may be presented to an Employment Tribunal (the additional information accompanying the practice direction encourages the use of the first):

(i)   online by using the online form submission service available at www.employmenttribunals.service.gov.uk;

(ii)   by post to Employment Tribunal Central Office (England and Wales) PO Box 10218, Leicester, LE1 8EG;

(iii)   in person to an Employment Tribunal Office listed in the schedule to the Practice Direction. The schedule to the Practice Direction sets out the addresses of the Tribunal offices by region.

A similar Presidential Practice Direction for Scotland (of the same date) provides for the same three methods of presentation (the postal address is Employment Tribunals Central Office (Scotland), PO Box 27105, Glasgow, G2 9JR).

Rule 85(2) underlines that a claim form may "only" be presented in accordance with the applicable practice direction. The three methods of presentation set out in the Presidential Practice Directions mark a significant shift away from the position under the previous Rules. The initial practice directions on the presentation of claims specified that presentation in person must be within tribunal business hours, but this has been removed from the 14 December 2016 version. Before the 2013 Rules, claims could be presented by fax and by personal delivery at the Tribunal offices up until midnight so as to present within the limitation period (see the cases of *Hutchinson 3G UK Ltd v Francois* [2009] ICR 1323 and *Post Office v Moore* [1981] ICR 623 respectively). In respect of personal presentation, the removal of specific permissible hours marks a return to such an approach. Older authorities should still be read in light of the new more limited list of permitted methods of presentation.

Where proceedings are transferred to a Tribunal by a Court, the *2013 Rules* still apply to proceedings as if the proceedings had been presented by the claimant: see *Rule 101*. In such cases the rules are applied mutatis mutandis.

19.32   *Date of Presentation*

The date of presentation of a claim form is an important date. It is by reference to that date that the question of whether the claim was presented within the statutory time limit will be resolved.

It has long been clear that a claim form is presented when it is received by the Tribunal, even if it is not dealt with immediately upon receipt: see *Hammond v Haigh Castle & Co Ltd* [1973] ICR 148. The Tribunal office will usually stamp the claim form with a date stamp showing the date of presentation (there is now a box for this date on the form). It is the claimant's responsibility to ensure that the Claim Form is in fact received by the tribunal. Whilst generally, acknowledgements of receipt of claims are sent out, it is important to check the position with the tribunal office as soon as practicable, if necessary by telephoning to confirm receipt.

It was formerly the position that where there was no authorised means by which a complaint could have been presented on a day when the tribunal office was closed, the time for presenting the complaint would be extended to the next working day (*Ford v Stakis Hotels and Inns Ltd* [1987] ICR 943). However, the availability of electronic submission of the claim form in accordance with the practice direction makes it difficult to see how there is room for this possibility in the great majority of cases. In *Sealy v Consignia plc* [2002] IRLR 624, Brooke LJ considered that the Tribunal office being closed was not a ground for extending the time limit to the next working day, but rather a situation where a tribunal would need to consider whether the absence of a means of physical delivery of a hard copy of the claim had rendered it not reasonably practicable to present the claim in time. Further, whilst *Rule 4(2)* makes provision for an extension of time to the next working day where a deadline falls on a non-working day, it is important to appreciate that this Rule only applies to a time specified by the Rules, a practice direction or an order made by the Tribunal – it cannot be relied upon in relation to a limitation date set by another enactment.

Many older authorities deal with when a claim form should be treated as having been presented in light of the particular way in which presentation was effected in that case. There is, for example, a substantial body of case law dealing with when a claim form sent by fax should be treated as having been presented. The previous case law is considered in previous editions of this work. Here, the focus is upon the three permitted methods of presentation under the *2013 Rules*. The *2013 Rules* provide for deemed dates of delivery of documents at *Rule 90* (see above). *Rule 90* also governs the presentation of a claim form to the Tribunal as this is expressly included within the scope of *Rule 85*: see sub-rule (2).

Where a claim form is sent by post, *Rule 90(a)* provides that it will be deemed to be presented, unless the contrary be proved, on the day on which it would be delivered in the ordinary course of post. This was also the position under the old rules. The Court of Appeal gave general guidance about presentation by post in *Sealy v Consignia plc* [2002] IRLR 624. The Court held that where a complainant chose to present his/her complaint by sending it by post, presentation will be assumed to have been effected, unless the contrary is proved, at the time when the letter would be delivered in the ordinary course of post. In the case of a first class letter, it was legitimate to adopt the approach from the *CPR* and conclude that the ordinary course of post would mean that it would be delivered on the second day after which it was posted (excluding Sundays, Bank Holidays, Christmas Day and Good Friday). This regime, which was expressly said by the Court to hold good until a simpler regime for the service of documents was introduced in respect of employment tribunals (see now *Rule 90*) was in fact the approach adopted within the new Rules.

Electronically submitted claim forms are deemed (unless the contrary is proved) to be presented on the day of the electronic transmission (see Rule 90(b)). Authority under the previous Rules dealt with the question of what constituted presentation when a claim is submitted by e-mail. In one case, *Mossman v Bray Management Ltd* [2005] All ER (D) 06 (Apr), EAT, it was held that where the claimant had clicked the 'submit' button for the completed form, but it had not been received on the tribunal website, it had not been presented. However in *Tyne and Wear Autistic Society v Smith* [2005] IRLR 336, the opposite conclusion was reached on the basis of only slightly different facts, and additional information. The claimant in that case had received an acknowledgement of receipt, and the Claim Form had reached the server of the company hosting the tribunals' website, but had not reached the tribunal office, for unknown reasons. The *Tyne and Wear* case was subsequently applied by analogy in other situations under the old rules (presentation by fax, which as noted above, is no longer permitted) and it is submitted that it is to be preferred to *Mossman*. This view is reinforced by the decision of the EAT in *Patel v South Tyneside Council* (UKEATPA/0917/11) that an appeal to the EAT was duly presented when sent by email to the correct address, followed by a notification of 'successful delivery' by the host server, Daemon, but did not (again for an unknown reason) reach the EAT's Inbox. The reasoning would seem to apply equally to the process of submitting a claim using the on-line submission form.

Under the previous *Rules*, a claim submitted electronically was treated as having been presented when it is received on the server used to receive claims and responses for the Tribunals Service. That may be a few seconds later than the time of sending. This may be important; in two cases the Court of Appeal and the EAT respectively upheld the dismissal of claims as out of time which were presented electronically, but received respectively 88 seconds and 8 seconds after midnight of the last day for presentation: *Beasley v National Grid* [2008] EWCA Civ 742, CA and *Miller v Community Links Trust* [2007] All ER (D) 196 (Nov), EAT. In the first case the delay was the result of incorrectly typing in the tribunal e-mail address; in the second, the claim had been submitted at one second before midnight but took nine seconds to arrive. This approach is likely to hold good under the *2013 Rules*.

If online transmission to an employment tribunal office is successful, an e-mail receipt is generated, and unless such a receipt is received, the claimant should contact the Tribunal service to check whether the Claim Form has in fact been received, and if necessary resubmit it.

The final method of presentation is by personal presentation at a Tribunal office. Unsurprisingly, *Rule 90(c)* provides that where the claim form is presented by this method, it will be deemed to be presented on the day of delivery. Until the Practice Direction was amended in December 2016, it was very precise about the times at which personal presentation could take place: it had to be within tribunal business hours of 9am – 4pm, Monday to Friday not including public holidays or weekends. This limitation has now been

19.32   Employment Tribunals – II

removed and it is perhaps likely that, like under the old rules, a Claim Form can be presented if it is placed through a letter-box or dealt with in some way held out by a Tribunal Office as a means whereby it will accept communications. Under the old rules, putting a claim form through the letterbox of the tribunal at any time prior to midnight counted as presentation on the day of posting.

Under the *2013 Rules*, the Tribunal is required to reject claim forms presented where they are not on the required form, do not contain the minimum specified information, are not accompanied by the appropriate fee, or where they suffer from substantive defects (see discussion below). Where, however, upon an application for reconsideration under *Rule 13(1)*, the Tribunal accepts that a defect in the claim form has been rectified, but that the original rejection decision was correct, *Rule 13(4)* provides that the claim is to be treated as having been presented on the date that the defect was rectified. In these circumstances, the actual date of presentation will be replaced by this later date.

19.33 *Presentation to the Wrong Office*

A claim form presented by post or electronically will be sent by the Tribunal service to the correct Tribunal office in order to be managed and determined. Where personal presentation takes place, and the claimant presents to the wrong office it will simply be forwarded to the correct office. As under the previous regime, the date of presentation will be the date it reaches the first office.

It should be remembered, however that the jurisdictions north and south of the border are separate, and if the Claim Form is presented in England and Wales when the correct venue for the claim is Scotland, or vice versa, the claim will not be regarded as having been presented within the correct jurisdiction; it cannot simply be transferred, and the claimant is at risk of being out of time if he or she subsequently presents a fresh Claim Form in the correct jurisdiction. This was confirmed under the old rules by the EAT in Scotland in *McFadyen v PB Recovery Ltd* (UKEATS/0072/08), where a claim had been completed online giving the postal address of the employer as Bristol, but not including the address in Glasgow where the claimant had worked; this had led to the claim being automatically routed to the Bristol tribunal. Following the rejection of that claim, the claimant presented a fresh claim in Scotland giving the correct details, but out of time, and the dismissal of that claim was upheld by the EAT.

In order to determine whether to present in England and Wales or Scotland, the tests set out in *Rule 8(2)* and *8(3)* should be followed (see discussion above). Where a claim is pending before an employment tribunal in England or Wales which could be determined by a tribunal in Scotland, and it is more convenient to do so, the claim can be transferred to Scotland, and vice versa (*Rule 99*). However this facility is only available if proceedings have been commenced in a tribunal which has jurisdiction to determine the claim, and could also have been commenced in the other jurisdiction in accordance with *Rule 8(2)* or *(3)* as the case may be. *Rule 99* indicates that such a transfer can take place of the Tribunal's own motion (acting through the President or Regional Employment Judge (England and Wales) or President or Vice President (Scotland)) or on application of a party. Depending on the direction of transfer, the consent of the President of Tribunals for England and Wales or Scotland must also be obtained.

19.34 *Multiple Claimants*

By *Rule 9*, two or more claimants may make their claims on the same claim form if their claims are based on the same set of facts. Where two or more claimants are wrongly included on the same claim form, this is treated as an irregularity falling within *Rule 6* (see above) and thereby allowing the Tribunal to take such action as it considers just, including the specific steps set out there (which notably include the making of a costs order).

19.35 *The Prescribed Form*

Rule 1(1) defines the "prescribed form" as "any appropriate form prescribed by the Secretary of State in accordance with" *Reg 12*. The current ET1 form is available on paper and on-line.

Fees

19.36 *Fees*

One of the major changes in Tribunal procedure since 29 July 2013 has been the introduction of the obligation on users of the Tribunal system to pay fees: see the *Employment Tribunals and Employment Appeal Tribunal Fees Order 2013*. There are fees to be paid on issue of a claim, a hearing fee, and various other fees for certain applications and judicial mediation. They are discussed further below.

Since their introduction, it would appear that fees have had a major impact in reducing the number of claims presented to the Employment Tribunals.

Since their introduction, UNISON has sought to challenge the fees regime in the Courts. The first challenge was *R (Unison) v Lord Chancellor (Equality and Human Rights Commission intervening)* [2014] ICR 498. Four grounds were advanced: (i) the requirement to pay fees violated the principle of effectiveness; (ii) the requirement also violated the principle of equivalence; (iii) in reaching the decision to introduce the new fees regime and making the 2013 Order the Lord Chancellor breached the public sector equality duty; and (iv) the imposition of higher rate fees for Type B claims (see below) had a disparate impact on minority groups and was thereby indirectly discriminatory. The Court rejected those challenges on the basis that (i) provided the fees were not so high that a prospective litigant was clearly unable to pay them, the fact that they imposed a burden on families with limited means was not enough to render them "excessive"; (ii) the new regime was not in breach of the principle of equivalence; (iii) it could not be said that the Lord Chancellor had failed to consider the relevant points in order to comply with the public sector equality duty – there had been a lengthy review prior to the introduction of the fees regime; and (iv) whilst there was a strong possibility that there would be some disparate impact on those who fell within a protected class who brought type B claims, on the evidence, it was not yet possible to gauge the extent of the impact of the new regime and thus it was not possible to reach a conclusion as to whether the imposition of higher rate fees for type B claims could be objectively justified. The Lord Chancellor had undertaken to keep the matter under review and would be under a duty to take remedial measures to remove any disparate effect that materialised. In relation to that point, it was notable that when the matter was before the Divisional Court, the reconciled quarterly statistics for October to December 2013 showing a 76% reduction in claims presented were not available to the Court (see **18.1** for the latest statistical position).

In September 2014, an appeal to the Court of Appeal was stayed pending a fresh judicial review application, relying on the statistics which had become available. That second challenge was, however, rejected by the divisional court in December 2014: *R (Unison) v Lord Chancellor (No 2)* [2015] ICR 390. The statistics were not enough to establish that the fees regime breached the EU principle of effectiveness or that they constituted unlawful indirect discrimination. There was no evidence that a particular claimant had been unable to bring a claim, and the statistics did not justify the conclusion that fees place women, the disabled and ethnic minorities at a substantial disadvantage, and in any event the regime was in pursuant of legitimate objectives and was proportionate.

The Court of Appeal gave its substantive views in a judgment handed down in August 2015. In *Regina (Unison) v Lord Chancellor (Equality and Human Rights Commission intervening) (Nos 1 & 2)* [2016] ICR 1, the Court held (i) that the union had failed to establish a breach by the Fees Order of the principle of effectiveness. Whilst the statistics showed a very significant decline in the number of claimants, that by itself did not evidence a breach of the effectiveness principles. Further, any breach might be capable of remedy by use of the 'exceptional circumstances' provision in §16 of *Schedule 3* of the *Fees Order*. When so deciding, the Court noted that remission should be afforded to those claimants who cannot realistically afford to pay the fee (see para 74). A very full and careful analysis of the causes of the decline in cases should be undertaken and if there are good reasons to think that part of it is due to claimants being unable to afford to bring proceedings, the level of fees and remission criteria will need to be revisited (see para 75). Further (ii) the indirect discrimination claim failed because although more women than men brought discrimination claims, type B claims were not limited to discrimination and there was no gender difference in respect of type B claims as a whole; also, the difference in fees between type A and type B claims could be justified by reference to how difficult they were for the Tribunal to deal with. (iii) The Equality Impact Statement prepared by the Lord Chancellor had given due regard to the impacts of the scheme, and there was no breach of the *Equality Act 2010, s 149* duty.

The latest twist in this saga is that the Court of Appeal's judgment has been appealed to the Supreme Court. Arguments were completed on 27-28 March 2017 and judgment is awaited. Meanwhile, the Ministry of Justice published its review of the introduction of fees. This accepted that there had been "a significant fall" in claims ("a dramatic change") but considered that the introduction of fees had broadly met its objectives and was a "positive outcome". It rejected the notion that people have been prevented from bringing claims. The government has made Proposals, however, to address a lack of awareness of the fee remission scheme and to make certain ET proceedings fee exempt where they relate to payments from the National Insurance Fund.

A similar challenge to that brought by UNISON in England has been brought by Scottish law firm Fox and Partners in the Court of Session and has been sisted (stayed) pending the outcome of the *UNISON* case: *Fox Solicitors Ltd v Lord Chancellor* [2013] CSOH 133.

19.37 *Fee Levels*

The *2013 Fees Order* distinguishes between two types of claim known as "type A" and "type B" claims. Type A claims are claims which are generally more straightforward and less involved. They are listed in a table 2 in *Schedule 2* of the *2013 Fees Order*. They include claims of: breach of contract, redundancy pay, unauthorised deductions from wages, written pay statement, written statement of reasons for dismissal, written statement of terms and conditions, and failure to pay compensation in pursuance of a Tribunal order under *Reg 15(7)* and *(8) TUPE*. Type B claims, by contrast, are the more complicated claims. They include those claims not listed in table 2 in *Schedule 2*, viz claims such as having suffered a detriment for enforcing the national minimum wage, discrimination claims, claims under the *Part Time Workers Regulations*, failure to inform and consult in redundancy cases, pregnancy cases and, notably, unfair dismissal.

When a claimant starts their claim, they must pay an "issue fee": *Art 4(1)(a)* of the *Order*; see also table 3 in *Schedule 2*. The issue fee is currently £160 for a type A claim, and £250 for a type B claim. Where a claim form contains more than one type of claim, only one issue fee is payable. If the claim consists of a mixture of type A and type B claims, then the issue fee for the higher, type B, claim is payable. An employer's contract claim is charged at the type A rate, irrespective of whether the employee's claim consists of a mixture of type A and type B claims: see *Art 11(3)* of the *Order*.

The issue fee can be paid on-line when presenting the claim, by debit or credit card. The Employment Tribunal Service encourages users, where possible, to pay their fees on-line. Alternatively, a claim can be posted with a cheque or postal to the relevant address depending on whether the claim is made in England and Wales or Scotland.

In addition to the issue fee, a claimant must pay a hearing fee: *Art 4(1)(b)* of the *Order*. At the appropriate time, the Tribunal will send the claimant a notice (pursuant to *Rule 40* – see below) requiring a hearing fee to be paid by a set date. The hearing fee is currently set at £230 for a type A claim and £950 for a type B claim: see table 3 in *Schedule 2*. Again, where more than one type of claim is advanced, the higher rate fee is payable.

Where claims are presented as a multiple (that is to say, where multiple claimants present claims in the same claim form), the fees that must be paid are different: see table 4 in *Schedule 2*. The issue and hearing fees vary depending upon the number of people named on the claim form and the type of claims presented. The fees due are currently as follows:

Number of people named on the claim form	Type A claims only	Mixture of type A and type B, or type B claims only
Between 2 and 10	£320	£500
Between 11 and 200	£640	£1,000
201 or more	£960	£1,500

Similarly, when it comes to hearing fees, fees for multiple claimants are altered as follows (again, see table 4 in *Schedule 2*):

Number of people named on the claim form	Type A claims only	Mixture of type A and type B, or type B claims only
Between 2 and 10	£460	£1,900
Between 11 and 200	£920	£3,800
201 or more	£1,380	£5,700

As well as fees for issue and for a hearing, there are other fees that are due under the *2013 Order, Art 4(2)* and *(3)*, for certain types of application, and for reconsideration. These fees are payable not only by claimants but by the relevant applicant party. They consist of:

(a)   A fee for reconsideration of a final judgment in the sum of £100 (type A) and £350 (type B).

(b)   A fee for an application to set aside a judgment in default in the sum of £100.

(c)   A fee for an application to dismiss a claim following settlement in the sum of £60.

(d)   A fee for bringing an employer's contract claim (made by way of application as part of the response to the employee's contract claim) in the sum of £160.

(e)   A fee for judicial mediation, payable by the Respondent, in the sum of £600.

The sums in question are set out in the table contained in *Schedule 1* to the *Fees Order 2013*.

19.38 *Help with Fees: Remissions*

It is possible to claim a remission for fees due if an applicant for a remission can pass both a disposable capital test, and an income test. The regime is set out within *Schedule 3* of the *Fees Order 2013*. Since 28 October 2015, the fees remission process has been called "Help with Fees" and a revised Help with Fees form EX160 and Guidance Booklet EX160A are available online from www.gov.uk.

The disposable capital test requires applicants to consider their total disposable capital and whether it is below a particular threshold set according to the age of the applicant and the level of fee in question: see Table 1 in *Schedule 3, paragraph 3*. To give a flavour, in order to pass the disposable capital test, a putative claimant (under 61 years) who is due to pay a fee of up to £1,000 must be able to certify that his/her disposal capital income is less than £3,000 per month. This increases to £16,000 if the putative claimant is 61 years of age or over. There are notable assets that fall to be excluded from disposable capital for these purposes, including a property which is the main or only dwelling occupied by the party (see *Schedule 3, paragraph 10* for the full list). If the putative claimant cannot satisfy the disposable capital test, the full fee will be payable.

If the disposable capital test is passed, then the applicant must also pass the disposable income test in order to claim a fee remission. A full remission is available where a specified benefit is being received by the applicant. The benefits in question include income based job-seeker's allowance, income related employment and support allowance, income support, universal credit (with gross average earnings of less than £6,000), state pension guarantee credit, and Scottish civil legal aid. Alternatively, if the applicant is not in receipt of one of those benefits, they will qualify for a full remission if their gross monthly income is less than the set threshold that is applicable to them. The thresholds vary depending upon whether the applicant is single, or in a couple, and is dependent upon the number of children that the applicant has: see *Table 2, Schedule 3, paragraph 11*. By way of example, a full remission will be obtained if a couple with two children receives £1,735 or less each month. A single person with no children may obtain a full remission if their monthly gross income is £1,085 or less. There is then a system of partial-remissions. For every £10 of income that an applicant has over the relevant threshold just mentioned, the applicant will have to pay £5 towards the fee. Where gross monthly income equates to the set gross monthly income cap threshold, then the applicant will not be eligible for a remission and will need to pay the full tribunal fee. These thresholds for those in a couple with two children are £5,735 per month, and for a single person without children, £5,085. As at February 2017, the Government was proposing to make changes so as to increase the gross monthly income threshold in order to target those who are most likely to find fees off-putting. The £1,085 gross monthly income threshold is proposed to be increased to £1,250

The disposable capital and gross monthly income of a party includes that of the partner of a party: see *Schedule 3, paragraph 14* (and *paragraph 1* for the definition of 'partner').

Under *Schedule 3, para 16*: "A fee specified in this Order may be remitted where the Lord Chancellor is satisfied that there are exceptional circumstances which justify doing so." The Court of Appeal considered that a broad view should be taken as to what might constitute exceptional circumstances: see *Regina (Unison) v Lord Chancellor (Equality and Human Rights Commission intervening) (Nos 1 & 2)* [2016] ICR 1 at para 73. Some examples are given in the EX160A leaflet.

19.39   *Fees and the Tribunal Rules*

A claimant must pay an issue fee when presenting his/her claim. Under *Rule 11(1)*, discussed in more detail below, the Tribunal must reject a claim if it is not accompanied by the fee or an application for remission. A claim is "accompanied" by an application for remission if the box on the form is ticked indicating that the claimant intends to apply for a fee remission, even if the EX160 form is returned later: see *Deangate Ltd v Hatley* [2015] UKEAT/0389/14. If a fee is paid but is not sufficient, then the Tribunal will issue a notice stating when the balance must be paid. The claim must be rejected if payment of the balance is not forthcoming by the date set. Where a remission application accompanies the presentation of a claim, rather than payment of the fee, and that remission application is ultimately unsuccessful, then the Tribunal will send the claimant a notice specifying the date for payment of the fee. If the fee is not paid by that date, then the Tribunal must reject the claim. Any claim rejected under *Rule 11* must be returned to the claimant with a notice explaining why it has been rejected.

For fees due at other times (see above), where a party does not pay a relevant Tribunal fee, or present a remission application in respect of that fee, the Tribunal will exercise its powers under *Rule 40* and send to the party a notice specifying a date for payment of the Tribunal fee or presentation of a remission application. In the case of the hearing fee, the High Court in *R (Unison) v Lord Chancellor* [2014] ICR 498 remarked that it would expect exchange of witness statements and documents to be exchanged before a hearing fee falls due to allow the claimant to make sensible decisions about continuing. If, at the date specified in a payment notice under Rule 40, the party has not paid the Tribunal fee, and no remission application has been presented, then, pursuant to *Rule 40(2)*, the Tribunal must: (a) in respect of a claim, dismiss it without further order; (b) in respect of an employer's contract claim, dismiss it without further order; (c) in respect of an application, dismiss the application without further order; and (d) in respect of judicial mediation ensure that the judicial mediation does not take place.

If a remission application is refused in part or in full, then the Tribunal will send the claimant a notice specifying the date for payment of the Tribunal fee (*Rule 40(3)*). If that payment has not been made by that date, *Rule 40(4)* states that the consequences will be as set out above in relation to *Rule 40(2)*.

To avoid injustice, the rules provide that where the consequence of dismissal is visited under *Rule 40(2)* or *40(4)*, a party may apply for the claim or response, or part thereof, to be reinstated, and the Tribunal may order a reinstatement. The discretion is at large, to be exercised in accordance with the overriding objective, however by *Rule 40(5)*, such a reinstatement shall be effective only if the Tribunal fee is paid, or a remission application presented and accepted by the date set in the order.

A party that has paid a fee can seek reimbursement of that fee by way of a costs order where they have been substantially successful. This is discussed in more detail at **19.130** (d) below.

Rejection of Claims

19.40   *The Bases for Rejection*

The *2013 Rules* provide for the Employment Tribunal to reject a presented claim in three different sets of circumstances.

Rule 10 deals with rejections for failure to use the prescribed form and failure to provide minimum information. Under *Rule 10(1)*, a Tribunal is required to reject a claim where (a) the claim has not been made on the prescribed form; and (b) where the minimum information is not supplied. The minimum information that must in all cases be included in the claim form is: (i) each claimant's name; (ii) each claimant's address; (iii) each respondent's name; (iv) each respondent's address; and (v) one of the following: (1) an early conciliation number, (2) confirmation that the claim does not institute any relevant proceedings, or (3) confirmation that one of the early conciliation exemptions applies. Where the claim is rejected under *Rule 10*, by *Rule 10(2)*, the form is to be returned to the claimant with a notice of rejection explaining why it has been rejected. The notice is to contain information about how to apply for a reconsideration of that rejection. In *Cranwell v Cullen* [2015] UKEATPAS/0046, the EAT held that a Tribunal had been right to reject a claim under *Rule 10* for failing to provide an early conciliation number when none of the EC exemptions applied. However, in *Mist v Derby Community NHS Trust* UKEAT/0170/15, the EAT took a broad view of the requirement to name the respondent so as not to require its full legal title and went on to point to the availability of *Rule 12(2A)* to correct minor errors (see below).

Rule 11 deals with rejections where the correct Tribunal fee has not been paid. Under *Rule 11(1)*, a Tribunal is required to reject a claim when it is not accompanied by a fee or a remission application. In *Deangate Ltd v Hatley* [2015] UKEAT/0389/14, the EAT held ticking the box indicating that an application for a remission would be made suffices even if the EX160 form is returned later. If the claimant has paid some money towards the fee, but the sum paid was lower than the amount that was due, the Tribunal must send the claimant a notice specifying a date for payment of the additional amount due and identifying the claim or part of the claim in respect of the relevant tribunal fee was not been paid in full (*Rule 11(2)*). In those circumstances, if the claimant does not pay the additional sum by the date specified, the claim must be rejected. If an application for a fee remission is refused in part or in full, the Tribunal must send the claimant a notice specifying the fee to be paid and the date for payment; where this is not paid by the date specified the Tribunal must reject the claim (*Rule 11(3)*). *Rule 11(4)* provides that where a claim or part of it has been rejected, the form is to be returned to the claimant with a notice of rejection explaining why it has been rejected. In contrast to *Rule 10(2)* and *Rule 12(3)* notices, the notice does not have to contain information about how to apply for a reconsideration of the rejection (because such a right for reconsideration is not granted by *Rule 13* – see below).

Rule 12 is concerned with substantive defects in the claim form. *Rule 12(1)* permits the staff of the Tribunal office to refer a claim form to an Employment Judge for a judicial decision concerning whether the claim form suffers from a substantive defect. Under *Rule 12(2)*, where the Judge considers that the claim, or part of it, is (a) one which the Tribunal has no jurisdiction to consider; (b) is in a form which cannot sensibly be responded to or is otherwise an abuse of process; (c) is one which institutes relevant proceedings and is made on a claim form that does not contain either an early conciliation number or confirmation that one of the early conciliation exemptions applies; or (d) is one which institutes relevant proceedings and is made on a claim form which contains information that one of the early conciliation exemptions applies, when none of those exemptions do apply; then the Judge must reject the claim. Under *Rule 12(2A)*, where the Judge considers that the claim, or part of it, is (e) one which institutes relevant proceedings and the name of the claimant on the claim form is not the same as the name of the prospective claimant on the early conciliation certification to which the early conciliation number relates; or (f) is one which institutes relevant proceedings and the name of the respondent on the claim form is not the same as the name of the prospective respondent on the early conciliation certificate to which the early conciliation number relates; then the Judge must reject the claim unless he or she considers that the claimant made a minor error in relation to a name or address and it would not be in the interests of justice to reject the claim. For an example where a minor error in the name of the respondent could have been rectified in this way, see *Mist v Derby Community NHS Trust* UKEAT/0170/15. Any rejected claim form under *Rule 12* must be returned to the claimant together with the notice of rejection giving the Judge's reasons for rejecting the claim or part of it. The notice must contain information about how to apply for a reconsideration of the rejection decision.

Rule 12 was considered in *Trustees of William Jones's School Foundation v Parry* [2016] ICR 1140. There, the ET1 form referred to attached sheets as containing the details of the claim, but the solicitor representing the claimant had mistakenly attached a document relating to a different case. The issue was whether the ET had been right to accept the claim, or whether it ought to have been rejected as being in a form which could not be sensibly responded to under *Rule 12(1)(b)*. Elisabeth Laing J held that although, contrary to the ET's finding, the claim could not sensibly be responded to, this was immaterial because *Rule 12(1)(b)* and *(2)* prescribed a procedure which allowed a claim to be rejected without hearing from any party (or only hearing one party) which was not authorised by primary legislation (*ETA, s 7*) and was accordingly ultra vires. The EAT held that the correct procedure for enforcing compliance with *Rule 12(1)(b)* was that set out in *Rule 27* – giving the parties the opportunity to make representations and then to have a hearing before a claim is dismissed. The Judge remarked that *Rule 12(1)(a)* was the only part of the rule that was authorised by *ETA, s 7*. Clearly this puts into doubt vires of the other provisions of *Rule 12(1)*, viz (c) to (f), concerning enforcement of the EC scheme.

or an explanation of why that is not possible, and if the Respondent wishes to request a hearing, this must be requested in the application. The claimant then has 7 days in which to give reasons in writing explaining why the application is opposed (if this is indeed the case): *Rule 20(2)*.

Applications under *Rule 20* may be determined by the Employment Judge either with or without a hearing: *Rule 20(3)* expressly states that the application may be determined without a hearing.

If the decision is to refuse an extension, any prior rejection of the response under *Rule 18* (see below) shall stand. If, conversely, the decision is to allow an extension, any judgment issued under *Rule 21* must be set aside: see *Rule 20(4)*.

The Tribunal is likely to approach an application made under *Rule 20* in light of the contents of the overriding objective and considering the balance of prejudice between the parties were it to grant, or not grant, the application.

Respondents are generally best advised to apply before the expiry of the time limit if this is possible, and as early as possible once the need to apply for an extension has become apparent. One obvious situation in which extensions will be sought is where the respondent did not receive the Claim Form until sometime after it was sent (either because of postal delays, or the respondent's absence, or because the claimant had given an incorrect address). If genuine, these reasons are likely to be compelling factors in favour of an extension of time: compare *Bone v Fabcon Projects Ltd*, above, where the claim was not received from the tribunal until, having heard of the claim through ACAS, the employer contacted the tribunal office and had it re-sent. However, as an alternative to applying for an extension, the respondent may be in a position to submit a response with the bare minimum of reasons for resisting the claim, and an offer to provide full particulars as soon as the necessary information can be obtained. This approach may also need to be adopted if there is insufficient information about the subject matter of the complaint in the Claim Form (although such cases might be less frequent now given the opportunity for the Tribunal to exercise powers under *Rule 12*); however in most cases this will not necessarily be regarded as a compelling reason for an extension of time, since in most cases the respondent will be fully aware of the point in dispute because it will have been considered as a grievance or have been the subject of disciplinary proceedings. If the respondent did not receive the form because it was incorrectly addressed, he or she may be able to argue that it was not 'sent'. In these circumstances if the respondent becomes aware of the claim soon enough, it may be possible to tell the tribunal the claim has not been received and ask for it to be re-served. The tribunal will not automatically accede to such a request, and if a judgment has already been issued under *Rule 21(2)* by the time the respondent contacts the tribunal, the only practical remedy for the respondent is to apply for a review of that judgment under *Rule 70*: see *Chowles (t/a Granary Pine) v West*, above, for an example.

19.46 *Acceptance of a Response*

Where the Tribunal accepts a response, it must send a copy of it to all other parties: *Rule 22*.

19.47 *Rejection of a Response*

There are two bases on which a Respondent's response can be rejected: (i) the failure to use the correct form or supply minimum information (*Rule 17*) and (ii) late presentation (*Rule 18*).

By *Rule 17*, the Tribunal is required to ("shall") reject a response where it is not made on a prescribed form or if it did not contain all of the minimum information. The minimum information required is (i) the respondent's full name, (ii) the respondent's address and (iii) whether the respondent wishes to resist any part of the claim. Where the Tribunal rejects a response under *Rule 17*, it must return the form to the respondent with a notice of rejection explaining why it has been rejected. The notice must also explain what steps may be taken by a Respondent, including the need (if appropriate) to apply for an extension of time, and how to apply for a reconsideration of the rejection.

If a Respondent's response is received outside the time limit set out in *Rule 16*, or any extension granted within the original limit, then it must be rejected by the Tribunal unless an application for an extension of time has already been made under *Rule 20* and the response includes or is accompanied by such an application: *Rule 18(1)*. In those circumstances, the response shall not be rejected pending the outcome of the application. Where the Tribunal rejects a response under this rule, it must return the response form to the respondent, together with a notice of rejection, explaining that the response was presented late. The notice sent to the Respondent must explain how the respondent can apply for an extension of time and how to apply for a reconsideration: *Rule 18(2)*.

19.48 *Reconsideration of Rejection*

A respondent has an entitlement under *Rule 19(1)* to apply for a decision to reject its response under *Rules 17* or *18* to be reconsidered on the basis that the decision to reject was wrong, or in the case of a rejection under *Rule 17* (failure to use the prescribed form or provide the minimum information) on the basis that the notified defect can be rectified. These constitute the same grounds for reconsideration as appear in *Rule 13* concerning the claim form (see above).

The respondent must apply in writing and present the application to the Employment Tribunal within 14 days of the date that the notice of rejection was sent. It must explain why the decision is said to have been wrong or must rectify the defect and must state whether the respondent requests a hearing: *Rule 19(2)*. If the respondent does not require a hearing, and the Employment Judge decides after considering the application to accept the response in full, then the Judge shall determine the application without a hearing; otherwise the application must be considered at a hearing attended only by the respondent: *Rule 19(3)*.

Where a judge allows an application for reconsideration in circumstances where the original decision to reject was correct, but where the defect has subsequently been rectified, the response is treated as having been presented on the date that the defect was rectified (*Rule 19(4)*). *Rule 19(4)* goes on to provide, expressly, that a Judge may nonetheless extend time under *Rule 5* (see above).

A number of cases were decided under the previous editions of the rules concerning the rejection of a respondent's response. In *Butlins Skyline Ltd v Beynon* [2007] ICR 121, the EAT held that an administrative decision to reject a response is also open to appeal (as well as, under the then rules, a review – now reconsideration). Whilst the *2013 Rules* now provide specifically and expressly for the reconsideration of rejection decisions and the grounds on which this can be done, and the new rules are likely to be the focus for any decision taken by a Tribunal, nonetheless, the old case law is helpful in showing the likely approach of the EAT. In *Jarretts Motors Limited v Wells* [2009] All ER (D) 350 (Jul), for example, Underhill P emphasised that tribunals were obliged to adopt as flexible an approach as possible in order to mitigate the injustice than can be caused by what he described as the then "complex and rigid rules" (para 9). The scope for review of the non-acceptance of a response under the old rules was clarified by the EAT in *Moroak (t/a Blake Envelopes) v Cromie* [2005] IRLR 535 and *Pendragon plc v Copus* [2005] ICR 1671.

The EAT in *Moroak* held that if it was in the interests of justice to extend time and admit a late response, the tribunal should do so. The test to be applied was that set out (in relation to earlier Rules) by the EAT in *Kwik Save Stores Ltd v Swain* [1997] ICR 49, which requires the tribunal to balance all relevant factors, with particular weight being given to whether the respondent would suffer greater prejudice by being denied relief than the claimant would suffer if relief were granted to the respondent. The merits of the defence, so far as readily ascertainable at this stage in the proceedings, may also be relevant. (The *Moroak* case concerned a response sent in 44 minutes late following a malfunction of the respondent's representative's computer, which the EAT unsurprisingly regarded as causing no prejudice to the claimant.) In *Pendragon*, the EAT makes it clear that the absence of a good reason for the failure by the respondent to submit a response in time, whilst clearly an important consideration, is not on its own a bar to granting relief from the consequences: see also to this effect *Thornton v Jones* (UKEAT/0068/11). A failure on the part of a tribunal to consider an application for review of the non-acceptance of a response was found to be an error of law in *South East Leisure Group Ltd v Vachoumis* (UKEAT/0270/10). As a general point, the latitude towards respondents shown in these decisions is clearly much greater than that shown towards claimants whose claims are presented out of time and seek an extension of time under the 'not reasonably practicable' dispensation, and, to a lesser extent, to those seeking an extension on just and equitable grounds. The simple explanation for the apparent discrepancy is that it is the claimant who seeks to invoke the powers of the tribunal, and can therefore be expected to do so promptly, whereas the respondent has not initiated, and probably does not want to be party to, the litigation; and these differences of context lead to different expectations as to compliance with the requirements of the tribunal. Once proceedings have been fully initiated, there is less evidence of a difference of approach to the parties' conduct, and in particular to failure to comply with directions.

As *Butlins Skyline Ltd* made clear, the non-acceptance of a response is a decision open to appeal, and although there were particular reasons under the old rules which made that outcome just, it is likely to remain the position under the *2013 Rules*. Careful consideration should be given to whether to appeal rather than seek reconsideration – usually the latter will be the more appropriate route given the need to show an error of law on appeal.

19.49 Effect of No Response

Rule 21(1) provides for the Tribunal to issue a default judgment and/or to limit further participation in proceedings where:

(a)   on the expiry of the time limit for presenting a response under Rule 16 no response has been presented; or

(b)   any response that has been presented has been rejected and no application for a reconsideration is outstanding; or

(c)   where the respondent has stated that no part of the claim is contested.

It is to be noted that the wording of *Rule 21(1)(a)* speaks of the time limit for presenting a response under *Rule 16* without adding reference to any extension granted under *Rule 20* (contrast *Rule 18(1)* which does contain this additional wording). That said, it is most unlikely that the Tribunal would visit the consequences in *Rules 21(2)* and *(3)* where the Respondent was still within an extended time limit, or where a response had been presented after the 28 days but within an extension granted by the Tribunal.

19.50 *Judgment in Default*

In the circumstances set out in *Rule 21(1)*, by *Rule 21(2)*, an Employment Judge is required to ("shall") decide whether, on the available material (including further information which the parties are required to provide by the Judge) a determination can properly be made of the claim or part of it. To the extent that a determination can be made, the Judge is required to issue a judgment accordingly. Otherwise a hearing must be fixed before a Judge alone.

It is clear that such a judgment may deal solely with liability, or also with remedy. Under the previous rules, in which the Tribunal had a discretion to issue a default judgment where no response was presented within time, it was common that default judgments were limited to liability; a default judgment on remedy was only appropriate where it is clear from the papers what the claimant is claiming, and this was unlikely except in claims for unlawful deductions or redundancy payments (and it was not be clear in many such cases what amount was being claimed). This is expected to the position under the *2013 Rules* also. The provision enabling Judges to order the provision of additional information is intended to enable more judgments under *Rule 21(2)* to deal also with remedy. In any case, a claimant who wishes to have a judgment covering remedy made is free to submit additional information without waiting for an Order to that effect, preferably by way of a Schedule of Loss; the Judge can necessarily only determine what remedy is appropriate in the light of the information available to him or her at the time of deciding.

As with the old rules, if the judgment under *Rule 21(2)* is for liability only, there is no provision in the *2013 Rules* for a second such judgment dealing with remedy. Rather *Rule 21(2)* provides for a hearing to deal with whatever matters are outstanding before a judge alone. The respondent will only be entitled to participate in any such hearing to the extent permitted by the judge: see *Rule 21(3)* below. It should be noted that even if a respondent is permitted to take part in a remedy hearing following a default judgment on liability, the tribunal cannot reopen any issues determined by the *Rule 21(2)* judgment, and issues relevant to remedy must therefore be decided on the basis of the claimant's claims as upheld in the earlier judgment. This was the position under the old rules: *Eaton v Spencer and others t/a/ Wiggles Experience* (UKEAT/0177/11).

Under the old rules, there was no requirement to give reasons for a default judgment issued under old *rule 8*. The *2013 Rules*, however, do not exempt judgments issued under *Rule 21(2)* from the general provisions of *Rule 62* – obligation to give reasons (see below). Either party may apply for reconsideration of the judgment in accordance with *Rule 70*. In the case of the claimant, this is likely to arise only in relation to remedy, if the tribunal has awarded less than he or she considers should have been awarded. The application must be made within 14 days of the date on which the judgment was sent to the parties (*Rule 71*). This time limit can be extended by the Judge under *Rule 5*. An example would be where the respondent only became aware of the proceedings, or the judgment, after the time limit for reconsideration had expired, because an incorrect address had been given by the claimant: see *Chowles (t/a Granary Pine) v West* (UKEAT/0473/08). The application must state the reasons for seeking the reconsideration (*Rule 71*). If it is the respondent who is applying, the application for reconsideration of the judgment issued under *Rule 21(2)* is likely to be accompanied by an application for an extension of time to present a response (or even in certain circumstances a reconsideration of the rejection of the response). It is important to remember the requirement of Rule 20(1) that an application for an extension after the time has expired must attach the proposed response to the claim as well as giving reasons for the applications made. Under the old rules, a failure to apply for an extension of time at the same time as a review of a default judgment was regarded as a technicality which should not be used to refuse an application for a review where there are good grounds for the review: *Bournemouth Borough Council v Leadbeater* (UKEAT/0010/11) (respondent had not received claim); and see *Jarretts Motors Ltd v Wells*, above, where a flexible approach by tribunals to applications for a review citing the wrong rule under the old rules was advocated by the EAT).

Please see **19.41** for commentary on the Rules regarding reconsideration generally. There are few criteria in the *2013 Rules* as to how applications for reconsideration of judgments issued under *Rule 21(2)* will be considered. The question under *Rule 70* is whether the interests of justice render it necessary to revoke the judgment. It is to be expected that Tribunals will have regard to the kinds of factors that were identified in the previous case-law, albeit with an eye to the fact that particular considerations under the old-rules have been removed. On a respondent's application, these are likely to include the reason for any delay in presenting a response, the extent to which the respondent can show there were reasonable prospects of successfully defending the claim (or, as the case may be, successfully disputing the amount of compensation, or any other remedy, awarded). None of these matters is likely to trump a broad consideration of what the interests of justice necessitate: see under the old rules *Pendragon plc v Copus* [2005] ICR 1671; *Pestle and Mortar v Turner* (UKEAT/0652/05), and *Thornton v Jones* (UKEAT/0068/11), where a default judgment was revoked despite a finding that there was no good reason for the respondent's failure to present its response on time. The general approach adopted in the earlier cases was also reiterated by the EAT in *Jarretts Motors Ltd v Wells* [2009] All ER (D) 350 (Jul). A point not addressed by the EAT in *Moroak* or *Pendragon* is what test has to be applied in determining whether the respondent has reasonable prospects of successfully defending the claim (or part of it). There is as yet no appellate authority on this point. A subsidiary point is whether it is enough that the respondent has reasonable prospects of disputing the amount of compensation claimed or likely to be claimed, even if there is no reasonable prospect of defending on the issue of liability. It would not make sense to deny a respondent the right to contest remedy where there are real issues in dispute, merely because liability will probably be established.

If it is the respondent who has applied for the reconsideration, the effect of a successful application is likely to be that the response will be accepted, and the respondent will be able to defend the claim in the normal way, but this is not automatic. When the application is by a claimant, the question is whether there are good grounds which necessitate the varying the original award in the interests of justice. As an alternative to a review application, a party may appeal against a judgment issued under *Rule 21(2)*. However, in practice it is difficult to envisage circumstances in which it would be preferable to appeal rather than apply for reconsideration. Since permissible grounds of appeal are limited to points of law, it would be much more likely in the majority of cases that grounds for reconsideration could be identified.

19.51 *Further Participation*

A further consequence is set out in *Rule 21(3)*: whilst the respondent is entitled to notice of any hearings and of the decisions made by the Tribunal, unless and until any extension of time is granted to the Respondent for presenting its response, it shall only be entitled to participate in any hearing "to the extent permitted by the Judge".

The discretion to permit participation by the respondent in circumstances where a response has not been submitted marks a major shift in the *2013 Rules*. This reflects the disquiet over *rule 9* of the old *Rules* which, read literally, prohibited a respondent from participating in proceedings (irrespective of the proportionality of that limitation on *Art 6* ECHR rights) other than by way of appearing as a witness or applying for a review of a default judgment. In *D&H Travel v Foster* [2006] ICR 1537, Elias P held that were it not for the availability of a review, there would be a real question as to the compatibility of the old *Rule 9* with *Art 6* of the ECHR. In *D&H Travel v Foster*, the respondent failed to serve a response in time, and a default judgment on liability was issued. The respondent attended at the remedy hearing, but the tribunal declined to hear it; the EAT held that this was an error. The respondent's attendance was an implied application to review the rejection of its late response, and it would have been proportionate as between the parties to have allowed the review and permitted the respondent to take part in the remedy hearing. The EAT also accepted under the old rules that the exclusion of the respondent from participating in a hearing convened at his or her request to review a default judgment would be absurd, and that the rules should be interpreted so as to permit the respondent to be heard at the hearing of the review, and not merely to permit the respondent to apply for a review: *Terry Ballard & Co (a firm) v Stonestreet* [2007] All ER (D) 176 (Mar); *Jarretts Motors Ltd v Wells*, above.

Rule 21(3) of the *2013 Rules* gives the Judge a discretion as to the future participation that the respondent might have. That discretion will have to be exercised not only in accordance with the overriding objective, but also in light of the fact that preventing a respondent from participating has the effect of limiting the respondent's ability to have access to the Tribunal to defend its civil rights (*Art 6 ECHR*). Under *HRA 1998, s 3* the Tribunal must interpret the rule to give effect to *Art 6*, and further under *HRA 1998, s 6*, the Tribunal is bound itself to give effect to Art 6 in its decision making. The upshot is that Tribunals will need to ensure that the extent of any limitation they impose is a proportionate one to give effect to the legitimate aim of the efficient and prompt resolution of employment claims.

It is also noteworthy that read literally *Rule 21(3)* would seem not to apply where a Respondent has been granted an extension of time, but has then failed to present its response within that extended period. It would be surprising if that were the result, and one would anticipate an interpretation of the Rule whereby it was avoided.

19.52 Employer's Contract Claim

If the claim, or one of the claims, brought by the claimant is for breach of contract, or for a sum due under a contract, the respondent may in addition to responding to the claim make an employer's contract claim. It is only in cases where the claim is made under the *Employment Tribunals Extension of Jurisdiction (England and Wales) Order 1994* or its Scottish equivalent, *Employment Tribunals Extension of Jurisdiction (Scotland) Order 1994*, that such a step is possible. Under the *2013 Rules*, an "employee's contract claim" is defined to be a claim brought by an employee in accordance with *articles 3* and *7* of the *1994 Order*. An "Employer's contract claim" means a claim brought by an employer in accordance with *articles 4* and *8* of the *1994 Order*. (See *Rule 1(1)*).

Rule 23 provides that any employer's contract claim must ("shall") be made as part of the response to the employee's contract claim and presented in accordance with *Rule 16*. It can be rejected on the same basis as a claimant's claim make be rejected under *Rule 12*, in which case the opportunity to seek reconsideration under *Rule 13* applies (see discussion above).

When the Tribunal sends a response containing an employer's contract claim to the other parties in accordance with *Rule 22*, it must notify the claimant that the response includes an employer's contract claim and include information about how to submit a response, the time limit for doing so, and what will happen if a response is not received by the Tribunal within that time limit: *Rule 24*.

The employee's response to an employer's contract claim must be submitted to the tribunal office within 28 days of the date that the response was sent to the claimant (*Rule 25*). *Rule 25* also provides that if no response is presented within that time limit, *Rules 20* and 21 apply (these allow the claimant to apply for an extension of time to present a response, and give powers to the Tribunal to issue a judgement in default under *Rule 21(2)* and limit the claimant's participation in the resolution of the claim under *Rule 21(3)*.

The *2013 Rules* do not contain any ability for a claimant's response to an employer's contract claim to be liable to be rejected under *Rules 17* or *18* (contrast *Rule 23*'s express reference to the potential for the employer's contract claim itself to be rejected under Rule 20).

19.53 INITIAL CONSIDERATION OF CLAIM FORM AND RESPONSE

The *2013 Rules* contain new provisions under which every claim and response will undergo initial screening by an Employment Judge to assess the prospects of success of the claims and the defences and in order to decide whether the claim ought to be permitted to proceed.

19.54 Initial Consideration

As soon as possible after the acceptance of the response, *Rule 26(1)* requires a Judge to consider "all of the documents held by the Tribunal in relation to the claim" in order to confirm whether there are arguable complaints and defences within the jurisdiction of the Tribunal.

Rule 26(1) empowers the judge to order a party to provide further information to allow him or her to carry out that initial screening.

The mandatory language of *Rule 26(1)* should be noted: it appears that the Tribunal must consider all the documents it holds – it cannot conduct a more summary review. Further the assessment must happen "as soon as possible after the acceptance of the response". Where an employer's contract claim is presented in the response, it is likely that the Judge will conduct the assessment after the employee's response to that contract claim has been presented, because it is at that stage that the pleadings will have 'closed'.

The first task of the Judge on initial consideration is to determine whether the claims and defences are within the jurisdiction of the Tribunal. This ought to be a reasonably straightforward exercise. The second task requires the Judge to consider whether the claims and defences are "arguable" (*Rule 26(1)*). No definition of "arguable" is contained within *Rule 26(1)*, however it is apparent from the circumstances in which the whole or parts of the claim or response may be dismissed by the judge, that s/he is assessing whether the claims and defences enjoy reasonable prospects of success. The use of the word "arguable" in *Rule 26(1)* is, however, sufficiently broad so as to allow the Judge conducting the initial consideration to make other observations as to the arguability of the claims and defences, which might be recorded in the case management order in accordance with *Rule 26(2)*, even where s/he is not satisfied that any part of the pleading should be dismissed at that stage as not enjoying reasonable prospects.

19.55 *Claims and Defences Arguable*

Where the Judge does not decide to dismiss the whole or part of a claim or response for not enjoying reasonable prospects of success, or not falling within the jurisdiction of the Tribunal, the Judge conducting the initial consideration must ("shall") make a case management order, unless one has already been made, which may deal with the listing of a preliminary or final hearing, and which may propose judicial mediation or other forms of dispute resolution (see *Rule 26(2)*). As noted above, it is likely that a Judge may at this stage make other observations as to the "arguability" of the claims and responses in this order.

The case management orders which might be made at this stage are considered in more detail below.

Where a devolution issue arises in the case, the Tribunal must as soon as practicable send a notice of that fact and a copy of the claim form and response to the bodies set out in *Rule 98*. It is likely that this will occur at the time of the initial consideration of claims.

19.56 *Dismissal of Claim or Response (or parts)*

If the Judge conducting the initial consideration considers either that the Tribunal has no jurisdiction to consider the claim (or part of the claim) or that the claim (or part of the claim) has no reasonable prospect of success, the Tribunal must sent a notice to the parties (a) setting out the Judge's view and the reasons for it; and (b) ordering that the claim, or part in question, shall be dismissed on such date as is specified in the notice, unless before that date, the claimant has presented written representations to the Tribunal explaining why the claim (or part of it) should not be dismissed: see *Rule 27(1)*.

Where no representations are received, the claim shall be dismissed from the date specified in the notice without further order, although the Tribunal must write to the parties to confirm that this has occurred: *Rule 27(2)*. If, however, representations are received within the specified time, an Employment Judge (the Rule does not require this to be the same Employment Judge who conducted the initial consideration) must consider them, and then will decide either to permit the claim (or part of the claim) to proceed, or to fix a hearing for the purpose of deciding whether the claim should be permitted to proceed: *Rule 27(3)*. A respondent is permitted to attend such a hearing, but *Rule 27(3)* expressly provides that it need not do so.

The question for the Judge either on receipt of the written representations, or at a hearing, per *Rule 27(3)* is whether the claim ought to be permitted to proceed (rather than a fresh consideration of the prospects of success of the claim). Whilst in most cases the two concepts are likely to be treated as identical, there is perhaps scope for claims with prospects falling below the threshold to be permitted to proceed for other reasons – for example, where the case is of particular importance, or where jurisprudence is developing.

Where, either after further written submissions, or after a hearing, the claim is permitted to proceed, the Judge must make a case management order: *Rule 27(4)*. It is likely that such an order will be similar in scope to that covered by *Rule 26(2)*.

A similar procedure applies to the response to the claim under *Rule 28*. Where an Employment Judge considers that the response or part of the response has no reasonable prospects of success, the Tribunal shall send a notice to the parties (a) setting out the Judge's view and reasons for it, (b) ordering the response (or part) to be dismissed on a specified date unless the respondent has presented written representations to the Tribunal explaining why the response (or part) should not be dismissed, and (c) specifying the consequences of the dismissal of the response. That consequence is specified by *Rule 28(5)*: if a response is dismissed the effect shall be as if no response had been presented as set out in *Rule 21* (see discussion above). This therefore needs to be specified in the Tribunal's notice.

A similar procedure for the consideration of written representations, and the holding of a hearing if necessary, applies following a notice given under *Rule 28(1)*: see *Rule 28(2), (3)* and *(4)*.

CASE MANAGEMENT ORDERS AND OTHER POWERS

Case Management Orders

19.57 *General Power*

Rule 29 provides that the Tribunal may at any stage of the proceedings, whether on its own initiative or on application, make a case management order. The Rule expressly states that the particular powers identified in the various following rules do not restrict that general power (subject to *rules 30A(2)* and *(3)* concerning postponements). A case management order may vary, suspend or set aside an earlier case management order where that is necessary in the interests of justice, and in particular where a party affected by the earlier order did not have a reasonable opportunity to make representations before it was made.

The approach under the *2013 Rules* represents a significant change from that in the old rules, which contained a list of the various orders that could be made. Under the *2013 Rules*, there is a general power to make appropriate case management orders, without the minutiae being specified. The Presidential Guidance on Case Management provides non-binding guidance (which nonetheless must be considered) covering some of these situations.

If an order is made against a party who has not had an opportunity to make representations before the order is made (as when the order is made on the Judge's own initiative, or is an order against a non-party), the order is subject to the right of the person subject to the order to apply to the tribunal to revoke or vary it. Any such application must be made in writing, (if possible) before the date for compliance with the order, and giving reasons for objecting to the order. In practice it can be expected that the tribunal will notify all parties of an application by a non-party to set aside an order against him or her (unless it is a witness order, in which case only the party requesting it would be advised of the application to set it aside). An application to set aside an order may be considered on the papers or at a hearing ordered for the purpose (see *Reddington v Straker & Sons Ltd* [1994] ICR 172).

In addition to applications to set aside orders made without notice to the party concerned, it is possible to apply for an order to be varied or revoked. The availability of the general power to vary or revoke orders made under *Rule 29* has been confirmed by the EAT: see *Onwuka v Spherion Technology UK Ltd* [2005] ICR 567 and *Hart v English Heritage* [2006] IRLR 915. This is distinct from the power of reconsideration, which these cases also confirm was not available for orders under the old rules. However it is important to note that as a matter of practice a tribunal or Judge will not vary or revoke an order unless there has been a material change of circumstances: *Goldman Sachs Services Ltd v Montali* [2002] ICR 1251, a decision affirmed in relation to the *2004 ET Rules* in *Hart v English Heritage* (above) and now under the *2013 Rules* in *Serco Ltd v Wells* UKEAT/0330/15. In the latter case, the EAT derived the applicable principles as follows (para 43 and 45): (i) that the *2013 Rules* must be taken to have been drafted with the principle of finality in mind such that challenges to an order would normally take place on appeal. Seeking the same Judge or another Judge of equivalent jurisdiction to look again at an order or decision, save in carefully defined circumstances, should be discouraged; (ii) the expression "necessary in the interests of justice" in *Rule 29* should be interpreted in light of that principle. Case-law under the CPR and in the Tribunal indicates that a variation or revocation of an order or decision may be necessary in the interests of justice where there has been a material change of circumstances after the order was made, or where the order has been based on either a misstatement, and there may be other occasions, which it is unwise to attempt to define but these will be "rare . . . [and] . . . out of the ordinary"; (iii) whether or not a subsequent event amounts to a material change in circumstances is a matter of "jurisdiction" and not a question of the exercise of discretion. It is to be decided from an objective standpoint.

Correspondence between a party or representative and the tribunal, such as an application for an order or a response objecting to the application, is afforded absolute immunity from claims based on it, in the same way as the claim and response are immune from being used as the basis of a further claim: *Dathi v South London and Maudsley NHS Trust* [2008] IRLR 350. Accordingly a letter from the respondent to the tribunal opposing an application for costs (and also a further letter to the claimant's representative declining to give voluntary disclosure) was immune from suit as an act of alleged victimisation.

19.58 *Applications for Case Management Orders*

Rule 30 governs the procedure under which the parties may apply for the Tribunal to make a case management order. *Rule 30(1)* provides that an application for a particular case management order may be made either at a hearing or by being presented in writing to the Tribunal. It is also clear from the ability of the Tribunal to make a case management order at any stage of the proceedings (*Rule 29*) that an application can similarly be made at any time. *Rule 30(3)* confirms that the Tribunal may determine the application in writing, or order it be dealt with at a preliminary or final hearing.

Even though an application can be made at any time, the Presidential Guidance on General Case Management encourages parties to make the application in writing or at a Preliminary Hearing and to do so as early as possible (paras 9 and 10). Where a hearing has been set, especially with the agreement of the parties, that fact must be considered by the judge who determines the application. Applications should state the reason why it is made, why it is considered to be in accordance with the overriding objective to make the case management order sought (para 12). All relevant documents should be provided with the application (para 13). If the parties are in agreement, and the application is made by consent, this should be indicated to the Tribunal (para 14). Where an application is made in writing, as well as sending a copy to all other parties and indicating to the Tribunal that this has been done (see *Rule 92*), *Rule 30(2)* requires the party making the application to notify the other parties that any objections to the application should be sent to the Tribunal as soon as possible. Prior to the *2013 Rules* a similar obligation only applied to legally represented parties.

The Presidential Guidance indicates that applications will be considered by the Employment Judge "as soon as practicable" (para 17) and the Judge may seek further information where this has not been supplied with the application (para 17). The decision of the Judge will be notified to all parties as soon as practicable after the decision has been made (para 18).

19.59 *Sanctions for Non-Compliance*

Any person (whether a party to the proceedings or not) who without reasonable cause fails to comply with a witness order or an order for disclosure commits a criminal offence punishable on summary conviction with a fine not exceeding £1,000 (*ETA 1996, s 7(4)*). This fact must be conveyed by a penal notice attached to any such order made under *ET Rules*). In practice the sanction of prosecution is not used (although it may be threatened for a recalcitrant recipient of an order for disclosure or to attend as a witness); this has given added weight to the sanctions available to the tribunal itself (as distinct from being dependent on other agencies for enforcement), but these are of necessity only available where the default is that of a party to the proceedings.

The sanctions (other than referring the case to the relevant authority for possible prosecution, if applicable) available to the tribunal if a party fails to comply (or is late in complying) with an order, or with any requirement laid down by the *Rules* or a Practice Direction, are that the tribunal may make an order for costs, or a preparation time order, against the offending party, or, in more serious cases, order that the party's claim or part thereof be struck out, or that a response or part thereof be struck out and/or that the respondent be debarred from defending the claim (see below). The potentially drastic consequences for a party of the powers to strike out a claim or response necessitate that such powers are used sparingly and only for extreme cases of disregard of orders or cases where the consequences for the possibility of a fair trial are significant. See further **19.76** et sec below. *Rule 38* introduces an intermediate option, long available to the courts, of the making of an 'unless' order: unless the party complies with an order by a stated date, his or her case is to be struck out on the date for compliance without further order (*Rule 38(1)*). In practice such an order will only normally be made after there has been a failure to comply with an earlier order, and the specific power in the rules to revisit the consequential striking out of the claim or, in the case of a response, to vary or revoke orders, can be used to relieve the party concerned of the consequences of an 'unless' order if it is shown that the party would otherwise suffer serious injustice. See further **19.81** below.

Disclosure and Information

19.60   *The Rule and Disclosure Generally*

Rule 31 enables the Tribunal to make an order that any person in Great Britain should disclose documents or information to a party (by providing copies or otherwise),or to allow a party to inspect such material as might be ordered by a county court or, in Scotland, by a sheriff. It is clear by the formulation of the *Rule* that it is apt to include orders made against non-parties as well as parties.

Rule 31 can only be used to require a person in Great Britain to disclose documents or information. Where the subject is in a European Union country, consideration should be given to *Rule 33* (see below).

Disclosure (formerly known as discovery) is the process in civil litigation where each party discloses to the other all documents relevant to the proceedings and not protected from disclosure. The tribunal's power to order disclosure is the same as that of the civil courts under *Part 31* of the *Civil Procedure Rules 1998* ('*CPR*'), or in Scotland that of the Sheriff Court. An important consequence of this is that the scope of disclosure should be consistent with the Overriding Objective of civil litigation.

There is no automatic disclosure in tribunals – unless given voluntarily or ordered by the tribunal it must be specifically asked for. However it has increasingly become the practice of tribunals in England and Wales, although not in Scotland, to order mutual disclosure at an early stage of the proceedings. In Scotland Practice Direction No 1 issued in December 2006 requires the mutual notification by the parties of the documents each intends to rely on at least 14 days before the Hearing (these are referred to as Productions, and the list of documents as an Inventory). The Presidential Guidance on General Case Management deals with disclosure of documents and the preparation of documents and provides that even where there is no formal disclosure order, the Tribunal generally will prefer that documentary evidence is presented in an easily accessible hearing bundle with everyone involved having an identical copy.

The formal process of disclosure involves supplying a list of all the documents in a party's possession and allowing the other party to inspect and take copies. In practice the parties may agree simply to supply copies of all the documents concerned.

An increasingly important element in disclosure of documents is the retrieval of e-mails and other electronic documents. These are equally documents, and are disclosable not only if paper copies have been put on a file, but also if retained electronically within the party's computer system (this extends to deleted or archived e-mails/documents, if they can still be accessed). The civil courts are developing more sophisticated procedures to deal with large electronic disclosure exercises (see e.g. *CPR PD 31B* and the use of predictive coding in *Pyrrho Investments Ltd v MWB Property Ltd* [2016] EWHC 256 (Ch)) which, although not directly applicable in the Employment Tribunal, might provide a suitable analogy in an appropriate case. Disclosure may be either general (ie covering the case as a whole) or specific (ie covering identified documents or classes of documents). Parties ordered to disclose documents need only undertake a reasonable search for relevant documents. A party giving voluntary disclosure need not disclose all documents; however, a document cannot properly be kept back if its non-disclosure would render a disclosed document misleading: *Birds Eye Walls Ltd v Harrison* [1985] ICR 278, where the claimant was permitted to amend his claim to add new grounds part way through the hearing after coming into possession of a relevant document in the possession of the employer that had not been included in its earlier disclosure. The same point probably applies to documents the concealment of which would render oral evidence misleading. Failure to disclose a relevant document can lead to very serious consequences, as shown by *Aslam v Barclays Capital Ltd* (UKEAT/0405/10), where the subsequent production by the respondent of a crucial document not disclosed before the hearing led to an order by the EAT for the re-hearing of the entire case.

The obligation to disclose documents is a continuing one, so that if further documents come to light, or come into existence, during the course of the proceedings, they must be disclosed if they are relevant to material already disclosed, or within the terms of an order for disclosure. This principle was applied by the Court of Appeal in *Scott v IRC* [2004] EWCA Civ 400, [2004] IRLR 713 in relation to a new policy on permitting employees to continue to work beyond the normal retirement age, which was adopted whilst the claim was proceeding and which affected the basis on which the claimant's claim for compensation for future loss of earnings would fall to be calculated.

The normal and recommended practice, where either disclosure has not been ordered by the tribunal at an early stage in the proceedings or the disclosure given appears to be incomplete, is for disclosure, or additional specific disclosure, to be requested by correspondence in the first instance. If this request is refused, ignored or not fully complied with, an application should be made to the tribunal for an order.

19.61   The test for whether disclosure of a particular document or class of documents should be ordered is whether disclosure is necessary for disposing fairly of the proceedings. This involves more than just relevance; an application for disclosure of a large quantity of documents of marginal relevance is likely to be refused on the ground of excessive burden on the other party, in accordance with the Overriding Objective, which includes the requirement to act proportionately to the importance and complexity of the case. A good example of a refusal of excessive disclosure is *British Aerospace plc v Green* [1995] ICR 1006, CA, where, in a case arising from a substantial redundancy selection exercise, disclosure of assessment records of several hundred employees was refused. See also *King v Eaton Ltd* [1996] IRLR 199.

The ambit of disclosure is likely to be widest in discrimination cases, because of the need to show evidence from which inferences can be drawn (*West Midlands Passenger Transport Executive v Singh* [1988] 1 WLR 730, [1988] ICR 614). However, even in discrimination cases a test of relevance still applies; further guidance is given in *Ministry of Defence v Meredith* [1995] IRLR 539, *Canadian Imperial Bank of Commerce v Beck* [2009] EWCA Civ 619, *HSBC Asia Holdings BV v Gillespie* [2011] IRLR 209 and *Kalu v Brighton & Sussex University Hospitals NHS Trust* (UKEAT/0609/12).

Confidentiality is not as such a reason for refusing disclosure. In a doubtful case the tribunal may inspect the documents before deciding whether they are sufficiently relevant to overcome the need to respect confidentiality (see *Science Research Council v Nasse* [1980] AC 1028, [1979] 3 All ER 673, [1979] 3 WLR 762, [1979] IRLR 465, [1979] ICR 921). If disclosure is ordered, it must be disclosure to the other party or parties; the tribunal cannot order disclosure to itself alone: *Knight v Department of Social Security* [2002] IRLR 249. If necessary in order to preserve confidentiality, the tribunal can order disclosure subject to anonymising the document and/or deleting passages which would or might reveal the identity of the author or source of a statement, a procedure known as redaction: *Asda Stores Ltd v Thompson* [2002] IRLR 245 (a case concerning disclosure of witness statements taken under terms of confidentiality in an investigation of alleged drug dealing). Further guidance as to the procedure to be followed where a party wishes to disclose documents subject to redaction is given in *Asda Stores Ltd v Thompson (No 2)* [2004] IRLR 598. The tribunal also has power to restrict disclosure to the party him or herself and his or her representative, and to limit the purpose for which disclosure is given to the conduct of the particular case: see the *Knight* case, above. This is in any event an implied condition of any non-voluntary disclosure of documents that are not subsequently put into the public domain by being referred to in the course of a public hearing. This point is made in the Presidential Guidance on General Case Management. When dealing with the confidentiality of disclosed documents, the Guidance emphasises that they can only be used for the hearing and must only be shown to a party and that party's advisor or representative or another witness (insofar as necessary). The documents "must not be used for any purpose other than the conduct of the case". One class of documents the disclosure of which is commonly made subject to restrictions is the claimant's medical records, and medical reports on the claimant; the tribunal may limit disclosure to the legal representatives and medical advisers of the respondent to protect the confidentiality of the claimant's medical history.

The EAT gave a summary of the above guidance for the correct approach on a disclosure application in *Plymouth City Council v White* (UKEAT/0333/13) as follows: (a) the judge must first consider if the document sought is relevant (if not, no disclosure should be ordered); (b) if it is relevant, the judge should consider if it is necessary for the fair trial of the case. In a case of objection, the Judge should examine the document itself: *Nassé*; (c) if the document is relevant and necessary and should be disclosed, the judge should consider whether there is a more nuanced way of disclosing so as to respect the confidentiality (e.g. using redaction); (d) if the judge has read the disputed documents, s/he should not conduct the full hearing unless the parties agree. See further *Birmingham City Council v Bagshaw & Others* [2016] UKEAT/0107/16.

If, exceptionally, a party cannot disclose a document without acting unlawfully, it is wrong in principle to order disclosure: *Barracks v Coles* [2006] EWCA Civ 1041, [2007] ICR 60, a case about a police officer refused security clearance for reasons the police force was unable lawfully to disclose. Disclosure can only be ordered of existing documents; it cannot be used to require the creation of a document (e.g. by compiling statistics): *Carrington v Helix Lighting Ltd* [1990] ICR 125. The restricting effect of this point is considerably eased by the tribunal's general power to order a party to provide information, which can include in an appropriate case a table, chart or schedule containing relevant information (including a Schedule of Loss, or a table giving numbers of staff classified by grade and ethnic origin – the issue in the *Carrington* case).

19.62 *Documents Privileged from Disclosure*

Certain documents are immune from disclosure. These include those subject to legal professional privilege and (with qualifications) public interest immunity. Legal professional privilege covers both legal advice privilege and litigation privilege. The former applies only to communications with and from professional legal advisers, not, for instance, an accountant, a trade union official, or lay adviser (including a professional but not legally qualified consultant): as confirmed by the Supreme Court in *R (on the application of Prudential Plc) v Special Commissioner of Income Tax* [2013] 2 All ER 247; see also *New Victoria Hospital v Ryan* [1993] ICR 201; *Howes v Hinckley and Bosworth Borough Council* [2008] All ER (D) 112 (Aug). Litigation privilege has wider application, covering communications with advisers who are not lawyers (see *Scotthorne v Four Seasons Conservatories (UK) Ltd* (UKEAT/0178/10)) but only in relation to communications the primary purpose of which is in relation to pursuing, defending or avoiding actual or anticipated litigation; for further details, specialist works on the subject should be consulted. Legal professional privilege can be waived; guidance was given by the EAT in *Brennan v Sunderland City Council* [2009] ICR 479 as to how to assess whether privilege has been waived. Public interest immunity is also a specialised area of law outside the scope of this work; the leading recent cases relevant to its application in tribunal proceedings are *Balfour v Foreign and Commonwealth Office* [1994] ICR 277 and *R v Chief Constable of West Midlands, ex p Wiley* [1995] 1 AC 274 (overruling *Halford v Sharples* [1992] 3 All ER 624, [1992] 1 WLR 736, [1992] ICR 583).

'Without prejudice' communications between the parties are in a slightly different category, as they are in their nature already known to both parties. They are, however, not admissible as evidence before the tribunal unless both parties agree, or to prove the contents of an agreement subsequently reached, or, exceptionally, where non-disclosure of the document would lead to the concealment of 'unambiguous impropriety' on the part of the party seeking to exclude the document, or where, if the content of the without prejudice communication was excluded, an abuse of the privileged occasion would occur. Something more is required than merely that one party would be put to a forensic disadvantage: see *Portnykh v Nomura International Plc* [2014] IRLR 251 in which the EAT confirmed that the exceptions to the without prejudice rule should not be applied too readily. See also *Savings and Investment Bank Ltd v Finken* [2004] 1 WLR 667. For an example where the exception was held not to be made out, and disclosure was refused, see *Brodie v Ward (t/a First Steps Nursery)* [2008] All ER (D) 115 (Feb). The same principle applies to evidence of oral communications conducted without prejudice. A distinction can be drawn between the fact of negotiations and their content and the former might be admissible where the latter is not: see *Faithorn Farrell Timms LLP v Bailey* [2016] ICR 1054.

However, the privilege against disclosure to the tribunal only applies to genuinely 'without prejudice' communications, i.e. those generated as or forming part of an attempt to settle a dispute. Usually, there must be a dispute, such that the parties must have contemplated that if not resolved, the matter might proceed to litigation, although it is not necessary that either party has actually threatened litigation. The dividing line has been described by the Court of Appeal as not always clear and highly dependent on the particular circumstances of each case: *Framlington Group Ltd v Barnetson* [2007] EWCA Civ 502, [2007] ICR 1439, [2007] IRLR 598.

By contrast, the EAT refused to interfere with a Tribunal's decision that a grievance meeting called by an employer which was then used as the occasion to put proposals to the employee for a severance package was not within the privilege (with the result that the employee could rely on what was said at the meeting to support a complaint of sex discrimination): *BNP Paribas v Mezzotero* [2004] IRLR 508. This was despite the fact that Ms Mezzotero was pursuing a grievance at the time, both because there was no dispute to which the proposals were directed, and also because it would be wrong to allow the employer to rely on the privilege when the status of the meeting was first raised unilaterally after it had begun, and had not been agreed in advance. However a subsequent analysis of the law by the EAT in *Woodward v Santander plc* [2010] IRLR 834 led it to the conclusion that Mezzotero does not lay down any new exception to the 'without prejudice' rule, but is better understood as an application of the 'unambiguous impropriety' exception, the impropriety being the act of discrimination committed in the course of the allegedly without prejudice meeting. In *Woodward* itself, the EAT upheld the exclusion by the tribunal of evidence that in the course of without prejudice negotiations the respondent's solicitors had said that the respondent would not provide a reference for the employee, a point she wished to use in evidence to support her claim of victimisation by the giving of poor references.

This area has been examined by the EAT in *Portnykh v Nomura International Plc* [2014] IRLR 251. There, Nomura announced an intention to dismiss Dr Portnykh for misconduct. Discussions then ensued as to whether the termination could be framed as redundancy; ultimately in open correspondence Nomura confirmed that it would structure the exit as a redundancy. Thereafter, there were exchanges of correspondence marked "without prejudice" about the terms of a potential settlement agreement. A draft settlement agreement was prepared by Nomura and sent to Dr Portnykh again marked "without prejudice"; it proposed to settle various listed heads of claim that Dr Portnykh might have. The negotiations broke down and Dr Portnykh brought a claim in the Tribunal for unfair dismissal contending that the real reason for his dismissal was that he had made protected disclosures. He relied on the inconsistent reasons for dismissal set out by Nomura. At a preliminary hearing, Nomura argued that it should be allowed to refer at trial to the "without prejudice" correspondence because it contended (and this remained in dispute) this would show that Dr Portnykh had asked for his dismissal to be characterised as a redundancy. The Tribunal allowed Nomura to do so, but the EAT reversed this ruling. The EAT held firm to the *Framlington* approach as to what amounts to a 'dispute' in law; it found that there was clearly a dispute on the facts: "If the employer announces an intention to dismiss the employee for misconduct and there are then discussions around the question of the alternative of the dismissal being for redundancy, no matter how amicable all that might be, it seems to me beyond argument that it either demonstrates a present dispute or contains the potential for a future dispute". The whole purpose of the proffered settlement agreement was to resolve Dr Portnykh's potential employment claims and preventing him having access to an Employment Tribunal to litigate about his dismissal. Whilst the draft agreement covered a wide breadth, it was about the termination of Dr Portnykh's employment. There was also no need for the allegation that made up the subsequent claim to have been made, nor was a degree of objection to the course proposed, or a degree of hostility to the other party an essential ingredient of a dispute. The EAT stated that where parties reach the stage of proffering and considering a settlement agreement it would very often be the case that there will be a dispute. The EAT also raised the issue of whether the without prejudice rule might also apply absent a dispute, but where there had been "negotiations between the parties" of the necessary type. This possibility arose from language used in earlier cases: see *Unilever plc v The Procter and Gamble Co* [2000] 1 WLR 2436 and In re *Daintry* [1893] 2 QB 116. Ultimately it was not necessary to consider the "outer limits" of the without prejudice rule in *Portnykh* and the matter is left for another case.

The privilege attached to without prejudice discussions may be waived by the conduct of a party (in a case where the other party also seeks to rely on the discussions): see *Brunel University v Vaseghi* [2007] EWCA Civ 482, [2007] IRLR 592 (privilege waived by making reference to discussions during grievance hearing before independent panel, and by referring to them in response form); *National Centre for Young People with Epilepsy v Boateng* (UKEAT/0440/10) (dispute about validity of agreement reached at mediation based on allegations against party's own solicitor constituted waiver of privilege by that party); and *Faithorn Farrell Timms LLP v Bailey* [2016] ICR 1054 (reference to privileged material in complaint and response without either party objecting). In *Gallop v Newport City Council* [2013] IRLR 23, the EAT considered a case in which, during evidence on remedy, one of the wing-members of the tribunal asked about negotiations over a proposed compromise agreement. The EAT held that the tribunal had erred: it was wrong in principle to have admitted evidence as to compromise negotiations absent a clear waiver by the parties. The Judge should have immediately intervened to cut off the wholly impermissible line of enquiry.

A separate but related statutory provision excludes disclosure of any communication made (orally or in writing) to an ACAS conciliation officer to a tribunal without the consent of the party who made the communication: *ETA 1996, s 18(7)*. In addition, parties engaging in mediation will almost always agree that if the mediation is unsuccessful, any documents produced for the purpose of the mediation, as well as anything said during it, is confidential; this confidentiality will not be overridden by an order for disclosure in the absence of the most compelling reasons. The obligation of confidentiality is applied as a matter of course to any judicial mediation conducted in the employment tribunal.

It is possible to restrict the 'without prejudice' nature of communications by adding the qualification 'save as to costs', to the effect that such communications may be relied on in any issue as to costs, after the tribunal has determined the claim itself. See further **19.22**.

In addition to the above, and relevant to unfair dismissal complaints only, the *Enterprise and Regulatory Reform Act 2013, s 14* inserted *section 111A* into the *ERA* which makes evidence of "pre termination negotiations" inadmissible in proceedings on a complaint under *s 111* (unfair dismissal). As HHJ Eady QC said in *Faithorn Farrell Timms LLP v Bailey* [2016] ICR 1054, *s 111A* must be viewed independently of common law without prejudice principles and a construction adopted that is informed by the language Parliament chose to use, not the language of the case law underpinning without prejudice privilege. "Pre-termination negotiations" are defined to mean "any offer made or discussions held, before the termination of the employment in question, with a view to it being terminated on terms agreed between the employer and employee". This definition includes negotiations and offers whether made by the employer or employee. It is designed to catch a wider range of discussions than those caught by the common law without prejudice rule set out above. The Explanatory Notes to the *Act* state (para 82): "The purpose of *section 14* is to provide a means for employers and employees to discuss settlement before any dispute has actually arisen, with certainty that the offer and any discussions about it cannot be used as evidence against them in a subsequent unfair dismissal claim." That said, if the common law rules includes "negotiations" absent a dispute (see *Portnykh* above) there might not be much clear blue water between the scope of the section and the common law rule in many cases. In *Faithorn Farrell Timms LLP*, the EAT held that pre termination negotiations extended both to the fact of the discussions (rather than just their content) and also to internal conversations within e.g. a corporate employer (rather than just discussions between the main protagonists).

There are three exceptions to the statutory provision: (i) the rule does not apply where, on the complainant's case, the circumstances are such that a provision of an Act of Parliament requires the complainant to be regarded as unfairly dismissed – in other words, where the claimant alleges automatically unfair dismissal. (ii) Where the tribunal considers anything said or done was "improper, or was connected with improper behaviour", then the rule only applies to the extent that the tribunal considers just. The ACAS Code of Practice No 4 on Settlement Agreements (July 2013) suggests (para 21) that the common law concept of unambiguous impropriety (relevant to the common law rules) is "narrower". This was addressed in *Faithorn Farrell Timms LLP*. HHJ Eady QC held that "improper behaviour" allowed a potentially broader approach than "unambigious impropriety": the ET had first to address the claimant's contention that the respondent had failed to engage in any genuine attempt to achieve a termination settlement (whether *s 111A* applied at all) and then the contention that its behaviour was improper. In that case, the latter issue was remitted. What is clear in relation to this exemption is that the Tribunal retains a great deal of discretion: it is for the Tribunal to consider whether what was said or done was improper and the exclusion is only to the extent that the Tribunal considers just. Finally, (iii) the rule does not affect the admissibility of evidence on the question of costs or expenses of evidence of an offer made on the basis that the right to refer to it on the question of costs or expenses is reserved. In other word, Calderbank offers can still be made and referred to on the question of costs.

One issue not covered by *s 14* is the issue of waiver. In *Faithorn Farrell Timms LLP*, the EAT held that where a conversation is protected pursuant to *s 111A*, that protection cannot be waived. This is because the statute prohibits admissibility in the circumstances specified. The EAT in *Faithhorn Farrell Timms LLP* also expressed the view that the correct reading of the statute meant that inadmissibility for the purposes of an unfair dismissal complaint did not mean that such evidence would be inadmissible for the purposes of any other proceedings before the ET (e.g. a claim of discrimination): "in such circumstances, the ET would allow the evidence to be admitted for one claim (e.g. discrimination) but still treat it as inadmissible for the other (the unfair dismissal claim) – see para 38.

It remains to be seen whether *ERA 1996, s 111A* will be an attractive source of protection for those wishing to have negotiations about termination. Given the limited scope of the provisions as compared with the common law rules, and the greater width and discretionary nature of some of the exceptions to the statutory scheme, it is suggested that the common law without prejudice rule will continue to play a dominant role, particularly where a dispute (in the *Framlington* sense) has become evident.

19.63 *Information*

Rule 31 also entitled the Tribunal to order a person in Great Britain to disclose "information" to a party. There has long been this power in a Tribunal and it is used to gain additional information about a claim or response which may be required because it fails to give sufficient details to enable the other party to know the case he or she has to meet; or the grounds stated may be ambiguous as to the facts or the basis in law of the claim. Orders to give additional information (previously referred to as 'further particulars') are designed primarily to spell out or clarify the party's case. The rules do not state particular criteria to operate when the Tribunal is considering making such an order, however, it is unlikely that there will be a particular change from the previous practice which involved considering how the provision of the information sought will assist the tribunal in dealing with the proceedings efficiently and fairly. This is wide enough to embrace the need for the applicant for the order to know the case he or she has to meet, since if that is not achieved it is difficult for the tribunal to deal with the proceedings fairly. A tribunal will not normally order the provision of additional information unless a written request has been made and either refused or ignored; the main exception is where an Employment Judge on reviewing the file considers that particulars or clarification are needed for the tribunal's own benefit as well as the parties'.

It should be noted that the Tribunal has the power at the initial consideration stage to order that additional information be provided concerning a claim or defence (see above). Under the old rules, similar orders against claimants before the response has been served were made, where the Judge reviewing the claim form considers that there is insufficient information to identify clearly the claims made or the issues raised by the claimant. These are likely to become more frequent following the initial consideration that must be given to all claims.

The EAT in *Byrne v Financial Times Ltd* [1991] IRLR 417 set out general principles governing the ordering of further particulars, which it is thought remain applicable to orders to provide additional information. These include the principle that the parties should not be taken by surprise at the last minute; that particulars should only be ordered when necessary to do justice in the case or to prevent adjournment; that the order should not be oppressive; that particulars are for the purposes of identifying the issues not for the production of evidence; and that complicated pleadings battles should not be encouraged.

Particulars of generalised allegations of discrimination may be ordered more readily than in other categories of case because of the potential seriousness of such allegations and the need for the tribunal to be able to identify clearly the allegations it is required to determine. In *Secretary of State for Work and Pensions (Jobcentre Plus) v Constable* [2010] All ER (D) 190 (Nov), where the claim was of automatically unfair dismissal for having made a protected disclosure under *ERA 1996, s 103A*, the EAT expressed the view that the respondent was entitled to know what the claimant claimed the disclosure was, when, how and to whom it had been made, and how it was alleged to have led to the dismissal, and ordered particulars to that effect to be provided. However the EAT has also held in an equal pay case that it was not appropriate for a tribunal to order the respondent to provide particulars of its material factor defence before the claimants had identified whom they intended to rely on as comparators: *Amey Services Ltd v Cardigan* [2008] IRLR 279.

Additional information may be ordered not only in relation to the claim or response as served, but in relation to any other matter relevant to the proceedings – for instance the claimant's losses or attempts to find alternative work, or, in equal pay or discrimination cases, the kind of information that was commonly sought by way of statutory questionnaires (see below). Even prior to the *2013 Rules*, the practice of ordering claimants to provide a Schedule of Loss had become relatively standard practice in all tribunal regions. This is now reinforced by the Presidential Guidance on General Case Management which, in the section on Remedies, provides that the Tribunal will usually order a statement of remedy; that Guidance sets out how such documents might be put together (see para 7ff).

19.64 *Questionnaires*

Prior to 6 April 2014, an alternative procedure for obtaining information from the respondent, or from a prospective respondent before proceedings are started, was available in discrimination cases. The claimant or prospective claimant could serve a statutory questionnaire on the respondent in accordance with regulations made under the *Equality Act 2010, s 138*. A questionnaire ought normally to have been served within 21 days following presentation of the Claim Form, or before proceedings had been started but within three months following the alleged discrimination: see the *Equality Act (Obtaining Information) Order 2010 (SI 2010/2194)*; the *Order* also enabled the tribunal to give permission for a further questionnaire to be served in the course of the proceedings, or extend time for the service of an initial questionnaire. The *2010 Order* also prescribed a form of questionnaire for use in equal pay cases. There was no obligation on respondents to reply to such questionnaires, and the tribunal had no power to order answers. Its only direct power was to grant an extension of the time limit laid down in each case for serving a questionnaire or to grant leave to serve a further questionnaire. The sanction for not answering within a reasonable time (set as eight weeks) or answering inadequately or evasively, was that in certain circumstances the tribunal hearing the case could draw adverse inferences against the respondent: *Equality Act 2010, s 138(4)*. A tribunal was not however obliged to infer discrimination from a deficient response to a questionnaire, and the EAT repeatedly warned tribunals that inferences should only be drawn from failure to answer questionnaires, or the nature of the replies, if this is justified in the particular circumstances, and not simply because of the respondent's default: see for further guidance on this *D'Silva v NATFHE* [2008] IRLR 412 and *Deer v Walford* (UKEAT/0283/10).

Following a consultation, the Government decided to repeal this route to further information – it considered that many employee hours per year were being spent in answering questionnaires, and that in many cases they amounted to a "fishing expedition". *Section 138* was repealed by *Enterprise and Regulatory Reform Act 2013, s 66(1)* with effect from 6 April 2014, except in relation to proceedings that relate to a contravention occurring before that date.

Notwithstanding the repeal of the statutory questionnaire procedure, it is still be open to claimants in discrimination cases to seek information from a respondent both prior to and after commencing proceedings. In *Dattani v Chief Constable of West Mercia Police* [2005] IRLR 327 the EAT held that the same power to draw adverse inferences from equivocal or evasive responses, or failure to respond, applied in discrimination cases in relation to questions outside the statutory questionnaire procedure. It could be argued that this still applies, although that case pre-dated the *Equality Act 2010* which enacted that principle in *s 138(4)*, and yet it is part of the section which has now been repealed as detailed above. The conclusions in this case might therefore (at least in theory) be vulnerable on reconsideration. A claimant can certainly still seek an order from the tribunal for the provision of further information where this is necessary (see above). ACAS has produced a Guide entitled "Asking and responding to questions of discrimination in the workplace" with suggestions as to how questions should be formulated and with an example form to use.

Similar procedures remain provided for part-time workers by the *Part-time Workers (Prevention of Less Favourable Treatment) Regulations 2000, reg 6*, and for fixed-term employees under the *Fixed-term Employees (Prevention of Less Favourable Treatment) Regulations 2002, reg 5*, to enable workers or employees respectively to ask their employers to explain the reasons for apparently less favourable treatment than that given to comparable full-time or, as the case may be, permanent workers. The consequences of failing to reply or deficient replies are as used to be the case under the *Equality Act 2010. Regulation 16* of the *Agency Workers Regulations 2010* makes similar provision for questions to be raised by agency workers of the agency or hirer, as appropriate, with similar consequences for failure to respond.

19.65   Requirement to Attend to Give Evidence

By *Rule 32*, the Tribunal may order any person in Great Britain to attend a hearing to give evidence, produce documents, or to produce information. Such orders are commonly referred to as a "witness order". By way of exception from the obligations imposed by *Rule 92*, an application for an order under *Rule 32* does not need to be notified to the other parties when it is made. This is because it may be inappropriate for the other party or parties to be aware that a witness order has been sought or granted in certain cases.

Rule 32 can only be used to require a person in Great Britain to produce documents, information or to give evidence. Where the subject is in a European Union country, consideration should be given to *Rule 33* (see below).

An order for the attendance of a witness can be sought if the witness is believed to have relevant knowledge or information to give and the party seeking the order believes he or she may not attend voluntarily. In practice a witness order can be needed where an employer would otherwise not be cooperative in releasing the witness. Orders are almost invariably required to secure the attendance of police officers. An ordered witness may apply before the hearing to set aside the order and the Tribunal has power to reconsider the Order granted without the witness having reasonable opportunity to make representations before it was made: see *Rule 29*. There is no minimum period of notice of the order that has to be given to the witness. It is normally for the party obtaining the order to ensure it is served on the intended witness, although some tribunal offices undertake the service of witness orders.

The granting of witness orders is a matter of discretion; the tribunal must consider whether the witness is likely to be able to give relevant evidence and whether the giving of that evidence is necessary, and may refuse unjustified requests as a part of the general power to control and manage the proceedings and in the interests of proportionality to the issues in dispute. In particular, the tribunal may properly limit the number of witnesses who are to be heard on a particular issue of fact, especially where the issue is not central to case: *Noorani v Merseyside TEC Ltd* [1999] IRLR 184. In *McBride v Standards Board for England* (UKEAT/0092/09), the EAT held that it is open to the tribunal as part of its general case management powers to impose restrictions in advance on the number or identity of witnesses to be called at the Hearing, not just as part of the process of managing the proceedings in the course of the Hearing itself.

Evidence is admissible only if relevant to an issue in the proceedings, and is generally relevant only if it relates to issues which are in dispute between the parties, and where issues of fact are agreed (for instance a note of a meeting is agreed by both parties) it is not necessary to call a witness to 'prove' that which is not in dispute. This may apply equally to issues of character: claimants often assume, for instance, that evidence of their good character is an important part of their case, but it would only be relevant in practice if good character is an issue in the case, and then only if it is disputed by the employer.

The use of genuinely reluctant witnesses is a matter requiring considerable care. The party calling the witness cannot normally prompt him or her, dispute what he or she says, or cross-examine him or her, and so may be faced with an unsympathetic witness giving unhelpful or damaging evidence that cannot effectively be challenged. There is no guarantee that the tribunal will intervene to probe the witness to rectify this, and the concept of a witness being formally treated as a 'hostile witness' is all but unknown in employment tribunal litigation. It may also be difficult to establish in advance what evidence a reluctant witness is in a position to give. For these reasons an application by a claimant for witness orders in respect of managers of the employer is nearly always inadvisable, and likely to be refused.

One way around this difficulty is for the tribunal to be asked to call the witness concerned itself; the witness can then be offered for cross-examination by both parties. The EAT has confirmed that tribunals had this power under the old rules (but there is no reason to think that the position is different under the *2013 Rules*: *Clapson v British Airways plc* [2001] IRLR 184, a case where the claimant himself was called by the tribunal after his representative indicated that he would not be called. However, the power is used very sparingly, and in general it remains the responsibility of the parties to put evidence before the tribunal and call any witnesses they rely on. It would be a serious matter, quite possibly amounting to contempt of court, for an employer to seek to prevent one of his or her employees from being called to give evidence or to influence his or her evidence (*Peach Grey & Co v Sommers* [1995] 2 All ER 513, [1995] ICR 549, [1995] IRLR 363), even if no witness order has been made. Any such attempt could also be regarded as scandalous or unreasonable conduct, entitling the tribunal to strike out the response in a sufficiently clear case. The employer may, however, seek to obtain a statement from such a witness as part of the preparation for the case; as a general principle, which applies to both parties, there is no 'property' in a witness.

The use of witness statements is discussed at **19.109** below.

Evidence from other EU Member States

19.66 *Introduction*

Rule 33 provides that the Tribunal may use the procedures for obtaining evidence prescribed in *Council Regulation (EC) No 1206/2001* of 28 May 2001 on cooperation between the courts of the Member States in the taking of evidence in civil or commercial matters (referred to in this section as the *Regulation*). Whilst the *Regulation* has always been directly effective before a tribunal, the *2013 Rules* introduce for the first time express reference to those procedures.

The Regulation prescribes procedures for judicial cooperation between the courts of the Member States for the taking of evidence. The *Regulation* was adopted in order to make it easier to take evidence in other Member States, for it was recognised that it will often be essential for a decision in a civil or commercial matter pending before a court in a Member State to take evidence in another Member State (see *recital 7*). The *Regulation* is applicable throughout the European Union with the exception of Denmark (*Art 1(3)*). The provisions of the Regulation prevail over other provisions contained in bilateral or multilateral agreements or arrangements concluded by the Member States and in particular the *Hague Convention of 1 March 1954 on Civil Procedure* and the *Hague Convention of 18 March 1970 on the Taking of Evidence Abroad in Civil or Commercial Matters*, in relations between the Member States party thereto (*Art 21*).

There are prescribed forms attached to the Regulation in an Annex which must be used when making, executing and refusing requests. These are referred to as applicable below. In addition, pursuant to *Art 19(1)*, the Commission has drawn up, and keeps updated, a Country Manual containing information provided by the Member States in accordance with *Art 22* relating to various of the articles of the *Regulation*. This is referred to where relevant   below   and   is   available   at   available   at http://ec.europa.eu/justice_home/judicialatlascivil/html/te_documents_en.htm. Further, in 2006, in order to give guidance on the operation of the *Regulation*, the European Commission published a Practice Guide for the Application of the Regulation on the Taking of Evidence (available at ec.europa.eu/civiljustice/publications/docs/guide_taking _evidence_en.pdf).

The procedures prescribed by the *Regulation* apply only in "civil or commercial matters". As the Practice Guide makes clear, that notion is an autonomous concept of Community Law designed to apply to all civil and commercial proceedings whatever the nature of the court or tribunal in which they are taking place. Litigation based on employment law is given as a specific example of disputes which are included within the concept (Practice Guide para 7). It is also a pre-requisite of applicability of the *Regulation* that the evidence obtained by the request is intended for use in judicial proceedings, commenced or contemplated (*Art 1(2)*).

It should also be noted at the outset that although the Regulation uses the concept of a "court" of a Member State, it is clear from the Practice Guide (para 9) that this should be given a broad interpretation, including all authorities in the Member States with jurisdiction in the matters falling within the scope of the *Regulation*. This plainly includes Employment Tribunals, as is recognised by *Rule 33*.

19.67 *The Two Types of Request*

The basic scheme of the *Regulation* is to permit two types of request to be made by a court or tribunal of a Member State (known in the *Regulation* as the "requesting court"):

(1)   A request that the competent court of another Member State (known in the Regulation as the "requested court") takes evidence on its behalf in that other Member State (*Art 1(1)(a)*); or

(2)   A request that the requesting court itself takes evidence within another Member State (*Art 1(1)(b)*).

The concept of "evidence" under the *Regulation* and relevant to both types of request, is not defined. The Practice Guide (para 8) refers to it including, by way of examples, "hearings of witnesses of fact, of the parties, of experts, the production of documents, verifications, establishment of facts, expertise on family or child welfare". This paragraph has been cited with approval by the ECJ in *Lippens v Kortekaas* [2013] CEC 618 (footnote 16) and *Prorail BV v Epedys NV* [2013] ILPr 18 (footnote 14). In The *MMR/MR Vaccination Litigation* [2004] EWHC 1098, Keith J also accepted (para 9) that a request could be limited to the inspection of documents and other objects, and referred to *Art 4(1)(f)* making express reference to such requests.

In respect of both types of request, *Art 1(1)* provides that the Regulation shall apply in civil or commercial matters "where the court of a Member State, in accordance with the provisions of the law of that State" makes the relevant request. In The *MMR/MR Vaccination Litigation* [2004] EWHC 1098, Keith J recorded that it was not disputed before him that this meant "that the courts of the foreign state can only be requested to make those orders which the courts of the requesting states can make against persons or bodies within its jurisdiction" (para 9). *Art 1(1)* mandates that it is the request which must be made "in accordance with the provisions of the law" of the Member State in which the requesting court is situated, but otherwise does not require that the content of the request is limited to orders which the requesting court could itself make against persons or bodies within its jurisdiction.

19.68 *Requirements of Requests of Either Type*

There are some common requirements for either type of request. First, requests must be made on Form A (which appears in an annex to the Regulation) and must contain the details set out in *Art 4*. These details are (a) the names of the requesting, and where appropriate, the requested court; (b) the names and addresses of the parties to the proceedings and their representatives, if any; (c) the nature and subject matter of the case and a brief statement of the facts; (d) a description of the taking of evidence to be performed; (e) where the request is for the examination of a person, the name(s) and address(es) of the person(s) to be examined, the questions to be put to the person(s) to be examined or a statement of the facts about which he is (they are) to be examined, where appropriate, a reference to a right to refuse to testify under the law of the Member State of the requesting court, any requirement that the examination is to be carried out under oath or affirmation in lieu thereof and any special form to be used, where appropriate, any other information that the requesting court deems necessary; (f) where the request is for any other form of taking of evidence, the documents or other objects to be inspected; (g) any request for the use of a special procedure or use of communications technology or for the presence and participation of the parties or representatives of the requesting court. Where the requesting court considers it necessary to enclose documents for the execution of the request, these should also be included with Form A.

Provided the request is on Form A and contains the necessary details, the request itself and all documents accompanying it are exempted from authentication or any equivalent formality by *Art 4(2)*.

Pursuant to *Art 5*, requests must be made in the official language of the requested Member State; or, if there are several official languages, in the official language (or one of the official languages) of the place where the requested taking of evidence is to be performed; or, alternatively, in another language which the requested Member State has indicated it can accept. The languages which each Member State has indicated it will accept are set out in the Country Manual maintained by the European Commission. Documents accompanying the request must also be translated into the language in which the request is written (*Art 4(3)*).

Requests (and other communications under the *Regulation*) must be transmitted by the swiftest possible means which the requested Member State has indicated it can accept (again, see the Country Manual): *Art 6*.

19.69 *(1) Requests under Art 1(1)(a)*

Requests under *Art 1(1)(a)* of the *Regulation* are made by the requesting court (in the present context, the Employment Tribunal) sending directly to the requested court the request on Form A, along with any other necessary documents and translations (see *Art 2(1)*). There is no involvement of third parties – the Tribunal communicates directly with the requested court. The appropriate requested court can be ascertained by consulting the appropriate Country Manual (see above) maintained by the European Commission and derived from the lists of competent courts provided by each Member State pursuant to *Art 2(2)* of the *Regulation*.

In addition to setting out in Form A the other details of the request required by *Art 4*, the requesting court may:

(a)   Call for the request to be executed in accordance with a special procedure provided for by the law of the requesting Member State (*Art 10(3)*).

(b)   Ask the requested court to use communications technology at the taking of evidence, in particular by using videoconference and teleconference (*Art 10(4)*).

In both cases, the requested court is obliged by the *Regulation* to comply with such a requirement unless the procedure is incompatible with the law of the Member State of the requested court, or by reason of "major practical difficulties" (see *Art 10(3)* and *(4)*). Whenever such a requirement is not complied with, the requested court must complete Form E attached to the Regulation.

The execution of a request "shall not give rise to a claim for any reimbursement of taxes or costs" (*Art 18(1)*). However, if the requested court so requires, the requesting court must ensure the reimbursement without delay of (i) fees paid to experts and interpreters; and (ii) costs occasioned by requesting the use of a special procedure or by using communications technology (Art 18(2)). Pursuant to *Art 18(2)*, the duty of the parties to bear these fees or costs is governed by the law of the Member State of the requesting court. Thus in a request emanating from an Employment Tribunal, any such fees or costs should be met by the party applying for a request to be made under *Rule 33*, subject to the application of the costs rules (discussed below). Where the opinion of an expert is required, the requested court is permitted to ask the requesting court for an adequate deposit or advance towards the expert's costs. In all other cases, however, a deposit or advance "shall not be a condition for the execution of a request" (*Art 18(3)*).

Where the law of the Member State of the requesting court provides for it, the parties and their representatives have the right to be present at the performance of the taking of evidence of the requested court (*Art 11(1)*). Thus save in exceptional cases where the presence of a party/representative is curtailed, a request from an Employment Tribunal will entitle the parties and their representatives to be present when the requested court takes evidence. The requesting court must inform the requested court that the parties/their representatives will be present and (where appropriate) that their participation is requested, either in Form A or at another appropriate time (*Art 11(2)*). It is for the requested court to determine, in accordance with *Art 10*, the conditions under which the parties/their representatives may participate (*Art 11(3)*). The requested court notifies the parties/their representatives of the time and place where the proceedings will take place and any conditions of participation using Form F (*Art 11(4)*). Even if not asked specifically by the requesting court, the requested court may ask the parties/their representatives to be present and participate in the taking of evidence where that possibility is provided for by the law of the requested Member State (*Art 11(5)*).

Similar provisions apply in respect of the presence and participation of representatives of the requesting court at the taking of evidence. Representatives are defined to include judicial personnel designated by the requesting court in accordance with the law of its Member State (*Art 12(2)*). Thus, if provided for by the law of the Member State of the requesting court, representatives of the requesting court have the right to be present (*Art 12(1)*). Thus the Employment Judge and Members of an Employment Tribunal have the right to be present at the taking of evidence performed by the requested court. The requesting court must inform the requested court that its representatives will be present and that their participation is requested, either in Form A or at another appropriate time (*Art 12(3)*). As with the parties/their representatives, it is for the requested court to determine, in accordance with Art 10, the conditions under which the representatives of the requesting court may participate (*Art 12(4)*). The requested court must notify the requesting court of the time when, and place where, the proceedings will take place and any conditions of participation using Form F (*Art 12(5)*).

Within 7 days of receipt of the request, the requested court must acknowledge receipt of the request on Form B (*Art 7(1)*). If the request is not in the correct language, or if the request or accompanying documents or translations are not legible, this must be noted on Form B (*Art 7(1)*). If the request is otherwise properly made, but has been sent to the wrong court in the foreign jurisdiction, viz the receiving court does not have jurisdiction to execute the request, the receiving court must forward the request to the competent court of its Member State and must inform the requesting court by completing the relevant section of Form A (*Art 7(2)*).

If a request cannot be executed because it does not contain all of the necessary information required by *Art 4*, the requested court must inform the requesting court "without delay and, at the latest, within 30 days of receipt of the request" using Form C (*Art 8(1)*). The requested court must request the missing information, which should be indicated as precisely as possible. If the request cannot be executed because a deposit or advance towards expert fees is necessary under *Art 18(3)* – see above – then the requested court shall inform the requesting court without delay and at the latest within 30 days of receipt of the request using Form C (*Art 8(2)*). It must also specify how the deposit or advance should be made. Once paid, the requested court must acknowledge receipt of the deposit or advance within 10 days of receipt, using Form D (*Art 8(2)*).

Pursuant to *Art 10(1)*, the requested Court "shall" execute the request "without delay and, at the latest, within 90 days of the receipt of the request". It must do so in accordance with the laws of the requested Member State (*Art 10(2)*). Any delay must be notified to the requesting court on Form G (*Art 15*). This must be accompanied by the grounds for the delay as well as an estimated time that the requested court expects it will need to execute the request. Where the requested court has informed the requesting court (under *Art 7(2)*) that the request is in the incorrect language or that the request/documents are not legible, or (under *Art 8(1)*) that the request does not contain all the necessary information under *Art 4*, the time limit pursuant to *Art 10* begins to run when the requested court receives the request duly completed (*Art 9(1)*). Similarly, where a deposit falls to be paid pursuant to *Arts 18(3)* and *8(2)*, the time runs from when the deposit or advance is made (*Art 9(2)*).

Where necessary, the requested court must apply the appropriate coercive measures in the instances and to the extent as are provided for by the law of the Member State of the requested court for the execution of a request made for the same purpose by its national authorities or one of the parties concerned (*Art 13*).

There are extremely limited circumstances in which the requested court can refuse to execute a request. As *recital 11* of the *Regulation* explains: "To secure the effectiveness of this *Regulation*, the possibility of refusing to execute the request for the performance of taking of evidence should be confined to strictly limited exceptional situations". *Art 14* specifies those limited situations. *Art 14(1)* is applicable to requests for the hearing of a person. It provides that such requests shall not be executed when the person concerned claims the right to refuse to give evidence or to be prohibited from giving evidence either (a) under the law of the Member State of the requested court; or (b) under the law of the

Member State of the requesting court, where that right has been specified in the request, or, otherwise confirmed by the requesting court (at the instance of the requested court). *Art 14(2)* is applicable to all requests and is additional to *Art 14(1)*. It provides that a request "may be refused only if" (a) the request does not fall within the scope of the *Regulation* as specified in *Art 1*; (b) the execution of the request under the law of the Member State of the requested court does not fall within the functions of the judiciary; (c) the requesting court does not comply with the request of the requested court to complete the request pursuant to *Article 8* within 30 days after the requested court asked it to do so; or (d) a deposit or advance asked for in accordance with *Article 18(3)* is not made within 60 days after the requested court asked for such a deposit or advance. The limited scope of the right to refuse is underlined by *Art 14(3)* which provides: "Execution may not be refused by the requested court solely on the ground that under the law of its Member State a court of that Member State has exclusive jurisdiction over the subject matter of the action or that the law of that Member State would not admit the right of action on it." If any of the grounds in *Art 14(2)* are relied upon by a requested court to refuse to execute a request, the requested court must notify the requesting court within 60 days of receipt of the request using Form H (see *Art 14(4)*).

In *Werynski v Mediatel 4B Spolka zoo* (C-283/09) [2012] QB 66, the ECJ held that the grounds on which a request could be refused were exhaustively listed in Art 14 (see §45). Similarly, the Practice Guide emphasises that "the refusal of a request should be absolutely exceptional" (§43).

Pursuant to *Art 16*, the requested court is obliged to send the requesting court without delay the documents establishing the execution of the request and, where appropriate, return the documents received from the requesting court. This should be accompanied by completed Form H.

19.70 *(2) Requests under Art 1(1)(b)*

Requests pursuant to *Art 1(1)(b)* are of a different nature. They involve the requesting court (here the Employment Tribunal) itself taking evidence directly in another Member State. Another qualitative difference is that whereas in respect of requests under *Art 1(1)(a)*, the requested court must, where necessary, apply appropriate coercive measures, the direct taking of evidence may only take place if it can be performed on a voluntary basis, without the need for coercive measures (see *Art 17(2)*).

Requests to take evidence pursuant to *Art 1(1)(b)* must be made by the requesting court sending Form I to the central body or competent authority specified by the target Member State (*Art 17(1)*). Each Member State is required by *Art 3(3)* to designate a central body or one or several competent authority(ies) to be responsible for making such determinations. These are maintained by the Commission within the relevant Country Manual.

The central body or competent authority of the requested Member State must inform the requesting court if the request is accepted within 30 days of receiving the request (*Art 17(4)*). If necessary it must specify under what conditions, according to the law of its Member State, such performance is to be carried out, using Form J. *Art 17(4)* provides, in particular, for the central body or competent authority to assign a court of its Member State to take part in the performance of the taking of evidence to ensure the proper application of *Art 17* and any conditions that have been set out. The central body or competent authority must encourage the use of communications technology.

By *Art 17(5)*, requests under *Art 1(1)(b)* may be refused "only if": (a) the request does not fall within the scope of the *Regulation* as set out in *Art 1*; (b) the request does not contain all of the necessary information pursuant to *Art 4*; or (c) the direct taking of evidence requested is contrary to "fundamental principles of law" in the requested Member State.

If the request is accepted, the taking of evidence must be performed by a member of the judicial personnel (or by any other person such as an expert) who is designated by the law of the Member State of the requesting court (*Art 17(3)*). Subject to any conditions set by the requested Member State's central body or competent authority, the request is executed by the requesting court in accordance with the law of its Member State. Accordingly, subject to any conditions, the Employment Tribunal would apply the *2013 Rules* when taking evidence in another Member State.

19.71 Expert Evidence

The use of expert witnesses in tribunal proceedings is still relatively rare, but has become somewhat more common, especially in cases where a claim that the applicant is disabled is disputed, or there is a claim for compensation for personal injury in a discrimination claim. In *Hampshire County Council v Wyatt* [2016] UKEAT/0013/16, the EAT reiterated that there was no requirement for expert evidence in order for a claim to claim personal injury damages arising from discrimination. That said, expert evidence in such cases can often identify "whether (i) all the injury or harm suffered by a claimant can be attributed to the unlawful conduct and (ii) that injury or harm is divisible. It may assist in determining the extent to which any treatment a claimant has undergone has been successful. It may also assist in dealing with questions of prognosis." (para 28). The EAT went on that where there are issues as to cause or divisibility of psychiatric or psychological harm it is advisable for medical evidence to be obtained and that a failure to produce such medical evidence risked a lower, or no, award being made. In unfair dismissal cases there may be technical issues affecting the computation of compensation, the calculation of pension loss in particular, which may on occasion require an expert witness. (In such cases it is advisable to apply to the tribunal for an order for issues of remedy to be heard separately, to avoid unnecessary costs being incurred on experts' fees.) Separate procedures apply in equal value cases, where the tribunal may be required to appoint an independent expert; details of the applicable rules are in *Sch 3* to the *2013 Regulations*.

The *2013 Rules*, like their predecessor rules, do not provide for how expert evidence should be dealt with in the Tribunal. The EAT has, however, given detailed guidance on the procedures to be adopted: de *Keyser Ltd v Wilson* [2001] IRLR 324. The main points are that there is no presumption that expert evidence will be allowed merely because one party wishes to call an expert; where appropriate the parties should use a joint expert, or at least if one party is calling an expert the other party should have an opportunity to agree to the terms of the instructions to the expert; and where there are experts on both sides, the tribunal should give directions setting out a timetable for the experts to meet to attempt to agree, or at least define, the issues in dispute. Guidance as to when a party may call its own expert to contradict the evidence of the joint expert was given by the EAT in *Hospice of St Mary of Furness v Howard* [2007] IRLR 944 (a case concerning medical evidence of the claimant's disability): the question for the tribunal is the same as that under *CPR 1998 Part 35* as explained in *Daniels v Walker* [2000] 1 WLR 1382.

An expert witness, even if instructed by one party and not jointly, has an overriding duty to the tribunal, which takes precedence over his or her duty to the party instructing him or her. There are also strict rules which govern how parties should interact with a joint expert: see *Peet v Mid-Kent Healthcare Trust: Practice Note* [2002] 1 WLR 210.

In practice, the use of joint experts may be inhibited by difficulties in agreeing who pays for the expert. As the EAT stated in *de Keyser*, the tribunal has no power, beyond its general powers to award costs, to order the parties to share the cost, or for one party to bear the cost, of an expert witness. This remains the case under the *2013 Rules*. In *City Facilities Management (UK) Ltd v Ling* (UKEAT/0396), the EAT confirmed that it is "wrong in law and perverse" for a Tribunal to have ordered a respondent to pay the full amount of fees due under a joint expert report. However the tribunal itself has limited powers to pay for an expert where a joint appointment has been ordered; any party seeking the appointment of an expert should make enquiries as to the availability of funds for this purpose.

For guidance as to the scope of admissible expert evidence in civil cases see *Kennedy v Cordia (Services) LLP* [2016] 1 WLR 597. There, in the context of a claim against an employer for injuries sustained by a home carer who slipped on an icy path, an engineering consultant provided expert evidence which, as well as unobjectionable parts, included statements as to how he would have carried out the risk assessment and as to the nature of the employer's legal duty. The Supreme Court held that the evidence was nonetheless admissible but that an experienced judge could readily treat the statements as the opinions of a skilled witness on health and safety practice, and make up his own mind on the legal question.

19.72 Amendments

There is no specific provision in the *2013 Rules* circumscribing the power that the Tribunal has to allow an amendment to a claim or response. This power forms part of the general case management power contained within *Rule 29*. Further, the Presidential Guidance on Case Management contains a section detailing the usual approach taken by the Tribunal to such applications.

It is open to any party to apply for permission to amend his or her claim or, as the case may be, response. Amendments may be necessary to correct or clarify details of the particulars already given, or to add information about a claim; sometimes amendments seek to go further, and to add to the claim, or put forward a new or different reason for resisting the claim. In practice it is also not uncommon that 'additional information' provided by a party, voluntarily or in response to a request, raises new allegations or heads of claim: in such cases the principles applicable to amendments apply. The same principles apply, with any necessary modifications, to applications by respondents to amend their response, for instance by adding a new ground of resistance to the claim or taking a point as to the tribunal's jurisdiction.

The principles applicable to amendments are summarised below. The leading case on the principles applicable is *Selkent Bus Co Ltd v Moore* [1996] ICR 836. In this case Mummery J set out general principles both as to the procedure to be followed in relation to amendments and the criteria governing the tribunal's exercise of discretion whether to allow the amendment. Points of procedure are covered below. In relation to discretion, Mummery J emphasised that the tribunal: "should take into account all the circumstances and should balance the injustice and hardship of allowing the amendment against the injustice and hardship of refusing it."

The relevant factors include those listed in the Presidential Guidance (para 5 concerning amendments), which in turn emanate from *Selkent*: the nature of the amendment, the applicability of time limits (as to which see (f) and (g) below) and the timing and manner of application. Amendments should not generally be denied punitively where no real prejudice will be done by them being granted: *Sefton NBC v Hincks* [2011] ICR 1357. When considering an amendment, a tribunal should consider the all the circumstances and carry out the balancing exercise identified in *Selkent* or risk making an error of law (see e.g. *Thomas v Samurai Incentives & Promotions Ltd* (UKEAT/0006/13). The Presidential Guidance highlights that Tribunals must balance the injustice and hardship of allowing the amendment against the injustice and hardship of refusing it (see paras 4 and 10(2) of the section dealing with amendments).

Further points relevant to the procedure for applying, and the criteria for the exercise of the tribunal's discretion, are set out below.

(a)   A party may only amend his or her claim or response with the permission of the tribunal. If permission is given on a written application without the other party having an opportunity to oppose the application, or without the amendment having been directly considered by the tribunal (as where permission to amend is given in general terms, although this practice is now disproved (see below)) the permission is provisional and the other party may apply to have it set aside: *Reddington v Straker & Sons Ltd* [1994] ICR 172, EAT. This is expressly confirmed by *Rule 29*. Guidance as to when an application to amend should be dealt with at a hearing (usually a preliminary hearing), and not simply on paper, is given in *Selkent* (above) and also now in the Presidential Guidance on General Case Management. Normally an application to amend should not be refused without affording the party applying the opportunity for an oral hearing of the application, but this is subject to any exceptional factors that may make it unnecessary to permit a hearing: *Mouteng v Select Services Partner Ltd* [2008] All ER (D) 25 (Jun). The Presidential Guidance envisages many decisions being taken on the papers after canvassing the views of the parties (para 1 concerning amendments); it acknowledges that "in some cases a hearing may be necessary".

(b)   It is important to appreciate that the tribunal only has jurisdiction to adjudicate on the acts complained of, so that it is necessary to amend the Claim Form to refer specifically to any further complaints (and to obtain permission to do so) if they are to be relied on: see *Chapman v Simon* [1994] IRLR 124, *Smith v Zeneca (Agrochemicals) Ltd* [2000] ICR 800 and *Ahuja v Inghams (A Firm)* [2002] ICR 1485. The EAT emphasised the importance of the pleadings in relation to the issues that are properly before the Tribunal in *Chandhok v Tirkey* [2015] IRLR 195 where the Judge had considered part of the issue by reference to a witness statement rather than a pleading. Langstaff P observed (para 16) " . . . such an approach too easily forgets why there is a formal claim, which must be set out in an ET1. The claim, as set out in the ET1, is not something just to set the ball rolling, as an initial document necessary to comply with time limits but which is otherwise free to be augmented by whatever the parties choose to add or subtract merely upon their say so. Instead, it serves not only a useful but a necessary function. It sets out the essential case. It is that to which a respondent is required to respond. A respondent is not required to answer a witness statement, nor a document but the claims made – meaning, under the *Rules of Procedure 2013 (SI 2013/1237)*, the claim as set out in the ET1." After acknowledging that Tribunals were designed to be accessible and that undue formalism should be avoided, he went on to say (para 17): "the starting point is that the parties must set out the essence of their respective cases on paper in respectively the ET1 and the answer to it. If it were not so, then there would be no obvious principle by which reference to any further document (witness statement, or the like) could be restricted. Such restriction is needed to keep litigation within sensible bounds, and to ensure that a degree of informality does not become unbridled licence. The ET1 and ET3 have an important function in ensuring that a claim is brought, and responded to, within stringent time limits. If a 'claim' or a 'case' is to be understood as being far wider than that which is set out in the ET1 or ET3, it would be open to a litigant after the expiry of any relevant time limit to assert that the case now put had all along been made, because it was 'their case', and in order to argue that the time limit had no application to that case could point to other documents or statements, not contained within the claim form. Such an approach defeats the purpose of permitting or denying amendments; it allows issues to be based on shifting sands; it ultimately denies that which clear-headed justice most needs, which is focus. It is an enemy of identifying, and in the light of the identification resolving, the central issues in dispute." And at para 18 he went on: "In summary, a system of justice involves more than allowing parties at any time to raise the case which best seems to suit the moment from their perspective. It requires each party to know in essence what the other is saying, so they can properly meet it; so that they can tell if a tribunal may have lost jurisdiction on time grounds; so that the costs incurred can be kept to those which are proportionate; so that the time needed for a case, and the expenditure which goes hand in hand with it, can be provided for both by the parties and by the tribunal itself, and enable care to be taken that any one case does not deprive others of their fair share of the resources of the system. It should provide for focus on the central issues. That is why there is a system of claim and response, and why an employment tribunal should take very great care not to be diverted into thinking that the essential case is to be found elsewhere than in the pleadings." These views were considered of importance by a subsequent division in *Remploy Ltd v Abbott & others* UKEAT/0405/14 in which it was recalled that a list of issues is not a pleading (see further at **19.86** and **19.97** below).

(c)   The tribunal has no power to amend a claim or response on behalf of a party; it can only grant or refuse permission on application being duly made: see *Margarot Forrest Care Management v Kennedy* (UKEATS/0023/10). Any application to amend should set out the precise wording of the amendment proposed, so that the other party can know the claim he or she has to meet: *Ladbrokes Racing v Traynor* (UKEATS/0067/06). Guidance as to the procedure to be adopted when an application to amend is made during the hearing is given in the *Ladbrokes* case, where the issue was the introduction of unpleaded allegations of procedural unfairness of the claimant's dismissal. Amongst other points, the decision in *Ladbrokes* emphasises the importance of any amendment being precisely formulated before a decision can be taken on whether to permit it, and, where an application to amend made during a hearing is disputed, of the tribunal giving reasons for its decision on the point. The EAT has emphasised that it is fundamental that any application to amend a claim must be considered in the light of the actual proposed amendment. In most cases this will require the amendment sought to be reduced to writing. Blanket permission to amend without the amendment having been drafted has now been depreciated. As the EAT put it, one of the dangers of permitting an amendment without seeing its terms is that, having been given the green light to draft an amendment, a party may go beyond the terms which the Judge was led to understand might be included in the amendment s/he was permitting. The EAT thought the position might be different if the amendment sought was very simple or a limited amendment was asked for by a litigant in person. See *Chief Constable of Essex Police v Kovacevic* UKEAT/0126/13 and *Remploy Ltd v Abbott & others* UKEAT/0405/14.

(d)   A distinction is made between amendments which add a new or different claim, and those which merely amend the factual or legal basis of an existing claim, for instance by adding further facts in support of a claim that a dismissal was unfair. Both can be made by way of amendment: the EAT in *Prakash v Wolverhampton City Council* [2006] All ER (D) 71 (Nov) held that a new claim can be "presented" by an application to amend an existing claim as well as by the issue of a separate originating application. Applications to amend the factual or legal basis of an existing claim are admissible whenever application is made, subject to the discretion of the tribunal, which is exercised in accordance with the principles laid down in the *Selkent* case. The timing of the amendment as well as its nature is likely to be of importance, but it is possible (and not uncommon in practice) for amendments to be allowed up to or even during the hearing, where no prejudice is caused to the other party; it is likely to be relevant to establish whether there was good reason for any delay in applying to amend. The same principles apply to an application by a respondent to amend the response: *Chadwick v Bayer plc* [2002] All ER (D) 88 (Jun) (a case involving an application to withdraw an admission of liability).

(e)   There is a fine line between a new claim and a claim implicit in the facts already pleaded, but not expressly identified as a claim. Examples of what is a new claim can be found in *Housing Corpn v Bryant* [1999] ICR 123, CA (victimisation in addition to a claim of direct sex discrimination); *Harvey v Port of Tilbury (London) Ltd* [1999] ICR 1030 (applicant alleging unfair dismissal seeking amendment to add claim that dismissal was disability discrimination); *Ali v Office of National Statistics* [2004] EWCA Civ 1363, [2005] IRLR 201 (complaint of direct racial discrimination does not cover indirect discrimination); and *Potter v North Cumbria Acute Hospitals NHS Trust* [2008] ICR 910, [2009] IRLR 22 (addition of new comparators for equal pay claim). A case on the other side of the line is *Eltek (UK) Ltd v Thomson* [2000] ICR 689, where an amendment to a claim of pregnancy-related discrimination against an employee was permitted to base the claim on her status as a contract worker; the distinction was based on the same pleaded facts and was still an allegation of sex discrimination. However, this decision is difficult to reconcile with the decisions cited above, and should be regarded as confined to its own facts. The earlier EAT decision of *Quarcoopome v Sock Shop Holdings Ltd* [1995] IRLR 353, that an allegation of discrimination encompassed both direct and indirect discrimination and victimisation has effectively been overruled by *Ali* (above). The Presidential Guidance (para 6 dealing with amendments) draws a distinction between amendments seeking to add or substitute a new claim arising out of the same facts as the original claim, and those which add a new claim entirely unconnected with the original claim. When determining which of the categories the instant case falls into, the entirety of the claim form must be considered (para 7). The Presidential Guidance (para 11 dealing with amendments) invites a Tribunal to look for a link between the facts described in the claim form and the proposed amendment. Where there is no such link, the claimant will be bringing an entirely new cause of action. In such cases, the Tribunal must then consider whether the new claim is in time in light of the relevant statutory formula including any extensions of time.

(f)   It used to be generally understood that an amendment to add a new claim could not be made outside the applicable time limit for the claim (subject to the tribunal's discretion to extend time in accordance with the relevant statutory criteria for the particular new claim). More recent cases have established that provided that the original claim was presented within the time limit for the claim to be added (or that time limit plus any extension the tribunal finds would have been justified on the facts of the case), the decision whether to amend is to be determined as a matter of discretion, applying the *Selkent* principles, but giving particular weight to the fact that at the time of the application for permission to amend, a fresh claim would be rejected as out of time. The principal relevant cases are *Lehman Brothers Ltd v Smith* [2005] All ER (D) 177 (Oct), EAT, *Transport and General Workers Union v Safeway Stores Ltd* [2007] All ER (D) 14 (Jun), EAT and *Evershed v New Star Asset Management* (UKEAT/0249/09). The position has now been made clear by the Court of Appeal, which dismissed an appeal against the last of these EAT decisions, upholding the reasoning of the EAT: *New Star Asset Management Holdings Ltd v Evershed* [2010] EWCA Civ 870. This position is now reflected in the Presidential Guidance. At para 5(2) of the section dealing with amendments, the Guidance explains that if the complaint to be added is out of time, the Tribunal "must" consider whether the time limit should be extended. Once this has been taken into account and the amendment allowed, the decision can only then be challenged on appeal. The Guidance goes on to explain that such applications to amend, with timing issues, should be dealt with at a preliminary hearing to allow all parties to attend to make submissions, and possibly to give evidence. It is not permissible to allow an amendment "subject to time bar" (i.e. on the basis that the limitation issue can be revisited later in proceedings): *Amey Services Ltd & Another v Aldridge & Others* [2016] UKEAT/0007/16.

The weight given to the competing considerations in each case will usually make it more difficult to persuade a tribunal to permit an amendment to be made after the time limit for a new claim has expired, if it would add a new claim, not least because in a case where the time limit has not yet expired, it is open to the claimant simply to present a second claim.

(g)   Where however the original claim was presented after the claim sought to be added would have been time-barred, there is no general jurisdiction to permit the time limit to be circumvented by adding the claim by amendment. This may only be done if the tribunal is persuaded that time would have been extended had the claim sought to be added been brought as part of the original claim, and then only if the balance of factors to be considered under *Selkent* favours giving permission.

(h)   The general view of practitioners was for some time that only matters which could have been the subject of a claim at the time of presentation of the originating application could be added by an amendment to the original claim: allegations of matters occurring after the claim was presented could not be added (since they could not have been included at the time), and a fresh application would be needed to pursue such matters as substantive claims. This view now appears to be incorrect in the light of the EAT's decision in *Prakash v Wolverhampton City Council* [2006] All ER (D) 71 (Nov), that an amendment could be made to a claim of unfair dismissal to add a complaint of dismissal occurring after the original claim had been presented. It was also suggested by the EAT that this reflected the practice in discrimination cases. Independently of this decision, in discrimination cases subsequent events may, if relevant, be relied on as evidence supporting the inference of discrimination sought to be made in relation to the substantive allegations, and an amendment to this effect may be permitted.

(i)   The EAT has applied a similar approach as discussed in (f) above to introducing new claims by amendment without those causes of action having been subject to the ACAS EC requirements. In *Science Warehouse v Mills* [2016] ICR 252, the EAT permitted a new claim of victimisation to be added without compliance with the EC requirements, but in circumstances where there had been compliance with the EC requirements in respect of the original claim. The EAT observed (para 31) that "had the subsequent claim been entirely unrelated to the existing proceedings . . . the tribunal might have declined to permit the amendment, but that decision would be informed by a variety of factors, not merely the fact that no early conciliation process could have been engaged in". See also *Drake International Systems Ltd v Blue Arrow Ltd* [2016] ICR 445 on substitution of parties.

(j)   It has been somewhat controversial whether the tribunal can take into account the underlying merits when an amendment is proposed. It is often said that this is an appropriate consideration for the tribunal under 'all the circumstances' when considering an amendment which would add a new claim. In *Woodhouse v Hampshire Hospitals NHS Trust* (UKEAT/0132/12), the EAT held that the balance of hardship and prejudice may in all the circumstances include an examination of the merits: "there is no point in allowing an amendment to add an utterly hopeless case" (para 15). However, otherwise it should be assumed that the case is arguable. There, the EAT held the tribunal had impermissibly taken into account the strength of the evidence relating to the proposed claims when at that stage there had been no disclosure given in relation to those claims. As to considering the merits of proposed claims, see also *Cooper v Chief Constable of West Yorkshire Police* (UKEAT/0035/06) at para 17.

(k)   One other category of amendment requiring mention is an amendment to add a party or alter the name of a party (see also below). The discretion of the tribunal in dealing with such amendments is governed by similar principles to those set out above, summarised in *Cocking v Sandhurst (Stationers) Ltd* [1974] ICR 650; and see

Drinkwater Sabey Ltd v Burnett [1995] ICR 328 and *Birch v Walsall Metropolitan Borough Council* (UKEAT/0376/10). A party may be added or substituted even at the hearing in an appropriate case, e.g. where a manager rather than the employing company had been identified as the employer in an unfair dismissal case: *Linbourne v Constable* [1993] ICR 698. Further, a respondent may be added even if his name and address had not been given to ACAS under the EC procedures: see *Drake International Systems Ltd v Blue Arrow Ltd* [2016] ICR 445. One point raised, but not decided, in the *Walsall* case is whether the effect of an amendment to add a respondent operates as from the time of permission to amend, or from when the claim was originally brought (as had generally been understood to be the position before this case). The point is of relevance to how far back claims for back pay can be made in equal pay cases (which Walsall was), as well as affecting whether a point on time limits can be taken by the party added by amendment.

(l)   All of the cases referred to in paragraph (k) are about the addition or substitution of a respondent. It might be thought that different principles apply to the addition of a claimant, since this amounts, for the new claimant, to the bringing of a claim for the first time, and if the applicable limitation period has expired, it should therefore only be possible to add the claimant if the circumstances justifying an extension of time are made out. However the EAT has held that a more liberal approach, effectively applying *Selkent* criteria as explained above, is appropriate: *Enterprise Liverpool Ltd v Jonas* (UKEAT/0112/09) (a case where a trade union applied to be substituted for the individual claimant in a claim of failure to consult over a proposed transfer of an undertaking).

Parties and Participation in Proceedings

19.73   *Addition, Substitution and Removal of Parties*

By *Rule 34*, the Tribunal may, on its own initiative, or on application of a party or any other person wishing to become a party, add any person as a party (by way of substitution or otherwise), if it appears that there are issues between that person and any of the existing parties falling within the jurisdiction of the Tribunal which it is in the interests of justice to have determined in the proceedings. The Tribunal may remove any party apparently wrongly included.

The Presidential Guidance (see from para 12–18 on the section concerning amendments) deals with adding or removing parties. The Guidance clarifies that asking to add a party is an application to amend the claim and the Tribunal will need to consider the type of amendment sought and particularly whether it is in response to a clerical error, an amendment which adds new labels to facts already set out, or whether it is a more fundamental amendment (para 14). The Guidance further indicates that applications to add parties should be done promptly. Applicants for such an order should set out in the application the name and the address of the party who it is wished to be added, and the application should say why they are liable for something that has been claimed. Also, the applicant should explain when s/he knew of the need to add the party and what action s/he took since that date (para 15). Similarly, applications to remove any party wrongly included should be made promptly after proceedings are served on them (para 16). A party can be removed from proceedings if the claimant has settled with them, or otherwise no longer wishes to proceed against them (para 17).

It is sometimes necessary for a claimant to apply to join one or more additional respondents to the claim. This may arise, for instance, where the respondent originally named disputes that it is or was the employer, or an issue arises as to whether the claimant's employment was transferred to a third party following a transfer of the former employer's undertaking.

For other examples, see para 13 of the Presidential Guidance. The addition or substitution of parties by amendment is discussed further at **19.72**(k) and (l) above; and see generally *Birch v Walsall Metropolitan Borough Council* (UKEAT/0376/10) and *Enterprise Liverpool Ltd v Jonas* [2009] All ER (D) 115 (Aug).

Under the previous rules, a distinction was drawn between the ability to add a person on the basis that that person may be liable for the remedy claimed, and also a related power to join a person as a party, even though no remedy is claimed against the person if they have an interest in the outcome of proceedings (*Rule 10(2)(k)* and *(r)* of the old *2004 Rules*). The latter option was used for special cases where, for example, it was thought in accordance with justice for an interested third party such as a trade union to be joined where a claim is in the nature of a test case with implications for its members generally, or for press organisations to be joined in order to apply for the revocation of a restricted reporting order (see **19.92**).

Under the old rules, the EAT held that a Judge could not join a third party on his/her own initiative; such a party could only be joined on an application by an existing party to the proceedings who wishes to make a claim against the party to be joined, or on application by the person seeking to be joined: *Beresford v Sovereign House Estates Ltd* [2012] ICR D9. (The position is different if a claim has been brought by the wrong claimant and there is an application to substitute the correct claimant: an example is *Enterprise Liverpool Ltd v Jonas* [2009] All ER (D) 115 (Aug), where the correct claimant for compensation for failure to consult employees affected by the transfer of an undertaking was the union, not the individual employee who had brought the initial claim: see further **19.72**(k).)

Under the *2013 Rules*, the position is now clear. There are no limits to the exercise of the power under *Rule 34*. Indeed, the Presidential Guidance (para 18) states that a Tribunal may permit any person to participate in proceedings on such terms as may be specified in respect of any matter in which that person has a legitimate interest. This could involve where they will be liable for any remedy awarded, as well as other situations where the findings made directly affect them. When either the employer or the complainant claims that dismissal was due to union pressure (see UNFAIR DISMISSAL – III (55)) a tribunal must grant an application to join the union as a party to proceedings if it is made before the hearing of the complaint, and may do so if the application is made after the commencement of the hearing but before an award is made (*TULRCA 1992, s 160(1), (2)*); the tribunal then has the power to order that the party joined pay some or all of any compensation awarded. A similar procedure operates under the *Transfer of Undertakings (Protection of Employment) Regulations 2006, reg 15(5)*), where a transferor facing a complaint of failure to inform employee representatives of measures envisaged by the transferee, who intends to allege that this was due to the default of the transferee in breach of *reg 13(4)*), must notify the transferee of this intention; in this case, notification automatically makes the transferee a party and no order of the tribunal is necessary (but the tribunal must be advised of the joinder so that the transferee can be informed of the hearing, etc).

Analogous issues can arise in discrimination cases, where a claim is brought against more than one respondent (typically the employer or former employer, and one or more individual managers said to have committed the acts of discrimination for which the employer is vicariously liable); the tribunal may in appropriate cases make an award against the respondents jointly and severally (see *Gilbank v Miles* [2006] EWCA Civ 543, [2006] IRLR 538 and *London Borough of Hackney v Sivanandan* [2013] IRLR 408, CA (see also the EAT's judgment at [2011] IRLR 740); the latter case establishes that unless the respondents are each responsible for clearly separate loss or damage suffered by the claimant, liability for compensation will always be joint and several). A joint and several award may be enforced in full against any of the respondents against whom it is made, a point of particular importance where (as in the cases cited) the employer has become insolvent. It is open to a respondent, as well as the claimant, to apply to have a further respondent joined, as was done in *Finlay v Cyron* (UKEAT/0121/11) (employer applying to join former manager alleged to have been the person responsible for the discrimination alleged by claimant).

A point which has posed difficulty is whether tribunals have power to make orders under the *Civil Liability (Contribution) Act 1978* for contribution between respondents who have been held jointly liable for an award of compensation. Although not the same as making a contribution order between respondents, a practice developed over time where tribunals did apportion liability between employer and employee respondents in discrimination claims so that each was separately liable to the claimant for that part of the compensation. In *Way v Crouch* [2005] IRLR 603, the EAT endorsed such apportionments as doing practical justice; however in *Sivanandan* (above), another division of the EAT disagreed, concluding that the tribunal had no power to make an apportionment (para 24). *Way* was ultimately overruled by the Court of Appeal in *Sivanandan* on this point (paras 82, 84). Following these decisions, the specific issue of contribution orders arose in *Brennan v Sunderland City Council* [2012] ICR 1183. The EAT held emphatically that the tribunal had no jurisdiction to entertain a claim under the *1978 Act* (para 19); such a claim should be made in the civil courts. It is therefore important for a claimant alleging discrimination to consider whether to claim against individuals in addition to the employer. An application to add an individual respondent after the proceedings have been started is subject to the considerations referred to above.

19.74 *Participation of Other Persons*

Rule 35 provides that the Tribunal may permit any person to participate in proceedings, on such terms as may be specified, in respect of any matter in which that person has a legitimate interest. This is a further power in the Tribunal to permit non-parties to participate in proceedings for particular purposes. It would be appropriate, for example, for non-parties potentially affected by orders sought to be permitted to make representations on the application, without necessarily needing to become a party to the action.

The Secretary of State is entitled to appear and be heard at any hearing in relation to proceedings which may involve a payment out of the National Insurance Fund and is to be treated as a party for the purposes of the *2013 Rules* in such cases: see *Rule 96*.

As to parties in claims relating to a term of a collective agreement under *Equality Act 2010, s 146(1)*, see *Rule 97* which deems persons to be respondents, whether or not identified in the claim. Such persons include the claimant's employer, every organisation of employers and organisation of workers which would negotiate a variation if the terms of the collective agreement were varied voluntarily.

19.75 *Multiple Parties and Lead Cases*

There are many cases which come to the Tribunal which involve more than two parties. These can span cases of a couple of claimants arising from the same facts, to claims brought by an entire workforce of many thousand employees against the same or a variety of Respondents. The Tribunal will have to decide how best to manage such cases in light of the overriding objective and the particular features of the cases in question.

Consolidation.

One option is for the tribunal to order that two or more claims be heard together. This power is part of the Tribunal's general case management power: *Rule 29*. This is often referred to as consolidation of the proceedings. In practice an order is likely to be made if the same question of law or fact arises in each case, or if the remedy claimed in them arises out of the same set of facts, such as if several workers claim redundancy payments on the closure of a business, or if for some other reason it is desirable to hear the claims together. Consolidation will also normally be appropriate if a claimant has brought more than one claim against the same respondent. The parties should have an opportunity to make representations before such an order is made.

Representative claimants or respondents.

Where many people have the same interest in defending a claim, one or more of them may be cited as the person or persons against whom relief is sought, or may be authorised by the tribunal, before or at the hearing, to defend on behalf of all the persons so interested. This was formerly expressly provided for by the *2001 Rules, rule 19(3)*. There is no equivalent express provision in the *2013 Rules*, but the general case management powers of the tribunal are sufficiently wide to cover the point (and see *Affleck v Newcastle Mind* [1999] IRLR 405 (claim against one member of a committee of unincorporated association on behalf of all the members of the committee)).

Lead test cases.

If there are a large number of claims raising the same question, some may be selected as lead, or test, cases. The large numbers of multiple claims for equal pay which have been brought against local authorities and NHS Trusts have usually required the selection of test cases, and a high level of active case management, to keep the issues to be heard by the tribunal within manageable limits. The general principles applicable to imposing a lead case regime can be found in *Ashmore v British Coal Corpn* [1990] ICR 485, and contrast *Department of Education and Science v Taylor* [1992] IRLR 308. These general principles are now subject to the express provision contained in *Rule 36*. Pursuant to *Rule 36(1)*, where a Tribunal considers that two or more claims give rise to common or related issues of fact or law, the Tribunal or the President may make an order specifying one or more of those claims as a lead case and staying (or in Scotland sisting) the other claims, which are known as "the related cases". When the Tribunal later makes a decision in respect of the common or related issue in the lead case(s), it must send a copy of that decision to each party in each of the related cases: *Rule 36(2)*. That determination is binding on the parties in the related cases (*Rule 36(2)*) except where, within 28 days of the date on which the Tribunal sent a copy of the decision, a party in the related cases applies in writing for an order that the decision does not apply to, and is not binding on the parties to, a particular related case (*Rule 36(3)*). For an example see *Engel v Ministry of Justice* [2017] ICR 277 rejecting an argument that the claim should be differentiated from the test case.

Rule 36(4) deals with lead cases dropping out during the course of group litigation. If a lead case is withdrawn before the Tribunal makes a decision in respect of the common or related issues, it shall make an order as to (a) whether another claim is to be specified as a lead case; and (b) whether any order affecting the related cases should be set aside or varied.

Striking Out

19.76 *The Rule in Outline*

Rule 37 permits a Tribunal to strike out all or part of a claim or a response, at any stage of the proceedings, and either on its own initiative or on the application of a party. The Tribunal can only however do so on one of the grounds set out in *Rule 37(1)*. The grounds are that:

(a)   the claim or response, (or part thereof) is scandalous or vexatious or has no reasonable prospect of success;

(b)   the manner in which the proceedings have been conducted by or on behalf of the claimant or the respondent (as the case may be) has been scandalous, unreasonable or vexatious;

(c)   there has been non-compliance with any of the Rules or with an order of the Tribunal;

(d)   that the claim or response has not been actively pursued;

(e)   that the Tribunal considers that it is no longer possible to have a fair hearing in respect of the claim or response (or the part to be struck out).

Rule 37(2) contains important procedural safeguards: a claim or response may not be struck out unless the party in question has been given a reasonable opportunity to make representations, either in writing or, if requested by the party, at a hearing (see *Beacard Property Management and Construction Ltd v Day* [1984] ICR 837). In practice any decision to strike out is likely to be taken at a preliminary hearing (although the issue may also arise at the hearing).

If a response is struck out, the effect is as if no response had been presented such that *Rule 21* applies (see above): *Rule 37(3)*. This provision is required because striking out a response does not by itself bring proceedings to an end.

It has been seen above that upon initial consideration, an Employment Judge is required to consider the arguability of every claim and defence. A dismissal notice may be given where the Judge considers that the claim or defence does not enjoy "reasonable prospects of success". This procedure might well have a knock-on effect on the frequency with which applications for strike out are put before a Tribunal, although there is nothing in principle to prevent this even where – on the material then available, and without submissions from all the parties – the judge on initial consideration did not make a proposal to dismiss the claim or defence.

19.77 *Prospects of Success*

The power to strike out a party's case as having no reasonable prospect of success was introduced by the *2001 Regulations*. The power is comparable to the power of the High Court under *Part 24* of the *CPR 1998* to give summary judgment where a case has no real prospect of success, as to which there is helpful guidance in *Swain v Hillman* [2001] 1 All ER 91, CA. The standard of "reasonable prospect of success" is, however, a higher threshold than that of a "real prospect". A tribunal is usually unlikely to entertain an application to strike out the claim or response at a preliminary hearing in factually contentious cases, since tribunals are reluctant to deny a party the opportunity to put his or her case to the tribunal except on the strongest grounds. The drastic nature of the power justifies caution in its exercise; the tribunal has a discretion to strike out, and is not required automatically to do so merely because it determines that the claim (or defence) has no reasonable prospects of success.

The importance of not striking out discrimination cases in particular in any but the clearest of cases has been reinforced by dicta in the House of Lords: *Anyanwu v South Bank Students' Union* [2001] UKHL 14, [2001] IRLR 305 (see Lord Steyn at para 24, Lord Hope at para 39). See also *Balamoody v UK Central Council for Nursing, Midwifery and Health Visiting* [2001] EWCA Civ 2097, [2002] ICR 646, paras 31–50; *HM Prison Service v Dolby* [2003] IRLR 694 and *Adebowale v Isban UK Ltd* (2015) UKEAT/0068/15, [2015] All ER (D) 127 (Aug) and, for a similar approach to whistleblowing cases, *Boulding v Land Securities Trillium Ltd*, [2006] All ER (D) 158 (Nov), EAT, and *Ezsias v North Glamorgan NHS Trust* [2007] EWCA Civ 330, [2007] 4 All ER 940, [2007] ICR 1126, [2007] IRLR 603. The Court of Appeal in *Ezsias*, which has come to be regarded as the leading case on striking out claims as misconceived, emphasised that it would only be in exceptional cases that it would be appropriate to strike out a claim where the central facts were in dispute and the evidence relating to them had not been heard; an example of an exceptional situation might be where the facts asserted by one party were clearly and directly contradicted by contemporaneous documentation. The Court therefore emphasised that what mattered was the nature of the dispute of fact.

The approach applied in *Ezsias* was affirmed by the Court of Appeal in *A v B and C* [2010] EWCA Civ 1378, where the court refused to strike the claim out despite evident weaknesses in it, because there were significant factual issues which could only be resolved by evidence.

In *Timbo v Grenwich Council for Racial Equality* (UKEAT/0160/12) the EAT overturned a decision to strike out in a discrimination claim as misconceived even though the application was made at the end of the Claimant's evidence at the final hearing and after the Respondent's statements had been read by the tribunal. The tribunal ought to have evaluated the core factual dispute in light of all the evidence. As the EAT said: "It is one thing to reach, at the half time stage, a provisional view that a witness's evidence is unsatisfactory and that it is unlikely to be accepted if there is evidence to the contrary. It is another thing altogether to reach a concluded view that a witness's evidence must inevitably be rejected in its entirety even if there is no evidence to contradict it" (para 48). In *Romanowska v Aspirations Care Limited* [2014] UKEAT/0015/14, there was an application to strike out a claim for automatic unfair dismissal based on the reason for the dismissal being the making of protected disclosures. The EAT held that "where the reason for dismissal is the central dispute between the parties, it will be very rare indeed that that dispute can be resolved without hearing from the parties who actually made the decision" (para 15).

An example of the striking out of a discrimination claim where the factual basis for inferring discrimination was considered to be simply too weak to establish an arguable case is *ABN AMRO Management Services Ltd v Hogben* (UKEAT/0266/09), where a claim of age discrimination (in selecting employees for alternative posts in a redundancy situation) relied on comparators both younger and older than the claimant. Where the claim as pleaded is legally misconceived, striking out is fully justified; good recent examples are *Hadfield v Health and Safety Executive* (UKEATS/0013/10) and *Hawkins v Atex Group Ltd* [2012] IRLR 807.

A possible solution to the problem in cases involving factual disputes is exemplified by *Eastman v Tesco Stores Ltd* [2012] All ER (D) 264. There, the tribunal heard evidence on the core area of factual dispute at the preliminary hearing dealing with the strike out application (the core issue was whether there had been express agreement to employment continuing through a four year career break). Having heard that evidence, and resolved it against the claimant, the tribunal struck out the complaint for having no reasonable prospects of success. The EAT endorsed that approach and distinguished the case from those where no evidence is heard at the preliminary hearing and the factual disputes remain unresolved at the preliminary hearing.

The Court of Appeal has held that where the central issue is the construction of a written contract, one must be careful not to take the suggestion that the case should be determined at trial with fuller investigation into the facts too far. Whilst the factual matrix is key to understanding what the parties must have intended by the words they used, it far from follows that the need to know what that matrix was requires a full trial with discovery, evidence and cross examination: see Jacob LJ at paras 4–5 in *Khatri v Cooperateive Centrale RaifeisenBoerenleenbank BA* [2010] IRLR 715 (a case involving summary judgment under the *CPR 1998*); see also *Qantas Cabin Crew (UK) Ltd v Alsopp* (UKEAT/0318/13).

As striking out is a more drastic remedy – what has been described as showing the 'Red card' (as compared to the 'Yellow card' of a deposit order and costs warning: see *HM Prison Service v Dolby* [2003] IRLR 694) – tribunals can be expected to consider the merits of the case more rigorously when considering that sanction. It is open to a party (and advisable in practice) to apply for both a deposit and strike out in the alternative. *Deer v University of Oxford* [2015] EWCA Civ 52 is an example of a case in which deposit orders were substituted by the Court of Appeal for a strike out of certain victimisation claims where there remained reasonable prospects of success.

19.78 *The Conduct of Proceedings; Compliance with Rules and Orders*

The Grounds for a strike out under *Rule 37(b)* and *(c)* are related: the former concerns the situation where the manner in which proceedings have been conducted by or on behalf of the claimant or respondent has been scandalous, unreasonable or vexatious, whereas the latter concerns specific identifiable non-compliance with Rules or Orders. As the EAT explained in *Harris v Academies Enterprise Trust* [2015] IRLR 208, "A party that does not observe an order is at the mercy of the tribunal. Though in many cases an unless order will be granted before there is a strike-out, it is not an essential prerequisite of an application to strike out and is no guarantee that one will not follow in an appropriate case." (para 35).

The conduct of a representative, as well as a party, may be grounds for striking out the party's case under *Rule 37(1)(b)* above, and it is not easily open to the party to 'disown' the representative: *Harmony Healthcare plc v Drewery* (EAT/866/00) (respondent's representative assaulting claimant's representative in waiting room). In *Harris*, the EAT reviewed the authorities (para 43) and noted that what is done in a party's name is done "presumptively, but not irrebuttably" on that party's behalf and that there were good reasons why a court should not ordinarily distinguish between a litigant and his advisors. There, the conduct of the respondent and representative viewed as a whole crossed the threshold for an award of costs, but the EAT upheld the judge's decision to distinguish between representative and client when it came to the exercise of discretion (see below).

The tribunal should only use the drastic sanction of striking out a claim or defence if this is a proportionate response to the offence: *Bennett v Southwark London Borough Council* [2002] EWCA Civ 223, [2002] IRLR 407, a case with helpful guidance on what constitutes 'scandalous' conduct. See also *Bolch v Chipman* [2004] IRLR 140, where guidance was given by the EAT both as to the procedure to be followed and the basis for making a strike-out order, in a case where the unreasonable conduct alleged was a threat of violence. The EAT stressed that the ground for striking out is not simply unreasonable behaviour but conducting the proceedings in an unreasonable manner. In *Gainford Care Homes Ltd v Tipple & Another* [2016] EWCA Civ 382, an employer was debarred from taking any further part in proceedings because of seriously intimidating conduct towards key witnesses. Whilst such a debarring order needed to be proportionate, an appeal to the EAT had only been based on a reasons challenge, and a subsequent appeal to the Court of Appeal could not go behind that limit. The reasons provided had been adequate.

Even where there has been unreasonable conduct on the part of a party or representative, the tribunal must still consider whether striking out the claim or response would be a proportionate sanction, and in particular whether a fair trial is still possible (in which case striking out would rarely be proportionate). The Court of Appeal has commented that it will only be in a very unusual case that it would be justified to strike out on procedural grounds a claim which has reached the point of trial: *James v Blockbuster Entertainment Ltd* [2006] EWCA Civ 684, [2006] IRLR 630. These sentiments were reiterated by the EAT in *Arriva London North Ltd v Maseya* [2016] UKEAT/0096/16. An example of a case where striking out was held to be justified because a fair trial was no longer possible (because of intimidation of the claimant by a director of the respondent outside the tribunal) is *Force One Utilities Ltd v Hatfield* [2009] IRLR 45, EAT. See also *Ahmed v Bedford Borough Council* (UKEAT/0064/13) where the EAT found an error of law where a Tribunal failed to consider whether a fair trial was still possible and whether a less draconian sanction was more appropriate in a case where the claimant in a multi-ground discrimination case failed to comply with an order that he undergo an examination by an appropriate expert relevant to the disability discrimination claim. In *Harris* (a case where witness statements in a discrimination case had not been exchanged in breach of the Tribunal's order), a judge's decision to separate the actions of the respondent teachers, facing serious allegations of discrimination, from the acts of their representative, when refusing to strike out the response was upheld by the EAT. There was evidential material before the judge that justified him concluding that the representative's actions were not a reflection of instructions from his clients and the prejudice of findings of discrimination without an opportunity to answer was seen as significant.

The Presidential Guidance on General Case Management (see paras 7–9 of the section concerning concluding cases without a hearing) emphasises that in some cases parties apply for a strike out of the opponent at every perceived breach of the rules. This is not a satisfactory method of managing a case and such applications are rarely successful. The Tribunal must exercise the power of strike out in light of the overriding objective and in proportion to what has occurred and the matters in dispute.

The question what amounts to unreasonable or vexatious conduct may arise in relation to the claimant's persistence in a claim when the respondent is prepared to concede all or part of the claim. In this connection it is important to remember that the remedies available to the claimant may include a declaration (that he or she has been unlawfully discriminated against, or unfairly dismissed) as well as compensation. Thus it has been held not to be vexatious for a claimant to pursue his or her claim for unfair dismissal even after the respondent has offered to pay the maximum sum which the tribunal could award, so long as the respondent has not admitted that the dismissal was unfair (*Telephone Information Services Ltd v Wilkinson* [1991] IRLR 148). In *Nicolson Highlandwear v Nicolson* [2010] IRLR 859, the EAT held in awarding expenses to the respondent that it was unreasonable of a claimant to pursue a claim of unfair dismissal leading to a finding that the dismissal was procedurally unfair but with a nil award of compensation, but the *Wilkinson* case was not cited and the authority of Nicholson on this point is therefore doubtful. On the other hand, a claimant who decides at the last moment to withdraw a claim, thereby causing the respondent unnecessary work and expense in preparing for the case, may well be held to have acted unreasonably in delaying the withdrawal: *McPherson v BNP Paribas (London Branch)* [2004] EWCA Civ 569, [2004] 3 All ER 266, [2004] IRLR 558 (a case on liability for costs in such circumstances).

Where res judicata or issue estoppel (see **19.127** below) does not apply, the party seeking an order to strike out the other party's case must show that there is a special reason why relitigation of the issue would be an abuse of process and therefore vexatious (*Department of Education and Science v Taylor* [1992] IRLR 308; and see *Blaik v Post Office* [1994] IRLR 280 and *Staffordshire County Council v Barber* [1996] ICR 379 on the principles applicable where a claimant who has failed in, or withdrawn, a claim under domestic law attempts to pursue the same point by way of a claim based on EU law).

19.79 *Not Actively Pursued; Fair Trial Not Possible*

The last two grounds for striking out are closely related. The fifth ground – that a fair trial is no longer possible – was introduced by the *2004 Regulations* and is carried over to the *2013 Rules*. The occasions when it would be appropriate to strike out a claim on either ground will be very rare. An example of when a fair trial is no longer possible would be where a case has been adjourned on several occasions, over such a period that witnesses are either no longer available or liable to have no recollection of relevant events. To this extent it overlaps with the power to strike out a claim which has not been actively pursued: it is unlikely that such a claim would be struck out whilst the possibility of a fair trial remains, unless the claimant has clearly indicated that he or she no longer intends to pursue the claim.

The leading authority on the test to be applied where it is asserted that the claim has not been actively pursued is *Evans v Metropolitan Police Comr* [1993] ICR 151, [1992] IRLR 570 which held that *Birkett v James* [1978] AC 297, in turn the leading case on the equivalent rule in civil cases, applied to employment tribunals. *Birkett v James* holds that claims should not be struck out unless there has either been intentional or contumelious default by the claimant, or inordinate and inexcusable delay leading to a substantial risk that a fair trial will not be possible, or to substantial prejudice to the respondent.

Four cases in which applications to strike the claim out because it had not been actively pursued are *Peixoto v British Telecommunications plc* [2008] All ER (D) 240 (May), where the hearing had been delayed for three years by the claimant's illness and there was no prognosis as to when she would be fit to give evidence; the EAT upheld the order striking out the claim made by the tribunal; *Rolls Royce plc v Riddle* [2008] IRLR 873, where the claimant failed to attend a hearing and was unable to support his claim to have been too ill to attend with medical evidence; in this case the EAT overruled the tribunal's decision not to strike out the claim; *Abegaze v Shrewsbury College of Arts and Technology* [2009] EWCA Civ 96, [2010] IRLR 238, where the claim had been struck out (both for this reason and because a fair trial was no longer possible) after a seven year delay, following a finding for the claimant on liability, caused in part by the claimant failing to take the steps necessary for the holding of a remedy hearing, but the Court of Appeal, reversing the EAT, held that the claim should not be struck out because rigorous case management orders could still achieve a fair hearing on remedy, and striking the claim out after liability had been established was therefore a disproportionate sanction; and B*alls v Downham Market High School & College* [2011] IRLR 217, where the EAT held that the tribunal had been in error in striking out a claim which had been combined with a claim by the claimant's wife, also employed by the same respondent; the wife's claim had been struck out after she was imprisoned for theft from the respondent, but the EAT accepted that the claimant's case was separate from his wife's, and that he had been trying unsuccessfully to reactivate it after being exonerated in relation to the theft.

The Court of Appeal's view in *Abegaze* was significantly influenced by the fact that the claimant had already secured a finding in his favour on liability, and would therefore be deprived of his remedy if the claim was struck out. Nevertheless the contrast between the extreme delay in *Abegaze* and the facts of *Rolls Royce*, above, suggests that the decision of the EAT in the latter case is out of line with the later Court of Appeal decision and should not now be regarded as authoritative.

The striking out of a claim or response for non-compliance with an order short of an 'unless' order has been described by the Court of Appeal as a 'draconic power', not to be too readily exercised: *James v Blockbuster Entertainment Ltd* [2006] EWCA Civ 684, [2006] IRLR 630. The Court of Appeal has twice ruled that striking out as a sanction should only be applied where it is proportionate to the offence: *Bennett v Southwark London Borough Council* [2002] EWCA Civ 223, [2002] IRLR 407, where the issue was a party's conduct during the Hearing; and *Blockbuster*, where it was failure to comply with orders.

The guiding principle in deciding whether or not to strike out a party's case for non-compliance with an order is the requirements of the Overriding Objective. These require the tribunal to consider all relevant factors, including in particular what prejudice the other party has suffered, the issue of proportionality of the sanction, whether a lesser sanction could cure the prejudice, and as an overriding consideration, whether a fair trial remains possible. These points were articulated by the EAT in *Armitage v Weir Valves & Controls (UK) Ltd* [2004] ICR 371, where the employers successfully appealed against the striking out of their notice of appearance because they had been 10 days late in complying with a direction to exchange witness statements. (See also *Hazelwood v Eagle* [2009] All ER (D) 55 (May), where the EAT set aside a strike-out made because the claimant was in persistent breach of an order to supply medical evidence of a claimed disability. A case going the other way on similar facts is *Bennett v London Probation Service* (UKEAT/0194/09); however in that case the claimant had indicated that she would never disclose the reports.) In *GCHQ v Bacchus* (UKEAT/0373/12) the EAT imposed an unless order rather than taking the draconian step of striking out where the claimant had refused to comply with an order requiring him to attend an appointment with a psychiatrist for the purpose of the respondent obtaining its own expert report, without which it would have been significantly disadvantaged in the litigation.

In *Maresca v Motor Insurance Repair Research Centre* [2004] 4 All ER 254, [2005] ICR 197, a case concerning the striking out of a claim for failure to comply with a case management order for mutual disclosure of documents, the EAT held that in considering whether to strike out a party's case, the tribunal should have regard to the factors listed in the pre-April 2013 version of *CPR 1998, rule 3.9*. (These included whether the application for relief was made promptly, whether the default was intentional, and whether the expected hearing date can still be met if the original order is now complied with.) The relevance of these considerations has been reiterated in several subsequent cases, but with the important proviso that it will not be an error of law for a tribunal to fail to refer to or consider each of the factors in the old *CPR rule 3.9* if the factors not considered are not relevant to the particular case. However, the more recent decision of the Court of Appeal in Neary, above, that it was not necessary to consider each of the factors in the old *CPR rule 3.9* where there had been a failure to comply with an 'unless' order is an indication that such an exercise is now rather less likely to be regarded as essential in other cases where the sanction for non-compliance with orders is under consideration. This position is further reinforced by the amendment of *CPR rule 3.9* post April 2013: the list of factors has been replaced by a requirement that the Court considers all the circumstances of the case, including the need for litigation to be conducted efficiently and at proportionate cost, and the need to enforce compliance with rules, practice directions and orders.

In *Blockbuster*, the Court of Appeal held that striking out could only be justified if either the offending party has been guilty of deliberate and persistent disregard of required procedural steps, or the unreasonable conduct of the case by that party (not necessarily deliberately so) has made a fair trial impossible. These are gateways to the exercise of the power; they do not necessitate the exercise of the power. Thus in *Osborne v Premium Care Homes Ltd* [2006] All ER (D) 272 (Oct), the sanction of debarring the respondent from defending the case on liability but permitting it to defend itself at the remedy stage was held to be a proper and proportionate response to breaches of orders that had made a fair trial on liability impossible (compare the similar sanction applied by the EAT where a response had not been submitted in time in *Foster v D & H Travel Ltd* [2006] ICR 1537). The incorporation of *art 6* of the *European Convention on Human Rights*, through the *Human Rights Act 1998*, provides a possible basis for challenges to striking-out decisions on the ground that the party (particularly a claimant) is deprived of the right to a determination of his or her civil rights by way of a fair and public hearing. However the case law of the European Court of Human Rights (which guides the decision-making of UK courts and tribunals) indicates that the proper judicial use of powers to control litigants, including striking out, does not in principle offend the *Convention*. (See also *Soteriou v Ultrachem Ltd* [2004] EWHC 983 (QB), [2004] IRLR 870 (striking out where contract of employment tainted by illegality not contrary to *art 6*).)

Elliott v The Joseph Whitworth Centre Ltd (UKEAT/0030/13) is a further example of a case that was permissibly struck out because a fair trial was impossible in circumstances where there had been a two year delay in the Tribunal Service taking action on the Claimant's ET1 claim form compounded by the inaction of his union representatives. The EAT considered the delay inexcusable and that it had made a fair trial impossible.

19.80 *Application to Set-Aside the Strike Out*

Rule 38(2) provides that a party whose claim or response has been dismissed, in whole or in part, may apply to the Tribunal in writing, within 14 days of the date the notice was sent to have the order set aside on the basis that it is in the interests of justice to do so. Such an application is determined on the basis of written representations unless the application contains a request to the contrary. As to the criteria to be applied when the Tribunal considers such an application, the Court of Appeal in *Neary* rejected the view expressed by the EAT that the tribunal must consider each of the factors listed in the pre April 2013 formulation of *CPR rule 3.9*, which set out the factors to be considered in the High Court where there is an application from relief from sanctions. The Court concluded that the decision whether to grant relief is simply a matter of discretion. This is now underlined by the formulation of the *2013 Rules* which renders the "interests of justice" the dominant test. As to what factors are likely to be relevant to the exercise of that discretion in particular cases, the fact that there has been a breach of the order will always be relevant, but not necessarily decisive. The principles in the *Blockbuster* case are relevant; in particular it will be important for the tribunal to determine whether a fair trial of the case is still possible; thus if (as in the *North Tyneside* case) the defaulting party has since complied with the 'unless' order, it may be disproportionate to deny that party a hearing, whether as claimant or respondent. However where there has been a persistent and unexplained failure to comply with orders, the tribunal is entitled to say 'enough is enough' (as the Court of Appeal held was the case in *Neary*).

19.81   Unless Orders

A less draconian option (as compared to striking out) for a Tribunal to secure compliance with rules and orders is for it to make an unless order. This is provided for by *Rule 38*. That *Rule* gives the Tribunal the power to make an order specifying "that if it is not complied with by the date specified the claim or response, or part of it, shall be dismissed without further order." Where such an order is made, and the party required to comply does not, the Tribunal must, by *Rule 38(1)* given written notice to the parties that dismissal has occurred. If a response is dismissed under the rule, the effect is to be as if no response had been presented, as set out in *Rule 21*.

As with strike out, under *Rule 38(2)*, a party whose claim or response has been dismissed, in whole or in part, as a result of an unless order, may apply to the Tribunal in writing, within 14 days of the date that the notice was sent, to have the order set aside on the basis that it is in the interests of justice to do so. Unless the application includes a request for a hearing, the Tribunal may determine it on the basis of written representations.

The operation of 'unless' orders under the old rules were described by the then President of the EAT, Underhill J, as a 'pig's breakfast': *North Tyneside Primary Care Trust v Aynsley* [2009] All ER (D) 125 (May). The effect of the decisions in *Uyanwa-Odu v Schools Office Services Ltd* (UKEAT/0294/05), *Neary v Governing Body of St Albans Girls' School* [2009] All ER (D) 30 (Jan), *EPI Coaches Ltd v Lafferty* [2009] All ER (D) 81 (Apr), the *North Tyneside case* and *Scottish Ambulance Service v Laing* (UKEATS/0038/12) was that if the order is not complied with by the due date (even if the non-compliance is partial), the claim, or as the case may be, response, was struck out automatically, without the need for further judicial intervention. The effect of the automatic strike-out of a claim, although not of a response, was that the original unless order was converted into a judgment, which then opened the door to a review under the then applicable rules: *Uyanwa-Odu, Neary*, (which reviews fully the relevant cases). *Neary* was the subject of a further appeal to the Court of Appeal, which reversed the decision of the EAT on the merits, but without disagreeing with the analysis of the effects of non-compliance with an 'unless' order (*Neary v Governing Body of St Albans Girls School* [2009] EWCA Civ 1190, [2010] ICR 473). Note that Smith LJ in *Neary* considered that the EAT's finding that the remedy of review was available in the case of a strike out taking effect for non-compliance with an unless order was not "wholly free from difficulty" (para. 5). In *Thind v Salvesen Logistics Ltd* (UKEAT/0487/09), the EAT applied the decision in *Neary*, but reached the opposite result, overturning the striking out of the claim, where the breach of an 'unless' order had resulted from a combination of delay by a medical expert in providing a report and inadvertence by the claimant's solicitors. As Lady Smith remarked in *Laing*, under the old rules, if the parties wished confirmation of their position in relation to an unless order, the onus was on them to communicate with the tribunal, but that ought not to be treated by the tribunal as an opportunity to revisit the question of whether the unless order should have been issued.

Under the *2013 Rules* the complications surrounding the availability of a 'review' (as it was called under the old rules) have been swept away by the ability of a party whose claim or response has been dismissed under an unless order to apply for the order set aside on the basis that it is in the interests of justice to do so. Similarly, to render that avenue of review available, tribunal must send a notice if the sanction under an unless order is applied. The same approach on such an application is likely to be taken as that under applications to set-aside a decision to strike out (see above).

A complicating factor in many cases where there has been an 'unless' order and it is asserted by the other party that there has been a failure to comply with it is that that point may itself be in dispute (for instance there may be a dispute about whether the party has complied fully with an order to give particulars or disclose documents). In such cases the issue can only be fairly resolved by a hearing, leading to a judgment on the disputed issue of non-compliance, which may in turn be open to appeal. These procedural complications may remove much of the value of 'unless' orders as orders of last resort. In *Johnson v Oldham Metropolitan Borough Council* (UKEAT/0095/13), the EAT held that the question of whether there has been compliance with an unless order needs to be determined qualitatively rather than quantitatively. Accordingly, the Tribunal's view that there had been "substantial compliance" adopted the wrong test. In *Wentworth-Wood & Others v Maritime Transport Ltd* [2016] UKEAT/0316/15, an unless order in a multiple-claimant claim was held to apply severally to each claimant such that an ET's decision to confirm dismissal of all claims because some claimants had not complied with the unless order could not stand.

Being able to tell whether an unless order has been complied with is important, and is a guiding feature of the judicial guidance on how unless orders ought to be framed. In *Mace v Ponders End International Ltd* [2014] UKEAT/0491/13, the EAT overturned a decision to strike out a claim on the basis of failure to comply with an unless order which required the claimant to "provide disclosure of all relevant documents" by a given date. The Claimant did not make a list, but did send some documents to the Tribunal and was informed at the last moment by the Tribunal that they should be sent to the Respondent. HHJ Richardson held that the order lacked the necessary quality of clarity and certainty to take effect as an order striking out the claim. Unless orders under *Rule 38(1)* must identify with clarity what is required for compliance. In *Mace*, it was unclear whether the order was intended to require the claimant to provide a list of documents or provide copies and if so to whom, and it was not remedied by reading the unless order against the original case management order. At para 25 the EAT held: "Employment Judges have to deal with a great deal of what is commonly known as "box work": that is, correspondence asking for the making of an order on paper when the Employment Judge does not have the luxury of a hearing and full argument. The making of an unless order is one such kind of box work, but it requires particular care. Unless orders must be clear in their terms and are especially likely to result in injustice and satellite litigation if they are not. It is important to pay detailed attention to the wording and also to consider carefully whether the sanction is proportionate."

19.82   Deposit Orders

Rule 39 permits a Tribunal to make a 'deposit order'. This is an order requiring a party (known in the rule as "the paying party") to pay a deposit not exceeding £1,000 as a condition of continuing to advance a particular allegation or argument. *Rule 39(1)* provides that if, at a preliminary hearing (under *Rule 53*), a Tribunal considers that any specific allegation or argument in a claim or response has "little reasonable prospects of success" then it can make a deposit order.

The question whether to make a deposit order must therefore be dealt with at a preliminary hearing. This may be held on the application of the other party or as a result of an order made by the tribunal of its own initiative, and the issue of a deposit order may be referred for hearing at a preliminary hearing together with any other issues in the case which are judged appropriate for determination at that stage, or as the sole issue for determination. The tribunal will consider the Claim Form and Response, the representations (which may include relevant documents) and argument. Usually no evidence is heard, but in some cases this can also be done. In practice a deposit order is made most often against claimants.

Rule 39 applies to "allegations" or "arguments", not just claims or responses viewed as a whole. Therefore there is scope for a Tribunal to take a robust view to the individual contentions that are advanced by the parties. If the Tribunal determines that an allegation or argument in a claim or response has little reasonable prospects of success, a deposit order not exceeding £1,000 can be made. The EAT has held that in deciding what prospects of success a claim or response may have, the tribunal can take into account the credibility of the facts asserted, and the likelihood that they can be established at a hearing: *Jansen van Rensburg v Royal Borough of Kingston-upon-Thames* (UKEAT/0096/07). This case was not cited in the later case of *Sharma v New College Nottingham* (UKEAT/0287/11), and the EAT's conclusion in that case that the same test should be applied for a deposit order as for the striking out of a claim as having no reasonable prospects of success is considered to be wrong, as it fails to give weight to the difference in wording between 'no' and 'little' reasonable prospect of success, and undermines the objectives of the deposit order procedure. The distinction between a deposit order and striking out was also highlighted in *H M Prison Service v Dolby* [2003] IRLR 694, where the EAT described the two sanctions respectively as 'the Yellow card' and 'the Red card'. There is no express power to reconsider a deposit order, however there is power to vary or revoke the deposit order (see *Rule 29* and, by analogy with the old rules, *Sodexho Ltd v Gibbons* [2005] IRLR 836). In *Sodexho*, the EAT upheld the use of this power to restart the time for payment of the deposit where it had transpired that the claimant had not received the order, having put an incorrect address for his solicitor on the Claim Form.

The tribunal must make reasonable enquiries in to the paying party's ability to pay the deposit. And must have regard to any such information when deciding the amount of the deposit (but not whether nor not to make the deposit per se): *Rule 39(2)*. The *Rule* does not make clear how the tribunal may ascertain the party's means, but in practice this does not appear to cause difficulty. In *Oni v NHS Leicester City* (UKEAT/0144/12) the EAT recommended the completion of the County Court means form EX140 by the party whose means are to be taken into account. A party's means may include a student loan: *Simpson v Chief Constable, Strathclyde Police* (UKEATS/0030/11). In *Hemdan v Ishmail & Another* [2017] ICR 486, the EAT underlined that the purpose of a deposit order was to identify at an early stage claims with little prospect of success and discourage their pursuit without making access to justice difficult or effecting a strike-out through the back door. The assessment of prospects should be made without a mini-trial of the facts and there should be a proper basis for doubting the likelihood of a party being able to establish essential facts at trial. Where misunderstandings as to the nature of allegations arose (e.g. where a party communicates through an interpreter) consideration of allowing an amendment might be appropriate when assessing prospects of success. It was further essential that a deposit order was proportionate and not set at a level that a party could not afford. In *Hemdan*, a victim of trafficking who received benefits with an income of around £125 per week was ordered by the ET to pay a deposit of £75 for each of three allegations. The EAT considered this was disproportionate and substituted an order of £1 per allegation.

The Tribunal must give its reasons for making a deposit order along with the order and the paying party must be notified about the potential consequences of the Order: *Rule 39(3)*. In *Akanu-Otu v Secretary of State for Justice* (UKEAT/0295/13), the EAT noted that there are differences of terminology and content in Rule 39 as compared with the previous rule. Under the old rule, in *Akanu-Otu* the EAT held that a deposit notice which stated that payment was required as a condition of being permitted to continue to take part in proceedings was adequate. Now the rule refers to the need to notify the paying party of the "potential consequences of the order" – in other words the content of *Rule 39(4)*. In *Akanu-Otu*, the EAT also held that regard could have been had to the guidance notes accompanying the order.

The consequence of not paying the deposit is set by *Rule 39(4)*: the specific allegation or argument to which the deposit order relates shall be struck out where the deposit is not paid by the date specified. This is a change to the old rules which provided for the party in question (whoever that was) not being permitted to take part in proceedings unless the deposit is paid.

What happens to the deposit is set by *Rule 39(5)*: if the Tribunal at any stage following the making of a deposit order decides the specific allegation or argument against the paying party for substantially the reasons given in the deposit order, then (i) the paying party shall be treated as having acted unreasonably in pursuing that specific allegation or argument for the purpose of costs, unless the contrary is shown, and rule 76, unless the contrary is shown; and (ii) the deposit shall be paid to the other party (or, if there is more than one, to such other party or parties as the Tribunal orders). In all other cases, the deposit is to be refunded. The amount of a deposit order will off-set any costs award applied for: *Rule 39(6)*. The value of the deposit order procedure for respondents is that many claimants who are warned that they are at risk of a costs order do not pursue their claim. Such applications can also be considered as a lesser alternative to the striking out of a claim or response as misconceived, if the order for the holding of a preliminary hearing provides for this.

19.83 Stay of Proceedings

The power to order a stay (or sist in Scotland) of proceedings is a general power within *Rule 29*. A stay operates to suspend the proceedings, not to end them. Applications to stay tribunal proceedings are often made, and frequently granted, where there are concurrent proceedings in the High Court (or Court of Session) and the employment tribunal arising out of the same employment. Tribunal proceedings may also be stayed pending the outcome of foreign litigation (*JMCC Holdings Ltd v Conroy* [1990] ICR 179). Conversely, the tribunal might be seen as the more appropriate venue to determine the complaints before it, ahead of proceedings elsewhere (see e.g. *BUQ v HRE* [2012] EWHC 2827 where the tribunal was acknowledged to be better placed than High Court to determine the truth or otherwise of disputed claims of sexual harassment). The EAT should only interfere with the tribunal's decision to postpone or continue with the proceedings before it if that decision resulted from an error of law or if it was perverse (*Carter v Credit Change Ltd* [1980] 1 All ER 252, [1979] ICR 908; *Automatic Switching Ltd v Brunet* [1986] ICR 542). An example of a case where the EAT was persuaded to overturn the refusal of a stay is *GFI Holdings Ltd v Camm* [2008] All ER (D) 74 (Sep), where the claimant was pursuing a claim in the High Court for unpaid bonuses, the determination of which would involve deciding issues that would also arise in his tribunal claim (for unfair dismissal). For further discussion of the factors to be taken into consideration, see *First Castle Electronics Ltd v West* [1989] ICR 72, *Bowater plc v Charlwood* [1991] ICR 798 and *Chorion plc v Lane* [1999] All ER (D) 194 (where the High Court proceedings had been brought by the former employer). The position has been restated by the EAT in *Mindimaxnox LLP v Gover* (UKEAT/0225/10) and *Paymentshield Group Holdings Ltd v Halstead* [2012] ICR D5, both cases where a stay was ordered by the EAT on the basis that there was a significant overlap between the issues to be decided in the tribunal and High Court proceedings (and, in the first case, with court proceedings in Cyprus). Other factors which may affect whether or not a stay of the tribunal proceedings should be granted are the delay that this may cause, the degree of complexity of the issues (complexity being a factor favouring giving priority to the High Court proceedings), the nature of the issues (see *BUQ* above), and the different costs regimes in the two jurisdictions, as well the relative importance of each set of proceedings and the stage each has reached. In *Paymentshield*, the fact that the High Court action had not been commenced (only a formal letter before action had been served) was held not to be a sufficient reason to displace the other factors favouring giving priority to the Court proceedings.

It may sometimes be appropriate for proceedings to be stayed pending the outcome of an appeal, or a reference to the CJEU, the result of which is likely to determine, or at least influence, the outcome of the particular case. In *Johns v Solent SD Ltd* [2008] IRLR 88, the EAT ordered a stay of a claim for unfair dismissal and age discrimination where the claimant alleged that she had been forced to retire, because the issue of the validity of the relevant provisions of the *Employment Equality (Age) Regulations 2006* had been referred to the CJEU in another case, and the EAT's decision was followed by a Practice Direction by the President of Tribunals that all similar cases should be stayed pending the CJEU's ruling.

A different reason for seeking a stay of the proceedings is that the parties wish to attempt to settle their dispute by alternative means, such as through mediation (see further **19.23**). Tribunals generally encourage the use of such alternatives to litigation, although they will be wary about adding delay if there is no realistic prospect of a settlement being achieved. In Scotland this encouragement has been formalised into a Practice Direction on the sisting of cases for mediation, issued in December 2006. One reason for staying tribunal proceedings where related proceedings between the parties are anticipated is that the doctrine of res judicata (ie that issues decided in one set of proceedings cannot be relitigated) may apply so as to bind the High Court later. This will only be true if precisely the same issue arises in both sets of proceedings (see *Munir v Jang Publications Ltd* [1989] ICR 1; *Crown Estate Comrs v Dorset County Council* [1990] Ch 297; *Soteriou v Ultrachem Ltd* [2004] EWHC 983 (QB), [2004] IRLR 870) and the decision of the tribunal on the particular point was necessary to the determination of the issues before it, and within its jurisdiction (see for both points *Bon Groundwork Ltd v Foster* [2012] IRLR 517, and for a discussion of the principles of res judicata see **19.127** below). A stay can necessarily only be granted once the proceedings to be stayed have been commenced, and there is no equivalent procedure to suspend the running of time limits for the bringing of tribunal proceedings. A claimant who wishes to bring both High Court (or county court) and tribunal proceedings, and to pursue the former first, should therefore present his or her claim to the tribunal within the statutory time limit and immediately apply for a stay pending the outcome of the other proceedings, explaining that the tribunal claim has been made at that time to ensure the claim is not time-barred (*Warnock v Scarborough Football Club* [1989] ICR 489).

19.84 References to the Court of Justice of the European Union

Rule 100 provides that where a Tribunal decides to refer a question to the Court of Justice of the European Union for a preliminary ruling under *Art 267* of the *Treaty on the Functioning of the European Union*, a copy of that decision shall be sent to the registrar of the CJEU.

Art 267 gives tribunals a discretion to refer questions concerning the interpretation of EU law to the CJEU where this is necessary. A reference is not appropriate where the issue is *acte clair* (as to the meaning of which, see *CILFIT Srl v Ministro Della Sanita* [1983] 1 CMLR 472). For guidance see the CJEU's Recommendations to National Courts and Tribunals on Initiation of Preliminary Ruling Proceedings (6.11.2012, OJ C338/1). The EAT has confirmed that in an appropriate case, a reference can be made on assumed facts: see *Attridge Law v Coleman* [2007] ICR 654.

HEARINGS

General Rules for All Types of Hearing

19.85 *General*

Rule 41 now gives voice to the general principle that Tribunals are free to regulate their own procedure to conduct the hearing in the manner it considers fair and having regard to the principles contained in the overriding objective. *Rule 41* specifically indicates that the following rules do not restrict that general power and that the Tribunal shall seek to avoid undue formality and may itself question parties or a witness so far as appropriate in order to clarify the issues or elicit the evidence. *Rule 41* also clarifies that the Tribunal is not bound by any rule of law relating to the admissibility of evidence in proceedings before the courts. Notwithstanding the apparent breath of the ability on the Tribunal to regulate its procedure, the procedure in fact adopted must comply with *ECHR, Art 6* by virtue of *HRA, s 6* and also be fair and comply with the rules of natural justice at common law. In *U v Butler* [2014] UKEAT/0354 (at para 72-3), the EAT recently applied the Supreme Court's dicta in *R (Osborn) v Parole Board* [2013] 3 WLR 1020 (a case involving parole decisions) to the effect that the procedural fairness of hearing is not merely reviewable on *Wednesbury* grounds, but "The Court must determine for itself whether a fair procedure was followed . . . its function is not merely to review that reasonableness of the decision maker judgment for what fairness requires".

In *Hak v St Christopher's Fellowship* [2016] IRLR 342, the EAT considered the duties of a Tribunal to ensure a fair hearing for a litigant whose first language was not English. In general, where a party wishes to have an interpreter present, the Tribunal should facilitate it as best it can and should "strive to do so" (para 38). However, there may be circumstances in which the command of English is so poor that a litigant cannot give the account which they would wish to give to the Tribunal. There is, in such cases, a powerful argument that the Tribunal must take all reasonable steps – including funding – to secure the services of an interpreter (para 39). By contrast, where a litigant had a well-demonstrated ability to speak, write and read English, an interpreter would be unnecessary and the request should be refused (but the Tribunal should "think long and hard" before so concluding in respect of a person whose mother tongue may well not be English (para 40). There were also cases, falling between these categories in which the Tribunal had to conduct an assessment of need, against achieving justice, fairness and equality of arms. This assessment was for the Judge bearing in mind that spoken and written language are different and that pressures in court are such that immediate comprehension and response are required (para 41). A useful test would be to ask whether the litigant's command of language was sufficient to enable him to give the best account to the tribunal which he would wish to give relating to the matters in dispute (para 45).

The broad discretionary powers do, however, result in considerable variation in the extent to which particular tribunals conduct cases in an inquisitorial way or leave it to the parties to present their case as they think best; much depends on the style of individual Judges. Under the previous *Rules*, the EAT has, however, stressed that a degree of formality and structure is necessary; informality can be counter-productive and tribunals should normally adhere to the generally recognised rules of procedure (*Aberdeen Steak Houses Group plc v Ibrahim* [1988] ICR 550). Although this case pre-dates the revisions of the *Rules* in 2001, 2004, and now 2013, it is still relevant. In particular, tribunals are required to observe such basic rules of fair conduct or natural justice as the rules against bias on the part of a Judge (*Laher v London Borough of Hammersmith and Fulham* (EAT/215/91), IDS Brief 531; for a more recent example of a case where there was found to be an appearance of bias on the part of the Judge see *Diem v Crystal Services plc* [2006] All ER (D) 84 (Feb), EAT (comment on colour of claimant's skin)). See also *Gill v Humanware Europe* (UKEAT/0312/08), where the EAT held that there was an appearance of bias when the judge (as it was alleged) had had a private conversation with counsel for the respondent in the course of the hearing.

It is a general principle that decisions which require to be taken in the course of the hearing on points of case management (such as whether to grant a party's application for an adjournment) should not be taken by the judge without consulting the lay members, if there are lay members sitting: *Jones v Corbin* (UKEAT/0504/10). The Judge should alert the parties before taking a point on which they have not addressed the tribunal (*Laurie v Holloway* [1994] ICR 32); and see *Launahurst Ltd v Larner* [2010] EWCA Civ 334 (error of law to base decision on point not raised by or with the parties during the hearing). It has also been held that the tribunal should not rely on cases discovered through its own researches without giving the parties an opportunity to make submissions on them: *Albion Hotel (Freshwater) Ltd v Maia e Silva* [2002] IRLR 200; but see also *Sheridan v Stanley Cole (Wainfleet) Ltd* [2003] EWCA Civ 1046, [2003] IRLR 885, adopting a less strict view on this point, and *Clark v Clark Construction Initiatives Ltd* [2008] EWCA Civ 1446, [2009] ICR 718, where it was held that the citation of cases was not in the circumstances material to the decision.

The Judge and members must also, unsurprisingly, remain attentive throughout the hearing: thus the Court of Appeal in *Stansbury v Datapulse plc* [2003] EWCA Civ 1951, [2004] IRLR 466 set aside the judgment of a tribunal reached after a hearing during which one of the lay members had fallen asleep after allegedly drinking alcohol during the lunch break. Contrast *Elys v Marks & Spencer Plc* [2014] ICR 1091 in which a lay member had apparently been sleeping for 15-20 seconds and had been observed to be drooling by the Judge (other instances of alleged sleeping by that member were rejected on the basis he had been attentive, but closing his eyes due to an eye condition). During the three week hearing the member had taken extensive notes, asked questions and had taken full part in discussions with the Tribunal. The EAT decided that it was for it to find facts as to what had happened and then consider whether a properly informed and impartial observer would regard there as having been inattention or the appearance of inattention. In that case, the EAT accepted that there was inattention during the 15-20 second incident (not otherwise) but this was not of sufficient materiality overall to amount to a procedural irregularity. More generally, the EAT emphasised the responsibility of those sitting in a judicial capacity for their own performance, and the entitlement of the parties to the attention of the entire panel for the entire case (trivial moments aside). If judges and members have any reason to think they might be subject to inattention for extraneous reasons they should make that plain to the Tribunal and, if necessary, the parties should be told enough to make an informed decision as to their position. In the instant case, the EAT doubted whether the appeal would have proceeded had the member explained that he suffered from the eye condition he did.

The Court of Appeal has expressed the view that it is always desirable that any irregularity in procedure, such as the Judge or a member falling asleep, or the making of inappropriate comments, should be raised at the time, but failure to do so (particularly if the party subsequently complaining was not represented at the time) is not necessarily a bar to raising the point on appeal: *Stansbury v Datapulse plc* [2003] EWCA Civ 1951, [2004] IRLR 466, para 23. Peter Gibson LJ acknowledged the difficulty that even a legal representative may have in raising such a point, since if the objection is unsuccessful the person complained about will continue to sit in the case.

The Court of Appeal has emphasised that despite the relative informality accorded to tribunal proceedings, employment tribunals are not inquisitorial bodies, so that where the burden of proof rests on a particular party, the onus is on that party to put evidence before the tribunal enabling that burden to be discharged: *McNicol v Balfour Beatty Rail Maintenance Ltd* [2002] EWCA Civ 1074, [2002] ICR 1498, a case where the claimant's status as a disabled person was in dispute. However, the Court indicated that the tribunal should use its case management powers to ensure that a claimant appreciated the kind of medical evidence that might be needed to establish disability. In *Joseph v Brighton & Sussex University Hospitals NHS Trust* UKEAT/0001/15, a litigant in person failed to prove that she met the statutory definition of disability in respect of two conditions she suffered from. The EAT rejected the notion that the Tribunal had erred by failing to seek out evidence in a 580 page bundle which the claimant did not refer to at the hearing. The duty to assist litigants in person did not extend to referring to all the documents in the bundle. Equally, Tribunals should not search out evidence on their own. In *East of England Ambulance Service NHS Trust v Sanders* [2015] ICR 293, after hearing evidence on disability, the Tribunal retired and conducted its own research as to the dosage of medication the claimant was taking by consulting Wikipedia and other websites. It then returned to the

Tribunal room and provided copies to the parties. Langstaff P rejected the suggestion that *Rule 41* permitted a Tribunal to make its own enquiries. At para 29 he said: "The Tribunal may, in an appropriate case, ask the parties whether they have thought about particular evidence or even, possibly, whether in an appropriate case the parties or one of them would wish an adjournment in order to obtain it. But it is not, as the Judge appeared to think, for the Tribunal itself to investigate the evidence and rely upon its own investigations. The Tribunal is, as we said at the start of this Judgment, to act as the adjudicator not as advocate." The Tribunal had assumed the truth of that which it discovered and had demonstrated it would place improper weight upon it. The EAT went on to emphasise that this should not prevent a Tribunal appropriately making allowance for a party appearing as a litigant in person even if the degree of intervention in a Tribunal would "raise some eyebrows in civil courts" (para 31). Non-leading questions should be the form of choice when the Tribunal invokes *Rule 41* to ask questions to elicit evidence.

More generally, tribunals are not under a duty to ensure that every allegation in a Claim Form is dealt with, regardless of whether the claimant puts forward evidence or argument in support of it (*Mensah v East Hertfordshire NHS Trust* [1998] IRLR 531, CA; and see *Hyde-Walsh v Ashby* [2008] All ER (D) 225 (Feb), EAT: tribunal has discretion whether to draw attention to a head of claim apparently overlooked by the claimant). This point is particularly important because of the general rule that arguments and points not taken at the tribunal hearing cannot be raised for the first time by way of appeal: see **20.15** below.

The EAT has held that the tribunal has discretion whether to permit a respondent to withdraw an admission: *Nowicka-Price v Chief Constable of Gwent Constabulary* (UKEAT/0268/09). The factors that should be taken into account in considering whether to exercise the discretion (and presumably also where it is the claimant who seeks to withdraw an admission or concession) are those listed for civil cases in *CPR Part 14*.

In some circumstances, it can be incumbent upon the Tribunal to grant a short adjournment of its own motion during a hearing. In *U v Butler* [2014] UKEAT/0354/13, the EAT held this applied where a claimant suffered from a mental disability, was a litigant in person and arrived after the hearing had started, and after the Tribunal had struck out his claims for failure to comply with case management orders. Although the judge told him he could apply for a review (which he did, only for it to be dismissed because his submissions were not supported by medical evidence), the EAT held it was incumbent upon the judge to have granted a short adjournment to allow the claimant to reflect and recover, and to gather material relevant to the review application. Further, the judge should also have informed him that the review application could have been made within 14 days of receiving the reasons rather than immediately.

More generally, Tribunals will take steps to assist litigants in person, but as the cases above show, when doing so, they must avoid stepping into the arena. The Court of Appeal in *Drysdale v Department of Transport* [2015] ICR D2 identified the following general propositions:

> "(1) It is a long-established and obviously desirable practice of courts generally, and employment tribunals in particular, that they will provide such assistance to litigants as may be appropriate in the formulation and presentation of their case.
>
> (2) What level of assistance or intervention is "appropriate" depends upon the circumstances of each particular case.
>
> (3) Such circumstances are too numerous to list exhaustively, but are likely to include: whether the litigant is representing himself or is represented; if represented, whether the representative is legally qualified or not; and in any case, the apparent level of competence and understanding of the litigant and/or his representative.

(4) The appropriate level of assistance or intervention is constrained by the overriding requirement that the tribunal must at all time be, and be seen to be, impartial as between the parties, and that injustice to either side must be avoided.

(5) The determination of the appropriate level of assistance or intervention is properly a matter for the judgment of the tribunal hearing the case, and the creation of rigid obligations or rules of law in this regard is to be avoided, as much will depend on the tribunal's assessment and "feel" for what is fair in all the circumstances of the specific case.

(6) There is, therefore, a wide margin of appreciation available to a tribunal in assessing such matters, and an appeal court will not normally interfere with the tribunal's exercise of its judgment in the absence of an act or omission on the part of the tribunal which no reasonable tribunal, properly directing itself on the basis of the overriding objective, would have done/omitted to do, and which amounts to unfair treatment of a litigant."

19.86 *Timetabling and Power to Control Proceedings*

Rule 45 provides that a Tribunal may impose limits on the time that a party may take in presenting evidence, questioning witnesses or making submissions, and may prevent the party from proceeding beyond any time so allotted. This, in conjunction with *Rule 41*, gives the Tribunal considerable ability to control the proceedings before it. Reference should also be made to the Presidential Guidance on General Case Management which contains a section on Timetabling. That Guidance underlines that the parties have a duty to conduct the case so that, wherever possible, the tribunal can complete the case within the time allowed.

In preparing for the hearing, a representative needs to consider whether he or she, or the other party's representative, will be required to open the case. The party bearing the burden of proof normally opens: in an unfair dismissal case this is the employer if dismissal is admitted, as he or she must show the reason; if dismissal is disputed (as often happens in constructive dismissal claims) the employee normally opens. The employee also normally opens in discrimination cases and claims for breach of contract or unlawful deduction of wages. Where there are claims which involve an initial burden of proof on each party, the tribunal will decide who should go first having regard to the wishes of the parties and any other factors appearing relevant (this may include in particular which party's evidence is more likely to assist the tribunal's initial understanding of the dispute). Tribunals do not normally permit the party who starts to make an opening statement, and if one is permitted it should be a reasonably brief introduction to the parties, the facts, the issues in dispute, the key documents and the principal contentions on any points of law that arise. Opening statements are not permitted at all in Scotland.

A party does not have the right to cross-examine come what may. The tribunal has a duty to keep the inquiry before it within reasonable bounds, and it does not have to allow lengthy and detailed cross-examination on matters that do not appear to it to be of assistance. These points were emphasised by the EAT in *Zurich Insurance Co v Gulson* [1998] IRLR 118. It is for the parties to determine what evidence they wish to put before the tribunal, however the EAT has confirmed the tribunal has a discretion to exclude even relevant evidence, where for instance the evidence is unnecessarily repetitive or of only marginal relevance: *Digby v East Cambridgeshire District Council* [2007] IRLR 585 (and see for the power of the tribunal to exclude irrelevant and marginally relevant evidence in advance of the hearing *HSBC Asia Holdings BV v Gillespie* [2011] ICR 192, EAT). This discretion must be exercised consistently with the parties' rights under *Art 6* of the *European Convention on Human Rights*, to a fair hearing of their respective cases. However Art 6 does not give unlimited protection to whatever a party may want. It has been confirmed, for instance, in *Power v Greater Manchester Police Authority* (UKEAT/0087/10), that there is no general right for a claimant to cross-examine the person alleged to have discriminated against him or her under *Art 6*, so that it was not a ground of appeal that the respondent had not called the decision-taker concerned as a witness, thereby preventing the claimant from cross-examining her. See also *Khan v Vignette Europe Ltd* (UKEAT/0134/09), where the EAT upheld a tribunal's refusal of a request by the claimant for an adjournment part-way through a hearing to enable him to undertake religious observances for Ramadan.

The tribunal may also, in the interests of devoting a proportionate amount of time to issues within the case, curtail unnecessarily lengthy evidence or cross-examination. However, that discretion must be exercised judicially and is open to challenge on appeal if exercised by reference to irrelevant considerations or perversely, as in the *Digby* case. Even before the introduction of *Rule 45*, it was an increasingly common practice for tribunals to set time limits on stages in the proceedings, such as cross-examination of a particular witness or the making of a closing submission, usually as part of a timetable set at the start of the hearing to ensure that it is concluded within the time available. Such restrictions should not be so restrictive as to deny a party the opportunity to put his or her case.

In his judgment in *Bache*, Mummery LJ made the following statement of the principles governing the conduct of tribunal hearings:

"(1) At the hearing the tribunal must follow a procedure which is fair to both sides. It must normally allow each party to call relevant evidence, to ask relevant questions of the other side's witnesses and to make relevant submissions on the evidence and the law.

(2) The tribunal is responsible for the fair conduct of the hearing. It is in control. Neither the parties nor their representatives are in control of the hearing.

(3) Procedural fairness applies to the conduct of all those involved in the hearing. Just as the tribunal is under a duty to behave fairly, so are the parties and their representatives. The tribunal is accordingly entitled to require the parties and their representatives to act in a fair and reasonable way in the presentation of their evidence, in challenging the other side's evidence and in making submissions. The rulings of the tribunal on what is and is not relevant and on what is the fair and appropriate procedure ought to be respected even by a party and his representative who do not agree with a ruling. If the party and his representative disagree with a ruling, an appeal lies against it if the tribunal has made an error of law."

As the Presidential Guidance on Timetabling makes clear, in simple cases it will be rare for a formal timetable to be issued, although the judge might set out and agree at the outset how the hearing will proceed. For longer cases, a written timetable may be created. Fairness will be the touchstone, but this does not always require an equal division of the time between the parties: it will depend on the issues. If an interpreter is required, additional time will be required. Once the timetable has been set, a Tribunal will expect the parties to keep to it as part of their duty to assist. The Presidential Guidance states that if time is exceeded, a Tribunal can ultimately guillotine the evidence. Tribunals do not, however, like to take that step.

The procedure in practice is that the Judge (who, along with the lay members (where they are present), will have read the Claim Form and Response Form) may first seek to clarify what issues are, or remain, in dispute between the parties. A list of issues might have been agreed or set as a result of a Preliminary Hearing for Case Management, or upon Initial Consideration of the Claim. If there is an agreed list of issues, that will, as a general rule, limit the issues at the substantive hearing to that list: see *Land Rover v Short* (UKEAT/0496/10) as approved in *Parekh v London Borough of Brent* [2012] EWCA Civ 1630. However, both the Court of Appeal in *Parekh* and the EAT in *Price v Sur-*

rey County Council (UKEAT/0450/10) (a judgment given, unusually, by the Senior President of Tribunals, Carnwath LJ, sitting as an EAT judge) have emphasised the importance of the tribunal that hears the case satisfying itself as to precisely what issues do require to be decided, and not simply accepting what the parties may have agreed as the issues or sticking slavishly to a list of issues. Nor was a list of issues to be construed as a formal contract, pleading, or statute; it is a useful took to allow a Tribunal to case manage a hearing so as best to ensure justice as between the parties: *Millin v Capsticks Solicitors LLP* [2014] UKEAT/0093/14. (See also *Remploy Ltd v Abbott & others* UKEAT/0405/14). Particular care is required where, as in Price, the list agreed between the parties was not a helpful framework for deciding the case. The list in Price was attached to the judgment as an illustration of how not to prepare a list of issues not least because it failed to distinguish clearly between the central issues and the detailed factual allegations. Having said that, the tribunal hearing the case does not have carte blanche to decide new points: it is confined to deciding the pleaded issues and cannot when considering the evidence adjudicate upon additional allegations or complaints: see *Chapman v Simon* [1994] IRLR 124, *Foster v Bon Groundwork* [2012] IRLR 517 and *Chandhok v Tirkey* [2015] IRLR 195. To do otherwise will deny the party affected a fair hearing: *British Gas Services Ltd v McCaull* [2001] IRLR 60. Further, where the issues have been properly identified and formulated, the hearing will focus upon and only upon the issues as so identified: see *Tucker v Partnership in Care Ltd* (UKEAT/0455/09). A Tribunal may also err in law when deciding issues that are not in dispute between the parties. An example can be seen in *Mr Clutch Auto Centres v Blakemore* [2014] UKEAT/0509/13 in whilst the parties disagreed as to how and when, they agreed that the employment relationship had ended. The EAT held in such circumstances it was not open to the Judge to find that the employment relationship was still continuing.

The judge will also deal at the start of the hearing with any preliminary points that have not been dealt with by paper adjudication or at a previous hearing. This might include correcting the name of the respondent, considering any applications to amend the Claim Form or Response Form and ruling on any disputes about disclosure of documents or attendance of witnesses either party wishes to raise. It should be noted that a substantive change in the name or identity of the respondent will necessitate an adjournment of the proceedings to enable the newly identified respondent to attend the hearing: *Johanson t/a Kaleidascope Child Care* (UKEAT/0541/10), where the claim was against a limited company, but (in its absence) the tribunal agreed to change the name of the respondent to that of an individual trading in the name of the company. In general it is better for all such applications to be dealt with in advance of the final hearing in order to avoid a risk of a postponement.

The usual procedure after any of the foregoing points that may arise have been addressed is as follows:

(a)   the party upon whom the burden of proof rests normally opens (the claimant in a discrimination case, the employer in an unfair dismissal claim where dismissal is conceded; if there are issues on which there is a burden of proof on both parties in turn, the tribunal is likely to hear submissions from the parties before deciding who should go first);

(b)   the party called upon to open: (i) may occasionally be permitted to make an opening statement giving an outline of the case (but this is increasingly rare except in the most substantial and complex cases and is not permitted in Scotland: see above); and (ii) calls his or her evidence, each witness giving evidence on oath or under affirmation (with the witness's statement normally being taken as his or her evidence-in-chief, and being read by the tribunal before the witness is called: see below) and being open to cross-examination by the other party, and questions by the members of the tribunal;

(c)   the other party:(i) calls his or her evidence; and (ii) makes a closing speech (usually called submissions); and

(d)   the party who opened the case then makes submissions (in Scotland the order of making submissions is reversed). See further as to the content of submissions, and the use of written submissions, below.

Procedural issues arising during the hearing will be ruled on by the judge, but should be decided by all members of the tribunal if it is a full tribunal, not the judge alone. If a party withdraws or abandons a claim or part of a claim, the tribunal should satisfy itself that the party (particularly if not professionally represented) understands the consequences of doing so, and does intend to withdraw or abandon the claim or contention: *Segor v Goodrich Actuation Systems Ltd* (UKEAT/0145/11).

The Presidential Guidance on General Case Management sets out in the section on timetabling these general steps in proceedings (see para 7).

Tribunal hearings are usually conducted in modern rooms with the three members of the tribunal sitting at a table on a slightly raised dais and the claimant and respondent sitting at tables facing the tribunal. There is a table at which the witness sits to give evidence. A full tribunal is composed of a legally qualified Employment Judge, one member with management experience and one member with trade union experience; as to cases where the Judge may sit alone or with just one other member, see **18.8** and **18.9** above. The proceedings are public (although in practice members of the public not connected with the proceedings attend relatively infrequently). For the power of the tribunal to sit in private, see **19.93** below.

Rule 46 of the *2013 Rules* provides that a hearing may be conducted, in whole or in part, by use of electronic communication (including by telephone) provided that the Tribunal considers that it would be just and equitable to do so and provided that the parties and members of the public attending the hearing are able to hear what the Tribunal hears and see any witness as seen by the Tribunal. Accordingly, hearings may be held by telephone or video link, so that it is possible, for instance, for evidence from a witness who is abroad to be heard by video link. In practice this happens infrequently, as most hearing centres are not equipped for video conferencing, and special arrangements therefore need to be made in advance; but if there are good reasons for such arrangements, an early application for a direction should be made to the tribunal. Some regions, such as London Central, have video conferencing facilities. At other hearing centres, directions can be made by the Tribunal for it to sit elsewhere so that the facilities are made available.

The Judge and members should be addressed as 'Sir' or 'Madam'. Proceedings are formal but considerably less so than in an ordinary court. Witnesses (including a party if giving evidence) are required to give their evidence on oath or under affirmation (see *Rule 43* below); the clerk will check on the preference of each witness in this respect. In Scotland, witnesses are excluded from the tribunal room until called to give their evidence (this does not apply to a party who is also a witness). Before the hearing starts, the clerk will speak to both parties and make a list of names of representatives and witnesses, and will collect copies of documents each party intends to rely on to give to members of the tribunal.

19.87 *Rights of representation*

The right of a party to be represented at a hearing by whoever he or she chooses (whether or not professionally qualified) is expressly given by *s 6, ETA 1996*. In *Bache v Essex County Council* [2000] IRLR 251, the Court of Appeal ruled that the tribunal therefore has no power to 'sack' a party's representative under its general power to control the proceedings. If it does so, this is a ground of appeal notwithstanding the acquiescence of the party at the time. However, denial of representation by the chosen person did not render the hearing a nullity, and on the facts the decision was upheld.

The EAT has applied the principle in *Bache* in a case where the employers unsuccessfully sought an order forbidding the claimant from using a particular firm of solicitors to represent him at the hearing because of a claimed conflict of interest: *Dispatch Management Services (UK) Ltd v Douglas* [2002] IRLR 389. However, if the party's chosen representative behaves inappropriately, the tribunal's powers to act in response to the misbehaviour of a party (in an extreme case extending to the striking out of the claim or defence, provided that this is a proportionate response: see *Bennett v Southwark London Borough Council* [2002] EWCA Civ 223, [2002] IRLR 407) are equally available in respect of conduct of the representative acting on behalf of the party: *rule 18(7)*. If the representative is acting for profit, the further sanction of a wasted costs order (see **19.133** for this) is available to the tribunal.

The tribunal has no power to impose a representative on an unrepresented party. This point was confirmed in *Johnson v Edwardian International Hotels Ltd* [2008] All ER (D) 23 (May), where the tribunal had sought to have the Official Solicitor appointed as the claimant's litigation friend, after he had made claims that he was the victim of a conspiracy involving the Prime Minister and the Jehovah's Witnesses to procure his dismissal. The EAT held that the tribunal's only recourse was to use its case management powers, including the power to strike out the claim on the ground that it had no reasonable prospects of success.

A person who is representing him or herself in a tribunal is known as a 'litigant in person'; this phrase is now to be preferred to 'self-represented litigant': see *Practice Guidance: Terminology for Litigants in Person* (issued by Lord Dyson MR, March 2013). The equivalent expression in Scotland is 'party litigant'.

19.88 *Written Representations and Skeleton Arguments*

Pursuant to Rule 42, the Tribunal shall consider any written representations from a party, including a party who does not propose to attend the hearing, if they are delivered to the Tribunal and to all other parties not less than 7 days before the hearing.

Written representations under *Rule 42* should not be confused with a skeleton argument that parties will often bring to a hearing setting out the central themes of their argument as to why they should succeed. Skeleton arguments are often provided to the Tribunal and other parties on the day of the hearing, sometimes at the outset of proceedings, and sometimes after the evidence has completed and the Tribunal is about to hear oral submissions. In the latter case, the Tribunal will often adjourn for a short period to read the written skeleton argument first and then proceed to hear oral submissions from the parties.

19.89 *Witnesses*

Rule 43 deals with witnesses. It provides that where a witness is called to give oral evidence, any witness statement of that person ordered by the Tribunal shall stand as that witness's evidence in chief unless the Tribunal orders otherwise. Acting under *Rule 43*, a Tribunal can decide to exclude parts of a witness statement (for example, if inadmissible in evidence). *Rule 43* requires witnesses to give their oral evidence on oath or affirmation.

Witnesses give their evidence seated at a table and should address the Judge as 'Sir' or 'Madam'. If, as is almost always required in England and Wales, a written witness statement has been prepared, the tribunal will normally have pre-read the statement themselves (for guidance as to the reading of witness statements see *Mehta v Child Support Agency* [2011] IRLR 305). Additional questions may then be asked if necessary, with the permission of the tribunal. Where a claimant is unrepresented, the Judge may ask more questions to elicit relevant matters. In Scotland, evidence-in-chief is given by way of answers to questions from the party's representative, or if the party has no representative, by way of narrative or in answer to questions from the tribunal.

Documents should be introduced in the witness statements in chronological or other systematic order by the witness who can best deal with them. It is desirable, if possible, to cross-refer in the written witness statements to the page numbers of any relevant documents, and to invite the tribunal to read the documents or relevant parts together with the witness statement.

Detailed guidance is now provided in the Presidential Guidance on General Case Management concerning how a witness statement should be prepared. That guidance stresses the need for witness statements to be typed if possible, for the statement to be in logical, numbered paragraphs and should cover all the issues in the case and set out fully what the witness has to tell the Tribunal about their involvement in chronological order. The Guidance also underlines the fact that, as additional questions are only allowed in limited circumstances, the statement should be as full as possible. A supplemental statement should be prepared if something has been left out of a witness statement and should be exchanged with the other party "immediately". Otherwise, mutual exchange of witness statements is usual, although sometimes the Tribunal can order sequential exchange.

When the representative of one party cross-examines a witness of the other party, he or she should put questions to the witness and not make comments or statements. It must be remembered that there is a dual purpose to cross-examination. One is to test the truthfulness and reliability of the witness; the other is to put the questioner's version of the facts to the witness so far as it concerns him or her, so that he or she has an opportunity of commenting on it. A failure to do this may prejudice the cross-examiner's case. It is a general principle that a party or representative may not cross-examine his or her own witness; the concept of a 'hostile witness' is in practice almost unknown.

Parties acting in person, and non-legally qualified representatives, often have difficulty in cross-examining witnesses, through inexperience or unfamiliarity with what is required. In these circumstances the Judge may assist in giving guidance as to what questions can be asked and how they may be put, but should not take over the cross-examination of the witness, as this may lead to an appearance of bias in favour of the party being assisted. How far a Judge will be prepared to go in assisting a party in these circumstances is very much a matter of personal style, and therefore dependent on the particular Judge.

Witnesses will not normally be permitted to refer to notes whilst giving evidence, unless these are agreed documents or a note taken by the witness at the time of an event or very soon thereafter; the witness may refer to such notes to refresh his or her memory of the event.

Rule 43 also gives the Tribunal a power to exclude from the hearing any person who is to appear as a witness in the proceedings until such time as that person gives evidence if it considers it in the interests of justice to do so. In Scotland it is the practice to require witnesses to wait outside the tribunal room until they are called to give their evidence; however, this is very infrequently done in English or Welsh proceedings.

The powers of the tribunal extend to a power to call witnesses of its own initiative (or at the request of a party who is for some good reason unable or unwilling to call the witness): *Clapson v British Airways plc* [2001] IRLR 184. The evidence given by a witness in tribunal proceedings carries absolute privilege in the law of defamation, and is also within the principle of judicial immunity from suit which applies generally to judicial proceedings. Thus in *Parmar v East Leicester Medical Practice* [2011] IRLR 641 it was held that statements in a witness statement prepared for tribunal proceedings could not be used to found a claim of victimisation. However the principle of judicial proceedings immunity is not wide enough to cover intimidating behaviour directed by a respondent at the claimant outside the tribunal room: *Nicholls v Corin Tech Ltd* (UKEAT/0290/07). The practice in the past has been that witnesses attending a hearing have been entitled to reclaim their travelling and subsistence expenses from the administration. However the repayment of witness expenses was discontinued from 6 April 2012, for cases presented on or after that date; instead the tribunal has power to order a party to pay the witness's expenses (the paying party may either be the party calling the witness or the opposing party): see below in relation to costs.

Rule 44 provides that, subject to any restrictive order the Tribunal makes on grounds of privacy or national security (under *Rules 50* and *94*), any witness statement which stands as evidence in chief shall be available for inspection during the course of the hearing by members of the public attending the hearing unless the Tribunal decides that all or any part of the statement is not to be admitted as evidence, in which case the statement or that part shall not be available for inspection. An illustration of *Rule 44* in operation is *Compass Group Plc v Guardian News and Media Ltd* [2014] UKEAT/0041/14 in which the EAT remitted to the Judge the issue of whether he had excluded the excised parts of the statement from evidence altogether, applying *Rule 43* (in which case those parts were not available for inspection by the public and media) or whether he had merely chosen to pay no attention to the parts in question (in which case inspection of the whole statement would be permitted under *Rule 44* with no further formality required).

19.90 *Non-Attendance and Postponements*

By *Rule 47*, if a party fails to attend or to be represented at the hearing, the Tribunal may dismiss the claim or proceed with the hearing in the absence of that party. Before doing so, it shall consider any information which is available to it, after any enquiries that may be practicable, about the reasons for the party's absence.

An alternative course either on the non-attendance of a party, or on application of a party, is to postpone (or if started, adjourn) the hearing to another date under the general case management power of *Rule 29*. Special provision has now been made in the *Rules* for applications for postponements (which term includes adjournments which cause the hearing to be held or continued on a later date): see *Rule 30A*. These provisions (which are applicable to all proceedings which are presented to a tribunal on or after 6 April 2016) restrict the scope of the general case management power under *Rule 29*. *Rule 30A* provides that:

(a)   Any application for a postponement must ("shall") be presented to the Tribunal and communicated to the other parties as soon as possible after the need for a postponement becomes known (*Rule 30A(1)*)

(b)   If a party applies to postpone a hearing less than 7 days before the date on which the hearing begins, the Tribunal is constrained in its ability to allow a postponement. It may only order a postponement in one of three circumstances (*Rule 30A(2)*):

    (i)   All the other parties consent to a postponement and it is practicable and appropriate for the purposes of giving the parties the opportunity to resolve their disputes by agreement, or it is otherwise in accordance with the overriding objective;

    (ii)   The application was necessitated by an act or omission of another party or the Tribunal; or

    (iii)   There are exceptional circumstances (which may include ill health relating to an existing long term health condition or disability).

(c)   Where a Tribunal has ordered two or more postponements of a hearing in the same proceedings on the application of the same party, and that party makes an application for a further postponement, such an application may only be granted in the three circumstances listed in (b) above (*Rule 30A(3)*).

Further, amendments have been made to *Rule 76(1)* to provide that where a postponement or adjournment has been granted on application of a party made less than 7 days before the date on which the relevant hearing begins, the Tribunal may make an award of costs against that party.

Subject to those provisions, there are a wide range of circumstances in which the Tribunal will be called upon to exercise its discretion as to whether or not to adjourn or postpone proceedings. When considering whether or not to postpone, the Tribunal must also have regard to the Presidential Guidance issued concerning seeking a Postponement of a Hearing. That guidance provides as follows.

Applications for a postponement should be made in writing and should state why the application is made and why it would be in accordance with the overriding objective to grant the postponement. (One might now add that parties applying in the circumstances captured by *Rule 30A* should set out why they contend those provisions have been satisfied.) Where application is made in writing, the party must notify the other parties that they should send any objections to the tribunal as soon as possible. It is important for parties to appreciate the need to enclose all documents relevant to the application with the application. If these requirements are not complied with, then the application will ordinarily not be considered absent exceptional circumstances. Where exceptional circumstances are relied upon, they should be detailed in the application. The guidance also states that the party wishing to make an application for postponement should wherever possible discuss the proposal either directly with the other parties or through their representatives. If this discussion has taken place, then the detail should be provided to the Tribunal. Where agreement is reached, the Tribunal should be told of this fact. The Guidance draws parties' attention to the fact that where the hearing has been fixed with the agreement of the parties, this will be a factor which is taken into account by the Judge when considering the postponement application.

The Guidance goes on to provide specific examples of additional information that would be of assistance to the Tribunal in different circumstances. This is referred to where relevant in the discussion of the case law below.

One situation which arises relatively frequently is the failure of a party (often, but not always the claimant) to attend coupled with an application for an adjournment of the hearing on the grounds of the absent party's ill-health. Guidance has been given by the Court of Appeal prior to *Rule 30A* in two cases – *Teinaz v Wandsworth London Borough Council* [2002] EWCA Civ 1040, [2002] IRLR 721 and *Andreou v Lord Chancellor's Department* [2002] EWCA Civ 1192, [2002] IRLR 728 – as to how a tribunal should apply the conflicting considerations of justice when such an application is made on or immediately before the date of the hearing. Where *Rule 30A(2)* applies, the main issue will be whether or not there are "exceptional circumstances" entitling the tribunal to permit the postponement. The definition of "exceptional circumstances" in *Rule 30A(4)* is inclusive, specifically referring to ill health relating to an existing long term health conditions or disabilities. Short term or sudden ill health is not, however, excluded and where applicable is likely to be regarded as capable of amounting to an exceptional circumstance. It would therefore seem unlikely that *Rule 30A(2)* will make a substantive change in relation to this class of postponement applications. The Court of Appeal's guidance in *Teinaz* and *Andreou* emphasises that the tribunal is entitled to require clear medical evidence to satisfy it that the impediment to attendance is genuine, the burden being on the party making the application. If there is clear and uncontradicted evidence that a party is medically unfit to attend the hearing, it will often be an error of law to proceed with the hearing in the absence of a party, even if this causes considerable inconvenience or delay to the proceedings, since the absent party is in effect denied a fair hearing of his or her case: see *Chang-Tave v Haydon School* (UKEAT/0153/10). The *Teinaz* case itself also relied expressly on *ECHR, Art 6* as demanding nothing less than an adjournment in those circumstances (see e.g. para 21). That said, in *Transport for London v O'Cathail* [2013] IRLR 310, the Court of Appeal held that it can be legitimate for a tribunal to take the exceptional step of rejecting an application for an adjournment on medical grounds, even in the face of unchallenged medical evidence supporting an adjournment. The Court emphasised that whilst the position of the potentially absent claimant is highly relevant, it is not determinative of every case. Overall fairness to both parties must be considered in the round and not pre-determined by the situation of one of the parties. *Art 6 of the ECHR* does not compel the tribunal to the conclusion that it is always unfair to refuse an application for an adjournment on medical grounds, if it would mean that the hearing would take place in the party's absence: the tribunal must balance the adverse consequences of proceeding with the hearing in the absence of one party against the right of the other party to have a trial within reasonable time and the public interest in prompt and efficient adjudication of cases.

The examples in the Presidential Guidance on Postponements, in line with this case law, states that where a party or witness is unable to attend for medical reasons, a medical certificate and supporting medical evidence should be provided in addition to an explanation of the nature of the health condition concerned. If medical evidence is supplied, it should include a statement from the medical practitioner that in their opinion, the applicant is unfit to attend the hearing, the prognosis of the condition and an indication of when that state of affairs may cease.

Where the evidence is unclear as to the applicant's fitness to attend or continue with the hearing, *Teinaz* emphasised that the tribunal has a power to give a direction to enable doubts to be resolved, e.g. by allowing for a short adjournment for further enquiries to be made. In *Iqbal v Metropolitan Police Authority* (UKEAT/0186/12), the EAT held that where an application for an adjournment on health grounds is made during the hearing, the tribunal should have regard to medical evidence including that in the bundle (e.g. expert and occupational health reports). Further, HHJ Richardson held when making further enquiries, a tribunal was entitled to entitled to ask the litigant to take with him a short letter drafted by the Tribunal explaining the assistance that the Tribunal can give to litigants in person and explaining what assistance and opinion it is that is required from the medical practitioner (para 20). Further enquiries will not, however always be required. In a "perhaps rare" case, the EAT in *Ejiofor t/a Mitchell & Co Solicitors v Sullivan* [2014] UKEAT/0268/13 upheld the judge's decision to proceed without more, despite a sick note being produced (the judge had found that a sick note had been "produced simply to add spurious weight to a weak and very late application for an adjournment"). Further guidance on the factors to be weighed up in determining last minute applications to adjourn was given in *D'Silva v Manchester Metropolitan University* (UKEAT/0336/09/LA) [2011] All ER (D) 05 (May), where the EAT upheld a decision to refuse an adjournment sought on the ground that the claimant claimed to be unfit to appear (but without supporting medical evidence) and sought an adjournment to arrange for representation, having lost his legal representation just before the hearing; the EAT held that the claimant was an educated and intelligent man with a full grasp of his claim and was therefore not sufficiently disadvantaged by the lack of representation to justify the cost and inconvenience to the respondent of an adjournment.

It is also not uncommon in practice that one party or the other does not attend without prior warning or explanation. The Court of Appeal has ruled that if the claimant fails to attend the hearing, the tribunal has a very wide discretion in the light of the available evidence whether to dismiss the claim, proceed in the claimant's absence or adjourn to another date: *Roberts v Skelmersdale College* [2003] EWCA Civ 954, [2003] ICR 1127. The usual procedure in such a case, whether it is the claimant or respondent who has failed to attend, is for a member of the tribunal staff to telephone the party concerned to seek an explanation for their absence. This practice was endorsed by the EAT in *Cooke v Glenrose Fish Co* [2004] ICR 1188, and the EAT has since held that a failure to attempt to contact the missing party would provide grounds for a review of any decision taken in that party's absence: *Euro Hotels (Thornton Heath) Ltd v Alam* (UKEAT/0006/09). The same approach was adopted by the

EAT in a case where the parties had been ordered to lodge written submissions, the claimant's had not been received, and the tribunal proceeded to reach its decision without any attempt to contact him to find out what had happened: *Quashie v Methodist Homes Housing Association* (UKEAT/0422/11). The EAT held that the tribunal was not entitled to assume that the claimant had decided not to make submissions, and its failure to investigate the matter deprived her of a fair hearing.

An option often adopted in practice when the claimant fails to attend, if the claim is of unfair dismissal, where the respondent has the initial burden of proof, is for the tribunal to hear the respondent's evidence and submissions before deciding the case on its merits, in the absence of the claimant. If the claimant does not attend for claimed medical reasons but without providing sufficient evidence of incapacity, the tribunal may refer the case to a PHR to consider striking the claim out as not being actively pursued; see *Rolls Royce Ltd v Riddle* [2008] IRLR 873; but see also *Abegaze v Shrewsbury College of Arts and Technology* [2009] EWCA Civ 96, [2009] All ER (D) 209 (Feb) and **19.17** above.

In the case of non-attendance of a respondent, if when contacted by the tribunal an excuse or explanation for non-attendance is offered, the respondent should be told of the right to apply for an adjournment, and any such application must be considered before the tribunal decides how to proceed: *Beswick Paper Ltd v Britton* (UKEAT/0104/09); this would presumably equally be so if it is the claimant who fails to attend but proffers an explanation. See also *Southwark London Borough Council v Bartholomew* [2004] ICR 358, EAT. If the respondent fails to appear without good reason having been given, the tribunal will usually agree to hear the claimant's case and give a decision in the respondent's absence.

If a representative for the party attends, the representative is entitled to be heard even though the party has not attended (see *Astles v A G Stanley Ltd* (UKEAT/1275/95), IDS Brief 588). It is also not uncommon that both parties attend the hearing but an application is made for an adjournment because of a last minute development affecting the conduct of the case, most commonly the sudden illness of an important witness. As indicated above, such applications are likely now to be caught by *Rule 30A(2)*. In such a case, the tribunal will consider the matter in the light of the views of both parties, and balancing the interests of justice as between the parties. Where *Rule 30A(2)* applies, one of the three bases on which the application may be allowed must be made out. A pre-Rule 30A(2) example can be found in *North Bristol NHS Trust v Harrold* (UKEAT/0548/11), where the EAT endorsed a tribunal's decision to refuse a respondent's application to adjourn a hearing on the final day of a three-day hearing in order to allow the respondent to call further witnesses; the EAT held a tribunal should not accede automatically to the wishes of one of the litigants, but rather balance the interests of both parties.

Turning to other grounds for seeking a postponement, in *Firouzian v Metroline Travel Ltd* (UKEAT/0233/12), the EAT held the tribunal was entitled to refuse to adjourn what is now a preliminary hearing on the question of disability until after the claimant's criminal trial. That trial was in respect of causing death by dangerous driving arising out of his employment as a bus driver. The claims of disability and race discrimination arose from how the claimant was allegedly dealt with under internal proceedings as a result of the same driving incident. The EAT held there was no risk of prejudicing the criminal trial because of the lack of overlap between the issues on the preliminary hearing and that trial. The tribunal had been entitled to refuse to postpone the preliminary hearing.

The Presidential Guidance now covers this situation. It indicates where there are other court proceedings (whether civil or criminal) details should be given as to when these proceedings were commenced, what they entail, and how it is said that they will affect the Tribunal case, or how the Tribunal proceedings will affect those other proceedings.

If the case is determined in the absence of a party and it later transpires that that party had not received notification of the hearing date, the tribunal may reconsider its decision: see **19.74–19.75** above. An application for reconsideration may also be made, and would need to be considered on its merits, if there is any other reason for the absence of the party which had not been known to the tribunal when a decision to proceed with the hearing had been taken. The issue for the tribunal will in each case be what is the balance of the interests of justice as between the decision reached standing or being set aside and the case being referred for a hearing, or re-hearing. It may be relevant to the determination of this point that the expense and inconvenience to the attending party of a re-hearing can be compensated by an order for costs; but it is generally a factor of little weight against ordering a re-hearing that the party whose representative failed to attend the hearing may recover any losses from the representative: see *Euro Hotels (Thornton Heath) Ltd v Alam*, above.

The Presidential Guidance considers other situations. Where parties and witnesses are not available this should be notified to the Tribunal as soon as possible stating the details of the witness or party concerned; what attempts have been made to make alternative arrangements; the reason for the unavailability and in the case of a witness, the relevance of their evidence. Any supporting documents should be provided. The same approach should be followed where a representative has become unavailable or a newly appointed representative is unavailable. It sometimes happens that a party's representative will withdraw shortly before a hearing. Where this has occurred, the Presidential Guidance indicates that details should be given as to when this has happened and whether alternative representation has been or is being sought.

If an outstanding appeal to the EAT or other appellant court is relevant to the hearing, details of the dates of the appeal and the matters being appealed should be provided. This is frequently encountered where, for example, a liability determination of the tribunal is appealed and a postponement is sought of a listed remedy hearing. In such circumstances, Tribunals are often keen to know when the appeal was lodged and whether the appeal has been considered by the EAT on the preliminary sift process under *Rule 3(7)* of the *EAT Rules*. If an appeal has passed through the EAT's sift, the Tribunal will know that the appeal has reasonable prospects of success and this is likely to affect the decision to postpone. However it does not always mean that a postponement will be granted. There can be situations where it is more appropriate for the case to complete all parts of the first instance decision making so that all appeals can be heard in one go.

If the basis of an application is late disclosure of information or documentation, then details of the failure to disclose, and the contents of the documents or information, should be given. The applicant should also explain how the documents/information are relevant to the issues in the case and how the late provision relates to Orders which have already been given in the case, and any requests made by the parties for such information or documents, and the responses to those requests that have been received.

Finally the Guidance indicates that Employment Judges are now encouraged to take a more pro-active approach to applications to postpone. If information has not been supplied, then an application may become the subject of a further enquiry from the Judge (although this will have the effect of delaying the determination of the application). Once all the relevant information is available, the Judge is to take into account all matters and information now available, and consider whether to grant or refuse the postponement. The decision remains in the discretion of the Judge concerned. The decision is notified to the parties as soon as possible after the decision has been made.

19.91 *Privacy and Restrictions on Disclosure: General*

Rule 50(1) gives a Tribunal a discretion, at any stage of the proceedings, on its own initiative or on application, to make an order with a view to preventing or restricting the public disclosure of any aspect of those proceedings so far as it considers necessary in the interests of justice or in order to protect the Convention rights of any person or in the circumstances identified in *ETA 1996, s 10A. Rule 50(2)* goes on to provide that in considering whether to make an order under this rule, the Tribunal shall give full weight to the principle of open justice and to the Convention right to freedom of expression.

The new formulation of *Rule 50* enables the Tribunal to make the orders that were previously available under the old rules, as well as widening the discretion to enable Tribunals to take action expressly to cover the protection of convention rights, albeit without losing sight of the principle of open justice. "Convention rights" within the meaning of this rule, has the same meaning as set out in *HRA 1998, s 1*: see *Rule 50(6)*. For the position prior to the enactment of *Rule 50* and the case law to similar effect, see the restricted reporting order section below.

Rule 50(3) contains a list of the types of Order that a Tribunal can now make:

(a)   an order that a hearing that would otherwise be in public be conducted, in whole or in part, in private;

(b)   an order that the identities of specified parties, witnesses or other persons referred to in the proceedings should not be disclosed to the public, by the use of anonymisation or otherwise, whether in the course of any hearing or in its listing or in any documents entered on the Register or otherwise forming part of the public record;

(c)   an order for measures preventing witnesses at a public hearing being identifiable by members of the public;

(d)   a restricted reporting order within the terms of *ETA 1996, s 11* or *12* (see section below).

The *Rule* permits any party – or a person with a legitimate interest – to make representations to the Tribunal before such an order is made. If no such opportunity was granted, then such a person has the right to apply to the Tribunal in writing for the order to be revoked or discharged either on the basis of written representations, or, if requested, at a hearing: *Rule 50(4)*.

19.92 *Restricted Reporting Orders*

Some employment tribunal cases involving allegations of sexual misconduct attract considerable publicity in the media, all too often prurient and embarrassing to those involved. In order to diminish the adverse effect on the parties of such publicity, the *ET* and *EAT Rules* contain powers for tribunals and the EAT respectively to restrict publication of material identifying those involved in such cases. These were first given by the *1993 ET Regulations* and *EAT Rules*, which introduced the power to make restricted reporting orders and register deletion orders. Equivalent powers were introduced by the *Disability Discrimination Act 1995* for cases where evidence of a personal nature is to be given (see now the *ETA 1996, ss 12* and *32*).

The provisions relating to restricted reporting orders are now contained in *rule 50* of the *2013 Rules* as we have seen and *rules 23* and *23A* of the *EAT Rules*. A restricted reporting order may be made by the tribunal of its own motion or on the application of a party. The precondition is that the case involves allegations of sexual misconduct. This is not limited to claims of discrimination by sexual harassment; it may include cases where the applicant's dismissal was for an alleged sexual offence (see eg *Securicor Guarding Ltd v R* [1994] IRLR 633) or any other proceedings in which allegations of sexual misconduct are expected to form part of the evidence, and regardless of whether or not the allegations can be substantiated: *X v Stevens* [2003] IRLR 411. 'Sexual misconduct' means a sexual offence, sexual harassment or other adverse conduct, of whatever nature, related to sex: *ETA 1996, s 11(6)*. The criterion in disability discrimination cases is whether 'evidence of a personal nature' is likely to be given (*ETA 1996, s 12(1)*). The primary purpose of a restricted reporting order is to protect parties, and sometimes witnesses, from being placed under inappropriate pressure when giving evidence by the fear of the publicity that may be given to their evidence. It prohibits, subject to criminal penalty, the publication in Great Britain of any matter likely to lead members of the public to identify a person as the person making, or a person affected by, the allegations of misconduct or, in a disability case, to identify the complainant or any other person named in the order (*ETA 1996, ss 11(2), 12(3)*). The scope of the power to make orders enables protection to be given not only to the alleged victim and miscreant in a sexual misconduct case, but also the employer, and individual employee respondents to the claim, if not directly covered otherwise. However, the EAT has ruled (departing from a previous decision) that a body corporate cannot be the subject of a restricted reporting order (*Leicester University v A* [1999] IRLR 352, following *R v London (North) Industrial Tribunal, ex p Associated Newspapers Ltd* [1998] ICR 1212 in preference to *M v Vincent* [1998] ICR 73).

When making a restricted reporting order, by *Rule 50(5)*, the Tribunal must (a) specify the person whose identity is protected; and may specify particular matters of which publication is prohibited as likely to lead to that person's identification – this is not in order to protect their identity but because identifying them would lead to the identification of those for whose protection the order is made: *Tradition Securities & Futures SA v Times Newspapers Ltd* [2009] IRLR 354; (b) specify the duration of the order; (c) ensure that a notice of the fact that such an order has been made in relation to those proceedings is displayed on the notice board of the Tribunal with any list of the proceedings taking place before the Tribunal, and on the door of the room in which the proceedings affected by the order are taking place; and (d) the Tribunal may order that it applies also to any other proceedings being heard as part of the same hearing.

Because of the wider public interest in justice being dispensed publicly, tribunals should not automatically order a restriction on publication simply – indeed especially – because both parties seek it: *X v Z Ltd* [1998] ICR 43, CA. The point was followed in *R v London (North) Industrial Tribunal, ex p Associated Newspapers Ltd* (above), in which Keene J stated that the words 'a person affected by the allegations of misconduct' should be interpreted narrowly, having regard to the principle of the freedom of the press to report court and tribunal proceedings fully and contemporaneously. In *Vatish v Crown Prosecution Service* (UKEAT/0164/11) the EAT set aside an order made to protect a witness who had not asked for protection and whose evidence had already been given by the time the order was made.

The wider interest in public justice is reflected in both *Rule 50(2)* – see above – and the fact that interested parties (in practice this will almost always be media representatives) have the right to make representations at the hearing at which the decision is made whether to impose an order or the right to ask for the order to be revoked: *Rule 50(4)*. In *Fallows and others v News Group Newspapers Ltd* [2016] ICR 801, Simler P held that *Rule 50(4)* had no temporal limitation and an application could be made even after the claim had been settled and withdrawn. A tribunal was not functus for these purposes after withdrawal of the claim. Under the old rules (which did not so provide), the Court of Session, overruling the EAT, held that tribunals can entertain applications from the press for an order to be revoked: *Davidson v Dallas McMillan* [2009] CSIH 70, [2010] IRLR 439. In addition, as the EAT noted in *Dallas McMillan*, it is open to press organisations to apply to be joined as parties to the proceedings for the purpose of making such an application; this was done in *Tradition Securities*, above.

Under the *2004 ET Rules* a new power was introduced enabling a Judge to make a temporary restricted reporting order, either on application by a party or of his or her own motion, and either without any hearing, or at a case management hearing. The parties were to be notified of a temporary order and informed of their right to apply for the continuance of the order; if no party applied within 14 days, the order lapsed, but if an application to continue it was made, the order remained in force until the question whether it should be continued could be determined at another hearing: see *Rule 50(2)–(5)* of the *2004 Rules*). Under the *2013 Rules* a tailored Order can still be made by the Tribunal creating the same effect: see the general discretion under *Rule 50*. This can be useful to deal with the situation where a party anticipates media interest in the case and seeks emergency protection from publicity.

A restricted reporting order remains in force until the promulgation of the final judgment in the case, unless revoked earlier. The EAT in the *Tradition Securities* case, above, held that an application to revoke, or vary the terms of, an order should only be entertained if there has been a change in the relevant circumstances since the order was made; but such changes may include the fact that a representative of the press, having become aware of the order, seeks to have the order revoked or varied (see now *Rule 50(4)*), or that a party for whose benefit the order was made now no longer wishes to have the protection afforded.

Once a final judgment has been given, the restriction on reporting the identities of those covered by the order falls away (unless the Tribunal has specified an earlier date in its order). This underlines the point that the purpose of the order is not to provide indefinite or permanent anonymity for the individuals covered by the order, but rather to ensure that they are not unduly pressured by the fear of publicity in giving their evidence. Where the judgment is given separately on liability and the tribunal will need to hold a further hearing to decide on remedy, the can order remains in force until the final remedy judgment is issued unless the Tribunal orders otherwise; see also *Chief Constable of West Yorkshire Police v A* [2001] ICR 128. Under the old rules it was established that the tribunal had no power to entertain an application for the revocation of an order once the proceedings are at an end: see *Davidson v Dallas McMillan*, above, where the point was expressly confirmed by the Court of Session. This had the consequence that if the claim is settled after liability has been determined but before a remedy hearing is concluded, or is withdrawn, the order can remain in force indefinitely. See now *Fallows and others*, above, which also confirms that an RRO does not automatically expire upon withdrawal under the new rules and that an application under *Rule 50(4)* can be made post withdrawal.

A notice drawing attention to the existence of the order must be placed on the tribunal door (*Rule 50(5)(c)*).

Guidance as to the scope and dissemination of orders has also been given by the High Court in *R v Southampton Industrial Tribunal, ex p INS News Group Ltd* [1995] IRLR 247.

Other Privacy Orders

Under the *2004 Rules*, the relatively narrow category of cases in which restrictive reporting orders can be made, and the limited duration of the protection conferred by an order, might have resulted in individuals being embarrassed, or subjected to harassment, if their identity was publicised, being deterred from bringing claims by the lack of protection available. Considerations of this kind led the tribunal in the *West Yorkshire* case, above, to hold that there is a further power to order restrictions on reporting tribunal proceedings in any case where this is necessary to ensure that a claimant seeking to assert enforceable rights under EU law (in this case a remedy for refusal to engage the claimant as a police officer because she was a transsexual) is not deterred from doing so by fear of publicity. The basis for this decision was the requirement of *art 6* of the *Equal Treatment Directive 1976* for member states to afford access to effective remedies for victims of unlawful sex discrimination. This point was expressly left open by the EAT in the *West Yorkshire* case, but in *X v Stevens*, above, it held that both the EAT under its inherent jurisdiction, and tribunals using their powers to regulate their own procedure, could make restricted reporting orders where this was necessary in order to prevent a claimant from being deterred from pursuing a claim, and regardless of whether the statutory conditions for a restricted reporting order or register deletion order were met and whether the respondent was or was not a state authority. The basis for this power was initially stated to be the effective enforcement of rights under EU law. An alternative, and wider power was derived from the obligation of a tribunal (and the EAT) as a public body to give effect so far as it can to the rights safeguarded by the *European Convention on Human Rights*: this is required by the *Human Rights Act 1998, s 6*. The rights protected include those to privacy under Art 8; in an appropriate case the conferring of anonymity on a party or witness may be justified as a means of safeguarding that person's *Art 8* rights. The EAT in *A v B* [2010] IRLR 844 (supplementary judgment at p 856) applied this principle to justify the making of a permanent anonymity order in relation to an appeal where the claimant had been the subject of unsubstantiated allegations of paedophile activities. A similar conclusion was reached in *B and C v A* [2010] IRLR 400, where the EAT considered a permanent anonymity order to be justified to protect a complainant of sexual violence (not the claimant in the case).The reliance in these cases on *Art 8* of the *Convention* provided a basis also for orders to be made protecting the identity of those who are not parties, or even witnesses, in the proceedings, where identification would be a sufficiently serious and unjustified interference with their privacy. This point was confirmed by the EAT in *F v G* [2012] ICR 246, where a permanent order was made to protect the identity of severely disabled students at the respondent college in circumstances where evidence about their sexual lives would be given in the course of the proceedings. The judgment of Underhill P in this case contains a full and helpful discussion of the range of orders that could be made and the basis for each.

This body of case law has affected the drafting of the 2013 Rules. It has been seen above that *Rule 50(1)* entitles the Tribunal to make wider orders than classic restricted reporting orders where to do would protect Convention rights of any person, or in circumstances under *ETA 1996, s 10A*. An example of a permanent order made under the *2013 Rules* can be seen in *EF v AB* [2015] IRLR 619, a case involving lurid revelations and allocations of sexual misconduct made by an ex-employee against the CEO and his wife. Slade J undertook a helpful review of the authorities and held that all the sexual conduct in question took place in private and there was a reasonable expectation of privacy which applied even though some of the information might have been true, and some false (para 59). On the balancing exercise between open justice and the *Art 8 ECHR* rights, she held the latter must prevail, relying on a number of factors including the effect on relevant children, and the reasonable expectation of privacy (para 84). A somewhat contrasting approach can be seen in *BBC v Roden* [2015] IRLR 627. There, during the course for an unsuccessful unfair dismissal complaint, allegations of sexual assault by the claimant emerged. A permanent anonymity order was made by the employment judge to protect the claimant's identity but this was lifted by the EAT. Simler J stressed the importance of open justice and that Art 6 ECHR guaranteed a publically proclaimed judgment. *Arts 8* and *10 ECHR* were also engaged. When values under different articles conflicted, an intense focus on the comparative importance of the specific rights being claimed in the particular case was required. In the present case the weight to be attached to the claimant's *Art 8* right was low and the Tribunal had failed to undertake the required balancing exercise. The only factor identified by the judge in that case as outweighing the principle of open justice was the risk of reputational damage to the claimant by public misunderstanding of the sexual allegations. However, Simler J held that the public should be "trusted to distinguish between an allegation and a finding of guilt" and there was no proper basis for the permanent anonymity order.

In practice it is relatively common that privacy is afforded to individuals who feature in the evidence in a case, such as children or medical patients, by a direction that they are not to be identified by name in the course of evidence, and avoiding identification in the judgment.

For discussion of the equivalent provisions governing appeals to the EAT, see **20.26** below.

Where allegations of a sexual offence are involved, there was prior to 2004 a separate power to make a 'register deletion order'. This had the effect of requiring that the public register of judgments and any other public documents generated in the proceedings were modified so as to prevent identification of persons making or affected by the allegation (*ETA 1996, s 11(1)(a)*).

Under the *2013 Rules*, it is no longer necessary to have such a separate rule. *Rule 67* is subject to *Rule 50* and the wide powers in that rule enable the Tribunal to take the necessary action, where appropriate, to delete matters from the register in appropriate cases.

19.93 *Private Hearings: Privacy and National Security*

Tribunal hearings are generally conducted in public and may be reported in the media. The requirement to sit in public applies to a final hearing (*Rule 59*) and to a preliminary hearing which determines a preliminary issue or a strike out application (*Rule 56*). Otherwise preliminary hearings are held in private.

The tribunal has power under *Rule 50* to direct that evidence or representations be heard in private if in the opinion of the tribunal it would be likely to consist of information which could not be disclosed without a breach of a statutory prohibition or which had been communicated to or obtained by the person concerned in confidence, or which if publicly disclosed could cause substantial damage to that person's undertaking or the undertaking in which he or she works, for reasons other than the effect of disclosure on collective bargaining (see *ETA 1996, s 10A*). The reference to information obtained in confidence may allow for medical evidence to be given in private. There is power to make an order in advance of the Hearing for particular evidence to be heard in private: *McBride v Standards Board for England* (UKEAT/0092/09). Prior to the new rules, which make this point expressly, the EAT had held that the relevant statutory provisions referred to in *rule 16* of the *2004 Rules* include the tribunal's duty under s 6 of the Human Rights Act 1998 not to act in such a way as to infringe protected human rights, so that there may be a duty to sit in private for the reception of evidence if the public reception of the evidence would be an impermissible violation of the right of privacy of an individual under Art 8 of the Human Rights Convention (*XXX v YYY* [2004] IRLR 137 (reversed by the Court of Appeal on other grounds [2004] IRLR 471), a case involving a video recording containing pictures of a young child). A less drastic way of protecting rights of privacy may be the giving of a direction that particular individuals (such as children or patients) are not to be identified by name in the course of the proceedings. The EAT has also held that where the tribunal has to determine whether particular evidence relied on by one of the parties is privileged as a without prejudice communication, the test for whether the tribunal should sit in private to hear this aspect of the case will depend on whether it is likely that evidence will be given which is covered by the confidentiality attaching to without prejudice communications; if so, that factor has to be balanced against the general public interest in open justice: *Eversheds LLP v Gray* (UKEAT/0585/11). If the tribunal decides to hold a hearing or part thereof in private, it will give reasons for doing so (*Rule 62(1)*); a decision to sit in private, or not to do so, is open to appeal, as occurred in the *Eversheds* case.

In addition, the tribunal may sit in private if directed to do so by a Minister of the Crown for reasons of national security. (*Rule 94*; and see *AB v Ministry of Defence*, UKEAT/0101/09.) *Rule 94* also contains more general powers to control the conduct of tribunal proceedings in national security cases. An example of such an order under equivalent provisions in previous *ET Rules* is *Fry v Foreign and Commonwealth Office* [1997] ICR 512 (order did not extend to excluding claimant's husband who was assisting the presentation of her case). The EAT has suggested that there may be good reasons for 'closed evidence' (ie evidence heard in private session) to be heard before open evidence in cases involving Crown employment and/or national security: *Farooq v Commissioner of Police of the Metropolis* [2008] All ER (D) 187 (Jun). This point was endorsed by the Court of Appeal in *Home Office v Tariq* [2010] EWCA Civ 462, a case in which the Court held that the procedure laid down for cases involving national security (*Sch 2* to the *ET Regulations 2004*), involving the exclusion of the claimant from part of the proceedings with a Special Advocate appointed to represent his interests during that part of the hearing, was not incompatible with *art 6* of the *European Convention on Human Rights*. The Court's decision in *Tariq* has subsequently been upheld by the Supreme Court: *Home Office v Tariq* [2011] UKSC 35, [2011] IRLR 843.

Subject to the provisions permitting a hearing in private, failure to hold the hearing at a place made accessible to the public renders any resulting judgment a nullity, even if no members of the public wished to attend the hearing: *Storer v British Gas plc* [2000] IRLR

495. There is no general power to exclude the press or public from a hearing where the power to sit in private does not apply but the evidence is of a sensitive or salacious nature: *R v Southampton Industrial Tribunal, ex p INS News Group Ltd* [1995] IRLR 247; and see as to the importance attached to tribunal hearings being conducted in public *R v London (North) Industrial Tribunal, ex p Associated Newspapers Ltd* [1998] ICR 1212. The reporting of proceedings in cases involving allegations of sexual misconduct or evidence of a personal nature in disability discrimination cases is subject to special procedures for the restriction of reports identifying the parties concerned: see **19.91** et sec above.

19.94 *Bias or conflict of interest*

A judgment or order of a tribunal will be open to appeal if the circumstances give rise to a perception of bias on the part of the judge or a lay member of the tribunal. The test is an objective one: would a reasonable independent observer, in full possession of the facts, consider that there was a real possibility of bias, arising either from the relationship between the judge or member and a party or witness, or the conduct of the hearing. The former aspect is considered in this section; as to allegations of bias in relation to the conduct of the hearing see **20.23–20.24** below. If any tribunal member has any connection with either of the parties, or the events in issue in the case, that fact should be made known to all concerned at the outset, and the case relisted before a fresh tribunal if necessary (*University College of Swansea v Cornelius* [1988] ICR 735). If a party raises an objection to the composition of the tribunal before the hearing commences, then unless that objection is irresponsible or frivolous it is preferable to reconstitute the tribunal if possible (*Halford v Sharples* [1992] ICR 146 at 171, EAT, a point not considered further when the case reached the Court of Appeal). See further on the circumstances in which participation by a particular Tribunal Judge or member in a hearing may be regarded as creating an appearance of bias *Locabail (UK) Ltd v Bayfield Properties Ltd* [2000] QB 451, [2000] 1 All ER 65, [2000] 2 WLR 870, [2000] IRLR 96, *Jones v DAS Legal Expenses Insurance Co Ltd* [2003] EWCA Civ 1071, [2004] IRLR 218, *Hamilton v GMB*, [2007] IRLR 391 and *Honey v Swansea City Council* [2008] All ER (D) 311 (Nov) (where failure by one of the lay members of the tribunal to disclose that he was, in his capacity as a trade union official, involved in a current dispute with the respondent local authority led to the judgment of the tribunal being set aside). The tests applied by the EAT in cases of alleged bias are discussed further at **20.23–20.24** below.

A finding of an appearance of bias was made in *Peninsula Business Services Ltd v Rees* (UKEAT/0335/08) where the (part-time) judge was in practice as a solicitor, and her firm had advertised its services as superior to those offered by consultants, of whom the appellant was one of the best known; by implication it could be thought her firm, and hence she, had an interest adverse to that of the appellant firm. It was also held that this point no longer applied in a second case involving the same judge and appellant heard after she had taken up a full-time appointment, as the conflict of interest could no longer apply. By contrast, the EAT rejected an allegation of apparent bias where the judge's daughter was a partner in the firm representing the claimant: *South Lanarkshire Council v Burns* (UKEATS/0040/12).

Whilst a connection between the judge (or a lay member) and a party or witness is likely, unless the parties consent to the judge or member sitting, to provide grounds for appeal, this is much less likely to be so where the connection is with a representative of one of the parties; see for instance *Williams v Cater Link Ltd* (UKEAT/0393/08): no perception of bias where (full-time) judge had whilst still in practice instructed counsel subsequently appearing for one of the parties in the case. A fundamental point is that the judge must not have any kind of financial interest in the proceedings. Technically, this would extend to minor interests such as holding a small shareholding in a large corporation that is the respondent to the proceedings; in practice parties would be unlikely to object to the judge sitting in these circumstances, but the interest should be disclosed. Interests held in common with large sections of the population, such as being a resident and Council Tax payer in the area of a local authority that is a respondent, or a user of the services of a utility or transport company, need not be declared.

The *Jones* case (above) makes the important point that if the Judge discloses an interest and invites the parties to indicate whether they agree to the case proceeding before him or her, and a party makes no objection, then provided that sufficient disclosure of the potential conflict of interest has been given, the party will be taken to have waived any right to challenge the fairness of the hearing on appeal by reference to the Judge's declared interest. The Court of Appeal also stressed the importance of giving the parties, particularly if unrepresented, a full explanation of the options available to them and time to consider their position, and of taking a full note of what the parties are told. These principles were applied by the EAT in *Adamson v Swansea University* (UKEAT/0486/09), where it was held that the claimant had given informed consent to the case being heard by an employment judge who had disclosed a personal acquaintance with a witness in the case. In *Bhardwaj v FDA & others* [2016] IRLR 789, the Court of Appeal held that an ET had provided the claimant with all material facts when it informed her that one of the respondents was a lay member in the same region and her waiver of her right to object was valid and irrevocable.

The fact that an accusation of bias has previously been made against a Judge by one of the parties, or that the Judge has in previous proceedings made adverse comments about a party or witness, is not of itself a reason for the Judge to withdraw from hearing a case (in technical language, to recuse him or herself): *Ansar v Lloyds TSB Bank plc* [2006] EWCA Civ 1462, [2007] IRLR 211, a case in which the Court of Appeal set out detailed guidance on the relevant principles to be applied. *WestLB AG London Branch v Pan* (UKEAT/0308/11) is an example of the application of *Ansar* by the EAT to overturn a decision by the employment judge to recuse herself after an objection by the claimant, taken without giving the other party a chance to be heard, and despite the judge considering that the objection was not justified. In *Papajak v Intellego Group Ltd* (UKEAT/0124/12) the EAT held, unremarkably, that an allegation of bias founded upon the judge having determined (different) issues against a litigant previously was without merit. However, note that where a firm conclusion on an issue is reached and the same issue is later re-heard by the same tribunal, the EAT has held that there is a real possibility of bias: *Menzies Distribution Ltd v Mendes* (UKEAT/0497/13). Whereas expressing a concluded view prior to the conclusion of proceedings can give grounds for a recusal application, the ET did not err in *Hussain v Nottinghamshire Healthcare NHS Trust* [2016] UKEAT/0080/16 where a costs warning was given to a claimant. An informed and impartial observer would not have thought the tribunal biased and the principles in *Oni v NHS Leicester City* [2013] ICR 91 had been complied with. As to the circumstances in which a tribunal should recuse itself where an allegation of bias in the conduct of the case is made by a party or his or her representative, see *Bennett v Southwark London Borough Council* [2002] EWCA Civ 223, [2002] IRLR 407. In sex discrimination cases, both sexes will normally be represented on the tribunal, and in race discrimination cases at least one member should have special knowledge of race relations; however, these are not mandatory requirements.

In *Begraj v Heer Manak Solicitors* (UKEAT/0496/13), the EAT gave guidance as to the appropriate response from a judge/tribunal who/that receives prejudicial information from a third party. In that case the Judge was approached by police officers part way through a lengthy hearing; the officers asked the judge to keep the approach secret from the parties, which the judge did for a week, but then revealed what had happened. Upon application the Tribunal recused itself. The EAT held that it was right to do so and offered the following guidance: (i) where a third party proffers information or opinion about the merits of a case, or the parties in it, to a Tribunal, without invitation, the parties must be made aware of what has happened without delay; (ii) judges may continue to receive advice or warnings about peculiar risks from the police, security services, security guards and other relevant personnel. The parties should expect Judges to put that information to one side when reaching a decision on the merits; (iii) judges must remain impartial and should re-buff and report approaches which interfere with their independence; (iv) in the event of doubt, judges should discuss the issue with a more senior judge (such advice should not relate to the merits of the case); (v) generally the Tribunal should not accept information on the basis that it remain confidential to the decision maker; (vi) there are exceptions to point (v) e.g. in national security cases; finally, (vii) there might be other exceptions to point (v) where there are serious risks to the security of an individual or where the revelation would be a significant breach of privacy to which a party might be entitled; usually, however, the approach should be mentioned to the parties with a request to keep it confidential.

The Different Types of Hearing

19.95 *General*

Under the *2004 Rules*, there were three types of hearing: Case Management Discussions, Pre-Hearing Reviews and Final Hearings. There were complex rules governing which orders could be made at which type of hearing. Under the *2013 Rules* there are now two principal types of hearing: a preliminary hearing and a final hearing.

19.96 *Preliminary Hearings: General*

Rule 53 defines the scope of a preliminary hearing. A preliminary hearing is a hearing at which the Tribunal may do one or more of the following things:

(a)   conduct a preliminary consideration of the claim with the parties and make a case management order (including an order relating to the conduct of the final hearing);

(b)   determine any preliminary issue;

(c)   consider whether a claim or response, or any part, should be struck out under *rule 37*;

(d)   make a deposit order under *rule 39*;

(e)   explore the possibility of settlement or alternative dispute resolution (including judicial mediation).

By *Rule 53(2)*, there may be more than one preliminary hearing in any case.

19.97 *Preliminary Hearings: Case Management*

Preliminary hearings are convened in many cases in order to conduct case management with the parties. Such preliminary hearings are often labelled by the Tribunal "preliminary hearings for case management". They are have much in common with Case Management Discussions under the *2004 Rules*, save that there are not the same restrictions on deciding points of substance that existed with CMDs (see *Way v Powercraft (Retail) Ltd* [2008] All ER (D) 151 (Aug): no general power to strike out claim at a CMD, and *Kerr v Ernst & Young Services Ltd* (UKEAT/0567/10) applying the principle to an order that particular claims within a discrimination case could only be treated as background, not substantive claims).

The Presidential Guidance for General Case Management includes an Agenda for Case Management at a Preliminary Hearing (set out in the Annex). Para 20 of the Guidance states that the agenda should be completed in advance of the Preliminary Hearing and sent to the Tribunal. If possible, it should be agreed by the parties.

The Court of Appeal has previously stressed the desirability of a directions hearing (a predecessor of the preliminary hearing for case management) in discrimination cases to enable the tribunal to deal with preliminary matters, identify the issues in dispute and establish a realistic time estimate for the hearing so that the case could be listed for long enough to avoid adjournments and delays in the substantive hearing: *Martins v Marks and Spencer plc* [1998] IRLR 326. These comments were reiterated, specifically in relation to claims based on the *Public Interest Disclosure Act 1998*, in *ALM Medical Services Ltd v Bladen* [2002] EWCA Civ 1085, [2002] ICR 1444. Under the 2004 Rules no uniform practice on the ordering of CMDs existed and it was often left to the parties to identify the need for a CMD, even in discrimination cases and some relatively complex claims. Under the *2013 Rules*, the initial consideration given to claims and responses in every case is likely to assist the Tribunal judiciary get an early grip on the issues within a case. As has been seen above, where a claim proceeds, the Tribunal must make a case management order, unless one has been made already. It is likely that in future judges will be able to identify at this stage where a preliminary hearing for case management is required, and make the necessary orders accordingly.

At a preliminary hearing for case management, the Tribunal will set out to identify the issues arising in the case with the parties. The parties are expected to attend with sufficient knowledge about the case to allow for this rigorous exercise to take place. Cost consequences might follow if the hearing cannot achieve its objectives (for an example, see *Wilsons Solicitors v Johnson* [2011] ICR D21). At many case management hearings, the issues will be reduced to writing and form an agreed list of issues. As the Court of Appeal explained in *Parekh v The London Borough of Brent* [2012] EWCA Civ 1630 (para 31), a list of issues is a useful case management tool developed by the tribunal to bring some semblance of order, structure and clarity to proceedings. If the list of issues is agreed, then that will, as a general rule, limit the issues at the substantive hearing to those in the list (on which see also *Land Rover v Short* (UKEAT/0496/10). However, the tribunal that hears the case is not required to stick slavishly to the list of issues where to do so would impair the discharge of the core duty to hear and determine the case in accordance with the law and the evidence (on which see also *Price v Surrey County Council* (UKEAT/0450/10); *Wilcox v Birmingham CAB Services Ltd* (UKEAT/0293/10); and *Millin v Capsticks Solicitors LLP* [2014] UKEAT/0093/14). The list of issues is not a substitute for the pleadings: see *Remploy Ltd v Abbott & others* UKEAT/0405/14, *Chandhok v Tirkey* [2015] IRLR 195 and the discussion at **19.86** above.

After the preliminary hearing for case management, the tribunal will send to the parties a copy of the orders made and a note of the discussion, which will include any list of issues. The Court in *Parekh* considered that where the issues were agreed, it would be difficult to see how the content of the list could ever be the proper subject of an appeal on a question of law. Alternatively, if the list was not agreed and it is contended that it is an incorrect record of the discussions, or there has been a material change in circumstances, the proper procedure is not to appeal, but to apply to the tribunal to reconsider the order in the interests of justice (para 32).

Orders for the preparation of chronologies, agreed facts, skeleton arguments etc are becoming increasingly common and parties should consider ahead of a case management hearing whether they would be appropriate to the circumstances of the individual case. Parties are prompted to do so on the Agenda for case management preliminary hearings which features in the Presidential Guidance.

One aspect of case management which is increasingly likely to be encountered, particularly in complex discrimination cases where numerous incidents have been raised by the claimant, is the application of the requirement in the Overriding Objective of proportionality: that the case be conducted in a manner proportionate to the importance and complexity of the issues in dispute. Employment Judges cannot arbitrarily limit the scope of the issues to be tried (see *McKinson v Hackney Community College* (UKEAT/0237/11) where an order limiting the number of incidents the claimant was permitted to rely on to six was set aside on appeal), but directions may be given limiting the number of documents to be put before the tribunal, or the time to be allowed for particular witnesses or for the hearing as a whole; or requiring a claimant to identify and put forward at the hearing only the most important incidents forming part of his or her case, with the other incidents stayed to a later hearing (in the hope that a decision on the selected issues will enable the parties to resolve their differences on the outstanding matters): see *HSBC Asia Holdings BV v Gillespie* [2011] ICR 192.

In certain cases, judicial assessment of a case as a means of facilitating ADR may take place at the end of a Preliminary Hearing for Case Management: see the discussion at **19.24A**.

19.98 *Preliminary Hearings: Substantive Issues*

Preliminary hearings are also frequently convened in cases in order to determine preliminary issues. By *Rule 53(3)* a "preliminary issue" is defined to mean, as regards any complaint, any substantive issue which may determine liability, for example, an issue as to jurisdiction or as to whether an employee was dismissed. Other preliminary issues may include such matters as whether a claim was presented in time (and if not, whether time should be extended); whether the claimant is or was an employee or a worker, where the status of the claimant is in dispute; whether he or she had sufficient service to qualify for the right claimed; whether the claimant is or has been disabled; or whether a transfer amounted to a relevant transfer for the purposes of the *Transfer of Undertakings (Protection of Employment) Regulations 2006*.

The House of Lords has however indicated strongly, albeit in obiter comments, that it is in many cases not appropriate to hold a preliminary hearing, particularly to determine issues that are not completely separate from the issues that will remain to be decided at any full hearing: *SCA Packaging Ltd v Boyle* [2009] UKHL 37, [2009] IRLR 746, per Lord Hope at paras 9–10, Lord Rodger at para 45 and Lord Neuberger at para 82. Their Lordships cautioned against the holding of a preliminary hearing unless there is 'a succinct knockout point' to be decided. In particular, as in the *SCA* case, the issue whether a claimant is disabled is not necessarily sufficiently separable from the other issues in a claim of disability discrimination to justify it being made the subject of a separate hearing; nor are time points in discrimination cases where part at least of the claim is in time, since evidence of earlier incidents is likely to be admissible even if those incidents are as such out of time, as supporting evidence in relation to the matters which are in time; thus it is unlikely that any time would be saved by having a separate preliminary hearing. See also *Rossetti Marketing Limited v Diamond Sofa Company Limited* [2012] EWCA Civ 1021 in which Lord Neuberger MR warned that "while often attractive prospectively, the siren song of agreeing or ordering preliminary issues should normally be resisted" (para 1) and *English v Thomas Sanderson Limited* [2009] ICR 543 in which the Court of Appeal held that a Tribunal should approach the use of a preliminary issue procedure with circumspection in any case where the result may be influenced by the details or nuance of the facts (paras 35, 36, 43). On the other hand in cases where it is arguable that the entire claim is out of time, a tribunal is likely to agree to that issue being addressed at a preliminary hearing because of the potential 'knockout' point involved.

Rule 56 governs when a preliminary hearing will be conducted in public. *Rule 53* provides that preliminary hearings must be conducted in private except where the hearing involves a determination of a preliminary issue or determination of a strike out application under *Rule 37*. In those circumstances, the part of the hearing dealing with such determinations is to be held in public (subject to the Tribunal having the ability to make orders for privacy reasons – *Rule 50* – and national security reasons – *Rule 94*). The Tribunal also may direct that the entirety of a preliminary hearing should be in public.

Rule 55 governs the constitution of the Tribunal for a preliminary hearing. It provides that preliminary hearings will be conducted by an Employment Judge sitting alone, except that where notice has been given that any preliminary issues are to be, or may be, decided at the hearing a party may request in writing that the hearing be conducted by a full tribunal. In such a case, an Employment Judge will then decide whether that would be desirable.

Unlike the old rules, there is no specific time limit for making the application for a full tribunal provided within *Rule 55*. Like the old rules, however, there would appear to be no power for the Judge on the day to convert the hearing to one before a full panel in the absence of a written application by a party. Any application for an adjournment to enable a party to make the necessary application is likely to be viewed with disfavour and may result in an application for the costs thrown away. It is therefore essential for a party wishing to have any preliminary issue decided by a full tribunal to apply promptly for an order to that effect. The fact that normally a preliminary hearing will be heard by an Employment Judge sitting alone is not generally regarded by tribunals as a good reason not to order the determination of factually complex preliminary points in this way.

The hearing of a preliminary hearing may be conducted by telephone or video link, provided that suitable arrangements are in place for members of the public to hear or see the proceedings: see above; however in practice this facility is very rarely used (as distinct from the practice of telephone preliminary hearings for case management, which is relatively common).

Preliminary hearings may be directed by a Tribunal on its own initiative following initial consideration under *Rule 26* or at any time thereafter, or as a result of an application by a party: *Rule 54*. When listing a preliminary hearing, the Tribunal shall give the parties reasonable notice of the date of the hearing and in the case of a hearing involving any preliminary issues at least 14 days' notice shall be given and the notice shall specify the preliminary issues that are to be, or may be, decided at the hearing.

19.99 *Interim Relief Hearings*

A Tribunal has the power to hear an application for interim relief (or to hear an application for its variation or revocation) under *TULRCA 1992, s 161* and *165* (cases of unfair dismissal where the claimant alleges the dismissal is unfair because it is principally on grounds related to union membership or activities); and *ERA 1996, s 128* and *131* (automatically unfair reasons for dismissal as listed in *s 128* including making protected disclosures).

If interim relief is granted, this involves either immediate reinstatement pending a full hearing, or if the employer will not reinstate, an order that the claimant be paid his or her normal pay until the hearing.

When such a hearing is held, *Rule 95* provides that *Rules 53* to *56* apply to the hearing, viz the rules relating to preliminary hearings: see above. This specifically includes the same rules for fixing a hearing – it must be done on reasonable notice, which may be very short if necessary. Under the primary legislation, a minimum of seven days' notice is required to hold an interim relief hearing: see the *ERA 1996 s 128(4)*, *TULRCA 1992, s 162(2)*). However, under *Rule 54*, 14 days' notice is required of a preliminary hearing which shall decide preliminary issues.

Rule 95 also provides that the Tribunal shall not hear oral evidence unless it directs otherwise. There is no set procedure for an interim relief application other than that Rule 95 provides that the default position is that evidence won't be heard. The practice as to whether the tribunal will agree to hearing witnesses varies as between tribunals. The exclusion of witness evidence may be regarded as a permissible exercise of case management powers in the interests of the expedition, which is given the highest priority in interim relief cases, but in an extreme case refusal to permit the calling of witnesses could be challenged on appeal as a procedural irregularity. The EAT has held that the tribunal is bound to hear and determine interim relief applications, however complex the underlying facts, if a timely application under one of the relevant jurisdictions has been presented: *Raja v Secretary of State for Justice* (UKEAT/0364/09); see also *London City Airport Ltd v Chacko* (UKEAT/0013/13).

19.100 *Final Hearing*

A final hearing is a hearing at which the Tribunal determines the claim or such parts as remain outstanding following the initial consideration (under rule 26) or any preliminary hearing: see *Rule 57*. A claim can have more than one final hearing to cover different issues (for example, liability, remedy or costs).

A Tribunal must give the parties not less than 14 days' notice of the date of a final hearing: *Rule 58*. All final hearings must be held in public, although that requirement (see *Rule 59*) is subject to the ability of the Tribunal to make an order under *Rules 50* and *94*.

The Judge is required to keep a full note of the evidence given; this is normally done in longhand, or occasionally on a laptop computer; the taking of notes sometimes results in a speed of proceedings which many observers not used to tribunal proceedings find rather slow. The notes are important not only to assist the tribunal in reaching its judgment (especially if the hearing is adjourned part-heard, or judgment is reserved) but also for the benefit of the EAT, if necessary, on any subsequent appeal.

Submissions, or closing speeches, are the opportunity to put to the tribunal the points the party considers should lead the tribunal to find in that party's favour, on each of the issues remaining in dispute. This may involve putting forward propositions as to what the relevant legal principles to be applied are, if necessary with the citation of relevant cases, as well as highlighting points of evidence, and reasons why it is submitted that the evidence of particular witnesses on disputed issues should be preferred. If cases are relied on, copies of the cases should be available to hand to the tribunal, and any particular passages in judgments that are relied on highlighted or drawn to the tribunal's attention. It is open to any party or representative to prepare written submissions or skeleton arguments and invite the tribunal to read them, and this is commonly done by legal representatives, particularly so in longer cases and cases where there are disputed points of law. Occasionally, the provision of written submissions may be directed in advance by the tribunal as part of its case management function, but this is rarely done except in lengthy cases. Written submissions are rarer in Scotland.

In addition, tribunals sometimes ask the parties to make their final submissions in writing, when there is not enough time to complete the case without an adjournment. The parties' representatives may sometimes suggest this. The EAT has given guidance to tribunals as to the procedure to be followed if written submissions are to be provided in place of, rather than in support of, oral submissions: *Barking and Dagenham London Borough Council v Oguoko* [2000] IRLR 179. The procedure should only be implemented with the consent of both parties, and each party must be served a copy of the other's submissions and given time to comment on them (comments being limited to correction of factual errors and responses to any new points of law not previously raised) before the tribunal proceeds to reach its decision. These points were reiterated by the EAT in *Blitz v Equant Integration Services Ltd (t/a Orange Business Services)* [2008] All ER (D) 203 (Jan), EAT, where the point was made that it is particularly important that each party should have the opportunity to comment, preferably orally, on the written submissions of the other. The EAT has held that where a tribunal ordered written submissions and those from the respondent were received in time, but the claimant's submissions were not (having gone astray) it was incumbent on the tribunal to make at least a telephone enquiry of the claimant before proceeding to reach a decision without her submissions: *Quashie v Methodist Homes Housing Association* (UKEAT/0422/11).

In a lengthy or legally complex case, the tribunal may ask for written submissions in addition to oral submissions. In such cases, adequate time must be allowed for the other party's representative, and the tribunal, to read and digest the written submissions before the oral submissions are made: *Sinclair Roche & Temperley v Heard* [2004] IRLR 763.

It is open to a party to submit at the conclusion of the other party's evidence that there is no case to answer. This should be done without prejudice to the right to call evidence if the submission is rejected. However, the making of such submissions has increasingly been discouraged by the higher courts, especially in discrimination cases where it is necessary to weigh the circumstantial evidence of discrimination with the employer's explanation in assessing whether the evidence justifies an inference of discrimination: see *British Gas plc v Sharma* [1991] ICR 19, where it was described as 'exceptional' for such a submission to be appropriate in a discrimination case. The principles were restated in *Clarke v Watford Borough Council* (EAT/43/99), in terms expressly approved by the Court of Appeal in *Logan v Customs and Excise Comrs* [2003] EWCA Civ 1068, [2004] IRLR 63, as follows:

(1)   There is no inflexible rule of law and practice that a tribunal must always hear both sides, although that should normally be done.

(2)   The power to stop a case at "half-time" must be exercised with caution.

(3)   It may be a complete waste of time to call on the other party to give evidence in a hopeless case.

(4)   Even where the onus of proof lies on the [claimant], as in discrimination cases, it will only be in exceptional or frivolous cases that it would be right to take such a course.

(5)   Where there is no burden of proof, as under *s 98(4)* of the *Employment Rights Act*, it will be difficult to envisage arguable cases where it is appropriate to terminate the proceedings at the end of the first party's case.

It should be noted that the reference above to the burden of proof in discrimination cases pre-dates changes in the burden introduced from 2001 onwards; however the point made at (4) above is if anything stronger where only an initial burden is placed on the claimant.

For the sake of certainty, it is best to obtain a clear indication from the employment tribunal at the commencement of the hearing of whether it will consider liability and remedy separately, and if so, when it will consider evidence and argument on contributory fault and/or on whether a *Polkey* reduction in compensation should be made if a dismissal is found to be procedurally unfair. The EAT has held that it is an error of law for the tribunal to deal with the *Polkey* point without giving the parties an opportunity to make submissions on it: *Market Force (UK) Ltd v Hunt* [2002] IRLR 863; *Grace v BF Components Ltd* (UKEAT/0006/05). By analogy this would apply equally to the issue of contribution, or the amount of any uplift or reduction in compensation under *s 207A, TULRCA 1992*. The point is an illustration of the more general point that it would be an error of law for the tribunal to decide a case on a point the parties have not raised or had an opportunity to deal with; see *Launahurst Ltd v Larner* [2010] EWCA Civ 334 for an example of a case where this was held to have occurred. The usual practice, in the absence of a direction to the contrary, is that the tribunal will proceed to deal with remedy, if time permits, immediately following its decision on liability (and assuming that that decision is in the claimant's favour). However, it is unusual (at least in England and Wales) for a tribunal to hear evidence relating solely to compensation before it has reached a decision on liability. In *Iggesund Converters Ltd v Lewis* [1984] ICR 544, the EAT suggested ways in which employment tribunals could deal with evidence and argument on the reduction of an award for contributory fault, and in *Ferguson v Gateway Training Centre Ltd* [1991] ICR 658 it suggested that the Judge should restate which issues are being considered prior to final submissions. The EAT has also emphasised that it is important that the tribunal gives the parties a chance to be heard on any issue of remedy before deciding the point: *Duffy v Yeomans & Partners Ltd* [1993] ICR 862. The EAT has held that in unfair dismissal cases, the tribunal must consider the issue of contributory fault if it appears to arise on the evidence: *Swallow Security Services Ltd v Millicent* [2009] All ER (D) 299 (Mar). If the point is to be considered, the tribunal would have to alert the parties to this, to enable them to make submissions on the point.

The practice in Scotland is that unless there has been a prior direction that issues of remedy be dealt with separately, the tribunal will hear evidence on all issues together, and will give a single judgment covering both liability and remedy; the usual practice in all but the most straightforward cases is for the judgment to be reserved and delivered in writing. If there is good reason for keeping the issue of remedy separate (such as that there will be insufficient time within the period listed for the hearing to deal with all issues, or expert evidence will be needed in relation to issues of remedy) an early application should be made for a direction for the hearing to deal in the first instance with liability only.

Sometimes in the course of the hearing the Judge will give an indication to the parties of the tribunal's provisional view as to the merits of the case, or more commonly a particular issue in the case. This may be done for a number of reasons: to encourage the parties to settle, or give them assistance to settle by giving an indication as to the likely outcome on a particular point or the case as a whole; to identify which issues should be focused on in evidence or cross-examination; or to identify the issues on which submissions are particularly sought. Caution is needed in giving any kind of preliminary indication of the tribunal's view, since this may be interpreted as indicating that the decision has already been reached, or provide a basis for a later appeal on grounds of apparent bias. However the Court of Appeal has confirmed that, provided that it is made quite clear that any views expressed are provisional, there is no objection in principle to the Judge expressing a view in the course of the case: *Jiminez v Southwark London Borough Council* [2003] EWCA Civ 502, [2003] IRLR 477. By contrast, in *Gee v Shell UK Ltd* [2002] EWCA Civ 1479, [2003] IRLR 82, the Court of Appeal held that there had been procedural unfairness where the Judge had warned the claimant (who was acting in person) that she was at risk of an award of costs against her, in circumstances where there was no real basis for an award of costs, and she felt obliged to withdraw her claim to avoid the costs sanction. Contrast the position in *Hussain v Nottinghamshire Healthcare NHS Trust* [2016] UKEAT/0080/16 where a costs warning had not represented a concluded view and was an appropriate way of pointing out potential danger to the claimant.

19.101 *Preparing for the hearing and Listing Arrangements*

The length of time from presentation of a claim to a Hearing varies considerably. HM Courts and Tribunals Service and its predecessors, the Tribunals Service, and before it the ETS, have for many years set performance targets for tribunals, one of which is that 75% of single cases will receive a first hearing within 26 weeks of receipt of the Claim Form, but success in achieving this figure has been variable, both over time and in different regions. For relatively simple cases many tribunal regions are now able to list a hearing date within a few weeks of the deadline for a response, but it is not unusual for there to be a delay of several months if a case needs to be listed for more than one day.

The tribunal must give the parties at least 14 days' notice of the date of a preliminary hearing which will decide preliminary issues and final hearing (see *Rules 54* and *58*). Otherwise reasonable notice of a preliminary hearing will be given (*Rule 54*). In practice, longer notice is usually (but not always) given. The usual practice for simple cases is to issue a notice of hearing without first checking with the parties whether the date is suitable (but in Scotland it is the practice to consult the parties before listing).

There is no automatic right to postponement of a hearing even if both parties request a postponement, and it is difficult on appeal to dispute a refusal to postpone (*Employment Service v Nathan* (EAT/1316/95), IDS Brief 568; *London Fire and Civil Defence Authority v Samuels* (EAT/450/00), IDS Brief 669); it is therefore important to apply as early as possible and with full reasons for the request. For an example of a successful appeal against the refusal of a postponement agreed by both parties, see *Chancerygate (Business Centre) Ltd v Jenkins* (UKEAT/0212/10). See postponements above at **19.90**.

Sometimes a listed hearing can be adjourned by the tribunal, often at short notice, for reasons of resource allocation (such as no judge being available to take the case). In *University of East Anglia v Amaik Wu* (UKEAT/0361/12), the tribunal had listed a multiple day hearing which had to be adjourned on the working day before it was due to start because of a lack of judges to hear it. The tribunal then relisted the hearing without reference to the parties' available dates. This impacted upon one of the respondent's witnesses who was due to attend a wedding abroad. The respondent therefore applied for a relisting which was refused by the tribunal judge. The EAT found the judge erred by taking into account irrelevant circumstances and failing to take into account the fact that the tribunal had not sought dates to avoid. The EAT recorded that "in general the understanding is that a prompt response [to a listing] asking for another date based on witness availability is dealt with sympathetically" (para 14). Deciding the point *de novo*, the EAT granted the adjournment; central were the facts that: the witness was crucial, the application prompt, the tribunal did not seek dates to avoid, the witness had a significant role at the wedding.

19.102 Listing arrangements are normally made at a preliminary hearing for case management in more complicated cases. Information is gathered ahead of that preliminary hearing by the completion of the Agenda Questionnaire found in the Presidential Guidance on Case Management. Otherwise, upon initial consideration of a claim, the case can be listed for an appropriate hearing length. If a case is likely to take longer than the allowed time it is important to apply at an early stage for a longer listing; otherwise the tribunal will have to reconvene, possibly months later, if the case is not completed within the allotted day (it is very rare indeed that the case would be continued the following day in those circumstances). For cases to be listed for more than a day without a preliminary hearing, most regions write to the parties advising them of the intention to list the case and requiring notification to the tribunal if a party considers the proposed time allocation to be inappropriate. It is important to respond to such an invitation, since the tribunal may hold the parties to a time allocation even if at the hearing they suggest that the time allowed is insufficient, and this is also an opportunity to give the tribunal dates to be avoided because eg a witness will not be available. In Scotland parties are asked to identify the witnesses they intend to call and how long the evidence of each will take to be heard, and the time allocated to the case is based on the parties' responses.

The basis on which cases are listed, unless otherwise indicated, is that sufficient time should be allowed not only to hear the evidence and submissions of the parties, but also for the tribunal to reach and announce its decision, and to deal if appropriate with remedies. Anecdotally, a figure often mentioned by judges as the time required for deliberations is around 25% of the time required to hear the evidence. Parties are now generally warned of this approach, and are advised also of the tribunal's power to set a timetable to ensure that the case is completed within the time available. Hearings are normally scheduled to take place at the Regional Office or other office of the tribunal at which the case has been presented (or to which the file has been transferred), but there are also a number of hearing centres at which cases are heard but which do not have a permanent staff presence. Increasingly, hearing centres shared with other tribunals are used, on the basis either of availability of tribunal rooms or of geographical convenience for the parties (the latter in particular in more rural areas); if travel to the tribunal office administering the case is likely to be difficult or expensive for a party, enquiries should be made of the tribunal as to whether it will be possible to list the case for hearing at a more convenient location. In Scotland, local Sheriff Courts are used for hearings in more remote locations.

Special priority is given to interim hearings of applications for interim relief (see **55.18** UNFAIR DISMISSAL – III). Only seven days' notice of the claim and of the hearing is required, and postponements will only be granted in exceptional cases (the statutory provisions stipulating this are *ERA 1996, s 128(4), (5)* and *TULRCA 1992, s 162(2), (4)*).

There are several steps a party should take prior to the hearing – preferably earlier rather than later. These are addressed in the following sections. The reader is also referred to the Presidential Guidance on General Case Management that has been issued.

19.103 A decision should be taken whether a legal or other representative is to be engaged; if so, this should be done in good time to enable the representative to prepare for the hearing and take any necessary interlocutory steps. There is no restriction on who may represent a party in the tribunal (see *Bache v Essex County Council* [2000] 2 All ER 847, [2000] IRLR 251).

In general no legal aid is now available. Legal assistance for the preparation of the case used to be available to claimants of limited means, but (apart from in limited circumstances in Scotland) this ceased to be so on the coming into force on 1 April 2013 of the *Legal Aid, Sentencing and Punishment of Offenders Act 2012*. There are now only very limited circumstances in which legal aid assistance is available in England and Wales. It is limited to telephone advice in discrimination cases (contact the Civil Legal Advice information line for details: 0345 345 4 345 or https://www.gov.uk/civil-legal-advice). In Scotland, a consultation is ongoing over plans to exclude civil legal assistance from various areas of civil law including employment law: see the paper "Legal Assistance in Scotland – Fit for the 21st Century".

Employers are often represented by an appropriate manager or a trade association official, employees by a union officer or a Citizens' Advice Bureau (CABx) or advice centre worker. The fact that no representative is given on the Claim Form or Response Form by no means necessarily indicates that the party concerned will not be represented. Whoever is to represent a party, it is desirable that the representative be consulted in good time before the hearing. It is also important that the tribunal is notified promptly of the appointment of a representative, with contact details, and of any change in arrangements for representation, to avoid the all too common situation that correspondence from the tribunal, including notice of hearings, does not reach the party or his or her current representative.

A number of organisations offer their services as representatives in tribunal proceedings, either as consultants offering a package of advice and representation to employers, or on a no win no fee basis for claimants. Concerns about the quality of representation offered by some of these organisations, and the lack of any professional or statutory regulation of their conduct, led to the introduction of a requirement, under the *Compensation Act 2006, Part 2*, for claims management services (including those providing representation in employment tribunals for reward) to be regulated. It is a criminal offence for a person or organisation who, or which, is not registered with the regulator (the Secretary of State for Justice) to provide representation for claimants (but not respondents) in employment tribunal proceedings for reward (including on a no win, no fee basis). In *Miller v Community Links Trust* [2007] All ER (D) 196 (Nov), the EAT referred an unregulated representative to the Regulator for possible action. A number of categories of representatives are exempt from regulation under the Compensation Act 2006, including lawyers, trade unions and the CABx; for full details see the *Compensation (Exemptions) Order 2007 (SI 2007/209)*. The *Compensation Act 2006* only applies to England and Wales, and there is no equivalent statutory regulation of representatives acting for reward in Scotland.

Before engaging a representative on a no win no fee basis, a prospective claimant needs to appreciate that the representative will normally have to be paid out of whatever compensation is awarded if the claim succeeds, since costs are not usually awarded, but compensation is assessed without regard to this liability. By way of further regulation of 'no win no fee' agreements, the *Damages-Based Agreements Regulations 2013 (SI 2013/609)*, which came into force on 1 April 2013, prohibit agreements in employment cases which provide for payment of more than 35% (including VAT) of the compensation recovered, whether by way of settlement or as an award of the tribunal: *reg 7*. This mirrored the provisions in the preceding *Damages-Based Agreements Regulations 2010*, which remain in force for agreements made before 1 April 2013. Neither set of Regulations extends to Scotland.

In an extreme case the conduct of a representative may lead to sanctions being imposed by the tribunal on the party represented, including striking out that party's case (see *Bennett v Southwark London Borough Council* [2002] EWCA Civ 223, [2002] IRLR 407). The tribunal also has the power to make a wasted costs order against a representative acting for profit (including under a no win, no fee agreement), i.e. an order that the representative must pay the other party's costs, or debarring the representative from recovering costs incurred from his or her client. See further **19.73**.

For those, particularly claimants, who cannot afford to pay for legal representation, free representation may be available through one or other of a number of organisations including the Citizens' Advice Bureaux (CABx) and the Free Representation Unit (5th Floor, Kingsbourne House, 229-231 High Holborn, London WC1V 7DA, tel. 020 7611 9555, www.thefru.org.uk), and in discrimination cases application may be made for legal assistance to the Equality and Human Rights Commission, although the Commission's budget for legal assistance is limited, and funding is concentrated on cases with wider implications or meeting priority criteria.

Most trade unions provide a free representation service for members, either through union officials or union-appointed solicitors, and usually subject to being satisfied that the claim has some merit. An increasing number of claimants are represented by lawyers paid for under legal expenses insurance (often provided as an optional addition to household insurance) and it is important that a claimant should check at as early a stage as possible whether this facility may be available. Further advice on possible sources of free professional representation can be obtained through CABx.

19.104 Consideration should be given to whether an application for any case management orders, or a preliminary hearing, is needed. Orders may be any of those discussed in this chapter. A preliminary hearing for case management may be listed by the tribunal of its own motion. Most commonly this happens in discrimination cases; where the issues appear complex; or where a party's application for an order has been opposed. It may also be necessary to apply to the tribunal for a preliminary hearing to determine a particular preliminary point (such as whether it has jurisdiction over the claim). A party may wish to apply for permission to amend the claim or response. An application which is likely to be contested should not be granted by the tribunal without the opposing party being given an opportunity to resist the application (in writing or, if the tribunal so orders, at a preliminary or other hearing) and if an amendment is allowed ex parte, without such an opportunity, the opposing party may apply to the tribunal to have the order set aside (see *Reddington v S Straker & Sons Ltd* [1994] ICR 172). A tribunal should not normally decide an application to amend a Claim Form which raises an issue of substance, without giving the parties an opportunity to make representations (*Smith v Gwent District Health Authority* [1996] ICR 1044). The practice in relation to applications to amend was restated by the EAT in *Selkent Bus Co Ltd v Moore* [1996] ICR 836. For more details, see **19.72** above.

19.105 It is sometimes necessary for a party to apply for a postponement of the hearing, either because a witness becomes unavailable or for a variety of other reasons. Any such application should if possible be made with the agreement of the other party. However even agreed applications are not necessarily granted by the tribunal. It is important to give full reasons for the application, especially if it is opposed. The earlier the application is made, the more likely it is to be granted and special rules now restrict the Tribunal's ability to accede to an application made shortly before the hearing or if the party applying has already applied twice for a postponement: see *Rule 30A*. If the application is made on grounds of ill-health, medical evidence will be required by the tribunal. In deciding applications, tribunals are entitled to have regard to the public interest in cases being heard as promptly as reasonably practicable, now reinforced by the incorporation into domestic law of the right under *art 6* of the *European Convention on Human Rights* to have a dispute decided within a reasonable time. In practice an application for a postponement of the hearing is made in quite a high proportion of cases, often very shortly before the hearing; although there are no statistics as to the percentage of applications granted and refused, experience suggests that the majority are refused. If a hearing was listed at a case management hearing, it is particularly difficult to persuade the tribunal to change the listing because a witness is not available: *London Fire and Civil Defence Authority v Samuels* (EAT/450/00). For the position where an application is made on the morning of the hearing or immediately before the hearing date, see **19.90**.

19.106 The relevant documentary evidence should be identified. Documentation likely to be relevant will include the contract of employment or letter of engagement, statutory statement of particulars of employment, relevant parts of any staff handbook (such as a disciplinary procedure), any written warnings, records of performance or attendance (if these are relevant issues), the letter of dismissal and any correspondence notifying the employee of the disciplinary investigation or hearing, notes or minutes of any relevant meetings, appeal documents if applicable, documents demonstrating the need for a redundancy, and documents relevant to quantification of the claim, such as payments made to the employee and pension documentation. The employee may need to produce documentation showing his or her attempts to mitigate his or her loss and any earnings since dismissal, as well as evidence of pay and benefits prior to dismissal, and social security benefits received after termination. In cases where a grievance has been raised, the documentation relating to the grievance, grievance hearings and any appeal will be required.

The parties will be expected, particularly if both have professional representation, to agree a bundle of documents including those to be relied on by both sides. It is now standard practice for the tribunal to make an order to this effect, however even if no order is made, the Presidential Guidance on General Case Management emphasises that a single bundle should be prepared and that the parties must cooperate to this end. Such a bundle may be referred to as an 'agreed' bundle or the 'hearing bundle'; the word 'agreed' here means that the authenticity of the documents is not disputed, but not that their relevance or accuracy is necessarily conceded. The bundle should be paginated (ie each page should be consecutively numbered) and, if substantial, indexed. Six copies will be needed for the hearing (three for the tribunal, or one if an Employment Judge is sitting alone, and one each for each party and for the witnesses). Some tribunal regions in England have adopted a practice of limiting the number of pages of documentation parties may include, but practice on this varies, and is subject to consideration of any reasoned case a party may make to put in more than the maximum number of pages.

Where the parties fail to cooperate over bundles, they are in principle at risk of costs orders (see below). In *Smith-Twigger v Abbey Protection Group Ltd* [2014] ICR D33 the EAT (dealing specifically with the bundling requirements in the EAT) held that "it is in general unacceptable that the parties should fail to co-operate over the contents of a bundle" (para 47).

In Scotland, documents produced to the tribunal are referred to as 'productions'. Parties with legal representation are required by a Practice Direction to notify each other of what productions each party intends to rely on, and provide copies, 14 days before the hearing; in straightforward cases it is unusual for any specific orders to be made for disclosure or exchange of productions, but it is nevertheless important to prepare sufficient copies of the documents, numbered and indexed (this is referred to as an 'inventory of productions'), as failure to do so will inevitably extend the length of the hearing; if possible there should be a joint bundle of productions. The usual practice is to number each document (which may be more than one page) separately.

As the rules of evidence do not apply fully in tribunals, it is not necessary formally to prove the documents in the tribunal bundle, unless the genuineness or accuracy of a document is disputed (e.g. in the latter case, minutes of a meeting). If there is a dispute, a witness who can confirm the accuracy of the document from personal knowledge should be called. Where there may be issues of authenticity, originals of any documents should wherever possible be available at the hearing.

There are no formal rules as to who should produce the sets of documents needed for the hearing. The usual practice is for the party advancing a case to take this responsibility (i.e. the claimant in discrimination or breach of contract cases, but the employer in unfair dismissal cases where the dismissal is admitted). However, it has in recent years become increasingly common for the respondent to accept the burden of preparing the bundles, and the requirement of the Overriding Objective that the parties should so far as possible be put on an equal footing has led to it becoming part of the common practice of tribunals, at least in cases with substantial documentation, to require respondents to undertake this task. Often the tribunal will encourage agreement on the question of the cost of preparing and duplicating the bundle, but its powers to award costs are limited to those in the rules.

19.107 One category of documents is not normally admissible before a tribunal; this is 'without prejudice' correspondence. This means correspondence conducted in an attempt to reach a settlement of a dispute; it is only admissible either to prove an agreement reached as a result or if both parties agree. For further details of the limits of the 'without prejudice' privilege see **19.13** above. Correspondence is sometimes conducted under the heading 'Without prejudice save as to costs'. This preserves the right of the party putting forward proposals to refer to the correspondence after the substantive issues have been decided by the tribunal, solely in support of an application for costs – see further **19.36** above. In unfair dismissal cases the effect of *ERA 1996, s 111A* should also be considered: pre-termination negotiations will, pursuant to that section become inadmissible in proceedings, subject to three exceptions. See further **19.13** above.

19.108 The relevant witnesses should be identified and their statements taken. An employer in an unfair dismissal case will usually need to call at least the manager who took the decision to dismiss the employee and, if applicable, the manager who decided the appeal. In a redundancy case, evidence of the redundancy situation, of the reasons for the decision to select the claimant, of consultation with the claimant and any recognised union, and of attempts to redeploy, may all be required. Where there has been a disciplinary hearing and the reason for the dismissal was that the manager decided on the evidence that the employee was guilty of misconduct, it is not the tribunal's function to re-try the case or decide for itself as to the employee's guilt; it should not therefore normally be necessary to call all those persons who were involved in the disciplinary hearing (apart from the manager conducting the hearing) or any earlier investigation. It may, however, be necessary to call the manager conducting any separate investigation prior to the disciplinary hearing, particularly so if there is any dispute as to the sufficiency or fairness of the investigation. In some cases it might be justifiable to call witnesses to the underlying allegations of misconduct as although this evidence does not go to liability for unfair dismissal, it can go to questions of contributory fault and liability for wrongful dismissal: see *London Ambulance Service v Small* [2009] IRLR 563, CA. As to the employee, whether any additional witness is to be called depends on the availability (and sometimes willingness) of those who have knowledge of relevant events.

Some caution should, however, be exercised when deciding whether to rely on a witness. Calling live evidence opens the door to cross examination and give the opponent the opportunity to elicit other evidence helpful to their case. A careful judgment call is often required. When making that call, advisors should consider whether the oral evidence is really necessary. In some cases it will be, but in other cases, the documents might tell their own story. Such considerations now take place against an increasing judicial trend towards recognising the unreliability of human memory; as Tom Bingham put it in The Business of Judging (OUP, 2000, p15): "the human capacity for honestly believing something which bears no relation to what really happened is unlimited" (cited with approval by Mostyn J in *A County Council v M and F* [2011] EWHC 1804 (Fam) (para 30) and Leggatt J in *Brogden v Investec Bank Plc* [2014] EWHC 2785 (Comm) (para 50)). More generally, see Leggatt J's longer analysis of the problems with relying on human memory in *Gestmin SGPS SA v Credit Suisse (UK) Ltd* [2013] EWHC 3560 (Comm) (paras 15 to 22). In *Suddock v Nursing and Midwifery Council* [2016] All ER (D) 53 (Jan), the Administrative Court cautioned against focusing overly on the demeanour of a witness when making findings. Whilst demeanour was not irrelevant, the way in which the person's evidence corresponded with non-contentious evidence or agreed facts, and with contemporaneous documents and the inherent probabilities and improbabilities of the account of events in question, as well as consistencies or inconsistencies, were likely to be far more reliable indicators of where the truth lay.

In most cases issues about the admissibility of particular evidence will be decided by the tribunal hearing the case in the course of the hearing. However it is open to the tribunal in the exercise of its case management powers to rule in advance of the hearing on the admissibility of particular evidence which a party proposes to call. This may be done where there is a dispute about admissibility based on legal arguments, such as whether the evidence is covered by legal professional privilege, but exceptionally a ruling may be based on proportionality. Thus in *HSBC Asia Holdings BV v Gillespie* [2011] ICR 192, [2011] IRLR 209, the EAT ruled that the tribunal should have excluded in advance evidence the claimant in a discrimination case intended to introduce at the hearing as background, in order to show a discriminatory culture within the respondent bank, covering a period of 10 years going back 18 years from the date of the claim, and involving departments of the bank, and individuals, who were not affected at all by the substantive allegations of harassment. Underhill P pointed out that whilst evidence that is irrelevant is inadmissible, relevance alone is not necessarily sufficient to justify admission; where the evidence is of marginal relevance, it may be disproportionate to admit it, as in this case where admission of the evidence would necessitate the calling of much additional evidence by the respondent to seek to rebut the allegations made, which were not the substantive complaints for which a remedy could be granted. See also now the EAT's judgment in *Kalu v Brighton & Sussex University Hospitals NHS Trust* (UKEAT/0609/12).

In *Vaughan v Lewisham Borough Council* [2013] All ER (D) 80, in a discrimination claim the claimant had sought permission to rely on some 39 hours of covert recordings she had made of her conversations with managers and colleagues which she asserted went to the pleaded issues. The claimant did not supply any transcripts to the tribunal. The EAT held that the judge had been correct to refuse to admit the recordings: it was not possible to form any view on the relevance or proportionality of the proposed evidence on the material that the claimant had produced. It was not enough to assert their centrality to pleaded allegations. The claimant was at liberty to make a fresh focused application to the tribunal, producing the transcripts and tapes which she wanted to rely on. The EAT went on to confirm that although the practice of making secret recordings is "to put it no higher, very distasteful", recordings are not inadmissible simply because of the way in which they were taken; see also *Dogherty v Chairman and Governors of Amwell View School* (UKEAT/0243/06); *Williamson v Chief Constable of Greater Manchester Police* (UKEAT/0346/09); and more recently *Punjab National Bank (International) Ltd v Gosain* (UKEAT/0003/14). For covert recordings conducted by the employer see *City and County of Swansea v Gayle* (UKEAT/0501/12).

19.109 For hearings in England and Wales, witnesses will need to be asked to prepare written statements of their evidence (legal representatives will normally prepare drafts themselves following an interview with each witness). These should be typed or legibly written, using short, numbered paragraphs. It is important that all relevant matters of which the witness has knowledge are covered. Whilst the practice as to timing is not consistent between tribunal regions, the almost universal practice is that the tribunal will direct the parties to prepare witness statements, and to exchange them prior to the hearing. Sometimes the tribunal will also direct that the witness statements will be taken as the evidence-in-chief of the witness. This means that the party calling the witness will not be able to ask him or her additional questions without the permission of the tribunal. If there is good reason why a statement cannot be produced for a particular witness, it is advisable to apply to the tribunal for an order exempting that witness from the general requirement for statements to be exchanged in advance.

The practice as to how witness statements are used at the hearing was in the past that in most cases the tribunal would invite the witnesses to give their evidence by reading the statement; sometimes (usually where the facts did not appear to be substantially in dispute, or in more lengthy cases) the tribunal would pre-read the statements and simply ask the witnesses to confirm the truth of their contents. The practice has now been changed. *Rule*

43 provides that if there is a witness statement, it stands as the witness's evidence-in-chief unless the tribunal directs otherwise. This means that the standard practice is that the witness will not have to read out the statement, but it will be read by the tribunal; and the witness will only be able to give additional evidence in chief if the tribunal agrees. The change reflects guidance given by the EAT in *Mehta v Child Support Agency* [2011] IRLR 305. In summary, Underhill P's guidance (which is likely to influence tribunals in deciding whether all or part of a statement should be read out) is that it is not a requirement of fairness that every witness statement is read out in full to the tribunal, but there may be cases where this is desirable, particularly if a party is unrepresented; it is not necessary for all statements to be treated in the same way: a witness may for instance be asked to read the key parts of his or her statement, the rest being read privately by the tribunal; and wherever possible, the tribunal should proceed with the agreement of the parties, taking care to ensure that any unrepresented party fully understands what is proposed, and agrees to the course proposed. In practice it will often be necessary for the tribunal to ask questions of the witness (or the representative of the party calling the witness) to clarify points in the statement, and to identify clearly documents referred to and the parts of documents the witness is referring to in the statement, so that these too can be read.

If it will not be possible to call a witness, evidence can be given by way of a signed statement, which should contain a statement confirming that the witness believes the facts stated in the statement to be true (a 'statement of truth'). Such evidence should be sent to the tribunal and the other party at least seven days before the hearing so that it can be considered as a written representation (see *Rule 42*) or by any other time limit set by the Tribunal for a witness statement. If tendered late, the tribunal may decline to consider it. In any case, however, the weight to be attached to evidence in this form is affected by the unavailability of the witness (for however cogent a reason) for cross-examination. Accordingly, unless the evidence is not in dispute, great caution should be used in relying on written evidence instead of a live witness.

The practice in Scotland is still that witness statements are not normally used as a means of giving evidence, or exchanged before the hearing. Instead, at least where there is legal representation, witnesses are usually interviewed before the hearing by the representative (a procedure known as 'precognosing' the witness), and a proof of evidence prepared, which can serve as a script for the advocate calling the witness. If there are particular reasons why it would be desirable for the evidence (or evidence of specific witnesses) to be given by way of written statements, early application should be made to the tribunal for directions on the point. Where witness statements are used, the new rules will apply equally.

19.110 It is open to any party to submit representations in writing to the tribunal; they must be submitted (and sent to each other party) at least seven days before the hearing date, unless the tribunal consents to a shorter period (*Rule 42*). Written representations may be made by a party attending the hearing, or in lieu of attendance. However, the latter course is extremely hazardous, since the absent party cannot deal with questions from the tribunal, points that arise unexpectedly or assertions made in evidence by the other party. In all but the simplest cases, attendance in person or by a representative is essential. The provision of written representations under the *ET Rules* outlined above is not to be confused with the practice of submitting a written skeleton argument; sometimes the tribunal will make an order for such skeletons to be exchanged and filed by a particular time, but otherwise, the parties are free to present them to the tribunal at the time of the hearing.

19.111 The current practice of tribunals in straightforward cases is to deal with all questions including, if appropriate, remedy, at one hearing. Accordingly, and unless the tribunal has directed that remedy will be dealt with subsequently, parties should come to the hearing prepared to deal with evidence relevant to remedy. This means that the claimant should include in his or her statement details of the earnings lost, any income received from new employment or state benefits, and information relevant to any claim that he or she has failed to take reasonable steps to mitigate his or her loss. In most regions the standard orders issued in unfair dismissal and discrimination cases include a requirement for the claimant to serve a Schedule of Loss detailing the amounts claimed, benefits received etc. The respondent should have the necessary information to put before the tribunal to establish take home pay (if disputed) and the value of any employment benefits. If there is likely to be a dispute about this, relevant documentation should be in the bundle. (It does not follow that the tribunal will have the time to deal with remedy, and it may agree to give the parties time to attempt to agree the remedy; however cases are listed on the basis that time is allowed for the tribunal to hear the case, reach and deliver its decision, and then deal with remedy if necessary.) If it is anticipated that additional evidence will need to be called in relation to remedy, particularly if expert evidence (e.g. on pension loss) will be needed, it may be advisable to apply well before the hearing for a direction that remedy will be dealt with separately at a second hearing. In Scotland the practice is that all issues including remedy will be dealt with together, before the decision on liability is given, if at all possible, although split hearings are becoming less uncommon, especially if expert evidence is required on the issue of remedy.

19.112 *Conversion from Preliminary Hearing to Final Hearing and vice versa*

By *Rule 48*, a Tribunal that is conduct a preliminary hearing may order that it be treated as a final hearing, or vice versa if the Tribunal is properly constituted for the purpose and if it is satisfied that neither party shall be materially prejudiced by the change.

DECISIONS, REASONS, THEIR ENFORCEMENT AND RECONSIDERATION

Decisions and Reasons

19.113 *Making and Recording Decisions*

The *2013 Rules* provide that decisions can be made by the Employment Tribunal both at or following a hearing and without a hearing.

If the Tribunal makes a decision without a hearing, by *Rule 60*, the decision must be communicated in writing to the parties, identifying the Employment Judge who has made the decision.

Where there is a hearing the Tribunal may either announce its decision in relation to any issue at the hearing or reserve it to be sent to the parties as soon as practicable in writing: *Rule 61(1)*. In Scotland the usual practice for all but the most straightforward cases is for the judgment to be reserved. If the Tribunal opts to announce the decision at the hearing, a written record (in the form of a judgment if appropriate) must still be provided to the parties (and, where the proceedings were referred to the Tribunal by a court, to that court) as soon as practicable: *Rule 61(2)*. *Rule 61(2)* goes on to clarify, however, that decisions concerned only with the conduct of a hearing need not be identified in the record of that hearing unless a party requests that a specific decision is so recorded.

Rule 61(3) requires the written record of decisions to be signed by the Employment Judge concerned. However, by *Rule 63*, if it is impossible or not practicable for the written record or reasons to be signed by the Employment Judge as a result of death, incapacity or absence, it shall be signed by the other member or members (in the case of a full tribunal) or by the President, Vice President or a Regional Employment Judge (in the case of a Judge sitting alone).

19.114 *Consent orders and judgments*

Rule 64 provides that where the parties agree in writing or orally at a hearing upon the terms of any order or judgment, a Tribunal may, if it thinks fit, make such order or judgment, in which case it shall be identified as having been made by consent. The rule makes clear that a Tribunal is not bound to make a consent order just because the parties have agreed, and it can still exercise its discretion to refuse to do so.

19.115 *Majority Decisions*

Rule 49 provides that where a Tribunal is composed of three persons any decision may be made by a majority and if it is composed of two persons the Employment Judge has a second or casting vote. The Court of Appeal in *Anglian Home Improvements Ltd v Kelly* [2004] EWCA Civ 901, [2005] ICR 242, [2004] IRLR 793 has given guidance that a tribunal should if at all possible avoid a majority decision, if necessary reserving its decision to give the members time to reflect and the Judge an opportunity to prepare reasons which accurately reflect the majority view (especially if he or she is in the minority).

19.116 *Effect of an Order or Judgment and Time for Compliance*

The normal rule is that a judgment or order takes effect from the day when it is given or made: *Rule 65*. However, *Rule 65* also provides that the Tribunal may specify a later date for it to take effect.

The *2013 Rules* introduce new provisions concerning compliance with judgments and orders.

If the order or judgment is for the payment of an amount of money, *Rule 66(1)* states that the party required to pay that sum must pay that amount within 14 days of the date of the judgment or order, unless (a) the judgment, order, or any of the *Rules*, specifies a different date for compliance; or (b) the Tribunal has stayed (or in Scotland sisted) the proceedings or judgment.

19.117 *Reasons*

Unlike the provisions of the old rules, the *2013 Rules* require a Tribunal to give reasons for a decision made on any disputed issue: *Rule 62(1)*. This is the case whether the issue is substantive or procedural. Rule 62(1) goes on to say that this includes any decision on an application for reconsideration, for orders for costs, preparation time or wasted costs.

Rule 62(2) goes on to specify how this duty should be discharged. If a decision has been given in writing, then the reasons must also be given in writing. In the case of a decision announced at a hearing the Tribunal may choose to give the reasons orally, or reserve them to be given in writing later. In the latter case, the reasons may (but need not be) part of the written record of the decision. Like the record of a decision, written reasons must be signed by the Employment Judge.

If oral reasons are given, the Judge must announce that written reasons will not be provided unless they are asked for by any party at the hearing itself, or by a written request presented by any party within 14 days of the sending of the written record of the decision. The written record of the decision must repeat that information: *Rule 62(3)*. If a request is received within that time period, the Tribunal will then produce, and send out, written reasons for the decision in question. If no request is received, the Tribunal will then only provide the written reasons if requested to do so by the Employment Appeal Tribunal or a court. The written reasons will normally be required as a prerequisite to an appeal against a judgment and so a litigant who intends to appeal against the decision in question should ask for written reasons in accordance with *Rule 62(3)* and the time limit mentioned above.

A proposal published in a December 2011 consultation for the introduction of a fee payable if reasons in writing are requested has been dropped. The provisions of *Rule 62* governing written reasons have the somewhat surprising consequence that if the judgment is not reserved, and neither party chooses to ask for reasons in writing, there will be no formal record of the reasons available to the press or other interested parties. Even in a case raising issues of wider public interest, there appears not only to be no duty, but even no power to give the reasons in writing, provided they have been given orally and none of the parties makes a request for written reasons and the matter is not appealed. This is particularly significant since judgments, and the written reasons for them, are matters of public record.

HM Courts and Tribunals Service sets a target for the promulgation of written judgments and reasons, which is currently that they must be promulgated within four weeks of the conclusion of the Hearing in 85% of cases; this target has been met consistently in recent years, although some tribunal offices have in some years fallen below the target. However occasionally there have been instances of serious delays in issuing the judgment in cases where the judgment was reserved at the end of the hearing. In one such case, *Bangs v Connex South Eastern Ltd* [2005] EWCA Civ 14, [2005] IRLR 389, the Court of Appeal, in the course of refusing to overturn the tribunal's decision, gave guidance as to how such delay is to be considered in the context of an appeal. Delay in issuing a judgment is not of itself an error of law and therefore not as such a ground of appeal. The key question, the Court held, is whether due to the delay there was a real risk that a party had been denied or deprived of the right to a fair trial.

In the related case of *Kwamin v Abbey National plc* [2004] IRLR 516, the EAT had taken a broader approach, which was disapproved by the Court of Appeal; it had also given strong guidance, which was implicitly approved by the Court of Appeal, as to the need to avoid lengthy delays in reaching and issuing reserved judgments. Three-and-a-half months is the longest acceptable time for the delivery of judgment following the conclusion of the hearing (or the delivery of written submissions, if later), and except in the most complex cases, longer delay without proper explanation (such as illness) would be regarded as culpable; it does not however follow that such delay justifies an appeal. An extreme example of delay occurred in *Carpenter v City of Edinburgh Council* (UKEATS/0038/07), where the judgment was issued over three years after the hearing had concluded; the EAT overturned the decision, not because of the delay itself, but because of a number of points on which it appeared from the terms of the reasons that the tribunal had forgotten relevant evidence.

In *Eyitene v Wirral Metropolitan Borough Council* [2014] EWCA Civ 1243, the Court of Appeal explained how Tribunals should prepare written reasons when sitting with lay members. At para 11, Underhill LJ approved the practice of: (i) the Tribunal having a full discussion after the close of submissions either on the same day or during a subsequent chambers day(s) (which are noted in the reasons); (ii) during the discussions, judges must identify with the lay members the issues that require determination and go through those issues in a structured fashion. Full notes of the decisions and essential reasoning, reflecting the view of all members and recording points of disagreement must be made. Some judges will type or record passages of the judgment there and then for agreement, but that depends on the case and judge in question. These materials form the basis of the Reasons, but it is not regarded as necessary for the detailed expression of the reasons to be agreed, which would substantially increase the time needed for deliberation. (iii) If the case is straight-forward then the discussion will be short and the decision and reasons can be delivered orally on the basis of the notes, and the reasons recorded on tape as they are delivered. The tape will form the basis of the written reasons if they are then requested, subject to any editing by the judge (see *The Partners of Haxby Practice v Collen* UKEAT/0120/12, discussed below). (iv) If the case is more complex, the reasons may have to be reserved and drafted by the Judge on the basis of the notes. The lay members are entitled to see the text of the reasons prior to final promulgation, but circulation is not routine without a request (save that where there is a split decision, the judge will always circulate a draft). Underhill LJ emphasised that "lay members should feel no inhibition about exercising that right if they wish to do so in a particular case".

19.118 *Adequacy of reasons*

Rules 62(4) and *(5)* contain some provisions concerning the nature of the reasons that Tribunals give. First, *Rule 62(4)* indicates that reasons for a decision must be proportionate to the significance of the issue and for decisions other than judgments may be very short. Case management decisions do not, therefore, require the judge to give expansive reasoning. Often in practice a judge will set out his/her reasoning on such a matter within a paragraph or so.

In the case of a judgment, *Rule 62(5)* provides a basic structure to the reasons. The reasons must identify the issues which the Tribunal has determined, state the findings of fact made in relation to those issues, concisely identify the relevant law, and state how that law has been applied to those findings in order to decide the issues. Further, where the judgment includes a financial award the reasons shall identify, by means of a table or otherwise, how the amount to be paid has been calculated. These requirements are similar to those which appeared in the previous rules – at *Rule 30(6)* of the *2004 Rules*.

There is an additional and specific duty to give an explanation of any award of interest, and reasons for any decision not to award interest, in discrimination and equal pay cases (*Employment Tribunals (Interest on Awards in Discrimination Cases) Regulations 1996 (SI 1996/2803), reg 7*); where the *Employment Protection (Recoupment of Jobseeker's Allowance and Income Support) Regulations 1996* apply, there is a requirement for the tribunal to state that they apply, and to specify the 'prescribed amount' (the part of the compensation covering the period during which benefits were received, which is then available for the DWP to recover the benefits before the balance is payable to the successful claimant).

The EAT has held that it is an error of law on the part of the tribunal not to give reasons meeting the requirements of *Rule 30(6)* of the *2004 Rules*: *Greenwood v NWF Retail Ltd* [2011] ICR 896. The logic of this decision applies equally to *Rule 62(5)* of the *2013 Rules*: see *Vairea v Reed Business Information Ltd* [2016] UKEAT/0177/15 and *Dutton v Governing Body of Woodslee Primary School* [2016] UKEAT/0305/15. In *Greenwood*, however, the EAT quoted with approval comments of Buxton LJ in *Balfour Beatty Power Networks Ltd v Wilcox* [2007] IRLR 63, at para 25, that: " . . . the rule is surely intended to be a guide and not a straitjacket. Provided it can be reasonably spelled out from the determination of the employment tribunal that what [now *Rule 62(5)* requires has been provided by that tribunal, then no error of law will have been committed."

The statutory requirements reflect and to some extent consolidate requirements increasingly emphasised by the appellate courts as a necessary part of the judicial process: see in particular *English v Emery Reimbold & Strick Ltd* [2002] EWCA Civ 605, [2003] IRLR 710. However in *Greenwood* the EAT said that the more relevant authority on sufficiency of reasons in employment tribunals is *Meek v City of Birmingham District Council* [1987] IRLR 250, CA.

The following statement by Bingham LJ in Meek is generally regarded as the leading statement of principle on inadequacy of reasons as a ground of appeal, and is regularly referred to for this purpose:

> "It has on a number of occasions been made plain that the decision of an [Employment] Tribunal is not required to be an elaborate formalistic product of refined legal draftsmanship, but it must contain an outline of the story which has given rise to the complaint and a summary of the Tribunal's basic factual conclusions and a statement of the reasons which have led them to reach the conclusion which they do on those basic facts. The parties are entitled to be told why they have won or lost. There should be sufficient account of the facts and of the reasoning to enable the EAT . . . to see whether any question of law arises; and it is highly desirable that the decision of an [Employment] Tribunal should give guidance both to employers and trade unions as to practices which should or should not be adopted."

Whilst the tribunal must reach a conclusion on all the issues required by the statute concerned to be decided, and at least consider all the relevant facts, its decision need only refer to the important and/or controversial points: *High Table Ltd v Horst* [1997] IRLR 513. It is, however, important that the tribunal properly identifies the legal rules and tests it has applied in reaching its decision: *Conlin v United Distillers* [1994] IRLR 169, para 6. Further guidance on the adequacy of reasons was given by the Court of Appeal in *Tran v Greenwich Vietnam Community Project* [2002] EWCA Civ 553, [2002] IRLR 735. Reasons need not be lengthy, but should be sufficient to explain to the parties how the tribunal got from its findings of fact to its conclusions (indeed, lengthy reasons can in certain circumstances still fail to tell the parties how the case was decided; for an example see *The Co-Operative Group Ltd v Baddeley* [2014] EWCA Civ 658). The reasons must explain why the evidence of one witness has been preferred over another on the relevant issue: see *Flannery v Halifax Estate Agents Ltd* [2000] 1 WLR 377 at 382 and *Kibirango v Barclays Bank plc* UKEAT/0234/14. In addition, whilst the reasons are primarily addressed to those already familiar with the context of the case, it is desirable that the reasoning can be ascertained from the face of the decision; in any case it is necessary that the decision is sufficiently reasoned to enable an appellate court or tribunal to ascertain what the tribunal's findings of fact and reasons for its conclusions were. The decision of the Court of Appeal in *Anya v University of Oxford* [2001] EWCA Civ 405, [2001] IRLR 377 contains important comments on the need for tribunals in discrimination cases to set out the findings reached on the issues of primary fact, and an explanation why the tribunal does or does not draw inferences of discrimination from the facts as found. A number of cases have highlighted the need for tribunals to give reasons for specific elements in their judgments; these include the exercise of the discretionary power to increase or reduce compensation under *Employment Act 2002, s 31* (the same point presumably applies to the replacement power under *TULRCA 1992, s 207A*), and decisions on contributory fault (in relation to which the Court of Appeal has suggested that the tribunal should make findings of fact separate from those made in relation to the fairness of the dismissal: *London Ambulance Service v Small* [2009] EWCA Civ 220, [2009] IRLR 563). The alleged inadequacy of the tribunal's reasons (often put as a complaint that the judgment was not 'Meek-compliant') is one of the most frequent grounds of appeal. However, the EAT is in practice rarely prepared to overturn a tribunal's judgment simply on the grounds that the reasons given are inadequate. The Court of Appeal in the English case stressed that it is not a good ground of appeal that the reasons for a judgment are inadequate if it is clear from reading the judgment with knowledge of the evidence given and submissions made why the point in question was decided as it was. However a rather stricter approach was taken by the Court of Appeal in *Bahl v Law Society* [2004] IRLR 799 (a discrimination case), emphasising that only in a limited class of cases will it be possible to make good in that way inadequate reasons given by the tribunal.

The EAT has adopted a practice, in many but not all of the cases where an appeal is brought on the ground of inadequate reasons, to remit the case to the tribunal for it to clarify or amplify its reasons, prior to the hearing of the substantive appeal. The legality of the practice (which had been in doubt because of conflicting decisions of the Court of Appeal on the EAT's powers) was initially confirmed by the EAT in *Burns v Consignia plc (No 2)* [2004] IRLR 425, and subsequently (but on a different basis) by the Court of Appeal itself in *Barke v SEETEC Business Technology Centre Ltd* [2005] EWCA Civ 578, [2005] IRLR 633, and the procedure is often referred to as a '*Burns/Barke* reference' accordingly. The power is to be found in the *2013 Rules* at *Rule 62(3)* which requires the tribunal to provide reasons for any order or judgment if requested by the EAT. The EAT also has the necessary power under a general provision giving it the power to regulate its own procedure (*ETA 1996, s 30(1)*). The Court added that the procedure should not be used in cases where the reasons were fundamentally deficient, or there is an allegation of bias, or a danger that the tribunal will tailor its response to shoring up the original decision rather than give its true reasons (a point taken up again by the Court in *Woodhouse School v Webster* [2009] EWCA Civ 91, [2009] IRLR 568, where it was stressed that the judge should not in responding go beyond clarification of reasons to advocacy for the original decision). See further on the use of the *Burns/Barke* procedure *Korashi v Abertawe Bro Morgannwg University Local Health Board* [2011] EWCA Civ 187, [2011] All ER (D) 09 (Mar).

A Tribunal can also err in law by making findings on matters not properly before it (as well as those findings not founding an issue estoppel): see *Baker v Peninsula Business Services Ltd* [2017] IRLR 394 at paras 81-82.

19.119 *Changing and correcting the decision and reasons*
A judgment given orally at the end of the hearing is a final decision. The powers of a tribunal to change its judgment subsequently, prior to promulgation in writing (eg where there is a subsequent change in the relevant case law), are very limited. In *Lamont v Fry's Metals Ltd* [1985] ICR 566 the Court of Appeal assumed, without deciding the point, that a tribunal can recall its judgment before it is entered in the Register. However, it should then give both parties an opportunity of addressing further argument to the tribunal (see also *Arthur Guinness Son & Co (Great Britain) Ltd v Green* [1989] ICR 241, EAT; *Gutzmore v J Wardley (Holdings) Ltd* [1993] ICR 581). More recent EAT decisions have emphasised the limits on the power of recall, and suggest that there is no power on recall to change the substantive judgment (*Spring Grove Services Group plc v Hickinbottom* [1990] ICR 111; *Casella London Ltd v Banai* [1990] ICR 215). However in *CK Heating Ltd v Doro* [2010] ICR 1449, the EAT held that a tribunal was entitled to recall for further consideration a decision, announced orally at the end of the hearing but which had not been issued as a written judgment, that the claimant's compensation would be reduced by 30% for contributory fault. Although in general the parties are entitled to regard an oral statement of the result of a hearing as final, until the written judgment is issued it is therefore open to the tribunal, if it considers it to be in the interest of justice to do so, to recall its decision. There is less objection to a decision being recalled in these circumstances if there will not be any requirement for reconsideration of the primary facts, or further evidence. A contrasting approach has been taken by the Court of Appeal to decisions reached by the Upper Tribunal where, under the different rules applicable there, decisions were effective as soon as the judge had uttered the words: see *Patel v Secretary of State for the Home Department* [2015] EWCA Civ 1175.

Rule 69 contains a power which can be used by an Employment Judge at any time to correct any clerical mistake or other accidental slip or omission in an order, judgment or any other document produced by a Tribunal. If such a correction is made, any published version of the document shall also be corrected. If any document is corrected under *Rule 69*, a copy of the corrected version, signed by the Judge, shall be sent to all the parties.

A similar power existed in the previous versions of the rules and has been held to be limited; thus in *Bone v Newham London Borough Council* [2008] EWCA Civ 435, [2008] IRLR 546 the Court of Appeal held that the tribunal did not have the power to 'correct' its judgment by inserting a finding that the dismissal of the claimant was an act of sex discrimination, having recorded the opposite in its original written judgment.

It has been held by the EAT that if the form of the correction under what is now *Rule 69* is the substitution of a complete corrected version of the judgment and reasons for the original version, time for appealing starts to run from the date of the correction: *Kennaugh v Lloyd-Jones (t/a Cheshire Tree Surgeons)* [2006] All ER (D) 363 (Nov). The better practice is therefore only to identify the words or passage corrected; this will not affect the running of time.

The issue of deviation in the written reasons for a judgment (as opposed to the judgment itself) from oral reasons delivered by the Tribunal was considered by the EAT in *The Partners of Haxby Practice v Collen* [2013] All ER (D) 11 (Feb). Whilst the EAT accepted that normally written reasons supplied pursuant to *rule 30(3)* will correspond closely to the oral reasons given at the conclusion of the hearing, it was acknowledged there will almost always be some degree of editing. Underhill J held that this editing process may, depending on the circumstances and temperament of the judge, be more or less substantial; every now and then there will be cases where the process of revision is so extensive that the reasoning in support of a conclusion differs in substance from the oral reasoning. The EAT held there was "no shame in this" and a departure from initially expressed reasoning does not involve any error of law. The written reasons, where supplied, are the sole authoritative statement of the tribunal's reasons and the oral reasons are superseded. The oral reasons might, however, still remain relevant to allegations of apparent bias or where they might elucidate some ambiguity in the written reasons. See further the discussion of the process of crafting the reasons in *Eyitene v Wirral Metropolitan Borough Council* [2014] EWCA Civ 1243 (above).

The power of reconsideration is considered at **19.124** below.

19.120 *The Register*

By *Rule 67*, a copy shall be entered in the Register of any judgment and of any written reasons for a judgment. In addition, where the proceedings were referred to the Tribunal by a court, a copy of any judgment and of any written reasons shall be provided to that court: *Rule 68*.

To give effect to this rule, there is a public register of tribunal judgments and written reasons: *Reg 14* of the *2013 Regulations*. All such judgments and reasons are entered in it and available for public (and press) scrutiny, except in cases of national security or where the tribunal has sat in private and it so orders (see *Rules 50* and *94*). The Tribunal has a discretion to delete matters from the public copy of a judgment and reasons by applying *Rule 50* see above. Necessarily only written reasons can be included in the Register, a factor which parties should consider before deciding whether to ask for written reasons where the reasons have been given orally.

In complaints under *sections 120, 127* or *146* of the *Equality Act 2010*, the Tribunal must also send a copy of all judgments and written reasons to the Commission for Equality and Human Rights. This obligation does not apply in proceedings where a direction or order under *Rule 94*, relating to national security, has been given and either the Security Service, the Secret Intelligence Service or the Government Communications Headquarters is a party to the proceedings.

For details about the on-line database of judgments and reasons see **18.5–18.6**.

Remedies and enforcement

19.121 *Generally*

The remedies available in the tribunal depend on the particular jurisdiction covering the case, and are discussed together with the substantive law elsewhere in this book. A number of additional points require mention.

A judgment ordering the payment of money made by a tribunal is enforceable as if it was a judgment of the County Court (or in Scotland the Sheriff Court). The fact that an appeal is pending does not itself suspend the remedy awarded, but if an application to enforce it is made to the County Court, the other party will usually be granted a stay of execution pending the appeal.

Tribunals have no power to enforce their own non-monetary judgments except by awards of compensation; the best examples are an additional award for failure to comply with an order for re-employment in an unfair dismissal case (*ERA 1996, s 117(3)–(5)*), and power to increase compensation if the employer has failed without reasonable justification to comply with a recommendation in a discrimination case (*Equality Act 2010, s 124(7)*). The absence of any enforcement machinery other than the County Court has led in a significant number of cases to real difficulties in the successful claimant recovering the compensation awarded, even disregarding cases where the employer is insolvent (in which case there may be a claim against the Secretary of State: see Insolvency of Employer (29)). Research commissioned by the Ministry of Justice (Research into the enforcement of employment tribunal awards in England and Wales, Ministry of Justice Research Series 9/09, May 2009) found that only 61% of those claimants interviewed who had received a tribunal award had received any payment; only 53% had been paid in full. Reasons for non-payment included

29% of non-paying employers simply refusing to pay, whilst 39% no longer existed or had gone bankrupt. The National Association of Citizens' Advice Bureaux had earlier proposed that awards of compensation should be paid by the state, with the right to recover the money from the employer passing to the Government (Hollow Victories, March 2005). This proposal was not accepted by the Government, but the *Tribunals, Courts and Enforcement Act 2007, s 142* (adding a new *s 19A* to the *ETA 1996*) has introduced some improvement in the position. Once the judgment has been formally registered with the County Court, any of the various means of enforcement of County Court judgments can be initiated without the need first to apply for the Court to order the respondent to pay the sum awarded and then to allow time for payment. A similar but simpler procedure applies in Scotland, where the enforcement of a payment ordered by a judgment is undertaken by the Sheriff Court on the authority of the judgment of the tribunal.

In order to incentivise the payment of employment tribunal awards, *Section 150* of the *Small Business, Enterprise and Employment Act 2015* provided for the amendment of the *ETA* to include a new *Part 2A*: financial penalties for failure to pay sums ordered to be paid or settlement sums. With effect from 6 April 2016, the relevant provisions are now to be found at *sections 37A to 37Q* of the *ETA 1996*. The provisions allow enforcement officers to issue warning notices to an employer in respect of defined sums awarded by a tribunal (including compensation and costs) and settlement sums that remain unsatisfied. If the sums remain unpaid, a penalty notice can then be issued requiring the employer to pay a financial penalty to the Secretary of State. The financial penalty will be 50% of the unpaid relevant sum, subject to a minimum of £100 and a maximum of £5,000. If, within 14 days of the penalty notice, the employer pays both the unpaid relevant sum and the penalty reduced by 50%, the employer will be treated as having complied with his obligations. If no payment is made, the full penalty will remain due and interest will be charged at the judgment rate. For the purposes of the statutory scheme, amounts in respect of financial awards are not regarded as outstanding during the time when the worker could make an application for costs (and if s/he has made that application, the period before it is finally determined) or where either party could appeal against the relevant tribunal judgment (and if a party has commenced appeal proceedings, the period before they have been finally determined). An employer to whom a penalty notice has been given may, before the end of the period within which the penalty must be paid, appeal against the penalty notice or the amount of a penalty to an employment tribunal on defined grounds (incorrect grounds stated on penalty notice, incorrect calculation or unreasonable for the enforcement officer to have issued the notice). The Department for Business, Innovation and Skills has published a form for claiming penalties which claimants can complete (see https ://www.gov.uk/government/uploads/system/uploads/attachment_data/file/ 524721/employment-tribunal-penalty-form.docx).

The Court of Appeal has held that failure to pay compensation awarded to a claimant in a discrimination case may be made the subject of a claim of victimisation: *Rank Nemo (DMS) Ltd v Coutinho* [2009] EWCA Civ 454, [2009] IRLR 672.

Where the tribunal has given judgment in favour of the claimant on liability but adjourned the question of remedy, it is open to the parties to reach a private agreement as to the remedy, subject to a formal consent judgment being made by the tribunal. Such an agreement, provided that it is embodied in a judgment, is binding without the need to comply with the requirements for a settlement agreement (as to which, see **19.19** et sec above): *Carter v Reiner Moritz Associates Ltd* [1997] ICR 881. Alternatively, if the parties wish to keep the terms of the agreement confidential, the tribunal may be asked to make a consent order staying (or in Scotland sisting) the proceedings for a period to allow for payment of the agreed sum (the amount of which need not be set out in the order), with provision for the case to be dismissed if no application is made to restore it within a stated period.

19.122 *Interest on awards*

Post-judgment interest is payable on any compensation ordered by a tribunal which has not been paid when due. Interest on unpaid tribunal awards accrues from the day after the decision unless the award is paid in full within 14 days (see *Employment Tribunals (Interest) Order 1990*, as amended, and *Rule 66*). Interest is payable at the rate fixed from time to time under *s 17* of the *Judgments Act 1838* applicable at the date it starts to accrue. The current rate is 8% (this has not been changed despite the general collapse in interest rates in 2008–9 and rates remaining low in the ensuing period). If compensation is subsequently increased or decreased on appeal, the new amount is subject to interest from the original date (*Employment Tribunals (Interest) Order 1990 (SI 1990/479)*).

Normally, tribunals cannot award pre-judgment interest as a remedy in its own right, however long the delay since the matters giving rise to the remedy. The principal exception to this is in discrimination and equal pay cases. The relevant regulations (which originate from regulations in sex discrimination and equal pay cases introduced in 1993 to give effect to a decision of the ECJ (*Marshall v Southampton and SW Hampshire Health Authority (No 2)* [1993] ICR 893)) are currently the *Employment Tribunals (Interest on Awards in Discrimination Cases) Regulations 1996 (SI 1996/2803)* (the '*1996 Interest Regulations*'). There is no automatic right to interest under the *1996 Interest Regulations*, but the tribunal is required to consider the question even if not asked to do so (*reg 2(1)(b)*). In practice, in any case where there is a significant time lag between the discrimination and the decision, a tribunal may be expected to award interest unless there are special reasons for not doing so.

The rate of interest is, since 29 July 2013, the rate fixed by *s 17* of the *Judgments Act 1838* and, in Scotland, the rate fixed by *section 9* of the *Sheriff Courts (Scotland) Extracts Act 1892*. The current rate is, as stated above, 8%. Prior to 29 July 2013, the rate was that laid down from time to time under *rule 27(1)* of the *Court Funds Rules 1987 (SI 1987/821)* as the rate of interest for the Special Investment Account (reg 3(2)); this had, since 1 July 2009, been 0.5%, having been reduced in stages in 2009 from the former rate of 6%. Where the calculation period covers periods of varying rates of interest, an average rate can be taken (*reg 3(3)*). There were detailed rules as to the period in respect of which interest should be awarded (*reg 6*) and the normal rules as to interest on the total sum (including interest) awarded by the tribunal are varied, so that interest on the sum awarded (at the higher Judgment Act rate) runs from the day after the day on which the decision on remedy is issued, unless the respondent pays in full within 14 days (*reg 8*). (See now the *Court Funds Rules 2011 (SI 2011/1734)*).

In an attempt to remedy the injustice to claimants that may arise from the lack of any power to award interest in, for instance, unfair dismissal cases, the Court of Appeal in *Melia v Magna Kansei Ltd* [2006] IRLR 117 held that compensation may be increased to reflect delay in receipt, by analogy with the reduction that may be made in calculating future loss to reflect accelerated payment. At the time of this case this was set at 2.5% a year, and the Court ruled that compensation could be increased at that rate for the delay between the date of dismissal and the date of the award. This principle applies primarily where there is also a discount for accelerated payment for future loss, but it is submitted that it is not limited to such cases, and thus amounts to a limited general power to award interest, at least where there has been significant delay between the dismissal and the decision on remedy. Since 20 March 2017, however, the Lord Chancellor reduced the discount rate from +2.5% to -0.75% (a reduction of 3.25%). This is likely to remove the incentive for claimants to pursue this line of argument.

19.123 *Recoupment of benefits received*

Where an employee has received Jobseeker's Allowance, Income Support or Income-related Employment and Support Allowance between the date of dismissal and the date of the award of compensation for unfair dismissal (and certain other forms of compensation such as a protective award in redundancy consultation cases, but not compensation for loss of earnings in discrimination cases), there is a procedure for the Department for Work and Pensions to recover whatever amount of these benefits has been paid to the claimant during that period. This is known as 'recoupment', and is regulated by the *Employment Protection (Recoupment of Jobseeker's Allowance and Income Support) Regulations 1996 (SI 1996/2349)* (the title of the *Regulations* has not been amended to reflect the addition of Income-related Employment and Support Allowance from November 2010). Recoupment only applies to the benefits listed above; other social security benefits are not affected. For details of how Employment and Support Allowance and other social security benefits may be taken into account in assessing compensation see **55.6 UNFAIR DISMISSAL – III**.

The system of recoupment is that the tribunal identifies the proportion of its award that relates to loss of income between dismissal and the date of the award; this is known as 'the prescribed element', and must be separately identified in the judgment and reasons. The employer should withhold this amount from any payment to the employee until notified by the Department for Work and Pensions how much it wishes to recoup from the award; notification must be given within 21 days, and the amount recoupable will be the amount of benefits paid, up to the maximum of the prescribed element. The employer must then pay the amount recouped to the DWP instead of the employee. If an award is made by the tribunal for future loss, the employee may lose relevant benefits during the period covered by the award, but this does not affect the amount or payment of the actual award.

The recoupment system applies only to an award by the tribunal. Whilst it ensures that neither the employer nor the employee benefits from the social security benefits paid to the employee, it may reduce quite considerably the value in the employee's hands of the tribunal's award. This does not apply to a payment agreed by the parties – a significant incentive to settle the amount of any compensation. Since recoupment does not apply to awards in discrimination cases, Jobseeker's Allowance, Income Support and Income-related Employment and Support Allowance do have to be taken into account (subject to rather complex rules affecting particular benefits) in calculating the employee's net losses in such cases.

Reconsideration

19.124 *General*

The previous position concerning the ability of a Tribunal to 'review' judgments it had made under the *2004 Rules* has been subject to rationalisation and simplification in the *2013 Rules*. The previous rules set out particular grounds on which judgments could be reviewed. The *2013 Rules* have opted simply for a test of the interests of justice.

By *Rule 70*, a Tribunal may now either on its own initiative (which may reflect a request from the Employment Appeal Tribunal) or on the application of a party, reconsider any judgment where it is necessary in the interests of justice to do so. When doing so, the decision (referred to in *Rule 70* and the subsequent rules dealing with reconsideration as "the original decision") may be confirmed, varied or revoked. If it is revoked it may be taken again.

There is a fee payable for making an application to reconsider a final judgment: see fees above.

There are separate powers of the Tribunal to reconsider decisions to reject claims and responses and to challenge decisions taken on initial consideration (see above).

As can be seen from the wording of *Rule 70*, it is also possible for a review to be instituted following an appeal to the EAT. The EAT has developed a practice in some cases of staying appeals to give the appellant an opportunity to apply for a review of the decision sought to be appealed. There is no obligation on the Judge who then receives a review application to grant a review, and each application will be considered on its merits; but in these circumstances, if the would-be appellant applies promptly for a review, it would be unlikely that the application would be refused solely on the ground that it is made out of time (see below). *Rule 70* also envisages a review request emanating directly from the EAT.

There is no power to reconsider orders other than judgments under *Rule 70*; in particular case management orders are not open to reconsideration. This will not normally present a problem, since there is a general power to vary or revoke such orders, which can be exercised without the formality of reconsideration (subject to there being a basis for varying or revoking a previous order: see **19.57** above). The power to vary case management orders that have been made, where this is necessary in the interests of justice, and in particular where a party affected by the earlier order did not have a reasonable opportunity to make representations before it was made, is contained in *Rule 29*. A similar power existed under the old rules (see *Onwuka v Spherion Technology UK Ltd* [2005] ICR 567, *Hart v English Heritage* [2006] ICR 655, [2006] IRLR 915 and *North Tyneside Primary Care Trust v Aynsley* [2009] All ER (D) 125 (May)). The EAT held that the power to vary an order (unless it was originally made without the party affected having had an opportunity to make representations before the order was made) should not be exercised unless there has been a material change in circumstances (see *Serco Ltd v Wells* UKEAT/0330/15; *Goldman Sachs Services Ltd v Montali* [2002] ICR 1251, where a preliminary hearing had been ordered on the issue of whether some of the claimant's complaints were out of time, but the tribunal appointed to hear the preliminary point instead directed that the issue should be determined at the substantive hearing; this decision was set aside by the EAT; *Sodexho Ltd v Gibbons* [2005] IRLR 836; and *Hart* (above) where the comment was made that there are stronger objections to reopening a decision taken after argument on the point than where the basis of the application is a point which had not been considered when the order was first made).

19.125 *Procedure*

Rule 71 requires an application for reconsideration to be presented in writing (and copied to all the other parties) within 14 days of the date on which the written record, or other written communication, of the original decision was sent to the parties or within 14 days of the date that the written reasons were sent (if later). The application must set out why reconsideration of the original decision is necessary. There is an exception for where an application for reconsideration is made in the course of a hearing. In such circumstances, it need not be presented in writing.

Once made, *Rule 72(1)* requires an application for reconsideration to be considered by an Employment Judge. If the Judge considers that there is no reasonable prospects of the original decision being varied or revoked (including, unless there are special reasons, where substantially the same application has already been made and refused), the application must be refused and the Tribunal must inform the parties of the refusal. Otherwise, *Rule 72(1)* requires that the Tribunal should send a notice to the parties setting a time limit for any response to the application by the other parties and seeking the views of the parties on whether the application can be determined without a hearing. The notice may also set out the Judge's provisional views on the application. This is a mandatory requirement as the EAT held in *The Practice Surgeries Ltd v Srivatsa* [2016] UKEAT/0212/15.

If the reconsideration application has not been refused, by *Rule 72(2)*, the original decision must be reconsidered at a hearing, unless the Employment Judge considers (having had regard to the views of the parties on whether the application can be determined without a hearing elicited under *Rule 72(1)*) that a hearing is not necessary in the interest of justice. If the reconsideration proceeds without a hearing, *Rule 72(2)* provides that the parties must be given a reasonable opportunity to make further written submissions. A failure to afford such an opportunity can give rise to an error of law: see e.g. *Srivatsa* (above).

Where a hearing is held, this will be a formal oral hearing at which if necessary evidence can be called. The test for whether fresh evidence should be admitted on reconsideration is the same as that laid down by the EAT in *Wileman v Minilec Engineering Ltd* [1988] ICR 318, adopting the established formulation as set out in *Ladd v Marshall* [1954] 1 WLR 1489; see **20.34** below. The EAT was clear that the *Ladd* test applied in *Outasight VB Ltd v Brown* [2015] ICR D11. HHJ Eady QC held that the change in the 2013 Rules (removing specified categories under which a review could be granted) did not introduce a broader discretion as to when fresh evidence could be admitted. The approach in *Ladd* would in most cases encapsulate what is meant by "the interests of justice" and provided a consistent approach across the civil courts. The EAT did recognise, however, a residual category of case where the requirements of *Ladd* were not strictly met and when, that notwithstanding, the interests of justice might still require the admission of fresh evidence. HHJ Eady held that Tribunals have always had the ability to review judgments in such circumstances. See also *Dundee City Council v Margaret Gennelli Malcolm* UKEATS/0019/15 in which Langstaff J held that a tribunal ought not to order reconsideration if its purpose was to permit a party to lead further evidence which could have been led earlier.

If the application is granted, the tribunal will either vary the decision or revoke it and order a re-hearing (*Rule 70*). If, on reconsideration, the tribunal concludes that the original decision was wrong, the power to vary is wide enough to allow variation by substitution of the opposite result, e.g. unfair rather than fair dismissal: *Stonehill Furniture Ltd v Phillippo* [1983] ICR 556. On the other hand, if the previous judgment is revoked, the matter must be re-decided, either without a hearing, if the judgment was originally issued without a hearing having been held, or at a fresh hearing.

The *2013 Rules* (*Rule 72(3)*) require, where "practicable", the initial consideration of an application to reconsider a judgment under *Rule 72(1)*, and the actual reconsideration under *Rule 72(2)*, to be taken by the Employment Judge who made the original decision, or, as the case may be, chaired the full tribunal which made it. Where that is not practicable, the President, Vice President or a Regional Employment Judge shall appoint another Employment Judge to deal with the application or, in the case of a decision of a full tribunal, shall either direct that the reconsideration be by such members of the original Tribunal as remain available or reconstitute the Tribunal in whole or in part. Under *Rule 35* of the *2004 Rules*, the EAT held that the similar requirement that where "practicable" the same judge should conduct a review application was intended to deal with cases where the original judge was physically unavailable, had died, or was too unwell to attend the application. "Practicable" meant feasible, not convenient; in that case, an allegation of bias against the judge did not render it impracticable for the original judge to consider the review application: see *Papajak v Intellego Group Ltd* [2013] UKEAT/0124/12. In *Benney v Department for Environment, Food and Rural Affairs* [2015] UKEAT/0252/13, the EAT held that the word "practicable" was to be properly construed by reference to dealing with the review application expeditiously, proportionately, fairly and in such a way as to save expense (i.e. by reference to the overriding objective). The word was not intended to be interpreted as it is in *ERA, s 111(2)(b)*, governing when extensions of time for unfair dismissal claims can be granted by the Tribunal. Whether it is practicable for the original judge to decide upon the application for a review is a question of fact to be decided in all the circumstances. In that case, the original judge had moved to a different region, the application for a review was made very late (approx. 2 years), the file had been destroyed and the application was made over 24 pages. The EAT found all of these to be legitimate factors justifying the Regional Judge determining the application. The EAT also commented in passing that it is possible that the merits of the application might also affect practicability: if an application is patently hopeless, it might be said to be impracticable to take up another Judge's time with what has already been considered by a Regional Employment Judge.

If a Tribunal proposes to reconsider a decision on its own initiative, *Rule 73* requires it to inform the parties of the reasons why the decision is being reconsidered and the decision shall then be reconsidered in accordance with *Rule 72(2)* as if an application had been made and not refused.

Under the old Rules, the EAT confirmed that the tribunal has no power to initiate a review of a judgment unless the procedural formalities are complied with: *CK Heating Ltd v Doro* [2010] ICR 1449. In *Srivatsa* (above) the EAT reached a decision to a similar effect under the *2013 Rules*.

19.126 *Commentary*

By *Rule 70*, a tribunal only has power to review a judgment. This will include any decision, including a determination of a preliminary point, which finally disposes of a particular issue, as well as a judgment on liability or remedy, or both. Under the old rules, it was held to include the striking out of a claim when a deposit was not paid (*Sodexho Ltd v Gibbons* [2005] IRLR 836), and on the same basis would include striking out a claim for other reasons such as unreasonable conduct. Under the *2013 Rules* the EAT has confirmed in *Trustees of the William Jones's School Foundation v Parry* [2016] ICR 1140, that a decision to whether or not to reject an ET1 taken under *Rule 12* does finally determine an issue which is capable of finally disposing of the claim and is therefore capable of reconsideration under *Rule 70*. Under the old rules, there was the ability to "review" where a claim was struck out for non-compliance with an unless order: see *Tisson v Telewest Communications Group Ltd*, [2008] All ER (D) 42 (May), EAT and *Neary v Governing Body of St Albans Girls' School* [2009] EWCA Civ 1190, [2010] ICR 473, EAT; where strictly, the effect of the striking out was to convert the conditional 'unless' order into a judgment, which could then be reviewed. See also *North Tyneside Primary Care Trust v Aynsley* [2009] ICR 1333. The approach is however different under the *2013 Rules* and the contortions seen under the previous rules are no longer necessary. *Rule 38(2)* provides the mechanism by which the unless order can be reconsidered and revoked if it is appropriate to do so: the interest of justice test applies there also.

The case law under the previous rules relating to 'review' must now be seen in light of the fact that the criteria for reconsideration have been reduced to one: that it is in the interests of justice. However, as the Court of Appeal held in *Ministry of Justice v Burton* [2016] ICR 1128, "the earlier case law cannot be ignored". The interests of justice include justice to the party which was successful at the hearing, and the public interest in the finality of litigation (see *Flint v Eastern Electricity Board* [1975] ICR 395). The reconsideration procedure enables errors which occur in the course of the proceedings to be corrected regardless of whether the error is major or minor (*Trimble v Supertravel Ltd* [1982] ICR 440), but it ought not to be used when an error of law was alleged after the parties have had a fair opportunity to present their case without procedural mishap. In a decision now endorsed by the Court of Appeal in *Burton*, the EAT held that the incompetence of a party's representative is not a sufficient reason for what was then a review of the decision: *Ironsides, Ray and Vials v Lindsay* [1994] ICR 384 (failure to argue that it was just and equitable to extend time in a discrimination case). See now *Burton* at para 21 and 24.

Where there is an obvious advantage in a mistake being addressed through reconsideration rather than requiring a party to appeal, it can be in the interests of justice to permit a review: *Williams v Ferrosan Ltd* [2004] IRLR 607 (a case where compensation had been awarded on a mistaken view on the part of both parties' representatives, and the Judge, as to whether it would be taxable); and see also *Sodexho Ltd v Gibbons* [2005] IRLR 836, in which *Williams* was strongly endorsed, and *Maresca v Motor Industry Repair Research Centre* [2005] ICR 197. A broad and non-technical approach to the power (then) to review a judgment in the interests of justice was also shown in the case of *Southwark London Borough Council v Bartholomew* [2004] ICR 358.

In *Council of the City of Newcastle upon Tyne v Marsden* [2010] ICR 743 the President of the EAT, Underhill J, reviewed the case law and concluded that the 'interest of justice' (as it featured as a ground of review under the old rules) confers a broad general discretion which should not be encrusted with too much case law, and that whilst the interests of finality in litigation remained important, this was not a conclusive argument. The President concluded that the principles underlying such decisions as *Trimble* and *Lindsay* remained valid as drawing attention to the underlying principles, which it would be wrong to ignore; but a liberal approach to the exercise of the discretion conferred by review (now reconsideration) in the interests of justice was nevertheless permissible.

This approach is reinforced by the framing of the new rules concerning reconsideration: it is open to the tribunal to review its decision if it considers that the interests of justice, broadly applied, justify such action.

Where a party wishes to rely on fresh evidence, the EAT has given very clear guidance to the effect that the most appropriate way to do so is by way of an application for (now) reconsideration of the tribunal's decision, rather than an appeal to the EAT, since the tribunal is better placed to decide whether the evidence would if available at the original hearing have made any difference to its conclusions: *Adegbuji v Meteor Parking Ltd* (UKEATPA/1570/09); *Korashi v Abertawe Bro Morgannwg University Local Health Board* [2012] IRLR 4. The President of the EAT, Langstaff J, has reinforced this point by a Practice Statement dated 17 April 2012 (available on the EAT website) which states that if an application to adduce fresh evidence is raised in an appeal to the EAT, the appeal will normally be stayed to allow the appellant to apply to the tribunal to reconsider its decision; if the tribunal refuses a reconsideration, that decision is of course open to appeal. Since *Outasight VB Ltd v Brown* [2015] ICR D11, it is clear that the same *Ladd v Marshall* test applies both on reconsideration and on appeal to the question of whether fresh evidence should be admitted. There is a separate power for the Judge to correct clerical errors or accidental slips (see above). This power is sometimes used to correct errors in the computation of compensation. It should not be used to make changes of substance to the judgment, such as the addition of a finding that the unfair dismissal of the claimant was also an act of unlawful discrimination: *Bone v Newham London Borough Council* [2008] EWCA Civ 435, [2008] ICR 923. As indicated above, the Court of Appeal has now emphasised the importance of finality of litigation in *Burton*.

ESTOPPEL, ABUSE OF PROCESS AND WITHDRAWAL

19.127 Estoppel and prevention of abuse of process

One important aspect of preventing abuse of the tribunal's process is the prevention of the relitigation of issues previously decided, or which could have been decided by the tribunal in earlier proceedings between the parties. This requires consideration of the legal doctrine of estoppel. There are a number of relevant forms of estoppel which may be relied on in tribunal proceedings: these are cause of action estoppel, which prevents the relitigation of a claim which has already been decided between the parties; issue estoppel, which may prevent a party from seeking to pursue a claim dependent on facts which are the subject of a prior and contrary finding in proceedings between the same parties; and a wider form of issue estoppel (sometimes referred to as the rule in *Henderson v Henderson* (1843) 3 Hare 100) which lays down that parties to litigation must bring forward their whole case and, except in special circumstances, will not be permitted to bring fresh proceedings in a matter which could and should have been litigated in earlier proceedings, but was omitted through negligence, inadvertence or accident. The first two forms of estoppel (often referred to collectively as res judicata) are considered further in **19.128**.

For an example of the operation of the rule in *Henderson v Henderson*, in the context of an employment tribunal claim, see *Sheriff v Klyne Tugs (Lowestoft) Ltd* [1999] IRLR 481 (action for personal injury allegedly caused by racial harassment struck out by the Court of Appeal, as this claim could and should have been pursued as part of the claimant's tribunal claim of racial discrimination against the same employers, which had been settled).

The principle to be applied in deciding whether it is an abuse of process to pursue a claim which could have been raised in prior proceedings was reviewed and restated by the House of Lords in *Johnson v Gore Wood* [2002] 2 AC 1, where Lord Bingham summarised the principles (at p 31) as being that the court or tribunal must consider whether in all the circumstances the bringing of proceedings is an abuse of process; the circumstances will include whether the proceedings are brought against the same defendant or respondent, why the claimant failed to include the issues now pursued in the earlier proceedings and whether the later action involves unjust harassment or oppression of the party sued. The EAT has confirmed that it is these principles that should be applied, not a narrower approach based on an earlier decision of the Court of Appeal, *Divine-Bortey v Brent London Borough Council* [1998] ICR 886: see *Parker v Northumberland Water* [2011] IRLR 652. The onus is on the respondent to establish abuse of process. See also *Thomas v Devon County Council* [2008] All ER (D) 236 (Feb), EAT (where after withdrawing one claim, the claimant was permitted to proceed with a second claim in the absence of any prejudice to the respondent).

A related but equally venerable doctrine, of the merger of causes of action, arose in *Fraser v HLMAD Ltd* [2006] EWCA Civ 738, [2006] IRLR 687, where it was held that a successful claim under the tribunal's contractual jurisdiction precluded the claimant from then bringing High Court proceedings to recover the balance of the damages for wrongful dismissal. His claim had been valued by the tribunal at some £80,000, but its power to make an award under the Extension of Jurisdiction Order 1994 was (and is) limited to £25,000, and the merger of his claim prevented him from pursuing the balance through separate proceedings.

The doctrines of cause of action and issue estoppel both apply to employment tribunals. The principle is that a decision on a specific claim or issue which has either not been appealed, or has been affirmed on appeal, is binding in any future litigation between the same parties, even if the decision was wrong in fact or law. Thus in *Watt (formerly Carter) v Ahsan* [2007] UKHL 51, [2008] 2 WLR 17, [2008] ICR 82, the House of Lords held that a tribunal was bound to follow a previous decision in earlier proceedings between the parties although in the meantime the Court of Appeal had held in unrelated proceedings that the interpretation of the relevant law which the tribunal had applied in the first case was wrong; in the result the tribunal was bound in law to apply an incorrect interpretation of the law in the second proceedings.

The doctrine of cause of action estoppel applies equally to a judicial decision by an Employment Judge to dismiss a claim; this prevents the relitigation of the claim between the same parties where it has already been the subject of a binding determination dismissing the claim, even though that may have been as a consequence of withdrawal by the claimant, and not a considered conclusion reached after the hearing of the case. This kind of estoppel has been the subject of three decisions of the Court of Appeal, which are not easily reconciled.

(1)   In *Lennon v Birmingham City Council* [2001] IRLR 826, the claimant had brought tribunal proceedings alleging sex discrimination resulting in a stress-related illness. She withdrew the proceedings before the hearing, and they were dismissed by the tribunal at her request. She then commenced county court proceedings in respect of stress-related ill health based on the same allegations (of offensive and intimidatory behaviour by fellow employees). The Court of Appeal, following *Barber v Stafford-shire County Council* [1996] 2 All ER 748, [1996] IRLR 209, held that the county court claim was rightly struck out as an attempt to relitigate matters which had been judicially determined by the tribunal's decision dismissing her earlier claim.

(2)   However in *Sajid v Sussex Muslim Society* [2001] EWCA Civ 1684, [2002] IRLR 113, a contrary conclusion was reached where the claimant had initially brought a breach of contract claim in the tribunal which he quantified well in excess of the maximum the tribunal could award, and then withdrew that claim specifically in order that he could pursue it in the High Court. Barber was distinguished because the withdrawal and subsequent dismissal of the claim was done with a view to pursuing the dispute elsewhere and not intended to determine the dispute.

(3)   Finally in *Ako v Rothschild Asset Management Ltd* [2002] EWCA Civ 236, [2002] 2 All ER 693, [2002] ICR 899, on facts materially indistinguishable from *Lennon*, the court nevertheless held that it was necessary and permissible to look at the surrounding circumstances; tribunals, unlike courts, did not have a procedure for discontinuance of proceedings (which does not trigger an estoppel), and if in substance the withdrawal was a discontinuance it should not bar fresh proceedings based on the same facts.

The gap in the *ET Rules* identified in *Ako* has since been rectified by a new provision originally in the *2004 Rules* and maintained in the *2013 Rules*, allowing for withdrawal without dismissal of the proceedings necessarily following: see **19.128** below for details. The EAT has held that these changes remove the basis for the exception to the general principles of cause of action estoppel created by *Ako*: see *Cokayne v British Association of Shooting and Conservation* [2008] ICR 185, discussed below. In any case where rights of future action may need to be preserved it is important for a claimant to make clear to the respondent and the tribunal why he or she is withdrawing his or her claim. Mummery LJ in *Ako* also recommends that tribunals ask claimants to state the reason for withdrawal before making an order dismissing the claim. This approach was further endorsed by the EAT in *Verdin v Harrods Ltd* [2006] IRLR 339 when discussing how the tribunals should approach cases where consent for an order dismissal a claim on withdrawal is not given (see para. 39).

Issue estoppel is a narrower principle: where a court or tribunal of competent jurisdiction has decided an issue of fact in proceedings between parties, those parties are then bound by that finding in any subsequent proceedings between them. The principle applies to decisions of employment tribunals which either have been upheld on appeal or not appealed, but only if the determination of the particular issue was within the jurisdiction of the tribunal and necessary to its decision. A case where neither of these conditions was satisfied is *Bon Groundwork v Foster* [2012] IRLR 517, where the tribunal in earlier proceedings between the parties had held that the claimant had not been dismissed for redundancy in circumstances where it had no jurisdiction to decide the point because the claimant had not been dismissed at all at the time of his claim. See also *Nayif v High Commission of Brunei Darussalam* [2014] EWCA Civ 1521 in which the Court of Appeal held the rejection of a race discrimination complaint on the jurisdictional time basis (claim out of time) did not prevent the claimant bringing a negligence claim in the high court based on the same matters.

The related Scots law doctrine of lis alibi pendens, under which a claim will be barred if it is the same as a claim already raised in litigation pending between the same parties, does not as such apply to employment tribunal proceedings: *Lynch v East Dunbartonshire Council* [2010] ICR 1094. However the fact of a second claim being brought in these circumstances may provide grounds for the striking out of the second claim under *Rule 37(1)(b)* as vexatious, a point which would apply equally in English proceedings. The case itself did not justify this characterisation, as the second proceedings had been brought to protect the claimants' position after the respondents had challenged the competency of the first proceedings on the question whether the claimants had complied with the statutory grievance procedure, as then required by the *Employment Act 2002, s 32*. For an example of the application of the principles of res judicata in Scots Law, and an explanation of the principles, see *Holmes v Greater Glasgow Health Board* (UKEATS/0045/11) (claim for sick pay struck out where previous claim in respect of an earlier period of the same absence had been dismissed).

In *Christou v London Borough of Haringey* [2013] EWCA Civ 178, the Court of Appeal held that a decision taken by an employer on an internal disciplinary complaint did not constitute a determination of an issue which establishes the existence of a legal right. Accordingly, the doctrine of res judicata is not applicable to such decisions.

19.128 Withdrawal and dismissal of claims

A claimant may choose to withdraw his or her claim because, for example, a settlement has been reached, or because the claimant does not want to proceed with the claim, or wishes to pursue the issue through other proceedings. Prior to the coming into force of the *2004 ET Rules*, the practice if a claimant withdrew the claim was for the tribunal to issue a formal order dismissing it. Some of the potential difficulties that this could cause are set out at **19.127** above. The *2004 Rules* introduced a new procedure under what was *Rule 25* of the *2004 Rules*, but this rule was drafted in terms described by the Court of Appeal as 'lamentable' (*Khan v Heywood & Middleton Primary Care Trust* [2006] IRLR 793). *Rules 51* and *52* of the *2013 Rules* are designed to meet the problems that were detected with the earlier formulation.

A claimant may withdraw his or her claim at any time in accordance with *Rule 51*. That rule provides what where a claimant informs the Tribunal, either in writing or in the course of a hearing, that a claim, or part of it, is withdrawn, the claim, or part, comes to an end, subject to any application that the respondent may make for a costs, preparation time or wasted costs order.

Accordingly, to comply with *Rule 51*, the claimant must notify the tribunal in writing of his or her wish to withdraw the claim or a particular part of it, and as against which respondent or respondents (if there are more than one) it is withdrawn. Alternatively, a claim or part thereof may be withdrawn orally at a hearing. A withdrawal takes effect immediately and (to the extent of the withdrawal) brings proceedings to an end without any further action by the Tribunal (see *Khan* under the previous rules). This remains the position under *Rule 51*. (As to withdrawal of part of a claim, see *Verdin v Harrods Ltd*, below.).

The fact that a claimant absents him or herself from a hearing does not necessarily amount to the withdrawal of the claim: *Smith v Greenwich Council* [2011] ICR 277, EAT. In that case the claimant had asked for an adjournment to give him time to work on the case; when this was (as he believed) refused, he indicated his intention to appeal and left the hearing. The EAT held that this was not withdrawal by conduct, not least because the statement that he intended to appeal was inconsistent with withdrawing the claim. The tribunal should only have treated the claim as withdrawn if the claimant had said expressly that he was withdrawing his claim. Tribunals have also been advised by the EAT not to treat a claimant as having withdrawn or abandoned part of his or her claim, or a particular contention, without making sure that that is the claimant's intention, and that he or she understands the consequences of doing so: *Segor v Goodrich Actuation Systems Ltd* (UKEAT/0145/11).Once notice of withdrawal of the claim has been given, it cannot be revoked by the claimant: Khan (above).

The test now endorsed by the EAT for withdrawal is that in *Segor* – did the claimant or his/her representative "clearly, unambiguously, and unequivocally" abandon the claim or part of the claim. This is a factual question. For an example of a withdrawal that meets this threshold, see *Osaghae v United Lincolnshire Hospitals NHS Trust* [2013] UKEAT/0576/12. See also *Drysdale v Department of Transport* [2015] ICR D2 in which the claimant's wife (his lay representative) told the Tribunal that she was making an application to withdraw the claim, after which the tribunal (on application by the respondent) dismissed the claim. Later, the representative, sought a review. The Court of Appeal held that the tribunal did not fail in its duty to assist a lay representative by ensuring that the decision to withdraw was fully considered and not taken in the heat of the moment.

Under the *2004 Rules*, the claim would only be dismissed if the respondent applied for an order to that effect within 28 days from the notice of withdrawal being sent by the Tribunal. Under the *Rule 52* of the 2013 Rules, however, the default position is that the Tribunal will dismiss a withdrawn claim. *Rule 52* provides that where a claim, or part of it, has been withdrawn under *Rule 51*, the Tribunal must issue a judgment dismissing it unless either of two exceptions can be made out. The *Rule* explains that an order dismissing the claim, or part of it, would mean that the claimant would be unable to commence a further claim against the respondent raising the same, or substantially the same, complaint. The two exceptions are: (a) the claimant has expressed at the time of withdrawal a wish to reserve the right to bring a further claim and the Tribunal is satisfied that there would be legitimate reason for doing so; or (b) the Tribunal believes that to issue such a judgment would not be in the interests of justice.

The effect of withdrawal of a claim under the old rules was explained by the EAT in *Verdin v Harrods Ltd* [2006] IRLR 339. The consequence of withdrawal, without more, is that the proceedings automatically come to an end, but the claimant is not precluded from pursuing the claim in other proceedings (including further proceedings in the tribunal, subject to the applicable time limits); if the tribunal claim has been dismissed, however, the bringing of further proceedings (in the tribunal or elsewhere) is likely to be regarded as an abuse of process. Indeed, as stated above *Rule 52* states in terms that the consequence of a dismissal judgment is that the same, or substantially similar, claim cannot be recommenced against the respondent.

In order to avoid the possibility of an order for dismissal of the claim being made in such circumstances, a claimant should explain to the tribunal when withdrawing the claim the basis on which it is being withdrawn, and whether there is any reason not to dismiss the claim. In *Cokayne v British Association for Shooting and Conservation* [2008] ICR 185, the claimant withdrew a constructive dismissal claim he had presented before the grievance procedure had been completed, and failed to explain that this was in order to re-present the claim after his grievance appeal was rejected. The first claim was dismissed and the EAT held that that presented a bar to the second claim, because the complaint of constructive dismissal was made res judicata by the dismissal of the first claim. It did not matter that the claimant had made clear to the respondent his intention to bring the second claim, or that the second claim was not in the general sense an abuse of process, since there are no exceptions to the operation of res judicata in this context. This clearly presents a trap for unwary claimants: the only solution in the particular case was for the claimant to apply for reconsideration of the dismissal of the withdrawn claim, a step encouraged by the EAT.

Under the old rules, the EAT in *Verdin* (above), identified the following two questions as being relevant to whether a dismissal order should be made. Is the withdrawing party intending to abandon the claim? If the withdrawing party is intending to resurrect the claim in fresh proceedings, would it be an abuse of process to allow that to occur? (see para 39). It is likely that these matters are likely to continue to be relevant to the Tribunal considering whether the exceptions to an order dismissing the claim (or part) in *Rule 52* are made out.

Where a claim is withdrawn but not dismissed, the file will be closed and retained for a period by the Tribunal before being destroyed; however it is open to any party to make an application for costs, preparation time or wasted costs (see *Rule 51*).

19.129 COSTS, PREPARATION TIME, AND WASTED COSTS ORDERS

Costs (referred to in Scotland as 'expenses') are awarded to a successful party only in relatively limited circumstances. However the range of circumstances was somewhat broadened by changes in the relevant provisions of the *ET Regulations* made in 2001. Further changes in the powers of the tribunal to award costs came into effect on 1 October 2004, under the 2004 Regulations. The maximum amount that may be awarded by a tribunal on summary assessment was increased by the *Employment Tribunals (Constitution and Rules of Procedure) (Amendment) Regulations 2012* ('the *2012 Regulations*') from £10,000 to £20,000, but only for cases first presented on or after 6 April 2012. The *2013 Rules* broadly recast the existing powers to make costs, preparation time and wasted costs orders. One notable change is the power for the Employment Tribunal now to conduct a detailed assessment of costs itself and order costs without limit after having done so. Whether this alternative to sending the case to the County or Sheriff Court for a detailed assessment will be used frequently remains to be seen, however anecdotal evidence suggests a willingness on the part of Tribunal judges to embrace this new power.

The powers available to a tribunal under the *2013 Rules* are:

(a)   to make a costs order;

(b)   to make a preparation time order; and

(c)   to make a wasted costs order against a party's representative

By *Rule 75(1)*, a costs order is an order that the paying party make a payment to the receiving party which is either (a) in respect of the costs that the receiving party has incurred whilst legally represented or while represented by a lay representative; (b) in respect of a tribunal fee paid by the receiving party; or (c) in respect of expenses incurred, or to be incurred for the purpose of, or in connection with, an individual's attendance as a witness at a Tribunal.

A preparation time order, by contrast, is an order that the paying party make a payment to the receiving party in respect of the receiving party's preparation time whilst not legally represented: *Rule 75(2)*. For these purposes, "preparation time" means time spent by the receiving party (including by employees or advisers) in working on the case, except for time spent at any final hearing.

A wasted costs order is an order made under *Rule 80* against a representative rather than a party, and in favour of any party (including the party that the representative represents).

A number of general points need to be made about these powers:

(a)   Orders may be made against or in favour of a respondent who has not had his or her response accepted, in relation to any part the respondent has taken in the proceedings. However if the respondent has not participated in the proceedings because it was prevented from doing so, having failed to have a response accepted, no costs can be awarded against it: *Sutton v The Ranch Ltd* [2006] ICR 1170; this is so even though the claimant may have incurred costs, e.g. in proving losses at a remedies hearing.

(b)   A costs order covering legal costs can only be made in favour of a receiving party whilst legally represented (i.e. by a barrister, advocate or solicitor with a current practising certificate).

(c)   It is not possible to make both a costs order and a preparation time order in the same proceedings and in favour of the same party (*rule 75(3)*). Thus a party represented initially by a non-practising solicitor, but by Counsel for the hearing, could only recover its costs of Counsel, and could not obtain a separate preparation time order for the cost of retaining the non-practising solicitor: *Ramsay v Bower cross Construction Ltd* (UKEAT/0534/07). This point may also cause difficulties if a party obtains orders on more than one occasion during the proceedings, and either becomes or ceases to be legally represented between the making of the orders. To meet this potential difficulty, *rule 75(3)* gives the tribunal power to make an order part way through the proceedings but to defer until the conclusion of the proceedings determining which category of order it should be. This will necessitate also deferring the decision as to the amount of the award; and it cannot meet the problem highlighted in *Ramsay*.

(d)   It is probable that a costs order cannot be made in respect of costs incurred before the claim or (in favour of the respondent) the response was presented. This was the view of the EAT in *Health Development Agency v Parish* [2004] IRLR 550. See further (e) below, and also *Sutton v The Ranch Ltd*, above.

(e)   Costs awards are intended to be compensatory, not punitive (a point confirmed by the Court of Appeal in *Lodwick v Southwark London Borough Council* [2004] EWCA Civ 306, [2004] IRLR 554). The EAT has held that this means that where costs are claimed because a party has acted unreasonably in conducting a case, the costs awarded should be no more than is proportionate to the loss caused to the receiving party by the unreasonable conduct: *Barnsley Metropolitan Borough Council v Yerrakalva* [2011] EWCA Civ 1255, [2012] IRLR 78.

(f)   Relevant definitions of "costs", "legally represented" and "represented by a lay representative" are to be found in *Rule 74*. In *Ladak v DRC Locums Ltd* [2014] ICR D39, the EAT has held that the definition of "costs" (there under the *2004 Rules*, but applicable to the *2013 Rules*) is wide enough to include costs in respect of the time spent by a qualified in-house legal representative. The costs of an in-house legal department was a charge or expense upon the employer.

(g)   In respect of costs generally, regard should now be had to the Presidential Guidance on General Case Management in which a section relation to costs is set out.

The award of costs is still relatively unusual. Following the broadening of the grounds on which costs could be awarded under the *2001 Regulations*, the frequency and amount of orders increased somewhat. The total number of awards (excluding orders for wasted costs, and preparation time orders) has historically averaged a little over 400 a year, with about three quarters of awards being made in favour of respondents. The sections below set out the provisions as to each of the categories of orders available to the tribunal. For simplicity, references to costs and costs orders are intended to encompass expenses and expenses orders in Scottish proceedings.

Where the Tribunal makes a costs, preparation time or wasted costs order, it may also make an order that the paying party (or, in the case of a wasted costs order, the representative) pay to the Secretary of State, in whole or in part, any allowances (other than allowances paid to members of the Tribunal) paid by the Secretary of State under *ETA 1996, s 5(2) or (3)* to any person for the purposes of, or in connection with, that person's attendance at the Tribunal: *Rule 83*.

19.130 Costs orders and Preparation Time Orders

A costs order, or a preparation time order, can be made in the circumstances of *Rule 76*. The relevant provisions of the *2013 Rules* governing the power to make, and the making and terms of, costs and preparation time orders are briefly as follows:

(a)   If the paying party has, in the opinion of the tribunal, acted vexatiously, abusively, disruptively or otherwise unreasonably in bringing or conducting proceedings, or his or her representative has so acted in bringing or conducting them, or if any claim or response had no prospects of success, the tribunal may make an order: *Rule 76(1)*. 'Conducting' proceedings applies equally to a respondent as to a claimant. Under the old rules, reference was made to the proceedings being "misconceived" which in turn was then defined as including 'having no reasonable prospect of success'. The *2013 Rules* now refer to the "no reasonable prospect of success" formulation directly, but it is helpful to note that references to claims or defences being "misconceived" in the older case-law refer to the same standard. For the meaning of 'vexatiously', see **19.131** below. Note that technically the tribunal is required to consider the award of costs, even if no application is made; but it has a discretion whether actually to make the award, and as to the amount (*Rule 76(1)*). In practice under the old rules it was unusual for a tribunal to exercise its discretion in favour of making a costs order in any case where the receiving party did not apply for costs.

Employment Tribunals – II   19.130

(b)   An order can be made where a party has been in breach of any order or practice direction: *Rule 76(2)*. This basis for awarding costs is often prayed in aid alongside the unreasonable conduct ground.

(c)   An order can also be made if a hearing has to be adjourned or postponed on the application of a party *(rule 76(2))*. In such cases, there is no requirement for this to be the fault of a party, although a costs order is more likely in those circumstances. Despite the wide discretion already present in this Rule, the Government has introduced, a new specific provision concerning postponements applicable to all proceedings which are presented on or after 6 April 2016. Where a hearing is postponed or adjourned on the application of a party made less than 7 days before the date on which the relevant hearing begins, the Tribunal "may" make an order and "shall" consider whether or not to make one (see *Rule 76(1)(c)* and the *Small Business, Enterprise and Employment Act 2015, s 151*). The *Rules* also provided that in respect of certain complaints of unfair dismissal, costs "must" be awarded where the claimant has expressed a wish to be reinstated or re-engaged which has been communicated to the respondent at least seven days before the hearing of the complaint, and a postponement or adjournment of the hearing has been caused by the respondent's failure, without good reason, to adduce reasonable evidence as to the availability of the job from which the claimant was dismissed, or of comparable or suitable employment *(rule 76(3))*.

(d)   A costs order to cover a tribunal fee can be made where a party has paid a Tribunal fee in respect of a claim, an employer's contract claim or application and that claim, counter claim or application is decided in whole or in part in favour of that party: *Rule 76(4)*. In such cases, the discretion of the Tribunal to order costs in order to reimburse the fees paid is entirely at large. Whilst in many cases this will follow the event, the rule indicates that this only opens the gateway to the exercise of discretion, rather than determining it. In *R (Unison) v Lord Chancellor (Equality and Human Rights Commission intervening)* [2014] ICR 498, the High Court noted (para 15) that the Lord Chancellor was to update his guidance stating that the general position is that a successful employee should expect to recover the fees he or she has incurred from the employer. The guidance, *Employment tribunal fees for individuals* (HMCTS, T435) was updated in March 2015 and states: "The general position is that, if you are successful, the respondent will be ordered to reimburse you, but the tribunal has no power to order reimbursement of fees paid if you lose your case. You can ask the tribunal to make an order to reimburse fees when it is considering the award due to you, or at any stage up to 28 days after the date on which your judgment was sent to you. Ultimately it is for the tribunal to decide whether it is appropriate that the respondent should reimburse you some or all of the fees you have paid, if you are successful."

EAT case law supports this general proposition, albeit that it is focused on appeal fees. In *Portnykh v Nomura International Plc (Costs)* (UKEAT/0448/13), the EAT made a conditional costs order covering the appeal fees in favour of a successful appellant despite the manner of his conduct of the appeal. HHJ Hand QC made clear that subject to specific exceptions arising from particular circumstances, where a party had succeeded, the unsuccessful party, after consideration of and subject to the means of the paying party to make such payment, should pay the fees incurred by the successful party. The order was conditional in that case because his application for a fee remission had not yet been determined. This approach was followed by the EAT in *Horizon Security Services Ltd v Ndeze* [2014] IRLR 854: whilst there is a broad discretion, the general expectation must be that a successful Appellant will be entitled to recover the sums paid from a Respondent that had actively sought to resist an appeal. The principle might need to be tempered to take account of particular facts or partial success (see e.g. *Old v Palace Fields Primary Academy* [2014]

UKEAT/0085/14 in which partial recovery was awarded to reflect the partial success in having the matter remitted to the same Judge for further consideration without a reversal of the finding). In *Look Ahead Housing and Care Ld v Chetty* [2015] ICR 375, Langstaff P gave guidance for future cases of partial success (para 53): "What the court centrally has to assess is whether it was necessary to incur the expense in order to bring the appeal – this includes asking whether the appeal, as in the present case, could have been avoided by the Appellant taking reasonable steps, or was made more likely to proceed by the behaviour of the Respondent to it; it should then recognise the fact, if it be the case, that an appeal has largely failed or for that matter largely succeed in deciding, in its discretion, exercised reasonably, whether it should award the full extent of the payment made by way of fees, or whether it should moderate that amount to a reasonable extent. A reasonable extent includes making no award at all, though in circumstances in which an appeal has been partly successful this would have to be carefully justified and is likely to be rare."

In a controversial decision, *Goldwater v Sellafield Ltd* [2015] IRLR 381, the EAT held, applying the EAT Rules that the appellants were not entitled to a costs order in respect of EAT fees paid by their union on their behalf. Whilst the judge confined his decision to the particular wording of *Rule 34A(2A)* (that a costs order based on fees will be in "an amount no greater than any fee paid by the appellant"), the decision is nonetheless of interest here because the similar wording of *Rule 76(4)* of the *2013 Rules* (permitting a costs order consisting of fees to be made "where a party has paid a Tribunal fee"). HHJ Shanks held that whilst the fees came within the definition of costs under the *EAT Rules*, as the appellants themselves, as opposed to their union, had aid no fees at all, *Rule 34A(2A)* limited the amount of a costs order which could be made to nil. The decision was controversial when made and since then, a subsequent division of the EAT (Wilkie J), this time after full argument, considered that the decision in *Goldwater* was wrong. In *Dr A W Ibarz v University of Sheffield* UKEAT/0018/15, it was held that the power to award fees was exercisable where the fee had not been paid personally by the Appellant but on his behalf by, for example, a union.

(e)   A costs order to cover witness expenses may be made on application of a party or witness, or of the Tribunal's own initiative where a witness has attended or has been ordered to attend to give oral evidence at a hearing: *Rule 76(5)*.

(f)   The procedure for making a costs or preparation time order is set out in *Rule 77*. An application may be made at any stage of proceedings up until 28 days after the date on which the final judgment is sent to the parties. No costs or preparation time order may be made until the paying party has had a reasonable opportunity to make representations in writing or at a hearing as the Tribunal orders, in response to the application.

(g)   A costs order may require the paying party to pay the whole or part of the other party's costs or expenses as assessed (by a County Court Costs Judge under the *CPR 1998* or by the Tribunal itself conducting a detailed assessment) if not otherwise agreed, or be for an agreed amount, or for a summarily assessed sum (not exceeding £20,000) fixed by the tribunal (*ET Rules, Rule 78(1)*). The limit on fixed costs was introduced by the *2001 Rules* and was retained in the *2004 Rules*; it does not apply to costs agreed between the parties or assessed by way of detailed assessment by the Tribunal itself or the County Court. When referring to the County Court for a detailed assessment, a Tribunal may specify that the assessment take place on an indemnity or standard cost assessment basis, however the Tribunal must properly consider the effect of the order it makes and the paying party's ability to pay when so doing (see *Howman v Queen Elizabeth Hospital King's Lynn* (UKEAT/0509/12); there the EAT held that an order for indemnity costs should be rare and the Tribunal failed to consider the effect of the order and the possibility of putting a cap on the overall order for costs). Similar considerations will no doubt apply to when the Tribunal itself conducts the detailed assessment. The maximum that can be awarded in a summary assessment was increased from £10,000 to £20,000 by the *Employment Tribunals (Constitution and Rules of Procedure) (Amendment) Regulations 2012 (SI 2012/468)* and has been retained in the *2013 Rules*. In assessing costs summarily, the tribunal is likely to refer to the guidelines used in summary assessments of costs in the High Court and County Court as to what are reasonable hourly rates for solicitors to claim in different parts of the country (these rates, which are published annually in the Supreme Court Practice, apply only to England and Wales). Similar criteria for the taxation of expenses in the Sheriff Court apply in Scottish proceedings. As stated above, the amount of costs awarded can include reimbursement of all or part of a Tribunal fee paid, or witness expenses "necessarily and reasonably incurred" in attending proceedings. The *Rules* provide that such sums do not count towards the £20,000 limit: see *Rule 78(3)*.

(h)   In deciding whether to make an order for costs or preparation time (and indeed wasted costs), and if so in determining the amount to be awarded, the tribunal is permitted but not required to have regard to the means of the party against whom the order is made (*rule 84*, reversing the decision of the Court of Appeal in *Kovacs v Queen Mary and Westfield College* [2002] EWCA Civ 352, [2002] IRLR 414 that there was no power to take means into account under an earlier iteration of the *Rules*). It was observed by Simon Brown LJ in *Kovacs* that logically, the discretion to have regard to the paying party's means would require the tribunal also to consider the means of the receiving party (para 10), and by Chadwick LJ that if means are a relevant factor, it would not be reasonable for a tribunal to make an award that it was satisfied the paying party could not meet (para 32). Neither of the points raised in *Kovacs* remains good law under the current *Rules*. Rule 84 is specific that it is the "paying party's" ability to pay that may be taken into account and not the means of the receiving party. This was made clear by the EAT (applying the *2004 Rules*): *Mardner v Gardner* [2014] UKEAT/0483/13 – there were good policy reasons why the means of the receiving party was irrelevant and therefore the tribunal ought to have disregarded the fact that the claimant (the applicant for costs) was funded by insurance and therefore not personally out of pocket as a result of bringing the claim. As to the second point, it is clear from the cases cited below, that means is only one consideration in the exercise of discretion, and there is no prohibition on making an award even if there is no ability to pay provided that has been considered.

Two further points were made by the EAT in *Jilley v Birmingham and Solihull Mental Health NHS Trust* [2008] All ER (D) 35 (Feb), EAT. First, the tribunal should state clearly whether or not it has taken the paying party's means into account in making its order as to costs. Secondly, if payment of all the receiving party's costs would be beyond the claimant's means, it may order payment of a specified proportion of the costs; this might presumably permit an order for costs to be assessed, subject to a maximum liability of a stated amount. In a subsequent decision the EAT has held that even if the claimant does not raise the issue of means, it should be raised by the tribunal, particularly before a very large order is made: *Doyle v North West London Hospitals NHS Trust* (UKEAT/0271/11), a case where an order to pay all the respondent's costs, estimated at £95,000, had been made. Contrast *Osonnaya v Queen Mary University of London* (UKEAT/0225/11) in which the EAT held that the tribunal is required, if the matter is raised, to consider ability to pay, but if the matter is not raised, there is no authority imposing a legal duty on the Judge to raise the question, even with a litigant in person. It is not necessary to take the claimant's means into account if she was voluntarily absent from the proceedings when the point arose (*Mirikwe v Wilson & Co Solicitors* (UKEAT/0025/11), or if the evidence of means given by the claimant is contradictory or unreliable (*Shields Automotive Ltd v Greig* (UKEATS/0024/10)). The last mentioned case is also authority for the point that 'means' can include equity in a home, even if not readily realisable. Similarly in *Chadburn v Doncaster and Bassetlaw Hospital NHS Foundation Trust* [2015] UKEAT/0259/14, the EAT upheld an award of costs even though the claimant currently could not afford to pay: affordability was "not the only criterion for the exercise of discretion". In that case there was also evidence that her financial position was likely to improve based on the realistic prospect of the claimant returning to employment. In *Oni v NHS Leicester City* (UKEAT/0144/12) the EAT held that there should be a proper consideration of means where the claimant asserted limited means and where the costs claimed were anticipated to be large. The EAT recommended the completion of the County Court means form EX140 by the party whose means are to be taken into account. In *Abaya v Leeds Teaching Hospital NHS Trust* [2017] UKEAT/0258/16, Singh J held that an ET had erred in taking into account the means of the claimant's ex-wife without explaining how that impacted the claimant's ability to pay. The ET also failed to explain how it had reached the sum it had decided to award.

(i)   It is not completely clear how far the power to take into account the paying party's means extends to taking the means of an organisation, such as a trade union, representing him or her into account. In a case decided before the *ET Rules* were amended to allow the conduct of a representative to be taken into account in deciding whether to make a costs order, the EAT held that the conduct of the case by a trade union representative did not entitle the tribunal to take the union's means into account in deciding the issue of a costs order against the claimant: *Omar v Worldwide News Inc* [1998] IRLR 291. This approach was however later doubted in *Beynon v Scadden* [1999] IRLR 700; it may in any case no longer be applicable following the change in the *ET Rules* permitting the award of costs on account of the unreasonable conduct of the proceedings by a party's representative. However any costs order would only be enforceable against the party against whom it is made, and it does not necessarily follow that a union would accept liability to reimburse its members in such a situation; this may make a tribunal reluctant to disregard the limited means of the claimant, even if permitted to do so.

(j)   If there has been a preliminary hearing, and a party was ordered to pay a deposit, and that party loses, *Rule 39(5)* imposes a presumption that the paying party is to be treated as having acted unreasonably in pursuing that specific allegation unless the contrary is shown and the deposit order shall be paid to the other party. However the tribunal is not required to make such an order solely on this ground unless, having considered the reasons given for the making of the deposit order, it considers that the reasons given were substantially the same as the reasons for finding against the party at the hearing. If costs are awarded, the deposit is used to pay, or in part payment of, the costs; if not, or if the costs awarded are less than the deposit, the deposit or balance is refunded to the party concerned (*rule 39(6)*). An example under the old rules is *Deer v Walford* [2011] UKEAT /0283/10. See, however, *Oni v Unison* [2015] UKEAT/0370/14 under the 2013 Rules in which the EAT held that a tribunal erred by assuming that once there was unreasonable conduct in persisting with proceedings following a deposit order, a costs order should follow subject only to considering means. Simler J held that even where unreasonable conduct has been found on that basis, a tribunal has a discretion as to whether or not costs should be awarded, and if so, in what amount; the tribunal must consider all relevant circumstances when exercising that discretion.

(k)   An application for costs may be made at any time at a preliminary hearing, or at the conclusion of a hearing, or subsequently in writing. If an application for costs is made after judgment is given finally determining the claim, it must be received by the tribunal no later than 28 days from the date the judgment was sent to the parties: *Rule 77*.

(l)   If an application for costs is made at the hearing, the other party will be given an opportunity to oppose the application orally. In any other case, an order cannot be made unless the intended paying party has been given an opportunity to give reasons why the order should not be made. This may be by way of a further hearing, or on paper, as the Judge may direct (*rule 77*). The EAT recently underlined that the putative paying party should be given a reasonable opportunity to oppose a costs award: see *Gwara v Mid Essex Primary Care Trust* (UKEAT/0074/13). The party claiming costs should, if the sum claimed is more than nominal, prepare a schedule showing the costs incurred and the amount claimed.

(m)   If within 14 days of the date of the order either party requests written reasons for a costs order, reasons must be given in writing (*rule 62*). This codifies the Court of Appeal's comments in *Lodwick v Southwark London Borough Council* [2004] EWCA Civ 306, [2004] IRLR 554 as to the importance of a tribunal giving sufficient reasons for both the fact and the amount of an award of costs.

(n)   There is in principle a power under rule 38 for the tribunal to make an 'unless' order for the payment of costs (*Criddle v Epcot Leisure Ltd* [2005] All ER (D) 89 (Aug)). The effect of this would be that if the costs are not paid by the date required, the party's case would automatically be struck out; for a claimant this means that the proceedings would be at an end, whilst a respondent in that position would be debarred from further participation in the case.

19.131

There have been several decisions on the scope of the power to award costs, when and how the discretion to do so should be exercised, and what costs should be awarded if an order is made. The leading cases are now *Barnsley Metropolitan Borough Council v Yerrakalva* [2011] EWCA Civ 1255, [2012] IRLR 78 and *Arrowsmith v Nottingham Trent University* [2011] EWCA Civ 797. A number of points can usefully be drawn from these and other relevant cases.

It is important to bear in mind that costs orders are relatively rare, but a tribunal is not obliged to refer to that fact in its reasoning, provided that it follows the statutory, two-stage procedure of first determining whether there has been unreasonable conduct etc, and then exercising a discretion whether to make an award, and if so of what amount or proportion of costs incurred: *Power v Panasonic (UK) Ltd* [2005] All ER (D) 130 (Jul), EAT, following *Salinas v Bear Stearns International Holdings Inc* [2005] ICR 1117. On the other hand, the mere fact that the tribunal makes an award of aggravated damages against the respondent does not justify making an order for costs: *Saiger v North Cumbria Acute Hospitals NHS Trust* (UKEAT/0325/10).

The bringing or maintaining of a claim which has no reasonable prospect of success is a sufficient reason for the tribunal to conclude that the party should be made liable for costs; this is equally so for a respondent which has presented, or maintained through the proceedings, a defence which had no reasonable prospect of success. It is a factor relevant to the exercise of the tribunal's discretion whether to award costs on this ground that the tribunal has warned the party concerned that he or she is at risk of a costs order, but such a warning is not a prerequisite to the making of an order; nor is it a prerequisite that the receiving party has put the paying party on notice that there may be an application for costs. (See *Millin v Capsticks Solicitors LLP* [2014] UKEAT/0093/14 (para 68) and *Deer v*

Walford (UKEAT/0283/10), where the respondent was awarded its full costs, following a four-day hearing, on the grounds both that the claim had been misconceived from the outset and that a deposit had been ordered on substantially the grounds that the claim failed; the award was upheld by the EAT.)

The conduct of a party's representative, as well as that of the party him or herself, can provide the basis for an award of costs; the party is in effect fixed with the consequences of his or her choice of representative. However, not all conduct of tribunal proceedings by a representative which causes additional cost to the other party is necessarily unreasonable; thus it was held by the EAT in *Francois v Castle Rock Properties Ltd* (UKEAT/0260/10) that the incompetent presentation of the claimant's case by her representative, an inexperienced solicitor, which had unnecessarily prolonged the hearing, was nevertheless on the facts not unreasonable conduct of the case, and there was therefore no justification for an award of costs. Where a party's unreasonable conduct, such as by failing to comply with orders for disclosure, exchange of witness statements or other case management orders, leads to a case having to be adjourned, the tribunal may award the other party its costs thrown away because of the 'lost' hearing. These are in effect wasted costs, but an order for costs thrown away is not the same as an order for 'wasted costs' under rule 80, which is an award against a representative; see **19.133**. Guidance as to the computation of costs thrown away has been given by the EAT in *Carruthers v London School of Economics Student Union* (UKEAT/0183/10). In *Schaathun v Executive & Business Aviation Support Ltd* UKEAT/0615/11 the EAT held that it was not unreasonable conduct of proceedings for a claimant whose first language was not English and whose command of English was good but not perfect to enquire by email a few days before a hearing as to whether an interpreter would be available. Even though the Tribunal postponed the hearing, the email could not have been read as an application for a postponement, nor was it foreseeable that a postponement would inevitably result. A good example of a finding of unreasonable conduct (by the respondent) leading to an unnecessary hearing is *Godfrey Morgan Solicitors Ltd v Marzon* (UKEAT/0465/11). It has been accepted by the Court of Appeal that deliberately delaying notification of a decision to withdraw a claim can constitute unreasonable behaviour (*McPherson v BNP Paribas (London Branch)* [2004] IRLR 558); the same would be true of unjustifiable delay in conceding liability, or an issue in the claim such as whether the claimant is disabled. This should not be relied on to penalise a party who, perhaps in the light of disclosure of documents or seeing the other party's witness statements, or the failure of settlement negotiations, takes a pragmatic decision to abandon a claim or defence. The unreasonable behaviour lies in then failing to inform the other party and the tribunal of the decision promptly, thereby allowing the other party to incur further costs (and possibly preventing the tribunal from listing another case for the date listed for the hearing). Whilst a litigant in person might receive a more sympathetic response from a tribunal considering whether conduct of litigation was unreasonable, they are not shielded from such a finding: see e.g. *Liddington v 2gether NHS Foundation Trust* [2016] UKEAT/0002/16.

A party may also be found to have acted unreasonably if he or she has rejected an offer to settle the proceedings, either made openly or 'without prejudice save as to costs', but it is not unreasonable behaviour to reject an offer simply because the tribunal's decision is more favourable to the party making the offer (eg the claimant is awarded less than the respondent had offered, or even nothing at all): *Kopel v Safeway Stores plc* [2003] IRLR 753. This decision has the effect that the tribunal may take into account offers made without prejudice save as to costs (often referred to as '*Calderbank*' offers; see **19.36** above), but costs do not automatically follow in the way that would be the case in equivalent situations in the High Court. See also *Power v Panasonic (UK) Ltd*, above, where a costs order was upheld on appeal in circumstances where the claimant was found by the tribunal to have put an unrealistically high value on her claims, rejected offers substantially in excess of what she was eventually awarded, and acted intransigently in negotiations; and see *G4S Security Services (UK) v Rondeau* (UKEAT/0207/09), where costs were awarded by the EAT on the basis of an appellant having unreasonably rejected offers to settle an appeal until he accepted the same offer on the morning of the hearing. A further recent example is *Sud v London Borough of Ealing* [2013] EWCA Civ 949, where offers were rejected out of hand by a claimant and the Court of Appeal noted that an argument that she was entitled to seek declarations or reinstatement did not have substantive credibility given her response to offers focussed on an exorbitant sum by way of suggested compensation.

In a case involving a claim of discrimination, one of the remedies is a declaration by the tribunal that the claimant was discriminated against. It will not necessarily be unreasonable conduct for a claimant to refuse a reasonable monetary offer where he or she is seeking such a declaration and the respondent is not prepared as part of the terms of settlement to admit liability. This principle was applied to unfair dismissal in *Telephone Information Services Ltd v Wilkinson* [1991] IRLR 148, EAT, but the opposite view was taken by the EAT in the later case of *Nicolson Highlandwear Ltd v Nicolson* [2010] IRLR 859, EAT, where the claimant had succeeded in obtaining a finding of unfair dismissal but the EAT considered that he had had no reasonable basis for pursuing the claim, since it was inevitable on the facts that he would not be awarded any compensation (he had admitted to defrauding his employers, and the tribunal had made a nil award). However *Wilkinson* was not cited, and the case cannot therefore be regarded as excluding the argument in other cases that it may be reasonable to pursue a claim of unfair dismissal purely to establish a finding to that effect.

Awards of costs on the basis that the paying party has acted vexatiously in the bringing or conduct of the proceedings are rare, since it is not necessary to show such extreme conduct in order to make a case for an award of costs. However a tribunal would be much more likely to exercise its discretion in favour of such an order if it found vexatious conduct. The essential difference between vexatious and merely unreasonable conduct is that the party concerned need not be aware that his or her claim has no reasonable prospect of success in order for it to be misconceived (and therefore the bringing of it to be unreasonable), but if a party pursues a claim knowing it has no reasonable prospect of success, or depends on false evidence, or pursues the claim out of malice towards the other party or for some other ulterior reason, his or her conduct may be found to be vexatious. See further *E T Marler Ltd v Robertson* [1974] ICR 72. For a party's conduct in bringing or pursuing a case to be labelled as 'vexatious', or even 'misconceived', it will normally be necessary, at least where the factual issues are disputed, for the tribunal to have heard and determined the dispute, and accordingly a tribunal should not award costs on this basis where the claim has been struck out on jurisdictional grounds: *Dean & Dean (a Firm) v Dionissiou-Moussaoui* [2011] EWCA Civ 1332. Further helpful guidance on what constitutes vexatious conduct of litigation can be found in the judgment of Lord Bingham CJ in *A-G v Barker* [2000] 2 FCR 1, [2000] 1 FLR 759, at 763–4, and in *A-G v Roberts* [2005] All ER (D) 138 (Jul).

The EAT has also held that where a tribunal finds on the evidence that a party has deliberately lied in evidence to the tribunal, that is necessarily at least unreasonable conduct, and should usually result in a costs order: *Daleside Nursing Home Ltd v Mathew* (UKEAT/0519/08) (a case where the tribunal had found that the racially abusive words alleged by the claimant had not in fact been used) and *Dunedin Canmore Housing Association Ltd v Donaldson* (UKEATS/0014/09). These cases were followed and applied in *Nicolson*, above, where the claimant had in evidence admitted what amounted to fraudulent conduct against his employer; the EAT held that it was an error of law for the tribunal not to award expenses. These cases must however now be read in the light of a number of subsequent decisions most notably, *Barnsley Metropolitan Borough Council v Yerrakalva* [2011] EWCA Civ 1255, [2012] IRLR 78, *Arrowsmith v Nottingham Trent University* [2011] EWCA Civ 797, [2012] ICR 159, *HCA International Limited v JL May-Bheemul* (UKEAT/0477/10) and *Kapoor v Governing Body of Barnhill Community School* (UKEAT/0352/13).

In *Yerrakalva*, the tribunal had awarded the respondent council all of its costs after the claimant withdrew her claim part-way through the Proceedings. It found that she had lied, in particular in exaggerating her claimed disability, but also criticised the council for the way it had defended the case. The Court of Appeal held that the tribunal was entitled to find the claimant's conduct was unreasonable, but not to award 100% of the council's costs, and reduced the award to 50%. Mummery LJ said (at para 41): "The vital point in exercising the discretion to order costs is to look at the whole picture of what happened in the case and to ask whether there has been unreasonable conduct by the claimant in bringing and conducting it, and in doing so, to identify the conduct, what was unreasonable about it and what effects it had." The costs awarded need not be precisely calculated to reflect the additional cost to the respondent caused by the claimant's unreasonable conduct, but should broadly reflect what had been caused by the erring party (the same points would apply equally to an unreasonable respondent). Mummery LJ also clarified that his Lord-ship's comments in *Macpherson v BNP Paribas (London Branch)* [2004] IRLR 558, which had been widely taken as indicating that a causal link need not be established, were not intended to have that effect but only to indicate that a precise correlation need not be established.

In *Arrowsmith*, the tribunal had applied the *Daleside* case on the basis that the fact that (as it had found) the claimant had told untruths as part of her case was evidence that she had conducted the case unreasonably. The Court of Appeal, in upholding a costs order against the claimant, emphasised that *Daleside* does not create a rule, and each case depends on its own facts; on the facts of this case, it was fully open to the tribunal to find her conduct to be unreasonable and award costs against her. In both of the Court of Appeal judgments the Court emphasises that it is a question of fact whether conduct is unreasonable, and therefore provided the tribunal correctly directs itself as to the law, its decision on that point, and equally on whether to exercise its discretion to award costs, will rarely be open to challenge on appeal.

It is also right to note that the EAT rejected the proposition that there was a general principle from the above cases that an award of costs must follow when a party fails to establish a central allegation in their case: *HCA International Ltd v May-Bheemul* [2009] All ER (D) 154 (Jun). That division of the EAT held that findings of perversity in the earlier cases arose because of their special facts. Similarly, in *Kapoor* (above), the EAT confirmed that giving false evidence is not, automatically, unreasonable conduct warranting a costs order.

Conversely, in *Topic v Hollyland Pitta Bakery* (UKEAT/0523/11), the EAT has confirmed that a claim can be found to have no reasonable prospects of success, and costs awarded, even in the absence of lying. There the claimant had genuinely believed she suffered discrimination, although her beliefs had no basis in reality. The genuineness of her beliefs was not relevant to whether the claim was misconceived but was relevant to the exercise of discretion whether or not to award costs, and if so, how much. Similarly, in *Ghosh v Nokia Siemens* (UKEAT/0125/12) the EAT confirmed that it was not necessary to have an express finding of dishonesty before making an award of costs in respect of a large number of failed allegations of discrimination. In *Millin v Capsticks Solicitors LLP* [2014] UKEAT/0093/14, the EAT noted that although discrimination cases have special difficulties for a claimant arising from the personal nature of the case and the difficulties of proof, they frequently involve the consideration over a long period of time by a tribunal of many allegations, facts and documents. The EAT held "Where a claim is truly misconceived and should have been appreciated in advance to be so, we see no special reason why the considerable expense to which a Respondent will needlessly have been put (or a claimant in a case win which a response is misconceived) should not be reimbursed in par tor in whole" (para 67).

19.132 Preparation time orders

Preparation time orders are intended to compensate a party who is not legally represented at the Hearing (or the conclusion of proceedings which do not reach a Hearing) for time spent preparing the case. This covers time spent by the receiving party personally, or (where applicable) by his or her employees, by a representative who is not a practising lawyer, or by a legal representative who was engaged at an earlier stage in the proceedings. Preparation time orders can be made in the same circumstances as an order for legal costs: see *Rule 76* and the commentary above.

The hourly rate is fixed by *Rule 79(2)*. The rate was initially fixed at £33 an hour, but subject to an automatic increase of £1 an hour each year. The same hourly rate applies regardless of whose time is being compensated; it will thus be the same for a claimant who had been dismissed from a job paid at the National Minimum Wage as for a solicitor engaged to prepare the case for hearing but not used to conduct the case at the Hearing.

By *Rule 79(1)*, the time allowed is what the tribunal assesses to be a reasonable and proportionate amount of time to spend on preparation having regard to such matters as the complexity of the case, the number of witnesses and the amount of documentation involved. Only time spent in preparation for the hearing will be compensated, not time spent attending the hearing itself: *Andrew v Eden College* (UKEAT/0438/10) and see *Rule 75(2)*.

Awards for preparation time were limited to a maximum of £10,000 but this sum was increased in line with the increase in the maximum award of costs to £20,000 (*Rule 78*). The principle that the tribunal may have regard to the paying party's means in deciding whether to make an order and if so the amount, applies equally to preparation time orders (*rule 84*); however it is not clear how this principle is to be applied in determining the amount – in particular whether the tribunal can reduce the hourly rate, or make an award for fewer hours' preparation time, or both.

19.133 Wasted costs orders

The power to make wasted costs orders was entirely new within the tribunal system when it was introduced in 2004. The power continues to exist in the *2013 Rules*: see *Rule 80*. Equivalent provisions have existed for many years in the civil courts, where experience has been that they are rarely made, no doubt in considerable part because of the necessary procedural safeguards for representatives potentially subject to such orders.

A wasted costs order is an order against a party's representative in favour of any party where the party has incurred costs as a result of any improper, unreasonable or negligent act or omission on the part of a representative or which, in the light of any such act or omission occurring after they were incurred, the Tribunal considers it unreasonable to expect the receiving party to pay (*rule 80(1)*). The need for causation between the act and the costs was stressed by Langstaff J in *Hafiz & Haque Solicitors v Mullick* [2015] ICR 1085. The term 'representative' is defined to exclude any representative who is not acting for profit, such as a trade union official or CAB adviser, or a representative who is employed by the party, such as a manager of the employing company (*Rule 80(3)*). However the term is not limited to legal representatives, and is expressly applied to a representative acting under a conditional fee agreement (*rule 80(2)*). A wasted costs order can be made in favour of a party whether or not that party is legally represented and can also be made in favour of a representative's own client (*Rule 80(3)*). The procedure is set out in *Rule 82*: the application for wasted costs can be made at any stage up to 28 days after the date of the final judgment in the proceedings. There is a requirement that the tribunal must give the representative a reasonable opportunity to make oral or written representations before making a wasted costs order. In addition the tribunal may (but is not obliged to) take into account the representative's ability to pay (*rule 84*); it is submitted that where the representative is a company or firm, it is the means of that entity, not the individual representative, that is to be considered, and it is the company or firm against which any order should be made, but these points are not made clear by the *Rules*. As with costs orders, reasons must be given if requested within 14 days of the order. The Tribunal must also inform the representative's client in writing of any proceedings for a wasted costs order and of any order made against the representative: *Rule 82*.

Wasted costs applications pose a number of potential practical difficulties. The first and most basic is that there may be a conflict of interest between a representative and his or her client. In these circumstances (eg where the tribunal is considering disallowing the representative's fees), the client will have to be advised to consider obtaining separate representation, and the representative will have to be given the opportunity to engage his or her own advocate; this will almost inevitably necessitate an adjournment of the hearing. Second, the question whether a representative was negligent may turn on what instructions were given by the client, and/or what advice was given by the representative. In the case of legal representatives, such matters are covered by legal professional privilege, which can only be waived by the client. (Non-lawyer representatives may also be subject to litigation privilege preventing them from disclosing their client's instructions without the consent of the client: *Scotthorne v Four Seasons Conservatories (UK) Ltd* (UKEAT/0178/10).) The client will be deemed to have waived privilege if he or she claims wasted costs against the representative, but not in other cases, such as where the other party has made the application. The tribunal will not be able to draw inferences against the representative from the refusal of the client to waive privilege.

The leading case on wasted costs in the civil courts is *Ridehalgh v Horsefield* [1994] Ch 205, [1994] 3 All ER 848. The EAT in *Mitchells Solicitors v Funkwerk Information Technologies York Ltd* [2008] PNLR 717, [2008] All ER (D) 99 (Apr) held that the guidelines laid down in *Ridehalgh* should equally be applied by a tribunal in considering whether the make a wasted costs order. The principles to be followed are:

(a)   The wasted costs jurisdiction should only be exercised with great caution and as a last resort

(b)   An order should only be made if the tribunal is satisfied that the representative's conduct was improper, unreasonable or negligent. (For an example of what constitutes such conduct see *Wilsons Solicitors v Johnson* [2011] ICR D21 (failure of claimant's solicitors to produce coherent particulars of his claims justified an order.)

(c)   A legal representative should not be held to have so acted simply because of having acted for a party who has pursued a hopeless case; an order can only be made on this basis if it is shown that the representative presented a case he or she regarded as bound to fail, and in doing so has failed in his or her duty to the court, and the proceedings amounted to an abuse of process.

(d)   The tribunal must take into account that unless the representative's client has waived privilege, the representative will be likely not to be able to explain why the case has been conducted in the manner it was. Accordingly, in *Hafiz & Haque Solicitors v Mullick* [2015] ICR 1085 the EAT held that a Tribunal should be slow to conclude that representatives have insufficient material to justify pleadings or schedules of loss where legal professional privilege prevents instructions from being revealed.

(e)   It must be shown that the representative's conduct caused the person applying for costs to incur unnecessary costs.

The tribunal must exercise a discretion at two stages: it must first decide whether the circumstances render the application justified and proportionate, in which case (but only if so) it can proceed to hear the application. Having done so, there is a further discretion to be exercised whether to make an order (and in what terms).

The judgment in *Mitchells Solicitors* contains a helpful and detailed analysis of both substantive and procedural issues likely to arise on a wasted costs application. The necessity to consider first whether the application should be entertained at all was emphasised by the Court of Appeal in *Gill v Humanware Europe Ltd* [2010] EWCA Civ 799, [2010] IRLR 877, where the Court concluded that the application (which had resulted in an award of only

£750) should not have been entertained at all on grounds of proportionality of the time and cost involved in determining the application. The decision is also authority for the points that normally there should be a hearing unless the parties agree to the matter being decided on the papers, particularly so where there are contested issues of fact; and that costs should only be awarded to compensate for additional costs incurred by the receiving party, not for costs that would have been incurred in any event (the costs in issue being of an appeal to the EAT). The strict causation requirement was highlighted by the EAT in *Isteed v London Borough of Redbridge* [2017] ICR D1, Simler P holding (at para 57): "As to causation, in *Ridehalgh* the Court of Appeal emphasised that the jurisdiction to make a wasted costs order extends only to impugned conduct that has caused a waste of costs and only to the extent of such wasted costs. The Court of Appeal held that demonstration of a causal link is essential and that where the conduct is proved but no waste of costs is shown to have resulted, the case may be referred to a disciplinary body or other authority, but it is not one for the exercise of the wasted costs jurisdiction."

Further helpful guidance on the procedure to be followed is given in *Godfrey Morgan Solicitors Ltd v Cobalt Systems Ltd* [2012] ICR 305 and more recently in *Single Homeless Project Ltd v Abu* (UKEAT/0519/12).

In contrast to an ordinary costs order, there is no express provision for the employment tribunal to refer the assessment of a wasted costs order made under rule 80 to the County Court. The tribunal itself must therefore deal with the assessment and make an order for a specified sum. So held the EAT in *Casqueiro v Barclays Bank* [2012] ICR D37, a decision under the old rules in which Slade J also observed that this may reflect a drafting oversight in the rules. It would appear likely therefore that a decision has been taken under the *2013 Rules* not to extend this power to the Tribunal.

19.134 VEXATIOUS LITIGANTS

The EAT has power, upon an application by the Attorney General, to make a restriction of proceedings order against a person who has habitually and persistently and without any reasonable ground either instituted vexatious proceedings in an employment tribunal or before the EAT (whether against the same person or against different persons), or made vexatious applications in tribunal or EAT proceedings. The effect of such an order, which may be for a limited or an indefinite period, is that employment tribunal and EAT proceedings may not be commenced or continued, and applications in such proceedings may not be made, without the leave of the EAT. The EAT may not give leave unless satisfied that the proceedings or application are not an abuse of process and that there are reasonable grounds for them; there is no appeal from a refusal of leave (*ETA 1996, s 33*). The first order made under s 33 was made in *A-G v Wheen* [2000] IRLR 461; the decision gives guidance as to the scope of the power and how the EAT should exercise the discretion conferred by it. The order was subsequently upheld by the Court of Appeal ([2001] IRLR 91); the court rejected an argument that an order was in breach of the litigant's rights under art 6 of the ECHR. A useful review of the criteria for making a restriction of proceedings order can be found in the judgment in *A-G v Roberts* [2005] All ER (D) 138 (Jul).

Rule 102 of the *2013 Rules* provides for the Tribunal to provide any information or documents requested by the Attorney General, the Solicitor General, or the Lord Advocate for the purpose of preparing an application or considering whether to make an application under *Senior Courts Act 1981, s 42* (see below); *Vexatious Actions (Scotland) Act 1898, s 1*; the *Courts Reform (Scotland) Act 2014, s 100*; or *ETA 1996, s 33*. As mentioned above, the right to petition the EAT for a restriction of proceedings order only lies with the Attorney General. This contrasts with the position in the High Court where civil restraint orders ("CROs") may be sought by litigants pursuant to *Civil Procedure Rules, r 3.11* and *Practice Direction 3C*. The High Court's power to make a CRO under those statutory provisions extends only to proceedings in the High Court or County Court (although in *Vidler v UNISON* [1999] ICR 746, an Employment Tribunal decided in relation to the power within the *Senior Courts Act 1981, s 42(1A)* that "any court" included a Tribunal so that the claimant was prevented by the High Court's order from bringing proceedings in the Tribunal).

In the important decision of *Nursing & Midwifery Council v Harrold* [2016] IRLR 250, however, Hamblen J decided that the High Court had an inherent jurisdiction to make a CRO covering proceedings before the Employment Tribunal. This decision followed that in *Law Society of England and Wales v Otobo* [2011] EWHC 2264 (Ch) which highlighted the Tribunal's status as an inferior court and the inherent jurisdiction of the High Court relating to proceedings before an inferior court. In the subsequent judgment in *Nursing & Midwifery Council v Harrold* [2016] EWHC 1078 (QB), Elisabeth Laing J applied the statutory provisions by analogy when making a CRO covering tribunal proceedings.

Civil Restraint Orders can be limited, extended or general civil restraint orders and can be made against a party who has issued claims or made applications which are totally without merit. For an example see *London Borough of Redbridge, Governing Body of Trinity Catholic High School v Johnson* [2012] EWHC 4224 (QB); *HM Attorney General v Johnson* [2017] EWHC 979 (Admin). For the meaning of "totally without merit" see *R (Grace) v Secretary of State for the Home Department* [2014] 1 WLR 3432. In *Harrold*, Elizabeth Laing J indicated that (para 139) " . . . it would be desirable for ETs, when they make decisions in weak claims, expressly to consider, and to make a finding on, the question whether the claim (or application) is TWM [totally without merit]. . . . It will greatly help to have the views of the ET on the TWM issue in any case in which a respondent to ET claims applies for a CRO in this court. It may also be that those who draft the rules governing the procedures in the ET and in the EAT may wish to give some thought to this topic."

19.135 PROCEDURE IN CERTAIN SPECIALIST JURISDICTIONS

The procedures described above apply to proceedings covered by *Sch 1* to the *ET Regulations 2013*. Other Schedules set out complementary rules of procedure in claims involving national security (*Sch 2*) and claims for equal pay for work of equal value (*Sch 3*; see EQUAL PAY (**22**)). These rules of procedure should be consulted if relevant.

The Employment Tribunal also has jurisdiction to determine a variety of statutory appeals. These include appeals against an assessment to levy imposed under *section 11* of the *Industrial Training Act 1982*; an improvement notice issued under *section 21* of the *Health and Safety at Work etc Act 1974* and a prohibition notice issued under *section 22* of that *Act*; an unlawful act notice issued by the Commission for Equality and Human Rights under section 21 of the Equality Act 2006; and a notice of underpayment issued under *section 19* of the *National Minimum Wage Act 1998*. In respect of such statutory appeals, *Rule 104* states that *Sch 1* applies to levy appeals for which purpose a reference to a claim and claimant shall be read as references to a levy appeal or to an appellant. *Rule 105* applies *Sch 1* to appeals against improvement and prohibition notices and *Rule 106* applies *Sch 1* to appeals against unlawful act notices. *Reg 12* of the *2013 Regulations* is clear that it is not necessary to use a prescribed ET1 form in such statutory appeals, however to enable the Tribunal to deal with appeals expeditiously and fairly, appellants should now use the form attached in the appendices to the Presidential Guidance on making a Statutory Appeal. Appellants should consult the relevant Presidential Guidance (for England and Wales, or for Scotland as appropriate) for details.

20   Employment Tribunals – III: Appeals

20.1   THE EMPLOYMENT APPEAL TRIBUNAL

Status and jurisdiction

Any appeal from a decision of an employment tribunal is heard by the Employment Appeal Tribunal ('EAT'), save for appeals in health and safety cases against improvement and prohibition notices, which go to the High Court or Court of Session, and in certain special jurisdictions outside the scope of this book. An appeal can only be brought on a point of law (see further below).

The EAT is a tribunal created by statute, and its substantive jurisdiction is statutory: *ETA 1996, s 21*. It also has both statutory (by *s 30(3) ETA 1996*) and (limited) inherent jurisdiction to regulate proceedings before it, as a superior court of record (ie of equivalent status to the High Court): see in particular *X v Stevens* [2003] IRLR 411, discussed at **20.26** below.

In addition to its appellate functions the EAT has certain limited jurisdictions as a court of first instance, in relation to information and consultation of employees; these rarely arise in practice and are not considered in detail in this chapter.

The EAT is not a 'court' within the meaning of *s 4* of the *Human Rights Act 1998*, and it therefore does not have the power to make a declaration that a statutory provision is incompatible with a Convention right guaranteed by the *Human Rights Act 1998:* see *Whittaker v Watson (P & D) (t/a P & M Watson Haulage)* [2002] ICR 1244, where it was suggested that in a case where there was a serious issue of compatibility the EAT should dispose of the appeal on paper, giving permission to appeal to the Court of Appeal. However the EAT is, like other public bodies, subject to the duty to give effect to Convention rights imposed by *section 3* of the *Act*: see e.g. *EF v AB* [2015] IRLR 619 (imposition of a permanent restriction on identifying parties to protect privacy rights).

The EAT is a single appellate court which sits in divisions and may sit anywhere in Great Britain (in fact, it normally sits in London and Edinburgh, and occasionally also in Cardiff). Both judicial and lay members may, and occasionally do, sit in both principal centres. Following questions being raised by some commentators as to how far a decision of the EAT given in Scotland binds English tribunals, and vice versa, the status and effect of decisions was the subject of a public statement by its then President, Morison J, on 3 April 1998 ([1998] IRLR 435). The statement makes it clear that all tribunals are equally bound by decisions of any division of the EAT wherever given.

Despite the foregoing, the EAT sitting in England or Wales is not formally bound by decisions of the Court of Session on appeals from the EAT sitting in Scotland, and the EAT sitting in Scotland is not bound by decisions of the Court of Appeal on appeals from the EAT in England or Wales. The consequences of this were starkly demonstrated in *Marshalls Clay Products Ltd v Caulfield* [2003] IRLR 552, a case on 'rolled up' holiday pay under the *Working Time Regulations 1998*, where the EAT refused to follow a decision of the Court of Session (*MPB Structures Ltd v Munro* [2002] IRLR 601); the Court of Appeal ([2003] IRLR 350) held that it had been entitled to do so, and that its decision was right, thereby raising the prospect of a different interpretation of the same legislation binding tribunals north and south of the border. A further example of an apparent conflict is between the decisions of the EAT sitting in England (on the interpretation of the *Fixed-term Employees (Prevention of Less Favourable Treatment) Regulations 2002*) in *Sharma v Manchester City Council* [2008]

IRLR 336 and *Carl v University of Sheffield* [2009] IRLR 616, and the earlier decision of the Inner House in *McMenemy v Capita Business Services plc* [2007] IRLR 400, reaching a different interpretation, which appears not to have been drawn to the attention of the EAT in *Sharma* but was in *Carl*. The only way to resolve such differences is by way of further appeal to the Supreme Court, a United Kingdom Court, whose decisions are binding in both jurisdictions, or, as happened in the *Marshalls Clay Products* case, by a reference to the CJEU (see *Robinson-Steele v RD Retail Services Ltd*: C-131/04 [2006] ECR I-2531, [2006] ICR 932, a decision supporting the Scottish approach).

Decisions of the EAT are not formally binding on the EAT itself. They are normally followed, even if in a later case the EAT has doubts about the correctness of the previous decision, unless the EAT is satisfied after argument that the first decision is clearly wrong, or there are exceptional circumstances; see for a full review of the circumstances in which a prior EAT decision may not be followed *British Gas Trading Ltd v Lock* (2016) UKEAT/0189/15, [2016] IRLR 316, [2016] All ER (D) 273 (Feb), EAT. However on occasion the EAT has overruled a previous decision; good examples are *Woodward v Abbey National plc* [2005] IRLR 782, overruling *Clark v Midland Packaging Ltd* [2005] 2 All ER 266, on the question when a Notice of Appeal is taken as received by the EAT, and *OTG Ltd v Barke* [2011] IRLR 272, overruling *Oakland v Wellswood (Yorkshire) Ltd* [2009] IRLR 250, on whether the exception in *reg 8(7)* of the *Transfer of Undertakings (Protection of Employment) Regulations 2006* applied to a company in administration. (The *Barke* decision was subsequently held by the Court of Appeal to be correct: *Key2Law (Surrey) LLP v De'Antiquis* [2012] IRLR 212.)

In addition, the range of representation means that the EAT's attention is not always drawn to relevant reported decisions, resulting on occasion in mutually inconsistent decisions, which the EAT in a subsequent case must choose between; this problem has become greater since the unreported decisions of the EAT have become publicly available on its website (http ://www.employmentappeals.gov.uk/public/search.aspx; in addition, all final judgments of the EAT issued since 1992 are now available on www.bailii.org).

20.2   The jurisdiction of the EAT to hear appeals from decisions of employment tribunals is conferred principally by *ETA 1996, s 21*. This provides that an appeal lies to the EAT on any question of law arising from any decision of, or arising in any proceedings before, an employment tribunal under any of a large number of statutory provisions listed in the section (see **20.10** below on the question who is entitled to institute an appeal). The statutory nature of the EAT's jurisdiction, the itemisation of the statutory provisions in s 21, and the proliferation of statutes and regulations conferring additional jurisdictions on employment tribunals, has led on occasions to errors of drafting being found to have failed to confer jurisdiction on the EAT over a particular class of appeal; most recently this was held to be so in relation to appeals concerning the statutory right of accompaniment under the *Employment Relations Act 1999, s 10* (*Refreshment Systems Ltd (t/a Northern Vending Services) v Wolstenholme* (UKEAT/608/03) ((2004) Times, 2 March). This oversight was corrected by the *Employment Relations Act 2004, s 38*.

However subject to this point (which has arisen only very infrequently) any decision of an employment tribunal or judge which determines a claim or issue in the case is in principle open to appeal, not just a formal judgment or decision given after a hearing. Even a failure to act, or delay in making a decision, may be the subject of an appeal: see *Paw v HM Revenue and Customs*, (UKEATPA/0703/11), where HHJ McMullen QC held that a letter written on the instructions of a judge stating that the tribunal could not give advice and stating the procedure for making a complaint could be the subject of an appeal if a point of law could be identified, as the letter arose in the course of proceedings before the tribunal. However the EAT has no jurisdiction to entertain an appeal against incidental findings of fact adverse to the appellant, as these are not 'decisions' within *s 21*: see *Wolfe v North Middlesex University Hospital NHS Trust* [2015] ICR 960, and **20.16** below. In addition an appeal which has become entirely academic is likely to be rejected as an abuse of process: *TIC International Ltd v Ali* (UKEAT/0284/15).

20.3   Fees

From its establishment in 1976 until July 2013, appeals to the EAT were free of charge. However, with effect for appeals presented since 29 July 2013, a fee is payable by the intending appellant, unless he or she qualifies for remission of the fee. The introduction of fees was brought into effect by the *Employment Tribunals and the Employment Appeal Tribunal (Fees) Order 2013, SI 2013/1893*, the same Order which introduced fees for claims to employment tribunals. The fee payable on presenting an appeal is £400; the conditions for full or partial remission of the fee are the same as for fees for presenting an employment tribunal claim, and are set out in a Schedule to the *Fees Order*.

However, unlike the procedure for tribunal claims, it is not necessary to pay the fee at the time of presentation of the appeal. Following receipt by the EAT of the appeal, the appellant is notified of the requirement to pay the fee, or apply for remission, and the latest date by which one or the other step must be taken; if the fee is not paid and no application for remission is made by that date, the appeal will be struck out, but with provision for the appeal to be reinstated if the fee is subsequently paid or an application for remission made. Reinstatement in these circumstances is however a matter for the discretion of the Registrar, not a right. If an application for remission of the fee is unsuccessful, a date will be notified for payment of the fee, with the same consequences if it is not paid in time. These points are set out in *Rule 17A* of the *Employment Appeal Tribunal Rules 1993*, added by amendment at the same time as the *Fees Order*.

A further fee, of £1,200, is payable for the appeal to proceed to a hearing; the same rules and procedures relating to applications for remission, and the striking out of the appeal, apply as for the initial appeal fee. There is no fee for issuing a cross-appeal. The EAT has power to order the respondent to an appeal to pay the fees incurred by the appellant as part of its jurisdiction to order the payment of costs; see **20.46** for details of the considerations likely to be taken in into account in deciding whether such an order should be made.

There is no provision for the repayment of fees once paid (other than by a subsequent, successful application for remission), even if the appeal is rejected at the initial sift, or not permitted to proceed, e.g. because the appeal was submitted out of time.

20.4   Composition

The composition of the EAT has traditionally mirrored that of the employment tribunals. Until recently this has meant that the great majority of full appeals have been heard by a panel of both judicial and lay members, but for appeals referred to a full hearing since 25 June 2013, all hearings are before a judicial member sitting alone unless the EAT has directed that there be a full panel with lay members; see further below.

The judicial members of the EAT are High Court or Circuit Judges, with one High Court Judge appointed as President for three years at a time. One Court of Session judge is also allocated to the EAT and presides over most Scottish, and some English, appeals. The lay members are formally appointed by the Queen on the recommendation of the Lord Chancellor and the Secretary of State (*ETA 1996, s 22(1)(c)*), and are selected for their experience in employment matters. They are generally very senior and experienced in their respective fields. The Judicial Appointments Commission has since 2006 been responsible for selection of candidates for lay membership in England and Wales.

20.5   The position before June 2013 was that the EAT normally sat in divisions of three, although there was (and still is) is provision for a panel of five (one judicial member and two from each of the panels of lay members). Full appeals from decisions of employment tribunals constituted of an employment judge sitting with lay members were required to be heard by a judge sitting with lay members. Where the decision under appeal was taken by an employment judge sitting alone, the appeal would usually be heard by a judge alone, but with a discretion, albeit rarely exercised, to constitute a full panel of three for such cases (*ETA 1996, s 28(4)*).

The Government in November 2011 announced a significant change in the composition of the EAT, as part of the package of reforms of the employment tribunal system which were the subject of consultations earlier that year. The change was implemented by the *Enterprise and Regulatory Reform Act 2013, s 12*, with effect from 25 June 2013 (with an exception for appeals 'in the process of being heard' on that date). *Section 12* removes the requirement for the EAT to be constituted with lay members altogether, replacing this with a discretion to convene a panel with lay members for specific cases. Even before this change, the increased number of cases heard in the employment tribunals by an employment judge sitting alone had already resulted in a considerable increase in the proportion of appeals heard by a judge sitting alone, a trend accentuated by the change in the composition of employment tribunals for hearings since 6 April 2012, whereby unfair dismissal cases are heard by an employment judge sitting alone, unless the discretion to order a full tribunal under *ETA 1996, s 4(5)* has been exercised or the claim includes another claim which requires to be heard by a full tribunal.

The practice of the EAT has been to use the power to order a full panel in cases where the judge considering the papers anticipates that the issues in the appeal are such that the judge hearing the appeal will be assisted by the contribution made by lay members with considerable experience of the working environment. An example of a case in which judicial discretion was exercised to order a full panel is *McGrath v Ministry of Justice* (UKEAT/0247/14), an appeal by a lay member of the employment tribunal claiming that his work was comparable with that of employment judges for the purposes of the *Part Time Workers (Prevention of Less Favourable Treatment) Regulations 2000*. Under provisions contained in the *Prisons and Courts Bill 2017*, the Senior President of Tribunals would be given powers to determine the composition of the EAT for particular classes of appeal. However this Bill lapsed on the dissolution of Parliament following the announcement of a General Election in June 2017.

In addition, issues arising in the EAT after a notice of appeal has been lodged but prior to the full hearing of an appeal have for many years been determined by a judicial member (often the President) sitting alone. Such matters include hearings for directions (when held) and appeals from decisions of the Registrar on preliminary points taken under *rule 20* (eg on extending time for a Notice of Appeal). References under *rule 3(10)* arising from a decision of the Registrar or a Judge that an appeal should not be admitted at the preliminary sift (see below for this) have since the introduction of this procedure also been required to be heard by a Judge alone; such cases have become increasingly common following a tightening of the practice of rejecting apparently hopeless appeals at the sift stage.

Where an appeal is required to be heard by a panel of three, the hearing may proceed in the absence of one of the lay members, but only with the agreement of all parties to the appeal (*ETA 1996, s 28(3)*). The Court of Appeal has ruled that it is a prerequisite to proceeding under this rule that the parties are informed as to which of the panels (employer or employee) the missing member belongs to: *De Haney v Brent Mind* [2003] EWCA Civ 1637, [2004] ICR 348.

Legal aid was in the past available to individuals for appeals from employment tribunals, subject to the normal conditions, although in practice it was very rarely granted. However with effect from 1 April 2013 the *Legal Aid, Sentencing and Punishment of Offenders Act 2012* removed this facility for cases in England and Wales. Legal aid is however still available for appeals in Scotland.

20.6   Practice and administration

The case-load of the EAT grew significantly during the 1990s, although not at the same rate as that of the employment tribunals, but the number of appeals declined somewhat in the early 2000s, reaching a low point of 1,728 potential appeals in 2005–6. The number of potential appeals then gradually increased to 2,172 in 2011–12 and 2,296 in 2012–13, the last full year before the introduction of fees. The impact of fees on numbers of appeals has not been quite as significant as the impact on numbers of claims presented in the employment tribunals, but has nevertheless been significant; potential appeals presented fell to 1721 in 2013–14, 1207 in 2014–15 and 970 in 2015–16.

A significant proportion of potential appeals are screened out at the preliminary sift (see **20.17** for an explanation of this) and are never registered as full appeals; thus the total numbers of cases dismissed as out of time, sifted out and withdrawn before registration in 2015-6 were, respectively, 117, 311 and 102; a further 68 appeals were withdrawn after registration, 87 struck out and 36 dismissed at a preliminary hearing. The total number of cases proceeding to a hearing in 2015–16 was 334. Figures for earlier years show a similar pattern.

20.7   The procedures of the EAT are regulated by *Rules* made under the *ETA 1996 s 30*; the current rules are the *Employment Appeal Tribunal Rules 1993 (SI 1993/2854)* (the '*EAT Rules*') as amended, most recently by the *Employment Appeal Tribunal (Amendment) Rules 2013 (SI 2013/1693)*. The changes made by the 2013 amendments address the introduction of fees for appeals (see **20.3** above) and a tightening of the procedure for further appeals after a Notice of Appeal has been rejected at the sift stage. As part of the process of regulating its own procedure, and also as a means to improve the appellate process, the EAT has from time to time issued Practice Directions. A significantly revised *Practice Direction* was issued on 9 December 2004 ([2005] IRLR 94). This in turn has been twice reissued with amendments, most recently in July 2013 ([2013] ICR 1382), referred to in this chapter as 'the *2013 Practice Direction*', or simply 'the *Practice Direction*'. The text of the *Practice Direction* is available on the EAT website (now part of the Judicial website, www.justice.gov.uk), and it is strongly advised that this be read carefully by anyone involved as a party to an appeal or as a representative. It applies to all appeals, whenever instituted. The EAT has however held that it is not mandatory for the EAT to follow the Practice Direction, and in the event of any inconsistency between its provisions and those of the EAT Rules, it is the latter which prevail: *Zinda v Governing Body of Barn Hill Community High* [2011] ICR 174.

The President of the EAT may also issue *Practice Statements* for the guidance of practitioners; most recently a *Practice Statement* issued by Langstaff P on 17 April 2012 gives guidance on applications to admit fresh evidence, and the citation of authorities, and a further *Practice Statement* was issued on 13 May 2015 dealing with the format and length of Notices of Appeal and Skeleton Arguments. *Practice Statements* are posted on the EAT's website. The 2012 *Statement* included the announcement that copies of the most commonly cited authorities would be available for reference at all EAT hearings and copies need not therefore be provided by the parties; a list of these authorities is annexed to the President's *Statement* on the EAT website. The 2015 Statement stresses the importance of representatives marking up bundles of authorities to highlight the passages to be relied on.

The *Practice Directions* of 2002 and 2004 introduced significant changes in procedure, including the adoption of the Overriding Objective (see **20.14** below and **19.1** above) and a duty for parties to co-operate with the EAT in achieving it, new obligations on the parties (rather than, as hitherto, the staff of the EAT) to prepare and submit the documentation to be considered at each appeal, and new 'tracks' to which different categories of appeal are allocated. All of these features are retained in the *2013 Practice Direction*. The Overriding Objective was formally incorporated into the *EAT Rules* in 2004.

Changes proposed in the *Prisons and Courts Bill 2017* include transferring the power to make Procedure Rules for the EAT to the Tribunal Procedure Committee, with a new *Schedule* to be added to the *Employment Tribunals Act 1996* setting out the matters that the *Rules* will be able to address, and including a new statement of the Overriding Objective; there will also be wider powers for the President of the EAT to issue Practice Directions, including for the conduct of cases by electronic means (such as video conferencing).

20.8 Administratively the EAT falls within the responsibilities of HM Courts and Tribunals Service (an agency of the Ministry of Justice and the successor to the Tribunals Service) but it remains separate from those appellate tribunals which have been grouped together into Chambers of the Upper Tribunal, starting from November 2008, under the reforms to the tribunal system generally introduced by the *Tribunals, Courts and Enforcement Act 2007*. Ministerial responsibility for the EAT Rules lies, rather confusingly, with BEIS; as noted above, this will transfer to the Tribunal Procedure Committee if the proposals in the *Prisons and Courts Bill 2017* are reintroduced and enacted after the June 2017 General Election.

The position of the EAT in Scotland is also somewhat anomalous, as HMCTS is responsible principally for the Courts and tribunals in England and Wales, but also for tribunals with jurisdiction in non-devolved areas of the law, including the EAT. One of the proposals made by the Smith Commission in November 2014 was for the devolution of the administration of reserved tribunals (including the EAT, as well as employment tribunals) to the Scottish Parliament. Powers to bring this proposal into effect by Order in Council are given in *s 39* of the *Scotland Act 2016*, which amends the restrictions on the powers of the Scottish Parliament contained in *Schedule 5* to the *Scotland Act 1998*. Initial proposals for the exercise of this power were issued for consultation by the Scottish Government in early 2016, but as at 1 May 2017 no firm proposals to make use of this power had been announced.

20.9 APPEALS

The procedure for appeals to the EAT is governed by the *EAT Rules*, as amended, supplemented by the *2013 Practice Direction*. The *EAT Rules* also contain modifications to the procedure for appeals in the (very infrequent) cases where the modified procedure for national security cases in *Sch 2* to the *ET Regulations* applies. These modifications are too specialised to be covered in detail in this chapter.

As part of the consultation preceding the making of the *2004 Amendment Rules*, the DTI solicited views on whether a statutory requirement should be introduced that permission would be required to appeal to the EAT; however this proposal was widely opposed and was not pursued (and was not resurrected in the January 2011 consultation paper on tribunal reform issued by its successor, BIS). Instead, however, a new procedure was introduced for weeding out obviously hopeless appeals without a hearing. This was introduced by amendments made in 2004 to the EAT Rules, with associated changes in the Practice Direction. This sifting procedure has been further tightened by amendments to the EAT Rules made in July 2013 (see **20.17** below for details of the sift); in addition, as explained at **20.3** above, a fee is now payable by the appellant as a condition of an appeal being entertained, unless the appellant can secure remission of the fee.

20.10 Who may appeal

Any party to the proceedings in an employment tribunal may appeal against an adverse decision (for the scope of what decisions may be the subject of an appeal see **20.2** above). Those who may appeal include a respondent to the original claim who has not presented a response, or whose response was not accepted by the tribunal (eg because it was out of time) and who has therefore not been permitted to take part in the proceedings: *Atos Origin IT Services UK Ltd v Haddock* [2005] ICR 277, [2005] IRLR 20, EAT; *Butlins Skyline Ltd v Beynon* [2007] ICR 121 (and see the *Practice Direction, para 19,* for the procedural steps required of such an appellant); and a claimant whose Claim Form has been rejected, either by an Employment Judge or by the secretariat, and who wishes to appeal against its rejection:

see respectively for appeals against rejection by an Employment Judge and by the secretariat *Richardson v U Mole Ltd* [2005] IRLR 668 and *Grant v In 2 Focus Sales Development Services Ltd* [2007] All ER (D) 281 (Jan), EAT. It is not yet clear whether it is possible to appeal against the rejection of a claim by the employment tribunal because of non-payment of the required fee, as it is arguable that this is a purely administrative act rather than a judicial decision; it is however possible to appeal against the striking out of a claim under *rule 40* of the *ET Rules of Procedure 2013* for non-payment of the hearing fee (*Aslam v Travelex Ltd* [2015] ICR D21), and the respondent to a claim can appeal against a decision to accept the claim (*Software Box Ltd v Gannon* [2016] ICR 148), and as an alternative to appealing, a prospective claimant whose claim is rejected for non payment of the required fee can present a second claim (and if necessary seek an extension of time for the second claim: see *Deangate Ltd v Hatley* [2015] ICR 890).

The right to appeal is not limited to parties to the proceedings from which an appeal is pursued. *Section 21* of the *Employment Tribunals Act 1996* gives the EAT jurisdiction to entertain appeals from decisions of employment tribunals, without specifying who may bring the appeal. The EAT confirmed in *Martineau v Ministry of Justice* [2015] ICR 1122 that this meant that a non party could in principle bring an appeal. The EAT commented that whilst it would usually be an abuse of process for a third party to bring an appeal (and any such appeal would be struck out for that reason) there could be circumstances in which a non-party had a sufficient interest to bring the appeal. In the instant case a large number of similar claims had been brought, and a lead claimant identified for a hearing. The lead claimant decided not to appeal against the rejection of his claim, but one of the other claimants, whose claim stood to be dismissed in consequence of the rejection of the lead claim, brought an appeal. The EAT held that it had jurisdiction to hear the appeal, and should do so in these circumstances. Another example of a non-party having a sufficient interest in the proceedings to be permitted to appeal would be a press organisation aggrieved at the terms of an order restricting the reporting of the tribunal's judgment.

20.11 Institution and content of appeals

Appeals to the EAT must be instituted by presenting a Notice of Appeal on, or substantially in accordance with the prescribed form (Form 1) to the EAT within 42 days from the date on which the written reasons were sent to the parties or, in a case where the reasons for the judgment were not reserved and written reasons were not requested when the judgment and reasons were given orally or within 14 days thereafter, within 42 days of the judgment being sent to the parties. An appeal from an order or other decision not in the form of a judgment must be presented within 42 days of the date of the order etc (*rule 3(3)*). For the purpose of calculating the 42 day period, the date of the judgment appealed against does not count, so that if for instance that date is a Friday, the last date for lodging an appeal is the Friday 6 weeks later (by 4 pm - see below).

The requirement for presentation means that the Notice of Appeal must be received by the EAT within the prescribed time. *Rule 37(1A)* requires that any act required to be done on or before a particular day must be done before 4 pm on that day; this includes the lodging of a Notice of Appeal: *Woodward v Abbey National plc* [2005] IRLR 782. It was also held in that case that the whole of the documentation required as part of a Notice of Appeal must be received by the EAT office by the deadline; this means that an appeal submitted by fax is only in time if the whole of the fax has been received on the EAT machine by 4 pm on the final day. With this important proviso, service may be by fax as well as by post or personal delivery; there is as yet no formal provision in the *EAT Rules* permitting a Notice of Appeal (or other documents) to be served by e-mail, but the EAT website confirms that appeals may be lodged by email (with the required accompanying documents attached) and this method of service is now routine. However appellants should be aware that the EAT has limited capacity to receive large scanned documents, and the alternative of sending an electronic link to the documents required to be lodged is not accepted: see further **20.14** below.

In *Patel v South Tyneside Council* (UKEATPA/0917/11) the EAT ruled that an appeal submitted by email was validly presented when the appellant received a 'successful delivery' notification from Daemon, the host server for the EAT, although no trace of the Notice of Appeal could be found at the EAT itself.

The EAT Rules permit service of notices, including a Notice of Appeal, at any office of the EAT (there are only two, in London and Edinburgh), so technically, and in contrast to the position governing presentation of a claim, a Notice of Appeal would be validly lodged if received in time at the Scottish office in respect of an appeal from a tribunal in England, and vice versa. However it is not sufficient that the Notice of Appeal is sent in error to the tribunal whose decision is to be appealed, if it is not in fact received by the EAT within the applicable time limit, and such an error is unlikely to be considered a sufficient reason to extend time: *Pierre-Davis v North West London Hospitals NHS Trust* (UKEATPA/1496/08). In practice appeals should always be sent to the office in the country in which the decision under appeal was taken, and are then administered by that office. There is no separate office in Wales, although a limited number of appeals from tribunals sitting in Wales are heard in Cardiff; the appropriate EAT office for appeals from Wales is the London office. The address of the London Office is Fleetbank House, 2–6 Salisbury Square, London EC4Y 8JX (tel: 020 7273 1041); the Edinburgh Office is at 52 Melville Street, Edinburgh EH3 7HF (tel: 0131 225 3963). The email addresses are respectively londoneat@hmcts.gsi.gov.uk and edinburgheat@hmcts.gsi.gov.uk.

The date from which time for appealing starts to run is the day after the date on which the judgment or reasons is or are sent (ie despatched, not received) to the parties or, in the case of an order, the day following the date of the order; the applicable date is recorded on the document containing the judgment, reasons or order itself. 'Sent' means sent and not received: *Gdynia America Shipping Lines (London) Ltd v Chelminski* [2004] EWCA Civ 871, [2004] ICR 1523. A decision is treated as having been sent on the day the document was actually sent by the tribunal office, even if is never received, for instance because it was sent to the wrong address: *Carroll v Mayor's Office for Policing and Crime* [2015] ICR 835. The only recourse of a party wishing to appeal who does not get to see the decision until very near the end of the 42 day period (as in the *Dodd* case: see **20.14** below), or after it has expired, is to apply for an extension of time, which will only be granted if the prospective appellant acted with due diligence when he or she became aware that the decision had been sent out.

The period for lodging an appeal is automatically extended to the next working day if it expires on a day on which the offices of the EAT are closed; in practice this will only apply to public holidays, since it is not the practice of tribunals to make orders or send out judgments on a Saturday or Sunday.

20.12 Format and Content of the Notice of Appeal

There is a prescribed form for Notices of Appeal, Form I, set out in the *Schedule* to the *EAT Rules*. It was stated in an early case that the use of a document other than the prescribed form will be permitted only in exceptional cases (*Martin v British Railways Board* [1989] ICR 24); however, in practice this requirement is no longer enforceable, not least since there is as yet no on line version of the Form; it is sufficient that the Notice of Appeal, in whatever format submitted, contains the information required to complete Form 1 and is accompanied by the required documents.

A *Practice Statement* issued by the President on 13 May 2015 ([2015] IRLR 542), and available on the EAT website, addresses the concerns of the Judges of the EAT about the increasing length of Notices of Appeal. It states that the Grounds of Appeal should be set out in numbered paragraphs briefly identifying each point, and except in cases alleging perversity or bias, where additional particulars are required, should 'usually occupy in total no more than two sides of A4 paper'. Any introductory or explanatory text considered necessary should also be brief. The *Practice Statement* warns that over-long Notices of Appeal may be sent back to be shortened, with adverse consequences, including a possible liability for costs, for any consequential delay; since the *Practice Statement* was issued the EAT has on a number of occasions returned Notices of Appeal to appellants' representative with instructions to shorten them.

It is however important that each of the grounds for the appeal that the appellant intends to rely on are clearly set out. The *Practice Direction* makes it clear (*para 3.10*) that there is no automatic right to add to or amend grounds of appeal, and permission to pursue a ground of appeal may be refused if it has not been set out in the original Notice of Appeal; even if permission to amend is given, there may be adverse costs consequences for the appellant. Delay in applying to amend a Notice of Appeal is likely to lead to permission to amend being refused; for a detailed review of considerations affecting applications to amend see **20.27** below. On the other hand a Notice of Appeal is not the same as the skeleton argument that is usually required for the appeal hearing itself.

20.13 Documentation to be submitted with the Notice of Appeal

In addition to the Notice of Appeal, the appellant must submit (i) a copy of the judgment or order which is the subject of the appeal; (ii) a copy of the written reasons for that judgment or order, if any; (iii) in the case of an appeal against a judgment, if written reasons are not enclosed, an explanation of why not; and (iv) also in the case of an appeal against a judgment copies of the claim and response forms (ET1 and ET3) or an explanation of why they are not included (*EAT Rules, rule 3(1)*). Form 1 also specifies the additional documentation required where there has been an application to review the decision the subject of the Notice of Appeal (see below). If there are no written reasons for the judgment being appealed, the appellant must include in the Notice of Appeal an application for the EAT to exercise its discretion to hear the appeal without written reasons, or to request the tribunal to supply them (*Practice Direction, para 3.4*).

A *Practice Statement* issued by the President in February 2005 ([2005] IRLR 189) makes it clear that all the required documentation must be received by the EAT in order for an appeal to be treated as lodged; so, for instance, if the judgment under appeal and any written reasons are not submitted by the deadline, the Notice of Appeal will be treated as out of time. If two or more cases initially presented on separate ET1s are heard together, each of the ET1s and, if applicable, ET3s, must be enclosed with the Notice of Appeal, or an explanation given for not enclosing them; if this is not done the Notice of Appeal will treated as not properly constituted, and will be rejected: see *Carroll v Mayor's office for Policing and Crime* [2015] ICR 835.

The requirement for all the documentation to be lodged within the time limit for appealing is very strictly applied: in *Woods v Suffolk Mental Health Partnership NHS Trust*, (UKEATPA/0360/06), an extension of time was refused where the Notice of Appeal was submitted on the last day with an incomplete copy of the claim form, and the missing pages were not received until after the time for appealing had expired; the refusal of an extension of time was subsequently upheld by the Court of Appeal ([2007] EWCA Civ 1180). Occasionally a more lenient view may be taken of failure to include all documents, as in *Singh-Rathour v Taylor* (UKEATPA/0879/10) [2011] All ER (D) 64 (May), where a respondent appealing a costs order failed to include the response forms of other respondents to the original proceedings who had no interest in the appeal, and *Hine v Talbot* (UKEATPA/1783/10), where the documents had been scanned and emailed to the EAT but two pages of the judgment had been fed through the scanner together; see also *Desmond v Cheshire West and Chester Council*, at **20.14** below. However, it would be very unwise to rely on such an exercise of leniency occurring. If the Notice of Appeal is submitted by email, the documents which are required to be sent together with it must be sent as an attachment; it is not acceptable to provide a link to documents contained in a file elsewhere, such as a Dropbox zip file: see *Majekodunmi v City Facilities Management UK Ltd* UKEATPA/0157/15 (25 September 2015, unreported), EAT.

If there has been an application for a reconsideration of the judgment under appeal, the application, and if available the judgment or order determining it, must be included with the Notice of Appeal (*Practice Direction, para 3.2*), but it appears from the wording of the *Practice Direction* that failure to do so will not lead to the appeal being treated as not validly lodged.

20.14   Time limits and extension of time

The time limit for instituting appeals is very strictly enforced (see eg *Mock v IRC* [1999] IRLR 785: last minute failure of computer of counsel preparing the Notice of Appeal not sufficient excuse for appeal being lodged one day late; *Woodward v Abbey National plc* [2005] IRLR 782: last page of faxed Notice not received until 4.06 pm on final day for appealing; extension only allowed because previous authority had suggested it was sufficient if the *first* page arrived in time). Every appeal lodged out of time must be accompanied by an application for an extension of time under *EAT Rules, rule 37* setting out the reasons for the delay. The time limit for an appeal applies even though there may be a pending application to the tribunal to reconsider its decision (*Practice Direction, para 5.4*). Nor is the fact that an application for public funding for the appeal is pending a reason for exceeding the time limit: *Practice Direction, para 5.8*.

The strict approach to the time limit adopted by the EAT has been upheld by the Court of Appeal, notwithstanding that a less rigorous approach applies to appeals to that court: *Aziz v Bethnal Green City Challenge Co Ltd* [2000] IRLR 111; *Jurkowska v Hlmad Ltd* [2008] EWCA Civ 231, [2008] IRLR 430 (where however a decision to grant an extension of time of 33 minutes in respect of a missing accompanying document was upheld on the particular facts: see further below for this).

General guidance as to the criteria for allowing appeals out of time has been given in *United Arab Emirates v Abdelghafar* [1995] ICR 65, a decision endorsed by the Court of Appeal in *Jurkowska* (and see *Practice Direction, para 5.7*). The principles have also been re-summarised by the EAT in *Muschett v Hounslow London Borough Council* [2009] ICR 424, and again more recently in *Hine v Talbot* (UKEATPA/1783/10).

In summary, the principles to be applied are that:

(a)   There is an interest in the finality of litigation, so stricter rules apply at the appeal stage than before a case has been heard.

(b)   The grant of an extension of time is an indulgence, and will only be granted in rare and exceptional cases (equally so where the appellant is a litigant in person).

(c)   The EAT must first be satisfied that it has been given a full, honest and acceptable explanation for the delay in submitting the appeal (or documents omitted).

(d)   The merits of the appeal are rarely relevant.

(e)   Lack of prejudice to the other party will not normally be a relevant factor in favour of extending time (but any prejudice to the proposed respondent *would* be a factor against an extension).

(f)   The foregoing points are guidelines, not intended to fetter the discretion of the Registrar and Judge in each case.

The EAT has rejected in terms an argument that these criteria for the application of the time limit for appeals are inconsistent with the Overriding Objective: *Waller v Bromsgrove District Council* (UKEATPA/0019/07).

The most recent reported decision of the Court of Appeal, *O'Cathail v Transport for London* [2012] EWCA Civ 1004, [2012] IRLR 1011, affirms the established approach, emphasising also that whilst the length of the extension of time sought is relevant, the primary focus is on whether there is a good excuse for the delay, that the strict requirement to lodge in time applies equally to the requirement to lodge all the specified accompanying documents as to the Notice of Appeal itself, and that the EAT must balance the interests of both parties. The Court in that case upheld the refusal by the EAT of a one day extension to validate the late submission of the judgment and reasons of the employment tribunal, despite the fact that the appellant, acting in person, was disabled and had suffered a panic attack on the final day for submission of the appeal.

For examples of exceptional circumstances held by the EAT to justify an extension of time, see *Dodd v Bank of Tokyo-Mitsubishi Ltd*, [2005] All ER (D) 74 (Dec) (tribunal judgment not received by appellant's solicitor until the 42nd day following its issue); *Jurkowska* (solicitors for appellant had not received judgment and mistakenly believed reasons, issued later, included the judgment; this decision was upheld by the Court of Appeal); *Hakim v Italia Conti Academy of Theatre Arts* (UKEATPA/1444/08) (application supported by medical evidence of claimant's dyslexia); *Hancocks v Cambian Education Services Ltd* (UKEATPA/0824/10) [2011] All ER (D) 64 (May) (combination of appellant's ignorance of right of appeal and misleading information given by employment tribunal office) and *Farmer v Heart of Birmingham Teaching Primary Care Trust* (UKEATPA/0896/14) (final attachment received 10 minutes late after a series of unusual and unforeseeable problems followed by internet failure).

A further example of the exercise of discretion on exceptional facts is *Desmond v Cheshire West and Chester Council* (UKEATPA/0027/12), where the appellant had tried to submit his appeal electronically on day 41 but it had been rejected because the attached files were too large for the EAT server to accept, and he then resubmitted the appeal with an electronic link to the ET1 and judgment, unaware of the EAT policy of not accepting documents sent via links (albeit the policy is stated on the EAT website). However in *Majekodunmi v City Facilities Management UK Ltd* UKEATPA/0157/15 (25 September 2015, unreported), EAT an extension of time was refused where the prospective appellant had submitted the Notice of Appeal by email with a link to a Dropbox zip file containing the required additional documentation; the documentation had not been 'received' at the point when the link was notified, as it would have been if sent in an attachment with the email attaching the Notice of Appeal.

In *Peters v Sat Katar Co Ltd* [2003] IRLR 574, the Court of Appeal allowed an appeal against a refusal to extend time where a litigant in person had posted her Notice of Appeal 14 days before the deadline but it had been lost in the post. It was, in the Court's view, not reasonable to expect an unrepresented party to realise the need to check with the EAT that the Notice had been received. However, it is very unlikely that this much indulgence would be shown to a professionally represented party.

Some indulgence may be given to an appellant who has greater difficulty appealing because of a disability, but even in such cases a very strict approach is taken: see *Lungu t/a Len Fowler Trophies v Shell (deceased)* (UKEATPA/1178/14) (appellant blind but had software that enabled him to 'read' Word documents: not entitled to extension so that time only ran from when a braille copy of judgment received).

An appeal out of time will not necessarily be permitted merely because a decision of a higher court has changed what was generally understood to be the law in favour of the intending appellant: *Setiya v East Yorkshire Health Authority* [1995] ICR 799.

Exceptionally a short extension may be granted where there is a wider public interest in the issue raised by the appeal: *Ministry of Justice v Burton* (UKEATPA/1215/14) (no good reason for being 11 minutes out of time, but case was a test case the outcome of which would determine a large number of other pending claims).

The Registrar of the EAT will determine any application for an extension of time to validate the Notice of Appeal or Respondent's Answer/cross-appeal (see below for these) on the basis of written representations from the parties (*Practice Direction, para 5.6*). Any party aggrieved by the Registrar's decision (including a respondent to the appeal, if the decision is to extend time) may appeal to a judge of the EAT within five days of the date the Registrar's decision is sent to the parties (*EAT Rules, rule 21; Practice Direction, para 6.3*). Appeals against decisions of the Registrar not to extend time are by way of a re-hearing, and evidence may be (and not uncommonly is) given, particularly where there is an issue as to the sufficiency of the explanation for the lateness of the appeal.

A more general power to extend time (used in relation to extending the time for compliance with later steps in the appeal process, including orders made on the sift) is given by *rule 37* of the *EAT Rules*; applications for extensions are considered in the first instance by the Registrar, with a right of appeal against a refusal. Time limits are not as strictly enforced at later stages of an appeal as in relation to the submission of the appeal, but are still applied relatively strictly, and failure to comply with a deadline without seeking an extension of time is highly risky, as the sanctions include the striking out of an appeal or debarring the respondent to the appeal from participating in the hearing; see further **20.15** below.

20.15 Responding to the Notice of Appeal

The procedure for responding to an appeal depends initially on how the appeal itself is treated by the EAT. All appeals are subject to a sift, as explained at **20.17** below, and only if the appeal is accepted at the sift, or subsequently on an appeal under *rule 3(10)* or after a preliminary hearing, is the respondent to the appeal required to respond formally. (There is an exception to this in some cases where a preliminary hearing has been ordered: the respondent may be directed to provide a concise statement giving reasons why the appeal should be rejected at the preliminary stage. However this is not the formal response to the appeal referred to below.)

If the appeal is allowed to proceed to a full hearing, a respondent to an appeal who wishes to resist the appeal must set out his or her grounds of resistance, and cross-appeal where applicable (see below), in or substantially in accordance with Form 3 (this is referred to as a 'Respondent's Answer') and deliver it to the EAT within the time specified by the Registrar (*EAT Rules, rule 6*; the form is set out in the *Schedule*, and the time limit for filing the response is usually set at 14 days). The respondent may rely on the reasons given by the tribunal, or (alternatively or additionally) other grounds put forward to the tribunal but not relied on by it in support of its findings. These should be set out fully at the outset; the same considerations as to amendments to the Notice of Appeal (as to which see **20.27** below) apply equally to any application to amend the Respondent's Answer.

If an appeal is registered, the respondent is given the opportunity to cross-appeal, that is, to appeal against any elements of the judgment or order under appeal that are adverse to him or her. Directions as to the time for filing the cross-appeal will be notified to the respondent at the same time that he or she is directed to file a Respondent's Answer. If there is a cross-appeal, the procedure applicable to appeals under *rule 3(7)* applies equally to the cross-appeal (*rule 6(12), (12A), (16)*); see **20.17** below for details. If the cross-appeal is accepted following scrutiny under *rule 3(7)*, it will be dealt with in accordance with directions given by a Judge or the Registrar; these can be expected to follow broadly the same procedures as for the appeal; further details are given in the *Practice Direction*. There is no separate fee for cross-appeals.

The EAT has confirmed that a cross-appeal may be made against any part of the decision of the tribunal which is the subject of the original appeal which is adverse to the cross-appellant, not just the part or parts of the decision that are the subject of the appeal: *Weerasinghe v Basildon & Thurrock NHS Foundation Trust* (2015) UKEAT/0397/14, [2016]

ICR 305 (a case where the claimant had succeeded in some but not all his claims, and following an appeal by the respondent against one of the findings in favour of the claimant, he cross appealed against some of the findings against him; this was held to be a valid cross-appeal). The same case also confirms that it is not a good ground of objection to a cross appeal that the time limit for appealing had expired by the time it was lodged. However it is not possible to use the device of a cross appeal to challenge a decision made in the proceedings on a different occasion to that on which the decision the subject of the original appeal was made; *Asda Stores Ltd v Thompson (No 2)* [2004] IRLR 598.

The time limit for submitting a Respondent's Answer is not as strictly enforced as that for submitting a Notice of Appeal, partly because the period for compliance is shorter, and partly because the debarring of a respondent to an appeal might lead to the appeal being allowed without the EAT being aware of the full picture, whereas striking out the appeal means that there is no decision on the merits of the appeal. However, the fact that there is a discretion to extend time does not mean that an extension will be granted readily; matters relevant to the exercise of the discretion include the length of and reasons for the delay, and the extent of any prejudice the other party would suffer if an extension is granted. If a response is not lodged in time and no extension is granted, the respondent will be debarred from taking any further part in the appeal. The prudent course is therefore always to comply with the deadline set, and if it is anticipated that that will not be possible, to apply as soon as possible for an extension of time. The principles are discussed in *Slingsby v Griffiths Smith Solicitors (a firm)* [2009] All ER (D) 150 (Feb); this case is also authority for the point that the principles applicable to extension of time for a Notice of Appeal apply equally stringently to any cross-appeal. The May 2015 *Practice Statement* (see **20.12** above) also gives guidance as to the importance of brevity in Respondent's Answers. Unless additional arguments are to be raised, it is usually sufficient to say that the respondent to the appeal relies on the reasoning of the employment tribunal.

20.16 Grounds of appeal

The EAT's jurisdiction is limited to appeals on points of law. In practice, one of the three most common grounds of appeal is 'perversity' (the other two are bias and insufficiency of reasons, both discussed below). Perversity is recognised to be a separate head of appeal but is narrowly construed and rarely successful. See *Piggott Bros & Co Ltd v Jackson* [1992] ICR 85, *East Berkshire Health Authority v Matadeen* [1992] ICR 723 and *Yeboah v Crofton* [2002] EWCA Civ 794, [2002] IRLR 634, and the discussion of these cases at **20.35**. It is not acceptable for an appellant to contend that 'the decision was contrary to the evidence' or that 'there was no evidence to support the decision', or to advance similar contentions, unless full and sufficient particulars identifying the particular matters relied upon are set out in the Notice of Appeal (*Practice Direction, para 3.8*). Equally however, the Notice of Appeal should avoid prolixity, and should not be as full as the skeleton argument which will generally be required for the full hearing of the appeal: see *Salmon v Castlebeck Care (Teesdale) Ltd* [2015] IRLR 191, [2015] ICR 735, and the May 2015 *Practice Statement*.

There are also specific requirements to be observed where a ground of appeal is bias or similar unfairness: see **20.23–20.25** for details. It is not a valid ground of appeal that the decision appealed against was a majority decision (even where the Employment Judge was the minority): *Chief Constable of Thames Valley Police v Kellaway* [2000] IRLR 170. However a serious procedural irregularity, leading to a hearing which was unfair to the appellant, may be the subject of an appeal on that ground, as may a failure to give adequate reasons for the tribunal's conclusions (see **20.36**).

The EAT will not normally entertain appeals which are, or have become, academic: for an example see *Evans v University of Oxford* (UKEATPA/1510/09) (appeal against refusal to adjourn hearing; by the time appeal due to be heard, hearing had been adjourned). Further, an otherwise successful party cannot appeal against an immaterial finding of the tribunal, or indeed any finding of fact; and if the prospective appellant considers that the tribunal has omitted to make a particular finding (having otherwise found for that party) the correct course is to apply to the tribunal to make a finding on the point, not to appeal: see *Wolfe v North Middlesex University Hospital NHS Trust* [2015] ICR 960.

20.17 Preliminary sifting of appeals

All Notices of Appeal are subject to a preliminary paper sift by either the Registrar or a Judge, in accordance with *rule 3(7)*. In practice the sifting is undertaken by a Judge in almost all cases. If it appears to the Judge reviewing the Notice that it discloses no reasonable grounds for bringing the appeal, or is an abuse of the EAT's process or otherwise likely to obstruct the just disposal of proceedings, the prospective appellant is notified that no further action will be taken on the appeal. Under the procedure in place before July 2013, a prospective appellant could either serve an amended Notice of Appeal (which would again be scrutinised under *Rule 3(7)*) or apply for a hearing before a judge. Changes in the *EAT Rules* as from 29 July 2013 have removed the former option. The only recourse for the prospective appellant whose Notice of Appeal has been rejected at the sift is therefore to apply within 28 days of the rejection for what is referred to as a 'Rule 3(10) hearing', before a judge sitting alone. This may (but rarely does) lead to the appeal being permitted to go forward to a full hearing.

In some cases, under a new provision in the EAT Rules (*Rule 3(7A)*) introduced in July 2013, a prospective appellant may be denied even the limited right to apply for a *Rule 3(10)* hearing, if the judge sifting the Notice of Appeal determines that the appeal is 'totally without merit' (this follows an equivalent procedure introduced some years ago in the Court of Appeal).

The time limit for appealing under *Rule 3(10)*, is enforced strictly, applying the same principles as for the time limit for the initial Notice of Appeal, a practice approved by the Court of Appeal in *Morrison v Hillcrest Care Ltd* [2005] EWCA Civ 1378. An example of a case where an extension of time for a *rule 3(10)* appeal was granted is *Mitchell v Barratt Homes (Leeds) Ltd* (UKEATPA/0903/08), where the delay was attributable to the appellant having erroneously appealed from the rejection of his appeal on the sift to the Court of Appeal, which had refused his appeal as premature. It is not permissible to circumvent the limits on challenging the rejection of an appeal under *rule 3(7)* by applying for a review of that decision: *Zinda v Governing Body of Barn Hill Community High* [2011] ICR 174.

As an indication of the prospects of a successful challenge to the refusal to allow an appeal to proceed under *rule 3(7)*, HHJ McMullen QC in the course of his judgment in *Haritaki v South East England Development Agency* [2008] IRLR 945 stated that in 2007–8, of a total of 917 appeals initially sifted out, there were applications under *rule 3(10)* in 210 cases, of which 29 were wholly or partly successful. An adverse decision of the Judge at a *rule 3(10)* hearing may be further appealed (with permission, either of the EAT or the Court of Appeal) to the Court of Appeal (in Scotland such an appeal would be to the Court of Session, also subject to obtaining permission to appeal). Applications for permission to appeal further are relatively frequent, but very rarely successful.

A hearing under *rule 3(10)* is effectively a re-hearing, and the judge will take a decision on the application on the basis of the material before him or her, not the more limited material that may have been available at the sift stage. It is open to the Judge hearing an application under *rule 3(10)* to permit only one, or some, of the grounds of appeal to proceed to a full or preliminary hearing, and this is in practice a common outcome of successful *rule 3(10)* hearings. In that event only the permitted ground or grounds will be entertained at the later hearing, and an appellant wishing to pursue further any of the grounds disallowed would have to seek permission to appeal to the Court of Appeal (or in Scotland to the Court of Session): see further **20.19** below. The judge may also permit the appellant to amend the

Notice of Appeal at this stage. Any such permission is provisional, and subject to the right of the respondent to apply to have the permission to amend set aside: see *Readman v Devon Primary Care Trus*t (UKEAT/0116/11) and **20.27** below.

A decision taken on the sift to allow an appeal to proceed to a full hearing is normally final; the respondent's opportunity to argue that the appeal has no merit is at the full hearing. However it is possible in exceptional circumstances for the EAT to review a decision taken on the sift, in the interests of justice; this was done (for the first and, to date only, recorded time) in *Jamieson v Nationwide Building Society* (UKEAT/0028/13), where the respondent complained that the decision to allow the appeal to proceed had been influenced by an untruthful statement made by the appellant about the facts of the case. (In the event the appeal was allowed to proceed, because it remained arguable even without the benefit of the false supporting statement.) Langstaff P pointed out that because a successful review would result in the appeal not being allowed to proceed further, the appellant in turn would be able to apply for a hearing under *rule 3(10)* – a reason why a review at this stage is likely to remain a rarity.

The Registrar also deals with interim applications, which must be made by notice in writing (*EAT Rules, rules 19, 20*). She disposes of such applications herself or refers them to a Judge, who may him or herself refer them for hearing before the EAT. An appeal lies against a decision of the Registrar (*EAT Rules, rule 21*). There are separate procedures for applications for restricted reporting orders; see further below for these.

20.18 For a period between 1997 and 2002, it was the practice for all appeals to be referred first to a preliminary hearing involving the appellant only. However this was replaced, following a recognition that it was not an efficient use of the EAT's resources to hold preliminary hearings in cases where there was clearly an arguable point of law, by a much greater use of the sift, as described above, to weed out hopeless cases, and a more sparing use of preliminary hearings for appeals which fall between being clearly arguable and clearly hopeless. The outcome, if a case is permitted to proceed on the sift, is therefore either that it is referred to a full hearing, or that it is to be considered at a preliminary hearing involving (usually) the appellant only (if there is a cross-appeal, or if so directed, the preliminary hearing may also be open to the respondent to the appeal).

If the appeal is permitted to go forward, whether to a full or preliminary hearing, directions for the steps needed to prepare the appeal for hearing will be given on paper. If the direction is that the appeal proceed to a full hearing, it will also be given a listing category. These (as set out at *para 11.19* of the *Practice Direction*) are:

P - recommended to be heard in the President's List

A - complex, and raising point(s) of public importance

B - other cases.

In an appropriate case the judge undertaking the sift may also direct that the appeal be expedited or fast-tracked; examples of the kinds of cases likely to be considered for expedition are given at *para 11.21* of the *Practice Direction*. Either or both parties may make a reasoned application for expedition of the appeal.

A number of other matters are routinely covered by directions given at the sift, including steps to be taken if either party wishes to rely on a note of any part of the evidence given in the tribunal, and arrangements for the lodging of appeal bundles and skeleton arguments. Directions made on paper are subject to the right of any party to the appeal to apply for a variation of the terms of the directions, an extension of time, or additional directions. If a party wishes to have directions varied, or seeks additional directions, the procedure is to apply by letter; see the final paragraph of **20.17** for how such applications are considered.

There has been a change in the EAT's practice in relation to listing appeals for hearing, following the introduction of fees. As explained in *Practice Direction para 12*, once a decision has been taken, whether on the sift, at a *rule 3(10)* hearing or at a preliminary hearing, that the appeal should proceed to a full hearing, the appellant will be required to pay the hearing fee or apply for remission, and only after this has been done will the case proceed to be listed for hearing, and the respondent be required to put in an answer to the Notice of Appeal; see also **20.29** below.

20.19 Preliminary hearings

Where a preliminary hearing is to be held, it is now the practice to order or invite the respondent to the appeal to make concise written submissions as to why the appeal should not be allowed to proceed to a full hearing (*Practice Direction, para 11.9*). The standard directions for preliminary hearings include a requirement for the respondent to lodge any cross-appeal, which will then also be considered at the preliminary hearing (with the consequence that both parties will have the opportunity to put their respective cases). In any case, the appellant will be required to submit a skeleton argument in support of the appeal in advance of the preliminary hearing. Standard directions for preliminary hearings also deal with such matters as applications to admit fresh evidence, or for notes of the evidence before the tribunal to be produced (see **20.21** below), and requiring an appellant alleging bias or a procedural defect to provide evidence on affidavit to support the allegation (see further **20.23–20.25** below). It is usual that the latter direction is expressed in terms that amount to an 'unless' order: if the appellant fails to comply within the time limit (typically 14 days from the date of the order) the relevant parts of the Notice of Appeal will be dismissed.

The outcome of a preliminary hearing may be that the appeal is dismissed, referred to a full hearing, or permitted to proceed but only on some of the grounds advanced in the Notice of Appeal. In the latter category of case, the EAT may not consider any other ground of appeal at the substantive hearing of the appeal, unless there are exceptional reasons to do so, but the appellant may seek permission to appeal to the Court of Appeal against what is effectively the dismissal of part of the appeal: *Miriki v General Council of the Bar* [2001] EWCA Civ 1973, [2002] ICR 505. Permission may also be given at this stage to amend the Notice of Appeal, but the respondent (unless present at the hearing and thus given an opportunity to object to the proposed amendment) will in such cases have the opportunity to apply to have the amendment set aside (see generally *Practice Direction, para 11.15*, and **20.33** below).

Hearings for directions may also be held under *EAT Rules, rule 24*, and there is a general power to give directions under *EAT Rules, rule 25* and to waive compliance with the normal rules under *EAT Rules, rule 39*. A new power to strike out a Notice of Appeal, or a Respondent's Answer, has been given by *rule 26(2)*, added from July 2013. This is subject to the right of the party affected to make representations, either on paper or, if requested, at a hearing. It is not yet clear in what circumstances this power will be used, but it is most likely to be used when there has been serious or persistent failure to comply with procedural requirements or orders.

20.20 Where a separate hearing is held by the employment tribunal on a preliminary issue and the tribunal gives a judgment, it is open to the losing party to appeal, and time for appealing runs from the date the reasons for the judgment on the preliminary issue are sent to the parties (or the date the written judgment is sent, if reasons have not been given in writing). However, the EAT has stated that it is only in exceptional cases that such an appeal will be *heard* before the final determination of the case by the tribunal: *Sutcliffe v Big C's Marine Ltd* [1998] ICR 913. One reason for this approach is that there may be a second appeal from the final decision of the tribunal, and in that event it is a better use of judicial resources for both appeals to be heard together. Appeals against interlocutory case management orders, by contrast, often need to be, and are, heard very speedily.

Conversely, where a party applies to the employment tribunal for a reconsideration of a judgment, and the application is refused, time for appealing against the original decision is not suspended, but if the refusal to reconsider, or the outcome of the reconsideration, is to be challenged a separate appeal must be lodged, with time for this running from the date of the refusal, or judgment, as the case may be. Such double appeals are not uncommon, and are whenever practicable taken together at a single hearing.

20.21 Notes of evidence

An issue often arising on an appeal is what evidence the tribunal had heard on a particular point. Normally, the only admissible evidence of this is the Employment Judge's note of the evidence given. These notes are not produced automatically or on the direct request of a party to the tribunal but only if ordered by the EAT. Reasons must be given in support of any application for an order for the production of the notes. The *Practice Direction, para 9*, sets out the procedure to be followed in, and the criteria applicable to, an application for production of the Employment Judge's notes. Applications must be made promptly, giving reasons in accordance with the criteria set out in the *Practice Direction*. Appellants should make their application together with the Notice of Appeal; if this is not done, and the case is referred to a preliminary hearing, the application for notes must be made at that hearing. In other cases, applications will be considered on paper by the Registrar or a Judge. The practice is that if an appeal is allowed through the sift, the directions given at that stage will include a standard direction which applies if either party intends to rely on notes of evidence (and whether or not any such application has been intimated). The Standard Direction requires the parties if possible to agree a note of the evidence in question; normally they are given 21 days to do so, and (if this does not prove to be possible) any further application for the Employment Judge's notes must be accompanied by evidence of the steps taken to agree the evidence (such as relevant correspondence).

There is no automatic right to production of the Employment Judge's notes simply because the appellant alleges that the decision was perverse: *Hawkins v Ball and Barclays Bank plc* [1996] IRLR 258, EAT. 'Fishing expeditions' are specifically disapproved by the *Practice Direction* (see *para 9.7*), with a warning that unreasonable applications may lead to an order for costs against the offending party.

20.22 Reference back to tribunal for clarification of reasons

A relatively recent innovation in the EAT's procedure is the reference back of appeals which are based on the inadequacy of the tribunal's reasons, for amplification or clarification of the reasons under challenge. It had been thought that there was no power for the EAT to refer a case back to the tribunal, whether for reconsideration of its findings or to clarify or amplify its reasons, except as part of the disposition of the case after hearing and deciding the appeal; this view was based on obiter comments by the Court of Appeal in *Tran (Kien) v Greenwich Vietnam Community Project* [2002] EWCA Civ 553, [2002] IRLR 735 on the ambit of *ETA 1996, s 35(1)*. However a different view was expressed, in relation to civil appeals generally, in the later case of *English v Emery Reimbold & Strick Ltd* [2002] EWCA Civ 605, [2002] 3 All ER 385, [2002] 1 WLR 2409, [2003] IRLR 710, and following that decision, the EAT held in *Burns v Consignia (No 2)* [2004] IRLR 425 that there is such a power.

This view was subsequently endorsed by the Court of Appeal, but on different grounds, in *Barke v SEETEC Business Technology Centres Ltd* [2005] EWCA Civ 578, [2005] IRLR 633. The view expressed in *Tran* was held to be correct, but it was held that there is power to remit derived from the provision (newly introduced in 2004) in the *ET Rules, rule 30(3)(b)*, for tribunals to be required to provide reasons if requested by the EAT (see now *rule 62(3)* of the *2013 Rules*); alternatively, the inherent jurisdiction of the EAT allowed this course to be adopted. The procedure for referral back has become known by reference to the leading cases as a '*Burns/Barke*' order. The power may be exercised on a Judge's initiative or at a preliminary hearing; the appeal then proceeds on the reasons as clarified or amplified. The Court of Appeal has stated that a *Burns/Barke* reference should not be made where the reasons given by the tribunal are too deficient to be remedied by amplification, and also that the judge responding to a request for clarification or amplification of reasons should limit him or herself to doing that, and should not attempt to justify or argue in support of the original decision: *Woodhouse School v Webster* [2009] EWCA Civ 91, [2009] IRLR 568. For further guidance on the use of procedure see *Korashi v Abertawe Bro Morgannwg University Local Health Board* [2011] EWCA Civ 187, [2011] All ER (D) 09 (Mar).

The most recent guidance given by the EAT, in *Wolfe v North Middlesex University Hospital NHS Trust* [2015] ICR 960, is that if it is claimed by the appellant that the tribunal has failed to deal at all with an issue which was before it, or to give adequate reasons for part of its decision, the proper course is to apply to the tribunal for it to rectify the failure (by way of reconsideration of its judgment and reasons), and it is the duty of advocates to take this course before appealing. If such a case is the subject of an appeal without the point having first been referred back to the tribunal, the EAT will adjourn the appeal for a reference to be made to the tribunal, and the appeal will not proceed until the tribunal has clarified its decision.

In a case where there is an appeal against a judgment or order for which the tribunal has not given written reasons, *ET Rules, rule 62(3)* implicitly gives the EAT power to ask the tribunal or Employment Judge to supply written reasons for the purpose of the appeal. This is frequently used where the appeal is against a decision taken without a hearing, for which written reasons may not be required by the *ET Rules*.

The EAT also has the power to stay an appeal; this is sometimes used (in addition to the circumstances covered by *Wolfe*, above) to enable the appellant to apply for a reconsideration of the tribunal's decision, where it is thought that a decision following reconsideration might obviate the need for an appeal; the procedure is formally sanctioned by the *Practice Direction, para 11.3*.

20.23 Allegations of bias

The EAT will not normally consider complaints of bias or of the conduct of an employment tribunal unless full and sufficient particulars are set out in the grounds of appeal. In any such case the Registrar may inquire of the party making the complaint whether it is the intention to proceed with the complaint, in which case the Registrar will give directions. Such directions may include the filing of affidavits dealing with the matters upon the basis of which the complaint is made, or for giving further particulars. The Employment Judge (and in appropriate cases the other members) will be given the opportunity of commenting upon the complaints made against him or her (*Practice Direction, para 13*). It has been held that this procedure should also be followed where a ground of appeal is that the tribunal refused or failed to adjourn the proceedings: *Knight v Central London Bus Co Ltd* (EAT/443/00).

The Court of Appeal has confirmed that the EAT has jurisdiction to hear an appeal based on an allegation of bias, unless the allegation was on its face so lacking in substance that it could not be said to amount to a real challenge: *Lodwick v Southwark London Borough Council* [2004] EWCA Civ 306, [2004] ICR 884, a case where the appellant had objected to the Judge but the latter had declined to recuse himself. Further detailed guidance as to how appeals alleging bias by the tribunal should be conducted, particularly where there is a dispute of fact as to what occurred at the hearing, has been given in *Facey v Midas Retail Security* [2001] ICR 287. The guidance provides for affidavits or witness statements to be served by each of the parties, comments to be provided by the judge and tribunal members, and if necessary the witnesses (but not the judge or tribunal members) to attend the EAT for cross-examination on their evidence.

A high proportion of appeals alleging bias are sifted out at the initial stage. Those allowed to proceed further are generally made subject to quite strict case management, including orders for the filing of affidavits within 14 days on an 'unless' basis. This means that the relevant parts of the appeal are automatically dismissed if the appellant fails to file an affidavit giving details of the allegations within the time allowed; however the appellant may apply retrospectively for a review of the original order: the criteria for reviewing such orders are considered in *Roberts v Carling* (UKEAT/0183/09).

20.24   Where there is an allegation of bias based on the conduct of the judge or one of the lay members of a tribunal at a hearing, the test is an objective one: whether, having regard to the relevant circumstances 'a fair minded and informed observer who had considered the facts would conclude that there was a real possibility that the tribunal was biased' (*Porter v Magill* [2001] UKHL 67, [2002] 2 AC 357, [2002] 1 All ER 465). Bias of this kind on the part of one tribunal member is sufficient (*Lodwick v Southwark London Borough Council*, above). Examples of cases where the EAT found that there was an appearance of bias are *Diem v Crystal Services plc* [2006] All ER (D) 84 (Feb), EAT, where, in a claim of race discrimination, the Employment Judge made comments about the colour of the claimant's skin, *Gill v Humanware Europe Ltd* (UKEAT/0312/08) [2009] All ER (D) 77 (Aug), where the employment Judge was alleged to have had private discussions about aspects of the case with counsel for the respondent in the absence of the claimant, who was representing himself (for the subsequent wasted costs proceedings in this case see [2010] IRLR 877) and *Governing Body of St Michael's Church of England Junior & Infant School v Smith* (UKEAT/0165/14) (excessive and confrontational questioning of witnesses by judge gave rise to a perception of bias).

In *Ansar v Lloyds TSB Bank plc* [2006] EWCA Civ 1462, [2007] IRLR 211, the Court of Appeal gave guidance on when the fact that a complaint of bias had been made against an Employment Judge makes it inappropriate for the Judge to continue to hear the case, or to deal with any later application by the person complaining. The mere fact of an allegation of bias having been made is not in itself a reason for the Judge to stand aside (the technical term is recusal). See also *Bennett v Southwark London Borough Council* [2002] EWCA Civ 223, [2002] IRLR 407 (allegations made against Judge during course of hearing). On the other hand if the tribunal has made comments, whether in the course of the hearing or in a judgment, which indicate that it has reached a conclusion on an issue still to be decided, it may be disqualified from continuing to deal with the case; a good example is *Oni v NHS Leicester City* [2013] ICR 91 (tribunal had made findings making it inappropriate for it to hear a costs application). See also *Begraj v Heer Manek Solicitors* [2014] IRLR 689, [2014] ICR 1020, in which the EAT held that a tribunal was right to recuse itself after the police had contacted the judge and given information about a party which they asked her not to disclose to the claimant; this rendered an unprejudiced hearing no longer possible.

For the position where a tribunal member is directly associated with a party to the case, or a body with an interest in the outcome of the proceedings (such as a pressure group) see *R v Bow Street Metropolitan Stipendiary Magistrate, ex p Pinochet Ugarte (No 2)* [2000] 1 AC 119, HL and *Helow v Secretary of State for the Home Department* [2008] UKHL 62, [2009] 2 All ER 1031. In *Honey v Swansea City Council* [2008] All ER (D) 311 (Nov), an appearance of bias was found to be established where one of the tribunal members was at the time of the hearing involved, in his capacity as a union official, in an unrelated dispute with the appellant local authority. The opposite conclusion was reached by the Court of Appeal in *Galloway v Barnet Enfield and Haringey Mental Health NHS Trust* [2010] EWCA Civ 1368 with respect to a lay member of the tribunal who had previously been employed for several years as HR Director of another NHS Trust; amongst other reasons for concluding that there was no basis for an allegation of apparent bias on these facts, Gross LJ made the point that the tribunal system benefits from the relevant knowledge and experience of lay members who have worked in the particular industry or sector to which the proceedings relate. See also *Taylor v Governing Body of the Potters Gate CE Primary School*

(UKEAT/0227/14) (fact that judge was a governor of another school in the same local education authority area as the respondent Governing Body, but had not had dealings with any of the persons involved in the case, did not create an appearance of bias).

A somewhat different situation which led to a finding of a perception of bias arose in *Peninsula Business Services Ltd v Rees* (UKEAT/0335/08) [2009] All ER (D) 134 (Sep), where the firm of solicitors for which the (part-time) employment judge worked had issued an advertisement for its services criticising the services offered by consultants, of which the appellant company was the best known. However in a second case heard together with *Rees*, it was held that there was no basis for a perception of bias where the judge had subsequently become full time and no longer worked for the firm concerned. A similar conclusion was reached in *Williams v Cater Link Ltd* (UKEAT/0393/08) [2009] All ER (D) 70 (Aug).

The foregoing examples are of cases where the connection with a party was either not disclosed or not fully disclosed; if a connection has been fully disclosed and the parties have consented to the judge or member concerned hearing the case, the relationship will normally not provide a ground of appeal: *Jones v DAS Legal Expenses Insurance Co Ltd* [2003] EWCA Civ 1071, [2004] IRLR 218. For an example where consent was held to have been given (which includes consideration of the requirements for informed consent) see *Adamson v Swansea University* (UKEAT/0486/09) [2010] All ER (D) 38 (May). Both cases stress the need for fully informed consent, and therefore a full disclosure by the judge or member of any relevant interest or connection.

20.25　Procedural unfairness to a party in the course of the hearing is also a permissible (and relatively common) ground of appeal: see further **20.37**. There have been conflicting decisions of the EAT as to whether any issue of allegedly improper conduct by the judge or a lay member arising in the course of the proceedings had to be raised at the time of its occurrence if it was to be the subject of an appeal (see *Peter Simper & Co Ltd v Cooke* [1986] IRLR 19 and *Red Bank Manufacturing Co Ltd v Meadows* [1992] ICR 204). The Court of Appeal reviewed the position and gave general guidance in *Stansbury v Datapulse plc* [2003] EWCA Civ 1951, [2004] IRLR 466, a case where the original decision was set aside for procedural irregularity on evidence that one of the lay members had fallen asleep during the proceedings after having consumed alcohol during the lunch break. The test where the issue was not raised with the tribunal at the time is one of reasonableness, recognising in particular that while it is desirable that the matter should be raised at the time, so that if possible corrective action can be taken, it is difficult even for a legal representative, let alone an unrepresented party, to raise a complaint against a member of the tribunal who, if the complaint is not accepted, will proceed to adjudicate on the case. Where it is claimed that there was procedural unfairness as a result of a ruling of the tribunal in the course of the hearing, the failure of the disadvantaged party to object at the time does not necessarily prevent the point from being taken on appeal, especially if the appellant had not been professionally represented: *Bache v Essex County Council* [2000] 2 All ER 847, [2000] IRLR 251.

It is for the EAT, not the tribunal itself, to decide any disputed issue as to whether a judge or lay member was asleep during the proceedings (or any other disputed issue about what was said or done during the hearing): *Elys v Marks and Spencer plc* [2014] ICR 1091.

Other circumstances may lead to allegations of procedural unfairness, which in principle is a permissible ground of appeal. One such was raised in *McGrath v Ministry of Justice* (UKEAT/0247/14), where the employment judge took into account his personal experience of working with lay members in deciding whether a lay member had a valid claim that his work was comparable to that of employment judges for the purposes of the *Part time Workers (Prevention of Less Favourable Treatment) Regulations 2000*; this was held not to be procedurally unfair as the judge had given the claimant a full opportunity to comment. In *East of England Ambulance Service NHS Trust v Sanders* [2015] IRLR 277, the EAT stated that the tribunal should not undertake its own researches on the internet to supplement the evidence adduced by the parties, particularly if the parties are not given an opportunity to comment on any material found in this way.

20.26   Restricted Reporting and Anonymity Orders

Rule 23 of the *EAT Rules* contains provisions which closely follow those of *rule 50* of the *ET Rules* conferring powers on tribunals to make restricted reporting orders and other orders protecting the identity of parties, witnesses and third parties. It should be noted that although the provisions of the *ET Rules* on this have been recast in the *2013 Rules*, there have been no corresponding amendments to the *EAT Rules*, which thus mirror the provisions formerly in the *ET Rules* more closely than the provisions in the new *ET Rules*. In particular *rule 23(2)* of the *EAT Rules* provides that if an appeal appears to involve allegations of the commission of sexual offence, the Registrar must withhold from the Register of judgments, and delete from other documents available to the public, any identifying matter likely to lead members of the public to identify any person making or affected by the allegations. The latter is treated as an administrative responsibility of the Registrar, and does not require an application by a party. This mirrors the procedure formerly applicable in employment tribunals under the *2004 ET Rules, rule 49*, now replaced by a wider power for the tribunal itself to grant anonymity to parties, witnesses or affected third parties.

In cases involving allegations of sexual misconduct (not amounting to an offence), a restricted reporting order, prohibiting the publication prior to the final judgment on the appeal of identifying matter likely to lead to the identification of any person named in the order, may be made either on a temporary basis or, on the application of a party or of the EAT's own motion, having given the parties an opportunity to be heard on the matter (*rule 23(3), (5)*). A temporary order lasts for 14 days unless a party applies for it to be extended, in which case the order continues in force until that application has been heard and determined (*rule 23(5A)–(5C)*).

There are other important differences in the scope of the powers of the EAT in comparison with those of the employment tribunal. There is no equivalent provision in *rule 23* to the provision in *rule 50* of the *ET Rules* enabling interested third parties such as press representatives to be given an opportunity to make representations before an order is made, or for it to be revoked. In addition, the power to make orders securing the permanent anonymity of a party is restricted by the express wording of the *ETA 1996, s 31* (which is the statutory authority for *rule 23*) to appeals against the making or refusal by a tribunal of restricted reporting orders and certain interlocutory appeals: appeals against final judgments of a tribunal are therefore not covered.

The last point has led to a series of cases in which the EAT has held that it nevertheless has power to order the anonymisation of public documents relating to the case, including judgments. In *Chief Constable of West Yorkshire Police v A* [2001] ICR 128 and *X v Stevens* [2003] IRLR 411 the reason for anonymity was that the claimant in each case would otherwise have been inhibited in pursuing a claim based on an EU right, and protection was thus considered necessary to ensure that that right could be given full effect. In the first case, the EAT under Lindsay P relied on the direct effect of the *EU Equal Treatment Directive*, while in the second, Burton P preferred to base the power on the inherent jurisdiction of the EAT as a superior court of record (see **20.1** above for this). In two further cases not involving any EU right, *B v A* [2010] IRLR 400 and *A v B* [2010] IRLR 844, the EAT, in both cases under Underhill P, held that where it was necessary to make an order in order to protect the rights of the party concerned to privacy under *art 8* of the *European Convention on Human Rights*, this could be done. The basis for doing so was clarified in a supplemental judgment in *A v B* [2010] IRLR 844 at 856) as the application of the EAT's general power to regulate its own procedure, conferred by *ETA 1996, s 30(3)*. The cases concerned claims of unfair dismissal; the dismissal in *A v B* had followed a report to the employer by the police of allegations that the claimant had been engaged in paedophile activities overseas and in *B v A* an allegation of rape made against the claimant by a fellow employee.

It is the duty of both the employment tribunal and the EAT, as public bodies, to ensure that effect is given to Convention rights: see *section 3* of the *Human Rights Act 1998*. This provides a basis for an order protecting the anonymity of a non-party whose privacy rights would otherwise be compromised by public disclosure of his or her identity: the anonymity requiring protection in *B v A* was that of the victim of the alleged rape, who was not herself a party to the proceedings but whose rights under *art 8* were asserted by the employer, which was. See further *F v G* [2012] ICR 246 (anonymity order made by tribunal on privacy grounds for the protection of vulnerable students of the respondent college upheld on appeal). In *EF v AB* [2015] IRLR 619 a permanent Restricted Reporting Order was made by the EAT on this basis to protect the privacy of the wife of a respondent in the original tribunal proceedings, and her young son, in the context of lurid allegations of sexual activity involving her having been made in the tribunal proceedings. In each of these cases, the countervailing rights of the press and the general public in the reporting of public judicial proceedings under *art 10* of the *Convention* had to be balanced against the individual interests of those whose privacy would be adversely affected by the reporting of the proceedings.

For further details of the scope of and case law relating to restricted reporting orders and other orders restricting publicity in employment tribunals, see **19.91–19.92**.

20.27 Amendments to the Notice of Appeal

Appellants frequently seek to amend their Notice of Appeal. This may be because they have advice that was not available before the Notice of Appeal was lodged, typically when an ELAAS representative (see **20.28** below) is made available to a previously unrepresented appellant at a preliminary or *rule 3(10)* hearing. Permission is required for any amendment, and the respondent to the appeal has the right to resist any application for permission. For this reason, if permission is given at a hearing at which the respondent is not present the permission is expressed as provisional, and is subject to the respondent's right within a set time (usually 14 days) to apply to have the permission set aside.

Permission to amend to add a ground of appeal will not be given unless the EAT is satisfied that the amendment raises a point of law which is at least arguable. There is also an important difference between amendments which clarify a ground of appeal already in the Notice of Appeal and amendments which raise entirely new points. The other factors the EAT will take into account in deciding whether to give permission to amend are set out in *Khudados v Leggate* [2005] ICR 1013, at para 86:

(a)   Whether the application for permission was made as soon as the need for amendment was known;

(b)   Whether a full, honest and acceptable explanation has been given for any delay in applying;

(c)   The extent to which permitting the amendment would delay the appeal;

(d)   Whether permitting the amendment will cause prejudice to the respondent (over and above the inevitable prejudice of having to deal with a ground of appeal that it would not otherwise have to meet), and conversely whether denying permission will cause prejudice to the appellant;

(e)   In some cases the merits of the proposed additional or amended ground will be relevant;

(f)   The public interest in the expeditious conduct of the EAT's business and efficient use of its resources.

These factors are further considered in *Readman v Devon Primary Care Trust* (UKEAT/0116/11), where Underhill P makes the point that a less stringent approach to permission to amend is taken at *rule 3(10)* hearings, since they are often the first point at which the appellant has legal advice about the potential points of law that could be pursued in the appeal, and because there will be no prejudice to the respondent since it will not up to that point have been required to take any action on the appeal. A similar point is made in *King v Royal Bank of Canada* [2012] IRLR 280 in relation to appeals by litigants in person, who should be given more latitude in relation to a failure to identify all the potential grounds of appeal at the outset, particularly in the light of the difficulty many lay persons have in obtaining legal advice. *King* contains a full and helpful summary of the considerations relevant to whether permission to amend should be given: see paras 31–44.

Whilst most applications to amend the Notice of Appeal are made, and determined, before the matter proceeds to a full hearing, there is in principle no restriction on how late in the proceedings an application for permission to amend may be made and granted. An extreme example of this is *BMC Software Ltd v Shaikh UKEAT/0092/16* (23 January 2017, unreported), where the appellant employer was given permission to amend its Notice of Appeal after the close of submissions. The issue raised by the amendment was a point of law affecting the jurisdiction of the tribunal whose decision was under appeal, and which had been raised by the EAT itself, and the EAT concluded that the balance of prejudice, including prejudice to the good administration of justice if permission was refused, was in favour of permitting the amendment.

20.28   CONDUCT OF THE APPEAL

Representation

As in employment tribunals, there is no restriction as to the persons who may represent a party to an appeal (*ETA 1996, s 29(1)*). In the nature of the proceedings, legal representation is more common than in the employment tribunals, but by no means universal. A scheme known as ELAAS has existed since 1996 for the provision of professional advice for, and, if desired, representation of, unrepresented appellants at preliminary hearings. This is operated with the active encouragement of the EAT by experienced barristers and solicitors who provide free representation on a rota basis. The Free Representation Unit and the Bar Pro Bono Unit also provide free representation in an increasing number of cases. There are as yet no equivalent services available for hearings in Scotland.

Concerns about the prevalence of organisations offering representation to parties in employment litigation, often on a no win no fee basis, but which were not subject to external scrutiny of their competence or professional standards, led to the introduction by the *Compensation Act 2006* of a scheme of regulation of claims management bodies, including those which provide representation in employment tribunals or the EAT for reward. It is a criminal offence for an unregulated person or body to undertake regulated claims management services for reward (including under conditional fee arrangements); those exempt from regulation include lawyers and trade unions, as well as those, such as the CAB, not acting for reward. The term 'regulated claims management services' covers the representation of claimants (but not respondents) in employment tribunal proceedings and any subsequent appeal to the EAT. The regulator is the Secretary of State for Justice. The *2006 Act* does not apply to Scotland, and there is currently no equivalent regulation of representatives who are not practising lawyers in Scotland.

20.29   Preparation for the hearing

It should first be noted that once an appeal is permitted to proceed to a full hearing (whether by a decision taken on the sift, or at a *rule 3(10)* or preliminary hearing) a hearing fee of £1,200 becomes payable by the appellant. This fee is additional to the fee for appealing (of

£400). The hearing fee must be paid, or an application for remission of the fee submitted, before the case will be referred to the Listing Department for listing for hearing. Failure to pay the fee, or to apply for remission (and pay the fee if the remission application is unsuccessful) may result in the appeal being struck out under *EAT rule 17A*. This is subject to a discretionary power to reinstate the appeal if the fee is subsequently paid, or remission granted following a further application, but reinstatement in these circumstances is not automatic, and will depend on the cogency of the appellant's explanation for not having paid the fee when originally required to do so.

Although normally the EAT will not hear an appeal until the relevant fees have been paid, or remission granted, some appeals may need to be heard so rapidly that it is not practicable to delay them until issues about the payment of fees have been resolved (particularly if an application for remission is made, as this may take some time to be decided). The EAT has confirmed that, exceptionally, it can hear an appeal before even the appeal fee has been paid or remitted: *Dozie v Addison Lee plc* (UKEAT/0328/13). The EAT has the power to do this since an appeal remains extant until it is struck out under *rule 17A*; but in the great majority of cases, where the appeal does not require to be heard almost immediately, it will not be entertained whilst fee issues remain outstanding. The appellant is still expected to pay the fees due (if not entitled to remission) following any hearing heard before the fee has been paid, although it is not clear what mechanism there is to enforce the obligation to do so; equally the EAT can order the respondent to the appeal to pay back the fees incurred by a successful appellant (see *rule 34A(2A)*, and an order to do so can be made conditional on the appellant having paid the fees (so that it will not apply if there is a successful remission application). See as to costs generally **20.42–20.46** below

20.30   The EAT will have before it at the substantive hearing the Notice of Appeal, the Respondent's Answer, the decision of the employment tribunal and any documents which were before the employment tribunal and which are relied on by the parties as relevant to the appeal. It is the responsibility of the appellant to lodge copies of a core bundle of documents (if possible this should be an agreed bundle, and it should be in the format set out in *para 8* of the *Practice Direction* and contain the documents listed there, together with any other documents relevant to the appeal). Irrelevant documents should not be included. Permission is required for the submission of a bundle exceeding 50 pages in addition to the documents required to be included under the *Practice Direction* (which include the Notice of Appeal and Respondent's Answer, the judgment under appeal and reasons, the ET1 and ET3, any orders made by the EAT, and a number of other documents specified in the *Practice Direction, para 8.2*). The Employment Judge's notes must be included in the appeal papers if their production was ordered.

It is not acceptable for the parties to fail to co-operate in agreeing the content of the appeal bundle. If however there is a dispute about what documents should be included, the appellant should prepare and lodge a core bundle containing the documents required under the *Practice Direction* to be included and any other documents the inclusion of which is agreed; any documents the relevance of which is disputed should also be included (within the overall limits set by the *Practice Direction*) but with the risk to a respondent to the appeal who insists on the inclusion of inappropriate or unnecessary documents that there may be a costs sanction. See *Smith-Twigger v Abbey Protection Group Ltd* (UKEAT/0391/13).

A party seeking to show that no reasonable tribunal could have reached the conclusion it reached on the evidence will almost certainly require the notes of evidence, or a jointly agreed note supplied by the parties (*Piggott Bros & Co Ltd v Jackson* [1992] ICR 85 at 96). (This view was qualified by the EAT in *Hawkins v Ball and Barclays Bank plc* [1996] IRLR 258, where the evidence was clearly recorded in the tribunal's decision and the issue was whether the conclusions reached from that evidence were perverse.) Any application for an order to produce all or part of the notes must be made in accordance with *para 9* of the *Practice Direction*; see **20.21** above.

Most cases are listed for a fixed date. It is the practice of the EAT that the listing office consults the parties, or as appropriate their representatives, over dates to avoid, and as a consequence once a hearing is listed, cogent reasons will be needed to secure a postponement. It is the duty of the parties to advise the EAT if for any reason the time estimate given for the hearing is likely to be inadequate or too long. Parties are also required to notify the EAT immediately of any settlement which results in the appeal being withdrawn; the Court of Appeal has stated that it is a strict professional duty of legal representatives to avoid waste of judicial time by notifying settlements of cases under appeal immediately, particularly if a settlement is achieved in the immediate run up to the hearing of the appeal: *Yell Ltd v Garton* [2004] EWCA Civ 87, (2004) Times, 26 February. Shorter, and urgent, appeals may be called on at short, sometimes very short, notice.

20.31 Skeleton arguments

In accordance with *para 16* of the *Practice Direction*, skeleton arguments are required to be lodged with the EAT and exchanged between the parties' representatives, normally 21 days in advance of the hearing (precise timing varies depending on the length of notice of the hearing and type of hearing); appellants may lodge a skeleton argument with the Notice of Appeal, and should prepare an agreed chronology of relevant events. Skeleton arguments are also required for preliminary hearings, and should be lodged 10 days in advance. The format and content of skeleton arguments are prescribed in some detail in *para 16* of the *Practice Direction*. This has been supplemented by guidance in the May 2015 *Practice Statement*, which explains that 'skeleton arguments are not expected to be full written arguments, but instead are intended to provide the framework within which oral submissions will be made, and should be as short as the nature of the case permits'.

The requirements for skeleton arguments do not apply in Scotland unless specifically directed; however it is increasingly common that skeleton arguments are directed in Scotland, and even when not directed, parties' representatives are encouraged to provide them.

Parties intending to rely on authorities are expected to provide copies for the use of the judge and (if present) members. The *Practice Direction, para 17* gives detailed guidance on the presentation of authorities. Parties are expected to co-operate in agreeing a joint list of authorities; the authorities should be presented in a ring binder, in chronological order and separately tabbed, using the officially reported versions with headnotes wherever available, and with the relevant passages highlighted; and only cases which are authority for a legal principle, rather than merely illustrative, should be relied on. Normally no more than 10 authorities should be cited unless the scale of the appeal warrants more extensive citation. If the EAT is presented with bundles of authorities which have not been marked up, it may require the party responsible to mark them up before the hearing begins, and if this results in additional costs for the other party, an order may be made against the party failing to provide marked up bundles in the first place: see *East of England Ambulance Service NHS Trust v Sanders* [2015] IRLR 277.

The EAT has available for reference its own copies of the most frequently cited cases, and it is not necessary to provide copies of any of the listed cases for the hearing. The full list of cases to which this practice applies is posted on the EAT website.

It is the practice of the EAT to read the papers, and skeleton arguments, in advance and representatives can expect to be asked questions arising from their and the other party's skeleton arguments as well as points arising in the course of their oral submissions.

20.32 The hearing

The hearing before the EAT consists of legal argument; it is not the practice to hear evidence again, and therefore witnesses who attended the tribunal do not need to attend the appeal. Exceptions to this, where witnesses may be required to give evidence, include where there is an appeal against a refusal by the registrar to extend time for a late notice of appeal: in such cases, evidence may be given to explain the delay in submitting the Notice of Appeal; and in relation to allegations of bias or improper conduct in the course of the hearing, where if the events in issue are disputed, the EAT may wish to hear live evidence from those present (other than the Employment Judge and members, who will never be required to give evidence). If fresh evidence is put forward this is done by way of affidavit, or a witness statement with a signed Statement of Truth.

20.33 Raising points not taken at the tribunal hearing

A party is not normally permitted to raise points of law which were conceded or abandoned, or never raised at all, before the employment tribunal, especially where such points would require further investigation of the facts. The law and practice on this issue was reviewed by the EAT in *Glennie v Independent Magazines (UK) Ltd* [1999] IRLR 719, following the decision of the Court of Appeal in *Jones v Governing Body of Burdett Coutts School* [1998] IRLR 521, which established that the EAT's discretion to allow a new point of law to be raised, or a conceded point to be reopened, should be exercised only in exceptional circumstances, for compelling reasons. This was especially so if the result would be to open up fresh issues of fact which, because the point was not in issue, were not sufficiently investigated before the employment tribunal. The facts that the point is of wider importance, or that the amount at stake in the claim is very significant, are not reasons to depart from the general practice: *UNISON v Leicestershire County Council* [2006] EWCA Civ 825, [2006] IRLR 810 (where the tribunal had made a protective award totalling several million pounds). An example of an exceptional case is *Lipscombe v Forestry Commission* [2007] EWCA Civ 428, [2007] All ER (D) 132 (May), where a litigant in person was permitted by the Court of Appeal to rely on a point not taken at the hearing, which involved undisputed facts and was decisive of whether the tribunal had jurisdiction.

The various authorities were again reviewed by the EAT, and the principles fully set out, in *Rance v Secretary of State for Health* [2007] IRLR 665. There is a discretion whether to allow the raising of new points or the reopening of conceded points, but it will be exercised only in exceptional cases, particularly so where the effect of taking the point would be that fresh issues of fact would have to be investigated; on the other hand the fact that the point goes to the tribunal's jurisdiction is not a trump card. Within these general principles, the earlier cases provide examples of the sort of case in which the discretion is, or is not, likely to be exercised in favour of the party seeking to raise the point.

In *London Borough of Wandsworth v Vining* (UKEAT/0234/13), the EAT allowed a new point to be taken by the respondent to the appeal (the claimant in the original hearing) because the point went to jurisdiction, involved no additional evidence if successful, and engaged the issue whether there had been a denial of an effective remedy by reference to *art 6* of the *European Convention on Human Rights*. The claimant had been successful in the employment tribunal but a subsequent decision of the Court of Appeal had effectively overruled the legal basis for the decision in his favour. The point was subsequently considered, and rejected, by the EAT at the full hearing of the appeal (see [2016] ICR 427).

20.34 Fresh evidence

Appellants not infrequently seek to put additional evidence before the EAT to undermine the basis for the decision under appeal. It is at least arguable that this is not a permissible ground of appeal, since the tribunal cannot be said to have erred in law in failing to take account of evidence which was not put before it; this point was noted, but not decided, by the EAT in *Adegbuji v Meteor Parking Ltd* (UKEATPA/1570/09). Irrespective of that point, the EAT has repeatedly urged that the usual way of seeking to have additional evidence considered is by applying to the tribunal itself to reconsider its decision: see for example *Korashi v Abertawe Bro Morgannwg University Local Health Board* [2012] IRLR 4.

The matter was made the subject of a Practice Statement by the President, Langstaff J, in 2012 which has now been incorporated in the *2013 Practice Direction*. This explains that there is a strong preference for fresh evidence applications to be pursued by way of reconsideration by the tribunal which took the decision under appeal since this is quicker than an appeal, which if successful would result in the matter being referred back to the tribunal to consider the evidence, and more suitable since the tribunal which took the original decision is better placed to assess whether the proposed fresh evidence would have affected its decision. Accordingly it is likely that if an appeal includes an application to admit fresh evidence, the appeal will be stayed for the appellant to apply to the tribunal to reconsider its original decision, based on the fresh evidence. This does not of course preclude a subsequent appeal on the ground that the tribunal erred in refusing to admit the evidence. Alternatively, if no application for a review has been made prior to the hearing of the appeal, the EAT may dismiss the appeal, leaving it to the appellant to apply to the tribunal for reconsideration of its decision, with the possibility of a further appeal to the EAT if that application is unsuccessful: see *Noor v Metroline Travel Ltd* (UKEAT/0059/14).

Despite the general approach, it may still exceptionally be more appropriate for an application for the admission of fresh evidence to be considered by the EAT, for instance if this is one of a number of issues in the appeal and it would delay or unnecessarily complicate matters for the fresh evidence point to be referred back to the tribunal for reconsideration.

Whether the point is dealt with by way of reconsideration by the tribunal, or appeal, the principles of the admissibility of fresh evidence are essentially the same. A party will not be permitted to adduce factual matters before the EAT which it chose not to put before the employment tribunal (*Bingham v Hobourn Engineering Ltd* [1992] IRLR 298). The test for the admission of fresh evidence is as set out in *Wileman v Minilec Engineering Ltd* [1988] ICR 318, adopting the established formula applied in appeals from the civil courts to the Court of Appeal, as set out in *Ladd v Marshall* [1954] 1 WLR 1489. The three requirements, which are cumulative, are set out in the *2013 Practice Direction, para 10.3*, as follows

> '10.3.1   the evidence could not have been obtained with reasonable diligence for use at the Employment Tribunal hearing;
> 10.3.2   it is relevant and would probably have had an important influence on the hearing;
> 10.3.3   it is apparently credible.'

The application of these requirements is fully reviewed in the judgment of the EAT in *Korashi v Abertawe Bro Morgannwg University Local Health Board* (above). A good example of a successful application to admit fresh evidence is *SQR Security Solutions Ltd v Badu* UKEAT/0329/15. The claimant in that case had given evidence that he had been unable to mitigate his loss because a number of job offers he had secured had been withdrawn. The appellant employers investigated these claims and sought to introduce evidence to show that they were false. The EAT accepted that this evidence could not reasonably have been adduced before the claimant had made the allegedly false claims, and that the evidence was material and important not just to rebut the claims but also as going to the credibility of the claimant's evidence as a whole.

The procedure if the issue is pursued before the EAT is that the evidence sought to be admitted should be submitted in the form of one or more sworn affidavits or witness statements with a signed Statement of Truth, or exhibited to an Affidavit or witness statement if the evidence is in documentary form. The evidence should normally be submitted together with the Notice of Appeal or Respondent's Answer (*Practice Direction, para 10*). If leave to admit the evidence is given, the case will usually be remitted for a rehearing, but the cogency of the evidence may occasionally be such that the original decision is simply reversed.

20.35 Errors of law and perversity

The EAT can only overturn the decision of an employment tribunal if the tribunal can be shown to have erred in law. Where an appeal succeeds, the point of law on which the tribunal erred should be identified in the EAT's decision (*British Gas plc v McCarrick* [1991] IRLR 305). The error of law may be an express misdirection or it may be inferred from the fact that the conclusion of the tribunal was one which no reasonable employment tribunal, properly directing itself as to the relevant legal principles, could have reached; in other words, that the decision of the tribunal was so inconsistent with the correct application of the law that it was either a perverse decision or reached applying incorrect legal principles.

Even if the EAT would have come to a different conclusion, it must not interfere with the decision of the employment tribunal unless an error of law is identified (*Retarded Children's Aid Society Ltd v Day* [1978] 1 WLR 763, [1978] ICR 437). Misunderstanding or misapplication of the facts does not of itself amount to an error of law unless the tribunal proceeds upon a basis contrary to the undisputed or indisputable facts (*British Telecommunications plc v Sheridan* [1990] IRLR 27).

Perversity is recognised as a separate ground of appeal, and is often relied on, but rarely successfully because of the high standard required to establish that a decision was perverse. Unless the employment tribunal has misdirected itself in law, its decision should not be disturbed on the ground of perversity unless the decision under appeal was not a permissible option (*Piggott Bros & Co Ltd v Jackson* [1992] ICR 85). In *Piggott*, the Court of Appeal held (at 92) that in concluding that the decision under appeal was not a permissible option, the EAT will almost always have to be able to identify a finding of fact which was unsupported by *any* evidence or a clear self-misdirection in law by the employment tribunal (see also *Hough v Leyland DAF Ltd* [1991] ICR 696, in which the EAT pointed out that a finding of fact was not perverse merely because the tribunal had reached it by way of inference and without any direct evidence). However, the EAT in *East Berkshire Health Authority v Matadeen* [1992] ICR 723 held that a conclusion drawn from unassailable facts could be attacked as perverse. The approach adopted in *Piggott* represented a departure from the test of whether one could say of a decision, 'My goodness, that was certainly wrong', formulated in *Neale v Hereford and Worcester County Council* [1986] ICR 471.

Subsequently, Mummery J has categorised perversity as including a decision that on the evidence before the tribunal is 'irrational', 'offends reason', 'must be wrong', 'is not a permissible option', or 'flies in the face of properly informed logic': *Stewart v Cleveland Guest (Engineering) Ltd* [1994] IRLR 440 at 443.

The Court of Appeal gave further guidance as to the correct approach to deciding perversity appeals in what has come to be regarded as the leading case on perversity appeals, *Yeboah v Crofton* [2002] EWCA Civ 794, [2002] IRLR 634:

> 'Such an appeal ought only to succeed where an overwhelming case is made out that the employment tribunal reached a decision which no reasonable tribunal, on a proper appreciation of the evidence and the law, would have reached.'

(Mummery LJ at para 93)

The court also warned of the danger of turning an appeal on a point of law into a rehearing of parts of the evidence.

20.36 Inadequacy of reasons

The alleged inadequacy of the reasons given by a tribunal is a frequently raised ground of appeal. A failure by an employment tribunal to give adequate (or any) reasons for a judgment or order, or a substantive finding in the proceedings, may amount to an error of law rendering the decision liable to be set aside on appeal. As to the adequacy of reasons, see the citation from *Meek v City of Birmingham District Council* [1987] IRLR 250, CA in **19.118** above and the cases cited there. It should be noted that the decision in *Meek* predates the introduction of a more prescriptive approach to the content of reasons for Judgments by *rule 30* of the *ET Rules 2004* (now replaced by similar wording in *rule 62(5)* of the *2013 ET Rules*), and a somewhat less tolerant approach to inadequately expressed reasons is apparent in EAT decisions, particularly in cases involving allegations of discrimination, than was formerly the case. In *Greenwood v NWF Retail Ltd* [2011] ICR 896, the EAT held that failure to comply with *ET Rule 30(6)* was in itself an error of law. However the EAT went on to confirm that this does not require the tribunal to follow precisely or rigidly the format prescribed by *Rule 30(6)*, provided that each of the matters specified in the rule was addressed. The EAT noted with approval the comment of Buxton LJ in *Balfour Beatty Power Networks v Wilcox* [2006] EWCA Civ 1240, [2007] IRLR 63 that:

> 'the rule is surely intended to be a guide and not a straitjacket. Provided it can be reasonably spelt out from the determination of the employment tribunal that what rule 30(6) requires has been provided by that tribunal, then no error of law will have been committed.'

These comments apply equally to the equivalent provisions of the *2013 ET Rules*. The EAT may also, if inadequacy of reasons is given as a ground of appeal, remit the case to the tribunal for it to clarify or amplify its reasons, prior to hearing the substantive appeal: see **20.22** above.

20.37 Procedural failures

A separate category of error of law is a failure by the tribunal to afford the parties a fair hearing, whether through some serious procedural failure or through bias, or where the circumstances have created a real danger, or a perception, of bias. Cases falling within this general categorisation would include, for instance, those where relevant evidence was unjustifiably excluded or a party was prevented from putting forward part of his or her case, or the tribunal failed to invite the parties to deal with a particular point before deciding it or relied on a point of law not canvassed at the hearing; the Employment Judge or a member sitting despite a potential conflict of interest; and inappropriate conduct by the Judge or a member in the course of the hearing (see generally as to these potential grounds **20.23–20.25** above). Excessive delay in delivering judgment following the hearing is not of itself an error of law, and will only provide grounds for appeal if in the circumstances there is a real risk that the appellant was deprived of the right to a fair trial: *Bangs v Connex South Eastern Ltd* [2005] EWCA Civ 14, [2005] 2 All ER 316, [2005] IRLR 389. Thus in *Grosvenor v Governing Body of Aylesford School* (UKEAT/0001/08) a delay of a year in promulgating the judgment was held not to provide a ground of appeal on the basis that the judgment, albeit excessively long, was adequately reasoned.

It may also be a ground of appeal that the tribunal has decided the case on a point not relied on by the parties and on which the losing party has not been given the opportunity to make submissions. An example is *Launahurst Ltd v Larner* [2010] EWCA Civ 334, where the tribunal held that the contract under which the claimant was held out to be self-employed was a sham, a point not advanced by him or raised with the respondent at the hearing. In addition, it may be a ground of appeal that the tribunal relied in reaching its decision on legal authorities not cited by the parties and on which they have not been given an opportunity to make submissions: *Clark v Clark Construction Initiatives Ltd* [2008] EWCA Civ 1446, [2009] ICR 718; however this does not prevent the citation of authority to support uncontentious or incidental points in the tribunal's judgment: *Stanley Cole (Wainfleet) Ltd v Sheridan* [2003] EWCA Civ 1046, [2003] ICR 1449. A further ground of appeal is that the tribunal supplemented the evidence presented to it by conducting its own researches on the internet, without giving the parties an opportunity to deal with the additional information thus discovered: *East of England Ambulance Service NHS Trust v Sanders* [2015] IRLR 277.

20.38 Disposal of the appeal

There are essentially two possible outcomes if an appeal is successful. Either the matter may be remitted (to the original tribunal or a fresh tribunal), to be considered further in the light of the EAT's judgment or for a complete rehearing; or the EAT may substitute a decision in favour of the appellant, eg that the dismissal was fair, rather than unfair. In cases not involving a specific point of statutory construction, which may necessarily determine the result, the EAT is careful not to usurp the tribunal's role as arbiter of facts. It will therefore not substitute a decision unless there is only one decision that a tribunal correctly directing itself in law could have reached (*Morgan v Electrolux Ltd* [1991] ICR 369).

Where an error of law is identified, the EAT must allow the appeal unless the conclusion of the employment tribunal was plainly and unarguably right, notwithstanding the misdirection (*Dobie v Burns International Security Services (UK) Ltd* [1984] 3 All ER 333, [1985] 1 WLR 43, [1984] ICR 812). Equally, unless the decision was plainly and arguably wrong, the EAT should not substitute a different decision but should remit the matter for rehearing.

Following conflicting decisions of the Court of Appeal as to the desirability of the EAT deciding a point rather than remitting it to the tribunal to decide (*Buckland v Bournemouth University Education Corporation* [2010] EWCA Civ 121, [2010] ICR 908 and *Tilson v Alstom Transport* [2010] EWCA Civ 1308, [2011] IRLR 169), the position was restated in two further decisions of the Court, *Jafri v Lincoln College* [2014] EWCA Civ 449, [2014] IRLR 544, [2014] ICR 920 and *Burrell v Micheldever Tyre Services Ltd* [2014] EWCA Civ 716, [2014] IRLR 630, [2014] ICR 935. The Court concluded (with reluctance) that it was bound by previous authority to hold that the EAT could only substitute a different conclusion from that reached by the tribunal if it considered that the result to be substituted followed from the findings made by the tribunal, supplemented by any undisputed or indisputable facts. The EAT cannot make additional findings of fact in order to avoid remitting the case to the tribunal (or a fresh tribunal).

However, as Underhill LJ pointed out in Jafri, the EAT can, if all parties consent, exercise the power conferred on it by *section 35(1)* of the *Employment Tribunals Act 1996* to decide the point itself rather than remit. It should also be noted that the Court in Burrell, whilst considering itself obliged to follow *Jafri*, explicitly encouraged the EAT to be robust in its approach to determining whether only one outcome of the original proceedings was possible, and if not, and if the parties were not willing to agree to the EAT determining the matter itself, to limit the scope of any necessary remission. This point was reinforced by Elias LJ in *Kuznetsov v Royal Bank of Scotland plc* [2017] EWCA Civ 43 (31 January 2017, unreported). It was suggested that the consent of the parties to the point being decided by the EAT rather than remitted should be sought before the hearing in any case where it was likely that the issue would arise; it was also noted that there is no advantage in remittal where the issue is not one of fact but of the correctness of a case management order (as in that case).

Nicholson v Hazel House Nursing Home Ltd UKEAT/0241/15 (12 May 2016, unreported) is an example of a case where the EAT, applying *Jafri*, concluded that it was able to substitute its own finding (that the appellant had been constructively dismissed) for that of the tribunal (that he had not been).

The same principles apply to appeals from interlocutory orders or judgments as to appeals from final judgments (*Adams and Raynor v West Sussex County Council* [1990] ICR 546). A good example of a case where an interlocutory order, fixing a hearing, was overturned because the employment judge had taken into account an irrelevant factor, is *Gillingham Football Club v McCammon* (UKEAT/0625/11); as often occurs in urgent appeals, in that case the EAT, with the parties' agreement, proceeded to re-decide the issue on the material before it rather than remit it to the tribunal.

The EAT in *Sinclair Roche & Temperley v Heard* [2004] IRLR 763 gave guidance which is frequently cited as to the factors to be considered in determining whether a case should or should not be remitted to the same tribunal. The principal factors to be taken into account are proportionality (it will almost always be more expensive and time consuming for a case to be remitted to a freshly constituted tribunal than to the tribunal which first decided the case); the passage of time (if a significant amount of time has passed since the hearing below, there may be a risk that that tribunal has forgotten the case); bias or partiality (remission to the same tribunal is inappropriate if there has been an issue of possible bias); whether the decision under appeal was totally flawed (in which case remission should be to a different tribunal); the risk of the tribunal having a second bite at getting to the same decision for different reasons; and a presumption of professionalism (favouring remission to the original tribunal, other things being equal). See para 46 of the judgment for details.

20.39 If a case is ordered by the EAT to be remitted (to the same or a fresh tribunal) following a successful appeal, the tribunal which hears the case on remission only has jurisdiction by reason of the remission. It cannot, therefore, even with the agreement of the parties, reopen or deal with issues other than those remitted for its consideration. This conclusion was reached by the Court of Appeal in *Aparau v Iceland Frozen Foods plc* [2000] 1 All ER 228, [2000] IRLR 196, where (in a constructive dismissal case) the issue remitted to the tribunal was whether a term had been incorporated in the contract of employment. This was then conceded, with the consequence that the constructive dismissal claim was made out, but the employers persuaded the tribunal to deal with the fairness of the dismissal, which had not been disputed at the original hearing. The Court of Appeal held that its decision on that point was a nullity. These principles would not, however, prevent the tribunal from dealing with a point affecting its jurisdiction to deal with the matters remitted.

20.40 Where both the parties to an application to an employment tribunal agree that the decision of the tribunal was in error and reach a proposed settlement, the parties may not themselves reverse that decision but must refer the matter to the EAT. The EAT is cautious about allowing an appeal without hearing argument on the issue of law, since any decision may have implications more generally than for the particular case. The parties should draw up a formal order and request the EAT to accept it, ratify it and make it part of the order of the Appeal Tribunal. However, unless the consent order is part of an overall settlement of the proceedings (in which case the EAT will usually agree to the order without hearing full argument – see *British Publishing Co Ltd v Fraser* [1987] ICR 517) a consent order will not be granted unless the EAT is persuaded by argument at a hearing that the decision appealed against was wrong in law; and if the effect of the proposed order is to remit the case to the tribunal for further consideration, the EAT will give a reasoned judgment on the appeal: *J Sainsbury plc v Moger* [1994] ICR 800; *Dozie v Addison Lee plc* (UKEAT/0328/13). See also *Practice Direction, para 18*. The *Practice Direction* also deals with withdrawal of appeals where there has been a settlement, and warns that if an application for permission to withdraw an appeal is made close to the hearing date, the appellant may be summoned to explain the delay in deciding not to pursue the appeal.

20.41 OTHER POWERS OF THE APPEAL TRIBUNAL

For the purpose of disposing of an appeal, the EAT may exercise any powers of the body or officer from whom the appeal was brought (*ETA 1996, s 35*). It also has the same general powers as the High Court in relation to production of documents, attendance of witnesses, contempt of court and other matters incidental to its jurisdiction (*ETA 1996, s 29(2)*). As to the EAT's powers to make restricted reporting orders, and orders preserving anonymity, see **20.26** above.

The *2002 Practice Direction* introduced new procedures regarding the transcription of judgments of the EAT, and these have been retained in the subsequent revisions. Unless the decision is reserved or the EAT so directs as part of its judgment given orally, or, in the case of a preliminary hearing, the judgment is given in the absence of the appellant, a transcript will only be drawn up if requested by one or both parties within 14 days, or the judge so directs (e.g. because of the public importance of the points decided) (*2013 Practice Direction, paras 21.3, 21.4*). The *Practice Direction* gives more detailed information about the arrangements for handing down reserved judgments and any consequential applications (for permission to appeal, for costs etc). In Scotland the practice is that judgments are normally reserved. Judgments given following full hearings which are ordered to be transcribed, or are reserved and handed down, are posted on the EAT website as are judgments given in appeals under *rule 3(10)*, but in this case only if a judge or the Registrar so directs: *Practice Direction, para 21.7.* The website address is http ://employmentappeals.decisions.tribunals.gov.uk/public/search.aspx; a new website, https ://www.gov.uk/employment-appeal-tribunal-decisions, was introduced in March 2017, but this has less useful search facilities than the older site. Most judgments are also available on http://www.bailii.org/.

20.42 COSTS

The powers of the EAT to award costs (expenses in Scotland) were significantly recast by the *2004 Amendment Rules*. The provisions are now contained in *rules 34–34D*. The scheme of the new provisions follows that of the *ET Rules* in providing separately for the costs incurred by unrepresented parties, and in introducing wasted costs orders. Additional powers to order a respondent to an appeal to pay as costs to the successful appellant the fees paid by the appellant to pursue the appeal were added as one of the changes in the EAT Rules consequential on the introduction of fees; see **20.46** for more details.

A party may apply for a costs order at any stage during the appeal, or within 14 days of the date the order finally disposing of the proceedings is sent to the parties (*rule 34(4)*). However, unless the paying party is given an opportunity at the hearing to make representations against the making of an order, it can only be made after an opportunity to make such representations has been afforded by notice to the party concerned (*rule 34(5)*). The representations will normally be dealt with on the papers, but if it is considered appropriate, they can be referred for a further hearing. Written reasons must be given for a costs order if a party so requests within 21 days of the date of the order (*rule 34(6)*).

The statistics published by the Ministry of Justice do not include details of the numbers and amounts of awards of costs or expenses; experience in practice is that awards are relatively uncommon but far from unknown.

20.43 Grounds for costs orders

The principal circumstances in which a costs order can be made against a party are that the paying party has brought proceedings that were unnecessary, improper, vexatious or misconceived, or that there has been unreasonable delay or other unreasonable conduct by the paying party. Without prejudice to the general application of those criteria, costs may be ordered in four specific cases, namely where the paying party has not complied with a direction of the EAT, or has amended a Notice of Appeal, Respondent's Answer or similar document, or has caused an adjournment of the proceedings (*rule 34A(1), (2)*; or, following the introduction of fees, where the receiving party has paid a fee, the paying party may be ordered to reimburse all or part of the fee (*rule 34A(2A)*; see further **20.46** below).

The most important of these conditions is the bringing of an appeal which is misconceived (ie has no reasonable prospect of success), and unreasonable conduct by a respondent, which may include resisting an appeal on misconceived grounds. In practice, however, there will rarely be grounds for an award of costs under either head, since misconceived appeals are likely to be screened out, at latest at the preliminary hearing, before the respondent to the appeal needs to incur significant costs in resisting it. It will also only very rarely be the case that it can be said that defending a decision of a tribunal against an appeal is as such unreasonable conduct (a view confirmed by the Court of Appeal in *Afolayan v MRCS Ltd* [2009] EWCA Civ 796).

The *manner* in which an appeal is pursued or defended may however be unreasonable even though the party concerned has a case with some merit. An example of a case where expenses were awarded on the ground that the appeal was so lacking in merit as to be misconceived is *Morgan v Greater Glasgow Health Board* (UKEATS/0044/11). In *Faithorn Farrell Timms LLP v Bailey* UKEAT/0025/16 (23 November 2016, unreported), costs were awarded against the appellant employer, which had succeeded in part of its appeal, because its unreasonable conduct of the appeal had put the respondent to the appeal to unnecessary expense.

One ground for an award of costs is that the appellant has pursued an appeal until just before it is due to be heard and then abandoned it, but this is less likely to occur following the introduction of a requirement to pay a hearing fee of £1,200 before the appeal is listed for a full hearing.

The EAT has no jurisdiction to make an order for costs incurred in the employment tribunal (unless in an appeal against the making or refusal to make such an order by the tribunal itself).

There are limits on the making of an order for costs against the respondent to an appeal who has not had an answer accepted by the EAT: in such a case *rule 34(3)* allows for a costs order in relation to his or her conduct of any part of the proceedings in which he or she has taken part; the necessary limitation implied by this is that if a respondent takes no part in the appeal, there is no power to award costs against that respondent (compare in relation to costs in the employment tribunal *Sutton v The Ranch Ltd* [2006] ICR 1170). It is not yet clear whether this reasoning will prevent awards of costs in relation to fees incurred by the appellant. Costs may be awarded in favour of a respondent who has taken only a limited part in the appeal, but in practice it is unlikely that such a respondent will have incurred significant costs, and only costs actually incurred can be claimed.

Further guidance on when the bringing or pursuit of an appeal can be categorised as unreasonable is given in *Iron and Steel Trades Confederation v ASW Ltd (in liquidation)* [2004] IRLR 926. In *G4S Security Services (UK) v Rondeau* (UKEAT/0207/09/DA), the EAT awarded costs against the respondent to the appeal, who had refused a reasonable offer of settlement by the appellant, only to accept it at the door of the court. An example of a case where costs were awarded against a successful appellant because the proceedings were 'unnecessary' is *Fowler v British School of Motoring* [2006] All ER (D) 93 (May), where the appellant employer had failed for no good reason to present its response to the original claim in time, and successfully appealed against the tribunal's refusal to review a decision that it should not be permitted to take part in the proceedings. The appeal was 'unnecessary' because the appellant could and should have submitted its response in good time.

The fact that the preconditions for an award of costs exist does not entitle the receiving party to an order. The EAT has a discretion whether to award costs (and its exercise of that discretion will rarely be disturbed on appeal: see *Afolayan*, above). If it decides to do so, it has a further discretion to take into account the means of the paying party (*rules 34A(3), 34B(2)*). The powers available subject to this discretion are to award a sum determined by the EAT itself by summary assessment, or an agreed sum, or to award costs subject to a detailed assessment by the High Court or taxation by the Auditor of the Court of Session (*rule 34B(1)*).

20.44 Litigants in person

There are separate rules as to the amount that may be awarded where the receiving party is a litigant in person (in Scotland a party litigant), equivalent to the powers of the tribunal to make a preparation time order. It should however be noted that, in contrast to the position in employment tribunals, the general power to award costs is not confined to an award to legally represented parties; any party who does not fall within the definition of a litigant in person or a party litigant is eligible for an award of costs in accordance with *rule 34B*. A litigant in person is defined to include a company or corporation which is acting without a legal representative, and a solicitor, barrister, advocate or other person qualified to conduct litigation who is appearing for him or herself (*rule 34D(7)*). This does not cover a company represented by an in-house lawyer, or an individual represented by a non-legal representative, including a relative or friend, or a professional consultant who is not a lawyer; the latter are therefore eligible for ordinary costs orders under *rule 34A*.

The conditions for an award of costs in favour of a litigant in person are the same as for any other party. The costs recoverable may not exceed two thirds of the costs that would be payable if the party had had legal representation (with an exception for any disbursements, such as a payment for legal advice, which may be recovered in full if a full award is made and the payment was of a reasonable amount) (*rule 34D(2)*). Within this overall restriction, the costs recoverable are payments for advice, and for expert assistance in assessing the claim for costs, and expenses incurred in the proceedings (eg for photocopying or travel to the hearing), and compensation for time spent preparing the case and attending the hearing (*rule 34D(3)*). In relation to this head, the rate of payment will either be the amount the party can prove he or she has lost (eg lost wages) or a flat rate of £36 an hour (from 6 April 2016; this rate increases annually by £1 an hour, in the same way as the equivalent rate for preparation time orders: see **19.132** for further details) (*rule 34D(4), (5)*). The amount awarded will be subject to the EAT's assessment of what was a reasonable and proportionate amount of time to spend preparing for the hearing. Litigants in person are treated no differently from legally represented litigants in relation to recovering fees paid to pursue the appeal.

20.45 Wasted costs orders

The powers to make wasted costs orders and the procedures to be followed are set out in new *rule 34C*. This is for all practical purposes in exactly the same terms, with necessary modifications of terminology, as *rule 48* of the *ET Rules*, and reference should therefore be made to the discussion of that *Rule* at **19.132** above for details. Guidance on the procedure to be followed in the EAT when considering a wasted costs application (as distinct from the hearing of an appeal against an order made by a tribunal) was given by the Court of Appeal in *Gill v Humanware Europe Ltd* [2010] EWCA Civ 799, [2010] ICR 1343, [2010] IRLR 877.

20.46 Reimbursement of fees

Following the introduction of fees, payable by the appellant, for appeals, the EAT Rules have been amended to give powers to the EAT to order a respondent to an appeal to pay all or part of the fees incurred by the appellant: see *rule 34A(2A)*. This, like the powers to award costs described above, is discretionary, and is subject to a power (but not an obligation) for the EAT to take into account the paying party's means - a point that is particularly important in cases where an employer pursues an appeal against an impecunious respondent who would as an appellant have qualified for remission of the fees.

The threshold requirements for making an order for costs under other provisions of *rule 34A* do not apply to an order for the reimbursement of fees paid. The EAT has a general discretion as to whether to make an order, and if whether of all or part of the fees paid. It first indicated the appropriate approach to applications for costs under *rule 34A(2A)* in

Portnykh v Nomura International plc (UKEAT/0448/13). The general principle is that if an appellant has substantially succeeded in the appeal, then subject to considering the means of the other party, an order should normally be made. The conduct of the appellant may be relevant but only to the extent that there has been conduct unnecessarily adding to the expense incurred by the other party in defending the appeal.

Subsequent decisions have refined the principles to be applied. Where there are three parties in the appeal, one of whom is a respondent to the appeal but has taken no active part in the proceedings, the appropriate order will normally be for the active respondent to reimburse the successful appellant: *Horizon Security Services Ltd v Ndeze* [2014] IRLR 854 and *Costain Ltd v Armitage* (UKEAT/0048/14).

Where an appeal succeeds only in part the position depends on the precise circumstances, and it may be appropriate either to refuse to make an order (as in *Perry's Motor Sales Ltd v Evans* (UKEAT/0275/14), where the appeal failed on the more important grounds and there was no evidence of the appellant having attempted to secure the other party's agreement to settle the one point on which the appeal did succeed) or to award only part of the fees. An important factor is whether it was necessary for the appellant to incur the fees: *Look Ahead Housing & Care Ltd v Chetty* [2015] ICR 375, where the EAT considered that the appellant should have first applied to the tribunal for reconsideration of its decision. The judgment of the President, Langstaff J, in this case includes useful general guidance on the application of the *rule*: see paras 51-54. See also *Colletti v Borealis Driver Services Ltd* UKEAT/0203/15, where the earlier cases were reviewed, and the additional point made that the way in which the claimant (the appellant before the EAT) had conducted the case in the tribunal was not relevant to whether the fees for the appeal were recoverable.

One specific issue raised by the wording of *rule 34A(2A)* is whether fees paid on behalf of the appellant by a third party, such as a trade union or insurer, are recoverable against the respondent to the appeal. The EAT initially held in *Goldwater v Sellafield Ltd* (UKEAT/0178/14) that the wording of the rule precluded an order for repayment of fees in such cases, but in the subsequent case of *Ibarz v University of Sheffield* (UKEAT/0018/15) a different division of the EAT reconsidered the point, concluded that the decision in Goldwater was wrong, and made an award to the successful applicant in respect of the fees paid on his behalf by his trade union. Subject to any contrary decision of the Court of Appeal it is thought likely that *Ibarz* will be followed in any future case raising this point.

A specific point in *Portnykh* was that the appellant had made an application for remission of the fee, which had not been determined by the time judgment was given on the appeal. The EAT held that as there is no power to order the repayment of costs paid, it could and should make a conditional order for the payment of costs, the condition being that the application for remission was refused, so that if the application succeeded there would be no costs to pay.

20.47 REVIEW

The EAT may review any order made by it on the grounds that:

(a)   the order was wrongly made as the result of an error on the part of the EAT or its staff;

(b)   a party did not receive proper notice of the proceedings leading to the order; or

(c)   the interests of justice require such review.

(*EAT Rules, rule 33.*)

(The terminology used has not changed in line with the change in the *2013 ET Rules* from 'review' to 'reconsideration'.) Orders which may be reviewed are not limited to final determinations of appeals; it may on occasion be appropriate for the EAT in the course of a hearing to review an order made earlier in the proceedings, such as an order specifying the grounds of appeal which may be considered (see *Khan v Vignette Europe Ltd* (UKEAT/0350/08)). The circumstances in which the review procedure can be invoked are rare (see *Stannard & Co (1969) Ltd v Wilson* [1983] ICR 86). In *Jenkins v P & O European Ferries (Dover) Ltd* [1991] ICR 652, the EAT on its own initiative was prepared to review its earlier decision on the ground that it recognised that there was a fundamental error of law in that decision, but in *Blockleys plc v Miller* [1992] ICR 749 it appeared to prefer a narrower approach. In *Digital Equipment Co Ltd v Clements (No 2)* [1997] ICR 237 the EAT reviewed, and reversed, its initial decision in circumstances where that decision had been given in ignorance of another decision on essentially the same point of law; the review thus enabled the EAT to resolve the law on a point on which there would otherwise have been conflicting authorities. There is as yet no reported decision of the EAT on whether its powers of review in the interests of justice have been enlarged by the addition to the *EAT Rules* of the Overriding Objective, but this would be consistent with the view taken by the EAT of the equivalent change in the *ET Rules* (see eg *Williams v Ferrosan Ltd* [2004] IRLR 607).

However there is no jurisdiction to review a decision not to register an appeal taken under *Rule 3(7)* on the sift; the appropriate course for an aggrieved appellant to take is to apply for a hearing under *Rule 3(10)*: see *Zinda v Governing Body of Barn Hill Community High* [2011] ICR 174. The EAT in that case accepted, however, that it might exceptionally be appropriate to permit a review of a decision taken under one of the procedures in *Rule 3* on the basis of fresh evidence having become available, if the point first arose after any time limit for appealing had expired. By contrast it has been held that there is power in exceptional circumstances to review a decision under *rule 3(7)* to allow the appeal to proceed to a hearing, where the decision to do so has been taken on the basis of false or misleading information given by the appellant: *Jamieson v Nationwide Building Society* (UKEAT/0028/13).

Where the EAT has not formally drawn up and issued the order embodying its decision, it has a wider power of review based on its inherent jurisdiction as a superior court of record, and need not confine itself to the *Blockleys* approach: *Bass Leisure Ltd v Thomas* [1994] IRLR 104 at 108–109. Exceptionally, the EAT may reach a provisional decision, notify the parties accordingly and invite further submissions before pronouncing final judgment; this was done in *Rubenstein and Roskin (t/a McGuffies Dispensing Chemists) v McGloughlin* [1997] ICR 318, [1996] IRLR 557.

20.48   FURTHER APPEALS

A further appeal may be taken to the Court of Appeal (or in Scotland, the Court of Session) on a point of law, but only with permission from the EAT or the Court of Appeal or Court of Session (*ETA 1996, s 37(1), (2)*). Permission should be sought initially from the EAT. If the EAT refuses permission, an application may be made to the Court of Appeal (or the Court of Session, as the case may be). The principles to be applied upon such an application were considered by the Court of Session in *Campbell v Dunoon and Cowal Housing Association Ltd* [1992] IRLR 528. The restrictions on 'second appeals' to the Court of Appeal introduced by the *Access to Justice Act 1999, s 55* do not apply to appeals from the EAT, and the introduction of more restrictive criteria in relation to other areas does not appear significantly to have affected the Court of Appeal's practice in granting permission to appeal in employment cases.

In appeals from the EAT, the Court of Appeal is a second-tier appellate court and is concerned with whether the decision of the employment tribunal was right, not with whether the EAT was right (*Hennessy v Craigmyle & Co Ltd* [1986] ICR 461; *Campion v*

Hamworthy Engineering Ltd [1987] ICR 966). However, the Court of Appeal itself expressed serious reservations about the correctness of this approach in *Gover v Propertycare Ltd* [2006] EWCA Civ 286, [2006] All ER (D) 408 (Mar), and it may fairly be regarded as arguable in the light of these reservations. Where the EAT has allowed an appeal from the original decision of the tribunal, the focus of a further appeal to the Court of Appeal is inevitably directed more to whether there was sufficient basis for that decision.

The time limit for lodging an appeal to the Court of Appeal with the permission of the EAT is 14 days from the date on which the order or judgment of the EAT was drawn up, unless the EAT gives a longer period; if permission is refused, an appellant's notice must be served on the court, by way of application for permission to appeal, within the same 14-day period (*Civil Procedure Rules 1998, r 52.3*).

The normal practice of the Court of Appeal is that costs follow the event, so that a successful appellant is usually entitled to, and will be awarded, his or her costs. Until 2013 this was equally the case for appeals from the EAT despite the general principle that the employment tribunals and EAT are costs-free jurisdictions in which an award of costs requires specific justification. However recent developments have reduced the risks to litigants of more modest means of the usual costs regime of the Court. In *Governing Body of St Albans Girls' School v Neary (No 2)* [2009] EWCA Civ 1214, the Court of Appeal refused to award costs to the employers, who had successfully appealed against the refusal of the EAT to strike out the claimant's claim for breach of an unless order. The fact that the employee had been taken to the Court by his ex-employer, rather than the other way round, coupled with the employee's impecuniosity, was considered by the Court to be in the circumstances a reason to depart from the normal rule that costs follow the event.

An amendment to the *Civil Procedure Rules 1998*, applicable from 1 April 2013, gives the court power on an appeal from a jurisdiction where costs are not normally awarded to make an order in advance of the appeal limiting the costs recoverable by the successful party, having regard to the means of the parties, the circumstances of the case and the interests of justice (*CPR Rule 52.9A*). The use of this power was foreshadowed by the decision in *Manchester College v Hazel* [2013] EWCA Civ 281 that the employee respondents to an appeal by the employer should be protected from an award of costs against them if the appeal succeeded (the employees having agreed not to seek costs if the appeal was refused). There is not as yet any equivalent provision protecting parties of limited means in appeals to the Court of Session.

A further appeal lies to the Supreme Court if the Court of Appeal, or the Supreme Court itself, gives permission. A number of special rules govern Supreme Court appeals.

In Scotland, the appeal from the EAT is to the Inner House of the Court of Session, and thence, with permission, to the Supreme Court. In Northern Ireland, appeals lie directly from the tribunal to the Northern Ireland Court of Appeal, and thence to the Supreme Court. Leave to appeal is required at each stage, except that appeals to the Northern Ireland Court of Appeal (which involve the stating of a case by the tribunal) are a matter of right.

20.49 ISSUES OF EU LAW

Where the outcome of an application or an appeal turns on a question of EU law, the answer to which is unclear, the tribunal or court may, or if it is a court of final appeal must, refer the question to the Court of Justice of the European Union (ECJ) under *art 234* of the *Treaty of Rome*. The parties to the application or appeal can request a reference in these circumstances. In *Enderby v Frenchay Health Authority and Secretary of State for Health* [1991] ICR 382, the EAT suggested that national appeals procedures ought normally to be exhausted before a reference was made, but the Court of Appeal ([1992] IRLR 15) decided to refer the case to the ECJ before making any order itself. A number of cases have been referred to the ECJ by employment tribunals, both before and after *Enderby*: see eg *Neath v Hugh Steeper Ltd*: C-152/91 [1994] 1 All ER 929, *Smith v Avdel Systems Ltd*: C-408/92 [1995] ICR 596, *P v S and Cornwall County Council*: C-13/94 [1996] IRLR 347, *Robinson-Steele v RD Retail Services Ltd*: C-131/04 [2006] ECR I-2531, [2006] ICR 932 and *Coleman v Atttridge Law*: C-303/06, [2008] IRLR 722. The incidence of referrals from employment tribunals appears to have increased since the *Coleman* case. The most recent reported referrals from an employment tribunal to the ECJ are the cases of *Lock v British Gas Trading Ltd*: C-539/12 [2014] IRLR 648, [2014] ICR 813 and *Greenfield v The Care Bureau Ltd*: C-219/14 [2016] IRLR 62, [2016] ICR 161.

The tribunal, and the EAT, should not refer a matter to the ECJ unless its ruling is 'necessary' for the determination of the case; if the case may turn on questions of fact, these should first be determined by the tribunal. However, in *Attridge Law v Coleman* [2007] IRLR 88, the EAT held, rejecting an appeal against an order of the tribunal referring an issue to the ECJ at a preliminary stage in the case, that a reference could be 'necessary' even if the point would not be determinative of the case, if the ruling sought was necessary to do justice. One important practical consequence of a reference to the ECJ being made by either the employment tribunal or the EAT, rather than a higher court, is that the costs of the proceedings before the ECJ are subject to the same rules as those applying to the referring court or tribunal, so that a party seeking a ruling from the ECJ is less at risk of an award of costs if the ruling is adverse if the reference is made before the case reaches the Court of Appeal or the Court of Session.

The UK Government's formal notification of intention to leave the EU does not affect the position as described above. It is not, at the time of writing, clear what the status will be of cases referred to, but not yet decided by, the ECJ when the UK leaves the EU.

21   Engagement of Employees

Cross-reference. See REFERENCES (40) for employment made conditional on references.

21.1   ADVERTISING

When advertising for prospective employees, an employer must be careful not to infringe the provisions of the equality legislation (see **13.12** DISCRIMINATION AND EQUAL OPPORTUNITIES – III). For example, the advertisement should avoid use of gender-specific phrases and should not indicate that applicants of a particular race or age are required (subject to this being a genuine occupational requirement). An example of this in the age discrimination field is *Canadian Imperial Bank of Commerce v Beck* [2011] 2 CMLR 82 where the EAT held that an advertisement seeking someone with a "younger, entrepreneurial profile" was sufficient to establish a prima facie case of age discrimination. *Section 39* of the *Equality Act 2010* provides that A must not discriminate against or victimise B in the arrangements made for deciding to whom to offer employment; as to the terms on which A offers B employment; or by not offering B employment. *Section 40* provides that an employer must not harass an applicant for employment.

However, it has been held that these provisions do not apply to an employee who is already in post and who is, for example, responding to an internally advertised vacancy: *Clymo v Wandsworth London Borough Council* [1989] ICR 250, EAT (c.f. *Timex Corpn v Hodgson* [1982] ICR 63, EAT). Moreover, the protection does not apply to an applicant who was not intending to take the job even if offered it, on the basis that there would have been no detriment in being rejected: *Keane v Investigo* (UKEAT/0389/09) (11 December 2009, unreported) and *Berry v Recruitment Revolution* (UKEAT/0190/10) (6 October 2010, unreported).

An advertisement indicating that a job is open only to persons who are or who are not union members will lead to a conclusive presumption that work has been refused on union membership grounds and thus, in general, unlawfully (see **21.3**(d) below, and the reference there cited).

21.2   INTERVIEWING AND SELECTION

An employer may use any interviewing and selection procedures he wishes, provided that they are not discriminatory within the meaning of the equality legislation (see DISCRIMINATION AND EQUAL OPPORTUNITIES – I (11), II (12), III (13)). Particular care should be exercised in wording job application forms and other documents in which applicants may be asked to provide personal information. There is no obligation on the candidate to disclose information potentially adverse to them as though there were a duty of good faith: *Nottingham University v Fishel* [2000] IRLR 471.

In *Cheltenham Borough Council v Laird* [2009] EWHC 1253 (QB), [2009] IRLR 621 an employer sued a former employee for having made allegedly fraudulent or negligent misrepresentations in her job application for a senior position and in particular in her responses to a pre-employment medical questionnaire. The claim was unsuccessful because the questions asked had been too ambiguous, not because no such cause of action could arise. *Section 60* of the *Equality Act* relates to enquiries about disabilities or health. *Subsection (1)* provides:

> "(1) A person (A) to whom an application for work is made must not ask about the health of the applicant (B) –

21.2   Engagement of Employees

(a)   before offering work to B, or

(b)   where A is not in a position to offer work to B, before including B in a pool of applicants from whom A intends (when in a position to do so) to select a person to whom to offer work."

Subsection (6) provides that enquiries about disability or health are allowed in so far as asking the question is necessary for the purpose of (a) establishing whether B will be able to comply with a requirement to undergo an assessment or establishing whether a duty to make reasonable adjustments is or will be imposed on A in relation to B in connection with a requirement to undergo an assessment, (b) establishing whether B will be able to carry out a function that is intrinsic to the work concerned, (c) monitoring diversity in the range of persons applying to A for work, (d) taking action to which *s 158* [positive action] would apply if references in that section to persons who share (or do not share) a protected characteristic were references to disabled persons (or persons who are not disabled) and the reference to the characteristic were a reference to disability, or (e) if A applies in relation to the work a requirement to have a particular disability, establishing whether B has that disability. The effect of subsection (6) is that employers may, and often do, ask applicants to complete a type of Equal Opportunities Monitoring Form, but that Form (or similar) must be detached or removed from the application before it is seen by those taking the hiring decision: *Patel v Lloyds Pharmacy Ltd* (UKEAT/0418/12/ZT) (6 February 2013, unreported).

Sections 158 and *159* relate to positive action. *Section 159* applies if a person (P) reasonably thinks that (a) persons who share a protected characteristic suffer a disadvantage connected to the characteristic, or (b) participation in an activity by persons who share a protected characteristic is disproportionately low. *Subsection (2)* provides that *Part 5* of the *Equality Act* (work) does not prohibit P from taking action within *subsection (3)* with the aim of enabling or encouraging persons who share the protected characteristic to (a) overcome or minimise that disadvantage, or (b) participate in that activity. Action within *subsection (3)* is treating a person (A) more favourably in connection with recruitment or promotion than another person (B) because A has the protected characteristic but B does not. *Subsection (4)* provides that *subsection (2)* applies only if (a) A is as qualified as B to be recruited or promoted, (b) P does not have a policy of treating persons who share the protected characteristic more favourably in connection with recruitment or promotion than persons who do not share it, and (c) taking the action in question is a proportionate means of achieving the aim referred to in *subsection (2)*.

Appendix 2 to the EHRC Statutory Code of Practice on Employment provides recommendations on the monitoring of diversity by employers.

21.3   In arranging an interview for a disabled person, it may be necessary for the employer to make reasonable adjustments to enable that person to attend. The employer is free to select for employment whomsoever he chooses, subject to the following:

(a)   the restrictions on the employment of CHILDREN AND YOUNG PERSONS (4);

(b)   the restrictions on the employment of FOREIGN EMPLOYEES (26);

(c)   the restriction on excluding a person from any office, profession, occupation or employment by reason of a spent conviction (see EMPLOYEE'S PAST CRIMINAL CONVICTIONS (17));

(d)   the bar on refusing a person employment because he is or is not a trade union member (see TRADE UNIONS – I (50)).

21.4

In *R (T & others) v Chief Constable of Greater Manchester & others* [2014] UKSC 35, [2015] AC 49 the Supreme Court considered the blanket requirement in the *Rehabilitation of Offenders Act 1974, section 113B* of the *Police Act 1997* and *articles 3* and *4* of the *Rehabilitation of Offenders Act 1974 (Exceptions) Order 1975* that criminal convictions and cautions must be disclosed in an enhanced criminal record check in the context of particular types of employment (such as with children or vulnerable adults), even if those convictions or cautions would otherwise be deemed spent by the *1974 Act*. The Supreme Court had no difficulty in finding that the criminal records regime pursued a legitimate aim, generally of protecting employers and children or vulnerable adults in their care, and particularly of enabling employers to make an assessment as to whether an individual is suitable for a particular kind of work. However, the Court held that that the disclosure of all convictions and cautions relating to recordable offences was disproportionate to that aim. The regime implemented by the *1997 Act* was declared incompatible with *Article 8 ECHR*, although the Court held that *articles 3* and *4* of the *1975 Order* should not have been declared ultra vires by the Court of Appeal because it was inconsistent with the non-effect on validity that a declaration of incompatibility is intended to have under the *Human Rights Act 1998* to declare void subordinate legislation made under the provision subject to that declaration. The Government had in any event enacted the *Rehabilitation of Offenders Act 1974 (Exceptions) Order 1975 (Amendment) (England and Wales) Order 2013* and the *Police Act 1997 (Criminal Record Certificates: Relevant Matters) (Amendment) (England and Wales) Order 2013*, which came into force on 29 May 2013, which applies a more nuanced filtering system distinguishing between offenders under and over the age of 18, types of offences which must always be disclosed relevant to safeguarding, the time elapsed and whether a custodial sentence resulted. That amended scheme has also been the subject of an adverse finding as to its compatibility with *Article 8, ECHR* in *R (P) v Secretary of State for Justice* [2017] EWCA Civ 321.

An employer may no longer avoid the non-disclosure of spent convictions through the Disclosure and Barring Service by requiring a prospective employee obtain a full criminal record through a subject access request. *Section 56* of the *Data Protection Act 1998* was brought into force on 10 March 2015 and makes it a criminal offence to require job applicants (or existing employees) to produce a copy of their criminal record through a subject access request.

Where an employment tribunal has made a finding in relation to an incident, it is not necessarily unreasonable for the police to form their own view, unrestricted by the tribunal, and to disclose the incident to a prospective employer: *R (W) v Chief Constable of Warwickshire* [2012] EWHC 406 (Admin).

21.5   ENGAGEMENT

An employer should inform a new employee of the terms and conditions under which he is to work and his commencement date and time. This should be done by letter (if not by a formal signed agreement), although a purely verbal agreement may be sufficient to found an employment relationship (as in *Ferguson v John Dawson & Partners (Contractors) Ltd* [1976] 1 WLR 1213). He is obliged by law to give the employee written particulars of those terms and conditions within two months of the commencement of his employment (see **8.6** Contract of Employment). An offer may be made 'subject to satisfactory references' and in *Wishart v National Association of Citizens Advice Bureaux Ltd* [1990] ICR 794 the Court of Appeal considered that this meant only satisfactory to the employer, subject to an obligation of good faith. If a conditional offer subject to satisfactory references is withdrawn upon receipt of that a reference, the decision to withdraw the offer is subject to challenge as an act of discrimination. For an example of a successful claim against both the former employer which provided a reference, and the putative employer which withdrew the offer of employment, under *section 15* of the *Equality Act 2010* arising out of a reference which had noted a high level of sickness absence, see: *Pnaiser v NHS England & Coventry City Council* [2016] IRLR 170, EAT.

21.5   Engagement of Employees

The actual day on which employment commences has importance under the rules for computing continuity of employment (see **7.3** CONTINUOUS EMPLOYMENT) irrespective of whether the employee actually performs any duties on that day, and determination of that day is a matter of fact (see *General of the Salvation Army v Dewsbury* [1984] ICR 498 and *Boufoy-Bastick v University of the West Indies* [2015] UKPC 27, [2015] IRLR 1014). The employment must start under the contract itself: *Koenig v Mind Gym Ltd* (2013) UKEAT/0201/12/RN, [2013] All ER (D) 261 (May), EAT.

21.6   EMPLOYMENT AGENCIES

For the law regulating employment agencies, and the status of those recruited through such agencies, see **47.2** TEMPORARY AND SEASONAL EMPLOYEES.

21.7   Data Protection Act 1998

If information about an applicant is stored on a computer or by way of paper records, the provisions of the *Data Protection Act 1998* must be complied with (see **10.13** *et seq* DISCLOSURE OF INFORMATION). An employer ought to be registered as a data controller with the Information Commissioner's Office.

21.8   WITHDRAWAL OF OFFERS OF EMPLOYMENT

Once an offer of employment has been made and accepted, a valid contract exists even though the date when the employee is due to start work may be delayed. If in these circumstances the employer retracts the offer or terminates the contract prior to the actual commencement of work, the employee will not be without a remedy. There are three remedies which may potentially be available to the employee depending on the circumstances. First, there may be a claim for wrongful dismissal (see WRONGFUL DISMISSAL **(58)**). Under ordinary contractual principles, such a scenario will be an anticipatory breach where one party has given unequivocal notice that it will not comply with the agreement: see the old authority of *Hochster v de la Tour* (1853) 2 E&B 678. That claim may be brought before the employment tribunal or the county court. Second, if the reason for the dismissal is an inadmissible reason, there may be a claim of unfair dismissal. No period of qualifying employment is necessary when the reason for dismissal is an inadmissible reason (see **54.3** UNFAIR DISMISSAL – **II**). The authority for both of these propositions is *Sarker v South Tees Acute Hospitals NHS Trust* [1997] ICR 673. Third, it may be possible to bring a claim alleging that the dismissal was discriminatory on grounds of age or sex or race or disability or religion or belief or sexual orientation (see DISCRIMINATION AND EQUAL OPPORTUNITIES – **I (11)**, **II (12)**, **III (13)**). An example in the discrimination context is *Mamedu v Hatten Wyatt Solicitors* [2008] All ER (D) 76 (Apr), EAT. The Court of Appeal has confirmed that obligations of trust and confidence can apply to both employer and employee from the outset of the contract where the agreement is one to take up employment at a future date (a so-called forward contract): *Tullett Prebon Plc v BGC Brokers LP* [2011] EWCA Civ 131, [2011] IRLR 420. In forward contract situations, an individual may have acquired contractual obligations to his future employer, but this does not absolve him of his contractual obligations (and fiduciary obligations if applicable) to his existing employer, even if those obligations are mutually inconsistent: *Imam-Sadeque v Bluebay Asset Management (Services) Ltd* [2012] EWHC 3511 (QB), [2013] IRLR 344; *Hilton v Barker Booth & Eastwood* [2005] UKHL 8, [2005] 1 WLR 567.

22 Equal Pay

22.1 Since the coming into force on 29 December 1975 of the *Equal Pay Act 1970* ('*EqPA 1970*'), women have been able to claim equal pay with men, and vice versa. The accession of Great Britain to the *Treaty of Rome* on 1 January 1973 also affected women's rights to equal pay since *art 157* (formerly *art 141*) provides that 'Each Member State shall ensure that the principle of equal pay for male and female workers for equal work or work of equal value is applied'. *Article 157* and *Directive No 75/117* ('the *Equal Pay Directive*') provide a European underpinning of the domestic rights to equal pay (see below **22.3**). The European Commission has also published a *Code of Practice on the Implementation of Equal Pay for Work of Equal Value for Women and Men* (COM(96)336). The provisions of domestic legislation which currently provide for equal pay between men and women are found in the *Equality Act 2010* ('*EA 2010*').

22.2 THE LEGISLATIVE FRAMEWORK

Domestic legislation

Discrimination in relation to pay (and other contractual terms) on grounds of age, disability, gender reassignment, marriage and civil partnership, race, religion or belief and sexual orientation is dealt with in the same way as discrimination in relation to other matters: see DISCRIMINATION AND EQUAL OPPORTUNITIES – I (11). However, sex discrimination in relation to pay (and other contractual terms) is generally dealt with separately. Prior to the coming into force of the *EA 2010*, sex discrimination in relation to contractual terms was 'carved out' of the *Sex Discrimination Act 1975* ('*SDA 1975*') by *s 6(5)* and *(6)* and instead covered by the *EqPA 1970*. As described further below, the *EqPA 1970* provided for a statutory equality clause to be implied into all contracts of employment. Thus, if a woman was engaged on like work or on work rated as equivalent to that of a man or on work of equal value to that of a man, a woman's contract was modified by the *EqPA 1970* so that she could claim pay equal to that which the man received.

EA 2010 consolidates the provisions previously found in the *EqPA 1970* into a single anti-discrimination statute alongside other aspects of discrimination law. The key provisions are found in *Chapter 3* of *Part 5* of the *EA 2010*. Although the *EqPA 1970* and the *SDA 1975* have been consolidated in the *EA 2010*, the same separation between discrimination in relation to pay and discrimination in relation to other matters is maintained in the *EA 2010* – with one important change. Differences in the contractual terms of men and women are covered by *ss 64–69* of the *EA 2010* (which effectively re-enact the provisions of the *EqPA 1970* by providing for a statutory implied sex equality clause in all contracts). Then, by virtue of *s 70* the 'ordinary' sex discrimination provisions are disapplied in circumstances where the claim relates to a term of the woman's contract that falls to be modified or included by virtue of the statutory sex equality clause, or would fall to be modified or excluded were it not for the fact that the employer is able to establish a defence of genuine material factor (see below), or because one of the various statutory exceptions in *Part 2* of *Sch 7* applies. They are also disapplied where the claim relates to contractual pay, but the statutory equality clause has no effect, unless – and this is the significant change on the position under the previous legislation - the difference in pay constitutes direct discrimination under *ss 13* or *14* of the *Act* (*s 71*). Complaints of direct discrimination in relation to contractual pay where there is no actual comparator and a hypothetical comparator only is relied on are thus dealt with under the 'ordinary' provision in relation to sex discrimination in s 13 of the Act (see DISCRIMINATION AND EQUAL OPPORTUNITIES – I (11)). All other complaints of sex discrimination in relation to contractual terms must be brought by reference to the sex equality clause in accordance with *ss 64–69* of the *Act* applying the statutory provisions and case law discussed in this chapter. Note that in *BMC Software Ltd v Shaikh* (UKEAT/0092/16/DM, 5 January 2017), Judge Hand considered it arguable that the effect of *EA 2010, s 70* was to preclude a complaint of constructive discriminatory dismissal where the repudiatory conduct relied upon was alleged to be a breach of the sex equality clause.

As with terms of a woman's employment related to pay, the right to equal treatment in respect of occupational pension schemes was 'carved out' of the *SDA 1975* and dealt with separately under the *Pensions Act 1995*. The same division is maintained in the *EA 2010*. Thus *EA 2010, s 75* creates a maternity equality rule that applies to all occupational pension schemes requiring them to treat time on maternity leave in the same way as time at work (save that any contributions may be reduced proportionate to any reduction in the pay that the woman receives during maternity leave). By *s 76* where a complaint concerns a matter that is covered by the maternity equality rule, no complaint of sex or pregnancy or maternity discrimination can be made in relation to it. Rather, the claim must be brought as an 'equal pay' claim based on the maternity equality rule under *s 75*.

Note that the *EA 2010* also contains a prohibition on pay confidentiality clauses which prevent employees from discussing their pay with colleagues (*EA 2010, s 77*) and a power to require employers with 250 or more employees to provide reports on the gender pay gap in their business (*EA 2010, s 78*), although the latter power has not yet been brought into force and the present Government has no plans to do so.

Prior to 1 October 2010 the *EqPA 1970* provided the domestic legal framework for the elimination of discrimination between the sexes in the terms of their contracts of employment. Because a large number of equal pay cases (including local authority 'multiples') continue to be heard under the *EqPA 1970*, and because the case law under *EqPA 1970* continues to be relevant under the *EA 2010*, this chapter continues to include reference to the *EqPA 1970* as well as *EA 2010*.

The *EqPA 1970* and the examples set out below are framed with reference to women but they are to be read as applying equally to men. The *EA 2010* is framed in gender neutral language.

Maternity and pregnancy

A similar exclusionary rule operates in respect of complaints about discrimination in relation to pay and pensions on grounds of maternity and pregnancy. Whilst an employee is absent from work on maternity leave, an employer may lawfully cease paying her anything other than pay to which she is entitled by statute or contract as a result of being pregnant or on maternity leave: *EA 2010, Sch 9, Part 3, para 17*. However, a woman remains entitled to any bonus in respect of a period when she is on compulsory maternity leave (*para 17(2)(c)*). She also remains entitled to be paid in accordance with the statutory maternity equality clause in *ss 73* and *74* of the *EA 2010* (see **22.13** below) and to be treated for the purposes of any occupational pension scheme in accordance with the statutory maternity equality rule in *s 75* of the *EA 2010* (dealt with at **12.35B** Discrimination and Equal Opportunities – II). The statutory maternity equality clause (broadly speaking) requires a woman who is paid during maternity leave by reference to her normal salary to receive any salary increases (proportionately adjusted) as she would have received if she were working, and likewise to be paid any bonus (proportionately adjusted where appropriate). By *s 76* it is then provided that where a term of a woman's employment relates to pay, no complaint of sex or pregnancy or maternity discrimination can be made in relation to it. Rather, the claim must be brought as an 'equal pay' claim based on the maternity equality clause under *ss 73* and *74* (see further below **22.13** and **22.28**).

Part-time workers

Discrimination against part-time workers was for some time (and is still to a certain extent) dealt with by way of the protection against indirect sex discrimination in the *SDA 1975* and now in *Chapter 1* of *Part 5 EA 2010* (see **11.34** DISCRIMINATION AND EQUAL OPPORTUNITIES – I). Part-time workers can also bring equal pay claims under the provisions discussed in this chapter (see especially **22.20** below). However, since 1 July 2000, part-time workers have also been specifically protected in relation to pay and other detriments by the *Part-time Workers (Prevention of Less Favourable Treatment) Regulations 2000 (SI 2000/1551)* (*'Part-time Workers Regulations'*) (PART-TIME WORKERS (33)).

Transsexuals

In 1996, the European Court of Justice, now the Court of Justice of the European Union (CJEU) decided that discrimination against transsexual employees constituted sex discrimination (*P v S and Cornwall County Council: C-13/94* [1996] IRLR 347). The *Sex Discrimination (Gender Reassignment) Regulations 1999 (SI 1999/1102)* inserted into the *SDA 1975* provisions relating to discrimination against those who intend to undergo, are undergoing or have undergone a gender reassignment (see, in particular, *SDA 1975, ss 2A and 4).* and these provisions were re-enacted in the *EA 2010* (see DISCRIMINATION AND EQUAL OPPORTUNITIES – I (11)). However, unlike for sex discrimination, there was no 'carve out' from the *SDA 1975* in respect of discrimination in relation to pay for transsexuals, which fell to be dealt with as an 'ordinary' discrimination rather than equal pay claim: see *SDA 1975, s 4(8).* The same is true under the *EA 2010.*

Code of Practice. Note that a code of practice prepared by the EOC came into force on 26 March 1997 and was re-issued by the Equal Opportunities Commission in 2003 and was admissible as evidence in *EqPA 1970* and *SDA 1975* proceedings. A new *Equal Pay: Statutory Code of Practice* has now been issued by the Equalities and Human Rights Commission under the *EA 2010.*

22.3   EU Provisions

The foundation of the right to equal pay in EU law is contained in what is now *art 157* of the *Lisbon Treaty* (formerly *art 141* of the *Treaty of Rome*) (the *'Treaty'*) which provides:

'Each Member State shall ensure that the principle of equal pay for male and female workers for equal work or work of equal value is applied.

For the purposes of this Article, "pay" means the ordinary basic or minimum wage or salary and any other consideration, whether in cash or in kind, which the worker receives, directly or indirectly, in respect of his employment from his employer.

Equal pay without discrimination based on sex means:

(a)   that pay for the same work at piece rates shall be calculated on the basis of the same unit of measurement;

(b)   that pay for work at time rates shall be the same for the same job.'

Article 157 and *Directive No 2006/54/EC* (*'the Recast Directive'* which replaced *Directive No 75/117* from 15 August 2009) provide a European underpinning to domestic rights to equal pay. These provisions have been relied upon as an aid to construction of domestic law and, increasingly, as a basis for disapplying inconsistent provisions of domestic legislation (cf *Scullard v Knowles* [1996] IRLR 344 and below). However, it is not possible in all circumstances to enforce *art 157* claims directly before the domestic courts (see EUROPEAN UNION LAW (23)).

The Council of the EU has also adopted *Directive 86/378/EEC* on the progressive implementation of the principle of equal treatment for men and women in occupational social security schemes, including pension schemes. *Directive 96/96/EC* (which came into effect on 1 July 1997) amended *Directive 86/378/EC* to take account of the CJEU's decision in *Barber v Guardian Royal Exchange Assurance Group* [1990] ICR 616. *Directive 86/378/EEC* has also been repealed and replaced by the provisions of the Recast Directive from 15 August 2009.

The *Recast Directive* provides at *Article 14* (which replaces *Article 5.1 of Directive No 76/207* (the '*Equal Treatment Directive*')):

> "There shall be no direct or indirect discrimination on grounds of sex in the public or private sectors, including public bodies, in relation to:
>
> ...
>
> (c) employment and working conditions, including dismissals, as well as pay as provided for in Article 141 (now *art 157*) of the Treaty..."

See also **11.2** DISCRIMINATION AND EQUAL OPPORTUNITIES – I and generally EUROPEAN UNION LAW (23).

The meaning of 'work' in EU law

Article 157 enshrines the right to equal pay for equal work. The definition of 'work' for this purpose has proven to be wider than might initially be imagined. In *Davies v Neath Port Talbot County Borough Council* [1999] ICR 1132, EAT, the issue was whether attending a union-organised course for elected health and safety representatives constituted 'work' for the purposes of *art 157*. Relying on an analogy with the CJEU cases of *Botel*: C-360/90 [1992] ECR I-3589 and *Lewark*: C-457/93 [1996] ECR I-243, the EAT determined that:

> 'Attending a training course organised by a recognised trade union is still related to the employment relationship and is safeguarding staff interests which is ultimately beneficial to the employer.'

The effect of this finding was that the complainant, who ordinarily worked part-time, was able to claim full-time pay as she was attending the course on a full-time basis. Reliance on *art 157* enabled the EAT to avoid applying *TULR(C)A 1992, s 169* which would otherwise have required her to be paid her normal part-time pay. *Section 169* had an indirectly discriminatory effect and was thus contrary to *art 157* and was not applied. Note, however, that not all trade union activities are 'work' for this purpose: see, eg, *Manor Bakeries Ltd v Nazir* [1996] IRLR 604 (attending trade union conference not 'work').

The meaning of 'pay' in EU law

It is now well established that 'pay' in *art 157* is to be given a broad meaning. In *Barber v Guardian Royal Exchange Assurance Group*: C-262/88 [1990] ICR 616, it was held that a benefit is in the nature of pay if the worker is entitled to receive it from his employer by reason of the existence of the employment relationship. Thus, it included benefits paid by the employer upon compulsory redundancy, even where they consisted of pension payments made after the termination of employment. It did not matter that the payment was received only indirectly from the employer (eg through the trustees of a pension scheme). The CJEU reached a similar decision in *Kuratorium Für Dialyse und Nierentransplantation eV v Lewark* [1996] IRLR 637, ruling that compensation paid pursuant to a German statute for loss of earnings whilst attending training sessions for participants in staff councils is pay. (Contrast, however, *Manor Bakeries Ltd v Nazir* [1996] IRLR 604, EAT: employee entitled to paid time off pursuant to a collective agreement to attend a trade union conference. The paid time-off was not 'pay' for the purposes of *art 157* as attending the conference was not 'work' and pay is remuneration for work.) In *Barber*, the CJEU also observed that pensions from both contributory and non-contributory schemes were 'pay' within *art 157*. (See also *Bilka-Kaufhaus GmbH v Weber von Hartz*: 170/84 [1987] ICR 110.) The CJEU, unusually, specifically limited the effect of its decision by stating that it could not be relied upon to claim entitlement to a pension prior to 17 May 1990 (the date of the decision). This matter is considered in greater detail at **22.14** *et seq* below.

A long-standing controversy over whether compensation for unfair dismissal is pay for the purposes of *art 157* was resolved by the decision of the CJEU in *R v Secretary of State for Employment, ex p Seymour-Smith and Perez*: C-167/97 [1999] ICR 447. The CJEU decided that the basic and compensatory awards (for which see **55.7** and **55.10** Unfair Dismissal – III) are deferred pay to which the worker is entitled (ultimately) by reason of his employment. The fact that the compensation consisted of a judicial award did not invalidate that conclusion. However, neither an order for reinstatement nor for re-engagement (for which see **55.2** and **55.3** Unfair Dismissal – III) is 'pay'. The CJEU does not seem to have considered the status of the monetary award made in cases where re-employment is ordered.

Pay includes sums paid in lieu of notice and also covers payments made by the Secretary of State on the insolvency of an employer in respect of the employee's contractual entitlement to notice (*Clark v Secretary of State for Employment* [1997] ICR 64, CA).

Further, 'pay' within *art 157* includes a statutory redundancy payment or an *ex gratia* payment upon redundancy (see *McKechnie v UBM Building Supplies (Southern) Ltd* [1991] ICR 710 for entitlement to equal statutory and contractual redundancy payments).

In *Rinner-Kühn v FWW Spezial-Gebäudereinigung GmbH & Co KG*: 171/88 [1989] IRLR 493, 'pay' was held to include the statutory sick pay which an employee was entitled to receive from her employer; see also *EC Commission v Belgium*: C-173/91 [1993] IRLR 404.

The CJEU also expanded the definition of 'pay' to cover contractual terms which relate to the calculation of entitlements or to requirements imposed as prerequisites to the granting of entitlements. In *Hill v Revenue Comrs and Department of Finance*: C-243/95 [1999] ICR 48, CJEU, the CJEU considered the employment conditions of certain Irish civil servants. Salary was dependent on length of service. Employees who worked half-time earned half of the full-time rate. However, when they moved to full-time employment their pay did not double. Instead, they were placed on the full-time pay spine at a level that gave them credit for only half of the actual period that they had worked for their employer. In other words, their length of service was pro-rated to reflect their previous part-time status. The CJEU decided that the method adopted by the employer for converting part-timers to full-time status constituted 'pay' within *art 157* and that it was, in the particular circumstances, discriminatory and not justified. However, terms with a less direct connection to pay rates may be treated differently. In *Gerster v Freistaat Bayern*: C-1/95 [1998] ICR 327, Bavarian civil service regulations, which required that periods of part-time service should (depending on the number of hours worked) either be entirely or partly discounted when assessing eligibility for consideration for promotion, were held not to offend *art 157*. The CJEU distinguished *Nimz*: C-148/89 [1991] IRLR 222, in which a complainant had successfully challenged a similar rule which gave part-time workers only partial credit for their periods of service. In *Nimz* promotion was practically automatic on completion of the relevant period of service. As the provision in *Gerster* was only concerned with eligibility for promotion, the connection to pay was insufficiently direct to bring the case within the scope of *art 157* which was not concerned with inequalities relating to 'access to career advancement'. The CJEU opined, however, that the rule was potentially contrary to the *Equal Treatment Directive (EEC/76/2007)*. It was left to the national court to decide whether or not the respondent's contention that the requirement was intended to ensure that employees had sufficient experience (and was therefore objectively justified) was made out.

The dividing line between what constitutes 'pay' and what is a 'working condition' that falls to be considered under the *Equal Treatment Directive* (and now, the *Recast Directive*) has been addressed by the CJEU in a number of cases. *Kording v Senator für Finanzen*: C-100/95 [1997] IRLR 710 concerned German legislation which exempted employees with sufficient length of service from having to take certain examinations. Part-time workers had to work a longer period which was pro-rated to the proportion of full-time hours that they worked. The CJEU considered that the provision was not 'pay', but that it was nevertheless indirectly discriminatory (though capable of objective justification). Similarly, the provision of subsidised nursery places to female staff only is to be regarded as a 'working condition' within the meaning of the *Equal Treatment Directive* rather than 'pay' within *art 157*: *Lommers v Minister van Landbouw Natuurbeheer en Visserij*: C-476/99 [2002] IRLR 430. The CJEU held that the fact that the fixing of certain working conditions may have pecuniary consequences is not sufficient to bring such conditions within the scope of *art 157*, which is a provision based on the close connection between the nature of the work done and the amount of pay. However, the CJEU went on to hold that measures giving a specific advantage to women with a view to eliminating inequality (such as providing nursery places for working mothers only) was not contrary to the *Equal Treatment Directive*, in particular where male single parents were given places on the same conditions. (See also *Steinicke v Bundesanstalt für Arbeit*: C-77/02 [2003] IRLR 892: schemes of membership that may have pecuniary consequences not 'pay', though they were indirectly discriminatory contrary to the *Equal Treatment Directive*).

22.4   THE RIGHT TO EQUAL PAY IN DOMESTIC LAW

The equal pay provisions in *Chapter 3* of *Part 5* of *EA 2010* apply by reason of *s 72 EA 2010* to persons who are employed or who hold "a personal or public office". Employment is defined by *s 83* of *EA 2010* as including "employment under a contract of employment, a contract of apprenticeship or a contract personally to do work" (cf **15.3** EMPLOYEE, SELF-EMPLOYED OR WORKER?) as well as Crown employment and employment as a "relevant member" of House of Commons or House of Lords staff. Service in the armed forces is deemed to be employment by *s 83(3)* of *EA 2010*. For the territorial scope of the *EA 2010*, see **12.18** DISCRIMINATION AND EQUAL OPPORTUNITIES – II.

The position under the *EqPA 1970* was similar. The right to equal pay applied:

(a)   to women employed in an establishment in Great Britain whether they were British or not and regardless of the law governing their contract of employment (*EqPA 1970, s 1(1), (11)*);

(b)   to men as well as women (*EqPA 1970, s 1(13)*).

'Employed' under *EqPA 1970* was defined as 'employed under a contract of service or of apprenticeship or a contract personally to execute any work or labour' (*EqPA 1970, s 1(6)(a)*).

Office-holders. As set out above, the equal pay provisions in *Chapter 3* of *EA 2010, Part 5* apply to personal or public office holders. Personal office holders are defined by *EA 2010, s 49* as those holding an office or post to which to which a person is appointed to discharge a function personally under the direction of another person, and in respect of which an appointed person is entitled to remuneration. Public office holders are defined by *EA 2010, s 50(2)* as those holding an office or post appointment to which is made by a member of the executive, or subject to the approval of a member of the executive, or in relation to which appointment is made on the recommendation of, or subject to the approval of the House of Commons, the House of Lords, the National Assembly for Wales or the Scottish Parliament. Following the decisions of the CJEU and Supreme Court in *O'Brien v Ministry of Justice* (respectively, C-393/10, [2012] ICR 955 and [2013] UKSC 6, [2013] 1 WLR 522) establishing that judges are 'workers' under European law, it is likely that many office holders will now also fall within the definition of 'employee' in *s 83* of the *EA 2010* and thus be covered by the standard rules on employees. However, the provisions in relation to office holders are likely still to remain relevant to such people, and also to those who are genuinely office holders and not employees or workers in European law.

The position under *EqPA 1970* was that statutory office-holders were formerly excluded from the provisions of the *EqPA 1970*. However, with effect from 1 October 2005, office-holders (with the exception of holders of political office) were expressly brought within the scope of the *Act: EqPA 1970, s 1(6A)–(6C)* as amended by *reg 35* of the *Employment Equality (Sex Discrimination) Regulations 2005*. Section *1(6A)* of the *Act* extended the right to equal pay to those holding an office or post to which persons were appointed to discharge functions personally under the direction of another person, and in respect of which they were entitled to remuneration, or any office or post to which appointments are made by (or on the recommendation of or subject to the approval of) a Minister of the Crown, a government department, the National Assembly for Wales or any part of the Scottish Administration. This amendment followed the decision of the Northern Ireland Court of Appeal in *Perceval-Price v Department of Economic Development* [2000] IRLR 380, holding that an identically worded provision in the *Equal Pay Act (Northern Ireland) 1970* was incompatible with *art 157* as the right to equal pay conferred by the *EC Treaty* extends to all 'workers' as defined by the CJEU in *Lawrie-Blum v Land Baden-Wurttemberg*: 66/85 [1986] ECR 2121 (a case about *art 48* of the *EC Treaty*). In *Lawrie-Blum*, the CJEU identified the 'essential feature' of an employment relationship as being that 'for a certain period of time a person performs services for and under the direction of another person in return for which he receives remuneration'. The NICA concluded that the tribunal chairmen fell within that definition despite their status as statutory office-holders, and disapplied the exclusion.

Employees posted abroad. Employment in an establishment in Great Britain formerly required that the employee should not work 'wholly or mainly outside Great Britain'. However, the *Equal Opportunities (Employment Legislation) (Territorial Limits) Regulations 1999 (SI 1999/3163)* removed the words 'or mainly' from the relevant provision. The effect is that the legislation now covers workers posted abroad. The *Regulations* came into effect on 16 December 1999. With effect from 1 October 2005, for the purposes of the *EqPA 1970*, employment is regarded as being at an establishment in Great Britain if (a) the employee does her work wholly or partly in Great Britain, or (b) if she does her work wholly outside Great Britain but her employer has a place of business at an establishment in Great Britain, her work is for the purposes of the business carried on at that establishment, and she is ordinarily resident in Great Britain at the time when she applies for or is offered the employment, or at any time during the course of the employment: *SDA 1975, s 10* as amended by the *Employment Equality (Sex Discrimination) Regulations 2005, reg 11(2)*.

For the current law and provisions dealing with the territorial extent of the *EA 2010* see generally **12.18** Discrimination and Equal Opportunities – **II**.

Women suspended on maternity grounds. Women whose pay is reduced when they are suspended on maternity grounds may not seek to challenge the reduction by bringing claims under the *EA 2010* or under the predecessor provisions in *EqPA 1970*. *ERA 1996, ss 66–70* represent a complete code governing the contractual entitlements of such women (*British Airways (European Operations at Gatwick) Ltd v Moore* [2000] IRLR 296, EAT) and see further **(32)** Maternity and Parental Rights. This position is now reflected in *paragraph 2* of *Schedule 7* to the *EA 2010* which provides that the 'sex equality clause' will not apply in respect of special treatment of women in connection with pregnancy or childbirth. However, there are circumstances in which women absent on maternity leave may bring challenges in relation to pay and benefits paid to them while on maternity leave: by virtue of the statutory maternity equality clause and rule in *ss 73* and *74* of the *EA 2010*: see further below **22.13** and **22.28** and **12.35**B Discrimination and Equal Opportunities – **II**

Members of the armed forces. Members of the armed forces were formerly expressly excluded from the scope of *EqPA 1970*. However, *EqPA 1970* was amended by the *Armed Forces Act 1996, s 24* to allow claims to be brought. This was brought into force on 1 October 1997 by the *Armed Forces Act 1996 (Commencement No 3 and Transitional Provisions) Order 1997 (SI 1997/2164)* and the *Equal Pay (Complaints to Employment Tribunals) (Armed Forces) Regulations 1997 (SI 1997/2162)*. The position under *EA 2010* is dealt with by a deeming provision, deeming members of the armed forces to be employees: see *EA 2010, s 83(3)*.

22.5 Equal Pay

22.5 The equality clause

Neither the *EqPA 1970* or the *EA 2010* straightforwardly prohibit direct and indirect discrimination in matters of contractual entitlement. Instead, the *EqPA 1970* adopted a rather oblique and artificial approach. By *s 1(2)* it implied an 'equality clause' into any contract of employment that does not already include one. The equality clause operated whenever a woman was doing like work, work of equal value or work rated as equivalent to that of a man (*s 2(1)*). The *EA 2010* adopts a similar approach. *Section 66(1)* creates a 'sex equality clause'. The clause has the effect that:

(a)   any term of a person's contract which is less favourable than that of an appropriate comparator is modified so as to be not less favourable (*s 66(2)(a)*);

(b)   where a person's contract does not have a term which corresponds to a beneficial term in the contract of an appropriate comparator, the person's contract is modified so as to include such a term: *(s 66(2)(b))*;

(c)   unless the employer does not seek to, or fails to, establish that the difference between the person's contract and the comparator's is genuinely due to a material factor which is not the difference of sex and which is not indirectly discriminatory and cannot be justified (*EA 2010, s 69*) (see **22.11** below).

Appropriate comparators are those doing "equal work" as defined in *EA 2010, s 65*, i.e. those doing:

(a)   *like work* (see below **22.6**); or

(b)   *work rated as equivalent* (see below **22.7**); or

(c)   work of *equal value* (see below **22.8**).

Thus, for example, if a man and a woman are engaged on like work and the man is paid £500 per week for that work, but the woman only £400, the equality clause will operate so as to entitle the woman to £500 per week. Also, if the man's contract contains a clause which entitles him to be paid during absence from work due to sickness, but the woman's contract contains no such clause, the woman's contract will be deemed by law to include such a clause. (For appropriate comparators see below **22.9**.)

The sex equality clause in *EA 2010* is framed in gender neutral language. That in the *EqPA 1970* was not, but by virtue of *s 1(13)* applied equally to men. It is also established in the case law that the operation of the equality clause allows 'piggyback' contingent claims. Thus, where a group of female claimants bring equal pay claims, male colleagues of those claimants may simultaneously bring 'piggyback' contingent claims using the female claimants as comparators and to recover sums equivalent to those awarded to such comparators (if they are successful) by way of arrears: *Llewellyn v Hartlepool Borough Council* [2009] ICR 1426, [2009] IRLR 796.

The equality clause applies to all terms and conditions of employment and not only to pay (eg *Sun Alliance and London Insurance Ltd v Dudman* [1978] ICR 551, relating to a contractual term granting a mortgage interest allowance). The provisions of the *SDA 1975* and the *EqPA 1970* were considered to contain an interlocking but mutually exclusive prohibition on discrimination on grounds of sex: *SDA 1975, s 6(6)* and *Peake v Automotive Products Ltd* [1977] ICR 480. The *EqPA 1970* applied where the contract regulated the provision of benefits in the form of money: *Grundy v British Airways plc* [2005] All ER (D) 94 (Aug), EAT; reversed on other grounds by the CA [2007] EWCA Civ 1020, [2008] IRLR 74). It was not necessary for the payment in question to be expressly provided for in the contract. Provided that the contract 'regulated' the payment it would fall under *EqPA 1970* and not under the *SDA 1975*: thus a so-called 'discretionary' bonus scheme would fall to have been considered under *EqPA 1970* if the discretionary element of it was in fact only as to the amount paid to all employees in any one year and not as to whether or not the employee is entitled to a bonus at all: *Hoyland v Asda Stores Ltd* [2006] IRLR 468. In that case the Court of Session expounded a 'but for' test in order to determine whether or not the payment fell to be considered under *EqPA 1970* or the *SDA 1975*, ruling that if the payment would not have been made 'but for' the existence of the contract of employment, then *EqPA 1970* applied. However, it is doubtful whether this is the correct approach since on that basis any benefit conferred on an employee *qua* employee would have to be regarded as covered by the *EqPA 1970*. The better approach is perhaps to be found in *Hosso v European Credit Management* [2012] ICR 547. In that case, Stanley Burnton LJ found that where the contract granted an employer a discretion as to whether and in what amount to confer a benefit, then the exercise of that discretion was not 'regulated' by the contract of employment and so any claim for discriminatory exercise of the discretion had to be pursued under the *SDA 1975* and not the *EqPA 1970*. Stanley Burton LJ considered that the difficulty with pursuing an equal pay claim where the term in question provided for a contractual discretion was that there was no difference in the terms of the complainant and the comparator's contracts of employment such that the equality clause could operate. Mummery LJ did not express a view on this reasoning preferring to confine his reasoning to the facts of *Hosso* which related to a share option scheme where the claimant and her comparator had the benefit of the same scheme (on the same terms). However, if Stanley Burnton LJ is correct, *Hoyland v Asda Stores Limited* has been effectively confined to its facts.

Section 70 of the *EA 2010* preserves the mutual exclusion of 'ordinary' sex discrimination and equal pay claims formerly contained in *s 6(6)* of the *EqPA 1970*, with one significant change. Where the 'sex equality clause' operates, or would operate but for the success of the employer's 'genuine material factor' defence (see below **22.10**) or the application of one of the exceptions in *Part 2* of *Sch 7* to the *Act* (see generally **12.11** DISCRIMINATION AND EQUAL OPPORTUNITIES - **II**), no claim for 'ordinary' sex discrimination may be made in relation to a contractual term relating to pay. However, and this is the significant change on the position under the *EqPA 1970*, where the 'sex equality clause' has no effect on a contractual term relating to pay (eg because no real comparator can be identified), then a direct (but not an indirect) discrimination claim may be brought in relation to that term under the 'ordinary' direct discrimination provisions: see *s 71* and DISCRIMINATION AND EQUAL OPPORTUNITIES - **I** (11). Note that in *BMC Software Ltd v Shaikh* (UKEAT/0092/16/DM, 5 January 2017), Judge Hand considered it arguable that the effect of *EA 2010, s 70* was to preclude a complaint of constructive discriminatory dismissal where the repudiatory conduct relied upon was alleged to be a breach of the sex equality clause.

It is however clear that the equality clause cannot operate so as to give the complainant a more favourable term than that contained in her comparator's contract. Where, for instance, qualified female employees are paid at the same rate as male trainees, the employee cannot rely on the clause to secure a premium over the rate paid to a trainee selected as a comparator (see *Enderby v Frenchay Health Authority (No 2)* [2000] ICR 612, CA), but a sex discrimination claim could now be brought using the male trainees as evidence to help establish the position for a hypothetical comparator.

In *Hayward v Cammell Laird Shipbuilders Ltd* [1988] ICR 464, the House of Lords rejected the argument that the 'total remuneration package' must be taken into account when making the comparison between a woman's pay and a man's. What must be compared is each distinct provision of the contract dealing with pay and benefits in kind. The applicant was thus entitled to the same rate of basic pay and overtime pay as her male comparator even if she was more favourably treated in other respects, in this case paid meal breaks, additional holidays and better sickness benefits. However, it can be difficult to determine what constitutes a distinct provision or term of the contract. In *Degnan v Redcar & Cleveland Borough Council* [2005] EWCA Civ 726, [2005] IRLR 615, the Court of Appeal held that attendance allowances paid to male employees were all part of a single term of the contract together with their hourly rate and fixed bonuses for the purposes of the comparison of the terms in the woman's contracts. This approach was held to be consistent with *Hayward* in that it did not lump together different terms but instead looked at the reality of the situation by classifying all these payments which related to the same subject-matter as coming under the same contractual term, being 'provision for monetary payment for the performance of the contract by employees during normal working hours'. All monetary payments received by the men should be aggregated and divided by the number of hours in the working week to give an hourly rate which, if lower for women than men, should be increased for women to eliminate the difference. This approach, of treating different payments as different elements of a single contractual term, does sit uneasily with the prohibition on taking a 'swings and roundabouts' approach in *Hayward*. This approach is also difficult to reconcile with the CJEU's decision in *Elsner-Lakeberg v Land Nordrhein-Westfalen* [2005] IRLR 209 in which it held that, in order to determine whether the principle of equal pay is being complied with, genuine transparency permitting an effective review is assured only if that principle applies to each aspect of remuneration, excluding any general overall assessment of the consideration paid. In that case, the CJEU held that it was necessary for there to be separate comparison in respect of the pay for regular hours and the pay for additional hours. Following *St Helens & Knowsley Hospital NHS Trust v Brownbill* [2011] IRLR 815 the scope for applying the approach taken in the *Degnan* case has been further limited. In *Brownbill* the Court of Appeal, upholding a decision of the EAT, held that the tribunal should have carried out a comparison between the rates paid to the complainants and their comparators for unsocial hours work. Broadly speaking, the comparators received lower rates of pay, but higher rates for unsocial hours. Overall, most of the complainants were better paid than their comparators. The tribunal noted that if the claims succeeded the complainants would be even more highly paid than their comparators and held that the claims failed. The EAT and Court of Appeal disagreed, holding that the pay for unsocial hours was a distinct term for distinct work, present in both the contracts of the claimants and their comparators, and the proper approach was to compare the pay received by the complainants and comparators for unsocial hours work and determine whether there was a genuine material factor other than the difference in sex justifying the inequality (see **22.11** below). The matter was remitted to the tribunal. In so deciding Maurice Kay LJ held that *Degnan* was not an exception to the principles set out in *Hayward*. It was merely a particular application of Hayward by looking at the reality of the contractual provisions on the facts of the particular case.

Section 66(2) of *EA 2010* appears to have accepted the analysis of the law as set out in *Hayward v Cammell Laird Shipbuilders Ltd* [1988] ICR 464 by requiring a comparison as between the term in a woman's contract and the "corresponding term" of the contract of the relevant comparator rather than by comparing the term in a woman's contract with "a term of a similar kind" as was required by *s 1* of *EqPA 1970*.

It was suggested in *Hayward* that the 'material factor' defence under *EqPA 1970, s 1(3)* and now found in *section 69 EA 2010* (see **22.10–22.12** below) might be available to an employer who could show that the unfavourable character of the term in the woman's contract was due to the more favourable character of the other terms. Broadly, the same approach is taken by the CJEU in relation to claims based upon *art 157* (see *Barber v Guardian Royal Exchange Assurance Group: C-262/88* [1990] ICR 616 and *Jämställdhetsombudsmannen v Örebro läns landsting*: C-236/98 [2000] ECR I-2189, [2001] ICR 249, CJEU).

Note, however, that once it has been established that there is a 'genuine material factor' (see **22.10–22.12** below) that justifies a difference in pay the equality clause will not operate so as to 'correct' a particular term of an employee's contract simply because that employee is, by the date of the hearing, a member of a group of women who are being paid less than a group of men: see *Armstrong v Newcastle Upon Tyne NHS Hospital Trust* [2005] EWCA Civ 1608, [2006] IRLR 124.

For indirect discrimination under the *EqPA 1970* and *EA 2010*, see below **22.11**.

22.6   Like work

A woman is regarded as employed on like work with men if, but only if, her work and theirs is of the same or of a broadly similar nature and the differences (if any) between the things she does and the things they do are not of practical importance in relation to the performance of her contract of employment. 'Like work' is defined by *s 65(2)* of *EA 2010* as meaning that "A's work and B's work are the same or broadly similar and such differences as there are between their work are not of practical importance in relation to the terms of their work". *Section 65(3)* of *EA 2010* states that in considering differences between the work of a claimant and her comparator, for the purposes of determining whether or not the two are engaged on 'like work' "it is necessary to have regard to the frequency with which differences between their work occur in practice and the nature and extent of the differences". Similar provisions were formerly contained in *s 1(4)* of the *EqPA 1970*.

Thus, although the job descriptions of male and female employees or their written job specifications may be different, if the differences in their duties are of no practical importance, the women will be considered to be employed on like work with the men. The question of what is or is not a difference of practical importance will always be one of fact and degree depending upon the particular circumstances of the case. If, for example, male guillotine operators in a paper mill are required once in two weeks to lift reams of paper whereas women are not, the lifting is purely incidental to their main employment and is not of practical importance. Accordingly, it is not a difference which would prevent the women's right to equal pay.

The EAT has stated in *Capper Pass Ltd v Lawton* [1977] ICR 83, that 'in deciding whether the work done by a woman and the work done by a man is "like work" the employment tribunal has to make a broad judgment. The intention is that the employment tribunal should not be required to undertake too minute an examination, or be constrained to find that work is not like work merely because of insubstantial differences. In order to be like work within the *Act*'s definition the work need not be of the same nature; it need only be broadly similar.' In that case, a cook in the directors' dining room was held to be engaged on like work with the assistant chefs of the company's factory canteen. The fact that women do their work at a different time of the day from men may not prevent them from claiming that they are engaged upon like work (*Dugdale v Kraft Foods Ltd* [1977] ICR 48; *National Coal Board v Sherwin* [1978] ICR 700; contrast with *Thomas v National Coal Board* [1987] ICR 757 in which the EAT held that a male canteen worker on permanent night-shift was not employed on like work with female day-shift canteen workers).

However, the duties actually performed are not the only considerations to be taken into account in deciding whether a woman is engaged on like work. In *Eaton Ltd v Nuttall* [1977] ICR 272, the EAT held that 'In considering whether there is like work, though the most important point is what the man does and what the woman does, the circumstances in which they do it should not be disregarded. One of the circumstances properly to be taken into account is the degree of responsibility involved in carrying out the job.'

Article 157 uses the term 'same work' rather than 'like work'. However, the case law on the European provision suggests that a tribunal should not simply confine its consideration to the duties actually performed. In *Angestelltenbetriebsrat der Wiener Gebeitskrankenkasse v Wiener Gebeitskrankenkasse* [1999] IRLR 804, the CJEU considered a case concerning psychotherapists. Whilst the psychotherapists were all engaged in 'seemingly identical activities', they could be divided into those who had had training in psychology to graduate level and those who had been trained as general practitioners. The graduate psychologists, the majority of whom were women, were paid less. The CJEU decided that training and qualifications could be matters which were relevant to the determination whether the work and/or job were the same and were not merely relevant to a possible material factor defence. It should be noted, however, that although the CJEU purported to proceed on the basis that the applicants and their comparators were engaged in the same activity, it also observed that

22.6 Equal Pay

the former general practitioners, who were better qualified, could be called on to perform 'different tasks or duties'. It is not a case, therefore, where it could be said that the applicants and their comparators necessarily performed identical tasks. The CJEU seems to have had a broader notion in mind when it referred to the 'activity' in which both groups were engaged. In *Brunnhofer v Bank der Osterreichischen Postsparkasse AG*: C-381/99 [2001] IRLR 571, CJEU, the CJEU followed *Angestelltenbetriebsrat*, to draw the conclusion that the existence of an identical collective agreement governing the employment of two employees was not in itself sufficient to show that they performed the same work, or work of equal value.

If a woman's work is more onerous or more responsible than a man's, she may not be considered to be engaged on like work, even though less well paid (*Waddington v Leicester Council for Voluntary Service* [1977] ICR 266). However, she may now be able to obtain equal pay by bringing a direct sex discrimination claim under *EA 2010, s 13* using a hypothetical comparator or in reliance on EU law as described in *Murphy v Bord Telecom Eireann* [1988] ICR 445 (see also **22.8** below).

22.7 Work rated as equivalent

A woman may claim equivalence with a man even though she is not engaged on like work, if a job evaluation study has been carried out in respect of his work and hers, and her job has been rated as equivalent to the man's in terms of the demands made on a worker, or would have been rated as equivalent but for the evaluation being made on a sex-specific system (*EA 2010, s 65(4)*). A system is sex-specific "if for the purposes of one or more of the demands made on a worker, it sets values for men different from those it sets for women" (*s 65(5)*). Similar provision was made in *EqPA 1970, s 1(5)*, although that Act gave examples of the ways in which demands made in jobs may differ in terms of "effort, skill, decision".

By *EA 2010, s 80(5)* a job evaluation study is 'a study undertaken with a view to evaluating, in terms of the demands made on a person by reference to factors such as effort, skill and decision-making, the jobs to be done (a) by some or all of the workers in an undertaking or group of undertakings, or (b) in the case of the armed forces, by some or all of the members of the armed forces'. By *EA 2010, s 131(5)–(7)* if under a job evaluation study the claimant's work has been given a different value to that of the comparator, a tribunal must determine that the work in question is not of equal value (see below **22.8**), unless 'it has reasonable grounds for suspecting that the evaluation contained in the study: (a) was based on a system that discriminates because of sex, or (b) is otherwise unreliable'. For these purposes, a system discriminates because of sex if a difference (or coincidence) between values that the system sets on different demands is not justifiable regardless of the sex of the person on whom the demands are made. Similar provision was previously contained in *s 2A(2A)* of the *EqPA 1970*. The validity of a job evaluation study may thus be challenged if reliance is placed on such a study to claim or to resist a claim for equal pay. There have been remarkably few such challenges. *Macdonald and ors v Glasgow City Council*, UKEATS/0008/14/BI, UKEATS/0009/14/BI and UKEATS/0011/14/BI provides a useful illustration of one such challenge, although ultimately the EAT concluded that the tribunal had taken an appropriate approach on the facts in that case (which involved a method of job evaluation which gave two values for each job).

Advice on job evaluation is set out in ACAS Advisory Booklet 'Job evaluation: Considerations and Risks' available at www.acas.org.uk. See also the *Equal Pay: Statutory Code of Practice* available at www.equalityhumanrights.com.

It has been held that the comparison of jobs must be done by reference to the same job evaluation study (*Paterson (KD) v Islington London Borough* (23 April 2004, UKEAT/0347/03/DA), but it is submitted that what is crucial is that the same system is applied, not that the evaluation is carried out by the same people or at the same time. A job evaluation must be carried out on an objective basis. The principles were set out in *Eaton Ltd v Nuttall* (see above **22.6**). The job of each worker covered by the study must be valued in terms of the demand made on the worker under various headings (eg effort, skill, responsibility) in the study (*Bromley v H & J Quick Ltd* [1988] ICR 623). Thus, it will not suffice simply to compare 'whole jobs'. The assessment should be qualitative, not quantitative – matters such as a difference in the number of hours worked go to the defence of material factor (see **22.10–22.12** below), not to evaluation of the job (*Leverton v Clwyd County Council* [1989] ICR 33). Whilst the study as a whole must be objective, it is permissible for it to contain certain subjective elements, so long as they are not themselves inadvertently discriminatory. It is for the employer to explain how any job evaluation study worked and what was taken into account at each stage (see also *Rummler v Dato-Druck GmbH* [1987] ICR 774).

In determining whether two jobs have been given an equal value by a job evaluation study, it is necessary to look at the full results of the study, including the allocation to grade or scale at the end of the evaluation process. Thus, in *Springboard Sunderland Trust v Robson* [1992] ICR 554, the EAT held that the applicant and a male comparator were employed on work rated as equivalent because each of their scores resulted in an allocation of the same grade, albeit their scores in a job evaluation study had been different.

If no job evaluation study has been carried out, there is no legal requirement for an employer to conduct one. However, once a job evaluation study has been undertaken and has resulted in a conclusion that the job of a woman is of equal value to that of a man, the woman may claim equal pay, despite the fact that the employers may not have implemented the scheme (*O'Brien v Sim-Chem Ltd* [1980] ICR 573). Where a valid job evaluation study has been carried out and a woman's job has been rated as slightly lower than her male comparator, it is not permissible for a tribunal, by reliance on extraneous expert evidence, to find that the difference is insignificant: *Home Office v Bailey* [2005] ICR 1057. But, for work to be rated as equivalent there must be a *completed* job evaluation study, and there is no complete job evaluation study unless and until the parties who have agreed to the carrying out of the study have accepted its validity (*Arnold v Beecham Group Ltd* [1982] ICR 744).

22.8   Work of equal value

Where a woman is employed on work which is not like work or work which has been rated as equivalent to that of a male comparator, she may claim equal pay with a man if her work is of equal value to his, in terms of the demands made on her, eg under such headings as effort, skill and decision (*EA 2010, s 65(1)(c)* and *(6)* and formerly *EqPA 1970, s 1(2)(c)*). Relying upon EU law, she may also claim equal pay where she is doing work of *greater* value (*Murphy v Bord Telecom Eireann*: 157/86 [1988] ICR 445 and *Bainbridge v Redcar & Cleveland Borough Council (No. 2)* [2008] EWCA Civ 885, [2009] ICR 13). Employees of one sex may use *EA 2010, s 65(1)(c)* to claim equal pay with those of the other sex doing a quite different job. Using this provision, a female cook employed as a canteen assistant succeeded in a claim for equal pay with male skilled tradesmen (see *Hayward v Cammell Laird Shipbuilders Ltd* [1988] ICR 464). The fact that one man is being paid the same as a woman for doing like work to hers is no longer a bar to the woman claiming equal pay with another man doing a different job of equal value to hers (see *Pickstone*). In that case, the House of Lords held that the construction of *EqPA 1970* which enabled them to achieve this result was consistent with EU law. (For the procedure to be adopted on claims based on work of equal value see **22.29** below.)

A woman will not be able to succeed in an equal value claim if a valid job evaluation study has concluded that she and her male comparator do work which is not of equal value (*EA 2010, s 2A(2)* and previously *EqPA 1970, s 2A(2)*). In such cases the employment tribunal must determine that the work is not of equal value unless it has reasonable grounds for suspecting that the study discriminated on the grounds of sex, or there are other reasons why it is not suitable to be relied upon *EA 2010, s 131(5)* and *(6)* (see previously *EqPA 1970, s 2A(2)* and *2A(2A)*). For these purposes, a system discriminates because of sex if a difference (or coincidence) between values that the system sets on different demands is not justifiable regardless of the sex of the person on whom the demands are made (*s 131(7)*).

It was suggested by the EAT in *Dibro Ltd v Hore* [1990] ICR 370 at 377 that a job evaluation study carried out at the request of the employer after the institution of proceedings which evaluates the jobs of the applicants and the comparator may be relied upon for the purposes of *s 2A(2)* (see also *Avon County Council v Foxall* [1989] ICR 407). In *McAuley v Eastern Health and Social Services Board* [1991] IRLR 467, the Northern Ireland Court of Appeal held that an employment tribunal had correctly concluded that the work of the applicants and that of their comparator could not be regarded as having been given different values under a job evaluation study so as to preclude their equal value claim, in circumstances in which the job evaluation study was prepared in respect of health boards in Great Britain and its results applied in Northern Ireland only through a policy of maintaining parity of remuneration with Great Britain.

A claimant may use a new job evaluation study which rates her as equivalent to a man as evidence in support of an equal value claim in relation to the period pre-implementation of the job evaluation study but a tribunal cannot necessarily work back from the fact that two jobs are now rated as equivalent to assume that they had equal value prior to implementation; see *Redcar & Cleveland BC v Bainbridge (No 2)* [2008] EWCA Civ 885 [2009] ICR 133. A job evaluation study is of evidential value only in an equal value claim and does not even raise a presumption of equal value for the employer to rebut: see *Hovell v Ashford and St Peter's Hospital NHS Trust* [2009] ICR 1545. However, it is not the case that an employment tribunal must always have the benefit of an independent expert report before finding equality where a woman's job has been marked lower than a comparator's job in a job evaluation study.

For guidance on how 'equal value' claims should be assessed where the woman's (or the man's) job has changed over time, see *Potter v North Cumbria Acute Hospitals NHS Trust* [2008] ICR 910, EAT.

22.9 Persons with whom an employee may claim equivalence

The man with whom a woman seeks to compare herself is known as the 'comparator'. Under the EA 2010 the comparator must be employed by the same employer or an associated employer and (a) work at 'the same establishment' (*s 79(3)*); or *(b)* if not working at the same establishment, 'common terms' must apply at each establishment (*s 79(4)*). For office holders (including police officers), the same person must be responsible for paying the claimant and her comparator (*s 79(5)* and *(8)*). There are also specific provisions for members of the House of Commons (*s 79(6)*) and House of Lords (*s 79(7)*). Similar provision was made in *EqPA 1970, s 1(6)* which allowed a complainant to compare herself with others in the 'same employment' which was defined as follows:

' . . . men shall be treated as in the same employment with a woman if they are men employed by her employer or any associated employer at the same establishment or establishments in Great Britain which include that one and at which common terms and conditions of employment are observed either generally or for employees of the relevant classes.'

The general principles about comparators developed in the case law under the *EqPA 1970* about comparators employed in the 'same establishment' thus remain relevant under the *EA 2010*. The questions of (i) what constitutes the 'same establishment' and (ii) in what circumstances employees at different establishments are to be regarded as employed on 'common terms and conditions of employment' are more complicated and are returned to below.

General rules about comparators

In contrast to direct and indirect discrimination cases brought under *SDA 1975* (now under *Chapter 1* of *Part 5 EA 2010*), the orthodox position prior to the coming into force of the *EA 2010* was that an employee could not use a 'hypothetical' comparator. In other words, she could not base a claim on an allegation that if a man were employed, for instance, on like work, he would be paid more (cf **11.15 DISCRIMINATION AND EQUAL OPPORTUNITIES – I**). Nor could a woman absent on maternity leave rely on an actual male comparator to bring a claim under the equal pay provisions in the *EqPA 1970* since there is no appropriate comparator for a pregnant woman, although in *Alabaster v Barclays Bank plc and Secretary of State for Social Security* [2005] EWCA Civ 508, [2005] IRLR 576 the CA held that in a claim for a pay increase received before the beginning of maternity leave to be taken into consideration when calculating statutory maternity pay, it was appropriate to disapply those parts of *s 1* of the *EqPA 1970* which impose a requirement for a male comparator (see further below **22.13** for maternity leave and pay arrangements). However, under the *EA 2010* a woman may bring a claim where there is no 'actual' comparator as a direct (but not an indirect) sex discrimination claim: see *EA 2010, s 71*. The previous case law on comparators for the purposes of the *EqPA 1970* will nevertheless remain relevant to the identification of 'evidential' comparators, whose circumstances may be considered by Tribunals in determining (i) whether or not the woman is being paid less than a hypothetical male comparator; and, if so (ii) whether the reason for the difference in treatment is sex such that a complaint of sex discrimination under *EA 2010, s 13* is made out.

It should be noted that although the *EA 2010* and the *EqPA 1970* on their face require a woman to identify an actual comparator if she wishes to bring an equal pay claim, there may be a class of cases where this requirement will need to be 'read down' in order to comply with EU law. Thus in *Allonby v Accrington and Rossendale College*: C-256/01 [2004] ICR 1328, the CJEU was asked to decide whether a male comparator with the right to join a pension scheme was necessary in a claim brought by part-time employees who had been dismissed and re-engaged as self-employed contractors to lecture at their former college. The complainant could not identify a male comparator who, like herself, was not an employee. The question was whether the statutory requirement that, in order to join the pension scheme, a teacher be employed under a contract of employment should, if found to have a differential impact on women, be set aside. The CJEU set out the orthodox position that a worker cannot rely on *art 157* in order to claim pay to which she could be entitled if she belonged to the other sex unless, now or in the past, there were workers in the undertaking concerned who perform or performed comparable work. However, where national legislation was the cause of the differential impact (the statutory requirement to be an employee in order to join the pension scheme being a provision of domestic law) the CJEU held there is no need to point to a comparator: it will be sufficient to show a statistical disadvantage. In the absence of objective justification for the national legislation, the requirement to be an employee should be set aside where it is shown that, among the teachers who are workers within *art 157* and fulfil all other conditions for membership of the pension scheme, a much lower percentage of women than men is able to fulfil that condition. In short, the CJEU held that where it is the national legislation that is the sole source of the different treatment, there is no need to identify a particular comparator, as the comparison can be done by examining the position nationally using statistics. This decision sits uncomfortably with the *EA 2010*, which requires an 'actual' comparator for equal pay claims. Further, although *s 70* of the *EA 2010* permits a claimant to bring an 'ordinary' direct sex discrimination claim in relation to pay under *s 13* of the *Act* where he or she has no actual comparator, the *EA 2010* does not permit recourse to be made to an 'ordinary' indirect sex discrimination claim under *s 19* in such circumstances.

Where a comparator is required, selection of an appropriate comparator is a matter for the employee (*Ainsworth v Glass Tubes and Components Ltd* [1977] ICR 347). She may select more than one individual, although tribunals have been warned by the House of Lords to be alert to prevent abuse of the procedure by applicants who 'cast their net over too wide a spread of comparators' (*Leverton v Clwyd County Council* [1989] ICR 33). There is no requirement that the comparator should be in any way 'typical' of his class (although the Court of Appeal in *North Yorkshire County Council v Ratcliffe* [1994] ICR 810 considered that such a requirement might be thought to be implicit in the *EqPA 1970*. The issue was not considered by the House of Lords when it heard the subsequent appeal: [1995] ICR 833.)

There is nothing to prevent a complainant from selecting as a comparator a male employee whom she believes is engaged in work of a lesser value than her own. However, if she is successful in her claim she will only receive the pay awarded to her comparator. A complainant cannot use the *EqPA 1970* to establish a salary differential in her favour (*Enderby v Frenchay Health Authority (No 2)* [2000] ICR 612, CA), (although a sex discrimination claim could now be brought under the *EA 2010* using the male employee as evidence to help establish the position for a hypothetical comparator).

In *Hartlepool Borough Council v Llewellyn* [2009] IRLR 796 the EAT found that male claimants could pursue contingent "piggyback" claims citing female comparators whose terms and conditions of employment had been modified by operation of *s 2(1)* of *EqPA 1970*. However, since the *EqPA 1970* required a real comparator, such claims could only be pursued in respect of periods where female comparators had actually received greater sums than the male claimants either by reason of terms found in the employment contract or alternatively by reason of a declaration of the employment tribunal.

Even under the *EqPA 1970* it was well-established that there is no requirement for contemporaneous employment between the complainant and her chosen comparator and express provision to this effect is made in *s 64(2) EA 2010*. Lindsay P, giving the judgment of the EAT in *Kells v Pilkington plc* [2002] IRLR 693, held that the effect of the CJEU's decision in *Macarthys Ltd v Smith* was that there was no requirement for contemporaneous employment and once the need for that has gone, there was, on the face of things, no specified period under the *EqPA 1970* within which comparisons can or cannot be made. This was confirmed by the Court of Appeal in *Gutridge v Sodexo* [2009] IRLR 721 where it was accepted that after a TUPE transfer, a transferring employee could continue to compare herself with a comparator whose employment did not transfer. The six-year period of limitation in *EA 2010, s 132* and *EqPA 1970, s 2(5)* (see **22.21** below) is concerned with the period of default which can be compensated for, rather than the period during which comparison is acceptable. Although considerable difficulties may arise in claims based on comparisons with predecessors from many years ago, these are difficulties of fact and evidence and not difficulties of law: see *Kells v Pilkington*. However, this does not mean that a complainant can compare herself with a successor in her role: see *Walton Centre for Neurology and Neurosurgery NHS Trust v Bewley* [2008] ICR 1047 in which the EAT held that an earlier decision of the EAT that had held that comparison with a successor was permissible (*Hallam Diocese Trustee v Connaughton* [1996] ICR 860) was wrongly decided. The comparison must involve a 'concrete appraisal' of the work actually performed and using a successor as a comparator would be akin to using a hypothetical comparator which is not permitted under Community law: *Bewley*.

The same establishment

As set out above, under *EA 2010, s 79(3)* (and formerly under *EqPA 1970, s 1(6)*) it is not sufficient for a complainant to be employed by the same employer as her comparator in order to claim equivalence. She must also either be employed at the 'same establishment' as her comparator or be able to show commonality of terms and conditions of employment (as to the latter see below). 'Establishment' was not defined in the *EqPA 1970*, and is not defined in the *EA 2010*, nor is it expressly used in *Art 157*. In *Defrenne v Sabena*: C-43/75 [1976] ICR 547 the CJEU stated that the then *Art 119* (now *Art 157*) applied where men and women carried out work 'in the same establishment or service'. In *South Ayrshire Council v Morton* [2002] IRLR 256 Lord Justice Clerk observed that it was apparent from this paragraph of *Defrenne* that 'the scope of the enquiry is not always confined to the claimant's own workplace or his own employer'. In *Edinburgh City Council v Wilkinson* [2012] IRLR 202 the Court of Session was of the view that whether or not a complainant and comparator worked at the same establishment was a question of fact requiring an evaluation of the relevant facts and circumstances. The term "establishment" was not intended to refer to a 'body' or an 'undertaking'. It was primarily directed to the place of work such as a particular complex or group of buildings and the organisational structure would also be a particularly important definitional element. The existence of a mobility clause in a contract of employment may suggest that the employer runs different establishments. On the facts of that case, where the complainants were local authority employees employed in schools, hostels and libraries and sought to compare themselves with male manual employees, the complainants and their comparators were employed in different physical locations and distinct entities. Those entities had a high degree of permanence and stability, different organisational structures and their own workforces which performed specific tasks. The employment tribunal was therefore entitled to conclude that the employees worked at different establishments.

Different establishments – common terms and conditions of employment

If the complainant and her comparator are employed at different establishments then in order to claim equivalence, the complainant must show that 'common terms and conditions of employment' are observed by the employer at the establishments in question 'either generally or for employees of the relevant classes' (*EA 2010, s 79(4)*, previously *EqPA 1970, s 1(6)*). Note that (as the Supreme Court has recently reminded: *North v Dumfries and Galloway Council* [2013] ICR 993) this requirement is not to be confused with the requirement for the complainant to identify a like term in the comparator's contract with which to claim equality (as to which see above **22.5**), nor with the requirement to establish that the work of claimant and comparator are equal (as to which see above **22.5**). The object is simply to identify where, notwithstanding the location of the claimant's and comparator's employments or particular features of their jobs (eg different hours or holiday allowances), the class of employees that includes the claimant and the class of employees that includes the comparator are employed on broadly similar terms and conditions. A simple example is where both groups of employees are covered by the same collective agreement, even if by slightly different provisions within that agreement: cf *Leverton v Clwyd County Council* [1989] ICR 33, CA. Whether or not there is a sufficient degree of similarity between the terms and conditions is a question of fact for the tribunal. Note that it is not necessary that there should be common terms and conditions applied at both establishments to the complainant's class of employee; what matters is that common terms apply to the claimant's class of employee at one establishment and to the comparator's class at another establishment, and that if the comparator were to be employed at the claimant's establishment, he would be employed on common terms (*North Yorkshire County Council v Ratcliffe* [1994] ICR 810 reversed on other grounds [1995] ICR 833).

A difficulty arises, however, where there are no employees doing the same job as the comparator who work in the establishment in which the complainant is employed. In those circumstances, it is necessary to show that if the male comparator was employed in the same establishment as the complainant, he would be employed on 'broadly similar' terms and conditions as he is in his current employment: see *British Coal Corpn v Smith* [1996] ICR 515 and *South Tyneside Metropolitan Borough Council v Anderson* [2007] EWCA Civ 654, [2007] ICR 1581 and *Beddoes v Birmingham City Council* [2011] EqLR 838, EAT (affd on other grounds [2012] EWCA Civ 585, [2012] EqLR 695). It was at one stage held (see *Dumfries and Galloway Council v North* [2009] ICR 1363, EAT) that it was necessary for a complainant to show that there was a 'real possibility' of the comparator actually being employed at the same establishment as the claimant. However, the Supreme Court in *North*

22.9 Equal Pay

([2013] UKSC 45, [2013] ICR 993) has now ruled that there is no such requirement: the claimant and comparator may be doing very different types of job which could never be carried out at the same establishment (because, eg, one is messy manual labour and the other involves working in an office). Nonetheless, the jobs may be of equal value or rated as equivalent and, if claimant and comparator are otherwise employed on common terms and conditions, the claimant's claim will succeed (subject to any material factor defence). See also *City of Edinburgh Council v Wilkinson* [2012] IRLR 202.

Associated employers

If two or more employers are associated (ie if one is a company of which the other directly or indirectly has control or if both are companies of which a third person directly or indirectly has control; see **7.9 CONTINUOUS EMPLOYMENT**) a woman working in a factory owned by Company A can claim equivalence with a man working in another factory owned by an associated company, Company B, provided that broadly similar terms and conditions of employment apply either generally or for employees of the class of which the comparator is a member (*EA 2010, s 79(3)(a)* and *79(4)(a)*; formerly *EqPA 1970, s 1(6)(c)*). It has long been established that, in the case of two companies controlled by a third person, it is not necessary for the third person to be a company. They may, for eg, be a local authority or government agency: see *Hasley v Fair Employment Agency* [1989] IRLR 106. Because the statutory language requires at least one of the allegedly associated employers to be a 'company' (see now *EA 2010, s 79(9)*), it appeared to exclude the possibility of two public sector employers being associated. However, in *Scullard v Knowles* [1996] IRLR 344 the EAT held that such an exclusion would be contrary to *art 157* and should be treated as 'displaced' by the broader European approach. Further, in *Fox Cross Claimants v Glasgow City Council* [2014] CSIH 27, [2014] EqLR 271, the Scottish Court of Session held that the word "company" was not limited to companies formed under the *Companies Act 2006*. The Court of Session followed the dictum of Lord Hoffmann in *O'Neill v Phillips* [1999] 1 WLR 1092 in holding that a company 'is an association of persons for an economic purpose, usually entered into with legal advice and some degree of formality' and therefore included a limited liability partnership and a community interest company.

The 'single source' test

Challenges made under European Union law to the validity of the requirement in *s 1(6)* of the *EqPA 1970* (reproduced in material respects in the *EA 2010, ss 79(3)* and *(4)*) that comparators be in the 'same employment' have resulted in the development of an additional 'single source' test for equal pay comparisons: *Lawrence v Regent Office Care Ltd* [2003] ICR 1092. The CJEU held that although there was nothing in the wording of *art 157* to suggest that its application was limited to situations in which men and women worked for the same employer, where, as in *Lawrence*, the differences in pay of workers of different sex performing equal work or work of equal value could not be attributable to a single source, such as a collective agreement, there was no one body responsible for the inequality which could restore equal treatment. Such a situation did not come within the scope of *art 157* and the work and pay of the different sets of workers could not be compared on the basis of *art 157*. See also *South Ayrshire Council v Morton* [2001] IRLR 28. This approach has been confirmed by the CJEU in *Allonby v Accrington and Rossendale College*: C-256/01 [2004] ICR 1328, CJEU. In *Allonby*, the applicant worked as a lecturer in the respondent college, but was a self-employed worker, hired by the college through an agency holding a database of lecturers. She claimed comparison with a named, salaried teacher at the college. The issue was whether working in the same establishment or service, for the benefit of a single employer, but under different contracts with different employers, was nevertheless working in the same employment for the purposes of *art 157*. The Court of Appeal ([2001] EWCA Civ 529, [2001] ICR 1189) referred the issue to the CJEU. The CJEU reiterated that *art 157* did not require the applicant to be employed by the same employer as her comparator and that a 'single source' would suffice. However, the CJEU considered on the facts of that case that there was no 'single source'. The fact that her pay as an employee of the agency was influenced by the rates of pay paid by the College did not mean that her pay and her comparator's was set by a 'single source'. This was so even though she may provide the same services as the man and for the benefit of the man's employer.

The 'single source' test was also considered by the Court of Appeal in *Robertson v Department for Environment, Food and Rural Affairs* [2005] EWCA Civ 138, [2005] ICR 750. In that case, the complainant and her comparator were both civil servants in common employment (all employed by the Crown). The CA held this was neither a necessary nor sufficient basis for an equal pay comparison. The bare fact of common employment is not enough: it is necessary in all circumstances to consider whether the terms and conditions were traceable to one source. The relevant body is the one which is responsible for the inequality and which could restore equal treatment. This will often, but not always, be the same employer. As responsibility for negotiating civil servant pay had been delegated down to the individual departments, an inter-department comparison did not involve comparison of pay from a single source and was not permissible. See also *Armstrong v Newcastle upon Tyne NHS Hospital Trust* [2005] EWCA Civ 1608, [2006] IRLR 124: in that case, although both sets of employees were employed by the same NHS Trust, which had endeavoured to a certain extent to harmonise terms and conditions across the hospitals for which it was responsible, the Court of Appeal held that the tribunal was right to find that the Trust had not assumed responsibility for the setting of terms and conditions of employment across all its hospitals and that therefore female employees in one hospital could not compare themselves with male employees in another. It remains to be seen what approach will be taken to employers hiving off their pay negotiations for different departments to different decision-making bodies or companies in order to avoid a 'single source' for cross-departmental comparison. Note, however, the cautionary observations of the Scottish EAT ([2013] ICR 954) and Court of Session in *Fox Cross Claimants v Glasgow City Council* [2014] CSIH 27, [2014] EqLR 27: careful consideration must be given to the power or authority alleged to be the 'single source' in order to ascertain whether it does constitute a 'single source' or whether the powers of the direct employer of claimant or comparator in relation to pay exclude or restrict the power of the alleged 'single source' in some material way. In this respect, it is immaterial that the alleged single source does not choose to exercise any power it has. What matters is whether it has the power.

In *Beddoes v Birmingham City Council* [2011] EqLR 838 the position of non-teaching staff was considered in community schools. The local authority employed those staff, but acting on the requirements of the governing body of the school. It was asserted, therefore, that there was no single source as between the complainants and their comparators, the terms and conditions of employment in relation to the comparators being set by the local authority. The EAT rejected the argument. First, the argument failed by reason of the decision in *North Cumbria Acute Hospitals NHS Trust v Potter* [2009] IRLR 176 where the EAT had held that it was not necessary to 'read down' *EqPA 1970, section 1(6)* so as to include the 'single source test': if complainant and comparator are in 'the same employment' for the purposes of *s 1(6)*, that is sufficient, their terms and conditions do not also have to emanate from a single source. Secondly, the argument failed on the facts (and on an application of the decision of the Court of Appeal in *South Tyneside MBC v Anderson* [2007] ICR 1581). Finally, the EAT considered that in most cases the requirement of a 'single source' was unlikely to be any different to the requirements of *EqPA 1970, s 1(6)* since in most cases, a complainant will be able to compare herself with the employer's other employees (subject to satisfying the establishment criterion) and there will be a 'single source' because the employer will have the power to determine the terms and conditions of each its own employees. This part of the EAT's decision was not appealed to the Court of Appeal ([2012] EWCA Civ 585, [2012] EqLR 695), which upheld the EAT's decision on other grounds.

22.9 Equal Pay

In all cases where the question of 'single source' arises it is important to remember that the principle as enunciated in *Lawrence* requires both that a single body is responsible for the inequality and that it is capable of restoring equal treatment: *North Cumbria Acute Hospitals NHS Trust v Potter* [2009] IRLR 176 and *Fox Cross Claimants v Glasgow City Council* [2014] CSIH 27, [2014] EqLR 27.

22.10 Material factor defence – general approach

Although a woman may establish that she is engaged on like work, work rated as equivalent to that of a man or work of equal value, she will not be able to claim equivalence with that man if the employer can establish a 'material factor' defence. By *s 69* of *EA 2010* a 'sex equality clause' will not have any effect where the 'responsible person' is able to show that the difference is because of a material factor. (A 'responsible person' is defined at *s 80* of *EA 2010* as the employer of a person or alternatively the person responsible for paying remuneration to that person.) That material factor must: (i) be a material difference between the claimant's case and her comparator's (s 69(6)); (ii) not be a factor which is directly discriminatory (*s 69(1)(a)* of *EA 2010*); nor (iii) one which is indirectly discriminatory (*s 69(1)(b)* and *(2)* of *EA 2010*). An indirectly discriminatory factor is defined as being a factor which results in "persons of the same sex doing work equal to A's" being "put at a particular disadvantage when compared with persons of the opposite sex doing work equal to A's" and where that factor is not "a proportionate means of achieving a legitimate aim". For this purpose, the long-term objective of reducing inequality between men's and women's terms of work is always to be regarded as a legitimate aim (*s 69(3)*).

Under the *EqPA 1970* a similar defence of 'genuine material factor' ('GMF') was available. It was a defence for the employer to show that the variation between the woman's contract and the man's contract was genuinely due to a material factor which was not the difference of sex (*EqPA 1970, s 1(3)*). In the case of equality claimed on the basis of *like work* or *work rated as equivalent*, that factor *must* be a material difference between the woman's case and the man's (*EqPA 1970, s 1(3)(a)*). In the case of equality claimed on the basis of *work of equal value*, that factor *may* be a material difference between the woman's case and the man's (*EqPA 1970, s 1(3)(b)*). Thus, in establishing a defence to a claim based on like work or work rated as equivalent, any difference in terms had to be explained (and, in some cases, objectively justified: see below) by a difference between the woman's case and the man's case. In a claim based on work of equal value the defence includes, but is not limited to, such differences.

The question whether an employer could succeed in a 'GMF' defence by relying upon a factor which did not objectively justify the difference in pay between the employee and her comparator received considerable judicial attention prior to the coming into force of the *EA 2010*. The 'old law' on this issue is set out below. The *EA 2010* has clarified the position. Under the *EA 2010* the employer will only be required to justify pay differentials where it relies, to explain such differentials, on a factor which is prima facie indirectly discriminatory, i.e. which puts persons of one sex at a particular disadvantage as compared to those of another sex doing the work (*s 69(1)(b)* and *(2)*). "Particular disadvantage" will likely be established by reference to statistical information. It remains to be seen, however, how the courts will now deal with the line of defence to an indirect discrimination equal pay claim identified in *Armstrong*, *Gibson* and *Hamilton* (see the 'Pre *EA 2010* approach' section below). In those cases, it was held that an employer can avoid the need to justify a pay differential if it is able to show that statistics which on their face establish a prima facie case of indirect sex discrimination are in fact wholly explained by factors unrelated to sex. This approach ought still to work under the *EA 2010* since an employer who establishes an *Armstrong*-type defence may be considered to have established that, contrary to initial appearances, no prima facie case of indirect discrimination arises because the arrangements in question do not put women at a disadvantage in comparison to men. On the other hand, it may be said that once a prima facie case of indirect discrimination is made out by reference to statistical evidence, then an employer has no alternative but to justify it in order to make out the defence in *s 69(1)(b)* and *(2)* of the *EA 2010*.

Pre EA 2010 approach

There was for some time a marked difference in the approach taken to the scope of the defence at European and domestic levels. The European approach was set out in *Enderby v Frenchay Health Authority* [1994] ICR 112: it requires that a difference in pay be objectively justified. Further, *Enderby* requires, subject to a de minimis principle, that the whole of the difference must be justified.

The approach taken by the UK courts has been, traditionally, less demanding. The domestic approach has been simply to require the employer to be able to account for the difference by reference to a factor which is material but is not the sex of the employee. Thus, in *Yorkshire Blood Transfusion Service v Plaskitt* [1994] ICR 74, the employer succeeded in establishing a defence in circumstances where the disparity in pay was due to a mistake. Whilst an error may explain an unlawful disparity, it clearly cannot be said to justify it. Nevertheless, if a factor provides no sensible basis for justifying the disparity, domestic tribunals have tended to conclude that the factor is not 'material'. In *Tyldesley v TML Plastics Ltd* [1996] ICR 356, the EAT made an ambitious attempt to reconcile the domestic and European approaches. The principle which the EAT developed may be summarised as follows: if the factor relied upon by the employer is one which may itself be tainted by sex discrimination, it must be shown that the factor objectively justifies the difference; however, if it is not tainted by sex discrimination, the factor need only explain the difference. The EAT decision in *Tyldesley* was approved by the House of Lords in *Strathclyde Regional Council v Wallace* [1998] ICR 205, HL and *Glasgow City Council v Marshall* [2000] ICR 196, HL) and applied by the EAT in *Parliamentary Comr for Administration v Fernandez* [2004] ICR 123; *King's College London v Clark* (2003) IDS Brief 747, p 11 (in which the EAT held that a mistake and a *TUPE* transfer adequately explained the difference in pay); and *Armstrong v Newcastle Upon Tyne NHS Hospital Trust* [2005] EWCA Civ 1608, [2006] IRLR 124. In *Armstrong* the Court of Appeal held that the need to provide objective justification does not arise in cases in which the bare *Enderby* statistics, taken in isolation, suggest *prima facie* discrimination but there are other factors which suggest that the statistics are not good evidence of such prima facie discrimination so that the pay differential can be said not to be the difference of sex. In *Sharp v Caledonia Group Services Ltd* [2006] ICR 218, the EAT, having cited the author of this chapter's then view that the issue 'remains vexed', proceeded to eschew the *Glasgow CC v Marshall* approach in favour of the more stringent European approach in the *Enderby* and *Brunnhofer* cases, the latter of which the EAT considered 'provides clear guidelines in equal pay cases as to the need for objective justification in all cases'. However, in *Armstrong* Lord Justice Buxton warned that, 'once the House of Lords has determined the meaning of [European Union rules] it is not open to domestic courts to resort to the decisions of the Court of Justice on which the House of Lords based its analysis in order to find a different or wider meaning'. Although Lord Justice Buxton does not appear to have been referred to the *Sharp* case, this would appear to be a condemnation of the approach taken by the EAT in that case and a reaffirmation that *Glasgow CC v Marshall* should continue to be applied unless and until the issue is reconsidered by the Supreme Court or the CJEU.

This the EAT did in *Villalba v Merrill Lynch & Co Inc* [2007] ICR 469 and *Surtees v Middlesbrough Borough Council* [2007] ICR 1644, holding that once an employer has established that a difference in pay was owing to factors other than sex, the employer is not required to go further and objectively justify the difference in pay. In *Villalba*, which concerned bonus payments based on performance assessments, it held it to be sufficient that the employer had shown that sex was not a factor in its decision-making. (Or, rather, that it was not a 'significant influence' on its decision-making, as per Lord Nicholls in *Nagarajan v London Regional Transport* [2000] 1 AC 501, HL.) In *Surtees* Elias P referred to the formulation set out in Villalba and observed that if the argument that 'the mere fact that a woman is making a comparison with a man whose job is of equal value itself automatically requires that any difference in pay is objectively justified, even though the employer shows that the difference has nothing to do with sex' is correct, then 'equal pay has broken loose from its moorings in discrimination law'. In that case, Elias P ruled that, where the employer has succeeded in explaining the difference in pay by reference to a factor that is not tainted by sex discrimination, he does not need to go further and objectively justify the use of that factor. On appeal from Elias P's judgment, the Court of Appeal in *Bainbridge/Surtees* [2009] ICR 133 considered arguments about the approach adopted by the Court of Appeal in *Armstrong* (supra) but held that it was not the right case to analyse that case. It did however express a tentative view that, in circumstances of apparent disparate impact, it was possible for an employer to satisfy a tribunal that a pay differential was not due to the difference of sex without having to show objective justification but only where the statistical evidence was not very strong or convincing.

In *Gibson v Sheffield City Council* [2010] EWCA Civ 63, [2010] ICR 708, the CA examined the issue again. That case concerned bonus schemes which had been introduced in the 1960s for manual workers in the Council (street cleaners, refuse collectors, maintenance, etc.) and subsequently consolidated into salary. As a result, the manual workers were paid over 30% more basic salary than the claimants who worked as care workers and school meals supervisors. The manual workers were overwhelmingly male, the care workers and school meals supervisors overwhelmingly female. The Tribunal found that the bonus schemes had initially been introduced for genuine productivity reasons, but since consolidation into basic pay the additional money was being paid without reference to productivity. The Tribunal found that it would not have been possible, because of the nature of their work, for similar bonus schemes to have been introduced for the claimants' roles and, in any event, that their work ethic had always been good. The Tribunal held that the reason for the difference in pay was the need to provide payments for increased productivity, and that this was unrelated to gender. Accordingly the Tribunal held, following *Marshall* and *Armstrong*, that it was not necessary for it to go on to determine whether the difference in pay was objectively justifiable. Smith LJ and Kay LJ in the Court of Appeal (although not Pill LJ) expressed the view that Armstrong was correct in principle and that an employer can avoid the need for objective justification if it can show that, notwithstanding that statistics have been produced which show that the pay practice in question has an adverse impact on women, the adverse impact has arisen as a result of factors wholly unrelated to gender. On the facts of the particular case, however, the CA ruled that the Tribunal had been wrong to find that the schemes were not sex-tainted. The matter was remitted to the Tribunal to consider the question of objective justification.

The cases show just how difficult it is for a Tribunal to determine whether or not a particular pay practice is 'tainted by sex discrimination'. In the *Armstrong* case (above) the Trust's explanation for the difference in pay between catering and portering staff was that the catering staff bonuses had been removed in order for the workforce to be competitively tendered in the market. A decision had been taken not to 'contract out' the portering contracts because portering was not subject to Compulsory Competitive Tendering and any decision to do so might therefore attract more controversy. The tribunal found that these reasons were 'tainted by sex discrimination'. However, the tribunal relied on its own experience to the effect that male workforces were more likely to be unionised and to object to contracting out and on that basis held the employer's explanation to be 'tainted by sex discrimination'. The CA ruled that it had not been open to the tribunal so to hold in the light of its findings of fact as to the Trust's reasons. The Court distinguished the *Ratcliffe* case (above) on the basis that in that case the tribunal had made an express finding as to the Council's reason for its decision to contract-out the domestic ancillary services and it was that express reason (rather than a further reason inferred by the Tribunal from its own experience) that the tribunal found was tainted by sex discrimination. Buxton LJ further observed that in the *Ratcliffe* case the House of Lords appeared to have been satisfied that the employer had failed to show any material difference between the comparator groups other than the difference in sex. In *Armstrong*, however, there were a number of differences between the two groups. The CA remitted the case to the Tribunal to determine again, in the light of its judgment, whether the bonus arrangements had a disparate impact on female employees, whether the decision to put domestic services out to tender, or to discontinue the domestic services' bonus scheme, was an act of discrimination and (if so) whether a GMF defence had been established. On remission (cf [2010] ICR 674) the Tribunal found (and the EAT upheld the decision) that there was a disparate impact and that the decision to withdraw the female catering staff bonuses to bring their pay into line with a labour market for domestics which was itself sexually discriminatory such that the arrangements were 'tainted by sex'. Objective justification was therefore required, but the Trust had failed to establish it.

In the *Gibson* case, by contrast to the first appeal in *Armstrong*, the CA overturned the Tribunal's decision that there was no sex taint on the grounds that it was perverse: the CA considered that the statistics were overwhelming and there had been a history of 'stereotyping' so (even though no similar bonus scheme could have been devised for the women's jobs) the 'sex taint' was present.

In *Newcastle-upon-Tyne NHS Hospitals Trust v Armstrong* [2010] ICR 674 and *Bury Metropolitan Borough Council v Hamilton* [2011] ICR 655, the EAT (Underhill P presiding) gave the clearest guidance to date on the approach that should be taken by tribunals to the GMF defence and the question of objective justification. The 'structured approach', as the EAT has termed it, is as follows (*Bury v Hamilton*, para 14):

- It is necessary first to identify the explanation for the differential complained of. The burden of proof is on the employer.

- It is then necessary to consider whether that explanation is 'tainted with sex'. What that not altogether happy metaphor means is that the explanation relied on must not itself involve sex discrimination, whether direct or indirect.

- In considering whether the explanation involves direct or indirect discrimination, the ordinary principles of the law of discrimination apply. That means that:

  - If the differential is the result of direct discrimination the defence under *s 1(3)* will fail;

  - If the differential involves indirect discrimination of either the PCP-type or the *Enderby*-type (as to this distinction, see **22.11** below) the defence will fail unless the employer proves that the differential is objectively justified as being a proportionate means of achieving a legitimate aim;

  - If the employer's explanation involves neither direct nor indirect discrimination the defence will succeed, even if the factor relied on cannot be objectively justified.

- In considering the employer's explanation, the ordinary principles governing the burden of proof in discrimination claims will apply. Thus if the claimant shows a prima facie case of discrimination (in the sense explained in *Madarassy v Nomura International plc* [2007] ICR 867), the burden shifts to the employer to prove the absence of such discrimination. (See generally DISCRIMINATION AND EQUAL OPPORTUNITIES – III (13)).

The 'structured approach' advanced by the EAT must, in this author's view, be correct as a matter of legal principle. It is also clear and readily capable of application by employment tribunals. However, it arguably does not deal with one strand of the case law, approved twice at Court of Appeal level in the *Armstrong* and *Gibson* cases (supra) (and accepted by the EAT in *Bury v Hamilton* as binding upon it), namely that there is an additional line of defence available to an employer in a case where a complainant has proved a *prima facie* case of indirect discrimination. In such cases, the Court of Appeal held that it was open to an employer at that stage to show that the apparent adverse impact on women is caused by factors other than sex so that there is then no need for the employer to go on to objectively justify the difference in pay.

See also, in this regard, *Sunderland City Council v Brennan* [2012] EWCA Civ 413, [2012] ICR 1216 and *Cooksey (GMB Claimants) v Trafford BC* [2012] Eq LR 744 and note that, in the latter case, the EAT observed that this 'no sex taint' *Armstrong* defence to indirect discrimination is unlikely to be available in practice where the *prima facie* case of indirect discrimination arises as a result of the application of a PCP applied by the employer (the first type of indirect discrimination described at **22.11** below). Rather, it will be relevant only where the indirect discrimination is to be found in the *Enderby*-type indirect discrimination, i.e. where there is a *prima facie* case of indirect discrimination arising as a result of a state of affairs (the second type of indirect discrimination case described below).

22.11   'Prima facie' indirect discrimination and the 'material factor' defence

The model adopted by the *EqPA 1970*, in which an employee compares her terms and conditions with those of a specific comparator, worked well enough in relation to cases of direct discrimination. Indeed, it favoured the complainant in that, once she had established that her male colleague enjoyed different and more favourable terms, the employer had then to establish that the difference was due to a material factor which was not a difference in sex. In effect, to use the language of *SDA 1975*, the employee needed only to establish that she had been 'less favourably treated'. She did not need to show that the less favourable treatment was 'on the ground of her sex'; it was for the employer to show that the difference in sex was not the ground of the difference in treatment (see **22.10** above and **11.34** DISCRIMINATION AND EQUAL OPPORTUNITIES – I.) Nonetheless, the 'structured approach' to the 'material factor' defence that was enunciated by the EAT in *Bury Metropolitan Borough Council v Hamilton* [2011] ICR 655 (above, **22.10**) required the tribunal, as a step in considering an employer's defence, to determine whether or not a 'prima facie' case of indirect discrimination had arisen. However, this issue has caused the courts and tribunals significant difficulties.

The *EA 2010* attempts to codify the law on indirect discrimination in equal pay claims. However, it does so through a circuitous route. First, a real comparator of the opposite sex must be identified by the complainant who is doing equal work (as defined by *s 65*), but being paid more: see *s 66*. The employer must then show both that the difference in treatment is not the difference in sex (*s 69(1)(a)*) and, if the factor that is causing the difference in pay puts persons of one sex at a particular disadvantage (*s 69(2)*), that the factor is a proportionate means of achieving a legitimate aim (*s 69(1)(b)*). See further above **22.10**.

Although there has been considerable doubt on the issue (cf, for eg, *Bailey v Home Office* [2005] EWCA Civ 327, [2005] ICR 1057) it is now generally recognised that there are two forms of indirect discrimination that arise in relation to equal pay (see *Bury Metropolitan Borough Council v Hamilton and ors* [2011] ICR 655, EAT):

- where the employer applies a provision, criterion or practice which puts or would put women at a particular disadvantage when compared with men (the 'PCP'-type of discrimination);

- where two groups of employees doing work of equal value receive different pay and there is a sufficiently substantial disparity in the gender break-down of the two groups (referred to as discrimination arising from a 'state of affairs', or *Enderby*-type discrimination, having first been recognised in the decision of the CJEU in *Enderby v Frenchay Health Authority* [1994] ICR 112).

These two forms are not mutually exclusive: *Cooksey (GMB Claimants) v Trafford BC* [2012] Eq LR 744.

In cases of the first type of indirect discrimination, the employee's terms will often be identical to those of her male comparator. In such cases, the issue will centre instead on a benefit which, whilst theoretically available to the complainant, is contingent on her satisfying a provision, criterion or practice ('PCP') which fewer women than men are able to satisfy. For instance, the contracts of both employees may provide that they are entitled to join their employer's pension scheme only if they work full-time. It is difficult to apply the equality clause to such cases. What is needed in order to eliminate the discrimination is not the addition to the complainant's contract of a clause already present in her comparator's, but the replacement of the term common to both contracts with one which does not have a discriminatory effect. For this reason, there was initially some doubt as to whether or not *EqPA 1970* prohibited indirect discrimination at all although it has now long been established that indirect discrimination is contrary to both UK and European law (*Jenkins v Kingsgate (Clothing Productions) Ltd* [1981] ICR 715, EAT, *Bilka-Kaufhaus GmbH v Weber von Hartz*: C-170/84 [1987] ICR 110, CJEU).

Thus, if pay criteria are adopted which apparently tend to favour men, it is for the employer to justify those criteria. Such criteria would include ones less favourable to part-time workers (see, eg *Arbeiterwohlfahrt der Stadt Berlin eV v Botel*: C-360/90 [1992] IRLR 423 and *Vroege v NCIV Institut voor Volkshuisvesting BV*: C-57/93 [1995] ICR 635, CJEU and generally **22.20** below).

In cases of the second type of indirect discrimination, it is not necessary for the complainant to follow the formal steps of identifying a provision, criterion or practice, choosing a pool for comparison and establishing a disparate impact. Thus in *Enderby v Frenchay Health Authority*: C-127/92 [1994] ICR 112, CJEU (the case in which the second type of discrimination was first recognised) the CJEU decided that the employer could be called upon objectively to justify a difference in pay once the complainant had demonstrated that 'significant statistics disclosed an appreciable difference in pay between two jobs of equal value, one of which was carried out almost exclusively by women and the other predominantly by men'. Whilst this approach focuses on disparities in pay, it plainly does not require the identification of any condition or requirement (now PCP). In *Ministry of Defence v Armstrong* [2004] IRLR 672, the EAT favoured the Enderby approach, holding that there is no need for a tribunal always to adopt the formulaic approach of the *SDA 1975* when considering whether there is a disparate impact for the purposes of *EqPA, s 1(3)*. Cox J stressed that the question in all cases is 'whether there is a causative link between the applicant's sex and the fact that she is paid less than the true value of her job as reflected in the pay of her named comparator'. Tribunals should 'focus on substance, rather than form and on the result, rather than route taken to arrive at it'.

Nonetheless, this has caused confusion in practice and the distinction between the two types of indirect discrimination has been doubted. Thus in *Bailey v Home Office* [2005] EWCA Civ 327, [2005] ICR 1057 the Court of Appeal held that the tribunal's attempt to fashion a condition or requirement out of the circumstances of the case had led it into error. It rejected the EAT's attempt to distinguish between condition and requirement/PCP cases on the one hand and cases which did not have an obvious condition or requirement/PCP but which involved a disparity of pay between two groups on the other. In each case, the Court of Appeal ruled that the tribunal is concerned to determine whether what on its face is a gender-neutral practice may be disguising the fact that female employees are being disadvantaged as compared with male employees to an extent that signifies that the disparity is *prima facie* attributable to a difference of sex. The Court of Appeal held that the statistical approach in *Seymour-Smith* could be used in either case. A common approach to both types of cases has the merit of ensuring that the Act is applied consistently to all forms of indirect discrimination. On the facts of *Bailey*, the Court of Appeal held that the tribunal could conclude that there was sufficient disparate impact requiring justification where there was one group of employees which contained a significant number, even though not a clear majority, of female workers whose work is rated as equal to that of another group of employees who are predominantly male and who receive greater pay. The fact that the disadvantaged group contained a significant number of men was not a bar to a claim.

It is certainly the case that in relation to both types of indirect discrimination there will often be an issue as to whether there is a sufficiently substantial disparity in the gender make-up of the two groups to give rise to a *prima facie* case of indirect discrimination.

In particular, the 'almost exclusively by women' formula used by the CJEU in *Enderby* has given rise to a number of difficulties of interpretation. The Court of Appeal in *British Road Services Ltd v Loughran* [1997] IRLR 92, CA, having carefully considered *Enderby*, took the view that it would suffice if there were a 'significant proportion of women' in the claimant's group. Later cases have attempted to establish a more precise formula, though with little success.

When it made its reference to the CJEU in *R v Secretary of State for Employment, ex p Seymour-Smith and Perez* [1999] ICR 447, the House of Lords asked for guidance on the circumstances in which a court is entitled to conclude that a provision has an indirectly discriminatory effect. Characteristically, in giving guidance, the CJEU posed as many questions as it answered. The CJEU declined to give any precise guidance as to the assessment of disparate impact; it merely observed that the national court must be satisfied that the proportion of women that can comply must be 'considerably smaller' than the proportion of men who can do so. In that case, which was concerned with the upper age limit on the availability of the right to claim unfair dismissal, the particular period with which the court was concerned was 1985, the date on which the former requirement of one year's service was increased to two years. At that point, the proportion of men who could comply with the requirement was 77.4%, whereas the proportion of women who could comply was 68.9%. Since that time the gap has narrowed. The CJEU observed that these figures did not suggest a sufficient disparity of impact to result in a discriminatory effect. However, the Court also observed that a small but persistent difference may result in a finding of discrimination. No guidance was given as to how this new, alternative test will operate. The majority of the House of Lords found the relevant provision to be discriminatory on the basis of this 'alternative' test. They do not appear to have seen it as an alternative, however (see **11.34** DISCRIMINATION AND EQUAL OPPORTUNITIES – I).

In assessing whether a statistically relevant difference in pay has been established, the CJEU in both *Enderby* (at para 17) and *Seymour-Smith* and *Perez* (at para 62) emphasised that it is for the national court to decide whether the pools of employees selected for comparison "cover enough individuals, whether they illustrate purely fortuitous or short-term phenomena and whether, in general, they appear to be significant". Further guidance on the proper test to be applied can be gleaned from *Barry v Midland Bank* [1999] ICR 859, HL. Lord Nicholls remarked at 869 that a comparison between the proportions of men and women disadvantaged by a particular provision could on its own be misleading, because those proportions would be affected by the comparative sizes of the disadvantaged and non-disadvantaged groups. (For an example of a case where the tribunal was so misled, see *Best v Tyne and Wear Passenger and Transport Executive (t/a Nexus)* [2007] ICR 523, EAT in which the EAT ruled that the tribunal had been wrong to find that a disparate impact had been established in circumstances where the disadvantaged group was mainly male, albeit that there were more women in the disadvantaged group than there were women in the advantaged group – in such circumstances there was no disparate impact on women generally.) In *Barry v Midland Bank*, Lord Nicholls suggested that the better guide would often be found by expressing the proportions of men and women in the disadvantaged groups as a ratio of each other. Moreover, the absolute size of numbers of those disadvantaged remains relevant, since a low ratio may be of little significance in a small company, but of considerable significance in a large company. Thus in *Audit Commission v Haq (S)* (UKEAT/0123/10/LA) (18 March 2011, unreported) the EAT held that the numbers involved were insufficient to give rise to a *prima facie* case of discrimination. In that case senior and junior administrative roles had been amalgamated and a pay protection policy implemented which meant that former senior administrators were paid more in the new role because they had previously been paid more. Two of the four former senior administrators were male (and both the senior administrators retained were male), whereas all nine former junior administrators were female. The tribunal found that there was unjustified indirect discrimination. The EAT overturned that decision, holding that the numbers involved were too small to give rise to a *prima facie* case of indirect discrimination on that ground alone. The CA ([2012] EWCA Civ 1621, [2013] IRLR 206) reversed the EAT on this point, upholding the Tribunal decision. The CA took the view that the numbers were sufficient. Post the amalgamation the numbers were sufficient to establish a prima facie case of discrimination. The employer could not rebut that case because, historically, the fact that all nine former junior administrators were female was itself evidence of a sex taint. In the absence of evidence of any other source of discrimination, the claims must fail. Cf also see *Armstrong v Newcastle Upon Tyne NHS Hospital Trust* [2005] EWCA Civ 1608, [2006] IRLR 124 where it was held that a failure by a tribunal to make a finding that the employer's arrangements have a 'considerable' impact on women prior to concluding that an arrangement is discriminatory will be an error of law: (although cf *Gibson v Sheffield City Council* [2010] EWCA Civ 63, [2010] ICR 708).

Care must also be taken in selecting the appropriate pools for comparison. In *Abbott v Cheshire & Wirral Partnership NHS Trust* [2006] EWCA Civ 523, [2006] IRLR 546 the Court of Appeal ruled that, while it was for the claimant in the first instance to select a pool for comparison, it was open to the employer to dispute the appropriateness of that pool, and it was for the tribunal to determine the appropriate pool for comparison purposes. The CJEU has noted that it is not permissible for a claimant to create the appearance of a difference in pay between groups of male and female employees by arbitrarily identifying as 'pools' a number of male employees who are paid more, and a number of female employees who are paid less. There has to be some connection between the employees in each group that means their circumstances can meaningfully be considered collectively: *Specialarbejder-forbundet i Danmark v Dansk Industri, acting for Royal Copenhagen A/S*: C-400/93 [1995] IRLR 648, CJEU, paragraph 36.

The proper approach to selection of the pool and statistical evidence was considered in *Secretary of State for Trade and Industry v Rutherford (No 2)*. This concerned a challenge to the upper age limit of 65 for unfair dismissal claims in *ss 109* and *156 ERA 1996* on the basis that it had a disparate impact on men which could not be objectively justified. The tribunal selected a pool consisting of those employees for whom retirement at 65 had 'some real meaning', being those aged 55 to 74. The Court of Appeal ([2004] EWCA Civ 1186, [2005] ICR 119) held that the tribunal had erred in law in concentrating on the 'disadvantaged group'. The Court of Appeal considered that the tribunal should have based its assessment of adverse impact on the statistics for the entire workforce to which the requirement of being under 65 applied and then primarily compared the respective proportions of men and women who could satisfy that requirement. Adopting this approach, the statistics clearly established that the difference in the working population between the proportion of men aged under 65 who could comply and the proportion of women under 65 who could comply was very small indeed. Accordingly, the complainants had failed to establish that there was any indirect sex discrimination against men in the imposition of the upper age limit. On appeal, the House of Lords ([2006] UKHL 19, [2006] IRLR 551) disagreed with the Court of Appeal's approach, but the judgments of their Lordships are not models of clarity as to the approach that is to be preferred. A majority of their Lordships rejected the classification of the case as one of (even potential) indirect discrimination. They each considered that this was not a case where one could speak coherently of those who are 'able to satisfy' a rule or requirement and those who are not. Since the rule in question simply imposes a disadvantage on those who stay in employment after the age of 65, there was therefore no comparison to be made since all men and all women over the age of 65 were equally disadvantaged. Lord Nicholls and Lord Walker, however, took a statistical approach as the Court of Appeal had done. However, unlike the Court of Appeal, they focused on the disadvantaged group (ie on the percentage of the workforce over 65), but emphasised how small this group was in comparison to the workforce as a whole. They noted that the proportion of the entire workforce affected by the age limit was 1.2%. 1.4% of the male workforce was affected, and 1% of the female workforce. Lords Walker and Nicholls considered that those proportions were simply too small to indicate a 'substantial' disadvantage to the male workforce.

In *Grundy v British Airways Plc* [2007] EWCA Civ 1020, [2008] IRLR 815 the Court of Appeal considered *Rutherford* and emphasised that the issue of whether or not there was a disparate impact was a question of fact in each case to be determined by the Tribunal. The Court observed that there was no rule as to what pool would or would not be appropriate, though care should be taken that the pool was not so small as to be unrepresentative or so large that like was not being compared with like. Similarly, there was no rule that one must always look at the advantaged or the disadvantaged groups. The job for the Tribunal is to identify a cohort within which the genuine material factor defence can be objectively tested. That means that employees within each pool chosen must share relevant characteristics and not exclude employees who also share those characteristics: *Cooksey (GMB Claimants) v Trafford BC* [2012] Eq LR 744 and *R (Unison) v Lord Chancellor (No 2)* [2015] ICR 390, DC.

While the Tribunal enjoys some latitude in its selection of pools, a Tribunal can still err in law by selecting the 'wrong' pool. In *Abbott v Cheshire* (supra), claims were brought by hospital domestic workers (almost entirely female) whose terms and conditions did not include a right to a bonus. They sought to compare themselves to hospital porters (entirely male) whose terms and conditions included a right to a bonus. The employers had argued that the proper comparator pool was not just the porters, but the porters and the catering staff. The catering staff were predominantly female and had also received bonuses. The Court of Appeal ruled that the tribunal had been wrong to reject the employer's argument as to pool: the three groups were plainly comparable. However, the Court of Appeal considered that the right result had been reached in any event because the porters and catering staff together were still 65% male in comparison to the domestic staff who were almost exclusively female: that was sufficient to establish a prima facie case of discrimination. The Court of Appeal also rejected an argument (based on *Specialarbejderforbundet i Danmark v Dansk Industri, acting for Royal Copenhagen A/S*: C-400/93 [1995] IRLR 648, CJEU) that the comparator group (of 37) was too small in order to establish a valid statistical difference in the proportions of male and female workers. The Court of Appeal considered that it would be wrong to set minimum numerical requirements because that would mean that indirect discrimination could never be established for small employers.

In *Pike v Somerset County Council* [2010] ICR 46, the CA considered a claim by a retired teacher who had returned to teaching part-time. She was unable to rejoin the Teachers' Pension Scheme and her service from then on did not count towards her pensionable employment. However, if she had returned to teaching full-time, she would have been able to rejoin the scheme. The competing pools comprised: (a) retired teachers who had returned to work, and (b) all members (whether or not retired) of the pension scheme. The CA held that the correct pool included retired teachers only. The pool was to be defined as a group in which all the members wanted a particular benefit, but the benefit was denied to some members because of a criterion applicable to the benefit. The members of the claimant's proposed pool, namely teachers returning after retirement, all wanted the benefit of their service being pensionable, but that benefit was denied to part-timers. Those who were members of the pension scheme but had not retired were uninterested in the post-retirement rules. They derived no advantage from the post-retirement rule favouring full-timers; it simply did not apply to them.

The introduction of equal pay questionnaires under the *Equal Pay (Questions and Replies) Order 2003* (see **22.29** below) assisted complainants with gathering appropriate statistics to show disparate impact and to enable complainants to pierce the culture of secrecy. However, the questionnaire procedure is not available for claims commenced after 25 April 2013 as *s 138* of the *EA 2010* was repealed by *s 66* of the *Enterprise and Regulatory Reform Act 2013*. The importance of transparency is nonetheless emphasised in the Equal Pay: Statutory Code of Practice published by the Equality and Human Rights Commission. Complainants may also find assistance in the results of 'equal pay audits' (see further below).

Note that under *s 77* of the *EA 2010* individuals are also protected from retaliation or victimisation where they seek, or provide, disclosures about the terms of their work (including how much they are paid) (*ss 77(4)* and *(5)*. Contractual terms purporting to restrict such disclosures will be void (*ss 77(1)* and *(2)*). In addition, *s 78* of the *EA 2010* makes provision (not yet in force, and the coalition government does not intend to bring it into force) requiring employers with 250 or more employees (and other employers who may be specified in delegated legislation) to publish information relating to the pay of employees for the purpose of showing whether there are differences in the pay of male and female employees.

22.12 Specific considerations in relation to the 'material factor' defence

The House of Lords in *Rainey v Greater Glasgow Health Board* [1987] ICR 129 resolved earlier doubts upon the matters which may be taken into account in considering a 'GMF defence under *s 1(3)* of the *EqPA 1970* in favour of holding that it is open to a tribunal to consider the merits of any factor advanced by an employer in support of such a defence, and the observations made in that case remain good law. At 140, Lord Keith stated:

> "The difference must be "material", which I would construe as meaning "significant and relevant", and it must be between "her case and his". Consideration of a person's case must necessarily involve consideration of all circumstances of that case. These may well go beyond what is not very happily described as "the personal equation", ie the personal qualities by way of skill, experience or training which the individual brings to the job. Some circumstances may on examination prove to be not significant or not relevant, but others may do so, though not relating to the personal qualities of the employee. In particular, where there is no question of intentional sex discrimination whether direct or indirect (and there is none here) a difference which is connected with economic factors affecting the efficient carrying on of the employer's business or other activity may well be relevant."

He held that the defence available in *EqPA 1970, s 1(3)* was equivalent in scope to the defence of justification held by the European court in *Bilka-Kaufhaus Gmbh v Weber von Hartz* C-170/84: [1987] ICR 110 to be available under *art 157*.

Although each case will therefore turn on its particular facts and circumstances, certain general points of principle have been considered in the cases as set out below.

Note that where, applying the 'structured approach' set out by the EAT in *Bury v Hamilton* (above, **22.10**), and now codified in *EA 2010, s 69*, it is necessary for the tribunal to consider whether a particular indirectly discriminatory situation or PCP is objectively justified, the approach to the question of justification should be the same as for any other case of discrimination, i.e. the employer must show that there is a legitimate aim and that the means used to achieve that aim are proportionate: see DISCRIMINATION AND EQUAL OPPORTUNITIES – II (12).

22.12   Equal Pay

Factors relevant to equal value as well as the 'material factor' defence

In *Davies v McCartneys* [1989] ICR 705, the EAT held that a defence was made out under s 1(3) despite the fact that some of the matters relied upon, such as circumstances in which the job was performed, were relevant to an assessment of whether the jobs were of equal value. In *Christie v John E Haith Ltd* [2003] IRLR 670, the EAT held that the mere fact that a particular factor may be relevant in the evaluation exercise to determine the question of equal value was not a ground for excluding it as part of a *s 1(3)* defence: the principle in *Davies v McCartneys* was not limited to cases where there had not actually been a determination of equal value taking into account the factors in question. Once an employee has shown that she is engaged on like work, work rated as equivalent to that of a man, or work of equal value to that of a man it is for the employer to prove that he has a defence under *s 1(3)* (*Financial Times Ltd v Byrne (No 2)* [1992] IRLR 163). See also *Kenny and ors v Minister for Justice, Equality and Law Reform* Case C 427/11 [2013] ICR D27 at §29 and *Angestelltenbetriebsrat der Wiener Gebeitskrankenkasse v Wiener Gebeitskrankenkasse* [1999] IRLR 804 at §29, where the CJEU holds that the fact that one group of employees doing a job has professional training and the other does not can both be a factor pointing to a finding that the employees are not doing 'like work' and a factor justifying any differential in pay.

The 'genuine' requirement

The factor relied upon must in fact be genuine and not a sham; see *Hartlepool Borough Council v Dolphin* [2009] IRLR 168 in which the EAT held the tribunal was entitled to find that productivity bonuses paid to men were a sham. The employer's assertion that an explanation was all that needed to be shown could not be accepted. The tribunal's task had been to determine whether the schemes had been genuine, by deciding whether they were intended to achieve and in fact achieved productivity improvements; its approach, in holding that the monitoring measures were not enough to satisfy it that the schemes were genuinely intended to improve productivity, was correct. Note, however, that tribunals should guard against using the word 'sham' unless there has actually been dishonesty on the part of the employer. If it is the case, for example, that productivity bonuses were justified when first introduced but cease to be so, that does not mean they are a 'sham', but merely that they are no longer justified: see *Bury Metropolitan Borough Council v Hamilton* [2011] ICR 655.

The 'genuine' requirement simply means that the factor relied on must truly be the reason for the difference in pay. Thus, for example, if there is evidence that women are systematically disadvantaged, it will not be acceptable to say simply that pay awards are based on the quality of work – it would be plain from the result that the system was being abusively applied (*Danfoss*).

Although the word 'genuine' (used in *EqPA 1970, s 1(3)*) does not appear in *EA 2010, s 69*, it is submitted that this is because the word is superfluous. Plainly an employer cannot establish a 'material factor' defence under the *EA 2010* unless there is genuinely (or truly) a material difference between a claimant's case and her comparator's that is not directly or indirectly discriminatory.

The distinction between the legitimate aim and the means used to achieve it

In considering whether a prima facie indirectly discriminatory measure is objectively justified (see above **22.11**), care must be taken in properly identifying and distinguishing the aim of the measure from the means used to achieve it. The fact that different measures with different aims could be introduced by an employer is not relevant in determining whether a particular measure with a legitimate aim is justified, what matters is whether there are more proportionate ways of achieving the aim of the measure in question: see *Blackburn v Chief Constable of West Midlands Police* [2008] EWCA Civ 1208, [2009] IRLR 135 (aim of rewarding those who did night work was legitimate and therefore it was proportionate to pay those persons more – it did not matter that other police forces had decided not to reward night workers). See also *Allen v GMB* [2008] IRLR 690. In that case the CA considered the situation of a union which had decided, in negotiating with an employer in relation to various pay issues, to adopt a policy whereby employees' interests in relation to future pay deals were prioritised over claims to back pay under the *EqPA 1970*. The result was that those employees who had equal pay claims (a predominantly female group) received less by way of settlement than they might otherwise have done. The Tribunal held that the union's objective (which it identified as being to achieve single status, avoiding privatisations, job losses, cuts in hours, and members receiving lower pay under the new system) was legitimate, but that the means used to achieve that aim amounted to 'manipulation' and were unjustified. One factor in the Tribunal's conclusion was that it was considered that the amount accepted by the Union in settlement of the equal pay claims was bordering on negligent. The EAT found that the Tribunal had taken the wrong approach to the question of objective justification. The EAT considered that, once it had been accepted that an aim was legitimate then if the means adopted to achieve that aim were the only means available then the policy would be justified. The CA disagreed and upheld the Tribunal's decision. The CA considered that the EAT had taken too narrow an approach to the concept of 'means'. The 'means' was not the balance struck by the union in the deal with the Council, but the methods used to persuade members to accept that deal. The Tribunal had been entitled to find that those methods had been manipulative and disproportionate to the legitimate aims pursued.

Timing of the justification/explanation

The material difference or factor relied upon must be one which exists throughout the period during which there is a difference in pay. For example, where a woman was appointed at a lower rate of pay than existing male employees because of financial constraints, there was no defence to her equal pay claim after those constraints had ceased to exist (*Benveniste v University of Southampton* [1989] ICR 617). However, where employees are on appointment placed at different points on a pay scale as a result of having different qualifications or experience, a continuing difference in pay as the employees move up that payscale as a result of annual increments will be lawful, provided that the continuing difference is wholly explained by the operation of the payscale and there was no discrimination in the initial decision as to where the employee was placed on the payscale on appointment: *Secretary of State for Justice (sued as National Offenders Management Service) v Bowling* [2012] IRLR 382. In that case the EAT said that that would even be the case if the employees' subsequent experience in the job meant that the man's initial advantage as a result of his qualifications and experience had been entirely wiped out by the woman's personal development in the role.

An initial difference in pay between male and female employees performing the same work cannot be justified on the basis of factors, such as a difference in performance levels, which become known only after the employees concerned have taken up their duties and which can only be assessed during the employment relationship (*Brunnhofer v Bank der Osterreichischen Postsparkasse AG*: C-381/99 [2001] IRLR 571, CJEU). However, such factors will obviously be relevant when what is complained about is the level of an annual bonus which is based on an assessment of an employee's performance during the year: *Villalba v Merrill Lynch & Co* [2006] IRLR 437.

'Red-circling' of existing pension entitlements will not amount to a genuine material factor where, although justifying an initial difference in pension entitlement, it does not provide justification for maintaining the differential over twenty years: *Home Office v Bailey* [2005] ICR 1057. See also *Cumbria County Council v Dow (No 1)* [2008] IRLR 91, EAT (difference in pay which arose from a bonus scheme originally designed to improve productivity was not objectively justified where the scheme had ceased to be effective and the bonus payments had in practice become automatic additions to the pay of the male comparators).

After-the-event justification

The Court of Appeal in *Cadman v Health and Safety Executive* [2004] EWCA Civ 1317, [2005] ICR 1546 reiterated that 'after the event' justification is permissible so that an employer may rely on matters which did not consciously and contemporaneously feature in its decision making at the time. The CJEU adopted the same approach in *Schönheit (Hilde) v Stadt Frankfurt am Main*: C-4/02 and C-5/02 [2003] ECR I-12575, [2004] IRLR 983. See also *Pulham v Barking and Dagenham London Borough Council* [2010] ICR 333 where the EAT held that an employer was not prevented from advancing a justification defence in respect of pay protection arrangements merely because they had not been "carefully costed and crafted" at the time of implementation.

Differences in hours worked

The House of Lords held in *Leverton v Clwyd County Council* [1989] ICR 33 that, if there was no significant difference between the hourly rates of pay of the applicant and her male comparator, it would be a legitimate, if not a necessary, inference that the difference between their total salaries was due to, and justified by, the difference in the number of hours worked. This approach was adopted by the CJEU in *Stadt Lengerich v Helmig* [1996] ICR 35 which held that, prima facie, there is unequal treatment wherever the overall pay of full-time employees is higher than that of part-time employees for the same number of hours worked. The CJEU determined that there was no discrimination where part-time employees only received pay at overtime rates once they had worked the equivalent of a full-time worker's ordinary weekly hours rather than once they had completed the number of hours which they themselves ordinarily worked each week.

Qualifications / training

In *Angestelltenbetriebsrat der Wiener Gebeitskrankenkasse v Wiener Gebeitskrankenkasse* [2000] ICR 1134 and *Kenny and ors v Minister for Justice, Equality and Law Reform* Case C 427/11 [2013] ICR D27 the CJEU accepted that differences in levels of professional training between the two groups of employees could justify differing levels of pay. Although a case concerned with alleged indirect race discrimination in relation to pay (and therefore not brought under the equal pay provisions of the *EA 2010*), *Greenland v Secretary of State for Justice* (UKEAT/0232/14/DA, 28 January 2015) is helpful here. That case concerned differences in pay between lay members of the Parole Board and the retired judges (all white males) who had been recruited to the Board. Among other things, the EAT considered that the differences in qualification, and the fact that the retired judges were able to chair oral hearings in a wider range of cases, meant that there were material differences between the retired judges and the lay members. See also the similarly unsuccessful case of *McGrath v Ministry of Justice* (UKEAT/0247/14/LA, 27 February 2015) concerning a claim by an employment tribunal lay member to a pension equivalent to that of the legally qualified tribunal judges.

The importance of transparency

The CJEU in *Danfoss* held that where an undertaking applies a system of pay which is totally lacking in transparency, it is for the employer to show that his practice concerning wages is not discriminatory. The Court of Appeal in *Calder v Rowntree Mackintosh Confectionery Ltd* [1993] ICR 811 apparently accepted that the transparency principle applied in English law, but held that it did not require the employer to explain exactly how a figure for shift premium was achieved. By contrast, in an important decision on City bonus payments, *Barton v Investec Henderson Crosthwaite Securities Ltd* [2003] ICR 1205, the EAT held that the tribunal erred in appearing to condone the lack of transparency in the employer's bonus system on the basis of its 'industrial knowledge' that the City 'bonus culture' was one of secrecy. Although the bonus claim was brought under the *SDA 1975*, the lack of transparency was also relevant to the material factor defence in the *EqPA* claim.

Note also that there have been obiter indications in UK authorities that, in cases where there is a challenge to a pay system which is alleged to be indirectly discriminatory, the clarity and simplicity of the system may amount to a material factor. Put another way, the material factor may consist of the 'administrative convenience' of operating a simple and straightforward system, or equally, the administrative inconvenience of having to alter it (cf Dillon and Hirst LJJ in *R v Secretary of State for Employment, ex p Equal Opportunities Commission* [1993] ICR 251, CA, and *Barry v Midland Bank plc* [1999] ICR 319, CA; the Court of Appeal's decision in *Barry* was upheld by the House of Lords ([1999] ICR 859), but on a different basis: their Lordships looked at the 'primary object' of the redundancy scheme in considering whether it was discriminatory, rather than reserving such issues to a consideration of whether the scheme could, if it had a disparate impact, be justified.

'Productivity bonuses' and attendance allowances

A number of cases have involved so-called 'productivity bonuses' and/or attendance allowances paid to male manual workers. See, for eg, *Degnan v Redcar & Cleveland Borough Council* [2005] EWCA Civ 726, [2005] IRLR 615; *Armstrong v Newcastle Upon Tyne NHS Hospital Trust* [2005] EWCA Civ 1608, [2006] IRLR 124; *South Tyneside Metropolitan Borough Council v Anderson* [2007] EWCA Civ 654, [2007] ICR 1581; *Bainbridge/Surtees* [2008] EWCA Civ 885; [2009] ICR 133; *Cumbria County Council v Dow and ors* [2008] IRLR 91; *Bury Metropolitan Borough Council v Hamilton* [2011] ICR 655; and *Gibson v Sheffield City Council* [2010] EWCA Civ 63, [2010] ICR 708; and *Sunderland City Council v Brennan* [2012] EWCA Civ 413, [2012] ICR 1216. Those cases show that in general employers have in practice found it difficult to justify bonuses that have applied to groups of (mainly) male workers but not to groups of (mainly) female workers. In such cases the tribunal will consider whether or not there was when the bonus was introduced, and whether there continues to be, a good reason for the payment of the bonus (e.g. performance improvement or maintaining productivity) or whether the bonus is in reality an 'attendance allowance' paid simply because the employee attends work (in which case it will not be justified). The tribunal will also consider whether or not a similar scheme could have been introduced for the female workers. However, even a finding that no similar scheme could have been introduced will not prevent the tribunal concluding that having the bonus for the male workers is not justified: see, eg, *Gibson v Sheffield City Council* [2010] EWCA Civ 63, [2010] ICR 708 (although note that in that case the tribunal had found that what were originally productivity bonuses had effectively become mere attendance allowances).

Seniority and length of service as factors

The CJEU has held that differences in seniority and length of service are generally material differences (not requiring special justification), at least where the employer is distinguishing between full-time workers (*Handels-Og Kontorfunktionaererernes Forbund i Danmark v Dansk Arbejdsgiverforening ('Danfoss')* [1991] ICR 74). In two subsequent cases, however, the CJEU appeared to doubt the correctness of *Danfoss* or at least have second thoughts as to its general application: see *Nimz v Freie und Hansestadt Hamburg*: C-184/89 [1991] ECR 1-297 and *Gerster v Freistaat Bayern*: C-1/95 [1998] ICR 327. In *Cadman v Health and Safety Executive* the Court of Appeal therefore referred the issue to the CJEU again. The CJEU (Case C-17/05, [2006] ICR 1623) affirmed that, as a general rule, an employer may rely on seniority and length of service as being genuine material differences not requiring special justification or (at least where pay is based on a job evaluation system) evidence that the individual in question has indeed acquired experience during his or her years in service. However, the CJEU made clear that, if the complainant provides evidence capable of giving rise to 'serious doubts' as to whether the criterion of length of service is, in the circumstances, appropriate to attain the legitimate objective of rewarding experience which enables the worker to perform his duties better, then the burden will shift to the employer to justify in detail reliance on the criterion of length of service by proving, as regards the job in question, that length of service goes hand in hand with experience and that experience enables the worker to perform his duties better. The CA in *Wilson v Health and Safety Executive* [2009] EWCA Civ 1074, [2010] ICR 302 clarified the approach that should be taken to domestic cases involving a length of service criterion in the light of the CJEU decision in *Cadman*. The CA ruled that, so far as domestic law is concerned, the "serious doubts" test put forward by the CJEU in *Cadman* is only of relevance before trial (presumably as a ground for 'strike out'). The CA said that what a claimant needs to show, pre-trial, is that there is evidence from which, if established at trial, it can properly be found that the general rule in *Danfoss* and *Cadman* (that seniority and length of service are generally material differences other than sex) does not apply. The CA confirmed, however, that a claim involving a length of service criterion is to be approached in essentially the same way as any other equal pay claim involving indirect discrimination. The burden is on the claimant to show disparate impact and, if that is established, the burden shifts to the employer either to explain or justify the difference as necessary (see further the discussion at 22.10 above). The CA noted (at 52) that the Tribunal had allowed the employer a 'margin of appreciation' in relation to objective justification in this case. The CA indicated that there was no error of law in that approach.

In *Secretary of State for Justice v Bowling* [2012] IRLR 382 the EAT (Underhill P presiding) held that a salary point scale applied by the civil service amounted to a good GMF defence. The salary scale explained the difference in pay between the claimant and her comparator. It continued to explain the differential throughout the claimant's employment and there was no reason to suppose that there was any sex taint in the application of the salary scale. A similar approach was adopted in *Skills Development Scotland Co Limited v Buchanan and others* [2011] EqLR 955 in which the EAT (Lady Smith presiding) held that transferred terms and conditions of employment which required future increases in salary amounted to a genuine material factor which explained the difference in pay throughout the period and which were not sex-tainted.

Market forces

One 'extrinsic factor' which may, in certain circumstances, justify a difference in pay is the scarcity of suitably qualified employees to fill a particular post. In such circumstances, an employer may be able to justify a resultant difference in pay as consisting of a necessary premium paid to obtain the scarce skills which the more highly paid employee has to offer (*Enderby v Frenchay Health Authority* [1994] ICR 112). See also *Greenland v Secretary of State for Justice* (UKEAT/0323/14/DA, 28 January 2015): although a claim in relation to race discrimination in pay, similar considerations apply to justification of 'prima facie' indirect discrimination. In that case, the EAT accepted that the higher pay paid to retired judges recruited to the Parole Board was justified by the urgent need to recruit more Board members with those qualifications in order to deal with the backlog of oral hearings.

Note that it is for the employer to show that the market dictated the higher rate of pay and not for the claimant to show that the pay was too high: see *Cumbria County Council v Dow and ors* [2008] IRLR 91, EAT. In *Ratcliffe v North Yorkshire County Council* (above) the women concerned, who were catering assistants, had been the subject of a job evaluation exercise. Their job had been rated as equivalent to that of certain other employees engaged in very different jobs and they had received the same pay. Their function was subject to competitive tendering. A competing company had much lower overheads as it paid its (largely female) staff lower wages than those paid by the Council. In order properly to compete, the Council believed it needed to reduce the pay of its own catering assistants. The majority of the tribunal found that whilst there was a material difference between the circumstances of the women and their comparators, namely that the women were employed in functions which had to be subjected to the market, the market itself was not sexually neutral and therefore the material difference was 'due to [a] difference in sex'. The catering sector was regarded as 'women's work' and the pay of those employed by the competing company, was discriminatorily low. The Court of Appeal disagreed (([1994] ICR 810). It found that the defence was made out on the controversial basis that even if the competing company's pay rates were discriminatory it did not follow that the Council discriminated if it lowered its own rates in order to compete. The decision of the House of Lords in *Ratcliffe* ([1995] ICR 833) is not a model of clarity. What is clear is that their Lordships found that the tribunal was entitled to reach the view that the defence had not been made out. It does not appear, however, that the basis of the decision was that the pay reduction was tainted by the competing company's discrimination. Lord Slynn noted (ibid, at 442): 'The fact, if it be a fact, that [the competing company] discriminated against women in respect of pay and that the [Council] had to pay no more than [the competing company] in order to be competitive does not however conclude the issue'. Unfortunately, it is not clear, from what follows, what their Lordships considered to be the conclusive factor. 'The basic question is whether the [Council] paid women less than men for work rated as equivalent. The reason they did so is certainly that they had to compete . . . The fact, however, is that they did pay women less than men engaged on work rated as equivalent. The employment tribunal found and was entitled to find that the employers had not shown that this was genuinely due to a material difference other than a difference of sex.' The decision does not, in the view of the author, mean that the need to establish or maintain a difference in pay will never found a successful *s 1(3)* defence, merely that the employer had not discharged the burden in the particular case.

Pay protection arrangements

In some cases where an employer has identified that there is an 'equal pay issue' as between two groups of employees, the employer has sought to equalise pay over the course of a number of years, by gradually reducing the pay of the highest-paid group, but in the meantime offering 'pay protection' to existing employees within that group. In *s 69(3)* of *EA 2010* a statutory basis for the lawfulness of 'pay protection' policies is provided. *Section 69(3)* provides that "the long-term objective of reducing inequality between men's and women's terms of work is always to be regarded as a legitimate aim". However, it does not follow that an employer who has made use of a pay protection policy will be able to succeed in the material factor defence. Employment tribunals are likely to scrutinise carefully a pay protection policy, in order to determine whether or not it is proportionate as to achieving any legitimate aim, particularly where the employer has already recognised that differentials in pay are tainted by historic discrimination.

In *Bainbridge v Redcar and Cleveland Borough Council/Surtees v Middlesbrough Borough Council (Bainbridge/Surtees)* [2008] EWCA Civ 885, [2009] ICR 133, the Council sought to justify a four-year 'pay protection' scheme introduced in the aforementioned circumstances on grounds that may broadly be described as cost (ie because it would have been too expensive to pay the predominantly female group more) and employee relations (ie in relation to the predominantly male group). However, the CA (and EAT) approved the Tribunal's finding that the Council had failed to establish the genuine material factor defence because the 'pay protection' policy was irredeemably tainted by sex discrimination as it amounted to perpetuating the benefit of the past sex discrimination. The Council's argument was that there was nothing inherently discriminatory in providing a 'soft landing' to protect employees from a sudden and drastic drop in pay. The Court of Appeal rejected the claimants' argument that as a matter of law, giving pay protection to the beneficiaries of past pay discrimination was always a breach of the *EqPA 1970*. However, the Court of Appeal also rejected the Council's argument that there was no *prima facie* sex discrimination in respect of the pay protection and held that the tribunal was right to look at the underlying reason for the pay protection and to find that it was causally related to historic unlawful sex discrimination. The burden of proof then shifted to the Council to objectively justify this *prima facie* discrimination. The Court of Appeal's judgment is not wholly clear as to when and how this can be justified, holding both that: (a) justification will be difficult where the employer knew or strongly suspected that there was past pay discrimination (see paragraph 133 of *Bainbridge/Surtees*), and/or (b) where the employer knows it is perpetuating past discrimination this can be justified if it considers the matter carefully and there is a good reason for pay protection to be offered only to the losers (paragraphs 149, 156 and 173 of *Bainbridge/Surtees*). Although the Court of Appeal in *Bainbridge/Surtees* was keen to stress the point made in the EAT that its decision did not rule out all 'pay protection' policies, its decision in practice left employers conducting a job evaluation scheme in a Catch 22 situation; the 'losers' will be unhappy if they do not receive 'pay protection' but the 'winners' will be unhappy at what they now see as historic pay discrimination.

In *Bury Metropolitan Borough Council v Hamilton* [2011] ICR 655 the EAT sought to clarify the approach that should be taken to pay protection cases. The EAT ruled that in any case where past direct discrimination has been 'recognised', the continuation for the future of such discrimination in the form of transitional or phasing-out arrangements cannot be justified. However, transitional arrangements that continue past indirect discrimination (as to which see below) will not be unlawful if they can be justified. In order to establish justification, the employer will need in all cases to advance cogent and specific reasons for the pay protection arrangements. Where cost is relied on as a reason for justifying the arrangements, evidence of the costs themselves and the financial context must be adduced. Mere assertions of unaffordability will not suffice. The tribunal will need to apply the proportionality test. In doing so it will be relevant to consider the employer's state of knowledge about the discriminatory effect of his provisions and the extent to which he tries to minimise that effect. See also *Macdonald and ors v Glasgow City Council* (12 May 2015), UKEATS/0008/14/BI, UKEATS/0009/14/BI and UKEATS/0011/14/BI.

Audit Commission v Haq (S) [2012] EWCA Civ 1621, [2013] IRLR 206 is another case in which pay protection arrangements were held to be pursuing a legitimate aim and to be justified. In that case, the EAT overturned the ET's decision on this point, and the EAT's judgment on this issue was upheld by the CA on appeal. The CA held that the ET had been wrong in law in rejecting the Commission's aims in this regard as illegitimate. The CA also considered that it was legitimate for an employer to take into account that without the pay protection arrangements the Commission might have been prejudiced as a result of losing the services of the employees in question.

See also *Naeem v Secretary of State for Justice* [2017] UKSC 27, [2017] 1 WLR 1343 which was a religious discrimination case rather than an equal pay case, but the Supreme Court's observations about the transitional pay protection arrangements for prison service chaplains are potentially relevant to equal pay too, albeit somewhat out of line with existing authority in this field. The Court observed (at paragraph 47) that where a case concerned the lawfulness of a transitional scheme, "the question was not whether the original pay scheme could be justified but whether the steps being taken to move towards the new system were proportionate. Where part of the aim is to move towards a system which will reduce or even eliminate the disadvantage suffered by a group sharing a protected characteristic, it is necessary to consider whether there were other ways of proceeding which would eliminate or reduce the disadvantage more quickly. Otherwise it cannot be said that the means used are "no more than necessary" to meet the employer's need for an orderly transition. . . . The burden of proof is on the respondent, although it is clearly incumbent upon the claimant to challenge the assertion that there was nothing else the employer could do. Where alternative means are suggested or are obvious, it is incumbent upon the tribunal to consider them."

Two CJEU cases on the justification of pay arrangements and transitional pay arrangements that are directly discriminatory on grounds of age also provide relevant guidance in this area. *Schmitzer v Bundesministerin für Inneres* (Case C-530/13) [2015] IRLR 331 concerned the pay scheme for Austrian civil servants. The CJEU accepted that on changing pay systems, pay protection arrangements intended to protect the rights of those acquired under the previous system pursued a legitimate aim. However, the CJEU emphasised that such arrangements would only be justified for a transitional period and that accordingly the Austrian arrangements (which perpetuated the previous discrimination indefinitely) were

Pay after the end of the protected period – Fourthly, where a term of a woman's work provides for pay after the end of the protected period, but does not provide for it to be subject to an increase to which it would have been subject had she not been on maternity leave, then the maternity equality clause modifies that term so as to provide for such an increase: *s 74(8)* (and see formerly *s 1(2)(f)* of the *EqPA 1970*).

The maternity equality clause as enacted in the *EqPA 1970* and the *EA 2010* is intended to reflect certain principles established by the case law under *art 157* decided prior to 2005. Other aspects of that case law have not been incorporated into the maternity equality clause and thus the case law discussed below remains relevant.

The story begins with the decision of the CJEU in *Gillespie v Northern Health and Social Services Board: C-342/93* [1996] ICR 498. At that time women whose pay was reduced when they were suspended on maternity grounds could not seek to challenge the reduction by bringing claims under *EqPA 1970*. The CJEU held that this position was compatible with *art 157*: a woman absent on maternity leave is not entitled to full pay. Women taking maternity leave are in a unique position which is not comparable with that of a man actually at work (see **11.9 DISCRIMINATION AND EQUAL OPPORTUNITIES – I**). However, the CJEU has confirmed that this does not mean that a woman is excluded from all equal pay rights while on maternity leave.

Thus increases in pay awarded during a woman's maternity leave must be taken into account when calculating the amount of maternity pay to which a woman is entitled, regardless of whether that increase is backdated to the reference period for calculating statutory maternity pay (as it was in *Gillespie*) or is awarded with only prospective effect at any time up until the end of the maternity leave (*Alabaster v Woolwich plc and Secretary of State for Social Security: C-147/02* [2005] ICR 695 and *Alabaster v Barclays Bank (No 2)* [2005] EWCA Civ 508, [2005] ICR 1246). This principle is reflected in the now statutory maternity equality clause.

In *Edwards v Derby City Council* [1999] ICR 114, the EAT considered an unusual case in which the male comparator was in receipt of full pay even though he was not at work. The complainant was a teacher absent on maternity leave and in receipt of half-pay. Her maternity leave overlapped with a half-term holiday. Had she not been absent on maternity leave, she would have received full pay without having to attend work. The EAT rejected her claim that she should have received full pay during the half-term period, relying on *Gillespie* as authority for the proposition that a woman absent on maternity leave was in a unique position which could not be compared with that of those working normally even if, in the particular circumstances, that might include periods in which no actual duties were performed. The decision was made, however, before the CJEU gave its ruling in *Boyle v Equal Opportunities Commission: C-411/96* [1999] ICR 360. In that case, EOC employees absent on maternity leave were entitled to three months' full pay and thereafter a period at a reduced rate. Those absent as a result of sickness were entitled to six months' full pay. In the fourth month of an absence, therefore, an employee absent through sickness would receive more than an employee absent on maternity leave. An employee fell sick during her maternity leave and wished to be put on sick leave. The EOC's contract of employment allowed the employee to move onto sick leave but only on the basis that the maternity leave was terminated. The CJEU decided that the provision was discriminatory. The employee had to be allowed to swap into a period of sick leave and then to swap back. *Boyle* is an example of a case where it has been decided, in effect, that though a pregnant woman is not comparable to a man with an illness, a pregnant woman with an illness may be treated as being comparable (see also *Handels-og Kontorfunktionaernes Forbund I Danmark, acting on behalf of Hoj Pederson v Faelesforeningen for Danmarks Brugsforninger, acting on behalf of Kvickly Skive: C-66/760* [1999] IRLR 55: national legislation providing that men who are unfit to work through illness should receive full pay but women absent from work as a result of a pregnancy-related condition should not, is contrary to *art 157*; *Osterreichischer*

22.13 Equal Pay

Gewerkschaftsbund v Wirtschaftskammer Osterreich (2004) 760 IDS Brief, p 9: period of voluntary parental leave not comparable to compulsory military or civilian service; cf also *P & O European Ferries (Dover) Ltd v Iverson* (1999) IDS Brief 640, p 6).

In *Abdoulaye v Regie National des Usines Renault SA*: C-218/98 [2001] ICR 527, the CJEU had to consider a provision in a collective agreement which governed the terms and conditions of Renault employees. Female employees not only continued to receive their full salary whilst on maternity leave but also received a lump sum to compensate them for the 'occupational disadvantages' that arose from their absence. Male employees argued that new fathers should receive the same bonus. However, the court decided that men were not subject to the same disadvantages. Unlike the women, they did not lose the chance of promotion or the right to performance-related pay for the period of maternity leave, nor did they suffer the resulting loss in the length of service.

The CJEU considered yet another variation on the theme of payments due or refused to those on maternity leave in *Lewen v Denda*: C-333/97 [2000] ICR 648. A firm paid Christmas bonuses to those in 'active' employment on 1 December each year. The complainant was absent on maternity leave on the relevant date. She was refused a bonus and claimed that her employers had breached *art 157*. The court felt that the result hinged upon the nature of the payment. A requirement that an employee should be in active employment was not discriminatory if the purpose of the payment was to encourage those at work to be loyal and to work hard in the following year. If, on the other hand, the purpose of the payment was to reward the employees for having worked hard in the previous year, it would be discriminatory to refuse to make any payment at all to those absent on parental leave. An employer could legitimately pro-rate the bonus to take account of the employee's absence from work, provided no account was taken of any period during which, by reason of her pregnancy, the employee was prohibited from attending work. For an example of a permissible proportionate reduction in bonus paid in recognition of work undertaken by the workforce during a period of ordinary maternity leave, see also, *Hoyland v Asda Stores Ltd* [2006] IRLR 468 (Court of Session). Specific provision in relation to bonuses is now made in the maternity equality clause.

Gruber v Silhouette International Schmeid GmbH & Co KG: C-249/97 [1999] ECR I-5295 was a case concerned with termination payments. In Austria, those who simply resign from employment receive no payment. However, those who resign for 'important reasons' and who have been employed for more than three years receive a payment. The European court determined that the 'important reasons' justifying payments had in common that they were all either concerned with poor working conditions or with misconduct on the part of the employer. Those who work for longer than five years and resign within a certain period after childbirth receive smaller payments. The complainant, who resigned after having had a child, argued that she should be entitled to compare herself with those who resigned for 'important reasons' and to pay her a reduced sum resulted in discrimination contrary to *art 157*. The court rejected her argument. Her situation was not analogous to that of someone who resigned because of poor working conditions or employer misconduct. That being so, her proposed comparison, and thus her claim, was ill-founded.

The suggestion in *Gillespie* that women absent on maternity leave are not entitled to receive pay is subject to an important qualification. The CJEU did suggest in *Gillespie* that 'the amount payable [to a woman absent on maternity leave] could not . . . be so low as to undermine the purpose of maternity leave, namely the protection of women before and after giving birth'. The *Pregnant Workers Directive EEC/92/85* requires member states to provide that women absent from work on maternity leave receive an 'adequate allowance' for 14 weeks (*arts 8(1)* and *11(2)(b)*). An allowance will be adequate provided that it is at least equivalent to what the employee would receive if she were absent through illness. In effect it requires that SMP should be at least as generous as SSP. A number of cases have since raised claims that sums received by the complainants during maternity leave did not amount to an 'adequate allowance'. In *Iske v P & O European Ferries (Dover) Ltd* [1997] IRLR 401, the EAT was asked to consider the adequacy of SMP. It declined to do so, although it suggested that it might have been prepared to consider the issue had the respondent been an emanation of the state. In *Gillespie v Northern Health and Social Services Board (No 2)* [1997] IRLR 410, the Northern Ireland Court of Appeal rejected a complaint that an employee's contractual maternity payments were less generous than contractual sick pay on the ground that the *Directive* merely required the payment to be more than SSP. In *Banks v Tesco Stores Ltd* [1999] ICR 1141, the EAT considered a case where an employee received no SMP at all. This was because, as her previous earnings were less than the lower earnings limit, she did not qualify for SMP. Notwithstanding that she was receiving nothing at all, the EAT declined to conclude that this was a case in which the amount received was so low as to undermine the purpose of maternity leave. The EAT relied on the fact that *art 11* of the *Pregnant Worker's Directive* allows member states to impose conditions upon entitlement to maternity pay. If the *Directive* allowed it, reasoned the EAT, it could not be read as contravening *art 157*. Where the maternity pay received by the employee is determined by reference to full pay, pay rises should be reflected in the level of maternity pay, even where the rises take place while the woman is away on maternity leave and after the reference period used to calculate the level of maternity pay (*Alabaster v Woolwich plc and Secretary of State for Social Security: c-147/02* [2005] ICR 695 and *Alabaster v Barclays Bank (No 2)* [2005] EWCA Civ 508, [2005] ICR 1246; though cf *Clark v Secretary of State for Employment* [1997] ICR 64, CA).

22.14   EQUAL PAY AND PENSIONS

The principles applicable to retirement and pensions have evolved slowly and continue to evolve. Prior to the decision in *Barber v Guardian Royal Exchange Assurance Group: C-262/88* [1990] ICR 616 domestic legislation on the matter was piecemeal. Following *Barber* (and the flurry of CJEU decisions which followed it: see below **22.5**) the UK was forced to rethink its approach. The fruits of this re-consideration were the *Occupational Pension Schemes (Equal Access to Membership) Amendment Regulations 1995 (SI 1995/1215)* and, subsequently, the *Pensions Act 1995*. Now those provisions are consolidated in the *EA 2010*. (For the position under the previous legislation, readers are referred to earlier editions of this book.)

The first part of this section is devoted to describing the statutory regime which was in force prior to the implementation of the *EA 2010* since a considerable number of cases are still in the employment tribunal system that relate to periods of service before either *SI 1995/1215* or *PA 1995* came into force or are based instead, like *Barber*, on *art 157*.

22.15   The legislation

There has, traditionally, been an inequality between men and women in the age at which they are expected to retire. The State pension was, until recently, payable to women who were aged 60 or older, whereas men did not receive corresponding benefits until aged 65. *PA 1995* provides for the progressive implementation of a common age of entitlement to State retirement benefits of 65 over a period of 10 years beginning on 6 April 2010 (*PA 1995, s 126*). Employers, however, have been prohibited from discriminating, either directly or indirectly, in relation to the age at which employees are required to retire since 7 February 1987 (*SDA 1986, s 2(1)*; see now *EA 2010, s 13* and Discrimination and Equal Opportunities – I (11)). If an employer chooses to adopt a retirement age (and many do not, given this is now direct age discrimination which must be justified: see generally Retirement (42)), an employer is not obliged to have a common retiring age for all its employees. It can provide for different ages to apply to different jobs if it can justify that direct age discrimination, but it should be aware that if the employees performing a particular job are predominantly of one sex, there is a risk of a claim of indirect sex discrimination (as well as direct age discrimination).

22.15 Equal Pay

Where an employer provides its employees with access to an occupational pension scheme (see RETIREMENT (42)), a 'non-discrimination rule' in *s 61* of the *EA 2010* prohibits discrimination in relation to access to membership of the scheme and to the benefits payable thereunder in respect of nearly all the protected characteristics covered by the *EA 2010*, i.e. age, disability, gender reassignment, marriage and civil partnership, race, religion or belief and sexual orientation. (See **12.35** DISCRIMINATION AND EQUAL OPPORTUNITIES – **II (12)** and *EA 2010, s 61*.) As with pay, however, slightly different provision is made in respect of sex and pregnancy/maternity discrimination in the operation of pension schemes. The legislation creates statutory sex equality and maternity equality rules as set out below. Where these rules apply (or would apply but for the exceptions in *Part 2* of *Sch 7*), the general non-discrimination rule does not: see *s 61(10)*). Thus the general non-discrimination rule only applies to occupational pension schemes where the sex equality rule under *s 67* or the maternity equality rule under *s 75* does not.

22.16 *Sex discrimination*

Section 67 of *EA 2010* provides for a 'sex equality rule' to be implied into all occupational pension schemes that do not already contain such a rule (*s 67(1)*). The sex equality rule applies both to terms on which people become members of the scheme, and the terms on which members of the scheme are treated, or any dependant who may benefit from the scheme (*s 67(3)* and *67(5)*). It also applies to the exercise of any discretion in relation to the way in which persons become members of the scheme or the way in which members of the scheme are treated, or any dependant who may benefit from the scheme (*s 67(4)* and *67(6)*).

The sex equality rule modifies any term of a scheme that would result in less favourable treatment of a man in comparison to woman (or vice versa) so as to ensure that the treatment is not less favourable (*s 67(2)(a)* and *s 64*). Similarly, it modifies any discretion so that it cannot be exercised in a way that would result in less favourable treatment (*s 67(2)(b)* and *s 64*).

As with the provisions relating to equal pay, the sex equality rule only operates where the man and woman are:

(i)   Employed in the same employment or on common terms and conditions: see *EA 2010, s 79* and above **22.9**; and

(ii)   Do equal work, i.e. like work, work rated as equivalent or work of equal value: see *ss 64* and *65* of the *EA 2010* and above **22.5**.

Again, as with the provisions relating to equal pay, the sex equality rule has no effect if the trustees or managers of the scheme in question are able to show that the difference in treatment between the man and the woman is because of a material factor that is not the difference of sex: *s 69(4)*. In other words, the material factor defence is available to a complaint of sex discrimination in relation to an occupational pension scheme as it is in relation to pay and the case law discussed above at **22.10–22.11** will apply equally here.

By *s 67(7)* it is expressly provided that if the effect of the term or the discretion differs according to a person's family, marital or civil partnership status, then the comparison for the purposes of the sex equality rule must be with persons of the opposite sex who share the same status (thus preventing the section from applying 'by the back door' to sexual orientation or marital status discrimination).

In accordance with the decisions of the CJEU in *Barber v Guardian Royal Exchange Assurance Group* (see below) and *Defrenne v Sabena* (see below) the sex equality rule does not operate on discriminatory terms relating to access to the pension scheme in respect of pensionable service prior to 8 April 1976 (*s 67(9)*) or on discriminatory terms relating to the way in which members of the scheme are treated in respect of benefits accruing from pensionable service prior to 17 May 1990 (*s 67(10)*). However, note that the CJEU has made it clear that the temporal limitation to 17 May 1990 in the Barber case does not apply to a 'benefits' claim which is made ancillary to an 'admissions' or 'access' claim (*Dietz v Stichting Thuiszorg Rotterdam*: C-435/93 [1996] IRLR 692). In the light of this decision, a question arises as to whether the *EA 2010* (and the *PA 1995* before that) properly implements EU law.

Section 68 of the *EA 2010* further provides a power for trustees and managers of an occupational pension scheme to make alterations to the scheme (including retrospective alterations: *s 68(4)*) to make it compliant with the sex equality rule. The power is available if the trustees and managers do not already have such power under the terms of the scheme, or if they do have such power under the terms of the scheme, but the procedure for using it would be unduly complex or protracted, or involve obtaining consents which cannot be obtained or which can be obtained only with undue delay or difficulty.

By virtue of *para 4* of *Part 2* of *Sch 7* to the *EA 2010* the Secretary of State may prescribe circumstances in which a man and woman may lawfully receive different amounts by way of pension where that difference is attributable only to differences in the state retirement pension to which men and women are entitled. The *Equality Act 2010 (Sex Equality Rule) (Exceptions) Regulations 2010/2132* duly prescribes for differences in pension to be permitted for bridging pensions and as a result of differences in indexation. Readers are referred to the text of *regs 2* and *3* of those *Regulations* for details.

Further, by virtue of *para 5* of *Part 2* of *Sch 7* to the *EA 2010*, a difference between men and women in relation to the calculation of employer's pension contributions or determination of benefits payable under the scheme is permitted if the difference results from the application of prescribed actuarial factors which differ for men and women. *Reg 4* of the *Equality Act 2010 (Sex Equality Rule) (Exceptions) Regulations 2010/2132* prescribes that different actuarial factors may be applied in respect of the average life expectancy of men and women where they are applied with a view to providing equal periodical pension benefits for men and women.

22.17 *Pregnancy and maternity discrimination*

The maternity equality rule in *EA 2010, s 75* has effect as follows in relation to any occupational scheme that does not already contain such a rule:

(a)   If a 'relevant term' of the scheme does not treat time when the woman is on maternity leave as it treats time when she is not, the term is modified so as to treat time when she is on maternity leave as time when she is not (*s 75(3)*);

(b)   If a term confers a 'relevant discretion' capable of being exercised so that time when she is on maternity leave is treated differently from time when she is not, the term is modified so as not to allow the discretion to be exercised in that way (*s 75(4)*).

A term is 'relevant' for this purpose if it is: (a) a term relating to membership of the scheme, (b) a term relating to the accrual of rights under the scheme, or (c) a term providing for the determination of the amount of a benefit payable under the scheme (*s 75(5)*). A discretion is 'relevant' for this purpose if its exercise is capable of affecting (a) membership of the scheme, (b) the accrual of rights under the scheme, or (c) the determination of the amount of a benefit payable under the scheme (*s 75(6)*).

The maternity equality rule does not, however, require the woman's contributions to the scheme in respect of time when she is on maternity leave to be determined otherwise than by reference to the amount she is paid in respect of that time (*s 75(7)*) (pay for this purpose includes statutory maternity pay: see *s 75(10)*).

There are also temporal limitations on the application of the maternity equality rule. First, so far as relating to time when she is on ordinary maternity leave but is not being paid by her employer, the maternity equality rule applies only in a case where the expected week of

22.17 Equal Pay

childbirth began on or after 6 April 2003 (i.e. after the coming into force of the *Maternity and Parental Leave (Amendment) Regulations 2002*) (*s 75(8)*). Secondly, so far as relating to time when she was on additional maternity leave but not being paid by her employer, the maternity equality rule (a) does not apply to the accrual of rights under the scheme in any case; and (b) applies for other purposes only in a case where the expected week of childbirth began on or after 5 October 2008 (ie after the amendments made on that date to the *Maternity and Parental Leave Regulations 1999* and the *Paternity and Adoption Leave Regulations 2002*).

22.18 *Enforcement and remedies*

Complaints of breach of the sex or maternity equality rules may be made in the same way as complaints of breach of the sex equality clause and the provisions in relation to enforcement set out below at **22.21**ff apply equally to pension complaints. In addition, by *s 127(4)* an employment tribunal has jurisdiction to determine an application by the trustees or managers of an occupational pension scheme for a declaration as to their rights and those of a member in relation to a dispute about the effect of an equality rule. In any proceedings before an employment tribunal relating to a breach of an equality rule, the employer is to be treated as a party (i.e. in addition to the trustees and managers of the occupational pension scheme) and is accordingly entitled to appear and be heard (*s 127(8)*).

The remedies available in a 'pensions case' are governed by *ss 133* and *134* of *EA 2010*. By *s 133(2)* if a court or tribunal finds there has been a breach of an equality clause or rule in relation to an occupational pension scheme, the court or tribunal may make a declaration as to the rights of the parties, but must not order arrears of benefits or damages or any other amount to be paid to the complainant unless the complainant is already a 'pensioner member' (i.e. in receipt of pension under the scheme): *s 133(3)*. Where the complainant is a pensioner member then they may be awarded arrears of benefits or compensation (*s 134(2)(b)*), provided that any such award is limited to the period of 6 years before the day on which the proceedings were commenced in a 'standard case', or the day on which the breach first occurred in a 'concealment' or 'incapacity' case (*s 133(4)* and *(5)* and see below **22.22**).

Where a declaration is made, it may relate to a specified period or time, provided that (in the case of declarations as to whether a person should be admitted to the scheme) the time in question is not before 8 April 1976 (*s 133(4)* and *(5)*), or (in the case of declarations as to terms on which a person may become a member of a scheme) the period in question does not begin before 17 May 1990 (*s 133(6)* and *(7)*). If the court or tribunal makes such a declaration, or awards arrears of benefit to a pension member, then the employer is required to contribute to the scheme whatever amount is necessary to enable the complainant to receive a pension on the declared terms, or to receive the arrears of benefit awarded, without the complainant or any other member being required to make further contribution: *s 133(8)* and *s 134(4)*.

See also **13.22** DISCRIMINATION AND EQUAL OPPORTUNITIES – III

22.19 Barber and claims based on art 157

The impetus for the statutory scheme described above, and now consolidated in the *EA 2010*, came from Europe. *Directive 86/378/EEC* required member states to introduce measures providing for equal rights to membership of occupational pension schemes by 1 January 1993. The UK had drafted legislation which was set out at *Social Security Act 1989, Sch 5* but before it could be brought into force it was overtaken by events, specifically the decision of the CJEU in *Barber*. The CJEU decided that pensions from both contributory and non-contributory schemes were 'pay' within the meaning of *art 157* in that they were deferred pay for services rendered during employment. The effect of the decision was that an obligation not to discriminate in relation to access to, or benefits under, a pension scheme was found already to exist without the need for implementing domestic legislation.

The potential consequences of the decision were so great that the CJEU took the unusual step of specifically limiting the effect of its decision by stating that it could not be relied upon to claim entitlement to a pension with effect from a date prior to 17 May 1990 (the date of the decision) unless the applicant had already commenced proceedings by that date. It was not initially clear whether the limitation excluded all claims relating to periods of service before the stipulated date or only those where the benefits arising out of such service were also payable prior to 17 May 1990. The precise scope of the limitation was later clarified in *Ten Oever v Stichting Bedrijfspensioenfonds voor het Glazenwassers- en Schoonmaakbedrijf*: C-109/91 [1995] ICR 74, in which the CJEU determined that *Barber* only applied to benefits payable in respect of periods of service after 17 May 1990 (but cf *Dietz v Stichting Thuiszord Rotterdam*: C-435/93 [1996] IRLR 692 below).

The *Barber* decision is now reflected in Protocol no. 33 to the consolidated (Lisbon) Treaty on the Functioning of the European Union as follows:

'For the purposes of Article 157 of the Treaty on the Functioning of the European Union, benefits under occupational social security schemes shall not be considered as remuneration if and in so far as they are attributable to periods of employment prior to 17 May 1990, except in the case of workers or those claiming under them who have before that date initiated legal proceedings or introduced an equivalent claim under the applicable national law.'

The *Barber Protocol* applies only to claims relating to the level of benefit provided and not to claims alleging denial of access to benefits. For instance, the formerly commonplace refusal of pension schemes to admit part-time workers was indirectly discriminatory on grounds of sex. Where a former part-time employee complains that she was refused access to membership, the *Protocol* does not apply and her claim may, subject to any other domestic limitations, go back as far as 8 April 1976, that being the date on which the CJEU gave its decision in *Defrenne* (*Deutsche Telekom AG v Schröder*: C-50/96 [2002] 2 CMLR 583) (see also below **22.21**). Surprisingly, the CJEU has also held that the *Barber* limitation does not apply to any ancillary claim for non-payment of benefits (*Dietz v Stichting Thuiszorg Rotterdam*: C-298/94 [1996] IRLR 692). A woman seeking a remedy in respect of such a denial of access to membership must pay the contributions which she would have paid had she been admitted to membership at the appropriate time if she is to be entitled to any benefits under the scheme in respect of the period of her exclusion (*Fisscher v Voorhuis Hengelo BV*: C-128/93 [1995] ICR 635).

The temporal limitations established in the *Barber* and *Defrenne* judgments are now reflected in specific provisions in the *EA 2010, ss 67(9)* and *(10)*. However, the principles established in the *Dietz* and *Fisscher* judgments have not been reflected in the *EA 2010* (nor were they reflected in the legislative scheme that preceded the *EA 2010*). A similar temporal limitation also applies to claims based on the *Part-time Workers Regulations* and governing *Directive 98/23*, which only enable equivalence to be claimed in respect of periods of service after those Regulations came into force on 7 April 2000: *Ministry of Justice v O'Brien* [2015] EWCA Civ 1000, [2016] ICR 182 (although note that the outcome of an appeal to the Supreme Court in that case is awaited).

Following the Barber decision, a number of cases were referred to the CJEU with the intention of clarifying the difficult issues left unresolved by the Barber decision itself. The following matters have now been settled. Benefits payable to survivors fall within *art 157* (*Ten Oever v Stichting Bedrijfspensioenfonds voor het Glazenwassers en Schoonmaakbedrijf*: C-109/91 [1995] ICR 74) as do benefits payable under non-contracted out supplementary schemes (*Moroni v Collo GmbH*: C-110/91 [1995] ICR 137). Benefits payable under schemes which have at all times been 'single sex' are not within art 157, nor are benefits payable as a result of contributions made by employees on a voluntary basis (*Coloroll Pension Trustees Ltd v Russell*: C-200/91 [1995] ICR 179).

22.19   Equal Pay

In *Quirk v Burton Hospitals NHS Trust* [2002] EWCA Civ 149, [2002] ICR 602, the Court of Appeal had to consider the effect of a provision in the *National Health Service Pension Scheme Regulations 1995* (*SI 1995/300*). Formerly, female members of the NHS Pension scheme could, in certain circumstances, retire early at 55. Men could only take early retirement once they were 60. The *1995 Regulations* corrected this discriminatory situation by providing that both men and women could retire at 55. However, whereas a woman retiring at 55 received a pension calculated by reference to her whole period of service, a man doing the same would receive a pension calculated by reference only to his service since 17 May 1990. Unsurprisingly, the woman's pension would be greater than that of a man with a comparable length of service. A male complainant sought to argue that the *1995 Regulations* were incompatible with *art 157*. He contended that the provision had the effect of precluding him from access to benefits in respect of his pre-1990 service. The Court of Appeal decided that, properly analysed, the case was not an 'access to benefits' case at all. The complainant was a member of the scheme. The contentious provision simply resulted in his receiving less money. It was, therefore, a 'level of benefit' case and the *Barber Protocol* applied. Lord Justice Buxton opined that the 'access'/'level of benefit' dichotomy was an unhelpful basis for analysis. The tribunal should ask itself whether the alleged discrimination relates to an age condition which varies according to sex. If it does, it is a case to which the *Barber Protocol* applies.

Where a member state provides for men and women to become entitled to a State pension at different ages (eg in the UK women used to become so entitled at 60 whereas men became entitled at 65, although the *Pensions Act 1995* provides for progressive implementation of a common age of entitlement of 65 over a period of 10 years beginning on 6 April 2010), occupational pension schemes sometimes provide for payment of a 'bridging pension', the purpose of which is to ensure that employees, of whichever sex, receive the same total sum by way of pension when their State entitlements are aggregated to their entitlements under the scheme. Between the ages of 60 and 65 in the UK male and female employees would, under such a scheme, receive the same total sum but the male employees would receive substantially more from their employers. It follows, therefore, that under a 'bridging pension' male employees will receive more 'pay' than their female colleagues over the period. However, the State pension is not 'pay' for the purposes of *art 157* (see further **22.3** above). In *Roberts v Birds Eye Walls Ltd*: C-132/92 [1994] ICR 338 the CJEU held that it is not contrary to *art 157* to take account of an employee's entitlement to a State pension when calculating benefits payable under a bridging pension; see also *Trustees of Uppingham School Retirement Benefit Scheme for Non-Teaching Staff v Shillcock* [2002] EWHC 641 (Ch), [2002] IRLR 702. Inequality of employer's contributions to a scheme (as opposed to the benefits payable to the employee under the scheme) which result from the use of different actuarial factors for men and women is not contrary to *art 157* (*Neath v Hugh Steeper Ltd*: C-152/91 [1995] ICR 158 and *Coloroll Pension Trustees Ltd v Russell*: C-200/91 [1995] ICR 179). See now *para 4* of *Part 2* of *Sch 7* to the *EA 2010* and the *Equality Act 2010 (Sex Equality Rule) (Exceptions) Regulations 2010/2132*, regs 2 and 3.

The CJEU has also given guidance on how a scheme should approach the task of modifying its rules so as to provide for equality. No action need be taken in relation to benefits payable in respect of periods of service prior to 17 May 1990 by reason of the temporal limitation established in *Barber*. Benefits payable in respect of the period between 17 May 1990 and the date on which the scheme is amended to provide for equality should be rounded up to the higher of the differential rates. After entitlements have been equalised, however, the scheme may reduce benefits overall provided that it is done in a way which involves no discrimination and which is consistent with the obligations of the employer and/or trustees under national laws and the contract of employment or rules of the scheme. Equalisation must be done in one step; it is not lawful for the employer or trustee to equalise benefits progressively over a transitional period (*Smith v Advel Systems Ltd*: C- 409/92 [1995] ICR 596). Schemes which reduced male entitlements to match female entitlements between 17 May 1990 and the date on which the discriminatory scheme was actually amended ('the

718

question of the compatibility of this limitation period was referred to the CJEU by the House of Lords in *Preston v Wolverhampton Healthcare NHS Trust* [1998] ICR 227. The CJEU decided (C–78/98, [2001] 2 AC 415) that the limitation was not, in principle, contrary to Community law. However, that decision was qualified in two respects. First, the CJEU stated that the national court would have to be satisfied that the limitation was not less favourable than the limitations applied to comparable domestic law claims. Second, the CJEU addressed the application of this limitation period to circumstances where an employee has been employed pursuant to a series of discrete contracts of employment. In *Preston* the CJEU held that the limitation should not apply from the date of termination of each employment contract in a case where the employee is engaged pursuant to a series of such contracts so that it can be said that a 'stable employment relationship' existed across the period of time covered by the individual contracts. On return to the House of Lords ([2001] UKHL 5, [2001] 2 AC 455), the six-month limitation period was held to be compatible with Community law but the issue of what constitutes a 'stable employment relationship' was remitted back to the employment tribunal: see **22.20** above for the progress of the *Preston* part-time workers pensions litigation.

With effect from 19 July 2003, *EqPA 1970* was amended by the *Equal Pay Act 1970 (Amendment) Regulations 2003* so that no claim in respect of an equality clause may be referred to an employment tribunal otherwise than by virtue of (*e*) above unless the proceedings are instituted on or before the 'qualifying date' (*EqPA 1970, s 2(4)*). These provisions have been replicated in tabular form in *EA 2010, ss 129–130*. The 'qualifying date' before which a claim must be brought varies depending on which of the following five categories applies to the circumstances of the claim (*EA 2010, s 129*; see previously *EqPA 1970, s 2ZA*):

A stable employment case

(a)   A 'stable employment case' means a case where the proceedings relate to a period during which a stable employment relationship subsists between the woman and the employer, notwithstanding that the period includes any time after the ending of a contract of employment when no further contract of employment is in force. In a stable employment case, the qualifying date is the date falling six months after the date on which the stable employment relationship ended. See *EA 2010, s 129* and *130(3)*. The CJEU in *Preston* indicated that a 'stable employment case' would be a case where the woman works regularly, but periodically or intermittently, for the same employer, under successive legally separate contracts. The CJEU indicated that in such cases the starting point for the limitation period should be fixed as 'the date on which the sequence of such contracts has been interrupted through the absence of one or more of the features that characterise a stable employment relationship of that kind, either because the periodicity of such contracts has been broken or because the new contract does not relate to the same employment or that to which the same pension scheme applies' (*ibid*, [70]). What is required is that there be a succession of contracts, with or without gaps between them: *North Cumbria University NHS Hospitals Trust v Fox* [2010] EWCA Civ 729, [2010] IRLR 804, *Slack v Cumbria County Council* [2009] EWCA Civ 293, [2009] 3 CMLR 8). In *Dass v College of Haringey Enfield and North East London* UKEAT/0108/12/MC, 27 November 2014, Slade J (sitting in the EAT) observed 'it is apparent that the CJEU considered that a stable employment relationship could continue beyond the end of a particular contract. It would however come to an end if no new contract were entered into by the time expected in accordance with the established pattern, or periodicity, of the parties entering into such contracts'. There is no requirement that there should be an 'umbrella contract' (express or implied) covering the whole period of the stable employment: that is a feature that is required to establish continuity of employment for the purposes of *s 212* of the *Employment Rights Act*

1996, but not to establish 'stable employment' for the purposes of the time limit for bringing an equal pay claim (*Slack* and *Dass* ibid). Nor is the concept of 'temporary cessation of work' in *s 212* of the *ERA 1996* relevant (*Dass*, ibid).

A concealment case

(b)   A 'concealment case' is a case where the employer deliberately concealed from the woman any fact (referred to as a 'qualifying fact') which is relevant to the contravention to which the proceedings relate, and without knowledge of which the woman could not reasonably have been expected to institute the proceedings, and the woman did not discover the qualifying fact (or could not with reasonable diligence have discovered it) until after the last day on which she was employed in the employment, or the day on which the stable employment relationship between her and the employer ended (as the case may be). In a concealment case, the qualifying date is the date falling six months after the day on which the woman discovered the qualifying fact in question (or could with reasonable diligence have discovered it). See *EA 2010, s 129* and *130(4)–(6)*.

A disability case (referred to as an incapacity case under EA 2010)

(c)   A 'disability case' means a case where the woman was under a disability at any time during the six months after the last day on which she was employed in the employment, the day on which the stable employment relationship between her and the employer ended, or the day on which she discovered (or could with reasonable diligence have discovered) the qualifying fact deliberately concealed from her by the employer (if that day falls after the day(s) referred to above, as the case may be). In a disability case, the qualifying date is the date falling six months after the day on which the woman ceased to be under a disability. See *EA 2010, s 129* and *130(7)–(9)*.

A case which is both a concealment and a disability case

(d)   In such a case, the qualifying date is the later of the two dates which would otherwise apply if it were just disability or just a concealment case. See *EA 2010, s 129*.

A standard case

(e)   A 'standard case' is a case which is not a stable employment case, a concealment case, a disability case or a case which is both a concealment and a disability case: see *EA 2010, s 139(2)*. In a standard case, the qualifying date is the date falling six months after the last day on which the woman was 'employed in the employment'. The meaning of that phrase was determined by the House of Lords in *Preston v Wolverhampton NHS Trust (No.1)* [1998] 1 WLR 280. Lord Slynn, with whose judgment Lords Goff, Lloyd, Nolan and Hope agreed, approved the analysis of Otton LJ delivering judgment in the Court of Appeal in that case ([1997] ICR 899) who said that the time limit runs 'from the end of the contract of employment alleged to contain the equality clause in respect of which the claim is made'. In *Slack v Cumbria County Council (Equality and Human Rights Commission intervening)* [2009] EWCA Civ 293, [2009] ICR 1217, CA (under the name of *Cumbria County Council v Dow (No.2)* in the EAT [2008] IRLR 109), the Court of Appeal upheld the EAT's decision that where it was clear from the contractual documents that employer and employee had agreed to effect a change to the contract by means not of a variation but rather by means of a termination and re-engagement (in contrast to the decision of the EAT in *Potter v North Cumbria Acute Hospitals NHS Trust* [2009] IRLR 900 where a change to contractual documents was found to be a variation) then time will start to run in respect of the previous contract from the date of termination where this is in accordance with the mutual intention of the parties. The potential harshness of this approach was alleviated in the Court of Appeal by the (new) argument that these were stable employment cases as there were a series of uninterrupted contracts and the cases were remitted back to the tribunal on this question: *Fox v North Cumbria University Hospitals NHS Trust* [2010] EWCA Civ 729, [2010] IRLR 804. See also *Winder v Aston University* [2007] All ER (D) 45 (Nov), EAT.

The tribunal has no discretion to extend time in a claim under *EqPA 1970* or under *EA 1010*. In this respect the time limit for sex discrimination claims is more generous as it allows for an extension of time where the tribunal considers it to be just and equitable: see **13.3** DISCRIMINATION AND EQUAL OPPORTUNITIES – **III**. Nor can the time limit be waived or varied by agreement between the parties: *Secretary of State for Health v Rance* [2007] IRLR 665. However, the time limit may be extended by the early conciliation procedures as set out below at **22.28**.

22.23 Compensation

Where a court (see **22.26** below for the jurisdiction of the civil courts) or tribunal upholds a complaint relating to a breach of an equality clause or rule (other than a breach with respect to membership of or rights under an occupational pension scheme) it may (a) make a declaration to that effect; and/or (b) order the employer to pay compensation to the employee in the form of an award by way of arrears of pay or damages (*EA 2010, ss 132(1)* and *(2)*). Note, however, that awards of damages or arrears of benefits are only available to pensioner claimants in pension cases: see above **22.18**.

If the claim is successful, the amount awarded will be the difference in pay between that of the claimant and the 'equal' or 'equivalent' employee. In certain cases, such as those involving performance-related pay or bonuses, that may require the tribunal to engage in the speculative exercise of devising an equivalent performance-related bonus scheme to apply to the group of workers to which the claimant belongs in order to determine the appropriate level of award: see *South Tyneside Metropolitan Borough Council v Anderson* [2007] All ER (D) 410 (Mar) (not appealed on this point: [2007] EWCA Civ 654, [2007] ICR 1581).

Compensation for non-economic loss was not recoverable in a claim under the *EqPA 1970*: *Degnan v Redcar and Cleveland Borough Council* [2005] ICR 1170. There is no reason to suppose that the position is any different under the *EA 2010*.

Note also, that the tribunal will not grant a declaration that there has been discrimination where in fact the employee has suffered no loss: see *Copple and others v Littlewoods Plc* [2011] EWCA Civ 1281, [2012] ICR 354. That case concerned a large number of part-time pensions claims. However, the EAT held that since most of the claimants would not actually have joined the scheme even if it had been open to them to do so, although there had been discrimination, no declaration would be granted since that would be to put the claimants in a better position than, say, a man who, despite having the option to join the scheme in his contract of employment, had not done so at the time.

The limitation provisions under the *EA 2010* now stipulate that a court or tribunal may not award compensation in respect of any time before the 'arrears day' (*s 132(3)*). The 'arrears day' in a 'standard case' (see above **22.22**) is the day falling 6 years before the day on which proceedings were instituted. The 'arrears day' in a concealment or incapacity (formerly, disability) case is the day on which the breach first occurred (*s 132(4)*).

Formerly, the *EqPA 1970* contained a two-year limitation period. This was held by the CJEU in *Preston v Wolverhampton Healthcare NHS Trust* to be incompatible with Community law. On return to the House of Lords ([1998] ICR 227, HL), it was held that the respondent employers could not rely on this two-year limitation which must be disapplied. The respondent employers could not therefore defeat a claim for periods prior to the two years to be taken into account, subject to the employee paying contributions owing in respect of the period for which membership was claimed retroactively. Future pension benefits had to be calculated by reference to full and part-time periods of service subsequent to 8 April 1976 as the date when the CJEU held in *Defrenne v Sabena*: 43/75 [1976] ICR 547 that *art 157* had direct effect. See now the *Equal Pay Act 1970 (Amendment) Regulations 2003*.

Following the CJEU's declaration of incompatibility in *Preston*, with effect from 19 July 2003, *EqPA 1970, s 2ZB* provided that arrears of pay may be recovered up to six years back from the 'arrears date'. As noted above, these provisions have now been replicated in the *EA 2010*.

However, note that where the claim is based on the job having been rated as equivalent by the employer, there can be no claim for back pay: the employee will be entitled to equal wages only from the date that the job was rated as equivalent: *Bainbridge v Redcar and Cleveland Borough Council* [2007] IRLR 494.

The meaning of the words "proceedings were instituted" which set the relevant arrears date in a 'standard case' was considered by the EAT in *Prest and others v Mouchel Business services and another* [2011] ICR 1345. The issue in that case was that proceedings had been amended so as to include new comparators. The tribunal found that the arrears date was the date on which the application to amend the ET1 had been made. The EAT disagreed, holding that the original and amended claims were, in substance, the same claims as both of the comparators were in one of the two classes of comparators named in the original claim. Consequently, proceedings were instituted on the date that the ET1 was originally presented to the employment tribunal. However, the matter may have been different in circumstances where the work done by the new comparator had been different from the work done by the comparators originally named in the ET1.

Exemplary damages are not available in cases under the *EqPA 1970* as such claims are contractual, rather than tortious (see *Allan v Newcastle-upon-Tyne City Council* [2005] IRLR 504, EAT).

The *Sex Discrimination and Equal Pay (Remedies) Regulations 1993 (SI 1993/2798)* (now replaced by the *Employment Tribunals (Interest on Awards in Discrimination Cases) Regulations 1996 (SI 1996/2803)*) conferred on the employment tribunal a power to award interest on sums awarded under the *EqPA 1970*. The tribunal is required to identify a 'mid-point date'. This date is the halfway point between the date on which the act of discrimination complained of occurred and the date on which the interest is being calculated (*reg 4*). Interest is then awarded in respect of the period from the mid-point date to the date of calculation (*reg 6(1)(b)*), except that interest on any sum for injury to feelings is to be awarded for the whole of the period from the date of the act of discrimination to the date of calculation (*reg 6(1)(a)*). Interest is simple interest and accrues from day to day (*reg 3(1)*). By *reg 3(2)* the rate to be applied in England and Wales is the rate fixed, for the time being, by *section 17* of the *Judgments Act 1838*. In Scotland the rate is the rate fixed, for the time being, by *section 9* of the *Sheriff Courts (Scotland) Extracts Act 1892*. Both rates are currently 8%.

If a respondent has made a payment to the complainant prior to the date of calculation, the date of payment is treated as if it were the date of calculation for the purposes of calculating the interest to be awarded (*reg 6(2)*).

The tribunal is given a discretion to calculate interest by reference to periods other than those set out above, or even to use different periods for different elements of the award (*reg 6(3)*). The discretion may be exercised only where the tribunal is of the opinion that:

(a)   there are exceptional circumstances, whether relating to the claim as a whole or to a particular element of the award; and

(b)   those circumstances have the effect that serious injustice would be caused if interest were to be awarded by reference to the period or periods specified in *reg 6(1)(a)* or *(b)* or *6(2)*.

22.24 Equal Pay Audits

Section 132 of the *EA 2010*, which deals with equal pay cases, contains no specific power to make a 'recommendation' such as is contained in *EA 2010, s 124(1)(c)* for other discrimination claims: see **13.21 Discrimination and Equal Opportunities – III**. However, it is arguable that equal pay cases also fall within the scope of *s 124(1)(c)* since that section applies to all contraventions of *Part 5* of the *Act*, which includes in principle contraventions of the equality clause: see *s 120(1)* and *124(1)*. Nonetheless, *s 98* of the *Enterprise and Regulatory Reform Act 2013* created a new power for employment tribunals to make a very specific type of 'recommendation' in an equal pay case. That *Act* inserts a new *s 139A* into the *EA 2010*. *Section 139A* gives the Secretary of State the power to make regulations requiring employment tribunals to order a respondent to carry out an equal pay audit in any case where the tribunal finds that there has been a breach of the equality clauses in the *EA 2010* or a contravention of the sex discrimination provisions relating to pay. This power is additional to the power to award compensation to the individual claimant (above), and to the power to impose a financial penalty on an employer (below). The purpose of such audits is 'to identify action to be taken to avoid equal pay breaches occurring or continuing' (*s 139A(3)*). The *Act* requires the regulations to provide for an equal pay audit not to be ordered where the tribunal considers that: (a) an audit completed by the respondent in the previous 3 years meets requirements prescribed for this purpose; (b) it is clear without an audit whether any action is required to avoid equal pay breaches occurring or continuing; (c) the breach the tribunal has found gives no reason to think that there may be other breaches; or (d) the disadvantages of an equal pay audit would outweigh its benefits (*s 139A(5)*). Otherwise, the *Act* allows for the regulations to make further provision as to the content of an audit, any circumstances in which an audit may be required to be published or disclosed to any person, the powers and duties of the tribunal for deciding whether an order has been complied with, and for the tribunal to have power, where a person fails to comply with an order to carry out an equal pay audit (*s 138A(2), (6)* and *(8)*). In the first regulations to be made under the section, the amount of such a penalty may not exceed £5,000 (*s 139A(8)*). That limit will not apply to subsequent regulations. Similarly, the statute gives power in the first regulations (but not in subsequent regulations) made under the section to provide for an exemption from the equal pay audit provisions for small and/or new businesses.

The *Equality Act 2010 (Equal Pay Audits) Regulations 2014 (SI 2014/2559)* made under that section came into force on 1 October 2014. Subject to certain exceptions, the Regulations require a tribunal, where it finds that there has been an equal pay breach, to order the respondent to carry out an audit (*reg 2*). There are exceptions where: (i) an audit covering the required matters has been carried out in the previous three years (*reg 3(1)(a)*); (ii) it is clear without an audit whether any action is required to avoid equal pay breaches occurring or continuing (*reg 3(1)(b)*); (iii) the breach which the tribunal has found gives no reason to think that there may be other breaches (*reg 3(1)(c)*); (iv) the disadvantages of an audit would outweigh its benefits (*reg 3(1)(d)*). There are also exceptions for existing micro-businesses and new businesses (*reg 4*). Micro-businesses are businesses with fewer than 10 full-time equivalent employees (*Sch, para 1*; full-time equivalence is calculated by reference to the formula in *para 6*), as determined immediately before the date of judgment (*Sch 1, para 2*). New businesses are businesses which are less than 12 months old when the claim is presented to the tribunal (*Sch, para 3(1)* and *reg 1(2)*). However, there is detailed provision in *Sch, para 3(2)–(8)* dealing with the circumstances where businesses have been transferred and are therefore not to be regarded as 'new businesses'. The exceptions for micro-businesses and new businesses are not going to be in force indefinitely. The Regulations only prohibit a tribunal from ordering such businesses to undertake an audit 'within the applicable exemption period' (*reg 4(1)*). The 'backstop' is ten years from the date the Regulations came into force (i.e. 1 October 2024) for both micro-businesses (*Sch, para 4*) and new businesses (*Sch, para 5*). Micro-businesses may lose the protection of the exception earlier if, during a six month 'assessment period', the number of days when their employees exceed 10 is greater than the number of days when they have fewer than 10 employees (see *Sch, para 4(2)* and *(3)* for the detailed provisions on 'assessment periods').

Where a tribunal makes an order under *reg 2* requiring an audit to be carried out, it must specify (by description) the employees who must be covered by the audit and the period of time to which the audit must relate (*reg 5(1)(a)*). The tribunal must also specify a date, which must be at least three months hence, by which the audit must be received by the tribunal (*reg 5(1)(b)* and *(2)*). The audit must then include relevant gender pay information for the categories of employees specified by the tribunal, identify any differences in pay between male and female employees and the reasons for those differences, including the reasons for any potential equal pay breach identified by the audit and must set out the respondent's plan to avoid equal pay breaches occurring or continuing (*reg 6*).

Where an audit is received by the tribunal by the time specified in the order, the tribunal must (of its own motion) determine whether the audit complies with the requirements of *reg 6* and, if so, make an order to that effect (*reg 7(1)* and *(2)*). If the tribunal is not satisfied that the audit complies, or if no audit has been received, then the tribunal must fix a hearing, and give the respondent notice of that (*reg 7(3)*). Where an audit has been received, the tribunal must also notify the respondent employer of the reasons why it is not satisfied with the audit and inform the respondent of its right to make representations at the hearing. If the employer does not provide the audit within the time specified, then the tribunal must specify a new date for compliance, which must be no later than the date fixed for the hearing (*reg 7(3)(c)*).

At the hearing, the tribunal must (if the audit has been received) determine whether it complies with the requirements of *reg 6*. If it does, it must make an order to that effect (*reg 8(3)(a)*). If the tribunal determines that the audit does not comply then the tribunal must notify the respondent of its reasons for that determination, make an order requiring the respondent to amend the audit and consider whether or not to order the respondent to pay a penalty under *reg 11* (*reg 8(4)*). Even if a compliant audit has been supplied by the date of the hearing, the tribunal may order the respondent to pay a penalty under *reg 11* if the respondent failed to provide the audit by the date originally set by the tribunal (*reg 8(3)(b)*). Where an audit has not been received by the date of the hearing, the tribunal must make an order specifying a new date by which the tribunal must receive the audit and consider whether or not to order the respondent to pay a penalty under *reg 11* (*reg 8(5)*). Where a respondent fails to comply with any of these orders, then the tribunal must fix a further hearing and notify the response of the date of the hearing and right to make representations (*reg 8(6)*, *(7)*).

Where a tribunal is satisfied that a compliant audit has been completed, and has made an order to that effect, the respondent must (not less than 28 days after the date of the order) publish the audit on its website (if it has one) for a period of three years and inform all people about whom gender pay information was included in the audit where they can obtain a copy (*reg 9(2)*). If the respondent considers that publication in this way would result in a breach of a legal obligation, then they must publish the report with such revisions as it considers necessary to ensure compliance with that legal obligation (*reg 9(3)(a)*). Only if it is not possible to make revisions that would avoid breach of the legal obligation is it permissible not to publish the audit (*reg 9(3)(b)*). Where the audit has been published, the respondent must, not more than 28 days after publication, send evidence of the publication to the tribunal and, where it has not published the report, or has published it in revised form, adequate written reasons why it considers that publication would result in breach of a legal obligation (*reg 9(5)* and *(6)*).

The tribunal must then consider (of its own motion) whether or not the respondent has complied with the publication requirements (*reg 10(2)*). If the tribunal concludes that the respondent has complied, or is not required to comply because of a legal obligation, it must issue a decision in writing to that effect (*reg 10(3)*). If the tribunal considers on the papers that the respondent has not complied, then it must fix a hearing to determine the matter, notifying the respondent of the reasons why it is not so satisfied and its right to make representations (*reg 10(4)*). If at the hearing, the tribunal determines that the respondent has complied, then it must issue a decision to that effect (*reg 10(6)*). If not, the tribunal must make an order setting a new date for compliance (*reg 10(7)*). If the respondent still does not comply, then a further hearing must be fixed (*reg 10(8), (9)*).

Where a tribunal finds that a respondent has failed to comply with an order to carry out an audit (under *reg 2*) or an order to amend an audit (under *reg 8*), then the tribunal may, if satisfied that the respondent has no reasonable excuse for failure to comply, order the respondent to pay a penalty to the Secretary of State under *reg 11*. Repeated penalties may be awarded for repeat offences (*reg 11(2)*). The maximum amount of any individual penalty is £5,000 (*reg 11(4)*). There is no limit on the number of penalties that can be awarded.

Guidance on equal pay audits is available on the Equalities and Human Rights Commission website.

22.25 Other financial penalties for employers

Section 16 of the *Enterprise and Regulatory Reform Act 2013* inserts a new *s 12A* into the *Employment Tribunals Act 1996* which, since coming into force on 25 April 2013, permits a tribunal to order an employer to pay a penalty to the Secretary of State if it concludes that the employer has breached any of the worker's rights to which the claim relates, and is also of the opinion that the breach has one or more aggravating features (*s 12A(1)*). This power may be used in addition to, or as an alternative to, awarding compensation to the employee or ordering the employer to carry out an equal pay audit (see above). However, where a tribunal has already decided to order the employer to pay compensation to the employee, the amount of any penalty awarded must be 50% of the value of the compensation awarded, except that if the amount of the financial award is less than £200, the amount of the penalty shall be £100, and if the amount of the financial award is more than £10,000, the amount of the award shall be £5,000 (*s 12A(5)*). In cases where two or more workers' claims have been considered together and the employer is ordered to pay a penalty in respect of any of those claims, the amount of the penalties in total shall be at least £100, the amount of a penalty in respect of a particular claim shall be no more than £5000 or no more than 50% of the amount of any compensation awarded to the employee (whichever is the lesser). If the total of the financial compensation awarded on all the conjoined claims is less than £200, then the penalty is capped at £100 (*ss 12A(6)* and *(7)*). In all other cases, the penalty must be at least £100 and no more than £5000 (*s 12A(3)*). In deciding whether to make a penalty order, and in deciding the amount of such order, the tribunal must have regard to the employer's ability to pay (*s 12A(2)*). Once a penalty order is made, it cannot be reviewed simply because the tribunal is subsequently called on to award compensation for failure a failure by the employer to comply with an order of the tribunal (such as an order for a recommendation under *s 124(7)* of the *EA 2010* or an order to carry out an equal pay audit) (*s 12A(9)*). This provision does not affect the Tribunal's general powers to review awards, however. Finally, it is to be noted that penalties awarded under these provisions operate like parking tickets: an employer who pays within 21 days of the order will have the amount of the penalty reduced by 50%: *s 12A(10)*.

22.26 Equal Pay Claims and the Civil Courts

Because the right to equal pay in the *EqPA 1970* and the *EA 2010* is given effect by way of the deemed inclusion of an equality clause in the worker's contract (see above **22.5**), it is possible for claims for equal pay to be brought in the civil courts by way of a claim for breach of contract. The *EA 2010* explicitly preserves the jurisdiction of the civil courts in respect of equal pay (*s 127(9)* of *EA 2010*), subject to provisions permitting the striking out of claims where such claims could be more conveniently dealt with by an employment tribunal and for the transferring of issues to the employment tribunal: see *s 128* of *EA 2010*. Note that there is not an equivalent power for the employment tribunal to transfer an equal pay claim to the County Court and the tribunal has no power to achieve the same ends by using its power to stay proceedings in *rule 29* of the *Employment Tribunals (Constitution and Rules of Procedure) Regulations 2013* even if it considers the High Court would be the more appropriate forum for the claim: *Asda Stores Ltd v Brierley and ors.*

The *EqPA 1970* contained identical provision to *s 128(2)* of the *EA 2010* at *s 2(3)* as follows: "Where it appears to the court in which any proceedings are pending that a claim or counter-claim in respect of the operation of an [equality clause] could more conveniently be disposed of separately by an [employment tribunal], the court may direct that the claim or counter-claim shall be struck out; and (without prejudice to the foregoing) where in proceedings before any court a question arises as to the operation of an [equality clause], the court may on the application of any party to the proceedings or otherwise refer that question, or direct it to be referred by a party to the proceedings, to an [employment tribunal] for determination by the tribunal, and may stay or sist the proceedings in the meantime." This section of the *EqPA 1970* suggested that the civil courts have jurisdiction over equal pay claims but raised the question of whether or not an equal pay claim which would be out of time in the employment tribunal, could be pursued by making use of the longer limitation periods permitted in contract claims in the civil courts or whether such claims fall to be struck out, under *EqPA 1970, s 2(3)* on the basis that it would be more convenient to hear them in the employment tribunal (having regard to the expertise of the employment tribunals in equal pay cases and the specialist rules of procedure).

In *Abdulla v Birmingham City Council* [2010] EWHC 3303 (QB), [2011] IRLR 309 Colin Edelman QC (sitting as a deputy High Court Judge) declined to strike out an equal pay multiple under *EqPA 1970, s 2(3)*. He considered that a construction of *EqPA 1970, s 2(3)* which permitted claims to be struck out on the basis that they could be more conveniently disposed of in the employment tribunal, even though they could not be heard in the employment tribunal (by reason of the time bar) would amount to the imposition of the employment tribunal time limit on claims in the civil courts even though Parliament had chosen not to enact the same time limit in the different sets of proceedings. He also considered that the European principle of equivalence was engaged and required that equal pay proceedings in the civil courts should have equivalent time limits to contract claims in the civil courts. A rather different approach was suggested by Slade J in *Ashby v Birmingham City Council* [2011] EWHC 424 (QB), [2012] ICR 1. Slade J drew on the jurisprudence which applied in the context of staying claims in this jurisdiction on an application of the *forum non conveniens* principles. She concluded that it was essential in applying *EqPA 1970, s 2(3)* to consider the reason why the claims had been pursued in the civil courts and why timely claims were not issued in the employment tribunal. Where the failure to issue a timely claim in the employment tribunal was reasonable, she opined that "the interests of justice are likely to be served by enabling claimants to continue litigating in a forum which has jurisdiction to hear their claims. Such considerations could affect the decision as to whether the claims could be more conveniently disposed of in the Employment Tribunal or, if a judge so concluded, whether discretion should be exercised to strike out the claims in the County Court." When the question came before the Court of Appeal in *Birmingham City Council v Abdulla* [2011] EWCA Civ 1412, [2012] ICR 20 the Court of Appeal preferred the approach of Colin Edelman QC to that of Slade J. Mummery LJ considered that the purpose of *section 2(3)* was to enable claims to be dealt with in the most appropriate forum and not to leave claimants without any remedy. Consequently, it would not be appropriate to strike out equal pay claims pursued in the civil courts exercising the section 2(3) power when the claims would be out of time such that the employment tribunal would have no jurisdiction to entertain them. The Court of Appeal did not therefore need to express an opinion upon the question of the European principle of equivalence. Mummery LJ did not find the comparison with the staying of claims on an application of to hold a Stage 1 or a Stage 2 equal value hearing does not preclude holding more than one of each of those types of hearing or other hearings from being held in accordance with the ordinary Tribunal rules of procedure in *Sch 1* to the *2013 Regulations: rule 12(2)* of *Sch 3* to the *2013 Regulations.*

The procedure for equal value claims provides as follows.

In making all directions in relation to equal value claims, the Tribunal is required to have regard to the indicative timetable (see *rule 2(2)* of *Sch 3* to the *2013 Regulations*).

Stage 1 Equal Value Hearing. Where there is a dispute as to whether one person's work is of equal value to another's (referred to as 'the question' in the *Regulations*), the Tribunal shall conduct a hearing called a 'Stage 1 Equal Value Hearing'. At this hearing the Tribunal must consider whether and how to exercise its powers under *EA 2010, s 131.* By *EA 2010, s 131(2),* where a dispute arises as to whether any work is of equal value, the Tribunal may proceed to determine that question itself. Alternatively, it may require a member of the panel of independent experts to prepare a report on that issue before the Tribunal determines the matter. (The panel of independent experts is appointed by ACAS: see *s 131(8)*). At the Stage 1 hearing the Tribunal shall (*rule 3* of *Sch 3* to the *2013 Regulations*):

(a)   strike out the claim if, by virtue of the claimant's and her comparator's work having been rated differently in a valid job evaluation study, their work is not of equal value;

(b)   determine whether or not the claimant and her comparator's work are of equal value, or alternatively require an independent expert to prepared a report on the question (and hear evidence and submissions for the purpose of deciding these issues);

(c)   if the Tribunal decides to require an independent expert to prepare a report on the question, the Tribunal must fix a date for a 'Stage 2 Equal Value Hearing';

(d)   if the Tribunal decides not to require an independent expert to prepare a report, then a date for a final hearing must be fixed.

Under the *2004 Regulations* there was also a specific power in *rule 4* to order disclosure to the expert of all documents and evidence relevant to the question of equal value disclosed between the parties. This power is now contained in *rule 2(1)(b)* of *Sch 3* to the *2013 Regulations. Rule 2* also gives the Tribunal specific power to limit the parties to facts that they have put in evidence and disclosed by a date set by the Tribunal (*rule 2(1)(a)*).

At the Stage 1 Equal Value Hearing, the tribunal shall also, unless it considers it inappropriate, make the following 'standard orders' (*rule 4* of *Sch 3* to the *2013 Regulations*):

(a)   before the end of the period of 14 days after the date of the Stage 1 hearing the claimant shall:

    (i)   disclose in writing to the respondent the name of any comparator, or, if the claimant is not able to name the comparator he shall instead disclose such information as enables the comparator to be identified by the respondent; and

    (ii)   identify to the respondent in writing the period in relation to which he considers that the claimant's work and that of the comparator are to be compared;

(b)   before the end of the period of 28 days after the date of the Stage 1 hearing:

    (i)   where the claimant has not disclosed the name of the comparator to the respondent, if the respondent has been provided with sufficient detail to be able to identify the comparator, he shall disclose in writing the name of the comparator to the claimant;

(ii)   the parties shall provide each other with written job descriptions for the claimant and any comparator;

(iii)   the parties shall identify to each other in writing the facts which they consider to be relevant to the question;

(c)   the respondent is required to grant access to the claimant and his representative (if any) to his premises during a period specified by the tribunal or chairman in order for him or them to interview any comparator;

(d)   the parties shall before the end of the period of 56 days after the date of the stage 1 equal value hearing present to the tribunal a joint agreed statement in writing of the following matters:

(i)   job descriptions for the claimant and any comparator;

(ii)   facts which both parties consider are relevant to the question;

(iii)   facts on which the parties disagree (as to the fact or as to the relevance to the question) and a summary of their reasons for disagreeing;

(e)   the parties shall, at least 56 days prior to the hearing, disclose to each other, to any independent or other expert and to the tribunal written statements of any facts on which they intend to rely in evidence at the hearing; and

(f)   the parties shall, at least 28 days prior to the hearing, present to the tribunal a statement of facts and issues on which the parties are in agreement, a statement of facts and issues on which the parties disagree and a summary of their reasons for disagreeing.

Where the Tribunal has decided to appoint an independent expert to prepare a report on the question, the Tribunal or a Chairman may if it or he considers it appropriate (for example where a party is not legally represented etc) at any stage of the proceedings order an independent expert to assist the tribunal in establishing the facts on which the independent expert may rely in preparing his report: *rule 5 of Sch 3 to the 2013 Regulations. Rule 2(1)(d) of Sch 3 to the 2013 Regulations* also makes specific provision in relation to joint reports being produced by experts where more than one expert is instructed in proceedings.

See generally the decision of the Scottish EAT in *Amey Services Ltd v Cardigan* [2008] IRLR 279 for discussion of the need for the claimant to identify comparators before the respondent is required to give details of any genuine material factor defence.

Stage 2 Equal Value Hearing. At the Stage 2 hearing the Tribunal shall make a determination of facts on which the parties cannot agree which relate to the question and shall require the independent expert to prepare his report on the basis of facts which have (at any stage of the proceedings) been agreed between the parties or determined by the tribunal (referred to as 'the facts relating to the question'): *rule 6(1) of Sch 3 to the 2013 Regulations.* The facts relating to the question shall be the only facts on which the tribunal shall rely at the hearing, subject to an application by the independent expert for some or all of the facts relating to the question to be amended, supplemented or omitted: *rule 6(2) and (3) of Sch 3 to the 2013 Regulations.*

At the Stage 2 hearing the Tribunal shall, unless it considers it inappropriate to do so, make the following 'standard orders' having regard to the indicative timetable (*rules 6(1)(b) and 7 of Sch 3 to the 2013 Regulations*):

(a)   make any orders which it considers appropriate;

(b)   fix a date for the hearing, having regard to the indicative timetable;

(c)   order, by a date specified by the Tribunal (with regard to the indicative timetable) the independent expert to prepare his report on the question and shall (subject to any special provision made in national security proceedings) have sent copies of it to the parties and to the tribunal; and

(d)   order the independent expert to prepare his report on the question on the basis of the facts relating to the question.

The merits hearing. In proceedings in relation to which an independent expert has prepared a report, unless the Tribunal determines that the report is not based on the facts relating to the question, the report of the independent expert shall be admitted in evidence in those proceedings: *rule 8(1) of Sch 3 to the 2013 Regulations.* If the Tribunal does not admit the report of an independent expert, it may determine the question itself or require another independent expert to prepare a report on the question: *rule 8(2) of Sch 3 to the 2013 Regulations.* The Tribunal may refuse to admit evidence of facts or hear argument as to issues which have not been disclosed to the other party as required by these rules or any order made under them, unless it was not reasonably practicable for the party to have so complied: *rule 8(3) of Sch 3 to the 2013 Regulations.*

The role of the independent expert. When a Tribunal requires an independent expert to prepare a report with respect to the question or to assist in establishing the facts, it shall inform that independent expert of the duties and powers he has under this rule: *rule 9(1) of Sch 3 to the 2013 Regulations.* The independent expert shall have a duty to the Tribunal to:

(a)   assist it in furthering the overriding objective in *rule 2 of Sch 1 to the 2013 Regulations*;

(b)   comply with the requirements of the rules and any orders made by the Tribunal in relation to the proceedings;

(c)   keep the Tribunal informed of any delay in complying with any order in the proceedings (with the exception of minor or insignificant delays in compliance);

(d)   comply with any timetable imposed by the Tribunal or chairman in so far as this is reasonably practicable;

(e)   inform the Tribunal or a chairman on request by it or him of progress in the preparation of the independent expert's report;

(f)   prepare a report on the question based on the facts relating to the question and (subject to the provisions for national security cases) send it to the Tribunal and the parties; and

(g)   attend hearings in the proceedings.

An expert is under a duty to assist the Tribunal on matters within his expertise and this duty overrides any obligation to the person from whom he has received instructions or by whom he is paid: *rule 10(2) of Sch 3 to the 2013 Regulations.* The independent expert may make an application for any order or for a hearing to be held as if he were a party to the proceedings: *rule 9(3) of Sch 3 to the 2013 Regulations.* An independent expert shall be given notice of all hearings, orders or judgments in those proceedings as if a party to those proceedings and when a party is required to provide information to another party, such information shall also be provided to the independent expert: *rule 12(1) of Sch 3 to the 2013 Regulations.* At any stage of the proceedings the Tribunal may, after giving the independent expert the opportunity to make representations, withdraw the requirement on the independent expert to prepare a report. If it does so, the Tribunal may itself determine the question, or it may determine that a different independent expert should be required to prepare the report: *rule 9(4)* of *Sch 3* to the *2013 Regulations*. When a Tribunal determines that an independent expert is no longer required, the expert shall provide the Tribunal with all documentation and work in progress relating to the proceedings by a date specified by the Tribunal in a form which the tribunal is able to use: *rule 9(5)* of *Sch 3* to the *2013 Regulations* (see also *EA 2010, s 131*). Such documentation and work in progress may be used in relation to those proceedings by the Tribunal or by another independent expert.

When it is alleged that the claimant's or comparator's jobs changed over the period in which equal value is claimed, a tribunal may, in the exercise of its case management powers, commission an expert's report based on the claimant's and comparator's jobs as they stood on the date the claims were presented and defer consideration of changes in job content to a later stage in the proceedings: see *Potter v North Cumbria Acute Hospitals NHS Trust* [2008] ICR 910, EAT.

Use of expert evidence. Expert evidence shall be restricted to that which, in the opinion of the tribunal, is reasonably required to resolve the proceedings: *rule 10(1)* of *Sch 3* to the *2013 Regulations*. No party may call an expert or put in evidence an expert's report without the permission of the Tribunal and no expert report shall be put in evidence unless it has been disclosed to all other parties and any independent expert at least 28 days prior to the hearing: *rule 10(3)* of *Sch 3* to the *2013 Regulations*. (See generally *Baines v Blackpool Borough Council* [2008] All ER (D) 95 (Jan), EAT, on the use of expert evidence in an equal value case.) In proceedings in which an independent expert has been required to prepare a report on the question, the Tribunal shall not admit evidence of another expert on the question unless such evidence is based on the facts relating to the question: *rule 10(4)* of *Sch 3* to the *2013 Regulations*. (See, in this regard, *Middlesbrough Borough Council v Surtees (No. 2)* [2008] ICR 349, EAT: this rule gives the discretion to admit the expert evidence of a second party's expert, but the words 'unless such evidence is based on the facts' mean that what the expert can give evidence about must exclude the facts which are not challenged and which represent a sacrosanct position following findings or agreement at an earlier stage in the proceedings.) Unless the Tribunal considers it inappropriate to do so, any such expert report shall be disclosed to all parties and to the Tribunal on the same date on which the independent expert is required to send his report to the parties and to the Tribunal: *rule 10(4)* of *Sch 3* to the *2013 Regulations*. If an expert (other than an independent expert) does not comply with these rules or an order made by the Tribunal or a chairman, the Tribunal may order that the evidence of that expert shall not be admitted: *rule 10(5)* of *Sch 3* to the *2013 Regulations*. Where two or more parties wish to submit expert evidence on a particular issue, the Tribunal may order that the evidence on that issue is to be given by one joint expert only. When such an order has been made, if the parties wishing to instruct the joint expert cannot agree who should be the expert, the Tribunal may select the expert: *rule 10(6)* of *Sch 3* to the *2013 Regulations*.

Written questions to experts. *rule 11* of *Sch 3* to the *2013 Regulations* makes provision for written questions to be put to experts (including an independent expert) on their report. The question must be: put once only; put within 28 days of the date on which the parties were sent the report; for the purpose only of clarifying the factual basis of the report; copied to all other parties and experts involved in the proceedings at the same time as they are sent to the expert who prepared the report; and answered within 28 days of receiving the question. An expert's answers to questions shall be treated as part of the expert's report: *rule 11(3)* of *Sch 3*. Where a party has put a written question to an expert instructed by another party and the expert does not answer that question, or does not do so within 28 days, the Tribunal may order that the party instructing the expert may not rely on the evidence of that expert: *rule 11(4)* of *Sch 3*.

Burden of proof

The same burden of proof provisions apply to equal pay claims as to other discrimination claims: see *EA 2010, s 136(1)–(4)*. The burden of proof is on the claimant. However, if there are facts from which the court could decide, in the absence of any other explanation, that the employer has contravened the provision concerned, the tribunal must hold that the contravention occurred, unless the employer shows that it has not contravened the provision. See further DISCRIMINATION AND EQUAL OPPORTUNITIES III, 13.3.

Help for complainants

With effect from 6 April 2003, claimants or potential claimants in equal pay claims were able to serve questionnaires in the same manner as under the other discrimination statutes. The *Equal Pay (Questions and Replies) Order 2003 (SI 2003/722)*, provided for such question-naires to be served before a claim was presented to a tribunal or within 21 days after such a claim or such longer period as the tribunal may on application allow. The tribunal could then draw adverse inferences, including an inference that the equality clause has been breached, where an employer deliberately and without reasonable cause failed to reply in the eight-week period specified by *reg 4* of the *Order* or where an employer's reply was evasive or equivocal: *EqPA 1970, s 7B*. Such questionnaires were particularly useful to complainants who bore the burden of establishing a disparate impact by reference to statistics: see *Nelson v Carillion Services Ltd* [2003] EWCA Civ 544, [2003] ICR 1256, CA.

These provisions were re-enacted in *s 138* of the *EA 2010*. However, the questionnaire procedure is not available for claims commenced after 25 April 2013 as *s 138* of the *EA 2010* was repealed by *s 66* of the *Enterprise and Regulatory Reform Act 2013*.

Note also that relevant information may be found in the gender pay gap information that employers with 250 or more employees are now required to publish as a result of regulations made under s *78* of the *EA 2010* (see further **22.32** below).

Further, the provisions in *EA 2010, s 132* in relation to equal pay audits have now been brought into force by the *Equality Act 2010 (Equal Pay Audits) Regulations 2014* (see above **22.24**).

In the meantime, employees of public sector employers may well be able to obtain relevant information about the pay of other employees by means of a request under the *Freedom of Information Act 2000*: see *South Lanarkshire Council v The Scottish Information Commissioner* [2013] UKSC 55, [2013] 1 WLR 2421.

Help may also be available by way of disclosure orders within proceedings: *rule 31* of the *Employment Tribunals Rules of Procedure 2013* provides that the tribunal has the same powers as the County Court to order any person to disclose documents. In *Birmingham City Council v Bagshaw and ors* [2017] ICR 263 the EAT held the ET had been entitled to use this power to get the Council (against whom proceedings by the claimants had been settled) to disclose judgments, orders and other material relating to those settled claims where that material was relevant to claims the claimants were still pursuing against an employer to whom they had transferred. See generally **19.60** EMPLOYMENT TRIBUNALS – II.

22.29 EFFECT ON CONTRACTS

A term in a contract which purports to exclude or limit any provision of the *EqPA 1970* is unenforceable by any person in whose favour the term would operate (*EA 2010, s 144(1)*; and see generally **13.32** DISCRIMINATION AND EQUAL OPPORTUNITIES – III). However, a contract settling a complaint to an employment tribunal will be upheld if it was made with the assistance of a conciliation officer and is a 'qualifying settlement agreement' (*EA 2010, s 144(4)(a)* and *(5)* and see **2.3** ADVISORY, CONCILIATION AND ARBITRATION SERVICE). It will also be upheld if it meets the statutory conditions for a compromise agreement or 'qualifying settlement agreement' entered into after the employee has had independent advice (*EA 2010, s 144(4)(b)* and *(5)* and *s 147*; and see **18.20** EMPLOYMENT TRIBUNALS and **13.33** DISCRIMINATION AND EQUAL OPPORTUNITIES – III). In other circumstances, an agreement by a complainant that he or she will not bring a claim for equal pay will be void, and the payment of any sum to compromise such a claim will not prevent her from continuing with her complaint.

22.30   Equal Pay

22.30 Collective agreements

Terms of collective agreements (whether they would otherwise be legally enforceable or not) are deemed automatically unenforceable and void insofar as they constitute, promote or provide for treatment that would contravene the *Act*: *EA 2010, s 145(1)* and see generally 12.32 DISCRIMINATION AND EQUAL OPPORTUNITIES – III. Employees (or persons seeking to be employees of) an employer who is party to the collective agreement or a member of an association/organisation of employers that is party (*s 146(5)*) have the right to complain to an employment tribunal about any term that is void or unenforceable under *s 145*. To be eligible to make a complaint the employee must be able to show that the term may affect them now or in the future (*s 146(2)*).

It was held that a tribunal may grant a declaration of incompatibility in existing proceedings before it under the *EqPA 1970* without the need to issue separate proceedings; see *UNISON v Brennan* [2008] ICR 955. The same must be true now of the tribunal's power under *s 146(3)*. In *Nimz v Freie und Hansestadt Hamburg*: C-184/89 [1991] IRLR 222, the CJEU held that where there is indirect discrimination in a provision of a collective agreement, the national court is required to disapply that provision, without requesting or awaiting its prior removal by collective negotiation (see also *Kowalska v Freie und Hansestadt Hamburg*: C-33/89 [1992] ICR 29, CJEU).

22.31 Protection for complainants

Under *s 77* of the *EA 2010* individuals are protected from retaliation or victimisation where they seek, or provide, disclosures about the terms of their work (including how much they are paid) (*ss 77(4)* and *(5)*). Contractual terms purporting to restrict such disclosures are void (*ss 77(1)* and *(2)*).

22.32 GENDER PAY GAP REPORTING

Section 78 of the *EA 2010* makes provision enabling the making of regulations requiring employers with 250 or more employees (and other employers who may be specified) to publish information relating to the pay of employees for the purpose of showing whether there are differences in the pay of male and female employees. Two sets of regulations have been made bringing these requirements into force: the *Equality Act 2010 (Gender Pay Gap Information) Regulations 2017*, SI 2017/172 (which apply to private sector employers) and the *Equality Act 2010 (Specific Duties and Public Authorities) Regulations 2017*, SI 2017/353 (which apply to public sector employers covered by the public sector equality duty in *EA 2010, s 149*: see 12.37 DISCRIMINATION AND EQUAL OPPORTUNITIES – II). The effect of the regulations is that employers with more than 250 employees must publish six metrics by April 2018, and annually thereafter, specifically: the difference between (1) the mean and (2) the median hourly rates of pay of male and female employees; the difference between (3) the mean and (4) the median bonus pay of male and female employees; (5) the proportions of male and female employees who are paid bonus pay; and (6) the proportions of male and female employees in the employer's lower, lower middle, upper middle and upper quartile pay bands. The regulations contain detailed provision as to how each of these metrics is to be calculated. Pay gap metrics are to be taken as at a 'snapshot date' of 31 March for public sector employers and 5 April for private sector employers. The bonus gap metrics refer to the 12-month period running up to that date. The information must be published on both the employer's own website and the government's website (the *Gender Pay Gap Viewing Service*) and must be left on the employer's website for a period of at least three years. The information must be accompanied by a report signed by director or other responsible person verifying report is accurate. Employers may publish a commentary with the data, but there is no requirement to do so. The regulations require the government to conduct a review of their operation at least every five years. Although *EA 2010, s 78(5)* permits the regulations to make provision for failure to comply with the regulations to constitute a criminal offence, punishable on summary conviction by a fine not exceeding level 5 on the standard scale, the regulations have made no such provision. There are therefore no specific penalties for non-compliance, although the Equality and Human Rights Commission would have power to take enforcement action under the *Equality Act 2006* (see generally **13.23** DISCRIMINATION AND EQUAL OPPORTUNITIES – **III**).

has since been used to disapply a number of the provisions of the *Equal Pay Act 1970* (now succeeded by *Chapter 3* of *Part 5* of the *Equality Act 2010*) including, by way of example, the provisions which excluded complaints by those indirectly discriminated against in relation to access to occupational pension schemes (*Preston v Wolverhampton Healthcare NHS Trust* [2001] 2 AC 455, CA) and which provided that two employers could be treated as 'associated' for the purposes of determining whether a complainant and her comparator are in the same employment only where one of the two employers was a company (*Scullard v Knowles and Southern Regional Council for Education and Training* [1996] IRLR 344, EAT). For further examples of provisions in domestic legislation being disapplied see *Perceval-Price v Department of Economic Development* [2000] IRLR 380, NICA, *Allonby v Accrington and Rossendale College*: C-256/01 [2004] IRLR 224, *Alabaster v Barclays Bank plc and Secretary of State for Social Security* [2005] EWCA Civ 508, [2005] IRLR 576 and *R (on the application of Manson (Finian)) v Ministry of Defence* [2005] EWCA Civ 1678, [2006] ICR 355.

A directive enters into force in the sense of producing legal effects in the member states from the date of its publication in the Official Journal of the European Communities or from the date of its notification to member states (*Adeneler v Ellinikos Organismos Galaktos*: C-212/04 [2006] IRLR 716). During the period prescribed for transposition of a directive, member states must refrain from taking any measure liable seriously to compromise the attainment of the result prescribed by it, whether or not the national measure is concerned with transposition of the directive: *Mangold v Helm*: C-144/04 [2006] IRLR 143 and *Adeneler v Ellinikos Organismos Galaktos* (above). During this period, domestic courts must refrain as far as possible from interpreting domestic law in a manner which might seriously compromise, after the period for transposition has expired, attainment of the objective pursued by the directive: *Adeneler v Ellinikos Organismos Galaktos*. Where the relevant provisions of the directive do not have direct effect (see below), the general obligation owed by national courts to interpret domestic law in conformity with the directive exists once the period for its transposition has expired.

What if the state has failed to introduce legislation which properly and fully implements the European law by the date specified in the directive? In those circumstances the Commission is empowered by *Art 258 [226, 169]* to bring enforcement proceedings against the defaulting member state (see for example *EC Commission v United Kingdom*: C-382/92 [1994] ECR I-2435, [1994] ICR 664). *Article 259 [227, 170]* contains a related but rarely used power for other member states to bring similar proceedings. Within our own jurisdiction legislation purporting to implement EU law has been successfully challenged using judicial review (for instance *R v Secretary of State for Employment, ex p Equal Opportunities Commission* [1994] ICR 317, HL and *Equal Opportunities Commission v Secretary of State for Trade and Industry* [2007] ICR 1234).

In addition, there are three mechanisms by which EU law may be given effect in British courts and tribunals, even where national law fails properly to implement it or would otherwise breach it: (1) a *Francovich* claim against the government for failure to implement; (2) reliance on the direct effect of EU law to bring a claim to enforce a European right; and (3) reliance on the direct effect of EU law to disapply an inconsistent domestic provision.

(1) *Francovich claims*

First, the landmark decision of *Francovich and Bonifaci v Italy*: C-6/90 and C-9/90 [1991] ECR I-5357, [1995] ICR 722, ECJ decided that an individual may have an EU law claim for damages against the state for failure properly to implement a directive. *Francovich* claims should be brought in the High Court; employment tribunals do not have jurisdiction to hear such claims (*Secretary of State for Employment v Mann* [1996] ICR 197, EAT, affirmed by the Court of Appeal [1997] ICR 209). The appropriate defendant is the Attorney General (*Mann; R v Secretary of State, ex p EOC* above). In order to bring a claim, the claimant will have to show that the unimplemented European provision is intended to confer rights on individuals. She must also establish that the breach is sufficiently serious and that the failure to implement the European provision is causally connected to the loss incurred (*Francovich* above). The ECJ's decision in *Brasserie du Pêcheur SA v Germany*: C-46/93 [1996] IRLR 267 provides useful guidance as to the scope of the substantive and procedural rights of an individual wishing to bring a *Francovich* claim. Where the relevant provision is enacted in an area of policy in relation to which a wide discretion is reserved to the member state the breach must be 'manifest' and 'grave'. Factors relevant to deciding whether a particular failure to implement is sufficiently serious include: the clarity and precision of the European provision, the breadth of the discretion reserved to the member state and the question whether the default was intentional. A breach will almost certainly be 'sufficiently serious' where a member state fails to implement a provision in circumstances where the ECJ has already ruled that there is an infringement or where it fails to take any steps to implement the directive before the date specified for implementation (*Dillenkofer v Germany*: C-178/94 [1997] IRLR 60, ECJ).

The member state cannot:

(a)   restrict the right to damages to cases where intentional or negligent default can be established;

(b)   adopt procedural rules governing the bringing of *Francovich* claims which are less favourable than those applying to analogous domestic claims or which have the effect of making it impossible or excessively difficult for individuals to obtain damages;

(c)   impose limits on the amount of damages recoverable which would have the effect that the compensation available was not commensurate with the loss suffered.

(2) Claims to enforce a directly effective European right

Secondly, the ECJ's doctrine of 'direct effect' means that, in some circumstances, an enforceable right may be conferred on an individual whether or not there has been any implementing legislation. There are three sources of directly effective rights: Articles of the Treaty, EU regulations and EU directives. An example of the first is the right to equal pay conferred by *Art 157 [141, 119]*. The ECJ decided that this particular provision was directly effective in the case of *Defrenne v Sabena*: 43/75 [1976] ICR 547.

Not all treaty provisions or directives are directly effective. The precise requirements for direct effect to be established are complex, but the provision concerned must be clear, unconditional and precise.

In *Gharehveran*: C-441/99 [2001] ECR I-7687 the ECJ established an exception to the rule that a directive may have direct effect only if it is clear, unconditional and precise. The problem in that case was that Swedish legislation excluded from employee protection on employer's insolvency (mandated under a directive) not only employees who owned the undertaking (permissible under the directive) but also those whose relatives owned the undertaking (impermissible). The ECJ held that, whilst the member state had a broad discretion as to the system of protection adopted, Sweden had fully exercised that discretion in the system that it had established. That meant that the individual had a precise and unconditional right, capable of being directly effective, to protection under that system. The principle therefore appears to be that, where a provision of EU law would lack direct effect because it offers too much choice to the member state to be clear, unconditional and precise, then if the state in question has in fact decided how it will exercise that choice, but has done so in some way that has a specific deficiency, direct effect can be used to remedy that deficiency. The *Gharehveran* principle has been discussed in a number of recent English cases (for example *Byrne v Motor Insurers' Bureau* [2009] QB 66, and *Duncombe v SoS for Children, Schools and Families* [2010] ICR 815, overturned on other grounds)).

A directly effective provision may be either horizontally or vertically directly effective. A provision which has only vertical direct effect is one which creates rights which an individual may enforce against the state but not against other individuals. A provision which has horizontal direct effect creates a right which may be enforced against other individuals.

Some, though not all, directly effective Treaty provisions have horizontal direct effect. An example of the application of horizontal direct effect is the case of *Barber v Guardian Royal Exchange Assurance Group*: C-262/88 [1990] ICR 616. When *Barber* was decided, domestic anti-discrimination legislation broadly excluded matters relating to pensions. In *Barber* the ECJ decided that occupational pensions were 'pay' within the meaning of *Art 157 [141, 119]*. As a result, individuals were able to bring a claim under *Art 157* if they suffered sex discrimination in relation to the benefits paid under a pension scheme. European law filled the gap left by the domestic legislation.

Where a member state fails properly to implement a directive by the due date, a directive may be the source of directly effective rights. However, these rights have only vertical direct effect (*Faccini Dori v Recreb Srl*: C-91/92 [1995] All ER (EC) 1; but cf *CIA Security International SA v Signalson*: C-194/94 [1996] ECR I-2201, [1996] All ER (EC) 557, ECJ in which a defendant to a counterclaim was entitled to have the domestic provision upon which the counterclaim was based disapplied on the basis that it had not been notified to the European Commission as required by *Directive 83/189/EEC*, thus arguably giving some limited horizontal effect to the directive). The rationale is that the state cannot rely on its own failure to implement the right to defend itself against those who might have been able to exercise the right against it. See also *R v Durham County Council, ex p Huddleston* [2000] 1 WLR 1484, [2000] 2 CMLR 229, CA.

For this purpose the 'state' includes any body, whatever its legal form, which has been made responsible by the state for providing a public service under the control of the state, and which has special powers for that purpose (*Foster v British Gas plc* [1991] ICR 84 and 463 and see *National Union of Teachers v St Mary's Church of England (Aided) Junior School (Governing Body)* [1997] ICR 334, CA – a voluntary aided school is an emanation of the state; see further **37.7 Public Sector Employees**). The individual seeking to rely upon the directive must be a citizen of an EU member state (*Bernstein v Immigration Appeal Tribunal* [1988] Imm AR 449), and must be a person of a kind within the scope of the directive (*Verholen*, above).

Direct effect can arise only after expiry of the time allowed for implementation of a directive (*Suffritti v Istituto Nazionale della Previdenza Sociale (INPS)*: C-140/91, C-141/91, C-278/91 and C-279/91 [1992] ECR I-6337, [1993] IRLR 289).

A directly effective right may, in theory, operate in one of two main ways. The right may be used in order to disapply a bar to an existing domestic remedy, or it may create a 'free-standing' right to a remedy. In many cases both types of operation may be appropriate. For instance, in a case similar to *Barber* (above) a claimant may argue either that the EU right works to disapply the exclusion of pension-related discrimination from the existing domestic legislation or that there is a free-standing right to an equal pension under *Art 157 [141, 119]* which, being horizontally directly effective, may be enforced against other individuals. The distinction between the two affects the question of what court or tribunal may consider cases based on European law, and what time limits apply to them.

It was at one point simply assumed that the employment tribunal had jurisdiction to hear claims based directly upon *Art 157* (*Stevens v Bexley Health Authority* [1989] IRLR 240; *Secretary of State for Scotland and Greater Glasgow Health Board v Wright and Hannah* [1993] 2 CMLR 257, [1991] IRLR 187, EAT). The difficulty was that employment tribunals have a statutory jurisdiction. In other words, they can hear only the cases which statute has specifically conferred jurisdiction upon them to hear. No statute has ever conferred jurisdiction on the employment tribunals to hear cases which are directly based upon *Art*

157. In two cases (*Biggs v Somerset County Council* [1996] IRLR 203 and *Barber v Staffordshire County Council* [1996] ICR 364) the Court of Appeal stated very clearly that the tribunal does not have jurisdiction to hear 'free-standing' *Art 157* claims. However, the ECJ and EAT have since held that, in the context of enforcing rights based on a directive, a national specialist court which is granted jurisdiction in matters relating to transposing legislation must have jurisdiction to hear claims arising directly from the directive thereby transposed: *Impact v Minister for Agriculture and Food*: C-268/06 [2008] IRLR 552 and *UNISON v Brennan* [2008] ICR 955, EAT. This is so provided that it is established that the obligation on the claimant to bring, at the same time, a separate claim based directly on the directive before an ordinary court would involve procedural disadvantages liable to render excessively difficult the exercise of the rights conferred on him by Community law. This principle probably applies to claims based directly on *Art 157*, since employment tribunals' equal pay jurisdiction is derived from domestic equal pay legislation which aims to transpose *Art 157*.

The question of what time limits apply to claims based directly on *Art 157* is not straightforward. Broadly speaking, European law has left the question of time limits to the member state subject to the following general principles of equivalence and effectiveness:

(i)   the time limits applied to the enforcement of EU law rights should be no more restrictive than those which apply to analogous domestic claims (see *Preston v Wolverhampton Healthcare NHS Trust* [2000] IRLR 506, ECJ and [2001] UKHL 5, [2001] IRLR 237);

(ii) the time limits should not make the enforcement of the rights impossible in practice (see *Rewe-Zentralfinanz GmbH v Landwirtschaftskammer für Saarland*: 33/76 [1977] 1 CMLR 533 and *Fisscher v Voorhuis Hengelo BV*: C-128/93 [1994] IRLR 662); and

(iii) provisions which seek to limit the amount of compensation recoverable by restricting the extent to which a claim may be back-dated are less likely to be considered to make enforcement of rights impossible than more straightforward time limits (*Steenhorst-Neerings v Bestuur van de Bedrijfsvereniging voor Detailhandel, Ambachten en Huisvrouwen*: C-338/91 [1993] ECR I-5475, [1994] IRLR 244; *Johnson v Chief Adjudication Officer (No 2)*: C-410/92 [1994] ECR I-5483, [1995] IRLR 157 and *Preston v Wolverhampton Healthcare NHS Trust* [2001] IRLR 237).

There was formerly thought to be a fourth principle, namely that where the right which the claimant seeks to enforce is a vertically directly effective right, time will not begin to run until the directive has been properly implemented (*Emmott v Minister for Social Welfare*: C-208/90 [1993] ICR 8). But in *Fantask A/S v Industriministeriet (Erhvervsministeriet)*: C-188/95 [1997] ECR I-6783, [1998] All ER (EC) 1 the ECJ decided that *Emmott* was restricted to its own facts and applied the *Rewe* criteria. See also *Danske Slagterier v Bundesrepublik Deutschland*: C-445/06 [2009] 3 CMLR 311.

(3) *Reliance on directly effective European legislation to disapply a domestic bar to a claim*

The third mechanism by which unimplemented European legislation may be given effect in domestic courts and tribunals derives from the decision in *Biggs v Somerset County Council* [1995] ICR 811 (affirmed by the Court of Appeal at [1996] ICR 364) which concerned a woman who did not qualify for protection against unfair dismissal because she worked part-time. The claim was prompted by the decision of the House of Lords in the *EOC* case (above) that the hours thresholds contained in *Employment Protection (Consolidation) Act 1978* were indirectly discriminatory and could not be justified, contrary to the *Equal Treatment Directive*. The claim was submitted many years after the relevant dismissal. An issue arose, therefore, as to what the relevant time limit was. The claimant argued, inter alia, that her claim was for equal pay under *Art 157 [141, 119]*. The 'pay' in question was compensation for unfair dismissal. Though once a matter of considerable controversy, the ECJ has now decided that unfair dismissal compensation is pay for the purposes of *Art 157 [141, 119]* (*Seymour-Smith* [1999] ICR 447, ECJ). The applicant relied upon *Rankin v British Coal Corpn* [1993] IRLR 69 to support an argument that there was no time limit for EU rights other than a requirement that they be brought within a reasonable time. In her submission this meant within a reasonable time of the decision in *EOC* which was the point at which it first became clear that she might have a claim.

The decision of the EAT in *Biggs* was to the effect that the claim was not brought under *Art 157 [141, 119]* but rather under the domestic legislation. The significance of the EU right was that it operated to override and disapply what would otherwise have been a bar to the bringing of proceedings under the domestic law. As the claim was under domestic law the domestic time limit (three months from the date of dismissal) applied unless it was itself inconsistent with EU law which it was not. A radically 'free-standing' European right of the sort argued for by the claimant would not have been enforceable in the employment tribunal as its jurisdiction is strictly defined by statute. No statute has conferred on the industrial tribunal any jurisdiction to consider claims based solely on EU law, which are independent of the operation of any domestic legislation (cf also *McManus v Daylay Foods Ltd* (unreported) EAT/82/95 and *Preston v Wolverhampton Healthcare NHS Trust* [1997] IRLR 233, CA for the application of the same reasoning to claims for a redundancy payment and in relation to the indirectly discriminatory exclusion of part-timers from access to membership of occupational pension schemes respectively). The decision was expressly limited to a consideration of cases based upon *Art 157 [141, 119]*. The EAT accepted that as a result of *Emmott*, cases based on a directive might fall to be treated differently.

The obligation of English courts to determine questions of EU law in accordance with the decisions of, and the principles laid down by, the ECJ is to be found in the *European Communities Act 1972, s 2(1)*. The national court is entitled to take a point of EU law of its own motion (see also *Verholen*, above, where the Advocate General suggested that it was under a positive obligation to do so). *Article 267 [234, 177]* of the *Treaty of Rome* provides a mechanism whereby national courts may, and sometimes must, refer questions to the ECJ for a preliminary ruling. The jurisdiction of employment tribunals to determine whether a domestic provision is in fact incompatible with EU law was confirmed by the Court of Appeal in *R (on the application of Manson (Finian)) v Ministry of Defence* [2005] EWCA Civ 1678, [2006] ICR 355.

The direct effect of 'general principles' of EU law

In *Mangold v Helm*: C-144/04 [2006] IRLR 143, the ECJ held that the domestic court was obliged to set aside provisions of national legislation which were incompatible with a directive even before the expiry date for implementation of the directive had passed. This conclusion was based in part on a controversial finding by the ECJ that non-discrimination on grounds of age is a 'general principle' of EU law, the source of which was held to be found in various international instruments and in the constitutional traditions common to the Member states.

There was considerable doubt amongst commentators as to whether *Mangold* was correct. The soundness of this approach and the existence of a general principle of non-discrimination on grounds of age were doubted expressly by the Advocate General in *Palacios de la Villa v Cortefiel Servicios SA* [2007] IRLR 989. However, in *Seda Kucukdeveci v Swedex GmbH & Co KG*: C-555/07 [2010] IRLR 346, [2010] All ER (D) 126 (Feb) the ECJ followed *Mangold*. It held that the *Equal Treatment Framework Directive* is a specific application of a general principle of EU law which prohibits age discrimination; and that this principle was breached by a German law providing that employment before the age of 25 was to be disregarded when calculating service-related notice periods. On this basis, the ECJ held that the national court was required, even in a dispute between private individuals, to disapply the offending national law which was incapable of interpretation in line with the directive. In effect, and controversially, because of the conflict with established principles, this decision gave horizontal direct effect to a directive.

The direct effect, in some circumstances, of the EU Charter of Fundamental Rights

As stated at **23.1** above, the *EU Charter on Fundamental Rights* is now given legal effect by *Art 6* of *TEU*. The *Charter* repeats many of the rights contained in the *European Convention on Human Rights* ('*ECHR*'), but also contains additional rights. *Art 6(3)* of the *TEU* provides that fundamental rights, as guaranteed by the *ECHR* and arising from the constitutional traditions of the member states, "shall constitute general principles of the Union's law". On the basis that the Charter expresses general principles of EU law, and in the light of the ECJ's decision in *Kucukdeveci* that general principles of EU law should be given horizontal direct effect, it now appears that domestic courts are, in some circumstances, obliged to give direct effect to the rights recognised in the *Charter*, even insofar as they are inconsistent with provisions of national law.

Many commentators initially believed, and the High Court stated at §§155 and 157 in *R (S) v SSHD* [2010] EWHC 705 (Admin), that the UK and Poland had negotiated an effective 'opt out' from the EU Charter, contained in *Protocol 30* to the *Treaty of Lisbon*. However, the ECJ in *NS v SSHD* (Case C-493/10) held that the opt-out has no legal effect (§§116-122), and that the *Charter* reflects pre-existing general principles of EU law which themselves have direct horizontal effect.

Art 51(1) of the *Charter* states that the *Charter* applies to member states only when they are implementing EU law. According to the EU Commission, the situations in which the application of the Charter is triggered under *Art 51(1)* include: (1) where national legislative activity and judicial and administrative practices are designed to fulfil obligations under EU law; (2) where a member state authority exercises a discretion which is vested in it by virtue of EU law; and (3) where national measures are linked to the disbursement of EU funds. (See the Commission's '2013 Report on the Application of the EU Charter of Fundamental Rights' (COM(2014) 224 final)). In *R (Zagorski) v BIS* [2010] EWHC 3110 (Admin) the High Court held that *Art 51(1)* requires consideration of whether, in taking a decision, a defendant is acting within the material scope of EU law. The case concerned exportation of drugs. The government had chosen not to legislate on the particular area in question. However, the fact that it was empowered to do so under EU law was a sufficient basis for finding that it was implementing EU law for the purposes of *Art 51(1)*.

It also seems that only some of the rights which are set out in the *Charter* have direct effect. In *Association de Mediation Sociale v Union Local Des Mediation Sociale Synidcats CGT* (case C-176/12) the ECJ found that *Art 27* of the *Charter*, on workers' right to information and consultation, did not have horizontal direct effect. It distinguished *Kucukdeveci* on the basis that *Art 27* is qualified by reference to "the conditions provided for by EU law and national laws and practices"; whereas *Art 21*, the right to non-discrimination on grounds of age, is not similarly qualified. There is now considerable uncertainty as to which Charter rights have direct effect, and which do not.

In *Benkharbouche v Embassy of Republic of Sudan* [2015] EWCA Civ 33, [2015] IRLR 301 the Court of Appeal disapplied the immunity from suit conferred by the *State Immunity Act 1978* on the ground that it was incompatible with *Art 47* of the *Charter*, which sets out the right to an effective remedy and a fair trial. This meant that the claimants were able to bring claims which, on their face, were expressly excluded by primary legislation. However, the *State Immunity Act* was disapplied only in relation to rights derived from EU Directives, in relation to discrimination and working time. The effect of the *Charter* was limited to claims "within the scope of EU law", which meant that it did not apply to employment rights, such as unfair dismissal, which are not derived from EU law.

The importance of the Charter was vividly illustrated in *Benkharbouche* by the fact that the Court of Appeal held that the *Statue Immunity Act 1978* also breached *Arts 6* of the *ECHR* (which is similar to *Art 47* of the *Charter*), as well as *Art 14* of the *ECHR*, but that *s 3* of *Human Rights Act 1998* ('*HRA*') (which requires legislation to be read compatibly with the ECHR so far as possible) did not enable it to be interpreted compatibly with *Art 6*. The *HRA* does not permit primary legislation to be disapplied; whereas the *Charter* does.

For an expression of judicial surprise at the far-reaching effects the Charter may now have, see §14 of Mostyn J's judgment in *R (AB) v SSHD* [2013] EWHC 3453: "The constitutional significance of this can hardly be overstated. The Human Rights Act incorporated into our domestic law large parts, but by no means all, of the European Convention on Human Rights. Some parts were deliberately missed out by Parliament. The Charter of Fundamental Rights of the European Union contains, I believe, all of those missing parts and a great deal more. Moreover, that much wider Charter of Rights would remain part of our domestic law even if the Human Rights Act were repealed."

23.4   EU REQUIREMENTS AFFECTING EMPLOYMENT LAW

EU employment legislation has been enacted or proposed in relation to a wide variety of different areas, notably the following:

(a)   free movement of labour;

(b)   equal access to social security benefits;

(c)   equal pay and equal treatment;

(d)   information on terms of employment;

(e)   redundancy procedure;

(f)   rights on the transfer of an undertaking;

(g)   health and safety at work;

(h)   information and consultation;

(i)   agency workers;

(j)   posted workers;

(k)   employees of insolvent employers;

(l)   fixed-term workers;

(m)   the regulation of pay in the financial services sector.

These are examined briefly in the following paragraphs. More detailed expositions of these areas may be found elsewhere in this book: see the cross-references below.

23.5   FREE MOVEMENT OF LABOUR

Articles 45–48 [39–42, 48–51] of the *TFEU* require member states to permit the free movement of workers between member states. No discrimination based on nationality may be exercised against EU nationals in relation to employment, remuneration or other conditions of work and employment. Free access to employment is a fundamental right, and there must be a judicial remedy against decisions which refuse the benefit of that right to EU nationals (*Union Nationale des Entraîneurs et Cadres Techniques Professionnels du Football (UNECTEF) v Heylens*: C-222/86 [1987] ECR 4097, [1989] 1 CMLR 901, ECJ).

Directives and regulations relating to these Articles have been passed. Great Britain has complied with these requirements so that EU nationals have a right to enter the country to take or seek work without the necessity of obtaining a work permit.

Article 45 [39, 48] of the *TFEU*, as a directly enforceable provision, was relied upon by the EAT in its decision in *Bossa v Nordstress Ltd* [1998] ICR 694 to disapply *ss 4* and *8(1)* of the *Race Relations Act 1976*. These sections had excluded those whose work was wholly or mainly outside Great Britain from bringing claims in the employment tribunal.

Directives regulate the mutual recognition of qualifications in member states for professions such as medicine and dentistry. *Directive 2005/36/EC* deals with mutual recognition of professional qualifications. EU nationals employed or seeking work here have the right to remain and to bring their families with them (see also FOREIGN EMPLOYEES (26)).

23.6 EQUAL ACCESS TO SOCIAL SECURITY BENEFITS

TFEU Art 48 [42, 51] provides for the passing by the Council and Parliament of the EU of such measures in the field of social security as are necessary to provide freedom of movement to workers. Such regulations, which provide for the aggregation of social security benefits which may have been paid in different member states, and for the payment of benefit in one member state where contributions have been made in another member state, have been passed (*Regulation 883/2004; Regulation 987/2009*). The regulations also ensure that the rules about liability to pay national insurance in the UK while working elsewhere in the EU are in line with the rules applied by the other Member States. Equal treatment between men and women in matters of social security, including occupational social security schemes, is largely dealt with by *Directive 79/7/EEC* and *Directive 2006/54/EC*; however, the ECJ has also held certain domestic social security provisions to be contrary to the *Equal Treatment Directive 76/207/EEC* (*Meyers v Adjudication Officer*: C-116/94 [1995] IRLR 498, a UK case about 'Family Credit'). A detailed account of this area is beyond the scope of this book.

23.7 EQUAL PAY AND EQUAL TREATMENT

Equality between men and women is an explicit objective of the EU (*Art 8 [3(2)]*). In all its activities, the EU must aim to eliminate inequalities, and to promote equality between men and women (*Art 8*). *Art 157 [141, 119]* obliges each member state to ensure and maintain the principle that men and women should receive equal pay for equal work. Further, *Council Directive 76/207/EEC* required member states to take the measures necessary to implement the principle of equal treatment for men and women in relation to the following stages of employment: engagement, training, promotion, working conditions and dismissal; and *Directive 75/117/EEC* required member states to take measures necessary to achieve equal pay between the sexes. *Directives 76/207/EEC* and *75/117/EEC* were repealed and replaced by *Directive 2006/54/EC*.

The UK sought to comply with the requirements imposed by *Art 157* and *Council Directives 75/117/EEC* and *76/207/EEC*. However, in a number of cases, the ECJ held that the UK had failed to comply fully with its EU obligations and further legislation has had to be introduced. See eg *EC Commission v United Kingdom of Great Britain and Northern Ireland*: 61/81 [1982] ECR 2601, [1982] ICR 578, ECJ. The domestic courts have also proven to be willing to find, without a reference to the ECJ, that domestic legislation is incompatible with European provisions. See eg *Equal Opportunities Commission v Secretary of State for Trade and Industry* [2007] IRLR 327. Domestic law protection from sex discrimination is now contained in the *Equality Act 2010*. See also EQUAL PAY (22) and DISCRIMINATION AND EQUAL OPPORTUNITIES – I (11).

In October 1992 a *Directive on the Protection of Pregnant Women at Work* (*Directive 92/85/EEC*) was adopted, which has led to the inclusion of a number of new and improved maternity rights provisions in the *Employment Rights Act 1996*. See also MATERNITY AND PARENTAL RIGHTS (32). In 2008 the EU Commission proposed a new directive, to replace the current one. However, the EU has, to date, still not been able to agree on a replacement directive.

Parental leave. The government sought to implement the *Parental Leave Directive (Directive 96/34/EC*, now replaced by *Directive 2010/18/EC*) by bringing into force the *Maternity and Parental Leave Regulations 1999 (SI 1999/3312)*. The domestic provisions confer a right to leave only on parents of children born on or after 15 December 1999. The compatibility of this restriction with EU law was referred to the ECJ (*R v Secretary of State for Trade and Industry, ex p Trades Union Congress* [2000] IRLR 565). Consequent amendments were made to ensure compliance with the directive: see the *Maternity and Parental Leave (Amendment) Regulations 2001 (SI 2001/4010)*. The *Parental Leave (EU Directive) Regulations 2013* implemented *Directive 2010/18/EC* by amending provisions relating to parental leave in the *Employment Rights Act 1996* and the *Maternity and Parental Leave Regulations 1999*.

Part-timers. The *Part-time Workers (Prevention of Less Favourable Treatment) Regulations 2000 (SI 2000/1551)* implement the *EU Part-time Work Directive (97/81/EC)*.

In December 1991 the Commission adopted a *Recommendation on the Protection of the Dignity of Men and Women at Work (92/131/EEC)*, which is not legally binding, but will be taken into account by courts and tribunals (see **23.1** above). It may be especially relevant to complaints of sex discrimination founded upon incidents of sexual harassment (see DISCRIMINATION AND EQUAL OPPORTUNITIES – I (11)). A further *Recommendation on Child Care* was adopted in March 1992.

Discrimination on grounds other than sex. Article 19 [13] of the TFEU confers a power on the EU to legislate against discrimination on grounds of racial or ethnic origin, religion or belief, disability, age and sexual orientation. The European Council has adopted two directives which are intended to give effect to the broad anti-discrimination principles found in *Art 19* of the *TFEU*.

The first is *Council Directive 2000/43/EC* of 29 June 2000 implementing the principle of equal treatment between persons irrespective of racial or ethnic origin. The directive prohibits direct and (unless it is objectively justified) indirect discrimination on grounds of racial or ethnic origin in both the public and private sectors. It does not prohibit discrimination on grounds of nationality. Harassment is expressly to be treated as an act of direct discrimination. Victimisation is also prohibited. There is a genuine occupational requirement defence. The provisions of the directive are now implemented by the *Equality Act 2010*.

The second directive is *Council Directive 2000/78/EC* of 27 November 2000 establishing a general framework for equal treatment in employment and occupation. The directive prohibits direct and unjustified indirect discrimination on grounds of 'religion or belief, disability, age or sexual orientation'. Like the *Race Discrimination Framework Directive* described above, it applies to both public and private sectors, prohibits harassment and victimisation, and includes an 'occupational requirement' defence. *Article 5* of the directive introduces a duty to take proportionate and appropriate measures to enable disabled persons to have access to, participate in or advance in employment or to undergo training which is analogous to the obligation imposed to by the *Equality Act 2010, ss 20* and *39(5)* to make reasonable adjustments: see *Navas (Chacon) v Eurest Colectividades SA*: C-13/05 [2006] ECR I-6467, [2007] ICR 1, ECJ. *Article 6* creates a defence of objective justification in cases of direct age discrimination. The directive is now implemented in Great Britain by the *Equality Act 2010*.

23.8 European Union Law

23.8 INFORMATION ON TERMS OF EMPLOYMENT

Directive 91/533/EEC (the *Information on Conditions of Employment Directive*) was adopted in October 1991. As a result of this directive, the United Kingdom, by means of amending the *Employment Protection (Consolidation) Act 1978* (now the *Employment Rights Act 1996*), extended the rights which already existed for employees to receive written particulars of the terms of their employment (see **8.4 CONTRACT OF EMPLOYMENT**).

23.9 REDUNDANCY PROCEDURE

Directive 98/59/EC contains requirements for the approximation of the laws of member states relating to collective redundancies. This was complied with by the enactment of provisions now to be found in *TULRCA 1992, ss 188–198*. See **39.2–39.6 REDUNDANCY – II**.

The ECJ found that by restricting the obligation to consult prior to collective redundancies to circumstances where the employer recognises a trade union in respect of the class of employees affected, the UK had failed properly to implement the predecessor to *Directive 98/59/EC, Directive 75/129/EEC (EC Commission v United Kingdom*: C-383/92 [1994] ECR I-2479, [1994] ICR 664, ECJ). In order to remedy this, the *Collective Redundancies and Transfer of Undertakings (Protection of Employment) (Amendment) Regulations 1995 (SI 1995/2587)* were enacted (see also **23.10** below).

23.10 RIGHTS ON TRANSFER OF BUSINESS

The *Transfer of Undertakings (Protection of Employment) Regulations 1981 (SI 1981/1794)* (now repealed and replaced by the *Transfer of Undertakings (Protection of Employment) Regulations 2006 (SI 2006/246)* were intended to implement the requirements of *Directive 77/187/EEC* (the *Acquired Rights Directive*). In fact, the *1981 Regulations* proved to be defective in several respects, and various amendments were made by the *Trade Union Reform and Employment Rights Act 1993* in an attempt to bring them into line with the directive. However, subsequent to those amendments being made, a further failure properly to comply was identified in *EC Commission v United Kingdom*: C-382/92 [1994] ECR I-2435, [1994] ICR 664 when the ECJ found that by restricting the obligation to consult prior to a transfer to circumstances where the employer recognises a trade union in respect of the class of employees affected, the UK had failed properly to implement *Directive 77/187/EEC*. In order to remedy this, the *Regulations* mentioned in **23.9** above *(SI 1995/2587)* were enacted.

On 12 March 2001, a new *Transfers Directive (2001/23/EC)* came into force. It is intended to codify the *Acquired Rights Directive (77/187/EEC)* and the amendments thereto adopted in 1998 (which are described in the main text). The *Transfer of Undertakings (Protection of Employment) Regulations 2006 (SI 2006/246)* came into force with effect from 6 April 2006 and are intended to implement the *Transfers Directive*.

(See **TRANSFER OF UNDERTAKINGS (52)**.)

23.11 HEALTH AND SAFETY

Between 1977 and 1986, the EU adopted directives on various aspects of health and safety, including safety signs, lead, asbestos and noise. A framework directive, *Directive 89/391/EEC* on the introduction of measures to encourage improvements in the safety and health of workers at work, was adopted in 1989. A number of statutory instruments have implemented the framework directive in national law (e.g. the *Management of Health and Safety at Work Regulations 1999 (SI 1999/3242)*, the *Health and Safety (Consultation with Employees) Regulations 1996 (SI 1996/1513)*, the *Control of Substances Hazardous to Health Regulations 2002 (SI 2002/2677)*).

The framework directive also provides for further directives, known as 'daughter' directives, to be made in particular areas (e.g. work equipment, personal protective equipment). A number of daughter directives have been made (e.g. *Directive 89/654/EEC* concerning the minimum safety and health requirements for the workplace, *Directive 2009/104/EC* concerning the minimum safety and health requirements for the use of work equipment by workers at work) and implemented in national law by health and safety regulations (e.g. the *Workplace (Health, Safety and Welfare) Regulations 1992 (SI 1992/3004)*).

(See **27.25** HEALTH AND SAFETY AT WORK – I.)

23.12 WORKING TIME

One directive which was adopted despite the objections of the UK is the *Working Time Directive 93/104/EC* (now repealed and replaced by *Directive 2003/88/EC*). It provided, with certain exceptions, for a maximum 48-hour week including overtime, averaged over four months. There was also provision for a minimum daily rest period of 11 consecutive hours, for a weekly break of not less than 35 consecutive hours, and for restrictions upon the length of night shifts. Finally there was provision for a minimum of four weeks' paid holiday per annum.

Whilst the directive was adopted under the provisions of the *TFEU* relating to Health and Safety at Work, the view of the UK government was that, in substance, it was an attempt to regulate conditions of employment, a matter which is outside the EU's competence. The UK brought a challenge to the directive in the European Court of Justice which was rejected by the Court (*United Kingdom v EU Council*: C-84/94 [1997] ICR 443).

In *Dominguez v Centre Informatique du Centre Ouest Atlantique* [2012] IRLR 321 the ECJ held that the right to four weeks' paid annual leave in *Art 7(1)* of the directive has vertical direct effect. Thus, the claimant was to be able to rely directly on *Art 7(1)*, but only if the referring court was satisfied that her employer, which dealt with social security, was an emanation of the state.

The *Working Time Regulations 1998 (SI 1998/1833)* came into force on 1 October 1998. The provisions of the *Regulations* relating to annual leave are summarised in HOLIDAYS **(29)**; as to the provisions relating to hours of work and rest breaks, see **28.15** HEALTH AND SAFETY AT WORK – II. In *R (on the application of the Broadcasting, Entertainment, Cinematographic and Theatre Union) v Secretary of State for Trade and Industry*: C-173/99 [2001] ICR 1152 the ECJ held that *reg 13* of the *Regulations*, restricting entitlement to paid annual leave to workers continuously employed for 13 weeks by the same employer, constituted an impermissible restriction on the rights conferred by the *Working Time Directive*. Consequential alterations to the *Regulations* were made by the *Working Time (Amendment) Regulations 2002 (SI 2002/3128)* with effect from 6 April 2003: see HOLIDAYS **(29)**. In *European Commission v United Kingdom*: C-484/04 [2006] ECR I-7471, [2007] ICR 592, the ECJ held that the UK had failed to fulfil its obligations under the *Working Time Directive* by issuing guidance on the *Regulations* which advised employers that they must make sure that workers can take their rest, but were not required to make sure they do take their rest.

The *Working Time Directive (93/104/EEC)* excluded employment in certain sectors from its scope. The sectors were: road, rail, air, inland waterway and lake transport, sea fishing, other work at sea, and doctors in training. *Directive 2000/34/EC* extended the application of the directive to non-mobile workers in the excluded sectors (with a special transitional period for its application to doctors in training). A consolidating *Directive 2003/88/EC* was adopted on 4 November 2003 and this is now the *Directive* governing this area (see WORKING TIME **(57)**). This has been implemented by the *Working Time (Amendment) Regulations 2003 (SI 2003/1684)*.

A specific directive covering the organisation of the working time of seafarers (*1999/63/EC*) was adopted on 21 June 1999. Domestic provision is made for sea fishermen and the inland water way sector by the *Fishing Vessels (Working Time: Sea Fishermen) Regulations 2004 (SI 2004/1713)* and the *Merchant Shipping (Working Time: Inland Waterways) Regulations 2003 (SI 2003/3049)*.

The *Working Time Directive 2003/88/EC* has recently been under review by the EU. However, in February 2013, the Commission announced that the European social partners had failed to come to an agreement on the review. As a result of this failure, it is expected that the Commission will draft a new legislative proposal.

23.13 INFORMATION AND CONSULTATION

The *European Works Councils Directive 94/45/EC* (now repealed and replaced by *Directive 2009/38/EC*) was adopted under the Social Protocol procedure. See EMPLOYEE PARTICIPATION **(16)**. The original *Directive* was implemented with effect from 15 January 2000 by the *Transnational Information and Consultation of Employees Regulations 1999 (SI 1999/3323)*. *Directive 2009/38/EC* was implemented by way of amendment to the *1999 Regulations*: see the *Transnational Information and Consultation of Employees (Amendment) Regulations 2010 (SI 2010/1088)*.

The *Directive of the European Parliament and of the Council 2002/14/EC* establishing a general framework for informing and consulting employees in the EU has been implemented in the UK by the *Information and Consultation of Employees Regulations 2004 (SI 2004/3426)*.

23.14 AGENCY WORKERS

The *EC Temporary Workers Directive (Directive 2008/104/EC)* provides for, amongst other things:

- equal treatment between temporary agency workers and permanent workers from the commencement of their work in terms of basic working and employment conditions (including working time, overtime, breaks, rest periods, night work, holidays and pay);

- the ability for member states to derogate from this by way of collective agreements or through agreements between social partners at national level (which the UK has done by implementing a 12-week qualifying period for agency workers' rights to equal basic working and employment conditions, which has been agreed by the TUC and the CBI); and

- temporary agency workers to be informed about permanent employment opportunities with the hirer.

The UK implemented the directive through the *Agency Workers Regulations 2010 (SI 2010/93)* which came into force in October 2011.

See TEMPORARY AND SEASONAL EMPLOYEES **(47)**.

23.15 POSTED WORKERS

The *Posted Workers Directive (Directive 96/71/EC)* aims to strike a balance between workers' rights on the one hand, and freedom of movement of services and freedom of establishment on the other. It aims to address lack of clarity about which law applies to workers who are posted from one undertaking within the EU to another; to avoid local terms and conditions being undermined by the use of "cheaper" foreign workers; and to avoid abuse of foreign workers. Broadly, it provides that temporarily posted workers should enjoy the same basic minimum employment rights as workers in the country to which they are posted. The rights covered by the directive include maximum work periods, minimum paid holidays, minimum rates of pay, health and safety and hygiene at work, and protective measures for pregnant women or those who have recently given birth. It does not cover all statutory employment rights; for example, the right not to be unfairly dismissed is outside the scope of the directive.

There are no UK Regulations which implement the *Directive*. Rather, UK legislation relevant to the directive (e.g. the *Working Time Regulations 1998* and the *National Minimum Wage Act 1998*) applies to all workers, whether they are employed on a temporary or a permanent basis in the UK.

The EU Commission has proposed that *Directive 96/71* be supplemented by a further directive, which would establish a common framework of provisions, including measures to prevent circumvention or abuse of the existing rules. The Commission's proposed new directive, which was published in March 2012, is yet to be approved by the European Council and the European Parliament.

See FOREIGN EMPLOYEES (**26.3**).

23.16 EMPLOYEES OF INSOLVENT EMPLOYERS

Minimum rights for the employees of insolvent employers were specified by *Directive 80/987/EEC*, which has now been repealed and replaced by *Directive 2008/94/EC* (see **31.1** INSOLVENCY OF EMPLOYER).

23.17 FIXED-TERM WORKERS

On 28 June 1999, the Council adopted a directive transposing into European law a framework agreement on fixed-term work (*1999/70/EC*). The directive was implemented in the UK by the *Fixed-term Employees (Prevention of Less Favourable Treatment) Regulations 2002 (SI 2002/2034)*. It prohibits less favourable treatment of fixed-term workers on account of their fixed-term status, save where such treatment is objectively justified; and restricts successive renewals of fixed-term contracts (see **47.8** TEMPORARY AND SEASONAL EMPLOYEES).

23.18 THE REGULATION OF PAY IN THE FINANCIAL SERVICES SECTOR

Pay in the financial services sector is regulated by remuneration codes in the Financial Conduct Authority Handbook and in Prudential Regulation Authority Rulebook. Most of the rules on pay contained in the handbooks are required by EU law, namely the *CRD IV Directive* (*2013/36/EU*) and accompanying *Capital Requirements Regulation* (*Regulation 575/2013*); the *Alternative Investment Fund Managers Directive* (*2011/61/EU*); and the *UCITS V Directive* (*Directive 2014/91/EU*).

The detailed rules contained in these instruments are beyond the scope of this chapter. Their overall purpose is to ensure that remuneration is consistent with and promotes sound and effective risk management. In other words, they are designed to de-incentivise excessively risky and short-termist behaviour by bankers and other financiers. One of the more important rules is the so-called 'bonus cap' for bankers. The cap is required by the *CRD IV Directive*. The value of a individual's variable pay (or bonus) should be no greater than the value of his or her fixed pay (or basic salary); in other words, the ratio of bonus to basic salary should not exceed 1:1. However, the ratio can be raised to 1:2 with the express permission of shareholders.

24   Financial penalties on employers

24.1 In relation to claims presented on or after 6 April 2014 a new power has been granted to employment tribunals to impose financial penalties on employers: *s 12A* of the *Employment Tribunals Act 1996*, introduced by *s 16* of the *Enterprise and Regulatory Reform Act 2013* (the implementation date being dealt with by *s 24* of that *Act*).

An employment tribunal may do so where it concludes that the employer has breached any of the worker's rights and it is of the opinion that the breach has 'one or more aggravating features'.

24.2 There is no guidance in the *Act* as to what is an aggravating factor. However, the explanatory notes suggested that a tribunal might consider 'the size of the employer; the duration of the breach; or the behaviour of the employer and employee', as well as whether the action was 'deliberate or committed with malice, the employer was an organisation with a dedicated human resources team, or where the employer had repeatedly breached the employment right concerned.' On the other hand, it might be less likely to find an aggravating factor where the business is new or small or the breach was the result of a genuine mistake.

24.3 Having found one or more aggravating factors, the tribunal must decide whether to order the employer to pay a penalty. In considering this question, it must have regard to the employer's ability to pay.

The level of the penalty is to be:

- Where no financial award is made against the employer on the claim, in the range £100 and £5,000;

- In relation to any other single claim where a financial award is made against the employer, the penalty is 50% of that award (subject to a minimum and maximum of £100 and £5,000); for these purposes:

  - the amount of the award to be taken into account ignores any uplift made by reason of a failure to comply with an order of the tribunal;

  - two or more claims in respect of the same act and the same worker are to be treated as a single claim;

- Where the tribunal considers two or more claims involving different workers (but the same employer), then the penalty shall be no more than £5,000 for each claim, provided that it should be no more than 50% of any financial award on that claim.

Any penalty which is imposed is payable to the Secretary of State. There is a discount of 50% for payment within 21 days after the day on which the penalty notice is sent to the employer.

24.4 A written Parliamentary question given on 4 January 2017, revealed that since April 2016 the Department for Business, Energy and Industrial Strategy had issued 60 penalty notices as a result of 164 warning notices to employers for failure to comply with employment tribunal orders to pay compensation to applicants. As a result of the employment tribunal penalty regime £83,000 in previously unpaid awards had been secured for claimants.

aspects of the affairs of the authorised person concerned which it is intended that the person will be responsible for managing in performing the function": *section 60(2A)* of *FSMA*. This is known as a "statement of responsibilities". Any significant change to the individual's responsibilities, such as addition, removal or re-allocation, will require the firm to submit a revised statement of responsibilities: SUP 10C.11.

Firms must also construct and keep up-to-date a management responsibility map, which comprehensively sets out the apportionment of responsibility, reporting lines and "reasonable details" about each senior manager: SYSC 4.5. Where responsibilities are shared, e.g. on a job share arrangement, the map should show this clearly. While one of the map's main purposes is to enable the regulators to know who is the appropriate person to speak to in respect of a specific matter, the regulators have emphasised that this is also a tool to help the firm itself understand its own business structure to identify potential failings or risks.

Some of the senior management responsibilities correspond to specific SMFs: e.g. the responsibility for safeguarding the independence of, and oversight of the performance of, the risk function ("Risk control") corresponds to SMF10, Chair of the Risk Committee. Others are less obvious, in particular the "overall responsibility" under SYSC 4.7.8 R. One senior manager may (and inevitably will) be responsible for more than one responsibility. An individual does not need to be on the governing body to have overall responsibility for a given matter, and so could in theory be someone quite junior, but the FCA does expect the person will be sufficiently senior and credible and will have sufficient resources and authority to be effective. The FCA is resistant to splitting responsibilities between more than one individual, it accepts that this could be justified as part of a job sharing arrangement or during a handover period: SYSC 4.7.

The "miscellaneous" SMF18 applies where an individual has a senior management responsibility which does not correspond to one of the specific SMFs identified by the regulators, and is not also approved for one of those SMFs. This will be particularly relevant where a firm has identified an activity, business area or management function which falls outside the responsibilities prescribed by the regulators. The "oversight SMFs", such as SMF10, must be carried out by a non-executive director, who (it is hoped) is in a more independent position to provide that oversight. The 12-week exemption, familiar from the APR, also applies to senior managers under the SMCR, so that a firm may appoint a non-approved individual to an SMF to provide up to 12 weeks' cover for a temporarily or unforeseeably absent senior manager: SUP 10C.3.13.

25.9   Certification

SMCR firms are required to certify that "employees" who carry out specified significant-harm functions ("SHFs") are "fit and proper" to carry out their roles. An employee for these purposes is someone who personally provides, or is under an obligation personally to provide, services to the firm in question under an arrangement made between the firm and the person providing the services or another person; and (b) is subject to (or to the right of) supervision, direction or control by the firm as to the manner in which those services are provided: *section 63E(9)* of *FMSA*. In other words, some distance from the definition of employment status familiar to employment lawyers.

SHFs are defined at *section 63E(5)* of *FSMA* as those which are not controlled functions, but (a) require the person performing it to be involved in one or more aspects of the firm's affairs, so far as relating to the activity, and (b) involve, or might involve, a risk of significant harm to the authorised person or any of its customers. The FCA has set out nine SHFs, including "significant management", "material risk takers" and "client–dealing" (the last of which being similar to the CF30 customer function under the APR), with explanations, at SYSC 5.2. The PRA has taken a slightly different approach: any function (other than a controlled function) that is performed by a significant risk taker for a firm is a certification function to the extent that the function requires the significant risk taker to be involved in one or more aspects of the firm's affairs, so far as relating to a regulated activity carried on by the firm: Certification 2.2.

FSMA sets out the same mandatory considerations for determining fitness and propriety as for a senior manager: the firm must have regard, in particular, to whether the person (a) has obtained a qualification, (b) has undergone, or is undergoing, training, (c) possesses a level of competence, or (d) has the personal characteristics, required by general rules made by the appropriate regulator in relation to employees performing functions of that kind: *section 63F(2)*. The firm should also follow the same regulatory guidance as if it was vetting a senior manager – always bearing in mind that the requirements of the certification role will almost inevitably be markedly different from that of a senior manager. The certificate is valid for only twelve months (*section 63F(5)* of *FSMA*), so must be renewed annually to allow an individual to continue carrying out his function. The regulators have endorsed the sensible approach of building the recertification process into any existing annual performance review procedure.

Under *section 63E*, such firms must take reasonable care to ensure that no employee of it performs a specified function under an arrangement entered into by it in relation to the carrying on by it of a regulated activity, unless the employee has a valid certificate. Both regulators do, however, allow a four-week grace period, where an appointment to a certification function is (PRA adds: "solely") to provide cover for a certified employee whose absence is reasonably unforeseen. The FCA also operates a "30-day rule", which allows individuals based outside the UK to perform most certification functions for up to 30 days in a year without being certified. As with approval, it is often prudent for the relevant contract (usually but not necessarily an employment contract) to expressly provide for termination in the event of a lack of certificate.

25.10 Code of Conduct

The SMCR also brings individuals who are neither approved nor certified within its regulatory scope, to the extent that "employees" of SMCR firms are bound by the "Code of Conduct", set out by the FCA at Handbook Chapter "COCON". Again, the definition of "employee" departs from employment law: section 64A defines an employee as someone who personally provides, or is under an obligation personally to provide, services to the firm in question under an arrangement made between the firm and the person providing the services or another person; and (b) is subject to (or to the right of) supervision, direction or control by the firm as to the manner in which those services are provided (identical to the definition in the context of certification employees). There are two sets of conduct rules: those which apply to all employees save for those in non-financial roles (e.g. post room staff, catering staff, HR, etc.), also referred to as "conduct rules staff", and those which apply to senior managers. The five basic conduct rules are:

Rule 1: You must act with integrity.

Rule 2: You must act with due skill, care and diligence.

Rule 3: You must be open and cooperative with the FCA, the PRA and other regulators.

Rule 4: You must pay due regard to the interests of customers and treat them fairly.

Rule 5: You must observe proper standards of market conduct.

Senior managers are subject to four further rules, which are (as one might expect) more onerous, in that they require the senior manager to take active steps:

SC1: You must take reasonable steps to ensure that the business of the firm for which you are responsible is controlled effectively.

SC2: You must take reasonable steps to ensure that the business of the firm for which you are responsible complies with the relevant requirements and standards of the regulatory system.

SC3: You must take reasonable steps to ensure that any delegation of your responsibilities is to an appropriate person and that you oversee the discharge of the delegated responsibility effectively.

SC4: You must disclose appropriately any information of which the FCA or PRA would reasonably expect notice.

Breach of these rules is misconduct (*sections 66A* and *66B* of *FSMA*), which may attract a disciplinary sanction from either regulator.

25.11 INVESTIGATIONS

The regulators have a broad range of investigatory powers, under *Part 11* of *FSMA*. These allow them to require firms and individuals to produce existing documents and to answer questions (both in writing and in compelled interviews). Usually this will be in the context of a formal investigation, but the regulators do have a power under *section 165* of *FSMA* to require, at any time, information or documents reasonably required in connection with the exercise of their functions under *FSMA*. More commonly, the regulator will appoint investigators (invariably internal staff) to carry out either "general investigations" into the nature, conduct or state of an authorised person's business under *section 167* or "investigations in particular cases" under *section 168* where it appears to the regulator that there has been a contravention of a specific provision. The nature of the suspected breach determines various aspects of the duties and powers of the investigators. For example, if a civil (as opposed to criminal or quasi-criminal) investigation is launched, the relevant regulator must give written notice to the subject of the investigation, specifying the suspected breach and reason for appointing investigators, unless such notification would frustrate the be likely to result in the investigation being frustrated: *section 170* of *FSMA*.

The regulators may become aware of potential breaches in a wide variety of ways. Very commonly, it will be self-reporting: Principle 11 of PRIN requires firms to deal with its regulators in an open and regulators cooperative way, and to disclose to the appropriate regulator appropriately anything relating to the firm of which that regulator would reasonably expect notice. Alternatively, a whistleblower from within a firm who has either exhausted internal processes or has no faith in them (assuming, indeed, that the firm has such internal processes) may tip the regulator off. The regulators may also respond to other bodies' findings, for example adverse judicial dicta in courts or tribunals, or to complaints from the public.

The investigators may use compulsory information-gathering powers against two groups of people: (1) the subject of the investigation and persons connected with them; and (2) any other person. If seeking information from the former category, the statutory threshold is lower: it merely requires that the investigator reasonably considers the question, provision of information or production of the document to be relevant to the purposes of the investigation: *section 171*. For these purposes, an individual is connected to the subject of the investigation if she is (depending on the corporate structure) an officer, manager, employee, agent or member – this includes being an employee or agent of an individual who is under investigation: *Schedule 15, Part I* of *FSMA*. Meanwhile, if the information is sought from someone unconnected to the subject of the investigation, a requirement may only be imposed if the investigator is satisfied that the requirement is necessary or expedient for the purposes of the investigation: *section 172* of *FSMA*.

Section 176 of *FSMA* sets out the consequences of non-compliance with a Part 11 information requirement. If someone subject to a requirement fails without reasonable excuse to comply with it, the regulator may refer that to the court who may in turn treat the defaulter as if he were in contempt. In the case of a body corporate, this would include a director or other officer: case-law on the Civil Procedure Rules contempt provision suggests that the individual in question must be aware of the order, and that failure to supervise or investigate, or wilful blindness, will be sufficient even in the absence of active participation in the breach: *Templeton Insurance Ltd v Thomas* [2013] EWCA Civ 35. Meanwhile, it is a criminal offence to falsify, conceal, destroy or dispose of a relevant document, or to permit or cause such behaviour, as well as to knowingly or recklessly provide false or misleading information.

Another option for the regulators is to obtain a "skilled persons" report under section 166. This involves a third party – usually one of the leading accountancy firms but occasionally solicitors or consultants – to independently review an authorised person's business or an aspect thereof. The scope of the review is set by the regulator but the costs (including those incurred by the FCA) are borne by the firm under review. Depending on the scope, this can be a substantial sum: the median cost of reviews in 2015/16 was £155,000, according to the FCA's annual report. The FCA and PRA both publish quarterly statistics on their use of this power describing the type of suspected misconduct and the type of firm (the FCA also includes the identity of the skilled person retained).

25.12 SANCTIONS

The regulators have a "toolkit" of powers under FSMA with which to carry out their functions. These can broadly be categorised as: (1) disciplinary or punitive; and (2) supervisory or protective. This is an important distinction for issues such as double jeopardy and limitation. They also arise in different ways: disciplinary responses tend to be where a person has breached a regulatory requirement which applies to them. For a firm, this could be a breach of any of the rules in the FCA Handbook or PRA Rulebook, including those set out in this Chapter, and including in particular the Principles for Business set out in PRIN. For an individual, this could be: a breach of the conduct rules; being knowingly concerned in a firm's contravention; a senior manager who breaches the "duty of responsibility" under Condition C of *sections 66A* or *66B* of *FSMA*; or market abuse. Protective measures, on the other hand, tend to be applied where a person is failing to reach a given standard of fitness and propriety. Depending on the context, this could be someone falling short of the very high standard required for a senior manager at a large bank, or (at the other end of the spectrum) so lacking in integrity that they cannot be permitted to perform any function in connection with regulated activities. Clearly, there will be cases where both are appropriate.

The lightest disciplinary measure is a public censure (i.e. a "statement of misconduct"), although this can have serious, and in some cases deleterious, effects on an individual's career. The regulators may also impose a condition, limitation or suspension in respect of an individual's approval, or a part thereof. By far the most common sanction is, however, the financial penalty, or "fine", imposed under *section 66* (for individuals) or *section 206* (for firms) of *FSMA*.

The amount of a financial penalty is decided according to set policies, in five steps: (1) disgorgement (i.e. ensuring that the wrongdoer retains no benefit from the breach); (2) seriousness of the breach (a fraction of the gross income from the breach up to 40%, depending on the seriousness); (3) mitigating and aggravating factors (which may relate to the nature of the breach or the conduct post-breach, including during the investigation); (4) a potential adjustment to ensure appropriate deterrence; and (5) a settlement discount (up to 30%, depending on the stage at which settlement is reached). There are similar policies in respect of the duration of conditions and suspensions. The regulators may also take into account serious financial hardship which might be caused by the fine, upon receipt of verifiable evidence that the subject is below the relevant threshold of income and capital holding.

The most draconian protective tool is a prohibition order under *section 56* of *FSMA* (or "ban"), whereby an individual is barred from carrying out = functions in relation to a regulated activity. This may be a "full ban" or it may be limited to specified functions, activities or firms. Individuals will be banned if they are deemed not to be fit and proper to perform functions. The purpose of this is not only to preclude those individuals from carrying out functions when they are unfit to do so, but may also be "*to send out messages to the financial services industry and to the public about unacceptable conduct in the financial markets and in order to deter others*": *Davies v Financial Services Authority* [2003] EWCA Civ 1128, [2004] 1 WLR 185 at [28]. Firms have a statutory duty to "take reasonable care to ensure that no function of his, in relation to the carrying on of a regulated activity, is performed by a person who is prohibited from performing that function by a prohibition order": *section 156(6)* of *FSMA*. As is clear from the statutory wording, this applies regardless of the relationship with the individual (i.e. whether the function is performed by an employee, worker, contractor etc.) but what is "reasonable" in the circumstances may vary. Meanwhile, it is a criminal offence for a banned individual to breach (or agree to breach) a prohibition order, punishable by a fine: *section 56(4)* of *FSMA*.

Senior managers and approved persons may also have their permissions removed or varied, either on the regulator's own initiative or voluntarily. Firms must therefore take reasonable steps to ensure that all controlled functions (whether under the SMCR or the APR) are at all times carried out by individuals with the appropriate approval. To this end, it is often advisable to include express contractual terms which provide for the eventuality that an individual becomes unable to perform his role due to his lack of approval.

A regulator may also require a bank, building society or MiFID investment firm to remove or replace a director or senior executive, and to take any necessary step to do so e.g. to call a shareholders' meeting: *section 71B*. It is subject to two conditions: (1) there is a significant deterioration in the firm's financial situation or serious infringement of a regulatory requirement or its own constitution; and (2) no less intrusive measure would be reasonably likely to reverse the deterioration or end the infringement. If merely removing or replacing the manager would itself not be sufficient to reverse the deterioration or bring the infringement to an end, the regulator may appoint a person to act (or one or more persons to act jointly) as a temporary manager of that firm: section 71C. These relatively new powers, implementing the *Banking Recovery and Resolution Directive 2014/59*, came into force on 16 December 2016.

The regulator will give the subject a "warning notice" in the first instance, following which the subject may make representations (the FCA would usually have furnished a preliminary investigation report prior to this, but that is not a statutory requirement). The relevant decision maker will then issue a "decision notice". If that is not appealed, a final notice is issued. Appeals go to the Upper Tribunal, which, depending on the nature of the reference, may either substitute its own decision or refer the matter back to the regulator with findings of fact. Where the notices identify a third party, they also have rights to see the notices, make representations and refer the matter to the Upper Tribunal: *section 393* of *FSMA*. The Supreme Court has held that a person may be identified by name or by a synonym, such as his office or job title, which makes it apparent from the notice itself that it could apply to only one person; extraneous information will be relevant where it enables one to interpret, but does not supplement, the language of the notice: *Financial Conduct Authority v Macris* [2017] UKSC 19.

Details of the measure taken, and the reasons for doing so, will usually be published by the relevant regulator pursuant to *section 391* of *FSMA*. This will involve publishing the final notice, and in some cases the warning notice as well. The regulator *must* publish such information about the matter as it considers appropriate, but *may not* publish information in certain circumstances, e.g. where it would be unfair to the subject of the action (FCA and PRA), prejudicial to the interests of consumers or detrimental to the stability of the UK financial system (FCA) or prejudicial to the safety and soundness of PRA-authorised persons (PRA).

Where the regulator decides not to take formal action using one of its statutory powers, it may issue a "private warning", i.e. a letter (identifying itself as a private warning) which sets out the concerns and reprimands the person in question. Other powers are the regulators' disposal include applying to the court for an injunction (*section 380 of FSMA*) or a restitution order (*section 382 of FSMA*), or requiring a firm to pay restitution without recourse to the courts (*section 384 of FSMA*).

25.13 REMUNERATION

One of the factors identified as contributing to the financial crisis was "inappropriate" remuneration policies, which allowed individuals to receive vast sums of money, often in the form of bonuses, irrespective of the eventual effects of their behaviour. It incentivised short-termism, since large profits in one fiscal year would yield large personal rewards, even if those profits were later revealed to be illusory or toxic. Accordingly, one of the earliest policy responses was a remuneration code, being the subject of an FSA Policy Statement in August 2009 (PS09/15), "Reforming remuneration practices in financial services", and one of the focuses of the G20 Pittsburgh Summit in September 2009 (which used the terminology of "compensation practices"). It is clear, however, from the PCBS report in 2013 that the problem remained unsolved: see especially Chapter 8 of that report, "Remuneration".

There are currently six remuneration codes applicable in the UK, depending on the type of investment firm. (In addition, insurance firms are subject to remuneration requirements pursuant to the directly applicable *Solvency II Regulation EU 2015/35*.) The codes are rules made by the FCA and PRA pursuant to their *Part 9A of FSMA* powers, appearing at Sections 19A-19E of the FCA Handbook Chapter "Systems and Controls", or "SYSC", and the "Remuneration" section of the PRA Rulebook as it applies to CRR firms (that is, banks, building societies and PRA-designated investment firms). It is beyond the scope of this chapter to adumbrate the differences between each of the various codes. The focus of this section will be on the rules applicable to dual-regulated firms, set out at SYSC 19D. (These are largely similar to two other codes: namely the PRA's and FCA's respective codes which relate to institutions covered by the *EU Capital Requirements Regulation 575/2013*.) The code contains three types of provisions: rules, indicated by the letter "R"; guidance, indicated by "G"; and evidential, indicated by "E", meaning that a contravention may be relied on as tending to establish contravention of such other rule made by that regulator as may be specified: *section 138C of FSMA*. Rules will also use the word "must", whereas guidance and evidential provisions will use "should".

Breach of the codes, given their status as regulatory rules, will render a firm liable for disciplinary action by the regulators but will not ordinarily render any transaction void or unenforceable: *section 138E(2) of FSMA*. The FCA has, however, carved out an exception for individuals who work at a firm which has total assets of greater than £50bn, whereby any provision which contravenes the rules on either guaranteed remuneration, deferral or clawback will be void. In addition, firms are required by the codes to take reasonable steps to remove contractual provisions which are incompatible with the codes.

The "general requirement" of the remuneration code is that firms "*must establish, implement and maintain remuneration policies, procedures and practices that are consistent with, and promote, sound and effective risk management.*" This is in order to achieve the codes' purpose of ensuring that policies are "*risk-focused,*" "*consistent with and promote effective risk management*" and "*do not expose [firms] to excessive risk.*"

The code then goes on to enumerate 12 "Remuneration Principles". Whereas the general requirement applies to all staff, the remuneration principles apply only to "material risk takers". An individual may be a material risk taker by virtue of her role or by virtue of the amount she is paid. She may, however, be exempt if she earns less than a "*de minimis*" amount (total remuneration of at least £500,000 or bonus more than 33% of total remuneration). Moreover, under the proportionality principle, smaller firms may disapply some of the remuneration rules.

(1)   Risk management and risk tolerance. A firm must ensure that its remuneration policy is consistent with, and promotes, sound and effective risk management and does not encourage risk-taking that exceeds the level of tolerated risk of the firm.

(2)   Supporting business strategy, objectives, values and long-term interests of the firm. A firm must ensure that its remuneration policy is in line with the business strategy, objectives, values and long-term interests of the firm.

(3)   Avoiding conflicts of interest. A firm must ensure that its remuneration policy includes measures to avoid conflicts of interest.

(4)   Governance. A firm must ensure that its management body in its supervisory function adopts and periodically reviews the general principles of the remuneration policy and is responsible for overseeing its implementation. It must ensure that the implementation of the remuneration policy is, at least annually, subject to central and independent internal review for compliance with policies and procedures for remuneration adopted by the management body in its supervisory function.

(5)   Control functions. This regulates the employment employees in control functions, who must be: (1) independent from the business units they oversee; (2) vested with appropriate authority; and (3) remunerated adequately both to attract qualified and experienced employees and commensurately with the importance of their role.

(6)   Remuneration and capital. This requires firms to ensure that total variable remuneration does not limit its ability to strengthen its capital base. A firm should have variable remuneration arrangements that are sufficiently flexible to allow it to direct the necessary resources towards capital building.

(7)   Exceptional government intervention. A firm that benefits from exceptional government intervention must ensure that: (1) variable remuneration is strictly limited as a percentage of net revenues when it is inconsistent with the maintenance of a sound capital base and timely exit from government support; (2) it restructures remuneration in a manner aligned with sound risk management and long-term growth, including (when appropriate) establishing limits to the remuneration of members of its management body; and (3) no variable or discretionary remuneration of any kind is paid to members of its management body unless this is justified. Guidance provides that this will normally apply only to members of the management body who were in office at the time that the intervention was required.

(8)   Profit-based measurement and risk adjustment. This requires firms to ensure that any measurement of performance used to calculate bonuses allows for risk adjustment. The guidance notes the importance of applying judgment and common sense.

(9)   Pension policy. This requires a firm's pension policy to be in line with its business strategy, objectives, values and long-term interests; and governs how discretionary pension benefits should be held (before retirement) and paid (after retirement).

(10)   Personal investment strategies. This requires a firm to ensure that its employees undertake not to use personal hedging strategies or insurance contracts to undermine the risk alignment effects embedded in their remuneration arrangements. Firms must also maintain effective arrangements designed to ensure that employees comply with their undertaking.

(11)   Non-compliance with the dual-regulated firms Remuneration Code. A firm must ensure that variable remuneration is not paid through vehicles or methods that facilitate non-compliance with remuneration obligations.

(12)   Remuneration structures. This is split into eight sections:

(a)   General requirement: A firm must ensure that the structure of an employee's remuneration is consistent with, and promotes, effective risk management.

(b)   Assessment of performance: This requires firms to take into account the performance of the business unit and firm as a whole, as well as the individual, and to take into account financial as well as non-financial criteria.

(c)   Guaranteed variable remuneration, buy-outs: Guaranteed bonuses are forbidden unless it is exceptional, the firm has a strong and sound capital base and it is limited to the first year of a new employee's service. Remuneration when buying out new employees' old contracts must align with the firm's long-term interests including appropriate retention, deferral and performance and clawback arrangements.

(d)   Ratios between fixed and variable components of total remuneration: i.e. the bonus cap. In general, the ratio of bonus to salary should not exceed 1:1, or 2:1 where approved by shareholders, owners or members.

(e)   Payments related to early termination: Payments relating to the early termination of a contract must reflect performance achieved over time and be designed in a way that does not reward failure or misconduct.

(f)   Retained shares or other instruments: At least 50% of a bonus must be an appropriate balance of (i) ownership interests in the firm and (ii) other instruments tied to the credit quality of the firm.

(g)   Deferral: At least 40% of a bonus (or 60% if the bonus is more than £500,000 or the firm is significant) must be deferred for a number of years (7 if PRA-designated SMF, 3-5 otherwise).

(h)   Performance adjustment (affordability, malus, clawback): Variable remuneration should be paid only if doing so is sustainable according to the financial situation of the firm as a whole, and justified on the basis of the performance of the firm, the business unit and the individual concerned. Firms must be able to clawback an amount equivalent to the bonus for at least seven years in appropriate circumstances. The firm must have policies for the application of malus and clawback which cover at least cover situations where the employee (i) participated in, or was responsible for, conduct which resulted in significant losses to the firm; or (ii) failed to meet appropriate standards of fitness and propriety.

When making decisions about malus and clawback, employers will be bound by ordinary principles of acting in good faith when exercising a contractual discretion: see Chapter X in this volume, but in particular *Keen v Commerzbank AG* [2006] EWCA Civ 1536, [2007] ICR

623; *Braganza v BP Shipping* [2015] UKSC 17, [2015] 1 WLR 1661. The courts will undoubtedly take into account the important policy considerations which underlie the remuneration codes, but an irrational or unfair decision may be the subject of a contractual claim for damages.

25.14 REGULATORY REFERENCES

The common law governing the contents of references, considered in detail at Chapter X of this volume, applies to the financial services sector just as it does to any other industry. This is explicitly acknowledged by both regulators in their latest policy statements. The FCA acknowledged in September 2016 that "Firms are subject to common law and employment law, which apply independently of regulatory requirements," and "a firm's compliance with the regulatory referencing requirements [needs] to be consistent with firms' common law duties." In addition to endorsing that acknowledgment, the PRA had also in February 2016 noted the employer's "duty to their former employees and to the recipient firm to exercise due skill and care in the preparation of the reference."

Indeed, it may be noted that many of the common law authorities in this area involved employers in the financial services industry. This should come as no surprise, given that it is sector in which the paramountcy of integrity and competence intersects with substantial amounts of compensation. This (as foreshadowed in the case-law) led to a chilling effect, whereby risk-averse employers have either toned down their references to the point of blandness or avoided giving them altogether (where possible). The regulators have therefore made it a priority to prevent "rolling bad apples" – individuals with poor conduct records who move from firm to firm undetected – with regulatory references. These are mandatory in two ways: first, certain firms are required to both seek and to give such reference; secondly, there are minimum requirements as to the contents of the reference. These requirements are set out in the PRA Rulebook Fitness and Propriety 2 and 5 and the FCA Handbook SYSC 22.

All SMCR firms are required to take reasonable steps to obtain appropriate references covering the previous six years of employment when assessing an individual's fitness and propriety. "Employment" in this context includes the broader definition used elsewhere in the SMCR (see above), as well as being an approved person or director (including non-executive director). References must be sought from all institutions, regardless of whether they are regulated or even in the financial services industry, and regardless of whether they are in the UK. Failure to obtain the reference will not in itself be a breach, as long as the requesting firm has taken reasonable steps.

Meanwhile, when receiving a request for a regulatory reference, any firm (i.e. not just SMCR firms) must provide one to another firm as soon as reasonably practicable, disclosing all information of which it is aware that it reasonably considers to be relevant to the requesting firm's assessment of whether the individual in question is fit and proper. The information only needs to go back six years before the date of the request, unless it relates to "serious misconduct", but nothing prevents a firm from disclosing more. SMCR firms are required to fill out a template, which prescribes certain categories of information which much be provided, regardless of whether the requesting firm is SMCR or not: SYSC 22.2.2 R. Non-SMCR firms are not subject to any requirements as to the form of the reference: SYSC 22.3.1 R.

SMCR firms are also required, up to six years after employing an individual, to update references where it becomes aware of matters, or reaches a conclusion or takes an action, which would have required them to draft their original reference differently. This will involve making reasonable inquiries as to the individual's current employer and forwarding details of those differences to the original requester as soon as reasonably practicable, unless the matter has become academic, for example because that firm is no longer the individual's employer.

25.14   Financial regulation in the UK

SYSC 22.5 governs what information should be included in the reference for FCA purposes. Firms are not required to disclose information that has not been properly verified, e.g. as a result of unfinished disciplinary proceedings. However, a firm *may* include such information if it wishes to. A firm should provide as complete a picture of an employee's conduct record as possible to new employers, while keeping within the bounds of its duty to exercise due skill and care in the preparation of the reference. The firm may give frank and honest views, but only after taking reasonable care both as to factual content, and as to the opinions expressed. References should be true, accurate, fair and based on documented fact.

A firm must not enter into any arrangements or agreements with any person that limit its ability to disclose information pursuant to its regulatory requirements. This will be most relevant in exit agreements and settlement agreements. While there should not be any problem with warranting that the firm is not aware of any disclosable information, if that is the position, the firm may not undertake not to revise a reference should new information or conclusions come to light.

25.15   WHISTLEBLOWING

Protection for whistleblowers is provided by the *Employment Rights Act 1996*, as amended by the *Public Interest Disclosure Act 1998*: see CHAPTER X of this volume. This statutory regime applies to workers in the financial services industry just as it does to any other worker. Given the importance of whistleblowing to the regulatory system, and by extension to the financial markets in general, there are various additional requirements which pertain to firms carrying our regulated activities.

First, firms are required to establish, implement and maintain appropriate and effective arrangements for the disclosure of reportable concerns by whistleblowers: PRA General Organisational Requirements 2A; SYSC 18.3. A "reportable concern" is, in fact, wider than a "qualifying disclosure" in the Employment Rights Act 1996, since it also includes (i) breaches of the firm's policies and procedures and (ii) behaviour that harms or is likely to harm the reputation or financial well-being of the firm. The firm's internal arrangements: must allow for confidentiality and a range of communication methods; must allow for effective assessment and escalation where appropriate; must ensure no victimisation; must provide feedback to the whistleblower where appropriate; and appropriate records must be kept. If a firm is found to have acted to the detriment of a whistleblower, the FCA says it could call into question the fitness and propriety of the firm or relevant members of its staff: SYSC 18.3.9 G.

One of the regulators' prescribed responsibilities is that of "Whistleblowers' Champion", who has responsibility for ensuring and overseeing the integrity, independence and effectiveness of the firm's policies and procedures on whistleblowing. This must therefore be allocated to a senior manager: the FCA expects that the firm will appoint a non-executive director as whistleblowers' champion if it has at least one.

26   Foreign Employees

26.1   ENTITLEMENT TO WORK IN THE UK

The first issue which arises in respect of employees who are not nationals of the UK is whether they are lawfully entitled to work in this country. The existing regime draws a broad distinction between nationals of Member States of the European Economic Area ('EEA'), which now comprises 27 Member-States, and others.

- *Migrant workers from within the EEA* — Employees who are nationals of countries within the EEA are generally entitled to work in the UK, see further the *Immigration (European Economic Area) Regulations 2016 (SI 2016/1052)* which came into force on 1 February 2017 (repealing and replacing the *Immigration (European Economic Area) Regulations 2006 (SI 2006/1003)* and clarifying the UK's implementation of more recent CJEU case law). Between 2004 and 2011, an exception to this general rule was in effect pursuant to the *Accession (Immigration and Worker Registration) Regulations 2004 (SI 2004/1219)* (as amended). Under the 2004 regulations, individuals who are nationals of recently acceded Member-States (apart from Cyprus and Malta) and who wanted to work in the UK for more than one month were required to register with the home office 'Worker Registration Scheme' as soon as they found work. The Worker Registration Scheme closed on 30 April 2011 and the 2004 Regulations were revoked. As from 1 January 2014, Bulgarian and Romanian nationals are no longer required to apply for permission to work. Croatian nations must obtain authorisation to work (see the scheme set out in the *Accession of Croatia (Immigration and Worker Authorisation) Regulations 2013, SI 2013/1460*).

- *Migrant workers from outside the EEA* — With the exception of Swiss nationals and Croatian nationals, individuals who are not nationals of a Member State of the EEA currently have their entitlement to work in the UK decided by the points-based system which came into force in the UK in November 2008. The points-based system largely replaced the long-standing work permits scheme. Swiss nationals are exempted from the points-based system and are accordingly free to work in the UK. See further below the discussion of the important changes to the points-based system introduced with effect from 6 April 2011.

The points-based system and the more limited work permit schemes applicable to nationals of newly acceded EU Member States was formerly administered by the UK Border Agency. However, the Agency was abolished in 2013, with the relevant decision making functions being returned to the Home Office. The relevant Home Office department is UK Visas and Immigration (UKUVI). Information for EEA nationals on working in another EEA country is available through the EURES network at europa.eu.

26.2   NATIONALS OF THE EUROPEAN ECONOMIC AREA

The principle of free movement of labour, which is now applicable to all members of the EEA, is derived principally from *art 45* of the *Treaty on the Functioning of the European Union (TFEU)*, and *Regulation 1612/68*. Other relevant pieces of European legislation include *Directive 68/360, Regulation 1251/70* (repealed by *Regulation 635/2006*), *Directive 90/365* and *Directive 90/364*. On 30 April 2006, the *Immigration (European Economic Area) Regulations 2006 (SI 2006/1003)* came into force in the UK. These regulations govern the freedom of movement of citizens of EU states and their families (including civil partners). Although Turkey and certain other states have Association Agreements with the EU, these confer no general right of free movement upon individuals (*R v Secretary of State for the Home Department, ex p Narin* [1990] 2 CMLR 233; but see also *Sevince v Staatssecretaris van Justitie*: C-192/89 [1992] 2 CMLR 57).

26.2   Foreign Employees

The family of an EEA worker may also come to this country without any restriction on their right of entry. EEA nationals are entitled to the same treatment as UK nationals with regard to pay, working conditions, access to housing and property, training, social security and trade union rights. They are free, if unemployed but seeking work, to claim jobseeker's allowance for up to three months if they have been claiming benefit in their own country for at least four weeks. There is also a considerable body of EU legislation directed towards establishing equivalence of mutual recognition of professional qualifications by member states (see 23.4 EUROPEAN UNION LAW). More restrictive rules however apply to the families of Croatian nationals.

Pursuant to the *Immigration (European Economic Area) Regulations 2016*, EEA nationals (and Swiss nationals) may, along with their families, reside in the UK for an initial period of three months, provided that they have a valid passport or identity card and do not become an unreasonable burden on the domestic social security system. After the initial three-month period has expired, the EEA/Swiss national may continue to reside in the UK along with their family for so long as they continue to be a 'qualified person'. A person will be a 'qualified person' for the purposes of the Regulations if he or she is: a job-seeker, a worker, a self-employed person, a self-sufficient person or a student. EEA and Swiss nationals will acquire a permanent right of residence if they have both resided and worked in the UK for more than five years.

Member states are entitled to except employment in the public service from the general requirement of free movement, and to reserve such employment for their own nationals (*TFEU, art 45(4)*); see also PUBLIC SECTOR EMPLOYEES (37). These provisions have given rise to a substantial number of reported cases in national courts and in the ECJ (now CJEU), a detailed discussion of which is beyond the scope of this book.

Collective agreements must take account of comparable employment completed in the public service of another member state for the purposes of seniority and promotion (*Schöning-Kougebetopoulou v Freie und Hansestadt Hamburg*: C-15/96 [1998] All ER (EC) 97). A clause in a collective agreement which treats foreign nationals differently in this respect breaches *art 45* of the *TFEU* and *Regulation 1612/68* on freedom of movement. For an ECJ ruling concerning the relationship between *art 45* and national legislation denying termination payments to a worker who left employment in order to take up work in another member state, see *Graf v Filzmoser Maschinenbau GmbH*: C-190/98 [2000] All ER (EC) 170.

See also EUROPEAN UNION LAW (23).

26.3   EUROPEAN UNION: POSTED WORKERS

Measures have been taken to implement in the UK the *Posting of Workers Directive (96/71)* which came into force on 16 December 1999. The *Directive* now applies to all EEA States. Broadly, it provides that minimum terms and conditions laid down by national laws, regulations or collective agreements should apply to workers posted temporarily by their employer to work in another State.

Article 1 provides that the *Directive* applies to undertakings which:

(a)   post workers to another member state on their account and under their direction under a contract concluded between the undertaking and a party in the other state for whom the services are intended;

(b)   make intra-company postings; or

(c)   are temporary employment undertakings or agencies which hire out workers to undertakings established or operating in an EU member state.

A further requirement in each case is that there must be an employment relationship between the undertaking making the posting and the worker during the period of posting. The terms and conditions of employment covered by the *Directive* are set out in exhaustively in *art 3(1)*, as follows:

(i)   maximum work periods and minimum rest periods;

(ii)   minimum paid annual holidays;

(iii)   minimum rates of pay, including overtime rates (but not supplementary occupational pension schemes);

(iv)   conditions of hiring out workers, in particular the supply of workers by temporary employment undertakings;

(v)   health, safety and hygiene at work;

(vi)   measures to protect at work pregnant women, new mothers, children and young people; and

(vii)   equality of treatment between men and women and other provisions on non-discrimination.

Various flexibilities are permitted under the *Directive*, such as not applying the minimum rate of pay to postings of less than one month. However, the UK Government has decided not to take advantage of any of the exemptions.

Workers may enforce their rights under the *Directive* in the territory of the member state to which they were posted without prejudice to their rights in the country where they are normally employed (*art 6*).

In *Mazzoleni*: C-165/98 [2001] ECR I-2189, the ECJ ruled (15 March 2001) that the principle of freedom of movement did not preclude one member state from requiring an undertaking established in another state which provides services in the territory of the first state to pay its workers the minimum remuneration fixed by the national rules of that state. However, application of these rules might prove to be disproportionate where the workers operate in a frontier region and are required to carry out their work, on a part-time basis and for brief periods, in more than one member state. It is for the host member state to decide the extent to which the imposition of a minimum wage is necessary and proportionate to protect the workers in question. In a number of cases emanating from Germany, the ECJ has examined the compatibility of certain domestic laws governing posted workers with the principle of freedom of movement. These cases include: *Finalarte Sociedade de Construcao Civil Lda v Urlaubs- und Lohnausgleichskasse der Bauwirtschaft*: C-49/98 [2001] ECR I-7831; *European Commission v Germany*: C-341/02 [2005] ECR I-2733, ECJ; *Ruffert (Dirk) v Land Niedersachsen*: C-346/06 [2008] ECR I-1989, [2008] All ER (EC) 902, ECJ; and *Hudzinski v Agentur fur Arbeit Wesel - Familienkasse*: C-611/10 [2012] 3 CMLR 23. For a recent guidance on the minimum rates of pay see *Sahkaolajen ammattilitto ry v Elektrobudowa Spolka Akcyjna*: C-396/13. The Posting of Workers Directive was considered by the High Court in *R (on the application of Low) v Secretary of State for the Home Department* [2009] EWHC 35 (Admin), [2009] 2 CMLR 539. In that case, an Irish company had hired non-EU nationals to work in certain catering establishments in the UK. The Secretary of State refused to confirm that these workers had a right to work under EU law. The applicants applied to have that decision judicially reviewed. They sought to argue that they had a right to work in the UK on an application of *art 49* of the Nice Treaty and/or under the *Posting of Workers Directive*, particularly because the Irish company which employed them had a right to provide services in the UK. The High Court rejected the claim. It held that the arrangements constituted an unlawful attempt to circumvent enforceable UK immigration laws. The Court of Appeal upheld the High Court's judgment, [2010] EWCA Civ 4.

26.3   Foreign Employees

The UK has sought to incorporate the *Directive* by making amendments to statutory employment rights. Most existing UK legislation relevant to the *Directive* applies to all workers, whether they are employed on a temporary or permanent basis in the UK (eg the *Working Time Regulations 1998*, the *National Minimum Wage Act 1998*, and health and safety legislation). For a discussion of the effect of the Directive on the application of the *Employment Rights Act 1996* see the Court of Appeal's judgment in *Lawson v Serco Ltd* [2004] EWCA Civ 12, [2004] ICR 204 and the opinion of Lord Hoffmann in the House of Lords [2006] UKHL 3, [2006] ICR 250 at 256 para 13.

In March 2012, the European Commission proposed new rules designed to increase the protection of posted workers. The rules are aimed in particular at improving levels of monitoring and compliance with the requirements imposed by the Directive. The new *Posting of Workers Enforcement Directive* was adopted by the EU's Council of Ministers in May 2014 (*Directive 2014/67*). The Directive has been implemented in England, Wales and Scotland by the *Posted Workers (Enforcement of Employment Rights) Regulations 2016, SI 2016/539* which entered into force on 18 June 2016. For the position in Northern Ireland see the *Posted Workers (Enforcement of Employment Rights) Regulations (Northern Ireland), SI 2016/242*. The 2016 Regulations make provision for a posted worker in the construction sector to have the right to make a claim, and bring proceedings before the Employment Tribunal or early conciliation, against their employer's contractor for the non-payment of wages (up to the national minimum wage).

26.4   NON-EEA NATIONALS

Up until November 2008, nationals from outside the EEA and Switzerland who were subject to immigration control were generally obliged to obtain work permits in order to be able to take up employment in the UK. On 26 November 2008, the work permit system was largely abolished and replaced by tier 2 of the points-based system (although work permit arrangements continue for employers wishing to recruit Croatian nationals). This system is operated by UK Visas and Immigration (UKVI), a department of the Home Office. Under the points-based system, migrant workers need to pass a points-based assessment before they are given permission to enter or remain in the United Kingdom. As originally constituted, the points-based system consisted of five tiers, with each tier having different points requirements. Points are awarded to reflect the migrant's ability, experience, age and, where appropriate, the level of need within the sector in which the migrant will be working.

(a)   tier 1 was concerned with highly skilled workers, for example scientists and entrepreneurs (this tier was effectively abolished with effect from 6 April 2011, for which see below);

(b)   tier 2 is concerned with skilled workers with a job offer, for example teachers and nurses;

(c)   tier 3 (currently suspended) is concerned with low skilled workers filling temporary shortages, for example construction workers for a particular project;

(d)   tier 4 is concerned with students; and

(e)   tier 5 is concerned with youth mobility and temporary workers, for example musicians coming to play in a concert.

A number of significant changes to the points-based system were introduced with effect from 6 April 2011. The key changes include the following: tier 1 is effectively closed, save that 1000 visas will be made available per annum under a new 'exceptional talent' route; the issuing of visas in respect of tier 2 skilled workers is subject to an annual cap; employers seeking to recruit tier 2 workers no longer have an annual allocation for the number of workers they can bring into the country but instead need to apply to UKVI for a certificate of sponsorship for each specific vacancy; the annual tier 2 cap does not apply in cases where the employer is seeking to fill a vacancy attracting a salary of £151,200 or more; tier 2 workers from outside the EU who want to come to the UK will need to have a graduate level job, speak an intermediate level of English, and meet specific salary and employment requirements. Guidance on the new approach to tier 2 visas along with other information about the points-based system can be found on UKVI website: www.gov.uk/visas -immigration. Organisations which apply to sponsor a migrant worker must agree to comply with a range of duties relating to the sponsoring arrangements, including duties relating to record-keeping, reporting (for example, where the sponsored worker fails to turn up to work) and allowing UKVI to make announced and unannounced site visits. For further information on the obligations of sponsor organisations see the UKVI guidance 'Sponsorship: Guidance for Employers and Educators', which can be found on the Home Office website. There have been suggestions that the UK's withdrawal from the EU may lead to changes to the points -based system.

26.5 IMMIGRATION, ASYLUM AND NATIONALITY ACT 1996

Since 27 January 1997, it has been an offence to employ a person who is not entitled, under the Immigration Rules, to work in the UK. Originally, this offence was provided for under *s 8* of the *Asylum and Immigration Act 1996* ('*AIA 1996*'). However, on 29 February 2008, AIA 1996, s 8 was repealed and replaced by provisions in the *Immigration Asylum and Nationality Act 2006* (IAN).

26.6   The statutory scheme governing the treatment of employers who employ persons not lawfully entitled to work in the UK is found in *sections 15–26* of *IAN*. Under *s 15*, the Secretary of State may issue a penalty notice to employers who employ persons: (a) who have no leave to enter or remain in the UK; or (b) whose leave is invalid, has ceased to have effect or does not entitle them to work in the UK. The penalty notice will require the employer to pay a specific amount subject to a statutory maximum. The employer will be excused from paying the penalty if he complied with certain 'prescribed requirements' relating to the employment, unless he knew at the time that the employment was unlawful despite his having complied with the requirements. The 'prescribed requirements' are provided for under the *Immigration (Restrictions on Employment) Order 2007*. The requirements imposed under the Order include that employers must scrutinise the passports and biometric immigration documents held by their potential employees and keep copies of those documents. Under *s 16*, the employer has a right to object to the notice by sending an objection to the Secretary of State. *Section 17* provides that the employer also has a right of appeal to the court against the penalty notice. The introduction of a penalty notice regime is one of the key novelties of the scheme introduced under *IAN*. Under *s 19*, the Secretary of State must issue a Code of Practice relating to the giving of penalties. Pursuant to s *21*, a person who employs someone who is subject to immigration control knowing that he or she is either in the UK unlawfully or is not lawfully entitled to work in the UK will be guilty of an offence and liable, on conviction, to imprisonment and/or a fine. *Section 22* provides that an employer (whether corporate or not) shall be treated as knowing a fact about an employee for the purposes of *s 21* if a person within the employing body has responsibility for an aspect of the employment and knows that fact. *Section 22(2)* makes provision for officers of the employer to be liable to conviction along with the employer itself in circumstances where the offence is committed with the consent or connivance of the officer. Under *s 23*, the Secretary of State is required to issue a Code of Practice to assist employers in avoiding racially discriminatory behaviour in the context of their complying with their obligations under *IAN*. The current 2014 versions of the codes of practice issued pursuant to *ss 19* and *23* can be found on the on the UKVI website, along with general guidance for employers on the application of *IAN*.

Foreign Employees

Claims under the ERA 1996

In order to bring a claim under the *Employment Rights Act 1996*, a claimant must show that he is an employee. A breach of immigration law may taint the contract of employment and deprive the individual of statutory protection. The crucial question is whether the claim arises out of or is so inextricably bound up with the employee's conduct that the court could not permit the claimant to recover without appearing to condone that conduct (see *Hall v Woolston Hall* [2000] IRLR 578; *Vakante v Governing Body of Addey & Stanhope School* [2004] EWCA Civ 1065, [2004] 4 All ER 1056). In *Blue Chip Trading Ltd v Helbawi (A)* (UKEAT/0397/08/LA) [2009] IRLR 128, a foreign student had breached the Immigration Rules by working more than 20 hours per week for his employer. The EAT held that the fact that some of the work done by the student was unlawful did not render the entire contract of employment illegal. Instead, the contract was severable from the unlawful arrangements so that the student could pursue a claim under the contract in respect of those times when he was working lawfully and in accordance with the Immigration Rules.

EEA nationals and their family members have an unqualified right to work in the UK. Therefore, their contracts of employment cannot be rendered void by reason of a failure to produce evidence of entitlement to work ((see *Okouimose v City Facilities Management (UK) Ltd*, UKEAT/0192/11 (13 September 2011, unreported); employee suspended without pay; claim for unlawful deduction from wages upheld). However, in *Kurumuth v NHS Trust North Middlesex University Hospital* UKEAT/0524/10/CEA, despite the fact that the employee had a right to work while awaiting the determination of a timely immigration application, the EAT held that it was acceptable for an employer to rely upon the Home Office guidance on preventing illegal working in deciding to dismiss the employee.

Discrimination claims

In *Vakante v Governing Body of Addey & Stanhope School* [2004] EWCA Civ 1065, [2004] 4 All ER 1056, the Court of Appeal considered the question of whether a claimant could pursue complaints of race discrimination against the respondent employer in circumstances where, as a person who was subject to immigration control, he had entered into an employment with the respondent knowing that the employment was unlawful. The Court of Appeal found that the claim was barred on an application of the 'inextricably linked' test. The Court also appeared to place reliance on the fact that the claimant had misled his employer as to his immigration status. The same result was reached by the Court of Appeal in *Allen v Hounga* [2012] EWCA Civ 609, [2012] IRLR 685 which concerned a race discrimination claim brought by a Nigerian national who had illegally posed as a member of the respondents' family in order to obtain entry into the United Kingdom. Compare those judgments with the judgment of the Employment Appeal Tribunal in *Wijesundera v Heathrow 3PL Logistics Ltd* (UKEAT/0222/13/DA) [2014] ICR 523. In that case, Langstaff P held that the crucial question is whether the form of the respondent's action giving rise to the claim is inextricably bound up with the illegal conduct. Whereas dismissal was inextricably linked to the claimant's employment status, sexual harassment was not.

The leading authority is now *Hounga v Allen* [2014] UKSC 47, [2014] IRLR 811 in which the Supreme Court reversed the Court of Appeal's decision and held that the claimant's race discrimination claim was not defeated by illegality. The Supreme Court split 3:2 on the reasoning. The majority judgment was delivered by Lord Wilson (with whom Lady Hale and Lord Kerr agreed). After reviewing the relevant authorities, Lord Wilson observed that the prevailing 'inextricable link' test has been subject to certain criticism but did not express a clear view on the matter. On the facts, all members of the Court agreed that the claim was not inextricably linked to the illegality. The illegal contract of employment provided no more than the context for the respondent's actions. However, the majority decided the appeal on the separate basis that the public policy aim of upholding immigration law was outweighed by the countervailing policy objective of supressing human trafficking. To allow the illegality defence to succeed would place the UK in breach of its international obligations under the United Nations 'Palermo Protocol' on forced labour and servitude, the Council of Europe Convention on Action against Trafficking in Human Beings and *Article 4* of the *ECHR*. The majority's failure to formulate a clear test introduces significant uncertainty. It is unclear whether the inextricable link test was disapplied in favour of an alternative public policy test or whether the inextricable link test is subject to policy exceptions.

26.7 JURISDICTION, APPLICABLE LAW AND THE TERRITORIAL SCOPE OF LEGISLATION DISTINGUISHED

Where a particular employment relationship has a foreign element, questions may arise as to whether the claim can be brought before English courts (the jurisdiction question). Depending on the circumstances, the allocation of jurisdiction between the courts of different states may be governed by EU law or common law rules.

The question may also arise as to what law governs the claim (the applicable law question). For example, where an employee who is based in France seeks to sue his British-based employer for breach of contract, a question may arise as to whether the claim is to be decided under English or French law. Alternatively, where a British-based employee is injured whilst travelling for work abroad, a question may arise as to whether any tortious claim for personal injury brought by the employee is governed by English law or the law of the country where the accident took place.

Importantly, the jurisdiction question is distinct from the applicable law question. For example, a contract may be governed by the laws of Saudi Arabia. This is not in itself determinative of whether the English courts have jurisdiction to hear the claim. Choice of law may, however, be a relevant factor in determining jurisdiction at common law, the logic being that courts are best placed to apply the domestic law of their own systems.

It is also important to be aware that, so far as statutory employment claims are concerned, the following additional question needs to be posed: 'Is this a claim which falls within the territorial scope of the particular legislation?' (the territorial scope question). Whether or not the statute applies to the facts of any given case is a question of statutory construction. Did Parliament intend that the relevant statutory protections should apply to a person in the relevant employee's specific circumstances? This issue is often said to concern the 'territorial jurisdiction' of the employment tribunals. However, the territorial scope question is entirely distinct from the jurisdiction question. Moreover, the territorial scope of legislation is not necessarily dependent on English law being the governing law of the contract of employment (although this is likely to be a relevant factor). These issues are examined in further detail below.

26.8 JURISDICTION

Where an employee brings a claim and the events about which the employee complains have a connection with more than one country, questions may arise as to whether the defendant can properly be served with proceedings and, further, whether England is the country in which claims can or must be brought.

In the context of claims brought against foreign defendants in the ordinary courts, reference must be made to *Part 6* of the *CPR* which contains detailed provisions on the question of when a foreign defendant may be served with proceedings. Service out of the jurisdiction will require the permission of the courts, save where the requirements of *CPR 6.33* have been met. If permission is required, the court will only consider granting permission in circumstances where the requirements contained in *CPR PD 6B paragraph 3.1* have been met. The courts will not grant permission where the domestic courts are clearly not the most appropriate forum for the claim. For an example of a case in which the domestic courts were considering whether they were the proper forum for tortious claims brought by foreign employees see *Lubbe v Cape plc* [2000] 4 All ER 268.

The employment tribunal rules contained in *Schedule 1* to the *Employment Tribunals (Constitution and Rules of Procedure) Regulations 2013*, which came into force in July 2013, contain specific provisions as to the circumstances in which an employment tribunal claim may lawfully be presented in England and Wales. If the requirements of these provisions are met then, in effect, the employment tribunal will have jurisdiction to hear the claim. In summary, a claim may lawfully be presented if: (a) the respondent or one of the respondents resides or carries on business in England or Wales; (b) one or more of the acts or omissions complained of took place in England or Wales; the claim relates to a contract under which the work is or has been performed partly in England or Wales; or (d) the Tribunal has jurisdiction to determine the claim by virtue of a connection with Great Britain and the connection in question is at least partly a connection with England and Wales. The proper application of *rule 8(2)*, which does not on its face expressly mirror the requirements as to service contained in the *CPR*, has yet to be considered in any detail by the appellate courts or tribunals.

Where the defendant is domiciled in an EU member state, the *Civil Jurisdiction and Judgments Act 1982* ("CJJA") applies. CJJA originally gave effect to the *Brussels Convention*. It was then amended to give effect to *Regulation 44/2001* (the '*Brussels I Regulation*'), which came into force on 1 March 2002. The *Regulation* covers all member states except Denmark, in respect of which the *Brussels Convention* still applies. More recently, the CJJA gives effect to *Regulation 1512/2012* (the '*Brussels I Regulation* (recast)') which came into force on 10 January 2015. Changes to the existing law in the UK required by the *Brussels I Regulation* and the *Brussels I Regulation* (recast) are contained in the *Civil Jurisdiction and Judgments Order 2001 (SI 2001/3929))*. The CJJA deals not only with jurisdiction, but also with the enforcement of judgments in other member states. Questions of interpretation arising under the *Convention*, the *Brussels I Regulation* or the *Brussels I Regulation* (recast) may be referred to the CJEU (see EUROPEAN UNION LAW (23)). Similar provisions apply under the *Lugano Convention* where the defendant is domiciled in an EFTA member state (*Civil Jurisdiction and Judgments Act 1991*).

Under the *Brussels I Regulation*, the normal rule is that the defendant must be sued in the state in which he is domiciled (*art 2*). However, special rules apply to claims relating to contracts of employment. These rules are contained in *s 5* (*arts 18–21*) of the *Brussels I Regulation* (see now *arts 20–23 Brussels I Regulation* (recast)). The terms "employer", "employee" and "employment" must be given an autonomous meaning. The phrase "relating to" should be given a broad interpretation. A dispute may "relate to" a contract of employment even though the claim itself is tortious in nature: see *Alfa Laval Tumba AB v Separator Spares International Ltd* [2013] 1 WLR 1110; *James Petter v . EMC Europe Ltd & Anor* [2015] IRLR 847.

Under *s 5* of the *Regulation*, an employer domiciled in a member state may be sued by his employee either: in the courts of the state where the employer is domiciled; or in the courts of the place where the employee habitually carries out his work or in the courts of the last place where he did so; or, if the employee does not or did not habitually carry out his work in any one country, in the courts of the place where the business which engaged the employee is or was situated (*art 19*) (In *Weber v Universal Ogden Services Ltd*: C-37/00 [2002] IRLR 365, the ECJ held that the relevant criterion for establishing the employee's habitual place of work was, having regard to the whole duration of employment, the place where he or she has worked the longest on the employer's business. See also: *Rutten v Cross Medical Ltd* [1997] IRLR 249, ECJ and *Mulox IBC Ltd v Geels*: C-125/92 [1994]

IRLR 422, ECJ. In *Harada Ltd (t/a Chequepoint UK) v Turner* [2001] EWCA Civ 599, [2001] All ER (D) 82 (Apr), the Court of Appeal held that an employment tribunal had jurisdiction to hear a wrongful dismissal claim made by an English employee working in Spain for an Irish offshore company since the central management and control of the company was exercised in England). Thus, the *Regulation* is fairly generous when it comes to claims brought against the employer by the employee (although compare *Powell v OMV Exploration & Production Ltd* [2014] IRLR 80: employee who resided in the UK but habitually carried out his work outside the EU was not entitled bring a claim in the English employment tribunal against an EU domiciled employer).

The *Regulation* is rather less generous when it comes to claims brought against the employee by the employer. The employer may bring proceedings only in the courts of the Member State in which the employee is domiciled, although he may counter-claim in the courts of another Member State in response to a claim brought by the employee (*art 20*). The *Brussels I Regulation* makes clear that exclusive jurisdiction clauses can only be enforced against an employee when those clauses are entered into after the particular dispute has arisen (*art 21(1)*). Under *art 18(2)* of the *Brussels I Regulation* an employer will be 'deemed to be domiciled' in a member state if it has a branch, agency or other establishment in that member state and the dispute arises out of the operations of that branch, agency or establishment.

In *Samengo-Turner v J & H Marsh & McLennan (Services) Ltd* [2007] EWCA Civ 723, [2007] 2 All ER (Comm) 813, [2008] IRLR 237, the Court of Appeal was called upon to apply the provisions of *s 5* of the *Brussels I Regulation* in a case where the employees were claiming that they were entitled to an anti-suit injunction to restrain breach of contract claims brought against them in New York. The employees were both domiciled and employed to work in the UK. When they notified their UK-based employer that they were terminating their employment in order to go and work for a competitor, claims were brought against them in New York for repayment of bonuses which had been awarded to them under a bonus agreement. The employees argued that they were entitled to the anti-suit injunction because, although the companies who could sue under the bonus agreement included US-based companies other than their employer, the reality was that the bonus agreement formed part of their contract of employment with the UK employer and, accordingly, on an application of *arts 18* and *20*, claims under that agreement would have to be brought in the UK, where the employees were domiciled. The Court of Appeal agreed with these arguments, holding that the employees were entitled to anti-suit injunctions restraining the New York proceedings.

For a decision on jurisdiction concerning proceedings involving employers located in two different Member states see *Glaxosmithkline v Rouard*: C-462/06 [2008] ICR 1375. In that case, the claimant was employed in the first instance by a French domiciled employer. His employment was then transferred to a UK domiciled employer, albeit that his contract with the UK employer imported certain entitlements which the claimant had enjoyed under his contract with the French company, including entitlements as to continuity of service. When the claimant was dismissed from his employment with the UK company, he sought to bring claims in France against both the French and the UK company. He asserted that he was entitled to proceed against the UK company on an application of *art 6(1)* of the *Brussels I Regulation* (*art 6(1)* entitles a claimant to sue a number of defendants in the place where any one of them is domiciled, provided that the claims are so closely connected that it is expedient to hear and determine them together to avoid the risk of irreconcilable judgments resulting from separate proceedings). The ECJ held that the claimant could not rely on *art 6(1)* to draw the UK company into the French proceedings for the simple reason that there was a comprehensive code to deal with claims brought in respect of employment contracts which was contained in *s 5* of the *Brussels I Regulation*; on an application of that code, no claim could be brought by the employee against the UK company in the French courts.

26.8 Foreign Employees

The rules for employment disputes under the *Brussels I Regulation* (recast) very closely mirror those in the *Brussels I Regulation*. However, employees' rights have been strengthened as a result of three important changes:

(a)   an employee is now able to sue an non-EU domiciled employer in the courts of the employee's habitual place of work or where the business which engaged the employee is situated (*art 21(2)*);

(b)   the place where an employee habitually works is clarified to include the place where or from where the employee carries out his work (*art 21(1)(b)(i)*). This clarification achieves consistency with the approach under the Rome I Regulation; and

(c)   the rules of jurisdiction on joining co-defendants have been extended to employment claims (art 20(1)). This change reverses the decision of the ECJ in *Rouard*.

In matters relating to tort, the *Brussels I Regulation* provides that the employer may be sued either in the courts of the member state where he is domiciled (*art 2(1)*) or in the courts of the place where the harmful event occurred (*art 5(3)*). These rules are maintained under the *Brussels I Regulation* (recast) (see *arts 4(1)* and *7(2)*).

Where proceedings involving the same cause of action and between the same parties ('parallel proceedings') are brought in the courts of different contracting states, a court other than the court 'first seised' is to stay proceedings and where the jurisdiction of the court first seised is established, other courts are to decline jurisdiction (*art 27* of the *Brussels I Regulation*). In the case of *Turner v Grovit*: C-159/02 [2004] All ER (EC) 485, the ECJ was called upon to decide whether it was possible under the Brussels Convention for the English courts to grant restraining orders in respect of proceedings in another Convention country on the ground of abuse of process. The ECJ concluded that the functioning of the Convention was underpinned by the necessity for the contracting state to place mutual trust in the judicial systems and institutions of other states and that, accordingly, it did not permit the jurisdiction of a court to be reviewed by a court in another contracting state other than in the special cases enumerated in *art 28*. These principles apply with equal force to the provisions of the *Brussels I Regulation*. However, in cases to which the *Brussels I Regulation* (recast) applies the first seised rule has been partly reversed by *art 31(2)*. The court designated in an exclusive jurisdiction agreement has priority to decide on the validity of the agreement and on the extent to which the agreement applies to the dispute pending before it.

A common law claim which is brought by an employee in the ordinary courts will usually be subject to the doctrine of forum non conveniens with the result that claim will not be allowed to proceed before the domestic courts if there is another more appropriate (foreign) forum for the claim (see further *Spiliada Maritime Corpn v Cansulex Ltd* [1987] AC 460, HL). It would seem that following a change in the *Employment Tribunal Rules of Procedure* wrought by the *Employment Tribunals (Constitution & Rules etc) Regulations 2004*, the doctrine can generally be applied equally by the Employment Tribunals in the context of breach of contract claims which are brought before them (see further *Crofts v Cathay Pacific* [2005] EWCA Civ 599, [2005] ICR 1436). However, following the judgment of the ECJ in *Owusu v Jackson* [2005] QB 801, it is strongly arguable that the *forum non conveniens* doctrine cannot be applied in a case where the English court automatically has jurisdiction to hear the claim under *s. 5* of the *Brussels I Regulation*.

The *Brussels I Regulation* (recast) introduced revised rules applicable where parallel proceedings have been initiated in the courts of a non Member State (*art 33*). In such cases, the English courts now have a discretion to stay proceedings if (a) it is expected that the court of the third State will give a judgment capable of recognition and, where applicable, of enforcement in that Member State; and (b) the court of the Member State is satisfied that a stay is necessary for the proper administration of justice. The court should take into account all the circumstances of the case including: the degree of connections between the facts and parties; how far advanced the third state proceedings are; and whether the third state's court can be expected to give a judgment within a reasonable time (*Recital (24)*). There are also new rules governing related proceedings in non Member State courts (*art 34*).

The employment tribunals have no jurisdiction to hear common law tortious claims brought by employees, whether foreign or domestic. However, they do have jurisdiction to hear breach of contract claims brought in respect of particular contracts of employment under the *Employment Tribunals Extension of Jurisdiction (England and Wales) Order 1994*. Article 3 of that *Order* provides that the tribunal will have jurisdiction to hear the particular claim in circumstances where, had the claim been brought in the ordinary courts, the courts would have been jurisdiction to hear and determine the claim. The effect and scope of *art 3* in respect of foreign employment was considered by the Court of Appeal in *Crofts v Cathay Pacific Airways Ltd* [2005] EWCA Civ 599, [2005] ICR 1436.

APPLICABLE LAW

26.9   Contract claims

Where an employer and employee are both English, and the work is done in England, it will generally be clear that the contract of employment is governed by English law, and there will normally be no doubt as to the jurisdiction of the English courts to deal with any contractual disputes which may arise. However, where there is a foreign element of some kind, difficult questions may arise concerning the system of law which governs the contract, and as to where any proceedings may be brought in this country. This is an extremely complicated area of law, and what follows is intended only as a simplified outline guide.

The *Contracts (Applicable Law) Act 1990* was enacted to give force in the United Kingdom to the *Rome Convention on the Law Applicable to Contractual Obligations* of 1980. That was a treaty between the EC member states, and provision is made for the ECJ to be given jurisdiction to determine questions concerning its interpretation (see EUROPEAN UNION LAW (23)). However, the Act applies to all contracts, not merely to those with an EC connection. With effect from 17 December 2009, the *Convention* ceased to apply in the UK and was replaced by a new *Regulation EC No 593/2008*, known as the *Rome I Regulation*. So far as "individual employment contracts" are concerned, the provisions of the *Rome I Regulation* broadly mirror those contained in the *Convention* (see in particular *art 8*). Therefore, the earlier case law on the interpretation and application of the *Convention* remains relevant.

A contract is governed by the system of law chosen by the parties, such choice being either expressed or demonstrated with reasonable certainty by the terms of the contract or the circumstances of the case (*art 3(1)*). However, in the case of a contract of employment, a choice of law made by the parties may not deprive an employee of the protection afforded to him by the "non-derogable provisions" or "mandatory rules" of the system of law which would apply if no such choice had been made (*art 9(2), Regulation* and *art 6(1), Convention*).

Mandatory rules are those which cannot be derogated from by contract in the law of the country concerned (*art 3(3)*). Mandatory rules consist not only of provisions relating to the contract of employment, but also provisions such as those concerning industrial safety and hygiene which are regarded in certain Member States as being provisions of public law. Hence, for example, under the *Convention*, if an English employee worked in Great Britain for an English employer, it is not possible to deprive him of the right to claim unfair dismissal (53), (54), (55) by providing that the contract shall be governed by, say, Hong Kong law (see further *Base Metal Trading Ltd v Shamurin* [2003] EWHC 2419 (Comm), [2004] 1 All ER (Comm) 159; see also *Employment Rights Act 1996, s 204*).

26.9 Foreign Employees

If the parties to a contract of employment have not chosen the system of law which is to govern the contract, then it will be governed by:

(a)   the law of the country in which or failing that from which the employee habitually carries out his work in performance of the contract, even if he is temporarily employed in another country (*art 8(2)* and *Recital (36)*); or

(b)   if the employee does not habitually carry out his work in any one country, the law of the country in which the place of business through which he was engaged is situated (*art 8(3)* and *Voogsgeerd v Navimer SA*: C-384/10, [2012] I.L.Pr 341, ECJ),

unless it appears from the circumstances as a whole that the contract is more closely connected with another country, in which case the contract shall be governed by the law of that country (*art 8(4)*).

The concept of the country in which the work is habitually carried out must be interpreted broadly (see *Koelzsch v Luxembourg*: C-29/10, [2012] 1 QB 210, [2011] ECR I-1593 at paras 43, 45 considering the narrower terms of *art 6(2)* of the Convention). As *art 8(2)* of the *Rome I Regulation* clarifies, this criterion must be understood as referring to the place in which or from which the employee carries out his working activities. For recent guidance on the application of *art 8(4)* see *Schlecker v Boedeker*: C-64/12, [2014] QB 320, CJEU.

The application of a rule of foreign law specified by *art 8* of the *Regulation* is subject to a number of limitations.

First, *art 8* does not restrict the application of overriding mandatory provisions of the law of the forum (*art 7(2), Convention* and *art 9(2), Regulation*). *Article 9* of the *Regulation* defines "overriding mandatory provisions" as provisions the respect for which is regarded as crucial by a country for safeguarding its public interests, such as its political, social or economic organisation, to such extent that they are applicable to any situation falling within their scope, irrespective of the law otherwise applicable to the contract under the *Regulation*.

Secondly, under *art 7(1)* of the *Convention*, even if one system of law applies (e.g. English law), effect could be given to the mandatory rules of the law of another country with which the contract has a close connection (e.g. France), provided that those mandatory rules would be applied under French law whatever system of law governed the contract, and depending upon the nature and purpose of those rules and the consequences of their application or non-application. However, importantly, *art 7(1)* did not have the force of law in the United Kingdom (*Contracts (Applicable Law) Act 1990, s 2(2)*). *Art 9(3)* of the *Regulation* adopts a narrower approach, providing that effect may be given to the mandatory rules of the law of the country where the obligations arising out of the contract have to be or have been performed, in so far as those mandatory rules render the performance of the contract unlawful.

Thirdly, in addition to showing deference to mandatory rules of the forum, the *Regulation* makes it clear that the application of a rule of foreign law specified by the *Regulation* may be refused if it is 'manifestly incompatible with the public policy (*ordre publique*) of the forum' (*art 21, Regulation* and *art 16, Convention*)). *Duarte v Black and Decker Corpn* [2007] EWHC 2720 (QB), [2008] 1 All ER (Comm) 401, the High Court was called upon to consider whether English common law principles relating to the enforcement of restrictive covenants in a contract of employment effectively overrode the governing law of the contract, which was in that case the law of Maryland. The court held that English common law rules relating to the enforcement of restrictive covenants in employment contracts did not constitute mandatory rules of the English forum and, hence, *art 6.1* of the *Convention* was not engaged in respect of the covenants. However, the court also decided that those common law rules enshrined public policy principles which should be applied to the contract under *art 16* of the *Convention*. As it happens, the court found that the law of Maryland in any event operated so as to ensure that the covenants were too wide to be enforceable.

Under *art 7(1)* of the *Convention*, even if one system of law applies (e.g. English law), effect could be given to the mandatory rules of the law of another country with which the contract has a close connection (e.g. France), provided that those mandatory rules would be applied under French law whatever system of law governed the contract, and depending upon the nature and purpose of those rules and the consequences of their application or non-application. However, importantly *art 7(1)* did not have the force of law in the United Kingdom (*Contracts (Applicable Law) Act 1990 Act, s 2(2)*).

Fourthly, *art 8* of the *Regulation* is without prejudice to the application of overriding mandatory provisions of the country to which a worker is posted in accordance with *Directive 96/71 (Recital (34), Regulation)*.

26.10 Tort claims

The rules determining what law applies to tortious claims arising out of employment disputes (such as conspiracy and unlawful interference) have evolved over time. Originally, non-statutory common law rules applied, see, eg *Sayers v International Drilling Co NV* [1971] 3 All ER 163 and *Johnson v Coventry Churchill International Ltd* [1992] 3 All ER 14. From 1 May 1996 until 11 January 2009, the common law rules were abolished and superseded by provisions contained in the *Private International Law (Miscellaneous Provisions) Act 1995 ('PILMPA')*. Under *PILMPA*, the general rule was that the applicable law would be the law of the country in which the events constituting the tort in question occur (*s 11(1)*). That rule was displaced where, viewed overall, it appeared that the tort was more closely connected to a country other than that which would be appropriate if the general rule were applied (*s 12(1)*). See further *Harding v Wealands* [2006] UKHL 32, [2006] 3 WLR 83 where the House of Lords decided, in respect of an accident which took place in New South Wales, that the provisions of *PILMPA* did not operate to enable the capping provisions contained in New South Wales personal injury legislation to apply to quantification by the UK courts of personal injury damages. However, with effect from 11 January 2009, the provisions of PILMPA, insofar as they relate to torts in the employment context were superseded by *Regulation EC No 864/2007*, known as the *Rome II Regulation*. Under *art 4* of *Rome II Regulation*, the general rule is that the law which applies to the tort is the law of the country where the damage occurred. This general rule may be displaced in circumstances where the parties are habitually resident in another country at the time the damage occurs (*art 4(2)*) or where it is clear from all the circumstances that the tort is manifestly more closely connected with another country (*art 4(3)*). Specific provision is made in the *Rome II Regulation* for particular non-contractual obligations in *arts 5–13*. Those relevant to the employment context are *art 6* (unfair competition), *art 8* (intellectual property rights, for example database rights) and *art 9* (industrial action).

TERRITORIAL SCOPE OF EMPLOYMENT LEGISLATION

26.11 Discrimination Claims

Where an employment relationship incorporates a foreign element (e.g. the employee has worked for his employer abroad), a question will often arise as to whether, in view of that foreign element, the employee has the right to bring a discrimination claim against his employer in the domestic employment tribunal. This question is often referred to as the 'territorial jurisdiction', 'territorial application' question. In order to distinguish the international jurisdictional question, the phrase 'territorial scope' is preferred here.

Until fairly recently, answering the territorial scope question entailed applying the express territorial scope provisions contained in the relevant anti-discrimination enactments see further: *s 1* of the *Equal Pay Act 1970*; *ss 6* and *10* of the *Sex Discrimination Act 1975* (as amended by the *Employment Equality (Sex Discrimination) Regulations 2005 (SI 2005/2467)*; ss *4* and *8* of the *Race Relations Act 1976*; ss *4(6)* and *68* of the *Disability Discrimination Act 1995*; and *reg 9* of the *Employment Equality (Religion and Belief) Regulations 2003*, *Employment Equality (Sexual Orientation) Regulations 2003* and *reg 10* of the *Employment Equality (Age) Regulations 2006*. Whilst there were some differences in how these provisions were framed across the different enactments, in general the employee would enjoy the protection of British anti-discrimination legislation provided that he or she worked 'wholly or partly in Great Britain'. On 1 October 2010, the new *Equality Act 2010* came into force. A principal aim of that Act was to consolidate all the myriad discrimination enactments into a single piece of legislation. One effect of the introduction of the Equality Act is that the territorial application question now has to be considered afresh. Below, consideration is given both to the territorial scope principles which applied under the original anti-discrimination enactments and to the position which now obtains under new *Equality Act*.

The Pre-Equality Act Position

As was indicated above, in cases involving an employment relationship which incorporated a foreign element, the question whether the employee could bring discrimination claims in Great Britain against his or her employer generally turned on whether the employee had done his work either 'wholly or partly in Great Britain'. In the case of *Saggar v Ministry of Defence* [2005] EWCA Civ 413, [2005] IRLR 618, the Court of Appeal was obliged to determine the meaning of the expression 'does his work wholly or partly in Great Britain' in the context of a claim brought under the *Race Relations Act 1976*. The issue arose in the context of certain complaints of racial discrimination which had been brought by an MOD employee who had initially been based in the UK for 16 years but had then been permanently stationed abroad. The issue for the Court of Appeal was whether the fact that the employee had, in the early phase of his employment, been based in the UK was sufficient to establish that he had worked 'wholly or partly in Great Britain' for the purposes of the Act. The Court of Appeal held that the correct approach was to focus not on the employment relationship as a whole, from its beginning to end, rather than merely on the time when the discrimination was alleged to have occurred. More recently, in *Tradition Securities and Futures SA v X* [2009] ICR 88, [2008] IRLR 934, the Employment Appeal Tribunal considered the concept of 'doing work wholly or partly in Great Britain' in the context of an employee who worked initially in France but then transferred to work in the UK. The employee went on to bring claims of sex discrimination in the English employment tribunal in respect of the period when she worked in France. The issue for the EAT was whether the *Sex Discrimination Act 1975* applied to the French phase of the employee's employment. The EAT concluded that it did not. It arrived at this conclusion based on the following analysis: during the period the employee was employed in France there would have been no question of her bringing claims under the *Sex Discrimination Act 1975* in the English employment tribunal as she would have not have worked wholly or partly in Great Britain during any part of this period; it could not be accepted that the right to claim discrimination in respect of this earlier period could, in effect, be retrospectively created as a result of the employee latterly coming and working in Great Britain. In *British Airways Plc v Mak* (UKEAT/0055/09/SM), a question arose as to whether certain cabin crew members who were based in Hong Kong could pursue claims of age and race discrimination against British Airways in the English employment tribunal. It was not in dispute that, as part of their duties, the claimants flew in and out of London airports and, further, that, whilst they were in the UK they performed certain airport duties and also undertook training. The employment tribunal decided that the work done by the claimants in Great Britain was sufficient to establish that they worked 'partly in Great Britain' and, hence, they could pursue their age and race discrimination claims. British Airways appealed the tribunal's judgment on the basis that the work done in Great Britain was *de minimis* and, hence, was insufficient to found jurisdiction. The EAT, having considered the Court of Appeal's judgment in *Saggar v Ministry of Defence*, accepted that jurisdiction could not be established if the work done here was *de minimis*. However, it rejected British Airways' case on the basis that the tribunal had properly found as a fact that the work done by the claimants had not been *de minimis* in all the circumstances. The Court of Appeal rejected British Airways' appeal against the EAT's judgment, [2011] EWCA Civ 184. The Supreme Court granted permission to appeal but the case subsequently settled.

Where employees have been working exclusively in another Member State of the European Union, a question may arise as to whether they may pursue discrimination claims in the domestic employment tribunals, notwithstanding that they have never actually done any work in the UK. This was an issue which arose in the case of *Ministry of Defence v Wallis & Grocott* [2011] EWCA Civ 231. In that case, two female claimants who had formerly been employed by the Ministry of Defence at NATO headquarters in Belgium brought claims of sex discrimination (and unfair dismissal) in the English employment tribunal. It was not in dispute before the tribunal that, whilst employed by the MOD, the claimants had worked exclusively in Belgium. The MOD argued that, in the circumstances and pursuant to the express provisions of the *Sex Discrimination Act 1975*, the tribunal had no jurisdiction to hear the claimant's sex discrimination claims as their employment with the MOD had not entailed them working 'wholly or partly in Great Britain'. The claimants, relying on a judgment of the EAT in *Bleuse v MBT Transport* (as to which see further below), argued that the tribunal did have jurisdiction to hear their discrimination claims, particularly because any other result would amount to an unlawful denial of the rights which they enjoyed under the directly effective *EU Equal Treatment Directive (No. 76/207)*. The tribunal accepted the claimants' arguments and held that it had jurisdiction to hear the discrimination claims (it also concluded that it had jurisdiction to hear the unfair dismissal claims – see further below). The tribunal's decision was upheld first by the EAT and then by the Court of Appeal. The Court of Appeal, agreeing with the EAT, held that the claimants enjoyed the protection of the directly effective rights afforded under the Directive and that, in order to give effect to those rights, the provisions of the SDA would have to be read down so as to afford the tribunal jurisdiction to hear the claims.

A related question faced the Supreme Court in *Duncombe v Department for Education & Skills* [2011] ICR 495. The Supreme Court considered the application of the *Fixed Term Employees (Prevention of Less Favourable Treatment) Regulations 2002* to employees of English employers, who had always worked in another EU country. Like the equality legislation explored above, the Regulations also enacted EU law. The Court found that it was unnecessary for it to reach a conclusion on whether the *Regulations* applied in this situation. However, it commented that if it had had to do so, it would have needed to make a reference to the CJEU. It found that, intuitively, employees ought to be protected in other EU countries, but that this issue was not yet *acte clair*.

See also *Williams v University of Nottingham* [2007] IRLR 660, where the EAT concluded that principles derived from the House of Lords' judgment in *Lawson v Serco* (discussed further below) should inform the Tribunal's approach to the application of certain express territorial scope provisions in the *Disability Discrimination Act 1995*.

Territorial scope of the Equality Act 2010

Whilst many practitioners may have expected the new *Equality Act 2010* to embody express territorial scope provisions similar to those contained in the original discrimination enactments, in fact the *Equality Act* contains no express territorial scope provisions at all. It is simply silent on the subject. The Explanatory Notes to the Act do not themselves shed much light on how the tribunals are to approach questions of territorial scope in respect of claims brought under the Act. They merely state that: 'the Act leaves it to tribunals to determine whether the law applies, depending for example on the connection between the employment relationship and Great Britain'. As matters currently stand, it is largely unclear what kind of 'connection' is needed to fall within the Equality Act's territorial scope. In a recent case, the Employment Appeal tribunal held that determining whether claims fell within the jurisdictional ambit of the *EA 2010* required the application of the test outlined by the House of Lords in *Lawson v Serco* (as to which see further below) – see *Bates Van Winklehoff v Clyde & Co LLP* (UKEAT/0169/12/RN). However, importantly the EAT reached this conclusion in circumstances where it was accepted by both parties that *Lawson v Serco* principles, which were devised in the context of a number of claims brought under the *Employment Rights Act 1996 ('ERA 1996')*, applied equally under the *EA 2010* as they did under *ERA 1996*. This decision was appealed to the Court of Appeal ([2012] EWCA Civ 1207), but there was no challenge to the judgment on this point. It remains to be seen whether this approach will be challenged in future cases. In *Ministry of Defence v Holloway* (2015) UKEAT/0396/14, [2015] All ER (D) 391 (Jul), EAT, a discrimination claim brought by civilian employees of the MOD in Cyprus, Langstaff P held that the applicable test depends upon the closeness of the connection, and raises much the same issue as raised by application of the *Ravat* principle regarding the *ERA 1996*.

Most recently, in *R (Hottak and AL) v Secretary of State for Foreign and Commonwealth Affairs and anor* [2016] QB 23, [2016] EWCA Civ 438, the Divisional Court considered a judicial review challenge to the protection redundancy package for Afghan nationals who had been employed as interpreters for British Forces in Afghanistan. The claimants claimed that the Afghan scheme was less generous than the equivalent scheme introduced when British Forces withdraw from Iraq. The claimants argued that their less favourable treatment amount to discrimination on grounds of nationality in relation to employee benefits and public functions, contrary to *sections 39(2)* and *29(6)* of the *Equality Act*. Both the claimants and the Foreign Secretary at least implicitly accepted that the approach to the territorial scope of the *ERA 1996* applied by analogy. The Court accepted this approach, reasoning that no intention may be imputed to Parliament that the territorial scope of the protection against discrimination be wider than unfair dismissal or other employment rights, and that there is much to be said for symmetry between the two statutes. Applying this approach, the Court held that *section 39(2)* did not apply on the facts since their employment relationship did not have a closer connection with Great Britain and with British employment law than with Afghanistan and Afghan law. The claimants could not be considered to be expatriate workers or peripatetic workers, however widely those terms might be understood. Their contracts of employment were not governed by English law. The connection with Great Britain was limited to the identity of their employer. Although they worked in and from both Camp Bastion and the British Embassy, this was far removed from operating in an international enclave. Their position was substantially the same as locally employed staff in a British embassy. The claimants continued to live and work in Afghanistan, and they did or could go home when not working. The Court of Appeal dismissed the claimants' appeal, finding that the Divisional Court's analysis correctly identified the principles, correctly assessed the relevant facts, was soundly based and arrived at a conclusion that was not only open to it on the evidence but was the correct one.

Claims under the Employment Rights Act 1996

Section 204 of the *ERA 1996* provides that the Act applies irrespective of the law which, apart from the *Act*, governs any person's employment. Accordingly, the *ERA 1996* contains non-derogable provisions for the purposes of *art 8(1)* of the *Rome I Regulation*. Where, in the absence of a choice, English law would be applicable the employee may not be deprived of rights under the *ERA 1996*.

The question whether foreign employees enjoy the rights afforded under the *ERA 1996*, particularly the right to claim unfair dismissal, was addressed by the House of Lords in the joined cases of *Lawson v Serco Ltd, Botham v MOD and Crofts v Veta Ltd* [2006] UKHL 3, [2006] ICR 250 ('*Lawson v Serco*'). The following principles were enunciated by the House of Lords in *Lawson v Serco*:

(a)   the question whether a particular claim falls within the territorial ambit of the unfair dismissal provisions contained in the Employment Rights Act 1996 will depend on the nature of the particular employment arrangements in issue in the case;

(b)   in 'standard cases' (ie cases where the employee works in Great Britain), the employee will be able to pursue their claim of unfair dismissal if they were 'working in Great Britain at the time of the dismissal';

(c)   in cases involving 'peripatetic employees' (eg airline pilots and international travelling salespersons), the employee will be able to pursue their claim of unfair dismissal if they were 'based in Great Britain' during the employment (cf. *Hunt v United Airlines Inc* [2008] ICR 934, EAT);

(d)   in cases involving 'expatriate employees' (ie employees who work and live abroad), the employee will not be able to pursue their claim of unfair dismissal in the absence of 'exceptional circumstances'. Those exceptional circumstances could include, for example: where the employee was posted abroad by a British-based employer to work on behalf of or as a representative of that employer (such a situation might arise in the case of a foreign correspondent posted to a foreign country by a British newspaper); or where the employee is working abroad but within a 'political or social enclave' (for example a British military base).

In practice, the greatest difficulties in applying the *Lawson v Serco* principles tend to arise in the context of 'expatriate employee' cases. However, see *Fuller v United Healthcare Services Inc* (UKEAT/0464/13/BA) in which the EAT held that a US citizen employed by a US company who worked in London almost half the time fell outside the territorial scope of the statutory protections against unfair dismissal and sexual orientation discrimination.

In *Duncombe v Department for Education & Skills (No. 2)* [2011] UKSC 36, [2011] 4 All ER 1020, the question arose whether teachers who were employed by the Department for Education and Skills to work in European schools throughout the European Union enjoyed the protection from unfair dismissal conferred by *ERA 1996*. The Supreme Court concluded that they did. The Supreme Court took the view that the test approved in *Lawson v Serco* was whether the employment had "much stronger connections" with Great Britain and with British employment law than with and any other system of law. In *Duncombe*, whilst the teachers were classic expatriate employees in that they lived and worked abroad, the facts of their cases were sufficiently exceptional to bring them within the scope of the legislation. Relevant factors here included that the teachers were employed to work in effect within international enclaves; they had no particular connection with the countries within which they were working and they did not pay local taxes.

The question was next considered by the Supreme Court in *Ravat v Halliburton Manufacturing & Services Ltd* [2012] UKSC 1. In *Ravat*, an English national was employed by a subsidiary of a multinational corporation. The subsidiary was based in Scotland. However, the employee discharged his duties in Libya. The work done by Mr Ravat was done for the benefit of a German subsidiary of the multinational corporation. Mr Ravat continued to live in England during the period of his employment and commuted to his work in Libya, spending 28 days there followed by 28 days in England. Consistent with his commuter status, Mr Ravat's contract of employment afforded him the same benefits which he would have enjoyed had he been employed in England. Moreover, his employer had assured him that English law would govern the contract. Mr Ravat was dismissed from his employment by a manager employed by another British-based subsidiary who was based in Cairo. The Supreme Court concluded that the Scottish employment tribunal had been entitled to conclude that it had jurisdiction to hear Mr Ravat's claim for unfair dismissal. On the wider question of when an expatriate employee's case would be sufficiently exceptional to fall within the scope of *ERA 1996*, the Supreme Court took the view that, in order to amount to an exceptional case, the employment would have to have a "stronger connection" with Great Britain than with the place where the employee worked. The place where the employee discharged his duties was highly relevant to but not necessarily determinative of the application of this test. Other relevant factors would include: the nationality of the employee; the place of recruitment and the location of the employer. In every case, it would be a question of fact and degree whether an expatriate employee's case was sufficiently exceptional such that it fell outside the general rule. In cases where the employee was. in effect, only a quasi-expatriate employee (i.e. because they worked abroad but continued to live in Great Britain) the general rule should in any event be applied more loosely. In cases where the employment involved a number of subsidiary companies of a larger multinational, it was important to be aware of the foreign elements which any foreign subsidiaries introduced into the employment relationship. However, those elements should not be relied upon so as to ignore the reality of the employee's situation. In Mr Ravat's case, it was unrealistic to treat his employment as falling outside the scope of *ERA*. This was particularly in view of the facts that: Mr Ravat was British and had been recruited in Great Britain; the employer's business was based in Great Britain; the employer had chosen to treat Mr Ravat as a commuter and, accordingly, had preserved all his contractual entitlements as though he had been employed in Great Britain; the employer had given Mr Ravat assurances to the effect that he would continue to enjoy the protection of English law; and, further, Mr Ravat had continued to live in England throughout his employment.

In *Bates Van Winklehoff v Clyde & Co LLP* [2012] EWCA Civ 1207, the Court of Appeal confirmed that it is only in the case of expatriate workers who both live and work wholly abroad that it is necessary to undertake an extensive comparative exercise to work out with which country the employment has the closest connection. Where the claimant lives and/or works for at least part of the time in the UK, a less strict test applies. The circumstances need not be truly exceptional before the connection with UK employment law can be identified. All that is required is that the tribunal should satisfy itself that the connection is sufficiently strong to enable it to be said that Parliament would have regarded it as appropriate for the tribunal to deal with the claim. Ms Bates van Winkelhof was a partner of a UK LLP who had been recruited to work in Africa but visited London for work on a regular basis. The Court of Appeal held that these facts involved a sufficient connection with the UK.

What *Lawson*, *Ravat* and *Duncombe* all confirm is that, whilst in the majority of cases expatriate employees will not fall within the scope of *ERA 1996*, there will be exceptional cases where the general rule does not apply. In *Duncombe*, Lady Hale emphasised that there is no hard and fast rule and that it is a mistake to try and torture the circumstances of one employment to make it fit one of the examples given in *Lawson*. In marginal cases, *Ravat* suggests it will be particularly important to consider a whole range of factors affecting the location of the employment relationship including not least: the nature and location of the employer's business, including whether the employer is a UK company and where the employment was administered; the nationality of the employee; where the employee was recruited; where the employee worked; where the employee lived during the period of the employment; whether the employee commuted from Great Britain; where the employee was taxed; whether the employee was paid in foreign currency; whether the contract was designed to afford the employee benefits which were peculiar to the foreign jurisdiction or to the domestic jurisdiction; whether the employee had any particular connection to the place where the duties were discharged and whether the employer gave assurances to the effect that the employee would be protected by domestic employment law. Considerable uncertainty remains regarding the relevance of particular factors, and the weight to be given to each factor, in any given case. Ultimately, the approach to the territorial scope question in *Ravat* resembles closely the *forum conveniens* stage of the jurisdiction question at common law. This conflation of methodology threatens to obscure the important conceptual distinction between the two questions. Moreover, not all of the connecting factors under the jurisdictional enquiry are (or should be) of equal relevance to the territorial scope question. Indeed, two of the factors relied on in *Ravat* are particularly problematic. First, absent any express statutory limitation, it is difficult to see why the employee's nationality should be of any relevance. Secondly, any reliance on the choice of law governing the contract of employment is seemingly precluded by *ERA 1996, s 204.*

The territorial scope question was recently considered in two recent cases. First, in *Dhunna v Creditsights Ltd* [2013] ICR 909, the EAT considered the case of an employee who lived and worked in Dubai for the UK subsidiary of a global organisation operated from the US and was line managed from Delhi and paid in US dollars. The EAT held that it was not enough that his employment had a greater connection with Great Britain and British employment law than with the foreign jurisdiction. The litmus test was whether the links were sufficiently strong to enable it to be said that Parliament would have regarded it as appropriate for the English tribunal to deal with the claim. The EAT rejected the argument that the tribunal should consider the substantive differences between any competing systems of law. The decision was upheld by the Court of Appeal who confirmed that the employee's connection with the UK were tenuous (see *Creditsights Ltd v Dhunna* [2014] EWCA Civ 1238). Secondly, in *Powell v OMV Exploration & Production Ltd* [2014] 1CR 63, Langstaff J reaffirmed that the starting point, which must not be forgotten, is that the statute will have no application to work outside the UK. There must be a 'sufficiently strong connection' to displace that position.

In *Olsen v Gearbulk Services Ltd & Anor* [2015] IRLR 818, the EAT held that a Danish national who was an 'internationally mobile' employee of a Bermudian company, living in Switzerland, who spent more time working in the UK than anywhere else, fell outside the territorial scope of *ERA 1996, s 204.* The EAT agreed with the ET's finding that the claimant had taken great steps to distance himself from having any permanence in the UK. After taking advice on his tax position, the claimant had freely chosen to be governed by a contract governed by Bermudian law and not to live in the UK.

Whilst the House of Lords in *Lawson v Serco* did not decide the point, it is generally accepted that the *Lawson v Serco* principles apply not merely to unfair dismissal provisions but also to all the other provisions of the *Employment Rights Act 1996* (see further *Bleuse v MBT Transport Ltd* [2008] IRLR 264 and, more recently, *Dhunna v Creditsights Ltd* (UKEAT/0246/12/LA), both of which concerned the application of provisions contained in the *Working Time Regulations 1998*. See also *Bates Van Winklehoff v Clyde & Co LLP* [2012] EWCA Civ 1207, in which the Court of Appeal accepted that the *Lawson v Serco* principles could apply to a whistleblowing case). See also *Netjets Management Ltd v CAC and Skyshare* [2012] IRLR 986, in which the High Court applied the *Ravat* test to a claim under the *Trade Union and Labour Relations (Consolidation) Act 1992.*

Additional Considerations

Where an employee works in another Member State of the European Union, a question may arise as to whether that employee can rely on directly effective EU rights in order to pursue claims in the domestic employment tribunals. This question has been considered in a number of recent cases. In *Bleuse v MBT Transport Ltd* [2008] IRLR 264, the EAT held that an expatriate employee who had worked in other Member States of the EU was entitled to bring claims under the *Working Time Regulations 1998* against his UK based employer. This was despite the fact that he had never worked in the UK. The EAT reached this conclusion on the basis that this was the result which was required by directly effective provisions of the *Working Time Directive 2003/88.* A similar conclusion was reached by the Court of Appeal in the context of a claim brought under the *Fixed-term Employees (Prevention of Less Favourable Treatment) Regulations 2002* ("the 2002 Regulations"): *Duncombe v Department for Education & Skills* [2009] EWCA Civ 1355, [2010] IRLR 331. However, the Court of Appeal's judgment in *Duncombe* was subsequently overturned by the Supreme Court, albeit on other grounds, *Duncombe v Department for Education & Skills* [2011] UKSC 14, [2011] 2 All ER 417. The Supreme Court found that it was unnecessary for it to reach a conclusion on whether the *Regulations* applied in this situation. However, it commented that, if it had had to do so, it would have needed to make a reference to the CJEU since this issue was not yet *acte clair*. In the circumstances, query whether the Court of Appeal's analysis in *Duncombe* can properly be relied upon. It should be noted that the *Duncombe* case subsequently came before the Supreme Court for a second time, *Duncombe v Department for Education and Skills (No. 2)* [2011] UKSC 36, [2011] 4 All ER 1020. On this second occasion, the claimant teachers succeeded in persuading the Supreme Court that their cases did fall within the scope of the *ERA 1996* on an application of *Lawson v Serco* principles (see above).

In *Holis Metal Industries Ltd v GMB and Newell Ltd* [2008] IRLR 187, the EAT concluded that the *Transfer of Undertakings (Protection of Employment) Regulations 2006* had the potential to apply to the transfer of undertakings which were situated in the UK prior to the transfer but were then transferred outside of the EU.

Following the judgment of the House of Lords in *Lawson v Serco*, it would seem that domestic employment tribunals cannot apply the common law doctrine of *forum non conveniens* in the context of statutory claims which come before it (see in particular per Lord Hoffmann at para 24). Thus, where the domestic employment tribunal has territorial jurisdiction to hear a particular statutory claim, it cannot then refuse to hear the claim on the basis that there is arguably some more appropriate forum in which the claim could be heard. This is simply because no foreign court has jurisdiction to hear a claim under UK employment legislation.

When bringing a claim against a foreign respondent in the Employment Tribunal, the rules of service provided for in *rule 8(2)* of the Tribunal Rules (as set out in *Schedule 1* to the *Employment Tribunals (Constitution & Rules etc) Regulations 2013*) must be considered. No authoritative guidance as to how this rule should be applied in the case of a foreign respondent has yet been provided by the appellate courts or tribunals. However, in the case of *Pervez v Macquarie Bank Ltd (London Branch)* (UKEAT/0246/10/CEA) [2011] ICR 266, [2011] IRLR 284, the EAT held that *rule 19(1)* of the predecessor to the current *Tribunal Rules*, could not be relied upon to oust the tribunal's jurisdiction in circumstances where that jurisdiction was afforded under primary legislation. Thus, in *Pervez*, the fact that the claimant's employer was based in Hong Kong and, hence, could not apparently be sued in the tribunal pursuant to *rule 19(1)* of the *Tribunal Rules*, did not operate to prevent the tribunal hearing the claimant's claims of unfair dismissal and race and religious discrimination. The tribunal had jurisdiction to hear these claims under the relevant primary enactments and that jurisdiction could not be excluded through the application of a rule contained in secondary legislation. For further discussion of *rule 19(1)* and *Pervez v Macquarie* see *Hasan v Shell International Shipping Services (PTE) Ltd & Ors* (UKEAT/0242/13/SM).

26.12 STATE IMMUNITY, DIPLOMATIC IMMUNITY AND DOMESTIC WORKERS

Particular problems of state immunity or diplomatic immunity may arise in cases where individuals are employed by foreign state embassies or foreign diplomatic agents. In practice, many of these posts are filled by foreign nationals. It is important to distinguish these two different types of immunity under international law. Difficult questions may also arise in the context of employment by international organisations but there is so far little English authority on this topic, which is beyond the scope of this book: for a recent decision of the EAT see *R Warner v B&M Europe, European Patent Office*, UKEAT/0139/16/RN finding that the grant of immunity to an international organisation does not engage *Article 6* of the *ECHR* insofar as such immunity is required by a rule of international law and/or is compatible with that provision.

State immunity

The law on state immunity is set out in the *State Immunity Act 1978*, which implements the *European Convention on State Immunity 1972*. The starting point under s 1 is that foreign states enjoy general immunity from suit before UK courts. *Section 4* introduces a specific exception for proceedings relating to a contract of employment where either (a) the contract was made in the UK, or (b) the work is to be wholly or partly performed in the UK (*s 4(1)*). However, this exception is itself subject to various exceptions. Two of these are of particular relevance to foreign employees. First, a state is immune if: (a) at the time when the proceedings are brought the individual is a national of the state concerned; or (b) at the time the contract was made the individual was neither a national of the UK nor habitually resident there (*SIA 1978, s 4(2)*). Secondly, a state is immune from proceedings concerning the employment of the members of the mission (*SIA 1978, s 16(a)*). This includes claims brought by administrative and technical staff and members of service staff in the domestic service of the mission such as cleaners and cooks (see *Vienna Convention on Diplomatic Relations 1961, Art 1*, which is incorporated in UK law by the *Diplomatic Privileges Act 1964*).

In the conjoined cases of *Benkharbouche v Embassy of the Republic of Sudan* and *Janah v Libya* [2015] EWCA Civ 33, the Court of Appeal considered the application of the *SIA 1978* to a range of claims under UK and EU law including unfair dismissal, racial discrimination and breach of the *Working Time Regulations 1998* brought by two Moroccan nationals employed as domestic service staff in foreign embassies. In the case of Ms Janah, the exception in *s 4(2)(b)* also applied as she was not habitually resident in the UK at the time the contract was made. Affirming the decision of EAT ([2013] IRLR 918), the Court of Appeal held that *ss 4(2)(b)* and *16(1)(a)* amounted to a disproportionate (and in the case of *s 4(2)(b)*, discriminatory) interference with the right of access to a court under *ECHR, Art 6* and *EU Charter, Art 47*. After conducting a comparative review, the Court of Appeal concluded that the breadth of immunity prescribed by *s 16(1)(a)* fell outside the range of tenable views of what is required by international law. Since the relevant provisions could not be read down, the Court of Appeal issued a declaration under *HRA 1998, s 4* for breach of *ECHR, Arts 6* and *14*. As far as the EU law claims were concerned, it was common ground that the substantive content of *Art 47* of the *EU Charter* is identical to that of *ECHR, Art 6* (see also *EU Charter, Art 52(3)*). However, relying on the CJEU's line of case law on the effect of general principles of EU law (see *Mangold v Helm*: C-144/04 [2005] ECR I-9981 and *Küküdeveci v Swedex*: C-555/07 [2010] IRLR 346), the Court of Appeal held that the right to an effective remedy guaranteed by *Art 47* has 'horizontal' direct effect. Thus, Ms Janah was able to rely on *Art 47* even though Libya is not an EU Member State. The Court of Appeal therefore disapplied *ss 4(2)(b)* and *16(1)(a)* of the *SIA 1978* to the extent necessary to enable employment claims (other than for recruitment, renewal or reinstatement) falling within the scope of EU law by members of the service staff, whose work does not relate to the sovereign functions of the mission staff. While the Court of Appeal's urge to confine state immunity to proceedings concerning core sovereign functions is understandable, state practice on the rule embodied in *s 16(1)(a)* remains mixed. The Court of Appeal's conclusion that the approach taken in the *SIA 1978* falls outside the tenable range of views is therefore a bold one. Similarly, the sweeping approach to 'horizontal direct effect' may be thought to apply to all fundamental rights found in the EU Charter. Unsurprisingly, the Court of Appeal has granted permission to appeal to the Supreme Court.

Diplomatic immunity

On the same day, the same bench of the Court of Appeal handed down its judgment in *Reyes and Anor v Al-Maliki and Anor* [2015] EWCA Civ 32. In that case, a domestic worker sued her Saudi diplomatic agent employer. In contrast to the result in *Benkharbouche*, the Court of Appeal held that Ms Reyes' claim was barred by diplomatic immunity pursuant to the

26.12 Foreign Employees

Vienna Convention on Diplomatic Relations 1961. The fact that the employer diplomat derived an economic benefit was not sufficient to bring the activity of employment within the *art 31(1)(c)* exception for commercial activities outside official functions. Indeed, the court found that the employment of domestic workers is incidental to a diplomat's official functions. The court therefore concluded that the international law obligation to grant diplomatic immunity represents a legitimate and proportionate restriction on the right of access to court under *art 6* of the *ECHR*. The case is currently on appeal before the Supreme Court.

Reyes confirms that, at least as far as serving diplomats are concerned, diplomatic immunity remains a jurisdictional bar to employment claims irrespective of the gravity of abuse alleged. It may, however, be possible to bring such claims against former diplomatic agents who enjoy residual immunity only. Where this is not an option, *Benkharbouche* suggests that claims should instead be pursued against the foreign embassy.

27 Health and Safety at Work – I: The Legal Framework

The law relating to health and safety is both long-established and rapidly developing. To that end, keeping track of it is difficult, like most other legal subject-matter. However, the Health and Safety Executive ('HSE') produces a wide range of free and priced information on health and safety in the workplace. See also www.hse.gov.uk.

Cross-reference. See HEALTH AND SAFETY AT WORK – II (28) for specific legislation and health and safety issues.

27.1 THE LEGISLATIVE FRAMEWORK

An employer is under a common law duty to have regard to the safety of his employees. He is also liable at common law for accidents caused by acts of his employees where the employees were acting in the course of their employment. The assessment of damages in personal injury actions is beyond the scope of this book. In addition to these common law duties, statutory obligations have been imposed upon employers in certain circumstances by such enactments as the *Occupiers' Liability Act 1957*, the *Occupiers Liability Act 1984* (see **27.12** below) and the *Health and Safety at Work, etc Act 1974* (see **27.16** below). An employer owes specific statutory duties to his own employees, members of the public who are affected by the activities of the employer, and other people's employees working on the employer's premises. A breach of an employer's statutory duties under the *Health and Safety at Work, etc Act 1974* (*'HSWA 1974'*) imposes only criminal liability, although a breach of health and safety regulations made thereunder, insofar as damage is caused, will give rise to civil liability unless the regulations provide otherwise (see **27.43** below). The *Enterprise and Regulatory Reform Act 2013*, by *section 69*, substantially amends *section 47* of the *1974 Act*. The consequence is that in cases where previously strict liability attached to an employer, it will become necessary for the claimant to show direct fault, i.e. negligence, on the part of the employer. The mere occurrence of an accident without more will not sound in liability. The reform was not retrospective and is only applicable to accidents after implementation, which was on 1 October 2013.

An employer is obliged to have in place insurance in respect of injury claims brought by employees .This duty was created by the *Employers' Liability (Compulsory Insurance) Act 1969*. In *Campbell v Gordon* [2016] UKSC 38 the Supreme Court decided, by a majority of 3 to 2, that the director of a company which had failed to take out cover was not personally liable to compensate an injured employee. The company would of course be liable to pay compensation but that would be subject to it having adequate assets to discharge the claim.

Under provisions in the *Employment Rights Act 1996*, employees are protected from dismissal or victimisation by the employer in health and safety cases (see **54.3** UNFAIR DISMISSAL – II and **28.8** HEALTH AND SAFETY AT WORK – II). In addition, an employer who fails to fulfil his legal duties may face a claim for constructive dismissal should an employee resign as a result of an alleged breach of the employer's duty of care. For example, in *British Aircraft Corpn v Austin* [1978] IRLR 332, an employer's obstinate and unjustified refusal to deal with a safety grievance was held to justify a complaint of constructive dismissal when the employee resigned (see **28.11** HEALTH AND SAFETY AT WORK – II).

27.2 THE COMMON LAW DUTY

An employer is obliged to take such steps as are reasonably necessary to ensure the safety of his employees. The definition of 'employee' is given a wide interpretation by the courts (*Lane v Shire Roofing Co (Oxford) Ltd* [1995] IRLR 493, [1995] PIQR P 417, CA). In

Autoklenz v Belcher (2011) UKSC 41 the Supreme Court explained that the question of status was to be determined by having regard to the true nature of the arrangement between the parties rather than by slavishly accepting documentation which might not be accurate. In *Cox v Ministry of Justice* [2016] UKSC 10, [2016] 2 WLR 806 the Supreme Court unanimously held that an employer was vicariously liable for injury inflicted upon the claimant, their employee, by a prisoner who was helping in the kitchens at the workplace, Swansea prison. The defendant contended that since the prisoner was not their employee it could not be held answerable for his clear negligence in dropping a heavy sack on Mrs Cox. The pragmatic view of the Court was that the prisoner was doing work which benefitted the claimant. In his absence a conventional employee would have been required to perform the task. It was fair, just and reasonable to extend liability.

The duty to ensure safety is not an absolute one and the mere occurrence of an accident does not of itself necessarily impose liability on the employer (see *McCook v Lobo* [2002] EWCA Civ 1760, [2003] ICR 89). All the circumstances of the accident will be investigated in deciding whether the employer acted reasonably or not. If an accident occurs as a result of the employer's failure to comply with his duty to his employees, he is liable for any resulting injury or damage.

Where a job has inherent risks to health and safety which are not commonly known but of which the employer is or ought to be aware, and if the employer cannot guard against those risks by taking precautionary measures, then he has a duty to inform prospective employees of the risks if knowledge of them would be likely to affect a sensible and level-headed person's decision on whether or not to accept the job (*White v Holbrook Precision Castings* [1985] IRLR 215). The employer must keep abreast of contemporary knowledge in the field of accident prevention (*Baxter v Harland and Wolff plc* [1990] IRLR 516; *Bowman v Harland and Wolff plc* [1992] IRLR 349). In *Williams v University of Birmingham* [2011] EWCA Civ 1242 the Court of Appeal emphasised that one must look to the knowledge of risk at the time of exposure, here to asbestos in the early 1970s, and must not make the error of applying hindsight.

The employer's compliance with his common law duty of care is usually tested under the following headings:

(a)   providing a safe place of work;

(b)   providing a safe means of access to the place of work;

(c)   providing a safe system of work;

(d)   providing safe plant and equipment;

(e)   employing competent fellow employees; and

(f)   protecting employees from unnecessary risk of injury.

However, these are simply specific aspects of the employer's overall general duty not to be negligent, and so should be viewed as examples of ways in which employers can take steps to ensure that their employees are reasonably safe at work.

27.3 Safe place of work

An employer is obliged to see that the place where his employees work is reasonably safe in all the circumstances. A place of work must be safely constructed and adequately maintained in a reasonable state of repair. An employer would be as guilty of failing to provide a safe place of work if, for example, a platform high above the ground on which men were required to stand was not adequately fenced as if one of the planks provided for the platform were rotten and liable to give way.

So far as construction of the workplace is concerned, it is not sufficient to show that the employer engaged a competent contractor to provide a safe place (*Paine v Colne Valley Electricity Supply Co Ltd and British Insulated Cables Ltd* [1938] 4 All ER 803, *per* Goddard LJ at 807). This reflects the general principle that the employer's duty of care to his employees is non-delegable. If, however, an employer maintains an adequate system of inspection of the workplace and despite inspection, a part of the workplace becomes inadequate or defective, the employer will probably not have been in breach of his common law duty. (He may nevertheless be in breach of a statutory provision which imposes a stricter duty.)

Temporary conditions affecting the workplace. A place of work which is intrinsically safe may become unsafe by the occurrence of certain events. Liquid may be spilt on a workshop floor making it slippery, a fence may be temporarily removed or an object placed in an unfamiliar position. All these events could cause accidents. The employer's liability will depend upon whether a reasonable employer would in the particular circumstances have taken measures to avoid the accident or different measures from those in fact taken. What is reasonable will vary according to the facts of the case. If a man slips on an oil slick at his workplace and thereby injures himself, his employer's potential liability may well vary according to how long the oil had been present (or according to the frequency with which such spillages occur, as in *Bell v Department of Health and Social Security* (1989) Times, 13 June). If the oil had been spilt just a few minutes before the accident there may well be no liability, whereas if it had been there for half a day, the position would be different. In *Thomas v Bristol Aeroplane Co Ltd* [1954] 2 All ER 1, an employer was held not to be in breach of the common law duty of care in failing to take steps to remove from the entrance to the factory frozen snow which had fallen about a quarter of an hour before the factory opened.

Employee working on other premises. An employer owes a general duty to his employee to provide him with a safe place of work whether he is employed on the employer's own premises or elsewhere; see the House of Lords judgment in *McDermid v Nash Dredging and Reclamation Co Ltd* [1987] AC 906, [1987] ICR 917. However, the extent of that duty when the employee is on other premises may well be less than when he is on his employer's premises. The test again is: did the employer in question act as a reasonable employer would have acted in the circumstances? Thus, if an employer sends a window-cleaner to premises he knows to be unsafe, he may well be held liable for any accident caused as a result of the state of the premises. If he does not know whether the premises are safe or not, then, depending on the convenience of inspection and the degree of risk involved, he may be held negligent in failing to inspect and, if necessary, make those premises safe (*General Cleaning Contractors Ltd v Christmas* [1953] AC 180).

The Supreme Court in *Kennedy v Cordia Services LLP* [2016] UKSC 6 gave an illuminating unanimous judgment as to risk assessment and avoidance. The claimant was a carer employed by the defendant. Her work entailed visiting patients at their homes. She was injured when, in the midst of a bitter spell of bad weather, she slipped on ice that had accumulated on the path leading up to the door of the patient upon she was about to call. The employer was aware of other similar incidents having occurred. A competent risk assessment would have lead to the issue of shoe attachments which could well have avoided the incident. The judgment is also helpful in explaining when and how expert evidence should be relied upon by a court.

The extent of an employer's duty in relation to employees working on other premises was considered by the Court of Appeal in *Square D Ltd v Cook* [1992] IRLR 34. An employer must take all reasonable steps to ensure the safety of his staff and this includes the premises where the staff are required to work (whether occupied by the employer or by a third party). This duty cannot be delegated. However, the duty is not an absolute one and considerations such as the place where the work is to be done, the nature of the building on the site concerned, the experience of the employee who is sent to work at such a site, the nature of the work he is required to do, the degree of control that the employer can reasonably be expected to exercise in the circumstances and the employer's own knowledge of the defective state of the premises are all factors to be taken into account. These considerations apply whether the third party's premises are in the UK or abroad. However, the court may take a different view of the employer's duty where staff are sent to work abroad for a considerable period of time. The Court of Appeal suggested that in such an instance, the employer may be expected to inspect the site personally and satisfy himself that the occupiers are conscious of their obligations concerning the safety of people working there.

27.4   Safe means of access

It is the duty of every employer to provide his employees with a safe means of access to their place of work. Thus, if access to a factory is by means of a footpath, that footpath should be kept in a reasonable state of repair.

Sometimes it is hard to distinguish the means of access to the place of work from the place of work itself. A painter may use a ladder to reach a position from where to carry on his decorating. The ladder may in certain circumstances be considered the means of access and in others the place of work. In any event the common law duty of care in relation to both is the same.

27.5   Safe system of work

A system of work is the method used for carrying out the work, the sequence of events followed. It includes such things as manning of operations, provision of equipment, and supervision. It may be that the system used by an employer is intrinsically unsafe or it may be that there is in existence a suitable system of work but that the system itself is applied unsatisfactorily. For example, an employer who provides insufficient workers to carry out a task may be held liable for any accident caused thereby.

One defect in an otherwise unimpeachable system may render the whole system unsafe. If, for example, the procedures for carrying out blasting in a quarry were adequate but the warning given to workers in the quarry to leave was too short, the whole system would thereby be rendered unsafe. Similarly, it would be considered an unsafe system to require men who had insufficient training or supervision to carry out a task which would otherwise be considered safe.

Where an operation is so inherently dangerous that it should not be performed at all, the employer must provide explicit instructions banning employees from carrying it out (*King v Smith* [1995] ICR 339). It would be incumbent upon the employer to police and uphold the prohibition.

Employers who require their workers to carry out manoeuvres which involve several actions should first check to see whether there are any relevant statutory requirements relating to the procedure. Before devising a system of working they should consult the employees who are to work the system or their representatives. Where the workforce is unionised, the employer has a duty to consult with union-appointed safety representatives. Non-unionised groups of workers or their representatives must also be consulted (see **28.20** HEALTH AND SAFETY AT WORK – **II**). If the procedure is at all complicated, employers should consult the Health and Safety Executive (see **27.26**).

Duty based on reasonable steps. The duty to provide a safe system of work is not an absolute one. The duty is to take reasonable steps to provide a system which will be reasonably safe, having regard to the dangers necessarily inherent in the operation. In deciding what is reasonable, long-established practice in the trade (although not necessarily conclusive) is generally regarded as strong evidence in support of reasonableness (*General Cleaning Contractors Ltd v Christmas* [1953] AC 180 *per* Lord Tucker at 195). Nevertheless, acceptable standards of safety change over the years and the courts will have regard to current best practice. In deciding the extent of the duty the courts will take into account: (i) the size of the danger; (ii) the likelihood of an accident occurring; (iii) the possible consequences of the occurrence of an accident; and (iv) the steps needed to eliminate all risk and the cost of doing so (*Edwards v National Coal Board* [1949] 1 KB 704).

Ensuring implementation of safety measures. It is not sufficient to provide a safe system of work. An employer should take such steps as are reasonably practicable to see that the system is implemented. If it is within his knowledge that a piece of safety equipment is persistently not used, he should take reasonable steps to encourage his workers to use it (*Bux v Slough Metals* [1974] 1 All ER 262). However, this duty is not so onerous as the duty to provide the safety equipment, etc in the first place. As Lord Radcliffe said in *Qualcast (Wolverhampton) Ltd v Haynes* [1959] AC 743 at 753: 'the courts should be circumspect in filling out that duty with the much vaguer obligation of encouraging, exhorting or instructing workmen or a particular workman to make regular use of what is provided'. In *Crouch v British Rail Engineering Ltd* [1988] IRLR 404 it was held to be insufficient on the facts merely to make safety goggles available for collection from a point about five minutes away. The failure to have them available where they were needed encouraged the taking of risks.

27.6   Safe equipment and materials

An employer is under a common law duty to provide equipment, materials and clothing to enable his workmen to carry out their duties in safety. As with the system of work, the duty is not an absolute one. It may be, for example, that goggles costing £300 per pair are marginally safer than those costing £50 per pair. In deciding whether an employer was in breach of his duty in failing to provide his employees with the more expensive goggles, the court would have regard to the difference in effectiveness between the cheaper and the more expensive goggles, the degree of risk involved, and the additional cost.

When an employer bought materials from a reputable supplier, and injury was caused by an undetected defect in those materials, his failure to examine the materials would not render him liable for the accident at common law. However, under the *Employers' Liability (Defective Equipment) Act 1969*, if an employee is injured by reason of a defect in the equipment, the injury is by statute deemed to be attributable to the fault of the employer. This does not affect the employer's right to allege that the accident was wholly or partly due to negligence on the part of the employee; nor does it affect any remedy the employer may have against his supplier. Thus, if an employee is injured by a piece of metal flying from a defective high-pressure hose, supplied to him by his employer, he could succeed in a claim against the employer for his injury. The employer could only seek to reduce the damages awarded against him by showing that the accident was caused or contributed to by the fault of the employee and/or by claiming against the supplier of the hose.

Under *s 1(3)* of the *Employers' Liability (Defective Equipment) Act 1969* 'equipment' includes any plant, machinery, vehicle, aircraft and clothing. A ship is 'equipment' for the purposes of *s 1(3)* (*Coltman v Bibby Tankers Ltd, The Derbyshire* [1988] ICR 67). 'Equipment provided by the employer' includes materials (in this case a flagstone) which an employee is given by the employer to do the job (*Knowles v Liverpool City Council* [1993] IRLR 588. The contention that 'equipment' was confined to the tools of the job was rejected; a nail, a brick and a piece of timber all amount to equipment.

27.7   Fellow workers

An employer is under a duty to provide competent fellow workers. Thus, if an employee of his is injured because of the known inadequacy of a fellow worker, the employer is liable to that employee in damages for the injury caused by the fellow worker. Even if the employee's action is untypical, the employer may nevertheless be held liable by reason of his

VICARIOUS LIABILITY (56). This principle also applies to the employer's duty not to engage or continue to employ employees who are known to indulge in dangerous 'horseplay' (*Hudson v Ridge Manufacturing Co Ltd* [1957] 2 QB 348). Liability on the part of an employer where one employee assaults another in the workplace has been considered in the conjoined appeals of *Wallbank v Wallbank Fox Designs Ltd* and *Weddall v Barchester* [2012] EWCA Civ 25. Lord Phillips in *The Catholic Care Child Welfare Society and others v Various claimants and The Institute of Brothers of the Christian Schools* [2012] UKSC 56 [at 19] wisely observed that the law was on the move. The absence of a conventional contract of employment between a religious body and some members of it who abused children did not prevent a finding of vicarious liability. The relationship was akin to employment and so the body was liable. One can anticipate interesting arguments about liability arising for the acts of volunteers and others who do not fulfil conventional employment criteria and yet, arguably, come within the ambit of quasi-employment.

The mere fact that an incident occurs at the premises of an employer will not in itself generate liability. In the Scottish case of *Vaickuviene v J Sainsbury plc* [2013] CSIH 67, [2013] IRLR 792, Ct of Sess, one employee murdered a workmate in the workplace. It was held that there was no liability on the part of the employer for he unprovoked and extreme act. This case was not addressed in the Supreme Court judgment of *Mohamud V WM Morrison Supermarkets plc* [2016] UKSC 11, [2016] 2 WLR 821. Mr Mohamud was the victim of an unprovoked attack perpetrated by an employee of the defendant. The incident occurred at a petrol station. The late claimant entered and asked if the employee manning the till could print off some documents for him from a USB stick. The employee chased Mr Mohamud out to his vehicle and assaulted him. A supervisor standing nearby implored the culprit to desist but to no avail. Having lost both at first instance and in the Court of Appeal, the claim succeeded before the Supreme Court. A close connection was held to exist between the job and the attack. The assailant was employed to attend to customers and was doing so, albeit in a despicable manner, when he carried out the attack.

An employer may not contract out of his liability to his employees for the negligence of fellow workers. The *Law Reform (Personal Injuries) Act 1948, s 1(3)* renders void any agreement to that effect.

27.8   Protection from risk of injury

An employer is under a duty to take reasonable care to see that his employees are not subjected to any unnecessary risks of injury. In *Charlton v Forrest Printing Ink Co Ltd* [1980] IRLR 331, the Court of Appeal held that an employer has a duty to take steps to eliminate a risk which he knows or ought to know is a real risk and not a mere possibility which would never influence the mind of a reasonable man. The Court of Appeal in *Coxall v Goodyear Great Britain Ltd* [2002] EWCA Civ 1010, [2003] ICR 152, considering whether or not an employer was under a duty to prevent an employee from doing work which he was willing to do because of a risk to his health, depended largely on the actual nature and extent of the risk. Consequently, if on the facts the employer were negligent in failing to either move the employee from the job in question or dismiss him in order to protect him from the danger, the employer would become liable.

Where a risk is not obvious, the employee will succeed only if he can show that the state of knowledge in the relevant industry at the relevant time was such that the employer knew or ought to have known of that risk. But an employer must keep reasonably abreast of developing knowledge, and if he has greater than average knowledge of the risks, he may have to take greater than average precautions (*Stokes v Guest Keen & Nettlefold (Bolts and Nuts) Ltd* [1968] 1 WLR 1776).

An employer may also be liable in certain circumstances for psychiatric illness caused by work if it is reasonably foreseeable (see *Page v Smith* [1996] AC 155 for the principles involved, and *Walker v Northumberland County Council* [1995] IRLR 35 and *Cross v*

Highlands and Islands Enterprise [2001] IRLR 336 at **28.24** Health and Safety at Work – II). The House of Lords in *White v Chief Constable of South Yorkshire Police* [1999] IRLR 110 overturned the ruling of the Court of Appeal in *Frost v Chief Constable of South Yorkshire Police* [1997] IRLR 173 relating to an employer's liability for work-related psychiatric illness. The case concerned police officers who sustained psychiatric damage as a result of tending to victims of the Hillsborough football stadium disaster which was caused by the employer's admitted negligence. Compensation for physical injury caused by negligence was recoverable if it was reasonably foreseeable that the conduct would cause such injury. Where this situation does not apply (ie the claimant is not within the range of foreseeable physical injury), individuals are 'secondary victims' and, in order to recover compensation for psychiatric injury, it was necessary that the conditions set out in *Alcock v Chief Constable of South Yorkshire Police* [1992] 1 AC 310 should be satisfied:

(a)   there must be a close tie of love and affection between the claimant and the victim;

(b)   the claimant must have been present at the accident or its immediate aftermath; and

(c)   the psychiatric injury must have been caused by direct perception of the accident or its immediate aftermath and not by hearing about it from someone else.

Since the officers did not have sufficiently close ties to the victims, their claim failed. The House of Lords concluded that the employment relationship did not put the officers in a special position in this regard. See also *Robertson and Rough v Forth Road Bridge Joint Board* [1995] IRLR 251, *Young v Charles Church (Southern) Ltd* (1997) 33 BMLR 101, CA and *Hunter v British Coal Corpn* [1999] QB 140, CA.

The House of Lords in *Corr (Administratrix of Corr dec'd) v IBC Vehicles Ltd* [2008] UKHL 13, [2008] ICR 372 held an employer liable for the suicide of their employee who had been badly injured in an accident at work six years before. Mr Corr had become severely depressed as a result of his injuries. His death was attributable to the accident for which the employer had been to blame. This is an example of the classic maxim that one must take the claimant as one finds him. Whilst extreme depression was not an inevitable consequence of injury it happened to have been so here and thus the defendant was liable.

In mainstream stress cases it had been the conventional approach to apportion liability where there were a combination of causes, some of which were non-tortious, that lead to injury. This would occur, for example, where it was accepted that the employer was culpable but the claimant had other non work related problems too. No more. In *Dickins v O2 Plc* [2009] IRLR 58 the Court of Appeal accepted, obiter, that stress was an injury incapable of division and so the claimant would be entitled to full compensation where the employer had made a material contribution to the injury.

In cases of industrial disease, it may often be difficult to determine whether the employee's illness was *caused* by the employer's breach of duty. The decision of the House of Lords in *Fairchild v Glenhaven Funeral Services Ltd* [2002] UKHL 22, [2003] 1 AC 32 contains a comprehensive review of the relevant authorities. The Supreme Court decided in *Sienkiewicz v Greif (UK) Ltd* [2011] UKSC 10, [2011] ICR 391 that the *Fairchild* principle can equally apply where there was only one relevant defendant and also that a claim may succeed without the need to prove that guilty exposure doubled the risk of harm. Here, the evidence was that the employer negligently exposed the victim to 18% more asbestos than would be found in the general environment. Accordingly, the employer was liable. In cases of mesothelioma only, *s 3* of the *Compensation Act 2006* enables a claimant to recover in full from any culpable employer even though the victim was exposed to asbestos in more than one job.

In *Chandler v Cape Industries Ltd* [2012] EWCA Civ 525 the Court of Appeal upheld a finding that a parent company was liable for the negligence of a subsidiary which was now defunct. The parent was liable because the respective businesses were similar (asbestos production), it had or ought to have had superior knowledge of health risks, it knew of an unsafe system of work at the subsidiary and it had intervened in the business of the subsidiary.

27.9 Vicarious liability for acts of employees

An employer is liable for the acts of his employee if they are committed in the course of the employee's employment. This is known as vicarious liability. The modern test is whether the incident was job related or job connected. An incident can be job related even if it forms no part of the employee's authorised work. In *Lister v Hesley Hall Ltd* [2001] 2 WLR 1311 it was found that a teacher who abused a pupil was acting in the course of employment even though what he did was criminal, unauthorised and something that no teacher should ever have done. Thus, if a van delivery driver drives negligently while in the normal course of his duties and causes an accident, his employer is held liable for the resulting damage or injury. Sexual abuse of a child by a priest was held to be the responsibility of the Archdiocese in *Maga v Roman Catholic Archdiocese of Birmingham* [2010] EWCA Civ 256. Likewise, the Court of Appeal held the employer liable when an employee stole silver bullion which was to be transported abroad from a secure compound which he was authorised to enter. This question is dealt with in more detail in VICARIOUS LIABILITY (56).

27.10 Employee working under direction of third party

The primary employer remains liable for the safety of an employee who is working under the direction of a third party. However, where the employee suffers an accident which is wholly due to the third party's negligence in breach of its duty of care, the primary employer may be able to recover full indemnity from the third party in accordance with the *Civil Liability (Contribution) Act 1978* (*Nelhams v Sandells Maintenance Ltd* (1995) Times, 15 June, CA).

27.11 Independent contractors

With the exception of the statutory occupier's liability (see **27.12** below), in general an employer is not liable for acts of an independent contractor engaged by him, provided that he exercised due diligence in selecting the contractor for the task. (For criminal liability in respect of the negligence of an independent contractor, see **27.19** below.)

27.12 OCCUPIERS' LIABILITY ACT 1957

Apart from the common law duties of an employer to provide his employees with a safe place of work, as an occupier of premises he owes his employees, and other visitors, the common duty of care imposed by the *Occupiers' Liability Act 1957* ('*OLA 1957*'). The extent of the duty which is owed to trespassers is defined by the *Occupiers' Liability Act 1984*. An outline is given below of the duties imposed on an employer, as the occupier of premises, to employees and other visitors by the *OLA 1957*.

27.13 Meaning of 'occupier'

An occupier of premises may be the owner, the lessor, or the licensee (a person who merely has permission to occupy). An occupier need not have exclusive control over premises in order to have a duty to persons who visit those premises; more than one person may owe a duty in respect of the same premises. For example, both an employer and an independent contractor may be held to be occupiers of premises where the employer has engaged the independent contractor to carry out work on the premises.

27.14 Duty of occupier

The extent of the duty of care is defined in *OLA 1957, s 2(2)* as:

'a duty to take such care as in all the circumstances of the case is reasonable to see that the visitor is reasonably safe in using the premises for the purposes for which he is invited or permitted by the occupier to be there.'

In defining the extent of the duty, the courts will take into account the *degree of control over the premises actually enjoyed* by the occupier and, if applicable, the division of duties between the two occupiers of the same premises. Thus, if a harbour authority leases a certain wharf to a shipping company and an employee of that company suffers an accident due to the state of repair of the wharf, the apportionment of blame will depend on the actual degree of control exercised by the harbour authority and the shipping company.

Children and persons pursuing a calling. OLA 1957, s 2(3) provides a little help in defining the extent of the duty of care to be exercised in relation to children and to persons on the premises in pursuance of a particular calling.

'The circumstances relevant for the present purpose include the degree of care, and of want of care, which would ordinarily be looked for in such a visitor, so that (for example) in proper cases:

(*a*)   an occupier must be prepared for children to be less careful than adults; and

(*b*)   an occupier may expect that a person, in the exercise of his calling, will appreciate and guard against any special risks ordinarily incident to it, so far as the occupier leaves him free to do so.'

The duty under *OLA 1957, s 2(2)* is to see that the visitor is reasonably safe in using the premises for the purpose for which he or she is there. This covers the static state of the premises and does not extend to dangers occurring to employees of contractors as a result of activities they are performing on the premises. The House of Lords, in its landmark ruling in *Fairchild v Glenhaven Funeral Services Ltd* [2002] UKHL 22, [2002] IRLR 533, overruled the Court of Appeal's decision ([2002] EWCA Civ 1881, [2002] IRLR 129) that claimants were not entitled to recover damages from their former employers in relation to mesothelioma, a form of cancer which develops as a result of negligent exposure to asbestos.

Unanimously, their Lordships held that the victim, on grounds of so-called 'justice', should not be deprived of a remedy because it cannot be established which of a series of different employers caused the alleged harm. As Lord Nicholls put it: '*Any other outcome would be deeply offensive to instinctive notions of what justice requires and fairness demands.*' Consequently, employers may now be held liable for damage which they did not cause. The House of Lords established a right to damages by departing from the orthodox test of causation where justice so requires, by establishing a notion of joint liability. For instance, on the facts of this case, it was sufficient that the employer's breach of duty materially increased the risk that the claimants would contract mesothelioma. Therefore, the *Fairchild* ruling presupposes negligence by all employers. Clearly, the impact of this historic ruling is that once a breach of duty can be established, then each employer becomes liable for the full damages.

27.15 Faulty work by independent contractor

If an accident occurs as a result of faulty work by an independent contractor employed at the premises which the employer occupies, *OLA 1957, s 2(4)(b)* provides that:

'the occupier is not to be treated without more ["without more" in the sense of "on those facts alone"] as answerable for the danger if in all the circumstances he had acted reasonably in entrusting the work to an independent contractor and had taken such steps (if any) as he reasonably ought in order to satisfy himself that the contractor was competent and that the work had been properly done.'

Thus, if injury is caused to a visitor to the premises by the fault of an independent contractor, the occupier will not be held liable for the injury or damage so caused if he can show that:

(a)   he acted reasonably in entrusting the work to the independent contractor (it may be held to be reasonable to employ an independent contractor where the work to be done is of a skilled or specialist nature and is beyond the capabilities of the employer);

(b)   he exercised a reasonable degree of care in selecting the independent contractor to see that he was competent to do the task entrusted to him; and

(c)   he checked so far as was possible to see that the work was properly carried out.

For example, an employer may need to have his factory rewired. He may have no electricians in his employ and, therefore, need to engage an outside firm. If he has reasonable grounds for regarding that firm as competent, he will not ordinarily be expected to supervise the firm's activities in order to ensure that a safe system of work is being used. But if he knows or has reason to suspect that the firm is using an unsafe system of work, it may well be reasonable for him to take steps to see that it is made safe. If he does not, he might be liable to one of his own or the firm's employees injured, eg by receiving an electric shock (*Ferguson v Welsh* [1988] IRLR 112, on different facts). He may also be liable to the employee for breach of other statutory provisions.

In 2011, a review entitled 'Reclaiming Health and Safety for All', of all existing health and safety legislation was undertaken by an advisory panel chaired by Professor Lofstedt, director of King's College Centre for Risk Management. The general consensus of the reports was that occupational health law – and the *Health and Safety at Work etc Act 1974* in particular – was not broken and was fit for purpose. Specifically, there have been several repeals/revocations of outdated legislation, e.g. *RIDDOR 1995*, consolidation of several pieces of legislation, e.g. Pressure Systems and Dangerous Substances, and reviews/discontinuation of certain Approved Codes of Practice (ACoPs), e.g. the ACoP associated to the *Management of Health and Safety at Work Regulations 1999*.

In essence, Lofstedt recommended a simplification of much of the guidance associated with primary legislation, rather than a root and branch change to what is working well in practice.

27.16   THE HEALTH AND SAFETY AT WORK, ETC ACT 1974

The *Health and Safety at Work, etc Act 1974* ('*HSWA 1974*') lays down general principles to be followed by employers governing the health and safety at work of employees. It also establishes the Health and Safety Commission ('the Commission') and the Health and Safety Executive ('the Executive') (note: he HSC has now been devolved; only the HSE now exists); gives powers to inspectors to issue improvement notices and prohibition notices; and imposes certain civil and criminal liabilities upon employers. The Executive publishes many explanatory guides and booklets. In the autumn of 2010 the Government published and accepted the report of Lord Young who concluded that the law was unduly onerous and a more proportionate approach should be taken. It is highly probable that the law will be simplified with lower burdens being imposed upon those in low risk environments. Rescue workers should also be put beyond the risk of prosecution where they take heroic actions when striving to save life and limb.

27.17   Health, safety and welfare

The provisions of *HSWA 1974, Part I* (as expressed in s *1(1)*) are designed to have the effect of:

(a)   securing the health, safety and welfare of persons at work;

(b)   protecting persons other than persons at work against risks to health or safety arising out of, or in connection with, the activities of persons at work; and

(c)   controlling the keeping and use of explosive or highly flammable or otherwise dangerous substances, and generally preventing the unlawful acquisition, possession and use of such substances.

Regulations and codes of practice are issued under *HSWA 1974* to give effect to the general principles set out and also to enforce the provisions of a large body of health and safety legislation which is set out in *Sch 1* to the *Act*. Among the more important regulations made under *HSWA 1974* are the *Health and Safety (First-Aid) Regulations 1981 (SI 1981/917)*, the *Reporting of Injuries, Diseases and Dangerous Occurrences Regulations 1995 (SI 1995/3163) (RIDDOR* has been amended/revised in 2013; *RIDDOR 2013* is *SI 2013/1471)* and the *Electricity at Work Regulations 1989 (SI 1989/635)*. There are also many regulations dealing with specific problems such as asbestos at work. From 1 October 1989 a large number of outdated Statutory Instruments were replaced upon the coming into force of the *Control of Substances Hazardous to Health Regulations 1988 ('COSHH')*. The *1988 Regulations* were subsequently amended and replaced by the *2002 Regulations (SI 2002/2675)* of the same name. *COSHH* has been described as 'the most far-reaching health and safety legislation since 1974'. Further important changes have taken place with the implementation of EC Directives on health and safety issues by regulations made under *HSWA 1974*. These regulations cover, *inter alia*, noise at work, management of health and safety, display screen equipment (VDUs), manual handling, work equipment, and workplace health, safety and welfare.

Further details of regulations made under *HSWA 1974* are contained in HEALTH AND SAFETY AT WORK – II (28) under specific subject headings.

As will be seen below, inspectors appointed under the *Act* have powers to enforce the legislation set out in *Sch 1* as well as the provisions of the *Act* itself, and health and safety regulations.

The protection of *HSWA 1974* is extended by *Health and Safety (Training for Employment) Regulations 1990 (SI 1990/1380)* to those receiving work experience provided pursuant to a training course or programme, or training for employment, or both, except if the training is received on a course run by an educational establishment.

27.18   Employer's obligations under HSWA 1974

HSWA 1974 contains provisions broadly equivalent to the common law duty of care of an employer to his employees (see **27.2** above) (*HSWA 1974, s 2(1), (2)*). Criminal liability under *HSWA 1974* can arise even where senior management has taken all reasonable steps to protect employees. A failure at local management level may be attributable to the employing organisation (*R v Gateway Foodmarkets Ltd* [1997] IRLR 189). A failure by an employer to comply with the requirements relating to the safety of his employees may also in certain circumstances constitute a fundamental breach of contract entitling the employee to resign and claim that he was constructively dismissed (*British Aircraft Corpn Ltd v Austin* [1978] IRLR 332).

Health and safety policy statement. Employers are obliged to prepare (and, if necessary, revise) a written statement of their general policy with respect to the health and safety at work of their employees and the organisation and arrangements for carrying out that policy. In addition, employers must bring such information to the notice of all of their employees (*HSWA 1974, s 2(3)*). The length and complexity of the notice required will depend on the nature of the employer's undertaking. Such information should in all cases be placed on an easily accessible notice board. In addition, information relating to health, safety and welfare must be given to employees by means of posters and leaflets approved and published by the Health and Safety Executive. From 1 July 2000 employers are required to use a revised version of the poster; additional detail is provided on aspects of the *Management of Health and Safety at Work Regulations 1999 (SI 1999/3242)* and new sections have been incorporated for the insertion of the names and locations of safety representatives and competent persons together with their health and safety responsibilities. Copies of the form of approved poster or leaflet may be obtained from HSE Books (see the *Health and Safety Information for Employees Regulations 1989 (SI 1989/682)*). Alternative health and safety posters may be approved by the HSE provided certain criteria are met (the *Health and Safety Information for Employees (Modifications and Repeals) Regulations 1995 (SI 1995/2923)*).

Employers who carry on undertakings in which for the time being they employ fewer than five employees are exempted from the requirement of *s 2(3)* by the *Employers' Health and Safety Policy Statements (Exception) Regulations 1975 (SI 1975/1584)*.

27.19 Employers and the self-employed

Employers and self-employed people are obliged to conduct their undertakings, so far as is reasonably practicable, in a way which will ensure that persons who may be affected, not being their employees, are not exposed to risks to health or safety (*HSWA 1974, s 3(1), (2)*). The conduct of the undertaking extends to the manner in which equipment is made available for use by employees outside business hours (*R v Mara* [1987] ICR 165). The Court of Appeal has ruled that it is not necessary to prove actual danger to members of the public for criminal liability to arise. It is sufficient to show that there is a risk which might be run (*R v Science Museum (Board of Trustees)* [1994] IRLR 25, 158 JP 39).

Subject to reasonable practicability, s *3(1)* creates an absolute prohibition on exposing non–employees to risk. It is no defence to argue that the employer is not liable because senior management was not involved in the incident (*R v British Steel plc* [1995] IRLR 310). It may not be sufficient to show that the employer has issued a code of instructions on a safe system of work. In certain circumstances tangible technical equipment may be necessary to ensure safety (*R v Rhône-Poulenc Rorer Ltd* [1996] ICR 1054, CA).

Nevertheless, employers should not necessarily be held criminally liable under s *3(1)* for an isolated act of negligence by the employee performing the work (*R v Nelson Group Services (Maintenance) Ltd* [1999] IRLR 646). It is a sufficient obligation to require the employer to show that everything reasonably practicable was done to see that the person doing the work had the appropriate skill and training, was adequately supervised and provided with safe equipment, and that a safe system of work was laid down.

In February 1997 Port Ramsgate, together with others, was convicted of a breach of *s 3(1)* and heavily fined following the collapse of a ferry passenger walkway which caused the death of six people. The port had employed highly reputable contractors and designers and made arrangements for safety checks but, according to the judge, it had not ensured that proper quality assurance provisions were included in the contract or given detailed thought to its own responsibilities for the design, construction and installation of the walkway.

In *R v Associated Octel Co Ltd* [1997] IRLR 123 the House of Lords held that an employer was criminally liable under s *3(1)* for the negligence of an independent contractor in respect of injuries sustained by an employee of the contractor while undertaking maintenance and repair work for the employer. The conduct of the employer's undertaking could cover ancillary activities carried out by independent contractors, particularly when the activity was carried out on the employer's premises.

Regulations may be introduced compelling employers and self-employed people to give information relating to health and safety to people (not being their employees) who may be affected by the way in which they conduct their undertakings (*HSWA 1974, s 3(3)*).

27.20 Duties of occupiers

Obligations are imposed on occupiers of 'non-domestic' premises in respect of persons who are not their employees but who are working on their premises or using plant or substances provided for use on the premises (*HSWA 1974, s 4*). They must take such measures as are reasonable for persons in their position to ensure, so far as is reasonably practicable, that the premises, plant and machinery are safe and without risks to the health of the non-employees working there. These provisions would apply to protect workers who were sent by their employer, for example, to re-decorate a client's factory. The nature of the duties imposed by *HSWA 1974, s 4* was considered by the House of Lords in *Austin Rover group Ltd v HM Inspector of Factories* [1990] ICR 133.

Operators in control of an establishment or installation which involves the use of dangerous substances are required to take all measures necessary to prevent major accidents and to limit their consequences to people and the environment, under the *Control of Major Accident Hazards Regulations 1999 (SI 1999/743)*, which came into force on 1 April 1999. Known as '*COMAH*', the *1999 Regulations* (which primarily affect the chemical industry) revoke and replace the *Control of Industrial Major Accident Hazards Regulations 1984 (SI 1984/1902)*. Under the *1999 Regulations*, operators are obliged to notify the competent authority about their activities and prepare a major accident prevention policy.

27.21 Duties of manufacturers

Manufacturers, designers, importers and suppliers of articles or substances for use at work are placed under a duty to ensure so far as is reasonably practicable that the design of their product is safe, to carry out necessary tests for so ensuring and to provide adequate information about the use of the product and the conditions necessary for its safe use (*HSWA 1974, s 6*, as amended by the *Consumer Protection Act 1987, s 36* and *Sch 3*). The manufacturers, designers, importers or suppliers of articles for use at work are exempt from such duties if they obtain a written undertaking from their customers that the customer will take specified steps sufficient to ensure, so far as is reasonably practicable, that the article will be safe and without risk to health when properly used (*HSWA 1974, s 6(8)*). This exemption is qualified where the goods are imported (*HSWA 1974, s 6(8A)*).

27.22 Duties of employees

Every employee while at work has the duty:

(a)   to take reasonable care for the health and safety of himself and of other persons who may be affected by his acts or omissions at work; and

(b)   to co-operate with his employer, or any other person, in ensuring that requirements or duties imposed by the relevant statutory provisions (including those specified in *Sch 1*) are complied with.

(*HSWA 1974, s 7*)

Thus, if an employer is required to provide his workers with goggles, supervisors should, if that task is delegated to them, ensure that adequate goggles are available. Also, the workers themselves are under an obligation to wear them.

There are additional duties placed on employees by the *Management of Health and Safety at Work Regulations 1999, regulation 14*.

27.23 Interference with safety measures

No person may intentionally or recklessly interfere with or misuse anything provided in the interests of health, safety or welfare in pursuance of any of the relevant statutory provisions (*HSWA 1974, s 8*). Thus, an employee who removes a safety guard provided by his employer, in breach of the regulations, is in breach of *s 8* and is guilty of an offence for which in a magistrates' court he may be fined up to level 5 on the standard scale and in the Crown Court there may be an unlimited fine (*HSWA 1974, s 33(1)(b), (3)(b)*; see **1.10** INTRODUCTION).

Such conduct may also justify dismissal, provided the employee was properly instructed about the safety measures and had been made aware that interference could lead to dismissal (*Martin v Yorkshire Imperial Metals Ltd* [1978] IRLR 440).

27.24 No charge for safety measures

An employer may not charge any employee of his for anything done or supplied in compliance with any specific requirement of the relevant statutory provisions (*HSWA 1974, s 9*). If, for example, an employer is required to provide an employee of his with a mask, he may not require that employee to contribute towards the cost of that mask. This applies to all personal protective equipment, including safety footwear.

27.25 EU LEGISLATION

The influence of European-derived legislation in the health and safety field is substantial. The original *Treaty of Rome*, as amended by the subsequent Treaties of Maastricht, Amsterdam and Nice (see **23.1** EUROPEAN UNION LAW), provides in *art 137* (formerly *art 118A*) for the adoption of Directives in connection with improvements to the working environment to protect workers' health and safety. Such Directives are subject to the co-decision procedure whereby the European Parliament jointly adopts proposals with the Council of Ministers. Health and safety directives are normally implemented in UK law by means of regulations made under *HSWA 1974*.

A surge in EU health and safety legislation occurred following the adoption of the so-called *Framework Directive (89/391)*, implemented on 1 January 1993. The *Directive* imposes a number of general obligations upon both employers and employees. Whereas much English legislation uses the standard of what is 'reasonably practicable', the EC approach is to set absolute standards and to permit a defence of *force majeure* for non-compliance (see *art 5(4)* of the *Directive*).

Five further Directives, laying down detailed requirements, were initially adopted pursuant to the *Framework Directive*. They relate to minimum requirements for safety and health in the workplace (*89/654*), the use of machines and equipment (*89/655*), the use of personal protective equipment (*89/656*), the use of visual display units (*90/270*) and the handling of heavy loads (*90/269*).

In addition, Directives have been adopted on, *inter alia*: carcinogens (*90/394, 97/42, 99/38*), biological agents (*90/679*), construction sites (*92/57*), health and safety signs (*92/58*), and protection of pregnant workers (*92/85*).

Regulations have been made by statutory instrument to implement the EC Directives referred to above. For further details of Regulations within the scope of this book, see HEALTH AND SAFETY AT WORK – II (28) under the specific subject heading.

27.26 THE HEALTH AND SAFETY COMMISSION AND EXECUTIVE

HSWA 1974, s 10 establishes the Health and Safety Commission and the Health and Safety Executive. The Commission is made up of both employer and employee representatives and the Executive is made up of three of the Commission's appointees approved by the Secretary of State for the Environment, one of whom is first chosen as the director of the

Executive and who is consulted as to the appointment of the other two members. The Commission's chief function is to advise, authorise research and make suggestions for the implementation of the provisions of the *HSWA 1974*. It may make suggestions for the passing of regulations. The Executive also has the duty of providing information and advice to any government minister who requests it.

The Commission may either direct the Executive or authorise any other person to investigate and make a special report on any accident, occurrence, situation or other matter that the Commission thinks is necessary or expedient to investigate, or (with the consent of the Secretary of State) direct an inquiry to be held into any such matter (*HWSA 1974, s 14(1)(2)*). The *Health and Safety Inquiries (Procedure) Regulations 1975*, as amended.

(SIs 1975/335; 1976/1246) lay down the procedure for the conduct of such inquiries. Since civil or criminal liability for an accident may depend on the outcome of such an inquiry, proper representation is essential.

The HSC and the HSE were merged on 1 April 2008 to form a single regulatory body called the Health and Safety Executive (HSE), formerly tasked with the general responsibilty of promoting improved health and safety in the workplace. The decision to merge followed consultation with interested parties and was arrived at pursuant to the process set out in the *Legislative and Regulatory Reform Act 2006*.

27.27 Information

HSWA 1974, s 27 enables the Commission to obtain information necessary for the discharge of its functions, or for provision to an enforcing authority (eg the Executive or an inspector) of information necessary to discharge its duties. Since April 2008, this has passed to the Executive (HSE).

27.28 Codes of Practice

The Commission is empowered by *HSWA 1974, s 16* to approve and issue Codes of Practice for the enforcement of *ss 2–7* or of health and safety regulations introduced under the *Act*, or any other existing statutory provisions. Approved Codes give guidance on methods of complying with regulations and on what is considered reasonably practicable.

27.29 ENFORCING AUTHORITIES AND INSPECTORS

The Health and Safety Executive and local authorities are responsible for the enforcement of the *Health and Safety at Work Act 1974*. From 1 April 1998 the *Health and Safety (Enforcing Authority) Regulations 1998 (SI 1998/494)* re-enact, with amendments, the *1989 Regulations* of the same name (*SI 1989/1903*) which are revoked. *Schedule 1* sets out the main activities which determine whether local authorities will be enforcing authorities.

The enforcement powers under *HSWA 1974* cover all the 'relevant statutory provisions', which comprise the provisions of *HSWA 1974, Part I*, all the enactments specified in *HSWA 1974, Sch 1* and regulations made under them, and any health and safety and agricultural health and safety regulations (*HSWA 1974, s 53(1)*).

In January 2002 the Health and Safety Commission published its revised enforcement policy statement which, for the first time, sets out specific criteria to enable enforcement officers to decide when to investigate health and safety incidents, and to prosecute breaches of the law. The statement may be viewed on the HSE's website at www.hse.gov.uk/pubns/. This policy provides clarity on offences and the penalties available, as well as the HSE's role in investigations and inquiries. Since 2001 the HSC has published a list of health and safety offenders convicted and a prosecutions database.

27.30 Powers of inspectors

Every enforcing authority has the power to appoint inspectors. An inspector has many powers to enforce the statutory provisions for which his enforcing authority has responsibility. He may enter premises, if necessary accompanied by a police constable, take measurements and photographs and make other records, and take samples of articles or substances found in any premises which he has power to enter and of the atmosphere in or near such premises. If he fears that an article or substance found on premises which he has power to enter has caused or is likely to cause danger to health or safety, he may have it dismantled or subjected to any process or test. He may not destroy it unless that action is necessary for the performance of his duties. The inspector may take possession of a dangerous or potentially dangerous article or substance to examine it, to ensure that it is not tampered with or to ensure that it is available for use as evidence in any proceedings under the *HSWA 1974*. When he takes possession of any article, the inspector must fix, in a conspicuous position, a notice giving particulars of the article or substance and stating that he has taken possession of it (*HSWA 1974, s 20(2)(a)–(i), (4)*).

An inspector may require persons to answer questions in the course of his investigations and to sign a declaration of the truth of their answers. He may require the production of books and documents and take copies of them. If he requires any facilities or assistance in the course of his investigations, he may require the person able to do so to provide him with such facilities (*HSWA 1974, s 20(2)(j)–(l)*). No answer given by a person to an inspector is admissible in evidence against that person or the husband or wife of that person (*HSWA 1974, s 20(7)*). The section does not compel a person to disclose a document which could be withheld on grounds of legal professional privilege in High Court proceedings (such as an opinion of counsel) (*HSWA 1974, s 20(8)*).

Where an inspector has reasonable cause to believe that an article or substance on premises he is empowered to enter is a cause of imminent danger of serious personal injury, he may seize it and cause it to be rendered harmless (*HSWA 1974, s 25(1)*).

27.31 IMPROVEMENT AND PROHIBITION NOTICES

Improvement notices

If an inspector is of the opinion that a person:

(a)   is contravening one or more of the relevant statutory provisions (see **27.29** above); or

(b)   has contravened one or more of those provisions in circumstances that make it likely that the contravention will continue or be repeated,

he may serve on that person a notice (referred to as 'an improvement notice') (*HSWA 1974, s 21*).

An improvement notice must: (i) state that he is of that opinion; (ii) specify the provisions which in his opinion are being or have been contravened; (iii) give particulars of the reasons for his opinion; and (iv) require that person to remedy the contravention within a specified period.

The specified period in (iv) above is not to be shorter than that allowed for an appeal to an employment tribunal (which is 21 days from the date of the service on the appellant of the notice appealed against; see *Employment Tribunals (Constitution and Rules of Procedure) Regulations 2001, Sch 5 (SI 2001/1171)*).

27.32 Prohibition notices

If an inspector regards any activities as involving or potentially involving *a risk of serious personal injury, or risk of imminent danger*, he may serve on the person in control of those activities a notice known as 'a prohibition notice' (*HSWA 1974, s 22*).

A prohibition notice must:

(a)   state the opinion of the inspector;

(b)   specify the matters which in his opinion give or, as the case may be, will give rise to the risks;

(c)   where in his opinion any of those matters involves or will involve a contravention of any of the relevant statutory provisions, state that he is of that opinion, specify the relevant provision or provisions, and give particulars of the reasons why he is of that opinion; and

(d)   direct that the activities to which the notice relates shall not be carried on by or under the control of the person on whom the notice is served unless the matters specified in the notice and any associated contraventions so specified have been remedied.

A direction given in pursuance of (*d*) above takes effect immediately if the inspector is of the opinion, and states it, that the risk of serious personal injury is or will be imminent. For example, in *BT Fleet Ltd v McKenna* [2005] EWHC 387 (Admin), (2005) Times, 5 April, QBD, Evans-Lombe J. held that an improvement notice served by a health and safety Inspector, pursuant to *HSWA 1974, s 21*, should be clear and easily understood for it to be operative.

Improvement and prohibition notices may make reference to any approved Code of Practice (see **27.28** above) (*HSWA 1974, s 23(2)(a)*).

27.33 Withdrawal of notices

Where an improvement notice or a prohibition notice which is not to take immediate effect has been served, the notice may be withdrawn by an inspector at any time before it takes effect and the period before it takes effect may be extended or further extended by an inspector at any time when an appeal against the notice is not pending (*HSWA 1974, s 23(5)*).

27.34 APPEALS AGAINST THE NOTICES

A person on whom an improvement or prohibition notice is served may, within 21 days, appeal to an employment tribunal (*Employment Tribunals (Constitution and Rules of Procedure) Regulations 2001 (SI 2001/1171), Sch 5, rule 2(1)*). A tribunal may extend the period for lodging an appeal (on an application made in writing to the Secretary of the Tribunals either before or after the expiration of the time limit) if it is satisfied that it is not or was not reasonably practicable for an appeal to be brought within that time (*rule 2(2)*).

One or more assessors may be appointed for the purposes of any such appeals brought before an employment tribunal (*HSWA 1974, s 24(4)*).

The tribunal may either cancel or affirm the notice and, if the tribunal affirms it, may do so either in its original form or with such modifications as the tribunal may in the circumstances think fit (*HSWA 1974, s 24(2)*).

27.35   Suspension of notices pending appeal hearing

Where an appeal is brought within the time limit allowed:

(a)   *Improvement notice*: the bringing of the appeal has the effect of suspending the operation of the notice until the appeal is finally disposed of or, if the appeal is withdrawn, until the withdrawal of the appeal (*HSWA 1974, s 24(3)(a)*); and

(b)   *Prohibition notice*: the bringing of the appeal will not affect the notice unless, on application by the appellant, the tribunal so directs, in which case the prohibition notice will be suspended from the time that the tribunal gives its direction (*HSWA 1974, s 24(3)(b)*).

27.36   Cost of remedy required

In deciding whether an improvement notice which required the cleaning and repainting of walls should be cancelled or not, an employment tribunal sitting at Shrewsbury held that the company's financial position was irrelevant and evidence relating to its financial position would not be admitted (*T C Harrison (Newcastle-under-Lyme) Ltd v Ramsey (K) (HM Inspector)* [1976] IRLR 135). It may therefore be no ground for appeal against such notices that the company cannot afford to remedy the defects.

27.37   CRIMINAL PROCEEDINGS

The HSE publishes an annual report naming companies and individuals convicted in the previous 12 months of flouting health and safety law. The names of those convicted are also listed on the HSE's website.

HSWA 1974, s 33 lists various offences including:

(a)   failure to discharge a duty under *ss 2–7* (see **27.18–27.22** above) (*HSWA 1974, s 33(1)(a)*);

(b)   contravention of any health and safety regulations or any requirement or prohibition imposed under such a regulation (*HSWA 1974, s 33(1)(c)*);

(c)   contravention of any requirement or prohibition imposed by an improvement notice or a prohibition notice (including any such notice as modified on appeal) (*HSWA 1974, s 33(1)(g)*);

(d)   intention to obstruct an inspector in the exercise or performance of his powers or duties (*HSWA 1974, s 33(1)(h)*).

Criminal offences are triable either summarily (ie in the magistrates' court) or on indictment (ie in the Crown Court) or 'either way' (ie where the defendant may normally elect the mode of trial). In respect of offences committed on or after 6 March 1992, *HSWA 1974, s 33(1A) and (2A)* (inserted by *Offshore Safety Act 1992, s 4*) empowers a magistrates' court to impose a fine of up to £20,000 for breaches of *HSWA 1974, ss 2–6* (see (*a*) above), failure to comply with an improvement or prohibition notice (see (*c*) above), and failure to comply with a court remedy order under *HSWA 1974, s 42* (see **27.39** below).

On indictment the penalty may be a fine unlimited in amount and/or, for certain offences, imprisonment for up to two years (*HSWA 1974, s 33(2)–(4); see* **1.10** INTRODUCTION).

In two cases, the courts have emphasised that where a company is convicted of offences under the *HSWA 1974* the financial penalties imposed should reflect the seriousness of the case. In *R v F Howe & Son (Engineers) Ltd* [1999] IRLR 434, the Court of Appeal indicated that the general level of fine for health and safety offences was too low and outlined some of the factors which should be taken into account by the courts when setting the level of fines. These observations were subsequently given unqualified support by the Court of Appeal in *R v Rollco Screw and Rivet Co Ltd* [1999] IRLR 439.

In *R v Davies (David Janway)* [2003] ICR 586, an employer was convicted and fined for being in breach of *ss 3(1)* and *33(1)* of the *HSWA 1974*, having failed to discharge the duty to conduct his undertaking in such a way as to ensure that he did not expose his employees to risks to their health and safety. The Court of Appeal, dismissing the employer's appeal, ruled that the *HSWA 1974* was regulatory and designed to protect and that the defence of 'reasonably practicable' was not incompatible with the *Human Rights Act 1998*. Consequently, £15,000 fine and £22,544.32 costs were upheld.

Current maximum penalties for offences specified in the Health and Safety at Work etc Act 1974, section 33 (HSWA)

HSWA SECTION	HSW(O)B, Schedule 6A, Item	CURRENT MAXIMUM
33(1)(a) Sections 2, 3, 4 and 6 – the general duties on employers and others	1	**Summary** - a fine not exceeding £20,000 **Indictment** - an unlimited fine
33(1)(a) Section 7 – duty on employees	2	**Summary** - a fine not exceeding £5,000 **Indictment** - an unlimited fine
33(1)(b) Section 8 – duty not to interfere with or misuse things provided for health and safety	3	**Summary** - a fine not exceeding £5,000 **Indictment** - an unlimited fine
33(1)(b) Section 9 – duty not to charge employees for things done to meet requirements of relevant statutory provisions	4	**Summary** - a fine not exceeding £5,000 **Indictment** - an unlimited fine

HSWA SECTION	HSW(O)B, Schedule 6A, Item	CURRENT MAXIMUM
33(1)(c) Contravening requirements of health and safety regulations, licences or authorisations	5	**Summary** – a fine not exceeding £5,000 **Indictment** – an unlimited fine
33(1)(d) Contravening requirements imposed specifically in relation to public inquiries or special investigations	6	**Summary only** – a fine not exceeding £5,000
33(1)(e) Contravening any requirement imposed by an inspector under section 20 (eg to give information for an investigation, or to leave premises undisturbed after an incident) or under section 25	7	**Summary** – a fine not exceeding £5,000 **Indictment (section 25 breaches only)** – an unlimited fine
33(1)(f) Preventing another person from appearing before an inspector, or from answering an inspector's question	7 (continued)	**Summary only** – a fine not exceeding £5,000
33(1)(g) Contravening an improvement or prohibition notice	7 (continued)	**Summary** – 6 months' imprisonment, or a fine not exceeding £20,000, or both **Indictment** – 2 years' imprisonment or an unlimited

(the director of a cleaning company). A director who fails to take out compulsory employers liability insurance is, however, not liable to a victim who is injured but unable to recover damages from the company which might have negligible assets or cannot otherwise satisfy a judgment.

Defining who is responsible. In *Tesco Supermarkets Ltd v Nattrass* [1972] AC 153, in a prosecution of a company for a breach of the *Trade Descriptions Act 1968*, Lord Reid observed that:

' . . . a board of directors can delegate part of their functions of management so as to make their delegate an embodiment of the company within the sphere of delegation.'

In that case, the company was held not to have delegated any of its functions, so that the acts or omissions of the store manager were not acts of the company itself; the House of Lords therefore quashed the company's conviction. However, the Court of Appeal decision in *R v British Steel plc* [1995] IRLR 310 has cast doubt on whether the approach of the House of Lords in a consumer protection case is sufficiently stringent for health and safety legislation.

In *R v Boal* [1992] IRLR 420, the Court of Appeal defined 'manager' in relation to personal liability under the *Fire Precautions Act 1971*. The court held that the relevant provision was intended:

' . . . to fix with criminal liability only those who are in a position of real authority, the decision-makers within the company who have both the power and responsibility to decide corporate policy and strategy. It is to catch those responsible for putting proper procedures in place; it is not meant to strike at underlings.'

Where directors have been convicted of offences under the *HSWA 1974*, the Court of Appeal has said that the penalties imposed should make it clear that directors had a personal responsibility which could not be shuffled off to the company (*R v Rollco Screw and Rivet Co Ltd* [1999] IRLR 439). See also, *R v Transco* [2006] All ER (D) 416 (Mar), CA, where in assessing the level of fine, the Court takes account of the employer's knowledge regarding their responsibility for any breach of health and safety.

Company Directors Disqualification Act 1986. A director found guilty of an indictable offence under *HSWA 1974* (whether on indictment or summarily) may be disqualified from holding office as a director under the *Company Directors Disqualification Act 1986, s 2(1)*. The first such disqualification occurred in 1992 when a director was disqualified for two years after being found guilty of serious breaches of *HSWA 1974*. The director had been fined £5,000 for refusing to comply with a prohibition notice in relation to dangerous rock falls where men were working. In September 1998, the managing director of a recycling company was disqualified under the *Company Directors Disqualification Act 1986* following a breach of the *Provision and Use of Work Equipment Regulations 1992* (see **28.12 HEALTH AND SAFETY AT WORK – II**) which had resulted in a serious injury to an employee operating an unguarded machine.

In July 2001 the HSC published guidance on health and safety responsibilities for company directors and board members (IND(G) 343, HSE) of public sector and voluntary organisations. In particular, the guidance specifies that Boards need to:

(a)   accept joint responsibility and leadership for their organisations' health and safety performance;

(b)   appoint one Board member as a health and safety director;

(c)   ensure that each Board member accepts his or her individual role in providing health and safety leadership;

(d)   ensure that all Board decisions reflect their health and safety intentions;

(e)   encourage the active participation of workers in improving health and safety; and

(f)   keep up-to-date with all health and safety issues affecting the organisation and review performance regularly.

27.39 Order to remedy default

If a person is convicted of an offence and it appears to the court that the matter is one which it is in his power to remedy, the court may, in addition to or instead of imposing any punishment, order him (within such time as may be fixed by the order) to take such steps as may be specified in the order to remedy the situation. The time fixed by such an order may be extended or further extended by order of the court on an application made before the end of the time originally fixed or as extended (*HSWA 1974, s 42(1), (2)*). Failure to comply with an order under *HSWA 1974, s 42* is an offence (*HSWA 1974, s 33(1)(o)*), which is punishable: (i) on summary conviction, by up to six months' imprisonment and/or a fine of up to £20,000; and (ii) on indictment, by up to two years' imprisonment and/or an unlimited fine (*HSWA 1974, s 33(2A)*, inserted by *Offshore Safety Act 1992, s 4*).

27.40 Time for bringing proceedings

Summary proceedings may be brought at any time within six months from the date on which there comes to the knowledge of an enforcing authority evidence to justify a prosecution (*HSWA 1974, s 34(3)*). A failure to do something required by the Act is treated as continuing until the requirement is complied with, so that the six-month period runs from the last day on which the requirement was not complied with (*HSWA 1974, s 34(2)*). The time limit is extended in cases where there is a special report under *s 14(2)(a)*, a report of an inquiry under *s 14(2)(b)*, a coroner's inquest, or a public inquiry (in Scotland) into a death, to three months from the making of the report or three months from the conclusion of the inquest or inquiry (*HSWA 1974, s 34(1)*).

27.41 Defence

Many of the statutory provisions contain the modification 'so far as is reasonably practicable', or 'practicable' or to use 'the best practicable means to do something'. In those cases the onus is on the accused to prove that it was not practicable or not reasonably practicable to do more than was in fact done to satisfy the duty or requirement, or that there was no better practicable means than was in fact used to satisfy the duty or requirement (*HSWA 1974, s 40*). However, where proceedings are brought under *HSWA 1974, s 33(1)(g)* for contravention of an improvement notice, the offence is established if there has been a non-compliance with a requirement of the notice irrespective of whether compliance was reasonably practicable (*Deary (HM Inspector of Factories) v Mansion Hide Upholstery Ltd* [1983] IRLR 195).

In addition, since 11 July 2001 the defence that UK health and safety provision did not apply in the part of the business outside the jurisdiction (ie not situated in the UK) was abolished by the *Health and Safety at Work etc Act 1974 (Application outside Great Britain) Order (SI 2001/2127)*.

27.42 Corporate killing

The successful prosecution for manslaughter following the death of 23 cocklers on Morecambe Bay in February 2004, and consequential sentencing on 21 counts of manslaughter, re-emphasised the need to tighten up existing laws on corporate manslaughter. Under the Common Law a conviction for corporate manslaughter is obtainable only where a senior individual in a company (the 'controlling mind') is shown to have been grossly negligent and thereby responsible for the fatal accident. This is difficult to prove where managerial responsibilities are divided as is typical in a large organisation. Tragic incidents involving major train crashes and the sinking of a cross-channel ferry failed to yield convictions.

The *Corporate Manslaughter and Corporate Homicide Act 2007*, implemented in April 2008, seeks to make it easier to secure convictions against organisations. The Act creates no new duties and nor does it render individuals liable to prosecution. Liability for the new offence depends on a finding of gross negligence in the way in which the activities of the organisation are run. In summary, the offence is committed where, in particular circumstances, an organisation owes a duty to take reasonable care for a person's safety and the way in which activities of the organisation have been managed or organised amounts to a gross breach of that duty and causes the person's death. How the activities were managed or organised by senior management must be a substantial element of the gross breach. The likely impact of the Act should not be exaggerated. The Government estimated that there would be about one prosecution a month. In fact, barely any prosecutions have been launched.

Section 1(1) defines the new offence, which is called corporate manslaughter in England and Wales and Northern Ireland and corporate homicide in Scotland.

The elements of the new offence are:

(a)   The organisation must owe a 'relevant duty of care' to the victim. The relevant duties of care are set out in *section 2*.

(b)   The organisation must be in breach of that duty of care as a result of the way in which the activities of the organisation were managed or organised. This test is not linked to a particular level of management but considers how an activity was managed within the organisation as a whole. *Section 1(3)* stipulates that an organisation cannot be convicted of the offence unless a substantial element of the breach lies in the way the senior management of the organisation managed or organised its activities.

(c)   The way in which the organisation's activities were managed or organised must have caused the victim's death. This means that the management failure need not have been the sole cause of death; it need only be a cause.

(d)   The management failure must amount to a gross breach of the duty of care. *Section 1(4)(b)* sets out the test for whether a particular breach is 'gross'. The test asks whether the conduct that constitutes the breach falls far below what could reasonably have been expected. *Section 8* sets out a number of factors for the jury to take into account when considering this issue. There is no question of liability where the management of an activity includes reasonable safeguards and a death nonetheless occurs.

Since only an organisation can be guilty the penalty upon conviction is a fine without limit. The court can also order that remedial measures be taken and it may make a publicity order requiring the defendant to publicise the conviction. The *Act* is extensive in application; employers, suppliers, Government departments, transport providers and others face liability. Valuable guidance may be found on the HSE website and the Government guidance notes upon the Act are exemplary.

In the first conviction under the *Act* in February 2011 Cotswold Geotechnics (Holdings) Ltd, a small company with 8 employees, was fined £385,000 after an employee was killed when a trench caved in. The company was allowed to pay the fine at the rate of £38,500 per annum as else it would have been forced out of business. This is a clear indication that massive penalties will be applied upon conviction.

Since the first case (above), there have been a further six cases brought by the Crown Prosecution Service (May 2014):

November 2011:	PS and JE Ward — Case pending
May 2012:	JMW Farms — £187,000 fine
July 2012:	Lion Steel Equipment — £480,000 fine
December 2012:	MNS Mingin — Case pending
February 2013:	Prince's Sporting Club — Case pending
March 2013:	Mobile Sweeperds (Reading) — Case pending

27.43 CIVIL LIABILITY

Breaches of *HSWA 1974*, ss 2–8 cannot form the basis of a civil action (*HSWA 1974, s 47(1)(a)*) but breach 'of a duty imposed by health and safety regulations . . . shall, so far as it causes damage, be actionable except in so far as the regulations provide otherwise' (*HSWA 1974, s 47(2)*). In other words, a civil action can be brought where a breach of the health and safety regulations causes damage, unless the regulations prevent such an action from being brought.

Any provision in any agreement to contract out of liability for such breaches is void unless the health and safety regulations provide otherwise (*HSWA 1974, s 47(5)*).

27.44 CONTRIBUTORY NEGLIGENCE

In any successful action against the employer for breach of duty at common law or under some enactment, the amount of damages may be reduced in proportion to the degree to which the employee failed to take reasonable steps for his own safety (*Law Reform (Contributory Negligence) Act 1945, s 1(1)*). The *Act* applies where both the employer and employee have contributed to the damage. For example, in *Bux v Slough Metals Ltd* [1974] 1 All ER 262 the employee's failure to use the goggles with which he was provided contributed to the extent of the injury he suffered and reduced his damages by 40%. It is for the employer to allege and establish contributory negligence. In *Dziennik v CTO Gesellschaft Fur Containertransport MBH* [2006] EWCA Civ 1456, [2006] All ER (D) 157 (Nov) the Court of Appeal held that since the employer had not pleaded the issue it was wrong of a Trial Judge to deduct 60%, of the compensation awarded even though there was overwhelming evidence to justify that decision. The Court of Appeal indicated in *Pitts v Hunt* [1991] 1 QB 24, [1990] 3 All ER 344 that there was no such thing as 100% contributory fault. The purpose of contribution was to apportion blame, not to put it all at the door of the claimant and the tenor of the *1945 Act* anticipated that, after deduction, the claimant would be left with something. This very point was reiterated by the same court in *Brumder v Motornet Services and Repairs Ltd* [2013] EWCA Civ 195.

27.45 CORONER'S INQUESTS

In some health and safety incidences, interaction with the coroner is necessary. A coroner enquires into reported deaths. It is the coroner's duty to find out the medical cause of the death, if it is not known, and to enquire about the cause of it if it was due to violence or otherwise appears to be unnatural. In most cases the deceased's own doctor, or a hospital doctor who has been treating him or her, is able to give a cause of death. However, there are a number of circumstances under which a death will be reported to the coroner. For example, when no doctor has treated the deceased during his or her last illness or when the death was sudden or unexpected or unnatural. Yet deaths are usually reported to the coroner by the police or by a doctor called to the death if it is sudden. A doctor will also report a patient's death if unexpected. In other cases, the local registrar of deaths may make the report. Whenever the death has been reported to the coroner the registrar must wait for the coroner to finish his or her enquiries before the death can be registered.

27.46 CORONER'S FINDINGS

The coroner may decide that death was natural and that there is a doctor who can sign a form saying so. In this case the coroner will advise the registrar. The coroner may ask a pathologist to examine the body. If so, the examination must be done as soon as possible. The coroner or his or her staff will, unless it is impracticable or cause undue delay, give notice of the arrangements to, amongst others, the usual doctor of the deceased and any relative who may have notified the coroner of his or her wish to be medically represented at the examination. If the examination shows the death to have been a natural one, there may be no need for an inquest and the coroner will send a form to the registrar of deaths so that the death can be registered by the relatives and a certificate of burial issued by the registrar. If the person is to be cremated, the certificate may be issued by the coroner.

27.47 INQUESTS

An inquest is not a trial. It is a limited inquiry into the facts surrounding a death. It is not the job of the coroner to blame anyone for the death, as a trial would do. The inquest is an inquiry to find out who has died, and how, when and where they died, together with information needed by the registrar of deaths so that the death can be registered. Most inquests are held without a jury. There are particular reasons when a jury will be called, including if the death occurred in prison or in police custody or if the death resulted from an incident at work. In every inquest which is held with a jury, it is the jury, and not the coroner, which makes the final decision. The High Court has decided in *Roach v Home Office* [2009] EWHC 312 (QB), [2009] NLJR 474 that in principle the costs of attending an inquest or indeed a Health and Safety prosecution may be recoverable in subsequent civil proceedings where a claim for damages is pursued. In *Lynch v Chief Constable of Warwickshire Police* [2014] JR 130517 it was declared that the inquest costs must be proportionate to the overall value of the subsequent civil claim. Consequently, significant inquest costs were disallowed as they were out of all proportion to the value and importance of the civil litigation.

27.48 'INTERESTED PERSONS'

An 'interested person' is someone who can question a witness at an inquest. They can be:

(a)   a parent, spouse, child and anyone acting for the deceased;

(b)   anyone who gains from a life insurance policy on the deceased;

(c)   any insurer having issued such a policy;

(d)   anyone whose actions the coroner believes may have contributed to the death, accidentally or otherwise;

(e)   the chief officer of police (who may only ask questions of witnesses through a lawyer);

(f)   any person appointed by a government department to attend the inquest;

(g)   anyone else who the coroner may decide also has a proper interest.

28   Health and Safety at Work – II: Specific Legislation and Health and Safety Issues

Cross-reference. See HEALTH AND SAFETY AT WORK – I (27) for safety duties at common law and the general legislative framework.

28.1   ACCIDENT REPORTING

Notification of accidents, diseases and dangerous occurrences. The current regulations governing the notification and recording of accidents are the *Reporting of Injuries, Diseases and Dangerous Occurrences Regulations 2013 (SI 2013/1471)*. The reporting rules have been amended with effect from 6th April 2012. Whereas before it was obligatory to report an occurrence, as defined below, where the individual was incapacitated for 3 days or more that period has been extended to only apply to incapacity for 7 days or more (excluding the day of the incident. The employer now has 15 days to report the incident from the date it occurred. Note that an incident involving incapacity must still be recorded albeit not reported by the employer. The HSE has issued explicit guidance that an entry in a workplace accident book will satisfy this obligation.

An employer must notify the Health and Safety Executive ('HSE') or local authority, whichever is in the circumstances the enforcing authority (see **27.29** HEALTH AND SAFETY AT WORK – I), of:

(a)   an accident arising out of or in connection with work resulting in:

   (i)   the death of any person;

   (ii)   a specific injury to any person at work:

   •   a fracture, other than to fingers, thumbs and toes

   •   amputation of an arm, hand, finger, thumb, leg, foot. or toe

   •   permanent loss of sight or reduction of sight

   •   crash injuries leading to internal organ damage

   •   serious burns (covering more than 10% of the body) or damaging eys, respiratory system or other vital organs

   •   scalpings (separation of skin from head) which require hospital treatment

   •   unconsciousness caused by head injury or asphyxia

   •   any other injury arising from working in an enclosed space which leads to hypothermia, heat-induced illness or requires resuscitation or admittance to hospital for more than twenty-four hours.

   (iii)   hospital treatment of a person not at work; or

   (iv)   major injury to a person not at work as a result of an accident in connection with work at a hospital;

(b)   a dangerous occurrence

   The list of reportable dangerous occurrences that have to be reported in all industrial and commercial sectors has been reduced and simplified. The full list is available at www.legislation.gov.uk/uksi/2013/1471/made. DOs removed include those involving the carriage of dangerous substances by road, failure of fairground equipment, and failure of load-bearing parts of freight containers. The revised list contains twenty-seven specified dangerous occurrences;

(c)   an accident connected with work as a result of which a person at work is incapacitated for work for more than seven days;

(d)   the death of an employee within one year of being injured as the result of a notifiable accident or notifiable dangerous occurrence (this applies whether or not the accident was reported at the time it occurred);

(e)   any person suffering from a reportable work-related illness as specified.

The former schedule of forty-seven industrial diseases has been replaced by eight categories of work-related illness: These include:

•   occupational dermatitis

•   occupational asthma

•   occupational cancer

•   diseases due to work exposure to biological events

•   carpel tunnel syndrome

•   severe cramp of the hand or forearm

•   hand/arm vibration syndrome

•   tendonitis or tenosynovitis of the hand or forearm.

These are reportable wherever at work they occur.

(f)   any 'gas incident' as specified.

(*Regulations 3–6.*)

In cases under (*a*) and (*b*) the enforcing authority must be notified by the fastest practicable means in the first instance, and a report on the prescribed form must be sent to that authority within 15 days (*reg 3*).

In cases under (*c*) a report must be sent on an approved form within 15 days of the accident. Category (*d*) requires notification in writing as soon as the employer becomes aware of the death. Under (*e*) a report on an approved form must be made forthwith and for cases falling within (*f*) notification is required immediately, followed by a report within 14 days. Accident reports must be made on Form F2508 and disease reports on Form F2508A. For notification to the HSE, an online notification regime is now in place. The HSE website contains links to the various report forms.

Road accidents are not covered by the *Regulations*, except where they result from exposure to a substance which is being transported, the loading or unloading of vehicles, specified roadworks or where a train is involved (*reg 10*). See *Road Safety Act 2005*.

The definition of 'accident' includes acts of non-consensual physical violence done to a person at work.

They must be kept at the place of work to which they relate, or at the usual place of business of the responsible person as defined in the *Regulations*, for a period of three years from the date the details were entered in the records.

Accidents to self-employed persons are covered if they were working under the control of someone else, in which case the obligations attach to the person in control of the premises where the accident occurred.

Major accident hazards. Operators of premises liable to major accident hazards are, in addition, subject to a special regime under the *Control of Major Accident Hazards Regulations 1999 (SI 1999/743)* from 1 April 1999 (see **27.20** HEALTH AND SAFETY AT WORK – I).

Notification of industrial injuries. An employee who suffers an 'industrial injury' must report the accident to his employer. Notice of the accident may be given orally or in writing, and may be given by someone else on the employee's behalf. It is sufficient notice if the accident is recorded in the accident book (see below). The employer is required to take reasonable steps to investigate the accident and must, on request, provide all information uncovered to the Department for Work and Pensions. Failure by an employee to notify an accident may jeopardise his entitlement to industrial injury benefits.

Accident book. Every employer who normally employs 10 or more persons on or about the same premises in connection with a trade or business must keep an accident book (Form BI 510) in which specified particulars of accidents may be recorded, as must (however few employees they have) all employers who are owners or occupiers of a mine or quarry or of a 'factory' within the meaning of the *Factories Act 1961, s 175* (*Social Security (Claims and Payments) Regulations 1979 (SI 1979/628), reg 25*). Part 3 of the *Data Protection Code of Practice (Employment)*, issued on 11 June 2003, sets out basic rules for employers to follow in relation to monitoring employee activities. Such activities may include accidents. Hence, accident books kept by employers will fall within these provisions.

28.2   ALCOHOL AND DRUG MISUSE

Problems arising from consumption of alcohol and misuse of drugs are seen as an increasing problem in the workplace. Employers have a duty of care, both at common law and under *HSWA 1974, s 2*, to ensure, so far as reasonably practicable, the health, safety and welfare at work of their employees. In addition, they are required to assess risks to health and safety under the *Management of Health and Safety at Work Regulations 1999* (see **28.17**). An employer who allows a person under the influence of drink or drugs to continue working could be in breach of its duty of care by putting the employee or others at risk.

Under the *Transport and Works Act 1992* it is a criminal offence for certain transport workers in safety-sensitive posts, primarily in the railway industry, to be unfit through drink or drugs while working. Transport system operators are required to show all due diligence in order to prevent an offence being committed.

It is an offence for occupiers of premises (such as employers) knowingly to allow the production or supply of controlled drugs on their premises or to permit the smoking of cannabis (*Misuse of Drugs Act 1971, s 8*).

Dependency on alcohol or drugs is an illness. Where an employee's performance or misconduct is found to be a result of alcohol dependency this should normally be handled as a capability issue (see **54.6** UNFAIR DISMISSAL – II). ACAS advises that drug dependency should be treated in the same way. However, the fact that use of non-prescription drugs is illegal may justify disciplinary action depending on the circumstances. One-off incidents of excessive consumption of alcohol by employees who are not alcohol-dependent would normally be dealt with according to disciplinary procedures. Off-duty use of alcohol or drugs is not normally the legitimate concern of the employer unless it has a connection with the workplace, damages the reputation of the employer's business or undermines trust and confidence in the employee.

As part of an overall health and safety policy, employers are advised to have a written policy on alcohol and drug misuse. Once a policy is in place, it should be applied consistently (*Angus Council v Edgley* EAT/289/99).

28.3   Drug testing

Drug testing is a controversial and sensitive issue. The HSE warns that testing is only likely to be acceptable if it is part of an organisation's health policy and is clearly designed to prevent risks to the misuser and others. Testing programmes should be introduced only with the consent of existing employees. Otherwise this may be seen as a breach of the implied term of trust and confidence, leading to constructive dismissal (see **53.7** UNFAIR DISMISSAL – I). Pre-employment testing where applicants are asked to take a test voluntarily raises fewer legal problems. In all cases individuals need to be assured of the integrity of the screening process and medical confidentiality. Company policies should indicate the action which will be taken if testing yields a positive result.

Drug testing (except in highly safety-critical areas) is unlikely to be justified unless there is a reasonable suspicion of drug use that has an impact on safety. Employers should also bear in mind the effect on protection of privacy of the *1950 European Convention on Human Rights* and the *Human Rights Act 1998* (see **30.6** HUMAN RIGHTS).

In *Swansea v Gayle* [2013] IRLR 768, an unfair dismissal claim, the EAT held it proper for an employer to have had an employee put under video surveillance. The claimant had been observed visiting a gym during working hours. The man was followed on 5 occasions and was surreptitiously filmed. At first instance this was found to be oppressive and dismissal was declared unfair. In a robust reversal, the EAT declared that the claimant had been watched whilst in public areas and the degree of surveillance demonstrated how thoroughly the local authority employer had investigated before electing to dismiss.

28.4   CONSTRUCTION SITE MANAGEMENT

Some 2.9 million workers make up the UK's construction industry. The *Construction (Design and Management) Regulations 1994 (SI 1994/3140)* gave effect to the EC Directive on temporary or mobile construction sites *(92/57)*. The *Regulations* impose detailed requirements with respect to design and management aspects of construction work, placing new obligations on all parties involved in construction projects. The *1994 Regulations* were amended by the *Construction (Design and Management) (Amendment) Regulations 2002 (SI 2002/2380)*. A revised Approved Code of Practice ('ACOP') and guidance on the *Construction (Design and Management) Regulations 1994 (SI 1994/3140)* have been published by the Health and Safety Commission and came into force on 1 February 2002. The revised ACOP is designed to clarify roles and responsibilities, placing emphasis on managing health and safety throughout the life of a project.

Further effect has been given to *Directive 92/57* by the *Construction (Health, Safety and Welfare) Regulations 1996 (SI 1996/1592)* as amended by *SI 1999/3242)* which also incorporate three sets of existing Regulations which have been modernised and simplified.

In 2007, the revised *Construction (Design and Management) Regulations* incorporated the *Construction (Health, Safety and Welfare) Regulations 1996* into one set of regulations: *CDM 2007 (SI 2007/320)*.

The HSE has recently announced a further review of the *CDM Regulations* and guidance which is due for completion during 2014.

Note that no statutory provision or rule of law is to be taken as imposing, upon a Sikh on a construction site, any requirement to wear a safety helmet at any time when he is wearing a turban (*EA 1989, s 11*). However, a Sikh who does not comply with a requirement that would otherwise have been imposed, and is injured, may recover damages in tort only to the extent that he would have suffered injury even if wearing a helmet (*EA 1989, s 11(5)*). A person who does require a Sikh to wear a safety helmet on a construction site will probably be guilty of indirect racial discrimination, and if he has no reasonable grounds to believe that the Sikh would not wear a turban at all times when on site, he will not be permitted to justify that requirement (*EA 1989, s 12(1)*). Nor will special treatment afforded to a Sikh in consequence of s *11* constitute racial discrimination against anyone else (*EA 1989, s 12(2)*). See *Construction (Head Protection) Regulations 1989 (SI 1989/2209)*.

28.5   DISPLAY SCREEN EQUIPMENT

The *Health and Safety (Display Screen Equipment) Regulations 1992 (SI 1992/2792)* give effect to the *EU Directive* relating to the use of display screen equipment (eg VDUs) (*90/270*). Broadly, the *Regulations* require every employer, after making a suitable and sufficient analysis of each workstation (ie display screen equipment, its accessories and the surrounding work environment) to ensure that it meets the detailed requirements set out in the *Schedule* to the *Regulations*. Users of display screen equipment must: (i) be provided with eye and eyesight tests on request, both initially and at regular intervals thereafter; (ii) be provided with adequate health and safety information relating to the equipment; and (iii) have their daily work routine planned in such a way that they have periodical interruptions from using the equipment. See also **28.29** on work-related upper limb disorders.

The ECJ has given a ruling on the application of *Directive 90/270* in *Dietrich v Westdeutscher Rundfunk*: C-11/99 [2000] ECR I-5589. *Article 2(a)* of the *Directive* and *reg 1(2)* of the *Health and Safety (Display Screen Equipment) Regulations 1992* provide that 'display screen equipment' means 'an alphanumeric or graphic display screen, regardless of the display process involved'. The court concluded that the term 'graphic display screen' had to be interpreted broadly and therefore included screens that display film recordings, whether in analogue or digital form. A film cutter in a television production studio was therefore entitled to the protection of the provisions of the Directive.

Regulation 3 of the *Health and Safety (Miscellaneous Amendments) Regulations 2002 (SI 2002/2174)*, by removing the limitation in relation to workstation users and operators, so as to widen the remit to all users, amends *reg 3* of the *DSE Regulations 1992*.

28.6   ELECTRICITY AT WORK

The *Electricity at Work Regulations 1989 (SI 1989/635)* place a duty on employers to assess all foreseeable risks associated with work activities involving electricity which might give rise to personal injury or danger. Electrical equipment covers everything from power lines to electric kettles.

Employers are required to install safe systems of working with well-maintained equipment (*reg 4*). Steps must be taken to avoid danger in the use of equipment where it is reasonably foreseeable that it will be exposed to adverse or hazardous environments (*reg 6*). Specific precautions are laid down with regard to the insulation and protection of conductors (*regs 7–9*).

Regulations 12 and *13* lay down requirements for cutting off the supply, isolation and for working on dead equipment. No person should be engaged in work near a live conductor except where it is reasonable in all the circumstances and suitable precautions are taken to prevent injury (*reg 14*). Special attention should be paid to adequate working space, means of access and lighting where work is to be done on electrical equipment (*reg 15*), and no person should work on electrical equipment unless he or she possesses appropriate technical knowledge or is adequately supervised (*reg 16*).

28.7   EMPLOYMENT PROTECTION

The *Employment Rights Act 1996* ('*ERA 1996*') provides that certain dismissals in health and safety cases are to be deemed automatically unfair (see **54.3** UNFAIR DISMISSAL – **II** below), and confers protection on employees in such cases from unfavourable treatment. Two recent

28.7 Health and Safety at Work – II

EAT decisions are illuminating. In *Oudahar v Esporta Group Ltd* [2011] IRLR 730 an employee refused to mop behind a fridge because maintenance work had taken place and electrical wires were protruding from the wall. It was no answer to his legitimate and reasonable belief in a danger being present for the employer to show objectively that the perceived danger did not exist. His refusal should have been taken seriously. In *Jaoa v Jurys Hotel Management Ltd* (2011) UKEAT/210/11 an employee was found to have a reasonable belief that it was dangerous to his health to require him to work on 9 successive night shifts even though this was strictly lawful and within the provisions of the *Working Time Regulations*.

28.8 Detriment in health and safety cases

ERA 1996, s 44 confers on an employee the right not to be subjected to any detriment by any act (short of dismissal), or any deliberate failure to act, by his employer done on the ground that:

(a) having been designated by the employer to carry out activities in connection with preventing or reducing risks to the health and safety of employees at work, he carried out, or proposed to carry out, any such activities;

(b) being a health and safety representative or member of a safety committee, in accordance with any statutory arrangements or by reason of being acknowledged as such by the employer, he performed or proposed to perform any functions as such a representative or member;

(c) he took part (or proposed to take part) in consultation with the employer in accordance with the *Health and Safety (Consultation with Employees) Regulations 1996 (SI 1996/1513)* or in an election for representatives of employee safety;

(d) where there is no representative or it is not possible to raise the matter by this means, he brought to his employer's attention, by reasonable means, circumstances which he reasonably believed were harmful or potentially harmful to health and safety;

(e) in circumstances of serious or imminent danger which he could not reasonably be expected to avert, he left, or proposed to leave, his place of work or any dangerous part of his place of work; or

(f) in circumstances of serious or imminent danger, he took, or proposed to take, appropriate steps to protect himself or other persons from the danger. 'Other persons' includes members of the public (*Masiak v City Restaurants (UK) Ltd* [1999] IRLR 780).

'Circumstances of danger' is not confined to dangers arising out of the workplace itself. It can include dangers caused by the misbehaviour of fellow employees (*Harvest Press Ltd v McCaffrey* [1999] IRLR 778). For the purposes of (*f*) above, whether the steps which the employee took, or proposed to take, were appropriate will be judged by reference to all the circumstances including, in particular, his knowledge and the facilities and advice available to him at the time (*ERA 1996, s 44(2)*). An employee will not be regarded as having suffered any detriment on the ground specified in (*f*) above if the employer shows that it was, or would have been, so negligent for the employee to take the steps which he took, or proposed to take, that a reasonable employer might have treated him as the employer did (*ERA 1996, s 44(3)*).

Provided a safety representative acts in good faith when pursuing a genuine health or safety matter, there is no duty to act reasonably (*Shillito v Van Leer (UK) Ltd* [1997] IRLR 495). In *Goodwin v Cabletel UK Ltd* [1997] IRLR 665 the Employment Appeal Tribunal held that the manner in which designated employees carry out health and safety activities can fall within the statutory protection. Tribunals must consider whether the way in which such employees approach their concerns about safety takes them outside the scope of health and safety activities.

28.9   Whistleblowing on safety

ERA 1996 provides further protection against victimisation by employers in specified circumstances if workers who ordinarily work in Great Britain raise concerns about, *inter alia*, health and safety issues (*ERA 1996, s 47B*, inserted by *Public Interest Disclosure Act 1998*, ('*PIDA 1998*'), *s 2*). The legislation protects not only direct employees but also most other workers including, specifically, agency workers, homeworkers, NHS practitioners and trainees on vocational or work experience schemes (*ERA 1996, s 43K* inserted by *PIDA 1998, s 1*). Provided certain conditions are met, workers will be protected against detrimental treatment or dismissal where they disclose information, they reasonably believe that disclosure is in the public interest and, further, they reasonably believe that the information tends to show that there has been, is, or will be a criminal offence; failure to comply with a legal obligation; a miscarriage of justice; endangering of health and safety; or damage to the environment. A full account of this protection may be found at **10.16** and following DISCLOSURE OF INFORMATION.

The *Public Interest Disclosure Act 1998* ('*PIDA 1998*'), which came into force 2 July 1999, provides further protection against victimisation by employers in specified circumstances if workers who ordinarily work in Great Britain raise concerns about, *inter alia*, health and safety issues (*ERA 1996, s 47B*, inserted by *PIDA 1998, s 2*). The legislation protects not only direct employees but also most other workers including, specifically, agency workers, homeworkers, NHS practitioners and trainees on vocational or work experience schemes (*ERA 1996, s 43K* inserted by *PIDA 1998, s 1*). Provided certain conditions are met workers will be protected against detrimental treatment (or dismissal, see **54.3** UNFAIR DISMISSAL – II) if they reveal information about the workplace relating to: a criminal offence; failure to comply with a legal obligation; a miscarriage of justice; endangering health and safety; or damage to the environment. Information disclosed which tends to show that any of the above matters is being deliberately concealed would also qualify for protection (*ERA 1996, s 43B* inserted by *PIDA 1998, s 1*). Workers are required to raise their concerns initially with the employer or prescribed regulator. External disclosures are protected only if stringent conditions are met; an exception is made for 'exceptionally serious cases' (*ERA 1996, ss 43C–43H*, inserted by *PIDA 1998, s 1*). In *Goode v Marks And Spencer plc* (2010) UKEAT/442/09 the mere expression of disquiet by way of opinion about what an employer was proposing to do (change certain employment terms and conditions) was held not to be a protected disclosure at all.

28.10   The remedy

An employee has the right to complain to an employment tribunal for a declaration and compensation if he has suffered a detriment by an act, or failure to act, done on any of the grounds specified in (*a*) to (*f*) in **28.9** above. On such a complaint it is for the employer to show the ground on which any act, or deliberate failure to act, was done (*ERA 1996, s 48(1), (2)*). Workers who have suffered detrimental treatment for making a protected disclosure are able to make a complaint to an employment tribunal (*ERA 1996, s 48(1A)*, inserted by *PIDA 1998, s 3*).

The employee may make a complaint within three months of the act, or failure to act, complained of (or the last act or failure, where that act or failure is part of a series of similar acts or failures). Where the tribunal is satisfied that it was not reasonably practicable for the complaint to be presented within three months, it may be presented within such further period as the tribunal considers reasonable (*ERA 1996, s 48(3)*; as to the meaning of 'the date of the act' and 'a deliberate failure to act', see *ERA 1996, s 48(4)*).

If the tribunal finds the complaint well-founded it will make a declaration to that effect and order compensation to be paid to the employee. The compensation will be such amount as it considers just and equitable in the circumstances, having regard to the right infringed and any loss which is attributable to the act or failure which infringed his right (*ERA 1996, s 49*). In the case of workers penalised for making a protected disclosure the tribunal may award such compensation as it considers just and equitable.

28.11 Breach of safety regulations and unfair dismissal

A failure by an employer to have regard for the safety of his employees can be considered a fundamental breach of contract entitling the employee to resign and claim that he has been constructively dismissed. In *British Aircraft Corpn Ltd v Austin* [1978] IRLR 332, the Employment Appeal Tribunal held that the employer's failure to give consideration to the employee's request that she should be provided with protective goggles incorporating the prescription lenses of her spectacles amounted to conduct entitling the employee to resign and, when she did resign, to claim that she had been constructively dismissed under what is now *ERA 1996, s 95(1)(c)*.

Where employees refuse to work with materials which in the past have adversely affected their health, and as a consequence are dismissed, the dismissals will be held to be unfair if the employer has not taken adequate steps to remedy the danger (*Piggott Bros & Co Ltd v Jackson* [1991] IRLR 309).

An employer may fairly dismiss an employee for breach of safety regulations if he brought the regulations to the attention of the employee and made clear to him the fact that such a breach would lead to dismissal (*Martin v Yorkshire Imperial Metals* [1978] IRLR 440).

28.12 EQUIPMENT FOR WORK

The law has been utterly transformed by *section 69* of the *Enterprise and Regulatory Reform Act 2013*. It is imperative to, appreciate that the *Act* only applies to accidents occurring on or after 1st October 2013 and so the authorities cited below remain good law for claims arising before that date.

What the *Act* does is to reverse the presumption that a breach of statutory duty such as the Manual Handling Regulations would be actionable as a breach of statutory duty. Now, no such claim is viable unless the legislative measure expressly provides that a civil claim is permitted. None of the key measures do so. Consequently, a claimant who would have been able to rely upon he strict duties imposed by workplace legislation is now compelled to prove fault. The claim for breach of statutory duty becomes a claim in common law negligence thus firmly putting the onus upon the claimant to establish breach, causation and foreseeability. Put simply, it will be harder for claimants to win.

The *Employers Liability (Defective Equipment) Act 1969* will become relevant again since it does expressly recognise a civil claim. Under the *Act*, an employer is held liable for injury caused by defective equipment which the employer has supplied. It matters not that the defect was incapable of detection. The scope of "equipment" has been held to be enormous. It captures a 90,000 ton ocean going tanker; *Coltman v Bibby Tankers Ltd* [1988] AC 276. Also, it includes materials used in performing a task such as paving slabs in the Law Lords decision of *Knowles v Liverpool City Council* [1993] 1 WLR 1428 where a submission that equipment ought to be confined to the tools of the trade, say a shovel or pick, was unanimously rejected.

The Lord Chancellor announced in early 2017 that the personal injury small claims limit would double to £2,000 whilst it would be raised to £5,000 in road traffic claims. The legislation to bring about these changes was abandoned as a result of the General Election but it is conceivable that measures will be brought forward again. Sir Rupert Jackson will be putting forward proposals to fix costs in claims worth , perhaps , up to £100,000. The likely implementation date is October 2018.

Every employer must, *inter alia*:

(a)   establish (and where necessary, give effect to) procedures to be followed in the event of serious and imminent danger to persons working in his undertaking; and

(b)   nominate a sufficient number of competent persons to implement such procedures in relation to the evacuation of the premises.

The procedures referred to in (*a*) above must:

(i)   so far as is reasonably practicable, require persons at work who are exposed to serious and imminent danger to be informed of the nature of the hazards and the steps to be taken to protect them from it;

(ii)   enable the persons concerned to stop work and proceed to a place of safety in the event of being exposed to serious, imminent and unavoidable danger; and

(iii)   require the persons concerned to be prevented from resuming work where there is still a serious and imminent danger.

(*Regulation 8.*)

Employers are required to ensure that any necessary contacts with external services are arranged, particularly as regards first aid, emergency medical care and rescue work (*reg 9*).

Employees must be provided with comprehensible and relevant health and safety information (*reg 10*), as must non-employees working in the employer's undertaking (*reg 12*) and temporary workers (*reg 15*). When employing school-age children, employers must inform their parents or guardians of the risks and control measures introduced (*reg 10*). Where two or more employers share a workplace, they must co-operate as necessary to enable them to comply with the applicable health and safety and fire precautions requirements, and co-ordinate measures they are taking to comply with such requirements (*reg 11*).

Employers must take into account employees' capabilities as regards health and safety in entrusting tasks to them. Employees must be provided with adequate health and safety training within working hours, which must be repeated where appropriate (*reg 13*). Employees must use all machinery and equipment in accordance with the training they have received. They must inform the employer of: (i) any work situation which represents an immediate danger to health and safety; and (ii) any shortcoming in the employer's protection arrangements for health and safety (*reg 14*).

An assessment must be made of workplace risks to new and expectant mothers, and measures must be taken to avoid any risk by altering working conditions or hours of work. Where it is not practicable to take these steps the woman should be suspended from work (subject to *ERA 1996, s 67*). Where it is necessary for her health and safety, a new or expectant mother must be removed from night work (*regs 16, 17*). (See also the *Suspension from Work (on Maternity Grounds) Order 1994 (SI 1994/2930).*) In *Day v T Pickles Farms Ltd* [1999] IRLR 217, the EAT emphasised that employers must undertake an assessment of the workplace risks to pregnant women as soon as a woman of child-bearing age is employed. It is not sufficient to wait until an employee becomes pregnant.

Young persons must not be employed in certain dangerous or harmful work activities unless it is necessary for their training, the risks are reduced to the minimum, and they are competently supervised. Children must never be permitted to do such work (*reg 19*).

In criminal proceedings employers have no defence for a contravention of their health and safety obligations by reason of any act or default caused by an employee or by a person appointed to give competent advice (*reg 21*).

Since October 2003, the *Management of Health and Safety at Work Regulations 1999 (SI 1999/3242)* have been amended to allow employees to claim damages from their employer if they suffer illness or injury as a result of a breach of the *Regulations*. Amending *reg 22*, the lifting of the civil liability exclusion will ensure full compliance with the *Health and Safety Framework Directive 89/391*. Guidance can be found at www.hse.gov.uk/services/education/information.htm.

28.18   MANUAL HANDLING OF LOADS

The HSE estimates that some 12.3 million working days have been lost due to work-related musculoskeletal disorders. As a result, some 1.1 million people a year are affected, making manual handling the most common cause of occupational illness in the UK. According to HSE statistics, some 37% of reported accidents are related to manual handling incidents. The *Manual Handling Operations Regulations 1992 (SI 1992/2793)* as amended by *SI 2002/2174*, give effect to the *EU Directive* relating to the manual handling of loads *(90/269)*. Broadly, the *Regulations* require each employer, so far as reasonably practicable, to avoid the need for his employees to undertake manual handling operations involving a risk of injury. That is a real risk, a foreseeable possibility of injury, not a probability (see *O'Neill v DSG Retail Ltd* [2002] EWCA Civ 1139, [2003] ICR 222). It is important to be able to show that consideration has been given to ways of avoiding such operations. Where it is not reasonably practicable, the employer is required to assess such operations and reduce the risk of injury arising from them to the lowest practicable level. For a case interpreting 'reasonably practicable' in this context, see *Hawkes v Southwark London Borough Council* (20 February 1998, unreported), CA. Emphasising the importance of providing, where practicable, information to employees on the weight of loads they are required to handle was noted in *Swain v Denso Marston Ltd* [2000] ICR 1079, CA.

Regulation 4 of the *Health and Safety (Miscellaneous Amendments) Regulations 2002 (SI 2002/2174)* amends the *1992 Regulations* by adding *reg 4(3)* by specifying factors to be taken account of, in determining whether operations involve risk, particularly of back injury to workers. The new regulation adds that particular regard should be given to: (a) the physical suitability of the employee to carry out the task; (b) the clothing and footwear the person is wearing; (c) the person's knowledge and training; and (d) the results of any relevant risk assessments. This amendment gives full effect to *Annex II* of *Directive 90/269/EEC* (OJ L156 25.6.90).

The *Regulations* also contain, in *Sch 1*, a list of the factors to which an employer must have regard (tasks, loads, working environment, individual capability and other factors) and the relevant questions which must be considered in each case when making an assessment of manual handling operations. Guidance on the *Regulations* has been published by the HSE (L23, revised 2004).

Since 31 December 1998, the *Merchant Shipping and Fishing Vessels (Manual Handling Operations) Regulations 1998 (SI 1998/2857)* give effect to *Directive 90/269* in respect of shipping activities in the UK. The *Regulations* apply to UK-registered ships and, in part, to ships registered outside the UK when they are in UK waters.

The HSE has developed an online manual handling chart tool (MAC Tool) to help identify high risk workplace manual handling activities.

28.19   NOISE AT WORK

According to the HSE, over 170,000 people in the UK suffer deafness, tinnitus or other ear conditions as a result of exposure to excessive noise at work. The *Control of Noise at Work Regulations 2005* (the *Noise Regulations*), in force since 6 April 2006 (except for the music and entertainment sectors where they come into force on 6 April 2008), replace the long-standing *Noise at Work Regulations 1989 (SI 1989/1790)* which came into force on 1 January 1990. The aim of these new *Noise Regulations* is to ensure that workers' hearing is protected from excessive noise at their place of work, which could cause them to lose their hearing and/or to suffer from tinnitus (permanent ringing in the ears). There has been a significant increase recently in the number of industrial deafness claims being made. In part this is due to the fact that legal costs remain at large in the event of success whereas fixed costs are now applicable to fast track public and employers liability claims worth up to £25,000. It is probable that the Government will publish proposals intended to fix costs in this type of claim. They are likely to be introduced in 2016 or 2017.

The level at which employers must provide hearing protection and hearing protection zones is now 85 decibels (daily or weekly average exposure) and the level at which employers must assess the risk to workers' health and provide them with information and training is now 80 decibels. There is also an exposure limit value of 87 decibels, taking account of any reduction in exposure provided by hearing protection, above which workers must not be exposed.

There is a general duty upon the employer to reduce the risk of damage to the hearing of his employees from exposure to noise to the lowest level reasonably practicable.

The Supreme Court has decided, by a bare 3–2 majority, that claimants exposed to noise levels of 85 decibels during the 1970s and 1980s could not recover damages for noise induced deafness since the employer was neither negligent nor in breach of the duty imposed by *section 29* of the *Factories Act 1961*. See *Baker v Quantum Clothing Group Ltd* [2011] UKSC 17.

In *Keefe v Isle of Man Steam Packet Co Ltd* [2010] EWCA Civ 683 the Court of Appeal declared that where an employer had failed to monitor noise levels, evidence of which would clearly determine whether exposure was unlawful, the evidence of the employer should be treated with some scepticism and that of the claimant should be treated benevolently.

The *Schedule* to the *Regulations* contains formulae for calculating an employee's 'daily personal noise exposure' and its weekly average. These are to be applied without taking into account the effect of ear protectors. If any employees are likely to be exposed to noise or sound pressure in excess of certain specified levels, the employer must ensure that a competent person makes a noise assessment identifying which employees are so exposed and providing such information with regard to the noise to which they may be exposed as will facilitate compliance with various duties imposed by the *Regulations*. Noise assessments must be reviewed if there is reason to suspect that they are no longer valid, or if there has been a significant change in the relevant work.

Where any employees are likely to be exposed to certain specified noise or sound pressure levels, their exposure to noise must so far as is reasonably practicable be reduced, other than by the provision of personal ear protection, and also so far as practicable be provided with suitable personal ear protectors to keep the risk of damage to below that arising from exposure to those levels. Employers must also, so far as reasonably practicable, identify by signs 'ear protection zones' where such exposure is likely and prevent employees from entering them without personal ear protectors.

At certain specified lower levels of noise, an employee must so far as practicable be provided with suitable and efficient personal ear protectors at his request.

There are also duties relating to ensuring the proper use and maintenance of equipment provided and to informing and training employees.

The HSE may grant exemptions from certain requirements where average weekly exposure does not exceed given levels.

Employees themselves are under a duty to use personal ear protectors and other protective measures and to report defects to the employer, and the self-employed are brought within the scope of the *Regulations*.

28.20 SAFETY REPRESENTATIVES

Employers are obliged to consult with employees over health and safety matters. Two different régimes operate: one for groups of workers in respect of which a union is recognised and the other where there is no union recognition.

For union-appointed safety representatives the *1977 Regulations* apply (*SI 1977/500* – see **28.21** below), and for non-unionised workers the *1996 Regulations* apply (*SI 1996/1513* – see **28.22** below)

28.21 Union-appointed safety representatives

Employers must recognise, afford facilities and allow time off for the training of safety representatives appointed in accordance with the *Safety Representatives and Safety Committees Regulations 1977 (SI 1977/500* as amended by *SI 1992/2051, SI 1996/1513, SI 1999/860)* made under the *HSWA 1974, s 2(4)*. Safety representatives are appointed by a trade union recognised by an employer from among the employees of a unionised workforce, with certain exceptions, eg members of the British Actors' Equity Association or of the Musicians' Union who need not be employees (*regs 3(1), 8(2)*). The representative should, if possible, either have been employed by his employer throughout the preceding two years or have had at least two years' experience in similar employment (*reg 3(4)*).

Safety representatives represent the employees in consultations with the employer over arrangements for their health and safety at work. Every employer is under a duty to consult safety representatives regarding such arrangements (*HSWA 1974, s 2(6)*); without prejudice to that general duty, employers are now required to consult safety representatives with regard to a number of specified health and safety matters, and to provide safety representatives with such facilities and assistance as they may reasonably require for the purposes of carrying out their functions under *HSWA 1974, s 2(4)* and the *Regulations (reg 4A*, inserted by the *Management of Health and Safety Regulations 1992 (SI 1992/2051))*. See also the Code of Practice and guidance notes, *Safety representatives and safety committees* (third edition 1996).

In addition, safety representatives have other functions, including the investigation of potential hazards and complaints about health, safety or welfare. They can make representations about such matters and attend meetings of safety committees (*reg 4(1)*). (See also **10.8** DISCLOSURE OF INFORMATION.) Employers must allow safety representatives time off with pay to perform these functions (*reg 4(2)*). An employer must also permit safety representatives time off with pay to undergo training to fulfil these duties. (See **49.9–49.10** TIME OFF WORK and the *Code of Practice on Time off for the Training of Safety Representatives*.) A safety committee must be established if two or more safety representatives request one in writing (*reg 9*). Safety representatives and others enjoy special protection from dismissal and action short of dismissal (see **28.9** above, **54.3** UNFAIR DISMISSAL – **II**).

28.22 Non-unionised workers

From 1 October 1996 the obligation on employers to consult over health and safety matters was extended to employees who are not covered by trade union-appointed safety representatives (*Health and Safety (Consultation with Employees) Regulations 1996 (SI 1996/1513)*).

Employers may consult either with their employees directly or through elected representatives (*reg 4*). Employees will be entitled to receive such information as is necessary to participate fully and effectively in the consultation process (*reg 5*). The functions of elected representatives are to make representations to the employer on health and safety issues and to represent employees in consultations with inspectors (*reg 6*). Elected representatives are entitled to time off with pay for training and to carry out their duties, and are protected against dismissal and victimisation (*regs 7, 8*).

28.23 SMOKING AT WORK

The EAT, in *Waltons and Morse v Dorrington* [1997] IRLR 488, held that there is a term implied into employment contracts that 'the employer will provide and monitor for his employees, so far as is reasonably practicable, a working environment which is reasonably suitable for the performance by them of their contractual duties'. In this particular case, a non-smoker was held to have been constructively dismissed when she was required, despite her protests, to work in a smoke-affected atmosphere.

The *Health Act 2006* prohibited smoking in the workplace from 2 April 2007 in Wales, from 30 April 2007 in Northern Ireland and from 1 July 2007 in England, (*SI 2006/3368*) via the *Smoke-Free (Premises and Enforcement) Regulations 2006*.

"Suitable 'smoking prohibited' notices should be displayed in accordance with the *Smoke-free (Signs) Regulations 2007 (SI 2007/923)*."

28.24 STRESS

Stress-related illness connected with work remains a controversial and topical issue for employers. According to the HSE, nearly 1 in 3 of workers across the EU (some 40 million people, estimated 5 million Britons) report that they are affected by stress at work (see www.hse.gov.uk/stress/resources.htm), losing an estimated 9.8 million working days in 2009–2010.

To tackle the problem of absence/ill-health caused or made worse by occupational stress, the HSE has produced a set of Management Standards that employers should achieve in practice. Compliance is not a legal requirement but will assist employers in reducing stress at source.

These Management Standards are based around six key areas:

Standard 1:	Demands — includes issues such as workload, work patterns and the working environment.
Standard 2:	Control — concentrates on how much or little) involvement or autonomy a person has in the way they work.
Standard 3:	Support — consider the level of encouragement and assistance provided by the organisation and the resources made available to provide support where additional assistance is needed.
Standard 4:	Relationships — promotes positive behaviours and co-operation at work and identifies if there are systems in place to respond to unacceptable behaviour.
Standard 5:	Role — considers how clearly job descriptions and organisational structures are defined, whether there are conflicts in workers' roles and whether there are clear and unambiguous reporting lines.
Standard 6:	Change — assess how organisational change is managed and communicated to the workforce.

28.25 Common law liability

'Many, alas, suffer breakdowns and depressive illnesses and a significant proportion could doubtless ascribe some at least of their problems to the strains and stresses of their work situation: be it simply overworking, the tension of difficult relationships, career prospect worries, fears or feelings of discrimination or harassment, to take just some examples. Unless, however, there was a real risk of breakdown which the claimant's employers ought reasonably to have foreseen and they ought properly to have averted there can be no liability.' This statement from Simon Brown LJ in *Garrett v Camden London Borough Council* [2001] EWCA Civ 395, [2001] All ER (D) 202 (Mar) sets out the relevant legal test to be applied by the Court when considering a common law action in negligence.

In *Sutherland v Hatton* [2002] EWCA Civ 76, [2002] IRLR 263 the Court of Appeal has set out guidelines for determining employer liability for psychiatric injury caused by stress at work, summarised below.

The ordinary principles of employers' liability apply. First, the kind of harm to the particular employee must be reasonably foreseeable. Foreseeability depends on what the employer knows (or ought reasonably to know) about the individual. It may be harder to foresee mental conditions than physical injury, but may be easier in a known individual. Unless the employer knows of a particular problem or vulnerability, it is usually entitled to assume that the employee can withstand normal job pressures. No occupations should be regarded as intrinsically dangerous to mental health. The court listed a number of factors likely to be relevant in establishing foreseeability, such as the nature and extent of the work done by the employee. In general, an employer does not need to make detailed inquiries of the employee or his or her medical adviser.

To trigger the employer's duty to take steps, the indications of likely harm to the employee's health must be obvious enough for the reasonable employer to realise that something should be done. An employer will only be in breach of duty if it fails to take steps which are reasonable in the circumstances. Where an employer offers a confidential advice service with referral to counselling, it is unlikely to be in breach of its duty. It will not amount to a breach of duty to allow a willing employee to continue in a job if the only reasonable step involves dismissal or demotion.

The steps an employer could and should have taken need to be identified. For the employee, it must be shown that the breach of duty caused or materially contributed to the harm suffered. So long as the breach by the employer was material rather than merely negligible the employer will be liable in full for the injury sustained. See the discussion in *Bailey (by her father and litigation friend) v Ministry of Defence* [2008] EWCA Civ 883, [2009] 1 WLR 1052, 103 BMLR 13.

Where stress risks are a feature of a particular job, a risk assessment should be made under the *Management of Health and Safety at Work Regulations 1992* (see **28.17** above) in the same way as for the risk of physical injury. It is important that complaints of working conditions or workloads causing stress are dealt with quickly and thoroughly and efforts made to reduce the risk of future health problems.

In cases of bullying the claimant might be able to rely on the civil cause of action established by *s 3* of the *Protection from Harassment Act 1997* as was the case in *Green v DB Group Services (UK) Ltd* [2006] EWHC 1898 (QB), [2006] IRLR 764. A secretary bullied by fellow employees established both negligence and breach of duty under the *1997 Act*. A significant advantage of the *Act* is that it provides for a six year limitation period. The common law time limit to institute proceedings is three years. However, the Court of Appeal in *Conn v Sunderland City Council* [2007] EWCA Civ 1492, [2008] IRLR 324, [2007] All ER (D) 99 (Nov) has taken a restrictive approach to civil claims under the *Act*. Conduct must be criminal in nature to found a valid civil claim. The same court took a more lenient approach in *Ferguson v British Gas Trading Ltd* [2009] EWCA Civ 46, [2009] 8 LS Gaz R 18 and refused to strike out a claim made under the *1997 Act* where the claimant alleged that she had been pursued aggressively by a utility company for payment of unjustified bills. In *Dowson v Chief Constable of Northumbria Police* [2010] EWHC 2612 (QB) a group of police officers failed in their claims. They alleged that a Detective Chief Inspector had constantly criticised and undermined them and subjected them to vulgar abuse. It was held that this was not sufficiently oppressive to cross the threshold on liability. Simon J did state, obiter, that unjustified and abusive arguments with an employee could be actionable. It is submitted that the court was influenced considerably by the notion that police officers are to be seen as robust and what might be acceptable here could well be unlawful in, say an office or hospital. In *Jones v Ruth* [2012] 1 All ER 490 the Court of Appeal awarded the claimant damages of £28,750 for harassment injury.

As well as claims for damages, it is also possible that employees whose complaints of excessive stress have gone unheeded could resign and claim constructive dismissal on the basis that the employer failed in the duty of care or breached the implied term to maintain the relationship of trust and confidence.

The High Court in *Sayers v Cambridgeshire County Council* [2006] EWHC 2029 (QB), [2007] IRLR 29 rejected a stress claim based upon a breach of the *Working Time Regulations*. The claimant established that she was working 55 hours a week and had never signed an individual opt –out agreement. Since a breach is a criminal matter the court decided that no civil remedy was intended by the legislature.

28.26 SUBSTANCES HAZARDOUS TO HEALTH

References in this section are to provisions of the *Control of Substances Hazardous to Health Regulations 2002 (SI 2002/2677)*, which replaced the *1999 Regulations* of the same name (except for *regs 4* and *20*, which came into force in 2004). Employers' duties remain unaffected. The main change is the removal of the *Schedule* listing maximum exposure limits ('MELs') from the *Regulations*. These appear instead in the HSE's publication *EH40* which is revised annually.

The definition of a substance hazardous to health is contained in *reg 2(1)*, and includes:

(a)   substances designated as very toxic, toxic, corrosive, harmful or irritant under product labelling legislation (the *CHIP Regulations*);

(b)   substances for which the Health and Safety Commission (now Executive) has approved a Workplace Exposure Limit (WEL);

(c)   biological agents (microorganisms, cell cultures or human endoparasites);

(d)   dust of any kind, when present at a concentrations in air equal to or greater than 10 mg/m^3 (inhalable dust) or 4 mg/m^3 (respirable dust) as a time-weighted average (twa) over an eight-hour period;

(e)   other substances creating a risk to health because of it chemical or toxicological properties and the way it is used or is present within the workplace.

Employers owe duties under *COSHH Regulations 2002* to their employees and, so far as reasonably practicable and with certain exceptions, to other persons who may be affected by the work which they carry on (*reg 3*). The Executive has powers to grant exemption certificates (*reg 14*).

An employer may not carry on any work liable to expose any employees to any substance hazardous to health unless he has made a suitable and sufficient assessment of the risks to their health and of the steps necessary to meet the requirements of *COSHH* (*Dugmore v Swansea NHS Trust* [2002] EWCA Civ 1689, [2003] ICR 574). The assessment must be reviewed forthwith if there is reason to suspect that it is no longer valid or if there has been a significant change in the work to which it relates (*reg 6*).

The employer must ensure that the exposure of his employees to hazardous substances is either prevented or, where this is not reasonably practicable, adequately controlled (*reg 7(1)*). So far as reasonably practicable, that objective is to be secured by measures *other* than the provision of personal protective equipment, although that is also to be provided where necessary. Special measures apply to exposure to carcinogens (*reg 7(2), (3), (4)*).

Employers are under a duty to take all reasonable steps to ensure that control measures, protective equipment etc. are properly used or applied, and employees are under a duty to make full and proper use of such facilities, to return them after use and to report any defects to their employer (*reg 8(1)*, *(2)*). The employer must maintain control measures and equipment in an efficient state, in efficient working order and in good repair, and keep records of tests carried out on them (*reg 9*).

In appropriate cases the employer must ensure that the exposure of employees to hazardous substances is monitored (*reg 10*) and/or that the relevant employees are under suitable health surveillance. In certain specified cases that must include medical surveillance, as a result of which the employer may be barred from engaging an employee for the work concerned (*reg 11*).

Employees whose work may expose them to hazardous substances are to be provided with suitable and sufficient information, instruction and training to enable them to know the risks of exposure and the precautions which should be taken (*reg 12*).

The Health and Safety Commission has approved a number of relevant Codes of Practice: 'Control of Substances Hazardous to Health', 'Control of Carcinogenic Substances' and 'Control of Biological Agents' are published in a single volume (L5 revised 2005). See also the COSHH Essentials website at www.coshh-essentials.org.uk. Codes of Practice on the control of vinyl chloride at work, control of substances hazardous to health in pottery production, prevention or control of legionellosis and on the safe use of pesticides for non -agricultural purposes are also available. The Executive has published 'COSHH assessments: a step by step guide to assessment and the skills needed for it' and 'Health Surveillance under COSHH'. EH40, which lists the occupational exposure limits for use in complying with *COSHH*, is updated annually.

The *COSHH Regulations 2002* do not cover asbestos or lead which are subject to specific legislation, including the *Control of Asbestos at Work Regulations 2006 (SI 2006/2793)* and the *Control of Lead at Work Regulations 2002 (SI 2002/2676)*.

The *COSHH Regulations* have been extended in Northern Ireland – see *COSHH (Amendment) Regulations (NI) 2005, SI 2005/165*.

28.27 VIBRATION AT WORK

The *Control of Vibration at Work Regulations 2005 (SI 2005/1093)* came into force on 6 July 2005. These *Regulations* will help both employers and employees to take preventive action from vibration risks in the workplace. These *Regulations* comply with *European Physical Agents (Vibration) Directive (Directive 2002/44)* which seeks to deal with the control of diseases caused by vibration at work from equipment, vehicles and machines.

Hand Arm Vibration (HAV) is a major cause of occupational ill health and it is estimated around five million workers are exposed to HAV in the workplace. Two million of these workers are exposed to levels of vibration where there are clear risks of developing disease.

See www.hse.gov.uk/vibration/index.htm. Also, see the HAV Health Surveillance scheme and vibguide.

Whole Body Vibration (WBV) has four principal effect:

•   health risks

•   impaired ability to perform duties

•   impaired comfort

•   motion sickness

Exposure to WBV causes a complex distribution of oscillatory motions and forces within the body. These may cause unpleasant sensations giving rise to discomfort or annoyance, resulting in impaired performance — e.g. loss of balance, degraded vision, or present a health risk. The most widely reported WBV injury is back pain.

The HSE has produced guidance on HAVS (L140, 2005) and WBV (L141, 2005).

28.28   VIOLENCE AND BULLYING AT WORK

The employer's duty of care at common law and under *HSWA 1974, s 2* means that an employer needs to provide adequate security precautions where it is reasonably foreseeable that employees may suffer violence in the course of their work (which, given the escalation of violent incidents at work, probably covers every workplace). When making the risk assessment required under the *Management of Health and Safety at Work Regulations 1992*, as amended in 1999, (see **28.17** above) the possibility of violence to employees must be evaluated. When an employee has been the victim of an attack and the employer has taken inadequate safety measures, the employee may resign and claim constructive dismissal (*Dutton & Clark Ltd v Daly* [1985] IRLR 363), or claim damages for negligence.

The HSE leaflet *Violence at Work: a guide for employers* sets out a strategy for the effective management of violence.

Employees must also be safeguarded against bullying or harassment at work either by members of the public or fellow employees. Such behaviour, if not causing actual physical harm, may have a detrimental effect on an employee's morale and health. Where insufficient action is taken to stamp out the problem it is possible that the employer may be held liable for personal injury even if psychological damage only is caused. Intentional harassment is a criminal offence under the *Public Order Act 1986, s 4A* (as inserted by the *Criminal Justice and Public Order Act 1994*). From 16 June 1997, the *Protection from Harassment Act 1997* creates two new criminal offences of harassment and provides a civil remedy whereby an individual can apply for an injunction and damages against the harasser. Racially aggravated harassment constitutes a separate offence from 30 September 1998 (*Crime and Disorder Act 1998, ss 31, 32*).

It is imperative that all complaints from employees of violence, bullying or harassment are investigated fully and prompt action taken where necessary. The failure to do so could provoke a constructive dismissal claim before the Employment Tribunal. It could also found the basis of a claim in negligence as it did in *Green v DB Group Services (UK) Ltd* [2006] EWHC 1898 (QB), [2006] IRLR 764 where allegations of workplace bullying were not acted upon and the victim was awarded over £800,000 in damages.

The Court of Appeal delivered a confused and confusing judgment in *Weddall v Barchester Healthcare Ltd* [2012] EWCA Civ 25. The case was conjoined with *Wallbank v Wallbank Fox Designs Ltd*. Both claimants were the unfortunate victims of assault perpetrated by a fellow employee. In the former case the court held that the act of violence was gratuitous and unconnected with employment so the defendant was not liable. With respect, it would appear that the assault arose because the claimant had given a fellow employee a lawful instruction to come in and work so as to cover someone who was absent. In the latter case the claimant was attacked after giving an employee a direction to turn on an oven in the factory where they worked. This incident was held to be one for which the employer was liable, it being job related. The distinction is fine if not imperceptible.

28.29   WORKPLACE STANDARDS

The *Workplace (Health, Safety and Welfare) Regulations 1992 (SI 1992/3004)* give effect to the EC Directive concerning the minimum health and safety requirements for the workplace (*89/654*). The *Regulations* came into force on 1 January 1993 in respect of any new workplace, and apply to any modification, extension or conversion of an existing workplace on or after that date. In respect of any other existing workplace, the requirements came into effect on 1 January 1996. *Regulation 6* of the *Health and Safety (Miscellaneous Amendments) Regulations 2002 (SI 2002/2174)* amends the *1992 Regulations* to give complete or clearer effect to the technical definitions of its key terms, such as the meaning of 'workplace'. These requirements supersede provisions in the *Factories Act 1961 (ss 1–7, 18, 28, 29, 57–60 and 69), Offices, Shops and Railway Premises Act 1963 (ss 4–16),* and *Agriculture (Safety, Health and Welfare Provisions) Act 1956 (ss 3, 5, 25(3) and (6)).*

The requirements under the *Regulations* are imposed on employers, persons having control of a workplace, and any person who is deemed to be the occupier of a factory by virtue of s *175(5)* of the *Factories Act 1961 (reg 4).* The requirements relate to the following matters:

(a)   maintenance of workplaces, and of equipment, devices and systems (*reg 5*);

(b)   ventilation of enclosed workplaces (*reg 6*);

(c)   temperature in indoor workplaces (including provision of thermometers) (*reg 7*);

(d)   lighting (*reg 8*);

(e)   cleanliness and waste materials/storage (*reg 9*);

(f)   room dimensions and space (*reg 10*);

(g)   workstations and seating (*reg 11*);

(h)   conditions of floors and traffic routes, and organisation of traffic routes (*regs 12, 17*);

(i)   falls or falling objects (*reg 13*);

(j)   windows, doors, gates, walls, skylights and ventilators (*regs 14–16, 18*);

(k)   escalators and moving walkways/travelators (*reg 19*);

(l)   sanitary conveniences (*reg 20*);

(m)   washing facilities (*reg 21*);

(n)   drinking water (*reg 22*);

(o)   accommodation for clothing, and facilities for changing clothing (*regs 23, 24*); and

(p)   facilities to rest and to eat meals (*reg 25*).

Regulation 24 requires facilities to be provided for changing clothes when workers have to wear special clothing for work and, for reasons of health or propriety, cannot be expected to change in another room. 'Special clothing' in this context means any clothing which would not ordinarily be worn other than for work, such as a distinctive uniform (*Post Office v Footitt* [2000] IRLR 243).

28.30   Safety signs

The *Health and Safety (Safety Signs and Signals) Regulations 1996 (SI 1996/341)* implements the EC Directive on safety signs and signals *(92/58)*. All workplace safety signs are required to be of a type referred to within the Regulations.

Basically, there are four recognised safety colours:

Red —   Prohibition sign: Danger, Firefighting equipment
Yellow/Amber —   Warning sign: Be careful, Take precautions

Blue —   Mandatory sign: Specific behaviour or action, Wear protective
                    equipment
Green —   Safe place, No Danger: Emergency Escape Routes, First Aid
                    Equipment.

28.31 WORK-RELATED UPPER LIMB DISORDERS ('WRULDS')

Work-related upper limb disorders or 'RSI' (repetitive strain injury) as they are commonly known, are becoming an increasingly worrying issue for employers, particularly in relation to keyboard users. Although there have only been a small number of claims successfully pursued through the courts, a number of employers have settled claims for large sums of money.

In 1996 a secretary who had developed 'writer's cramp' (a WRULD disorder) as a result of an excessive typing workload succeeded before the Court of Appeal in a claim that her employer had been negligent in allowing her to type for long periods on a word processor without breaks. The court held that it was reasonably foreseeable that a WRULD condition could occur with the amount of typing involved and that the company had negligently failed to warn the employee of the need to take breaks. This ruling was overturned by the House of Lords in *Pickford v Imperial Chemical Industries plc* [1998] IRLR 435, primarily because of inconclusive medical evidence. In addition the employer was held not to be in breach of the duty of care in failing to warn of the need to take breaks because, unlike a typist, a secretary could organise the workload to avoid continuous working on a word processor. (A statutory requirement to provide information to workers on health and safety risks associated with VDUs is contained in the *Health and Safety (Display Screen Equipment) Regulations 1992 (SI 1992/2792)* (see **28.6** above).)

The possibility of contracting WRULDs can be minimised by paying attention to posture, ergonomics, job design and working methods and conditions.

More recently, the term musculoskeletal disorders (MSDs) has been introduced to cover a range of conditions including WRULDs and RSI which adversely affect the skeletal system and its associated muscles, tendons and ligaments.

These conditions are usually separated into those affecting the upper limbs (from the shoulder to the fingertips), the lower limbs (from the hip to the toes) and the back.

Among people who have ever worked, 2.7% suffer from some form of musculoskeletal disorder, resulting in 10.7 million lost working days (2006–07). On average, each affected person took 16.7 days off in a twelve-month period.

The HSE has produced a useful guidance publicaiton – HSG60, 2nd Edition, 2002 – entitled *Upper Limb Disorders in the Workplace.*

28.32 MINERS KNEE

This osto-arthritic condition is not one for which the employer was liable, held the Court of Appeal in 2012. The claims have been abandoned.

Miners Knee is an example of a lower limb disorder, similar to beat knee (bursitis).

29 Holidays

29.1 The right of an employee to a period of paid holiday is regulated by his contract of employment (see **29.8** below) and the *Working Time Regulations 1998 (SI 1998/1833)* (see **29.2–29.6** below). The *Deduction from Wages (Limitation) Regulations 2014* amended *reg 16* of the *Working Time Regulations* to confirm that the *Working Times Regulations* do not confer a contractual right to paid holiday: the regime under the *Regulations* is simply statutory (although a contract of employment could, in principle, expressly incorporate the *Regulations*). In addition, in certain fields of employment, separate statutory provision is made (see **29.7** below).

29.2 STATUTORY RULES

Working Time Regulations 1998

The *Working Time Regulations 1998 (SI 1998/1833)* came into force on 1 October 1998. They implemented the *Working Time Directive 93/104/EC* which has now been replaced by the *Working Time Directive 2003/88/EC*. The *Regulations* confer a right on workers to take paid annual leave (*reg 13(1)*). There is no continuous service requirement to qualify for paid annual leave. Initially, *reg 13(7)* did specify that only workers with 13 weeks' continuous service qualified. However, this limitation was ruled contrary to European law by the European Court of Justice ('ECJ') in *R (on the application of the Broadcasting, Entertainment, Cinematographic and Theatre Union) v Secretary of State for Trade and Industry ('BECTU')*: C-173/99 [2001] IRLR 559. As a consequence of this decision, *regs 13(7)* and *13(8)* were revoked with effect from 25 October 2001.

'Worker' is defined in the *Regulations* to include employees and those employed under a contract pursuant to which they undertake personally to provide services. However, those who are in business on their own account and whose 'employer' is in reality their customer or client are not workers (*reg 2(1)*). There is a constant stream of case law on the definition of worker and a detailed review can be found earlier in this book in EMPLOYEE, SELF-EMPLOYED OR WORKER **15.9**.

Children under the age for compulsory schooling are not workers and, therefore, are not entitled under the *Regulations* to paid holiday: *Ashby v Addison* [2003] ICR 667, [2003] IRLR 211, EAT.

Originally in *Gibson v East Riding of Yorkshire Council* [2000] IRLR 598 the Court of Appeal held that *art 7* of the *Working Time Directive*, which sets out a right to paid holiday, does not have direct effect. This meant that employees could not rely directly on *art 7* of the *Directive* before the domestic courts, but only on their rights under the *Regulations*. However in *Dominguez v Centre Informatique du Centre Ouest Atlantique*: C-282/10 [2012] IRLR 321 the ECJ suggested that *art 7* of the *Directive* did have direct effect and could be relied upon by workers where their employer was an emanation of the state. Subsequently, in *NHS Leeds v Larner* [2012] ICR 1389, [2012] IRLR 825, the Court of Appeal confirmed that *art 7* of the *Directive* was directly effective. As the employer in that case was an emanation of the state the Claimant was entitled to rely directly on *art 7* to support her claim.

For further discussion of the *Working Time Regulations* and *Directive* see WORKING TIME **(57)**, EUROPEAN UNION LAW **(23)** and HEALTH AND SAFETY AT WORK – II **(28)**.

29.3 Holidays

29.3 Period of leave – Number of Days' Leave in a Leave Year

Annual Entitlements: Annual Leave and Additional Annual Leave

Annual entitlements under the *Regulations* are based upon the concept of a 'leave year'. A leave year commences on the date set out in a relevant agreement. A relevant agreement means a workforce agreement, a collective agreement which is incorporated into the contract of employment, or any other agreement in writing which is legally enforceable as between the worker and his employer (normally this will simply be the contract of employment). In the absence of such an agreement, the leave year commences on 1 October 1998 and on the anniversary of that date for those workers already in employment on that date, and, for workers who started work after 1 October 1998, on the date their employment commenced (*reg 13(3)*).

When the *Regulations* were introduced, they entitled a worker to four weeks' annual leave in each leave year (*reg 13(1)*). For a worker working a five day week this amounted to 20 days' annual holiday. Public holidays (of which there are normally eight each year) may count towards the worker's annual leave entitlement. The fact that an employer could count public holidays towards the four week entitlement was much criticised by workers and trade unions. The Department for Trade and Industry (as it then was) sought to address this criticism by introducing the concept of additional annual leave (*reg 13A*).

The total entitlement to annual leave (*reg 13*) and additional annual leave (*reg 13A*) is 5.6 weeks per year. For a person working five days a week, this increases the entitlement to 28 days' annual leave per year. *Reg 13A(3)* further provides that the aggregate entitlement to annual leave and additional annual leave is subject to a maximum of 28 days. So an employee working six days a week would only be entitled to a total of 28 days' annual leave. When considering the entitlement to leave under the *Regulations*, it should not be forgotten that the *Regulations* set only minimum requirements: more generous provision relating to annual leave may be, and often is, made in the contract of employment.

The distinction between annual leave and additional annual leave is also relevant to the treatment of leave at the end of the leave year. A worker may not carry forward from one leave year to the next any of the four weeks' annual leave (*reg 13(9)(a)*) (save in cases of sickness absence, or various types of maternity and parental leave – see **29.3A** below). Nor may an employer pay a worker in lieu of permitting him to take annual leave except on termination of his employment (*reg 13(9)(b)*). The prohibition of payment in lieu of annual leave is intended to remove any incentive for workers to accept additional payment rather than taking leave as this would undermine the health and safety objectives of the *Directive*: see *Federatie Nederlandse Vakbeweging v Netherlands State*: C-124/05 [2006] ECR I-3423, [2006] ICR 962, ECJ. The position with additional annual leave is different. A relevant agreement may provide for any additional annual leave to be carried forward into the immediately following leave year (ie leave carried over under this regulation should not then be carried over into the subsequent leave year)(*reg 13A(7)*). However, an employer is not permitted to make a payment in lieu of additional annual leave.

Finally, to add to the complexity of the current statutory provisions, *reg 26A* provides that the entitlement to additional annual leave under *reg 13A* does not apply where, subject to certain conditions, as at 1 October 2007, a relevant agreement provided that all workers engaged by an employer were entitled to annual leave of at least the equivalent to the now extended statutory entitlement (ie 5.6 weeks or 28 days).

Accruing Annual Leave

The leave entitlement is based on the entire leave year. However, save for workers in their first year of employment, the *Regulations* do not make provision for leave to be accrued incrementally on a month by month basis. So, for example, subject to agreement with the employer (which is discussed at **29.5** below), a worker would be entitled under the *Regulations* to take all his or her annual and additional annual leave at the very start of the leave year. By contrast, workers in their first year of employment accrue entitlement to leave at the rate of one-twelfth of their entitlement on the first day of each month and leave under the *Regulations* may only be taken after it has been accrued (*regs 13(5)* and *13A(5)*).

In *Zentralbetriebsrat der Landeskrankenhauser Tirols v Land Tirol*: C–486/08 [2010] IRLR 631 the ECJ gave important guidance on dealing with accrued annual leave when a worker changes from full time to part time employment during the leave year. It held that the combined effect of the *Part Time Workers Directive* and the *Working Time Directive* was that a reduction of working hours when moving from full time to part time employment does not reduce the right to annual leave that the worker has accrued during the period of full time employment if the worker did not have the opportunity to take that accrued leave. In *Land Tirol* it was rather unclear what the ECJ meant by referring to a worker 'not having the opportunity to exercise the right' to take accrued leave. More recently in *Greenfield v The Care Bureau Ltd*: C-219/14, [2016] ICR 161, [2016] IRLR 62, the facts of which are considered in more detail below, the ECJ affirmed that "annual leave accrued during a reference period can be taken during a subsequent period" without referring to a need to enquire into whether a worker "had the opportunity to exercise the right" to take accrued leave. In the circumstances, it now seems clear that annual leave accrued as a full time worker may be carried over into a period of part time employment (provided it is in the same leave year).

The facts of *Greenfield* were that an employee took 7 days' annual leave early in the leave year at a time when she was working one day a week. Accordingly, the leave taken was equivalent to 7 weeks' leave, and so above the annual leave entitlement under the *Regulations*. Around 2 months into the leave year, she significantly increased her days of work to 12 days every 2 weeks. Later in the leave year she asked to take annual leave, but this was refused on the basis that she had exhausted her entitlement by taking 7 days' leave earlier in the leave year. The employer's argument was that as she had exhausted her annual leave entitlement while working one day a week, she could take no more annual leave that year, irrespective of her hours of work for the rest of the leave year. The ECJ, unsurprisingly in view of the decision in *Land Tirol*, held that a new calculation of annual leave entitlement must be carried out for periods when working time is increased. Accordingly, the calculation of the employee's annual leave entitlement in that case should have been based upon the entitlement accrued while working one day a week, plus the leave accrued while working 12 days out of 14. The 7 days' leave she had taken early in the leave year would be deducted from that total.

To give another example, based on simple facts, a worker working 5 days a week for 6 months of the leave year will accrue 2 weeks – or 10 days – paid annual leave under the *Regulations* (the leave accrued would be 14 days including additional annual leave; this example, however, refers only to on annual leave as the ECJ decisions would not technically apply to additional annual leave as additional leave reflects a domestic policy decision rather than the implementation of the *Directive*). If the worker then chose to take that accrued leave at a time when he or she had changed to working 3 days a week, he or she would still be entitled to 10 days' paid leave, rather than just 6 days' (which would be two weeks' leave based on the worker's reduced hours). The same principles would apply in the reverse situation. While working 3 days a week for 6 months, the worker would accrue 6 days' leave. If the worker then changed to full time work, he or she would only be entitled to carry over the leave actually accrued but untaken as a part time worker. The accrued but untaken holiday would not be recalculated based on the new full time hours.

The question of how entitlement to leave is accrued is particularly relevant to workers who do not work for the entire leave year. How is leave entitlement calculated in these cases? Three particular scenarios are commonly encountered in the workplace. First, as mentioned above, a worker may commence employment part-way through the leave year. Where this happens, in that leave year the worker is entitled to the proportion of the annual leave entitlement equal to the proportion of the leave year for which he is employed (*regs 13(5) and 13A(5)*).

The second scenario is that the worker leaves the employment part way through the leave year. In this situation, *reg 14* provides a mechanism to compare the amount of leave taken by a worker in that part of the leave year which he worked with the amount of leave accrued. So, for example, if a worker left the employment exactly six months through the leave year, he would have accrued half his annual leave entitlement; this can be compared to the amount of leave actually taken. *Reg 14* then sets out procedures for dealing with any difference between leave accrued and leave taken. These procedures are discussed at **29.4A** below.

29.3A   Annual Leave, Absence from Work and Illness

The third scenario occurs where, although the worker remains employed throughout the leave year, he is absent for part or all of the year due to, for example, illness. Neither the *Regulations* nor the *Directive* expressly address this situation or the relationship between illness and annual leave. Accordingly, it has been left to the courts to seek a solution. In 2011, the Government's Modern Workplaces consultation proposed that these issues would be addressed in amended *Regulations*. However it is not clear if, or when, such amendments will be introduced.

Until clarification is provided in amended *Regulations*, employers, workers and Tribunals will need to find answers from an increasingly complex collection of decisions of both the ECJ and the domestic courts on the relationship between annual leave and sick leave. A detailed review of those cases is beyond the scope of this chapter. However the summary below seeks to draw out the key principles of those cases.

The key points to be taken from the decisions of the ECJ in relation to interpretation of the *Working Time Directive* are:

- Paid annual leave "is a particularly important principle of Community social law from which there can be no derogations".

- The purpose of the right to paid annual leave (i.e. to provide a period of rest, relaxation and leisure) is different from the purpose of sick leave (i.e. to enable a worker to recover from illness): recently reaffirmed in *Sobczyszyn v Szkola Podstawowa w Rzeplinie*: C-178/15 [2016] IRLR 725. As a result entitlement to annual leave continues to accrue during sickness absence.

- Workers must be given the opportunity to take annual leave. Accordingly, workers should not lose their entitlement to annual leave simply because they are unable to take that annual leave as a result of sickness. This was initially decided by the ECJ's decisions in the joined cases of *HM Revenue and Customs v Stringer and Schultz-Hoff v Deutsche Rentenversicherung Bund*: C-502/06, [2009] ICR 932, [2009] IRLR 214. The ECJ specifically noted that the aims of the *Directive* could be achieved in more than one way. For example, workers could be permitted to take annual leave while they are on sick leave. In addition or alternatively, where a worker has been unable to take annual leave because he is sick, he could be permitted to take that leave later, even if that meant carrying the untaken leave over into the next leave year.

- In *Pereda v Madrid Movilidad SA*: C-277/08, [2009] IRLR 959 the ECJ held that where a worker does not wish to take annual leave during a period of sick leave, the employer must grant him annual leave for a different period, if necessary, by permitting him to carry leave over to a new leave year. Subsequently in *Asociación*

Nacional de Grandes Empresas de Distribución (ANGED) v Federación de Asociaciones Sindicales (FASGA) and others: C-78/11, [2012] ICR 1211, [2012] IRLR 779 the ECJ held that a worker who falls ill during a period of annual leave must be permitted to interrupt that annual leave and take the untaken annual leave at a later date (even if that resulted in the leave being carried over to a new leave year). In such a case the employer would clearly be entitled to require the worker to provide proof of illness during the holiday.

• Entitlement to annual leave cannot be made conditional on a worker carrying out a minimum amount of work in the leave year. In *Dominguez v Centre Informatique du Centre Ouest Atlantique*: C-282/10, [2012] IRLR 321 the ECJ held that a French provision making entitlement to paid annual leave conditional upon an employee doing one month of actual work during the leave year was inconsistent with the *Directive*.

• Where a worker's employment terminates, he is entitled to be paid in lieu for annual leave which has accrued but which the worker was unable to take due to sickness (even where that is annual leave accrued over more than one leave year): see *HM Revenue and Customs v Stringer*.

• Issues also commonly arise in relation to carrying over annual leave while on maternity and parental leave. For example in *Zentralbetriebsrat der Landeskranken-hauser Tirols v Land Tirol*: C-486/08, [2010] IRLR 631 the ECJ held that the effect of the *Working Time Directive* and the *Framework Agreement on Parental Leave* was that a worker who took parental leave could carry over, until after the parental leave, any annual leave accrued prior to the worker taking parental leave.

A major difficulty thrown up by the ECJ's decisions is the apparent inconsistency between the decision in *Pereda* (recognising that in certain cases workers must be permitted to carry leave over into the next leave year) and *reg 13(9)* of the *Regulations* which provides that leave cannot be carried over from one leave year to the next.

In *NHS Leeds v Larner* [2012] ICR 1389, [2012] IRLR 825, the Court of Appeal (Mummery LJ) suggested that *reg 13(9)* of the *Regulations* could be interpreted consistently with the ECJ decisions referred to above in the following way (the words in italics have been added by the Court of Appeal to ensure consistency with the *Directive*):

"Leave to which a worker is entitled under this regulation may be taken in instalments, but— (a) it may only be taken in the leave year in respect of which it is due, *save where the worker was unable or unwilling to take it because he was on sick leave and as a consequence did not exercise his right to annual leave . . . .*"

While the *Larner* case was decided by the direct application of *art 7* of the *Working Time Directive* (as the Claimant was employed by an emanation of the state) rather than under the *Regulations*, the approach of the Court of Appeal in *Larner* was followed by the EAT in *Sood Enterprises Ltd v Healy* [2013] ICR 1361, [2013] IRLR 865. Accordingly, employers should permit workers to carry over annual leave if they have not been able to, or have chosen not to, take it due to illness. In this regard, in *Plumb v Duncan Print Group Ltd* [2016] ICR 125, [2015] IRLR 711 the EAT emphasised that a worker who is absent from work on sick leave is entitled to choose not to take annual leave while on sick leave; he is not required to demonstrate that he is physically unable to take annual leave by reason of his medical condition before being permitted to carry it over into the next leave year.

A further issue then arises in relation to how long a worker will retain the right to carry over leave, before that entitlement lapses. In *KHS AG v Schulte*: C-214/10 [2012] IRLR 156 the ECJ held that national rules or relevant agreements could limit the period for which annual leave could be accrued during long term absence. In *Schulte* a provision of a German Collective Agreement provided that any entitlement to annual leave which accrued during sickness absence would lapse 15 months after the end of the leave year in which it was accrued. The ECJ gave guidance that any carry over period must be "substantially longer" than the leave year but accepted that the period of 15 months in the case before it was permissible. In a subsequent case, *Neidel v Stadt Frankfurt am Main*: C-337/10, [2012] ICR 1201, [2012] IRLR 607 the ECJ held that a 9 month carry over period was insufficient.

The *Regulations* do not address the issue of the period of carry over in respect of annual leave which cannot be taken in the leave year in which it accrued (although they do provide in *reg 13A(7)* that a relevant agreement may permit additional annual leave to be carried over into the immediately following leave year). However, in *Plumb v Duncan Print Group Ltd* [2016] ICR 125, [2015] IRLR 711 the EAT concluded by reference to the International Labour Organisation - Holiday and Pay Convention, that a carry-over period of 18 months should be read into *reg 13(9)*: see paragraph 45 of the decision. Accordingly, until there is an amendment to the *Regulations*, or a further judicial decision, workers should be permitted to carry over for 18 months from the end of the leave year any annual leave that they were unable or unwilling to take in that leave year because of illness.

Annual Leave and Giving Notice during Illness

As explained in **29.5** below, *reg 15* of the *Regulations* sets out a procedure for the employer and worker to agree or determine when annual leave is taken. Where a worker wishes to claim entitlement to be paid in respect of annual leave during a period of sickness absence, the worker would have to give notice to the employer and would then be entitled to receive paid annual leave: see *Larner* at paragraph 87 and *Fraser v Southwest London St George's Mental Health Trust* [2012] ICR 403, [2012] IRLR 100 at paragraph 30. A worker on long term sick leave who has exhausted sick pay may well want, or need, to be paid in respect of annual leave while they remain ill, rather than carrying that annual leave over.

In other cases, as the ECJ noted in *Stringer*, a worker may simply wish to keep annual leave which she could not take because she was ill until after she has recovered (even if that means carrying it over into a new leave year). It has now been confirmed that the worker is not required to give notice of the intention to carry that annual leave over to the next leave year: see *NHS Leeds v Larner* [2012] ICR 1389, [2012] IRLR 825 and *Sood Enterprises Ltd v Healy* [2013] ICR 1361, [2013] IRLR 865.

Taking Annual Leave on Return to Work after Sick Leave

A further difficulty arises in cases where a worker is unable to take leave due to sickness but returns to work in the same leave year. In such a case, is the worker permitted to carry leave over, or is she required to take her leave in the current leave year? In *NHS Leeds v Larner* Mummery LJ hinted, by reference to the EAT decision in *Fraser v Southwest London St George's Mental Health Trust*, that there would be no entitlement to carry over annual leave where the worker was able to take it in the current leave year. Accordingly, the focus in such cases is likely to be on whether the worker was reasonably able to do so. This will be fact specific and will depend on the amount of accrued but untaken leave and the period between the worker returning to work from sickness absence and the end of the leave year.

Annual Leave and Additional Annual Leave: Should they be treated in the same way?

As explained below, the government has proposed that annual leave under *reg 13* and additional annual leave under *reg 13A* should be treated differently when considering the right to carry over annual leave which cannot be taken due to illness. This reflects that the leave under *reg 13* is the leave required by the *Directive*, while leave under *reg 13A* goes beyond the *Directive* and is a national policy. Pending amendment of the *Working Time Regulations*, how should the current provisions – as interpreted in *Larner* – be applied? In *Neidel v Stadt Frankfurt am Main*: C-337/10, [2012] ICR 1201, [2012] IRLR 607, the ECJ confirmed that the *Directive* did not require national law to permit additional leave to be carried over in cases of illness. The ECJ made a similar point in *Dominguez v Centre Informatique du Centre Ouest Atlantique*: C-282/10 [2012] IRLR 321. In *Larner* the Court of Appeal refused to determine this point, but strongly hinted that it considered that *Neidel* had already provided the answer. In *Sood Enterprises Ltd v Healy* [2013] ICR 1361, [2013] IRLR 865, the EAT took up the Court of Appeal's hint and expressly held that a worker could not carry over additional annual leave accrued while off sick, unless there was a relevant agreement with the employer which permitted this.

However, one further caveat must be borne in mind in relation to the treatment of annual leave and additional annual leave. Where other Directives are also in play such as those governing maternity leave, it would appear to be unlawful not to permit the carryover of additional annual leave. For example in *Gomez (Merino) v Continental Industrias del Caucho SA*: C-342/01 [2004] ECR I-2605, [2005] ICR 1040, the ECJ held that, in relation to maternity leave, where a Member State had provided for a longer entitlement to annual leave than the minimum prescribed by the *Working Time Directive*, the Pregnancy *Directive 92/85* also applied to the entitlement to that additional annual leave. Accordingly that additional annual leave could not be operated in a way which undermined the taking of maternity leave (see further discussion of the *Merino Gomez* case at **29.5** below).

Proposed Amendments

As the above summary illustrates, the relationship between annual leave and sick leave is complex. Part of the difficulty has been that neither the *Directive* nor the *Regulations* provided any guidance on these issues. As a result the ECJ and domestic courts were left to provide solutions on a case by case basis – typically in response to cases with relatively unusual facts.

Amendment of the *Regulations* was proposed as part of the Modern Workplaces consultation. In summary, the initial key proposals in the consultation document were:

- The 4 weeks' annual leave under *reg 13* and the 1.6 weeks' additional annual leave under *reg 13A* will continue to accrue during sickness absence.

- The *Regulations* will allow annual leave to be rescheduled where the worker has been unable to take annual leave due to illness (whether he fell ill before or during the leave). This will include a right to carry over untaken leave where there is no opportunity to reschedule that annual leave in the current leave year.

- However the right to reschedule and carry over will be limited to the 4 weeks' annual leave under *reg 13*. It will not apply to the 1.6 weeks' additional annual leave under *reg 13A* (or any further contractual leave to which a worker is entitled). This will require employers and workers to know under which provision each particular period of leave is being taken. The government has proposed that this could be determined by a local agreement, failing which the amended *Regulations* will specify the order in which leave is deemed to be taken (the suggestion is that *reg 13* leave would be deemed to be taken first followed by all other types of annual leave).

- The carry over rights will also apply where leave cannot be taken due to maternity, paternity, parental or adoption leave. However this right will extend to both annual leave under *reg 13* and additional annual leave under *reg 13A*.

The implementation of these proposed amendments has stalled (perhaps due, initially, to the need to take into account the on-going stream of cases from the ECJ and domestic courts and more recently as a result of Brexit). However at some future point amended *Regulations* will hopefully resolve many of the issues considered above (as well as those considered below in relation to calculation of holiday pay).

29.3A   Holidays

Conclusion on Annual Leave and Illness

Until the *Regulations* are amended, to avoid costly legal disputes, it would be prudent for employers to give a worker, who is sick during a period of annual leave, the option of still taking annual leave during the period of sickness or taking annual leave at a later date, even if this means carrying the annual leave missed through sickness over to the next leave year, and beyond where the worker is absent for a very long time.

One source of comfort for employers and workers is that while complex issues do arise when considering sickness absence and annual leave, the reality is that these issues will only arise in exceptional cases: typically where workers are on long term sick leave, or they have left taking their annual leave until the end of the leave year and then fallen ill. In most cases, where workers fall sick during or shortly before a period of annual leave, and request that the period be treated as sick leave, they will be able to take the annual leave which they missed as a result of sickness later in the same leave year.

29.3B Annual Leave and Reasons for Absence other than Illness or Maternity etc

Workers may be absent from work for reasons other than illness, maternity leave, paternity leave, parental leave or adoption leave etc. For example, a worker may agree a period of unpaid leave or a sabbatical. Do they continue to accrue annual leave entitlement during such absences? Again the *Directive* and *Regulations* do not provide an answer. However, some guidance can be found in the ECJ decision in *Heimann and another v Kaiser GmbH*: C-229/11 [2013] IRLR 48. In that case, the employer dismissed a number of employees due to financial difficulties. However it then agreed with its works council to extend the employment contracts of the dismissed workers for one year from the date of their dismissal on a zero hours short-time working basis. This suspended the workers' obligation to work and the employer's obligation to pay them a salary. The purpose of that extension was to give the workers the opportunity of receiving, for the year following their dismissal, a statutory allowance payable during periods of zero hours short-time working. The ECJ held that the *Working Time Directive* permitted national law or relevant agreements to provide that annual leave accrued in proportion to the time actually worked during the leave year (as it would for part time workers). Accordingly, such a law or agreement could provide that annual leave did not accrue during periods where no work was being performed. In reaching this conclusion the ECJ explained that the situation of a worker unable to work as a result of an illness, and that of a worker on short-time working, are fundamentally different. In particular, the ECJ noted, during the period of short-time working, the worker was free to rest or to devote himself to recreational and leisure activities, whereas a worker on sick leave would be subject to physical or psychological constraints caused by illness.

The reasoning of the ECJ in *Heimann* ought to apply equally to other absences not caused by illness, or maternity or paternity leave, such as unpaid leave and sabbaticals. However in such cases employers should be advised expressly to agree with the worker that he will not accrue annual leave during the period of absence (and to record that agreement in writing).

29.3C Carry Over of Annual Leave in Cases other than Illness or Maternity etc

As explained above, in *NHS Leeds v Larner* [2012] ICR 1389, [2012] IRLR 825, the Court of Appeal suggested that *reg 13(9)* of the *Regulations* could be interpreted to allow annual leave to be carried over to a new leave year "where the worker was unable or unwilling to take it because he was on sick leave and as a consequence did not exercise his right to annual leave . . . ." This will also apply to maternity and other parental leave.

To what extent might a similar analysis apply where a worker is prevented from taking annual leave due to reasons other than illness or maternity etc? In *Sash Window Workshop Ltd v King* [2015] IRLR 348 the EAT suggested that annual leave could be carried over in cases where a worker was "unable or unwilling because of reasons beyond his control, to take annual leave and as a consequence did not exercise his right to annual leave." In that case the employer refused to pay holiday pay to Mr King on the erroneous belief that he was not a worker, and so not entitled to annual leave under the *Regulations*. The EAT held that the Tribunal should have considered whether the employer's refusal to pay holiday pay meant that Mr King was unwilling or unable to take annual leave for a reason beyond his control. This approach clearly extends the scope of *Larner* to situations where the reason for not taking leave is unrelated to illness, maternity etc. *Sash Window Workshop* was appealed to the Court of Appeal which has referred certain questions to the ECJ (C-214/16). The Advocate General's Opinion is due to be handed down in June 2017, with the judgment of the ECJ to follow.

Subject to any clarification from the ECJ (or Court of Appeal on remission), the decision in *Sash Window Workshop* leaves open the question of the circumstances in which a Tribunal would conclude that a worker was unable or unwilling to take annual leave for reasons beyond his control: the employer's refusal to pay holiday pay may be one such situation but waiting until the very end of the leave year before trying to take leave and then being unable to do so is unlikely to satisfy this test. This is illustrated by the EAT decision in *Shannon v Rampersad* [2015] IRLR 982 in which the EAT upheld the Tribunal's conclusion that the claimant was not entitled to accrued holiday pay for previous years because he could have requested annual leave but had chosen not to. That approach could put workers in a difficult position where the employer has indicated that it will not look favourably at requests for paid annual leave: if the worker chooses not to rock the boat by not requesting leave, should his entitlement lapse? It is suggested that in such cases the Tribunal should look into whether the worker's right to request leave was undermined by the employer's attitude towards such requests.

29.4   Payment for Annual Leave

A worker is entitled to be paid for any period of leave at the rate of a week's pay for each week of leave. In *British Airways plc v Noble* [2006] EWCA Civ 537, [2006] ICR 1227, [2006] IRLR 533 the Court of Appeal reiterated that pay while on holiday should be the same as pay while at work. The application of this simple principle to various employment situations is not, however, as straightforward as it sounds.

Calculating a Week's Pay

Calculating the amount of holiday pay a worker should receive has become the new area of substantial, sustained litigation under the *Working Time Regulations*, following hot on the heels of the cases discussed above which dealt with the relationship between sickness and annual leave entitlements. In fact, calculation of holiday pay is likely to be far more significant than the holiday/sickness issues as it will potentially affect all workers who currently receive lower holiday pay than their normal pay (because for example when working they work overtime or receive shift premia), not just those few who are on long term sick leave.

The starting point is that under the *Regulations* a week's pay is calculated in accordance with the rules in *ERA 1996, ss 221–224 (reg 16)*. These rules distinguish between workers who have normal working hours and those that do not. The provisions are themselves complex and are discussed in more detail in Redundancy – I (38) and Pay– I (34)).

Where, a worker does not have normal working hours a week's pay is calculated under *ERA 1996, s 224*, by averaging his pay over the last 12 weeks in which he worked.

However, it is important to note that, in certain situations, pay as determined under *ERA 1996, ss 221–224* may not be the same as the actual pay earned by a worker in a typical working week. For example, where an employee does have normal working hours, overtime only qualifies as part of a week's pay where the overtime is fixed under the contract of employment. The effect is that only contractual hours are included when calculating a week's pay and, for example, non-contractual overtime hours are not. This is illustrated by the decision in *Bamsey v Albion Engineering and Manufacturing plc* [2004] EWCA Civ 359, [2004] ICR 1083, [2004] IRLR 457 in which the employee worked significant overtime. However as his contractual hours were only 39 this lower number of weekly hours formed the basis of his entitlement to holiday pay. He argued that this was contrary to the *Working Time Directive* which required workers to be paid during holiday periods at the same or similar level to their normal income when actually at work and that the *Working Time Regulations, reg 16* should be interpreted purposively to ensure that this was achieved. The Court of Appeal rejected this argument and confirmed that non-contractual overtime did not form a part of a week's pay for workers. It also concluded that this interpretation was not contrary to the purpose of the *Directive* which did not require member states to guarantee more pay during a holiday period than a worker was contractually entitled to even if the worker regularly worked periods of non-contractual overtime.

A further impact of the application of the rules in *ERA 1996, ss 221–224* is that commission payments were, in many cases, not taken into account when determining a week's pay: see *Evans v Malley Organisation Ltd* [2002] EWCA Civ 1834, [2003] ICR 432, [2003] IRLR 156. As explained below, *Bamsey v Albion Engineering* and *Evans v Malley* no longer represent the law in relation to calculating holiday pay under the *Regulations*.

The long standing approach to calculating holiday pay in accordance with *ERA 1996, ss 221–224* was thrown into doubt by the ECJ's decision in *Williams v British Airways*: C-155/10, [2011] IRLR 948. In that case, the claimant pilots argued that while on holiday they should receive basic salary plus 2 supplements which they received while working. The first was a flying pay supplement (or 'FPS') which was an additional payment of around £10 per hour spent flying. The second was a time away from base allowance (or 'TAFB') which British Airways regarded as a payment to cover expenses (but which HMRC regarded as overgenerous for this purpose and a portion of which was taxable as remuneration). The ECJ decided that pay during annual leave must be comparable or equivalent to pay normally received when working but that remuneration intended to cover expenses incurred while working need not be paid during annual leave. That strongly suggested that payments such as overtime needed to be included when calculating holiday pay, as overtime is a part of normal remuneration for work done.

The ECJ's decision was considered by the Supreme Court [2012] ICR 1375, [2012] IRLR 1014, which remitted the case to the Employment Tribunal to determine (i) the average value of the FPS over a representative period (as the FPS was clearly part of normal remuneration); and (ii) whether the TAFB was genuinely intended exclusively to cover expenses (in which case it would not be payable during annual leave). Although *Williams* was brought under the *Civil Aviation (Working Time) Regulations 2004*, the ECJ's reasoning applies equally to cases under the *Working Time Regulations* and *Directive*.

Subsequently in *Lock v British Gas Trading Ltd*: C-539/12, [2014] ICR 813, [2014] IRLR 648, the ECJ decided that holiday pay should take into account commission payments (effectively meaning that the Court of Appeal decision in *Evans v Malley Organisation Ltd* was inconsistent with the *Directive*). In *Lock*, as is typical in commission cases, Mr Lock's pay was not affected while he was on holiday because during that period he was paid commission for earlier sales. However his future commission payments were affected as he made no sales during his period of leave. The ECJ, following *British Airways v Williams*, noted that the sales which earned Mr Lock commission were an intrinsic part of the work he performed. Accordingly that commission needed to be taken into account when calculating remuneration in respect of annual leave. In reaching this conclusion the ECJ was influenced by the fact that losing future commission payments as a result of sales not being made during a period of annual leave could deter workers from taking annual leave. Accordingly, following *Lock*, commission that would notionally have been earned during a period of annual leave should be treated as being payment "in respect of" the period of annual leave, and this commission will fall to be paid at a later date. The ECJ went on to state that it was for the national court or Tribunal to determine how to calculate the amount that should be paid in respect of the commission that would have been earned but for annual leave. However, based on comments of Advocate General Bot, it seems likely that one lawful approach would be to calculate the commission payable on sales that would notionally have been made during a period of leave by reference to the average commission over a representative period (such as 12 months).

Following the ECJ decisions in *Williams* and *Lock*, the expected challenge that the *Regulations* did not correctly implement the *Directive* was considered by the EAT in *Bear Scotland Ltd v Fulton* [2015] ICR 221, [2015] IRLR 15. The EAT concluded that:

- The *Directive* required that a worker should receive normal pay during periods of annual leave. Normal pay will need to be determined by considering average remuneration over a reference period determined by each member state (paragraph 44). Remuneration will amount to normal pay where there is an intrinsic or direct link between the remuneration and the tasks which a worker is required to carry out (paragraph 45). This effectively draws the distinction identified in *Williams* between payment for work and payment of expenses.

- Pay for non-guaranteed overtime was part of normal pay and, therefore, the *Directive* required this to be taken into account when calculating holiday pay.

- The *Regulations* could be interpreted to achieve this result by adding words to *reg 16(3)(d)* so that it reads: "(d) as if the references to *sections 227* and *228* did not apply and, in the case of the entitlement under *regulation 13*, *sections 223(3)* and *234* do not apply." The EAT also commented that as long as the *Regulations* are interpreted to implement the *Directive*, it did not matter exactly what words were read into the *Regulations*.

The decision in *Bear Scotland* was followed in March 2015 by the Employment Tribunal decision in *Lock*, reported at [2015] IRLR 438 (following remission from the ECJ). As in *Bear Scotland*, the Employment Tribunal in *Lock* felt able to construe the *Regulations* purposively so that they were compatible with the *Directive*. In doing so, the Tribunal could not simply adopt exactly the same approach as the EAT in *Bear Scotland* (as the words added to *reg 16(3)(d)*) in *Bear Scotland* dealt only with the overtime issues relevant to that case). In order to ensure that commission was taken into account when calculating holiday pay the Tribunal in *Lock* concluded that a new *reg 16(3)(e)* should be added to the *Regulations* which reads: "as if, in the case of the entitlement under *regulation 13*, a worker with normal working hours whose remuneration includes commission or similar payment shall be deemed to have remuneration which varies with the amount of work done for the purpose of *section 221*".

The EAT decision in *Bear Scotland* was not appealed to the Court of Appeal. However the Employment Tribunal decision in *Lock* was appealed to the EAT ([2016] IRLR 316). In that appeal, the EAT held that although *Lock* and *Bear Scotland* concerned commission and overtime respectively, it was not possible to distinguish the cases. Further the EAT held that, while it had been argued that *Bear Scotland* was wrongly decided and should not be followed, the EAT would not depart from its practice that it would normally follow one of its earlier decisions. As the EAT stated at the end of its judgment in *Lock*, "if *Bear Scotland* was wrongly decided, then it must be for the Court of Appeal to say so."

The Court of Appeal in *British Gas v Lock* [2017] ICR 1, [2016] IRLR 946, agreed with the EAT's decisions in that case, and also in *Bear Scotland*, and held that the *Working Time Regulations 1998* can be interpreted compatibly with the *Directive*, with the result that the holiday pay of a worker should include an element referable to the amount of contractual results-based commission the worker normally earned that he would otherwise not earn during his holiday period: as the Court of Appeal explained the *Regulations* must be interpreted on the presumption that the UK Government intended "to fulfil *entirely* the obligations arising under the *Directive*". The Supreme Court has refused permission for British Gas to appeal against this decision. However that is not the end of the matter for two reasons. First, the Court of Appeal expressly stated that its decision was limited to the facts before it: i.e. where Mr Lock had a contractual results based entitlement to commission and the same approach would not necessarily apply to other forms of commission scheme. So there will almost certainly be future cases which consider different forms of commission scheme. Secondly, *Lock* has now returned to the Employment Tribunal so that it can determine the actual financial impact of including commission in Mr Lock's holiday pay (which will also require consideration of the appropriate reference period). The fact that the Court of Appeal, EAT and ET have all felt able to interpret the *Regulations* consistently with the *Directive* means that there is no immediate requirement for the government to revisit how holiday pay is calculated under the *Working Time Regulations*. In addition, a clear principle has now been established by the ECJ, willingly followed and applied by the domestic Courts and Tribunals, that holiday pay should be the same as normal pay for tasks intrinsically or directly linked to work performed.

Nonetheless, a number of uncertainties remain, which will need to be clarified in future decisions or by amendment of the *Regulations*. These areas of uncertainty include:

•   What forms of variable pay should be treated as normal pay? Normal pay clearly includes overtime which the employee was required to perform if offered (*Bear Scotland*) and contractual results based commission (*Lock*). Similarly, in *Patterson v Castlereagh Borough Council* [2015] IRLR 721, the Court of Appeal in Northern Ireland held that, in principle, voluntary overtime could be included when determining holiday pay. However it will be a question of fact for each tribunal to determine whether or not that voluntary overtime was normally carried out by the worker with sufficient permanency to be included in the calculation of holiday pay. It is suggested that, in addition, normal pay would include, shift-premia, unsocial hours payments, acting up payments, most forms of commission and certain types of bonuses. As made clear in the Court of Appeal's decision in *Lock*, this will need to be decided on a case by case basis.

•   As noted above, in *Bear Scotland* and *Lock* the EAT and the Employment Tribunal had to read different words into the *Regulations* to ensure that overtime and commission respectively were included in the calculation of holiday pay. Other types of variable payment may need additional amendments to be read into the *Regulations*. It is far from ideal for Employment Tribunals to have to engage in a constant process of rewriting the *Regulations* in order for them to correctly implement the *Directive*.

•   As both the EAT in *Bear Scotland* and the ET in *Lock* were able to construe the *Regulations* consistently with the Directive, the calculation of a week's pay is still based on the rules in *ERA 1996, ss 221–224* (albeit with some amendments). Accordingly it is suggested that, where it is necessary to calculate a week's pay using a reference period, that period would remain 12 weeks. However some commentators have suggested that the reference period will need to be revisited. While, the Court of Appeal in *Lock* did not address the question of the appropriate reference period, the Employment Tribunal will have to do so at the remitted hearing.

In the circumstances, notwithstanding the clarification provided by the decisions in *Bear Scotland* and *Lock*, the full implications of the ECJ decisions in *Williams* and *Lock* are still in the process of being worked out at a domestic level. What is now clear beyond doubt is

In addition, in *Revenue and Customs v Stringer* [2009] UKHL 31, [2009] ICR 985, [2009] IRLR 677, the House of Lords confirmed that that a claim for holiday pay to which a worker was entitled under the *Regulations* could be brought as a claim for unlawful deduction of wages under *ERA 1996, Part II*. In reaching this conclusion the House of Lords overturned the decision of the Court of Appeal ([2005] ICR 1149, [2005] IRLR 465) who had held that *reg 30* was intended to provide a single and exclusive regime for the enforcement of the statutory rights in the *Regulations*.

The right to bring a claim for unlawful deductions of wages under *ERA 1996, Part II* in relation to holiday pay was significant as *ERA 1996, Part II* provides that the time limit for presenting a claim where there has been a series of deductions of pay is 3 months from the date of the last deduction in the series (see *ERA 1996, s 23(3)*). Accordingly a worker could potentially have brought a claim for a number of failures to permit paid holiday stretching back over a significant period of time (up to 6 years if the *Limitation Act 1980* applied or, if it didn't, all the way back to introduction of the *Regulations* in 1998 – there was no clear answer on this issue). By contrast to unauthorised deductions claims, *reg 30* does not have a provision dealing with a series of failures to pay holiday pay, so a separate claim has to be brought within 3 months of each failure.

There are, however, now two limits on the extent to which a worker is entitled to recover the failure to pay for holidays over a period of time as a "series of deductions". These limits are:

•   In *Bear Scotland Ltd v Fulton* [2015] ICR 221, [2015] IRLR 15 the EAT held that, for there to be a series of deductions, there had to be "a sufficient factual, and a sufficient temporal, link" between the deductions (paragraph 79). Accordingly if there is a gap of 3 months or more between deductions, the passage of time will break the "temporal link" with the result that there is no "series" of deductions and the Tribunal's jurisdiction to consider the earlier deduction or deductions will be extinguished. This interpretation of "series of deductions" was novel, and it potentially greatly reduces the retrospective liability of employers for unpaid holiday pay (or indeed any other unauthorised deductions of pay). The Claimants in these appeals (supported by their trade unions) did not seek to appeal this point to the Court of Appeal. However, given its ramifications, it is almost certain that the Court of Appeal (and possibly the Supreme Court) will be asked to consider this issue in the future.

•   The *Deduction from Wages (Limitation) Regulations 2014 (2014/3322)* amended *ERA 1996, s 23* to provide that a Tribunal can only consider unauthorised deductions claims in relation to holiday pay (and certain other payments including claims for fees, bonuses, commission, or other emoluments referable to employment) where payment fell due within the 2 year period prior to the presentation of the claim. In effect this introduced a two-year cap on recovery of unauthorised deductions from wages. This new rule came into force for any claims presented to the Employment Tribunal on or after 1 July 2015. It has been suggested that this amendment may be either ultra vires (as the *Regulation* amending the *ERA 1996* was made under *European Communities Act 1972, s 2(2)* and it is arguable that these amendments do not arise out of the UK's obligations under European law) and/or that it is unlawful because it undermines the EU law principle of effectiveness.

In addition, as mentioned above, an unlawful deductions claim must be made within 3 months of the last in the series of deduction. Accordingly in a holiday pay claim a Tribunal will need carefully to consider when the last deduction of holiday pay was made. The Employment Tribunal decision in *Khan v Martin McColl* (ET/1702926/09) (22 March 2010, unreported) illustrates the point. Mr Khan had been on long term sick leave. He resigned due to his illness in mid-2009 (at which point he had accrued but not taken leave from 2008 and 2009). The employer paid him in respect of his accrued but untaken leave for 2009. He brought a claim for payment of his untaken leave from 2008. The Tribunal held that Mr Khan's claim for unlawful deductions from wages in respect of the 2008 leave was out of time. As the employer had paid Mr Khan his 2009 holiday entitlement on termination of employment, the last of the series of deductions was prior to the start of 2009. This issue has not yet been tested on appeal. However it is suggested that the argument that the last deduction was made on 31 December 2008 is questionable, given that under the *Regulations* payment in lieu of annual leave may only be made on the termination of employment. On that basis, the date for the payment of Mr Khan's leave which he could not take in 2008 due to illness (and which therefore could have been carried over to 2009) was the date his employment ended, rather than 31 December 2008.

A further issue arises in relation to whether unauthorised deductions claims can only be made where a worker has taken holiday and not been properly paid for it or whether such claims can also be made where a worker is not permitted to take holiday at all. The House of Lords in *Stringer* plainly envisaged that a worker could bring an unlawful deduction of wages claim in the former category – ie if the worker had taken holiday but not been paid for it. However it is less clear whether such a claim should be available where the employer refuses to permit a worker to take paid holiday and the worker decides to work rather than take the holiday in order to avoid a loss of earnings. In such a case, as the worker has continued to attend work and be paid for doing so, he will earn the same as normal and there would be no deduction from wages. Instead the loss suffered by the worker would be the loss of the health, relaxation and other benefits associated with taking a period of annual leave. The *Regulations* recognise the distinction between these two scenarios and in the latter a Tribunal is entitled to award just and equitable compensation (see *regs 30(1)(a)* and *30(4)* of the *Regulations*). Where, however, a worker is not paid for holiday which is actually taken, the *Regulations* provide that the compensation must be the amount of money which ought to have been paid to the worker during the period of leave (see *regs 30(1)(b)* and *30(5)*).

Despite this distinction, in *Canada Life Ltd v Gray* [2004] ICR 673 the EAT concluded that a worker could bring an unlawful deductions claim in respect of his or her annual leave entitlement regardless of whether or not the leave had actually been taken, and that the series of deductions could extend back into previous leave years. More recently in *Fraser v Southwest London St George's Mental Health Trust* [2012] ICR 403 the EAT took a different approach and suggested that a worker could not recover unpaid holiday as a deduction from wages where he or she had not actually taken the leave in question. A similar analysis was also adopted by the EAT in *Sash Window Workshop Ltd v King* [2015] IRLR 348: at paragraphs 37 and 38 the EAT noted that it was not obvious that an unauthorised deductions claim could be made in relation to a complaint based on refusal to permit a worker to take annual leave as the worker would have been paid his wages for the periods he worked which he would otherwise have taken as annual leave, and what had been lost was the health and welfare benefits of taking annual leave, not wages. It is suggested that the EAT's conclusions in *Fraser* and *Sash Window Workshop* on this issue were correct.

In addition to claims based on entitlements to annual leave under the *Regulations*, a worker may also be entitled to bring a claim for unlawful deduction of wages or breach of contract on the basis that, under his contract of employment, he was entitled to holiday pay or payment in lieu of accrued but untaken holiday. This will depend on the interpretation of the contract of employment and is discussed at paragraph **29.9** below.

29.7 Civil aviation, shipping and agricultural workers

Statutory leave entitlements for crew members employed in civil aviation are governed by the *Civil Aviation (Working Time) Regulations 2004* which implement the *Aviation Working Time Directive (2000/79/EC)*.

Regulation 4 provides that 'a crew member is entitled to paid annual leave of at least four weeks, or a proportion of four weeks in respect of a period of employment of less than one year'. As with the *Working Time Regulations*, this leave may be taken in instalments and may not be replaced by a payment in lieu, except where the crew member's employment is terminated, and the right is enforceable through a claim to the Employment Tribunals.

However the *Civil Aviation (Working Time) Regulations 2004* do not contain any of the detailed mechanisms in the *Working Time Regulations* for determining when annual leave may be taken and the rate of pay during leave. They also have different provisions in relation to remedies.

These lacunae have been the source of a number of claims, most notably, *Williams v British Airways plc*: C-155/10 [2011] IRLR 948 (ECJ) and [2012] ICR 1375; [2012] IRLR 1014 (Supreme Court) (referred to in **29.4A** above) which concerned a claim by pilots who only received basic pay when they took annual leave despite the fact that when they were actually working they had a contractual entitlement to additional remuneration in the form of 2 supplements. The issue was what payment the pilots should receive during annual leave given that the *Civil Aviation (Working Time) Regulations 2004* did not make any provision for how pay should be calculated (unlike the *Working Time Regulations 1998* which expressly refer to *ERA 1996, ss 221–224*). The ECJ concluded that during annual leave workers must receive comparable or equivalent pay to what they receive when actually working, but that this did not include payments to cover expenses.

A further consequence of the lack of detailed provisions for calculating pay in the *Civil Aviation (Working Time) Regulations 2004* is that there is no definition of the period over which average or normal pay should be calculated (under the *ERA 1996*, the reference period is 12 weeks). However the Supreme Court in *Williams* gave guidance that in cases under these *Regulations* the relevant reference period could be determined by the employer (and/or included a relevant agreement) provided that it was representative. Failing that, the Employment Tribunal should determine the length of the representative reference period so that the level of "normal" remuneration to be paid during annual leave could be calculated.

Specific regulations have also been made for certain other industries: see the *Fishing Vessels (Working Time: Sea-fishermen) Regulations 2004 (SI 2004/1713);* the *Merchant Shipping (Working Time: Inland Waterways) Regulations 2003 (SI 2003/3049)*; and the *Merchant Shipping (Hours of Work) Regulations 2002 (SI 2002/2125).* In relation to agricultural workers, historically their holiday entitlements were set by the *Agricultural Wages Board* under the *Agricultural Wages Act 1948, s 3*, as substituted by *EPA 1975, s 97(1), Sch 9 Pt 1.* However the Agricultural Wages Board was abolished in 2013 pursuant to the provisions of the *Enterprise and Regulatory Reform Act 2013.* Currently there are different provisions governing holiday entitlements for agricultural workers in each of England, Wales, Scotland and Northern Ireland.

29.8   CONTRACT

The *Working Time Regulations 1998* lay down a minimum paid annual holiday entitlement. The contract of employment may, however, make more generous provision than provided for by the *Regulations*. In such circumstances, the contract will determine the employee's rights in respect of that more generous provision. Authorities on the common law on employee's rights to holidays which were decided before the *Regulations* came into force must now be read subject to those *Regulations*.

Particulars of holiday entitlement are among those the employer is obliged by the *Employment Rights Act 1996, s 1(4)(d)(i)* to supply in writing to the employee (see **8.7(g)** CONTRACT OF EMPLOYMENT). In the absence of express provisions, certain terms relating to holidays have been implied by the courts.

29.8 Holidays

It is thought likely that in most industries, in the absence of express provision, it will be held to be an implied term of the contract of employment that bank holidays may be taken as paid holiday: see *Tucker v British Leyland Motor Corpn Ltd* [1978] IRLR 493 at 496, in which a County Court judge decided that ' . . . if no express contractual provision or regular usage to the contrary is established an hourly paid employee is entitled to a day's holiday on recognised public holidays without fear of dismissal as an absentee; and that if he is entitled to a guaranteed minimum weekly wage he is entitled to be paid for that day without having to work additional hours in that week.'

It was held in *Hurt v Sheffield Corpn* (1916) 85 LJKB 1684, that the right to a holiday accrued only at the end of the year in the absence of any express provision to the contrary. Although this does not accord with the normal modern practice, the Court of Appeal in *Morley v Heritage plc* [1993] IRLR 400 declined to disapprove the decision in *Hurt*.

In *Morley*, it was held that there was no implied term in the contract that the employee should be paid for accrued but untaken leave when he left part-way through the year. However, in an appropriate case it might be possible to imply such a term as a matter of custom and practice. The decision of the EAT in *Janes Solicitors v Lamb-Simpson* (1996) 541 IRLB 15 suggests that in the case of an oral contract where there is nothing in writing, there is a wide area over which terms could be implied on the basis of business efficacy, including one as to accrued holiday pay. In addition, in *Wang v Beijing Ton Ren Tang (UK) Ltd* (UKEAT/0024/09/DA) [2010] All ER (D) 84 (Jan), the EAT held that a provision in a worker's contract that, on the termination of her employment, the worker could recover pay in lieu of all untaken holiday (i.e. not just untaken holiday from the final leave year) was valid and not contrary to the *Regulations* (which, as explained above, prohibit in most cases the carrying over of leave from one year to the next), Accordingly, where a worker's contact includes such a term, and the worker has untaken leave from a number of leave years, he or she should claim under the contract rather than the *Regulations*. However, in the absence of any term on the payment of accrued but untaken leave, a claim could be brought under the *Regulations* in respect of untaken leave in the last leave year (see **29.4** above).

The contract may also provide that the employer is entitled, on the termination of employment, to claw back payment for holidays taken by the worker but not accrued. However in the absence of an express provision of the contract of employment, no term can be implied which would allow such a claw back: see *Hill v Chapell* [2003] IRLR 19, EAT. Not only would a deduction in the absence of express agreement be contrary to the *Regulations*, it could also be an unlawful deduction from wages under *section 13* of the *Employment Rights Act 1996*, and a breach of contract.

Where there is a contractual entitlement to pay due under the contract for accrued but untaken holiday the contract may also make express provision as to how that entitlement is calculated. In the absence of such provision, there is inconsistent EAT authority as to how the rate of a day's pay should be calculated where the worker is paid an annual salary. The two approaches adopted have been to divide annual salary by 365 or to divide it by the actual number of working days. Obviously the former calculation will mean that the worker is entitled to lower payment for each untaken day of accrued holiday. In *Thames Water Utilities v Reynolds* [1996] IRLR 186 the EAT concluded that the *Apportionment Act 1870* applied with the result that a day's pay was to be calculated by dividing annual salary by 365. In *Taylor v East Midlands Offender Employment Consortium* [2000] IRLR 760 the EAT accepted that the *Apportionment Act* did apply in calculating a day's pay. However on the facts of the case, the pay for the employee's 10 days accrued but untaken holiday were 'grossed up' to 14 days pay to take account of weekends necessarily included in the 10-day holiday period. Thus the EAT found a way to mitigate the apparent harshness of the decision in *Thames Water*.

Subsequently (at a preliminary hearing) in *Leisure Leagues UK Ltd v Maconnachie* [2002] IRLR 600 the EAT concluded that the approach in *Thames Water* was wrong for two reasons. First, the approach was at odds with the virtually universal practice in industry in respect of the calculation of holiday pay in respect of holiday entitlement which is by reference to a day's work rather than calendar days per year. Second, *Thames Water* predated the *Working Time Regulations*. The issue was resolved by *Yarrow v Edwards Chartered Accountants* [2007] All ER (D) 118 (Aug), in which HHJ Peter Clarke (who had also sat on *Thames Water*) declined to follow his own decision in *Thames Water* and, instead, applied *Maconnachie*. His reasons for doing so were that: (i) judicial comity required him to follow the more recent decision, and (ii) in any event the advent of the *Regulations* required a different approach than that which had been adopted in *Thames Water*.

30   Human Rights

30.1   INTRODUCTION

The employment relationship may give rise to issues involving human rights law. At the individual level, human rights law may give an employee important protection against acts of discrimination or protect the employee's privacy or right to a fair hearing. Similarly, in relation to collective labour relations, human rights law is relevant to the right of members of a trade union to associate, to join a trade union of their choice and to take part in industrial action.

From 2 October 2000, with the coming into force of the *Human Rights Act 1998*, the domestic courts have been required to interpret United Kingdom law in accordance with the provisions of the European Convention on Human Rights and Fundamental Freedoms ('the Convention'). Prior to the *Act* coming into force, the Convention did not form part of the domestic law of the UK but was an international obligation which could, in appropriate cases, be used as an aid to the interpretation of unclear UK statutory provisions. An aggrieved individual seeking to rely upon the Convention was required to seek to present a case to the European Court of Human Rights for the determination of that court. This process could be expensive and very slow. Whilst the right of petition to the European Court remains as the final source of determination and jurisprudence on Convention Rights, issues of Convention rights may now be determined directly in the UK domestic courts.

This chapter presents an overview of the Convention and the historical development of the rights most relevant to the employment relationship, identifying some of the key decisions of the European Court of Human Rights and instances where Convention principles have assisted the UK courts in interpreting statutory provisions. The chapter goes on to consider, in outline, the key provisions of the *Human Rights Act* and its application and recent UK decisions in the employment sphere raising issues under the *Act*.

30.2   THE CONVENTION

Effect of the Convention

The European Convention on Human Rights and Fundamental Freedoms is an international treaty which was drawn up in 1950 and came into force in 1953. The Convention sets out in broad terms a number of fundamental rights and freedoms. It also established the European Commission of Human Rights and the European Court of Human Rights, both based in Strasbourg. It should be emphasised that the Convention and its institutions are entirely separate from the law and institutions of the European Community. The subscribing states are the members of the Council of Europe. Also, unlike European Community Law, the provisions of the Convention are not part of domestic law; they only bind the Government. The main text of the Convention, which has been amended by several protocols, can be found in Command Paper *Cmd 8969* (1953), published by the Stationery Office.

If a state which is a party to the Convention interferes with or abrogates any of the rights or freedoms enshrined in the Convention, a complaint may be made by any other party state. More importantly, the Convention allows for a right of direct complaint by an *individual* affected by an alleged breach of the Convention (such an individual right of complaint is very rare in international law). The Government of the United Kingdom ratified the Convention in 1950. However, it was not until 1966 that the UK Government recognised the jurisdiction of the European Court of Human Rights and accepted the right of an individual in the UK to petition the court.

30.3 Human Rights

30.3 Procedure for petition by an individual

In outline the procedure is as follows. The aggrieved individual must pursue every remedy available under UK law. When he has exhausted these 'domestic' remedies, without having his complaint satisfactorily resolved, he may present his petition to the European Commission of Human Rights. The Commission investigates the complaint. If it decides that there is, or may be, a breach of the Convention and that the complaint is admissible, it will endeavour to obtain a settlement between the parties. If no settlement is reached, the Commission will refer the case, together with its report, to the European Court of Human Rights. The court will then proceed to decide on the complaint.

UK legal aid is not available for petition, but limited legal aid is available from the Council of Europe. ECHR cases are now also among the limited categories of litigation in which English lawyers are now permitted to work on a conditional fee basis.

30.4 KEY DECISIONS OF THE ECHR ON FREEDOM OF ASSOCIATION, THE RIGHT TO PRIVATE LIFE AND OTHER RELEVANT PROVISIONS

One of the most significant cases concerning UK collective employment law to reach the European Court of Human Rights was the British Rail closed shop case, *Young, James and Webster v United Kingdom* [1981] IRLR 408, [1983] IRLR 35.

Article 11 of the Convention provides:

'1.   Everyone has the right to . . . freedom of association with others, including the right to form and to join trade unions for the protection of his interests.

2.   No restrictions shall be placed on the exercise of these rights . . . [certain exceptions permitted].'

In the *Young, James and Webster* case, the court held that the requirement on the applicants to join one of the unions specified in the closed shop agreement between British Rail and the railway unions, in circumstances where there had been no such requirement at the time when they were engaged, amounted to a restriction on the freedom guaranteed by *art 11* because the alternative to their joining was that they would lose their jobs ([1981] IRLR 408 at 409). The court made substantial monetary awards to the applicants.

The decision left the general question of the consistency of closed shop agreements with *art 11* unclear. Now that the right of individuals not to join a specified trade union has been entrenched and the pre-entry closed shop has been outlawed (see TRADE UNIONS – I (50)), it has become less important to resolve that issue. However, in *Sibson v United Kingdom* (1993) 17 EHRR 193, the court held that there was no breach of *art 11* where the complainant had no objection based on conviction to being a member of the union concerned, and where non-membership would not lead to dismissal (but rather to a move to another depot at which he could be required to work under his contract); contrast *Sigurjonsson v Iceland* (1993) 16 EHRR 462.

In a further important decision of collective employment rights (*Wilson and NUJ v United Kingdom*; *Palmer, Wyeth and RMT v United Kingdom*; *Doolan v United Kingdom* [2002] IRLR 568) the ECHR ruled that the UK was in breach of the right of freedom of association under *art 11* by permitting employers to use financial incentives to persuade employees to surrender trade union rights (see *TULRCA 1992, s 146(1)(a)*). This is the first case in which the ECHR has upheld a claim relating to trade union rights under *art 11*. (For example, in the past, a complaint by workers at GCHQ that they were not permitted to belong to trade unions was not referred to the court by the Commission, which accepted the Government's argument based upon national security.) The *Wilson* decision prompted the introduction of *s 29* of the *Employment Relations Act 2004* which introduced new sections into *TULRCA 1992* conferring a right upon workers not to have an offer made by the employer for the purpose of inducing the worker not to be a member of a union or to take part in the activities of the union.

30.6   HUMAN RIGHTS ACT 1998

The *Human Rights Act 1998* (which received the Royal Assent on 9 November 1998) came into force on 2 October 2000 and is a radical reform of the status of the Convention in domestic law. The *Act* requires that the courts interpret United Kingdom law in accordance with the Convention. *Section 1* of the *HRA 1998* lists those articles of the Convention to which the *Act* is to apply and those articles are set out as *Sch 1* to the *Act*. By *HRA 1998, s 2* a court or tribunal determining a question in connection with a Convention right must take into account relevant judgments, decisions, declarations and opinions made or given by the Commission and Court of Human Rights and the Committee of Ministers of the Council of Europe. Primary and subordinate legislation are to be read, wherever possible, as being compatible with Convention rights but are not rendered void if incompatible (*HRA 1998, s 3*). Certain courts will be given the power to make a declaration of incompatibility when satisfied that the provision of primary legislation is incompatible with a Convention right (*HRA 1998, s 4*). This power does not, however, extend to an employment tribunal or the EAT. Accordingly, a detailed consideration of the *Act* is beyond the scope of this work.

The effect of the *Act*, as more cases are brought in domestic law relying upon Convention rights, is likely to be considerable in many fields; not least employment law, where *art 6* (the right to a fair hearing), *art 8* (the right to respect for private and family life), and also *arts 10, 11* and *14* (considered in **30.4** above) are likely to be of the greatest importance. The *Act* makes it unlawful for a 'public authority' to act in contravention of the Convention (*HRA 1998, s 6*). Those aggrieved will be able to bring proceedings against the authority in question (*HRA 1998, s 7*). The definition of 'public authority' is broad and includes any body whose function is of a public nature (*HRA 1998, s 6(3)*) and includes, expressly, courts and tribunals. The definition would appear to be sufficiently broad to apply to, for example, privatised public utilities.

The *Act* provides for remedies including an award of damages analogous to the principles applied by the European Court of Human Rights in relation to compensation (*HRA 1998, s 8*). Ministers of the Crown are given the power to amend offending legislation following a declaration of incompatibility (*HRA 1998, s 10*). Finally, in relation to any new legislation, a Minister of the Crown is required in either House prior to the second reading of the Bill to make a statement that the provisions of the Bill are compatible with the Convention rights or to state that, despite incompatibility, the Government wishes the House to proceed with the Bill in any event (*HRA 1998, s 19*).

30.7   THE APPLICATION OF THE HUMAN RIGHTS ACT 1998 IN EMPLOYMENT CASES

A number of cases have arisen in employment law raising issues under the *Human Rights Act 1998* particularly in relation to the right to a fair hearing (*art 6*) and the right to private and family life (*art 8*). The paragraphs below provide illustrations. As a point of procedure, it is to be observed that the Court of Appeal has sought to discourage a perceived tendency for Employment Tribunals to treat EC and human rights issues as appropriate for determination as preliminary issues (see *Barracks v Coles (Secretary of State for the Home Department intervening)* [2006] EWCA Civ 1041, [2007] ICR 60). In the light of this, it is likely that such arguments will have to be raised as part of the full hearing of the claim rather than at a preliminary point.

(a) Article 6

Article 6 provides for "a fair and public hearing within a reasonable time by an independent and impartial tribunal". Its application has been considered in a variety of employment related contexts with the issue of its application to disciplinary proceedings in particular generating a substantial body of law. In summary the majority of internal disciplinary proceedings will not engage *art 6* if the employee has the right to bring proceedings in the employment tribunal in satisfaction of the requirements of *art 6*.

A-G v Wheen [2001] IRLR 91 concerned *s 33* of the *Employment Tribunals Act 1996* which permitted the Attorney General to make a restriction of proceedings order against a litigant barring him from bringing further proceedings without the leave of the EAT on the grounds of vexatious institution of proceedings. The Court of Appeal held that *s 33* did not conflict with the right to a fair hearing under *art 6(1)* of the *Convention*. The Court of Appeal stated that the right under *art 6(1)* was not an absolute right but was to be balanced between the rights of the citizen to use the courts and the rights of others (and the court) to avoid wholly unmeritorious claims. Further, the order made *did* provide for access to the Employment Tribunal system but required permission first. As access was not prohibited, but was provided on terms, there could be no breach of *art 6(1)*.

In *Tehrani v United Kingdom Central Council for Nursing, Midwifery and Health Visiting* [2001] IRLR 208, 2001 SLT 879, the issue was to what extent *art 6* of the *Convention* (namely, the entitlement 'to a fair and reasonable public hearing within a reasonable time by an independent and impartial tribunal established by law') applied to disciplinary proceedings other than in a court of law. Whilst *art 6* may not apply to purely internal disciplinary inquiries, it was held in *Tehrani* that, when disciplinary proceedings determine the right to practice a profession, *art 6* may apply, as the decision of the Council's Professional Conduct Committee fell within a 'determination' of 'civil rights and obligations' for the purposes of *art 6*. It followed that there was an entitlement to a hearing before an independent and impartial tribunal. However, the Court of Session held that a professional disciplinary tribunal was not required to meet all the requirements of an independent and impartial tribunal if the disciplinary procedures provided for a right of appeal to a court of law. The Court of Session, following a review of relevant authorities, concluded that the case law of the ECHR established that there was no breach of the Convention if the disciplinary tribunal is subject to the control of a court of full jurisdiction, which court complies with the requirements of *art 6(1)*. This case raises important questions in relation to professional disciplinary bodies which do not have a statutory right of appeal to a court. If the disciplinary body is not sufficiently independent or important to satisfy *art 6(1)*, it is not clear whether a right to present subsequent complaints in an Employment Tribunal will be sufficiently akin to a statutory right of appeal to satisfy the exception recognised in the jurisprudence of the ECHR.

In *Kulkarni v Milton Keynes Hospital NHS Trust* [2009] IRLR 829 the Court of Appeal held, in the context of a doctor facing serious disciplinary charges, that the doctor was entitled to be represented by a lawyer instructed by Medical Protection Society. The facts of the case were unusual in that there was an express contractual term permitting representation by various persons, including a legally qualified person who "will not be representing the practitioner formally in a legal capacity". Holding the words quoted above to be devoid of meaning the court of Appeal concluded that the doctor was entitled contractually to be represented by a lawyer instructed by the MPS. Of broader significance, it appeared, were Lady Justice Smith's (*obiter*) observations on *art 6*. Whilst *art 6* would not be engaged in ordinary disciplinary proceedings, where the effect of the disciplinary proceedings could deprive the employee of the right to practice his or her profession *art 6* could, in Smith LJ's view, be engaged conferring the right to legal representation. Thus where the outcome could be effectively barring from employment in the NHS the right would be engaged. This reasoning if correct would, *prima facie*, be applicable to a large number of occupations where a decision to dismiss by an employer would have the effect of freezing the employee out of employment in his chosen field. See, however, the discussion of *Mattu v University Hospitals of Coventry and Warwickshire NHS Trust* [2012] EWCA Civ 641 below.

The scope of application of *Kulkarni* was, in practice, very limited (and see, in *R (on the application of Kirk) v Middlesbrough Borough Council* [2010] IRLR 699, a case involving a disciplinary hearing in relation to a social worker, *art 6* was held not to be engaged).

Similarly, in *Hameed v Central Manchester University Hospital NHS Foundation Trust* [2010] EWHC 2009 (QB) the High Court held that *Kulkarni* (above) was exceptional and that each case must be considered on its own facts in the light of the gravity of the charge, the likelihood of dismissal and the individual's chance of practising their profession in the future if dismissed. On the facts this was not a case where the practising of the profession would be lost. Accordingly, there was no right to rely upon *art 6* in relation to the disciplinary process. Leave to appeal on the *art 6* point was, however, granted.

In an important decision, *R (on the application of G) v Governors of X School* [2011] IRLR 766, the Supreme Court effectively limited the expansion of the *Kulkarni* principle. The case involved disciplinary proceedings against a teacher accused of misconduct. If the charges were upheld there was an obligation to report the findings to the Independent Safeguarding Authority ("ISA") (see Employee's Past Criminal Convictions 17.8) for consideration whether the teacher was to be included on the list of persons considered to be unsuitable to work with children. The decision was to be taken by the ISA but the outcome of the disciplinary process would have a significant influence or effect on the ISA's decision. On this basis the Court of Appeal concluded that *art 6* was engaged so as to entitle the teacher to legal representation. This was overturned by the Supreme Court which did not consider that there was a sufficient connection between the disciplinary proceedings and the ISA proceedings for *art 6* to apply at the disciplinary hearing concluding that the ISA would exercise its independent judgment on the issue of barring. Although the case appears restrictive of further development in this area it is important to note that the reasoning in *Kulkarni* was not expressly disapproved and was explained as involving circumstances where the employer's disciplinary process would be determinative of the employee's right to work in his chosen profession.

A number of further cases have considered the extent to which the composition of a disciplinary panel can be challenged relying upon art 6 and the right to an independent and impartial tribunal established by law. Applying the same principles as articulated in *Kulkarni*, reliance on *art 6* on this basis has proved unsuccessful. See *R (on the application of Puri) v Bradford Teaching Hospitals NHS Foundation Trust* [2011] IRLR 582; *Hameed v Central Manchester University Hospital NHS Foundation Trust* [2010] EWHC 2009 (QB) (above).

The most recent example is *Mattu v University Hospitals of Coventry and Warwickshire NHS Trust* [2012] IRLR 661 in which the Court of Appeal concluded that an NHS trust's disciplinary decision to dismiss an employee under his contract of employment did not determine any civil right of his within the meaning of *Art 6*. The case is particularly significant in that the majority of the Court of Appeal expressly disapproved Smith LJ's *obiter dicta* in *Kulkarni* (above) that *art 6* could be engaged where the effect of upholding the disciplinary charges would, effectively or in practice, bar the practitioner from practising his chosen profession in the future. The Court of Appeal held that a contractual decision to dismiss did not determine civil rights and obligations (which could only be determined by public or professional bodies; compare *Tehrani* above) even if the practical effect of that contractual decision was to "freeze-out" the employee from his chosen employment. *Article 6* would only be engaged at the stage of determination of the question of whether the dismissal was in breach of contract or unfair (ie at the judicial determination stage). Leave to appeal to the Supreme Court in *Mattu* has been refused. Accordingly, it is now clear that the "*Kulkarni* principle" of the potential application of *art 6* in disciplinary decisions simply has no application to contractual disciplinary decisions by employers (which are, of course, the vast majority of cases).

In the context of disciplinary procedure, *R (on the application of Bonhoeffer) v General Medical Council* [2011] EWHC 1585 (Admin), High Court is significant in that the Court concluded, drawing upon *art 6* jurisprudence, that a professional conduct body erred in law in admitting hearsay evidence in relation to serious allegations of child abuse. The Court concluded that the more serious the allegation, the more important it was to ensure that the accused be afforded fair and proper procedural safeguards. This is a potentially important development and it remains to be seen how broadly it may be applied in other disciplinary proceedings involving serious allegations of wrongdoing.

As to the Employment Tribunal system itself and *art 6(1)*, it had been suggested in *Smith v Secretary of State for Trade and Industry* [2000] IRLR 6 that the Employment Tribunals may not be independent when determining matters on redundancy payments from the DTI as the DTI appointed lay members of the tribunals. The case was not appealed. In *Scanfuture UK Ltd v Secretary of State for Trade and Industry* [2001] IRLR 416, the EAT revisited the question of whether the mechanism of appointment of lay members to the Employment Tribunal breached *art 6(1)* of the *Convention*. It is significant to note that the procedures for the appointment of lay members have changed since the procedures which were in place in 1999 (the time of the Employment Tribunal decision in *Scanfuture*). The EAT found that the new procedures complied with the ECHR. As to the position in 1999, the EAT concluded that the procedures for the appointment of lay members breached *art 6(1)* of the *Convention*. The application of *art 6* has also led to successful appeals against decisions of the employment tribunal which have been issued after a lengthy period of delay. See also the consideration of *art 6* in the context of allegations of bias in relation to an employment tribunal in *Jones v DAS Legal Expenses Insurance Co Ltd* [2003] EWCA Civ 1071, [2004] IRLR 218. In *Kwamin v Abbey National plc* [2004] IRLR 516 the EAT emphasised that it is a fundamental principle of natural justice that a fair trial includes the absence of excessive or avoidable delay by the tribunal and that the same principle is enshrined in the right to a fair trial within a reasonable period in *art 6*. In *Kwamin* the decisions under appeal had been delivered 7.5, 12 and 14.5 months after the end of the hearings respectively. The EAT gave guidance that, whilst it remained for an appellant to show that the result was unfair as a consequence of delay, employment tribunal decisions must be delivered within 3.5 months (after which there would, in the view of the EAT be 'culpable delay'). The issue of whether *arts 6* and *8* may require certain tribunal hearings to be conducted in private (beyond the categories of cases for which statutory provision for the tribunal sitting in private is already made) has been raised in *XXX v YYY*. The EAT had held that *arts 6* and *8* required the tribunal to sit in private. On appeal (*XXX v YYY* [2004] EWCA Civ 231, [2004] IRLR 471) the Court of Appeal reached its decision on different grounds relating to relevance of the evidence in issue. Accordingly the *art 6* and *8* points on the need for a tribunal to sit in private (outside the existing categories of claims) remain undecided at Court of Appeal level.

In *Home Office v Tariq* [2011] UKSC 35 the Supreme Court considered whether the use of closed proceedings in an employment law context was compatible with *art 6*. The claimant, an immigration officer, brought claims of race and religious discrimination following his suspension because of national security concerns. The employment tribunal adopted the closed material procedure in the interests of national security under *rule 54(2)* of *Schedule 1* of the *ET Rules* and the claimant contended that the procedure was contrary to art 6. The Supreme Court concluded that he closed material procedure did not violate *art 6* and was necessary on grounds of national security. Further there was no absolute requirement that the claimant see the allegations against him in order to challenge them. *Art 6* did not prescribe a uniform approach to all cases and the character of the proceedings (eg a civil claim as opposed to criminal charges) and the circumstances of a particular case can justify derogating from the right to see the allegations in issue. *Rule 49* of the *Employment Tribunal Rules of Procedure* (permitting anonymity orders) was considered in *A v B* [2010] IRLR 844 and the EAT concluded that it also had the power to anonymise a judgment if the loss of a claimant's anonymity would involve a breach of his *art 8* rights. See also *B and C v A* [2010] IRLR 400.

In *R v Securities and Futures Authority, ex p Fleurose* [2002] IRLR 297 the Court of Appeal held, in relation to disciplinary proceedings of the SFA (which could result in a fine and/or suspension), that such proceedings were not a criminal charge or offence for the purposes of *art 6* of the Convention. Nevertheless, the SFA were required to prove the allegations, to permit the accused to prepare a defence in the knowledge of the 'charges' and to allow a proper opportunity to give evidence and call evidence and to question witnesses giving evidence in support of the allegations.

In *R (on the application of Wright) v Secretary of State for Health* [2009] UKHL 3, [2009] 2 All ER 129 a declaration of incompatibility with the HRA was issued in relation to *Part VII* of the *Care Standards Act 2000*. That *Act*, for the purposes of protection vulnerable persons, made provision for a list to be kept of persons considered unsuitable to work with vulnerable adults. The *Act* also provided for workers to be placed provisionally on the list where concerns arose about their conduct pending final determination in relation to their conduct. The Court held these provisions, for provisional listing without the right to be heard, to be incompatible with the workers' right to a fair hearing under *art 6* of the Convention and also the right to respect for private and family life under *art 8*. The House of Lords subsequently confirmed on appeal that these so called POVA and POCA lists were indeed incompatible with *art 6* (see *R (on the application of Wright) v Secretary of State for Health* [2009] UKHL 3, [2009] 2 All ER 129). The POCA and POVA lists are to be replaced by new provisions under the *Safeguarding Vulnerable Groups Act 2006* but their Lordships in *Wright* ventured no opinions as to whether the new system would be less vulnerable to challenge under *art 6* than the old.

In *Dispatch Management Services (UK) Ltd v Douglas* [2002] IRLR 389, the EAT considered the situation where an application was made to remove representatives in Employment Tribunal proceedings on the grounds of conflict of interest. The Court of Appeal in *Bache v Essex County Council* [2000] IRLR 251 had held that there was no power in an Employment Tribunal to interfere with a party's choice of representative. In *Douglas*, the EAT held that this principle of non-interference was not inconsistent with the right to a fair hearing under *art 6* of the Convention.

In *Whittaker v Watson (P & D) (t/a P & M Watson Haulage)* [2002] ICR 1244, 67 BMLR 28 the EAT confirmed that it was not a 'court' for the purposes of hearing a submission that domestic legislation was incompatible with Convention rights. Referring to the definition of 'court' in *s 4(5)* of the *Human Rights Act 1998*, the EAT held that the conclusion was clear but puzzling (not least when the EAT was composed of a High Court judge sitting with lay members) and was, perhaps, a result which had not been intended in the drafting of the legislation.

On the issue of adjournment of hearings, the Court of Appeal held in *Teinaz v Wandsworth London Borough Council* [2002] EWCA Civ 1040, [2002] IRLR 721 that, in order to comply with the right to a fair trial under *art 6*, a litigant whose presence is needed for the fair trial of a case and who is unable to attend through no fault of his own will usually have to be granted an adjournment regardless of the inconvenience of such adjournment to the court or other parties (see also *Andreou v Lord Chancellor's Department* [2002] EWCA Civ 1192, [2002] IRLR 728). The practice of part-time EAT judges appearing as counsel before lay members of the EAT with whom they had previously sat in a judicial capacity and the compatibility of that practice with *art 6* reached the House of Lords in *Lawal v Northern Spirit Ltd* [2003] UKHL 35, [2003] IRLR 538. Overturning the decision of the Court of Appeal (which had upheld the decision of the EAT), the House of Lords held that such a practice tended to undermine confidence in the judicial system and ought to be discontinued. In determining whether there is bias in terms of the right to a hearing before an impartial tribunal under *art 6(1)* or the common law test of bias, the principle to be applied was that stated by the House of Lords in *Porter v Magill* [2001] UKHL 67, [2002] 2 AC 357 namely whether a fair minded and informed observer, having considered the given facts, would conclude that there was a real possibility that the tribunal was biased. The key to this test is public perception of the possibility of unconscious bias. On apparent bias of tribunal members and *art 6* see *City and County of Swansea v Honey* UKEAT/0465/09.

The principle that illegal contracts will not be enforced by the Courts was the subject of an *art 6* challenge in *Soteriou v Ultrachem Ltd* [2004] EWHC 983 (QB), [2004] IRLR 870. A claim of wrongful dismissal was struck out by reason of illegality. The Claimant contended that this contravened the right to a fair hearing and also that the strike out was contrary to *art 1* of the *First Protocol* to the *Convention*. These arguments were rejected. The Court held that *art 6* was not breached as the issue of illegality was part of the substantive law of contract and not a mere procedural bar and that, in any event, the strike out would have been legitimate under *art 6(2)*. As to the claim based upon the *First Protocol* right (in relation to 'possessions'), it was held that, although a claim of breach of contract could indeed be a 'possession', there was no deprivation of a possession here as the contract was unenforceable (on the grounds of illegality) and therefore conferred no 'possession' which the claimant could complain that he was deprived and that the claimant had had his case considered substantively as part of the strike out application.

(b) Article 8

In relation to the right to private life, in the context of employment litigation, this right must be balanced with the right of the parties to have a fair trial of the issues between them. In *De Keyser Ltd v Wilson* [2001] IRLR 324, the EAT considered the *art 8* right to respect for private and family life in the context of an unfair dismissal claim in which the applicant alleged she suffered from a depressive illness caused by stress at work. In the course of the proceedings, the applicant agreed to be seen by the employer's medical expert and a letter of instruction was drafted on behalf of the employer to the expert which letter included certain details of the applicant's private life. The employment tribunal struck out the employer's notice of appearance on the basis that the employer's conduct of the proceedings was scandalous and in breach of the applicant's Convention right to privacy. Allowing the employer's appeal, the EAT held that there was no breach of *art 8* and that in relation to the need, in the context of the case, for a medical examination, the right to privacy was qualified as far as necessary by the right of both parties to have a just trial of the issues between them. In judicial review proceedings, the provisions of the *Employment Equality (Sexual Orientation) Regulations 2003* were found to be compatible with the convention rights in *art 8* and *art 14* (see *R (on the application of Amicus – MSF section) v Secretary of State for Trade and Industry* [2004] EWHC 860 (Admin), [2004] IRLR 430).

In *Whitefield v General Medical Council* [2002] UKPC 62, [2003] IRLR 39 the Privy Council considered the extent to which *art 8* was engaged in circumstances where the respondent, the General Medical Council, made it a condition of the applicant's continued practice as a doctor that he 'abstain absolutely from the consumption of alcohol'. The Privy Council held that the condition was not a breach of *art 8(1)* and in any event would, in the circumstances, have been justified under *art 8(2)*.

The provisions of the *Human Rights Act* are only directly applicable against public authorities. However, in the context of proceedings before the employment tribunal, Convention rights (and in particular the rights contained in *art 8*) may nonetheless be relevant in proceedings before the employment tribunal even where the employer is in the private sector. This is illustrated by the decision of the Court of Appeal in *X v Y* [2004] EWCA Civ 662, [2004] IRLR 625. The case concerned a dismissal by the employer for the employee's failure to disclose a caution. The employee contended that the dismissal was unfair as breaching the Convention right to respect for family life. While the claim failed on the facts, the Court of Appeal accepted that, if a dismissal was on grounds of an employee's private conduct within *art 8*, and was an interference with the right to respect for private life, that fact would be relevant to the determination of a claim of unfair dismissal whether the employer was a public authority or not. This is because the employment tribunal must, under *s 3* of the *Human Rights Act* read and give effect to relevant legislation (in this case the general provisions as to fairness of dismissal in *s 98* of the *ERA*) in a way which is compatible with Convention Rights such as *art 8*. In such circumstances there is no basis to treat a public employer differently from a private employer. Accordingly, say the Court of Appeal, it would not normally be fair to dismiss an employee for a reason which was an unjustified interference with the employee's private life. For a consideration of the role of *art 8* in relation to the fairness of the dismissal of a employee employed by a public sector employer see *Pay v Lancashire Probation Service* [2004] IRLR 129, EAT where the EAT held that a tribunal should effect consideration of Convention rights in the context of the fairness or otherwise of a dismissal by interpreting the words 'reasonably or unreasonably' in *s 98(4)* of the *ERA* as including the words 'having regard to the applicant's Convention rights'. Accordingly, in assessing the fairness in all the circumstances, consideration must be given to whether there had been an interference with the applicant's Convention rights and also any matters advanced by the employer as justification for such an interference. On the facts of *Pay*, in the EAT the applicant was unsuccessful in establishing that the *art 8* right to private life was engaged and, in relation to the *art 10* right of freedom of expression, the interference in issue was found to be justified in the circumstances. Notwithstanding the outcomes on the facts of both *X v Y* and *Pay*, the cases provide important indications of the likely relevance of Convention rights to the issue of the substantive fairness of dismissals both in the private and public sector. See **30.4** above in relation to *Pay* in the ECHR.

On the (generally limited) relevance of *art 8* to the general enquiry as to fairness of dismissal under *ERA 1996, s 98(4)* see *Turner v East Midlands Trains Ltd* [2012] EWCA Civ 1470 in which the Court of Appeal held that the application of *art 8* (where engaged) did not result in any higher standard of procedural fairness than that which was required under the range of reasonable responses test. See also *X v Y* [2004] IRLR 625 (CA), *Leach v OFCOM* [2012] IRLR 839 (CA) and *Garamukanwa v Solent NHS Trust* [2016] IRLR 476 (below) which each suggest, in summary, that art 8 arguments will add little to the application of the test under *art 8* arguments will add little to the application of the test under *ERA 1996, s 98(4)*.

Issues of surveillance of employees arose in *McGowan v Scottish Water* [2005] IRLR 167, EAT. The employee, suspected of falsely claiming on time sheets, was put under surveillance by private investigators engaged by the employer. The employee was dismissed in the light of evidence obtained on the surveillance. In an unfair dismissal claim the employee alleged the surveillance was a breach of *art 8*. This was rejected by the Scottish EAT on the facts of the case. The EAT held that *art 8* was indeed engaged in circumstances of covert surveillance but the central issue was that of proportionality. In the circumstances of suspected serious fraud, the surveillance was undertaken for legitimate reasons and was held to be proportionate. The case is significant in illustrating that, where employers do engage in covert surveillance of employees by whatever means, *art 8* is engaged and a 'strong presumption' (per Lord Johnston) of invasion of the right to family life will arise. Accordingly, it will be of central importance for an employer to be able to show that the interference arising was for a legitimate purpose and also 'proportionate' in all the circumstances which will involve consideration of the seriousness or gravity of the issue which prompted the surveillance and the extent of the surveillance exercise undertaken. Consider, however, the ECHR's recent decision in *Vukota-Bojic v Switzerland* [2017] IRLR 94 (at **[30.4]** above) in which the ECHR held that covert surveillance by an insurance company was not on the facts of that case "in accordance with law" and so the claim succeeded without the need to consider the issue of proportionality at all. This has potential application in the employment context as well.

The admissibility of covert recordings of a disciplinary hearing was considered in *Chairman and Governors of Amwell View School v Dogherty* [2007] IRLR 198. On the facts the EAT held that an employment tribunal had not, in allowing some of the covert recordings to be admitted in evidence, breached the school's governors' *art 8* rights. Recording of the private deliberations of the panel were, however, excluded on public policy grounds. In *City and Council of Swansea v Gayle* [2013] IRLR 768 the EAT further considered covert video surveillance evidence of a claimant in the context of an unfair dismissal appeal. The ET had held the dismissal unfair by reason of the use of covert surveillance. This was held by the EAT to be an error of law, holding that an employee has no right of privacy when doing acts which were defrauding the employer. In *Garamukanwa v Solent NHS Trust* [2016] IRLR 476 an employer was provided by the police with copies of malicious emails sent by an employee to other employees from, it appeared, the employee's private mobile telephone. The claimant was dismissed for gross misconduct and contended that the employer had breached his *Art 8* rights. This was rejected by the EAT which held that *Art 8* was not engaged on the facts as the employee had no reasonable expectation of privacy in relation to such communications.

Rule 49 of the Employment Tribunal Rules of Procedure (permitting anonymity orders) was considered in *A v B* [2010] IRLR 844 and the EAT concluded that it also had the power to anonymise a judgment if the loss of a claimant's anonymity would involve a breach of his *art 8* rights. See also *B and C v A* [2010] IRLR 400.

Closely related to the right to family and private life is the right to peaceful enjoyment of possessions. In *Nerva v United Kingdom* [2002] IRLR 815 the ECHR held that the decision of the UK High Court and the Court of Appeal that tips included in cheque and credit card payments were the property of the employer and could be used by them to discharge their statutory obligations to pay the applicant waiters a minimum level of remuneration did not amount to a breach of the applicants' rights under *art 1* of the *First Protocol to the Convention* to the peaceful enjoyment of their possessions (see **34.21 Pay – I**). See also *Legal & General Assurance Ltd v Kirk* [2001] EWCA Civ 1803, [2002] IRLR 124 in which the Court of Appeal held that a right to seek a particular employment cannot constitute a possession for the purposes of *art 1* of the *First Protocol to the Convention*. Similarly, in *R (Malik) v Waltham Forest NHS Primary Care Trust (Secretary of State for Health, interested party)* [2007] EWCA Civ 265, [2007] 4 All ER 832, [2007] ICR 1101, the Court of Appeal (reversing the decision of the Administrative Court at [2006] IRLR 526) held, in essence, that the right to practice a profession cannot be regarded as a 'possession' for the purposes of *art 1* of the *First Protocol*. In that case a medical practitioner had been unlawfully suspended and contended that his inclusion on a NHS medical performers list was a possession (inclusion on the list being a requisite for practice akin to a licence) and the suspension had interfered with the peaceful enjoyment of that 'possession'. The Court of Appeal rejected the contention that inclusion on the list was a possession for the purposes of *art 1*. *Art 1*, the Court of Appeal held does not cover an anticipated future right to income and thus the decision represents a substantial limitation upon the applicability of *art 1* in employment claims.

(c) Other Convention rights in the employment context

Article 9 protects freedom of thought, conscience and religion and the right to manifest religion or belief in worship, teaching, practice and observance. Its application to the requirement of Sunday working was considered in *Copsey v WWB Devon Clays Ltd* [2005] EWCA Civ 932, [2005] IRLR 811. In that case a change in shift pattern giving rise to an obligation to work on a Sunday led to the dismissal of the claimant for whom Sunday working was incompatible with his religious beliefs. The claimant brought a claim for unfair dismissal and alleged a breach of *art 9*. His claim was dismissed by the employment tribunal. On appeal to the Court of Appeal the decision of the Tribunal was upheld. Mummery LJ held that *art 9* was not in any event engaged as the employee was not compelled to work on a Sunday – he could always leave and get alternative employment (*Stedman v United Kingdom* [1997] 23 EHHR CD 168 applied). Rix and Neuberger LJJ held that *art 9* might be engaged but, applying the test of reasonableness and *s 98(4)* of the *ERA*, reasonable steps had been taken to accommodate the employee and accordingly the employment tribunal had not erred in reaching the decision which it did. This approach to human rights issues being engaged at the level of the general fairness of a dismissal under *s 98(4)* of the *ERA* is consistent with the approach adopted in relation to *art 8* in *Pay v Lancashire Probation Service* [2004] IRLR 129 and in *X v Y* [2004] EWCA Civ 662, [2004] IRLR 625 (see **30.7**(b) above).

In *Eweida v British Airways plc* [2010] ICR 890 the Court of Appeal held that an employer's policy forbidding visible jewellery, which prevented displaying a cross on a necklace while at work, had not amounted to indirect discrimination under the *Employment Equality (Religion or Belief) Regulations 2003 SI 2003/1660* (see now *s 19* of the *EqA 2010*). The Court rejected the argument that art 9 was relevant to the employee's case. Relying on *Kalac v Turkey* [1997] 27 EHRR 552, the Court held that *art 9* did not protect all acts motivated or inspired by religion or belief. If there are other ways in which an employee can practise or observe his or her religion then a breach of *art 9* is unlikely. In *Wasteney v East London NHS Foundation Trust* [2016] IRLR 388, which involved a complaint of direct discrimination on grounds of religion or belief, the EAT observed that, where the issues was whether treatment was because of manifestation of religion or because of "inappropriate" manifestation of that religion, the issue of "inappropriateness" could be tested by reference to *art 9(2)* and the relevant case law under that article.

Art 9 has been relied on, so far without success, in cases of employees refusing to carry out certain aspects of their work on the ground that it conflicted with their religious beliefs and where that refusal conflicted with the rights of others and thus could not be accommodated. In *Ladele v London Borough of Islington* [2010] ICR 532, CA the claimant refused to conduct civil partnership services in relation to same-sex couples. The Court of Appeal held that the employer Council did not discriminate against the claimant on the ground of religion when it threatened her with dismissal for refusing to carry out the services. The claimant's *art 9* rights should not override the Council's need to ensure equality. A similar conclusion was reached in *McFarlane v Relate Avon Ltd* [2010] ICR 507 which raised very similar issues. In *McClintock v Department for Constitutional Affairs* [2008] IRLR 29 the EAT held that a Justice of the Peace, who resigned from the Family Panel when his request to be excused from cases that might lead to the adoption of a child by a same-sex couple was rejected, was not discriminated against on the ground of his religious belief and nor were his *art 9* rights infringed and/or any infringement would have been justified under *art 9(2)*.

In *Eweida v United Kingdom* [2013] IRLR 231 the ECHR has given judgment in relation to the claims in *Eweida*, *Ladele*, *McFarlane* and also in relation to *Chaplin* (a case involving a nurse who was prohibited from wearing a cross at work in accordance with hospital policy). In Ms Eweida's case the ECHR held that the prohibition in issue did breach her *art 9* rights. The wearing of the cross was a manifestation of religion and the interference was not justified or proportionate. Conversely in *Chaplin*, although interference with religious manifestation was made out, the prohibition in a nursing content of jewellery on health and safety grounds was justified. The claims in *Ladele* and *McFarlane* each failed before the ECHR, with the court concluding that the interference in issue was justified. The ECHR stressed that the aim of the employer was to secure the implementation of its policy of providing a service without discrimination to others. This was considered by the ECHR to be the most important factor in justifying the requirements in issue, given that the ECHR generally allows national authorities a wide margin of appreciation when striking the balance between competing Convention rights. Thus, where the manifestation of religious belief will conflict with the rights of others (or where eg health and safety obligations are engaged) a prohibition on the manifestation is likely to be justified. Where, however, there is no such competing interest or right it is likely (as in Ms Eweida's case) to fail to be a justified interference with the *art 9* rights of the complainant. Similarly, in *Mba v Mayor and Burgesses of the London Borough of Merton* [2014] IRLR 145 a requirement to work on a Sunday was held by the Court of Appeal to be justified. Whilst the size of the group affected by a particular measure was relevant to indirect discrimination it was not a relevant consideration in a case where *art 9* was engaged and the question was whether the policy in question can be justified in the light of the difficulty or otherwise of accommodating the particular religious practices of the individual claimant.

Articles 10 and *11* on freedom of expression and association respectively were engaged in *Gate Gourmet London Ltd v Transport and General Workers Union* [2005] EWHC 1889 (QB), [2005] IRLR 881. This case involved applications for injunctions restraining picketing at Heathrow Airport. Fulford J held that in deciding whether to grant such an injunction appropriate weight must be given to the 'right to picket' (as a consequence of the *art 10* and *art 11* rights). On the facts of the case an order was granted limiting the number of pickets but the decision is significant in its express recognition in the domestic courts of effectively the right to picket in relation to an employment dispute (see also *Unison v United Kingdom* [2002] IRLR 497 above at **30.4**). *Redfearn v Serco Ltd (t/a) West Yorkshire Transport Service)* [2006] EWCA Civ 659, [2006] IRLR 623 involved the dismissal of an employee because of him standing as a candidate for the British National Party. The claim was brought under the *Race Relations Act 1976* (the claimant having insufficient continuous employment to bring an unfair dismissal claim) raising claims of direct and indirect discrimination which were both rejected. Issues of freedom of expression were raised under the *Human Rights Act* relying upon *art 10* but these were rejected by the domestic court on the basis of applying *art 17* of the Convention which provides that nothing in the Convention gives a right to engage in activities which themselves are aimed at destroying Convention rights and freedoms. See however *Redfearn v United Kingdom* (above) in which the ECHR has held the dismissal in *Redfearn* and the absence of effective remedy in UK law was a breach of *art 10* and *art 11* rights of the complainant. Confidentiality provisions in a contract of employment have been held by the ECHR to be in violation of the right to freedom of expression under *art 10* (*Matuz v Hungary* [2015] IRLR 74).

In *Hill v Governing Body of Great Tey Primary School* [2013] IRLR 274 *art 10* was in issue in an unfair dismissal claim. In that case a school employee had contacted parents and the press in relation to a child being hurt in the playground. An employment tribunal found her subsequent dismissal unfair having regard to *art 10*. On appeal the EAT confirmed that *art 10* was engaged and an employment tribunal must adopt a structured approach to the issue including making a structured assessment of proportionality.

In *Ministry of Justice v Prison Officers Association* [2008] EWHC 239 (QB), [2008] ICR 702, [2008] IRLR 380 the issue of the 'right to strike' in the context of *art 11* was considered by a domestic court. The Prison Officers Association had been subject to an injunction restraining their strike action (in circumstances of a no strike agreement being in force). In seeking to discharge the injunction various arguments based on *art 11* were unsuccessful before the Court. The Court held that *art 11*, whilst protecting freedom of association, contains no express right to strike and, even if it did, *art 11(2)* gave considerable freedom to a member state to restrict such a right. Accordingly the injunction restraining strike action was maintained. In the context of the statutory process for trade union recognition by the Central Arbitration Committee, *s 178* and *Schedule 1* of the *Trade Union and Labour Relations (Consolidation) Act 1992 (TULR(C)A)* has been construed purposively to give effect to *art 11* rights by reading a limitation into the exclusion of a recognition application where another trade union is recognised for very limited collective bargaining purposes (*Pharmacists' Defence Association Union v Boots Management Services* [2013] IRLR 262).

The question of whether the complex balloting and notice provisions contained in *Part V* of the *Trade Union and Labour Relations (Consolidation) Act 1992 (TULR(C)A)* infringe the right to freedom of association under *art 11* has been considered in *Metrobus Ltd v Unite the Union* [2010] ICR 173. The Court of Appeal rejected the Union's contention that the provisions of *TULR(C)A* presented obstacles so numerous and so complex that errors by unions were almost inevitable, and that for this reason the rights under *art 11* were so constrained as not to be effectively exercisable in respect of industrial action. A similar argument was rejected in *EDF Energy Powerlink Ltd v National Union of Rail, Maritime and Transport Workers* [2010] IRLR 114. The ECHR has now considered some *art 11* issues in a trade union context in *National Union of Rail, Maritime and Transport Workers v United Kingdom* [2014] IRLR 467. The union contended that its ability to protect its members interests was subject to excessive statutory control and this, it was alleged, gave rise to breach of the *art 11* right of freedom of association. Two key matters were under consideration. First the complexity of strike ballot requirements (arising from the *EDF Energy Powerlink Ltd* case above) and, second, the prohibition on secondary action. The first issue was determined to be inadmissible on the facts and, accordingly, was not the subject of a substantive determination. As to secondary action, the ECHR held that strike action was clearly protected by *art 11* and that secondary action by its nature may well have broader ramifications than primary action and effect upon persons not party to the dispute. The court held that the ban on secondary action did not strike at the core of trade union activity and thus member stated were to be afforded a wide margin of appreciation and that the ban was not an unjustified interference with the union's right of freedom of association.

30.8   OTHER INTERNATIONAL OBLIGATIONS RELEVANT TO HUMAN RIGHTS

The Council of Europe has also promulgated, and the United Kingdom has ratified, the *European Social Charter*, which contains provisions relating to, for example, annual holidays and the right to strike. This should not be confused with the Social Charter and the Social Chapter to the Maastricht Treaty agreed by the EC (see **23.3** EUROPEAN UNION LAW). There is an Additional Protocol which has not been signed by the UK.

The International Labour Organisation ('ILO') is a specialist body of the United Nations. It has issued a number of conventions, some of which have been ratified by the United Kingdom. They deal with matters such as health and safety, freedom of association and racial discrimination. UK law has been held by the ILO to infringe these conventions in a number of respects. However, there is no remedy for any such breaches in English courts or tribunals.

from the sum payable *after* it has been capped, rather than deducting them from the total sum owing to the employee and then applying the cap (*Morris v Secretary of State for Employment* [1985] ICR 522, [1985] IRLR 297, EAT, followed in *Titchener v Secretary of State for Trade and Industry* [2002] ICR 225, [2002] IRLR 195, EAT).

The eight-week limit in respect of which an employee may claim arrears of pay under *s 184(1)(a)* is a permitted derogation to the *EC Directive* and, as a derogation, it must be interpreted restrictively, so as to afford maximum benefit to the employee. Accordingly, it must be construed as permitting an employee to choose the eight weeks in respect of which his claim is most valuable: see *Mann v Secretary of State for Employment* [1999] IRLR 566, HL and *AGR Regeling v Bestuur van der Bedrijfsvereniging voor de Metaallnijverheid*: C-125/97 [1998] ECR I-4493, [1999] ICR 605, ECJ (a case on the meaning of the *EC Directive* which *ERA 1996, s 182* partly implements). See further *Mau v Bundesanstalt fur Arbeit*: C-160/01 [2003] ECR I-4791, [2004] 1 CMLR 1113.

Where an employee claims notice pay under *s 184(1)*, the amount he may recover depends on whether he worked out his notice or was unlawfully dismissed without notice. In the former case, he may recover his arrears of pay from the Secretary of State as a liquidated sum. In the latter case, he is subject to the normal rules on mitigating his loss. Thus, the Secretary of State may in those circumstances, in assessing the amount he is liable to pay, take into account any earnings of the employee during the notice period, or, where the employee has failed to mitigate his loss properly, any earnings he should have received (*Secretary of State for Employment v Cooper* [1987] ICR 766, EAT; *Secretary of State for Employment v Stewart* [1996] IRLR 334, EAT). He may also deduct from the amount payable the amount of state benefits the employee has received during the notice period, which he would not have received but for his dismissal (see *Westwood v Secretary of State for Employment* [1985] ICR 209, HL).

The liability of the Secretary of State to make payments under *s 182* cannot exceed that of the insolvent employer. Thus, where the insolvent employer would be entitled to set-off against the debt owed by him to the employee sums owed by the employee to him, the Secretary of State is entitled to deduct from the amount he pays the employee the amount of the employer's set-off (see *Secretary of State for Employment v Wilson* [1997] ICR 408, [1996] IRLR 330, EAT).

Where an insolvency practitioner such as a trustee in bankruptcy, liquidator, administrator or receiver has been (or is required by law to be) appointed, the Secretary of State will not normally make any payment from the National Insurance Fund until the insolvency practitioner sends the Secretary of State a statement of what is due to the employee. The Secretary of State may, however, at his discretion, satisfy himself that the employee's claim is valid and that he does not need a statement before paying the claim *(ERA 1996, s 187)*. Once payment has been made to the employee by the Secretary of State, the employee's rights to claim the debt against his employer are transferred to the Secretary of State. In addition, any sums payable as the result of a subsequent decision of an employment tribunal requiring an employer to pay the debt to the employee must be paid to the Secretary of State *(ERA 1996, s 189)*. Following an application under *s 183*, the Secretary of State has the power to request in writing that the employer provide information and documents to allow the Secretary of State to decide whether the application is well founded. Failure to comply with such a request without reasonable excuse is a criminal offence *(ERA 1996, s 190)*.

31.6   Remedy under ERA 1996 Part XII

A person who has applied for payment of other guaranteed debts may, within the period of three months beginning with the date on which the decision of the Secretary of State on that application was communicated to him (or if that is not reasonably practicable, within such further period as is considered reasonable), present a complaint to an employment tribunal that:

31.6 Insolvency of Employer

(a)   the Secretary of State has failed to make any such payment; or

(b)   any such payment by him is less than the amount which should have been paid.

(*ERA 1996, s 188.*)

If the employment tribunal finds the complaint well-founded, it will make a declaration to that effect and state the amount due from the Secretary of State. See *Secretary of State for Employment v Reeves* [1993] ICR 508 for the law relating to interest upon the tribunal's award in such a case (for interest generally, see **18.28** EMPLOYMENT TRIBUNALS − I).

31.7 Unpaid contributions to occupational pension schemes

The Secretary of State may make payments out of the National Insurance Fund into an occupational pension scheme if he is satisfied that an employer has become insolvent and that, at the time he became insolvent, there remained unpaid relevant contributions falling to be paid by him to the scheme. Application for payment is to be made by the person competent to act in respect of the pension scheme (*Pension Schemes Act 1993 ('PSA 1993'), s 124(1)*). 'Relevant contributions' are defined as contributions to be paid by the employer on his own behalf or on behalf of a worker from whose pay a deduction has been made for that purpose (*PSA 1993, s 124(2) and 124(6)*).

The amount payable in respect of contributions of an employer on his own behalf is the least of the following:

(a)   the balance of relevant contributions remaining unpaid on the date when the employer became insolvent and payable by the employer on his own account to the scheme in respect of the 12 months immediately preceding that date;

(b)   the amount certified by an actuary to be necessary for the purpose of meeting the liability of the scheme on dissolution to pay the benefits provided by the scheme to or in respect of the workers of the employer;

(c)   an amount equal to 10% of the total amount of remuneration paid or payable to those workers in respect of the 12 months immediately preceding the date on which the employer became insolvent.

The sum payable is the lesser of the amounts in (a) and (c) above in any case where the scheme is a defined contributions scheme, a shared risk scheme under which all the benefits that may be provided are money purchase benefits, or a shared risk scheme under which all the benefits that may be provided are money purchase benefits or collective benefits.

(*PSA 1993, ss 124(3) and (3A)* (as inserted by the *Pension Schemes Act 2015*).)

The sum payable in respect of unpaid contributions on behalf of a worker may not exceed the amount deducted from the pay of the worker in respect of the worker's contributions to the occupational pension scheme during the 12 months immediately preceding the date on which the employer became insolvent (*PSA 1993, s 124(5)*).

The liquidator, receiver or trustee in bankruptcy (or other 'relevant officer', as defined) must make a statement to the Secretary of State of the amounts so owing before any payment out of the National Insurance Fund may be made (*PSA 1993, s 125(3), (4)*). However, the Secretary of State may make a payment from the National Insurance Fund if he is satisfied that he does not require such a statement in order to determine the relevant amounts (*PSA 1993, s 125(5)*).

The rights and remedies of the persons competent to act in respect of the scheme will be transferred to the Secretary of State (*PSA 1993, s 127(1)*).

A person who has applied to the Secretary of State for payment of pension contributions may present a complaint to the Employment Tribunal that the Secretary of State has failed to make any such payment or that any such payment by him is less than the amount which should have been paid *(PSA 1993, s 126)*. The provisions in relation to remedy are the same as those for claims for payment of guaranteed debts under *ERA 1996, Part XII:* see **31.6** above.

Following the decision of the ECJ in *Robins and another v Secretary of State for Work and Pensions* C-278/05 [2007] 2 CMLR 269, [2007] IRLR 270, that UK legislation did not provide the minimum degree of protection of accrued occupational pension rights required by *Article 8* of *EC Directive 80/987*, the *Financial Assistance Scheme (Miscellaneous Amendments) Regulations 2007/3581* (and subsequent regulations made under *s 286* of the *Pensions Act 2004* (as amended by the *Pensions Acts 2007, 2008* and *2011*)) were enacted to determine the pension protection provided for qualifying employees upon an 'insolvency event' occurring in respect of their employer.

31.8 Pensions Act 2004

The *Pensions Act 2004* provides protection for employees of employers which become insolvent. The Act established a new body corporate, the Pensions Regulator, together with the Pension Protection Fund, the Board of the Pension Protection Fund and the Pension Protection Fund Ombudsman.

Chapter 3 of *Part 2* to the *Act (ss 126–181A)* provides for pension protection for 'eligible' pension schemes in the event that the employer suffers an 'insolvency event'. The complex details of the protection offered are set out in detail in the Act and also in the *Pension Protection Fund (Compensation) Regulations 2005 (SI 2005/670)*, the *Financial Assistance Scheme (Miscellaneous Amendments) Regulations (SI 2007/3581)* and subsequent regulations made under *s 286* of the *Pensions Act 2004* (as amended by the *Pensions Acts 2007, 2008* and *2011*). However, in summary the Board of the Pension Protection Fund will, in defined circumstances, be under a duty to assume responsibility for eligible schemes following an insolvency event. The Board may pay compensation to members of the pension scheme whose pensions are affected by the insolvency pursuant to the pension compensation provisions set out in *Sch 7*.

The *Pension Protection Fund and Occupational Pension Scheme (Levy Ceiling and Compensation Cap) Order 2016 (SI 2016/82)* caps the relevant compensation at £37,420.42, with effect from 1 April 2014.

31.9 Statutory maternity, paternity, adoption and sick pay

An employee who, due to the insolvency of his or her employer, is unable to obtain statutory maternity pay, paternity pay, adoption pay, sick pay or statutory shared parental pay may claim such payment from HM Revenue and Customs: see *Statutory Maternity Pay (General) Regulations 1986 (SI 1986/1960), regs 7* and *30, the Statutory Paternity Pay and Statutory Adoption Pay (General) Regulations 2002 (SI 2002/2822), reg 43, the Statutory Sick Pay (General) Regulations 1982 (SI 1982/894), reg 9B*, and the *Statutory Shared Parental Pay (General) Regulations 2014, reg 45*, respectively. See also Maternity and Parental Rights **(32)** and Sickness and Sick Pay **(44)**.

31.10 OTHER CONSEQUENCES OF INSOLVENCY AND RELATED EVENTS

Insolvency frequently necessitates the dismissal of the employees formerly engaged by the insolvent business. Insolvency itself does not absolve employers from the duty to have consultation with the unions and employees before the dismissal notices are sent out (see the cases cited in **39.6** Redundancy – **II**).

The *Transfer of Undertakings (Protection of Employment) Regulations 2006 (SI 2006/246)*, *regs 8 and 9* make special provision with regard to employee rights where at the time of a relevant transfer the transferor is subject to relevant insolvency proceedings. See **52.11** TRANSFER OF UNDERTAKINGS. The special provision for the (partial) disapplication of *TUPE* in insolvency situations applies only when the *TUPE* transfer occurs after insolvency proceedings have been formally 'instituted' and when the insolvency practitioner is acting in that capacity and has been appointed as such; see *Secretary of State for Trade and Industry v Slater and others* [2007] IRLR 928. The effect of *TUPE* is partially disapplied where the employer is in insolvency proceedings which are 'relevant insolvency proceedings' within *reg 8(6)* of *TUPE*. The effects of *TUPE* are disapplied almost in their entirety (NB but not in respect of the information and consultation obligations in *regs 11* and *13–16* of *TUPE*) if the insolvency proceedings fall within *reg 8(7)* of *TUPE*. Whether insolvency proceedings are 'relevant' insolvency proceedings within *reg 8(6)* or *(7)* of *TUPE* depends on whether they were instituted 'with a view to the liquidation of the assets' of the employer.

The EAT held that as the primary object of an administration is to rescue the company as a going concern that purpose is inconsistent with the liquidation of the assets of the company so that an administration can never fall within *reg 8(7)* of *TUPE*; *OTG Ltd v Barke* [2011] IRLR 272. The Court of Appeal in *Key2Law (Surrey) LLP v De'Antiquis* [2011] EWCA Civ 1567, [2012] IRLR 212 has confirmed that the "absolute" approach to administration proceedings applies and not the "fact-based" approach. Administration proceedings instituted pursuant to *Insolvency Act 1986, Sch B1* never fall within *TUPE, reg 8(7)*. *TUPE* applies to companies in administration and there is no scope for argument on the individual facts of each case.

Reg 8(7) does not apply to the purchase of a business or assets from a company in administration, including sales using pre-pack arrangements, so that in such a case the employees of the insolvent transferor will transfer to the purchaser. In *Pressure Coolers Ltd v Molloy* [2011] IRLR 630 the EAT considered the effect of *TUPE* on liability to pay compensation in a pre-pack administration, where the claimant, after having been dismissed by the transferee on redundancy grounds, had brought successful employment tribunal claims. Adopting a purposive approach to *TUPE, reg 8(3)*, the EAT concluded that liability lay with the transferee, not the Secretary of State, because the dismissal had occurred after the transfer date. The same reasoning was used by the EAT in *Dobrucki v Secretary of State for Business, Innovation and Skills* ([2015] All ER (D) 30 (Apr)).

Subject to the application of the *Transfer of Undertakings (Protection of Employment) Regulations* (see TRANSFER OF UNDERTAKINGS (**52**)), the effect of a winding-up order made by the court is to terminate the contracts of employment made by the company (*Re General Rolling Stock Co* (1866) LR 1 Eq 346; *Measures Bros Ltd v Measures* [1910] 2 Ch 248). The same occurs where a receiver is appointed by the court (*Reid v Explosives Co Ltd* (1887) 19 QBD 264; *Midland Counties District Bank Ltd v Attwood* [1905] 1 Ch 357), and if employees continue to work for the business they will be deemed to have entered into new contracts of employment with the receiver.

However, a voluntary winding-up does not terminate contracts of employment, because the liquidator is an officer of the company and the personality of the employer does not change (*Midland Counties District Bank*, above). Nor does the appointment of a (contractual) receiver who is an agent of the company otherwise than by the court (eg under a loan security agreement) have that effect, at any rate unless the employees concerned are directors or managers who could not continue to perform their functions without a conflict with the exercise of the receiver's powers (*Re Foster Clark Ltd's Indenture Trusts* [1966] 1 WLR 125; *Re Mack Trucks (Britain) Ltd* [1967] 1 WLR 780; *Griffiths v Secretary of State for Social Services* [1974] QB 468; *Nicoll v Cutts* [1985] PCC 311; *Re Ferranti International plc* [1994] 4 All ER 300 (Ch D), [1995] 2 All ER 65 (HL)). See also *Deaway*

Trading Ltd v Calverley [1973] 3 All ER 776; and *Pambakian v Brentford Nylons Ltd* [1978] ICR 665, 122 Sol Jo 177, EAT. The appointment of an administrator, as agent of the employer, does not automatically terminate contracts of employment.

The institution of insolvency proceedings gives rise to a statutory moratorium on commencing or pursuing proceedings against the insolvent employer without the consent of the insolvency practitioner or the court; *Insolvency Act 1986, Sch B1*. Exceptional circumstances will be required before the courts will only lift the moratorium to permit employees seeking to enforce money claims for protective awards, unfair dismissal etc; see *Unite the Union v Nortel Networks UK Ltd (in administration)* [2010] EWHC 826 (Ch), [2010] IRLR 1042.

31.11 Liability of administrative receivers and administrators

An administrative receiver is, essentially, a receiver or manager of substantially the whole of a company's property appointed on behalf of the holders of debentures secured by a floating charge (*Insolvency Act 1986, s 29(2)*). By contrast, a person may be appointed as the administrator of a company by an administration order of the court, by the holder of a floating charge or by the company or its directors (*Insolvency Act 1986, Sch B1 paras 10, 14 and 22* respectively). The administrative receiver or administrator will be treated as adopting the contract of employment of an employee if he continues the employment relationship for 14 days after appointment (*Insolvency Act 1986, s 44(2)* and *Sch B1, para 99(5)(a)*). An administrative receiver or administrator will not be able to avoid adoption of the contract simply by writing to employees expressly to state that he is not adopting the contracts. If he takes advantage of the services of existing employees without negotiating new contracts of employment for more than 14 days he will be regarded as having adopted their contracts (*Powdrill v Watson* [1995] 2 AC 394; see also *Re Antal International Ltd* [2003] EWHC 1339 (Ch), [2003] 2 BCLC 406).

An administrative receiver will be personally liable on any contract of employment adopted by him in carrying out his functions. Any such liability is limited to 'qualifying liabilities', essentially contractual liabilities for payment of a sum by way of wages or salary or contribution to an occupational pension scheme where that liability is incurred while the administrative receiver is in office and in respect of services rendered wholly or partly after the adoption of the employment contract. However, the administrative receiver is entitled to be indemnified out of the company's assets (*Insolvency Act 1986, s 44* as amended by *Insolvency Act 1994*). For the law prior to 15 March 1994, see *Powdrill v Watson* [1995] 2 AC 394.

An administrator does not undertake a personal liability. 'Qualifying liabilities' for wages, salary and pension contributions after the adoption of the contract are, however, given 'super priority' in that they are charged on the company's property in their custody or control in priority to most other charges and securities including the fees and expenses of the administration (*Insolvency Act 1986, Schedule B1, para 99*; see also *Re Allders Department Stores Ltd (in administration)* [2005] ICR 867). In *Krasner v McMath* [2005] EWCA Civ 1072, [2006] ICR 205 the Court of Appeal concluded that an administrator's liabilities to employees of a company in administration for protective awards and payments in lieu of notice were not payable in priority to the expenses of the administration (save that any payments in lieu of notice where an employer did not require an employee to work during his notice period and paid his wages attributable to that period in a lump sum would be payable in priority as such payments constitute wages as set out in *Delaney v Staples (RJ) (t/a De Montfort Recruitment)* [1992] 1 AC 687, [1992] ICR 483, HL).

31.11   Insolvency of Employer

In *Larsen v Henderson* [1990] IRLR 512 an important suggestion was made by the Scottish Court of Session that a receiver owes a duty of care to the employees of a company in receivership to adopt such method of achieving his desired end as will have the least adverse effect upon them. There is considerable doubt as to whether this suggestion is, in fact, correct.

32   Maternity and Parental Rights

Cross-references. See Unfair Dismissal – **I (53)** and **II (54)** for the general rules on unfair dismissal; Equal Pay **(22)** and Discrimination and Equal Opportunities – **I (11)** for the rules prohibiting discrimination on the ground of pregnancy and maternity.

INTRODUCTION

32.1   Chapter structure and scope
This chapter has the following structure:

(i)   Introduction [**32.1**].

(ii)   Ante-natal care & adoption appointments [**32.9**].

(iii)   Maternity-related suspension, dismissal and detriment [**32.24**].

(iv)   Maternity Leave [**32.35**].

(v)   Statutory maternity pay [**32.54**].

(vi)   Unpaid parental leave [**32.62**].

(vii)   Shared parental leave and pay [**32.68**].

(viii)   Paternity and adoption leave & pay [**32.106**].

32.2

This chapter provides an overview of maternity and parental rights in UK law, concentrating on those aspects that are most often litigated in the employment tribunal. Topics that are not addressed in this chapter in detail include:

* Discrimination on the grounds of pregnancy and maternity under the *Equality Act 2010 (EA 2010)* (but see [**32.25**] and Discrimination and Equal Opportunities – **I (11)**, **II (12)**, and **III (13)**).

* Specific health & safety requirements relating to pregnancy & maternity rights, such as risk assessments (however, see *O'Neill v Buckinghamshire County Council* [2010] IRLR 384).

* The detail and practicalities of administering statutory payments to entitled individuals.

* Equal pay (see Equal Pay **(22)**).

32.3   *Summary of maternity and parental rights*
Parents and adopters enjoy the following rights:

* *Ante-natal care & adoption appointments*: pregnant women are entitled to paid time off to attend ante-natal appointments, and their partners are entitled to unpaid time off work to accompany the mother. A similar scheme applies for adoption appointments; one parent may take paid time off, and the other unpaid time off.

* *Maternity-related suspensions* must be justified, employers must offer suitable alternative work and generally must continue to remunerate the employee. Dismissal on grounds relating to maternity, pregnancy or the exercise of other family-leave rights will usually be automatically unfair, and any detriment imposed for any of those reasons will be unlawful.

32.3   Maternity and Parental Rights

- *Maternity leave*: mothers are entitled to 52 weeks of maternity leave (26 weeks ordinary maternity leave ("**OML**"), 26 weeks additional maternity leave ("**AML**")), without any need for a qualifying period of service. The first two weeks of maternity leave are 'compulsory maternity leave' ("**CML**") and an employer cannot allow a mother to return to work within that period.

- *Statutory maternity pay*: mothers with at least 6 months continuous service generally qualify for 39 weeks of statutory maternity pay ("**SMP**"), at the rate of 90% of average weekly earnings for the first six weeks and the remaining 33 weeks at the lower of the statutory rate of £140.98 or 90% of normal weekly earnings. Many employers provide enhanced contractual maternity entitlements. Mothers who do not qualify for SMP may quality for maternity allowance ("**MA**"), a social security benefit.

- *Shared parental leave and pay*: mothers with at least six months continuous service may generally curtail their statutory maternity leave and and SMP, and (flexibly) share the balance of leave and pay between herself and her partner as shared parental leave ("**SPL**") and statutory shared parental pay ("**SSSP**"). The rate of SSPP is the lower of the statutory rate of £140.98 or 90% of normal weekly earnings. SPL and SSPP is also available to adopters, surrogate parents and others, and replaces 'additional paternity leave' ("**APL**")

- *Unpaid parental leave*: employees with a year's service may take up to 18 weeks of unpaid leave for each natural or adopted child up to the child's 18th birthday, but such leave can only be taken in blocks of one week at a time (unless the contract of employment provides otherwise).

- *Paternity and adoption leave and pay*: statutory paternity leave (birth) is two weeks in length, with a qualifying requirement for 26 weeks' continuous service. Statutory paternity pay, with the same qualifying requirement, is payable at either £140.98 per week or 90% of the employee's normal weekly earnings. Adoption leave for a primary adopter is 52 weeks in length with no qualifying period of service. Statutory adoption pay ("**SAP**"), which generally requires six months' continuous service, is set at 90% of average weekly earnings for the first six weeks, then the remaining 33 weeks are paid at the lower of the statutory rate of £140.98 or 90% of normal weekly earnings. There is also shared parental leave and pay in adoption cases which confer essential the same entitlements as in the case of birth.

32.4   *Abbreviations*

Abbreviations peculiar to this chapter include:

- AML – additional maternity leave.

- APL – additional paternity leave.

- ACAS Guide – 'Shared Parental Leave: a good practice guide for employers and employees' (14 October 2014), ACAS.

- BIS Guide – 'Employer's Technical Guide to Shared Parental Leave and Pay' (December 2014), Department for Business, Innovation and Skills.

- EWC – expected week of childbirth.

- Leave Curtailment Regulations – the *Maternity and Adoption Leave (Curtailment of Statutory Rights to Leave) Regulations 2014 (SI 2014/3052)*.

- MA – maternity allowance.

- MA Curtailment Regulations – the *Maternity Allowance (Curtailment) Regulations 2014 (SI 2014/3053)*.

- MPL Regulations – the *Maternity and Parental Leave etc. Regulations 1999 (SI 1999/3312)*.

- OML – ordinary maternity leave.

- PAL Regulations – *Paternity and Adoption Leave Regulations 2002 (SI 2002/2788)*.

- Pay Curtailment Regulations – the *Statutory Maternity Pay and Statutory Adoption Pay (Curtailment) Regulations 2014 (SI 2014/3054)*.

- SAL – standard adoption leave.

- SAP – statutory adoption pay.

- SMP – statutory maternity pay.

- SMP Regulations – the *Statutory Maternity Pay (General) Regulations 1986 (SI 1986/1960)*.

- SML – statutory maternity leave.

- SPL – shared parental leave.

- SPL Regulations – the *Shared Parental Leave Regulations 2014 (SI 2014/2050)*.

- SSPP – statutory shared parental pay.

- SSPP Regulations – the *Statutory Shared Parental Pay (General) Regulations 2014 (SI 2014/3051)*.

- SSCBA 1992 – *Social Security Contributions and Benefits Act 1992*.

32.5   *The development of maternity & parental rights*

Historically, the *Employment Protection Act 1975* created statutory rights for female employees. These provisions were re-enacted in the *Employment Protection (Consolidation) Act 1978*. An additional right, the right to paid time off for ante-natal care, was conferred by the *Employment Act 1980*, which also amended the existing provisions, and statutory rights were further extended by the *Trade Union Reform and Employment Rights Act 1993*.

With the exception of the law relating to statutory maternity pay (which is contained in the *Social Security Contributions and Benefits Act 1992*), all the relevant legislation was consolidated into the *Employment Rights Act 1996* ("**ERA 1996**"). Most of the rights and principles set out in the *ERA 1996* which relate to maternity leave have found their way into the *Employment Relations Act 1999* ("**ERA 1999**"), or appear in the regulations made under the *ERA 1999*, principally the *Maternity and Parental Leave etc. Regulations 1999 (SI 1999/3312)*.

The *Employment Act 2002* ("**EmA 2002**") and accompanying regulations ushered in significant changes to the law on maternity and paternity rights, extending the period of ordinary maternity leave from 18 weeks to 26 weeks, and the period of additional maternity leave to 26 weeks from the date when ordinary maternity leave has ended. The *Work and Families Act 2006*, and accompanying regulations, introduced further changes, including a right (now abolished) to additional paternity leave to enable parents, in effect, to share the right to additional leave to care for their child (see **32.63** below), a move which has recently been taken a step further by the introduction of shared parental leave and pay under the *Children and Families Act 2014* ("**CFA 2014**") (see **32.68** below).

The *Social Security Act 1989, Sch 5 paras 2, 5, 6*, contains provisions which deal with unfair maternity and family leave provisions in employment-related benefits schemes. These provisions are intended to implement *Directive 86/378/EEC* (see **23.5** EUROPEAN UNION LAW) and were brought into force to a limited extent on 23 June 1994 (*Social Security Act 1989 (Commencement No 5) Order 1994 (SI 1994/1661)*).

32.6 Maternity and Parental Rights

32.6 The law as to sex discrimination (see DISCRIMINATION AND EQUAL OPPORTUNITIES – I (11), II (12), and III (13)) has also historically been extremely important in defining the extent of the protection which the law confers on women in connection with pregnancy or childbirth and, indeed, in connection with IVF treatment (on which see *Mayr v Backerei und Konditorei Gerhard Flockner OHG*: C-506/06 [2008] IRLR 387 and *Sahota v Home Office* [2010] ICR 772).

32.7 In 2008, the European Commission proposed a number of new rights in relation to maternity leave as part of proposed revisions to the *Pregnant Workers Directive EC 1992/85*. The Government consulted on those proposals during 2009 and published a response in 2010. In October 2010 the European Parliament adopted amendments to the *Directive* which went beyond even those proposed by the Commission, including a right to 20 weeks' paid maternity leave, two weeks' paid paternity leave and breastfeeding leave. These were politically controversial and were broadly rejected by the European Council in late 2010. It remains to be seen how or if the proposed revisions will be taken forward.

In June 2010 the European Parliament agreed a new *Directive 2010/41/EU* to provide for increased protections for self-employed workers, including a right to maternity leave for self-employed women and their partners. The UK has taken the view that existing domestic legislation already provides sufficient compliance for the purposes of the new Directive. As to the right to maternity allowance in UK law, see **32.61** below.

32.8 In December 2009, EU Charter of Fundamental Rights (the "**Charter**") came into effect. Article 33 of the Charter provides:

Family and professional life

1. The family shall enjoy legal, economic and social protection.

2. To reconcile family and professional life, everyone shall have the right to protection from dismissal for a reason connected with maternity and the right to paid maternity leave and to parental leave following the birth or adoption of a child.

Similarly, Article 34(1) provides:

Social security and social assistance

1. The Union recognises and respects the entitlement to social security benefits and social services providing protection in cases such as maternity, illness, industrial accidents, dependency or old age, and in the case of loss of employment, in accordance with the rules laid down by Community law and national laws and practices.

It remains to be seen what, if any role the Charter will play in the development of maternity and paternity rights. It is suggested that, given the prominence of EU law in this field, it is likely to have a significant role to play. See *R(NS) v Secretary of State for the Home Department* [2010] EWCA Civ 990 and *Association De Mediation Sociale v Union Locale Des Syndicats Cgt*; (Case C-176/12) [2014] as to the applicability of the Charter.

On 13 March 2014, the *Children and Families Act 2014* received Royal Assent. It made three important changes to the law:

• *Part 7* provides for statutory rights to shared parental leave and pay;

• *Part 8* provides for a new right to time off to accompany on ante-natal appointments; and

• *Part 9* abolishes the requirement to be a carer in order to request flexible working (see [**49.17**]).

Shared parental leave is discussed in detail below at **[32.68]**. Accompanying on ante-natal appointments is discussed at **[32.14]** and the new right to request flexible working is addressed at **[49.17]**.

In March 2016 the Equality and Human Rights Commission and HM Government published 'Pregnancy and maternity-related discrimination and disadvantage: Experiences of mothers', which set out stark findings. Some 77% of women reported a potentially discriminatory or negative experience, 10% of mothers said that their employer discouraged them from attending antenatal appointments and 11% of mothers reported being dismissed, made compulsorily redundant or treated so poorly they had to leave their job. On 12 July 2016, the House of Commons Women and Equalities Committee published a report entitled 'Pregnancy and maternity discrimination', noting that the March 2016 research, when compared with equivalent research in 2005, showed that pregnancy and maternity discrimination was getting worse. The report set out a range of recommendations. The Government's response notably included a commitment to review the position in relation to making new and expectant mothers redundant, as well as commenting on a range of other practical measures.

ANTE-NATAL CARE & ADOPTION APPOINTMENTS

32.9   Paid time off for ante-natal care

An employee who is pregnant and who has, on the advice of a registered medical practitioner, registered midwife or registered nurse, made an appointment to attend at any place for the purpose of receiving ante-natal care, is entitled: (a) not to be unreasonably refused time off during her working hours to enable her to keep the appointment (*ERA 1996, s 55(1)* and *57(1)*); and (b) to be paid for the period of absence at the appropriate hourly rate (*ERA 1996, s 56(1)*). (See also *art 9* of the *Pregnant Workers Directive 92/85/EEC.*) See **[32.14]** below in relation to the right to accompany a pregnant woman to an ante-natal appointment and **[32.19]** in relation to adoption appointments.

32.10 *Qualifying requirements*

There is no minimum qualifying period of employment for the enjoyment of this right. However, in respect of all save the first appointment for ante-natal care for which she seeks time off work, the employee must, if requested to do so by her employer, produce for his inspection:

(a)   a certificate from a registered medical practitioner, registered midwife or registered nurse stating that she is pregnant; and

(b)   an appointment card or some other document showing that the appointment has been made.

(ERA 1996, s 55(2)–(3) and s 55(5).)

If an employer could reasonably refuse to allow an employee time off to attend an ante-natal appointment – for example, if she were a part-time employee and could arrange to attend during her time off – yet he allows her time off, it is thought that he is not obliged to pay her during the period of her absence provided that he obtains her agreement and makes it clear that the time is not being given in satisfaction of a statutory obligation. This qualification is an important one: if an employee is entitled to take time off in accordance with the provisions of *ERA 1996, s 55(1)*, she is automatically entitled to be paid for the time taken (*ERA 1996, s 56(1)*). (See *Gregory v Tudsbury Ltd* [1982] IRLR 267.)

32.11 *Right to remuneration*

The employee is entitled to payment from her employer for the period of her absence, at the appropriate hourly rate. That rate is the amount of one week's pay divided by:

(a)   the number of normal working hours in a week for that employee when employed under the contract of employment in force on the day when the time off is taken;

(b)   where the number of such normal working hours differs from week to week or over a longer period, the average number of such hours, calculated by reference to the hours worked during the period of 12 weeks ending with the last complete week before the day on which the time off is taken; or

(c)   where the number of hours worked in a week differs, but the employee has not been employed long enough for the 12-week calculation to be made, a number which fairly represents the number of normal working hours in a week taking into account (as appropriate in all the circumstances) the average number of hours which the employee could expect under her contract and the average number of hours worked by other employees of the same employer in comparable employment.

(*ERA 1996, ss 56(2)–(6) and 225(3)*; and see PAY – I (34).)

32.12 *Remedies*

An employee may present a complaint to an employment tribunal to the effect that her employer has unreasonably refused her time off as required by *s 55(1)* of the *ERA* or has failed to pay her the whole or part of any amount to which she is entitled under *s 56(1)* (see *ERA 1996, s 57(1)*). Such a complaint must be presented within the period of three months beginning with the date of the appointment concerned, or within such further period as the tribunal considers reasonable in a case where it is satisfied that it was not reasonably practicable for the complaint to be presented within the period of three months (*ERA 1996, s 57(2)*; for reasonable practicability see 18.7 EMPLOYMENT TRIBUNALS – I). The extension of time limits under *section 207B*, to facilitate conciliation before institution of proceedings, apply. By analogy with the time limit in unfair dismissal cases, it is thought that it will not be considered to be reasonably practicable for an employee to present a claim until she is aware or ought reasonably to be aware of her rights (see *Nu-Swift International Ltd v Mallinson* [1978] IRLR 537, [1979] ICR 157). Where an employment tribunal finds a complaint well-founded, it will make a declaration to that effect and make an order for payment of twice the amount of money due under the statutory provisions (*ERA 1996, s 57(3)–(5)*). The employee's statutory right to remuneration does not affect her contractual right, but any contractual remuneration will go to discharge her statutory entitlement, and vice versa (*ERA 1996, s 56(5)–(6)*).

A dismissal for a reason for a reason relating to ante-natal appointments may relate to pregnancy, and so be automatically unfair under *ERA 1996, s 99*. See [32.31].

32.13 *Agency Workers*

From 1 October 2011 agency workers who have worked for the qualifying period prescribed in *reg 7* of the *Agency Workers Regulations 2010 (SI 2010/93)* (i.e. working in the same role with the same hirer for 12 continuous calendar weeks), have comparable rights as against both their temporary work agency and their hirer (*ERA 1996, ss 57ZA–57ZD*). Following the *CFA 2014, s 129*, agency workers also have the right not to be subject to detriment for exercising their rights to attend ante-natal care appointments.

32.14 ACCOMPANYING FOR ANTE-NATAL CARE: UNPAID TIME OFF

The *CFA 2014* by *Part 8* created a new right for certain employees to take unpaid time off work to attend up to two ante-natal appointments if they have a "qualifying relationship" with a pregnant woman, by inserting new *sections 57ZE–57ZI* into the *ERA 1996*. In September 2014 the Department for Business, Innovation and Skills published an employer guide entitled 'Time off to accompany a pregnant woman to ante-natal appointments'. The government brought *ERA 1996, ss 57ZE–57ZI* into force on 1 October 2014.

32.29 *Agency Workers*

From 1 October 2011 agency workers who have worked for the qualifying period prescribed in *reg 7* of the *Agency Workers Regulations 2010 (SI 2010/93)* (i.e. working in the same role with the same hirer for 12 continuous calendar weeks), have comparable protections where the supply of that worker to a hirer is ended on maternity grounds pursuant to one of the measures in **32.26** above or *reg 20* of the *Conduct of Employment Agencies and Employment Businesses 2003* (*ERA 1996, ss 68A–68D, 69A* and *70A*).

32.30 *Pregnant Workers Directive*

In *Parviainen v Finnair Oyj* (Case C-471/08) [2011] ICR 99, the CJEU has held that where an employer transfers a pregnant employee to another job to avoid health risks during her pregnancy, *art 11* of the *Pregnant Workers Directive* requires that she receive her basic pay together with any compensation or allowances related to her status (e.g. related to her seniority, qualifications or length of service). *Gassmayr v Bundesminister fur Wissenschaft und Forschung* (Case C-194/08) [2010] ECR I-6281 held that *art 11* is directly enforceable in national courts.

32.31 Protection from dismissal by reason of pregnancy

An employee will automatically be held to have been unfairly dismissed if the reason or principal reason for his or her dismissal relates to any of the following:

(a)   her pregnancy;

(b)   the fact that she has given birth to a child, where her ordinary or additional maternity leave period is ended by the dismissal;

(c)   the application of a requirement or recommendation such as is referred to in *ERA 1996, s 66(2)* (suspension from work on maternity grounds; see **32.9** above);

(d)   the fact that she took, sought to take or availed herself of the benefits of ordinary or additional maternity leave;

(e)   the fact that he or she took or sought to take parental leave or time off under the *ERA 1996, s 57A* (time off to care for dependants);

(f)   the fact that she failed to return to work after a period of ordinary or additional maternity leave in circumstances where her employer did not notify her of the date on which the period in question would end, and she reasonably believed that the period had not ended, or he gave her less than 28 days' notice of the relevant end date, and it was not reasonably practicable for her to return on that date;

(g)   the fact that she undertook, considered undertaking or refused to undertake work during her statutory maternity leave period in accordance with *reg 12A* of the *MPL Regulations*;

(h)   the fact that he or she declined to sign a workforce agreement for the purposes of the *MPL Regulations*;

(i)   the fact that he or she performed (or proposed to perform) any functions or activities as a workforce representative or as a candidate to be such a representative;

(j)   relates to taking time off under *section 57ZE* (accompanying to ante-natal appointments);

(k)   relates to time off under *sections 57ZJ* or *57ZL* (adoption appointments);

(l)   relates to shared parental leave (see [**32.68**]).

(*Reg 20* of the *MPL Regulations*; *ERA 1996, s 99*.)

An employee will also be treated as having been unfairly dismissed if the reason for the dismissal is that he or she is redundant, but where the circumstances constituting the redundancy applied equally to one or more employees in the same undertaking who held similar positions and who have not been dismissed, and it is shown that the reason or the principal reason for which he or she was selected for dismissal is a reason connected with the above matters (*reg 20(2)*).

In addition, a woman will be treated as having been automatically unfairly dismissed even if there is a genuine redundancy situation if the employer fails to comply with the requirements set out in *reg 10* for dealing with redundancies during ordinary or additional maternity leave (*reg 20(1)(b)*, and see *Simpson v Endsleigh Insurance Services Ltd* [2011] ICR 75). The dismissal for redundancy must, however, end the maternity leave period. See [**32.50**].

There is no longer a small employers' exemption for automatically unfair dismissal. However, there is an exemption in non-redundancy situations, if the employer can show that it is not reasonably practicable (for a reason other than redundancy) to permit the employee to return to a job which is both suitable for her and appropriate for her to do in the circumstances; and an associated employer offers her a job of that kind, and she accepts or unreasonably refuses that offer (*reg 20(7)*). It is for the employer to establish that he has satisfied this statutory defence (*reg 20(8)*).

Even though the dismissal may not be treated as automatically unfair, however, it may still be unfair according to ordinary principles of the law of unfair dismissal. If the employee is dismissed because another employee has been engaged in her position, that will not be an acceptable reason for her dismissal (*McFadden v Greater Glasgow Passenger Transport Executive* [1977] IRLR 327).

Under the previous legislation, it was held that the words 'or any other reason connected with her pregnancy' were to be interpreted broadly (*Clayton v Vigers* [1989] ICR 713). This included a pregnancy-related illness, such as post-natal depression arising in the period of maternity leave following childbirth (*Caledonia Bureau Investment and Property v Caffrey* [1998] ICR 603, [1998] IRLR 110, EAT). The same broad interpretation is likely to apply under the present legislation, but see also *Atkins v Coyle Personnel plc* [2008] IRLR 420, EAT in relation to paternity leave (see below, **32.63**).

In *Ramdoolar v Bycity Ltd* [2005] ICR 368, the EAT held that for a dismissal to be automatically unfair for a reason connected with pregnancy, the employer must know, or believe in the existence, of the pregnancy. It is not sufficient that symptoms of pregnancy existed which the employer ought to have realised meant that the employee was pregnant. The EAT left open the possibility, however, that a dismissal may be automatically unfair if an employer, detecting the symptoms of pregnancy and fearing the consequences, dismisses the employee before his suspicion could be proved right.

A dismissal in connection with pregnancy and the taking of maternity leave may also amount to sex discrimination (see DISCRIMINATION AND EQUAL OPPORTUNITIES – 1 (11)) and, for an example, *Eversheds Legal Services Ltd v De Belin* [2011] IRLR 448, [2011] ICR 1137 where a man succeeded in a sex discrimination claim in respect of preferential treatment given to a woman on maternity leave in redundancy selection scoring which went beyond what was reasonably necessary to compensate a woman for the disadvantages occasioned by her pregnancy/maternity leave.

32.32 *Qualifying period for protection from dismissal*

There is no qualifying period for a complaint of unfair dismissal where the dismissal is for any of the reasons set out in *ERA 1996, s 99* (see above, **32.31**), nor (although less common!) is there any upper age limit (*ERA 1996, s 108(3)*). See also **48.14** TERMINATION OF EMPLOYMENT for the obligation to give reasons for dismissal of pregnant employees.

32.33 Protection from detriment by reason of pregnancy

Reg 19 of the *MPL Regulations* (and the *ERA 1996, s 47C*) confers a statutory right protecting a woman from being subject to any detriment (other than dismissal) by any act, or any deliberate failure to act, by her employer if it is done for the reason that:

(a)   she is pregnant;

(b)   she has given birth to a child, if the act or failure to act takes place during the employee's ordinary or additional maternity leave period;

(c)   she is the subject of a relevant requirement, or a relevant recommendation, as defined by s *66(2)* of the *ERA 1996*;

(d)   she took, sought to take or availed herself of the benefits of, ordinary or additional maternity leave; or

(e)   she took or sought to take parental leave or time off under the *ERA 1996, s 57A*;

(f)   she failed to return to work after a period of ordinary or additional maternity leave in circumstances where her employer did not notify her of the date on which the period in question would end, and she reasonably believed that the period had not ended, or he gave her less than 28 days' notice of the relevant end date, and it was not reasonably practicable for her to return on that date;

(g)   she undertook, considered undertaking or refused to undertake work during her statutory maternity leave period;

(h)   the fact that she declined to sign a workforce agreement for the purposes of the *MPL Regulations*;

(i)   the fact that she performed (or proposed to perform) any functions or activities as a workforce representative or as a candidate to be such a representative.

(j)   relates to taking time off under *section 57ZE* (accompanying to ante-natal appointments);

(k)   relates to time off under *sections 57ZJ* or *57ZL* (adoption appointments);

(l)   relates to shared parental leave (see [**32.68**]).

CFA 2014, s 129 also introduces new protections from detriment for agency workers by inserting a new *subsection (5)* into *section 47C* of the *ERA 1996*.

A woman is treated as availing herself of the benefits of ordinary or additional maternity leave if, during that period, she avails herself of the benefit of any of the terms and conditions of her employment preserved by s *71* or s *73* of *ERA 1996: reg 19(3)–(3A)*.

The failure of an employer to pay a woman on maternity leave wages, salary or a bonus which she would have earned had she been at work cannot be a 'detriment' within the meaning of *reg 19*: see *Hoyland v Asda Stores Ltd* [2005] IRLR 438, [2005] ICR 1235.

32.34 *Remedies*

Where an employee has suffered such a detriment, she may claim to an employment tribunal pursuant to *ERA 1996, s 48*. On such a complaint, it is for the employer to show the ground on which any act, or deliberate failure to act, was done. The complaint must be presented within the period of three months beginning with the date of the act or failure to act, or the last of the series of similar such acts. Time for presenting a complaint can be extended where (as in the case for unfair dismissal) the employment tribunal is satisfied that it was not reasonably practicable for the complaint to be presented within the period of three months.

If the complaint is well-founded, the employment tribunal shall make a declaration to that effect, and may make an award of compensation. The amount of compensation shall be such as the tribunal considers to be just and equitable in all the circumstances, having regard to the infringement to which the complaint relates, and any loss attributable to the act in question (*ERA 1996, s 49*).

32.35 MATERNITY LEAVE

ERA 1996, Pt VIII (ss 71–75), and the *MPL Regulations* made thereunder, provide for a statutory right to maternity leave. It is necessary to distinguish between three types of maternity leave: (a) compulsory maternity leave; (b) ordinary maternity leave ("OML"); and (c) additional maternity leave ("AML").

In summary, compulsory maternity leave is a two-week period in which a mother is not permitted to return to work; OML is a 26 week period; and AML is an additional 26 week period of leave. Taken together, these periods of leave are known as 'statutory maternity leave'.

Church of England clergy have the right to maternity, paternity, parental and adoption leave in accordance with directions given by the Archbishops' Council: see the *Ecclesiastical Offices (Terms of Service) Regulations 2009 (SI 2009/2108), reg 23* and the *Ecclesiastical Offices (Terms of Service) Directions 2010 (SI 2010/1923)*.

See [32.54] in relation to statutory maternity pay. This section concerns statutory maternity leave only.

32.36 Compulsory maternity leave

An employee entitled to OML in accordance with *ERA 1996* shall not be permitted by her employer to work for a period of two weeks commencing with the day on which childbirth occurs. (This is described as 'compulsory maternity leave' (*ERA 1996, s 72*, and the *MPL Regulations, reg 8*). Failure to comply with this prohibition renders the employer liable on summary conviction to a fine (*ERA 1996, s 72(5)*).

Note that an occupier of a factory will be subject to a fine if he knowingly allows a woman to be employed therein within four weeks after she has given birth: *Public Health Act 1936, s 205*.

32.37 Ordinary maternity leave

The OML period commences with the date which the employee notifies as the date on which she intends her absence to commence (see below **32.39**), or if earlier, the first day on which she is absent from work wholly or partly because of pregnancy or childbirth after the beginning of the 4th week before the EWC (*reg 6(1)–(2)*). If childbirth occurs before the relevant date, OML commences on the day after the day of the birth (*reg 6(2)*). 'Childbirth' means the birth of a living child or the birth of a child whether living or dead after 24 weeks of pregnancy (*reg 2(1)*).

32.38 The OML period continues for 26 weeks or until the latest of the end of the compulsory maternity leave period, the expiry of any period during which there is any statutory prohibition on the employee working by reason of her recently having given birth, or upon her dismissal (*reg 7*).

32.39 In order to enjoy the right to OML, the employee must generally:

(a)   notify her employer of:

(i)   her pregnancy;

(ii)   the EWC'; and

(iii)   the date on which she intends her OML period to start;

no later than the 15th week before her EWC or, if that is not reasonably practicable, as soon as is reasonably practicable; and

(b)   if requested to do so by her employer, produce for his inspection a certificate from a registered medical practitioner or a registered midwife stating the EWC (*reg 4(1)*).

The notification of the date on which the employee intends her OML period to start must be in writing, if the employer so requests (*reg 4(2)*). Note that OML cannot start any earlier than the beginning of the 11th week before the EWC (*reg 4(2)*). As to these notification provisions, and for an example of a case in which it was found to have been not reasonably practicable for the employee to comply with *reg 4*, see the decision of the EAT in *St Alphonsus RC Primary School v Blenkinsop* (UKEAT/0082/09) [2009] All ER (D) 54 (Aug).

However:

(a)   where the period of OML commences the day following the first day after the beginning of the 4th week before the EWC on which she is absent from work wholly or partly because of pregnancy, by *reg 6(1)(b)*, the employee must notify her employer as soon as is reasonably practicable that she is absent wholly or partly because of pregnancy and of the date on which her absence on that account began (*reg 4(3)*); and

(b)   where childbirth occurs before the notified leave date or before the employee has notified such a date (see *reg 6(2)*), the employee must notify her employer that she has given birth (and on which date) as soon as is reasonably practicable after the birth (*reg 4(4)*).

Such notice must be given in writing if the employer so requests (*reg 4*).

The date upon which the employee commences OML may be varied if she gives 28 days' notice before the date that is being varied, or 28 days' notice before the new date, whichever is earlier (or if those dates cannot be complied with, she gives notice as soon as it is reasonably practicable to do so) (*reg 4(1A)*). Such notice must be in writing if the employer so requests.

There is no service requirement for OML.

32.40 An employee who is absent from work at any time during her OML period is entitled to the benefit of the terms and conditions of employment which would otherwise have been applicable to her, such as holiday entitlement, even if they do not arise under her contract of employment, although this does not confer any entitlement to remuneration (*ERA 1996, s 71* and *reg 9*). The *MPL Regulations* define 'remuneration' as wages or salary only (*reg 9(3)*).

In *Peninsula Business Services v Donaldson* (UKEAT/0249/15) (9 March 2016) the EAT held that *reg 9* of the *MPL Regulations* did not require a salary sacrifice scheme for childcare vouchers, whereby a portion of a person's remuneration was diverted in exchange for the aforesaid vouchers, to be continued during maternity leave. The vouchers provided under the scheme were not a benefit as such, but remuneration that had been diverted for the tax-efficient provision of childcare. The EAT disapproved HMRC guidance providing to the contrary in its judgment. However, the EAT noted *obiter* at [35] that if the vouchers had merely been given as such, as an additional benefit, *reg 9* would require the continued provision of the vouchers. Clearly, the distinction drawn by the EAT is of significance for all salary sacrifice benefits during maternity leave.

The employee is also bound during this period by any obligations arising under these same terms and conditions (*ERA 1996, s 71* and *reg 9*).

In *Gomez (Merino) v Continental Industrias del Caucho SA* (C-342/01) [2004] ECR I-2605, [2004] IRLR 407, [2005] ICR 1040, the ECJ held that a worker must be able to take the paid annual leave to which she is entitled under the *Working Time Directive* during a period other than the period of her maternity leave.

32.41 An employee returning after an isolated period of OML is ordinarily entitled to return to the job in which she was employed before her absence (*reg 18*). 'Job' means the nature of the work that she is employed to do in accordance with her contract, and the capacity and place in which she is so employed (*reg 2(1)*). See **32.50** below for the considerations relating to a redundancy situation.

The purpose of this provision is to put the returning employee back into a situation as near as possible to that which she left: see *Blundell v Governing Body of St Andrews Catholic Primary School* [2007] ICR 1451, EAT. In that case, it did not mean that the returning teacher had to be offered the job of teaching the particular class that she had taught before her maternity leave. The work that she was employed to do was that of a teacher, her capacity was viewed as a class teacher rather than the teacher of a particular reception class, and her place of work was the school and not a particular classroom. Note that the right to return to the job carries with it the right to return on terms and conditions no less favourable than those that the employee would have enjoyed had she not been absent, and with her seniority, pension and similar rights as they would have been had she not been absent (*reg 18A*).

32.42 An employee who has a contractual or other right to maternity leave may not exercise both that and the statutory right separately, but may take advantage of whichever right is in any particular respect more favourable. The provisions of *ERA 1996* and of the *Regulations* then apply, modified as necessary, to the exercise of the composite right (*reg 21*).

32.43 The position in relation to surrogacy arrangements, up to 5 April 2015, was that in two cases (*Z v A Government Department* (Case C-363/12) and *CD v ST* (Case C-167/12)) the CJEU held that women who receive children under a surrogacy arrangement are not entitled to maternity leave, even where the receiving mother breast feeds the child. However, the CJEU also held that this does not prevent a member state introducing more provision that is more favourable to commissioning mothers who receive babies through surrogacy. The *CFA 2014* did just that from April 2015: it provided for surrogacy parents to receive the same rights to leave and pay as those adopting children (see [**32.68**]).

32.44 Additional maternity leave

An employee who qualifies for OML now qualifies automatically for AML as well (*reg 4*). There is no qualifying period of employment for this right. She will continue to have the benefit of her terms and conditions of employment during AML (and is bound by any obligations), in the same way as during OML (*reg 9* and see above **32.29**).

The AML period commences on the day after the last day of the employee's OML period (*reg 6(3)*). Importantly, where the employee notifies her employer under reg 4 of the date on which her OML period will commence or has commenced, the employer shall notify her of the date on which her AML period shall end either 28 days of the date on which he received the notification (where the notification is under *reg 4(1)(a)(iii), (3)(b)* or *(4)(b)*) or within 28 days on which the employee's OML period commenced (where the notification is under *reg 4(1A)*) (*reg 7(6),(7)*).

The right to AML continues until the end of the period of 26 weeks from the date upon which it commences, unless the employee is dismissed before that date (*reg 7(4)*).

32.45 An employee who is entitled to AML may return to work before the end of the AML period. To do so, she has to give her employer not less than eight weeks' notice of the date on which she intends to return (*reg 11(1)*). If she does give this notice, then it would appear that her employer cannot seek to postpone her return date.

Where an employee does not give eight weeks' notice of her intended return date and attempts to return to work earlier than the end of her AML period, then her employer is entitled to postpone her return to such a date as will mean that he has eight weeks' notice of her return (*reg 11(2)*). The only exception to this is that the postponement cannot extend beyond the date of the end of the AML period (*reg 11(3)*). During the period of postponement, the employer is under no contractual obligation to pay any remuneration until the date to which the employee's return was postponed, save where he has failed to notify her of when the AML period was due to end (*reg 11(4)–(5)*).

An employee is entitled to change her mind as to when to return to work during the AML period, if she has already given notice of return before the end of that period or if the employer has (in line with the procedure above) postponed her return date (*reg 11(2A)–(2B)*). If the employee wishes to return to work later than the original return date, she must give her employer not less than eight weeks' notice ending with the original return date. If she wishes to return earlier than the original return date, she must give at least eight weeks' notice of the new return date.

The employee does not need to inform her employer that she intends to exercise her right to return at the end of the AML period unless she is specifically requested to do so by her employer. In addition, an employer is no longer entitled to request confirmation that the employee will be returning to work at the end of the AML period (the former *reg 12* has been revoked).

32.46 The right on redundancy is the same as for employees seeking to return after OML (see **32.50** above).

32.47 The returning employee has the right to return to the job in which she was employed before her absence or, if it is not reasonably practicable for the employer to permit her to return to that job, to another job which is both suitable for her and appropriate for her to do in the circumstances (*reg 18(2)*). The definition of 'job' is the same as for returnees from OML: see *Blundell v Governing Body of St Andrews Catholic Primary School* [2007] ICR 1451, EAT and see above **32.40**. The right is also to return on terms and conditions no less favourable than would have applied if the employee had not been absent. She is entitled to the same seniority, pension rights and similar rights as she would have enjoyed if she had not taken any AML (*reg 18A*). There is no right as such to return to work on a part-time basis, or on terms preferable to the returning employee: see *British Telecommunications plc v Roberts* [1996] IRLR 601, [1996] ICR 625, EAT. Nevertheless, an employer's refusal to permit an employee to job share or return part-time might constitute indirect sex discrimination (*Hardys & Hansons plc v Lax* [2005] IRLR 726, [2005] ICR 1565, CA).

32.48 Save for the limited circumstances described by *regulation 20* of the *MPL Regulations*, the legislation has nothing to say about the difficult question of mothers who do not return to work on the return date. *Regulation 20* states that a mother will be automatically unfairly dismissed if the reason for the dismissal relates to the fact that she failed to return to work after a period of ordinary or additional maternity leave in circumstances where her employer did not notify her of the date on which the period in question would end, and she reasonably believed that the period had not ended, or he gave her less than 28 days' notice of the relevant end date, and it was not reasonably practicable for her to return on that date

In other circumstances, it may well be that the law under the previous legislation will prevail. It may be useful therefore to consider the decision of the House of Lords in *Halfpenny v IGE Medical Systems Ltd* [2001] IRLR 96, [2001] ICR 73, construing the former legislation.

The facts of *Halfpenny* are relatively straightforward. The employee failed to return to work on the notified return date for reasons of ill-health, supported by a medical certificate. As she had not exhausted her contractual entitlement to sick leave and had a good reason for her absence, her employer was found to have dismissed her wrongfully by refusing to extend her period of leave. In addition, the employer was found to have discriminated against the employee on grounds of her sex as it would have allowed a male employee to continue sick leave with pay.

In the Court of Appeal ([1999] IRLR 177, [1999] ICR 834), it was held (confirming the earlier decision of *Crees v Royal London Mutual Insurance Society Ltd* [1998] IRLR 245, [1998] ICR 848) that to avail herself of the right not to be unfairly dismissed following maternity leave, an employee need not physically return to work on the notified day of return. An employee was held to have exercised the right to return to work following maternity leave (and also preserved her continuity of employment) merely by giving the appropriate notice of return before the notified date of return.

This aspect of the decision was overturned by the House of Lords, where it was held that an employee did not avail herself of the 'return to work' merely by giving the appropriate notice of return if she did not actually return to work on the notified day. Rather, the employee had to give the appropriate notice and also demonstrate that, on the notified date for return, she had done something consistent with the due performance by her of her revived contract of employment. Normally, this would mean that she actually returned to work physically. If, however, under the contract she would not be bound to return on that day (eg as a result of an accident, a strike, or poor weather conditions) she merely had to have done something to demonstrate that she would have returned to work otherwise. If she were ill, she would have to provide the necessary certificates that would be required of her under the contract.

The House of Lords went on to decide that where the employee had demonstrated the appropriate conduct for a 'return to work', she would be treated as having been 'dismissed' by her employer if he refused to let her return, for the purposes of the law of unfair dismissal only. She had no right, however, to claim that she had been wrongfully dismissed as the contract of employment would be treated as having been suspended until her actual return. This aspect of the decision may have been overtaken by the fact that the period of AML during which the contract continues ends pursuant to the legislation.

See *Rashid v Asian Community Care Services Ltd* (EAT/480/99, 16 November 2000) [2000] All ER (D) 2344 for a case in which an employment tribunal found that a mother had terminated the contract of employment by failing to return to work, a finding reversed by the EAT.

32.49 An employee who has both a statutory and a contractual right to return to work may not exercise the two rights separately, but may take advantage of whichever right is the more favourable in any particular respect (*reg 21*).

32.50 Redundancy during maternity leave

If, during the OML or AML period, redundancy makes it impracticable to continue to employ an employee under her existing contract, she is entitled to be offered alternative employment with her employer, his successor (as defined by *ERA 1996, s 235(1)*) or an associated employer (see **7.9(a)** CONTINUOUS EMPLOYMENT) if a suitable available vacancy exists. The offer must be made before the old employment ends, and the new employment must commence immediately the old employment ends. It must involve work of a kind suitable in relation to the employee and appropriate for her to do in the circumstances, and the terms and conditions as to capacity, place of employment and otherwise must not be substantially less favourable than under the old contract (*MPL Regulations, reg 10*).

These provisions have been considered by the EAT in *Simpson v Endsleigh Insurance Services Ltd* [2011] ICR 75. Amongst other things, the EAT indicated that: (i) the requirement of suitability in *reg 10(2)* can only sensibly be tested by the requirement that it is coupled with a new contract of employment which complies with *reg 10(3)* – the provisions should not be looked at in isolation; (ii) there is no requirement on the employee to engage in this process and it is up to the employers, knowing what they do about the employee, to decide whether or not a vacancy is suitable; and (iii) the EAT was "by no means satisfied" that an employer could choose to test suitability by assessment and interview, contrary to the suggestion in the IDS Handbook on Redundancy. More recently, in *Wainwright v Sefton Borough Council* [2015] IRLR 90, [2015] ICR 652, the EAT considered how *regulation 10* may operate depending upon the particular redundancy process chosen. The EAT reiterated that the obligation under *regulation 10* arises once the employee is redundant within the meaning of *ERA 1996, s 139*, and does not depend on any label imposed by the employer (such as 'displacement' or 'redeployment'). The tribunal also emphasised that a breach of *regulation 10* does not necessarily also entail discrimination under *section 18* of the *EqA*.

More favourable treatment of a woman for a reason related to her pregnancy can be less favourable treatment of a man for sex-related reasons and unlawful discrimination: *Eversheds Legal Services v De Belin* [2011] IRLR 448, [2011] ICR 1137. In that case the EAT considered that the protection of special treatment afforded to women in connection with pregnancy or childbirth under *paragraph 2* of *Schedule 7* to the *2010 Act* must be proportionate, and in *De Belin* the employer could have compared periods for the purposes of redundancy scoring where both employees had been at work.

In *Riezniece v Zemkopibas ministrija (Republic of Latvia)* (Case C-7/12) the CJEU held that the Framework Agreement on Parental Leave precluded a worker being put in a less favourable position in a redundancy selection exercise because they had taken parental leave; and stated that a person returning from parental leave cannot be dismissed merely because the post to which the person would be returning to work is due to be abolished.

32.51 Dismissal of replacement

Where an employer engages an employee to take the place of one who is absent due to pregnancy, the subsequent dismissal of that employee upon the resumption of work by the original employee will be considered to be a dismissal for a (potentially fair) some other substantial reason (see **54.14** UNFAIR DISMISSAL – **II**) only if the employer informs the employee in writing, on engaging her, that her employment will be terminated on the resumption of work by another employee who is, or will be, absent wholly or partly because of pregnancy, childbirth, adoption leave, APL or SPL, or the end of a period of suspension from work on maternity grounds, and if the employee is dismissed in order to make it possible to give work to the returning employee (*ERA 1996, s 106*). The language used in the written information must be clear and unambiguous: see *Victoria and Albert Museum v Durrant* [2011] IRLR 290.

However, this fact does not, in itself, make the dismissal fair. The employment tribunal will consider whether the dismissal was fair in all the circumstances (see further **54.4** UNFAIR DISMISSAL – **II**). The EAT in *Victoria and Albert Museum v Durrant* also indicated, *obiter*, that *s 106* does not operate in all cases to deem the reason for dismissal to be for some other substantial reason. In some cases the reason for dismissal might be (for example) redundancy, notwithstanding that *s 106* is engaged.

32.52   Right to written statement of reasons for dismissal

Without having to request it, and irrespective of how long she has been employed, an employee is entitled to a written statement giving particulars of the reason for her dismissal if she is dismissed whilst pregnant, or after childbirth in circumstances in which her OML or AML period ends by reason of the dismissal: *ERA 1996, s 92(4)*.

32.53   Work during statutory maternity leave

An employee may carry out up to 10 days' work for her employer during her statutory maternity leave period without bringing her maternity leave to an end (*reg 12A(1)*), known as 'keeping in touch' or 'KIT' days. Work means any work done under the contract of employment and may include training or any activity undertaken for the purposes of keeping in touch with the workplace (*reg 12A(3)*). Such work does not extend the total duration of the statutory maternity leave period (*reg 12A(7)*).

Any work carried out on any date constitutes a day's work for these purposes (*reg 12A(2)*). However, reasonable contact from time to time between an employee and her employer (eg to discuss her return to work) does not bring the maternity leave period to an end (*reg 12A(4)*). There is no right for an employer to require that an employee work during the statutory maternity leave period, and no right for an employee to work during this period (*reg 12A(6)*). The employee does not lose her entitlement to SMP during the 10 keeping in touch days and any additional payment for the work done is a matter of contract between her and the employer.

32.54   STATUTORY MATERNITY PAY

The statutory provisions relating to the system of statutory maternity pay ("**SMP**"), first introduced by the *Social Security Act 1989*, have been consolidated into the *Social Security Contributions and Benefits Act 1992* ("**SSCBA 1992**"). The relevant provisions have been the subject of significant amendments to reflect the *Pregnant Workers Directive* (*Directive 92/85/EEC*). The general position is that the employer pays SMP, but the employer may recoup a significant proportion of the SMP paid from the government (see [**32.60**]).

The legislative scheme governing payment of SMP and, in particular, the rules on when the SMP period commences were considered by the Upper Tribunal in *Wade v North Yorkshire Police Authority* [2011] IRLR 393, UT (TCC).

It is not possible to contract out of the obligation to pay SMP. Consequently, for the purposes of a settlement agreement, it is not sufficient to settle 'all claims' (in the normal way) by the payment of a sum unless the part of the total sum constituting SMP is specifically identified in the settlement agreement: see *Campus Living Villages UK Ltd v Commissioners for HMRC* [2016] UKFTT 0738 (TC). In that case, despite making a payment of £60,000 by way of settlement, the FTT held that a further £42,325.26 was payable by way of SMP due to the drafting of the settlement agreement.

There may also be a contractual right to maternity pay under a woman's contract of employment. This is often known as 'enhanced' maternity pay. If the employee fails to return to work and contractual maternity pay becomes repayable to the employer pursuant to a term of the contract, either the employer or the employee may be able to recover the National Insurance contributions on such pay from the Secretary of State.

32.55   Qualifying requirements

An employee must normally satisfy the following conditions before she can qualify for SMP:

(a)   She must have been continuously employed by her employer for at least 26 weeks ending with the week immediately preceding the 14th week before the EWC, but have ceased to work for him (see CONTINUOUS EMPLOYMENT (7)). (Note that she will have normally have 'ceased to work for him' by reason of her pregnancy, but there is no requirement to prove this (see further the repealing provisions in the *Employment Act 2002, Sch 8, para 1*));

(b)   her normal weekly earnings, for the period of 8 weeks ending with the week immediately preceding the 14th week before the EWC, must be not less than the lower limit for the payment of National Insurance contributions (£113 per week from 6 April 2017);

(c)   she must have become pregnant and reached, or been confined before reaching, the start of the 11th week before the expected week of confinement.

(SSCBA 1992, s 164(1), (2).)

'Confinement' is defined as labour resulting in the issue of a living child, or labour after 24 weeks of pregnancy resulting in the issue of a child whether alive or dead *(SSCBA 1992, s 171(1))*. 'Employee' is defined as meaning a woman who is gainfully employed in Great Britain either under a contract of service or in an office (including elective office) with general earnings *(SSCBA 1992, s 171(1))*. (Note that this definition is subject to various other statutory provisions, including those in *s 171(1)* itself and in *reg 17* of the *Statutory Maternity Pay (General) Regulations 1986 (SI 1986/1960)* (the "**SMP Regulations**")).)

There are certain exceptions to the above requirement of continuous employment. For example, the employer remains liable to pay SMP if the period of continuous employment was not less than eight weeks and he brought the contract of employment to an end solely or mainly for the purpose of avoiding his liability for SMP *(reg 3 of the SMP Regulations)*. In addition, the right to SMP survives if the woman is confined more than 14 weeks before the expected date of confinement, and would, but for her confinement, otherwise have qualified *(reg 4 of the SMP Regulations as amended by SI 1994/1367, reg 3)*.

For the purpose of calculating continuity of employment, it is the existence of the contract of employment which is crucial, and not whether the employee is in fact working. In *Secretary of State for Employment v Doulton Sanitaryware Ltd* [1981] ICR 477, EAT (decided under the previous law relating to maternity pay), it was held on the facts that the parties intended the contract to continue even though the employee had stopped working (she had been put on a list of 'prolonged absentees'). In *Rosselle v Institut national d'assurance maladie-invalide* (Case C-65/14) the CJEU held that the six month period of employment required to establish entitlement to a maternity allowance could not be re-started merely because a worker's employment status or the post of the worker has changed at that particular employer.

It is clearly intended that the right to SMP should not be conditional upon an intention to return to work after the confinement.

There is no entitlement to SMP in respect of any week in which the employee is in legal custody or sentenced to a term of imprisonment, other than a suspended sentence, or in respect of any subsequent week within the maternity pay period *(reg 9 of the SMP Regulations)*.

Members of Her Majesty's forces are excluded from the right to SMP *(SSCBA 1992, s 161(2))*. The right extends to persons working for the Crown *(s 161)*, within the EU, to employees who are absent from Great Britain on holiday or for business purposes at any time during the maternity pay period, as well as to certain mariners (see the *Statutory Maternity Pay (Persons Abroad and Mariners) Regulations 1987 (SI 1987/418)*, as amended by *Social Security Contributions, Statutory Maternity Pay and Statutory Sick Pay (Miscellaneous Amendments) Regulations 1996 (SI 1996/777), reg 4)*.

SSCBA 1992, s 164(6) provides that any agreement is void in so far as it purports to exclude or limit the right to SMP.

32.56 Procedure for making a claim

The employee must give her employer (or the person liable to make payments of SMP) 28 days' prior notice of the date from which she expects his liability to pay SMP to begin, or if that is not reasonably practicable, such notice as is reasonably practicable (*s 164(4)* and *reg 23* of the *SMP Regulations*). That notice must be in writing if the liable person so requests (*SSCBA, s 164(5)*).

The employee must also provide the liable person with a maternity certificate signed by a doctor or midwife as evidence of her pregnancy and of the expected date of confinement and there is a prescribed form for such certificates (*reg 22 of the SMP Regulations; Social Security Administration Act 1992, s 15; Statutory Maternity Pay (Medical Evidence) Regulations 1987 (SI 1987/235)*).

32.57 Period of entitlement

SMP is payable in respect of each week during the 'maternity pay period'. The maternity pay period will be a period of 39 consecutive weeks (*reg 2(2)* of the *SMP Regulations*). In general, when it starts depends upon when the employee gives notice and stops work (*reg 2(1)* of the *SMP Regulations*). However, ordinarily the first day of the period will not be earlier than the 11th week before the expected week of confinement, nor later than the day immediately following the day of confinement. Note that *reg 2* of the *SMP Regulations* contains other specific rules on the start of the maternity pay period. The *SMP Regulations* do not permit payment to cease upon dismissal.

These rules were considered by the Upper Tribunal in *Wade v North Yorkshire Police Authority* [2011] IRLR 393, UT (TCC). The UT provided detailed guidance the start date for SMP and observed that a woman could nominate a date from which she wished to claim SMP and would be ceasing to work "in conformity with [a] notice" for the purposes of *reg 2(1)* even if she has previously ceased to work on some other basis (in a way analogous to her right to claim statutory maternity leave from a date of her choosing, even if she had previously been away from work for e.g. annual leave or sick leave).

SMP is not ordinarily payable by an employer in respect of a week during any part of which the woman works under a contract of service with him (*SSCBA, s 165(4)*).

32.58 Amount of payments

SSCBA 1992, s 166 provides for two rates of payment. (Note: the application of *s 166* is modified by *SI 1986/1960, reg 4(3)* (as amended by *SI 1994/1367, reg 3*) where the employee is confined more than 14 weeks before the expected date of confinement, and would, but for her confinement, otherwise have qualified; see **32.48** above.)

For the first six weeks of the maternity pay period, the rate is calculated as being 90% of the employee's normal weekly earnings for the period of 8 weeks immediately preceding the 14th week before the EWC (there is no minimum rate of payment) (*SSCBA, s 166(2)*). The calculation is made by reference to actual earnings, regardless of any abnormal amounts in those eight weeks. After the first six weeks, the payment for the remaining 33 weeks is set at the lesser of £140.98 per week or the rate payable during the first six weeks (*SCCBA, s 166(1)(b)*; *reg 6* of the *SMP Regulations*). The rate of SMP is amended annually, and the stated rate is correct as of 6 April 2017.

In any case where a woman is awarded a pay increase (or would have been awarded such an increase had she not then been absent on statutory maternity leave) and the pay increase applies to the whole or any part of the period between the beginning of the relevant period

For the purposes of presentation, throughout this chapter the person who shares in SPL or pay who but who is not the mother or primary adopter is referred to as the mother or primary adopter's **"partner"**. The partner is referred to in the masculine gender throughout. It is also assumed that the primary adopter is female. The following key abbreviations are used:

- **"SPL"** – shared parental leave.

- **"SSPP"** – statutory shared parental pay.

The right to shared parental leave and pay respectively were created by inserting new *sections 75E to 75K* into the *ERA 1996*, and *sections 171ZU to 171ZZ5* into the *Social Security Contributions and Benefits Act 1992* (**"SSCBA 1992"**). Those sections came into effect on 30 June 2014, primarily for the purpose of making regulations. The substance of the SPL and SSPP schemes are set out in those regulations. The principal regulations, and the abbreviations used for them in this chapter, are:

- The *Shared Parental Leave Regulations 2014 (SI 2014/3050)*: the **"SPL Regulations"**;

- The *Statutory Shared Parental Pay (General) Regulations 2014 (SI 2014/3051)*: the **"SSPP Regulations"**.

- The *Maternity and Adoption Leave (Curtailment of Statutory Rights to Leave) Regulations 2014 (SI 2014/ 3052)*: the **"Leave Curtailment Regulations"**.

- The *Maternity Allowance (Curtailment) Regulations 2014 (2014/3053)*: the **"MA Curtailment Regulations"**;

- The *Statutory Maternity Pay and Statutory Adoption Pay (Curtailment) Regulations 2014 (SI 2014/3054)*: the **"Pay Curtailment Regulations"**.

The Department for Business, Innovation and Skills published 'Employer's Technical Guide to Shared Parental Leave and Pay' in December 2014 (the **"BIS Guide"**), the majority of which is helpfully set out in a 'Frequently Asked Questions' format. ACAS has also published 'Shared Parental Leave: a good practice guide for employers and employees' (the **"ACAS Guide"**). Both are referred to below.

Shared parental leave

32.69   *Eligibility for shared parental leave: birth cases*

If both partners are to take up SPL, both partners must fulfil the relevant qualification criteria set out in the *SPL Regulations*. The criteria for a mother's entitlement to SPL is set out at *regulation 4* of the *SPL Regulations*, and the partner's entitlement to SPL is set out in *regulation 5* of the *SPL Regulations*. The criteria for the mother under *regulation 4* are:

- The mother is an employee (see *sections 75E to 75K* of the *ERA 1996*, under which 'employee' is defined by *ERA 1996, s 230(1)*).

- The mother satisfies the continuity of employment test set out in *regulation 35* of the *SPL Regulations*. *Regulation 35* requires the mother to have been in continuous employment with the same employer for 26 weeks immediately before the 'relevant week' (which is the 15th week before the EWC), and to have remained in continuous employment at that employer until the week before any period to be taken as SPL. Note that by contrast, there is no such requirement for statutory maternity leave.

- The mother has the main responsibility for the care of the child (along with her partner). This requirement is not further defined.

32.69   Maternity and Parental Rights

- The mother is entitled to SML in respect of the child (see **[32.35]**).

- The mother has curtailed her SML (see **[32.73]** below) and complied with the relevant notice and evidential requirements (see **[32.81]** below]).

- The mother's partner (a) fulfils the employment and earnings test set out in *regulation 36* of the *SPL Regulations* (**[32.70]** below)), (b) with the mother, the partner has the main responsibility for the care of the child, and (c) falls within the relevant class of persons under the definition of 'P' in *regulation 4* of the *SPL Regulations* (see the next paragraph)

A mother may share her leave with the child's father, her spouse, civil partner or her **"partner"** (see the definition of "P" in *regulation 3* of the *SPL Regulations*). Partner is defined in *regulation 3* of the *SPL Regulations* as someone of either sex who lives with the mother and child "in an enduring family relationship" but is not the mother's child, parent, grandchild, grandparent, sibling, aunt, uncle, niece or nephew. There is no indication in the *SPL Regulations* of what an 'enduring family relationship' is.

32.70 The employment and earnings test under *regulation 36* requires the partner to fulfil two conditions:

- To have been an employed earner or self-employed earner (see *section 2* of *SSCBA 1992*) for at least 26 weeks of the last 66 weeks before the EWC (which do not need to be continuous); and,

- To have average weekly earnings of not less than the amount specified in *section 35(6A)* of the *SSCBA 1992* in the tax year before the tax year in which the EWC falls, which is currently £30.

See *regulation 36* and the relevant sections of the *SSCBA 1992* referred to therein for further details.

32.71 It is also possible for the partner of a mother or primary adopter to take SPL, notwithstanding the fact that the mother or primary adopter cannot take SPL (see FAQ 10 of the BIS Guide). The requirements for a partner to take SPL in such a situation (and indeed, generally) are set out in *regulation 5* of the *SPL Regulations*. An example of this situation, in the case of birth parents, is where the mother is entitled to SMP or MA which she curtails, and the partner fulfils the criteria set out in *regulation 36* of the *SPL Regulations* (employment and earnings test), the partner may take SPL even if the mother or primary adopter does not fulfil the requirements of *regulation 35* (continuity of employment test). This may be the case if the mother is self-employed or her employment terminated after she acquired the right to SMP. The possibility of the partner being eligible for SPL despite the mother's ineligibility for SPL arises from the differences between *regulation 4(2)* and *5(3)* in the *SPL Regulations*. Generally, if the mother qualifies for SML, the partner will be entitled to SPL; but if the mother only qualifies for SMP or MA, she cannot receive SPL but the partner may be entitled to it.

32.72 *Eligibility for shared parental leave: adoption, surrogacy and special cases*

Part 3 of the *SPL Regulations* (*regulations 20* to *34*) sets out the entitlement of adopters (*Part 2, regulations 4* to *19*, makes equivalent provision in respect of birth mothers and their partners). The criteria for adopters under regulation 20 are much the same as those for mothers under *regulation 4* of the *SPL Regulations*, as is the scheme for adoptive parents generally. The primary adopter (defined as 'A' in *regulation 3* of the *SPL Regulations*) is the person with whom the child is or is expected to be placed for adoption; special provision is made in *regulation 3* for cases in which two people have been matched jointly.

The provisions in respect of adopters include local authority foster parents who have a child placed with them with a view to adoption in accordance with *section 22C* of the *Children Act 1989*: see the definition of 'placed for adoption' in *regulation 3* of the *SPL Regulations*.

The following regulations make special provision for adoptions from overseas:

- the *Employment Rights Act 1996 (Application of Sections 75G and 75H to Adoptions from Overseas) Regulations 2014 (SI 2014/3091)*;

- the *Shared Parental Leave and Paternity and Adoption Leave (Adoptions from Overseas) Regulations 2014 (SI 2014/3092)*, and

- the *Statutory Shared Parental Pay (Adoption from Overseas) Regulations 2014 (SI 2014/3093)*.

The *Statutory Shared Parental Pay (Persons Abroad and Mariners) Regulations 2014 (SI 2014/3134)* makes provision for certain individuals who work outside the UK and seafarers.

Finally, the *Paternity, Adoption and Shared Parental Leave (Parental Order Cases) Regulations 2014 (2014/3096)* extend the right to adoption leave to intended parents under a surrogacy agreement, and by that route also extend to them the right to SPL. The conditions for taking SPL are the generally same as those for adoptive parents, albeit modified by the regulations. Surrogate parents are not mentioned again in respect of SPL in this chapter. Note that the birth mother of a child given up for adoption or under a surrogacy agreement may also be entitled to SPL. See further the following regulations:

- The *Social Security Contributions and Benefits Act 1992 (Application of Parts 12ZA, 12ZB and 12ZC to Parental Order Cases) Regulations 2014 (SI 2014/2866)*;

- The *Employment Rights Act 1996 (Application of Sections 75A, 75B, 75G, 75H, 80A and 80B to Parental Order Cases) Regulations 2014 (SI 2014/3095)*;

- The *Statutory Paternity Pay and Statutory Adoption Pay (Parental Orders and Prospective Adopters) Regulations 2014 (SI 2014/2934)*;

- *Statutory Shared Parental Pay (Parental Order Cases) Regulations 2014 (SI 2014/3097)*.

32.73 *Curtailment of leave*

In order to take SPL, a mother must curtail her entitlement to SML, or in the case of adoption, the adopter must curtail her entitlement to statutory adoption leave ("SAL"). There are two methods of doing so: (1) returning to work early, with the relevant notice requirements (see next paragraph); or (2) giving a curtailment notice in accordance with the *Maternity and Adoption Leave (Curtailment of Statutory Rights to Leave) Regulations 2014 (SI 2014/3052)*: the "**Leave Curtailment Regulations**". Note that the first two weeks of SML are compulsory for a mother: see *section 72(1)* of the *ERA 1996*, *regulation 8* of the *MPL Regulations*, and *regulation 6(2)(a)* of the *Leave Curtailment Regulations*.

32.74 Returning to work early entails following the relevant notice requirements under the regulations for SML or statutory adoption leave. The relevant regulations are *regulation 11* of the *MPL Regulations*, and *regulation 25* of the *PAL Regulations*. Generally, those regulations provide that the employee must give the employer at least eight weeks' notice of the date that she intends to return to work.

32.75 A leave curtailment notice must be issued in accordance with the procedure set out *Part 2* (in the case of SML; *regulations 5–8*) or *Part 3* (in the case of statutory adoption leave; *regulations 9–12*) of the *Leave Curtailment Regulations*.

A leave curtailment notice must be in writing, and state the date on which the mother or adopter's leave is to end. That date is known as the 'leave curtailment date': see the definition in *regulation 3(1)* of the *SPL Regulations*. The leave curtailment date must be at least eight weeks after the date on which the leave curtailment notice was given to the employer: *regulations 6(2)(b)* and *10(2)(a)* of the *Leave Curtailment Regulations*. See *regulations 6(2)* and *10(2)* for further conditions. If the person is employed by more than one employer, the leave curtailment notice must be given to all her employers at the same time: *regulation 5(3)* and *9(3)* of the *Leave Curtailment Regulations*.

When a leave curtailment notice is provided to an employer, the notice and evidential requirements must be complied with: specifically, a notice of entitlement to SPL, or a declaration of consent and entitlement must be provided. A notice of entitlement to SPL is required where the mother herself wishes intends to take SPL. The evidential requirements relating to a notice of entitlement are burdensome; the declaration of consent and entitlement provides a less burdensome option that permits the partner to take SPL (as the mother's leave will be curtailed), even though the mother will have to give a notice of entitlement later if she wishes to take SPL herself. See [32.82] for further details.

A leave curtailment notice may be revoked only in accordance with *regulations 8* (birth) or *12* (adoption) of the *Leave Curtailment Regulations*, by means of a 'revocation notice'. Those regulations set out three circumstances in which a leave curtailment notice may be revoked: (1) neither parent are entitled to SPL or SSPP; (2) the death of the mother or adopter's partner; (3) in the case of birth only, the notice was provided before the birth of the child. See the BIS Guide for further detail.

32.76 *Rules on how SPL may be taken*

Regulations 7 and *23* of the *SPL Regulations* for birth and adoption cases respectively make general provision as to how SPL must be taken. First, SPL may only be taken between the date of birth or adoption and the first birthday/anniversary of the child's adoption. Consequently, a partner could take SPL from the date of birth of a child, so long as a mother has fixed her curtailment date (and even though the mother would still be on SML until the curtailment date). Second, SPL must be taken in complete weeks. Third, SPL may be taken in continuous or discontinuous periods (see [32.78] below). Fourth, the minimum amount of time taken as SPL is one week. Fifth, SPL may be taken concurrently. Specifically, one parent may be absent on SPL whilst the other is absent for the particular child on any of the types of parental leave provided for under *Part 8* of the *1996 Act* (i.e. SPL, SML, SAL, statutory paternity leave or unpaid parental leave) or in receipt of pay under *section 35* or *Part 12, 12ZA* or *12ZC* of the *SSCBA 1992* in respect of the same child (i.e. MA, SMP, SAP, statutory paternity pay or SSPP).

32.77 The total amount of leave available to be taken as SPL is determined by *regulations 6* (in the case of birth) and *22* (in the case of adoption) of the *SPL Regulations*. In both the calculations set out below, the following must also be deducted from the total SPL available: (a) any periods of leave booked or taken by the other parent; (b) any periods of leave required to be taken under *regulation 18* or *33* (see [32.80]); (c) any weeks of SSPP to which the other parent is entitled but during which the other parent is not absent on SPL. In other words, the amount of SPL available to a particular parent / adopter depends to a large degree on what is agreed between them.

Where a mother or adopter returns to work early, the amount of SPL available is 52 weeks minus the number of weeks of SML or statutory adoption leave already taken: *regulations 6(1)(b)* and *22(1)(b)* of the *SPL Regulations*. The total amount of SPL available in the case of birth cannot be more than 50 weeks, because the first two weeks of SML are compulsory for a mother: see *section 72(1)* of the *ERA 1996, regulation 8* of the *MPL Regulations*, and *regulation 6(2)(a)* of the *Leave Curtailment Regulations*. The period is four weeks in the circumstances described by *s 205* of the *Public Health Act 1936*.

Where a mother or adopter curtails her SML or statutory adoption leave, the total amount of SPL available is 52 weeks minus the number of weeks between the first day of SML or statutory adoption leave and the date specified in the leave curtailment notice: *regulations 6(1)(a)* and *22(1)(a)* of the *SPL Regulations*. The total amount of SPL available in the case of adoption is 50 weeks: see *regulation 10(2)(b)* of the *Leave Curtailment Regulations* and *regulation 22(1)(b)* of the *SPL Regulations*.

Employees are also entitled to work for 20 'keeping in touch' or SPLiT days: see [**32.101**] for details.

32.78   *Regulations 12* to *19* (birth) and *28* to *34* (adoption) make provision in respect of the methods for booking leave. Leave must be booked through a period of leave notice: see [**32.81**] below as to the formal requirements relating to period of leave notices.

The crucial limiting issue in respect of booking leave is that an employee may only issue three period of leave notices to each of his or her employers: *regulation 16(1)* of the *SPL Regulations*. That limit includes variation of period of leave notices (see [**32.79**] below). However, the limit in *regulation 16(1)* may be waived by agreement between the employer and employee, and the limit does not include: (a) notices given in response to an employer request to vary the period of leave (*regulations 16(2)(c)* and *32(2)(c)*); (b) notices given due to changes in the expected birth date or date of adoption (*regulations 16(2)(b)* and *32(2)(b)*); (c) notices withdrawn within 15 days and before being agreed by the employer in respect of discontinuous leave (*regulations 16(2)(a)* and *32(2)(a)*). The fact that three notices may be given means that an employee may take three separate (continuous) blocks of leave.

An employee may book either a continuous or discontinuous period of leave. There is considerable flexibility as how discontinuous periods of leave may be structured. An employee may propose a 'week-on, week-off' arrangement, or that they take two-months leave, work for four weeks, then take another two-months of leave (with the partner taking the balance of the leave at various times arranged with his own employer). However, employers do not have to accept an employee's proposal of discontinuous leave: *regulation 14* and *30* of the *SPL Regulations* (see below for further details). Employers are, however, required to accept the employee's request for continuous leave: *regulations 13* and *29* of the *SPL Regulations*.

After an employee requests discontinuous leave, the employer has two weeks to decide whether to: (a) consent to the periods of leave requested; (b) propose alternative dates for the periods of leave; (c) refuse the periods of leave without proposing alternative dates (*regulations 14(2)* and *30(2)* of the *SPL Regulations*). If no agreement is reached between the employee and employer, the employee is entitled to take the total amount of leave requested (in the period of leave notice) as continuous block of leave: *regulations 14(4)* and *30(4)*. The start date of that continuous period of leave must be nominated by the employee within 5 days of the end of the two-week negotiation period (and that date must be eight weeks before the period of leave notice was given to the employer), failing which the original start-date will have effect: *regulations 14(5)* and *30(5)*. However, if alternative dates are agreed during the two-week negotiation period, the employee is entitled to take that leave (*regulations 14(3)* and *30(3)*). The employee may also withdraw the period of leave notice requesting discontinuous leave if there is no agreement so long as it is withdrawn before the two week period ends: *regulations 14(6)* and *30(6)*. (That withdrawal will not count towards the three permitted period of leave notices: *regulations 16(2)(c)* and *32(2)(c)*).

However, as the employee may give three notices to take continuous leave, the fact that an employer can refuse (other types of) discontinuous leave may be of limited significance: the employee is entitled to take three 'blocks' of leave, making the total SPL period 'discontinuous' in that the employee can insist on returning to work for two periods during the SPL period (see further FAQ 46 of the BIS Guide). For discontinuous leave proper (i.e. within the meaning of *regulations 14* and *30*), the difficulty for employers will be likely to be ensuring they are consistent as between employees in responding to requests for discontinuous leave.

32.79   After the employee has given notice of a continuous period of leave or a discontinuous period of leave has been agreed with the employer, the employee may submit a notice to vary those periods of leave (a 'variation notice'): see *regulations 15* and *31* of the *SPL Regulations*. A variation notice may request changes to continuous leave, in which case *regulations 13* and

Maternity and Parental Rights

29 of the *SPL Regulations* apply. In other words, so long as the dates to be varied are more than eight weeks away (including the start and end date, even if that cancels a period of leave), the employer cannot refuse the variation. However, the employer can refuse a request to convert continuous leave into discontinuous leave, or to vary the dates of discontinuous leave, in accordance with the process set out in the paragraph above relating to *regulations 14* and *30* of the *SPL Regulations*. A variation notice must state the periods of leave which the employee is already entitled to (whether continuous or discontinuous: *regulations 15(3)* and *31(3)*, and the rules relating to the number of notices that may be given by the employee apply to the variation notice (see [**32.78**]). If the amount of SPL to be taken by each of the parents / adopters changes, a variation notice of entitlement will be have to be submitted to the employer: see [**32.85**] below.

32.80 *Regulations 18-19* and *33-34* make provision for certain changes of circumstances.

Regulations 18 and *33* relate to an employee ceasing to care for a child or the mother/primary adopter revoking their notice of curtailment. In such circumstances, if those events occur more than eight weeks before the SPL in question, the leave need not be taken. If those events occur less than eight weeks before SPL is due to be taken, the employer may require the employee to take the period of leave as SPL if it is not reasonably practicable for the employer to accommodate the change in circumstances by allowing the employee to work during the planned period of SPL. Note that as the period is taken as SPL, the leave reduces the overall amount of SPL that is available to be taken.

Regulations 19 and *34* relate to the death of the child or one of the parents/adopters. *Regulation 19* and *Part 1* of the *Schedule* to the SPL Regulations make provision for circumstances in which the mother, partner or child dies before the end of the period in which SPL may be taken. *Regulation 34* and *Part 2* of the *Schedule* make equivalent provision in the case of death or disruption of the child's placement for adoption.

32.81 *Notice and evidential requirements*

The main notice and evidential requirements relating to SPL are as follows:

* A notice of entitlement must be provided with certain signed declarations: *regulations 8, 9* (birth) and *24, 25* (adoption) of the *SPL Regulations*. (Alternatively, a declaration of consent and entitlement may be provided by the mother so as to enable her partner to take SPL: see *regulation 5* and *9* of the *Leave Curtailment Regulations*.)

* Certain additional information must be provided upon request: *regulations 10* (birth) and *28* (adoption) of the *SPL Regulations*.

* A variation notice of entitlement must be given to the employer if the amounts of SPL to be taken by each of the parents changes: *regulations 11* and *27* of the *SPL Regulations*.

* A period of leave notice must be provided to book the periods of leave: *regulations 12* (birth) and *28* (adoption) of the *SPL Regulations*.

32.82

The requirements to provide a notice of entitlement and signed declarations are set out in *regulations 8, 9* (birth) and *24, 25* (adoption) of the *SPL Regulations*. *Regulations 8* and *24* address the mother or primary adopter's notice of entitlement, and *regulations 9* and *25* address the partner's notice of entitlement. The notice of entitlement serves also as the notice that the employee intends to take SPL: see the subtitle of each of the regulations cited in this paragraph. A notice of entitlement must be provided to the employer at least eight weeks before the first period of SPL, and must be in writing.

A declaration of consent and entitlement may be provided by the mother/adopter to her employer to curtail her SML or SAL (which she would do so as to enable her partner to take SPL) without complying with the onerous requirements of a notice of entitlement. See *regulations 5* and *9* of the *Leave Curtailment Regulations*. A declaration of consent and entitlement means a written declaration signed by the mother or primary adopter stating that (a) her partner has given a notice of entitlement to his or her employer and (b) that the mother / primary adopter consents to the amount of leave her partner proposes to take. See the definition provided by *regulation 3* of the *Leave Curtailment Regulations*.

In the case of birth, the notice of entitlement must contain the following information (*regulations 8(2)* and *9(2)* of the *SPL Regulations*):

• The names of the mother and partner;

• The start and end dates of any SML taken or to be taken;

• The total amount of SPL available;

• The expected week of birth and the date of birth (to be provided as soon as reasonably practicable after the child's birth and in any event before the first period of SPL is taken);

• A binding indication of how much SPL each of the mother and partner each intend to take (a notice to vary entitlement may later be provided under *regulation 11*: see [**32.85**]);

• A non-binding indication of when the employee intends to take SPL, including specific dates.

In the case of adoption, the notice of entitlement must contain the following information (*regulations 24(2)* and *25(2)* of the *SPL Regulations*):

• The names of the primary adopter and his or her partner;

• The date that the primary adopter was notified that she was matched for adoption;

• The date that the child is expected to be placed, and the date the child was placed (to be provided as soon as reasonably practicable after the child is placed and in any event before the first period of SPL is taken);

• The start and end dates of any statutory adoption leave or pay taken or to be taken by the primary adopter;

• The total amount of SPL available;

• A binding indication of the amount of SPL each adopter intends to take (a notice to vary entitlement may later be provided under *regulation 27*: see [**32.85**]);

• A non-binding indication of when the employee intends to take SPL, including specific dates.

32.83

The signed declarations that must accompany the notice of entitlement must contain the following:

• **Declarations accompanying mother's notice of entitlement to her employer:** in the case of birth, a mother must provide a signed declaration from her and must also provide a signed declaration from the mother's partner (herein, the partner). The mother's signed declaration must state that: (A) she satisfies or will satisfy the conditions in *regulation 4(2)* of the *SPL Regulations*, that is, that she is entitled to take SPL; (B) that the information in her notice is accurate; (C) that she will immediately inform her employer if she ceases to care for the child. A signed declaration from the partner must be provided to the mother's employer stating: (A) his name, address, and national insurance number (or a declaration that he does not have one); (B) that he satisfies or will satisfy the conditions in *regulation 4(3)* of the *SPL Regulations* which enable the mother to take SPL; (C) that he is the father / spouse / civil partner / partner of the mother; (D) that the partner consents to the amount of SPL which the mother intends to take; (E) that he consents to the mother's employer processing the information in the declaration.

- **Declarations accompanying partner of mother's notice of entitlement to his employer:** in the case of birth, the partner of a mother (herein, the partner) must provide to his employer a signed declaration from him and a signed declaration from the mother. The partner's signed declaration must: (A) state that he satisfies or will satisfy the conditions set out in *regulation 5(2)* of the *SPL Regulations*, that is, that he is entitled to take SPL; (B) that the information in his notice is accurate; (C) that he is the father / spouse / civil partner / partner of the mother; (D) that he will immediately inform his employer if the mother tells him that she has revoked her curtailment notice; (E) that that he will immediately inform his employer if he ceases to care for the child. A signed declaration from the mother must be provided to the partner's employer: (A) stating the mother's name, address and national insurance number (or a declaration that she has none); (B) that the mother satisfies the conditions in *regulation 5(3)* which enable the partner to take SPL; (C) that the mother consents to the amount of SPL which the partner intends to take; (D) that the mother will immediately inform the partner if she revokes her curtailment notice; (E) that the mother consents to the partner's employer processing the information in the mother's declaration.

- **Declarations accompanying a primary adopter's notice of entitlement to her employer:** in the case of adoption, the primary adopter must provide a signed declaration from her and must also provide a signed declaration from her partner (herein, the partner). The primary adopter's signed declaration must state that: (A) she satisfies the conditions in *regulation 21(2)*, that is, that she is entitled to take SPL; (B) the information given in her notice is accurate; (C) she will immediately inform her employer if she ceases to care for the child. The primary adopter must also provide a signed declaration from her partner: (A) that states his name, address, and national insurance number (or a declaration that he has none); (B) that that the partner satisfies the conditions in *regulation 20(3)* which entitle the primary adopter to take SPL; (C) that the partner is the spouse / civil partner / partner of the primary adopter; (D) that the partner consents to the amount of leave which the primary adopter intends to take; (E) that the partner consents to the primary adopter's employer processing the partner's information.

- **Declarations accompanying notice of entitlement from the partner of the primary adopter to his employer:** in the case of adoption, the partner of the primary adopter (herein, the partner) must provide a signed declaration from him and must also provide a signed declaration from the primary adopter. The partner's signed declaration must: (A) state that the partner satisfies the conditions set out in *regulation 21(2)* that entitle him to take SPL; (B) that the information given in his notice is accurate; (C) the partner is the primary adopter's husband / civil partner / partner; (D) that the partner will immediately inform his employer if he ceases to care for the child or if the primary adopt revokes her notice of curtailment. The partner must also provide to his employer a signed declaration from the primary adopter that: (A) specifies the primary adopter's name, address and national insurance number (or a declaration that he has none); (B) that the primary adopter satisfies or will satisfy the conditions in *regulation 21(3)* which entitle the partner to take SPL; (C) that the primary adopter consents to the amount of leave which the partner intends to take; (D) that the primary adopter will immediately inform her partner if she revokes her notice of curtailment; (E) that the primary adopter consents to the partner's employer processing the primary adopter's information.

Clearly, those declarations are very complicated and bureaucratic. The dangers are as follows. For the parents / adopters, if they fail to provide the requisite declarations, the right to SPL falls away. For the employer, a failure to hold the correct paperwork leaves them open to their rebate of SSPP being challenged by HMRC if there is an audit. Overall, perhaps, the dangers are greater for the employees, and it is difficult to see what justification there is for entitlement to SPL to depend on the completion of such complex paperwork.

32.84   Additional information that may be requested by the employer in the case of birth includes the following (see *regulation 10* of the *SPL Regulations*):

- A copy of the child's birth certificate;

- The name and address of the mother/adopter's or partner's employer (as the case may be).

The employer may must make the request within 14 days of receiving the relevant notice, and the employee must provide the information within 14 days of receiving the request.

In the case of adoption, the additional information that may be requested includes the following (see *regulation 26* of the *SPL Regulations*):

- The name and address of the adoption agency;

- The date that the adopter was notified of having been matched for adoption with the child;

- The date on which the adoption agency expects to place the child; and,

- The name and address of the partner's employer.

The timescales are the same as above.

32.85   A variation notice of entitlement is required if the parents intend to change the amount of SPL to be taken by either of the parents: *regulations 11* and *27* of the *SPL Regulations*. A variation notice of entitlement must contain the following:

- A description of the periods of SPL notified by each of the parents under a period of leave notice or variation notice;

- A non-binding indication of when the employee giving the notice to his or her employer intends to take the SPL, including specific dates;

- A description of the periods of SSPP that have been notified by each of the parents;

- A declaration signed by both parents or adopters that they agree the variation.

There is no limit to the number of notices that may be given.

32.86   A period of leave notice must meet the requirements of *regulation 12* (in the case of birth) or *28* (in the case of adoption) of the *SPL Regulations*. The period of leave notice must be in writing, and contain the start and end dates of each period of leave requested. It must be given to the employer at least eight weeks before the start dates of the first period of leave requested. The period of leave notice may also specify a date relative to the birth or adoption of the child: see *regulations 12(4)(c)* and *28(4)(c)* of the *SPL Regulations*. The period of leave notice cannot be given before the notice of entitlement, and cannot state dates outside the range in which SPL may be taken: *regulations 12(5)* and *28(5)* of the *SPL Regulations*.

32.87 Statutory shared parental pay

Statutory shared parental pay or "**SSPP**" is governed by *sections 171ZU to 171ZZ5* of the *SSCBA 1992*, and the *Statutory Shared Parental Pay (General) Regulations 2014 (2014/3051)* (the "**SSPP Regulations**"). The general principles applicable to SSPP are much the same as SPL: a mother or primary adopter must curtail her entitlement to SMP, maternity allowance or statutory adoption pay, and the remaining balance may be taken by either parent as SSPP.

A government rebate of 92% applies to payments by the employer of SPPP: see the *Statutory Shared Parental Pay (Administration) Regulations 2014 (2014/2929)*, which make equivalent provision for SSPP as for SMP (see [**32.60**]).

32.88 *Eligibility for SSPP*

The conditions of eligibility for SSPP for a particular employee are very similar to those for SPL. See in particular the *SSPP Regulations* at *regulation 4* and *5* (birth cases), *17* and *18* (adoption cases), and *29-31* (general provisions).

- The individual must be an employee, although the term is defined more widely than for SPL. *Section 171ZZ4(2)* of the *SSCBA 1992* provides the relevant definition: "in this Part, "employee" means a person who is gainfully employed in Great Britain either under a contract of service or in an office (including elective office) with general earnings (as defined by *section 7* of the *Income Tax (Earnings and Pensions) Act 2003)*". *Regulation 33* of the *SSPP Regulations* make provision for certain special cases and *section 171ZZ2* provides that Crown servants are to be treated as employees for these purposes.

- The employee must have 26 weeks continuous employment with the same employer by the end of the 'relevant week' (immediately before the 14th week before the EWC, or in adoption cases, the week on which the adopter is matched with the child): *regulations 4(2)(a), 5(2)(a)* and *30* in the case of birth and *regulations 17(2)(a), 18(2)(a)* and *31* in the case of adoption. See regulations 34-38 as to 'continuous employment'.

- The employee must have normal weekly earnings of at least £113 a week (the applicable rate from from 6 April 2017) for eight weeks immediately proceeding the relevant date: *regulations 4(2)(a), 5(2)(a)* and *30(1)(b)* (birth) and *17(2)(a), 18(2)(a)* and *31(1)(b)* (adoption).

- The employee must share the main caring responsibility for the child with the other parent at the date or birth or adoption: *regulations 4(2)(b), 4(3)(a), 5(2), 5(3)(a)* in the case of birth and *regulations 17(2)(b), 17(3)(a)* and *18(3)(a)* in the case of adoption.

- The employees must have complied with the relevant notice requirements eight weeks before leave begins (see [**32.92**] below).

- The mother/adopter must be entitled to SMP or statutory adoption pay and have curtailed that entitlement: *regulations 4(2)(d), 4(3), 5(3)(c)* and *5(3)(d)* in case of birth, and *17(2)(d), 17(2)(e)* and *18(3)(c)* in case of adoption.

- During each week of SSPP, the individual must intend to care for the child, and be absent from work (although see *regulations* 15 and 27 for certain exceptions). If the individual is an employee within the meaning of *section 230* of the *ERA 1996* (as opposed to the wider meaning for the purposes of SSPP), he or she must be absent from work by means of SPL. See *regulations 4(2)(f)-(h), 5(2)(d)-(f)* in case of birth, and *17(2)(f)-(h), 18(2)(d)-(f)* in case of adoption.

- The other parent must satisfy the 'employment earnings test' set out in *regulation 29* of the *SSPP Regulations: regulations 4(3)(b), 5(3)(b)* in case of birth, and *17(3)(b), 18(3)(b)* in case of adoption. This test is identical to that which applies under SPL: see [**32.70**] above.

Women who do not qualify for SMP but who do qualify for the social security benefit of MA cannot create a shared entitlement to SSPP. However, a woman who is eligible for MA may create an entitlement to SSPP for her partner by curtailing her MA (see *regulation 5(3)(d)* of the *SSPP Regulations*); she will not herself be entitled to SSPP because one of the conditions of entitlement for her is eligibility for SMP or SAP (see *regulations 4(2)(d)* and *17(2)(d)* of the *SSPP Regulations*).

32.89 *Curtailing maternity pay or allowance*

A mother must curtail her SMP or MA for each parent to be entitled to SSPP. The procedures for doing so in the case of SMP and SAP are set out in *regulations 7* and *12* respectively of the *Statutory Maternity Pay and Statutory Adoption Pay (Curtailment) Regulations 2014 (2014/3054)* (the "**Pay Curtailment Regulations**") and for MA, they are set out in *regulation 5* of the *Maternity Allowance (Curtailment) Regulations 2014 (2014/3053)* (the "**MA Curtailment Regulations**").

Those provisions require the provision of a 'maternity pay period curtailment notice', 'adoption pay period curtailment notice' or a 'maternity allowance period curtailment notification' respectively, which all have the following requirements:

- They must be given to the prescribed person: in the case of SMP and SAP, the person liable to pay the SMP or SAP, and in the case of MA, the Secretary of State. In the cases of SMP and SAP, they must be in writing.

- They must specify the date on which the SMP, SAP or MA is to end, which must be the last day of a week.

- The date chosen for the curtailment must be at least eight weeks after the curtailment notice was given.

- If the mother has the right to ordinary maternity leave under *section 71* of the *ERA 1996*, then the date chosen to curtail must be at least one day after the end of the period of compulsory maternity leave, and if not, at least two weeks after the end of the pregnancy or adoption date.

- The curtailment date must be at least one week before the last day or the SMP, SAP or MA period.

Readers should consult the regulations referred to above for information as to their detailed operation, such as where a curtailment notice is provided when the employee has already returned to work.

Provisions as to the revocation of a curtailment notice may be found at *regulations 8* and *13* of the *Pay Curtailment Regulations* (in respect of birth and adoption respectively), and *regulation 6* of the *MA Curtailment Regulations*. In short, in the case of SMP or MA a revocation notice may only be provided if the curtailment notice was provided before the birth of the child (and given within six weeks of the child's birth), or the mother's partner dies. In the case of SAP, a revocation notice may only be provided if the primary adopter's partner dies.

32.90   *SSPP: how much and when?*

The weekly rate of payment of SSPP is the smaller of (a) £140.98 or (b) 90% of the normal weekly earnings of the individual claiming SSPP: see *regulation 40(1)* of the *SSPP Regulations*. *Regulation 43* provides that payments of SSPP may be made in a "like manger to payments or remuneration but shall not include payment in kind of by way of the provision of board and lodgings". Payments are normally to be made on the day on which it was normal practice for the employee to be paid, or if there is no such practice, on the last day of a calendar month: *regulation 44(5)*. *Subsection 171ZY(6)* of the *SSCBA 1992* provides that SSPP may be calculated at a daily rate (see also regulation 40(2) of the SSPP Regulations). *Section 171ZX* makes provision for the person liable to make payments, and see *regulations 44* and *45* of the *SSPP Regulations* as to determinations by HMRC as to an employer and HMRC's liability to pay SSPP. *Regulation 41* provides that any contractual remuneration (including sick pay) goes towards discharging an employer's liability to pay SSPP. See *regulation 42* in respect of dismissals and SSPP; *regulation 48* as to issues relating to the capacity of the person receiving SSPP; and *regulation 39* as to issues relating to an individual being employed in two or more separately jobs.

32.91   The amount of SSPP available to be shared depends on the remaining SMP, SAP or MA, and is governed by *regulation 10* and *22* of the *SSPP Regulations*. The maternity pay period for SMP is 39 weeks, but due to the requirements relating to curtailment set out above, the maximum SMP that may be taken as SSPP is 37 weeks. The same applies to SAP. The minimum amount of SSPP that may be taken is one week: *regulations 7(2)(d)* and *12(2)(d)* of the *Pay Curtailment Regulations*. It should be noted that it is not sufficient for the mother merely to return to work to curtail her entitlement, because her maternity pay period will continue to 'run in the background'. Rather, she must specifically curtail her SMP or SAP: see the BIS Guide at FAQ 30. See similarly *regulation 10(1)(a)* in respect of MA. *Regulations 11* and *23* of the *SSPP Regulations* provide that SSPP will not be payable after the first birthday of the child or the first anniversary of the adoption. Finally, SSPP cannot be taken by a mother or primary adopter when they are receiving SMP/SAP/MA, but if the curtailment date has been set, her partner may receive SSPP even whilst the mother/primary adopter is in receipt of SMP/SAP/MA.

Section 171ZY(4) of the *SSCBA 1992* provides that SSPP is not payable in respect of a week during any part of which the employee works for an employer, with the exception provided by *regulation 12* and *24* of the *SSPP Regulations* relating to 'keeping in touch' or SPLiT days (see those regulations more generally as to obligations that arise when work is undertaken for an employer). See *subsection 171ZY(3)* and *regulations 13* to *15*, and *25* to *27* of the *SSPP Regulations* as to other circumstances in which SSPP is not payable due to the actions of the employee.

32.92   *Notice and evidential requirements*

The notice and evidential requirements for SSPP are much the same as those for SPL. However, as the length of time the SSPP is shorter than for SPL, parents and adopters must make a separate decision as to how to divide their SSPP. Whilst the regulations are silent on the matter, the ACAS Guide suggests that the notice of claim for SSPP may be included in the notice of entitlement for SPL. The relevant regulations within the SSPP Regulations are *regulation 6* for claims by a mother; *regulation 7* for claims by the partner; *regulation 19* for claims by the primary adopter; and *regulation 20* for claims by the partner of the adopter.

One of the purposes of the notice and evidential requirements is to prevent both parents fraudulently taking (up to) 50 weeks of SPL, rather than sharing that pay / leave. There is, however, no provision in the regulations for communication between the respective employers of the two employees. The BIS Guide states at FAQ 67 that employers are not expected to perform detailed checks, and specifically, that they are not expected to contact the employer of the other employee to satisfy themselves regarding the eligibility of the partner to SPL. However, whilst the BIS Guide then states *"[e]mployers are entitled to rely on the information about the other parent provided to them by their employee"*, it goes on to say (in accordance with the regulations) that *"employers who want to check can ask their employee for the name of the other parent's employer and contact them if they wish."* The BIS Guide also states that HMRC will attempt to identify any parents defrauding the system.

32.93   The requirements in respect of birth are as follows (for convenience, the person liable to pay the mother's SSPP is refereed to below as her 'employer'):

- **Notice provided by a mother to her employer**: the mother must provide her employer with notice of: (A) the total number of weeks that the mother would be entitled to claim SSPP if no claim for SSPP were made by her partner; (B) the number of those weeks that each of the mother and her partner intend to take as SSPP; (C) the period or periods during which the mother intends to claim SSPP; (D) a written and signed declaration from the mother's partner that consents to the mother's intended claim for SSPP; that the partner meets the required conditions for the mother's eligibility for SSPP under *regulation 4(3)*; that sets out the partner's name, address, and national insurance number (or a declaration that he has no national insurance number); and consents to the mother's employer processing the partner's information; (E) the child's EWC, and as soon as is reasonably practicable, the child's date of birth; (F) the mother's name; (G) a written declaration from the mother stating that the information in the notice is correct; that the mother meets the conditions for eligibility for SSPP; that the mother will immediately inform the person who will be liable to pay SSPP if she ceases to curtail her SMP or maternity allowance; the date on which the maternity pay period or maternity allowance period began and the number of weeks by which it is or will be reduced.

- **Notice provided by a partner of a mother to his employer**: the partner of the mother (the 'partner') must provide his employer with notice of: (A) the total number of weeks that the partner would be entitled to claim SSPP if no claim for SSPP were made by the mother; (B) the number of those weeks that each of the mother and her partner intend to take as SSPP; (C) the period or periods during which the mother intends to claim SSPP; (D) a written and signed declaration from the mother that consents to the partner's intended claim for SSPP; states that the mother meets the required conditions for the partner's eligibility for SSPP under *regulation 5(3)*; that the mother will immediately inform the partner if she ceases to curtail her SMP or MA; specifies the mother's name, address and national insurance number (or a declaration that she has no national insurance number); specifying the date on which the mother's SMP period or MA period began and the number of weeks by which it is or will be reduced; and consents to the partner's employer processing the mother's information; (E) states the EWC, and as soon as reasonable practicable after the birth, the child's date of birth; (F) the partner's name; (G) a written declaration signed by the partner that the information given by the partner is correct; that the partner meets the conditions for eligibility of SSPP in *regulation 5(2)* SSPP; and that the partner will immediately inform his employer if the mother ceases to curtail her SMP or maternity allowance.

Save where otherwise specified above, the employer must receive this information at least eight weeks before the beginning of the first period of SSPP.

The employer may also request a copy of the child's birth certificate (or if one has not been issued, a declaration signed by the mother which states that one has not been issued); and the name and address of the partner's employer (or if the partner has no employer, a written declaration signed by the mother that states the partner has no employer). In both cases, the information must be provided to the employer within 14 days of the information being requested; and the employer has only 14 days from the date of the notice to request that information.

32.94 The requirements in respect of adoption (set out in *regulation 19* and *20* of the *SSPP Regulations*) are the same as those in respect of birth, with the following adjustments: (1) the date of placement, rather than of birth, is required; (2) the date on which the primary adopter was matched with the child, rather than the EWC; (3) the date of placement for adoption, instead of the date of birth; and finally, (4) in respect of the information that may be requested by the employer, that information is the name and address of the adoption agency; the date on which the primary adopter was notified that she had been matched with the child; the date on which the adoption agency was expecting to place the child with the primary adopter; and this is in place of the child's date of birth as set out above.

32.95 Parents and adopters may vary a notice to claim SSPP in accordance with *regulations 8* (birth) and *21* (adoption) of the *SSPP Regulations*. Such a variation notice must be given at least eight weeks before the first period of SSPP specified in the original notice. A variation notice may vary the number of weeks that they intend to claim SSPP in the notice, under the same time constraints, if the notice sets out how many weeks both parents have claimed SSPP and includes a signed declaration from both parents/adopters to the effect that they consent to the variation.

Employment protection and SPL / SSPP

32.96 *Introduction*

Employees taking SPL enjoy the following protections (see *regulations 37* to *44* of the *SPL Regulations*):

- Protection from dismissal;

- Protection from detriment;

- Protection from discrimination;

- Redundancy protection;

- Keeping in touch or 'SPLiT' days;

- Protections in resect of terms and conditions of employment during SPL;

- Returning to work after SPL.

Each is addressed in turn below.

32.97 *Protection from dismissal*

Section 99(1) of the *ERA 1996* makes provision that an employee will be regarded as unfairly dismissed if the principal reason for dismissal is one of a prescribed kind, known as 'automatically unfair dismissal'. See generally UNFAIR DISMISSAL – I (53) and II (54). *Section 99(3)(bb)* of the *ERA 1996* provides that reasons relating to SPL are of that prescribed kind.

Regulation 43 of the *SPL Regulations* makes further provision in respect of the reasons that will result in an employee being unfairly dismissed for the purposes of *section 99* of the *ERA 1996*. *Regulation 43(1)* states that the employee will be regarded as unfairly dismissed if the reason or principal reason is of a kind specified in *regulation 43(3)*, or where the employee is redundant, that regulation 39 of the *SPL Regulations* has not been complied with (see [32.100] in respect of redundancy).

Regulation 43(3) states that if the reason for the dismissal are reasons relating to any of the following, the employee will be unfairly dismissal:

•   That the employee took, sought to take, or made use of the benefits of, SPL;

•   That the employer believed that the employee was likely to take SPL;

•   That the employee undertook, considered undertaking, or refused to undertake work in accordance with regulation 37 (in respect of keeping in touch or 'SPLiT' days; see [**32.101**]).

Regulation 43(2) also provides that an employee who is dismissed will be regarded as unfairly dismissed for the purposes of *Part 10* of the *ERA 1996* if they were dismissed for redundancy because of one of the matters set out in *regulation 43(3)*, and the circumstances constituting the redundancy applied equally to one or more employees in the same undertaking who held positions similar to that held by the dismissed employee who had not been dismissed by the employer.

Regulation 42 of the *SSPP Regulations* provides that a former employer will be liable to pay SSPP to a former employee where the employee was employed on a continuous basis for at least eight weeks and the employee's contract of services was brought to an end solely or mainly for the purpose of avoiding liability to pay SSPP.

32.98 *Protection from detriment*

Section 47C(2)(bb) of the *ERA 1996* provides that an employee has a right not to be subjected to any detriment by any act or deliberate failure to act by his employer for a reason set out in *regulation 42(1)* of the *SPL Regulations*. Those reasons are:

•   the employee took, sought to take, or made use of the benefits of, SPL;

•   the employer believed that the employee was likely to take SPL; or

•   the employee undertook, considered undertaking, or refused to undertake work in accordance with regulation 37 ('keeping in touch' or SPLiT days).

Regulation 42(2) states that an employee makes use of the benefits of SPL if during a period of SPL the employee benefits from any of the terms and conditions of employment persevered by *regulation 38* during that period (see [**32.102**]).

32.99 *Protection from discrimination*

There are a range of potential claims arising from SPL under the *Equality Act 2010*. The most difficult relate to indirect discrimination on grounds of sex, and is discussed below at [**32.105**]. There is also the possibility of discrimination on grounds of material or civil partnership status as well as sexual orientation. Finally, there is also a range of more common but less legally novel complaints that may arise from the introduction of SPL, such as harassment, direct discrimination on grounds of sex and so on. See generally DISCRIMINATION AND EQUAL OPPORTUNITIES – I (11), II (12), and III (13).

32.100 *Redundancy protection*

Regulation 39 makes provision in respect of redundancy during a period of SPL. *Regulation 39(2)* requires an employer to offer any suitable alternative vacancy with the employer, the employer's successor or an associated employer under a new contract of employment that takes effect immediately after the end of the employee's previous employment contract. *Regulation 39(3)* requires the new contract of employment to be suitable in relation to the employee and appropriate work for the employee to do in the circumstances; and that the terms and conditions and provisions as to the capacity and place in which the employee are employed are not substantially less favourable to the employee than if she had not been redundant. A failure to fulfil this duty will result in a finding of unfair dismissal, but subject to *section 141* of the *ERA 1996*.

32.101　Maternity and Parental Rights

32.101 *Keeping in touch or 'SPLiT' days*

Regulation 37 makes provision for 'keeping in touch' days (equivalent to those in respect of maternity leave), which are labelled 'SPLiT' ('shared parental leave in touch') days in the BIS Guide at FAQ 85. The nature of SPLiT days is set out in *regulation 37(1)*: they permit the employee to carry out work for the employer without the employee bringing the period of SPL to an end. The employee has no right to undertake such work, and the employer no right to require that the employee undertake the work: *regulation 37(6)*. The employee may work for up to 20 keeping in touch or 'SPLiT' days "for each employer" (*regulation 37(2)*), but such days do not have the effect of extending SPL (*regulation 37(7)*). *Regulation 37(4)* provides that keeping in touch or 'SPLiT' days constitute work under the contract of employment, which may create an entitlement to pay for that work depending on the terms of the contract (that may in turn be set off against entitlement to SSPP). However, contact to discuss an employee's return to work or any reasonable contact from time to time between the employer and employee does not constitute work: *regulation 37(5)*.

32.102 *Terms and conditions during SPL*

Regulation 38 provides that during SPL an employee is entitled to the benefit of all of his or her terms and conditions of employment, within the meaning of *ERA 1996, s 751(2)* (in other words, excluding the right to remuneration by way of wages and salary). The employee is also bound by any obligations arising from those terms and conditions, subject to *ERA 1996, s 751(1)(b)*.

32.103 *The effect of more favourable contractual rights*

If the employee has a contractual right to SPL in addition to his or her statutory rights, *regulation 45(a)* of the *SPL Regulations* provides that the employee may not exercise those rights separately, but may take advantage of whichever right is more favourable, "in any particular respect", in taking leave. *Regulation 45(b)* provides that the provisions in the *SPL Regulations* as regards the *ERA 1996* are modified to protect the 'composite right' (i.e. presumably, the contractual and statutory rights combined).

32.104 *Returning to work after SPL*

Regulations 40 and *41* make provision in respect of returning to work after SPL. *Regulation 41(1)* provides that an employee has the right to return to work to the job that he or she had before the absence if:

- the employee's statutory leave in respect of the particular child is less than 26 weeks; and,

- if the period of SPL was the last or two or more consecutive periods of statutory leave (under *Part 8* of the *1996 Act*), there was no additional maternity leave, additional paternity leave or unpaid parental leave of more than four weeks.

Otherwise, the employee's right to return to the same job is subject to whether it is reasonably practicable for the employer to permit to the employee to return to that job; if it is not reasonably practicable, the employee has only a right under *regulation 40(2)* to a job which is both suitable for the employee and appropriate for the employee to do in the circumstances.

Note that by *regulation 41(1)*, the job is the one specified in the contract of employment (which is not necessarily precisely what the employee was doing before taking SPL), and the capacity and place the employee was employed before the absence. However *regulation 41(3)* provides that the right under *regulation 40* is a right to return:

- with the employee's seniority, pension rights and similar rights as they would have been if there was no absence; and

- on terms and conditions not less favourable than those which would have applied if there had been no absence.

A refusal to permit the employee to return in accordance with her *regulation 40* rights may constitute a detriment or a (unfair) dismissal.

32.105 Litigation issues in respect of SPL

Many employers provide enhanced contractual rates of maternity pay for their female employees. One of the most important questions of the SPL legislation is whether a failure to enhance shared parental pay to the level of enhanced maternity pay will leave an employer open to claims of sex discrimination.

A similar issue was litigated in *Shuter v Ford Motor Co* [2014] EqLR 717 in respect of a failure to enhance additional paternity leave ("APL"). The tribunal rejected the man's claim, but not in a way that will provide employer with much comfort as regards SPL. A direct discrimination claim was rejected on the basis that the correct comparator for the male on APL was not a woman on enhanced maternity pay, but a woman receiving APL. In the indirect claim, however, the employer succeeded by making out its defence of justification on the facts, due to the need to recruit and retain women in a largely male industry. Whether employers will generally be able to make out such a defence remains to be seen (see also *Hofman v Barmer Ersatzkasse* (Case 184/83) [1984] ECR 3047 for examples of other potential legitimate aims).

One issue in respect of SPL/SSPP is whether the finding in *Shuter* in respect of direct discrimination will stand further scrutiny, because (it might be argued) parental rights under SPL/SSPP are no longer associated with the biological aspects of childbirth and pregnancy (see *section 13(6)(b)* of the *EqA*), and consequently the comparator point is no longer a good one. See, in particular, *Pedro Manuel Roca Alvarez v Sesa Start Espana ETT SA*: C-104/09, [2011] All ER (EC) 253, in which the CJEU held that the principle of equal treatment in *Directive 76/207/EEC* and *Directive 2006/54/EC* (see *recital 24* in particular) precluded a Spanish law which allowed mothers to take "breastfeeding leave" in the first nine months following the birth of their child irrespective of the employment status of the child's father, but only allowed fathers to take such leave if the child's mother was also in employment (the appellant's wife was self-employed). See also *Eversheds Legal Services Ltd v De Belin* [2011] IRLR 448, [2011] ICR 1137.

On the other hand, the CJEU considered a shared parental leave scheme in *Montull v Instutio Nacional de la Seguridad Social (INSS)* (Case C-5/12) and appeared to depart from *Roca Alverez*. The Court held that the *EU Pregnant Worker's Directive* does not preclude a system of shared maternity leave under which an employed mother can let her child's employed father take all or part of her maternity leave once the compulsory two-week period under *Article 8(2)* of the *Directive* is completed. Nor (as in the facts of the case) does the Directive preclude a system whereby mothers who are self-employed are not entitled to share their leave with an employed father, on the grounds that the mother does not meet the relevant criteria for a primary right to leave. The Court also held that the principle of equal treatment is not breached by giving the right to leave to each parent of an adopted child in their own right. It will be interesting to see how the CJEU reconciles *Montull* with *Roca Alvarez* in future cases.

In *Maistrellis v Ypourgos Dikaiosynis* (Case C-222/14) – which referred to *Roca Alvarez* but not *Montull* – the CJEU considered a Greek system of parental leave whereby nine months' leave is provided to female civil servants, and to male civil servants only if the mother of their child works or exercises a profession. The CJEU found such a system to be directly discriminatory on grounds of sex, and that it was *"liable to perpetuate a tradition distribution of the roles of men and women"* (para 50). Query therefore whether, given that the SPL entitlement for a father depends on the entitlement of the mother, SPL might also be contrary to EU law.

So far, it seems that the only UK decision concerning shared parental leave is *Snell v Network Rail Infrastructure Limited* (2016), an uncontested decision of the Scottish Employment Tribunal. Obviously, as an uncontested decision, at first-instance, ti s not binding on any other Employment Tribunal. Further, this account of the case is based only on an online report of the case written by Millie Kempley of EMW LLP (see https ://www.emwllp.com/latest/shared-parental-leave/), the judgment not being uploaded to the database of online Employment Tribunal decisions. Nevertheless, in that case, Mr and Mrs Snell were Network Rail employees. Network Rail's SPL policy provided for the statutory rate of pay for partners (such as Mr Snell) for 39 weeks, but 26 weeks of full pay for mothers (followed by 13 weeks at the statutory rate, and 13 weeks unpaid leave). Network Rail did not contest the claim at Tribunal, leaving remedy as the only issue. With the agreement of the parties, the Tribunal made a declaration that Mr Snell was indirectly discriminated against in relation to his sex on account of Network Rail's SPL policy.

For employment protections in respect of SPL, see [32.96], and in relation to discrimination generally, see DISCRIMINATION AND EQUAL OPPORTUNITIES – I (11), II (12), and III (13).

PATERNITY AND ADOPTION LEAVE & PAY

32.106 Paternity Leave

The law in relation to 'paternity leave' has changed dramatically in recent years:

(a)   The *Employment Act 2002* introduced an entitlement to a short period of 'paternity leave'. This is described in this chapter as 'ordinary' paternity leave. The details are set out in the *Paternity and Adoption Leave Regulations 2002 (SI 2002/2788)* (the **"PAL Regulations"**).

(b)   There was a right, now abolished, to 'additional' paternity leave under the *Additional Paternity Leave Regulations 2010 (SI 2010/1055)* (the **"Additional PL Regulations"**), which came into force on 6 April 2010 (in relation to children whose expected week of birth begins on or after 3 April 2011). The *Additional PL Regulations* implement powers in the *Work and Families Act 2006*. In effect they allow parents to share additional leave between them. The rights to additional paternity leave and pay were abolished from 5 April 2015, but remain available for EWCs before that date. The material set out below is retained for the transitional period and in respect of historical cases.

(c)   See [32.68] above in relation to the introduction of shared parental leave from 5 April 2015;

32.107 Entitlement to 'ordinary' paternity leave

An employee is entitled to paternity leave under *reg 4* of the *PAL Regulations* (i.e. to be absent from work for the purpose of caring for a child or supporting the child's mother) if:

(a)   he has been continuously employed for a period of not less than 26 weeks ending with the week immediately preceding the 14th week before the expected week of the child's birth (note the provisions in *reg 4(3), (5)* where the child is born early or is stillborn);

(b)   he is either the child's father or is married to or is the civil partner or partner of the child's mother (note that this definition may include a female civil partner or partner of the child's mother);

(c)   he has or expects to have responsibility for bringing up the child (main responsibility, if he is not the child's father); and

(d)   he has complied with the requirements to give notice (and, in certain cases, provide evidence) set out in *reg 6* of the *PAL Regulations*.

An employee is not entitled to take paternity leave if the employee has taken any shared parental leave in respect of the child: *regulation 4(1A)* of the *PAL Regulations*.

32.108 *'Ordinary' paternity leave*

The employee may take either one week's leave, or two consecutive weeks' leave: *reg 5(1)*. This leave may only be taken during the period commencing with the child's birth or the date on which the child is placed with the adopter and ending either 56 days' later or, if the child is born before the first day of the expected week of its birth, 56 days after that date: *reg 5(2)*.

Before taking 'ordinary' paternity leave, the employee must notify his employer that he intends to do so, specifying the expected week of childbirth, the length of leave that he has chosen to take (see *reg 5(1)*), and the date on which he has chosen to take such leave (see *reg 5(3)–(4)*): *reg 6(1)*. Such notice must be given in or before the 15th week before the expected week of the child's birth or as soon as reasonably practicable if notice could not have been given sooner: *reg 6(2)*. In addition, if requested by the employer, the employee must sign a declaration that he is taking leave for the purpose of caring for the child or supporting the child's mother (per *reg 4(1)*) and that he satisfies the eligibility requirements in *reg 4(2)(b)–(c)*: *reg 6(3)*.

There is a mechanism in the *PAL Regulations* to vary the date on which 'ordinary' paternity leave will begin, including where the birth is late: *reg 6(4)–(8)*.

32.109 *Benefits during 'ordinary' paternity leave*

During the course of paternity leave, an employee is entitled to the benefit of all the terms and conditions that would have applied if he or she had not been absent (save for those in relation to remuneration, ie. wages or salary), and remains bound by the obligations that arise out of those terms and conditions: *reg 12*.

An employee is entitled to return to the same job at the end of an isolated period of paternity leave or the last of two or more consecutive periods of statutory leave which did not include any period of statutory leave which when added to any other periods of statutory leave (excluding parental leave) taken in relation to the same child means that the total amount of statutory leave taken in relation to that child totals more than 26 weeks, or a period of parental leave of more than four weeks (*reg 13(1)*). In all other cases, he or she is entitled to return to the same job or, if this is not reasonably practicable, to another job which is suitable and appropriate for him or her to do in the circumstances (*reg 13(2)*). The employee's return to work broadly carries with it the same seniority, pension and similar rights and the right to no less favourable terms and conditions than he would have enjoyed had he not taken leave (*reg 14*).

32.110 Additional paternity leave: entitlement

As noted above, the rights to additional paternity leave ("APL") and pay were abolished from 5 April 2015, but remain available for EWCs before that date.

32.111 APL is available for the purpose of caring for a child whose expected week of birth falls on or after 3 April 2011 (*regs 3* and *4* of the *Additional PL Regulations*). In short, so long as the mother returns to work, her partner may take up to 26 weeks of leave. The short period of ordinary paternity leave under the *PAL Regulations*, extends in addition to absence for the purpose of caring for the child's mother (*reg 4* of the *PAL Regulations*).

By *reg 4* of the *Additional PL Regulations*, an employee is entitled to APL if:

(a)   he has been continuously employed for a period of not less than 26 weeks ending with the week immediately preceding the 14th week before the child's expected week of birth (note the provisions in relation to early births in *reg 4(4)*);

(b)   he remains in continuous employment with that employer until the week before the first week of his APL;

(c)   he is either the child's father or, if he is not the child's father, he is married to or is the partner or civil partner of the child's mother (again, this definition could include the female partner or civil partner of the child's mother);

(d)   he has, or expects to have, the main responsibility for the child's upbringing (apart from any responsibility that the mother may have);

(e)   he has complied with the applicable notification and evidence requirements in *regs 6* and *7* of the *Additional PL Regulations*;

(f)   the child's mother is entitled, because of becoming pregnant with the child, to maternity leave, SMP or maternity allowance and has returned to work (or is treated as having returned to work) as defined in *reg 25* of the *Additional PL Regulations*; and

(g)   the child's mother has signed the mother declaration referred to in *reg 6* of the *Additional PL Regulations*.

Separate provision is made for APL in the event of the mother's death: see *regs 10–13* of the *Additional PL Regulations*.

32.112 *Additional paternity leave*

A person may take a continuous period of APL of any multiple of complete weeks between two and 26 weeks, and may take that leave at any time within the period beginning 20 weeks after the child's birthdate and ending on the child's first birthday (*reg 5*). In addition, *regs 7* and *9* of the *Additional PL Regulations* govern the commencement, variation or cancellation of APL, *reg 29* governs the termination of APL where the person is dismissed during that period, *reg 30* contains provisions for the early return from a period of APL and *reg 24* applies where the child in question dies.

APL cannot begin until eight weeks after the date the person gave leave notice to his employer under *reg 6* of the *Additional PL Regulations* (*reg 5(4)*). Reg 6 requires that, not less than eight weeks before his chosen start date for APL, the person give his employer:

(a)   "leave notice" (a written notice specifying the child's expected week of childbirth, the child's date of birth, and the dates the person has chosen under *reg 5* as the start and end dates of his APL);

(b)   an "employee declaration" (a signed written declaration stating that the purpose of the period of leave will be to care for the child, and that the person satisfies the eligibility conditions in *reg 4(2)(c)–(d)* of the *Additional PL Regulations*); and

(c)   a "mother declaration" (a written declaration by the mother giving the information specified in *reg 6(2)(c)* of the *Additional PL Regulations*).

The person must provide a copy of the child's birth certificate and the name and address of the employer of the child's mother (or, if the mother is self-employed, her business address) within 28 days of any request to that effect from his or her employer, provided that the request is made within 28 days of receipt of the "leave notice": see *reg 6(3)*.

An employer who receives leave notice from an employee under *reg 6(1)* or a subsequent notice under *reg 7(1)* must confirm the relevant dates to the employee in writing within 28 days: *reg 8(1)*. The employer must also give such confirmation in certain circumstances under *reg 8(2)*.

In addition, the person must give his employer written "withdrawal notice" under *reg 6(4)* as soon as reasonably practicable if he no longer satisfies the conditions in *reg 4(2)(c)* or *(d)* or if the child's mother no longer satisfies the conditions in *reg 4(5)* of the *Additional PL Regulations*. An employer has a number of rights when an employee gives such "withdrawal notice": see *reg 6*.

32.113 *Benefits during additional paternity leave*

During the course of APL, a person is entitled to the benefit of all the terms and conditions that would have applied if he had not been absent (save for those in relation to remuneration, ie. wages or salary, as to which see **[32.116]**), and remains bound by the obligations that arise out of those terms and conditions: see *reg 27* of the *Additional PL Regulations*. He will gain special protection where, during his APL period, it is not practicable by reason of redundancy for the employer to continue to employ him under his existing contract: see *reg 28*.

In addition:

(a)   A person taking APL of no more than 26 weeks will be entitled to return to the same job at the end of an isolated period of paternity leave or the last of two or more consecutive periods of statutory leave which did not include any period of AML, or additional adoption leave or a period of parental leave of more than four weeks (*reg 31(1)*). Otherwise, the person is entitled to return to the same job or, if this is not reasonably practicable, to another job which is suitable and appropriate for him to do in the circumstances (*reg 31(2)*). The employee's return to work broadly carries with it the same seniority, pension and similar rights and the right to no less favourable terms and conditions than he would have enjoyed had he not taken leave (*reg 32*).

(b)   A person who has the benefit of both a statutory right to APL and a corresponding contractual right may not exercise both separately but may take advantage of whichever right is, in any particular respect, the more favourable (and the relevant statutory provisions shall apply, modified as necessary to give effect to more favourable contractual terms, to the exercise of such a composite right: *reg 35*).

In addition, a person may carry out up to ten days' work for his employer during an APL period without bringing that period to an end, but his employer cannot require that he do so (and he cannot demand to do so): see *reg 26* of the *Additional PL Regulations*.

32.114 Adoption Leave

Entitlement to adoption leave has been introduced:

(a)   under the *PAL Regulations*, both as adoption leave per se (see especially *regs 8–14*) and as a form of paternity leave in relation to an adopted child (see especially *regs 15–27*);

(b)   under the *Additional PL Regulations*, as a form of APL in relation to adopted children who are matched to a person who is notified of having been matched on or after 3 April 2011 (see especially *reg 3* and *regs 14–23*), although these rights are abolished as of 5 April 2015 in favour of shared parental leave. See **[32.68]** above;

(c)   under the *Additional Paternity Leave (Adoptions from Overseas) Regulations 2010 (SI 2010/1059)* (the "**Overseas Adoptions Additional PL Regulations**") and the *Employment Rights Act 1996 (Application of Section 80BB to Adoptions from Overseas) Regulations 2010 (SI 2010/1058)*, as APL in relation to employees married to or the civil partner or partner of an adopter whose child enters Great Britain on or after 3 April 2011, but these rights are abolished as of 5 April 2015 in favour of shared parental leave. See **[32.68]** above;

(d)   the *CFA 2014* and accompanying regulations make provision for shared parental leave. See [**32.68**] above;

(e)   the *Paternity and Adoption Leave (Amendment) (No. 2) Regulations 2014 (2014/3206)* create new rights to adoption leave and paternity leave for local authority foster parents who are prospective adopters if they have been notified that a child is to be placed with them under *section 22C* of the *Children Act 1989* following consideration in accordance with *section 22C(9B)(c)* of that *Act*.

An employee is not entitled to take adoption leave if the employee has taken any shared parental leave in respect of the child or exercised a right to take time off under *section 57ZJ* of the *1996 Act* (adoption appointments): *regulation 8(1A)* of the *PAL Regulations*.

The detailed rules applicable to adoption leave are broadly similar to those applicable to the comparable provisions for ordinary and additional maternity leave. Those applicable to paternity leave in relation to adopted children are broadly similar to those applicable to ordinary and additional paternity leave.

32.115 Protection against detriment in relation to paternity or adoption leave

As with employees taking maternity leave, employees are protected against suffering detriment in certain circumstances in relation to paternity or adoption leave: *reg 28* of the *PAL Regulations*, *reg 33* of the *Additional PL Regulations*, *reg 23* of the *Overseas Adoptions Additional PL Regulations* and *ERA 1996, s 47C*. Dismissal of an employee for a reason connected with the fact that he took, or sought to take, paternity or adoption leave, or for a series of other specified related reasons, will be an automatically unfair dismissal, save in prescribed circumstances, as will the dismissal of a person on APL for the reason that he is redundant where *reg 28* of the *Additional PL Regulations* or *reg 18* of the *Overseas Adoptions Additional PL Regulations* as appropriate have not been complied with: *reg 29* of the *PAL Regulations*, *reg 34* of the *Additional PL Regulations*, *reg 24* of the *Overseas Adoptions Additional PL Regulations* and *ERA 1996, s 99*. The protections in relation to APL in the *Additional PL Regulations* came into effect on 6 April 2010; and those of the *Overseas Adoptions Additional PL Regulations* on 9 April 2010 (and the same applies to the protection from detriment/dismissal provisions therein).

In *Atkins v Coyle Personnel plc* [2008] IRLR 420, the EAT observed that there had to be a causal connection between the dismissal and the taking of paternity leave in a claim under *reg 29* of the *PAL Regulations*, rather than some vague, less stringent connection. The mere fact that a dispute between employee and manager originated in an incident when the employee was on paternity leave will not be sufficient by itself to establish the causal connection.

32.116 Statutory paternity and adoption pay

Employees who satisfy certain qualifying conditions are entitled to statutory paternity pay for up to two weeks in the sum of the lesser of £140.98 per week as of 6 April 2017 or 90% of his normal weekly earnings, and employees adopting children after 5 April 2015 are entitled to 90% of their gross average weekly earnings for the first six weeks, after which the same position as statutory paternity pay applies (see the *Statutory Paternity Pay and Adoption Pay (General) Regulations 2002 (SI 2002/2822)*): *Statutory Paternity Pay and Statutory Adoption Pay (Weekly Rates) Regulations 2002 (SI 2002/2818)*, as regularly amended.

In addition, employees who satisfy the relevant qualifying conditions are entitled to additional statutory paternity pay in accordance with the detailed requirements of the *Additional Statutory Paternity Pay (General) Regulations 2010 (SI 2010/1056)* or the

Additional Statutory Paternity Pay (Adoptions from Overseas) Regulations 2010 (SI 2010/1057) and the *Additional Statutory Paternity Pay (Weekly Rates) Regulations 2010 (SI 2010/1060)*. See also variously the *Additional Statutory Paternity Pay (Birth, Adoption and Adoptions from Overseas) (Administration) Regulations 2010 (SI 2010/154)*, the *Statutory Paternity Pay (Adoption), Additional Statutory Paternity Pay (Adoption) and Statutory Adoption Pay (Adoptions from Overseas) (Persons Abroad and Mariners) Regulations 2010 (SI 2010/150)* and the *Additional Statutory Paternity Pay (National Health Service Employees) Regulations 2010 (SI 2010/152)*.

33 Part-Time Workers

33.1 LEGAL FRAMEWORK

Part-time workers are protected from discrimination under both European and domestic law.

- *Directive 97/81/EC* on part-time work (implementing 'the *Framework Agreement*') was concluded by the European Social Partners and adopted by the European Council on 15 December 1997. It was given force in the United Kingdom by *Directive 98/23/EC*. The *Framework Agreement* is aimed at eliminating discrimination against part-time workers and contributing to the encouragement, development and quality of part-time work.

- The prohibition on discrimination in *cl 4* of the *Framework Agreement* is a specific expression of the principle of equality, which is a fundamental principle of EU law. See, for example paragraph 58 of the judgment of the CJEU in: *Istituto Nazionale della Previdenza Sociale v Bruno*: C-395/08 & C-396/08, [2010] IRLR 890.

- The Directive is implemented domestically in the *Part-Time Workers (Prevention of Less Favourable Treatment) Regulations 2000 (SI 2000/1551)* ('the Regulations'), as since amended. Note, however, that the *Regulations* were made under *s 19* of the *Employment Relations Act 1999* and not *s 2* of the *European Communities Act 1972* and that, in some respects, the protections in the *Regulations* go beyond those mandated by the *Directive* (see further **33.20** below).

The *Regulations* provide a relatively simple, gender-neutral route for tackling discrimination against part-time workers. A part-time worker may still, however, have a claim in the alternative under the *Equality Act 2010*. In *Voss v Land Berlin*: C-300/06 [2007] ECR I-10573, [2008] 1 CMLR 49, for example, the ECJ held that a difference in treatment which is detrimental to part-time workers could be contrary to the principle of equal pay and therefore require objective justification. See also, for example, *Pike v Somerset County Council* [2009] EWCA Civ 808, [2010] ICR 46, [2009] IRLR 870 (in relation to a provision of the *Teachers' Superannuation (Consolidation) Regulations 1988* which disadvantaged part-time workers); *Meerts v Proost NV*: C-116/08 [2010] All ER (EC) 1085, ECJ (in relation to notice pay for workers who are taking part-time parental leave); and *Copple v Littlewoods plc* [2012] ICR 354 (in relation to occupational pension schemes). This chapter is concerned with the *Regulations* only.

As to the application of sex discrimination legislation to part-time workers, see DISCRIMINATION AND EQUAL OPPORTUNITIES I (11), II (12), and III (13) and EQUAL PAY (22).

33.2 Guidance Material

Sections 20 and *21* of the *Employment Relations Act 1999* empower the Secretary of State to issue a Code of Practice in relation to part-time work and the *Framework Agreement*. To date, however, no Code has been issued. BERR (as it then was) issued Guidance Notes to accompany the *Regulations* which provide advice on the law as well as on how employers can widen access to part-time work, although these do not appear to have been updated (webarchive.nationalarchives.gov.uk/20121212135622/http://www.bis.gov.uk/files/file 23861.pdf). Some limited guidance is provided in the Explanatory Note to the *Regulations*.

33.3 Part-Time Workers

33.3 Direct effect

In *Zentralbetriebsrat der Landeskrankenhauser Tirols v Land Tirol*: C-486/08 [2010] IRLR 631, the ECJ held that *cl 4(1)–(2)* of the *Framework Agreement* (i.e. the non-discrimination provision) is unconditional and sufficiently precise for individuals to be able to rely upon it before a national court (see paragraphs 21–25). This is consistent with the approach taken in *R (on the application of Manson (Finian)) v Ministry of Defence* [2005] EWHC 427 (Admin), [2005] All ER (D) 270 (Feb), in which Moses J considered, *obiter*, that *cl 4* of the *Framework Agreement* has direct effect. In *Christie v Department for Constitutional Affairs and Department for Work and Pensions* [2007] ICR 1553, however, an appeal against a decision that there was no directly enforceable right did not get through the EAT 'sift'. The President did not express any opinion on the point (see [23]).

33.4 WHO HAS THE RIGHT?

Workers

The majority of rights under the *Regulations* are granted to 'workers'. The definition of 'worker' in *reg 1(2)* is the same as that in *s 230(3)* of the *Employment Rights Act 1996*. It covers individuals who have entered into, work or worked under a contract of employment or any other contract, whether express or implied and (if it is express) whether oral or in writing, whereby the individual undertakes to do or perform personally any work or services for another party to the contract, whose status is not by virtue of the contract that of a client or customer of any profession or business undertaking carried on by the individual (see Employee, Self-Employed or Worker? (15)).

Applicants for employment are not within the scope of the *Regulations*. In addition, it is important to note that *reg 7(1)* (unfair dismissal) applies only to 'employees' (see **33.21**).

The *Regulations* apply to those in Crown employment and to House of Lords and House of Commons staff: *regs 12, 14* and *15*. They also apply to persons appointed as police cadets or holding the office of constable other than under a contract of employment, who are treated as employed under a contract of employment for these purposes: *reg 16*. Special provisions apply to constables who are seconded to the Serious Organised Crime Agency: *regs 16(1A)–(1B)*.

The *Framework Agreement* applies to 'workers who have an employment contract or employment relationship as defined by the law, collective agreement or practice in force in each Member State'. In *O'Brien v Ministry of Justice*: C-393/10 [2012] IRLR 412 the CJEU explained:

- None of the terms 'worker', 'employment contract' or 'employment relationship' are defined in the *Framework Agreement*. The *Directive* and the *Framework Agreement* do not aim at complete harmonisation of national laws in this area, but only to establish a general framework for eliminating discrimination against part-time workers. Member States are free to define those terms in accordance with national law and practice. It is for national law to determine whether a person in part-time work has a contract of employment or an employment relationship.

- However, Member States may not apply rules which are liable to jeopardise the achievement of the objective pursued by the *Framework Agreement* and deprive it of its effectiveness. In particular, a Member State cannot remove certain categories of people from the scope of the protection offered by the *Framework Agreement* at will, violating its effectiveness.

- The exclusion of fee-paid judges from the protection of the Regulations would be permitted only if the nature of the employment relationship concerned is *"substantially different"* from that between employers and their employees who are 'workers' under national law.

In *Ministry of Justice (formerly Department for Constitutional Affairs) v O'Brien* [2013] UKSC 6, [2013] 1 WLR 522, the Supreme Court held that fee-paid judges are 'workers' for the purposes of the *Regulations*. Recorders were not self-employed free agents who could make their own choices as to the work they would do, and where and when that work was to be done.

33.5 **Casual workers and members of the armed forces**

In *Wippel v Peek & Cloppenburg Gmbh & Co Kg*: C-313/02 [2004] ECR I-9483, [2005] ICR 1604, the ECJ considered the status of 'framework contracts of employment' or 'work on demand' contracts, which set out applicable rates of pay, but provide no fixed working hours, no guarantee of income, and that the worker can accept or refuse the job offered each week without having to give any reason for doing so. The ECJ considered that such contracts do fall within the scope of the *Directive*, provided that the following conditions are met: (a) that such workers have a contract or employment relationship recognised by law, collective agreement or practices in force in the member state; (b) that they work 'part-time', ie their normal working hours are less than those of a comparable full-time worker; and (c) that in regard to part-time workers working on a casual basis, the member state has not excluded them from the benefit of the terms of the *Framework Agreement*, pursuant to *cl 2(2)*.

Under UK law, a framework contract would probably lack the mutuality of obligation necessary to amount to a contract of employment (see EMPLOYEE, SELF-EMPLOYED OR WORKER? **(15)**). Depending on the precise terms of the framework contract, an individual may also fall outside the domestic definition of a 'worker' if he or she has not 'undertaken to perform any work or services', e.g. if the individual is not obliged to accept any work offered to her under the framework contract.

As to the armed forces:

•   The *Regulations* apply to members of the armed forces, subject to specific exceptions: *reg 13(1)*. They apply to individuals employed by Reserve Associations established for the purposes of *Part XI* of the *Reserve Forces Act 1996* ('the 1996 Act'): *reg 13(1)*. However, they do not apply to service as a member of the reserve forces in so far as that service consists of undertaking training obligations under *ss 38, 40* or *41* of the *Reserve Forces Act 1980*, *s 22* of the *Reserve Forces Act 1996* ('the 1996 Act'), regulations made under *s 4* of the *1996 Act* or voluntary training or duties under *s 27* of the *1996 Act*: *reg 13(2)*.

•   *Reg 7(1)* (unfair dismissal) does not apply to members of the armed forces: *reg 13(1)*. In addition, a complaint concerning the service of any person as a member of the armed forces may only be presented to an employment tribunal under *reg 8* of the *Regulations* if that person has already made a complaint in respect of the same matter to an officer under the service redress procedures, and that complaint has not been withdrawn: *reg 13(3)–(6)*.

Is the exclusion in respect of reservists in *reg 13(2)* compatible with the Directive? At first instance in *R (on the application of Manson (Finian)) v Ministry of Defence* [2005] EWHC 427 (Admin), [2005] All ER (D) 270 (Feb), Moses J expressed the obiter view that it is compatible. *Cl 2(2)* of the *Framework Agreement* permits member states to exclude part-time workers who work on a casual basis from the protections of the *Framework Agreement*, provided that they do so for objective reasons and after prescribed consultation. Moses J noted that 'casual worker' is not defined: it is a term left to member states to define pursuant to *recital 16* and to the *Framework Agreement* (although any definition must not diminish the class of part-time worker so as to deprive the *Directive* of any force).

33.6   Part-Time Workers

33.6   Fee-paid holders of judicial office

The *Regulations* do not apply to any individual in his capacity as the holder of a judicial office if he is remunerated on a daily fee-paid basis: *reg 17*.

The scope and effect of *reg 17* has been extensively litigated in the past five years, both domestically and in Europe, in the ongoing 'judicial pensions' proceedings.

In 2010, the Supreme Court (in *O'Brien v Department for Constitutional Affairs* [2010] UKSC 34, [2010] IRLR 883) referred the compatibility of *reg 17* with European law to the CJEU. The Supreme Court noted: (1) that there was no single definition of "worker" for all Community law purposes; (2) that in contrast to the position under other Directives (where references to workers have an autonomous European meaning), the effect of *cl 2(1)* of the *Framework Agreement* read with *recital 16* of the *Directive* was to make domestic law relevant to the interpretation of the expression 'worker'; but also (3) that domestic law must respect the underlying purposes of the EU legislation and must not oust or "trump" the principles underlying that legislation in such a way as to frustrate them. It considered, however, that the application of these principles to *reg 17* required a reference.

In 2012, the CJEU gave judgment in (*O'Brien*: C-393/10 [2012] IRLR 412), holding that:

- It is for each Member State to define the concept of 'workers who have an employment contract or an employment relationship' for the purposes of the *Framework Agreement*. However, Member States may not apply rules which are liable to jeopardise the achievement of the objective pursued by the *Framework Agreement* and deprive it of its effectiveness, by arbitrarily excluding a category of persons from the protection the *Framework Agreement* offers.

- The exclusion of fee-paid judges from the protection of the *Regulations* would be permitted only if the nature of the employment relationship concerned is *"substantially different"* from the hat between employers and their employees who are 'workers' under national law.

- The term "worker" is used in the definition of the scope of the *Framework Agreement* to draw a distinction from a self-employed person, and the national court would have to bear in mind that this distinction is part of the spirit of the *Framework Agreement*. It would be necessary for the national court to consider the rules for appointing and removing judges, and the way in which their work is organised. For example, judges are expected to work during defined times and periods, and are entitled to sick pay, maternity or paternity pay and other similar benefits. The CJEU also noted that the fact that judges are subject to terms of service and might be regarded as workers within the meaning of cl 2.1 of the *Framework Agreement* does not undermine the principle of the independence of the judiciary or the right of Member States to provide a particular status for the judiciary. It merely aims to extend to those judges the scope of the principle of equal treatment and to protect them against discrimination as compared with full-time workers.

- Full-time judges and recorders perform essentially the same activity. Accordingly, if fee-paid judges are workers for these purposes, the *Framework Agreement* precludes discrimination between full-time judges and fee-paid part-time judges for the purposes of access to the relevant retirement pension scheme, unless such a difference in treatment can be justified by objective reasons. Again, whether or not that is so would be a matter for the national court. However, the CJEU noted that *"budgetary considerations cannot justify discrimination"*.

In 2013, the Supreme Court held in light of the CJEU's judgment, that fee-paid judges are 'workers' for the purposes of the *Regulations* (in *Ministry of Justice (formerly Department for Constitutional Affairs) v O'Brien* [2013] UKSC 6, [2013] 1 WLR 522. Recorders are not self-employed free agents who can make their own choices as to the work they do, and where and when they do that work. They are expected to observe the terms and conditions of their appointment, and may be disciplined if they fail to do so. The Court noted that the very fact that most recorders are self-employed barristers or solicitors merely serves to underline the different character of their commitment to the public service when they undertake the office of recorder. They are in an employment relationship within the meaning of cl 2.1 of the *Framework Agreement* and so must be treated as "workers" for the purposes of the *Regulations*.

On 27 March 2014, the Ministry of Justice announced the steps it proposed to take in response to the *O'Brien* litigation: www.gov.uk/government/news/ministry-of-justice -statement-in-fee-paid-judicial-cases.

33.7   QUALIFYING PERIOD

There is no qualifying period for entitlement to the rights conferred by the *Regulations*. In *O'Brien v Ministry of Justice* [2016] IRLR 100, the Court of Appeal held that when calculating the pension rights of a part-time Recorder, the tribunal should consider only sitting days after 7 April 2000 (ie. the date by which the UK was required to transpose the *Directive*). Pension rights attributable to a particular period of service were acquired during that period and the legal situation created by that period of service was "definitively fixed", as a matter of EU law, and to ensure legal certainty, when that period expired.

33.8   DISCRIMINATION

Less favourable treatment

A part-time worker has the right not to be treated by his employer less favourably than a comparable full-time worker: (a) as regards the terms of his contract; or (b) by being subjected to any other detriment by his employer: *reg 5(1)*. However, the right applies only if the treatment is on the ground that the worker is a part-time worker, and if it is not objectively justified: *reg 5(2)*.

A person is being treated less favourably 'as regards the terms of his contract' if those contractual terms are less favourable. He or she does not have to wait until that term is triggered to his detriment before beginning proceedings: see *Sharma v Manchester City Council* [2008] ICR 623, at [45].

It is likely that the same approach will be taken to 'detriment' as has been adopted in relation to other anti-discrimination provisions (see DISCRIMINATION AND EQUAL OPPORTUNITIES – I (11)). Pressuring an individual to work full time, issuing an ultimatum to that effect, or selecting him or her for redundancy are all examples of potential less favourable treatment. Requiring a part-time worker to work a higher proportion of 'standby' to rostered hours than a full-time worker can also constitute a detriment: *Gibson v Scottish Ambulance Service* (EATS/0052/04) (16 December 2004) at [13].

33.9   *The pro rata principle*

The *Regulations* require that the 'pro rata principle' be applied to determine whether a part-time worker has been treated less favourably than a comparable full-time worker unless it is inappropriate: *reg 5(3)*. That principle – which is defined in *reg 1(2)* – means that where a comparable full-time worker receives or is entitled to receive pay or some other benefit, a part-time worker is to receive or be entitled to receive not less than the proportion of that pay or other benefit that the number of his weekly hours bears to the number of weekly hours of the comparable full-time worker. 'Weekly hours' means, by *reg 1(3)*: (a) the number of hours a worker is required to work under his contract of employment in a week in which he has no absences from work and does not work any overtime; or (b) where the number of such hours varies according to a cycle, the average number of such hours.

The original source for the 'pro rata principle' is *cl 4(2)* of the *Framework Agreement*.

A tribunal considering *reg 5* should always consider whether it is 'appropriate' to apply the pro rata principle. It will usually be appropriate to do so where the claim is based on a difference in pay for hours worked in the ordinary course of events: *James v Great North Eastern Railway* [2005] All ER (D) 15 (Mar), EAT. However, in *Matthews v Kent and Medway Towns Fire Authority*, a tribunal held that it was inappropriate to apply the pro rata principle over the whole range of a financial package for fire fighters which included pension benefit, sick pay and pay for additional duties. This conclusion was not challenged on appeal (House of Lords decision reported at [2006] ICR 365).

The role of the pro rata principle was further considered by the EAT and then the Court of Session in *McMenemy v Capita Business Services Ltd* [2007] IRLR 400 (CS). Employees at a call centre which operated seven days a week were entitled to public holidays which 'fell on [their] normal working day'. The claimant worked part-time, Wednesday to Friday. He was not allowed time off in lieu when public holidays fell on a Monday, although full-time workers in his team who normally worked on Mondays were given the day off. He argued that he had a stand-alone right to pro rata treatment as regards holidays, and that he could demonstrate that he received less holiday than a comparable full-time worker. The tribunal, EAT and Court of Session dismissed his claim. The EAT held that the tribunal had been entitled to conclude that the reason that the claimant was receiving the treatment complained of was not because he was a part-time worker but because he did not work on a Monday. The tribunal did not err in failing to have regard to the pro rata principle because *reg 5(3)* is not an independent right, and is not something that a tribunal must have in mind when considering whether any less favourable treatment is on the ground that the employee is a part-time worker (see **33.16** below). The Court of Session agreed: the pro-rata principle relates only to the logically first question whether or not a part-time worker has been treated less favourably than a full-time worker.

33.10   *Overtime*

Where part-time workers only receive overtime rates once they have worked the equivalent of a full-time worker's weekly hours, not once they have completed the hours they themselves ordinarily work each week, there is no less favourable treatment: *reg 5(4)*. This reflects the orthodox position with regards to equal pay: see *Stadt Lengerich v Helmig* [1996] ICR 35, CJEU and **22.12** EQUAL PAY. It does not affect the right of part-time workers to receive other payments such as unsocial hours payments, weekend payments or other forms of enhanced pay on comparable terms to full-time workers.

In James v Great North Eastern Railways [2005] All ER (D) 15 (Mar), the EAT held that the *reg 5(4)* exception did not apply to an 'additional hours payment' made to full-time workers. Full-time employees were contractually obliged to work a 40 hour week judged over the length of an 8-week roster cycle. Employees could also be required to work overtime. Pay for the first 35 hours was paid at basic rate; they then received an 'additional hours payment' for the next five hours, being 1¼ times basic pay, and any overtime over and above the 40 hours was paid at 1¼ times basic pay. Pay for the set hours for part-time workers was at the same basic rate as full-time equivalent posts, with pay for any overtime up to 35 hours being at the same basic rate. Pay for additional hours over 35 hours was at 1¼ times basic pay but part-time workers did not receive an 'additional hours payment'. The EAT held that the payment in question must amount to a 'true' overtime payment to fall within the *reg 5(4)* exception. The 'additional hours payment' made to full-time workers was pay for the contractual rostered hours that they worked and, accordingly, the *reg 5(4)* was not applicable.

33.11 *Paid annual leave*

In *Zentralbetriebsrat der Landeskrankenhauser Tirols v Land Tirol* C-486/08, [2010] IRLR 631 the CJEU held that the pro rata principle in *cl 4(2)* of the *Framework Agreement* could not be applied to reduce ex post facto annual leave which had been accumulated (but not yet taken) during a period of full-time work. EU law, and in particular *cl 4(2)*, precluded a national provision under which a worker who moved from full- to part-time either suffered a reduction in the paid annual leave which he had accumulated but not been able to exercise while working full-time, or was required to take that leave with a reduced level of pay. *Land Tirol* was endorsed by the CJEU in *Heimann v Kaiser GmbH*: C-229/11 [2013] IRLR 48. As to the converse situation, see the similar approach in *Greenfield v The Care Bureau Ltd* [2016] IRLR 62.

33.12 *Occupational Pensions*

In *Istituto Nazionale della Previdenza Sociale v Bruno* C-395/08 & C-396/08, [2010] IRLR 890, the CJEU held that the *Framework Agreement* precluded national legislation under which part-time vertical-cyclical workers (i.e. workers working only during certain periods of the year) were treated less favourably than comparable full-time workers in relation to the qualifying period for accruing pension rights, unless that treatment could be objectively justified. The Court held, in particular, that the prohibition of discrimination in relation to "employment conditions" found in the *Framework Agreement* and *Directive* extended to occupational pensions dependent on an employment relationship (and the ECJ gave guidance as to when social-security type pensions would fall within that definition) and confirmed that that prohibition extended to the future effects of situations which arose prior to the *Framework Agreement* and *Directive* coming into force (e.g. periods of employment before the *Directive* came into force which were qualifying service requirements for future retirement pensions).

In *O'Brien v Ministry of Justice* [2016] IRLR 100, however, the Court of Appeal held that when calculating the pension rights of a part-time Recorder, the tribunal should consider only sitting days after 7 April 2000 after 7 April 2000 (ie. the date by which the UK was required to transpose the Directive). See **33.7** above.

33.12A *Allowances*

In *Österreichischer Gewerkscaftsbund v Verband Österreichischer Banken und Bankiers*: C-467/12 [2015] IRLR 67, the CJEU held that a dependent child allowance paid by employers in Austria pursuant to a collective agreement fell within the scope of Clause 4 of the Framework Agreement and could be paid pursuant to the principle of *pro rata temporis*. Such allowance was "pay", not a social security benefit.

33.12B *Discretion*

In *Ministry of Justice v Burton* [2016] IRLR 100, the EAT held that there was less favourable treatment where part-time judges of the Residential Property Tribunal were paid for writing-up time as a matter of discretion, whilst full-time tax judges received such payments as a matter of entitlement.

33.13 Comparators

The *Regulations* involve the making of a comparison between a part-time worker and a 'comparable' full-time worker, unless *regs 3* and *4* apply. Special provisions apply in relation to a full-time worker who drops down to part-time, or someone returning from less than 12 months' maternity leave.

33.14 *Actual comparator*

Do the *Regulations* require an 'actual' comparator (as is ordinarily the case under the *Equal Pay Act 1970*: see **22.9** EQUAL PAY), or will a hypothetical comparator suffice (as under the *Equality Act 2010*: see **11.15** DISCRIMNATION AND EQUAL OPPORTUNITIES – I)?

33.14 Part-Time Workers

• The wording of the *Regulations* suggests that a narrow comparison is all that is envisaged, and that if there is no full-time comparator employed by the same employer, any claim will fail. However, the wording of the *Directive* is somewhat wider, stating that 'where there is no comparable full-time worker in the same establishment, the comparison shall be made by reference to the applicable collective agreement or, where there is no applicable collective agreement, in accordance with national law, collective agreements or practice'.

• In *Carl v University of Sheffield* [2009] ICR 1286, the EAT confirmed that a part-time worker must show that he or she has been treated less favourably than an *actual* full-time comparator. The definition of a comparable full-time worker in *reg 2(4)* does not include the "or would" formula found in *s 1(1)(a)* of the *Sex Discrimination Act 1975* or *s 1(1)(a)* of the *Race Relations Act 1976* (i.e. "*a person discriminates against a woman if ... on the ground of her sex he treats her less favourably than he treats or would treat a man*"). The EAT noted that a hypothetical comparator is expressly permitted in certain circumstances under *regs 3* and *4* and that this suggests that these two exceptional categories are the only cases in which reliance on a hypothetical comparator is permissible. In addition, the EAT endorsed the dicta of Lady Smith in *McMenemy v Capita Business Services Ltd* [2006] IRLR 761 to the effect that a hypothetical comparator was probably 'not apposite' under the *Regulations* and that the *Framework Agreement* does not require any other conclusion. In *McMenemy*, Lady Smith had noted that the ECJ had held in *Wippel v Peek & Cloppenburg GmbH & Co KG* [2005] ICR 1604 that a particular part-time contract was not in breach of the *Directive* when there was no full-time worker in the establishment with the same type of contract or employment relationship to enable a comparison and had not gone on to construct a hypothetical comparator.

• The decision in *Carl* is consistent with the early observations of the EAT in *Tyson v Concurrent Systems Inc Ltd* [2003] All ER (D) 09 (Sep) and *Lynch v Royal Mail Group plc* [2003] All ER (D) 11 (Sep). In *Advocate General for Scotland v Barton* [2016] IRLR 210, recently, the Inner House of the Court of Session held that a comparator who had worked only 70% of available hours was not a permissible comparator, even though he had been treated by the Secretary of State as working "full time" for certain pension purposes. The effect of this restriction is likely to be that the *Regulations* will not provide protection for the many part-time workers who do jobs only done by part-timers.

33.15 *Identifying 'part-time' and 'full-time' workers*

The first step is to identify 'full-time workers' and 'part-time workers'.

• A worker is a part-time worker if he is 'paid wholly or in part by reference to the time he works and, having regard to the custom and practice of the employer in relation to workers employed by the worker's employer under the same type of contract, is not identifiable as a full-time worker': *reg 2(2)*.

• By contrast, he is a full-time worker if he is 'paid wholly or in part by reference to the time he works and, having regard to the custom and practice of the employer in relation to workers employed by the worker's employer under the same type of contract, is identifiable as a full-time worker': *reg 2(1)*.

These definitions are structured by reference to workers employed under "*the same type of contract*". *Reg 2(3)* provides that each of the following groups shall be regarded as being employed under different types of contract, for the purposes both of determining whether a worker is full- or part-time in the first place and of comparing the treatment of full- and part-time workers: (a) employees employed under a contract that is not a contract of apprenticeship; (b) employees employed under a contract of apprenticeship; (c) workers who are not employees; and (d) any other description of worker that it is reasonable for the employer to treat differently from other workers on the ground that workers of that description have a different type of contract. As to the authorities on the meaning of "*the same type of contract*" in this context, see further 33.16 below.

The *Regulations* used to provide that those working under fixed term contracts were employed under different types of contract to those who worked under permanent contracts. However, the distinction between fixed-term and permanent contracts was removed by the *Part-Time Workers (Prevention of Less Favourable Treatment) Regulations 2000 (Amendment) Regulations 2002, SI 2002/2035* with effect from 1 October 2002 in order to give effect to the *Fixed-Term Employees (Prevention of Less Favourable Treatment) Regulations 2002, SI 2002/2034*, which prohibit discrimination between fixed term employees and comparable permanent employees.

In *Hudson v University of Oxford* [2007] EWCA Civ 336, [2007] All ER (D) 356 (Feb) the Court of Appeal allowed an appeal against a tribunal decision to strike out Mr Hudson's claim of less favourable treatment on the basis that it had no reasonable prospects of success. Mr Hudson was employed by the University under two part-time contracts. He claimed that, in reality, he had had one full-time job and that he had been less favourably treated when compared with other full-time employees. The Court of Appeal considered it arguable that (1) his contention that the reality was that he had a single full-time job did not necessarily preclude him from having been a part-time worker as defined in *reg 2(2)* of the *Regulations*; (2) to the extent that he was a part-time worker under one of his contracts, he was, on account of his job, treated less favourably than relevant full-time comparators; and (3) he was so treated on the ground that he was contractually and within the terms of *reg 2* a part-time worker. He was therefore permitted to pursue his claims under the *Regulations*. The Court of Appeal left open the question whether the comparison should be between a part-time worker doing two jobs and a full-time worker doing both jobs together, or whether each part-time contract had to be looked at separately and compared with a full-time worker under separate contracts.

33.16 *Identifying a 'comparable full-time worker'*

The second step is to determine whether the part-time workers' full-time colleagues are 'comparable full-time workers' within the meaning of *reg 2(4)*.

A full-time worker will be a 'comparable full-time worker' in relation to a claimant part-time worker within the meaning of *reg 2(4)* where, at the time that the less favourable treatment occurs:

(a)   both workers are employed by the same employer under the same type of contract, and both are engaged in the same or broadly similar work (having regard, where relevant, to whether they have a similar level of qualification, skills and experience); and

(b)   the full-time worker works or is based at the same establishment as the part-time worker.

If there are no full-time workers who satisfy the requirements in (a) above, a full-time worker who satisfies those requirements but who works or is based at a different establishment may be considered: *reg 2(4)(b)*.

In *O'Brien v Ministry of Justice*: C-393/10 [2012] IRLR 412 the CJEU noted that 'comparable full-time worker' is defined in *cl 3* of the *Framework Agreement* as 'a full-time worker in the same establishment having the same type of employment contract or relationship, who is engaged in the same or a similar work/occupation, due regard being given to other considerations which may include seniority and qualification/skills' and that "*those criteria are based on the content of the activity of the persons concerned*". Accordingly, the CJEU concluded that full-time judges and recorders were in a comparable situation, notwithstanding that they have different careers as recorders retain the opportunity to practise as barristers, because they perform essentially the same activity.

33.17   *'Same type of contract'*

What does the requirement that a comparable full-time worker be employed by the same employer as the part-time worker *"under the same type of contract"* actually mean?

Reg 2(3) provides that the following categories of workers are employed under different types of contract: (a) *"employees employed under a contract that is not a contract of apprenticeship"*; (b) *"employees employed under a contract of apprenticeship"*; (c) *"workers who are not employees"*; and (d) workers in a long-stop category - *"any other description of worker that it is reasonable for the employer to treat differently from other workers on the ground that workers of that description have a different type of contract"*.

The leading authority is *Matthews v Kent and Medway Towns Fire Authority* [2004] ICR 257 (in the EAT); [2005] ICR 84 (in the Court of Appeal) and [2006] ICR 365 (in the House of Lords). This was a test case brought by part-time ('retained') firefighters who claimed that they were treated less favourably than comparable full-time firefighters in that they were denied access to statutory pension arrangements, they were denied increased pay for additional responsibilities and their sick pay arrangements were calculated on a less favourable basis. The Courts decided as follows:

(a)   The ET and the EAT considered that the retained firefighters were employed under a different type of contract from full-time firefighters, as it was reasonable for the employer to treat them differently within the meaning of *reg 2(3)(d)*. The ET had found many differences and special features in working patterns as between the two groups.

(b)   The Court of Appeal took a different approach. It held that both retained and full-time firefighters belonged to category (a) in *reg 2(3)*, being employees employed under a contract that was not a contract of apprenticeship.

(c)   A majority of the House of Lords (Lord Mance dissenting) upheld the approach of the Court of Appeal. They held that the requirement that the part-time worker and the full-time worker proposed as a comparator be employed under the same type of contract is directed to comparable types of employment relationship rather than comparable terms and conditions of employment. The categories set out in *reg 2(3)* are defined broadly in a way that allows for a wide variety of different terms and conditions within each category. The categories are mutually exclusive. Under *reg 2(3)(d)* the courts are asked to examine a type of worker who is different from any of those previously mentioned in *reg 2(3)(a)–(c)*. While it is difficult to think of a type of contract which is different to those mentioned in *reg 2(3)(a)–(c)*, a contract will only fall within *reg 2(3)(d)* if a worker does not fall into one of the other categories. It is a long-stop or residual category. It is not designed to allow employers to single out particular kinds of part-time working arrangements and treat them differently from the rest.

In *Wippel v Peek & Cloppenburg GmbG & Co KG* [2005] ICR 1604 (see **33.4**), the ECJ considered the position of part-time workers who worked according to need under 'framework contracts'. It held that as there was no full-time worker who worked according to need under a 'framework contract', there was no comparable full-time worker who worked under the same type of employment contract or relationship as the part-time worker within the meaning of the *Framework Agreement*. The employment relationship differed, as to subject matter and basis, between a full-time worker (working under a 'traditional' contract) and the claimant (working under a 'framework contract').

33.18 *'The same or broadly similar work'*

Matthews v Kent and Medway Towns Fire Authority (see **33.17**) also provided guidance on what is meant by *"the same or broadly similar work"*. The tribunal had held that retained firefighters were not engaged in the same or broadly similar work as full-time firefighters. That finding was upheld by the EAT and the Court of Appeal, but then rejected by the House of Lords:

(a)   The EAT and Court of Appeal found that full-time firefighters carried out measurable additional job functions, such as educational, preventive and administrative tasks which were not carried out by retained firefighters. There were differences in entry standards, probationary standards and on-going training, which led to differences in the level of qualification and skills. They noted that differences in recruitment procedures and promotion prospects also served to illustrate the different work carried out by full-time firefighters compared to retained firefighters, as full-time firefighters are recruited to do a job with measurable additional functions and overwhelmingly constitute the recruitment pool for promotion to higher grades. In short, the EAT and Court of Appeal did not accept that firefighting was the central role of all operational fire fighters, such that retained and full-time firefighters must be engaged in broadly similar work.

(b)   The House of Lords disagreed. The majority (Lord Nicholls, Lord Hope and Baroness Hale) held that the tribunal had erred in concentrating on the differences in the work carried out by retained and full-time firefighters, rather than assessing the weight to be given to the similarities in such work. The question is not whether the work is different, but whether it is the same or broadly similar. The *Regulations* are inviting a comparison between two types of workers whose work will almost inevitably be different to some extent. The tribunal must look at the work that both the full-time and part-time worker are engaged in, and ask whether it is the same work or if not, whether it is broadly similar. To answer that question, the tribunal must look at the whole of the work, leaving nothing out of account. Regard must be had to the question whether they have a similar level of qualification, skills and experience when judging whether work which at first sight appears to be the same or broadly similar does indeed satisfy the test in the *Regulations*. But this question must be directed to the whole of the work that the two kinds of workers are actually engaged in at the relevant time, not to some other work for which they may be qualified. In carrying out the assessment, particular weight should be given to the extent to which the work of part-time and full-time workers is exactly the same. If a large component of the work is exactly the same, the question is whether any differences are of such importance as to prevent the work of the two groups being regarded overall as 'the same or broadly similar'. Where both full- and part-timers do the same work, but the full-timers have extra activities with which to fill their time, this does not mean that the work under consideration is not nevertheless the same or broadly similar overall. The importance of the work which the workers do to the work of the enterprise as a whole is also of great importance in this assessment. If full-timers do the more important work and part-timers are brought in to do the more peripheral tasks, it is unlikely that the work of the two groups is the same or broadly similar. However, where full-timers and part-timers spend much of their time on the core activity of the enterprise, the fact that full-timers may do some extra tasks will not prevent their work being the same or broadly similar to that of the part-timers.

The case was remitted to the tribunal for reconsideration of whether the retained and full-time firefighters are engaged in the same or broadly similar work, where the ET determined that the part-time firefighters were carrying out the same or broadly similar work to the full-time firefighters. There was a substantial body of work comprising the firefighter's 'central duties' that were the same for both roles, and the full-timers' additional skills and experience, while relevant, did not contribute 'something different to the work'.

These issues have been explored recently in two cases in relation to part-time Judges and lay members: *Moultrie v Ministry of Justice* [2015] IRLR 264 and *McGrath v Ministry of Justice* (UKEAT/0247/14/LA; permission to appeal refused – [2016] EWCA Civ 379). In *Matthews v Kent and Medway Towns Fire Authority*, Lord Hope had said, at paragraph 15 that:

> "It is important to appreciate that it is the work on which the workers are actually engaged at the time that is the subject matter of the [regulation 2(4)] comparison. So the question whether they have a similar level of qualification, skills and experience is relevant only insofar as it bears on that exercise. An examination of these characteristics may help to show that they are each contributing something different to work that appears to be the same or broadly similar, with the result that their situations are not truly comparable. But the fact that they may fit them to do other work that they are not yet engaged in, in the event of promotion for example, would not be relevant."

Against that backdrop, in *Moultrie*, Lewis J held in the EAT that a Tribunal had been entitled to conclude that the position of part-time fee-paid medical members of tribunals such as the mental health tribunal (who were not entitled to an occupational pension) was not the same or broadly similar to the work of full-time, salaried regional members (who were so entitled). Some 85% of the work done by the two groups was the same, that work was of the highest importance to the work of the relevant tribunals, and there was no different between the two groups' respective levels of qualifications, skills and experience. Nevertheless, the Tribunal had been entitled to conclude that full-timers performed a role which was qualitatively different from that of part-timers. The additional work performed by full-timers, including appraisal, recruitment and training work, and other tasks delegated by chief medical members of the tribunals and Chamber Presidents, was sufficiently important to mean that the two groups' work was not the same or broadly similar. In *McGrath*, decided shortly afterwards, the EAT (HHJ Peter Clark presiding) held that the situation of an Employment Judge and the lay members of an Employment Tribunal were, similarly (indeed, a fortiori), not truly comparable for the purposes of *regulation 2(4)*.

33.19   *The scope of the comparison*

The EAT in *Matthews v Kent and Medway Towns Fire Authority* [2004] ICR 257, EAT (see 33.12 above) followed the approach of the House of Lords in *Hayward v Cammell Laird Shipbuilders Ltd* [1988] AC 894 and held that each specific term of the contract must be compared, rather than a 'broad brush' comparison. In the House of Lords in *Matthews*, Baroness Hale (with whom Lord Nicholls and Lord Hope agreed) did not rule out the possibility that a less favourable term might be so well balanced by a more favourable one that it could not be said that part-timers were treated less favourably overall. Nor did she rule out the possibility that more favourable treatment on one point might supply justification for less favourable treatment on another. On the facts, however, she found it difficult to see how a differently structured pay package for retained fire-fighters could justify total exclusion from the pension or sick pay schemes, unrelated to the hours actually worked.

33.20   *Specific circumstances where a comparator is not required*

There are two circumstances in which *Regulations* do not require a strict comparative approach.

First, if an individual becomes a part-time worker having previously worked in a job on a full-time basis, he can compare his part-time conditions with his previous full-time contract. *Reg 3* applies where the worker was a full-time worker within the meaning of *reg 2(1)* but, following a termination or variation of his contract, he continues to work under a new or varied contract, whether of the same type or not, that requires him to work for a lower number of weekly hours than the number he was required to work immediately before the termination or variation. The effect of *reg 3(2)* is that *reg 5* applies to such a worker as if he were a part-time worker and as if there were a comparable full-time worker employed under the terms that applied to him immediately before the termination or variation.

Secondly, if an individual who had previously worked in a job on a full-time basis returns to a part-time role after a period of absence of up to twelve months, such as maternity leave, he or she can compare their new part-time conditions with their previous full-time contract: *reg 4*.

- This regulation applies where the worker was a full-time worker within the meaning of *reg 2(1)* immediately before the period of absence (irrespective of whether the absence followed a termination of her contract), and where she returns to work for the same employer within 12 months of the date on which her absence started. The worker must return to the same job or a job at the same level under a contract in which she is required to work for a number of weekly hours that is lower than the number she was required to work immediately before the period of absence, regardless of whether the new contract is a different contract or a varied contract, or whether it is of the same type as the original contract or not: *reg 4(1)*.

- *Reg 5* applies to such a worker as if she were a part-time worker and as if there were a comparable full-time worker employed under: (a) the contract under which she was employed immediately before the period of absence; or (b) where it is shown that, had she continued to work under the original contract, a variation would have been made to its term during the period of absence, the original contract including that variation: *reg 4(2)*.

33.21 'On the ground that the worker is a part-time worker'

It is not sufficient for a tribunal to be satisfied that a claimant part-time worker has been less favourably treated than his or her full-time comparator. Liability will lie only if the less favourable treatment is "*on the ground that the worker is a part-time worker*": *reg 5(2)(a)*.

Unfortunately, there is a division between English and Scottish authority as to the meaning of "*on the ground that*" in *reg 5* of the *Regulations*. In England and Wales, the EAT held in *Carl v University of Sheffield* [2009] ICR 1286 that 'on the ground that' means that part-time work must be the effective and predominant cause of the less favourable treatment complained of; it need not be the only cause. This had similarly been the conclusion of the EAT in *Sharma v Manchester City Council* [2008] ICR 623, but the EAT in *Sharma* had not had cited to them a contrary decision of the Court of Session, *McMenemy v Capita Business Services Ltd* [2007] IRLR 400. In Scotland, *McMenemy* remains authority for the proposition that the less favourable treatment of part time workers will only be prohibited where it is for the sole reason that the workers work part-time (following an earlier decision of the Scottish EAT in *Gibson v Scottish Ambulance Service* (EATS/0052/04)). In *Carl*, the EAT noted that it was not bound by decisions of the Court of Session and declined to follow the approach taken in *McMenemy*. Judge Peter Clark noted that the expression "on the ground that" or "on the grounds of" appears frequently in domestic legislation and agreed with Elias J in *Sharma* that domestic legislation may go further than the protection contained in the *Framework Agreement*. The uncertainty has been further deepened by the decision of the EAT in *Engle v Ministry of Justice* UKEAT/337/15, [2017] ICR 277. The decision appears to have been reached without reference to any of the previous authorities. The learned judge noted that the language of the *Framework Directive* suggested that a remedy was to be available to those who were treated less favourably "solely because they work part-time"; acknowledged that the wording of the *Regulations* was wider but then held that their purpose was the same: "the purpose of the legislation is not to redress any and all injustices that may exist; it is to redress the less favourable treatment of part-time workers if and only if that treatment occurs because they are part-time workers". It is unclear what the EAT has decided. On one view it has taken the *McMenemy* line but the reference to "because of" echoes the test for direct discrimination in *EA 2010, s 13* which only requires that the protected characteristic should be a substantive and not the sole cause of the less favourable treatment.

It is respectfully submitted that the approach in *Carl* and *Sharma* is to be preferred. It was conceded in *McMenemy* that the *Regulations* should be construed consistently with the *Framework Agreement* and that they did not go further than the *Framework Agreement*. The Court of Session referred to the wording of *cl 4(1)* of the *Framework Agreement* to the effect that 'part-time workers shall not be treated in a less favourable manner than comparable full-time workers solely because they work part-time . . . ' and held that 'solely' means that less favourable treatment must be for the reason that workers work part-time and for that reason alone. It is submitted that the EAT in *Carl* was right to doubt the correctness of the original concession. The *Regulations* were made under *s 19* of the *Employment Relations Act 1999* and not under *s 2* of the *European Communities Act 1972*. It was therefore open to Parliament to go further than the *Framework Agreement*. It is further submitted that the absence of the word 'solely' in the *Regulations* is crucial to the analysis and that, properly construed, the *Regulations* do go further than the *Directive* in this regard. The phrase 'on the grounds that' in the *Regulations* should be interpreted in the same way as the 'on the prohibited grounds' test in other discrimination legislation (see **11.3–11.11** DISCRIMINATION AND EQUAL OPPORTUNITIES – **I** for application of the 'on the prohibited grounds' test in other contexts).

In *Komeng v Sandwell MBC* [2011] EqLR 1053 the EAT commented, at [45], that tribunals should take care before accepting an explanation that the reason for less favourable treatment lies merely in general poor administration, because of the risk that this masks discrimination on prohibited grounds.

33.22 Objective justification

Any less favourable treatment may be justified on objective grounds: *reg 5(2)(b)*.

The concept of objective justification is treated in the same way under the *Regulations* as in other anti-discrimination contexts (see **12.9** DISCRIMINATION AND EQUAL OPPORTUNITIES – **II** and **22.11** EQUAL PAY). Less favourable treatment will be objectively justified only if it can be shown that the treatment: (1) has a legitimate objective, such as a genuine business objective; (2) is necessary to achieve that objective; and (3) is an appropriate way of achieving that objective.

In *O'Brien v Ministry of Justice*: C-393/10 [2012] IRLR 412 the CJEU commented that the concept 'objective grounds' within the meaning of cl 4 of the *Framework Agreement* must be understood as not permitting a difference in treatment between part-time workers and full-time workers to be justified on the basis that the difference "*is provided for by a general, abstract norm*" and, on the contrary, that the unequal treatment must "*respond to a genuine need be appropriate for achieving the objective pursued and be necessary for that purpose*" (see paragraph 64). The CJEU added, in this context, that "*budgetary considerations cannot justify discrimination*" (see paragraph 66).

When *O'Brien* was remitted to the Supreme Court, the Court rejected the Ministry of Justice's attempts to justify a difference in treatment in pension provision for part-time and full-time judges, holding that they were not made out on the evidence. It adopted the guidance given by Advocate General Kokott [2012] ICR 955 to the effect that the unequal treatment at issue must be justified "*by the existence of precise, concrete factors, characterising the employment condition concerned in its specific context and on the basis of objective and transparent criteria for examining the question whether that unequal treatment responds to a genuine need and whether it is appropriate and necessary for achieving the objective pursued"*. It concluded that the aims of giving a greater reward to those who are thought to need it most or to those who make the greatest contribution, or recruiting a high quality judiciary might all be legitimate aims – but that the Government had failed to make out the specific basis for such justification on the evidence. For example, an employer might devise a scheme which rewarded its workers according to need rather than to their contribution, but the criteria would have to be precise and transparent, but that was not the case in relation to the provision for part-time judges, some of whom would need occupational pension provision, others of whom would not. Equally, the proper approach to differential contributions is to make special payments for extra responsibilities – which was not the case here. There was (the Court found) blanket discrimination between part-time and full-time judges which had not been justified. *O'Brien* concerned a recorder, but the Court noted that it seemed unlikely that the ministry's argument could be put any higher than it has been in relation to any other holder of part-time judicial office.

33.23 RIGHT TO RECEIVE A WRITTEN STATEMENT OF REASONS FOR LESS FAVOURABLE TREATMENT

A worker who considers that his employer may have treated him in a manner which infringes a right conferred upon him by *reg 5* may request in writing from his employer a written statement giving particulars of the reasons for the treatment: *reg 6*. The employer must provide such a statement within 21 days of the worker's request and such written statements will be admissible as evidence in any proceedings under the *Regulations*. A tribunal may draw inferences from an employer's refusal to answer or provision of an evasive or equivocal response: *reg 6(3)*.

Reg 6 does not apply where the treatment in question consists of the dismissal of an employee, and that employee is entitled to a written statement of reasons for his dismissal under *s 92* of the *Employment Rights Act 1996* (see **48.14, 48.15** TERMINATION OF EMPLOYMENT).

33.24 PROTECTION FROM DETRIMENT

A worker has the right, by *regs 7(2)–(3)*, not to be subjected to any detriment by an act, or deliberate failure to act, by his employer done on the ground that:

(i)   he has brought proceedings against the employer under the *Regulations*;

(ii)   he has requested a written statement under *reg 6*;

(iii)   he has given evidence or information in connection with any proceedings under the *Regulations* brought by any worker;

(iv)   he has done anything under the *Regulations* relating to his employer or any other person;

(v)   he has alleged that his employer has infringed the *Regulations*;

(vi)   he has refused or proposed to refuse to forego any right under the *Regulations*; or

(vii)   the employer believes or suspects that he has done or intends to do any of these things.

However, neither *reg 7(1)* (unfair dismissal) nor *reg 7(2)* (protection from detriment) applies in relation to an allegation that the employer has infringed the *Regulations* (or that the employer believes or suspects that the worker has made or intends to make such an allegation) if the allegation made by the worker is false and not made in good faith: *reg 7(4)*.

33.25 RELATIONSHIP WITH UNFAIR DISMISSAL

Reg 7(1) provides that an employee who is dismissed is to be regarded as unfairly dismissed for the purposes of *Part X* of the *Employment Rights Act 1996* if the reason or principal reason for his dismissal is that:

(i)   he has brought proceedings against the employer under the *Regulations*;

(ii)   he has requested a written statement under *reg 6*;

(iii)   he has given evidence or information in connection with any proceedings under the *Regulations* brought by any worker;

(iv)   he has done anything under the *Regulations* relating to his employer or any other person;

(v)   he has alleged that his employer has infringed the *Regulations*;

(vi)   he has refused or proposed to refuse to forego any right under the *Regulations*; or

(vii)   the employer believes or suspects that he has done or intends to do any of these things.

Save as set out in *reg 7*, a breach of the *Regulations* does not make any dismissal automatically unfair: *Pipe v Hendrickson Europe Ltd* [2003] All ER (D) 280 (Apr), EAT. In such cases, a tribunal must ascertain the reason for the dismissal, and then determine whether the dismissal was unfair within the terms of *s 98(4)* of the *Employment Rights Act 1996* (see UNFAIR DISMISSAL – II (54)). The act of discrimination may be an important factor for the tribunal to take into account when carrying out this evaluation, but it does not automatically follow that the dismissal is unfair.

33.26 APPLICATIONS TO AN EMPLOYMENT TRIBUNAL

A worker may present a complaint to an employment tribunal that his employer has infringed a right conferred on him by *reg 5* (less favourable treatment) or *reg 7(2)* (victimisation): *reg 8(1)*. Where a worker presents a complaint to a tribunal under the *Regulations*, it is for the employer to identify the ground for the less favourable treatment or detriment: *reg 8(6)*. A claim for breach of the *Regulations* that includes an allegation that the *Regulations* themselves are incompatible with *Directive 97/81* cannot be brought by way of judicial review, and must be brought in the tribunal: *R (on the application of Manson) v Ministry of Defence* [2005] EWCA Civ 1678; [2006] ICR 355.

33.27 TIME LIMITS

A claim must ordinarily be presented to a tribunal before the end of the period of three months beginning with the date of the less favourable treatment or detriment to which the complaint relates, save that the time limit will be extended as set out in *reg 8A* of the *Regulations* to reflect the rules on early conciliation: *reg 8(2)*, *reg 8(2A)*, *reg 8A* and CHAPTER 3: ACAS CONCILIATION. A six month time limit applies to complaints by members of the armed forces: *reg 8(2)*.

Where an act or failure to act is part of a series of similar acts or failures comprising the less favourable treatment, the time runs from the last of those acts. For the purposes of calculating the date of the less favourable treatment or detriment, *reg 8(4)* and *8(5)* provides that:

(a)   where a term in the contract is less favourable, that treatment shall be treated, subject to (b) below, as taking place on each day of the period during which the term is less favourable;

(b)   where an application relies on *regs 3* or *4* the less favourable treatment shall be treated as occurring on, and only on, in the case of *reg 3*, the first day on which the applicant worked under the new or varied contract and, in the case of *reg 4*, the day on which the applicant returned; and

(c)   a deliberate failure to act contrary to *reg 5* or *7(2)* shall be treated as done when it was decided on. In the absence of evidence establishing the contrary, a person shall be taken to decide not to act when he does an act inconsistent with doing the failed act, or if he has done no such inconsistent act, when the period expires within which he might reasonably have been expected to have done the failed act if it was to be done.

A tribunal may consider a complaint which is out of time if, in all the circumstances of the case, it considers that it is just and equitable to do so: *reg 8(3)*. In *Miller v Ministry of Justice* UKEAT/0003/15/LA and UKEAT/0004/15/LA, the EAT upheld the decision of an employment judge to refuse extensions of time in the judicial pensions litigation. The fact that other litigation was proceeding as a test case did not relieve these claimants of their own duty to make a claim in time; nor did a Moratorium which had been established by the Secretary of State after these claims were issued. (See **33.6** above).

33.28 REMEDIES

Where an employment tribunal finds that a complaint presented to it under *reg 8* is well-founded, it shall take such of the following steps as it considers just and equitable:

(a)   *Making a declaration as to the rights of the complainant and the employer in relation to the matters to which the complaint relates: reg 8(7)(a).*

(b)   *Ordering the employer to pay compensation to the complainant: reg 8(7)(b).*

Where a tribunal orders compensation, the amount of the compensation awarded shall be such as the tribunal considers just and equitable in all the circumstances having regard to (a) the infringement to which the complaint relates, and (b) any loss which is attributable to the infringement having regard, in the case of an infringement of the right conferred by *reg 5*, to the pro rata principle, except where it is inappropriate to do so: *reg 8(9)*. The loss shall be taken to include any expenses reasonably incurred by the complainant in consequence of the infringement and loss of any benefit which he might reasonably be expected to have had but for the infringement: *reg 8(10)*. In *Ministry of Justice v Burton* [2016] IRLR 100, the EAT held that an employment judge was entitled to make a "broad brush assessment" when calculating the appropriate compensation.

Compensation in respect of less favourable treatment on the grounds of part-time status (i.e. less favourable treatment contrary to *reg 5* of the *Regulations*) will *not* include compensation for injury to feelings: *reg 8(11)*.

In *Tyson v Concurrent Systems Inc Ltd* [2003] All ER (D) 09 (Sep), EAT, the appellant sought to argue that stigma damages and stigma compensation were not excluded by *reg 8(11)*. The EAT doubted whether stigma damages which did not include loss of earnings produced by the stigma could be brought within the provisions of *reg 8*.

Normal principles of mitigation apply: *reg 8(12)*. Where the tribunal finds that the act, or failure to act, to which the complaint relates was to any extent caused or contributed to by the action of the complainant, it shall reduce the amount of the compensation by such proportion as it considers just and equitable having regard to that finding: *reg 8(13)*.

(c) *Recommending that the employer take, within a specified period, action appearing to the tribunal to be reasonable, in all the circumstances of the case, for the purpose of obviating or reducing the adverse effect on the complainant of any matter to which the complaint relates: reg 8(7)(c).*

If the employer fails, without reasonable justification, to comply with a recommendation made by an employment tribunal under *reg 8(7)(c)* the tribunal may, if it thinks it just and equitable to do so, increase the amount of compensation required to be paid to the complainant in respect of the complaint where an order for compensation has already been made, or may make such an order for the first time: *reg 8(14).*

(For a more detailed discussion of these rules in relation to other anti-discrimination legislation, see DISCRIMINATION AND EQUAL OPPORTUNITIES – III (13).)

33.29 RESTRICTION ON CONTRACTING OUT

The restriction on contracting out of employment rights contained in *s 203* of the *Employment Rights Act 1996* applies in relation to the *Regulations* as if they were contained in the *1996 Act: reg 9* (see **53.19, 53.20** UNFAIR DISMISSAL – I).

(The requirements for a valid compromise agreement which satisfies the statutory conditions are addressed at **19.18–19.20** EMPLOYMENT TRIBUNALS – II.)

33.30 LIABILITY OF EMPLOYERS AND PRINCIPALS

As in other anti-discrimination legislation, anything done by a person in the course of his employment is treated for the purposes of the *Regulations* as also done by his employer, whether or not it was done with the employer's knowledge or approval: *reg 11(1)*. Anything done by a person as agent for the employer with the authority of the employer is treated as also done by the employer: *reg 11(2).*

In proceedings under the *Regulations* against any person in respect of an act alleged to have been done by a worker of his, it shall be a defence for that person to prove that he took such steps as were reasonably practicable to prevent the worker from (a) doing that act, or (b) doing, in the course of his employment, acts of that description: *reg 11(3).*

(See further **11.54** DISCRIMINATION AND EQUAL OPPORTUNITIES – I.)

34   Pay – I: Payments, Pay Statements and Miscellaneous Statutory Pay Rights

Cross-references. See PAY – II (35) for statutory deductions from pay; EQUAL PAY (22) for the rules against sex discrimination in pay; TRADE UNIONS – II (51) for deduction of trade union subscriptions.

34.1   INTRODUCTION

An employee's right to payment for his services is, of course, fundamental to the employment relationship and is principally governed by the particular terms of the contract of employment between the individual employee and employer. For example, the rate of pay and the intervals at which payment is made are governed by the individual employee's contract of employment, which also provides for any bonuses, commission, overtime, holiday pay or sick pay which may be payable. Such matters must be included in the written particulars of the contract of employment given by the employer to the employee (see 8.4 CONTRACT OF EMPLOYMENT). There is, however, a substantial overlay of statutory rights and protection afforded to employees in relation to payment for their services in the form of the right not to suffer unauthorised deductions from wages, the right to a National Minimum Wage and the right to itemised pay statements. These important rights are considered below.

Various other statutory rights to payment, such as statutory sick pay (see SICKNESS AND SICK PAY (44)) and statutory maternity pay (see MATERNITY AND PARENTAL RIGHTS (32)) are considered in other chapters in this work. Certain miscellaneous statutory rights to payment, namely, guarantee payments and medical suspension payments are outlined towards the end of this chapter. In addition there is an overview of the principles applicable to the calculation of 'a week's pay' – a statutory concept relevant to calculation of the sums payable under a number of the statutory employment rights such as the right to a redundancy payment and the payment of a basic award in a claim for unfair dismissal.

34.2   PAYMENT OF WAGES AND DEDUCTIONS FROM WAGES

Deductions from employees' pay were originally regulated by the *Wages Act 1986 ('WA 1986')*. The *WA 1986* had replaced the *Truck Acts*, which had formerly restricted payment of wages other than in cash (but see **34.3** below). The *WA 1986* made special provision for employees in retail employment affording them greater protection against deductions from their wages. The provisions of the *WA 1986* are all consolidated in *Part II* of the *Employment Rights Act 1996*. In this section of this chapter, references below are to the *Employment Rights Act 1996 ('ERA')* unless otherwise stated. In very rare cases, involving contracts of employment predating 1987, it may be necessary to have regard to the previous law as set out in **34.3** and **34.4** below. In the vast majority of cases the position will be governed exclusively by the provisions of *Part II* of the *ERA* as discussed in **34.6** *et seq* below.

34.3   PAYMENT OF WAGES

WA 1986, s 11 (now repealed) removed restrictions on the way in which payment of wages to manual and other workers may be made. The method of payment is now to be determined solely by the terms of the contract. It will be either the subject of express agreement or determined by an implied term. If no express agreement is reached it is likely that the method of payment impliedly agreed will be that which is customary in the industry.

The provisions of *WA 1986* replaced the old restrictions on the payment of wages contained in the *Truck Acts* and the *Payment of Wages Act 1960*. *Section 11* came into force on 1 January 1987 (*The Wages Act 1986 (Commencement) Order 1986 (SI 1986/1998)*). However, because s *1* of the *Truck Act 1831* operated by implying into the contract of employment a term that wages were payable in coin and not otherwise, it would appear that the contractual terms thus created survived the repeal of the *Act*. In other words, where the worker was employed pursuant to an unamended contract of employment created before 1 January 1987, it may be necessary on rare occasions to refer to the provisions set out in **34.4** and **34.5** below, but the requirement of pay in coin is now contractual rather than statutory and may be varied by consent. Such consensual variation will be implied if payment has in fact been other than in coin for a lengthy period.

34.4 PAYMENT OF WAGES: PRE-1987 POSITION

Until 1 January 1987, all wages payable to a manual labourer for work done by him, with certain exceptions, had to be paid to him in current coin of the realm or, if he so requested, by payment into a bank account or by cheque, postal order or money order (*Truck Act 1831, s 3; Payment of Wages Act 1960, s 1*). Any agreement to the contrary was illegal, null and void. If an employer acted in breach of the *Truck Acts*, for example, by payment in kind by the delivery of goods, or by payment by cheque against the employee's wishes:

(a)   the employee could sue for the wages due, no allowance being made for the value of the goods supplied; and

(b)   the employer was guilty of an offence.

(*Truck Act 1831, s 9.*)

A foreman did not fall within the protection of the *Truck Acts* (*Brooker v Charrington Fuel Oils Ltd* [1981] IRLR 147).

34.5 Exceptions

These are:

(i)   The provision of medicine or medical attendance, fuel materials, tools and accommodation could form part of the consideration for the employee's services (*Truck Act 1831, s 23*).

(ii)   Payments to domestic servants did not need to comply with the requirements as to payment in coin (*Truck Act 1831, s 20*).

(iii)   Contracts for the provision for agricultural workers of food, non-intoxicating drink, a cottage or other similar allowances or privileges were not illegal if money wages were paid in addition to these benefits (*Truck Amendment Act 1887, s 4*).

34.6 DEDUCTIONS FROM WAGES: THE CURRENT PROVISIONS

No deduction from a worker's wages may be made unless either:

(a)   it is required or permitted by a statutory or contractual provision; or

(b)   the worker has given his prior written consent to the deduction.

(*ERA 1996, ss 13(1), 15(1).*)

It is extremely important that deductions are not made in breach of this provision. Not only may sums wrongfully deducted be ordered to be repaid, but the employer may lose the right to recover the sums which he was seeking to deduct by any means at all (see **34.8** below).

If the deduction is made pursuant to a contractual provision, the terms of the contract must have been shown to the worker or, if not in writing, its effect notified in writing to the worker before the deduction is made (*ERA 1996, ss 13(2), 15(2)* and see *Kerr v Sweater Shop (Scotland) Ltd; Sweater Shop (Scotland) Ltd v Park* [1996] IRLR 424, EAT). In *Mennell v Newell & Wright (Transport Contractors) Ltd* [1997] IRLR 519 the Court of Appeal held that an employment tribunal had no jurisdiction to deal with *threatened* deductions from wages as the *Act* stated that a tribunal could only hear complaints where an employer had actually made a deduction. Accordingly, a threat of dismissal in order to impose a variation of the contract of employment so as to enable an employer to make deductions from wages did not amount to a breach of the relevant wages provisions of the *ERA 1996*. In *Discount Tobacco and Confectionery Ltd v Williamson* [1993] ICR 371, it was held that for there to be prior written consent, the consent must precede not only the deduction itself, but also the event or conduct giving rise to the deduction. What has to appear in writing in either case is not merely provision for repayment of the sum concerned but for it to be deducted *from wages* (*Potter v Hunt Contracts Ltd* [1992] ICR 337).

The above provisions do not apply to deductions:

(i)   made in order to reimburse the employer for any overpayment of wages or expenses made for any reason;

(ii)   made pursuant to any statutory disciplinary proceedings;

(iii)   which are statutory payments due to a public authority. In *Patel v Marquette Partners (UK) Ltd* [2009] IRLR 425, [2009] ICR 569, EAT, the (unsurprising) application of this exclusion to a deduction in the form of a taxation decision in relation to a bonus was considered. The policy underlying the exclusion of such matters from the general provision of *s 13* of the *ERA* is that challenges to a statutory authority's decision that money is owing must be made under the specific legislation empowering the deduction (e.g. the tax legislation) and thus the exclusion in *s 14(3)* was to be generally construed in an non technical way;

(iv)   payable to third parties, for example, trade union dues, made either pursuant to a contractual term to the inclusion of which the worker has agreed in writing, or otherwise with his prior written agreement or consent (but as to union dues, see **49.1** TRADE UNIONS – **II** for restrictions on the deduction of union dues);

(v)   made from a worker's wages for taking part in a strike or other industrial action; or

(vi)   made, with the worker's prior written agreement or consent, for the purpose of satisfying an order of a court or tribunal for the payment of an amount by the worker to the employer.

(*ERA 1996, ss 14, 15.*)

It is irrelevant whether deductions made for a purpose falling within these exceptions are in fact lawful and justified. Such issues are outside the jurisdiction of the tribunal under the *ERA 1996* in any event (*Sunderland Polytechnic v Evans* [1993] ICR 392, in which the EAT disapproved its own earlier reasoning in *Home Office v Ayres* [1992] ICR 175; see also *SIP (Industrial Products) Ltd v Swinn* [1994] ICR 473). In an important clarification, however, in *Gill v Ford Motor Co Ltd; Wong v BAE Systems Operations Ltd* [2004] IRLR 840, the EAT held that where an exception provided by *s 14* is relied upon by an employer, the employment tribunal must make findings of fact as to whether the *s 14* ground is actually engaged on the facts of the case. This does not, however, oblige the tribunal to make findings as to whether, as a matter of contract, such deductions are lawful as the enquiry is limited to whether the factual basis for reliance upon a *s 14* exception is made out. On the scope of the "industrial action" exception see *Norris v London Fire and Emergency Planning Authority* [2013] IRLR 428. An employee refusing to carry out a task which he did not believe he was obliged under his contract to do is not, without more, "industrial action". Industrial action also connotes action taken by more than one worker acting together. Accordingly, a lone employee cannot "take part" in industrial action for the purposes of the exclusion under *ERA 1996, s 14(5)*.

Equivalent restrictions apply to the receipt of payments by an employer, from a worker employed by him, in his capacity as the worker's employer (*ERA 1996, s 15(1), (5)*).

The scope of the wages provisions of the *ERA 1996* is dependent upon the meaning given to the crucial terms 'wages', 'deduction' and 'worker'.

Wages. Wages are defined by *ERA 1996, s 27(1)* to mean any sums payable to the worker by his employer in connection with his employment, including:

(A)   any fee, bonus, commission, holiday pay or other emolument referable to his employment (or unpaid commission; see *Robertson v Blackstone Franks Investment Management Ltd* [1998] IRLR 376, CA below);

(B)   sums payable pursuant to orders for reinstatement or re-engagement (see UNFAIR DISMISSAL – III (55));

(C)   sums payable pursuant to interim orders for the continuation of a contract of employment (see 55.21 UNFAIR DISMISSAL – III);

(D)   PAY – I (34), guarantee payments, medical suspension payments (see further below), remuneration on suspension on maternity grounds (see MATERNITY AND PARENTAL RIGHTS (32)), certain payments for TIME OFF WORK (49) and remuneration under protective awards (see 39.6 REDUNDANCY – II);

(E)   statutory sick pay (see SICKNESS AND SICK PAY (44)); and

(F)   statutory maternity pay, paternity pay and adoption pay (see MATERNITY AND PARENTAL RIGHTS (32)).

A non-contractual bonus also counts as wages when payment is made (*ERA 1996, s 27(3)*). The EAT in *Kent Management Services Ltd v Butterfield* [1992] ICR 272 appeared to suggest that the *WA 1986* extended to any sums of the relevant kinds which would normally be expected to be paid, even if there was no strict contractual entitlement to receive them (see also *Farrell Matthews & Weir v Hansen* [2005] IRLR 160 below). Further, an employment tribunal has no jurisdiction, in relation to a claim of unlawful deduction from wages, to determine an applicant's *entitlement* to statutory sick pay where that entitlement was disputed by the employer. In relation to statutory sick pay, the exclusive jurisdiction for the determination of disputes as to entitlement rests with the Inland Revenue and, on appeal, the Inland Revenue Commissioners. The employment tribunal only has jurisdiction in relation to statutory sick pay where the employer admitted entitlement to statutory sick pay but had withheld all or part of that pay. The same limitation will apply in relation to statutory maternity, paternity or adoption pay. See *Taylor Gordon & Co Ltd v Timmons* [2004] IRLR 180, EAT.

However, the following payments are excluded from the definition of wages by *s 27(2)*:

(I)   advances under loan agreements or by way of an advance of wages;

(II)   payments in respect of expenses incurred in carrying out the employment (for example a car mileage allowance; see *Southwark London Borough v O'Brien* [1996] IRLR 420 EAT but compare *Mears v Salt* UKEAT/0522/11 EAT where it was held on the facts that a longstanding "travel allowance" was in fact the payment of an emolument and not caught by the exclusion for expenses);

(III)   payments by way of pension, allowance or gratuity in connection with the worker's retirement or as compensation for loss of office;

(IV)   any payment referable to the worker's redundancy; and

(V)   any payment otherwise than in his capacity as a worker.

Benefits in kind are not treated as wages unless they are vouchers, stamps or similar documents of a fixed monetary value capable of being exchanged for money, goods or services (*ERA 1996, s 27(5)*). This would embrace, for example, luncheon vouchers.

Particular doubts arose as to whether a payment in lieu of notice amounts to wages. However, the House of Lords in *Delaney v Staples* [1992] ICR 483 held that it did not. Wages were payments in respect of the rendering of services during the employment, so all payments in respect of the termination of the contract are excluded, save to the extent that they are expressly caught by *s 27(1)*.

In *Robertson v Blackstone Franks Investment Management Ltd* [1998] IRLR 376, the Court of Appeal, upholding the decision of the EAT, held that commission payments which become payable after the termination of employment are 'wages' within the definition of *ERA 1996, s 27* and, accordingly, are protected against unauthorised deductions made by the employer. The statutory requirement was that the sum was payable 'in connection with the employee's employment' but it did not require the sum to be payable *during* the currency of the employee's contract. The Court of Appeal further held that the employer was entitled to set off sums paid as an advance against future commission in assessing the amount payable. To hold to the contrary would contravene *ERA 1996, s 25(3)* which obliges a tribunal to take into account sums 'already paid or repaid' by the employer to the worker. In *New Century Cleaning Co Ltd v Church* [2000] IRLR 27, the Court of Appeal held that the employer did not breach the provisions of *Part II* of the *ERA 1996* in reducing the amount of money paid to teams of employees for each job done by the team. On the facts of the case, which concerned a window-cleaning business, there was no express or implied contractual term for identifying the amount of money which each team would be paid nor any such term relating to the distribution of the money among the team. Accordingly, there was no breach of *ERA 1996, s 13(3)* which relates to the amount of wages 'properly payable' to each employee. The amount payable to each member of the team was not sufficiently certain to allow the wages to be ascertained prior to allocation of the money to each individual.

In *Farrell Matthews & Weir v Hansen* [2005] IRLR 160 the issue of discretionary bonuses as 'wages' was further considered. In that case a solicitor was paid an annual discretionary bonus in instalments. The claimant left her employer in circumstances where £9,000 of the bonus was still outstanding. The EAT held that a deductions from wages claim under s 13 had been rightly allowed. The employer's argument relying upon *ERA 1996, s 27(3)* that non-contractual bonus could only become wages when actually paid was rejected by the EAT which held that once the bonus payable had been declared by the employer the sum became payable and amounted to wages within the meaning of *ERA s 27(1)*. Similarly, in *Tradition Securities and Futures SA v Mouradian* [2009] EWCA Civ 60, [2009] All ER (D) 100 (Feb) it was held by the Court of Appeal that claims for deductions from bonus payments could be brought under the unlawful deductions jurisdiction, even where there is a dispute over alleged variations to the bonus scheme, provided the employer has fully exercised its discretion to make a payment under the scheme and the amount claimed is quantified, and payment is due.

The issue of quantification of the sum in issue is crucially relevant to whether a claim may be brought under the deduction from wages provisions of the *ERA*. In *Adcock v Coors Brewers Ltd* [2007] EWCA Civ 19, [2007] All ER (D) 190 (Jan), *sub nom Coors Brewers Ltd v Adcock*, the Court of Appeal considered whether a claim in relation to an *unquantified* discretionary bonus could be advanced under the provisions of *Part II* of the *ERA*. While such claims could be brought under the Employment Tribunal's *contractual* jurisdiction after termination of employment (by analogy with the discretionary bonus cases such as

Clark v Nomura plc [2000] IRLR 766 which had been brought as a contractual claim in the High Court) that jurisdiction is limited to £25,000 whilst the jurisdiction under the provisions of *Part II* of the *ERA* is unlimited. The Court of Appeal held (applying *Delaney v Staples* [1992] ICR 483, HL) that the jurisdiction under *Part II* of the *ERA* is limited to claims brought on the premise that a *specific amount of money* by way of wages is owing. Accordingly, the jurisdiction does not extend to an unquantified claim in relation to an unidentified sum (such as a claim to a discretionary bonus). Such claims will remain limited to the contractual jurisdiction and, in relation to claims with a potential value of in excess of £25,000, or whether the employee remains in the employer's employment, will still have to be brought in the Courts rather than the employment tribunal. See also, applying the principle of the requirement of quantifiability as a precondition to a claim under *s 13* of the *ERA*, *Mouradian v Tradition Securities and Futures SA* [2009] EWCA Civ 60, *Allsop v Christiani and Neilsen Ltd* (UKEAT/0241/11) and *Kingston-upon-Hull CC v Schofield* UKEAT/0616/11 (6 November 2012).

Deductions. A broad definition of deductions is contained in *ERA 1996, s 13(3), (4)*. Where the total amount of any wages that are paid on any occasion by an employer to any worker employed by him is less than the total amount of the wages properly payable on that occasion (after deductions), the amount of the deficiency counts as a deduction, unless it is attributable to an error of computation as defined by *s 13(4)*. A conscious decision not to pay a particular sum which is caused by the employer's mistaken interpretation of the contract of employment is not such an error of computation (*Yemm v British Steel plc* [1994] IRLR 117; *Morgan v West Glamorgan County Council* [1995] IRLR 68).

In determining whether there been a deduction it is necessary to calculate the sum "properly payable" to the worker considering the definition of wages in *s 27* of the *ERA* and then compare it to the sum actually paid. It is an error to apply the "week's pay" calculation provisions in *Chapter II* of *Part XIV* of the *ERA* in this exercise as *s 13(3)* of the *ERA* has its own calculation regime (*Davies v Droylsden Academy* (UKEAT/0044/16)).

There were originally doubts as to whether *s 13(3), ERA 1996* applies only to cases where there is some amount due as wages and the employer has sought to recover some *other* sum allegedly due to him by setting it off against those wages, or whether it also extends to the case where the employer has simply refused to pay the wages allegedly due or some part of them (usually because he denies that they are due at all). In *Delaney v Staples* [1991] ICR 331, the Court of Appeal held that a total non-payment *was* a deduction. The House of Lords ([1992] ICR 483) did not have to consider this point on appeal. In *Francis v Elizabeth Claire Care Management Ltd* [2005] IRLR 858 the EAT held that 'deduction' had a wide meaning and can include a case of failure to pay wages on time (rejecting robustly the employer's argument that there was no right to be paid on time). In that case, the employee was dismissed for complaining about the late payment. Unsurprisingly, that dismissal was held to be automatically unfair as a dismissal for asserting a statutory right (ie the right not to suffer deductions from wages. See also *s 104* of the *Employment Rights Act 1996* and **54.3**(d) Unfair Dismissal – **II.**). In *Lucy v British Airways plc* [2009] All ER (D) 58 (Jan) the distinction between a claim to a deduction from wages and a breach of contract claim was helpfully illustrated. The issue was whether a claim for loss of a flying pay supplement was an unlawful deduction from wages or a breach of contract claim which should be pursued in the civil courts. The claimant had previously been paid a supplement when carrying out flying duties. Following closure of the base at which the claimants worked, they continued to be paid basic pay but not flight supplements (as they were not flying). The EAT held that for the claims to fall within *Part II* of the *ERA* they must be quantifiable and held that the claims could be quantified. The claimants failed, however, on the issue whether the sums in question were wages. The EAT held they were not as they were only payable when the claimants were actually undertaking flying duties. Accordingly, there could be no claim to a deduction from wages but there might be a claim for contractual loss based upon breach of contract arising from the withdrawal of a contractual scheme.

In *Bruce v Wiggins Teape (Stationery) Ltd* [1994] IRLR 536, the *WA 1986* (as it then was) was held to cover a situation in which the employer, in breach of contract, reduced the employee's wages. In *Morgan* (above), the wages provisions of the *ERA 1996* were similarly applied where the employer had demoted the employee without having power to do so. In *Hussman Manufacturing Ltd v Weir* [1998] IRLR 288, the employer had a contractual right to change the employee's working hours. After the employee was moved from night shift he was worse off as a result of loss of unsocial hours pay. The EAT held that a reduction in income which is the result of a lawful act by the employer is not a deduction. The EAT acknowledged, however, that in exceptional cases the unilateral exercise of such a contractual right by the employer might breach the implied term of mutual trust and confidence. In a situation where there is no contractual right to change the hours of work, a unilateral change by the employer, without the consent of the workers, to short-time working and, consequently, a reduction in remuneration, will amount to an unlawful deduction from wages: *International Packaging Corpn (UK) Ltd v Balfour* [2003] IRLR 11. In *Beveridge v KLM UK Ltd* [2000] IRLR 765, the EAT considered whether it was an unlawful deduction from wages to fail to pay any salary to an employee (who, following a period of sickness absence, claimed to be fit and willing to return to work) during a six-week period when the employer wished to satisfy itself that the employee was in fact fit to return. The EAT held that, in the absence of express provision to the contrary, an employee who offers his services is entitled to be paid wages. Accordingly there was an unlawful deduction from wages for the purposes of *Part II* of *ERA 1996* (see 53.7 UNFAIR DISMISSAL – I.).

An illustration of the sometimes complicated exercise of determining entitlement to payment for the purposes of *s 13* of the *ERA 1996* is the Court of Appeal decision in *Dunlop Tyres Ltd v Blows* [2001] EWCA Civ 1032, [2001] IRLR 629 which involved the construction of ambiguous contractual terms in a collective agreement as to rates of pay. The Court of Appeal concluded that, on the proper construction of the agreement, the employees were entitled to triple pay for public holidays and, accordingly, the claim for unlawful deduction of wages was well founded. See also *Henry v London General Transport Services Ltd* [2002] EWCA Civ 488, [2002] IRLR 472. An example of the requirement of employee consent to variations to the rate of remuneration is provided by *Davies v MJ Wyatt (Decorators) Ltd* [2000] IRLR 759. In that case, the employer, in an attempt to meet its obligations to provide paid holiday under the *Working Time Regulations*, unilaterally reduced the employees' hourly pay in order to fund the holiday payment. Unsurprisingly, this amounted to an unlawful deduction from wages. In relation to holiday pay to which an employee is entitled under the *Working Time Regulations*, there may be an overlap between the right to recover these sums (in the event of non payment) under the *Working Time Regulations* and under the *ERA 1996, s 13*. In *List Design Group Ltd v Douglas* [2003] IRLR 14 it was held that even though the claim to holiday pay was out of time under the relevant provisions of the *Working Time Regulations*, it was recoverable pursuant to the *ERA 1996* as an unauthorised deduction from wages. This conclusion was upheld by the House of Lords in *HM Revenue and Customs v Stringer* [2009] IRLR 667 which confirms that failure to pay holiday pay under the WTR can constitute an unauthorised deduction from wages under the *ERA 1996*.

In *Mears v Salt* UKAT/0522/11 the EAT had held that, in determining whether there had been an unlawful deduction from wages, as the employment tribunal was required by *s 13(3)* of the *ERA* to determine the "total amount of wages properly payable" this required the tribunal to construe and interpret the relevant contract including identifying any applicable implied terms. The argument, by analogy with the provisions in *Part I* of the *ERA* (to the effect that, in relation to statements of terms and conditions, the tribunal may only declare the terms and conditions but not interpret them) was accordingly rejected. See also *Fairfield Ltd v Skinner* [1992] ICR 836. More recently, however, in *Agarwal v Cardiff University* (UKEAT/0210/16) the EAT held, relying upon *Southern Cross Healthcare v Perkins* [2011] IRLR 247 (which held that there was no power of interpretation under *Part I* of the *ERA*) that the same principle applies equally to *s 13* of the *ERA* and *Part II*. Thus, whilst a Tribunal may for the purposes of a deductions from wages claim identify the relevant term applicable in order to determine the sum properly payable it was held that it is impermissible to construe or interpret the relevant term so identified in a deduction from wages claim. Such a process of interpretation or construction is only permissible under the Tribunal's contractual jurisdiction and not under the statutory provision of *Part II* of the *ERA*. It is respectfully suggested that *Agarwal* is likely to be followed in subsequent cases.

Even if the contract provides for an express power to make a deduction then the deduction will not be lawful if it is in fact a penalty and not a genuine pre-estimate of loss (*Cleeve Link Ltd v Bryla* [2014] IRLR 86). It must be determined as a matter of construction if the provision in issue was intended to deter breach or to compensate for it. The EAT gave helpful guidance on the process to be adopted by tribunals in addressing this issue. The contract must be construed at the time it was entered into on an objective basis. In assessing the question of deterrence and compensation it is relevant to have regard to the difference between the sum to be deducted and that which could be recovered in an action for breach. If the difference is extravagant then this may indicate that it is only explicable as a penalty. See also *Murray v Leisureplay plc* [2005] IRLR 946 (CA) which was applied and analysed in *Cleeve Link Ltd v Bryla*.

Finally, the fact that the government declares a public holiday does not necessarily give rise to a right to additional payment for that day. In *Campbell and Smith Construction Group Ltd v Greenwood* [2001] IRLR 588, the EAT held that the failure by an employer to pay an additional day's pay for the Millennium public holiday (which, on the facts, the employees were already contractually entitled to take as holiday) was not an unlawful deduction from wages. The EAT stated that a government declaration of an additional so-called public holiday does not, of itself, entitle employees to an additional day's paid holiday.

Worker. By *s 230(3), ERA 1996* those entitled to the protection from deductions from wages include persons working under contracts of apprenticeship and contracts for services as well as contracts of employment (see EMPLOYEE, SELF-EMPLOYED OR WORKER? (15)). The contract for services must be one whereby the individual undertakes to do or perform personally any work or services for another party to the contract whose status is not, by virtue of the contract, that of a client or customer of any profession or business undertaking carried on by the individual.

34.7 Deductions from wages of, and receipt of payments from, workers in retail employment

Special provisions apply to deductions from the wages of workers in retail employment and to payments by such workers, on account of cash shortages or stock deficiencies. Retail employment is defined as employment involving the carrying out by workers of retail transactions – the sale or supply of goods, or the supply of services (including financial services) – directly with members of the public (*ERA 1996, s 17(1)–(3)*).

The employer of a worker in retail employment may not deduct for cash shortages or stock deficiencies more than one-tenth of gross wages payable to the worker on a particular pay day (*ERA 1996, s 18(1)*). The employer must make such a deduction not more than 12 months after the date when he discovered or ought reasonably to have discovered the shortage or deficiency (*ERA 1996, s 18(2), (3)*).

If such a worker's pay is calculated by reference to cash shortages or stock deficiencies, the difference between the payment made when there are shortages and when there are not is treated as a deduction and the difference may not be more than one-tenth on any pay day (*ERA 1996, s 19(1)*).

In addition, the employer of a worker in retail employment may not receive from the worker any payment on account of a cash shortage or stock deficiency, unless certain requirements are met. The employer must:

(a)   notify the worker in writing of his total liability to him in respect of that shortage or deficiency; and

(b)   make a demand for payment which is:

   (i)   in writing; and

   (ii)   on a pay day.

(*ERA 1996, s 20(1), (2).*)

The demand must be made not earlier than the first pay day on or after the date of the written notification and not later than 12 months after the date when the employer discovered or ought reasonably to have discovered the shortage or deficiency (*ERA 1996, s 20(3)*).

The amount demanded on a particular pay day must not exceed one-tenth of the gross wages payable to the worker on that day, or the balance of that one-tenth remaining after any deductions on account of cash shortages or stock deficiencies (*ERA 1996, s 21(1)*).

The restriction of deductions and payments to one-tenth of gross wages (and the requirements referred to in (*a*) and (*b*) above) do not apply to deductions or payments made from the final payment of wages. Nor do *ss 20* and *21* apply to payments made after the final payment of wages (*ERA 1996, ss 20(5), 21(3), 22(1)–(4)*). However, after the 12-month time limit referred to above has expired, the employer may neither receive payments (even after the final payment of wages), nor bring legal proceedings for recovery unless he has made a demand in accordance with *ss 20* or *21* within that time limit (*ERA 1996, ss 21(3), 22(4)*).

Even if legal proceedings are taken against a worker still in retail employment, a court which finds him liable to pay sums in respect of a shortage or deficiency must make provision so that the rate of payment does not exceed that which the employer could recover under *s 20* or *s 21* (*ERA 1996, ss 21(3), 22(4)*).

34.8 Remedies

The worker's exclusive remedy for breach by his employer of the statutory provisions outlined above is to present a complaint to an employment tribunal (*ERA 1996, s 23(1)*). The remedy of a worker for any contravention of *ss 13(1), 15(1), 18(1)* or *21(1)* is by way of a complaint to an employment tribunal under *s 23(1)* and not otherwise (*ERA 1996, s 205(2)*). However, the Court of Appeal has held in *Rickard v PB Glass Supplies Ltd* [1990] ICR 150 that what is now *s 205(2)* was not intended to prevent an employee from pursuing a claim in contract before the county court or High Court for moneys due to him where the non-payment is alleged by the employer to be due to the fact that no payment is due at all. Such a claim may now also be brought in the employment tribunal, within certain limits (see **8.23 Contract of Employment**).

A complaint may be made that:

(a)   an unauthorised deduction has been made contrary to *s 13(1)* or *s 15(1)*;

(b)   an unauthorised payment has been received by the employer contrary to *ss 15(1)* or *20(1)*;

(c)   deductions exceeding the limit set by *s 18(1)* have been made; or

(d)   the employer has received more than the limit set by *s 21(1)*.

(*ERA 1996, s 23(1).*)

The time limit for presenting a complaint to an employment tribunal under these provisions is three months beginning with the date of the deduction or the receipt of which complaint is made. The tribunal has jurisdiction to extend the time limit where it is satisfied that it was not reasonably practicable for the complaint to be presented within the relevant period of three months (see **18.8 EMPLOYMENT TRIBUNALS – I**). Guidance on dealing with limitation points arising under those provisions was given by the EAT in *Taylorplan Services Ltd v Jackson* [1996] IRLR 184. It is to be noted that the right to make a complaint relates only to 'unauthorised' deductions. Deductions made by an employer in accordance with a direction given by a public authority pursuant to statute are authorised deductions, therefore the right not to suffer unlawful deductions does not apply, and a tribunal has no jurisdiction to hear a claim in respect of them (*Patel v Marquette Partners (UK) Ltd* [2009] ICR 569).

Where a series of deductions or payments are made, in certain circumstances, the time limit runs from the date of the last payment (*ERA 1996, s 23(3)*). A complaint may then be made about the entire unlawful series (*Reid v Camphill Engravers* [1990] IRLR 268). See also *Group 4 Nightspeed Ltd v Gilbert* [1997] IRLR 398, EAT. In *Arora v Rockwell Automation Ltd* [2006] All ER (D) 112 (May), EAT the EAT held (applying *Group 4 Nightspeed Ltd v Gilbert*) that, in relation to an unlawful deductions claim, time starts to run, not from the date of termination of the contract, but from the date of the payment of wages containing the shortfall. In *Bear Scotland Ltd v Fulton* [2015] IRLR 15 (the much publicised holiday pay case) the EAT held that for the purposes of a series of deductions claim under *ERA 1996, s 23(2)* and *23(3)* that a previous underpayment which occurred more than three months before the next in the alleged series could not form part of the series of deductions for the purposes of *s 23(3)*. As Langstaff P explained (at paragraph 81): "The sense of the legislation is that any series punctuated from the next succeeding series by a gap of more than three months is one in respect of which the passage of time has extinguished the jurisdiction to consider a complaint that it was unpaid." This is a significant limitation of the historic application of *s 23(3)* to a series of deductions claim. Further, by the *Deduction from Wages (Limitation) Regulations 2014 (SI 2014/3322)* which came into force on 8 January 2015 a further limitation upon claims for a series of deductions is imposed. By *Reg 4* new *subsections 4A* and *4B* are added to *ERA 1996, s 23* to the effect that for deductions from wages falling within the definition of wages contained in *ERA 1996, s 27(1)(a)* any series of deductions is limited to the maximum period of two years preceding the date of presentation of the complaint to the employment tribunal. Thus this "longstop" provision will apply to all claims for "any fee, bonus, commission, holiday pay or other emolument referable to his employment, whether payable under his contract or otherwise" (*ERA 1996, s 27(1)(a)*) but will not apply to the other categories of wages as listed in *ERA 1996, s 27(1)(b)–(j)* (see *ERA 1996, s 23(4B)*). Moreover, the new provisions are subject to transitional arrangements as set out in *Reg 4* of *Deduction from Wages (Limitation) Regulations* so that the two year "longstop" provision will only apply to claims presented to the employment tribunal on or after 1 July 2015.

Where an employment tribunal finds that a complaint under *s 23(1)* is well-founded, it will make a declaration to that effect and, where an unlawful deduction or payment has been made, will order the employer to pay (or, as the case may be, repay) to the worker the amount of the deduction or payment (*ERA 1996, s 24*).

If the wages provisions of the *ERA 1996* have been satisfied in respect of an amount less than the deduction, the employer will be ordered to pay the worker the difference between the amount actually deducted and that which could lawfully have been deducted (*ERA 1996, s 25(1), (2)*).

In making the order, the tribunal will take into account payments or repayments already made to the worker (*ERA 1996, s 25(3)*). Section 25(3) applies to any payment made by an employer in respect of a deduction at any time prior to the date on which the tribunal makes its order and is not limited to amounts paid *before* the deduction (see *Robertson v Blackstone Franks Investment Management Ltd* [1998] IRLR 376).

Where a tribunal has ordered an employer to pay or repay a worker any amount (the relevant amount), the amount which the employer is entitled to recover by whatever means in respect of the matter which gave rise to the deduction or payment (including cash shortages or stock deficiencies) is reduced by the relevant amount (*ERA 1996, s 25(4), (5)*). In other words, sums wrongfully deducted cannot later be recovered at all, even if they were properly owing to the employer. The correctness of this far-reaching proposition was confirmed by the EAT in *Potter v Hunt Contracts Ltd* [1992] ICR 337.

Where an order is made under *ERA 1996, s 11* and *ss 23–25* (see **34.20** below) the aggregate of the amount ordered to be paid by the employer to the worker will not exceed the amount of the deduction (*ERA 1996, s 26*).

Parties cannot, by agreement, exclude or limit the operation of *ERA 1996, ss 23–25* except where agreement has been reached to refrain from presenting or continuing with a complaint where a conciliation officer has taken action in accordance with *s 18(2)* or *(3)* of *ERA 1996* or where the employee has entered into a compromise agreement which meets certain conditions, principally that legal advice has been taken (*ERA 1996, s 203(1), (2)*; for compromise agreements, see **18.22** Employment Tribunals – **I**).

These provisions do not apply to employment where under his contract the person employed ordinarily works outside Great Britain (*ERA 1996, s 196(2), (3)*; and see **53.15** Unfair Dismissal – **I**).

34.9   THE NATIONAL MINIMUM WAGE ACT 1998

The *National Minimum Wage Act 1998* ('*NMWA 1998*') received the Royal Assent on 31 July 1998 and came fully into force on 1 April 1999. The majority of the detailed provisions as to the operation of the National Minimum Wage ('NMW') are contained in the relevant Regulations. The *National Minimum Wage Regulations 1999 (SI 1999/584)* ("the 1999 Regs") were issued in March 1999 and came into force on 1 April 1999. The *1999 Regs* have now been replaced by the *National Minimum Wage Regulations 2015 (SI 2015/621)* ("the *2015 Regs*") with effect from 6 April 2015. The *1999 Regs* will continue to apply to any issue relating to the NMW arising prior to 6 April 2015 and so there is likely to be a considerable transitional period during which the *1999 Regs* will continue to be applicable. In the text below reference is made to the relevant provisions of the *1999 Regs* and also to the equivalent provisions of the *2015 Regs*. The *2015 Regs* are not intended to make substantive changes to the relevant law but are, according to the explanatory note to the *2015 Regs*, a "remake" of the *1999 Regs* consolidating the amendments to those Regs. Accordingly they involve a rewriting of the existing law as contained in the *1999 Regs* and not merely a renumbering of the relevant regulations.

All 'workers' (see *NMWA 1998, s 54* and below) are to be paid at a rate which is not less than the NMW. As to the level of the NMW, the main points as now enacted in the *Regulations* are as follows:

(a)   with effect from 1 April 2017 workers aged 25 and over qualify for the National Living Wage of £7.50 per hour (*Reg 4 of the 2015 Regs* as substituted by the *National Minimum Wage (Amendment Regulations 2017 (SI 2017/465))* and *section 1(3)* of the *NMWA 1988*);

(b)   from 1 April 2017 the NMW for workers aged 21 and over (but less than 25) is £7.05 per hour (previously £6.95 per hour) (*Reg 4A(1)(a)* of the *2015 Regs* as substituted by the *National Minimum Wage (Amendment Regulations 2017 (SI 2017/465))*);

(c)   from 1 April 2017 the NMW for workers aged 18–20 is £5.60 (previously £5.55 per hour) (*Reg 4A(1)(b)* of the *2015 Regs* as substituted by the *National Minimum Wage (Amendment Regulations 2017 (SI 2017/465))*);

(d)   from 1 April 2017 the NMW for workers under 18 is £4.05 per hour (previously £4.00 per hour) (*Reg 4A(1)(c)* of the *2015 Regs* as substituted by the *National Minimum Wage (Amendment Regulations 2017 (SI 2017/465)*);

(e)   workers aged under 19 engaged on a contract of apprenticeship or workers aged over 19 but employed on the first 12 months of a contract of apprenticeship are now entitled, from 1 April 2017, to the new rate of £3.50 per hour (previously £3.40) (*Reg 5* of the *2015 Regs* determines when the apprenticeship rate applies).

Certain categories of workers are expressly excluded by *reg 12* of the *1999 Regs* (as amended) from entitlement to the NMW. In summary, the excluded categories for the purposes of the *1999 Regs* are as follows:

(i)   workers engaged on certain "Government arrangements" (such as "Programme Led Apprenticeships") and schemes designed to provide training, work experience or temporary work (such as "Apprenticeships or Advanced Apprenticeships"). See *reg 12(4A)–12(7)* of the *1999 Regs*;

(ii)   workers engaged in work experience of less than one year pursuant to a course of higher education are excluded from the NMW by *reg 12(8)*, *(9)* and *(9A)* of the *1999 Regs*;

(iii)   workers who were homeless persons working in return for shelter and benefits pursuant to a not for profit scheme are not entitled to the NMW provided all of the conditions of *reg 12(10),(11)* and *(12)* of the *1999 Regs* are satisfied; and

(iv)   workers participating in the European Community Leonardo da Vinci programme or the European Community Youth in Action Programme or the European Community Erasmus Programme or Comenius Programme are not entitled to the NMW (*reg 12(13)–(16)* of the *1999 Regs*).

Part 6 of the *2015 Regs* sets out the rewritten categories of exclusions from the right to the NMW in *regs 51–56* and comprises: schemes for training, work experience, temporary work or obtaining work (*reg 51*); schemes for trial periods of work (*reg 52*); work experience as part of a higher or further education course (*reg 53*); government funded traineeships in England not exceeding six months (*reg 54*); work schemes for provision of accommodation to the homeless (*reg 55*); and European Union programmes (*reg 56*).

Guidance and up to date information on the NMW may be found from links on the gov.uk website at www.gov.uk/national-minimum-wage.

Detailed provisions are contained in each of the *1999* and *2015 Regulations* for the purpose of calculating whether a worker has been paid the NMW. Thus, the individual's hourly rate of pay must be determined by reference to total remuneration over a 'relevant pay reference period' and the hours worked during that period. The pay reference period is one month or a shorter period if the worker is paid by reference to such shorter period (eg a week) (see *reg 10* of the *1999 Regs* and *reg 6* of the *2015 Regs*). Regulations exist for allocation of pay to relevant periods (*reg 30* of the *1999 Regs* and *regs 8* and *9* of *Part 4* of the *2015 Regs*). As to determining the actual remuneration received in the relevant period, *regs 30–37* of the *1999 Regs* (and *Regs 9–15* of the *2015 Regs*) set out in detail the treatment of various types of payment. Gross pay must be determined and the following payments will be included for the purpose of calculation:

(i)   incentive payments including commission; and

(ii)   bonuses.

It is important to note that since 1 October 2009 tips, service charges, gratuities and cover charges cannot be used to make up National Minimum Wage pay by amendments made to the *NMW Regulations* by the *National Minimum Wage Regulations 1999 (Amendment)*

Regulations 2009 (SI 2009/1902). See also *reg 10(m)* of the *2015 Regs* which is to the same effect. Previously it had been held that tips and gratuities paid through the payroll system could be used in discharge of the *NMWA 1998* remuneration obligations (see *Nerva v United Kingdom* [2002] IRLR 815, ECtHR, (see **30.7 HUMAN RIGHTS**) but that tips distributed through a "tronc" system (and not directly through the employer's payroll) did not count towards the national minimum wage (*Annabels (Berkeley Square) Ltd v Revenue and Customs Comrs* [2009] EWCA Civ 361). The position has now been simplified (and helpfully clarified) so that eligible workers will receive at least the National Minimum Wage in base pay with any tips being paid in addition. In addition a voluntary code of best practice on service charges, tips, gratuities and cover charges has been introduced with the aim to improve the information provided to customers and workers. The code is intended to provide practical guidance to businesses on how to operate in a fair and transparent way and aims to ensure that businesses are able to provide their customers with sufficient information to make an informed choice before they leave a tip or gratuity or pay a service charge. The relevant guidance and code of practice may be accessed from www.bis.gov.uk/policies/employment-matters/rights/nmw.

A worker's basic pay, from which enhancements such as time and a half payments are calculated, must comply with the NMW and the enhanced rate of pay is not the relevant hourly rate of pay for the purposes of the *Regulations*. This remains that case even if the worker never receives only the basic pay, but is always paid at the enhanced rate, for example where the worker always works night shifts which are remunerated at the enhanced rate (*Hillier v Hamilton House Medical Ltd* (2009) EAT Appeal No. UKEAT/0246/09), [2009] All ER (D) 319 (Nov)

Certain deductions are ignored for the purpose of calculating the remuneration in the relevant period (eg tax and National Insurance deductions, deductions in respect of the worker's conduct in relation to which he is contractually liable, deductions in respect of loans or overpayment, deductions in relation to accidental overpayment and deductions in relation to the purchase of shares, options or other securities (*reg 33* of the *1999 Regs* and *reg 12* of the *2015 Regs*). The general principle is that benefits in kind are not to be included for the purpose of calculating the remuneration (*reg 9* of the *1999 Regs* and *reg 10* of the *2015 Regs*). The exception to this is living accommodation provided by the employer. The 'value' of the accommodation is set by *reg 36* of the *1999 Regs* (as amended by the *National Minimum Wage (Amendment) Regulations 2017 (SI 2017/465)* and cannot exceed, with effect from 1 April 2017, £6.40 for each day the accommodation is provided, giving a maximum of £44.80 per week. This is reflected in *regs 14–16* of the *2015 Regs*. Travel expenses to a temporary workplace and related subsistence costs paid by an employer and eligible for tax relief are also excluded from the calculation of payments for the purposes of the NMW with effect from 1 January 2011 by amendments made to *reg 31* of the *1999 Regs* by the *National Minimum Wage (Amendment) (No. 2) Regulations 2010 (SI 2010/3001)* and see *reg 10(n)* of the *2015 Regs*.

Regulations 31 and *36* of the *1999 Regs* (and see now *regs 14–16* of the *2015 Regs*) in relation to accommodation and deductions have been considered by the Court of Appeal in *Leisure Employment Services Ltd v Revenue and Customs Comrs* [2007] EWCA Civ 92, [2007] IRLR 450. Upholding the decision of the EAT, the Court of Appeal held that, in relation to holiday resort workers living on site in accommodation provided by the employer, it was not permissible to count a £6 sum per fortnight which they had agreed to pay for gas and electricity as counting towards the minimum wage as the total permitted by *reg 36* in relation to accommodation had already been exhausted by their rent payments. Accordingly, the employer was in breach of the NMW. Conversely, a "sleep-in payment" paid to a care worker was held not to amount to an allowance within the meaning of *reg 31 (1)(d)* of the *1999 Regs* and could therefore be taken into account when calculating whether the worker had received the minimum wage (*Smith v Oxfordshire Learning Disability NHS Trust* (2009) EAT Appeal No. UKEAT/0176/09), [2009] ICR 1395, [2009] All ER (D) 170 (Aug)

The provisions for the calculation of the number of hours worked by the worker in the relevant pay reference period are similarly complicated. There are four types of work which can be carried out:

(A)   time work (*reg 3* of the *1999 Regs* and *reg 17(b)* and *regs 30–35* of the *2015 Regs*) which is paid by reference to the time which a worker works;

(B)   salaried hours work (*reg 4* of the *1999 Regs* and *reg 17(a)* and *regs 21–29* of the *2015 Regs*) which deals with the situation where a worker is paid under the contract for a fixed number of hours a year and is paid an annual salary in instalments;

(C)   output work (*reg 5*) which covers piece-work and commission-related working (as amended by the *National Minimum Wage Regulations 1999 (Amendment) Regulations 2004 (SI 2004/1161)* with effect from 1 October 2004 with further amendments coming into force on 6 April 2005). Output work is addressed in the *2015 Regs* in *reg 17(c)* and *regs 36–43*); and

(D)   unmeasured work (*reg 6* of the *1999*) which provides a residual category. Unmeasured work is addressed in the *2015 Regs* in *reg 17(d)* and *regs 44–50*)

The actual hours worked must be calculated in accordance with the detailed calculation provisions of the *1999 Regulations* or the *2015 Regulations* (for matters after 6 April 2015). A detailed consideration of these provisions is beyond the scope of this work. For the detail of the provisions and the methods of calculation the reader is referred to *Tolley's National Minimum Wage: A Practical Guide* (ISBN: 075450 226-0).

34.10 Coverage of the Act

Section 54(3) defines 'worker' for the purpose of the *NMWA 1998* as 'an individual who has entered into or works under (or where employment has ceased worked under):

(a)   a contract of employment (which is defined to include a contract of apprenticeship);

(b)   or any other contract, whether express or implied and (if it is express) whether oral or in writing, whereby the individual undertakes to do or perform personally any work or services for another party to the contract whose status is not by virtue of the contract that of client or customer of any profession or business undertaking carried on by the individual.'

Regulation 12 of the *National Minimum Wage Regulations 1999 (SI 1999/584)* and *s 54* (the definition of Worker) of the *National Minimum Wage Act 1998* were considered by the Court of Appeal in the context of a pupil barrister in *Edmonds v Lawson* [2000] IRLR 391. The claimant was a pupil in the defendant's chambers and was over the age of 31. Accordingly, she did not fall within *reg 12(2)* which, at that time, excluded only workers under the age of 26 on the first 12 months of a contract of apprenticeship from the NMW. At first instance Sullivan J held that the applicant was entitled to the NMW on the basis that during her pupillage there was a contract of apprenticeship between the applicant and the barristers' chambers (see [2000] IRLR 18). On appeal, the Court of Appeal held that the pupillage arrangement between the applicant and the chambers had the essential characteristics of an intention to create legal relations and, accordingly, there was a legally binding contract between the applicant and the chambers. The Court of Appeal held, however, allowing the appeal, that the contract was not a contract of apprenticeship and did not fall within the definition of a contract of employment within *s 54(3)* of the *NMWA 1998*. In relation to *s 54(3)(b)* (which relates to any other contract whereby the individual undertakes to do or perform personally any work or services for another party) the Court of Appeal held that the pupil did not undertake to perform work or services for the members of the chambers and in the event that the pupil did any work for which she was paid, the person for whom the work was done was the pupil's professional client. Accordingly, the pupil was not entitled to the benefit of the National Minimum Wage. In *Lee v Chassis & Cab Specialists Ltd* (UKEAT/0268/10/JOJ) [2011] All ER (D) 178 (Feb) the EAT held that apprentice status at common law (not a case where the specific exceptions for government arrangements in *reg 12* applied) was not negated by the involvement of a third party in the provision of training and, accordingly, the claimant worker was properly subject to the (then) exception excluding apprentices from the coverage of the NMW. See also *Flett v Matheson* [2006] IRLR 277.

Prisoners, share fisherman and voluntary workers working for no remuneration are expressly not covered (*NMWA 1998, ss 43–45*). Persons who are covered by the Act include Crown employment (*NMWA 1998, s 36*), most work on board ships registered in the United Kingdom (*NMWA 1998, s 40*), work in the armed services (*NMWA 1998, s 37*) and in the House of Commons and House of Lords (*NMWA 1998, ss 38, 39*). Additionally (and importantly), home workers are expressly included in the coverage of the *Act* (*s 35*) as are agency workers (*NMWA 1998, s 34*). The definition of 'home worker', in *s 35* of the *NMWA 1998*, is intended to cover persons whose place of work is not materially under the control of the person for whom the work is being done: *IRC v Post Office* [2003] IRLR 199.

The coverage of the *NMWA* was further considered in *James v Redcats (Brands) Ltd* [2007] IRLR 296 in which the EAT had to determine if a parcel courier was a 'worker' or a 'home worker' or not covered by the *NMW* at all (as had been held by the employment tribunal). The decision of the EAT provides important and helpful guidance on the issue of 'worker' generally, the requirement of mutuality of obligation, and emphasises that in marginal cases a person is *presumed* to qualify for the *NMW* unless the contrary is established (*NMWA s 28*). As to the issue of 'homeworker', a submission that to qualify a person must have some identified 'place' from which they work (albeit not necessarily their own home) was rejected in the light of the general policy of the *NMWA*. Thus a person engaged in delivery or distribution of items could nevertheless be a 'homeworker' for the purposes of the *NMWA*.

By *Reg 2(2)* of the *National Minimum Wage Regulations 1999* an employer is exempt from the obligation to pay the NMW where the worker lives with the family and is treated as a family member "in particular as regards to the provision of accommodation and meals and the sharing of tasks and leisure activities", so long as there is no deduction from wages for food or accommodation. This exclusion is now contained in the similarly worded *regs 57* and *58* of the *2015 Regs*. The provision was intended to apply to eg au pairs, nannies and companions. In *Julio v Jose* [2012] IRLR 180, the EAT considered this exemption for live-in domestic workers. The claimants were foreign domestic workers employed in the respondents' households. The EAT held that the exemption must be narrowly interpreted and it must be shown that the relevant individual was genuinely being treated as a family member. On the facts *reg 2(2)* of the *1999 Regs* applied in respect of all the claimants and accordingly they were not entitled to the NMW. In *Nambalat v Taher* [2012] IRLR 1004 (Court of Appeal), on appeal from the decision of the EAT in *Julio v Jose* [2012] IRLR 180, the Court of Appeal upheld the decision of the EAT that the claimants fell within the exclusion in *reg 2(2)* of the *1999 Regs*. Pill LJ confirmed that the exception should be carefully and narrowly construed and cautioned that employment tribunals must be astute to ensure that the exception was not used as a device for obtaining cheap domestic labour. The same result would appear to arise under *reg 57* of the *2015 Regs*.

The Secretary of State is afforded an additional power to make regulations applying the minimum wage to persons not otherwise covered (*NMWA 1998, ss 41* and *42*). By the *National Minimum Wage (Offshore Employment) Order 1999 (SI 1999/1128)* the operation of the *NMWA 1998* has been extended to workers in offshore employment, defined as employment in United Kingdom territorial waters, exploring or exploiting natural resources in the UK sector of the continental shelf or (in a foreign sector) a cross boundary petroleum field. *Section 22* of the *Employment Relations Act 1999* inserted a new *s 44A* into the *NMWA 1998*. By this section the exclusion from the entitlement to the NMW (see *ss 43–45*) is extended to cover residential members of religious communities. Accordingly, it would appear that nuns and monks will be excluded from entitlement to the NMW. The relevant provisions came into force on 25 October 1999.

The power to set the rate is conferred by *NMWA 1998, s 2* (for the current rates, see above). *NMWA 1998, s 3* gives the power to the Secretary of State to exclude persons under 26 from the operation of the National Minimum Wage or to apply a different hourly rate to such persons. The statutory role of the LPC and the obligations of the Secretary of State to refer matters to the LPC are set out in *ss 5–8* and *Sch 1*.

34.11 Written records and pay statements

In addition to the fixing of the minimum wage, the *Act* casts further obligations upon employers of maintaining records in relation to hours worked and payments made to workers in a manner to be prescribed by the regulations (*NMWA 1998, s 9*). By *reg 38(1)* of the *1999 Regs* the employer is obliged to keep records 'sufficient to establish that [the worker] is remunerated at a rate at least equal to the national minimum wage'. This is reflected in the *2015 Regs* in *reg 59* generally and *reg 59(1)* in particular. The records must be kept in such a way that the information about a worker in respect of a pay reference period may be produced in a single document (*reg 38(2)* of the *1999 Regs* and see to like effect *reg 59(2)* of the *2015 Regs*). The relevant records must be kept for a period of three years (*reg 59(8)* of the *2015 Regs* formerly *reg 38(7)* of the *1999 Regs*). The records may be stored on computer (*reg 59(9)* of the *2015 Regs* and *reg 38(8)* of the *1999 Regs*). Workers may require the employer to produce the records and the worker may take a copy in order to determine if the worker is in fact being paid the minimum wage (*NMWA 1998, s 10*). Failure to comply with such a request may lead to a complaint being made to an employment tribunal (*NMWA 1998, s 11*). If the tribunal upholds the complaint it shall make a declaration to that effect and order that the employer pay the worker a sum equivalent to 80 times the hourly rate of the relevant National Minimum Wage then in force (*NMWA 1998, s 11(2)*). The *Act* in *s 12* provides a power for regulations to be made to provide workers with a National Minimum Wage statement which would be similar to the right an itemised statement under the provision of *ERA 1996* (see below). Following widespread opposition to this proposal the *Regulations* in their present form contain no obligation to provide a National Minimum Wage statement.

34.12 Failure to pay the National Minimum Wage: individual remedies

A failure to pay to an employee the National Minimum Wage entitles the employee to commence proceedings in the employment tribunal or the county court to recover the difference between what has been paid and what ought to have been paid under the National Minimum Wage. By amendments to *s 17* of the *NMWA* (introduced by the *Employment Act 2008, s 8*), where a worker has been paid at a rate less than the national minimum wage he can claim the difference based upon the rate of the national minimum wage applying at the time of the arrears being determined as if it had been at that rate throughout the periods the employer was in default. The claim may be brought either as a breach of *Part II* of the *ERA 1996* as an unlawful deduction from wages or as a breach of contract claim. For claims of unlawful deductions of wages presented after 1 July 2015 the claim will be subject to a cap of two years back pay by the *Deduction from Wages (Limitation) Regulations 2014 (SI 2014/3322)* (see, further, **34.8** above). In relation to workers (as defined in *NMWA 1998, s 54(3)*) who are not covered by the provisions of *Part II* of the *ERA 1996* (see above) because they do not satisfy the particular definition of worker in *ERA 1996, s 230(3)*, they are deemed to be covered by the provisions by *s 18* of the *National Minimum Wage Act 1998*. An employee has a right not to suffer a detriment (*NMWA 1998, s 23*) nor to be dismissed by reason of bringing proceedings relating to the enforcement of the National Minimum Wage (*NMWA 1998, s 25* which inserts *ERA 1996, s 104A*). (See also **54.3** UNFAIR DISMISSAL – II.) As to proceedings in the employment tribunal, claims relating to non-payment of the NMW, may be heard by an employment tribunal chairman sitting alone (*NMWA 1998, s 27* amending *ETA 1996, s 4*). The burden of proof in such cases is unusual: it will be presumed that the employee is paid less than the minimum wage unless the employer establishes the contrary (*NMWA 1998, s 28*). This principle applies whether the proceedings are brought in the employment tribunal under *Part II* of the *ERA 1996* or for breach of contract claims whether in the county court or in the employment tribunal. Accordingly, this will be an added incentive for employers to keep proper records as required in order to be able to establish that a worker has in fact been paid, at least, the National Minimum Wage. The worker's right to present a complaint that he has been subjected to a detriment in contravention of *s 23* is contained in *s 24* which extends the powers in *ss 48* and *49* of the *ERA 1996* to detriment cases arising in relation to the National Minimum Wage. On a related point, the EAT held in *Paggetti v Cobb* [2002] IRLR 861 that, in assessing a compensatory or basic award for unfair dismissal, calculations pursuant to *ss 221–229* of the *ERA 1996* were automatically subject to the NMW. This principle applies even if the claimant has not made a specific NMW claim as it is sufficient if, prior to the dismissal, he was remunerated at a rate less than the NMW. On the facts of the instant case, the applicant was only paid £120 for a 63-hour week. Compensation was, accordingly, to be assessed based upon the NMW rate. In *Blue Chip Trading Ltd v Helbawi* [2009] IRLR 128 a student subject to immigration restrictions on working was only permitted to work up to 20 hours per week during term time but could work without restriction during vacations. He knowingly worked more than the 20 hours he was permitted to work during term time. He claimed that he had not been paid the NMW. The EAT held that it would be contrary to public policy to allow the claimant to recover for any work done during the period he was knowingly in breach of the working limits. However, he could recover the NMW in relation to those periods when he was not subject to limitations on periods of work (such as the vacations) as in that case the unlawful elements of his performance could be severed.

Devices adopted by employers to attempt to meet the minimum wage obligation without additional expenditure are unlikely to succeed in practice. In *Laird v AK Stoddart Ltd* [2001] IRLR 591, the EAT considered whether there was a breach of the *NMWA 1998* or an unlawful deduction from wages contrary to *s 13(1)* of *ERA 1996* in circumstances where the employer consolidated part of an employee's attendance allowance into the basic hourly rate for the job in order to comply with the NMW requirement (at that time £3.60 per hour). By *reg 31* of the *National Minimum Wage Regulations 1999 (Amendment) Regulations 2000 (SI 2000/1989)*, certain payments are not to be taken into account in calculating the total remuneration. This exclusion includes an attendance allowance. Accordingly, the employer sought to reduce the attendance allowance and increase the basic pay to comply with the NMW. The employees were not consulted. The EAT held that there was no breach of the *NMWA 1998*. The EAT went on, however, to hold that the reduction in the attendance allowance was an unlawful deduction from wages for the purposes of *s 13* of the *ERA 1996* as there was no consent to the change and *s 27* of the *ERA 1996* required attendance allowances to be taken into account in determining whether there was any unlawful deduction from wages. Moreover, an employer cannot minimise his obligations by attempting to exclude certain work time from the calculation of hours worked. By way of example, in *British Nursing Association v Inland Revenue (National Minimum Wage Compliance Team)* [2002] IRLR 480, the Court of Appeal upheld the decision of the EAT ([2002] EWCA Civ 494, [2001] IRLR 659) that nurses providing a night service by telephone from home were working throughout the shift period for the purposes of the *NMWA 1998*, although free to do whatever they wanted between telephone calls. The fact that there was an obligation to be ready to answer the call throughout the night shift meant that the nurses were working throughout the shift and were engaged on 'time work' within the meaning of the *NMWA 1998* (see **34.9** above). It is also worthy of note that this case was an appeal from an enforcement notice served by the Inland Revenue – an example of a State as opposed to individual remedy in relation to the *NMWA 1998* (see below). The *British Nursing Association* case was followed by the Court of Session in *Scottbridge Construction Ltd v Wright* [2003] IRLR 21. That case concerned a nightwatchman, who was permitted by his employer to sleep on the employer's premises whilst at work. It was held that he was engaged on 'time work' for the purposes of the *NMWA 1998* and, accordingly, was entitled to the NMW for all the hours he was required to be on the premises, including time asleep as, even if asleep, he could respond to an alarm when he awoke and was thus liable to perform functions at every stage during the night. Conversely, in *Walton v Independent Living Organisation Ltd* [2003] IRLR 469 the Court of Appeal held that a live-in carer, required to be on the client's premises for a consecutive period of 72 hours each week, was only entitled, under the *NMWA 1998*, to payment in respect of the time that she was actually carrying out her duties as her work was properly characterised as 'unmeasured work' (with a daily average agreement falling within *reg 28* of the *1999 Regs*) and not 'time work' and, accordingly, *British Nursing Association* and *Scottbridge Construction* (above) were distinguished (see **34.9** above). In *McCartney v Oversley House Management* [2006] ICR 510 (EAT) *British Nursing Association* was applied in relation to 'on-call' work holding that a manager at a residential home with 'on call' obligations was engaged on 'salaried hours work' with the result that it was found that the employee was remunerated at a rate below that permitted by the *NMW*. In *Burrow Down Support Services Ltd v Rossiter* [2008] ICR 1172, the EAT applied the *British Nursing Association* decision and *Scottbridge Construction Ltd v Wright* to conclude that notwithstanding changes introduced to *reg 15* of the *NMW Regulations 1999* the previous cases remained good law so that a night sleeper at a care home who was permitted to sleep but had to be available throughout the night shifts to deal with emergencies was entitled to the NMW for each hour of the shift. The issue of time asleep was further considered in *South Manchester Abbeyfield Society Ltd v Hopkins* (UKEAT/0079/10/ZT) [2011] ICR 254, [2011] IRLR 300. The Claimants were employed in housekeeping roles with "on call" periods overnight. The EAT held that such periods when the employee was sleeping did not qualify for the NMW (although the same periods might count for the purposes of the working time regulations). The provision of *regs 15(1A)* and *16(1A)* of the *1999 Regs* would only apply to the periods that the worker was "awake for the purposes of working". This is reflected in the *2015 Regs* in *reg 32* which provides that time work includes hours when a worker is available and required to be available but that hours when a worker is "available" only includes hours when the worker is awake for the purposes of working, even if a worker by arrangement sleeps at or near a place of work" (*reg 32(2)* of the *2015 Regs* and see also *Reg 27*). In *City of Edinburgh Council v Lauder UK* EATS/0048/11 the EAT held that "on-call" time of a sheltered housing residential warden provided with accommodation was not time which qualified for the NMW, applying *British Nursing Association, Scottbridge Construction Ltd v Wright* and *South Manchester Abbeyfield Society Ltd v Hopkins* (above). In *Whittlestone v BJP Support Ltd* [2014] IRLR 176 the issue of "sleep over" work was further considered. The EAT held, applying *Burrow Down Support Services Ltd v Rossiter* (above) that the claimant qualified for the NMW. The EAT gave guidance on the approach to be adopted in distinguishing between an employee working (but permitted to sleep) and the different situation of being "on call". See also *Esparon v Slavikovska* (UKEAT/0217/12) in which the EAT observed the difficulty in reconciling the previous case law but reached a decision consistent with that in *Whittlestone v BJP Support Ltd*. The issue returned to the EAT in *Shannon v Rampersad* [2015] IRLR 982. The claimant was employed as an on-call night care assistant and was permitted to sleep during the period of attendance. Applying *Reg 16(1A)* the EAT concluded that this was an "on-call" situation and, accordingly, the time spent sleeping did not qualify for the NMW. In *Governing body of Binfield Chuch of England Primary School v Roll* [2016] IRLR 670 the EAT emphasised that the key issue in such MMW cases was the determination of the relevant terms of the contract.

In *Royal Mencap Society v Tomlinson Blake (and other appeals)* UKEAT/0290/16/DM the EAT heard appeals from three employment tribunal decisions each involving similar issues of whether carers performing a sleep-in shift were working during the shift and entitled to receive the NMW. The EAT, following an extensive review of the previous authorities, concluded that it was not possible to provide "bright line" clarity on when the NMW was payable in such cases. It was held that a multifactorial approach was appropriate emphasising the fact-sensitive nature of enquiry that must be conducted on a case by case basis. As to matters relevant to the multifactorial test, there is a helpful summary at paras 42-44 of the Judgement which include:

(1)   The employer's particular purpose in engaging the worker may be relevant to the extent that it informs what the worker might be expected or required to do: for example, if the employer is subject to a regulatory or contractual requirement to have someone present during the particular period the worker is engaged to be present, that might indicate whether and the extent to which the worker is working by simply being present;

(2)   The extent to which the worker's activities are restricted by the requirement to be present and at the disposal of the employer may be relevant. This may include considering the extent to which the worker is required to remain on the premises throughout the shift on pain of discipline if he or she slips away to do something else;

(3)   The degree of responsibility undertaken by the worker;

(4)   The immediacy of the requirement to provide services if something untoward occurs or an emergency arises

34.13 Failure to pay the National Minimum Wage: state remedies

The *Act* also provides a system whereby the right to minimum wage may be enforced by state officials rather than individuals. The enforcement mechanisms were substantially modified by the *Employment Act 2008* which introduced new *s 19–19H* into the *NMWA* replacing the old *ss 19–22F* with a new regime of enforcement notices with effect from 6 April 2009. The relevant officers are HM Revenue & Customs (see *NMWA 1998, s 13*). Officers may require an employer to produce records, allow access to premises and provide information in order to determine an issue under the *Act* (*NMWA 1998, s 14*). Officers may take copies of records produced. Information which is so obtained may be used only for the purposes of the *Act* or for criminal or civil proceedings relating to the *Act* if authorised by the Secretary of State (*NMWA 1998, s 15*). By a further amendment contained in the *Employment Act 2008* the information may, however, be supplied to officers acting for the purposes of the *Employment Agencies Act 1973* and may thereafter be used for the purposes of that Act. Similarly, the information may be disclosed to a relevant worker or agency worker for the purpose of assisting the officer in the enforcement of the obligations under the *Act*.

In cases where it appears that an employer is paying less than the National Minimum Wage *s 19* of the *NMWA* provides for the issue of a 'notice of underpayment' requiring the employer to pay to the worker, within a 28-day period, sums due in accordance with the provision for calculation of arrears of the NMW under *s 17* of the *Act*.

By *s 19A*, the employer may be required to pay a financial penalty because of the failure to pay the NMW within 28 days. The amount of the penalty was originally 50% of the arrears of the NMW as calculated subject to a minimum of £100 and a maximum of £5000 (*s 19(6), (7)*) but this has increased substantially in recent years. First, in March 2014 the penalty increased to 100% of the total arrears and a cap of £20,000 per notice of underpayment (*National Minimum Wage (Variation of Financial Penalty) Regulations 2014 (SI 2014/547)*). The penalty has increased now to 200% of the arrears from 1 April 2016 (see the *National Minimum Wage (Amendment) Regulations 2016 SI 2016/68, reg 2* amending *NMWA 1998, s 19A(5A)*). Further, from 26 May 2015 the cap of £20,000 now only applies per affected worker (and not per notice of underpayment) (see the *Small Business, Enterprise and*

Employment Act 2015, s 152 and *Small Business, Enterprise and Employment Act 2015 (Commencement No 1) Regulations 2015 (SI 2015/1329)* which amended *NMWA 1998, s 19A).* The combination of the increase in the percentage penalty (to 200%) and the modifications to the applicable cap to a per worker cap is intended to have a strong deterrent effect on any employer failing to pay the NMW and the quantum of penalty for those who continue to fail to do so is likely to be severe. If, however, the employer complies with the notice within 14 days of its service the financial penalty is reduced by 50% (*NMWA 1998, s 19A).*

An HMRC policy document on enforcement and prosecution in relation to the NMW (up to date as at May 2015) can be downloaded at: www.gov.uk/government/publications/enforcing-national-minimum-wage-law.

It is Government policy since 2011 to "name and shame" employers who break NMW Law. A policy document titled "*Policy on HM Revenue & Customs Enforcement, Prosecutions And Naming Employers Who Flout National Minimum Wage Law*" was first promulgated with effect from January 2011 by BIS in relation to the operation of the regime introduced by the *Employment Act 2008* and can be found at www.gov.uk/government/uploads/system/uploads/attachment_data/file/316652/bis -14-621-national-minimum-wage-policy-on-hm-revenue-and-customs-enforcement -prosecutions-and-naming-employers-who-break-national-minimum-wage-law -updated.pdf. The Policy was intended to identify when employers who have breached the NMW will be publicly named and is intended to raise awareness of the NMW enforcement mechanisms and to deter employers who may seek to breach the NMW obligations. The policy in sections 5.2 and 5.3 set out the general criteria to be applied for naming employers (eg knowing breach, failure to keep NMW records, obstruction of compliance officers or previous failure to pay arrears) and provision was made for employers to make representations before they were named (section 5.5).

A tougher and simpler policy was introduced in late 2013 whereby all employers who have been issued with a notice of underpayment and have not appealed or have had an appeal dismissed are to be considered for naming by means of a press release. Employers have 14 days to identify exceptional circumstances why they should not be named. The exceptions are narrowly circumscribed and limited to a risk of personal harm to an individual or their family; national security; or that naming would not be in the public interest. It follows that in a normal case naming will follow as a matter of course.

A right of appeal against a notice of underpayment lies to the employment tribunal (*s 19C*). In the event of non-compliance with a notice of underpayment, an officer may present a complaint for unlawful deduction of wages on behalf of relevant workers (*s 19D*). Non-compliance with a notice to pay a penalty may be enforced in the county court by the relevant officer (*s 19E*). Provision is also made for withdrawal and replacement of notices of underpayment (*ss 19F, 19G*).

In *IRC v Bebb Travel plc* [2002] IRLR 783 the EAT had held that, on a proper construction of the legislation, compliance officers were not entitled, pursuant to *s 19* of the *NMWA 1998*, to serve an enforcement notice on the respondent employer requiring it to pay arrears of wages in respect of employees who had ceased employment before the notice was issued. This unsatisfactory result was reversed by the passage of the *National Minimum Wage (Enforcement Notices) Act 2003* which came into force on 8 July 2003. As a result *s 19* of the *NMWA 1998* provides that an enforcement notice may be served on an employer who has not paid an employee a rate of pay at least equal to the NMW whether or not the worker is still employed. The further revisions introduced by the *Employment Act 2008* maintained this position. Thus *s 19(1)* provides that a notice of underpayment may relate to any period for which the worker *at any time* qualified for the NMW.

Finally, if the preceding enforcement measures are to no avail, there is a criminal offence created for employers who wilfully breach their obligations to workers under the Act. It is an offence:

(i)   to fail to refuse or wilfully neglect to pay the minimum wage (*NMWA 1998, s 31(1)*);

(ii)   to fail to keep records as required by *s 9* (*NMWA 1998, s 31(2)*);

(iii)   to falsify *s 9* records (*NMWA 1998, s 31(3)*);

(iv)   to knowingly provide false information to an officer (*NMWA 1998, s 31(4)*); or

(v)   to obstruct or delay an officer or to refuse to answer questions or furnish information (*NMWA 1998, s 31(5)*).

Each offence under *s 31* was originally only punishable on summary conviction with a fine not exceeding level 5 on the Standard Scale (see **1.10** INTRODUCTION) (*NMWA 1998, s 31(9)*). In the case of a body corporate, if an offence is committed with the consent, connivance or by the neglect of an officer of the company, that officer, as well as the body corporate, is guilty of the offence (*NMWA 1998, s 32*). Proceedings for offences under the *Act* were limited to the Magistrates Court but with amendments introduced by the *Employment Act 2008*, the potential for greater penalties is introduced as the offence, in serious cases, may be tried on indictment as well as summarily.

The ability to effectively police whether employers are abiding by their obligations to pay the NMW is enhanced by the provisions of *s 39* of the *Employment Relations Act 1999* which permits revenue officials to disclose information which comes into their possession in the course of carrying out the function of Commissioners of the Inland Revenue to other agencies for the purposes of the *National Minimum Wage Act 1998*. The information may be disclosed to the Secretary of State for any purpose relating to the *National Minimum Wage Act 1998*. That information may be supplied by the Secretary of State for any purpose relating to the *National Minimum Wage Act 1998*. That information may be supplied by the Secretary of State to any person acting under *s 13(1)(b)* of the *NMWA 1998* or to the agricultural wages inspectors.

34.14 OTHER DEDUCTIONS FROM WAGES

In *Sim v Rotherham Metropolitan Borough Council* [1986] ICR 897, it was held that the principle of equitable set-off applied to contracts of employment. In other words, where an employee's breach of contract has caused the employer loss, the employer is in principle entitled to retain for himself sums representing the amount of that loss when he pays the employee's wages. This saves the employer from paying the full wage and suing for damages for breach of contract. However, the court retains a discretion to disallow the set-off. Further, if there is no contractual provision or written consent permitting a deduction by way of set-off, for the employer to make such a deduction may contravene the wages provisions of the *ERA 1996* (see **34.6** above; this will not be an obstacle where the deduction is made for taking part in industrial action).

The leading authority on the employer's right to pay less than the full contractual wage where the employee refuses to carry out all his contractual duties is the decision of the House of Lords in *Miles v Wakefield Metropolitan District Council* [1987] ICR 368. A superintendent registrar with a normal working week of 37 hours, including three hours on Saturday mornings, took industrial action and refused to conduct weddings on Saturdays. He worked normally during the rest of the week. It was held that the council was entitled to deduct $^3/_{37}$ths from his normal salary, even though the registrar would have been willing to perform duties other than the conduct of weddings on Saturdays (in fact, the council instructed him to work normally or not at all).

Lord Brightman and Lord Templeman took the view that a worker not performing the full range of his contractual duties was not entitled to his full wages but to a *quantum meruit* payment based upon the value of the work actually done. The other law Lords in *Miles* did not, however, express a view on the *quantum meruit* point. An employer placed in such a position by a partially performing employee must make it clear to the employee that he is not waiving that employee's breach of contract in failing to perform the full range of his contractual duties. He should state that, whilst the breach continues, he will make a specified adjustment to the employee's wages.

However, an employer cannot be *compelled* to accept and pay for something significantly less than the efficient performance of all the employee's contractual duties (*MacPherson v Lambeth London Borough Council* [1988] IRLR 470). In *Wiluszynski v Tower Hamlets London Borough Council* [1989] IRLR 259 the Court of Appeal, dealing with a council employee who had refused to perform a material part of his duties, held that the council was entitled to withhold the whole of his pay. This decision was arrived at only because the council had clearly informed the employee that if he attempted to undertake limited work, he would not be paid for it. See also *British Telecommunications plc v Ticehurst* [1992] ICR 383. Recently, in *Spackman v London Metropolitan University* [2007] IRLR 744 (Co Ct) a test case relating to claimant lecturers some of the issues raised by *Sim*, *Miles* and *Wiluszynski* arose again for consideration. In *Spackman* recovery was sought of deductions made by the university in respect of days in which the lecturers participated in industrial action short of strike and thus provided partial performance. Rejecting the claim to full pay on the basis that an employer is not obliged to accept partial performance, the judge went on to hold that employees participating in collective industrial action have no right to remuneration at all by way of *quantum meruit* and if they present for work and undertake some duties or even the substantial majority of those duties they run the risk of being paid nothing by the employer. The fact that the university had paid anything at all was more than the employees wee legally entitled to expect. In *Luke v Stoke-on-Trent City Council* [2007] EWCA Civ 761, [2007] ICR 1678, [2007] IRLR 777 an employee refused to return to their job unless conditions were met and refused a temporary transfer to a different location, following an investigation into the employees allegations of bullying. The employers decision to stop wages was upheld by the court of Appeal on the application of the principle, recognised in *Miles* (above) of 'no work, no pay'.

In *Ekwelem v Excel Passenger Services* (UKEAT/0438/12) the EAT considered the effect of the inability to work due to a criminal charge. The orthodox position is that wages are payable to an employee if the employee is ready and willing to work but is prevented from doing so by reason of unavoidable impediment. In *Burns v Santander UK plc* [2011] IRLR 639 an employee was not entitled to wages during a period on remand which had resulted in conviction as the impediment was avoidable. In *Ekwelem* the employee was, however, acquitted. The EAT remitted the case to the tribunal for further consideration on the issue of whether the employee was entitled to wages for the relevant period he was unable to work due to the pending charge. From the EAT's judgment it appears possible that different conditions may apply so as to distinguish Burns in cases where the employee is acquitted of the charge which caused the inability to carry out work.

Where an employee is actually required to work only on, say, 245 days in the year, and that employee participates in a one-day strike, the question frequently arises as to whether the employer is entitled to deduct $1/_{245}$ or only $1/_{365}$ of the annual salary in respect of that day. It is thought that this may depend upon the precise terms of the contract of employment, and upon the nature of the work done (eg does it require extensive preparation outside actual working hours?). In *Smith v Bexley London Borough Council*, IDS Brief 448, p 5, a county court judge took the approach more favourable to the employer. However, in *Re Bank of Credit and Commerce International SA* [1994] IRLR 282, Evans–Lombe J, although approving this approach where the question was what a lost day had cost the employer, held that, when considering what part of a monthly salary had accrued by the date of a dismissal, the total number of days in that month had to be taken into account, and not merely working days; this point was not considered on appeal. (See also *Thames Water Utilities v Reynolds* [1996] IRLR 186, EAT applying *Re Bank of Credit and Commerce International SA*.) In

Leisure Leagues UK Ltd v Maconnachie [2002] IRLR 600, however, in the context of holiday pay, the EAT held that the correct denominator was the number of working days in the year (in this case, 233 days) and the *Thames Water* decision was distinguished on the basis it predated the *Working Time Regulations*. The issue of holidays working days and deductions arose for determination in *Cooper v Isle of Wight College* [2007] EWHC 2831 (QB), [2008] IRLR 124 in the context of apportioning annual salary in order to calculate a day's pay for the purpose of deductions to be made for participation in days of industrial action. The employer contended that the employees only provided actual services on 228 days of the year (deducting 32 days of statutory and contractual holiday) and that this should be used for calculating the value of a day's pay. Rejecting this argument it was held that the paid holidays had to be brought into account for the apportionment exercise so that the wage payable for any one day was $^1/_{260}$th of the annual wage and not $^1/_{228}$th as the employer had contended. In *Amey v Peter Symonds College* [2014] IRLR 206 (QBD) the issue arose again in the context of industrial action. The case involved a teacher who had participated in two days of strike action. The employer made deductions based on 1/260th for each strike day (based on working days). The teacher contended, relying on the *Apportionment Act 1870, s 2* and *Leisure Leagues UK Ltd v Maconnachie* and *Re BCCI* (above), that $^1/_{365}$ths should be used. It was held, applying both *s 2* and *s 7* (stipulations that apportionment does not apply) of the *Apportionment Act 1870* and applying *Cooper v Isle of Wight College* (above) that *s 7* would apply where the terms of the contract were inconsistent with apportionment on a calendar day basis under *s 2*. Here the contract expressly stipulated the working hours and days and holidays. Accordingly, the employer was correct to use $^1/_{260}$ths as the basis for deductions. The Court of Appeal has now had the opportunity to consider the effect of the *Apportionment Act 1870* in *Hartley v King Edward VI College* [2015] IRLR 650. This was another strike case and the issue was whether pay should be deducted for strike days at the rate of $^1/_{365}$ or $^1/_{260}$ (reflecting the number of working days). At first instance it was determined that $^1/_{260}$ths should be used applying *Amey v Peter Symonds College* (*supra*). This was the correct result said the Court of Appeal but for different reasons. The Court of Appeal held that the Apportionment Act 1870 applied to employment and remuneration (applying Item *Software (UK) Ltd v Fassihi* [2004] EWCA Civ 1244, [2004] IRLR 928) but that *s 2* of the *Act* does not compel appointment on a calendar day basis (i.e $^1/_{365}$ths). The form of appointment to be applied was to be determined in each case from the proper construction of the contract. In that case the proper construction required a $^1/_{260}$ths apportionment.

The court will not normally make mandatory interlocutory orders for the payment of wages; in clear cases, the employee's remedy is to apply for summary judgment (*Jakeman v South West Thames Regional Health Authority and London Ambulance Service* [1990] IRLR 62).

34.15 OVERPAYMENT

Payments made under a mistake of law or fact are, in principle, recoverable by the party who made the payment. This would extend to a mistaken overpayment of wages. However, if the employee in good faith changes his position by incurring expenditure which he would not otherwise have incurred, he may have a defence in whole or part to any subsequent claim to recover the overpayment (*Lipkin Gorman (a firm) v Karpnale Ltd* [1991] 2 AC 548; see also *Avon County Council v Howlett* [1983] 1 All ER 1073, [1983] 1 WLR 605).

34.16 ITEMISED PAY STATEMENTS

An employer must give any employee of his, at or before the time at which any payment of wages or salary is made to him, a pay statement in writing containing the following particulars:

(a)   the gross amount of the wages or salary;

(b)   the amounts of any variable and any fixed deductions from that gross amount and the purposes for which they are made, unless a statement of fixed deductions has been given to the employee (see **34.17** below);

(c)   the net amount of wages or salary payable; and

(d)   where different parts of the net amount are paid in different ways, the amount and method of payment of each part payment.

(*ERA 1996, s 8.*)

Tips paid by customers to a waiter in a restaurant were held not to be wages within the meaning of *EPCA, s 8* (now *ERA 1996, s 8*), and his employers were therefore not required to give particulars of such tips or of payments from them to the manager of the restaurant (*Cofone v Spaghetti House Ltd* [1980] ICR 155).

34.17   Statement of fixed deductions

Provided that the employer has given in writing a standing statement of fixed deductions, there is no need to itemise fixed deductions on an employee's pay statement, but simply to state the total amount of the deductions. This standing statement should give the following information:

(a)   the amount of each deduction;

(b)   the intervals at which the deduction is to be made; and

(c)   the purpose for which it is made.

(*ERA 1996, s 9(1)–(3).*)

A statement of fixed deductions may be amended, whether by the addition of a new deduction or by a change in the particulars or cancellation of an existing deduction, by notice in writing containing particulars of the amendment given by the employer to the employee (*ERA 1996, s 9(3)*).

It must be remembered that a standing statement of fixed deductions only remains effective for 12 months from the date on which it is given to the employee. Before the expiry of the 12-month period, the employer must re-issue the statement, together with any amendments, in consolidated form (*ERA 1996, s 9(4)*).

34.18   Exclusions

The requirement for an employer to provide an employee with a pay statement does not apply:

(a)   to persons engaged in police service (*ERA 1996, s 200(1)*);

(b)   to employment as a merchant seaman, or as a master or member of the crew of a fishing vessel where the employee is remunerated only by a share in the profits or gross earnings of the vessel (*ERA 1996, s 199(2)(4)*).

34.19   Application to an employment tribunal

If an employer does not give any employee of his a pay statement, the employee may refer the matter to an employment tribunal to determine what particulars ought to have been included in a statement so as to comply with the requirements in **34.11** above (*ERA 1996,* *s 11(1)*). An employee may also apply to a tribunal, as may an employer, to determine provisions which should have been included in a pay statement or a standing statement of fixed deductions, but which have been omitted (*ERA 1996, s 11(2)*).

Any application concerning a pay statement must be brought while the employee is still employed by the relevant employer, or within three months of the date on which the employment ceased (*ERA 1996, s 11(4)*) or within such further period as the tribunal consider treasonable where satisfied that it was not reasonably practicable for the application to be made before the end of the period of three months (*ERA s 11(4)(b)*).

34.20 Tribunal order

Where, on a reference under these provisions, an employment tribunal finds that an employer has failed to give an employee a pay statement or that a pay statement or standing statement of fixed deductions does not, in relation to a deduction, contain the particulars required to be included in that statement, the tribunal will make a declaration to that effect.

Where the tribunal further finds that any unnotified deductions have been made from the pay of the employee during the period of 13 weeks immediately preceding the date of the application (whether or not such deductions were made in breach of the contract of employment), the tribunal may order the employer to pay the employee a sum not exceeding the aggregate of the unnotified deductions so made (*ERA 1996, s 12(3)–(5)*; see **34.8** above for the relationship between *ERA 1996, s 11* and *ss 23–25*).

For example, an employee may be required by his contract of employment to pay subscriptions to a sports club of £1 per week. If the employer does not notify the employee of this deduction, either in a note with his pay packet or in a statement of fixed deductions, then, on an application to an employment tribunal, the tribunal may order the employer to repay the employee a sum of up to £13, which is equivalent to the employee's subscriptions for the previous 13 weeks.

In *Milsom v Leicestershire County Council* [1978] IRLR 433, an employment tribunal held that an employer was in breach of the requirement to give an itemised pay statement. A sum had been deducted from the employee's wages, the only explanation being that it was a 'miscellaneous deduction/payment'. The tribunal ordered the employer to pay £25 to the employee for the failure to give a proper statement, despite the fact that the employee was well aware of the reason for the deduction and that the employer was entitled under the contract between the parties to make such a deduction.

However, in *Scott v Creager* [1979] ICR 403, the EAT held that where an employer had made unnotified deductions, an employment tribunal had not erred in awarding a sum to the employee equal to the amount by which the pay she actually received fell short of the net pay she should have received.

34.21 GRATUITIES AND TRONCS

The authorities relating to a system whereby customers' gratuities are pooled in a 'tronc' and distributed among employees (typically, restaurant staff) were reviewed by the Court of Appeal in *Nerva v RL & G Ltd* [1996] IRLR 461. This was a case dealing with whether payments out of a tronc counted towards the minimum remuneration required under a Wages Council order; it establishes that a gratuity left by a customer as a cash tip is normally held on trust for the benefit of the restaurant's employees, whereas payments received by those employees in respect of such a gratuity added to a customer's cheque or credit-card payment are not held on trust, but instead form part of their remuneration. The case, under the name *Nerva v United Kingdom* (Application 42295/98) [2002] IRLR 815, went to the European Court of Human Rights (see **30.7** Human Rights). The ECHR upheld the decision of the Court of Appeal concluding that an employer could use such payments in discharge of remuneration obligations to the waiter employees and that such a practice did not amount to a breach of the applicants' rights (under Article 1 of Protocol No 1 to the European Convention on Human Rights) to peaceful enjoyment of their possessions. On the exclusion with effect from 1 October 2009 of such payments from the calculation of whether there has been compliance with the NMW and for the government's code of practice on such payments. See **34.9** above.

34.22 PAY ON TERMINATION OF EMPLOYMENT

Upon termination of employment, an employer should pay to the former employee any of the following sums which may be due, depending upon the circumstances: wages in lieu of notice (see **48.9** TERMINATION OF EMPLOYMENT); accrued holiday pay (see **29.4A** HOLIDAYS); reimbursement of expenses; other contractual payments; and redundancy pay (see REDUNDANCY – I (**38**)).

If the employee is paid weekly or monthly and the employment has terminated part-way through the week or month, he will be taken to have earned a rateable proportion of his wages or salary for that period. This is the result of applying the *Apportionment Act 1870*, which provides by *s 2* that (*inter alia*) all annuities and other periodical payments in the nature of income shall be considered as accruing from day to day, and shall be apportionable in respect of time accordingly. 'Annuities' are defined by *s 5* to include salaries and pensions. It is possible to exclude apportionment by an express stipulation to the contrary (*Apportionment Act 1870, s 7*). The *Act* is also capable of being applied to a payment such as an annual bonus when the employee leaves part-way through the year (see, on the application of the *Apportionment Act 1870, Thames Water Utilities v Reynolds* [1996] IRLR 186, EAT and *Re Bank of Credit and Commerce International SA* [1994] IRLR 282) and compare *Leisure Leagues UK Ltd v Maconnachie* [2002] IRLR 600 and *Amey v Peter Symonds College* [2014] IRLR 206 (QBD) at **34.14** above. See also *Item Software (UK) Ltd v Fassihi* [2004] EWCA Civ 1244, [2004] IRLR 928 and now *Hartley v King Edward VI College* [2015] IRLR 650 (at **34.14** above).

34.23 GUARANTEE PAYMENTS FOR WORKLESS DAYS

The *Employment Protection Act 1975* created certain rights to payment when no work is done owing to circumstances beyond the control of the employee. These provisions are now contained in the *Employment Rights Act 1996 ('ERA 1996')*. These are of benefit, chiefly, to hourly paid employees and to workers on piece rates.

34.24 RIGHT TO GUARANTEE PAYMENT

Workless day

Where any employee, throughout a day during any part of which he would normally be required to work in accordance with his contract of employment, is not provided with work by his employer by reason of:

(a)   a diminution in the requirements of the employer's business for work of the kind which the employee is employed to do; or

(b)   any other occurrence affecting the normal working of the employer's business in relation to work of the kind which the employee is employed to do,

he is, subject to certain exceptions, entitled to a guarantee payment (*ERA 1996, s 28(1)–(3)*).

A threatened power cut is such an occurrence (*Miller v Harry Thornton (Lollies) Ltd* [1978] IRLR 430).

If a worker can turn down work given to her she is not normally 'required to work' within the meaning of the section and is not entitled to a guarantee payment when not provided with any work (*Mailway (Southern) Ltd v Willsher* [1978] ICR 511; *York and Reynolds v Colledge Hosiery Co Ltd* [1978] IRLR 53). It had been held in a series of old cases at employment tribunal level that variations to the contract to reduce the days worked may mean that the employee would no longer normally be required to work on the workless days. See *Clemens v Peter Richards Ltd (t/a John Bryan)* [1977] IRLR 332 and *Daley v Strathclyde Regional Council* [1977] IRLR 414. Until recently there was no consideration of these provisions by the higher courts. In *Abercrombie v Aga Rangemaster Ltd* [2013] IRLR 953 this issue was, for the first time, considered by the Court of Appeal. In that case there was a formal agreed variation to the employees' contracts of employment, albeit for a fixed temporal period (in that case a 6 month period in which Fridays were not to be worked with an equivalent reduction in pay). The EAT had held that the effect of this was that Friday ceased to be a day on which the employees would be normally be required to work for the purposes of *ERA 1996, ss 28(1)* and *30(1)* and that there was no requirement in *s 28(1)* of the *ERA 1996* for any variation of the employees' contract to be permanent in order to change the employees' normal working hours and thus disentitle the employees to guarantee payments. Reversing the EAT the Court of Appeal held that the issue under *s 28(1)* was that of "normally". On the facts, notwithstanding a temporary, albeit formal, variation of the contracts, Friday remained a day on which the employees were "normally required to work" and thus were entitled to guarantee payments.

If an employer provides some although not the usual amount of work during a day, that is not considered a 'workless day' for which an employee is entitled to a guarantee payment. Examples of situations which may cause a day to be 'workless' are a lack of orders, under (*a*), or any other occurrence such as a power cut affecting the normal working of the employer's business in relation to work of the kind which the employee is employed to do, under (*b*).

Where employment begins before midnight and extends into the next day, the period of employment for the purpose of deciding which is the workless day is defined as follows:

(i)   if the employment before midnight is, or would normally be, of longer duration than that after midnight, that period of employment is treated as falling wholly on the first day; and

(ii)   in any other case, that period of employment is treated as falling wholly on the second day.

(*ERA 1996, s 28(4), (5)*.)

34.25 Qualifying period

In order to qualify for the entitlement, an employee must have been continuously employed for one month ending with the day before the workless day (*ERA 1996, s 29(1)*). (See CONTINUOUS EMPLOYMENT (7).)

An employee who is employed:

(a)   under a contract for a fixed term of three months or less; or

(b)   under a contract made in contemplation of the performance of a specific task which is not expected to last for more than three months,

is not entitled to a guarantee payment unless he has been continuously employed for a period of more than three months ending with the day before that in respect of which the guarantee payment is claimed (*ERA 1996, s 29(2)*).

34.26 Exclusions

Trade disputes. An employee is not entitled to a guarantee payment in respect of a workless day if the failure to provide him with work occurs in consequence of a strike, lock-out or other industrial action involving any employee of his employer or of an associated employer (*ERA 1996, s 29(3)*; for 'associated employer' see **7.9**(a) CONTINUOUS EMPLOYMENT). Thus, a dispute with his employer involving members of another union at his workplace or of employees of his employer at a factory in another part of the country, which causes a halt in production, disentitles an employee from receiving a guarantee payment.

Offer of suitable alternative work. An employee is not entitled to a guarantee payment in respect of a workless day if:

(a)   his employer has offered to provide alternative work for that day which is suitable in all the circumstances (whether or not it is work which the employee is employed to perform under his contract) and the employee has unreasonably refused that offer; or

(b)   he does not comply with reasonable requirements imposed by his employer with a view to ensuring that his services are available.

(*ERA 1996, s 29(4), (5)*.)

Both objective and subjective tests are involved in deciding what is 'suitable' and 'reasonable' within the meaning of (*a*) above. No general rules can be laid down, but what tribunals will have in mind are pay, hours, geographical location and skill required. So far as (*b*) is concerned, clearly, if an employer asked an employee to telephone to find out whether work was available, that would be considered a reasonable requirement. It has been held that a wide variety of alternative work may be suitable if it is only temporary. See *Purdy v Willowbrook International Ltd* [1977] IRLR 388, IT; *Meadows v Faithful Overalls Ltd* [1977] IRLR 330, IT.

34.27 Amount of payment

The amount of the guarantee payment payable in respect of any day is the sum produced by multiplying the *number of normal working hours* in that day by the *guaranteed hourly rate* (*ERA 1996, s 30(1)*).

The 'guaranteed hourly rate' is the amount of one week's pay (see below **34.34**) divided by the number of normal working hours in that week. In calculating 'normal working hours' where the number of working hours in a week fluctuate, one takes the average number of working hours over the 12 weeks ending with the last complete week before the day in respect of which the guarantee payment is payable. If the employee has not been employed for 12 weeks, a calculation is made having regard to:

(a)   the average number of normal working hours in a week which the employee could expect in accordance with the terms of his contract; and

(b)   the average number of such hours of other employees engaged in relevant comparable employment with the same employer.

(*ERA 1996, s 30(2)–(4)*.)

If any employee's contract has been varied or a new contract has been entered into for short-time working, the calculation is made by reference to the last day that the original contract was in force (*ERA 1996, s 30(5)*).

The amount of a guarantee payment payable to an employee in respect of any day will not exceed £27.00 (with effect from 6 April 2017: *Employment Rights (Increase of Limits) Order 2017 (SI 2017/175)*). The previous maximum was £26.00. Further, such payments cannot exceed five days in any period of three months. The present maximum annual liability is therefore £540.00 (*ERA 1996, s 31*). Any contractual remuneration paid to an employee in respect of a workless day goes towards discharging any statutory liability of the employer to pay a guarantee payment in respect of that day and, conversely, any guarantee payment paid in respect of a day goes towards discharging any liability of the employer to pay contractual remuneration in respect of that day (*ERA 1996, s 32*). Thus, if any employee is paid on a weekly or monthly basis, irrespective of the work actually done, these payments will go towards discharging any statutory liability. Contractual payments made in respect of any workless days are to be taken into account when calculating the maximum number of days within the three-month period for which the employee is entitled to a payment (*Cartwright v G Clancey Ltd* [1983] ICR 552).

The Secretary of State may by order exempt certain industries from these provisions where there is in force a collective agreement or an agricultural wages order which complies with certain conditions (*ERA 1996, s 35*).

34.28 Remedy for failure to make payment

An employee may present a complaint to an employment tribunal that his employer has failed to pay the whole or any part of a guarantee payment to which he is entitled. The tribunal, if it finds the complaint well-founded, will order the employer to pay the complainant the amount of guarantee payment which it finds due to him (*ERA 1996, s 34(1), (3)*). Such a complaint must be presented to a tribunal before the end of the period of *three months* beginning with the workless day (or within such further period as the tribunal considers reasonable, when it is satisfied that it was not reasonably practicable for the complaint to be presented within the period of three months; see **18.20** EMPLOYMENT TRIBUNALS – I) (*ERA 1996, s 34(2)*).

34.29 MEDICAL SUSPENSION PAYMENTS

Statutes and regulations safeguard workpeople from exposure to health hazards. They may provide, for example, that a factory be closed when the atmosphere in it becomes contaminated. At common law, if a factory closed down in compliance with regulations relating to the health of the factory workers, the workers were not entitled to be paid for the time lost unless their contracts provided otherwise. However, now where an employee is suspended from work by his employer on medical grounds in compliance with any law or regulation concerning the health and safety of workers, he may be entitled to be paid remuneration by his employer while he is so suspended for a period not exceeding 26 weeks. The provision which leads to him being suspended must be one of those for the time being specified in *ERA 1996, s 64(3)*. At present only the *Control of Lead at Work Regulations 1980 (SI 1980/1248), reg 16*, the *Ionising Radiations Regulations 1985 (SI 1985/1333), reg 16* and the *Control of Substances Hazardous to Health Regulations 1988 (SI 1988/1657), reg 11*, are so specified. (See also **32.47** MATERNITY AND PARENTAL RIGHTS for an employee's right to remuneration when suspended on maternity grounds.)

34.30 Qualifying conditions

An employee will be regarded as suspended from work only if, and so long as, he continues to be employed by his employer but is not provided with work or does not perform the work he normally performed before the suspension (*ERA 1996, s 64(5)*).

In order to be entitled to claim a medical suspension payment, the employee must have been continuously employed for a period of one month ending with the day before that on which the suspension begins (*ERA 1996, s 65(1)*).

An employee who is employed:

(a)   under a contract for a fixed term of three months or less; or

(b)   under a contract made in contemplation of the performance of a specific task which is not expected to last for more than three months,

is not entitled to a medical suspension payment unless he has been continuously employed for a period of more than three months ending with the day before that on which the suspension begins (*ERA 1996, s 65(2)*).

For continuity of employment, see CONTINUOUS EMPLOYMENT (7).

34.31   Exclusions from right to payment

These are:

(a)   An employee will not be entitled to a medical suspension payment in respect of any period during which he is incapable of work by reason of disease or bodily or mental disablement (*ERA 1996, s 65(3)*).

(b)   An employee is not entitled to a medical suspension payment in respect of any period during which:

(i)   his employer offered to provide him with suitable alternative work, whether or not it was work the employee was engaged to perform; and

(ii)   the employee unreasonably refused to perform that work.

(*ERA 1996, s 65(4)(a)*.)

If, for example, an employee is engaged as a machine operator in the toolroom of a factory and the toolroom has to be closed for medical reasons for a few weeks, it may be considered unreasonable for the operative to refuse to work on a similar type of machine in a different part of the factory, provided he is offered the same rate of pay as that which he had previously received.

(c)   An employee is not entitled to a medical suspension payment in respect of any period during which he did not comply with reasonable requirements imposed by his employer with a view to ensuring that his services were available (*ERA 1996, s 65(4)(b)*).

Therefore, if an employer sent a man home because his workplace was medically unsafe but asked him to telephone each day to find out whether his services were required, and the employee failed to do so, he may be deprived of his right to a medical suspension payment.

34.32   Amount of payment

The employee is entitled to a week's pay in respect of every week of suspension (with proportionate reduction for part of a week) (*ERA 1996, s 69(1)*). A week's pay is calculated in accordance with *ERA 1996, ss 220–229* (see below **34.34**). If an employee is entitled to payment during suspension on medical grounds by a term of his contract, he will only be able to claim from the employer the additional amount by which his statutory entitlement exceeds the contractual entitlement. Any payment under a contract goes to discharge the statutory liability and vice versa (*ERA 1996, s 69(2), (3)*). Thus, if an employee's week's pay is £489 (the same as the statutory week's pay; see the *Employment Rights (Increase of Limits) Order 2017 (SI 2017/175)* with effect from 6 April 2017) and, on suspension from work on medical grounds, he is contractually entitled to £300, he can claim £189 as a statutory medical suspension payment. If, however, the week's pay is £600 and the contractual entitlement £300, the statutory medical suspension payment will still be capped at £189.

34.33 Remedy for failure to make payment

If an employer fails to make a medical suspension payment, an employee may present a complaint to an employment tribunal in respect of that payment (*ERA 1996, s 70(1)*).

The complaint must be presented to the tribunal within three months beginning with the day in respect of which the claim is made (or within such further period as the tribunal considers reasonable, in a case where it is satisfied that it was not reasonably practicable for the complaint to be presented within the period of three months) (*ERA 1996, s 70(2)*; for reasonable practicability, see **18.20** EMPLOYMENT TRIBUNALS – I).

Where an employment tribunal finds a complaint well founded, it will order the employer to pay the complainant the amount of remuneration which it finds is due to him (*ERA 1996, s 70(3)*).

34.34 'A WEEK'S PAY'

The amount of money payable under several of the statutory employment protection rights depends upon a calculation based on the week's pay of the employee concerned. For example, a week's pay is the basis for the calculation of a redundancy payment and of the basic award in a claim for unfair dismissal.

The calculation of a week's pay differs according to whether the employee is in employment for which there are normal working hours or whether he is in employment for which there are no normal working hours.

The statutory rules governing 'a week's pay' are set out in *ERA 1996, ss 221–229*.

34.35 EMPLOYMENTS FOR WHICH THERE ARE NORMAL WORKING HOURS

If the employee's normal working hours are the same every week and his remuneration for employment in normal working hours does not vary with the amount of work done in the period, the amount of a week's pay is the amount which is payable by the employer under the contract of employment in force on the calculation date if the employee works throughout his normal working hours in a week (*ERA 1996, s 221(2)*). One possible complication is illustrated by *Agard v Westminster Kingsway College* (UKEATPA/0767/10/SM) (14 December 2010, unreported). Here the employee worked 20 hours per week for 40 weeks of the year but could not take holiday during this (term-time) 40 week period. The holiday was 5.39 weeks. The EAT held that in such circumstances the calculation of a week's pay should add in the holiday weeks giving 45.39 working weeks by which the annual salary would be divided. See also *Gilbert v Barnsley Metropolitan Borough Council* (UKEAT/674/00) [2002] All ER (D) 45 (Apr).

Where the amount of the remuneration varies with the amount of work done but the number of normal working hours does not vary, the amount of a week's pay is the amount of remuneration for the number of normal working hours in a week calculated at the *average* hourly rate of remuneration payable by the employer to the employee in respect of the period of 12 weeks:

(a)   where the calculation date is the last day of a week, ending with that week;

(b)   in any other case, ending with the last complete week before the calculation date.

(*ERA 1996, s 221(3)*.)

This is the provision which must be applied even where the variation may be attributable to the amount of work done by other employees (*Keywest Club Ltd (t/a Veeraswamys Restaurant) v Choudhury* [1988] IRLR 51, EAT).

Where the employee is required under his contract to work during normal working hours on days of the week or at times of the day which differ from week to week or over a longer period so that the remuneration payable for or apportionable to any week varies, the amount of a week's pay is based upon the average remuneration paid and the average number of hours worked in the last 12 weeks before the calculation date (*ERA 1996, s 222*).

For the purposes of these calculations, weeks in which the employee was not paid because he was not working are excluded, and a previous working week is brought into account (*ERA 1996, s 223(1), (2)*).

34.36 Overtime

In a case where remuneration for employment in normal working hours is unaffected by any variable element in the pay structure, overtime hours and payment for them only fall within the calculation if the employer is obliged to provide, and the employee is obliged to work, the overtime (*Tarmac Roadstone Holdings Ltd v Peacock* [1973] 2 All ER 485, [1973] 1 WLR 594, [1973] ICR 273; *Gascol Conversions Ltd v Mercer* [1974] ICR 420). Thus, where overtime is voluntary and there is no such variable element, a week's pay is simply the contractual amount payable for the normal working hours in a full week, excluding overtime (*ERA 1996, ss 221(2), 234(1), (2)*). The same definition of a week's pay applies where a minimum number of hours of overtime is fixed by the contract of employment except that, in such a case, 'normal working hours' include that minimum number of hours of compulsory overtime (*ERA 1996, s 234(3)*).

However, where there is a variable element in the employee's remuneration dependent on results, eg piece rates, productivity bonus, or commission, the amount of a week's pay is to be calculated in accordance with *ERA 1996, s 221(3)* and *223(3)*. *Section 223(3)* provides as follows:

'Where, in arriving at the (average) . . . hourly rate of remuneration, account has to be taken of remuneration payable for, or apportionable to, work done in hours other than normal working hours, and the amount of that remuneration was greater than it would have been if the work had been done in normal working hours (or, in a case within *s 234(3)* falling within the number of hours without overtime), account shall be taken of that remuneration as if –

(a)   the work had been done in normal working hours, falling within the number of hours without overtime in a case within *s 234(3)*; and

(b)   the amount of that remuneration had been reduced accordingly.'

In *British Coal Corpn v Cheesbrough* [1990] 2 AC 256, [1990] 1 All ER 641, [1990] 2 WLR 407, [1990] ICR 317, the House of Lords had to consider the situation where there was a variable element, namely, a weekly bonus paid to the employee for work done during normal working hours. The employee also regularly worked voluntary overtime, which was paid at time and a half, but no additional bonus was paid in respect of overtime. In such a case, the effect of *ERA 1996, s 223(3)* was that the total hours worked in the relevant weeks (including overtime) had to be taken into account, but the overtime premium was to be disregarded, and the overtime was to be treated as having been worked in normal working hours. The House of Lords held that the overtime was to be treated as having been paid at the basic hourly rate, without the addition of an amount to reflect the employee's weekly bonus. On the particular facts, this worked against the employee because his bonus had to be spread over more hours, thereby reducing his average rate of remuneration and the amount of his 'week's pay'.

34.37 EMPLOYMENTS FOR WHICH THERE ARE NO NORMAL WORKING HOURS

The amount of a week's pay is the amount of the employee's average weekly remuneration in the period of 12 weeks:

(a)   where the calculation date is the last day of a week, ending with that week;

(b)   in any other case, ending with the last complete week before the calculation date.

In arriving at the average weekly rate of remuneration no account shall be taken of a week in which no remuneration was payable by the employer to the employee, and remuneration in earlier weeks is brought in so as to bring the number of weeks of which account is taken up to 12 (*ERA 1996, s 224*).

34.38 THE CALCULATION DATE

In ascertaining the 'calculation date' for the purpose of the calculations described above, it is necessary to look to *ERA 1996, ss 225, 231*. Different calculation dates apply for the various purposes for which it may be necessary to ascertain the amount of a week's pay.

34.39 THE AMOUNT OF A WEEK'S PAY

For the purposes of calculating the amount of a week's pay, remuneration includes wages, salaries and expenses insofar as they represent profit in the employee's hands (*S & U Stores Ltd v Wilkes* [1974] 3 All ER 401). It also includes an incentive bonus, irrespective of whether the bonus is identifiably related to the particular employee's efforts (*British Coal Corpn v Cheesbrough* [1990] 2 AC 256, [1990] 1 All ER 641, [1990] 2 WLR 407, [1990] ICR 317). The amount of remuneration without deduction of tax is taken into account for the purposes of calculating a basic award and a redundancy payment (*Secretary of State for Employment v John Woodrow & Sons (Builders) Ltd* [1983] ICR 582). In *W A Armstrong & Sons v Borril* [2000] ICR 367, the EAT held that a week's pay for the purpose of a redundancy payment payable to an agricultural worker was the amount specified in the *Agricultural Wages Order* without deduction of board and lodging.

The amount of a week's pay for certain calculations is subject to statutory maxima. The present limit on the amount of a week's pay for the purpose of calculating a basic award of compensation for unfair dismissal and for calculating a redundancy payment is, with effect from 6 April 2017, £489 (*Employment Rights (Increase of Limits) Order 2017 (SI 2017/175)*). The previous limit, for matters arising prior to 6 April 2017, was £479.

35   Pay – II: Attachment of Earnings

35.1   An *attachment of earnings order* is a means of enforcing a court order that a person must pay a sum of money. The order is made by the court and operates as an instruction to that person's employer to deduct sums from his earnings and pay them directly to the court office. The employer must also notify the court of certain matters. The *Attachment of Earnings Act 1971* ('*AtEA 1971*'), as amended, sets out the obligations of employers and the methods of calculating the deductions. Similar systems for attachment of earnings have been introduced in order to assist with the enforcement of the council tax (see **35.10** below) and of child support maintenance under the *Child Support Act 1991* or the *Child Support, Pensions and Social Security Act 2000* ('*CSPSSA 2000*') as the case may be (see **35.11** below).

An attachment of earnings order may be made by a court if it appears to it that a person has failed, or is likely to fail, to pay in a satisfactory way sums due from him. Orders may be made for the payment of:

(a)   **maintenance:**

    (i)   if under a High Court maintenance order, an attachment of earnings order may be made in the High Court or the county court;

    (ii)   if under a county court maintenance order, an order may be made in the county court;

    (iii)   if under a magistrates' court maintenance order, an order may be made in a magistrates' court;

(b)   **payments under an administration order** (dealing with a number of debts owed by the same person) – county court;

(c)   **payment under a legal aid contribution order** pursuant to *section 17(2)* of the *Access to Justice Act 1999* and Regulations under that Act. – magistrates' court.

(*AtEA 1971, s 1(1)–(3)* as amended.)

Where a county court makes an administration order in respect of a debtor's estate, it may also make an attachment of earnings order to secure the payments required by the administration order (*AtEA 1971, s 5(1)*).

The person who is obliged to make the deduction is the employer. No obligation rests on someone who as servant or agent makes payments to the employee (*AtEA 1971, s 6(2)*).

35.2   EARNINGS FROM WHICH THE DEDUCTIONS ARE MADE

Earnings, for the purposes of attachment of earnings, include wages or salary together with bonuses, commission, overtime pay and other emoluments payable under a contract of employment in addition to wages or salary. Pensions, annuities and compensation for loss of office are also included as is statutory sick pay (*AtEA 1971, s 24(1)* as amended by, *inter alia, Social Security Act 1985, s 21, Sch 4 para 1; Social Security Act 1986, Sch 10 para 102; Pension Schemes Act 1993, s 190, Sch 8 para 4*).

The following payments are not treated as earnings:

(a)   sums payable by any public department of the Government of Northern Ireland or a territory outside the United Kingdom;

(b)   income or allowances payable to the debtor as a member of Her Majesty's forces other than pay or allowances payable by his employer to him as a special member of a reserve force (see the *Reserve Forces Act 1996*);

(c)   pensions, allowances or benefits payable under any social security enactment (including, in particular, statutory maternity pay);

(d)   pensions or allowances payable in respect of disablement or disability;

(e)   except in relation to a maintenance order, wages payable to a person as a seaman, other than wages payable to him as a seaman of a fishing boat;

(f)   guaranteed minimum pension within the meaning of the *Pensions Schemes Act 1993*;

(g)   a tax credit within the meaning of the *Tax Credits Act 2002*.

(*AtEA 1971, s 24(2)* as amended by, inter alia, *Social Security Pensions Act 1975, s 65; Merchant Shipping Act 1979, s 39; Merchant Shipping Act 1995, s 314(2), Sch 13 para 46; Pension Schemes Act 1993, s 190, Sch 8 para 4; Tax Credits Act 2002, s 47, Sch 3, para 1*).

In order to determine whether payments made by him are earnings, an employer may apply to the court which made the order (*AtEA 1971, s 16(1), (2)*). While such an application, or an appeal from the finding on such an application, is pending, an employer will not incur any liability for non-compliance with the order to which the application relates (*AtEA 1971, s 16(3)*).

35.3   DEDUCTIONS FROM PAY

Where an employer receives an attachment of earnings order which relates to one of his employees, he must make such deductions from his employee's pay as are specified in the order (*AtEA 1971, s 6* as amended by *Courts and Legal Services Act 1990, Sch 17 para 5; Access to Justice Act 1999, s 90, Sch 13 paras 64, 66, Tribunals, Courts and Enforcement Act 2007; Collection of Fines (Final Scheme) Order 2006 (SI 2006/1737)*).

The court may use the following terms.

(a)   '*Attachable earnings*': that part of the employee's earnings to which an attachment of earnings order applies (usually income after statutory deduction).

(b)   '*Normal deductions*': the sum to be deducted from the employee's income on each pay day.

(c)   '*Protected earnings*': the earnings below which no deduction may be made.

35.4   Calculating the deduction

If an attachment of earnings order is made, then the employer must, on pay day:

(a)   if the attachable earnings are greater than the protected earnings:

    (i)   deduct the lesser of the normal deduction and the amount of the excess; and

    (ii)   in the case of orders *not* made to secure the payment of a judgment debt or payments under an administration order, deduct any *arrears* still outstanding, insofar as the excess allows;

(b)   if the attachable earnings are equal to or less than the protected earnings, take no action (but the arrears are increased by the amount due).

(*AtEA 1971, Sch 3 Pt I; ERA 1996, s 240, Sch 1 para 3.*)

Example. A part-time employee earns, on average, £90 per week after tax, National Insurance, etc but because the employee is on piece-work his weekly earnings may vary. The court has ordered the employee to pay £300 at a *normal deduction rate* of £15 per week, and has decided that his *protected earnings rate* is to be £60 (ie, the employee will always be allowed to take home £60, provided that he earns that much). The order does not relate to a judgment debt or an administration order.

The following table shows his pay, and the deductions over a five-week period.

Week no.	Attachable earnings	Deductions under the order	Take home	Comments
	£	£	£	
1	90	15	75	Normal deduction
2	95	15	80	Normal deduction
3	70	10	60	Only £10 deducted, Jones takes home his protected earnings
4	95	20	75	Normal deduction plus £5 of arrears
5	100	15	85	Normal deduction

See also *Pepper v Pepper* [1960] 1 WLR 131.

35.5   Priority of orders

Where there are two or more orders in existence, which are not to secure either the payment of judgment debts or payments under an administration order, then the employer must deal first with the first in time and apply the residue of the debtor's earnings over and above his protected earnings to subsequent orders, dealing with them in date order. Where there are several types of orders in existence, those to satisfy judgment debts or administration orders must be dealt with after the rest (*AtEA 1971, Sch 3 Pt II paras 7, 8*).

35.6   Time limits

It should be noted that the following notices should be complied with, within seven days:

(a)   an attachment of earnings order (*AtEA 1971, s 7(1)*);

(b)   a variation (*AtEA 1971, s 9(2)*);

(c)   a notice of cessation or discharge (*AtEA 1971, s 12(3)*).

35.7   EMPLOYER'S OBLIGATIONS TO NOTIFY COURT

An employer must notify the relevant court as follows.

(a)   Where a person is served with an attachment of earnings order directed to him and the debtor is not in his employment, *or* subsequently ceases to be in his employment, he must within 10 days give notice of that fact to the court (*AtEA 1971, s 7(2)*). In relation to a deductions from earnings order (see 33.11 below) there is a similar obligation to notify the Secretary of State (*SI 1992/1989 Reg 16(1), (2)*).

(b)   If the court orders him to do so, the employer must give the court, within a specified period, a statement signed by him or on his behalf of the debtor's earnings and anticipated earnings (*AtEA 1971, s 14(1)(b)*). In relation to a deductions from earnings order (see **35.11** below) similar requirements are imposed by the *Child Support Information, Evidence and Disclosure Regulations 1992 (SI 1992/1812)*

(c)   If he becomes the debtor's employer and knows that the order is in force and by what court it was made, he must within seven days of his becoming the debtor's employer or acquiring that knowledge (whichever is the later) notify that court in writing that he is the debtor's employer and include in his notification a statement of the debtor's earnings and anticipated earnings (*AtEA 1971, s 15(c)*). In relation to a deductions from earnings order (see **35.11** below) similar obligations are imposed (*SI 1992/1989 Reg 16(3)*).

35.8 PENALTIES FOR NON-COMPLIANCE

If an employer, required to comply with any of the above provisions relating to deductions or notice, fails to do so, he may be liable on conviction in a magistrates' court to a fine of not more than level 2 on the Standard Scale (see **1.10** INTRODUCTION) or he may be fined up to £250 by a judge of the High Court or the county court (*AtEA 1971, s 23*, as amended). Furthermore, if he gives a notice or makes any statement on these matters which he knows to be false in a material particular then, in addition to being fined, he may be imprisoned for not more than 14 days. It should be noted that the *Legal Aid, Sentencing and Punishment of Offenders Act 2012* makes provision in *ss 86–87* for the Secretary of State to increase the levels 1–4 of the standard scale fines to such sums considered appropriate. These provisions are, however, not yet in force (see **1.10** INTRODUCTION).

It will be a defence for an employer to prove:

(a)   that he took all reasonable steps to comply with the attachment of earnings order; or

(b)   that he did not know and could not reasonably be expected to know that the debtor was not in his employment, or had ceased to be so, and that he gave the required notice as soon as reasonably practicable after that fact came to his knowledge.

(*AtEA 1971, s 23(5)*.)

35.9 OTHER MATTERS

Clerical costs. When an employer makes a deduction in compliance with an order from an employee's earnings, he is entitled to deduct £1 (or such sum as is currently applicable) for clerical and administration costs (*AtEA 1971, s 7(4)(a); Attachment of Earnings (Employer's Deduction) Order 1991 (SI 1991/356), art 2*). The employer must give the employee a statement in writing of the deduction (*AtEA 1971, s 7(4)(b)*).

Pay statements. The employee must be given a pay statement showing, among other things, deductions from his pay. An employer need not, on each occasion upon which a payment of wages is made, give separate particulars of a fixed deduction. It is sufficient if he supplies a statement of the aggregate amount of fixed deductions having supplied a standing statement in writing of each fixed deduction stating:

(a)   the amount of the deduction; and

(b)   the intervals at which the deduction is to be made; and

(c)   the purpose for which it is made.

Any such standing statement is valid for 12 months. It may be amended (by adding a new deduction or altering or cancelling an existing one) by a written notice to the employee, detailing the amendment. If the employer wishes to continue to rely on the statement, it must be reissued in a consolidated form, incorporating any amendments previously notified to the employee, at intervals not exceeding 12 months.

(*ERA 1996, ss 8, 9*.) (See further **34.17** PAY – I.)

If an employer requires advice or information concerning an attachment of earnings order or subsequent procedures he should contact the court where the order was made.

35.10 COUNCIL TAX

Attachment of earnings for failure to pay the council tax is provided for by the *Council Tax (Administration and Enforcement) Regulations 1992 (SI 1992/613)*, as amended (by, inter alia, the *Local Government Changes for England (Community Charge and Council Tax, Administration and Enforcement) Regulations 1995 (SI 1995/247)*, the *Local Authorities (Contracting Out of Tax Billing, Collection and Enforcement Functions) Order 1996 (SI 1996/1880)*, the *Community Charge and Council Tax (Administration and Enforcement) (Amendment) (Jobseeker's Allowance) Regulations 1996 (SI 1996/2405)*, the *Council Tax (Administration and Enforcement) (Amendment) Regulations 1998 (1998/295)* and the *Council Tax (Administration and Enforcement) (Amendment) (England) Regulations 2004 (SI 2004/927)* and the *Council Tax (Administration and Enforcement) (Amendment) (No. 2) (England) Regulations 2012 (SI 2012/3086)*. There must first be an outstanding sum in respect of which the relevant billing authority (in general, a district or borough council) has obtained a liability order from magistrates pursuant to *reg 34*. The authority is then itself empowered by *reg 37(1)* to make an attachment of earnings order to secure the payment of any outstanding sum covered by the liability order.

The attachment order is directed to the debtor's employer, and is in a prescribed form (*reg 37(2)*). A duty to comply with an order served upon him is imposed on the employer by *reg 37(3)*. Non-compliance is an offence unless the employer proves that he took all reasonable steps to comply with the order, and is punishable by a fine not exceeding level 3 on the Standard Scale (*reg 56(2)*; and see **1.10** INTRODUCTION).

The amount to be deducted under the order is regulated by *reg 38* and *Sch 4*. An amount is specified for any given level of net earnings. 'Earnings' has the same meaning as in the *AtEA 1971* (see **35.2** above and see *reg 32(1)*), and the net earnings are arrived at by the deduction of income tax, primary class 1 contributions under the *Social Security Act 1975* and certain amounts deductible for the purposes of a superannuation scheme (*reg 32(1)*).

The employer must notify the debtor in writing of the total sum deducted up to the date of each notification (*reg 39(2)*). The notice should be provided at the same time as a pay statement (*reg 39(3)*) The employer may deduct the sum of £1 towards administrative costs for each deduction made (*reg 39(1)*).

While such an order is in force, the debtor is under a duty to notify the authority of changes in his employment pursuant to *reg 40*. The ex-employer is under a similar duty (*reg 39(4)*), as is the new employer if he knows of the order (*reg 39(6)*).

If two or more orders are made under these provisions (or such an order is made following the making of an order under the *AtEA 1971*), the priority between them is governed by *reg 42*.

35.11 CHILD SUPPORT MAINTENANCE

A similar system to that under the *AtEA 1971* operates in relation to the enforcement of the payment of child support maintenance by an absent parent, under the *Child Support Act 1991* ('*CSA 1991*') and under the *Child Support, Pensions and Social Security Act 2000* ('*CSPSSA 2000*'). Orders under the *CSA 1991* or *CSPSSA 2000* (which apples to orders made after 3 March 2003) are referred to as 'deduction from earnings orders', and the procedure is set out in the *Child Support (Collection and Enforcement) Regulations 1992 (SI 1992/1989)*, as amended by, inter alia, the *Child Support (Collection and Enforcement and Miscellaneous Amendments) Regulations 2001 (SI 2001/162)* and the *Child Support (Miscellaneous Amendments) (No. 2) Regulations 2008 (SI 2008/2544)* and the *Child Support Collection and Enforcement (Deduction Orders) Amendment Regulations 2009 (SI 2009/1815)* and the *Child Support (Deduction Orders and Fees) (Amendment and Modification) Regulations 2016 (SI 2016/439)*. The regime is similar to that under the *AtEA 1971* and is therefore not dealt with separately in this chapter. Priority between deduction from earnings orders, and between one or more such orders and one or more attachment of earnings orders, is governed by *reg 24* of the *Child Support (Collection and Enforcement) Regulations 1992*. See also **35.7** ante.

36   Probationary Employees

36.1   LEGAL STATUS

Many employers when engaging new employees state that they will initially be employed for a 'probationary' period. An employee may have reduced contractual rights (for example, a shorter contractual notice period) during their probationary period, but their status as a probationer has no effect on their statutory rights. For example, unless their employment continues for less than a month, a probationer will have to be given written particulars of the main terms of their employment (see **8.4** CONTRACT OF EMPLOYMENT). During the probation period, it is an implied contractual term that the employer will take reasonable steps to maintain an appraisal, giving guidance by advice or warning where necessary: *White v London Transport Executive* [1981] IRLR 261.

36.2   DISMISSING A PROBATIONER

It is a commonly held but mistaken belief that giving a new employee the status of probationer enables the employer to dispense with that employee's services, if he is found to be unsatisfactory, without the normal hazards of dismissal, such as a claim for unfair dismissal. The labelling of an employee as a 'probationer' has virtually no effect on the employer/employee relationship. If a probationer with the necessary length of service is dismissed, he may bring a claim for unfair dismissal as may any other employee in a similar situation. The fact that he only had probationer status will not automatically make the dismissal fair. It is merely a circumstance which the tribunal will take into account in deciding whether the dismissal was fair or unfair.

In *Post Office v Mughal* [1977] ICR 763 at 768, the Employment Appeal Tribunal laid down guidelines for employment tribunals considering the fairness of the dismissal of an employee during a probationary or trial period. They considered that the following question should be asked: 'Have the employers shown that they took reasonable steps to maintain appraisal of the probationer throughout the period of probation, giving guidance by advice or warning when such is likely to be useful or fair; and that an appropriate officer made an honest effort to determine whether the probationer came up to the required standard, having informed himself of the appraisals made by supervising officers and any other facts recorded about the probationer?'. In *Anandarajah v Lord Chancellor's Department* [1984] IRLR 131, the EAT cautioned against reliance on previous authority – in that case Mughal – in assessing the fairness of a dismissal. The preferred approach was to apply the statutory test now set out in *Employment Rights Act 1996, s 98(4), (6)* to the circumstances of each case. However, in *British Heart Condition v Harrison* EAT/1354/96 the EAT found the *Mughal* guidelines useful. In particular, in *Harrison* the EAT noted that a probationer must be taken to know that they are on trial and that they can expect to be judged strictly against a reasonable standard. Where a probationer has been unfairly dismissed, there may be particular Polkey issues for the Employment Tribunal to consider when assessing the compensatory award. For example, would the probationer have passed the probation period if they had not been unfairly dismissed and, if so, what difference would that have made to their employment prospects if they had subsequently resigned: *Davidson-Hogg v Davis Gregory Solicitors and Howarth* (UKEAT/0512/09/ZT) (15 November 2010, unreported).

The above considerations apply where a probationer has the qualifying length of service to bring an unfair dismissal claim. Note that in the case of dismissals for certain impermissible reasons (including trade union activities, union membership or non-membership, health and safety activities, pregnancy or childbirth, refusal of a protected shop worker or betting worker or opted-out shop worker or betting worker to do shop work on a Sunday, the assertion of a statutory right) there is no qualifying period (see UNFAIR DISMISSAL – I (53)). Further, employees who claim that their dismissal was discriminatory, can bring claims under the *Equality Act 2010* without establishing any qualifying period of employment.

36.3   EXTENDING A PROBATION PERIOD

If the end of the contractual probation period is approaching and an employer is not yet sure whether to dismiss the employee or not, the probation period can be extended if the contract includes an express right for the employer to do so or if the employee agrees to an extension. If the employer fails to exercise any such right before the end of the probation period, then the employee automatically passes the probation period; an employer does not have an implied right to extend an employee's probationary period for a reasonable time in order to assess their suitability (*Przybylska v Modus Telecom Ltd* (UKEAT/0566/06/CEA) [2007] All ER (D) 06 (May)). If an employee is placed on garden leave before the end of their probation period and subsequently dismissed without having been formally confirmed in post, they have nevertheless passed their probation period: *Cornell (Lynne) v Revenue and Customs Comrs* (TC00108) [2009] UKFTT 140 (TC), [2009] STI 2199.

Note that as a probationer often has different terms and conditions, status and benefits, the extension of an employee's probationary period of employment is generally a detriment: *N v Lewisham London Borough Council* (UKEAT/156/09) [2009] ICR 1538.

In *Millbank Financial Services v Crawford* [2014] IRLR 18, an employee who complained to her employer about the extension of her probationary period, asserting that there had been no feedback during the probationary period, no consultation with the person recruited to carry out the HR function, no consultation with the director and just a single meeting at the end of the probation period with no plan of action and no idea how long the probation period would last, was held to have disclosed "information" for the purpose of a whistleblowing claim (see paragraph **10.16**: DISCLOSURE OF INFORMATION BY EMPLOYEES).

37   Public Sector Employees

37.1   Many people are employed in the public sector, for example in the Civil Service, the police, as teachers or by local authorities. Much of the law described in other chapters of this book applies equally to such people. However, there may sometimes be special factors to bear in mind when dealing with or advising upon public sector employment.

In many cases, there are specific statutory provisions which affect employment in particular areas of the public sector. The provisions set out below are among the most important, but it will be important to look carefully at all the relevant statutes and Statutory Instruments when dealing with an individual case.

37.2   CROWN SERVANTS

The civil service is made up of all permanent but non-political offices and employments (except for those in the armed forces) held under the Crown. Crown servants have a special status in the eyes of the law, albeit that the common law position has been much changed by statute. At common law, the Crown servant is employed at the pleasure of the Crown. That is, he can be dismissed at will – without notice and without the need to show cause or to follow any particular procedure (see *Dunn v R* [1896] 1 QB 116; *Council of Civil Service Unions v Minister for the Civil Service* [1985] AC 374).

There has for many years been a controversy as to whether Crown servants in fact have a CONTRACT OF EMPLOYMENT (8) at all. The question was considered by the Divisional Court in *R v Civil Service Appeal Board, ex p Bruce* [1988] 3 All ER 686, [1988] ICR 649 (the Court of Appeal did not express an opinion when it considered the case). It was suggested that there was nothing unconstitutional in a Crown servant having a contract of employment: the question was whether that was the intention of the Crown when the employment began. In *Bruce*, it was said that the evidence suggested no such intention in relation to civil servants prior to 1985 (which was the case in question), but a likelihood that future civil service appointments *would* be on the basis of contract. However, in *R v Lord Chancellor's Department, ex p Nangle* [1992] 1 All ER 897, [1991] ICR 743, the Divisional Court upon similar facts concluded that *Bruce* was wrong and that a contract *did* exist for current civil servants. This decision was applied by the High Court to civil servants appointed by the Postmaster General: in *British Telecommunications Plc v Royal Mail Group Ltd* [2010] EWHC 8 (QB), [2010] All ER (D) 10 (Jan). See also *McClaren v Home Office* [1990] ICR 824.

The employment statutes avoid the question of whether there is an employment contract, by deeming that there is such a contract for specific purposes or by explicitly including or excluding civil servants. An example of the former approach is *TULRCA 1992, s 245*, which deems Crown servants to have a contract of employment for the purpose of liability for torts involving the inducement or threatened inducement of a breach of contract (see **45.2 STRIKES AND INDUSTRIAL ACTION**), and of certain provisions of *TULRCA 1992*.

Civil servants enjoy most of the normal statutory rights by virtue of *ERA 1996, s 191*. This provision applies many of the sections of *ERA 1996* to individuals employed under or for the purposes of a government department or any officer or body exercising on behalf of the Crown functions conferred by a statutory provision (see *Adult Learning Inspectorate v Beloff* (UKEAT/0238/07/RN) [2008] All ER (D) 254 (Jan) for the wide scope of this expression), including the right to pursue a claim for UNFAIR DISMISSAL – I (53). The main exceptions are the right to a minimum notice period (because of the doctrine that employment by the Crown is terminable at will) and the right to a statutory redundancy payment (although redundancy payments are in fact made to civil servants when appropriate: see *R (Public and Commercial Services Union) v Minister for the Civil Service* [2010] EWHC 1027 (Admin),

37.2 Public Sector Employees

[2010] ICR 1198. Further, a civil servant's right under a scheme to a redundancy payment can constitute a possession for the purposes of Article 1 Protocol 1 of the ECHR: *R (Public and Commercial Services Union) v Minister for the Civil Service* [2011] EWHC 2041 (Admin), [2012] 1 All ER 985, [2011] IRLR 903. However, compulsory retirement has been found not to engage Article 1 Protocol 1, as it does not deprive the employee of any accrued rights: *The Police Superintendents Association of England and Wales and others v Chief Constable of Bedfordshire Police* [2013] EWHC 2173 (Admin) at [89]–[93]). Not only does *ERA 1996, s 191* fail to apply the statutory redundancy payment rights to such employees, any employee whose employment is treated for the purposes of pensions and other superannuation benefits as being in the civil service of the state, is explicitly prevented from claiming a statutory redundancy payment by *ERA 1996, s 159*. For continuity of employment see *ERA 1996, s 191*.

Similarly to the approach regarding rights under *ERA 1996*, civil servants have rights by virtue of *TULRCA 1992, s 273*, with the exception of the collective redundancy procedures in *Chapter 2* of *Part IV* of that Act.

The *Transfer of Undertakings (Protection of Employment) Regulations 2006 (SI 2006/246)* (*TUPE*) apply to transfers of undertakings from the public sector to the private sector, but not to the administrative reorganisation of public administrative authorities or to the transfer of administrative functions between public administrative authorities (*reg 3(5)*). However, the Cabinet Office's non-statutory Statement of Practice 'Staff Transfers in the Public Sector' in effect guarantees 'TUPE-equivalent' treatment for public sector employees who are transferred within the public sector. In addition, from 2005 until 13 December 2010, the Code of Practice on Workforce Matters in Public Sector Service Contracts required private sector employers to provide the same terms and conditions for new employees as for employees who had transferred from the public sector. This Code has been replaced by six voluntary Principles of Good Employment Practice. Further, the *Employment Relations Act 1999, s 38* enables the Secretary of State to make regulations extending the *TUPE* protections to other staff. To date, this power has been exercised in relation to the creation of OFCOM, the Greater London Authority, the Rent Officer Service, the Research Councils UK Shared Services Centre, some staff transferring to the Department for Work and Pensions and various staff in public health units.

The *Equality Act 2010, s 83(2)* provides that "employment" includes Crown employment for the purposes of *Part 5, Work*. The *Equality Act 2010, s 83(5)* provides that in the case of a person in Crown employment a reference to the person's dismissal is a reference to the termination of the person's employment. *Paragraph 5* of *Schedule 22* to the *Equality Act 2010* makes various exceptions to the prohibitions on discrimination for rules restricting Crown Employment to persons of particular birth, nationality, descent or residence. The applicable rules are the *Race Relations (Prescribed Public Bodies) (No. 2) Regulations 1994 (SI 1994/1986)*.

In relation to industrial action in the public sector, there is an extension to the statutory immunity from claims in tort for action taken in contemplation or furtherance of a trade dispute (see **45.3 STRIKES AND INDUSTRIAL ACTION**). Whereas the dispute must normally be between the workers concerned and their employer in order to attract the immunity, a dispute between a Minister of the Crown and any workers is treated as a dispute between those workers and their employer if the dispute relates to matters which:

(a)   have been referred for consideration by a joint body on which statutory provision is made for the Minister to be represented, or

(b)   cannot be settled without the Minister exercising a statutory power.

(*TULRCA 1992, s 244(2)*.)

37.3   ARMED FORCES

The armed forces are not part of the civil service and, to date, the statutory protections have not been applied to them so extensively. The main statutory provisions specific to service in the armed forces include the *Armed Forces Acts 1991, 1996, 2001, 2006* (the repeal of the 2006 Act was due to come into effect in November 2013, but was delayed until May 2018 by *SI 2013/2603, Art 2, SI 2014/1882, Art 2, SI 2015/1766, Art 2*, and then *SI 2017/569, Art 2) 2011* and *2016*, the *Armed Forces Redundancy Scheme Order 2006 (SI 2006/55)* (as amended by *SI 2011/208* and *2011/3013*), the *Armed Forces (Redundancy, Resettlement and Gratuity Earnings Schemes) (No. 2) Order 2010 (SI 2010/832)*, and the *Armed Forces (Service Complaints and Financial Assistance) Act 2015*.

Members of the armed forces have the protection of the equality legislation by virtue of the *Equality Act 2010, s 83(3)*, which provides that *Part 5, Work* applies to service in the armed forces as it applies to employment by a private person. *Paragraph 4 of Schedule 9* to the *Equality Act 2010* provides for various exceptions relating to the armed forces. In particular, the armed forces are not prohibited from discriminating in specified respects in relation to service in armed forces if they can show that requiring the employee to be male or not transsexual is a proportionate means of ensuring the combat effectiveness of the armed forces. *Part 5* of the *Equality Act 2010* does not apply to service in the armed forces at all in relation to age or disability.

Interesting issues concerning the territorial scope of the law have arisen from recent cases about the rights of those employed by the British armed forces abroad: *R (Hottak) v Secretary of State for Foreign and Commonwealth Affairs* [2015] IRLR 827; *Ministry of Defence v Holloway* UKEAT/0396/14/BA (see **[26.11]** FOREIGN EMPLOYEES

Members of the armed forces have the right to make a complaint about any matter relating to their service (*Armed Forces (Redress of Individual Grievances) Regulations 2007 (SI 2007/3353)*). The High Court has considered the scope of this right, including human rights issues: *Crosbie v Secretary of State for Defence* [2011] EWHC 879 (Admin), see also *Clayton v Army Board of the Defence Council* [2014] EWHC 1651 (Admin). The *Armed Forces (Service Complaints and Financial Assistance) Act 2015* introduced a new complaints ombudsman. Under *s 121* of the *Equality Act 2010*, if a member of the armed forces fails to exercise a right to apply to the Defence Council to determine their complaint, this will bar the jurisdiction of the Employment Tribunal to determine that complaint: *Equality Act 2010, s 121* and *Duncan v Ministry of Defence* (UKEAT/0191/14/RN).

If and when *ERA 1996, s 192* comes into force, on a date to be fixed by regulations (*ERA 1996, Sch 2, para 16*), most of the rights enjoyed by other Crown servants, eg unfair dismissal, will be extended to members of the armed forces, although not any rights associated with trade union membership.

37.4   POLICE

Police officers are officers of the peace and, as such, are not Crown servants. The main statutes are the *Police Act 1996* (a consolidating statute), the *Police Reform Act 2002*, the *Police Reform and Social Responsibility Act 2011* and the *Police (Complaints and Conduct) Act 2012*. The *Police Act 1996* includes provisions barring membership of trade unions other than the Police Federation (*s 64*) and making it a criminal offence to induce or attempt to induce breaches of discipline, which would include the taking of industrial action (*s 91*). Police officers are generally excluded from the benefit of various statutory rights, including the right to complain of UNFAIR DISMISSAL – I, II, III (53, 54, 55) and the right to complain of an unlawful deduction of wages (see *Metropolitan Police Comr v Lowrey-Nesbitt* [1999] ICR 401), by *ERA 1996, s 200(1)*. They may, however, claim in relation to detriment on the ground that, or dismissal by reason that, they made a protected disclosure: *ERA 1996, s 43KA* (and see *Lake v British Transport Police* [2007] EWCA Civ 424, [2007] ICR 1293).

Police officers also have the protection of the discrimination legislation by virtue of the *Equality Act 2010, s 42* which provides that holding the office of constable and appointment as police cadet (with some exceptions) are treated as employment by the chief officer or relevant authority for the purposes of *Part 5, Work.*

It should be noted that judicial proceedings immunity prevents employment tribunal challenges to the way in which decisions are arrived at by the Police Misconduct Board (including on the grounds that the decisions were discriminatory), but does not prevent challenges to the decisions themselves: *P v Commissioner of Police of the Metropolis* [2016] EWCA Civ 2.

Some other bodies, such as local authorities, employ constables who are not subject to the general statutory scheme for police officers. These constables still have no remedy for unfair dismissal if they are "maintained by virtue of an enactment" (see *Redbridge LBC v Dhinsa* [2014] EWCA Civ 178 and *Wandsworth LBC v Vining* UKEAT/0234/13/LA, which is subject to an outstanding appeal).

37.5   LOCAL GOVERNMENT

Local government employees generally have a contract of employment (with the exception of some officers such as coroners) and therefore have the normal employment rights (except where the statute provides otherwise). However, it should be remembered that the local authority is a creature of statute, which limits its powers to those provided by statute. Local authorities have the power to appoint such staff as they think are necessary for the proper discharge of their statutory functions on such reasonable terms and conditions as the local authority thinks fit, under the *Local Government Act 1972, s 112.* This power is subject to the *Localism Act 2011, s 41* which requires local authorities to comply with its pay policy statement. Terms and conditions are agreed at a national level (with some scope for local variations) with the National Joint Council, incorporated in the collective agreement known as the Green Book. Also see the *Local Authorities (Standing Orders) (England) Regulations 2001 (SI 2001/3384).*

Local authorities face some restrictions on who they can appoint. By *s 116* of the *Local Government Act 1972*, members of an authority may not be appointed to any paid office with that authority. Further restrictions are contained in the *Local Government and Housing Act 1989*: certain posts are 'politically restricted', which means that their holders may not be members of *any* local authority without express exemption (*ss 1–3*); with certain exceptions, all appointments must be made on merit (*s 7*); and authorities must ensure so far as practicable that they are not represented in negotiations about terms and conditions of employment by members of the authority who are also in local authority employment or who are officials or employees of trade unions whose members include local authority employees (*s 12*). The *Local Government Officers (Political Restrictions) Regulations 1990 (SI 1990/851)* have been held not to contravene the European Convention on Human Rights (*Ahmed v United Kingdom* (Application 22954/93) (1998) 29 EHRR 1, [1999] IRLR 188, European Court of Human Rights).

There are further rules in relation to specific posts (chief officers), including the local authority's Head of the Paid Service and monitoring officer. All employees of a local authority are also officers, but an officer (including a chief officer) does not have to be an employee: *Pinfold North Ltd v Humberside Fire Authority* [2010] EWHC 2944 (QB). The *Local Authorities (Standing Orders) Regulations 1993 (SI 1993/202)* require local authorities to incorporate in standing orders provision relating to their staff. These must include provision for the appointment of chief officers and for investigation by a designated independent person (known as a DIP) in case of alleged misconduct by a chief officer.

The *Transfer of Undertakings (Protection of Employment) Regulations 2006 (SI 2006/246)* do not apply to the administrative reorganisation of public administrative authorities or to the transfer of administrative functions between public administrative authorities (*reg 3(5)*). Note that the Code of Practice on Workforce Matters in Local Authority Service Contracts was abolished on 23 March 2011. See **52.9 TRANSFER OF UNDERTAKINGS**.

The position is more complicated in respect of school staff. School teachers' pay and conditions of employment are subject to control by the Secretary of State for Education and Employment by virtue of the *Education Act 2002, ss 119–130*; and compensation for redundancy is subject to regulations made under the *Public Service Pensions Act 2013*, and now the *Compensation for Redundancy and Premature Retirement) Regulations 2015 (SI 2015/601)*. The identity of the employer (in practice) depends on which of the following two categories the school falls within: (*a*) community, voluntary controlled, community special and maintained schools; or (*b*) foundation, voluntary aided and foundation special schools. The former category have delegated budgets and, by virtue of the *Education (Modification of Enactments Relating to Employment) (England) Order 2003 (SI 2003/1964)*, the *ERA 1996* generally applies as if the governing body were the employer. More detail is given on the complicated interrelationship of the employment responsibilities of the local education authority and the governing body in the *School Staffing (England) Regulations 2009 (SI 2009/2680)*. These relationships were considered by the Court of Appeal in *Murphy v Slough Borough Council* [2005] EWCA Civ 122, [2005] ICR 721 and (in relation to comparators under the *EqPA*) by the CA in *South Tyneside Metropolitan Borough Council v Anderson* [2007] EWCA Civ 654, [2007] ICR 1581 (considered by the Inner House of the Court of Session, Scotland, in *North v Dumfries and Galloway Council* [2011] CSIH 2). *Murphy* was considered by the Employment Appeal Tribunal in *Butt v Bradford Metropolitan District Council* (UKEAT/0210/10/ZT) [2010] All ER (D) 92 (Oct) and *Birmingham City Council v Akhtar* [2011] 3 CMLR 42, [2011] Eq LR 838 *Davies v London Borough of Haringey* [2014] EWHC 3393 (QB), [2015] ELR 18.

37.6 AVAILABILITY OF JUDICIAL REVIEW

Generally, an employment tribunal will be the appropriate forum for an employee to bring a claim against a public sector employer. However, those who work in the public sector may sometimes seek to assert their rights, not simply in an employment tribunal or in an action for tort or breach of contract in the ordinary courts, but by way of an application for judicial review. This is a means of challenging the unlawful actions and decisions of public authorities and bodies exercising statutory power. The possible grounds for such challenge include procedural unfairness, acting outside the statutory powers and irrationality. Applications are heard in the Administrative Court and the procedure is governed by the *Civil Procedure Rules, Part 54* (note also the *Practice Direction* and the *Pre-Action Protocol*). Its features include a need to obtain permission to proceed from the court and a strict time limit (applications must be brought promptly, and *in any event* within three months of the action challenged).

Historically there has been much academic debate about the circumstances in which a claim must (or cannot) be brought by way of judicial review (see eg *O'Reilly v Mackman* [1983] 2 AC 237 and *Roy v Kensington and Chelsea and Westminster Family Practitioner Committee* [1992] 1 AC 624, [1992] 1 All ER 705, [1992] 2 WLR 239, [1992] IRLR 233). Whilst in recent years (and particularly since the introduction of the *Civil Procedure Rules*), the categorisation of claims has become less important, it remains the case that only claims involving a public law element can proceed by way of judicial review.

A helpful statement of the position in the employment context is to be found in the judgment of Woolf LJ in *McClaren v Home Office* [1990] ICR 824. He concluded that judicial review was generally an unnecessary and inappropriate remedy for public sector employees, but that there were two types of case where it might be available. One was where the decision impugned was that of a tribunal or other body (such as the Civil Service Appeal Board) which had a sufficient public law element and was not wholly domestic or informal. The other was where the employee was adversely affected by a decision of *general* application which was alleged to be flawed (the decision to bar trade union membership at GCHQ was an example of this).

This decision was applied in *R (Davies) v Pennine Acute Hospitals* [2010] EWHC 2887 (Admin) and *R (Kirk) v Middlesbrough Borough Council* [2010] EWHC 1035 (Admin), [2010] IRLR 699 and in both cases the High Court found that judicial review was not available because the issues were essentially private law matters. However, see the Court of Appeal's important decision in *R (Shoesmith) v Ofsted* [2011] EWCA Civ 642, [2011] PTSR D13, 154 Sol Jo (no 17) 27 which related to the dismissal of the Director of Children's Services, Haringey Council. The Claimant issued a claim for judicial review challenging an Ofsted report, the action of the Secretary of State in removing the Claimant from her statutory office based upon that report and the actions of Haringey in subsequently dismissing her from its employment. In this case, the Court of Appeal found that the issues were amenable to judicial review because the position of Director of Children's Services had been created, required and defined by statute. In *R (Lock) v Leicester City Council* [2012] EWHC 2058 (Admin), the High Court distinguished *Shoesmith*. The claimant applied for judicial review of the defendant local authority's decision to dismiss her from her post as chief executive. The Court found that it could consider the decision to terminate her statutory role as designated head of paid service. However, it could not consider the termination of her contractual role as chief executive.

An application for judicial review was also considered in *Crosbie v Secretary of State for Defence* [2011] EWHC 879 (Admin), where the claimant was an army chaplain whose fixed term contract had not been renewed and who (unsuccessfully) alleged various breaches of public law principles and *Article 6, ECHR*.

It should also be remembered that the court hearing an application for judicial review has an overriding discretion as to whether any relief should be granted. One possible reason for refusing to consider a claim or to grant relief is that some alternative remedy was available and should have been pursued. Thus, in *Bruce* (see above) the Divisional Court accepted that there was a sufficient public law element for an unsuccessful appeal against dismissal to the Civil Service Appeal Board to be judicially reviewable, but held that only in exceptional cases would it be right not to confine the applicant to his remedy in an industrial tribunal. The Court of Appeal upheld the refusal of relief on the facts without expressing a view on the general proposition. In *R v Hammersmith and Fulham London Borough Council, ex p NALGO* [1991] IRLR 249, it was held that a local authority's redundancy selection policy should be tested by way of cases brought in the tribunal alleging unfair dismissal or discrimination, and not by way of judicial review. In *R (Shoesmith) v Ofsted* [2011] EWCA Civ 642, the Court of Appeal confirmed that in the great majority of cases proceedings in the employment tribunal will be the better, if not the only, remedy where a local authority employee has been dismissed. It suggested that the exceptions would be cases where the remedy available in the employment tribunal was inadequate because of the statutory cap on compensation or where the case raised significant issues falling out with the scope of an employment tribunal's inquiry. On the facts of this case, the Court of Appeal found that there was a benefit in the Claimant being able to bring all her claims (against Ofsted, the Secretary of State and her local authority employer) in one set of proceedings and that success in judicial review proceedings would be more valuable in financial and reputational terms, due to the cap on compensation in the employment tribunal. For these reasons, the right to bring an unfair dismissal claim in the employment tribunal was not an equally convenient and effective alternative remedy for the Claimant.

If available, judicial review can provide a powerful remedy to the employee, as it did in *R v Civil Service Appeal Board, ex p Cunningham* [1991] 4 All ER 310, [1992] ICR 816, where a decision of the Board was struck down because of the Board's failure to give adequate reasons. In the case of *R (Shoesmith) v Ofsted* [2011] EWCA Civ 642, the Court of Appeal declared that the Claimant's dismissal had been unlawful and ordered the local authority to pay compensation.

37.7   LITIGATING AGAINST PUBLIC AUTHORITIES

A local authority has an express power under the *LGA 1972, s 222* to prosecute, defend or appear in legal proceedings, and an implied power to compromise litigation. However, a public body can lawfully compromise a dispute with an employee (or ex employee) only in circumstances where it is acting within the scope of its statutory powers in doing so. One application of the *ultra vires* doctrine is that any sum paid to settle a claim must not be excessively generous. See *Gibb v Maidstone and Tunbridge Wells NHS Trust* [2009] EWHC 862 (QB), [2009] All ER (D) 209 (Apr) where an NHS Trust paid its Chief Executive £100,000 in excess of what she could have been awarded by an employment tribunal in return for her leaving its employment. The High Court found that this was excessive generosity, which led to a finding that the payment was irrational and therefore the compromise agreement was void. However, this decision was overturned by the Court of Appeal, which found that the sum was not excessively generous because the NHS Trust was entitled to take into account the employee's length of service and chances of re-employment: [2010] EWCA Civ 678.

In litigation against public authorities, in particular government departments, attempts to obtain documents by way of an order for disclosure may sometimes be met by a claim that those documents should not be disclosed because they are subject to public interest immunity. This means that the interest in preventing the disclosure of such documents outweighs the interest in the court or tribunal having all the relevant evidence. The court may itself examine the documents in order to decide whether they ought to be disclosed. See in particular *Conway v Rimmer* [1968] AC 910, *Air Canada v Secretary of State for Trade* [1983] 2 AC 394, *R v Chief Constable of West Midlands Police, ex p Wiley* [1995] 1 AC 274, *R (Corner House Research) v Director of the Serious Fraud Office (BAE Systems plc, interested party)* [2008] UKHL 60, [2009] AC 756, *R (Mohamed) v Secretary of State for Foreign and Commonwealth Affairs* [2010] EWCA Civ 65, [2010] 4 All ER 91, *R (on the application of Evans) v Secretary of State for Defence* [2013] EWHC 3068 (Admin) and *Amin v Director General of the Security Service* [2014] EWCA Civ 598.

Occasionally employment disputes will also raise questions of national security (see, eg *Council of Civil Service Unions v Minister for the Civil Service* [1985] AC 374). Provision is made for requiring or enabling tribunals and the EAT to sit in private in cases involving national security or confidential information (*ETA 1996, ss 10* and *10A* respectively). See also *Employment Tribunals (Constitution and Rules of Procedure) Regulations 2013 (SI 2013/1237), reg 10* and *para 94* of *Sch 1, Sch 2*, and *para 13* of *Sch 3* and *Employment Appeal Tribunal Rules 1993 (SI 1993/2854), rule 30A*. The Supreme Court held that the former Employment Tribunal Rules were not intrinsically unlawful, provided that sufficient safeguards were in place and the procedure was used flexibly in the context of the case, as it progressed: *Home Office v Tariq* [2012] 1 AC 452. The Employment Appeal Tribunal gave guidance on the correct approach when an application is made for a closed hearing before the EAT on national security grounds in *AB v Ministry of Defence* [2010] ICR 54, [2009] All ER (D) 135 (Sep). The application of *Tariq* was considered by the Court of Appeal in *Kiani v Secretary of State for the Home Department* [2016] 2 WLR 788.

Where in the opinion of any Minister of the Crown the disclosure of any information would be contrary to the interests of national security, disclosure of that information will not be required by certain provisions of *ERA 1996*, and no person may disclose that information in any court or tribunal proceedings relating to any of those provisions (*ERA 1996, s 202*). The rights generally available to employees who have made a protected disclosure do not apply in relation to employment in the Security Service, the Secret Intelligence Service, or the Government Communications Headquarters. (*ERA 1996, s 193*).

37.8 EUROPEAN UNION LAW

All employment relationships are currently affected by EUROPEAN UNION LAW (23). However, public sector employees may find themselves in a special position because of the way in which the doctrine of 'direct effect' is applied.

Some categories of EC legislation (the Treaties themselves, and regulations) become applicable once promulgated without any need for further action by member states. In the case of *Directives*, however, the intention is that member states should, within a given time, take such steps as they consider appropriate to implement the *Directive* in their territory. The European Court of Justice has frequently held that, if a member state fails to comply with its obligation (either because it does nothing or because what it does is held not to achieve all that the *Directive* requires), then, although that *Directive* cannot be relied upon in proceedings against private persons, provided that the *Directive* is clear and uncondi- tional, it may be relied upon against that State. The State may not take advantage of its own wrong in failing to introduce measures to implement the *Directive*. In order for a person to be able to rely on a *Directive* against the State, the terms of the *Directive* must be clear and it must be unconditional, ie it must require no further implementing measures or time before it is intended to have effect.

It was this doctrine which enabled the applicant in *Marshall v Southampton and South West Hampshire Area Health Authority (Teaching)* [1986] ICR 335 to succeed in her claim of unlawful sex discrimination based on discriminatory retiring ages at a time before the *Sex Discrimination Act 1986* was passed. The health authority which employed her was agreed to be an organ of the state, so that she could rely directly upon *Directive 76/207/EEC*, unlike private sector employees (see 23.6 EUROPEAN UNION LAW).

The question of whether a nationalised industry (since privatised) is the state for these purposes fell to be considered in *Foster v British Gas plc*. The House of Lords referred the question to the European Court of Justice, which held ([1991] ICR 84) that the doctrine applies to 'a body, whatever its legal form, which has been made responsible, pursuant to a measure adopted by the state, for providing a public service under the control of the state and has for that purpose special powers beyond those which result from the normal rules applicable in relations between individuals'. The House of Lords ([1991] ICR 463) went on to hold that British Gas before privatisation fell within this definition. However, mere control by the state is not enough, and so the doctrine did not apply to a manufacturing company which was wholly owned by the state but which did not provide a public service and possessed no special powers (*Rolls-Royce plc v Doughty* [1992] ICR 538). The doctrine did apply to a water company privatised under the *Water Act 1989* and *Water Industry Act 1991* (*Griffin v South West Water Services Ltd* [1995] IRLR 15), and to the governing body of a voluntary aided school (*National Union of Teachers v St Mary's Church of England Aided Junior School (Governing Body)* [1997] ICR 334, [1997] IRLR 242, CA). In *Hillman v London General Transport Services Ltd* (14 April 1999, unreported), the EAT held that the respondent company was simply a commercial concern and was not an emanation of the state, applying *Foster v British Gas plc*.

38   Redundancy – I: The Right to a Redundancy Payment

Cross-references. Transfer of Undertakings (52). See 54.11 Unfair Dismissal – II for dismissal on grounds of redundancy, and Pay – I (34) for details of the calculation of the employee's weekly pay. See Contract of Employment (8) for principles applicable to enhanced redundancy payments claimed under the contract of employment.

38.1   The *Redundancy Payments Act 1965* ('*RPA 1965*') introduced the right of employees who lost their jobs in certain circumstances to a payment from their employers irrespective of whether they had another job to go to. The *RPA 1965* was amended by the *Employment Protection Act 1975* ('*EPA 1975*') and the provisions, as amended, were re-enacted in the *Employment Protection (Consolidation) Act 1978* ('*EPCA 1978*'). The provisions are now contained in the *Employment Rights Act 1996* ('*ERA 1996*').

38.2   PRE-CONDITIONS FOR PAYMENT

The conditions which must be fulfilled for a person to be entitled to a redundancy payment are:

(a)   that he was an employee;

(b)   that he had been continuously employed for the requisite period;

(c)   that he was dismissed (as defined); and

(d)   that the dismissal was by reason of redundancy.

(*ERA 1996, ss 135, 155.*)

Certain employees are excluded from the right to a redundancy payment (see **38.10** below).

38.3   APPLICANT MUST HAVE BEEN AN EMPLOYEE

Only 'employees' are entitled to claim a redundancy payment. Thus, those engaged under a contract for services are not entitled to make such a claim. 'Employee' is defined as:

> '   . . .   an individual who has entered into or works under (or, where the employment has ceased, worked under) a contract of employment.'
>
> (*ERA 1996, s 230(1)*)

See Employee, Self-Employed or Worker? (15).

If the respondent to an application for a redundancy payment (ie the employer) disputes the fact that the applicant was an employee, it is for the applicant to prove that he was.

38.4   Continuous employment for the requisite period

In order to be entitled to a redundancy payment, an applicant must have been *continuously employed for a period of two years ending with the relevant date* (see below for 'relevant date') (*ERA 1996, s 155*).

The rules for computing continuous employment are dealt with in detail in Continuous Employment (7).

The relevant date. The relevant date in relation to the dismissal of an employee:

38.4 Redundancy – I: The Right to a Redundancy Payment

(a) where his contract of employment is terminated by notice, whether given by his employer or by the employee, means the date on which that notice expires;
(b) where his contract of employment is terminated without notice, means the date on which the termination takes effect; and
(c) where he is employed under a limited-term contract which terminates by virtue of the limiting event without being renewed under the same contract, means the date on which the termination takes effect.
(*ERA 1996, s 145.*)

This provision corresponds to the definition of the 'effective date of termination' for the purposes of unfair dismissal contained in *ERA 1996, s 97(1)*; for a discussion of its application see **53.13 UNFAIR DISMISSAL – I**.

If an employee is dismissed with no notice or less than the statutory minimum period of notice, for the purposes, *inter alia*, of calculating the qualifying period of employment, the relevant date will be the date upon which the statutory minimum period of notice would have expired had it been given (*ERA 1996, s 145(5)*). (See **48.7 TERMINATION OF EMPLOYMENT**.) However, this provision does not affect the employer's right to dismiss without notice for an employee's gross misconduct (*ERA 1996, s 86(6)*). In the event of such a dismissal, the statutory minimum period of notice will not be added on for the purpose of computing the length of continuous employment.

38.5 Changes in the ownership of the business

The *Transfer of Undertakings (Protection of Employment) Regulations 2006 (SI 2006/246)* are discussed fully in **TRANSFER OF UNDERTAKINGS (52)**. By virtue of the *Regulations*, on a 'relevant transfer' of an undertaking, the existing employees' contracts of employment are not terminated. On completion of such a transfer all the transferor's rights, powers, duties and liabilities under or in connection with any such contract are transferred to the transferee (*Transfer of Undertakings Regulations, reg 4(2)(a)*). Therefore, such an employee will be deemed not to have been dismissed by the transferor and the continuity of his employment will be preserved.

38.6 The employee must have been 'dismissed'

There is no presumption of dismissal and, if the employer disputes the fact, it is for the employee to prove it. For redundancy payments purposes, dismissal has a statutory meaning instead of merely meaning termination of the contract by the employer. Sub-paragraph (*a*) below reflects the common law position (see **48.5 TERMINATION OF EMPLOYMENT**), and occurs most frequently in practice, while (*b*) would not be a dismissal at common law. In addition, certain forms of termination of the contract at common law are disregarded for redundancy payments purposes (see below).

An employee will be taken to be dismissed by his employer if, but only if:

(a) the contract under which he is employed by the employer is terminated by the employer, whether it is terminated by notice or without notice;
(b) where under that contract he is employed for a limited term, the contract terminates by virtue of the limiting event without being renewed under the same contract; or
(c) the employee terminates that contract with or without notice in circumstances such that he is entitled so to terminate it without notice by reason of the employer's conduct (not being termination by reason of a lock-out).
(*ERA 1996, s 136(1), (2).*)

The statutory definition of dismissal for redundancy payments purposes is the same as for the purposes of unfair dismissal (see **UNFAIR DISMISSAL – I (53)**).

Where in accordance with any enactment or rule of law any act on the part of an employer, or any event affecting an employer, operates so as to terminate a contract of employment, that is treated for redundancy payments purposes as a termination by the employer, even if it would not otherwise amount to such a termination (*ERA 1996, s 136(5)*; and see *Pickwell v Lincolnshire County Council* [1993] ICR 87).

Situations where no dismissal occurs. An employee is deemed not to have been dismissed in certain circumstances where a dismissal by reason of redundancy has in fact taken place. Two examples are given below.

(i)   *Renewal or re-engagement.* If an employee's contract is renewed or he is re-engaged under a new contract of employment and:

(A) the offer, whether in writing or not, is made before the ending of the existing contract; and
(B) it is to take effect either immediately on the ending of the original employment or within a period of not more than four weeks thereafter (if the contract ends on Friday, Saturday or Sunday, the new employment must take effect four weeks from the following Monday),

no dismissal will be deemed to have taken place in respect of the termination of the original contract (*ERA 1996, s 138(1)*).

If the terms and conditions of the new employment differ wholly or in part from the original contract, the employee has a trial period of four weeks from the ending of the original employment, or such longer period as may be agreed in writing, within which to decide whether to accept or reject the offer (see **38.12** below). If he rejects the offer or if the employer terminates or gives notice to terminate the contract for a reason connected with the change in contractual terms, within that period, the employee will be taken to have been dismissed on the date of termination of the original contract for the reason that contract was terminated (*ERA 1996, s 138(2)–(6)*).

(ii)   *Offers of employment by associated companies.* It should be noted that where the employer is a company, any reference to re-engagement by the employer is construed as including a reference to re-engagement by *that company or by an associated company*, and any reference to an offer made by the employer is construed as including a reference to an offer made by an associated company (*ERA 1996, s 146(1)*). For the meaning of 'associated company', see **7.9(a)** CONTINUOUS EMPLOYMENT.

Employee who leaves prematurely. An employee who leaves his employment before his employer's notice of dismissal expires may lose his right to a redundancy payment. If the employee gives written notice to terminate his employment on a date earlier than that given by his employer, he will not lose his right to a redundancy payment if the employer does not object to his premature departure. If, however, the employer does object and serves on the employee a written request to withdraw his notice, warning him that if he does not do so the employer will contest any liability to make a redundancy payment, he may lose the right to such a payment. If the employer withholds the redundancy payment, the employee may apply to an employment tribunal which will decide whether the employee is entitled to the full payment, or no payment, or part of the payment. The tribunal will consider whether the employee's action in leaving prematurely was reasonable or unreasonable in the circumstances (*ERA 1996, ss 136(3), 142(1), (2)*). If, however, the parties agree by mutual consent to substitute some other date of termination for the date specified by the employer, no such question arises (*CPS Recruitment Ltd v Bowen and Secretary of State for Employment* [1982] IRLR 54).

38.7 Redundancy must be the reason for dismissal

In order to be entitled to a redundancy payment, the employee must be dismissed by reason of redundancy. An employee who has been dismissed by his employer is, unless the contrary is proved, presumed to have been dismissed by reason of redundancy for the purposes of any claim for a redundancy payment (*ERA 1996, s 163(2)*). There is, however, no formal burden of proof upon the employer. The tribunal must decide whether the presumption has been rebutted on the basis of all the evidence before them: see *Greater Glasgow Health Board v Lamont* UKEATS/0019/12.

'Redundancy' is defined as follows:

> 'For the purposes of this Act an employee who is dismissed shall be taken to be dismissed by reason of redundancy if the dismissal is wholly or mainly attributable to –
>
> (*a*)   the fact that his employer has ceased or intends to cease:
> (i) to carry on the business for the purposes of which the employee was employed by him, or
> (ii) to carry on that business in the place where the employee was so employed, or
> (*b*)   the fact that the requirements of that business:
> (i) for employees to carry out work of a particular kind, or
> (ii) for employees to carry out work of a particular kind in the place where the employee was employed by the employer,
> have ceased or diminished or are expected to cease or diminish.'

(*ERA 1996, s 139(1)*; note that a different definition applies for the purposes of the redundancy consultation provisions of *TULCRA 1992* (see **39.3** REDUNDANCY – II).)

Sub-paragraph (*a*) covers the closure of the employer's business as a whole, or, alternatively, just at the place where the employee is employed. The test for determining 'the place where the employee was employed' is primarily a factual one, although the employee's contractual terms may provide evidence of the place of work where the employee did go from place to place (see *High Table Ltd v Horst* [1998] ICR 409, CA). Thus, if an employee had as a matter of fact worked in only one location, then the existence of a contractual mobility clause (entitling the employer to transfer him) will not widen the definition of the place where the employee was employed under *ERA 1996, s 139(1)* (see also *Bass Leisure Ltd v Thomas* [1994] IRLR 104).

Under sub-para (*b*) it must be considered whether the business requires so many employees to carry out certain work. In deciding whether there has been a cessation or diminution in the requirements of the business for employees to carry out 'work of a particular kind', it was uncertain whether the work is defined by what is required under an employee's contract of employment ('the contract test'), or by what an employee is actually doing ('the function test'), or by a blend of the two. Until 1997, it was assumed that the Court of Appeal in *Cowen v Haden Ltd* [1983] ICR 1 had established that the proper test was the contract test. However, the EAT in *Safeway Stores plc v Burrell* [1997] ICR 523 disagreed with this interpretation of *Cowen v Haden* and stated that the terms of an employee's contract of employment were irrelevant when determining whether there was a redundancy situation within the meaning of *ERA 1996, s 139(1)*. The House of Lords confirmed in the case of *Murray v Foyle Meats Ltd* [2000] 1 AC 51, [1999] 3 All ER 769, [1999] 3 WLR 356, [1999] ICR 827 that both the 'contract test' and the 'function test' are an unnecessary gloss on the plain wording of the statute. Further, the Court of Appeal held in *Shawkat v Nottingham City Hospital NHS Trust (No 2)* [2001] EWCA Civ 954, [2001] IRLR 555 that whether there was less need for employees to carry out work of a particular kind was always a question of fact for a tribunal to decide.

The House of Lords in *Murray* approved the reasoning of the EAT in *Safeway Stores v Burrell* (see above), one of whose conclusions was that 'bumped employees' will be dismissed by reason of redundancy. A 'bumping' situation will exist where Smith, whose job is no longer required, is put by his employer into Brown's position, so that Brown is dismissed instead of Smith. The reasoning in *Safeway Stores v Burrell* would mean that Brown was redundant, because the employer's requirement for work of a particular kind had diminished, and because Brown was dismissed as a result. It is not necessary that any reduction in the employer's requirements for work of a particular kind should be a reduction in the type of work that Brown himself carried out. *Safeway Stores v Burrell* follows earlier authority (see *W Gimber & Sons Ltd v Spurrett* (1967) 2 ITR 308; applied by the EAT in *Elliott Turbomachinery Ltd v Bates* [1981] ICR 218) in reaching this conclusion. The EAT decision in *Church v West Lancashire NHS Trust* [1998] ICR 423 initially created some uncertainty as to whether *Safeway Stores* was correct, but those doubts were dispelled by *Murray*, and more recently, by the EAT in *Stankovic v City of Westminster* [2001] All ER (D) 340 (Oct), EAT. Indeed, the EAT specifically stated in *Stankovic* that *Church* was no longer good authority on the point.

A redundancy situation within the meaning of *ERA 1996, s 139(1)(b)* will also exist where the amount of work available for the same number of employees has reduced. So, for example, where an employer offers employees reduced working hours following a downturn in business, and an employee is dismissed for refusing to accept reduced working hours, the dismissal is for redundancy: see *Packman v Fauchon* [2012] ICR 1362. (In *Packman*, Langstaff P considered in detail the EAT's decision to the opposite effect in *Aylward v Glamorgan Holiday Homes Ltd* UKEAT/167/02, and declined to follow it.)

Where an employee is employed on a succession of fixed-term contracts this can, in principle, give rise to a dismissal by reason of redundancy on the expiration of each fixed-term contract (*Pfaffinger v City of Liverpool Community College* [1997] ICR 142).

38.8   Redundancy payments for lay-off and short time

Special provisions relating to redundancy claims by piece-workers who are laid off or put on short time are contained in *ERA 1996*. An employee is considered to be *laid off* during a particular week if under his contract he gets no pay of any kind from his employer for that week because there is no work for him to do although he is available for work (*ERA 1996, s 147*). An employee is considered to be on short time for a week if during that week he gets less than half a week's pay (*ERA 1996, s 147(2)*).

A redundancy payment may only be claimed by a worker laid off or on short time if he gives notice in writing to his employer of his intention to claim and the claim is submitted within four weeks of:

(a) the end of a continuous period of lay-off or short time of four or more weeks' duration; or
(b) the end of a period of six weeks' lay-off or short time out of 13 weeks (where not more than three weeks were consecutive).
(*ERA 1996, s 148.*)

He must then terminate his contract of employment by giving the contractual period of notice or one week's notice, whichever is the greater (*ERA 1996, s 150(1)*).

The notice to terminate must be given within the following time limits:

(a) if the employer does not give a counter-notice (see **38.9** below) within seven days after the service of the notice of intention to claim, that period is three weeks after the end of those seven days;
(b) if the employer gives a counter-notice within those seven days, but withdraws it by a

subsequent notice in writing, that period is three weeks after the service of the notice of withdrawal; and
(c) if the employer gives a counter-notice within those seven days and does not so withdraw it, and a question as to the right of the employee to a redundancy payment in pursuance of the notice of intention to claim is referred to a tribunal, that period is three weeks after the tribunal has notified to the employee its decision on that reference.
(*ERA 1996, s 150(3)*.)

Even if an employee fails to comply with these statutory requirements, he may claim that he has been constructively dismissed for redundancy if he is laid off in fundamental breach of his contract of employment (*A Dakri & Co Ltd v Tiffen* [1981] ICR 256; cf *Kenneth McRae & Co Ltd v Dawson* [1984] IRLR 5). However, no term should be implied into an employee's contract that any period of lay-off will be for no longer than is reasonable, in circumstances where Parliament has provided a detailed scheme which sets out the appropriate balance between the rights of the employee and the interests of the employer: *Craig v Bob Lindfield & Son Ltd* (UKEAT/0220/15) (20 November 2015, unreported).

38.9   Counter-notice

An employee who gives a notice of intention to claim pursuant to *ERA 1996, s 148* will not be entitled to a redundancy payment if, on the date of service of that notice, it was reasonably to be expected that he would (if he continued to be employed by the same employer), not later than four weeks after that date, enter upon a period of employment of not less than 13 weeks during which he would not be laid off or kept on short time (*ERA 1996, s 152(1)*).

However, an employer cannot take advantage of this rule unless, within seven days after service of the notice of intention to claim, he gives the employee notice in writing that he will contest liability to make a redundancy payment (*ERA 1996, s 152(1)(b)*). If the employee wishes to pursue his claim after the service of a counter-notice, an employment tribunal must be asked to determine whether he is entitled to a redundancy payment (*ERA 1996, s 149*).

38.10   Exclusions from right to payment

The following are excluded from the right to a redundancy payment.

(a)   Masters or crew of a fishing vessel who are not remunerated otherwise than by a share of the profits or gross earnings of the vessel (*ERA 1996, s 199(2)* (see *Goodeve v Gilsons (a firm)* [1985] ICR 401)).

(b)   Civil servants and other public employees (*ERA 1996, s 159*).

(c)   Persons employed in any capacity under the Government of any territory or country outside the United Kingdom (*ERA 1996, s 160*).

(d)   Domestic servants in a private household where the employer is the parent (or step-parent), grandparent, child (or step-child), grandchild or brother or sister (or half-brother or half-sister) of the employee. References to step-parent or step-child include relationships arising through civil partnership: see the *Civil Partnership Act 2004, ss 246, 247, Sch 21* (*ERA 1996, s 161*).

(e)   Employees who have been offered employment on the same terms and conditions as their original employment or offered *suitable alternative employment* and in either case have *unreasonably refused the offer* (see **38.12** below) (*ERA 1996, s 141(1)–(3)*).

(f)   Employees who have been offered suitable alternative employment, and have unreasonably terminated their contracts during the statutory trial period (see **38.12** below) (*ERA 1996, s 141(4)*).

(g)   Employees who are dismissed for misconduct. If notice is given for this reason it must be accompanied by a statement in writing that the employer would, because of the employee's conduct, be entitled to terminate the contract without notice. If the employee is dismissed without notice, there is no need to give any statement in writing that dismissal was on the ground of misconduct (*ERA 1996, s 140(1)*). The employer is entitled to terminate when the employee has been in fundamental breach of his contract of employment (*Bonner v H Gilbert Ltd* [1989] IRLR 475). This provision does not apply where the dismissal is for taking part in a strike (*ERA 1996, s 140(2)*). The tribunal, in any event, has a discretion to award the whole or part of a redundancy payment to the dismissed employee where it is just and equitable to do so (*ERA 1996, s 140(3)*).

(h)   Employees who are dismissed if an *exemption order* is in force (*ERA 1996, s 157*). An exemption order is an order made by the Secretary of State for Business, Innovation and Skills exempting an employer or a group of employers from liability to make redundancy payments under the *Act* where they have similar or more advantageous agreements with their employees for making payments on redundancy.

38.11 Time limit for claims

Employees are not entitled to a redundancy payment unless, before the end of the period of six months beginning with the relevant date:

(a) the payment has been agreed and paid;
(b) the employee has made a claim for the payment by notice in writing given to the employer;
(c) a question as to the right of the employee to the payment, or as to the amount of the payment, has been referred to an employment tribunal; or
(d) a complaint of unfair dismissal has been presented by the employee to a tribunal.
(*ERA 1996, s 164(1)*.) (For the meaning of 'relevant date', see **38.4** above.)

If, however, within the *next* six months, the employee takes the action in (*b*), (*c*) or (*d*), a tribunal may award a redundancy payment if it considers it just and equitable to do so having regard to the reason for the delay (*ERA 1996, s 164(2)*).

An application for a redundancy payment is 'referred' to an employment tribunal when it is received by the tribunal office and not when it is sent by the employee (*Secretary of State for Employment v Banks* [1983] ICR 48).

See also **38.14** below.

38.12 UNREASONABLE REFUSAL OF SUITABLE ALTERNATIVE EMPLOYMENT

An employee who is dismissed by reason of redundancy loses his right to a redundancy payment if he unreasonably refuses an offer of suitable alternative employment. The offer of alternative employment:

(a)   must be made by his original employer or an associated employer (*ERA 1996, s 141(1)*; and see **7.9**(a) Continuous Employment);

(b)   must be made before the ending of his employment under his previous contract (*ERA 1996, s 141(1)*);

(c)   may be oral or in writing;

(d)   must take effect either immediately on the ending of the employment under the previous contract or after an interval of not more than four weeks thereafter (*ERA 1996, s 141(1)*). The alternative employment will be treated as taking effect immediately on the ending of the employment under the previous contract if that employment ends on a Friday, Saturday or Sunday, and the alternative employment is to commence on or before the next Monday. The interval of four weeks is calculated accordingly (*ERA 1996, s 146(2)*). An offer which is not ongoing and which would take effect prior to the dismissal will not satisfy *ERA 1996, s 141(1)* (*McHugh v Hempsall Bulk Transport Ltd*, IDS Brief 480, p 6); and

(e)   must be either:
(i) on the same terms and conditions as the previous contract; or
(ii) suitable employment in relation to the employee.
(*ERA, s 141(3)*.)

If the terms and conditions of the renewed or new contract of employment differ (wholly or in part) from the corresponding provisions of his previous contract, the employee has a statutory trial period of four weeks, beginning with the ending of his previous employment, in which to decide whether the alternative employment is suitable for him. The four-week trial period means four calendar weeks. Thus, 11 days when the factory was closed over Christmas had to be taken into account (*Benton v Sanderson Keyser Ltd* [1989] ICR 136). This four-week period may be extended by agreement, for the purpose of retraining the employee for employment under the new or renewed contract. Such an agreement must:

(i) be made before the employee starts work under the renewed or new contract;
(ii) be in writing;
(iii) specify the date of the end of the trial period; and
(iv) specify the terms and conditions of employment which will apply in the employee's case after the end of that period.
(*ERA 1996, s 138(6)*.)

Although the employer is no longer required, in making the offer, to give the employee details of the changes in terms and conditions in writing, where applicable, employers may still find it useful to do so. The employer, however, remains obliged to give written particulars of the main terms of an employee's employment within one month of the change (*ERA 1996, s 4(1)*). (See **8.7 Contract of Employment**.)

An employee whose contract was repudiated by his employers is entitled, in accordance with the common law, to a reasonable period in which to decide whether to enter into a new contract or to treat himself as dismissed (see **Termination of Employment (48)**). So an employee whose contract is repudiated, and who is given alternative employment which does not fall within the terms of *ERA 1996, s 138(1)*, has a reasonable period within which to decide whether to accept the repudiation and claim a redundancy payment: see *Turvey v C W Cheney & Son Ltd* [1979] ICR 341. However, the *Turvey* case should not be seen as authority for the proposition that the common law can operate to extend the statutory four-week period under *ERA 1996, s 136*. If alternative employment is offered within the terms of *ERA 1996 s 138(1)*, the four-week period cannot be extended save under *s 138(6)*: see *Optical Express Ltd v Williams* [2008] ICR 1.

If the employee accepts the alternative employment, which was offered before the termination of his original employment and which takes effect not more than four weeks thereafter, he is deemed not to have been dismissed on the termination of the original employment for the purposes of determining any liability of the employer for redundancy payments (*ERA 1996, s 138(1)*; see *Jones v Governing Body of Burdett Coutts School* [1997] ICR 390, EAT, cf *Ebac Ltd v Wymer* [1995] ICR 466). If, during the trial period, the employee terminates the contract or gives notice to terminate it, or if the employer, for a reason connected with or arising out of any difference between the renewed or new contract and the previous contract, terminates the contract or gives notice to terminate it, the employee is treated as having been dismissed on the date on which his original contract came to an end (*ERA 1996, s 138(2), (4)*).

If, during the trial period, the employer dismisses the employee for a reason unconnected with or not arising out of the change, the employee can bring an unfair dismissal claim on the basis of the fairness of the dismissal in the trial period (*Hempell v W H Smith & Sons Ltd* [1986] ICR 365).

If the terms of the new contract are suitable and the employee unreasonably terminates the contract during the trial period, he will not be entitled to a redundancy payment by reason of his dismissal under the original contract (*ERA 1996, s 141(4)*).

The question of the suitability of an offer of alternative employment is an objective matter, whereas the reasonableness of the employee's refusal depends on factors personal to him and is a subjective matter to be considered from the employee's point of view. This means that the importation of a "reasonable band of responses" test analogous to that used in unfair dismissal is not appropriate: see *Readman v Devon Primary Care Trust* [2013] IRLR 878. So, for example, the offer to a butcher's shop manager of a job as a supermarket butchery department manager may be suitable alternative employment, but his perceived loss of status may make it reasonable for him to refuse it (*Cambridge & District Co-operative Society v Ruse* [1993] IRLR 156). The Court of Appeal in *Spencer and Griffin v Gloucestershire County Council* [1985] IRLR 393 has said that in evaluating the separate questions of suitability of employment and reasonableness of refusal, the employment tribunal is entitled to look at factors which may prove, on analysis, to be common to both. In that case, the Court of Appeal, in upholding a decision of an employment tribunal, considered that a refusal by an employee to do work of a lower standard than the employee considered reasonable, may be a reason for holding that the work offered is not suitable or has been reasonably refused. Before the tribunal, an employee can rely on a reason for refusal that he or she has not expressly raised with the employer when refusing the offer: see *Dunne v Colin & Avril Ltd* UKEAT/0293/16 (8 March 2017).

38.13 AMOUNT OF THE PAYMENT

The amount of the redundancy payment is based upon the employee's age, length of continuous employment and gross average wage.

The calculation of continuity is made in accordance with rules set out in *ERA 1996, ss 210 to 219*; see **38.4** above and Continuous Employment **(7)**.

Contractual agreements relating to continuity of employment cannot affect an employer's statutory liability to make a redundancy payment (*Secretary of State for Employment v Globe Elastic Thread Co Ltd* [1980] AC 506, [1979] 2 All ER 1077, [1979] 3 WLR 143, [1979] ICR 706). Therefore, if an employer agrees to preserve an employee's continuity of employment where there is no continuity in accordance with the statutory provisions, he will be contractually liable to make a redundancy payment calculated in accordance with his agreement, but not liable to make any payment under statute.

The amount of the redundancy payment is calculated by reference to the period, ending with the relevant date, during which the employee has been continuously employed. (For the meaning of 'relevant date' see **38.4** above.) There is then allowed:

(a) one and a half week's pay for each such year of employment which consists wholly of weeks in which the employee was not below the age of 41;
(b) one week's pay for each such year of employment (not falling within (*a*) above) which consists wholly of weeks in which the employee was not below the age of 22; and
(c) half a week's pay for each such year of employment not falling within either of the preceding sub-paragraphs.

38.13 Redundancy – I: The Right to a Redundancy Payment

(*ERA 1996, s 162(1), (2)*.) Where an employee has been continuously employed for 20 years ending with the relevant date, no account is taken of any year of employment earlier than those 20 years (*ERA 1996, s 162(3)*). In other words, the maximum number of years to be taken into account in calculating a redundancy payment is 20, reckoning back from termination of his contract. A previous redundancy payment breaks continuity for this purpose (*ERA 1996, s 214(2)*).

A week's pay is calculated in accordance with *ERA 1996, ss 221–229*. The calculation is based on average wages without deduction of tax, not taking into account overtime, unless the employer is contractually bound to provide and the employee to work such overtime. Where an employee is on short-time working on the calculation date, "a week's pay" should be that provided for by the original contract of employment, notwithstanding the short-time working: see *Dutton v Jones* UKEAT/0236/12. (See PAY – I (34) for full details.)

With effect from 6 April 2017, the maximum amount of a week's pay allowed in computing a statutory redundancy payment is £489 (*ERA 1996, s 227* and the *Employment Rights (Increase of Limits) Order 2017 (SI 2017/175)*). Thus, the current maximum statutory redundancy payment is £14,670.

38.14 REFERENCES TO EMPLOYMENT TRIBUNAL AND RESTRICTION ON CONTRACTING OUT

Any question arising as to the right of an employee to a redundancy payment, or as to the amount of a redundancy payment, is to be referred to and determined by an employment tribunal (*ERA 1996, s 163(1)*). Where an employment tribunal determines that an employee has a right to a redundancy payment, it may also order the employer to pay to the employee such amount as it considers appropriate in all the circumstances to compensate him for any financial loss which is attributable to the non-payment of the redundancy payment (*ERA 1996, s 163(5)*).

Any provision in any agreement (whether a contract of employment or not) is *prima facie* void insofar as it purports to exclude or limit any provisions relating to redundancy, or to preclude any person from bringing any proceedings in respect of a redundancy payment before an employment tribunal (*ERA 1996, s 203(1)*).

However, an employee will be bound by a settlement agreement reached following action by a conciliation officer, or by a compromise contract which satisfies the statutory conditions, including that the employee should have had independent advice (*ERA 1996, s 203(2)*; and see **2.4 ADVISORY, CONCILIATION AND ARBITRATION SERVICE** and **18.20 EMPLOYMENT TRIBUNALS – I**).

38.15 Ready Reckoner for Redundancy Payments

To use the Table — Read off employee's age and number of complete years' service. The Table will then show how many weeks' pay the employee is entitled to. It should be noted that although the Table runs only between the ages of 20 and 64, service before and after these ages does count for redundancy purposes, and there is no age below or above which redundancy payments cannot be claimed.

The Table may also be used to calculate the basic award for unfair dismissal.

AGE (years)	SERVICE (years)																		
	2	3	4	5	6	7	8	9	10	11	12	13	14	15	16	17	18	19	20
20	1	1½	2	2½															
21	1	1½	2	2½	—														
22	1	1½	2	2½	3	—													
23	1½	2	2½	3	3½	4	—												
24	2	2½	3	3½	4	4½	5	—											
25	2	3	3½	4	4½	5	5½	6	—										
26	2	3	4	4½	5	5½	6	6½	7	—									
27	2	3	4	5	5½	6	6½	7	7½	8	—								
28	2	3	4	5	6	6½	7	7½	8	8½	9	—							
29	2	3	4	5	6	7	7½	8	8½	9	9½	10	—						
30	2	3	4	5	6	7	8	8½	9	9½	10	10½	11	—					
31	2	3	4	5	6	7	8	9	9½	10	10½	11	11½	12	—				
32	2	3	4	5	6	7	8	9	10	10½	11	11½	12	12½	13	—			
33	2	3	4	5	6	7	8	9	10	11	11½	12	12½	13	13½	14	—		
34	2	3	4	5	6	7	8	9	10	11	12	12½	13	13½	14	14½	15	—	
35	2	3	4	5	6	7	8	9	10	11	12	13	13½	14	14½	15	15½	16	—
36	2	3	4	5	6	7	8	9	10	11	12	13	14	14½	15	15½	16	16½	17
37	2	3	4	5	6	7	8	9	10	11	12	13	14	15	15½	16	16½	17	17½
38	2	3	4	5	6	7	8	9	10	11	12	13	14	15	16	16½	17	17½	18
39	2	3	4	5	6	7	8	9	10	11	12	13	14	15	16	17	17½	18	18½
40	2	3	4	5	6	7	8	9	10	11	12	13	14	15	16	17	18	18½	19

Age	2	3	4	5	6	7	8	9	10	11	12	13	14	15	16	17	18	19	20
41	2	3	4	5	6	7	8	9	10	11	12	13	14	15	16	17	18	19	19½
42	2½	3½	4½	5½	6½	7½	8½	9½	10½	11½	12½	13½	14½	15½	16½	17½	18½	19½	20½
43	3	4	5	6	7	8	9	10	11	12	13	14	15	16	17	18	19	20	21
44	3	4½	5½	6½	7½	8½	9½	10½	11½	12½	13½	14½	15½	16½	17½	18½	19½	20½	21½
45	3	4½	6	7	8	9	10	11	12	13	14	15	16	17	18	19	20	21	22
46	3	4½	6	7½	8½	9½	10½	11½	12½	13½	14½	15½	16½	17½	18½	19½	20½	21½	22½
47	3	4½	6	7½	9	10	11	12	13	14	15	16	17	18	19	20	21	22	23
48	3	4½	6	7½	9	10½	11½	12½	13½	14½	15½	16½	17½	18½	19½	20½	21½	22½	23½
49	3	4½	6	7½	9	10½	12	13	14	15	16	17	18	19	20	21	22	23	24
50	3	4½	6	7½	9	10½	12	13½	14½	15½	16½	17½	18½	19½	20½	21½	22½	23½	24½
51	3	4½	6	7½	9	10½	12	13½	15	16	17	18	19	20	21	22	23	24	25
52	3	4½	6	7½	9	10½	12	13½	15	16½	17½	18½	19½	20½	21½	22½	23½	24½	25½
53	3	4½	6	7½	9	10½	12	13½	15	16½	18	19	20	21	22	23	24	25	26
54	3	4½	6	7½	9	10½	12	13½	15	16½	18	19½	20½	21½	22½	23½	24½	25½	26½
55	3	4½	6	7½	9	10½	12	13½	15	16½	18	19½	21	22	23	24	25	26	27
56	3	4½	6	7½	9	10½	12	13½	15	16½	18	19½	21	22½	23½	24½	25½	26½	27½
57	3	4½	6	7½	9	10½	12	13½	15	16½	18	19½	21	22½	24	25	26	27	28
58	3	4½	6	7½	9	10½	12	13½	15	16½	18	19½	21	22½	24	25½	26½	27½	28½
59	3	4½	6	7½	9	10½	12	13½	15	16½	18	19½	21	22½	24	25½	27	28	29
60	3	4½	6	7½	9	10½	12	13½	15	16½	18	19½	21	22½	24	25½	27	28½	29½
61	3	4½	6	7½	9	10½	12	13½	15	16½	18	19½	21	22½	24	25½	27	28½	30
62	3	4½	6	7½	9	10½	12	13½	15	16½	18	19½	21	22½	24	25½	27	28½	30
63	3	4½	6	7½	9	10½	12	13½	15	16½	18	19½	21	22½	24	25½	27	28½	30
64	3	4½	6	7½	9	10½	12	13½	15	16½	18	19½	21	22½	24	25½	27	28½	30

39   Redundancy – II: Practice and Procedure

(See ACAS advisory booklet "How to manage collective redundancies" (published April 2013)).

Cross-reference. See REDUNDANCY – I (38) for the right to a redundancy payment.

39.1   If an employer dismisses an employee by reason of redundancy, he has a number of statutory obligations in addition to that of making the employee a redundancy payment.

He may be liable in a claim of unfair dismissal unless he acts fairly. He must allow the employee reasonable time off work to look for alternative employment. If the proposed dismissal is of 20 or more employees at one establishment within 90 days, the employer must consult 'appropriate representatives' of the employees concerned. For the meaning of 'appropriate representatives' in this context, see **39.4** below.

This chapter considers the following.

(a)   The requirements for consultation before making an employee redundant (see **39.2**–**39.7** below).

(b)   The requirement for notification to the Department for Business, Innovation and Skills (see **39.8** below).

(c)   The basic 'fair dismissal' considerations relating to proposed redundancies (see **39.9** below).

The chapter ends with a checklist of redundancy dismissal procedure (see **39.10** below).

39.2   CONSULTATION AND NOTIFICATION REQUIREMENTS

The *Trade Union and Labour Relations (Consolidation) Act 1992* (*'TULRCA 1992'*), as amended by the *Trade Union Reform and Employment Rights Act 1993* (*'TURERA 1993'*) and relevant regulations, imposes far-reaching obligations on employers to notify and consult appropriate employee representatives about proposed redundancies. *TULRCA 1992, s 193* imposes obligations on employers to notify the Secretary of State for Employment about proposed redundancies. The statutory provisions give effect to the *EC Collective Redundancies Directive 98/59/EC*, amending *Directive 75/129/EEC* and *Directive 92/56/EEC* (see **23.8** EUROPEAN UNION LAW). For the use of the Directive as an aid to construction of the statute, see *Hough v Leyland DAF Ltd* [1991] ICR 696; but cf *Re Hartlebury Printers Ltd* [1993] 1 All ER 470, [1992] ICR 559. Above and beyond the requirements of the *Directive*, *TULRCA 1992* also empowers employers to whom employees will, or are likely to, transfer under the provisions of the *Transfer of Undertakings (Protection of Employment) Regulations 2006* (*"TUPE"*) to engage in consultation with the representatives of those employees prior to transfer: see *TULRCA 1992, ss 198A, 198B*.

39.3   Meaning of 'redundancy' and 'dismissal'

In *TULRCA 1992, Part IV Chapter II*, which contains the statutory consultation and notification requirements, references to 'dismissal as redundant' are references to dismissal for a reason not related to the individual concerned or for a number of reasons all of which are not so related (*TULRCA 1992, s 195(1)*). This is a substantially different definition from that which applies for redundancy payments purposes (see **38.7** REDUNDANCY – I). A reason 'relates to' an individual if it is something to do with him such as something he is or something he has done, and is to be distinguished from a reason relating to the employer, such as his need to effect business change in some respect: see *University and College Union* *v University of Stirling* [2015] UKSC 26, [2015] ICR 567. For the purposes of any proceedings under *TULRCA 1992*, where an employee is or is proposed to be dismissed, it shall be presumed that he is or is proposed to be dismissed as redundant unless the contrary is proved (*TULRCA 1992, s 195(2)*). It follows from the definition of 'dismissal as redundant' in *TULRCA 1992, s 195(1)* that the collective consultation and notification provisions in *TULRCA 1992* can apply to proposed dismissals, notwithstanding the fact that there is no intention to lose jobs or workers. Thus, where an employer seeks to change the terms and conditions of employment of a part or group of the workforce by giving notice of termination to the employees concerned and offering them re-engagement on new terms, the employer may be under a duty to consult in accordance with *TULRCA 1992, s 188* (*GMB v MAN Truck & Bus UK Ltd* [2000] IRLR 636).

A 'redundancy' within the meaning of *Directive 58/59/EC* means the declaration by an employer of its intention to terminate the contract of employment rather than the actual cessation of the employment relationship upon the expiry of the period of notice. See *Junk v K Kühnel*: C-188/03 [2005] IRLR 310. This affects the timing of collective consultation under *TULRCA 1992* (see further **39.5** below).

The term 'dismissal' in *TULRCA 1992* is to be construed in accordance with *Part X* of *ERA 1996* (see *TULCRA 1992, s 298*). So the applicable definition of "dismissal" includes a constructive dismissal (see *ERA 1996, s 95(1)(c)*). This is consistent with EU law. A constructive dismissal can in principle amount to a dismissal for the purposes of *art 1(1)* of *Directive 98/59/EC*: see *Pujante Rivera v Gestora Clubs Dir SL and another* C-422/14 [2016] ICR 227. In *Pujante*, the CJEU stated that where an employer made significant unilateral changes to an employee's contract for reasons not related to the individual concerned, and the individual resigned as a consequence, the circumstances would fall within the definition of "redundancy" in the *Directive*.

The provisions of *TULRCA 1992, Part IV, Chapter II* do not apply to employment under a contract for a fixed term, unless the employer proposes to dismiss an employee on a fixed-term contract before the term has expired: see *TULRCA 1992, s 282* as amended with effect from 6 April 2013. That position is consistent with *Directive 98/59/EC*: see *Rabal Canas v Nexea Gestion Documental* C-392/13 [2015] IRLR 577.

39.4 Notification to appropriate representatives

Where an employer is proposing to dismiss as redundant at least 20 employees at an establishment within a period of 90 days or less, he must consult about the dismissals 'appropriate representatives' of the affected employees (*TULRCA 1992, s 188(1)*). The class of 'affected employees' includes not only those who may be dismissed, but also any employee affected by the proposed dismissals or who may be affected by measures taken in connection with those dismissals (*TULRCA 1992, s 188(1)*). An employer has to include employees whom it is hoped to redeploy in calculating the number it proposes to dismiss as redundant, if what is proposed amounts to a termination of the employee's existing contract of employment (*Hardy v Tourism South East* [2005] IRLR 242, EAT). This is because the applicable definition of dismissal for the purposes of *TULRCA s 188* (that in *ERA 1996, s 95*) refers to the termination of an employee's contract, with or without notice. Employees who volunteer for redundancy pursuant to an invitation from the employer should be included in the numbers of those the employer proposes to dismiss as redundant: see *Optare Group v Transport and General Workers' Union* [2007] IRLR 931.

The 'appropriate representatives' of any affected employees are:

(a)   if the employees are of a description in respect of which an independent trade union is recognised, representatives of the trade union; or

(b)   in any other case, either:

(i)   employee representatives appointed or elected by the affected employees for other purposes but who have authority to receive information and to be consulted about the proposed dismissals on their behalf; or

(ii)   employee representatives elected by the affected employees for the purposes of *TULRCA 1992, s 188* and in accordance with the statutory procedure set out in *TULRCA 1992, s 188A*.

(*TULRCA 1992, s 188(1B)* as amended by *SI 1999/1925*.)

'Representatives of a trade union' are officials or other persons authorised by the union to carry on collective bargaining with the employer (*TULRCA 1992, s 196(2)* as substituted by the *Collective Redundancies and Transfer of Undertakings (Protections of Employment) (Amendment) Regulations* (*SI 1995/2587*)). 'Recognition', in relation to a trade union, is defined by *TULRCA 1992, s 178(3)* as meaning the recognition of the union by an employer, or two or more associated employers, to any extent, for the purpose of collective bargaining (as defined by *TULRCA 1992, s 178(1)*). In *National Union of Gold, Silver and Allied Trades v Albury Bros Ltd* [1979] ICR 84, the Court of Appeal held that recognition should not be held to be established unless there was clear and unequivocal evidence of an express agreement, or conduct from which recognition should be inferred which involved not a mere willingness to discuss but a positive decision to negotiate on one or more of the issues specified in what is now *TULRCA 1992, s 178(2)*. See also *Working Links (Employment) Ltd v Public and Commercial Services Union*: UKEAT/0305/12 (12 March 2013).

39.5   The timing and content of the consultation

It has long been understood that, in order to comply with the requirements of *TULRCA 1992, s 188*, the employer must begin consultations before giving individual notices of dismissal (*National Union of Teachers v Avon County Council* [1978] IRLR 55). However, in *Junk v Kühnel*: C-188/03 [2005] IRLR 310, the CJEU ruled that, for the purposes of *Directive 98/59/EC*, consultation must in fact already have been completed before employees are given notice of dismissal. This is because a 'redundancy' for the purposes of the Directive means the declaration of an employer of its intention to terminate the contract of employment (ie the giving of notice), rather than actual dismissal on the expiry of notice.

Consultation must not be a sham exercise; there must be time for the representatives, who are consulted, to consider properly the proposals that are being put to them (*Transport and General Workers' Union v Ledbury Preserves (1928) Ltd* [1985] IRLR 412). Fair consultation involves giving the body consulted a fair and proper opportunity to understand fully the matters about which it is being consulted, and to express its views on those subjects, with the consulting employer thereafter considering those views properly and genuinely. The process of consultation is not one in which the employer is obliged to adopt any or all of the views expressed by the person or body whom he is consulting (*R v British Coal Corpn and Secretary of State for Trade and Industry, ex p Price* [1994] IRLR 72). Further, the consultation envisaged by *s 188* cannot begin until the information required by the section, as set out below, has been given (*E Green & Son (Castings) Ltd v Association of Scientific, Technical and Managerial Staffs* [1984] ICR 352; see also *GEC Ferranti Defence Systems Ltd v MSF* [1993] IRLR 101 and [1994] IRLR 104).

The employer does not 'propose' to dismiss until he has reached the stage of having formulated a specific proposal (*Hough v Leyland DAF Ltd* [1991] ICR 696). Thus, the word 'propose' connotes an intention in the mind of the employer (*Scotch Premier Meat Ltd v Burns* [2000] IRLR 639). Significantly, the EAT held in the *Burns* case that where an employer had determined a plan of action which had two alternative scenarios only one of which necessarily included redundancies then this was capable of amounting to the employer 'proposing to dismiss' employees. It was, however, emphasised that this was essentially a question of fact for the employment tribunal to determine. In addition, a 'proposal' to dismiss does not necessarily have to be made by the person with power to carry out the dismissal (*Dewhirst Group v GMB Trade Union* [2003] All ER (D) 175 (Dec), EAT). For further consideration of what is meant by a 'proposed' dismissal, and for the application of *TULRCA 1992, s 188* where administrators have been appointed, see *Re Hartlebury Printers Ltd* [1993] 1 All ER 470, [1992] ICR 559, *R v British Coal Corpn, ex p Vardy* [1993] ICR 720 and *MSF v Refuge Assurance plc* [2002] IRLR 324. In *MSF* the EAT held that *s 188* did not have the same meaning as *Directive 75/129* (now, *Directive 98/59*), which requires consultation when collective redundancies are first 'contemplated'. 'Contemplation' means 'having a view', and refers to a relatively early stage in the decision-making process, whereas 'proposes' relates to a state of mind which is much more certain (see also *Scotch Premier Meat Ltd v Burns* [2000] IRLR 639 and *R v British Coal Corpn, ex p Vardy* [1993] ICR 720). More recently the EAT in *Unison v Leicestershire County Council* [2005] IRLR 920 approved the tribunal's finding that a 'proposal' meant 'something less than a decision that dismissals are to be made and more than a possibility that they might occur'. While not inconsistent with *Vardy* or *MSF*, this ruling suggests that an employer may "propose" to dismiss employees at an earlier stage of the decision-making process than previously understood. Of course, insofar as there is any difference between the requirements of the *Directive* and that of *TULRCA 1992*, employees of 'the State' may be able to rely directly on the *Directive* (cf *Griffin v South West Water Services Ltd* [1995] IRLR 15) (see 23.2 European Union Law; 37.7 Public Sector Employees).

In circumstances where decisions on collective redundancies are taken within a group of companies with a parent company and subsidiaries, the obligation to consult always lies with the subsidiary company which employs the workers, and never with the parent, irrespective of whether the decision in connection with collective redundancies is made by the parent or the subsidiary. Where the parent company makes decisions on redundancy across the group, consultation obligations are only triggered once the subsidiary in which collective redundancies would be made has been identified: see *Akavan Erityisalojen Keskusliitto AEK ry v Fujitsu Siemens Computers Oy*: C-44/08 [2010] ICR 444, CJEU.

Where a consultation is required, it must begin 'in good time', and in addition:

(a)   if an employer is proposing to dismiss *at least 100* employees at any one establishment within a period of 90 days or less, the consultation must begin at least 45 days before the first of the dismissals takes effect; and

(b)   in any other case in which consultation is required, consultation must begin at least 30 days before the first of the dismissals takes effect.

(*TULRCA 1992, s 188(1A)*, as substituted by *SI 1995/2587*, and as amended by *SI 2013/763* with effect from 6 April 2013.)

The phrase 'before the first of the dismissals takes effect' obviously refers to the proposed date of the first dismissal, not the actual date, otherwise the provisions would be unworkable (see *E Green & Son (Castings) Ltd v ASTMS* [1984] IRLR 135, following *GKN Sankey Ltd v National Society of Motor Mechanics* [1980] IRLR 8). On the basis of *Junk v Kühnel*: C-188/03 [2005] IRLR 310, consultation for the purposes of *Directive 98/59/EC* must be completed before notice of dismissal is given (see above). The EAT in *Unison v Leicestershire* [2005] IRLR 920 held that it was possible to read *TULRCA 1992 s 188(1)* consistently with EC law by construing the phrase "proposing to dismiss" as meaning "proposing to give notice of dismissal". The effect of this construction is that the full consultation must be completed before notices of dismissal are issued. Whether consultation has begun 'in good time' is a matter of fact and degree for the employment tribunal: see *UNISON v Leicestershire County Council* [2006] EWCA Civ 825, [2006] IRLR 810, CA.

The term 'establishment' for the purposes of *TULRCA 1992, s 188* is to be interpreted in line with its meaning in *Article 1(1)(a)* of *Directive 98/59*: see *MSF v Refuge Assurance plc* [2002] IRLR 324 and *Renfrewshire Council v Educational Institute of Scotland* [2013] IRLR 76.

The CJEU held in *Rockfon A/S v Specialarbejderforbundet i Danmark*: C-449/93 [1996] ICR 673 that the word 'establishment' under *Directive 75/129* (the predecessor to *Directive 98/59*) referred to the local employment unit, that is the unit to which the workers made redundant are assigned to carry out their duties. Thus, for example, the fact that a contract contains a mobility clause allowing the worker to be moved elsewhere is not relevant: see *Renfrewshire Council v Educational Institute of Scotland* [2013] ICR 172. Although the term 'establishment' connotes a distinct entity assigned to perform particular tasks, an 'establishment' need not have any legal, economic, or administrative autonomy, nor have a management that can independently effect collective redundancies, nor be geographically separate from other units of the undertaking in question: see *Athinaiki Chartopoiia AE v Panagiotidis*: C-270/05 [2007] IRLR 284, interpreting Directive 98/59.

The CJEU confirmed in *USDAW and Ethel Austin Ltd and ors* C-80/14 [2015] ICR 675 and in *Lyttle v Bluebird UK Bidco 2 Ltd* C-182/13 [2015] IRLR 577 that the interpretation of 'establishment' in the *Rockfon* case is correct; that the same interpretation applies wherever the term 'establishment' is used in Directive 98/59; and that the threshold test in *TULRCA 1992, s 188(1)* that proposed dismissals concern at least 20 employees at a single establishment is consistent with EU law. Thus, no reliance can be placed on the controversial decision of the EAT in *USDAW v Ethel Austin Ltd* [2013] ICR 1300 that the phrase 'in one establishment' in *TULRCA, s 188(1)* should effectively be ignored in order properly to reflect EU law.

For the purposes of the consultation, the employer must disclose in writing to the appropriate representatives:

(i)   the reasons for his proposals;

(ii)   the number and descriptions of employees whom it is proposed to dismiss as redundant;

(iii)   the total number of employees of any such description employed by the employer at the establishment in question;

(iv)   the proposed method of selecting the employees who may be dismissed;

(v)   the proposed method of carrying out the dismissals with due regard to any agreed procedure, including the period over which the dismissals are to take effect;

(vi)   the proposed method of calculating the amount of any redundancy payments otherwise than in compliance with a statutory obligation;

(vii)   the number of agency workers working temporarily for and under the supervision and direction of the employer,

(viii) the parts of the employer's undertaking in which those agency workers are working, and

(ix)   the type of work those agency workers are carrying out.

(TULRCA 1992, s 188(4).)

Where the employer has invited affected employees to elect representatives, but the affected employees fail to do so within a reasonable time, then the employer must give the requisite information to each affected employee individually (*TULRCA 1992, s 188(7B)*).

The information must be provided in proper form: it will not do to say that it may be gleaned from the surrounding circumstances and from a number of documents (*Sovereign Distribution Services Ltd v TGWU* [1990] ICR 31).

The consultation must include consultation about ways of avoiding the dismissals, reducing the number of employees to be dismissed and mitigating the consequences of the dismissals, and must be undertaken by the employer with a view to reaching agreement with the appropriate representatives (*TULRCA 1992, s 188(2)*). The fact that consultation must be undertaken with a view to reaching agreement means that it is tantamount to negotiation (*Junk v Kühnel*: C-188/03 [2005] IRLR 310). An employer must consult on all the matters set out in *TULRCA 1992, s 188(2)*, which are to be viewed disjunctively. Furthermore, it is not open to an employer to argue that consultation would, in the circumstances, be futile or useless (*Middlesbrough Borough Council v TGWU* [2002] IRLR 332).

Until relatively recently, the domestic courts held that *TULRCA 1992, s 188* did not require consultation about the reasons for the redundancy, including whether or not a plant should close (see *Vardy*, and two cases following *Vardy*: *Middlesbrough v TGWU* and *Securicor Omega Express Ltd v GMB* [2004] IRLR 9). However, the EAT took a different approach in *UK Coal Mining Ltd v National Union of Mineworkers (Northumberland Area)* [2008] ICR 163, [2008] IRLR 4. In the *UK Coal Mining* case, the Employment Appeal Tribunal observed that at the time *Vardy* was decided, *TULRCA 1992, s 188* required consultation only 'about the dismissal'. After amendments made in 1995, *TULRCA 1992, s 188* now required consultation over 'ways of avoiding dismissals'. This inevitably involved engaging with the reasons for dismissals. So, where dismissals were inextricably linked with the closure of a plant, a duty to consult over the closure would arise. The EAT in *UK Coal Mining* followed *Vardy* and *MSF* in holding that the wording 'proposing to dismiss' in *TULRCA 1992, s 188* connoted a more certain state of mind than the wording 'contemplating dismissals' in *Directive 98/59*. Nevertheless, the EAT indicated that this would not prevent the consultation obligation from extending to the closure of a plant: in a closure context where it is recognised that dismissals will inevitably, or almost inevitably, result from the closure, dismissals will be proposed at the point when closure itself is proposed.

The question whether the *Vardy* or *UK Coal* approach should be preferred is at present unclear. In *United States of America v Nolan (Christine)* [2011] IRLR 40, the Court of Appeal referred to the CJEU the issue whether *Directive 98/59* gives rise to consultation obligations when the employer is proposing, but has not yet made, a strategic business decision that will inevitably lead to redundancies; or whether it gives rise to consultation obligations only when such a strategic decision has actually been made, and the employer then proposes consequential redundancies. The Court of Appeal stated that it was referring the question because it was unclear from the CJEU's judgment in *Akavan Erityisalojen Keskusliitto Alek RY and others v Fujitsu Siemens Computers OY* C-44/08 [2009] IRLR 944 which approach was to be preferred. The Court also stated that *TULRCA 1992, s 188* was not intended to impose a wider consultation obligation than that contained in *Directive 98/59* (so that the proper approach to *TULRCA 1992, s 188* would be determined by the meaning of the *Directive*). The CJEU, however, declined to rule on the reference on the basis that *Directive 98/59* did not apply to workers employed by public administrative bodies or by establishments governed by public law, and this included civilian staff at a military base: *United States of America v Nolan* C-583/10 [2013] ICR 193 (Note that the Court of Appeal on remission from the CJEU, and the Supreme Court on appeal, have nevertheless held that *TULRCA 1992, s 188* should not be interpreted so as to mirror the exclusion of public administrative bodies from *Directive 98/59*: *United States of America v Nolan* [2014] EWCA Civ 71 [2014] ICR 685 CA, [2015] ICR 1347 SC.)

Specified employers may also be obliged to inform and consult appropriate representatives about economic decisions likely to lead to changes in work organisation or contractual relations under the *Information and Consultation of Employees Regulations 2004, SI 2004/3426.*

Failure to consult with the appropriate representatives, or to do so within the stipulated time when it was reasonably practicable to do so, may lead to the employer being held liable to pay each redundant employee a protective award (see **39.7** below). Such a failure is also likely to render the dismissals unfair (*Kelly v Upholstery and Cabinet Works (Amesbury) Ltd* [1977] IRLR 91; *North East Midlands Co-operative Society Ltd v Allen* [1977] IRLR 212; *Polkey v A E Dauton (or Dayton) Services Ltd* [1988] AC 344, [1988] ICR 142, HL; but cf *Hough*, above).

39.6 Election of employee representatives

If elections are held for employee representatives they must be held in accordance with the provisions of *TULRCA 1992, s 188A*. This provides that:

(a) the employer shall make such arrangements as are reasonably practical to ensure that the election is fair;

(b) the employer shall determine the number of representatives to be elected so that there are sufficient representatives to represent the interests of all the affected employees having regard to the number and classes of those employees;

(c) the employer shall determine whether the affected employees should be represented either by representatives of all the affected employees or by representatives of particular classes of those employees;

(d) before the election the employer shall determine the term of office as employee representatives so that it is of sufficient length to enable information to be given and consultations under this section to be completed;

(e) the candidates for election as employee representatives are affected employees on the date of the election;

(f) no affected employee is unreasonably excluded from standing for election;

(g) all affected employees on the date of the election are entitled to vote for employee representatives;

(h) the employees entitled to vote may vote for as many candidates as there are representatives to be elected to represent them or, if there are to be representatives for particular classes of employees, may vote for as many candidates as there are representatives to be elected to represent their particular class of employee; and

(i) the election is conducted so as to secure that:

(i) so far as is reasonably practicable, those voting do so in secret; and

(ii) the votes given at the election are accurately counted.

(*TULRCA 1992, s 188A(1)*.)

Further, if after an election held in accordance with this procedure, an elected representative ceases to act as a representative so that employees are no longer represented then they shall elect another representative by an election held in accordance with the requirements at (*a*), (*e*), (*f*) and (*i*) above (*TULRCA 1992, s 188A(2)*).

An employer is not necessarily obliged to hold a formal election if it simply accepts all candidates as appropriate representatives: *Phillips v Xtera Communications Ltd* [2012] ICR 171. An "election" for the purposes of *s 188A(1)* occurs when, pursuant to fair arrangements, the number of candidates matches the number of representatives to be elected, and no further candidates are proposed. In such circumstances, there is no need for a ballot or vote.

39.7 Pre-transfer consultation

With effect from 31 January 2014, the provisions of *TULRCA* were amended by the addition of new *ss 198A* and *198B*, permitting an employer to whom employees will, or are likely to, transfer under *TUPE* to engage in pre-transfer consultation with the representatives of those employees (see TRANSFER OF UNDERTAKINGS (52)).

Where there is to be, or is likely to be, a relevant transfer, and the transferee is proposing to dismiss as redundant 20 or more employees at one establishment within a period of 90 days or less, and the individuals who work for the transferor and who are to be (or are likely to be) transferred to the transferee's employment under the transfer include one or more individuals who may be affected by the proposed dismissals or by measures taken in connection with them, the transferee may elect to consult, or to start to consult, representatives of affected transferring individuals before the transfer takes place ("pre-transfer consultation"): *TULRCA 1992, s 198A(1)–(2)*. A "relevant transfer" is a transfer under *TUPE*, or any other transfer which by virtue of any enactment is either deemed to be a TUPE transfer, or is of the same or similar effect: see *TULRCA 1992, s 198A(7)*.

An election to engage in pre-transfer consultation may be made only if the transferor agrees to it, and must be made by way of written notice to the transferor: *TULRCA 1992, s 198A(3)*. On any complaint, if a question arises as to whether notice of an election has been given or agreed to by the transferor, it is for the transferee to show those matters: *TULRCA 1992, s 198B*.

If the transferee elects to carry out pre-transfer consultation, the consultation requirements in *TULRCA 1992, ss 188–198* apply from the time of the election as if the transferee were already the transferring individuals' employer, and as if any transferring individuals affected by the proposed dismissals were already employed at the relevant establishment: *TULRCA 1992, s 198A(4)*. The transferor is empowered to provide information or other assistance to help the transferee meet those consultation requirements. However, a failure on the part of the transferor to provide information or other assistance to the transferee does not constitute special circumstances rendering it not reasonably practicable for the transferee to comply with any consultation requirement: *TULRCA 1992, s 198B(1)(d)*.

A transferee who elects to carry out pre-transfer consultation may cancel that election at any time by written notice to the transferor. However, if he does so, nothing he has done prior to that cancelation is of any effect for the purposes of *TULRCA 1992, ss 188–198*, and he cannot make another election: *TULRCA 1992, ss 198A(5)–(6)*.

The appropriate representatives of transferring individuals for the purposes of *TULRCA 1992, s 188(1B)* are, where the transferor recognises an independent trade union, representatives of that union: *TULRCA 1992, s 198B(1)(a)*.

39.8 Protective award

If an employer fails to comply with any of the statutory requirements for consultation or fails to do so within the appropriate time, a complaint may be made to an employment tribunal by the trade union where the failure relates to trade union representatives, or by any of the affected employees or by any of the employees who have been dismissed as redundant where the failure relates to the election of employee representatives, or in the case of any other failure relating to employee representatives, by any of the employee representatives to whom the failure related and, in any other case, by any of the affected employees or by any of the employees who have been dismissed as redundant (*TULRCA 1992, s 189*).

A protective award is an award in respect of employees in respect of whose dismissal or proposed dismissal the employer has failed to comply with a requirement of *s 188*: *TULRCA 1992, s 189(3)*. So, for instance, it cannot cover employees whom the employer originally proposed to dismiss, but subsequently decided to keep on (whether as a result of consultation or otherwise). They may be employees whom it was originally proposed to dismiss, but they are not employees whom it "is proposed" to dismiss: see *Securicor Omega Express v GMB* [2004] IRLR 9.

A protective award can only be made in favour of those in respect of whom a complaint of breach has been proved by themselves or their representative. So, where a claim is made by a trade union, the protective award will benefit only those employees within the bargaining unit in respect of which the union is recognised: *TGWU v Brauer Coley Ltd (in administration)* [2007] IRLR 207. Similarly, where a claim is made by an individual employee, the employment tribunal can only make an award in the individual claimant's favour, and cannot make an award that benefits other redundant employees: *Independent Insurance Company Ltd v Aspinall* [2011] IRLR 716. Note also that an individual employee who is not an employee representative cannot bring a claim in respect of a failure relating to employee representatives (other than a failure relating to the election of representatives): see *Northgate HR Ltd v Mercy* [2007] EWCA Civ 1304, [2008] ICR 410, [2008] IRLR 222.

If a question is raised on any such complaint as to whether or not any employee representative was an appropriate representative for the purposes of *s 188*, the burden of proof will be on the employer to show that the employee representative had the authority to represent the affected employees (*TULRCA 1992, s 189(1A)*). Also, where the alleged failure relates to the election of employee representatives, the burden will be on the employer to show that the statutory election procedure in *s 188A* has been complied with.

The complaint must be presented before the date on which the last of the dismissals to which the complaint relates takes effect, or during the period of three months beginning with that date, or within such further period as the tribunal considers reasonable in a case where it is satisfied that it was not reasonably practicable for the complaint to be presented during the period of three months (*TULRCA 1992, s 189(5)*; and see **18.20** EMPLOYMENT TRIBUNALS – I).

It is a defence to such an application for an employer to show that there were special circumstances which rendered it not reasonably practicable for him to comply with the requirements, and that he took all such steps as were reasonably practicable in those circumstances (*TULRCA 1992, s 188(7)*). For example, an unforeseen financial crisis may make it necessary to close down a plant at short notice so that consultations can only take place during a shorter period than that prescribed by law. The test focuses upon the actual events that occurred, and not upon what an employer might have thought about consultation if it had addressed its mind to the question at the relevant time: see *E Ivor Hughes Educational Foundation v Morris* [2015] IRLR 696.

In *Clarks of Hove Ltd v Bakers' Union* [1979] 1 All ER 152, [1978] 1 WLR 1207, [1978] ICR 1076, the Court of Appeal held that insolvency is not on its own a special circumstance and that it depends entirely on the course of the insolvency whether the circumstances can be described as special or not. (See also *Angus Jowett & Co Ltd v National Union of Tailors and Garment Workers* [1985] ICR 646, [1985] IRLR 326, EAT; *Re Hartlebury Printers Ltd* [1993] 1 All ER 470, [1992] ICR 559.) The employer may not neglect his duty under *TULRCA 1992, s 188* merely because he considers that consultation will achieve nothing (*Sovereign Distribution Services Ltd v TGWU* [1990] ICR 31).

Section 188(7) precludes the employer from relying upon a failure to provide information by the person whose decision led to the proposed dismissals if that person directly or indirectly controls the employer. The meaning of this provision was considered in *GMB and Amicus v Beloit Walmsley Ltd* [2004] IRLR 18. The EAT determined that: (i) the mischief at which this provision is aimed is a controlling entity's delay in providing the employer with information. Any period of delay in providing information must therefore count against the employer, for the purposes of determining whether or not the duty under *TULRCA 1992, s 188* could have been complied with; (ii) there must be a causal link between the decision, and the proposed dismissals. However, it is not necessary that the person making the decision contemplates any particular number of dismissals, at any particular establishment; (iii) the 'information', required to be provided by *TULRCA s 188(7)*, is not confined to the 'information' required to be disclosed by *TULRCA s 188(4)*. It includes information necessary to begin the process of consultation.

An employer would appear to escape its information and consultation obligations under *s 188* if he invites any affected employees to elect representatives and has given enough time to allow for an election but such election is not organised (*TULRCA 1992, s 188(7A)*; and see *R v Secretary of State for Trade and Industry, ex p UNISON* [1996] IRLR 438).

Where a tribunal finds the complaint well-founded it makes a declaration to that effect and may also make a protective award (*TULRCA 1992, s 189(2)*). A protective award is an order that an employer make payments for the protected period in respect of specified employees who have been dismissed, or whom it is proposed to dismiss, as redundant without complying with the statutory requirements for consultation. The length of the period will be what is considered to be just and equitable by the tribunal in the circumstances having regard to the seriousness of the employer's default and will be up to 90 days, beginning on the date on which the first of the dismissals to which the complaint relates was proposed to take effect, or the date of the award, whichever is the earlier (*TULRCA 1992, s 189(4)*). See *Transport and General Workers' Union v Ledbury Preserves (1928) Ltd* [1986] ICR 855; *E Green & Son (Castings) Ltd v Association of Scientific, Technical and Managerial Staffs* [1984] ICR 352. The purpose of the award is to provide a sanction for breach by the employer of the obligations in *TULRCA s 188*, not to compensate employees for any loss suffered: hence the futility of consultation is not relevant to the making of a protective award (*GMB v Susie Radin Ltd* [2004] EWCA Civ 180, [2004] 2 All ER 279, [2004] ICR 893, reversing *Spillers-French (Holdings) Ltd v USDAW* [1980] 1 All ER 231, [1980] ICR 31, [1979] IRLR 339). Nor is the employer's insolvency relevant to the size of any protective award: the employment tribunal should focus simply upon the seriousness of the employer's default in failing to comply with its statutory duty (*Smith v Cherry Lewis Ltd* [2005] IRLR 86). In the *Susie Radin* case, the Court of Appeal stated that how the length of the protected period is assessed is a matter for the tribunal, but a proper approach in a case where there has been no consultation is to start with the maximum period and reduce it only if there are mitigating circumstances justifying a reduction. Mitigating circumstances may, however, include any steps taken by the employer before proposals have crystallised in relation to keeping employees informed or consulted, even if there has been no consultation under *TULRCA s 188* itself (*AMICUS v GBS Tooling Ltd (in administration)* [2005] IRLR 683). A union's obstructive approach to statutory consultation may also be taken into account when assessing the correct level of a protective award: see *GMB v Lambeth Service Team; TGWU v Lambeth Service Team* [2005] All ER (D) 153 (Jul), EAT. Furthermore, when assessing the seriousness of the default, it is relevant to consider both the culpability of the employer and the harm or potential for harm of the default: see *Shanahan Engineering Ltd v Unite the Union* UKEAT/0411/09. There is no connection between the length of the statutory consultation period, and the length of the protective award. Even if the employer proposed to dismiss fewer than 100 employees, so that the minimum consultation period was 30 days before the first dismissal took effect, the proper protective award for a complete failure to consult is 90 days: see *Hutchins v Permacell Finesse Ltd (In Administration)* [2008] All ER (D) 112 (Jan).

Where a tribunal has made a protective award, every employee to whom it relates is entitled to be paid remuneration by the employer for the protected period at the rate of a week's pay (see PAY – I (34)) for each week of the period (*TULRCA 1992, s 190(1), (2), (5)*). There is no upper limit on the amount of a week's pay for this purpose.

If an employee, specified in the award, receives payments under his contract of employment during the protected period, those payments do not go to discharge his employer's liability under the protective award, nor vice versa: see *Cranswick Country Foods plc v Beall* [2007] ICR 691.

Liability for protective awards will transfer as a result of a transfer of an undertaking under the *Transfer of Undertakings (Protection of Employment) Regulations 2006 (SI 2006/246)* (*Alamo Group (Europe) Ltd v Tucker* [2003] ICR 829, following *Kerry Foods Ltd v Creber* [2000] ICR 556 and not following *TGWU v McKinnon* [2001] ICR 1281 – see also TRANSFER OF UNDERTAKINGS (52)).

Disallowance of payment under award. If an employee remains employed during a protected period and:

(i)   he is fairly dismissed by his employer for a reason other than redundancy;

(ii)   he unreasonably terminates the contract of employment; or

(iii)   he unreasonably refuses an offer of suitable alternative employment made to take effect before or during the protected period,

he will not be entitled to payment under the protective award in respect of any period during which he would have been employed but for the dismissal, termination or refusal of employment (*TULRCA 1992, s 191(1)–(3)*). If the offer of alternative employment embodies terms which differ from those under which he previously worked, the employee has a trial period of four weeks beginning with the commencement date of the new contract (or by agreement in writing, a longer period) (*TULRCA 1992, s 191(4)–(6)*; see also **38.6** REDUNDANCY – I). If during the trial period, the employment is terminated by the employer for a reason connected with the change to the new or renewed employment, or by the employee, the employee remains entitled to his protective award unless he acted unreasonably in terminating or giving notice to terminate the contract (*TULRCA 1992, s 191(7)*).

Remedy for non-payment of award. If an employer fails to pay a protective award, the employee concerned may present a complaint to an employment tribunal which will order the employer to make the payment (*TULRCA 1992, s 192(1), (3)*). The time limit for the presentation of a complaint by an individual employee for failure to pay a protective award is three months from the day or last day of the failure to make the payment, or such further period as the tribunal considers reasonable in a case where it is satisfied that it was not reasonably practicable for the complaint to be presented within the period of three months (*TULRCA 1992, s 192(2)*; and see **18.20** EMPLOYMENT TRIBUNALS – I).

The Employment Appeal Tribunal held in *Howlett Marine Services Ltd v Bowlam* [2001] IRLR 201 that the three months' time limit for bringing a complaint in respect of non-payment of a protective award under *TULRCA 1992, s 192(2)* runs from the last day of the protected period. Moreover, this remains the case even when the protective award was made by a tribunal well after the expiry of the protective period. However, the EAT held in *Howlett* that in these circumstances it would obviously not have been 'reasonably practicable' to present a complaint within the three months' time limit so that the tribunal would still have jurisdiction to hear it provided that it was presented in such further period of time as was reasonable.

39.9   NOTIFICATIONS TO THE DEPARTMENT FOR BUSINESS, INNOVATION AND SKILLS

An employer must send written notification of certain redundancies to the Redundancy Payments Service, (an executive agency of the Department for Business, Innovation and Skills, 'BIS'). If he proposes to make 100 or more employees redundant at one establishment within a period of 90 days or less, the employer must notify the Secretary of State in writing at least 45 days before giving notice to terminate an employee's contract in respect of any of those dismissals (*TULRCA 1992, s 193(1)*). If he proposes to make 20 or more employees redundant at one establishment within a period of 90 days or less, the employer must give at least 30 days' notice (*TULRCA 1992, s 193(2)*).

The notice must be in a prescribed form and sent to the specified office. The applicable form (Form HR1) is available on the government's website. If consultation with appropriate representatives is required, the representatives concerned must be identified and the date when consultations began must be stated (*TULRCA 1992, s 193(4)*). Where consultation with appropriate representatives is required, he must give a copy of the notice to those representatives (*TULRCA 1992, s 193(6)*). If there are special circumstances which make it impossible for the employer to comply with any of the requirements of notifying BIS or the representatives concerned, he must take such steps to comply as are reasonably practicable in the circumstances (*TULRCA 1992, s 193(7)*). Ignorance of the statutory obligation to notify BIS cannot constitute such special circumstances (*Secretary of State for Employment v Helitron Ltd* [1980] ICR 523); see also **39.8** above.

In *Vauxhall Motors Ltd v TGWU* [2006] IRLR 674, the employer sent written notification of proposed redundancies twice in respect of a single redundancy exercise, because the length over which redundancy proposals were considered (approximately two years) meant that the first notification had expired. The union argued that following the second notification, fresh consultation should have occurred under *TULRCA 1992, s 188*. The EAT disagreed, stating that the lodging of notification was immaterial to the question of whether the employers were in breach of *TULRCA 1992*.

Failure to notify BIS may lead to a conviction and fine of up to level 5 on the Standard Scale in a magistrates' court (*TULRCA 1992, s 194(1);* and see **1.10** INTRODUCTION).

(The cap of £5,000 on fines at level 5 was removed in March 2015 by *Legal Aid, Sentencing and Punishment of Offenders Act 2012, s 85*, so that a fine under *TULRCA 1992, s 194(1)* may in principle be of an unlimited amount.)

39.10   FAIRNESS OF THE DISMISSAL

Where redundancy is the reason for a dismissal the employer will be liable in a claim for unfair dismissal in addition to the redundancy payment if he fails to act fairly. The principles governing the fairness of dismissals for redundancy are set out in full in UNFAIR DISMISSAL – II **(54)**, and in particular in **54.11**. The main points to bear in mind are that the dismissal may either be automatically unfair, or unfair because the employer has failed to act reasonably in all the circumstances.

Automatic unfairness arises, subject to certain exceptions, where an employee is selected for an inadmissible reason. Circumstances where the employer may be held to have acted unreasonably include where he has failed to consult the trade unions or individuals involved (his obligations in this respect may go beyond the express statutory obligations dealt with in **39.4** above), where selection criteria are inadequate or have been improperly applied, or where inadequate efforts have been made to find alternative employment for those whose jobs have disappeared.

39.11 CHECKLIST OF REDUNDANCY DISMISSAL PROCEDURE

In practical terms, the first step in the redundancy dismissal procedure is the business decision on the necessity of making one or more employees redundant. Thereafter the following actions should be considered and undertaken as necessary.

(a)   *Preliminary procedure* (not necessarily in chronological order)

    (i)   Where the proposal is to issue notices of dismissal for redundancy to at least 20 employees at an establishment within 90 days or less, consult with the appropriate representatives of the employees concerned within the appropriate time limits on the measures to be taken which are set out below. Provide them with all necessary information. (Provide each affected employee with the necessary information where the affected employees fail to elect representatives within a reasonable time.)

    (ii)   Decide on the number of employees to be made redundant.

    (iii)   Invite volunteers for redundancy.

    (iv)   Consider whether alternative jobs are available within the organisation or group. If it should be necessary to retrain employees for those jobs, consider the practicability of doing this.

    (v)   Select employees to be made redundant in accordance with any customary arrangement or agreed procedure. If no such arrangement or procedure exists, establish, if possible with the agreement of the relevant unions or employee representatives, objective criteria for selection, and apply them.

    (vi)   Consult with individuals affected before a final decision is taken.

    (vii)   Inform those employees as soon as possible of their impending redundancies.

    (viii)   Allow them time off to look for other employment.

    (ix)   Notify BIS of impending redundancies within the appropriate time limits.

(b)   *Dismissal notices* (taking due note of the time limits – see below)

NB Consultations must be completed before notices of dismissal are sent out.

Time limits. The date on which the dismissal is to take effect should be fixed having regard to the obligations of the employer as regards notice (see TERMINATION OF EMPLOYMENT (48)) and with an eye on the following time limits.

For step (*a*)(i):

(A)	'in good time'	in all cases in which consultation is required and in any event:
(B)	45 days before first notice of dismissal	100+ employees in one establishment to be dismissed within 90 days
(C)	30 days before first notice of dismissal	20–99 employees in one establishment to be dismissed within 90 days

For step (*a*)(ix), as (B) and (C) for step *(a)*(i) above.

40   References

40.1   An employer may be requested to provide a general reference or specific details about an employee or ex-employee. The request may come from the employee, a prospective employer or any other person interested in obtaining such information. (For example, the employee may need a reference in order to obtain a mortgage or a lease of residential premises.) The request may be for a reference to be given over the telephone, but more usually it will be for a written document. In certain sectors, in particular financial services, detailed regulatory requirements in respect of giving and obtaining references on certain types of employees apply.

40.2   THE EMPLOYER'S OBLIGATION

An employer is not obliged to provide such a reference, regardless of whether the employee was dismissed: see for example *Ros and Angel v Fanstone* [2007] UKEAT/0372/07 (unreported). As one of the terms of settlement of a claim or a potential claim before an employment tribunal, an employer may agree to provide a reference, and he will then be bound to do so, assuming the agreement to be enforceable (see **40.8** below).

40.3   CONTENTS

If the enquiry for a reference poses certain questions, then clearly those issues should be dealt with. If, however, the request is a general one, for example, from a prospective employer, the following matters will commonly be dealt with.

(a)   Length of service.

(b)   Positions held.

(c)   Competence in the job.

(d)   Honesty.

(e)   Time-keeping.

(f)   Reason for leaving.

(g)   Any other particular remarks about the employee, such as long periods of absence due to sickness.

(h)   Any relevant remarks of a more personal nature about the employee.

For references relating to a certain level of employee, some employers complete a form dealing with these matters. However, for a more senior employee such a form may give an inadequate picture and a full letter may be more appropriate.

40.4   EMPLOYER'S LIABILITIES

To the employee

References given by one employer to a prospective employer may not be made the grounds for a libel action by the employee even if the information given proves to be inaccurate, provided that the employer believes the information to be correct and gives it without malice. This is because the employer (or ex-employer) and the prospective employer have a common interest in the statement made about the employee, and the statement is protected by what is known as 'qualified privilege'. As Lord Ellenborough CJ said in 1818: 'In the case of master and servant, the convenience of mankind required that what is said in fair communication between man and man, upon the subject of character, should be privileged, if made *bona fide* and without malice. If, however, the party giving the character knows what he says to be untrue, that may deprive him of the protection which the law throws around such communications' (*Hodgson v Scarlett* (1818) 1 B & Ald 232; see also *Sutherland v British Telecommunications plc* (1989) Times, 30 January). The defence of qualified privilege may, however, be lost if the statement is not merely passed between people having a mutuality of interest in the subject matter but falls into the hands of a third person. Thus, all references should be carefully marked 'private and confidential'.

In *Spring v Guardian Assurance plc* [1994] ICR 596, the House of Lords (Lord Keith dissenting) held that an employer owes a duty of care to an employee about whom he writes a reference. The employer's duty is to take reasonable care in the preparation of the reference, and he will be liable to the employee in negligence if he fails to do so and the employee thereby suffers damage.

The obligation on the employer is to provide a true, accurate and fair reference. The reference must not give a misleading impression. However, as long as the reference is accurate and does not tend to mislead, there is no obligation on the employer to set great detail or to be comprehensive. In *Bartholomew v London Borough of Hackney* [1999] IRLR 246, the employer stated that the employee had been suspended and was subject to disciplinary action, which action ceased upon an agreed termination of the employee's employment. The employee complained that a reference was negligent because it failed to say that he strongly disputed the charges. The reference was held not to be negligent. It was accurate and fair and did not cease to be so simply because it did not recite chapter and verse.

In *Kidd v Axa Equity and Law Life Assurance Society plc* [2000] IRLR 301, the High Court held that the duty of care on an employer did not require the employer to provide a reference which was fair, full and comprehensive. The duty is to take reasonable care. That means not giving misleading information whether by selective provision of information or by the inclusion of information in a manner that would lead a reasonable recipient to draw a false or mistaken inference. However, there is no duty to give a full or comprehensive reference, nor to refer to all material facts. See also *Byrnell v British Telecommunications Plc* [2009] EWHC 727 (QB), where the High Court rejected an argument that a purely factual reference (referring only to dates of employment and the former employee's role) was so inadequate as to constitute no "reference" at all.

Subsequent to *Bartholomew*, the Court of Appeal has further considered the requirements of accuracy and fairness in a reference for an employee who has resigned while under investigation, so that the investigation was never completed: *Cox v Sun Alliance Life Ltd* [2001] EWCA Civ 649, [2001] IRLR 448. In *Cox*, the employer provided an inaccurate and unfair reference, suggesting that it would have had a reasonable basis for dismissing the employee on the grounds of dishonesty amounting to corruption. Mummery LJ drew an analogy between the principle to be applied and the proper approach of a tribunal to dismissal for misconduct, as set out in *British Home Stores Ltd v Burchell* [1978] IRLR 379. If an employee is to be fairly dismissed for misconduct, the employer must genuinely believe in the employee's guilt, must have reasonable grounds for that belief, and must have carried out a reasonable investigation. The same principles will render negligent a reference that alludes to an employee's misconduct, when the employer has not carried out an investigation, and does not have reasonable grounds for believing in his misconduct.

On this latter issue, see *Jackson v Liverpool* [2011] IRLR 1009. The ex-employer had provided a partial reference, in that it had not answered two of the questions posed by the prospective new employer. The ex-employer had a telephone conversation with the prospective new employer in which he explained that there were certain unresolved allegations concerning discrepancies in the ex-employee's record-keeping, but had made it clear that these were only allegations. Contrary to the finding of the first-instance judge, the Court of Appeal held that the ex-employer had not behaved unfairly or otherwise negligently.

In order to succeed in an action based on an allegedly negligent reference, a claimant will have to show first that the information contained in the reference is misleading, second, that it would be likely to have a material effect on a reasonable recipient and, third, that the defendant was negligent in compiling the reference. In *Bullimore v Pothecary Witham Weld Solicitors* (UKEAT/0189/10/JOJ) [2011] IRLR 18, an employer gave a former employee an unfairly adverse reference which led to the withdrawal of a subsequent offer of employment. The EAT held that the employee's loss was not too remote from the employer's actions, and the employee could recover for loss of earnings and injury to feelings. Compare this with *Brown v Baxter (T/A Careham Hall)* UKEAT/0354/09/SM (7 July 2010, unreported), where it was found that the employer would have given an unfavourable reference even if it had not dismissed the employee. The unfavourable reference therefore was not "a consequence" of the dismissal, and should not have been reflected in the damages awarded to the employee. The employee sought to rely on the "stigma damages" principle arising from *Chagger v Abbey National plc* [2009] EWCA Civ 1202, [2010] ICR 397, [2010] IRLR 47 (see CONTRACTS OF EMPLOYMENT (8)), but this was dismissed as irrelevant: the usual principles of causation applied.

In *McKie v Swindon College* [2011] IRLR 575, the High Court extended the principle established in *Spring* to hold that a former employer could be liable to a former employee in damages for negligent misstatement where it had sent an e-mail about him to a subsequent employer which resulted in his dismissal.

The EAT has held that the implied term of trust and confidence in a contract of employment requires the employer to provide a reference that is 'fair and reasonable'. If the employer fails to do so, the employee may resign and claim constructive dismissal (see *TSB Bank plc v Harris* [2000] IRLR 157). However, that case was decided prior to *Kidd*, and *Bartholomew* was not referred to.

A former employee who is refused a reference or given a bad reference because he or she had made a complaint of discrimination or done some other protected act under the *Equality Act 2010* would be entitled to sue for victimisation provided that the claim arose out of the incidents of the employment relationship or was sufficiently proximate to the employment or that there was a substantive connection between the complaint and the employment. This entitlement was first recognised in the context of sex discrimination law by the decision of the European Court of Justice in *Coote v Granada Hospitality Ltd: C-185/97* [1999] ICR 100. It was there held that an employer who refused to provide a reference to an ex-employee on the grounds that the employee had brought legal proceedings to enforce the right to equal treatment of men and women would be liable for victimisation. At the time of this decision the position under domestic law was that the discrimination legislation only applied to events occurring during employment and not afterwards: *Adekeye v Post Office (No 2)* [1997] IRLR 105. The EAT has held that the *Sex Discrimination Act 1975* ('*SDA 1975*') can be construed consistently with this decision (*Coote v Granada Hospitality Ltd (No 2)* [1999] IRLR 452). More recently the House of Lords has overturned *Adekeye* and held that the protection afforded to employees by the discrimination legislation is not coterminous with the existence of a contractual relationship. Therefore claims may be brought by former employees so long as there is a substantive connection between the discriminatory conduct

40.4 References

alleged and the employment relationship, whenever the discriminatory conduct arises: *Relaxion Group plc v Rhys-Harper* [2003] UKHL 33, [2003] 4 All ER 1113. See also *Metropolitan Police Service v Shoebridge* UKEAT/0234/03.

An employee who was refused a reference after employment had ended or who was provided with a poor reference because he had made a protected disclosure under *Part IVA* of the Employment Rights Act 1996 (see DISCLOSURE OF INFORMATION (10)) would be able to allege that that the failure to provide the reference to or the content of it involved the employee being subjected to a detriment on the ground that the employee had made a protected disclosure, contrary to *s 47B*: *Woodward v Abbey National plc* [2006] IRLR 677, CA.

In *Pnaiser v NHS England* [2016] IRLR 170, the EAT held that giving a negative reference in connection with absence arsing from disability could constitute an unlawful act of discrimination.

40.5 To the recipient

The recipient of a negligent reference may also be able to sue the person giving the reference for any loss suffered. It is reasonably foreseeable that the recipient of a reference will act on its contents and if he relies on a reference which is inaccurate because it was carelessly drawn up and thereby suffers loss, the giver of the reference may be held liable to pay the recipient damages on account of his negligence (cf *Hedley Byrne & Co Ltd v Heller & Partners Ltd* [1964] AC 465).

There is no sure way of avoiding the possibility of liability for negligent mis-statements in references since the *Unfair Contract Terms Act 1977* ('*UCTA 1977*'). Disclaimers such as 'The above information is given in confidence and in good faith. No responsibility, however, can be accepted for any errors, omissions or inaccuracies in the information or for any loss or damage that may result from reliance being placed upon it' may have been effective to exclude liability before the *UCTA 1977* came into force, but now such a disclaimer will only be effective insofar as it 'satisfies the requirement of reasonableness' (*UCTA 1977, s 2(2)*). The 'explanatory provisions' of the *Act* state that such a notice of disclaimer will satisfy this requirement of reasonableness where it is 'fair and reasonable to allow reliance upon it, having regard to all the circumstances obtaining when the liability arose or (but for the notice) would have arisen' (*UCTA 1977, s 11(3)*). If the reference purports to give facts which are ordinarily within the knowledge of an employer, it is thought that liability cannot now be excluded for negligent mis-statement of those facts. If, however, it contains an opinion as to the employee's suitability for a certain post which he has not filled in the past, it may be considered reasonable to insert a disclaimer for such a statement of opinion.

40.6 Data Protection Act 1998

If information about an employee is stored on a computer, the provisions of the *Data Protection Act 1998* must be complied with (see **10.13** *et seq* DISCLOSURE OF INFORMATION).

40.7 LIABILITY OF PERSONS OTHER THAN THE EMPLOYER

It is frequently the case that employment will be dependent on a satisfactory medical report being presented to the prospective employer. In *Kapfunde v Abbey National plc and Daniel* [1998] IRLR 583, the claimant was refused employment on the basis of a medical report. She sought to sue the author of the report alleging that it was negligent. The Court of Appeal dismissed the claim holding that a medical practitioner who compiles a report about a prospective employee does not owe a duty of care to the prospective employee. There is insufficient proximity between the author of the report and the prospective employee. It may well be, however, that the medical practitioner owes a duty of care to the prospective employer.

40.8   REFERENCES AND EMPLOYMENT PROTECTION RIGHTS

Although employees do not have a statutory right to a reference, references may affect proceedings in employment tribunals. A good reference may be powerful evidence against an employer who tries to justify the dismissal of an employee on grounds of misconduct or incompetence. Similarly, a reference which is inconsistent with written reasons for a dismissal supplied to an employee may be persuasive in enabling the employee to show that those written reasons were inadequate or untrue, thus entitling him to an award under *ERA 1996, s 93* (see **48.15** TERMINATION OF EMPLOYMENT).

A reference may sometimes be used to compromise a claim for unfair dismissal. If a reference is given in such circumstances, care should be taken to ensure that the reference is accurate and complete and the compromise reached with the assistance of a conciliation officer (see **2.4** ADVISORY, CONCILIATION AND ARBITRATION SERVICE).

40.9   EMPLOYMENT CONDITIONAL UPON REFERENCES

Sometimes, a contract of employment may be offered 'subject to satisfactory references'. In *Wishart v National Association of Citizens' Advice Bureaux Ltd* [1990] ICR 794, the Court of Appeal was strongly of the opinion that such a provision was satisfied only if the references supplied were subjectively satisfactory to that particular employer. However, it recognised that it was arguable that the requirement was an objective one.

41   Restraint of Trade and Confidential Information

41.1   INTRODUCTION

Considerations of restraint of trade operate in employment law in two distinct ways: first, there is the common law doctrine of restraint of trade comprising a body of rules under which certain contractual restraints must be justified before the court will enforce them. Secondly, a court will have regard to the impact of restraints on trade in any form in situations where the common law doctrine does not apply, or cannot be applied in accordance with its rules, as a factor influencing its discretion to grant or withhold the remedy of an injunction and in framing the terms of any injunction granted. The latter operation of what may be called 'considerations' of restraint of trade is seen most clearly in so-called 'garden leave' and 'springboard' injunction cases. Confusion between restraint of trade as a narrow doctrine of the law of contract and as a factor in the exercise of judicial discretion as to whether or not to grant an injunction, has led to considerable confusion in the law and, on occasion, to judicial error: see *J A Mont (UK) Ltd v Mills* [1993] IRLR 172. That confusion still persists: see *Tullett Prebon plc v BGC Brokers LP* [2010] IRLR 648 and *JM Finn & Co Ltd v Holliday* [2014] IRLR 102.

Obligations of confidentiality that arise in the employment situation are also apt to cause confusion and, again, a clear distinction must be drawn between those obligations which underpin, in part, the doctrine of restraint of trade and those which give rise to relief and remedies which lie outside that doctrine altogether.

It is impossible in a work of this nature to do more than briefly sketch the main principles of these large and partially interlocking fields of law which apply specifically to the employment relationship. Hence we do not deal in this chapter with restraint of trade principles as they apply to business sale agreements, shareholder agreements or partnerships, etc, even where there may be partial overlaps of principle. It should, however, be noted that the statutory regulation of competition in the United Kingdom has recently undergone major changes to bring it into line with European models: see *Competition Act 1998* and *Enterprise Act 2002*. These reforms affect the common law doctrine of restraint of trade and, in certain circumstances, displace it altogether: see *Days Medical Aids Ltd v Pihsiang Machinery Manufacturing Co Ltd* [2004] EWHC 44 (Comm), [2004] 1 All ER (Comm) 991. The domestic statutory controls, over restraints ancillary to mergers and acquisitions of businesses, however, apply to individuals only if they may be treated as 'undertakings', i.e. if they have a controlling interest in the business merged or acquired. The vast majority of employees will not, therefore, fall within the provisions of *Part I* of the *Competition Act 1998* or *Art 101* of the *Lisbon Treaty*. For this reason, we do not attempt a review of competition law in this chapter. However, although the principles of competition law do not apply directly to most employees, they may have an indirect impact in shaping public policy, from which the common law doctrine itself springs (see further below **41.5**).

Proceedings in relation to the enforcement or breach of covenants in restraint of trade must in almost all cases be brought in the ordinary courts, and not in the employment tribunals. This is because most disputes in relation to the enforcement or breach of such covenants will fall outside the jurisdiction of the employment tribunals, since any claim in respect of such a covenant will not (as a general rule) be one that 'arises or is outstanding' on the termination of the employee's employment so as to bring it within the scope of the *Employment Tribunals Extension of Jurisdiction (England and Wales) Order 1994*. (This Order extended the jurisdiction of the employment tribunals so as to encompass breach of contract claims by employees and, where the employee has brought such a claim, counterclaims for breach of contract by the employer: see *Peninsula Business Services Ltd v Sweeney* [2004]

IRLR 49 and generally **8.22c** and **8.22d** Contract of Employment). Further, the employment tribunals' contractual jurisdiction (as set out in the *Extension of Jurisdiction Order*) only extends to the power to award damages for breach of contract: the employment tribunals have no power to issue injunctions, which is the usual remedy sought by the claimant in restraint of trade cases (see below **41.16**).

There have been a handful of cases in which the question of the enforceability of covenants in restraint of trade has been raised as part of a claim falling within the jurisdiction of the employment tribunals, for example where an employee's refusal to sign up to covenants in restraint of trade is relied on by an employer as a reason for dismissing an employee, or where sums deducted pursuant to a covenant in restraint of trade are claimed as an unlawful deduction from wages. However, the Court of Appeal has now confirmed that, in both those situations, the employment tribunal need not determine whether or not the covenant in question is reasonable and enforceable. Thus in *Willow Oak Developments Ltd (t/a Windsor Recruitment) v Silverwood* [2006] EWCA Civ 660, [2006] IRLR 607 the Court of Appeal confirmed previous authority to the effect that a refusal on the part of an employee to sign up to new terms and conditions of employment that included covenants in restraint of trade was capable (whether or not the restraints were reasonable) of being a potentially fair reason for dismissing an employee. However, the Court of Appeal observed that the reasonableness (or otherwise) of the restraints was a (non-determinative) factor which the employment tribunal could take into account when determining whether or not it was in fact fair to dismiss the employee for that reason under *ERA 1996, s 98(4)* (see generally **54.14** Unfair Dismissal – II). The Court of Appeal disapproved the earlier decision of the EAT in *Forshaw v Archcraft Ltd* [2006] ICR 60 in which it was held that, if the new term sought to be imposed by the employer was in fact an unreasonable restraint of trade, then an employee dismissed for failing to sign up to that term had been unfairly dismissed. As to unlawful deductions from wages claims under *s 23* of the *Employment Rights Act 1996*, the EAT in *Peninsula Business Services* (above) confirmed that deductions pursuant to clauses in restraint of trade are to be treated in the same way as deductions pursuant to any other clause in the employee's contract: provided the covenant is set out in writing, and the employee has agreed to it in writing, the employer will have a defence to any such claim in the employment tribunal. The employee's remedy in such circumstances lies in a claim for breach of contract in the ordinary courts: see generally Pay – I: Payments, Pay Statements and Miscellaneous Statutory Pay Rights (34).

We propose to review first the law in relation to the common law doctrine of restraint of trade (below **41.2**), then to review confidential information (below **41.13**) and to consider restraint of trade as a discretionary element in granting injunctive relief outside of the narrow common-law doctrine of restraint of trade (including so-called 'garden leave' and 'springboard' injunctions) (below **41.14, 41.15**). Finally, we consider procedural issues and remedies (below **41.16**).

41.2 THE COMMON LAW DOCTRINE OF RESTRAINT OF TRADE

Although of ancient origin the doctrine in its modern form may be traced to the speech of Lord McNaghten in *Nordenfelt v Maxim Nordenfelt Guns and Ammunition Co Ltd* [1894] AC 535, 565:

> 'All interference with individual liberty of action in trading, and all restraints of trade of themselves, if there is nothing more, are contrary to public policy, and therefore void. That is the general rule. But there are exceptions: restraints of trade and interference with individual liberty of action may be justified by the special circumstances of a particular case. It is a sufficient justification, and indeed it is the only justification, if the restriction is reasonable – reasonable, that is, in reference to the interests of the parties concerned and reasonable in reference to the interests of

the public, so framed and so guarded as to afford adequate protection to the party in whose favour it is imposed, while at the same time it is in no way injurious to the public.'

It follows that in applying the common law doctrine of restraint of trade it is necessary to consider the following fundamental issues:

(1)   what restraints of trade are covered by the doctrine?

(2)   what are the legitimate interests of the parties?

(3)   is the restraint injurious to the public interest?

41.3   What restraints are covered?

A very large number of contracts or contractual provisions will impose some limits on a person's freedom to trade (for example, a contract to sell specific goods or a lease of a property prohibiting the use of the premises for business purposes). Such contracts or provisions are not subject to the restraint of trade doctrine: see *Esso Petroleum Co Ltd v Harper's Garage* [1968] AC 269.

Various tests have been propounded to identify restraints which do, or do not, fall within the doctrine. The best of these tests, it is submitted, is contained in the speech of Lord Pearce in the *Esso* case:

'The doctrine does not apply to ordinary commercial contracts for the regulation and promotion of trade during the existence of the contract, provided that any prevention of work outside the contract, viewed as a whole, is directed towards the absorption of the parties' services and not their sterilisation. Sole agencies are a normal and necessary incident of commerce and those who desire the benefits of a sole agency must deny themselves the opportunities of other agencies. So, too, in the case of a film star who may tie herself to a company in order to obtain from them the benefits of stardom   . . .   parties habitually fetter themselves to one another.

When a contract only ties the parties during the continuance of the contract and the negative ties are only those which are incidental and normal to the positive commercial arrangements at which the contract aims, even though those ties exclude all dealing with others, there is no restraint of trade within the meaning of the doctrine and no question of reasonableness arises. If, however, the contract ties the trading activities of either party after its determination, it is a restraint of trade and the question of reasonableness arises. So, too, if *during* the contract one of the parties is too unilaterally fettered so that the contract loses its character of a contract for the regulation and promotion of trade and acquires the predominant character of a contract in restraint of trade. In that case   . . .   the question whether it is reasonable arises.'

Applying this to a contract of employment, it is clear that the doctrine will apply to restraints imposed on the employee's working activities or fields of work after the original contract has ended. It is also clear from that test, however, that the doctrine can apply to some employment contracts, or provisions within those contracts, intended to operate during the currency of the employment relationship. Thus extravagantly oppressive and one-sided employment contracts may be held unenforceable during their lifetime: see *Young v Timmins* (1831) 1 Cr & J 331. The doctrine may also apply where, for example, other contractual provisions may be imposed which have the substantive effect of restraining the freedom of the employee to move jobs (for example, provisions clawing back bonuses if an employee goes to work for a rival or depriving an employee of commission which he has earned during the currency of his employment if he leaves to work for a rival). Some cases have considered such clauses solely by reference to the common law penalty doctrine (eg *Imam-Sadeque v BlueBay Asset Management (Services) Ltd* [2012] EWHC 3511 (QB)). Where the restraint of trade doctrine has been relied upon, the courts have not been consistent in their treatment of these kinds of provisions. In *Sadler v Imperial Life Assurance Co of Canada Ltd* [1988] IRLR 388, HC the doctrine was held to apply to a covenant depriving an employee of commission payable post termination of his employment if he went to work for a rival. The provision in question was held unenforceable and severed from the agreement, thereby entitling the employee to recover the commission payments (see also *Marshall v NM Financial Management Ltd* [1997] 1 WLR 1527, [1997] IRLR 449, CA). However, in *Peninsula Business Services Ltd v Sweeney* [2004] IRLR 49 the EAT held that a provision in an employee's contract denying him post-termination commission was not a restraint of trade since it did not impose any restraint on him as to whom he might work for or what he might do: it was merely an 'economic disincentive' to discourage the employee from leaving his employment. The EAT's decision in *Peninsula* seems far too restrictive in its refusal to apply the doctrine of restraint of trade to the provision in question. The doctrine is not based upon the form of the contractual restraint, but upon its substantive effect: 'whether a particular provision operates in restraint of trade is to be determined not by the form the stipulation wears but . . . by its effect in practice. . . . The clause in question here contains no direct covenant to abstain from any kind of competition or business, but the question to be answered is whether, in effect, it is likely to cause the employee to refuse business which otherwise he would take or, looking at it in another way, whether the existence of this provision would diminish his prospects of employment' (*per* Lord Wilberforce, *Stenhouse Australia Ltd v Phillips* [1974] AC 391, PC at 402F-H). In the *Stenhouse* case the clause held to be unenforceable as an unreasonable restraint of trade was a profit-sharing clause imposed on an employee of an insurance broker as part of a settlement agreement entered into on the termination of his employment. The clause provided that, in the event that any client of the employer within a period of five years from the date of termination of the employment placed any insurance business (of the type transacted by the employer) with the departing employee, the departing employee would be entitled to a one-half share of the commission received in respect of such transaction. See also **21.20** *London Ltd v Reilly* [2012] EWHC 1912 (Ch) where the judge refused to follow *Peninsula v Sweeney* (ibid).

It is of crucial importance to distinguish between post-termination restraints and garden leave provisions. An exclusive services provision in an employment contract operating during the currency of the employment relationship will not have the doctrine applied to it. Nonetheless, if, during the currency of the employment contract, the employer puts the employee on garden leave and seeks an injunction to prevent the employee, during that notice period, from working for a competitor, the court will pay heed to the restrictive effect of the exclusive services provision in determining whether to grant such an injunction and, if so, for what period. This is not the application of the doctrine of restraint of trade but the application of considerations of restraint of trade in the exercise of a judicial discretion: see *Symbian Ltd v Christensen* [2001] IRLR 77, *Provident Financial Group plc and Whitegates Estate Agency Ltd v Hayward* [1989] 3 All ER 298, [1989] ICR 160, CA and *Mont v Mills* (supra).

It is a cardinal principle of the application of the common law doctrine of restraint of trade that the court must determine the enforceability of the contract or contractual provision concerned as at the date the contract was entered into, not at the date when it comes to be enforced (see *Gledhow Autoparts Ltd v Delaney* [1965] 1 WLR 1366, *Home Counties Dairies Ltd v Skilton* [1970] 1 WLR 526, *Commercial Plastics Ltd v Vincent* [1965] 1 QB 623, *Allan Janes LLP v Balraj Johal* [2006] EWHC 286 (Ch), [2006] ICR 742 and *Patsystems Holdings Ltd v Neilly* [2012] EWHC 2609 (QB)). Thus if a restrictive covenant is adjudged to be invalid at the date it was entered into, it cannot be saved by a subsequent renegotiated contract of employment referring to an agreement or general acknowledgment by an employee that his previous terms 'remain unchanged' (*Patsystems*, ibid). It is accordingly apparent that the restraint of trade doctrine in its pure form may be readily applied to an employee's post-termination restraints, but cannot in its 'pure' form be applied to disputes which arise in relation to garden leave injunctions. In the case of exclusive service provisions in contracts of employment their reasonableness at the date the contract is entered into is obvious: they are there to provide the employer with the means of ensuring that the employee's skills and endeavours are fully absorbed. Thus they satisfy Lord Pearce's test at that stage. It is only when they are deployed during notice periods as the basis for seeking injunctive relief to enforce garden leave that they cease to have the character of a provision to absorb skills and endeavours and take on the character of a provision aimed at sterilising the employee. At that stage the doctrine of restraint of trade still cannot be applied in its pure form. The court embarks on a more flexible exercise of determining what, if any, harm the employee on garden leave may do to the employer's business if freed during his notice period to work for a rival and weighing against that harm considerations of restraint of trade in imposing an injunction restricting what the employee is permitted to do during his notice period or part of it (see *Symbian Ltd v Christensen* above). Because the court is engaged on a more flexible exercise than that permitted under the doctrine of restraint of trade it is able, for example, to impose injunctions for a period of time less than the contractual period of notice and, it would seem, can take into account interests of the employer that would not be considered legitimate under the doctrine of restraint of trade (see below **41.14**). In *JM Finn & Co* (above), the judge, Simler J, recognised the distinction between the judicial approach to enforcing contractual post-termination restraints and exercising a discretion to enforce by injunction negative contractual obligations of employee during notice periods. However, it appears that she believed that the latter exercise was an application of the restraint of trade doctrine. The danger of this confusion is that the courts will become less flexible in relation to discretionary relief in garden leave cases or will become too flexible in relation to granting relief in post-termination restraint cases, in effect re-writing the contractual restraint as happened in the *Tullett* case (see below). It appears that the Court of Appeal decision in the *Symbian* case (above) was not cited to the Court in the *JM Finn* case.

It also follows from the aforementioned cardinal principle that in judging the reasonableness of contractual restraints the court cannot consider events occurring after the contract containing the restraints is entered into. There is a limited exception to this rule in relation to events or matters subsequent to the outset of the contract where such events or matters throw a general light on what might have been fairly contemplated on a reasonable view of the meaning of the restrictive covenant in question (see *Coppage v Safety Net Security Ltd* [2013] IRLR 970). In *Coppage* the Court of Appeal upheld the first instance judges' approach to the issue of the enforceability of a covenant where he had taken into consideration the stability of the customer base of the employer during the last 12 months of the employee's employment as one factor in holding the covenant to be reasonable. However, when judging whether a covenant has been breached the court will, of course, look at the circumstances at the date of the alleged breach. A good illustration of the distinction between judging whether a covenant is valid and judging whether it is breached is furnished by *Phoenix Partners Group LLP v Asoyag (Maurice)* [2010] EWHC 846 (QB), [2010] IRLR 594. In that case (an interim injunction application) the judge held that it was likely that the restrictive covenants would, at trial, be held enforceable. However, those restrictive covenants prohibited the covenantor from joining a business "which competes with" the business of the covenantee and from soliciting or dealing with clients "in competition with" the business of the covenantee. At the date of the alleged breach, as the judge held, the covenantee had discontinued doing business of the particular kind covered by the covenants and, accordingly, the judge held that there was no breach of the covenant. A further example of this approach is to be found in *Stallergenes (UK) Ltd v Stern & Anor* [2013] EWCA Civ 1249.

There is one area of potential difficulty in applying this rule as to the date when the court must consider the reasonableness of any covenant in restraint of trade, namely that caused by the effect of the *Transfer of Undertakings (Protection of Employment) Regulations 2006* ('the *2006 TUPE Regulations*', which replace the *1983 TUPE Regulations* with effect from 6 April 2006: see generally TRANSFER OF UNDERTAKINGS **(52)**). The effect of those *Regulations* is that, where there is a 'relevant transfer' of an undertaking or part of one, employees whose contracts would otherwise be terminated by that transfer are instead subject to a statutory novation of their existing employment contract so that the transferee company is substituted for the transferor company. *Regulation 4(1)* of the *TUPE Regulations* provides that, following a transfer, an employee's contract of employment 'shall have effect after the transfer as if originally made between the person so employed and the transferee'. If *reg 4(1)* were to be applied literally then it would have the effect of rendering certain restrictive covenants (which prohibit dealing with customers of a specified business) imposed by the specified business (the transferor) upon its employees nugatory if the transfer that takes place had the result of substituting in every respect (and at all material times) the transferee for the transferor. In *Morris Angel & Son Ltd v Hollande* [1993] IRLR 169 the court considered the effect of *reg 5(1)* of the *1983 TUPE Regulations* (now *reg 4(1)* of the *2006 TUPE Regulations*) on a restrictive covenant in the employee's contract of employment which prohibited him, for a period of one year after the contract came to an end, from seeking 'to procure orders from or do business with any person, firm or company who has, at any time during the one year immediately preceding the cesser done business with [Group Y]'. The business of Group Y was sold to X Ltd and on the date of sale the employee's contract of employment with Group Y was terminated. The employee sought to contend that the effect of the transfer was to substitute in the restrictive covenant for clients of Group Y the clients of X Ltd. Accordingly, the employee contended that he could not be in breach of the covenant by canvassing or soliciting persons who had been clients of group Y during the period one year prior to the termination of his contract because the effect of the old *reg 5(1)* was to alter the wording of the covenant 'clients of X Ltd' which, as a matter of fact, he had not solicited or dealt with after the termination of his employment. At first instance, it was held that the old *reg 5(1)* applied so that, although the transferee company could enforce the covenant, the customers with whom he was prohibited from doing business after termination were those of the transferee X Ltd. It followed that there was no breach of the covenant in question. On appeal, the Court of Appeal preferred a construction of the rules under which the transferee company was deemed to have been the owner of the transferor's business during the relevant 12-month period (i.e. the 12 months prior to the termination of the employment contract). Thus, the customers with whom the employee was prohibited from dealing under the covenants were those of the part of the business transferred (ie those of Group Y prior to the transfer). It followed that the employee was in breach and an interim injunction was ordered.

Any attempt to impose a new restrictive covenant upon employees following a *TUPE* transfer was, prior to 6 April 2006, almost bound to fail. Such variations to an employee's contract of employment were unenforceable under *reg 5(1)* of the *1983 TUPE Regulations* even if they formed part of a 'package' which was to the overall benefit of the employee (see *Credit Suisse First Boston (Europe) Ltd v Lister* [1998] IRLR 700). However, under the *2006 TUPE Regulations* variations to an employee's contract that are implemented for 'economic, technical or organisational' reasons entailing changes in the workforce will be valid even if the reason for the variation is connected to the transfer. So if in a particular case the reason for seeking to change the restrictive covenants is an 'ETO' reason, then such a variation will be valid. Under the *2006 TUPE Regulations* employees should be informed of the identity of the transferee employer prior to the transfer. If they are not, then their entitlement to object under *reg 4(7)* may be exercised after the transfer so that the transferee cannot enforce post-termination restrictive covenants in their contracts of employment (see *New ISG Ltd v Vernon* [2007] EWHC 2665 (Ch), [2008] ICR 319). See also TRANSFER OF UNDERTAKINGS **(52)**.

41.4 The interests of the parties

In order to justify a contract or provision in restraint of trade it must be proved that it is reasonable in the interests of the parties. This does not mean that the provision in question must support the interests of both parties equally. Rather, it means: 'For a restraint to be reasonable in the interests of the parties it must afford *no more than* adequate protection of the party in whose favour it is imposed . . . though in one sense no doubt it is contrary to the interests of the covenantor to subject himself to any restraint, still it may be for his advantage to be able so to subject himself in cases where, if he could not do so, he would lose other advantages, such as . . . the possibility of obtaining employment or training under competent employers' (*Herbert Morris Ltd v Saxelby* [1916] 1 AC 688, 707 *per* Lord Parker). It is now firmly established that the burden of proof in relation to this first step in the justification process is on the party seeking to enforce that covenant: see *Mason v Provident Clothing and Supply Co Ltd* [1913] AC 724 *per* Viscount Haldane, LC at 733 and Lord Shaw at 741 and *Herbert Morris*, above, at 700, 707 and 715. This will normally, but not invariably, be the employer (see, for example, *Wyatt v Kreglinger and Fernau* [1933] 1 KB 793, where it was the employee who sought to enforce the covenant in question because that covenant was the sole consideration supporting the employee's pension entitlement).

The courts will not enforce any provision against mere competition (such covenants are generally referred to as 'covenants in gross'). It is of the essence that an employer demonstrates that he has a legitimate interest to protect. Preventing competition *per se* is not a legitimate interest. Covenants in restraint of trade are upheld not on the ground that the employee 'would, by reason of his employment or training, obtain the skill and knowledge necessary to equip him as a possible competitor in the trade, but that he might obtain such personal knowledge of and influence over the customers of his employer or such an acquaintance with his employer's trade secrets as would enable him, if competition were allowed, to take advantage of his employer's trade connection or utilise information confidentially obtained' (*per* Lord Parker in *Herbert Morris*, above, 709). This quotation from Lord Parker demonstrates that, historically, the courts had recognised two legitimate interests of the employer justifying the imposition of a reasonable restraint: (a) trade secrets (and confidential information); and, (b) customer connection.

The categories of legitimate interest that may be protected by an employer are not, however, confined to the two interests mentioned by Lord Parker. The modern approach to the identification of interests justifying provisions in restraint of trade is not based on a narrow categorisation: ' . . . the employer's claim for protection must be based upon the identification of some advantage or asset inherent in the business which can properly be regarded as, in a general sense, his property and which it would be unjust to allow the employee to appropriate for his own purposes, even though he, the employee, may have contributed to its creation. For while it may be true that an employee is entitled and is to be encouraged to build up his own qualities of skill and experience, it is equally his duty to develop and improve his employer's business for the benefit of his employer. These two obligations interlock during his employment: after its termination they diverge and mark the boundary between what the employee may take with him and what he may legitimately be asked to leave behind to his employers' (per Lord Wilberforce *Stenhouse Australia Ltd v Phillips*, ibid at p 400). Thus, in recent years new interests of an employer have been identified by the courts as justifying the protection of provisions in restraint of trade. In *Office Angels Ltd v Rainer-Thomas* [1991] IRLR 214, CA the court recognised as a legitimate interest of an employment agency the pool of workers on the agency's books. See also *East England Schools CIC (t/a 4MySchools) v Palmer and anor* [2014] IRLR 191. In *Dawnay, Day & Co Ltd v de Braconier d'Alphen* [1997] IRLR 285, affd [1998] ICR 1068, CA the court recognised as a legitimate interest the stability of an employer's workforce, holding that a covenant imposed on an employee prohibiting him from soliciting his former colleagues to leave their employment was a reasonable restraint. Nevertheless, some caution needs to be exercised in framing contractual provisions in restraint of trade. Client connection is an important aspect of the goodwill of any business, but it is not the exclusive component of that goodwill. A competent and hard-working employee who does not have any dealings with clients may enhance the reputation of his employer's business, and the reputation of the business is part of its goodwill, but an employer cannot prohibit an employee from going to work for a competitor upon termination of his employment merely to protect the enhanced reputation of his business to which the employee has contributed: the employee is entitled to take with him his own skills and knowledge, even where those skills and knowledge have contributed to the reputation enjoyed by the employer (see *Countrywide Assured Financial Services Ltd v Smart* [2004] EWHC 1214 (Ch)).

Another interest that in practice one frequently sees employers seeking to protect are their suppliers. Thus one sees covenants aimed at prohibiting a former employee from dealing with suppliers of his former employer or, in extreme cases, from seeking to solicit or entice the supplier to cease to be a supplier of the former employer. The latter kind of covenant was considered in *Landmark Brickwork Ltd v Sutcliffe and ors* [2011] IRLR 976. In that case Slade J granted an interim injunction to enforce it, without giving reasons. However, while an employer is of course entitled to restrain an employee from inducing a supplier to break an existing contract with the employer (since that is in any event a tort to induce or procure the breach of a contract), it is hard to see what legitimate interest an employer has in preventing its employees from dealing with its suppliers generally. Such a covenant merely inhibits the suppliers' ability to trade and has no impact on the employer's business. The only situation in which an employer might have a legitimate interest in protecting its suppliers would be if the supplies in question were scarce so that if an employee took supplies from the supplier there would be insufficient to supply the employer. Even a covenant such as that considered in the *Landmark* case (ie prohibiting the employee from seeking to dissuade a supplier from continuing to supply the employer) might not be protecting a legitimate business interest if the supplies were readily obtainable elsewhere and the employee was not (in approaching the supplier) misusing the employer's confidential information. In *Energy Renewals Ltd v Borg* [2014] IRLR 713, a restriction on contacting suppliers of the former employer was considered to be too wide to be enforceable where those suppliers comprised all of the six national energy suppliers in the energy brokerage sector and would effectively preclude the employee from acting in competition.

Having identified a legitimate interest to protect, the contract or contractual provision in question must be no more than adequate to protect that interest. Clearly the reasonableness of the ambit or duration of any restraint is tied to the nature of the interest in question. If it is sought by an employer to protect his customer connection, that may be achieved by post-termination restraints which prohibit for a reasonable period of time the ex employee from soliciting or dealing with those customers with whom the employee had contact during the course of his employment. *Prima facie* there would be no justification for imposing on that employee a post-termination restraint which prohibited him from entering into employment with a competitor. However, if an employer wishes to protect trade secrets or confidential information he may be justified in imposing a post-termination restraint prohibiting the employee from joining a competitor for a reasonable period of time. It is dangerous for an employer to seek too wide a protection for a limited interest because a court is entitled to look at the nature of the restraints imposed with a view to determining whether a lesser restraint would have been adequate to protect the employer's interest: see *Office Angels*, above. We return to the various forms of restraint and issues of reasonableness in more detail below.

Difficulties can arise in relation to corporate groups. Sometimes the employer company within the group will be a mere holding company which does not itself conduct any business. In such an instance, provided that the group is vertically aligned, the court will readily hold that the holding company has a legitimate interest to protect arising from the business conducted by its subsidiaries and can therefore enforce the covenant if valid (see *Stenhouse v Phillips*, ibid and *Beckett Investment Management Group Ltd v Hall* [2007]

EWCA Civ 613, [2007] ICR 1539). In such cases the parent or holding company is treated as conducting its business through the agency of its subsidiaries. However, in relation to horizontally organised groups, such an analysis is not possible (see *Henry Leetham & Sons Ltd v Johnstone-White* [1907] 1 Ch 322). In light of the fact that many persons employed within corporate groups are employed by a service company, close attention should be paid to the drafting of any restrictive covenants in employment contracts entered into by the service company to ensure that they properly embrace the legitimate interests of the subsidiaries for whom the employees will in fact be working.

Another case on restructuring of a business arose in *Towry EJ Ltd v Barry William Prosser Bennett and ors* [2012] EWHC 224 (QB). In that case Company A purchased shares of Company B. A number of employees then left. Company B was restructured and ceased to have any employees. It then commenced proceedings against the departed employees seeking to enforce post-termination restrictive covenants, both for the period whilst it was still in business and also for a period after that. Counsel for the employees submitted that there is a free-standing principle that a covenantee cannot enforce a covenant if he no longer has a legitimate business interest to protect. There is some force in that submission since the doctrine of restraint of trade is one founded in public policy (see above **41.2**) and it is hard to see why as a matter of public policy a covenant in restraint of trade should be enforceable in the absence of a protectable legitimate interest. At least, where an employer is no longer trading it should be the case that neither interim nor final injunctions will be granted since if the employer is not trading it can be suffering no more than nominal damage. However, in *Towry* Cox J held that the covenant was enforceable and that there was no free-standing principle that a restrictive covenant only remained enforceable for as long as the employer continued to have a legitimate business interest to protect. However, that case concerned only claims for breach of contract and inducement (which failed on the facts) and there was no claim for an injunction. (Cf *Phoenix Partners Group LLP v Asoyag* [2010] IRLR 594 for a case in which a post-termination covenant was not enforceable where an employer had ceased to do business because it was framed in terms preventing the employee from competing; since the employer had ceased to do business, the employee was not competing; see also *BFCA Ltd v Butt* [2013] EWHC 326 (QB)).

It is important to note that an interest of an employer in his customer connection can be protected even if the employee is not moving to a competitor business. Recent cases such as *Caterpillar Logistics Services (UK) Ltd v Paul Huesca de Crean* [2012] EWCA Civ 156, *[2012] ICR 981* and *Generics (UK) Ltd v Yeda Research and Development Co Ltd and anor* [2012] EWCA Civ 726, [2012] CP Rep 39 support, in principle, the protection of customer connection by prohibiting employees on reasonable terms from going to work with a customer. Such covenants are important in the area of service industries where employees are seconded to, or spend substantial periods of time, working for, or within the premises of, clients and can therefore establish strong relationships with those clients who may choose to poach those employees to save themselves the costs of paying the employer's fees for providing services through those employees. It may also be that these kind of 'customer' covenants can be justified on the basis of confidential information (although it must be recognised that there will be a substantial overlap, or sharing, of information between the customer and employer in these kinds of cases).

41.5   The public interest

Much confusion has arisen about the second step in the justification process enunciated by Lord McNaghten in the *Nordenfelt* case (see above, **41.2**). Problems arise for two reasons: first, the doctrine of restraint of trade is a creation of public policy which collides head on with another public policy, namely the sanctity of contract; secondly, in some cases (particularly those decided in the early part of the 20th century) judges tend to use the expressions 'public policy' and 'public interest' interchangeably (see for example Cozens-Hardy MR in *Sir WC Leng & Co Ltd v Andrews* [1909] 1 Ch 763). This confusion has led in more recent times to judicial debate about whether the doctrine of restraint of trade has been properly applied in the past in distinguishing between the private interest of the parties and public policy in the sense of public interest (see, for example, *per* Lord Reid in the *Esso Petroleum* case (above, at p 300E)). It is submitted that the true analysis of the doctrine is as follows:

(a)   It is contrary to public policy for parties to a contract to enter into restraints which go beyond the reasonable protection of legitimate private interests (the first limb of Lord McNaghten's test).

(b)   It is also contrary to public policy for parties to a contract to enter into restraints which are no more than adequate to protect a private legitimate interest recognised by the law, if those restraints are contrary to the public interest (the second limb of Lord McNaghten's test).

(c)   It follows that, in theory at least, a covenant which satisfies public policy to the extent that it is no more than adequate to protect a private legitimate interest may fail to satisfy public policy because it is not in the public interest.

Unfortunately, it is not possible to identify any cases in the employment field which clearly illustrate proposition (c). In a number of cases, eg *Sir WC Leng* (above), *Herbert Morris v Saxelby* (above), *Strange (SW) Ltd v Mann* [1965] 1 WLR 629, *Countrywide Assured Financial Services Ltd v Smart* (above) and *Commercial Plastics Ltd v Vincent* [1965] 1 QB 623, the courts have held covenants to be against 'public policy' (and sometimes against the 'public interest') where, it is submitted, the real basis for the decisions in those cases is that there is no legitimate interest of the covenantee to protect or, alternatively, that the restraints go beyond what is reasonable to protect that interest. This is against public policy in the sense set out in (a) above, but is not illustrative of the principle in (c) above. (The only exception in these cases would appear to be the, (perhaps) *obiter*, statement of Farwell LJ in the *Sir WC Leng* case above at p 334.)

In a number of cases the public interest (as distinct from public policy) has been raised as a discrete ground of attack on contractual restrictions, but with a marked lack of success. Although Lord Denning MR in *Oswald Hickson Collier & Co v Carter-Ruck* [1984] AC 720n appeared to hold that it was contrary to 'public policy' that a fiduciary (a solicitor) should be precluded by a restrictive covenant from acting for a client who wanted him to act, that decision was swiftly departed from: see *Edwards v Worboys* [1984] AC 724n; *Bridge v Deacons* [1984] AC 705 and *Allan Janes LLP v Balraj Johal* [2006] EWHC 286 (Ch), [2006] ICR 742. See also, in relation to the medical profession, *Kerr v Morris* [1987] Ch 90, [1986] 3 All ER 217.

Probably the real reason why issues of public interest do not generally arise for decision, at least in employment cases, is because restraints which customarily appear in employment contracts normally have no impact on the public at large and hence the public interest. Moreover the onus of proving that a restraint is injurious to the public interest is upon the person (normally the employee) who is making that allegation. The burden is a heavy one: *A-G Commonwealth of Australia v Adelaide Steamship Co Ltd* [1913] AC 781 at 797 *per* Lord Parker. It is, however, submitted that one area in which the issue of public interest is of great significance in the employment field is where an employee challenges an indirect restraint upon his freedom. These kind of restraints arise where the employee has no direct restraint imposed upon him in his contract of employment but nonetheless is fettered by contractual restraints which his employer has entered into with other parties. In these cases the private interests of the parties are not in issue because the parties are not challenging the enforceability of the restraints: a third party (the employee) is challenging the restraints in so far as they affect him and not the parties to the contract. (See *Eastham v Newcastle United Football Club Ltd* [1964] Ch 413 and *Greig v Insole* [1978] 3 All ER 449 and compare *Kores Manufacturing Co Ltd v Kolok Manufacturing Co Ltd* [1957] 3 All ER 158 which involved an agreement between two employers not to employ each other's employees for a period of five years after their leaving the employment of the respective parties. In fact, however, in that case, the challenge to the agreement was not made by an employee but by one of the parties. Nonetheless, the Court of Appeal opined, *obiter*, that such an agreement could not be justified under the restraint of trade doctrine because of its indirect effect upon employees.)

It was suggested by Lord Hodson in the *Esso* case that issues of the burden of proof in relation to the interests of the parties and the public interest will seldom arise because, once the agreement is before the court, it is open to the scrutiny of the court in all its surrounding circumstances 'as a question of law': *Esso*, above, 319. It is submitted that this is not right. In the employment situation the employer must (if he seeks to enforce a restraint) establish that the covenant is in the interests of the parties in the narrow sense required by the doctrine. If the employee wishes to challenge the restraint on the ground that it is injurious to the public interest he cannot rely on the employer to furnish the court with the evidence required to prove injury to the public: the onus is on him to do that. The evidence which would require the court to consider the impact of a restraint upon a particular market is likely to be voluminous and to require expert opinion. Most employees would lack the financial means to undertake the provision to the court of that kind of evidence themselves. It is therefore extremely improbable that a court will have furnished to it in an employment case all the evidence that is required to deal properly with the issue of the public interest. It may be, however, that restraint of trade law is entering into a new era where issues of public interest will become more prominent. In the case of *Dranez Anstalt v Hayek (Zamir)* [2002] EWCA Civ 1729, [2003] 1 BCLC 278 restrictive covenants entered into by the inventor of a new ventilator for use in hospitals were held to constitute unreasonable restraints of trade by the Court of Appeal amongst other grounds on the basis that they offended against the public interest in restricting the inventor from making further developments which would be of great benefit to the public. There are, too, the developments in competition law to which reference has already been made (see above **41.1**). Competition law will not normally have any relevance to employees as they are not 'undertakings' for the purposes of competition law. However, the European Commission has issued guidance in Commission Notice [2005] OJ C-56/24 as to its position in relation to ancillary restraints taken upon the merger or acquisition of a business as follows: "*Non-competition clauses are justified for periods of up to three years, when the transfer of the undertaking includes the transfer of customer loyalty in the form of both goodwill and know-how. When only goodwill is included, they are justified for up to two years.*" This Guidance was adopted by the OFT in its previous Mergers Assessment Guidance, but the most recent joint OFT / Competition Commission guidance does not refer to this. Nonetheless, it is possible that these periods may be taken as a 'benchmark' for public policy in cases involving the common law of restraint of trade.

41.6   Judging the reasonableness of restraints

Construction of covenants in restraint of trade

The principles which a court should apply to the construction of covenants in restraint of trade do not materially differ from the principles applicable to the construction of any other written terms. Those principles are derived from the speech of Lord Hoffmann in *Investors Compensation Scheme v West Bromwich Building Society* [1998] 1 WLR 896 at 912H–913E (see *Beckett Investment Management Group Ltd v Hall*, ibid). The approach of the Court is exemplified in the case of *Clarke v Newland* [1991] 1 All ER 397. In that case, the Court concluded that the following approach should be adopted. First, the court should consider the construction of the term in question without having regard to the issue of validity or invalidity of the covenant, ie the court must decide what the contractual provision means before it decides whether the provision is reasonable or not. Second, the court must have regard to the object of such restraints, namely the protection of one of the parties against trade rivalry. Finally, the court must construe the provision in context, that is to say, having regard to the factual matrix at the date when the contract was made. By following this approach, a court ought to avoid the worst excesses of an over-literal construction or of an over-purposive approach. The vice inherent in the over-literal construction of a covenant in restraint of trade is that the court ignores the intent of the parties and construes the covenant so that it extends to situations not contemplated by the parties:

> 'Another matter which requires attention is whether a restriction on trade must be treated as wholly void because it is so worded as to cover cases which may possibly arise, and to which it cannot be reasonably applied . . . Agreements in restraint of trade, like other agreements, must be construed with reference to the object sought to be obtained by them. In cases such as the one before us, the object is the protection of one of the parties against rivalry in trade. Such agreements cannot be properly held to apply to cases which, although covered by the words of the agreement, cannot reasonably be supposed ever to have been contemplated by the parties, and which on a rational view of the agreement are excluded from its operation by falling, in truth, outside and not within its real scope.'

Haynes v Doman [1899] 2 Ch 13, CA, *per* Lindley LJ at 24–25. (See also *Coppage v Safety Net Security* (above) where the Court of Appeal decried the use, in attacking a covenant as too wide, of arguments based on merely theoretical or fanciful possibilities.)

In this respect much criticism has been levelled at the decision in *Commercial Plastics v Vincent* [1965] 1 QB 623. A purposive approach to construction is well illustrated by the following cases. In *Moenich v Fenestre* (1882) 67 LT 602 the expression 'any trade or business' in a restrictive covenant was held to mean, contextually, 'any trade or business as commission merchant'. In *G W Plowman & Son Ltd v Ash* [1964] 1 WLR 568 a covenant requiring an employee after termination of the employment 'not [to] canvass or solicit for himself or any other person . . . any farmer or market gardener who shall . . . have been a customer of the employers' was construed by the court as meaning, in the context of the employment agreement read as a whole, 'not to canvass or solicit with respect to the goods which the employee dealt with during his employment'. In *Home Counties Dairies Ltd v Skilton* [1970] 1 WLR 526 the words 'dairy produce' were construed by the court as being limited to only that sort of dairy produce with which the employee had been concerned whilst in employment. (See also *Hollis & Co v Stocks* [2000] IRLR 712.) In *TFS Derivatives Ltd v Morgan* [2004] EWHC 3181 (QB), [2005] IRLR 246 'business' was held to refer to a particular business activity of the investment company in question, and not to the whole of the 'business entity' that was the company: see also *Dyson Technology Ltd v Strutt* [2005] EWHC 2814 (Ch), [2005] All ER (D) 355 (Nov), but compare the approach taken in *Wiggle Ltd v Burge* which appears to be out of line with these authorities (9 May 2012, QB, unreported). In the recent case of *Croesus Financial Services Ltd v Bradshaw and anor* [2013] EWHC 3685 (QB) the judge held that the expression 'personal contact in the course of their duties' (in relation to defining a class of clients which the employees were barred from dealing with by a restrictive covenant) when properly construed meant business contact that was more than trivial or de minimis and was personally undertaken by the employee covenantee. Compare this generous approach to construction with the approach adopted by Andrew Smith J in *Ashcourt Rowan Financial Planning Ltd v Hall* [2013] IRLR 637 which was far more restrictive.

However, the Court can be guilty of, in effect, re-writing a covenant by an over-purposive approach (see *Littlewoods Organisation Ltd v Harris* [1977] 1 WLR 1472, CA). The court ought not to be over indulgent when faced with ill-drafted and ambiguous provisions in restraint of trade. In *J A Mont (UK) Ltd v Mills* [1993] IRLR 172, CA a sales and marketing director of a paper mill entered into a severance agreement with his employer to terminate his employment. Under this agreement the employee received one year's remuneration although he was not required to work for the employer during that period. The severance agreement contained the following restraint: 'This total payment is made on

Nature of the restraint

The approach of the court is first to identify the legitimate interest or interests which the employer is seeking to protect by the restraints in question. Restraints can take a wide variety of forms, but broadly fall into two categories:

(a)   Restraints against conducting or being engaged or interested in a competing business (whether specifically identified or not in the covenant) for a period of time; and

(b)   Restraints which prohibit a limited kind of competitive activity, such as soliciting or dealing with customers.

The former category of restraint (a non-compete restraint) may be in a wide form prohibiting an employee from joining a competitor's business regardless of the field of that business in which he is proposing to work, or it may be limited to prohibiting him working for a competitor in the particular field in which the employee has been engaged by the former employer imposing the covenant. The more limited form of non-compete provision is now more frequently encountered in modern contracts of employment, but the wider form of restraint is sometimes still upheld by the courts: see *Norbrook Laboratories (GB) Ltd v Adair* [2008] EWHC 978 (QB), [2008] IRLR 878. It is to be observed that considerable care must be taken in drafting even the more limited form of non-compete restraint: see *Ashcourt Rowan Financial Planning v Hall* (above).

The court, having identified an interest of the employer justifying protection, is entitled to look at the <u>nature</u> of the restraint deployed to determine whether the legitimate interest could have been protected by a narrower restraint than, for example, either a wide or narrow non-compete provision (see *Office Angels Ltd v Rainer-Thomas* [1991] IRLR 214, CA). In identifying the legitimate interest to be protected the court is entitled to look at any express words in the contract which may identify that interest (*Office Angels*). If the employer has categorically identified the interest he seeks to protect (for example, client connection) he cannot, when the covenant comes to be tested in court, claim that the restraint in fact is aimed at protecting a different interest (for example, confidential information: see *Office Angels*). This, however, is a matter of construction: see *Patsystems Holdings Ltd v Neilly* [2012] EWHC 2609 (QB). Again, if the interest to be protected is, for example, client connection or the stability of the employer's workforce a covenant in the nature of a non-compete provision risks being held to be disproportionate for such interests may be protected by a covenant directed at the prohibition of specific competitive acts, such as the soliciting or dealing with customers, or the soliciting or enticing away of staff. It follows that the nature of the interest to be protected will dictate the nature of the restraint which should be employed by the employer to protect the interest. Non-compete provisions are generally only justifiable if the nature of the interest to be protected is trade secrets and confidential information: see *per* Simon Brown LJ in *J A Mont (UK) Ltd v Mills* [1993] IRLR 172. This is because it is notoriously difficult to police covenants which merely restrain the disclosure or use of confidential information. Moreover, it is notoriously difficult for a covenantee to know what information is truly confidential and which he cannot use or disclose and what information is merely part of his stock of accumulated knowledge and experience which he is entitled to disclose or use. Accordingly an employer may protect his trade secrets and confidential information by imposing on an employee a covenant restraining that employee for a reasonable period of time from joining a competitor, at least in the same field of activity in which he was engaged for the former employer (see *Littlewoods Organisation Ltd v Harris* [1977] 1 WLR 1472, CA; *Printers & Finishers Ltd v Holloway* [1964] 3 All ER 54n, [1965] RPC 239; and *David (Lawrence) Ltd v Ashton* [1991] 1 All ER 385, [1989] ICR 123, CA). Nevertheless, caution must be exercised in drafting non-compete restraints so as to ensure that the definition of 'competitor' is not too widely drawn, thereby rendering the covenant unenforceable: see *Norbrook Laboratories*, ibid.

In some cases the court has upheld non-compete provisions where the interest to be protected is client connection. The basis for this is that in some instances it may be impossible, or, at least, very difficult for the employer to 'police' a more limited covenant restraining soliciting or dealing with clients (see *Scorer v Seymour-Johns* [1966] 1 WLR 1419, *per* Salmon LJ, p 1427C-E, *Turner v Commonwealth and British Minerals Ltd* [2000] IRLR 114, *per* Waller LJ at para 18 and *TFS Derivatives Ltd v Morgan* [2004] EWHC 3181 (QB), [2005] IRLR 246).

It is, however, submitted that the courts should be suspicious of assertions that it is difficult to police non-solicitation and non-dealing covenants. If it is difficult to do so, it is likely to be because there is no firm connection between the client and the employer in the first place, and the justification sometimes advanced for area non-compete restraints (namely that they are intended to protect what is in effect passing trade) is surely, for that reason, wrong in principle. If trade is passing it is difficult to see how the employee can gain any material knowledge of, or influence over, such clientele. In the *TFS Derivatives* case the court appeared to assume that it would be difficult to police non-solicitation and non-dealing covenants in circumstances in which the only evidence proffered by the employer to support this assertion was their experience of losing clients when an employee had previously left their employment. However, the employer did not at the same time suggest that that other employee had surreptitiously breached his non-solicitation and non-dealing covenants. If clients leave an employer in circumstances in which the employer is not asserting that their departure is consequent upon breaches of restrictive covenants by a former employee, it is difficult to see how the conclusion may be drawn that the covenants in question cannot be effectively policed. It is equally, if not more, plausible that the covenants were simply ineffective to achieve their purpose.

In *Thomas v Farr Plc* [2007] EWCA Civ 118, [2007] IRLR 419 the Court of Appeal held that a covenant prohibiting the solicitation of clients would not be sufficient to protect confidential information relating to those clients because such a covenant could not be policed. This was because the covenantor did not, in his work for the competitor company which he had joined, actually deal with clients himself. Prohibiting him from soliciting clients would not in any way inhibit his ability to pass on confidential information about those clients learnt whilst working for the covenantee to those members of staff in the competing company who *were* actually dealing with clients. Whereas it is extremely difficult to police covenants merely restraining the disclosure or use of confidential information, it is submitted that it is very far from self-evident that non-solicitation or non-dealing covenants taken to protect customer connection cannot be policed and no such assumption ought to be made without evidence of some sort to that effect. The fact is that breaches (or alleged breaches) of non-solicitation/-dealing covenants are regularly uncovered by covenantees: see for example *Allan Janes LLP v Johal (Balraj)*, above, and *Advantage Business Systems Ltd v Hopley (James)* [2007] EWHC 1783 (QB), [2007] All ER (D) 399 (Jul). See also the cautious approach taken by the court to 'policing' arguments in *Ashcourt Rowan* (above) and *Brake Brothers Ltd v Ungless* [2004] All ER (D) 586.

The court also held in the *TFS Derivatives* case that a non-compete provision was justified to protect confidential information. However, the court does not appear to have fully analysed the restraint in question to determine whether its duration was in fact commensurate with the length of time in which such information may have been of continuing use to a competitor. Compare *Duarte v Black and Decker Corpn*, ibid, where the judge, in determining that a two-year restraint on joining a competitor to protect confidential information would be unlawful under English law, considered the likely 'shelf-life' of the confidential information in question (cf *Norbrook Laboratories*, ibid).

Recently, however, the rationale adopted in the TFS Derivatives case, was adopted by Foskett J in *Tradition Financial Services v Gamberoni* [2017] EWHC 768 (QB). In that case, he stated, in broad terms, that he agreed with Counsel for Tradition that "*the necessity for non-compete provisions arises where non-solicitation and non-dealing covenants and confidential information restrictions are difficult to police or where there are material disputes as to what information is confidential".*

The ambit of the restraint

The ambit of a restraint will comprise the following elements:

(a)   the geographical area within which the restraint is to operate;

(b)   the proscribed actions (eg non-solicitation or non-dealing with clients and the class of client not to be solicited or dealt with).

Geography

Restraints may be worldwide (and will be so construed) if they contain no express or, perhaps, implied geographical limitation (see *Commercial Plastics Ltd v Vincent*, above). Worldwide non-compete restraints may be justifiable on the basis that they are necessary to protect trade secrets or confidential information: see *Scully UK Ltd v Lee*, above. Conversely, a restraint against soliciting or dealing with clients will not require an express geographical limitation (see *G W Plowman & Son Ltd v Ash* [1964] 1 WLR 568), even if clients may be located throughout the world, because the restraint is limited by the class of proscribed person. In many employment contracts radial or other area restraints are frequently employed. These are extremely clumsy instruments and appear to be a hang-over from the old common-law 18th and 19th-century rules about 'general' and 'partial' restraints. Area restraints must have a functional correspondence with the legitimate interest to be protected (see *Office Angels* and *Landmark Brickwork Ltd v Sutcliffe and Ors* [2011] IRLR 976). Thus, a local business whose customers are drawn exclusively or substantially from a radius of, say, five miles from the place of that business cannot justify a radial restraint of ten miles. Equally, the area in which a restraint is to operate will be considered carefully by the court. Thus, a radial restraint of five miles, for example, may be justifiable in rural or lightly populated areas, but could not be justified in a major conurbation where it may cover populations of a million or more: see *Fellowes & Son v Fisher* [1976] QB 122 and *Spencer v Marchington* [1988] IRLR 392. The real difficulty with radial or area restraints is that they are unnecessary if the protection is sought for the purposes of, say, customer connection because a non-solicit or non-compete covenant will suffice. It is difficult to see how they can be justified on the basis that they are necessary to protect confidential information or trade secrets since such interests are not confined to territorial boundaries (see *Scully UK Ltd v Lee*, above). Neither can radial restraints be justified on the basis of an interest in the stability of the workforce because solicitation of employees can readily be conducted from outside the radius imposed and, again, a more focused form of protection is afforded by a non-solicitation/non-enticement of staff covenant. The only practical effect of an area restraint, over and above that of a more limited non-solicitation or non-dealing covenant, is that it will prevent an ex employee from competing with his ex employer for new customers, ie customers who have not dealt with the former employer before (see *Allan Janes LLP v Balraj Johal*, above). Accordingly, radial restraints of the non-compete provision variety extend the protection afforded to an employer beyond that element of good will, namely existing client connection which he is entitled to protect. In business sale agreements it may be legitimate for the purchaser to protect himself against the vendor acquiring future business which ought otherwise to go to the business sold (see *Allied Dunbar (Frank Weisinger) Ltd v Weisinger* [1988] IRLR 60). The acquisition of new clients by reason of recommendation of existing clients is, however, based on the reputation of the business which, although it forms part of the goodwill on a business sale, forms no part of a legitimate interest to protect in the case of employer/employee covenants (see *Countrywide Assured Financial Services Ltd v Smart* [2004] EWHC 1214 (Ch)). See also *Merlin Financial Consultants Ltd v Cooper* [2014] IRLR 610, where a UK-wide restriction was upheld in circumstances where the employer's clients were predominantly in London and the South East, on the basis that the financial market was a single geographical market which was particularly true in the age of electronic communication. The latter point does highlight the increasingly outmoded nature of geographical restraints in some sectors.

The proscribed actions

If the proscription is against conducting, or joining, or being employed in (or being otherwise interested in) another business then the covenant will be too wide if the proscribed business is described as 'a similar business' to that of the employer. An employer may be entitled to protect himself from unfair competition by the employee, but he is not permitted to prohibit the ex employee from joining or setting up a business which is merely 'similar' and not competitive (see *Scully v Lee* [1998] IRLR 259, CA, but cf *Spafax Ltd v Harrison* [1980] IRLR 442, CA, where the court reached the opposite conclusion). It is sometimes held by the courts that it is not legitimate to bar an employee from working in a competitive business in an area of work in which he has not been engaged in the employer's business (see, for example, *Commercial Plastics v Vincent*, above) or in a part of a competitor's business which does not compete with the former employer. Given, however, that a non–compete covenant may generally only be justified on the basis that it protects trade secrets or confidential information, it is difficult to see the logic behind such decisions: a former employee may impart confidential information of his former employer to a competing business after he leaves his employment and joins that competing business, regardless of the capacity in which he is working with the competitor or the department in which he may be engaged: see *Symbian Ltd v Christensen* [2001] IRLR 77 and *Norbrook Laboratories* ibid at para 81.

Lesser forms of restraint, such as non-solicitation or dealing with customers, may be too wide if the class of customer with which the ex employee may not deal is drawn too widely. For example, covenants which prohibit soliciting or dealing with any client of the employer will be too wide if the employer has many hundreds or thousands of customers and the employee covenantor has dealt with only a limited number of them whilst employed: see *Marley Tile Co Ltd v Johnson* [1982] IRLR 75 and *Office Angels*, above. However, courts have upheld covenants that are not limited to dealings with clients which the employee has dealt with whilst employed: see *Gilford Motor Co. Ltd v Horne* [1933] Ch 935, CA, *Plowman v Ash* (above), *Business Seating (Renovations) Ltd v Broad* [1989] ICR 729, *Allan Janes LLP v Balraj Johal*, above, *Thurstan Hoskin & Partners v Jewill Hill & Bennett* [2002] EWCA Civ 249, [2002] All ER (D) 62 (Feb) and *Safetynet Security Ltd v Coppage* [2013] IRLR 970. The better view is, however, that proscribed classes of customers should be limited to those that the employee has dealt with or, at least, may have knowledge about because the employee in question has overseen the work of other employees dealing with them (see *Spafax v Harrison*, above). Similarly, the class of customer ought to be limited to those persons who were clients of the employer for a defined period of time prior to the termination of the employee's contract of employment. In this way the covenant will not embrace persons who may have been clients prior to the employment of the employee, but were not clients of the employer at any time during the period of the employee's employment. However, in *Plowman v Ash* (above) the Court of Appeal held that an employer is entitled to protect by a non-dealing covenant customers who have ceased to deal with that employer during the currency of the employment contract in which that restraint appeared. This seems contrary to principle. It is of the essence of a reasonable restraint that it should protect the employer only against unfair competition by the employee, which means the exploitation by the employee of his knowledge about, and influence over customers that he has acquired during his employment (see *per* Lord Parker in *Herbert Morris v Saxelby*, above). The recent case of *White Digital Media Ltd v Weaver and anor* [2013] EWHC 1681 (QB) emphasises the danger of not restricting non–solicitation or non–dealing covenants to those clients about whom the covenantee has knowledge or over whom he can exercise influence. A covenant will be too wide in its ambit if it purports to prohibit the ex employee from soliciting or dealing with persons who only become customers of the employer after the employee has left his employment (see *Konski v Peet* [1915] 1 Ch 530). There is a limited exception to this, namely prospective customers. An employer is entitled to protect himself against solicitation or dealing with prospective customers, at least where those prospective customers have been in negotiation with the employer prior to the employee leaving his employment and the employee has had contact with that prospective customer in the course of the negotiations (see *International Consulting Services (UK) Ltd v Hart* [2000] IRLR 227 and *Advantage Business Systems Ltd v Hopley* ibid, but compare *Associated Foreign Exchange Ltd v International Foreign Exchange UK Ltd* [2010] EWHC 1178 (Ch), [2010] IRLR 964).

The problem posed by the existence of contradictory authorities on whether the class of clients not to be solicited or dealt with ought to be closed by reference to clients actually dealt with by the employee remains to be resolved, the Court of Appeal having failed to grapple with the issue in *Dentmaster (UK) Ltd v Kent* [1997] IRLR 636. It would seem from the recent decisions cited above that ultimately the reasonableness of non-solicitation and non-dealing covenants is so fact sensitive that authorities can provide little guidance. The Court of Appeal in the *Coppage* case (above) observed that cases in this area turn so much on their own facts that the citation of precedent is not of assistance.

Difficulty can arise even with limited restraints on dealing with customers where the market may be small and the customers therefore limited in number. This difficulty may be exacerbated by the use of ambiguous phraseology (see *Austin Knight (UK) Ltd v Hinds* [1994] FSR 52). The courts regard a non-solicitation covenant as being the least form of restraint and therefore more readily justifiable (see *Stenhouse Australia Ltd v Phillips*, above, *Scully v Lee*, above and also *Premier Model Management Ltd v Bruce* [2012] EWHC 3509 (QB)). Similarly, a restriction on dealing with suppliers of the employer was not upheld where all of the principal suppliers in the market were covered and it had the effect of preventing any competition: see *Energy Renewals Ltd v Borg* [2014] IRLR 713.

There is remarkably little authority on what constitutes 'solicitation'. In *Wessex Dairies Ltd v Smith* [1935] 2 KB 80 a milkman, prior to the termination of his employment contract, informed his customers, that he was leaving his existing employment, but would be available to do business with them again after a specified date in the future. The Court of Appeal held that this constituted solicitation of his employer's customers. In *Taylor Stuart & Co v Croft (Timothy)* (1998) 606 IRLB 15 an employee subject to a non-solicitation restraint despatched a letter to clients on the headed notepaper of a new firm he was proposing to establish as follows:

> 'Dear X,
>
> This is to inform you that I left the Partnership of Taylor Stuart & Co on 18 November 1994. With effect from 1 December 1994 I shall be establishing my own professional practice and can be contacted as above.'

The court held that it was of the essence of solicitation that the client should be requested to transfer his custom. Accordingly, the letter would have been unobjectionable if it had been limited to its first sentence, but constituted a solicitation because of the second, which invited the addressees to contact him. Other forms of solicitation less direct than that involve advertising. In *Trego v Hunt* [1896] AC 7 it was held that an advertisement not directed specifically to the clients of the business concerned, but more generally, did not constitute 'solicitation'. In *Towry EJ Ltd v Bennett and ors* [2012] EWHC 224 (QB) the learned judge held, as must be right, that solicitation can occur even though a client or customer makes the first approach to the employee. It is of the essence of a solicitation that the employee engages in requesting, persuading or encouraging a person to place business with them or on behalf of their employer. It is plain that a customer who makes a first approach to the employee along the lines of 'what are you doing now, having left your former employer?' can be solicited with the response 'I'm in the same line of business as before. Have you got any work that my new employer could do for you?' In that situation who makes the first approach is irrelevant, it is the substance of the conversation that matters. See *Croesus Financial Services Ltd* (above). See also the discussion of the meaning of 'solicitation' in *QBE Management Services (UK) Ltd v Dymoke* [2012] IRLR 458 at paragraphs 184 to 185. There must be a 'direct and specific' appeal, whether by advertisement or otherwise.

Further difficulties arise where, in addition to a prohibition on 'solicitation', a draughtsman of a restrictive covenant adds other expressions such as: 'enticing away' or 'interfering with' the clients or customers of the employer. The word 'canvass' is synonymous with soliciting (see *QBE Management Services ibid and Customer Systems Plc v Ranson* [2012] EWCA Civ 841, [2012] IRLR 769). In other such cases, it is difficult for the court to know whether the covenant merely prohibits solicitation in the sense of making the first approach or whether acts beyond making the first approach are also prohibited such as to render the covenant a prohibition against dealing with customers even if those customers make the first approach to the employee: see *Austin Knight (UK) Ltd v Hinds* [1994] FSR 52 and *Hanover Insurance Brokers v Schapiro*, above, *per* Dillon LJ, but *cf* Nolan LJ. In *Hydra plc v Anastasi* [2005] EWHC 1559 (QB), [2005] All ER (D) 276 (Jul) Royce J held in respect of a covenant 'not to solicit or entice away any employee of the employer for a period of twelve months following the termination of the covenantor's employment' that the word 'entice' meant 'tempt, lure, persuade and inveigle'. In that case the facts established were that the covenantee employer company was a small business with few employees and it was therefore entitled to protect the entirety of its employees from poaching by a former employee and, further, on the facts the employee who had left to join the covenantee's rival business had himself approached the covenantor and sought to persuade him to let him join the new venture. In those circumstances, there was no breach of the covenant not to entice away an employee. It seems therefore that, even in the extended meaning of the word 'entice' given by Royce J, the essential ingredient of that term is making the first approach.

It is to be observed that the views of the client cannot affect or influence the court in determining whether to enforce a non-solicitation or non-dealing covenant. In *John Michael Design plc v Cooke* [1987] ICR 445 a client intervened in an application by a claimant employer for interim injunctive relief against former employees to restrain them from dealing with former clients of the employer. The client protested that the interim injunction should not extend to prohibit the former employees from dealing with the intervenor because the intervenor had no intention whatsoever of doing any further business with the claimant. At first instance, the judge acceded to the intervenor's argument. The Court of Appeal, however, held that there should be no qualification of the interim injunction to enforce the restrictive covenants in question so as to exclude from its ambit an individual client. Rather, the Court of Appeal held that the restrictive covenant was most necessary to the claimant in the cases of clients refusing to do future business because, manifestly, if a client proposed to remain loyal to the claimant employer there was no need for the protection of the restrictive covenant.

Until the case of *Dawnay, Day & Co Ltd v de Braconier d'Alphen* [1998] ICR 1068 there was conflicting authority at Court of Appeal level as to whether an employer could justify a restraint on soliciting his employees to leave his employment. In the *Dawnay, Day* case it was held that an employer had a legitimate interest in the stability of his workforce, at least so far as senior employees were concerned. However, in *Dawnay, Day* there were two restraints relating to the protection of the workforce in the employment contracts in question. The first restraint prohibited soliciting senior employees to leave their employment. The second restraint prohibited the covenantor employing the covenantee's senior employees. The claimants sought relief only in respect of the first of these covenants which the judge held to be reasonable. The judge, however, opined *obiter* that the second form of restraint would be too wide to be enforceable. This *obiter* opinion was followed by Tugendhat J in *White Digital Media Ltd* (above) where he held a covenant restricting one former employee from employing another former employee unenforceable. The objection to any form of restraint prohibiting an ex employee from employing in his business, or in a business that he has joined, a colleague of his at his former employers is that it amounts to a restraint on that colleague from seeking or obtaining work with whom he pleases. In *Kores Manufacturing Co Ltd v Kolok Manufacturing Co Ltd* (above) two employers in the same industry entered into an agreement that they would not employ members of each other's staff for a period of time after those employees had left their respective employment. The Court of Appeal held that this provision was unenforceable because it was not limited to senior employees who might carry away trade secrets or confidential information to the competitor. However, the Court of Appeal also opined, *obiter*, that the covenant was against public policy because it would prevent employees of each of the parties from seeking employment with the other in circumstances in which those individual employees did not have in their employment contracts any restraint prohibiting them from joining a competitor. The effect of the covenant in *Kores Manufacturing Co Ltd v Kolok Manufacturing Co Ltd* was to enable the two employers to achieve through the back door what they had failed to achieve through the front.

However, in *TFS Derivatives* (above) one of the restrictive covenants in the employee's contract was as follows: '[you will not] for six months employ, engage or work with an employee for the purpose of the supply of relevant services or a business which competes, or which plans to compete with, or is similar to a relevant business'. The learned judge held that this covenant went 'no further than is reasonably necessary in all the circumstances to protect [a legitimate interest] of the employer'. The judge did not, however, grant an injunction to enforce this restraint on the grounds that there was no evidence of breach. However, the judge's attention does not appear to have been drawn to the decision in *Dawnay, Day* (above) or to *Kores Manufacturing Co Ltd v Kolok Manufacturing Co Ltd* (above). Employers seeking to impose restrictions on the solicitation of their staff should be cautious about distinguishing for the purposes of such protection those staff occupying positions of importance to the covenantor's business or have training or business or technical knowledge and experience from those members of staff who do not: see *TSC Europe (UK) Ltd v Massey* [1999] IRLR 22. In small organisations, however, it may be that all the staff will have the necessary qualities or importance to justify protection against solicitation by an ex employee.

Duration

Whether the length of any restraint renders it unreasonable is a matter of impression for the judge. In *Stenhouse Australia Ltd v Phillips* [1974] AC 391 (above) Lord Wilberforce stated that the question of a reasonable duration for a covenant in restraint of trade could not 'advantageously form the subject of direct evidence. It is for the judge, after informing himself as fully as he can of the facts and circumstances relating to the employer's business, the nature of the employer's interest to be protected, and the likely effect on this of solicitation, to decide whether the contractual period is reasonable or not. An opinion as to the reasonableness of elements of it, particularly of the time during which it is to run, can seldom be precise, and can only be formed on a broad and commonsense view' (*Stenhouse*, 402). The question that the court must ask itself is: 'what is a reasonable time during which the employer is entitled to protection against solicitation of clients with whom the employee had contact and influence during employment and who were not bound to the employer by contract or by stability of association' (ibid). Thus even limited restraints, such as non-solicitation of client covenants, will be subject to close scrutiny to determine whether their duration is too long given the circumstances of the covenantee's business and the covenantor's role in that business: see *Associated Foreign Exchange Ltd v International Foreign Exchange UK Ltd* [2010] EWHC 1178 (Ch), [2010] IRLR 964. So far as the protection of confidential information is concerned acute problems are likely to arise in relation to fixing a reasonable duration for a post-termination covenant restraining an employee from engaging in competition with the employer. Logically, if the covenant is designed to protect trade secrets or equivalent confidential information in the sense of information that would never be disclosed by the employer and could not be 'reverse engineered' by a rival then it would be reasonable to impose a lifetime prohibition on the employee working for a competitor. Yet the courts constantly refer to the necessity, even when protecting trade secrets and equivalent confidential information, of keeping the non-compete provision to a reasonable duration: see, for example, *per* Cross J in *Printers and Finishers Ltd v Holloway (No 2)* [1965] 1 WLR 1. Where a covenant over a limited geographical area is taken to protect confidential information, the courts have, in the past, accepted a non-compete provision of unlimited duration: *Haynes v Doman* [1899] 2 Ch 13, CA. But, as the Court of Appeal has recently observed in *Scully v Lee* (above), confidential information knows no territorial boundaries and, accordingly, the imposition of an area blanket restraint to protect confidential information is, in itself, illogical. All that can be said about the duration of covenants to protect confidential information is that it must be an issue of fact in every case as to the reasonableness of the duration of the covenant and it is submitted that the covenant's duration must necessarily be a function of how long the information to be protected is likely to remain confidential, or, at least, useful to a competitor (see *Norbrook Laboratories v Hopley* ibid and *Duarte v Black and Decker Corpn* ibid). Thus, if the confidential information to be protected is information relating to a proposed business strategy the covenant cannot endure for longer than the period during which the strategy is to remain confidential before being implemented (in effect, made public) by the employer. This, however, does not resolve the essential problem presented by extremely confidential technical information (for example, the secret of the recipe for the manufacture of Coca-Cola – anecdotally the most treasured and most protected trade secret in the world). Would it be permissible for that company to impose a lifetime ban on an employee who knew what the recipe was from joining a competitor like Pepsi-Cola? The law has yet to grapple with this problem. It is, however, clear that a judge is <u>not</u> bound by precedent to uphold as reasonable a restraint of the same duration and in the same field as a previous judge: see *Dairy Crest Ltd v Pigott* [1989] ICR 92, CA. It is equally clear that the more limited the ambit of the restraint, the greater the period of duration that will be upheld: see *Stenhouse v Phillips*, above, and *Fitch v Dewes* [1921] 2 AC 158. However, it must be doubtful that the latter case would, on the same facts, nowadays be followed (see, for example, *Allan Janes LLP v Balraj Johal*, above). It seems clear that where both the ambit of the restraint is narrow and the duration is short the covenant will a fortiori be held enforceable. Thus a non-solicitation restraint for a period of six months was upheld by the Court of Appeal in the *Coppage* case (above). Moreover there seems to be a trend toward upholding covenants where the duration of the covenant appears to be an industry standard, for example non-solicitation and non-dealing covenants imposed on insurance brokers for 12 months (see for example *Romero Insurance Brokers Ltd v Templeton and anor* [2013] EWHC 1198 (QB) and *Tradition Financial Services v Gamberoni* [2017] EWHC 768 (QB)). Such industry 'standards' for restrictive covenants should be approached with suspicion by the Courts. The fact that an industry imposes similar restraints does not mean that they will be justifiable. It remains the case that the court must scrutinise each case on its own facts.

(Subject always to the caveat that judges should not slavishly follow precedent in restraint of trade cases, but rather examine the reasonableness of covenants in the light of the facts of each case, for a convenient compendium of cases where covenants have been upheld, or not, see *Restrictive Covenants Under Common and Competition Law* (4th edn, Sweet & Maxwell), Kamerling & Osman, p 381ff.)

41.9   *What is the consequence of a finding of unreasonableness?*

Many judges (see, for example, Lord McNaghten in *Nordenfelt*, above, and Cox J in *TFS Derivatives*, above) have erroneously described a covenant in restraint of trade which is not justifiable as being 'void'. This is not correct. A covenant in unreasonable restraint of trade is merely unenforceable. The significance of this distinction is that a covenant in restraint of trade is not illegal in the sense of it being a criminal offence to enter into or perform the obligations so imposed: *Apple Corpn Ltd v Apple Computer Inc* [1992] FSR 431, Ch D. Accordingly, covenants in restraint of trade, the proper law of which is English law will be enforced by an English court by, for example, a worldwide injunction even if the restraint may be invalid under the law of other jurisdictions. Equally, whole contracts may be found to be in restraint of trade (see, for example, *A Schroeder Music Publishing Co Ltd v Macaulay* [1974] 1 WLR 1308).

41.10   Other elements

Consideration

There is considerable debate as to whether a court is permitted to look at the adequacy of the consideration which supports any contract or provision in restraint of trade as part of the court's investigation into the reasonableness of the covenant. Authorities against the court considering adequacy of consideration include: *M and S Drapers (a firm) v Reynolds* [1957] 1 WLR 9, CA *per* Hodson LJ and *Allied Dunbar (Frank Weisinger) Ltd v Weisinger* [1988] IRLR 60, paras 30–32 *per* Millett J. Contradicting these authorities are: Lord McNaghten in *Nordenfelt* (above) at 565, Lord Hodson (apparently dissenting from his own earlier judgment in *M and S Drapers*) in *Esso Petroleum v Harper's Garage* (above) at 318D-F and Lord Pearce in the same case at 323E-F. (See also *Reuse Collections Ltd v Sendall* [2015] IRLR 226 at [71], where HHJ Stephen Davies considered, *obiter*, that the adequacy of the consideration was a factor relevant to the reasonableness of the restrictive covenant.) The better view, it is submitted, is that the court cannot look to the adequacy of the consideration in the sense of determining whether the value of the bargain to the party restrained is the same as the value imparted to the covenantee. The court does not ask 'whether the consideration is equal in value to that which the party gives up or loses by the restraint under which he has placed himself . . . it is impossible for the court . . . to say whether, in any particular case, the party restrained has made an improvident bargain or not'. Rather the test is whether 'the restraint of a party from carrying on a trade is larger and wider than the protection of the party with whom the contract is made can possibly require': (*per* Tindale CJ, *Hitchcock v Coker* (1837) 6 Ad & El 959). It is therefore submitted that the issue of consideration has become confused because in many cases the courts have elided the issue of consideration in the technical sense of the contractual rule that there must be adequate consideration to support a bargain enforceable by the courts with consideration in the sense of a balance of benefit between the parties bestowed under a contract. The latter form of consideration may be considered only to the extent that the covenantee does not under the bargain struck extract more protection from the covenantor than is reasonable to protect the covenantee's legitimate interests. If it were legitimate to consider the adequacy of consideration, then it would follow that covenants in restraint of trade could be purchased outright, which is clearly not the law (see *Mont v Mills* ibid). The more money paid to the covenantor, either specifically as consideration to support a restrictive covenant, or by way of salary or other emoluments of employment, the longer the restraint that could be imposed upon him. This cannot be right because the nature, ambit and duration of a covenant can never be greater than is merely adequate to protect a legitimate interest. The legitimate interest does not change as a function of the amount of money paid to a covenantor. Equally, taking into account the adequacy of consideration would mean that low-paid employees could never have valid restrictions imposed upon them, even although the employer might have legitimate interests to protect. The court has rejected in a recent case the notion that low pay vitiates a restrictive covenant: see *Norbrook Laboratories* ibid. Extreme cases do, however, arise in which the courts will indulge in balancing the benefit and burden as between the two parties: see *Schroeder v Macaulay* (above) and *M and S Drapers (a firm) v Reynolds* [1957] 1 WLR 9, CA. There must be some consideration to support the restraint and it should be noted that in this respect a deed will not be sufficient if it is a seal alone: see *Hutton v Parker* (1839) 7 Dowl. 739. Equally, restrictive covenants cannot be supported where the only consideration for them is a promise to perform an existing contract: see *WRN Ltd v Ayris* [2008] EWHC 1080 (QB), [2008] IRLR 889. The introduction of restrictions after the commencement of employment should normally be supported by consideration. In *Reuse Collections Ltd v Sendall* (*ibid*), the

High Court held that a restrictive covenant introduced during employment was unenforceable for want of consideration in that there was no express benefit or payment associated with the variation, and continued employment did not suffice as consideration where the variation was not proposed on the basis that a failure to accept would lead to dismissal or other sanction.

41.11 *Repudiatory breach*

An employer in repudiatory breach of an employment contract, where that breach is accepted as terminating the same by the employee, cannot enforce any post-termination restraints: *General Billposting Co Ltd v Atkinson* [1909] AC 118. However, the fact that a restrictive covenant purports to apply upon termination of the contract of employment, 'howsoever caused, whether lawfully or unlawfully', does not itself render the covenant too wide and unenforceable: cf *Rock Refrigeration v Jones and Seward Refrigeration Ltd* [1997] 1 All ER 1, [1996] IRLR 675. There was a period when this proposition was doubted by the courts and it was held that restrictive covenants purporting to apply upon termination of the contract of employment 'howsoever caused, whether or lawfully or unlawfully' were held to be too wide. However, in the *Rock Refrigeration* case this argument was resolved in favour of upholding covenants expressed to apply even to a termination of the employment contract occasioned by a repudiatory breach by the employer. The Court of Appeal held that the doctrine of restraint of trade does not become engaged unless and until the contract of employment containing the restraints is lawfully terminated. Thus, if the employer repudiates the contract, which is then terminated by the acceptance of that repudiation by the employee, the restrictive covenant does not fall to be considered at all under the restraint of trade doctrine because both parties to the contract which has been repudiated are discharged from future performance of their express contractual obligations: see *Photo Production Ltd v Securicor Transport Ltd* [1980] AC 827. The principle of *Securicor* is that upon acceptance of repudiatory breach express future obligations upon both parties (the innocent and the guilty) to a contract are discharged, whereupon implied secondary obligations (such as the obligation to pay damages for breach) come into force. However, despite the (minority) views expressed by Phillips LJ in *Rock Refrigeration* (above), it is submitted that the court cannot at this stage imply obligations in restraint of trade because they are, *prima facie*, contrary to public policy and unenforceable (see *Wallace Bogan & Co v Cove* [1997] IRLR 453). (To this principle there are the very narrow exceptions of an implied obligation in business sale agreements on the part of the vendor not to solicit customers of the business sold (see *Trego v Hunt*, above) and an implied obligation on the part of employees not to make use of or disclose trade secrets or equivalent confidential information of their employers after the termination of the employment contract (see *Faccenda Chicken v Fowler*, above).) It is inconceivable beyond these two implied obligations that a court will impose by implication any other provisions in restraint of trade because it is contrary to public policy in the broad sense to do so. The decision in *Rock Refrigeration* does, however, reveal a real danger for employers (identified by Phillips LJ). If an employer accepts a repudiatory breach by an employee as terminating the contract of employment he will (under the principle in the *Securicor* case) be in danger of losing the protection of any post-termination restraints in the contract of employment. It should be noted, however, that the majority of the court in *Rock Refrigeration* considered that a repudiatory breach did not discharge an employee from his obligations of confidentiality (see also *Campbell v Frisbee* [2002] EWHC 328 (Ch), [2002] EMLR 656). It is for this reason that it is crucial for employers to provide expressly in any contract of employment for a right to terminate the contract (ie in accordance with its terms) in the event of any conduct of the employee which would constitute a repudiatory breach (for example, gross misconduct). If the contract of employment is terminated in accordance with an express term of that kind then the rules relating to repudiatory breach do not apply because the employer will have terminated the contract in accordance with its express terms and will not have to rely on any implied obligation arising under common law but can rely instead on the obligations expressed in the contract of employment as applying post-termination of the same. It should be noted that an employer's decision to cease paying an employee who had failed to give due notice of resignation under the contract does not necessarily amount to an acceptance of the employee's repudiatory breach so as to bring the contract to an end: see *Sunrise Brokers LLP v Rogers* [2014] IRLR 780, where the High Court held that the employer had the option of affirming the contract where an employee had refused to continue working and that the failure to pay the employee did not automatically bring the contract to an end. The employer was therefore entitled to seek injunctive relief to keep the employee on garden leave notwithstanding the absence of the usual requirement that the employee continues to be paid for the duration of the notice period.

Controversially, in *RDF Media Group Plc v Clements* [2007] EWHC 2892 (QB), [2008] IRLR 207, the judge held that an employee against whom the employer had committed a breach of the implied duty of trust and confidence was not entitled to treat the contract as repudiated because that employee had committed a prior breach of that same implied duty which was not known to the employer at the date on which the employer breached that duty. Because the employee could not treat the contract as repudiated, covenants he had entered into in a shareholders agreement continued to operate. Not only does this decision fly in the face of long-established principles of repudiatory breach of employment contracts (see *Healey v Francaise Rubastic SA* [1917] 1 KB 946, which was upheld in the House of Lords in *Ramsden v David Sharratt & Sons Ltd* (1930) 35 Com Cas 314, HL, and *Howard v Pickford Tool Co Ltd* [1951] 1 KB 417), but it is based upon an authority relating to commercial arbitrations (*Bremer Vulkan Schiffbau und Maschinenfabrik v South India Shipping Corpn Ltd* [1981] AC 909, HL) which although a decision of the House of Lords was much criticised at the time and has subsequently been superceded in any event by statutory reforms of arbitration. In *Food Corpn of India v Antclizo Shipping Corpn, The Antclizo* [1988] 2 All ER 513, [1988] 1 WLR 603, HL Lord Goff commented on the *Bremer* case as follows: 'It is not understating the position to record that the effect of this decision and, indeed, the reasoning upon which it is based, has provoked serious disquiet among the whole commercial community. In particular, it has been suggested that the mutual obligation resting upon both parties to proceed with their reference to arbitration, as expressed by Lord Diplock, bears no relation to commercial reality . . . '. In *Tullett Prebon plc v BGC Brokers LP* [2010] EWHC 484 (QB), [2010] IRLR 648 the judge refused to follow the *RDF* case (decision affd on appeal [2011] EWCA Civ 131; [2011] IRLR 420). The same judge (Jack J) again refused to follow the RDF case in a more recent decision: *Brandeaux Advisers (UK) Ltd v Chadwick* [2010] EWHC 3241 (QB), [2011] IRLR 224 holding that an unaccepted repudiation was a "thing writ in water" (see the *Howard* case supra). Subsequently, judges sitting in the Court of Session and the EAT have declined to follow the *RDF* case: see *McNeill v Aberdeen City Council (no. 2)* [2014] IRLR 113 and *Atkinson v Community Gateway Association* [2014] IRLR 834.

In *Lonmar Global Risks Ltd v West* [2011] IRLR 138 an employee was subject to 12 months post termination non-solicitation and dealing covenants set out in clause 14A of his employment contract. Clause 14B stated: "Clause 14A shall apply in the event of termination of the . . . employment in all circumstances except unlawful termination by [the employer]". It was argued on behalf of the employee that an unfair dismissal by the employer would fall within the expression "unlawful termination". At trial the judge ruled that "unlawful termination" meant unlawful termination at common law ie a wrongful dismissal not a mere unfair dismissal. The judge went on to hold the covenants enforceable.

41.12 Conflict of laws

Because the law of restraint of trade arises as a matter of public policy, foreign law, even if it is the proper law of the contract, cannot dictate the validity or invalidity of a provision in restraint of trade. Contracts of employment the proper law of which is a foreign law will not be enforced by an English court if the restraints in question are unenforceable under the public policy of England and Wales: see *Rousillon v Rousillon* (1880) 14 Ch D 351. A distinction must be made between principles relating to mandatory rules of English law and English public policy. The restraint of trade doctrine is not a mandatory rule for the purposes of Article 6(1) of the Rome Convention. Rather, it falls under Article 16 of that Convention: see *Duarte v Black and Decker Corpn* [2007] EWHC 2720 (QB), [2008] 1 All ER (Comm) 401 and *BGC Capital Markets (Switzerland) LLC v Rees* [2011] EWHC 2009 (QB). Accordingly, where covenants in restraint of trade are expressed to be governed by a proper law other than the law of England, and would be enforceable under that proper law, but not under the English doctrine of restraint of trade, then the result of the application of the specified foreign law would be 'manifestly incompatible with English public policy': *Duarte*, ibid. It follows that the approach that should be taken to covenants expressed to be governed by foreign law is for the English court first to determine whether those covenants would be valid under that foreign law. If not, then there is no need to apply the doctrine of restraint of trade to them. If however, the court decides that the covenants would be valid under the chosen foreign law, then the English court must go on to apply its own doctrine of restraint of trade to those covenants. If invalid under the English doctrine of restraint of trade, then the English law 'trumps' the chosen foreign law.

41.13 TRADE SECRETS AND CONFIDENTIAL INFORMATION

On 28 November 2013 the European Commission proposed a Draft Directive for the protection of trade secrets. This was followed by a new Council proposal published on 19 May 2014. The proposal is for a comprehensive codification of the law on confidential information as it applies to trade secrets such as chemical formulae or recipes, techniques of manufacture or technological developments and 'soft' trade secrets such as information about customers and suppliers, business processes, business plans and market research are, under the proposed *Directive*, to be dealt with together as, in effect, a discrete species of intellectual property akin to copyright, design rights, patents and trade marks. It is anticipated that the *Directive* will be adopted by the Commission in due course. If so, thereafter there will thereafter be a transposition period during which member states will be required to incorporate the *Directive* into their national law. For the time being, however, the position regarding the protection of trade secrets and confidential information remains a matter of common law and equity. (The European Court of Human Rights has held that there was a violation of a Hungarian journalist's right to freedom of expression under *Art 10, ECHR*, in circumstances where he was dismissed for breaching express confidentiality clauses in his contract by publishing a book about his employer's practices: *Matúz v Hungary* [2015] IRLR 74.)

The courts have long recognised that trade secrets are a legitimate interest which an employer may protect by imposing a covenant limiting the field of activity in which an ex employee may engage after leaving his employment (see, for example, Lord Parker in *Herbert Morris v Saxelby*, above, and *Printers and Finishers Ltd v Holloway* [1964] 3 All ER 54, [1965] RPC 239). In this respect, therefore, obligations of confidentiality that an employee owes his employer have an important role to play in the doctrine of restraint of trade. However, obligations of confidentiality, if breached by an employee either during or after the employment contract has ended, may give rise to claims for relief which lie outside any claim for breach of restrictive covenants in employment contracts, specifically the so-called 'springboard injunction'. In recent years, decisions of the court have led to much confusion in these areas, such that discussions of the principles of the law of confidentiality now resemble medieval theological debates about how many angels can dance on pinheads.

It is necessary, therefore, to identify certain basic principles relating to the obligations of confidence owed by employees to their employers. The obligation of good faith and fidelity (now transmuted into an obligation of trust and confidence: see generally **8.13 CONTRACT OF EMPLOYMENT**) implied into all contracts of employment has as an incident of that larger duty a specific obligation that the employee shall not make use of, or disclose, for the benefit of a competing business information acquired by the employee about his employer's business in the course of his employment (see *Robb v Green* [1895] 2 QB 1). In that case an employee during his contract of employment made a list of the names and addresses of his employer's clients and, following the termination of his employment, used that list to canvas the clients of the former employer for a rival business established by the employee. The employee was held to have breached the implied duty of good faith and fidelity in so acting and was ordered by injunction to hand over the list he had made to his former employer and to pay damages. The decision was affirmed on appeal ([1895] 2 QB 315). It is of the greatest significance to observe that the defendant contended that the information contained on the list which he had made was information that could be obtained from sources within the public domain. The trial judge (Hawkins J) did not accept that all the information could have been so sourced, but added (p 18) that even were that true the employee had nonetheless acted in breach of his duty in creating a convenient compilation of material for the purpose of assisting an intended competitor. (For a more recent case on the scope of the employee's obligations of good faith and fidelity while in employment, see *Helmet Integrated Systems Ltd v Tunnard* [2006] EWCA Civ 1735, [2007] IRLR 126, in which the Court of Appeal accepted that the employee had not breached his obligations to his employer by taking, during his employment and unbeknownst to his employer, steps preparatory to competing with his employer; see also *Khan v Landskerr Childcare Ltd* UKEAT/0036/12/DM, *Imam-Sadeque v BlueBay Asset Management (Services) Ltd* [2012] EWHC 3511 (QB) and **8.16** CONTRACT OF EMPLOYMENT. Note, however, that the position is otherwise for company directors and very senior employees: see *Crowson Fabrics Ltd v Rider and ors* [2007] EWHC 2942 (Ch), [2008] IRLR 288; *Reuse Collections Ltd v Sendall* [2015] IRLR 226; and **9.16** DIRECTORS.)

Some ninety years after *Robb v Green* [1895] 2 QB 1 the Court of Appeal embarked on an analysis of the duties of confidentiality owed by an employee: see *Faccenda Chicken Ltd v Fowler* [1986] ICR 297, CA. At first instance in that case, Goulding J had analysed the position thus ([1984] ICR 589 at 598–599):

> 'Let me now deal with the alleged abuse of confidential information. I must make it clear that anything I say about the law is intended to apply only to cases of master and servant. In my view information acquired by an employee in the course of his service, and not the subject of any relevant express agreement, may fall as regards confidence into any of three classes. First, there is information which, because of its trivial character or its easy accessibility from public sources of information, cannot be regarded by reasonable persons or by the law as confidential at all. The servant is at liberty to impart it during his service or afterwards to anyone he pleases, even his master's competitor. An example might be a published patent specification well known to people in the industry concerned . . . Secondly, there is information which the servant must treat as confidential (either because he is expressly told it is confidential, or because from its character it obviously is so) but which once learned necessarily remains in the servant's head and becomes part of his own skill and knowledge applied in the course of his master's business. So long as the employment continues, he cannot otherwise use or disclose such information without infidelity and therefore breach of contract. But when he is no longer in the same service, the law allows him to use his full skill and knowledge for his own benefit in competition with his former master; and . . . there seems to be no established distinction between the use of such information where its possessor trades as a principal, and where he enters the employment of a new master, even though the latter case involves disclosure and not mere personal use of the information. If an employer wants to protect information of this kind, he can do so by an express stipulation restraining the servant from competing with him (within reasonable limits of time and space after the termination of his employment). Thirdly, however, there are, to my mind, specific trade secrets so confidential that, even though they may necessarily have been

learned by heart and even though the servant may have left the service, they cannot lawfully be used for anyone's benefit but the master's. An example is the secret process which was the subject matter of *Amber Size & Chemical Co Ltd v Menzel* [1913] 2 Ch 239.'

Goulding J went on to hold that the information that had been used by the defendants upon leaving the plaintiff company's employment and setting up a rival business fell into the second of the three categories and, accordingly, there was no breach of duty involved in its use by the defendants. This was not a case in which there were any post-termination restraints in the defendants' contract of employment with Faccenda limiting their business activities in any way. Goulding J, however, opined (above, 599E) that an employer can protect the use of information in the second category, even though it does not include any information in the third category (ie a trade secret or its equivalent) by means of a restrictive covenant. The Court of Appeal held:

(1)   That in contracts of employment confidentiality obligations of the employee are to be determined by that contract.

(2)   Absent any express term relating to confidential information in an employment contract, the obligations of the employee in respect of the use and disclosure of information are the subject of implied terms.

(3)   During the currency of the employment relationship the obligations in relation to the use and disclosure of information are included in the implied term imposing a duty of good faith and fidelity (or trust and confidence) on the employee. The Court of Appeal declined to consider the precise limits of the confidentiality obligation arising out of that implied term during the currency of the employment contract, but observed:

(a)   that the extent of the duty of good faith will vary according to the nature of the contract; and

(b)   that that duty would be broken if an employee makes a list of customers, or memorises such a list, for use after his employment ends, even though there is no legal impediment on the employee soliciting or doing business with those customers after he leaves his employment. For this proposition the Court of Appeal returned to and relied on *Robb v Green* (above).

(4)   The implied term imposing an obligation on the employee not to use or disclose information learnt during his employment after the determination of the same is more restricted in its scope than the obligation during the currency of the employment contract and arising from the general duty of good faith and fidelity. Specifically, the implied post-termination obligation does not extend to all information given to, or acquired by, the employee while in his employment, and may not cover information which is only 'confidential' in the sense that it falls within the broader category of information that is protected during the currency of the employment contract as an incident of the obligation of good faith and fidelity. For this proposition the Court of Appeal relied upon the judgment of Cross J in *Printers and Finishers Ltd v Holloway* [1965] RPC 239 at 253:

'In this connection one must bear in mind that not all information which is given to a servant in confidence and which it would be a breach of his duty for him to disclose to another person during his employment is a trade secret which he can be prevented from using for his own advantage after the employment is over, even though he has entered into no express covenant with regard to the matter in hand. For example, the printing instructions were handed to Holloway to be used by him during his employment exclusively for the plaintiffs' benefit. It would have been a breach of duty on his part to divulge any of the contents to a stranger while he was employed, but many of these instructions are not really 'trade secrets' at all. Holloway was not, indeed, entitled to take a copy of the instructions away with him; but in so far as the instructions cannot be called 'trade secrets' and he carried them in his head, he is entitled to use them for his own benefit or the benefit of any future employer.'

(See also *E Worsley & Co Ltd v Cooper* [1939] 1 All ER 290.)

Accordingly, the Court of Appeal (*obiter*) disagreed with Goulding J's judgment where he stated that an employer can protect 'category 2' information (not also falling within 'category 3') by means of an express post-termination restraint. The Court said:

'In our view the circumstances in which a restrictive covenant would be appropriate and could be successfully invoked emerge very clearly from the words used by Cross J in *Printers & Finishers Ltd v Holloway* [ibid] . . . If the managing director is right in thinking that there are features in the plaintiffs' process which can fairly be regarded as trade secrets and which their employees will inevitably carry away with them in their heads, then the proper way for the plaintiffs to protect themselves would be by exacting covenants from their employees restricting their field of activity after they have left their employment, not by asking the court to extend the general equitable doctrine to prevent breaking confidence beyond all reasonable bounds.'

On this analysis, as the Court of Appeal pointed out, it is impossible to provide a comprehensive list of those things which constitute trade secrets, or equivalent confidential information, that will be protected by the implied obligation of confidence operating post-termination and which would therefore form a legitimate interest justifying an express post-termination restraint limiting the fields of activity in which the ex employee may work for a period of time. Secret processes of manufacture are an obvious example of such information but 'innumerable other pieces of information are capable of being trade secrets, though the secrecy of some information may be only short lived . . . the fact that the circulation of certain information is restricted to a limited number of individuals may throw light on the status of the information and its degree of confidentiality'.

(5)   The Court of Appeal went on to hold that in order to determine whether any particular item of information falls to be protected under the implied obligation of confidentiality operative <u>after</u> the termination of the employment contract a court must consider all the circumstances of the case, including the following matters:-

(a)   the nature of the employment (ie was the employee engaged in a capacity where confidential material was habitually handled by him and he might, accordingly, be expected to realise its sensitivity);

(b)   the nature of the information itself (ie only information which is a 'trade secret' or the equivalent of a trade secret is protected by the post-termination implied obligation);

(c)   whether the employer impressed on the employee the confidentiality of the information;

(d)   whether the relevant information can be easily isolated from other information which the employee is free to use or disclose.

41.13   Restraint of Trade and Confidential Information

The decision by the Court of Appeal in *Faccenda Chicken* has been criticised by some judges and by some textbook writers. In *Balston Ltd v Headline Filters Ltd* [1987] FSR 330 Scott J doubted the Court of Appeal's opinion that information falling within Goulding J's second category which did not also fall within his third category (termed by some textbook writers as 'mere confidential information') could not be protected by an express post-termination restraint. Similarly, in *Systems Reliability Holdings plc v Smith* [1990] IRLR 377, Harman J refused to follow this part of the Court of Appeal's judgment in *Faccenda*. See also *Lancashire Fire Ltd v SA Lyons & Co Ltd* [1997] IRLR 113, CA, per Bingham LJ, para 16 and *A T Poeton (Gloucester Plating) Ltd v Horton* [2001] FSR 169, [2000] ICR 1208, CA.

It is respectfully submitted that these doubts are erroneous. First, it is unquestionably a matter of principle that it is against public policy to restrain the use by an ex employee of knowledge and skills that he has acquired in the course of his employment: see *Herbert Morris v Saxelby*, above, per Lord Parker and *Commercial Plastics Ltd v Vincent* [1965] 1 QB 623. If the employer is to have a legitimate interest to protect in confidential information that information must fall into a special category of sensitivity beyond the mass of more mundane information that an employee will necessarily accumulate during his employment. Second, the Court of Appeal's decision in *Faccenda* does not warrant the criticism that has been levelled against it that it constitutes an excessively narrow view of the obligations of confidentiality in employment contracts or the class of information that may legitimately be protected by an express post-termination restraint or by the implied obligation of confidence operating after the contract of employment has come to an end. As the Court of Appeal pointed out, innumerable other pieces of information besides secret processes of manufacturing may constitute trade secrets, or their equivalent, and thus fall within the protection of express or implied post-termination obligations. Thus in one industry the identity of clients or customers may constitute the equivalent of a trade secret, as will information about the prices charged to those customers by the employer. In other businesses (as in *Faccenda* itself) the same kind of information will constitute only information protectable during the currency of the employment contract, but not afterwards. To an extent, confusion that has arisen since *Faccenda* is the product of quibbles about vocabulary: the expression 'trade secrets' is no doubt more apt to describe information relating to secret processes of manufacture than it is to describe information such as the identity of customers, but there is no sensible reason why one should not describe the latter information as 'information the equivalent of a trade secret' where it is treated as so equivalent in certain industries or businesses. It would, perhaps, be better if the use of the expression 'trade secrets' was abandoned altogether and replaced with the expression 'protectable confidential information'. It was certainly the view of Staughton LJ in *Lansing Linde Ltd v Kerr* [1991] 1 WLR 251, 260B that the problem was one of vocabulary: 'It appears to me that the problem is one of definition: what are trade secrets, and how do they differ (if at all) from confidential information? [It has been] suggested that a trade secret is information which, if disclosed to a competitor, would be liable to cause real (or significant) harm to the owner of the secret. I would add, first, that it must be information used in a trade or business and, secondly, that the owner must limit the dissemination of it or at least not encourage or permit widespread publication.'

There are reasons to doubt the test there propounded by Staughton LJ for identifying protectable confidential information, not least because it appears to place too much emphasis on the subjective view of the employer as to the status of information as distinct from the correct test which must needs be based upon the objective view of the court, but Staughton LJ, nonetheless, correctly identified the confusion that can arise from the terminology that abounds in these cases.

A second area of confusion arises from the difference between the implied obligation of confidentiality which survives after the employment contract has come to an end and the protection that may be afforded by an express post-termination restraint. The implied obligation is limited to an obligation not to disclose or make use of 'protectable confidential information'. This obligation should not be extended to prohibit an employee who possesses such information from going to work for a competitor of his former employer: see *Caterpillar Logistics Services (UK) Ltd v Paula Huesca de Crean* [2012] EWCA Civ 156, [2012] ICR 981 and *Generics (UK) Ltd v Yeda Research and Development Co Ltd* [2012] EWCA Civ 726, [2012] C.P. Rep. 39. It merely restrains him, when working for that competitor, from disclosing or using, the protectable confidential information. (Note that the position is different for self-employed professionals such as lawyers, accountants and patent attorneys who may be made the subject of so-called 'barring-out' orders preventing them from acting in litigation against a former client where it is necessary in order to avoid a significant risk of disclosure of 'protectable confidential information': see *Bolkiah v KPMG* [1999] 2 AC 222 and note the view of Sir Robin Jacobs in *Generics (UK)* ibid that the same principle might apply to in-house lawyers.)

As has been pointed out above (**41.8**), an obligation not to disclose or make use of confidential information in the course of new employment is virtually impossible to police. Accordingly, employers frequently resort to an express post-termination restraint limiting the fields of activity in which the former employee may be involved for a period following the termination of the employment (ie a non-compete provision or, at least, an obligation not to join that part of a competitor's business which competes with the former employer). It is respectfully submitted that Scott J's reservations in *Balston* about the Court of Appeal's decision in *Faccenda* were based on confusion between the scope of the implied obligation of confidentiality and the more practical protection that can be afforded by post-termination non-compete restraints. Equally, in the *Systems Reliability* case, it should be observed that the learned judge had characterised the restraints that he was dealing with as having arisen with respect to a business sale agreement, and not an employment contract. As has also been pointed out above (**41.8**), the court's approach to business sale agreements and the restraint of trade doctrine is very different to the approach adopted to restraints in employment contracts.

The Court of Appeal re-stated the *Faccenda* principle in *Thomas v Farr plc* [2007] EWCA Civ 118, [2007] IRLR 419 and held that only information the equivalent of a trade secret can be protected by a post-termination non-compete restraint.

In conclusion, it is submitted that the law on an employee's obligations of confidentiality may be stated as follows:

(a)   During the currency of the employment contract the employee is bound as an incident of his implied obligation of trust and confidence not to disclose or make use of the mass of information he acquires about his employer's business. The information covered by that obligation is limited so as to exclude only information which is trivial or in the public domain. However, it should be noted that if the employee sources and removes lists of customers or other information from the records of his employer for use in a rival business it does not matter that that information may be available in the public domain or that that information was originally compiled by the employee in the service of the employer. That information belongs to the employer and the employee cannot use it without breaching the implied obligation of confidentiality that existed during the life of his employment contract: see *Crowson Fabrics Ltd v Rider* [2008] IRLR 288 and *Pennwell Publishing (UK) Ltd v Ornstien* [2007] EWHC 1570 (QB), [2007] IRLR 700. NB many compilations of information contained within an employer's computer systems will independently attract protection as databases under the *Copyright, Designs and Patents Act 1988 (as amended)*, but this lies outside the scope of this chapter.

(b)   After the contract of employment comes to an end the employee is subject to an implied obligation not to disclose to, or make use for the benefit of, a competitor information which constitutes protectable confidential information, ie information which has the status of a trade secret or its equivalent. It is an issue of fact, in every case, depending on all the circumstances and applying the various guidelines, whether or not information falls into this category. Certain information, such as the identity of clients or customers is capable of falling into this category, but not necessarily in all businesses. The same is true of price information and many other kinds of information. No comprehensive list can therefore be drawn up of this kind of information. It is, however, clear that technical information regarding manufacturing processes and high level strategic business plans (for example, whether and, if so, when old models are to be replaced by new) will be likely to fall into this third category of protectable confidential information regardless of the nature of the business concerned.

(c) The protection afforded by the implied confidentiality obligation operating after the employment contract has come to an end is limited to disclosing or making use of the information concerned. This implied obligation is therefore of limited practical use to an employer because it does not prevent the employee from going to work for a rival and, once within a rival's business, it is impossible for the employer to monitor whether or not the employee is disclosing or making use of the concerned information.

(d) Accordingly, an employer who rightly considers that an employee may in the course of his employment acquire information falling within the class of protectable confidential information (ie a trade secret or equivalent confidential information) has a legitimate interest to protect under the doctrine of restraint of trade and may justify imposing a covenant restricting the field of activity of that employee when he leaves his employment. The covenant must, however, be reasonable as to its ambit and duration. Although 'category 3' confidential information can, in certain circumstances, justify worldwide restraints because confidentiality knows no territorial limitations (see *Scully v Lee*, above), in other cases, the evidence may show that a worldwide restraint will be held to be too wide to be enforceable (see *Lansing Linde Ltd v Kerr*, above and *Commercial Plastics Ltd v Vincent*, above). It may also be the case that a non-compete provision, ie one prohibiting an employee who possesses confidential information in the third category from working in any capacity for a competitor will also be held to be too wide in its ambit: see *Commercial Plastics v Vincent*. The contrary argument, however, is that it is legitimate to restrain an employee with 'category 3' confidential information from working in any capacity for a competitor because he is still in a position, at the very least, to reveal that information to the competitor that he joins even where he may be employed by that competitor in the part of its business which does not compete with the former employer or he joins it in a capacity in which he does not need to make use of or disclose that information in order to perform his new duties. These are difficult considerations which the court must weigh in considering the reasonableness of any post-termination restraint taken to protect 'category 3' confidential information.

(e) An express restrictive covenant in an employment contract not to make use of the employer's confidential information during or after the employment will be construed so as to apply to 'Faccenda Category 2' information during the contract but only 'Faccenda Category 3' information after the contract has ended: see *SBJ Stephenson Ltd v Mandy* [2000] IRLR 233.

(f) The duration of an express restrictive covenant is frequently unlimited in time, but this is not fatal to the validity of such an express covenant: *SBJ Stephenson v Mandy* (ibid) and *Caterpillar Logistics Services (UK) Ltd v Huesca de Crean* [2012] EWCA Civ 156, [2012] ICR 981.

The action for breach of confidence in relation to trade secrets by employees will normally be based on breach of contract. A claim for breach of contract will not normally require any form of *mens rea* on the part of the employee. It is, however, clear that an employee cannot be in breach of an express or implied obligation not to make use of or disclose confidential information if:– (a) they had never acquired that information in the first place and/or (b) they had not themselves used or disclosed the information or (c) had cause to know that the information in question had been used or disclosed. So much, one might have thought, was axiomatic. However, in a recent case, *Vestergaard Frandsen A/S and ors v Bestnet Europe Ltd and ors* [2013] 1 WLR 1556 an attempt was made to persuade the Supreme Court that a former employee who was not privy to confidential information of the former employer, nor had any knowledge that it was being used in a rival business which she had joined as a director was nonetheless liable for misuse of that information because she information because she had entered a common design, one element of which was the misuse of her former employers' confidential information. Unsurprisingly, the attempt failed. Some useful propositions about the mens rea required for primary and secondary liability for breach of confidence in relation to trade secrets may be extracted from the decision of the Supreme Court, viz:

(a)   The classic case of breach of confidence involves the claimants' confidential information being used inconsistently with its confidential nature by a defendant who received it in circumstances where he/she had agreed or ought to have appreciated that it was confidential. Thus the mens rea for the classic case of breach is that the defendant must have agreed (expressly or impliedly) or must know that the information is confidential. Thus a defendant who receives information imparted in confidence who then goes on to use that information even unconsciously and under a mistake as to their legal obligations will be liable for breach of confidence (see *Seagar v Copydex Ltd* [1967] 1 WLR 923) and a defendant who is found to have received information in confidence has no defence if he uses that information that he did not realise that he was breaching confidence or even using the information in question;

(b)   A defendant who receives information not knowing that it is a trade secret and where there is no reasonable basis for suspecting that it is, he/she will nonetheless be liable to maintain confidentiality in that 'secret' from the moment he/she is told or otherwise becomes aware that it is in fact confidential;

(c)   Secondary liability for breach of confidence can arise where a person assisting the recipient of confidential information to misuse it. However such secondary liability would 'normally' require the assistant either to know or to be reckless (by turning a 'blind eye') to the recipient's misuse of that information;

(d)   A third party who does not know and does not turn a blind eye to a recipient's misuse of confidential information may nonetheless be liable for that misuse by virtue of vicarious liability (eg if the third party employs the recipient who then abuses confidentiality obligations);

(e)   A person who has not received and has not used confidential information nor assisted a breach of confidence by another knowing that it is a breach of confidence or being reckless as to whether it is cannot be liable for that breach either as a primary or a secondary party.

In *Brandeaux Advisers (UK) Ltd v Chadwick* [2010] EWHC 3241 (QB), [2011] IRLR 224, the defendant employee transferred by email from her work computer to her personal computer vast quantities of confidential materials concerning the Claimants' investment funds. It appears that the employee was "storing" the materials for the purposes of using them in the event that litigation ensued between her and her employer and/or in case there was a dispute with Regulators (she had been chief compliance officer for the Claimants' Group).

The Claimant bought proceedings against the defendant for breach of express confidentiality terms in her contract and for breach of the implied duty of fidelity. The defendant contended that there were implied terms in her contract of employment which entitled her to use her employer's confidential information or disclose it to third parties where such use or disclosure was "fairly required for her legitimate interests or to protect her legal rights or to defend herself" and that she was so entitled where the use or disclosure was in the public interest including use or disclosure in relation to financial regulators.

The judge held that this was not a case involving legitimate whistleblowing (and even if it had been he doubted whether using confidential information in reporting matters to a regulator could ever justify the wholesale transfer of an employer's information onto an employee's personal computer). Moreover the judge doubted that the possibility of future litigation could ever justify an employee so transferring confidential information of their employer. An employee should, in the event of a dispute, rely upon the court's disclosure process to provide relevant documents. In the event, on the facts, the judge held that the employee was not entitled to transfer the information and in so doing was in repudiatory breach of her contract of employment. (Note that documents disclosed in the course of tribunal proceedings cannot be used in separate High Court proceedings without the permission of the Court: see *IG Index Ltd v Cloete* [2015] ICR 254.)

41.14   RESTRAINT OF TRADE AS A DISCRETIONARY ELEMENT IN GRANTING INJUNCTIVE RELIEF

Garden leave injunctions

It is now clear (see *Symbian v Christensen*, above) that considerations of restraint of trade play an important part in influencing the court's discretion to grant injunctive relief to enforce express or implied negative obligations of employees during notice periods. This is not the application of the 'classic' doctrine of restraint of trade. It differs in the following fundamental respects from the classic doctrine:-

(a)   the court is enforcing contractual rights which at the time the contract is made would not be subject to the restraint of trade doctrine in its classic form because those rights of the employer (namely the right to exclusive service by the employee) would not, under the classic doctrine, be considered a restraint of trade;

(b)   the court looks to the position as at the date when garden leave is imposed rather than the position when the contract was first entered into;

(c)   the court is able to temper the relief granted, both as to the ambit of any injunction and as to its duration; the court is not obliged to impose injunctive relief which exactly mirrors the contractual provisions in question (see *GFI Group Inc v Eaglestone* [1994] IRLR 119);

(d)   it would seem that the court can take into account interests of the employer which go beyond the legitimate interests that the court would uphold in enforcing post-termination restraints under the restraint of trade doctrine. In *Provident Financial* Dillon LJ considered it legitimate, in principle, to grant garden leave injunctions not only when there was a risk to the employer's confidential information or client connection from the departing employee, but also where the employee would merely enhance a competitor's business if he joined it during his notice period. This appears to come perilously close to supporting covenants in gross (ie covenants against mere competition). (See also *Elsevier v Munro* [2014] IRLR 766, where the risk of unconscious use of confidential information by an employee provided additional justification for the grant of an injunction to support a prohibition on working for a competitor during the notice period.)

Thus, the court can impose injunctions restraining an employee on garden leave from joining or assisting a competitor of the employer for a period less than the notice period stipulated in the contract of employment (*GFI v Eaglestone*, above). Equally, the court may limit the injunctive relief granted – and will so limit it – to restrain the employee only from working for a competitor during the whole or part of the notice period, but will not restrain an employee during his notice period from working for a new employer <u>not</u> in competition with the existing employer: see *Provident Financial Group plc v Hayward* [1999] ICR 160. There is no principle which requires a court to refuse to enforce a covenant in restraint of trade operating post termination of a contract of employment where a court has, during the notice period of the employee under that contract, granted a 'garden leave' injunction: see *Credit Suisse Asset Management Ltd v Armstrong* [1996] ICR 882, CA. However, the Court of Appeal in that case opined that the position might be different, and the post-termination restraint not enforced, in circumstances where it was preceded by a very lengthy period of garden leave, ie of a year or more. It should also be observed that the decision in *Armstrong* does not prevent a court, when judging the reasonableness of a covenant operating post-termination, from taking into account a period of garden leave. Thus, if an employee is subject to a post-termination restraint prohibiting him from joining a competitor after termination of his employment and that employee is also subject to a garden leave provision during his notice period the court may conclude (looking at the contract from the date it was entered into) that the combination of the garden leave period and the non-compete period would involve too lengthy a 'sterilisation' of the employee in question. This is particularly so where the employee is subject to other post-termination restraints such as a non-solicitation or non-dealing covenant. Such an argument was considered and rejected on the facts in *Tradition Financial Services v Gamberoni* [2017] EWHC 768 (QB). In that case, the combined period of garden leave and covenant was only 9 months, however. The court may strike down the non-competition covenant but uphold the non-solicitation and non-dealing provisions: see *Credit Suisse First Boston (Europe) Ltd v Padiachy* [1999] ICR 569, [1998] IRLR 504. Nevertheless, it should not be supposed that a period of garden leave is to be regarded as a desirable alternative to post-termination restraints: in *TFS Derivatives Ltd v Morgan* [2004] EWHC 3181 (QB), [2005] IRLR 246, counsel for the employee sought to argue that a three-month non-compete clause was unlawful because the interest to be protected (client connection) could more appropriately and reasonably have been protected by a 'garden leave' clause of six months. He invited Cox J to make general observations as to the reasonableness and greater attraction of garden leave clauses generally. Cox J declined, observing that a six-month garden leave clause could legitimately be regarded as more onerous for the employee than a three-month non-compete because it prevented the employee from working at all. She also noted that the employer may understandably not wish to pay the employee for six months of no work and, further, that such a clause may not, in any case, be adequate to protect the employer's interests because it would not operate on summary termination of the contract by either party. In *Elsevier Ltd v Munro* (*ibid*), it was held that the public policy underlying garden leave injunctions was not engaged in a case where the employer did not seek to place the employee on garden leave but the employee had instead sought to work for a competitor in breach of his contractual obligations. It was not open to an employee in those circumstances to complain that that the relief sought by the employer would compel the employee to a period of idleness.

In *Tullett Prebon plc v BGC Brokers LP* [2010] EWHC 484 (QB), [2010] IRLR 648 Jack J held that as a matter of discretion in imposing injunctive relief he could enforce fully by injunction for the full term of notice garden leave provisions and then enforce, but for a duration shorter than the contractual term, post-termination restraints. This is impermissible because it amounts to re-writing the post-termination restraints by reducing the duration thereof by means of an injunction. In so doing, he clearly overlooked *Mont v Mills* (supra) and *Provident Financial v Hayward* (supra). This point was not considered on appeal in *Tullett*: [2011] EWCA Civ 131, [2011] IRLR 420. However, in *QBE Management Services (UK) Ltd v Dymoke and ors* [2012] EWHC 80 (QB), [2012] IRLR 458 Haddon-Cave J confirmed the orthodox position.

41.15 Restraint of trade and springboard relief

Employees who commit breaches of duty to their employer whilst employees by copying or removing customer lists or other confidential information for use in a rival business either during or after the termination of their employment contracts may be restrained by 'springboard injunction' from dealing with the customers whose details they have filched from their employer (see *Roger Bullivant Ltd v Ellis* [1987] ICR 464 and *PSM International plc v Whitehouse* [1992] IRLR 279, CA).

Recently the court has also shown itself to be willing to grant springboard relief to counteract the effect of breaches of duty other than the duty of confidentiality. Thus in *Midas IT Services Ltd v Opus Portfolios Ltd* (21 December 1999, unreported), Ch D, springboard relief injuncting a company which it was alleged had procured breaches of the duty of trust and confidence by a senior employee of the claimant for a period of six months from acquiring a licence to distribute software was granted. The breaches of duty allegedly induced by the enjoined company were not breaches of the obligations of confidentiality. This authority was followed in *UBS Wealth Management (UK) Ltd v Vestra Wealth LLP* [2008] EWHC 1974 (QB), [2008] IRLR 965, the court holding explicitly that springboard relief was not limited merely to breach of confidence cases. Where there has been mass poaching by illicit means of employees and/or clients, springboard injunctions may issue to restrain the poacher from employing employees illicitly poached or from dealing with clients illicitly solicited. The ambit and duration of such springboard injunctions are necessarily fact sensitive and it is not possible to formulate guidelines.

However, in all cases the ambit and duration of springboard injunctions will be influenced by considerations of restraint of trade. A springboard injunction necessarily interferes with the enjoined parties' right to do certain kinds of business with certain people and judges appreciate that the effect of imposing such injunction will be to impose restraints of trade in circumstances in which an employee may not have any express post-termination restraints in his contract of employment:

'I am acutely conscious of the fact that competition should be encouraged and I am acutely conscious of the fact that it must be quite wrong to impose a restraint which is effectively only going to operate to stop a man using his acquired skills rather than to stop him using confidential information which he ought never to have taken into use at all.'

Fisher-Karpark Industries Ltd v Nichols [1982] FSR 351.

Nonetheless, the judge granted the springboard injunction in that case against employees who it was alleged had misused confidential information of their employer in a rival business.

'Interim injunctions can be granted to prevent defendants . . . from obtaining an unjust headstart in, or a springboard for, activities detrimental to the person who provided them with confidential information. . . . However, in relation to that type of information, as distinct from that concerning real trade secrets, the court should be concerned that it does not, in granting such an injunction, give the injured party more protection than he realistically needs and, in particular, discourage or prohibit what in the course of time becomes legitimate competition.'

per May LJ in *Bullivant v Ellis*, above, at 481G-H.

'The [springboard] injunction is directed to fairness of competition. Because the policy of the law is to encourage and certainly not to restrain fair competition the injunction is limited in duration to that period in which, in the court's estimation, the person injuncted could reasonably be expected to have assembled the confidential information using lawful means if earlier the assembled information comes as such into the public domain'

per Blackburn J in *Midas IT Services Ltd v Opus Portfolios Ltd* (unreported, Ch D, 21 December 1999, pp 13–14)

In one springboard case at least (*Bullivant v Ellis*, above), the Court of Appeal considered that the appropriate duration of springboard relief in respect of an employee who had removed a card index of clients from his employer prior to the termination of his contract which he afterwards used in a rival business ought to be limited to the same period of a post-termination restraint in his contract of employment prohibiting dealing with his former employer's customers. It is submitted, however, that this direct correlation between springboard relief and the period of any post-termination restraint will not be invariably be adopted by the courts. Some forms of activity by employees in breach of their duties of trust and confidence whilst employed either in respect of the removal or misuse of confidential information or in respect of other wrongdoings, such as the canvassing or soliciting of the employer's customers during their employment for a rival business will cause serious harm requiring periods of restraint by springboard injunction of a longer duration than any post-termination restraint in the employment contract. After all, post-termination restraints are framed at the outset of a contract to protect a limited class of interests and in the expectation that the employee will abide by his contractual duties during his employment. The employer cannot, in framing covenants which are no more than adequate to protect his interests, anticipate and build into such covenants protection against any possible breach of trust and confidence which might be committed by the employee during his contract of employment.

In *Tullett Prebon plc v BGC Brokers LP* [2010] EWHC 484 (QB), [2010] IRLR 648 the court was invited to grant springboard relief against the defendant restraining it from recruiting any of the claimants' staff for a period of 18 months from the first grant of interim injunctive relief in the proceedings. The judge determined that an appropriate period for such form of relief would be approximately 12, not 18, months and that the basis on which it should be granted was not springboard relief, but as a *quia timet* injunction. The judge held that the recruitment of the claimant's staff had been achieved by illicit means and that the claimant was entitled to fear that such means might be deployed again. Since those means were difficult to detect it was necessary to injunct the defendants from any recruitment of the Claimant's staff. The difficulty with this approach is that the logic of it points not to a limited period of relief but, rather, to a permanent injunction. Moreover, there seems no principled basis upon which this form of *quia timet* relief can be subject to a limited duration. The judge appears to have held that he could limit the period of this form of relief to 14 days from the delivery of his judgment in this case. He stated "There is no justification for any further substantial extension of the relief. The court must assume that the exposure of BGC's conduct as set out in the judgment will curb unlawful recruitment in the future. BGC is a substantial and ostensibly responsible company. The relief against BGC will be continued for 14 days from the delivery of the judgment so the judgment may be absorbed. It will then end." The learned judge did not explain upon what basis it could be assumed that the defendant would, by reason of having absorbed his judgment, cease to pursue its illicit poaching operations. It is respectfully submitted that springboard relief is to be preferred in these kinds of case because it is relief which is intrinsically subject to limitations of duration. This point was not considered on appeal in *Tullett*: [2011] EWCA Civ 131; [2011] IRLR 420. However, *QBE Management Services (UK) Ltd v Dymoke and ors* [2012] EWHC 80 (QB), [2012] IRLR 458 restores what it is submitted are the proper principles of springboard relief in this area, in particular, that the length of springboard relief must be a function of how long it would have taken the defendants to achieve the springboard advantage had they employed lawful means to do so.

PROCEDURAL MATTERS

41.16 Pleading

Because the common law doctrine of restraint of trade requires contractual provisions falling within it to be justified before they are enforceable, employers seeking to enforce such provisions ought to plead in their particulars of claim the grounds justifying the restraint. Equally, a defendant who wishes to attack a covenant as unenforceable should raise in his defence the grounds upon which he claims the covenant is unenforceable. It would appear that a court cannot of its own motion raise issues of unenforceability of covenants under the restraint of trade doctrine: see *Petrofina (Great Britain) Ltd v Martin* [1966] Ch 146. Accordingly, the parties must raise these issues themselves. It is to be observed, however, that there have been instances in which a court has, of its own volition, taken the point that a covenant is in unlawful restraint of trade: see *Marion White Ltd v Francis* [1972] 1 WLR 1423.

In cases which raise issues of confidential information (whether as justifying a covenant in restraint of trade or otherwise) the information claimed to be confidential must be properly and fully particularised in any statement of case and as early as possible (see *Ocular Sciences Ltd v Aspect Vision Care Ltd* [1997] RPC 289). In particular, where injunctions restraining disclosure or use of confidential information are sought the confidential information to be protected must be fully particularised: see *Caterpillar Logistics Services (UK) Ltd v Huesca de Crean* [2012] EWCA Civ 156, [2012] ICR 981. In order to protect highly confidential information from public disclosure in the course of proceedings orders should be sought from the court at the earliest possible stage that particulars of confidential information contained in any statement of case should not be available on the court file for public inspection. The best practice is to plead the details of any confidential information at issue between the parties in a confidential annexure to the statement of case.

41.17 Injunctions

It has long been recognised by the courts that the proof of loss and damage arising from a breach of a post-termination restraint in an employment contract is a difficult, if not impossible, matter. Accordingly, in the vast majority of cases, the covenantee will seek to enforce restraints by way of injunction. However, it must be remembered that an injunction is a discretionary remedy and, even where a court holds a restraint to be valid, it will retain a residual discretion as to whether to enforce that contractual restraint by injunction or not. Thus, if an employer delays before seeking an injunction, such that a substantial part of the period of the restraint sought to be enforced has elapsed before injunctive relief is sought, then the court may not grant an injunction at all: see *Wincanton Ltd v Cranny* [2000] IRLR 716, CA and *Legends Live Limited v Harrison* [2017] IRLR 59 (where an injunction was refused in the entertainment industry after some delay and where it appeared that the injunction was being sought as a weapon to cause disruption). That said, delay in and of itself, will be unlikely to result in a judge refusing injunctive relief: see *Law Society of England and Wales v Society for Lawyers* [1996] FSR 739. The personal circumstances of the defendant in injunction cases may also be relevant in that the court will weigh any hardship that might be occasioned by the imposition of an injunction (see *Corporate Express Ltd v Day* [2004] EWHC 2943 (QB), [2004] All ER (D) 290 (Dec)). It is, however, submitted that injunctions should not be refused merely because the defendant is likely to be impoverished by them for that would create a licence to breach contractual duties based upon a means test. Some special or exceptional hardship would need to be shown for an injunction to be refused by a court: see the observations of Colman J in *Insurance Co v Lloyd's Syndicate* [1995] 1 Lloyd's Law Reports 272, 276-7 which were endorsed by the Court of Appeal (save that Rimer J did not think a test of exceptionality to be helpful) in *D v P* [2016] EWCA Civ 87.

For the purposes of interim injunction, there is no special rule applicable to restrictive covenants in employment contracts. The principles in *American Cyanamid Co v Ethicon Ltd* [1975] AC 396 will apply and if the covenantee raises serious issues to be tried as to the enforceability of that covenant an interim injunction will almost invariably be granted: see *Lawrence David Ltd v Ashton* [1991] 1 All ER 385, [1989] ICR 123. The court will, if requested by the defendant against whom an interim injunction has been granted, generally order a 'speedy trial'. In the event that a 'speedy trial' is not possible before the period of the restraint in question elapses, however, a different approach might be taken by the court to the grant of an interim injunction. In such a case, the court might go beyond deciding whether there is a serious issue to be tried and attempt some assessment of the claimant's prospect of success at trial: see *Lansing Linde Ltd v Kerr* [1991] 1 WLR 251, *per* Staughton LJ at 258. The court should not, however, allow the hearing of an application for interim injunctions in these circumstances to degenerate into a prolonged battle based upon evidence which cannot be tested at that stage by cross-examination. It is to be noted that issues as to the proper construction of a restrictive covenant (see above **41.6**) should normally be resolved at the interlocutory stage, unless the construction of the covenant depends on disputed facts that cannot properly be resolved without a trial: see *Arbuthnot Fund Managers Ltd v Rawlings* [2003] EWCA Civ 518, [2003] All ER (D) 181 (Mar). (See also *Le Puy v Potter* [2015] EWHC 193 (QB), where the possibility of a speedy trial resulting in a judgment five or six months before the expiry of a 12-month restraint meant that the *American Cyanamid* approach was appropriate and *Allfiled UK Limited v Eltis* [2016] FSR 11 where Hildyard J suggested that the *American Cyanamid* test should only be "departed from in extreme circumstances where a trial is rendered plainly and obviously otiose".) The decision in *Landmark Brickwork Ltd v Sutcliffe and ors* [2011] IRLR 976 seems to be a departure from the *Arbuthnot* guidance. It is respectfully submitted that construction issues must be resolved by the Court on an interim application, unless (and this will be a rare case) there is a dispute as to the factual matrix from which the contract arose. It cannot be right for a Court to impose an injunction based on a contract in restraint of trade without the Court determining what the true ambit of the restraint may be. The approach in *Landmark*, it is respectfully submitted, cannot be correct.

For the procedure on obtaining interim injunctions see *Parts 23* and *25* of the *Civil Procedure Rules*. Injunctions can also be sought as final relief at trial.

When considering whether to make, and making, an application for an interim injunction without notice or on short notice, it is vital to take note of the guidance given by Silber J in *CEF Holdings Ltd v Mundey* [2012] EWHC 1524 (QB), [2012] IRLR 912. That case well illustrates the dangers of short notice and without notice applications. It should never be forgotten by practitioners that an action to restrain by injunction employees or former employees may have the effect of destroying a nascent business or otherwise seriously damaging a person's ability to earn a living in the manner of their choosing. To take such a step without affording the employee an opportunity properly to be represented and resist such an application should really only be contemplated in extreme cases, for example where there is clear evidence that a former employee has obtained and is misusing or proposing to misuse confidential information of his former employer or where there is clear evidence that former employees are engaged in surreptitious efforts to suborn the loyalty of other employees or surreptitious efforts illicitly to capture or divert work from former employer's customers. In any event, in all cases where an application for injunctive relief is made without notice or on short notice the applicant must have carried out as full an investigation as possible into the circumstances of alleged misconduct and relayed to the Court those circumstances together with any other factual or legal defence that may be available to the defendant to the Court asked to grant an injunction. Fundamental to the obligation to make full and frank legal disclosures as well as factual disclosures is the obligation to alert the Court to any matters which may go to whether or not the Court has a jurisdiction to grant the injunctive orders sought or any of them, as well as to alert the Court if the interim injunction may effectively dispose of the injunction part of the case such that the Court should consider whether to apply the principles in *Lansing Linde Ltd v Kerr* rather than the 'standard' *American Cyanamid* test.

Often where interim injunctions are sought, supporting orders are also sought such as interim delivery-up and computer destruction orders (see *Arthur J Gallagher Services UK Limited v Skriptchenkov* (11 February 2016, unreported) or interim disclosure orders (see *Aon Limited v JLT Reinsurance Brokers* [2010] IRLR 600).

41.18   Declaration

It is, of course, open to a covenantor (employee) to challenge the enforceability of a covenant in restraint of trade by initiating legal proceedings seeking a declaration that the covenant in question is unenforceable. It is not clear, and must be open to doubt, whether a defendant could obtain an interim declaration to this effect pending trial, even a speedy trial. Alternatively, where a court refuses a claimant an injunction on the basis that there is only a very short period left for the restraint to run, it may nonetheless grant the claimant a declaration that the covenant in question is reasonable and enforceable (see *Corporate Express Ltd v Day* [2004] EWHC 2943 (QB), [2004] All ER (D) 290 (Dec); and see *Petter v EMC Europe Ltd* (16 April 2015, unreported), for a case where a speedy trial was considered appropriate in a claim brought by an employee for a declaration as to the enforceability of a restrictive covenant).

41.19   Damages where confidential information or trade secrets are involved

As for damages, there is a dearth of reported cases upon how damages for breach of a post-termination restraint are to be calculated. On ordinary principles, however, an employer can only recover for loss of any profit that he might have made had the covenant not been breached rather than his loss of revenue. In the event that customers have been filched by an ex employee in breach of a restraint against soliciting or dealing with them, the court may be able to assess at trial the loss of profits incurred by the employer up to the date of trial, but will be faced with the difficult task of assessing future loss which must be based on the employer's chance of retaining those customers: see *SBJ Stephenson Ltd v Mandy* [2000] IRLR 233. In *Merlin Financial Consultants Ltd v Cooper* [2014] IRLR 610 HHJ Peter Hughes QC was prepared to take a 'broad brush' approach as to the question of which clients the employer would have retained had the post-termination restraint been complied with. In that case, the judge held that the employer would have retained 70% of the clients in the first year, and 40% in the second year (see paragraph 83 of the judgment).

It may be possible to obtain damages for breach of a post-termination restraint on the basis set out in *Wrotham Park Estate Co Limited v Parkside Homes Limited* [1974] 1 WLR 798 (that is, in the context of post-termination restraints, the notional fee that the parties would have agreed for the defendant to purchase his way out of the restraints). That proposition was accepted by Phillips J in *One Step (Support) Limited v Morris-Garner* [2015] IRLR 215 who held that it was just to order the payment of *Wrotham Park* damages where there had been a breach of restrictive covenants in circumstances where it was difficult for the claimant to show any loss "Not least because there was a degree of secrecy in the establishment of [the Defendants'] business which has not been fully reversed by the disclosure process...". Phillips J's judgment in One Step was upheld on appeal to the Court of Appeal [2017] QB 1 but as at the date of writing, the Supreme Court has granted permission to appeal, but has yet to hand down any judgment. Previously, in *BGC Capital Markets (Switzerland) LLC v Rees* [2011] EWHC 2009 (QB) Jack J had held that *Wrotham Park* damages were not payable: "In my judgment the award of release payment damages is not available as a substitute for conventional damages to compensate a claimant for damage he has not suffered. Nor should it be used to award a larger sum than a conventional calculation of loss provides."

Similar issues can arise in the assessment of loss for breach of confidence. There are cases where the breach of confidence gives rise to a loss of profit which can be assessed on ordinary principles. However, in other cases, courts have awarded damages to compensate for the loss of a 'notional licence fee' which ought to have been paid for use of the confidential information (in place of or in addition to damages for loss of profit): see *Seager v Copydex Limited (No. 2)* [1969] 1 WLR 809; *Force India Formula One Team Limited v 1 Malaysia Racing Team SDN BHD* [2013] EWCA Civ 780; *Vestergaard Frandsen A/S v Bestnet Europe Limited* [2014] EWHC 3159 (Ch). The law as to the assessment of licence fee damages is developing. In *Marathon Asset Management LLP v Seddon* [2017] EWHC 300 (Comm) it was suggested that the proper approach was to distinguish between cases where the claimant would have sold its confidential information to the defendant for a fee and such cases where it was unrealistic to suppose that the claimant might have licenced its confidential information. In the first type of case, the court should seek to estimate the 'licence fee'. In the second type of case, Leggatt J considered, "*Such a method makes no sense because in such a context the negotiation is not merely fictional in the sense that it did not actually happen but fictional in the stronger sense that it lacks any verisimilitude. The law ought not to employ fictions of the latter sought.*" In the latter case, the court should order an account of profits, or payment of a percentage of the defendant's profits as licence fee damages.

Licence fee damages will only be payable for such period as the confidential information is actually used. Where the use of confidential information has given rise to a 'derived product' which is subsequently sold in the marketplace resulting in increased competition for the claimant, then damages will be assessed to compensate the claimant for the fact that he will face such competition sooner than he otherwise would have done. Licence fee damages would only be appropriate, on this analysis, for the period of time in which the confidential information is used to derive the new product: *Vestergaard Frandsen A/S v Bestnet Europe Limited* [2017] FSR 5.

41.20   Accounts of profits

Where an employee has breached a post-termination restraint prohibiting him from joining a competitor and it can be demonstrated that he has revealed to that competitor confidential information or trade secrets of the employer, an account of profits may be ordered by the court. This will, however, be an account of profits for breach of confidence rather than for breach of the negative covenant not to join a competitor. Despite the House of Lords' decision in *A-G v Blake* [2001] 1 AC 268 that accounts of profits can, in certain circumstances, be ordered against an employee for breach of a negative restraint, it is submitted that this principle cannot and should not be applied in the case of ordinary employees outside government security services. That was certainly the view of of Phillips J in *One Step (Support) Limited v Morris-Garner* [2015] IRLR 215.

The award of an account of profits for breaches of confidence is a discretionary one. Unlike in cases of breach of fiduciary duty, the claimant does not have an automatic entitlement to an account of profits for such breaches: *Walsh v Shanahan, Leonard and SLH Properties Ltd* [2013] EWCA Civ 411.

42   Retirement

42.1   RETIREMENT AGE

The age at which an employee must retire was once a matter solely to be determined by the contract of employment. In the past, employers and employees were free to agree a contractual retirement age, when employment would terminate without the need for further action.

However, in recent years, any "retirement" dismissal is unlawful unless it can be objectively justified (since the revocation of the "national default retirement age" of 65 by the *Employment Equality (Repeal of Retirement Age Provisions) Regulations 2011 (SI 2011/1069)* ('*Repeal Regulations*').

The state pension age is not of itself a contractual retiring age. Indeed it would be unlawful sex discrimination for an employer to require employees to retire at state pension age, since this disadvantages women whilst pension age differs according to sex. Under the *Pensions Act 1995*, the state pension age is being equalised at age 65. This was being phased in over a 10 year period which commenced on 6 April 2010. The *Pensions Act 2011* amended the timetable and state pension age is being equalised at 65 by November 2018. The state pension age will then increase to 66 for both men and women from December 2018 to October 2020. The government has also announced its intention to introduce further rises to 67 (between 2034 and 2036) and to 68 (between 2044 and 2046). However, the *Pensions Act 2014* provides for a regular review of the state pension age, at least once every five years, to take account changes to life expectancy. The government is currently considering a report commissioned from John Cridland which was published in March 2017 which makes recommendations of further changes.

Pensionable age under an occupational pension scheme is distinct from both the contractual retirement age and the state pension age (although each may be the same). It is unlawful to provide different pensionable ages for men and women in an occupational pension scheme following the decision of the ECJ in *Barber v Guardian Royal Exchange Assurance Group*: C-262/88 [1991] 1 QB 344 that pension benefits were 'pay' within *art 141* of the *Treaty of Rome* (formerly *art 119*): see further EQUAL PAY (**22**) for the UK legislation giving effect to this decision; note that this does not affect pensions earned by service prior to 17 May 1990 (the date of the *Barber* decision). It follows that, so long as pensionable age under the statutory provisions is different according to sex, (ie 60 for women and 65 for men), an employer cannot simply use the state pension age for an occupational pension scheme (see, for example, the ECJ's decision in *Kleist v Pensionsversicherungsanstalt*: C-356/09 [2010] All ER (D) 37 (Dec)). The courts have on occasion allowed rectification of pension schemes to equalise the retirement age for men and women where the trustees have intended but failed to amend the relevant scheme (see, for example, *Pioneer GB Ltd v Webb* [2011] EWHC 2683 (Ch) and *Industrial Accoustics Ltd v Crowhurst*, Ch (15 May 2011, unreported)).

The question as to whether an individual has retired (eg for the purposes of a pension scheme) is usually one of fact and degree; thus the House of Lords has held that a managing director who withdrew from active involvement in the running of a company but remained in office as an unpaid non-executive director had retired: *Venables v Hornby* [2003] UKHL 65, [2004] ICR 42. The Court of Appeal has held that a provision in a pension scheme conferring enhanced benefits on employees who 'retire at the request of' the employer applies to those employees who take voluntary redundancy or early retirement, but not those who are made compulsorily redundant: *AGCO Ltd v Massey Ferguson Works Pension Trust Ltd* [2003] EWCA Civ 1044, [2004] ICR 15.

42.2   Retirement

42.2   EMPLOYMENT PROTECTION AND RETIRING AGE

The enforced retirement of an employee is often a source of resentment, and may provoke a claim for unfair dismissal and for age discrimination. (If there is no provision in the contract for retirement and contractual notice is not given, there could also be a claim for wrongful dismissal.)

Until October 2006, most employees were unable to bring claims for unfair dismissal if, on or before the effective date of termination, they had attained the 'normal retiring age' or, if none, the age of 65. The *2006 Regulations* removed the age ceiling on the right to complain of unfair dismissal as of 1 October 2006. They added 'retirement' as a potentially fair reason for dismissal in certain circumstances and set out the circumstances in which a dismissal was deemed to be by reason of retirement and when such a dismissal was fair.

Similarly, the *2006 Regulations* revoked a provision which previously restricted the right to a redundancy payment to those who had attained the 'normal retiring age' or, where there was no such age, the age of 65.

There was also an exception from the prohibition on age discrimination for dismissals by reason of retirement at or above the age of 65 (the 'National Default Retirement Age').

The above was unaffected by the coming into force of the *Equality Act 2010*. However, the *Repeal Regulations* changed the situation entirely. "Retirement" is no longer listed as a potentially fair reason for dismissal. Further, the National Default Retirement Age was also repealed. This means that, unless the employer can prove that the retirement is "some other substantial reason" for the dismissal, the dismissal will be unfair within the meaning of *s 98* of the *Employment Rights Act 1996*. Also, unless the employer can objectively justify the dismissal, the dismissal will additionally constitute discrimination on the grounds of age.

An employee required to retire in breach (or in the absence) of a contractual retirement age will be able to make a claim for breach of contract. However, if the employer gives the notice required under the contract, the fact that the reason for giving notice is to enforce retirement will not render an otherwise lawful dismissal a breach of contract. This is so even where the employer has an equal opportunity policy which includes provisions excluding age discrimination: *Taylor v Secretary of State for Scotland* [2000] ICR 595.

42.3   Retirement dismissals

The separate chapters on discrimination (**Discrimination and Equal Opportunities** I (11), II (12), and III (13)) set out further detail of the provisions of the *2006 Regulations* and the *Equality Act 2010*. In particular, those chapters address questions relating to matters such as objective justification.

In summary, law on retirement dismissals can be summarised as follows:

(a)   A retirement dismissal at any age constitutes a potentially age discriminatory act unless it can be objectively justified by showing that the decision is a proportionate means of achieving a legitimate aim.

(b)   Retirement is not a potentially fair reason for dismissal (*s 98(2)(ba)* of the *Employment Rights Act 1996* has been removed). An employer has to show that such a dismissal is for "some other substantial reason" and fairness will be determined in accordance with the usual principles under *s 98(4)* (see **Unfair Dismissal (52)**).

42.4   JUSTIFYING RETIREMENT DISMISSALS

Employers can no longer rely simply on compulsory contractual retirement ages as a defence to claims for age discrimination or unfair dismissal. They are instead required objectively to justify any and all retirement dismissals. If a retirement dismissal cannot be justified, it will constitute discrimination on the grounds of age and would also be likely to be unfair.

Since the retirement exception never applied to contract-workers, office-holders, barristers, advocates and partners, there has always been a requirement to justify any "retirement" of those non-employees. There have therefore been a few domestic authorities which have addressed whether such retirements can be justified. In *Hampton v Lord Chancellor* [2008] IRLR 258, an employment tribunal held that the compulsory retirement of a part-time Recorder at the age of 65 could not be objectively justified.

In *Seldon v Clarkson Wright & Jakes* [2012] UKSC 16, [2012] ICR 716 a firm of solicitors sought to justify the compulsory retirement of a partner at the age of 65. The tribunal at first instance accepted that the retirement was a proportionate means of achieving the legitimate aims of ensuring that associates were given a reasonable opportunity to become partners, facilitating the planning of the partnership and limiting the need to expel underperforming partners. The EAT held that, although the tribunal was entitled to find that having a compulsory retirement age was justified, there was no evidence to support the justification of fixing the retirement age at 65. The Court of Appeal disagreed. The Supreme Court dismissed a further appeal. In doing so, the following useful guidance was given as to how the courts will assess the justification of retirement dismissals (see paragraphs [50] to [58] per Lady Hale):

(1)   The justification of direct age discrimination is different from the justification of indirect discrimination. Only certain kinds of aim are capable of justifying direct age discrimination. The aims must be social policy objectives of a public interest nature rather than purely individual reasons particular to the employer's situation such as cost reduction or improving competitiveness.

(2)   A certain amount of flexibility is permitted to employers in the pursuit of legitimate social policy aims.

(3)   The ECJ has identified a number of different legitimate aims in the context of justifying direct age discrimination. The following are those most likely to be relevant in the context of justifying a retirement dismissal:

- promoting access to employment for younger people,

- the efficient planning of the departure and recruitment of staff,

- sharing out employment opportunities fairly between the generations,

- ensuring a mix of generations of staff so as to promote the exchange of experience and new ideas,

- rewarding experience,

- facilitating the participation of older workers in the workforce,

- avoiding the need to dismiss employees on the ground that they are no longer capable of doing the job which may be humiliating to the employee concerned, and

- avoiding disputes about the employee's fitness for work over a certain age.

(4)   These legitimate aims form two broad groups: inter-generational fairness and dignity.

(5)   It is necessary to ask whether an aim is legitimate in the particular circumstances of the employment concerned;

(6)   Even if there is a legitimate aim, it is still necessary to enquire whether that aim was in fact being pursued, although the aim need not have been articulated or even realised at the time when the measure was first adopted.

(7)   The means chosen must also be both appropriate and necessary to achieve the end.

(8)   The gravity of the effect upon the employees discriminated against has to be weighed against the importance of the legitimate aims in assessing the necessity of the particular measure.

(9)   Where a general rule was justified, the existence of that rule would usually justify the treatment which resulted from it.

(10)   In the context of intergenerational fairness, it is relevant that at an earlier stage of life, a partner or employee might have benefited from the rule.

On the facts of *Seldon*, the Supreme Court held that:

(1)   staff retention and workforce planning were both directly related to the legitimate social policy aim of sharing out professional employment opportunities fairly between generations;

(2)   limiting the need to expel partners by way of performance management was directly related to dignity aims;

(3)   the matter would be remitted to the employment tribunal because it was possible that the tribunal would have regarded the choice of a mandatory retirement age of 65 as a proportionate means of achieving the first two aims.

When *Seldon* was remitted back to the tribunal, it was found that the compulsory retirement age of 65 was justified on the facts. Upon a further appeal ([2014] ICR 1275), it was held that the task for the tribunal was to determine the balance between the discriminatory effect of having a particular age and its success in achieving the legitimate aims. The fact that an employee could point to a different age which would also meet those aims does not mean that the age chosen could not be justified. Employers are entitled to select a "bright line" age. In addition, it was held that the agreement of the parties to a particular age can be a relevant consideration.

The Irish Equality Court ("IEC") considered the justification of compulsory retirement in two cases. In *Doyle v ESB International Ltd* [2013] 1 CMLR 48, the IEC held that the compulsory retirement of a graphic designer shortly after his 65th birthday was lawful. That Court held that the dismissal was justified by reason of the aims of avoiding the embarrassment of compulsory medical examinations, offering career pathways to new employees and having a consistent rule across the workplace. By contrast, in *Sweeny v Aer Lingus TEO* [2013] 1 CMLR 51, the IEC held that a compulsory retirement at aged 65 was not justified. The only justification put forward by the employer was that it would be perverse for the complainant to receive a pension while still working. The IEC held that it was well established that receipt of a pension entitlement did not necessitate retirement and so no legitimate aim had been put forward.

The Court of Justice of the European Communities has also considered the justification of retirement dismissals in a number of cases.

In *Fuchs v Land Hessen* [2012] ICR 93, the CJEU held that a law providing for a compulsory retirement age was not precluded by the *Equal Treatment Directive* and that legitimate aims would include establishing an age structure that balances younger and older employees, encouraging the recruitment and promotion of young people and preventing disputes about employees' fitness to work beyond a certain age. By contrast, in *Prigge v Deutsche Lufthansa AG* [2011] IRLR 1052, the ECJ held that a compulsory retirement age of 60 for pilots set out in a collective agreement was unlawful. It was not "necessary for the protection of health" within the meaning of *Article 2(5)* and nor was it justified under *Article 6(1)* as an aim such as air traffic safety does not fall within the aims as it was not a "social policy objective". The CJEU has recognised that the automatic retirement of employees at an age when they are entitled to draw a pension has, for a long time, been a feature of employment law in many Member States and that it is widely used in employment relationships (see especially *Rosenbladt v Oellerking Gebaudereinigungsgesellschaft mbH*: C-45/09 [2011] 1 CMLR 32, [2011] IRLR 51; *Félix Palacios de la Villa v Cortefiel Servicios SA*: C-411/05 [2008] All ER (EC) 249, [2007] IRLR 989, and has noted that retirement issues require a balance to be struck between political, economic, social, demographic and/or budgetary considerations and the choice to be made between prolonging people's working lives or, conversely, providing for early retirement. It has repeatedly accepted that in such social policy matters the national authorities enjoy a wide margin of discretion (see also *Mangold v Helm*: C-144/04 [2005] ECR I-9981, [2006] 1 CMLR 43). The CJEU has in these cases accepted that the aim of sharing employment between the generations, with its associated benefits, should, in principle, be regarded as objectively and reasonably justifying differences in treatment on grounds of age. However, the proportionality of the retirement or measure in question will be considered carefully, in particular whether it actually serves that legitimate aim, or whether the aim could be achieved in another way or without 'catching' the particular employee or employee group in issue.

In *Hörnfeldt v Posten Meddelande AB*: C-141/11 [2012] 3 CMLR 37, [2012] IRLR 785, [2012] Eq LR 892, the CJEU held that a Swedish law, under which compulsory retirement below 67 was prohibited but it was permissible above 67, was not precluded, despite not taking into account the amount of an employee's retirement pension, The CJEU reiterated the need for a balance to be struck and considered that promoting access of young people to a profession was a legitimate aim. The Court held that the measure was appropriate and necessary as it reduced obstacles for those who wished to work beyond 65, made it easier for young people to enter and/or remain in the labour market and made it possible to avoid situations in which elderly workers are terminated in humiliating circumstances. It was necessary, despite not taking into account the amount of retirement pension an individual would receive as it conferred an unconditional right to work until 67, did not provide a mandatory scheme of automatic retirement in that the contracting parties could agree to a fixed term contract beyond the age of 67 and took into account the availability (if not the amount) of a retirement pension.

On references to the CJEU, the CJEU has in some cases ruled that the question of proportionality is one that must be addressed by the national court. Thus it was in the 'Heyday' challenge [2009] ICR 1080, CJEU. On its return to the Administrative Court (*R (on the application of Age UK) v Secretary of State for Business, Innovation & Skills* [2010] ICR 260), Blake J held that the national default retirement age was based upon a social policy aim of certainty, clarity and maintaining confidence in the labour market and that it was proportionate for there to be such a blanket exception. The judge further held that the choice of age of 65 was within the margin of appreciation when it was adopted in 2006 but that the conclusion might have been different had there been no suggestion of an upcoming government review. Blake J also indicated that he did not see how 65 could remain as the appropriate age after that review. It was this decision that led to the removal of the *reg 30* exception to the *AR 2006* and the end of the national default retirement age.

In *Palacios* (above), however, the CJEU went so far as to find the measure in question actually justified and did not leave the matter to the national court. The significant difference between 'Heyday' and *Palacios* was that in *Palacios* the default retirement provision was contained in a collective agreement. The CJEU considered it important that it had specifically been considered and agreed by the social partners that a default retirement age (corresponding to the age at which individuals become entitled to a state pension) was appropriate and necessary in the context of the particular labour market at issue. In *Rosenbladt* (above), too, the CJEU held the compulsory retirement provision to be justified and did not leave the matter to the national court. Again, the provision in question was in a collective agreement which the CJEU considered enabled specific account to be taken of the nature of the labour market in question (cleaning in this case). The CJEU also considered it to be important that although there was a provision for automatic retirement at 65, German law also prohibited anyone over the age of 65 from being refused employment on grounds of age. This was thought important since it struck an appropriate balance between the aim of maintaining access to the labour market for younger people, whilst also permitting those who wished to work beyond 65 to do so. Similarly, in *Fuchs v Land Hessen*, Joined Cases C-159/10 and C-160/10: [2011] IRLR 1043 the CJEU found provisions of regional German law which required state prosecutors to retire at age 65 unless it was in the interests of the service for their employment to be extended by periods of up to one year, up to a maximum retirement age of 68, was justified. The factors that the CJEU held to be particularly important were: (i) that this was a profession in which the number of posts available was limited and accordingly there was a particular need to have a compulsory retirement age in order to allow the recruitment of younger workers; (ii) that the workers would not suffer financial hardship as they could continue working as independent legal advisers with no age limit, or they could draw a pension upon retirement; (iii) although budgetary considerations could not themselves provide justification, they could support the decision made about the age at which to draw the line; (iv) political considerations could also be taken into account; (v) the fact that the measure in question related only to one region of Germany was not significant; (vi) nor was the fact that there was (temporarily) a slight mismatch between the measure and the national retirement age (which had risen to 67 for workers other than civil servants). The CJEU emphasized the importance of the national authority adducing specific evidence of justification and not relying on assertions, as the CJEU considered had happened in the *Age UK* case (above).

Cases where compulsory retirement ages have been held not to be justified include:

Prigge v Deutsche Lufthansa AG: C-447/09 [2011] IRLR 1052 where the CJEU found that German legislation requiring pilots to retire at 60 was not justified in the interests of safety because, although the physical capabilities required of pilots did tend to become impaired in older age, there was no evidence that pilots ceased to possess the necessary physical capabilities at 60.

In *European Commission v Hungary*: C-286/12 [2013] CMLR 44, the CJEU held that a Hungarian law which created an abrupt change from a retirement age of 70 to one of 62 for judges, notaries and prosecutors was not justified and went beyond what was necessary. Although the aims (standardising age limits and facilitating access for young lawyers) were legitimate, the measure was not appropriate and necessary as there was no evidence that more lenient provisions could not have achieved the same ends.

Certain retirement-related measures have also been approached by the courts in the same way as retirement. See, eg *Georgiev v Tehnicheski universitet – Sofia, filial Plovdiv*: C-250/09 and C-268/09 [2011] 2 CMLR 179 (provision for university professors to have 12-month contracts only after 65 and to be compulsorily retired at 68 held by CJEU to be capable of justification, although it was for the national court to decide whether it was a proportionate means of pursuing the legitimate aim pursued), *Kraft Foods UK Ltd v Hastie* [2010] ICR 1355 (provisions capping redundancy pay at the level that would have been received had employment ceased at 65 proportionate and justified) and compare *Ingeniorforeningen i Danmark v Region Syddanmark*: C-499/08 [2011] 1 CMLR 35 (measure providing severance payments for all long-serving employees but not those over 65 was disproportionate because it applied to all employees over 65 regardless of whether they were actually drawing a pension).

For a detailed analysis of the law on objective justification outside the retirement context, see further DISCRIMINATION AND EQUAL OPPORTUNITIES **II (12)** at 12.9.

42.5   EARLY RETIREMENT

There is no legal impediment to employees voluntarily retiring early, subject only to the giving of any notice required under the contract of employment. Where there is a pension scheme, of which the employee is a member, the scheme may provide for the drawing of a pension on early retirement, generally with the consent of the employer. Occupational pension schemes which meet the requirements for Inland Revenue approval (the vast majority do, since this is a condition for favourable tax treatment) are precluded from paying a pension earlier than age 55 except where retirement is on grounds of ill-health. For employees over 55, early retirement may be used as an inducement to accept redundancy, and pension scheme rules typically offer one or more of the following benefits:

(a)   immediate payment of the pension that would have been payable at pensionable age, without reduction for early payment;

(b)   commutation of part of the pension to a lump sum;

(c)   conferment of additional years of service in computing the pension; and

(d)   permitting the employee to divert all or part of a severance payment into the pension scheme to purchase added years.

The position of individuals depends on the detail of usually complex scheme rules, operating within limits defined by Inland Revenue requirements. The European Court of Justice has ruled (*Beckmann v Dynamco Whicheloe Macfarlane Ltd:* C-164/00 [2002] All ER (EC) 865) that benefits by way of payment of an immediate and/or augmented pension on termination of employment for redundancy are not 'old age, invalidity or survivors' benefits' within the meaning of the *Acquired Rights Directive 1977*, and accordingly the right to such benefits is preserved when an employee is transferred to a new employer as a result of a relevant transfer of the former employer's undertaking, or part thereof. The ECJ has reiterated these conclusions, in relation to voluntary early retirement, and confirmed their application to public sector pension schemes regulated by statutory provisions: *Martin v South Bank University:* C-4/01 [2004] 1 CMLR 472. See also *reg 10* of the *Transfer of Undertakings (Protection of Employees) Regulations 2006* (see TRANSFER OF UNDERTAKINGS (52)). This has particular practical significance where employees transfer from public sector employers such as the NHS as a result of the contracting out of services, since the responsibility for funding often very expensive early retirement or redundancy terms will fall on the transferee employer. However, in *Procter & Gamble Co v Svenska Cellulosa Aktiebolaget SCA* [2012] EWHC 1257 (Ch), it was held that benefits first triggered as early retirement benefits became "old age benefits" at normal retirement age. Accordingly, the transferee was liable to meet the cost of early retirement up to normal retirement age but not afterwards.

Where an employer offered employees the opportunity to take early retirement and received too many applicants, it may be permissible to apply a "cheapness criteria" to select those whose applications would be successful, despite any indirect age discrimination: *HM Land Registry v Benson* [2012] IRLR 373.

Ill-health retirement is frequently provided for in pension scheme rules. There is no standard set of criteria or procedures. Rules typically require medical evidence sufficient to satisfy the employer, the trustees or both that the employee is incapacitated from either performing any work or from his usual occupation. The requirement may be that the incapacity is expected or likely to be permanent, and rules may provide for the suspension of the payment of a pension (during the period until the employee reaches pensionable age) on evidence that he or she is again capable of work. For guidance as to the interpretation and application of criteria in scheme rules determining eligibility for ill-health retirement, see *Derby Daily Telegraph Ltd v Pensions Ombudsman* [1999] IRLR 476.

42.5 Retirement

The benefits provided under the rules of pension schemes also vary considerably, but typically include immediate payment of an unreduced pension, sometimes with added years. The statutory pension schemes for police officers and firefighters provide for enhanced benefits, known as 'injury awards', where members retire on ill-health grounds as a result of an injury sustained in the course of duty. There are defined procedures for assessing the degree of incapacity (beyond incapacity for active police or fire service) and elaborate rights of appeal under each set of regulations.

Despite the pension advantages of ill-health retirement, if the employee objects to retiring, and if he or she is disabled within the meaning of the *Equality Act 2010*, the possibility that enforced retirement constitutes disability discrimination needs to be considered. See *Trustees of Swansea University Pension & Assurance Scheme v Williams* [2015] ICR 1197 for a case in which the Employment Appeal Tribunal overturned a tribunal's finding that ill-health retirement provisions discriminated on the grounds of disability since they were based on the disabled employee's final salary when he was by then working part time by reason of his disability.

See further DISCRIMINATION AND EQUAL OPPORTUNITIES II (12) at 12.9. Ill-health retirement may also constitute age discrimination, see further DISCRIMINATION AND EQUAL OPPORTUNITIES I (11) at 11.40.

In *Palmer v Royal Bank of Scotland* [2014] ICR 1288, an employer had permitted employees who were at risk of redundancy and over 50 to opt for early retirement. This was held not to constitute age discrimination against a 49 year old as there was no appropriate comparator.

Decisions whether to grant or refuse an ill-health pension are subject to limited control by the courts; good examples are *Harris v Shuttleworth (Lord)* [1994] ICR 991, CA on the correct interpretation of the definition of incapacity and *Mihlenstedt v Barclays Bank International Ltd* [1989] IRLR 522 on the employer's duty to act in good faith in assessing medical evidence of incapacity (discussed further at 42.12 below) and the *Derby Daily Telegraph* case (above) on the duty to construe the rules in a purposive and practical way.

42.6 CHANGING THE RETIREMENT AGE

Where the contract provides for a particular retirement age, the legal principles governing changes in terms of the contract of employment apply equally to any attempt to change the retirement age. In the absence of consent by the employees, or incorporation of an agreement reached through collective bargaining, a change cannot be unilaterally imposed through the contract. The failure of an employee to object to a change notified to him, as by a new statement of particulars of terms, does not amount to acceptance of the change by silence. This is most clearly so where the change has no immediate practical effect on the employee: *Aparau v Iceland Frozen Foods plc* [1996] IRLR 119.

This may have no practical consequences where the employer seeks to increase the retirement (as distinct from pension) age, since this would be no more than a promise to defer enforced retirement. Nor would a lowering of the age by unilateral notification, not accepted by the employee, prevent the employer from retiring an employee at the lower age by giving the contractual notice of termination (as a matter of contract). However, such a dismissal would in all probability be open to challenge as unfair and, might also amount to unlawful age discrimination (see above).

A variation to a contractual retirement age agreed between an employee and the transferee following a TUPE transfer is enforceable by the employee against the transferee. However, the employee would also be able to hold the transferee to the pre-transfer contractual position. In effect, such an employee can choose which he prefers: *Regent Security Services Ltd v Power* [2007] EWCA Civ 1188, [2008] 2 All ER 977, [2008] IRLR 66.

1102

A term of a contract is unenforceable against a person in so far as it constitutes, promotes, or provides for treatment of that or another person that constitutes discrimination contrary to the *Equality Act 2010*, including age discrimination (*s 142*).

Different considerations apply to changes in pensionable age under an occupational pension scheme. In relation to past service, such changes may be precluded by the rules of the scheme unless they are in all respects advantageous to the members affected. Changes designed to equalise pension ages between men and women following the ECJ's decision in *Barber v Guardian Royal Exchange Assurance Group:* C-262/88 [1991] 1 QB 344 are, in addition, subject to restrictions arising from principles of EU law: *Smith v Avdel Systems Ltd*: C-408/92 [1995] All ER (EC) 132; see further EQUAL PAY (**22**). Whilst these requirements do not prohibit a change that would have the effect, as regards future service, of 'levelling down' rights as a matter of European law, this is subject to the requirements of national law as to the validity of any change. The consent of individual employees would be required for a change in the pensionable age, even for benefits derived from future service, where that age is expressly or impliedly a term of the contract.

42.7   BENEFITS AFTER RETIREMENT

Employers may provide certain benefits to employees which continue beyond retirement. Even if the benefits are expressly provided to be discretionary they will nevertheless almost certainly be 'pay' in EU law: *Garland v British Rail Engineering Ltd* [1983] 2 AC 751, ECJ (concessionary travel facilities for families of retired employees); such benefits must therefore be provided without discrimination on grounds of sex.

If a benefit is contractual it must be provided, even if it becomes unduly expensive to continue its provision: *Baynham v Philips Electronics (UK) Ltd* (1995) IDS Brief 551 (private medical insurance during retirement). As there is no basis for compelling a former employee, who cannot be dismissed, to agree to abandon a continuing contractual right, the employer has no option but to 'buy out' the benefit or continue to provide it. The inclusion of such provisions in the contract of employment is therefore a matter requiring great caution.

42.8   PENSIONS

The law of pensions is outside the scope of this book. It is a large and complex area which it would not be practicable to cover in detail. Pensions law rests mainly on the principles of the law of trusts (most pension schemes are administered, and the funds held, by trustees) and increasingly detailed statutory regulation. The principal legislation governing pension schemes is the *Pension Schemes Act 1993*, a consolidating Act, together with the *Pensions Act 1995*, the *Pensions Act 2004*, the *Pensions Act 2011* and, most recently, the *Pensions Act 2014*. In addition, stakeholder pension schemes are the subject of *Part I* of the *Welfare Reform and Pensions Act 1999* and supporting Regulations: see **42.10** below for brief details.

The *Pensions Act 2004* was a major piece of legislation. Among other things, it established a new Pensions Regulator (replacing the Occupational Pensions Regulatory Authority) with a remit including the prevention of fraud and ensuring the proper funding of pension schemes as well as a Board of the Pension Protection Fund. The Board is responsible for administering a compensation scheme for employees in private sector pension schemes, who risk losing accrued pension rights if their employer becomes insolvent and the pension scheme is insufficiently funded. Other provisions include a requirement for the transferee employer following a transfer within the *Transfer of Undertakings (Protection of Employment) Regulations 2006* to provide those employees who have transferred with pension benefits for future service broadly comparable with those previously enjoyed.

42.8 Retirement

Reform to the state pension was introduced in the *Pensions Act 2007* and to the private pension system in the *Pensions Act 2008*. The latter was aimed at enabling and encouraging more people to build up a private pension income to supplement the basic state pension. The *Pensions Act 2008* was followed by the *Workplace Pensions Reform Regulations 2010*. These reforms focused on the introduction of "automatic-enrolment" into workplace pensions schemes, from which an individual would need actively to opt-out, combined with a minimum employer contribution and the creation of a pension scheme, now known as the National Employment Savings Trust ("NEST") that could be used by any employer.

The *Pensions Act 2011*, which gained Royal Assent on 3 November 2011, made a number of changes including:

(a)   increasing the state pension age to 66 between 2018 and 2020, to be applied to both men and women; and

(b)   an expansion of the requirement for automatic enrolment.

In January 2013, the government published a new draft Pensions Bill which became the *Pensions Act 2014* ("*2014 Act*"). This act contains provisions to introduce a single-tier pension which will for future pensioners, replace the current two-component State Pension with a single component flat-rate pension, a "singe-tier pension". This single-tier pension replaces the current basic State Pension and additional State Pension with a flat-rate pension that is set above the basic level of means-tested support for people who reach State Pension Age on or after 6 April 2016. The act also provided for a new type of voluntary National Insurance contributions, Class 3A, to allow pensioners who reach State Pension Age before 6 April 2016 to top up their additional state pension. It also brought forward the increase in the State Pension age to 67 and set out a framework for a regular review of the State Pension age at least every five years. Such a review would be based around the principle that people should expect to spend a certain proportion of their adult life in retirement and would be informed by actuarial reports. The *2014 Act* also contains a number of mainly technical amendments to auto enrolment and contains powers to allow the government to introduce minimum governance and administration standards and restrict charges in workplace pensions. The government has announced that it intends to use these powers to restrict high and unfair charges and to strengthen governance in defined contribution workplace schemes. Finally, the *2014 Act* contains a number of other measures relating to private pensions which are outside the scope of this book.

Recent changes, enacted in the *Taxation of Pensions Act 2014*, which were effective from 6 April 2015, permit much greater flexibility for pensioners. They allow, in principle, any person over the minimum pension age to access the funds in any money purchase scheme without constraint.

Finally, the *Pension Schemes Act 2015* received royal assent on 3 March 2015. It did two main things. First, it introduced a new category of pension scheme, "Defined Ambition", described further below. Second, it introduced further provisions supporting the increase in flexibility including rights to transfer pension funds between schemes.

Areas of particular relevance to employment are dealt with below: stakeholder pensions; discrimination and pension rights and benefits; the rights of members to elect trustees under the *Pensions Act 1995* and the legal protection of employee trustees; employers' duties in respect of pension schemes; and the machinery available to resolve employees' disputes and grievances about pension rights. Brief notes about some of the principal features of pension schemes, and pension terminology are given first.

Pension schemes may be described as occupational or personal. *Personal pension schemes* are money purchase funds invested by the pension provider on behalf of the individual and used to purchase an annuity at retirement. Within statutory limits employee contributions are tax deductible. Employers may agree to make contributions, but are under no obligation to match contributions they would have made on the employee's behalf to the *occupational pension scheme*.

Occupational pension schemes may be *statutory* (the major public sector schemes covering a quarter of the employed workforce, principally the civil service and armed forces, local government and NHS workers, teachers and the police and fire service, under the *Superannuation Act 1972* and specific statutory regulations) or established by trust deed, to which the scheme rules are usually appended. They may be either *defined benefit*, also referred to as *final salary*, schemes, or *money purchase* schemes (sometimes referred to as *defined contribution* schemes). The former provide benefits based on pensionable salary and years of service, normally either 1/60 or 1/80 of pensionable salary for each year of pensionable service. A lump sum retirement benefit may be provided, in addition to pension based on 1/80 of salary, or by commuting the capital value of part of the pension in 1/60 schemes (subject to limits imposed by the Inland Revenue). All the principal statutory public sector schemes are final salary schemes. Following the coming into force of the *Pensions Schemes Act 2015*, there will also be a third category of pension schemes, defined ambition schemes.

All major public sector schemes and most private sector schemes also provide for a (usually reduced) pension to be payable to a surviving spouse, often referred to as *survivor's benefit*. Some schemes extend the coverage of survivors' benefits to unmarried partners. In such cases, it would be unlawful to limit the benefit to partners of the opposite sex to the member concerned; but the restriction of benefits to the deceased member's spouse where the right to the benefit accrued or the benefit is payable in respect of periods of service prior to the coming into force of the *Civil Partnership Act 2004* is lawful, as is the conferring of a benefit on married persons and civil partners to the exclusion of other persons: see *Equality Act 2010, para 18* of Part 3 of Sch 9; or, prior to 1 October 2010, *reg 25* of the *2003 Regulations*. In *R (ota Cockburn) v Secretary of State for Health* [2011] EWHC 2095 (Admin), Supperstone J held that disregarding the period of pensionable service prior to a certain date when calculating widower's but not a widow's pension was lawful having regard to the cost of retrospective equalisation. See also *Innospec Ltd v Walker* [2014] IRLR 334 for an equivalent decision in relation to same sex partners and *O'Brien v Ministry of Justice (No 2)* [2014] IRLR 40 in relation to part-time workers.

Money purchase schemes (also referred to as *defined contribution* schemes) have fixed rates of contribution, and benefits are purchased according to market conditions from the investment yield of the contributions. Following *Bridge Trustees Ltd v Yates* [2011] UKSC 42, [2011] 1 WLR 1912, [2011] ICR 1069, (in which the Supreme Court held that an equilibrium of assets and liabilities was not a requirement of a money purchase scheme), the government introduced a new clearer definition of a money purchase scheme (see *ss 181, 181A* and *181B* of the *Pension Schemes Act 1993* as amended/inserted).

Defined benefit schemes are funded by employer and employee contributions. Employees contribute a fixed percentage of salary and other pensionable earnings. Some schemes are non-contributory. The employer contributes the balance required to fund the scheme sufficiently, in accordance with an actuarial review of the liabilities of the scheme conducted at regular intervals. If the scheme is in surplus, the employer's contributions may be temporarily suspended (a 'pensions holiday'). There are complex rules, largely outside the scope of this book, as to the permissible uses of pension fund surpluses; see **42.16** for the most important cases on this.

Defined ambition schemes have recently been introduced in this country. In this new type of scheme, risks are shared between the employee and the employer, an insurance provider or the scheme itself. The aim is to provide greater certainty for members about the final value of their pension benefits than a defined contribution pension and to provide more cost predictability for employers than a defined benefit pension.

42.8 Retirement

Pensionable salary is the reference point for the calculation both of benefits under a defined benefit scheme and employee contributions. What earnings fall to be treated as pensionable is primarily a matter for the rules of the particular scheme; normally this will cover basic salary, but the position may be more complex where total pay is made up of a number of additional components such as shift allowances, production bonuses and other allowances. In *Newham London Borough Council v Skingle* [2003] EWCA Civ 280, [2003] 2 All ER 761, the Court of Appeal held that pensionable salary for the purpose of the *Local Government Pension Scheme Regulations 1997* included overtime payments, but only where, as in the instant case, the overtime was in effect obligatory on the employee, a school caretaker, who had been required to perform duties out of normal working hours by the nature of his job.

Schemes generally provide for employees to purchase additional years of pensionable service, up to the scheme maximum, by making *additional voluntary contributions* ('AVCs') up to an overall permitted maximum of 15% of pensionable earnings. (These are distinct from *free-standing additional voluntary contributions* ('FSAVCs') which are either single payment or periodic contribution personal pension schemes marketed by pension companies and purchased direct by employees, using the balance of tax relief available to the employee and not used up by contributions to the employer's occupational scheme.)

Pension schemes may provide additional benefits, including (as well as survivors' benefits as described above) pensions for surviving children or other dependants. Death in service benefit, in effect life insurance, of up to a maximum of four times pensionable salary, is commonly provided. The availability of these benefits, and of increases in benefits provided, is a matter primarily for the rules of the particular scheme, but increasingly the statutory framework of approved pension schemes lays down not only maximum benefits permitted within the framework of a favourable tax regime, but minimum standards that must be met.

Contributions to personal pension schemes attract tax relief up to limits. The annual allowance is 100% of earnings or £40,000, subject to a lifetime limit of £1,000,000.

The value of pension funds is necessarily dependent on the underlying value of investments in which the funds are held, and the amount of pension that can be bought from a fund of a given value depends on current annuity rates, which are lower for women than for men owing to differences in life expectancy. In a case relating to the *Goods and Services Directive*, the ECJ held, in *Association belge des Consommateurs Test-Achats ASBL v Conseil des ministres*: C-236/09 [2011] NLJR 363, [2011] Pens LR 145, that the use of gender based insurance premiums was contrary to the principle of equal treatment. In its decision, the ECJ did not refer to the *Equal Treatment Directive* (which prohibits occupational pension schemes from discriminating on the grounds of sex) or to its own previous case law such as *Coloroll Pension Trustees Ltd v Russell*: C-200/91 [1995] All ER (EC) 23, in which it held that the use of gender based actuarial factors does not contravene *art 157* of the *Treaty on the Functioning of the EU* (formerly *art 141* and, prior to that, *art 119* of the *Treaty of Rome*). The effect of *Test-Achats* remains to be seen. However, it would seem that it is difficult to see why the use of gender-based actuarial factors would be contrary to the principle of equal treatment in relation to insurance premiums but not in relation to pensions.

Sharp falls in the values of equities, following a steady decline in the rate of annuities which can be purchased on the realisation of pension fund investments, led many major employers to conclude that the provision of defined benefit pension schemes had become too expensive. Accordingly employers, in significant numbers, adopted policies of closing their defined benefit schemes to new entrants, offering instead to contribute to new defined contribution schemes. Less commonly but more controversially, some employers have sought the closure of their defined benefit schemes in relation to future service of current members. The legality of such a step may be open to challenge, but whether it is challengeable in any particular case will depend on the precise terms of the employees' contracts, and of the pension scheme rules. A further distinction is that the rights earned by past service are likely to be protected by the rules of the Scheme from any retrospective adverse change, whereas rights to be accrued by future service are likely only to be protected (if at all) as a matter of contract. There is a general consensus that the benefits available under a defined benefit scheme are of greater value to employees than the alternative of money purchase scheme membership.

In *R (ota Staff Side of the Police Negotiating Board) v Secretary of State for Work and Pensions* [2011] EWHC 3175 (Admin), a judicial review of the Government's decision to alter the basis upon which public service pensions were adjusted to take account of inflation was unsuccessful. This change was likely to reduce the value of benefits to pension scheme members over time. In *R (ota Public and Commercial Services Union) v Minister for the Civil Service* [2011] EWHC 2041 (Admin), [2011] IRLR 903, McCombe J held that the rights of civil servants under the Civil Service Compensation Scheme which included redundancy and early retirement benefits, constituted possessions within the meaning of *Article 1* of the *First Protocol of the European Convention on Human Rights 1950*. However, the introduction of a new Scheme that reduced those benefits was a lawful proportionate interference with those rights.

A different but related matter of concern has arisen in a number of cases where a pension scheme has been wound up following the insolvency of the employer. The rules of each scheme determine the order in which claims on the scheme must be met in such circumstances; typically these require that the claims of those already in receipt of a pension must be met first. If the scheme is in deficit (which is possible up to a permitted margin, and more likely at a time of declining share prices) this may leave a serious shortfall for employees who were active (ie contributing) members of the scheme at the date of its closure, whose pensions may be dramatically reduced as a result. The *Pensions Act 2004* addressed this problem in two ways, by changing the priorities required to be followed in distributing the scheme assets, and by creating a compensation scheme for employees who lose accrued pension rights.

The *members* of a pension scheme are those employees who, being eligible, have elected to join the scheme, retired employees in receipt of a pension, and those former employees who have retained the right to a deferred pension payable at pensionable age. Employees who leave the service of the employer may withdraw their contributions, but only if pensionable service is under two years, or transfer the value to another employer's scheme or a personal pension. In either case the employee ceases to be a member of the first scheme. *Transfer values* are calculated by reference to actuarial valuations, but actual criteria depend on the rules of each scheme. A lump-sum payment is made to the new scheme which gives credit for years of service depending on its own advisers' computations of the cost of purchasing service. *Transfer values* may not therefore fully reflect accrued service. Further, the actuarial factors used include mortality tables reflecting the different life expectancy of, and therefore different cost of providing pensions for, each sex, so that transfer values may differ according to sex. The ECJ has held that this does not contravene *art 157* (formerly *art 141* and before that *art 119*) of the *Treaty of Rome* (*Coloroll Pension Trustees Ltd v Russell*: C-200/91 [1995] All ER (EC) 23). This exception is preserved by the UK legislation giving effect to EU law (see **22.19 Equal Pay** for details) (but see above concerning the uncertain effect of the *Test-Achats* case). The same consequences, and legal exceptions, apply to the value attributed, in terms of additional years of service, to AVCs.

The *State Earnings Related Pension Scheme* ('SERPS'), established in 1975, was designed as a fallback for employees who do not benefit from occupational pensions. Pension schemes which met prescribed minimum standards could apply to be *contracted out* of SERPS. *Contracting out* was the norm for larger schemes, not least because both employer and employee paid lower rates of National Insurance if the employee was in a contracted-out scheme. In place of the SERPS pension the scheme was required to assure a *Guaranteed Minimum Pension*, protected by more stringent rules as to indexation and preservation where benefits are transferred or commuted. SERPS was replaced in April 2002, but for future

42.8 Retirement

earnings only, by the *State Second Pension*. Because the change is not retrospective, rights under SERPS will exist, in preserved form, for very many years. The State Second Pension accrues at different rates on banded earnings between the National Insurance lower earnings limit and the National Insurance upper earnings limit. Additionally, there are some credits for earnings for people with a long-term illness or disability.

The *Pensions Act 2007* provided for the abolition of contracting out on a money-purchase basis. Since 6 April 2012, it is no longer possible to contract out of the State Second Pension through a money-purchase scheme or a personal pension or stakeholder pension scheme. Those who already contract out will be able to continue to make their own contributions and benefit from any employer contributions but will not be able to benefit from any rebate of National Insurance contributions. It is, however, possible to contract out in a final salary or career average scheme.

The *Pensions Act 2014* has replaced the two-component state pension with a single component flat-rate pension that will be set above the basic level of means-tested report for those who reach State Pension age on or after 6 April 2016.

42.9 Stakeholder pensions

The legislation for this form of pension is *Part I* of the *Welfare Reform and Pensions Act 1999* (which is largely enabling) and the *Stakeholder Pensions Scheme Regulations 2000 (SI 2000/1403)* as amended. The intention behind these pensions was to encourage individuals, particularly those with modest earnings, and who are not members of occupational pension schemes, to make provision for their retirement. Stakeholder pensions are private sector schemes but subject to registration, minimum standards of performance and approved schemes of governance. Schemes are required to be flexible, so that contributions can be suspended or varied, and any individual who is not contributing to a contracted out occupational pension scheme, including minors and those not in employment, can contribute up to a fixed amount per year. Contributions are made net of standard rate income tax, which is made up by the State, even if the individual is not a taxpayer. If earnings are sufficient, contributions in excess of the fixed amount a year gross can be made, with corresponding tax relief.

In the past, employers could, but could not be obliged to, contribute to individual employees' pensions. However, with the coming into force of the *Pensions Act 2008*, employers are required to enrol eligible workers into a qualifying workplace pension arrangement, see further below for details.

42.10 Automatic enrolment under the Pensions Act 2008

The *Pensions Act 2008* ("*2008 Act*") puts into law reforms to the private pension system set out in the White Paper "Personal Accounts: a new way to save" published in December 2006. It contains a number of measures aimed at encouraging greater private pension saving.

The regime requires employers to enrol "eligible jobholders" automatically into an "automatic enrolment scheme" with effect from the date upon which such jobholders become eligible. Once an "eligible jobholder" is enrolled, the employer is under an obligation either to make minimum contributions (if it is a defined contribution scheme) or to offer a minimum level of benefits (if it is a defined benefit scheme). Employers are also under an obligation to provide certain information to eligible jobholders including information about automatic enrolment, what it means and their right to opt out.

The key duties to be imposed are contained in *sections 2 to 8* of the *Pensions Act 2008*, as amended ("*2008 Act*"). They were imposed month by month over a multiple year "staging period" depending on the size of the employer. Employers with the most employees were required to comply with the duties first. The relevant date in relation to each employer is called the "staging date".

The first task is to identify who is an "eligible jobholder". A "jobholder" is defined in *section 1* of the *2008 Act* as a worker:

(a)   who is working or ordinarily works in Great Britain under the worker's contract;

(b)   who is aged at least 16 and under 75; and

(c)   to whom "qualifying earnings" are payable in the relevant pay reference period.

"Worker" is defined in *s 88(3)* as an individual who has entered into or works under a contract of employment or any other contract by which the individual undertakes to do work or perform services personally for another party to the contract. "Contract of employment" is defined as a contract of service or apprenticeship, whether express or implied and (if it is express) whether oral or in writing (*s 88(1)*). These definitions are very similar to those set out in *s 230* of the *Employment Rights Act* (see EMPLOYEE, SELF-EMPLOYED OR WORKER? (15)). However, contracts of a client or customer of a profession or business undertaking are excluded (*s 88(4)*).

In relation to agency workers, in the absence of a workers' contract between the worker and either the agent or the principal, then the regime applies as if there was a workers' contract and whichever of the agent or the principal is responsible for paying the agency worker in respect of the work (or which of them does actually pay (*s 89*). Further, that person is treated as the employer for the purposes of automatic enrolment.

"Qualifying earnings" are defined in *s 13(1)* as the part, if any, of the gross earnings payable to that person in that period that is within a range which has been amended by order annually. For the period from 6 April 2016, "qualifying earnings" were more than £5,824 but not more than £43,000, and from 6 April 2017 more than £5,876 but not more than £45,000.

"Earnings" is defined to mean:

(a)   salary, wages, commission, bonuses and overtime;

(b)   statutory sick pay;

(c)   statutory maternity pay;

(d)   statutory paternity pay;

(e)   statutory adoption pay;

(f)   statutory shared parental pay; and

(g)   sums prescribed for the purposes of the section.

       (2008 Act, s 13)

Where the pay reference period is less than 12 months, the figures are adjusted proportionately (*s 13(2)*).

Workers who receive gross earnings of more than the maximum figure will still qualify as jobholders. However, contributions will only be payable on the qualifying earnings.

A "jobholder" is "eligible" for the purposes of automatic enrolment:

(a)   who is aged at least 22,

(b)   who has not reached pensionable age, and

(c)   to whom earnings of more than £10,000 are payable by the employer in the relevant pay reference period.

42.10 Retirement

(*2008 Act, s 3*, as amended)

Further guidance has been published by the Pensions Regulator, see the Pensions Regulator's Guidance Note No. 1 "Employer duties and defining the workforce" as to who will count as a worker. The guidance states, for example, that office-holders such as non-executive directors, company secretaries, board members and trustees are not workers but that casual or zero hours workers are likely to be if the other conditions are satisfied.

Section 3 of the *Pensions Act* is the provision imposing the automatic enrolment duty. Employers must enrol eligible jobholders in an automatic enrolment scheme with effect from the "automatic enrolment date" (*s 3(2)*). This is defined as the first day on which the *section 3* duty applies to the jobholder (*s 3(7)*). This means either the staging date for the employer or, if later, the date upon which the individual becomes an eligible jobholder. There are, however, provisions for deferral for up to three months upon written notice in accordance with detailed rules set out in *section 4*.

Employers have only been required to comply with the key duties from the applicable staging date. The staging dates for employers with a PAYE scheme of over 40 as of 1 April 2012 have all passed. For smaller employers, the information on staging dates can be found on the pension regulator's website at www.thepensionsregulator.gov.uk.

In order to be a "qualifying automatic enrolment scheme", a pension scheme must be an "automatic enrolment scheme" which "qualifies" by meeting certain quality requirements. To be an "automatic enrolment scheme":

- it must **not** prevent the employer from making the requirements for a jobholder automatically to become an active member of the scheme; or

- require the jobholder to express a choice in relation to any matter or to provide any information, in order to remain an active member.

(*section 17*)

In order to be a "qualifying scheme" it must:

- be an occupational pension scheme or a personal pension scheme;

- be registered under *Chapter 2* of *Part 4* of the *Finance Act 2004* (ie be registered for tax purposes); and

- satisfy the minimum "quality requirement" in relation to that a particular jobholder whilst that jobholder is an active member.

(*section 16*)

The "quality requirement" is defined differently for different pension scheme types (money purchase, defined contribution etc) and for UK and non-UK schemes. The detailed provisions are set out in *sections 20* to *28* of the *2008 Act* with further guidance in the Pensions Regulator's detailed guidance Note No. 4 "Pension Schemes".

If an employer does not wish to use an existing pension scheme or set up a new pension scheme, then it may use the National Employment Savings Trust ("NEST"). NEST is a central pension scheme established by a corporation set up by the Government. NEST is an occupational direct contribution scheme. Employers who use it must meet the minimum contribution requirements for such schemes to satisfy the minimum "quality requirement". For more information, see the NEST website at www.nestpensions.org.uk.

In addition to the requirement of automatic enrolment, employers are also obliged not to take any action by which a jobholder would cease to be an active member of a qualifying scheme or by which the scheme would cease to be a qualifying scheme (*section 2(1)*,

2008 Act). Employers are not in breach of the section if the jobholder remains an active member of another qualifying scheme or if he or she requests to leave the scheme *(section 2(2)).* Nor are they in breach if an eligible jobholder ceases to be a member of a scheme for a prescribed period before joining another scheme.

Employers are also required automatically to re-enrol jobholders who were but are no longer members of the scheme for particular reasons. For details, see *section 5* of the *2008 Act* and *Parts 2* and *3* of the *Occupational and Personal Pension Schemes (Automatic Enrolment) Regulations 2010, SI 2010/772* (*"2010 Regulations"*).

Finally, the Secretary of State may make provisions to require employers to provide employees with prescribed information in relation to their rights under *sections 2* to *8* of the *2008 Act* (see *section 10* of the *2008 Act*). The details are clearly set out in the Pension Regulator's detailed guidance Note No. 10 "Information to workers: the new duties".

Opting out

Eligible jobholders are entitled to opt out of the scheme under *section 8* of the *2008 Act.* However, this is only possible during an "opt-out" period. This is a one month period following the later of the date on which the jobholder first became an active member of the pension scheme and the date upon which he or she was provided with written enrolment information (see *regulation 9* of the *2010 Regulations*). The notice is only valid if it must also includes the following:

(a)   (a) A statement set out in schedule 1 to the Regulations as follows:

"WHAT YOU NEED TO KNOW

Your employer cannot ask you or force you to opt out.

If you are asked or forced to opt out you can tell the Pensions Regulator – see www.thepensionsregulator.gov.uk/

If you change your mind you may be able to opt back in – write to your employer if you want to do this.

If you stay opted out your employer will normally put you back into pension saving in around 3 years.

If you change job your new employer will normally put you back into pension saving straight away.

If you have another job your other employer might also put you into pension saving, now or in the future. This notice only opts you out of pension saving with the employer you name above. A separate notice must be filled out and given to any other employer you work for if you wish to opt out of that pension saving as well."

(b)   statements from the jobholder to the effect that the jobholder wishes to opt out of pension saving and understands that, in so doing, he or she will lose the right to pension contributions from the employer and may have a lower income upon retirement;

(c)   the jobholder's name;

(d)   the jobholder's national insurance number or date of birth;

(e)   a signature by the jobholder or, if electronic, a statement confirming that the jobholder personally submitted the notice; and

(f)   the date.

(*reg 9(6)* of the *2010 Regulations*)

Jobholders who have opted out can choose to opt back in but they may only do so once in the 12 month period from when they first choose to opt back in (*2008 Act, section 7*).

There are also detailed obligations to keep records.

Enforcement

Employers who willfully fail to comply with the automatic enrolment duty, the automatic re-enrolment duty or the duty to allow jobholders to opt in commit a criminal offence. The officers of a body corporate which commits such an offence may be liable to a fine or prison term of up to two years if the offence has been committed with the consent or connivance of an officer or is attributable to any neglect on the part of the officer (see *sections 45 to 47* of the *2008 Act*).

Employers are prohibited from making any statement or asking any question directly or by an agent for the purposes of recruitment which indicates (expressly or impliedly) that an application for employment may be determined by reference to whether or not an applicant might opt out of automatic enrolment (*s 50(1), 2008 Act*).

Pursuant to *section 55*, employees have a right not to be subjected to any detriment by an act, or a deliberate failure to act, by the worker's employer, done on the ground that

(a)   any action was taken, or was proposed to be taken, with a view to enforcing in favour of a worker one of the specified employers' duties,

(b)   the employer was prosecuted under *s 45* as a result of action taken for the purpose of enforcing in favour of the worker one of the specified employers' duties, or

(c)   any of the specified employers' duties apply or will or might apply to the worker.

It is immaterial whether or not the requirement does apply or whether or not it has in fact been contravened but any claim that the requirement applies or has been contravened must be made in good faith (*s 55(2)*).

A dismissal cannot be a detriment within the meaning of *s 55*. However, a new *section 104D* has been inserted into the *Employment Rights Act 1996* ("*ERA*") (by *s 57* of the *2008 Act*) which provides that an employee is unfairly dismissed if the reason or principal reason for the dismissal is that:

(a)   any action was taken, or was proposed to be taken, with a view to enforcing in favour of a worker one of the specified employers' duties,

(b)   the employer was prosecuted under *s 45* as a result of action taken for the purpose of enforcing in favour of the worker one of the specified employers' duties, or

(c)   any of the specified employers' duties apply or will or might apply to the worker.

Again, it is immaterial whether or not the requirement does apply or whether or not it has in fact been contravened but any claim that the requirement applies or has been contravened must be made in good faith (*s 104D(2), ERA*).

A worker may present a complaint to an employment tribunal that he or she has been subjected to a detriment in contravention of *section 55*. Where the complaint is in relation to the termination of a contract which is not a contract of employment, the limits on compensation which apply to unfair dismissal compensation apply (see *ss 56(3)* and *(4)*).

There are restrictions on agreements to limit the operation of the scheme (*section 58, 2008 Act*) which are similar to those familiar from the *Equality Act 2010*.

42.11 Discrimination and occupational pension schemes

The *Equality Act 2010* ("*EA 2010*") contains provisions which prohibit discrimination in relation to pensions. Occupational pension schemes are deemed to include a "non-discrimination rule" (*s 61(1)*). A "non-discrimination rule" is a provision by virtue of which a responsible person (A) must not discriminate against another person (B) in carrying out any of A's functions in relation to the scheme, and must not, in relation to the scheme, harass or victimise B (*s 61(2)*).

The provisions of an occupational pension scheme have effect subject to the non-discrimination rule. A "responsible person" is a trustee or manager of the scheme, an employer whose employers are, or may be, members of the scheme and a person responsible for appointing a person to an office, where the office holder is or may be a member of the scheme (*s 61(4)*).

A discriminates against B for the purposes of *EA 2010* if A treats B less favourably than A treats or would treat others "because of a protected characteristic" (*s 13*). Disability, sex, and age are among the protected characteristics. A discriminates against B indirectly by applying a provision, criterion or practice which A applies or would apply to others with whom B does not share the characteristic, but puts those sharing the characteristic at a particular disadvantage, puts B to that disadvantage and which A cannot show to be a proportionate means of achieving a legitimate aim (*s 19*). A also discriminates against a disabled person, B, if A treats B unfavourably because of something arising in consequence of B's disability, and A cannot show that the treatment is a proportional means of achieving a legitimate aim (*s 15*). Harassment and victimisation are defined in *ss 26* and *27* respectively.

A duty to make reasonable adjustments also applies to a responsible person (*s 20*).

Section 62 provides trustees and managers of occupational pension schemes the power, by resolution, to alter their scheme's rules to conform to the non-discrimination rule.

Where there is a breach of a non-discrimination rule, it is possible to bring proceedings under *Part 9* of *EA 2010* in the employment tribunal. (This does not prevent the investigation or determination of any matter by the Pensions Ombudsman.) The tribunal, if it finds a complaint well-founded, may make an order declaring that the complainant has a right to be admitted to the scheme or to membership of the scheme without discrimination (*EA 2010, s 124(2)*). Such an order may have effect in relation to a period before the order was made (*s 124(4)*). In such cases, the tribunal may not make an order for compensation for age discrimination except for injury to feelings or where a respondent fails to comply with a recommendation (*s 124(3)*).

The particular position in relation to each of sex and age discrimination is addressed further below.

41.12 *Maternity leave and pension benefits*

Pursuant to section 75 of *EA 2010*, a 'maternity equality rule' is deemed to be included in occupational pension schemes. This is the rule that any term of the scheme, or any discretion capable of being exercised under it, that purports to treat a woman differently in respect of time when she is on maternity leave compared to time when she is not, is modified so that both period fall to be treated in the same way (*s 75(3)* and *(4)*). Any term or discretion relating to membership of the scheme, accrual of rights or determination of benefits payable under the scheme falls within the scope of the rule.

The effect of this rule is that any period when a woman is on paid maternity leave must be treated as if she was not on leave. It must be treated as if it were a period during which she was attending work for the purposes of the occupational pension scheme.

The maternity equality rule does not require the woman's contributions to the scheme while she is on maternity leave to be determined other than by reference to the amount she is actually paid (ie statutory or contractual maternity pay). It is not clear from the statue whether or not the employer is required to pick up the shortfall. The Explanatory Notes to *EA 2010* state that 'a woman who is paid while on maternity leave will entitled to accrue rights in a scheme as though she were paid her usual salary but she will only be required to make contributions based on her actual pay. The Guidance from the 'Pensions Trust" in its 'Pensions Bulletin – Fact Sheet 3' states that 'the employer is required to pay the shortfall in the member's contributions to ensure that the scheme receives the right amount of funding for the benefits being accrued." It is fair to say that different commentators take different views and there is no authority on point.

Section 75 of *EA 2010* applies to unpaid ordinary maternity leave as well as paid ordinary maternity leave. This means that employers should continue making contributions to any occupational pension scheme during unpaid ordinary maternity leave as if the employee was working normally and earning her normal remuneration.

It is noted that *section 27* replaced *para 5* of *Schedule 5* to the *Social Security Act 1989*. The repealed provision applied to all 'service related benefits' and not just occupational pensions. It is no clear whether or not that change was deliberate.

This accords with the ECJ's ruling in *Boyle v Equal Opportunities Commission*: C-411/96 [1999] ICR 360 that it is a breach of the *Pregnant Workers Directive (92/85)* to exclude from pensionable service any part of the core 14 weeks' maternity leave conferred by the *Directive*, whether it is paid or unpaid.

Section 75 of *EA 2010* provides that the maternity equality rule does not apply to the accrual of rights under an occupational pension scheme in respect of unpaid period of additional maternity leave (*s 75(9)(a)*). It is unclear whether or not this distinction in treatment between paid and unpaid additional maternity leave is sustainable in the light of the ECJ's decisions in *Boyle* and in *Lord Brandenburg v Sass* [2005] IRLR 147, ECJ. In *Sass*, the ECJ held that the fact that domestic law grants women maternity leave of more than 14 weeks does not preclude that leave from being considered to be maternity leave within the meaning of the Pregnant Workers Directive. That would suggest that there is no basis for differentiating the first 14 weeks from the remainder of the maternity leave period such that the Boyle ruling would apply in respect of the entirety of the period. The High Court in *R (Equal Opportunities Commission) v Secretary of State for Trade and Industry* [2007] ICR 1234 held that Sass meant that there is no justification for giving employees on additional maternity leave any less protection from sex discrimination than those on ordinary maternity leave. However, the effect of the ECJ's decision in *Gillespie v Northern Health and Social Services Board*: C-342/93 [1996] All ER (EC) 284 appears to be that exclusion of unpaid leave from service does not contravene either *art 157* or the *EU Equal Pay* or *Equal Treatment Directives*.

Section 75 of *EA 2010* provides that a woman's paid maternity leave (whether ordinary or additional) should be treated as if it were a period during which she was working normally for the purposes of occupations schemes. In other words, maternity leave is included within the period of pensionable service. The Maternity and Parental Leave Regulations make specific provision for an employee's seniority, pension rights and similar rights to be preserved during ordinary and additional maternity leave (*reg 18* and *18A(1)(a)*). However, since this is subject to what is now *s 75(7)* to *(9)* of *EA 2010*, a period of unpaid ordinary maternity leave does count as pensionable service but a period of unpaid additional maternity leave does not. In the case of unpaid additional maternity leave, even though the period is not counted as pensionable service, continuity is preserved. The employee is not treated as having left and rejoined the scheme.

Similar but not identical provisions with respect to paid paternity, adoption and shared parental leave are set out in *paras 5A, 5B* and *5C* of *Sch 5* to the *Social Security Act 1989* as inserted and amended.

The ECJ has also ruled that a reduction in the pension of civil servants who have worked part time contravened *art 157* since it affected a considerably higher proportion of women than men, if the reduction in the pension was greater than the proportion of the reduction of working hours: *Schönheit (Hilde) v Stadt Frankfurt am Main*: C-4/02 and C-5/02 [2003] ECR I-12575.

However, where it is established that the denial of access to an employer's pension scheme indirectly discriminated against part-time workers on the grounds of sex, the part-time employees are not entitled to a declaration of entitlement if they would have opted out of the scheme even if they had been eligible to join: *Copple v Littlewoods Plc* [2011] EWCA Civ 1281, [2012] ICR 254.

42.13 *Age discrimination and pension benefits*

EA 2010 does not itself contain exemptions specifically for age. However, there is a power for a Minister of the Crown to make exceptions in relation to rules, practices, actions or decisions relating to age. The relevant Order is the *Equality Act (Age Exceptions for Pension Schemes) Order 2010 (SI 2010/2133)*. That Order provides that it is not a breach of the non-discrimination rule:

(a) for the employer, or trustees or managers of a scheme to maintain or use in relation to the scheme the rules, practices, actions or decisions:

    (i) which are set out in *Schedule 1* to the *Order* (see the *Order* itself for the detail); or

    (ii) as they relate to rights accrued or benefits payable in respect of periods of pensionable service prior to 1 December 2006;

(b) for the employer to maintain or use practices, actions or decisions set out in *Schedule 2* to the *Order* in relation to the payment of contributions (see the *Order* itself for the detail);

(c) for the trustees or managers to follow certain rules, practices, actions or decisions in relation to length of service (see *art 6*, as amended for the detail).

42.14 Employee pension trustees

Most pension schemes provide for the appointment by the employer of the trustees of the scheme. Many schemes provide for the appointment of a trustee company as sole trustee; its directors are in such cases usually nominated by the employer. Despite the stringent legal obligations of trustees to the members of the scheme, concern that in practice trustees are often vulnerable to pressure from the employer to take decisions in the employer's interest led to a significant change in the law.

Sections 241–242 of the *Pensions Act 2004* require at least one third of the trustees of a pension scheme established under a trust to be member-nominated, and the same minimum proportion of member-nominated directors where a trust company is the sole trustee. Further, the Secretary of State now has the power (by order) to increase the proportion to a half.

The *Occupational Pension Schemes (Member-nominated Trustees and Directors) Regulations 2006 (SI 2006/714)* set out detailed exceptions to the requirement for member-nominated trustees and member-nominated directors of corporate trustees for certain schemes, including small schemes and those that have few members.

The *Pensions Act 2004* also contains provisions requiring all individual trustees and corporate trustees to have knowledge and understanding of certain specified documents and legal principles.

Member-nominated trustees need not all be employees, but in practice most will be. Those who are employees have the right to be permitted to take reasonable time off for training in their duties and for the performance of those duties, and to be paid for such time off (*ERA 1996, ss 58–59*, consolidating provisions introduced by the *Pensions Act 1995*). They may bring a claim to the employment tribunal if the employer does not permit them to take the time off or pay them for it: *s 60, ERA 1996*. There is no equivalent right for candidates for election. Employee trustees are also protected from suffering detriment short of dismissal by reason of their performance or proposed performance of their functions as such (*ERA 1996, s 46*) and from dismissal for that reason (*ERA 1996, s 102*). The ambit of these provisions is similar to, but not identical to, the statutory rights and protection given to officials of an independent trade union and to statutory safety representatives and representatives of employee safety; see **49.2** and **49.9 TIME OFF WORK**.

Member-nominated trustees have the same duties in law to the beneficiaries of the trust funds as other trustees. Where (as will often be the case in practice) the nominated trustees have been put forward as candidates by trade unions there is a potential for conflict between their obligations as trustees and advocacy of union policy on such matters as ethical investment of funds or non-investment in competitor industries: see for a good practical example *Cowan v Scargill* [1985] Ch 270 (resolving the conflict in favour of the trustee obligations).

42.15   Employers' duties in respect of pension schemes

The obligations of pension trustees in relation to the management of funds, the alteration of rules and decisions as to individual cases are outside the scope of this book. A helpful judicial discussion of the position is to be found in *Stannard v Fisons Pension Trust Ltd* [1992] IRLR 27 (and see *Hillsdown Holdings plc v Pensions Ombudsman* [1997] 1 All ER 862, where the employer was ordered to return to the pension fund a surplus improperly paid out by the trustees). Further, it was held in *Power v Trustees of the Open Text (UK) Ltd Group Life Assurance Scheme* [2009] EWHC 3064 (Ch), [2010] SWTI 567 that the obligation of pension trustees does not extend to proposing benefit improvements.

There have also been a number of important decisions dealing with the rights and obligations of employers as opposed to trustees.

In *Mihlenstedt v Barclays Bank International Ltd* [1989] IRLR 522, the Court of Appeal held that, where a contract of employment provides for membership of a pension scheme, there is an implied obligation upon the employer to discharge his functions under the scheme in good faith and, so far as lies within his power, to procure the scheme's benefits for the employee. However, as emphasised in *Prudential Staff Pensions Ltd v The Prudential Staff Assurance Co* [2011] EWHC 960 (Ch), this implied duty does not go so far as to require an employer to arrive at a decision which is substantially fair or reasonable, see discussion below.

In *Mettoy Pension Trustees Ltd v Evans* [1991] 2 All ER 513, it was held that, where an employer was given a discretion under the rules of the scheme as to how certain surplus funds were to be applied, that was to be treated as a fiduciary power: the employer was under a duty to the objects of the power (the beneficiaries under the scheme) to consider whether and how to exercise it, and (presumably) to do so fairly and in good faith. Similarly, it was held in *Imperial Group Pension Trust Ltd v Imperial Tobacco Ltd* [1991] 2 All ER 597 that an employer's power under the rules of the scheme to give or withhold consent to an amendment of the rules had to be exercised in good faith, and the employer could only have regard to his own financial interests to the extent that to do so was consistent with that obligation of good faith. Thus the employer's rights had to be exercised with a view to the efficient running of the scheme, and not for the collateral purpose of forcing its members to give up their accrued rights. The Vice-Chancellor based this conclusion upon the employer's implied obligation to maintain the trust and confidence of its employees (see **8.15**

CONTRACT OF EMPLOYMENT). However, in *British Coal Corpn v British Coal Staff Superannuation Scheme Trustees Ltd* [1995] 1 All ER 912, Vinelott J held that whilst the duty to act in good faith in relation to amendments was related to the duty applicable in cases of distribution of a surplus, it was not a fiduciary duty in the full sense. He found that it could not be said that *any* exercise of the relevant power of amendment had to be invalid if and insofar as the amendment might benefit the employer directly or indirectly. Further, in *Prudential Staff Pension Scheme, Re* (above), Newey J reiterated that the obligation of good faith was not to be taken as requiring an employer to arrive at a decision which was "fair" when exercising a power given to him in apparently unfettered terms by the scheme rules. In deciding to award pension increases on a less generous basis than previously, the employer was entitled to have regard to his own interests. Finally, in *IBM United Kingdom Pensions Trust Ltd v IBM United Kingdom Holdings Ltd* [2012] EWHC 3540 (Ch), [2013] Pens. L.R. 33, it was held that the scope of the duties set out in *Imperial* was controversial. Four principles could be confidently identified: (a) discretion had to be exercised in favour of consent to a change in rules if a refusal of consent would be irrational or perverse; (b) The correct test was not one of fairness – assessing whether a decision was irrational or perverse was not to be equated with the application of an objective standard of reasonableness; (c) the test was a "severe" one; (d) the test was an objective one (see [18]). In *Bradbury v BBC* [2015] EWHC 1368 (Ch), [2015] All ER (D) 153 (May), Warren J held that the pensions ombudsman was entitled to find that the BBC's decision to impose a 1% cap on increases to pensionable salary was not in breach of the implied term of trust and confidence.

The question of recovery by the employer of surplus pension funds was considered in *National Grid Co plc v Mayes* [2001] UKHL 20, [2001] 2 All ER 417, upholding the right of the employer to appropriate a substantial surplus in the pension fund to meet debts owed by it to the fund. This case turned principally on the construction of the particular rules, and does not lay down any new general principles.

Where the pension scheme rules afford a benefit to employee members which is only available subject to the employee making an application or taking steps which necessitate being aware of the availability of and conditions for the benefit, the employer is under an applied contractual duty to draw to employees' attention the benefit and the necessity to take action to obtain or preserve it: *Scally v Southern Health and Social Services Board* [1992] 1 AC 294. An extension of this approach was shown in *Aspden v Webbs Poultry and Meat Group (Holdings) Ltd* [1996] IRLR 521, where the High Court held that an express term permitting dismissal on notice was subject to an implied term that it would not be used so as to defeat the employee's claim to disability benefits also provided for by the contract. This reasoning would apply equally to ill-health pension benefits. The implied term applied in *Aspden* received support, *obiter*, in the Court of Appeal in *Brompton v AOC International Ltd* [1997] IRLR 639 at 643, but was given a more limited construction in *Hill v General Accident Fire and Life Assurance Corpn plc* [1998] IRLR 641. See also *Villella v MFI Furniture Centres Ltd* [1999] IRLR 468.

The limits to the principle established by *Scally* are shown in *University of Nottingham v Eyett* [1999] 2 All ER 437: where an employee is aware of his entitlement to a benefit and is taking a decision as to how to maximise it, the employer is not under a positive duty to warn him that he has not chosen the most advantageous way. *Eyett* was approved and applied in the Court of Appeal in *Outram v Academy Plastics* [2000] IRLR 499, where a claim that employers owed a duty of care to an employee who had resigned after 20 years' service and later re-joined the employer, to advise him to re-join the employer's pension scheme, was struck out as having no prospect of success. Two points were emphasised: the established law that trustees of a pension scheme do not owe a duty of care to advise scheme members faced with choices about pension matters; and the principle (confirmed in *Scally*) that there cannot be any wider duty owed by an employer to an employee in tort than that owed in contract.

42.15 Retirement

An employer answering queries from pension scheme trustees about a former employee's work record owes no duty of care to that employee which could make him liable for damages in negligence (*Petch v Customs and Excise Comrs* [1993] ICR 789; but cf *Spring v Guardian Assurance plc* [1995] 2 AC 296, referred to in **40.4 REFERENCES**).

42.16 Claims and disputes over pension rights

Some employees' claims in relation to pension rights may be taken to an employment tribunal. These include claims in respect of membership or benefits made under the *Equality Act 2010*. Such claims may be made in appropriate cases against the trustees as well as (or instead of) the employer.

In addition, employees' rights against employers in relation to pensions are in their nature contractual, and the Court of Appeal has held this to be so in principle also for the member's relationship to the trustees (*Harris v Shuttleworth (Lord)* [1994] ICR 991, CA). Accordingly, pension disputes may be taken to an employment tribunal by an aggrieved employee, if they arise on or are outstanding at the termination of his employment, under the *Employment Tribunals Extension of Jurisdiction (England and Wales) Order 1994 (SI 1994/1623)* or the parallel Scottish Order. Claims against the trustees based on the contract of membership are permissible because the Order applies to claims under contracts connected with employment, and does not limit claims to those against the former employer. (This jurisdiction may not apply where the scheme is a statutory public sector scheme with the right to membership conferred, and benefits prescribed, by statute.)

However, there are important limitations to the tribunal's contractual jurisdiction. The only remedy it can award is damages, with a statutory maximum of £25,000. Claims can also be brought only following termination of employment, and within a three-month time limit. Claims must arise out of, or be outstanding on, the termination of the employment.

In pension claims, remedies such as a declaration of rights or a direction to the employer or trustees to determine a claim in accordance with law are often important. Further, claims frequently have values far in excess of £25,000, for example, where a pension payable for the rest of the claimant's life is in issue. For these reasons, such claims are typically brought in the ordinary courts.

However, there are other avenues to pursue claims and disputes, of increasing practical importance. The *Pensions Act 1995, s 50* created a statutory requirement for all occupational pension schemes (except those with only one member or where all the members are trustees) to establish a procedure for the internal resolution of all disputes raised by or on behalf of members or their dependents or prospective members. (This requirement applies equally to stakeholder pension schemes.) *Sections 50 to 50B of the Pensions Act 1995*, inserted by the *Pensions Act 2004*, set out requirements which these procedures must meet. Secondary legislation made under *s 50* sets out further detailed provisions.

A remedy of growing importance is a complaint to the Pensions Ombudsman (11 Belgrave Road, London SW1V 1RB, tel: 020 7630 2200; www.pensions-ombudsman.org.uk). The Pensions Ombudsman is a statutory body constituted under *ss 145–151* of the *Pension Schemes Act 1993* (as amended by the *Pensions Act 1995*), and his decisions are enforceable in law, subject to a right of any aggrieved party to appeal on a point of law to the High Court. For an example of a case exploring the extent of the right to appeal, see *Dolland v Trustees of BTG Pension Fund* [2011] All ER (D) 247 (Apr). The Pensions Ombudsman may determine any question of fact or law, or claim of maladministration raised by or on behalf of a scheme member, against either the employer or the scheme trustees, or the managers or administrators of a pension scheme. There are limited exceptions to this jurisdiction in relation to public sector schemes and he cannot normally act where the complainant has instituted court or tribunal proceedings (but the fact that such proceedings could be brought has no bearing on his jurisdiction). The High Court has held that the sanctions available to him include the award of compensation for distress and inconvenience, but the Court of Appeal expressly left this point open: *Westminster City Council v Haywood* [1998] Ch 377. Subsequent cases such as *Maclaine v Prudential Assurance Co Ltd* [2006] EWHC 2037 (Ch) have awarded compensation for this.

There is a time limit of three years for lodging complaints (extendable at his discretion in limited circumstances): *reg 5* of the *Personal and Occupational Pension Schemes (Pensions Ombudsman) Regulations 1996 (SI 1996/2475)*. Complaints should first be referred to the Pensions Advisory Service (TPAS) for possible informal resolution, and this step needs to have been completed, so that the complaint can be lodged before the expiry of the three-year time limit. TPAS can be contacted at 11 Belgrave Road, London SW1V 1RB, tel 0845 601 2923; further information is available on its website (www.opas.org.uk). There is a right of appeal to the High Court against final, but not preliminary, decisions of the Pensions Ombudsman. (However, in cases where there is no right of appeal an application for judicial review may be possible: see on both these points *Legal & General Assurance Society Ltd v Pensions Ombudsman* [2000] 2 All ER 577.) The Pensions Ombudsman is not automatically a party to an appeal, but may apply to appear in the appeal; in that event, if his decision is not upheld, the successful party may obtain an order for the Ombudsman to pay its costs on the appeal (*Moores (Wallisdown) Ltd v Pensions Ombudsman (Costs)* [2002] 1 All ER 737).

The Pensions Ombudsman has issued a number of determinations of far-reaching significance, particularly in relation to the use by employers of surpluses in pension funds; this has been accompanied by an increase in the number of appeals against his determinations, which have highlighted restrictions in the powers conferred on him by the *1993 Act*: see, eg *Westminster City Council v Haywood* (above) and *Edge v Pensions Ombudsman* [2000] Ch 602, [1999] 4 All ER 546, holding that the Pensions Ombudsman cannot entertain complaints which could only be remedied by steps which would adversely affect the interests of third parties not party to the determination. (See also on this point *Marsh & McLennan Companies UK Ltd v Pensions Ombudsman* [2001] IRLR 505.)

The Pensions Regulator is the principal regulatory body controlling the activities of pension funds and trustees. It was established under the *Pensions Act 2004*, replacing the Occupational Pensions Regulatory Authority. Individual complaints continue to be dealt with by the Pensions Advisory Service.

43   Service Lettings

43.1   Some employers provide residential accommodation for their employees. They may do so because the nature of the work is such that the job can be done more efficiently if the employee is close at hand. Another reason may be that the work is in a part of the country in which there is a shortage of accommodation, and the only way in which the employer can attract workers is to provide them with somewhere to live.

The provision of such accommodation poses a dilemma for both employee and employer when the employment relationship comes to an end. The interest of the employee in retaining security of tenure in his home conflicts with the interest of the employer in regaining the accommodation so that he can use it for the employee's replacement. Another question is the extent to which rent controls apply.

It is not possible to give more than a broad outline of this area of law in a book on employment law, and those wishing to find more detailed discussion should consult such works as *Woodfall's Landlord and Tenant* or *Hill and Redman's Law of Landlord and Tenant*. That is particularly true of some of the complex transitional provisions associated with the change from the regime of the *Rent Act 1977* ('*RA 1977*') to that of the *Housing Act 1988* ('*HA 1988*'). Nor have we sought to deal here with matters such as the scope of the landlord's and the tenant's respective repairing obligations. A summary of the law as it affects employees is set out below. It has been assumed that situations such as that of a resident landlord are unlikely to arise in the employment context.

43.2   NATURE OF THE OCCUPANCY

It is of the greatest importance to distinguish between a *service tenancy* and a *service licence*. The grounds on which possession may be recovered from a tenant as opposed to a licensee are limited by statute (see below).

The test for distinguishing between a tenancy and a licence has been re-stated by Lord Templeman, giving the decision of the House of Lords in *Street v Mountford* [1985] AC 809 (see also *Bruton v London and Quadrant Housing Trust* [2000] 1 AC 406, HL). In *Street v Mountford*, Lord Templeman also gave guidance about the position of service occupiers.

> 'To constitute a tenancy the occupier must be granted exclusive possession for a fixed or periodic term certain in consideration of a premium or periodical payments' (p 818E).

> 'A service occupier is a servant who occupies his master's premises in order to perform his duties as a servant. In those circumstances the possession and occupation of the servant is treated as the possession and occupation of the master and the relationship of landlord and tenant is not created; see *Mayhew v Suttle* (1854) 4 E. & B 347. The test is whether the servant requires the premises he occupies in order the better to perform his duties as a servant:

> "Where the occupation is necessary for the performance of services, and the occupier is required to reside in the house in order to perform those services, the occupation being strictly ancillary to the performance of the duties which the occupier has to perform, the occupation is that of a servant";

> per Mellor J in *Smith v Seghill Overseers* (1875) LR 10 QB 422, 428'. (p 818G–H).

A requirement that the employee live in certain accommodation for the better performance of his duties (so that he is a licensee and not a tenant) may be expressed in his contract of employment or may be implied. A chauffeur who is given a flat above the garage, or a housekeeper who is given accommodation in the premises she is charged with looking after, would, save in exceptional circumstances, be considered to be occupying that accommodation for the better performance of his or her duties. (Employers should be aware that certain duties associated with residency, e.g. sleep-in care duties at a residential care home, might attract national minimum wage for sleep-in hours: See e.g. *Shannon v Rampersad* [2015] IRLR 982 and *Royal Mencap Society v Tomlinson-Blake* UKEAT/0143/16/DM, 21 April 2017; (See PAY – I (34)). Employers may consider it wise to state expressly in any contract of employment or letter of offer of employment (where it is the case) that the employee will be required to occupy certain premises for the better performance of his duties and that his occupation is to cease upon the termination of the employment. But such a statement will not avail the employer if it does not accurately reflect the reality of the situation: cf *Aslan v Murphy* [1989] 3 All ER 130. An employee will be a licensee rather than a tenant where he exclusively occupies an employer's residential accommodation in anticipation that, at a reasonable time in the future, the employment will benefit from that occupation; this applies notwithstanding that at the time when the employee entered into occupation, the occupation was irrelevant to his existing duties (*Norris v Checksfield* [1991] 4 All ER 327).

If the employee is not a service licensee in this sense, he may still be a lodger and not a tenant if the employer provides attendance or services which require him or his servants to exercise unrestricted access to, and use of, the premises. Otherwise, however, the agreement to grant exclusive possession for a term at a rent points to the creation of a tenancy. Indeed, in *Ashburn Anstalt v Arnold* [1989] Ch 1, the Court of Appeal held that even a rent was not an essential constituent of a lease (although this case was overruled by the House of Lords in *Prudential Assurance Co Ltd v London Residuary Body* [1992] 2 AC 386; and cf *Bostock v Bryant* (1990) 61 P & CR 23). Two cases illustrate the application of these principles in employment cases.

In *Postcastle Properties Ltd v Perridge* [1985] 2 EGLR 107, the plaintiffs brought a possession action for an estate cottage. The occupant, a man of 80 years, had been employed by the plaintiffs' predecessor in title. He remained in occupation, and continued to work for and to pay £1.50 per week rent to the plaintiffs after they purchased the premises. He was held to have a tenancy. Strong evidence was needed to rebut the presumption of tenancy, which was not forthcoming in that case.

In *Royal Philanthropic Society v County* [1985] 2 EGLR 109, the defendant was employed as a houseparent at the plaintiff's school. Initially he was provided with furnished accommodation in the school building. He was a licensee of the room. On marrying, he was provided with a house some miles from the school. Approximately one year later his employment came to an end, whereupon a notice to quit was served. Possession was successfully claimed in the county court. This was overturned on appeal, the Court of Appeal holding that the defendant was a tenant. Fox LJ said:

> 'The overall effect of *Street v Mountford* as we understand it is that an occupier of residential accommodation at a rent for a term is either a lodger or a tenant . . . ' (p 1071).

> 'The employment, it seems to us, is material only if there is a true service occupancy, ie where the servant requires the premises for the better performance of his duties as a servant . . . ' (p 1072).

Referring to a variety of factors put forward by counsel for the plaintiffs in his attempt to show that no tenancy was created, such as the informality of the paperwork, the relationship of the parties, and the fact that the previous occupancy was that of lodger, Fox LJ said:

> ' . . . it seems to us that they amount really to an attempt to go back to the approach, disapproved by the House of Lords in *Street v Mountford*, of examining the circumstances with a view to ascertaining the intention of the parties. The only

intention that is relevant under the law as it now stands "is the intention demonstrated by the agreement to grant exclusive possession for a term at a rent" (*Street v Mountford* at p 891).' (p 1072)

These decisions serve to demonstrate that, although the employment relationship continues as before, the nature of the employee's occupancy of premises may change.

Somewhat different considerations may apply in cases of joint occupation (see, eg *Mikeover Ltd v Brady* [1989] 3 All ER 618; *Stribling v Wickham* [1989] 2 EGLR 35).

43.3   RECOVERY OF POSSESSION

In order to recover possession from an occupying employee or ex-employee, the employer/landlord will first have to ensure that the employee's *contractual* right to occupy, whether under a licence or a tenancy, is brought to an end. If the employee does not leave voluntarily, it will then be necessary to obtain an order for possession, generally in the county court. In the case of a tenancy, the court's powers to make such an order are restricted by statute.

It is important that the employer does not seek to regain possession, whether by forcible eviction or by harassment without recourse to court proceedings. Such a course of action will contravene the *Protection from Eviction Act 1977* ('*PFEA 1977*').

Where premises are let as a dwelling under a tenancy or licence, even under a tenancy which is not statutorily protected, it is not lawful for the owner to exercise a right of re-entry or forfeiture under the lease, or to enforce his right to recover possession, otherwise than by court proceedings (*PFEA 1977, ss 2, 3(1), (2B)*). 'Let as a dwelling' means 'let wholly or partly as a dwelling', so *PFEA 1977, s 2* applies to premises which were let for mixed residential and business purposes (*Patel v Pirabakaran* [2006] EWCA Civ 685, [2006] 4 All ER 506). However, premises let for such mixed purposes are not 'let as a separate dwelling' within *Rent Act 1977, s 1* (*Tan v Sitkowski* [2007] EWCA Civ 30, [2007] All ER (D) 16 (Feb)). It has been held that *article 6* of the *European Convention on Human Rights* (ie. the right to a fair hearing before an independent and impartial tribunal for the determination of civil rights) was satisfied where *PFEA 1977, s 3* was invoked by a local authority (*Coombes v Waltham Forest London Borough Council* [2010] 2 All ER 940).

There is a deemed tenancy for these purposes whenever a person has exclusive possession of any premises under the terms of his employment (*PFEA 1977, s 8(2)*).

It is a criminal offence unlawfully to deprive the employee of his occupation (*PFEA 1977, s 1(2)*). It is also an offence if a person, with the intention of causing the residential occupier to give up occupation or to refrain from exercising any rights or pursuing any remedy open to him, does acts which are likely to interfere with the peace and comfort of the occupier, or his family, or persistently withdraws or withholds services normally required for the occupation of the premises as a residence (*PFEA 1977, s 1(3)*, as amended by *HA 1988, s 29*). Where that intent cannot be shown, an offence is nonetheless committed if the employer or his agent, without reasonable grounds, does acts likely to interfere with the peace or comfort of the residential occupier or members of his household or persistently withdraws or withholds services reasonably required for the occupation of the premises as a residence, knowing or having reasonable cause to believe that that conduct is likely to cause the occupier to give up occupation or to refrain from exercising a right or remedy (*PFEA 1977, s 1(3A),(3B)*, as inserted by *HA 1988, s 29*). The offence of harassment under *PFEA 1977, s 1(3)* may be committed even if the actions complained of do not otherwise amount to a civil wrong (*R v Burke* [1991] 1 AC 135). As to whether occupiers are 'residential occupiers' for the purposes of *PFEA 1977, s 1(3A)*, see *Prosecution Appeal (No 28 of 2007); R v Harris* [2008] All ER (D) 190 (Feb).

43.3 Service Lettings

Further, a right to damages for unlawful eviction (in addition to any existing rights to claim in tort or for breach of contract) is created by *HA 1988, s 27* (see *Tagro v Cafane* [1991] 2 All ER 235, *Sampson v Wilson* [1996] Ch 39, *Osei-Bonsu v Wandsworth London Borough Council* [1999] 1 All ER 265 and *Lambeth London Borough Council v Loveridge* [2014] 1 WLR 4516). Where a landlord obtained an order for possession from the court and applied for a warrant for possession against a tenant, the tenant remained protected under *PFEA 1977, s 3(1)* (see above) until the warrant had been executed and was therefore entitled to damages for unlawful eviction under *HA 1988, s 27* when the landlord forcibly evicted the tenant before such execution (*Haniff v Robinson* [1993] QB 419, [1993] 1 All ER 185).

Once the licence or tenancy has been brought to an end and the employer is seeking to recover possession, the employer ought not to accept further payments of rent (at least without making clear in writing the basis on which he does so), because the acceptance of such payments may lead to the creation of a fresh tenancy. If the employee continues to occupy the premises after he should have left, compensation will eventually be recoverable by order of the court (called 'mesne profits'). As to the liability of a former secure tenant (who had become a 'tolerated trespasser') for mesne profits, see *Jones v Merton London Borough Council* [2008] EWCA Civ 660, [2008] 4 All ER 287. (However, note that provisions in *Schedule 11* to the *Housing and Regeneration Act 2008* (which, with some exceptions, came into force on 20 May 2009) will in effect prevent the creation of 'tolerated trespassers' in future, by amending the *Housing Acts 1985, 1988* and *1996* so as to provide that a possession order made against (inter alia) a secure or assured tenant will not end the tenancy until the tenant is evicted.)

43.4 Service licence

A true *service licence* can be determined on termination of the relevant employment contract, with the notice period provided for in the contract. If the contract is silent on this point, then reasonable notice should be given. It is unlikely that a period of less than four weeks would be reasonable. If the licence is a *periodic licence* (ie one which continues from week to week or month to month, rather than for a fixed term), a minimum of four weeks' notice to terminate it must be given in the prescribed form (*PFEA 1977, s 5(1A)* as inserted by *HA 1988, s 32*; *Notices to Quit, etc (Prescribed Information) Regulations 1988 (SI 1988/2201)*). The termination of a licence which is expressed to come to an end with the termination of the employee's employment need not comply with the requirements of *PFEA 1977, s 5(1A)* as to notice, because such a licence is not a 'periodic licence' for the purposes of that provision (*Norris v Checksfield* [1991] 4 All ER 327).

On the termination of a *service licence* the employer can take proceedings for possession. He will have to show:

(a)   that the premises were occupied by the employee for the duration of his employment (or for some agreed lesser period), and for the better performance of his duties;

(b)   that the employment (or the lesser period) has ended, or that proper notice to determine the licence has been given;

(c)   that either the agreed notice has been given or the former employee has been given an adequate period in which to vacate the premises;

(d)   that no new arrangement has been created since the contract ended (therefore it is unwise to accept further payments of rent without specifying the basis on which this is done).

In *Whitbread West Pennines Ltd v Reedy* [1988] ICR 807, the former employee sought to argue that possession should not be ordered against him because there was pending an unfair dismissal claim in which he sought reinstatement (see **55.2 UNFAIR DISMISSAL – III**).

The argument failed. The Court of Appeal held that for the replacement employee to move into the accommodation would not make reinstatement any less practicable, and that in any event the employer could elect not to reinstate but to pay enhanced compensation instead. In a case where the licence to occupy terminates along with the employment, it does so notwithstanding that the dismissal is wrongful (*Ivory v Palmer* [1975] ICR 340) or contractually lawful but statutorily unfair (*Carroll v Manek*, (1999) 79 P & CR 173).

43.5   Service tenancy

Tenancies in existence prior to 15 January 1989 continue to be governed by *RA 1977* or *Housing Act 1980* ('*HA 1980*'). Tenancies entered into on or after that date, however, are governed by *HA 1988*. Tenancies entered into on or after 28 February 1997 are affected by amendments made to *HA 1988* by the *Housing Act 1996* ('*HA 1996*'). Various kinds of tenancy therefore fall to be considered.

(i)   *Protected tenancies under RA 1977.* These are automatically converted into *statutory tenancies* when the original, contractual tenancy expires through effluxion of time or a notice to quit is served.

(ii)   *Protected shorthold tenancies under HA 1980.* These arose where, before the grant of the tenancy, the landlord served a prescribed notice indicating that this was the nature of the tenancy. The term must have been between one and five years, with the landlord having no right to end it sooner whilst the tenant complied with his obligations (*HA 1980, s 52*).

(iii)   *Assured tenancies under HA 1988.* This will now be the normal basic type of tenancy (but see (v) below). The tenant must be an individual who occupies the dwelling as his only or principal home, and the letting must not be one which is specifically excluded from protection (*HA 1988, s 1*). As to the meaning of 'dwelling' in *HA 1988, s 1*, see *Uratemp Ventures Ltd v Collins* [2001] UKHL 43, [2002] 1 AC 301.

(iv)   *Assured shorthold tenancies under HA 1988 (pre-HA 1996 tenancies).* These are similar in concept to the old protected shorthold tenancies, but their scope is less restricted. They must be for a fixed term of not less than six months, contain no landlord's right to terminate during the first six months if the tenant complies with his obligations, and the grant must be preceded by service of a notice in the prescribed form (*HA 1988, s 20*). The notice may be served on the tenant's authorised agent (*Yenula Properties Ltd v Naidu* [2002] EWCA Civ 719, [2003] HLR 229). A notice not in the prescribed form nor 'substantially to the same effect' is invalid (*Manel v Memon* (2000) 33 HLR 235 — applied in *Kahlon v Isherwood* [2011] EWCA Civ 602, [2011] All ER (D) 205 (May), a case on *HA 1988, s 19A* and *Sch 2A* (see (v) below)). Also invalid is a notice which fails to state correctly the landlord's name (*Gill v Cremadez* [2000] CLY 3876); see also *Ravenseft Properties v Hall* [2001] EWCA Civ 2034, [2002] HLR 624 and *Osborn & Co Ltd v Dior* [2003] EWCA Civ 281, [2003] HLR 649.

(v)   *Assured shorthold tenancies under HA 1988 (post-HA 1996 tenancies).* Any assured tenancy which is entered into on or after 28 February 1997 (otherwise than pursuant to a contract entered into before that date) will be an assured shorthold tenancy, unless it falls within one of the exceptions set out in *HA 1988, Sch 2A* (as to which, see *Andrews v Cunningham* [2007] All ER (D) 343 (Jul)) (*HA 1988, s 19A*, inserted by *HA 1996, s 96*). Unlike pre-*HA 1996* assured shorthold tenancies, no notice need be served by the landlord on the tenant prior to the grant, and the tenancy need not be for a fixed term. However, if requested to do so in writing, a landlord under a post-*HA 1996* assured shorthold tenancy has a duty to provide a tenant with a written statement of the principal terms of the tenancy where these are not evidenced in writing (*HA 1988, s 20A*, inserted by *HA 1996, s 97*).

43.5 Service Lettings

In order to recover possession from a service tenant, the contractual tenancy must be terminated. This will occur if (in the case of a fixed-term tenancy) the term of the tenancy expires without being renewed, if the landlord claims to forfeit the lease where the lease makes provision for forfeiture for breach of certain terms in it, or (in the case of a periodic tenancy) if the landlord serves a notice to quit.

Expiry of term. If the tenancy is for a fixed term of, for example, two years, the contractual tenancy will automatically terminate on the expiry of the two-year period and it is not necessary for a notice to quit to be served.

Forfeiture for breach of a term of the lease. Except in the case of forfeiture for the non-payment of rent, the landlord must serve a notice under the *Law of Property Act 1925, s 146* on the tenant, specifying the breaches complained of and requesting him to remedy the same within a reasonable period of time and to pay reasonable compensation.

Notice to quit. A notice to quit should be in writing and some acknowledgement of receipt should be asked for. If sent by post, it should be sent by recorded delivery. To be valid the notice to quit must expire on the proper day. The notice to quit must expire at the end of the period of the tenancy. Because specifying a wrong date is fatal to a notice to quit, landlords should add the following saving clause in the notice to quit after the specified date: 'or at the expiration of the (week/month) of your tenancy which shall expire next after the expiration of four weeks from the service upon you of this notice'. The notice to quit must be served not less than four weeks before the date on which it is to take effect (*Protection from Eviction Act 1977, s 5*). Information prescribed by the *Notices to Quit, etc (Prescribed Information) Regulations 1988 (SI 1988/2201)* must be included in the notice to quit; otherwise it will be invalid.

No rent must be accepted after discovery of a breach of a term in the lease which gives the landlord the right to forfeit, such as unlawful sub-letting. Accepting rent may be construed as waiving the breaches complained of or creating a new tenancy.

43.6 Situations in which possession may be claimed from tenant

Where a *protected shorthold tenancy* or an *assured shorthold tenancy* comes to an end, the court *must* grant the landlord possession if the proper procedure is followed. In the case of an assured shorthold tenancy, this involves giving the tenant not less than two months' notice in writing that possession is required. The notice must specify a date that is the last date of a period of the tenancy (*Fernandez v McDonald* [2003] EWCA Civ 1219, [2003] 4 All ER 1033; see also *Notting Hill Housing Trust v Roomus* [2006] EWCA Civ 407, [2006] 1 WLR 1375). In the case of a post-*HA 1996* assured shorthold tenancy (see category (v) in **43.5** above), a possession order may not be made so as to take effect earlier than six months after the beginning of the tenancy (where the tenancy is a replacement tenancy, the six-month period runs from the beginning of the *original* tenancy) (*HA 1988, s 21*, as amended by *HA 1996, ss 98, 99*). The procedural requirements in relation to the old protected shorthold tenancy were somewhat more complex: see *HA 1980, s 55; RA 1977, s 98(2), Sch 15 Case 19*. Possession of properties let on shorthold tenancies can also be recovered on the same grounds as are available in the case of ordinary tenancies.

In the case of a *protected tenancy* under *RA 1977*, the landlord must bring himself within one of a number of specified 'Cases' set out in *Sch 15*. Those Cases in *Sch 15 Part I* are 'discretionary' grounds, in that they require the court to be satisfied also that it is reasonable to grant possession; they include grounds such as arrears of rent or the causing of a nuisance. Those Cases in *Sch 15 Part II* constitute mandatory grounds for possession. In addition, the court may make an order, if it is reasonable to do so, where suitable alternative accommodation is or will be available for the tenant. See generally *RA 1977, s 98*.

The ground particularly relevant to pre-1989 service lettings is *Case 8* (a discretionary ground): this arises if the landlord requires the premises for a whole-time employee, the existing tenant was granted a tenancy in consequence of his employment, and he has ceased to be in that employment.

A similar approach governs recovery of possession under *assured tenancies* under *HA 1988*. Again, there are both mandatory and discretionary grounds, and where one of the latter is established the court will have to be persuaded that it is reasonable to order possession (*HA 1988, s 7, Sch 2*). *Ground 16* is a discretionary ground which applies where the dwelling-house was let to the tenant in consequence of his employment by the landlord or a previous landlord, and the tenant has ceased to be in that employment. It will be seen that this is less stringent, from the landlord's point of view, than *Case 8* under *RA 1977* (see above), because it is not necessary to show that the accommodation is required for another employee. However, to do so would obviously assist the argument that it was reasonable to order possession. The availability of suitable alternative accommodation is another discretionary ground (*Ground 9*).

As in the case of RA 1977 (see s 100), the court has a wide discretion under HA 1988, s 9 to adjourn possession proceedings and to suspend the execution of orders; see generally *White v Knowsley Housing Trust* [2008] UKHL 70, [2008] All ER (D) 115 (Dec).

43.7   Tenants of public authorities

Under *HA 1985*, security of tenure was conferred upon tenants of local authorities and of certain other public bodies. However, various categories are excluded from security of tenure. Those which are pertinent to employment include:

(a)   Cases where the tenant is an employee of the landlord; or of:

    (i)   a local authority;

    (ii)   a development corporation;

    (iii)   the governors of an aided school;

    (iv)   an urban development corporation;

    (v)   a housing action trust;

    (vi)   a Mayoral Development Corporation;

and his contract of employment requires him to reside in the dwelling for the better performance of his duties.

In *Surrey County Council v Lamond* [1999] 1 EGLR 32 (see also [1999] 2 CLY 3736), the Court of Appeal held that in deciding whether for this reason a tenancy was not a secure tenancy, the court needed to ascertain what duties the employee was to perform and then determine whether it was genuinely practicable for the employee to perform them if he did not occupy the dwelling concerned; see also *Hughes v Greenwich London Borough Council* [1994] 1 AC 170, HL, *Elvidge v Coventry City Council* [1994] QB 241, [1993] 4 All ER 903 and *Brent London Borough Council v Charles* (1997) 29 HLR 876, CA. In *Wragg v Surrey County Council* [2008] EWCA Civ 19, [2008] All ER (D) 09 (Feb), the Court of Appeal construed this provision as laying down two distinct conditions: (i) that 'his contract of employment requires him to occupy the dwelling-house'; (ii) that the requirement was 'for the better performance of his duties'. Condition (i) looked only to the terms of the contract: did the contract contain such a requirement or not? However, condition (ii) raised an issue of fact outside the contract: 'the question was not whether the contract stated that the requirement was for the better performance of his duties, but whether the requirement was in fact for the better performance of his duties'.

(b)   Where the tenant is a member of the police force, and the dwelling is provided rent-free by regulations made under the *Police Act 1996*. (See *Holmes v South Yorkshire Police Authority* [2008] EWCA Civ 51, [2008] HLR 532.)

(c)   Where the tenant is employed by a fire and rescue authority; and

   (i)   he is contractually bound to live close to a particular fire station; and

   (ii)   the dwelling-house was let to him by the authority so that he could comply with the condition.

(d)   Cases where temporary accommodation is granted in order to assist employees who are new to an area to find permanent accommodation there, provided that it is linked to an offer of employment to a person who was not resident in the district immediately before the grant, that it does not exceed one year and that the tenant is informed, in writing, of the circumstances in which the exception applies and that the landlord is of the opinion that it falls within that exception.

(*Housing Act 1985, Sch 1 paras 2(1), (2), (3), 5(1)*, as amended.) (See also *Nicholas v Secretary of State for Defence* [2015] EWCA Civ 53, [2015] 1 WLR 2116 where it was held that there was no violation of *Art 8, ECHR* rights in seeking possession of Crown property from the former spouse of a member of the RAF who had a license to occupy the property for the better performance of his duties.)

43.8   RENT CONTROL

Occupation under a *licence* is not subject to rent control.

Where the employee went into occupation under a *RA 1977 protected tenancy* or a *protected shorthold tenancy*, he could apply under *Part IV* of that *Act* for a fair rent to be registered, and the landlord was not then entitled to charge a greater rent (*RA 1977, s 44*). Now that new protected tenancies cannot be created, that provision will be of diminishing importance, although the possibility of such an application remains.

A tenant under an *assured tenancy* under *HA 1988* has no right to challenge the contractual rent which he has agreed to pay, whether the rent demanded of him is that originally agreed upon, or has subsequently been varied pursuant to a rent review clause. However, if the contractual tenancy comes to an end and the landlord wishes to increase the rent, he must serve notice of the proposed increase upon the tenant in a prescribed form (*HA 1988, s 13*). The tenant may then go before a Rent Assessment Committee and seek a determination that the proposed new rent exceeds that which might reasonably be expected to be obtained in the open market, by a willing landlord, on the same terms of letting (*HA 1988, s 14*). There are strict time limits within which any reference by the tenant to the Rent Assessment Committee must be made.

A tenant under an *assured shorthold tenancy* may refer the rent charged to the Rent Assessment Committee, during the initial fixed term of the tenancy (in the case of a pre-*HA 1996* assured shorthold tenancy) or during the first six months of the tenancy (in the case of a post-*HA 1996* assured shorthold tenancy). However, the Committee may reduce the rent only if:

(i)   there is a sufficient number of similar dwelling-houses in the locality let on assured tenancies (whether shorthold or not) for a proper determination to be possible; and

(ii)   the rent charged is *significantly* higher than the rent which the landlord might reasonably be expected to obtain having regard to the rents payable under other assured tenancies in the locality.

(*HA 1988, s 22*, as amended by *HA 1996, s 100*.)

43.9   AGRICULTURAL TIED HOUSES

Where the employee is or was engaged in agriculture or forestry, special rules may apply. A discussion of these rules is beyond the scope of this book. They are to be found in the *Rent (Agriculture) Act 1976* as amended by *HA 1988*, and in *HA 1988, ss 24, 25* (as amended by *HA 1996, s 103*).

44   Sickness and Sick Pay

Cross-references. See Termination of Employment (48) for sickness and frustration of contract of employment; for sickness and unfair dismissal, see **54.8** Unfair Dismissal – II.

44.1   In relation to pay for periods of sickness, the following may apply:

(a)   contractual provisions for sick pay (see **44.2** below);

(b)   the statutory right to a specified level of sick pay ('statutory sick pay', see **44.3** –**44.8** below).

As in many areas of employment law, statutory payments are offset against contractual payments and vice versa. This 'offsetting' of payments during sickness is considered in **44.9** –**44.11** below.

Employers may now opt out of the statutory sick pay scheme, so long as they provide the same minimum level of remuneration as an employee would be entitled to as a matter of statute. (See **44.3** below.)

Persistent illness may constitute such incapacity for work as to warrant dismissal (see **54.8** Unfair Dismissal – II).

In rare circumstances, sickness may render performance of the contract so radically different from that contemplated by the parties as to amount to a frustration of the contract (see **48.3** Termination of Employment).

44.2   CONTRACTUAL PROVISIONS FOR SICK PAY

An employer may agree to pay his employees while they are absent due to ill-health. Such payments commonly run for a specified period of time and are subject to conditions.

The written particulars given to an employee setting out the terms and conditions of his employment must state whether or not the employer makes payments for periods of absence due to sickness and, if so, upon what terms (see **8.4** Contract of Employment). In *Mears v Safecar Security Ltd* [1983] QB 54, [1982] 2 All ER 865, [1982] 3 WLR 366, [1982] ICR 626, the Court of Appeal held that where such a term is not specified or agreed, the tribunal must consider all the facts and circumstances to ascertain the term to be implied. There is no presumption of a contractual right to sick pay. An employment tribunal must look to all the facts and circumstances, and to the conduct of the parties since the contract began.

Where there is a contractual right to sick pay, but no provision as to its duration, the court will imply a reasonable term (*Howman & Son v Blyth* [1983] ICR 416).

For the failure to comply with the statutory duty to specify in the written particulars of terms of employment what provisions for sick pay apply, see **8.7** Contract of Employment.

44.3   STATUTORY SICK PAY

(For further details see HMRC's booklet 'Employer Handbook for Statutory Sick Pay' (28th March 2014).

Since 1983, all employees, subject to certain specified exceptions (see **44.4** below), have been entitled to receive statutory sick pay ('SSP') from their employers. The entitlement limit is, generally, 28 weeks in a three-year period. The basic provisions are now consolidated into the *Social Security Contributions and Benefits Act 1992* ('*SSCBA 1992*'). The main set of regulations is the *Statutory Sick Pay (General) Regulations 1982 (SI 1982/894)* as amended, principally by the *Statutory Sick Pay (General) Amendment Regulations 1986 (SI 1986/477)*, the *Statutory Sick Pay (General) Amendment (No 2) Regulations 1987 (SI 1987/868)* and the *Social Security Contributions, Statutory Maternity Pay and Statutory Sick Pay (Miscellaneous Amendments) Regulations 1996 (SI 1996/777)*.

The essential requirements for qualification are that an employee must:

(a)   have four or more consecutive days of sickness (including Sundays and holidays) during which he is too ill to be capable of doing his work (see further **44.5** below); and

(b)   notify his absence to his employer, subject to certain statutory requirements and any agreement between them; and

(c)   supply evidence of incapacity – this is also a matter for the employer: a common example of an employer's requirement would be:

(i)   a 'self-certificate' for periods of four to seven days;

(ii)   a doctor's certificate or other evidence of sickness for periods after the first seven days.

(*SSCBA 1992, ss 151, 152, 156; Statutory Sick Pay (General) Regulations 1982, reg 7.*) The medical evidence that can be required of an employee is prescribed by the *Statutory Sick Pay (Medical Evidence) Regulations 1985*, as amended in 2010 (*SI 2010/137*).

Employers cannot require employees to contribute towards payments (*SSCBA 1992, s 151(2)*).

Employees may still be entitled to SSP even if they are absent from Great Britain on holiday or for business purposes at any time during the incapacity (*SI 1996/777, reg 3*).

An employer may choose to opt out of the statutory sick pay scheme, provided that he continues to pay contractual remuneration to his employees at or above the SSP rate and does not make his employees contribute to the cost of their sick pay up to that rate. Such employers still have to comply with certain documentary and record keeping requirements (see **44.7** below).

44.4 Excluded employees

The following categories of employee are not entitled to receive SSP. These are an employee:

(a)   having average weekly earnings less than the weekly lower earnings limit for National Insurance ('NI') contribution liability (currently £113 per week);

(b)   going sick within 57 days of having previously been entitled to incapacity benefit;

(c)   going sick within 85 days of having previously been entitled to an employment and support allowance;

(d)   who has done no work for his employer under the contract of service;

(e)   going sick during a stoppage of work at his place of employment due to a trade dispute, unless he proves that at no time has he had a direct interest in that dispute;

(f)   who is pregnant and goes off sick during the maternity pay period (see **32.26** MATERNITY AND PARENTAL RIGHTS);

(g)   who has already been due 28 weeks' SSP from his employer in any one 'period of incapacity for work' (or any two or more 'linked' periods) (see **44.5** below);

(h)   who, subject to certain provisions, has already been due 28 weeks' SSP from his former employer, and the gap between the first day of incapacity with the new employer and the last day on which SSP was paid by the former employer is eight weeks or less;

(i)   who is in legal custody at any time on the first day of incapacity.

(*SSCBA 1992, Sch 11*, as amended by the *Statutory Sick Pay Act 1994, s 1*; *Social Security Act 1985, s 18(2)(d)*; *Statutory Sick Pay (General) Regulations 1982 (SI 1982/894)*; *Statutory Sick Pay (General) Amendment Regulations 1986 (SI 1986/477)*.)

Where the employer is notified that an excluded employee has been absent for four consecutive days or more, he is legally bound to send a form to the employee not later than seven days after being so notified (or, where this is impracticable, not later than the first pay day in the following tax month). This form provides the explanation to the employee and the DWP of why SSP is not being paid, and allows the employee to claim state sickness benefit instead (*Statutory Sick Pay (General) Regulations 1982 (SI 1982/894), reg 15*, as amended).

It should also be noted that agency workers on assignments of less than three months are not entitled to SSP. The repeal of the previous exclusion from SSP for those whose 'contract of service was entered into for a specified period of not more than three months' did not apply to agency workers: see *Revenue and Customs Comrs v Thorn Baker Ltd* [2007] EWCA Civ 626, [2008] ICR 46.

44.5   The payment period

The period of four or more days of sickness (see **44.3** above) is called a 'period of incapacity for work' ('PIW'). Two or more PIWs which are separated by eight weeks or less are said to be 'linked' and are counted as one PIW (*SSCBA, s 152; Statutory Sick Pay (General) Amendment Regulations 1986 (SI 1986/477)*).

During a PIW, SSP is payable *only*:

(a)   while there is a 'period of entitlement', as defined (eg payment will cease, in the normal case, if the employment ends); *and*

(b)   for days within the PIW which are 'qualifying days'.

The intention behind the idea of 'qualifying days' was that they would be the days on which the employee would normally be required to work, but it is open to employers in all cases to specify the pattern of qualifying days by agreement with the employees concerned. Each week must have at least one qualifying day, and qualifying days must not be defined by reference to the days of sickness (*Statutory Sick Pay (General) Regulations 1982 (SI 1982/894); Statutory Sick Pay (General) Amendment Regulations 1985 (SI 1985/126)*).

SSP is not payable for the first three qualifying days in a PIW (*SSCBA 1992, s 155(1)*). It is paid for the fourth qualifying day onwards until either the employee becomes well again or the maximum payment period is reached (*SSCBA 1992, s 155(2)*).

The maximum entitlement to SSP is now 28 weeks in any period of entitlement. A period of entitlement, as between an employee and his employer, is a period beginning with the commencement of a period of incapacity for work and ending with the earliest of:

(i)   the termination of that period of incapacity for work;

(ii)   the day on which the employee reaches, as against the employer concerned, his maximum entitlement to statutory sick pay;

(iii)   the day on which the employee's contract of service with the employer concerned expires or is brought to an end;

(iv)   in the case of an employee who is, or has been, pregnant, the day immediately preceding the beginning of the disqualifying period (as defined by *SSCBA 1992, s 153(12)*) (*SSCBA 1992, s 153(2)*).

A period of entitlement ends after three years if it has not otherwise ended (*Statutory Sick Pay (General) Regulations 1982 (SI 1982/894), reg 3(3)*, inserted by *SI 1986/477*).

Employees who are still sick when their entitlement to SSP terminates may be entitled to state benefits. Employers of such employees must inform them in a prescribed form of the reason for the termination of SSP (*Social Security Administration Act 1992, s 130; Statutory Sick Pay (General) Regulations 1982 (SI 1982/894), reg 15*, as amended by *Statutory Sick Pay (General) Amendment Regulations 1986 (SI 1986/477)*, and by *Statutory Sick Pay (General)(Amendment) Regulations 2008 (SI 2008/1735)*). *SSCBA 1992, Sch 12* deals with the relationship between statutory sick pay and other benefits and payments.

44.6   The amounts payable and recoverable

Employees who earn less than the lower weekly earnings limit for NI liability (£112) are excluded from SSP (*SSCBA 1992, Sch 11 para 2(c)*). In all other cases, the amount of SSP payable is £89.35. Thus, the maximum amount payable over 28 weeks is £2,501.80 (*SSCBA 1992, s 157(1)*, as amended by the *Social Security (Incapacity for Work) Act 1994, s 8(1)*).

SSP is considered as earnings for PAYE, income tax and NI contribution purposes (*SSCBA 1992, s 4(1); Income and Corporation Taxes Act 1988, s 150*).

Right of recovery. The right of employers to recover from their NI contributions amounts paid by way of SSP was abolished by the *Statutory Sick Pay Act 1994*. The right of employers to recover SSP paid above a certain threshold has also been abolished.

44.7   Records

Until recently, employers were statutorily obliged to keep records for SSP purposes, and to retain certain information for at least three years, stored in such a way that inspectors could have access to them. This requirement has now been abolished by the *Statutory Sick Pay (Maintenance of Records) Revocation Regulations 2014 (SI 2014/55)*.

It is still necessary, however, to keep accounting records, *inter alia*, details of all SSP payments made, along with those of pay, NIC and PAYE income tax. Revenue records must be retained for seven years.

Employers may also find it useful to keep fuller records, eg self-certification forms, medical certificates, dates of all absences and the reasons for them. Such records can be used for the purposes of audit, and may also help to identify personnel problems.

44.8   Disputes

If an employer does not pay an employee SSP, the employee may ask him to give written reasons for the decision, and the employer must comply within a reasonable time (*Social Security Administration Act 1992, s 14(3)*).

If the employee wishes to challenge the employer's decision as to whether he is entitled to sick pay, he may ask for a determination of the issue by Her Majesty's Revenue and Customs (*Statutory Sick Pay and Statutory Maternity Pay (Decisions) Regulations 1999 (SI 1999/776)*). A challenge to HMRC's decision can be made to the First-Tier Tax Tribunal (Tax). For a recent example of a dispute as to whether an employee was entitled to sick pay, see *Mitre Plastics v Revenue and Customs Comrs* (TC00720) [2010] UKFTT 455 (TC). An employment tribunal does not have jurisdiction to determine whether an employee is entitled to statutory sick pay, although it would have jurisdiction to determine a claim of unlawful deduction from wages if the employer admitted entitlement but withheld payment of SSP: *Taylor Gordon & Co Ltd (t/a Plan Personnel) v Timmons* [2004] IRLR 180, EAT; *Sarti (Sauchiehall St) Ltd v Polito* [2008] ICR 1279.

The First-Tier Tax Tribunal does not have power to order payment of any sick pay to which an employee is entitled. Payment must be enforced through the Courts: see *Cleaver (t/a B.R.E. Cleaver Fruit & Veg Wholesaler) v R&C Commrs* [2014] UKFTT 1075 (TC).

As far as evidence of incapacity is concerned, the employer cannot require the employee to produce a medical certificate from a doctor for the first seven days of sickness. With that qualification, he can request the employee to provide reasonable evidence of incapacity, such as a self-certificate for absences of up to seven days (*Social Security Administration Act 1992, s 14; Statutory Sick Pay (Medical Evidence) Regulations 1985 (SI 1985/1604)*).

44.9   OFFSETTING PAYMENTS MADE DURING SICKNESS AGAINST SSP

Any contractual remuneration paid to an employee for a day of sickness is to be offset against the SSP due for the *same day* (*SSCBA 1992, Sch 12 para 2*). An employer can never pay the employee an amount in total which is *less* than the SSP due.

In personal injury actions, any special damages claimed will be subject to a deduction for SSP paid (*Palfrey v Greater London Council* [1985] ICR 437). The same principle was applied to payments under a non-contributory permanent health insurance scheme in *Hussain v New Taplow Paper Mills Ltd* [1987] 1 All ER 417, [1987] 1 WLR 336, [1987] ICR 28.

44.10   Contributory sickness schemes

An employee must not contribute to his own SSP. Thus, in the case of a jointly funded, ie 'contributory', sickness scheme, the amount of sick pay which will be offset against SSP must be in the proportion that the employer's contribution bears to the joint contributions to the scheme.

44.11   Contributory pension schemes

In the case of contributory pension schemes, offsetting will depend on how the pension scheme defines salary for calculation purposes: if salary is defined as 'earnings subject to PAYE income tax', then any SSP paid should be included in earnings for pension purposes. In that case the employee's pension contribution would be deducted from his full gross sick pay, ie including the SSP element. (See, in particular, the *Occupational Pensions Board Announcement No 2 (March 1983)*.)

44.12   PERMANENT HEALTH AND SALARY CONTINUANCE BENEFITS

It is increasingly common for employers to provide their employees with permanent health or salary continuance benefits during periods of long-term sickness or incapacity, lasting usually more than six or twelve months. Employers will normally provide these benefits by taking out insurance coverage for the benefit of their employees.

The right of an employee to receive permanent health or salary continuance benefits will usually depend on the terms of the insurance policy entered into by the employer, as the contract of employment will probably state that the benefits payable to the employee in the event of long-term incapacity are 'subject to' or 'governed by' the rules of the insurance policy. However, where the employer makes no reference to its insurance policy in documents provided to an employee, then the employer cannot rely upon the terms of the policy as against the employee. The employer will be bound by the words of its own contractual documentation with the employee: see *Jowitt v Pioneer Technology (UK) Ltd* [2003] EWCA Civ 411, [2003] ICR 1120. Also, where the insurance policy provides for significant exemptions to the payment of benefits (eg disentitling employees to benefits on leaving service), the employer will not be able to rely on these exemptions as against the employee if the employee was not shown the policy itself or was not told that he should read it (*Villella v MFI Furniture Centres Ltd* [1999] IRLR 468).

In *Briscoe v Lubrizol Ltd* [2002] EWCA Civ 508, [2002] IRLR 607, the Court of Appeal held that the claimant's entitlement to disability benefit depended upon his satisfying the definition of 'disablement' contained in the employer's insurance policy ('totally unable . . . to perform his normal occupation'), rather than the definition set out in the company information handbook ('unable to follow any occupation'). The court referred to the decision in *Villella*, and held that 'the court looks unfavourably upon an employer who seeks to restrict his contractual obligation as described in a handbook in reliance upon a policy which he has not brought to the attention of his employee; but that does not mean, by way of corollary, that where the handbook expressly or by implication refers to such a policy and purports to summarise its effect upon the employee's rights in a manner which is disadvantageous to the employee, the court will similarly regard the handbook as definitive of those rights'. The court looked at all the facts and determined that it was the clear contractual intention of the parties to bestow upon the employee the benefits provided for in the insurance policy, rather than the handbook.

As the employee will not be a party to the insurance policy, he will ordinarily not be entitled to enforce his rights to receive these benefits directly against the insurer. Rather, he will have to enforce those rights against the employer, who in turn will probably seek to join the insurer as a third party (*Rutherford v Radio Rentals Ltd* 1993 SLT 221). Where, under the contract of employment, the employer is obliged to pay over to the employee such sums as it receives from the insurer, then the employer will be under a duty to take all reasonable steps to secure that the insurance benefits are paid. This may include the pursuit of litigation against the insurer if necessary (*Marlow v East Thames Housing Group Ltd* [2002] IRLR 798).

An employee is not automatically deprived of his entitlement to receive salary continuance benefits from his employer merely because the employer ceases to pay his insurance premiums or terminates the policy (*Bainbridge v Circuit Foil UK Ltd* [1997] IRLR 305).

44.13   Effect on the right to terminate the contract of employment

The existence of these benefits may restrict the employer's ability to terminate the contract of employment. In circumstances where the insurance policy provides that benefits will only be paid in respect of employees who continue to be employed by the policy-holder (ie the employer), the courts may imply a term into the contract of employment to the effect that the employer cannot bring the contract to an end solely with a view to terminate those benefits, or for a specious or arbitrary reason or for no reason at all, while the employee was incapacitated for work (see *Hill v General Accident Fire and Life Assurance Corpn plc* [1998] IRLR 641; compare *Aspden v Webbs Poultry and Meat Group (Holdings) Ltd* [1996] IRLR 521 and see *Lloyd v BCQ Ltd* [2013] 1 CMLR 1166) (see **8.22B** CONTRACT OF EMPLOYMENT). In *Lloyd*, the EAT held that such a term would not be implied where the contract of employment made no reference to permanent health insurance benefits, and the contract expressly permitted termination for long-term absence. Relying on *Reda v Flag Ltd* [2002] UKPC 38, the EAT held that an *Aspden*-type term could not be implied.

In *Briscoe v Lubrizol Ltd* [2002] EWCA Civ 508, [2002] IRLR 607, the Court of Appeal had to determine whether the employer was justified in terminating a contract of employment, the effect of which would be to deprive the employee of his entitlement to disability benefit.

The Court of Appeal reviewed the case law and held that 'the employer ought not to terminate the employment as a means to remove the employee's entitlement to benefit but the employer can dismiss for good cause whether that be on the ground of gross misconduct or, more generally, for some repudiatory breach by the employee'. On the facts, the Court of Appeal held that the employer was entitled to treat the contract as having come to an end: the employee, who had been off work for a prolonged period of time, had disobeyed the employer's lawful instruction to attend so as to discuss his long-term absence; he was in breach of an instruction to return the employer's calls to re-arrange that appointment; and his continued absence from work was unexplained by any current medical report. In the circumstances, he was held to have been in breach of the duty of trust and confidence, which justified the employer in treating the contract of employment as having been terminated.

44.14 Effect of permanent health benefits on the calculation of damages

Payments made by an employer under a permanent health insurance plan are not treated as remuneration or earnings from employment within the meaning of the *Administration of Justice Act 1982, s 10(i)*. Rather, they are to be regarded as a 'contractual' pension or benefit and are therefore not taken into account so as to reduce damages to an employee suing in respect of injuries sustained as a result of an accident at work (*Lewicki v Brown and Root Wimpey Highland Fabricators Ltd* [1996] STC 145, [1996] IRLR 565).

44.15 'Unable to follow any occupation'

Permanent health insurance schemes often require the employee to show that he is unable to follow his own occupation for a period of time and thereafter that he is 'unable to follow any occupation' if he is to obtain long-term benefits. In *Walton v Airtours plc* [2002] EWCA Civ 1659, [2003] IRLR 161, the Court of Appeal held that the words 'unable to follow any occupation' had to be read in a common sense practical way and any inability must be assessed realistically. It was held that the phrase connoted being engaged in regular work for a substantial or indefinite period. It was enough that an employee could work on a temporary basis, or was able to start a new job for a few days but not continue thereafter to earn income. See also *Jowitt v Pioneer Technology (UK) Ltd* [2003] EWCA Civ 411, [2003] ICR 1120, [2003] IRLR 356.

45   Strikes and Industrial Action

Cross-references. See Trade Unions – I (49) for the liability of unions for industrial action and Human Rights (29).

45.1   LIABILITY FOR INDUSTRIAL ACTION – BACKGROUND

The right to take industrial action takes the form, in this country, of statutory *immunity* for action which would otherwise attract legal liability at common law. The statutory immunity first appeared in something like its present form in the *Trade Disputes Act 1906, s 3*, and its scope has varied frequently since then.

This area of the law has been and is likely to continue to be influenced by the right to freedom of association embodied in *art 11* of the *ECHR*, which was incorporated into domestic law by the *Human Rights Act 1998*. In *Demir v Turkey* (App no 34503/97) (2008) 48 EHRR 1272, [2009] IRLR 766, the European Court of Human Rights held for the first time that the right to bargain collectively should in general form part of the right to freedom of association. In addition, the requirements of European law may impact on the ability of workers to take industrial action. In *International Transport Workers' Federation v Viking Line ABP*: C-438/05 [2008] All ER (EC) 127, [2008] ICR 741 the European Court of Justice held that the right to freedom of establishment embodied in Article 43 of the EC Treaty could in principle be unlawfully restricted by industrial action aimed at preventing a ferry operator from registering one of its vessels in a different country in order to lower its labour costs. However, it was also held that such a restriction might be justified by an overriding public interest (such as the protection of workers) provided that it was proportionate to the objective in question. The ECJ adopted a similar approach to the potential impact of industrial action on the right of freedom to provide services under Article 49 of the EC Treaty in *Laval un Partneri Ltd v Svenska Byggnadsarbetareforbundet*: C-341/05 [2008] All ER (EC) 166, [2008] IRLR 160. The part-French owned claimant railway operating company in *Govia GTR Railway Ltd v ASLEF* [2017] ICR 497 failed before the Court of Appeal in an argument that the union in calling strike action was acting in breach of its rights of establishment under Article 49 of the EC Treaty and its right to provide and receive services under Article 56, even though the strike affected the rail link to Gatwick Airport.

The current basic immunity and the qualifications upon it are contained in the *Trade Union and Labour Relations (Consolidation) Act 1992* ('*TULRCA 1992*'), and were significantly amended with effect from 1 March 2017 when the *Trade Union Act 2016* came into force. In *Metrobus Ltd v Unite the Union* [2009] EWCA Civ 829, [2010] ICR 173 the Court of Appeal rejected the argument that the notification provisions contained in TULRCA 1992 were so difficult or onerous as to give rise to a breach of *art 11* of the *ECHR*. This approach was followed by the European Court of Human Rights in *National Union of Rail, Maritime and Transport Workers v United Kingdom* (App no 31045/10) [2014] IRLR 467, in which the applicant union's complaint that the strike-ballot notice requirements had violated *art 11* was held to be inadmissible. All that the union had been required to do was comply with the procedural requirements laid down by UK law. Moreover, it was significant that the union, having initially been restrained by injunction from calling a strike, subsequently was able to comply with the notice requirements and had successfully called a strike.

In deciding whether legal proceedings can be taken against individuals (or unions) carrying on industrial action, it first must be ascertained whether a tort is being committed, for example, inducing a breach of contract (see **45.2** below). Then it must be ascertained whether the act amounting to the commission of that tort attracts the immunity conferred by *TULRCA 1992*.

45.1 Strikes and Industrial Action

This will involve consideration of whether the act was done in contemplation or furtherance of a trade dispute, whether the industrial action has the support of a ballot, whether the industrial action has been properly initiated, and whether the immunity has been lost because the action is unlawful secondary action or for some other reason.

The law relating to trade disputes is extremely complex. What appears below is an outline of the principles involved.

45.2 LIABILITY AT COMMON LAW

The law relating to the so-called 'economic torts' has developed gradually over the years; it is a difficult area which in many respects is still unclear. The most frequently encountered of the torts relate, broadly, to interference with contractual relations (note that *TULRCA 1992, s 245* deems Crown servants to have contracts of employment for these purposes). They include:

(a) direct inducement of a breach of contract. A union which calls a strike will almost always induce the relevant employees to breach their contracts of employment;

(b) the indirect inducement or procurement of a breach of contract by unlawful means. For example, A may be able to sue the union if his contract to obtain goods from B is breached by B when the union induces B's employees to go on strike in breach of their contracts of employment;

(c) interference with business by unlawful means. This may include the case where the performance of contracts is impeded but there is no actual breach;

(d) intimidation. This is designed to deal with the situation where the harm results, directly or indirectly, not from the actual using of unlawful means, but from the threat of such use;

(e) conspiracy, ie an agreement either to do an unlawful act or to do a lawful act by unlawful means. The effect of the second limb is that an act done by two or more people may be unlawful even though it would have been lawful if done by one person acting alone.

Apart from the usual requirements of causation and foreseeability, it will usually be necessary to show that the defendant knows of the relevant contract and intends to procure its breach or the interference with its performance. Conspiracy is made out only where the agreement is to do an unlawful act, or where the defendant's predominant purpose is to injure the plaintiff, and not to further his own legitimate interests (see *Lonrho plc v Fayed* [1992] 1 AC 448).

Some of the most important of the many authorities on the economic torts are *D C Thomson & Co Ltd v Deakin* [1952] Ch 646, *J T Stratford & Son Ltd v Lindley* [1965] AC 269, *Torquay Hotel Co Ltd v Cousins* [1969] 2 Ch 106, *Merkur Island Shipping Corpn v Laughton* [1983] ICR 490, *News Group Newspapers Ltd v SOGAT '82 (No 2)* [1987] ICR 181, *Middlebrook Mushrooms Ltd v TGWU* [1993] ICR 612; *Timeplan Education Group Ltd v National Union of Teachers* [1997] IRLR 457; *OBG Ltd v Allan* [2008] 1 AC 1; and *Total Network SL v Revenue & Customs Comrs* [2008] UKHL 19, [2008] 1 AC 1174, [2008] 2 All ER 413.

Although it is usually a breach of contract which is ultimately at the root of liability, that is by no means necessarily the case. See, eg *Lonrho plc v Fayed*, above (allegation of intentional infliction of harm by unlawful means based upon fraudulent misrepresentation made to, but not causing loss to, third party). Doubt surrounds the extent to which breach of a statutory duty or a penal statute may be relied upon as unlawful means if the breach is not itself actionable. See *Lonrho Ltd v Shell Petroleum Co Ltd (No 2)* [1982] AC 173; *Barretts & Baird (Wholesale) Ltd v Institution of Professional Civil Servants* [1987] IRLR 3; *Associated British Ports v TGWU* [1989] 1 WLR 939 (point not argued in the House of Lords); and *OBG Ltd v Allan* [2008] 1 AC 1.

Any successful picket will almost certainly involve the *prima facie* commission of the tort of inducing a breach of contract or of interference with contract by unlawful means (see *Union Traffic Ltd v TGWU* [1989] ICR 98). Picketing may also involve the torts of nuisance and intimidation (especially if it is mass picketing), or of trespass (see *Mersey Dock and Harbour Co v Verrinder* [1982] IRLR 152, *Thomas v National Union of Mineworkers (South Wales Area)* [1985] ICR 886, *News Group Newspapers Ltd v SOGAT (1982)* [1987] ICR 181) (see **45.9** below).

45.3   THE IMMUNITY FOR LIABILITY

TULRCA 1992, s 219 provides as follows:

'(1)   An act done by a person in contemplation or furtherance of a trade dispute shall not be actionable in tort on the ground only:

(*a*)   that it induces another person to break a contract or interferes or induces any other person to interfere with its performance; or

(*b*)   that it consists in his threatening that a contract (whether one to which he is a party or not) will be broken or its performance interfered with, or that he will induce another person to break a contract or to interfere with its performance.

(2)   An agreement or combination by two or more persons to do or procure the doing of any act in contemplation or furtherance of a trade dispute shall not be actionable in tort if the act is one which, if done without any such agreement or combination, would not be actionable in tort.'

This formula provides immunity from actions based upon the most common of the economic torts. However, it is possible to formulate a cause of action which falls outside *s 219* (see, eg *Prudential Assurance Co Ltd v Lorenz* (1971) 11 KIR 78 (inducing breach of fiduciary duty); *Associated British Ports v TGWU* [1989] 1 WLR 939 (inducing breach of statutory duty; the point was not argued in the House of Lords)). In such cases it is probably irrelevant that the act complained of may also constitute an inducement to breach of contract which does fall within the immunity.

The statutory immunity does not protect employees from actions by their employers for breach of contract. However, in practice it is unlikely to be worthwhile for an employer to sue individual employees for losses arising from industrial action (see **45.16**(d) below).

45.4   'A TRADE DISPUTE'

'Trade dispute' is given a statutory definition for this purpose by *TULRCA 1992, s 244(1)*, namely:

' . . . a dispute between workers and their employer which relates wholly or mainly to one or more of the following, that is to say:

(*a*)   terms and conditions of employment, or the physical conditions in which any workers are required to work;

(*b*)   engagement or non-engagement, or termination or suspension of employment or the duties of employment, of one or more workers;

(*c*)   allocation of work or the duties of employment as between workers or groups of workers;

(d)   matters of discipline;

(e)   a worker's membership or non-membership of a trade union;

(f)   facilities for officials of trade unions; and

(g)   machinery for negotiation or consultation, and other procedures, relating to any of the above matters, including the recognition by employers or employers' associations of the right of a trade union to represent workers in any such negotiation or consultation or in the carrying out of such procedures.'

In *s 244* 'employment' includes any relationship whereby one person personally does work or performs services for another (*TULRCA 1992, s 244(5)*).

'Worker', in relation to a dispute with an employer, means:

(a)   a worker employed by that employer; or

(b)   a person who has ceased to be employed by that employer where:

(i)   his employment was terminated in connection with the dispute; or

(ii)   the termination of his employment was one of the circumstances giving rise to the dispute.

(*TULRCA 1992, s 244(5)*.)

The test of whether there is a trade dispute is an *objective* test (*NWL Ltd v Woods* [1979] ICR 867). A dispute for political reasons which is unconnected with terms and conditions of employment is not considered to be a trade dispute. One such case involved a refusal by broadcasting technicians to make a broadcast to South Africa during the apartheid era (*BBC v Hearn* [1977] IRLR 273). Similarly, a proposed strike intended as a protest against Government policies was held not to be in contemplation or furtherance of a trade dispute (*Express Newspapers v Keys* [1980] IRLR 247). However, in *Secretary of State for Education v NUT* [2016] IRLR 512, the High Court held that a dispute between a teaching union and the Secretary of State in relation to the funding of sixth form colleges did give rise to a trade dispute between the union and the Secretary of State, despite the fact that the sixth form colleges set teachers' pay on an individual basis.

In *Mercury Communications Ltd v Scott-Garner* [1984] ICR 74, an injunction was granted to restrain industrial action since the court held that the risk to jobs did not appear to be the major factor in the dispute. However, if the union genuinely wishes to achieve its demands relating to terms and conditions of employment (or any other matter falling within *TULRCA 1992, s 244(1)*, it is not relevant to establish whether those demands are realistic (*Associated British Ports v TGWU* [1989] 1 WLR 939, a point not argued on appeal). See also *Newham London Borough Council v NALGO* [1993] ICR 189. In *ISS Mediclean Ltd v GMB* [2015] IRLR 96, the High Court rejected an application for an injunction based on the employer's contention that the matters in issue had essentially been resolved. It was clear that certain matters remained in dispute.

If workers take industrial action in this country in order to further a trade dispute abroad, then, provided that the outcome of the dispute relating to matters occurring outside the UK is likely to affect them in one or more of the aspects specified in *s 244(1)*, it will be considered to be a trade dispute for the purpose of the immunity conferred by *s 219* (*TULRCA 1992, s 244(3)*).

Although the dispute must be between workers (not merely the union) and their employer, it will be sufficient to show that it results from the breakdown of negotiations in which the union was acting on behalf of those workers; and in any event a 'Yes' vote in the strike ballot will amount to an adoption of the dispute by the workers (*Associated British Ports v TGWU* [1989] 1 WLR 939, a point not argued on appeal).

Where a dispute relates to terms and conditions, a strike will be treated as 'in furtherance of a trade dispute' even if some of those balloted and who may be called out are not themselves affected by the terms and conditions in dispute: see *British Telcommunications plc v Communications Workers Union* [2003] EWHC 937 (QB), [2004] IRLR 58. However, in *University College London Hospitals NHS Trust v Unison* [1999] ICR 204, the Court of Appeal upheld an injunction granted against the defendant union following a dispute relating to the future terms and conditions of the employees of a number of private companies which it was proposed should take over the activities of the claimant hospital trust. It was held that a dispute about the terms and conditions of employees of third party employers, who had never been employed by the subject of the proposed strike action, was not a trade dispute within the meaning of *TULRCA 1992, s 244(1)*. Nor was a dispute that was mainly concerned with the terms and conditions of existing employees with an unidentified future employer a trade dispute within the meaning of the section. This approach was held by the European Court of Human Rights to be in accordance with the right to freedom of association contained in *art 11(1)* of the European Convention of Human Rights in *Unison v United Kingdom* [2002] IRLR 497. The European court accepted in that case for the first time that the prohibition on the right to strike was an interference with the *art 11(1)* right which required justification under *art 11(2)*, albeit the restriction was justified in that case.

In contrast with the approach in the *University College London Hospitals NHS Trust* case, in *Westminster City Council v Unison* [2001] EWCA Civ 443, [2001] ICR 1046, the Court of Appeal held that a dispute which was predominantly about the change in the identity of the employer consequent on the transfer of employees from a local authority to a private company did fall within the definition of trade dispute.

In *P (a minor) v National Association of School Masters/Union of Women Teachers* [2003] UKHL 8, [2003] ICR 386, the House of Lords held that a dispute as to the reasonableness of an order by the head teacher of a school that the staff should teach an excluded pupil, who had subsequently been reinstated, did amount to a trade dispute as to the teachers' terms and conditions of employment. The dispute related to the teachers' terms and conditions in the sense that it concerned the nature and extent of their contractual obligation to teach the pupil.

Thus, subject to the limits outlined above and to the further restrictions considered below, a person or a trade union may take part in industrial action so long as it is in contemplation or furtherance of a trade dispute as defined.

45.5   'In contemplation or furtherance . . . '

If there is a trade dispute, the question whether a particular act is in contemplation or furtherance of it is to be judged *subjectively*. In *Express Newspapers Ltd v McShane* [1980] ICR 42, the House of Lords held that 'If the party who does the act honestly thinks at the time he does it that it may help one of the parties to the trade dispute to achieve their objectives and does it for that reason, he is protected by the section' (*per* Lord Diplock at 57). The House of Lords reversed the decision of the Court of Appeal which had applied a more objective test. The subjective test was also applied by the House of Lords in *Duport Steels Ltd v Sirs* [1980] IRLR 116. It is sufficient if one purpose of the strike is the furtherance of the dispute, even though there may be other purposes not within the immunity (*Associated British Ports v TGWU* [1989] 1 WLR 939, a point not argued on appeal).

45.6   LIMITS IMPOSED ON SECONDARY ACTION

In non-legal language, 'secondary action' is the term used to describe industrial action taken by workers where the real dispute is not between themselves and their own employer. The typical example is the 'sympathy strike'.

45.6 Strikes and Industrial Action

Nothing in *TULRCA 1992, s 219* prevents an act from being actionable in tort where one of the facts relied upon for the purpose of establishing liability is that there has been secondary action which is not lawful picketing (*TULRCA 1992, s 224(1)*). Lawful picketing means acts done in the course of such attendance as is declared lawful by *TULRCA 1992, s 220* by a worker employed or last employed by the employer who is party to the dispute, or by a trade union official whose attendance is lawful by virtue of *s 220(1)(b)*. There is secondary action in relation to a trade dispute when, and only when, a person:

(a)   induces another to break a contract of employment or interferes with or induces another to interfere with its performance, or

(b)   threatens that a contract of employment under which he or another is employed will be broken or its performance interfered with, or that he will induce another to break a contract of employment or to interfere with its performance,

and the employer under the contract of employment is not the employer party to the dispute (*TULRCA 1992, s 224(2)*). An employer cannot be party to a dispute between another employer and his workers, and if more than one employer is in dispute with his workers, each dispute is to be treated as separate (*TULRCA 1992, s 224(4)*). A contract of employment is defined to include any contract for personal service, and is thus not confined to the contracts of those who are employees in the strict sense (*TULRCA 1992, s 224(6)*; cf EMPLOYEE, SELF-EMPLOYED OR WORKER? (15)).

The effect of *TULRCA 1992, ss 220* and *224(1)* is that it will not be actionable if, for example, strikers in dispute with their own employer and picketing their workplace induce a lorry-driver not to cross the picket-line, and thus to breach his contract of employment with his own employer who is not a party to the dispute. Subject to this limited type of exception, however, it will be tortious to organise any form of secondary action, including secondary picketing. Unlike under earlier legislation, there is no exception where the aim of the secondary action is to disrupt the supply of goods and services to or from the employer who is party to the dispute or an associated employer of that party.

However, if a particular act constitutes primary action in relation to a trade dispute, the same act may not be relied upon as constituting secondary action so as to evade the immunity in tort. Primary action means the same as secondary action but where the employer under the contract of employment *is* party to the dispute (*TULRCA 1992, s 224(5)*).

In *National Union of Rail, Maritime and Transport Workers v United Kingdom* (App no 31045/10) [2014] IRLR 467 the RMT union argued before the European Court of Human Rights that the UK's blanket ban on secondary action amounted to an infringement of its rights under *art 11* of the ECHR. The court accepted that the ban on secondary action, as it applied in that case, constituted an interference with the RMT's rights under *art 11*. However, that interference was in pursuit of a legitimate aim. Secondary action may well have much broader ramifications than primary action. It may impinge on the rights of persons not party to the dispute, cause broad disruption to the economy and affect the delivery of services to the public. Further, the restriction was proportionate, particularly as a ban on secondary action did not strike at the very substance of the right of freedom of association. It is not wholly clear from the court's decision whether this is its final word on the point, or whether it considered the position might be different on different facts.

45.7   PRESSURE TO IMPOSE UNION MEMBERSHIP OR RECOGNITION

Under *TULRCA 1992, ss 222* and *225*, certain industrial action taken to impose union membership or recognition requirements does not have the protection of *s 219* and will therefore be unlawful. Specifically, there is no immunity from actions in tort for individuals who induce or attempt to induce another:

(a)   to incorporate in a contract to which that other person is a party, or proposed contract to which that other person intends to be a party, a term or conditions which would require that a party to the contract should recognise one or more trade unions for the purpose of negotiating on behalf of workers employed by him, or that he should negotiate with or consult with an official of one or more trade unions;

(b)   on grounds of union exclusion (that is, that the supplier or prospective supplier does not or is not likely to recognise, negotiate or consult as set out in (a) above), to:

   (i)   exclude a person from a list of approved suppliers of goods and services or persons from whom tenders for the supply of goods or services are invited;

   (ii)   exclude a person from the group of persons from whom tenders for the supply of goods or services are invited;

   (iii)   fail to permit a particular person to submit such a tender; or

   (iv)   terminate or determine not to enter into a contract with a particular person for the supply of goods or services.

(*TULRCA 1992, ss 186, 187, 225.*)

Nor is there any immunity where the act concerned is done because, or partly because, a particular employer is employing, has employed or might employ a person who is not a member of any, or any particular, trade union, or because a particular employer refrains from discriminating against such a person, or because it is believed that any of these things has occurred (*TULRCA 1992, s 222(1)*).

Nor is there any immunity where the act concerned is, or is part of, an inducement or an attempted inducement of a person:

(a)   to incorporate in a contract to which that person is party or intends to be party a term or condition which would require that the whole, or some part, of the work done for the purposes of the contract be done only by persons who are or are not members of trade unions or a particular trade union; or

(b)   on union membership grounds (that is, that if the proposed contract were entered into with the person concerned, work for the purposes of the contract would be or would be likely to be done by persons who were or were not members of trade unions or a particular trade union; or in the case of the termination of a contract that such work has been or is likely to be done by such persons), to

   (i)   exclude a person from a list of approved suppliers of goods and services or persons from whom tenders for the supply of goods and services may be invited;

   (ii)   exclude a person from the group of persons from whom tenders for the supply of goods or services are invited;

   (iii)   fail to permit a particular person to submit such a tender;

   (iv)   determine not to enter into a contract with a particular person for the supply of goods or services; or

   (v)   terminate a contract with a particular person for the supply of goods or services.

(*TULRCA 1992, ss 144, 145, 222(3).*)

See also **51.19 TRADE UNIONS – II**.

45.8 Strikes and Industrial Action

45.8 Action in response to dismissal of unofficial strikers

The immunity under *TULRCA 1992, s 219* is lost where the reason, or one of the reasons, for doing the act in question (such as an inducing of breaches of contract by organising a strike) is the fact or belief that an employer has dismissed one or more employees in circumstances such that by virtue of *TULRCA 1992, s 237* they have no right to complain of unfair dismissal (*TULRCA 1992, s 223*).

TULRCA 1992, s 237, which is discussed in detail in 53.18 UNFAIR DISMISSAL – I, provides that an employee has no right to complain of unfair dismissal if at the time of dismissal he was taking part in an unofficial strike or other unofficial industrial action.

45.9 PICKETING

As noted above, any successful picket will be liable to involve the commission of a tort. The statutory immunity for picketing is contained in *TULRCA 1992, s 220*. A person acts lawfully if he attends:

(a)   in contemplation or furtherance of a trade dispute; *and*

(b)   at a specified place, namely:

    (i)   at or near his own place of work; or

    (ii)   if he is unemployed and either his last employment was terminated in connection with a trade dispute or if the termination was one of the circumstances giving rise to a trade dispute, at or near his former place of work; or

    (iii)   if he does not work or normally work at any one place or if the place where he works or normally works is in a location such that attendance there for picketing is impracticable, at any premises of his employer from which he works or from which his work is administered; or

    (iv)   if he is an official of a trade union, at or near the place of work or former place of work of a member of that union whom he is accompanying and whom he represents; and

(c)   for the purpose only of peacefully obtaining or communicating information or peacefully persuading any person to work or abstain from working.

The requirements for a lawful picket have been expanded with effect from 1 March 2017 by *s 10* of the *Trade Union Act 2016*, which has inserted a new *s 220A* into *TULRCA 1992*, imposing additional duties on trade unions to supervise pickets. In particular, it is now a requirement of a lawful picket: that the union appoints someone to supervise the picketing, who is an official or other member of the union; that the supervisor must wear something that readily identifies him (such as an armband) and have a letter stating that the picketing is approved by the union, which he must show as soon as reasonably practicable if asked by a representative of the employer; that the union or supervisor must tell the police the supervisor's name and how to contact them, and where the picketing will be taking place; and that the supervisor must be present or readily contactable and able to attend at short notice while the picketing is taking place.

Any person who pickets outside these limits will lose the immunity from actions in tort. By reason of *TULRCA 1992, s 219(3)* he cannot rely upon the general immunity conferred by *s 219* upon acts done in contemplation or furtherance of a trade dispute unless *s 220* is also satisfied. Accordingly, he will be liable to a claim for an injunction and/or damages if, in the course of such picketing, he commits a tort.

The purpose of condition (*b*) above is to remove the immunity from 'flying pickets'. The Court of Appeal considered its effects in *Union Traffic Ltd v Transport and General Workers Union* [1989] ICR 98 in which it was held that lorry drivers were not entitled to picket depots at which they frequently called for deliveries, repairs and the like, because they were not the bases from which the drivers worked. In *Rayware Ltd v Transport and General Workers Union* [1989] ICR 457 a gate leading to a private trading estate but some way from the employer's premises on that estate was held to be 'near' the place of work since it was the nearest the pickets could get to their place of work without committing a trespass.

Further, *s 220* only serves to give immunity from actions in tort where the tort arises out of the mere act of attendance at the place concerned. If the picket commits further torts, such as inducing breaches of the contracts of employment of those whom he seeks to dissuade from crossing the picket line, he will be liable unless he has the protection of *s 219*, which is discussed more fully elsewhere in this chapter. In *Thames Cleaning v United Voices of the World* [2016] IRLR 695 the High Court held that, when a union organised a protest, which did not amount to picketing in the sense of seeking to dissuade workers from entering their employer's premises, it was not appropriate to grant an injunction to prevent picketing. However, an injunction was granted imposing an exclusion zone around the entrance to the employer's premises, so as to prevent individuals with no connection to the employer harassing the employer through their protesting activities. The statutory immunity which applies to picketing does not extend to demonstrations which amount to harassment.

One of the circumstances in which the protection of *TULRCA 1992, s 219* is lost is where one of the facts relied on for the purpose of establishing liability is that there has been secondary action which is not lawful picketing (*TULRCA 1992, s 224(1)*) (see **45.6** above). Any picket is liable to involve secondary action, because the pickets will try to turn back the employees of third parties, hence the exception in *s 224(1)* for lawful picketing. Lawful picketing is defined in *TULRCA 1992, s 224(3)* as acts done, in the course of attendance declared lawful by *s 220*, by a worker employed (or, if not in employment, last employed) by the employer party to the dispute or by a trade union official whose attendance is lawful by virtue of *TULRCA 1992, s 220(1)(b)*. The effect of these provisions is to remove the immunity from secondary picketing whilst retaining it for direct picketing of the employer who is a party to the dispute, even if that involves pickets trying to turn back the employees of third parties.

45.10 Broome's case

In *Broome v DPP* [1974] ICR 84, the defendant, a picket during an industrial dispute, stood holding a placard in front of a vehicle on a highway, urging the driver not to go to a nearby site and preventing him from so doing for some nine minutes. The Divisional Court reversed the decision of the Stockport magistrates acquitting the defendant and convicted him of obstructing the highway. The House of Lords affirmed the conviction. The law which their Lordships had to consider was *Industrial Relations Act 1971, s 134* (which was framed, for these purposes, in similar terms to the present *TULRCA 1992, s 220*). Lord Reid said of the defendant's conduct (at 89):

> ' . . . his attendance there is only made lawful by subsection (2) if he attended only for the purpose of obtaining or communicating information or "peacefully persuading" the lorry driver. Attendance for that purpose must I think include the right to try to persuade anyone who chooses to stop and listen, at least in so far as this is done in a reasonable way with due consideration for the rights of others. A right to attend for the purpose of peaceful persuasion would be meaningless unless this were implied.
>
> But I see no ground for implying any right to require the person whom it is sought to persuade to submit to any kind of constraint or restriction of his personal freedom.'

Lord Salmon made similar observations.

Thus, police officers acted within their powers when they prevented pickets from approaching a lorry carrying 'strike breakers' during an industrial dispute because they feared an obstruction or a breach of the peace (*Kavanagh v Hiscock* [1974] ICR 282).

45.11 Code of Practice

The Secretary of State for Employment has issued a Code of Practice on picketing under his statutory powers (see **5.4 CODES OF PRACTICE**). The original Code was revised and reissued by virtue of the *Employment Code of Practice (Picketing) Order 1992 (SI 1992/476)*.

The most notable provisions of the *Code* include the recommendation that there should not generally be more than six pickets at any one entrance (*para 51*), recommendations as to the functions of the picket organiser (*paras 54* to *57*), and recommendations concerning avoiding impediments to the movement of essential supplies, services and operations (*paras 62* to *64*).

45.12 CRIMINAL LIABILITY

Action taken by pickets may give rise to criminal liability. For example, they may be prosecuted under *TULRCA 1992, s 241(1)(d)*, which provides that a person who:

' . . . with a view to compelling another person to abstain from doing or to do any act which that person has a legal right to do or abstain from doing, wrongfully and without legal authority . . . watches or besets the house or other place where that person resides, or works, or carries on business, or happens to be, or the approach to such house or place',

shall, on summary conviction, be liable to a fine not exceeding level 5 on the Standard Scale, or up to six months' imprisonment, or both (*TULRCA 1992, s 241(2)*; see **1.10 INTRODUCTION**).

However, compulsion of the other person, and not mere persuasion of him, must be the object of the watching and besetting (*DPP v Fidler* [1992] 1 WLR 91). The watching and besetting is not wrongful unless tortious (*Thomas v National Union of Mineworkers (South Wales Area)* [1985] ICR 886), but it appears that it may be wrongful even if no action in tort could be brought because of the statutory immunity (*Galt v Philp* [1984] IRLR 156). Other criminal charges for assault, criminal damage and offences under the *Public Order Act 1986* (especially ss 1–5) may arise if the pickets behave unlawfully. In such cases *TULRCA 1992, s 220* cannot provide them with a defence. *Public Order Act 1986, Part II* gives the police certain powers to impose conditions upon public processions and assemblies, in addition to their common law powers to take such action as may be necessary to prevent a breach of the peace.

The House of Lords held in *DPP v Jones* [1999] 2 AC 240 that the public have the right to use the highway for such reasonable and usual activities, including peaceful assembly, as are consistent with the primary right of passage. This important decision was plainly influenced by *art 11* of the European Convention on Human Rights (the right to freedom of peaceful assembly).

Any action which does not fall within the provisions of *TULRCA 1992, s 220* constitutes an offence if the obstruction takes place on the public highway, since the *Highways Act 1980, s 137(1)* provides:

'If a person, without lawful authority or excuse, in any way wilfully obstructs the free passage along a highway he is guilty of an offence . . . '.

For the definition of obstruction, see *Cooper v Metropolitan Police Comr* (1985) 82 Cr App Rep 238. However, picketing may take place outside factory gates which are on private property. In such a case, the pickets cannot be guilty of obstructing the highway but may be liable for a private trespass or nuisance.

45.13 THE LIABILITY OF TRADE UNIONS

Trade unions are no longer, as they once were, immune from all proceedings in tort arising from industrial action. They are now liable for tortious acts which they are taken to have authorised or endorsed (see **50.16** Trade Unions – I). They enjoy the same statutory immunity as individuals, but only if they fulfil the ballot requirements of *TULRCA 1992*. The liability of trade unions in actions in tort is subject to statutory financial limits (see **50.17** Trade Unions – I).

45.14 BALLOTS BEFORE INDUSTRIAL ACTION

In order to enjoy immunity from actions in tort for acts inducing persons to take part or continue to take part in industrial action, trade unions must be supported by a ballot (*TULRCA 1992, s 226(1)*). The ballot must comply with the complex procedural obligations contained in *Part V* of *TULRCA 1992*. The requirements of *Part V* have been substantially amended, and made more exacting, with effect from 1 March 2017, by the *Trade Union Act 2016*. Notwithstanding the onerous nature of these requirements, the Court of Appeal held in *Metrobus Ltd v Unite the Union* [2009] EWCA Civ 829, [2010] ICR 173 that they were not incompatible with the right to freedom of association contained in *Article 11* of the *European Convention on Human Rights*. A similar challenge raised in *National Union of Rail, Maritime and Transport Workers v United Kingdom* (App no 31045/10) [2014] IRLR 467 was ruled inadmissible by the European Court of Human Rights. The following are the prerequisites of a ballot before industrial action.

(a)   All of those members whom it is reasonable for the union to believe will be called upon to take part in the industrial action, and no others, must be balloted (*TULRCA 1992, s 227(1)*). Those "taking part" in the industrial action are not confined to members who will in fact be called upon to breach their contracts of employment; they may participate in other ways: see *London Underground Ltd v ASLEF* [2011] EWHC 3506. Moreover, since 18 September 2000, this requirement has been mitigated by a new *TULRCA 1992, s 232B* which provides that a failure to comply which is accidental and on a scale which is unlikely to affect the result of the ballot will be disregarded. In *British Airways plc v Unite the Union* [2009] EWHC 3541, [2010] IRLR 423, the High Court held that the union had failed to comply with the requirement to ballot only those whom it reasonably believed would be called upon to take action, in circumstances where several hundred members had been balloted whom the union knew would no longer be employed by the employer at the time of the ballot. The union could gain no assistance from *TULRCA 1992, s 232B*, since the failure, though unintentional, could not properly be described as accidental. The Court of Appeal considered the requirement that a relevant failure must be "accidental" for *s 232B* to come into play in *London & Birmingham Railway Ltd v ASLEF; Serco Ltd v RMT* [2011] EWCA Civ 226, [2011] ICR 849, and held that the union's actions in permitting two members to vote who should not have been should be disregarded. The mistake was due to human error, and it did not matter that it could have been avoided if reasonable steps had been taken to keep the union's records up to date. Moreover, the Court of Appeal went on to express the view that a general de minimis principle applies in the context of the balloting procedures. By virtue of *TULRCA 1992, s 232A*, industrial action will not be regarded as having the support of a ballot if any member whom it was reasonable at the time of the ballot for the union to believe would be induced to take part in the action is induced to take part. However, the union is not confined to balloting and inducing to take part in the action only those who will be directly affected by the subject matter of the trade dispute: see *United Closures and Plastics Ltd* [2012] IRLR 29. It was held by the Court of Appeal in *London Underground Ltd v National Union of Rail, Maritime and Transport Workers* [1996] ICR 170 that the defendant union could induce members who had not been balloted to take part in industrial action if those members had joined the union since the ballot. It was also recognised that a union may induce non-members to participate, even though they will not have been balloted. In *P (a minor) v National Association of School Masters/Union of Women Teachers* [2003] UKHL 8, [2003] ICR 386 the House of Lords held that the union's failure to send ballot papers to two teachers who had recently joined the staff did not invalidate the ballot. In particular, the failure to send those teachers ballot papers did not necessarily mean that they had not been accorded entitlement to vote within the meaning of *TULRCA 1992, s 232A(c)*. The requirement to send out ballot papers to those defined as entitled to vote in *s 227(1)* is subject to the caveat 'so far as is reasonably practicable' in *s 230(2)*. Further, *s 232B* makes the requirement to send out ballot papers subject to the disregard of small accidental errors. Accordingly, the ballot was valid. By contrast, in *Midline Mainline Ltd v National Union of Rail, Maritime and Transport Workers* [2001] EWCA Civ 1206, [2001] IRLR 813 the failure to ballot 25 union members in a ballot of 91 members was held by the Court of Appeal to be too significant to be disregarded.

If the persons balloted have different places of work, *TULRCA 1992, s 228* requires a separate ballot for each workplace, unless those balloted share a common feature of terms and conditions of employment or occupational description which is not shared by other members with the same employer who are not balloted and, in a case where there are such other members, is not a factor which employees of that employer have in common by virtue of having the same place of work. A new *TULRCA 1992, ss 228* and *228A*, enable unions to hold a ballot across separate workplaces if the dispute affects at least one member of the union in each workplace, or if the ballot is limited to all members whom the union reasonably believes to have particular kinds of occupation and are employed by a particular employer or employers with whom the union is in dispute, or if entitlement to vote is given only to members of the union who are employed by an employer or employers with whom the union is in dispute. 'Workplace' is defined as the premises at which an employee works or, where an employee does not work at a particular premises, the premises with which his employment has the closest connection (*TULRCA 1992, s 228(4)*). Where separate workplace ballots are not required, the ballot may legitimately include employees of more than one employer, if a number of employers are party to the dispute (*University of Central England v NALGO* [1993] IRLR 81). Employees of different employers may be held to have the same place of work even if their respective employers each have only a licence over the premises at which they work (*Intercity West Coast Ltd v National Union of Rail, Maritime and Transport Workers* [1996] IRLR 583).

(b)   So far as is reasonably practicable, every person entitled to vote must have a voting paper sent to him by post at his home address (or other address which he has requested the union to treat as his postal address), and must be given a convenient opportunity to vote by post (*TULRCA 1992, s 230(2)*). Special provisions apply to merchant seamen. It was held in *British Railways Board v National Union of Railwaymen* [1989] ICR 678 that the words 'reasonably practicable' mean that inadvertent errors such as missing some members off the list will not necessarily invalidate the ballot. This principle was given statutory force by *TULRCA 1992, s 232B* which provides for small-scale, accidental failures to be disregarded (see (*a*) above).

(c)   The voting paper must contain at least one of the following questions –

(i)   a question which requires the voter to say, by answering 'Yes' or 'No' whether he is prepared to take part, or to continue to take part, in a strike;

(ii)   a question which requires the voter to say, by answering 'Yes' or 'No', whether he is prepared to take part, or as the case may be to continue to take part, in industrial action falling short of a strike.

(*TULRCA 1992, s 229(2).*)

This means that a strike and action short of a strike must be the subject of separate questions on the ballot paper (*Post Office v Union of Communications Workers* [1990] ICR 258). The requirements for the voting paper will be augmented when *s 5* of the *Trade Union Act 2016* comes into force, at a date yet to be fixed, so as to require the inclusion of a summary of the matters in issue in the trade dispute, specifying the types of industrial action short of strike which are contemplated, and indicating the periods within which the industrial action of each type is expected to take place.

TULRCA 1992, s 229(2A) provides that an overtime ban and a call-out ban constitute action short of a strike for the purposes of the strike ballot provisions.

With effect from 1 March 2017, the voting paper must also include: a summary of the matters in issue in the relevant trade dispute; the types of any industrial action short of a strike proposed; and the period within which each relevant type of industrial action is expected to take place: *TULRCA 1992, ss 229(2B), (2C)* and *(2D)*.

(d)   The following statement must appear without comment on every voting paper:

'If you take part in a strike or other industrial action, you may be in breach of your contract of employment.

However, if you are dismissed for taking part in strike or other industrial action which is called officially and is otherwise lawful, the dismissal will be unfair if it takes place fewer than twelve weeks after you started taking part in the action, and depending on the circumstances may be unfair if it takes place later.'

(*TULRCA 1992, s 229(4).*)

(e)   The voting paper must clearly specify the address to which, and the date by which, it is to be returned, and must be numbered (*TULRCA 1992, s 229(1A)*).

(f)   The voting paper must specify who, in the event of a vote in favour of action, is authorised for the purposes of *TULRCA 1992, s 233* (see **45.15** below) to call upon members to take part or continue to take part in the industrial action (*TULRCA 1992, s 229(3)*). The specified person need not be authorised under the rules of the union, but must be within *TULRCA 1992, s 20(2)* (ie a person empowered by the rules to call for the action, or the principal executive committee, president or general secretary, or any other committee or official of the union; see also TRADE UNIONS – I (50)). It is thought that the voting paper may specify alternative persons as having the authority to call for action. Further, in a case where an independent scrutineer is required (see (*k*) below), the ballot paper must state his name (*TULRCA 1992, s 229(1A)(a)*).

(g) So far as is reasonably practicable those voting must vote in secret (*TULRCA 1992, s 230(4)(a)*). They must be allowed to vote without interference from the union, and so far as is reasonably practicable, without incurring direct costs to themselves (this presumably means that reply-paid envelopes must be used for the postal ballot) (*TULRCA 1992, s 230(1)*). For reasonable practicability, see (*b*) above.

(h) The votes must be fairly and accurately counted, although an inaccuracy in counting is to be disregarded if it is accidental and on a scale which could not affect the result of the ballot (*TULRCA 1992, s 230(4)*).

(i) The majority of those voting in the ballot must have answered 'Yes' to the appropriate question (*TULRCA 1992, s 226(2)*). Where a ballot poses two separate questions, one relating to strike action and the other to industrial action short of a strike, the relevant majority is a majority of those voting on the specific question. It is not necessary that the majority voting 'Yes' in response to the particular question also comprise a majority of those taking part in the ballot (*West Midlands Travel Ltd v Transport and General Workers' Union* [1994] ICR 978). Further, with effect from 1 March 2017, at least 50% of those who were entitled to vote in the ballot must have done so.

(j) Since 1 March 2017, an additional requirement has applied where the majority of those entitled to vote in the ballot are normally engaged in the provision of "important public services". In such cases, 40% of those entitled to vote in the ballot must have voted in favour of taking industrial action (*TULRCA 1992, s 226(2C)*). Services falling within health services, education of those aged under 17, fire services, transport services, decommissioning of nuclear installations and management of radioactive waste and border security may be specified by the Secretary of State by statutory instrument as falling within the definition of "important public services". The Secretary of State has issued regulations specifying such "important public services" in all these sectors (except decommissioning of nuclear installations and management of radioactive waste). The Department of Business, Energy and Industrial Strategy also issued non-statutory guidance on the application of this additional threshold in January 2017.

(k) In a case where the number of members entitled to vote in the ballot (the aggregated number is taken where there are separate workplace ballots in accordance with (*a*) above) exceeds 50, a qualified scrutineer must be appointed. The union must ensure that he duly carries out his functions without interference, and must comply with all his reasonable requests. The scrutineer will make a report as soon as reasonably practicable after the ballot, and in any event within four weeks, stating whether he is satisfied that there are no reasonable grounds for believing that there was any contravention of statutory requirements, that the ballot arrangements included all reasonably practicable security arrangements to minimise the risk of unfairness or malpractice, and that he has been able to carry out his functions without interference from the union. Any person entitled to vote in the ballot, and the employer of any such person, is entitled (upon request made within six months of the ballot and upon payment of any reasonable fee specified by the union) to be provided with a copy of the report (*TULRCA 1992, ss 226B, 226C, 231B*). The persons qualified to be scrutineers are those satisfying the requirements of the *Trade Union Ballots and Elections (Independent Scrutineer Qualifications) Order 1993 (SI 1993/1909)*.

(l) The union must take such steps as are reasonably necessary to secure that every person whom it is reasonable for the union to believe will be the employer of persons entitled to vote in the ballot receives both notice that the ballot will take place, and a sample voting paper. In *English, Welsh & Scottish Railway Ltd v National Union of Rail, Maritime and Transport Workers* [2004] EWCA Civ 1539, 148 Sol Jo LB 1246 the Court of Appeal held that, where a notice of intention to hold an industrial action ballot was addressed to only one of two very closely related employers involved in an industrial dispute with the union, the notice should be treated as having been given to both companies. The notice must be received not later than the seventh day before the opening of the ballot, and must specify the anticipated opening day and identify the categories of employees of that employer whom the union believes will be entitled to vote. The sample voting paper must be received not later than the third day before the opening day (*TULRCA 1992, s 226A*).

A valid notice must contain lists of the categories of employee whom the union reasonably believes will be entitled to vote in the ballot and the workplaces at which they work. The notice must also state the total number of employees to be balloted and the number in each category, together with an explanation of how those figures were arrived at (*TULRCA 1992, s 226A*). The Court of Appeal held in *National Union of Rail, Maritime & Transport Workers v Serco Ltd* [2011] EWCA Civ 226, [2011] IRLR 399 that the duty to provide such an explanation is not an onerous one, usually requiring only an indication of the sources of the information and highlighting any major known deficiencies. Unions are expressed not to be under a duty to supply an employer with the names of the employees concerned. By *s 226(2D)*, the lists and figures supplied must be as accurate as is reasonably practicable in the light of the information in the possession of the union. In *London & Birmingham Railway Ltd v ASLEF; Serco Ltd v RMT* [2011] EWCA Civ 226, [2011] ICR 849 the Court of Appeal held that this obligation does not require unions to seek out additional information or set up systems to improve their record keeping. In *British Airways plc v Unite the Union* [2009] EWHC 3541, [2010] IRLR 423, the High Court held that the union had failed to comply with the notice provisions in circumstances where it had included in the ballot notice a substantial number of employees whom it could not reasonably have believed would be entitled to vote in the ballot, since they would no longer be employed by the employer by the time the strike was called. In *Metrobus Ltd v Unite the Union* [2009] EWCA Civ 829, [2010] ICR 173, a majority of the Court of Appeal held that, in respect of non-check off employees, the union is obliged to provide a list of the numbers of employees who will be entitled to vote, the numbers in each workplace, the numbers in each category of worker and an explanation of how the figures were worked out. However, a misstatement of the number of relevant check off employees (by 10 out of nearly 800) was held not to be sufficiently material to invalidate the ballot. As noted above, in *London & Birmingham Railway Ltd v ASLEF; Serco Ltd v RMT* [2011] EWCA Civ 226, [2011] ICR 849, the Court of Appeal endorsed the view (obiter) that a general de minimis principle applies in the context of the balloting notification procedures, such that a very small error in the notice will not generally invalidate a ballot. By contrast, in *Metroline Travel Ltd v Unite the Union* [2012] EWHC 1778 (QB), [2012] IRLR 749 a notice was held to be invalid when it referred to balloting certain grades of employee working on the contract for a particular client "on a full time or part basis". This was too imprecise, as it was unclear whether this included employees who might be expected to work for the client, or who were associated with the client, and whether they had to be working for the client directly or indirectly. As noted above, the European Court of Human Rights held in *National Union of Rail, Maritime and Transport Workers v United Kingdom* (App no 31045/10) [2014] IRLR 467 that the notification requirements in relation to ballots were compatible with the right of freedom of association under *art 11* of the ECHR, notwithstanding their relatively onerous nature.

(m)   As soon as is reasonably practicable after the holding of the ballot, the union must take such steps as are reasonably necessary to ensure that all persons entitled to vote, and their employers, are informed of the number of votes cast, the number of 'Yes' and 'No' votes, and the number of spoiled voting papers (*TULRCA 1992, s 231*, *s 231A*). Since 1 March 2017, the information to be provided has been extended to include whether at least 50% of those entitled to vote have voted and, in cases relating to important public services, whether at least 40% have voted in favour of the industrial action. In *Metrobus Ltd v Unite the Union* [2009] EWCA Civ 829, [2010] ICR 173 the Court of Appeal held that the union had acted in breach of *TULRCA 1992, s 231A(1)* by delaying just two days in notifying the employer of the result of a strike ballot. It further held that the duty to provide such information applies irrespective of whether the union proposes to initiate industrial action. However, not every technical challenge will succeed. In *British Airways plc v Unite the Union* [2010] EWCA Civ 669, [2010] ICR 1316, a majority of the Court of Appeal held that the trade union had taken such steps as were reasonably necessary to comply with the duty to inform members of the results of the ballot by providing them on its website, on union notice boards and via news sheets, even though each member had not been sent an individual email or text message with the results.

Where there are separate ballots for different workplaces, paras (*b*) to (*l*) are to be tested in relation to the ballot for the workplace of the person whose inducement to take part in the action is relied upon to found the liability in tort (*TULRCA 1992, s 226(3)*). This means in particular that a 'Yes' vote is required at every workplace where the members are to be called upon to take action.

If there is a suspension of industrial action for negotiations, a further ballot need not be held before industrial action is resumed, provided that the terms of the original ballot cover the reason for the resumed action (*Monsanto plc v Transport and General Workers Union* [1987] ICR 269). However, this will not apply where there is a substantial interruption of the action as opposed to a mere suspension; where the action is irregular and spasmodic, it is a question of fact and degree whether it is sufficiently continuous and self-contained to be covered by a single ballot (*Post Office v Union of Communications Workers* [1990] ICR 258). In *London Underground Ltd v National Union of Railwaymen* [1989] IRLR 341 it was held that at the time of the ballot there must be a genuine, definite, substantial dispute (actual or reasonably foreseeable) between the parties, and that the ballot question must relate wholly to matters capable of constituting a trade dispute. However, in *Associated British Ports v TGWU* [1989] 1 WLR 939 it was held that there was no need for the ballot information to describe or define every issue with which the dispute was concerned, provided that it was possible to identify the strike which was called with the strike which was voted for (the point was not argued on appeal).

Special provisions apply to overseas members and to members in Northern Ireland (*TULRCA 1992, s 232*). A union which is a federation, and which does not have individual members whom it will call out on strike, cannot comply with the relevant provisions of *TULRCA 1992* and therefore will enjoy no immunity from action when calling a strike (*Shipping Co Uniform Inc v International Transport Workers Federation* [1985] ICR 245).

The Secretary of State is empowered by *TULRCA 1992, ss 203, 204* to issue codes of practice relating to the conduct by trade unions of ballots and elections (see CODES OF PRACTICE (5)). The original *Code on Trade Union Ballots on Industrial Action* has been revised and reissued (*Employment Code of Practice (Industrial Action Ballots and Notice to Employers) Order 2005 (SI 2005/2420)*). The *Code* deals with, among other things, the situations in which an industrial action ballot is appropriate, establishment of the balloting 'constituency', preparation and distribution of voting papers, and the conduct and counting of the ballot.

45.15   CALLING FOR INDUSTRIAL ACTION

In order for the action to be treated as supported by the ballot, there must have been no call by the union to take part in or continue to take part in the action to which the ballot relates, or any authorisation or endorsement of such action (see **50.16** TRADE UNIONS – I), *before* the date of the ballot (*TULRCA 1992, s 233(3)(a)*).

The call for industrial action must be made by the person specified on the ballot paper (see **45.14**(*f*) above). It is permissible for the specified person to call for action subject to some condition whose fulfilment is a matter for the judgment of local officials, although he may not simply delegate his authority (*Tanks and Drums Ltd v TGWU* [1992] ICR 1).

The call for action must be made, and the action must commence, before the end of the period of four weeks beginning with the date of the ballot (*TULRCA 1992, ss 233, 234(1)*). However, *TULRCA 1992, s 234(1)* provides that this period may be extended up to a maximum of eight weeks by agreement between the union and the employers. There are provisions which enable the union to apply to the court for an extension of time, up to a maximum of 12 weeks from the date of the ballot, where for the whole or part of that period action is prohibited by a court order or an undertaking given to the court which subsequently ceases to have effect (*TULRCA 1992, s 234(2)–(6)*). Since 1 March 2017 *s 9* of the *Trade Union Act 2016* has amended *TULRCA 1992, s 234(1)* so as to provide that the mandate for industrial action shall automatically expire six months after the date of the ballot, or up to nine months after that date if so agreed between the union and the employer.

The union must take such steps as are reasonably necessary to give notice to an employer whose employees it reasonably believes will be or have been induced to take part in the action, describing the categories of employees concerned and specifying whether the action is intended to be continuous (in which case it must state the intended commencement date for any of those employees) or discontinuous (in which case it must state the intended dates for any of them to take part). A valid notice must contain lists of the categories of employee whom the union reasonably believes will be induced to take part in industrial action. The notice must also state the total number of employees to be induced to participate and the number in each category. Unions are expressed not to be under a duty to supply an employer with the names of the employees concerned. The notice must be received within the period beginning with the day when the requirement to notify employers of the ballot result is satisfied (see **45.14**(*m*) above) and ending with (since the coming into force of *s 8* of the *Trade Unions Act 2016* on 1 March 2017) the fourteenth day before the first day specified in the notice, unless the union and employer agree that only seven days' notice need be given (*TULRCA 1992, s 234A*). Thus the union is effectively required to give an employer at least two weeks' notice of industrial action.

45.16   EMPLOYER'S RIGHTS AND REMEDIES

The withdrawal of labour will usually amount to a breach of the contracts of employment of the individuals concerned. A strike notice may, however, at least in theory, be construed as due notice to *terminate* the contracts of employment of the strikers. Whether this is so depends upon the words used and on the circumstances (*Boxfoldia Ltd v National Graphical Association* [1988] ICR 752). Action taken in a go-slow or work-to-rule may also be considered a breach by each individual participant of his contract of employment. In *Secretary of State for Employment v Associated Society of Locomotive Engineers and Firemen* [1972] ICR 7 at 56 Lord Denning MR said:

> 'If [an employee] with   . . .   others, takes steps wilfully to disrupt the undertaking, to produce chaos so that it will not run as it should, then each one who is a party to those steps is guilty of a breach of his contract. It is no answer for any one of them to say "I am only obeying the rule book", or "I am not bound to do more than a 40-hour week". That would be all very well if done in good faith without any wilful disruption of services; but what makes it wrong is the object with which it is done.'

See also *British Telecommunications plc v Ticehurst* [1992] ICR 383.

The courses of action open to an employer, and others affected by industrial action, include the following:

45.16   Strikes and Industrial Action

(a)   An employer may try to conciliate, if necessary with the assistance of the ADVISORY, CONCILIATION AND ARBITRATION SERVICE (2).

(b)   If employees are on strike or their work is disruptive within the meaning of Lord Denning's statement above, they do not have to be paid for the period during which industrial action persists. If employees are refusing to perform part of their contractual duties, employers may deduct an appropriate sum from their salaries (*Sim v Rotherham Metropolitan Borough Council* [1986] ICR 897; *Miles v Wakefield Metropolitan District Council* [1987] ICR 368; *Wiluszynski v Tower Hamlets London Borough Council* [1989] ICR 493; and see PAY – I (34)). In *Spackman v London Metropolitan University* [2007] IRLR 744 the claimant complained at having been paid only 70% of her contractual salary in respect of a period during which she had been performing only some of her contractual duties as part of industrial action being taken against her employer. The county court rejected her argument that she was entitled to a *quantum meruit* payment for some or all of the balance of her salary. Such an approach was inappropriate in circumstances where the contract of employment continued to govern the relationship between the parties. Moreover, it was held that employees participating in this type of industrial action are taking the risk of recovering no pay at all when they carry out only some of their contractual duties.

(c)   If employees or unions are taking disruptive industrial action which is not in contemplation or furtherance of a trade dispute or is unprotected secondary action or action for a purpose not within the statutory immunities, or is action by trade unions taken without a ballot, an employer affected may apply to the High Court for an *injunction* to prevent them from continuing such action. He may sue either the individuals involved or the union responsible, or both. Note that *TULRCA 1992, s 221(1)* requires that any application for an injunction must be brought to the attention of the other party if it seems likely that he may claim that he is acting in contemplation or furtherance of a trade dispute. Unless the court is satisfied that all reasonable steps have been taken, an injunction will not be granted. However, it is important to apply to the court speedily.

In deciding whether or not to grant the injunction, a court must have regard to the likelihood of the defendant succeeding in establishing a defence under *TULRCA 1992, s 219* or *s 220 (TULRCA 1992, s 221(2))*. Although the likelihood of establishing the defence is only one factor to be considered in deciding where the 'balance of convenience' lies (that being the test of whether to grant an interim injunction if the plaintiff has an arguable case and an ultimate award of damages would not be an adequate remedy for either party), the injunction will normally be refused if it appears more likely than not that the statutory defence will be made out (*NWL Ltd v Woods* [1979] ICR 867). The court will also have regard to whether it is likely that in practice the grant or refusal of the injunction will be decisive in determining the legal proceedings for an injunction (if so, it becomes more important to try to form a view of the ultimate chances of success); it will compare the disadvantage to the workers in being unable to strike while the iron is hot with the potential losses to the employer. In a proper case it may have regard to the public interest, and if all other considerations are evenly balanced it will usually attempt to preserve the status quo (see, eg *Dimbleby & Sons Ltd v NUJ* [1984] ICR 386; *Union Traffic Ltd v TGWU* [1989] ICR 98; *Associated British Ports v TGWU* [1989] 1 WLR 939 (point not argued in the House of Lords)). The court will, however, under no circumstances grant an injunction if its effect would be to compel the employees to work (*TULRCA 1992, s 236*).

In proceedings arising out of an act which is by virtue of *TULRCA 1992, s 20* is taken to have been one by a trade union (as to which see **50.16** TRADE UNIONS – I), the court's power to grant an injunction includes power to require the union to take such steps as the court considers appropriate for ensuring that there is no, or no further, inducement of persons to take part in industrial action or to continue to do so, and that no person engages in any conduct after the granting of the injunction by virtue of such inducement prior to the injunction (*TULRCA 1992, s 20(6)*). This represents a statutory development of the decision in *Solihull Metropolitan Borough v National Union of Teachers* [1985] IRLR 211, that where industrial action was called without a ballot, union leaders could be required to rescind the instruction.

If the union or the individuals against whom a court order is obtained act in breach of the order, proceedings may be taken for contempt of court (see, eg *Richard Read (Transport) Ltd v National Union of Mineworkers (South Wales Area)* [1985] IRLR 67; *Express and Star Ltd v NGA* [1986] ICR 589;*Kent Free Press v NGA* [1987] IRLR 267). The penalties which a court may impose if it finds a contempt proved are a fine, sequestration and imprisonment. A writ of sequestration will not affect the separate funds of a branch which is an unincorporated association (see *News Group Newspapers Ltd v Society of Graphical and Allied Trades 1982* [1986] ICR 716). Note that the union will not be able to use its funds to indemnify individuals penalised for contempt of court, nor for certain criminal offences (*TULRCA 1992, s 15*; and see **50.18 TRADE UNIONS – I**).

(d)   The employer may also claim damages against those taking part in or organising the industrial action, or against the union (see **50.16 TRADE UNIONS – I**). A claim in *tort* for inducing breaches of contract (the most common cause of action) will only succeed if the statutory immunity does not apply. However, the immunity does not extend to straightforward actions for *breach of contract*, and individual strikers may be sued on that basis. In practice, this is rarely likely to be worthwhile for an employer. Notwithstanding the absence of a statutory immunity for breach of contract, an employer is precluded from obtaining an injunction to restrain a breach of contract where the effect of the order would be to compel the employee to work (*TULRCA 1992, s 236*). Damages are limited to the loss actually caused by the individual striker (*National Coal Board v Galley* [1958] 1 WLR 16), which may be difficult to prove, or confined to the extra cost of hiring a substitute; and to seek to enforce a substantial award of damages against ordinary employees, even if practicable, will clearly have industrial relations implications. In certain circumstances it may also be possible to recover money which the employer has been forced to pay under duress of unlawful industrial action (see, eg *Dimskal Shipping Co SA v ITWF* [1992] IRLR 78). The damages which may be awarded against a trade union in tort are limited (by reference to the number of members) by *TULRCA 1992, s 22*.

(e)   If necessary, an employer may in limited circumstances dismiss all employees on strike (or taking other industrial action) and try to engage a new labour force. In the case of unofficial action, he may dismiss selectively. The employment tribunal's unfair dismissal jurisdiction is also *prima facie* excluded in respect of workers dismissed during official industrial action (subject to the significant exception contained in *s 238A* – see below) if two conditions are met: *first*, all the employees in the employer's establishment who were taking part in the industrial action at the date when the complainant was dismissed must also be dismissed; *secondly*, none of those employees can be offered re-engagement by the employer until *after* the expiry of the period of three months beginning with the date of the dismissal, or else all of them must be offered re-engagement within that period (see further **53.17 UNFAIR DISMISSAL – I**) (*TULRCA 1992, ss 237, 238*).

However, the exclusion from the right to claim unfair dismissal contained in *TULRCA 1992, s 238* does not apply where the employee is taking part in 'protected industrial action' and if certain other conditions are satisfied (*TULRCA 1992, s 238A*). 'Protected industrial action' is defined as action which was induced by an act protected by *TULRCA 1992, s 219*. An employee will be treated as having been automatically unfairly dismissed if the reason or principal reason for his dismissal was that the employee has taken part in protected industrial action and:

(i)   the dismissal took place within twelve weeks of the start of the protected industrial action by the employee (or within such further period as falls to be added to the twelve weeks to reflect any period during which the employee was locked out by his employer); or

(ii)   the dismissal took place more than twelve weeks (or such longer period as results from a lock-out period) after the start of the protected industrial action and the employee had ceased taking part in the industrial action within the twelve-week period; or

(iii)   the dismissal took place more than twelve weeks (or such longer period as results from a lock-out period) after the start of the protected industrial action, the employee had not ceased to take part in the industrial action within the first twelve weeks but the employer had failed to take such procedural steps as would have been reasonable for the purposes of resolving the dispute.

(See further **54.3** UNFAIR DISMISSAL – **II**.)

45.17 UNION MEMBERS' RIGHT TO A BALLOT

TULRCA 1992, s 62 gives a remedy to a trade union member whose union seeks to involve him in industrial action without the support of a ballot. This includes all those members who work under contracts for personal services, and not merely those who are employees in the strict sense (*TULRCA 1992, s 62(8)*). Such a person may apply to the High Court (or the Court of Session in Scotland), which will make an order (see below) if he can demonstrate that:

(a)   the union has, without the support of a ballot, authorised or endorsed any industrial action; and

(b)   that members of the union, including the applicant, have been or are likely to be induced by the union to take part in or continue to take part in that action.

Again, any application should be made without undue delay.

For the purpose of deciding whether the members are induced by the union and whether action is authorised or endorsed by the union, reference is made to the test of liability of unions for official action contained in *TULRCA 1992, s 20* (*TULRCA 1992, s 62(5)* and see **50.16** TRADE UNIONS – **I**). The fact that the inducement is ineffective is immaterial (*TULRCA 1992, s 62(6)*).

The action is authorised or endorsed without the support of a ballot unless, not more than four weeks (or such longer period as may be agreed in accordance with *TULRCA 1992, s 234(1)*) before the commencement of the action, there has been a ballot complying with *TULRCA 1992, ss 226B to 233* (see **45.14** and **45.15** above) in respect of the action, in which the applicant was entitled to vote. The majority of those voting must have answered 'Yes' to a question asking them whether they are prepared to strike or take part in the industrial action concerned (*TULRCA 1992, s 62(2)*).

If the court upholds the complaint, it will make such order as it considers appropriate for requiring the union to take steps to ensure that there is no further inducement of members to take part in the action and that no member engages in any further conduct resulting from the prior inducement. The steps so required may include the withdrawal of any relevant authorisation or endorsement (*TULRCA 1992, s 62(3)*). Disobedience to such an order will, of course, be a contempt of court.

45.18 THIRD PARTIES' RIGHTS AND REMEDIES

At common law, parties whose contracts were interfered with by unlawful industrial action could apply to the High Court for an injunction and damages, provided that the loss caused was not too remote or unforeseeable. The holder of a train ticket was able to recover damages from the rail unions for wrongfully interfering with his contract with British Rail (*Falconer v ASLEF and NUR* [1986] IRLR 331).

There is a statutory right under *TULRCA 1992, s 235A*, for an individual to apply to the High Court where he claims that any trade union or other person has done or is likely to do an unlawful act to induce any person to take part or continue to take part in industrial action, if a likely effect of the industrial action is to prevent or delay the supply of goods or services to the applicant, or to reduce the quality of goods or services supplied to him (*TULRCA 1992, s 235A(1)*). For these purposes an act is unlawful if it is actionable in tort by any one or more persons (which need not include the applicant himself), or in the case of an act by a trade union, if it could form the basis of an application by a member under *TULRCA 1992, s 62* (see **45.17** above) (*TULRCA 1992, s 235A(2)*). It is immaterial whether the applicant has any entitlement to be supplied with the goods or services in question (*TULRCA 1992, s 235A(3)*).

If the court is satisfied that the claim is well-founded, it must make such order as it considers appropriate for requiring the person by whom the act of inducement has been or is likely to be done to take steps for ensuring that no or no further act of inducement is done by him, and that no person engages in further conduct by virtue of his prior inducement (cf **45.16**(*c*) above) (*TULRCA 1992, s 235A(4)*). The court also has power to grant interlocutory relief (*TULRCA 1992, s 235A(5)*).

45.19 CONSEQUENCES FOR EMPLOYEES

For any industrial action, whether or not in contemplation or furtherance of a trade dispute:

(a)   the employee loses his right to pay during the industrial action (see **45.16**(b) above and **Pay – I (34)**);

(b)   he is not entitled to receive jobseeker's allowance or income support, although his family may in some circumstances receive income support (see *Cartlidge v Chief Adjudication Officer* [1986] ICR 256) subject to the deduction of a prescribed sum in respect of notional strike pay (see *Tolley's Social Security and State Benefits Handbook* for further details);

(c)   he is not entitled to any guarantee payment in respect of the days on which he is engaged in industrial action;

(d)   if dismissed during a strike, a participant in that strike may not be able to claim compensation for unfair dismissal (although he will be treated as automatically unfairly dismissed in the circumstances outlined in **45.16**(e) above);

(e)   so far as the computation of periods of continuous employment is concerned (for example, for redundancy and unfair dismissal claims), absence due to participation in a strike will not break continuity, but the period of absence is not counted in the computation. The start of the period of employment will be deemed to be postponed by the appropriate number of days (see **7.11 Continuous Employment**).

45.20 EMPLOYEES WHO MAY NOT STRIKE

Some employees are forbidden by law to strike. These include members of the armed services, prison officers and police officers. In *Ministry of Justice v Prison Officers Association* [2008] EWHC 239 (QB), [2008] ICR 702 Wyn Williams J rejected an argument by the

Prison Officers' Union that he should refuse to grant an injunction to restrain strike action on the basis of the right to freedom of association conferred by *Article 11(1)* of the Convention. That article, as he found, does not confer any right to strike. Whilst that proposition must be regarded as requiring further analysis following the European Court of Human Rights' decision in *Demir v Turkey* (App no 34503/970) (2008) 48 EHRR 1272, [2009] IRLR 766, the European Court since held in *Professional Trades Union for Prison, Correctional and Secure Psychiatric Workers v United Kingdom* (App No 59253/11) (2013) 57 EHRR SE9 that the application challenging the UK's statutory ban on industrial action by prison officers was inadmissible, on the grounds that the matter had already been considered by the Committee on Freedom of Association of the International Labour Organisation.

Attempts have been made to argue that, given that inducement of a breach of statutory duty does not fall within the *TULRCA 1992, s 219* immunity (see **45.3** above), such provisions effectively prohibit organised strike action. But the decisions of the House of Lords in *Associated British Ports v TGWU* [1989] 1 WLR 939 at 970 and of Mantell J in *Wandsworth London Borough Council v NASUWT* [1994] ICR 81 (the point was not argued on appeal), suggest that the courts will be reluctant to construe the relevant statutes so as to reach such a result.

It is a criminal offence for a person 'wilfully and maliciously [to break] a contract of service or of hiring, knowing or having reasonable cause to believe that the probable consequences of his so doing, either alone or in combination with others, will be to endanger human life, or cause serious bodily injury, or to expose valuable property whether real or personal to destruction or serious injury' (*TULRCA 1992, s 240(1)*). The penalty is a fine not exceeding level 2 on the Standard Scale (see **1.10** INTRODUCTION) or imprisonment for not more than three months (*TULRCA 1992, s 240(3)*).

46   Taxation

OUTLINE

46.1   ITEPA 2003

The employment tax legislation is contained in the main in the *Income Tax (Earnings and Pensions) Act 2003* which is referred to in this chapter as *ITEPA 2003*. This is supported by various regulations, including the *Income Tax (Pay As You Earn) Regulations 2003* (*SI 2003/2682*).

46.2   Employment income

For income tax purposes, income from employment includes 'general earnings' and 'specific employment income'.

(a)   General earnings include (in each case, excluding exempt amounts):

   (i)   earnings which are defined by *ITEPA 2003, s 62* as including any salary, wage or fee, gratuities or other profit or benefit obtained if it is money or money's worth, or anything else constituting an emolument of employment ('money's worth' means something of direct monetary value to the employee or capable of being converted into money or something of direct monetary value to the employee); and

   (ii)   amounts treated as earnings which include amounts paid to agency workers (*ss 44–47*), amounts paid through intermediaries (*ss 48–61*) and managed service companies (*s 61A*), benefits in kind (*ss 63–220*), sickness and disability pay (*s 221*), payments of tax by the employer (ss 222, 223), payments to non-approved personal pension arrangements (*s 224*), payments or valuable consideration given for restrictive undertakings (*ss 225, 226*), shares of employee shareholders *(ss 226A–226D)* or balancing charges treated as earnings (*Capital Allowances Act 2001, s 262*).

(b)   Specific employment income includes (in each case, excluding exempt amounts):

   (i)   other non-share related income including benefits from employer-financed retirement benefit schemes (*ss 393–400*) and payments on termination of employment (*ss 401–416*);

   (ii)   share related payments and benefits (*ss 417–554*); and

   (iii)   payments which count as employment income under any other enactment.

(*ITEPA 2003, s 7.*)

General earnings include 'benefits in kind' as per (*a*)(ii) above (see **46.21** et seq below). The taxation of benefits and expenses was reformed with effect from 2016/17. From 6 April 2016 onwards, the tax treatment of expenses and benefits in kind is the same regardless of the earnings level of the employee (subject to an exception for certain lower-paid ministers of religion. However, 2015/16 and earlier tax years, different rules applied depending on whether the employee was a director or earned at a rate of above £8,500 a year or whether the employee was a 'lower-paid employee' earning at a rate of less than £8,500 inclusive of any benefits in kind. From 2016/17 onwards (other than in relation to certain lower-paid ministers of religion) the benefits code applies in its entirety to all employees irrespective of their earnings level (*FA 2015, s 13(1)* (omitting *ITEPA 2003, Pt 3 Ch 11* with effect from 6 April 2016).

In general terms, the amount assessable to tax in respect of a benefit is its cash equivalent value. Unless specific rules apply to determine the calculation of the cash equivalent value of the benefit (as, for example in the case of company cars and fuel, living accommodation, employment-related loans etc), the cash equivalent value is simply the cost to the employer less any amount made good by the employee (*ITEPA 2003, ss 203–206*) (see **46.28** The charging provisions also cover the provision of benefits to the family or household of the employee or director. The benefit is essentially taxed in the same way as if were provided to the employee.

46.3   'Directors and lower-paid employees' – 2015/16 and earlier tax years

The concept of a 'lower-paid employee' was abolished from 6 April 2016. From that date the benefits code applies in its entirety to all employees regardless of their earnings rate, subject to a limited exception for certain lower-paid ministers of religion.

For 2015/16 and earlier tax years, the rules governing the taxability of benefits in kind recognised two categories of employers – directors, and employees earnings at the rate of at least £8,500 a year (P11D employees), and lower-paid employees (P9D employees). P9D employees were only taxed on a limited range of benefits.

As far as directors are concerned, the rules applying for 2015/16 and earlier tax years for P11D employees and directors applied to all 'directors', irrespective of the level of their earnings unless they:

(a)   earned less than £8,500 per year (including all benefits in kind and before deduction of any necessary expenses of the employment); and

(b)   had no material interest (ie the interest does not exceed 5% with or without associates) in the company; and

(c)   were either working full-time as a director or the company was non-profit making and did not hold investments, or was a charity.

Lower-paid employees were employees whose earnings were at the rate of less than £8,500 per year, including all benefits in kind and before deduction of any necessary expenses of the employment.

The distinction between lower paid (or P9D) employees and P11D employees was withdrawn from 6 April 2016. From that date, the benefits code applies in its entirety to all employees regardless of their earnings rate (*FA 2015, s 13(1)*, omitting *ITEPA 2003, Pt 3 Ch 11* with effect from 6 April 2016).

(*ITEPA 2003, ss 63, 67, 68, 216–220.*)

PAY AS YOU EARN (PAYE)

46.4   Definition and earnings limits

PAYE is the statutory system of deducting income tax from the employment income (see **46.2** above) of an employee at the time that the employee is paid by the employer so as to secure, as far as possible, that the income tax liability in respect of the employment income is satisfied by the deductions made. The employer effectively acts as a tax collector for HM Revenue and Customs. In addition, the PAYE system collects National Insurance contributions of both employee and employer. It is also used for the operation of Statutory Sick Pay (SSP). Statutory Maternity Pay (SMP), Statutory Paternity Pay (SPP), , Statutory Adoption Pay (SAP) and Shared Parental Pay (ShPP), to collect student loan repayments and to collect charitable donations under Payroll Giving (see **46.33** below).

Under Real Time Information (RTI) employers are required to send details of pay and deductions to HM Revenue and Customs electronically each time that an employer is paid.

The PAYE system applies to all payments of employment income assessable to income tax in excess of certain defined limits. These limits (the 'PAYE thresholds') are as laid down from time to time by HM Revenue and Customs. For a person with one employment only, the PAYE threshold is broadly aligned with the weekly/monthly equivalent of the personal allowance for income tax.

For 2017/18 the PAYE thresholds are as follows:

Weekly	£221
Monthly	£958
Annual	£11,500

The regulations governing the operation of PAYE are the *Income Tax (Pay As You Earn) Regulations 2003 (SI 2003/2682)*.

46.5   Sources of information

Guidance on PAYE is available on the GOV.UK website (www.gov.uk). HMRC publish guidance for employers on PAYE, which can be found on the GOV.UK website (see www.gov.uk/topic/business-tax/paye). Detailed instructions on the operation of PAYE can also be found in the HM Revenue and Customs booklet 'Employer's Further Guide to PAYE and NICs' (CWG2). The 2017/18 edition is available to download from the GOV.UK website (see www.gov.uk/government/publications/cwg2-further-guide-to-paye-and-national-insurance-contributions).

Guidance on the operation of PAYE is also contained in the HM Revenue and Customs guidance manuals – PAYE Instructions (collection) manual and PAYE Online Manual. Guidance on employment income generally is found in the Employment Income Manual. The manuals are also available on the GOV.UK website (see www.gov.uk/government/collections/hmrc-manuals).

HMRC also publish an online magazine for employers, Employer Bulletin, which is available to download from the GOV.UK website (see www.gov.uk/government/collections/hm-revenue-and-customs-employer-bulletin). The bulletin is published bi-monthly and aims to provide employers and agents with the latest information on payroll topics and other issues that affect them.

To help small employers to work out their PAYE and NIC liabilities, HMRC also publish a free RTI-compatible software package, Basic PAYE Tools, which is available to download from the GOV.UK website (see www.gov.uk/basic-paye-tools). The product is designed for employers with nine or fewer employees and can be used to work out payroll deductions and to produce and send RTI submissions to HMRC.

See also the *Payroll Management Handbook 2008* (or later edition).

46.6   Method of deduction

Employers must maintain (among other documents) a deductions working sheet (P11 or equivalent) for each employee known to be earning amounts above the PAYE threshold. This will generally be maintained electronically by means of a payroll software package as the introduction of real time information (RTI) has effectively rendered manual payrolls obsolete. The employee's tax code determines the amount that the employee is able to earn before paying tax and is used to work out the appropriate amount of tax to be deducted from that employee's wages. The employee's tax code must be recorded on the P11 or equivalent. A tax code will vary to reflect the circumstances of the employee. The tax code number will be the appropriate amount of personal allowances less the final digit. For example, an employee who receives the basic personal allowance for 2017/18 of £11,500 would have a code number of 1500. A suffix or prefix is then added to the code.

The suffix code letter indicates how the code should be updated to reflect changes announced in the Budget. The suffix code letters in use for 2017/18 are as follows:

L = Personal allowance

M = Individual has received 10% of their partner's personal allowance

N = Individual has transferred 10% of their personal allowance to their partner

Y = Personal allowance (born before 6 April 1938)

T = Specific notification required from HM Revenue and Customs.

Sometimes a code will have a prefix instead of a suffix:

D0 = Higher rate tax and no personal allowances)

D1 = Additional rate (and no personal allowances)

K = Where state pension or benefits in kind exceed personal allowances

BR = Basic rate tax and no personal allowances

0T = No personal allowances

NT = No tax to be deducted

Therefore, a person who receives the basic personal allowance for 2017/18 and who has no other adjustments to his or her code has a tax code for 2017/18 of 1150L.

A K code requires an addition to be made to the employee's pay (or to a pension) in order to arrive at taxable pay. This enables the correct amount of tax to be deducted where emoluments such as benefits in kind exceed personal allowances. There is an overriding regulatory limit to ensure that the maximum amount deducted from emoluments in any pay period does not exceed 50% of cash pay after allowing for deductions such as pension contributions and payroll giving.

From 6 April 2016 taxpayers who live in Scotland will pay the Scottish Rate of Income Tax (SRIT). UK rates are reduced by ten percentage points for people who live in Scotland. Scottish taxpayer will pay the reduced UK rate plus the SRIT. For2017/18, the SRIT is 10%, meaning that the basic rate of tax for Scottish taxpayers is the same as the rest of the UK (e.g. a basic rate of 20% applies in the rest of the UK, whereas Scottish basic rate taxpayers pay 10% UK tax plus 10% SRIT – a total of 20%). Scottish taxpayers are identified by a tax code that starts with a letter 'S'. Employers must apply the SRIT to employees with an 'S' tax code.

For 2017/18 the basic rate limit for the UK excluding Scotland is set at £33,500. For Scottish taxpayers, the basic rate band applying to non-savings and non-dividend income is set at £31,500.

The calculation of tax due is generally performed using computerised payroll systems. However, the correct results will only be obtained if the software is up to date and reflects current tax rates. The introduction of RTI and the requirement to report pay and deductions details to HMRC electronically means that manual payrolls are no longer an option. However, employers with nine or fewer employees can use HMRC's free RTI-compatible software package, Basic PAYE Tools.

From May 2017 tax codes will be updated in-year to reflect changes in an employee's circumstances.

Contributions to registered pension schemes and charitable donations through Payroll Giving (see **46.33** below) are deducted from the gross pay before calculation of tax due and in this way the associated tax relief is given at source.

46.7   Employees joining after 6 April

Employees joining after 6 April 2016:

(a)   *Employees holding form P45 from previous employer.* If an employee starts work with a P45 from a previous employer, it may be possible to work out the code from that shown on the P45. If the leaving date is in the 2017/18 tax year, the code is that shown on the P45. If the employee left their previous job in the 2016/17 tax year, the tax code tool on the GOV.UK website (see www.gov.uk/new-employee-tax-code) can be used to ascertain the tax code. If the employee left their previous job before 6 April 2016, the P45 should not be used to work out the tax code. Instead the employee should complete a new starter checklist (see www.gov.uk/government/publications/paye-starter-checklist).

(b)   *New employees, with no form P45.* New employees who join without a P45 will need to provide starter details (which can be provided using the optional starter checklist which is available on the GOV.UK website: see www.gov.uk/government/publications/paye-starter-checklist and declare which of the following statements applies to them:

(A)   This is my first job since 6 April and they have not been receiving taxable Jobseeker's Allowance, Employment and Support Allowance, taxable Incapacity Benefit, State or Occupational Pension.

(B)   This is now my only job, but since last 6 April I have had another job, or received taxable Jobseeker's Allowance, Employment or Support Allowance or taxable Incapacity Benefit. I do not receive a State or Occupational Pension.

(C)   As well as my new job, I have another job or receive a State or Occupational Pension.

The tax code used depends on which statement applies, as indicated in the table below.

Starting statement	Tax code
A	1150L cumulative
B	1150L on week 1/month 1 basis
C	BR cumulative
Starter declaration not completed	0T week 1/month 1

Under RTI, employers must supply details of new starters to HM Revenue and Customs electronically as part of the Full Payment Submission (FPS).

46.8   Employee leaving or dismissed

Form P45 must still be issued to an employee who leaves the employer's employment. Form P45 is the mechanism by which details of the employee's pay to date and tax deducted are transferred from one employer to the next.

Under RTI the employer is not required to send form P45 to HM Revenue and Customs. Instead, leaver details notified to HM Revenue and Customs as part of the FPS.

Where payments are made to the former employee after the form P45 has been issued, tax must be deducted using the 0T code rather than by reference to the employee's normal tax code. Where payments are made after the P45 has been issued, under no circumstances should a further form P45 should be issued. Code 0T must also be used for share-based payments made after the issue of form P45.

If the amount of the payment made after the leaving date is known before the employee leaves, it must be entered on the deductions working sheet by reference to the date of the future payment. In this situation, the amount is therefore included within the amount shown on form P45.

Pay in lieu of notice. Where an employee is dismissed with pay in lieu of notice, the taxation treatment is dependent on the nature of the payment. The tax treatment of pay in lieu of notice is complex and the term is often used to describe payments with varying characteristics. As a general rule, pay in lieu of notice is treated in the same way as a payment of wages or salary if the employee was contractually entitled to it or had an expectation of receiving it. A contractual PILON is one which has its source in the contractual arrangements between the employer and the employee. For a PILON to be contractual, it does not have to be set out in the main employment contract. It may be contained in another document, such as a side letter to the contract, the staff handbook, the letter of appointment, a redundancy agreement or an agreement with the relevant union. In determining whether a PILON is contractual (and therefore the appropriate tax treatment) it is important to check all relevant documents, not just the main contract of employment. However, HM Revenue and Customs accepts that where a contract or other supporting documentation makes no reference to pay in lieu of notice and the employee has no expectation of receiving pay in lieu of notice, a payment of such compensation would generally be for an employer's breach of contract. In that case, the payment will come within the charging provisions relating to termination payments (*ITEPA 2003, ss 401–403*) and so the first £30,000 of the payment would be exempt from tax. HM Revenue and Customs' views on what constitutes a contractual payment are set out in HM Revenue and Customs' Employment Income Manual EIM 12975ff.

In *Delaney v Staples* [1992] 1 All ER 944 it was held that *non-contractual* payments in lieu of notice were not to be regarded as wages for the purposes of what is now *ERA 1996, s 27*. However, HM Revenue and Customs takes the view that 'what constitutes wages under employment law is not the same as what constitutes emoluments under tax law'.

In *Richardson v Delaney* [2001] STC 1328 it was held that a discretionary PILON was taxable as earnings. The contract was brought to an end by mutual consent and a payment agreed in lieu of notice. The court found that there was no breach of earnings and consequently the payment was taxable as earnings.

In *EMI Group Electronics Ltd v Coldicott* [1999] STC 803 the Court of Appeal confirmed the HM Revenue and Customs' long-standing practice that *contractual* payments in lieu of notice are assessable as employment income but it was accepted that payments made to junior employees were not taxable since those employees had no contractual right to them. See HM Revenue and Customs' Employment Income Manual EIM 12977

Care should be taken when drafting termination letters and ambiguous language can cause confusion as to the correct tax treatment. This was illustrated in the decision in *Ibe v McNally (Inspector of Taxes)* [2005] EWHC 1551 (Ch), [2005] STC 1426.

Legislation is to be introduced to treat all payments in lieu of notice, regardless of whether they are contractual or non-contractual, as payments of earnings with effect from 6 April 2018. This will mean that from that date, all payments in lieu of notice will be taxed in full without the benefit of the £30,000 exemption. Also from 6 April 2018, employer's National Insurance contributions will be payable on termination payments in excess of the £30,000 exempt limit. However, no employee contributions will be due on payments taxed as termination payments rather than as earnings and the first £30,000 of a termination payment will remain free from income tax.

46.9   Employee retiring on pension from employer

The employer must notify the tax office within 14 days and continue operating the code but on the non-cumulative basis until revised instructions are received from the tax office. However, if the pension is to be paid by the trustees of a pension scheme etc, the employee should be treated as leaving (see **46.8** above).

46.10   Death of employee

If an employee dies the employer must complete a form P45. Under RTI, the death of an employee is notified to HM Revenue and Customs electronically as for starters and leavers as part of the FPS. The same procedure applies if a pensioner dies.

The same rules apply in the case of payments made after the date of death as for payments made after the date an employee leaves (see **46.8** above).

46.11   Students employed during vacation

A student is treated in the same way as any other employee, even if the student only works during the holidays.

46.12   Employees working abroad

The general rule is an employer must continue to operate PAYE in the normal way in respect of payments made to employees who go abroad to work. An employee who works abroad for a year or more may be able to obtain UK tax relief on their earnings and the employer may be permitted to use special PAYE arrangements. Where an employee has an overseas contract, tax may be deducted in that country. The employer is advised to contact both HM Revenue and Customs and the overseas authority to ensure that he is clear as to his obligations.

The residence status of an individual for tax purposes is determined by reference to the statutory residence test.

An employer who has a place of business in the UK must pay Class 1 National Insurance contributions on all earnings paid during the first 52 weeks that an employee is working abroad where the employee is ordinarily resident in the UK and was resident in the UK immediately before starting the employment abroad.

Further guidance on the procedures that should be followed in respect of employees going abroad to work can be found on the GOV.UK website at www.gov.uk/paying-employees -working-abroad.

46.13   Refunds of tax when employee is away from work

Because of the cumulative nature of the PAYE system, periods during which no emoluments are received may give rise to a right to repayments of tax. In the case of such an absence, eg unpaid leave, a repayment may be made by the employer to the employee. This procedure is unlikely to apply to short absences caused by sickness as any statutory sick pay (see **44.6** Sickness and Sick Pay) paid to the employee is taxable in the usual way. Tax is also chargeable on any payment made by the employer (or by a third party under arrangements made by the employer) through a sick pay scheme.

An employer must not refund tax to an employee who is absent from work in consequence of a trade dispute in which the employee is involved, until the dispute has ended unless the employer is authorised to make a tax refund on form P48, or the employee leaves during a trade dispute.

Where an employee becomes unemployed (see **46.8**) and claims jobseekers' allowance or employment support allowance or receives universal credit, any tax refund due to him will be made by the Jobcentre Plus. However, because these benefits are taxable, payment of any refund will be withheld until the person obtains a new job or, if earlier, until the end of the tax year. Where the employee does not claim either jobseekers allowance or income support and sends Part 2 and 3 of form P45 to HM Revenue and Customs with a declaration that he/she will remain unemployed for the rest of the tax year, any tax refund due will be paid by HM Revenue and Customs.

REAL TIME PAYE INFORMATION (RTI): REPORTING INFORMATION TO HM REVENUE AND CUSTOMS

46.13a Real Time Information (RTI) requires employers to submit pay and deductions information to HMRC electronically each time that an employee is paid. As information must be reported electronically, RTI necessitates the use of a computerised payroll. Small employers with nine or fewer employees can use HM Revenue and Customs Basic PAYE Tools software package, which is free to download from the GOV.UK website (see www.gov.uk/basic-paye -tools).

Under RTI, employers report payments to HMRC as part of their normal payroll activity. The same procedure applies irrespective of whether the payments made via the payroll are payments of pay or pension. The legislation imposes a requirement on employers to report pay and deductions details to HM Revenue and Customs 'on or before' the time at which payment is made to the employee. Penalties apply where RTI returns are made late in more than one month in the tax year. However, HMRC allow a three-day period of grace before levying a penalty for a late return, although it should be noted that if an employer habitually files returns within this three-day period, HMRC may charge a penalty. The employer may need to complete an Employer Payment Summary (EPS) in addition to or instead of the FPS. An EPS is made in various circumstances including where no payments are made to employees in the period or where the employee have received funding from HM Revenue and Customs.

Under RTI, employers supply starter and leaver details as part of the FPS process. However, they must also still provide an employee who leaves with a P45 as this remains the mechanism by which pay and tax details are transferred from one employer to another. If an employee joins without a form P45 the employer will need to collate the starter details required for the FPS submission (see **46.7**).

At the end of the tax year, employers must comply with the RTI end of year procedures, for which see **46.15**).

Detailed guidance on the reporting obligations under RTI can be found on the GOV.UK website at www.gov.uk/running-payroll/reporting-to-hmrc.

46.13b Penalties for late RTI returns

Penalties may be charged for late RTI returns. Under RTI, employers must submit a FPS to HM Revenue and Customs on or before making a payment to an employee. Where no payments are made in a particular tax month, the employer must submit an EPS instead. A penalty may be charged where HM Revenue and Customs have not received a FPS or an FPS for a particular tax month as expected.

The penalty is a monthly late filing penalty, but no more than one penalty will be charged each month regardless of the number of submissions made. Employers are allowed to make returns late for one month in the tax year without being penalised as no penalty is charged for the first month in the tax year in which the returns are filed late. Thereafter a fixed penalty will be charged each time that a return if filed late. The size of the penalty will depend on the number of employees within the PAYE scheme, as shown in the table below.

Number of employees	Monthly late filing penalty
1 – 9	£100
10 – 49	£200
50 – 249	£300
250 or more	£400

An additional penalty of 5% of the tax and NIC which should have been shown on the return may also be charged if the return is more than three months late.

The penalties are charged in-year and are issued quarterly (July, October, January and April). HM Revenue and Customs will issue electronic warnings where expected information has not been received. The FPS includes a RTI 'late reporting reason' data item to enable employers to tell HM Revenue and Customs why they are filing a submission late. HMRC allow a three-day period of grace before a submission is regarded as 'late'.

46.14 PAYE – PAYMENT OF TAX BY EMPLOYER

The employer must pay to the Collector of Taxes, within 17 days (ie by the 22nd of each month) where the payment is made by an approved electronic method or within 14 days of the end of every tax month (ie by the 19th of each month) where payment is made by post, all tax and National Insurance contributions deducted together with the employer's National Insurance contributions; plus any student loan deductions; less any recoveries of statutory maternity pay, statutory paternity pay, statutory adoption pay or shared parental pay (see **32.30 Maternity and Parental Rights** and **44.6 Sickness and Sick Pay**) (where applicable including an amount to compensate for employer's National Insurance contributions thereon). A single remittance is sufficient. Where the deadline falls on a non-banking day, such as weekend or bank holiday, postal payments must reach HM Revenue and Customs on the previous banking day and in the case of electronic payment, cleared funds must reach HM Revenue and Customs' bank account on the previous banking day. If these deadlines are missed the payment will be treated as being made late.

Employers with 250 or more employees are required to make their monthly payments of PAYE electronically. Penalties are charged where PAYE is paid late on more than one occasion during the tax year (see **46.14a**).

Employers who have reasonable grounds for believing that the average monthly total tax and National Insurance to be paid to the Collector will be less than £1,500 are able to make payments quarterly instead of monthly (*reg 70* (before 6 April 2004, *regs 41, 42*)). New employers must notify HM Revenue and Customs if they wish to make quarterly payments, but existing employers need not do so unless a demand is received from HMRC.

46.14   Taxation

Under RTI, where an employer makes no payments to employees during a tax month, the employer must submit an employer payment summary (EPS) to HM Revenue and Customs to advise them of this. In this way, the EPS acts as a nil declaration telling HM Revenue and Customs that no PAYE or NIC is due for the tax month in question.

HM Revenue and Customs has the power under *reg 80* of the PAYE regulations to determine the amount of tax payable where it appears to it that tax may have been payable but has not been paid; and interest at the prescribed rate on unpaid tax in respect of *reg 80* determinations can be charged under *reg 82*.

Interest at the prescribed rate is charged automatically on late payments of PAYE. Interest is charged in-year once the outstanding payment has been made. Interest is charged from the due date to the date on which payment is made. A repayment supplement at the prescribed rate is also available where overpaid deductions are later refunded (*regs 82, 83*).

46.14A   PENALTIES FOR LATE PAYMENT OF PAYE

Employers may suffer a penalty if they do not pay the PAYE they owe on time and in full on more than one occasion in the tax year. The penalty regime applies to all employers including large employers who are required to make payments of PAYE electronically. The penalty amount is a percentage of the amount of PAYE that is owed. No penalty is charged if payment is made late only on one occasion in the tax year and the first late payment is not counted as a default. Thereafter, the penalty rate depends on the number of occasions on which payment is made late. Each late payment after the first one is regarded as a default The penalty rate starts at 1% (2 to 4 defaults), rising to 2% (5 to 7 defaults) then to 3% (8 to 10 defaults) with a top penalty rate of 4% applying to 11 or more defaults. A further penalty of 5% will apply if the any of the PAYE remains unpaid after six months and again after 12 months.

Late payment penalties are levied in-year on a quarterly basis.

Penalties will not be charged if HMRC accept that the employer had a reasonable excuse for the late payment.

46.15   PAYE – END OF YEAR PROCEDURE

RTI end of year procedures.

Under RTI employers supply pay and deductions information to HM Revenue and Customs progressively throughout the tax year. As a result there is no need to file annual returns at the year end. Instead, the employer must indicate on their final Full Payment Submission (FPS) for the tax year that it is the last FPS for the tax year. The final FPS must be submitted on or before the date on which the last payment in the tax year is made to an employee. The final submission can be made either as part of the last FPS, or by means of an EPS or an earlier year update (EYO). Where the submission is made by means of an EPS it must be made by 19 April after the end of the tax year. If the submission is made after that date (of if changes are made to an earlier submission after 19 April), it must be made by means of an EYO. If the final submission is not made before 20 May, a late filing penalty may be charged. The penalty is charged at the rate of £100 for each group or part group of 50 employees for each month or part month that the final submission remains outstanding after 19 May.

Certificate of Pay and Tax Deducted (P60)

The employer is required to provide each employee employed on 5 April at the end of the tax year with a certificate of pay and tax deducted (form P60) by 31 May following the end of the tax year. The P60 (which is usually provided by the payroll software package) can be given to the employee in paper format or electronically.

46.16 Forms P11D and P11D(b)

For 2016/17 onwards, the benefits code in its entirety applies to all employees regardless of their earnings rate (subject to a limited exception for certain lower paid ministers of religion).

Where non-cash benefits and expenses have been provided to employees or directors, a return of those benefits must be made to HM Revenue and Customs by 6 July after the end of the tax year unless (for 2016/17 onwards) those benefits have been taxed via the payroll in a process known as payrolling).

For 2016/17 and later tax years, benefits which have not been payrolled must be notified to HMRC on form P11D. The employer must also submit form P11D(b) by 6 July following the end of the tax year to which it relates. Form P11D is a return of 'Expenses and Benefits' and return P11D(b) is a 'Return of Class 1A National Insurance Contributions' which declares the total amount of Class 1A contributions due to be paid on P11D benefits (see **46.17** below) and includes a declaration that all the required forms P11D have been completed and submitted to HM Revenue and Customs. Form P11D(b) is required regardless of whether of benefits are payrolled.

For self-assessment purposes, employers must provide to each employee or director either a copy of the form P11D or a statement of their benefits by 6 July after the end of the tax year. Where benefits have been payrolled, the employee must be given details of payrolled benefits as well as those returned on form P11D.

Items covered included within a PAYE settlement agreement do not need to be returned on form P11D (or for 2015/16 and earlier years, form P9D). Similarly, items covered by an exemption, including that for qualifying paid and reimbursed expenses which replaced the dispensation regime from 6 April 2016 onwards. See **46.18** in relation to PAYE settlement agreements.

Forms P11D and P11D(b) can be submitted electronically using commercial software packages or via HM Revenue and Customs' Expenses and Benefits Online Service or PAYE Online service. Forms can also be submitted in paper format as electronic submission is not compulsory. They can also be filed using electronic data interchange (EDI) or magnetic media for 2016/17 returns and earlier years. From 2017/18, electronic P11Ds will need to be filed in XML format via the Government Gateway.

46.16a Payrolling

Since 2016/17, employers have been able to choose to account for the tax on a limited range of benefits in kind via the payroll (a process known as 'payrolling') rather than reporting them on form P11D. Employers wishing to payroll benefits must register to do so before the start of the tax year in question using HMRC's online Payrolling Benefits in Kind service (see   https://www.gov.uk/government/publications/payrolling-benefits-in-kind-draft-guidance/payrolling-benefits-in-kind). Employers who wished to payroll benefits for 201718 needed to register before 6 April 2017. The deadline for registering to payroll 2018/19 benefits is 5 April 2018. Where the deadline is missed, HMRC may allow the employer to payroll informally but where this is the case, the employer will still need to report the benefit on form P11D after the year end. Employers choosing to payroll benefits must ensure that they have a payroll software package which is able to support payrolling.

Payrolling is voluntary and employers can choose what benefits are payrolled and for which employees. For 2016/17 employers could payroll all benefits except for vouchers and credit tokens. Employer-provided living accommodation and low interest and interest-free loans. From 2017/18 onwards, the list of benefits which can be payrolled is extended to include non-cash vouchers and credit tokens.

Once an employer has registered to payroll benefits for particular employees, they must continue to do so throughout the tax year unless the employee has insufficient pay to cover the tax on the benefit or the employer stops providing that benefit to the employee. Employers can continue to payroll registered benefits in later tax years – it is not necessary to re-register the benefits before the start of the next tax year. However, employers can change the mix of payrolled benefits before the start of each tax year.

The amount that is payrolled in respect of a non-cash benefit is the cash equivalent of the benefit divided by the employee's pay frequency. For example, if an employee was paid monthly and received private medical insurance with a cash equivalent value of £480, the employee would include £40 as 'pay' each month in respect of the benefit, being the annual cash equivalent value of £480 divided by the number of pay days in the year (12). The tax on the 'pay' of £40 in respect of the benefit is deducted from the employee's cash pay each month.

Employers who choose to payroll must provide employees with a letter explaining what payrolling is and what it means for them. Before 1 June following the end of the tax year, employers must also provide employees with a description of the benefits that have been payrolled and the associated cash equivalent value. Benefits that are taxable and which have not been payrolled must be notified to HMRC by 6 July following the end of the tax year on form P11D. Employers must also make a return of Class 1A National Insurance contributions due on form P11D(b) by the same date, regardless of whether the benefits have been payrolled or returned on form P11D.

Where employers have opted to payroll car and fuel benefits, from 2017/18 changes to these benefits can be notified via the Full Payment Submission (FPS) rather than on form P46(Car). It will become compulsory to notify car and fuel benefits via the FPS from April 2018.

Guidance on payrolling is available on the gov.uk website at www.gov.uk/government/publications/payrolling-benefits-in-kind-draft -guidance/payrolling-benefits-in-kind.

(*Income Tax (Pay As You Earn) Regulations 2003 (SI 2003/2682), Pt 3 Ch 3A* (as inserted by *SI 2015/1927, reg 6*.)

46.17 Class 1A National insurance contributions

Class 1A National Insurance contributions are employer-only contributions payable on most taxable benefits in kind. For 2016/17 a Class 1A liability arises where a benefit is taxable regardless of the earnings level of the employee, unless that benefit is specifically exempt from the Class 1A charge or within the scope of Class 1. For 2015/16 and earlier tax years, a Class 1A liability only arose in respect of taxable benefits provided to P11D employees and directors. For 2015/16 and earlier tax years, no Class 1A National Insurance liability arose in respect of benefits provided to P9D employees, even if the benefit was taxable.

Class 1A National Insurance contributions must be paid by 22 July following the end of the tax year to which they relate if paid electrically (or by 19 July otherwise) and must be reported to HM Revenue and Customs on form P11D(b) (see **46.16** above) by 6 July following the end of the tax year. Employers are still required to submit form P11D(b) where they opt to payroll benefits in kind. Returns filed late may attract a penalty and interest is charged on Class 1A National Insurance contributions paid late. As with PAYE, if the deadline falls on a non-banking day, payment must reach HM Revenue and Customs by the previous banking day.

Class 1A National Insurance contributions are employer-only contributions chargeable at the Class 1A rate (13.8% for 2016/17 and 2017/8). Where an item that would otherwise attract a Class 1A charge is included within a PAYE settlement agreement (see **46.18**), Class 1B contributions are payable instead.

(*Social Security Contributions and Benefits Act 1992, ss 10, 10ZA; Child Support, Pensions and Social Security Act 2000, ss 74, 75*). For further details of Class 1A contributions, see *Tolley's National Insurance Contributions 2006/07* (or later edition).

46.18 PAYE Settlement Agreements

A PAYE Settlement Agreements is an agreement with HM Revenue and Customs whereby the employer can settle, in a single payment, the income tax and National Insurance liability on certain expenses payments and benefits provided to employees. Such expenses payments and benefits do not then need to be processed through the PAYE system or recorded on forms P11D. A formal written agreement to make such a payment must be made with HM Revenue and Customs by 6 July following the end of the tax year.

The benefits which are covered by the agreement are subject to tax and Class 1B National Insurance contributions which must be paid by 22 October where payment is made electronically (or by 19 October otherwise). Class 1B National Insurance contributions are payable on the benefits that would otherwise be subject to Class 1 or Class 1A contributions if they were not included in the agreement. The rate of Class 1B contributions is 13.8% for 2016/17 and 2017/18. The tax payable must be 'grossed-up' at either the basic or higher rate of tax depending on the liability of the employees concerned since the payment of the tax liability is itself a benefit subject to tax.

Class 1B National Insurance contributions are payable on the aggregate of the total value of the benefits and the grossed-up amount of income tax due.

A PAYE Settlement Agreement is not suitable for all benefits in kind. The items which may be included within a PAYE Settlement Agreement are set out in HM Revenue and Customs Statement of Practice 5/96.

The procedures for setting up a PAYE Settlement Agreement are to be simplified from 6 April 2018. From that date it will no longer be necessary to agree the PAYE Settlement Agreement with HMRC in advance.

46.19 PAYE ONLINE

The PAYE online service was used to provide information to HMRC electronically prior to the introduction of RTI. It can also be used to send and receive payroll information and can be used by employers, agents and payroll bureaux alike. Since the introduction of RTI, PAYE Online can be used for P11Ds and P11D(b)s and for a range of other forms, notices and reminders. Expenses and benefits forms can also be submitted using the HM Revenue and Customs' Expenses and Benefits Online Service.

Before using the service, employers and agents must register on the HM Revenue and Customs' web page and then activate the service using the activation PIN that is sent through the post. Employers must be registered for PAYE Online in order to be able to send pay and deductions information to HMRC electronically under RTI.

46.19A SECURITY FOR PAYE

Since 6 April 2012, HM Revenue and Customs have been to ask employers to pay a security where there is a serious risk that the employer in question will not pay over PAYE and NIC to HMRC. The required security will usually take the form of a cash deposit from the business or director, which will be held in a joint taxpayer/HMRC bank account, or in the form of a bond from an approved financial institution which is payable on demand.

The power to require a security will only be exercised for employers who deliberately seek to defraud the Government. This includes employers who deliberately choose not to pay, who engage in pheonixism (whereby the business evades tax by becoming insolvent and then setting up a new company almost immediately to continue trading), companies that have no qualms about building up large PAYE and NIC debts and companies that do not respond to HMRC's attempts contact them to address their tax issues.

The amount of security required will be calculated on a case-by-case basis depending on the amount of tax that is at risk and the previous behaviour of the employer, Employers who are asked for a security for PAYE can appeal against this decision. Employers who are asked for a security and who fail to provide it risk prosecution by HMRC and may be fined.

46.20 RECORDS

The PAYE regulations stipulate various records that employers must keep for PAYE purposes. The records that the employer is required to maintain, but which do not need to be sent to HM Revenue and Customs, must be retained for not less than three years after the end of the year to which they relate. Under self-assessment, regulations require employees to keep sufficient records to enable them to make a correct and complete return.

46.21 TAXABLE BENEFITS – GENERAL RULES

Detailed information on the tax treatment of benefits in kind is to be found in *Tolley's Income Tax 2017/18*. Concise factual information, in tabular form, is contained in *Tolley's Tax Data 2017/18*. A brief account of general principles in relation to those benefits most commonly derived from employment is given in this paragraph and in **46.22–46.28** below. Special rules applying to employee share schemes are outlined briefly in **46.29–46.33** below.

The regime for taxing expenses and benefits was fundamentally reformed from 2016/17 onwards. From that date, the benefits code in its entirety applies to all employees irrespective of their earnings rate (subject to a limited exception for certain lower paid ministers of religion). For 2015/16 and earlier tax years, 'lower paid' employees (i.e. those earning at a rate of less than £8,500 inclusive of the cash equivalent of benefits in kind) were only taxed on a limited range of benefits, whereas the full benefits code applied to directors (irrespective of their earnings rate) and to employees earning at a rate of at least £8,500 a year. The £8,500 threshold and the concept of a 'lower paid' employee were abolished from 6 April 2016.

Some of the main taxable benefits are as follows.

(a) Expense payments and allowances – taxable subject to exemption for actual expenses incurred in the performance of the duties; see **46.28** below (*ITEPA 2003, ss 70–72*).

(b) Cash vouchers – taxed on their redemption value.

Non-cash vouchers and transport vouchers – taxed on the cost to the employer of providing them less any contribution from employee (unless used to obtain certain non-taxable benefits).

Credit tokens – taxed on the cost to the employer of the money, goods or services obtained less any contribution from employee (unless used to obtain certain non-taxable benefits).

(*ITEPA 2003, ss 73–96.*)

(c) 'Living accommodation' – taxed on the annual value (as defined) or the actual rent paid by the employer if greater, subject to exemptions (eg where the employee is a representative occupier). For accommodation costing in excess of £75,000 an additional charge is made on the excess value over £75,000 (*ITEPA 2003, ss 97–113*).

(d) Cars, vans and related expenses – taxed on the cash equivalent values, see **46.24** to **46.27** below *(ITEPA 2003, ss 114–172)*. For cars the cash equivalent depends on the level of CO2 emissions and the list price, and for car fuel, the determinant is the level of CO2 emissions (which determines the appropriate percentage) and the multiplier set by HMRC. Vans are taxed by reference to a scale charge. A separate fuel charge also applies to vans.

(e) Interest-free or reduced interest employment-related loans – the taxable benefit is the difference between the interest paid (if any) and the 'official rate' of interest at a rate prescribed by the Treasury. There are certain reliefs for loans made at fixed rates not below market value when made, and loans for some specified purposes. No tax charge arises on loans made to employees on commercial terms where the employer lends to the general public. Nor is there any charge where the aggregate value of beneficial loans does not exceed £10,000 at any time in the tax year..

Loans written off are taxed on the amount written off.

(ITEPA 2003, ss 173–191.)

(f) Shares and securities – an employee who is given shares or securities or options over shares and securities, or is allowed to acquire them on terms more favourable than those available to the public, is taxed on the value of the benefit he receives. Tax and National Insurance advantages are available in relation to certain approved share option and share incentive schemes *(ITEPA 2003, ss 192–200)*.

(g) Assets gifted – if new, charged at cost to employer and if used, generally taxed at market value *(ITEPA 2003, ss 203, 204)*.

(h) Mileage allowances paid to employees using their own vehicles for business journeys– taxed on excess over approved amounts *(ITEPA 2003, ss 229–232, 235, 236)*.

(i) Medical treatment or insurance premiums, unless for treatment outside the UK while the employee is working abroad or the treatment is 'recommended medical treatment' the cost of which is no more than £500 a year *(ITEPA 2003, ss 320C, 325)*.

(j) Relocation expenses – non-qualifying expenses and benefits and qualifying expenses and benefits exceeding £8,000 per move *(ITEPA 2003, ss 271–289)*.

(k) Use of employer's assets – land taxable at annual value, other assets at 20% of market value when first lent or rental charge if higher *(ITEPA 2003, ss 203–205)*. Exemptions are available for computers loaned prior to 6 April 2006 (costing up to £2,500) and bicycles. Special rules apply to company cars, company vans, and living accommodation. No charge arises in respect of employer-provided mobile phones (limited to one per employee).

(l) Services supplied by employer, such as in-house goods or services provided at less than cost – taxed on the direct extra (marginal) cost the employer incurs, less any payments made by the employee or director. This was found to be the correct way of computing such benefits in *Pepper (Inspector of Taxes) v Hart* [1993] AC 593, [1993] ICR 291, HL.

46.22 Benefits taxable on 'lower-paid' employees – 2015/16 and earlier tax years

The taxation of benefits and expenses was reformed from 6 April 2016. From that date, the benefits code in its entirety applies in its entirety to all employees regardless of their earnings rate (subject to a limited exception for certain lower paid ministers of religion). The concept of a 'lower paid employee' and the £8,500 threshold were abolished from 6 April 2016 *(FA 2015, s 13(1)* (omitting *ITEPA 2003, Pt 3, Ch 11* with effect from 6 April 2016).

For 2015/16 and earlier tax years, lower-paid employees were only taxed on a limited range of benefit and the majority of benefits that may be provided to an employee were not taxable when provided to those employees in an excluded employment, ie employees who are not directors and who earn at a rate of less than £8,500 per annum including expenses payments and benefits. However, some benefits were taxable on all employees irrespective of the level of the employee's earnings. The benefits that fell into this category are as follows:

(a)   Vouchers and credit tokens – as per **46.21**(b) above.

(b)   'Living accommodation' – as per **46.21**(c) above.

(c)   Loans written off – taxed on amount written off.

(d)   Non-business related expenses and personal expenses paid on the employee's behalf – expenses under £25 can be ignored.

(e)   Relocation expenses – as per **46.21**(j) above.

(f)   Assets gifted to employee – taxed at second hand value.

Where for 2015/16 and earlier tax years, these benefits were provided to an employee earning at a rate of less than £8,500 a year, they had to be returned to HM Revenue and Customs on form P9D by 6 July following the end of the tax year to which they relate (see **46.16**).

46.23 Tax-free benefits

A number of exemptions exist which enable a benefit to be provided free of tax. However, in the majority of cases, the exemption is conditional on certain conditions being met. It should be noted that from 6 April 2017 onwards, the majority of exemptions do not apply where the benefit is made available under an optional remuneration scheme, such as a salary sacrifice or flexible remuneration scheme, or where a cash alternative is offered instead. See **46.27A** for the rules applying to salary sacrifice schemes.

(a)   Meals provided in a canteen – not assessable, but taxable if not provided for the staff generally *(ITEPA 2003, s 317)*. From 6 April 2011 the exemption does not apply if the meals are made available under salary sacrifice arrangements.

(b)   Contributions to registered pension schemes – contributions by an employer are not taxable.

(c)   Medical insurance premiums or medical treatment outside the UK where the employee performs duties abroad but not including the cost of an air ambulance back to or treatment in the UK *(ITEPA 2003, s 325)*. Medical check-up, health screening, eye tests and corrective appliances (such as glasses) can also be provided tax-free as long as certain conditions are met. With effect from 1 January 2015, the provision medical treatment recommended to an employee as part of occupational health services designed to help the employee to return to work sooner is exempt, subject to a cap of £500 per employee per tax year *(ITEPA 2003, s 320C)*.

(d)   Childcare facilities, such as workplace nurseries, for employees' children under 18 provided by the employer alone or with other employers, local authorities etc. Since 6 April 2005 the exemption has also applied (subject to qualifying conditions) to the provision of childcare at or away from the workplace at registered, non-residential facilities provided by the employer (either alone or in partnership with other parties but financed and managed wholly by the employer). Care provided by means of a workplace nurseries is tax-free without limit as long as the associated conditions are met. Employers can also provide childcare vouchers and/or employer supported childcare tax-free up to certain limits. Certain conditions must be met. The exemption applies (subject to the conditions) to the provision of childcare vouchers up to the weekly limit (plus the cost of supplying the vouchers) used to obtain qualifying childcare and to the provision of employer-supported childcare. (*ITEPA 2003, ss 84(2A), 270A, 318–318D; FA 2004, s 78, Sch 13*). The tax-free weekly limit depends on the date that the employee joined the childcare or voucher scheme and the employee's marginal rate of tax. The limit for employees who joined before 6 April 2011 is set at £55 per week, regardless of their marginal rate of tax. For 2015/16 and 2016/17 the limit is £55 per week for a basic rate taxpayer, £28 per week for a higher rate taxpayer £25 per week for an additional rate taxpayer The relief is worth £11 per week to all employees who join the scheme after 6 April 2011 regardless of their marginal rate of tax. The exemptions for employer supported childcare and childcare vouchers is being phased out as a result of the Government-supported childcare scheme which was introduced from 28 April 2017. Under this scheme, parents are able to open an online account to cover the cost of childcare with a registered provider. The Government will provide a 20p top-up for every 80p that the parents pay into the account. The top-up is capped at £2,000 per child per tax year (or £4,000 per year where the child is disabled). The top-up will be tax-free. Employees will be able to join tax-exempt voucher and employer-supported schemes offered by their employer until April 2018 and once in a scheme will be able to remain in it as long as the employer continues to offer the scheme. Alternatively, the employee can opt to leave the scheme and join the Government top-up scheme instead. The exemption for employer-supported childcare and childcare vouchers remain available beyond April 2017 where provision is made under a salary sacrifice or other optional remuneration arrangement.

(e) Work-related training (*ITEPA 2003, ss 250–260*) and outplacement counselling services for employees who are or become redundant. Also welfare counselling (*SI 2000/2080*).

(f) For employees starting a new job or moving with their existing employer, qualifying relocation expenses and benefits up to the value of £8,000 per move (*ITEPA 2003, ss 271–289*).

(g) In-house workplace sports and recreational facilities provided by employers for use by the staff generally, provided overnight accommodation is not available and the facilities are not on domestic premises. The exemption does not cover the use of assets such as yachts, cars and aircraft for private use (*ITEPA 2003, ss 261–263*).

(h) The provision of living accommodation for employees (but not directors) in certain circumstances where it is necessary for their job. This exemption extends to the employer's payment of employees' council tax. Accommodation provided as a result of a security threat is also exempt (*ITEPA 2003, ss 99, 100*).

(i) The provision of accommodation, supplies or services used by the employee in performing the duties of the employment, provided that any private use is insignificant, and that the sole purpose of providing the benefit is to enable the employee to perform the duties (from 6 April 2000) (*ITEPA 2003, s 316*).

(j) Alterations and additions to premises of a structural nature or landlord's repairs to premises of living accommodation which is provided by reason of a person's employment (*ITEPA 2003, s 313*).

(k) The provision of parking facilities at or near the workplace for a car, cycle or motorcycle (*ITEPA 2003, s 237*).

(l) Provision of travel, accommodation and subsistence during public transport disruption caused by industrial action (*ITEPA 2003, s 245*).

(m)   Provision of transport between home and place of employment or the provision of cars for severely disabled employees (*ITEPA 2003, ss 246, 247*).

(n)   Provision of transport for occasional late night journeys from work to home (*ITEPA 2003, s 248*).

(o)   Private use of mobile phones provided by the employer (from 6 April 1999) – limited to one phone per employee from 6 April 2006 (*ITEPA 2003, s 319*). The exemption applies equally to smartphones (Business Brief 02/12).

(p)   The loan of certain computer equipment provided prior to 6 April 2006 with a value not exceeding £2,500 (equating to a cash equivalent of £500) by the employer to the employee (providing that loans are not restricted to senior employees) (from 6 April 1999). The exemption does not apply to computer equipment loaned to the employee after 5 April 2006.

(q)   Provision of works buses with a seating capacity of nine or more, provided for employees to travel to and from work. Additionally, (from 6 April 2002) where employees benefit from their employer's subsidy of a bus service by receiving free or reduced-price travel, there is no tax charge on this benefit (*ITEPA 2003, ss 242, 243*). Also (from 6 April 2002) there is an exemption for the provision of buses for local shopping services (*SI 2002/205*).

(r)   The loan of bicycles and cycling safety equipment provided for employees to travel from home to work (from 6 April 1999) (*ITEPA 2003, s 244*). This exemption remains available beyond April 2017 where provision is made under a salary sacrifice or other optional remuneration agreement.

(s)   The cost of an annual Christmas party or similar event, providing that it is open to all staff generally and the cost per person attending does not exceed £150. (*ITEPA 2003, s 264*).

(t)   Paid and qualifying reimbursed expenses which would be deductible if the employee met the expense him or herself (from 6 April 2016, replacing the dispensation regime that applied prior to that date) (*ITEPA 2003, s 289A–289E*);

(u)   Trivial benefits costing not more than £50 (subject to an annual cap of £300 where provided to directors of close companies and their families (from 6 April 2016) (*ITEPA 2003, s 323A to 323C*).

46.24 COMPANY CARS, VANS AND FUEL

The provision of company cars, vans and fuel are taxable benefits when available for the private use of the employee.

From 2016/17 onwards, the liability arises regardless of the employee's earnings rate. However, for 2015/16 and earlier tax years, the provision of cars, vans and fuel was not taxable on 'lower-paid employees as defined, see **46.3** above). However, the cash equivalent of the benefit had to be taken into account in determining whether the employee is 'lower paid' and in the case of a company car this may be sufficient to breach the £8,500 threshold.

For 2016/17 onwards the tax charge on company cars, van and fuel available for private arises whenever these are provided to an employee (subject to the availability of any specific exemptions).

46.25 Company cars

The cash equivalent of the benefit derived from the private use of a company car is based on a percentage of the car's list price, graduated according to the level of the vehicle's carbon dioxide (CO_2) emissions. The percentage is set for petrol cars with an adjustment for diesel cars.

The relevant threshold is set at 95g/km for 2013/14 onwards. Where the CO_2 emissions figure is equal to the relevant threshold, the appropriate percentage is set at 18% for 2017/18. Thereafter, the appropriate percentage is increased by 1% for every 5g/km increase in carbon dioxide emissions until the maximum appropriate percentage is reached (37% for 2017/18)). For 2017/18, the maximum charge (of 37%) applies to company cars with CO_2 emissions of 190g/km and above. The actual CO_2 emissions are rounded down to the nearest 5g/km for the purposes of determining the appropriate percentage. However, actual CO_2 emissions are used to determine whether a car is a low or zero emission car.

The appropriate percentage for cars which have emissions below the relevant percentage but of 76g/km or above, have an appropriate percentage of 17% for 2016/17.

For cars which have CO_2 emissions of 75g/km or less, the appropriate percentage depends on whether the emissions fall in the 0-51g/km band or the 51-75g/km band. The appropriate percentage for the lowest band is set at nine per cent in 2017/18. The appropriate percentage for the 51–75g/km band is set at 13 per cent in 2017/18. The government have also provided a commitment to d a two percentage point differential between those bands in 2018/19 and 2019/20. Cars which have no CO_2 emissions are charged as follows for 2017/18:

Engine size	Registration pre 1 January 1998	Registration 1 January 1998 to 30 September 1999
1400cc or less	16%	16%
1401cc to 2000cc	27%	27%
2001cc or more	37%	37%
No cylinder capacity	37% otherwise	37% otherwise

Diesel cars attract a supplement of 3%, subject to the maximum charge of 37%. The supplement was to be removed from 6 April 2016, but it was announced at the time of the 2015 Autumn Statement that it would be retained until 2020.

The 'list price' is the price published by the manufacturer, importer or distributor (inclusive of delivery charges and taxes) at the time of registration. It is important to note that this is unlikely to be the price actually paid by the employer for the car. The list price for the car includes any standard accessories provided with the car, but the price of any optional extras supplied with the car when first made available to the employee, together with any further accessory costing £100 or more must be added in. Where an employee makes a capital contribution to the initial cost of the car, the price of the car for the year of contribution and subsequent years is reduced by that contribution or £5,000 if less. The list price is always used in calculating the cash equivalent value, even if the car was purchased second-hand.

The value of the benefit is reduced proportionately if the car is 'unavailable' for part of the year. The benefit is further reduced (or extinguished) by the amount of contributions which an employee is required to make for private use. Cars more than 15 years old and worth over £15,000 are taxed by reference to their open market value in accordance with special rules for classic cars.

(*ITEPA 2003, ss 114–148.*)

46.26 Car fuel

The benefit on car fuel provided for private motoring in a company car is calculated by applying the car benefit appropriate percentage ascertained in **46.25** above to a multiplier. For 2017/18 the multiplier is set at £22,600 (for 2016/17 the multiplier was set at £22,200). The multiplier is increased annually by inflation.

The value of the fuel benefit is proportionately reduced if the car is not available for part of the year. No charge applies if the employee is required to, and does, make good to the employer the cost of all fuel used for private purposes (including travel between home and work). The charge is proportionately reduced if the employee begins to meet the cost of the fuel provided for private use, or fuel ceases to be provided for private use, from a date part way through the year, provided this condition continues to be met for the rest of the year. However, if the provision of fuel is withdrawn and then reinstated before the end of the year, the charge applies in full.

Before providing fuel for private motoring in a company car, employers and employees should consider whether this is a worthwhile benefit. At current levels of taxation it is unlikely to be a tax-efficient benefit unless private mileage is very high, especially in a climate of falling fuel prices.

Where the employer does not provide a company car driver with fuel and the company car driver uses the company car for business purposes, the employer will usually reimburse the cost of that fuel. HM Revenue and Customs publish 'advisory' fuel rates for company cars which can be used to reimburse employees tax-free mileage payments for business motoring in company cars. The figures may also be used for reimbursement by employers of fuel used for private motoring. The advisory rates will not be binding where the employer can demonstrate that the cost of business motoring is higher than the advisory rates. With effect from 1 March 2017, the rates are as follows:

Engine size	Petrol	LPG
1,400cc or less	11p	7p
1,401 to 2,000cc	14p	9p
Over 2,000cc	22p	14p

Engine size	Diesel
1,600cc or less	9p
1601cc to 2000cc	11p
Over 2,000cc	13p

The rates are revised quarterly (*ITEPA 2003, ss 149–153.*)

46.27 Vans

The provision of a company van weighing no more than 3.5 tonnes for the private use of employees is taxed by reference to an annual scale charge. For 2017/18 the charge is £3,230 a year. It was set at £3,170 for 2016/17. It is increased annually in line with inflation. The charge is reduced proportionately if the van is not available for the whole year, or is unavailable for 30 consecutive days or more. Payments by an employee towards private use of the van will also reduce the tax charge. Special provisions apply where vans are shared between several employees. Since 6 April 2005, no charge has applied to employees who have to take their van home and are not allowed, and do not make, any private use of the van (insignificant use being disregarded).

The zero charge for electric and other zero-emission vans that applied for a five-year period from 6 April 2010 came to an end on 5 April 2015. Following the abolition of the zero charge, the charge for zero-emission vans is being increased progressively, with the charge being set at 20% of the full van benefit charge for 2015/16, 2016/17 and 2017/18, 40% for 2018/19, 60% for 2019/20, 800% for 2020/21 and 90% for 2021/22. Zero emission vans available for private use will pay the full van benefit charge from 2022/23 Consequently, the charge for electric and other zero-emission vans is set at £646 (20% of £3,230) for 2017/18.

A separate fuel scale charge applies where fuel is provided for private mileage in the company van. For 2017/18 the charge is set at £610 (for 2016/17 the charge was set at £598) (*ITEPA 2003, s 248A*).

46.27A   SALARY SACRIFICE ARRANGEMENTS

Salary sacrifice arrangements have in the past been a popular way of enabling employees to take advantages of the tax exemptions available in respect of certain benefits in kind without passing the cost of providing those benefits onto the employer.

Under a salary sacrifice arrangement, the employee gives up an amount of cash salary in return for a benefit in kind. Where the benefit in kind is exempt from tax and National Insurance, under the rules applying prior to 6 April 2017 there is no tax or National Insurance to pay on the benefit in kind. The employee saves tax and primary Class 1 National Insurance on the salary given up in exchange for the benefit and the employer saves secondary Class 1 National Insurance. Salary sacrifice arrangements were often used to take advantage of the tax and National Insurance exemptions available for childcare vouchers and mobile telephones.

However, new valuation rules introduced from 6 April 2017 seriously reduce the advantages associated with salary sacrifice arrangements and mean that for all but a handful of protected benefits, the benefit of any associated tax exemption is lost where the benefit is provided through a salary sacrifice or other optional remuneration arrangement, or where a cash alternative to a benefit is offered instead.

Under the new valuation rules, the amount charged to tax where the benefit is provided under a salary sacrifice or other optional remuneration agreement or where a cash alternative is offered instead is the amount of salary foregone or the cash alternative offered where this is higher that the cash equivalent value computed in accordance with normal rules. As the cash alternative is nil where an exemption applies, under these valuation rules the amount charged to tax will be the cash foregone or the cash alternative, as appropriate.

The new valuation rules do not apply to the following protected benefits:

- pension savings;
- employer-provided pension advice;
- childcare and childcare vouchers;
- cycles and cyclists' safety equipment under cycle to work schemes; and
- ultra-low emission cars.

As such, they continue to benefit from associated tax exemptions where provided via a salary sacrifice or other optional remuneration scheme or where a cash alternative is offered. In the cash of a low emission car, the benefit is taxed according to the cash equivalent value calculated under the company car rules rather than by reference to any cash alternative offered where this is higher than the cash equivalent.

Where an arrangement is in place on 5 April 2017, the start date of the new rules is delayed until the earlier of the date on which the contract ends, is modified or renewed, and 6 April 2021 where the benefit taken in exchange is a car (other than an ultra low emissions car) living accommodation or school fees, and 6 April 2018 in all other cases.

TAX RELIEF FOR EXPENSES AND EXEMPTION FOR QUALIFYING PAID AND REIMBURSED EXPENSES

46.28 Tax relief for expenses

Tax relief is available for expenses incurred wholly, exclusively and necessarily in the performance of the duties. This is an especially difficult test to satisfy and it must be shown that the employee is obliged to incur and pay the expense as the office holder. Similarly, reimbursements to employees (other than employees in an excluded employment, as defined in **46.3** above) in respect of expenses, or any sum put at their disposal to cover expenses (such as for business travel and subsistence), are treated as earnings and relief can be claimed for the allowable part (*ITEPA 2003, ss 333–336*, previously *ICTA 1988, s 198*).

For 2016/17 and later tax years, expenses that are fully deductible are exempt from tax if paid or reimbursed by the employer (see **45.28A**). The exemption replaced the dispensation regime applying for 2015/16 and earlier tax years.

46.28a Exemption for qualifying paid and reimbursed expenses

An exemption, which applies for 2016/17 and later tax years, is available where the expense that is paid or reimbursed is fully deductible by the employee (*ITEPA 2003, s 289A*). The exemption is conditional on two conditions being met. Condition A is that the payer or another person operates a system for checking that the employee is incurring and paying amounts in respect of expenses of the same kind and a deduction would be allowed in respect of those expenses. Condition B is neither the payer nor any other person operating the system knows or suspects or could reasonably be expected to know or suspect that the employee had not incurred and paid an amount in respect of the expenses or that a deduction would not be allowed in respect of the amount. The exemption is not be available if the payment or reimbursement is provided pursuant to a salary sacrifice arrangement.

Also from 6 April 2016 the employer can instead apply to HMRC to pay expenses tax-free in accordance with an agreed flat rate (*ITEPA 2003, s 289B*).

46.28b Dispensations – 2015/16 and earlier tax years

To avoid unnecessary administration, where expenses payments or benefits did no more than cover expenses incurred wholly, exclusively and necessarily in the performance of the duties, for 2015/16 and earlier years, the employer could obtain a dispensation from HM Revenue and Customs. Such a dispensation avoided the need for employer to include the expenses payments and benefits on the employee's form P11D for tax and Class 1A National Insurance purposes or the expenses payments in the employee's gross pay for tax and Class 1 National Insurance purposes. The employee was relieved from the need to make an associated claim for relief to offset the taxable benefit that would otherwise arise.

The dispensation regime is abolished for 2016/17 and later tax years (*FA 2015, s 12*). It is replaced by an exemption for qualifying paid or reimbursed expenses.

46.29 EMPLOYEE SHARE SCHEMES

Tax advantages are available where employees are provided with shares or share options via an approved share or share option scheme.

Shares and share options can also be made available to employees by means of unapproved schemes. Although these lack the tax advantages available to approved schemes, they are not bound by the associated conditions and offer more flexibility.

46.29a Savings-related share option schemes

Savings-related share option schemes are tax-advantaged schemes established in accordance with *ITEPA 2003 ss 516–520, Sch 3* (amended by *FA 2003, Schs 21, 22*) whereby a company may establish a scheme for its employees to obtain options to acquire the company's shares without charge to income tax either on the value of the options or on any subsequent increase in the value of the shares before the options are exercised. The scheme must be linked to an approved savings scheme (subject to a monthly limit of £500 (£250 prior to 6 April 2014)) to provide the funds for the acquisition of the shares when the option is exercised. For capital gains tax purposes, the market value is not substituted for the consideration given so the base cost is the amount paid for both the shares and the option. For further details of the scheme rules, see *Tolley's Income Tax 2005/06* (or later edition).

46.30 Company share option schemes

A company share option plan (CSOP) is a tax-advantaged share option plan set up in accordance with *ITEPA 2003, ss 521–526, Sch 4* (as amended by *FA 2003, Sch 21 para 16*). The scheme applies to options granted from 17 July 1995 (before that date, options were granted under what was known as the 'executive share option scheme' which provided more generous tax relief). The aggregate market value of shares acquired under the option and any other approved options held by the employee (other than savings-related schemes) must not exceed £30,000. There is no tax charge when the options are granted, if all the conditions have been complied with. Options under the scheme have to be exercised between three and ten years after being granted but may be exercised within three years of the grant where the individual ceases to be an employee due to injury, disablement redundancy or retirement. Options granted before 9 April 2003 must be exercised between three and ten years after being granted (without exception), and not more frequently than once in every three years. For capital gains tax purposes, the base cost is the amount paid for both the shares and the option. For further details of the plan rules, see *Tolley's Income Tax 2005/06* (or later edition).

46.31 Share incentive plans

Share incentive plans were introduced by *FA 2000, s 47, Sch 8*, and were originally known as the all-employee share ownership plan. The legislation is now found in *ITEPA 2003, ss 418, 488–515, Sch 2* (amended by *FA 2003, Schs 21, 22*). Share Incentive Plans (SIPs) are intended to be available to all employees, and were designed to replace profit-sharing schemes. Employees can receive up to £3,600 (£3,000 prior to 6 April 2014) worth of free shares per year, with the option of purchasing shares up to £1,800 per year (£1,500 per year prior to 6 April 2014) by deductions from salary. For every share purchased, the employee can be given two free shares. To remain free of tax and National Insurance, all shares acquired must be held in the plan for a specified period of time, normally at least three years. Dividends of up to £1,500 per employee per tax year can be reinvested tax-free in additional shares in the company. Withdrawals of shares from the plan are not subject to capital gains tax and they are treated as acquired by the employee at their market value at that time. For further details of the plan rules, see *Tolley's Income Tax 2005/06* (or later edition).

46.32   Enterprise management incentives

The 'enterprise management incentive scheme' was introduced by *FA 2000, s 62, Sch 14* and amended by *FA 2001, s 62, Sch 14*. The legislation is now contained within *ITEPA 2003, ss 527–541, Sch 5*. The scheme allows small independent trading companies to reward employees with tax-advantaged share options worth up to £120,000 per employee. Any gain on the sale of such shares is chargeable to capital gains tax. The company must be an independent UK company carrying on a qualifying trade, and its gross assets must not exceed £15,000,000. For further details *Tolley's Income Tax 2005/06* (or later edition).

The availability of enterprise management incentives is now limited to companies with fewer than 250 employees.

For a thorough discussion of the schemes outlined in **46.29–46.32**, see *Tolley's Tax Planning 2005/06* (or later edition).

46.32A   EMPLOYEE SHAREHOLDER STATUS

Employee shareholder status is an employment status which has been available since 1 September 2013. Employee shareholders have fewer employment rights than employees, but enjoyed tax advantages as compensation for the lost employment rights. The income tax and capital gains tax advantages associated with employee shareholder status were abolished in relation to employee shareholder agreements made on or after 1 December 2016.

Employee shareholders receive a minimum of £2,000 in their employer's company or their employer's parent company. Where the agreement was made before 1 December 2016, there are no tax or National Insurance contributions to pay on the award of the shares. However, any shares awarded to the employee shareholder in excess of £2,000 are taxed in accordance with the normal rules for employment-related securities. Employee shareholders are also able to dispose of up to £50,000 worth of shares received by virtue of being an employee shareholder under an agreement made before 1 December 2016 free of capital gains tax, as long as they do not have a material interest in the employer company. Employee shareholders do not have unfair dismissal rights (unless the dismissal is automatically unfair) or the right to statutory redundancy pay, the right to request flexible working or certain rights to request time off to train. They are also required to give more notice (16 weeks rather than 8) if they intend to return to work early from statutory maternity, paternity, adoption or shared parental leave. See www.gov.uk/employee-shareholders for more details on employee shareholder status.

46.33   PAYROLL GIVING SCHEME

Employees can authorise their employers to deduct charitable donations from their earnings before tax, for passing on to nominated charities approved through agency charities with which the employer has made arrangements. Deductions must be made under a scheme authorised by HM Revenue and Customs and subject to regulations made by Statutory Instrument. National Insurance contributions remain payable on the gross earnings.

46.34   PROVISION OF SERVICES THROUGH AN INTERMEDIARY (IR35)

Provisions were introduced with effect from 6 April 2000 by *FA 2000, Sch 12* which are designed to counter what the Government considers to be tax avoidance where services are provided through an intermediary, ie typically single workers contracting out their services to a client via their own personal services company. The provisions are generally referred to as IR35 after the Budget Press Release in which they were announced. The legislation is now found within *ITEPA 2003, ss 48–61* (as amended by *FA 2003, s 136*).

The measures were introduced following 'concern about the hiring of individuals through their own service companies so that they can exploit the fiscal advantages offered by a corporate structure'. The rules were extended from 10 April 2003 so they not only apply to services provided for another person's business but now also to those engaged in a domestic capacity, such as nannies. For an example of a case where, before the enactment of these provisions, personal service companies were used to avoid PAYE, see *Sports Club v HM Inspector of Taxes (and related appeals)* (Sp C 253) [2000] STC (SCD) 443.

The rules are designed to ensure that a comparable amount of PAYE and NIC is payable on contractors' income in circumstances where, if the service company did not exist, the worker would be an employee of the client as would be payable if the contractor were employed directly by the client. There are corresponding NIC provisions, contained in the *Welfare Reform and Pensions Act 1999, s 75 (SI 1999/3420)* and the *Social Security Contributions (Intermediaries) Regulations 2000*.

The provisions apply to 'relevant engagements'. To be a relevant engagement, the terms of all the contracts applying to the engagement will be reviewed, including the contract between an agency and the client, and between the worker's personal service company and the agency. If the terms of the contracts would have created a contract of employment had they been entered into directly between the client and the worker, the IR35 rules apply. The provisions do not introduce any statutory definition of employment or self-employment, so the existing case law will still apply to decide employment status.

For further details of the provisions, see *Tolley's Income Tax 2010/11*. A substantial library of information about these provisions is available on the gov.uk website and a list of the available resources of relevance can be found at https://www.gov.uk/guidance/ir35-find-out-if-it-applies.

The Court of Appeal confirmed the legality of the provisions in the judicial review case of *R (on the application of Professional Contractors Group Ltd) v IRC* [2001] EWCA Civ 1945, [2002] STC 165 employee-like services will be taxed as if there was a real employment situation.

The corresponding NIC provisions (contained in the *Social Security Contributions (Intermediaries) Regulations 2000 (SI 2000/727)*) were held to apply in *Battersby v Campbell (Inspector of Taxes)* (Sp C 287) [2001] STC (SCD) 189 and *FS Consulting Ltd v McCaul* (Sp C 305) [2002] STC (SCD) 138.

Services provided to public sector bodies

From 6 April 2017 the IR35 rules were reformed where the end client is a public sector body. The new rules apply to contracts for work after 5 April 2017 and to payments made after 5 April 2017 in respect of work done before that date. Under the rules, where the services are provided to a public sector body, it is the public sector body rather than the intermediary who is responsible for deciding whether the IR35 rules apply. Where IR35 is in point, the fee payer, which may be the public sector body or which may be an agency, is responsible for deducting payments of tax and primary Class 1 National Insurance contributions from payments made to the worker. Guidance on the application of the rules can be found in a technical note available on the GOV.UK website at https://www.gov.uk/government/publications/off-payroll-working-in-the-public-sector-reform-of-the-intermediaries-legislation-technical-note.

46.35 MANAGED SERVICE COMPANIES

Managed service companies are intermediary companies through which the services of a worker are provided to an end client. They are not the same as personal service companies and in contrast to a personal service company the worker is not usually in business on his own account and does not exercise control over the business. The control is with the provider of the managed service company.

Legislation was introduced to counter the use of managed service companies to avoid tax and National Insurance contributions. The tax legislation, which is contained in *FA 2007*, *s 25* and *Sch 3*, applies from 6 April 2007. Corresponding National Insurance provisions, contained in the *Social Security Contributions (Managed Service Companies) Regulations 2007 (SI 2007/2070)*, apply from 6 August 2007.

Under the rules all payments made by a managed service company to a worker are treated as payments of employment income, regardless or the nature of the payment or how it is described. This means that PAYE and NIC must be applied, even if the payment is described as a dividend. The managed service company is responsible for the operation of PAYE and NIC.

The managed service company rules also reduced the scope for the worker to claim deductible travel expenses.

From 6 August 2007, where the PAYE and NIC debts of a managed service company cannot be recovered from the company, HMRC may transfer the debt personally to the company director or to the managed service company provider. Debts may be transferred to third parties from 6 January 2008.

46.36 DISGUISED REMUNERATION

Provisions were introduced from 6 April 2011 (*ITEPA 2003, Pt 7A*) to tackle arrangements that use trusts and other vehicles to reward employees in a way that is designed to avoid, defer or reduce tax and National Insurance liabilities by disguising what is in effect remuneration. The rules also target arrangements that are designed to be used as a tax-advantaged way to save for retirement by using an employer financed retirement benefit scheme as an alternative to, or a top up to, savings in a registered pension scheme.

The rules provide for an income tax charge to apply where trusts or other intermediate vehicles are used in arrangements aimed at providing value to an individual in what is in substance a reward or recognition in connection with the individual's employment. Although the rules are not limited to arrangements involving employee benefit trusts (EBTs), in practice many of the arrangements that fall within their scope will feature EBTs. A charge will also apply where a loan is provided in connection with the employee's arrangement. The tax charge will operate in the following ways.

- Sums or assets that are earmarked for employees by trusts or other intermediaries will be treated as if the amount of the sum or the value of the asset earmarked for the employee is a payment of PAYE income provided by the employer's employee to the employee.

- Loans provided to employees by trusts and other intermediaries will be treated as if the value of the loan is a payment of PAYE income provided by the employee's employer to the employee.

- Assets provided to employees by trusts or other intermediaries will be regarded for tax purposes as a payment of PAYE income by the employer where certain conditions (as specified in the legislation) are met.

- Sums or assets that are earmarked by the employer with a view to a trust to other intermediary providing retirement benefits to the employee are treated as if the amount of the sum or value of the asset earmarked for the employee is a payment of PAYE income provided by the employee's employer to the employee.

The disguised remuneration rules apply from 6 April 2011 in relation to rewards which are earmarked for an individual employee or otherwise made available on or after that date. Anti-forestalling rules applied in certain situations in relation to sums paid or assets provided between 9 December 2010 and 6 April 2011, where if provision had been made on or after 6 April 2011, the new rules would be in point.

Regulations impose a National Insurance charge on the amounts chargeable to tax from the same date.

47   Temporary and Seasonal Employees

Cross-references. See **15.3** EMPLOYEE, SELF-EMPLOYED OR WORKER? for the distinction between a contract for services and a contract of service/employment. See TAXATION **(46)** for vacation employment of students. See also ENGAGEMENT OF EMPLOYEES **(21)** and PROBATIONARY EMPLOYEES **(36)**.

47.1   An employer may sometimes engage workers on a temporary basis. This might be to take over work while a permanent employee is away or to cope with fluctuating workloads (eg due to seasonal work requirements). In this chapter, the description 'temporary' is applied to a worker who is referred to an employer by an employment agency (the kind of worker commonly referred to as a 'temp') and also to an employee who is employed for a limited period. 'Seasonal worker' is applied to a person who enters into the direct employment of the employer for a limited period at a busy time of the year. Employees who are engaged for a limited period (including seasonal workers) may be fixed-term employees and accordingly will qualify for protection under the provisions of the *Fixed-Term Employees (Prevention of Less Favourable Treatment) Regulations 2002 (SI 2002/2034)* (these *Regulations* are considered below at **47.14**).

As to employment of part-time workers or job-sharers, their employment rights are not dependent on their working a specified number of hours in a week: see CONTINUOUS EMPLOYMENT **(7)**. See also the *Part-time Workers (Prevention of Less Favourable Treatment) Regulations 2000 (SI 2000/ 1551)* as amended by *SI 2002/2035* (see **22.12** EQUAL PAY).

47.2   TEMPORARY WORKERS

Employment agencies

Employment agencies fulfil two main functions: they effect introductions of permanent staff to employers and they supply temporary staff for a short period of time. So far as the first category is concerned, after the introduction has been made, the employment agency drops out of the picture, and the employer enters into a direct relationship with the employee with all the attendant duties and responsibilities of a normal employment contract. If, however, the worker is supplied on a temporary basis – the agency charging its client a weekly fee out of which it pays the worker – the client is more accurately to be regarded in most circumstances as a user of that worker's services and not his employer (here called the 'quasi employer'). Because the quasi employer controls not only what the agency worker does but how he does it, the quasi employer may be vicariously liable for any wrong done by the worker while working for him (see VICARIOUS LIABILITY **(56)**) and be liable to the worker for any claim by him for damages for personal injuries (*Mersey Docks and Harbour Board v Coggins and Griffiths (Liverpool) Ltd* [1947] AC 1; *Denham v Midland Employers' Mutual Assurance Ltd* [1955] 2 QB 437). However, it was for a considerable period doubtful whether the quasi employer would be liable to the worker for unfair dismissal or redundancy if the employment agency could be regarded as the primary employer who lends the worker's services to other employers (*Cross v Redpath Dorman Long (Contracting) Ltd* [1978] ICR 730, EAT). In *Ironmonger v Movefield Ltd* [1988] IRLR 461, it was held that the contract with the employment agency was one *sui generis*, somewhere between a contract of employment and a contract for services. A similar approach was taken in *Wickens v Champion Employment* [1984] ICR 365 where there was held to be no contract of employment between a worker and an employment agency.

In *McMeechan v Secretary of State for Employment* [1997] IRLR 353 the Court of Appeal held that an agency worker *may* have the status of an employee in relation to a *particular engagement* actually worked even if there is no such status as an employee under the *general*

47.2   Temporary and Seasonal Employees

terms of engagement between the worker and the employment agency. In this case, the appellant's claim to employee status was limited to a specific contract in relation to which he was owed money. The Court of Appeal held, despite an express term describing the appellant as 'a self-employed worker' that he was in fact an employee in relation to the specific engagement under consideration. It was, accordingly, unnecessary for the Court of Appeal to determine whether the appellant was to be considered an employee under the general terms of the engagement with the employment agency.

The issue of the employment status of temporary and agency workers has been a difficult and ongoing problem with conflicting judicial decision and bursts of judicial activism and then retreat as the cases summarised below illustrate. What is clear is that it will be a matter for Parliament to address ultimately and not the courts – a point made with particular clarity by the Court of Appeal in *James v Greenwich London Borough Council* [2008] EWCA Civ 35, [2008] ICR 545, [2008] IRLR 302 (below).

47.3   *Similar facts different results*

In *Costain Building and Civil Engineering Ltd v Smith* [2000] ICR 215, the EAT had reversed a finding by an Employment Tribunal that a worker supplied by an agency and appointed by a trade union as a safety representative was an employee. The worker was paid without deduction of tax or National Insurance. The EAT held that the only contracts were between the employment agency and the worker and between the employment agency and the company. By way of contrast, in *Motorola Ltd v Davidson* [2001] IRLR 4, the EAT held that a worker supplied by an agency was an employee of the hiring company (Motorola) and could, accordingly, present a complaint of unfair dismissal. The EAT held that Motorola exercised sufficient control in reality over the worker to give rise to employee status, rejecting Motorola's argument that the worker was controlled by the agency. This was a significant decision in that there was no express contract between the worker and Motorola, a factor which had previously been fatal to the contention that the worker was an employee of the quasi employer. The facts of the case should also be noted in that the employee was specifically selected to work at Motorola and had done so permanently for over two years.

While each case may turn upon its own facts, in the area of employment status of agency workers even on similar facts, wholly different conclusions have been reached by different courts. This left agency workers in a very unsatisfactory and uncertain position with regard to employment protection rights. A clear illustration of the problem was provided by *Johnson Underwood Ltd v Montgomery* [2001] EWCA Civ 318, [2001] IRLR 269. In that case the claimant had worked for the client of the employment business for some two and a half years. Upon the termination of her 'employment' she presented a claim for unfair dismissal. The issue of who was the employer arose as a preliminary issue. The case eventually reached the Court of Appeal which concluded, applying the tests of control and mutuality of obligation, that, on the particular facts, the claimant was not an employee of the employment business. The unfortunate consequence of this decision was that the claimant was left without a remedy as the original employment tribunal decision (to the effect that she was not an employee of the client business at which she had worked for two and a half years) had not been appealed. A striking example of very long term agency workers being found not to have employment status was provided by *Esso Petroleum Co Ltd v Jarvis* [2002] All ER (D) 112 (Jan). In that case, agency workers who had worked for the same client for 9 and 11 years, respectively, were found not to be employees of the client on the basis of the absence of a contractual relationship between the workers and the client. This may be contrasted with the *Motorola* decision above. In *Hewlett Packard Ltd v O'Murphy* [2002] IRLR 4 it was held that there was no contractual nexus between the worker (who had worked for six years) and the appellant client. Accordingly, he was not an employee. *Motorola* was not, however, referred to in the *Hewlett Packard* case.

47.4   *Activism – the search for an implied contract of employment*

The lack of certainty in this area of the law and the apparently conflicting decisions at EAT level lead to a trilogy of decisions of the Court of Appeal which developed the concept of an *implied contract of employment* arising between the worker and the client using his services. In *Franks v Reuters Ltd* [2003] EWCA Civ 417, [2003] IRLR 423 the claimant entered into a temporary worker agreement with an employment agency and was supplied to Reuters where he worked for five years working hours fixed by Reuters but paid by the employment agency. The Court of Appeal held that the worker was an employee of Reuters. The question to be addressed by an employment tribunal was whether a contract of employment could be implied between the worker and Reuters from the circumstances of his work and what was said by the parties at the time work commenced and subsequently. The Court of Appeal explained that although a person cannot become an employee simply by reason of length of the time which they have worked, the length of 'service' was not irrelevant evidence in the context of a person who was allowed to stay working in the same place for the same client for over five years because dealings between parties over a period of years, as distinct from weeks or months, are capable of generating implied contractual relationships.

The principles in *Franks* were developed in *Dacas v Brook Street Bureau (UK) Ltd* [2004] EWCA Civ 217, [2004] IRLR 358. In *Dacas* the applicant had worked exclusively as a cleaner at a hostel run by Wandsworth Council for at least four years until the engagement was terminated. Mrs Dacas brought proceedings for unfair dismissal against the supplying agency and, alternatively, the Council. In a striking illustration of the unsatisfactory nature of the law in this area the Employment Tribunal concluded that she was employed by neither the agency not the council. This result – that Mrs Dacas was employed by nobody – was described in the Court of Appeal (by Sedley LJ) as 'simply not credible'. The Court of Appeal concluded that the agency was not the employer of the claimant as the necessary mutuality of obligation or control was not present. As to the Council, Mummery LJ concluded that employment by that body would accord with 'practical reality and commonsense' and in Sedley LJ's view there was an inference to be drawn that the Council was the employer. The Court of Appeal in *Dacas* stressed that, in proceedings before an Employment Tribunal where the status of a claimant is in issue, the Tribunal is required as a matter of law to consider whether there is an *implied* contract between the parties who are not in an express contractual relationship with each other. (On the facts of *Dacas* there was a contract between Mrs Dacas and the agency and between the agency and the Council. The relationship between Mrs Dacas and the Council was considered by the majority (Munby J dissenting) to be an *implied* contract of employment).

In *Cable and Wireless plc v Muscat* [2006] EWCA Civ 220, [2006] IRLR 354 the implied contract approach was again considered but on somewhat atypical facts. The Court of Appeal held for the first (and only) time that there was *in fact* an implied contract of employment between the worker and the client end-user (in *Franks* the issue had been remitted to the Employment Tribunal and the observations in *Dacas* as to implied contract status of the claimant were, on the particular facts of that appeal, *obiter*). The facts of *Muscat* were complicated and somewhat unusual. The worker had originally been an employee who was then required to go to agency provided services followed by a *TUPE* transfer. As such, the case did not illustrate the more common factual circumstances of a worker providing services to a client consistently through an agency for a period of time in excess of, say, one year. Further the Court held that the guidance of the majority in *Dacas* was to be applied and followed by Employment Tribunals in future cases. On the issue of the fact that payment of the worker was made by the agency rather than the client end user (which factor was one of the main reasons for Munby J's dissent in *Dacas*), the Court held that this is not a particularly strong factor against employee status if the other factors point to employment by the end user client.

47.5 Temporary and Seasonal Employees

47.5 *The retreat from the implied contract: the need for 'necessity'*

The later authorities show that an implied contract will rarely be found and it appears that *Cable & Wireless plc v Muscat* is likely to be a case confined to its own facts. In a number of EAT decision culminating with an important test case decision of the Court of Appeal in *James v Greenwich London Borough Council* [2008] IRLR 302 it has been made clear that an implied contract between the worker and the end user will only arise when it is necessary to imply such a contract. In *James v Greenwich London Borough Council* [2007] ICR 577, [2007] IRLR 168 the claimant was an agency worker who had worked for the local authority for a number of years acting under the direction of the council without intervention from the employment agency. She was treated like a permanent member of staff on the staff rota. When she went off work by reason of sickness the agency replaced her with another worker. On her return the claimant was informed her services were no longer required and she brought a claim for unfair dismissal. The EAT ([2007] ICR 577, [2007] IRLR 168) held that the issue is whether it is *'necessary'* to imply a contract of employment between the worker and the end-user. The EAT (Elias P) held that it was not sufficient that the arrangements are *consistent* with a contract of employment as in order to imply such a contract it must be necessary in that the way in which the contract is performed is only consistent with an implied contact between the worker and the end-user and not consistent with another contractual relationship. The EAT held that mere passage of time will not justify such an implication but that there must be some words or conduct after commencement of the working relationship entitling the Tribunal to conclude that the agency relationship no longer adequately reflects the reality of the relationship. The EAT observed that 'we suspect that it will be a rare case where there will be evidence entitling the tribunal to imply a contract between the worker and end user'. In *Cairns v Visteon UK Ltd* [2007] IRLR 175 the facts engaged were somewhat unusual in that there *was* a contract of employment between the worker and the employment agency. The issue before the EAT was whether, in such circumstances, a contract of employment could nevertheless also be implied between the worker and the end-user client as well. The EAT held, following *James*, that there was no business necessity to make such an implication (nor any policy reason) to extend parallel protection under the *ERA* to an employee who was already protected by the employment relationship between the employer and the employment agency employer. Similar decisions of differently constituted EAT's followed in *Astbury v Gist Ltd* [2007] All ER (D) 480 (Mar), EAT, *Heatherwood and Wexham Park Hospitals NHS Trust v Kulubowila* [2007] All ER (D) 496 (Mar), EAT and *Wood Group Engineering Ltd v Robertson* UKEAT0081/06 (6 July 2007, unreported) and see *Wood v National Grid Electricity Transmission plc* [2007] All ER (D) 358 (Oct), EAT.

The Court of Appeal in *James v Greenwich London Borough Council* [2008] IRLR 302 has now confirmed the correctness of the EAT's approach in that case. The crucial test in relation to the end use is whether it is necessary to imply a contract of employment in order to explain the relationship. It is not enough for the claimant to show that the relationship looks like that of employer and employee. The guidance given by the EAT in James ([2007] IRLR 168) was specifically approved by the Court of Appeal. In *Dacas*, Sedley LJ had stated that conduct which was maintained over 'weeks or months' as opposed to 'a brief time' might rise to a finding that there was an implied contract of employment between the client and the worker which had appeared to suggest that a agency worker providing services for a substantial period of time to one end user would be likely to be considered an employee on the basis of an implied contract of employment. The EAT in *James* had disagreed with Sedley LJ on this point and the Court of Appeal in *James* firmly agrees with the EAT that mere length of time does not justify implication of a contact of employment. See also, on the proper approach to the test of necessity, *Cave v Portsmouth City Council* [2008] All ER (D) 313 (May), EAT.

The effect of *James v Greenwich London Borough Council* is that it will be very difficult for a claimant to show that it is necessary to imply a contract of employment between the worker and the end user as the relationship is explicable by the contract of agency between the agency and the worker which of course may not be a contact of employment between the worker and the agency. Whilst this is a substantial limitation upon atypical workers obtaining employment protection rights the judgment of the Court of Appeal (Mummery LJ and see Thomas LJ) concludes with express recognition of compelling policy arguments favouring agency workers having employment rights against the end user but emphasises that it is unrealistic, absent Parliament legislating on the issue, for litigants to hope or expect the Courts to be able to create such rights. By way of illustration, in *Muschett v HM Prison Service* [2010] IRLR 451 the Court of Appeal applying James, held that a temporary agency worker was unable to being a claim for discrimination and unfair dismissal against either the end user client or the supplying agency. This represents a considerable gap in the protection against discrimination which might be expected to apply to agency workers both as a matter of general principle and as a matter of European law. More recently in *Tilson v Alstom Transport* [2010] EWCA Civ 1308, [2011] IRLR 169, CA, it was held applying *James* that a senior manager engaged by the end user for two years through a third parry contractor was unable to claim unfair dismissal against the end user as he was not an employee. On the facts it was simply not necessary to imply a contract of employment. The Court of Appeal observed that the use of agencies was not contrary to public policy even if the aim was to avoid employment rights and "disapproval" of the arrangements by a tribunal could not justify implication of a contract of employment. Further, the conduct of the parties may be relevant in determining mutual expectations and the legal relationship subsisting. In *Tilson* the fact that the claimant had refused permanent employment because the agency work was more remunerative was a powerful factor against the implication of an employment contract. Similarly, in *Smith v Carillon (JM) Ltd* [2015] EWCA Civ 209, [2015] IRLR 467, in rejecting the arguments in favour of implying a contract of employment, the Court of Appeal observed (per Elias LJ) that it was not against public policy for a contractor to obtain services in this way even where the purpose was to avoid legal obligations which would arise if the workers were employed directly and, further, that a court could not imply a contract because it disapproves of the conduct of the employer.

The *James v Greenwich London Borough Council* line of cases considers the possibility of employment by the client end-user. The issue of employment by the employment agency was revisited by the Court of Appeal in *Bunce v Postworth Ltd (t/a Skyblue)* [2005] EWCA Civ 490, [2005] IRLR 557. In that case the Court of Appeal held that an agency welder was not employed by the agency who supplied him. In this case the worker did not work for only one end user and a claim against the end user was not pursued. The absence of control exercised by the agency was held to be fatal to the claim against the agency and the Court of Appeal distinguished its earlier decision in *McMeechan* (above) in relation to the possibility of an overall contract with the agency and separate contracts in relation to each assignment. The legal position of such workers remains uncertain and unsatisfactory with a large number of people not enjoying the full range of employment rights solely because of their agency work arrangements as opposed to more typical 'employment'; a point stressed by Keene LJ in the Court of Appeal. The answer, however, was said to lie in the need for new legislation and not judicial creativity.

In a series of cases it has been made clear by the courts that the parties may not avoid employee status by the use of contractual definitions even if apparently unequivocal and recorded in a written agreement. In *Royal National Lifeboat Institution v Bushaway* [2005] IRLR 674, the EAT held that a written agreement, which defined the claimant as a 'temporary worker' supplied by an employment agency, was not conclusive as to the relationship between the parties notwithstanding a provision that the written agreement constituted the entire agreement between the parties. The EAT considered that as the relationship was not accurately reflected in the contractual document it was permissible to go beyond the terms of the document and examine the employment status of the claimant. On the facts the claimant was found to be an employee even though engaged on quite different terms and conditions to those of other employees.

47.5 Temporary and Seasonal Employees

In *Protectacoat Firthglow Ltd v Szilagyi* [2009] IRLR 365 and in *Autoclenz Ltd v Belcher & Others* [2010] IRLR 70 the Court of Appeal held that it was not necessary for a term to be properly characterised as a "sham" before it could be not applied. *Protectacoat* and *Autoclenz* established that where there is a dispute as to the genuineness of an express term there is no need to show a common intention to mislead. Instead it is enough if the written term did not represent the intentions or expectations of the parties. The court or tribunal was to consider whether or not the words of the written contract represented the true intentions or expectations of the parties (and therefore their implied agreement and contractual obligations) not only at the inception of the contract but at any later stage where the evidence shows that the parties have expressly or impliedly varied the agreement between them. The focus of the enquiry had to be to discover the actual legal obligations of the parties and to carry out that exercise the tribunal had to examine all the relevant evidence including the written term itself as read in the context of the whole agreement. It would include evidence of how the parties conducted themselves in practice and what their expectations of each other were. This approach gave rise to what was perceived to be a conflict with the earlier Court of Appeal decision in *Consistent Group Limited v Kalwak* [2008] IRLR 505 which had suggested that the term must be a "sham" before it could be disapplied.

The matter has now been resolved beyond doubt by the decision of the Supreme Court in *Autoclenz Ltd v Belcher* [2011] UKSC 41. The Supreme Court approved the judgments of the Court of Appeal in *Autoclenz* and *Protectacoat* (as well as that of the EAT in *Kalwak* so that the decision of the Court of Appeal in *Kalwak* is, effectively, overruled). The real question for the court is what was the true agreement between the parties? The concept or requirement of "a sham" was unhelpful in the employment context where a broader enquiry was required into the true terms of the agreement as the agreements in issue were frequently drafted by the employer and where inequality of bargaining power was present. The enquiry permitted consideration to be given to the subsequent conduct of the parties as evidence of what was originally agreed between them. The court must consider the relative bargaining power of the parties in deciding whether the terms of any written agreement in truth represented what was agreed and this required a purposive approach to the problem.

47.6 *The Temporary Agency Work Directive (2008/104/EC) and the Agency Worker Regulations 2010 (SI 2010/93)*

In May 2008 the then Government announced that it had reached agreement with the TUC and the CBI on legislating to give agency workers the right to terms and conditions of employment comparable to those enjoyed by permanent employees.

Under the agreement, agency workers were to be entitled to equal treatment with comparable permanent workers after 12 weeks of employment. The agreement defines equal treatment as 'at least the basic working and employment conditions that would apply to the workers concerned if they had been recruited directly by that undertaking to occupy the same job'. The agreement does not cover occupational social security schemes. The agreement also requires that these arrangements be reviewed after a suitable period to establish how they are working in practice.

In June 2008 the Council of the European Union announced that a common position had been reached on the draft Directive on agency work resulting in the *Temporary Agency Work Directive (2008/104/EC)*. The *Directive* is limited to temporary *agency* workers and thus does not affect the employment status of temporary workers but permits the UK to implement the agreement between the Government, the CBI and the TUC.

The purpose of the *Directive* is to ensure the protection of temporary agency workers by applying the principle of equal treatment (*art 5*) so that, after 12 weeks in a given job, the basic working and employment conditions (duration of working time, overtime, breaks, rest periods, night work, holidays and public holidays and pay) of temporary agency workers shall be, for the duration of their assignment at a hirer, at least those that would apply if they had been recruited directly by that undertaking to occupy the same job. There are also other entitlements that aim to improve the situation for agency workers in other areas, for example, in terms of improved access to permanent employment and training. Member states had until 5 December 2011 to implement the *Directive*.

In the first case on the construction of the *Directive Auto- ja Kuljetusalan Työntekijäliitto AKT ry v Öljytuote ry* [2015] IRLR 502, the ECJ held that restrictions on the use of temporary agency workers imposed by a collective agreement were not contrary to the provisions of *art 4* of the *Directive*. In *Betriebsrat der Ruhrlandklinik gGmbH v Ruhrland-klinik gGmbH* [2017] IRLR 194 the ECJ held that the characterisation of the relationship under national law is not determinative of worker status and that a "worker" is not limited to persons with a contract of employment with the temporary work agency. The issue is whether there is an "employment relationship" which is determined by whether a person for a period of time "performs services for and under the direction of another person, in return for which he receives remuneration".

The Agency Worker Regulations 2010 (SI 2010/93)

Following consultation in relation to the implementation of the *Directive*, the *Agency Worker Regulations 2010 (SI 2010/93)* were passed by the previous Government and were due to come into force on 1 October 2011. The *Regulations* were, however, further amended prior to their coming into force by the *Agency Workers (Amendment) Regulations 2011 (SI 2011/1941)*. Accordingly, particular care should be taken to ensure that the most up to date version of the *Regulations* is consulted. References to the *Regulations* below are to the amended *Regulations*. In May 2011 the Government's 51 page guidance document on the *Regulations* and their effect was published. See the "Agency Workers Regulations Guidance" which may be obtained from www.bis.gov.uk/assets/biscore/employment-matters/docs/a/11-949-agency-workers-regulations-guidance.pdf. The Guidance is not a Code of Practice and does not, accordingly, have any specific legal status but it is likely that it will be used by the employment tribunals in interpreting and applying the Regulations as a body of relevant case law is developed.

In summary, the *Regulations* introduce, with effect from 1 October 2011, a right to equal treatment in relation to terms and conditions of employment for agency workers in comparison to the permanent employees and workers of the hirer.

Definitions

Under the *Regulations* (*reg 3*) an "agency worker" means an individual who is supplied by a "temporary work agency" to work temporarily for and under the supervision and direction of "a hirer" and who has a contract with the temporary work agency which is a contract of employment or any other contract to perform work and services personally for the agency. The meaning of "temporary" is not defined in the *Regulations* (or the *Directive*) but has been considered by the EAT in *Moran v Ideal Cleaning Services Ltd* [2014] IRLR 172. In that case the claimants had worked as cleaners for between 6 and 25 years employed as agency workers on contracts of indefinite duration. On termination of their engagements they brought claims under the *Regulations*. The EAT held that the arrangements under which the claimants worked were indefinite in duration and permanent and that "temporary" meant not permanent. A purposive construction to the effect that all agency workers satisfying the *Regulations'* 12 week qualifying period were agency workers benefiting from the protection of the *Regulations* was rejected as giving no meaning or effect to the word "temporary" at all. Insofar as that construction left a lacuna of protection, that lacuna, the EAT held, was a deliberate consequence of the drafting of the *Directive* as limited to temporary workers.

"Worker" (as opposed to an agency worker) is subject to the usual statutory definition of a person who has entered into or works under (or where the employment has ceased, worked under) a contract of employment, or any other contract, whether express or implied and (if it is express) whether oral or in writing, whereby the individual undertakes to do or perform personally any work or services for another party to the contract whose status is not by virtue of the contract that of a client or customer of any profession or business undertaking carried on by the individual (*Reg 2*). The Guidance addresses "agency worker" at page 7 with examples of those who are considered to fall inside and outside that definition. *Reg 4* defines "temporary work agency" as a person engaged in the economic activity, public or private, whether or not operating for profit, and whether or not carrying on such activity in conjunction with others, of supplying individuals to work temporarily for and under the supervision and direction of hirers or paying for, or receiving or forwarding payment for, the services of individuals who are supplied to work temporarily for and under the supervision and direction of hirers. A "hirer" (*reg 2*) means a person engaged in "economic activity, public or private, whether or not operating for profit, to whom individuals are supplied, to work temporarily for and under the supervision and direction of that person".

The Rights

Under *reg 5(1)* the agency worker is entitled to the same basic working and employment conditions as he would be entitled to for doing the same job had he been recruited by the hirer. The "relevant terms and conditions" which must be provided equally are terms as to (a) pay; (b) the duration of working time; (c) night work; (d) rest periods; (e) rest breaks; and (f) annual leave (*reg 6(1)*). "Pay" (*reg 6(2)*) means any sums payable to a worker of the hirer in connection with the worker's employment, including any fee, bonus, commission, holiday pay or other emolument referable to the employment, whether payable under contract or otherwise but excludes the "payments or rewards" listed in *reg 6(3)*. The excluded payments include sick pay, pension payments, maternity payments, redundancy payments, any payment or reward made pursuant to a financial participation scheme (as defined in *reg 6(5)* as profit share and share option schemes), loyalty and long service bonuses, statutory time off payments for trade union duties, guarantee payments, any payment by way of an advance under an agreement for a loan or by way of an advance of pay, payment in respect of expenses incurred by the worker in carrying out the employment and any payment to the worker otherwise than in that person's capacity as a worker.

The rights under *reg 5* do not arise until the agency worker has completed the qualifying period (*reg 7*) whereby he must work in "the same role" with the same hirer for 12 continuous calendar weeks, during one or more assignments. The agency worker will be considered to work in the same role (*reg 7(3)*) unless he starts a new role with the hirer in relation to which the work making up the whole or main part of the new roles is "substantively different" from the previous role and the agency has informed the worker in writing of the type of work required in the new role. By *reg 7(3)* any week during the whole or part of which an agency worker works during an assignment is counted as a calendar week. *Regs 7(4)–(12)* make provision for determination if the work is executed for 12 continuous weeks and makes provision in *Reg 7(8)* for the effect of breaks in work by reason of sickness or injury, jury service, strike or lockout or maternity absence. If the qualifying period is satisfied the worker acquires the *reg 5* rights until the worker is no longer working in the same role, within the meaning of *reg 7(3)*, with that hirer (*reg 8(a)*) or there is a break between assignments, or during an assignment, when the agency worker is not working, to which *reg 7(8)* does not apply. *Reg 9* is an anti avoidance measure which provides that the agency worker will be treated as having satisfied the qualifying period if she or he is prevented from otherwise satisfying the requirements of *reg 7* by reason of "structure of assignments". Where the worker has worked in two or more substantively different roles for the hirer, if the most likely explanation for the adoption of that arrangement was to avoid the worker acquiring the qualifying period (and hence rights under *reg 5*), then the worker shall be treated by *reg 9* as having completed the qualifying period. Thus shifting workers around without legitimate purpose will not prevent the rights accruing and, if a hirer or temporary work agency is found to be engaged in such avoidance practices, the *Regulations* make provision for an additional award of up to £5000 (*reg 18(14)*).

Under *reg 10*, headed "Permanent contracts providing for pay between assignments", there is an important exception to the operation of at least part of the *Regulations*. To the extent to which it relates to pay, *reg 5* does not have effect in relation to an agency worker who has a permanent contract of employment with a temporary work agency if certain specific and stringent conditions set out in *reg 10* are satisfied (in summary, where the written contract provides for terms as to remuneration, location and hours of work and as to the type of work as may be offered and express exclusion of *reg 5* and where the agency is obliged to take reasonable steps to seek and provide work to the agency worker and where the agency is obliged during periods where the worker is not working for a hirer to make payment of a minimum amount). This is the so called "Swedish Derogation" as it was introduced into the *Temporary Agency Work Directive* (2008/104/EC) at the request of the Swedish government. By *reg 10(1)(a)* the relevant contract must be entered into before the first assignment and must include terms and conditions in writing relating to:

(i)   the minimum scale or rate of remuneration or the method of calculating remuneration;

(ii)   the location or locations where the agency worker may be expected to work;

(iii)   the expected hours of work during any assignment;

(iv)   the maximum number of hours of work that the agency worker may be required to work each week during any assignment;

(v)   the minimum hours of work per week that may be offered to the agency worker during any assignment, provided that it is a minimum of at least one hour; and

(vi)   the nature of the work that the agency worker may expect to be offered, including any relevant requirements relating to qualifications or experience.

Further, the relevant contract of employment must contain a statement that the effect of entering into it is that the employee does not, during the currency of the contract, have any entitlement to the rights conferred by *reg 5* insofar as they relate to pay. In addition, by *reg 10(c)*, the temporary work agency must take reasonable steps to seek suitable work for the agency worker, to provide suitable work as available and to pay minimum remuneration. The contract is not terminable unless the temporary work agency has complied with its obligations under *reg 10(c)* for not less than an aggregate of 4 weeks. These provisions have been considered at tribunal level in *Bray and others v Monarch Personnel Refuelling (UK) Ltd* ET/1801581/2012. That case considered agency workers who had undertaken the same work (tanker driving for BP) prior to the introduction of the *Regulations* but who entered into new contracts starting on 1 December 2011. The claimants contended that the new contracts did not comply with *reg 10* as they had not been entered into "before the first assignment". Rejecting the claims, the tribunal concluded that the contracts had been entered into before the beginning of the first assignment under the contract, even though the agency workers had actually worked for BP throughout a longer period. The assignment which started on 1 December 2011 was the "first assignment" under the new contract. The tribunal considered that "assignment" did not mean the entire continuous period that an agency worker works for a hirer and the absence of a gap in provision of the work did not prevent the workers being engaged on separate assignments. Accordingly, the contracts were compliant with *reg 10* and the workers were not entitled to the same rate of pay pursuant to *reg 5*.

Reg 11 makes provision for the calculation of the minimum amount of payment required under *reg 10(1)(c)*. It is important to note that even where a contract satisfying reg 10 exists, the agency worker is still entitled to the protection afforded by *reg 5* in relation to working time, night work, rest periods and holidays and the rights to access to collective facilities and job information.

47.6 Temporary and Seasonal Employees

In contrast to the *reg 5* rights which are subject to the *reg 7* qualifying period, all agency worker during an assignment are entitled to immediate equal access to "collective facilities and amenities" provided by the hirer (*reg 12*) as are available to a comparable worker. The facilities include canteen, childcare and transport services (*reg 12(3)*) and a "comparable worker" is and employee or worker of the hirer engaged in broadly similar work for the hirer with (where relevant) a similar level of qualification and skills working at the same establishment (*reg 12(4)*). Agency workers also have the right to be informed by the hirer of any relevant vacant posts with the hirer, to give that agency worker the same opportunity as a comparable worker to find permanent employment with the hirer (*reg 13*). This does not amount to a right of preference in selection for the position – it is an obligation to provide information and no more. An argument that *reg 13* should be construed to give the relevant agency worker preference in the permanent appointment or, alternatively, a guaranteed interview was robustly rejected by the EAT in *Coles v Ministry of Defence* (2015) UKEAT/0403/14, [2015] IRLR 872.

Liability for Breach

Under *reg 14* breach of *reg 5* will lead to liability in the temporary work agency and/or the hirer to the extent each is liable for breach. Under *reg 16* an agency worker may make a written request to the temporary work agency for a written statement containing information relating to a suspected breach of *reg 5* and a similar right exists in relation to a hirer in suspected breach of *reg 12* or *reg 13*. Failure to provide the information will permit adverse inferences to be drawn by an employment tribunal (*reg 16(9)*). Where the agency worker is an employee the usual protection against detriment in employment is provided along with provision for automatically unfair dismissal if the reason for the detriment or dismissal was the doing of any of a number of protected acts (see *reg 17*). The rights under the *Regulations* may be enforced in the employment tribunal subject to the normal time limits (*reg 18*) and just and equitable extension (*regs 18(4)* and *(5)*). Compensation is assessed on the just and equitable basis and is not subject to a statutory limit but excludes an injury to feelings award (*reg 18(15)* but an additional sum of up to £5000 may be awarded for seeking to avoid the rights under the Regulations accruing (*reg 18(14)* and *reg 9(4)*). An award may be made against the temporary work agency and/or the hirer. The issue of assessment of compensation under *Reg 18* was considered by the EAT in *Amissah v Trainpeople.Co.UK Ltd* [2017] IRLR 318 which provides useful guidance on the approach to compensation, particularly in a case of joint liability of the temporary work agency and the hirer.

The *Regulations* make provision for consequential amendment to the relevant primary (principally *TULR(C)A* and *ERA*) and secondary legislation as set out in *Sch 2* to the *Regulations*.

47.7 Statutory control of employment agencies

Persons who carry on employment agencies or employment businesses had formerly to be licensed by the Secretary of State. The licensing provisions have now been replaced by a system under which the Secretary of State may apply to an Employment Tribunal for an order prohibiting a person from carrying on, or being concerned with the carrying on, of any employment agency or employment business or any specified description of such agency or business. The Tribunal may make the order if it is satisfied that the person concerned is unsuitable, on account of misconduct or for other sufficient reason, to do what the order prohibits; there are detailed provisions concerning the application of this test to companies and partnerships. There is an appeal on a question of law to the Employment Appeal Tribunal.

The prohibition, which may be for a maximum period of 10 years, may be absolute or it may be on carrying on the business otherwise than in accordance with specified conditions. Non-compliance with a prohibition order without reasonable excuse is an offence punishable by a fine. The person to whom the order applies may apply to the tribunal to have it varied or revoked where there has been a material change in circumstances.

(*Employment Agencies Act 1973, ss 3–3D*, as inserted by *Deregulation and Contracting Out Act 1994, Sch 10 para 1.*)

It is a criminal offence to charge a person a fee for finding or seeking to find him employment, save in such cases as the Secretary of State prescribes (*Employment Agencies Act 1973, s 6*). The classes which have been prescribed relate to occupations in the entertainment industry, to modelling and to *au pairs*.

The *Employment Act 2008* introduced with effect from 6 April 2009 a strengthening of the enforcement regime. Certain offences under the Act are now triable on indictment as well as summarily (*s 15* of the *Employment Act 2008*). The offences affected are those of: (i) failure to comply with a prohibition order, (ii) contravention of any regulations made under the *1973 Act* and (iii) requesting or receiving a fee for providing work-finding services (except in those sectors such as entertaining and modelling where agencies are entitled to charge for these services under certain circumstances). As a result of the option of trial on indictment the Employment Agency Standards Inspectorate ('EAS') will be able to prosecute for 'attempting' to commit offences under the 1973 Act (eg attempting to obtain money for providing work-finding services). The EAS will be able to bring a prosecution for attempting to commit one of these offences on the basis of evidence obtained from the agency's records, without the need for agency workers to give evidence as witnesses.

If tried on indictment the penalty is a fine but may exceed that which may be imposed on summary conviction (see **1.10** Introduction for the Standards Scale of fines applicable to summary offences). In addition, significant amendments are made to *s 9* of the *Employment Agencies Act 1973* in relation to rights of inspection and disclosure of documents to officers by *s 16* of the *Employment Act 2008*. The EAS is now able to require a person carrying on an agency to provide financial records and documents and information at such time and place as the inspector may specify. In addition, banks may be required to provide financial information regarding agencies (where the agency has been asked to provide the information specified and has not done so). The inspectors are also given powers to remove documents from an agency in order to take copies. By *s 18* of the *Employment Act 2008* enforcement of the National Minimum Wage and employment agency standards is enabled by allowing officers appointed under the relevant legislation to share information with each other for the purpose of their respective enforcement functions. *Section 18* now allows minimum wage and employment agency officers to pass information about an employer's compliance to each other for the purposes of their enforcement functions.

In *First Point International Ltd v Department of Trade and Industry* (1999) 164 JP 89 the Court of Appeal, considered the scope of the unamended *s 6*. The section provides that a person 'shall not demand or directly or indirectly receive from any person a fee for finding him employment or seeking to find him employment'. The facts of *First Point International* were as follows. A person interested in work in Thailand contacted First Point International which sent him promotional materials and details of a 'personal client appraisal service' which required payment of almost £100 for an 'appraisal pack' containing appraisal questionnaires to be completed by the potential employee. The potential employee duly paid the fee, completing the questionnaires. First Point International then offered to identify suitable employment for him, for which service they would charge £3,150. The potential employee did not avail himself of this opportunity but First Point International was convicted of two offences under *s 6*. The £100 payment was found to be a fee for seeking to find employment; the £3,150 was found to be a 'demand' for payment for seeking to find employment. On appeal, the Court of Appeal upheld the convictions concluding that the fee for the appraisal documents was, as a matter of law, part of the 'seeking of employment'. As to the invitation to pay £3,150, the Court of Appeal concluded that *s 6* was not limited to cases where there was an enforceable legal right to payment but extended to invitations to make payments.

The *Employment Relations Act 1999* clarifies the application of *s 6* by providing that the prohibition on the charging of fees will extend to 'requests' for payment or the provision of information. The relevant amendments came into force on 25 October 1999.

The conduct of employment agencies was further regulated by the *Conduct of Employment Agencies and Employment Businesses Regulations 1976 (SI 1976/715)*. These *Regulations* have now been replaced with the *Conduct of Employment Agencies and Employment Businesses Regulations 2003 (SI 2003/3319)* with effect from 6 April 2004 (as amended) (see below **47.9**).

47.8   Statutory control of employment agencies: the 2003 reforms

As far back as 1999, the Government published a consultation paper, 'Regulation of the Private Recruitment Industries', proposing the replacement of, *inter alia*, the *Conduct of Employment Agencies and Employment Businesses Regulations 1976 (SI 1976/715)*. The key proposals in that document sought to clarify the legal rights and obligations of agencies, their workers and clients, to require checks to be made upon the relevant qualifications of workers and, in certain cases, to require references and to prevent workers engaging in hazardous work for which they were not qualified. Consultation of the proposed changes had a lengthy history continuing into 2002–2003. From 6 April 2004 the *Conduct of Employment Agencies and Employment Business Regulations 2003 (SI 2003/3319)* ('the *2003 Regulations*') have been in force.

The Department for Trade and Industry (now BIS) consulted on new measures to protect vulnerable agency workers in 2007. As a consequence of the responses to that consultation the Government made amendments to the *Regulations* by the *Conduct of Employment Agencies and Employment Businesses (Amendment) Regulations 2007 (SI 2007/3575)* ('the *2007 Regulations*') which came into force on 6 April 2008.

The government engaged in further consultation which closed in June 2009 in relation to the *Regulations* with particular regard to vulnerable categories of agency workers in the entertainment and modelling field and the use of upfront fees and umbrella companies in the employment of temporary workers. New regulations, the *Conduct of Employment Agencies and Employment Business Regulations (Amendment) Regulations 2010 (SI 2010/1782)*, came into force on 1 October 2010. The *2010 Regulations* take effect by amendment to the *2003 Regulations*. The amendments increase the protection of performers seeking work through employment agencies and employment businesses by limiting when upfront fees can be charged and by extending cooling off periods. In addition the changes made by the amendments in the *2010 Regulations* purport to reduce the administrative burden placed on employment agencies and business expect in situations where the person seeking work will be working with or caring for vulnerable groups. The *2003 Regulations* were most recently amended by the *Conduct of Employment Agencies and Employment Businesses (Amendment) Regulations (SI 2016/510)* with effect from 8 May 2016 which in summary matters removes *Regulations 9, 11* and *17*, amends *Regulations 23* and *27A*, amends *Schedules 4* and *5* (on various record keeping obligations) and removes altogether *Schedule 6*.

The *2003 Regulations* (as amended by the *2010 Regulations* and the *2016 Regulations*) are considered below.

47.9   The Conduct of Employment Agencies and Employment Businesses Regulations 2003 (SI 2003/3319) (as amended)

The majority of provisions of the *2003 Regulations* came into force with effect from 6 April 2004 Transitional provisions dealt with engagements which were in place prior to the coming into force of the *2003 Regulations*. At the outset it is important to identify the precise terminology used by the *Regulations*. Under the *2003 Regulations* a person seeking work through an agency or employment business is a 'work-seeker'. The client to whom the services are supplied is the 'hirer' (*reg 2*). As to the agencies, the relevant definitions are found in the *Employment Agencies Act 1973* as follows. An 'employment agency' finds work-seekers employment with hirers or supplies hirers with work-seekers for employment (*s 13(2)*). An 'employment business' engages work seekers directly and supplies them on a temporary basis to the hirer (*s 13(3)*). Thus in ordinary usage headhunters are employment *agencies* and temping agencies are employment *businesses*.

Under the *2003 Regulations*, an employment agency or business (as the case may be) must on the first occasion of offering to provide or arrange the provision of a service to a work-seeker provide certain notice to the work seeker in relation to the service and fee calculations (*reg 13(1)*). However, it is important to note that *reg 13(1)* only applies where one or more services or goods referred to in *reg 13(1)(b)* for which the work-seeker will or may be charged a fee may be provided to the work-seeker. By *reg 13(1)(b)* (as amended by the *2007 Regulations* and the *2010 Regulations*) where an employment agency or business offers to provide or arrange additional charged for services they are required to provide (i) the amount or method of calculation of the fee (ii) the identity of the person to whom the fee is or will be payable(iii) a description of the services or goods to which the fee relates and a statement of the work-seeker's right to cancel or withdraw from the service and the notice period required and (iv) the circumstances, if any, in which refunds or rebates are payable to the work-seeker, the scale of such refunds or rebates, and if no refunds or rebates are payable, a statement to that effect.

By *reg 12* there are prohibitions on employment businesses withholding payment to work-seekers on certain grounds. By *reg 14* employment businesses are required to obtain agreement to terms with work-seekers, which terms must be recorded in documentary form. In relation to a work-seeker, terms must be agreed in advance of provision of services in one document or a number of documents given at the same time (*reg 14(2)*). The terms of engagement can only be varied with the work-seeker's consent and the variation must be agreed in writing (*reg 14(4), (5)*). When terms have been agreed, the employment business cannot threaten to withdraw its services in order to induce the work-seeker to accept a variation to the terms of business (*reg 14(6)*). It should be noted that the obligations under *reg 14* no longer apply to employment agencies after 1 October 2010. This was one of the amendments to ease administrative burdens introduced by the *2010 Regulations*.

Also in the case of employment businesses, the written terms must state whether the work-seeker is to be an employee of the business (*reg 15*). The terms must also specify the terms of employment, including notice periods, holidays and holiday pay and remuneration intervals. There must be an undertaking from the employment business to pay the agreed rate of pay (even if the hirer does not pay) and the level of remuneration must be specified (or at least the minimum rate expected to be obtained) (*reg 15*).

By *reg 16* employment agencies are required to obtain agreement from the work-seeker as to the terms which will apply, including details of services to be provided, the agency's authority to act for the work-seeker and details of fees. It should be noted that this provision only applies to any work-finding services for which the employment agency is permitted by *reg 26(1)* to charge a fee.

The *2003 Regulations* (as amended) contain detailed provisions in relation to the charging for the services of an employment agency or employment business. In general, employment agencies and businesses are prohibited from charging a fee to work-seekers for finding a job.

Under the *Employment Agencies Act 1973* it is not unlawful to charge for certain services such as training or assistance with CV drafting and the like. By *reg 5* it is, however, unlawful to insist that a work-seeker avails themselves of such additional services as a condition for the provision of employment business services. Where the worker uses such services as are not unlawful under the *Act* by *reg 5(2)* (added by the *2007 Regulations*), the agency or business must ensure that the work-seeker is able to cancel or withdraw from those services at any time without incurring any detriment or penalty, subject to the work-seeker giving to the provider of those services in paper form or by electronic means notice of five business days or, for services relating to the provision of living accommodation, notice of ten business days. In the case of employment as an actor, background artist, dancer, extra, musician, singer or other performer or as a photographic or fashion model, where that work-seeker uses a service for which the *Act* does not prohibit the charging of a fee, then *reg 5(3)* provides for a 30 day cooling off period during which the agency or the employment business shall not charge a fee to a work-seeker for that part of the service which consists of providing photographs, audio or video recording of the work-seeker. Further, the work-seeker shall be entitled without detriment or penalty to cancel or withdraw from any contract with the agency or employment business for such a service with immediate effect by informing the agency or employment business of cancellation or withdrawal. Where the work-seeker informs the agency or employment business of cancellation or withdrawal the work-seeker has no obligation to make any payment under the contract.

Reg 6 restricts an employment business or agency from taking detrimental action relating to work-seekers working elsewhere and *reg 7* restricts employment businesses from providing work-seekers in cases of industrial disputes. *Reg 8* restricts agencies and employment businesses from purporting to act on a different basis (eg purporting to be an agency when in fact acting as a business). *Reg 10* restricts the charging of certain fees to hirers and *reg 11* limits the entering into of contracts on behalf of clients.

Limited exceptions to the general principles apply in relation to employment agencies who deal with actors, musicians, models, sportspersons and those engaged in the creative arts, film or theatrical businesses such as composers, writers, artists, directors, production managers and the like (see *Sch 3* to the *Regulations* as amended). Even in these categories, the practice of demanding payment of fees in advance of securing an engagement is, in the main, prohibited (see *regs 26(3), (5)* and *(6)* as amended) along with the practice of charging both the work-seeker and the hirer a fee. The *2007 Regulations* add a seven day 'cooling off period' in which work seekers may cancel or withdraw from any contract to include their details in a publication without detriment or penalty. Agencies thus cannot take a fee for including a work seeker in a publication until after seven days from the work seeker entering into a contract with the agency (*reg 26(5)(d)*).

The *2003 Regulations* permit charges to be made to hirers on a broader basis. One important area of limitation is, however, in relation to 'transfer fees' (ie where a hirer wishes to permanently engage a temporary worker supplied by an employment business or where the hirer wishes to re-engage the worker through a different employment business). In the light of concerns about such fees being an unhelpful restriction on the provision of labour, the *Regulations* limit transfer fees as follows: in cases of workers becoming permanent employees, transfer fees may only be charged if the hirer employs the worker within eight weeks of the end of the engagement or within 14 weeks of the start of the assignment. Further, the contract between the employment business and the hirer must provide the option for the hirer to extend the period of the original hire on no less favourable terms (*reg 10*).

Part IV of the *2003 Regulations* makes provision for requirements to be satisfied in relation to the introduction or supply of a work-seeker to a hirer (see *regs 18–22*). The *Regulations* impose minimum obligations on the employment agency or employment business to take steps to ensure that the work-seeker is suitable and also that the hirer is suitable (see *reg 20*).

In relation to the work-seeker the employment business or agency must obtain confirmation of identity and willingness to perform the role *(regs 19, 21(1)(a)(i))*. Where an employment business receives information relevant to the suitability of a worker supplied it must inform the hirer or terminate the engagement *(reg 20(2), (3), (4))*. Similar provisions apply in relation to an employment agency *(reg 20(5), (6))*. Further obligations arise in relation to checking professional qualifications *(reg 22)* and in relation to suitability for working with vulnerable persons *(reg 22)*. Information about the post, health and safety risks, qualifications required and rates payable and other terms of engagement must be obtained by the agency or employment business from the hirer *(reg 18)* and the employment business or agency should ensure that the hirer has carried out an adequate risk assessment for health and safety purposes. In relation to assignments of five consecutive days or less the administrative burden in relation to provision of information is reduced *(regs 21(4) and (5))*. Written notifications must still however be provided to the hirer in relation to the name of the work-seeker and confirmation of identity and experience and to the work-seeker in relation to the identity of the hirer, the nature of the business and the duration or likely duration of the work.

Further, an employment business or agency must not withhold pay due to a work-seeker in a number of circumstances (including that the hirer has not paid the employment business) (see *reg 12*) and must not disclose information relating to the work-seeker without prior consent, save for the purposes of providing the job finding services or for legal proceedings or to professional bodies relevant to the work-seeker *(reg 28)*. An employment agency or business may not subject a work-seeker to any detriment on the ground that the work-seeker has terminated the contract or given notice to terminate the contract and cannot require a work-seeker to provide information as to the identity of future employers *(reg 6)*.

As to work-seekers who provide their services via limited companies, the provisions of the *Regulations* were, by *reg 32(1)*, extended to this category of work-seeker with effect from 6 July 2004. The work-seeker is the limited company providing the individual's services and the individual is termed the 'person supplied by the work-seeker to carry out the work'. In this category the worker with a service company may opt out of the application of the *Regulations*. Any such opt out must be signed by the individual and the company before any assignment starts *(reg 32(9))*. By an amendment made by the *2007 Regulations* the agency or employment business must inform the hirer that such an opt-out agreement exists so that the *Regulations* do not apply. The opt-out option does not apply to engagements which involve working with vulnerable groups such as children and the elderly *(reg 32(12))*.

Breach of the *Regulations* (or breach of the *Employment Agencies Act 1973*) resulting in damage is actionable in the civil courts *(reg 30(1))* and an employment agency or employment business which breaches the *Regulations* may be liable to prosecution and a fine *(Employment Agencies Act 1973, s 5(2))*. By *reg 31(1), (2)* contractual terms in agreements with work-seekers or hirers which are prohibited by the *Regulations* are unenforceable and transfer fees which are in breach of the *Regulations* are liable to be repaid.

47.10 The application of the National Minimum Wage

The *National Minimum Wage Act 1998*, applies to all workers (as defined in *s 54(3)*). By *s 34* of the *National Minimum Wage Act 1998*, agency workers shall have the right to the National Minimum Wage in relation to whichever of the parties (agent or principal) is responsible for paying or actually pays the worker (see further PAY – I (34)). On the power to share relevant information between enforcement officers under the Employment Agency and NMW regimes see *s 18* of the *Employment Act 2008* and **47.7** above.

47.11 Temporary and Seasonal Employees

47.11 Employees

A temporary employee may accrue sufficient qualifying employment to present a complaint of unfair dismissal. If at the outset of his employment it was made clear to him that he was only engaged on a temporary basis, the employer's refusal to renew his temporary contract should be considered to be for a substantial reason falling within *ERA 1996, s 98(1)(b)* and may well be considered fair. (See *Fay v North Yorkshire County Council* [1986] ICR 133 approving *Terry v East Sussex County Council* [1977] 1 All ER 567.) The dismissal of replacement employees, taken on in place of permanent employees on medical suspension or absent because of pregnancy or confinement, will be considered to be for a reason falling within *s 98(1)(b)* provided that the dismissal is effected so as to allow the permanent employee to resume his original work, and provided that the dismissed employee was informed in writing at the time of the engagement that the employment was temporary and would be terminated when the permanent employee returned (*ERA 1996, s 106*). The Tribunal will then go on to decide whether the dismissal was fair within the meaning of *ERA 1996, s 98(4)(b)*. See also the provisions of the *Fixed-Term Employees (Prevention of Less Favourable Treatment) Regulations 2002 (SI 2002/2034)* (below at **47.13**).

47.12 SEASONAL WORKERS

Workers taken on for a limited period of time, such as seasonal sales staff or extra staff taken on to deal with the tourist season, are considered to be employees for all purposes. They enjoy all the normal employment protection rights provided that they have the necessary qualifying periods of employment.

Where such an employee is dismissed when the seasonal demand has ended, the fact that he was only taken on as a seasonal worker will not automatically make the dismissal fair. It is merely one of the circumstances which must be taken into account by an Employment Tribunal in deciding whether the employer acted reasonably (see Unfair Dismissal – II (52)). Also, a seasonal worker must be given at least the statutory minimum period of notice to terminate his contract of employment, unless the contract was for a fixed term (see **48.7** Termination of Employment).

If the period of unemployment between seasons is short and the employee is habitually re-engaged, his continuity of employment may be preserved during the period of his absence due to the temporary cessation of work (*ERA 1996, s 212(3)(b)*). (See **8.6** Continuous Employment, *Fitzgerald v Hall, Russell & Co Ltd* [1970] AC 984, *Ford v Warwickshire County Council* [1983] ICR 273 *Sillars v Charringtons Fuels Ltd* [1989] ICR 475, *Prater v Cornwall County Council* [2006] EWCA Civ 102, [2006] IRLR 362 and see also *Hellyer Bros Ltd v McLeod* [1987] ICR 526.)

Employers should therefore take just as much care to comply with all the applicable employment rules regarding seasonal staff as they do in the case of their permanent staff. See also the provisions of the *Fixed-Term Employees (Prevention of Less Favourable Treatment) Regulations 2002 (SI 2002/2034)* (below at **47.13**).

47.13 FIXED-TERM EMPLOYEES (PREVENTION OF LESS FAVOURABLE TREATMENT) REGULATIONS 2002 (SI 2002/2034)

In the case of employees who are engaged for a fixed period or for a particular task the *Fixed-Term Employees (Prevention of Less Favourable Treatment) Regulations 2002 (SI 2002/2034)* ('the Regulations') provide important rights to ensure that these employees are not less favourably treated than employees who are permanent or employed for an unlimited duration. The provisions of the Regulations came into force on 1 October 2002 and are derived from the *Fixed-Term Work Directive 99/70/EC*.

A fixed term contract is defined under the *Regulations* (*reg 1*) as a contract of employment that under its provisions will terminate (a) on the expiry of a specific term (b) on the completion of a particular task or (c) on the occurrence or non occurrence of any other specific event other than the attainment by the employee of any normal and bona fide retirement age. Thus (a) covers, say, an engagement for six months, (b) covers engagement to undertake a specific task (cf **47.11** above) and (c) is apt to cover the situation where an employee is engaged to cover for an absent employee until their return to work (eg following, say, a period of maternity absence). If a contract is to terminate on expiry of a specific term then the fact that there is also provision for earlier termination by notice does not prevent the contract being a fixed term contract for the purpose of the Regulations (*Allen v National Australia Group Europe Ltd* [2004] IRLR 847, EAT).

Certain employments are excluded from the protection afforded by the *Regulations* including apprentices, those on work experience and the armed forces (*regs 14, 18, 20*). The most significant exclusion, perhaps, is contained in *reg 19* whereby 'agency workers' are excluded from the protection of the *Regulations*. Agency worker means any person who is supplied by an employment business to do work for another person under a contract or other arrangements made between the employment business and the other person. 'Employment Business' for the purpose of the *Regulations* means 'the business . . . of supplying persons in the *employment* of the person carrying on the business, to act for, and under the control of, other persons in any capacity' (emphasis added (*reg 19(3)*). In the light of the complexity of the law relating to the issue of when an agency worker is employed by the agency (see **47.2** above) it appears likely that the ambit of this exclusion will be uncertain and highly likely to lead to continued litigation of the issue of who in fact employs an agency worker. In relation to agency workers the extent of the exclusion and its relationship with rights to statutory sick pay (SSP) was considered by the Court of Appeal in *Revenue and Customs Comrs v Thorn Baker Ltd* [2007] EWCA Civ 626, [2008] ICR 46. In the result agency workers engaged on a contract for less than three months continue to be excluded from the right to SSP.

The *Regulations* introduce the concept of a 'comparable permanent employee' (*reg 2*) who is, in relation to the fixed term employee, employed by the same employer and engaged in the same or broadly similar work having regard, where relevant, to whether they have a similar level of qualification or skill. The comparable permanent employee is to be employed at the same establishment as the fixed term employee or, if no suitable comparator exists at the establishment at which the fixed term employee is engaged, at another of the employer's establishments.

By *reg 3* the fixed term employee has the right not to be treated less favourably by the employer than a comparable permanent employee as regards terms of the contract or by being subjected to any detriment by the employer. The right includes the right not to be less favourably treated in relation to any period of service qualification relating to any particular condition of service, any opportunity to receive training or the opportunity to secure any permanent position in the establishment (*reg 3(2)*). The Court of Appeal in *Department of Work and Pensions v Webley* [2004] EWCA Civ 1745, [2005] IRLR 288 held that the non-renewal of a fixed-term contract, of itself, is not capable of involving less favourable treatment for the purpose of the Regulations. In that case fixed term workers had their contracts terminated after 51 weeks as a matter of policy regardless of whether there was an ongoing need for work or not.

Guidance on the structured approach to be taken by employment tribunals under the *Regulations* is provided by *Manchester College v Cocliff* (UKEAT/0035/10/CEA) [2010] All ER (D) 92 (Sep). The claimant employee had worked as a part-time lecturer at the employer college on a succession of fixed-term contracts since March 2005. He claimed that the terms of his employment were less favourable than those of a comparator employed on a permanent basis. The EAT held that an employment tribunal must first determine if the claimant and comparator were engaged in the same or broadly similar work. If so, it must then consider whether the less favourable treatment was on the ground that the claimant was a fixed term employee. Only if the second question is answered affirmatively is there a need to consider objective justification. In *Cocliff* the tribunal erred in considering the question of whether the less favourable treatment was justified before it had considered the reason for the treatment. Further the tribunal erred in rejecting justification based on differences in the jobs. The finding that the work was broadly similar does not preclude justification based upon such differences as do exist. The question is whether they are sufficient to justify the different treatment.

In relation to the opportunity to secure permanent positions, the fixed term employee has the right to be informed of available vacancies in the establishment by the employer (*reg 3(6), (7)*). The protection against less favourable treatment applies only if the treatment in issue is on the grounds that the employee is a fixed term employee and the treatment is not justified on objective grounds (*reg 3(3)*). Thus, for example, if an employer pays a fixed term employee at a lower rate than comparable permanent employees by reason of the fixed term status, this may (but not must) be less favourable treatment which the employer may have to objectively justify. On the application of the *Fixed-Term Work Directive 99/70/EC* and, hence, the *Regulations* (as a matter of purposive construction) to issues of inequality of pay see the ECJ's decision in *Del Cerro Alonso v Osakidetza-Servicio Vasco de Salud*: C-307/05 [2007] 3 CMLR 1492, [2008] ICR 145. In *Impact v Minister for Agriculture and Food*: C-268/06 [2008] IRLR 552 ECJ the principles in *Del Cerro* are developed, holding that *cl 4* of the Directive must be interpreted to cover not only pay but also pensions and thus exclusion from such rights will require objective justification. The ECJ in *Impact* (and in *Zentralbetriebsrat der Landeskrankenhäuser Tirols v Land Tirol*: C-486/08 [2010] IRLR 631) also held that *cl 4* was precise enough to be directly effective at national level but *cl 5* (on successive contracts) was not directly effective but nevertheless provided a guide to interpretation. Also, the ECJ held that employment adjudicating bodies (ie the employment tribunals in the UK) must have jurisdiction to hear directly arguments based on the Directive. See also *Gavieiro v Conselleria de Educacion e Ordinacion Universitaria del la Xunta de Galicia*: C-444/09 [2011] IRLR 504 (ECJ) in which an argument that the inevitably temporary nature of fixed term employment could itself objectively justify unequal treatment was (unsurprisingly) rejected but which also upheld the direct effect of *art 4* of the Framework Agreement on fixed term work so that it could be relied upon during a period of failure to implement the Directive.

Similarly, if, say, the employer limits certain facilities to permanent staff such as health care or other benefits, this may (but not must) be less favourable treatment of the fixed term employee which may require objective justification if it is to be permissible. It is not every difference in treatment, however, that will amount to less favourable treatment. *Regulation 3(5)* is an important provision which provides that, in order to determine whether a fixed term employee has been treated less favourably than a comparator, the 'pro rata' principle shall be applied unless it is inappropriate. The pro rata principle is defined in *reg 1* as follows:

> "where a comparable permanent employee receives or is entitled to pay or any other benefit, a fixed term employee is to receive or be entitled to such proportion of that pay or other benefit as is reasonable in the circumstances having regard to the length of his contract of employment and to the terms on which the pay or other benefit is offered."

The less favourable treatment in issue under *reg 3* must, however, be the act of the employer (or his agent). Less favourable treatment of a fixed term worker by a third party (e.g. an insurer in relation to the provision of less favourable health care insurance in comparison to permanent employees) will not render the employer liable unless the relationship of principal and agent is established (*Hall v Xerox UK Ltd* UKEAT/0061/14).

Regulation 4 provides an important gloss on objective justification providing that, in the event of less favourable treatment of a fixed term employee as regards any term in his contract, that treatment is to be regarded as objectively justified if the terms of the fixed term employee's contract 'taken as a whole' are at least as favourable as the comparator's contract of employment. Thus it is appropriate to look at the whole employment package afforded to the fixed term employee and not to concentrate on any single term when considering objective justification of contractual differences.

By *reg 5* a fixed term employee has the right to request in writing a statement from the employer setting out the reasons for any treatment in issue. That statement is to be provided within 21 days of the request (*reg 5(1)*). The statement is admissible in evidence before an employment tribunal (*reg 5(2)*) and failure to provide a statement without reasonable excuse or provision of an evasive or equivocal statement permits the tribunal to draw such inferences as appear just and equitable including an inference that the right in question has been infringed (*reg 5(3)*).

By *reg 6* a fixed term employee who is dismissed by reason of (i) bringing proceedings or (ii) giving evidence in relation to proceedings under the *Regulations*, or (iii) requesting a statement of reasons or (iv) alleging that the employer had contravened the *Regulations* or (v) doing anything under the *Regulations* or (vi) refusing forego a right conferred by the *Regulations*, is to be regarded as having been unfairly dismissed for the purposes of *Part 10* of the *ERA*. (See *reg 6(3)*). If the fixed term employee is dismissed in contravention of *reg 6*, then no qualifying period of service applies for the purposes of the *ERA*: see *ERA s 108(3)(j)*. By *reg 6(2)* a fixed term worker has the right not to be subjected to any detriment for like reasons to those applying to dismissal (see *reg 6(3)*).

The right to present complaints to the employment tribunal is set out in *reg 7* and the normal three month time limit subject to just and equitable extension applies (*reg 7(2), (3)*). Time runs from the act of less favourable treatment but can also apply when the act in question is the last in a series of similar acts or failures. In *Ibarz v University of Sheffield* (UKEAT/0018/15) the series concept was found to be capable, in an appropriate case, of applying where a claimant had worked on a series of separate contracts for a period of years with gaps between the contracts. If, as a matter of fact, the less favourable treatment satisfied the test of a "series of acts similar to each other" then a claim of less favourable treatment over the whole period of the successive contracts could be advanced. By *reg 7(6)* it is for the employer to identify the ground for the less favourable treatment or detriment. If an employment tribunal finds a complaint well founded it may provide a declaration as to the claimant's right and may award compensation assessed on the just and equitable basis including compensation for any loss suffered by the claimant (*reg 7(8), (9)*). Infringement of *reg 3* (Less favourable treatment) shall not, however, include an injury to feelings award (*reg 7(10)*). The employment tribunal also has power to make recommendations for the purpose of obviating or reducing the adverse effect on the complainant (*reg 7(7)(c)*). Failure without reasonable justification to comply with such recommendations may lead to an increase in the award of compensation (*reg 7(13)*).

An important right arises under *reg 8* to deal with the situation of persons employed on a succession of purported fixed-term contracts or a lengthy fixed term contract which is renewed. *Regulation 8* provides that, where a fixed term employee has been continuously employed under (i) a single fixed-term contract which is renewed or (ii) a number of fixed term contracts for a total period of four years or more and where continuity of employment is preserved, then the employee will become a permanent employee unless the employer can show objective justification (*reg 8(2)*). For the purposes of determining continuous employment *Chapter 1* of *Part 14* of the *ERA* is applied (*reg 8(4)*) (See also CONTINUOUS EMPLOYMENT (7)).

In *Duncombe and Fletcher v Secretary of State for Children Schools and Families* [2011] UKSC 14 the Supreme Court considered the applicability and effect of *reg 8* of the *Regulations*. The case involved employment at European Schools in other member States. Such schools have a rule that teachers may only be employed for nine years (a two year contract followed by contracts of three and four years). In the EAT and Court of Appeal the decision of the tribunal that objective justification for the nine year rule was not made out was upheld on appeal. In the Supreme Court it was held that the case had proceeded on the wrong basis. The purpose of the *Regulations* was not to prevent fixed term contracts but to prevent discrimination against fixed term workers. The focus of *reg 8* was whether the use of the current fixed term contract (if that current contract took the overall period of employment over four years) was objectively justifiable. The issue was not whether the "nine year rule" as a maximum period for employment of the teachers was objectively justified. Indeed it would have been wholly permissible to have engaged the teachers on one nine year fixed term contract from the outset. Understood in this way objective justification of the final (current contract) was made out: "It is not [the nine year rule] which requires to be justified, but the use of the latest fixed-term contract bringing the total period up to nine years. And that can readily be justified by the existence of the nine year rule. The teachers were employed to do a particular job which could only last for nine years. The Secretary of State could not foist those teachers on the schools for a longer period, no matter how unjustifiable either he or the employment tribunals of this country thought the rule to be" (per Baroness Hale at para 25). Given this finding it was not necessary to determine the subsidiary issue as to whether the *Regulations* in fact could apply to employees engaged in other member States, although Baroness Hale stated (para 33) that she "would be inclined to agree with the Tribunals and the Court of Appeal that Mr Duncombe and other teachers employed by the Secretary of State in European schools abroad are covered by the Fixed-term Regulations". Finally, the case raised issues of unfair dismissal jurisdiction and the application of *Lawson v Serco* principles and on these issues the Supreme Court reserved judgment.

It should be noted, in the context of the application of *reg 8*, that any period of continuous employment prior to 10 July 2002 does not count for the purposes of *reg 8*. The effect is that from 10 July 2006 and thereafter those who have been employed on two or more successive fixed term contracts for four or more years will be deemed to be permanent employees absent objective justification. On objective justification see the judgment of the ECJ in *Adeneler v Ellinikos Organismos Galaktos*: C-212/04 [2006] IRLR 716 in which the compatibility of Greek legislation on fixed–term work with the *Fixed-Term Work Directive 99/70/EC* and Framework Agreement was considered. The ECJ held that 'objective reasons' requiring the use of fixed-term contacts required justification by specific factors relating to the particular activity carried out and the conditions under which it is carried out. What is required is 'precise and concrete circumstances characterising a given activity, which are therefore capable in that particular context of justifying the use of successive fixed term contracts'. The ECJ explained that these 'circumstances' may arise from the specific nature of the tasks undertaken or their inherent characteristics or from the pursuit of a legitimate social policy objective of a Member State. See also *Zentralbetriebsrat der Landeskrankenhäuser Tirols v Land Tirol*: C-486/08 [2010] IRLR 631 and *Marquez Samohano v Universitat Pompeu Fabra*: C-190/13 [2014] IRLR 459. In *Secretary of State for Children, Schools and Families v Fletcher* [2008] 3 CMLR 1462, [2009] ICR 102 the issue of objective justification was considered in relation to *reg 8* in a domestic context where a teacher at a European School succeeded in establishing permanent status by the use of *reg 8* despite provisions to the effect that, under the relevant treaty provisions setting up the school, a teacher's secondment could not exceed nine years. In *Hudson v Department for Work and Pension* [2013] IRLR 32 (CA) the claimant relied on a series of fixed term contracts with the DWP in order to claim a declaration in accordance with *reg 8* that she had become a permanent employee. The final contract in the series was not covered by *reg 18* (which disapplies the *Regulations* in cases of employment on a scheme to provide training) but the earlier contracts fell within the *reg 18* exclusion. The EAT had held that, as *reg 18* used the present tense, it only applied to a current contract and not the earlier ones with the result that they could count towards the requisite four year period of service for the purposes of *reg 8*. Reversing the EAT ([2012] IRLR 900) the Court of Appeal by majority held that that *reg 18* when engaged totally disapplies the *Regulations* so that any period of employment falling under *reg 18* cannot count towards the period of four years continuous employment required to convert the contract into a permanent one under *reg 8*.

Reg 8 may be modified or excluded by a collective agreement or workforce agreement (*reg 8(5)*). A fixed term worker, however, may not individually contract out of his rights under the Regulations save as is permitted under *s 203* of the *ERA*.

By *reg 9* an employee who considers that by application of *reg 8* he is a permanent employee may request a written statement from the employer confirming his permanent employee status. Such a statement is to be provided within 21 days and must either confirm the change in status or provide reasons why it is said the employee remains a fixed term employee (*reg 9(1)*, *(2)*). If the employer intends to rely upon objective justification the grounds must be specified in the statement (*reg 9(2)*). The statement is admissible in any court proceedings (*reg 9(3)*) and failure to provide a statement or evasive or equivocal replies permit adverse inferences to be drawn (*reg 9(4)*). An employee who considers himself to be a permanent employee by virtue of *reg 8* may apply to the employment tribunal for a declaration to that effect (*reg 9(5)*) but prior to making an application for the declaration the employee must have sought or obtained a statement pursuant to *reg 9(1)* (*reg 9(6)(a)*). Finally, at the time of the application for the declaration the employee must be employed by the employer and accordingly 'historical' applications for a declaration by former employees are not to be entertained (*reg 9(6)(b)*).

The *Regulations* make provision for vicarious liability of the employer for the acts of its employees and agents (*reg 12(1)*, *(2)*) subject to a defence for the employer to prove that it took such steps as were reasonably practicable to prevent the employee doing the act or acts of that description in the course of his employment (*reg 12(3)*).

48   Termination of Employment

48.1   A contract of employment may be terminated in several ways: by mutual agreement; by frustration; by expiry; by dismissal by the employer; by notice given by the employee; or by acceptance of a fundamental repudiatory breach of contract by the employer or the employee. The distinction between these different modes of termination may be of importance in determining whether the employee may bring a claim for UNFAIR DISMISSAL – I (53), WRONGFUL DISMISSAL (58) or REDUNDANCY – I (38).

The death of either party terminates the contract of employment, unless the contract expressly or impliedly provides otherwise. The bankruptcy of the employer does not operate as a dissolution of the contracts of employment between himself and his employees, but in general the winding-up of a company and the dissolution of a partnership do operate to terminate the contract (see, eg *Briggs v Oates* [1990] ICR 473, holding that the expiration of the partnership represented a breach of the employee's contract, but suggesting that mere departures from, and additions to, a body of partners would not have such an effect). This is subject to the effect of the *Transfer of Undertakings (Protection of Employment) Regulations 2006 (SI 2006/246)* (see TRANSFER OF UNDERTAKINGS (52)).

It may be held in a particular case that, where an employee starts to work for his old employer in a new capacity, then the old contract has come to an end and has been replaced by a new one. Whether or not this is so is a question of degree (*Hogg v Dover College* [1990] ICR 39; *Alcan Extrusions v Yates* [1996] IRLR 327; and, more recently, *Smith v Trafford Housing Trust* [2013] IRLR 86 where the demotion of an employee, and a reduction in his salary, as a disciplinary sanction for posting a comment about gay marriage on his Facebook wall was held to be a (wrongful) termination of the earlier contract).

48.2   MUTUAL AGREEMENT

Termination by agreement between employer and employee may be effected either orally or in writing. The agreement to terminate may take effect on any day in the month or year, and does not have to coincide with a pay-day.

The courts will scrutinise an apparent agreement to terminate if the employee alleges that he was given no choice but to consent to the ending of his employment. The general principle which the courts will apply is that if the cause of the employee's willingness to agree to the termination of his employment is the threat of dismissal, he will be held to have been dismissed. If, however, other additional factors, such as financial inducements, affected his decision he will be taken to have resigned by mutual agreement. He will then not be entitled to bring any claim for unfair or wrongful dismissal.

In *Sheffield v Oxford Controls Co Ltd* [1979] ICR 396, the employee was told that if he did not resign he would be dismissed. He signed an agreement to resign in return for certain financial benefits. The Employment Appeal Tribunal found that he had resigned and had not been dismissed because his resignation had been brought about not by the threat of dismissal but by other factors such as the offer of financial benefits. See also *Birch v University of Liverpool* [1985] ICR 470, *Scott v Coalite Fuels and Chemicals Ltd* [1988] ICR 355, *Hellyer Bros Ltd v Atkinson and Dickinson* [1992] IRLR 540 and *Optare Group Ltd v Transport and General Workers' Union* [2007] IRLR 931.

The authorities were reviewed in *Sandhu v Jan de Rijk Transport Ltd* [2007] ICR 1137. On the facts of that case, the Court of Appeal held that the employee had not resigned even though he had entered into a severance agreement. The employee had been invited to a meeting at which he was told, without prior warning, that he was being dismissed. During

48.2   Termination of Employment

the course of the meeting, the parties agreed severance terms. However, the employee had not received any legal advice and had no opportunity to reflect on matters. In reaching an agreement, he had simply done his best to 'salvage what he could from the inevitable fact that he was going to be dismissed'. Furthermore, the severance terms were not particularly favourable to him (three months' salary, and the short term retention of the use of the employer's car and mobile phone).

Also, in *Caledonian Mining Co Ltd v Bassett* [1987] ICR 425, an employer who dishonestly persuaded his employees to resign was treated as having dismissed them. The dishonesty in that case was held by the employment tribunal to consist of a preconceived arrangement designed by the employers to avoid liability for redundancy payments.

An agreement for the automatic termination of a contract of employment on the occurrence of a certain event may be ineffective to exclude entitlement to statutory employment protection rights because of *ERA 1996, s 203(1)* (see **53.19** Unfair Dismissal – I).

48.3   FRUSTRATION

Frustration occurs where the performance of the contract of employment becomes impossible or substantially different from that which the parties contemplated at the time of entering into the agreement by reason of an unforeseen and unprovided for event which has occurred without the fault or default of either party to the contract (*Paal Wilson & Co A/S v Partenreederei Hannah Blumenthal* [1983] 1 AC 854 at 909). A contract will be terminated by frustration if performance becomes unlawful (eg by the passing of a statute after the contract is made). The question of termination of a contract of employment by reason of frustration most frequently arises in cases of absence of the employee because of illness or imprisonment. Where the contract is frustrated, there is no dismissal (the essence of frustration is that in law termination is *automatic*), and hence no possible claim for wrongful or unfair dismissal or redundancy. The employee will be able to recover for services rendered prior to the frustrating event, relying if necessary upon *Law Reform (Frustrated Contracts) Act 1943, s 1(3)*.

In *Williams v Watsons Luxury Coaches Ltd* [1990] ICR 536, the EAT drew together the principles of the doctrine of frustration as they apply to contracts of employment. At 541, Wood J held that the following principles applied to cases of frustration by reason of illness:

'First, that the court must guard against too easy an application of the doctrine, more especially when redundancy occurs and also when the true situation may be a dismissal by reason of disability. Secondly, that although it is not necessary to decide that frustration occurred on a particular date, nevertheless an attempt to decide the relevant date is far from a useless exercise as it may help to determine in the mind of the court whether it really is a true frustration situation. Thirdly, that there are a number of factors which may help to decide the issue as they may each point in one or other direction. These we take from the judgment of Phillips J in *Egg Stores (Stamford Hill) Ltd v Leibovici* [1977] ICR 260, 265:

" . . . Among the matters to be taken into account in such a case in reaching a decision are these: (1) the length of the previous employment; (2) how long it had been expected that the employment would continue; (3) the nature of the job; (4) the nature, length and effect of the illness or disabling event; (5) the need of the employer for the work to be done, and the need for a replacement to do it; (6) the risk to the employer of acquiring obligations in respect of redundancy payments or compensation for unfair dismissal to the replacement employee; (7) whether wages have continued to be paid; (8) the acts and the statements of the employer in relation to the employment, including the dismissal of, or failure to dismiss, the employee; and (9) whether in all the circumstances a reasonable employer could be expected to wait any longer."

1212

To these we would add the terms of the contract as to the provisions for sickness pay, if any, and also, a consideration of the prospects of recovery. Fourthly – see *FC Shepherd & Co Ltd v Jerrom* [1986] ICR 802 – the party alleging frustration should not be allowed to rely upon the frustrating event if that event was caused by that party – at least where it was caused by its fault.'

For earlier cases of frustration of the contract due to illness, see *Marshall v Harland and Wolff Ltd* [1972] ICR 101; *Hart v AR Marshall & Sons (Bulwell) Ltd* [1977] ICR 539; *Egg Stores (Stamford Hill) Ltd v Leibovici* [1977] ICR 260; and *Notcutt v Universal Equipment Co (London) Ltd* [1986] ICR 414.

The principles set out in *Leibovici* must be added to where the employee is suffering from a disability. In *Warner v Armfield Retail & Leisure Ltd* [2014] ICR 239, it was held that before the doctrine of frustration can apply there is an additional factor: namely, whether the employer is in breach of the duty to make reasonable adjustments. While there is something which it is reasonable to expect the employer to have to do in order to keep the employee in employment, the doctrine of frustration can have no application.

For frustration of the contract of employment due to imprisonment, see *FC Shepherd & Co Ltd v Jerrom* [1986] ICR 802, in which the Court of Appeal held that a contract of employment was capable of being frustrated by the imposition of a custodial sentence.

In *Four Seasons Healthcare Ltd (formerly Cotswold Spa Retirement Hotels Ltd) v Maughan* [2005] IRLR 324, on the other hand, the EAT held that bail conditions which effectively prevented a registered mental nurse from attending work at a care home did not constitute a 'frustrating event'. The EAT noted that it was unaware of similar cases which supported an argument for 'frustration', and further that the employer had the opportunity, of dismissing the employee, if it so wished.

The rule that frustration could not be induced by a party's own default applied only to the party alleging that frustration had occurred.

The doctrine of frustration was analysed by Gray J in *Gryf-Lowczowski (Jan) v Hinchingbrooke Healthcare NHS Trust* [2005] EWHC 2407 (QB), [2006] IRLR 100. The case concerned a consultant general and colorectal surgeon who, following a referral to the National Clinical Assessment Authority, had been on special leave from work for almost two years and could not resume his duties at the employing trust until he had undergone a period of training at another trust. The employer sought to argue that the contract of employment had been frustrated. This was rejected by Gray J who stressed that, in looking at point (9) (in the *Leibovici*) case, where the employment was of such a nature that its termination by frustration would have a 'catastrophic' effect on the employee of making it highly unlikely that he would find work again as a medical practitioner within the NHS, it would be reasonable to expect an employer to wait rather longer than might be the case in other circumstances before the contract was held to be frustrated.

On the facts of that case, Gray J held that the crucial question for the Court was whether there remained a realistic possibility that a placement could be found to enable the employee to be re-skilled and thereafter to resume his former duties with the employer. Gray J held that there was such a possibility, and so the contract was not frustrated.

Where a contract of employment has been brought to an end by reason of 'frustration' (ie performance of the contract becomes impossible or substantially different from that contemplated by the parties at inception without fault on either side), the parties cannot thereafter agree that the contract continues to subsist: see *G F Sharp & Co Ltd v McMillan* [1998] IRLR 632. In that case, a joiner lost the use of his left hand and could never work for his employer in that capacity again. Although the parties agreed to keep the employee 'on the books' so that he could gain access to greater pension benefits, the EAT held that this did not amount to a continuation of the contract of employment. The contract had been nullified by the employee's injury. As a consequence, the employee was not entitled to notice of termination of his employment or payment in lieu.

48.4   EXPIRY

If a contract is for a fixed period, it will automatically terminate at the end of that period. No notice need be given. It should be noted that, for the purposes of a claim for redundancy pay or in respect of unfair dismissal, the expiry of a fixed-term contract may nevertheless constitute a dismissal (see **38.7** REDUNDANCY – I and **53.4–53.6** UNFAIR DISMISSAL – I). If an employee remains in his employment after the expiry of the term, he will be considered to be working under the same terms and conditions as before, save only that his employment is subject to an implied term that it can be terminated by either party upon giving reasonable notice (see **48.6** below).

48.5   DISMISSAL BY THE EMPLOYER

'Dismissal' is here used in its popular sense, to mean termination of a contract of employment by the employer. For the purposes of the unfair dismissal and redundancy payments legislation, the concept of dismissal is given a special statutory meaning which includes both the expiry of a fixed-term contract without its renewal and 'constructive dismissal' (see **38.7** REDUNDANCY – I and **53.4** UNFAIR DISMISSAL – I).

Sometimes there may be a dispute as to whether the words used by the employer (or the employee in the case of a resignation) in fact amount to a dismissal. Where those words are ambiguous, the court or tribunal should ask how they would have been understood by a reasonable listener in the circumstances (*Sothern v Franks Charlesly & Co* [1981] IRLR 278).

A party who has used unambiguous words cannot normally be heard to say that he did not mean what he appeared to mean. There are 'special circumstances', however, in which the words used will not be treated as definitive. In those circumstances, the person purportedly giving notice should be given an opportunity to satisfy the recipient that he did not intend to bring the employment relationship to an end (*Willoughby v CF Capital Ltd* [2011] IRLR 985). See, for instance, *Barclay v City of Glasgow District Council* [1983] IRLR 313, where a mentally handicapped employee purported to resign and the EAT held that there are circumstances where words are spoken under emotional stress, which the other party ought to know are not meant to be taken seriously. Similarly, where words are spoken in the heat of the moment: see *Sovereign House Security Services Ltd v Savage* [1989] IRLR 115. See also *Kwik-Fit (GB) Ltd v Lineham* [1992] ICR 183.

Dismissal may be either *summary* or with *notice*. At common law, either party to the contract of employment is always free to terminate the relationship by giving the proper notice provided that the contract is one which, whether expressly or impliedly, is terminable upon giving notice. Thus, if such notice is given, there can be no claim for WRONGFUL DISMISSAL (**58**). To be effective in law, the notice must expire on a certain specified day (*Morton Sundour Fabrics Ltd v Shaw* (1966) 2 ITR 84), or upon the occurrence of a specified event (*Burton Group Ltd v Smith* [1977] IRLR 351). There is no dismissal on notice where an employer informs an absent employee that if he does not return to work by a particular date he will be treated as having terminated his employment, even if the employee does not turn up on that date and the employer treats the employment as having been terminated (*Rai v Somerfield Stores Ltd.* [2004] ICR 656).

For the date at which termination takes effect, see **53.13** UNFAIR DISMISSAL – I. The parties may by agreement either advance or postpone the date of termination (*Mowlem Northern Ltd v Watson* [1990] ICR 751; and see also *Palfrey v Transco plc* [2004] IRLR 916).

The contract of employment may provide for summary termination in certain circumstances. Summary dismissal in other circumstances is *prima facie* a breach of contract, unless the employee is in fundamental breach of the contract (see **48.13** below). Whether the dismissal is or is not fair is an entirely separate question. A dismissal may be fair even though proper notice is not given, and a dismissal on notice may nonetheless be unfair (see *Treganowan v Robert Knee & Co Ltd* [1975] ICR 405; *BSC Sports and Social Club v Morgan* [1987] IRLR 391; and Unfair Dismissal – **II (54)**).

Where an employer is expressly permitted to terminate the contract of employment by making a payment in lieu of notice, there is an implied obligation on the employer to notify the employee in clear and unambiguous terms that such payment has been made and that it is made in the exercise of the contractual right to terminate the employment with immediate effect (*Société Générale v Geys* [2013] ICR 117).

Where an employer exercises the power to terminate the contract of employment by making a payment in lieu, a debt will accrue, and it will not be open to the employer to resile from making the necessary payment on discovering conduct which would otherwise have justified a wrongful dismissal. There has been no wrongful dismissal, but a termination in accordance with the contract's own terms: see *Cavenagh v William Evans Ltd* [2012] ICR 1231. The principle set out in *Boston Deep Sea Fishing and Ice Co v Ansell* 39 Ch D 339 did not go as far as to say that after-discovered misconduct provided an employer with a defence to an action for payment of an accrued debt. Where an employer gives notice of termination, however, no debt for the notice monies accrues and, if the employer dismisses the employee summarily during the notice period, the principle in *Boston Deep Sea Fishing* can be relied upon by the employer to resist a claim for damages: see *Williams v Leeds United Football Club* [2015] IRLR 383.

A 'dismissal' by the employer can result from the termination of one contract and its replacement by another: see *Hogg v Dover College* [1990] ICR 39; and *Smith v Trafford Housing Trust* [2013] IRLR 86 (see **48.1**).

48.6   Termination on notice – the contractual notice period

The contract of employment will usually specify the period of notice to be given to terminate the contract; indeed, the written particulars given to the employee must include the length of notice which the employee is obliged to give or entitled to receive (see **8.7** Contract of Employment).

If the contract is not for a fixed term and the notice period has not been expressly agreed, there is an implied term that it may be terminated upon reasonable notice (see *Reda v Flag Ltd* [2002] UKPC 38, [2002] IRLR 747). The court will determine what amounts to reasonable notice. Factors taken into account include the seniority and remuneration of the employee, his age, his length of service and what is usual in the particular trade. As a very rough guide, a period of two weeks or one month might be appropriate in the case of a manual worker, three months in the case of senior skilled workers or middle management, and between three months and one year in the case of more senior managers. However, the period of notice must be determined on the particular facts of each case. (For a discussion of the factors, see *Clarke v Fahrenheit 451 (Communications) Ltd* (EAT 591/99) (1999) IDS Brief 666, p 11.)

48.7   Termination on notice – statutory minimum notice

Whatever may be the contractual provisions – whether express or implied – for termination of the contract, the notice actually given must not be less than the statutory minimum period of notice. The contractual notice must be given if that is longer. The statutory rules are as follows:

48.7 Termination of Employment

(a)   an employee who has been continuously employed for one month or more but less than two years is entitled to not less than one week's notice;

(b)   an employee who has been continuously employed for two years or more but less than 12 years is entitled to one week's notice for each year of continuous employment;

(c)   any employee who has been employed for 12 years or more is entitled to not less than 12 weeks' notice.

(ERA 1996, s 86(1).)

This results in the following:

Table of statutory minimum notice

Period of continuous employment (years)	Minimum period (weeks)
Less than 2 (but 1 month or more)	1
At least 2 but less than 3	2
At least 3 but less than 4	3
At least 4 but less than 5	4
At least 5 but less than 6	5
At least 6 but less than 7	6
At least 7 but less than 8	7
At least 8 but less than 9	8
At least 9 but less than 10	9
At least 10 but less than 11	10
At least 11 but less than 12	11
12 or more	12

For example, if a clerk has been employed for 12 years under a contract which does not specify the period of notice to which he is entitled, a term of reasonable notice would be implied which in his case may well be one month. However, his length of service entitled him to 12 weeks' notice and that is the minimum notice he must be given.

An employee cannot contract out of his right to the statutory minimum period of notice *(ERA 1996, s 203)*. However, he may waive his right to notice on a particular occasion, or accept a payment in lieu of notice *(ERA 1996, s 86(3); Trotter v Forth Ports Authority* [1991] IRLR 419).

48.8 Exceptions

Certain seamen do not have the right to be given the statutory minimum period of notice: *(ERA 1996, s 199)*.

48.9 Pay in lieu of notice

An employer who intends to dismiss an employee may consider it desirable that the employee should cease work immediately and not work out his notice period. For example, some employers consider it unwise to let a sales representative, who knows that he is to be dismissed, have any further contact with the employer's customers, for fear of endangering their goodwill. If an employee is dismissed without notice or with short notice it is usual to give him pay in lieu of notice. It would be possible, although unusual, to give an employee notice to expire halfway through the contractual or statutory notice period and to make a payment in lieu of notice in respect of the remainder of the period. Another possibility is to continue to pay the employee as usual, but to ask him to remain at home. This will not normally represent a breach of contract by the employer (but see **8.13** CONTRACT OF EMPLOYMENT). Even if he makes a payment in lieu of notice, an employer will nevertheless in theory be guilty of a breach of contract (unless the contract provides for this possibility – as, for example, in *Cavenagh v William Evans Ltd* [2012] ICR 1231). However, the employee will not normally have a right of action in damages unless, through the premature determination of his contract, he has been deprived of valuable statutory rights. (See observations in *Robert Cort & Son Ltd v Charman* [1981] ICR 816; *Delaney v Staples* [1992] IRLR 191; and *Abrahams v Performing Rights Society* [1995] IRLR 486, CA.) However, in certain circumstances, the employee may be able to obtain an injunction to restrain a termination before the expiry of the contractual notice period. Such relief may be obtained where, by the employer's breach, the employee will suffer loss for which he cannot be compensated in damages, as where during the notice period the employee would have been able to exercise a share option in respect of which a claim in damages has been excluded.

The practice of giving pay in lieu of notice is virtually universal, but it does not fit easily into the traditional legal framework. Two connected problem areas are:

(a)   whether pay in lieu of notice is taxable (see **48.10** below);

(b)   if tax-free, whether it should be paid gross or net (see **48.11** below).

48.10

Taxation of pay in lieu of notice. The contract of employment may expressly empower the employer to dismiss the employee summarily on making a payment in lieu of notice. If the contract does set out such a right then the payment in lieu constitutes an 'emolument' of the employment, and tax should be deducted under PAYE in the usual way (see *EMI Group Electronics Ltd v Coldicott (Inspector of Taxes)* [1999] IRLR 630). The employee is not entitled to the benefit of the £30,000 exemption referred to below. It is probable that any appropriate National Insurance contributions should be paid as well.

Normally, there is no express contractual term relating to the making of payments in lieu of notice, but the employer may have an almost invariable custom of giving pay in lieu of notice. The House of Lords has held that such a payment is a payment of compensation for the employer's breach of contract in not giving due notice (*Delaney v Staples* [1992] ICR 483). Accordingly, the payment escapes the general Schedule E charge. It follows that neither the frequency with which such payments are made nor any expectation on the part of the employee would affect this. Since a non-contractual payment in lieu of notice falls to be regarded as compensation, it will be tax-free under the general rules. It may nevertheless be taxable under the special rules on compensation payments for loss of office (eg 'golden handshakes'), but only if the *total* amount paid to the employee, including any redundancy payment and any other termination payments, exceeds £30,000 (*Income Tax (Earnings and Pensions) Act 2003, ss 401, 403*). A non-contractual payment in lieu of notice is not subject to National Insurance contributions.

Where the employer and employee genuinely negotiate an agreement to terminate the employment contract, and no question of breach of contract by the employer arises, then any lump sum payable as part of the agreement will be treated as an 'emolument' from employment and will be taxable under Schedule E. The £30,000 exemption will not apply: see *Richardson (HM Inspector of Taxes) v Delaney* [2001] IRLR 663.

48.11 *Payment gross or net?* Most employers who make a payment in lieu of notice which is tax-free, pay over to the employee his full gross wages or salary. Legally, however, if pay in lieu of notice is to be regarded as compensation for breach of contract (see above), it would follow that the employer is only liable to pay the net amount that the employee would have

Termination of Employment

received after deduction of tax and National Insurance. This is because the measure of damages for breach of contract is calculated on the basis of *the amount lost* by the employee in not being allowed to work his notice. However, there is nothing to prevent an employer from paying the gross amount and there may be sound reasons for doing so, eg to maintain good industrial relations or public relations. It is also conceivable, although unlikely, that an employer who had a consistent practice of making payments gross might be held liable to pay the gross amount to an employee on the ground that the consistent practice had given rise to an implied contractual term (see, eg *Gothard v Mirror Group Newspapers Ltd* [1988] ICR 729). (To avoid the tax charge it would be necessary to establish that this term related only to the manner of calculating pay in lieu and not to the employer's liability to make the payment.) Pay in lieu of notice does not amount to wages for the purposes of the provisions relating to protection of wages (*ERA 1996, ss 13–27*) (see **34.6 Pay – I**).

48.12 Employee's rights during period of notice

Where an employee has been continuously employed for one month or more (see Continuous Employment (7)), and his employment is terminated either by the employer giving notice, or by notice given by himself, the employee is given certain rights during the statutory minimum notice period, ie the period shown in **48.7** above where the employer gives notice, and one week where the employee gives notice (*ERA 1996, s 87(1), (2)*). This does not apply, however, where notice is given by the employer and the contractual notice period exceeds the statutory minimum by at least one week (*ERA 1996, s 87(4)*), as illustrated in the case of *Budd v Scotts Co (UK) Ltd* [2004] ICR 299, [2003] IRLR 145, EAT.

The rights in question are set out in *ERA 1996, ss 87–91*. Although it will not be possible to rely upon them directly if the statutory minimum notice is not given by the employer, they are to be taken into account in assessing damages in a Wrongful Dismissal (58) action (*ERA 1996, s 91(5)*).

The principal right conferred is to be paid in cases where the employee is ready and willing to work, but no work is provided for him by his employer, or where the employee is incapable of work because of sickness or injury, or where the employee is absent from work wholly or partly because of pregnancy or childbirth, or is absent in accordance with the terms of his employment relating to holidays. Where there are normal working hours, the amount payable is arrived at by taking the number of hours covered by the above situations and applying to them the hourly rate of remuneration produced by dividing a week's pay by the number of normal working hours (*ERA 1996, s 88*). Where there are no normal working hours, the employer must pay a week's pay in each week of the notice period, provided that the employee is ready and willing to do work of a reasonable nature and amount to earn a week's pay (*ERA 1996, s 89*). In each case, any payments in fact made (including holiday pay and sick pay) go towards meeting the employer's liability.

Accordingly, an employee who has been dismissed on account of prolonged sickness absence is entitled to receive full salary during his notice period if his sickness continues during that period. This is the case even if the employee had by the time of his dismissal exhausted his rights to sick pay, and would have received no payment from his employer if his contract had not been terminated.

The employer is not liable to make payments in respect of a period during which the employee is on leave at his own request (*ERA 1996, s 91(1)*), nor where the employee has given notice and thereafter takes part in a strike (*ERA 1996, s 91(2)*).

Where the employer breaks the contract during the notice period, payments made under *ERA 1996, ss 87–91* go to mitigate the damage suffered (*ERA 1996, s 91(3)*). Where the employer terminates the contract during the notice period and is entitled to do so because of the employee's breach of contract (see **48.13** below), there is no liability under *ERA 1996, s 88* or *s 89* in respect of the subsequent part of the full notice period (*ERA 1996, s 91(4)*).

48.13 Summary dismissal

If the employee acts in a way which is incompatible with the faithful discharge of his duty to his employer he may be dismissed instantly, without notice or wages in lieu of notice. Examples of misconduct which can in certain circumstances give rise to the right to dismiss summarily are wilful disobedience of a lawful order from the employer, theft of the employer's property, and drunkenness such as to impair the performance of his duties. The misconduct must be gross or grave, seen in the light of all the circumstances of the case. In general, employees should be given a clear indication of the type of conduct which the employer regards as warranting summary dismissal (*ACAS Code of Practice 1, para 23*).

Summary dismissal for misconduct which is not gross is a breach of contract rendering the employer liable in damages for WRONGFUL DISMISSAL (**58**).

For a discussion of the exact moment when a dismissal without notice takes effect, see *Octavius Atkinson & Sons Ltd v Morris* [1989] ICR 431.

48.14 Written statement of reasons for dismissal

An employee is entitled to be provided by his employer, on request, within 14 days of that request, with a written statement giving particulars of the reasons for his dismissal if:

(a)   he is given by his employer notice of termination of his contract of employment; or

(b)   his contract of employment is terminated by his employer without notice; or

(c)   where he is employed under a contract for a fixed term, that term expires without being renewed under the same contract.

(*ERA 1996, s 92(1)*.)

The reasons given by an employer are admissible in evidence in any proceedings. The employer's reply to a request may refer to full reasons given in an earlier written communication, a copy of which should be sent with the reply. Where a legal adviser is appointed by the employee, as a duly authorised agent to receive the information, it is sufficient to communicate the information to the legal adviser (*Kent County Council v Gilham* [1985] ICR 227).

An employee is not normally entitled to written reasons unless he has been continuously employed for a period of two years ending with the effective date of termination (*Unfair Dismissal and Reasons for Dismissal (Variation of Qualifying Period) Order 2012 (SI 2012/989)*) (an exception is made for employees whose continuous period of employment commenced before 6th April 2012: for these employees, only one year's continuous employment is required).

Special rules apply if an employee is dismissed at any time while she is pregnant, or after childbirth in circumstances in which her maternity leave period ends by reason of her dismissal (for the maternity leave period, see **32.38** MATERNITY AND PARENTAL RIGHTS). She is entitled to a written statement of reasons for the dismissal, irrespective of the length of her employment, and without having to make any request (*ERA 1996, s 92(4)*).

48.15 Remedy for failure to give reasons

A complaint may be made by the employee to an industrial tribunal on the grounds:

(a)   that his employer unreasonably failed to provide a written statement under *ERA 1996, s 92* of the reason for dismissal; or

(b)   that the particulars given in purported compliance with that section are inadequate or untrue.

48.15 Termination of Employment

(ERA 1996, s 93(1).)

The obligation is, of course, to give the actual reason for dismissal; the question is not whether that reason is in fact well-founded.

In *Daynecourt Insurance Brokers Ltd v Iles* [1978] IRLR 335, the company failed to answer an employee's request for written reasons for his dismissal. Its justification for doing so was a general request by the police officer who investigated the alleged theft of company funds by the employee, that the company should not answer any correspondence or deal with any matter that related to the police investigations of the company's records. The EAT held that the industrial tribunal's finding, that the company should not have simply ignored the employee's statutory request but should have sought further advice of the police officer, was not wrong in law. A failure to provide written reasons may be unreasonable even if the employee knows perfectly well why he has been dismissed, since one purpose of the provision is that the employee should be able to show the reasons to third parties (*McBrearty v Thomson*, IDS Brief 450, p 15).

Except in maternity cases (see **48.14** above), there cannot be a complaint to the tribunal that the reasons given are inadequate if there has been no request for proper reasons by the employee pursuant to *ERA 1996, s 92(1)* (*Catherine Haigh Harlequin Hair Design v Seed* [1990] IRLR 175).

In *Banks v Lavin*, IDS Brief 410, p 6, the EAT held that the statement 'many jobs not being done' was an inadequate reason, because it was not sufficiently specific.

The time limit for presentation of the complaint is three months from the effective date of termination of employment. This period can be extended if the industrial tribunal is satisfied that it was not reasonably practicable to present it within the three-month period (*ERA 1996, s 93(3);* and see **18.20** EMPLOYMENT TRIBUNALS – **I**).

If the tribunal finds the complaint well-founded, it will make an award that the employer pay to the employee a sum equal to the amount of two weeks' pay. It may also make a declaration as to what it finds that the employer's reasons were for dismissing the employee (*ERA 1996, s 93(2)*). A week's pay is calculated in accordance with the provisions of *ERA 1996, ss 221–229*, formerly *EPCA 1978, Sch 14* and the calculation date is:

(i)   where the dismissal was with notice, the date on which the employer's notice was given; or

(ii)   in any other case, the effective date of termination.

(ERA 1996, s 226(2).)

(See further REDUNDANCY – **I** (38).)

The amount of a week's pay is not subject to a statutory maximum for this purpose.

48.16 RESIGNATION BY THE EMPLOYEE

As in the case of dismissal by the employer, the employee may resign with or without notice. For the question of whether the words used will amount to a resignation, see **48.5** above. No particular terms of art are required for resignations (*Walmsley v C&R Ferguson Ltd* [1989] IRLR 112). A failure to give due notice is *prima facie* a breach of contract, but may be justified where the employee resigns in response to a repudiatory breach of contract by the employer (see **48.18** below).

A failure by an employee to give proper notice of resignation is *prima facie* a breach of contract. The more difficult question will usually be what, if any, are the damages payable by the employee. In *Giraud UK Ltd v Smith* [2000] IRLR 763, the Employment Appeal

Tribunal struck down a clause in an employment contract which provided that 'failure to give the proper notice and work it out will result in a reduction from your final payment equivalent to the number of days short'. This was held to be an unlawful penalty clause rather than a lawful liquidated damages clause. There was evidence to suggest that the employer could easily find replacements for the employee in question (he worked as a driver), so that it was not a genuine pre-estimate of loss. Furthermore, the clause was oppressive, as there was no limitation on the right of the employers to recover damages for actual loss if this was greater than that specified in the clause. Therefore, the employee was in a position where if the actual loss turned out to be nil, he would be liable for the sum set out in the clause, but if the actual loss was greater than the sum set out in the clause, he could face an unlimited claim for the balance. The clause enabled the employer to say, 'Heads I win, tails you lose'.

48.17 Termination by the employee giving notice

The statutory minimum period of notice to be given by an employee, who has been continuously employed for one month or more, is one week (*ERA 1996, s 86(2)*). However, the contractual period of notice to be given will, in many cases, be longer. The contractual notice may be either expressly agreed upon or implied. If it is implied, the notice to be given is that which is a reasonable period in all the circumstances (see **48.6** above).

48.18 Summary termination by the employee

If an employer is in breach of a fundamental term of the contract of employment, the employee is entitled to leave the employment forthwith. Leaving the employment in these circumstances is known as 'constructive dismissal' for redundancy payments and unfair dismissal purposes, since although the employee takes the initiative in leaving his employment he will be considered to have been dismissed within the meaning of *ERA 1996, s 136(1)* (see **38.6** REDUNDANCY – I) and *ERA 1996, s 95(1)* (see **53.4** UNFAIR DISMISSAL – I). In such circumstances, the employee would also be able to claim damages for WRONGFUL DISMISSAL (**58**).

48.19 REPUDIATORY CONDUCT

It has already been seen (see **48.13** and **48.18** above) that a repudiatory breach of contract by either the employer or the employee entitles the other party to terminate the relationship without giving notice or by giving short notice. A dismissal in such circumstances is not necessarily fair, nor a constructive dismissal following the employer's breach necessarily unfair, although they often will be.

The courts have sometimes gone further, and suggested that a repudiatory breach *automatically* brings a contract of employment to an end (see, eg *Marriott v Oxford and District Co-operative Society Ltd (No 2)* [1970] 1 QB 186). The 'automatic' theory has now been rejected by the Supreme Court in *Société Générale v Geys* [2013] ICR 117. This means that (leaving aside questions of frustration and expiry at a specified time or upon the occurrence of a specified event) there is no such thing as an automatic termination because of one party's conduct. There must always be an acceptance of the breach constituting a dismissal by the employer or a resignation by the employee.

However, it is of the nature of the employment relationship that, where one party is unwilling to perform the contract, it will be very difficult for the other party to say that the relationship remains alive. An acceptance of the breach by the innocent party will readily be inferred from his conduct. See also *Marsh v National Autistic Society* [1993] ICR 453.

The Court of Appeal in *Weathersfield Ltd (t/a Van & Truck Rentals) v Sargent* [1999] IRLR 94 overruled the decision of the EAT in *Holland v Glendale Industries Ltd* [1998] ICR 493 that an employee must make plain to his employer the reason for leaving if he is to rely upon his employer's repudiatory conduct as justifying his resignation and subsequent claim of constructive dismissal. The court held that whether there has been an 'acceptance' of the employer's repudiatory conduct is for the employment tribunal (or court) to determine on the facts and evidence in each case. On the facts of that case (where an employee had been instructed to discriminate against black and Asian customers), the employee had been put in 'an outrageous and embarrassing position', and so did not want to confront her employers with the reason for leaving. She just left the job a few days after being issued with the instruction. This did not prevent her from claiming successfully that she had been constructively dismissed on the grounds of the instruction.

It is always a question of fact for the court or tribunal as to whether the employee resigned in consequence of the employer's repudiatory breach of contract. In *TSB Bank plc v Harris* [2000] IRLR 157, the Employment Appeal Tribunal upheld a finding of constructive dismissal where the employee was considering leaving her job in any case before the repudiatory breach of contract occurred (the breach arose out of the contents of a reference supplied to a prospective employer). See also *White v Bristol Rugby Ltd* [2002] IRLR 204. In *Ishaq v Royal Mail Group Ltd* [2017] IRLR 208, on the other hand, the Employment Appeal Tribunal held that there was no constructive dismissal where the 'true' or 'real' reason for a postal worker's resignation was not a repudiatory breach (failure to make adjustments for his disability and putting him on unsuitable postal routes), even though that breach was referred to in his letter of resignation. Rather, the EAT found that the postal worker had really resigned to avoid a disciplinary hearing that was due to take place the day after he wrote his resignation letter.

In *Da'Bell v NSPCC* [2010] IRLR 19, the Employment Appeal Tribunal observed that where a person reacts to offensive conduct by writing a letter the next day, this will easily lead to a finding that he resigned in response to that conduct. If he leaves the matter for a year, however, and digs it up again, his resignation at that point is less likely to be treated as directly related to the breach.

48.20 RETRACTION OF RESIGNATION OR DISMISSAL

The general rule is that words of resignation or dismissal, once communicated to the other party and accepted by him, cannot unilaterally be withdrawn (*Riordan v War Office* [1959] 3 All ER 552, *Willoughby v CF Capital plc* [2011] IRLR 985). However, the EAT has suggested that good industrial relations practice requires that an employer should be able to withdraw words of dismissal provided that he does so almost immediately (*Martin v Yeoman Aggregates Ltd* [1983] ICR 314). If this view is correct, it should apply equally to a case of resignation by the employee.

In *Wallace v Ladbrokes Betting and Gaming Ltd* (UKEAT/0168/15/JOJ), the EAT discussed the so-called 'cooling off period' following a resignation made in the 'heat of the moment'. This was regarded as a period during which the employer might be satisfied that its understanding that there has been an unequivocal resignation is correct. It was not a period in which the employee was given the opportunity to unilaterally withdraw her resignation.

48.21 REMEDIES FOR WRONGFUL TERMINATION

An employee who has been dismissed, or who has resigned in circumstances amounting to a constructive dismissal, may complain of UNFAIR DISMISSAL – I (53) to an employment tribunal, whether or not proper notice was given to him. If proper notice was not given, or if he resigned summarily in response to the employer's repudiatory breach, he may bring a claim for WRONGFUL DISMISSAL (58) in the ordinary courts. Where the employee fails to give proper notice, the employer may also in principle sue for damages. Also, either party may in certain, limited circumstances be able to obtain an injunction restraining an unlawful termination. See further 8.23 CONTRACT OF EMPLOYMENT.

49   Time Off Work

Cross references. See CHILDREN AND YOUNG PERSONS (4.8), EDUCATION AND TRAINING (14), HOLIDAYS (29), MATERNITY AND PARENTAL RIGHTS (32), SICKNESS AND SICK PAY (44) and STRIKES AND INDUSTRIAL ACTION (45).

49.1   In addition to the rights to take time off work covered elsewhere in this book, there are several distinct rights in exercise of which an employee may take time off work in specific circumstances.

— Trade union officials and members may take time off work for certain duties and activities (see **49.2–49.5** below).

— Employees have the right to take time off work to perform certain public duties (see **49.4–49.5** below).

— An employee under notice of redundancy may take time off to look for work, etc (see **49.6–49.7** below).

— Safety representatives, and elected representatives, must be given time off to perform their duties (see **49.8–49.9** below).

— Employees who are trustees of occupational pension schemes have a right to time off for performing their duties (see **49.10–49.11** below).

— Employee representatives must be given time off to perform their functions (see **49.12–49.13** below).

— Employees have the right to time off for European Works Council duties (see **49.14** below).

— Employees have the right to time off to care for dependants (see **49.15–49.16** below).

— Employees have the right to request flexible working to care for children (see **49.17** below).

This chapter also considers the obligation to reinstate members of the reserve forces in employment after military service (see **49.18** below). For the question of whether such time off (at least in the trade union and health and safety representative context) amounts to "working time" for the purposes of the *Working Time Regulations* see *Edwards v Encirc Ltd* [2015] IRLR 528 and **56.5** WORKING TIME

49.2   TRADE UNION OFFICIALS

An employer is obliged to permit an employee, who is an official of an independent trade union recognised by the employer, to take time off during working hours to:

(a)   carry out duties, as such an official, which are concerned with:

   (i)   negotiations with the employer that are related to or connected with any matters that fall within *TULRCA 1992, s 178(2)* (see **39.4** REDUNDANCY – II) and in relation to which the trade union is recognised by the employer, or

   (ii)   the performance, on behalf of employees of the employer, of any functions that are related to or connected with any matters falling within *TULRCA 1992, s 178(2)* that the employer has agreed may be so performed by the trade union, or

(iii)   receipt of information from the employer and consultation with the employer under *TULRCA 1992, s 188* or under the *Transfer of Undertakings (Protection of Employment) Regulations 2006 (SI 2006/246)* (see REDUNDANCY – **II (39)** and TRANSFER OF UNDERTAKINGS **(52)**);

(iv)   negotiations with a view to entering into an agreement under *regulation 9* of the *Transfer of Undertakings (Protection of Employment) Regulations 2006 (SI 2006/246)* that applies to employees of the employer, or the performance on behalf of employees of the employer of functions related to or connected with the making of an agreement under that regulation.

(b)   undergo training in aspects of industrial relations which is:

(i)   relevant to the carrying out of any such duties as are mentioned in (*a*); and

(ii)   approved by the Trades Union Congress or by the independent trade union of which he is an official.

(TULRCA 1992, s 168(1), (2).)

The Court of Appeal in *British Bakeries (Northern) Ltd v Adlington* [1989] ICR 438 held that it was a question of fact, dependent on the particular circumstances of the case, whether a preparatory meeting was sufficiently proximate to carrying out duties concerned with (at that time) industrial relations to come within the statutory predecessor of *TULRCA 1992, s 168*. Although the section has been amended since *Adlington*, it is thought that the decision is equally applicable to whether attendance at a meeting is sufficiently proximate to carrying out the duties now specified in *s 168*. See also *London Ambulance Service v Charlton* [1992] ICR 773.

It is to be noted that the right accrues only to officials of independent trade unions recognised by the employer (see **50.19** TRADE UNIONS – **I**). There is no right to time off if, for example, the purpose is to attend a demonstration in support of a dispute with another employer or to carry out internal union duties. Nor would *s 168* extend to, say, taking part in a course on pension schemes if the employer does not consult or bargain with the union about pensions and has not agreed to it performing any pension-related functions on behalf of his employees.

In *Ashley v Ministry of Defence* [1984] ICR 298, the EAT held that unless it can be shown that the recognised union expressly or impliedly required the attendance of its official at a meeting, the attendance of the official at such a meeting cannot constitute the carrying out by the official of a duty within the meaning of *s 168*. The EAT further held that attendance at an advisory meeting could be a duty within the meaning of *s 168*; whether it is, is a question of fact.

The amount of time a trade union official is permitted to take off in the exercise of his statutory right, the purposes for which, the occasions on which, and any conditions subject to which, time off may be so taken are those that are reasonable in all the circumstances, having regard to any relevant provisions in the ACAS Code of Practice (*TULRCA 1992, s 168(3)*).

In considering whether the request for time off is reasonable in all the circumstances, tribunals will take into account such matters as the nature, extent and purpose of time off already being taken by that employee (*Wignall v British Gas Corpn* [1984] ICR 716; *Borders Regional Council v Maule* [1993] IRLR 199). *Section 168(3)* assumes that a request for time off has been made and that such request has come to the notice of the employer. It is only if these two conditions are satisfied that the employee can have a remedy for an employer's failure to permit him to take time off (see *Ryford Ltd v Drinkwater* [1996] IRLR 16 and **49.5** below).

In deciding whether the right to time off is being exercised reasonably within the meaning of *s 168(3)*, the EAT in *Depledge v Pye Telecommunications Ltd* [1981] ICR 82, considered that where comprehensive arrangements existed for the discussion of industrial relations matters it would be reasonable for trade union officials to use them.

An employee who is a member of an independent trade union recognised by the employer and who is a learning representative of the trade union is entitled to time off under *s 168A, TULRCA 1992*. An employee who is a learning representative is entitled to time off in order to undertake, in relation to qualifying members of the trade union, the analysis of learning and training needs, the provision of information and advice on learning and training matters, the promotion of the values of learning and training, the consultation of the employer on learning and training activities, and preparation for the learning representative's activities. The right to time off arises only where the trade union has provided the employer with written notice that the employee is a learning representative and that (a) he has undergone sufficient training for his learning representative activities within the last six months and the trade union has given the employer notice in writing of this fact; (b) the trade union has given the employer notice in the last six months that the employee will be undergoing such training; or (c) within six months of such notice, the employee has undergone the training and the trade union has given the employer notice of that fact. The employer is also required the permit the employee time off for training that is relevant to his functions as a learning representative. The employer's obligation to permit time off is subject to a reasonableness test.

The trade union official who is entitled to take time off work to perform his duties under *section 168* or *168A, TULRCA 1992* is entitled to be paid for the period of his absence. Where his pay does not vary with the amount of work done, he is paid as if he had worked during the period of absence. Where his pay does vary according to the amount of work done, the amount he is to be paid during his absence is calculated by reference to the average hourly earnings for that work. The average hourly earnings are those of the employee concerned unless they cannot fairly be estimated, in which case the tribunal will take the average earnings of persons in comparable employment with the same employer or (if there are no such persons) a reasonable figure (*TULRCA 1992, s 169*).

The employee is entitled to paid time off only at a time when he would otherwise be working, and not to paid time off in lieu if the trade union duties are performed at a time when he would not otherwise be working (*Hairsine v Kingston upon Hull City Council* [1992] ICR 212, [1992] IRLR 211 and *Diamond v Park Lane College* UKEAT/0249/05/LA). However, a part time worker is entitled to receive pay for the actual hours attended on a training course, rather than just for the part time hours that they normally worked; a failure to pay for the actual hours worked would be unjustifiable indirect sex discrimination: *Davies v Neath Port Talbot County Borough Council* [1999] ICR 1132, [1999] IRLR 769, EAT.

If an employer is obliged under a contract of employment to pay an employee for time off taken to perform trade union duties, then those payments will go to discharge any statutory liability he may have to make such payments, and vice versa (*TULRCA 1992, s 169(4)*).

Trade union officials are statutorily entitled to a reasonable amount of paid time off to accompany a worker at a disciplinary or grievance hearing, provided that they are certified by the union as being capable of acting as the worker's companion (*ERA 1999, s 10(6)*). This right applies whether or not the union is recognised by the employer, but the worker must be employed by the same employer as the union official.

See also the ACAS Code of Practice 3: Time off for trade union duties and activities which lays down guidelines. The Code is to be taken into account in determining what is reasonable and the current version came into force on 1 January 2010.

It should be noted that since October 2012, civil servants who are trade union representatives have been obliged to spend at least 50% of their working hours delivering their civil service role, with any exemptions requiring specific agreement. According to a Cabinet

Office report published on 29 September 2014, as a result of this the number of full-time union representatives in government departments has gone down from 200 in November 2011 to less than 10, and resulted in approximately £6m of savings per year.

49.3   TRADE UNION ACTIVITIES

An employer is obliged to permit an employee of his, who is a member of an independent trade union recognised by him, to take part in certain trade union activities during working hours. The activities are defined as:

(a)   any activities of the trade union of which the employee is a member; and

(b)   any activities in relation to which the employee is acting as a representative of such union;

(*TULRCA 1992, s 170(1)*). This excludes activities which themselves consist of industrial action whether or not in contemplation or furtherance of a trade dispute (*TULRCA 1992, s 170(2)*).

The right in *TULRCA 1992, s 170(1)* does not include a right to time off for the purpose of acting as, or having access to services provided by, a learning representative of a trade union (*TULRCA 1992, s 170(2A)*). However, where the trade union learning representative in question is carrying out activities for which he is entitled to time off under *TULRCA 1992, s 68A*, the employer is obliged to permit an employee to take time off in his working hours to access those services (*TULRCA 1992, s 170(2B)–(2C)*).

In *Luce v Bexley London Borough Council* [1990] ICR 591, the EAT held that whether trade union activity fell within the definition was a matter of fact and degree, but that it must in a broad sense be linked to the employment relationship; the tribunal had been entitled to hold that teachers were not entitled to time off to lobby Parliament against the *Education Reform Bill*. See also **54.3(a)** Unfair Dismissal – II.

The amount of time that may be taken, and the purposes for which and the occasions on which it may be taken, are those that are reasonable in all the circumstances; the same test applies to the imposition of conditions by the employer (*TULRCA 1992, s 170(3)*). The employee is not entitled to be paid for time he takes off to participate in trade union activities unless he is a trade union official and the time is taken in accordance with **49.2** above.

49.4   PUBLIC DUTIES

An employer is obliged to permit an employee of his who is:

(a)   a justice of the peace;

(b)   a member of a local authority (within the meaning of the *Local Government Act 1972*), the Common Council of the City of London, a National Park Authority or the Broads Authority;

(c)   a member of any statutory tribunal;

(d)   a member of an independent monitoring board for a prison;

(e)   a member of the NHS Commissioning Board, a clinical commissioning group, an NHS Trust, an NHS foundation trust, the National Institute for Health and Care Excellence, the Health and Social Care Information Centre, a Local Health Board, or a Special Health Authority;

(f)   a member of the managing or governing body of an educational establishment maintained by a local authority, a further education corporation, sixth form college corporation or higher education corporation, or the General Teaching Council for England or Wales;

(g)   a member of the Environment Agency;

(h)   various similar bodies in Scotland.

to take time off work during the employee's contractual working hours for certain specified purposes (*ERA 1996, s 50*). There is no right to be paid for this time off work.

The right does not extend to specified classes of employees (*ERA 1996, ss 191–195, 199* and *200*). Clergy of the Church of England also have a right to time off work for public duties by virtue of the *Ecclesiastical Offices (Terms of Service) Regulations 2009 (SI 2009/2108)*.

In deciding when and how much time is to be taken off, regard will be paid to:

(i)   how much time off is required for the performance of the duties of the office, or as a member of the body in question, and how much time off is required for the performance of the particular duty;

(ii)   how much time off has already been permitted for the performance of any relevant public duty, union duty or activity;

(iii)   the circumstances of the employer's business and the effect of the employee's absence on the running of that business;

and these considerations will be applied in deciding what is reasonable in the circumstances (*ERA 1996, s 50(4)*). (See *Borders Regional Council v Maule* [1993] IRLR 199 and *Riley-Williams v Argos Ltd* EAT/811/02, (2003) 147 SJLB 695.)

Local authorities may not allow their employees more than 208 hours' paid time off in any financial year for the purpose of performing duties as councillors (other than council chairmen) (*Local Government and Housing Act 1989, s 10*).

Although there is no statutory provision entitling an employee to time off for jury service, prevention of a person from attending as a juror is a contempt of court and employees are protected from being subjected to a detriment or dismissal as a result of jury service (*ERA 1996, ss 43M, 98B*).

49.5   EMPLOYEE'S REMEDIES IN RESPECT OF TIME OFF FOR TRADE UNION AND PUBLIC DUTIES

An employee may present a complaint to an employment tribunal that (*a*) he has not been allowed time off to carry out public duties or trade union duties or activities, or (*b*) in the case of a trade union official's duties that he has not been paid for time he has been permitted to take off (*ERA 1996, s 51(1); TULRCA 1992, ss 168(4), 168A(9), 169(5), 170(4)*). An employee can only bring a complaint under *TULRCA 1992, s 168(4)* that an employer has failed to permit him to take time off, in circumstances where a request for time off has been made by the employee and that request has come to the notice of the employer (see *Ryford Ltd v Drinkwater* [1996] IRLR 16).

If it finds such a complaint well-founded, the tribunal will make a declaration to that effect and may order the employer to pay the employee compensation for the default and for any loss caused thereby (*ERA 1996, s 51(3); TULRCA 1992, s 172(1), (2)*). In the case of a union official who has not been paid for time taken off, the tribunal will order the employer to make the appropriate payment (*TULRCA 1992, s 172(3)*; see **49.2** above). In *Skiggs v South West Trains Ltd* [2005] IRLR 459 a union official was prevented by his employer from attending meetings in the capacity of union representative pending the outcome of a grievance investigation into his behaviour. The EAT held that although he had suffered no financial loss nor injury to feelings, he was entitled to recover compensation to reflect the fact that a wrong was done to him, because *TULRCA 1992, s 172(2)* makes reference to both the employer's default and any loss sustained by the employee.

An employment tribunal does not have the power to impose conditions upon the parties as to the way in which the time off shall be taken or to specify the amount of time off which should be allowed (*Corner v Buckinghamshire County Council* [1978] IRLR 320).

The time limit for presenting such complaints is three months from the date of the failure complained of, but pre-action conciliation (see **ACAS Conciliation (3)**) is compulsory and time spent on this does not count towards this period (*ERA 1996, s 51(2)–(2A)*; *TULRCA 1992, s 171(1)–(2)*). If the tribunal is satisfied that it was not reasonably practicable for the complaint to be presented within the time limit (see **18.2 Employment Tribunals – I**), then it may be extended (*ERA 1996, s 51(2)*; *TULRCA 1992, s 171(2)*). Time may also be extended for claims under *ERA 1996* where there is mediation in certain cross-border disputes (*ERA 1996, s 51(2A)*).

In *Gayle v Sandwell and West Birmingham Hospitals NHS Trust* [2011] EWCA Civ 924, [2011] IRLR 810, [2012] ICR D3, the statutory rights to unpaid time off for trade union activities were not relied upon but the employer had a recognition agreement whereby it would permit accredited representatives such time off for trade union activities as was reasonable and subject to the needs of the service. The employee attended a trade union meeting without complying a management instruction to resolve the issue of time off under the recognition agreement and was disciplined. The Court of Appeal upheld the tribunal's finding that this was on the basis of her failure to comply with the management request and not her trade union activities therefore there was no breach of *TULRCA 1992, s 146*.

49.6   TIME OFF TO LOOK FOR WORK OR MAKE ARRANGEMENTS FOR TRAINING

An employee who has been given notice of dismissal by reason of redundancy must be allowed reasonable time off by his employer, during his working hours before the end of his notice period, to look for new employment or to make arrangements for training for future employment (*ERA 1996, s 52(1)*). In order to qualify for this right, the employee must have been continuously employed for a period of at least two years, by the date on which (*a*) the notice is due to expire, or (*b*) the date on which it would expire had the statutory minimum period of notice been given, whichever is the longer (*ERA 1996, s 52(2)*). (See **Continuous Employment (7)**.) For an employee's general rights relating to education and training, see **Education and Training (14)**.)

An employee who is so allowed time off is entitled to be paid for the time taken off at the appropriate hourly rate, which is calculated by the amount of one week's pay divided by the number of normal working hours in a week or, where the number of those hours varies, by taking the average of the 12 weeks ending with the last complete week before the notice was given (*ERA 1996, s 53(1)–(3)*). The maximum amount payable cannot exceed 40% of a week's pay (*ERA 1996, s 53(5)*). The right to be paid is dependent upon the right to take time off. Thus, if an employee with less than two years' continuous service is given time off to seek other employment, there is no statutory obligation on the employer to pay him for time so taken.

An employee who is under notice of redundancy is entitled to time off to look for work irrespective of whether he has an appointment to attend a specific interview (*Dutton v Hawker Siddeley Aviation Ltd* [1978] ICR 1057, [1978] IRLR 390).

49.7   Remedy

If an employer has unreasonably refused the employee time off or has failed to pay him, the employee may present a complaint to an employment tribunal (*ERA 1996, s 54(1)*). The time limit for the presentation of such a complaint is three months beginning with the day on which it is alleged that time off should have been allowed, but pre-action conciliation is compulsory (see **49.17**) and time spent on this does not count towards this period (*ERA 1996, s 54(2)–(2A)*). If the tribunal is satisfied that it was not reasonably practicable for the complaint to be presented within the time limit (see **18.21** EMPLOYMENT TRIBUNALS – I), then it may be extended (*ERA 1996, s 54(2)*). Time may also be extended where there is mediation in certain cross-border disputes (*ERA 1996, s 54(2A)*).

The employer may be made liable to pay (i) remuneration for the period of absence or (ii) remuneration for the period during which he should have allowed time off, or both. The maximum amount, where both these provisions are applicable together, cannot exceed 40% of a week's pay (*ERA 1996, s 54(4)*).

If an employer unreasonably refuses to allow an employee time off work when statutorily obliged to do so, the employee is entitled to be paid the remuneration to which he would have been entitled if he had been allowed time off, in addition to his normal pay (*ERA 1996, s 53(4)–(6)*).

Any contractual remuneration paid to an employee for a period of time which he takes off to seek or train for new employment when he is under notice of dismissal for redundancy goes towards discharging the employer's statutory liability, and vice versa (*ERA 1996, s 53(7)*).

49.8   SAFETY REPRESENTATIVES AND ELECTED REPRESENTATIVES

The *Safety Representatives and Safety Committees Regulations 1977 (SI 1977/500)*, as amended, impose a duty upon employers to allow safety representatives time off with pay for the performance of their duties as safety representatives, and to undergo training in health and safety matters. Such persons are only entitled to be paid for time given off: in *Howlett v Royal Mail Group Ltd* (UKEAT/0368/13/DA) an engineer who had 60% release from a shift pattern that permitted (but did not require) one Sunday per month paid at overtime rates but then became a full-time safety representative working from Monday to Friday was only entitled to be paid as he would have been for working as an engineer from Monday to Friday. In relation to the right to time off for training, the 1978 Code of Practice approved by the Health and Safety Commission on time off for the training of safety representatives remains in force. The two questions are (1) whether the proposed training was reasonable in all the circumstances, and (2) whether it was necessary for the employee to take paid time off work: *Duthie v Bath and North East Somerset Council* [2003] ICR 1405 and *Walker v North Tees and Hartlepool NHS Trust* UKEAT/0563/07/RN. Also see *Coats v Strathclyde Fire Board* UKEATS/0022/09/BI, where an employee failed to establish that it was necessary for him to take time off to perform any of the specified health and safety functions on the dates and at the times in relation to which he was refused permission. On the rights of part-time employees, see *Calder v Secretary of State for Work and Pensions* UKEAT/0512/08/LA.

The *Health and Safety (Consultation with Employees) Regulations 1996 (SI 1996/1513)* impose a similar duty upon employers who, pursuant to those *Regulations* (see **28.22** HEALTH AND SAFETY AT WORK – II), consult with elected employee representatives. In addition to the duty to allow such representatives time off with pay to perform their duties as such and to undergo training, an employer must also permit a candidate for election as such a representative time off with pay to perform his functions as such a candidate.

49.9   Remedy

If an employer refuses a safety representative or elected representative time off for these purposes or if he does not pay him for the time taken, the safety representative or elected representative may present a complaint to an employment tribunal (*1977 Regulations, reg 11(1); 1996 Regulations, Sch 2 para 2*). The time limit within which a complaint must be presented is three months from the date where the failure occurred, but pre-action conciliation is compulsory (see ACAS CONCILIATION (3)) and time spent on this does not count towards this period (*1977 Regulations, reg 11(2)–(2A); 1996 Regulations, Sch 2, para 3–3A*). If the tribunal is satisfied that it was not reasonably practicable for the complaint to be presented within the time limit then it may be extended (*1977 Regulations, reg 11(2); 1996 Regulations, Sch 2 para 3*; see (18) EMPLOYMENT TRIBUNALS – I). Where an employment tribunal finds the complaint well-founded, it may make an award of such an amount as the tribunal considers just and equitable in all the circumstances, having regard to the employer's default in failing to permit time off to be taken by the employee and to any loss sustained by the employee which is attributable to the employee's complaint (*1977 Regulations, reg 11(3); 1996 Regulations, Sch 2 para 4*). Where the complaint is based upon the failure of the employer to pay remuneration due, the employment tribunal will order that sum to be paid to the employee (*1977 Regulations, reg 11(4); 1996 Regulations, Sch 2 para 5*). Compensation can be awarded having regard to the employer's default even without proof of loss to the employee; equally whilst it might be unusual for there to be no award of compensation the discretionary nature of *reg 11(3)* allows for that possibility: *Rowe v London Underground Ltd* (UKEAT/0125/16/JOJ). In the same case, it was said (although strictly *obiter*) that *reg 11(3)* does not permit an award for injury to feelings.

49.10   TIME OFF FOR OCCUPATIONAL PENSION SCHEME TRUSTEES

Employees who are trustees of an occupational pension scheme, or directors of trustee companies, have a right to time off during working hours (*ERA 1996, ss 58–60* and also see the *Occupational Pension Schemes (Member-Nominated Trustees and Directors) Regulations 2006, SI 2006/714*). Such employees will have a right to time off for the purpose of performing any of their duties as trustees or undergoing training relevant to such performance (*ERA 1996, s 58(1)*). This right is not subject to a period of continuous employment which an employee may have with an employer. The amount of time off which an employee is to be permitted to take and the conditions under which time off may be taken are those that are reasonable in all the circumstances having regard, in particular, to (*a*) the amount of time off required for the performance of the duties of a trustee of the scheme and undergoing training, and (*b*) the circumstances of the employer's business and the effect of the employee's absence on the running of that business (*ERA 1996, s 58(2)*).

An employee who is so allowed time off is entitled to be paid for the time taken off. The amount to be paid is the amount which he would have been paid if he had worked during the time taken off or, if his remuneration varies with the amount of work done, an amount calculated by reference to his average hourly earnings (*ERA 1996, s 59(1)–(3)*). If the work is such that no fair estimate can be made of the employee's average hourly earnings, then the amount to be paid will be calculated by reference to the average hourly earnings of similar work of a person in comparable employment with the same employer as the employee in question, or if there are no such persons, a figure of average hourly earnings which is reasonable in the circumstances (*ERA 1996, s 59(3)(4)*).

49.11   Remedy

If an employer has failed to permit the employee to take time off, or has failed to pay him, the employee may present a complaint to an employment tribunal (*ERA 1996, s 60(1)*). The time limit for the presentation of such a complaint is three months beginning with the date when the failure occurred but pre-action conciliation (see **ACAS Conciliation (3)**) is compulsory and time spent on this does not count towards this period (*ERA 1996, s 60(2)–(2A)*). If the tribunal is satisfied that it was not reasonably practicable for the complaint to be presented within this period (see **18.21 Employment Tribunals**), then it may be extended (*ERA 1996, s 60(2)*). Time may also be extended where there is mediation in certain cross-border disputes (*ERA 1996, 60(2A)*).

Where an employment tribunal finds the complaint as to failure to permit time off to be well-founded, it will make an order to that effect and may award such an amount as the tribunal considers just and equitable in all the circumstances, having regard to the employer's default in so failing and any loss sustained by the employee which is attributable to the complaint (*ERA 1996, s 60(3), (4)*). Where the complaint is that the employer has failed to pay the employee for time taken off, the employment tribunal will order the employer to pay the sum found to be due (*ERA 1996, s 60(5)*).

Any contractual remuneration paid to an employee for a period of time off for the purpose of performing his duties as a trustee of an occupational pension scheme or for related training, goes towards discharging the employer's statutory liability, and vice versa (*ERA 1996, s 59(6)*).

49.12 TIME OFF FOR EMPLOYEE REPRESENTATIVES

An employee who is an employee representative for the purposes of *TULRCA 1992, Part IV Chapter II* (see **39.4 Redundancy – II**) or *Transfer of Undertakings (Protection of Employment) Regulations 2006 (SI 2006/246), regs 9, 12* and *15* (see **Transfer of Undertakings (52)**), or a candidate in an election for such an employee representative, has the right to reasonable time off during contractual working hours in order to perform his functions as such an employee representative or candidate, or in order to undergo training to perform such functions (*ERA 1996, s 61*).

This right is not subject to a period of continuous employment which the employee may have with an employer. The employee is entitled to be paid for time taken off during working hours. The amount of pay is calculated in accordance with the provisions governing a week's pay and *Part XIV* of *ERA 1996* (*ERA 1996, s 62(1)*) (see **Pay – I (34)**).

An employee who is a negotiating representative or an information and consultation representative is entitled to take reasonable time off during his working hours in order to perform his representative functions (*Information and Consultation of Employees Regulations 2004, reg 27 (SI 2004/3426)*). He is entitled to be paid remuneration for the time off at the appropriate hourly rate (*reg 28*).

An employee who is a member of a special negotiating body, a member of a representative body, an information and consultation representative, an employee member on a supervisory or administrative organ, or a candidate in an election in which any person elected will, on being elected, be such a member or representative, is entitled to take reasonable time off during working hours in order to perform the functions of member, representative or candidate (the *European Public Limited-Liability Company (Employee Involvement) (Great Britain) Regulations 2009 (SI 2009/2401), reg 26*). Where an employee takes time off in this way, he is entitled to be paid remuneration at the appropriate hourly rate (*reg 27*).

The *Occupational and Personal Pension Schemes (Consultation by Employers and Miscellaneous Amendment) Regulations 2006 (SI 2006/349)* provide (*para 2, Sch*) that an employee who is a representative falling within *reg 12(2)(a)* or *(3)* or *13(2)*, and is consulted under the *Regulations* about a listed change by a relevant employer is entitled to be permitted by his employer to take reasonable time off during the employee's contractual working hours in order to perform his functions as such a representative. He is entitled to be paid for such time off at the appropriate hourly rate (*para 3, Sch*).

49.12 Time Off Work

The *European Cooperative Society (Involvement of Employees) Regulations 2006 (SI 2006/2059)* give under *reg 28* a right to reasonable time off to an employee who is a member of a special negotiating body or representative body, an information and consultation representative, an employee member of a supervisory or administrative organ, an election candidate or meeting participant under *reg 17(2)(h)* or *para 11(2)(h)* of *Sch 1* or *para 7(4)* of *Sch 2*. *Regulation 29* entitles the employee to payment at the appropriate hourly rate and *reg 30* gives the employee the right to present an employment tribunal claim where time off or payment are denied.

The *Companies (Cross-Border Mergers) Regulations 2007 (SI 2007/2974)* give an employee who is a member of a special negotiating body, a director of a transferee company, or a candidate in an election for a director or member, a right to take reasonable time off during working hours in order to perform his functions as such a member, director or candidate (*reg 43*). The right to remuneration at the appropriate hourly rate is provided by *reg 44*. The right to present a claim to an employment tribunal where time off or payment are denied is provided by *reg 45*.

Note that some of the above rights only apply where there is a minimum number of employees.

49.13 Remedy

All of the above regulations enable an employee to complain to an employment tribunal that his employer has denied him the rights conferred thereunder. In all cases the claim must be presented within three months of the day on which time off was taken, or which it is alleged time off should have been allowed but pre-action conciliation (see ACAS CONCILIATION (3)) is compulsory and time spent on this does not count towards this period. The tribunal may extend time if it was not reasonably practicable to present the claim within this period. Where the complaint is that time off has unreasonably been denied, the tribunal may order payment at the appropriate rate for the period which should have been allowed.

49.14 TIME OFF FOR EUROPEAN WORKS COUNCIL DUTIES

An employee who is a member of a European Works Council, a member of a special negotiating body, an information and consultation representative, or a candidate for election to be such a representative, is entitled to paid time off in order to carry out his or her duties (*Transnational Information and Consultation of Employees Regulations 1999, regs 25* and *26 (SI 1999/3323)*). An employee who is a member of a special negotiating board or a European Works Council has the right to take reasonable time off during working hours to undertake training (*regs 19B* and *25*). An employee who is unreasonably refused such time off, or denied payment in accordance with the formula contained in *reg 26*, may bring a complaint to an employment tribunal under *reg 27*. The claim must be presented within three months of the day on which time off was taken, or which it is alleged time off should have been allowed but pre-action conciliation (see ACAS CONCILIATION (3)) is compulsory and time spent on this does not count towards this period (*regs 27* and *27A*). The tribunal may extend time if it was not reasonably practicable to present the claim within this period (*reg 27*). Where the complaint is that time off has unreasonably been denied, the tribunal may order payment at the appropriate rate for the period which should have been allowed (*reg 27*).

49.15 TIME OFF FOR DEPENDANTS

Under *ERA 1996, s 57A* employees are entitled to be permitted by their employer to take a reasonable amount of time off during working hours in order to take action which is necessary:

(a)   to provide assistance when a dependant falls ill, gives birth, is injured or assaulted;

(b)   to make arrangements for the provision of care for a dependant who is ill or injured;

(c)   in consequence of the death of a dependant;

(d)   because of the unexpected disruption or termination of arrangements for the care of a dependant; or

(e)   to deal with an incident which involves the employee's child which occurs unexpectedly in a period during which an educational establishment which the child attends is responsible for him.

(*ERA 1996, s 57A(1)*.) Any disruption caused to the employer is irrelevant in determining whether the employee's circumstances trigger the right: *Qua v John Ford Morrison Solicitors* [2003] ICR 482.

An employee must inform his employer as soon as reasonably practicable of the reason for his absence, and, where he is able to inform his employer in advance of his absence, how long he expects to be absent (*ERA 1996, s 57A(2)*). In *Ellis v Ratcliff Palfinger Ltd* (UKEAT/0438/13/BA) the employee whose wife was taken into hospital to give birth on Tuesday but did not inform his employer of his absence or the reason until Wednesday evening was held not to have done so as soon as reasonably practicable.

"Dependant' is defined as a spouse or civil partner, child or parent of the employee, or a person who lives in the same household as the employee (excluding live-in employees, tenants, lodgers and boarders). In addition, for the purposes of (*a*), (*b*) and (*d*) above, a dependant includes any person who reasonably relies on the employee to assist him if ill or injured, or who reasonably relies on the employee to make arrangements to provide care for him (*ERA 1996, s 57A(3), (4)* and *(5)*). Illness and injury are defined to include mental illness and injury (*ERA 1996, s 57A(6)*).

In a case concerning a childminder's unavailability, of which the employee had 16 days' notice during which period she had tried and failed to make alternative childcare arrangements, the EAT considered whether, given the length of time, she had been entitled to take a day off and provide childcare herself (*Harrison v Royal Bank of Scotland plc* [2009] IRLR 28). The EAT held that the relevant question was whether the action taken by the employee was necessary because of the unexpected disruption or termination in the care of her dependant. The length of notice of the disruption was significant, because it enabled the employee to explore alternative arrangements, however, there were no hard and fast rules.

A period of a month or more for a parent to care for a child would almost never fall within *ERA 1996 s 57A*: *Cortest Ltd v O'Toole* UKEAT/0470/07/LA.

Sick leave taken because of a bereavement reaction does not qualify as time off in consequence of the death of a dependant (*Forster v Cartwright Black* [2004] ICR 1728, [2004] IRLR 781).

48.16 Remedy

An employee who has unreasonably been refused permission to take time off in accordance with his right under *s 57A* may complain to an employment tribunal (*ERA 1996, s 57B(1)*). The time limit for such complaints is three months beginning with the date the refusal occurred, but pre-action conciliation is compulsory (see ACAS CONCILIATION (3)) and time spent on this does not count towards this period (*ERA 1996, s 57B(2)–(2A)*). The tribunal has a discretion to extend time where it was not reasonably practicable for the employee to present his claim in the three-month period (*ERA 1996, s 57B(2)*). Time may be extended where there is mediation in certain cross-border disputes (*ERA 1996, s 57B(2A)*). If a tribunal finds the complaint well-founded, it may make a declaration to that effect, and may award such compensation as it considers just and equitable, having regard to the employer's default in refusing to permit time off to be taken by the employee, and any loss sustained by the employee (*ERA 1996, s 57B(3)* and *(4)*).

49.17 TIME OFF TO CARE FOR CHILDREN

Maternity, paternity, adoption leave and leave for ante-natal care are covered in detail in MATERNITY AND PARENTAL RIGHTS (32).

FLEXIBLE WORKING

An employee who has been continuously employed for 26 weeks has the right to apply in writing to his or her employer to request a change in hours, times or location of work (*Employment Rights Act 1996, ss 80F–80I*; *Flexible Working Regulations 2014 (SI 2014/1398)*. Only one such statutory request can be made in any 12 month period (*ERA 1996, s 80F(4)*). The employer must deal with the application in a reasonable manner, notify the employee of the decision within 3 months (or such longer period as may be agreed) and may refuse such an application only on grounds of the burden of additional costs, detrimental effect on the ability to meet customer demand, inability to re-organise work among existing staff, inability to recruit additional staff, detrimental impact on quality, detrimental impact on performance, insufficiency of work during the periods during which the employee proposes to work, or planned structural changes (*ERA 1996, s 80G(1)*). An employer can notify the employee that the application is treated as withdrawn if the employee fails to attend meetings arranged to discuss the application (*ERA 1996, s 80G(1D)*). Guidance on the obligation to handle such requests in a reasonable manner is contained in "Code of Practice 5 – Handling in a reasonable manner requests to work flexibly", published by ACAS in June 2014.

An employee is protected against detriment (*ERA 1996, s 47E*) and dismissal (*ERA 1996, s 104C*) on the ground that he or she made (or proposed to make) an application under *section 80F* or brought proceedings under *section 80H* or alleged the existence of any circumstance which would constitute a ground for bringing such proceedings.

An employee may complain to an employment tribunal that an employer has failed to deal with his or her flexible working application as required by *section 80G* or has rejected the application on the basis of incorrect facts or has wrongly treated the application as having been withdrawn (*ERA 1996, s 80H*). The time limit for such a complaint is three months but pre-action conciliation is compulsory (see **ACAS CONCILIATION (3)**) and time spent on this does not count towards this period (*ERA 1996, s 80H(5)–(7)*). The tribunal has a discretion to extend time where it was not reasonably practicable for the employee to present his claim within this period (*ERA 1996, s 80H(5)*). Time may be extended where there is mediation in certain cross-border disputes (*ERA 1996, s 80H(7)*).

If the complaint is upheld the employment tribunal may order the employer to reconsider the application and may award compensation of up to eight weeks' pay. The employment tribunal does not have the power to order the employer to implement the employee's request for flexible working.

49.18 REINSTATEMENT AFTER MILITARY SERVICE

The *Reserve Forces (Safeguard of Employment) Act 1985* provides two basic types of employment protection for reservists in the armed forces: (1) protection (on pain not just of liability to pay compensation but also of criminal prosecution) against dismissal on account of the reservist's liability to be mobilised, and (2) a right to reinstatement when the reservist returns to his civilian job after a period of mobilisation.

49.19 So far as the right of reinstatement is concerned, the following is a short summary of the main provisions in the *1985 Act.*

Where a person has entered upon a period of whole-time service in the armed forces of the Crown, and has done so in pursuance of a notice or directions for the calling out of reserve or auxiliary forces, or for the recall of service pensioners, or in pursuance of an obligation or undertaking to serve as a commissioned officer, then he has certain rights to be reinstated in employment by his former employer.

The former employee must apply in writing to his former employer after the period of military service ends and not later than the third Monday after the end of that period, or as soon afterwards as reasonably possible (*s 3*). He must also notify the employer of a date, not later than 21 days after the latest date allowed for the application, when he will be available for employment (*s 4*).

The employer must then reinstate the former employee in his old occupation on terms no less favourable than would have applied but for the military service, or (if that is not reasonable and practicable – as to which, see *s 5*), in the most favourable occupation and on the most favourable terms and conditions which are reasonable and practicable in his case (*s 1(2)*). The person concerned must then be employed for at least 13, 26 or 52 weeks, depending on the length of his continuous employment prior to the military service, or for so much of that time as is reasonable and practicable (*s 7*; see *Slaven v Thermo Engineers Ltd* [1992] ICR 295).

Complaints that a person's statutory rights have been infringed may be made to a Reinstatement Committee, which may order employment to be made available to the applicant, and order the payment of compensation to him (*s 8*). There are rights of appeal in certain circumstances to an umpire sitting with assessors (*s 9*). Non-compliance with an order is a criminal offence (*s 10*). The procedure upon applications and appeals is governed by the *Reinstatement in Civil Employment (Procedure) Regulations 1944 (SI 1944/880).*

It should also be noted that there is no qualifying period of employment for the purposes of a claim for unfair dismissal where the reason for the dismissal is, or is connected with, the employee's membership of a reserve force (*Employment Rights Act 1996, s 108(5)*).

50 Trade Unions – I: Nature and Liabilities

Cross-references. See also STRIKES AND INDUSTRIAL ACTION **(44)**; TIME OFF WORK **(48)** for time off for trade union duties or activities; TRADE UNIONS – II **(50)** for individual rights and union membership; 53.3 UNFAIR DISMISSAL – **II** for dismissal for participation in union activities.

50.1 THE STATUS OF A TRADE UNION

The present law on the status and liability of trade unions is governed by the *Trade Union and Labour Relations (Consolidation) Act 1992* ('*TULRCA 1992*'). 'Trade union' is statutorily defined in *TULRCA 1992, s 1* as an organisation (whether permanent or temporary) which either –

(a)   consists wholly or mainly of workers of one or more descriptions and is an organisation whose principal purposes include the regulation of relations between workers of that description or those descriptions and employers or employers' associations; or

(b)   consists wholly or mainly of –

(i)   constituent or affiliated organisations which fulfil the conditions specified in para (*a*) above (or themselves consist wholly or mainly of constituent or affiliated organisations which fulfil those conditions), or

(ii)   representatives of such constituent or affiliated organisations;

and in either case is an organisation whose principal purposes include the regulation of relations between workers and employers or between workers and employers' associations, or include the regulation of relations between its constituent or affiliated organisations.

In *British Association of Advisers and Lecturers in Physical Education v National Union of Teachers* [1986] IRLR 497, the Court of Appeal construed this definition broadly so as to include an association 'concerned with the professional interests of its members'.

Several of the larger trade unions are made up of a number of constituent sections. The definition in *TULRCA 1992, s 1* ensures that both the conglomerate organisation and its constituent parts are considered to be trade unions. The National Union of Mineworkers is made up of a number of areas such as the National Union of Mineworkers (South Wales area), all of which are, under *TULRCA 1992*, to be considered trade unions. Similarly, a branch of a trade union may be held to be a trade union (see *News Group Newspapers Ltd v Society of Graphical and Allied Trades '82 (No 2)* [1987] ICR 181).

50.2 Legal capacity

Unless a trade union is a special registered body as defined by *TULRCA 1992, s 117* (such bodies are mostly incorporated professional associations), it is not, nor to be treated as if it were, a corporate entity (*TULRCA 1992, s 10*). However, *TULRCA 1992, s 10(1)* gives a trade union a statutory legal personality which it would otherwise lack so that it can:

(a)   make contracts;

(b)   sue or be sued in its own name (see **50.16** and **50.17** below for certain immunities enjoyed by trade unions); and

(c)   be a defendant in criminal proceedings.

All property belonging to a trade union must be vested in trustees in trust for the union (*TULRCA 1992, s 12(1)*).

50.3   CERTIFICATION OFFICER

The Secretary of State appoints a Certification Officer in consultation with ACAS under *TULRCA 1992, s 254*. He makes an annual report to the Secretary of State, who presents it to Parliament and publishes it (*TULRCA 1992, s 258*). His functions include:

(a)   dealing with complaints relating to the keeping of the register of a union's members (see **50.13** below);

(b)   dealing with complaints relating to trade union internal elections (see **50.14** below);

(c)   dealing with complaints relating to political fund ballots (see **50.15** below);

(d)   maintaining a list of trade unions (see **50.21** below);

(e)   certifying whether trade unions are independent (see **50.22** below);

(f)   certain supervisory functions in relation to trade union amalgamations (see **50.39** below); and

(g)   administering the scheme for financial contributions towards trade union ballots.

The Certification Officer may at any time, if he thinks there is good reason to do so, require a trade union (or any person who appears to be in possession of the documents) to produce specified documents which are accounting documents or which may be relevant in considering the union's financial affairs (*TULRCA 1992, s 37A*). He may also appoint inspectors to investigate and report upon a union's financial affairs if there are circumstances suggesting fraud, misconduct or a breach of statutory obligations or union rules in relation to those affairs, and all past and present officials and agents of the union and other persons appearing to be in possession of relevant information must then co-operate with the investigation, including by producing documents and attending before the inspectors (*TULRCA 1992, s 37B*). Reports made will be published by the Certification Officer, and there are various other administrative provisions, as well as criminal sanctions for contravention of statutory requirements (*TULRCA 1992, ss 37C–37E; TULRCA 1992, ss 45, 45A*).

The Certification Officer has jurisdiction to consider applications by members or former members of a trade union claiming that there has been a breach or threatened breach of the union's rules, pursuant to a new *TULRCA 1992, s 108A*. The Certification Officer may consider such a claim only if it relates to:

(a)   the appointment or election of a person to, or their removal from, any office;

(b)   disciplinary proceedings (including expulsion);

(c)   the balloting of members on any issue other than industrial action;

(d)   the constitution or proceedings of any executive committee or of any decision-making meeting; and

(e)   such other matters as the Secretary of State may specify.

With effect from 1 March 2017, the Certification Officer gained a range of new and additional powers in relation to investigations and enforcement by virtue of *ss 17–21* of the *Trade Union Act 2016* coming into force.

In *UNISON v Gallagher* (2005) IDS Brief No 791 the Employment Appeal Tribunal found that the Certification Officer had exceeded his jurisdiction in holding that the appellant union had breached its disciplinary rules by excluding a member, who had previously been disciplined and debarred from holding office for five years, from is annual delegate conference. The exclusion followed a decision by the union that all those who had been expelled or debarred from holding office should no longer be allowed to attend the conference. Although the exclusion was consequent upon the previous disciplinary determination, it was held to be administrative in nature, and therefore fell outside the Certification Officer's jurisdiction.

The limited nature of the Certification Officer's jurisdiction was again emphasised in *Irving v GMB* [2008] IRLR 202. In that case, the EAT upheld the decision of the Certification Officer that he had no jurisdiction to consider the applicant's complaint about the way in which a complaint against him had been handled. This was because the matter was dealt with by way of grievance proceedings rather than disciplinary proceedings, and so fell outside the Certification Officer's jurisdiction.

The complaint must be made within six months of either the alleged breach or threatened breach, the conclusion of an internal complaints procedure relating to the breach or the expiry of one year from such a complaints procedure being invoked. *TULRCA 1992, s 108B* provides that the Certification Officer must accept an application only if satisfied that the applicant has taken all reasonable steps to resolve the claim through internal complaints procedures. If he accepts an application, he may make a declaration and an enforcement order requiring steps to be taken to remedy the breach. By *TULRCA 1992, s 108C* an appeal lies to the Employment Appeal Tribunal. Since 1 March 2017, such an appeal has no longer been confined to appeal on a point of law.

50.4   CENTRAL ARBITRATION COMMITTEE

The Central Arbitration Committee ('CAC') was established pursuant to the *Employment Protection Act 1975* and continues by virtue of *s 259* of the *Trade Union and Labour Relations (Consolidation) Act 1992* ('*TULRCA 1992*').

50.5   Constitution

The Secretary of State for Trade and Industry is responsible for appointing members of the CAC whom he selects from persons nominated by ACAS as being experienced in industrial relations and who include both employers' and workers' representatives. In addition, the Secretary of State appoints a chairman and may appoint one or more deputy chairmen after consultation with ACAS (*TULRCA 1992, s 260*).

50.6   Functions

These are:

(a)   Arbitration in trade disputes (see **50.7** below).

(b)   Resolution of complaints that an employer has failed to disclose information which he was required to disclose by *TULRCA 1992, s 181* (*TULRCA 1992, s 183*) (see **50.8** below).

(c)   Determination of questions previously referred to the Industrial Arbitration Board (*TULRCA 1992, Sch 3 para 7*). (The Board was the successor of the Industrial Court created by the *Industrial Courts Act 1919*, to which trade disputes of various kinds could be referred.)

(d)   Union recognition disputes (see **50.11** below).

(e)   Resolution of complaints that an employer has failed to comply with its duty to provide data requested under the *Information and Consultation of Employees Regulations 2004 (SI 2004/3426)* (see EMPLOYEE PARTICIPATION (16)).

50.7   Arbitration

The CAC may arbitrate on trade disputes at the request of one or more parties to the dispute, provided that all parties consent to the arbitration. The request for arbitration is made to ACAS in the first instance, which may refer the matter to the CAC (*TULRCA 1992, s 212(1)(b)*; and see **2.6 ADVISORY, CONCILIATION AND ARBITRATION SERVICE**).

50.8   Complaint of failure to disclose information

The CAC may hear and determine complaints made by an independent trade union recognised for collective bargaining purposes that the employer by whom it is recognised has not disclosed information to which the union is statutorily entitled (see **10.3 DISCLOSURE OF INFORMATION**) (*TULRCA 1992, ss 181, 183*). The CAC is only empowered to make a declaration if the union is recognised by the employer for the particular purpose to which the information relates (*R v Central Arbitration Committee, ex p BTP Tioxide Ltd* [1981] ICR 843). The CAC will refer the complaint for conciliation by ACAS if it considers that it is reasonably likely to be settled in that way (*TULRCA 1992, s 183(2)*). Any person with a proper interest in the complaint is entitled to be heard by the CAC (*TULRCA 1992, s 183(4)*). If the CAC finds the complaint well-founded, it will make a declaration specifying the information which must be disclosed, the date upon which the employer refused or failed to disclose it and the period within which it must be disclosed (*TULRCA 1992, s 183(3), (5)*).

If the employer fails to comply with the order of the CAC, the union may present a further complaint which may be coupled with, or followed by, a claim that certain terms and conditions should be included in the contracts of one or more descriptions of employees in respect of whom the union is recognised by the employer (*TULRCA 1992, ss 184, 185*).

If the CAC finds the further complaint wholly or partly well-founded, it may make an award that, in respect of any description of employees specified in a claim for the inclusion of terms and conditions, the employer shall from a certain date observe either the terms and conditions specified in the claim or other terms and conditions which the CAC considers appropriate (*TULRCA 1992, ss 184(2), (4), 185(3)*). These terms and conditions have effect as part of the contract of employment of any such employee, unless superseded or varied by a further award, a collective agreement, or an agreement with the employee which improves those terms (*TULRCA 1992, s 185(5)*).

An award may only be made in respect of a description of employees, and may only comprise terms and conditions relating to matters in respect of which the trade union making the claim is recognised by the employer (*TULRCA 1992, s 185(4)*). The right to present a claim for terms and conditions expires if the employer discloses, or confirms in writing, the information specified in the declaration, and a claim presented shall be treated as withdrawn if the employer does so before the CAC makes an award on the claim (*TULRCA 1992, s 185(2)*).

50.9   No contracting out

Any provision in an agreement is void insofar as it purports to prevent a person from bringing proceedings before the CAC, unless a conciliation officer has taken action pursuant to his statutory duties or unless the agreement varies or supersedes an award under *TULRCA 1992, s 185 (TULRCA 1992, s 288)*.

50.10   Appeal

There is no appeal against an award of the CAC, but its decision may be challenged by judicial review proceedings in the High Court (or, in Scotland, the Court of Session) and set aside if it can be shown that the CAC:

(a)   misdirected itself in law or exceeded its jurisdiction;

(b)   failed to take into account relevant considerations or took into account irrelevant ones; or

(c)   acted unreasonably or in breach of natural justice.

For an example of the very limited basis on which the Court of Session was prepared to intervene in a decision of the CAC, see *Fullarton Computer Industries Ltd v Central Arbitration Committee* [2001] IRLR 752.

50.11 Statutory trade union recognition

With the coming into force of *s 70A* and *Sch A1* of *TULRCA 1992*, introduced by the *Employment Relations Act 1999* ('*ERA 1999*'), the role of the CAC was considerably expanded and enhanced. With effect from 6 June 2000, trade unions gained a statutory right to be recognised by employers for collective bargaining purposes. See further **50.19–50.38**.

The CAC, under the chairmanship of Sir Michael Burton, plays a central role in relation to the recognition procedures. Applications to the CAC in relation to recognition are heard by a panel of three members, including the chairman or a deputy chairman.

50.12 OBLIGATIONS

Trade unions have statutory obligations to keep accounting records (for members' rights of inspection, see **51.2 TRADE UNIONS – II**), to make annual returns, to appoint auditors and to make arrangements for the inspection of their members' superannuation schemes (*TULRCA 1992, ss 28, 32, 32A, 32ZA, 33, 40*). Additional requirements in relation to the making of annual returns were introduced by *ss 7* and *12* of the *Trade Union Act 2016* which came into force on 1 March 2017. In particular, if industrial action has been taken during the return period details of that must be set out (*TULRCA 1992, s 32AZ*). Similarly, details for expenditure out of a union's political fund must be included if they exceed £2,000 for the year (*TULRCA 1992, s 32ZB*). Unions must keep an up-to-date register of members (see **50.13** below), hold periodic elections for membership of the principal executive committee and for certain other positions (see **50.14** below), and hold ballots on the continued application of trade union funds for political purposes (see **50.15** below) (*TULRCA 1992, ss 24, 46, 71*). In *Paul v NALGO* [1987] IRLR 43 the Certification Officer considered several of these obligations. A trade union must, at the request of any person, supply him with a copy of its rules either free or on payment of a reasonable charge (*TULRCA 1992, s 27*).

50.13 Register of members

Every trade union is obliged by *TULRCA 1992, s 24* to compile and keep up to date a register of members. A member has a right to a copy of any register entry relating to him (*TULRCA 1992, s 24(3)*).

A member of the union may apply to the Certification Officer, or to the High Court in England or the Court of Session in Scotland, for a declaration that these requirements have not been complied with (*TULRCA 1992, ss 25, 26*). The court or (since 25 October 1999) the Certification Officer may also make an enforcement order requiring the union to compile or update the register (*TULRCA 1992, ss 25(5A), 26(4)*). There is a right of appeal against this Certification Officer's decisions under this section to the Employment Appeal Tribunal pursuant to *TULRCA 1992, s 45D*. Since 1 March 2017, such an appeal has no longer been confined to appeal on a point of law. Elections and disqualification

50.14 Elections and disqualification from office

Trade unions are obliged to secure that, with certain exceptions, all members of its principal executive committee, and its president and general secretary, stand for election at least every five years (*TULRCA 1992, ss 46(1), 119*). Members of the principal executive committee are those who, under the rules or practice of the union, may attend at some or all of its meetings (other than merely to provide factual information or professional advice) (*TULRCA 1992, s 46(3)*). The position of president or general secretary is exempted from the election requirement if its holder is not an employee of the union, is not a voting member of the executive and holds the position for not more than 13 months (*TULRCA 1992, s 46(4)*). The position of president is also exempted if the incumbent was appointed or elected in accordance with the union's rules, at the time of such appointment or election he or she held a designated executive position by virtue of having been elected in accordance with the election requirements under the section and continues to hold such a designated position, and has held such a position for no more than five years (*TULRCA 1992, s 46(4A)*).

In *GMB Union v Corrigan* [2008] ICR 197 the claimant alleged that *TULRCA 1992, s 46* had been breached because, following the suspension of its general secretary, the union had appointed an acting general secretary but failed to hold an election for over a year, pending the completion of an internal investigation. The EAT held that there had been no breach of the statutory duty, since the acting general secretary continue to play an acting role only, and the investigation was a legitimate reason for postponing the election of a new general secretary.

The ballot must, as far as is reasonably practicable, be secret. An independent scrutineer must be appointed to oversee the ballot, and his name must appear on the voting paper. Among his other duties, the scrutineer is obliged to make a report on the ballot to the union which must send it or notify its contents to members. Handling of voting papers and counting of votes must also be independently undertaken. Candidates must, so far as reasonably practicable, be enabled to distribute election addresses without cost to themselves. The members entitled to vote must, so far as is reasonably practicable, be given a convenient opportunity to vote by post. Members may not be unreasonably excluded from standing as candidates, and may not be required, directly or indirectly, to belong to a political party. There are detailed provisions governing the circumstances in which particular classes of members may be excluded from voting (*TULRCA 1992, ss 47–52; Trade Union Ballots and Elections (Independent Scrutineer Qualifications) Order 1993 (SI 1993/1909)*). In *Thompson v NUM* (2015) IDS Brief No 1019 the EAT held that union rules which permitted only current members of the union's national executive committee to stand for national office did not unreasonably exclude other members from standing, even though this in practice reduced the number of potential candidates to a very small pool of 10 or 11.

Although *TULRCA 1992, s 51(6)* requires the election result to be determined solely by counting the number of votes cast, this did not invalidate a rule limiting the number of members of the National Executive Council ('NEC') who could be elected from any one geographical division (*R v Certification Officer for Trade Unions and Employers' Associations, ex p Electrical Power Engineers' Association* [1990] ICR 682, HL). The House of Lords took the view that the statutory provision was intended only to exclude weighted or block votes and electoral colleges.

The Certification Officer has held that it is permissible for ballot papers to contain information, such as the names of nominating branches, other than that prescribed by the statute (*Decision D/3/89*).

A person who claims that his union is in breach of the election provisions may apply to the Certification Officer, or to the High Court in England or to the Court of Session in Scotland. He must have been a member of the union at the date of the election, and at the date of the application. The application must be made within one year of the date on which the result of the election was announced (*TULRCA 1992, s 54*). The Certification Officer or the court may make a declaration specifying the provisions with which the trade union has failed to comply (*TULRCA 1992, ss 55(2), (3), 56(3)*). If it makes a declaration, the court or the Certification Officer must also, unless it is considered that to do so would be inappropriate, make an enforcement order to secure the holding of an election specified in the order (*TULRCA 1992, ss 55(5A), 56(4)*). There is a right of appeal to the Employment Appeal Tribunal against a decision of the Certification Officer, or a question of law, under *TULRCA 1992, s 56A*.

The Secretary of State is empowered by *TULRCA 1992, ss 203* and *204* to issue a Code of Practice relating to the conduct by trade unions of ballots and elections (see CODES OF PRACTICE (5)). Codes of Practice have been issued, which deal with ballots on industrial action (see STRIKES AND INDUSTRIAL ACTION (45)) and access to workers during recognition and derecognition ballots.

In the event that the executive council of a union seeks to breach the union's election rules, individual members of the union have a contractual right by virtue of their contracts of membership to challenge the validity of the council's decision (*Wise v Union of Shop, Distributive and Allied Workers* [1996] ICR 691). It was held by the High Court in *Ecclestone v National Union of Journalists* [1999] IRLR 166 that a union's exclusion of a candidate for election on the basis that he did not have the confidence of the NEC was both a breach of the union's rules and contrary to the prohibition on unreasonably excluding candidates within *TULRCA 1992, s 47*.

Persons who have previously been convicted of certain offences under *TULRCA 1992, s 45* as amended (which deals in particular with failure to comply with statutory obligations, and with dishonest falsification or destruction of documents) are disqualified from membership of the principal executive committee and from being president or general secretary (subject to the same exemptions as set out above). The disqualification is for five or ten years, depending upon the offence committed (*TULRCA 1992, s 45B*). If a union allows a disqualified person to hold office, a member of the union may apply to the Certification Officer or to the court for a declaration to that effect. They have the power to require the union to take steps to remedy the position (*TULRCA 1992, s 45C, 45C(5A)*). There is a right of appeal against the Certification Officer's decisions under this section to the Employment Appeal Tribunal on any question of law, under *TULRCA 1992, s 45D*.

In *AB v CD* [2001] IRLR 808, the Court of Appeal considered the appropriate mechanism for resolving a tied vote in the second round of the election, by single transferable vote, of a regional union representative. The rules of the union, the RMT, were silent as to how such a tie should be resolved. In the absence of any express rule, the candidate who had received the most votes in the first round was declared elected.

The Court of Appeal upheld this decision. A term was to be implied into the union rules that a tie would be resolved in this way, in order to give efficacy to the contract, as an obvious inference from the express terms of the rules and in order to complete the contract between the members. However, such a term was not to be implied from custom and practice. In order for custom and practice to warrant the implication of a contractual term in the rules of a trade union, the relevant custom must be known, or at least readily ascertainable, by all members.

50.15 Political levy

A trade union may not apply its ordinary funds in the furtherance of political objects as defined by *TULRCA 1992, s 72*, which deals mainly with support for political parties and with attempts to influence the outcome of elections. Payments for such purposes may only be made out of a separate political fund, and then only if there is a political resolution in force approving the furtherance of those objects (*TULRCA 1992, s 71*). Union members have a right to apply to the Certification Officer for a decision that funds have been applied in breach of *s 71* (*TULRCA 1992, s 72A*). Such a resolution must be passed at least every 10 years by a ballot held in accordance with union rules which have been approved by the Certification Officer as complying with the relevant statutory requirements (*TULRCA 1992, ss 73, 74*). Those requirements, found in *TULRCA 1992, ss 75–78* are very similar to those which apply to ballots for union elections (see **50.14** above). Complaints of non-compliance with the ballot requirements may be made either to the Certification Officer or to the court within a year after the announcement of the result (*TULRCA 1992, ss 79–81*).

A union member is entitled to give notice that he objects to contributing to the political fund, and he is then to be exempted from making such contributions, and must not be put at any disadvantage or excluded from the union as a result (*TULRCA 1992, s 82*). A member who complains of a breach of these requirements may complain to the Certification Officer, who may make such order for remedying the breach as he thinks just under the circumstances (*TULRCA 1992, s 82(2), (3)*). A notice of objection should be in the form set out in *TULRCA 1992, s 84(1)* or to like effect. When a political resolution is adopted, members must be notified of their right to object and be given the opportunity to obtain exemption notice forms from union offices or from the Certification Officer (*TULRCA 1992, s 84(2)*). *Section 11* of the *Trade Union Act 2016*, which came into force on 1 March 2017, imposes additional restrictions in relation to trade union political funds. By *s 84* of *TULRCA 1992*, as amended, a member must have been given an "opt in" notice before he can be required to contribute to a political fund. However, these amendments apply only from 1 March 2018 (i.e. a year after the section comes into force), and then apply only to persons who join the union after that date or where the union establishes its political fund for the first time after that date.

If a union member certifies to his employer that he is exempt from making political contributions, the employer must ensure that they are not deducted from his wages (*TULRCA 1992, s 86*). There is a right to apply to an employment tribunal for a declaration that the employer has breached this obligation, and for an order that the employer repay sums deducted and, if considered appropriate, require the employer to take specified steps in relation to emoluments payable to the union member. If the member considers that the employer has failed to comply with an order to take such specified steps, he may present a further complaint to the tribunal (*TULRCA 1992, ss 86, 87*; and see Pᴀʏ – I (34)).

50.16 LIABILITY IN TORT

The immunity of trade unions in proceedings in tort arising out of strikes or industrial action is now similar to that of individuals (see Sᴛʀɪᴋᴇꜱ ᴀɴᴅ Iɴᴅᴜꜱᴛʀɪᴀʟ Aᴄᴛɪᴏɴ (45)). Such immunity only applies to action taken in contemplation or furtherance of a trade dispute. With certain narrowly defined exceptions, it does not protect secondary action or action taken to enforce trade union membership. Further, a trade union does not enjoy immunity from liability in tort for inducing breaches of contracts of employment unless its action has the support of a ballot (see **45.14** Sᴛʀɪᴋᴇꜱ ᴀɴᴅ Iɴᴅᴜꜱᴛʀɪᴀʟ Aᴄᴛɪᴏɴ). However, where proceedings in tort are brought against a trade union:

(a)   for a reason specified in *TULRCA 1992, s 219* (inducing breach of, and interference with, contracts; see **45.2** Sᴛʀɪᴋᴇꜱ ᴀɴᴅ Iɴᴅᴜꜱᴛʀɪᴀʟ Aᴄᴛɪᴏɴ); or

(b)   in respect of an agreement or combination by two or more persons to induce or do an unlawful act;

then that act will only be taken to have been done by the union if it is taken to have been authorised or endorsed by the union (*TULRCA 1992, s 20(1)*). An act will only be taken to have been authorised or endorsed if it was done, authorised or endorsed by one of the following:

(i)   the principal executive committee; or

(ii)   any person who is empowered by the rules to do, authorise or endorse acts of the kind in question; or

(iii)   the president or general secretary as defined in *TULRCA 1992, s 119*; or

(iv)   any other official of the union (whether employed by it or not), or by any member of a group to which such an official belongs and whose purposes include organising or co-ordinating industrial action; or

(v)   any other committee of the union, by which is meant any group of persons constituted in accordance with the rules of the union.

(*TULRCA 1992, s 20(2), (3)*).

An act will not be taken to have been endorsed by a person in category (iv) or (v) above if it was repudiated by the principal executive committee or the president or general secretary as soon as reasonably practicable after coming to the knowledge of any of them (*TULRCA 1992, s 21(1)*).

In order to be effective, written notice of the repudiation must be given without delay to the committee or official in question, and the union must also do its best to give individual written notice without delay to every member who it has reason to believe is taking part in, or might otherwise take part in, industrial action as a result of the repudiated act, and to the employer of every such member. The written notice must contain a statement in statutorily prescribed form (*TULRCA 1992, s 21(2)–(4)*).

The union will not be able to rely upon such a repudiation if the principal executive committee, or president or general secretary, has subsequently behaved in a way which is inconsistent with the purported repudiation (*TULRCA 1992, s 21(5)*). They will be treated as so behaving if, upon a request made within three months of the purported repudiation by a party to a commercial contract whose performance has been or may have been interfered with by the repudiated act and to whom written notice of the repudiation has not been given, they do not forthwith confirm in writing that the act has been repudiated (*TULRCA 1992, s 21(6)*). (See also *Express and Star Ltd v National Graphical Association* [1985] IRLR 455; upheld on other grounds, [1986] ICR 589.)

The liability of trade unions in such actions in tort is subject to financial limits, considered below.

50.17 Limits on damages awarded against a trade union, enforcement of judgments and protected property

With the exception of amounts awarded in actions for personal injury or for breach of duty in connection with the ownership, occupation, possession, control or use of property, the amount of damages awarded (not including interest; see *Boxfoldia Ltd v National Graphical Association* [1988] ICR 752) in any proceedings in tort brought against a trade union must not exceed the following limits:

(i)   £10,000, if the union has fewer than 5,000 members;

(ii)   £50,000, if it has 5,000 or more members but fewer than 25,000 members;

(iii)   £125,000, if it has 25,000 or more members but fewer than 100,000 members;

(iv)   £250,000, if it has 100,000 or more members.

(*TULRCA 1992, s 22(2)*.)

The Secretary of State may by order vary any of these sums (*TULRCA 1992, s 22(3)*).

A judgment, order or award made in proceedings of any description brought against a trade union is enforceable against any property held in trust for the union (see **50.2** above) to the same extent and in the same manner as if it were a body corporate (*TULRCA 1992, s 12(2)*). However, no award of damages, costs or expenses is recoverable by enforcement against protected property (*TULRCA 1992, s 23(1)*). Protected property includes the property of individual members, officials and trustees, the contents of a political fund which cannot, under the rules, be used to finance industrial action (see **50.15** above), and the contents of separate provident benefit funds (*TULRCA 1992, s 23(2)*).

50.18 LIABILITY OF INDIVIDUAL MEMBERS

The individual participants in industrial action have the same immunity as trade unions. Such immunity only applies to action taken in contemplation or furtherance of a trade dispute. There is, however, no limit on the damages which may be awarded if an individual is found liable. With certain narrowly defined exceptions, secondary industrial action is not protected. (See **45.6** STRIKES AND INDUSTRIAL ACTION.)

TULRCA 1992, s 15 renders unlawful the application of the property of a trade union towards the payment of any penalty imposed upon an individual for an offence or for contempt of court, or towards any indemnity in respect of such liabilities. This applies to all kinds of offences unless designated otherwise by order made by the Secretary of State (*TULRCA 1992, s 15(5)*). However, the prohibition does not extend to civil liabilities, provided that the indemnity or contribution is otherwise lawful and *intra vires* the union. The union is given the right to recover property or its value applied in contravention of these provisions from the individual concerned (*TULRCA 1992, s 15(2)*), and in the event of its unreasonable failure to take proceedings to this end, the court may order, upon application by a union member, that that member shall be authorised to do so in the union's name and at its expense (*TULRCA 1992, s 15(3)*).

50.19 RECOGNITION, INDEPENDENCE AND RIGHTS

The most far-reaching change in the law brought about by the *Employment Relations Act 1999* was the new recognition machinery for collective bargaining purposes contained in *Sch 1* to that *Act*. The relevant provisions, which are now contained in *Sch A1* to *TULRCA 1992*, confer a right upon trade unions to be recognised by employers for collective bargaining purposes, provided various (extremely complex) conditions are fulfilled. Thus, whilst the new procedures encourage employers and unions to agree on recognition wherever possible, they bring about a fundamental change in the law in providing for compulsory recognition in certain circumstances. The new provisions came into force on 6 June 2000. The principal features of the recognition machinery are summarised at **50.25–50.38** below.

The European Court of Human Rights held in *Wilson and National Union of Journalists v United Kingdom* (Applications 30668/96, 30679/61 and 30678/96) [2002] IRLR 568 that *art 11* of the European Convention of Human Rights did not impose a requirement for compulsory collective bargaining. However, in *Demir v Turkey* (Application No 34503/97) (2008) 48 EHRR 1272, [2009] IRLR 766, the European Court held that the right to bargain collectively is one of the essential elements of the right to form and join trade unions for the protection of workers' interests and so should in general (and subject to any lawful restrictions) be recognised as forming part of the right to freedom of association.

Previous provisions in the *Employment Protection Act 1975* ('*EPA 1975*'), covering the statutory procedure by which independent trade unions could refer recognition issues to ACAS, were repealed in 1980. Although the previous statutory recognition machinery in the *EPA 1975* was repealed, the concepts of 'independence' and 'recognition' discussed below continue to be relevant for some purposes. One is the procedure for handling redundancies laid down in *TULRCA 1992, Part IV* (see **39.2** REDUNDANCY – **II**). Others are disclosure of information for collective bargaining purposes under *TULRCA 1992, s 181* (see **10.2** DISCLOSURE OF INFORMATION), the information and consultation requirements contained in the *Transfer of Undertakings (Protection of Employment Regulations 2006 (SI 2006/246)* (see **52.22** TRANSFER OF UNDERTAKINGS) and the right to time off for trade union duties and activities (see **49.2, 49.3** TIME OFF WORK). In addition, the concept of 'independence' is central to the new procedures for recognition for collective bargaining purposes (see below).

50.20 Voluntary recognition

The recognition provisions contained in *TULRCA 1992, Sch A1* provide specifically for voluntary recognition. Even before those provisions came into effect, however, an employer could voluntarily agree to recognise a trade union. Recognition can be express or implied. An employer need not have entered into a formal recognition agreement in order to be considered to have recognised a particular trade union. 'Recognition' is defined in *TULRCA 1992, s 178(3)* as 'the recognition of the union by an employer . . . to any extent, for the purpose of collective bargaining', and 'collective bargaining' means negotiations relating to or connected with: terms and conditions of employment; physical conditions of work; recruitment, dismissal and suspension; allocation of work; matters of discipline; union membership; facilities for officials of trade unions; and bargaining machinery and other procedures (*TULRCA 1992, s 178(1)(2)*). A different definition of collective bargaining applies under the new recognition machinery (see below).

If management in fact consult a trade union about some or all of these matters they may be taken to have recognised that trade union (*Joshua Wilson & Bros Ltd v Union of Shop, Distributive and Allied Workers* [1978] IRLR 120). In *National Union of Gold, Silver and Allied Trades v Albury Bros Ltd* [1979] ICR 84, the Court of Appeal held that an act of recognition is such an important matter that it should not be held to be established unless the evidence is clear, either by actual agreement for recognition or clear and distinct conduct showing an implied agreement to recognise the trade union for the purposes of collective bargaining. In that case, the Court of Appeal held that an attempt by the union to negotiate with the management increased wages for one man did not establish recognition by the employer. Recognition will not be inferred from the fact that a union has been given a right of representation in pay bargaining where that right is given by a third party over whom the employer has no control (*Cleveland County Council v Springett* [1985] IRLR 131).

50.21 Listing

A list of trade unions is maintained by the Certification Officer (*TULRCA 1992, s 2*). Any trade union whose name is entered on the list may apply to the Certification Officer for a certificate that it is independent (*TULRCA 1992, s 6(1)*). A union which is not on the list maintained by the Certification Officer will automatically be refused a certificate of independence (*TULRCA 1992, s 6(3)*).

50.22 Independence

If the union is listed, the Certification Officer will proceed to determine whether the applicant is an independent trade union. An independent trade union is defined in *TULRCA 1992, s 5* as:

' . . . a trade union which –

(a) is not under the domination or control of an employer or a group of employers or of one or more employers' associations; and (*b*)   is not liable to interference by an employer or any such group or association (arising out of the provision of financial or material support or by any other means whatsoever) tending towards such control.'

In *Squibb UK Staff Association v Certification Officer* [1979] ICR 235, CA, the Certification Officer refused to grant a certificate of independence to a staff association which relied to a considerable extent upon facilities provided by the employers. He considered that the association could not be said to be free from liability to interference by the employers. The Court of Appeal upheld the refusal of the grant of the certificate. For a more recent example, see *Government Communications Staff Federation v Certification Officer* [1993] ICR 163.

In *Bone v North Essex Partnership NHS Foundation Trust* [2014] ICR 1053, the Court of Appeal held that a certificate of independence is retrospective for a reasonable period prior to the issue of the certificate. In those circumstances, a union representative's claim for detriment on grounds of trade union activities could be heard, even though the certificate of independence was not issued until after the events of which he complained.

50.23 Factors implying independence

In *Blue Circle Staff Association v Certification Officer* [1977] 1 WLR 239, some of the principles upon which the Certification Officer acts are set out (at 245–246):

'1   *Finance*: If there is any evidence that a union is getting a direct subsidy from an employer, it is immediately ruled out.

2   *Other assistance*: The Certification Officer's inspectors see what material support, such as free premises, time off work for officials, or office facilities a union is getting from an employer, and attempt to cost them out.

3   *Employer interference*: If a union is very small and weak and gets a good deal of help, then on the face of it its independence will be considered to be in danger and liable to employer interference.

4   *History*: The recent history of a union   . . .   is considered. It was not unusual for a staff association to start as a "creature of management and grow into something independent".

5   *Rules*: The applicant union's rule book is scrutinised to see if the employer can interfere with or control it, and if there are any restrictions on membership. If a union is run by people near the top of a company it could be detrimental to rank and file members.

6   *Single company unions*: While they are not debarred from getting certificates, because such a rule could exclude unions like those of miners and railwaymen, they are considered to be more liable to employer interference. Broadly based multi-company unions are considered more difficult to influence.

7   *Organisation*: The Certification Officer's inspectors then examine the applicant union in detail, its size and recruiting ability, whether it is run by competent and experienced officers, the state of its finance, and its branch and committee structure. Again, if the union was run by senior men in a company, employer interference was a greater risk.

8   *Attitude*: Once the other factors have been assessed, inspectors looked for a "robust attitude in negotiation" as a sign of genuine independence, backed up by a good negotiating record   . . . '

Before making a determination on the question of independence, the Certification Officer makes such inquiries as he sees fit and takes into account any relevant information submitted to him (*TULRCA 1992, s 6(4)*). In general, he should not be cross-examined upon his reasons for his decision (*Squibb* at **50.22** above).

50.24 Withdrawal of certificate of independence and appeals against Certification Officer's decision

The Certification Officer may at any time withdraw a certificate, after giving notice to the trade union affected and determining the relevant questions, if he is of the opinion that the trade union in question is no longer independent (*TULRCA 1992, s 7(1)*).

A trade union aggrieved by the refusal of the Certification Officer to issue it with a certificate, or by a decision of his to withdraw its certificate, may appeal to the Employment Appeal Tribunal. If the appeal is successful the Employment Appeal Tribunal will give directions to the Certification Officer to act according to its findings (*TULRCA 1992, s 9*).

50.25 RECOGNITION FOR COLLECTIVE BARGAINING PURPOSES

The current procedure for the recognition of trade unions by employers for the purposes of collective bargaining was introduced by *ERA 1999, Sch 1*. This recognition machinery came into effect on 6 June 2000 and is contained in *TULRCA 1992, Sch A1*. The new law represented a fundamental change in industrial relations in the United Kingdom, since it conferred upon trade unions a right to be recognised by employers for collective bargaining purposes, provided various conditions are satisfied. The new regime does, however, seek to promote voluntary recognition wherever possible. Also significant is the enhanced role for the Central Arbitration Committee ('CAC') (see **50.4**) in determining a range of issues relating to recognition. In carrying out these functions, the CAC is under a duty to have regard to the object of encouraging and promoting fair and efficient practices in the workplace. The provisions relating to the membership of the CAC contained in *TULRCA 1992, s 260* were amended by *ERA 1999, s 24* so as to require the Secretary of State to appoint only persons experienced in industrial relations, having first consulted with ACAS and such other persons as he may choose to consult (*TULRCA 1992, Sch A1 para 171*) (see **50.11** above). The new recognition procedures are extremely complex. Below is set out a summary of the principal provisions.

50.26 The scope of the recognition procedure

The recognition procedures apply only to employers which, taken with any associated employers, employ either at least 21 workers on the day on which a request for recognition is received, or have employed an average of at least 21 workers in the 13 preceding weeks (*TULRCA 1992, Sch A1 para 7(1)*). For this purpose, the definition of 'worker' contained in *TULRCA 1992, s 296(1)* applies. In *R (on the application of the BBC) v Central Arbitration Committee* [2003] EWHC 1375 (Admin), [2003] ICR 1542 it was held that an application for recognition should not have been entertained by the CAC in respect of freelance cameramen and women working for the BBC, since they were excluded from the definition of 'workers' as 'professionals'. The CAC had erred in finding that the cameramen and women were not 'professionals' merely because they had no regulatory body.

Only unions which have been certified as independent under *TULRCA 1992, s 6* may make a request for recognition.

The territorial reach of the CAC union recognition procedures was considered in *Netjets Management Ltd v CAC* [2012] EWHC 2685 (Admin), [2012] IRLR 986. The employer, which ran private business flights throughout Europe, sought to argue that the union's application for recognition in respect of all pilots fell outside the CAC's remit because most of the pilots were based outside the United Kingdom. The High Court upheld the CAC's decision that it had jurisdiction. There were "sufficiently strong" connections with Great Britain. In particular, the pilots' contracts were governed by English law and subject to the exclusive jurisdiction of the English Courts. No other EU states have been put forward as a more appropriate forum for collective bargaining. Moreover, if there was no collective bargaining on pay, hours and holidays in Great Britain, the pilots would be prevented from exercising their right to collective bargaining under Article 11 of the Convention.

50.27   Collective bargaining

The definition of collective bargaining contained in *TULRCA 1992, s 178* does not apply to the new recognition provisions. Instead, collective bargaining is defined as negotiations relating to pay, hours and holidays, subject to the parties agreeing that additional matters may also be the subject of collective bargaining (*Sch A1, paras 1–4*). For the purposes of this provision, the CAC has held that pension benefits fall within the definition of pay (see *UNIFI v Union Bank of Nigeria* [2001] IRLR 713).

50.28   The request for recognition

A union or unions seeking recognition must apply first to the employer. The request must be made in writing, identify the relevant unions and bargaining unit and state that it is made under *TULRCA 1992, Sch A1 para 8*. If the parties agree within 10 working days on the appropriate bargaining unit and further agree that the union is (or unions are) to be recognised to conduct collective bargaining on behalf of that unit, then the union is (or unions are) deemed to be recognised, and no further steps need be taken. If the employer does not accept the request, but agrees to negotiate, then the union will be deemed to be recognised if the parties are able to agree within a further 20-day period. The parties may request ACAS to assist in conducting such negotiations (*Sch A1, para 10*).

50.29   Reference to the CAC

If the employer either rejects or fails to respond to the request within 10 days, or if negotiations break down during the subsequent 20-day period, the union may apply to the CAC to decide on the appropriate bargaining unit and whether the union has the support of a majority of workers within that unit. The union may ask the CAC to determine the question of majority support if the parties have agreed on the appropriate bargaining unit, but have not agreed on whether the union should be entitled to conduct collective bargaining on its behalf. However, the union may not apply to the CAC if it has rejected or failed to respond to a proposal by the employer that ACAS be requested to assist in negotiations (*Sch A1, paras 11, 12*).

TULRCA 1992, Sch A1 sets out a detailed procedure for the various sequential steps that must be taken by the CAC once it has received an application for union recognition. This procedure is subject to a relatively strict timetable, with the CAC generally being given 10 days to reach a determination at each stage of the procedure. The time limits within the recognition procedure are subject to extension by the CAC in most cases, although in some circumstances the CAC is under a duty to give reasons for such an extension to the parties.

The CAC must decide whether any application for recognition is 'valid' within the meaning of *TULRCA 1992, Sch A1 paras 5–9* and 'admissible' within the meaning of *TULRCA 1992, Sch A1 paras 33–42*, having considered any evidence provided by the employer or the union (*Sch A1, para 15*). The criteria of 'validity' are essentially the requirements as to union independence and number of workers employed referred to above. On the literal wording of *Sch A1*, an application may be 'inadmissible' if there is already in force a collective agreement under which a union is recognised for collective bargaining purposes (*Sch A1, para 35*). This exclusion can have far-reaching consequences. In *R (on the application of National Union of Journalists) v Central Arbitration Committee* [2005] EWCA Civ 1309, [2006] ICR 1 the Court of Appeal upheld the decision of the High Court that the

NUJ's application to the CAC was inadmissible, because the employer already had a recognition agreement with another union. This was the case notwithstanding that that agreement had not been used to determine the terms and conditions of workers within the bargaining unit and the other union had at most one member working in the relevant division of the employer's business. Similarly, in *Transport and General Workers' Union v Asda* [2004] IRLR 836 the CAC held the union's application inadmissible because the employer had a 'partnership agreement' in place with another union. This was despite the fact that the 'partnership agreement' provided for only limited representational rights, and specifically excluded collective bargaining on terms and conditions of employment, including pay.

However, this approach was challenged by the CAC in *Pharmacists' Defence Association v Boots Management Services Ltd* [2013] IRLR 262. The employer had a long-standing relationship with a listed trade union, but the union was not recognised for the purposes of collective bargaining in relation to terms and conditions of employment. On the literal wording of *Sch A1, para 35*, the application by a rival union for recognition was precluded, because another union was already recognised for some collective bargaining purposes. The CAC held that a literal reading of the paragraph would be incompatible with Article 11 of the Convention. Accordingly, it re-wrote *Sch A1, para 35*, so that a recognition application by another union will be precluded only if another union is already recognised as entitled to conduct collective bargaining "*in respect of pay, hours and holidays*". The employer successfully applied for judicial review of the CAC's decision, on the basis that this interpretation of *Sch A1, para 35* was not properly open to the CAC, even applying the interpretive duty contained in *Human Rights Act 1998, s 3(1)*: see *R (Boots Management Services Ltd) v CAC* [2014] IRLR 278. However, in *R (Boots Management Services Ltd) v CAC* [2014] IRLR 887, following intervention by the Government, the High Court reversed its decision and held that the plain wording of *Sch A1, para 35* was compatible with the ECHR after all. This was because the derecognition procedures contained in *Part VI* of *Sch A1* permitted a union to apply for the incumbent union to be derecognised, even if the incumbent union had very limited collective bargaining rights. The Court of Appeal upheld the decision of the High Court: [2017] IRLR 355.

An application will be inadmissible unless members of the relevant union (or unions) constitute at least 10% of workers within the bargaining unit and a majority of the workers within that unit are likely to favour recognition (*Sch A1, para 36*). Further, where an application is made by more than one union, the application will be inadmissible unless they show that they will co-operate with each other so as to secure and maintain a stable and effective collective bargaining arrangement, and further that they will act together for collective bargaining purposes if the employer wishes (*Sch A1, para 37*). An application will also be inadmissible if brought within three years of a previous application by the same union or unions in respect of the same or substantially the same bargaining unit (*Sch A1, paras 39–40*). If the application does not fulfil the criteria of 'validity' and 'admissibility', it must not be accepted by the CAC.

If the CAC accepts an application, it must first try to assist the parties in seeking to agree on the appropriate bargaining unit within a period of 20 working days (which may be extended). In the absence of agreement, the CAC must decide on the appropriate bargaining unit (*Sch A1, paras 18, 19*).

In *Prison Officers' Association and Securicor Custodial Services Ltd*, Re (2000) IDS Brief 670, the CAC accepted that the employer's recognition of a non-independent staff association precluded the application by an independent trade union for recognition pursuant to *Sch A1, para 35*. Where such an association is recognised, therefore, the independent union may well have to seek to initiate derecognition proceedings.

50.30 The appropriate bargaining unit

In deciding on the appropriate bargaining unit, the CAC must take into account the need for the unit to be compatible with effective management and, in so far as they do not conflict with that primary need, the following additional factors:

(a)   the views of the parties;

(b)   existing national and local bargaining arrangements;

(c)   the desirability of avoiding small fragmented bargaining units within an undertaking;

(d)   the characteristics of the workforce falling within and outside of the unit; and

(e)   the location of workers (*Sch A1, para 19*).

In *R (on the application of Kwik-Fit (GB) Ltd) v Central Arbitration Committee* [2002] EWCA Civ 512, [2002] ICR 1212, the Court of Appeal considered the approach to be adopted by the CAC when considering competing contentions by the union and employer as to the appropriate bargaining unit. Buxton LJ rejected the employer's contention that the CAC has a duty to treat on equal terms the unit proposed by the union and any alternative proposed by the employer. The recognition machinery is put in motion by a request from the union. Provided the CAC finds that the unit put forward by the union is 'appropriate', it need not go further and consider whether there is a more appropriate unit that might be identified. It must take into account the employer's views, but should not weigh up whether an alternative unit put forward by the employer might be better than that proposed by the union, provided that that proposed by the union meets the requirement of being 'appropriate'. The decision highlights the way in which the recognition process is essentially union-driven.

In *Re Benteler Automotive UK and ISTC* (Central Arbitration Committee, 17 October 2000) (IDS Brief 677), the CAC broadly accepted the union's argument that the relevant bargaining unit was shop-floor employees only. Although the employer argued that supervisory, technical and administrative staff should be included, so as to reflect their 'whole company' ethos, the CAC noted that this did not reflect the existing management organisation and practice at the company. Although the CAC did not wish to impede the employers in achieving a 'whole company' approach, existing economic realities determined the appropriate bargaining unit.

In *Graphical Paper and Media Union v Derry Print Ltd* [2002] IRLR 380, the CAC considered the proper approach to determining the appropriate bargaining unit where a single business was run through two separate companies, with members of the workforce being allocated to one business or the other. The CAC concluded that, under the recognition machinery in *TULRCA 1992, Sch A1*, a bargaining unit could not include the employees of more than one employer. The language and scheme of the recognition provisions envisaged the determination of a bargaining unit by reference to a single employer.

However, the CAC went on to hold that, on the facts of the case, it was permissible to treat the two companies in question as a single employer. A more liberal approach to lifting the corporate veil in this way was appropriate here than in some other legal contexts. The CAC accordingly determined that the appropriate bargaining unit comprised the production workers of both companies. The CAC thereby recognised the importance of determining the bargaining unit by reference to the economic realities on the shop floor.

In *R (on the application of Cable & Wireless Services UK Ltd) v Central Arbitration Committee* [2008] EWHC 115 (Admin), [2008] IRLR 425, [2008] ICR 693 Collins J upheld a decision of the CAC that the smallness of a bargaining unit would not in itself necessary lead to fragmentation. Whilst small fragmented bargaining units were undesirable, the mischief underlying this criterion was avoiding the proliferation of such units resulting from the creation of a unit lacking in any obviously identifiable boundary. In *R (Lidl) v Central Arbitration Committee* [2017] EWCA Civ 328 the Court of Appeal held that the specific criterion of the desirability of avoiding small fragmented bargaining units applies only where there is more than one potential bargaining unit in play.

If the parties have agreed, or the CAC has decided on, a bargaining unit which differs from that originally proposed, the CAC must consider whether the application is valid by reference to further criteria of 'validity' set out in *paras 43–50 (Sch A1, para 20)*. These further criteria of validity closely mirror those of 'admissibility' set out above (see *paras 33–42*). Where there is no such disparity, and where the CAC is satisfied that the criteria of validity are satisfied, the CAC must proceed with the application for union recognition.

50.31 Union recognition

The central provisions of the new recognition procedure are those which provide for the compulsory recognition of unions for collective bargaining purposes. Such recognition may or may not be preceded by a secret ballot of the workers within the relevant bargaining unit. Where the CAC is satisfied that a majority of the workers within the bargaining unit are members of the union, it must issue a declaration that the union is recognised as entitled to conduct collective bargaining on behalf of the workers within the bargaining unit, unless:

(a)   it is satisfied that a ballot should be held in the interests of good industrial relations; or

(b)   there is credible evidence from a significant number of union members within the bargaining unit that they do not want the union to conduct collective bargaining on their behalf; or

(c)   evidence about the circumstances in which members joined the union or about the length of time they have been members is produced, which leads the CAC to conclude that there are doubts about whether a significant number of members wish the union to conduct collective bargaining on their behalf.

If any of those circumstances apply, the CAC must give notice that it intends to arrange for the holding of a secret ballot in which the workers will be asked whether they want the union to be recognised. Equally, the CAC must give notice of its intention to arrange for the holding of a secret ballot if it is not satisfied that a majority of workers within the bargaining unit are members of the union. The CAC must then arrange for the holding of a ballot unless it receives notification within 10 working days (or such longer period as the CAC specifies) from the union (or from the union and employer jointly) that they do not want a ballot to take place (*Sch A1, paras 20–24*).

In *Fullarton Computer Industries Ltd v Central Arbitration Committee* [2001] IRLR 752, the Court of Session upheld the CAC's decision that a trade union should be recognised without a ballot on the grounds that a ballot would not be in the interests of good industrial relations. The Court of Session approached the case on the basis that the CAC was under no obligation to give reasons for its decision. (The CAC is obliged by the statute to give reasons for some of its decisions, particularly those relating to the extension of time limits within the recognition procedure, but not, ironically, for those substantive decisions, such as this one, which are likely to be determinative of the outcome of the recognition application.) If reasons were given, the decision could be set aside only if they disclosed some manifest error or flaw on the face of the record. This case highlights the difficulty inherent in challenging the CAC's decision as to whether a ballot is likely to be in the interests of good industrial relations.

50.32   The recognition ballot

The recognition ballot, which must be conducted by a qualified independent person appointed by the CAC, may be conducted in the workplace, by post or, exceptionally, by some combination of the two. A 'qualified independent person' is defined for these purposes as someone who fulfils the conditions of either being a practicing solicitor or being eligible for appointment as a company auditor. In addition, a number of organisations providing electoral services are specified by name to be such persons (*Recognition and Derecognition Ballots (Qualified Persons) Order 2000 (SI 2000/1306)*). The costs of the ballot are divided equally between the employer on the one hand and the union (or unions) on the other. In deciding on the appropriate method, the CAC must take into account the risk of unfairness or malpractice if the ballot is conducted in the workplace, costs and practicality, and such other matters as it considers appropriate (*Sch A1, paras 25, 28*).

The employer is placed under five duties in relation to a recognition ballot:

(a)   it must co-operate generally with both the union and the person appointed to conduct the ballot;

(b)   it must give the union such reasonable access to the workers within the bargaining unit as will enable it to inform the workers of its object and seek their support and opinions;

(c)   it must give the CAC the names and home addresses of the workers within the bargaining unit, including any workers who join the unit after the initial list has been provided, and must further inform the CAC if any such workers have ceased to be within the unit. The CAC passes this information on to the person appointed to conduct the ballot;

(d)   it must refrain from unreasonably seeking to induce workers to refrain from attending meetings with a union regarding recognition;

(e)   it must refrain from taking or threatening action against a worker because he has attended or intends to attend a meeting with a union regarding recognition

A new code of practice on access to workers during recognition and derecognition ballots came into effect on 1 October 2005 pursuant to *TULRCA 1992, ss 203–204* and the *Employment Code of Practice (Access to Workers during Recognition and Derecognition Ballots) Order 2005 (SI 2005/2421)*.

It the employer fails to comply with any of these duties, the CAC may order the employer to take remedial steps. If the employer fails to comply with such an order, the CAC may cancel the ballot (or ignore it if it has taken place) and make a declaration of recognition (*Sch A1, paras 26, 27*).

The person appointed to conduct the ballot must send all relevant workers any information supplied by the union, provided that the union bears the cost of sending such information.

The most important (and controversial) provision in the union recognition procedure is that which determines the effect of the outcome of the recognition ballot. If union recognition for collective bargaining purposes is supported by:

(a)   a majority of the workers voting, and

(b)   at least 40% of the workers within the bargaining unit,

then the CAC must issue a declaration that the union is recognised for collective bargaining purposes. If those conditions are not satisfied, then the CAC must declare that the union is not so recognised. The Secretary of State may by order amend this provision so as to specify a different degree of requisite support (*Sch A1, para 29*). It follows that, even if a majority of those voting support recognition, the union will not be recognised if a low turnout entails that those in favour constitute less than 40% of the workforce within the bargaining unit.

In *R (on the application of Ultraframe (UK) Ltd) v Central Arbitration Committee* [2005] EWCA Civ 560 [2005] ICR 1194 the Court of Appeal upheld a decision of the CAC directing a re-run of a recognition ballot. Although a majority of those voting had supported recognition, the 40% requirement had not been achieved by four votes. The unions complained that a number of employees had not received ballot papers, and the CAC concluded that five employees, who would have voted in favour of recognition, had not been given a reasonable opportunity to vote. The Court of Appeal concluded that the CAC had jurisdiction to investigate and, if appropriate, to annul the ballot, and so had acted within its powers in ordering a re-run.

All parties informed by the CAC of a recognition ballot must refrain from using unfair practices in relation to such a ballot (*Sch A1, para 27A*). 'Unfair practices' are defined so as to include; making inducements to vote in a particular way; coercion; undue influence; and dismissal, disciplinary action or detriment, or threats of such actions, aimed at influencing the outcome of the ballot. A party may complain to the CAC if it believes that unfair practices have been used (*Sch A1, para 27C*). If the CAC finds a complaint well-founded, it must make a declaration to that effect, and may order the party concerned to take specified action, or give notice that it intends to arrange a secret ballot in which the workers are asked whether they want the union to conduct collective bargaining on their behalf (*Sch A1, para 27C*). The CAC's further powers upon such a finding also include a power in certain circumstances to cancel or annul a ballot.

50.33 The method of collective bargaining

Once a declaration of recognition has been made, the parties may seek to negotiate an agreement as to the method by which they will conduct collective bargaining during a 30-day period or such longer period as they agree. If no agreement is reached, the parties may apply to the CAC for assistance. The CAC must try to help the parties to reach an agreement. If after a further 20 days (or such further period as the CAC agrees with the parties) still no agreement has been reached, the CAC must specify the method by which the parties will conduct collective bargaining. A detailed 'specified method' is set out in the *Trade Union Recognition (Method of Collective Bargaining) Order 2000 (SI 2000/1300)*. This must be taken into account by the CAC when specifying a method of collective bargaining for the parties. In those circumstances, unless the parties agree otherwise, the specified method has effect as if made in a legally enforceable contract between parties. However, specific performance will be the only remedy available for any breach of the specified method. If the parties have agreed the method by which they will conduct collective bargaining, but one or more of the parties fails to carry it out, the parties may apply to the CAC for assistance (*Sch A1, paras 30–32*).

In *British Airline Pilots' Association v Jet2.com Ltd* [2017] IRLR 233 the Court of Appeal held that the specified method in that case, which provided for collective bargaining relating to 'pay, hours and holidays', included collective bargaining over rostering. The language of *Sch A1, para 3(3)* was not confined to collective bargaining over proposals which, if agreed, would give rise to individual contractual rights.

50.34 Voluntary recognition

TULRCA 1992, Sch A1 Part II contains additional provisions relating specifically to voluntary recognition. These provisions apply where the parties reach agreement that the union should be recognised as entitled to conduct collective bargaining at some point before the compulsory recognition procedure summarised above has been exhausted. Agreement may have been reached either before or after an application to the CAC has been made (*Sch A1, para 52*). Any party to such an agreement may apply to the CAC for a decision whether or not the agreement is indeed an 'agreement for recognition' as defined (*Sch A1, para 55*).

If the CAC decides that the agreement is an 'agreement for recognition', the employer may not terminate the agreement for a period of three years. The union, however, may terminate such an agreement at any time, with or without the consent of the employer. It follows that an employer, but not a union, who enters into a recognition agreement may be bound by that agreement for up to three years (but see below for the provisions relating to changes in the bargaining unit and derecognition) (*Sch A1, para 56*).

Where the parties have entered into a recognition agreement, but have failed to agree on a method for conducting collective bargaining, they may apply to the CAC for assistance. Equally, if the parties have agreed on a method, but one or more of the parties fails to carry it out, they may apply to the CAC for assistance. The CAC must not accept either type of application unless the requirements as to number of workers employed and union certification are satisfied. Once it has decided that an application is admissible, the CAC must try to help the parties to reach an agreement. If after a period of 20 days (or such further period as the parties agree) still no agreement has been reached, the CAC must specify the method by which the parties will conduct collective bargaining, taking into account the 'specified method' set out in the *Trade Union Recognition (Method of Collective Bargaining) Order 2000 (SI 2000/1300)*. As in the case of compulsory recognition, unless the parties agree otherwise, the specified method has effect as if made in a legally enforceable contract between parties. Again, however, specific performance is the only remedy available for any breach of the specified method (*Sch A1, paras 58–63*).

50.35   Changes in the bargaining unit

If either party believes that the original bargaining unit is no longer appropriate, it may apply to the CAC for a decision as to the appropriate bargaining unit. Such an application is admissible only if the CAC decides that the original unit is likely to be no longer appropriate, either because the organisation or structure of the employer's business or the employer's business activities have changed, or because there has been a substantial change in the number of workers employed in the original unit (*Sch A1, paras 64–68*). Once the CAC has accepted the application, the parties may agree on a new bargaining unit. If no such agreement is reached, the CAC must decide whether the original unit is appropriate and, if not, decide on a new unit or units. Again, in deciding whether the original unit is appropriate, the CAC must take into account only changes in the organisation or structure of the employer's business or the employer's business activities, or any substantial change in the number of workers employed in the original unit. In deciding what new unit might be appropriate, the CAC must adopt similar criteria to those outlined above in respect of an initial application for recognition (*Sch A1, paras 69–73*).

If an employer believes that the original bargaining unit has ceased to exist and wishes the collective bargaining arrangements to cease to have effect, it must give notice to the union, copied to the CAC. Provided proper notice is given, the collective bargaining arrangements will cease to have effect unless the union applies to the CAC within 10 days for a decision on whether the original unit has ceased to exist and whether it is no longer appropriate in any event. If such an application is made, the CAC must determine these questions, having given the employer and the unions an opportunity to put forward their views on whether the unit has ceased to exist or is no longer appropriate. Again, in deciding whether the original unit is no longer appropriate, the CAC must take into account only any changes in the organisation or structure of the employer's business or the employer's business activities, or any substantial change in the number of workers employed in the original unit. If the CAC decides that the original unit has ceased to exist, the collective bargaining arrangements cease to have effect. If it decides that it has not ceased to exist and remains an appropriate bargaining unit, the collective bargaining arrangements remain in place. If, however, the CAC decides that the original unit has not ceased to exist, but that it is no longer an appropriate unit, it must decide what other bargaining unit is (or units are) appropriate by reference to the same criteria as apply when initially deciding on the appropriate bargaining unit (see above) (*Sch A1, paras 74–81*).

The CAC must further decide whether the difference between the original unit and the new unit is such that the level of support for the union within the new unit needs to be assessed. If not, then the CAC simply issues a declaration that the union is recognised as entitled to conduct collective bargaining on behalf of the new unit. If, however, the CAC decides that the level of support needs to be assessed, it must carry out a procedure similar to that in respect of an initial application for recognition before determining whether to make a recognition declaration. This procedure may require the holding of a secret ballot. The threshold for recognition is the same as in the case of an initial application for recognition (ie a majority of those voting and 40% of workers within the unit voting in favour of union recognition) (*Sch A1, paras 85–89*).

50.36 Derecognition

The procedure set out in *TULRCA 1992, Sch A1* also contains detailed provisions relating to the derecognition of unions for collective bargaining purposes. Following the expiry of three years from a declaration of recognition by the CAC, the employer may apply for derecognition if he believes that he (taken with any associated employers) has employed an average of fewer than 21 workers over a period of 13 weeks (*Sch A1, paras 99–103*). Further, an employer may issue a request to the unions to agree to end the collective bargaining arrangements, again following the expiry of three years from a declaration of recognition. If the union rejects or fails to respond to such a request, or the parties enter negotiations but fail to reach agreement, the employer may apply to the CAC with a view to a secret ballot being held to decide whether the bargaining arrangements should be ended (*Sch A1, paras 104–111*). A specific derecognition procedure applies where a declaration of recognition has been made automatically by the CAC on the basis that it is satisfied that a majority of the workers within the bargaining unit are members of the union, and the basis of the employer's request for an end to the bargaining arrangements is that fewer than half of the workers within the unit are, in fact, union members (*Sch A1, paras 122–133*).

Any worker falling within the bargaining unit similarly may apply to the CAC to have collective bargaining arrangements ended once three years have expired after a declaration of recognition. However, such an application is inadmissible unless the CAC decides that at least 10% of the workers within the bargaining unit favour ending the collective bargaining arrangements *and* that a majority of the workers within the unit would be *likely* to favour ending the arrangements. In the absence of agreement through negotiation (or withdrawal of the application), the CAC must arrange for the holding of a secret ballot to decide whether the bargaining arrangements should be ended (*Sch A1, paras 112–116*). A specific derecognition procedure applies where an employer and a union which has not been certified as independent have agreed that the union should be recognised as entitled to conduct collective bargaining purposes and a worker wishes to apply to the CAC to have the bargaining arrangements ended (*Sch A1, paras 134–147*). In *R (Boots Management Services Ltd) v CAC* [2014] IRLR 887 held that the derecognition procedures contained in *Part VI* of *Sch A1* permitted a union to apply for the incumbent union to be derecognised, even if the incumbent union had very limited collective bargaining rights.

The provisions relating to the conduct of a derecognition ballot mirror closely the provisions summarised above in relation to a recognition ballot (*Sch A1, paras 117–121*).

If a union which the CAC has declared to be recognised as entitled to conduct collective bargaining has its certificate of independence withdrawn (or, where, several unions are parties, they all have their certificates withdrawn), the relevant bargaining arrangements shall cease to have effect and the parties shall be taken to have agreed that the union is entitled to conduct collective bargaining on behalf of the bargaining unit concerned. However, if the union (or one of the unions) succeeds in an appeal against the decision to withdraw its certificate, the bargaining arrangements are reinstated (*Sch A1, paras 149–153*).

50.37 Detriment

TULRCA 1992, Sch A1 Part VIII creates a right on the part of workers not to be subjected to a detriment on union recognition-related grounds. In particular, a worker has a right not to be subjected to a detriment by any act, or any deliberate failure to act, by his employer on grounds that the worker:

(a)   sought to obtain or prevent recognition of a union;

(b)   indicated support for, or opposition to, recognition;

(c)   sought to secure or prevent the ending of collective bargaining arrangements;

(d)   indicated support for, or opposition to, the ending of collective bargaining arrangements;

(e)   influenced or sought to influence the way in which votes would be cast in a recognition ballot;

(f)   influenced or sought to influence other workers to vote or abstain in such a ballot;

(g)   voted in such a ballot;

(h)   proposed to do, failed to do, or proposed to decline to do, any of the matters set out above.

However, an unreasonable act or omission by the worker is not capable of falling within these grounds. If subjected to such a detriment, the worker may complain to an employment tribunal (*Sch A1, para 156*).

There is a parallel right not to be dismissed on union recognition-related grounds. Such dismissal will be automatically unfair (see **54.3** Unfair Dismissal – **II**) (*Sch A1, paras 161–165*).

The worker may make a complaint to an employment tribunal within three months of the act or failure to act complained of, or within such further period as the tribunal considers reasonable in a case where it is satisfied that it was not reasonably practicable for the complaint to be presented within three months (*Sch A1, para 157*).

It is for the employer to show the ground on which he acted or failed to act (*Sch A1, para 158*). If the tribunal finds the complaint well-founded, it will make a declaration to that effect and may order compensation to be paid. The compensation will be such amount as it considers just and equitable in all the circumstances, having regard to the infringement complained of and any loss sustained by the complainant. Compensation may be reduced on account of a failure to mitigate, or on account of the applicant's contributory fault (*Sch A1, para 159*). By analogy with the principles applied to action short of dismissal on trade union grounds (see **51.18** Trade Unions – **II**), it is likely that such compensation may include an award in respect of injury to feelings (compare *Adams v Hackney London Borough Council* [2003] IRLR 402).

50.38 Training

The *Employment Relations Act 1999* also imposed training obligations upon employers where a union is recognised for collective bargaining purposes in accordance with *TULRCA 1992, Sch A1* in circumstances where the CAC has specified to the parties the method for conducting collective bargaining (*ERA 1999, s 5*). In those circumstances, an employer is under a duty to invite trade union representatives to meetings, to be held at least once every six months, for the purpose of:

(a)   consulting about the employer's policy on training workers within the bargaining unit;

(b)   consulting about the employer's plans for such training in the following six months; and

(c)   reporting about training provided since the previous meeting.

The employer must provide to the union any information without which the union representatives would be materially impeded in participating, and which it would be in accordance with good industrial relations practice to provide, at least two weeks before such a meeting. The employer must also take into account any written representations submitted by the union within four weeks of a meeting (*TULRCA 1992, s 70B*).

A trade union may complain to an employment tribunal if an employer fails to comply with the obligation to consult on training. Such a complaint must be presented within three months of the alleged failure complained of, or within such further period as the tribunal considers reasonable in a case where it is satisfied that it was not reasonably practicable for the complaint to be presented within three months. Where a complaint is upheld, the tribunal shall make a declaration to that effect and may award compensation to each person who was, at the time when the failure occurred, a member of the bargaining unit. The maximum amount of compensation is two weeks' pay per worker (subject to the limit on a week's pay set out in *ERA 1996, s 227(1)*, currently £489).

50.39   AMALGAMATIONS AND TRANSFERS OF ENGAGEMENTS

One trade union may amalgamate with or transfer its engagements to another trade union. However, it may not do so unless a resolution which approves the amalgamation or transfer, in a form approved by the Certification Officer, has been passed by a vote of members. The right to be balloted may not extend to members who are not full members of the union (see *National Union of Mineworkers (Yorkshire Area) v Millward* [1995] ICR 482). *TULRCA 1992, ss 97–105* and the *Trade Unions and Employers' Associations (Amalgamations, etc) Regulations 1975 (SI 1975/536)*, as amended, regulate amalgamations and specify the information which must be given to union members and the manner in which the ballot must be taken. *TULRCA 1992, s 103* provides a remedy, by way of complaint to the Certification Officer, to a union member dissatisfied with the way in which the vote on the resolution was taken.

51   Trade Unions – II: Individual Rights and Union Membership

51.1   RIGHTS OF UNION MEMBERS IN RELATION TO EMPLOYER

An employee who is a member of a trade union has the following rights in relation to his employer.

(a)   He may not be refused employment because of his membership of a trade union (see **51.3** below).

(b)   Dismissal for membership of, or for taking part in the activities of, an independent trade union is automatically unfair, as is dismissal on union recognition-related grounds (see **54.3** UNFAIR DISMISSAL – **II**).

(c)   Subjection to detriment by his employer for membership of, or for taking part in the activities of, or using the services of, an independent trade union, or on union recognition-related grounds, gives the employee the right to complain to an employment tribunal which may award him compensation (see **51.18** below).

(d)   The right to time off from work to take part in trade union activities (see **49.3** TIME OFF WORK).

(e)   The right not to suffer the deduction of unauthorised or excessive union subscriptions from his wages (see **51.21** below).

(f)   Where a trade union is recognised for collective bargaining purposes within *TULRCA 1992, Sch A1, TULRCA 1992, s 70B* imposes upon the employer a duty to consult with trade union representatives on training for workers within the bargaining unit (see TRADE UNIONS – **I (50)**);

(g)   A worker who is required or invited to attend a disciplinary or grievance hearing by his employer has the right to be accompanied by a trade union official (see **51.22** below).

In addition, a trade union *official* has the right to take time off with pay for his trade union duties (see **49.2** TIME OFF WORK).

51.2   RIGHTS OF UNION MEMBERS OR INTENDING MEMBERS IN RELATION TO UNION

A trade union member or would-be member has the following rights in relation to his union.

(a)   The right not to be excluded or expelled save on certain specified grounds and in accordance with the rules of the union (see **51.11** to **51.14** below).

(b)   The right under *TULRCA 1992, s 69* to terminate his membership with the union on giving reasonable notice and complying with any reasonable conditions.

(c)   The right not to have disciplinary action taken against him by the union save in accordance with the rules of the union and to be protected from disciplinary action taken on certain grounds (see **51.15** and **51.16** below).

(d)   The right under *TULRCA 1992, s 62* to apply to the High Court (or, in Scotland, the Court of Session) if members of his union, including himself, have been called on to take industrial action which has not received prior ballot approval (see **45.18** STRIKES AND INDUSTRIAL ACTION).

(e)   The right under *TULRCA 1992, s 30* to inspect the union's accounting records, in the company of an accountant if he so desires.

(f)   The right under *TULRCA 1992, s 16* to apply for relief to the High Court (or, in Scotland, the Court of Session) where the trustees of the union's property permit it to be applied unlawfully or comply with unlawful directions from the union.

He or she is also protected against unlawful discrimination (see **12.29 DISCRIMINATION AND EQUAL OPPORTUNITIES – II**). For example, in *Allen v GMB* [2008] EWCA Civ 810, [2008] ICR 1407, [2008] IRLR 690 the Court of Appeal held a trade union to be liable to affected members when it negotiated a pay deal the effect of which was indirectly discriminatory against women members. Nationals of other EU member states are entitled to equal rights as members of trade unions (*Regulation 1612/68/EEC, art 8*; and see EUROPEAN UNION LAW (23)).

An attempt to bring a common law claim against a union which had not achieved a result favouring a particular member was struck out as having no prospect of success in *Iwanuszezak v General Municipal Boilermakers and Allied Trades Union* [1988] IRLR 219. The union had to put the collective interests of its whole membership first.

51.3   CLOSED SHOP

The *Industrial Relations Act 1971* gave the right to employees to belong to the trade union of their choice or not to belong to a trade union at all. That *Act* was repealed by the *Trade Union and Labour Relations Act 1974* ('*TULRA 1974*'), which enabled an employer lawfully to enforce a closed shop by a 'union membership agreement' made with a trade union or trade unions. The *Employment Acts 1980* and *1982* subsequently imposed certain restrictions and conditions on the closed shop. The *Employment Act 1988* effectively outlawed dismissals to enforce a closed shop. Dismissals to enforce a union membership agreement are automatically unfair. The *Employment Act 1990* made it unlawful to refuse a person employment on grounds of membership or non-membership of a trade union. The relevant provisions are now all to be found in the *Trade Union and Labour Relations (Consolidation) Act 1992* ('*TULRCA 1992*').

(See also **30.4 HUMAN RIGHTS**.)

51.4   The pre-entry closed shop

Where an employer has a policy of offering employment only to members of a particular trade union, this is known as a pre-entry closed shop. Until 1991 such a policy remained lawful.

TULRCA 1992, s 137(1) now provides that it is unlawful to refuse a person employment because he is, or is not, a member of a trade union. The refusal is also unlawful if it is because the person is unwilling to accept a requirement to become or remain (or to cease to be or not to become) a member, or to make payments or suffer deductions in the event of his not being a member. References in this context to being or not being a member of a trade union are to being or not being a member of any trade union, of a particular trade union or of one of a number of particular trade unions, or of a particular branch or section of a trade union (*TULRCA 1992, s 143(3)*). In *Harrison v Kent County Council* [1995] ICR 434, it was held that an employer's refusal to employ an applicant because of his previous union *activities* could amount to an unlawful refusal of employment on grounds of union membership. In *Miller v Inserverve Industrial Services Ltd* (UKEAT/0244/12/SM) the EAT held that there had been no breach of *TULRCA 1992, s 137(1)* where a trade union official had pressurised an employer to recruit three named employees, with a view to their acting as shop stewards. The relevant manager declined to recruit them because he resented being "bullied" by the union. It was not the individuals' trade union membership *per se* that led him to refuse to recruit them, but his dislike of the union's approach.

These provisions do not apply where the employee would ordinarily work outside Great Britain (*TULRCA 1992, s 285(1)*; **53.15**(e) UNFAIR DISMISSAL – I). Nor do they apply to cases where a person may not be considered for appointment to an office in a trade union unless he is a member of the union, even though as a holder of the office he would be employed by the union (*TULRCA 1992, s 137(7)*). For the meaning of 'office', see *TULRCA 1992, s 137(7)(a), (b)*.

A deliberate omission to offer employment is considered to be a refusal for these purposes, as are a refusal or deliberate omission to deal with the application or the causing of its withdrawal, a spurious offer of employment (that is, one the terms of which are such as no reasonable employer who wished to fill the post would offer and which is not accepted) and an offer of employment which is withdrawn or which the offeror causes the prospective employee not to accept, or an offer which is not accepted because it includes a requirement of union membership or non-membership (*TULRCA 1992, s 137(5), (6)*).

There are two situations where the refusal of employment is deemed to have been on union membership grounds:

(a)   where an advertisement is published which indicates or might reasonably be understood as indicating that the employment is only open to union members or non-members, or that a requirement of the sort referred to in *s 137(1)(b)* will be imposed, and a person who does not satisfy that condition or is unwilling to accept that requirement is refused employment to which the advertisement relates (*TULRCA 1992, s 137(3)*); or

(b)   where there is an arrangement or practice under which employment is offered only to persons put forward or approved by a union which puts forward or approves only its members, and a person who is not a member of the union is refused employment in pursuance of the arrangement or practice (*TULRCA 1992, s 137(4)*).

In *Miller v Interserve Industrial Services Ltd* [2013] ICR 445 the EAT drew a distinction between a refusal of employment on trade union grounds, on the one hand, and a refusal based on the overbearing conduct of a union official. The latter having been found to been the true reason for the refusal to employ, the claims under *TULRCA 1992, s 137* failed.

A person who is refused employment on unlawful grounds has a right of complaint to an employment tribunal, and no other remedy (*TULRCA 1992, s 143(4)*). The complaint must be presented within three months of the refusal or other conduct complained of, unless the tribunal considers that it was not reasonably practicable to do so (*TULRCA 1992, s 139(1)*; and see **18.20** EMPLOYMENT TRIBUNALS – I). Where the respondent has acted under pressure from a third party such as a trade union, there is provision for that third party to be joined into the proceedings and to be ordered to pay all or part of any compensation awarded (*TULRCA 1992, s 142*).

If the tribunal finds the complaint well-founded, it will make a declaration to that effect, and may (if it considers it just and equitable to do so) order the respondent to pay compensation assessed on the same basis as damages for breach of statutory duty, which may include compensation for injury to feelings (*TULRCA 1992, s 140(1), (2)*). The tribunal will presumably ask itself whether the applicant would have obtained the job had it not been for his membership or non-membership of a union, or the percentage chance of his doing so, and will compensate him for lost earnings if so. The maximum award of compensation is the same as for unfair dismissal, currently £80,541 (*ERA 1999, s 34*; *Employment Rights (Increase of Limits) Order 2017 (SI 2017/175)*).

The tribunal may also, or alternatively, make a recommendation that the respondent take within a specified period action appearing to the tribunal to be practicable for the purpose of obviating or reducing the adverse effect on the applicant of the conduct complained of, and may make or increase an award of compensation (up to the statutory maximum) if the respondent fails without reasonable justification to comply (*TULRCA 1992, s 140(1)(b), (3)*).

An appeal on a question of law lies from the decision of the tribunal to the Employment Appeal Tribunal (*TULRCA 1992, s 291(2)*).

Any agreement purporting to exclude the right to complain under these provisions is void, unless reached as part of a settlement after a conciliation officer has taken action, or where the statutory conditions governing compromise contracts have been satisfied, including that the complainant should have had advice from a relevant independent advisor (*TULRCA 1992, s 288*; and see **2.4** ADVISORY, CONCILIATION AND ARBITRATION SERVICE and **18.22** EMPLOYMENT TRIBUNALS – I).

There are also provisions dealing similarly with cases where an employment agency acts on behalf of an employer, or where such an agency refuses its services on unlawful grounds (*TULRCA 1992, s 138*; see also *TULRCA 1992, ss 141* and *143(2)*).

51.5   Dismissal and the closed shop

The dismissal of an employee or his selection for redundancy will automatically be regarded as unfair if the principal reason for the dismissal or selection was that he was not a member of any trade union, or of a particular trade union, or of one of a number of particular trade unions, or had refused or proposed to refuse to become or remain a member (*TULRCA 1992, ss 152(1)(c), 153*) (see **54.3** UNFAIR DISMISSAL – II). References to trade union membership include membership of any trade union, or of a particular trade union or one of a number of particular trade unions, or of a particular branch or section of a trade union (*TULRCA 1992, s 152(4)*).

'Proposing to refuse to remain a member' covers the situation where the proposed refusal is contingent upon a particular event (*Crosville Motor Services Ltd v Ashfield* [1986] IRLR 475).

For the relevance of the employer's belief in the employee's membership or non-membership, see *Leyland Vehicles Ltd v Jones* [1981] ICR 428.

Compensation for the dismissal is assessed as described in **51.7** below.

Note that there is no minimum qualifying period of employment before an employee is entitled to make such a complaint of unfair dismissal, nor is there any upper age limit (*TULRCA 1992, s 154*).

51.6   FAILURE TO MAKE PAYMENTS

Instead of being a member of a trade union, an employee may be subject to a requirement to make a payment, eg to a charity. If such an employee who is not or ceases to be a union member refuses, in breach of a requirement, to make such a payment and is dismissed for that reason, he will be treated as dismissed for failure to become or remain a member of a trade union. The same is true if he is dismissed for objecting to a provision which entitles his employer to deduct such a payment from his wages (*TULRCA 1992, s 152(3)*). A dismissal for failure to make such a payment or for objecting to such a provision will be regarded as automatically unfair, and will be compensated as described in **51.7** below.

An employer may only deduct a trade union subscription from an employee's pay if certain statutory requirements are complied with (see **51.21** below).

51.7 COMPENSATION FOR CLOSED SHOP DISMISSALS

For the detailed rules on compensation, see **55.6–55.19** UNFAIR DISMISSAL – **III**. Note in particular, however, that *in addition* to the general rules governing unfair dismissal awards, the following apply to 'automatically' unfair dismissals to enforce a closed shop.

(a)   There is a minimum basic award of £5,970, although the compensatory award is calculated in the normal way.

(b)   There is provision that conduct of the employee in refusing to join a union or to make payments in lieu of joining, or in objecting to such payments, should be disregarded in assessing contributory fault for possible reduction of any part of the award (*TULRCA 1992, s 155*). However, it seems that confrontational conduct by the employee could form the basis for a finding of contributory fault provided that the immediate circumstances constituting the principal reason for dismissal are excluded from consideration (*TGWU v Howard* [1992] ICR 106).

(c)   The employee may request that a third party (eg a union) be joined in the unfair dismissal proceedings if pressure by it has induced the dismissal and the award may be made wholly or partly against that third party.

(*TULRCA 1992, ss 155–156, 160.*)

51.8 DETRIMENT

Every worker has the right not to be subjected to detriment by his employer for the purpose of compelling him to be or become a member of a trade union or a particular trade union, or for the purpose of enforcing a requirement that in the event of his failing to become or ceasing to be a member he must make one or more payments (*TULRCA 1992, s 146(1)(c), (3)*). Infringement of this right entitles the employee to complain to an industrial tribunal and seek a declaration and compensation (*TULRCA 1992, s 146(5)*; and see **51.18**, **51.19** below).

51.9 INDUSTRIAL ACTION, TRADE UNION DISCIPLINE AND THE CLOSED SHOP

The statutory immunity for industrial action is inapplicable where the purpose of the action is to impose union membership requirements or to enforce a closed shop. For a more detailed account of the relevant provisions, see **45.7** STRIKES AND INDUSTRIAL ACTION.

An individual member of a trade union may not be disciplined either for proposing to resign from the union, or for working with non-union members or for an employer who employs non-union labour (*TULRCA 1992, s 65(2)* as amended; for further details, see **51.16** below).

51.10 TRADE UNION 'BLACKLISTS'

The *ERA 1999* contains provisions to prohibit the compilation of trade union 'blacklists'. The Secretary of State is empowered to make regulations prohibiting the making of lists which relate to trade union members or those who have taken part in trade union activities with a view to such lists being used by employers or employment agencies for discriminating in relation to recruitment or treatment of workers. The Secretary of State may further make regulations prohibiting the use, sale and supply of such lists. (*ERA 1999, ss 3, 4*). The *Employment Relations Act 1999 (Blacklists) Regulations 2010 (SI 2010/493)* came into force on 2 March 2010, prohibiting the use of blacklists to deny employment to or dismiss or cause detriment to employees as a result of their trade union membership or activities.

These regulations introduced a general prohibition on compiling, using, selling or supplying lists which contain details of union members or participants in trade union activities, and are compiled with a view to being used by employers or employment agencies for the purposes of discrimination in relation to the recruitment or treatment of workers (*reg 3*). A person who has been refused employment has a right to complain to the employment tribunal against another person who has refused him employment if that other person has contravened the prohibition contained in *reg 3* or has relied on information provided by a person in contravention of *reg 3*, in circumstances where he knows or ought reasonably to know that the information relied upon is supplied in contravention of that regulation (*reg 5*). In *Miller v Inserverve Industrial Services Ltd* [2013] ICR 445 the EAT held that there had no breach of *reg 5* where a trade union official had pressurised an employer to recruit three named employees, with a view to their acting as shop stewards, but the relevant manager had declined to recruit them because he resented being "bullied" by the union. Even if it could be said that the manager had compiled a "mental list" of the three individuals, it was not a prohibited list because it had not been prepared for the purposes of discriminating against the individuals on grounds of their trade union membership or activities. His disinclination to recruit them arose from his dislike of the union's approach.

There is an equivalent right to complain against an employment agency which refuses to provide its services on such grounds (*reg 6*). If the claim is upheld, the tribunal must make a declaration to that effect, and make order compensation and make recommendations (reg 8). Where an award of compensation is made, the amount shall be not less than £5,000 (subject to certain increases and deductions) (*reg 8(3)*). An equivalent right to bring a claim before the employment tribunal is given to any person who is subjected to a detriment for a reason relating to a prohibited list (*reg 9*). In addition, *reg 12* amends the *ERA 1996* so as render it automatically unfair to dismiss an employee for a reason related to a prohibited list (*ERA 1996, s 104F*). In those circumstances, the minimum basic award again shall not be less than £5,000 (*ERA 1996, s 120(1C)*).

51.11   EXCLUSION OR EXPULSION FROM A UNION – GENERAL

TULRCA 1992, s 174 confers upon persons seeking or in employment, in respect of which a closed shop agreement is in force, the right not to be unreasonably excluded or expelled from a trade union. However, since it is unlawful for an employer to refuse employment on grounds of non-membership of a trade union, this provision is of little practical importance. *TURERA 1993, s 14* introduced a right not to be excluded or expelled, save on certain grounds, which is not dependent upon the existence of a closed shop. This right is considered in **51.13** below.

The common law also provides a remedy for members expelled from a trade union in breach of an express or implied provision of the rules (see **51.12** below).

51.12   The common law

Since there is no contract in existence between an applicant for membership and a trade union, the only right he may have in certain circumstances at common law is not to have his application rejected arbitrarily or capriciously (see *Nagle v Feilden* [1966] 2 QB 633). However, this right was developed in cases where a closed shop or the equivalent was in force (which is no longer likely to be a practical problem, for the reasons given in **51.3** above), and there may be little need to invoke it in future in view of the new statutory right discussed in **51.13** below.

Once a person has been accepted as a member of a union he may not be expelled except in accordance with the rules (see, for example, *Edwards v Society of Graphical and Allied Trades* [1971] Ch 354). In *Goring v British Actors Equity Association* [1987] IRLR 122, the court took the view that the sole common law rights of a union member against the union were those conferred by its rules (including the implied obligation not to act capriciously or arbitrarily). Further, in *Hamlet v General Municipal Boilermakers and Allied Trades Union* [1987] ICR 150, the court held that where a member of a union complained of the decision of a union, the court's function was not to review that decision but merely to ensure that the internal procedures of the union had been complied with. However, in addition to any implied term that a member is not to be expelled arbitrarily or capriciously, a member whose expulsion is being considered is entitled to be dealt with in accordance with the rules of natural justice (*Lee v Showmen's Guild of Great Britain* [1952] 2 QB 329 and see also *Hudson v GMB* [1990] IRLR 67). See also **51.15** below.

The common law remains important in relation to expulsions because, unlike the statutory right (see **51.13** below), it provides a means of controlling the procedure which is followed. Further, the common law right may be used, by means of an application for an injunction, to prevent the expulsion taking place at all.

51.13 The statutory right

A union member has a statutory right not to be excluded or expelled from a trade union except on certain specified grounds (*TULRCA 1992, ss 174–177*) (see **51.3** above).

The exclusion or expulsion of an individual from a union is only permissible in the following circumstances:

(a)   he does not satisfy an enforceable membership requirement contained in the rules (ie one which restricts membership solely by reference to one or more of the following criteria: employment in a specified trade, industry or profession; occupational description; or possession of specified qualifications or work experience);

(b)   he does not qualify for membership because the union only operates in particular parts of Great Britain;

(c)   the union's purpose is to regulate relations between its members and a particular employer (or particular associated employers; for associated employers see **7.9**(a) Continuous Employment), and he is not employed by such an employer;

(d)   the exclusion or expulsion is entirely attributable to his conduct, provided such conduct does not include either conduct consisting of being, ceasing to be or having been or ceased to be a member of another trade union or employed by a particular employer or at a particular place or conduct to which *TULRCA 1992, s 65* applies (see **51.16** below); and the conduct to which his exclusion or expulsion is wholly or mainly attributable is not conduct consisting of being or ceasing to be or having been or ceased to be a member of a political party, unless membership of that party is contrary to the rules or objectives of the trade union (provided that the relevant objective is reasonable ascertainable). However, exclusion or expulsion for membership of a political party will not be permissible if it was done contrary to the union's rules, if the decision was taken unfairly, or if the individual would lose his livelihood or suffer exceptional hardship by reason of not being, or ceasing to be, a member of the union.

(*TULRCA 1992, s 174(1)–(4).*)

The earlier provision in *s 174* preventing a trade union from excluding or expelling a member for being or ceasing to be a member of a political party was held by the European Court of Human Rights in *Associated Society of Locomotive Engineers & Firemen v United Kingdom (Application No 11002/05)* [2007] IRLR 361, ECtHR to infringe the right to freedom of association under Article 11 of the European Convention. The Court found that the UK law did not strike the right balance between the member's rights and those of the union in so far as it prevented the union from expelling the member on grounds of his membership of the British National Party. As a result, with effect from 6 April 2009 *s 174* was amended by *EA 2008, s 19* so as to permit expulsion on grounds of membership of a political party in the circumstances set out in the legislation.

For these purposes, if an application for membership of a trade union is neither granted nor rejected, it will be treated as having been refused on the expiry of the period within which it might reasonably have been expected to have been granted or refused. In addition, if under the rules of a trade union any person ceases to be a member of the trade union on the happening of an event specified in the rules, he will be treated as having been expelled from the union (*TULRCA 1992, s 177(2)*).

An employee, who had voluntarily surrendered his membership of a union, could not make a complaint under the predecessor of *s 174* on the basis that his resignation had been forced on him by the conduct of union officials, although there might be cases where the resignation was not truly voluntary (*McGhee v Midlands British Road Services Ltd* [1985] ICR 503). Furthermore, an employee who had been suspended from a union beyond the six-month period allowed in the union's rule book was held to have been neither excluded nor expelled within the meaning of *s 174* (*NACODS v Gluchowski* [1996] IRLR 252).

These rights are additional to common law rights in relation to expulsion or exemptions (see **51.12** above) (*TULRCA 1992, s 177(5)*).

51.14 The remedy

TULRCA 1992 provides for a two-stage remedy for an employee who complains that he has been expelled or excluded in breach of *s 174*. He must begin by presenting a complaint to an employment tribunal against the union in question, within the period of six months from the refusal or expulsion. Applications outside this time limit can only be heard if the tribunal is satisfied that it was not reasonably practicable to present the complaint in time and the complaint was presented within such further period as the tribunal considers reasonable (*TULRCA 1992, ss 174(4), 175;* and see **18.20** Employment Tribunals – I).

At the first stage, the tribunal's function is limited to rejecting the application or finding that it is well-founded, and, if the latter, making a declaration to that effect (*TULRCA 1992, s 176(1)*).

Where the tribunal declares that the applicant has been wrongly refused or expelled from union membership, he will be entitled to compensation. However, he cannot apply for compensation until four weeks have elapsed after the declaration. This four-week period is designed to give the trade union an opportunity of admitting or readmitting the applicant to membership. The application must be made to an employment tribunal, however, within six months of the declaration. (*TULRCA 1992, s 176(2), (3)*).

Amount of compensation. Compensation will be of such amount as is considered just and equitable in all the circumstances, but the minimum award is £9,118. The maximum award of compensation is equal to the aggregate of:

(a)   30 times the current limit on the amount of a week's pay for the purposes of calculating the basic award in unfair dismissal cases, which is at present £489; and

(b)   the current maximum compensatory award in unfair dismissal cases, which is at present £80,541.

(See Unfair Dismissal – III (55).) Thus the present maximum award is £95,211. Since it will now be unusual, because the closed shop has been outlawed, for the inability to belong to a union to cause financial loss, it is unclear how the assessment of compensation should be approached. In *Bradley v NALGO* [1991] ICR 359, the EAT indicated that, assuming compensation for injury to feelings to be available, it should be on a modest scale. However, in *Adams v Hackney London Borough Council* [2003] IRLR 402 the EAT held, in the context of action short of dismissal by an employer on trade union grounds, that in principle awards for injury to feelings should not be approached any differently whatever the ground of discrimination relied upon, although each case will depend on its own facts. (See also *Beaumont v Amicus MSF* (2004) 148 Sol Jo LB 1063 in which an award for injury to feelings was made in a claim for unjustifiable discipline by a trade union).

Compensation may be reduced where the exclusion or expulsion was, to any extent, caused or contributed to by the action of the applicant (*TULRCA 1992, s 176(5)*). It appears that this step should precede the application of the statutory maximum or minimum.

Where a complaint of expulsion under *s 174* succeeds, the applicant cannot also complain of the expulsion under *TULRCA 1992, s 66* (unjustifiable disciplining; see **51.16** below).

51.15 DISCIPLINING BY A TRADE UNION – COMMON LAW

A member of a trade union has a right to be dealt with in accordance with the rules of his union and in accordance with natural justice (see also **51.12** above). If a union acts in breach of the rules or in breach of natural justice, the member affected may apply to the High Court for an injunction and a declaration of his rights. Members of the National Union of Mineworkers ('NUM'), disciplined for breach of a union instruction given in breach of the rules, were held to be entitled to a declaration of the invalidity of the instruction and the unlawfulness of the disciplinary action (*Taylor v National Union of Mineworkers (Derbyshire Area)* [1984] IRLR 440). Injunctions were granted to NUM members to restrain their union from instructing or seeking to persuade them or others not to work. The NUM had described the strike as official, where it had been called without a ballot as required by the rules, and had threatened disciplinary action. However, the courts will not review a decision of a trade union which is taken in accordance with the rules but which is attacked on the basis that it is one which no reasonable trade union could have reached in the circumstances (*Hamlet v General Municipal Boilermakers and Allied Trades Union* [1987] ICR 150). Nevertheless, the rules may be subject to an implied obligation not to act capriciously or arbitrarily (*Goring v British Actors Equity Association* [1987] IRLR 122). For examples of the courts intervening where there has been a breach of natural justice (ie the right to a fair hearing before an unbiased decision-maker), see *Roebuck v National Union of Mineworkers (Yorkshire Area)* [1977] ICR 573 and *Stevenson v United Road Transport Union* [1977] ICR 893. However, the rules of natural justice are not generally applicable in the context of a union's contractual relations with its officials, in its capacity as an employer (*Meacham v Amalgamated Engineering and Electrical Union* [1994] IRLR 218). The court may imply into a union's rule-book a power to discipline its members where no express power exists (*McVitae v UNISON* [1996] IRLR 33).

The court will ignore any provision of the union's rules which purports to provide that his only remedy is by way of some form of determination or conciliation in accordance with the rules (*TULRCA 1992, s 63(1)*). It will also ignore any provision which requires or permits such determination or conciliation, provided that the member has made a valid application to the union for determination or conciliation more than six months before bringing court proceedings (*TULRCA 1992, s 63(2)*), unless the member has himself unreasonably delayed matters (*TULRCA 1992, s 63(4)*). Applications are deemed valid unless the union informs the member of invalidity within 28 days of receipt (*TULRCA 1992, s 63(3)*).

51.16 DISCIPLINING BY A TRADE UNION – STATUTORY PROVISIONS

TULRCA 1992, s 64(1) confers an important right 'not to be unjustifiably disciplined' by a union of which a person is or has at any time been a member. This right is conferred in addition to any existing rights and the only remedies for any infringement are those conferred by *ss 66* and *67* (*TULRCA 1992, s 64(4), (5)*). In *Unison v Kelly* (UKEAT/0188/11/SM) the EAT rejected an argument put forward by the union that the statutory right not to be unjustifiably disciplined amounted to an unlawful interference with Article 11 of the Convention. Union members have a right to hold their unions to account in this regard.

A person is unjustifiably disciplined if the conduct or supposed conduct for which he is disciplined falls within, or is believed by the union to amount to conduct which falls within, any of the 12 categories which may be summarised as follows:

(a)   failing to participate in or support, or opposing, any industrial action;

(b)   failing to break a contract of employment or other agreement with the employer for the purposes of industrial action;

(c)   asserting, including by bringing proceedings, that the union or any of its officials or representatives is in breach of its obligations under the general law, its rules or any agreement (although false assertions made in bad faith are excluded by *s 65(6)*);

(d)   encouraging or assisting another person to fulfil obligations to the employer or to make or to attempt to vindicate assertions of the kind described in para (*c*);

(e)   failing to comply with any requirement imposed as a result of unjustifiable disciplinary action taken against himself or another;

(f)   failing to agree to the deduction of union dues from his wages;

(g)   resigning or proposing to resign from the union or another union, or being or becoming, or proposing or refusing to become, a member of another union;

(h)   working or proposing to work with individuals who do not belong to the union, or who are or are not members of another union;

(i)   working or proposing to work for an employer of such individuals;

(j)   requiring the union to do an act which any provision of *TULRCA 1992* requires it to do on a member's requisition;

(k)   consulting or requesting assistance from the Certification Officer (see **50.3** Trade Unions – I), or from any other person in relation to assertions of the kind described in para (*c*);

(l)   proposing to do any of these things, or doing acts which are preparatory or incidental to them,

unless that conduct would independently and justifiably lead to disciplinary action (*TULRCA 1992, s 65(2)–(5)*).

The disciplinary action against which members are protected includes expulsion, fines, deprivation of benefits or facilities, encouragement to another union not to accept him as a member, or subjection to any other detriment (*TULRCA 1992, s 64(2)*). This extends to suspension from membership, and to naming a strike-breaker in a branch circular with the intention of causing embarrassment (*NALGO v Killorn and Simm* [1991] ICR 1).

Complaints of unjustifiable disciplinary action are to be made to an employment tribunal within three months of the determination complained of (*TULRCA 1992, s 66(1), (2)*). A mere recommendation is not a determination (*TGWU v Webber* [1990] ICR 711). Time may be extended for such period as the tribunal considers reasonable, either where it was not reasonably practicable to present the complaint within three months (see **18.20** Employment Tribunals – I), or where any delay is wholly or partly attributable to a reasonable attempt to pursue an appeal or otherwise to have the decision reconsidered (see *NALGO v Killorn* *and Simm*, above). If the complaint is well-founded, the tribunal will make a declaration to that effect (*TULRCA 1992, s 66(3)*). If such a declaration is made, the complainant may make an application to the employment tribunal to seek compensation and/or the repayment of any sums paid by him as the result of the disciplinary action (*TULRCA 1992, s 67(1)*). Applications for compensation are to be made not less than four weeks or more than six months after the disciplinary action is declared unjustifiable (*TULRCA 1992, s 67(3)*).

The compensation awarded will be that sum which is just and equitable in all the circumstances, taking account of the duty to mitigate loss and of any contributory fault (*TULRCA 1992, s 67(5)–(7)*). The Court of Appeal considered the principles to be applied in awarding compensation for unjustified discipline by a trade union in *Massey v Unifi* [2007] EWCA Civ 800, [2008] ICR 62. Among other matters, the approach to injury to feelings in *Vento v Chief Constable of West Yorkshire Police* [2002] EWCA Civ 1871, [2003] ICR 318 was applied and it was accepted in principle (although not on the facts of the case) that aggravated damages could be awarded. Before dealing with mitigation or contribution, however, the tribunal is required by *TULRCA 1992, s 67(9)* to apply the statutory maxima and minima contained in *s 67(8)*. The maximum is the aggregate of (*a*) 30 times the maximum week's pay for calculating the basic award in unfair dismissal cases (*ERA 1996, s 227*), and (*b*) the maximum compensatory award in such cases (*ERA 1996, s 124*). These figures are at present £489 and £80,541, respectively, giving a maximum award under *s 67(8)* of £95,211. If the determination has not been revoked, or the union has failed to take all reasonable steps to reverse the determination, the minimum award is the amount for the time being specified in *TULRCA 1992, s 176(6A)*, which is at present £8,868. (See also **55.14 Unfair Dismissal – III.**)

51.17   DETRIMENT ON GROUNDS OF UNION MEMBERSHIP OR ACTIVITIES

TULRCA 1992, s 146 concerns detriment caused by an employer against a worker as an individual:

(a)   to prevent or deter him from, or to penalise him for, belonging to an independent trade union; or

(b)   to prevent him or deter him from taking part in the activities of an independent union at an appropriate time (ie a time outside working hours or a time when the employer has consented to him taking part in union activities), or to penalise him for doing so; or

(c)   from 1 October 2004, to prevent him or deter him from making use of trade union services at an appropriate time, or to penalise him for doing so; or

(d)   to compel him to join any trade union.

The Court of Appeal held in *Bone v North Essex Partnership NHS Foundation Trust* [2014] ICR 1053 that it was not necessary in a claim under *s 146* for the independence of the trade union to be established in order for an employment tribunal to have jurisdiction. Having failed to dispute independence at the employment tribunal, it was too late for the employer to argue that the trade union was not independent at the EAT.

There was previously considerable doubt as to whether omissions could constitute 'action' for those purposes. In *Associated Newspapers Ltd v Wilson; Associated British Ports v Palmer* [1995] ICR 406, a majority of the House of Lords held that withholding a salary increase from employees who refused to sign personal contracts and give up collectively bargained terms and conditions did not amount to a breach of *s 146*.

However, the *ERA 1999, Sch 2* had the effect of reversing this aspect of the House of Lords' decision in *Wilson/Palmer* with effect from 25 October 1999. In particular, *TULRCA 1992, s 146(1)* now prohibits subjecting an individual to a detriment by any act, or any deliberate failure to act, by the employer on grounds of trade union membership or activities.

Wilson/Palmer subsequently went to the European Court of Human Rights in *Wilson and National Union of Journalists v United Kingdom* (Applications 30668/96, 30679/61 and 30678/96) [2002] IRLR 568. The Court held that, by permitting employers to use financial incentives to induce employees to surrender the right to union representation (as opposed to deterring union membership altogether), the United Kingdom had failed in its positive duty to secure the enjoyment of the right to freedom of association under *art 11* of the *European Convention on Human Rights*. In response to that decision, *s 29* of the *Employment Rights Act 2004* inserted new *ss 145A–145F* into *TULRCA 1992* which from 1 October 2004 conferred upon workers a right not to have an offer made to them by their employer for the sole or main purpose of inducing the worker:

(a)   not to be or seek to become a member of a trade union;

(b)   not to take part, at an appropriate time, in trade union activities;

(c)   not to make use, at an appropriate time, of trade union services; or

(d)   to be or become a member of a trade union (*s 145A*).

In addition, a worker who is a member of an independent trade union which is recognised, or is seeking to be recognised, by his employer, has the right not to have an offer made to him by his employer if:

(a)   acceptance of that offer, together with other workers' acceptance of similar offers, would result in the workers' terms and conditions no longer being determined by collective bargaining with the union; and

(b)   the employer's sole or main purpose in making the offers is to achieve that result (*s 145B*).

In *Davies v Asda Stores Ltd* (IDS Brief 801) an employment tribunal held that the employer had breached *s 145B* of *TULRCA 1992* by offering new terms and conditions to union members provided they relinquished collective bargaining. The 340 members were each awarded £2,500.

In *Department of Transport v Gallacher* [1994] ICR 967, the Court of Appeal held that an employer's advice that an employee's prospects of promotion would be improved if he returned to a line management position, instead of engaging in full-time trade union duties, was not given for the purpose of deterring the employee from taking part in union activities within the meaning of *TULRCA 1992, s 146*. The relevant purpose is the object which the employer desires or seeks to achieve – in *Gallacher*, his purpose was to assist the employee in obtaining promotion.

In *FW Farnsworth Ltd v McCoid* [1998] IRLR 362, it was held that the derecognition of a shop steward by an employer could amount to action taken against the shop steward as an individual for the purpose of preventing or deterring him from taking part in trade union activities or penalising him for doing so within the meaning of *TULRCA 1992, s 146*.

A worker also has the right not to be subjected to a detriment in order to require him to make payments in lieu of union subscriptions when he is not (or is no longer) a union member (*TULRCA 1992, s 146(3)*). In addition, *ERA 1999, Sch 1* introduced a new right not to be subjected to a detriment on union recognition-related grounds (see **50.37** TRADE UNIONS – I).

See also **53.3** UNFAIR DISMISSAL – II.

51.18 The remedy

The employee may make a complaint to an employment tribunal within three months of the action complained of, or within such further period as the tribunal considers reasonable in a case where it is satisfied that it was not reasonably practicable for the complaint to be presented within three months (see **18.20** EMPLOYMENT TRIBUNALS – I) (*TULRCA 1992, ss 146(5), 147*).

It is for the employer to show the purpose for which action was taken against the employee (*TULRCA 1992, s 148(1)*). However, notwithstanding this statutory language, the tribunal should not apply the approach to the burden of proof applicable in discrimination cases: see *Serco Ltd v Dahou* [2015] IRLR 30. If the tribunal finds the complaint well-founded, it will make a declaration to that effect and may order compensation to be paid. The compensation will be such amount as it considers just and equitable in all the circumstances, having regard to the right infringed and any loss sustained by the complainant. Compensation may be reduced on account of the applicant's contributory fault (*TULRCA 1992, s 149*). It would appear that compensation for an action short of dismissal may include an award in respect of injury to feelings (*Cleveland Ambulance NHS Trust v Blane* [1997] ICR 851). In *Adams v Hackney London Borough Council* [2003] IRLR 402 the EAT held that in principle awards for injury to feelings should not be approached any differently in cases of discrimination on trade union grounds than in other cases of discrimination. However, the level of award will depend on the individual applicant. Some may feel deeply hurt by trade union discrimination, whilst other more robust characters may suffer little, if any, distress. Since the aim is to compensate and not to punish, the compensation ought not to be the same in each case.

Joinder of third parties. Where the employer was induced to take the action complained of by industrial action or threat of such action, although no account is to be taken by the tribunal of such pressure when deciding the complaint, the union (or unions) may be joined as a third party to the proceedings and may be ordered to pay all or part of the compensation as the tribunal considers just in the circumstances (*TULRCA 1992, ss 148(2), 150*).

51.19 PROHIBITION ON UNION MEMBERSHIP AND UNION RECOGNITION REQUIREMENTS IN CONTRACTS FOR GOODS OR SERVICES

Any term or condition of a contract for the supply of goods or services is void insofar as it purports:

(a)   to require that the whole, or some part, of the work done for the purposes of the contract is to be done only by persons who are or who are not members of trade unions or of a particular trade union (*TULRCA 1992, s 144*);

(b)   to require any party to the contract to recognise one or more trade unions (whether or not named in the contract) for the purpose of negotiating on behalf of workers, or any class of worker, employed by him or to negotiate or consult with, or with any official of, one or more trade unions (whether or not so named) (*TULRCA 1992, s 186*).

(For the prohibition of industrial action to impose union membership or recognition requirements, see **45.7** STRIKES AND INDUSTRIAL ACTION.)

Further, it is unlawful for a person to refuse to deal with a supplier or prospective supplier of goods or services on union membership grounds (*TULRCA 1992, s 145(1)*). Refusing to deal with a person means excluding that person's name from a list of approved suppliers or of persons from whom tenders may be or are invited, or if he fails to permit that person to submit a tender, decides not to enter into a contract with that person, or terminates an existing contract (*TULRCA 1992, s 145(2), (3), (4)*). Such a refusal is on union membership grounds if the ground or one of the grounds for it is that work done for the purposes of any contract would be done, or would be likely to be done, by persons who were or were not members of a trade union or of a particular union (*TULRCA 1992, s 145(2)*).

It is also unlawful to refuse to deal with such a person on the ground that he does not, or is not likely to, recognise one or more trade unions for negotiating purposes or negotiate or consult with one or more trade unions or their officials (*TULRCA 1992, s 187*).

In the case of an unlawful refusal to deal, an action for breach of statutory duty may be brought by the person with whom the defendant has refused to deal or by any other person adversely affected (*TULRCA 1992, ss 145(5), 187(3)*).

51.20 DEDUCTION OR SUBSCRIPTIONS: THE 'CHECK-OFF'

The following provisions are to be found in *TULRCA 1992, ss 68* and *68A* as amended by the *Deregulation (Deduction from Pay of Union Subscriptions) Order 1998 (SI 1998/1529)*.

Where arrangements exist between an employer and a union relating to the making of deductions from wages in respect of union subscriptions (commonly known as the 'check-off'), the employer must ensure that deductions are only made in accordance with an authorisation signed and dated by the worker concerned (*TULRCA 1992, s 68(1), (2)*). A worker has the same meaning as in *Part II* of the *Employment Rights Act 1996* (see PAY – I (34)), and is thus not confined to employees in the strict sense (*TULRCA 1992, s 68(4)*). If the worker subsequently withdraws the authorisation in writing, the employer must cease to make deductions as soon as is reasonably practicable (*TULRCA 1992, s 68(2)*).

In *Cavanagh v Secretary of State for Work & Pension* [2016] ICR 826 the High Court held that employees within a government department had gained a contractual right to have their union subscriptions deducted through the 'check-off' by virtue of the clear and specific provisions to that effect in the civil service code.

The signing of an authorisation does not oblige the employer to maintain or continue to maintain the arrangements for making deductions (*TULRCA 1992, s 68(3)*).

If the employer makes a deduction in contravention of these provisions, the worker may present a complaint to an employment tribunal within the period of three months beginning with the date of payment of the wages from which the deduction (or the last deduction, if the complaint relates to more than one) was made (*TULRCA 1992, s 68A(1)*). If the tribunal is satisfied that it was not reasonably practicable for the complaint to be presented within that period, it may extend time for such further period as it considers reasonable.

Where the tribunal finds a complaint well-founded, it will make a declaration to that effect, and will order the employer to repay the amount improperly deducted and not already repaid (*TULRCA 1992, s 68A(2)*). Provision is made to avoid double recovery where the same deduction also contravenes other statutory provisions (*TULRCA 1992, s 68A(3)*). It is not clear whether, if the sums deducted had already been paid by the employer to the union, the employer would be able to recover them from the union in a common law claim for restitution.

Prior to 23 June 1998, the 'check-off' provisions further required that the worker's authorisations must have been signed within the last three years. They also required that an increased subscription could only be deducted if the employer had given the worker at least one month's written notice. These requirements were removed by the *Deregulation (Deduction from Pay of Union Subscriptions) Order 1998 (SI 1998/1529)* made under the *Deregulation and Contracting Out Act 1994*.

The repealed requirements continue to apply to authorisations given before 23 June 1998 (*reg 3(1)*). However, by *reg 3(2), (3)*, an employer may give a worker notice in a form prescribed in the *Schedule* to the *Regulations* that such an authorisation is to be treated as having been given under the new provisions (and so will be treated as of unlimited duration until withdrawal, and as not requiring advance notice of any increase in the amount deducted). Provided the worker does not object by written notice within 14 days, the new provisions will apply.

With effect from 1 March 2017, additional restrictions have been imposed on the use of the 'check-off' in the public sector, by virtue of *s 15* of the *Trade Union Act 2016*. In particular, deductions from a workers' wages in respect of union subscriptions may be made only if the workers have been given the option to pay by other means, and only if the arrangements have been made for the union to make reasonable payments to the employer in respect of making the deductions. An employer is a relevant public sector employer if specified as such in regulations made by a Minister of the Crown (*TULRCA 1992, s 116B*).

51.21 THE RIGHT TO BE ACCOMPANIED

A new right to be accompanied by a trade union official (or a fellow employee) was introduced by *s 10* of the *Employment Relations Act 1999*. Any worker who is required or invited to attend a disciplinary or grievance hearing by his employer is now entitled to be accompanied either by a trade union official (as defined in *TULRCA 1992, ss 1, 119*) or fellow worker of his choice. The employer must permit the companion to put the worker's case, respond to any views expressed and confer with the worker during the hearing. However, the employer is not required to permit the companion to answer questions on the worker's behalf (*ERA 1999, s 10(2B), (2C)*). If the worker's chosen companion is not available at the time of the hearing, and the worker proposes a reasonable alternative time within the subsequent period of five working days, the employer must postpone the hearing to the time proposed (*ERA 1999, s 10(4), (5)*). The employer must also give the worker's companion time off for the purpose of accompanying the worker to the meeting (*ERA 1999, s 10(6)*). Guidance on the application of this right is given in the ACAS Code of Practice on Disciplinary and Grievance Procedures (2009).

A 'disciplinary hearing' is defined for these purposes so as to include a hearing which could result in a formal warning (*ERA 1999, s 13(4)*). For these purposes, the test of whether a warning is 'formal' is one of substance. If the warning will become part of the worker's disciplinary record, then the right to be accompanied applies (*Ferenc-Batchelor v London Underground Ltd* [2003] ICR 656). However, the right is confined to disciplinary or grievance matters. It therefore did not apply to a meeting which led to an employee's dismissal on grounds of redundancy: see *Heathmill Multimedia ASP Ltd v Jones* [2003] IRLR 856. The EAT held in *Skiggs v South West Trains Ltd* [2005] IRLR 459 that an investigative interview regarding a grievance raised by another employee against the claimant was not a disciplinary hearing at which the claimant had a right to be accompanied.

This new statutory right does not require a union to provide representation to an employee. However, a member may have a contractual right to representation deriving from the union rule-book. In *English v UNISON* (2000) IDS Brief 668, the county court held that a qualified right to representation arose as a matter of contract from the union's guide to disciplinary hearings.

A worker denied the right to be accompanied may complain to the employment tribunal within three months of the employer's failure (or such further period as is considered reasonable where it was not reasonably practicable to present the complaint within three months) (*ERA 1999, s 11(1), (2)*). Where a complaint is upheld, the tribunal may make an award of up to two weeks' pay, subject to the statutory maximum contained in *ERA 1996, s 227(1)*, currently £489. In addition, a worker has a right not to be subjected to a detriment or dismissed for seeking to exercise the right to be accompanied. Dismissal on this ground will be automatically unfair (*ERA 1999, s 12*).

51.22 ADVICE BY TRADE UNIONS TO MEMBERS

The scope of a trade union's duty of care towards its members in giving advice was considered by the High Court in *Friend v Institution of Professional Managers and Specialists* [1999] IRLR 173. It was held that a trade union advising or acting for a member in an employment dispute owed the member a duty of care in tort to use ordinary skill and care. However, once solicitors had been engaged on the member's behalf, any duty there might previously have been on the union to advise on the dispute came to an end.

The EAT held in *Unite the Union v Nailard* [2017] ICR 121 that a union was liable as principal under the *Equality Act 2010* for acts of sexual harassment of a member carried out by two elected branch officials.

52   Transfer of Undertakings

52.1   Far-reaching rules for the protection of employees' rights on the transfer of an undertaking are contained in the *Transfer of Undertakings (Protection of Employment) Regulations 2006 (SI 2006/246)* ('the *Regulations*'). These came into force on 6 April 2006. They replace entirely the previous legislation, the *Transfer of Undertakings (Protection of Employment) Regulations 1981 (SI 1981/1794)* as amended by the *Transfer of Undertakings (Protection of Employment) (Amendment) Regulations 1987 (SI 1987/442)*, by the *Trade Union Reform and Employment Rights Act 1993*, by the *Collective Redundancies and Transfer of Undertakings (Protection of Employment) (Amendment) Regulations 1995 (SI 1995/2587)* and by the *Collective Redundancies and Transfer of Undertakings (Protection of Employment) (Amendment) Regulations 1999 (SI 1999/1925.)* With effect from 31 January 2014 the *Regulations* were amended by the *Collective Redundancies and Transfer of Undertakings (Protection of Employment) (Amendment) Regulations 2014 (SI 2014/16)*.

The purpose of the original 1981 Regulations was to fulfil the United Kingdom's obligations under European Community law to give effect to *EC Council Directive 77/187*, generally known as the *Acquired Rights Directive*. A new *Directive* was adopted on 29 June 1998 which amends *Directive 77/187* by wholly replacing the texts of *arts 1–7*. Member states had three years within which to bring into force measures which implement the amended *Directive*. See *Official Journal, 17 July 1998 (L201/88)*. The provisions of the original and the amending *Directive* have been consolidated in a further *Directive* adopted on 12 March 2001: *Directive 2001/23/EC*, Official Journal, 22 March 2001 (L82/16). It was the need to transpose the new provisions into UK law which prompted the introduction of the *Regulations*. However, the *Regulations* go further than is required by European law and introduce an additional concept, that of 'a service provision change'. That they go further than European law is emphasised by the fact that the *Regulations* are made not only under *s 2(2)* of the *European Communities Act 1972* but also under *s 38* of the *Employment Relations Act 1999*, which empowered the Secretary of State to make regulations in circumstances other than those to which the Community obligation applies. In addition, the *Regulations* seek to clarify the meaning of certain terms by incorporating concepts developed by the courts.

Historically, English courts and tribunals have so far as possible construed the *Regulations* consistently with the *Directive*, even to the extent of reading in additional words (see **52.10** below, and **23.2** Eᴜʀᴏᴘᴇᴀɴ Uɴɪᴏɴ Lᴀᴡ). However, when considering the meaning of a service provision change, they may not feel obliged so to do, although the concepts of 'service provision change' and 'transfer of an undertaking' are not mutually exclusive.

References below are to provisions of the *Regulations* unless stated otherwise.

52.2   Where there is a 'relevant transfer', that is either where there is a 'service provision change' (see **52.3** below) from person *A* to person *B*, or where an 'undertaking' (see **52.4** below) is 'transferred' (see **52.5** below) from person *A* to person *B*:

(a)   individuals who are employed by *A* 'immediately before the transfer' (see **52.14** and **52.12** below) automatically become the employees of *B* from the time of the transfer, on the terms and conditions they previously held with *A* (see **52.13** below);

(b)   *B* inherits *A*'s rights and liabilities in relation to those individuals (see **52.18** below);

(c)   collective agreements, made by or on behalf of *A* with a trade union recognised by *A*, are inherited by *B* (see **52.20** below);

(d)   where *A* recognises a union in respect of employees in the undertaking to be transferred and, following the transfer, the undertaking transferred maintains an identity distinct from any other undertaking owned by *B*, *B* must recognise the union in respect of those employees (see **52.21** below);

(e)   *A* must inform recognised trade unions or employee representatives about the consequences of the transfer, and *B* must provide *A* with sufficient information in this regard (see **52.22** below);

(f)   in certain circumstances, it may be necessary for *A* or *B* to consult with recognised trade unions or elected employee representatives concerning the transfer (see **52.23** below); and

(g)   dismissal of any employee (whether before or after the transfer) where the reason for dismissal is the transfer is automatically unfair unless the reason is 'an economic, technical or organisational reason entailing changes in the workforce' in which case the dismissal is for a fair reason and the question is whether it is fair in all the circumstances, applying the normal principles of unfair dismissal (see **52.24** below).

52.3   WHAT IS A 'RELEVANT TRANSFER'?

Service provision change

There are three situations which may amount to a service provision change (*reg 3(1)(b)*):

(a)   Activities cease to be carried out by a person ('a client') on his own behalf and are carried out instead by another person on the client's behalf ('a contractor'). This situation is sometimes referred to as contracting out or outsourcing.

(b)   Activities cease to be carried out by a contractor on a client's behalf (whether or not those activities had previously been carried out by the client on his own behalf) and are carried out instead by another person ('a subsequent contractor') on the client's behalf. This situation is sometimes referred to as reassigning.

(c)   Activities cease to be carried out by a contractor or a subsequent contractor on a client's behalf (whether or not those activities had previously been carried out by the client on his own behalf) and are carried out instead by the client on his own behalf. This situation is sometimes referred to as contracting in or insourcing.

In any of these three situations there will be a relevant transfer if immediately before the service provision change:

(a)   There is an organised grouping of employees situated in Great Britain which has as its principal purpose the carrying out of the activities concerned on behalf of the client; and

(b)   The client intends that the activities will, following the service provision change, be carried out by the transferee other than in connection with a single specific event or task of short-term duration (*reg 3(3)(a)*). The focus here is on the intention of the client, rather than on that of the transferee: *SNR Denton UK LLP v Kirwan* [2013] ICR 101. It is possible for "client" to refer to a group of clients, and for there to be more than one contract, provided that there is some common intent between the members of that group with regard to the provision of the service in question: *Ottimo Property Services Ltd v Duncan* [2015] ICR 859. There are conflicting views on whether activities are excluded if they relate to either a single specific event or task of short-term duration or whether they must relate to both: see *SNR Denton* and *Liddell's Coaches v Cook* [2013] ICR 547. In *Swanbridge Hire & Sales Ltd v Butler* (UKEAT/0056/13) the EAT preferred the approach in *SNR Denton*. The event or task must be intended to be of short-term duration: it is not enough that this was the client's hope (*Robert Sage Ltd v O'Connell* [2014] IRLR 428). The question is one of fact almost invariably requiring the tribunal to draw an inference from all the relevant surrounding circumstances, including both contemporaneous events and subsequent matters which might throw light on the relevant party's intention at the relevant date: *ICTS UK Ltd v Mahdi* [2016] ICR 274.

The activities before and after the transfer must be fundamentally the same (*reg 3(2A)* and see *QLog Ltd v O'Brien* UKEAT/0301/13).

However, a service provision change will not be a relevant transfer if the activities concerned consist wholly or mainly of the supply of goods for the client's use (*reg 3(3)(b)*). The application of this exception is essentially one of fact: the supply of sandwiches and drinks to a client's canteen for sale to its staff would fall within the exception, but if the supplier also provided the canteen staff to dispense the goods, then this might not fall within the exception: *Pannu v Geo W King Ltd* [2012] IRLR 193.

There is no service provision change where there is a change of both contractor and of client; the activities carried out by different contractors before and after the transfer must be carried out for the same client: *Hunter v McCarrick* [2012] EWCA Civ 1399, [2013] ICR 235. For these purposes, client means an organisation that is in a position to carry out activities either itself or by commissioning them from others to carry out those activities on its behalf: *CT Plus (Yorkshire) CIC v Black* UKEAT/0035/16. In deciding whether there is a single client for these purposes, it may be relevant that "contractor" is defined to include a "sub-contractor": see *Jinks v London Borough of Havering* UKEAT/0157/14; cf *Horizon Security Services Ltd v Ndeze* [2014] IRLR 854.

The requirement for an organised grouping of employees involves consideration of four steps. The first is to identify the service which the putative transferor was providing to the client. The next is to list the activities which the staff of that company performed in order to provide that service. The term "activities" should be given its ordinary, everyday meaning, defined in a common sense and pragmatic way without excess generality (*Arch Initiatives v Greater Manchester West Mental Health NHS Foundation Trust* [2016] ICR 607 as approved in *Salvation Army Trustee Co v Bahi* UKEAT/0120/16). The third is to identify the employee or employees of that company who ordinarily carried on those activities. The fourth is to consider whether that company organised that employee or those employees into a 'grouping' for the principal purpose of carrying out the listed activities. See *Rynda (UK) Ltd v Rhijnsburger* [2015] EWCA Civ 75, [2015] ICR 1300. These principles were drawn from the following earlier EAT authorities. The requirement for an organised grouping of employees connotes that the employees be organised in some sense by reference to the requirements of the client in question, a deliberate putting together of a group of employees for the purpose of the relevant client work: *Seawell Ltd v Ceva Freight (UK) Ltd* [2012] IRLR 802). The client work need not be the sole purpose, provided it is the principal purpose: *Argyll Coastal Services Ltd v Stirling* (UKEATS/0012/11, 15 February 2012). There is no such grouping where a group of employees happen to work mostly on tasks for a particular client only from a combination of circumstances such as shift patterns and working practices, where there was no deliberate planning or intent: *Eddie Stobart Ltd v Moreman* [2012] ICR 919. A director involved in a mainly strategic role and spending little time on actual service delivery may not be part of an organised grouping: *Edinburgh Home-Link Partnership v The City of Edinburgh Council* (UKEATS/0061/11, 10 July 2012). Whilst there may be more than one purpose, the carrying out of the activities in question has to be the principal purpose of the grouping, whether or not it is in fact carrying them out at any particular time; on the other hand, the activities undertaken may change to such an extent that the principal purpose of the grouping has changed by the date of the transfer (*Tees, Esk & Wear Valleys NHS Foundation Trust v Harland* UKEAT/0173/16).

52.3 Transfer of Undertakings

The EAT has considered the question of service provision change in three cases in particular: *Kimberley Group Housing Ltd v Hambley* [2008] ICR 1030; *Churchill Dulwich Ltd (in liq) v Metropolitan Resources Ltd* [2009] ICR 1380; and *OCS Group Ltd v Jones* (UKEAT/0038/09). From these cases, the following principles can be drawn:

(a)   Service provision change is a wholly new statutory concept. The circumstances in which one is established are comprehensively and clearly set out in *reg 3(1)(b)* itself and *reg 3(3)*. The new provisions appear straightforward and their application to an individual case is essentially a question of fact.

(b)   There is no need to adopt a purposive construction as opposed to a straightforward and common sense application of the relevant statutory words. See also *Hunter v McCarrick* [2012] EWCA Civ 1399, [2013] ICR 235.

(c)   Under *reg 3(1)(b)*, the first question for the Tribunal is to identify the relevant activity or activities, since only then can one consider whether those activities cease to be carried on by the contractor on a client's behalf and are carried out instead by another person on the client's behalf. See further *SNR Denton UK LLP v Kirwan* [2013] ICR 101.

(d)   The conditions in *reg 3(3)* cannot be considered until a decision is made as to whether or not there is a service provision change falling within *reg 3(1)(b)*.

(e)   Whether the activities carried out by the putative transferee are fundamentally or essentially the same as those carried out by the putative transferor is a question of fact and degree. Some minor differences between the nature of the tasks carried on after what is said to have been a service provision change as compared with before it, or in the way in which they are performed as compared with the nature or mode of performance of those tasks in the hands of the alleged transferor, does not mean that there is no service provision change. Further, a substantial change in the amount of the particular activity required by the client could show that the post-transfer activity was not the same as it was pre-transfer: *Department for Education v Huke* (UKEAT/0080/12, 17 October 2012). The focus for this purpose is the work done on the ground, not the work which might be done under the contract (*Lorne Stewart plc v Hyde* (UKEAT/0408/12)).

(f)   It is possible for a transferor to transfer the provision of a service to more than one transferee. It is also possible for some activities carried out by the putative transferor to be transferred, whilst others are not: *Arch Initiatives v Greater Manchester West Mental Health NHS Foundation Trust* [2016] ICR 607.

(g)   However, there may be some circumstances in which a service which is being provided by one contractor to a client is in the event so fragmented that nothing which one can properly determine as being a service provision change has taken place.

(h)   In considering whether an employee is assigned to the part of the provision of the service transferred to a particular transferee, the tribunal applies the same approach as to a transfer under *reg 3(1)(a)*.

In *Ankers v Clearsprings Management Ltd* [2009] All ER (D) 261 (Feb) the tribunal found that there was no discernible pattern in the transfer of accommodation services to asylum seekers from one service provider to another. The EAT determined that where the service provided is so fragmented, a tribunal may be entitled to find that no relevant transfer took place. The EAT subsequently rejected a tribunal's finding that there was no service provision change based upon a combination of 'fragmentation' and a finding that 15% of the work done by the original contractor would not be required by the new contractor and so the "activities" undertaken before and after the contract would not be essentially or fundamentally the same: *Enterprise Management Services Ltd v Connect-Up Ltd* [2012] IRLR 190.

In *Ward Hadaway Solicitors v Love* (UKEAT/0471/09) the EAT refused to interfere with a tribunal's judgment that there was no service provision change following a competitive tender for future solicitors' regulatory services in circumstances in which none of the work in progress was handed over and no employee transferred. Similarly, in *Johnson Controls Ltd v Campbell* (UKEAT/0041/12) the EAT refused to interfere with a tribunal's judgment that there was no service provision change where a client ceased to use a centralised taxi administration service, but instead arranged for its secretaries to book taxis with taxi firms directly, since the activity undertaken by the contractor was not continued by the client.

Where there is a service provision change which is a relevant transfer, 'the transferor' means the person who carried out the activities prior to the service provision change and 'the transferee' means the person who carries out the activities as a result of the service provision change (*reg 2(1)*).

52.4   Transfer of an undertaking or business

Undertaking or business

The *Regulations* apply to the transfer of an undertaking or of a business situated immediately before the transfer in the United Kingdom.

The *Regulations* also cover the transfer of part of an undertaking or business. A 'part' of an 'undertaking' means a unit which is to some extent separate and self-contained from the remainder of the enterprise such as an operating division which is autonomous from the remainder of the business by virtue, for example, of having its own accounts, management structure, and product specialisation. However, the *Regulations* may apply even where the part does not retain its organisational autonomy, provided that the functional link between the various elements of production transferred is preserved and that functional link enables the transferee to use those elements to pursue an identical or analogous economic activity: see *Klarenberg v Ferrotron Technologies GmbH*: C-466/07 [2009] ICR 1263.

In *Fairhurst Ward Abbotts Ltd v Botes Building Ltd* [2004] EWCA Civ 83, [2004] ICR 919 the Court of Appeal ruled that, provided that there is an identifiable stable economic entity before the transfer takes place, the law does not require that the particular part transferred should itself, before the date of the transfer, exist as a discrete and identifiable economic entity: it is sufficient if a part of the larger entity becomes identified for the first time as a separate economic entity on the occasion of the transfer separating a part from the whole. This approach was applied in *Transport & General Workers Union v Swissport (UK) Ltd (in administration)* [2007] ICR 1593.

'Undertaking' would appear to include a professional practice, such as that of an NHS doctor (see *Jeetle v Elster* [1985] ICR 389), the activities of a charitable foundation (*Redmond (Dr Sophie) Stichting v Bartol*: C-29/91 [1992] ECR I-3189, [1992] IRLR 366), and the carrying out of an activity pursuant to a contract (see **52.5** below). An undertaking which is carried out on a non-profit making basis but is contracted out to be carried out on a commercial basis may still transfer where all the other characteristics of the activity remained the same before and after the alleged transfer: *Alderson v Secretary of State for Trade and Industry* [2003] EWCA Civ 1767, [2004] ICR 512.

However, an economic entity is not defined only by the employment status of a group of employees, but also by the function which that group undertakes: *Wynnwith Engineering Co Ltd v Bennett* [2002] IRLR 170. In *Wain v Guernsey Ship Management Ltd* [2007] EWCA Civ 294, [2007] ICR 1350 the Court of Appeal rejected the contention that a group of short-term contract employees comprised an economic entity.

52.5 Transfer of Undertakings

52.5 *Transfer*

A relevant transfer occurs where there is a transfer of an economic identity which retains its identity (*reg 3(1)(a)*).

Thus, in deciding whether there has been a transfer of an undertaking, the critical question is whether the undertaking retains its identity and is carried on by the transferee. In answering that question, all the factual circumstances must be considered, but particular factors include: the type of undertaking or business concerned; whether tangible assets such as buildings and moveable property are transferred; the value of intangible assets at the time of the transfer; whether the majority of employees are taken over by the new employer; whether customers are transferred; the degree of similarity between the activities carried on before and after the alleged transfer; and the period, if any, for which those activities are suspended (*Spijkers v Gebroeders Benedik Abbatoir CV*: 24/85 [1986] 2 CMLR 296; *Redmond (Dr Sophie) Stichting v Bartol*: C-29/91 [1992] ECR I-3189, [1992] IRLR 366; *Rask and Christensen v ISS Kantineservice A/S*: C-209/91 [1993] IRLR 133, ECJ).

The ECJ has considered the application of this test in a number of cases involving the contracting out of services and changes of contractors. The importance within the UK of this line of authority is likely to be limited in the future since such cases are likely to constitute service provision changes, whether or not there is a transfer of an undertaking.

In *Schmidt v Spar und Leihkasse der Früheren Ämter Bordersholm, Kiel und Cronshagen*: C-392/92 [1995] ICR 237 it was held that there could be a transfer of contracted-out cleaning services, even where the services are performed by a single employee and there is no transfer of tangible assets; and *Merckx v Ford Motors Co Belgium SA*: C-171/94 and C-172/94 [1996] IRLR 467. The ECJ held in *Ledernes Hovedorganisation (acting for Rygard) v Dansk Arbejdsgiverforening (acting for Sto Molle Akustik A/S)*: C-48/94 [1995] ECR I-2745, [1996] ICR 333, however, that the transfer of an undertaking must involve the transfer of a 'stable economic entity' and went on to hold in *Süzen v Zehnacker Gebäudereingung GmbH Krankenhausservice*: C- 13/95 [1997] ICR 662 that an activity does not, in itself, constitute such an entity. It follows, the ECJ stated, that the mere fact that a similar activity is carried on before and after a change of contractors does not mean there is a transfer of an undertaking. In the case of a labour-intensive undertaking with no significant assets (eg contract cleaning), there will generally be no transfer unless the new contractor takes on a majority of the old contractor's staff. This approach was reinforced in *Vidal (Francisco Hernandez) SA v Gomez Perez*: C-127/96, C-229/96 and C-74/97 [1999] IRLR 132, ECJ and in *Sánchez Hidalgo v Asociación de Servicios Aser*: C-173/96 [2002] ICR 73. The ECJ again emphasised the requirement for a stable economic entity, adding that 'an organised group of wage earners who are specifically and permanently assigned to a common task may, in the absence of other factors of production, amount to an economic entity'. Examples of the application of this approach include *Oy Liikenne Ab v Liskojarvi*: C-172/99 [2002] ICR 155 (the absence of a transfer of assets conclusive where the activity required substantial tangible assets) and *Jouini v Princess Personal Service GmbH*: C-458/05 [2008] ICR 128 (the possibility of a transfer of a part of a temporary employment agency). In order to be a 'stable economic entity', the economic entity must have a sufficient degree of functional autonomy, the concept of autonomy referring to the powers granted to those in charge of the group of workers concerned to organise, relatively freely and independently, the work within that group, including to give instructions and allocate tasks to subordinates within the group without direct intervention from other organisational structures of the employer; such autonomy must exist before the transfer (*Amatori v Telecom Italia SpA*: C-458/12 [2014] IRLR 400).

The importance of the distinction between a labour-intensive undertaking and an asset reliant undertaking was crucial in *Abler v Sodexho MM Catering Betriebsgesellschaft mbH*: C-340/01 [2004] IRLR 168, in which the ECJ found that the catering sector was based essentially on equipment. Thus, where a new contractor took over the use of that equipment then there was a transfer, even though the equipment was in fact owned by neither the transferor nor the transferee but by the party contracting out the activity. The ECJ specifically held that the degree of importance to be attached to each factor will vary according to the activity carried on. (See also *Guney-Gorres v Securicor Aviation (Germany) Ltd*: C-232/04 and C-233/04 [2006] IRLR 305 and *ADIF v Aira Pascual*: C-509/14 [2016] IRLR 156.) A further pronouncement, again in relation to the labour-intensive cleaning of premises, was in *CLECE SA v Valor*: C-463/09 [2011] ICR 1319. In *Ferreira da Silva v Estado Portugues*: C-160/14 [2015] IRLR 1021 the CJEU emphasised the importance of "the functional link of interdependence and complementarity" of the various elements of production (eg staff and assets) rather than the retention of the specific organisation of those elements.

The Court of Appeal has emphasised that the correct approach is 'multi-factorial': *Balfour Beatty Power Networks Ltd v Wilcox* [2006] EWCA Civ 1240, [2007] IRLR 63. No single aspect need determine the question. All factors must be balanced before a decision is reached. The CA considered that there could be a relevant transfer even in an industry which was asset reliant and where there was no transfer of tangible assets: the ECJ had not, the CA considered, laid down any stark rule to the contrary in *Oy Liikenne*. On the facts, the assets were in any event leased and so they could be better characterised as tools and equipment. The CA also observed that an enterprise may be 'stable' as a matter of practical and industrial reality, even though its long-term future is not assured. A similar, multi-factorial approach had been followed by the EAT in *P & O Trans European Ltd v Initial Transport Service Ltd* [2003] IRLR 128 and in *NUMAST v P&O Scottish Ferries Ltd* [2005] ICR 1270.

A number of cases involving contracting out and changes of contractors have also come before the UK courts, many arising out of local government compulsory competitive tendering. The courts have held in this context that if similar activities are carried on before and after a change of service provider, there can be a transfer of an undertaking notwithstanding that no assets are transferred (*Dines v Initial Health Care Services Ltd* [1995] ICR 11) or that neither assets nor staff are transferred (*BSG Property Services v Tuck* [1996] IRLR 134). See also *Kenny v South Manchester College* [1993] IRLR 265, *Isles of Scilly Council v Brintel Helicopters Ltd* [1995] ICR 249 and *Kelman v Care Contract Services Ltd* [1995] ICR 260. The reasoning of these cases must now, however, be reconsidered in the light of *Betts v Brintel Helicopters Ltd* [1997] IRLR 361, in which the Court of Appeal followed *Süzen* (see above) and held that there was no transfer on a change of contractor providing helicopter services to a company, where the new contractor took over no staff, and only a limited part of the old contractor's assets. The court distinguished labour intensive undertakings, where the key factor is whether the majority of employees are taken over by the new employer, and other types of undertaking, where a broader range of factors must be considered.

The Court of Appeal reconsidered the scope of *Süzen* (with express reference to *Sánchez Hidalgo*) in *ECM (Vehicle Delivery Service) v Cox* [1999] IRLR 559. The court stated that the importance of *Süzen* had been overstated: the ECJ had not overruled its previous interpretive rulings. It is for the national court to make the necessary factual appraisal, considering in particular the factors identified in *Spijkers*. One relevant factor is whether the majority of employees are taken over by the new employer to enable it to carry on the activities of the undertaking on a regular basis. The mere loss of a service contract to a competitor does not of itself indicate the existence of a transfer. This appeal was followed by Lindsay J in *RCO Support Services Ltd v Unison* [2000] ICR 1502 and in *Cheesman v R Brewer Contracts Ltd* [2001] IRLR 144.

The Court of Appeal's judgment in *RCO Support Services Ltd v Unison* [2002] EWCA Civ 464, [2002] ICR 751 appeared to accept that *Süzen* represented a shift on the previous position, such that a mere similarity in the activities of the entity before and after the transfer cannot be enough to establish a transfer. However, the additional factors required need not amount to a transfer of a majority of the workforce (in terms of numbers and skills) as had been the case in *Süzen*. On the facts of *RCO* a similarity in operating methods and training within the activities was found to be enough, even where the location of the activity had moved.

As to the question of the relevance of an intention of the transferee to avoid the application of TUPE, the Court of Appeal in *RCO* stated that a subjective motive of the putative transferee to avoid the application of TUPE is not the real point. However, in deciding whether or not there is a transfer, it may be relevant to take into account the objective circumstances surrounding a decision not to take on the workforce. It is far from clear how that distinction will be drawn in practice. Some guidance is to be found in the decision in *Astle v Cheshire County Council* [2005] IRLR 12. The EAT held that if a tribunal finds that the reason or principal reason of the transferee was to avoid the application of TUPE then it is a relevant factor to take into account in the *Spijkers* exercise, and may be decisive.

In *RCO* the Court of Appeal made reference to its earlier decision in *ADI (UK) Ltd v Willer* [2001] EWCA Civ 971, [2001] IRLR 542 in which it had recognised that *Süzen* represented something of a retreat by the ECJ from its earlier decisions. In *ADI* it concluded that, in a labour-intensive operation, the absence of a transfer of staff from the outgoing contractor to the incoming contractor should lead to the conclusion that there is no transfer of an undertaking, even though the work, the equipment used, the location and the ultimate customers are the same. However, in such cases, the balance would be tipped the other way if the reason why there was no transfer of staff was that the parties wished to avoid the application of the *Regulations*. If such an intention is established, then there will be deemed to have been a transfer. This ruling substantially supersedes the decisions in *Whitewater Leisure Management Ltd v Barnes* [2000] ICR 1049, EAT and *Lightways (Contractors) Ltd v Associated Holdings Ltd* [2000] IRLR 247, Ct of Sess.

In *Rygaard v Stro Molle Akustik* [1996] IRLR 51, the ECJ held that existing authorities presuppose that the transfer relates to a stable economic entity whose activity is not limited to one specific works contract. However, the scope of this ruling was restricted to its facts (ie single contracts for building works) by the EAT in *Argyll Training Ltd v Sinclair* [2000] IRLR 630, in which it stated that there is no basis for automatically excluding all single-contract undertakings from the possibility of being transferred. Indeed, it is possible (though not common) for a single employee to constitute a stable economic entity, provided that the entity can be said to be sufficiently structured and autonomous: *Dudley Bower Building Services Ltd v Lowe* [2003] ICR 843.

52.6   Other concepts defining 'relevant transfer'

General

The *Regulations* apply to public and private undertakings engaged in economic activities, whether or not they are operating for gain (*reg 3(4)(a)*).

The *Regulations* apply even if the transfer is governed or effected by foreign law, or if the employees in the undertaking, business or activities work outside the UK or if their employment is governed by foreign law (*reg 3(4)(b)*). The *Regulations* have the potential to apply to a transfer from the UK to a non-EU entity in the event that on the transfer the undertaking did not remain within the jurisdiction: *Holis Metal Industries Ltd v GMB and Newell Ltd* [2008] ICR 464, [2008] IRLR 187, EAT.

In *Allen v Amalgamated Construction Co Ltd*: C-234/98 [1999] ECR I-8643, [2000] ICR 119, the ECJ held that the *Acquired Rights Directive* can apply to a transfer between two subsidiary companies in the same group, provided that they are distinct legal persons each with specific employment relationships with their employees. This was so even though the two companies had the same management, were in the same premises, and were engaged in the same works. Where the putative transfer is to a number of group companies which includes the original employer, there is no relevant transfer: *Hyde Housing Association Ltd v Layton* [2016] ICR 261.

On the other hand, where an individual is employed by one group company but works on a permanent basis in an undertaking run by another company within the group, the latter company may be the 'transferor' for the purposes of the *Directive*, even though there is no contractual relationship between that company and the individual: *Albron Catering BV v FNV Bondgenoten*: C-242/09 [2011] ICR 373.

In *Foreningen af Arbejdsledere i Danmark v Daddy's Dance Hall A/S*: 324/86 [1988] IRLR 315 the European Court of Justice held that there was a relevant transfer where a lessee of restaurant premises gave notice to its employees upon the determination of the lease, and the lessor then granted a new lease to a third party which continued to run the business without any interruption. Where the identity of the economic unit was retained, it did not matter that the transfer took place in two phases. The same result was reached on similar facts in *Litster v Forth Dry Dock and Engineering Co Ltd* [1989] ICR 341 and in *P Bork International A/S v Foreningen af Arbejdsledere i Danmark*: 101/87 [1989] IRLR 41 (owner of leased undertaking repossessed it after forfeiture of the lease and then sold it on to a third party who resumed operation of the business). These decisions will be important where businesses are operated on a franchise (see also *LMC Drains Ltd v Waugh* [1991] 3 CMLR 172).

If the agreement pursuant to which the transfer occurred is rescinded, there may be a relevant 'retransfer' back to the original transferor (*Berg and Busschers v Besselsen*: 144/87 and 145/87 [1990] ICR 396).

52.7 *More than one transaction*

A relevant transfer may be affected by a series of two or more transactions (*reg 3(6)(a)*). In construing the *1981 Regulations* purposively, it has been held that the court will seek to identify whether there is in truth a single transfer and will look beyond an 'ingenious device' whereby an intermediary company is introduced for the sole purpose of achieving the contracting parties' mutual wish to transfer an undertaking between them which is stripped of liability to the employees (see *Re Maxwell Fleet and Facilities Management Ltd (No 2)* [2000] ICR 717). In *Temco Service Industries SA v Imzilyen*: C-51/00 [2002] IRLR 214 the ECJ confirmed that the absence of a contractual link does not in itself prevent the application of the *Directive*; it was enough if the transferor and transferee were part of the web of contractual relations.

52.8 *Transfer of property*

A transfer may take place whether or not any property is transferred to the transferee by the transferor (*reg 3(6)(b)*).

52.9 *Administrative functions carried out by a public body*

'A relevant transfer' does not include an administrative reorganisation of public administrative authorities, or the transfer of administrative functions between public administrative authorities (*reg 3(5)*). This limited exclusion was originally explained by the European Court of Justice in *Henke v Gemeinde Schierke*: C-298/94 [1996] IRLR 701 and was then recognised in *art 1(1)(c)* of *Directive 2001/23*. It was further clarified in two subsequent decisions of the European Court of Justice: *Mayeur v Association Promotion de l'Information Messine*: C-175/99 [2002] ICR 1316 (transfer where the work of a non-profit making tourist agency was taken over by the municipality); and *Collino v Telecom Italia SpA*: C-343/98 [2002] ICR 38 (transfer on a reorganisation of telephone service providers). In *Viggosdottir v Islandspostur HF* [2002] IRLR 425, the EFTA Court held that the *Directive* could apply to the conversion of a state entity into a wholly state-owned limited liability company, and that it is for the national court to decide whether the individuals fall under the protection of national employment law in accordance with the principles set out by the ECJ in *Collino*. The *Henke* exception was applied by the High Court in *Law Society of England and Wales v Secretary of State for Justice* [2010] EWHC 352 (QB), [2010] IRLR 407, [2010] All ER (D) 10 (Mar) to extend to the Legal Complaints Service on the basis that it was a body which had exercised public authority in that it carried out regulatory and quasi-judicial functions which are subject to judicial review. However, the exception did not apply to auxiliary services within Italian State schools, such as cleaning, caretaking and administrative assistance: *Scattolon v Ministero dell'Istruzione, dell'Università e della Ricerca*: C-108/10 [2012] ICR 740.

52.10 *Share transfers*

The *Regulations* apply only to the transfer of an undertaking from one legal person to another. They do not apply, for example, to the transfer of shares in a company which carries on the undertaking (*Initial Supplies Ltd v McCall* 1992 SLT 67). This is so even though this form of transaction was adopted with the purpose of avoiding the *Regulations* (*Brookes v Borough Care Services* [1998] IRLR 636).

In *Millam v Print Factory (London) 1991 Ltd* [2007] EWCA Civ 322, [2007] ICR 1331 the Court of Appeal reiterated this principle, but went on to uphold a tribunal's conclusion that the business nevertheless transferred to the acquiring company. The CA also rejected the EAT's analysis that it could pierce the corporate veil. An issue of piercing the corporate veil arises only when it is established that activity X is carried on by company A, but for policy reasons it is sought to show that in reality the activity is the responsibility of the owner of company A, company B; to pierce the corporate veil it must generally be shown that the subsidiary company is a sham or façade. In the present case, the activity was in fact carried on by company B, and so there was a relevant transfer from A to B.

52.11 *Insolvency*

The ECJ held in *Abels v Administrative Board of the Bedrijfsvereniging voor de Metaalindustrie en de Electrotechnische Industrie*: 135/83 [1985] ECR 469 that the *Directive* does not apply to the transfer of an undertaking, business or part of a business in the course of insolvency proceedings. In *Jules Dethier Equipment SA v Dassy*: C-319/94 [1998] ICR 541, it ruled that it does apply in the event of the transfer of an undertaking which is being wound up by a court if the undertaking continues to trade. It also applies where the undertaking transferred is being wound up voluntarily (*Europièces SA (in liq) v Sanders*: C-399/96 [1998] ECR I-6965, ECJ). The distinction drawn in *Donaldson v Perth & Kinross Council* [2004] ICR 667 was between an 'irretrievable insolvency and cessation of business' and 'the sale of the business as a going concern', but this was not followed in *Transport & General Workers Union v Swissport (UK) Ltd (in administration)* [2007] ICR 1593.

Clarification is now given in *reg 8(7)*, which provides that *reg 4* (effect of relevant transfer on contracts of employment) and *reg 7* (dismissal of employee because of relevant transfer) do not apply to any relevant transfer where the transferor is the subject of 'bankruptcy proceedings or any analogous insolvency proceedings which have been instituted with a view to the liquidation of the assets of the transferor and are under the supervision of an insolvency practitioner'.

Furthermore, *regs 8(1)* to *(6)* apply to 'relevant insolvency proceedings', that is insolvency proceedings which have been opened in relation to the transferor not with a view to the liquidation of the assets of the transferor and which are under the supervision of an insolvency practitioner. They extend the statutory regimes for payments by the Secretary of State (under chapter VI of *Part XI* and *Part XII* of the *Employment Rights Act 1996*) to transfers in such cases. The relevant debts (those falling within *s 184* of the *Employment Rights Act 1996*) have to arise before the transfer in order to come within that state guarantee: *Pressure Coolers Ltd v Molloy* [2012] ICR 51 (applied in *Secretary of State for BIS v Dobrucki* (UKEAT/0505/13)).

52.17 What the transferee acquires

As noted above, the transferee inherits those employees employed by the transferor immediately before the transfer on their existing terms and conditions, assuming that they do not object in accordance with **52.16** above. He has no power to impose, without the agreement of the individual employee (see **52.28** below), any different terms and conditions from those he has inherited from the transferor (see **52.26** below). Equally, the transferred employee has no right to insist that he be given the benefit of any superior terms and conditions enjoyed by the transferee's existing staff (see *Jackson v Computershare Investor Services plc* [2007] EWCA Civ 1065, [2008] ICR 341) (except possibly by means of a claim for EQUAL PAY **(22)**).

For the effect of a transfer upon restrictive covenants expressed in terms of the transferor's customers, see *Morris Angel & Son Ltd v Hollande* [1993] ICR 71; see also **52.29** below and RESTRAINT OF TRADE, CONFIDENTIALITY AND EMPLOYEE INTERVENTIONS **(41)**. For the effect of a transfer on the question whether employees are redundant, see *Chapman and Elkin v CPS Computer Group plc* [1987] IRLR 462. For the effect of a transfer on an employee's normal retiring age, see *Cross v British Airways* [2006] EWCA Civ 549, [2006] ICR 1239.

52.18 The transferee inherits all accrued rights and liabilities connected with the contract of employment of the transferred employee. This includes liability for negligence and breach of statutory duty (*Taylor v Serviceteam Ltd* [1998] PIQR P201). If, for example, the transferor was in arrears with wages at the time of the transfer, the employee can sue the transferee as if the original liability had been the transferee's. The transferor is relieved of his former obligations without any need for the employee's consent (*Berg and Busschers v Besselsen* [1990] ICR 396). Equally, the transferee can sue an employee for a breach of contract committed against the transferor prior to transfer. The transferee will also inherit all the statutory rights and liabilities which are connected with the individual contract of employment. The transferred employee's period of continuous employment will date from the beginning of his period of employment with the transferor, and the statutory particulars of terms and conditions of employment, which every employer is obliged to issue, must take account of any continuity enjoyed by virtue of the *Regulations* (a proposition approved by the Court of Justice in *Unionen v Almega Tjänsteförbunden* C-336/15). (As to continuity of employment when a school transfers to grant-maintained status, see *Pickwell v Lincolnshire County Council* [1993] ICR 87.)

Liability for (for example) sex discrimination transfers to the transferee, even though the employee was employed part-time at the time of the transfer and the discrimination concerned the termination of a previous full-time contract (*DJM International Ltd v Nicholas* [1996] IRLR 76). In *Bernadone v Pall Mall Services Group* [2001] ICR 197, the Court of Appeal held that an employee's claim for personal injuries against his former employer was transferred to the new employer, together with the right of the former employer to an indemnity from its insurers: it was an implied term of the employee's contract of employment that he would be protected by insurance, as required by statute and that right to an indemnity fell within *reg 4(2)*. It did not matter whether the employee's claim was pleaded in contract, tort or breach of statutory duty.

Where a contract provides that nationally agreed pay rates will normally be paid by an employer, it is an implied term that the employer must give notice if it intends to depart from that normal situation. That implied term will transfer, so that if a transferee employer fails to give such notice it will be bound to pay a nationally agreed pay increase, even though it is not itself part of the transferor's bargaining structure: *Glendale Managed Services v Graham* [2003] EWCA Civ 773, [2003] IRLR 465.

However, in *French v MITIE Management Services Ltd* [2002] IRLR 512 the EAT accepted the transferee's argument that the employees' right to benefit from a profit sharing or share option scheme required only that the transferee provide the right to participate in a scheme of 'substantial equivalence, but one which is free from unjust, absurd or impossible features'. That concept cannot be applied to a mobility clause which operates within a defined geographic area: *Tapere v South London and Maudsley NHS Trust* [2009] ICR 1563.

52.19 Rights and liabilities which are not assigned under the Regulations

The *Regulations* do not have the effect of assigning:

(a)   criminal liabilities (*reg 4(6)*); or

(b)   rights and liabilities relating to provisions of occupational pension schemes which relate to benefits for old age, invalidity or survivors (*reg 10*).

In *Walden Engineering Co Ltd v Warrener* [1993] ICR 967, the EAT rejected arguments that employees should be entitled to equivalent pension benefits after the transfer. Moreover, it was held by the Court of Appeal in *Adams v Lancashire County Council* [1997] ICR 834 that the *Regulations* and the *Directive* do not cover transfer of future pension rights, that the exclusion of pension rights from the *Regulations* is consistent with the *Directive*, and that therefore there was no duty on a private contractor to provide an occupational pension scheme for former local government catering workers; see *Eidesund v Stavanger Catering A/S*: C-2/95 [1996] IRLR 684. Since the term relating to pension does not transfer under the *Regulations*, time to bring a claim under the *Equal Pay Act 1970* starts to run from the time of the transfer: *Preston v Wolverhampton Healthcare NHS Trust (No 3); Powerhouse Retail Ltd v Burroughs* [2004] EWCA Civ 1281, [2005] ICR 222 (applied to all pay terms in *Gutridge v Sodexo Ltd* [2009] EWCA Civ 729, [2009] ICR 1486, [2009] IRLR 721).

However, these exceptions are to be interpreted strictly: *Beckmann v Dynamco Whicheloe Macfarlane Ltd*: C-164/00 [2003] ICR 50. The ECJ ruled that early retirement benefits and benefits intended to enhance the conditions of such retirement did not fall within the meaning of rights to old-age pension schemes and so the obligation to pay such benefits did transfer to the new employer. These principles were applied by the ECJ in *Martin v South Bank University*: C-4/01 [2004] IRLR 74.

Moreover, *ss 257* and *258* of the *Pensions Act 2004* (together with the *Transfer of Employment (Pension Protection) Regulations 2005 (SI 2005/649)*) require a transferee to provide certain pension benefits to employees for whom there was an occupational pension scheme with the transferor.

The application of the distinction as to what does and does not transfer is illustrated by *Procter & Gamble Co v Svenska Cellulosa Aktiebolaget SCA* [2012] IRLR 733: the High Court held that the employees' right to be considered for early retirement benefits transferred under TUPE, whereas benefits payable after normal retirement age (including those first triggered as early retirement benefits) do not transfer.

52.20 TRANSFER OF AN UNDERTAKING AND THE TRADE UNION

Collective agreements

Under *reg 5*, a collective agreement, which:

(a)   is made between the transferor and a union recognised by the transferor; and

(b)   applies to an employee whose contract has become automatically assigned to the transferee by virtue of the transfer,

is automatically transferred to the transferee in its application to that employee. Further, anything done by or under or in connection with that agreement by the transferor before the transfer is deemed to have been done by the transferee.

The practical effect of this provision is probably minimal, since collective agreements are in English law presumed to be unenforceable (see *TULRCA 1992, s 179* and **6.2 COLLECTIVE AGREEMENTS**) unless, which is rare, the contrary is stated in the agreement. It is only in this rare case where a binding agreement is entered into that *reg 5* will pass any legal obligation to the transferee. If the terms of a collective agreement are incorporated into the contract of employment of an individual, whose service is automatically assigned on the transfer, then its terms will bind the transferee simply by virtue of the general rule that the transferee inherits the rights and liabilities in the individual's contract: *Whent v T Cartledge Ltd* [1997] IRLR 153. However, a contract which incorporates a collective agreement will not transfer any rights or liabilities in relation to a provision of a collective agreement where that provision is agreed after the date of the transfer and the transferee is not a participant in the collective bargaining for that provision (*reg 4A*). This regulation (introduced in the 2014 amendments) effectively applies the judgment in *Alemo-Herron v Parkwood Leisure Ltd*: C-426/11 [2013] ICR 1116 (see also *ÖGB v WKO*: C-328/13 [2014] ICR 1152).

Regulation 5(b) provides that any order made in respect of a collective agreement transferred under *reg 5* takes effect as if the transferee were a party to the agreement. In effect, this means that awards of the Central Arbitration Committee ('CAC') made against the transferor are binding against the transferee to the extent that they previously bound the transferor.

52.21 Recognition

Where the transferor recognises a union in respect of employees in the undertaking or part of the undertaking to be transferred and, following the transfer, the undertaking or part of the undertaking transferred maintains an identity distinct from the rest of the transferee's business or businesses, the transferee must recognise the union in respect of those employees (*reg 6*). The underlying provision within the *Directive* was considered by the ECJ in *Federación de Servicios Públicos de la UGT (UGT-FSP) v Ayuntamiento de La Línea de la Concepción*: C-151/09 [2010] ICR 1248.

The general provisions applicable to recognition are to be found in *s 70A* of and *Schedule A1* to the *Trade Union and Labour Relations (Consolidation) Act 1992* (see **50.11 TIME OFF WORK**).

52.22 Information and consultation

Employee Liability Information

Regulations 11 to 16 provide an important code for the provision of information by the transferor to the transferee, and by employers to affected employees.

Regulation 11 imposes a duty on the transferor to notify the transferee of certain information relating to any person employed by him who is assigned to the activity which is the subject of the relevant transfer. The information must be in writing or some other readily accessible form.

That information, defined as 'employee liability information' is:

(a)   the identity and age of the employee;

(b)   the information specified in *s 1* of the *Employment Rights Act 1996* (see **8.6 CONTRACT OF EMPLOYMENT**); if further information is given than required (for example, whether a bonus is contractual or not, then the recipient has no claim if that additional information is wrong: see *Born London Ltd v Spire Production Services Ltd* UKEAT/0255/16;

(c)   information of any disciplinary action taken against the employee and of any grievance raised by them within the previous two years to which a Code of Practice issued under *Part IV* of the *TULR(C)A 1992* applies;

(d)   information relating to actual or potential claims against the transferor;

(e)   information of any collective agreement which will apply to the employee pursuant to *reg 5*.

This information must also be provided in relation to an employee who has resigned because of the transfer: *reg 11(4)*.

This information must be provided not less than 28 days before the relevant transfer, unless there are special circumstances which mean that this is not reasonably practicable, in which case it must be given as soon as reasonably practicable thereafter: *reg 11(6)*.

If the transferor fails to comply with this obligation, the transferee may present a complaint to an employment tribunal. If successful, the tribunal may make an award of compensation to the transferee, such as is just and equitable in particular having regard to any loss sustained by the transferor which is attributable to the breach and the terms of any contract between transferor and transferee which provide for the payment of such a sum in any event. The minimum level of such an award is, however, fixed at £500 per employer (subject to a discretion to award a lower figure if the tribunal considers that just and equitable).

52.23 *Information and consultation of employees*

Under *reg 13*, the employer of employees affected by the transfer, whether he is the transferor or transferee, must inform all the appropriate representatives of any of the affected employees, long enough before the transfer to enable consultations to take place between the employer and those representatives, of the following:

(a)   the fact that a relevant transfer is to take place;

(b)   when it is to take place;

(c)   the reasons for it;

(d)   the legal, economic and social implications of the transfer for affected employees;

(e)   the measures which he envisages taking in relation to those employees (and if no measures are envisaged, that fact);

(f)   if the employer is the transferor, the measures which the transferee envisages that he will take in relation to those employees who are to be automatically assigned to him on the transfer (or if no measures are envisaged, that fact).

If a transfer does not in fact take place, then the duty to inform and consult will have not arisen: *I Lab Facilities Ltd v Metcalfe* [2013] IRLR 605.

Where such information is provided, the employer must also include specified information relating to the use of agency workers (if any) by that employer: *reg 13(2A)*.

The obligation under sub-para (*d*) is satisfied where the employer states a genuine belief, even if that belief is wrong in law: *Communication Workers Union v Royal Mail Group Ltd* [2010] ICR 83.

Appropriate representatives are representatives of an independent trade union recognised by the employer for employees of that description. If there is no such union then the appropriate representatives are, at the employer's choice, either (i) employee representatives elected by the affected employees for this purpose in an election complying with the requirements of *reg 14*, or (ii) employee representatives appointed or elected by the affected employees for some other purpose but who have authority from those employees to receive information and to be consulted about the proposed dismissals on their behalf (*reg 13(3)(b)*). If there are no appropriate representatives at the relevant time, the employer

In *Kerry Foods Ltd v Creber* [2000] ICR 556, receivers dismissed all of the employees of an undertaking prior to its transfer. The employment tribunal found that the reason for this dismissal was the transfer. The EAT ruled that the tribunal should then have concluded that (by reason of the *Litster* principle – see **52.10** above) the employees were employed in the undertaking immediately before the transfer, that their employment was transferred and the transferee was then treated as having dismissed them. However, if the main reason for the dismissal is an ETO reason within *reg 7(1)(b)*, then the employee is not deemed to have been employed immediately before the transfer, his employment does not transfer and his only remedy for unfair dismissal is against the transferor. If the dismissal is in fact effected by the transferee, then the employee's remedy lies against the transferee, which may itself invoke an ETO reason.

In *Wilson v St Helens Borough Council* [1999] 2 AC 52 the House of Lords (reversing the decision of the Court of Appeal) held that an actual dismissal before, on or after the transfer is effective, even where the transfer was the reason for the dismissal. The dismissal is not a nullity and the employee cannot compel the transferee to employ him on the same terms and conditions as those on which the transferor employed him.

For the transfer to be the reason for dismissal within *reg 7(1)*, it is not necessary that the employer had in mind a specific transferee at the time of the dismissal (*Morris v John Grose Group Ltd* [1998] ICR 655, an approach approved in *Spaceright Europe Ltd v Baillavoine* [2011] EWCA Civ 1656, [2012] ICR 520).

The passage of time may increase the chances that the chain of causation between the transfer and the reason for the dismissal has been broken; however, the mere passage of time without anything happening does not in itself constitute a weakening to the point of dissolution of the chain of causation: *Taylor v Connex South Eastern Ltd*, IDS Brief 670, p 10.

The reason for dismissal may be connected with the transfer, even though the employee dismissed was never employed in the undertaking or part transferred (*reg 7(4)*). If, for example, the transferee dismisses his existing staff to accommodate the employees he is to inherit from the transferor, or if the job of an existing employee disappears following a reorganisation consequent upon the transfer, the dismissal will nonetheless be connected with the transfer.

It appears that a transferor may not invoke the defence of an 'organisational' or 'economic' reason where a transferee is willing to acquire the undertaking only on terms that the transferor's staff are first dismissed, because the reason must relate to the conduct of the business for those words to apply (*Wheeler v Patel* [1987] ICR 631 and *Gateway Hotels Ltd v Stewart* [1988] IRLR 287, not following *Anderson v Dalkeith Engineering Ltd* [1985] ICR 66, EAT. See also *Ibex Trading Co Ltd v Walton* [1994] ICR 907).

Whitehouse v Blatchford & Sons Ltd [2000] ICR 542 concerned a transfer following the award of a new contract for the provision of services to a hospital. It was a stipulation of that contract that the number of employees be reduced. The applicant was dismissed following the transfer. The Court of Appeal held that the employment tribunal had been entitled to find that the applicant's dismissal was for an economic, technical or organisational reason. If the transferee had not complied with the stipulation then it would not have won the contract. The court followed *Wheeler v Patel*: the reason must be connected with the future conduct of the business as a going concern. See also *Thompson v SCS Consulting Ltd* [2001] IRLR 801. A transferor cannot dismiss and then rely upon the future conduct of the business by the transferee after the transfer in an attempt to establish an ETO reason; the transferor itself has no intention of continuing the business and so the reason for the dismissal does not relate to its future conduct of the business: *Hynd v Armstrong* [2007] CSIH 16, [2007] IRLR 338 (Court of Session, Inner House). Similarly, an administrator may not rely upon an ETO reason where it dismisses an employee to make the business of the company a more attractive proposition to prospective transferees as a going concern, since here the intention is not to continue to conduct the business but to sell it: *Spaceright Europe Ltd v Baillavoine* [2011] EWCA Civ 1656, [2012] ICR 520, applied in *Kavanagh v Crystal Palace FC (2000) Ltd* [2013] IRLR 291.

The EAT has held that when a transferor gives notice of termination to employees before a transfer takes place and the notice expires after the transfer, it is the transferor's reasons for the dismissals which should be examined in determining whether the transferee can be held to have unfairly dismissed the employees (*BSG Property Services v Tuck* [1996] IRLR 134).

The words 'entailing changes in the workforce' impose important limitations on the defence of 'economic, technical or organisational reason'. It is only when the employer sets out to change the structure of his workforce, by reducing numbers or changing the functions which individuals perform (or now by changing the place where people work), that the reason will entail a change in the workforce. Hence, the employer cannot fairly dismiss transferred employees who will not agree to changes in their old terms and conditions of employment (see *Berriman v Delabole Slate Ltd* [1985] ICR 546; *Crawford v Swinton Insurance Brokers Ltd* [1990] ICR 85; *Porter and Nanayakkara v Queen's Medical Centre (Nottingham University Hospital)* [1993] IRLR 486; *The Manchester College v Hazel (No 2)* [2014] IRLR 392). It is not a requirement that the whole workforce be affected (see *Nationwide Building Society v Benn* [2010] IRLR 922, a case which also makes it clear that an employer can raise the ETO defence even in cases of constructive dismissal). A change from using employees to franchisees who were limited companies to carry out meter reading work entailed changes to the workforce; the word 'workforce' connotes the whole body of employees as an entity and does not include limited companies: *Meter U Ltd v Ackroyd* [2012] ICR 834.

There is, however, no limitation on the defence of 'economic, technical or organisational reason' that the dismissal would have been made in any case, for instance pursuant to a decision taken before there was any question of transferring the undertaking (*Trafford v Sharpe & Fisher (Building Supplies) Ltd* [1994] IRLR 325, not following Advocate-General Van Gerven in *D'Urso v Ercole Marelli Elettromeccanica Generale SpA*: C-362/89 [1992] IRLR 136, ECJ).

In determining the reason for dismissal, the tribunal must consider the reasons of the employer. Where an administrator has been appointed, it is his reasons which are relevant and any earlier stratagem of a director cannot be attributed to the administrator: *Amicus v Dynamex Friction Ltd* [2008] EWCA Civ 381, [2009] ICR 511.

If an employer brings the case within the category of economic, technical or organisational reason entailing changes in the workforce, it will remain to be considered whether he acted reasonably in the circumstances (applying the ordinary approach to unfair dismissal cases). The considerations which will be relevant must vary with the circumstances of the individual case. It is fair to assume, however, that a failure to offer the employee an available job in some part of the business not affected by the economic technical or organisational problem in question, or a failure to consult the employee, will be grounds on which such dismissals may sometimes be considered unfair.

Whilst each case turns on its facts, it is unlikely to be unreasonable for an employee to refuse an offer from a transferee who refuses to acknowledge the effect of TUPE, but offers engagement on a self-employed basis or on less favourable terms: *F&G Cleaners Ltd v Saddington* [2012] IRLR 892.

52.27 Redundancy payments

An employee dismissed by reason of redundancy is, subject to various qualifying conditions, entitled to a redundancy payment (see REDUNDANCY – I (38)). He is dismissed by reason of redundancy if the principal reason is that his employer has ceased or intends to cease carrying on business in the place where the employee was employed or if there is a diminution in the requirements of the employer's business for the work of the particular kind for which the employee is employed.

An employee whose contract is automatically assigned under the *Regulations* will not be dismissed by the transferor and cannot therefore become entitled to a redundancy payment unless and until he is dismissed by the transferee by reason of redundancy.

If, however:

(a)   an employee is dismissed by the transferor in advance of the transfer by reason of the fact that the transferor is to go out of business in the place where the employee was employed or no longer requires work of the particular kind done by the employee; or

(b)   following the transfer, the transferee dismisses the employee for either of these reasons,

the employee is, on the face of it, entitled to a redundancy payment.

Despite decisions of the EAT in Scotland to the contrary, the Employment Appeal Tribunal in England has now confirmed that the employee will, in these circumstances, qualify for a redundancy payment even though the reason for his dismissal may qualify as an economic, technical or organisational reason entailing changes in the workforce. In *Gorictree Ltd v Jenkinson* [1985] ICR 51, it was held that the dismissal does not cease to be by reason of redundancy merely because it also qualifies as an economic, technical or organisational reason under the *Regulations*. It is likely that this decision, and not the earlier Scottish decisions, will be followed in future.

52.28 AVOIDING THE REGULATIONS AND THEIR CONSEQUENCES

An agreement to exclude or limit the application of the *Regulations* is invalid (*reg 18*). The transferor and transferee may, however, validly agree that one shall indemnify the other for sums payable in consequence of the operation of the *Regulations*. In practice, it is quite common for transferees to take such indemnities from transferors.

The principle of automatic transfer may not be derogated from by a collective agreement with a trade union (*D'Urso v Ercole Marelli Elettromeccanica Generale SpA*: C-362/89 [1992] IRLR 136, ECJ), nor on account of the business being in critical difficulties (*Spano v Fiat Geotech SpA*: C-472/93 [1995] ECR I-4321, ECJ).

Where an employee's employment contract is brought to an end, a compromise agreement will be effective and is not an agreement which purports to exclude or limit the operation of the *Regulations*: *Solectron Scotland Ltd v Roper* [2004] IRLR 4.

52.29 Variation of employees' contracts after transfer of an undertaking

Although an employee cannot waive the benefit of the *Regulations*, there may be an agreed variation to the terms and conditions of employment following the transfer provided that the reason for the change is not the transfer itself (unless the reason for the variation is an economic, technical or organisation reason entailing changes in the workforce) (*reg 4(4)* and *(5)*, as amended, developing principles established in *Martin v South Bank University*:

C-4/01 [2004] IRLR 74; *Foreningen af Arbejdsledere i Danmark v Daddy's Dance Hall A/S*: 324/86 [1988] IRLR 315); cf the judgment of the CA in *Power v Regent Security Services Ltd* [2007] EWCA Civ 1188, [2008] ICR 442, applying the *1981 Regulations*, which did not have provisions equivalent to *reg 4(4)* and *(5))*. For this purpose, changes to the workforce include a change in the place where they are employed (*reg 4(5A)*). In addition, even where the reason for the variation is the transfer itself, a variation is effective where the terms of the contract permit the employer to make such a variation (*reg 4(5)(b)*) or where the variation is to a term or condition incorporated from a collective agreement, provided that the variation takes effect more than one year after the transfer and overall the employee's rights and obligations are no less favourable to him (*reg 4(5B)*).

The ECJ has ruled that the *Directive* does not preclude a public body, as a transferee, from reducing the pay of its incoming staff where it is necessary to do so in order to comply with national rules in force for public employees. However, if the variation is sufficiently detrimental, then the employees will be entitled to resign and claim that the employer was responsible for their dismissal (under *art 4(2)*).

In *Cornwall County Care Ltd v Brightman* [1998] ICR 529, employees were dismissed by the transferee after the transfer and re-employed on less favourable terms and conditions. The EAT held that they had been unfairly dismissed since the reason for the dismissals had been the transfer. However, the employees had 'accepted' the new terms and conditions by continuing to work for the transferee. They were unable to continue to claim a right to their original terms and conditions – that claim was 'bought out' by the compensation for unfair dismissal. A change in terms and conditions brought about merely because of the expiry of employees' fixed-term contract may be effective: *Ralton v Havering College of Further and Higher Education* [2001] IRLR 738. The tribunal had been right to apply the test of whether the variation was solely by reason of the transfer. In *Enterprise Managed Services Ltd v Dance* (UKEAT/0200/11) a variation in terms was effective where it was introduced in order to achieve improved performance and efficiency, and so the harmonisation of terms amongst employees was simply a by-product of the variation, rather than the principal reason for it. The question is not whether the variation would not have happened 'but for' the transfer, but what the operative reason in fact was and so where the reason was a mistaken view that the employee was being overpaid, then this was not a reason connected with the transfer: *Smith v Trustees of Brooklands College* (UKEAT/0128/11).

53   Unfair Dismissal – I: The Right to Make a Claim

Cross-references. See Termination of Employment (48) for the various ways of terminating the contract at common law; Unfair Dismissal – II (54) for whether the dismissal was fair; Unfair Dismissal – III (55) for remedies for unfair dismissal; Wrongful Dismissal (58) for dismissals in breach of contract.

53.1   The *Industrial Relations Act 1971* originally created the right not to be unfairly dismissed. The right was then re-enacted in the *Employment Protection (Consolidation) Act 1978* and then in the *Employment Rights Act 1996* ('*ERA 1996*'). *ERA 1996* is a consolidation Act, so the rights thereunder are exactly the same as those which previously existed under the earlier statutes and the old case law remains relevant.

An employer who dismisses an employee without good reason or without following a fair procedure lays itself open to a claim for unfair dismissal. When such a claim is brought, the employer bears the burden of proof in establishing the reason for the dismissal. The employment tribunal will then consider whether the dismissal was fair in all the circumstances, neither party having the evidential burden in this enquiry. If the dismissal is held to be unfair, the employer can be ordered to re-engage, reinstate or to pay compensation to the ex-employee. The parties to a claim for unfair dismissal are known as the *claimant* (employee) and the *respondent* (employer). The claimant was formerly called the applicant.

53.2   PRE-CONDITIONS OF A CLAIM

A complaint of unfair dismissal must be presented to an employment tribunal before the end of the period of three months beginning with the effective date of termination of the employment (or within such further period as the tribunal considers reasonable in a case where it is satisfied that it was not reasonably practicable for the complaint to be presented within the period of three months) (*ERA 1996, s 111(2)*).

Prior to 6 April 2009, an employee benefited from a limitation period of six months from the effective date of termination of the employment (*EmA 2002, s 32* and *Employment Act 2002 (Dispute Resolution) Regulations 2004, reg 15*) in certain circumstances. The provisions for the extension of time in this way were repealed by the *Employment Act 2008, s 1*. (See further 18.24–18.25 Employment Tribunals-I and also 53.13 below for effective date of termination.) This chapter used to contain detailed reference to the statutory dispute resolution procedures. These references have now been removed on the assumption that few if any cases remain live where the trigger date was before 6 April 2009. Readers should consult earlier editions of this work if required.

Leaving aside the now almost universal requirement for an early conciliation certificate (dealt with elsewhere in this work at 3.1) a claimant must also satisfy the conditions set out below if he wishes to bring a claim for unfair dismissal. If these conditions are not disputed by the respondent, no evidence need be brought by the claimant to establish them. If, however, there are grounds for suspecting that any of those necessary prerequisites is absent, the employment tribunal will inquire into the matter, as it affects their jurisdiction to hear the case. The burden is on the claimant to show that he satisfies those conditions. The conditions are:

(a)   that the claimant was employed by the respondent under a contract of employment (see **53.3** below);

(b)   that the claimant was dismissed, as defined (see **53.4** below);

(c)   in most cases, that the claimant was employed for the necessary qualifying period (see **53.11** below). (The employer may sometimes argue that a claim cannot be brought because the employee did not work for the qualifying period under a *lawful* contract (see **53.16** below).)

The exclusion of employees over retirement age from the right to complain of unfair dismissal was removed on 1 October 2006. Special rules used to apply to dismissals by reason of retirement but these too have been repealed (see **53.14**).

Certain employees are excluded from the right not to be unfairly dismissed:

(i)   certain specified classes of employees (see **53.15** below);

(ii)   those dismissed in connection with a lock-out or unofficial strike and, in some cases, persons dismissed in connection with an official strike, provided certain conditions are satisfied (see **53.17–53.18** below).

53.3   EMPLOYMENT BY THE RESPONDENT

In order to bring a claim for unfair dismissal, a claimant must show that he was employed by the respondent under a contract of employment (*ERA 1996, ss 94(1), 230(1)*). Therefore, sub-contractors or consultants under contracts for services are not protected by the unfair dismissal provisions even though they may work regularly for one person or organisation. See EMPLOYEE, SELF-EMPLOYED OR WORKER? **(15)**.

The *Employment Relations Act 1999, s 23* gives the Secretary of State the power to extend the right not to be unfairly dismissed to individuals who do not fit the current definition of 'employee'.

53.4   DISMISSAL BY THE RESPONDENT

An employee is treated as having been dismissed if, but only if:

(a)   the contract under which he is employed by the employer is terminated by the employer, whether it is so terminated by notice or without notice;

(b)   where he is employed under a limited-term contract, and the contract terminates by virtue of the limiting event without being renewed under the same contract; or

(c)   the employee terminates that contract with or without notice in circumstances such that he is entitled to terminate it without notice by reason of the employer's conduct (usually called 'constructive dismissal').

(*ERA 1996, s 95(1)*.)

The contract of employment of an employee who is on ordinary or additional maternity leave or parental leave is deemed to continue whilst he or she is on leave, with appropriate amendments (*ERA 1996, s 71* and *Maternity and Parental Leave, etc Regulations 1999 (SI 1999/3312), reg 17*). It follows that if an employer does not permit the employee to return at the end of the leave or acts in repudiatory breach of contract during the leave period (and the employee accepts the repudiation), the employee will be treated as having been dismissed (see further **32.33** MATERNITY AND PARENTAL RIGHTS).

53.5   Termination by the employer

Notice of dismissal, once accepted, cannot generally be withdrawn (*Riordan v War Office* [1959] 1 WLR 1046). Thus, an employer who gives notice to an employee which is accepted cannot thereafter withdraw that notice without the consent of the employee. The same principle applies to notice of resignation given by the employee. In *Willoughby v CF Capital* [2011] EWCA Civ 1115; [2011] IRLR 985 the Court of Appeal discussed the so called 'special circumstances exception' to the rule in *Riordan* and concluded that it was not truly an exception to the rule but rather "*a cautionary reminder to the recipient of the notice that, before accepting or otherwise acting upon it, the circumstances in which it is given may require him first to satisfy himself that the giver of the notice did in fact really intend what he had apparently said by it.*"

Where an employer gives notice to an employee to terminate his contract of employment and, at a time within the period of that notice, the employee gives notice to the employer to terminate the contract of employment on a date earlier than the date on which the employer's notice is due to expire, the employee will nevertheless be taken to have been dismissed by his employer for the purposes of an unfair dismissal claim. The reasons for the dismissal are then taken to be the reasons for which the employer's notice was given (*ERA 1996, s 95(2)*). According to the EAT, an employer may vary the notice of dismissal which determines the effective day of termination, with the effect of bringing forward that date (*Palfrey v Transco plc* [2004] IRLR 916). If an employee gives notice to terminate his employment and, during that period of notice, the employer summarily dismisses him, the employee will be considered to have been dismissed despite the fact that he first gave notice to terminate his contract (*Harris and Russell Ltd v Slingsby* [1973] 3 All ER 31). However, if, after the employee has given notice, the employer takes advantage of a contractual right to make a payment in lieu of notice, there is no dismissal (even if the employee is thereby deprived of commission income) (*Marshall (Cambridge) Ltd v Hamblin* [1994] ICR 362, [1994] IRLR 260).

A contract of employment is only terminated by an employer if there is a specified or ascertainable date on which the contract is to cease (*Haseltine Lake & Co v Dowler* [1981] ICR 222). Dismissal, to be effective, must be communicated to the employee (*Hindle Gears Ltd v McGinty* [1985] ICR 111 and *Gisda Cyf v Barratt* [2010] UKSC 41, [2010] ICR 1475, contrasted with *Kirklees MBC v Radecki* [2009] EWCA Civ 298, [2009] IRLR 555). In *Sandle v Adecco UK Ltd* [2016] IRLR 941, the EAT accepted that a dismissal could be inferred from an employer's conduct, but held that it still had to be communicated to the employee in a sufficiently unequivocal way to be effective.

An employer is not entitled to deny that there was a dismissal merely because the individual who dismissed the employee did not in fact have the authority to do so (*Warnes v Trustees of Cheriton Oddfellows Social Club* [1993] IRLR 58).

A very substantial departure by an employer from an original contract of employment may amount to termination of that contract of employment and its replacement by the offer of a different and inferior contract. In such cases, there is a termination by the employer, rather than a constructive dismissal (see **53.7** below; *Alcan Extrusions v Yates* [1996] IRLR 327; but see *Robinson v Tescom Corp* [2008] IRLR 408 for circumstances in which a contract remains extant although the employee works under protest).

53.6   Expiry of a fixed-term contract

It used to be thought that a fixed-term contract was one which did not contain a provision for prior determination by notice. However, in *Dixon v BBC* [1979] ICR 281, the Court of Appeal held that the words 'a fixed term' include a specified stated term even though the contract is determinable by notice within its term. *Regulation 1* of the *Fixed-term Employees (Prevention of Less Favourable Treatment) Regulations 2002 (SI 2002/2034)* provides that a fixed-term contract is a contract of employment that, under its provisions determining how it will terminate in the normal course, will terminate – (a) on the expiry of a specific term, (b) on the completion of a particular task, or (c) on the occurrence or non-occurrence of any other specific event other than the attainment by the employee of any normal and *bona fide* retiring age in the establishment for an employee holding the position held by him. (see Part-Time Workers (33)).

53.7 Constructive dismissal

In order to establish that he has been constructively dismissed, an employee must show the following:

(i) His employer has committed a repudiatory breach of contract. A repudiatory breach is a significant breach going to the root of the contract (*Western Excavating (ECC) Ltd v Sharp* [1978] ICR 221). In *Tullett Prebon Plc v BGC Brokers LP* [2011] EWCA Civ 131, [2011] IRLR 420 the Court of Appeal applied the orthodox contractual test for a repudiatory breach in holding that it is one in which the contract-breaker has shown an intention, objectively judged, to abandon and altogether refuse to perform the contract. In *Leeds Dental Team Ltd v Rose* [2014] ICR 94, the EAT rejected a submission to the effect that *Tullett* had changed the law. It follows that – at least in a case based on a breach of the implied term of mutual trust and confidence – it is not necessary for a tribunal to make a factual finding as to the employer's actual (subjective) intention with regards to the contract, simply a finding as to whether, objectively, the conduct complained of was likely to destroy or seriously damage the relationship of trust and confidence. It is not enough to show merely that the employer has behaved unreasonably although *"reasonableness is one of the tools in the employment tribunal's factual analysis kit for deciding whether there has been a fundamental breach"* (*Buckland v Bournemouth University Higher Education Corporation* [2010] EWCA Civ 121, [2010] IRLR 445). The line between serious unreasonableness and a breach of the implied term of trust and confidence (see **8.13** CONTRACT OF EMPLOYMENT) is a fine one (see eg *Sheridan v Stanley Cole (Wainfleet) Ltd* [2003] ICR 297, [2003] IRLR 52). Likewise, there is no rule that an act of direct or indirect discrimination by an employer will constitute a repudiatory breach, but the line between repudiatory and non-repudiatory acts of discrimination is narrow (see eg *Shaw v CCL Ltd* [2008] IRLR 284). Every breach of the implied term of trust and confidence is a repudiatory breach of contract (*Morrow v Safeway Stores* [2002] IRLR 9, *Ahmed v Amnesty International* [2009] ICR 1450). The breach of contract may be an *anticipatory* rather than an *actual* one, i.e. even though no breach has yet occurred, it is sufficient if the employer has indicated a clear intention not to fulfil the terms of the contract in the future, and the employee accepts that intention to commit a breach as bringing the contract to an end (*Norwest Holst Group Administration Ltd v Harrison* [1985] ICR 668; *Greenaway Harrison Ltd v Wiles* [1994] IRLR 380). However, in *Kerry Foods Ltd v Lynch* [2005] IRLR 680 the EAT held that an employee had resigned prematurely in response to his employer's notice that it intended to terminate his employment and re-engage him on varied terms to which he had refused to agree. The EAT considered that the giving of lawful notice of termination could not by itself constitute a repudiatory breach of contract.

(ii) He has left because of the breach (*Walker v Josiah Wedgwood & Sons Ltd* [1978] ICR 744; *Holland v Glendale Industries Ltd* [1998] ICR 493). It was also suggested in *Walker* that the employee must make clear when he resigns that he regards himself as having been constructively dismissed. Note that it is an error of law for the tribunal to focus on the question of whether the repudiatory breach of contract was the main, predominant or 'effective' cause of the employee's resignation. The question is whether a repudiatory breach has played a part in the employee's resignation (*Wright v North Ayrshire Council* [2014] ICR 77)

(iii) He has not waived the breach (also known as 'affirming' the contract). In other words, he must not delay his resignation too long, or do anything else which indicates acceptance of the changed basis of his employment. See the discussion in *WE Cox Toner (International) Ltd v Crook* [1981] ICR 823, [1981] IRLR 443. Merely to protest at the time will not prevent such acceptance being inferred. An express reservation of rights may in certain circumstances be effective (see *Bliss v South East Thames Regional Health Authority* [1987] ICR 700; *Waltons & Morse v Dorrington* [1997]

IRLR 488) but not in others (see *Robinson v Tescom Corp* [2008] IRLR 408). Where there has been a repudiatory breach of contract by a party to a contract of employment, the breach is not capable of remedy in such a way as to preclude acceptance by the other party (*Buckland v Bournemouth University Higher Education Corporation* [2010] EWCA Civ 121, [2010] IRLR 445). The wronged party has an unfettered choice whether to accept the breach or not, whatever his motives. All the defaulting party can do is to invite affirmation of the contract by making amends.

Examples of breaches of contract upon which a complaint of constructive dismissal might be founded include: a reduction in pay (*Industrial Rubber Products v Gillon* [1977] IRLR 389); a complete change in the nature of the job (*Ford v Milthorn Toleman Ltd* [1980] IRLR 30; *Pedersen v Camden London Borough Council* [1981] ICR 674; *Land Securities Trillium Ltd v Thornley* [2005] IRLR 765); a failure to follow the prescribed disciplinary procedure (*Post Office v Strange* [1981] IRLR 515); an act of sex discrimination (*Shaw v CCL Ltd* [2008] IRLR 284). In *Crawford v Suffolk Mental Health Partnership* [2012] EWCA Civ 138, [2012] IRLR 402 Elias LJ observed, *obiter*, that suspending an employee as a 'knee-jerk' reaction would be a breach of the implied term of mutual trust and confidence. See also CONTRACT OF EMPLOYMENT (8).

A complaint of constructive dismissal may be based upon the conduct of a fellow employee even though that employee would not have had the authority to dismiss the complainant; the test is whether the employer is vicariously liable for the conduct complained of (*Hilton International Hotels (UK) Ltd v Protopapa* [1990] IRLR 316; see also *Warnes v Trustees of Cheriton Oddfellows Social Club* [1993] IRLR 58; and VICARIOUS LIABILITY (56)).

The employer may be held to be in repudiatory breach of contract not only if he breaks an express term but also if he infringes an implied term. The most common term relied upon is, of course, the implied term of mutual trust and confidence. Even if the employer's act which was the proximate cause of an employee's resignation was not by itself a fundamental breach of contract, the employee may be able to rely upon the employer's course of conduct considered as a whole in establishing that he was constructively dismissed. The 'last straw' must contribute, however slightly, to the breach of trust and confidence (*Omilaju v Waltham Forest London Borough Council* [2004] EWCA Civ 1493, [2005] IRLR 35). Glidewell LJ conveniently summarised some of the relevant principles in *Lewis v Motorworld Garages Ltd* [1986] ICR 157 at 169D–170A:

> "If the employer is in breach of an express term of a contract of employment, of such seriousness that the employee would be justified in leaving and claiming constructive dismissal, but the employee does not leave and accepts the altered terms of employment, and if subsequently a series of actions by the employer might constitute together a breach of the implied obligation of trust and confidence, the employee is entitled to treat the original action by the employer which was a breach of the express terms of the contract as a part – the start – of the series of actions which, taken together with the employer's other actions, might cumulatively amount to a breach of the implied terms."

In *BG plc v O'Brien* [2001] IRLR 496, the EAT rejected an argument that the implied duty of trust and confidence could not impose a positive obligation upon an employer; it held that the employer in that case had breached the duty of trust and confidence by failing to offer him a revised contract of employment when all his colleagues were offered a revised contract. This is a somewhat surprising decision, because it means that the duty of trust and confidence can impose a contractual obligation to vary a contract, but it was upheld by the Court of Appeal ([2002] IRLR 444). In *Visa International Service Association v Paul* [2004] IRLR 42 the duty of trust and confidence was breached by a failure to notify an employee on maternity leave of a new post, for which she was not shortlistable but for which she would have applied.

53.7 Unfair Dismissal – I: The Right to Make a Claim

There is a line of demarcation, however, between an employee's common law cause of action for breach of contract through destroying the relationship of trust and confidence and the employee's statutory complaint of unfair dismissal (see further *Eastwood v Magnox Electric plc* [2004] UKHL 35, [2004] IRLR 733; *Triggs v GAB Robins (UK) Ltd* [2008] EWCA Civ 17, [2008] IRLR 317, and *Edwards v Chesterfield Royal Hospital NHS Foundation Trust* [2011] UKSC 58, [2012] ICR 201 and **8.13 Contract of Employment**).

Where there is a genuine dispute between parties about the terms of a contract of employment, it is not an *anticipatory breach* of the contract for one party to do no more than argue his point of view (*Financial Techniques (Planning Services) Ltd v Hughes* [1981] IRLR 32; see also *Bridgen v Lancashire County Council* [1987] IRLR 58).

However, there can be a constructive dismissal even where the employer acts on a genuine, although mistaken, belief. So, for example, an employer's action in appointing a replacement for the claimant and in telling customers that the claimant was no longer employed is capable of amounting to a constructive dismissal, even in circumstances where the employer genuinely, although mistakenly, believed that the employee had left (*Brown v JBD Engineering Ltd* [1993] IRLR 568).

The offer of a new contract on less favourable terms upon the expiry of a fixed-term contract cannot amount to a constructive dismissal, because when the offer is made, there is no contract in existence (*Pfaffinger v City of Liverpool Community College* [1997] ICR 142).

A constructive dismissal is not necessarily unfair (*Savoia v Chiltern Herb Farms Ltd* [1982] IRLR 166, *Buckland v Bournemouth University Higher Education Corporation* [2010] EWCA Civ 121, [2010] IRLR 445). In practice, however, it will be harder to demonstrate that a particular action is reasonable where it contravenes the contract of employment. The tribunal will look at the conduct of the employer which amounted to the breach of contract, at which stage the test is objective and the range of reasonable responses test should not be used; and then tribunal will ask whether the employer acted reasonably, in the same way as any other case of unfair dismissal (see **Unfair Dismissal II (54)**). The Court of Appeal clarified the correct test in *Buckland*: (i) in determining whether or not the employer is in fundamental breach of the implied term of trust and confidence the unvarnished *Malik* test applies; (ii) if acceptance of that breach entitled the employee to leave, he has been constructively dismissed; (iii) it is open to the employer to show that such dismissal was for a potentially fair reason; and (iv) if he does so, it will then be for the employment tribunal to decide whether the dismissal for that reason, both substantively and procedurally, fell within the range of reasonable responses and was fair.

53.8 Forced resignation

If an employee resigns in circumstances where he is given no alternative but to resign or be dismissed, he will be considered to have been dismissed for the purposes of unfair dismissal. The question of whether the conduct of the employer caused the employee to leave is one of fact for the employment tribunal (*Martin v Glynwed Distribution Ltd* [1983] ICR 511, CA). However, telling an employee that he will be dismissed at some unspecified date in the future does not give the employee the right to resign and claim that he has been constructively dismissed if the employer is guilty of no anticipatory breach of contract – the employer may intend to give due notice, and a dismissal giving contractual notice is not, of course, a breach of contract (*Haseltine Lake & Co v Dowler* [1981] ICR 222; see also *Norwest Holst Group Administration Ltd v Harrison* [1985] ICR 668).

If an employee decides to leave because he has negotiated satisfactory terms for his departure, he will be considered to have resigned. Nevertheless, in *Sheffield v Oxford Controls Co Ltd* [1979] ICR 396, Arnold J said, at 402:

> "It is plain, we think, that there must exist a principle . . . that where an employee resigns and that resignation is determined upon by him because he prefers to resign

rather than to be dismissed (the alternative having been expressed to him by the employer in the terms of the threat that if he does not resign he will be dismissed), the mechanics of the resignation do not cause that to be other than a dismissal. The cases do not in terms go further than that. We find the principle to be one of causation."

Sheffield v Oxford Controls was endorsed by the Court of Appeal in *Jones v Mid-Glamorgan County Council* [1997] ICR 815. Again, in *Sandhu v Jan de Rijk Transport Ltd* [2008] EWCA Civ 430, [2007] IRLR 519, the Court of Appeal construed a forced resignation during one meeting as a dismissal, holding that resignation implies some form of negotiation and discussion and must be a genuine choice on the part of the employee. The Court of Appeal observed that none of the authorities treated as a resignation a decision made during a single meeting, and placed weight on the facts that the employee had had no warning that the purpose of the meeting was to dismiss him, had had no advice, and had had no time to reflect.

In considering these authorities regard must now be had to the terms of *ERA 1996, s 111A*. That section (inserted by *Enterprise and Regulatory Reform Act 2013, s 14*) provides that pre-termination negotiations will not be admissible as evidence in a complaint of unfair dismissal unless the tribunal considers that there has been improper behaviour. The precise implications are yet to be fully worked out, but one potential effect of the section is that the circumstances of many 'forced resignations' which hitherto might have founded a complaint of constructive dismissal will not now be admissible before a tribunal at all. The leading case on *section 111A* is now *Faithorn Farell Timms v Bailey* [2016] ICR 1054.

53.9   Repudiatory conduct by the employee

Employers sometimes consider that an employee has 'dismissed himself' by breaching some fundamental term of his contract of employment, such as failing to attend work. This is almost certainly not a correct approach. In *Thomas Marshall (Exports) Ltd v Guinle* [1978] ICR 905, Megarry VC held that an employee's repudiation of his contract of employment had to be accepted by the employer to bring the contract to an end. This 'acceptance' view was approved by a majority of the Court of Appeal in *Gunton v Richmond-upon-Thames London Borough Council* [1980] ICR 755, and by a majority of the Court of Appeal in *London Transport Executive v Clarke* [1981] ICR 355. Similarly, in *Boyo v Lambeth London Borough Council* [1994] ICR 727, the Court of Appeal endorsed the 'acceptance' view of the termination of a contract of employment. The Court of Appeal took this approach in *Triggs v GAB Robins (UK) Ltd* [2008] EWCA Civ 17, [2008] IRLR 317 in respect of a requirement for an employee to accept an employer's repudiatory breach, making a conceptual distinction between the repudiatory breach and the acceptance which effects the dismissal (see TERMINATION OF EMPLOYMENT (48)).

There is now an authoritative exposition of the law in this area in the Supreme Court's decision in *Société Générale v Geys* [2012] UKSC 63, [2013] ICR 117. By a majority, the Supreme Court approved the *Gunton/Boyo* 'acceptance' approach which it described as the 'elective theory' (as opposed to the 'automatic theory'). It remains the case, therefore, that an unaccepted repudiatory breach of contract by an employee is a 'thing writ in water'.

53.10   Situations of no dismissal

There is *no dismissal* in the following cases.

(a)   *Termination of the contract of employment by consent of both parties* (see **52.8** above).

(b)   *Termination by the employee whether with or without notice* in the absence of 'constructive dismissal' or forced resignation (see **53.7** and **53.8** above). A valid notice given by an employee cannot usually be withdrawn without the employer's consent

(*Riordan v War Office* [1959] 3 All ER 552, [1960] 3 All ER 774; *Sothern v Franks Charlesly & Co* [1981] IRLR 278). However, it may be that words of resignation (or dismissal) spoken in the heat of the moment can be regarded as not being a true resignation, or else can be withdrawn if this is done very quickly (*Martin v Yeoman Aggregates Ltd* [1983] ICR 314; *Barclay v City of Glasgow District Council* [1983] IRLR 313 and *Willoughby v CF Capital* [2011] EWCA Civ 1115, [2011] IRLR 985 (above **53.5**)).

(c)   *Termination of employment by 'frustration'.* If the contract of employment cannot be performed or if its performance becomes radically different from that contemplated when the contract was entered into, it may be considered to have been terminated by frustration. The doctrine of frustration continues to apply to contracts of employment, though the EAT has recently let it be known that that is only due to binding Court of Appeal authority and its application is "not beyond question" (*Warner v Armfield Retail & Leisure Ltd* [2014] ICR 239; see further **48.3** TERMINATION OF EMPLOYMENT).

(d)   *Termination on the occurrence of an external event.* A contract for a voyage may be terminated 'automatically' when the voyage is completed (*Ryan v Shipboard Maintenance Ltd* [1980] ICR 88). An appointment for 'as long as sufficient funds are provided either by the Manpower Services Commission or by other firms/sponsors to fund it' was held to come to an end automatically when the specified event took place (*Brown v Knowsley Borough Council* [1986] IRLR 102). See also **53.6** above.

53.11   EMPLOYMENT FOR QUALIFYING PERIOD

From 1 June 1999, the qualifying period for claims of unfair dismissal was reduced from two years to one year (*ERA 1996, s 108(1)* and the *Unfair Dismissal and Statement of Reasons for Dismissal (Variation of Qualifying Period) Order 1999 (SI 1999/1436)*). For persons whose period of continuous employment begins on or after 6 April 2012, the qualifying period is once again two years (*Unfair Dismissal and Statement of Reasons for Dismissal (Variation of Qualifying Period) Order 2012 (SI 2012/989)* and *ERA 1996, s 108(1)* as amended).

The original two-year qualifying period was challenged in *R v Secretary of State for Employment, ex p Seymour-Smith (No 2)* [2000] IRLR 263 on the basis that it had a disproportionately adverse effect on women and was inconsistent with the *EC Treaty, art 119*, now *TFEU, art 157* (equal pay). This battleground has not been re-entered following the recent reversion to a two-year qualifying period.

The qualifying period is calculated from the beginning of the employee's employment under the relevant contract of employment. This could be earlier than the date the employee starts performing duties under the contract (*General of the Salvation Army v Dewsbury* [1984] ICR 498; but in *Wood v Cunard Line Ltd* [1991] ICR 13 the Court of Appeal expressed some doubt as to whether *Dewsbury* was correctly decided. See also *Koenig v Mind Gym Ltd* (UKEAT/0201/12)). The first day on which the employee started work is included, so that an employee who has worked 365 days (and whose period of continuous employment commenced prior to 6 April 2012) is protected against unfair dismissal (*O'Brien v Pacitti Jones (a firm)* [2005] CSIH 56, [2005] IRLR 888).

If an employee is dismissed on medical grounds in compliance with any law, regulation or code of practice providing for health and safety at work, the qualifying period for a claim is only one month (*ERA 1996, s 108(2)*).

An employee who is wrongfully dismissed in breach of the contractual notice entitlements and whose dismissal has the effect of preventing him or her from attaining the qualifying period for a complaint of unfair dismissal may not in an action for wrongful dismissal recover damages representing the loss of the chance to bring unfair dismissal proceedings (*Harper v Virgin Net Ltd* [2004] EWCA Civ 271, [2004] IRLR 390).

if an employer dismisses an employee without notice after 51 weeks, the effective date of termination will be taken to be one week later, as the minimum period of notice after more than one month's employment is one week (see **48.7** TERMINATION OF EMPLOYMENT). The employee will thus be entitled to claim compensation for unfair dismissal (assuming the period of continuous employment commenced prior to 6 April 2012). However, the extra time will not be added where an employee is summarily dismissed in circumstances where the employer is entitled to dismiss summarily, eg for gross misconduct (see **48.13** TERMINATION OF EMPLOYMENT). An employer is not entitled simply to define a dismissal as being for gross misconduct without the tribunal investigating whether that description is justified (*Lanton Leisure Ltd v White and Gibson* [1987] IRLR 119). The statutory extension of the effective date of termination applies even where the employee waives his right to notice (*Secretary of State for Employment v Staffordshire County Council* [1989] IRLR 117, the Court of Appeal holding that the fact that an employee has waived his right to notice or has accepted a payment in lieu of notice under *ERA 1996, s 97(4)* is relevant only to his rights in contract).

For the purpose of calculating the qualifying period of employment where an employee terminates his contract of employment in circumstances in which he is entitled to do so by reason of his employer's conduct, the effective date of termination will be considered to be the date on which the statutory minimum notice required of the employer would have expired (*ERA 1996, s 97(4)*).

53.14 RETIRING AGE

The *Employment Equality (Age) Regulations 2006 (SI 2006/1031)* came into force on 1 October 2006 and were largely repealed with effect from 1st October 2010 by *Equality Act 2010, s 211(2), Schedule 27, Part 2.*

The upper age limit for complaining of unfair dismissal, contained in *ERA 1996, s 109*, was removed and was replaced by a byzantine statutory process contained in *ERA 1996, sections 98ZA–98ZH*. With effect from 6 April 2011 however, those provisions were repealed and the concept of default retirement age abolished by the *Employment Equality (Repeal of Retirement Age Provisions) Regulations 2011 (SI 2011/1069)* (subject to savings in *regulation 5*). See **54.4** UNFAIR DISMISSAL II (54), RETIREMENT (42). Retirement is no longer a potentially fair reason for dismissal under *ERA 1996, section 98*.

53.15 EXCLUDED CLASSES OF EMPLOYEES

Certain classes of employment are excluded from the protection of the unfair dismissal provisions. If a respondent wishes to show that a claimant falls within an excluded class, the burden of proof is on him to do so (*Kapur v Shields* [1976] ICR 26). The excluded cases are defined by *ERA 1996, ss 199* and *200*.

(a)   Dismissal from any employment as a master or as a member of the crew of a *fishing vessel* where the employee is not remunerated otherwise than by a share in the profits or gross earnings of the vessel (*ERA 1996, s 199(2)*).

(b)   Dismissal from employment under a contract of employment in police service or to persons engaged in such employment (*ERA 1996, s 200* and see *Spence v British Railways Board* [2001] ICR 232 and *Redbridge LBC v Dhinsa* [2014] EWCA Civ 178, except for unfair dismissals on health and safety grounds (contrary to *ERA 1996, s 100)*, or because the employee has made a protected disclosure (contrary to *ERA 1996, s 103A*);

(c)   Dismissal from employment where the employee is an "employee shareholder" within the meaning of *ERA 1996, s 205A*. Such individuals (of whom there are thought to be very few) retain the protection of the automatically unfair dismissal provisions.

Certain other employees may also, for a variety of reasons short of an absolute statutory bar be excluded from the right to complain of unfair dismissal:

(a)   Dismissal from employment in respect of which the employee has validly contracted out of his right to claim compensation for unfair dismissal (*ERA 1996, s 203(2)* and see **53.19, 53.20** below);

(b)   Those whose employment lacks a sufficient connection with Great Britain. *Section 196 of the ERA 1996 was repealed in its entirety by s 32(3) of the Employment Relations Act 1999* and so, with effect from 25 October 1999, the territorial limits were removed. For those dismissed before 25 October 1999, any employment where under his contract of employment the employee ordinarily worked outside Great Britain was an excluded case.

The position is now governed by a series of decisions of the appellate courts. In *Lawson v Serco Ltd* [2006] UKHL 3, [2006] IRLR 289 the House of Lords gave guidance on the circumstances in which the right not to be unfairly dismissed applies. A claimant will generally be protected if he was working in Great Britain at the time of his dismissal and peripatetic employees are subject to a 'base' test. It is a question of law where an employee is based. The EAT applied the *Serco* test in *Williams v University of Nottingham* [2007] IRLR 660, *Bleuse v MBT Transport Ltd* [2008] IRLR 264, *Ministry of Defence v Wallis* [2010] ICR 1301 (and see [2011] EWCA Civ 231) and *Pervez v Macquarie* [2011] ICR 266. The Supreme Court revisited the *Serco* test in *Duncombe v Secretary of State for Children, Schools and Families (No 2)* [2011] ICR 1312 and *Ravat v Halliburton & Manufacturing & Services Ltd* [2012] ICR 389 and examples of the synthesis of these authorities and their application are to be found in the Court of Appeal's decisions in *Bates van Winkelhof v Clyde & Co LLP* [2013] ICR 883 and *Dhunna v Creditsights Ltd* [2015] ICR 105. In *Smania v Standard Chartered Bank* [2015] ICR 436, the EAT held that the test was no different if the complaint was of automatically unfair dismissal on whistleblowing grounds.

The factual examples within the case law on *ERA 1996, s 196* remain of relevance to cases where it is asserted that an employment tribunal has jurisdiction over certain employment, even though the legal test for jurisdiction over unfair dismissal claims changed with the repeal of *s 196*. Where an employee worked both inside and outside Great Britain, one would look at the terms of the contract, express or implied, and how the contract operated in practice, in order to ascertain where the employee's base was (cf *Wilson v Maynard Shipbuilding Consultants AB* [1978] ICR 376, and per Lord Denning MR and Sir David Cairns in *Todd v British Midland Airways Ltd* [1978] ICR 959). See also *Jackson v Ghost Ltd* [2003] IRLR 824, *Crofts v Cathay Pacific Airways Ltd* [2005] EWCA Civ 599, [2005] IRLR 624 and *Diggins v Condor Marine Crewing Services Ltd* [2009] EWCA Civ 1133, [2010] IRLR 119. In *Windstar Management Services Ltd v Harris* [2016] ICR 847 Elisabeth Laing J rejected the suggestion that she should follow the approach taken to place of work for a seafarer adopted by Leggatt J in *R (Fleet Maritime Services Bermuda Ltd) v Pensions Regulator* [2016] IRLR 199 (a case concerned with pension auto-enrolment under the Pensions Act 2008) and instead applied the approach in *Lawson, Duncombe* and *Ravat*.

The contract to be considered is that subsisting at the time of dismissal, and not any previous contract between the parties *(Weston v Vega Space Systems Engineering Ltd* [1989] IRLR 429). Where the contract of employment is of little assistance, the tribunal should go by the conduct of the parties and the way they have operated the contract (per Lord Denning MR in *Todd* at 964).

The relevant location used to be the employer's operational base, not the actual place of work (*Addison v Denholm Ship Management (UK) Ltd* [1997] IRLR 389).

A person employed to work on board a ship registered in the United Kingdom (not being a ship registered at a port outside Great Britain) used to be regarded as a person who under his contract ordinarily worked in Great Britain unless:

(i)   the employment was wholly outside Great Britain; or

(ii)   the employee was not ordinarily resident in Great Britain.

(*ERA 1996, s 196(5)* now repealed); see, eg *Wood v Cunard Line Ltd* [1991] ICR 13.)

Employees engaged upon certain activities connected with offshore drilling were given employment protection rights by the *Employment Protection (Offshore Employment) Order 1976 (SI 1976/766)*. See *Addison*, above, and *ERA 1996, s 201*.

53.16 EMPLOYEE CANNOT ENFORCE RIGHTS IF CONTRACT ILLEGAL

The courts will not enforce an illegal contract. Thus, if it appears to an employment tribunal that, for example, a contract of employment was entered into with an agreement that no tax be paid on some part or all of the remuneration, the tribunal may consider the agreement to be a fraud on the Inland Revenue and may dismiss the claim. The position will normally be different if the employee was innocent of any wrongdoing, or if he merely performed some unlawful act in the course of an otherwise lawful employment. The leading case is *Colen v Cebrian (UK) Ltd* [2004] IRLR 210 and reference should also be made to *Enfield Technical Services v Payne* [2008] ICR 1423, *ParkingEye Ltd v Somerfield Stores Ltd* [2013] QB 840 and *Patel v Mirza* [2016] 3 WLR 399. For a fuller discussion, see **8.24** CONTRACT OF EMPLOYMENT.

53.17 DISMISSAL IN CONNECTION WITH A LOCK-OUT OR STRIKE

Official action

The law relating to unfair dismissals in the context of official industrial action was changed substantially by *Employment Relations Act 1999, s 16* and *Sch 5*, which introduced a new *TULCRA 1992, s 238A* from 24 April 2000. (See *Employment Relations Act 1999 (Commencement No 5 and Transitional Provision) Order 2000, art 3 (SI 2000/875)*) (*TULRCA 1992, s 238*, as amended by *TURERA 1993, Sch 8 para 77* and *ERA 1996, Sch 1 para 56*). *Section 238A* was amended further by the *Employment Relations Act 2004*.

Prior to the changes introduced by *Sch 5* and the *Employment Relations Act 2004*, employees who took part in lawful industrial action lost their right to claim unfair dismissal if they were dismissed whilst the industrial action was taking place and all other employees who were taking part in the industrial action were similarly dismissed. The main consequences of the changes were that:

(a)   the right to claim unfair dismissal is restored for many employees who are taking part in lawful, official, industrial action, provided that the reason for their dismissal is their participation in the industrial action; and

(b)   dismissal for such a reason will, in such cases, be automatically unfair.

TULRCA 1992, s 238, as amended by *Sch 5*, provides that the exclusion from the right to claim unfair dismissal if dismissal takes place during industrial action will not apply where the employee is regarded as unfairly dismissed by reason of *TULRCA 1992, s 238A*. An employee will be treated as being unfairly dismissed by reason of *s 238A* if the employee is taking part in protected industrial action and if certain other conditions (set out below) are satisfied.

53.17 Unfair Dismissal – I: The Right to Make a Claim

Section 238A defines 'protected industrial action' as meaning action which was induced by an act protected by *TULRCA 1992, s 219* (see **45.3 STRIKES AND INDUSTRIAL ACTION**). In effect, 'protected industrial action' is official industrial action in respect of which the trade union concerned and its officials enjoy immunity from suit.

An employee will be treated as having been automatically unfairly dismissed if the reason or principal reason for dismissal was that the employee has taken part in protected industrial action and:

(i)   the date of dismissal is within the protected period; or

(ii)   the date of dismissal is after the end of protected period and the employee had stopped taking protected industrial action before the end of that period; or

(iii) the date of dismissal is after the end of the protected period, the employee had not stopped taking protected industrial action before the end of that period, and the employer had not taken such procedural steps as would have been reasonable for the purposes of resolving the dispute to which the protected industrial action relates.

An employee may be taking part in industrial action even though he is not in breach of his contract of employment, eg by refusing to work overtime (*Power Packing Casemakers Ltd v Faust* [1983] ICR 292). Industrial action will generally exist where there is concerted action involving the application of pressure in the search for some advantage (*Glenrose (Fish Merchants) Ltd v Chapman*, IDS Brief 438, p 5). One person may be involved in industrial action on his own (*Lewis and Britton v E Mason & Sons* [1994] IRLR 4).

In deciding whether the employer has taken reasonable procedural steps, the tribunal must consider whether the employer complied with procedures set out in any relevant collective bargaining agreement, whether the employer or the union agreed to take part in negotiations after the industrial action had commenced, and whether the employer or the union had unreasonably refused to take part in conciliation or mediation. *TULCRA 1992, s 238A(7)* provides that in deciding whether the employer has taken reasonable procedural steps, the tribunal should take no account of the merits of the dispute which gave rise to the industrial action.

The above provisions represented a major change in the law relating to unfair dismissal in the context of official industrial action. It should be emphasised that not that every employee who is dismissed whilst taking part in official industrial action will be deemed to be unfairly dismissed. It is only if the reason for dismissal is that the employee was taking part in the protected industrial action that the dismissal will be automatically unfair. If the employee is dismissed for some other reason, such as misconduct or redundancy, during the relevant period, the dismissal will not be automatically unfair; rather, the tribunal will consider whether the dismissal was fair applying normal principles. Similarly, if the employee is dismissed for inducing the industrial action, rather than being induced, the dismissal will not be automatically unfair under *s 238A*.

There may still be cases in which the right to claim unfair dismissal will be excluded, namely, if the whole of the part of the workforce which is taking part in industrial action is dismissed and the conditions set out in *s 238A* are not satisfied, for example because the industrial action has lasted for more than the protected period and the employer has taken reasonable procedural steps to resolve the dispute. In practice, however, *TULRCA 1992, s 238A* is likely to deter employers from dismissing all employees who are taking part in industrial action, because of the risk that this will lead to a finding that each of the employees concerned has been automatically unfairly dismissed.

TULRCA 1992, s 239(4) provides that if a claim for unfair dismissal arising out of protected industrial action succeeds, a tribunal should not consider the question of reinstatement or re-engagement until after the end of the employee's participation in the protected industrial action.

1318

53.18 Unofficial action

TULRCA 1992, s 237 provides that an employee has no right to complain of unfair dismissal if at the time of dismissal he was taking part in an unofficial strike or other unofficial industrial action (see *Sehmi v Gate Gourmet* [2009] IRLR 807). This bar to jurisdiction is different from that contained in *TULRCA 1992, s 238*. The effect of the change is that, where the employees take part in unofficial industrial action, the employer can dismiss selectively without the tribunal thereby acquiring jurisdiction to hear a complaint of unfair dismissal. It is immaterial whether participation in the unofficial action was in fact the reason for the dismissal.

The time of dismissal means:

(a)   where the employee's contract is terminated by notice, when the notice is given;

(b)   where the contract is terminated without notice, when the termination takes effect; and

(c)   where the employee is employed under a fixed-term contract which expires without renewal, when that term expires.

(*TULRCA 1992, s 237(5)*.)

The test of whether a person is taking part in unofficial action at a particular time will presumably be the same as in cases under *TULRCA 1992, s 238* (see **53.17** above).

Industrial action will be unofficial in relation to the dismissed employee unless:

(i)   that employee is a member of a union which has authorised or endorsed the action;

(ii)   the employee is not a union member, but those taking part in the action include members of a union which has authorised or endorsed it; or

(iii)   none of those taking part in the action are union members.

(*TULRCA 1992, s 237(2)*.)

Thus, if the employee is a union member, his own union *must* have authorised or endorsed the action if it is not to be unofficial. If he is not, then if there are *any* union members among the participants, at least one union whose members are involved must have authorised or endorsed the action if it is not to be unofficial.

For the purposes of determining whether industrial action is to be taken to have been endorsed by a union, *TULRCA 1992, s 20(2)* is to be applied, by reference to the facts as at the time of dismissal (see **48.16 TRADE UNIONS – I**). However, a repudiation under *TULRCA 1992, s 21* does not make action unofficial before the end of the next working day (*TULRCA 1992, s 237(3), (4)*).

For the purposes of *s 237*, membership of a union for purposes unconnected with the employment in question shall be disregarded. But an employee who is a union member when he starts to take part in action will be treated as such throughout the action even if he ceases to be a member (*TULRCA 1992, s 237(6)*).

Again, the exclusion of jurisdiction does not apply if the reason for the dismissal is one specified in *ERA 1996, ss 98B,99, 100, 101A(d), 103, 103A, 104, or 104C* (jury service, family, health and safety, working time or redundancy or transfer of undertaking employee representative, protected disclosure cases, or assertion of statutory right to take time off work for dependants).

53.19 NO CONTRACTING OUT

With certain exceptions (see **53.20** below), any agreement to prevent any person from presenting or pursuing a complaint of unfair dismissal is void (*ERA 1996, s 203(1)*). A clause in a contract of employment purporting to exclude this right will be ineffective, leaving the employee free to pursue a claim for unfair dismissal in the employment tribunal. In *Igbo v Johnson Matthey Chemicals Ltd* [1986] ICR 505, the Court of Appeal held that a variation of an employment contract which provided that if an employee failed to return from a period of leave on a certain date, her contract would be automatically terminated, converted a right not to be unfairly dismissed into a conditional right not to be dismissed; accordingly, it was void by reason of *EPCA 1978, s 140(1)* (the predecessor section of *ERA 1996, s 203(1)*). However, in *Scott v Coalite Fuels and Chemicals Ltd* [1988] ICR 355, an employee who had agreed to accept voluntary retirement as an alternative to redundancy was not successful in putting forward a similar argument. In *Salton (Logan) v Durham County Council* [1989] IRLR 99, EAT, a case where an employee under threat of dismissal agreed terms for termination, *Igbo* was distinguished on the grounds that this was a separate contract from the contract of employment, entered into without duress, after proper advice and for good consideration, and that termination was not contingent upon the happening of future events in circumstances which the parties might not have envisaged. In *M&P Steelcraft Ltd v Ellis* [2008] ICR 578 the EAT suggested that the conditions necessary for an infringement of *ERA 1996, s 203* were (i) that 'but for' the clause in question the employee would have enforceable statutory rights and (ii) that the only purpose of the clause must be to alter, or seek to alter, what would, absent the clause, be the legal effect of the contractual arrangements.

Similarly, any agreement to pay an ex-employee money in consideration for his refraining from presenting or pursuing a complaint in an employment tribunal is normally unenforceable, subject to the exceptions considered in **53.20** below.

53.20 Exceptions

An agreement restricting the right to claim for unfair dismissal is enforceable if it is contained in the following agreements:

(a)   a valid settlement agreement satisfying the statutory conditions, including that the employee should have taken independent legal advice (see **19.20** EMPLOYMENT TRIBUNALS – I and note *Hinton v University of East London* [2005] EWCA Civ 532, [2005] IRLR 552 and *Industrious Ltd v Horizon Recruitment Ltd (in liq)* [2010] IRLR 204) (*ERA 1996, s 203(2)*);

(b)   a dismissal procedure agreement reached between employers and one or more independent trade unions which has been approved by the Secretary of State;

(c)   any agreement to refrain from presenting a complaint that he was unfairly dismissed where the conciliation officer has taken action in accordance with his statutory duties (see **2.3** ADVISORY, CONCILIATION AND ARBITRATION SERVICE (ACAS));

(d)   any agreement to refrain from proceeding with a complaint where the conciliation officer has taken action in accordance with his statutory duties (see **2.3** ADVISORY, CONCILIATION AND ARBITRATION SERVICE (ACAS)). Where there has been a transfer of an undertaking for the purposes of the *Transfer of Undertakings (Protection of Employment) Regulations 2006 (SI 2006/246)*, such an agreement if made by the transferor and not finalised until after the transfer will not prevent an employee from claiming against the transferee (*Thompson v Walon Car Delivery* [1997] IRLR 343).

54   Unfair Dismissal – II: The Fairness of the Dismissal

Cross-references. See Unfair Dismissal – I (53) for the right to make a claim; Unfair Dismissal – III (55) for remedies for unfair dismissal.

54.1   REASONS FOR DISMISSAL

Once the fact of dismissal has been established, it is for the employer to show (*ERA 1996, s 98(1)*):

(a)   what was the reason (or, if there was more than one, the principal reason) for the dismissal; and

(b)   that it was one of the reasons set out in **54.2** below.

An employment tribunal will investigate the real reason for the dismissal of the employee. The fact that an employer told an employee that the reason for his dismissal was redundancy will not preclude the tribunal from deciding that, for example, the real reason for dismissal was lack of capability. A reason for dismissal is a set of facts known to the employer or of beliefs held by it, which cause it to dismiss the employee (*Abernethy v Mott, Hay and Anderson* [1974] ICR 323). The same approach applies even where the organisation in question did not believe at the time that it was the employee's employer, though this may of course impact on the issue of fairness when the procedure followed comes to be assessed (*Dye v Royal Free London NHS Foundation Trust* (UKEAT/0350/15/DA) (14 September 2016, unreported)). The facts which cause the employer to act as he does are to be treated as the reason for the dismissal even if the employer does not realise that his actions amount to a dismissal (*Ely v YKK Fasteners (UK) Ltd* [1994] ICR 164). The tribunal should not find for the employer on a ground not argued before it if this would prejudice the employee who, for example, might have put his case differently if he was aware that the argument was being run (*Hannan v TNT-Ipec (UK) Ltd* [1986] IRLR 165). Whether or not it does so is a fact-sensitive question for the Tribunal (*Secretary of State for Justice v Norridge (UKEAT/0443/13/LA)* (10 March 2014, unreported) and see further **54.2**).

If there is a dispute over the reason for the dismissal, the burden of proving which one of the competing reasons for the dismissal was the principal reason is on the employer (*Maund v Penwith District Council* [1984] ICR 143). Additionally, the employer will only be allowed to rely upon facts known to him at the time of the dismissal to establish what the reason for the dismissal was. Thus, facts which come to light after the dismissal cannot be relied upon to justify the dismissal, although they may affect the level of compensation (*W Devis & Sons Ltd v Atkins* [1977] ICR 662; and see **55.13** Unfair Dismissal – III).

When a dismissal is by notice, the employer's reason for the dismissal must be determined both by reference to the reason for giving the notice to terminate and by reference to the reason when dismissal occurs (*Parkinson v Marc Consulting Ltd* [1998] ICR 276).

Complexities can arise in cases where a dismissing officer has to obtain authorisation for his or her decision. Whose reasons should be treated as determinative will depend upon the facts of each case. Helpful guidance has been given by the EAT in *GM Packaging (UK) Ltd v Haslem* (UKEAT/0259/13/LA29) (29 January 2014, unreported). The Court of Appeal reiterated the importance of identifying the correct decision-maker(s) when ascertaining the reason for dismissal, and considered how the motives of other employees may be attributed to the correct decision-maker(s), in *Co-operative Group Ltd v Baddeley* [2014] EWCA Civ 658.

54.1 Unfair Dismissal – II

Where the dismissal in question is constructive, the reason for dismissal is determined by asking why the employer behaved in the way that gave rise to the fundamental breach (or breaches) of contract. That is determined by analysis of the employer's reasons for so acting, no the employee's perception (*Wyeth v Salisbury NHS Foundation Trust* (UKEAT/0061/15/JOJ) (12 June 2015, unreported)).

54.2 Acceptable reasons for dismissal

The following are acceptable reasons for dismissal (*ERA 1996, s 98(1), (2)*):

(a) reasons related to the capability or qualifications of the employee for performing work of the kind which he was employed to do;

(b) reasons related to the conduct of the employee;

(c) that the employee was redundant (for the definition of 'redundancy' see **38.7 REDUNDANCY – I**);

(d) that the employee could not continue to work in the position which he held without contravention (either on his part or on that of his employer) of a duty or restriction imposed by or under an enactment; or

(e) some other substantial reason of a kind such as to justify the dismissal of an employee holding the position which that employee held.

Until 6th April 2011, retirement was an additional potentially fair reason for dismissal under *ERA 1996, s 98(2)(ba)*. This has been repealed by the *Employment Equality (Repeal of Retirement Age Provisions) Regulations 2011*. Retirement is no longer a potentially fair reason for dismissal and will have to be brought under one of the other headings (most likely the "some other substantial reason" category). This will be considered further at **54.4** below.

It is a question for the tribunal to determine under which, if any, of the acceptable reasons the employer's reason for dismissal falls. This was emphasised by the EAT in *UPS Ltd v Harrison* (UKEAT/0038/11/RN) (16 January 2012, unreported). The tribunal should first make findings as to the employer's own reasons for dismissal. It should then ask itself how those reasons are best characterised in terms of *ERA 1996, s 98*. Whilst the tribunal is not bound by the employer's label, it must seek to characterise the employer's own reasons (i.e. the reasons which the tribunal finds, as a matter of fact, led the employer to dismiss), rather than substitute its own view as to the reason for the dismissal. To take an example of this approach in practice, where the reason for dismissal put forward by the employer was 'incapability by reason of unsatisfactory attendance record', but it was clear that the reason for the dismissal was the claimant's poor attendance and not the ill health which caused this attendance, the tribunal erred in law in characterising the reason for the dismissal as 'capability' rather than 'some other substantial reason' (*Wilson v Post Office* [2000] IRLR 834).

Whilst the tribunal needs to consider whether the reason for dismissal falls within any of the acceptable categories, when it comes to assess whether the dismissal was reasonable in all the circumstances (and therefore fair) it needs to do so by reference the live, operative reason, rather than the statutory label. To take a common instance, in a misconduct case, the tribunal should assess the fairness of the dismissal by reference to the conduct which caused the employer to dismiss, rather than by reference to an abstract notion of misconduct (*Vodafone Ltd v Nicholson* (UKEAT/0605/12/SM) (17 May 2013, unreported)). The tribunal should focus on the whole of the conduct which caused the employer to dismiss, not just part of it (*GM Packaging (UK) Ltd v Haslem* (UKEAT/0259/13/LA29) (29 January 2014, unreported) and *Marl International Ltd v Dickinson* (UKEAT/0447/12/KN) (22 February 2013, unreported)). However, it remains possible for a dismissal being found to be fair by reference to part of the reason for dismissal, even if the employer could not reasonably have dismissed in reliance upon some other part of the reason (*Robinson v Combat Stress* (UKEAT/0310/14/JOJ) (5 December 2014)). The EAT has confirmed that the same analysis applies in relation to reasons for dismissal other than misconduct, such as capability (*Devon & Cornwall Police and Crime Commissioner v Weavin* (UKEAT/0215/14/DA) (13 November 2014)).

In *Choksi v Royal Mail Group Ltd* (UKEAT/0280/15/LA) (21 January 2016, unreported), the EAT considered the following situation: (i) a dismissing officer dismisses for two instances of misconduct (A and B), but accepts that A, by itself, would not have justified the dismissal; (ii) an appeal officer upholds the dismissal, but also states that in his view, A by itself justified dismissal; (iii) the Employment Tribunal finds that the employer did not act reasonably in dismissing the employee for B, but acted reasonably in dismissing in relation to A. Is that approach permissible? As the EAT noted, if it is, it leads to an odd result; the employee would have been better placed having not appealed and gone straight to the Employment Tribunal, as the dismissal based on B would have been found to be unfair, and the dismissing officer would not have dismissed for A alone. That said, the reasonableness of a decision to dismiss is usually be scrutinised by reference to the process as a whole, including any appeal hearing (*West Midland Co-operative Society Ltd v Tipton* [1986] ICR 192). The EAT did not provide an absolute answer to this issue. Rather it found that the Employment Tribunal erred in law by failing to consider the differences in the reasoning of the dismissing and appeal officers on its decision, and remitted the matter for further consideration. As the EAT noted, the issue no doubt requires further analysis. In the meantime, it is submitted that the orthodox approach remains that the Employment Tribunal should examine the process as a whole, including the appeal, by reference to *ERA 1996, s 98(4)*. The view taken by the appeal officer remains relevant. That said, the fact that the dismissing officer did not consider dismissal justified for a certain act will is likely to impact significantly upon the Employment Tribunal's analysis of whether or not the dismissal was ultimately within the range of reasonable responses or not.

If a claimant positively asserts a different and inadmissible reason for dismissal, he must produce some evidence to support his case (see *Kuzel v Roche Products Ltd* [2008] ICR 799 where the claimant asserted that he had been dismissed because he made a protected disclosure). The claimant does not bear the burden of proving that reason, but some evidence must be put before the tribunal in support of his assertion. As the Court of Appeal stated in *Kuzel*, if the tribunal finds that the reason put forward by the employer was not, in fact, the reason for the dismissal, it is not correct to say, as a matter of law or logic, that it must find that the reason was that asserted by the employee (though as the court also noted, this will often be the case, and the conclusion that the reason advanced has not been proved may well support the employee's case as to the true reason). The same analysis applies outside the context of whistleblowing to other automatically unfair reasons for dismissal (see, in the context of trade union activities, the recent decision in *Serco Ltd v Dahou* [2015] IRLR 30)). In cases where the employee asserts a different reason for dismissal, the tribunal should first consider the potentially fair reason advanced by the employer, since it bears the primary burden, before considering the alternative reasons for dismissal, including those advanced by the employee (*Whitelock and Storr v Khan* (UKEAT/0017/10/RN) (26 October 2010, unreported)), though note the view of the EAT in *Governing Body of John Loughborough School v Alexis* (UKEAT/0583/10/JOJ) (16 December 2011, unreported) to the effect that if an employer's reason is rejected, it has failed to discharge the burden placed upon it by *ERA, s 98(1)* and the dismissal must therefore be unfair (see also *Earl v Slater and Wheeler (Airlyne) Ltd* [1973] 1 WLR 51, observation of Sir John Donaldson *obiter* at 149). In *Secretary of State for Justice v Norridge* (UKEAT/0443/13/LA) (10 March 2014, unreported)) detailed consideration was given to whether a dismissal can be fair where the reason relied upon is not the one pleaded or argued by the employer. The EAT was of the view that it could. The issue is whether or not the difference is one of substance, or is merely a matter of labelling. The question is a fact-sensitive one for the Tribunal to take in the circumstances of each case.

The fact that an employer has a prior reason for wishing to dismiss an employee (such as poor performance) does not by itself mean that, if a different ground for dismissal arises (such as the employee committing an act of gross misconduct), this cannot be the reason or principal reason for a subsequent dismissal. The fact that the employer welcomes the opportunity to dismiss does not mean that, in this example, misconduct was not the sole or principal reason for the dismissal having occurred (*Governing Body of John Loughborough School v Alexis* (UKEAT/0583/10/JOJ) (16 December 2011, unreported), following *ASLEF v Brady* [2006] IRLR 576). These principles have been confirmed by the Court of Appeal in *Co-operative Group Ltd v Baddeley* [2014] EWCA Civ 658. However, as the Court of Appeal emphasised, in such a case, determining the reason or principal reason will be a complex factual question for the tribunal and the employer's case is likely to be subject to a significant degree of scrutiny.. The latter point is well illustrated by the facts in *Governing Body of John Loughborough School v Alexis*, where the EAT upheld the tribunal's finding that the principal reason for the dismissal was not misconduct as alleged by the employer, but the employer's pre-existing views about the claimant's inadequate performance.

This chapter first considers the unacceptable reasons for dismissal (see **54.3** below), followed by the criteria for assessment of the fairness of a dismissal where the reason is acceptable (see **54.4** below). Finally, each of the acceptable reasons listed above are addressed in more detail in turn (see **54.5** and onwards below).

54.3   DISMISSALS WHICH ARE DEEMED UNFAIR

The *Employment Rights Act 1996* sets out a number of circumstances in which a dismissal will be deemed to be unfair automatically. Additionally, most of the following automatically unfair reasons for dismissal will render the dismissal unfair if they constitute the reason for which an employee was selected for redundancy (see **54.11**(a) below). In most cases, where an employee has been dismissed for an automatically unfair reason it will also be possible for the tribunal to hear the claim and pronounce the dismissal unfair when it would not normally have jurisdiction to do so because the employee lacked sufficient continuous service though significantly, this is not the case in relation to dismissals rendered unfair by the *Transfer of Undertakings (Protection of Employment) Regulations 2006 (SI 2006/246)* (see UNFAIR DISMISSAL – I (53)). However, in such cases the burden of proving that the reason for dismissal was the inadmissible reason rests on the employee (*Smith v Hayle Town Council* [1978] ICR 996; *Maund v Penwith District Council* [1984] ICR 143; *Ross v Eddie Stobart Ltd* (UKEAT/0068/13/RN) (8 August 2013, unreported).

(a) Employer's failure to follow statutory dismissal and disciplinary procedures

The *Employment Act 2002, s 34* inserted a new *s 98A* into the *Employment Rights Act 1996*, concerning statutory dismissal and disciplinary procedures. These procedures were repealed on 6 April 2009. They continued to apply, during a transitional period, to cases where the trigger event occurred prior to the date of repeal. The number of cases to which they are relevant is now low, although there continue to be some, mostly at appellate level, where they fall to be considered.

Section 98A(1) rendered a dismissal automatically unfair if: (i) one of the statutory disciplinary procedures set out in Sch 2 applied in relation to the dismissal; (ii) the procedure had not been completed; and (iii) the non-completion of the procedure was wholly or mainly attributable to failure by the employer to comply with its requirements. The *Employment Act 2002 (Dispute Resolution) Regulations 2004 (SI 2004/752)* ("the

Dispute Resolution Regulations") described the circumstances and manner in which the statutory dismissal and disciplinary procedures applied. These procedures will not be considered further in this chapter due to their diminishing significance in practice. Previous editions may be referred to for a detailed discussion of their operation.

(b) Union-membership, participation and non-membership dismissals

The dismissal of an employee will automatically be regarded as unfair if the reason or principal reason for it was that the employee (*TULRCA 1992, s 152*):

(i) was, or proposed to become, a member of an independent trade union;

(ii) had taken part, or proposed to take part, in the activities of an independent trade union at an appropriate time;

(iii) had made use, or proposed to make use, of trade union services at an appropriate time;

(iv) had failed to accept an inducement contrary to *TULRCA 1992, s 145A* or *145B;* or

(v) was not a member of any trade union, or of a particular trade union, or of one of a number of particular trade unions, or had refused, or proposed to refuse, to become or remain a member.

There is no need for an employee to have been employed for any qualifying period to present a complaint on this ground (*TULRCA 1992, s 154*). Where the employee has not been employed for the qualifying period, the burden of proving that the reason for dismissal was union-related is upon the employee (*Smith v Hayle Town Council* [1978] ICR 996; *Maund v Penwith District Council* [1984] ICR 143).

An 'independent trade union' is defined as any union which is not under the control or domination of an employer (*TULRCA 1992, s 5*) (see **50.22** Trade Unions – I).

'Membership of a trade union' within the meaning of *TULRCA 1992, s 152* was construed broadly by the EAT in *Discount Tobacco and Confectionery Ltd v Armitage* [1995] ICR 431 to include approaching a trade union officer to enlist his help in elucidating and attempting to negotiate terms and conditions of employment. *Discount Tobacco v Armitage* was followed by the EAT in *Speciality Care plc v Pachela* [1996] ICR 633.

Such action may, alternatively, be considered to be taking part in the activities of a trade union (*Dixon and Shaw v West Ella Developments* [1978] ICR 856; see also *British Airways Engine Overhaul Ltd v Francis* [1981] ICR 278). For an employee to be taking part in the activities of a trade union, the activity must be that of the union and not merely that of an individual who happens to belong to a union (*Drew v St Edmundsbury Borough Council* [1980] ICR 513, holding also that trade union activity within *s 152* did not include the taking of industrial action). The dismissal of an employee because of union activities with a previous employer can come within *s 152*, although dismissing an employee for failing to tell the truth about past activities would not (*Fitzpatrick v British Railways Board* [1992] ICR 221).

'An appropriate time', in relation to an employee taking part in the activities of a trade union, means a time which either (*TULRCA 1992, s 152(2)*):

(A) is outside his working hours; or

(B) is a time within his working hours at which, in accordance with arrangements agreed with or consent given by his employers, it is permissible for him to take part in those activities or make use of trade union services.

'Working hours', in relation to an employee, means any time when, in accordance with his contract of employment, he is required to be at work (*TULRCA 1992, s 152(2)*). Consent for these purposes may be express or implied (*Marley Tile Co Ltd v Shaw* [1980] ICR 72).

It is not necessary for the employee to show that the employer's actions were motivated by malice or anti-union hostility (*Dundon v GPT Ltd* [1995] IRLR 403).

Dismissal for conduct which on its own would justify dismissal, such as assault, may not become automatically unfair simply because it took place in the course of union activities, though in *Bass Taverns v Burgess* [1995] IRLR 596 the Court of Appeal held a dismissal to be automatically unfair under *s 152* even though the employee had gone 'over the top' in making critical remarks about the employer. A similar point was made in relation to the retention of unlawfully obtained information by the EAT in *Metrolink Ratpdev Ltd v Morris* (UKEAT/0113/16/RN) (15 December 2016, unreported).

Closed shop. Under the relevant provisions of *TULRCA 1992*, all dismissals to enforce a closed shop are now automatically unfair (see Trade Unions – II (51) for more detail on the issue of closed shops).

(c) Health and safety-related dismissals

The dismissal of an employee will automatically be regarded as unfair if the reason or principal reason for it was that the employee (*ERA 1996, s 100(1)*, as amended):

(i)   having been designated by the employer to carry out activities in connection with preventing or reducing risks to health and safety at work, carried out, or proposed to carry out, any such activities;

(ii)   being a representative of workers on matters of health and safety at work, or a member of a safety committee in accordance with arrangements established under or by virtue of any enactment, or by reason of being acknowledged as such by the employer, performed or proposed to perform any functions as such a representative or a member of such a committee;

(iii) took part (or proposed to take part) in consultation with the employer pursuant to the *Health and Safety (Consultation with Employees) Regulations 1996 (SI 1996/1513)* (see 28.22 Health and Safety at Work – II) or in an election of representatives within the meaning of those *Regulations*, whether as a candidate or otherwise;

(iv)   being an employee at a place where there was no such representative or safety committee, or where it was not reasonably practicable for the employee to raise the matter by means of the representative or safety committee, brought to his employer's attention by reasonable means circumstances connected with his work which he reasonably believed were harmful or potentially harmful to health or safety;

(v)   in circumstances of danger which he reasonably believed to be serious and imminent and which he could not reasonably have been expected to avert, left or proposed to leave or (while the danger persisted) refused to return to his place of work or any dangerous part of his place of work; or

(vi)   in circumstances of danger which he reasonably believed to be serious and imminent, took or proposed to take appropriate steps to protect himself or other persons from the danger.

In the case of (vi) above, whether the steps in question were appropriate will be judged by reference to all the circumstances, including in particular the employee's knowledge and the facilities and advice available to him at the time. The dismissal will not be unfair if the

(vi)   time off for dependants under *ERA 1996, s 57A*.

(vii)   time off for ante-natal appointments under *ERA 1996, s 57ZE*

(viii)   time off for adoption appointments under *ERA 1996, s 57ZJ or s 57ZL*

and which reason has been prescribed by the Secretary of State in regulations.

Given recent steps to provide parents with great flexibility in relation to time off, it is important that employers and practitioners give careful consideration to the various regulations which give effect to these rights. A full discussion of these complicated provisions is outside the scope of this chapter, which are instead considered in detail at **32.7** Maternity and Parental Rights.

(f) Pension scheme trustees

An employee's dismissal will automatically be regarded as unfair if the reason or principal reason for it is that, being a trustee of a trust scheme which relates to his employment, the employee performed (or proposed to perform) any functions as such a trustee (*ERA 1996, s 102*).

(g) Employee representatives

An employee's dismissal will automatically be regarded as unfair if the reason or principal reason for it is that the employee, being (*ERA 1996, s 103*):

(i)   an employee representative for the purposes of *TULRCA 1992, Part IV Chapter 2* (see **39.4** Redundancy – **II**) or *Transfer of Undertakings (Protection of Employment) Regulations 1981 (SI 1981/1794)*, and from 6 April 2006 the *2006 Regulations (SI 2006/246)* (see **52.18** Transfer of Undertakings); or

(ii)   a candidate in an election for such an employee representative,

performed, or proposed to perform, any functions or activities as such an employee representative or candidate. A dismissal will also be automatically unfair if the reason or principal reason is the employee's participation in an election for employee representatives in a redundancy or transfer of undertakings context.

Similarly, dismissals of employee representatives contrary to the *Occupational and Personal Pension Schemes (Consultation by Employers and Miscellaneous Amendment) Regulations 2006 (SI 2006/349) (para 5, Sch)* are automatically unfair, as are dismissals contrary to the *European Cooperative Society (Involvement of Employees) Regulations 2006 (SI 2006/2059) (reg 31)*.

(h) Shop workers and betting workers who refuse Sunday work

These provisions were introduced by the *Sunday Trading Act 1994* (shop workers) and the *Deregulation and Contracting Out Act 1994* (betting workers) and are now contained in *ERA 1996, s 101* (see **8.48** Contract of Employment). The dismissal of an employee who is a shop worker or betting worker will automatically be regarded as unfair if the reason or principal reason for the dismissal is that the employee:

(i)   being a protected shop worker or an opted-out shop worker, or a protected betting worker or an opted-out betting worker, refused (or proposed to refuse) to do shop work, or betting work, on Sunday or on a particular Sunday, except (in the case of an opted-out shop worker or an opted-out betting worker) in respect of any Sunday or Sundays falling before the opting-out notice expired; or

(ii)   gave (or proposed to give) an opting-out notice to the employer.

(j) Working time cases

An employee's dismissal will automatically be regarded as unfair if the reason or principal reason for the dismissal is that the employee (*ERA 1996, s 101A*):

(i)   refused (or proposed to refuse) to comply with a requirement which the employer imposed (or proposed to impose) in contravention of the *Working Time Regulations 1998* (or the *Merchant Shipping (Working Time: Inland Waterways) Regulations 2003*; the *Fishing Vessels (Working Time: Sea-fishermen) Regulations 2004*; the *Cross-border Railway Services (Working Time) Regulations 2008* and the *Merchant Shipping (Hours of Work) Regulations 2002*).

(ii)   refused (or proposed to refuse) to forgo a right conferred on him by those regulations;

(iii)   failed to sign a workforce agreement for the purposes of those regulations, or to enter into, or agree to vary or extend, any other agreement with his employer which is provided for in those *Regulations*; or

(iv)   being a representative of members of the workforce for the purposes of *Sch 1* to those regulations, or a candidate in an election for such a representative, performed (or proposed to perform) any functions or activities as such a representative or candidate.

(k) Unfair selection for redundancy

A dismissal for redundancy will be unfair if the circumstances constituting the redundancy applied equally to one or more other employees in similar positions and the sole or principal reason for dismissal was automatically unfair. These are set out in *ERA 1996, s 105* (see below) and are broadly aligned with the automatically unfair reasons for dismissal.

(l) Dismissals on a transfer of an undertaking

Where either before or after a relevant transfer, any employee of the transferor or transferee is dismissed, that employee shall *prima facie* be treated as unfairly dismissed if the transfer or a reason connected with it is the reason or principal reason for his dismissal (*Transfer of Undertakings (Protection of Employment) Regulations 2006 (SI 2006/246), reg 7(1)(a)*)). However, the dismissal is not *automatically* unfair if the reason for it falls within *reg7(1)(b)*, that is if it is for an economic, technical or organisational reason entailing changes in the workforce. This is a complicated area of law outside the scope of this Chapter. It is considered in detail in Transfer of Undertakings (52).

(m) Spent convictions

A spent conviction or a failure to disclose it is not a proper ground for dismissal (see **17.3** Employee's Past Criminal Convictions).

(n) National Minimum Wage cases

This provision was inserted into *ERA 1996* by the *National Minimum Wage Act 1998, s 25* (see **34.9** Pay – I). A dismissal will automatically be regarded as unfair if the reason or principal reason for the dismissal is that (*ERA 1996, s 104A*):

(i)   any action was taken, or was proposed to be taken, by or on behalf of the employee with a view to enforcing, or otherwise securing the benefit of, specified rights granted under the *National Minimum Wage Act 1998* (namely any right for which the remedy for its infringement is a complaint to the Employment Tribunal and any right conferred by *section 17*);

(ii)   the employer was prosecuted for any offence under the *National Minimum Wage Act 1998, s 31*, by reason of any action taken by or on behalf of the employee; or

(iii)   the employee qualifies, or will or might qualify, for the National Minimum Wage or for a particular rate of the National Minimum Wage.

It is immaterial whether the employee in fact has the right to the National Minimum Wage or that right has been infringed, provided that the claim made by or on behalf of the employee was made in good faith.

(o) Public interest disclosure cases

This provision was inserted into *ERA 1996, ss 103A and 105(6A)* by the *Public Interest Disclosure Act 1998, s 5* (see **10.17 Disclosure of Information** for a detailed discussion of this complicated topic). An employee's dismissal will automatically be regarded as unfair if the reason or principal reason for the dismissal is that the employee made a protected disclosure as defined in *ERA 1996, ss 43A–43L* (*ERA 1996, s 103A*). There is no statutory maximum cap upon compensation in public interest disclosure cases (*ERA 1996, s 124(1A)*). In *Stolt Offshore Ltd v Miklaszewicz* [2002] IRLR 344, the Scottish Court of Session upheld the EAT's ruling that it was possible to bring a claim under *ERA 1996, ss 103* and *105(6A)* even if the disclosure itself took place many years before the *Public Interest Disclosure Act 1998* came into force, provided that the dismissal itself took place after 2 July 1999.

(p) Dismissals connected with union recognition

Dismissals connected with union recognition are automatically unfair (*TULRCA 1992, Sch A1, para 161*, inserted by *Employment Relations Act 1999, s 1(2)* and *Sch 1*). This applies to dismissals where the reason or main reason is that the employee: (i) acted with a view to obtaining or preventing recognition; (ii) indicated that he supported or did not support recognition; (iii) acted with a view to securing or preventing the ending of bargaining arrangements; (iv) indicated that he supported or did not support the ending of bargaining arrangements; (v) influenced or sought to influence whether other employees voted or how they voted; (vi) voted in such a ballot; or (vii) proposed to do or failed to do or proposed to decline to do, any of the above acts. A dismissal for one of the above reasons will not be automatically unfair, however, if the reason was an unreasonable act or omission by the employee.

(q) Right to be accompanied at disciplinary and grievance hearings

This set of automatically unfair dismissals consists of dismissals of employees because they exercised or sought to exercise the right under *s 10* of the *ERA 1999* to be accompanied at disciplinary and grievance hearings, or because they accompanied a fellow worker to such a hearing (*Employment Relations Act 1999, s 12*). *Sections 10–12* do not apply only to employees in the normal sense used for the purposes of the *ERA 1996* (*ERA 1996, s 230(3)*), but to a wider group of workers set out in *Employment Relations Act 1999, s 13* and include agency workers and home workers.

(r) Protected industrial action

Employment Relations Act 1999, s 16 and *Sch 5* provide that the dismissal of employees who are taking part in protected (ie official) industrial action will be automatically unfair if the conditions set out in the new *TULRCA 1992, s 238A* are satisfied.

(s) Dismissals for asserting the rights of part-time workers

Regulation 7 of the *Part-time Workers (Prevention of Less Favourable Treatment) Regulations 2000* provides that an employee who is dismissed for any of the following reasons will automatically be regarded as having been unfairly dismissed:

(i)   if the employee has brought proceedings against his employer under the *Regulations* or requested a written statement of reasons under the *Regulations*;

(ii)   if the employee has given evidence or information in connection with such proceedings brought by a worker or otherwise done anything under the *Regulations* in relation to the employer or any other person, or alleged that the employer had infringed the *Regulations*;

(iii)   if the employee refused (or proposed to refuse) to forgo a right conferred on him by the *Regulations*; or

(iv)   if the employer believes or suspects that the employee has done or intends to do any of the above things.

(See Part-Time Workers (33))

(t) Action to enforce rights under the Tax Credits Act 1999

ERA 1996, s 104B provides that a dismissal will be automatically unfair if the reason, or principal reason, is that the employee took, or proposed to take, action with a view to enforcing or securing the benefit of a right under *section 25* of the *Tax Credits Act 1999*, or that a penalty was imposed upon the employer or proceedings for a penalty brought as a result of action taken by or on behalf of the employee for the purpose of enforcing that right, or that the employee is entitled, or will or may be entitled to working tax credit.

(u) Activities as a member of special negotiating body, European Works Council, etc

The *Transnational Information and Consultation of Employees Regulations 1999, reg 28* provides that a worker will be automatically unfairly dismissed if the reason or principal reason for the employee's dismissal was that:

(i)   the employee had performed any functions or activities as a member or representative of, or a candidate for, a special negotiating body, a European Works Council, or as an information and consultation representative or as a candidate for such a position; or

(ii)   the employee or a person acting on his behalf asked, or proposed to ask, for time off in relation to such activities; or

(iii)   the employee took specific steps in relation to such activities specified in *reg 28(6)*, including taking proceedings before the Employment Tribunal, the Employment Appeal Tribunal or the CAC, acting with a view to securing that a relevant body did or did not come into existence, voting in a ballot, or seeking to influence others' votes.

The *European Public Limited-Liability Company Regulations 2004, reg 42* and the *Information and Consultation of Employees Regulations 2004, reg 30* create similar protections for employee representatives and candidates, as do the *Companies (Cross-Border) Mergers Regulations 2007.*

(v) Dismissals for asserting the rights of fixed-term employees

Regulation 6 of the *Fixed-term Employees (Prevention of Less Favourable Treatment) Regulations 2002* provides that a dismissal will be automatically unfair if the reason or principal reason was that:

(i)   the employee brought proceedings against his employer under the *Regulations* or requested a written statement of reasons under the *Regulations;*

(ii)   the employee gave evidence or information in connection with such proceedings brought by an employee or otherwise did anything under the *Regulations* in relation to the employer or any other person, or alleged that the employer had infringed the *Regulations*;

(iii)   the employee refused (or proposed to refuse) to forgo a right conferred on him by the *Regulations*;

(iv)   the employee declined to sign a workforce agreement for the purpose of the *Regulations;*

(v)   the employee, being a workforce representative or candidate for the purpose of the *Regulations*, performed (or proposed to perform) any functions or activities in that capacity; or

(vi)   the employer believes or suspects that the employee has done or intends to do any of the above things.

(w) Dismissals for asserting the right to request flexible working

Section 104C of the *ERA 1996* renders a dismissal automatically unfair where the reason (or if more than one, the principal reason) was that the employee:

(i)   made (or proposed to make) an application for a contract variation (see *ERA 1996, s 80F*);

(ii)   (prior to 30 June 2014) exercised (or proposed to exercise) a right conferred on him by *ERA 1996, s 80G* (procedural entitlements);

(iii)   brought proceedings against his employer to enforce the right to request flexible working under *ERA 1996, s 80H*; or

(iv)   alleged the existence of any circumstance which would constitute a ground for bringing such proceedings against his employer.

(See **49.17 Time Off Work**)

(x) Jury service

ERA 1996, s 98B makes a dismissal automatically unfair where the reason or principal reason was that the employee was summoned to do jury service, or was absent from work because he attended at any place in pursuance of being called to perform jury service. The dismissal is not unfair if the employer shows that the circumstances were such that the employee's absence in pursuance of being summoned was likely to cause substantial injury to the employer's undertaking, that the employer brought those circumstances to the attention of the employee, and the employee unreasonably failed or refused to apply to the appropriate officer for excusal from or deferral of the obligation to attend in pursuance of being so summoned.

(y) Participation in Education or Training

ERA 1996, s 101B makes a dismissal automatically unfair where the reason or principal reason was that, being entitled to be permitted to participate in education or training by the *Education and Skills Act 2008, s 27* or *s 28*, the employees exercised or proposed to exercise that right. This provision is yet to be brought into force.

(z) Pension Enrolment

ERA 1996, s 104D makes a dismissal automatically unfair where the reason or principal reason was that:

(i)   any action was taken or was proposed to be taken with a view to enforcing in favour of the employee a requirement to which *ERA 1996, s 104D* applied;

(ii)   the employer was prosecuted for an offence under *Pensions Act 1998, s 45* as a result of action taken for the purpose of enforcing in favour of the employee a requirement to which *ERA 1996, s 104D* applied; or

(iii)   any provision of *Chapter 1* of *Part 1* of the *Pensions Act 1998* applied to the employee or would apply or might have applied.

It is immaterial whether or not the statutory requirement applied in the favour of the employee or whether or not the requirement had been contravened, but the claim that the requirement applied or had been contravened must have been made in good faith (*ERA 1996, s 104D(2)*).

(A) Study and Training

ERA 1996, s 104E makes a dismissal automatically unfair where the reason or principal reason was that the employee:

(i)   made (or proposed to make) an application for time off for study and training under *ERA 1996, s 63D*,

(ii)   exercised (or proposed to exercise) a right conferred on the employee under *ERA 1996, s 63F*,

(iii)   brought proceedings against the employer under *ERA 1996, s 63I*, or

(iv)   alleged the existence of any circumstance which would constitute a ground for bringing such proceedings.

(See EDUCATION AND TRAINING (14)). This does not apply to "small employers" as defined in *Schedule 3* of the *Apprenticeships, Skills, Children and Learning Act 2009 (Commencement No. 2 and Transitional and Saving Provisions) Order 2010*.

(B) Blacklists

ERA 1996, s 104F makes a dismissal automatically unfair where the reason or principal reason relates to a prohibited list and either:

(i)   the employer contravenes *Employment Relations Act 1999 (Blacklists) Regulations 2010, reg 3* in relation to that prohibited list, or

(ii)   the employer—

    (a)   relies on information supplied by a person who contravenes that regulation in relation to that list, and

    (b)   knows or ought reasonably to know that the information relied on is supplied in contravention of that regulation.

(See **51.10** Trade Unions **II**: Individual Rights And Union Membership)

A reverse burden of proof, similar to that used in discrimination claims, applies, so that if there are facts from which the tribunal could conclude, in the absence of any other explanation, that the employer:

(i)   contravened *Employment Relations Act 1999 (Blacklists) Regulations 2010, reg 3*, or

(ii)   relied on information supplied in contravention of that *Regulation,*

the tribunal must find that such a contravention or reliance on information occurred, unless the employer shows that it did not (*ERA 1996 s 104F(2)*).

(C) Agency Workers

Under the *Agency Workers Regulations 2010, reg 17*, a dismissal will be unfair where the reason or principal reason is that:

(i)   the agency worker brought proceedings under the *Agency Workers Regulations 2010*,

(ii)   the agency worker gave evidence or information in connection with such proceedings brought by any agency worker,

(iii)   the agency worker made a request for a written statement under *Agency Workers Regulations, reg 16*,

(iv)   the agency worker otherwise did anything under the *Regulations* in relation to a temporary work agency, hirer or any other person,

(v)   the agency worker alleged that a temporary work agency or hirer had breached the *Regulations*, provided that the allegation is not false and is made in good faith; or

(vi)   the agency worker refused or proposed to refuse to forgo a right conferred by the *Regulations*,

(vii)   the a hirer or a temporary work agency believes or suspects that the agency worker has done or intends to do any of the above protected acts.

(See Temporary and Seasonal Employees (**47**))

(D) Employee Shareholder status

From 1 September 2013, an employee will be regarded as being unfairly dismissed if the reason or principal reason for the dismissal is that the employee refused to accept an offer by the employer for the employee to become an employee shareholder within the meaning of *ERA, s 205A* (*ERA, s 104G*).

54.4   FAIRNESS IN THE CIRCUMSTANCES

If the employer establishes that the reason for the dismissal is an acceptable reason, the tribunal will proceed to determine whether the dismissal was fair or unfair in all the circumstances (which expressly include the size and administrative resources of the employer's undertaking), having regard to equity and the substantial merits of the case (*ERA 1996, s 98(4)*). Whereas the burden of establishing the reason for the dismissal rests on the employer, the burden in relation to this second limb of the tribunal's inquiry is neutral.

A number of principles apply to tribunals' assessment of whether an employer has acted reasonably in dismissing an employee regardless of the reason for dismissal relied upon. This will be discussed in this section. The chapter will then go on to consider the issues which commonly arise when assessing reasonableness in relation to each of the acceptable reasons for dismissal. However, practitioners should have in mind, as the appellate courts frequently reiterate, that the overall question for the tribunal remains whether or not the employer has acted reasonably in dismissing the employee for the reason established, in accordance with *section 98(4)*.

Previously, where an employer could show that the reason for dismissal was retirement, the dismissal was presumed to be fair provided that the employer had followed the procedure set out in *Schedule 6* to the *Employment Equality (Age) Regulations 2006 (ERA 1996, s 98(3A)* and *98ZG)*. Subject to transitional provisions applicable to employees to whom notice of retirement was given prior to 6th April 2011, these provisions have now been repealed by the *Employment Equality (Repeal of Retirement Age Provisions) Regulations 2011*. Employers continuing to operate a retirement age in their workplace will now need to objectively justify the policy, to avoid the dismissal being an act of age discrimination. Further, for the purposes of unfair dismissal, it seems likely that employers will rely upon the dismissal being for "some other substantial reason". If that dismissal is to be fair, it must be procedurally and substantively reasonable. Whilst awaiting authority on the question of what is required in such circumstances, the consultation provisions detailed in *Schedule 6* to the *Employment Equality (Age) Regulations 2006* would seem to be a sensible place for an employer to start.

When addressing fairness in the circumstances, the tribunal will consider whether the employer acted reasonably or unreasonably in treating the reason for the dismissal as a sufficient reason for dismissing the employee. The EAT has reiterated that the tribunal must focus on whether the employer acted reasonably in dismissing for the reason(s) for which the tribunal has found that the employee has been dismissed (see for example *Beaumont v Costco Wholesale UK Limited* (UKEAT/0080/15/DA) (7 July 2015, unreported)). The tribunal should not add or exclude certain reasons based upon its own view or findings when it comes to consider whether the employer acted reasonably in dismissing for those reasons for the purposes of *ERA 1996, s 98(4)* (*O'Hanlon v Post Office Ltd* UKEAT/0202/12/LA (15 October 2012, unreported) and *Nejjary v Aramark Ltd* UKEAT/0054/12/CEA (31 May 2012, unreported)). The Tribunal should look at the totality of the reasons which caused the employer to dismiss (*Governing Body of Beardwood Humanities College v Ham* UKEAT/0379/13/MC (4 April 2014, unreported)). That said, a dismissal may be found to be fair by reference to part of the reason for dismissal, even if the employer could not reasonably have dismissed in reliance upon some other part of the reason (*Robinson v Combat Stress* (UKEAT/0310/14/JOJ) (5 December 2014), though it is important in assessing this question to consider why the employer did in fact dismiss the employee (*Broecker v Metroline Travel Ltd* (UKEAT/0124/16/DM) (unreported, 27 July 2016)).

The tribunal will take into account not only whether the employer had reasonable grounds for dismissing the employee, but also whether it adopted a fair procedure in dismissing him. The correct approach for a tribunal, when applying *ERA 1996, s 98(4)*, is to consider whether the employer's actions, including its decision to dismiss, fell within the band of responses which a reasonable employer could adopt (*Iceland Frozen Foods Ltd v Jones* [1983] ICR 17; *British Leyland (UK) Ltd v Swift* [1981] IRLR 91, CA; *Gilham v Kent County Council (No 2)* [1985] ICR 233; *Neale v Hereford and Worcester County Council* [1986] ICR 471). The tribunal must not substitute its view for that of the employer and judge whether the employer has taken the "correct" approach. Rather it should recognise that different employers may reasonably react in different ways to a particular situation. A finding of unfair dismissal should only be made where an employer's conduct and decision making fell outside the range of reasonable responses. The question is not whether a reasonable employer "would" have dismissed, but whether dismissal was within the range of reasonable responses taking into account that different employers might reach different decisions (see *Mundangepfupfu v Penning Care NHS Foundation Trust* (UKEAT/0109/15/DA) (17 December 2015, unreported)). This approach is different to the approach taken by courts or tribunals in cases of wrongful dismissal (see for instance *Cossington v C2C Rail Ltd* (UKEAT/0053/13/BA) (12 September 2013, unreported)). With this in mind, tribunals have been encouraged by the EAT to make clear in their Reasons what findings of fact they have made about the employer's knowledge and view at the time of the decision to dismiss and what findings they have made for themselves having heard oral evidence. Likewise, the question of fairness for the purpose of *ERA 1996, s 98(4)* does not turn on whether the dismissal is summary or on notice, as recently affirmed in *Savigar v Stoke on Trent City Council* (UKEAT/0228/14/BA) (15 May 2015, unreported).

The 'band of reasonable responses' test does not apply solely to the decision to dismiss. It applies also to the procedure followed by the employer (*Whitbread plc v Hall* [2001] ICR 699; *Sainsbury's Supermarkets Ltd v Hitt* [2003] ICR 111). This includes, in a conduct case, the investigation and the employer's findings and conclusions (*Cossington v C2C Rail Ltd* (above)). Whether or not a procedural defect is sufficient to undermine the fairness of the dismissal as a whole, for the purposes of *ERA 1996, s 98(4)*, is a question for the Tribunal. Not every procedural error will do so. The fairness of the whole process should be looked at, alongside the other relevant factors (*Fuller v Lloyds Bank plc* [1991] IRLR 336); *South London and Maudsley NHS Foundation Trust v Balogun* (UKEAT/0212/14/BA) (17 November 2014, unreported)).

Doubt was cast upon the correctness of the band of reasonable responses approach by the EAT in *Haddon v Van den Bergh Foods Ltd* [1999] ICR 1150. However, the matter was reconsidered by the Court of Appeal in *Foley v Post Office and HSBC Bank (formerly Midland Bank) v Madden* [2000] ICR 1283 and the orthodox position was restored. The Court of Appeal held that tribunals were not to approach the issue of reasonableness by reference to their own judgment of what would have been done if they had been the employer. The test has been applied consistently since Foley (see, for example, *Sarkar v West London Mental Health NHS Trust* [2010] IRLR 508). In *Tuner v East Midlands Trains Ltd* [2013] ICR 525 the Court of Appeal confirmed that the range of reasonable responses test is compatible with *ECHR, Art 8* and reiterated that it should not be equated with the *Wednesbury* unreasonable test applied in administrative law. The Court of Appeal emphasised that the range of reasonable responses is not limitless in *Newbound v Thames Water Utilities Ltd* [2015] IRLR 734. In *O'Brien v Bolton St Catherine's Academy* [2017] EWCA Civ 145 the Court of Appeal reiterated that the range of reasonable responses test was different to that of *Wednesbury* unreasonableness and doubted whether the range of reasonable responses test should yield a different result to the proportionality test in *section 15* of the *Equality Act 2010*.

Before deciding to dismiss, the employer must have investigated the relevant facts adequately. Whether seen as part of following a fair procedure, or as a stand-alone requirement, failing to conduct a reasonable investigation is highly likely to render the dismissal unfair. What is required will of course depend upon the context in each case, as considered in more detail in relation to the different reasons for dismissal below. Provided that requirement is met, however, the reason for, and the fairness of, the action taken by the employer is determined by examining the circumstances known to it at the time of the dismissal or when he maintains that decision at the conclusion of an internal appeal (*West Midlands Co-operative Society Ltd v Tipton* [1986] ICR 192). In *Orr v Milton Keynes Council* [2011] ICR 704, the Court of Appeal (Sedley LJ dissenting) held that the knowledge of an employee is not to be attributed to the dismissing officer for the purposes of deciding whether or not dismissal was fair in the circumstances (though the claimant employee is likely to argue that the employer would have uncovered that knowledge had it conducted a reasonable investigation) (see also **54.10, 54.15** below). An employer cannot be criticised for failing to have regard to material which came to light for the first time as evidence during the tribunal hearing (*Dick v Glasgow University* [1993] IRLR 581).

With regards procedural matters, even if the employer has complied with its own dismissal procedures, or the ACAS Code, the tribunal may nevertheless consider that the employer did not adopt a fair procedure in dismissing the employee. It is therefore important to consider in each case what procedural requirements fairness called for. In this context, the paragraphs in the *ACAS Code of Practice* relating to disciplinary practice and procedures provide useful guidelines but are not prescriptive or exhaustive (*Lock v Cardiff Rly Co* [1998] IRLR 358). The main point of these provisions is that *there should be a known disciplinary procedure which should be followed*. If there is a complaint against an employee, he should be informed in detail and preferably in writing of the complaint, and be given an opportunity to make representations, if necessary through, or in the presence of, an employee representative. (If the employee is a union member, his representative may be his shop steward.) In *Clark v Civil Aviation Authority* [1991] IRLR 412 at para 20, the EAT gave guidance as to how a disciplinary hearing should be conducted. A failure to follow the ACAS Codes of Practice, or internal procedures, is not determinative of the fairness of a dismissal (see *UPS Ltd v Harrison* (UKEAT/0038/11/RN) (16 January 2012, unreported) emphasising that the tribunal must address whether the procedure followed, overall, was reasonable, it being insufficient to simply find that the employer did not follow its own policy). That said, it is important to bear in mind that such a failure can affect the outcome (and frequently does so in practice), and, with the shift of the burden of proof in discrimination cases, a failure to follow a relevant Code of Practice or internal procedure may lead an employment tribunal to infer unlawful discrimination **11.21** Discrimination and Equal Opportunities – I). In that regard, as a general rule, whether a dismissal has been carried out in breach of contract is a relevant factor in assessing its fairness, but is not conclusive (*Hooper v British Railways Board* [1988] IRLR 517; *Post Office v Marney* [1990] IRLR 170; and see *Stoker v Lancashire County Council* [1992] IRLR 75). However, see *Johnston v Welsh National Opera Ltd* [2012] EWCA Civ 1046 for an example of a case where a failure to follow a contractual disciplinary procedure played a very significant role in a finding of unfair dismissal which was upheld by the Court of Appeal. In *Shevlin v Innotech Advisers Ltd & Ors* ((UKEAT/0278/14/BA) (17 July 2015, unreported)), after a detailed analysis of the above authorities and others, the EAT held that the link between a contractual obligation and fairness arises where there can be said to be a coincidence between the right in question and the statutory right not to be dismissed unfairly. A similar approach to a university's statute was applied by the EAT in *Dronsfield v University of Reading* [2016] ICR 1107.

The employee should also be given the opportunity, where practicable, to appeal to a level of management not previously involved (although cf *Robinson v Ulster Carpet Mills Ltd* [1991] IRLR 348). The tribunal must have regard to the appeal process when considering the unfair dismissal claim before it. The Court of Appeal has emphasised that there is no rule of law that earlier unfairness can be cured only by an appeal by way of a rehearing and not by way of a review. The Tribunal should examine the fairness of the disciplinary process as a whole and each case will depend upon its own facts (*Taylor v OCS Group Ltd* [2006] ICR 1602). There are no limitations on the nature and extent of the deficiencies which a thorough and effective appeal can cure (*Khan v Stripestar Ltd* (UKEAT/0022/15/SM) (10 May 2016, unreported)). Two examples illustrate the important role which an appeal can play depending on those facts. In *Scott v Northumbria Probation Board* UKEAT/0451/11/RN (22 May 2012, unreported) a substantial aspect of the original decision to dismiss was overturned by an internal appeal board, but the dismissal was upheld. The EAT held that in such circumstances the individual hearing the appeal necessarily puts itself in the position of being the principal decision-maker and the tribunal must focus carefully upon its decision. The EAT reiterated that whether the appeal was classified as a review or a re-hearing was irrelevant in this regard. In *First Hampshire & Dorset Ltd v Parhar* UKEAT/0643/11/LA (10 May 2012, unreported), the EAT reminded tribunals to consider the whole process, including the appeal, when examining ill-health capability dismissals, particularly where new facts or evidence were available by the time of the appeal (see also *Fox v British Airways Plc* (UKEAT/0315/14/RN) (22 April 2015, unreported)). This applies whether the new facts or evidence assist the employee or, as they did on the facts of *Parhar* (above), and, the employer (see also *Holt v Res On Site Limited* (UKEAT/0410/13/BA) (27 February 2014, unreported) in which the EAT again emphasised the importance of assessing the process as whole). Where an employer uses an independent third party to conduct an appeal, its refusal to implement the third party's decision to uphold the appeal will not necessarily render the dismissal unfair (*Kisoka v Ratnpinyotip* (UKEAT/0311/13/LA) (11 December 2013, unreported)), though in practice it seems likely that that would often be the case.

In an appropriate case, it may fall to the Employment Tribunal to consider whether any human resources department had an improper degree of influence over the decisions made by the officers in question (see *Ramphal v Department for Transport* [2015] IRLR 985 where the Employment Tribunal erred in failing to consider adequately whether such influence had been exerted improperly over an investigating officer's report and see also *Dronsfield v University of Reading* [2016] ICR 1107.

Although notice once given cannot unilaterally be withdrawn, it may be withdrawn by agreement. The result is that the tribunal has regard, in appropriate cases, to what takes place between the giving of notice and the ultimate termination of employment in determining whether a dismissal was reasonable in all the circumstances. Dismissal is better analysed as a process than an event as highlighted, for example, by the fact that tribunals take internal appeals into account in assessing fairness (*South Tyneside Council v Ward* (UKEAT/0358/10/RN) (12 July 2011, unreported)).

The most common procedural failings in practice include: a failure to give warnings when shortcomings in an employee's performance first emerge, or to record them properly in writing; failure to give adequate advance notice of a disciplinary hearing, or to inform the employee before the hearing of the substance of the complaint to be considered or the fact that, if the complaint is found proved, the employee may be dismissed; failure to inform the employee of or to permit him to exercise the right to be accompanied to a disciplinary hearing; managers acting on evidence on which the employee has had no chance to comment; decisions being taken or influenced by persons other than those who have considered what the employee has to say; and appeals being determined by persons with a prior involvement in the matter. Procedural requirements in particular contexts are dealt with in more detail in **54.6–54.14** below.

For several years it was thought that if an employer had adopted an unfair procedure in dismissing an employee, but established that if he had adopted a fair procedure the employee would still have been dismissed, the dismissal could be held to be fair. However, in *Polkey v A E Dauton (or Dayton) Services Ltd* [1988] ICR 142, the House of Lords confirmed that the sole question for the tribunal was whether the employer acted reasonably at the time. In the vast majority of cases, there was no scope to consider what might have happened if the employer had acted differently, except at the stage of assessing compensation (see **55.13** UNFAIR DISMISSAL – III). However, the House of Lords also stated that where the employer could reasonably have concluded in the light of circumstances known to him at the time of dismissal that it would have been utterly useless to follow the normal procedure, he might well have acted reasonably if he did not follow the procedure. In *Duffy v Yeomans & Partners Ltd* [1995] ICR 642, the Court of Appeal said that it was not necessary, in order to come within this exception, that the employer actually applied his mind to the question whether normal procedures would be utterly useless. It will, however, be an unusual case where following procedures would meet this high threshold (see *Nabili v Norfolk Community Health and Care NHS Trust* (UKEAT/0039/16/RN) (21 June 2016, unreported) for a recent example of a case which did not). For an example of a case where the significance of the procedural defect was relevant to the decision on liability see *London Central Bus Company Ltd v Manning* (UKEAT/0103/13/DM) (11 December 2013, unreported).

EmA 2002, s 34, introduced a new *s 98A(2)* into *ERA 1996* which had the effect of overturning *Polkey*. Failure to follow a procedure in relation to the dismissal of an employee was not regarded – by itself – as making the employer's action unreasonable if he showed that he would have decided to dismiss the employee if he had followed the procedure. This provision was repealed with effect from 6 April 2009 and the position is now as set out in the paragraph above.

54.5 GROUNDS FOR DISMISSAL – LACK OF CAPABILITY OR QUALIFICATIONS

Capability means capability assessed by reference to skill, aptitude, health, or any other physical or mental quality. *Qualifications* means any degree, diploma or other academic, technical or professional qualification, *relevant to the position which the employee held* (*ERA 1996, s 98(3)*).

54.6 Capability

As with other reasons for dismissal, the employer is not required to prove that the employee was incapable of performing his job in order to defeat a claim for unfair dismissal. The employer need only establish an honest belief on reasonable grounds that the employee was incapable (*Taylor v Alidair Ltd* [1978] ICR 445).

In cases of lack of capability, it has long been established that before dismissal an employer should inform the employee what is required, inform the employee of the ways in which he is failing to perform his job adequately, warn him of the possibility that he may be dismissed because of this, and provide him with an opportunity to improve (see, for example, *James v Waltham Holy Cross UDC* [1973] ICR 398). Where warnings have been given, an employee will only be able to reopen them in exceptional circumstances. The approach applicable in the context of misconduct dismissals (see the detailed discussion of *Davies v Sandwell MBC* at **54.9** below) will apply equally to warnings issued in good faith on prima facie grounds for capability reasons (*General Dynamics Information Technology Limited v Carranza* [2015] ICR 169).

There are some cases where a tribunal might be prepared to accept that a warning was not required. For example, in *James v Waltham Holy Cross UDC* itself, it was suggested that a capability defect may be so extreme that there is an irredeemable incapability, with the result that a warning would be of no benefit to the employee. Equally, in *Taylor v Alidair Ltd* (above), the Court of Appeal stated that the potential consequences of incompetence may be so serious that one failure to perform may justify dismissal e.g. a failure committed by a passenger-carrying airline pilot. However, in practice such cases are likely to be very rare, and should be treated as exceptional departures from the general rule that a warning, and time for improvement, are likely to be seen as pre-requisites for a fair dismissal (though of course the extent of the procedural steps which are necessary will be very context dependent).

54.6A Procedure for capability dismissals

(See also **54.10** below.) In regard to capability and performance management, employers should follow procedures agreed with or notified to their employees. Such procedures may include the following steps.

(i)   If an employee falls short of the performance required of him, a meeting (of which the employee is given prior written notice containing an outline of the matters to be considered) should be arranged with him and his representative at which he is informed of:

    (a)   the respects (in detail) in which he falls short of the required standards;

    (b)   the time within which his performance must improve; and

    (c)   the fact that if he fails to improve he will receive a written warning and if he still fails to improve within a reasonable time he may be dismissed.

If possible, a note taker should attend this meeting and take a contemporaneous note of what is said. If this cannot be done, a written record of what was said should be made as soon as possible after the meeting. The employee and his representative/companion (if appropriate) should be sent a letter setting out a brief summary of the meeting and of the conclusions reached, including any warning given.

(ii)   If the employee's performance fails to improve, he should be sent a letter:

    (a)   setting out the respects in which he has failed to improve; and

    (b)   inviting him and his representative to another meeting to explain this failure.

(iii)   At the second meeting, at which again there should be a witness and a record kept:

    (a)   the complaints against the employee should be reiterated; and

    (b)   he should be given an opportunity to explain.

If he has no satisfactory explanation for his failure to improve, he should be informed that:

    (c)   he has a further time in which to improve; and

    (d)   failure to improve within this time will result in dismissal.

    The employee and his representative should again be sent a summary of the meeting.

(iv)   If there is no improvement, repeat step (ii), warning him that his dismissal will be considered.

(v)   At the third meeting, repeat steps (iii)(a) and (b) and if no satisfactory explanation is given, give notice of dismissal if the circumstances warrant such a sanction.

(vi)   If practicable, and in any event if the contract or any disciplinary or grievance procedure requires it, if the employee wishes to challenge his dismissal, a manager or managers not involved in the original decision to dismiss should conduct an appeal hearing.

Other steps which may be taken are the offer of training to assist the employee's performance, and consultation with his union representative. Consideration should be given to whether the employer has other work available to which the employee would be better suited.

The importance of these steps will vary according to the circumstances. They should not be treated as a checklist of steps which must be taken in every case, but simply represent a suggested approach to managing performance issues. For example, it may be that a senior employee ought to be well aware of what is required of him and the consequences of failing to perform his duties adequately. It might be that the context of a particular case takes a less formal approach within the range of reasonable responses. However, where possible it is best to give formal warnings in cases of incapability, irrespective of the seniority of the employee.

The ACAS Code does not apply to ill health dismissals not involving allegations of culpable conduct (*Holmes v Qinetiq Ltd* [2016] ICR 1016. The decision in *Holmes* leaves open precisely which cases involving culpable actions will and will not attract the application of the ACAS Code.

54.7   Qualifications

Dismissal for lack of qualifications is not common since an employer will have difficulty in convincing a tribunal that an employee whom he engaged with full knowledge of his qualifications is not qualified for the job. If, however, the employee misled the employer into believing that he possessed certain qualifications which were essential for the performance of the task to which he was appointed, he may be dismissed for his lack of qualifications. Some of the cases on lack of qualifications have arisen where a man employed as a driver is disqualified from driving and therefore is no longer able to perform his duties (see, for example, *Appleyard v F M Smith (Hull) Ltd* [1972] IRLR 19). Consideration should be given to offering a disqualified employee suitable alternative employment.

54.8   Lack of capability due to ill-health

In cases of ill-health which make future performance of the contract of employment impossible, the contract may be considered to have been frustrated and the employee not to have been dismissed (see **48.3 TERMINATION OF EMPLOYMENT**). However, instances of frustration of the contract of employment are extremely rare in practice.

Before dismissing an employee for reasons of ill-health, an employer should find out the current medical position. This will usually involve obtaining, with the employee's consent, a report from the employee's general practitioner and, if appropriate, his consultant (see **10.15 DISCLOSURE OF INFORMATION** for the *Access to Medical Reports Act 1988* and the *Access to Health Records Act 1990*). In some cases, it may be thought necessary to have the employee examined, with his consent, by a doctor appointed by the employer (increasing numbers of employers have access to either internal or external occupational health advice for such purposes).

In *D B Schenker Rail (UK) Ltd v Doolan* (UKEATS/0053/09/BI) (13 April 2011, unreported), the Scottish EAT reiterated that whilst employers were obliged to take steps to inform themselves of the employee's medical position, this should be judged against a standard of reasonableness. The Scottish EAT, by analogy with the *Burchell* test applied to cases of misconduct, considered that a tribunal should ask whether a reasonable employer could find, from the material before it, that the employee was not capable of returning to his post (or could reasonably believe in whatever other reason for dismissal was proved). The tribunal was not to substitute its own answer to that question for that given by the employer. The Scottish EAT further emphasised that whilst medical and expert reports may assist the employer, the question is ultimately managerial, rather than medical.

Once the employer has properly informed himself of the employee's state of health and the prognosis, he should consider the requirements of his business, the employee's past sickness record and whether the employee could be offered an alternative position more suitable to his state of health (*Spencer v Paragon Wallpapers Ltd* [1977] ICR 301). The employer should also consider whether the employee should be regarded as disabled and, if so, whether any reasonable adjustments should be made for the employee. The employer should consult the employee and any representative before dismissing him (*East Lindsay District Council v Daubney* [1977] ICR 566; *Merseyside and North Wales Electricity Board v Taylor* [1975] ICR 185). The central question is whether a reasonable employer would have waited longer to dismiss and, if so, how long (*Harris v Monmouthshire County Council* (UKEAT/0332/14/DA) (23 October 2015, unreported), *BS v Dundee City Council* [2014] IRLR 131 and *Spencer* (above)).

Having properly informed itself of the position and consulted with the employee, the employer must decide what action to take. The EAT in *Lynock v Cereal Packaging Ltd* [1988] ICR 670 stated that whilst each case will turn on its facts, some factors which may be important include: (i) the nature of the illness; (ii) the likelihood of it recurring or some other illness arising; (iii) the length of the various absences and the spaces of good health between them; (iv) the need of the employer for the work done by the particular employee; (v) the impact of the absences on others who work with the employee; (vi) the adoption and the carrying out of the policy; (vii) the emphasis on a personal assessment in the ultimate decision and of course, (viii) the extent to which the difficulty of the situation and the position of the employer has been made clear to the employee so that the employee realises that the point of no return, the moment when the decision was ultimately being made may be approaching. The EAT also held that the mere fact that an employee is fit at the time of dismissal will not render the dismissal unfair, as the tribunal has to look at the history as a whole.

Whilst it is important to consider whether an employee can be offered an alternative position, an employer will not act unreasonably if he offers the employee alternative employment at a reduced rate of pay where this is the only suitable alternative employment which is available for him (*British Gas Services Ltd v McCaull* [2001] IRLR 60). Fairness requires the employer to consider eligibility under an ill-health early retirement scheme before dismissing an employee for long-term ill-health (*First West Yorkshire Ltd t/a First Leeds v Haigh* [2008] IRLR 182). The employee, on the other hand, has no duty to volunteer information about his prospects of recovery to his employer (*Mitchell v Arkwood Plastics (Engineering) Ltd* [1993] ICR 471), though if he elects not to do so this may reduce the information which the employer has to take into account if it is to have acted reasonably; it will be difficult for the employee to later criticise the employer for not discovering information that he could have provided if he takes this course of action.

Where the problem consists of persistent short absences caused by unconnected minor ailments, rather than a long absence for a common cause, a medical examination has little purpose. The employee should be told what level of attendance he is expected to attain, the period within which that is to be achieved and that dismissal may follow if there is no sufficient improvement. The situation should then be monitored to see whether absence is reduced below a reasonable level. A second warning would be appropriate in borderline cases (see *International Sports Co Ltd v Thomson* [1980] IRLR 340; *Rolls-Royce Ltd v Walpole* [1980] IRLR 343; *Lynock v Cereal Packaging Ltd* [1988] ICR 670).

Whether the ill health was caused by the employer's actions will not determine fairness. The issue of responsibility for the illness or injury is tangential to the question of fairness of the dismissal (*London Fire and Civil Defence Authority v Betty* [1994] IRLR 384; *Edwards v Governors of Hanson School* [2001] IRLR 733; *McAdie v Royal Bank of Scotland* [2008] ICR 1087). The question can, however, arise where the employer is in some sense responsible for the incapacity, rather than merely where it can be found to have caused it (*L v M* (UKEAT/0382/13/DXA) (16 May 2014, unreported).

In *H J Heinz Co Ltd v Kenrick* [2000] IRLR 144, the EAT held that it would be an error of law for a tribunal to proceed on the basis that a disability-related dismissal which is not 'justified' under the *Disability Discrimination Act 1995* is, without more, automatically unfair under the *ERA 1996*. Separate consideration must be given to the question of unfairness (see the recent confirmation of this in *Perratt v City of Cardiff Council* (UKEAT/0079/16/RN) (28 June 2016, unreported), though see the recent observations of the Court of Appeal in *O'Brien v Bolton St Catherine's Academy* [2017] EWCA Civ 145 which emphasise the undesirability of the range of reasonable responses test and the proportionality test in *section 15* of the *Equality Act 2010* yielding different results).

54.9   GROUNDS FOR DISMISSAL – CONDUCT

It is worth noting that in order to prove a potentially fair reason for dismissal, an employer need only show that the reason for the dismissal related to the employee's conduct. Tribunals should not be drawn into the trap of construing the concept of "conduct" too narrowly. This point has been reiterated by the Scottish EAT, which has held that the conduct need not be of any particular character, and finding that the tribunal had erred in that case by asking whether the conduct was "reprehensible" (*Royal Bank of Scotland v Donaghay* (UKEATS/0049/10/BI) (11 November 2011, unreported)). This was an impermissible gloss on the statutory language.

The starting point in most cases where misconduct is the reason for dismissal is the approach formulated by Arnold J in *British Home Stores Ltd v Burchell* [1980] ICR 303n. At 304 he stated:

> 'What the tribunal have to decide every time is, broadly expressed, whether the employer who discharged the employee on the grounds of misconduct in question (usually, though not necessarily, dishonest conduct) entertained a reasonable suspicion amounting to a belief in the guilt of the employee of that misconduct at that time. That is really stating shortly and compendiously what is in fact more than one element. First of all, there must be established by the employer the fact of that belief; that the employer did believe it. Secondly, that the employer had in his mind reasonable grounds upon which to sustain that belief. And thirdly, we think, that the employer, at the stage at which he formed that belief on those grounds, at any rate at the final stage at which he formed that belief on those grounds, had carried out as much investigation into the matter as was reasonable in all the circumstances of the case.'

In *Boys and Girls Welfare Society v McDonald* [1997] ICR 693, the EAT pointed out that *Burchell* had been decided when the burden of proving reasonableness rested with the employer rather than neutrally as is the position today. The above passage must be read subject to this qualification to avoid the tribunal falling into error and requiring the employer to prove reasonableness (see also *Singh v DHL Services Ltd* (UKEAT/0462/12/LA) (4 September 2013, unreported)).

The EAT in *McDonald* added that (i) in any event, *Burchell* may not be appropriate where there is no real conflict on the facts; and (ii) *Burchell* does not mean that an employer who fails one or more of the three tests is, without more, guilty of unfair dismissal. The tribunal should focus upon the question whether the employer's action fell within the range of reasonable responses open to a reasonable employer. Notwithstanding the comments made by the EAT in *McDonald*, the *Burchell* test was approved by the *Court of Appeal in Foley v Post Office, HSBC Bank (formerly Midland Bank) v Madden* [2000] ICR 1283 (amongst other cases), and is applied almost as a matter of course by tribunals considering misconduct dismissals in practice.

In addition to the test set out in *Burchell*, if the dismissal is to be fair it must have been reasonable for the employer to have dismissed the employee for the misconduct in question. In other words, dismissal must be a fair sanction. As with other aspects of the law on unfair dismissal, the tribunal will again focus on whether or not the sanction imposed fell within the band of responses which a reasonable employer might have adopted (see *Foley* above) (the same test will be applied when the tribunal assesses the reasonableness of the investigation undertaken by the employer (see *Sainsbury's Supermarkets Ltd v Hitt* [2003] ICR 111, above)). The test should not be confused with the different question about whether or not the employer was contractually entitled to dismiss without notice for gross misconduct (a question determined by the tribunal making findings of its own on the balance of probabilities). The tribunal should focus upon the sufficiency of the conduct in which the employer found the employee to have engaged as a reason for dismissal (*Weston Recovery Services v Fisher* (UKEAT/0062/10) (7 October 2010, unreported); *Vodafone Ltd v Nicholson* (UKEAT/0605/12/SM) (17 May 2013, unreported)).

The final point follows from the fact that the range of reasonable responses test is being applied. The consequence of this objective approach is that the tribunal should not substitute its own factual findings about events giving rise to the dismissal for those of the dismissing officer, nor should it impose its view of the appropriate sanction in exchange for that of the employer. Instead that tribunal should ask (i) whether there were reasonable grounds upon which the employer could believe that the employee had committed the misconduct in question; (ii) whether the employer completed a reasonable investigation prior to dismissal; and (iii) whether the decision to dismiss for the misconduct in question fell within the band of reasonable responses (*London Ambulance Service NHS Trust v Small* [2009] IRLR 563). The Court of Appeal emphasised this principle in *Boardman v Nugent Care Society* [2013] EWCA Civ 198, [2013] ICR 927, in which the Court drew a clear distinction between the tribunal's fact-finding role in unfair and wrongful dismissal claims. An example of this principle in practice is *Quadrant Catering Ltd v Smith* (UKEAT/0362/10/RN) (10 December 2010, unreported), where the EAT held that the tribunal erred by suggesting that dismissal should have been used only as a last resort, and substituting its view of the facts for those of the employer.

In *Tayeh v Barchester Healthcare Ltd* [2013] EWCA Civ 29, [2013] IRLR 387 the Court of Appeal emphasised the point above that it is for the employer to judge the severity of offence. In that case the tribunal's decision was overturned as it had substituted its own mistaken view of the severity of the offence for that of the employer. Equally, however, the EAT should not substitute its view for that of the employment tribunal, and should avoid an overly "pernickety" scrutiny of the tribunal's reasons (*Fuller v Brent London Borough Council* [2011] ICR 806).

The ACAS Guidance on disciplinary proceedings suggests the following factors may be relevant when determining what, if any, disciplinary penalty to impose: whether the employer's rules indicate the likely penalty; the penalty imposed in similar cases in the past; the employee's disciplinary record, work record, experience and length of service; whether there are any special mitigating circumstances which might make it appropriate to adjust the severity of the penalty; and whether the proposed penalty is reasonable in all the circumstances. An employment tribunal is likely to have similar factors in mind when determining whether or not dismissal was a reasonable sanction in the circumstances of the case.

When deciding what sanction to impose, it is important to consider the circumstances of the individual case, and not simply to apply an inflexible policy (*Post Office v Marney* [1990] IRLR 170; *Rentokil Ltd v Mackin* [1989] IRLR 286, EAT). For example, even where an employee is dismissed for misconduct such as dishonesty which is referred to in the employer's disciplinary code as being misconduct which would normally lead to dismissal, the duty on an employer to act fairly and reasonably requires that they should investigate the seriousness of the offence in the particular case (*John Lewis plc v Coyne* [2001] IRLR 139). It cannot be assumed that an instance of what would usually be seen as serious misconduct will automatically result in a fair dismissal (*Centrewest London Buses Ltd v Spencer* (UKEAT/0481/12/DM) (16 May 2013, unreported)). Indeed, a finding of gross misconduct does not automatically justify dismissal as a matter of law (*Brito-Babapulle v Ealing Hospital NHS Trust* [2013] IRLR 854). Taking an example to illustrate the above point, it is important to consider any mitigating features which might justify a lesser sanction for reasons specific to the employee, or the incident in question (see *Department for Work and Pensions v Coulson* (UKEAT/0572/12/LA) (15 May 2013, unreported) for an example of a case where the failure by the employer to give any weight to mitigating features rendered the dismissal unfair).

Although employers should consider each disciplinary case on its individual merits, on occasion a dismissal may be held unfair on the ground that the dismissed employee has been treated inconsistently, in that the employer has on other occasions dealt more leniently with similar instances of misconduct (*Cain v Leeds Western Health Authority* [1990] ICR 585, *Post Office v Fennell* [1981] IRLR 221). In *Hadjioannous v Coral Casinos Ltd* [1981] IRLR 352, the EAT held that evidence of inconsistency is relevant in a limited range of circumstances, namely: (i) it may be evidence as to how an employee has been led to be believe that certain categories of conduct will be viewed by his employer; (ii) it may suggest that the purported reason for dismissal advanced by the employer is not real or genuine; and (iii) it may support an argument that the sanction of dismissal was unreasonable. However, this should only be the case if the two cases in question were, to adopt the language used by the EAT in *Hadjioannous*, "truly parallel", as the emphasis should be on the individual employee's case. Tribunals should generally be cautious in finding a dismissal to have been unfair on grounds of inconsistent treatment (*Hadjioannous* (above); *Paul v East Surrey District Health Authority* [1995] IRLR 305; *Harrow London Borough Council v Cunningham* [1996] IRLR 256, EAT). The EAT continues to apply a test of strict parity in cases where comparators are relied upon (see *Honey v City and County of Swansea* (UKEAT/0465/09/JOJ) (16 April 2010, unreported) where a difference in seniority and job description justified a difference in sanction). The EAT has emphasised that the appropriate question remains whether a reasonable employer could properly, within the bounds of a range of reasonable responses, have decided to deal with the two cases differently. Where the tribunal accepts the employer's reason for having treated the two cases differently, the dismissal will only be unfair if that reason can be said to have been outside the range of responses open to the employer (*General Mills (Berwick) Ltd v Glowacki* (UKEAT/0139/11/ZT) (22 September 2011, unreported) and see also *SPS Technologies Ltd v Chughtai* UKEAT/0204/12/SM (3 December 2012, unreported) where the employer was held to have drawn a reasonable distinction between two cases because it reasonably found on the evidence that charges were made out against one employee but not another). It follows from the above that it is in practice difficult (though by no means impossible) for an employee to succeed on a claim for unfair dismissal by reference to a comparator.

Whilst the employer's policy on conduct which will and will not be treated as gross misconduct is of course relevant to the reasonableness of the dismissal, the fact that the employee is dismissed for conduct not set out in a handbook or similar document will not inevitably lead to a finding that the dismissal is unfair. For example, the tribunal is entitled to take into account whether the employee should have been aware of the gravity of the misconduct in question in determining whether a reasonable employer would necessarily have warned the employee of the consequences of his actions (*Royal Bank of Scotland v Nwosuagwe-Ibe* (UKEAT/0594/10/ZT) (February 2010, unreported) provides an example of such reasoning).

If an employee has recently been given a disciplinary warning (especially if it was for a similar offence), this may make it more reasonable to dismiss for the act of misconduct. The EAT in *Auguste Noel Ltd v Curtis* [1990] ICR 604 confirmed that previous warnings for dissimilar conduct may also be relevant. In *Wincanton Group Plc v Stone & Ors* [2013] IRLR 178 the EAT emphasised that the misconduct for which the employee is dismissed need not necessarily be of the same nature as the conduct which led to the warning being imposed. The EAT further noted that a final written warning always implies, subject only to the individual terms of a contract, that any misconduct of whatever nature will often, and usually, be met with dismissal, and it is likely to be by way of exception that that will not occur. Where an appeal against a prior warning is pending, the employer should take into account both the warning and the fact that it is subject to an undetermined appeal in considering whether to dismiss, although he is not precluded from dismissing before the appeal is heard (*Tower Hamlets Health Authority v Anthony* [1989] ICR 656, see also *Wincanton Group Plc v Stone & Ors* [2013] IRLR 178 in which the EAT further suggested that an employer ought to take account of any challenge to the warning being made in legal proceedings). Both of those authorities were applied by the EAT in *Rooney v Dundee City Council* (UKEATS/0020/13/BI) (15 October 2013, unreported). Nor is it necessarily unfair to take into account a warning which was not extant at the time of the misconduct in question; the question remains what is reasonable in all the circumstances (*John-Charles v NHS Business Services Authority* (UKEAT/0105/15/BA) (12 October 2015, unreported), though note the need, made clear by the EAT's Judgment, for the employee to have an opportunity to make representations on the relevance of the warning). In *Davies v Sandwell Metropolitan Borough Council* [2013] EWCA Civ 135, [2013] IRLR 374 the Court of Appeal doubted, albeit *obiter*, whether the EAT had been correct in that case to suggest that it was unreasonable for the employer to take into account the fact that an appeal against historic disciplinary sanction had been abandoned.

In *Diosynth Ltd v Thomson* [2006] CSIH 5, [2006] IRLR 284 the Court of Session concluded that it had been unreasonable for an employer to dismiss an employee for breaches of safety procedures after a fatality, because the employer had treated an expired warning for breach of safety procedures as a determining factor in the decision to dismiss. In *Webb v Airbus UK Ltd* [2008] ICR 561, however, the Court of Appeal held that it is open to an employment tribunal to find a dismissal fair even where an employer has taken into account a spent warning. Diosynth was distinguished on the basis that in that case the expired warning tipped the balance towards the decision to dismiss, but in *Airbus* the employer had shown that the reason for dismissal was the later misconduct, and the previous misconduct affected the decision as to what sanction to impose. The EAT has confirmed that the Court of Appeal's decision in *Webb* correctly articulates the legal position (*Stratford v Auto Trial VR Ltd* (UKEAT/0116/16/JOJ) (31 October 2016, unreported)).

In recent years there has been a great deal of litigation concerning the circumstances in which it will be appropriate for a tribunal to consider the reasonableness of an earlier written warning during an unfair dismissal hearing. In *Nunn v Royal Mail Group* [2011] ICR 162 the EAT considered a case where an employee was dismissed because he failed to accept a demotion sanction imposed on him following disciplinary proceedings. The EAT held that unless there is a glaringly obvious reason why the demotion (or, presumably, any other previous sanction) was unfair, the tribunal is not required to examine in detail the precise nature of the allegations and procedure involved. If the employee is dissatisfied with the demotion, his proper remedy is a claim for constructive unfair dismissal. In *Davies v Sandwell Metropolitan Borough Council* [2013] EWCA Civ 135, [2013] IRLR 374 the Court of Appeal considered in detail the approach employers and tribunals should take to previous warnings in unfair dismissal cases. The Court of Appeal approved the central principle laid down in earlier authorities to the effect that it is legitimate for an employer to rely on a final warning, provided that it was issued in good faith, that there were at least prima facie grounds for imposing it and that it was not manifestly inappropriate to issue it. The Court of Appeal added that in answering that question it is not for the tribunal to re-open the warning and consider the adequacy of the evidence in detail. There need to be exceptional circumstances before a tribunal should go behind an earlier disciplinary process (see also *Wincanton Group Plc v Stone & Ors* [2013] IRLR 178). Whilst the issue for the tribunal is therefore relatively narrow, it remains necessary for the tribunal to apply its mind to that question and consider and decide whether the warning given was manifestly inappropriate (*Simmonds v Milford Club* UKEAT/0323/12/KN [2013] ICR D14. In *Simmonds*, the EAT held that if an Employment Tribunal has cause on the facts to consider that a previous disciplinary sanction may have been manifestly inappropriate, it should hear evidence and decide on the relevant facts whether the sanction applied was manifestly inappropriate. Likewise, in *Way v Spectrum Property Care Ltd* [2015] EWCA Civ 381, [2015] IRLR 657, the Court of Appeal emphasised that a warning given in bad faith ought not to be taken into account in deciding if a dismissal was fair, even if an internal appeal against the warning had rejected the employee's assertion of bad faith. The Court of Appeal allowed the Claimant's appeal following the Employment Tribunal's failure to consider if the warning had been issued in bad faith. However, even where the warning is manifestly inappropriate, the extent to which the employer relied upon it in reaching the decision to dismiss must be considered when deciding whether or not the ultimate dismissal if unfair (*Bandara v BBC* (UKEAT/0335/15/JOJ) (9 June 2015, unreported)).

Where, during a disciplinary process, the employee raises an issue of bad faith, lack of prima facie grounds, or manifest impropriety in relation to an earlier warning, the employer may be required to examine that issue, though that is unlikely to extend to an obligation to conduct a full reinvestigation (*Appiah v Compass Group UK & Ireland Ltd* (UKEAT/0129/16/DM) (8 September 2016, unreported)).

What of the different position where an employer conducts a second disciplinary process in relation to the same matter? Or, having addressed an issue first as a customer complaint (for example), then brings disciplinary proceedings in relation to the same issue? There is no absolute answer to this question. It is, in effect, a matter for the Employment Tribunal to consider in all the circumstances, by reference to *ERA 1996, s 98(4)* and the range of reasonable responses test. The civil law doctrines of res judicata and abuse of process should not be imported into this consideration, nor should an "exceptional circumstances" test be applied (see *Northamptonshire Healthcare NHS Foundation Trust v Chawla* (UKEAT/0075/15/JOJ) (8 January 2016, unreported), applying *Christou v London Borough of Haringey* [2013] IRLR 379). The decision in *Chawla* obtains useful practical guidance on the types of issues which will be relevant to the Employment Tribunal's consideration of fairness on this issue, such as whether the employee had been assured that no further action would be taken, or whether there was such a delay that the employee could reasonably have considered the matter resolved.

Is a concession by the employee during cross examination that the sanction of dismissal was reasonable determinative of this issue? No, held the EAT in *Adama v Partnerships in Care Limited* (UKEAT/0047/14/MC) (12 June 2014, unreported). The tribunal must consider for itself if the sanction is within the range of reasonable responses. The concession is clearly relevant to that decision, but it is not determinative.

An employer is entitled to take into account both the actual impact of the impugned conduct, and the potential impact of that conduct when determining whether dismissal was a reasonable sanction (*Wincanton Plc v Atkinson* (UKEAT/0040/11/DM) (19 July 2011, unreported)). In that case, two employees failed to renew their HGV licences with the effect that they had been driving the employer's vehicles in breach of regulations and without valid insurance. The tribunal took the view that as they had not caused an accident, and the employer had not been subject to regulatory sanctions, no harm had resulted and their dismissals were unfair. The EAT overturned the tribunal on the grounds that insufficient weight have been given to the very serious potential consequences of the misconduct.

If the employer reasonably believes that one of a number of employees is guilty of dishonesty and, despite proper investigation, cannot identify the culprit, it may be reasonable to dismiss all those who could have been responsible (*Monie v Coral Racing Ltd* [1981] ICR 109; *Whitbread & Co plc v Thomas* [1988] ICR 135; *Parr v Whitbread & Co plc* [1990] ICR 427; *Frames Snooker Centre v Boyce* [1992] IRLR 472). In *John Lewis plc v Coyne* [2001] IRLR 139, the EAT gave useful guidance on what type of misconduct can be said to amount to 'dishonesty', holding that the best working test is that set out in *R v Ghosh* [1982] QB 1053. In summary, there are two aspects to dishonesty – the objective and the subjective – and judging whether or not there has been dishonesty involves going through a two-stage process. First, it must be decided whether according to the ordinary standards of reasonable and honest people, what was done was dishonest. If so, then second, consideration must be given to whether the person concerned must have realised that what he or she was doing was by those standards dishonest. The question, of course, remains whether or not the employer could reasonably have believed that the employee was guilty of fraud, by reference to that definition (*Brito-Babapulle v Ealing Hospital NHS Trust* [2013] IRLR 854). See also *Panama v Hackney London Borough Council* [2003] IRLR 278 on proof of fraudulent conduct and

Centrewest London Buses Ltd v Spencer (UKEAT/0481/12/DM) (16 May 2013, unreported) on the application of the *Theft Act 1968* in the employment context). Notwithstanding the above, doubt has recently been cast upon the appropriateness of referring to definitions from the field of criminal law in *Gondalia v Tesco Stores Ltd* (UKEAT/0320/14/JOJ) (20 January 2015, unreported). In that case the EAT emphasised that the employee's state of mind is important, but so are other factors. In the light of the above, and until there is clear guidance to the contrary, employers would be well advised to continue to exercise care when using the labels of dishonesty or theft as a justification for a dismissal. However, where they have done so *Gondalia* may allow room for argument that a more flexible approach should be taken by the tribunal.

Where an employer relies upon the employee's conduct in refusing to obey an instruction, the lawfulness of that instruction was not decisive when considering the reasonableness of the dismissal under *ERA 1996, s 98(4)*, although it is a relevant factor: *Farrant v Woodroffe School* [1998] ICR 184. The same principle applies where an employee is dismissed for breach of an absence policy (*Sakharkar v Northern Foods Grocery Group Ltd* (UKEAT/0442/10/ZT) (8 March 2011, unreported)) or for failing to comply with an instruction given pursuant to a contractual mobility clause (*Kellogg Brown & Root (UK) Ltd v Fitton* (UKEAT/0205/16/BA) (21 November 2016, unreported).

Length of service is a factor which an employment tribunal may properly take into account in deciding whether the decision of an employer to dismiss in reaction to the employee's conduct was an appropriate one (*Strouthos v London Underground Ltd* [2004] IRLR 636).

The conduct for which an employee is dismissed usually relates to behaviour during working hours, but in certain cases an employee may be dismissed fairly for other behaviour, if it is likely to affect the performance of his contract. If, for example, a playgroup leader is convicted of an indecent assault on a child outside his hours of work, his conviction for such an offence may make him unsuitable for carrying on his employment (eg *Nottinghamshire County Council v Bowly* [1978] IRLR 252, in which the EAT held to be fair the dismissal of a teacher after his conviction for an offence of gross indecency with a man and similarly the Court of Appeal in *X v Y* [2004] ICR 1634 including consideration of *art 8* of the *ECHR*). *Article 8* arose again, in a slightly different way, in *Garamukanwa v Solent NHS Trust* [2016] IRLR 476. In that case the employer (which was a public authority for the purposes of the *HRA 1998*, used in its internal disciplinary process material seized from the employee's home by the police in the course of a criminal investigation which the police provided to the employer. The police had specifically informed the employer that it was entitled to use the information. This was argued by the Claimant to have been contrary to *Article 8*. The EAT reiterated that, following *X v Y*, the first question is whether the circumstances of the dismissal are such that they fall within the ambit of *Article 8*. The EAT held that the Employment Tribunal had been entitled to conclude that the Claimant had no reasonable expectation of privacy in relation to the material and that *Article 8* was not therefore engaged. It is clear from the EAT's judgment, however, that questions of this nature require a careful analysis of the facts of the case. At the time of writing, it is understood that an application to the Court of Appeal for permission to appeal is outstanding.

The issue of employee's privacy away from the workplace has taken on renewed importance in the context of dismissals involving employee's use of social media, which frequently occurs after hours. This matter came before the EAT in *Game Retail Ltd v Laws* (UKEAT/0188/14/DA) (3 November 2014, unreported). The EAT refused to lay down general guidance for dismissals in such cases. The EAT agreed that the existence of a policy, the nature and seriousness of the misuse in question, any previous warning, and any actual or potential damage to the business were likely to be relevant. The EAT considered them to be so obvious that they did not constitute helpful points of guidance but they do, with respect, at least provide a starting point. On the issue of the use being in the employee's own time, the EAT also accepted that the extent to which the usage was "private" was a relevant question, owing to employees having the right to express themselves. Ultimately, however, the question is whether the decision to dismiss was reasonable. That will depend upon the particular employment and the circumstances. The EAT's view was that the range of reasonable responses test was sufficiently flexible to meet the challenge of social media dismissals. The EAT's judgment provides a timely reminder that in this context, as in any other, the Employment Tribunal must not substitute its own view, but must objectively scrutinise that of the employer. As an until there is further authority on this matter, those involved in cases involving a dismissal for use of social media should give careful consideration to the EAT's full judgment.

What if the misconduct in question occurs during the course of an investigation into the employee's other misconduct? The EAT considered this in *Kids City Limited v Gayle* (UKEAT/0106/13/MC) (24 February 2014, unreported) and held that it is open to the employer to have regard to such matters, subject to the usual requirement of fairness that the employee has the opportunity to answer its concerns.

Even in a case of misconduct justifying dismissal from the employee's existing job, it may sometimes be necessary to consider whether the employee could still be employed in some other capacity. However, it may be reasonable to leave investigation of that possibility until after the time when notice is given (*P v Nottinghamshire County Council* [1992] ICR 706). The EAT gave further consideration to this point in *Wincanton Group Plc v Stone & Ors* [2013] IRLR 178. The EAT consider it "highly arguable" that when an employee is dismissed from a job he has been employed to do in circumstances in which he cannot be expected legally to continue doing it, the employer may owe no duty to seek alternative employment. However, as both sides accepted that was such a duty in that case, the EAT declined to resolve the point conclusively.

Cases in which an employee is arrested by the police and charged with theft of his employer's property pose particular difficulties. Even if the employee may be charged with a criminal offence, he must be given an opportunity by his employer to state his case (*Read v Phoenix Preservation Ltd* [1985] ICR 164). In *Leach v Office of Communications* [2012] ICR 1269 the Court of Appeal upheld the EAT's decision to the effect that an employer which receives information from a third party must, as far as practicable, assess for itself the reliability of the information. For example, it should check the integrity of the informant body and the safeguards within the body's internal processes to assess the accuracy of the information supplied. The employer should not simply take an uncritical view of the information provided. However, the Court acknowledged that there will be cases where an employer cannot be expected to carry out his own independent investigation in order to test the reliability of the information provided by a responsible public authority. The EAT has emphasised that a tribunal is not bound to hold that because the policy have reported an allegation without endorsing it, a dismissal based on that report is fair (*Z v A* [2014] IRLR 244). The EAT went on to explain that the applicable principles are those set out in *Leach v Office of Communications*, but reiterated that those principles leave room for a tribunal to draw its own conclusions as to the reasonableness of the dismiss. The issues which arise in cases such as these are complex and those advising on such matters should consider the judgments of the EAT in *Z v A* and of the EAT and Court of Appeal in *Leach v Office of Communications* in full.

Is it proper for the employer to conduct his own investigation and question the employee whilst the police investigations are proceeding? In *Harris v Courage (Eastern) Ltd* [1982] ICR 530, the Court of Appeal approved the decision of the EAT that there is no absolute rule that once an employee had been charged with an offence and advised to say nothing until his criminal trial, an employer could not dismiss him for the alleged offence. Because of the long delay before a criminal prosecution is finally disposed of, it will often be necessary or desirable for the employer to act before its conclusion. Employers frequently carry out their own investigations and dismiss for dishonest conduct before a prosecution is concluded. If the employer awaits the outcome of a criminal trial and the employee is acquitted, he may find it harder to justify a subsequent dismissal, although the burden on the prosecution at the criminal trial is heavier than upon the employer in showing that he acted reasonably. The evidence which it is permissible for the employer to rely upon is less restricted than that which is admissible in the criminal trial, but how far it is reasonable for the employer to rely upon evidence which has been ruled inadmissible in a criminal trial depends on the facts in each case (*Dhaliwal v British Airways Board* [1985] ICR 513). In *Close v Rhondda Cynon Taff Borough Council* [2008] IRLR 868, the EAT held that it was not outside the range of reasonable responses for the employer to choose not to conduct its own independent questioning of witnesses during its disciplinary process but instead to rely on statements given by the witnesses to the police, even though the statements had been given in a police investigation into different allegations against the employee. According to the EAT, the focus of the police investigation was irrelevant and there was no duty on the employer to allow cross examination of the witnesses.

54.10 Procedure for misconduct dismissals

Employers are no longer under a legal obligation to follow the statutory dismissal procedures but they are advised to adopt and use rigorous internal procedures instead. It is important to have a known disciplinary procedure. Employers are also advised to consult the ACAS Code of Practice. The statutory dismissal and disciplinary procedures, although repealed from 6 April 2009, may still affect some ongoing cases.

If an employee is suspected of misconduct, the employer should investigate the matter fully and give the employee an opportunity to explain himself.

An employer will often wish to suspend an employee during the course of an investigation, for example where it suspects that an employee has engaged in dishonest or fraudulent conduct. However, as Elias LJ has pointed out in *obiter* (but nevertheless important) remarks, employers should not automatically suspend employees and assume that this action will be justified. A suspension which amounts to nothing more than a knee jerk reaction will be a breach of the implied term of mutual trust and confidence. Elias LJ further doubted the cogency of the widely expressed view that suspension is in the best interest of both the employer and the employee (*Crawford & Ors v Suffolk Mental Health Partnership NHR Trust* [2012] IRLR 402). However, in both *Graham v Secretary of State for Work and Pensions* [2012] IRLR 759 and *Tayeh v Barchester Healthcare Ltd* [2013] EWCA Civ 29, [2013] IRLR 387 the Court of Appeal was of the view that a tribunal could take into account the fact that an employee had not been suspended promptly when assessing the reasonableness of the employer's decision to dismiss for misconduct. This places employers in a difficult position where, on the one hand, any suspension should not be a knee jerk reaction on their part but, on the other, the decision not to suspend might later be taken to indicate that they did not regard the offence as serious.

An employer has no right to suspend an employee without pay unless this is expressly provided for in the contract of employment. A suspension without pay in the absence of a contractual right to do so may be a serious breach of contract enabling the employee to resign and claim constructive dismissal (*Morrison v Amalgamated Transport and General Workers Union* [1989] IRLR 361). It is also important to make sure that the employee understands that the suspension is not a disciplinary sanction, and that the employer has not yet decided whether he committed the alleged acts.

The extent of the investigation will depend on the circumstances. In *Royal Society for the Protection of Birds v Croucher* [1984] ICR 604, the EAT held that in a case in which an employee admitted offences of dishonesty there was very little scope for the kind of investigation referred to in *Burchell* (see **54.9** above) (see also *CRO Ports London Ltd v Wiltshire* (UKEAT/0344/14/DM) (unreported 23 January 2015) for a recent illustration of this principle). However, in certain cases, the admission itself will not be sufficient and the employer will need to investigate further. For instance, it might be necessary to make findings on the employee's culpability even where the fact that the conduct in question did occur is admitted (see *Burdett v Aviva Employment Service Ltd* (UKEAT/0439/13/JOJ) (14 November 2014) in which the misconduct had been admitted, but the employee said it was attributable to his mental illness). The employer does not have to prove beyond reasonable doubt that the employee was guilty of the misconduct, but merely that he had acted reasonably in treating the misconduct as sufficient for dismissing the employee in the circumstances known to him at the time. Where, however, the facts are disputed, it is of great importance that employers take seriously their responsibility to conduct a fair investigation, particularly where the employee's ability to work in his/her chosen career could be blighted by a finding of misconduct (*Salford Royal NHS Foundation Trust v Roldan* [2010] ICR 1457 and see recently *Tykocki v Royal Bournemouth and Christchurch Hospitals NHS Foundation Trust* (UKEAT/0081/16/JOJ) (17 October 2016, unreported)). Serious allegations of criminal misbehaviour should also be investigated very carefully and conscientiously, albeit tribunals should remember that the investigation is being conducted by an employer and it is inappropriate to require the safeguards found in a criminal trial (*A v B* [2003] IRLR 405). The Court of Appeal applied the decisions in *Roldan* and *A v B* in *Crawford v Suffolk Mental Health Partnership NHS Trust* [2012] IRLR 402. In *Tuner v East Midlands Trains Ltd* [2013] ICR 525, the Court of Appeal again reiterated that when determining whether an employer has acted within the range of reasonable responses, it will be relevant to have regard to the nature and consequences of the allegations, as a reasonable employer should have regard to the gravity of those consequences when determining the nature and scope of the appropriate investigation. The Court of Appeal went on to hold that where an employee's rights under *ECHR, Art 8* are engaged, matters bearing on the culpability of the employee must be investigated with a full appreciation of the potentially adverse consequences to the employee and that the band of reasonable responses test allows for a heightened standard to be adopted where those consequences are particularly grave (see also *Miller v William Hill Organisation Ltd* (UKEAT/0336/12/SM) (21 June 2013, unreported) in which the EAT overturned a finding of a fair dismissal because the employer had failed to check CCTV footage which would have exculpated the claimant, as well as that which incriminated her, before finding that the employee had committed a criminal offence, even though it could have done so at no additional cost). In *Stuart v London City Airport* UKEAT/0273/12/BA (9 November 2012, unreported) the EAT rejected an argument that the "heightened scrutiny" test set out in *A v B* did not apply to a case where an employee was alleged to have dishonestly taken goods from premises without paying for them. The EAT considered that such an allegation was always serious and required careful investigation which includes gathering evidence which might potentially be viewed as exculpatory or consistent with the Claimant's explanation. The EAT overturned the Tribunal's decision on the basis that it had failed in a number of respects to investigate the Claimant's explanations or exculpatory information. However, the Court of Appeal ([2013] EWCA Civ 973) in turn reversed the EAT's decision and reinstated that of the tribunal. This shows that the trend evident in *Roldan* and the cases following it should not be taken too far. The Court of Appeal considered there to be no basis for finding that the tribunal overlooked the gravity of the allegation when assessing the extent of the investigation.

In *Stuart v London City Airport* (above), the Court of Appeal held that the reasonableness of the investigation can be assessed by reference to the way in which the employee put his/her case during the internal procedure. In particular, if it is debatable whether or not an investigatory step was required, whether or not the employee asked for it to be undertaken is an important consideration. The Court of Appeal provided a strong reminder that the question remains whether the investigation was a reasonable one in *Shrestha v Genesis Housing Association Limited* [2015] EWCA Civ 94, [2015] IRLR 399, in which it refused to hold that each line of an employee's defence must be investigated unless it is manifestly false or unarguable. That approach was said to be too narrow and, the Court of Appeal held, it is always necessary to have regard to the context when assessing the reasonableness or otherwise of the investigation.

For certain professions, where internal disciplinary procedures are likely to lead to external statutory procedures, the standards of procedural fairness required for the internal disciplinary process may be higher than in the general case, in order to ensure that the employee's rights under *ECHR, Art 6* are respected. In *Kulkarni v Milton Keynes Hospital NHS Trust* [2010] ICR 101 the Court of Appeal held that a doctor facing allegations of sexual misconduct was entitled to legal representation during his internal disciplinary hearing. Likewise, in *R(G) v Governors of X School* [2010] 1 WLR 2218, which involved a teaching assistant at a primary school who was accused of sexual misconduct, the Court of Appeal held that he was entitled to legal representation at the school's disciplinary hearing, because *ECHR, Art 6* applied to an internal disciplinary process which was determinative of the employee's civil right to practise his profession. In *Mattu v University Hospitals of Coventry and Warwickshire NHS Trust* [2013] ICR 270 the Court of Appeal again considered the impact of *Art* 6 to disciplinary proceedings, concluding that the *NHS Trusts'* decision to dismiss an employee under his contract of employment did not determine his civil rights as defined in *Art* 6 (see HUMAN RIGHTS (30.7(a)) for a more detailed discussion of the authorities in this area).

The circumstances known to the employer for these purposes are those known to the dismissing officer, and those known to other senior officers who are not party to the decision to dismiss will not be attributed to that office (*Orr v Milton Keynes Council* [2011] ICR 704 (Sedley LJ dissenting)), though the employee might argue that an investigation which failed to uncover those facts was unreasonable. It does not matter if the employer's view, if reasonable at the time, is subsequently found to be mistaken (*St Anne's Board Mill Co Ltd v Brien* [1973] ICR 444; *British Home Stores Ltd v Burchell* [1980] ICR 303n). Equally, if the employer did not have reasonable grounds to dismiss at the time, the dismissal will be considered to be unfair even if evidence subsequently comes to light which proves him right (*W Devis & Sons Ltd v Atkins* [1977] ICR 662). In such a case, however, the employee may be awarded little or no compensation (see UNFAIR DISMISSAL – III (55)). The reasonableness of the decision will be scrutinised at the time of the final decision to dismiss, namely, at the conclusion of any appeal hearing (*West Midland Co-operative Society Ltd v Tipton* [1986] ICR 192).

In *Salford Royal NHS Foundation Trust v Roldan* [2010] ICR 1457, Elias LJ gave guidance, albeit *obiter*, about the approach an employer should take to allegations of misconduct where the evidence consists of diametrically conflicting accounts of an alleged incident with little other evidence to provide corroboration to either account. Employers are not obliged to believe one employee and disbelieve the other. It may be, for example, that the parties are both seeking to be truthful, but perceive events differently. Alternatively, in some cases the employer will be entitled to find that they are not satisfied that they can resolve the conflict of evidence and simply find the case not proved and give the employee the benefit of the doubt. This need not mean that they do not believe the complainant.

An employer's disciplinary procedures should follow the principles of natural justice, although a breach of the rules of these principles does not automatically make a dismissal unfair (*Slater v Leicestershire Health Authority* [1989] IRLR 16). Each case will turn on its facts and, as with the extent of the investigation, what is required will depend upon the relevant circumstances, such as the resources of the employer and the nature of the allegation.

It is important to frame the disciplinary charge carefully in order to ensure that a misconduct dismissal is for a matter charged, which has been fully investigated and to which the employee has had a proper opportunity to respond (*Strouthos v London Underground Ltd*

[2004] IRLR 636). Whilst in some cases it might be arguable that the employee knows the essence of the case against him, and the dismissal is accordingly fair, an employee is entitled to know the specific charge against him. For example, where money has gone missing, an employee is entitled to know whether the employer is alleging fraud or mere incompetence, as these are likely to lead to different reactions from the employee (*Celebi v Scolarest Compass Group UK & Ireland Ltd* (UKEAT/0032/10/LA) [2010] All ER (D) 136 (Sep), where additional matters came to light during the process, and allegations were added to the charge with the employee's consent). A further example of this principle is found in *Royal Mail Group Ltd v Lall* UKEAT/0228/12/ZT (15 October 2012, unreported) in which the employee was disbelieved as to his integrity without being given the opportunity to address the allegation. This issue should not be looked at over-technically by tribunals. The important point is that the employee knows the charge he is facing. The substance of the allegation is more important than the precise label that is attached to it (see, for instance, *Brito-Babapulle v Ealing Hospital NHS Trust* [2014] EWCA Civ 1626). The importance of substance over form in this context has recently been emphasised by the Court of Appeal in *Adeshina v St George's University Hospitals NHS Foundation Trust & Ors* [2017] EWCA Civ 257.

In *Khanum v Mid-Glamorgan Area Health Authority* [1979] ICR 40, it was held that natural justice required that the employee should know the accusations made against her, that she should be given an opportunity to state her case and that the members of the management team and the appeals panel should act in good faith. Further, in *Bentley Engineering Co Ltd v Mistry* [1979] ICR 47, the EAT held that natural justice required not merely that an employee should have a chance to state his own case but that he must know sufficiently what was being said against him so that he could put forward his own case properly. This principle was reaffirmed in *Louies v Coventry Hood and Seating Co Ltd* [1990] ICR 54: if heavy reliance is placed upon the statements of witnesses, the dismissal will almost always be unfair unless the employee has sight of the statements or is told exactly what is in them. However, in *Hussain v Elonex plc* [1999] IRLR 420, the Court of Appeal stressed that there is no hard and fast rule that in all cases an employee must be shown copies of witness statements obtained by an employer about the employee's conduct. Whether a failure to disclose information renders a dismissal unfair will be a fact-sensitive question (*Old v Palace Fields Primary Academy* (UKEAT/0085/14/BA) (17 October 2014, unreported).

Nor is there a rule obliging an employer to make witnesses available for cross examination by the employee (*Santamera v Express Cargo Forwarding* [2003] IRLR 273). It is a matter of what is fair and reasonable in each case; the gravity of the allegation and the consequences for the employee might allow a tribunal to find that an employer's refusal to allow the employee to question a witness was unreasonable (*TDG Chemical Ltd v Benton* (UKEAT/0166/10/DM) (10 September 2010, (unreported). For guidance in cases where an informant does not wish to be identified, see *Linfood Cash and Carry Ltd v Thomson* [1989] ICR 518 and *Asda Stores Ltd v Thompson (No 2)* [2004] IRLR 598. The EAT has held that unjustifiable delay in carrying out disciplinary proceedings can render unfair a dismissal which would otherwise have been held fair (*Royal Society for the Prevention of Cruelty to Animals v Cruden* [1986] ICR 205). If possible, the employer should avoid a situation where the same members of management act as witnesses or complainants and as judges (Slater, above, but the Court of Appeal recognised that avoidance of this might sometimes prove impracticable, especially where the employer is a very small organisation). The focus in such cases is on the impartiality (or otherwise) of the decision maker. The tribunal needs to consider how the decision maker might have been influenced by the allegedly improper involvement of a given employee in some part of the process (*UCATT v Dooley* (UKEAT/0346/12/JOJ) (3 May 2013, unreported)).

Other points to bear in mind are: that the employee should be given reasonable advance warning of the hearing and that disciplinary action is under consideration; that the employee should be given the opportunity to call witnesses if appropriate; and that the decision to dismiss should be taken by those who conduct the hearing, and not by someone who had only received a report of the disciplinary hearing (this was held to be an essential requirement of fairness by the EAT in *Budgen & Co v Thomas* [1976] ICR 344 though see *Parker v Clifford Dunn Ltd* [1979] ICR 463 to the effect that that will not inevitably be the case). A failure to keep adequate notes of a disciplinary hearing may amount to a procedural defect (*Vauxhall Motors Ltd v Ghafoor* [1993] ICR 376). A clandestine recording of a disciplinary hearing may be admissible evidence during an unfair dismissal claim, as in *Chairman and Governors of Amwell View School v Dagherty* [2007] ICR 135, although the EAT held that those parts of the secret recording which contained the disciplinary panel's private deliberations were not admissible. A finding that a member of a disciplinary panel fell asleep might justify a finding of procedural unfairness (*UCATT v Dooley* (UKEAT/0346/12/JOJ) (3 May 2013, unreported)).

It is often alleged that decision makers were biased against the employee. In *O'Adeshina v St George's University Hospitals NHS Foundation Trust* (2015) UKEAT/0293/14, [2015] IRLR 704, the EAT conducted a detailed review of the authorities in this area (a decision from the Court of Appeal in this case is expected imminently). In short, the strict rules of apparent bias do not apply, though the appearance of bias remains a relevant consideration for the purpose of *ERA 1996, s 98(4)*, whilst actual bias is more likely to give rise to a breach of natural justice fundamental to the question of fairness. Ultimately, the question remains one of fact for the Employment Tribunal, and it should not be approached as it would be in judicial proceedings.

If the decision is being taken by a panel, the employee is entitled to expect that the composition of the panel will remain the same from the start of the proceedings to the end. However, there may be circumstances where it is fair to proceed with reduced numbers. Where the expectation is not met, this may, though not inevitably, justify a finding of serious procedural unfairness sufficient to render the dismissal unfair. The reason for the change in the composition of the panel, and the prejudice to the employee of the change, are both relevant to the seriousness of the defect (*UCATT v Dooley* (UKEAT/0346/12/JOJ) (3 May 2013, unreported)).

The EAT considered the fairness of a dismissal founded in part upon covert surveillance conducted by an employer in *City and County of Swansea v Gayle* [2013] IRLR 768. There the employer used a private investigator who found the claimant at a sports centre during hours for which he was being paid. The tribunal found the dismissal unfair, on the basis that the employer should not have used covert surveillance in circumstances where the claimant's colleagues had already said that they had seen him at the centre. The EAT overturned the decision. It gave detailed consideration to *Article 8* of the *ECHR*, noting that in this case it was not breached because the photographs were taken in a public place during the employer's time whilst the claimant was engaged in wrongdoing. More generally, the EAT emphasised that in such cases the central question remains that posed by *s 98* of the *ERA*, and that only faults relevant to the dismissal were likely to render it unreasonable. The EAT went on to comment that the tribunal in this case had essentially found that the investigation was too thorough, which was unlikely to lead to the conclusion that the dismissal was unfair.

In *Bailey v BP Oil (Kent Refinery) Ltd* [1980] ICR 642, the Court of Appeal held that the failure by employers to comply with a disciplinary procedure agreement was a factor to be taken into account, but that the weight to be given to it depended upon the circumstances; see also *Stoker v Lancashire County Council* [1992] IRLR 75. Similarly, in *Westminster City Council v Cabaj* [1996] ICR 960, the Court of Appeal held that failure by an employer to follow its own contractually enforceable disciplinary procedure does not inevitably mean that the dismissal was unfair. In *Sarkar v West London Mental Health NHS Trust* [2010] IRLR 508 an employee's misconduct was initially dealt with under one procedure (under which an employee could receive, at most, a written warning) but it was later dealt with by a disciplinary panel when the more informal procedure broke down, and the employee was dismissed. The Court of Appeal held that the employer had not fettered its disciplinary options by using the first procedure, and was entitled to revise its approach to the misconduct following a detailed assessment of the evidence of the employee's conduct and its impact. However, the tribunal had been entitled to conclude that the use of the first procedure indicated a view on the employer's part that the misconduct alleged was relatively minor, and that it was inconsistent with this approach to later make a finding of gross misconduct based on the same matters.

Defects in the original procedure may be capable of being cured by a fair appeal, depending upon the seriousness of any allegations made against the employee, how bad the initial unfairness was and whether the appeal takes the form of a complete rehearing. The Court of Appeal has emphasised that there is no rule of law that earlier unfairness can be cured only by an appeal by way of a rehearing and not by way of a review, because the examination should be of the fairness of the disciplinary process as a whole. Each case will depend upon its own facts (*Taylor v OCS Group Ltd* [2006] ICR 1602)

Section 10 of the *Employment Relations Act 1999* gives an employee a right to be accompanied at a disciplinary hearing by a trade union official or another of the employer's workers. If the employee is denied this right, he may present a claim to the employment tribunal and may be awarded up to two weeks' pay (*ERA 1999, s 11*).

54.11   GROUNDS FOR DISMISSAL – REDUNDANCY

Redundancy is a potentially fair reason for dismissal. However, where the reason or the principal reason for the dismissal of an employee was that he was redundant (see REDUNDANCY – I (38)), the dismissal may be automatically unfair under *ERA 1996, s 105*. The dismissal will be automatically unfair if the circumstances constituting the redundancy applied equally to one or more employees in the same undertaking who held positions similar to that held by the dismissed employee and who have not been dismissed by the employer, and the reason for dismissed employee's selection was an automatically-unfair reason. The automatically unfair reasons for redundancy selection are in largely similar terms to the automatically unfair reasons for dismissal (see **54.3** above) and so are summarised in relatively brief fashion here:

(i)   the reason (or if more than one, the principal reason) for which the employee was selected was one of the reasons related to jury service specified in *ERA 1996, s 98B(1)*, provided that *s 98B(2)* does not apply;

(ii)   the reason (or, if more than one, the principal reason) for which he was selected was one of the health and safety-related reasons specified in *ERA 1996, s 100*;

(iii)   the reason (or, if more than one, the principal reason) for which he was selected was one of those related to shop/betting shop workers refusing to work Sundays set out in *ERA 1996, s 101*;

(iv)   the reason (or, if more than one, the principal reason) for which he was selected was one of those related to working time set out in *ERA 1996, s 101A*;

(v)   the reason (or, if more than one, the principal reason) for which he was selected was related to his role as a trustee of an occupational pension scheme, as specified in *ERA 1996, s 102(1)*;

(vi)   the reason (or, if more than one, the principal reason) for which he was selected related to his work as an employee representative (see **39.4** REDUNDANCY – **II**) as specified in *ERA 1996, s 103*;

(vii)   the reason (or, if more than one, the principal reason) for which he was selected was that he had made a protected disclosure, as specified in *ERA 1996, s 103A*;

(viii) the reason (or, if more than one, the principal reason) for which he was selected related to his assertion of a statutory right as specified in *ERA 1996, s 104(1)*;

(ix)   the reason (or, if more than one, the principal reason) for which he was selected was one of those relating to the national minimum wage set out in *ERA 1996, s 104A*;

(x)   the reason (or, if more than one, the principal reason) for which he was selected was one of those relating to tax credit specified in *ERA, s 104B*;

(xi)   the reason (or, if more than one, the principal reason) for which he was selected related to a flexible working request as specified in *ERA, s 104C*;

(xii)   the reason (or, if more than one, the principal reason) for which he was selected was one of those related to studying and training specified in *ERA, s 104E*;

(xiii)   the reason (or, if more than one, the principal reason) for which he was selected was one of those relating to official industrial action mentioned in *Trade Union and Labour Relations (Consolidation) Act 1992 s 238A(2)*, and *s 238A(3), (4)* or *(5)* applies to the dismissal;

(xiv)   the reason (or, if more than one, the principal reason) for which he was selected was one related to his activities as a member of a special negotiating body as specified in *regulation 28(3)* or *(6)* of the *Transnational Information and Consultation of Employees Regulations 1999*;

(xv)   the reason (or, if more than one, the principal reason) for which he was selected was one related to his assertion of his rights as a part-time worker, as detailed in *reg 7(3)* of the *Part-time Workers (Prevention of Less Favourable Treatment) Regulations 2000*;

(xvi)   the reason (or, if more than, the principal reason) for which he was selected was one related to his assertion of his rights as a fixed-term employee as specified in *reg 6(3)* of the *Fixed-term Employees (Prevention of Less Favourable Treatment) Regulations 2002*;

(xvii)   the reason (or, if more than, the principal reason) for which he was selected was one specified in the *European Public Limited-Liability Company Regulations 2004, reg 42(3)* or *(6)*;

(xviii)   the reason (or, if more than one, the principal reason) for which he was selected related to his activities as an employee representative (see **51.18 TRANSFER OF UNDERTAKINGS**) as detailed in *Information and Consultation of Employees Regulations 2004, reg 30*;

(xix)   the reason (or, if more than one, the principal reason) for which he was selected was one specified in *paragraph 5(3)* or *(5)* of the *Schedule* to the *Occupational and Personal Pension Schemes (Consultation by Employers and Miscellaneous Amendment) Regulations 2006*;

(xx)   the reason (or, if more than one, the principal reason) for which the employee was selected was one specified in *para (3)* or *(6)* of *regulation 31* of the *European Cooperative Society (Involvement of Employees) Regulations*;

(xxi)   the reason (or, if more than one, the principal reason) for which the employee was selected was one specified in the *Companies (Cross-Border Mergers) Regulations 200 reg 46(2)* or *47(2)*;

(xxii)   the reason (or, if more than one, the principal reason) for which the employee selected was one specified in *European Public Limited-Liability Company (Em Involvement) (Great Britain) Regulations 2009, reg 29(3)* or *(6)*;

(xxiii)   the reason (or, if more than one, the principal reason) for which the empl selected related to a prohibited black list as specified in *ERA 1996, s 104* the condition in either *104F(1)(a)* or *(b)* is met;

(xxiv)   the reason (or, if more than one, the principal reason) for which the employee was selected was one specified in the *Agency Workers Regulations 2010, reg 17(3)*.

(xxv)   the reason (or, if more than one, the principal reason) for which he or she was selected related to pregnancy, maternity leave etc within the meaning of *ERA 1996, s 99* and the *Maternity and Parental Leave etc Regulations 1999, reg 20* or the *Shared Parental Leave Regulations 2014, reg 43*.

(xxvi)   the reason (or, if more than one, the principal reason) for which the employee was selected for dismissal related to trade union membership or activities under the *Trade Union and Labour Relations (Consolidation) Act 1992, s 153*.

(xxvii)   the reason (or, if more than one, the principal reason) for which the employee was selected for dismissal was one of those specified in *ERA 1996, s 104D(1)* (pension enrolment).

An employer should not, however, give preferential consideration to an employee in a redundancy selection process on the ground that he or she is a health and safety representative (*Smiths Industries Aerospace and Defence Systems v Rawlings* [1996] IRLR 656).

A redundancy dismissal which is not automatically unfair may nevertheless be unfair 'in all the circumstances' within the meaning of *ERA 1996, s 98(4)*. Whilst a tribunal will not investigate the commercial merits of an employer's decision that redundancies were required (*James W Cook & Co (Wivenhoe) Ltd (in liq) v Tipper* [1990] ICR 716, CA; *Campbell v Dunoon and Cowal Housing Association* [1993] IRLR 496), there are other ways in which a dismissal by reason of redundancy might be found to be unfair. The position was summarised by Lord Bridge in *Polkey v A E Dayton Services Ltd* [1988] ICR 142 at 162–163:

> " . . . in the case of redundancy, the employer will normally not act reasonably unless he warns and consults any employees affected or their representative, adopts a fair basis on which to select for redundancy and takes such steps as may be reasonable to avoid or minimise redundancy by redeployment within his own organisation . . . It is quite a different matter if the tribunal is able to conclude that the employer himself, at the time of dismissal, acted reasonably in taking the view that, in the exceptional circumstances of the particular case, the procedural steps normally appropriate would have been futile, could not have altered the decision to dismiss and therefore could be dispensed with."

TULRCA 1992, s 188 (as amended by *TURERA 1993, s 34* and *SI 1995/2587*) imposes a duty on employers to consult appropriate representatives of the employees concerned. A failure to comply with that requirement will probably – although not necessarily – render the dismissal unfair (*Hough v Leyland DAF Ltd* [1991] ICR 696). In order to comply with the requirements of *s 188*, the employer must begin consultations before giving individual notices of dismissal (*National Union of Teachers v Avon County Council* [1978] ICR 626). See **39.2–39.5** REDUNDANCY – **II** for further details on this topic and the specific remedies for breach of the collective consultation provisions.

Even where no trade union is recognised for bargaining purposes, in respect of dismissals taking effect on or after 1 March 1996, employers must (by virtue of *SI 1995/2587*) consult with employee representatives before deciding which employees should be made redundant, where at least 20 or more employees are proposed to be made redundant at one establishment within 90 days or less (see **39.2** et seq REDUNDANCY – **II**).

The EAT in *Williams v Compair Maxam Ltd* [1982] ICR 156 listed the principles which, in the experience of the two lay members, reasonable employers adopted when dismissing for redundancy employees who are represented by an independent trade union recognised by them. The EAT stressed that the principles would not stay unaltered forever, and that they the fairness of foreshortening a notice period in circumstances where there is a potential for alternative work to arise in *Missirlis v Queen Mary University of London* (UKEAT/0038/15/LA) (16 May 2016, unreported), though as the case was remitted to the Employment Tribunal, the guidance is not definitive, save for reiterating the importance of *section 98(4)* of the *ERA*.

In *Lloyd v Taylor Woodrow Construction* [1999] IRLR 782, the EAT held that, as with conduct and capability cases, a defect in a redundancy consultation process could be cured on appeal, provided that the appeal is a rehearing and not merely a review of the original decision. The Court of Appeal, however, has ruled that the appeal need not take the form of a rehearing (see *Taylor v OCS Group Ltd* above).

> 'If the employer can establish that had he taken reasonable steps to consult with the employee or find him other employment, he would still have been dismissed, an employment tribunal may find the dismissal to be unfair but award no compensation, or compensate only for the wages and benefits which would have been received while consultation was taking place. (See also **54.4** above; and **55.13**.) The question to be asked in the exceptional case contemplated by *Polkey* (above) where consultation would be pointless is not whether the employer in fact made a conscious decision not to consult, but whether a reasonable employer could have decided not to consult in the light of the facts that were known at the time (*Duffy v Yeomans & Partners Ltd* [1993] IRLR 368; cf *Dick v Boots the Chemists Ltd* IDS Brief 451, p 12; see also *Heron v Citylink – Nottingham* [1993] IRLR 372).'

It is worth noting that the significance of *Polkey* was changed for a period by *EmA 2002, s 34*, which introduced a new *s 98A(2)* into *ERA 1996*. This provision, however, was repealed in April 2009. *Section 98A(2)* provided that failure to follow a procedure in relation to the dismissal of an employee should not be regarded as, by itself, making the employer's action unreasonable if he showed that he would have decided to dismiss the employee if he had followed the procedure. The purpose of the subsection was to deter employees from bringing unfair dismissal claims if they were relying upon a technical breach of procedure by the employer, which had no effect on the outcome (see further *Kelly-Madden* above).

54.12 Dismissal procedure

From decided cases (see **54.11** above) the following guidelines emerge:

(a)   consult with employee representatives;

(b)   consider possible alternatives to redundancies, eg short-time working, work sharing, other costs savings, etc;

(c)   if redundancy becomes necessary, in consultation with employee representatives, agree objective criteria for selection for redundancy;

(d)   apply the criteria objectively;

(e)   inform the employees affected at the earliest opportunity and give the employees an opportunity to contest the scores they are given;

(f)   investigate the possibilities of offering them alternative employment within the company or group, continuing the investigation until the employment has come to an end;

(g)   give them time off to seek employment;

(h)   pay all moneys due;

(i)   conduct an appeal; and

(j)   keep careful records and minutes of these steps.

Whilst the failure to follow the above will not necessarily render a dismissal unfair, they provide a useful starting point for an employer undertaking a redundancy exercise. As emphasised above, they should not be treated as a statutory checklist for achieving a fair dismissal.

54.13 GROUNDS FOR DISMISSAL – CONTRAVENTION OF ANY ENACTMENT

If an employer dismisses an employee because the employee could not continue to work in the position which he held without contravention (either on his part or on that of his employer) of a duty or restriction imposed by or under an enactment, the reason for the dismissal falls within *ERA 1996, s 98(2)(d)*.

The fact that an employer genuinely but erroneously believes that he would be breaking the law by continuing to employ an employee does not make the reason for the dismissal of that employee a reason falling within *ERA 1996, s 98(2)(d)*, but it could be 'some other substantial reason' justifying the dismissal within *ERA 1996, s 98(1)(b)* (see **54.14** below) (*Bouchaala v Trusthouse Forte Hotels Ltd* [1980] ICR 721).

Procedure. In these cases employers should:

(a)   arrange a formal meeting at which the employee (ideally with an accompanying person) should be informed of the situation and invited (himself or through a representative) to express his views; and

(b)   in appropriate cases, find out if the company or an associated company has a suitable vacancy which the employee can be offered instead.

54.14 GROUNDS FOR DISMISSAL – 'SOME OTHER SUBSTANTIAL REASON'

These reasons need not be of the same type as those that are specified in the *Act*. If the reason for dismissal is not one of those set out in *ERA 1996, s 98(2)* (see **54.2** above), it may nevertheless be an acceptable reason if the employer can show that it was 'some other substantial reason of a kind such as to justify the dismissal of an employee holding the position which that employee held' (*ERA 1996, s 98(1)(b)*). Examples of such reasons are the following.

(a)   *Necessary re-organisation of the business* (*Hollister v National Farmers' Union* [1979] ICR 542; *Richmond Precision Engineering Ltd v Pearce* [1985] IRLR 179; *Catamaran Cruisers Ltd v Williams* [1994] IRLR 386; *Cobley v Forward Technology Industries plc* [2003] ICR 1050). This may also apply in cases where changes in terms and conditions have led the employee to claim constructive dismissal (*Genower v Ealing, Hammersmith and Hounslow Area Health Authority* [1980] IRLR 297). But note that the employee must be fairly considered for any new job created by the reorganisation (*Oakley v Labour Party* [1988] ICR 403). An employer does not need to establish that the change in terms of employment in such cases is essential in order to show that the reason falls within *ERA, s 98(1)(b)*. There is no principle of law that the survival of the business must depend upon the adoption of the terms (*Garside and Laycock Ltd v Booth* [2011] IRLR 735). If ostensibly the reason could justify the dismissal, it is a substantial reason and the enquiry moves to the fairness of the dismissal. It is at this later stage when the balancing exercise between the needs of the employer and the detriment to the employee falls to be considered (*Roberts v Acumed Ltd* (UKEAT/0466/09/DA) (25 November 2010, unreported). This balancing exercise requires a focus on the words "in accordance with equity" in *ERA 1996, s 98(4)*, as well as a careful scrutiny of the procedure followed (*Garside and Laycock v Booth* (above)). For an example of a successful dismissal followed by re-engagement on new terms, see *Slade & Ors v TNT (UK) Ltd* (UKEAT/0113/11/DA) (13 September 2011, unreported). See also *Taylor v Crockford* (UKEAT/0370/13/SM) (28 February 2014, unreported) for an example of a case involving a failure to agree upon a change of hours.

(b)   *Economic, technical or organisational reasons entailing changes in the workforce* of the transferor or the transferee before or after a relevant transfer within the meaning of the *Transfer of Undertakings (Protection of Employment) Regulations 2006 (SI 2006/246), reg 7(3)(b)* (see **52.26** Transfer of Undertakings).

(c)   Reasons of *necessary economies* such as in *Durrant and Cheshire v Clariston Clothing Co Ltd* [1974] IRLR 360 in which a tribunal held that it was reasonable for a company to dismiss two employees who were earning £25.87 per week each but for whom they had to provide transport costing the company £24 per week each. See also *Buckland v Bournemouth University Higher Education Corporation* [2010] IRLR 445, in which the Court of Appeal speculated about a case of constructive dismissal which could be characterised as a fair dismissal for some other substantial reason, where a major customer of the employer had defaulted on a payment with the consequence that the employer had an unexpected lack of funds and had, in repudiatory breach of contract, failed to pay the employee.

(d)   *Protection of the interest of the business* such as in *RS Components Ltd v Irwin* [1974] 1 All ER 41 in which the company was held to have fairly dismissed an employee for refusing to sign a reasonable restrictive covenant which was considered necessary. In considering the fairness of a dismissal for a refusal to accept new terms and conditions, it is material to consider what proportion of the workforce had accepted the change when the decision to dismiss was taken (*St John of God (Care Services) Ltd v Brooks* [1992] ICR 715). The Court of Appeal has now gone further in *Willow Oak Developments Ltd (t/a Windsor Recruitment) v Silverwood* [2006] EWCA Civ 660, [2007] IRLR 607 and held a dismissal lawful for refusal to sign restrictive covenants, where the new covenants were provided to the employee earlier on the same day and were unreasonably wide, on the basis that the employer's reliance on the refusal to sign was lawful because the reliance was on a reason of the 'kind' capable of justifying dismissal.

(e)   *An employee's personality* cannot, by itself, be a fair reason for dismissal, however, in certain circumstances the manifestations of that personality can give rise to 'some other substantial reason' for dismissal (*Perkin v St George's Healthcare NHS Trust* [2005] EWCA Civ 1174, [2005] IRLR 934).

(f)   *Expiry of a fixed-term contract* when it is shown that the contract was adopted for a genuine purpose and that fact was known to the employee, and it is also shown that the specific purpose for which the contract was adopted has ceased to be applicable (*North Yorkshire County Council v Fay* [1986] ICR 133. See also *Terry v East Sussex County Council* [1976] ICR 536 and *Tasneem v Dudley Group of Hospitals NHS Trust* (UKEAT/0232/10/CEA) (29 June 2011, unreported)). Note, however, the *Fixed-term Employees (Prevention of Less Favourable Treatment) Regulations 2002*.

(g)   The imposition of a *sentence of imprisonment* (*Kingston v British Railways Board* [1984] ICR 781). In some cases, this may have the effect of *frustrating* the contract, thus bringing it to an end without a dismissal (see **48.3** Termination of Employment).

(h)   *Dismissal of the replacement of an employee suspended on medical or maternity grounds (ERA 1996, s 106(3))*. Where an employer suspends an employee on medical grounds in compliance with a statutory requirement and engages another in his place, he should inform the replacement employee in writing when engaging him that his employment will be terminated at the end of the suspension of the original employee. If he dismisses the replacement employee in order to allow the original employee to resume work, the dismissal will be regarded as having been for a reason falling within *ERA 1996, s 98(1)(b)*.

(i)   *Dismissal of the replacement of an employee absent due to pregnancy or childbirth (ERA 1996, s 106(2))*. Where an employer engages an employee to replace another employee who is absent due to pregnancy and on engaging the replacement employee the employer informs him in writing that his employment will be terminated on the return to work of the pregnant employee, a dismissal of the replacement employee to give work to the original employee will be considered as a dismissal for a reason falling within *ERA 1996, s 98(1)(b)*.

(j)   *Relationship breakdown.* In *Ezsias v North Glamorgan NHS Trust* [2011] IRLR 550 the EAT accepted the employment tribunal's finding that the employer had dismissed the employee because of a breakdown in relationship, rather than the employee's conduct which led to that breakdown. The result was that the employer was not required to follow a contractual disciplinary hearing. However, the EAT noted that tribunals would be on the lookout for an employer using the rubric of "some other substantial reason" as a pretext to conceal the real reason for dismissal. This was reiterated by the Court of Appeal in *Leach v Office of Communications* [2012] ICR 1269 which stated that "breakdown of trust" is not a mantra that can be mouthed by an employer faced with difficulties in establishing a more conventional conduct reason for dismissal. The seniority of the individual and the size of the employer are both likely to be relevant to the question of whether or not the breakdown justifies dismissal (*Phoenix House Ltd v Stockman & Ors* [2017] ICR 84).

As usual, dismissal for such a reason will be fair if it was within the 'range of reasonable responses' (see **54.4** above) and a fair procedure was followed. In *Alboni v Ind Coope Retail Ltd* [1998] IRLR 131, the Court of Appeal held that an employment tribunal is bound to have regard to events between notice of dismissal and the date that dismissal took effect, both in determining the reason for dismissal and whether the employers acted reasonably in the circumstances in treating it as a sufficient reason for dismissal.

When breakdown of trust and confidence is given as the reason for the dismissal, what is the scope of the tribunal's examination of the facts which resulted in that position having been reached? This was considered by the EAT in *Governing Body of Tubbenden Primary School v Sylvester* UKEAT/0527/11/RN [2012] ICR D29. The EAT held that where, as in that case, the reason was essentially a consequence of conduct, it made sense for the tribunal to have regard to the immediate history leading up to the dismissal when assessing reasonableness. The EAT made it clear that it was not holding that in every case in which there is a dismissal because of a breakdown of trust and confidence the tribunal must have regard to how that situation came about. Tribunals are, however, entitled to do so in an appropriate case, of which that was an example.

The fact that a client which procures the dismissal of an employee may have acted unfairly does not mean the dismissal is unfair (*Henderson v Connect (South Tyneside) Ltd* [2010] IRLR 468). If the employer has done everything he reasonably can to avoid or mitigate the injustice brought about by the stance of the client, most obviously by trying to get the client to change his mind and, if that is impossible, by trying to find alternative work for the employee, but has failed, the eventual dismissal will be fair. The employer does, however, need to take into account the injustice and take the steps which it can to remedy it. See *Dobie v Burns International Security Services (UK) Ltd* [1984] ICR 812 for a discussion of factors to be considered when assessing the question of injustice for these purposes. *Bancroft v Interserve (Facilities Management) Ltd* UKEAT/0329/12/KN (13 December 2012, unreported) is an example of such a case. The employee in that case was dismissed because of third party pressure from a client. The EAT applied Henderson and found that the tribunal had failed to grapple properly with the question of whether or not the employer had done everything it could to mitigate the injustice caused by the third party's request. The EAT also raised an interesting question as to whether the employer was required to have taken steps earlier in the employment history to seek to remedy a problem before it became an insuperable problem leading to dismissal at the behest of the client, but did not find it necessary to resolve the issue in its decision.

In *Jefferson (Commercial) LLP v Westgate* UKEAT/0128/12/SM (19 July 2012, unreported) the EAT considered the question of procedural fairness in the context of an SOSR dismissal. Westgate was recently applied by the EAT in *Express Medicals Ltd v O'Donnell* (UKEAT/0263/15/DA) (9 February 2016, unreported).In Westgate both the employer and employee were found to have lost trust and confidence in each other, the employee having stated that he did not intend to return to work. The EAT overturned the tribunal's finding that the resulting dismissal was unfair because of a failure on the employer's part to hold a meeting. The EAT held that whilst the ACAS Code might extend beyond pure misconduct and poor performance scenarios, it had little to say in the present context of an irretrievable breakdown, where a further meeting would not have achieved anything. The EAT reiterated that in every case it is necessary for the tribunal to consider *ERA 1996, s 98(4)* and apply it sensibly to the facts of the case. The EAT in *Phoenix House Ltd v Stockman & Ors* [2017] ICR 84 came to the same conclusion in relation to the applicability of the ACAS Code in the context of a dismissal following a breakdown in trust and confidence. The EAT held that what is required in such a case is that the employer fairly considers whether or not the relationship has deteriorated to such an extent that the employee cannot be reincorporated into the workforce without unacceptable disruption. Elements of the ACAS Code incorporate basic common sense principles of fairness, which are capable of being and should be applied to such a decision, such as giving the employee the chance to show that he can return to work. The EAT emphasised, however, that this does not mean that the ACAS Code applies in term.

In certain circumstances, it may be necessary to consider suitable alternative employment before dismissing for "some other substantial reason", though it is not an automatic requirement of a fair dismissal (see *USDAW v Burns* (UKEAT/0557/12/DA) (1 April 2014, unreported)).

54.15 DISMISSAL FOLLOWING AN INTERNAL APPEAL

If an employee uses an internal appeal procedure to challenge a decision to dismiss him, and his appeal is rejected, he will be regarded as having been dismissed from the date of his original dismissal, unless his contract provides otherwise (see, eg *J Sainsbury Ltd v Savage* [1981] ICR 1, approved in *West Midlands Co-operative Society Ltd v Tipton* [1986] ICR 192).

In *Tipton*, the House of Lords decided that the fairness of a dismissal is judged at the time of the final decision to dismiss, which, if there is an internal appeal, will be at the conclusion of such an appeal. Lord Bridge said at 204D:

> 'A dismissal is unfair if the employer unreasonably treats his real reasons as a sufficient reason to dismiss the employee, either when he makes his original decision to dismiss, or when he maintains that decision at the conclusion of an internal appeal.'

In other words, facts and matters that come to light during the appeal hearing, whether in favour of the employee or against him, ought to be taken into account (see **54.4** above for a detailed discussion about the role of the appeal).

54.16 PRESSURE ON AN EMPLOYER TO DISMISS UNFAIRLY

In determining the reason for a dismissal, or whether it was fair in the circumstances, no account is taken of any pressure which by calling, organising, procuring or financing a strike or other industrial action, or threatening to do so, was exercised on the employer to dismiss the employee. Any question relating to dismissal will be determined as if no such pressure had been exercised (*ERA 1996, s 107*).

However, a trade union or an individual who induced the employer to dismiss an employee may, in certain circumstances, be joined in the proceedings and be ordered to pay all or part of any compensation awarded for unfair dismissal (*TULRCA 1992, s 160*). (See **55.17** UNFAIR DISMISSAL – III.)

55   Unfair Dismissal – III: Remedies

55.1   When an employment tribunal finds that a complaint of unfair dismissal is well-founded, it may make an order for the reinstatement or re-engagement of the complainant, or an order for compensation. This chapter deals with the remedies for unfair dismissal and the settlement of claims, as follows.

—   Reinstatement (see **55.2** below) and re-engagement (see **55.3** below) and related rules (see **55.4**, **55.5** below).

—   Awards of compensation (see **55.6–55.16** below), comprising the following:

•   Basic award (see **55.7–55.9** below).

•   Compensatory award (see **55.10–55.13** below).

•   Additional award in case of non-compliance with order for reinstatement or re-engagement (except union-related, health and safety, pension scheme trustee and employee representative cases) (see **55.14** below).

•   Maximum awards (see **55.16** below).

•   Union-related, health and safety, pension scheme trustees and employee representative dismissals – special award (see **55.16–55.18** below) and reduction of total award (see **55.19** below).

—   Joinder of parties (see **55.17** below).

—   Interim relief (see **55.18** below).

—   Settlement (see **55.19** below).

For the enforcement of, and interest upon, tribunal awards, see **19.121** and **19.122** Employment Tribunals – **II**.

In practice, a successful complainant will in most cases receive an award of compensation which is made up of a basic award and a compensatory award. Orders for reinstatement and re-engagement are rare. Other payments are restricted to special circumstances as indicated in the relevant paragraphs.

The tribunal's first step on finding a dismissal to be unfair should be to explain to the employee the possibility of an order for reinstatement or re-engagement, and to ask him whether he wishes such an order to be made (*ERA 1996, s 112(1)*). This question should be asked even if the employee has indicated his preferred remedy in his originating application. Although the tribunal's failure to ask the claimant whether he wishes to be reinstated or re-engaged does not render its decision on remedies a nullity, at least where the claimant was legally represented (*Cowley v Manson Timber Ltd* [1995] ICR 367), an appeal tribunal should be very ready to remit a case for further consideration of remedy in these circumstances (*Constantine v McGregor Cory Ltd* [2000] ICR 938).

Even where an employer has offered to pay the maximum possible award of compensation, but has not admitted that the dismissal was unfair, the employee is entitled to proceed with his complaint (*Telephone Information Services Ltd v Wilkinson* [1991] IRLR 148; see also *NRG Victory Reinsurance Ltd v Alexander* [1992] ICR 675).

55.2   REINSTATEMENT

An order for reinstatement is defined as *an order that the employer shall treat the complainant in all respects as if he had not been dismissed*. In deciding whether to make such an order, the tribunal must consider:

(a)   whether the complainant wishes to be reinstated;

(b)   whether it is practicable for an employer to comply with an order for reinstatement; and

(c)   (in a case where the complainant wholly or partially caused or contributed to the dismissal) whether it would be just to order his reinstatement.

(ERA 1996, s 116(1).)

In *McBride v Scottish Police Authority* [2016] ICR 788, the Supreme Court held that an order for reinstatement requires the reinstatement of "the contractual rights, the terms and conditions of the employment" but does not require "the recreation of the precise factual conditions at the point of dismissal". Differing from the EAT's view in *British Airways v Valencia* [2014] IRLR 683, the Court held that an employer could, for example, give a reinstated employee a new line manager in order to avoid further conflict.

In deciding whether to make an order for reinstatement, the tribunal will consider the effect that such an order would have on the respondent's business. If, as in *Coleman and Stephenson v Magnet Joinery Ltd* [1974] ICR 25, such an order would inevitably lead to industrial unrest, it should not be made. Nor should it be considered practicable where it would lead to a redundancy situation or to significant overmanning (*Cold Drawn Tubes Ltd v Middleton* [1992] ICR 318; see also *Port of London Authority v Payne* [1994] ICR 555). A finding on the practicality or otherwise of ordering re-employment is one which is obviously within the tribunal's exclusive territory as an 'industrial jury' and an appeal against such a finding on grounds of perversity alone was described as 'virtually impossible' in *Clancy v Cannock Chase Technical College* [2001] IRLR 331 (however for a recent successful example see *British Airways Plc v Valencia* [2014] IRLR 683).

If the tribunal orders reinstatement, it must specify:

(i)   any amount payable by the employer in respect of any benefit which the complainant might reasonably be expected to have received but for the dismissal, including arrears of pay, for the period between the date of termination of employment and the date of reinstatement;

(ii)   any rights and privileges, including seniority and pension rights, which must be restored to the employee; and

(iii)   the date by which the order must be complied with.

(ERA 1996, s 114(1).)

Moreover, if the complainant would have benefited from an improvement in his terms and conditions of employment had he not been dismissed, the order for reinstatement will require him to be treated as if he had benefited from that improvement from the date on which he would have done so had he not been dismissed. Thus, if an order for reinstatement is made, the claimant must be restored to his original job and receive back pay and benefits from the date of his dismissal (*ERA 1996, s 114(3)*).

Where there is a breakdown in trust and confidence, the remedy of reinstatement or re-engagement has very limited scope and will only be practicable in the rarest of cases. In *Wood Group Heavy Industrial Turbines Ltd v Crossan* [1998] IRLR 680, the Scottish EAT overturned an order for re-engagement made by a tribunal in a case in which the employee had been unfairly dismissed for dealing in drugs in the workplace and the employer genuinely believed in the guilt of the employee.

Where an employee is unfairly dismissed both by the transferor and then (after being re-engaged) again by the transferee of a business, the transferee may be liable to pay two basic awards because of the provisions of the *Transfer of Undertakings (Protection of Employment) Regulations 2006 (Fenton v Stablegold Ltd (t/a Chiswick Court Hotel)* [1986] ICR 236) (see also Transfer of Undertakings **(52)**).

55.8   Exceptions

The amount of the basic award is *two weeks' pay* where the tribunal finds that the reason or the principal reason for the dismissal of the employee was that he was redundant and that:

(a)   he unreasonably refused or left suitable alternative employment (contrary to *ERA 1996, s 141)*; or

(b)   his employment was renewed or he was re-engaged and he was therefore not considered dismissed under *ERA 1996, s 138(1)*.

(ERA 1996, s 121.)

The above provision has the curious effect that an employee is entitled to a basic award of compensation notwithstanding the fact that he is not considered as dismissed for the purposes of claiming a redundancy payment (see **39.6** Redundancy – **I**).

Where a dismissal is to be regarded as unfair by virtue of:

(i)   *TULRCA 1992, s 152* or *153* (ie for a 'union-related' reason); or

(ii)   *ERA 1996, s 100(1)(a)* or *(b)* (health and safety activities as a representative, committee member or designated employee; note that this does not apply to all the circumstances in which a health and safety dismissal is automatically unfair); or

(iii)   *ERA 1996, s 101A(1)(d)* (activities as a workforce representative in a 'working time' case; note that this does not apply to all the circumstances in which a 'working time' dismissal is automatically unfair); or

(iv)   *ERA 1996, s 102(1)* (activities as a pension scheme trustee); or

(v)   *ERA 1996, s 103* (activities as an employee representative),

then the amount of any basic award (before any reduction) will be not less than £5,970 *(TULRCA 1992, s 156(1); ERA 1996, s 120(1))*.

Where a dismissal is unfair by virtue of *ERA 1996, s 104F* (blacklisting) the amount of any basic award will be not less than £5,000 *(ERA 1996, s 120(1C))*.

55.9   Reduction of basic award

Where the tribunal considers that any conduct of the complainant before the dismissal (or, where the dismissal was with notice, before the notice was given) was such that it would be just and equitable to reduce or further reduce the amount of the basic award to any extent, the tribunal will so reduce the award *(ERA 1996, s 122(2); TULRCA 1992, s 156(2))*. The exercise required by *s 122(2)* is to be undertaken by the tribunal in three stages: (i) identification of the conduct said to give rise to contributory fault (ii) assessment of whether that conduct was blameworthy (iii) decision on whether it is just and equitable to reduce the award. In making the assessment at stages (i) and (ii) the tribunal's focus should be on what the employee has done, not the employer's assessment of how wrongful the conduct is (*Steen v ASP Packaging Ltd* [2014] ICR 56). See also **55.13** below. However, a basic award can never be reduced on the basis of a failure to mitigate (*Lock v Connell Estate Agents* [1994] IRLR 444).

The amount of the basic award will not be reduced by virtue of the above provisions where the reason or principal reason for the dismissal was that the employee was redundant, unless the dismissal is to be regarded as unfair (*a*) by virtue of *TULRCA 1992, s 153* (selection for redundancy for a 'union-related' reason), or (*b*) because the reason for selecting the employee for dismissal was one of those specified in *ERA 1996, s 100(1)(a)* or *(b)*, *101A(1)(d), 102(1)* or *103* (see (ii)–(v) in **55.8** above). In that event, the reduction will apply only to so much of the basic award as is payable because of *TULRCA 1992, s 156(1)* or *ERA 1996, s 120* (see **55.8** above) (*ERA 1996, s 122(3); TULRCA 1992, s 156(2)*).

Where the tribunal finds that the complainant has unreasonably refused an offer by the employer which, if accepted, would have the effect of reinstating the complainant in his employment in all respects as if he had not been dismissed, the tribunal will reduce or further reduce the amount of the basic award to such extent as it considers just and equitable having regard to that finding (*ERA 1996, s 122(1)*).

The basic award may also be reduced where the employee has been awarded any amount in respect of the dismissal under a designated dismissal procedures agreement, to such extent as the tribunal considers it just and equitable having regard to that award (*ERA 1996, s 122(3A)* inserted by the *Employment Rights (Dispute Resolution) Act 1998, s 15, Sch 1, para 22*).

The amount of the basic award will be reduced or, as the case may be, further reduced, by the amount of any redundancy payment awarded by the tribunal in respect of the same dismissal or of any payment made by the employer to the employee on the ground that the dismissal was by reason of redundancy, whether in pursuance of statutory provisions or otherwise (*ERA 1996, s 122(4)*). No reduction of the basic award will be made, however, when the employer makes a payment in respect of redundancy but, objectively viewed, the employee was not redundant (*Boorman v Allmakes Ltd* [1995] IRLR 553).

Note that, where an employee had received an *ex gratia* payment from his former employers which included his statutory entitlement and which was sufficient to cover any basic or compensatory award, the EAT held that an employment tribunal was not obliged to make a basic award (*Chelsea Football Club and Athletic Co Ltd v Heath* [1981] ICR 323; cf *Barnsley Metropolitan Borough Council v Prest* [1996] ICR 85).

See also **55.14** below for reduction in union-related cases.

55.10   COMPENSATORY AWARD

The compensation recoverable on a complaint of unfair dismissal increased dramatically in 1999, but, in the current job market, the maximum award is often criticised as being unrealistically low. There are some calls substantially to increase or even remove the cap, though such calls are very unlikely to be heeded in the present political climate.

For dismissals before 25 October 1999, the maximum amount of the compensatory award was £12,000. With effect from 25 October 1999, the maximum amount of the compensatory award was increased to £50,000, and was abolished altogether in a small number of cases (*Employment Relations Act 1999, ss 34(4)* and *37(1)*; *SI 1992/2830*). For dismissals on or after 6th April 2016, the maximum compensatory award has again increased from £78,962 to £80,541 (*SI 2017/175*). Note, however, that pursuant to *ERA 1996, s 124(1ZA)* the maximum compensatory award is the lower of £80,541 and "52 multiplied by a week's pay" of the individual employee. For these purposes, a 'week's pay' is to be calculated in accordance with the provisions of *ERA 1996, ss 221–229 (s 227* is of course not applicable).

There is no maximum compensatory award in health and safety cases (*ERA 1996, s 100*), protected disclosure cases (*ERA 1996, s 103A*), selection for redundancy on health and safety grounds (*ERA 1996, s 105(3)*), and selection for redundancy on protected disclosure grounds (*ERA 1996, s 105(6A)*): *ERA 1996, s 124(1A)*. In the case of a refusal to reinstate or re-engage (see **55.5** above), the tribunal may exceed the normal maximum to the extent necessary fully to reflect the sums which would have been payable under its original order (*ERA 1996, s 124(4)*).

The application of the statutory limit is the last step in the calculation, applied after assessing the amount of loss and after taking into account any payments made by the respondent to the claimant and after any increase or reduction required by any statute or rule of law (*ERA 1996, s 124(5)*). For example, if a claimant's loss was assessed at £90,000 and the tribunal found that he was 50% to blame for the dismissal, he would be awarded £45,000 and not 50% of the statutory maximum (*Walter Braund (London) Ltd v Murray* [1991] ICR 327). Similarly, an employment tribunal must first deduct an *ex gratia* payment and then apply the statutory maximum (*McCarthy v British Insulated Callenders Cables plc* [1985] IRLR 94).

The order in which deductions should be made is further considered at **55.13** below.

For the relationship between compensation for unfair and wrongful dismissal, see **58.33** Wrongful Dismissal.

55.11 Amount

The amount of compensation is such amount as the tribunal considers just and equitable in all the circumstances, having regard to the loss sustained by the complainant in consequence of the dismissal insofar as that loss is attributable to action taken by the employer (*ERA 1996, s 123(1)*).

The loss shall be taken to include:

(a)   any expenses reasonably incurred by the complainant in consequence of the dismissal; and

(b)   loss of any benefit save for the contingent right to a redundancy payment which he might reasonably be expected to have had but for the dismissal.

(*ERA 1996, s 123(2), (3)*.)

55.12 Assessment of compensatory award

Since the decision in *Norton Tool Co Ltd v Tewson* [1972] ICR 501, the tribunal has a duty to show how compensation is made up. The most common heads of compensation are those set out below. Whereas the basic award is based upon *gross* pay, the compensatory award depends upon the *net* value of wages and other benefits.

Immediate loss of wages. This is the sum of the loss of wages from the date of termination until the date of the hearing. Account will be taken of wages paid in lieu of notice and earnings in other employments (see also **55.13** below). If the employee has obtained new permanent employment, but has then lost it again, the original employer should not be taken as having caused the loss of earnings after the second dismissal (*Mabey Plant Hire Ltd v Richens*, IDS Brief 495, p 13).

In *Burlo v Langley* [2006] EWCA Civ 1178, [2007] IRLR 145 the Court of Appeal confirmed that *Norton Tool* is authority only for the proposition that compensation for unfair summary dismissal should include full pay for the notice period, without any requirement for the claimant to mitigate his loss during the notice period or to give account of earnings from other employers during the notice period. The observation in *Norton Tool* that it was good industrial relations practice to pay full notice pay whenever an employee was dismissed without notice had to be considered in the light of the House of Lords judgment in *Dunnachie v Kingston-Upon-Hull City Council* [2004] UKHL 26, [2005] 1 AC 226, and a claimant was only entitled to receive compensation for his actual losses. This meant that the claimant nanny was not entitled to receive full pay in respect of the notice period following her unfair dismissal during which she was in fact unable to work after accidental injury; her loss during the notice period was her sick pay entitlement only.

In *Stuart Peters Ltd v Bell* [2009] EWCA Civ 938, [2009] IRLR 941, the Court of Appeal explained that the *Norton Tool* principle does not apply to cases of constructive unfair dismissal. They held that good industrial relations practice requires that an employer who chooses to bring a contract of employment to an end without a notice period should, in the absence of gross misconduct by the employee, offer the employee pay in lieu of notice, and the *Norton Tool* principle ensures that an employer who fails to comply with that good practice is not in a better position than the employer who does comply, since the employee need not give credit for sums earned in mitigation during the notice period. In cases of constructive dismissal, however, there is no principle of industrial relations requiring the employer to offer a payment in lieu. Indeed, the employer may wish to retain the services of the employee and be hoping that the employee will affirm the contract. The employee may also wish to remain in employment but claim damages for the repudiatory breach of contract. Therefore, in cases of constructive unfair dismissal, an employee must give credit for sums earned in mitigation during the notice period.

Future loss of earnings. If the claimant is unemployed at the time of the hearing or is in less remunerative employment than that from which he was dismissed, he will be awarded a sum for future loss of earnings. The award will be based upon the claimant's net loss of earnings for such period as the tribunal considers reasonable, bearing in mind such matters as the length of time he may be unemployed. Compensation must be assessed on the basis of what has actually occurred by the time of the hearing, rather than what might have been expected to occur at the time of the dismissal (*Gilham v Kent County Council (No 3)* [1986] ICR 52). Nevertheless, the exercise of assessing future loss involves predicting what might have happened if the Claimant had not been dismissed and what might happen in the future, and the tribunal will have to make an assessment based on uncertainties and sometimes speculation (*Scope v Thornett* [2006] EWCA Civ 1600, [2007] IRLR 155). Future loss of earnings does not necessarily cease when an employee obtains employment of a permanent nature at an equivalent or higher salary than he previously enjoyed. If the employee obtains another job but then loses the new job within a short time with no right to compensation, the loss from the first dismissal may continue (*Dench v Flynn & Partners* [1998] IRLR 653, overruling *Whelan (t/a Cheers Off Licence) v Richardson* [1998] IRLR 114, EAT). In *Wardle v Crédit Agricole Corporate and Investment Bank* [2011] EWCA Civ 545, [2011] ICR 1290 the Court of Appeal, overturning a tribunal's decision to award career-long loss to the Claimant, held that it would be a rare case in which awarding compensation for such a period would be appropriate. The rare case would be one where the evidence showed that there was no real prospect of the employee obtaining another job. In other cases – which would be the vast majority – the tribunal should only award damages to the time when the employee was "likely to obtain an equivalent job".

The award will take into account any increase in salary or any other benefit the claimant would have enjoyed had he not been dismissed, even beyond his contractual entitlements (*York Trailer Co Ltd v Sparkes* [1973] ICR 518 and for a recent example *Kapoor v Balfour Beatty Group Employment Ltd* UKEAT/0011/15). It will take account not only of regular wage or salary payments but also, for example, commission or bonus payments.

If the employee has obtained new employment which is more remunerative than the original job, it may be that the overall result by the time of the hearing is that he has suffered no loss at all (*Ging v Ellward Lancs Ltd* [1991] ICR 222). But where there has been a great delay in assessing the loss suffered, it may not be just and equitable to apply *Ging* (*Fentiman v Fluid Engineering Products Ltd* [1991] ICR 570; *Lytlarch Ltd v Reid* [1991] ICR 216).

The tribunal may award damages for loss of earnings in relation to a period in which the claimant is unfit for work and in receipt of incapacity benefit, if the inability to work is itself attributable to the actions of the employer in unfairly dismissing him. So, for example, if the claimant is receiving invalidity benefit because of depression caused by unemployment, which in turn was caused by the unfair dismissal, the claimant may receive compensation for the period in which he was unfit to work (*Hilton International Hotels (UK) Ltd v Faraji* [1994] ICR 259; *Devine v Designer Flowers Wholesale Florists Sundries Ltd* [1993] IRLR 517). The invalidity benefit received will, however, be taken into account (*Puglia v C James & Sons* [1996] ICR 301). Where there has been a constructive dismissal, however, losses flowing from repudiatory breach of contract are not recoverable in unfair dismissal proceedings, even where the repudiatory breach reduced the employee's earning capacity post-dismissal (*Triggs v GAB Robbins (UK) Ltd* [2008] IRLR 317).

Loss of use of a company car. If the employee had the use of a company car not only for the purposes of his employment but also for private use, he will be compensated for the loss of that benefit. The tribunal will take into account whether or not the employer paid for the petrol for private motoring. The incidence of tax will be taken into account as it is in the assessment of loss of all benefits in kind. In assessing the value of a car, petrol and running costs, reference is sometimes made to annual estimates published by the AA (*Shove v Downs Surgical plc* [1984] ICR 532).

Loss of benefits in kind. In assessing compensation, the tribunal will take into account other benefits in kind such as free accommodation, medical insurance and subsidised meals. It may do so even where there was no strict contractual entitlement to such benefits. A claimant is not entitled to receive compensation in respect of life insurance (and, logically, any other insurance) for a period following dismissal during which he did not take out replacement cover and the risks insured did not occur (*Knapton v ECC Card Clothing Ltd* [2006] IRLR 756). This is because to make a payment in respect of that period would give the claimant a windfall.

Loss of reputation. It had long been believed that the claimant is not entitled to damages for the loss to his reputation which has resulted from the dismissal (*Addis v Gramophone Co Ltd* [1909] AC 488). However in *Malik v BCCI* [1997] ICR 606, the House of Lords held that the claimant will be entitled to 'stigma damages' to compensate for difficulties in finding work which may result from the poor reputation of the employer at the time of dismissal, on the basis that the employer breached its duty of trust and confidence to the employee by acting in a manner which gave rise to its poor reputation. A claimant may not receive damages for the stress or injury to feelings resulting from the manner of dismissal (*Bliss v South-East Thames Regional Health Authority* [1987] ICR 700, *French v Barclays Bank plc* [1998] IRLR 646, CA and *Dunnachie v Kingston-Upon-Hull City Council* [2004] UKHL 36, [2004] IRLR 727 in which the HL ended the uncertainty created by Lord Hoffman's comments in *Johnson v Unisys Ltd* [2001] UKHL 13, [2001] IRLR 279 and the CA's decision [2004] EWCA Civ 84, [2004] IRLR 287). If an employee suffers from a reactive depression following a dismissal, which renders him unfit for employment between the date of dismissal and the date on which compensation is determined, the employment tribunal must ask what caused his loss. It may be just and equitable to compensate him for all or part of his loss of earnings, despite his unfitness for work, depending on the degree to which the dismissal caused his loss (*Dignity Funerals v Bruce* [2005] IRLR 189).

Pension rights. If, prior to his dismissal, the complainant was a member of a company pension scheme, and fails to obtain new employment, or obtains new employment where there is no company pension scheme, he will almost certainly suffer financial loss because any deferred pension payable will be based on the employee's salary at the date of dismissal (subject to statutory uplifting) instead of on the salary he would have received at normal retiring age. Even if he has obtained employment in another company which operates such a scheme, so that he is able to transfer his accrued rights under the previous scheme to the new scheme, it is likely that this will still involve a degree of loss because the transfer value will only reflect the value of those accrued rights at the date of leaving rather than reflecting the enhanced value which would have been added to those accrued rights, had the complainant remained with the previous company until retirement age instead of being dismissed. In any of these circumstances, the task of assessing compensation for loss of pension rights is a hard one. Some guidance is provided by a booklet prepared by a committee of employment tribunal judges in consultation with the Government Actuary's Department ('Employment Tribunals – Compensation for Loss of Pension Rights', 3rd ed. TSO, 2003). The booklet is not binding upon tribunals (*Bingham v Hobourn Engineering Ltd* [1992] IRLR 298; see also *Manpower Ltd v Hearne* [1983] ICR 567; *Tradewinds Airways Ltd v Fletcher* [1981] IRLR 272; *Willmont Bros Ltd v Oliver* [1979] ICR 378; *Mono Pumps Ltd v Froggatt and Radford* [1987] IRLR 368 and at the time of writing it is understood that it has been formally withdrawn by the President of Employment Tribunals. In *Griffin v Plymouth Hospital NHS Trust* [2015] ICR 347 Underhill LJ recognised the value of the booklet but cautioned that it is not to be regarded as gospel and observed that it will not yield the appropriate approach in every case. Following *Griffin*, in March 2016 a working group of Employment Judges published a consultation paper which recommended that the booklet be replaced by Presidential Guidance in a similar form. The consultation was due to close on 20 May 2016, but since then nothing further appears to have happened.

In the meantime, an alternative approach may be for the tribunal to assess the period for which the employee should be compensated for loss of pension rights, and to make an award based upon the cost of purchasing a policy to make up the difference between the pension which he will receive and the amount he would have received had he remained in employment until the end of the period. An award for loss of pension rights which is based solely on the value of the employer's contributions is not appropriate in assessing loss of pension rights under a scheme which yields not only an income benefit but also a lump sum arising as of right rather than by commutation (see for example *Lund v St Edmund's School* [2013] ICR D26). In *Bentwood Bros (Manchester) Ltd v Shepherd* [2003] EWCA Civ 380, [2003] IRLR 364 the Court of Appeal held that an employment tribunal had erred in applying only a 5% discount for accelerated receipt, even though the sum represented two and a half years' future earnings and ten years' pension payments. In some cases it may be appropriate to use the Ogden tables to calculate pension loss and is not an error of law for a tribunal so to do: *Chief Constable of West Midlands Police v Gardner* [2012] Eq LR 20.

Payments received by an employee under an occupational or private pension scheme, whether contributory or not, should not be offset against compensation awarded for unfair dismissal. This is because pensions are deferred pay and a decision by an employee to take an early pension after unfair dismissal is a personal decision about money management, rather than a factor which reduces the loss suffered in consequence of the unfair dismissal (*Knapton v ECC Card Clothing Ltd* [2006] IRLR 756).

Loss of statutory rights. The tribunal will assess a nominal figure for loss of protection from unfair dismissal for the first two years (the period for acquiring unfair dismissal protection) of any new employment. A few years ago, the appropriate figure was normally £100 (*SH Muffett Ltd v Head* [1987] ICR 1). It is now common for tribunals to award £250–£350.

It will also award compensation for loss of the accrued right to the statutory minimum period of notice. The loss was assessed in *Daley v AE Dorsett (Almar Dolls) Ltd* [1982] ICR 1 as half the wages due during that period, but it is thought that this may be too high in the ordinary case. See also *Arthur Guinness Son & Co (Great Britain) Ltd v Green* [1989] ICR 241.

Frequently, employment tribunals will award just one sum for loss of statutory rights, commonly in the region of £300–£350, to cover loss of protection from unfair dismissal and loss of accrued right to statutory notice.

55.13 FACTORS REDUCING OR INCREASING THE COMPENSATORY AWARD

Just and equitable. The tribunal has a discretion to make an award which is less than the full amount of the claimant's loss if the tribunal considers it just and equitable to do so (*ERA 1996, s 123(1)*). Thus, if the employee has been guilty of misconduct which was only discovered after the dismissal, and therefore could not be relied upon to establish contributory fault (see below), a reduced award or no award may be made (*W Devis & Sons Ltd v Atkins* [1977] ICR 662; *Tele-Trading Ltd v Jenkins* [1990] IRLR 430; *Chaplin v H J Rawlinson Ltd* [1991] ICR 553). See *Slaughter v C Brewer & Sons Ltd* [1990] ICR 730 for reductions under *s 123(1)* in cases of ill-health.

The fact that an employer could have dismissed an employee fairly for poor attendance when he dismissed her unfairly for ill-health was held by the Court of Appeal not to justify a reduction in the compensatory award on just and equitable grounds where the employer, in full knowledge of the facts, chose not to dismiss her on grounds of poor attendance (*Devonshire v Trico-Folberth Ltd* [1989] ICR 747).

It is only events which took place before dismissal which can render it just and equitable to reduce the compensatory award. A tribunal may not, for example, take account of a breach of a duty of confidentiality which took place after dismissal (*Soros v Davison* [1994] ICR 590).

In *Simrad Ltd v Scott* [1997] IRLR 147, the EAT held that it was not just and equitable to assess the compensatory award by reference to the lower rate of pay which the applicant was receiving because of her decision to change career and train as a nurse. The change of career was too remote to be linked to the dismissal.

Contributory fault. Where the tribunal finds that the dismissal was to any extent caused or contributed to by any action of the complainant, it will reduce the amount of the compensatory award by such proportion as it considers just and equitable having regard to that finding (*ERA 1996, s 123(6)*). The same percentage of deduction will usually apply to both basic and compensatory awards. The precise method by which deductions for contributory fault should be made differs, however, between basic and compensatory awards (*Steen v ASP Packaging Ltd* [2014] ICR 56).

If, therefore, an employee was guilty of misconduct which was grave, but did not justify dismissal, or if the procedures used to dismiss him were unfair, but his own conduct to a certain extent contributed to his misfortune, the amount of compensation may be reduced. The reduction may be as much as 100% in an appropriate case (*W Devis & Sons Ltd v Atkins* [1977] ICR 662). The EAT has recently said that whilst a 100% reduction for contributory fault is a permissible finding, it is still an unusual one (*Steen v ASP Packaging Ltd* [2014] ICR 56). See also **55.19** below for reduction in union-related cases.

In order for a deduction for contributory fault to be made for the employee's misconduct, that conduct must be culpable or blameworthy in the sense that, whether or not it amounted to a breach of contract or tort, it was foolish or perverse or unreasonable in the circumstances (*Nelson v BBC (No 2)* [1980] ICR 110 recently re-affirmed in *Frith Accountants v Law* (below)).

Where the tribunal has jurisdiction in the case of a dismissal for taking part in industrial action (see **53.17** UNFAIR DISMISSAL – I), it is not open to the tribunal to hold that participation in the industrial action in itself amounts to contributory fault: *Crossville Wales Ltd v Tracey* [1997] ICR 862, overruling *TNT Express Ltd v Downes* [1994] ICR 1.

Lack of capability is unlikely to be blameworthy in the *Nelson* sense unless it involves, for example, laziness or obstructive behaviour. However, in a case, say, of incapability due to ill-health, it may be appropriate to make a reduction under the general 'just and equitable' formulation referred to above (*Slaughter v C Brewer*, above).

A reduction for contributory fault may be made in the case of constructive dismissal and where the employer has failed to establish an acceptable reason for the dismissal (*Morrison v Amalgamated Transport and General Workers Union* [1989] IRLR 361; *Polentarutti v Autokraft Ltd* [1991] ICR 757). In *Frith Accountants v Law* [2014] ICR 805 Langstaff J held that it would be unusual, particularly in a case of breach of the implied term of mutual trust and confidence, for a reduction to be made for contributory fault on a constructive dismissal complaint.

In *Optikinetics Ltd v Whooley* [1999] ICR 984, the EAT held that where a tribunal found that there was contributory fault on the part of a claimant, it was obligatory for the tribunal to make a reduction in the compensatory award by such proportion as it considered just and equitable, but there was no similar obligation in respect of the basic award.

The Court of Appeal in *London Ambulance Service NHS Trust v Small* [2009] EWCA Civ 220, [2009] IRLR 563 advised employment tribunals that it was desirable to keep separate their findings of fact on the fairness of the dismissal from their findings on other questions, such as contributory fault, constructive dismissal, discrimination and victimisation. This is because the fairness of the dismissal is decided on the basis of an objective view of the employer's decision making process, without the need for a rehearing on the question of misconduct. By contrast, other disputed facts, such as whether the employee's fault had contributed to the dismissal, required a decision by the tribunal based upon the evidence which it had heard.

The Court of Session in Scotland has held that it is an error of law for a tribunal to fail to give reasons for a reduction in an award for contributory fault (*Nairne v Highlands and Islands Fire Brigade* [1989] IRLR 366). In *Steen v ASP Packaging Ltd* [2014] ICR 56 the EAT remarked that it is "all too often" an error of law for a tribunal simply to state its conclusion on contributory fault and the amount of reduction without addressing seriatim the questions which arise out of the statutory provisions (and which the EAT there analysed). On this point see also *Look Ahead Housing & Care Ltd v Chetty* [2015] ICR 375.

Failure to provide written particulars. Under *EmA 2002, s 38*, an employment tribunal which finds in favour of an employee after hearing a complaint of unfair dismissal but makes no award to the employee, and which has noticed that when the proceedings began the employer was in breach of its duty to provide the employee with a written statement of initial employment particulars or particulars of change, must make an award of at least two weeks' pay (up to £978) and may, if it considers it just and equitable in all the circumstances, make an award of four weeks' pay (*EmA 2002, s 38(2)*) (up to £1,956). Where the employment tribunal makes an award to the employee for unfair dismissal in such a case, that award must be increased by at least two and up to four weeks' pay (*EmA 2002, s 38(3)*). The duty to award at least two and up to four week's pay in such a case does not arise if there are exceptional circumstances which would make the award or increase unjust or inequitable (*EmA 2002, s 38(5)*).

Failure to follow 2009 ACAS Code of Practice 1 on Disciplinary and Grievance Procedures. Section 1 of the *Employment Act 2008* repealed *ss 29–33* of the *EmA 2002*, namely the statutory dispute resolution provisions, with effect from 6 April 2009. *Section 3 of the EA 2008* inserted a new *s 207A* into *TULRCA 1992* which came into force on 6 April 2009. The effect in unfair dismissal cases to which the new rules apply is that where an employment tribunal concludes that an employer has unreasonably failed to comply with the 2009 ACAS Code of Practice 1 on disciplinary and grievance procedures, it may increase any award which it makes to the employee by up to 25%, if it is just and equitable in all the circumstances. Conversely, if the employee has unreasonably failed to comply with the ACAS Code, the tribunal may reduce the award by up to 25%, if it considers it to be just and equitable in all the circumstances. In *Lund v St Edmund's College* [2013] ICR D26 the EAT held that the facts that the employee had been dismissed for some other substantial reason and that the tribunal had found that he had contributed to his dismissal did not mean that *TULRCA 1992, s 207A* should be disapplied. The provision was penal in effect and the employee had done nothing to contribute to the employer's failure to follow the Code.

In *Holmes v Qinetiq Ltd* [2016] ICR 1016 the EAT held that the ACAS Code did not apply to situations in which an employee was dismissed for ill-health capability. Although a capability procedure involved an assessment of poor performance it could not properly be characterised as a 'disciplinary situation'. In *Phoenix House Ltd v Stockman* [2017] ICR 84, Mitting J held that the ACAS Code does not apply to dismissals for some other substantial reason, disagreeing with certain observations to the contrary by Elisabeth Laing J in *Hussain v Jurys Inn Group Ltd* (UKEAT/0283/15).

Whether the unfairness made any difference. It was initially thought that, if the employee would have been dismissed even if the employer had done all that he ought to have done, the dismissal ought not to be regarded as unfair. That approach was held to be wrong in *Polkey v AE Dayton Services Ltd* [1988] ICR 142 (see **54.4** UNFAIR DISMISSAL – **II**) which introduced an approach requiring the tribunal to reduce compensation by a percentage to take account of the possibility that the employee would have been dismissed even if a fair procedure had been followed.

The Scottish Court of Session in *King v Eaton (No 2)* [1998] IRLR 686 said that it was open to a tribunal to decline to permit an employer at a remedies hearing to lead additional evidence to show that the result would have been the same even if fair procedures had been followed. If it is not realistic or practicable to embark upon such an exercise or the exercise would be highly speculative, the tribunal should not do so. To ask what would have happened if the employer had acted fairly is still relevant to compensation. For example, if the company shut down and all the employees were made redundant a few weeks after the claimant was unfairly dismissed, his compensatory award ought not to run beyond that date (see *James W Cook & Co (Wivenhoe) Ltd v Tipper* [1990] ICR 716, holding also that the tribunal cannot investigate the commercial and economic reasons behind the closure). The tribunal may take account of the fact that an employee with a short period of service is more at risk of being selected for redundancy if job losses occur (*Morris v Acco Ltd* [1985] ICR 306). Again, it may be that the tribunal considers that an employee dismissed for misconduct without a hearing could not, in fact, have said anything effective in his own defence, or that an employee dismissed without warning for lack of capability was not capable of improvement in any event. In a different context, it has been suggested that it ought not to be assumed too readily that a failure to observe the principles of natural justice made no difference to the result (*John v Rees* [1970] Ch 345 at 402).

The tribunal ought also to consider *when* that dismissal would have taken place, eg even if it is certain that a fair procedure would have led to the same result, it may be that its adoption would have prolonged the period of earning for a number of weeks (see *Mining Supplies (Longwall) Ltd v Baker* [1988] ICR 676) or perhaps not at all (*Robertson v Magnet Ltd (Retail Division)* [1993] IRLR 512). If the employee could only have hoped for continued employment in a different and less well-paid job, the calculation of his loss ought to be based upon those lower earnings (*Red Bank*, above).

In *O'Donoughue v Redcar and Cleveland Borough Council* [2001] EWCA Civ 701, [2001] IRLR 615, the Court of Appeal made it clear that it was not always necessary or appropriate to make a percentage assessment as to whether the claimant would have been dismissed fairly if there had been no unfair dismissal. This was especially the case if the tribunal was assessing the likelihood that the claimant might have been fairly dismissed, not at the time of dismissal, but at some time in the future. In such circumstances, it may not be possible to identify an overall percentage risk, because there may be, say, a 20% chance of dismissal in six months but a 30% chance in a year. In Miss O'Donoughue's case the tribunal concluded that her divisive and antagonistic approach was such that she would have been bound to be dismissed fairly within six months, and so the tribunal limited compensation for future loss to the six-month period. The Court of Appeal held that the tribunal had approached the matter correctly and that it had been appropriate to assess a safe date by which the tribunal was certain that that dismissal would take place and then to make an award of full compensation in respect of the period prior thereto. See also *Scope v Thornett* [2006] EWCA Civ 1600, [2007] IRLR 155.

The EAT in *Chagger v Abbey National plc* [2009] IRLR 86 advised tribunals that even where the dismissal was unfair because of discriminatory grounds, it is necessary to conduct a *Polkey* exercise, to consider what would have happened if the claimant had not been dismissed for discriminatory reasons and whether there would have been a lawful dismissal for a fair reason. The Court of Appeal [2009] EWCA Civ 1202, [2010] IRLR 47, however, held that the EAT had erred in limiting the future loss to that period during which the claimant would have been employed by the respondent, observing that an employee's success in finding new employment is influenced by the particular job market at the time when he finds himself seeking work and that it is generally easier for someone who is still working to find a new job than someone who has been unemployed or out of the industry. Most notably, the Court held that a discriminatory dismissal can alter someone's career path, by necessitating his bringing an employment tribunal claim against the employer, which can create a stigma making him unattractive to future employers, for which the original employer must remain liable. Such future loss flowing from stigma would be equally recoverable in a general unfair dismissal claim as in a claim of a discriminatory dismissal.

In *Andrews v Software 2000 Ltd* [2007] IRLR 568 the EAT explained that *s 98A(2)* (which was then in force) should be applied first, and then *Polkey* questions fall to be addressed. The following principles emerged from the relevant case law:

(a)   In assessing compensation the task of the tribunal is to assess the loss flowing from the dismissal, using its common sense, experience and sense of justice. In the normal case, that requires it to assess for how long the employee would have been employed but for the dismissal.

(b)   If the employer seeks to contend that the employee would or might have ceased to be employed in any event had fair procedures been followed, or alternatively would not have continued in employment indefinitely, it is for him to adduce any relevant evidence on which he wishes to rely. However, the tribunal must have regard to all the evidence when making that assessment, including any evidence from the employee himself.

(c)   There will, however, be circumstances where the nature of the evidence which the employer wishes to adduce, or on which he seeks to rely, is so unreliable that the tribunal may take the view that the whole exercise of seeking to reconstruct what might have been is so riddled with uncertainty that no sensible prediction based on that evidence can properly be made.

(d)   Whether that is the position is a matter of impression and judgment for the tribunal; but in reaching that decision the tribunal must direct itself properly. It must recognise that it should have regard to any material and reliable evidence which might assist it in fixing just compensation, even if there are limits to the extent to which it can confidently predict what might have been; and it must appreciate that a degree of uncertainty is an inevitable feature of the exercise. The mere fact that an element of speculation is involved is not a reason for refusing to have regard to the evidence.

(e)   An appellate court must be wary about interfering with the tribunal's assessment that the exercise is too speculative. However, it must interfere if the tribunal has not directed itself properly and has taken too narrow a view of its role.

(f)   Even if a tribunal considers some of the evidence or potential evidence to be too speculative to form any sensible view as to whether dismissal would have occurred on the balance of probabilities, it must nevertheless take into account any evidence on which it considers it can properly rely and from which it could in principle conclude that the employment may have come to an end when it did, or alternatively would not have continued indefinitely.

(g)   Having considered the evidence, the tribunal may determine:

   (i)   that if fair procedures had been complied with, the employer has satisfied it – the onus being firmly on the employer – that on the balance of probabilities the dismissal would have occurred when it did in any event;

   (ii)   that there was a chance of dismissal but less than 50%, in which case compensation should be reduced accordingly;

   (iii)   that employment would have continued but only for a limited fixed period. The evidence demonstrating that may be wholly unrelated to the circumstances relating to the dismissal itself, as in the *O'Donoghue* case; or

   (iv)   employment would have continued indefinitely.

However, this last finding should be reached only where the evidence that it might have been terminated earlier is so scant that it can effectively be ignored.

Note that in *Ministry of Justice v Parry* [2013] ICR 311 the EAT pointed out that the part of the *Software 2000* guidance relating to *section 98A(2)* should no longer be followed in light of the repeal of that subsection.

In *Eversheds v De Belin* [2011] ICR 1137 the EAT followed *Andrews v Software 2000* and *Scope v Thornett* [2006] EWCA Civ 1600, [2007] IRLR 155 in holding that tribunals should not decline to undertake a *Polkey* exercise merely because it involves 'speculation'. It is only in circumstances where the evidence is 'so scant that it can effectively be ignored' that the tribunal could safely hold that the exercise would be too speculative. In both *Ministry of Justice v Parry* [2013] ICR 311 and *Hill v Governing Body of Great Tey Primary School* [2013] ICR 691 the EAT has laid some emphasis on the importance of the tribunal adopting a percentage chance approach to the *Polkey* exercise, though in *Stonehouse Coaches Ltd v Smith* [2014] ICR D14 has sought to explain the distinctions between the percentage chance approach and that which looks at the period of time before which the employee would fairly have been dismissed.

In illustration of the fact that *Polkey* reductions continue to perplex both litigants and tribunals, Langstaff J was driven once again in *Contract Bottling Ltd v Cave* [2015] ICR 146 to explain the nature of the intellectual exercise it is necessary for tribunals to carry out.

In *Compass Group v Ayodele* [2011] IRLR 802 the EAT held that although the primary burden of proving loss lies on a Claimant, that would initially be discharged by showing that he has been unfairly dismissed. If an employer seeks to argue a *Polkey* point it must be properly raised and supported by evidence. The need for evidence in support of a *Polkey* argument is a point often overlooked by employers.

If a percentage reduction is being made on the basis that employment may have terminated fairly during the period for which compensation is being assessed and also on account of contributory fault, the two reductions should be applied sequentially (*Rao v Civil Aviation Authority* [1994] ICR 495). Thus, if there was a 50% chance that the employee would have been dismissed in any event, and he was 30% to blame for his dismissal, he should be awarded only 35% of his actual loss (ie half of 70%). If the employee receives a termination payment, the payment should be deducted after this process has been carried out (*Digital Equipment Co Ltd v Clements (No 2)* [1998] ICR 258; *Heggie v Uniroyal Englebert Tyres Ltd* [1998] IRLR 425).

In *Steel Stockholders (Birmingham) Ltd v Kirkwood* [1993] IRLR 515, the EAT held that it was only where the defect was procedural rather than substantive that a percentage reduction may be made. The distinction between procedural and substantive defects was however easier to state than to apply and in *O'Dea v ISC Chemicals Ltd (t/a as Rhône-Poulenc Chemicals)* [1995] IRLR 599, the Court of Appeal held that employment tribunals should not attempt to categorise defects in this manner. In *Secretary of State for Justice v Lown* [2016] IRLR 22 the EAT again noted that the *Polkey* principle does not only apply to 'procedurally' unfair dismissals.

There is no magic in the word 'Polkey' and it is not an error of law for a Tribunal not to use the term if it has dealt in substance with the principle: *Look Ahead Housing & Care Ltd v Chetty & anr* [2015] ICR 375.

Mitigation of loss. The employee is under a duty to mitigate his loss, but is under no duty to prove that he has done so. He must take reasonable steps to obtain alternative employment. A compensatory award is intended to compensate the employee for loss and is not a penal award against the employer. What employment he will be under a duty to accept is a matter to be determined by the tribunal. He must be realistic in his job expectations. He may not demand a salary or status higher than that which he previously enjoyed, and may have to accept some reduction. If the employee has not made reasonable efforts to find other work, his compensation will be reduced to reflect the tribunal's view of what would have happened if he had mitigated his loss. However, the burden of proving a failure to mitigate is on the employer, and the standard of what is reasonably required of the employee should not be set too high (*Fyfe v Scientific Furnishings Ltd* [1989] ICR 648, *Look Ahead Housing & Care Ltd v Chetty* [2015] ICR 375 and *Cooper Contracting Ltd v Lindsey* [2016] ICR D3 (which contains a helpful review of the authorities on where the burden of proof lies and the extent of the duty)).

Where an unfairly dismissed employee had unreasonably refused an employer's offer of reinstatement, he was rightly held only to be entitled to a basic award (*Sweetlove v Redbridge and Waltham Forest Area Health Authority* [1979] ICR 477). In *Wilding v British Telecommunications plc* [2002] EWCA Civ 349, [2002] IRLR 524, the Court of Appeal held that the duty to mitigate which is imposed on an employee requires him when considering an offer of re-employment to act as a reasonable person unaffected by the prospect of compensation, that the onus is on the employer to show that the employee had failed in that duty, that the test of reasonableness was objective, that the circumstances in which an offer of re-employment was made and refused, the attitude of the employer, the way in which the employee had been treated, and all the surrounding circumstances should be taken into account by the tribunal, and that the tribunal must not be too stringent in its expectations of the injured party.

There is no duty to mitigate until the dismissal has actually taken place (*Trimble v Supertravel Ltd* [1982] IRLR 451). Failure by the employee to activate the internal appeals procedure after the dismissal cannot, as a matter of law, amount to a failure to mitigate (*Lock v Connell Estate Agents* [1994] IRLR 444, not following *Hoover Ltd v Forde* [1980] ICR 239).

In *Daley v AE Dorsett (Almar Dolls) Ltd* [1982] ICR 1, the EAT did not interfere with an employment tribunal's finding that an employee's decision not to accept full-time employment at a rate of earnings less than the amount of unemployment benefit was reasonable. It stressed, however, that employment tribunals should be very slow indeed in finding reasonable a decision of a dismissed employee not to accept subsequent employment because he would be receiving less than unemployment benefit.

Expenses incurred in seeking to mitigate the loss suffered (eg the cost of travelling to job interviews) are recoverable as part of the compensatory award. That could include the cost of starting up a business of the employee's own, if that was a reasonable thing to do (see *Aon Training Ltd (formerly Totalamber plc) v Dore* [2005] EWCA Civ 411, [2005] IRLR 891; *Gardiner-Hill v Roland Beiger Technics Ltd* [1982] IRLR 498). Legal expenses incurred in pursuing the unfair dismissal claim are not recoverable (for the award of costs see **18**: EMPLOYMENT TRIBUNALS – I).

Payments made by the employer. Payments made by the claimant's former employer, whether under a contractual liability or *ex gratia*, will generally be taken into account (*Rushton v Harcros Timber and Building Supplies Ltd* [1993] ICR 230). In *Simrad Ltd v Scott* [1997] IRLR 147, however, the EAT held that a loan which was to be repaid by way of work need not be taken into account for these purposes as it would not be just and equitable to do so since the employee had been deprived of the opportunity to carry on working.

It was formerly understood that the employee must give credit for pay in lieu of notice and other benefits received from the old employer during the notice period (*Addison v Babcock FATA Ltd* [1987] ICR 805) and for earnings from any new employment during the notice period, because the contractual right to notice pay does not create a debt owed by the employer which must be paid irrespective of the employee's real loss, but gives rise merely to a claim in damages or compensation where the employer breaches his contractual or statutory notice obligations (*Rowley v Cerberus Software Ltd* [2001] EWCA Civ 78, [2001] IRLR 160). Similarly, neither pension payments (*Hopkins v Norcros plc* [1994] ICR 11), nor an educational grant received in connection with a course embarked upon after dismissal (*Justfern Ltd v D'Ingerthorpe* [1994] ICR 286) were taken into account. The full amount of invalidity benefit was deducted in *Puglia v James & Sons* ([1996] IRLR 70), which did not follow *Hilton International Hotels (UK) Ltd v Faraji* ([1994] ICR 259). *Puglia v James* was itself not followed in *Rubenstein and Roskin (t/a McGuffies Dispensing Chemists) v McGloughlin* [1996] IRLR 557, in which the EAT deducted only half the amount of invalidity benefit. In a further variation, the EAT in *Sheffield Forgemasters International Ltd v Fox* [2009] ICR 333, [2009] IRLR 192 held that receipt of incapacity benefit did not preclude a claimant from obtaining compensation for loss of earnings during such a period, because some people can lawfully claim incapacity benefit while performing light work.

There were subsequently conflicting decisions at EAT level concerning the deductibility from the compensatory award of monies which the employee earns or receives during the notice period. In *Hardy v Polk (Leeds) Ltd* [2004] IRLR 420 the EAT held that the same duty to mitigate arises as there is at common law and account should be taken of earnings from new employment. A differently-constituted EAT in *Voith Turbo Ltd v Stowe* [2005] IRLR 228 held that it was open to an employment tribunal not to deduct earnings from new employment from the pay in lieu of notice, in accordance with good industrial practice. A more recent EAT decision, however, in *Morgans v Alpha Plus Security* [2005] IRLR 234, held that incapacity benefit received following a dismissal was properly deducted from the compensatory award, in order to ensure that the employee was compensated for his actual loss only. The Court of Appeal has now concluded that an employee is not required to give credit against his unfair dismissal compensatory award for earnings from another employer during the notice period, when unfairly dismissed without pay in lieu of notice, but that his entitlement for compensation in respect of the notice period is limited to his actual loss (see *Burlo v Langley* above [2006] EWCA Civ 1178, [2007] IRLR 145).

Jobseeker's allowance received will not be taken into account (but see **55.6** above for the rules on recoupment).

The payments made by the employer are deducted by the employment tribunal from the gross sum after compensation has been reduced to take account of contributory fault and/or the fact that dismissal might have taken place anyway: *Digital Equipment Co Ltd v Clements (No 2)* [1998] IRLR 134.

Delayed Payment. In *Melia v Magna Kansei Ltd* [2005] EWCA Civ 1547, [2006] IRLR 117, the Court of Appeal held that when assessing a claimant's loss, an employment tribunal may make an allowance for delayed payment. According to the Court, this is distinct from a tribunal awarding interest, which it may not do.

The order in which deductions should be made. The Court of Appeal in *Digital Equipment v Clements (No 2)* [1998] IRLR 134 and the Scottish Court of Session in *Leonard v Strathclyde Buses Ltd* [1998] IRLR 693 have considered the order in which deductions should be made from the compensatory award. The position is now clear, except where non-statutory redundancy payments are concerned. The order of deduction is as follows:

(a)   calculate the total loss actually suffered by the claimant;

(b)   deduct amounts received in mitigation and any payment made by the former employer (other than a non-statutory redundancy payment);

(c)   make any adjustment for failure on the part of the employee or employer to follow statutory procedures;

(d)   make any reduction for contributory fault;

(e)   apply the statutory maximum.

The controversy as regards non-statutory redundancy payments is as to whether the effect of *ERA 1996, s 123(7)* is that such payments should be deducted after the reduction for contributory fault but before the statutory maximum is applied, or whether they should only be deducted after the statutory maximum is applied. It is not clear from the judgments in *Digital Equipment v Clements (No 2)* which of the two alternative approaches should be followed. In *Leonard v Strathclyde Buses*, however, the Court of Session held that non-statutory redundancy payments should be deducted before the statutory maximum is applied and said that there was nothing in *Digital Equipment v Clements (No 2)* which points to any different view.

The approach taken by the Court of Appeal in *Digital Equipment v Clements (No 2)* was adopted once again by the Scottish Court of Session in *Heggie v Uniroyal Englebert Tyres Ltd* [1999] IRLR 802.

55.14   ADDITIONAL AWARD – NON-COMPLIANCE WITH AN ORDER

Additional compensation in cases where an order for reinstatement or re-engagement is made but not complied with (see **54.5** above) consisting of not less than 26 weeks' and not more than 52 weeks' pay (except union-related, health and safety, pension scheme trustee and employee representative cases where a special award may be made, see **55.16** below) (*ERA 1996, s 117*).

The tribunal may not simply make the maximum award in order to force compliance with its order. It must consider factors such as the employer's conduct and the extent to which the compensatory award has met the actual loss suffered (*Morganite Electrical Carbon Ltd v Donne* [1988] ICR 18).

Where the employer has made an *ex gratia* payment which exceeds the amount of any loss suffered, it may be possible to set off the surplus against any additional award (*Darr v LRC Products Ltd* [1993] IRLR 257).

55.15   REDUCTION OF AWARD – 'UNION-RELATED' CASES

Where an award of compensation is made in respect of a dismissal which is to be regarded as unfair by virtue of *TULRCA 1992, s 152* or *s 153*, a tribunal, in considering whether it would be just and equitable to reduce or further reduce the amount of *any part* of the award, will disregard any conduct or action which constitutes:

(a)   a breach or proposed breach of a requirement that the complainant should:

(i)   be or become a member;

(ii)   cease to be or refrain from becoming a member; or

(iii)   not take part in the activities; or

(iv)   not make use of the services which are made available to him

of any trade union or a particular trade union or one of a number of particular trade unions;

(b)   acceptance of or failure to accept an offer by the employer made to induce the employee not to become a member or participate in activities of a trade union (contrary to *TULRCA 1992, s 145A*) or not to participate in collective bargaining (contrary to *TULRCA 1992, s 145B*); or

(c)   an objection or proposed objection (however expressed) to the operation of a provision for the deduction of union subscriptions from his remuneration (under *TULRCA 1992, s 152(3)*).

(*TULRCA 1992, s 153.*)

However, it seems that confrontational conduct by the employee could form the basis for a finding of contributory fault provided that the immediate circumstances constituting the principal reason for dismissal are excluded from consideration (*Transport and General Workers' Union v Howard* [1992] ICR 106).

55.16 MAXIMUM AWARDS

Maximum awards:

(i)   The maximum amount of a 'week's pay', which determines the maximum amount of a basic award, is reviewed annually and linked to the RPI (*ERelA 1999, s 34(1)*) (but see *SI 2009/1903, Art 3*, which excluded the operation of *ERelA 1999, s 34* following the increase to £380 from 1 October 2009) (see Pay– I (**34**)). The current maximum is £489.

(ii)   The minimum basic award in a case of dismissal unfair under *TULRCA 1992, s 152* or *s 153* or *ERA 1996, s 100(1)(a)* and *(b)*, *101A(d)*, *102(1)* or *103* is £5,970.

(iii)   The maximum basic award is 20 × 1½ × £489 = £14,670.

(iv)   An employee may also receive an award in respect of unfair dismissal which is increased by £978 –£1,956 under *EmA 2002, s 38* (see **55.13** above).

(v)   The maximum compensatory award is £80,541 (see **55.10** above).

(vi)   Note the exceptions in which the ceiling on compensation does not apply (*ERA 1996, s 124(1A)*). There is no statutory maximum compensatory award in cases in which a person is regarded as automatically unfairly dismissed by reason of *ERA 1996, s 100* (health and safety cases), *s 103A* (public interest disclosure cases), *s 105(3)* (selection for redundancy on grounds of health and safety activity) or *s 105(6A)* (selection for redundancy on the ground of public interest disclosure) (*ERelA 1999, s 37(1)*).

(vii)   The additional award will, in all cases, be not less than 26 and not more than 52 weeks' pay, giving a maximum of £25,428 (see **55.14**).

55.17 JOINDER OF THIRD PARTIES

If, in any proceedings before an employment tribunal on a complaint of unfair dismissal, either the employer or the complainant claims:

(a)   that the employer was induced to dismiss the complainant by the actual or threatened calling, organising, procuring or financing of a strike or other industrial action; and

(b)   that such pressure was exercised because the complainant was not a member of any trade union or of a particular trade union or of one of a number of particular trade unions,

the employer or the complainant may request the tribunal to direct that the person whom he claims exercised the pressure, be joined as a party to the proceedings (*TULRCA 1992, s 160(1)*).

A tribunal must grant such a request if it is made before the hearing of the complaint begins, but it may be refused if it is made after that time. The tribunal will refuse to hear such a request if it is made after the tribunal has made an award of compensation (*TULRCA 1992, s 160(2)*).

If the tribunal makes an award of compensation and considers that the complaint of pressure is well-founded, it may make an order that the third party (joined according to the procedure outlined above) pay all or such part of the award as the tribunal may consider just and equitable in the circumstances (*TULRCA 1992, s 160(3)*).

55.18 INTERIM RELIEF IN RESPECT OF CERTAIN DISMISSALS

An employee who complains that he has been dismissed for:

(a)   being or proposing to become a member of an independent trade union;

(b)   taking part or proposing to take part in the activities of an independent trade union at an appropriate time;

(c)   not being a member of any trade union, or of a particular trade union, or of one of a number of particular trade unions, or refusing or proposing to refuse to become or remain a member;

(d)   carrying out, or proposing to carry out, activities which he has been designated by the employer to carry out in connection with preventing or reducing risks to health and safety at work;

(e)   performing or proposing to perform any functions as a representative of workers on matters of health and safety at work, or as a member of a safety committee;

(f)   performing or proposing to perform any functions or activities as (i) a representative of members of the workforce for the purposes of *Sch 1* to the *Working Time Regulations 1998* or (ii) a candidate for election as such a representative;

(g)   performing or proposing to perform any functions as a trustee of a relevant occupational pension scheme which relates to his employment;

(h)   performing or proposing to perform any functions as (i) an employee representative for the purposes of *TULRCA 1992, Part IV, Chapter II* (redundancies) or *regs 9, 13 and 15* amnof *Transfer of Undertakings (Protection of Employment) Regulations 2006* or (ii) a candidate for election as such a representative;

(i)   activities relating to union recognition or bargaining arrangements; or

56   Vicarious Liability

56.1   'Vicarious liability' describes the principle of law which allows an employer to be held liable for the tortious acts of his employees committed in the course of their employment. Such liability would extend, for example, to the case of a van driver who drives negligently in the normal course of his duties and causes an accident; his employer will be held liable for any resulting injury. The employer may also be held vicariously liable where one employee injures another at work, or where an employee steals from a customer, again providing that the act is done in the course of employment.

There are some instances of vicarious liability imposed by statute, eg by the *Equality Act 2010, s 109(1) (see* **12.26** DISCRIMINATION AND EQUAL OPPORTUNITIES – **II**).

The common law tests (see below) for vicarious liability are not applicable where there is express statutory provision in relation to vicarious liability (*Jones v Tower Boot Co Ltd* [1997] IRLR 168). This principle finds illustration in the case of *Mahood v Irish Centre Housing* (2011) (appeal no UKEAT/0228/10/ZT). In *Mahood*, the Employment Appeal held that an employer was not vicariously liable for the alleged harassment of an employee by a temporary agency worker under the *RRA 1976*. Even if the employer exerted a sufficient degree of control over the agency worker to render the employer tortiously liable at common law for his actions, that did not impact on the question of whether the employer was vicariously liable under statutory provisions contained in the *RRA 1976*. The relevant provisions on vicarious liability did not create liability for third parties. If, however, the tribunal found that the agency worker, as a matter of implication, could be deemed to be an employee of the employer or alternatively, if the harassment occurred in circumstances where the agency worker was exercising authority conferred on him by the employer, and therefore was acting as the employer's agent, then the employer may yet be vicariously liable for the agency worker's actions. However, the common law tests remain relevant to whether or not an employer may be vicariously liable for an employee's contravention of a statute that does not make any express provision as to vicarious liability: *Majrowski v Guys and St Thomas' NHS Hospital Trust* [2006] UKHL 34, [2006] 3 WLR 125, [2006] ICR 1199. In that case, the House of Lords held that an employer may be vicariously liable for harassment committed by its employee that was unlawful by virtue of s 3 of the Protection from Harassment Act 1997 (a provision that on its face only applies to individuals). The judgment in *Majrowski* should be compared with the judgment of the Court of Appeal in *NHS Manchester v Fecitt & Ors* [2011] EWCA Civ 1190. In *Fecitt*, an employee had been subject to victimising behaviour on the part of her colleagues in response to the fact she had made a protected disclosure. The Court of Appeal held that the employer was not liable for the acts of victimisation. This was because the *Employment Rights Act 1996*, which affords protection to employees who have made protected disclosures, does not prohibit victimisation of a whistle-blower by co-workers. In the circumstances, the co workers victimisation of the employee, whilst being morally repugnant, was not unlawful per se. It followed that there was no unlawful act in respect of which the employer could be held vicariously liable (*Cumbria CC v Carlisle-Morgan* [2007] IRLR 314 overruled). The approach adopted in *Fecitt* should be contrasted with the approach taken to personal liability and vicarious liability under the *Equality Act 2010*. *Section 109* of that *Act* renders the employer vicariously liable in circumstances where the employer's employee or agent engages in acts of discrimination or victimisation in the course of their employment, subject to the defence provided for in *s 109(4)*, namely that the employer has taken all reasonable steps to avoid the unlawful conduct. *Section 110* of that *Act* operates to render employees and agents of the employer personally liable for any act of discrimination or victimisation undertaken in the course of their employment. Importantly, these provisions make clear that there will be no liability either for the employer or for the employee where the unlawful discrimination or victimisation occurs outside the course of the employee's employment.

Vicarious Liability

At common law, a key consideration when applying the doctrine of vicarious liability is the degree of connection which the wrongful act has with the particular employment. Following *Lister v Helsley Hall Ltd* [2001] UKHL 22, [2002] 1 AC 215 and the more recent judgment of the Supreme Court in *Mohamud v WM Morrison Supermarkets plc* [2016] UKSC 11, [2016] 2 WLR 821, the core question is whether there is a sufficiently close connection between the relevant wrongful conduct and the employment such that it would be fair and just to hold the employer vicariously liable. In *Mohamud*, the Supreme Court held that the court was required to consider two matters: first, what was the field of activity entrusted by the employer to the employee, looked at broadly? Second, whether there was a sufficient connection between that field of activity and the wrongful conduct to make it right for the employer to be held liable to the claimant under the principle of social justice.

In *Mohamud* itself the Supreme Court held that the employer was vicariously liable for the employee's assault on a customer essentially because the field of activity which had been entrusted to the employee included dealing with customers and the assault came about in the context of the employee dealing with a particular customer on behalf of the employer, albeit that the manner in which he dealt with the customer was an abuse of his position. In *Axon v Ministry of Justice* [2016] EWHC 787 (QB), the High Court considered whether the Ministry of Defence was vicariously liable for the actions of an employee who had disclosed information concerning a commanding officer of a naval ship to a newspaper. The Court held that there was no liability because the employee's actions were not in themselves wrongful, as the disclosed information was neither private nor confidential. However, it also held on an *obiter* basis that, had the employees' actions amounted to an unlawful disclosure of private or confidential information, then, on the approach approved by the Supreme Court in *Mohamud*, the Ministry of Defence would have been vicariously liable in respect of that disclosure. This was because the functions entrusted to the employee included protecting the confidentiality of any confidential information to which she had access as an employee.

As will be apparent from the analysis of the relevant jurisprudence in this area set out above and below, there is no single litmus test for determining whether the conduct and the employment are sufficiently closely connected such that there is vicarious liability. Instead, the courts have tended to approach the issue of sufficiency of connection on a case by case basis, with reference to the specific factual circumstances of the case. However, the courts will inevitably also be heavily influenced by judgments in previous cases which rested on similar facts. The implications of this judicial approach to vicarious liability is that determining whether an employer is likely to be vicariously liable in any one case will require close examination of how the courts have approached factually similar cases in the past.

A number of the cases in this area have focussed on the issue of the employer's liability where an employee assaults a colleague or a third party. In *Gravil v Carroll* [2008] EWCA Civ 689, [2008] ICR 1222, [2008] IRLR 829, the Court of Appeal concluded that a rugby club was vicariously liable when one of its players assaulted another player. The Court of Appeal found that the club was liable because the assault was so closely connected to the player's employment with the club that it would be fair and just to hold the club liable. More recently, in *Mohamud*, referred to supra, the Supreme Court held that a supermarket was vicariously liable for the violent attack by one of its sales assistants on a customer. The fact that the assault amounted to a gross abuse of the employee's position and was directly contrary to instructions which the supermarket had given to him did not prevent the supermarket being vicarious liable. The assault, which came about in circumstances where the employee was responding to a customer query, fell squarely within the field of his employment activities and it was otherwise. The wrongful conduct was accordingly sufficiently closely connected with the employee's employment to make it fair and just that the employer be held liable. Compare *Clive Bellman v Northampton Recruitment Ltd* [2016] EWHC 3104 (QB): employer not liable for assault by director/employee on fellow employee which took place outside of the workplace after a work Christmas party. In *Fletcher v*

Chancery Lane [2016] EWCA Civ 1112, the Court of Appeal held that the first instance judge had erred when he concluded that an employer was vicariously liable in negligence in circumstances where its employee had crossed the road and collided with a cyclist. The evidence was such that it was impossible to conclude that the employee's act of crossing the road was sufficiently connected with his employment so as to render the employer vicariously liable.

For an example of a case where the court has held an employer liable for an employee's thieving conduct see *Brink's Global Services Inc v Igrox Ltd* [2010] EWCA Civ 1207, [2011] IRLR 343. In *Brink's* the Court of Appeal held that an employer who had employed an individual to fumigate the vaults of a third party was vicariously liable when the employee stole a number of silver bars from the vaults in question. The Court held that the theft from the very vault which he had been instructed to fumigate was reasonably incidental to the purpose for which the employee was employed and it was otherwise fair and just to hold the employer liable. Similarly, in *Morris v C W Martin & Sons Ltd* [1966] 1 QB 716, the House of Lords held that the employer was vicariously liable in circumstances where its employee had stolen a fur coat which had been entrusted to the employer by a third party.

Both *Igrox* and *Morris* concerned cases where the third party affected by the criminal conduct had a direct commercial relationship with the employer. Different considerations may arise where no such relationship exists between the wronged party and the employer, as was the case in *Dubai Aluminium Co Ltd v Salaam* [2002] UKHL 48, [2003] 2 AC 366. In *Dubai Aluminium*, the question was whether a law firm was vicariously liable in a case where a partner of the firm was alleged to have knowingly drafted various legal agreements in support of a fraudulent enterprise. The persons who were the target of that enterprise had themselves had no dealings with the firm in question. The House of Lords held that vicarious liability was established. This was particularly on the basis that, although the partner was alleged to have drafted the agreements for dishonest purposes, his acts of drafting the agreements were so closely connected with the acts that he was authorised to undertake by the firm that it was fair and just to treat the firm as being vicariously liable for those acts. The approach adopted in *Dubai Aluminium* approved by the Supreme Court in *Mohamud*.

For a recent example of how the courts approach cases where the wrong-doing has resulted from employees engaging in 'horseplay', see *Paul Graham v Commercial Bodyworks Ltd* [2015] EWCA Civ 47. In this case, the employee had been engaging in horseplay with his colleague whilst both were working with highly flammable thinning agents in the employer's repair shop. In the course of their interaction, the employee accidentally set his colleague alight, causing terrible burns. The facts that the incident occurred whilst both employees were at work and the employees had been required to work with highly flammable substances were not sufficient to render the employer vicariously liable for the employee's acts. Query whether the court would have reached the same conclusion had it had the benefit of the Supreme Court's judgment in *Mohamud*.

The question of whether an employer may be held vicariously liable for the actions of an employee who has unlawfully misused third party personal data is due to be considered by the High Court in the forthcoming group litigation case: *Various Claimants v WM Morrison Supermarkets plc.*

An important and controversial question which arises in connection with vicarious liability is the question of whether churches which are caught up in child sex abuse cases can be held vicariously liable for abuses committed by their priests. In *Maga v Birmingham Roman Catholic Archdiocese Trustees* [2010] EWCA Civ 256, [2010] 1 WLR 1441, the Court Appeal held that church trustees were vicariously liable for the sexual abuse of a minor by an assistant priest (overturning the judgment of the High Court ([2009] EWHC 780 (QB)). In *Maga*, the Court of Appeal concluded it was fair and just to impose vicarious liability for the sexual abuse on the trustees because there were a number of factors which, when taken together, showed that there was a sufficiently close connection between the employment at the church of the assistant priest (C) and the abuse which C had inflicted on M. The factors relied upon by the Court of Appeal included in particular that: through being employed by the church as a priest, C had been able to hold himself out to M as being particularly trustworthy and authoritative; C had also used his functions as a priest, including his duty to evangelize, to get to know M; the church had given C particular responsibilities for youth work and C had been able to 'groom' M through that work; moreover, C had developed his relationship with M in the course of a disco which had been organised by the church, took place on church premises and which C attended as a priest. It is clear that central to the Court of Appeal's analysis was the fact that it was C's role as a priest in the archdiocese which gave him the status, authority and opportunity to draw M into his sexually abusive orbit (compare *JGE v Trustees of the Portsmouth Roman Catholic Diocesan Trust* [2012] EWCA Civ 938 where the Court of Appeal held that the fact that the relationship between the Trust and the priest was not an employment relationship per se did not prevent the Trust being vicariously liable for the priest's conduct). The Supreme Court has since taken a similar approach in *Catholic Child Welfare Society & Ors v Institute of the Brothers of Christian Schools* [2012] UKSC 56, [2012] 3 WLR 1319, [2013] IRLR 219. In that case, a lay Roman Catholic order provided education to children. The diocesan bodies responsible for the Institute and the Institute itself were found vicariously liable for sexual abuse by the teachers. Having reviewed the cases on vicarious liability, the Court took the view that establishing vicarious liability required the application of a two stage test. At the first stage, the question was whether the relationship between the defendant and the tortfeasor was one which was capable of giving rise to vicarious liability, for example was it akin to an employer/employee relationship. At the second stage, the question was whether the defendant had not only used the tortfeasor to carry on its own business but had done so in a manner which created or significantly increased the risk that the victims would be subject to the relevant unlawful act. In other words, there had to be a strong causative link between the relationship between the defendant and the tortfeasor on the one hand and the unlawful act on the other. It was this 'close connection' which was required between the relationship and the unlawful act which established the defendant's vicarious liability. The Court held that, on the facts of the case before it, the element of vicarious liability was made out.

The principles approved in Catholic Child Welfare have since been applied outside the religious sphere. Thus, in the case of *Cox v Ministry of Justice* [2016] UKSC 10, [2016] 2 WLR 806, the Supreme Court held that the Ministry of Justice was vicariously liable for injuries sustained by a catering manager employed in one of Her Majesty's prisons, where the injuries were inflicted by a prisoner working in the prison kitchens. Key factual considerations here included that the prisoner had been integrated into the operation of the kitchen; the prisoner's activities were of benefit to the prison; the prisoner had been bound to engage in the work and received a nominal wage for that work and the prisoner had been placed by the Ministry in a position where he could commit negligent acts within the fields of activities assigned to him. The facts that the Ministry did not profit from the arrangement and that the Ministry was under a statutory duty to provide the prisoner with useful work did not militate against the imposition of vicarious liability.

Difficult questions on vicarious liability may arise where the individual who has committed the relevant wrong is not directly employed by the defendant. In the case of *Hawley v Luminar Leisure Ltd* [2006] EWCA Civ 18, [2006] IRLR 817, the Court of Appeal decided that the owners of a nightclub could be held vicariously liable for an assault carried out by a doorman on a member of the public, even though the doorman had been supplied to the nightclub by a third party company. Though the doorman was not directly employed by the nightclub, he could properly be deemed to be an employee of the nightclub for the purposes of vicarious liability principles. See also on the question of dual vicarious liability, *Viasystems (Tyneside) Ltd v Thermal Transfer (Northern) Ltd* [2005] EWCA Civ 1151, [2006] 2 WLR 428, [2006] ICR 327. In this case, the Court of Appeal held that both the employer and the third party exercising day-to-day control over the employee could be vicariously liable for the employee's negligence. The *Viasystems* decision was considered by the Court of Appeal in *Hawley*. The Court of Appeal concluded that, on the facts of the *Hawley* case, only the nightclub and not the doorman's employer should be liable for the assault on the basis that there had been a total transfer of control to the nightclub. In *Colour Quest Ltd v Total Downstream UK plc* [2009] EWHC 540 (Comm), [2009] 2 Lloyd's Rep 1, the High Court considered questions of vicarious liability in connection with the widely reported explosions at the Buncefield oil storage depot. In that case, the oil tank which caused the explosion was part of the operations of a particular oil storage company (H). The explosion had been caused by the negligence of an employee (N) who had been seconded to H by an oil company (T). T sought to argue that it was not vicariously liable for the explosion and that vicarious liability lay with H as the company to which N had been seconded and, further, as the company which directed and controlled tank filling operations. The court held that T was vicariously liable for N's negligence because, as a matter of fact, it was T rather than H which controlled both tank filling operations and the activities of on-site staff. These conclusions were not challenged when the case went on appeal to the Court of Appeal: [2010] EWCA Civ 180, [2010] QB 86.

In general, there is no vicarious liability for the torts of persons other than employees, such as independent contractors engaged by the employer (but see **56.3** below). Provided that the employer has exercised due care in the choice of the contractor, he should not be held liable for acts of negligence committed by that contractor. This principle was confirmed in by the Court of Appeal in *Biffa Waste Services Ltd v Maschinenfabrik Ernst Hese GMBH* [2008] EWCA Civ 1257, [2009] BLR 1. In that case, the Court of Appeal held that the appellant company (B) was not vicariously liable for the negligence of a sub-contractor (P) who had negligently caused a fire in part of a recycling plant which B was contracted to provide. In reaching this conclusion, the court took into account in particular that: P's men were skilled workers; B did not exercise control over the way they worked; the men had not become part of B's business; their work had been temporary (taking place over a couple of days); and B was not based in the UK and had no presence at the site. The fact that B had supervisory rights in respect of the work did not mean it exercised control in respect of the work, particularly as the right to supervise did not, by itself, carry with it the entitlement to instruction how to do the work. The court emphasised that the burden to show transfer of liability for an employee was a heavy one. The court also rejected arguments that B should be held vicariously liable for P's negligence because the work in question was extra-hazardous. The court held that such an argument would only succeed where the work was exceptionally dangerous whatever precautions were taken. The Court of Appeal thereby distinguishing the earlier and much criticised Court of Appeal judgment in *Honeywill & Stein Ltd v Larkin Bros (London's Commercial Photographers) Ltd* [1934] 1 KB 191. However, where the employer owes a personal duty to safeguard others from harm (as he does in relation to the safety of his employees), he may not escape responsibility by delegating that duty, and will thus have to answer for harm caused by the negligent act of a contractor engaged for the purpose of discharging the duty (see, eg *McDermid v Nash Dredging and Reclamation Co Ltd* [1987] ICR 917; although, this is a case not so much of vicarious liability as a failure to discharge the employer's own primary duty). See also the statutory occupier's liability for independent contractors. (**27.15** HEALTH AND SAFETY AT WORK – I) and statutory liability under *HSWA 1974* (**27.16** HEALTH AND SAFETY AT WORK – I).

For a case in which a town council was held vicariously liable for the behaviour of a councillor towards a council employee, see *Moores v Bude Stratton Town Council* [2000] IRLR 676. The reasoning in *Moores* was applied by the EAT in *De Clare Johnson v MYA Consulting Ltd* [2007] All ER (D) 58 (Dec), EAT. In that case, the EAT found that a company was vicariously liable for the acts of the managing director's partner where the partner lived in the business premises.

An employer which is liable to a third party for damages resulting from the negligence of its employee may seek to recover those damages from the negligent employee. See for example: *Lister v Romford Ice and Cold Storage Co Ltd* [1957] AC 555, HL.

56.2 Vicarious Liability

56.2 'IN THE COURSE OF HIS EMPLOYMENT'

The essential precondition of vicarious liability is that the act complained of should have been done in the course of the employment. This concept extends beyond, although it will almost invariably also include, acts which the employee is in fact instructed or authorised to perform. In 2001, the principle was refined by the House of Lords in *Lister v Hesley Hall Ltd* [2001] UKHL 22, [2002] 1 AC 215, [2001] IRLR 472 (see below).

In *Aldred v Nacanco* [1987] IRLR 292, the Court of Appeal approved the following test (taken from *Salmond on Torts*, 18th edn, p 437):

> 'If a servant does negligently that which he was authorised to do carefully, or if he does fraudulently that which he was authorised to do honestly, or if he does mistakenly that which he was authorised to do correctly, his master will answer for that negligence, fraud or mistake. On the other hand, if the unauthorised and wrongful act of the servant is not so connected with the authorised act as to be a mode of doing it, but is an independent act, the master is not responsible; for in such a case the servant is not acting in the course of his employment but has gone outside of it.'

Thus, there may be vicarious liability for the consequences of an act which has been expressly forbidden, eg *Rose v Plenty* [1976] 1 WLR 141 (milk roundsman allowing boy to help with deliveries despite contrary instruction, and boy injured through roundsman's negligence), or which is clearly unauthorised, eg *Morris v CW Martin & Sons Ltd* [1966] 1 QB 716 (dry-cleaning company held liable to owner of fur coat stolen by employee to whom the goods had been entrusted); see also *Brink's Global Services Inc v Igrox Ltd* [2010] EWCA Civ 1207 discussed above. The employer may be vicariously liable for fraud even where the employee acts purely for his own benefit and not to advance the interests of the employer, if the employee is ostensibly authorised to act on the employer's behalf (*Lloyd v Grace, Smith & Co* [1912] AC 716).

In *Lister v Hesley Hall Ltd* [2001] UKHL 22, [2002] 1 AC 215, [2001] IRLR 472, the House of Lords pointed out that the *Salmond* test also states that an employer:

> ' . . . is liable even for acts which he has not authorised, provided they are so *connected* with acts which he has authorised that they may rightly be regarded as modes – although improper modes – of doing them.'

The *Lister* case concerned acts of sexual abuse committed by a school warden on boys in his care. Previously, in *Trotman v North Yorkshire County Council* [1999] IRLR 98, a case with similar facts, the Court of Appeal had held that acts of indecent assault on a pupil were too far removed from being an unauthorised mode of carrying out a teacher's duties as to make the employer vicariously liable. This had been followed by the lower courts in *Lister*. However, the House of Lords in *Lister* held that this was the wrong approach. The correct test is to ask whether the employee's torts were so closely connected with the employment that it would be fair and just to hold the employer vicariously liable. On the facts in *Lister* the answer was that they were. See also *Fennelly v Connex South Eastern Ltd* [2001] IRLR 390, CA; *Mattis v Pollock (t/a Flamingo Nightclub)* [2003] EWCA Civ 887, [2003] 1 WLR 2158, CA; *Bernard v A-G of Jamaica* [2004] UKPC 47, [2005] IRLR 398. *Sidhu v Aerospace Composite Technology Ltd* [2000] IRLR 602; *Wilson v Exel UK Ltd (t/a Exel)* [2010] CSIH 35; *Brink's Global Services Inc v Igrox Ltd* [2010] EWCA Civ 1207; *Maga v Birmingham Roman Catholic Archdiocese Trustees* [2010] EWCA Civ 256 and *Richard Weddall v Barchester Healthcare Ltd: Wallbank v Wallbank Fox Designs Ltd* [2012] EWCA Civ 25, discussed above. *Lister* indicates that the details of the relationship between employer and victim, not the precise terms of the tortfeasor employee's employment, will determine whether vicarious liability exists. If the employee's torts took place in the discharge of the employer's duties to the victim, the employer will be vicariously liable: see *Balfron Trustees Ltd v Peterson* [2001] IRLR 758. See also *Dubai Aluminium Co Ltd v Salaam* [2002]

UKHL 48, [2003] 2 AC 366, discussed supra. The approach adopted in Lister was specifically approved by the Supreme Court in *Mohamud v WM Morrison Supermarkets plc* [2016] UKSC 11, [2016] 2 WLR 821, as discussed supra.

In *Catholic Child Welfare Society & Ors v Institute of the Brothers of Christian* (see above), the Supreme Court considered the test in Lister. Lord Phillips, giving the judgment of the Court, commented that *Lister* had not given clear guidance on the nature of the 'close connection' which was required in order to establish vicarious liability. He stressed that the creation of a risk that the unlawful act would take place was likely to be an important element in the facts which gave rise to vicarious liability, although it would not be sufficient to establish vicarious liability without more. This explained why many of the cases where vicarious liability had been established involved employment relationships where the tortfeasor was responsible for care of the victim.

In *Sidhu*, the employer was not vicariously liable for direct racial discrimination for a racist attack on Mr Sidhu which was carried out by a fellow employee out of hours at a racetrack. The attack took place during a social event organised by the company. The Court of Appeal held that the Tribunal had been entitled to find that such behaviour did not fall within the 'course of employment' for the purposes of *s 32(1)* of the *Race Relations Act 1976*. The fact that the majority of those attending the event were friends and family rather than employees was a significant factual consideration in the case. In *Mohamud*, the Supreme Court held that a supermarket was vicariously liable for an employee's assault on a customer. This was on the basis that the assault occurred in the context of the employee dealing with the customer, an activity which fell firmly within the field of his activities as an employee.

There may be vicarious liability for acts done even whilst the employee is not working, if at the time that employee is being paid for his time, is carrying out the instructions of his employer or is subject to the employer's directions. In *Smith v Stages* [1989] ICR 272, the House of Lords held an employer vicariously liable for injuries sustained in a crash caused by the negligent driving of an employee driving his workmate (the injured claimant) home to Staffordshire after completing a job in Pembroke. The speeches of Lord Goff and Lord Lowry contain extensive analyses of vicarious liability for the acts of employees travelling to and from work. Generally, an employer will not be held vicariously liable for any accident caused by the negligent driving of an employee travelling between his home and his regular place of work, because such a journey is not 'in the course of employment'. However, liability for an accident may be established where the employee is travelling in the employer's time in the course of the employer's business (as in *Smith v Stages*). This will depend on the employee's status, and the nature of his occupation; employees in peripatetic occupations (such as engineers or sales representatives) are likely to come within this category.

It is a different matter if the tortious act is so far removed from what the employee is in fact authorised to do that he can be said to be on 'a frolic of his own'. However, as is made clear by the Supreme Court's judgment in *Mohamud*, the court may be slow to conclude that the employee was on a frolic of his own where the impugned conduct had a degree of connection with functions entrusted to the employee. In *General Engineering Services Ltd v Kingston and St Andrew Corpn* [1989] ICR 88, the court held that there was no vicarious liability where firemen pursuing a go-slow drove at a snail's pace to a fire. The court reached this conclusion on the basis that their act was not a mere mode of performance, but was the very antithesis of what they were engaged to do. Query whether the court's conclusions would withstand scrutiny in the light of *Mohamud*.

In two cases involving police officers, the courts have found the relevant authority to be vicariously liable for the acts of police officers on the basis that the officers in question had, at the time of the unlawful act, held themselves out to the complainant as being police officers. The first of those cases, *Weir v Bettison (sued as Chief Constable of Merseyside Police)* [2003] EWCA Civ 111, [2003] ICR 708, concerned the vicarious liability of the

Chief Constable under *s 88* of the *Police Act 1996*. In that case an off-duty police officer had told the claimant he was a police officer before violently assaulting him and locking him in a police van (taken by the officer without authority). The Court of Appeal held that the Chief Constable was vicariously liable: at the time of the incident the police officer was 'apparently acting as a constable, albeit one behaving very badly'. The second case, *Bernard v A-G of Jamaica* [2004] UKPC 47, [2005] IRLR 398, concerned the Attorney General's vicarious liability at common law. Applying the principles enunciated in *Lister*, the Privy Council held that the Attorney-General was vicariously liable for the acts of a police officer who, after announcing that he was a policeman, shot the claimant and subsequently purported to arrest the claimant for interfering with his duties as a policeman. Compare *Hartnell v A-G of the British Virgin Islands* [2004] UKPC 12, [2004] 1 WLR 1273 in which the Privy Council held that the Attorney-General was not vicariously liable where a police officer had used his police gun to open fire, without warning, in a bar. The Privy Council did, however, hold that the Attorney General was primarily liable in negligence for entrusting someone of Mr Hartwell's character and disposition with a gun. See also *N v Chief Constable of Merseyside Police* [2006] EWHC 3041 (QB), [2006] All ER (D) 421 (Nov), the Chief Constable was not vicariously liable where a police officer wearing his uniform and holding himself out as a police officer took an intoxicated woman to his home and raped her. The fact that the officer had used his uniform and position to secure the trust of the woman in question did not by itself render the Chief Constable vicariously liable. The Chief Constable was not liable from the point where the officer put the woman in his car. The judge made clear that the circumstances as whole must be looked at and that the result may have been different if he had been exercising a police functions such as making an arrest. In *Allen & Ors v Chief Constable of Hampshire* [2013] EWCA Civ 967, a claimant had entered into a relationship with one of the Chief Constable's officers and had then been subject to harassment by that officer. She went on to claim that the Chief Constable was vicariously liable for the harassment. The Court of Appeal concluded that the first instance judge had been right to strike out the claim. This was because both the relationship between the claimant and the officer and the harassment to which she had been subject had no connection with the officer's employment by the Chief Constable.

As will be seen from the above examples, the dividing line between what is and what is not within the course of employment is a fine one, and will often depend upon what the court considers that justice requires in the particular case.

56.3   'PRO HAC VICE' EMPLOYMENT

Sometimes an employer (the general employer) may lend or hire his employee to another employer (the special employer) for a particular task or transaction. Although the employee continues to be employed by the general employer under his contract of employment, he may in certain circumstances be treated as the employee of the special and not of the general employer for the purposes of establishing vicarious liability. One term for this situation is *pro hac vice* ('for this occasion') employment.

Whether the potential liability has in fact been transferred from the general to the special employer must depend upon the arrangements that exist between them, and in particular upon which of them has the right to control the way in which the work is done. It will not be easy to show such a transfer (see, eg *Mersey Docks and Harbour Board v Coggins and Griffith (Liverpool) Ltd* [1947] AC 1), but it was established in the case of *Sime v Sutcliffe Catering Scotland Ltd* [1990] IRLR 228 where the special employer had complete control over day-to-day management and the way the work was carried out. The question of whether potential liability has transferred from the general employer to the special employer was considered by the Court of Appeal in *Hawley v Luminar Leisure Ltd* [2006] EWCA Civ 18, [2006] IRLR 817. In that case, a company which owned a nightclub ('L') contracted with a third party supplier of personnel ('S') for the supply of a doorman. The doorman went on to assault a member of the public whilst working at the nightclub. The Court of Appeal found that the doorman should be deemed to be a temporary employee of L for the purposes of determining vicarious liability. The Court of Appeal went on to find that vicarious liability should be attributed to L rather than S even though S employed the doorman. The Court of Appeal concluded that L, and not S, should be held vicariously liable for the assault, first, because, in obtaining the doorman's services, L had not been seeking to gain access to trained specialists on whose skill and expertise it depended and, second, because control of the doorman had rested with L; thus, there had been an effective transfer of both control and responsibility from S to L. Note, however, that while control is the paramount test, 'entire and absolute control' is not a necessary precondition of vicarious liability in such cases: *Viasystems (Tyneside) Ltd v Thermal Transfer (Northern) Ltd* [2005] EWCA Civ 1151, [2006] 2 WLR 428, [2005] IRLR 983. In the case of *Biffa Waste Services Ltd v Maschinenfabrik Ernst Hese GMBH* [2008] EWCA Civ 1257 [2009] BLR 1, the Court of Appeal held that a contractor (B) who enjoyed supervisory rights in respect of work done by a sub-contractor (P) lacked the necessary control over the sub-contractor's employees to be vicariously liable for their negligence. Factors influencing the Court of Appeal's conclusion on this issue included that the contractor was not present at the site where the negligence occurred (*Viasystems* distinguished); P's workers were skilled workers; B did not control the way they worked; and the work was done over a very short period (a couple of days).

Where it is the subcontracted employee himself who is injured, the 'pro hac vice' doctrine does not apply and there is a right of action against the general employer. The question of who controls the subcontracted employee is only relevant to the issue of liability if the subcontracted employee injures a third party (*Morris v Breaveglen Ltd* [1993] IRLR 350).

It was, until the decision of the Court of Appeal in the *Viasystems* case, generally assumed that it was not possible for both the general employer and the special employer to be vicariously liable for the same act of the same employee. *Viasystems* concerned the installation of air conditioning in a factory. The first defendants were engaged to do the work. They subcontracted ducting work to the second defendants, who in turn contracted with the third defendants for the provision of fitters and fitters' mates. A fitters' mate (S) negligently damaged part of the ducting system, causing the factory to flood. At the time he was under the supervision of both the fitter (employed, like S, by the third defendants) and the second defendants' supervisor. At first instance, the County Court found the third defendants alone to be vicariously liable for the negligence of S. It was assumed (apparently by all parties) that it was not possible to have dual vicarious liability. On appeal to the Court of Appeal, however, the Court reviewed the authorities that were said to support that assumption. They found that, in most of those cases, the possibility of dual vicarious liability had not been argued or considered (as, indeed, it had not in *Viasystems* at first instance). May LJ observed that 'the core question is who was entitled, and in theory obliged, to control the employee's relevant negligent act so as to prevent it'. He concluded that, if there were (as there were in *Viasystems*) genuinely two 'employers' who could have controlled the employee, then both could be vicariously liable. Rix LJ agreed that two 'employers' could be vicariously liable, but he put the test slightly differently. He said dual vicarious liability would be found in a 'situation where the employee in question, at any rate for relevant purposes, is so much a part of the work, business or organisation of both employers that it is just to make both employers answer for his negligence'. The Court noted that such situations would be rare, and that dual vicarious liability would be redundant where one of the 'employers' was itself primarily liable. The Court determined that the second and third defendants were equally responsible and that the second and third defendants should each contribute 50% of the damages awarded to the claimant pursuant to ss 1(1) and 2 of the *Civil Liability (Contribution) Act 1978* (which provide, respectively, that 'any person liable in respect of any damage suffered by another person may recover contribution from any other person liable in respect of the same damage (whether jointly with him or otherwise)' and that the amount of recoverable contribution 'shall be such as may be found by the court to be just and equitable having regard to the extent of the person's responsibility for the damage in question'.

The Supreme Court has now approved Rix LJ's approach and disapproved that of May LJ. It found two 'employers' vicariously liable in *Catholic Child Welfare Society & Ors v Institute of the Brothers of Christian Schools* (see above). In that case, the institute was a Roman Catholic order providing education to children. The diocesan bodies with statutory responsibility for managing a school left it to the institute to nominate a brother to act as headmaster and appoint other brothers to teach there. The question was whether the Diocesan bodies or the institute itself should be held liable for sexual abuse by the brothers teaching in the institute. The Supreme Court held them both liable. In doing so, it expressly preferred Rix LJ's approach. It found that: 'where two defendants were potentially vicariously liable for the act of a tortfeasor, it was necessary to give independent consideration to the relationship between the tortfeasor and each defendant in order to decide whether that defendant was vicariously liable. The test for liability was not whether both defendants had exercised control over the tortfeasor but whether the tortfeasor had been so much a part of the work, business or organisation of both defendants that it was fair to make both answer for his acts. In considering that question in relation to each defendant the approach of Rix LJ is to be preferred to that of May LJ.'

57   Working Time

57.1   THE WORKING TIME DIRECTIVE

Until relatively recently working hours were not regulated by statute for the vast majority of workers in the UK. Special provisions have applied to specific groups in the past but most were swept away in the 1980s and 1990s. For example, restrictions on the employment of retail workers contained in the *Shops Act 1950* were repealed by the *Deregulation and Contracting Out Act 1994*, although some protection against enforced Sunday working has remained (now contained in *ss 36–43 Employment Rights Act 1996*).

This situation changed in 1998 as a result of European legislation, but only after a protracted battle. In November 1993 *EC Directive 93/104* 'concerning certain aspects of the organisation of working time' ('the *Working Time Directive*') was adopted; it came into force in member states on 23 November 1996. The legal basis for the *Directive* was as a health and safety measure under *art 118A* of the *Treaty of Rome* (the current equivalent is *art 154* of the *Treaty on the Functioning of the European Union*), which requires only qualified majority voting. Hence it could be, and was, adopted without the assent of the UK Government. However, the Conservative Government of the day refused to accept the legitimacy of the *Directive* on the grounds that it could not be categorised as health and safety legislation. No attempt was made by the UK to comply with the 1996 deadline for implementation, pending the outcome of a challenge to the *Directive* in the ECJ.

In the event the Court ruled, in *United Kingdom v EU Council*: C-84/94 [1997] ICR 443, that (with one minor exception) the UK's objections should be rejected. Following a change of government, implementation of the *Directive* eventually took place on 1 October 1998, by means of the *Working Time Regulations 1998 (SI 1998/1833)*. The *1998 Regulations* have been supplemented by guidance published by the Department of Trade and Industry (now the Department for Business, Innovation and Skills (BIS)), in accordance with a duty imposed on the Secretary of State by *reg 35A* (a provision added in 1999). It should, however, be noted that this guidance has no formal legal status as an interpretation of the *Regulations*. For further details see **57.26**.

The *Directive*, which covers working hours, rest breaks and holidays, initially did not apply to a number of sectors of activity. The exceptions were: air, rail, road, sea, inland waterway and lake transport, sea fishing, other work at sea and the activities of doctors in training. (For the scope of these exceptions see further **57.3** below.)

However, agreement was reached in 2000 on the extension of the *Directive* to excluded sectors and activities. The *Working Time Directive* was amended by *Directive 2000/34* to cover all non-mobile workers in the excluded sectors, doctors in training, and offshore and railway workers (including mobile railway workers). The *Directive* was implemented domestically by amendments to the *Working Time Regulations* with effect from 1 August 2003, with implementation for doctors in training phased over several years but finally completed from 1 August 2011. The *Directive*, as amended by the *2000 Directive*, was in turn replaced by *Directive 2003/88/EC*, a purely consolidating measure, which came into force on 2 August 2004. References in this chapter to the *Directive* apply equally to the 2003 version.

In addition to this general extension of the original *Directive*, further *Directives* have been adopted for those specific categories of workers still not covered by the principal provisions. The working time of seafarers engaged on merchant ships was covered in *Directive 99/63*, which was given effect in the UK by the *Merchant Shipping (Hours of Work) Regulations 2002*; see **57.31** below for more details. Comparable provisions covering workers on sea fishing vessels, and on inland waterway and lake transport, are summarised at **57.31** and **57.32**.

Mobile workers in the civil aviation sector were covered by a separate *Directive, 2000/79*, in turn implemented domestically by the *Civil Aviation (Working Time) Regulations 2004, SI 2004/756*, discussed at **57.33** below.

A further *Directive, 2002/15* 'on the organisation of working time of persons performing mobile road transport activities', which applies to drivers covered by *Regulation EEC 3820/85* (now *Regulation 561/2006*) or the AETR agreement, was implemented by the *Road Transport (Working Time) Regulations 2005, SI 2005/639*. For further details see **57.34** and **57.35** below. Self-employed owner-drivers were not initially covered by the *Regulations*. However in April 2012 amendments were made to the *2005 Regulations* by the *Road Transport (Working Time) (Amendment) Regulations 2012, SI 2012/991*, extending the application of the *2005 Regulations* to self-employed drivers, with effect from 11 May 2012.

The provisions of the original *Working Time Directive* permitting derogations from its provisions, in particular those permitting individual opt-outs from the 48 hour week, were expressly made subject to a review by the European Council on a report from the Commission. The principal areas considered for amendment of the *Directive* were a tightening up (or the removal) of the provision permitting member states to allow individual opt-outs from the maximum 48 hour working week (a provision the UK has adopted: see **57.7** below) and a change in the status under the *Directive* of time spent on call but not actually working.

The Commission's initial report was issued in December 2003. This was then followed by various rounds of consultations on proposals and counter-proposals, eventually ending in April 2009 in deadlock between the Parliament, the Council and the Commission, and abandonment of the attempt to amend the *Directive*.

A fresh initiative by the Commission to secure agreement to amendments to the *Directive* was announced in March 2010. After an initial decision by the Social Partners not to attempt to produce a Framework Agreement, their agreement to negotiate a Framework Agreement was eventually announced in November 2011, but these negotiations failed to produce an agreed proposal. Eventually in December 2014 the Commission initiated a fresh round of consultations with a view to putting forward new proposals for reform, but it appears unlikely that a consensus will be found easily or speedily on the form of any amendments to the *Directive*. Changes to the *Directive* did not feature in the package of reforms to the EU negotiated by the British Government with other EU heads of Government in March 2016.

57.2   WORKING TIME REGULATIONS 1998

As noted above, the *Working Time Directive* was implemented in Great Britain by the *Working Time Regulations 1998 (SI 1998/1833)*, which came into force on 1 October 1998. The *1998 Regulations* also brought into force certain provisions in the EC *Directive on the Protection of Young People at Work (94/33)* ('the *Young Workers' Directive*) relating to rest periods, breaks and night work in respect of young people. See also **4.6 CHILDREN AND YOUNG PERSONS**. The *1998 Regulations* have subsequently been amended several times; details are given below. The *1998 Regulations*, as amended, govern hours of work, night work, breaks and holidays.

Since the *1998 Regulations* (as amended) are the domestic implementation of the *Directive*, courts and tribunals will approach the interpretation of the *Regulations* on the basis that they should so far as possible be so interpreted as to give effect to the stated purposes of the *Directive*. In this context it is important to appreciate that the *Directive* was adopted as a health and safety measure, as one of the 'daughter' directives under the 1989 *Framework Health and Safety Directive 89/391*. It should therefore be interpreted so as to promote the protection of workers' health and safety whenever such an interpretation is possible. In addition, of course, the case law of the ECJ on the interpretation and application of the *Directive* is likely to be a decisive guide to the interpretation of equivalent provisions in the *1998 Regulations*.

The position following the UK Government's formal notification to the EU of its intention that the UK will cease its membership of the EU has in part been clarified by a White Paper issued in March 2017. This confirms the Government's intention to legislate, via a 'Great Reform Bill' to preserve in force following Brexit the provisions of legislation passed under the *European Communities Act 1972*, and the effect of decisions of the ECJ on the interpretation of the EU legislation implemented by such domestic provisions. Thus it is expected that the *Working Time Regulations* will remain in force, and continue to be interpreted so far as possible consistently with the *Working Time Directive* as interpreted by the ECJ, unless and until Parliament legislates to change the position.

The ECJ has held that *art 7* of the *Directive*, which gives workers the right to paid annual leave, is sufficiently unconditional and precise to be directly enforceable in national courts, against state authorities in their capacity as employers: *Dominguez v Centre informatique du Centre Ouest Atlantique*: C-282/10 [2012] IRLR 321. This means that in claims made under the *Regulations* against those public sector employers which are, in EU terms, state authorities, the *Directive* can be relied on as a source of rights if the *Regulations* cannot be interpreted to give full effect to the equivalent provision of the *Directive*. Even if the employer is not a state authority, however, courts and tribunals are expected to interpret the *Regulations* consistently with the *Directive* as interpreted by the ECJ, if necessary 'reading down' the provisions of the *Directive* into the relevant provisions of the *Regulations*; a good example of this is *Sood Enterprises Ltd v Healy* [2013] IRLR 865, a case on entitlement to holiday pay for periods of long-term sickness absence. Further clarification of how far the *Regulations* can be modified to ensure compliance with the requirements of EU law was given by the Court of Appeal in the case of *British Gas Trading Ltd v Lock* [2016] EWCA Civ 983, [2016] IRLR 946, [2017] ICR 1.

The ECJ has also held that *art 6(b)* of the *Directive*, which sets a limit on the working week of an average of 48 hours, is directly enforceable in national courts and tribunals against state authorities as employers: see *Pfeiffer v Deutsches Rotes Kreuz, Kreisverband Waldshut eV*: C-397/01 to 403/01, [2005] IRLR 137.

An example of the general approach of the ECJ to the interpretation of the *Working Time Directive* is its decision in *European Commission v United Kingdom*: C-484/04 [2006] IRLR 888. In this case, the European Commission had issued a Reasoned Opinion that the United Kingdom had failed fully to implement the *Directive* in two respects, including with respect to the terms of the official Guidance issued by the Department of Trade and Industry, which (at that time) stated that 'employers must make sure that workers *can* take [rest breaks and rest periods], but are not required to make sure that they *do* take their rest' (the emphasis was in the original text). The UK Government declined to act on the Reasoned Opinion, and the Commission brought enforcement proceedings.

On this issue, the Court found against the UK. Whilst accepting that the *Directive* did not require member states to go so far as requiring employers to force their workers to take rest entitlements, the Guidance was 'liable to render the rights [to rest periods and rest breaks] meaningless' and was thus incompatible with the objective of the directive, which required minimum rest periods to be treated as 'essential for the protection of workers' health and safety'. The Court added that 'Member States are under an obligation to guarantee that each of the minimum requirements laid down by the directive is observed'. The DTI amended the passage in the Guidance criticised by the Court, by deleting the second half of the quoted passage.

57.3   Coverage

Workers covered by the *1998 Regulations* include employees working under a contract of employment and other individuals who work under a contract personally to perform work or provide services for the 'employer' (except for people genuinely in business on their own account who are in a client or customer relationship with the 'employer') (*reg 2(1)*). *Regulation 36* provides that an agency worker who would not otherwise fall within the definition of a worker under these provisions will be treated as being employed by whichever of the agent or principal is responsible for paying him or her or, if that is not ascertainable, by whichever in fact pays the worker (see further for the position of agency workers generally **57.37** below). The extended definition of 'worker' has been held to include self-employed building subcontractors who in practice worked exclusively for one employer: *Byrne Bros (Formwork) Ltd v Baird* [2002] IRLR 96. (See further on this *Wright v Redrow Homes (Yorkshire) Ltd* [2004] EWCA Civ 469, [2004] IRLR 720, and, for a fuller discussion of these and subsequent cases on this much-litigated issue, see EMPLOYEE, SELF-EMPLOYED OR WORKER? **15.9**.)

The *Regulations* also apply, by express provision, to those in Crown service and the armed forces, and to police officers (who would otherwise fall outside the definition of 'workers'): *regs 37–41*. Certain non-employed trainees are also covered by the *Regulations* (*reg 42*). The breadth of the application of the *Regulations* reflects the point that the ECJ has repeatedly held that the term 'worker', 'has an autonomous meaning specific to European Union Law' applicable to the scope of the *Working Time Directive*, which 'may not be interpreted differently according to the law of member States': see most recently *Union syndicale Solidaires Isère v Premier Ministre*: C-428/09 [2011] 1 CMLR 1206, [2011] IRLR 84, para 28 and *Fenoll v Centre d'Aide par le Travail "la Jouvenne"*: C-316/13 [2016] IRLR 67, para 29, where the Court stated that 'The essential feature of an employment relationship is that for a certain period of time a person performs services for and under the direction of another person in return for which he receives remuneration'.. The court in these cases held in turn that casual or seasonal workers working no more than 80 days a year, and disabled individuals attending rehabilitation centres performing work for modest pay as part of a rehabilitation programme, could potentially fall within the terms of this definition.

The *Regulations* also apply, with separate provisions in relation to several important points, to young workers. Those requirements of the *Young Workers' Directive* which were not implemented by the *1998 Regulations* were implemented by amendments to the *1998 Regulations* introduced by the *Working Time (Amendment) Regulations 2002*. The principal changes are the imposition of a maximum working day of 8 hours, and a maximum working week of 40 hours (neither of which is subject to averaging over a longer period) for workers below the age of 18 (but above compulsory school age: see below). See further **57.6**.

In addition, the *2002 Regulations* restrict the employment of a young worker during the 'restricted period', which is normally 10 pm to 6 am, but 11 pm to 7 am if the worker is contractually required to work later than 10 pm: for details of these restrictions see **57.10** below.

There are separate provisions in the *Children and Young Persons Act 1933, s 18(1)*, as amended in compliance with *Directive 94/33*, which regulate the working hours and holiday entitlements of children below the maximum compulsory school age. (For Scotland, the equivalent provisions are in the *Children and Young Persons (Scotland) Act 1937*.) The EAT has held, by reference to these provisions, that such children are not 'workers' for the purposes of the *1998 Regulations*, and accordingly not covered by them: *Ashby v Addison (t/a Brayton News)* [2003] ICR 667, a case involving a claim for holiday pay by a 15 year old paper boy.

Following amendments made by the *Working Time (Amendment) Regulations 2003*, the *1998 Regulations* now apply to all workers (with the exclusion of school age children) other than those mobile workers in certain transport sectors, who are now all covered by separate legislation. Doctors in training were brought fully within the scope of the *Regulations* with effect from August 2009, subject to limited and specific exemptions from the 48 hour working week the last of which expired on 31 July 2011.

The *Regulations* do not apply to 'certain activities of the armed forces, police or other civil protection services', but only to the extent that certain characteristics of the particular service concerned 'inevitably conflict' with the *Regulations: reg 18*. This exception mirrors a provision in *art 1(3)* of the *Directive*, which was narrowly construed by the ECJ in *Pfeiffer v Deutsches Rotes Kreuz, Kreisverband Waldshut eV*: C-397/01 to C-403/01 [2005] IRLR 137 as applying to the emergency services only in the context of the provision of services essential for the protection of public health, safety or order in situations of exceptional gravity, and thus not excluding from the *Directive* the routine operation of a public ambulance service. The same conclusion was reached in relation to a public fire service in *Personalrat der Feuerwehr Hamburg v Leiter der Feuerwehr Hamburg*: C-52/04, unreported, with the proviso that the 48 hour limit on weekly working time could be exceeded 'in exceptional circumstances of such gravity and scale that the aim of ensuring the proper functioning of services essential for the protection of public interests, such as public order, health and safety, must temporarily prevail over the aim of guaranteeing the health and safety of workers assigned to intervention and rescue teams'. This interpretation is very likely to be followed in the construction of the exception in the *1998 Regulations*.

With regard to the former exclusion of transport workers, the position initially was that all workers, whether mobile or non-mobile, within undertakings in the excluded sectors, were excluded from the *Directive*: *Bowden v Tuffnells Parcels Express Ltd*: C-133/00 [2001] IRLR 838. This is still relevant to the exclusion of mobile workers in the civil aviation and road transport sectors referred to at (i) and (iii) below, but non-mobile workers in these sectors were brought within the scope of the *Regulations* by the amendments made in 2003. The Court in *Pfeiffer*, above, held that emergency ambulance services were outside the road transport sector. It was accepted that bus drivers engaged in the provision of scheduled services fall within the provisions of the *1998 Regulations*, rather than the *Road Transport (Working Time) Regulations 2005*, in *Feist v First Hampshire & Dorset Ltd* [2007] All ER (D) 180 (Feb), EAT.

In summary, the position as to the coverage of the *1998 Regulations* is now as follows:

(a) all workers in Great Britain are covered save for those in exempted categories listed below; see below for the application of the *Regulations* outside Great Britain;

(b) the *Regulations* do not apply to those of compulsory school age, but do apply with modifications to those above compulsory school age but below 18;

(c) the *Regulations* do not apply to merchant seafarers to whom *Directive 99/63* applies;

(d) the *Regulations* do not apply to workers on board sea-going fishing vessels or ships or hovercraft operating inland waterway or lake transport (of goods or passengers); see further below.

In addition, the provisions of the *Regulations* limiting working time and night work, relating to monotonous work, and conferring rights to rest periods and rest breaks, do not apply:

(i) to mobile workers in the civil aviation sector, who are covered by the legislation implementing *Directive 2000/79*;

(ii) to the extent that characteristics peculiar to the armed forces, the police and civil protection services inevitably conflict with any such provisions;

(iii) to mobile workers in the road transport sector, who are covered by legislation under *Directive 2002/15*.

(For those in categories (i) and (ii), but not (iii), entitlements regarding health assessments and paid annual leave are also excluded.)

For the specific application of the *1998 Regulations* to mobile workers on railways see **57.29**; for seafarers see further **57.31**, for mobile workers in the lake and inland waterway transport sectors see further **57.32**, for the aviation sector see further **57.33** and for mobile workers in road transport see **57.34** and **57.35**. One further exclusion, in respect of hours of work, restrictions on night work, rights to health assessments and protection from monotonous work, but not in respect of rest breaks, rest periods or rights to annual leave, is for workers employed as domestic servants in a private household: *reg 19*. See further **57.30** below.

The *1998 Regulations* apply to Great Britain. The territorial scope of the *Regulations* was extended by the *Working Time (Amendment) Regulations 2003 (SI 2003/1684)* to 'offshore work', as defined, and from 1 October 2006 their territorial scope was further extended to cover workers on oil and gas rigs in UK territorial waters and the UK and cross-border oil and gas fields within the UK sector of the Continental Shelf (see the *Working Time (Amendment No 2) Regulations 2006, SI 2006/2389*); the EAT has since confirmed the view of the DTI (as it then was) that this amendment was simply declaratory of the effect of the *2003 Regulations*: *Transocean International Resources Ltd v Russell* (UKEATS/0074/05) (4 October 2006, unreported).

In *Bleuse v MBT Transport Ltd* [2008] IRLR 264, the EAT had to consider whether the *1998 Regulations* can apply outside Great Britain and its associated waters. The claim in issue was brought by a German national, resident in Germany, who worked as a lorry driver, principally in Austria, for a company registered in the UK but owned by an Austrian national. The Claimant never worked within Britain, but his contract of employment was expressed to be governed by English law. In the context of a claim for holiday pay, the EAT held that the claim could be maintained in an employment tribunal as this was necessary in order to give effect to a directly enforceable EU right.

The status and scope of what has become known as the '*Bleuse* principle' is however far from clear. It is unclear from the EAT's reasoning in *Bleuse* itself whether the decision would apply equally to other rights under the *1998 Regulations*, or what difference it would make if there was a clear right to pursue the claim in another EU member state, if the Respondent was not a UK company, or the contract was not governed by English law (or some combination of these factors). The Court of Appeal in *Duncombe v Secretary of State for Children, Schools and Families* [2009] EWCA Civ 1355, [2010] IRLR 331 held that *Bleuse* was correctly decided, and enunciated a general principle that tribunals have jurisdiction under statutory provisions implementing EU Directives in any case where it is necessary to assume jurisdiction to give effect to an EU right, at least where the contract in issue is governed by English (or Scots) law.

However when the case reached the Supreme Court (under the name *Secretary of State for Children, Schools and Families v Fletcher* [2011] UKSC 14, [2011] ICR 495), it was decided on a different point, making it unnecessary to decide the correctness of the *Bleuse* principle. Lady Hale, giving the only reasoned judgment, indicated that the Court was favourably inclined to the principle, but that had it been necessary to decide whether the claimants could rely on rights conferred by a Directive in relation to employment in another EU member state, the Court would have considered it necessary to refer the point to the CJEU for an opinion. The applicability of the '*Bleuse* principle' is therefore unclear pending a decision on the point by the ECJ.

It is in any case clear that the *Bleuse* principle does not confer rights under the *1998 Regulations* on a worker outside the EU; this was confirmed by the Court of Appeal in *Dhunna v Creditsights Ltd* [2014] EWCA Civ 1238, [2014] IRLR 953, [2015] ICR 105 in relation to a worker based in Dubai; see also *Wittenborg v Sunset Personnel Services* UKEATS/0019/13 (31 January 2017, unreported), holding that the Regulations did not apply to the employment by a company registered in Scotland of a German national to work on a ship based off the coast of Nigeria.

57.4 Agreements: definition

Where flexibility and modifications are permitted under the *Working Time Regulations*, employers may conclude agreements to cover the situation. Depending on the circumstances, these may take the form of a collective agreement, a workforce agreement or a relevant agreement.

Regulation 2(1) provides that a *collective agreement* is an agreement or arrangement made by or on behalf of one or more independent trade unions and one or more employers or employers' associations relating to any of the matters set out in *TULRCA 1992, s 178(2)*; see **6 COLLECTIVE AGREEMENTS**. For the purposes of the Working Time Regulations, a collective agreement may include an award made under a collective agreement providing for binding third party arbitration: *Bewley v HM Prison Service* [2004] ICR 422.

A *workforce agreement* means an agreement between an employer and its workers or their elected representatives in respect of which certain conditions are satisfied as set out in *Sch 1*:

(a)   the agreement is in writing;

(b)   it has effect for a specified period of five years or less;

(c)   it applies to all the relevant members of the workforce or to all of the relevant members who belong to a particular group (eg who undertake a particular function, work at a particular workplace or belong to a particular department);

(d)   it is signed by representatives of the workforce (or particular group, as applicable). If the employer has 20 or fewer workers, the agreement may be signed either by appropriate representatives or by the majority of workers employed by the employer, but note that the limit is on the total number of workers employed, not the number covered by the agreement, if that is only a section of the workforce;

(e)   before the agreement was signed, the employer provided all workers to whom the agreement applies with copies and such guidance as is reasonable to understand it fully.

Requirements concerning the election of representatives are set out at *Sch 1 para 3*.

A *relevant agreement* includes both collective and workforce agreements and, in addition, any other agreement in writing which is legally enforceable as between worker and employer. This definition may therefore include the written terms of a contract of employment.

Where a provision of the *Regulations* is modified or excluded by a workforce or collective agreement and a worker is thereby required to work during what would be a rest period or break, the employer must allow, where possible, an equivalent period of compensatory rest. In exceptional cases where it is not possible for objective reasons to grant compensatory rest, the employer must provide appropriate protection to safeguard the worker's health and safety (*reg 24*). The scope of the concept of compensatory rest is considered more fully at **57.29** below.

57.5   WORKING TIME

In relation to a worker, 'working time' is defined in *reg 2(1)* as:

(a)   any period during which the individual is working, at the employer's disposal and carrying out his or her activity or duties;

(b)   any period during which he or she is receiving 'relevant training'; and

(c)   any additional period which is to be treated as working time for the purpose of the *Regulations* under a relevant agreement.

'Relevant training' means work experience or training provided on a training course or programme of training for employment, other than courses run by educational institutions or organisations whose main business is the provision of training (see further as to the position under the Directive of training provided by third parties *European Commission v Ireland*: C-87/14 [2016] IRLR 77).

According to the BIS Guidance (now provided on the www.gov.uk website), the definition of working time includes: working lunches, business travel time, and 'in some [unspecified] cases' time spent working abroad. It does not include: home-to-work travel, rest breaks when no work is done, time spent travelling outside normal working time or non-job-related training.

The position in relation to travelling time has been clarified by a decision of the ECJ, *Federacion de Servicios Privados del Sindicato Comisiones Obreras v Tyco Integrated Security SL*: C-266/14 [2015] IRLR 935 (*'Tyco'*). The case concerned security equipment engineers who had formerly worked from a depot at which they collected instructions and a company vehicle, which they used to visit customers' premises, returning to the depot at the end of the working day. The employer closed the depots and the employees thereafter worked from home, receiving daily schedules by mobile phone and travelling from home to the first customer of the day, and returning from the last, in company provided transport. On these facts the ECJ held that the time spent travelling to the first customer, and home from the last, met all three elements of the definition of working time. It is not yet clear whether there are any particular features of this work pattern the absence of which would affect the position, but it is likely to be the case that time spent travelling between the worker's home and customers' premises, as well as between customers, where the worker performs work at the premises of different customers during the working day or from day to day, will always be working time for the purposes of the *reg 2(1)(a)* of the *Regulations*, which reproduce verbatim the wording in the *Directive*. The position for travel between customers' premises is a fortiori: see *Kennedy v Cordia (Services) LLP* [2016] UKSC 6, [2016] 1 WLR 597 (10 February 2016) (a health and safety case).

The EAT has held that time spent by workers who are also trade union representatives or health and safety representatives, attending meetings at the request of the employer but outside their normal working hours, is working time for the purposes of the *Regulations*: *Edwards v Encirc Ltd* [2015] IRLR 528. The principal practical consequence of this in the particular case was that the claimants were entitled to the minimum daily rest period of 11 hours between the conclusion of the meeting and the start of the following working day.

There is no corresponding definition of 'rest', and a rest period is defined in such a way as to exclude any period of working time from being treated as a rest period, but not otherwise more specifically. In effect the two concepts are mutually exclusive, and any time that is not working time or annual leave can be attributed as part of an entitlement to a rest period, including (subject to the *Tyco* case) time spent on such activities as travel between the workplace and the worker's home. See further **57.14–57.17**, below.

One important issue as to the ambit of the definition of working time is the status of time 'on call'. This has been the subject of three decisions of the ECJ, to the effect that 'on-call' time constitutes working time where the worker is required to be at his or her place of work during this period. If the worker is away from the workplace when on call and can pursue leisure activities, on-call time is not working time (*Sindicato de Médicos de Asistencia Pública (Simap) v Conselleria de Sanidad y Consumo de la Generalidad Valenciana*: C-303/98 [2000] IRLR 845). The Court has subsequently confirmed that time spent on call and at the workplace, but not actually performing the worker's duties, was to be regarded as working time in circumstances where the worker (a hospital doctor) was permitted to rest when his services were not required, and rest facilities were provided for this purpose by the employer: *Landeshauptstadt Kiel v Jaeger*, above: C-151/02 [2003] IRLR 804.

This conclusion was reiterated in *Vorel v Nemocnice Český Krumlov*: C-437/05 [2007] ECR-I 331, but with the important additional qualification that this did not prevent national law from providing for a lower rate of pay for the inactive parts of periods on-call (as the Czech law under reference did).

However, in *Dellas v Premier Ministre*: C-14/04 [2006] IRLR 225 the ECJ held to be incompatible with the *Directive* a French law which provided for time spent on call and at the employer's premises, but not actually working, to count at the rate of only a half or a third of actual time; the principal objection of the Court was that it was (at least theoretically) possible for workers subject to this law to work in excess of the 48 hour week, although France has adopted a lower maximum of 44 hours. Thus whilst the rate of pay for time on call may be lower (subject, in the UK context, to the application of the National Minimum Wage), time on call itself must be taken into account fully.

These decisions of the ECJ have been controversial for their implications for the staffing of hospital medical services in particular, and would have been affected by the implementation of the Commission's proposals for revision of the *Directive*, referred to at **57.1** above. The failure of negotiations between the Social Partners on amendments to the *Directive* however precludes any immediate change in the position.

The EAT has held that the effect of the decision in *Jaeger* is that a warden employed at a sheltered housing complex on 24 hour call is to be regarded as working throughout the period on call although she was provided with a flat to occupy at the premises, and was free to use her time as she pleased subject to remaining in the vicinity to be available for call-outs. Accordingly the employer was in breach of the requirement to permit a daily rest period for the warden: *MacCartney v Oversley House Management* [2006] ICR 510, EAT, not following the earlier case of *Stamp v South Holland District Council* [2003] All ER (D) 19 (Jun), which the EAT regarded as inconsistent with the reasoning and decision in *Jaeger*. *MacCartney* has since been followed in a further EAT decision on similar facts, *Hughes v Graham (t/a Graylyns Residential Home)* [2008] All ER (D) 137 (Oct), EAT.

In a further decision on this point, the EAT in *Truslove v Scottish Ambulance Service* [2014] ICR 1232 held that time spent by ambulance drivers on call, who were required to be available and within a defined distance of the ambulance station (which was a considerable distance from their homes), counted as working time. However not all time spent on call is working time, as confirmed by the decision of the Northern Ireland Court of Appeal in *Blakley v South Eastern Health & Social Services Trust* [2009] NICA 62 that time spent on call by an Estates Officer, who was required to be contactable to be called out but not required to be at his workplace, or at home, was not 'working time'; only the time during which he was actually on a call-out met the requirements of the definition. The difference between these two cases is the effect of the restriction on the whereabouts of the worker.

The English Court of Appeal has also considered the application of the definition of 'working time' to 'down time': *Gallagher v Alpha Catering Services Ltd* [2004] EWCA Civ 1559, [2005] IRLR 102. The employees delivered catering supplies to aircraft at Gatwick Airport. They often had to wait for an aircraft to be ready for servicing; during these periods they had to remain at the airport and in radio contact with the employer, but could use the time eg to take refreshment. It was held that all three limbs of the definition of 'working time' were satisfied on these facts, and the down time or waiting time counted as working time.

On the other hand, an employment tribunal in a test case on the rights of workers on North Sea oil rigs has held that the time between each working shift whilst the worker is offshore is not working time, and accordingly can constitute a rest period, despite the necessary restrictions on what activities can be undertaken whilst on the oil rig and the fact that the worker cannot in practice leave the oil rig between shifts: *Russell v Transocean International Resources Ltd* (Case S/104056/04) (May 2005, unreported). This point was not directly in issue in the subsequent appeals to the EAT, Court of Session and Supreme Court in this case (see *Russell v Transocean International Resources Ltd* [2011] UKSC 57, [2012] IRLR 149), but the tribunal's view was implicitly endorsed in the approach to the case adopted by Lord Hope in the Supreme Court.

The issue of what constitutes 'working time' may also arise as a matter of contract. An example is *Alexander v Jarvis Hotels plc* (EATS/0062/05) (30 May 2006, unreported) where the EAT held that time spent by a hotel manager overnight at the hotel was working time, although he was free to sleep. His work consisted of being present at the hotel to respond to any emergency, an arrangement required of the hotel for health and safety reasons.

There have also been a number of cases about what constitutes time for which payment is due under the *National Minimum Wage Act 1998*, but these relate to different definitions and do not necessarily assist in interpreting the definition of 'working time' in the *1998 Regulations* (and nor do decisions on the meaning of 'working time' under the *Working Time Regulations* assist in the interpretation of the *National Minimum Wage Regulations*: see *Wray v J W Lees & Co (Brewers) Ltd* [2012] IRLR 43, EAT).

57.6 Maximum weekly working time

An employer is required to take all reasonable steps, in keeping with the need to protect health and safety, to ensure that each adult worker works no more than 48 hours on average in each working week, averaged over reference periods of 17 weeks. Such periods are extended to 26 weeks for certain workers – see 'special case' exemptions at **57.29** below. The reference period may also be extended to a maximum of 52 weeks where a collective or workforce agreement so provides, on the basis of objective or technical reasons concerning the organisation of work (*regs 4(1), (2), (5), 23(b)*). The possible extension to 52 weeks is the technical basis on which 'annualised hours' agreements are most appropriately made. *Regulations 25A* and *25B* of the *1998 Regulations* make specific provision for the reference periods applicable respectively to doctors in training (26 weeks) and offshore workers (52 weeks).

A relevant agreement may stipulate when the reference period begins. Otherwise, the reference period will be a rolling 17-week (or 26 or up to 52 week) period (*reg 4(3)*). Where a worker has been employed for less than 17 weeks, the reference period will be the number of weeks which have elapsed since he or she started work (*reg 4(4)*).

Average working time is calculated according to the formula:

$$\frac{A + B}{C}$$

where:

'A' is the total number of hours of working time in the reference period;

'B' is the total number of hours worked immediately after the reference period during extra days equivalent to the number of 'excluded days' (see below for this) in the reference period; and

'C' is the number of weeks in the reference period (*reg 4(6)*).

For the purpose of calculating average hours, certain days are to be excluded: days taken as basic statutory annual leave under the *1998 Regulations* (but not days of annual leave taken under a contractual provision over and above the statutory entitlement, or days taken as part

57.10 Length of night work

Employers are required to take all reasonable steps, in keeping with the need to protect workers' health and safety, to ensure that night workers' normal hours of work do not exceed an average of eight in each 24 hours during a 17-week reference period (*reg 6(1), (2)*). This will be a rolling 17-week period unless a relevant agreement specifies successive periods (*reg 6(3)*). For individuals who have worked for less than 17 weeks, the average is calculated over the period since they started work for the employer (*reg 6(4)*).

Regulation 6(5) provides that average normal hours of work for a night worker are calculated according to the formula:

$$\frac{A}{B-C}$$

where:

'A' is the number of normal working hours during the reference period;

'B' is the number of days during the reference period; and

'C' is the total number of hours during the reference period spent by the worker in statutory weekly rest periods (see **57.17** below) divided by 24. The effect of the formula is to create a maximum of 48 hours a week (8 hours in each of the 6 days a week, excluding one weekly rest day).

Normal hours of work do not include overtime hours unless overtime is guaranteed; therefore it is not a breach of the *Regulations* if a night worker exceeds the permissible maximum hours only by virtue of working voluntary overtime (subject to compliance with the general 48-hour week). Further restrictions on working hours for night work involving special hazards or heavy mental or physical strain are summarised in **57.11** below.

Limits on the length of night work and the 17-week reference period may be excluded or modified by collective or workforce agreement (*reg 23*). Exclusions also apply to workers whose working time is 'unmeasured' and those covered by the 'special case' exceptions (see **57.28, 57.29** below).

The foregoing restrictions on night work apply to adult workers. For young workers under 18, there are much stricter restrictions, introduced by the *2002 Regulations*. Young workers are prohibited from working at all between midnight and 4 am, with very limited exceptions applicable to workplaces such as hospitals, or in connection with cultural, artistic, sporting or advertising activities, where the work is required to provide continuity of service, and no adult worker is available to perform the work. For most young workers there is a restricted period, which is either 10 pm to 6 am, or, if the worker is contractually required to work later than 10 pm, 11 pm to 7 am. Young workers are not permitted to work at all during this period, except as mentioned above, and subject to further exceptions in relation to work in agriculture, retail trading, postal and newspaper delivery, catering, hotels, restaurants and similar establishments, and bakeries; workers in these sectors are permitted to work during the restricted period, but not between midnight and 4 am, in the same limited circumstances of necessity mentioned above. These provisions are contained in *regs 6A* and *27A* of the *1998 Regulations*.

57.11 Special hazards

Where a night worker's job involves special hazards or heavy physical or mental stra[?] averaging of hours is permitted. The employer must ensure that the worker does n[?] for more than eight hours in any 24-hour period which includes night work (*reg 6(7[?]* maximum applies separately to each 24-hour period, without averaging, and inc[?] hours actually worked.

57.11 Working Time

Regulation 6(8) provides that work will be regarded as involving special hazards or heavy strain if it is identified as such in a collective or workforce agreement which takes account of the specific effects and hazards of night work, or alternatively if it has been recognised as involving significant risk in a risk assessment made under the *Management of Health and Safety at Work Regulations 1999 (SI 1999/3242)*: see **28.17** Health and Safety at Work – II. A collective or workforce agreement may modify or exclude the application of *reg 6(7)* (*reg 23*). Exceptions apply as for length of night work (see **57.10** above).

57.12 Health assessments

Before assigning an adult worker to night work, the employer must ensure that the worker has the opportunity of a free health assessment (*reg 7(1)*). However, if the worker has previously had an assessment and there is no reason to believe that it is no longer valid, a further assessment is not necessary. Free assessments must also be offered at regular intervals thereafter. The length of time between assessments should be whatever is appropriate to the particular circumstances. The BIS Guidance suggests that a yearly assessment will often be appropriate.

Young persons are to have the opportunity for a free assessment of health and capacities before being assigned to work during the restricted period (see **57.10**) and at regular intervals (*reg 7(2)*). It is not necessary to offer a further assessment if the young person has previously had an assessment and there is no reason to believe that it is no longer valid. BEIS advises that special consideration should be given to young workers' suitability for night work, taking account of physique, level of maturity and experience. The requirement to offer an assessment to a young worker does not apply where the work is of an exceptional nature (*reg 7(4)*).

An assessment, whether of an adult or young worker, does not necessarily entail a full medical examination. BIS suggests that employers ask workers to complete a questionnaire which asks about health issues which are relevant to the particular type of night work. If the employer is then unsure about a worker's fitness for night work, he or she should be asked to undergo a medical examination.

Regulation 7(5) provides that the assessment may not be disclosed, except to the worker in question, unless he or she has given consent in writing to the disclosure. This may cause difficulties for the employer if a medical adviser identifies that a worker has a medical condition which could expose him or her to a risk to health. It would be the duty of the employer to safeguard the worker against such a risk, but the employer has no practical means of knowing of the risk unless the information is volunteered by the worker or there is consent to disclosure of the medical assessment. The medical adviser who has evaluated the information supplied or conducted the examination can however make a simple statement (if applicable) to the effect that the assessment shows the worker to be fit, or not fit, to take up, or continue, a night work assignment.

57.13 Transfer to day work

If an employer is advised by a registered medical practitioner that a worker is suffering from health problems which are connected with night working, the employer is required to transfer the worker, if possible, to work which does not qualify as 'night work' (see **57.9** above) (*reg 7(6)*). Normally this will be day work but could involve some night work, provided this is less than 3 hours in any 24 hours. Such work must be work 'to which the worker is suited'. Unlike the comparable provisions in relation to pregnant employees (under *s 6* of *ERA 1996* and *reg 17* of the *Management of Health and Safety at Work Regulations 1999*), there is no provision for the protection of enhanced rates of pay for night work for a worker who is transferred to other work under *reg 7(6)*. However, employers may also need to take into consideration their obligations under the *Equality Act 2010* where a worker's lack of fitness amounts to a disability.

Employers are required to maintain, and retain for two years, records which are adequate to show compliance with the provisions on length of night work and health assessments (*reg 9*).

57.14 REST PERIODS AND REST BREAKS

Under the *1998 Regulations* workers are entitled to daily and weekly rest periods totalling 90 hours per week and to rest breaks during the working day. A 'rest period' is defined in *reg 2(1)* as a period which is not working time, other than a rest break or statutory annual leave. It therefore includes time spent in travelling between a worker's home and the normal workplace (but not travel to or from customers' premises - see the *Tyco* case at **57.5** above). However it does not include time spent on call at the employer's premises, even if the worker is in fact able to rest between times when his or her services are required, and is provided with facilities for resting: *Landeshauptstadt Kiel v Jaeger*: C-151/02 [2003] IRLR 804, ECJ. See further the discussion of what constitutes 'working time' at **57.5** above.

The Supreme Court has confirmed that there is no qualitative requirement for rest periods other than the absence of a requirement to work: see *Russell v Transocean International Resources Ltd* [2011] UKSC 57, [2012] IRLR 149, a case holding that it was permissible for employers to require oil rig workers, who worked a pattern of two weeks offshore and two weeks onshore, to take their annual leave entitlement during the periods onshore, notwithstanding that these were periods during which they would not otherwise be required to work, and provided that there was also sufficient time during onshore 'field breaks' for rest periods and any compensatory rest.

57.15 Daily rest periods

Adult workers are entitled to a rest period of at least 11 consecutive hours in each 24-hour working period (*reg 10(1)*). It is not necessary for the 11 hours to fall within the same calendar day provided they are consecutive.

The 11-hour rule does not apply to shift workers when they change shifts and cannot take a daily rest period between the end of one shift and the start of the next (*reg 22(1)(a)*). Similarly it does not apply to workers whose activities involve periods of work split up over the day, such as cleaning or catering staff working split shifts (*reg 22(1)(c)*). 'Shift work' means 'any method of organising work in shifts whereby workers succeed each other at the same workstations according to a certain pattern, including a rotating pattern, and which may be continuous or discontinuous, entailing the need for workers to work at different times over a given period of days or weeks'.

Compensatory rest must normally be offered to shift workers who have to work during what would otherwise be a rest period. If this is not possible, 'appropriate protection' is required to safeguard health and safety (*reg 24*). The ECJ has held (*Landeshauptstadt Kiel v Jaeger*: C-151/02 [2003] IRLR 804; *Union syndicale Solidaires Isère v Premier Ministre*: C-428/09 [2011] 1 CMLR 1206, [2011] IRLR 84) that compensatory rest must be provided immediately following the period of work without a rest period or rest break for which it compensates. See further the discussion of compensatory rest in relation to rest breaks at **57.17** below.

There is a separate provision in *reg 24A* for those mobile workers not excluded from the right to rest periods generally (see as to this **57.33–57.36** below), excluding the right to rest periods provided that 'adequate rest' is afforded, the requirements of which are defined in *reg 24A(3)*. The right to adequate rest in such cases is in substitution for, not cumulative with, the right to compensatory rest under *Reg 24*: *Feist v First Hampshire & Dorset Ltd* [2007] All ER (D) 180 (Feb), EAT.

Adult workers whose time is 'unmeasured' (see **57.28** below) and those who are considered 'special case' exceptions under *reg 21* (subject to certain conditions, see **57.29** below) are not covered by the entitlement to daily rest. The entitlement may also be modified or excluded by collective or workforce agreement under *reg 23*. The second and third of these exceptions are subject to the provision of compensatory rest, or 'appropriate protection' in default.

Subject to these exceptions, where a daily rest period is interrupted, for instance by an out-of-hours call-out, or a requirement to attend a health and safety meeting with the employer (as in *Edwards v Encirc Ltd* [2015] IRLR 528, EAT; see **57.5** above) there is an entitlement to a full 11 hour rest period before the individual resumes work.

For young workers (ie those over compulsory school age but under 18) the requirement is to provide not less than 12 consecutive hours' rest in any 24-hour period (*reg 10(2)*). Where activities involve periods of work that are split up over the day or are of short duration, the 12-hour rest period may be interrupted (*reg 10(3)*). In addition a *force majeure* clause applies, which gives the employer leeway to require a young worker to work during the 12-hour minimum where work has to be done which no adult worker is available to do and the requirement:

(a)   is due to unusual and unforeseeable circumstances beyond the employer's control or exceptional events which could not have been avoided despite all due care by the employer;

(b)   is of a temporary nature; and

(c)   must be carried out straight away.

An equivalent period of compensatory rest must be allowed within the following three weeks (*reg 27*). This concession is designed to cope with exceptional circumstances which cannot be handled in any other way.

Entitlement to rest periods entails at the least that the employer must *allow* employees who wish to do so to take their rest period. The extent to which it also entails an obligation on the employer to *ensure* that rest periods are *taken* is more contentious. The DTI (as BEIS then was) view, as expressed in the original Guidance on the *Regulations*, was that it does not. This view was, however, successfully challenged by the Commission in proceedings before the European Court (*European Commission v United Kingdom*: C-484/04 [2006] IRLR 888). (For further details see **57.2** above.)

Despite this, the EAT initially held that there is no breach of *reg 10* until the worker requests that he or she be allowed rest periods and the employer refuses: *Miles v Linkage Community Trust Ltd* [2008] IRLR 602 and *Carter v Prestige Nursing Ltd* (UKEAT/0014/12) (11 May 2012, unreported). However this gives little weight to the obligation to afford rest periods and rest breaks set out in the Working Time Directive. A different approach appeared to be taken in *Scottish Ambulance Service v Truslove* UKEATS/0028/11 (12 January 2012, unreported), a case on time limits. The authorities were thoroughly reviewed by the EAT in *Grange v Abellio London Ltd* [2017] IRLR 108, [2017] ICR 287, a case on the identically worded provisions of reg 12 on rest breaks. The EAT declined to follow *Miles* and *Carter*, and held that *reg 12* must be read as imposing an obligation on employers to ensure proactively that workers are in fact able to take the required rest breaks, although a worker could not be forced to take a break. 'Refusal to permit' the taking of a rest break, the statutory condition for a remedy for an infringement of the right to take rest breaks, must be read as covering denial of the right by the practical effect of the way that the worker's work is organised, without the need for a positive request. This position applies equally to rest breaks under *reg 12* and to rest periods under *regs 10* and *11* (as to which see below). *Miles* and *Carter* should not now be regarded as correctly stating the law.

57.16 Weekly rest periods

Adult workers are normally entitled (as to the meaning of this see the final paragraph of **57.15**) to an uninterrupted rest period of at least 24 hours in each seven-day period of working. This may be arranged as two uninterrupted rest periods of not less than 24 hours in each 14-day period, or one uninterrupted period of not less than 48 hours in each 14-day period (*reg 11(1)*, *(2)*). The minimum weekly rest period must not run concurrently with any part of a daily rest period (see **57.15** above) except where this is justified by objective or technical reasons, or reasons 'concerning the organisation of work' (*reg 11(7)*). Thus the combined effect of the daily and weekly rest entitlements is to create a minimum entitlement of 35 consecutive hours each week, or 59 hours in each 14-day period. See **57.15** for the correct approach to when the right to weekly rest periods is infringed.

For young workers the minimum weekly rest period is 48 hours. This may be interrupted where activities involve periods of work that are split up over the day or are of short duration, and may be reduced where this is justified by technical or organisational reasons. However the period may not be reduced to less than 36 consecutive hours (*reg 11(3)*, *(8)*).

A seven or 14-day period for these purposes begins on the day provided for in a relevant agreement (see **57.4** above) or, failing this, at the start of each week (or every other week, as the case may be). A 'week' for this purpose starts at midnight between Sunday and Monday (*reg 11(4)*, *(6)*).

In the case of shift workers, the weekly rest requirement in respect of adults does not apply when workers change shift and cannot take a weekly rest period between the end of one shift and the start of another. Neither does it apply to workers whose activities involve periods of work split up over the day (*reg 22(1)*). Cleaning and catering staff may provide examples. For the definition of 'shift working' see **57.15** above. Compensatory rest must normally be offered to shift workers who have to work during what would otherwise be a rest period. If this is not possible, 'appropriate protection' is required to safeguard the worker's health and safety (*reg 24*). (See as to these concepts the discussion at **57.17** below.)

The right to rest periods may also be modified or excluded by a collective or workforce agreement, but subject to the workers concerned being afforded compensatory rest: *regs 23*, *24*. The right is also excluded, subject to the same conditions as to compensatory rest, for certain categories of work: see *reg 21*, discussed at **57.29**. The position for mobile workers not excluded from the *Regulations* altogether is the same in relation to weekly rest periods as for daily rest periods: see *reg 24A* and **57.15** above.

Adult workers whose time is 'unmeasured' (see **57.28** below) are not subject to the weekly rest requirements.

57.17 Rest breaks

After a working period of six hours, an adult worker is entitled to a rest break (*reg 12(1)*). The length of the break and any conditions which apply to it are to be determined by collective or workforce agreement. In the absence of such an agreement, the break is to be at least an uninterrupted period of 20 minutes which the worker is entitled to take away from the workstation where applicable (*reg 12(2)*, *(3)*). If a worker works a single shift of 12 hours, the entitlement is still to one rest break, not two: *Hughes v Corps of Commissionaires Management Ltd (No 1)* [2009] ICR 345, [2009] IRLR 122, EAT. Whilst workers cannot be forced to take rest breaks, the right is not dependent on the worker requesting to exercise it, but also applies to the way in which the worker's work is organised, so that the employer has a duty proactively to ensure that a worker who wishes to take a rest break has the opportunity to do so: see *Grange v Abellio London Ltd*, discussed at **57.15** above.

Regulation 12(1) may be modified or excluded by collective or workforce agreement, subject to the provision of compensatory rest (*regs 23*, *24*). The right is also excluded, subject to the same conditions as to compensatory rest, for certain categories of work: see *reg 21*, discussed at **57.29** below. Those mobile workers not excluded altogether from the *1998 Regulations*, as summarised in **57.15** above, are subject to the same limitations on the right to rest breaks as described above. Adult workers whose time is 'unmeasured' are not entitled to rest breaks (see **57.28** below).

It has been held that for a period to count as a rest break, the worker must be able to know at the beginning of the period that it will not be interrupted by the demands of work. Accordingly, 'down time', and periods during time on call, at least where the worker is required to be at his or her workplace, cannot be counted as a rest period, even if it transpires that there was a continuous period of at least 20 minutes during which the worker was not called on to perform any work: *Gallagher v Alpha Catering Services Ltd* [2004] EWCA Civ 1559, [2005] IRLR 102; *MacCartney v Oversley House Management* [2006] ICR 510, EAT.

A case the other side of the line is *Martin v Southern Health & Social Care Trust* [2010] NICA 31, [2010] IRLR 1048; the claimant, a nurse, was expressly entitled to an uninterrupted (and unpaid) break unless an emergency arose, in which case she was entitled to claim time off in lieu by way of compensation. The Northern Ireland Court of Appeal held that this was sufficient to constitute the breaks as 'rest breaks' despite relatively frequent interruptions in practice (but for which compensatory time off was always given if claimed). The crucial distinction from the facts in *Gallagher* was that in that case there was no presumption that there would be an uninterrupted break. As to the meaning of 'entitled', see the final paragraph of **57.15**.

As to compensatory rest, the ECJ has twice held that this must be afforded immediately after the period of work without the required rest period or rest break for which it is intended to compensate: *Landeshuptstadt Kiel v Jaeger*: C-151/02, [2003] IRLR 804, and *Union syndicale Solidaires Isère v Premier Ministre*: C-428/09 [2011] 1 CMLR 1206, [2011] IRLR 84. In the latter case the Court observed that in order to be effective to enable the worker to rest effectively, the compensatory rest must entail the worker 'being able to remove himself from his working environment for a specific number of hours' immediately following the period of work in issue.

The application of the requirement to afford compensatory rest has been considered domestically in a number of cases. The first case was *Hughes (No 1)*, above. The EAT held that compensatory rest must be of equivalent length to the break foregone, and afforded at a time which would otherwise be part of the worker's working time. Such compensatory rest must be offered if at all possible, and it is only if it is not possible for 'objective reasons' that the employer may instead provide 'appropriate protection' to the employee. The precise scope of 'appropriate protection' is a matter of considerable uncertainty, and the EAT did not find it necessary to set out further what the concept requires.

Hughes (No 1) also raised the question whether the worker is entitled to be paid for any period of compensatory rest. The EAT concluded that this was not required by the *Regulations*, and whether it was required as a matter of contract would depend on the terms of the worker's contract; this was remitted to the tribunal to consider, but with the EAT indicating a provisional view that generally there would be an entitlement to be paid. This however is far from clear, since there is no requirement for rest breaks themselves to be paid – this too is a matter of contract between the parties – and if payment for compensatory rest was required where the break compensated for would not have attracted a right to be paid, it could be said that the worker would be overcompensated for the loss of the break.

The second case, *Hughes v Corps of Commissionaires Management Ltd (No 2)* [2011] EWCA Civ 1061, [2011] IRLR 915, was an appeal from the decision of the tribunal hearing the remission of certain issues in *Hughes (No 1)*, which had rejected Mr Hughes' claims. The EAT upheld that decision, but on different grounds; it decided that on the facts compensatory rest had been granted: Mr Hughes, a security guard, was permitted to re-commence any rest break which had been interrupted by a requirement to resume his duties (the risk of which had led to the finding that he had not been permitted to take the required rest breaks). Compensatory rest did not have to mirror exactly the requirements of the break for the denial of which it compensated, provided the arrangements were 'equivalent'. As the alternative arrangements were within the time for which he was in any case paid, the issue whether there is any separate right to be paid for compensatory rest did not in the event arise. The case then proceeded to the Court of Appeal, which upheld the EAT's decision. An equivalent period of compensatory rest had to have the characteristics of rest, in the sense of being a break from work, and as far as possible must ensure that the period free from work was at least the 20 minutes required for a rest break; however on the facts these requirements had been met.

The issue of compensatory rest did not fall directly for decision in *Martin*, above, but it is implicit in the decision in that case that a right to claim time off in lieu (it appears without loss of pay) for any break which in the event was interrupted did satisfy the requirements for compensatory rest. The judgment does not indicate when time off in lieu was in practice taken. As noted above, the ECJ has twice held that compensatory rest must be afforded immediately following the period of work without the required rest break for which it is compensation; however as the point did not arise directly in the light of its decision on what constitutes a rest break, the Court in *Martin* did not have to consider whether the requirements of timing of the compensatory rest were met by these arrangements.

If in exceptional cases it is not possible 'for objective reasons' to afford compensatory rest, 'appropriate protection' must if possible be offered instead (*reg 24(b)*; the phrase is taken directly from the wording of the *Directive*). This provision was considered, obiter, in *Hughes (No 2)*; the EAT suggested that it could include a range of measures other than the provision of rest such as the way that work is organised or health checks for affected workers. The ECJ subsequently expressed the view in *Union syndicale*, above, that 'only in absolutely exceptional circumstances' could resort be had to 'appropriate protection', and that limiting the number of days in a year that seasonal workers could work to a maximum of 80 was not a permissible means of affording 'appropriate protection' for the denial of daily rest periods. This judgment was not cited to the Court of Appeal when the appeal in *Hughes (No 2)* reached the Court, which rejected the argument that there must be 'exceptional circumstances' in addition to objective reasons for not providing compensatory rest: it would be exceptional that there were objective reasons, and that was sufficient. Whether the Court would have reached this conclusion if it had been aware of the decision in *Union syndicale* is unclear. The Court of Appeal did not consider in any detail the range of what could constitute protection under *reg 24(b)*, as it was satisfied that the arrangements for a deferred break were sufficient; but it did reject, as had the EAT, a submission that the employer would have to conduct a risk assessment to assess the sufficiency of the protection afforded.

An example of a situation where objective reasons might make it impossible to afford compensatory rest, given in an Advisory Opinion by the EFTA Court in *M'Bye v Stiftelsen Fossumkollektivet*: E-5/15 [2016] IRLR 227, is where therapists were providing treatment for young people with drug or alcohol problems which entailed the therapists living together with their patients, to the extent that continuity of service by the same therapists was regarded as beneficial for the patients.

In the case of young workers, there is an entitlement to a break of at least 30 minutes, consecutive if possible, if the individual's daily working time exceeds four and a half hours. The worker is entitled to take the break away from the workstation if applicable. When a young worker has more than one employment, the daily working time must be calculated by aggregating the number of hours worked for each employer (*reg 12(4), (5)*). There is an exception to the entitlements of young workers under a *force majeure* clause (*reg 27*). This specifies that *reg 12(4)* does not apply where work has to be done which no adult worker is available to do and:

57.17 Working Time

(a)   the requirement is due to unusual and unforeseeable circumstances beyond the employer's control or exceptional events which could not have been avoided despite all due care by the employer;

(b)   is of a temporary nature; and

(c)   must be carried out straight away.

An equivalent period of compensatory rest must be allowed within the following three weeks.

57.18 Monotonous work

Apart from the specific obligations to provide rest breaks described in **57.17**, an employer is required to ensure that workers are given adequate rest breaks where the work pattern puts workers' health and safety at risk, in particular because the work is monotonous or the work rate pre-determined (*reg 8*). This appears to be a requirement which is additional to the basic entitlement to rest breaks set out in *reg 12*. The wording of the regulation is a paraphrase of *art 13* of the *Directive*, and it has not to date been the subject of judicial interpretation. Apart from those in excluded sectors to whom the *Regulations* do not apply at all, there are no exceptions to the application of *reg 8*.

57.19 ANNUAL LEAVE

Workers within the *1998 Regulations* are entitled to a total of 5.6 weeks' statutory holiday in respect of each leave year (subject to a maximum entitlement of 28 working days (*regs 13* and *13A*). This entitlement was increased from the original three weeks to four weeks in 1999, to 4.8 weeks from 1 October 2007, and to 5.6 weeks from 1 April 2009; the latter increases were made by the *Working Time (Amendment) Regulations 2007, SI 2007/2079*, which give workers a separate right to the additional annual leave under slightly different conditions, rather than simply increasing the basic entitlement. The *Regulations* also cover statutory holiday pay, notice requirements in respect of taking annual leave, and pay in lieu on termination. Full details of the annual leave provisions in the *1998 Regulations*, including accrual of leave during sick leave and how holiday pay is to be calculated, are set out in **29 – Holidays**.

Special rules as to the timing of the holiday year apply to agricultural workers in Wales and Scotland, and those in England first employed before 1 October 2013 (*reg 43, Sch 2*). The equivalent Regulations for workers in civil aviation also have different provisions as to the computation of holiday pay: see *British Airways plc v Williams* [2012] UKSC 43, [2012] IRLR 1014, [2012] ICR 1375.

57.20 ENFORCEMENT AND REMEDIES

Different enforcement arrangements operate according to the nature of the breach of the *1998 Regulations*. Working time limits are enforced by the Health and Safety Executive ('HSE') and local authorities, and within their areas of responsibility the Civil Aviation Authority ('CAA') and the Driver and Vehicle Standards Agency ('DVSA', the successor to the Vehicle and Operator Services Agency) and the Office of Rail and Road ('ORR', formerly the Office of Rail Regulation). The HSE enforces the limits in factories, building sites, mines, farms, fairgrounds, quarries, chemical plants, nuclear installations, schools and hospitals. Local authority officers have the same role in respect of shops and retailing, offices, hotels and catering, sports, leisure and consumer services. The enforcement powers of the various agencies are essentially the same as those provided for in the *Health and Safety at Work etc Act 1974*. For technical reasons the addition of the CAA and DVSA to the list of enforcing authorities was considered to necessitate the restatement of the enforcement powers within the *1998 Regulations*, and these can be found in *regs 28–29E* and *Sch 3*. These provisions were then applied to the ORR when it was given enforcement responsibilities in relation to rail staff by the *Railways Act 2005* and regulations made under that Act. For further details of enforcement powers and penalties see **57.21** below and **27.29–27.41** HEALTH AND SAFETY AT WORK – I.

The other method of enforcement is that workers who are not receiving their entitlements or are penalised for insisting on their rights can pursue claims in employment tribunals: see **57.22–57.24** below.

57.21   Health and safety

Regulation 28 provides that the relevant enforcing authority, ie the HSE, local authority or the CAA, DVSA or ORR, is responsible for enforcing the following provisions: weekly working time (*reg 4(2)*); length of night work (*reg 6(2), (7)*); health assessments for night workers (*reg 7(1), (2)*) and transfers to day work (*reg 7(6)*); rest breaks for monotonous work (*reg 8*); record-keeping (*reg 9*); and compensatory rest in relation to night work (*reg 24*). Enforcing authorities are also responsible for the enforcement of the additional restrictions on working hours and night work for young workers in *regs 5A(4)* and *27A(4)(a)*, and for the provisions on adequate rest for mobile workers under *reg 24A*.

An employer who fails to comply with any of these requirements commits an offence (*reg 29*). The offences are punishable on summary conviction by a fine not exceeding £5,000 (the limit on the maximum fine will be removed when the relevant part of the *Legal Aid, Sentencing and Punishment of Offenders Act 2012* comes into force). On conviction on indictment the punishment is an unlimited fine. *Regulations 29A–29E* contain provisions equivalent to those in the *Health and Safety at Work etc Act 1974* in relation to offences due to the default, etc of another person, offences by bodies corporate, powers to prosecute and powers of courts to require the remedying of causes of offences. Provisions as to the appointment and powers of inspectors, including the making of improvement and prohibition notices and rights of appeal against such notices, and restrictions on disclosure of information, are contained in *Sch 3*.

Additionally, the High Court has held that *reg 4(1)*, which specifies that a worker's average hours per week should not exceed 48, imposes a contractual obligation on an employer. Contracts should therefore be read as providing that an employee should work no more than an average of 48 hours during the reference period (*Barber v RJB Mining (UK) Ltd* [1999] IRLR 308). Consequently, employees who are asked to work over the 48-hour limit without their agreement may be able to bring proceedings in the civil courts for a declaration of rights and seek an injunction barring the employer from requiring them to work additional hours. However, this does not confer any right to claim compensation in an employment tribunal for being required to work more than 48 hours a week: the jurisdiction of the tribunals does not extend to claims for breach of *reg 4* (see **57.22** below). It remains to be determined judicially whether the position thus summarised sufficiently meets the requirements of EU law, in the light of the judgment of the ECJ in *Fuss v Stadt Halle (No 2)*: C-429/09 [2011] IRLR 176 that the right not to work more than a 48 hour week conferred by *art 6(b)* of the *Working Time Directive* is directly enforceable domestically, at least as against those employers which are state authorities, so that a worker whose right has been infringed must have the right to secure reparation for any infringement once the scope of the law has been made clear at ECJ level (as was the case on the facts, which related to time spent on call at the workplace). It may be that the remedy of an action for breach of contract would be regarded in EU law as sufficient to meet the requirements of the Court in *Fuss (No 2)*, but if not, it is considered that a claim against a state authority as employer based on the *Directive* rather than the *Regulations* could be brought in an employment tribunal despite the lack of jurisdiction to hear such claims under the *Regulations* themselves, by analogy with equal pay claims.

There is as yet no reported case in which a worker has successfully claimed damages for personal injury resulting directly from being made to work hours in excess of those permitted under the *Regulations*, but in two cases in which the Court of Appeal has upheld awards of damages for psychiatric injury, the fact that the employee had worked well in excess of the 48 hour limit without his agreement was regarded as an evidentially relevant factor in favour of the point that the damage ought to have been foreseen by the employer: *Hone v Six Continents Retail Ltd* [2005] EWCA Civ 922, [2006] IRLR 49; *Pakenham-Walsh v Connell Residential* [2006] EWCA Civ 90, [2006] 11 LS Gaz R 25. However, in *Sayers v Cambridgeshire County Council* [2006] EWHC 2029 (QB), [2007] IRLR 29 (a case where a claim for damages for personal injury failed on the facts) the High Court held that a breach of *reg 4* by the employer does not as such confer a right for the worker to sue for damages for breach of statutory duty.

57.22 Individual remedies

Under *reg 30(1)(a)* a complaint may be made to an employment tribunal that the employer has refused to permit a worker to exercise his or her rights in connection with: daily rest (*reg 10(1), (2)*); weekly rest (*reg 11(1), (2), (3)*); rest breaks (*reg 12(1), (4)*); entitlement to annual leave (*reg 13(1)*); entitlement to compensatory rest (except in relation to night work) (*regs 24, 25, 27*) or to adequate rest (*reg 24A*).

Reg 30(1)(b) makes similar provision for complaints of failure to pay any sums due as payments in respect of annual leave entitlement or accrued holiday pay on termination under *reg 16(1)* or *14(2)* respectively. The House of Lords has ruled that claims for holiday pay can in the alternative be brought as claims for unlawful deductions from wages under *Part II* of the *Employment Rights Act 1996*, which are subject to somewhat less strict time limits (*Stringer v HM Revenue and Customs* [2009] UKHL 31, [2009] IRLR 677, reversing the decision of the Court of Appeal (*IRC v Ainsworth* [2005] EWCA Civ 441, [2005] IRLR 465). However this is only possible for claims for unpaid holiday pay or pay in lieu; other claims can in their nature only be brought under *reg 30*.

It should be noted that (apart from complaints of failure to pay sums due), the basis for complaints is of a refusal to permit the worker to exercise a relevant right. It is not enough that the right was not in fact exercised, unless this was attributable to the employer.

Tribunals have no express jurisdiction to hear claims by individuals for breach of the 48-hour limit on weekly working time. (See **57.20** above as to possible claims under the Directive itself for infringement of a worker's right not to work more than 48 hours a week). Following the lead given by the High Court in *Barber v RJB Mining (UK) Ltd* [1999] IRLR 308 (see **57.21**), tribunals may accept that a term is implied into a contract of employment that the employer must not require the employee to work more than 48 hours a week in the reference period. The effect of this is, however, limited. An employee complaining of constructive dismissal could rely on being required to work excessive hours as a breach of contract, but the tribunal has no power to award compensation for excessive hours as such, unless overtime is required under the terms of the employee's contract to be paid, in which case a claim for unlawful deductions could be made (*Forbouys Ltd v Rich* [2002] All ER (D) 156 (Apr), EAT), or there is a claim under the *National Minimum Wage Act 1998*.

Claims brought under *reg 30* must normally be presented within three months of the date on which the right should have been permitted or the payment should have been made. This period is extended to six months for complaints by members of the armed forces (who are required to utilise internal redress procedures before commencing tribunal proceedings).

Where a tribunal is satisfied that it was not reasonably practicable to present a claim within the time limit, it may extend the period to a date it considers reasonable. In relation to claims for refusal to permit the claimant to take rest breaks or rest periods, the time limit for making a complaint runs from the date of each refusal: *Scottish Ambulance Service v Truslove* (UKEATS/0028/11), 12 January 2012, unreported. The EAT in that case rejected an argument that where the employee had raised a grievance, time ran from the date on which the grievance was rejected, or on the date (if later, of the first refusal of a rest period, holding that each refusal was a fresh cause of action with its own time limit (and thus the claims were in time so far as relating to refusals occurring within three months prior to the claims being presented). It follows that claims presented more than three months after any particular refusal of rest will be out of time (subject to any extension of time); there is no provision in *reg 30* for time not to run during a series of refusals.

Claims brought under *reg 30* were initially classed as Category A claims for the purposes of fees, with the consequence that the lower rate of fees, £160 on presentation of the claim and £230 on listing for a hearing, were payable (subject to any entitlement to remission of the fee). However an amendment to the *Employment Tribunals and the Employment Appeal Tribunal (Fees) Order 2013* has reclassified claims under *reg 30* (other than claims in relation to annual leave and holiday pay) as Category B, attracting the higher rates of fees (£250 on issuing a claim and £950 for the hearing). The change applies to any claim presented on or after 6 April 2014. Claims under *reg 30* (and under *Part II* of the *Employment Rights Act 1996*) are subject to the Early Conciliation procedure, so that a reference to ACAS, and the issuing of an Early Conciliation Certificate is required before a claim can be presented; consequential extensions to the time limit for presenting claims in certain circumstances are provided for by *reg 30B*, or as the case may be *section 207B* of the *1996 Act*.

Following an amendment to the *Employment Tribunals Act 1996, s 4*, claims for holiday pay, and for pay in lieu of holiday not taken prior to the termination of employment, may be heard by an employment judge sitting alone: see *SI 2009/789*. This amendment is intended to facilitate tribunals dealing with claims for holiday pay speedily together with claims for unpaid wages, as the two are often brought together, and frequently not defended (usually because the employer is insolvent). Other claims made under *reg 30* of the *Working Time Regulations* require to be heard by a full tribunal of three.

Where a complaint is considered to be well-founded, the tribunal will make a declaration to that effect and may make an award of such compensation (if any) as it considers to be just and equitable in all the circumstances, having regard to the employer's default and any loss sustained by the worker. It should be emphasised that the award of compensation is discretionary, and a nil award is permissible; such an award was upheld by the EAT in *Miles v Linkage Community Trust Ltd* [2008] IRLR 602, and the fact that the reasoning in this case as to what constitutes a refusal by an employer to afford a rest period or rest break has since been disapproved (see *Grange v Abellio London Ltd* [2017] IRLR 108, [2017] ICR 287, and **57.15** above) the possibility of no compensation being awarded remains open. However, insofar as the reasoning in that case is based on the claimant's failure to complain for some time about the denial of his rights, it is of doubtful authority following the subsequent decision of the CJEU in *Fuss v Stadt Halle (No 2)*: C-429/09 [2011] IRLR 176 that a right to reparation for an infringement of rights under the Directive (in that case by a requirement to work more than 48 hours a week) could not be made conditional on the worker having first complained about the continuing infringement of rights.

The heads of loss for which compensation can be awarded on a successful complaint under *reg 30* do not include injury to feelings; this was finally confirmed by the EAT in *Santos Gomes v Higher Lever Care Ltd* [2016] IRLR 678, [2016] ICR 926.

Where the complaint involves failure to pay holiday pay or pay in lieu of holiday not taken prior to termination of employment (the issues arising in the vast majority of claims under the *1998 Regulations*), the tribunal will order the employer to pay the amount owed.

57.23 Victimisation

ERA 1996, s 45A (as inserted by *reg 31* of the *1998 Regulations*) provides that a worker has the right not to be subjected to any detriment by any act, or any deliberate failure to act, by his or her employer on the ground that the worker:

(a)   refused (or proposed to refuse) to comply with a requirement of the employer imposed in contravention of the *Regulations*;

(b)   refused (or proposed to refuse) to forgo a right conferred by the *Regulations*;

(c)   failed to sign a workforce agreement, or to enter into or agree to vary or extend any other agreement provided for in the *Regulations*;

(d)   being a representative of members of the workforce for the purposes of *Sch 1* or a candidate in an election for such a representative, performed (or proposed to perform) any functions or activities as such a representative or candidate;

(e)   brought proceedings against the employer to enforce a right conferred by the *Regulations*; or

(f)   alleged that the employer had infringed such a right.

So far as (*e*) and (*f*) are concerned, it is immaterial whether or not the worker has the right or whether or not the right has been infringed, but the claim must be made in good faith. In respect of (*f*), it is sufficient for the worker to make it reasonably clear to the employer what the right was that he or she alleges has been infringed. However for claims under paragraph (a) or (b), it is a necessary element of the claim that the worker has in fact refused, or proposed to refuse, to comply with an unlawful requirement or to forgo a right, as the case may be, and similarly for paragraph (c) there must be an actual failure to sign an agreement (such as an opt-out from the 48 hour week under *reg 5*), so there must have been a request by the employer: see for the points made in relation to each of these paragraphs *Gale v Mid & West Wales Fire Service* (UKEAT/0365/14).

There is separate protection, for employees only, from unfair dismissal (see **57.24** below) and dismissal is excluded from the definition of detriment for employees (but by necessary implication, dismissal of a worker who is not an employee is within the scope of detriment); for a worker who is not an employee, a complaint of subjection to detriment can be brought to cover the comparable situation of termination of his or her contract. It is at least arguable that *s 45A* covers detriments suffered after the termination of employment, by analogy with the Court of Appeal's reasoning in *Woodward v Abbey National plc* [2006] EWCA Civ 822, [2006] ICR 1436 on the equivalent provision in relation to 'whistleblowers' (*ERA 1996, s 47B*).

The remedy for a contravention of *s 45A* is a complaint to an employment tribunal under *s 48*. Normally the complaint must be presented within three months of the act or failure to act the subject of the complaint but tribunals have discretion to extend the time limit where it was not reasonably practicable to present the claim in time. Where the complaint is of an act or omission 'extending over a period', time does not start to run until the last day of the period. Claims made under *section 48* are subject to the higher rate of fees, £250 on presentation and a further £950 for the hearing (subject to any right to remission).

It is for the employer to show the reason for any detriment to which the worker was subjected: *s 48(2)*. The EAT in *Fecitt v NHS Manchester* [2011] IRLR 111 held that the standard of proof thus placed on the employer is the same as in discrimination cases where the burden of proof has been reversed in accordance with *Igen Ltd v Wong* [2005] EWCA Civ 142, [2005] IRLR 258. On a further appeal to the Court of Appeal ([2011] EWCA Civ 1190, [2012] IRLR 64), the Court acknowledged that strictly *Igen v Wong* had no application as no EU derived right was involved, but nevertheless upheld the correctness of the general approach, noting that this created an anomaly by comparison with the burden of proof in a claim for automatically unfair dismissal under *Employment Rights Act 1996, s 103A*. The correctness of the approach in *Fecitt* in cases of detriment under *s 45A* was confirmed by the EAT in *Gale v Mid & West Wales Fire Service*, above.

An example of a claim based on detriment under *s 45A* is *Arriva London South Ltd v Nicolaou* (UKEAT/0280/10), where the claimant, a bus driver, was denied access to lucrative rest day working because he had refused to opt out of the 48 hour week. The EAT remitted the case to the tribunal to consider whether the employer had acted reasonably in the light of its explanation that it was concerned to comply with its duty under *reg 4(2)* not, so far as reasonably practicable, to permit a worker who had not opted out to work more than 48 hours a week, a point not fully addressed by the tribunal. In a second appeal, *Arriva London South Ltd v Nicolaou (No 2)* [2012] ICR 510, the EAT upheld the tribunal's second rejection of Mr Nicolaou's complaint. The tribunal had held that the employer had been acting reasonably to ensure that it complied with its duty not to permit an employee who has not opted out to work more than an average of 48 hours a week. The EAT accepted the argument that any resulting disadvantage to the employee was not a detriment, because it did not entail a legitimate sense of grievance, and that the reason for denying the claimant access to rest day working was not causally connected to his having opted out, but rather to the employer's desire to take steps to ensure compliance with its statutory obligations.

In well-founded cases, the tribunal will make a declaration to that effect and may also award such compensation as it considers just and equitable. The amount of compensation which may be awarded is unlimited, except that where the detrimental action suffered by a worker (who is not working under a contract of employment) is termination of contract, the compensation must not exceed the maximum amount which could be awarded to an employee who has been unfairly dismissed for a similar reason (*ERA 1996, s 49*). Compensation may include compensation for injury to feelings.

For workers in sectors covered by specific regulations, and who are either wholly or partially excluded from the application of the *1998 Regulations*, the position is inconsistent. *Section 45A* also applies in the same way in relation to the equivalent provisions of the *Merchant Shipping (Working Time: Inland Waterways) Regulations 2003* and the *Fishing Vessels (Working Time: Sea-fishermen) Regulations 2004*, but not (either through legislative oversight or to reflect differences in the parent *Directives*) to the comparable provisions for workers in civil aviation and road transport: see further **57.33** and **57.34**. Merchant seamen (see **57.31**) are also not covered by the provisions of *s 45A*.

57.24 Unfair dismissal

It is automatically unfair to dismiss an employee for certain reasons connected with rights and entitlements under the *1998 Regulations* (*ERA 1996, s 101A*, as inserted by *reg 32(1)*). Employees may present a claim under this provision regardless of length of service. *Section 101A* does not cover employees asserting the equivalent rights under the *Road Transport (Working Time) Regulations 2005*: see *Ross v Eddie Stobart Ltd* (UKEAT/0085/10), 16 May 2011, unreported. An alternative basis of claim may be that the employee has raised concerns about health and safety in relation to working time: see *ERA 1996 s 100*, and *Joao v Jurys Hotel Management UK Ltd* (UKEAT/0210/11), 11 October 2011, unreported (reasonableness of employee's objection to working nine successive night shifts not dependent on the shift pattern being a breach of the *Working Time Regulations*). For further details see **54.3(h)** UNFAIR DISMISSAL – **II**.

It is also automatically unfair to dismiss an employee for 'asserting a statutory right' (*ERA 1996, s 104*). The rights conferred by the *1998 Regulations* are included within the definition of 'statutory rights' under *s 104* (as amended by *reg 32(2)*). Therefore where an employee has been dismissed for bringing proceedings to enforce a working time right, or for alleging that the employer has infringed such a right, this will be considered automatically unfair. Employees may present a claim under this provision also regardless of length of service. In *Ajayi v Aitch Care Homes (London) Ltd* (UKEAT/0464) (3 February 2012, unreported), the EAT held that the assertion of a statutory right such as the right to take a rest break had to be communicated to the employer, so that employees dismissed for sleeping on duty could not claim that they were thereby asserting their right to a rest break. See also **54.3(c)** UNFAIR DISMISSAL – **II**.

The points made in **57.23** above about the application of *s 45A* to workers covered by equivalent legislation for particular sectors apply equally to protection from unfair dismissal.

57.25 Restrictions on contracting out

A provision in an agreement which purports to exclude or limit the operation of any part of the *1998 Regulations* or to prevent a person from making a tribunal claim connected with the *Regulations* will be void, except, of course, where the *Regulations* themselves permit exclusion or modification (*reg 35*). The general rule does not apply where worker and employer have entered into an ACAS-conciliated settlement or a settlement agreement. For comments on the potential breadth of the restrictions on contracting out, see the contrasting reasoning of the Court of Session in *MPB Structure Ltd v Munro* [2003] IRLR 350 and the Court of Appeal in *Caulfield v Marshalls Clay Products Ltd* [2004] EWCA Civ 422, [2004] IRLR 564, and the views of the ECJ in *Robinson-Steele v RD Retail Services Ltd*: C-131/04 [2006] IRLR 386, broadly endorsing the approach of the Court of Session.

57.26 GUIDANCE

The Secretary of State for Business, Energy and Industrial Strategy is responsible for arranging publication of information and advice on the *1998 Regulations* after consultation with both sides of industry (*reg 35A*). The Guidance was updated in August 2003 to reflect the changes made in the *Regulations* by the *2003 Amendment Regulations*, and was further amended following the decision of the ECJ in *European Commission v United Kingdom*: C-484/04 [2006] IRLR 888 that the guidance on workers' rights to rest periods and rest breaks put the UK in breach of its obligations to implement the *Directive* (see **57.2**). For a time, separate guidance for employers and employees was given via separate websites, but these have been replaced by (much less detailed) guidance on the website www.gov.uk. It should be noted that the Guidance does not have the force of law, and is not necessarily entirely accurate (both because of brevity and specific inaccuracies, such as the that the 48 hour limit on the working week applies to the total working time of those who work for more than one employer). Useful additional guidance for enforcing authorities has been issued by the Health and Safety Executive: see www.hse.gov.uk/lau/lacs/95-1.htm.

57.27 EXCEPTIONS

In addition to sectors of activity wholly excluded from the ambit of the *1998 Regulations* (see **57.3** above) various categories of worker are excepted from the full scope of the *Regulations*.

57.28 Unmeasured working time

The limit on the average working week, requirements as to daily and weekly rest periods and breaks for adults, and restrictions on hours of work for night workers are disapplied for workers whose working time is not measured or pre-determined or can be determined by the workers themselves, on account of the specific characteristics of their job (*reg 20(1)*). *Regulation 20* suggests that this may be the case for:

(a)   managing executives or other persons with autonomous decision-taking powers;

(b)   family workers; or

(c)   workers officiating at religious ceremonies in churches and religious communities.

(Annual leave entitlements nevertheless apply to workers within the exemptions created by *reg 20*.)

Following the enforcement proceedings by the Commission described in **56.2** above, the partial exemption from *reg 20* for those whose working time is partially unmeasured (*reg 20(2)*) was revoked by the *Working Time (Amendment) Regulations 2006 (SI 2006/99)* with effect from 6 April 2006.

There have as yet been no reported cases in the UK courts on the scope of the exception. The scope of the exception was briefly considered by the ECJ in *Union syndicale Solidaires Isère v Premier Ministre*: C-428/09 [2011] 1 CMLR 1206, [2011] IRLR 84, but the Court went no further than concluding that as there was no indication in the papers before it that the workers concerned could decide the number of hours they worked, they did not fall within the exception. In some other EU member states the domestic legislation specifies particular categories or levels of management as being within the exemption, but in the UK the approach has been simply to reproduce the rather imprecise wording of the *Directive* itself. In consequence the contractual arrangements in each case, and not just the individual's job title, would need to be considered to determine whether the individual falls within the exemption.

57.29 Special cases

Regulation 21 provides that in relation to certain specified situations or types of activity, the *Regulations* relating to daily and weekly rest periods and breaks (in respect of adults only) and hours of work for night workers are disapplied. This is subject to workers being permitted to take compensatory rest or, if that is not possible, being provided with appropriate protection; see for a discussion of this **57.17** above. The following groups fall within the *reg 21* exception:

(a)   where the worker's activities are such that the place of work and home are distant from one another or different places of work are distant from one another, including cases where the worker is involved in offshore work;

(b)   where the worker is engaged in security and surveillance activities requiring a permanent presence in order to protect property and persons, as may be the case for security guards and caretakers or security firms;

(c)   where the worker's activities involve the need for continuity of service or production, as may be the case in relation to:

   (i)   services relating to the reception, treatment or care provided by hospitals or similar establishments (including the activities of doctors in training), residential institutions and prisons;

   (ii)   work at docks or airports;

   (iii)   press, radio, television, cinematographic production, postal and telecommunications services and civil protection services;

   (iv)   gas, water and electricity production, transmission and distribution, household refuse collection and incineration;

   (v)   industries in which work cannot be interrupted on technical grounds;

   (vi)   research and development activities;

   (vii) agriculture;

      (viii)   the carriage of passengers on regular urban passenger services;

(d)   where there is a foreseeable surge of activity, as may be the case in relation to agriculture, tourism and postal services;

(e)   where the worker's activities are affected by:

      (i)   an occurrence due to unusual and unforeseeable circumstances, beyond the control of the worker's employer;

      (ii)   exceptional events, the consequences of which could not have been avoided despite the exercise of all due care by the employer; or

      (iii) an accident or the imminent risk of an accident;

(f)   where the worker works in railway transport and –

      (i)   his or her activities are intermittent;

      (ii)   he or she spends his working time on board trains; or

      (iii) his or her activities are linked to transport timetables and to ensuring the continuity and regularity of traffic.

Additionally, for workers falling within these categories the reference period for the weekly working time limit is extended from 17 weeks to 26 weeks (*reg 4(5)*).

The list of exclusions, which the regulation has copied largely verbatim from the *Directive*, is open to differences of interpretation. In particular, it should be noted that the categories listed in (*c*) are neither necessarily within the exemption (the wording is 'as may be the case in relation to') nor exhaustive of possible exempt activities.

The application of these exceptions was considered by the Court of Appeal in *Gallagher v Alpha Catering Ltd* [2004] EWCA Civ 1559, [2005] IRLR 102, a case concerning workers engaged in delivering and uplifting catering supplies to and from aircraft at Gatwick Airport, whose complaint was that they were refused rest breaks during the working day in breach of *reg 12*. The employers relied on two points in *reg 21* as providing exemption from their liability to afford rest breaks. These points were (*c*)(ii) and (*d*) above. As to the first, the Court emphasised that the emphasis in (*c*) was placed squarely on the activity of the worker, not of the employer, so that the test was not whether the employer had to maintain continuity of service but whether the particular worker's activity involved such continuity; on the facts it did not. The same approach was applied by the Court of Appeal to the work of security guards under (*b*) in *Hughes v Corps of Commissionaires Management (No 2)* [2011] EWCA Civ 1190, [2011] IRLR 915, but on the facts it was held that the work did require a continuous presence of the worker. In *Martin v Southern Health & Social Care Trust* [2010] NICA 31, [2010] IRLR 1048, the work of nurses providing care to in-patients in a hospital were held to fall within the exception at (c) above. Subsequently, in *Associated British Ports v Bridgeman* [2012] IRLR 639, the EAT referred to the ECJ the question whether the *Directive* requires a separate assessment of whether continuity of service is required with respect to rest breaks and to daily rest periods, or a single assessment covering both. The point arose in a case brought by a ship's pilot, the employment tribunal having held that the need for continuity of service was made out for rest breaks (since the pilot could not take a break whilst piloting a ship) but not daily rest periods between duties. The case was however settled before the ECJ could rule on the point.

The Court in *Gallagher* also rejected an argument that the variations in the numbers of aircraft requiring servicing at different times of the week, and increases in numbers during holiday periods, amounted to a 'foreseeable surge of activity' for the purposes of *reg 21(d)*.

The exception for the carriage of passengers on urban bus services was considered in *Feist v First Hampshire & Dorset Ltd* [2007] All ER (D) 180 (Feb), EAT, where it was held that the entitlement to compensatory rest attaching to the exemptions under *reg 21* applied only where the workers concerned were excluded from the right to rest solely by *reg 21*. In the case of bus drivers, who are also excluded as mobile workers by the effect of *reg 24A*, the corresponding right is limited to the right to 'adequate' rest conferred by *reg 24A*; the rights are not cumulative.

For a discussion of the requirement for compensatory rest when one of the exceptions in *reg 21* applies, see **57.17** above.

57.30 Domestic servants

Workers who are employed as domestic servants in a private household are excluded from the scope of the *Regulations* relating to: the 48-hour week; length of night work; health assessments and transfers to day work; and breaks for monotonous work. Such domestic workers are, however, covered by provisions on rest periods, breaks and annual leave (*reg 19*). The basis in the *Directive* for this exclusion appears to be that workers in domestic service are specifically excluded from the definition of 'worker' in the framework *Health and Safety Directive 89/391, art 3(a)*, and it appears that this limitation is considered to be incorporated by reference into the *Working Time Directive* itself by *art 1(4)*. However it is not entirely clear whether this is in fact the position; the point has yet to be tested.

57.31 SEAFARERS AND WORKERS ON INLAND WATERWAYS

A separate set of rules regulating the working time of seafarers on sea-going United Kingdom flagged vessels is laid down by the *Merchant Shipping (Hours of Work) Regulations 2002*. These implement EC *Directive 99/63*, which was adopted to fill one of the gaps in the coverage of the *Working Time Directive*. (Equivalent legislation is required of other member states in relation to the crews of ships flying their respective flags, but the inspection and enforcement provisions of the *2002 Regulations* extend to such vessels whilst in a UK port or UK waters: *reg 3(1)*). The *2002 Regulations* do not apply to fishing vessels, pleasure vessels, static offshore installations or most tug boats, or their respective crews. The *1998 Regulations* do not apply at all to those seafarers covered by *Directive 99/63*, or to the crews of fishing vessels: *reg 18(1)*.

The principal features of the *Merchant Shipping Regulations* are:

(a)   a minimum of 10 hours' daily rest (divided into not more than two periods);

(b)   a minimum of 77 hours' rest in any seven-day period;

(c)   provision for (a) and/or (b) to be made subject to exceptions by way of a collective or workforce agreement;

(d)   provision for the suspension of scheduled working hours and rest periods in an emergency;

(e)   maintenance of records of hours worked;

(f)   a prohibition on night work for those under 18;

(g)   entitlement to paid annual leave (which may be taken in instalments);

(h)   powers of inspection and enforcement, including penalties.

Directive 99/95 provides a mechanism for the verification and enforcement of compliance with *Directive 99/63* by ships calling at ports of member states. *Directive 99/63* has been extensively amended by a later *Directive, 2009/13*, which gives effect to the *International*

Labour Organisation Maritime Labour Convention 2006, which came into force in August 2013. The annual leave entitlement conferred by the Merchant Shipping Regulations has been extended, and a right to complain to an employment tribunal over denial of the right or failure to pay holiday pay conferred, by the *Merchant Shipping (Maritime Labour Convention) (Hours of Work) (Amendment) Regulations 2014, SI 2014/308*. Neither the *Directive* nor the *Merchant Shipping Regulations* apply to the crews of vessels registered in non-EU states. This has the (surprising) consequence that the *1998 Regulations* apply to some such seafarers, such as those based in the UK and working on non-EU flagged vessels operating from British ports: see by way of analogy *Diggins v Condor Marine Crewing Services Ltd* [2009] EWCA Civ 1133, [2010] IRLR 119 and *Harris v Windstar Management Services Ltd* (2016) UKEAT/0001/16, [2016] All ER (D) 189 (May), EAT.

Separate regulations, the *Fishing Vessels (Working Time: Sea-fishermen) Regulations 2004 (SI 2004/1713)* apply to the crews of UK registered fishing vessels. The *1998 Regulations* do not apply at all to those workers covered by the *2004 Regulations: 1998 Regulations, reg 18(1)(b)*.

The *2004 Regulations* apply to those employed on sea fishing vessels registered in the UK, wherever the vessel may be, and also (but in relation only to rights to rest periods and certain enforcement provisions) to those working on vessels registered in an EU member state whilst in UK waters. They apply only to those employed under a contract of employment, not to workers in the wider sense; that point apart, the definitions used are essentially the same as those used in the *1998 Regulations*. The principal rights conferred are:

(a)   a maximum 48 hour working week (averaged over 52 weeks, but with no facility for individual opt-outs);

(b)   adequate rest (with minimum entitlements of 10 hours in 24, in no more than two separate periods, and 77 hours in any week);

(c)   health assessments, and transfer from night work if the health assessment discloses health problems associated with night work;

(d)   paid annual leave; and

(e)   to make a complaint to an employment tribunal if denied adequate rest or paid leave.

The rights not to be subjected to detriment, or dismissed, for asserting rights under the *Regulations*, are conferred by amendments to the *ERA 1996*. Other enforcement provisions include powers for the Maritime and Coastguard Agency to inspect records and detain vessels. The Secretary of State has a limited power to grant exemptions from the limits on working time and the minimum required periods of rest, and there is a general exemption for emergencies.

A further *Directive, N.o 2017/159*, was adopted by the EU in April 2017; this will give effect to a framework agreement between representatives of employers and unions to implement the International Labour Organisation *Convention on Work in Fishing*. However the Directive is not required to be given domestic effect until November 2019, and as it is expected that the UK will by then have left the EU, it is as yet unclear whether its provisions will require to be implemented domestically. The UK has not (as at 1 May 2017) ratified the *Work in Fishing Convention*.

57.32   Workers employed on UK vessels operating under certificates limiting the vessel to inland waterways and lakes, or not requiring to be certificated, or on non–UK registered vessels operating solely within such waters, are covered by the *Merchant Shipping (Hours of Work: Inland Waterways) Regulations 2003 (SI 2003/3049)*, made under *s 85* of the *Merchant Shipping Act 1995*. In summary, these *Regulations* provide for a maximum of 48 hours working time a week, averaged in the same way as under the *1998 Regulations*, rights for night workers to free health assessments and to be transferred to other work if available if the worker's health is prejudiced by night working, rights to adequate rest, which must be of at least 77 hours in total in any week, and to four weeks' paid annual leave in each leave year. Other rights conferred by the *1998 Regulations* are however not mirrored in these *Regulations*.

There are limited exceptions for workers whose working time is unmeasured, and in certain cases the averaging period for the 48 hour week is extended to 26 weeks and may be further extended by a collective or workforce agreement. Employers are under a duty to maintain records. Breach of the provisions relating to maximum working time, health assessments and record keeping are offences, whilst the remedy for breaches of the provisions on rest periods and annual leave is by way of complaint to an employment tribunal. The *2003 Regulations* contain the usual prohibition on contracting out, except by way of a compromise agreement. The *2003 Regulations* mirror the *1998 Regulations* very closely in terminology; the *1998 Regulations* are excluded completely for those workers covered by the *2003 Regulations: 1998 Regulations, reg 18(1)(c)*.

In February 2012 a Framework Agreement was made by the sectoral social partners which will form the basis of a revised Directive for the Inland Waterways sector, but the Directive had not been adopted by 1 May 2017.

57.33 AVIATION SECTOR

In November 2000 the Social Affairs Council formally adopted a *Directive* implementing the social partners' agreement on working time in the aviation sector, *Directive 2000/79* on the organisation of working time of mobile workers in civil aviation. The domestic implementation of this *Directive* has been effected by the *Civil Aviation (Working Time) Regulations 2004 (SI 2004/756)*. The *2004 Regulations* apply to crew members of civil aircraft flying for the purposes of public transport, and confer the following rights:

(a)   paid annual leave of at least four weeks, as to which see *British Airways plc v Williams* [2012] UKSC 43, [2012] IRLR 1014, [2012] ICR 1375;

(b)   free health assessments;

(c)   right of transfer from night work to day work where possible if health problems are caused by night work;

(d)   appropriate health and safety protection;

(e)   maximum working time of 2,000 hours a year, calculated on a rolling basis;

(f)   a maximum of 900 hours block flying time in any one (rolling) year;

(g)   at least seven local days (ie days at the crew member's home base) each month and at least 96 local days each year free of all duty and standby.

Infringements of the rights at (a), (b) and (c) may be made the subject of a complaint to an employment tribunal; however there is no equivalent to the protection from detriment or dismissal for asserting rights under the *1998 Regulations* for workers covered by the *Civil Aviation Regulations*; the reason for this omission is unclear. In other respects the *Regulations* are enforceable by the Civil Aviation Authority, following the model of the *1998 Regulations*.

Workers covered by *Directive 2000/79* are excluded from the operative provisions of the *1998 Regulations* governing adult workers: *reg 18(2)(b)*. However, unlike those in the sectors discussed in **57.31** and **57.32** above, this is not an exclusion of the *Regulations* in their entirety; the principal practical difference appears to be that specific provisions on young workers' hours in the *1998 Regulations* and the provisions for their enforcement by the CAA, do apply to the civil aviation sector. One issue which has arisen under the *2004 Regulations* is the treatment in calculating an individual's total annual working time (see (e) above) of standby duty. The *Regulations* were amended, following consultations by the Department for Transport, by the *Civil Aviation (Working Time) (Amendment) Regulations 2010, SI 2010/1226*, to provide that standby time counts in full towards the permitted annual working hours, subject to certain exceptions the effect of which is that time counts at half the rate of actual time.

57.34   MOBILE WORKERS IN ROAD AND RAIL TRANSPORT

Mobile workers are defined as 'any worker employed as a member of travelling or flying personnel by an undertaking which operates transport services for passengers or goods by road or air': *1998 Regulations, reg 2(1)*. (See **57.36** below for rail workers.)

Most such mobile workers are excluded from the application of the *1998 Regulations* by *reg 18*, by virtue of their falling within the terms of either *Directive 2000/79* (as to which, see **57.33** above) or *Directive 2002/15*, which requires member states to enact parallel provisions as to working time, etc for mobile workers in road transport. Any mobile workers (as defined above) who fall outside these categories are subject to *reg 24A*, which excludes the provisions of the *Regulations* as to night work, rest breaks and rest periods, but not those relating to the working week, health assessments, monotonous work, or paid annual leave. The exclusions are subject to rights to periods of adequate rest, which are required to be sufficiently long and continuous to ensure that the worker's health is protected. The EAT has held that the right to adequate rest is in effect in substitution for rights under *reg 24* to compensatory rest, rather than cumulative with that right: *Feist v First Hampshire & Dorset Ltd* [2007] All ER (D) 180 (Feb), EAT.

57.35   *Directive 2002/15* applies to mobile workers employed in the road transport industry who are covered by the *Drivers' Hours Regulations (Regulation 3820/85)*, which cover maximum driving hours for drivers of most commercial freight and passenger vehicles within the EU or the European Economic Area, or by the AETR Agreement 1970, which makes equivalent provisions covering road transport across the outer boundaries of the EU and EEA. (Note that following the introduction of *Directive 2002/15*, the *Drivers' Hours Regulations* were replaced by an updated equivalent, *Regulation 561/2006*, which came into force on 11 April 2007.) The *Directive* covers maximum working hours, breaks, rest periods and restrictions on night work, and the maintenance of records. It does not cover annual leave entitlement or rights to health assessments, or the rights in relation to working time, daily rest periods and rest breaks of young workers, in respect of which the *1998 Regulations* apply equally to workers otherwise governed by the *2002 Directive* (insofar as those provisions affecting only young workers are capable of applying to mobile workers in road transport).

The implementation of this *Directive* was effected by the *Road Transport (Working Time) Regulations 2005 (SI 2005/639)*. The *2005 Regulations* apply to those mobile workers who in the course of their work drive, or travel in vehicles to which either the *Drivers' Hours Regulations* or the AETR agreement apply. They are thus not limited in their application to drivers as such, but may cover, for instance, attendants on long distance coaches. However, in line with the *Directive, Regulations* did not initially cover self-employed owner-drivers. Under *Art 2(1)* of the *Directive* the exclusion of self-employed drivers was due to lapse on 23 March 2009, but the *Directive* also made provision for the Parliament to decide, on the basis of a report by the Commission, whether the exemption should continue. Initially in September 2009 the Parliament rejected a report by the Commission which would have had the effect of extending the *Directive* to self-employed drivers; however, the Parliament subsequently reversed its position on the point, and the *2005 Regulations* have been amended accordingly, with effect from 11 May 2012, to apply to self-employed drivers in accordance with the *Directive*: see the *Road Transport (Working Time) (Amendment) Regulations 2012, SI 2012/991*.

The *2005 Regulations* impose a limit on working time of an average of 48 hours a week, averaged over either rolling or fixed periods of 17 weeks, with an absolute limit of 60 hours in any week. In limited circumstances the averaging period may be extended to 26 weeks. Working time is broadly defined to include all working time, not just the time spent driving or travelling, but excluding breaks and certain periods on standby (referred to as 'periods of availability'). See further *Vehicle and Operator services Agency v Wright* [2011] EWHC 1389, 27 May 2011, unreported, Div Ct (driving a 23-seat coach for private purposes counted as 'driving'). The *2012 Regulations* include an extended definition of 'working time' which makes it clear that the performance of general administration by self-employed drivers does not count as working time.

The *Regulations* do not contain any provision for individual opt-outs from the limits on working hours. In addition to limits on working hours, there are provisions for rest breaks and rest periods, and additional limits on night working. However the *Regulations* do not confer entitlements to paid annual leave. This is because the *1998 Regulations* apply in this respect; enforcement of rights to paid leave is by way of individual complaint to an employment tribunal under *reg 30* of the *1998 Regulations* or *Part II* of the *ERA 1996*.

Employers (and self-employed drivers, from 11 May 2012) are required to ensure compliance with the *Regulations*, and enforcement is by inspectors appointed by the Department for Transport, using sanctions similar to those under the equivalent provisions of the *1998 Regulations*. The *2005 Regulations* do not make provision for individual workers to complain to an employment tribunal if not afforded the required rest breaks or rest periods, or dismissed or subjected to detriment for asserting their rights. This omission was challenged by way of Judicial Review in *R (oao United Road Transport Union) v Secretary of State for Transport* [2013] IRLR 890 (CA). The challenge was rejected on the ground that the Regulations are intended to impose an obligation on drivers to take the specified breaks; this reflected the purpose of the *Regulations*, which was to promote the safe operation of road transport. Drivers' interests were in the Court's view protected by the fact that they could not be required to work without the mandatory breaks, and any attempt by an employer to require them to do so would be a breach of an implied term of their employment.

The *Drivers' Hours Regulations* apply directly as part of domestic law without the need for separate implementing legislation. The restrictions on the maximum permitted hours of work, and minimum rest periods, for drivers covered by the *Regulations*, are underpinned by criminal liability: an example of a successful prosecution for taking an insufficiently long rest break between shifts is *Harding v Vehicle and Operator Services Agency* [2010] EWHC 713 (Admin).

57.36 Mobile workers in the rail sector are covered by the *1998 Regulations*, and fall outside the exclusions applied by *reg 24A*, as they are outside the definition of 'mobile workers' quoted above; however they are subject to the effects of *reg 21*: see **57.29** above for this. Separate Regulations govern various aspects of the working time of rail workers working on services through the Channel Tunnel: see the *Cross-Border Railway Services (Working Time) Regulations 2008, SI 2008/1660*.

57.37 AGENCY WORKERS

Agency workers are covered by the *1998 Regulations* whether or not they satisfy the test to be workers under the *Regulations*: see *reg 36*. In addition, the *Agency Workers Regulations 2010 (SI 2010/93)*, which implement the EU *Agency Workers Directive 2009*, confer on temporary agency workers (within the definition in *reg 3*) rights to equality of treatment with comparable directly employed staff of the end user of their services: *reg 5*. This right applies to contractual terms relating to working time, including night work, rest periods, rest breaks and annual leave (*reg 6(1)*). Thus if a comparable directly employed employee is entitled to an hour's paid break during a shift, the agency worker will have the same entitlement, although this is more generous than the statutory minimum stipulated by the *Working Time Regulations*. The entitlement is to the terms and conditions that would have applied to the agency worker had he or she been directly recruited to do the same job as an employee of the end user, and is subject to a number of conditions, of which the most significant is a qualifying period of 12 weeks working for the end user (*reg 7*).

57.38   CHURCH OF ENGLAND CLERGY

By virtue of the *Ecclesiastical Offices (Terms of Service) Regulations 2009*, which came into force on 1 January 2010, the holders of certain ecclesiastical offices in the Church of England (who are neither employees nor workers for the purposes of the *1998 Regulations*) are given rights to a weekly rest day (but it may be stipulated by the relevant Church authorities that this must not be taken on a Sunday or any of the principal feast days of the Church of England) and to annual leave without loss of stipend. Enforcement of these rights is a matter of internal Church procedures: there is no right of recourse to an employment tribunal. The rights conferred by the *2009 Regulations* do not apply to ministers of any church other than the Church of England; the position in other cases will therefore depend on whether the individual is held to be a worker within the *1998 Regulations*.

58   Wrongful Dismissal

58.1   INTRODUCTION

A wrongful dismissal occurs when an employer dismisses an employee in a way which is in breach of the employee's contract of employment. Most commonly, this arises when the employer dismisses the employee summarily (ie without any notice at all) or with short notice, and has no sufficient justification for doing so. However, there may also be a wrongful dismissal in other situations: for example, if the employer terminates the employment without following some procedure prescribed by the contract. Further, if the employee resigns in response to some repudiatory breach of contract by the employer, that will give rise to a claim which is in effect for wrongful dismissal.

Thus, wrongful dismissal is a common law cause of action based upon a breach of contract. The right not to be wrongfully dismissed, unlike the right not to be unfairly dismissed, is not one which depends upon statute. A dismissal which is wrongful need not necessarily be unfair, and vice versa. This is because an employer may behave unreasonably in dismissing an employee even though he has observed the letter of their contract, whilst a decision to dismiss may be reasonable even if it involves a breach of contract (although failure to comply with contractual procedures is one factor to be taken into account in deciding whether a dismissal is unfair). See *Treganowan v Robert Knee & Co Ltd* [1975] ICR 405; *BSC Sports and Social Club v Morgan* [1987] IRLR 391 and *Westminster City Council v Cabaj* [1996] ICR 960.

The primary remedy for an employee who is wrongfully dismissed is an action for damages for breach of contract. In certain circumstances, however, the employee may seek the assistance of the court in keeping the contract of employment alive.

58.2   Contracts whose breach may give rise to wrongful dismissal claims

The wrongful termination of any normal contract of employment will give rise to an action for wrongful dismissal. Certain special categories of employment are dealt with below (see **58.43** and **58.44**). Where the contract pursuant to which a self-employed person provides services is wrongfully terminated, the action for breach of contract is not strictly speaking one for wrongful dismissal but similar principles will apply.

58.3   WHAT CONSTITUTES A DISMISSAL

The fundamental precondition for a wrongful dismissal claim is that the employee should have been dismissed. This will usually occur in one of the following ways:

(a)   dismissal upon notice by the employer (see **58.5** below), although there will normally be no wrongful dismissal if full notice has been given;

(b)   summary dismissal by the employer; and

(c)   constructive dismissal (see **58.6** below).

However, there may also be a deemed dismissal in certain other circumstances (see **58.8–58.10** below).

58.4 Wrongful Dismissal

58.4 Dismissal contrasted with other modes of termination

The employee will have no right to claim damages if the contract is brought to an end by mutual agreement or by his own resignation (unless in response to the employer's repudiatory breach), by frustration, or through the automatic operation of provisions in the contract (for example, expiry of a fixed term contract, or a provision that the employment will end as soon as the employee reaches a certain age).

For a fuller discussion of these possible modes of termination, see UNFAIR DISMISSAL – I (53). Note that expiry of a fixed term contract without renewal constitutes a deemed dismissal for the purposes of unfair dismissal but not for the purposes of wrongful dismissal.

58.5 Dismissal upon notice

Unless the contract otherwise provides, an effective notice may be given either orally or in writing. However, a notice is of no effect unless and until it is communicated to the employee (*Brown v Southall and Knight* [1980] ICR 617; *Hindle Gears Ltd v McGinty* [1985] ICR 111).

A purported notice is ineffective unless it is expressed to expire on a certain specified or ascertainable day, or upon the occurrence of a specified event (*Morton Sundour Fabrics Ltd v Shaw* (1966) 2 ITR 84; *Burton Group Ltd v Smith* [1977] IRLR 351). Accordingly, there will be no dismissal if the employee is merely warned that his job will come to an end at some point in the future (*Devon County Council v Cook* [1977] IRLR 188; *International Computers Ltd v Kennedy* [1981] IRLR 28), or if it is not possible to tell from the notice when the employment will end (*Haseltine Lake & Co v Dowler* [1981] ICR 222).

Usually, the employer's intention to dismiss will be clear. Sometimes, however, the language of a letter or conversation may leave room for doubt as to whether the employer is actually dismissing the employee, or whether he is merely warning or threatening that he may do so, or indeed whether he is simply expressing frustration or anger. In such circumstances, the court will consider, not the employer's subjective intention, but rather the objective meaning of the words used, considered against the background of the circumstances in which they are used. The ultimate question is how the words should reasonably have been regarded by the other party to the contract (*Tanner v DT Kean Ltd* [1978] IRLR 110; *Sovereign House Security Services Ltd v Savage* [1989] IRLR 115).

In order to decide whether due notice has been given, or whether the employee has been wrongfully dismissed, it may be important to decide on what date the notice takes effect. The day on which the notice is given will not normally be counted in calculating any period to which the notice refers (*West v Kneels Ltd* [1987] ICR 146).

Once notice has been given by one party to the contract, it may not be withdrawn except by mutual consent (*Riordan v War Office* [1959] 1 WLR 1046). Therefore, if an employer gives short notice to an employee, and later realises his mistake and seeks to retract that notice, the employee is entitled to refuse to agree to the retraction and to sue for wrongful dismissal (although the employer might then argue that the employee had failed to mitigate his loss).

58.6 Constructive dismissal

The employee will be treated as having been constructively dismissed if he resigns in response to a repudiatory breach of contract by the employer. This means that the employer must have breached some term of the contract, whether express or implied (or have indicated a clear intention to do so – see **58.22** below), and the breach must be sufficiently serious to 'go to the root of the contract'. (This will be the case if, for instance, the employer has breached the duty of trust and confidence: see *Morrow v Safeway Stores plc* [2002] IRLR 9). It is enough if the breach played a part in the resignation: *Wright v. North Ayrshire Council* [2014] ICR 77.

The employee must accept the breach by resigning, and he must not take so long to do so that he is deemed to have affirmed the contract or waived the employer's breach: affirmation can be implied from prolonged delay (*Mari v Reuters Ltd*, UKEAT/0539/13/MC). Furthermore, at common law, if the employee gives any notice (including short notice) of termination this will be treated as an affirmation of the contract: *Cockram v Air Products plc* [2014] IRLR 672; *Elsevier Ltd v Munro* [2014] IRLR 766.

For a full discussion of the different factual circumstances which may amount to a constructive dismissal, see UNFAIR DISMISSAL – I (53). Note, however, that in the unfair dismissal context it has been held to be necessary for the employer's breach of contract to be the true cause of the resignation. It is not thought that this applies to an action for wrongful dismissal (cf *Boston Deep Sea Fishing and Ice Co v Ansell* (1888) 39 Ch D 339; and see *RDF Media Group plc v Clements* [2007] EWHC 2892 (QB), [2008] IRLR 207).

58.7 Need for employer's breach of contract to be accepted

Where one party commits a repudiatory breach of contract, it is necessary for that breach to be 'accepted' by the other, innocent party before the contract can be brought to an end. That is because the innocent party may instead choose to keep the contract in existence, and simply to sue for damages if the breach of contract has caused him loss.

This rule applies to a contract of employment where the employer's breach of contract consists of some act or omission falling short of a purported dismissal. For instance, if the employer persists in withholding some significant benefit in kind, the employee may choose whether to resign and bring the contract to an end (thereafter suing for wrongful dismissal), or whether to remain in employment and simply sue for damages for the loss of the benefit.

This rule also applies where the employer purports to dismiss the employee in breach of contract (for example, in breach of a contractual procedure, or by purporting to dismiss summarily where there is no justification for doing so). In such a situation, the employee will normally simply accept his dismissal and sue for damages for wrongful dismissal. However, in some cases, the employee may wish to keep the contract alive — perhaps because there is an advantage to him in still being employed at a particular date (eg to receive a bonus or to invoke the benefits of an insurance policy), or because he hopes for a different outcome if the employer is obliged to go through a proper disciplinary procedure.

The Supreme Court has rejected the proposition that the act of wrongful dismissal brings the employment to an end without any need for acceptance of the breach by the employee: the 'automatic termination' theory (see *Société Générale v Geys* [2013] ICR 117).

Nonetheless, it is clear that in the employment context such acceptance will be readily inferred from the employee's words or conduct. For instance, an employee who seeks other work, or signs on for jobseeker's allowance, or even one who simply does not return to work and says nothing, will very probably be held to have ceased to be employed. (However, see *Brompton v AOC International Ltd* (above) where, on the facts of that case, the employee's request for his P45 did not amount to acceptance of the repudiatory breach; and see *Geys v Société Générale, London Branch* [2010] EWHC 648 (Ch), [2010] IRLR 950, where a request by an employee's solicitors for delivery of 'termination documentation' was treated by the Court as the employee keeping his options open, rather than affirmation of the breach.) To be on the safe side, an employee who wishes to argue that his employment continues should assert clearly and quickly that he regards himself as still employed, and that he is available for work if required.

58.8 Employer changing identity or ceasing to exist

If the employer is an individual, the death of that individual will bring the contract to an end. However, it appears that this will be regarded as a case of termination pursuant to an implied term of the contract, and not of wrongful dismissal (see *Farrow v Wilson* (1869) LR 4 CP 744).

58.8   Wrongful Dismissal

If the employer is a partnership, then the dissolution of that partnership or a major change in its composition amounts to a dismissal of the employee (*Tunstall v Condon* [1980] ICR 786; *Briggs v Oates* [1990] ICR 473). It was held in *Brace v Calder* [1895] 2 QB 253 that the same applied when there was any change in the identity of the partners. However, it is not thought that this approach would be taken by the courts in modern cases of large partnerships whose membership frequently fluctuates. Firms should insert appropriate express terms into their contracts of employment to deal with this situation.

The permanent closure of the workplace amounts to a termination of the contracts of those employed there (*Glenboig Union Fireclay Co Ltd v Stewart* (1971) 6 ITR 14). This is not true of a temporary shutdown, although that might, depending upon the circumstances, amount to a repudiatory breach of contract.

58.9   Insolvency

Where the employer is a company, then an order for the compulsory winding up of that company has the immediate effect of terminating the contracts of employment of the company's employees (*Re General Rolling Stock Co* (1866) LR 1 Eq 346; *Measures Bros Ltd v Measures* [1910] 2 Ch 248, CA). However, contracts of employment continue during a voluntary winding up (*Midland Counties District Bank Ltd v Attwood* [1905] 1 Ch 357).

Again, contracts of employment are treated as coming immediately to an end if the employing company is put into receivership by an order of the court (*Reid v Explosives Co Ltd* (1887) 19 QBD 264; *Re Foster Clark Ltd's Indenture Trusts* [1966] 1 WLR 125). By contrast, the employment continues if the receiver is appointed otherwise by the court and as agent for the company, as typically occurs under, say, a creditor bank's debenture (*Hopley-Dodd v Highfield Motors (Derby) Ltd* (1969) 4 ITR 289; *Griffiths v Secretary of State for Social Services* [1974] QB 468). However, even a receivership of this latter kind may have the effect of terminating the contract of employment of a senior manager, if there is a fundamental inconsistency between the continuation of that individual's employment and the receiver's power and duty to conduct the business of the company (*Re Mack Trucks (Britain) Ltd* [1967] 1 WLR 780).

(See INSOLVENCY OF EMPLOYER (31).)

58.10   Removal from board of directors

In principle, a person's status as a director of the company and his status as an employee of that company are separate and distinct. Accordingly, the employee may cease to be a director without any impact upon his contract of employment.

Sometimes, however, it may be an express or implied term of the contract of employment that the employee is to be a director, either of the employing company itself, or of some associated company. In such a case, removal from the board will amount to a repudiation of the contract of employment, allowing the employee to sue for wrongful dismissal (*Shindler*, below).

However, even in a case where removal from the board brings the employment to an end, it may be contended that the company's articles of association were incorporated into the contract of employment when it was made, and have the effect of ending the employment without any breach on the company's part (see eg *Read v Astoria Garage (Streatham) Ltd* [1952] Ch 637; cf *Southern Foundries (1926) Ltd v Shirlaw* [1940] AC 701; *Shindler v Northern Raincoat Co Ltd* [1960] 1 WLR 1038).

(See DIRECTORS (9).)

In this situation, there are three principal options open to the employer (assuming that there are no grounds for a summary dismissal). The first is to negotiate an early termination with the employee. Some financial incentive may be offered, or the employee may simply be happy to be released from his obligations sooner rather than later. There is no legal obstacle to this course, because *s 86(3)* of the *ERA 1996* permits the employee to waive his right even to the statutory minimum period of notice (or to accept a payment in lieu of notice).

The second option is for the employer to pay the employee wages in lieu of notice. This course is frequently adopted. However, it should be borne in mind that to dismiss an employee with pay in lieu rather than to give due notice is in fact to dismiss wrongfully. The true legal analysis of this situation is that there is a summary dismissal carried out in breach of contract, and the wages paid in lieu in fact represent a payment of damages for that breach of contract (see *Gothard v Mirror Group Newspapers Ltd* [1988] IRLR 396). In some cases, the fact that the dismissal is theoretically wrongful may be of no practical significance. But that will not always be so. For instance, the dismissed employee may have a residual claim for the value of lost benefits in kind during the notice period. (See, for example, *Silvey v Pendragon plc* [2001] IRLR 685, where the early termination deprived an employee of enhanced pension rights. Even though the employee had accepted pay in lieu of notice, the Court of Appeal held that the loss of these pension rights was recoverable as damages for wrongful dismissal). The wrongful dismissal may also prevent the employer from relying upon restrictive covenants in the contract of employment (see **58.34** below).

An employee has no statutory or common law right to be paid in lieu of notice (*Rowley v Cerberus Software Ltd* [2001] EWCA Civ 78, [2001] ICR 376; *Hardy v Polk (Leeds) Ltd* [2004] IRLR 420. However, provision may be made by contract. In order to avoid the problems of the 'theoretically wrongful' dismissal described above, many service agreements now incorporate a clause which gives the employer the option of terminating the contract lawfully by making a payment in lieu of notice instead of actually giving notice. Such a clause ought to define clearly whether the payment is to be based upon basic pay only, or whether the calculation is also to have regard to other elements of the remuneration package, and whether the payment is to be made gross or net of tax. Where the contract of employment does not expressly define the payment that will be made in lieu of notice the Court will interpret the contract 'holistically', without any preconception that it necessarily seeks to give the employee what he would have earned had he remained in employment during the notice period (*Locke v. Candy & Candy Ltd* [2010] EWCA Civ 1350, [2011] IRLR 163.

Summary termination pursuant to a payment in lieu (PILON) provision does not constitute a breach of contract (*Rex Stewart Jeffries Parker Ginsberg Ltd v Parker* [1988] IRLR 483). Where payment in lieu has been made in accordance with a PILON provision, this will bring the contract of employment to an end, so long as the employer notifies the employee in clear and unambiguous terms that such payment has been made and that it is made in the exercise of the contractual right to terminate the employment with immediate effect (*Société Générale v Geys* [2013] ICR 117).

Where the employer exercises the right to terminate the contract with a payment in lieu of notice, the employee is under no obligation to give credit for actual or imputed earnings during what would have been the notice period. In other words, there is no duty on the employee to mitigate loss (as to which, see **58.30** below). He is entitled to claim for the full sum due to him under the contract as a debt (*Abrahams v Performing Rights Society* [1995] ICR 1028).

The sum paid to the employee in lieu of notice will be taxable in his hands under Schedule E (*EMI Group Electronics Ltd v Coldicott (Inspector of Taxes)* [1999] IRLR 630).

Merely because a contract of employment contains a payment in lieu clause, however, does not mean that every termination will be treated as if the employer exercised the right to dismiss and then make the payment in lieu without any deduction for mitigation. Much will depend on the precise wording of the contract. In *Gregory v Wallace* [1998] IRLR 387, the Court of Appeal held that, on the facts, the employer did not exercise the right to make a payment in lieu, where notice of termination had to be in writing and termination had been oral. Instead, the employer was treated as having dismissed the employee wrongfully and in breach of contract.

In *Cerberus Software Ltd v Rowley* [2001] ICR 376, on the other hand, where the contract stated that the employer 'may' make a payment in lieu of notice to the employee. The Court of Appeal held that this gave the employer the choice whether or not to make the payment.

There is no breach of contract even if it is the employee who has originally given notice, and the employer who then brings the employment to an immediate end with a payment in lieu (*Marshall (Cambridge) Ltd v Hamblin* [1994] IRLR 260). In *Hamblin* it was also held that the employment could be lawfully terminated with a payment in lieu of salary only, notwithstanding that the employee typically received a high proportion of his remuneration from commission; however, the EAT's reasoning is hard to follow and may depend upon the fact that the payment of commission was held to be discretionary and not a contractual right.

The third option is for the employee to be put on so-called 'garden leave'. This means that notice is duly given and the employee continues to be paid and to receive his full contractual benefits but he is not required or permitted to attend for work. This may be achieved by an express garden leave clause or, in certain circumstances, by 'implying' such a clause into the contract.

The power to place an employee on garden leave will not be implied if the refusal to provide work would constitute a repudiatory breach of contract. There will be a repudiatory breach if the contractual consideration moving from the employer includes an obligation to permit the employee to perform work but not if the contractual consideration is confined to payment of remuneration only (*Collier v Sunday Referee Publishing Co Ltd* [1940] 2 KB 647).

The Court of Appeal has acknowledged that employees increasingly regard work itself as important to them, and not just remuneration (*William Hill Organisation Ltd v Tucker* [1999] ICR 291). Moreover, it held that whether there is an obligation to provide work, rather than merely pay, will depend on a careful construction of the contractual arrangements. Of particular importance will be whether the position of the employee was 'specific and unique'; and whether the employee has some skill which will be lost if not practised. Other factors may be whether the contractual remuneration consists in part of a commission which depends upon work actually done (see eg *Devonald v Rosser & Sons* [1906] 2 KB 728). See also *Langston v Amalgamated Union of Engineering Workers* [1974] ICR 180, 510, CA; *Breach v Epsylon Industries Ltd* [1976] ICR 316; *Spencer v Marchington* [1988] IRLR 392; *SBJ Stephenson Ltd v Mandy* [2000] IRLR 233 (no obligation to provide work to a divisional director of an insurance brokerage).

In *SG&R Valuation Service Co LLC v Boudrais* [2008] IRLR 770, the court held that the Defendant employees had a right to work, based on the *Tucker* analysis. However, this right was qualified, and was subject to the employees being ready and willing to work. The employees' wrongdoing (removal of confidential information, solicitation of staff and diversion of business opportunities) demonstrated that they were not ready and willing to work, and so the employer was entitled to withhold work from them during their notice period.

It should be borne in mind, however, that the existence of an express garden leave clause may be taken into account by a court in determining the validity of any post-termination restraints on the employee (*Credit Suisse Asset Management Ltd v Armstrong* [1996] ICR 882; see further RESTRAINT OF TRADE (41)).

58.22 ANTICIPATORY BREACHES OF CONTRACT

It is important to remember that a breach of contract, in this as in other contexts, may be either *actual* or *anticipatory*. An anticipatory breach of contract occurs where there has not yet been any actual breach, because the time for performance of the relevant obligation has not yet arrived, but one party has indicated a clear refusal to perform the contract, or has made it impossible for himself to fulfil his obligations when the time comes. In the case of an employment contract, this might occur, for example, if the employer announced that the employee's salary would be unilaterally reduced by a significant amount the following month.

Where an anticipatory breach of contract occurs, and it is sufficiently serious to be repudiatory, the innocent party is faced with a choice. First, he may immediately accept the breach as bringing the contract to an end, and sue for damages. Secondly, he may keep the contract alive, and continue to call for performance by the other party. Thus, in the example above, the employee could immediately resign and sue for damages for wrongful dismissal. Alternatively, he could continue to assert his right to be paid a full salary the following month, which would give the employer an opportunity to change his mind; if the salary was indeed reduced, then the employee would at that point have to choose between resigning and affirming the contract, as discussed in **58.6** above. In the latter event, he might also be able to sue in debt for arrears of salary, as discussed in **58.24** below.

It has been suggested that an anticipatory breach, as opposed to an actual breach of contract, will not be repudiatory if it stems from an innocent mistake on the part of the party in breach as to what the contract requires of him (see *Frank Wright & Co (Holdings) Ltd v Punch* [1980] IRLR 217, EAT; *United Bank Ltd v Akhtar* [1989] IRLR 507; and *Brown v JBD Engineering Ltd* [1993] IRLR 568).

58.23 REMEDIES FOR WRONGFUL DISMISSAL

Remedies other than claims for damages

Injunctions

If the employee moves swiftly, he may be able to obtain an injunction restraining the employer from dismissing him wrongfully. However, it is unusual for the court to agree to insist upon performance of a contract of employment, because of the personal relationship between employer and employee without which the contract cannot properly function. Nevertheless, the breakdown of the relationship of trust and confidence will not automatically prevent an employee from obtaining injunctive relief (see *Gryf-Lowczowski (Jan) v Hinchingbrooke Healthcare NHS Trust* [2005] EWHC 2407 (QB), [2006] IRLR 100 (see further CONTRACT OF EMPLOYMENT (8)).

58.24 *Claims in debt*

If the employer's breach of contract consists of the failure to pay a sum of money that is due, for example by imposing a reduction in salary, the employee's sole choice is not between resigning and claiming to have been wrongfully dismissed on the one hand, and accepting the reduced salary on the other. Rather, he may choose to affirm the contract of employment despite the employer's breach, yet continue to assert his entitlement to the unpaid moneys, and sue in debt for those moneys if they remain unpaid. For examples, see the decisions of the House of Lords in *Rigby v Ferodo Ltd* [1988] ICR 29 and the EAT in *Bruce v Wiggins Teape (Stationery) Ltd* [1994] IRLR 536.

58.25   Actions for damages for wrongful dismissal

General approach to assessment of damages

The basic principle in assessing the damages payable for wrongful dismissal is that the employee must be put into the same position as if the employer had properly performed the contract. However, it is to be assumed for these purposes that the employer would have performed the contract in the way least burdensome to himself, and would have minimised his obligations to the employee by giving due notice to terminate the contract at the earliest opportunity (see *Lavarack v Woods of Colchester Ltd* [1967] 1 QB 278 and *Clark v BET plc* [1997] IRLR 348, though see *Horkulak v Cantor Fitzgerald International* [2004] EWCA Civ 1287, [2005] ICR 402. In that case, the Court of Appeal held that the rule did not apply to the failure to make discretionary bonus payments where the employer is contractually obliged to exercise his discretion rationally and in good faith. In those circumstances, the Court will look to see what bonus the employee probably would have received if he had continued in employment, rather than the minimum sum that his employer might have awarded him consistent with his contractual obligation to act rationally and in good faith).

Two main consequences follow from this basic principle. First, the court will have to ask itself how much better off the employee would have been if he had been given proper notice on the date when he was wrongfully dismissed (or if notice which had already been given had been allowed to run its course). This will normally mean that the *prima facie* measure of the damages is the net amount of the employee's salary and benefits for the notice period. In the case of a fixed term contract, the equivalent period is of course the unexpired portion of the term remaining as at the date of dismissal.

Second, the court (unlike an employment tribunal assessing compensation for unfair dismissal) will only compensate the employee for the loss of benefits to which he was contractually entitled, and not for those which he would probably have received in practice but to which he had no legal right (*Lavarack*, above). It may also be necessary to consider questions of causation arising upon the particular facts of a given case. For example, the employer may be able to prove upon a balance of probabilities that the employee would have left his job voluntarily within the notice period in any event, or that an employee dismissed because of long-term absence through sickness would have remained off work throughout the notice period and would therefore have earned nothing during that period.

Where the wrongfulness of the dismissal stems from a failure to follow a proper procedure (see **58.18** above), the traditional view has been that damages should be awarded on the basis that notice could lawfully have been given on the day when the necessary procedures, if followed, could have been concluded (*Gunton v Richmond-upon-Thames London Borough Council* [1980] ICR 755; see also *Alexander v Standard Telephones and Cables Ltd (No 2)* [1991] IRLR 286 and *Boyo v Lambeth London Borough Council* [1994] ICR 727). The court will not speculate as to whether or not the employee would have remained in employment if the disciplinary procedure had been followed (*Focsa Services (UK) Ltd v Birkett* [1996] IRLR 325; *Janciuk v Winerite Ltd* [1998] IRLR 63; *Wise Group v Mitchell* [2005] ICR 896). The Supreme Court in *Edwards v Chesterfield Royal Hospital NHS Foundation Trust* [2012] ICR 201 declined to consider whether *Gunton* was properly decided.

58.26   *'Liquidated damages' clauses and other provisions for termination payments*

Sometimes a service agreement may contain a provision that the employer is to pay a specified sum, or a sum calculated in a specified way, to the employee if the employment comes to an end in particular circumstances.

If the employee seeks to enforce such a provision, a basic question which may arise is whether the clause is a penalty clause. If so, the court will not give effect to it, and the employee will simply have to sue for damages in the normal way (assuming that he has been wrongfully dismissed). In order to decide whether a particular provision is indeed a penalty clause, it is necessary to apply a two-stage test.

of past performance by that employee, and performance by other employees during the relevant period as compared with their own past performance. In yet other cases, the court may be required to assess the employer's likely profits in years which are yet to come, in which case expert evidence is likely to be required if the claim is of any size. Where an employer operates a discretionary bonus scheme an employee who has a contractual entitlement to participate in that scheme is entitled to a bona fide and rational exercise of discretion by his employer as to whether or not he receives his bonus and in what sum (*Clark v Nomura International plc* [2000] IRLR 766, EAT; *Horkulak v Cantor Fitzgerald International* [2004] EWCA Civ 1287, [2005] ICR 402). In deciding how much compensation to award an employee where his employer has failed to exercise its discretion rationally and in good faith, the court may take into account the range of bonus payments made to other employees. The court is not obliged to award the employee the minimum bonus that the employer could lawfully have paid if it is not fair and reasonable to do so (see *Horkulak*).

Share options. The effect of dismissal may be that the employee loses the right to exercise share options which he holds, or that he is compelled to exercise them within a shorter timescale than would otherwise have been the case, with adverse implications for the differential between the exercise price and the market price of the shares. Where this is so, and where there is no valid exclusion clause in respect of liability for such loss (see **58.37** below), the court will have to assess the value of the shares which the employee could otherwise have obtained, less what it would have cost him to acquire them.

Cars. Company cars often represent a substantial head of loss, although for any damages to be recoverable it is obviously essential that the claimant should have been permitted to make some personal use of the car.

There are a number of possible ways in which the loss may be assessed. If the employee has actually had to hire a replacement car, and has acted reasonably in doing so, then the hire charges should be recoverable. Alternatively, a fairly rough and ready lump sum may be awarded.

More commonly, however, the court will be invited to have regard either to the value which the Inland Revenue places upon the car for tax purposes, or to the AA's estimated running costs. The Revenue scales, which are based on size or value, age and mileage, were formerly not much relied upon by employees, because the tax treatment of such benefits was generous, and did not reflect their true value. More recently, changes in policy have made the Revenue scales a better and fairer guide.

The AA estimates provided the basis of valuation adopted by the court in *Shove v Downs Surgical plc* [1984] ICR 532. They are annual figures comprising standing charges and running costs per mile for various sizes of car and a given annual mileage.

Clearly, whatever basis of valuation is adopted, it is necessary to examine the terms of the contract (either express, or implied through practice) as to what costs associated with running the car were to be met by the employer, and which by the employee. In particular, it is necessary to know which party was responsible for meeting the cost of petrol for private use.

Pensions. The loss of pension contributions, or pension rights, is also in many cases an extremely important head of damages.

Insurance cover. It is commonplace for employees to be contractually entitled to the benefit of free medical insurance, permanent health insurance and the like, both for themselves and for their families.

The value of such benefits is frequently assessed as if it could be equated with the cost to the employer of providing the insurance cover, and this may be convenient when the sums at stake are small. However, it is not a strictly accurate approach. If the employee has in fact obtained replacement cover, then the loss suffered is the reasonable cost to him of doing so (and an individual may have to pay more than a company purchasing the same cover on a group basis). However, if the employee has chosen not to take out such insurance himself, then he suffers no loss (save, perhaps for the 'peace of mind' which the employee previously enjoyed, knowing that insurance coverage was in place) unless during the relevant period some event occurs which would have led to the making of a payment under the policy, had it still been in force. In that event, there may be arguments as to whether the whole amount of the lost payment is recoverable, or whether the employee should have mitigated his loss by obtaining replacement cover.

It is also necessary to bear in mind that, depending upon the basis on which the insurance is arranged and paid for, the period for which cover is lost through the wrongful dismissal (or replacement cover has to be purchased) may not exactly correspond to the period between the dismissal and the date when due notice would have expired.

Holidays. The conventional view is that the right to paid holiday is not a separate compensatable head of loss, since the pay which would have been received is covered by the claim for lost salary. However, it is at least arguable that the opportunity to receive that salary, without having to work for it, is itself a valuable benefit, and that the salary payable in respect of the relevant period is the appropriate measure of that value. The counter-argument is that the wrongfully dismissed employee in effect finds himself enjoying a good deal of holiday time, whether he likes it or not. On the other hand, he is not truly on holiday (because he has a continuing duty to look for ways of mitigating his loss), and he may find other employment which offers the same pay but less generous holiday arrangements.

Accommodation. If it was a contractual benefit that the employee should be provided with free or cheap accommodation, and the employee has had to vacate that accommodation as a result of the dismissal, then the cost of finding alternative accommodation for the duration of the notice period is a recoverable head of loss.

Sometimes employees who have lost accommodation seek to claim for their removal expenses. However, it is unlikely that such expenses are properly recoverable in most cases, since the employee would have had to leave the accommodation in due course even if proper notice had been given.

Miscellaneous. In advising employees with wrongful dismissal claims, it is important to ensure that all contractual benefits have been identified and claims made for their value. Other than the common and valuable benefits discussed above, benefits in kind may include, for example, meals, payment of telephone bills and the use of a mobile phone, discounts on particular products (such as mortgages for bank employees), and personal use of credit cards offering preferential interest rates. See also **58.33** below for loss of the right to complain of unfair dismissal.

However, a right to reimbursement of expenses only represents a head of loss if the expenses in question were not confined to expenditure incurred for the purposes of the job (the point being that such expenditure will cease to be incurred once the job is lost).

In all cases, it is wise to be sure that benefits have been properly declared to tax before they are introduced into the calculation of loss, lest an argument be put forward that the contract is void for illegality (see **58.35** below).

A claim for damages for wrongful dismissal will often be combined with a claim in debt for wages accrued to the date of dismissal, and for accrued holiday pay if that is a contractual right. Claims in debt are not subject to the obligation to mitigate. Nor can the employer avoid paying accrued wages even if there was misconduct prior to the dismissal which justified summary termination (*Healey v Française Rubastic SA* [1917] 1 KB 946). Wages accrue on a daily basis and an employee will normally be entitled to claim an apportionment of wages for a period worked even where he has been summarily dismissed before his salary became due under the terms of his contract: *Item Software (UK) Ltd v Fassihi* [2002] EWHC 3116 (Ch), [2003] IRLR 769.

58.29 *Compensation for distress and other intangible loss*

The normal rule is that in an action for breach of contract, including an action for wrongful dismissal, it is not possible to recover damages for distress or injured feelings for the manner of the breach (*Addis v Gramophone Co Ltd* [1909] AC 488; *Johnson v Unisys Ltd* [2001] UKHL 13, [2001] ICR 480).

Further, while an employee may recover damages at common law for a breach of the implied term of trust and confidence occurring prior to a dismissal, the House of Lords has held that such a claim cannot be made in respect of the dismissal itself, for this would impinge on the statutory right not to be unfairly dismissed, the jurisdictional and compensatory limits for which have been determined by Parliament (*Johnson*, ibid). Their Lordships considered this boundary, which they called 'the *Johnson* exclusionary area', again in *McCabe v Cornwall County Council* [2004] UKHL 35; [2004] IRLR 733. Their Lordships affirmed the decision in *Johnson*, but expressed dissatisfaction with the boundary line drawn. Lord Steyn, noting that the reasoning of a number of their Lordships in *Johnson* had been underpinned by an assumption that compensation for non-pecuniary loss was available in unfair dismissal, suggested that the issue ought to be revisited in the light of the decision of the House in *Dunnachie v Kingston-Upon-Hull City Council* [2004] UKHL 36, [2004] IRLR 727. (In *Dunnachie*, their Lordships ruled that compensation for unfair dismissal was strictly limited to compensation for pecuniary loss: see generally **55.12** UNFAIR DISMISSAL – **III**.) Lord Nicholls, however, observed (at para 33) that the whole issue required the 'urgent attention' of Parliament.

In *Gibb v Maidstone & Tunbridge Wells NHS Trust* [2009] IRLR 707, the Court held that the employing trust had been in breach of the implied term of trust and confidence in giving assurances to its former chief executive that the necessary approvals were or would be in place for the compromise agreement that they were entering into. However, the Court held that this did not give rise to a cause of action in damages, as it fell within 'the Johnson exclusion area'. The inaccurate assurances had been given by the employer as part of the steps leading up to the employee's dismissal. The case has recently been considered by the Court of Appeal ([2010] EWCA Civ 678, [2010] IRLR 786), and the decision overturned on other grounds. On this point, however, Laws LJ held that if he was required to decide it, he would have held that the breach did not fall within 'the Johnson exclusion area', as the employee entered into the compromise agreement before the termination of her contract, and the fact that the loss fell in after it does not show that the termination caused the loss.

It is possible, however, to recover damages for loss of reputation or future prospects on the labour market (in actions for wrongful dismissal or breach of contract – where the breach is not known until after termination) where the employer is in breach of the duty of trust and confidence: so-called 'stigma damages' (*Malik v BCCI SA* [1997] ICR 606). Recovery of stigma damages will probably be rare, however, as the employee is required to establish not only that there was a breach of the duty, but that the requirements of causation and remoteness are also satisfied. In the *Malik* case it was assumed for the purposes of argument that the employer bank operated its business in a corrupt and dishonest way; that its corruption and dishonesty were widely known; and that the employees were at a handicap on the labour market as they were tainted by their connection with the employer. At trial, however, none of the former employees were able to establish that the employer's breach caused them any financial loss, as they could not demonstrate that the bank's wrongdoing blighted their job prospects (*Bank of Credit and Commerce International SA v Ali* [1999] IRLR 508).

Damages for the loss of future employment prospects may be more readily available where the contract is one of apprenticeship (*Dunk v George Waller & Son Ltd* [1970] 2 QB 163), or where (as with the engagement of an actor) part of its purpose is to provide publicity for the employee (*Clayton (Herbert) and Jack Waller Ltd v Oliver* [1930] AC 209, HL).

58.30 *Mitigation and collateral benefits*

An employee who has been wrongfully dismissed is under a duty to mitigate his loss by seeking alternative sources of income. Any other income received during the notice period in relation to which the employee is being compensated will normally have to be taken into account so as to reduce the loss suffered.

The dismissed employee's obligation is to act reasonably. The principles applied in wrongful dismissal cases are very similar to those applicable in assessing compensation for unfair dismissal, and reference should also be made to the discussion in UNFAIR DISMISSAL – III (55).

The claimant's obligation to mitigate ought not to be treated as imposing too heavy an obligation upon him, and the burden of proving a failure to mitigate is upon the defendant (*Fyfe v Scientific Furnishings Ltd* [1989] ICR 648). In the first instance, it will probably (depending upon all the circumstances) be reasonable for the employee to seek to find employment of a status and at a salary commensurate with that which he lost upon being dismissed. However, if time goes by without other work being found, the court will expect him to lower his sights. Employees must certainly expect to provide cogent justification for refusing any jobs which are actually offered to them. How far afield in geographical terms a dismissed employee must seek for work in order to be acting reasonably will depend upon his age, the nature of his work, and his personal and domestic circumstances.

It is often advisable for the claimant employee to be able to show that he has pursued all the available avenues of job-seeking, such as registration with agencies and Jobcentres, perusal of job advertisements in general and specialist publications, and use of consultants or outplacement services; not all these possibilities will be appropriate in all cases, however. Copies of all letters written and other relevant documents should be retained, and a record kept of relevant telephone conversations.

It has become increasingly common in large wrongful dismissal claims for expert evidence to be given by recruitment consultants, who use their experience of the relevant industrial sectors to estimate when, and with what remuneration package, a person in the claimant's position should have been able to obtain alternative employment (see, for example, *Clark*, above).

Seeking employment is not the only reasonable means by which a dismissed employee may seek to mitigate his loss. In an appropriate case he may seek to set up his own business or to work in a self-employed or freelance capacity (*Gardiner-Hill v Roland Beiger Technics Ltd* [1982] IRLR 498). Only in an exceptional case, however, would it be held that a claimant had acted unreasonably in *failing* to go into business on his own account. It is more doubtful that there has been proper mitigation where a claimant chooses to undertake further education or retraining instead of seeking work, unless his or her existing skills are very unlikely to lead to a new job.

If the circumstances of the dismissal have been acrimonious, or have involved bad faith or unreasonable conduct on the part of the employer, it is unlikely that the employee will be held to have acted unreasonably if he rejects an offer of new employment made by that employer (see eg *Shindler v Northern Raincoat Co Ltd* [1960] 1 WLR 1038). Nor, it appears, is it an unreasonable failure to mitigate if the employee fails to invoke an internal appeal procedure (*Lock v Connell Estate Agents* [1994] IRLR 444). However, a failure to complete the statutory grievance procedure in Sch 2 to the *Employment Act 2002* will mean that a tribunal will reduce any damages awarded (*s 31*) or even prevent the employee from bringing a claim altogether (*s 32*). See generally **55.9** UNFAIR DISMISSAL – III.

Expenses reasonably incurred in attempting to mitigate loss may be deducted from the fruits of the mitigation or added to the loss suffered as the case may be.

Moneys received during the notice period which have to be deducted from wrongful dismissal damages include not only income from a new job, but also any payments already made by the defendant on account of the dismissal, and state benefits (*Parsons v BNM*

Laboratories Ltd [1964] 1 QB 95; but it was held in *Westwood v Secretary of State for Employment* [1985] ICR 209 that unemployment benefit should not be taken into account if the entitlement to it runs out whilst the employee is still out of work after the end of the notice period). However, the employee does not have to give credit for any benefits received from insurance policies which pay out in the event of unemployment, or for a pension which becomes payable upon the dismissal (*Hopkins v Norcros plc* [1994] ICR 11). Nor does the employee have to give credit for the fact that he works shorter hours in his new job, or receives longer holidays than beforehand (*Potter v Arafa* [1995] IRLR 316).

58.31 *Interest and accelerated receipt*

Depending upon the length of the notice period or fixed term contract, and how long it takes for the wrongful dismissal claim to be brought to trial, the claimant may find either that he has suffered a loss through being deprived of the use and benefit of his salary for the period between the dismissal and the trial, or that he gains because the award of damages is in his pocket much sooner than the salary which it represents would have been paid.

Accordingly, that part of the award of damages which represents salary which ought to have been paid in the past will normally carry an award of interest. The discretionary power of the High Court to award interest is found in *s 35A* of the *Supreme Court Act 1981*, and that of the county court in *s 69* of the *County Courts Act 1984*. The rate and period of interest, as well as whether to award it at all, are in the court's discretion. However, the award will always be of simple interest; it will generally run from the date when payment should have been made until the date of judgment, unless the claimant has been culpably slow in prosecuting the proceedings; and it will frequently reflect the judgment rate of interest over the relevant period (currently 8%).

Where damages are being received earlier than the payments for whose loss they compensate were due, it is normal for a percentage discount to be applied on account of accelerated receipt, generally reflecting the anticipated rate of inflation over the relevant period.

Sometimes, where the award of damages covers a very long period, the percentage discount may be increased (or a further discount applied) to take account of the so-called 'vicissitudes of life' – in other words, the intangible chance that the claimant might never have served the full notice period because he fell ill, chose to depart, or encountered the proverbial number 57 bus. It is not thought that any very large discount is generally appropriate on this score.

58.32 *Taxation of damages*

The ultimate objective of the award of damages, as explained above, is to put the claimant into exactly the same position as if the contract had been duly performed. In that event, he would of course have been paid his salary net of tax and national insurance contributions, and would have had to pay tax upon most benefits in kind. However, simply to deduct tax and national insurance from the gross loss would be too simplistic an approach, because the award of damages will itself be subject to tax in the hands of the employee. A further complication is that the damages will only be taxed insofar as they exceed the tax-free allowance of £30,000 which applies to compensation payments for loss of office The principal relevant taxing provisions are contained in *Part 6* of the *Income tax (Earnings and Pensions) Act 2003*. Employers are required to report to the Inland Revenue details of any award of payment and/or benefits upon termination of an employment contract where the total amount of the award exceeds £30,000 (*Income Tax (Pay as You Earn) Regulations 2003 (SI 2003/2682), regs 91 to 93*).

The correct approach is therefore for the court to ascertain the net sum which the employee ought ultimately to receive, and to gross that amount up until it has arrived at a grossed-up sum which, when the damages are taxed, will reduce again to the correct net sum. Authority for this grossing-up procedure is to be found in *Stewart v Glentaggart* 1963 SLT 119 and *Shove v Downs Surgical plc* [1984] ICR 532. In order to ensure the correct application of tax rates, bands and allowances, it may be necessary to have details of the employee's income from all sources.

Similar principles should apply where one is calculating a settlement figure rather than an award of damages. It will be necessary to look at each element that makes up the overall settlement sum.

An employer who pays a grossed-up sum by way of settlement should first ensure either that the Inland Revenue is content for moneys to be paid gross and taxed in the employee's hands, or that the employee has agreed as part of the settlement to reimburse the employer for any demand for tax upon the sums paid which may subsequently be made.

58.33 *Relationship with compensation for unfair dismissal*

An employee who has been both wrongfully and unfairly dismissed cannot be compensated twice for the same loss. However, there are a number of important respects in which the rules governing the compensatory award for unfair dismissal differ from those governing damages for wrongful dismissal. In particular: damages for wrongful dismissal are essentially limited to the notice period, whereas compensation for unfair dismissal may in principle extend indefinitely; in wrongful dismissal only strict contractual rights are taken into account, whereas the employment tribunal may allow for other benefits and heads of loss (eg likely future pay increases, discretionary bonuses, loss of statutory rights); and the compensatory award in unfair dismissal may not exceed a statutory maximum.

Therefore, if an employee who has already received damages for wrongful dismissal goes on to obtain a ruling from an employment tribunal that he has been unfairly dismissed, he may ask for compensation (up to the statutory maximum) representing his loss beyond the notice period and his non-contractual benefits within the notice period.

If an employee who has already been compensated for unfair dismissal brings an action for wrongful dismissal, the court must examine the way in which that compensation has been calculated, and deduct from the wrongful dismissal damages those elements already covered by the tribunal award. The same will apply where the unfair dismissal claim has been settled by payment of a sum to the former employee (*Aspden* — see **58.19** above). However, if the sum actually awarded by the tribunal has been capped at the statutory maximum, it will frequently not be possible to say whether the award actually received represents one sort of loss rather than another. In that situation, the court will therefore not make any deduction from the damages which it awards (*O'Laoire v Jackel International Ltd (No 2)* [1991] ICR 718).

A summary dismissal, albeit wrongful, is nonetheless effective to terminate the employment at once (subject to the question of acceptance of the breach, as to which see **58.7** above). It is not generally possible for an employee to complain of unfair dismissal unless he has been continuously employed for two years prior to the effective date of termination (see UNFAIR DISMISSAL – I (53)). Hence it is possible that the effect of a wrongful dismissal may be to deprive the employee of an unfair dismissal claim, if the absence of due notice or proper application of contractual disciplinary procedures makes the difference to whether there is the necessary period of service prior to termination. However, an employee cannot claim that lost right of complaint as a head of damages in the wrongful dismissal proceedings (*Harper v Virgin Net Ltd* [2004] EWCA Civ 271, [2005] ICR 921; applied in *Wise Group v Mitchell* [2005] ICR 896).

58.34 EFFECT OF A WRONGFUL DISMISSAL UPON OTHER CONTRACTUAL OBLIGATIONS

If the employee is wrongfully dismissed, the effect will normally be to release him from any further performance of his own contractual obligations, even those which are expressed to continue after the termination of the employment. In particular, this means that the employer will be unable to enforce any restrictive covenants contained in the contract of employment (*General Billposting Co Ltd v Atkinson* [1909] AC 118; *Rock Refrigeration Ltd v Jones* [1996] IRLR 675).

However, an arbitration clause will normally remain enforceable even after a wrongful dismissal.

58.35 POSSIBLE DEFENCES TO A WRONGFUL DISMISSAL CLAIM

Illegality

No action may be brought upon a contract which is treated as illegal upon grounds of public policy. In the employment context, this most frequently applies to situations where the employer and employee have colluded to evade the payment of income tax. For a fuller account, see CONTRACTS OF EMPLOYMENT (8) and UNFAIR DISMISSAL – I (53).

58.36 Invalidity of contract

The employer may seek to argue that the contract, or some of its terms, were never validly entered into. This might arise, for example, if the employer was a local authority, and contended that entry into the contract had for some reason been *ultra vires*. Alternatively, a limited company might contend that a director's contract of employment had been concluded in a way which was not in accordance with the company's articles of association, or that the contract had been concluded for an improper purpose (for example, if members of the board of directors voted to grant each other long fixed term contracts in order to protect their own positions in advance of an anticipated takeover). See *Re W and M Roith Ltd* [1967] 1 WLR 432; *Guinness plc v Saunders* [1990] 2 AC 663; and *Runciman v Walter Runciman plc* [1992] BCLC 1084.

58.37 Exclusion clauses

It is not common to find in a contract of employment provisions purporting to exclude or limit the employer's liability for wrongful dismissal (although share option schemes often provide that no sum in respect of lost opportunities under the scheme is to be awarded by way of compensation for dismissal). Although no such provision could effectively exclude compensation for statutory rights (see UNFAIR DISMISSAL – I (53)), there is no reason in principle why a contract should not seek to exclude or limit liability for wrongful dismissal or other possible contractual claims.

An employee faced with such an exclusion clause, however, might seek to argue that it was subject to the controls laid down by the *Unfair Contract Terms Act 1977* (*UCTA*). If *UCTA* applied, then the clause would be upheld only insofar as it satisfied the requirement of reasonableness at the time when the contract was made. Nevertheless, in *Commerzbank AG v Keen* [2007] ICR 623, the Court of Appeal held that *UCTA* did not apply to contracts for the remuneration of employees.

58.38 PROCEDURAL ASPECTS OF WRONGFUL DISMISSAL CLAIMS

Choice of court

Until recently, and subject to the possibility of arbitration, it had been necessary to bring an action for wrongful dismissal in the ordinary courts – that is, the High Court (in London or in a district registry) or the county court. Those courts remain the primary forum for such actions, certainly those of substantial value. However, as discussed below, employment tribunals also now have a contractual jurisdiction which extends to wrongful dismissal claims.

The choice of whether to proceed in the High Court or county court depends principally upon the value of the claim. In a wrongful dismissal action, there is no absolute bar to commencing proceedings in either court. However, the trial of the action will normally take place in the county court if the value of the action (ie the amount, exclusive of interest, which the claimant reasonably expects to recover) is less than £50,000, and will normally take place in the High Court if that value is £50,000 or more.

Employees are also able to bring proceedings in the employment tribunal in respect of claims for (inter alia) damages for breach of a contract of employment arising or outstanding on the termination of employment, which would of course include claims for wrongful dismissal (*Employment Tribunals Act 1996, s 3*; *Employment Tribunals Extension of Jurisdiction (England and Wales) Order 1994 (SI 1994/1623)* – see *SI 1994/1624* in relation to Scotland). However, the tribunal is not empowered in such proceedings to order the payment of an amount exceeding £25,000. Nor does the tribunal have any jurisdiction to award interest (although the award once made will carry interest if not satisfied within 42 days). Employees should bear in mind that where wrongful dismissal (or any breach of contract) proceedings are issued in the employment tribunal, the employer is entitled to counterclaim for any breach of contract committed by the employee which arises or is outstanding on the termination of employment (*art 4 of the 1994 Order*).

Occasionally, a contract of employment may contain an arbitration clause capable of applying to a wrongful dismissal claim. In such a case, the employee is entitled to refer the claim to arbitration rather than commencing proceedings in the ordinary courts or the employment tribunal. If the employee instead chooses to begin proceedings in the High Court or county court, the employer may seek to have those proceedings stayed under *s 94* of the *Arbitration Act 1996* so that the matter can be referred to arbitration. The court is obliged to grant a stay unless satisfied that the arbitration agreement is null and void, inoperative, or incapable of being performed (*section 9(4)*).

It would appear that wrongful dismissal proceedings brought in the employment tribunal could also be stayed so as to give effect to an arbitration clause. Although any provision in an agreement purporting to preclude the presentation of a complaint to a tribunal is normally void, this does not apply where (as here) the tribunal's jurisdiction is founded upon an order made under *s 3* of the *Employment Tribunals Act 1996*.

There is also the possibility for wrongful dismissal claims to be considered by the Companies Court (part of the Chancery Division of the High Court, within an unfair prejudice petition pursuant to the *Companies Act 2006, s 994*. In *Wootliff v Rushton-Turner* [2016] EWHC 2802 (Ch), it was held that a shareholder and former employee of a company could pursue such a claim, and that it would be inefficient, disproportionate and a waste of resources for the claims to be heard in separate proceedings.

58.39 Relationship with tribunal proceedings

Where a claim for wrongful dismissal is commenced in the High Court or county court, and at the same time a complaint of unfair dismissal is presented to an employment tribunal, an application may be made for one or other set of proceedings (usually the tribunal claim) to be stayed pending the outcome of the other litigation.

Where the claim of wrongful dismissal has been brought in the employment tribunal and judgment has been reached by the tribunal, it is not open to the employee to recover damages in excess of the tribunal's jurisdiction (£25,000) by proceedings in the county court or High Court. The common law doctrine of merger of causes of action will be held to apply (see *Fraser v HLMAD Ltd* [2006] EWCA Civ 738, [2006] IRLR 687). Therefore, where the employee's potential recovery is greater than £25,000, the appropriate forum in which to proceed with an action must be thought through with some care.

An employee may be able to withdraw an employment tribunal claim for wrongful dismissal, however, and proceed instead in the county court or High Court without being barred by the operation of the principle of cause of action estoppel, if it is made clear that the withdrawal from the employment tribunal is for this very purpose (see *Sajid v Sussex Muslim Society* [2001] EWCA Civ 1684, [2002] IRLR 113).

58.40 Limitation periods

A wrongful dismissal action in the High Court or county court is a claim for breach of contract, and as such is subject to a limitation period of six years from the accrual of the cause of action (*Limitation Act 1980, s 5*). Hence, proceedings must be commenced before the sixth anniversary of the dismissal.

In the employment tribunal, the complaint will have to be presented within the period of three months beginning with the effective date of termination of the contract of employment, or (where the tribunal is satisfied that it was not reasonably practicable for the complaint to be presented within that period) within such further period as the tribunal considers reasonable (*Employment Tribunals Extension of Jurisdiction (England and Wales) Order 1994 (SI 1994/1623), art 7* – see *art 7* of *SI 1994/1624* in relation to Scotland).

58.41 Summary judgment, interim payments, payments into court, and hearings on liability and quantum

In the High Court and county court, although not the employment tribunal, the claimant employee who considers that the defendant employer has no real prospect of successfully defending the claim may apply for summary judgment on written evidence alone (*Civil Procedure Rules 1998, Part 24*). This is particularly important in wrongful dismissal claims, where the true issue between the parties is often not whether the employer was entitled to dismiss without due notice, but what loss the employee has suffered, and in particular the extent to which that loss could or should have been mitigated. In such a case the court may be persuaded to enter judgment for damages to be assessed, or at least to make the granting of leave to defend the action conditional upon the defendant making a payment into court (which will act as an incentive to settlement of the claim, and should ensure that the claimant is able to enforce any judgment ultimately obtained).

The application for summary judgment will often be combined with an application for an interim payment (*CPR 1998, rule 25.6*), which will also be appropriate in a case where the employer has admitted liability but contests the amount of damages.

If the defendant employer believes that the claimant is likely to succeed on the issue of whether he was wrongfully dismissed, but that he is claiming damages substantially in excess of those to which he is truly entitled, then it may be appropriate for that defendant to make a payment into court in satisfaction of the claimant's cause of action (*CPR 1998, Part 36*). If the claimant accepts the payment in within a specified period, the proceedings will come to an end, and the claimant will automatically be entitled to his costs up until the date of payment in. If the claimant does not do so, and ultimately recovers less at trial than the sum paid in, then he will have to pay the defendant's costs since payment in.

Where both liability and quantum are in dispute, the parties will wish to consider (especially where the calculation of loss raises complex points of detail) whether liability should be tried as a preliminary issue, with a hearing on quantum to follow only if the claimant establishes that he has been wrongfully dismissed and the parties are still unable to compromise their differences at that point.

Save for the possibility of separate hearings on liability and quantum, none of these procedural opportunities will be available if the claim is brought in the employment tribunal.

58.42 Compromise of claims

The various statutory restrictions, which prescribe that an employee may compromise claims based upon his statutory rights only in certain specified ways, do not apply to wrongful dismissal claims (*Sutherland v Network Appliance Ltd* [2001] IRLR 12). Any compromise contained in a binding contract will do, and a binding contract requires only offer and acceptance, an intention to create legal relations and consideration. There is good consideration for a contract of compromise even if the claimant's claim is in fact ill-founded, because the defendant is spared the expense and vexation of resisting it. However, it may in certain circumstances be possible to set aside a compromise on the grounds of mistake or misrepresentation (see eg *Bell v Lever Bros Ltd* [1932] AC 161).

Once High Court or county court proceedings have actually been commenced, it is not unusual for terms of settlement to be incorporated into an order of the court. In particular, the order may give the parties liberty to apply to the court for the purpose of enforcing those terms.

58.43   SPECIAL CATEGORIES OF EMPLOYMENT

Crown servants

This category covers, principally, civil servants and (probably) NHS employees. Although Crown servants have the right to complain of unfair dismissal (*ERA 1996, s 191*), it does not appear that it is possible for them to bring an action for wrongful dismissal. This is because it is a rule of law that Crown service is determinable by the Crown at will (*Riordan v War Office* [1959] 1 WLR 1046). Consistently with this principle, Crown servants do not enjoy the right to a statutory minimum period of notice.

58.44   Apprentices

The employer's right of summary dismissal is more restricted in a contract of apprenticeship than in a normal contract of employment. It appears that nothing short of conduct which makes it impossible for the employer to carry out the essential purpose of the contract (to teach the apprentice his trade) will justify termination without notice (see *Learoyd v Brook* [1891] 1 QB 431; *Newell v Gillingham Corpn* [1941] 1 All ER 552).

By the same token, an employer will generally be precluded from terminating a contract of apprenticeship solely on the ground of redundancy where the business is not closed down, or there is no change in the character of the business (*Wallace v CA Roofing Services Ltd* [1996] IRLR 435).

For special considerations applying to the assessment of damages for wrongful dismissal of an apprentice, see **58.29** above. For Modern Apprenticeships, see generally **14** EDUCATION AND TRAINING.

Index

Index

Age discrimination – *cont.*
applications to Employment Tribunal – *cont.*
  questionnaire, 13.9
  recommendations, 13.21
  remedies, 13.12–13.22
  time limits, 13.4–13.7
assistance for persons discriminated
  against, 13.31
barristers, 12.27
'because of the protected characteristic', 11.25
benefits provided to public, 12.20
burden of proof, 13.3
careers guidance, 12.32
Codes of Practice, and
  legal effect, 5.12
  power to issue, 5.11
  revision, 5.18
  revocation, 5.18
combined discrimination, 11.29
comparators, 11.15
compensation
  aggravated damages, 13.18
  discrimination, 13.19
  exemplary damages, 13.18
  general principles, 13.13
  indirect discrimination, 13.14
  injury to feelings, 13.16
  interest, 13.20
  introduction, 13.12
  pecuniary loss, 13.15
  personal injury, 13.17
  unfair dismissal, 13.19
conciliation, 13.10
contract workers, 12.24
Crown, 12.36
detriment, 11.50
direct discrimination
  'because of the protected characteristic', 11.25
  generally, 11.13
  less favourable treatment, 11.14–11.16
disclosure, 13.9
dismissal, 11.49
duty to make reasonable adjustments, 11.37
education needs, 12.10
employed at establishment in GB, 11.42
employment agencies, 12.32
employment, in
  advertisements, 11.43
  dismissal, 11.49
  'employment', 11.41
  engagement, 11.44–11.46
  harassment, 11.51
  introduction, 11.40

Age discrimination – *cont.*
employment, in – *cont.*
  opportunities, 11.47–11.48
  post-employment behaviour, 11.52
  subjection to other detriment, 11.50–11.51
  territorial jurisdiction, 11.42
employment outside Great Britain, 12.18
employment-related services, 12.33
employment service-providers, 12.34
enforcement
  applications to Employment Tribunal, 13.2–13.22
  assistance for persons discriminated against, 13.31
  EHRC, by, 13.23–13.24
  injunctions, 13.29–13.30
  introduction, 13.1
  settlement, 13.33
  void contract terms, 13.32
enforcement by the EHRC
  formal inquiries and investigations, 13.25–13.27
  generally, 13.23–13.24
  introduction, 12.38
  unlawful act notices, 13.28
engagement, 11.44
equal opportunities, and
  enforcement, 12.38
  general exceptions, 12.17–12.23
  genuine occupational requirement or qualification, 12.2–12.8
  introduction, 12.1
  justification, 12.9
  non-employees/employers covered, 12.24–12.36
  positive discrimination, 12.10
  public authorities, and, 12.37
  specific exceptions, 12.15
Equality Act 2010, 11.1
exceptions
  child care, 12.15
  genuine occupational requirement, 12.8
  length of service, 12.15
  life assurance cover to retired workers, 12.15
  national minimum wage, 12.15
  pension schemes, 12.15, 12.35D
  redundancy benefits, 12.15
  retirement, 12.15
extension of time, 13.7
financial penalties, 13.20A
formulation of complaint, 13.8
general exceptions
  benefits provided to public, 12.20
  employment outside Great Britain, 12.18
  illegal contracts, 12.19

Index

Index

Index

Index

Index

Index

Index

Index

Index

Index

Index

Index

Index

Index

Index

Index

Index

Index

Index

Index

Index

Index

Index

Index

Index

Index

Index

Index

Index

Index

Index

Index

Index

Index

Index

Index

Index

Index